LEFT: ROOMAJI, MIDDLE: HIRAGANA, RIGHT: KATAKANA

kya	きゃ	キャ			kyu	きゅ	キュ			kyo	きょ	キョ
gya	ぎゃ	ギャ			gyu	ぎゅ	ギュ			gyo	ぎょ	ギョ
sha	しゃ	シャ			shu	しゅ	シュ	she*	シェ	sho	しょ	ショ
ja	じゃ	ジャ			ju	じゅ	ジュ	je*	ジェ	jo	じょ	ジョ
cha	ちゃ	チャ			chu	ちゅ	チュ	che*	チェ	cho	ちょ	チョ
ja	ぢゃ	ヂャ			ju	ぢゅ	ヂュ			jo	ぢょ	ヂョ
nya	にゃ	ニャ			nyu	にゅ	ニュ			nyo	にょ	ニョ
hya	ひゃ	ヒャ			hyu	ひゅ	ヒュ			hyo	ひょ	ヒョ
bya	びゃ	ビャ			byu	びゅ	ビュ			byo	びょ	ビョ
pya	ぴゃ	ピャ			pyu	ぴゅ	ピュ			pyo	ぴょ	ピョ
mya	みゃ	ミャ			myu	みゅ	ミュ			myo	みょ	ミョ
rya	りゃ	リャ			ryu	りゅ	リュ			ryo	りょ	リョ
tsa*		ツァ	tsi* ti*	ツィ ティ	tu*		トゥ	tse*	ツェ	tso*		ツォ
			di*	ディ	dyu* du*		デュ ドゥ					
fa*		ファ	fi*	フィ	fyu*		フュ	fe*	フェ	fo*		フォ

*Used in borrowed words

KODANSHA'S Basic English-Japanese Dictionary

Seiichi Makino
Seiichi Nakada
Mieko Ohso
Editorial Adviser Wesley M. Jacobsen

KODANSHA INTERNATIONAL
Tokyo · New York · London

Distributed in the United States
by Kodansha America, Inc.,
and in the United Kingdom and continental Europe
by Kodansha Europe Ltd.,

Published by Kodansha International Ltd.,
17-14, Otowa 1-chome, Bunkyo-ku, Tokyo 112-8652,
and Kodansha America, Inc.

ISBN-13: 978-4-7700-2895-2
ISBN-10: 4-7700-2895-4
CIP data available

First edition, 1999
First paperback edition, 2002
15 14 13 12 11 10 09 08 07 06 10 9 8 7 6 5 4

www.kodansha-intl.com

PREFACE

This is an English-Japanese dictionary primarily for students and teachers of the Japanese language, but anyone who is interested in the basic vocabulary of the English language and its corresponding vocabulary in the Japanese language should find this dictionary useful. We have chosen approximately 4,500 basic English words as entries, so that the user will have access to a Japanese vocabulary sufficient for the purposes of speaking and writing about most topics arising in daily life.

The following are some of the unique features of this English-Japanese dictionary.

(1) Although it has the appearance of a regular English-Japanese dictionary, this dictionary is actually a bilingual dictionary in the sense that the index of basic Japanese words provided at the end allows it to be used as a Japanese-English dictionary as well.

(2) Each entry in English is followed by a description of its basic meaning and a set of Japanese words which fall within the range of meaning of the English entry. Each of these Japanese words is in turn followed by a description of its basic meaning, allowing one to see readily what the crucial differences are in meaning between the English and Japanese words.

(3) Unlike typical English-Japanese dictionaries intended for use by native speakers of Japanese, the present dictionary provides numerous example sentences written in both Japanese script (i.e., *hiragana*, *katakana* and *kanji*) and romanization.

(4) Noteworthy information on the grammatical behavior and correct usage of Japanese words and of important differences between Japanese and English are provided throughout the dictionary for the benefit of those studying the Japanese language.

More than ten years have now passed since one of the writers, Seiichi Makino, initially proposed the idea of a new type of English-Japanese dictionary to Mr. Shinji Ichiba of

Kodansha International, who very kindly accepted the proposal. For the first few years there were only two of us, Seiichi Makino of Princeton University and Seiichi Nakada of Aoyama Gakuin University, working on the dictionary, but owing to the busy schedule of Seiichi Nakada, we decided to ask Mieko Ohso of Nagoya University to join us in the project.

Makino wrote the initial draft for half of the entries and Nakada and Ohso the other half, but we have carefully checked each other's drafts and corrected them wherever necessary. So in effect every part of this dictionary has been written by the three of us.

Naturally we owe a great deal to our predecessors in the field of English-Japanese dictionaries, but the notion of basic meaning which we rely on crucially owes itself to Professor Shiro Hattori's original notion of sememe (*igiso*). We would like to express our deep gratitude to Mr. Shinji Ichiba, the former editor-in-chief of Kodansha International, who has been so understanding of our project and has been so patient with the slow pace of our work, and to Mr. Hitoshi Wakayama of Kodansha International, Mr. Taro Hirowatari of Parastyle, Inc. and Ms. Midoriko Iio of Parastyle, Inc. who have given us editorial advice and ideas, and done the actual editing of our work. And last but not least, our thanks to Professor Wesley M. Jacobsen of Harvard University, who kindly provided a native check of our manuscripts. Without his most conscientious native check, the dictionary would not have seen the light.

Since this dictionary is the first of its kind we are aware that there is ample room for improvement. It is our hope that you as users of the dictionary will forward to us your comments, suggestions and criticisms so they may be incorporated in future editions of the work.

Seiichi Makino
Seiichi Nakada
Mieko Ohso

CONTENTS

HOW TO USE THIS DICTIONARY

This dictionary is an English-Japanese dictionary written primarily for students and teachers of the Japanese language. However, the meaning of basic Japanese vocabulary can be looked up in the index, so in effect this dictionary combines the characteristics of both an English-Japanese and a Japanese-English dictionary.

Each entry consists of the following parts:

(1) Vocabulary item entry. (e.g. drink)

(2) Specification of part of speech. (e.g. v.t.)

(3) Definition of the basic meaning of the entry word in square brackets. (e.g. **[**to take liquid into one's stomach**]**)

(4) Japanese translation(s) of the entry word in both romanization and Japanese script. (e.g. 〈*-o*〉 *nomu* 〈〜を〉飲む)

(5) Pitch accent markers on the romanized form of the Japanese word.

(6) Information on the derivation of certain Japanese words.

(7) Specification of the verbal/adjectival conjugation of the Japanese word.

(8) Specification of the origin of the Japanese word, i.e., whether it is a Sino-Japanese word or a loan word.

(9) Definition of the basic meaning of each Japanese word in square brackets. (e.g. **[**to take s.t. into one's stomach without chewing《fig. "accept s.o.'s demand"》**]**)

(10) Other English translations in double parentheses for each Japanese word. (e.g. ((swallow, accept)))

(11) The antonym of the Japanese word, if necessary.

(12) Example sentences along with their translations in Japanese script and romanization.

(13) Note(s) on usage and unusual grammatical behavior.

(14) Special notes on *kanji* orthography marked by ㊮. (e.g. "leave space vacant"▷空ける, otherwise ▷開ける)

(15) Phrase(s) including idioms, if any.

This dictionary is written not only for you to use as a regular dictionary in looking up appropriate Japanese words that correspond to an English word, but for you to browse through without any specific purpose, as if you were in a library of basic words. In the first case, that is, when you use this dictionary to look up Japanese words, you should read every part of the particular entry you are interested in.

You should pay special attention, first, to the description of the basic meaning of words, because that description should tell you how an English word intersects in meaning with its Japanese counterpart. It is never the case that a given English word and its corresponding Japanese word cover the same area of meaning. However, when an English word and its corresponding Japanese word mean virtually the same thing, no basic meaning is provided. The basic meaning is otherwise provided for you so that you will be aware of the various uses of the word.

Secondly, you should read the example sentence translations very carefully so that you can learn how to use each word in a given context. The Japanese translation of an English sentence may have more than one Japanese word in it, sometimes with an asterisk. The asterisk means that the Japanese word is not acceptable in that sentence, although it is acceptable in other sentences. If you know a sizable number of *kanji* already, you may encounter cases in which different *kanji* are used for one and the same Japanese word to represent slight differences in meaning, as shown in (14) above.

Thirdly, check the conjugation type, especially of verbs. Each verb is classified according to whether it is an intransitive verb or a transitive verb and whether it is of conjugation type ① (i.e. the so-called U-Verbs) or type ② (i.e. the so-called RU-Verbs) or type ③ (i.e. *kuru* and *suru*).

Fourthly, read the notes carefully, because important grammatical information is given there. This dictionary is not a dictionary of grammar, but we have tried our best to make it close to one.

As explained earlier, this dictionary can be used as a Japanese-English dictionary as well. To use it that way you will need to look up a Japanese word in the index. There all the English words that correspond to the Japanese word are listed. All you have to do is to go to any one of the English word entries (or all the English word entries, if you have time) and find the Japanese word there.

To use this dictionary properly you should understand the abbreviations and symbols employed in it. Here is a list of the abbreviations and symbols.

Abbreviations

adj. / adj. = adjective

adj(*i*). / adj(*i*). = *i*-type adjective

adj(*i*). *ku* = adverbial form of *i*-type adjective (e.g. *ookiku* of *ookii* "big")

adj(na). / adj(*na*). = *na*-type adjective (= *keiyoo dooshi*)

adj(*na*). *ni* = adverbial form of *na*-type adjective (e.g. *shizukani* of *shizukana* "quiet")

adj.*te* = *te*-form of adj(*i*). and adj(*na*). (e.g. *samukute* "cold and...," *shizukade* "quiet and...")

adv. = adverb

aux. = auxiliary

Br. E = British English usage

•**c** = Chinese origin word (= Sino-Japanese word)

•**c+f** = a word partly of Chinese and partly of other origin (e.g. *Nihongo- tesuto* "Japanese test")

comp. prt. = compound particle (e.g. *ni-tsuite, ni kanshite*)

conj. / conj. = conjunction

cop. = copula (= *da/ desu/ dearu*)

cop.*te* = *te*-form of copula (= *de*)

•**f+c** = a word partly of non-Chinese and partly of Chinese origin (e.g. *Furansu-go* "French language")

•**f** = foreign word (= loan word)

fig. = figurative extension

⟨**fml**⟩ = formal form

int. = interjection

n. / N = noun
neg. = negative
pot. = potential
prep. = preposition
pron. = pronoun
prt. / prt. = particle (= *joshi*)
⟨s⟩ = used primarily in the spoken language
S = sentence
s.a. = some animal
Sinf. = sentence that ends with an informal predicate (e.g. *Nihon ni iku* of *Nihon ni iku n desu* "It is that I am going to Japan")
s.o. = someone
s.t. = something
suf. = suffix (e.g. *-sa* "-ness," *-ya* "store")
V = verb
Vcond. = conditional stem of Group 1 verb (= U-Verb, e.g. *hanase* of *hanaseba* "if s.o. speaks")
vi. = intransitive verb
Vinf. = informal form of verb (e.g. *kaku* "write," *kaita* "wrote")
Ving = progressive form of verb
V*masu* = *masu*-stem of verb (e.g. *kaki* of *kakimasu* "write")
Vneg. = informal negative form of Group 1 verb (= U-Verb, e.g. *kaka* of *kakanai* "s.o. doesn't write s.t.")
Vstem = stem of Group 2 verb (= RU-Verb, e.g. *tabe* of *taberu* "eat")
vt. = transitive verb
Vvol. = volitional form of verb (e.g. *kakoo* "let's write it," *tabeyoo* "let us eat it")
V*te* = *te*-form of verb (e.g. *kaite* "write and…," *mite* "see and…")
⟨w⟩ = used primarily in the written language

Symbols
( ) = optional part
① = Group 1 verb (= U-Verb, e.g. *kaku* "write," *yomu* "read")
② = Group 2 verb (= RU-Verb, e.g. *taberu* "eat," *miru* "see")
③ = Irregular verb (e.g. *suru* "do")
《x, y, z》 = English translations
[xxxx**]** = xxxx is basic meaning
[xxxx ⟨s⟩**]** = the word is used primarily in the spoken language
[xxxx ⟨w⟩**]** = the word is used primarily in the written language
[xxxx 《fig. "yyy"》**]** = yyy is a figurative extension from the basic meaning
/ = or (e.g. s.o./s.t. = someone or something)
x /⟨ y / = x comes from y (e.g. *mizu-asobi* 水遊び /⟨*mizu* water + V*masu* of *asobu* ① play/)
x ↔ y = y is an antonym of x
* = ungrammatical or unacceptable
? = of questionable acceptability, though not totally ungrammatical; the degree of unacceptability is indicated by the number of question marks, two being the highest
ø = zero, i.e., nothing should be used in the position where ø occurs.
㊥ = special note on *kanji* orthography

A

a adj. **[indefinite article (an before a vowel), used to mean oneness, a generic term, sameness, "a person called," and "per"]**

1. hi⌈to⌉tsu no N 一つのN [one (thing)], hi⌈to⌉ri no N 一人のN [one (person)], ø

NOTE: Often not expressed in Japanese. When expressed, counters are commonly used such as *koohii ip-pai* for "a cup of coffee." SEE APPENDIX II

EX. (**a**) Bob is a student at the University of Tokyo.
ボブは東大の({ø/*一人の/*一つの})学生です。
*Bobu wa Toodai no ({ø/*hitori no/*hitotsu no}) gakusei desu.*
(**b**) There lived an old man in the village.
その村に{一人の/*一つの/*ø}老人が住んでいた。
*Sono mura ni {hitori no/*hitotsu no/*ø} roojin ga sunde ita.*
(**c**) That's surely a possibility, isn't it?
それは確かに{一つの/?ø/*一人の}可能性でしょうね。
*Sore wa tashikani {hitotsu no/?ø/*hitori no} kanoo-sei deshoo ne.*

NOTE: The example below shows that counters normally follow the nouns they modify; more specifically, they are found before the verb. *Is-satsu* may be omitted, and yet the sentence is perfectly acceptable in Japanese. *Boku wa hon o (is-satsu) katta.* "I bought a book."

2. ⟨-to⟩ i⌈u mono⌉ ⟨〜と⟩いうもの [thing which is called]

EX. A car can be a lethal weapon.
車というものは凶器にもなり得る。
Kuruma to iu mono wa kyooki ni mo nari-uru.

3. -goto ni 〜ごとに [at each recurring occurrence of s.t., without exception], ni-tsuki につき [per]

EX. The rental rate is 20 cents a mile.
レンタル料金は一マイル{ごとに/につき}二十セントです。
Rentaru-ryookin wa ichi-mairu {-goto ni/ni-tsuki} ni-jus-sento desu.

4. ⟨-to⟩ i⌈u hito ⟨〜と⟩いう人 [a person called]

EX. A Miss Cornwell came to see you while you were out.
あなたの留守中にコーンウエルさんという人が会いに来ましたよ。
Anata no rusu-chuu ni Koon'ueru-san to iu hito ga ai ni kimashita yo.

abandon vt. **[for s.o. to give up s.t. completely]**
⟨-o⟩ **su⌈teru** ⟨〜を⟩捨てる ② **[for s.o. to let go of s.t. that has become unnecessary or to sever a relationship]**《throw away, dump, give up》, ⟨-o⟩ **ya⌈meru** ⟨〜を⟩やめる ② **[for s.o. to discontinue s.t. that he/she has been doing, including a plan to do s.t.]**《stop, quit, cancel》, ⟨-o⟩ **da⌈nne⌉n-suru** ⟨〜を⟩断念する ③ •c **[for s.o. to give up hope, etc. unwillingly]**《give up》
㊿ "resign" ▷辞める, otherwise ▷やめる

EX. (**a**) Yoko abandoned any hope of becoming a flight attendant.
よう子はスチュワーデスになる希望を{捨てた/断念した/*やめた}。
*Yooko wa suchuwaadesu ni naru kiboo o {suteta/dannen-shita/*yameta}.*
(**b**) Has John abandoned his plan to teach English in Japan?
ジョンは日本で英語を教える計画を{やめた/捨てた/断念した}のか。
Jon wa Nihon de eigo o oshieru keikaku o {yameta/suteta/dannen-shita} no ka.

NOTE: *Yameru* may be used when the object is a nominalized sentence followed by *no* (such as

A

-ni naru no o) or when the object denotes planning, such as *keikaku*.

abbreviation n. **[a shortened form of a word/phrase]**

1. sho⌈oryaku 省略 •c [an act of omitting/deleting s.t.]

2. rya⌈ku-go 略語 •c [a word that is shortened]

ability n. **[the skill/qualities necessary to do s.t.]**

1. no⌉oryoku 能力 •c [the capability to be able to perform a given task] ((capacity, faculty))

2. sa⌈inoo 才能 •c [innate intellectual or artistic capability, esp. of an outstanding kind] ((talent, gift))

EX. (**a**) I do not doubt his ability to do the job.
彼にその仕事をする{能力/?才能}があることは疑いない。
Kare ni sono shigoto o suru {nooryoku/?sainoo} ga aru koto wa utagai nai.
(**b**) She has a son of great musical ability.
彼女には非常に音楽の{才能/*能力}のある息子がいる。
*Kanojo ni wa hijooni ongaku no {sainoo/*nooryoku} no aru musuko ga iru.*

NOTE: While *nooryoku* refers to a general ability, *sainoo* emphasizes talent in a specific field such as music, art, etc.

abnormal adj. **[not normal]**

fu⌈tsuu dena⌉i (N) 普通でない(N) [not ordinary] ((unusual)), i⌈joona 異常な adj(*na*). **•c [different from the ordinary state of affairs] ((extraordinary)) ↔ seijoona 正常な** adj(*na*). **•c**

EX. The old man began to show abnormal behavior from time to time.
その老人はときどき{普通でない/異常な}行動を見せるようになった。
Sono roojin wa toki-doki {futsuu denai/ijoona} koodoo o miseru yooni natta.

aboard adv./prep. **[on/in/onto an airplane, ship, etc.]**

({hi⌈ko⌉o-ki/fu⌉ne} nado ni) not⌈te ({飛行機/船}などに)乗って /⟨V *te* of *noru* ① ride/

EX. (**a**) All aboard.
皆さん、乗ってください。
Mina-san notte kudasai.
(**b**) Is there a doctor aboard this plane?
この飛行機に医者が乗っていますか。
Kono hikoo-ki ni isha ga notte imasu ka.

about prep. **[concerning, having to do with]**

ni-tsuite について comp. prt.

EX. Do you know anything about that?
それについて何か知っていますか。
Sore ni-tsuite nani-ka shitte imasu ka.

—— adv. **[expressing approximation]**

1. ya⌉ku 約 •c ((approximately)), o⌈yoso およそ ((approximately))

EX. About two hundred people came to the lecture.
{約/およそ}二百人の人が講演会に来ました。
{Yaku/Oyoso} ni-hyaku-nin no hito ga kooen-kai ni kimashita.

2. -gurai 〜ぐらい ((approximately))

EX. I saw about fifty cars in the parking lot when I arrived at the office.
事務所に着いたとき、駐車場に五十台ぐらい車がとまっているのを見ました。
Jimu-sho ni tsuita toki, chuusha-joo ni go-juu-dai-gurai kuruma ga tomatte iru no o mimashita.

3. -goro 〜ごろ ((around, toward))

EX. The farewell party is going to start at about 6:30.
送別会は六時半ごろ(に)始まります。
Soobetsu-kai wa roku-ji-han-goro (ni) hajimarimasu.

NOTE: *Yaku* denotes approximation in number, but *-goro* (or *koro*) refers only to time.

above prep./adv. **[existing at a higher point than some standard]**

⟨-no⟩ u⌈e {ni/de/o} ⟨〜の⟩上{に/で/を} n.+prt. **[a position which is higher than s.t./s.o./s.a. or which is in contact with the surface of s.t.] ((on, over, top)), ⟨-no⟩ u⌈e no ho⌉o {ni/de/o} ⟨〜の⟩上の方{に/で/を}** n.+prt. **[in an upward direction]**

EX. (**a**) The moon appeared above the horizon.
地平線の上に月が出た。

A

Chihei-sen no ue ni tsuki ga deta.
(**b**) Look at the airplane flying above.
上の方を飛んでいるあの飛行機をご覧なさい。
Ue no hoo o tonde iru ano hikoo-ki o gorannasai.

absence n. **[the state of not being/existing at a place]**
1. ru⌉su 留守 •c [being away from home/the office]
EX. Did anyone call in my absence?
僕の留守中にだれか電話してきましたか。
Boku no rusu-chuu ni dare-ka denwa-shite kimashita ka.
2. ⟨-ga⟩ na⌉i ko⌈to⌉ ⟨～が⟩ないこと [s.t. not existing]
EX. The absence of freedom is a major problem in this country.
自由がないことがこの国の一大問題だ。
Jiyuu ga nai koto ga kono kuni no ichidai-mondai da.

absent adj. **[not existing]**
1. kes⌈seki-shite 欠席して /⟨V *te* of *kesseki-suru* ⓪ be absent/ •c [not being in class, a meeting, etc.], ya⌈su⌉nde 休んで /⟨V *te* of *yasumu* ① rest/ [resting] 《repose》
EX. Taro is absent from school with the flu.
太郎は流感で学校を{欠席して/休んで}いる。
Taroo wa ryuukan de gakkoo o {kesseki-shite/yasunde} iru.
2. na⌉i 無い adj(*i*). **[for s.t. not to exist]**
EX. Diligence is absent from his character.
彼の性格には勤勉さが無い。
Kare no seikaku ni wa kinben-sa ga nai.

absolutely adv. **[completely and totally/certainly]**
ze⌈ttai ni 絶対に •c [an adverb that indicates the speaker/writer's strong assertion about s.t.] 《by all means》
EX. (**a**) It is absolutely impossible to learn 1,000 kanji in a week.
漢字を一週間で1,000覚えるなんて絶対に不可能だ。
Kanji o is-shuukan de sen oboeru nante zettai ni fu-kanoo da.
(**b**) It is absolutely crucial that Japan and the U.S. share good relations.
日米関係が良好であることは絶対に重要だ。
Nichi-Bei-kankei ga ryookoo dearu koto wa zettai ni juuyoo da.

absorb vt. **[to suck up s.t. completely]**
1. ⟨-o⟩ mu⌈chuu ni saseru ⟨～を⟩夢中にさせる ③ [to take up the entire attention, energy, or time of s.o.]
EX. The study of Japanese absorbed John.
日本語の勉強はジョンを夢中にさせた。
Nihon-go no benkyoo wa Jon o muchuu ni saseta.
NOTE: The above is more naturally expressed as follows: *Jon wa Nihon-go no benkyoo ni muchuu datta.*
2. ⟨-o⟩ kyu⌈ushuu-suru ⟨～を⟩吸収する ③ •c [to take liquid, light, etc. in 《fig. "assimilate"》]
EX. Black is a color which absorbs light well.
黒は光をよく吸収する色です。
Kuro wa hikari o yoku kyuushuu-suru iro desu.
PHRASE: be absorbed in ⟨*-ni*⟩ *muchuu da* ⟨～に⟩夢中だ
EX. Ms. Sakamoto is absorbed in horse racing.
坂本さんは競馬に夢中だ。
Sakamoto-san wa keiba ni muchuu da.

abundance n. **[more than sufficient quantity]**
ho⌈ofu-sa 豊富さ •c

abundant adj. **[more than sufficient]**
yu⌉takana 豊かな adj(*na*). **[to be filled with what is necessary and to spare] 《rich, plentiful》, ho⌈ofuna 豊富な** adj(*na*). **•c [for monetary possessions/experiences/varieties of a thing to be plentiful] 《rich》**
EX. The U.S. is abundant in natural resources.
アメリカは天然資源が{豊か/豊富}だ。
Amerika wa tennen-shigen ga {yutaka/hoofu} da.

academy n. **[a school for special training or a society of famous/important scientists, artists, etc.]**

A

1. a⌈ka⌉demii アカデミー •f
2. ga⌈kuin 学院 •c [an educational institution]
3. ga⌈kushi⌉-in 学士院 •c [a society of learned people]

accent n. [a particular pronunciation associated with an area/social class or stress/high pitch given to (part of) a word]
1. na⌈mari⌉ なまり [a pronunciation which deviates from that of the standard language]
2. kyo⌈osei 強勢 •c [stress], a⌉kusento アクセント •f [stress/high pitch given to (part of) a word]

accept vt. [for s.o. to take/receive s.t. willingly]
⟨-o⟩ u⌈ke-toru ⟨〜を⟩受け取る ① [for s.o. to take s.t. that is offered and hold it in one's hand] ⟪receive, get, take⟫, ⟨-o⟩ u⌈ke-ireru ⟨〜を⟩受け入れる ② [for s.o. to admit s.t./s.o.] ⟪admit, receive⟫, ⟨-ni⟩ o⌈ojiru ⟨〜に⟩応じる ② [for s.o. to answer yes to s.t.] ⟪respond, answer, consent, satisfy, meet⟫

EX. (a) Please accept this present.
この贈り物{を受け取って/*を受け入れて/*に応じて}下さい。
*Kono okuri-mono {o uke-totte/*o uke-irete/*ni oojite} kudasai.*
(b) I am happy to accept your invitation.
喜んでご招待{に応じます/*を受け取ります/*を受け入れます}。
*Yorokonde go-shootai {ni oojimasu/*o uke-torimasu/*o uke-iremasu}.*
(c) Our proposal was not accepted.
我々の提案は{受け入れられなかった/*受け取られなかった/*応じられなかった}。
*Ware-ware no teian wa {uke-ire-rarenakatta/*uke-tora-renakatta/*ooji-rarenakatta}.*

acceptable adj. [for s.t. to be worth taking/receiving]
u⌈ke-ire-rareru 受け入れられる /⟨pot. of *uke-ireru* ② accept/ [can be accepted] ⟪admissible⟫

EX. The terms of payment were not acceptable to us.
その支払い条件は我々にとって受け入れられるものではなかった。
Sono shiharai-jooken wa ware-ware ni-totte uke-ire-rareru mono dewanakatta.

acceptance n. [the action/instance of accepting s.t. or agreement with approval of s.t. or belief in s.t.]
ju⌈daku 受諾 •c [an act of accepting s.o.'s proposal or offer as it is] ⟪approval⟫, yo⌈onin 容認 •c [an act of admitting s.t. that is not entirely satisfactory] ⟪admission, permission⟫

access n. [an instance/means of approaching]
se⌈kkin 接近 •c [an act/instance of coming closer], chi⌈kazu⌉ku ho⌈ohoo 近付く方法 •c [a manner of approaching s.t.]

accident n. [an unexpected occurrence of s.t.]
ji⌉ko 事故 •c [a happening caused by human carelessness, etc.] ⟪happening, incident⟫

EX. Hanako had an accident last night.
花子は昨夜事故にあった。
Hanako wa sakuya jiko ni atta.

PHRASE: by accident *guuzen (ni)* 偶然(に) •c ⟪by chance⟫

EX. I met Prof. Gold in Kobe quite by accident.
僕は全く偶然(に)神戸でゴールド先生に会った。
Boku wa mattaku guuzen (ni) Koobe de Goorudo-sensei ni atta.

accidentally adv. [happening unexpectedly/by chance]
gu⌈uzen ni 偶然に •c [happening unexpectedly without any reason] ⟪by accident, by chance⟫

accompaniment n. [in music, a part, usually instrumental, played with the main part for richer effect ⟪fig. "s.t. that accompanies s.t. else"⟫]
ba⌈nsoo 伴奏 •c [an act of playing a musical instrument in an ancillary manner to increase the effectiveness of another instrument/voice]

EX. I want to sing with her piano accompaniment.

彼女のピアノの伴奏で歌いたい。
Kanojo no piano no bansoo de utai-tai.

accompany vt. **[to go with s.t./s.o. 《fig. "play a musical accompaniment"》]**
1. 〈-to〉 **i⌈ssho ni i⌈ku** 〈〜と〉一緒に行く ① **[for s.o./s.a. to go with s.o.]**, 〈-ni〉 **do⌈okoo-suru** 〈〜に〉同行する ③ •c **[for s.o. to go with s.o.]**

EX. Taro accompanied Hanako to the bus stop.
太郎はバス停まで花子{と一緒に行った/に同行した}。
Taroo wa basu-tei made Hanako {to issho ni itta/ni dookoo-shita}.

2. (**u⌈ta no**) **ba⌈nsoo o suru** (歌の)伴奏をする ③ •c **[for s.o. to play a musical accompaniment]**

EX. Her mother accompanied Masako's singing on the piano.
母親はピアノで正子の歌の伴奏をした。
Haha-oya wa piano de Masako no uta no bansoo o shita.

accomplish vt. **[for s.o. to succeed in doing s.t.]**
〈-o〉 **ya⌈ri-toge⌉ru** 〈〜を〉やり遂げる ② **[for s.o. to carry s.t. to successful completion]** **《complete, achieve, carry out》**

EX. Don accomplished the difficult assignment.
ドンは困難な課題をやり遂げた。
Don wa konnanna kadai o yari-togeta

according to [based on a reliable source]
〈-ni〉 {**yore⌉ba/yo⌈ru to**} **Sinf. so⌉oda** 〈〜に〉{よれば/よると}Sinf.そうだ

EX. According to this morning's paper, there was a terrible train accident in Kyushu yesterday.
今朝の朝刊に{よれば/よると}、昨日九州でひどい列車事故があったそうだ。
Kesa no chookan ni {yoreba/yoru to}, kinoo Kyuushuu de hidoi ressha-jiko ga atta sooda.

accordion n.
a⌈ko⌉odeon アコーデオン •f

EX. Can you play the accordion?
アコーデオンが弾けますか。
Akoodeon ga hike-masu ka.

account n. **[a counting or reporting]**
1. ko⌈oza 口座 •c **[a sum of money kept in a bank]**

EX. Excuse me. I would like to open an account with your bank.
すみません。おたくの銀行で口座を開きたいんですが。
Sumimasen. Otaku no ginkoo de kooza o hiraki-tai n desu ga.

2. ha⌈nashi⌉ 話 **[an act/instance of speaking 《fig. "rumor"》]** **《story》**, **se⌈tsumei** 説明 •c **[an act/instance of explaining the content of/reason for/significance of s.t.]**

EX. (**a**) Elizabeth gave me an interesting account of her trip.
エリザベスは私に旅行の面白い{話/?説明}をしてくれた。
Erizabesu wa watashi ni ryokoo no omoshiroi {hanashi/?setsumei} o shite kureta.
(**b**) I want to hear his account of what happened.
何があったのか彼の{説明/話}を聞きたい。
Nani ga atta no ka kare no {setsumei/hanashi} o kiki-tai.

—— vt. [for s.o./s.t. to explain s.t.]
〈-ni〉 {〈-o〉/〈-ni-tsuite〉} **se⌈tsumei-suru** 〈〜に〉{〈〜を〉/〈〜について〉}説明する ③ •c **[for s.o. to give an explanation of s.t. to s.o.]**

EX. One cannot account for a person's tastes.
人の好き嫌い{を/について}説明することはできない。
Hito no suki-kirai {o/ni-tsuite} setsumei-suru koto wa dekinai.

NOTE: A similar Japanese proverb is *Tade kuu mushi mo suki-zuki.*

accuracy n. **[the state of being correct/exact]**
se⌈ikaku-sa 正確さ /〈stem of *seikakuna* adj(*na*). accurate + suf. *sa* ness/ •c **[the degree to which s.t. is correct and free from error]**

EX. Grammatical accuracy is important.
文法の正確さは重要です。
Bunpoo no seikaku-sa wa juuyoo desu.

accurate adj. **[exact and precise]**
se⌈ikakuna 正確な adj(*na*). **[in accord with fact and reliable]**

A

EX. Is your watch accurate?
あなたの時計は正確ですか。
Anata no tokei wa seikaku desu ka.

accurately adv. **[exactly/precisely]**
se⌈ikakuni 正確に /⟨adj(*na*). *ni* of *seikakuna* accurate/ •c [without any mistake]

EX. Speaking accurately is more important than speaking fluently.
正確に話すことは流暢に話すことよりも重要です。
Seikakuni hanasu koto wa ryuuchooni hanasu koto yori mo juuyoo desu.

accuse vt **[for s.o. to find fault with s.o.]**
⟨-o⟩ hi⌉nan-suru ⟨～を⟩非難する ③ •c [for s.o. to criticize s.o./s.t.], ⟨-o⟩ se⌈me⌉ru ⟨～を⟩せめる ③ [for s.o. to press s.o. hard verbally/physically] ⟪blame, attack, criticize⟫
㊥ "striking an opponent in order to beat him" ▷攻める, otherwise ▷責める

EX. Mary accused Morris of drinking her coke.
マリーはモーリスが彼女のコーラを飲んだと{責めた/非難した}。
Marii wa Moorisu ga kanojo no koora o nonda to {semeta/hinan-shita}.

accustom vt. **[to make s.t. familiar]**
⟨-ni⟩ na⌈ra⌉su ⟨～に⟩慣らす ① [for s.o. to make s.o. get used to s.t.] ⟪habituate⟫
PHRASE: accustom oneself to ⟨*-ni*⟩ *nareru* ⟨～に⟩慣れる ③

EX. Try to accustom yourself to driving on the left side of the road.
道路の左側を運転することに慣れるように努力して下さい。
Dooro no hidari-gawa o unten-suru koto ni nareru yooni doryoku-shite kudasai.

ache vi. **[for a part of the body to have pain]**
i⌈ta⌉mu 痛む ①, i⌈ta⌉i 痛い adj(*i*). **[for s.o./s.a. to experience an unpleasant physical sensation, often in a particular part of the body] ⟪painful, sore, hurt⟫**

EX. My tooth aches.
歯が{痛む/痛い}。
Ha ga {itamu/itai}.

achieve vt. **[for s.o. to do s.t. successfully]**
⟨-o⟩ na⌈shi-toge⌉ru ⟨～を⟩成し遂げる ② ⟪accomplish, carry out⟫, ⟨-o⟩ ta⌈ssei-suru ⟨～を⟩達成する ③ •c [for s.o. to attain s.t.] ⟪attain⟫

EX. The scientist achieved his plan.
科学者はその計画を{成し遂げた/達成した}。
Kagaku-sha wa sono keikaku o {nashi-togeta/tassei-shita}.

achievement n. **[what s.o. achieves/achieved]**
gyo⌈oseki 業績 •c [what one has accomplished] ⟪result⟫, ko⌈oseki 功績 •c [some accomplishment which is to s.o.'s great credit] ⟪contribution⟫, ta⌈ssei 達成 •c [an act/instance of achieving s.t.] ⟪accomplishment, attainment⟫

EX. (**a**) That is a great scientific achievement.
それは科学上の偉大な{功績/?業績/*達成}だ。
*Sore wa kagaku-joo no idaina {kooseki/?gyooseki/*tassei} da.*
(**b**) The achievement of her goal was difficult.
彼女の目的{達成/*功績/*業績}は困難だった。
*Kanojo no mokuteki-{tassei/*kooseki/*gyooseki} wa konnan datta.*
(**c**) His achievements in this field are highly regarded.
彼のこの分野における{業績/功績/*達成}は高く評価されている。
*Kare no kono bun'ya ni okeru {gyooseki/kooseki/*tassei} wa takaku hyooka-sarete iru.*

acid n. **[any of a class of substances containing hydrogen that can be replaced by a metal to form a salt]**
sa⌉n 酸 •c
—— adj. **[having a bitter, sharp taste]**
san⌈mi ga a⌉ru (N) 酸味がある(N) [having a sour taste]
PHRASE: acid rain *sansei-u* 酸性雨 •c

acknowledge vt. **[for s.o.to accept/admit as]**
⟨-o⟩ mi⌈tomeru ⟨～を⟩認める ② [for s.o. to perceive or consent to the value or correctness of s.t./s.o./s.a.] ⟪see, notice,

recognize, appreciate, approve)), ⟨-o⟩ **sho⌈onin-suru** ⟨〜を⟩承認する ③ •c **[to recognize or approve s.t./s.o.]** ((recognize, approve))

EX. Country A acknowledged the sovereignty of Country B.
A国はB国の主権を{認めた/承認した}。
Ei-koku wa bii-koku no shuken o {mitometa/shoonin-shita}.

acknowledg(e)ment n. **[an act of acknowledging s.t./s.o.]**
sho⌈onin 承認 •c ((approval, recognition))

acquaint vt. **[for s.o.to cause s.o. to know]**
⟨-ni⟩ ⟨-o⟩ **shi⌈raseru** ⟨〜に⟩⟨〜を⟩知らせる ② **[for s.o. to cause s.o. to become aware of s.t.]** ((inform, notify, tell))

PHRASE: be acquainted with ⟨-o⟩ *shitte iru* ⟨〜を⟩知っている ② ((know))

EX. I have long been acquainted with the man.
その男のことは前から知っています。
Sono otoko no koto wa mae kara shitte imasu.

acquaintance n. **[s.o. known]**
shi⌈ri-ai 知り合い

EX. Dr. Nishitani is an old acquaintance of our family.
西谷博士は私たちの古くからの知り合いです。
Nishitani-hakase wa watashi-tachi no furuku kara no shiri-ai desu.

acquire vt. **[for s.o. to get/gain/learn s.t. by one's own efforts/actions]**
⟨-o⟩ {**e⌉ru/u⌉ru**} ⟨〜を⟩得る ② **[for s.o. to get s.t. ⟨w⟩]** ((obtain, get, gain, win)), ⟨-o⟩ **shu⌈utoku-suru** ⟨〜を⟩習得する ③ •c **[for s.o. to learn and internalize s.t.]** ((learn)), ⟨-o⟩ **ka⌈kutoku-suru** ⟨〜を⟩獲得する ③ •c **[for s.o. to succeed in getting hold of s.t. valued and abstract with effort]** ((get, obtain))

NOTE: *Uru* is a classical form and can be used only in this form. That is, it does not have any conjugation.

EX. (**a**) John worked hard to acquire a good knowledge of Japanese.
ジョンは日本語の十分な知識を{得る/習得する/?獲得する}ために一生懸命(に)勉強した。
Jon wa Nihon-go no juubunna chishiki o {{eru/uru}/shuutoku-suru/?kakutoku-suru} tame ni isshoo-kenmei (ni) benkyoo-shita.
(**b**) The museum acquired a rare painting.
美術館は珍しい絵画を{得た/獲得した/*習得した}。
*Bijutsu-kan wa mezurashii kaiga o {eta/kakutoku-shita/*shuutoku-shita}.*

acquisition n. **[an acquiring]**
ka⌈kutoku 獲得 •c

EX. Child language acquisition is a hot area of linguistic research today.
幼児の言語獲得は今日の言語研究の先端分野だ。
Yooji no gengo-kakutoku wa konnichi no gengo-kenkyuu no sentan-bunya da.

acre n.
e⌉ekaa エーカー •f (=4,046.8m²)

across prep. **[from one side to the other side of]**
⟨-no⟩ **mu⌈koo(-gawa) ni** ⟨〜の⟩向こう(側)に **[at/to a point opposite an intervening object]** ((beyond))

EX. The bank is across the street.
銀行は道の向こう側にあります。
Ginkoo wa michi no mukoo-gawa ni arimasu.

PHRASE: go across *oodan-suru* 横断する ③ •c

act vt. **[to do s.t., including playing a role]**
1. **ko⌈odoo-suru** 行動する ③ •c **[for s.o./s.a. to behave in a certain way]** ((behave))

EX. Think before you act.
行動する前に考えよ。
Koodoo-suru mae ni kangaeyo.

2. ⟨-no⟩ **ya⌈ku⌉ o tsu⌈tome⌉ru** ⟨〜の⟩役を務める ② **[for s.o. to play some role]** ((serve as))

EX. Mr. Henderson acted as chairperson of the new committee.
ヘンダーソン氏は新しい委員会の議長の役を務めた。
Hendaason-shi wa atarashii iin-kai no gichoo no yaku o tsutometa.

— n. **[part of a play that comes between curtains]**

A

ma⌈ku⌉ 幕 •c **[a drapery concealing the stage, etc., from the audience 《fig. "part of a play that comes between curtains"》]**

EX. The play has three acts.
劇は三幕ものです。
Geki wa san-maku-mono desu.

PHRASE: between acts *maku-ai* 幕あい

acting n. **[performing]**
e⌉ngi 演技 •c [an act of performing by actors, athletes, acrobats, etc.]

—— adj. **[temporarily taking over the position of]**
-dairi ～代理

EX. Prof. Ichiro Morita is acting chairman of the English Department.
森田一郎先生は英語学科の学科長代理です。
Morita Ichiroo-sensei wa eigo-gakka no gakka-choo-dairi desu.

action n. **[the doing of s.t.]**
ko⌈odoo 行動 •c [the act of moving one's body for a purpose] 《behavior》, ka⌈tsudoo 活動 •c [active movement], ko⌉oi 行為 •c [s.t. one does willfully]

EX. (**a**) The President took prompt action on the matter.
大統領はその件で迅速な{行動/*活動/*行為}を取った。
*Daitooryoo wa sono ken de jinsokuna {koodoo/*katsudoo/*kooi} o totta.*
(**b**) The new director took action.
新しいディレクターは{活動/行動/*行為}を開始した。
*Atarashii direkutaa wa {katsudoo/koodoo/*kooi} o kaishi-shita.*
(**c**) Richard's action left no room for excuse.
リチャードの{行為/行動/*活動}は弁解の余地がなかった。
*Richaado no {kooi/koodoo/*katsudoo} wa benkai no yochi ga nakatta.*

active adj. **[characterized by positive activity]**
1. ka⌈tsudoo-tekina 活動的な adj(*na*). **•c**

EX. Hanako is a very active housewife.
花子はとても活動的な主婦だ。
Hanako wa totemo katsudoo-tekina shufu da.

PHRASE: active volcano *kak-kazan* 活火山 **•c**, active voice *noodoo-tai* 能動態 **•c** ↔ passive voice *judoo-tai* 受動態 **•c**, *uke-mi* 受け身

2. (⟨-ni⟩) se⌈kkyoku-tekina (⟨～に⟩)積極的な adj(*na*). **•c [inclined to act on one's own initiative 《fig. "agreeable"》] 《positive》**

EX. Yoshio played an active part in the event.
良男はその催し物で積極的な役割を演じた。
Yoshio wa sono moyooshi-mono de sekkyoku-tekina yakuwari o enjita.

activity n. **[the state/instance of being active]**
ka⌈tsudoo 活動 •c [active movement]

EX. Club activities start at 3:30.
クラブ活動は三時半から始まる。
Kurabu-katsudoo wa san-ji-han kara hajimaru.

actor n. **[a person who acts in a play/movie/TV drama]**
ha⌈iyuu 俳優 •c [a person who acts in dramatic performances as a profession] 《player》, ya⌈kusha 役者 •c [a person who plays a role in a dramatic performance 《fig. "a person who can pretend to be s.o. else"》] 《player》

actress n. **[a female actor]**
jo⌈yuu 女優 •c [a female actor in a movie, TV drama, etc.], ya⌈kusha 役者 •c [a person who plays a role in a dramatic performance 《fig. "a person who can pretend to be s.o. else"》]

actual adj. **[existing in reality]**
ji⌈ssai no N 実際のN •c 《real》

EX. Show us a few actual examples.
私たちに実際の例をいくつか見せて下さい。
Watashi-tachi ni jissai no rei o ikutsu-ka misete kudasai.

actually adv. **[really/in fact]**
ji⌈ssai wa 実際は •c 《in reality》

EX. He looks like a teenager but he's actually 25.
彼はティーンエージャーのように見えるけれど、実際は二十五歳なんですよ。
Kare wa tiin-eijaa no yooni mieru keredo, jissai wa ni-juu-go-sai na n desu yo.

acute adj. **[severe and sharp]**
su⌈rudo⌉i 鋭い adj(*i*). **[for a knife/pen/light/attack/mind/behavior/pain/sound/eyes/ears/observation/words/judgment to be capable of cutting/piercing s.t. (figuratively)]** ⟪sharp, pointed, keen⟫, **ha⌈geshi⌉i** 激しい adj(*i*). **[of an action/state/character/emotion being extremely strong in force/degree]** ⟪violent, vehement, fervent⟫ ↔ **nibui** 鈍い adj(*i*).

EX. John felt an acute pain in his left leg.
ジョンは左足に{鋭い/激しい}痛みを感じた。
Jon wa hidari ashi ni {surudoi/hageshii} ita-mi o kanjita.

A.D.
{ki⌉gen/se⌈ireki} {紀元/西暦} •c ↔ **kigen-zen** 紀元前 •c

EX. The temple was built in 780 A.D.
そのお寺は{紀元/西暦}780年に建てられた。
Sono o-tera wa {kigen/seireki} nana-hyaku-hachi-juu-nen ni tate-rareta.

adapt vt. **[for s.o. to make s.t. (more) suitable by changing it]**
⟨-o⟩ ⟨-ni⟩ te⌈kioo-saseru ⟨〜を⟩⟨〜に⟩適応させる ② •c /⟨causative of *tekioo-suru* ③ adapt oneself/

EX. Anyone living for the first time in a foreign country should adapt his behavior to that of the host country.
初めて外国で暮らす人は、自分の行動をその国の様式に適応させるべきだ。
Hajimete gaikoku de kurasu hito wa, jibun no koodoo o sono kuni no yooshiki ni tekioo-saseru-beki da.

adaptation n. **[an act/instance of adapting s.t.]**
te⌈kioo 適応 •c ⟪accommodation⟫, **ho⌈n'an** 翻案 •c **[a writing adapted from an original work]** ⟪an adapted version⟫

adapter n.
a⌈da⌉putaa アダプター •f

add vt. **[for s.o. to put together so as to increase s.t./s.o.]**
⟨-o⟩ ku⌈waeru ⟨〜を⟩加える ②, **⟨-o⟩ ta⌈su** ⟨〜を⟩足す ① **[for s.o. to join s.t. to s.t. else so as to increase the total amount or as a supplement]**, **⟨-ni⟩ ⟨-o⟩ i⌈reru** ⟨〜に⟩⟨〜を⟩入れる ② **[for s.o./s.a. to cause s.t./s.o./s.a. to move into an enclosed space]** ⟪put in, join, insert, include⟫

EX. (a) Did you add the sales tax?
消費税を{加えました/足しました/入れましたか}か。
Shoohi-zei o {kuwaemashita/tashimashita/iremashita} ka.
(b) Shall I add some sugar to your coffee?
コーヒーに砂糖を少し{入れましょう/?加えましょう/?足しましょう}か。
Koohii ni satoo o sukoshi {iremashoo/?kuwaemashoo/?tashimashoo} ka.
(c) Please add sugar to the shopping list.
買い物のリストに砂糖を{加えて/入れて/*足して}下さい。
*Kai-mono no risuto ni satoo o {kuwaete/irete/*tashite} kudasai.*

addition n. **[an adding of numbers]**
ta⌈shi⌉-zan 足し算 **[an adding as an arithmetic operation]**, **tsu⌈ika** 追加 •c **[an act of adding s.t. to s.t. else]**, **ka⌈san** 加算 •c **[an adding of numbers and figures]**

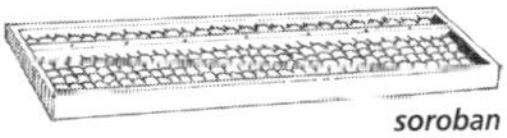

soroban

EX. Keiko is quick at addition when using the abacus.
恵子はそろばんを使っての{足し算/?加算/*追加}が早い。
*Keiko wa soroban o tsukatte no {tashi-zan/?kasan/*tsuika} ga hayai.*

PHRASE: in addition *sono ue* その上, *sarani* さらに ⟪further, moreover⟫

EX. Tony is taking a full load of classes at the university. In addition, he works nights as a security guard at the local factory.
トニーは大学で目一杯授業をとっている。{その上/さらに}夜は地元の工場でガードマンとして働いている。
Tonii wa daigaku de me-ippai jugyoo o totte iru. {Sono ue/Sarani} yoru wa jimoto no koojoo de gaadoman to-shite hataraite iru.

A

PHRASE: in addition to ⟨*-no*⟩ *hoka ni* ⟨〜の⟩ほかに ⟪besides⟫

EX. In addition to *unagi*, Jim also ate *tenpura.*
うなぎのほかに、ジムはてんぷらも食べた。
Unagi no hoka ni, Jimu wa tenpura mo tabeta.

additional adj. **[added/extra]**
tsu⌈ika no N 追加のN •c

EX. How much was the additional charge for that?
その追加(の)費用はいくらでしたか。
Sono tsuika (no) hiyoo wa ikura deshita ka.

address n. **[a place where one lives or a speech]**
1. ju⌉usho 住所 •c [a place where one lives] ⟪**abode**⟫

EX. What is your address?
あなたの住所はどこですか。
Anata no juusho wa doko desu ka.

2. e⌈nzetsu 演説 •c [an act of speaking one's (political) belief/opinion in public]

EX. The Premier made an address to the nation on TV.
総理はテレビで国民に演説をした。
Soori wa terebi de kokumin ni enzetsu o shita.

— vt. **[for s.o. to speak to s.o. or on a topic]**
1. ⟨-ni⟩ ha⌈nashi⌉ o suru ⟨〜に⟩話をする ③ [for s.o. to speak to s.o.]

EX. The dean addressed the students.
学部長は学生に話をした。
Gakubu-choo wa gakusei ni hanashi o shita.

2. ⟨-ni-tsuite⟩ ha⌈na⌉su ⟨〜について⟩話す ① [for s.o. to speak on a topic]

EX. The ambassador addressed the question of peace.
外交官は平和の問題について話した。
Gaikoo-kan wa heiwa no mondai ni-tsuite hanashita.

adequate adj. **[sufficient or suitable]**
1. ju⌈ubu⌉nna 十分な adj(*na*). **•c [as much as necessary]** ⟪**enough, plentiful**⟫

EX. It is said that the city has an adequate supply of water.
市には十分な水の供給量があるそうだ。
Shi ni wa juubunna mizu no kyookyuu-ryoo ga aru sooda.

2. te⌈kisetsuna 適切な adj(*na*). **•c [proper for a purpose]** ⟪**proper, pertinent, fit, suitable, appropriate**⟫

EX. He couldn't come up with adequate evidence to support his theory.
彼は自分の理論を裏付けるのに適切な証拠をあげることができなかった。
Kare wa jibun no riron o urazukeru no ni tekisetsuna shooko o ageru koto ga dekinakatta.

adjacent adj. **[next to each other]**
to⌈nari-a⌉tta N 隣あったN /⟨Vinf. past of *tonari-au* ① become next to each other/

EX. We reserved two adjacent rooms.
私たちは隣あった二部屋を予約した。
Watashi-tachi wa tonari-atta futa-heya o yoyaku-shita.

adjective n.
ke⌈iyo⌉o-shi 形容詞 •c

adjust vt. **[for s.o. to alter s.t. so as to make it fit]**
⟨-o⟩ cho⌈osei-suru ⟨〜を⟩調整する ③ •c [for s.o. to make an adjustment to] ⟪**change**⟫

EX. The photographer adjusted the camera angle.
写真家はカメラ・アングルを調整した。
Shashin-ka wa kamera-anguru o choosei-shita.

adjustment n. **[an act of adjusting s.t.]**
cho⌈osei 調整 •c

administration n. **[management of an institution]**
ka⌉nri-u⌈n'ei 管理運営 •c [an act of seeing that s.t. is managed well] ⟪**management, control, supervision**⟫, **gyo⌈osei 行政 •c [management of governmental affairs]** ⟪**government**⟫

EX. (**a**) The college expanded under his able administration.
大学は彼の巧みな{管理運営/*行政}のもとに発展した。
Daigaku wa kare no takumina {kanri-

*un'ei/*gyoosei} no moto ni hatten-shita.*
(**b**) Administration, legislation, and judicature constitute three independent powers of government.
{行政/*管理運営}、立法、司法が、統治の分立する三権を構成する。
*{Gyoosei/*Kanri-un'ei}, rippoo, shihoo ga, toochi no bunritsu-suru sanken o koosei-suru.*

admiral n.
ka⌈igun-ta⌉ishoo 海軍大将 •c

admiration n. **[an act/target of admiring s.t./s.o.]**
sho⌈osan 賞賛 •c ⟪praise⟫, **sho⌈osan no ma⌈to 賞賛の的 [a target of admiring]**

EX. Noam has the admiration of the entire class.
ノームはクラス全員の{賞賛の的/*賞賛}だ。
*Noomu wa kurasu zen'in no {shoosan no mato/*shoosan} da.*

NOTE: *Shoosan* 賞賛 is sometimes written as 称賛 with the same meaning.

admire vt. **[for s.o. to regard s.o./s.t. with wonder]**
⟨-o⟩ **sho⌈osan-suru ⟨～を⟩賞賛する** ③ •c ⟪praise⟫

EX. Everybody admired Yumi's charm.
だれもが由美の魅力を賞賛した。
Dare-mo ga Yumi no miryoku o shoosan-shita.

NOTE: *Shoosan* 賞賛 is sometimes written as 称賛 with the same meaning.

admission n. **[allowing s.o. to enter somewhere or an entrance fee]**
1. **kyo⌉ka 許可** •c **[an act of allowing s.o. to do s.t. he/she wants to do]** ⟪permission⟫

EX. Taro was given admission to the college of his choice.
太郎は自分が入りたかった大学から入学許可をもらった。
Taroo wa jibun ga hairi-takatta daigaku kara nyuugaku-kyoka o moratta.

2. **nyu⌈ujo⌉o-ryoo 入場料** •c **[an entrance fee]**

EX. Admission to the concert is ¥5,000.
音楽会の入場料は五千円です。
Ongaku-kai no nyuujoo-ryoo wa go-sen-en desu.

admit vt. **[for s.o. to permit s.o. to enter somewhere ⟪fig. "allow s.o.'s accusation to enter into one's own mind," "acknowledge"⟫]**
1. ⟨-ni⟩ **ha⌉iru ko⌈to⌉ o yu⌈ru⌉su ⟨～に⟩入ることを許す** ① **[for s.o. to allow s.o. to enter somewhere]**

EX. Bill was admitted to the Japanese School at Middlebury.
ビルはミドルベリーの日本語学校に入ることを許された。
Biru wa Midoruberii no Nihon-go-gakkoo ni hairu koto o yurusa-reta.

2. ⟨-o⟩ **mi⌈tomeru ⟨～を⟩認める** ② **[for s.o. to perceive or consent to the value or correctness of s.t./s.o./s.a.]** ⟪see, notice, recognize, acknowledge, appreciate, approve⟫

EX. Jiro admitted his mistake.
次郎は自分の誤りを認めた。
Jiroo wa jibun no ayamari o mitometa.

adopt vt. **[for s.o. to take s.t./s.o. as one's own]**
1. ⟨-o⟩ **sa⌈iyoo-suru ⟨～を⟩採用する** ③ •c **[for s.o. to decide to use s.t./s.o. after careful consideration]** ⟪employ, use, take⟫

EX. The publisher adopted our ideas.
出版社は我々のアイデアを採用した。
Shuppan-sha wa ware-ware no aidea o saiyoo-shita.

2. **yo⌈oshi ni suru 養子にする** ③ **[for s.o. to take s.o. into one's own family as a child]**

EX. After the war, Chinese families adopted many Japanese children.
戦後、中国人の家庭が多くの日本人の子供を養子にした。
Sengo, Chuugoku-jin no katei ga ooku no Nihon-jin no kodomo o yooshi ni shita.

adorn vt. **[for s.o. to serve as an ornament to s.t.]**
⟨-o⟩ **ka⌈zaru ⟨～を⟩飾る** ① **[for s.o. to arrange s.t. effectively so as to make it appear**

A

A

beautiful 《fig. "embellish," "exhibit"》] 《decorate, ornament, embellish》
EX. The girl adorned her room with flowers.
少女は部屋を花で飾った。
Shoojo wa heya o hana de kazatta.

adult n. **[grown to full size/strength or matured mentally/physically]**
o⌈tona 大人 [s.o./s.a. that is grown up], se⌈ijin 成人 •c [s.o. that is grown up]
EX. (**a**) You are already an adult, so you should know better.
もう{大人/??成人}なんだから、もう少し分別がなくちゃ。
Moo {otona/??seijin} na n da kara, moo sukoshi funbetsu ga nakucha.
(**b**) This is a movie for adults.
これは{成人/?大人}向きの映画です。
Kore wa {seijin/?otona}-muki no eiga desu.

advance vt. **[for s.o. to cause s.o./s.t. to move forward 《fig. "suggest," "promote"》]**
〈-o〉 te⌈ian-suru 〈〜を〉提案する ③ •c [for s.o. to put s.t. forward for discussion or adoption] 《propose, suggest》
EX. The professor advanced a new scheme.
教授は新構想を提案した。
Kyooju wa shin-koosoo o teian-shita.

— vi. **[to go forward 《fig. "progress," "increase"》]**
1. sho⌈oshin-suru 昇進する ③ •c [for s.o. to be promoted to a higher position] 《be promoted》
EX. Saburo advanced to the position of department manager.
三郎は部長に昇進した。
Saburoo wa buchoo ni shooshin-shita.
2. shi⌉npo-suru 進歩する ③ •c [to make steady improvement] 《progress》
EX. Teresa has advanced in her Japanese ability.
テレサの日本語力は進歩した。
Teresa no Nihon-go-ryoku wa shinpo-shita.
3. su⌈sumu 進む ① [to go forward of one's/its own accord 《fig. "make progress," "become advanced," "to feel inclined"》] 《march forward, progress》
EX. The troops advanced against the enemy.
軍隊は敵に向かって進んだ。
Guntai wa teki ni mukatte susunda.

— n.
shi⌉npo 進歩 •c [moving ahead in knowledge, ability, social conditions, etc.]
EX. Computer science has made rapid advances recently.
コンピューター科学は最近長足の進歩を遂げた。
Konpyuutaa-kagaku wa saikin choosoku no shinpo o togeta.
PHRASE: in advance *mae-motte* 前もって
EX. You have to pay in advance.
代金は前もって支払って下さい。
Daikin wa mae-motte shiharatte kudasai.
PHRASE: advance sale *mae-uri* 前売り

advantage n. **[a more favorable position]**
1. yu⌉urina ta⌈chiba 有利な立場 [an advantageous position]
EX. The French have an advantage over the Japanese in studying Spanish.
フランス人は日本人よりスペイン語の学習で有利な立場にある。
Furansu-jin wa Nihon-jin yori Supein-go no gakushuu de yuurina tachiba ni aru.
2. a⌈dobante⌉eji アドバンテージ •f [the point after deuce in tennis]
PHRASE: take advantage of 〈-o〉 *riyoo-suru* 〈〜を〉利用する ③ •c
EX. Take advantage of every opportunity to speak Japanese.
あらゆる機会を利用して日本語を話しなさい。
Arayuru kikai o riyoo-shite Nihon-go o hanashinasai.

advantageous adj. **[giving advantage to s.o./s.t.]**
yu⌉urina 有利な adj(*na*). **•c [having an advantage or giving an advantage to s.o.] 《profitable, gainful, lucrative》 ↔ furina 不利な** adj(*na*). **•c; yu⌈uekina 有益な** adj(*na*). **•c [yielding profit/benefit] 《profitable, beneficial》 ↔ muekina 無益な** adj(*na*). **•c**

EX. (a) I don't believe that it is an advantageous policy for the people.
それは国民にとって{有益な/*有利な}政策であるとは思えない。
*Sore wa kokumin ni totte {yuuekina/ *yuurina} seisaku dearu to wa omoe-nai.*
(b) The court passed a sentence more advantageous to the wife.
裁判所は妻の方に{有利な/*有益な}判決を下した。
*Saiban-sho wa tsuma no hoo ni {yuurina/*yuuekina} hanketsu o kudashita.*
(c) Buying tax-free national bonds is more advantageous than putting money in the bank.
銀行に預けるより、無税の国債を買う方が{有利/?有益}だ。
Ginkoo ni azukeru yori, mu-zei no kokusai o kau hoo ga {yuuri/?yuueki} da.

adventure n. **[a dangerous undertaking]**
bo⌈oken 冒険 •c [the act of doing s.t. dangerous or s.t. that may not be successful] ⟪risk⟫

EX. Tom likes adventure.
トムは冒険が好きだ。
Tomu wa booken ga suki da.

adventurous adj. **[fond of adventure]**
bo⌈oken-zuki no N 冒険好きのN

EX. Mark Twain wrote a lot about adventurous boys.
マーク・トゥエーンは冒険好きの少年の話をたくさん書いた。
Maaku Tueen wa booken-zuki no shoonen no hanashi o takusan kaita.

adverb n.
fu⌈kushi 副詞 •c

advertise vt. **[for s.o. to make generally/publicly known]**
⟨-o⟩ ko⌈okoku-suru ⟨〜を⟩広告する ③ •c

advertisement n. **[a public notice offering merchandise, service, etc.]**
ko⌈okoku 広告 •c [PR]

EX. We put an advertisement for our car in the newspaper.
私たちは車の広告を新聞に出した。
Watashi-tachi wa kuruma no kookoku o shinbun ni dashita.

advice n. **[an opinion given as to what to do]**
chu⌈ukoku 忠告 •c [s.t. which s.o. tells the other to do or not to do out of consideration for the other], a⌈doba⌉isu アドバイス •f [a personal suggestion to do or not to do s.t. given usually by s.o. higher in rank or older in age such as a professor to s.o. lower in status or younger in age such as a student]

EX. Follow your teacher's advice.
先生の{忠告/アドバイス}に従いなさい。
Sensei no {chuukoku/adobaisu} ni shitagainasai.

advise vt. **[for s.o. to give advice to s.o.]**
⟨-ni⟩ {⟨-yooni⟩/⟨-to⟩} chu⌈ukoku-suru ⟨〜に⟩{⟨〜ように⟩/⟨〜と⟩}忠告する ③ •c [for s.o. to tell s.o. to do or not to do s.t. out of consideration for the other], ⟨-ni⟩ {⟨-yooni⟩/⟨-to⟩} chu⌉ui-suru ⟨〜に⟩{⟨〜ように⟩/⟨〜と⟩}注意する ③ •c [for s.o. to pay/cause s.o. to pay close attention to s.t. or to tell s.o. to be careful so that s.t. undesirable does not occur] ⟪warn⟫

EX. The doctor advised my father not to drink.
医師は父に酒を飲まないように{忠告/注意}した。
Ishi wa chichi ni sake o nomanai yooni {chuukoku/chuui}-shita.

affair n. **[a thing to do ⟪fig. "love affair"⟫]**
ko⌈to⌉ こと [s.t. intangible or a nominalizer forming a noun clause expressing s.t. perceived indirectly by means of one's rational faculties rather than directly through the five senses] ⟪thing, matter⟫, **ko⌈to-gara⌉ 事柄 [s.t. which concerns s.o.]** ⟪matter⟫, **gyo⌉omu 業務 •c [s.t. that must be done as a matter of official business]** ⟪business matters, business, work⟫

EX. (a) This is a private affair.
これはプライベートな{こと/事柄/*業務}です。
*Kore wa puraibeetona {koto/koto-gara/ *gyoomu} desu.*

(**b**) The Ministry of Foreign Affairs manages Japan's affairs with foreign countries.
外務省は日本と外国との{こと/業務/?事柄}を取り扱う。
Gaimu-shoo wa Nihon to gaikoku to no {koto/gyoomu/?koto-gara} o tori-atsukau.

affect vt. **[to produce an effect]**
1. **⟨-ni⟩ e⌈ikyoo-suru ⟨〜に⟩影響する** ③ **•c [to have an effect on s.o./s.t./s.a.]** **⟪influence⟫**

EX. The drought affected the crops.
干ばつが農作物に影響した。
Kanbatsu ga noosaku-butsu ni eikyoo-shita.

2. **⟨-o⟩ ka⌈ndoo-saseru ⟨〜を⟩感動させる /⟨causative of *kandoo-suru* ③ be moved/** ② **•c [to move s.o. emotionally]** **⟪impress, move⟫**

EX. Miki was much affected by the action.
美樹はその行為にとても感動した。
Miki wa sono kooi ni totemo kandoo-shita.

affection n. **[a warm feeling of caring for or loving]**
a⌈ijoo 愛情 •c [an instinctive feeling of loving or wanting to be loved] **⟪love, attachment, fondness⟫**

EX. Many animals show a deep affection for their young.
多くの動物が自分の子供に対して深い愛情を示します。
Ooku no doobutsu ga jibun no kodomo ni taishite fukai aijoo o shimeshimasu.

affirm vt. **[for s.o. to say positively/assertively]**
1.⟨-o⟩ ko⌈otei-suru ⟨〜を⟩肯定する ③ **•c [for s.o. to acknowledge s.t. to be true]** ↔ **⟨-o⟩ hitei-suru ⟨〜を⟩否定する** ③ **•c**

EX. He affirmed the rumor.
彼はそのうわさを肯定した。
Kare wa sono uwasa o kootei-shita.

2. **⟨-to⟩ da⌈nge⌉n-suru ⟨〜と⟩断言する** ③ **•c [for s.o. to declare decisively on the basis of evidence that s.t. is true]**

EX. Masao affirmed that he had never lied to anybody.
政夫は自分はだれにもうそをついたことがないと断言した。
Masao wa jibun wa dare ni mo uso o tsuita koto ga nai to dangen-shita.

affirmation n. **[the act of affirming s.t.]**
1. **ko⌈otei 肯定 •c [an act of acknowledging s.t. to be true]** **⟪acknowledgment⟫**, **da⌈nge⌉n 断言 •c [an act of declaring s.t. decisively]** **⟪declaration⟫**

Africa n.
A⌈furika アフリカ •f

African adj.
A⌈furika no N アフリカのN •f

after prep. **[later in time than ⟪fig. "in search of s.t.," "according to"⟫]**
1. **⟨-no⟩ a⌉to de ⟨〜の⟩後で** n.+prt. **[later in time than]**

EX. After supper I watched TV.
夕食の後でテレビを見た。
Yuushoku no ato de terebi o mita.

2. **⟨-o⟩ mo⌈to⌉mete ⟨〜を⟩求めて /⟨V *te* of *motomeru* ② seek for/ [in search of s.t.]**

EX. I am after a better position in the company.
私は会社でよりよい地位を求めている。
Watashi wa kaisha de yori yoi chii o motomete iru.

3. **⟨-no⟩ na⌈ni china⌉nde ⟨〜の⟩名にちなんで /⟨V *te* of *chinamu* ① be related/ [in imitation of]**

EX. The parents named their son Hideyo after the famous doctor.
両親は有名な医者の名にちなんで、息子を英世と名付けた。
Ryooshin wa yuumeina isha no na ni chinande, musuko o Hideyo to na-zuketa.

—— conj. **[following the time when s.o. has done s.t.]**
Vinf. past a⌉to de Vinf. past後で

EX. After Taro came home from school, he left again to go to his cram school.
太郎は学校から帰宅した後で、塾へ行くためにまた外出した。
Taroo wa gakkoo kara kitaku-shita ato de, juku e iku tame ni mata gaishutsu-shita.

PHRASE: after all *kekkyoku* 結局 •c [finally after various developments along the way], *tootoo* とうとう [some state/situation arises as a final result of s.t.] ((at last)), *yappari* やっぱり [as expected]

EX. Taro married Hanako after all.
太郎は{結局/とうとう/やっぱり}花子と結婚した。
Taroo wa {kekkyoku/tootoo/yappari} Hanako to kekkon-shita.

NOTE: "Vinf. past *ato ni*" may also be used in a limited set of cases where the verb in the main sentence semantically "fills the vacuum" left by (the meaning of) the verb in the subordinate sentence containing *ato*. For example, *Taroo ga kaetta ato ni Hanako ga yatte-kita.* "Hanako came after Taro had left." Here, Taro's leaving is interpreted as "the vacuum" mentioned above and Hanako's coming interpreted as "filling that vacuum."

afternoon n.

go⌉go 午後 •c

EX. (a) The children went swimming in the afternoon.
子供たちは午後泳ぎに行った。
Kodomo-tachi wa gogo oyogi ni itta.
(b) I'll be free in the afternoon.
午後は暇です。
Gogo wa hima desu.

afterward(s) adv. **[later]**

a⌉to de 後で n.+prt. **((later))**

EX. I'll do it afterward(s).
後でします。
Ato de shimasu.

again adv. **[once more or back to a former position/condition]**

1. ma⌈ta また, mo⌈o ichi-do⌉ もう一度 [one more time] ((once more)), fu⌈tatabi 再び [once more ⟨w⟩]

EX. (a) I'd like to see you again soon.
近いうちに{また/もう一度/再び}お目にかかりたいです。
Chikai uchi ni {mata/moo ichi-do/futatabi} o-me ni kakari-tai desu.
(b) He was elected to the position again.
彼は{また/もう一度/再び}その役に選出された。
Kare wa {mata/moo ichi-do/futatabi} sono yaku ni senshutsu-sareta.

2. mo⌉to no yooni もとのように [as before]

EX. Soon after her operation she felt well again.
彼女は手術を受けたけど、すぐもとのように元気になりました。
Kanojo wa shujutsu o uketa kedo, sugu moto no yooni genki ni narimashita.

PHRASE: again and again *nan-do-mo* 何度も

against prep. **[in opposition to/contrast with/contact with s.t./s.o.]**

1. ⟨-ni⟩ ha⌉n-shite ⟨～に⟩反して /⟨V *te* of *han-suru* ③ be contrary to/ [to oppose s.t.] ((contrary to))

EX. Masato married Hiromi against his parents' wishes.
雅人は両親の望みに反して博美と結婚した。
Masato wa ryooshin no nozomi ni han-shite Hiromi to kekkon-shita.

2. ⟨-ni⟩ yo⌈ri-kaka⌉tte ⟨～に⟩寄り掛かって /⟨V *te* of *yori-kakaru* ① lean against/ [leaning on s.t./s.o.]

EX. You must not lean against this white wall.
この白壁に寄り掛かってはいけません。
Kono shira-kabe ni yori-kakatte wa ikemasen.

3. ⟨-o⟩ ha⌈ikei ni ⟨～を⟩背景に n.+prt. **[having s.t. as background]**

EX. Waikiki beach looked beautiful against the setting sun.
沈む太陽を背景にワイキキの浜辺は美しかった。
Shizumu taiyoo o haikei ni Waikiki no hamabe wa utsukushikatta.

age n. **[how old s.o./s.t. is]**

1. to⌈shi⌉ 年 [a 12-month period as measured by the Gregorian calendar], ne⌈nrei 年齢 •c

EX. George looks young for his age.
ジョージは{年/年齢}の割に若く見える。
Jooji wa {toshi/nenrei} no warini wakaku mieru.

2. ji⌈dai 時代 •c [a subinterval on the continuum of past, present, and future

designated for some historical purpose] **⟪period, era⟫**

EX. We live in the electronic age today.
我々は今エレクトロニクスの時代に生きている。
Ware-ware wa ima erekutoronikusu no jidai ni ikite iru.

aged adj. **[old in years]**
to⌈shi-to⌉tta N 年取ったN [(for an animate being) to have existed for a relatively long time], to⌈shi⌉ o ⌈to⌉tte i⌈ru (N) 年を取っている(N) /⟨V *te iru* of *toshi o toru* ① gain years/ [for s.o./s.a. to have existed for a relatively long time] ⟪old⟫

EX. The winner turned out to be an aged woman.
優勝したのは{年取った/年を取っている}女の人だった。
Yuushoo-shita no wa {toshi-totta/toshi o totte iru} onna no hito datta.

agency n. **[a business providing a specified service]**
da⌈iri⌉-ten 代理店 •c [a commercial office doing business usually on behalf of its host company], e⌉ejenshii エージェンシー •f [a company performing a specified service such as travel reservations]

EX. Akiko works for a travel agency.
章子は{旅行代理店/トラベルエージェンシー}に勤めている。
Akiko wa {ryokoo-dairi-ten/toraberu-eejenshii} ni tsutomete iru.

agent n. **[s.o. empowered to act for another]**
da⌈iri-nin 代理人 •c [s.o. who takes the place of s.o. else in an official capacity], e⌉ejento エージェント •f

EX. The negotiation of my contract is left to my agent.
契約交渉は{代理人/エージェント}に任せてある。
Keiyaku-kooshoo wa {dairi-nin/eejento} ni makasete aru.

PHRASE: real estate agent *fu-doosan-gyoosha* 不動産業者 •c

ago adv. **[in the past]**
-ma⌉e (ni) ～前(に) [at an earlier time or in front of] ⟪before, in front of⟫

EX. Sue came to Japan five years ago.
スーは五年前(に)日本へ来た。
Suu wa go-nen-mae (ni) Nihon e kita.

PHRASE: a little while ago *sakki* さっき, *saki-hodo* さきほど, *shibaraku mae ni* しばらく前に

EX. I saw Mr. Tanaka a little while ago.
私は{さっき/さきほど/しばらく前に}田中さんに会いました。
Watashi wa {sakki/saki-hodo/shibaraku mae ni} Tanaka-san ni aimashita.

NOTE: *Saki-hodo* sounds more formal and polite than *sakki*, which is most commonly used in conversation.

agree vi. **[to be in accord with s.o./s.t.]**
1. ⟨-ni⟩ do⌈oi-suru ⟨～に⟩同意する ③ •c [for s.o. to have the same opinion as] ⟪consent to, comply with⟫, ⟨-ni⟩ sa⌈nsei-suru ⟨～に⟩賛成する ③ •c [for s.o. to think that s.o.'s opinion is good and express that openly] ⟪approve of, subscribe to, support⟫ ↔ ⟨-ni⟩ hantai-suru ⟨～に⟩反対する ③ •c; ⟨-to⟩ i⌉ken ga i⌈tchi-suru ⟨～と⟩意見が一致する ③ •c [for one's opinions to match with] ⟪accord⟫

EX. (**a**) The president agreed to the proposal.
社長はその提案{に同意/に賛成/*と意見が一致}した。
*Shachoo wa sono teian {ni dooi/ni sansei/*to iken ga itchi}-shita.*
(**b**) We agreed to work on the project.
我々はその計画を実行することで{同意/賛成/意見が一致}した。
Ware-ware wa sono keikaku o jikkoo-suru koto de {dooi/sansei/iken ga itchi}-shita.
(**c**) I agreed with the manager on game tactics.
試合の作戦に関して監督{に同意/に賛成/と意見が一致}した。
Shiai no sakusen ni kanshite kantoku {ni dooi/ni sansei/to iken ga itchi}-shita.

2. {⟨-to⟩/⟨-ni⟩} a⌉u {⟨～と⟩/⟨～に⟩}あう ① [for two people/objects to come face to face or in contact with each other or to fit each other] ⟪meet, experience, fit, be suitable to⟫

A

NOTE: The particle *to* is chosen when mutuality is under focus, and the particle *ni* is chosen when non-mutuality or unilateral directionality is under focus.

EX. (**a**) The food did not agree with me.
その食物は私には合わなかった。
Sono tabe-mono wa watashi ni wa awanakatta.
(**b**) His statement doesn't agree with the witness's testimony.
彼の供述は目撃者の証言と合わない。
Kare no kyoojutsu wa mokugeki-sha no shoogen to awanai.

㊈ "meet"▷会う, otherwise ▷合う

agreement n. **[being in harmony or accord]**
1. do⌈oi 同意 •c [having the same opinion as others]《**accord, consent**》
2. i⌈tchi 一致 •c [for two or more things to match or be in harmony]《**consensus**》
3. kyo⌈otei 協定 •c [an arrangement agreed upon between people]《**contract, treaty, accord**》

agriculture n. **[work of cultivating soil, producing crops and raising livestock] no⌉ogyoo 農業 •c**《**farming**》

ah int. **[an exclamation expressing pain, delight, regret, disgust, surprise, etc.] a⌉a ああ**

EX. Ah, that feels good!
ああ、気持ちがいい。
Aa, kimochi ga ii.

ahead adv. **[in/to the front]**
sa⌈ki 先 n. **[the end of a stick/stick-like object**《**fig. "future," "the other party"**》**]**《**up, end, first**》, **ze⌈npoo 前方 •c [space in front of the speaker]**《**front**》

EX. (**a**) A: Where's the washroom?
トイレはどこですか。
Toire wa doko desu ka.
B: Straight ahead.
まっすぐ{先/?前方}です。
Massugu {saki/?zenpoo} desu.
(**b**) Construction ahead.
{前方/*先}工事中
*{Zenpoo/*Saki} kooji-chuu*
(**c**) You should always plan ahead.
いつも先を考えて計画を立てるべきだ。
Itsu-mo saki o kangaete keikaku o tateru-beki da.

PHRASE: ahead of *mae ni* 前に

EX. The plane landed ahead of schedule.
飛行機は予定より前に到着した。
Hikoo-ki wa yotei yori mae ni toochaku-shita.

PHRASE: Go ahead. *Doozo (o-saki ni).* どうぞ(お先に)。《After you.》

aid vt. **[for s.o. to help s.o. do s.t.]**
⟨-o⟩ ta⌈suke⌉ru ⟨〜を⟩助ける ② [for s.o./s.a. to provide resources or one's own time/energy to s.o./s.a. to enable it/him/her to escape danger/death/difficulty or to ensure that s.t. goes well]《**help, assist, save**》, **⟨-o⟩ e⌉njo-suru ⟨〜を⟩援助する ③ •c [for s.o. to help s.o. in trouble, esp. financially]**《**assist, support, help**》

EX. Japan should aid economically weaker countries more.
日本は経済的に弱い国をもっと{助ける/援助す}べきだ。
Nihon wa keizai-tekini yowai kuni o motto {tasukeru/enjo-su}-beki da.

—— n. **[assistance]**
e⌉njo 援助 •c [an act/instance of helping s.o. in a troubled situation]《**help, assistance, support**》

EX. The student needed financial aid to continue his education.
学生は学業を続けるため財政的援助を必要としていた。
Gakusei wa gakugyoo o tsuzukeru tame zaisei-teki-enjo o hitsuyoo to shite ita.

aim vt. **[for s.o. to point a weapon so as to hit s.o./s.a./s.t.**《**fig. "direct one's ambition/goal"**》**]**
ne⌈rai o sa⌈dame⌉ru ねらいを定める ② [for s.o. to point a weapon so as to hit s.o./s.a./s.t.《**fig. "direct one's eyes to some target"**》**]**《**target**》

EX. The detective aimed his gun at the fugitive.
刑事は逃走犯に銃のねらいを定めた。
Keiji wa toosoo-han ni juu no nerai o sadameta.

A

— n. **[the act of pointing a weapon so as to hit s.o./s.a./s.t. 《fig. "a goal/target one makes efforts to reach"》]**
mo⌈kuhyoo 目標 •c [s.t. one wishes to achieve] 《target, goal, object, objective》
EX. A: What is your aim in life, Zhang?
張さん、君の人生の目標は何だ。
Chan-san, kimi no jinsei no mokuhyoo wa nan da.
B: My aim is to become a Japanese-speaking lawyer.
僕の目標は日本語の話せる弁護士になることさ。
Boku no mokuhyoo wa Nihon-go no hanase-ru bengo-shi ni naru koto sa.

air n.
ku⌉uki 空気 •c
EX. The air in the cities is polluted.
都会の空気はよごれている。
Tokai no kuuki wa yogorete iru.
PHRASE: on the air *hoosoo-chuu* 放送中

aircraft n.
hi⌈ko⌉o-ki 飛行機 •c 《airplane》

air force n. **[the aviation branch of the armed forces]**
ku⌈ugun 空軍

airline n.
ko⌈okuu-ga⌉isha 航空会社 •c
EX. A: Which airline are you taking to Honolulu?
ホノルルへはどの航空会社を使うの。
Honoruru e wa dono kookuu-gaisha o tsukau no.
B: I'll take Japan Air Lines.
日本航空だよ。
Nihon Kookuu da yo.
NOTE: *Nihon Kookuu* is often abbreviated as *Nikkoo.*

airmail n. **[mail sent by airplane]**
ko⌈okuu-bin 航空便 •c
— vt. **[to send mail by airplane]**
⟨-o⟩ ko⌈okuu-bin de o⌈kuru ⟨～を⟩航空便で送る ①

airplane n.
hi⌈ko⌉o-ki 飛行機 •c 《aircraft》
EX. The airplane crashed in the mountains.
飛行機が山の中に墜落した。
Hikoo-ki ga yama no naka ni tsuiraku-shita.

airport n. **[a place where aircraft can land and take off with facilities for passengers]**
ku⌈ukoo 空港 •c, hi⌈koo-joo 飛行場 •c
NOTE: Always use *kuukoo* with the airport name, for example, *Narita Kuukoo.*
EX. I had my carry-on bag inspected at Haneda Airport.
羽田空港で手荷物の検査を受けた。
Haneda Kuukoo de te-nimotsu no kensa o uketa.

Alabama n.
A⌈rabama アラバマ •f

alarm n. **[a warning sound 《fig. "call to arms"》]**
ke⌈ihoo 警報 •c [a warning of danger] 《warning》
EX. The city hall sent out an alarm.
市役所は警報を発した。
Shi-yakusho wa keihoo o hasshita.
PHRASE: fire alarm *kasai-hoochi-ki* 火災報知器 •c
— vt. **[to make s.o. suddenly afraid or anxious]**
⟨-o⟩ o⌈doroka-se⌉ru ⟨～を⟩驚かせる /⟨causative of *odoroku* ① be surprised/ ② [to surprise and frighten] 《surprise, astonish, astound》
EX. The news alarmed my father.
その知らせは父を驚かせた。
Sono shirase wa chichi o odoroka-seta.
PHRASE: alarm clock *mezamashi-dokei* 目覚まし時計
EX. I set my alarm clock before going to bed.
目覚まし時計をかけて寝た。
Mezamashi-dokei o kakete neta.

alas int. **[an exclamation expressing sorrow/anxiety]**
a⌉a ああ [an exclamation expressing surprise, sorrow, joy, etc.]
EX. Alas, poor David!
ああ、かわいそうなデービッド。
Aa, kawai-soona Deebiddo.

Alaska n.
A⌈rasuka アラスカ •f

A

Albany n.
O⌉orubanii オールバニー •f
album n. **[a book containing a collection of pictures, stamps, etc. or a record, tape, CD, etc. with several pieces by the same performer]**
a⌈rubamu アルバム •f
EX. (**a**) I took out an old album to show him a photograph of my father.
彼に父の写真を見せるために、古いアルバムを出してきた。
Kare ni chichi no shashin o miseru tame ni, furui arubamu o dashite-kita.
(**b**) Celine Dion's new album is to be released next month.
セリーヌ・ディオンの新しいアルバムが来月発売になる。
Seriinu Dion no atarashii arubamu ga raigetsu hatsubai ni naru.
alcohol n.
a⌈rukooru アルコール •f
alcoholic adj. **[containing alcohol]**
a⌈rukooru no ha⌉itta N アルコールの入ったN /⟨Vinf. past of ***hairu*** ① contain/
PHRASE: alcoholic beverage *sake* 酒
— n. **[s.o. addicted to alcohol]**
a⌈rukooru-chu⌉udoku アルコール中毒 •f+c [the state of being addicted to alcohol]
alcove n. **[a small space in a room formed by a recession in the wall]**
to⌈ko-no-ma 床の間 [a recessed section of a Japanese-style guest room where artistic ornaments are displayed]
alert adj. **[observant and watchful]**
yu⌈dan na⌉ku ki o kuba⌉tte iru (N) 油断なく気を配っている(N) /⟨***yudan naku*** **attentively + V*te iru* of *ki o kubaru*** ① **pay attention**/ **[showing no lack of attention]** ⟪**vigilant**⟫, **ki⌈binna 機敏な** adj(*na*). **•c [to be quick in mind and physical movement]** ⟪**smart, quick, quick-witted**⟫, **shi⌈kka⌉ri-shite iru (N) しっかりしている(N)** /⟨**V*te iru* of *shikkari-suru*** ③ **be firm**/ **[for a person/body/structure to be physically/psychologically not easily broken/changed]** ⟪**strong, conscious**⟫
EX. (**a**) Mr. Li Ziyang was always an alert pilot.
李紫陽さんはいつも{油断なく気を配っている/機敏な/?しっかりしている}パイロットだった。
Ri Shiyoo-san wa itsu-mo {yudan naku ki o kubatte iru/kibinna/?shikkari-shite iru} pairotto datta.
(**b**) Grandmother was alert till her last day.
祖母は最期まで{しっかりしていた/*機敏だった/*油断なく気を配っていた}。
*Sobo wa saigo made {shikkari-shite ita/ *kibin datta/*yudan naku ki o kubatte ita}.*
alien adj. **[foreign ⟪fig. "very different and difficult to accept"⟫]**
ga⌈ikoku no N 外国のN •c [foreign]
— n.
ga⌈ikoku⌉-jin 外国人 •c ⟪foreigner⟫
EX. Ms. Wang has lost her alien registration card.
王さんは外国人登録証をなくしてしまった。
Wan-san wa gaikoku-jin-tooroku shoo o nakushite shimatta.
alike adj. **[similar to one another]**
ni⌈te iru (N) 似ている(N) /⟨**V*te iru* of *niru*** ② **resemble**/ **[showing resemblance]** ⟪**similar, resemble**⟫
EX. Jack and Jill are very much alike.
ジャックとジルは大変よく似ている。
Jakku to Jiru wa taihen yoku nite iru.
— adv. **[in the same manner]**
byo⌈odooni 平等に /⟨**adj(*na*). *ni* of *byoodoona* equal**/ **•c [in equal parts and without discrimination]** ⟪**equally, impartially**⟫
EX. Everyone is treated alike here.
ここでは、みんな平等に扱われます。
Koko de wa, minna byoodooni atsukawa-remasu.
alive adj. **[not dead]**
i⌉kite iru (N) 生きている(N) /⟨**V*te iru* of *ikiru*** ② **live**/ ⟪**living**⟫
EX. A: Is the dog dead?
その犬は死んでいますか。
Sono inu wa shinde imasu ka.

A

B: No, it's still alive.
いや、まだ生きています。
Iya, mada ikite imasu.

all adj. **[the entire amount of]**
su˥bete no N すべてのN **[exhaustively inclusive], ze˥nbu no N** 全部のN •c **[covering the whole of], a˥rayu˥ru N** あらゆるN **[all that can be thought of]**

EX. All things being equal, most people desire peace.
{すべての/全部の/あらゆる}条件が同じなら、ほとんどの人は平和を望む。
{Subete no/Zenbu no/Arayuru} jooken ga onaji nara, hotondo no hito wa heiwa o nozomu.

— n. **[without any exception]**
ze˥nbu 全部 •c **[everything/everybody], mi˥nna˥** みんな **[extending to all things/persons/animals concerned]**

EX. (**a**) All of the employees of the company are women.
社員は{全部/みんな}女性です。
Shain wa {zenbu/minna} josei desu.
(**b**) All that we received in inventory yesterday has been sold.
きのう仕入れたのは{全部/みんな}売れた。
Kinoo shi-ireta no wa {zenbu/minna} ureta.

PHRASE: not at all. *doo-itashimashite.* どういたしまして。

EX. A: Thank you very much.
ありがとうございます。
Arigatoo gozaimasu.
B: Not at all.
どういたしまして。
Doo-itashimashite.

NOTE: *Doo-itashimashite* is used in response to "thank you."

PHRASE: all right *daijoobuna* だいじょうぶな adj(*na*)., *ii* いい adj(*i*).

EX. Is tomorrow all right?
明日でも{だいじょうぶ/いい}ですか。
Ashita demo {daijoobu/ii} desu ka.

alley n. **[a narrow street/walk between buildings or a lane in a garden/park]**
ro˥ji 路地 •c **[a narrow street/walk between buildings]** ⟪**lane, alleyway**⟫, **ko-˥michi** 小道 **[a lane in a garden/park]** ⟪**path, lane, trail**⟫

alligator n.
wa˥ni ワニ ⟪**crocodile**⟫

allow vt. **[to permit s.o. to do/have s.t.]**
1. ⟨-o⟩ **yu˥ru˥su** ⟨〜を⟩許す ① **[for s.o. to allow s.o. else to do s.t. freely ⟪fig. "forgive"⟫]** ⟪**let, permit, forgive, excuse, pardon**⟫

EX. They do not allow you to use English at that Japanese school.
あの日本語学校では英語を使うことを許さない。
Ano Nihon-go-gakkoo de wa eigo o tsukau koto o yurusanai.

2. ⟨-ni⟩ ⟨-o⟩ **a˥taeru** ⟨〜に⟩⟨〜を⟩与える ② **[for s.o. to cause/let s.o. have s.t.]**

EX. Mrs. Sato allowed 5,000 yen per month to her son in high school.
佐藤夫人は、高校生の息子に毎月五千円を与えていた。
Satoo-fujin wa, kookoo-sei no musuko ni mai-tsuki go-sen-en o ataete ita.

allowance n. **[an amount of money given regularly]**
ko˥-zukai 小遣い **[an amount of money allocated to a member of the family for his/her own spending]** ⟪**pocket money, spending money**⟫

EX. I got my allowance from my mother instead of from my father.
私は父からではなく母から小遣いをもらった。
Watashi wa chichi kara dewanaku haha kara ko-zukai o moratta.

almost adv. **[very nearly]**
1. **ho˥to˥ndo** ほとんど **[not entirely but very close to so]** ⟪**all but, most, nearly**⟫

EX. (**a**) John got an A in almost all the courses that he took at the university.
ジョンは大学で取った科目のほとんど全部にAをもらった。
Jon wa daigaku de totta kamoku no hotondo zenbu ni ei o moratta.
(**b**) Jim calls his girl friend almost every day.

ジムはガールフレンドにほとんど毎日電話をかけている。
Jimu wa gaaru-furendo ni hotondo mainichi denwa o kakete iru.

2. V*masu* -so˥oni naru V*masu*そうになる ① [to come very close to Ving]

EX. I almost got killed in a car accident.
僕は車の事故で死にそうになったことがある。
Boku wa kuruma no jiko de shini-sooni natta koto ga aru.

alone adj./adv. **[without others]**
hi˦to˥ri de 一人で n.+prt. **[without any other person]** ⟪**by oneself**⟫

EX. (**a**) George was alone at home when the hurricane struck.
ジョージは、ハリケーンが襲ったとき、家に一人でいた。
Jooji wa, harikeen ga osotta toki, ie ni hitori de ita.
(**b**) My ninety-year-old aunt still lives alone.
私の九十歳の叔母はまだ一人で住んでいる。
Watashi no kyuu-jus-sai no oba wa mada hitori de sunde iru.

along prep./adv. **[over or through the length of]**

1. ⟨-ni⟩ **so˥tte** ⟨〜に⟩**沿って /**⟨**V*te* of *sou* ① go parallel with/ [on a line parallel to the length of s.t.]**

EX. Japanese cherry trees were planted along the Potomac River.
日本の桜の木がポトマック川に沿って植えられた。
Nihon no sakura no ki ga Potomakku-gawa ni sotte ue-rareta.

2. (sa˦ki e) **su˦sunde** (先へ)**進んで /**(**V*te* of *susumu* ① advance/ [progressively forward]**

EX. Please move along.
先へ進んでください。
Saki e susunde kudasai.

PHRASE: get along *yatte-iku* やっていく, *kurashite-iku* 暮らしていく

EX. I wonder how Mr. Morishita will get along from now on?
森下さんはこれからどうやって{やって/暮らして}いくんだろう。
Morishita-san wa kore-kara doo yatte {yatte/kurashite}-iku n daroo.

aloud adv. **[speaking/reading with the normal voice]**
ko˥e ni ˦da˥shite 声に出して /(**V*te* of *dasu* ① put out/**

EX. Try and read Japanese aloud as much as possible.
出来るだけ、日本語は声に出して読んでごらんなさい。
Dekiru dake, Nihon-go wa koe ni dashite yonde gorannasai.

alphabet n.
a˦rufabe˥tto アルファベット •f

alphabetically adv.
a˦rufabetto-jun ni アルファベット順に n.+prt. **•f+c**

EX. The names are listed alphabetically.
名前はアルファベット順に載せてあります。
Namae wa arufabetto-jun ni nosete arimasu.

Alps n.
A˦rupusu-sa˥nmyaku アルプス山脈 •f+c

already adv. **[by/before the implied time]**
mo˥o もう [to be no longer in the same state as at some previous time] ⟪**not any more, not any longer, yet, now**⟫, **su˥deni すでに** ⟪**previously**⟫

EX. Tom has already left for Japan.
トムは{もう/すでに}日本へ発ちました。
Tomu wa {moo/sudeni} Nihon e tachimashita.

also adv. **[likewise]**
…mo ma˥ta …もまた ⟪**too, besides, in addition, as well**⟫

EX. Seiichi likes cats. Reiko also likes cats.
清一は猫が好きだ。玲子もまた猫が好きだ。
Seiichi wa neko ga suki da. Reiko mo mata neko ga suki da.

alter vt. **[to make s.t. different]**
⟨**-o**⟩ ⟨**-ni**⟩ **ka˦eru** ⟨〜を⟩⟨〜に⟩**かえる ② [to cause s.o./s.t./s.a. to change]** ⟪**change, modify, replace**⟫

A

㊉ "replace"▷代える, otherwise ▷変える

EX. Hiroko altered her life style when she went to the States.
浩子はアメリカへ行って生活様式を変えた。
Hiroko wa Amerika e itte seikatsu-yooshiki o kaeta.

alternate adj. **[succeeding each other in turn]**
ko˥ogo no N 交互のN •c [occurring by turns]
—— vt. **[to do s.t. by turns]**
⟨-to⟩ ⟨-o⟩ ko˥ogo ni su⌈ru ⟨〜と⟩⟨〜を⟩交互にする ③ •c [to interchange regularly or in succession]

EX. John alternated study and play.
ジョンは勉強と遊びを交互にした。
Jon wa benkyoo to asobi o koogo ni shita.

alternative n. **[a choice between two or more things]**
da⌈ian 代案 •c [another choice]

EX. The alternative was to drop the intensive English course.
代案は英語集中コースをなくすことだった。
Daian wa eigo-shuuchuu-koosu o nakusu koto datta.

PHRASE: have no alternative but Vinf. nonpast affirmative *shika nai* Vinf. nonpast affirmative しかない

EX. We had no alternative but to agree to the proposal.
その提案に同意するしかなかった。
Sono teian ni dooi-suru shika nakatta.

although conj. **[in spite of the fact that]**
ga が [a disjunctive coordinate conjunction that combines two sentences] ⟪but⟫, ke(re)do(mo) け(れ)ど(も) [a disjunctive subordinate conjunction that combines two sentences] ⟪though⟫, Sinf. noni のに [contrary to everybody's expectation based on the sentence preceding *noni*, the proposition in the sentence following *noni* is the case]

NOTE: When the nonpast affirmative form of adj(*na*). or N+cop. occurs before *noni*, {adj(*na*). stem/N} *na* is used.

EX. (**a**) Although he is rich, he is not happy.
彼は金持ち{だが/だけ(れ)ど(も)/?なのに}幸福ではない。
Kare wa kanemochi {da ga/ dake(re)do(mo)/?na noni} koofuku dewanai.
(**b**) Although he went to the show, he could not get in.
彼はショーに行った{が/け(れ)ど(も)/?のに}入れなかった。
Kare wa shoo ni itta {ga/ke(re)do(mo)/ ?noni} haire-nakatta.
(**c**) Although it was freezing cold outside, Fred went out without a jacket on.
外はいてつくほど寒い{のに/け(れ)ど(も)/が}フレッドは上着も着ないで出かけてしまった。
Soto wa itetsuku hodo samui {noni/ ke(re)do(mo)/ga} Fureddo wa uwagi mo kinai de dekakete shimatta.

altogether adv. **[to a complete/exhaustive degree or in all]**
1. su⌈kka˥ri すっかり ⟪completely⟫, ka⌈nzenni 完全に /⟨adj(*na*). *ni* of *kanzenna* complete/ •c [in a manner absolutely free from any lack or imperfection] ⟪wholly, completely, perfectly⟫

EX. The factory was destroyed altogether by the fire.
工場はその火事で{完全に/すっかり}焼けてしまった。
Koojoo wa sono kaji de {kanzenni/ sukkari} yakete shimatta.

2. zenbu de 全部で •c ⟪in all⟫

EX. Altogether there were six ping pong balls.
ピンポンの球は全部で六個あった。
Pinpon no tama wa zenbu de rok-ko atta.

aluminum n.
a⌈ruminyu˥umu アルミニウム •f

NOTE: There is a gap between its pronunciation ([aruminyuumu]) and *katakana* representation (アルミニウム [aruminiumu]).

always adv. **[at all times]**
i˥tsu-mo いつも [no matter when] **((invariably, usually))**, **tsu˥ne ni 常に** n.+prt. **[without break or not changing ⟨w⟩]** **((habitually))**

EX. (**a**) Masao is always late for class.
正夫は{いつも/常に}授業に遅れる。
Masao wa {itsu-mo/tsune ni} jugyoo ni okureru.
(**b**) She always wears a black sweater.
彼女は{いつも/常に}黒いセーターを着ている。
Kanojo wa {itsu-mo/tsune ni} kuroi seetaa o kite iru.

am vi. **[affirmative nonpast tense of the first person singular of the copula and of the existential verb "to be"]**
1. de˥su です cop. **[formal affirmative nonpast tense of the copula *da*]** **((is, are))**, **da だ** cop. **[informal/written style affirmative nonpast tense of the copula]** **((is, are))**, **de˥a˥ru である** cop. **[written style affirmative nonpast tense of the copula]** **((is, are))**, **dego˥zaima˥su でございます [very formal affirmative nonpast tense of the copula]** **((is, are))**

NOTE: *Degozaimasu* is always used in its formal form.

EX. I am a student at Kyushu University.
私は九州大学の学生{です/だ/である/でございます}。
Watashi wa Kyuushuu-daigaku no gakusei {desu/da/dearu/degozaimasu}.

2. i˥ru いる ② [for s.o./s.a. to exist] **((is, are, exist))**, **o˥rima˥su おります [for the speaker or s.o./s.a. the speaker empathizes with to exist ⟨fml⟩]**

NOTE: *Orimasu* is almost always used in its formal form.

EX. (**a**) Where am I now?
僕は今どこに{いる/*おります}んだろう?
*Boku wa ima doko ni {iru/*orimasu} n daroo?*
(**b**) I am at the airport now.
私は今空港に{います/おります}。
Watashi wa ima kuukoo ni {imasu/orimasu}.

—— aux. **[an auxiliary verb used in the passive or progressive construction]**
1. {Vneg. reru/Vstem rareru/sa˥re˥ru} {Vneg.れる/Vstemられる/される} ② [for s.t./s.o./s.a. acting as the subject of the sentence to be affected by the action of the verb of that sentence]

EX. I am often bullied because I am different from others.
僕は人と違うのでよくいじめられる。
Boku wa hito to chigau node yoku ijime-rareru.

2. V*te* iru V*te*いる ② [to be in the middle of doing s.t. or in a state resulting from s.t. that happened earlier]

EX. I am studying Japanese now.
私は今日本語を勉強しています。
Watashi wa ima Nihon-go o benkyoo-shite imasu.

a.m. n. **[before noon]**
go˥zen 午前 •c [during the morning hours] **↔ gogo 午後 •c**

EX. The store is open from 7:00 A.M. to 10:00 P.M.
あの店は午前七時から午後十時まで開いている。
Ano mise wa gozen shichi-ji kara gogo juu-ji made aite iru.

amateur n. **[s.o. who engages in an activity or a sport without being paid for it]**
a˥machua アマチュア •f [a lay, non-professional person] ↔ puro プロ •f; shi˥rooto 素人 •c [s.o. who is not trained as an expert at s.t.] **((layman)) ↔ kurooto くろうと •c**

EX. (**a**) He is a suprisingly good singer for an amateur.
彼は{アマチュア/素人}にしてはびっくりするほど歌がうまい。
Kare wa {amachua/shirooto} ni shite wa bikkuri-suru hodo uta ga umai.
(**b**) Not only amateurs but professionals can take part in the Olympics.
オリンピックには{アマチュア/??素人}だけでなくプロも出られる。

A

Orinpikku ni wa {amachua/??shirooto} dake denaku puro mo de-rareru.

amaze vt. **[to fill s.o. with great surprise]** **⟨-o⟩ bi⌈kku⌉ri-sa⌈seru** ⟨～を⟩びっくりさせる **/⟨causative of *bikkuri-suru* ③ be surprised/ ② [to cause s.o./s.a. to be surprised at a sudden or unexpected event], ⟨-o⟩ o⌈doroka-se⌉ru** ⟨～を⟩驚かせる **/⟨causative of *odoroku* ① be surprised/ ② ⟪astonish, astound⟫**

EX. Ritsuko's actions always amaze us.
律子の行動はいつも我々を{びっくりさせる/驚かせる}。
Ritsuko no koodoo wa itsu-mo ware-ware o {bikkuri-saseru/odoroka-seru}.

amazing adj. **[causing surprise]** **o⌈doroku-be⌉ki N** 驚くべきN **⟪astonishing⟫, bi⌈kku⌉ri-suru yoona** びっくりするような adj(*na*).

EX. That is really an amazing story, isn't it?
それは本当に{驚くべき/びっくりするような}話ですね。
Sore wa hontoo ni {odoroku-beki/bikkuri-suru yoona} hanashi desu ne.

Amazon n.
A⌈ma⌉zon アマゾン **•f, A⌈mazo⌉n-gawa** アマゾン川 **[the Amazon river]**

ambassador n.
ta⌉ishi 大使 **•c**

EX. The current Australian ambassador to Japan is a nice person.
今度の駐日オーストラリア大使はいい人だ。
Kondo no chuu-Nichi-Oosutoraria-taishi wa ii hito da.

ambition n. **[strong desire to achieve s.t.]** **ya⌉shin** 野心 **•c [strong desire to attain an objective], ta⌈imoo** 大望 **•c ⟪aspiration, desire⟫**

EX. Liz had an ambition to become a great actress.
リズは大女優になりたいという{野心/大望}をいだいていた。
Rizu wa dai-joyuu ni nari-tai to iu {yashin/taimoo} o idaite ita.

ambitious adj. **[full of or showing ambition]**
1. ta⌈imoo a⌉ru N 大望あるN **[having an ambition]**

EX. Bob is an ambitious young man.
ボブは大望ある若者だ。
Bobu wa taimoo aru waka-mono da.

2. ya⌈shin-tekina 野心的な adj(*na*). **•c [for a plan/project to necessitate extraordinary effort/ability]**

EX. It's a highly ambitious project.
それは大変野心的な計画だ。
Sore wa taihen yashin-tekina keikaku da.

America n. **[North and South America, esp. the U.S.A.]**
A⌈merika アメリカ **•f [U.S.A.], Be⌈ikoku** 米国 **•c [the United States of America ⟨w⟩]**
PHRASE: South America *Minami-Amerika* 南アメリカ, *Nanbei* 南米 **•c**; North America *Kita-Amerika* 北アメリカ, *Hokubei* 北米 **•c**; Central America *Chuubei* 中米 **•c**, the United States of America *Amerika-Gasshuukoku* アメリカ合衆国 **•f+c**

American adj.
A⌈merika no N アメリカのN **•f ⟪of America⟫, Be⌈ikoku no N** 米国のN **•c ⟨w⟩**
—— n.
A⌈merika⌉-jin アメリカ人 **•f+c, Be⌈ikoku⌉-jin** 米国人 **•c ⟨w⟩**

amid prep. **[among/in the middle of]**
1. ⟨-no⟩ na⌉ka {ni/de/o} ⟨～の⟩中{に/で/を} n.+prt. **[located inside (a three-dimensional space)] ⟪among, in, at, within, into, inside⟫**

EX. Jim stood amid the crowd.
ジムは人込みの中に立った。
Jimu wa hito-gomi no naka ni tatta.

2. ⟨-no⟩ saichuu ni ⟨～の⟩最中に **[while s.t. is taking place] ⟪in the midst of⟫**

EX. Father had to go out amid the storm.
父は嵐の最中に出かけなければならなかった。
Chichi wa arashi no saichuu ni dekakenakereba naranakatta.

ammunition n. **[bullets, bombs, explosives, etc.]**
da⌈n'yaku 弾薬 **•c**

among prep. **[in the midst of or group of]**
1. ⟨-no⟩ na⌉ka {de/ni} ⟨～の⟩中{で/に} n.+prt.

[located inside (a three-dimensional space)] ((in, inside, into, in the midst of, in the company of))

EX. The scholar found the writer's new manuscript among her letters.
学者はその作家の手紙の中に新しい原稿を見つけた。
Gakusha wa sono sakka no tegami no naka ni atarashii genkoo o mitsuketa.

2. ⟨-no⟩ a⌈ida de ⟨〜の⟩間で n.+prt. **[to or for each of] ((between))**

EX. The money was divided among the four children.
その金は四人の子供たちの間で分けられた。
Sono kane wa yo-nin no kodomo-tachi no aida de wake-rareta.

3. ni に prt. **[indicating a spatial/temporal point of contact, often construed as a location where s.t./s.o./s.a. exists, a goal, or an indirect object] ((to, at, in, for, by))**

EX. The professor is very popular among the students.
その教授は学生に人気がある。
Sono kyooju wa gakusei ni ninki ga aru.

PHRASE: among other things *sono hoka ni mo (iroiro) aru ga toriwake* その外にも(いろいろ)あるがとりわけ ((especially))

EX. Among other things, Hideo is a good painter.
英男は(その外にも)いろいろな才能があるが、とりわけ絵が上手だ。
Hideo wa (sono hoka ni mo) iroirona sainoo ga aru ga, toriwake e ga joozu da.

amount n. **[total cost or quantity]**

1. ga⌉ku 額 **•c [amount of money] ((sum))**

EX. The amount of the purchase came to $1,000.
買い物の額は千ドルになった。
Kai-mono no gaku wa sen-doru ni natta.

2. ryo⌉o 量 **•c [quantity]**

EX. The factory requires a large amount of water.
この工場は多量の水を必要とする。
Kono koojoo wa taryoo no mizu o hitsuyoo to suru.

(**b**) Do you know the average amount of water the Japanese use per day?
日本人が一日に使う平均的な水の量を知っていますか。
Nihon-jin ga ichi-nichi ni tsukau heikin-tekina mizu no ryoo o shitte imasu ka.

Amsterdam n.
A⌈musute⌉rudamu アムステルダム **•f**

amuse vt. **[to entertain s.o. or keep s.o. pleasantly occupied]**
⟨-o⟩ ta⌈noshima-se⌉ru ⟨〜を⟩楽しませる **/⟨causative of *tanoshimu* ① enjoy/ ②, ⟨-o⟩ o⌈moshiro-gara-se⌉ru** ⟨〜を⟩面白がらせる **/⟨causative of *omoshiro-garu* ① regard s.t. as entertaining/ ② ((entertain))**

EX. Mary amused her granddaughter with funny stories.
マリーは笑い話をして孫娘を{楽しませた/面白がらせた}。
Marii wa warai-banashi o shite mago-musume o {tanoshima-seta/omoshiro-garu-seta}.

amusement n. **[s.t. that entertains]**
ta⌈noshi⌉mi 楽しみ **/⟨V*masu* of *tanoshimu* ① enjoy/, go⌈raku** 娯楽 **[s.t. one does for fun during one's free time] ((entertainment))**

EX. Karen's chief amusement is music.
カレンの主な{楽しみ/娯楽}は音楽だ。
Karen no omona {tanoshimi/goraku} wa ongaku da.

and conj. **[in addition to]**

1. N to N NとN prt. **[a conjunction that lists items exhaustively] ((along with, in addition to))**

EX. I bought carnations and roses for my mother.
母親にカーネーションとバラを買った。
Haha-oya ni kaaneeshon to bara o katta.

2. N ya N NやN prt. **[a conjunction that lists two or more items non-exhaustively]**

EX. We have beer, sake, juice and so forth.
ビールや酒やジュースなどがあります。
Biiru ya sake ya juusu nado ga arimasu.

3. N ni N NにN prt. **[a particle that lists**

A

two or more items cumulatively]

EX. John, Mary, and Tom came to visit the house.
ジョンにマリーにトムが家にたずねて来た。
Jon ni Marii ni Tomu ga uchi ni tazunete-kita.

NOTE: *To, ya* and *ni* combine only nouns.

4. so⌈shite そして conj. **[later in a sequence of events]** ⟪**and then**⟫

EX. Megumi said goodbye and drove away.
恵はさよならを言い、そして車で去った。
Megumi wa sayonara o ii, soshite kuruma de satta.

5. {V/adj./cop.}*te* {V/adj./cop.}*te* [two (or more) events/states occurring at the same time or in succession]

EX. (**a**) Haruo played the piano, and Akiko sang a song.
春雄がピアノを弾いて、亜希子が歌を歌った。
Haruo ga piano o hiite, Akiko ga uta o utatta.
(**b**) Tom went to the library and studied.
トムは図書館へ行って勉強した。
Tomu wa tosho-kan e itte benkyoo-shita.
(**c**) The kitten was small and lovely.
その子猫は小さくてかわいかった。
Sono ko-neko wa chiisakute kawaikatta.
(**d**) My older brother is a businessman and my younger brother is a teacher.
兄はビジネスマンで、弟は教師です。
Ani wa bijinesu-man de, otooto wa kyooshi desu.

6. s⌈oo-sure⌉-ba そうすれば **[if one does s.t., then (after an imperative sentence)]**

EX. Use this dictionary and you will be able to master Japanese.
この辞書を使いなさい。そうすれば、日本語がマスターできます。
Kono jisho o tsukainasai. Soo-sure-ba, Nihon-go ga masutaa-dekimasu.

7. **na⌉ndo-mo** 何度も **[to emphasize frequency/intensity]** ⟪**many times**⟫

EX. John tried and tried, but he could not solve the problem.
ジョンは何度もやってみたが、問題は解けなかった。
Jon wa nando-mo yatte mita ga, mondai wa toke-nakatta.

PHRASE: and so on/forth *-nado* 〜など

EX. I bought stationery goods such as pencils, ballpoint pens, erasers, and so forth.
私は鉛筆やボールペンや消しゴムなどの文房具を買った。
Watashi wa enpitsu ya booru-pen ya keshi-gomu nado no bunboo-gu o katta.

PHRASE: and then *sore-kara* それから

EX. Jerry graduated from school, and then he went to Japan.
ジェリーは学校を卒業した。それから、彼は日本へ行った。
Jerii wa gakkoo o sotsugyoo-shita. Sore-kara kare wa Nihon e itta.

Andes n.
A⌈ndesu-sa⌉nmyaku アンデス山脈 **•f+c**

angel n.
te⌉nshi 天使 **•c, {e⌉nzeru/e⌉njeru}** {エンゼル/エンジェル} **•f**

angle n. **[the space between two straight lines that diverge from a common point or between two planes that extend from a common line]**
ka⌉kudo 角度 **•c**

EX. A: This problem is very difficult.
この問題はとても難しい。
Kono mondai wa totemo muzukashii.
B: Why don't you look at it from another angle?
別の角度から見てみたらどうですか。
Betsu no kakudo kara mite mitara doo desu ka.

Anglo-Saxon n.
A⌈nguro-Sa⌉kuson アングロサクソン **•f**

angry adj. **[feeling/expressing annoyance, animosity or resentment]**
⟨-o⟩ o⌈ko⌉tte iru (N) ⟨〜を⟩怒っている**(N)** **/⟨V *te iru* of *okoru* ① get angry/ ⟪enraged⟫, {⟨-ni⟩/⟨-de⟩} ha⌈ra⌉ ga tatsu** {⟨〜に⟩/⟨〜で⟩} 腹が立つ, **{⟨-ni⟩/⟨-de⟩} ha⌈ra⌉ o tatete iru (N)**

{(〜に)/(〜で)}腹を立てている(N) /⟨Vte iru of *hara o tateru* ② get angry/ ⟪mad⟫
NOTE: *Hara ga tatsu* and *hara o tateru* are idioms.
EX. (a) The teacher is very angry with me.
先生は僕のこと{をとても怒っている/{に/で}とても腹を立てている/*{に/で}腹が立つ}。
*Sensei wa boku no koto {o totemo okotte iru/{ni/de} totemo hara o tatete iru/ *{ni/de} hara ga tatsu}.*
(b) Mother got angry over my dirty room.
母は私のきたない部屋のこと{{に/で}腹を立てていた/を怒っていた/*{に/で}腹が立った}。
Haha wa watashi no kitanai heya no koto {{ni/de} hara o tatete ita/o okotte ita/{ni/de} hara ga tatta}.*
(c) I was angry at her irresponsible attitude.
彼女のいいかげんな態度{に腹が立った/に腹を立てていた/を怒っていた}。
Kanojo no iikagenna taido {ni hara ga tatta/ni hara o tatete ita/o okotte ita}.
NOTE: The subject of *hara ga tatsu* must be first person.

animal n. **[a living organism which, unlike plants, takes in food and is capable of movement or sensation]**
do⌈obutsu 動物 •c [living things other than plants]
EX. The zoo has many animals.
動物園にはたくさんの動物がいる。
Doobutsu-en ni wa takusan no doobutsu ga iru.

ankle n. **[the joint connecting the leg and the foot]**
a⌈shi⌉-kubi 足首 [the narrow part above the joint connecting the leg and the foot], ku⌈rubushi くるぶし [the joint connecting the foot with the leg]
EX. I fell and hurt my ankle.
転んで{足首/?くるぶし}を痛めた。
Koronde {ashi-kubi/?kurubushi} o itameta.

announce vt. **[for s.o. to make s.t. known publicly]**
⟨-ni⟩ ⟨-o⟩ shi⌈raseru ⟨〜に⟩⟨〜を⟩知らせる /⟨causative of *shiru* ① come to know/ ② [for s.o. to cause s.o. to know s.t.] ⟪inform⟫, ⟨-o⟩ ha⌈ppyoo-suru ⟨〜を⟩発表する ③ •c [for s.o. to let the public know s.t. tangible] ⟪publish, express, release⟫
EX. (a) The company announced a new product.
会社は新製品を{発表した/*知らせた}。
*Kaisha wa shin-seihin o {happyoo-shita/ *shiraseta}.*
(b) The butler announced the arrival of a visitor.
執事が客の到着を{知らせた/*発表した}。
*Shitsuji ga kyaku no toochaku o {shiraseta/*happyoo-shita}.*

announcement n. **[a statement which makes s.t. known publicly]**
ha⌈ppyoo 発表 •c [the act of announcing s.t. in public] ⟪publication, statement, communique⟫, ko⌈ohyoo 公表 •c [an official public statement] ⟪proclamation⟫

annoy vt. **[to irritate/displease s.o.]**
⟨-o⟩ ko⌈mara-se⌉ru ⟨〜を⟩困らせる /⟨causative of *komaru* ① be in an unpleasant situation/ ② [to cause s.o. to be in an unpleasant or troubled situation] ⟪trouble, worry⟫
EX. Taro always annoys the teacher by interrupting her class.
太郎はいつも授業の邪魔をして先生を困らせる。
Taroo wa itsu mo jugyoo no jama o shite sensei o komara-seru.
PHRASE: be annoyed ⟨*-de*⟩ *komaru* ⟨〜で⟩困る ①
EX. We are annoyed by the constant traffic noise.
ひっきりなしに通る車の騒音で困っている。
Hikkiri-nashi-ni tooru kuruma no sooon de komatte iru.

annoyance n. **[the feeling of being annoyed]**
me⌉iwaku 迷惑 •c [an act/instance of causing s.o. a feeling of unpleasantness/loss of profit] ⟪nuisance, trouble⟫
EX. Unexpected visitors are an annoyance.
不意の訪問客は迷惑だ。
Fui no hoomon-kyaku wa meiwaku da.

A

annoying adj. **[irritating]**
ya⌉kkaina 厄介な adj(*na*). •c **[causing trouble, difficulty and annoyance]** ((**troublesome**)), **me⌈ndo⌉ona** 面倒な adj(*na*). •c **[causing trouble for s.o. including oneself]**

EX. We have an annoying situation on our hands.
{厄介な/面倒な}情況になった。
{Yakkaina/Mendoona} jookyoo ni natta.

annual adj. **[occurring, done, etc., once a year]**
ma⌈i-toshi no N 毎年のN **[occurring, done, etc., every year]** ((**yearly**))

EX. The speech contest is an annual event at this school.
この学校では、弁論大会は毎年の行事です。
Kono gakkoo de wa, benron-taikai wa mai-toshi no gyooji desu.

PHRASE: annual events *nenchuu-gyooji* 年中行事 •c, annual income *nenshuu* 年収 •c

annually adv. **[yearly]**
ma⌈i-toshi 毎年 **[every year]**

another adj. **[one more or a different one]**
1. mo⌈o hito⌉tsu もう一つ adv. **[an additional thing]** ((**additional**)), **mo⌈o hito⌉ri** もう一人 adv. **[an additional person]**

EX. (**a**) May I have another piece of cake?
お菓子を{もう一つ/*もう一人}いただけませんか。
*O-kashi o {moo hitotsu/*moo hitori} itadake-masen ka.*
(**b**) I need another assistant.
助手が{もう一人/*もう一つ}要ります。
*Joshu ga {moo hitori/*moo hitotsu} irimasu.*

2. be⌈tsu no N 別のN, **ho⌈ka no N** 外のN **[different]** ((**alternative, other**))

EX. (**a**) Will you show me another word processor?
{別/外}のワープロを見せて下さい。
{Betsu/Hoka} no waapuro o misete kudasai.
(**b**) I will ask another person.
{別/外}の人に聞いてみます。
{Betsu/Hoka} no hito ni kiite mimasu.

3. a⌉to あと **[more]**

EX. The second semester will start in another two weeks.
あと二週間で二学期が始まる。
Ato ni-shuukan de ni-gakki ga hajimaru.

— pron.
be⌈tsu no mono 別のもの **[a different thing]**

EX. To know Japanese is one thing, and to teach it is another.
日本語を知っていることと教えることは別のものである。
Nihon-go o shitte iru koto to oshieru koto wa betsu no mono dearu.

answer vt. **[for s.o. to respond verbally to a question, letter, etc]**
⟨-ni⟩ ko⌈tae⌉ru ⟨〜に⟩こたえる ② **[for s.o. to react to s.t. such as a question, demand, expectation, temperature]** ((**reply, respond, solve, react**))
㊅ "respond verbally"▷答える, otherwise ▷こたえる

EX. A: Were you able to answer all the questions?
全部の質問に答えられましたか。
Zenbu no shitsumon ni kotae-raremashita ka.
B: Yes, fortunately I was.
はい、おかげ様で。
Hai, o-kage-sama de.

PHRASE: answer the phone *denwa ni deru* 電話に出る ②

EX. Will someone answer the phone, please?
だれか電話に出てくれませんか。
Dare-ka denwa ni dete kuremasen ka.

— n. **[a reply to s.t.]**
ko⌈ta⌉e 答え **[an act/instance of responding verbally to a question or statement]** ((**response, reply, solution**)), **he⌈nji⌉** 返事 •c **[the act/instance of responding to a statement/letter/written question]** ((**reply**))

EX. (**a**) I'm waiting for an answer to my letter.
私は手紙の{返事/*答え}を待っています。
*Watashi wa tegami no {henji/*kotae} o matte imasu.*

(b) Is this answer correct?
この{答え/*返事}は合っていますか。
*Kono {kotae/*henji} wa atte imasu ka.*

ant n.
a⌈ri あり

Antarctic adj.
Na⌈nkyoku no N 南極のN •c

Antarctica n.
Na⌈nkyoku-ta⌉iriku 南極大陸 •c ((the Antarctic Continent))

antenna n. [an apparatus to send/receive radio waves or a sensory organ located on the head of insects]
a⌈ntena アンテナ •f [an apparatus to send/receive radio waves] ((aerial)), sho⌈kkaku 触角 •c [a sensory organ located on the head of insects] ((feeler))

antique n.
ko⌈ttoo-hin 骨とう品 •c

anxiety n. [an uneasy feeling due to fear, worry, etc.]
shi⌈npai 心配 •c [an uncomfortable feeling caused by uncertainty or by the expectation of danger/evil/s.t. troublesome] ((concern, apprehension, uneasiness, fear, worry)), fu⌈an 不安 •c [an uncomfortable feeling caused by uncertainty or by expectation of the worst] ((uneasiness, uncertainty))

EX. (a) The exam is a source of anxiety.
試験が{心配/不安}の種です。
Shiken ga {shinpai/fuan} no tane desu.
(b) Sorry to have caused you so much anxiety.
{心配/*不安}をかけてすみません。
*{Shinpai/*Fuan} o kakete sumimasen.*

anxious adj. [full of/causing anxiety or eager anticipation]
1. 〈-o〉 shi⌈npai-shite iru (N) 〈〜を〉心配している(N) /〈V*te iru* of *shinpai-suru* ③ worry/ •c [causing worry to s.o.] ((worried, concerned))

EX. Teruko is anxious about her son's safety.
輝子は息子の安否を心配している。
Teruko wa musuko no anpi o shinpai-shite iru.

2. shi⌈kirini…V*masu* ta-⌈ga⌉tte iru (N) しきりに…V*masu*たがっている(N) /〈V*te iru* of *ta-garu* ① show signs of Ving/ ② [eagerly wishing] ((eager to)), se⌈tsuboo-shite iru (N) 切望している(N) /〈V*te iru* of *setsuboo-suru* ③ want badly to/ ② •c

EX. (a) The student is anxious to know the result of the entrance exam.
学生は入学試験の結果を{しきりに知りたがって/*切望して}いる。
*Gakusei wa nyuugaku-shiken no kekka o {shikirini shiri-ta-gatte/*setsuboo-shite} iru.*
(b) I was anxious to go to Japan.
私は日本へ{行くことを切望して/*しきりに行きたがって}いた。
*Watashi wa Nihon e {iku koto o setsuboo-shite/*shikirini iki-ta-gatte} ita.*

NOTE: When the subject is first person *watashi*, use *…-tai to omotte iru* instead, as in *Watashi wa Nihon e iki-tai to omotte ita.* In this case, *shikirini* cannot be used.

anxiously adv.
shi⌈npai-shite 心配して /〈V*te* of *shinpai-suru* ③ worry/ •c ((with anxiety))

any adj./pron. [one/some/every]
1. do⌈nna…demo どんな…でも [any kind of object/person/animal]

EX. A: Do I have to use special sheets of paper for the report?
レポートには特別な紙を使わなければなりませんか。
Repooto ni wa tokubetsuna kami o tsukawanakereba narimasen ka.
B: No, any kind of paper will do.
いいえ、どんな紙でもいいですよ。
Iie, donna kami demo ii desu yo.

2. i⌈kura-ka いくらか [to some extent in quantity/number/degree], na⌉ni-ka 何か [a thing/situation/animal which the speaker/writer cannot specify] ((something)), da⌉re-ka だれか [a person whom the speaker/writer cannot specify] ((someone))

EX. (a) Did you have any money then?
その時{いくらか/*何か/*だれか}お金を持っていたのですか。
*Sono-toki {ikura-ka/*nani-ka/*dare-ka}*

o-kane o motte ita no desu ka.
(**b**) Did you meet any person you knew at the party?
パーティーで{だれか/*いくらか/*何か}知っている人に会いましたか。
*Paatii de {dare-ka/*ikura-ka/*nani-ka} shitte iru hito ni aimashita ka.*
(**c**) Do you have any question?
{何か/*いくらか/*だれか}質問がありますか。
*{Nani-ka/*Ikura-ka/*Dare-ka} shitsumon ga arimasu ka.*

3. na⌈ni-mo…neg. 何も…neg. [for what is being described not to apply to anything mentioned] ((**thing**)), **da⌈re-mo…neg. だれも…neg. [for what is being described not to apply to any person mentioned]** ((**person**)), **su⌈ko⌉shi-mo…neg. 少しも…neg. [not even the least amount]** ((**quantity**))

EX. (**a**) John didn't eat any fish.
ジョンは魚は{少しも/何も/*だれも}食べなかった。
*Jon wa sakana wa {sukoshi-mo/nani-mo/*dare-mo} tabenakatta.*
(**b**) I didn't see any student.
学生は{だれも/?少しも/*何も}見かけなかった。
*Gakusei wa {dare-mo/?sukoshi-mo/*nani-mo} mi-kakenakatta.*

— adv.

su⌈ko⌉shi wa 少しは [to a degree or extent]

EX. Has Glen's grandmother gotten any better recently?
グレンのおばあさんは最近少しは良くなっていますか。
Guren no o-baa-san wa saikin sukoshi wa yoku natte imasu ka.

PHRASE: at any rate *tonikaku* とにかく

EX. At any rate, let's try.
とにかくやってみよう。
Tonikaku yatte miyoo.

PHRASE: any more/longer *moo…nai* もう…ない

EX. Misako is already eighteen. She is not a child any more.
美佐子はすでに十八だ。もう子供じゃない。
Misako wa sudeni juu-hachi da. Moo kodomo janai.

anybody pron. **[any person]**

1. da⌉re-ka だれか [a person whom the speaker/writer cannot specify]

EX. Is anybody home?
だれか家にいますか。
Dare-ka ie ni imasu ka.

2. da⌈re-mo…neg. だれも…neg. [for what is being described not to apply to any person mentioned]

EX. There wasn't anybody at school on Sunday.
日曜日にはだれも学校にいなかった。
Nichiyoo-bi ni wa dare-mo gakkoo ni inakatta.

3. da⌈re-demo だれでも [any/every person in an affirmative sentence]

EX. Anybody can learn to speak Japanese.
だれでも日本語が話せるようになる。
Dare-demo Nihon-go ga hanase-ru yooni naru.

anyhow adv. **[in any case]**

to⌉nikaku とにかく [in spite of other things] ((**anyway**))

EX. A: What happened then?
それでどうしたの。
Sore-de doo-shita no.
B: Well, anyhow, I called the police.
うん。とにかく警察に電話をかけた。
Un. Tonikaku keisatsu ni denwa o kaketa.

anyone pron. **[any person]**

1. da⌉re-ka だれか [a person whom the speaker/writer cannot specify]

2. da⌈re-mo だれも SEE anybody

3. da⌈re-demo だれでも SEE anybody

anything pron. **[any object, event, fact, etc.]**

1. na⌉ni-ka 何か [a thing/situation/animal which the speaker/writer cannot specify]

EX. Is there anything you want to say?
何か言いたいことがありますか。
Nani-ka ii-tai koto ga arimasu ka.

2. na⌈ni-mo…neg. 何も…neg. [for what is being described not to apply to anything mentioned]

EX. Bob didn't eat anything this morning.

ボブは今朝何も食べなかった。
Bobu wa kesa nani-mo tabenakatta.

3. na⌉n-demo 何でも [any kind of thing, event, fact, etc. in an affirmative sentence]

EX. A: What would you like to eat?
何が食べたいですか。
Nani ga tabe-tai desu ka.
B: Anything except *nattoo* will do.
なっとう以外なら何でもいいですよ。
Nattoo igai nara nan-demo ii desu yo.

anyway adv.
to⌉nikaku とにかく ⦅at any rate⦆ SEE the example for anyhow

anywhere adv. **[in/at/to any place]**
do⌉ko {ni/e} demo どこ({に/へ})でも, do⌉ko ({ni/e}) mo どこ({に/へ})も, do⌉ko-ka {ni/e/de} どこか{に/へ/で}

EX. (a) Sit anywhere you like.
{どこ({に/へ})でも/*どこ({に/へ})も/*どこか{に/へ/で}}好きなところに座ってください。
*{Doko ({ni/e}) demo/*Doko ({ni/e}) mo/*Doko-ka {ni/e/de}} sukina tokoro ni suwatte kudasai.*
(b) I didn't go anywhere during the summer break this year.
今年の夏休みは{どこ({に/へ})も/*どこ({に/へ})でも/*どこか{に/へ/で}}行かなかった。
*Kotoshi no natsu-yasumi wa {doko ({ni/e}) mo/*doko ({ni/e}) demo/*doko-ka {ni/e/de}} ikanakatta.*
(c) Did you go anywhere on Sunday?
日曜日に{どこか{に/へ/*で}/*どこ({に/へ})も/*どこ({に/へ})でも}行きましたか。
*Nichiyoo bi ni {doko-ka {ni/e/*de}/*doko ({ni/e}) mo/*doko ({ni/e}) demo} ikimashita ka.*

apart adv. **[separated by a distance]**
be⌈tsu-betsu ni 別々に •c [aside, away in place/time] ⦅separately⦆

EX. Philip decided to live apart from his family.
フィリップは家族と別々に暮らすことにした。
Firippu wa kazoku to betsu-betsu ni kurasu koto ni shita.

PHRASE: apart from… …*wa betsu ni shite* …は別にして

EX. He was a good student apart from a few absences.
何回か休んだことは別にして、彼はいい学生でした。
Nan-kai ka yasunda koto wa betsu ni shite, kare wa ii gakusei deshita.

apartment n. **[a set of rooms rented in a building]**
a⌈pa⌉ato アパート •f [a rented room/set of rooms in a building containing rooms for the purpose of being rented out or such a building itself] ⦅flat⦆, ma⌉nshon マンション •f [a condominium either rented or purchased]

apiece adv. **[to/for/from each]**
hi⌈to⌉tsu (ni-tsu⌈ki) 一つ(につき) ⦅per piece⦆

EX. The nectarines cost 15 cents a piece.
ネクタリンは一つ(につき)十五セントする。
Nekutarin wa hitotsu (ni-tsuki) juu-go-sento suru.

Apollo n.
A⌉poro アポロ •f

apologize vi. **[for s.o. to express regret for a fault]**
wa⌈biru わびる ① [for s.o. to express regret for a fault] ⦅beg pardon, beg forgiveness⦆, ⟨-ni⟩ ⟨-o⟩ a⌈yama⌉ru ⟨〜に⟩⟨〜を⟩あやまる ① [for s.o. to go off the right track physically or ethically (and to express regret for it)] ⦅mistake, err, beg pardon⦆
㊥ "err"▷誤る, otherwise ▷謝る

EX. (a) Masao apologized to the teacher for being late.
正雄は先生に遅れたことを{わびた/謝った}。
Masao wa sensei ni okureta koto o {wabita/ayamatta}.
(b) What kind of attitude is that? You should apologize to your father.
何ですかその態度は。お父さんに{謝りなさい/*わびなさい}。
Nan desu ka sono taido wa. O-too-san

A

| *ni {ayamarinasai/*wabinasai}.*

apostrophe n.
a⌈posutoro⌉fi アポストロフィ •f

Appalachian adj.
A⌈parachia-sa⌉nmyaku no N アパラチア山脈のN •f+c

apparatus n. **[a complex machine/device/system]**
so⌉ochi 装置 •c **((device, gadget, equipment))**

EX. | A new device to record one's voice made its debut.
人の声を録音する新しい装置が出た。
Hito no koe o rokuon-suru atarashii soochi ga deta.

apparent adj. **[s.t. is readily seen/visible]**
1. a⌈ki⌉rakana 明らかな adj(*na*). **[readily seen so that there is no doubt or ambiguity] ((evident, obvious, clear)), me⌈ihakuna** 明白な adj(*na*). •c **[accepted as such without doubt/suspicion by every body] ((evident, obvious, clear))**

EX. | It was apparent that Hitomi was ill.
瞳が病気なのは{明らか/明白}だった。
Hitomi ga byooki na no wa {akiraka/meihaku} datta.

2. ga⌈iken-joo dake no N 外見上だけのN **[visible only on the surface] ((seeming, superficial))**

EX. | The problem was more apparent than real.
その問題は、どちらかと言えば外見上だけのものであった。
Sono mondai wa, dochira-ka to ieba gaiken-joo dake no mono deatta.

apparently adv. **[in an apparent way]**
a⌈ki⌉rakani 明らかに /〈**adj**(*na*). ***ni*** **of *akirakana* apparent/ [without any doubt] ((obviously, clearly, evidently)), mi⌉ta-tokoro…yo⌉oda** 見たところ…ようだ **((seemingly))** SEE the note for seem

EX. | That person was apparently a woman.
{明らかに/見たところ}あの人は女のようだった。
{Akirakani/Mita-tokoro} ano hito wa onna no yoodatta.

appeal vt. **[to address oneself/itself to s.o.]**
〈-ni〉〈-o〉 u⌈ttaeru 〈〜に〉〈〜を〉訴える ② **[for s.o. to bring civil action against s.o. else ((fig. "communicate s.t. very strongly," "take recourse in s.t."))] ((sue, complain, plead))**

EX. | (**a**) The refugees appealed to the authorities for assistance.
難民は当局に援助を訴えた。
Nanmin wa tookyoku ni enjo o uttaeta.
(**b**) This music has nothing that appeals to me.
この音楽は私に訴えるものが何もない。
Kono ongaku wa watashi ni uttaeru mono ga nani-mo nai.

—— n.
1. u⌈ttae 訴え **[a request for help] ((suit))**
2. mi⌈ryoku 魅力 •c **[s.t. beautiful, excellent, superb that catches the heart and mind of s.o. who comes in contact with it and eventually captivates him] ((attraction, charm)), a⌈pi⌉iru** アピール •f **[an urgent request which is felt deeply or attraction or interest]**

EX. | (**a**) The man rejected her appeal.
男は彼女の{訴え/*魅力/*アピール}を退けた。
*Otoko wa kanojo no {uttae/*miryoku/*apiiru} o shirizoketa.*
(**b**) This album by Thelonious Monk still has not lost its appeal.
このセロニアス・モンクのアルバムはまだその{魅力/?アピール/*訴え}を失っていない。
*Kono Seroniasu Monku no arubamu wa mada sono {miryoku/?apiiru/*uttae} o ushinatte inai.*
(**c**) The referee refused the player's appeal.
審判は選手の{アピール/?訴え/*魅力}を退けた。
*Shinpan wa senshu no {apiiru/?uttae/*miryoku} o shirizoketa.*

appealing adj. **[able to move the feelings]**
mi⌈ryoku-tekina 魅力的な adj(*na*). •c **((attractive, charming))**

EX. | The idea of spending Christmas vacation on an island in the South Pacific is very appealing.

南太平洋の島でクリスマス休暇を過ごすという案はとても魅力的だ。
Minami-Taiheiyoo no shima de Kurisumasu-kyuuka o sugosu to iu an wa totemo miryoku-teki da.

appear vi. **[to comes into one's sight ⟪fig. "conjecture based on what comes into one's sight"⟫]**
1. a⌈raware⌉ru 現れる ② **[to become exposed/visible] ⟪come out, emerge⟫**
EX. A completely new computer appeared on the market.
全く新しいコンピューターが市場に現れた。
Mattaku atarashii konpyuutaa ga shijoo ni arawareta.
2. Sinf. yo⌉ona Sinf.ような aux. adj(*na*). **[an auxiliary adj(*na*). which expresses the likelihood of s.t. or the likeness of s.t./s.o./s.a. to s.t./s.o./s.a.] ⟪look like, appear, seem⟫**
EX. (**a**) That house appears to be empty.
あの家は空いているようだ。
Ano ie wa aite iru yooda.
(**b**) He appears to be inexperienced.
彼は新米のようだ。
Kare wa shinmai no yooda.
NOTE: Note the following exceptional forms when *yoona* connects with a preceeding nonpast affirmative form: {adj(*na*). stem + *na*/ N *no*} *yoona*.

appearance n. **[coming out or outward looks of s.t.]**
1. shu⌈tsugen 出現 •**c [appearing of s.t. new] ⟪emergence, coming out, appearing, apparition, arrival⟫**
EX. The appearance of the computer did not necessarily mean the end of the abacus.
コンピューターの出現は、必ずしもそろばんの終わりを意味するわけではなかった。
Konpyuutaa no shutsugen wa, kanarazu-shimo soroban no owari o imi-suru wake dewanakatta.
2. ga⌈iken 外見 •**c [outward aspect of anything] ⟪face⟫**
EX. Don't judge people by their appearance.
人を外見だけで判断してはいけない。
Hito o gaiken dake de handan-shite wa ikenai.

appetite n. **[desire for food]**
sho⌈kuyoku 食欲 •**c**
EX. (**a**) I don't have much of an appetite today.
今日はあまり食欲がない。
Kyoo wa amari shokuyoku ga nai.
(**b**) Wine increases your appetite.
ワインは食欲を増進する。
Wain wa shokuyoku o zooshin-suru.

applaud vt./vi. **[for s.o. to show approval of s.t./s.o. by clapping one's hands]**
⟨-ni⟩ ha⌉kushu o o⌈kuru ⟨〜に⟩拍手を送る ① **[for s.o. to send a hand-clap to] ⟪clap⟫, ⟨-o⟩ sho⌈osan-suru** ⟨〜を⟩賞賛する ③ •**c ⟪praise, admire⟫**
EX. The audience applauded the performance of the violinist.
聴衆はそのバイオリニストの演奏{に拍手を送った/を賞賛した}。
Chooshuu wa sono baiorinisuto no ensoo {ni hakushu o okutta/o shoosan shita}.
NOTE: *Shoosan* 賞賛 is sometimes written as 称賛 with the same meaning.

applause n. **[approval, esp. as shown by clapping hands]**
ha⌉kushu 拍手 •**c [clapping of hands], sho⌉osan** 賞賛 •**c [an act/instance of expressing high regard or approval of s.o./s.t.] ⟪praise, admiration⟫**
NOTE: *Shoosan* 賞賛 is sometimes written as 称賛 with the same meaning.

apple n.
ri⌈ngo りんご
PHRASE: apple-polishing (flattery) *goma-suri* ごますり

applicant n. **[s.o. who applies for s.t.]**
o⌈obo⌉-sha 応募者 •**c ⟪entrant, contestant⟫, shi⌈ga⌉n-sha** 志願者 •**c**
EX. (**a**) Applicants for national universities appear to be on the decline.
国立大学の入学{志願者/*応募者}は減ってきているらしい。

A

*Kokuritsu-daigaku no nyuugaku-{shigan-sha/*oobo-sha} wa hette-kite iru rashii.*
(**b**) How many applicants were there for the contest?
今度のコンテストの{応募者/*志願者}は何人ぐらいですか。
*Kondo no kontesuto no {oobo-sha/*shigan-sha} wa nan-nin-gurai desu ka.*

application n. **[an act/instance of applying to or for s.t.]**
1. mo⌈oshi-komi 申し込み [applying for a position, admission, etc.]
EX. Please send me an application form.
申し込み用紙を送って下さい。
Mooshi-komi-yooshi o okutte kudasai.
2. o⌈oyoo 応用 •c [applying theory, etc. to s.t., usually practical]
EX. I am doing research on the application of linguistics to language teaching.
私は言語学の言語教育への応用を研究しています。
Watashi wa gengo-gaku no gengo-kyooiku e no ooyoo o kenkyuu-shite imasu.

apply vt. **[for s.o. to put s.t. in contact with s.t. else 《fig. "put s.t. to practical/special use"》]**
1. ⟨-ni⟩ ⟨-o⟩ tsu⌈ke⌉ru ⟨〜に⟩⟨〜を⟩つける ① [for s.o./s.a. to cause s.t./s.o. to adhere to s.t./s.o./s.a. else] 《fix, put, attach, spread》
㊈ "wear"▷着ける, "attach, spread, fix" ▷付ける, otherwise ▷つける
EX. Do you have any medicine to apply to a burn?
やけどに付ける薬はありませんか。
Yakedo ni tsukeru kusuri wa arimasen ka.
2. ⟨-o⟩ ⟨-ni⟩ o⌈oyoo-suru ⟨〜を⟩⟨〜に⟩応用する ③ •c [for s.o. to put s.t. to practical or specific use]
EX. You should apply the theory to practical problems.
理論を実際的問題に応用すべきだ。
Riron o jissai-teki-mondai ni ooyoo-su-beki da.

—— vi. **[for s.t. to be relevant or for s.o. to make a request for employment/admission]**
1. a⌈tehama⌉ru あてはまる ① [for s.t., esp. a rule, to be true of] 《hold true, conform to》
EX. That grammar rule does not apply here.
あの文法規則はここにはあてはまらない。
Ano bunpoo-kisoku wa koko ni wa atehamaranai.
2. ⟨-o⟩ mo⌈oshi-ko⌉mu ⟨〜を⟩申し込む ① [for s.o. to (formally) convey a request or desire to s.o. else or to an institution in the hopes of having it granted] 《propose, offer, request, ask, challenge》
EX. Barbara applied for a scholarship to study in Japan.
バーバラは日本留学の奨学金を申し込んだ。
Baabara wa Nihon-ryuugaku no shoogaku-kin o mooshi-konda.

appoint vt. **[for s.o. to name s.o. for an office or set a date, place, etc.]**
ni⌈nmei-suru 任命する ③ •c [for s.o. to name s.o. for an office/post], shi⌈mei-suru 指名する ③ •c [for s.o. to nominate s.o. for an office/post] 《nominate, designate, call on》
EX. Mr. Han was appointed chairman of the committee.
ハンさんは委員会の委員長に{任命/指名}された。
Han-san wa iin-kai no iin-choo ni {ninmei/shimei}-sareta.

appreciate vt. **[for s.o. to set a high value on s.t.]**
1. ⟨-o⟩ mi⌈tomeru ⟨〜を⟩認める ② [for s.o. to perceive or consent to the value or correctness of s.t./s.o./s.a.] 《notice, spot, recognize, approve, judge, admit, permit, allow》
EX. Charlie's work was appreciated by all.
チャーリーの業績は皆に認められた。
Chaarii no gyooseki wa mina ni mitome-rareta.
2. ⟨-o⟩ ka⌈nshoo-suru ⟨〜を⟩鑑賞する ③ •c [for s.o. to admire the quality of an artistic

A

object] ((enjoy, admire))

EX. More and more Americans have come to appreciate "haiku."
ますます多くのアメリカ人が俳句を鑑賞するようになった。
Masu-masu ooku no Amerika-jin ga haiku o kanshoo-suru yooni natta.

3. {⟨-o⟩/⟨-ni⟩} ka˥nsha-suru {⟨〜を⟩/⟨〜に⟩} 感謝する ③ •c [for s.o. to recognize s.t. gratefully] ((thank))

EX. We appreciate your cooperation.
ご協力{を/に}感謝します。
Go-kyooryoku {o/ni} kansha-shimasu.

appreciation n. **[an act/instance of appreciating s.t./s.o.]**

1. ka˥nshoo 鑑賞 •c [admiration of the quality of an artistic object] ((admiration, enjoyment))

2. ka˥nsha 感謝 •c [feeling thankful to s.o. for s.t.] ((gratitude, thankfulness, thanks))

approach vt./vi. **[to come closer to s.t./s.o./s.a.]**

1. ⟨-ni⟩ chi˥kazu˥ku ⟨〜に⟩近付く ① [to move closer to s.o./s.a./s.t.] ((near, draw near, go near, come near)), ⟨-ni⟩ se˥kkin-suru ⟨〜に⟩接近する ③ •c [for s.o./s.a./s.t. non-temporal to move closer to s.t./s.o./s.a. ((fig. "be intimately related"))] ((come near))

EX. (a) A typhoon is approaching Japan.
台風が日本に{近付いて/接近して}いる。
Taifuu ga Nihon ni {chikazuite/sekkin-shite} iru.
(b) Summer is approaching.
夏が{近付いて/*接近して}いる。
*Natsu ga {chikazuite/*sekkin-shite} iru.*
(c) My yearly income is approaching ¥20,000,000.
私の年収は二千万円に{近付いた/*接近した}。
*Watashi no nenshuu wa ni-sen-man-en ni {chikazuita/*sekkin-shita}.*

2. ⟨-ni⟩ Vinf. nonpast hanashi o mo˥chi-kakeru ⟨〜に⟩Vinf. nonpast話を持ちかける ② [for s.o. to make a proposal to s.o.]

EX. My friends approached me about starting a new business.
友達が新しい事業を始める話を僕に持ちかけてきた。
Tomodachi ga atarashii jigyoo o hajimeru hanashi o boku ni mochi-kakete kita.

—— n.

1. se˥kkin 接近 •c [an act/instance of coming closer]

EX. The imminent approach of the typhoon put the village in a state of panic.
台風の急接近で村はパニック状態になった。
Taifuu no kyuu-sekkin de mura wa panikku-jootai ni natta.

2. ho˥ohoo 方法 •c [a way to do s.t.] ((method)), a˥puro˥ochi アプローチ •f

EX. What is the best approach to solving this problem?
この問題を解決する最善の{方法/アプローチ}は何でしょうか。
Kono mondai o kaiketsu-suru saizen no {hoohoo/apuroochi} wa nan deshoo ka.

appropriate adj. **[being proper to a task/situation]**

te˥kitoona 適当な adj(*na*). **•c ((suitable, fit, proper))**

EX. Put an appropriate word in the parentheses.
かっこの中に適当なことばを入れなさい。
Kakko no naka ni tekitoona kotoba o irenasai.

approval n. **[an act/instance of considering s.t. to be okay]**

1. sa˥nsei 賛成 •c [an agreement with s.o.'s opinion] ((agreement)) ↔ hantai 反対 •c

2. sho˥onin 承認 •c [a formal consent to s.t.] ((okaying))

approve vt. **[for s.o. to consider s.t. good, satisfactory, or agreeable]**

⟨-ni⟩ sa˥nsei-suru ⟨〜に⟩賛成する ③ •c [for s.o. to think that s.o.'s opinion is good and express that openly] ((agree, support)) ↔ ⟨-ni⟩ hantai-suru ⟨〜に⟩反対する ③ •c; ⟨-o⟩ sho˥onin-suru ⟨〜を⟩承認する ③ •c [for s.o. to give an okay to s.t.] ((okay, recognize))

EX. We cannot approve the plan to construct a

A

nuclear power plant.
原子力発電所を建設する計画{に賛成/を承認}することはできない。
Genshi-ryoku-hatsuden-sho o kensetsu-suru keikaku {ni sansei/o shoonin}-suru koto wa dekinai.

approximate adj. **[more or less correct, exact, or similar]**
o⌈oyoso no N おおよそのN **[nearly correct]** **《rough》**

EX. (**a**) Give us an approximate figure.
おおよその数字を出して下さい。
Ooyoso no suuji o dashite kudasai.
(**b**) I gave our boss an approximate account of the event.
上司に催しのおおよその説明をした。
Jooshi ni moyooshi no ooyoso no setsumei o shita.

approximately adv. **[about]**
da⌈itai 大体 **•c [for the most part 《fig. "nearly"》]** **《about, roughly, generally》,**
ya⌉ku 約 **•c [about (used with a quantity)]** **《about》**

EX. It takes approximately twenty minutes to walk to the university.
大学まで歩いて{大体/約}二十分かかる。
Daigaku made aruite {daitai/yaku} ni-jup-pun kakaru.

April n.
shi-⌈gatsu⌉ 四月 **•c**

NOTE: 四月 is never pronounced **yon-gatsu*.

apron n. **[a cloth worn over the front part of the body and tied around the waist to keep one's clothes clean while cooking, etc.]**
e⌉puron エプロン **•f, ma⌈e-kake** 前掛け

EX. Mother is the one in the kitchen wearing an apron.
{エプロン/前掛け}をして台所にいるのが母です。
{Epuron/Mae-kake} o shite daidokoro ni iru no ga haha desu.

apt adj. **[tending to do s.t. or suitable for s.t.]**
1. V*masu* gachina V*masu*がちな adj(*na*). **[tending or inclined to do s.t.]** **《likely, tend to, be inclined to》**

EX. People are apt to think ill of others.
人は他人を悪く思いがちである。
Hito wa tanin o waruku omoi-gachi dearu.

2. te⌈kisetsuna 適切な adj(*na*). **•c [proper for a purpose]** **《pertinent, fit, adequate, appropriate, suitable, proper》**

EX. Donald's remark was apt for the situation.
ドナルドの発言はその情況に適切であった。
Donarudo no hatsugen wa sono jookyoo ni tekisetsu deatta.

aquarium n. **[a glass tank to keep fish, etc. alive or a building containing such tanks]**
su⌈izoku⌉-kan 水族館 **•c [a building that has fish or other water animals on exhibit],**
su⌈isoo 水そう **•c [a water tank]**

Arab n.
A⌈rabu⌉-jin アラブ人 **•f+c, A⌈rabia⌉-jin** アラビア人 **•f+c**

Arabia n.
A⌈rabia アラビア **•f**

Arabian adj. **[of Arab/Arabia]**
A⌈rabia no N アラビアのN **•f [of Arabia],**
A⌉rabu no N アラブのN **•f [of Arab],**
{A⌈rabu⌉/A⌈rabia⌉}-jin no N {アラブ/アラビア}人のN **[of the people of Arabia]**

—— n.
A⌈rabu⌉-jin アラブ人 **•f+c, A⌈rabia⌉-jin** アラビア人 **•f+c**

Arabic n.
A⌈rabia-go アラビア語 **•f+c**

arc n.
ko⌉ 弧 **•c**

architect n. **[s.o. who designs buildings and supervises their construction]**
ke⌈nchiku-ka 建築家 **•c**

architecture n. **[the art and science of designing and constructing buildings or the design/style of a building/buildings]**
ke⌈nchiku 建築 **•c** **《construction, building》**

EX. I am interested in Gothic architecture.
ゴシック建築に興味があります。
Goshikku-kenchiku ni kyoomi ga arimasu.

Arctic adj. **[of the most northern part of the earth]**

Ho⌈kkyoku no N 北極のN •c ↔ Nankyoku no N 南極のN •c; Ho⌈kkyoku-chi⌉hoo 北極地方 n. •c **[the most northern district of the world]** ⟪the Arctic⟫

are vi. **[affirmative nonpast tense of the second person singular or plural/first or third person plural of the copula and of the existential verb "to be"]**

1. de⌉su です cop. **[formal affirmative nonpast tense of the copula *da*]** ⟪is, am⟫, **da だ** cop. **[informal/written style affirmative nonpast tense of the copula]** ⟪is, am⟫, **de⌈a⌉ru である** cop. **[written style affirmative nonpast tense of the copula], dei⌈rassha⌉ru でいらっしゃる** cop. **[affirmative nonpast tense of the copula showing deference to the person in subject position]** ⟪is⟫, **dego⌈zaima⌉su でございます** cop. **[very formal affirmative nonpast tense of the copula]** ⟪is, am⟫

NOTE: *Degozaimasu* is always used in its formal form.

EX. (a) You are an American, aren't you?
アメリカ人{です/だ/でいらっしゃいます/*である/*であります/*でございます}ね。
*Amerika-jin {desu/da/deirasshaimasu/*dearu/*dearimasu/*degozaimasu} ne.*
(b) You are a promising scholar.
君は有望な学者{です/だ/である/*であります/*でいらっしゃいます/*でございます}。
*Kimi wa yuuboona gakusha {desu/da/dearu/*dearimasu/*deirasshaimasu/*degozaimasu}.*
(c) Whales are mammals.
鯨はほ乳類{です/だ/である/であります/でございます/*でいらっしゃいます}。
*Kujira wa honyuurui {desu/da/dearu/dearimasu/degozaimasu/*deirasshaimasu}.*

2. i⌈ru いる ② [for s.o./s.a. to exist] ⟪is, am, exist⟫, **a⌉ru ある ① [for s.t. to exist]** ⟪exist⟫, **i⌈rassha⌉ru いらっしゃる ① [for s.o. to the speaker shows deference to to exist]** ⟪is, exist⟫, **go⌈zaima⌉su ございます [for s.o. to exist ⟨fml⟩]** ⟪am, is, exist⟫, **o⌈rima⌉su おります [for the speaker or s.o./s.a. the speaker empathizes with to exist ⟨fml⟩]** ⟪am, is, exist⟫

NOTE: Both *gozaimasu* and *orimasu* are almost always used in their formal forms.

EX. (a) Where are you now?
今どこに{いる/いらっしゃる/*ございます/*おります}の。
*Ima doko ni {iru/irassharu/*gozaimasu/*orimasu} no.*
(b) There are many parks in this town.
この町には公園がたくさん{ある/ございます/*いる/*おります/*いらっしゃる}。
*Kono machi ni wa kooen ga takusan {aru/gozaimasu/*iru/*orimasu/*irassharu}.*
(c) My father and mother are in Hokkaido now.
父と母は今北海道に{います/おります/*あります/*いらっしゃいます/*ございます}。
*Chichi to haha wa ima Hokkaidoo ni {imasu/orimasu/*arimasu/*irasshaimasu/*gozaimasu}.*

— aux. **[an auxiliary verb used in the passive or progressive construction]**

1. {Vneg. reru/Vstem rareru/sa⌈re⌉ru} {Vneg.れる/Vstemられる/される} ② [for s.t./s.o./s.a. acting as the subject of the sentence to be affected by the action of the verb of that sentence]

EX. You are often praised by your teacher, aren't you?
先生によくほめられるんでしょ?
Sensei ni yoku home-rareru n desho?

2. V*te* iru V*te*いる ② [to be in the middle of doing s.t. or in a state resulting from s.t. that happened earlier]

EX. Are you still studying Japanese?
まだ日本語を勉強していますか。
Mada Nihon-go o benkyoo-shite imasu ka.

area n. **[a region/part of the world, a country, a city, etc.]**

A

chi⌉iki 地域 •c [a geographic division characterizable in terms of climate/culture/natural environment] ((region, district)), **chi⌈ta⌉i 地帯 •c [a belt-like geographical part/division with certain characteristics]** ((zone, belt))

EX. (a) The residents in this area are strongly oppossed to the construction of a new golf course.
新しいゴルフ場の建設には{地域/*地帯}の住民の反対が強い。
*Atarashii gorufu-joo no kensetsu ni wa {chiiki/*chitai} no juumin no hantai ga tsuyoi.*
(b) That is an industrial area.
あそこは工業{地帯/*地域}です。
*Asoko wa koogyoo-{chitai/*chiiki} desu.*

PHRASE: in this area *kono hen* この辺, residential area *juutaku-chi* 住宅地

aren't vi. **[negative nonpast tense of the second person singular or plural of the copula and of the existential verb "to be"]**
1. **{dewaa⌈rimase⌉n/jaa⌈rimase⌉n}** {ではありません/じゃありません} **[formal negative nonpast tense of the copula *da*]** ((isn't, am not)), **{dewa⌈na⌉i/ja⌈na⌉i}** {ではない/じゃない} **[informal/written style negative nonpast of the copula]** ((isn't, am not))

EX. You are not a student, are you?
あなたは学生{ではありません/じゃありません/ではない/じゃない}よね。
Anata wa gakusei {dewaarimasen/jaarimasen/dewanai/janai} yo ne.

2. **i⌈nai** いない adj(*i*). **[for s.o./s.a. not to exist]** ((isn't, am not, not exist)), **na⌉i** ない adj(*i*). **[for s.t. not to exist]** ((isn't, there isn't))

EX. (a) You aren't here until five, are you?
ここに五時まで{いません/いない}よね。
Koko ni go-ji made {imasen/inai} yo ne.
(b) These dictionaries aren't in the library.
これらの辞書は図書館にはない。
Kore-ra no jisho wa tosho-kan ni wa nai.

NOTE: The formal nonpast form of *nai* is either *nai desu* or *arimasen.* The informal past form of *nai* is *nakatta* and its formal version is either *nakatta desu* or *arimasen deshita.* Similarly the formal nonpast form of *inai* is either *inai desu* or *imasen.* The informal past form of *inai* is *inakatta* and its formal version is either *inakatta desu* or *imasen deshita.*

— aux. **[an auxiliary verb used in the passive or progressive construction]**
1. **{Vneg. renai/Vstem rarenai/sarenai}** **{Vneg.れない/Vstemられない/されない}** **[for s.t./s.o./s.a. acting as the subject of the sentence not to be affected by the action of the verb of that sentence]**

EX. You aren't bullied by your classmates, are you, Joe?
ジョーはクラスメートにいじめられないよね。
Joo wa kurasu-meeto ni ijime-rarenai yo ne.

2. **V*te* inai V*te* いない [for s.o./s.a./s.t. not to be in the middle of doing s.t. or not to be in a state resulting from s.t. that happened earlier]**

EX. You aren't writing a novel any longer?
もう小説を書いていないの?
Moo shoosetsu o kaite inai no?

Argentina n.
A⌈ruze⌉nchin アルゼンチン •f

argue vt./vi. **[for s.o. to dispute (about) s.t. with s.o.]**
{⟨-o⟩/⟨-ni-tsuite⟩} **gi⌉ron-suru** {⟨～を⟩/⟨～について⟩}議論する ③ **•c [for s.o. to exchange opinions on some topic]** ((discuss, dispute, debate)), ⟨-ni-tsuite⟩ **ku⌈chi-araso⌉i-suru** ⟨～について⟩口争いする ③ **[for s.o. to fight verbally]**, ⟨-ni-tsuite⟩ **ko⌉oron-suru** ⟨～について⟩口論する ③ **•c** ((dispute))

EX. (a) We argued about the question of war and peace.
我々は戦争と平和の問題について{議論/?口論/*口争い}した。
*Ware-ware wa sensoo to heiwa no mondai ni-tsuite {giron/?kooron/*kuchi-arasoi}-shita.*
(b) The brothers argued in a loud voice.
兄弟は大声で{議論/口論/口争い}した。
Kyoodai wa oo-goe de {giron/kooron/

| *kuchi-arasoi}-shita.*

argument n. **[an act/instance of disputing (about) s.t. with s.o.]**
gi⌉ron 議論 •c [an exchange of opinions on some topic] ((discussion, dispute, debate)), **ku⌈chi-araso⌉i 口争い [a verbal fight]** ((dispute, quarrel)), **ko⌉oron 口論 •c**

EX. | Sachiko always starts arguments.
佐智子はいつも{議論/口争い/口論}を始める。
Sachiko wa itsu-mo {giron/kuchi-arasoi/kooron} o hajimeru.

arise vi. **[for s.t. to come into being or result from s.t.]**
o⌈ko⌉ru 起こる ① [for an unusual/disturbing event to take place] ((happen, occur, break out)), **o⌈ki⌉ru 起きる ② [for s.o./s.a./s.t. that has been lying horizontally dormant to stand up vertically ((fig. "wake up," "occur"))]** ((get up, happen, transpire, break out)), **sho⌈ojiru 生じる ② [for s.t. to come to exist]** ((stem, be born, be formed, occur))

EX. | (a) Difficulties arose in the course of negotiation.
交渉の途中で困難が{起こった/起きた/生じた}。
Kooshoo no tochuu de konnan ga {okotta/okita/shoojita}.
(b) We discussed problems arising from the changes in the immigration law.
移民法の改正によって{生じた/起こった/起きた}問題について話し合った。
Imin-hoo no kaisei ni yotte {shoojita/okotta/okita} mondai ni-tsuite hanashi-atta.

arithmetic n.
sa⌈nsu⌉u 算数 •c

Arizona n.
A⌈rizona アリゾナ •f

Arkansas n.
A⌈akanso⌉o アーカンソー •f

arm n. **[a bodily part between the shoulder and hand]**
u⌈de⌉ 腕 ((ability, skill))
NOTE: The Japanese word *te* can refer to arms as well as hand.

EX. | She has long arms.
彼女は{腕/手}が長い。
Kanojo wa {ude/te} ga nagai.

armed forces n.
gu⌉ntai 軍隊 •c

armor n.
yo⌈roi-ka⌉buto よろいかぶと, ka⌈tchu⌉u 甲ちゅう •c

yoroi-kabuto, katchuu

arms n. **[weapons used in war]**
bu⌉ki 武器 •c [an instrument used in combat] ((weapon))

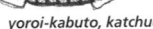

EX. | Have you read Hemingway's *A Farewell to Arms*?
ヘミングウエイの『武器よさらば』を読みましたか。
Heminguuei no "Buki yo saraba" o yomimashita ka.

army n.
ri⌈ku⌉-gun 陸軍 •c [armed forces deployed on land]

around prep. **[so as to encircle or envelop, etc. ((fig. "approximately"))]**
1. N no ma⌈wari {ni/de/o} Nの周り{に/で/を} n.+prt. **[surrounding s.t.]**

EX. | There are lots of trees around our house.
我が家の周りには木がたくさんある。
Waga-ya no mawari ni wa ki ga takusan aru.

NOTE: *Mawari* 周り is sometimes written as 回り with the same meaning.

2. a⌈chi⌉-kochi (to) あちこち(と) [in various places] ((here and there, from place to place))

EX. | Kaoru traveled around the world.
薫は世界をあちこち(と)旅行した。
Kaoru wa sekai o achi-kochi (to) ryokoo-shita.

3. ⟨-o⟩ ma⌈gatta⌉ to⌈koro⌉ ni ⟨～を⟩曲がったところに [at a place after one turns]

EX. | The telephone office is just around the corner.
電話局はすぐそこの角を曲がったところにあります。

A

Denwa-kyoku wa sugu soko no kado o magatta tokoro ni arimasu.

4. **{koro/-goro}** {ころ/〜ごろ} **[indicating approximate (point of) time]**

EX. Hideko usually comes here around 7:00.
英子はたいてい七時ごろここに来ます。
Hideko wa taitei shichi-ji-goro koko ni kimasu.

NOTE: With a specific time such as 7:00 P.M., use *-goro*. In a broader time frame such as the Meiji Era or at that time, use *koro* as in *Meiji no koro* or *ano koro*.

—— adv. **[in an encircling fashion]**

1. **ma⌈wari {ni/o}** 周り{に/を} n.+prt. **[one's surroundings]**

EX. Ken thought he heard someone call him and looked around, but saw no one.
健はだれかに呼ばれたと思い周りを見回したがだれもいなかった。
Ken wa dare-ka ni yoba-reta to omoi mawari o mi-mawashita ga dare-mo inakatta.

2. **a⌈chi⌉-kochi ({de/ni/o})** あちこち({で/に/を}) n.+prt. **[in every direction/here and there]**

EX. I took Mr.Wang around Tokyo.
私は東京で王さんをあちこち案内した。
Watashi wa Tookyoo de Wan-san o achi-kochi annai-shita.

3. **ma⌈wari** n. 周り **[the way or area s.t./s.o./s.a. goes around] ((circumference, surroundings, tour)), shu⌉ui** 周囲 **•c**

EX. Tony ran twice around the school.
トニーは学校の{周り/周囲}を二回走った。
Tonii wa gakkoo no {mawari/shuui} o ni-kai hashitta.

arouse vt. **[to let or cause s.t./s.o. to arise]**

1. **⟨-o⟩ o⌈ko⌉su** ⟨〜を⟩おこす ① **[to cause s.o./s.t./s.a. that is dormant or lying to be more active or to stand/wake up] ((set upright, begin, create, wake up, establish, restore))**

EX. The policeman aroused the old man from his sound sleep.
警官がぐっすり寝ていた老人を起こした。
Keikan ga gussuri nete ita roojin o okoshita.

NOTE: The above is more naturally expressed as follows: *Roojin wa gussuri nete ita tokoro o keikan ni oko-sareta.*

㊥ "restore" ▷おこす, otherwise ▷起こす

2. **⟨-o⟩ ka⌉nki-suru** ⟨〜を⟩喚起する ③ **•c [to evoke s.t.] ((awaken, stir up))**

EX. It may be a difficult task to arouse interest in the audience.
聴衆の関心を喚起するのはたいへんな作業でしょう。
Chooshuu no kanshin o kanki-suru no wa taihenna sagyoo deshoo.

arrange vt. **[for s.o. to put s.t. in proper order ((fig. "make plans"))]**

1. **⟨-o⟩ to⌈tonoe⌉ru** ⟨〜を⟩整える ② **[for s.o. to put s.t. in due order ((fig. "prepare"))]**

EX. Emi arranged her dress before going out.
恵美は出かける前に衣服を整えた。
Emi wa dekakeru mae ni ifuku o totonoeta.

2. **⟨-o⟩ to⌈ri-kimeru** ⟨〜を⟩取り決める ② **[for s.o. to make plans/preparations for s.t. or decide on s.t.] ((agree on/upon, decide on, fix, settle))**

EX. The diplomats arranged the schedule for the summit conference.
外交官は首脳会談の日程を取り決めた。
Gaikoo-kan wa shunoo-kaidan no nittei o tori-kimeta.

NOTE: In the case of arranging flowers, the proper verb in Japanese is *ikeru* ②, as in *hana o ikeru. Ikebana* is "flower arrangement."

arrangement n. **[an act/result of arranging]**

1. **se⌉iri** 整理 **•c [an act/result of putting things/people in order], se⌉iton** 整とん **•c [an act/result of putting concrete things in order], na⌈rabe-kata** 並べ方 **[the way one arranges things]**

EX. (a) Nowadays we use computers for the arrangement of documents.
今では書類の{整理/?整とん/*並べ方}にコンピューターを使う。
*Ima de wa shorui no {seiri/?seiton/ *narabe-kata} ni konpyuutaa o tsukau.*

(**b**) This example illustrates an awkward arrangement of words.
この例は語のまずい{並べ方/*整理/*整とん}を示しています。
*Kono rei wa go no mazui {narabe-kata/ *seiri/*seiton} o shimeshite imasu.*

2. to⌈ri-kime 取り決め [an act/result of making plans/preparations for s.t. or deciding on s.t.] ⟪agreement, settlement, decision⟫

EX. By prior arrangement, Misato is the first speaker.
以前からの取り決めにより、美里が最初の講演者です。
Izen kara no tori-kime ni yori, Misato ga saisho no kooen-sha desu.

3. (usually pl.) **yo⌉oi 用意 •c [an act of preparing for s.t. that will take place fairly soon] ⟪preparations⟫, ju⌉nbi 準備 •c [an act of carefully making s.t. ready for some purpose well ahead of time] ⟪preparation, provision⟫, shi⌈taku 支度 [an act of making ready s.t. that is necessary for some purpose, esp. a meal/outing/trip] ⟪preparation⟫**

EX. (**a**) Sam is making arrangements for Keiko's birthday party.
サムは啓子の誕生パーティーの{用意/準備/支度}をしている。
Samu wa Keiko no tanjoo-paatii no {yooi/junbi/shitaku} o shite iru.
(**b**) The student is making arrangements for an exam.
学生は試験の{準備/?用意/*支度}をしている。
*Gakusei wa shiken no {junbi/?yooi/ *shitaku} o shite iru.*

arrest vt. **[for s.o. to seize a criminal in the name of the law]**
⟨-o⟩ ta⌉iho-suru ⟨〜を⟩逮捕する ③ •c

EX. The police arrested the suspect.
警察は容疑者を逮捕した。
Keisatsu wa yoogi-sha o taiho-shita.

arrival n. **[an act of arriving]**
to⌈ochaku 到着 •c [an arriving]

EX. I am waiting for the arrival of the flight from Tunisia.
チュニジアからの飛行機の到着を待っています。
Chunijia kara no hikoo-ki no toochaku o matte imasu.

arrive vi. **[to come to some destination]**
⟨-ni⟩ tsu⌈ku⌉ ⟨〜に⟩つく ① [for s.o./s.t./s.a. to attach himself/herself/itself to s.o./s.t./ s.a. else ⟪fig. "come/turn on"⟫] ⟪get to, reach, become attached, touch, engage in, study under, follow, come/turn on⟫, ⟨-ni⟩ to⌈ochaku-suru ⟨〜に⟩到着する ③ •c [for s.o. to reach a destination] ⟪get to, reach⟫

EX. Their bus has just arrived.
彼らのバスは今{着いた/到着した}ところだ。
Kare-ra no basu wa ima {tsuita/ toochaku-shita} tokoro da.

㊉ "arrive"▷着く, "become attached"▷付く, "take a position in a company, etc."▷就く, otherwise ▷つく

arrow n. **[an object shot from a bow or a sign similar to it in shape]**
ya⌉ 矢 •c [an object shot from a bow], ya⌈ji⌉rushi 矢印 •c [a sign similar in shape to an object shot from a bow]

art n. **[skill in the making/doing of s.t., esp. s.t. beautiful]**
ge⌈ijutsu 芸術 •c [skill applied to creative work or creative work itself], bi⌉jutsu 美術 •c [the making of drawings, paintings, statues, etc.]

EX. (**a**) Sachiko is an art history major.
祥子は{美術/*芸術}史を専攻している。
*Sachiko wa {bijutsu/*geijutsu}-shi o senkoo-shite iru.*
(**a**) He has no sense of art.
彼は{芸術/?美術}が分からない。
Kare wa {geijutsu/?bijutsu} ga wakaranai.

PHRASE: art gallery *bijutsu-kan* 美術館 •c, *garoo* 画廊 •c

article n. **[a piece of writing on a particular subject in a magazine, etc., or a particular thing/object, or a part of speech, or a section of a legal agreement]**
1. ki⌉ji 記事 •c [a complete piece of writing,

A

as in a newspaper, etc.]

EX. I always read articles on trade problems in the major newspapers.
僕はいつも主要新聞の貿易問題に関する記事を読みます。
Boku wa itsu-mo shuyoo-shinbun no booeki-mondai ni kansuru kiji o yomimasu.

2. shi⌈na-mono 品物 [an item for sale] ⟪goods, wares, commodity⟫

EX. That store carries articles of high quality.
あの店はいい品物を売っている。
Ano mise wa ii shina-mono o utte iru.

3. ka⌈nshi 冠詞 •c [the grammatical term referring to a, an, and the]

4. jo⌈okoo 条項 •c [one of the sections of a legal document such as a contract]

EX. I was asked to translate the articles of a technical agreement.
技術契約の条項を翻訳するように頼まれた。
Gijutsu-keiyaku no jookoo o hon'yaku-suru yooni tanoma-reta.

artistic adj. **[of art/artists]**
ge⌈ijutsu-tekina 芸術的な adj(*na*). **•c**

as adv. **[equally, like]**
o⌈naji-ku⌉rai 同じくらい [to about the same extent] ⟪equally⟫

EX. Lisa is just as good as Carol at Japanese.
リサはキャロルと同じくらい日本語が上手だ。
Risa wa Kyaroru to onaji-kurai Nihon-go ga joozu da.

—— conj. **[in the way or manner that]**

1. Sinf. yo⌉oni Sinf.ように, Vinf. ⌈toori⌉ ni Vinf.とおりに [in exactly the same manner that]

EX. When in Rome, do as the Romans do.
ローマではローマ人がする{ように/とおりに}しなさい。
Rooma de wa Rooma-jin ga suru {yooni/toori ni} shinasai.

NOTE: A similar Japanese proverb is *Goo ni itte wa goo ni shitagae.*

2. Vinf. nonpast ni tsu⌈rete Vinf. nonpast につれて /(V*te* of *tsureru* ② take s.o. along/ [a change occurs in accordance with another simultaneously occurring change] ⟪with, in proportion to⟫

EX. As it grew dark, I became more and more uneasy.
暗くなるにつれて、ますます不安になってきた。
Kuraku naru ni tsurete, masu-masu fuan ni natte-kita.

3. Sinf. no⌉de Sinf.ので [a subordinate conjunction expressing reason or cause. The speaker believes that the information he/she provides in "S1 node" as cause/reason for "S2" is valid and is also evident and acceptable to the listener] ⟪because, since⟫, Sinf. kara Sinf.から [a subordinate conjunction expressing reason or cause] ⟪so, since, because⟫

NOTE: When the non-past affirmative of adj(*na*). or N+cop. occurs before *node,* {adj(*na*). stem/N} *na* is used.

EX. As the rent is reasonable, Tim will probably take the apartment.
家賃がそう高くない{ので/から}、ティムは多分そのアパートを借りるでしょう。
Yachin ga soo takakunai {node/kara}, Timu wa tabun sono apaato o kariru deshoo.

4. ke⌉(re)do(mo) け(れ)ど(も) [a disjunctive subordinate conjunction that combines two sentences] ⟪although⟫, Sinf. noni Sinf. のに [contrary to everybody's expectation based on the sentence preceding *noni*, the proposition in the sentence following *noni* is the case] ⟪even though, despite the fact that⟫

NOTE: When the nonpast affirmative form of adj(*na*). or N+cop. occurs before *noni*, {adj(*na*). stem/N} *na* is used.

EX. (**a**) Late as it was, we decided to go out.
遅かった{け(れ)ど(も)/?のに}私たちは外出することにした。
Osokatta {ke(re)do(mo)/?noni} watashi-tachi wa gaishutsu-suru koto ni shita.
(**b**) Child as she was, Rie knew a lot about physics.

子供{だったけ(れ)ど(も)/なのに}、理恵は物理学をよく知っていた。
Kodomo {datta ke(re)do(mo)/na noni}, Rie wa butsuri-gaku o yoku shitte ita.

— prep. **[in the role/function of]**
to-shite として comp. prt. **[in the capacity of]**

EX. You can use this box as a chair.
この箱はいすとして使えます。
Kono hako wa isu to-shite tsukae-masu.

— pron. **[(when used together with "such" or "the same") a relative pronoun which introduces a sentence modifying the preceding noun in the meaning "similar or identical to"]**
Sinf. yo⌉ona Sinf.ような awx. adj(*na*). **[like s.o./s.a./s.t. that...]**

NOTE: When the nonpast affirmative form of adj(*na*). or N+cop. occurs before *yooni*, the form changes to adj(*na*). stem *na* or N *no*, respectively.

EX. I'd like to buy a car such as Ed has.
エドが持っているような車を買いたい。
Edo ga motte iru yoona kuruma o kai-tai.

PHRASE: as is *sono mama de* そのままで

EX. The price of this bicycle is $20 as is.
この自転車の値段はそのままで二十ドルです。
Kono jitensha no nedan wa sono mama de ni-juu-doru desu.

PHRASE: as soon as possible *dekiru dake hayaku* 出来るだけ早く

EX. Would you pay me as soon as possible?
できるだけ早く私にお支払いいただけますか。
Dekiru dake hayaku watashi ni o-shiharai itadake-masu ka.

ash n.
ha⌈i 灰

ashamed adj. **[feeling inferior or unworthy due to consciousness of guilt]**
ha⌈zukashi⌉i 恥ずかしい adj(*i*). **[feeling shame/fear of appearing in front of others]** **((be ashamed, shameful, bashful, embarrassed))**

EX. I was really ashamed that I had failed the exam.
試験に落ちて本当に恥ずかしかった。
Shiken ni ochite hontoo ni hazukashikatta.

ashore adv.
ki⌈shi⌉ {ni/de/e} 岸{に/で/へ} n.+prt. **[to/on the shore]**

ashtray n.
ha⌈i-zara 灰皿

Asia n.
A⌉jia アジア •f

aside adv. **[away or apart]**
wa⌈ki⌉ ni わきに n.+prt. **[on the side of s.o./s.t./s.a.]** **((beside, by))**, **ha⌈na⌉rete** 離れて /⟨V*te* of *hanareru* ② separate/ **[to be separated from a place/person]** **((apart from))**

EX. (a) Tomoko put the cat aside and stood up.
知子は猫を{わきに/*離れて}置いて立ち上がった。
*Tomoko wa neko o {waki ni/*hanarete} oite tachi-agatta.*
(b) The man stood aside to let the lady pass.
女性を通すために男は{離れて/わきに}立った。
Josei o toosu tame ni otoko wa {hanarete/waki ni} tatta.

ask vt. **[for s.o. to inquire/request]**
1. **(⟨-ni⟩) ⟨-o⟩ ta⌉zune⌉ru** (⟨〜に⟩)⟨〜を⟩たずねる ② **[for s.o. to put a question to s.o.]** **((inquire))**, **(⟨-ni⟩) ⟨-o⟩ ki⌈ku** (⟨〜に⟩)⟨〜を⟩きく ① **[for s.o./s.a. to focus one's attention on a sound so that it is perceived by the ears or to request/receive information from s.o. about s.t. orally or to take notice and accept s.t. said by another]** **((listen, inquire))**

㊅ "ask"▷尋ねる, "visit"▷訪ねる
㊅ "listen to s.t. seriously"▷聴く, otherwise ▷聞く

EX. Dorothy asked Nick when he'd returned from Japan.
ドロシーはニックにいつ日本から戻ったか{尋ねた/聞いた}。
Doroshii wa Nikku ni itsu Nihon kara modotta ka {tazuneta/kiita}.

A

2. ⟨-ni⟩ ⟨-o⟩ ta⌈no⌉mu ⟨〜に⟩⟨〜を⟩頼む ① **[for s.o. to request s.t. of s.o.]** ⟪beg, implore, request⟫

EX. The students asked the teacher to postpone the test.
学生は先生にテストを延期するよう頼んだ。
Gakusei wa sensei ni tesuto o enki-suru yoo tanonda.

PHRASE: ask…a favor ⟨*-ni*⟩ *o-negai-suru* ⟨〜に⟩お願いする ③

EX. John asked his father a favor.
ジョンはお父さんにお願いした。
Jon wa o-too-san ni o-negai-shita.

PHRASE: ask…a question ⟨*-ni*⟩ *shitsumon-suru* ⟨〜に⟩質問する ③ •c

asleep adj./adv.

ne⌈mutte 眠って **/⟨V*te* of *nemuru* ① sleep/ ⟪sleeping⟫**

EX. The dog was fast asleep.
犬はぐっすり眠っていた。
Inu wa gussuri nemutte ita.

aspect n. **[the way s.t. appears/looks ⟪fig. "phase"⟫]**

1. yo⌈osu 様子 **•c [the way s.o./s.t./s.a. looks] ⟪state, condition, appearance⟫**

EX. The office was changed in aspect.
オフィスは様子が変わった。
Ofisu wa yoosu ga kawatta.

2. kyo⌈kumen 局面 **•c [one of a number of different appearances to a situation depending on one's vantage point in space or time] ⟪situation, phase⟫**

EX. We must consider the matter from different aspects.
本件は違う局面から考慮しないといけない。
Honken wa chigau kyokumen kara kooryo-shinai to ikenai.

3. so⌉o 相 **•c [a grammatical term referring to phenomena such as perfective and progressive]**

assembly n. **[the meeting together of a group of people for a specific purpose]**

shu⌈ukai 集会 **•c [an act/instance of many people gathering in a place at a certain time to talk] ⟪rally, meeting, gathering, congregation⟫, ka⌈igoo** 会合 **•c [an act/instance of many people gathering for consultation] ⟪meeting, gathering, get-together⟫**

EX. (**a**) They held an assembly at school to debate the issue.
彼らはその問題を討議するため学校で{集会/*会合}を持った。
*Kare-ra wa sono mondai o toogi-suru tame gakkoo de {shuukai/*kaigoo} o motta.*
(**b**) The college called a faculty assembly.
大学は教授たちの{会合/集会}を開いた。
Daigaku wa kyooju-tachi no {kaigoo/shuukai} o hiraita.

assert vt. **[for s.o. to declare/maintain s.t.]**

1. {⟨-to⟩/⟨-o⟩} **shu⌈choo-suru** {⟨〜と⟩/⟨〜を⟩}主張する ③ **•c [for s.o. to state one's opinion firmly with a view to making others agree with it or accept it] ⟪maintain, defend, hold, claim, insist⟫**

EX. (**a**) Toshihiko asserted his rights at the hearing.
俊彦は公聴会で自分の権利を主張した。
Toshihiko wa koochoo-kai de jibun no kenri o shuchoo-shita.
(**b**) She asserted that she was innocent.
彼女は無実だと主張した。
Kanojo wa mujitsu da to shuchoo-shita.

2. ⟨-to⟩ **da⌈nge⌉n-suru** ⟨〜と⟩断言する ③ **•c [for s.o. to declare decisively on the basis of evidence that s.t. is true] ⟪state positively, declare, affirm⟫**

EX. The politician asserted that the bill was for the good of the country.
政治家はその法案が国のためであると断言した。
Seiji-ka wa sono hooan ga kuni no tame dearu to dangen-shita.

assign vt. **[for s.o. to set/mark for a specific purpose]**

⟨-o⟩ **wa⌈ri-ate⌉ru** ⟨〜を⟩割り当てる ② **⟪allot, allocate⟫**

EX. The professor assigned a different task to each of the students.

教授は各々の学生に違った課題を割り当てた。
Kyooju wa ono-ono no gakusei ni chigatta kadai o wari-ateta.

assignment n. **[s.t. allotted]**
1. wa⌈ri-ate 割り当て ⟪allotment, allocation⟫
2. ka⌈dai 課題 •c [s.t. given to a person as a task to accomplish] •c ⟪task⟫, shu⌈kudai 宿題 [school work to be done at home] •c ⟪homework⟫

EX. Taro has to do many homework assignments during the summer.
太郎は夏にたくさんの{課題/宿題}をしなければならない。
Taroo wa natsu ni takusan no {kadai/shukudai} o shinakereba naranai.

assist vt. **[usually for a subordinate to help his/her superior]**
⟨-o⟩ ta⌈suke⌉ru ⟨〜を⟩助ける ② [for s.o./s.a. to provide resources or one's own time/energy to s.o./s.a. to enable it/him/her to escape danger/death/difficulty or to ensure that s.t. goes well] ⟪help, aid, save⟫, ⟨-o⟩ te⌈tsuda⌉u ⟨〜を⟩手伝う ① [for s.o. to do part of s.o.'s work for him/her] ⟪help⟫

EX. (**a**) Kazuko assisted her husband in carrying out the project.
和子は夫を{助けて/*手伝って}任務を全うさせた。
*Kazuko wa otto o {tasukete/*tetsudatte} ninmu o mattoo-saseta.*
(**b**) The research fellow assisted the professor in translating the article into English.
助手は教授の論文の英訳を{手伝った/*助けた}。
*Joshu wa kyooju no ronbun no ei-yaku o {tetsudatta/*tasuketa}.*

assistance n. **[an act/instance of assisting a person/group]**
e⌉njo 援助 •c [an act/instance of helping s.o. in a troubled situation] ⟪aid, support, help⟫, jo⌈ryoku 助力 •c [an act/instance of helping s.o. in need] ⟪help, aid, support⟫

EX. (**a**) Many African countries require food assistance.
アフリカの国の多くは食糧{援助/*助力}を必要としている。
*Afurika no kuni no ooku wa shokuryoo-{enjo/*joryoku} o hitsuyoo to shite iru.*
(**b**) She needs my assistance.
彼女は私の{助力/援助}を必要としている。
Kanojo wa watashi no {joryoku/enjo} o hitsuyoo to shite iru.

associate vt./vi. **[to connect or combine s.t./s.o. with another]**
1. ⟨-o⟩ re⌈nsoo-suru ⟨〜を⟩連想する ③ •c [for s.o. to connect s.t./s.o./s.a. with another in one's mind] ⟪remind…of⟫

EX. We associate peace with prosperity.
平和と聞くと繁栄を連想する。
Heiwa to kiku to han'ei o rensoo-suru.

2. ⟨-to⟩ ko⌈osai-suru ⟨〜と⟩交際する ③ •c [for s.o. to keep company with s.o. as a friend] ⟪keep company with, go out with⟫

EX. Try to associate only with good people.
善良な人間とのみ交際するようにしなさい。
Zenryoona ningen to nomi koosai-suru yooni shinasai.

—— n. **[a fellow worker]**
na⌈kama⌉ 仲間 [a person in one's in-group with whom one frequently spends time, excluding one's relatives, spouse, and offspring ⟪fig. "the same kind"⟫] ⟪partner, colleague, friend⟫, do⌉oryoo 同僚 •c [a person of same status in a place of work] ⟪colleague⟫, kyo⌈odoo-keiei⌉-sha 共同経営者 •c [a person with whom one runs a business] ⟪partner⟫

association n. **[an act/result of associating or a group of people joined together for a shared purpose]**
1. kyo⌈okai 協会 •c [an organization established and maintained by a group of people cooperating together for some public purpose] ⟪organization, society⟫

EX. The association for international understanding to which I belong will have its annual meeting next Saturday.
私が所属している国際理解のための協

会は、次の土曜日に年次大会を開催する。
Watashi ga shozoku-shite iru kokusai-rikai no tame no kyookai wa, tsugi no doyoo-bi ni nenji-taikai o kaisai-suru.

2. ko⌈osai 交際 •c [the act of associating with persons other than your family/relatives] **《fellowship, partnership, companionship, dating》, ka⌈kawari-ai かかわりあい [a relationship/connection]** **《connection, ties》**

EX. The president denied any association with the gangster.
社長は暴力団員との{交際/かかわりあい}を否定した。
Shachoo wa booryoku-dan-in to no {koosai/kakawari-ai} o hitei-shita.

3. re⌈nsoo 連想 •c [a mental connection between ideas]

assume vt. **[for s.o. to take s.t. on oneself or take on an appearance, role 《fig. "presume"》]**

1. 〈-o〉 hi⌈ki-uke⌉ru 〈〜を〉引き受ける ② [for s.o. to take on the responsibility for s.t./s.o./s.a.] 《undertake》

EX. The Personnel Manager assumed full responsibility for the training of the new employees.
人事部長は新入社員研修の全責任を引き受けた。
Jinji-buchoo wa shinnyuu-shain-kenshuu no zen-sekinin o hiki-uketa.

2. Sinf. fu⌈ri⌉ o su⌈ru Sinf.ふりをする ③ [to pretend to do s.t.] 《feign》, 〈-o〉 yo⌈soo⌉u 〈〜を〉装う ① [to pretend as if s.t. were true] 《pretend, affect, be dressed in》

EX. Saburo assumed ignorance of the incident.
三郎はその事件に関して{知らないふりをした/無知を装った}。
Saburoo wa sono jiken ni kanshite {shiranai furi o shita/muchi o yosootta}.

NOTE: When the nonpast affirmative form of adj(*na*). or N+cop. occurs before *furi o suru*, the form changes to adj(*na*). stem *na* or N *no*, respectively.

3. 〈-to〉 ka⌈tei-suru 〈〜と〉仮定する ③ •c [for s.o. to suppose, presume] 《suppose, presume, hypothesize》

EX. The grammarian assumed that in the language he was studying the verb always came at the end of the sentence.
文法家は、研究中の言語では動詞がいつも文末に来ると仮定した。
Bunpoo-ka wa, kenkyuu-chuu no gengo de wa dooshi ga itsu-mo bun-matsu ni kuru to katei-shita.

assumption n. **[an act/instance of assuming]** **ka⌈tei 仮定 •c 《supposition》, hi⌈ki-uke⌉ru koto 引き受けること 《acceptance, undertaking》, ka⌈setsu 仮説 •c 《hypothesis》, mi⌈sekake 見せかけ 《pretense》**

PHRASE: on the assumption that… *…to iu katei no moto ni* …という仮定のもとに

assure vt. **[for s.o. to give confidence to s.o. that s.t. is certain]**

{〈-to〉/〈-o〉} ho⌈shoo-suru {〈〜と〉/〈〜を〉}保証する ③ •c [for s.o. to give a formal promise that s.t. will be done] 《guarantee, ensure, certify》, ta⌈shikani…to i⌈u 確かに…と言う ① [for s.o. to say that s.t. is certainly the case] 《ensure》

EX. (**a**) I assure you that there is enough money to carry it out.
それを実行するお金は{十分あることを保証します/*確かに十分あると言います}。
*Sore o jikkoo-suru o-kane wa {juubun aru koto o hoshoo-shimasu/*tashikani juubun aru to iimasu}.*
(**b**) He assured me that he was coming.
彼は{確かに来ると言いました/*来ることを保証しました}。
*Kare wa {tashikani kuru to iimashita/*kuru koto o hoshoo-shimashita}.*

astonish vt. **[to fill s.o. with sudden surprise]**

〈-o〉 o⌈doroka⌉-su 〈〜を〉驚かす /〈the shorter causative of *odoroku* ① be surprised/ ① [to shock s.o./s.a. unawares] 《surprise》, 〈-o〉 o⌈doroka-se⌉ru 〈〜を〉驚かせる /〈causative of *odoroku* ① be surprised/ ② [to cause s.o./s.a. to be surprised at a sudden or

unexpected event], 〈-o〉 bi⌈kku⌉ri-saseru 〈〜を〉びっくりさせる /〈causative of *bikkuri-suru* ③ be surprised/ ②

EX. The news astonished my father.
そのニュースは父を{驚かせた/驚かした/びっくりさせた}。
Sono nyuusu wa chichi o {odoroka-seta/odoroka-shita/bikkuri-saseta}.

NOTE: The above is more naturally expressed as follows: *Sono nyuusu o kiite chichi wa {odoroita/bikkuri-shita}.*

astonishing adj. **[causing great surprise] o⌈doroku-be⌉ki N 驚くべきN 〈w〉 《surprising, amazing》, bi⌈kku⌉ri-suru yoona びっくりするような** adj(*na*). **《surprizing》**

EX. It was an astonishing event.
それは{驚くべき/びっくりするような}出来事だった。
Sore wa {odoroku-beki/bikkuri-suru yoona} deki-goto datta.

astonishment n. **[great surprise] o⌈doroki⌉ 驚き /〈V*masu* of *odoroku* ① be surprised/ 《surprise》**

astringent adj. **[severe, bitter] shi⌈bu⌉i 渋い** adj(*i*). **[said of unripe fruit, etc., with a taste causing a numbing sensation in the tongue 《fig. "sullen," "refined"》] 《puckery, glum, sulky, tasty》**

astronaut n.
u⌈chuu-hikoo⌉ shi 宇宙飛行士 •c

astronomer n.
te⌈nmon-gaku⌉sha 天文学者 •c

astronomy n.
te⌈nmo⌉n-gaku 天文学 •c

at prep. **[denotes a spatio-temporal location]**

1. de で prt. **[a particle indicating location of an activity or event] 《in, on》, ni に** prt. **[a particle indicating a spatial/temporal point of contact, often construed as a location where s.t./s.o. exists, a goal, or an indirect object] 《in, on》**

EX. (**a**) Hideo and Yukari had their wedding at a church in Honolulu.
英夫と夕加里はホノルルの教会{で/*に}結婚式を挙げた。
*Hideo to Yukari wa Honoruru no kyookai {de/*ni} kekkon-shiki o ageta.*
(**b**) The plane arrived at Kennedy Airport on time.
飛行機は定刻にケネディー空港{に/*で}到着した。
*Hikoo-ki wa teikoku ni Kenedii Kuukoo {ni/*de} toochaku-shita.*
(**c**) Classes at this school begin at 8:00.
この学校の授業は八時{に/*で}始まります。
*Kono gakkoo no jugyoo wa hachi-ji {ni/*de} hajimarimasu.*
(**d**) My sister got married at age twenty-two.
妹は二十二の時{に/*で}結婚した。
*Imooto wa ni-juu-ni no toki {ni/*de} kekkon-shita.*

2. 〈-ni〉 mu⌈katte 〈〜に〉向かって /〈V*te* of *mukau* ① head/ [to or toward/in the direction of], ni に prt. **[a particle indicating a spatial/temporal point of contact, often construed as a location where s.t./s.o. exists, a goal, or an indirect object] 《to, toward》**

EX. The child threw a stone at the dog.
子供は犬{に向かって/に}石を投げた。
Kodomo wa inu {ni mukatte/ni} ishi o nageta.

3. V*te* V*te* [of perception verbs such as *mite, kiite, shitte* used with emotive verbs expressing a cause/reason] 《because of》

EX. Akemi will be elated at the news.
朱美はその知らせを聞いて大喜びするでしょう。
Akemi wa sono shirase o kiite oo-yorokobi-suru deshoo.

4. de で prt. **[a particle expressing rate, quantity, degree, price, speed, etc.]**

EX. This train runs at 230 km per hour.
この列車は時速230キロで走る。
Kono ressha wa jisoku ni-hyaku-san-juk-kiro de hashiru.

PHRASE: at last *tsuini* ついに [s.t. expected/feared arises after a long time and long thinking] 《finally》, *tootoo* とうとう [some state/situation arises as a final result of s.t.] 《finally》, *yatto* やっと [at the end after having

A

tried hard or waited for a long time] ((finally))

EX. At last, Bob entered the school of his choice.
ボブは{ついに/とうとう/やっと}志望校に入れた。
Bobu wa {tsuini/tootoo/yatto} shiboo-koo ni haire-ta.

PHRASE: at any rate *tonikaku* とにかく ((anyway))

EX. It was a boring play, but at any rate there was one outstanding individual performance.
たいくつな芝居だが、とにかく一人きわだった演技者がいた。
Taikutsuna shibai da ga, tonikaku hitori kiwa-datta engi-sha ga ita.

Athens n.
A|tene アテネ •f

athlete n. **[s.o. trained to compete in sports, etc.]**
u|ndoo-se|nshu 運動選手 •c

athletic adj. **[relating to sports and physical exercises or physically strong]**
kyo|ogi no N 競技のN •c, **su|pootsu-man rashi|i** スポーツマンらしい adj(*i*). **[characteristic of an athlete]** ((**sportsmanlike**))

Atlantic adj.
Ta|ise|iyoo no N 大西洋のN •c

PHRASE: the Atlantic Ocean *Taiseiyoo* 大西洋 •c

atmosphere n. **[the mixture of gases that surround the earth or a feeling in the mind created by people/a place]**
ta|iki-ke|n 大気圏 •c **[the air surrounding the earth], fu|n'i|ki** 雰囲気 •c **[a temporary state of mind evoked by an artistic work or an environment]**

EX. (**a**) This coffee shop has a good atmosphere.
この喫茶店は{雰囲気/*大気圏}がいい。
*Kono kissa-ten wa {fun'iki/*taiki-ken} ga ii.*
(**b**) Chlorofluorocarbon destroys the ozone layer in the atmosphere.
フロンガスは{大気圏/*雰囲気}のオゾン層を破壊する。
*Furon-gasu wa {taiki-ken/*fun'iki} no ozon-soo o hakai-suru.*

atmospheric adj. **[for/relating to the earth's atmosphere]**
ta|iki no N 大気のN •c, **ta|iki-chuu no N** 大気中のN •c **[in the atmosphere]**

atom n.
ge|nshi 原子 •c

atomic adj.
ge|nshi no N 原子のN •c

EX. The atomic bomb was first dropped on Hiroshima.
原子爆弾は初めて広島に落とされた。
Genshi-bakudan wa hajimete Hiroshima ni otosa-reta.

attach vt. **[for s.o. to fasten/join/connect s.t. by some means]**
1. ⟨**-ni**⟩ ⟨**-o**⟩ **tsu|ke|ru** ⟨〜に⟩⟨〜を⟩つける ② **[for s.o./s.a. to cause s.t./s.o. to adhere to s.t./s.o./s.a. else]** ((**fix, fasten, spread**)), ⟨**-ni**⟩ ⟨**-o**⟩ **to|ri-tsukeru** ⟨〜に⟩⟨〜を⟩取り付ける ② **[for s.o. to set an apparatus into position onto s.t.]** ((**join, fix, install**))
㊊ "attach/fix/spread"▷付ける, "wear"▷着ける, otherwise ▷つける

EX. (**a**) Be sure to attach this label to your suitcase.
このラベルをスーツケースに{付ける/*取り付ける}のを忘れないで下さい。
*Kono raberu o suutsukeesu ni {tsukeru/*tori-tsukeru} no o wasurenaide kudasai.*
(**b**) We attached an air-conditioner to the wall.
壁にエアコンを{取り付けた/?付けた}。
Kabe ni eakon o {tori-tsuketa/?tsuketa}.

2. ⟨**-o**⟩ **a|ishite i|ru** ⟨〜を⟩愛している /⟨V *te iru* of {*aisuru* ③/ *aisu* ①} love/ ② **[to connect to s.t. by ties of affection, etc.]**, ⟨**-ni**⟩ **a|ichaku o mo|tte iru** ⟨〜に⟩愛着をもっている /⟨V *te iru* of *motsu* ① have/ ② **[to feel an attachment to]** ((**be very fond of**))

EX. Ethel is deeply attached to Japan.
エセルは日本{を深く愛している/に愛着をもっている}。
Eseru wa Nihon {o fukaku aishite iru/ni aichaku o motte iru}.

attack vt. **[for s.o./s.a. to use verbal or physical force against s.o./some area in order to cause harm** ((**fig. "s.t. beyond**

human control assails s.o./some area"》] ⟨-o⟩ ko⌈ogeki-suru ⟨〜を⟩攻撃する ③ •c 《to charge, criticize, assault, condemn》, ⟨-o⟩ o⌈so⌉u ⟨〜を⟩襲う ① [to initiate harmful action upon s.o./s.a./some place] 《assault, strike, hit》

EX. (a) The British Navy attacked the Falkland Islands.
英国海軍がフォークランドを{攻撃した/襲った}。
Eikoku-kaigun ga Fookurando o {koogeki-shita/osotta}.
(b) The girl was suddenly attacked with a high fever.
少女は突然高熱に{襲われた/*攻撃された}。
*Shoojo wa totsuzen koonetsu ni {osowa-reta/*koogeki-sareta}.*

—— n.
ko⌈ogeki 攻撃 •c 《assault, offense》 ↔ boogyo 防御 •c

attempt vt. [for s.o./s.a. to try to do s.t.] Vvol. to su⌈ru Vvol.とする ③ [for s.o./s.a. to try to do s.t.], ⟨-o⟩ ko⌈koromi⌉ru ⟨〜を⟩試みる ② [for s.o. to do s.t. on an experimental basis ⟨w⟩] 《try》, ⟨-o⟩ ku⌈wadate⌉ru ⟨〜を⟩企てる ② [for s.o. to plan s.t. and try to put it into practice] 《plan, plot, design》

EX. The prisoner attempted to escape.
囚人は逃走{しようとした/を試みた/を企てた}。
Shuujin wa toosoo {-shiyoo to shita/o kokoromita/o kuwadateta}.

—— n. [an act of trying to do or making an effort to succeed at s.t.]
ku⌈wadate⌉ 企て /⟨V*masu* of *kuwadateru* ② plan/ [an act/instance of planning s.t. and trying to put it into practice] 《plan, plot, project》, ko⌈koromi⌉ 試み /⟨V*masu* of *kokoromiru* ② try/ [an act of doing s.t. on an experimental basis] 《plan, plot, endeavor》

PHRASE: attempted murder *satsujin-misui* 殺人未遂 •c

attend vt./vi. [for s.o./s.a. to be present at s.t. or to be with s.o. esp. to give protection/care or to give s.t. one's attention]

1. ⟨-ni⟩ shu⌈sseki-suru ⟨〜に⟩出席する ③ •c [for s.o. to be present at some event], {⟨-ni⟩/⟨-o⟩} de⌉ru {⟨〜に⟩/⟨〜を⟩}出る ② [for s.o. to come out for or present oneself at some event] 《participate》

EX. Many foreign students attended the lecture.
多くの留学生が講演会に{出席した/出た}。
Ooku no ryuugaku-sei ga kooen-kai ni {shusseki-shita/deta}.

2. ⟨-no⟩ se⌈wa⌉ o su⌈ru ⟨〜の⟩世話をする ③ •c [for s.o. to give care to s.o.] 《look after》, ⟨-no⟩ ka⌉ngo o su⌈ru ⟨〜の⟩看護をする ③ •c [for s.o. to provide nursing aid to] 《nurse, care for》

EX. Which nurse is attending this patient?
どの看護婦がこの患者の{世話/看護}をしていますか。
Dono kango-fu ga kono kanja no {sewa/kango} o shite imasu ka.

3. ⟨-ni⟩ se⌉i o dasu ⟨〜に⟩精を出す ① [for s.o. to apply oneself to one's work] 《busy oneself with one's work, work hard》, ⟨-ni⟩ ha⌈ge⌉mu ⟨〜に⟩励む ① [for s.o. to be diligently engaged in one's work] 《strive, labor, devote oneself to》

EX. Terry is attending to his new business very diligently.
テリーは自分の新しい事業に一生懸命{精を出して/励んで}いる。
Terii wa jibun no atarashii jigyoo ni isshoo-kenmei {sei o dashite/hagende} iru.

4. ⟨-ni⟩ chu⌉ui o ha⌈ra⌉u ⟨〜に⟩注意を払う ① [to give attention to s.t./s.o.] 《watch》

EX. I will attend to the speaker.
その発言者に注意を払います。
Sono hatsugen-sha ni chuui o haraimasu.

attendance n. [an act of being present at s.t. or the number of people present] shu⌈sseki 出席 •c [an act of attending a class/meeting], shu⌈sseki-sha⌉-suu 出席者数 •c [the number of persons present]

A

attention n. **[an act of attending to s.t.]** **chu⌉ui 注意 •c [an act of fixing the mind on s.t. ⟪fig. "warning," "advice"⟫] ⟪caution⟫**

EX. The teacher drew everyone's attention to a section in the book.
先生は本のある部分に関して、みんなの注意を促した。
Sensei wa hon no aru bubun ni kanshite, minna no chuui o unagashita.

attic n. **[a space/room immediately below the roof of a house]**
ya⌈ne-ura 屋根裏

attitude n. **[manner/feeling toward s.o./s.t./s.a.]**
ta⌉ido 態度 •c

EX. (**a**) The government took a wait-and-see attitude on the matter.
政府はその件を静観する態度を取った。
Seifu wa sono ken o seikan-suru taido o totta.
(**b**) His arrogant attitude offended the female worker.
彼の横柄な態度は女子社員の反感を買った。
Kare no ooheina taido wa joshi-shain no hankan o katta.

attract vt. **[to draw s.t./s.o. to itself or oneself]**
⟨-o⟩ hi⌈ki-tsuke⌉ru ⟨～を⟩引き付ける ② ⟪draw near oneself⟫

EX. The musical *CATS* attracted a large audience.
ミュージカル『キャッツ』は多くの観衆を引き付けた。
Myuujikaru "Kyattsu" wa ooku no kanshuu o hiki-tsuketa.

attraction n. **[s.t. which draws s.t. to itself]** **hi⌈ki-tsuke⌉ru mo⌈no⌉ 引き付けるもの [s.t. that attracts or draws] ⟪charm⟫, mi⌈ryoku 魅力 •c [s.t. beautiful, excellent, or superb that captivates the heart and mind of s.o. who comes in contact with it] ⟪charm, appeal⟫, a⌈tora⌉kushon アトラクション •f [entertainment of some sort]**

EX. (**a**) What's the attraction of that profession?
その仕事の{魅力/*引き付けるもの/*アトラクション}は何ですか。
*Sono shigoto no {miryoku/*hiki-tsukeru mono/*atorakushon} wa nan desu ka.*
(**b**) There was a mystical attraction in his speech.
彼のスピーチは不思議な{魅力/引き付けるもの/*アトラクション}があった。
*Kare no supiichi wa fushigina {miryoku/hiki-tsukeru mono/*atorakushon} ga atta.*
(**c**) The attraction of the party was a string quartet playing Mozart.
パーティーの{アトラクション/魅力/*引き付けるもの}はモーツアルトの弦楽四重奏だった。
*Paatii no {atorakushon/miryoku/*hiki-tsukeru mono} wa Mootsaruto no gengaku-shijuu-soo datta.*
(**d**) The Olympic Games have no attraction for me.
オリンピック大会は私にはまったく{魅力/引き付けるもの/*アトラクション}がない。
*Orinpikku-taikai wa watashi ni wa mattaku {miryoku/hiki-tsukeru mono/*atorakushon} ga nai.*

attractive adj. **[having the power to attract or pleasing]**
mi⌈ryoku-tekina 魅力的な adj(*na*). **•c [⟨usually said of a person⟩ having charm] ⟪appealing, charming⟫**

EX. Rumiko is a very attractive woman.
留美子はとても魅力的な女性だ。
Rumiko wa totemo miryoku-tekina josei da.

audible adj. **[able to be heard]**
⟨-ga⟩ ki⌈koeru ⟨～が⟩聞こえる ② [for a sound to be passively and spontaneously perceived by the ears] ⟪hear, sound⟫

EX. The teacher's voice was hardly audible due to the children's cheers.
子供たちの歓声で先生の声はほとんど聞こえなかった。
Kodomo-tachi no kansei de sensei no koe wa hotondo kikoenakatta.

audience n. **[those gathered to hear and see s.t. or those reached by radio/TV]**
cho⌈oshuu 聴衆 •c [those who hear], ka⌈nshuu 観衆 •c [a mass of people watching a sports game/a festival], shi⌈cho⌉o-sha 視聴者 •c [those listening to or watching a radio or TV program]

EX. (**a**) The audience applauded the performance.
{聴衆/観衆/視聴者}は演奏に拍手を送った。
{Chooshuu/Kanshuu/Shichoo-sha} wa ensoo ni hakushu o okutta.
(**b**) The audience in the theater was quiet.
劇場の{観衆/*聴衆/*視聴者}は静かだった。
*Geki-joo no {kanshuu/*chooshuu/ *shichoo-sha} wa shizuka datta.*
(**c**) We had a telephone call from the TV audience.
テレビの{視聴者/*観衆/*聴衆}から電話があった。
*Terebi no {shichoo-sha/*kanshuu/ *chooshuu} kara denwa ga atta.*

August n.
ha⌈chi-gatsu⌉ 八月 •c

aunt n. **[the sister of one's father/mother]**
o⌈ba おば [the sister of one's own father/mother], o⌈ba-san おばさん [the sister of s.o. else's father/mother or a middle-aged woman]

㊈ "aunt older than one's parent"▷伯母, "aunt younger than one's parent"▷叔母

EX. A: How is your aunt doing?
おばさんはいかがですか。
Oba-san wa ikaga desu ka.
B: She's fine, thank you.
おかげ様で、おばは元気にしております。
O-kage-sama de, oba wa genki ni shite orimasu.

Australia n.
O⌈osutora⌉ria オーストラリア •f

Australian n.
O⌈osutoraria⌉-jin オーストラリア人 •f+c

Austria n.
O⌈osuto⌉ria オーストリア •f

Austrian n.
O⌈osutoria⌉-jin オーストリア人 •f+c

author n. **[a writer of books, etc.]**
sa⌉kka 作家 •c [one who creates artistic work as an occupation, such as a novelist, a painter, etc.] ((artist, writer, novelist)), sa⌉kusha 作者 •c [the creator of a particular poem/novel/painting/sculpture, etc.] ((writer, playwright)), cho⌉sha 著者 •c [the writer of a particular book/thesis/essay] ((writer))

EX. (**a**) The author of this novel is a woman.
この小説の{作者/著者/*作家}は女性です。
*Kono shoosetsu no {sakusha/chosha/ *sakka} wa josei desu.*
(**b**) She is a well-known author and also a popular actress.
彼女はよく知られた作家であり、人気女優でもある。
Kanojo wa yoku shira-reta sakka deari, ninki-joyuu de mo aru.

authority n. **[the power to give orders, enforce obedience, take action, or make final decisions or a person with much knowledge/experience in a given field]**
ke⌉n'i 権威 •c [reliability resulting from knowledge, prestige, power, etc.] ((power)), ke⌉nryoku 権力 •c [the (political) right to command one's subordinates]

EX. (**a**) This is a dictionary of great authority.
これは大変{権威/*権力}のある辞書です。
*Kore wa taihen {ken'i/*kenryoku} no aru jisho desu.*
(**b**) Those in authority must always think about the people.
{権力/*権威}の座にある人はいつも国民のことを考えねばならない。
*{Kenryoku/*Ken'i} no za ni aru hito wa itsu-mo kokumin no koto o kangaeneba naranai.*

2. **ke⌈n'i⌉(-sha) 権威(者) •c [a person with much knowledge/experience] ((expert))**

EX. George is an authority on child psychology.
ジョージは児童心理学の権威である。

Jooji wa jidoo-shinri-gaku no ken'i dearu.

auto n. **[a car]**
ji⌈do⌉osha 自動車 •c [a vehicle driven by an engine and used on the road for transportation] 《car》, **ku⌈ruma 車 [wheel 《fig. "car"》]** 《car》

automatic adj. **[moving/operating by itself]**
ji⌈doo no N 自動のN •c [working by itself], o⌈otomachi⌉kku no N オートマチックのN •f

EX. (**a**) I can only drive an automatic shift.
私は{オートマチックの/?自動の}車しか運転できない。
Watashi wa {ootomachikku no/?jidoo no} kuruma shika unten-dekinai.
(**b**) This is an automatic door.
これは{自動(の)/オートマチックの}ドアです。
Kore wa {jidoo (no)/ootomachikku no} doa desu.

automatically adv.
ji⌈doo-tekini 自動的に •c

automobile n. **[an automatic vehicle]**
ji⌈do⌉osha 自動車 •c [a vehicle driven by an engine and used on the road for transportation], ku⌈ruma 車 [wheel 《fig. "car"》]

EX. (**a**) An automobile plant is scheduled to be built here.
ここには{自動車/*車}工場が建設される予定です。
*Koko ni wa {jidoosha/*kuruma}-koojoo ga kensetsu-sareru yotei desu.*
(**b**) They shut out all automobiles from the park.
公園からすべての{自動車/車}を締め出した。
Kooen kara subete no {jidoosha/kuruma} o shimi-dashita.

autumn n. **[fall season]**
a⌉ki 秋 [the season between summer and winter] 《fall》

EX. In Japan, autumn covers the months of September through November.
日本では秋は九月から十一月までの月です。
Nihon de wa aki wa ku-gatsu kara juu-ichi-gatsu made no tsuki desu.

available adj. **[may be used/gotten]**
1. ri⌈yoo-deki⌉ru (N) **利用できる(N) ② •c [can be utilized], te⌉ ni ⌈ha⌉iru** (N) **手に入る(N) ① [can be obtained]**

EX. (**a**) The company used all available means to rescue its manager.
会社は部長救出のため{利用できる/*手に入る}すべての手段を講じた。
*Kaisha wa buchoo-kyuushutsu no tame {riyoo-dekiru/*te ni hairu} subete no shudan o koojita.*
(**b**) This dictionary is available at the college store.
この辞書は大学の購買部で{手に入る/*利用できる}。
*Kono jisho wa daigaku no koobai-bu de {te ni hairu/*riyoo-dekiru}.*

2. te⌉ ga a⌈ite iru (N) **手が空いている(N) /《V*te iru* of *te ga aku* ① become free/ [free and not tied up]**

EX. Is Mr. Nomoto available now?
野本さんは今手が空いていますか。
Nomoto-san wa ima te ga aite imasu ka.

avenue n. **[a wide street lined with trees/tall buildings]**
o⌈o-do⌉ori 大通り [a broad street] 《street, big road》

average n. **[an arithmetical mean, i.e., the result of dividing the sum of two or more quantities by the number of quantities]**
he⌈ikin 平均 •c 《mean》

EX. Students must maintain an above average grade to qualify for a fellowship.
学生は奨学金をもらうためには平均以上の成績を維持しなければならない。
Gakusei wa shoogaku-kin o morau tame ni wa heikin-ijoo no seiseki o iji-shinakereba naranai.

—— adj. **[having the characteristic of being average]** 《mean》
he⌈ikin no N 平均のN •c

EX. The average life span of the Japanese is

probably the longest in the world.
日本人の平均(の)寿命はおそらく世界最長であろう。
Nihon-jin no heikin (no) jumyoo wa osoraku sekai-saichoo dearoo.

avoid vt. **[for s.o./s.a. to keep away from s.t./s.o./s.a.]**
⟨-o⟩ sa⌈ke⌉ru ⟨〜を⟩避ける ② **⟪avert, duck, ward off, shun, skirt⟫**, **⟨-o⟩ ka⌉ihi-suru** ⟨〜を⟩回避する ③ **•c [for s.o. to try to go around s.t. for fear of being negatively affected by it] ⟪avert, skirt⟫**

EX. (**a**) To lose weight, you should avoid sweets.
体重を減らすには、甘いものを{避ける/*回避す}べきです。
*Taijuu o herasu ni wa, amai mono o {sakeru/*kaihi-su}-beki desu.*
(**b**) The government avoided confusion by banning demonstrations.
政府はデモを禁止して混乱を{避けた/回避した}。
Seifu wa demo o kinshi-shite konran o {saketa/kaihi-shita}.

aw int. **[a sound expressing disappointment or pity]**
o⌉o! おお!

awake vt. **[to rouse s.o. from sleep]**
⟨-de⟩ me⌉ ga sa⌈me⌉ru ⟨〜で⟩目が覚める ② **[for the first person to wake up (because of s.t.)]**, **⟨-de⟩ me⌉ o sa⌈ma⌉su** ⟨〜で⟩目を覚ます ① **[for s.o./s.a. to wake up (because of s.t.)]**

EX. (**a**) The emergency bell ringing awoke me .
非常ベルの音で{目が覚めた/目を覚ました}。
Hijoo-beru no oto de {me ga sameta/me o samashita}.
(**b**) A big noise awoke the child in the middle of the night.
子供は夜中に大きな音で{目を覚ました/??目が覚めた}。
Kodomo wa yonaka ni ookina oto de {me o samashita/??me ga sameta}.

NOTE: The subject of *me ga sameru* is the speaker himself/herself or s.o. the speaker empathizes with.

—— vi. **[for s.o./s.a. to wake up]**
o⌈ki⌉ru 起きる ① **[for s.o./s.a./s.t. that has been lying horizontally dormant to stand up vertically ⟪fig. "wake up," "occur"⟫] ⟪get up, happen⟫**

EX. Kotaro awoke one morning to find himself famous.
光太郎はある朝起きると有名になっていた。
Kootaroo wa aru asa okiru to yuumei ni natte ita.

—— adj. **[not asleep]**
me⌉ o sa⌈ma⌉shite iru (N) 目を覚ましている **(N) /⟨V *te iru* of *me o samasu* ① wake up/** ②

EX. The baby was wide awake even at midnight.
赤ん坊は真夜中なのにぱっちりと目を覚ましていた。
Akanboo wa ma-yonaka na noni patchiri to me o samashite ita.

awaken vt./vi. SEE awake

award vt. **[for s.o. to give s.o. a prize, etc.]**
⟨-ni⟩ ⟨-o⟩ a⌈taeru ⟨〜に⟩⟨〜を⟩与える ② **[for s.o. to cause/let s.o. have s.t.] ⟪give, present, bestow, provide, allot⟫**, **⟨-ni⟩ ⟨-o⟩ ju⌉yo-suru** ⟨〜に⟩⟨〜を⟩授与する ③ **•c [for s.o. to bestow s.t. on s.o. in a formal way] ⟪bestow⟫**

EX. Professor Smith was awarded the Japan Foundation prize.
スミス教授は国際交流基金賞を{与えられた/授与された}。
Sumisu-kyooju wa Kokusai-kooryuu-kikin-shoo o {atae-rareta/juyo-sareta}.

—— n. **[prize]**
sho⌉o 賞 **•c [s.t. officially given to one in recognition of an accomplishment] ⟪prize⟫**

EX. Dr. Yuasa received an award for her many years of service to the university.
湯浅博士は大学への長年の功績によって賞を受けた。
Yuasa-hakase wa daigaku e no naga-nen no kooseki ni yotte shoo o uketa.

aware adj. **[conscious and knowing]**
⟨-ni⟩ ki-⌈zu⌉ite iru (N) ⟨〜に⟩気付いている **(N) /⟨V *te iru* of *ki-zuku* ① notice/ [knowing, realizing, conscious]**

A

EX. Harumi was aware that she had to make up her mind.
治美は決心をしなければならないことに気付いていた。
Harumi wa kesshin o shinakereba naranai koto ni ki-zuite ita.

awareness n. **[the state of knowing or realizing]**
ki-⌈zu⌉ite iru koto 気付いていること [the fact of knowing or realizing], ji⌈kaku 自覚 •c [self-realization] ⟪consciousness⟫

away adv. **[on the way or removed from some place]**
1. ha⌈na⌉rete 離れて /⟨V *te* of *hanareru* ② become separate/ [to be separated from a place/person], ru⌉su ni suru 留守にする ③ [for s.o. to be absent from]

EX. (**a**) The campus is two kilometers away from the station.
キャンパスは駅から二キロ{離れて/*留守にして}います。
*Kyanpasu wa eki kara ni-kiro {hanarete/*rusu ni shite} imasu.*
(**b**) Please take care of our cats while we are away.
{留守にして/*離れて}いる間、猫の世話をお願いします。
*{Rusu ni shite/*Hanarete} iru aida, neko no sewa o o-negai-shimasu.*

2. a⌈chira e あちらへ n.+prt. **[in another place/direction], a⌈tchi⌉ e あっちへ** n.+prt. **⟨s⟩**

EX. Go away! I don't like dogs.
あっちへ行け。ぼくは犬が苦手なんだ。
Atchi e ike. Boku wa inu ga nigate na n da.

NOTE: *Atchi* is a more colloquial form of *achira.*

3. sa⌉tte 去って /⟨V *te* of *saru* ① leave/ [disappearing]

EX. Old soldiers fade away.
老兵は消え去っていく。
Roohei wa kie-satte-iku.

PHRASE: right away *sugu ni* 直ぐに ⟪at once⟫, *tadachini* 直ちに ⟨w⟩ ⟪immediately⟫

EX. We will do it right away.
{直ぐに/直ちに}致します。
{Sugu ni/Tadachini} itashimasu.

awe n. **[a mixed feeling of reverence, fear, and wonder]**
i⌈kei い敬 •c [feeling of reverence]

awful adj. **[terrible for its kind] ⟪dreadful, appalling⟫**
o⌈soroshi⌉i 恐ろしい adj(*i*). **[for s.o. to be afraid of s.t./s.o./s.a. which is unusual or mysterious or for s.t./s.o./s.a. to cause such fear] ⟪dreadful, fearful⟫, mo⌈no-sugo⌉i ものすごい** adj(*i*). **[causing great fear] ⟪fearful, terrible, fierce⟫, hi⌈do⌉i ひどい** adj(*i*). **[of a frightening kind/degree or cruel] ⟪terrible, cruel, rough, merciless, outrageous, frightful⟫, i⌈ya⌉na 嫌な** adj(*na*). **[very displeasing to s.o.] ⟪disagreeable, unpleasant, disgusting, offensive⟫**

EX. (**a**) There was an awful earthquake in Izu last week.
先週、伊豆で{恐ろしい/ものすごい/ひどい/?嫌な}地震があった。
Senshuu, Izu de {osoroshii/mono-sugoi/hidoi/?iyana} jishin ga atta.
(**b**) I stopped eating as the food at the cafeteria smelled awful.
食堂の食べ物は{嫌な/ひどい/?ものすごい/*恐ろしい}においがしたので、食べるのをやめた。
*Shokudoo no tabe-mono wa {iyana/hidoi/?mono-sugoi/*osoroshii} nioi ga shita node, taberu no o yameta.*

awfully adv. **[to an awful degree]**
to⌈temo とても [to a great extent (in affirmative contexts) or no matter what one does (in negative contexts)], su⌉goku すごく /⟨adj(*i*). *ku* of *sugoi* awful/ [to an extent that s.t. causes fear ⟪fig. "terribly"⟫] ⟪terribly, terrifically⟫

EX. This chicken curry is awfully hot.
このチキンカレーは{とても/すごく}辛い。
Kono chikin-karee wa {totemo/sugoku} karai.

awkward adj. **[causing difficulty or unable to handle things]**
1. bu-⌈ki⌉yoona 不器用な adj(*na*). **•c [not**

being able to handle things skillfully]** ⟪clumsy, unskilled⟫ ↔ kiyoona 器用な adj(*na*). •c; **gi⌈kochina⌉i** ぎこちない adj(*i*). **[for a movement/expression to lack smoothness]** ⟪clumsy⟫

EX. (**a**) My sister is awkward with her hands.
妹は手先が{不器用だ/??ぎこちない}。
Imooto wa te-saki ga {bu-kiyoo da/ ??gikochinai}.
(**b**) The boy is awkward in his walk.
その少年は歩き方が{ぎこちない/*不器用だ}。
*Sono shoonen wa aruki-kata ga {gikochinai/*bu-kiyoo da}.*

2. ya⌉kkaina 厄介な adj(*na*). •c **[causing trouble, difficulty and annoyance]** ⟪troublesome, cumbersome, burdensome, complicated⟫

EX. I was in a very awkward position then.
私はその時大変厄介な状況にあった。
Watashi wa sono-toki taihen yakkaina jookyoo ni atta.

ax n. **[a tool for chopping trees and splitting wood]**
o⌉no おの
PHRASE: get the ax *kubi ni naru* 首になる ①

EX. I tried to work harder, but I got the ax anyway.
がんばって働くようにしたけれど、やっぱり首になった。
Ganbatte hataraku yooni shita keredo, yappari kubi ni natta.

axis n. **[a line around which s.t. rotates]**
ji⌈ku⌉ 軸 •c

axle n. **[a rod on which or with which a wheel turns]**
sha⌈jiku 車軸 •c **[axis for a wheel]**

B

baby n. **[a very young child/animal]**
a⌉ka-chan 赤ちゃん **[an term of endearment for akanboo ⟪fig. "s.o. who knows little about what society is like"⟫]** ⟪infant⟫, **a⌈kanboo** 赤ん坊 **[a child recently born or still in the mother's womb]** ⟪infant⟫

EX. (**a**) How old is your baby?
お宅の{赤ちゃん/*赤ん坊}はおいくつですか。
*Otaku no {aka-chan/*akanboo} wa o-ikutsu desu ka.*
(**b**) A baby suddenly started to cry on the train.
電車の中で{赤ちゃん/赤ん坊}が急に泣き出した。
Densha no naka de {aka-chan/akanboo} ga kyuuni naki-dashita.

baby-sitting n. **[an act of looking after a child for a short time while the parents are out]**
be⌈bii-shi⌉ttaa ベビー・シッター •f **[taking care of s.o. else's child/children for a fee or s.o. who does that]**

EX. Helena did baby-sitting to earn some spending money.
ヘレナはお小遣いを稼ぐためベビー・シッターをした。
Herena wa o-kozukai o kasegu tame bebii-shittaa o shita.

back n. **[the rear part of the body from the nape of the neck to the end of the spine

B

《fig. "the rear part or reverse of s.t."》]
1. se⌈naka 背中 [the rear part of the body from the nape of the neck to the end of the spine]

EX. Masayoshi injured his back while playing volleyball.
正芳はバレーボールをやっている最中に背中を痛めた。
Masayoshi wa baree-booru o yatte-iru saichuu ni senaka o itameta.

2. u⌈shiro 後ろ [the area opposite to or farthest from the front]

EX. Students seem to want to sit in the back of the classroom.
学生は教室の後ろに座りたがるようだ。
Gakusei wa kyooshitsu no ushiro ni suwari-ta-garu yooda.

— adv.

1. u⌈shiro e 後ろへ n.+prt. **[toward the rear]**

EX. Please stand back, everybody.
皆さん、後ろへさがってください。
Mina-san, ushiro e sagatte kudasai.

2. mo⌉to no i⌉chi e 元の位置へ n.+prt. **[to a former position]**

EX. Put the book back on the shelf.
本を棚の元の位置へ戻しなさい。
Hon o tana no moto no ichi e modoshinasai.

background n. **[the scenery located behind s.t.]**
ha⌈ikei 背景 •c [s.t. that exists behind a focused item], ba⌈kku-gura⌉undo バックグラウンド •f

backward adv. **[toward the back 《fig. "in reverse order," "opposite to usual"》]**
u⌈shiro muki ni 後ろ向きに n.+prt. **[facing toward the back], gya⌈ku ni 逆に** n.+prt. **[in reverse order]**

EX. A boy was riding his bike backward.
男の子が自転車を{後ろ向き/逆}に乗っていた。
Otoko-no-ko ga jitensha o {ushiro muki/gyaku} ni notte ita.

backyard n. **[the area in the back of a house]**
u⌈ra-niwa 裏庭

EX. We had a barbecue in our backyard.
私たちは裏庭でバーベキューをした。
Watashi-tachi wa ura-niwa de baabekyuu o shita.

bacon n.
be⌉ekon ベーコン •f

bacteria n.
ba⌈kuteria バクテリア •f

bad adj. **[not good or unacceptable]**

1. wa⌈ru⌉i 悪い adj(*i*). **[not good]**

EX. Staying up late is a bad habit.
夜更かしは悪い習慣です。
Yo-fukashi wa warui shuukan desu.

2. ⟨-ga⟩ he⌈ta⌉na ⟨～が⟩下手な adj(*na*). **[not skilled at doing s.t.] ↔ ⟨-ga⟩ joozuna ⟨～が⟩上手な** adj(*na*).

EX. Sam is very bad at doing figures.
サムはすごく計算が下手だ。
Samu wa sugoku keisan ga heta da.

3. ku⌈sat⌉ta N 腐ったN /⟨Vinf. past of *kusaru* ① rot/ [deteriorated to the point of being useless] 《spoiled, stale, rotten》, i⌈tan⌉da N 傷んだN /⟨Vinf. past of *itamu* ① become damaged/ [suffering from damage]

EX. Harry ate some bad shrimp on the Ginza last night and got sick.
ハリーは夕べ銀座で{腐った/傷んだ}えびを食べて病気になりました。
Harii wa yuube Ginza de {kusatta/itanda} ebi o tabete byooki ni narimashita.

4. i⌈kenai N いけないN [not acceptable] 《wicked, immoral》

EX. It's bad to tell a lie.
うそをつくのはいけないことです。
Uso o tsuku no wa ikenai koto desu.

5. hi⌈do⌉i ひどい adj(*i*). **[of a frightening kind/degree or cruel] 《awful》**

EX. Prof. Suzuki has a bad cold.
鈴木教授はひどい風邪です。
Suzuki-kyooju wa hidoi kaze desu.

PHRASE: too bad *zannenna* 残念な adj(*na*). •c

EX. It was too bad that you couldn't make it to the Boston Philharmonic concert.
ボストン・フィルの演奏会に行けなかったとは残念でしたね。
Bosuton-firu no ensoo-kai ni ike-

nakatta to wa zannen deshita ne.

badly adv. **[in a bad manner or very much]**

1. ma⌈zu⌉i まずい adj(*i*). **[having bad flavor ⟪fig. "ugly," "unskillful," "awkward"⟫] ⟪poorly⟫, ⟨-ga⟩ he⌈ta⌉na ⟨〜が⟩下手な** adj(*na*). **[poor at s.t.] ⟪unskillfully⟫ ↔ ⟨-ga⟩ joozuna ⟨〜が⟩上手な** adj(*na*).

EX. (**a**) My older sister writes well but types badly.
姉は文は上手なんですが、タイプは{下手/??まずい}です。
Ane wa bun wa joozuna n desu ga, taipu wa {heta/??mazui} desu.
(**b**) He handled the situation (a bit) badly.
彼のその事態の取り扱いはちょっと{まずかった/下手だった}。
Kare no sono jitai no toriatsukai wa chotto {mazukatta/heta datta}.

2. hi⌈jooni 非常に [to a great degree/extent] ⟪very much⟫

EX. My younger brother badly wants a word processor.
弟はワープロを非常に欲しがっています。
Otooto wa waapuro o hijooni hoshigatte imasu.

bag n. **[a non-rigid container made out of paper, plastic, etc.]**
ka⌈ban かばん ⟪satchel, suitcase, briefcase⟫, fu⌈kuro⌉ 袋 ⟪paper, cloth, or plastic container⟫

PHRASE: brown bag (containing a lunch) *bentoo* 弁当

baggage n. **[bags, etc. of a traveler]**
te-⌈ni⌉motsu 手荷物 [bags, etc. of a traveler that are transportable by hand] ⟪luggage⟫

bait n. **[food put on a hook as a lure for fish, etc.]**
e⌈sa⌉ えさ [food given to s.a. to catch/raise it]

bake vt. **[to cook food in an oven]**
⟨-o⟩ ya⌈ku ⟨〜を⟩焼く ① [for s.o. to cause a change in s.t. through exposure to heat/fire/sunlight] ⟪broil, grill, roast, fry, toast, burn, tan⟫

EX. Mother bakes us delicious bread.
母は我々においしいパンを焼いてくれます。
Haha wa ware-ware ni oishii pan o yaite kuremasu.

bakery n. **[a store where bread, etc. is baked/sold]**
pa⌉n-ya パン屋

balance n. **[a state of equilibrium in weight, value, etc. or a weighing instrument]**

1. tsu⌈ri-ai 釣り合い /⟨Vmasu of *tsuri-au* ① balance/, ba⌈ransu バランス •f [a state of equilibrium in weight, value, etc.]

EX. World peace is maintained by the balance of power.
世界平和は力の{釣り合い/バランス}で維持されている。
Sekai-heiwa wa chikara no {tsuri-ai/baransu} de iji-sarete iru.

2. ha⌈kari⌉ はかり /⟨Vmasu of *hakaru* ① measure, time/, te⌈nbin 天びん •c [an instrument for weighing, esp. one with two matched hanging scales]

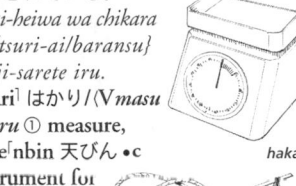

hakari

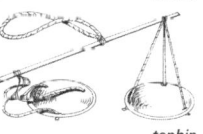

tenbin

balcony n.
ba⌈ruko⌉nii バルコニー •f

bald adj. **[lacking hair on the head]**
ha⌉geta N はげたN /⟨Vinf. past of *hageru* ② get bald/ [not covered by hair]

EX. That bald person over there is Yul Brynner.
あそこの(頭が)はげた人はユル・ブリンナーです。
Asoko no (atama ga) hageta hito wa Yuru Burinnaa desu.

ball n. **[a spherical or almost spherical]**

1. ta⌈ma⌉ たま, bo⌈oru ボール •f [a spherical or almost spherical object used in playing a game, such as baseball]
㊥ "ball"▷球, "gem"▷玉, "bullet"▷たま

2. ya⌈kyuu 野球 •c [baseball]

EX. Did you watch the ball game on TV last night?
ゆうべテレビで野球の試合を見ましたか。

Yuube terebi de yakyuu no shiai o mimashita ka.

3. bo⌈oru ボール •f [a pitched ball in baseball that is not hit and is not a strike]

B

4. bu⌈to⌉o-kai 舞踏会 •c [formal social dance], da⌈nsu-pa⌉atii ダンスパーティー •f

ballet n.

ba⌉ree バレエ •f

NOTE: "Volleyball" is also abbreviated as *baree* in Japanese.

balloon n. [an airtight bag containing gas which floats in the air]

fu⌈usen 風船 •c [a small inflatable bag used as a toy], ki⌈kyuu 気球 •c [a large, airtight bag that rises and floats above the earth when filled with hot air or a gas lighter than air such as hydrogen/helium, often with an attached car or gondola for carrying passengers/instruments]

ball-point pen n.

bo⌈orupen ボールペン •f

Baltimore n.

Bo⌈ruchi⌉moa ボルチモア •f

bamboo n.

ta⌈ke 竹

banana n.

ba⌉nana バナナ •f

band n. [s.t. that binds/ties objects together or a group of musicians playing together]

1. ba⌈ndo バンド •f, ga⌈kutai 楽隊 •c [a group of musicians playing together]

EX. Allan plays the sax in the band.
アランは{バンド/楽隊}でサックスを吹いている。
Aran wa {bando/gakutai} de sakkusu o fuite iru.

2. hi⌈mo ひも [a fine cord that binds/ties together] ((cord, lace)), o⌉bi 帯 [a Japanese-style strip of cloth used with kimono] ((sash, girdle)), ba⌈ndo バンド •f [a strip of leather, cloth, etc. for wearing around the waist or an object similar in shape] ((belt))

EX. We need some bands to tie these things together.
これらを縛るのに{ひも/帯/ベルト}が要る。
Kore-ra o shibaru no ni {himo/obi/beruto} ga iru.

PHRASE: rubber band *wa-gomu* 輪ゴム

bang n. [a loud, sudden noise]

do⌈su⌉n どすん, ba⌈ta⌉n ばたん, do⌈shi⌉n どしん, zu⌈do⌉n ずどん [onomatopoeia denoting a hard, noisy blow or impact]

EX. It went bang!
{ドスン/バタン/ドシン/ズドン}という音がした。
{Dosun/Batan/Doshin/Zudon} to iu oto ga shita.

—— vt. [for s.o. to shut/put s.t. somewhere hard and noisily]

⟨-o⟩ ba⌈ta⌉n to shi⌈me⌉ru ⟨～を⟩ばたんと閉める ② [for s.o. to shut s.t. with a loud, sudden noise], ⟨-o⟩ do⌈shi⌉n to o⌈ku ⟨～を⟩どしんと置く ① [for s.o. to put s.t. somewhere with a loud, sudden noise]

EX. He banged the door shut.
彼は戸をバタンと閉めた。
Kare wa to o batan to shimeta.

bank[1] n. [an establishment for receiving, keeping, lending, or sometimes issuing money, etc., or the office or building of such an establishment]

gi⌈nkoo 銀行 •c

EX. I deposited some money in the bank.
銀行にお金を少々預けた。
Ginkoo ni o-kane o shoo-shoo azuketa.

PHRASE: bank employee *ginkoo-in* 銀行員

EX. He is a bank employee.
彼は銀行員だ。
Kare wa ginkoo-in da.

bank[2] n. [a rise of land along a river]

ka⌈wa-gishi 川岸 [land along either side of a river] ((embankment))

EX. Our school is on the right bank of Chikuma River.
私たちの学校は千曲川の右の川岸にあります。
Watashi-tachi no gakkoo wa Chikuma-gawa no migi no kawa-gishi ni arimasu.

bar n. [a long, narrow, hard object; a place where alcoholic drinks are served; lawyers in general]

1. **yo⌈ko-boo 横棒 [a horizontal (wooden) barrier], ka⌈nnuki⌉ かんぬき [a lock]**

EX. Remember to lock the door using the bar.
扉を{横棒/かんぬき}で閉めるのを忘れないように。
Tobira o {yoko-boo/kannuki} de shimeru no o wasurenai yooni.

2. **-ko ～個 •c [counter for solid objects]**

EX. I bought a bar of soap.
僕は石けん一個を買った。
Boku wa sekken ik-ko o katta.

3. **[a place where alcoholic drinks are served], ba⌉a バー •f, sa⌈ka-ba 酒場 [a drinking place] ((pub, tavern))**

PHRASE: bar exam *shihoo-shiken* 司法試験 •c

barber n. **[s.o. who cuts men's hair as an occupation]**
to⌈ko-ya 床屋 [s.o./a shop that renders service in hair cutting, shampooing and shaving as a business], ri⌈hatsu⌉-ten 理髪店 •c ((barbershop))

EX. (a) I went to a barber yesterday to get a haircut.
きのうは{床屋/理髪店}に行って髪を刈ってもらった。
Kinoo wa {toko-ya/rihatsu-ten} ni itte kami o katte moratta.
(b) I'll just run over to the barber.
ちょっと{床屋/?理髪店}へ行ってくる。
Chotto {toko-ya/?rihatsu-ten} e itte kuru.

bare adj. **[not covered or clothed]**
ha⌈daka no N 裸のN [without clothes] ((naked))

barefoot adj./adv. **[without shoes/stockings]**
ha⌈dashi no N はだしのN, ha⌈dashi de はだしで n.+prt.

EX. It is dangerous to walk around barefoot here.
ここは、はだしで歩くと危険です。
Koko wa, hadashi de aruku to kiken desu.

barely adv. **[only just, scarcely]**
ya⌈tto やっと [at the end after having tried hard or waited for a long time] ((narrowly, at last, finally))

EX. It was dark, and his face was barely visible.
暗くて彼の顔がやっと見えるほどだった。
Kurakute kare no kao ga yatto mieru hodo datta.

bargain n. **[a mutual agreement/contract or s.t. sold at a price favorable to the buyer]**

1. **to⌈ri⌉-hiki 取引 [a business transaction] ((trade, transaction))**

EX. We made a bargain with Pacific Corporation.
太平洋商事と取引をした。
Taiheiyoo-shooji to tori-hiki o shita.

2. **to⌈kka-hin 特価品 •c [specially priced merchandise], ba⌈agen-hin バーゲン品 •f+c [s.t. sold at a price favorable to the buyer] ((sale))**

EX. Bargains are usually found in the basement of a department store.
{特価品/バーゲン品}は通常デパートの地下売り場にある。
{Tokka-hin/Baagen-hin} wa tsuujoo depaato no chika-uriba ni aru.

barge n. **[a large, flat-bottomed boat for transporting freight on rivers, etc.]**
ha⌈shike はしけ

bark vi. **[for a dog to make a sharp, abrupt cry]**
ho⌈e⌉ru ほえる ② [for a dog, wolf, etc. to utter a loud, rambling sound]

EX. Our dog does not bark even at the sight of a burglar.
うちの犬はどろぼうを見てもほえない。
Uchi no inu wa doroboo o mite mo hoenai.

barley n.
o⌈omu⌉gi 大麦

barn n. **[a farm building for sheltering harvested crops, livestock, etc.]**
na⌉ya 納屋 •c [a hut for storing agricultural implements, etc.] ((shed)), mo⌈no-oki⌉ 物置 [a storage place] ((storeroom, lumber closet))

barrel n. **[a large, cylindrical container with slightly bulging sides and flat ends or a unit of capacity]**

ta⌈ru たる **[a wooden cylindrical container with a lid for the storage of liquid or powder], {ba⌉reru/ba⌉areru} {バレル/バーレル} •f [a unit of capacity equal to 31.5 gallons]**

B

barren adj. **[for land to be unproductive]**
fu⌈moo no N 不毛のN •c [not productive] ⟪not fertile⟫ ↔ hiyokuna 肥沃な adj(*na*). **•c**

EX. The farmer turned the barren land into fertile farmland.
農民は不毛の土地を豊かな農地に変えた。
Noomin wa fumoo no tochi o yutakana noochi ni kaeta.

barrier n. **[anything that hinders/blocks]**
sho⌈oga⌉i-butsu 障害物 •c [s.t. which hinders smooth progress of s.t.] ⟪obstacle, obstruction⟫, sho⌈oheki 障壁 •c [a wall of partition ⟪fig. "bottleneck"⟫] ⟪wall⟫

EX. (**a**) Tariff barriers are detrimental to trade.
関税の{障壁/*障害物}は貿易に対して害になる。
*Kanzei no {shooheki/*shoogai-butsu} wa booeki ni taishite gai ni naru.*
(**b**) There was a barrier on the highway.
高速道路に{障害物/*障壁}があった。
*Koosoku-dooro ni {shoogai-butsu/*shooheki} ga atta.*

base n. **[the part of s.t. on which s.t. rests ⟪fig. "a headquarters," "source of supply," "any of the four goals a baseball player must reach to score a run"⟫]**
1. ki⌈so⌉ 基礎 •c [that on which s.t. more complex is built] ⟪foundation, basis⟫

EX. Christianity forms the base of his belief.
キリスト教が彼の信念の基礎です。
Kirisuto-kyoo ga kare no shinnen no kiso desu.

2. ki⌈chi⌉ 基地 •c [a place from which military operations or explorations are conducted], be⌉esu ベース •f

EX. They established a base in the Antarctic.
彼らは南極に{基地/ベース}を設置した。
Kare-ra wa Nankyoku ni {kichi/beesu} o setchi-shita.

3. ru⌉i 塁 •c, be⌉esu ベース •f [any of the four goals a baseball player must reach to score a run]

— vt. **[for s.o. to establish as a foundation for s.t.]**
⟨-ni⟩ ki⌈so⌉ o o⌈ku ⟨〜に⟩基礎を置く ① [to set a foundation on s.t.], ⟨-ni⟩ mo⌈to-zu⌉ku ⟨〜に⟩基づく ① [to use s.t. as a foundation/basis for s.t. else]

EX. His arguments are based on experimental results.
彼の議論は実験の結果に{基礎を置いて/基づいて}いる。
Kare no giron wa jikken no kekka ni {kiso o oite/moto-zuite} iru.

— adj. **[mean-spirited, cowardly]**
hi⌈retsuna 卑劣な adj(*na*). **•c [despicable, low] ⟪mean, dirty⟫**

EX. That was a base act.
それは卑劣な行為だった。
Sore wa hiretsuna kooi datta.

baseball n.
ya⌈kyuu 野球 •c, be⌈esu-bo⌉oru ベースボール •f

EX. (**a**) Baseball is the most popular team sport in Japan.
{野球/ベースボール}は日本で一番人気のあるチームスポーツです。
{Yakyuu/Beesu-booru} wa Nihon de ichiban ninki no aru chiimu-supootsu desu.
(**b**) Children are playing baseball in the field.
子供たちが野原で{野球/??ベースボール}をしている。
Kodomo-tachi ga nohara de {yakyuu/??beesu-booru} o shite iru.

basement n. **[a floor below the main floor of a building, usually underground]**
chi⌈ka⌉-shitsu 地下室 •c [a room in a house, etc. below the main floor], chi⌈kai 地階 •c [an underground floor below the main floor of a building]

bashful adj. **[easily embarrassed]**
ha⌈zukashi-gari-ya no N 恥ずかしがりやのN [easily embarrassed] ⟪shy⟫, u⌈chikina 内気な adj(*na*). **[of a personality that is**

withdrawn and reserved] ⟪timid⟫, **ha⌈nikami-ya no N** はにかみやのN **[showing embarrassment]** ⟪shy⟫

EX. Ichiro is a very bashful boy.
一郎はとても{恥ずかしがりやの/内気な/はにかみやの}少年です。
Ichiroo wa totemo {hazukashi-gari-ya no/uchikina/hanikami-ya no} shoonen desu.

basic adj. **[forming a base for s.t.]**
ki⌈hon-tekina 基本的な adj(*na*). •c **[forming a prototype which is common to all its variations]** ⟪fundamental⟫, **ki⌈so-tekina** 基礎的な adj(*na*). •c **[forming the base on which to build s.t. more complex]** ⟪fundamental⟫

EX. A year's intensive study of Japanese will give you a basic knowledge of the language.
日本語を一年間集中的に勉強すれば{基本的な/基礎的な}知識が身につく。
Nihon-go o ichi-nenkan shuuchuu-tekini benkyoo-sureba {kihon-tekina/kiso-tekina} chishiki ga mi ni tsuku.

basin n. **[a wide, shallow container for liquid ⟪fig. "round valley"⟫]**
1. **ta⌈rai** たらい **[a larger liquid container for washing s.t.]**, **se⌈nme⌉n-ki** 洗面器 •c **[a smaller liquid container for washing one's face]**
2. **bo⌈nchi** 盆地 •c **[a depression in the earth's surface]** ⟪valley, hollow⟫

basis n. **[the basic supporting element]**
ki⌈so⌉ 基礎 •c **[that on which s.t. more complex is built]** ⟪base, foundation⟫, **ko⌉nkyo** 根拠 •c **[the facts/conditions that provide a base for a rumor, accusation, etc.]** ⟪ground⟫, **ki⌉hon** 基本 •c **[a base upon which to start s.t.]** ⟪fundamental⟫

EX. (**a**) On what basis can you say that?
何を{根拠/*基礎/*基本}にそう言えますか。
*Nani o {konkyo/*kiso/*kihon} ni soo iemasu ka.*
(**b**) The result was obtained on the basis of a large-scale survey.
その結果は大掛かりな調査を{基礎/*基本/*根拠}として得られた。
*Sono kekka wa oogakarina choosa o {kiso/*kihon/*konkyo} to-shite e-rareta.*
(**c**) Freedom and equality are the bases for democracy.
自由平等は民主主義の{基本/?基礎/*根拠}です。
*Jiyuu-byoodoo wa minshu-shugi no {kihon/?kiso/*konkyo} desu.*

basket n. **[a container made of straw, strips of wood, etc. woven together]**
ka⌈go かご **[a woven container made of straw, bamboo, etc.]**, **ba⌈suke⌉tto** バスケット •f **[a container made of straw, etc. woven together]**

EX. I took many pictures of kittens in a basket.
僕は{かご/バスケット}に入った子猫の写真をたくさん撮った。
Boku wa {kago/basuketto} ni haitta ko-neko no shashin o takusan totta.

bass n. **[the tonal range of the lowest male voice/musical instruments]**
1. **ba⌉su** バス •f **[the tonal range of the lowest male voice]**
2. **be⌉esu** ベース •f **[a musical instrument that produces low-pitched tones]**

bat n. **[a club with which to hit a ball in baseball or a turn at hitting]**
1. **ba⌉tto** バット •f **[a club with which to hit a ball in baseball, etc.]**
2. **da⌈jun** 打順 •c **[the order in which a baseball player hits the ball]**

EX. Sadaharu is at bat now.
今は貞治の打順だ。
Ima wa Sadaharu no dajun da.

bat n. **[a nocturnal, mouselike, flying mammal with a furry body and membranous wings]**
ko⌉omori こうもり

bath n. **[a washing, esp. of the body, in a tub of hot water]**
fu⌈ro⌉ ふろ **[hot water in which to wash oneself or a bathroom]**, **nyu⌈uyoku** 入浴 •c

furo

B

[immersing oneself in hot water to wash oneself]

EX. Grandfather is very fond of taking baths.
祖父は{ふろ/入浴}が大好きだ。
Sofu wa {furo/nyuuyoku} ga dai-suki da.

B

bathe vt./vi. **[to give a bath to/to take a bath]**
⟨-o⟩ nyu⌈uyoku-sa⌈seru ⟨〜を⟩入浴させる /⟨causative of *nyuuyoku-suru* ③ take a bath/ ② •c [for s.o. to cause s.o. to take a bath], fu⌈ro⌉ ni ha⌉iru ふろに入る ① [for s.o. to take a bath], nyu⌈uyoku-suru 入浴する ③ •c

bathroom n. **[a room with a bathtub, toilet, etc.]**
fu⌈ro-ba ふろ場 [a room with a bathtub, but usually no toilet], yo⌈kushitsu 浴室 •c ⟨w⟩, (o-)⌈tea⌉rai (お)手洗い [a lavatory], to⌉ire トイレ •f [toilet]

EX. (**a**) Where is the bathroom?
{(お)手洗い/トイレ/ふろ場/浴室}はどちらですか。
{(O-)tearai/Toire/Furo-ba/Yokushitsu} wa dochira desu ka.
(**b**) The bathroom in this apartment doesn't have a shower.
このアパートの{ふろ場/浴室/*(お)手洗い/*トイレ}にはシャワーが付いていない。
*Kono apaato no {furo-ba/yokushitsu/ *(o-)tearai/*toire} ni wa shawaa ga tsuite inai.*

bathtub n. **[a tub for holding hot water to bathe in]**
yu⌉bune 湯舟 [a vessel for holding hot water to take a bath in], yo⌈kusoo 浴槽 •c [a container for hot water to bathe in]

batter n. **[the baseball player whose turn it is to bat]**
ba⌉ttaa バッター •f, da⌉sha 打者 •c

battery n.
1. [a cell which generates an electric current]
de⌉nchi 電池 •c [a device for generating electricity by means of chemical reactions], ba⌉tterii バッテリー •f [a cell which generates an electric current, usually rechargeable]

EX. The battery has run down.
{電池/バッテリー}が切れてしまった。
{Denchi/Batterii} ga kirete shimatta.

2. [the pitcher and the catcher in baseball]
ba⌉tterii バッテリー •f

batting n. **[the act of using a bat in a game of ball]**
ba⌉ttingu バッティング •f

battle n. **[a fight between armies, ships, or planes]**
ta⌈takai 戦い /⟨V*masu* of *tatakau* ① fight/ [an act/instance of fighting/competing]

EX. The Genji clan won the battle.
源氏がその戦いに勝った。
Genji ga sono tatakai ni katta.

—— vi. **[to fight]**
⟨-to⟩ ta⌈takau ⟨〜と⟩戦う ① [for s.o. to try in a determined way to prevent/stop s.t. from happening or to get/achieve s.t.] ⟪fight⟫

EX. The people battled against poverty.
国民は貧困と戦った。
Kokumin wa hinkon to tatakatta.

bay n. **[a body of water forming an indentation in the shoreline]**
wa⌉n 湾 •c [a place where seawater forms an indentation into the land]

B.C. [before Christ]
ki⌈gen-ze⌉n 紀元前 •c [before the base year in history] ↔ kigen 紀元 •c

be vi. **[to exist/copula]**
1. a⌉ru ある ① [for s.t. to exist], i⌉ru いる ② [for s.o./s.a. to exist], go⌈zaima⌉su ございます [for s.t. to exist ⟨fml⟩], o⌈rima⌉su おります [for the speaker or s.o./s.a the speaker empathizes with to exist ⟨fml⟩], i⌈rassha⌉ru いらっしゃる ① [for s.o. the speaker shows deference to to exist] ⟪is, are⟫

NOTE: Both *gozaimasu* and *orimasu* are almost always used in their formal forms.

EX. (**a**) There are many temples in Kyoto.
京都にはお寺がたくさん{あります/ございます/*いらっしゃいます/*います}。
Kyooto ni wa o-tera ga takusan

*{arimasu/gozaimasu/*irasshaimasu/ *imasu}.*
(**b**) There are many people in Tokyo.
東京には人がたくさん{います/??おります/??いらっしゃいます/*あります/*ございます}。
*Tookyoo ni wa hito ga takusan {imasu/ ??orimasu/??irasshaimasu/*arimasu/ *gozaimasu}.*
(**c**) The cat you're looking for is on the roof.
あなたが探している猫は屋根の上に{います/??おります/*いらっしゃいます/*あります/*ございます}。
*Anata ga sagashite iru neko wa yane no ue ni {imasu/??orimasu/*irasshaimasu/ *arimasu/*gozaimasu}.*
(**d**) Our guests are in the living room.
お客様は居間に{いらっしゃいます/います/*おります/*あります/*ございます}。
*O-kyaku-sama wa ima ni {irasshaimasu/imasu/*orimasu/ *arimasu/*gozaimasu}.*

2. da だ cop. **[informal/written style affirmative nonpast tense of the copula]** ((is, am, are)), **de⌉su** です cop. **[formal affirmative nonpast tense of the copula *da*]** ((is, am, are)), **de⌈a⌉ru** である cop. **[written style affirmative nonpast tense of the copula]** ((is, am, are)), **dei⌈rassha⌉ru** でいらっしゃる cop. **[affirmative nonpast tense of the copula showing deference to the person in subject position]** ((is, are)), **dego⌈zaima⌉su** でございます cop. **[very formal affirmative nonpast tense of the copula]** ((is, am, are))

EX. (**a**) Dr. Chomsky is a famous linguist.
チョムスキー博士は著名な言語学者{です/だ/である/でいらっしゃいます/??でございます}。
Chomusukii-hakase wa chomeina gengo-gakusha {desu/da/dearu/ deirasshaimasu/??degozaimasu}.
(**b**) We are happy.
私たちは幸福{だ/です/である/でございます/*でいらっしゃいます}。
*Watashi-tachi wa koofuku {da/desu/ dearu/degozaimasu/*deirasshaimasu}.*

3. V*te* i⌈ru V*te*いる ② [to be in the middle of doing s.t. or in a state resulting from s.t. that happened eariler]

EX. (**a**) Chako the dog is already dead.
犬のチャコはもう死んでいる。
Inu no Chako wa moo shinde iru.
(**b**) The door is open.
ドアが開いています。
Doa ga aite imasu.

— aux. **[an auxiliary verb used in the passive or progressive construction]**

1. V*te* i⌈ru V*te*いる ② [to be in the middle of doing s.t. or in a state resulting from s.t. that happened earlier]

EX. (**a**) We are writing a dictionary.
我々は辞書を書いている。
Ware-ware wa jisho o kaite iru.
(**b**) What are you doing now?
あなたは今何をしていますか。
Anata wa ima nani o shite imasu ka.

2. {Vneg. reru/Vstem rareru/sa⌈re⌉ru} {Vneg.れる/Vstemられる/される} ② [for s.t./s.o./s.a. acting as the subject of the sentence to be affected by the action of the verb of that sentence]

EX. (**a**) The fish was eaten by the cat.
魚は猫に食べられた。
Sakana wa neko ni tabe-rareta.
(**b**) The child was praised by the teacher.
子供は先生にほめられた。
Kodomo wa sensei ni home-rareta.
(**c**) *The Tale of Genji* was written by Murasaki Shikibu.
『源氏物語』は紫式部によって書かれた。
"Genji Monogatari" wa Murasaki Shikibu ni yotte kaka-reta.

NOTE: The verb *suru* "do" changes to *sareru* in the passive construction.

beach n. **[an expanse of sand or pebbles along a shore]**
ha⌈ma⌉ 浜 **[a flat sandy area along an ocean/ lake], ka⌉igan** 海岸 •c **[the land next to the ocean], bi⌉ichi** ビーチ •f **[a place where the land meets an ocean/lake used for bathing and other recreation]**

EX. | Many tourists go to the beach at Waikiki.
多くの観光客がワイキキの{浜/海岸/ビーチ}へ行く。
Ooku no kankoo-kyaku ga Waikiki no {hama/kaigan/biichi} e iku.

bead n. **[a small ball of glass, etc. pierced for stringing]**
bi⌉izu ビーズ **•f, ju⌈zu-dama** 数珠玉 **[a Buddhist rosary]**

juzu-dama

beak n. **[the bill of a bird]**
ku⌈chibashi くちばし

bean n. **[a seed or pod of a plant of the legume family]**
ma⌈me⌉ 豆

EX. | *Jack and the Bean Stalk* is a famous story.
『ジャックと豆の木』は有名なお話です。
"Jakku to mame no ki" wa yuumeina o-hanashi desu.

beanpaste n. **[fermented paste made from soya beans for miso soup]**
mi⌉so 味そ

bear¹ n.
ku⌈ma⌉ 熊

kuma

bear² vt. **[to bring forth or to carry ⟪fig. "withstand," "have"⟫]**

1. ⟨-o⟩ u⌈mu ⟨～を⟩うむ ① **[to give birth to s.t./s.o./s.a.]**

㊇ "give birth to an offspring"▷産む, "give birth to an offspring/s.t. such as artistic work, rumor, interest, etc."▷生む

EX. | Yoshiko bore a child in Tokyo.
美子は東京で子供を生んだ。
Yoshiko wa Tookyoo de kodomo o unda.

PHRASE: be born *umareru* 生まれる ②

EX. | I was born in Kanazawa.
僕は金沢で生まれた。
Boku wa Kanazawa de umareta.

2. (mi o) mu⌈subu (実を)結ぶ ① **[to produce fruit, etc.]**

EX. | Her effort bore fruit.
彼女の努力が実を結んだ。
Kanojo no doryoku ga mi o musunda.

3. ⟨-ni⟩ ta⌈e⌉ru ⟨～に⟩耐える ② **[to not succumb to pain/pressure/distress]**

EX. | Rumi cannot bear being alone.
留美は一人でいることに耐えられない。
Rumi wa hitori de iru koto ni tae-rarenai.

4. a⌉ru ある ① **[for s.t. to exist]**

EX. | (**a**) This check bears the president's seal.
この小切手には社長の印がある。
Kono kogitte ni wa shachoo no in ga aru.
(**b**) His left hand bears a scar.
彼の左手には傷あとがある。
Kare no hidari-te ni wa kizu-ato ga aru.

beard n. **[the hair growing on the lower part of a man's face]**
a⌈go⌉-hige あごひげ **[the hair growing on the chin]**

bearing n. **[the way in which s.t. is carried or s.t. relates to s.t. else ⟪fig. "attitude," "any part of a machine in/on which another part revolves, slides, etc."⟫]**

1. ho⌈ogaku 方角 **•c [the line or course on which s.t. exists as relative to some reference point, esp. the location of the speaker], i⌉chi** 位置 **•c [the place occupied by s.t./s.o./s.a.] ⟪location⟫**

EX. | When I came up to the street level from the subway, I lost my bearing.
地下鉄から通りへ上がってきたら、{方角/位置}が分からなかった。
Chika-tetsu kara toori e agatte-kitara, {hoogaku/ichi} ga wakaranakatta.

2. ta⌉ido 態度 **•c [verbal and nonverbal manifestations of what one thinks/feels], mo⌈no⌉-goshi** 物腰 **[an attitude in dealing with people]**

EX. | His haughty bearing is unbearable.
彼の横柄な{態度/物腰}には我慢できない。
Kare no ooheina {taido/mono-goshi} ni wa gaman-dekinai.

3. ka⌈nkei 関係 **•c [a quality by which two or more things are considered to be connected or joined together] ⟪relationship⟫**

EX. | The document had no bearing on the matter.

その書類は本件に何の関係もなかった。
Sono shorui wa honken ni nan no kankei mo nakatta.

4. be⌈aringu ベアリング **•f, ji⌈ku-uke** 軸受け **[the part of a machine in/on which an axle revolves]**

beast n. **[any large, four-footed animal]**
yo⌈tsu-ashi no do⌈obutsu 四足の動物 **•c [four-footed animal], ke⌈mono** 獣 **[animal], ke⌈damono** けだもの **[animal** ⟪**fig. "a despicable person"**⟫**]**

beat vt. **[for s.o. to hit/strike s.t./s.o./s.a. repeatedly** ⟪**fig. "outdo"**⟫**]**
1. ⟨**-o**⟩ **na⌈gu⌉ru** ⟨〜を⟩殴る ① **[for s.o. to bring one's fist or to use s.t. against s.o./s.a. hard with the intention of causing harm]** ⟪**hit, pound**⟫**,** ⟨**-o**⟩ **ta⌈ta⌉ku** ⟨〜を⟩たたく ① **[for s.o. to bring the hand/s.t. held in the hand against s.o./s.t./s.a., usu. repeatedly** ⟪**fig. "criticize"**⟫**]**

EX. The naughty boy beat the poor dog.
わんぱく坊主はかわいそうな犬を{殴った/たたいた}。
Wanpaku-boozu wa kawai-soona inu o {nagutta/tataita}.

2. ⟨**-o**⟩ **ma⌈kasu** ⟨〜を⟩負かす ① **[for s.o. to cause s.o. to lose]** ⟪**defeat**⟫

EX. The University of Michigan beat Ohio State in football.
ミシガン大学はフットボールでオハイオ州立大学を負かした。
Mishigan-daigaku wa futto-booru de Ohaio-shuuritsu-daigaku o makashita.

—— vi. **[for s.t. to strike/hit/dash repeatedly and hard or to move rhythmically]** ⟪**hit**⟫
1. ⟨**-ni**⟩ **ha⌈ge⌉shiku u⌈chi-tsuke⌉ru** ⟨〜に⟩激しく打ちつける ② **[for s.t. to hit s.t. else violently over and over again]** ⟪**hit**⟫

EX. The heavy rain beat against the windows.
ひどい雨が窓に激しく打ちつけた。
Hidoi ame ga mado ni hageshiku uchi-tsuketa.

2. ko⌈doo-suru 鼓動する ③ **•c [for s.t. (usually the heart) to throb/pulsate rhythmically]** ⟪**throb, pulsate, vibrate, tick**⟫

EX. My heart began to beat fast when I saw her.
彼女に会ったとき、私の心臓は速く鼓動し始めた。
Kanojo ni atta toki, watashi no shinzoo wa hayaku kodoo-shi-hajimeta.

NOTE: The above is more naturally expressed as follows: *Shinzoo no kodoo ga hayaku natta.*

beautiful adj. **[having beauty (which causes admiration)]**
1. u⌈tsukushi⌉i 美しい adj(*i*). **[aesthetically very pleasing to the eye, ear, mind, etc.]** ⟪**lovely, pretty**⟫**, ki⌉reina** きれいな adj(*na*). **[pleasantly attractive due to having beauty or orderliness or due to being free from dirt]** ⟪**clean, pretty, tidy, neat**⟫

EX. Listening to beautiful music cleanses our heart.
{美しい/きれいな}音楽を聞くと心が清らかになる。
{Utsukushii/Kireina} ongaku o kiku to kokoro ga kiyorakani naru.

2. su⌈barashi⌉i すばらしい adj(*i*). **[causing great wonder/admiration/pleasure due to being extremely good]** ⟪**wonderful, splendid, marvelous, great**⟫**, su⌈tekina** すてきな adj(*na*). **[giving a favorable impression to the observer on the basis of outward appearance such as dress, color, pattern, etc.]** ⟪**neat**⟫

EX. Aunt Lucie made me a beautiful dress.
ルーシーおばさんは私に{すばらしい/すてきな}ドレスを作ってくれた。
Ruushii-oba-san wa watashi ni {subarashii/sutekina} doresu o tsukutte kureta.
(**b**) The opening ceremony was blessed with beautiful weather.
開会式は{すばらしい/*すてきな}晴天に恵まれた。
*Kaikai-shiki wa {subarashii/*sutekina} seiten ni meguma-reta.*

beautifully adv. **[in a beautiful manner]**
u⌈tsuku⌉shiku 美しく **/**⟨**adj(*i*).** ***ku*** **of** ***utsukushii*** **beautiful/ [in a beautiful manner], ki⌉reini** きれいに **/**⟨**adj(*na*).** ***ni*** **of** ***kireina*** **pretty, clean/ [in a beautiful/clean manner]**

B

beauty n. **[the quality of pleasing the senses or mind or s.o. or s.t. beautiful]**

1. bi⌉ 美 •c[the quality of being beautiful; an object of aesthetics], u⌈tsuku⌉shi-sa 美しさ /⟨adj(*i*). stem of *utsukushii* beautiful + suf. *sa*/ [the quality of being beautiful]

EX. Japanese architecture makes good use of the beauty of symmetry.
日本建築は対称の{美/美しさ}をうまく生かしている。
Nihon kenchiku wa taishoo no {bi/utsukushi-sa} o umaku ikashite iru.

2. u⌈tsukushi⌉i hito 美しい人 [a beautiful person, almost always a woman], bi⌈jin 美人 •c [a beautiful lady]

EX. Elizabeth had great beauty.
エリザベスは{美しい人/美人}だった。
Erizabesu wa {utsukushii hito/bijin} datta.

3. ki⌉reina mo⌈no⌉ きれいなもの [s.t. which is beautiful or attractive to look at]

EX. I didn't know that the night-blooming cereus was such a beauty.
月下美人があんなにきれいなものとは知らなかった。
Gekka-bijin ga annani kireina mono to wa shiranakatta.

beauty parlor n.
bi⌈yo⌉o-in 美容院 •c ⟪hair dresser⟫

beaver n.
bi⌉ibaa ビーバー •f

because conj. **[for the reason/cause that]**
Sinf. node Sinf.ので prt. **[a subordinate conjunction expressing reason or cause. The speaker believes that the information he/she provides in "S1 node" as cause/reason for "S2" is valid and is also evident and acceptable to the listener] ⟪since, so, as⟫, S kara Sから** prt. **[a subordinate conjunction expressing reason or cause] ⟪since, so, as⟫**

NOTE: When the nonpast affirmative form of adj(*na*). or N + cop. occurs before *node*, {adj(*na*). stem/N} *na* is used.

EX. (**a**) I went to bed early because I was tired.
疲れた{ので/から}、早く寝た。
Tsukareta {node/kara}, hayaku neta.
(**b**) A: Why didn't you come to the party?
どうしてパーティーに来なかったんですか。
Dooshite paatii ni konakatta n desu ka.
B: Because I had lots of work to do.
仕事がたくさんあった{から/*ので}です。
*Shigoto ga takusan atta {kara/*node} desu.*
(**c**) It's correct because I told you so.
僕がそう言うんだ{から/*ので}間違いはないよ。
*Boku ga soo iu n da {kara/*node} machigai wa nai yo.*
(**d**) I didn't go because I had a cold.
風邪をひいていた{から/ので}行きませんでした。
Kaze o hiite ita {kara/node} ikimasen deshita.
(**e**) Because it's raining hard outside, why don't you stay home?
外は雨がひどい{から/*ので}、うちにいたら?
*Soto wa ame ga hidoi {kara/*node}, uchi ni itara?*
(**f**) Because tomorrow's game is very important, please come to cheer us on.
明日はすごく大事な試合{だから/??なので}、是非応援に来てくれ。
Ashita wa sugoku daijina shiai {da kara/??na node}, zehi ooen ni kite kure.
(**g**) Because Professer Nonaka is very much concerned about you, you'd better write to him.
野中先生が君のことをすごく心配していらっしゃる{から/?ので}、お手紙を差し上げたほうがいいですよ。
Nonaka-sensei ga kimi no koto o sugoku shinpai-shite irassharu {kara/?node}, o-tegami o sashi-ageta hoo ga ii desu yo.
(**h**) Because I've bought some superb Australian wine, shall we drink it together?
すばらしいオーストラリアワインを買ってきた{から/*ので}、一緒に飲まない?
*Subarashii Oosutoraria-wain o katte kita {kara/*node}, issho ni nomanai?*

NOTE: It is better to avoid using *node* if S2 is an advice, request, suggestion or invitation as in examples (e), (f), (g), (h). Use *kara* instead, but in a formal public announcement or other formal speech, *node* may be used even in such examples.

become vi. **[to come to be or change into]**
{⟨-ni⟩/adj(*i*). *ku*/adj(*na*). *ni*} na⌉ru {⟨〜に⟩/adj(*i*). *ku*/adj(*na*). *ni*}なる ① [to change into]

EX. (**a**) Robin became a doctor.
ロビンは医者になった。
Robin wa isha ni natta.
(**b**) Naomi has become famous in Japan.
ナオミは日本で有名になった。
Naomi wa Nihon de yuumeini natta.
(**c**) My son has become tall.
息子は背が高くなった。
Musuko wa se ga takaku natta.

bed n.
be⌉ddo ベッド •f, shi⌈ndai 寝台 •c
PHRASE: go to bed *neru* 寝る ② ⟪retire at night⟫

bedroom n.
bed⌈doruu⌉mu ベッドルーム •f, shi⌈nshitsu 寝室 •c

bee n.
ha⌈chi はち

beef n. **[the meat of an ox, cow, or bull]**
gyu⌈uniku 牛肉 •c, bi⌉ifu ビーフ •f

beefsteak n.
su⌈te⌉eki ステーキ •f , bi⌈futeki ビフテキ •f

beer n.
bi⌉iru ビール •f

beet n.
te⌈nsai てん菜 •c, bi⌉ito ビート •f

before prep. **[ahead of in time/space/order/rank/importance]**
⟨-no⟩ ma⌉e ni ⟨〜の⟩前に [at an earlier time or in front of]

EX. (**a**) I made a phone call before departure.
出発の前に電話をかけた。
Shuppatsu no mae ni denwa o kaketa.
(**b**) I had never stood before so many people in my life.
生まれて初めてあんなに多くの人の前に立った。
Umarete hajimete annani ooku no hito no mae ni tatta.

—— conj. [earlier than the time that]
Vinf. nonpast ma⌉e ni Vinf. nonpast前に [prior to the time when]

EX. (**a**) Please let me know before you come.
来られる前に知らせて下さい。
Ko-rareru mae ni shira-sete kudasai.
(**b**) I had a little whiskey before I went to bed.
寝る前にウィスキーを少し飲んだ。
Neru mae ni uisukii o sukoshi nonda.

—— adv. [in advance or in the past]
ma⌉e ni 前に [at an earlier time or in front]

EX. John has been to Korea before.
ジョンは前に韓国に行ったことがある。
Jon wa mae ni Kankoku ni itta koto ga aru.

beg vt. **[to ask for earnestly]**
⟨-o⟩ ko⌉u ⟨〜を⟩請う ① [for s.o. to ask s.o. to do s.t. earnestly], ⟨-o⟩ se⌈ga⌉mu ⟨〜を⟩せがむ ① [for s.o. to press/beseech s.o. to do s.t. for him/her] ⟪press, pester⟫
NOTE: Note that the V*te* and Vinf. past forms of *kou* are *koote* and *koota* respectively.

EX. (**a**) The man begged for money.
その男は金を{請うた/せがんだ}。
Sono otoko wa kane o {koota/seganda}.
(**b**) The child begged his father to take him to Disneyland.
子供は父親にディズニーランドに連れて行ってと{せがんだ/?請うた}。
Kodomo wa chichi-oya ni Dizunii-rando ni tsurete-itte to {seganda/?koota}.

PHRASE: I beg your pardon. *E?* えっ?, *Gomennasai.* 御免なさい。[I am sorry./Excuse me.], *Moo ichi-do osshatte kudasai.* もう一度おっしゃって下さい。[Please say that again.]

beggar n.
ko⌈jiki⌉ こじき

begin vt. **[for s.o. to start s.t.]**
1. ⟨-o⟩ ha⌈jimeru ⟨〜を⟩始める ② [for s.o./s.a. to perform the first part of an activity] ⟪commence⟫

EX. The researcher began her work right away.
その研究者は直ちに仕事を始めた。

B

Sono kenkyuu-sha wa tadachini shigoto o hajimeta.

2. V*masu* ha⌈jime⌉ru V*masu*始める ② [to start doing s.t.] ⟪**start**⟫

EX. Finally, the child began to talk.
やっと子供は話し始めた。
Yatto kodomo wa hanashi-hajimeta.

— vi. **[for s.t. to start]**

ha⌈jimaru 始まる ① [for the first part of s.t. to take place] ⟪**commence**⟫

EX. In Japan, school begins in April, not in September.
日本では九月ではなく四月に学校が始まります。
Nihon de wa ku-gatsu dewanaku shi-gatsu ni gakkoo ga hajimarimasu.

beginning n. **[a starting or commencing]**

1. ha⌈jime 初め /⟨V*masu* of *hajimeru* ② begin/ [the starting point or origin of s.t.] ↔ **owari 終わり**

EX. (**a**) Charlie came to Japan at the beginning of October.
チャーリーは十月の初めに来日した。
Chaarii wa juu-gatsu no hajime ni rai-Nichi-shita.
(**b**) I watched the incident from beginning to end.
私は事件を初めから終わりまで見た。
Watashi wa jiken o hajime kara owari made mita.

2. ha⌈jimari 始まり [the point from which a series of actions/incidents start]

EX. (**a**) A kiss was the beginning of their romance.
キスが二人のロマンスの始まりだった。
Kisu ga futari no romansu no hajimari datta.
(**b**) The lower stock market index was the beginning of the collapse of the bubble economy.
株価指数の低下がバブル経済崩壊の始まりだった。
Kabuka-shisuu no teika ga baburu-keizai-hookai no hajimari datta.

behave vi. **[to conduct oneself or itself in a specified way]**

1. fu⌈ruma⌉u 振るまう ① [for s.o. to act in a certain way in front of others or to entertain s.o. with food or drink] ⟪**conduct oneself, demean oneself**⟫

EX. None of the children of the school behaved badly abroad.
外国で行儀悪く振る舞った生徒はいなかった。
Gaikoku de gyoogi-waruku furumatta seito wa inakatta.

2. gyo⌈ogi-yo⌉ku suru 行儀よくする ③ [for s.o./s.a. to show good manners]

EX. Did the children behave themselves while we were out this evening?
子供たちは今晩私たちの留守中に行儀よくしていましたか。
Kodomo-tachi wa konban watashi-tachi no rusu-chuu ni gyoogi-yoku shite imashita ka.

3. u⌈go⌉ku 動く ① [to change in location or position ⟪fig. "shake," "be affected," "change," "be transferred"⟫] ⟪**stir, shift, shake, operate, vary**⟫

EX. The machine behaved well.
機械は調子よく動いた。
Kikai wa chooshi-yoku ugoita.

behavior n. **[the way s.o./s.t. acts or functions]**

fu⌈ruma⌉i 振るまい /⟨V*masu* of *furumau* ① behave/ [the way one acts in front of others or the entertainment of a guest with drinks and/or food etc.] ⟪**demeanor, conduct, action**⟫, **ko⌈odoo 行動 •c [the act of moving one's body for a purpose]** ⟪**action**⟫, **ta⌉ido 態度 •c [verbal and nonverbal manifestations of what one thinks/feels]** ⟪**posture, bearing**⟫

EX. (**a**) The gracious behavior of the lady left a good impression on him.
その女性の上品な{振る舞い/態度/*行動}が彼にいい印象を与えた。
*Sono josei no joohinna {furumai/taido/ *koodoo} ga kare ni ii inshoo o ataeta.*
(**b**) His vulgar behavior cannot be dismissed lightly.
彼の粗野な{振る舞い/態度/行動}を見

過ごすことはできない。
Kare no soyana {furumai/taido/koodoo} o mi-sugosu koto wa dekinai.

behind prep. **[spatially/temporally in the back of s.t./s.o. 《fig. "supporting," "hidden"》]**

1. ⟨-no⟩ u⌈shiro ni ⟨〜の⟩後ろに n.+prt. **[in the back of] 《in the rear of》**

EX. The lady sat behind me in the bus.
その婦人はバスで私の後ろに座った。
Sono fujin wa basu de watashi no ushiro ni suwatta.

2. ⟨-ni⟩ o⌈kurete ⟨〜に⟩遅れて /⟨Vte of *okureru* ② be late/ [be later than] 《delayed, after》

EX. The plane arrived behind schedule.
飛行機は予定に遅れて到着した。
Hikoo-ki wa yotei ni okurete toochaku-shita.

3. ⟨-o⟩ shi⌉ji-shi⌈te ⟨〜を⟩支持して /⟨Vte of *shiji-suru* ③ support/ [in support of s.t./s.o.]

EX. Prof. Smith has the dean behind him.
スミス教授は学部長が支持している。
Sumisu-kyooju wa gakubu-choo ga shiji-shite iru.

4. ⟨-no⟩ ha⌉igo ni ⟨〜の⟩背後に n.+prt. **[in back of]**

EX. What is behind all this?
この背後に何が隠されていますか。
Kono haigo ni nani ga kakusa-rete imasu ka.

—— adv. **[at/toward the rear 《fig. "delayed"》]**

1. a⌉to ni 後に n.+prt. **[remaining after] 《after, back》**

EX. The father went to Osaka, but the family stayed behind.
父親は大阪へ行ったが、家族は後に残った。
Chichi-oya wa Oosaka e itta ga, kazoku wa ato ni nokotta.

2. o⌈kurete 遅れて /⟨Vte of *okureru* ② be late/ [late] 《be tardy, overdue, in arrears》

EX. (**a**) Max was running ten minutes behind schedule.
マックスは予定より十分遅れていた。
Makkusu wa yotei yori jup-pun okurete ita.
(**b**) Yoichiro is behind in his rent.
陽一郎は家賃の支払いが遅れている。
Yooichiroo wa yachin no shiharai ga okurete iru.

being n. **[existence of s.o./s.a./s.t.]**

1. so⌈nzai 存在 •c [the fact of being present (in some significant way)]

2. i⌈ki⌉-mono 生き物 [a living thing], ni⌈ngen 人間 •c [a human]

PHRASE: come into being *umareru* 生まれる ②, for the time being *toobun* 当分 •c

EX. This will do for the time being.
当分これで間に合う。
Toobun kore de ma-ni-au.

Belgium n.

Be⌈rugi⌉i ベルギー •f

belief n. **[s.t. believed/an opinion/ conviction]**

shi⌈nkoo 信仰 •c [believing in a religion] 《faith》, shi⌉nnen 信念 •c [what s.o. believes in beyond reason], shi⌈nrai 信頼 •c [trusting s.o. completely and leaving everything to that person] 《confidence, trust》

EX. (**a**) Yasuhiro didn't attempt to change his belief in materialism.
康弘は物質主義への{信念/信仰/*信頼}を変えようとしなかった。
*Yasuhiro wa busshitsu-shugi e no {shinnen/shinkoo/*shinrai} o kaeyoo to shinakatta.*
(**b**) A child's belief in his parents is not to be betrayed.
親に対する子供の{信頼/*信念/*信仰}は裏切ってはいけない。
*Oya ni taisuru kodomo no {shinrai/ *shinnen/*shinkoo} wa uragitte wa ikenai.*
(**c**) His belief in Christianity is not to be doubted.
彼のキリスト教の{信仰/*信念/*信頼}は疑ってはいけない。
*Kare no Kirisuto-kyoo no {shinkoo/ *shinnen/*shinrai} wa utagatte wa ikenai.*

B

B

believe vt. **[to have confidence or faith in the truth of s.t./s.o.]**
⟨-o⟩ shi⌈nji⌉ru ⟨～を⟩信じる ② [for s.o. to have confidence in the truth of] ((think to be true)), ⟨-to⟩ o⌈mo⌉u ⟨～と⟩思う ① [for s.o. to spontaneously perceive s.t. in one's mind or to have an opinion about s.t.] ((think, feel))

EX. (**a**) I believe you.
僕は君を信じるよ。
Boku wa kimi o shinjiru yo.
(**b**) I believe that Hanako is telling the truth.
私は花子が真実を語っていると{信じる/思う}。
Watashi wa Hanako ga shinjitsu o katatte iru to {shinjiru/omou}.
(**c**) A: Will it snow tomorrow, too?
明日も雪が降るかな?
Asu mo yuki ga furu ka na?
B: I believe so.
降ると{思う/*信じる}よ。
*Furu to {omou/*shinjiru} yo.*

bell n. **[a hollow cup-shaped instrument of cast metal suspended from the vertex and rung by the stroke of a clapper, hammer, etc.; the stroke or sound of such an instrument]**
ka⌈ne 鐘 [a hollow, metal, cup-shaped instrument that rings when struck, often seen in Japanese temples], be⌉ru ベル •f [an instrument that rings when pushed or struck, often found on the door of residences]

EX. (**a**) The bell is ringing now.
{鐘/ベル}が今鳴っている。
{Kane/Beru} ga ima natte iru.
(**b**) The temple bell is a hundred years old.
お寺の{鐘/*ベル}は百年前のものだ。
*O-tera no {kane/*beru} wa hyaku-nen mae no mono da.*

belly n. **[the stomach with its adjuncts]**
ha⌈ra⌉ 腹, o-⌈naka おなか ((tummy))

NOTE: *Hara* is not usually used by women or children.

belong vi. **[to be a member of, adherent to, inhabitant of, etc.]**
⟨-ni⟩ zo⌈kusu⌉ru ⟨～に⟩属する ③ •c [to be a member of an institution/group/genre] ((be counted among, appertain to)), ⟨-ni⟩ sho⌈zoku-suru ⟨～に⟩所属する ③ •c [for s.o. to be a member of some institution] ((be affiliated with, be attached to))

EX. (**a**) I belong to the judo club at college.
僕は大学の柔道部に{属して/所属して}います。
Boku wa daigaku no juudoo-bu ni {zokushite/shozoku-shite} imasu.
(**b**) The whale belongs to the mammal class.
鯨は哺乳類に{属する/*所属する}。
*Kujira wa honyuu-rui ni {zokusuru/*shozoku-suru}.*

beloved adj. **[greatly loved, dear to the heart]**
sa⌈iai no N 最愛のN •c [most loved], i⌈toshi⌉i いとしい adj(*i*). **[for s.o./s.t./s.a. to arouse in one a desire to be loving to him/her/it] ((darling, dear, pitiful))**

EX. Takashi lost his beloved daughter.
孝は{最愛の/いとしい}娘を亡くした。
Takashi wa {saiai no/itoshii} musume o nakushita.

below prep. **[lower in rank, degree, amount, rate, etc. than]**
-ika ～以下 •c [lower than] ((under, less than))

EX. The store is selling tapes below cost.
あの店はテープを原価以下で売っている。
Ano mise wa teepu o genka-ika de utte iru.

—— adv. **[in a lower place]**
shi⌈ta no ho⌉o ni 下の方に n.+prt. **[in a lower place than]**

EX. The hot spring is down below.
温泉は下の方にあります。
Onsen wa shita no hoo ni arimasu.

belt n. **[a band of flexible material, such as leather, for encircling the waist]**
o⌉bi 帯 [a Japanese-style strip of cloth used with kimono] ((sash)), be⌈ruto ベルト •f, ba⌈ndo バンド •f [a strip of leather, cloth, etc., for wearing around the waist or an

object similar in shape]

EX. (a) Fasten your seat belt please.
座席の{ベルト/*バンド/*帯}を締めて下さい。
*Zaseki no {beruto/*bando/*obi} o shimete kudasai.*
(b) Simon has a black belt in judo.
サイモンは柔道で黒{帯/*ベルト/*バンド}だ。
*Saimon wa juudoo de kuro-{obi/*beruto/*bando} da.*
(c) I got a leather belt for my birthday.
誕生日に革の{ベルト/バンド/*帯}をもらった。
*Tanjoo-bi ni kawa no {beruto/bando/*obi} o moratta.*

obi

bend vt. **[to force s.t. into a curved/crooked form]**
⟨-o⟩ ma⌈geru ⟨～を⟩曲げる ② **[for s.o. to cause s.t. to be curved/twisted]** ⟪**curve, bow, flex**⟫, **⟨-o⟩ o⌈ri-mageru** ⟨～を⟩折り曲げる ② **[for s.o./s.a. to cause s.t. straight or flat to become curved or angular by directly exerting force on it]**

EX. (a) Do not bend this envelope.
この封筒は{折り曲げない/??曲げない}で下さい。
Kono fuutoo wa {ori-magenai/??magenai} de kudasai.
(b) They say he has the supernatural power to bend a spoon without touching it.
彼はスプーンに触れないでそれを{折り曲げる/曲げる}ことが出来る神通力の持ち主だそうだ。
Kare wa supuun ni furenai de sore o {ori-mageru/mageru} koto ga dekiru jintsuuriki no mochi-nushi da sooda.

— vi. **[for s.o./s.t. to turn/be turned from a straight line or from some direction/position]**
ma⌈garu 曲がる ① **[to become not straight]** ⟪**curve, turn, wind, twist, crook**⟫

EX. The road bends north at that point.
道路はその地点で北へ曲がっている。
Dooro wa sono chiten de kita e magatte iru.

beneath adv. **[in a lower place, below]**
shi⌈ta no ho⌉o {ni/de/o} 下の方{に/で/を} n.+prt. **[in a place lower than]** ⟪**below**⟫

EX. An expressway runs beneath.
高速道路が下の方を走っている。
Koosoku dooro ga shita no hoo o hashitte iru.

— prep. **[below, lower than]**
⟨-no⟩ shi⌈ta {ni/de/o} ⟨～の⟩下{に/で/を} n.+prt. **[in a place below]** ⟪**below**⟫

EX. Buds are growing beneath the snow.
雪の下でつぼみが育っている。
Yuki no shita de tsubomi ga sodatte iru.

benefit n. **[s.t. that brings help/advantage/profit]**
ri⌉eki 利益 •c **[an increase in (monetary) wealth generated by an excess of returns over costs]** ⟪**interest, gains, profit**⟫, **o⌈nkei** 恩恵 •c **[love and blessing combined]** ⟪**boon, favor**⟫

EX. (a) Mr. Yoshida did that for the benefit of the Japanese people.
吉田氏は日本国民の{利益/*恩恵}のためにそれをやった。
*Yoshida-shi wa Nihon-kokumin no {rieki/*onkei} no tame ni sore o yatta.*
(b) Mankind received a great deal of benefit from the invention of electricity.
人類は電気の発明により多大な{恩恵/利益}を受けた。
Jinrui wa denki no hatsumei ni yori tadaina {onkei/rieki} o uketa.

— n. (pl.) **[payments made by a public agency]**
kyu⌈ufu-kin 給付金 •c **[payments from an official agency]**

EX. He qualifies for medical benefits.
彼は医療給付金を受ける資格がある。
Kare wa iryoo-kyuufu-kin o ukeru shikaku ga aru.

— vt. **[to be profitable to]**
to⌉ku o suru 得をする ③ **[for s.o. to make a profit (by paying nothing or an amount**

B

B

less than normally required)]

EX. The new tax law will benefit singles.
新しい税法は独身者が得をする。
Atarashii zeihoo wa dokushin-sha ga toku o suru.

Berlin n.
Be⌉rurin ベルリン •f

berry n. **[any small, juicy, fleshy fruit]**
be⌉rii ベリー •f
NOTE: "Strawberry" is *ichigo.*

beside prep. **[by/at the side of]**
⟨-no⟩ so⌉ba {ni/de/o} ⟨〜の⟩そば{に/で/を} n.+prt. **[near s.t./s.o./s.a. the speaker empathizes with], ⟨-no⟩ chi⌈ka⌉ku {ni/de/o} ⟨〜の⟩近く{に/で/を}** n.+prt. **[in the vicinity of s.t./s.o./s.a.] ⟪near⟫**

EX. A small mill stands beside the lake.
湖の{そば/近く}に小さな水車小屋が立っている。
Mizuumi no {soba/chikaku} ni chiisana suisha-goya ga tatte iru.

besides adv. **[in addition]**
so⌈re ni それに [in addition to what has been mentioned in the preceding context] ⟪moreover⟫, so⌈no ue その上 [on top of that] ⟪as well, in addition⟫

EX. I am not interested in golf; besides it's awfully expensive.
ゴルフには興味がない。{それに/その上}おそろしく高い。
Gorufu ni wa kyoomi ga nai. {Sore ni/Sono ue} osoroshiku takai.

—— prep. **[in addition to, as well as]**
⟨-no⟩ ho⌈ka ni ⟨〜の⟩外に n.+prt. **[excepting the thing/topic mentioned] ⟪other than⟫**

EX. Besides a typewriter, he also has a word processor.
彼はタイプライターの外にワープロも持っている。
Kare wa taipuraitaa no hoka ni waapuro mo motte iru.

best adj. **[of the most excellent kind]**
i⌈chiban i⌉i 一番いい adj(*i*). **[of the most excellent kind] ⟪top⟫, sa⌈ijoo no N 最上のN •c [highest in rank/degree/quality, esp. in degree of pleasure/satisfaction produced], sa⌈iryoo no N 最良のN •c [of the most excellent kind] ⟪ideal⟫, sa⌈ikoo no N 最高のN •c [highest in location/quality]**

EX. (a) Honesty is the best policy.
正直は{一番いい/最上の/最良の/最高の}策である。
Shoojiki wa {ichiban ii/saijoo no/sairyoo no/saikoo no} saku dearu.

NOTE: A similar Japanese proverb is *Shoojiki wa sairyoo no saku.*

(b) She is my best friend.
彼女は僕の{一番いい/最高の/?最良の/?最上の}友達だ。
Kanojo wa boku no {ichiban ii/saikoo no/?sairyoo no/?saijoo no} tomodachi da.
(c) Yesterday's game was the best of this season.
昨日の試合は今季で{一番いい/最高の/*最上の/*最良の}ゲームだった。
*Kinoo no shiai wa konki de {ichiban ii/saikoo no/*saijoo no/*sairyoo no} geemu datta.*

—— adv. **[superlative of well; in the highest degree]**
i⌈chiban 一番 •c [number 1 ⟪fig. "the marker of the superlative degree"⟫]

EX. A: What kind of pet do you like best?
ペットは何が一番好きですか。
Petto wa nani ga ichiban suki desu ka.
B: I like cats best of all.
私は猫が一番好きです。
Watashi wa neko ga ichiban suki desu.

—— n. **[the thing, condition, circumstance, action, etc. that is most excellent, most suitable, etc.]**
sa⌈ijoo no mo⌈no⌉ 最上のもの [the thing that is most excellent], sa⌈ikoo no mo⌈no⌉ 最高のもの [the thing of the highest quality], sa⌈izen 最善 •c [the utmost effort], be⌉suto ベスト •f [the most one can do]

EX. (a) I want my son to have the best.
私は息子に{最上のもの/最高のもの/*最善/*ベスト}を持たせたい。
*Watashi wa musuko ni {saijoo no mono/saikoo no mono/*saizen/*besuto} o mota-se-tai.*

(**b**) I did my best.
{最善/ベスト/*最上のもの/*最高のもの}を尽くした。
*{Saizen/Besuto/*Saijoo no mono/*Saikoo no mono} o tsukushita.*

bet n. **[an agreement between two people that the person who proves wrong about the result of a future event will pay a predetermined amount to the other]**
ka⌈ke⌉ かけ **《wager》**

EX. Jack lost a bet with Jill.
ジャックはジルとのかけに負けた。
Jakku wa Jiru to no kake ni maketa.

—— vt. **[for s.o. to declare in, or as in, a wager]**
1. ⟨-ni⟩ (ka⌈ne o) ka⌈ke⌉ru ⟨〜に⟩(金を)かける ② **[for s.o. to wager money on s.t.]** **《wager, stake, gamble》**

EX. Taro bet ¥50,000 on the race.
太郎はそのレースに五万円かけた。
Taroo wa sono reesu ni go-man-en kaketa.

2. ki⌈tto きっと adv. **[with a high level of certainty]** **《surely, certainly》**

EX. I bet it will snow tonight.
今晩はきっと雪だよ。
Konban wa kitto yuki da yo.

PHRASE: You bet. *Mochiron.* もちろん。《of course, certainly》

between prep. **[in or through the space that separates two things]**
⟨-no⟩ a⌈ida {ni/de/o/etc.} ⟨〜の⟩間{に/で/を/etc.} n.+prt. **[in/at/through the space separating two or more things]**

EX. (**a**) The bullet train travels between Tokyo and Osaka in about three hours.
新幹線は東京と大阪の間を約三時間で走る。
Shinkansen wa Tookyoo to Oosaka no aida o yaku san-jikan de hashiru.
(**b**) The accident happened between 10:00 and 11:00 P.M.
その事故は午後十時から十一時の間に起こった。
Sono jiko wa gogo juu-ji kara juu-ichi-ji no aida ni okotta.
(**c**) What are some of the problems now pending between Japan and the U.S.?
今、日本とアメリカの間で懸案になっているのは例えばどんな問題ですか。
Ima, Nihon to Amerika no aida de ken'an ni natte iru no wa tatoeba donna mondai desu ka.

PHRASE: Just between you and me. *Koko dake no hanashi da keredo.* ここだけの話だけれど。

beverage n. **[a liquid for drinking such as juice, tea, coffee, alcohol, but not including ordinary water]**
no⌈mi⌉-mono 飲物 **[s.t. one takes in through one's mouth without chewing]**

EX. I don't take any alcoholic beverages.
私はアルコールの入った飲物はいただきません。
Watashi wa arukooru no haitta nomimono wa itadakimasen.

beyond prep. **[in/on/to the farther or other side of 《fig. "surpassing"》]**
⟨-no⟩ mu⌈koo {ni/de/no} ⟨〜の⟩向こう{に/で/の} n.+prt. **[over, on the other side of]**, **⟨-o⟩ ko⌈eta tokoro {ni/de/no}** ⟨〜を⟩こえたところ{に/で/の} n.+prt. **[in a place over, on the other side of]**, **⟨-o⟩ ko⌈ete iru** ⟨〜を⟩こえている /⟨V*te iru* of *koeru* ② surpass/ ② **[surpassing/exceeding/out of reach of]**
㊥ "go over s.t. spatially"▷越える, "surpass/exceed"▷超える

EX. (**a**) There is an interesting village beyond this mountain.
この山{の向こうに/を越えたところに}面白い村があります。
Kono yama {no mukoo ni/o koeta tokoro ni} omoshiroi mura ga arimasu.
(**b**) The matter is quite beyond me.
その件ははるかに私の能力を超えている。
Sono ken wa harukani watashi no nooryoku o koete iru.

bicycle n. **[a vehicle with two wheels operated by pushing on the pedals]**
ji⌈te⌉nsha 自転車 •c **[self-propelling vehicle]**

EX. Shinobu went on an errand by bicycle.
忍は自転車に乗ってお使いに行った。

B

Shinobu wa jitensha ni notte o-tsukai ni itta.

bid vt. **[for s.o. to express a greeting to s.o. or to offer as the price one will pay or accept for s.t.]**

1. {⟨-o⟩/⟨-to⟩} i⌈u {⟨〜を⟩/⟨〜と⟩}言う ① [for s.o. to verbally express s.t.]

EX.| I will have to bid him farewell.
彼にさよならを言わなければならない。
Kare ni sayonara o iwanakereba naranai.

2. nyu⌈usatsu-suru 入札する ③ [for s.o. to set a price on]

EX.| Four companies have bid for the construction of the new football stadium.
新しいフットボールスタジアムの建設に四社が入札した。
Atarashii futtobooru-sutajiamu no kensetsu ni yon-sha ga nyuusatsu-shita.

big adj. **[of large size, extent, capacity, importance, etc.]**

o⌈oki⌉i 大きい adj(*i*). **[greater than usual in size or degree], o⌉okina N 大きなN** ((large))

NOTE: *Ookina* is more impressionistic and less objective sounding than *ookii.*

EX.| Mr. Tanaka lived in a big house in Australia.
オーストラリアで田中さんは{大きい/大きな}家に住んでいた。
Oosutoraria de Tanaka-san wa {ookii/ookina} ie ni sunde ita.

biggest adj. **[largest in size]**

{i⌈chiban/mo⌈tto⌉mo} o⌈oki⌉i {一番/最も}大きい adj(*i*). **[largest in size], {i⌈chiban/mo⌈ttomo} o⌉okina N {一番/最も}大きなN [greatest in size], sa⌈idai no N 最大のN •c [largest in scale]**

EX.| This banyan tree is the biggest tree around here.
このバニヤンの木がこの辺で{{一番/最も}{大きい/大きな}/最大の}木です。
Kono baniyan no ki ga kono-hen de {{ichiban/mottomo}{ookii/ookina}/saidai no} ki desu.

bike n. **[a short form of bicycle]**

ji⌈te⌉nsha 自転車 •c [self-propelling vehicle]

NOTE: In Japanese, the word *baiku* refers to a motor bike rather than to a bicycle.

bill n. **[a bank note or an itemized statement of charges for goods or services]**

1. sa⌈tsu 札 •c [paper money, bank note]

EX.| Could you give me ten thousand-yen bills for this ten-thousand-yen bill?
この一万円札を千円札十枚に両替してくれませんか。
Kono ichi-man-en-satsu o sen-en-satsu juu-mai ni ryoogae-shite kuremasen ka.

2. ka⌈njoo 勘定 •c [an act/instance of counting] ((reckoning, calculation, accounts, check)), **se⌈ikyuu-sho 請求書 •c [a written document which requests payment, bill in general]**

EX.| The bill comes to ¥50,000.
{勘定/請求書}は五万円になる。
{Kanjoo/Seikyuu-sho} wa go-man-en ni naru.

billion n. **[a figure ten times a hundred million]**

ju⌉u-oku 十億 •c

biology n. **[a branch of science having to do with living things such as humans, animals, and plants]**

se⌈ibutsu⌉-gaku 生物学 •c [scholarship in living things]

EX.| There has been an increasing interest in biology among college students.
大学生の間で生物学への関心が高まっている。
Daigaku-sei no aida de seibutsu-gaku e no kanshin ga takamatte iru.

birch n.

shi⌈ra-kaba 白かば

bird n. **[any of a class of warmblooded, two-legged, egg-laying vertebrates with feathers and wings]**

to⌈ri 鳥

EX.| I wish I could fly in the sky like a bird.
鳥のように空を飛べたらなあ。
Tori no yooni sora o tobetara naa.

birth n. **[the act of bringing forth offspring or of being born]**

ta⌈njoo 誕生 •c [being born]

EX.| The birth of a new baby is often likened to

the launching of a vessel.
新しい赤ちゃんの誕生は、よく船の進水にたとえられる。
Atarashii aka-chan no tanjoo wa, yoku fune no shinsui ni tatoe-rareru.

PHRASE: date of birth *seinen-gappi* 生年月日 •c

birthday n. **[the day of s.o.'s birth or the anniversary of that day]**
ta⌈njo⌉o-bi 誕生日 •c
EX. When is your birthday?
誕生日はいつですか。
Tanjoo-bi wa itsu desu ka.

biscuit n. **[a crisp, unleavened wafer; cracker or cookie]**
bi⌈suke⌉tto ビスケット •f

bit n. **[a small piece/quantity]**
su⌈ko⌉shi 少し [(in) a small number/quantity or (to) a small degree], sho⌉o-shoo 少々 •c [a little], cho⌉tto ちょっと [for a short time or in a small quantity or to a small degree]
EX. It's a bit strange.
{少し/少々/ちょっと}変ですね。
{Sukoshi/Shoo-shoo/Chotto} hen desu ne.
NOTE: *Chotto* is the most colloquial of the three.
PHRASE: bit by bit *sukoshi-zutsu* 少しずつ
EX. I have come to understand Japan bit by bit.
日本が少しずつ分かってきた。
Nihon ga sukoshi-zutsu wakatte-kita.

bite vt. **[for s.o./s.a. to seize/pierce/cut with the teeth or jaws]**
⟨-o⟩ ka⌉mu ⟨～を⟩かむ ① [for s.o./s.a. to pinch s.t. between the upper and lower teeth and cut/crush it] 《chew》, ⟨-o⟩ ka⌈ji⌉ru ⟨～を⟩かじる ① [for s.o./s.a. to chew at s.t. with the teeth 《fig. "know s.t. superficially"》] 《gnaw》
EX. (**a**) A big dog bit the child in the hand.
大きい犬が子供の手を{かんだ/かじった}。
Ookii inu ga kodomo no te o {kanda/kajitta}.
(**b**) She was biting an apple.
彼女はりんごを{かじって/?かんで}いた。
Kanojo wa ringo o {kajitte/?kande} ita.

—— n. **[amount of food bitten off; mouthful or morsel]**
hi⌈to⌉-kuchi 一口 •c [a mouthful]
EX. Do you want a bite of this apple?
このりんご、一口どうですか。
Kono ringo, hito-kuchi doo desu ka.

biting adj. **[cutting/sharp]**
ha⌉da o sa⌉su yoona 肌を刺すような adj(*na*). **[as if piercing the skin]**
EX. A biting wind was blowing all day.
一日中肌を刺すような風が吹いていた。
Ichi-nichi-juu hada o sasu yoona kaze ga fuite ita.

bitter adj. **[having a sharp, often unpleasant taste 《fig. "severe," "harsh"》]**
1. ni⌈ga⌉i 苦い adj(*i*). **[acrid, hard, having a sharp taste]**
EX. (**a**) I had a bitter experience.
私は苦い経験をした。
Watashi wa nigai keiken o shita.
(**b**) Good medicine tastes bitter.
いい薬は苦い。
Ii kusuri wa nigai.
NOTE: A similar Japanese proverb is *Ryooyaku wa kuchi ni nigashi.* This proverb means that advice given for s.o.'s good is beneficial, but not sweet; it is painful and hard.
2. tsu⌈uretsuna 痛烈な adj(*na*). **•c [critical or attacking in nature, painfully severe/sharp] 《biting, sharp, incisive, fierce》, shi⌈nratsuna 辛らつな** adj(*na*). **•c [critical or satirical in nature, very harsh] 《sharp, biting, acid, harsh, severe, poignant, caustic》**
EX. John received bitter criticism over his conduct.
ジョンは自分の行いに対して{痛烈な/辛らつな}批判を受けた。
Jon wa jibun no okonai ni taishite {tsuuretsuna/shinratsuna} hihan o uketa.

bitterly adv. **[in a bitter manner]**
hi⌉doku ひどく /⟨adj(*i*).*ku* of *hidoi* awful/ [to the extent that one feels awful 《fig. "very"》] 《terribly, badly, awfully, very much》, ha⌈ge⌉shiku 激しく /⟨adj(*i*).*ku* of *hageshii* violent/ [in a fierce manner] 《violently, heavily》

B

EX. The man was bitterly attacked in the press.
その男はマスコミに{ひどく/激しく}たたかれた。
Sono otoko wa masukomi ni {hidoku/hageshiku} tataka-reta.

black adj. **[of the color of coal/pitch]**
ku⌈ro⌉i 黒い adj(*i*).

EX. Mary keeps a black dog.
メリーは黒い犬を飼っている。
Merii wa kuroi inu o katte iru.

PHRASE: black tea *koocha* 紅茶 •c

EX. The Japanese drink black tea as well as green tea.
日本人は緑茶のほか紅茶も飲みます。
Nihon-jin wa ryokucha no hoka koocha mo nomimasu.

— n. **[the name of the color describing coal/pitch《fig. "black people"》]**
1. ku⌉ro 黒 **[the name of the color describing coal/pitch《fig. "be guilty of a crime"》]**

EX. Black is the opposite of white.
黒は白の反対だ。
Kuro wa shiro no hantai da.

2. ko⌈kujin 黒人 •c **[a person with dark-colored skin]**

EX. The candidate has the support of both blacks and whites.
その候補者は黒人からも白人からも支持されている。
Sono kooho-sha wa kokujin kara mo hakujin kara mo shiji-sarete iru.

blackboard n. **[a large, smooth, usually dark surface of slate or other material on which to write/draw with chalk]**
ko⌈kuban 黒板 •c

EX. The teacher wrote a Chinese character on the blackboard.
先生は黒板に漢字を書いた。
Sensei wa kokuban ni kanji o kaita.

blacksmith n. **[one who makes and repairs iron objects, including horseshoes]**
ka⌈ji-ya かじ屋

blade n. **[the cutting part of a tool/instrument/weapon]**
ha⌉ 刃 •c

EX. May I use one of your razor blades?
かみそりの刃を一枚拝借してもいいですか。
Kamisori no ha o ichi-mai haishaku-shite mo ii desu ka.

blank adj. **[not written on/empty]**
ha⌈kushi no N 白紙のN •c **[of white paper]** **《not marked》, ku⌈uhaku no N** 空白のN •c **[of s.t. empty or not written on]**

EX. There were two blank pages in the book.
本には{白紙の/空白の}ページが二ページあった。
Hon ni wa {hakushi no/kuuhaku no} peeji ga ni-peeji atta.

— n. **[an empty space]**
1. yo⌈haku 余白 •c **[an area of paper where there is no writing/printing/painting/drawing]** **《margin》**

EX. Leave some blank space on the left.
左側に少し余白を残しなさい。
Hidari-gawa ni sukoshi yohaku o nokoshinasai.

2. ku⌈uran 空欄 •c **[a blank area that is expected to be filled out]**

EX. Please fill in all the blanks on the application form.
申し込み用紙の空欄は全部書き込んでください。
Mooshi-komi-yooshi no kuuran wa zenbu kaki-konde kudasai.

blanket n. **[a large piece of cloth, often of soft wool, used as a bed cover for warmth]**
mo⌉ofu 毛布 •c

blast vt. **[for s.o./s.t. to blow up s.t.]**
⟨-o⟩ **ba⌈kuha-suru** ⟨～を⟩爆破する ③ •c **[to explode s.t.]**

EX. Dynamite blasted the old building to pieces.
ダイナマイトがその古い建物を爆破して、粉々にした。
Dainamaito ga sono furui tate-mono o bakuha-shite, kona-gona ni shita.

blaze vi. **[for s.t. to burn/shine brightly]**
a⌈ka-a⌉ka-to ka⌈gaya⌉ku 明々と輝く ① **[for s.t. to shine brightly]** **《glare》, a⌈ka-a⌈ka-to mo⌈eru** 明々と燃える ② **[for s.t. to burn brightly]** **《flame》**

EX. (a) In their house, lights were blazing late into the night.
彼らの家では夜遅くまで明かりが明々と{輝いて/*燃えて}いた。
*Kare-ra no ie de wa yoru osoku made akari ga aka-aka-to {kagayaite/*moete} ita.*
(b) As a sign of welcome, a fire was blazing in the fireplace.
歓迎の印として暖炉では火が明々と{燃えて/*輝いて}いた。
*Kangei no shirushi to-shite danro de wa hi ga aka-aka-to {moete/*kagayaite} ita.*

bleed vi. **[for s.o./s.a. to emit/lose blood]**
chi ⌈ga de⌉ru 血が出る ② [for blood to come out], shu⌈kketsu-suru 出血する ③ •c
EX. Atsushi was bleeding in the mouth.
敦は口から{血が出て/出血して}いた。
Atsushi wa kuchi kara {chi ga dete/shukketsu-shite} ita.

blend vt. **[to mix/mingle]**
⟨-o⟩ ma⌈ze⌉ru ⟨～を⟩混ぜる ② [for s.o. to cause two or more objects to be combined] ⟪**mix, mingle**⟫
EX. My father always blends Blue Mountain with a bit of mocha.
父はいつもブルー・マウンテンとモカを少々混ぜます。
Chichi wa itsu-mo buruu-maunten to moka o shoo-shoo mazemasu.

—— n. **[a mixture of varieties]**
ko⌈ngo⌉o-butsu 混合物 •c [mixture], bu⌈rendo ブレンド •f [a mixture of different varieties of coffee, tea, alcohol spirits, etc.]
EX. (a) This coffee is a blend of Blue Mountain and Mocha.
このコーヒーはブルー・マウンテンとモカの{ブレンド/*混合物}です。
*Kono koohii wa buruu-maunten to moka no {burendo/*kongoo-butsu} desu.*
(b) The new fuel is a blend of gasoline and corn oil.
新しい燃料はガソリンとコーンオイルの{混合物/*ブレンド}だ。
*Atarashii nenryoo wa gasorin to koon-oiru no {kongoo-butsu/*burendo} da.*

blind adj. **[unable to see]**
me⌉ ga mi⌈e⌉nai 目が見えない [for the eyes to be unable to see] ⟪**sightless**⟫**, mo⌈omoku no N 盲目のN •c [sightless]** ⟨**fml**⟩
EX. Helen Keller was blind.
ヘレン・ケラーは{目が見えなかった/盲目だった}。
Heren Keraa wa {me ga mienakatta/moomoku datta}.

—— n. **[s.t. that keeps out light]**
bu⌈raindo ブラインド •f, hi-⌈yoke 日よけ [sun visor]
EX. Please close the blinds as we want to turn on the light.
電気を付けますから{ブラインド/日よけ}をおろして下さい。
Denki o tsukemasu kara {buraindo/hi-yoke} o oroshite kudasai.

block n. **[any large, solid piece of wood/stone/metal, often with flat surfaces or a group of buildings regarded as a unit]**
1. ka⌈tamari 塊 [a piece of solid substance] ⟪**lump, mass, chunk**⟫**, bu⌈ro⌉kku ブロック •f**
EX. The movie set was made of concrete blocks.
その映画のセットはコンクリートの{塊/ブロック}でできていた。
Sono eiga no setto wa konkuriito no {katamari/burokku} de dekite ita.
PHRASE. building block *tsumi-ki* 積み木
2. bu⌈ro⌉kku ブロック •f, ku⌈kaku 区画 •c [a unit of s.t. clearly marked off from others ⟨**fml**⟩**]**
EX. (a) The station is a couple of blocks from here.
駅はここから二、三{ブロック/?区画}先です。
Eki wa koko kara ni-san-{burokku/?kukaku} saki desu.
(b) A block is normally 50 yards long.
一{ブロック/区画}とは普通五十ヤードです。
Ichi-{burokku/kukaku} to wa futsuu go-juu-yaado desu.

—— vt. **[to impede passage/progress by occupying s.t.]**
⟨-o⟩ fu⌈sagu ⟨～を⟩ふさぐ ① [to close an

opening] ⟪hinder, stop up⟫, ⟨-o⟩ bo⌈ogai-suru ⟨〜を⟩妨害する ③ •c [to keep s.t. from occurring or s.o./s.a. from doing s.t., esp. by forcible means] ⟪stop, obstruct the passage of⟫

B

EX. (**a**) Do not block the emergency exit.
避難路を{ふさいで/?妨害して}はいけません。
Hinan-ro o {fusaide/?boogai-shite} wa ikemasen.
(**b**) The senator blocked the passage of the trade bill.
議員は貿易法案の通過を{妨害した/*ふさいだ}。
*Giin wa booeki-hooan no tsuuka o {boogai-shita/*fusaida}.*

blond adj. **[yellow/yellowish-brown, said of hair]**
ki⌈npatsu no N 金髪のN •c, bu⌈rondo no N ブロンドのN •f

blood n. **[the red fluid circulating in the heart, arteries and veins of vertebrates]**
chi 血, ke⌈tsu⌉eki 血液 •c ⟨fml⟩

EX. (**a**) Kentaro deposited some blood in a blood bank.
健太郎は{血液/血}を{血液/*血}銀行に預けた。
*Kentaroo wa {ketsueki/chi} o {ketsueki/*chi}-ginkoo ni azuketa.*
(**b**) Blood is thicker than water.
{血/*血液}は水よりも濃い。
*{Chi/*Ketsueki} wa mizu yori mo koi.*
(**c**) Oh, it's blood!
あっ、{血/*血液}が出た。
*A, {chi/*ketsueki} ga deta.*

bloody adj. **[involving bloodshed]**
chi-⌈namagusa⌉i 血なまぐさい adj(*i*). **[smelling of blood]**

EX. There are still many bloody wars going on in the world today.
今日世界ではまだ血なまぐさい戦争が続いている。
Konnichi sekai de wa mada chi-namagusai sensoo ga tsuzuite iru.

bloom vi. **[for s.t. to bear a flower or flowers]**
sa⌈ku 咲く ① [to blossom, come out]

EX. These flowers blossom in early spring.
この花は春先に咲く。
Kono hana wa haru-saki ni saku.

—— n. **[the state/time of flowering or a flower]**
1. sa⌈kari 盛り [the height of s.t.] ⟪height, summit, peak⟫

EX. Cherry blossoms are in bloom now.
桜の花は今が盛りです。
Sakura no hana wa ima ga sakari desu.

2. ha⌈na⌉ 花 [flower ⟪fig. "height," "peak"⟫]

blossom n. **[a flower/bloom, esp. of a fruit-bearing plant]**
ha⌈na⌉ 花 [flower ⟪fig. "height," "peak"⟫]

EX. Masao and Mika went to see the cherry blossoms in Ueno Park.
正夫と美香は上野公園に桜の花を見に行った。
Masao to Mika wa Ueno-kooen ni sakura no hana o mi ni itta.

NOTE: *Hana* in expressions such as *o-hana-mi* (flower-viewing) typically refers to cherry blossoms.

blouse n. **[a loose, shirtlike garment extending to the waist line or just below, worn by women]**
bu⌈ra⌉usu ブラウス •f

EX. Reiko is wearing a white blouse and a black skirt.
玲子は白いブラウスを着て、黒いスカートをはいている。
Reiko wa shiroi burausu o kite, kuroi sukaato o haite iru.

blow vi. **[for s.t. to move with some force, said of wind or a current of air ⟪fig. "make/give sound"⟫]**
1. (ka⌈ze ga) fu⌈ku (風が)吹く ① [for the wind to move]

EX. The wind was blowing hard on that day.
その日は、風がひどく吹いていた。
Sono hi wa, kaze ga hidoku fuite ita.

2. na⌈ru 鳴る ① [for a musical instrument/telephone/bell/thunder/stomach/ears, etc. to emit a sound]

EX. The train pulled out as the whistle blew.
笛が鳴って汽車が出て行った。
Fue ga natte kisha ga dete-itta.

—— vt. **[for s.o./s.t. to cause s.t. to fly away by the application of a sudden movement of air or to sound a wind instrument by forcing air into it 《fig. "clear/clean the nose by forcing air through," "cause to burst/break by an explosion"》]**

1. 〈-o〉 fu⌈ki-toba⌉su 〈〜を〉吹き飛ばす ① **[to cause s.t. to fly away by the application of wind or breath]**

EX. Sachiko had her hat blown off by a strong wind.
祥子は強風に帽子を吹き飛ばされた。
Sachiko wa kyoofuu ni booshi o fuki-toba-sareta.

2. 〈-o〉 fu⌈ku⌉ 〈〜を〉吹く ① **[for s.o. to cause air to come out of one's mouth 《fig. "perform music on a wind instrument"》]**

EX. Mr. Suzuki blew his trumpet in front of me.
鈴木さんは僕の前でトランペットを吹いた。
Suzuki-san wa boku no mae de toranpetto o fuita.

3. (ha⌈na o) ka⌈mu (鼻を)かむ ① **[for s.o. to clear the nose by forcing air through]**

EX. Johnny, blow your nose!
ジョニーちゃん、鼻をかみなさい。
Jonii-chan, hana o kaminasai.

4. 〈-o〉 ba⌈kuha-suru 〈〜を〉爆破する ③ •c **[for s.o. to explode s.t.]**

EX. The soldiers blew up the station with dynamite.
兵隊はダイナマイトで駅を爆破した。
Heitai wa dainamaito de eki o bakuha-shita.

—— n. **[a hard hit or shock]**

da⌈geki 打撃 •c **[an act of hitting or the resulting damage]** 《**hit, damage**》

EX. The death of Yujiro's father was a big blow to him.
父の死は裕次郎にとって大きな打撃だった。
Chichi no shi wa Yuujiroo ni-totte ookina dageki datta.

blue adj. **[of the color of the clear sky or gloomy]**

1. a⌈o⌉i 青い adj(*i*). **[of the color of the sky on a clear day and also that of newgrown grass and the leaves of most plants and trees]**

NOTE: In Japanese, *aoi* refers to both blue and green. A traffic signal is said to be *aoi*. There is also another word, *midori*, for green.

EX. She always wears a blue hat.
彼女はいつも青い帽子をかぶっている。
Kanojo wa itsu-mo aoi booshi o kabutte iru.

2. yu⌈uutsuna 憂うつな adj(*na*). •c **[showing sadness and depression of spirit]** 《**gloomy, melancholy**》, **ge⌉nki ga na⌉i (N)** 元気がない **(N) [lacking in spirit]** 《**depressed, low in spirits**》

EX. Jim looked blue the last time I saw him.
僕がこの前会ったとき、ジムは{憂うつそうな/元気がない}顔をしていた。
Boku ga kono mae atta toki, Jimu wa {yuuutsu-soona/genki ga nai} kao o shite ita.

—— n. **[the color of a clear sky]**

a⌉o 青 **[the color of a clear sky or green]**

EX. Mark all additions in blue.
追加分はすべて青でマークして下さい。
Tsuika-bun wa subete ao de maaku-shite kudasai.

board n. **[a long, flat piece of sawed wood or daily meals or a group of administrators or persons who direct or supervise some activity]**

1. i⌉ta 板 **[a flat piece of wood, normally sawed rather thin]** 《**plank, sheet, metal plate**》

EX. Get me a few boards for the bookshelf.
本棚用に板を二、三枚持ってきて下さい。
Hon-dana-yoo ni ita o ni-san-mai motte-kite kudasai.

2. sho⌈kuji 食事 •c **[the act of a person's eating in order to sustain oneself]** 《**meal, dinner, diet**》, **ma⌈kana⌉i** 賄い /〈V*masu* of *makanau* ① provide s.o. with meals/ **[meal**

B

provided in a lodging house or dormitory] ⟪meal⟫

EX. How much do you charge a month for room and board?
{食事/賄い}つきで部屋代は月いくらになりますか。
{Shokuji/Makanai}-tsuki de heya-dai wa tsuki ikura ni narimasu ka.

3. ka˥i 会 [a meeting or society], i˥i˥n-kai 委員会 •c [a committee meeting] ⟪committee, council⟫

EX. (**a**) The board of directors met to discuss the issue.
{理事会/役員会}はその問題を討議するため会合を持った。
{Riji-kai/Yakuin-kai} wa sono mondai o toogi-suru tame kaigoo o motta.
(**b**) The board of education will convene a meeting on Monday at 1:00 P.M.
教育委員会は月曜日の午後一時より会を開く。
Kyooiku-iin-kai wa getsuyoo-bi no gogo ichi-ji yori kai o hiraku.

— vt. **[for s.o. to get on a train, bus, etc.] ⟨-ni⟩ no˥ru ⟨〜に⟩のる ① [to get onto s.t./s.o./s.a. that can support one's weight ⟪fig. "be recorded"⟫] ⟪get on, ride, take⟫**

㊥ "ride"▷乗る, "be recorded"▷載る

EX. The pilot boarded the plane and took off immediately.
パイロットは飛行機に乗ると、ただちに離陸した。
Pairotto wa hikoo-ki ni noru to, tadachini ririku-shita.

PHRASE: on board ⟨*-ni*⟩ *notte* ⟨〜に⟩乗って /⟨V*te* of *noru* ① ride/

EX. The jet had 400 passengers on board.
そのジェット機には乗客四百人が乗っていた。
Sono jetto-ki ni wa jookyaku yon-hyaku-nin ga notte ita.

boat n. **[a vehicle for transportation on water, esp. a small, open watercraft]**

1. fu˥ne 船 [a vehicle for transportation on water] ⟪ship, vessel, watercraft⟫

EX. Joseph Hiko returned to Japan by boat.
ジョーゼフ彦は船で日本に戻った。
Joozefu Hiko wa fune de Nihon ni modotta.

2. bo˥oto ボート [a small, open watercraft] •f ⟪rowboat⟫

EX. The children enjoyed rowing the boat on the lake.
子供たちは湖でボートをこいで楽しんだ。
Kodomo-tachi wa mizuumi de booto o koide tanoshinda.

body n. **[the physical structure and substance of a man/animal/plant/vehicle] ka˥rada 体 [the whole physical substance of s.t. which has life] ⟪physique, constitution, frame, statue, figure, health⟫, shi˥ntai 身体 •c [the physical structure of a human] ⟪physique⟫, ni˥ku-tai 肉体 •c [flesh of a human]**

EX. (**a**) In order not to get sick, one must keep one's body clean.
病気にならないためには{体/身体/*肉体}を清潔にしておかなければならない。
*Byooki ni naranai tame ni wa {karada/shintai/*niku-tai} o seiketsuni shite okanakereba naranai.*
(**b**) A sound mind in a sound body.
健康な{体/身体/肉体}に健康な精神。
Kenkoona {karada/shintai/niku-tai} ni kenkoona seishin.

boil vi. **[for s.t. to bubble up and vaporize by being heated]**
wa˥ku わく ① [to bubble up from heat or spring up spontaneously as from under the ground]

㊥ "bubble up from heat"▷沸く, "spring up spontaneously as from under the ground"▷わく

EX. On the mountain, water boiled at below 100 °C.
山の上では摂氏百度以下で湯が沸いた。
Yama no ue de wa sesshi hyaku-do-ika de yu ga waita.

— vt. **[for s.o. to cause water, etc. to reach the bubbling stage by heating or to cook** s.t. by putting it in hot water]

1. ⟨-o⟩ wa⌈kasu ⟨〜を⟩沸かす ① [to cause s.t. to bubble by heating it] ⟪heat, make hot⟫

EX. I boiled some water to make coffee.
私はコーヒーを入れるため湯を沸かした。
Watashi wa koohii o ireru tame yu o wakashita.

2. ⟨-o⟩ yu⌈de⌉ru ⟨〜を⟩ゆでる ② [for s.o. to cook s.t. by putting it in hot water for some time and then removing it from the hot water]

EX. Mother boiled some eggs for the children.
母親は子供たちのために卵をゆでた。
Haha-oya wa kodomo-tachi no tame ni tamago o yudeta.

3. ⟨-o⟩ ni⌈ru ⟨〜を⟩煮る ② [for s.o. to prepare food by heating it until it is soft in a seasoned liquid and retaining the liquid] ⟪cook⟫

EX. Please boil this meat well.
この肉はよく煮て下さい。
Kono niku wa yoku nite kudasai.

boiler n. [a tank in which water is turned to steam or one for heating water and storing it]

bo⌉iraa ボイラー •f [a device to make hot water], ka⌈ma かま [a pot to make hot water or to cook rice]

bold adj. [showing or having fearlessness]

da⌈ita⌉nna 大胆な adj(*na*). •c [having the capacity to do things daringly which ordinary people cannot do due to fear/hesitation/reservation] ⟪daring, courageous, fearless, impudent⟫

EX. One has to be bold at times.
人は大胆でなければならないときがある。
Hito wa daitande nakereba naranai toki ga aru.

boldly adv. [daringly]

da⌈ita⌉nni 大胆に /⟨adj(*na*). *ni* of *daitanna* bold/ •c

bolt n. [a threaded metal rod used together with a nut to hold parts together]

bo⌈ruto ボルト •f

bomb n. [an explosive, incendiary, or chemical-filled container for dropping, hurling, or exploding]

ba⌈kudan 爆弾 •c

EX. An old bomb was found in the underground tank.
地下のタンクから古い爆弾が見つかった。
Chika no tanku kara furui bakudan ga mitsukatta.

bond n. [anything that binds s.t. ⟪fig. "debenture"⟫]

1. ki⌉zuna きずな [a positive connection between things which are hard to separate, such as between kin] ⟪ties, yoke, bondage⟫, so⌈kubaku 束縛 •c [limitation of freedom of activity] ⟪restraint, restriction, fetters⟫

EX. (**a**) All the members of the Takeda family are tied together by a strong bond of affection.
武田家の家族全員は強い愛情の{きずな/*束縛}で結ばれている。
*Takeda-ke no kazoku zen'in wa tsuyoi aijoo no {kizuna/*sokubaku} de musubarete iru.*
(**b**) It is extremely difficult to break the bonds of convention in this society.
この社会では因襲の{束縛/*きずな}を破ることが非常に困難だ。
*Kono shakai de wa inshuu no {sokubaku/*kizuna} o yaburu koto ga hijooni konnan da.*

2. sa⌈iken 債券 •c [an interest-bearing certificate issued by a government or corporation, redeemable on a specific date] ⟪debenture, a financial instrument⟫

bone n. [the hard tissue forming the skeleton of most vertebrates]

ho⌈ne⌉ 骨

EX. John broke a bone in his left foot when he fell.
ジョンは転んだ際に左足の骨を折ってしまった。
Jon wa koronda sai ni hidari-ashi no hone o otte shimatta.

bonus n. [anything given in addition to the customary amount, esp. extra

B

compensation above one's salary]
bo˥onasu ボーナス •f [extra compensation above salary usually paid twice a year by Japanese companies to their employees], sho˥oyo 賞与 •c [money or other compensation given in recoguition of s.o. ⟨w⟩]

EX. (**a**) This summer's bonus was especially good.
今年の夏の{ボーナス/賞与}は特によかった。
Kotoshi no natsu no {boonasu/shooyo} wa tokuni yokatta.
(**b**) This vase was given to my grandfather by the company as a bonus.
この花瓶は会社が祖父に{賞与/*ボーナス}としてくれたものです。
*Kono kabin wa kaisha ga sofu ni {shooyo/*boonasu} to-shite kureta mono desu.*

book n. **[a printed work of some length on consecutive sheets of paper bound together in a volume or a record/account of business transactions]**
1. ho˥n 本 •c [a printed work of some length on consecutive sheets of paper bound together in a volume]

EX. I have to return these books to the library.
この本を図書館に返さなければならない。
Kono hon o tosho-kan ni kaesanakereba naranai.

2. cho˥obo 帳簿 •c [a record/account of business transactions]

EX. My father keeps the books every day.
父は毎日帳簿を付けています。
Chichi wa mai-nichi choobo o tsukete imasu.

—— vt. **[to reserve rooms, seats, etc. ahead of time]**
⟨-o⟩ yo˥yaku-suru ⟨〜を⟩予約する •c [for s.o. to make formal arrangements in advance to have s.t. set apart for a particular person or use] ⟪**reserve, speak for**⟫

EX. Ethel booked two seats for the Kabuki performance.
エセルは歌舞伎の席を二つ予約した。
Eseru wa kabuki no seki o futatsu yoyaku-shita.

bookcase n. **[a set of shelves for holding books]**
ho˥n-bako 本箱 [a box ⟨lit.⟩ or case for books]

bookshelf n. **[a shelf on which books are kept]**
ho˥n-dana 本棚 [a shelf for books]

bookstore n. **[a store where books are sold]**
ho˥n-ya 本屋 [a shop for books] ⟪**bookshop**⟫**, sho˥ten 書店 •c**

EX. (**a**) I ordered a copy of this dictionary from the Sato bookstore.
私はこの辞書を一冊佐藤{書店/*本屋}に注文しました。
*Watashi wa kono jisho o is-satsu Satoo-{shoten/*hon-ya} ni chuumon-shimashita.*
(**b**) There are a couple of good bookstores in my neighborhood.
うちの近所にいい{本屋/書店}が数軒ある。
Uchi no kinjo ni ii {hon-ya/shoten} ga suuken aru.

boom n. **[swift growth; a period of prosperity]**
bu˥umu ブーム •f [s.t. growing/becoming suddenly popular] ⟪**a rapid increase in popularity**⟫

EX. It was about ten years ago that the so-called cat boom started.
いわゆる猫ブームが始まったのは今から約十年前です。
Iwayuru neko-buumu ga hajimatta no wa ima kara yaku juu-nen mae desu.

booming adj. **[flourishing]**
bu˥umu no N ブームのN [flourishing] ⟪**growing, prosperous**⟫

EX. Hawaii benefits from a booming tourist industry.
ハワイはブームの観光産業の恩恵を受けている。
Hawai wa buumu no kankoo-sangyoo no onkei o ukete iru.

boot n. **[a covering of leather, rubber, etc. for the foot and lower part of the leg]**
bu⌉utsu ブーツ •f, na⌈ga-gutsu 長靴 [long shoes]

EX. (**a**) My wife bought an expensive pair of leather boots.
妻は値段の高い革の{ブーツ/?長靴}を買った。
Tsuma wa nedan no takai kawa no {buutsu/?naga-gutsu} o katta.
(**b**) Few people wear rubber boots in the rain these days.
雨の日にもゴムの{長靴/*ブーツ}をはく人は少なくなった。
*Ame no hi ni mo gomu no {naga-gutsu/*buutsu} o haku hito wa sukunaku natta.*

booth n. **[a stall for selling goods; a small structure to house a public telephone, etc.]**
bu⌉usu ブース •f [a stall for display purposes at a fair, etc.], bo⌉kkusu ボックス •f [a box/small compartment]

EX. (**a**) Someone left a purse in the telephone booth.
だれかが電話{ボックス/?ブース}に財布を忘れた。
Dare-ka ga denwa-{bokkusu/?buusu} ni saifu o wasureta.
(**b**) The booths in our language lab are air-conditioned.
うちのランゲージ・ラボの{ブース/*ボックス}には空調がある。
*Uchi no rangeeji rabo no {buusu/*bokkusu} ni wa kuuchoo ga aru.*

border n. **[an edge/dividing line]**
ko⌈kkyoo 国境 •c [a dividing line between countries], fu⌈chi⌉ 縁 [the outer part of an extended object/space that is farthest from its center] ⟪**edge, verge, side, shore, margin, brink, brim, rim, hem**⟫

EX. (**a**) This is the border of the country.
これがその国の{国境/*縁}です。
*Kore ga sono kuni no {kokkyoo/*fuchi} desu.*
(**b**) Our carpet has an orange border.
うちのじゅうたんにはオレンジ色の{縁/*国境}がついている。
*Uchi no juutan ni wa orenji-iro no {fuchi/*kokkyoo} ga tsuite iru.*

bore vt. **[to make s.o. weary by being dull]**
⟨-o⟩ ta⌈ikutsu-saseru ⟨〜を⟩退屈させる /⟨causative of *taikutsu-suru* ③ get bored/ ② •c [to make s.o. lose patience, zeal, etc. by being uninteresting]

EX. Don't make movies which bore the audience.
観客を退屈させるような映画は作らないで下さい。
Kankyaku o taikutsu-saseru yoona eiga wa tsukuranaide kudasai.

PHRASE: be bored with ⟨*-ni*⟩ *taikutsu-suru* ⟨〜に⟩退屈する ③ •c

EX. I was utterly bored with the movie.
あの映画には全く退屈した。
Ano eiga ni wa mattaku taikutsu-shita.

bored adj. **[weary due to monotony or dullness]**
ta⌈ikutsu-shite iru (N) 退屈している(N) /⟨V*te iru* of *taikutsu-suru* ③ be bored/ [feeling weary because one has nothing to do or because s.t. is monotonous and lacks interest]

EX. The guy looked bored.
奴は退屈しているようだった。
Yatsu wa taikutsu-shite iru yoo datta.

boring adj. **[causing s.o. to get bored]**
ta⌈ikutsuna 退屈な adj(*na*). **•c [causing s.o. to get bored]** ⟪**dull**⟫, **tsu⌈mara⌉nai つまらない** adj(*i*). **[causing dissatisfaction due to lack of worth or interest]** ⟪**dull, tedious, uninteresting**⟫

EX. The book turned out to be boring.
その本は{つまらない/退屈だ}ということが分かった。
Sono hon wa {tsumaranai/taikutsu da} to iu koto ga wakatta.

born adj. **[brought into life]**
u⌈mareru 生まれる ② [to come into existence]

EX. I was born in 1980.
私は1980年に生まれた。

Watashi wa sen-kyuu-hyaku-hachi-juu-nen ni umareta.

borrow vt. **[to take/receive s.t. from s.o. with the intention of returning it]**
⟨-o⟩ ka⌈riru ⟨〜を⟩借りる ② [for s.o. to be allowed to use s.o. else's possession temporarily] ⟪take s.t. intending to return it; use, rent⟫

EX. I borrowed a car from my friend.
友達に車を借りた。
Tomodachi ni kuruma o karita.

B

boss n. **[one in authority over employees]**
u⌈wa-yaku 上役 [one's superior in a company/office], bo⌉su ボス •f [a superior, employer ⟨s⟩]

EX. Our boss is a strict person.
うちの{上役/ボス}は厳格な人です。
Uchi no {uwa-yaku/bosu} wa genkakuna hito desu.

Boston n.
Bo⌉suton ボストン •f

both adj./pron. **[the two]**
ryo⌈oho⌉o no N 両方のN •c [of the two], ryo⌈ohoo-tomo 両方共 [the two of them]

EX. (**a**) He held the precious tea cup in both hands.
彼は貴重な茶わんを両方の手で持った。
Kare wa kichoona chawan o ryoohoo no te de motta.
(**b**) Hisashi brought two friends with him. Both were very tall.
久士は友達を二人連れてきた。両方共背が高かった。
Hisashi wa tomodachi o futari tsurete-kita. Ryoohoo-tomo se ga takakatta.

bother vi./vt. **[to annoy/disturb/worry/pester s.o.]**
⟨-ni⟩ me⌉iwaku o ka⌈ke⌉ru ⟨〜に⟩迷惑をかける ② •c [for s.o. to cause s.o. to feel unpleasant/inconvenienced] ⟪trouble, disturb, bother, annoy, inconvenience⟫, ⟨-o⟩ ka⌈ma⌉u ⟨〜を⟩構う ① [for s.o. to pay attention to s.t./s.o./s.a.]

EX. (**a**) I'm sorry to bother you.
{ご迷惑をおかけして/*構って}すみません。
*{Go-meiwaku o o-kake-shite/*Kamatte} sumimasen.*
(**b**) Will it bother you if I turn off the heater?
ヒーターを切っても{構いません/*迷惑をかけません}か。
*Hiitaa o kitte mo {kamaimasen/ *meiwaku o kakemasen} ka.*

PHRASE: Don't bother. *Doozo o-kamai naku.* どうぞお構いなく。

EX. A: Can I bring you some coffee?
コーヒーでもお持ちしましょうか。
Koohii demo o-mochi-shimashoo ka.
B: No. Don't bother.
いえ。どうぞお構いなく。
Ie. Doozo o-kamainaku.

bottle n. **[a narrow-necked container, usually of glass, for holding liquids]**
bi⌉n 瓶 •c [a slender, glass container with a narrow mouth normally used for holding liquids]

EX. I dropped the bottle of champagne by mistake.
あやまってシャンペンの瓶を落としてしまった。
Ayamatte shanpen no bin o otoshite shimatta.

bottom n. **[the lowest part or place]**
1. so⌈ko 底 [the lowest inside part of s.t. which itself is lower than other places] ⟪depths, bed⟫

EX. They found the Titanic at the bottom of the ocean.
彼らは海の底でタイタニック号を見付けた。
Kare-ra wa umi no soko de Taitanikku-goo o mitsuketa.

2. shi⌈ta no ho⌉o 下の方 [the side underneath], fu⌈moto⌉ ふもと [the foot of a mountain]

EX. (**a**) Sign your name at the bottom of this form.
この用紙の{下の方/*ふもと}に署名して下さい。
*Kono yooshi no {shita no hoo/*fumoto} ni shomei-shite kudasai.*

(**b**) We have a house at the bottom of Mt. Fuji.
我々は富士山の{ふもと/??下の方}に家を持っています。
Ware-ware wa Fuji-san no {fumoto/ ??shita no hoo} ni ie o motte imasu.

bounce vi. **[to rebound upon striking a surface]**
ha⌈ne-kaeru 跳ね返る ① [for s.t. to be thrown back from a surface] ⟪**rebound, recoil, spring or jump back**⟫, **ha⌈zumu 弾む ① [for s.t. which falls to spring back due to its resilience]** ⟪**spring, bound, rebound**⟫

EX. (**a**) The ball bounced off the wall.
ボールは壁に当たって{跳ね返った/弾んだ}。
Booru wa kabe ni atatte {hane-kaetta/ hazunda}.
(**b**) This tennis ball bounces well.
このテニスボールはよく{弾む/?跳ね返る}。
Kono tenisu-booru wa yoku {hazumu/ ?hane-kaeru}.

boundary n. **[anything marking a limit or bound]**
sa⌈ka⌉i 境 [a dividing line between two or more adjacent areas] ⟪**border**⟫, **kyo⌈okai 境界 •c** ⟪**border**⟫

EX. This river marks the boundary between the two cities.
この河が2つの市の{境/境界}になっている。
Kono kawa ga futatsu no shi no {sakai/ kyookai} ni natte iru.

bounded [limited by or having a boundary with]
⟨-to⟩ sa⌈ka⌉i o se⌈ssuru ⟨〜と⟩境を接する ③ [to have a boundary with]

EX. Switzerland is bounded on the north by Germany and France.
スイスは北側でドイツおよびフランスと境を接している。
Suisu wa kita-gawa de Doitsu oyobi Furansu to sakai o sesshite iru.

bound for [headed for or about to go to some place]
⟨-e⟩ i⌈ku ⟨〜へ⟩行く ①, {-iki/-yuki} 〜行き [going to/headed for]

EX. This train is bound for Kumamoto.
この列車は{熊本へ行きます/熊本行きです}。
Kono ressha wa {Kumamoto e ikimasu/ Kumamoto-iki desu}.

B

bow vi. **[to bend the head/body to show respect, agreement, etc.]**
⟨-ni⟩ o-⌈jigi o suru ⟨〜に⟩お辞儀をする ③ •c [for s.o. to bend the body/head as a salutation or as an expression of respect to s.o.] ⟪**show obeisance**⟫

EX. The students bowed to the teacher.
学生たちは先生にお辞儀をした。
Gakusei-tachi wa sensei ni o-jigi o shita.

—— n. **[an inclination of the body/head as a salutation]**
o-⌈jigi お辞儀 •c [a bending of the body/head as a salutation]

o-jigi

EX. Taro made a bow.
太郎はお辞儀をした。
Taroo wa o-jigi o shita.

bowl n. **[a deep, rounded dish or s.t. similar in shape to that]**
1. ha⌈chi⌉ 鉢 [tableware with an opening at the top and deeper inside than a plate], **do⌈nbu⌉ri どんぶり [a deep and thick ceramic container]** ⟪**pot, basin**⟫, **wa⌈n わん [a container made of wood, porcelain, or metal in which to put cooked food]**, **bo⌈oru ボール •f [a deep (metallic/plastic) container for mixing/ washing ingredients for cooking]**

wan

EX. (**a**) Miso soup is usually served in a bowl.
みそ汁は通常{おわん/*鉢/*どんぶり/*ボール}で出す。
*Miso-shiru wa tsuujoo {o-wan/*hachi/ *donburi/*booru} de dasu.*
(**b**) We usually eat *udon* in a bowl.

B

うどんは大抵{どんぶり/*わん/*鉢/*ボール}で食べる。
*Udon wa taitei {donburi/*wan/*hachi/*booru} de taberu.*
(**c**) I washed the rice in a stainless bowl.
ステンレスの{ボール/*わん/*鉢/*どんぶり}で米をといだ。
*Sutenresu no {booru/*wan/*hachi/*donburi} de kome o toida.*
(**d**) As we had six American guests, we served salad in a big Imari bowl.
アメリカ人のお客さんが六人いらしたので、伊万里焼きの大きな{鉢/*ボール/*おわん/*どんぶり}にサラダをもって出した。
*Amerika-jin no o-kyaku-san ga roku-nin irashita node, imari-yaki no ookina {hachi/*booru/*o-wan/*donburi} ni sarada o motte dashita.*

2. e⌈nkei-ge⌉kijoo 円形劇場 •c [a round athletic stadium] ⟪amphitheater⟫

bow-wow n. **[the sound of a dog barking]**
wa⌉n-wan ワンワン [the sound of a dog barking or a dog in baby-talk]

box n. **[a container, usually rectangular and lidded]**
ha⌈ko 箱 ⟪case, crate, carton⟫

EX. Would you put it in a box for me?
それを箱に入れて下さいませんか。
Sore o hako ni irete kudasaimasen ka.

boy n. **[a male child]**
sho⌈onen 少年 •c [a male person ranging in age from grade school to high school ⟨fml⟩], o⌈toko⌉-no-ko 男の子 [a male child]

EX. (**a**) Boys, be ambitious.
{少年/*男の子}よ、大志を抱け。
*{Shoonen/*Otoko-no-ko} yo, taishi o idake.*
(**b**) Many boys prefer soccer to baseball these days.
最近は野球よりサッカーの好きな{少年/男の子}のほうが多い。
Saikin wa yakyuu yori sakkaa no sukina {shoonen/otoko-no-ko} no hoo ga ooi.
(**c**) Our kids are all boys.
うちの子供はみんな{男の子/*少年}です。
*Uchi no kodomo wa minna {otoko-no-ko/*shoonen} desu.*

PHRASE: boy friend *booi-furendo* ボーイフレンド •f

brain n. **[the part of the central nervous system enclosed in the cranium of vertebrates, serving to control and coordinate mental and physical actions ⟪fig. "intelligence"⟫]**
1. no⌉o 脳 •c [the part of the central nervous system enclosed in the cranium of vertebrates]

EX. Wear a helmet so your brain won't be harmed if you should fall from a high place.
高い所から落ちても脳に損傷を与えないようにヘルメットをかぶりなさい。
Takai tokoro kara ochite mo noo ni sonshoo o ataenai yooni herumetto o kaburinasai.

2. zu⌉noo 頭脳 •c [the function of the part of the central nervous system enclosed in the cranium of vertebrates]

EX. We have to use our brains in a more creative manner.
我々は頭脳をもっと創造的に使わねばならない。
Ware-ware wa zunoo o motto soozoo-tekini tsukawaneba naranai.

brake n. **[any device for slowing/stopping a vehicle/machine, usually by pressing a block/band against a moving part]**
bu⌈re⌉eki ブレーキ •f

EX. (**a**) We have to apply the brakes on inflation.
このインフレにブレーキをかけるべきだ。
Kono infure ni bureeki o kakeru-beki da.
(**b**) I slammed on the brakes, and the car skidded to the side.
急にブレーキをかけたら、車が横に滑ってしまった。
Kyuuni bureeki o kaketara, kuruma ga yoko ni subette shimatta.

B

branch n. **[any woody extension from a tree/shrub; hence, any part or extension of a main body, as a separately located unit of a business]**

1. e⌈da 枝 [that part of a tree which comes out from the trunk/stem]

EX. During the Tanabata Festival people hang their wishes on a branch of a bamboo tree.
七夕祭りには、願い事を竹の枝につるす。
Tanabata-matsuri ni wa, negai-goto o take no eda ni tsurusu.

2. shi⌈ten 支店 •c [an auxiliary office of a company, bank, etc. set up in a different location for the convenience of customers]

EX. Mr. Yamada was transferred to the Osaka branch office.
山田さんは会社の大阪の支店に転勤になった。
Yamada-san wa kaisha no Oosaka no shiten ni tenkin ni natta.

brand n. **[kind, grade, or make, as indicated by a stamp, trademark, etc.]**
bu⌈rando ブランド •f, sho⌉ohyoo 商標 •c [a mark/label identifying the manufacturer] ⟪trademark⟫

EX. Many people buy goods by brand rather than by their actual quality.
実際の品質より{ブランド/?商標}で品物を買う人が多い。
Jissai no hinshitsu yori {burando/?shoohyoo} de shina-mono o kau hito ga ooi.

brass n. **[a yellow metal alloy of copper and zinc]**
shi⌈nchuu 真ちゅう •c

brave adj. **[having courage]**
i⌈samashi⌉i 勇ましい adj(*i*). **[not fearing enemies or difficulties and determined to fight to the finish] ⟪courageous, bold⟫, yu⌈ukanna 勇敢な** adj(*na*). **•c [having courage and undaunted by difficulties] ⟪bold, courageous⟫**

EX. (**a**) His brave act saved the life of the drowning child.
彼の{勇敢な/*勇ましい}行為がおぼれかかっていた子供を救った。
*Kare no {yuukanna/*isamashii} kooi ga obore-kakatte ita kodomo o sukutta.*
(**b**) The movie depicted the life of a brave warrior.
その映画は{勇ましい/勇敢な}戦士の一生を描いた。
Sono eiga wa {isamashii/yuukanna} senshi no isshoo o egaita.

brazier n. **[a metal container to hold burning coals]**
hi⌉bachi 火鉢 [a charcoal-burner made of wood/bronze/iron/brass/copper/porcelain]

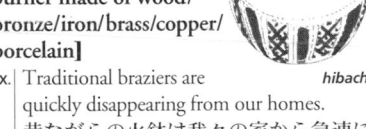

hibachi

EX. Traditional braziers are quickly disappearing from our homes.
昔ながらの火鉢は我々の家から急速になくなりつつある。
Mukashi-nagara no hibachi wa ware-ware no ie kara kyuusokuni nakunari-tsutsu aru.

bravely adv. **[in a courageous manner]**
yu⌈ukanni 勇敢に /⟨adj(*na*), *ni* of *yuukanna* brave/ •c, i⌈sama⌉shiku 勇ましく /⟨adj(*i*), *ku* of *isamashii* brave/

bread n. **[a baked food made from flour or ground grain and mixed with water, etc. ⟪fig. "livelihood"⟫]**

1. pa⌉n パン •f

EX. Man cannot live by bread alone.
人はパンだけでは生きられない。
Hito wa pan dake de wa iki-rarenai.

2. se⌈ikei 生計 •c [daily living, livelihood] ⟪living⟫

EX. He is the bread winner of the family.
彼が家族の生計を担っている。
Kare ga kazoku no seikei o ninatte iru.

break vt. **[to make unusable by cracking or to cut open the surface of s.t.] ⟪smash⟫**

1. ⟨-o⟩ ko⌈wa⌉su ⟨〜を⟩壊す ① [to forcibly change the shape of s.t. and thereby render it useless; to separate s.t. into pieces forcibly and suddenly] ⟪destroy⟫

EX. My little brother broke the computer I had bought.

僕が買ったコンピューターを弟が壊してしまった。
Boku ga katta konpyuutaa o otooto ga kowashite shimatta.

B

2. ⟨-o⟩ **ya⌈bu⌉ru** ⟨〜を⟩破る ① **[to apply force to a part of s.t. thin and flat such as paper/cloth/a wall and thereby damage it ⟪fig. "break a promise/law/silence," "beat"⟫] ⟪tear, tear up, destroy⟫**

EX. (a) The baby kept breaking one *shoji* paper screen after another for fun.
赤ん坊は面白がって障子を次々に破っていた。
Akanboo wa omoshiro-gatte shooji o tsugi-tsugini yabutte ita.
(b) John never breaks his promise.
ジョンは決して約束を破らない。
Jon wa kesshite yakusoku o yaburanai.
(c) The skater broke the record.
そのスケート選手は記録を破った。
Sono sukeeto-senshu wa kiroku o yabutta.

PHRASE: break down *koshoo-suru* 故障する ③ •c ⟪become out of order⟫

EX. Our car broke down on the expressway.
私たちの車は高速道路で故障した。
Watashi-tachi no kuruma wa koosoku-dooro de koshoo-shita.

3. ⟨-o⟩ (⟨-ni⟩) **wa⌈ru** ⟨〜を⟩(⟨〜に⟩)割る ① **[to apply force to a hard substance and render it into two or more pieces ⟪fig. "(in mathematics) find how many times a given number is contained in another"⟫] ⟪split, divide⟫**

EX. Sam broke an expensive vase by accident.
サムは誤って高価な花瓶を割ってしまった。
Samu wa ayamatte kookana kabin o watte shimatta.

4. ⟨-o⟩ (⟨-ni⟩) **o⌉ru** ⟨〜を⟩(⟨〜に⟩)折る ① **[for s.o. to render a long solid object into two or more parts by bending/separating it] ⟪snap, fracture⟫**

EX. The ping-pong player could not take part in the final match because he had broken his right arm in an accident.
卓球の選手は事故で右腕を折ってしまったので決勝戦に出場できなかった。
Takkyuu no senshu wa jiko de migi-ude o otte-shimatta node kesshoo-sen ni shutsujoo-dekinakatta.

— vi. **[to become cracked or divided and thereby rendered unusable, to burst or to become fractured]**

1. ko⌈ware⌉ru 壊れる ② **[for s.t. to lose its original shape and thereby be rendered unusable because of some force applied to it] ⟪be wrecked, become out of order⟫**

EX. The lamp fell and broke.
スタンドが倒れて壊れた。
Sutando ga taorete kowareta.

2. ya⌈bure⌉ru 破れる ② **[for s.t. thin and flat to be cut/damaged] ⟪burst⟫**

EX. The paper bag got wet and broke.
紙袋がぬれて破れた。
Kami-bukuro ga nurete yabureta.

3. ki⌈re⌉ru 切れる ② **[for s.t. to be cut] ⟪be severed⟫**

EX. The rope broke in the middle.
綱は真ん中で切れた。
Tsuna wa mannaka de kireta.

4. (⟨-ni⟩) **wa⌈re⌉ru** (⟨〜に⟩)割れる ② **[for s.t. hard to be rendered into two or more pieces by the application of force ⟪fig. "for opinions to be divided"⟫] ⟪crack⟫**

EX. An eggshell broke and a chick came out.
卵が割れてひよこが出てきた。
Tamago ga warete hiyoko ga dete kita.

5. (⟨-ni⟩) **o⌈re⌉ru** (⟨〜に⟩)折れる ② **[for s.t. long and solid to be rendered into two or more parts by bending/separating]**

EX. My leg broke when I fell.
転んだら足が折れた。
Korondara ashi ga oreta.

breakfast n. **[the first meal of the day]**
a⌈sa-go⌉han 朝ご飯 **[morning meal], cho⌈oshoku** 朝食 •c **[morning meal ⟨fml⟩]**

EX. Yoshihiko always has an egg for breakfast.
義彦はいつも{朝食/朝ご飯}に卵を食べます。
Yoshihiko wa itsu-mo {chooshoku/asa-gohan} ni tamago o tabemasu.

breath n. **[air taken into the lungs and then let out]**
i⌉ki 息, **ko⌈kyuu** 呼吸 **•c [inhaling and exhaling of air by an organism to stay alive]** ((**air, respiration**))

EX. (**a**) I ran at full speed and got out of breath.
私は全速力で走ったので{息/*呼吸}が切れた。
*Watashi wa zen-sokuryoku de hashitta node {iki/*kokyuu} ga kireta.*
(**b**) They recovered their breath by resting a little.
彼らは少し休んで{呼吸/息}を整えた。
Karera wa sukoshi yasunde {kokyuu/iki} o totonoeta.

breathe vi. **[for s.o./s.a. to take air into the lungs and let it out again]**
i⌉ki o suru 息をする ③, **ko⌈kyuu o suru** 呼吸をする ③ **•c** ⟨**fml**⟩

EX. Put on the mask and breathe normally.
マスクをして普通に{息/呼吸}をして下さい。
Masuku o shite futsuu ni {iki/kokyuu} o shite kudasai.

breathing n. **[respiration]**
ko⌉kyuu 呼吸 **•c [inhaling and exhaling of air by an organism to stay alive]** ((**air, respiration**))

breed vt. **[to bring forth offspring or raise, rear, and train animals]**
1. ⟨**-o**⟩ **u⌈mu** ⟨〜を⟩うむ ① **[to give birth to s.t./s.o./s.a.]** ((**give birth to, bear, produce**))
㊕ "give birth to an offspring"▷産む, "give birth to an offspring/s.t. such as artistic work, rumor, interest, etc."▷生む

EX. Pigs often breed five piglets in a litter.
豚はよく一度に五匹の子豚を生む。
Buta wa yoku ichi-do ni go-hiki no ko-buta o umu.

2. ⟨**-o**⟩ **shi⌈iku-suru** ⟨〜を⟩飼育する ③ **•c [for s.o. to rear living things such as domestic animals]** ((**rear, raise**))

EX. They breed horses on the farm.
あの農場では馬を飼育している。
Ano noojoo de wa uma o shiiku-shite iru.

—— vi. **[to reproduce]**
ha⌈nshoku-suru 繁殖する ③ **•c [for s.a./vegetation to be born one after another and multiply]** ((**self-propagate**))

EX. Rabbits breed rapidly.
うさぎは急速に繁殖する。
Usagi wa kyuusokuni hanshoku-suru.

—— n. **[a minimum unit of classification of agricultural products or domestic animals established on the basis of hereditary characteristics, morphology, etc.]**
hi⌈nshu 品種 **•c** ((**sort, kind, variety, grade**))

EX. The laboratory recently developed a new breed of lilies.
研究所は最近ユリの新しい品種を開発した。
Kenkyuu-jo wa saikin yuri no atarashii hinshu o kaihatsu-shita.

breeze n. **[a gentle wind]**
so⌈yo⌉-kaze そよ風 **[a gentle and pleasant wind]**

EX. I went outside in order to feel the breeze.
そよ風に吹かれに外に出た。
Soyo-kaze ni fuka-re ni soto ni deta.

brick n. **[an oblong block of baked clay used in building, etc.]**
re⌉nga れんが

EX. Jack works in an office building made of brick.
ジャックはれんが造りの建物のオフィスで働いています。
Jakku wa renga-zukuri no tate-mono no ofisu de hataraite imasu.

bride n. **[a woman just married or about to be married]**
ha⌈na⌉yome 花嫁 ↔ **hanamuko** 花婿; **shi⌉npu** 新婦 **•c** ⟨**fml**⟩ ↔ **shinroo** 新郎 **•c** ⟨**fml**⟩; **o-⌈yome-san** お嫁さん ↔ **o-muko-san** お婿さん

EX. The bride looked rather tired.
{花嫁/新婦/お嫁さん}は少し疲れた様子だった。
{Hanayome/Shinpu/

hanayome

B

O-yome-san} wa sukoshi tsukareta yoosu datta.

PHRASE: the bride and bridegroom *shinroo-shinpu* 新郎新婦 •c

B

bridge[1] n. **[a structure built over a river, etc. to provide a way across]**

1. ha⌈shi⌉ 橋

EX. Let's cross this bridge.
この橋を渡りましょう。
Kono hashi o watarimashoo.

bridge[2] n. **[a card game of two pairs of players in which the players bid for the right to name the trump suit or declare no-trump]**

bu⌈ri⌉jji ブリッジ **•f**

brief adj. **[to be short in time or content, concise]**

mi⌈jika⌉i 短い adj(*i*). **[to have little spatial or temporal length]** ⟪short⟫, **ka⌈nketsuna** 簡潔な adj(*na*). **•c [for a verbal expression to be short and to the point]** ⟪concise, compendious⟫

EX. (**a**) A brief explanation will do.
{短い/簡潔な}説明でいいです。
{Mijikai/Kanketsuna} setsumei de ii desu.
(**b**) Please write brief answers; long ones won't do.
{短い/簡潔な}答えを書いて下さい。長いのは駄目です。
{Mijikai/Kanketsuna} kotae o kaite kudasai. Nagai no wa dame desu.

—— vt. **[for s.o. to supply s.o. with all pertinent information]**

⟨-ni⟩ {⟨-o⟩/⟨-ni-tsuite⟩} se⌈tsumei-suru ⟨〜に⟩ {⟨〜を⟩/⟨〜について⟩}説明する ③ **•c [for s.o. to give an explanation of s.t. to s.o.]**

EX. The aide briefed the President on the current situation.
補佐官は大統領に現状{を/について}説明した。
Hosa-kan wa daitooryoo ni genjoo {o/ni-tsuite} setsumei-shita.

briefcase n. **[a flat case for carrying papers, books, etc.]**

bu⌈riifuke⌉esu ブリーフケース **•f, sho⌈rui-ka⌉ban** 書類かばん **[a bag for documents]**

EX. He lost his briefcase at the airport.
彼は空港で{ブリーフケース/書類かばん}をなくしてしまった。
Kare wa kuukoo de {buriifukeesu/shorui-kaban} o nakushite shimatta.

briefly adv. **[in a short or concise manner]**

te⌈mijikani 手短に **/⟨adj(*na*). *ni* of *temijikana* brief/ [in a short and simple fashion]** ⟪in short⟫, **ka⌈nketsuni** 簡潔に **/⟨adj(*na*). *ni* of *kanketsuna* brief/ •c [in a simple way and to the point]** ⟪simply, in short⟫

bright adj. **[shining with light, brilliant in color, or mentally quick and clever]**

1. **a⌈karui** 明るい adj(*i*). **[for there to be enough light to do s.t. or for s.t. to be not dark in color ⟪fig. "cheerful," "be versed in"⟫]** ⟪light, cheerful⟫ ↔ **kurai** 暗い adj(*i*).

EX. A: Do you see the bright star up there?
あの上の方に明るい星が見えるでしょう。
Ano ue no hoo ni akarui hoshi ga mieru deshoo.
B: Which one?
え、どの星ですか。
E, dono hoshi desu ka.

2. **a⌈tama⌉ ga i⌉i** 頭がいい **[for s.o./s.a. to have a well-developed ability to learn, reason, and understand], ri⌈koona** 利口な adj(*na*). **[quick in thinking and understanding]** ⟪clever, wise, intelligent, smart⟫

EX. Jim was so bright that he went to Princeton.
ジムは{頭がよかった/利口だった}のでプリンストンへ行った。
Jimu wa {atama ga yokatta/rikoo datta} node Purinsuton e itta.

brightly adv. **[in a bright manner]**

a⌈karuku 明るく **/⟨adj(*i*). *ku* of *akarui* bright/ [in a bright manner]** ⟪lightly⟫

brightness n. **[the state or quality of being bright]**

a⌈karu-sa 明るさ **/⟨the stem of adj(*i*). *akarui* bright + suf *sa* ness/ [the state or quality of being light or cheerful]**

EX. The brightness of the star has increased over the past couple of days.
この二、三日でその星の明るさが増した。
Kono ni-san-nichi de sono hoshi no akaru-sa ga mashita.

brilliant adj. **[shining brightly or vivid or very intelligent]**
1. ki˥ra-kira hi˹ka˥tte iru (N) きらきら光っている(N) **/⟨V*te iru* of *hikaru* ① shine/ [to emit or reflect light in such a way as to appear shiny and bright]** ⟪**glittering, dazzling, twinkling, sparkling, glistening**⟫

EX. The jewels she bought are brilliant.
彼女が買った宝石はきらきら光っている。
Kanojo ga katta hooseki wa kira-kira hikatte iru.

2. su˹barashi˥i すばらしい adj(*i*). **[causing great wonder/admiration/pleasure due to being extremely good]** ⟪**splendid, wonderful, grand, great, magnificent, superb**⟫, **a˹tama˥ ga i˥i** 頭がいい adj(*i*). **[for s.o./s.a. to have a well-developed ability to learn, reason, and understand]** ⟪**smart**⟫

EX. (**a**) Serge had brilliant talents when it came to language.
サージはことばとなると素晴らしい能力を持っていた。
Saaji wa kotoba to naru to subarashii nooryoku o motte ita.
(**b**) Mary's son was so brilliant that he went to college at the age of 12.
マリーの息子は十二歳で大学へ行ったほど{素晴らしかった/頭がよかった}。
Marii no musuko wa juu-ni-sai de daigaku e itta hodo {subarashikatta/atama ga yokatta}.

bring vt. **[to carry or lead s.o./s.t. to the place where the speaker is or will be or to cause to happen]**
1. ⟨-o⟩ mo˹tte-ku˥ru ⟨〜を⟩持って来る ③ **/⟨V*te* of *motsu* ① hold + *kuru* ③ come/ [for s.o./s.a. to come having s.t. on oneself], ⟨-o⟩ tsu˹rete-ku˥ru** ⟨〜を⟩連れて来る ③ **/⟨V*te* of *tsureru* ② be accompanied by + *kuru* ③ come/ [to come being accompanied by s.o.]**

EX. (**a**) Bring your own drinks to the party.
パーティーには自分の飲物を{持って/*連れて}来て下さい。
*Paatii ni wa jibun no nomi-mono o {motte/*tsurete}-kite kudasai.*
(**b**) May I bring my wife to the meeting?
会に家内を{連れて/*持って}来てもいいですか。
*Kai ni kanai o {tsurete/*motte}-kite mo ii desu ka.*

2. ⟨-ni⟩ ⟨-o⟩ {mo˹tara˥su/hi˹ki-oko˥su} ⟨〜に⟩⟨〜を⟩{もたらす/引き起こす} ① **[to come to some place with s.t. or to cause some situation, usually undesirable, to occur]** ⟪**carry, produce, cause**⟫

EX. The drought brought heavy losses to the region.
かんばつはその地域に大きな損害を{もたらした/引き起こした}。
Kanbatsu wa sono chiiki ni ookina songai o {motarashita/hiki okoshita}.

PHRASE: bring up ⟨-o⟩ *sodateru* ⟨〜を⟩育てる ② ⟪foster, train, grow, breed⟫

EX. Our cat was brought up by a dog.
うちの猫は犬に育てられました。
Uchi no neko wa inu ni sodate-raremashita.

Britain n. **[England, Scotland, Wales and Northern Ireland]**
Da˥i-buriten-too 大ブリテン島 **•c+f+c**

British adj. **[of Great Britain or its people]**
I˹girisu no N イギリスのN **•f, E˹ikoku no N** 英国のN **•c [of Britain], I˹girisu˥-jin no N** イギリス人のN **•f+c, E˹ikoku˥-jin no N** 英国人のN **•c [of a person/persons of Britain]**

EX. (**a**) It's a British airline.
それは{イギリス/英国/*イギリス人/*英国人}の航空会社です。
*Sore wa {Igirisu/Eikoku/*Igirisu-jin/*Eikoku-jin} no kookuu-gaisha desu.*
(**b**) An Australian actor played a British detective in the movie.
あの映画ではオーストラリア人の俳優

が{イギリス人/英国人/イギリス/英国}の探偵を演じた。
Ano eiga de wa Oosutoraria-jin no haiyuu ga {Igirisu-jin/Eikoku-jin/Igirisu/Eikoku} no tantei o enjita.

B

— n. **[the people of Great Britain]**
I⌈girisu⌉-jin イギリス人 •f+c, **E⌈ikoku⌉-jin** 英国人 •c **[a person/persons of Britain]**

broad adj. **[large in extent from side to side]**
ha⌈ba ga hi⌈ro⌉i 幅が広い adj(*i*). **[having width that is great in extent]** ((wide across)) ↔ **semai** 狭い adj(*i*).

EX. There is a broad road running through the center of the town.
その町の中心には道幅の広い道路が一本通っている。
Sono machi no chuushin ni wa michi-haba no hiroi dooro ga ip-pon tootte iru.

broadcast vt. **[for s.o. to transmit by radio or television]**
⟨-o⟩ ho⌈osoo-suru ⟨〜を⟩放送する ③ •c **[for s.o. to transmit (a program) by means of radio or television]**

EX. Nowadays the Olympic Games are broadcast by satellite.
今ではオリンピック競技は衛星で放送される。
Ima dewa Orinpikku-kyoogi wa eisei de hoosoo-sareru.

— n. **[transmission of a radio/television program]**
ho⌈osoo 放送 •c

EX. This is a live broadcast.
これは生放送です。
Kore wa nama-hoosoo desu.

broadcasting n. **[the act of going on the air]**
ho⌈osoo 放送 •c **[transmission of a radio/television program]**

Broadway n. **[street in New York City with many theaters, etc.]**
Bu⌈roodoue⌉i ブロードウエイ •f

EX. I saw *Cats* on Broadway.
私はブロードウエイで『キャッツ』を見た。
Watashi wa Buroodouei de "Kyattsu" o mita.

broil vt. **[for s.o. to cook by direct exposure to heat]**
⟨-o⟩ ya⌈ku ⟨〜を⟩焼く ① **[to cause a change in s.t. through exposure to heat/fire/sunlight]** ((grill, barbecue, bake, roast, toast, burn))

EX. The cook broiled the meat.
コックは肉を焼いた。
Kokku wa niku o yaita.

— vi. **[for s.t. to be cooked by direct exposure to heat]**
ya⌈keru 焼ける ② **[to be transformed into a state different from the original state through exposure to heat/fire/sunlight]** ((be burned, be grilled, be baked, be roasted, be toasted, be tanned))

EX. I can smell the steak broiling in the oven.
オーブンでステーキの焼けるにおいがする。
Oobun de suteeki no yakeru nioi ga suru.

brook n. **[a small stream]**
o⌈gawa 小川 •c **[small river]**

broom n. **[a bundle of fibers or straws attached to a long handle used for sweeping]**
ho⌈oki ほうき **[an instrument for sweeping floors]**

brother n. **[a male related to one by having the same parent(s)]**
1. kyo⌉odai 兄弟 •c **[a person related to one by having the same parent(s)]** ((sister, brethren, sibling))

EX. They are brothers.
彼らは兄弟です。
Kare-ra wa kyoodai desu.

2. a⌉ni 兄 **[an older male related to one by having the same parent(s)]** ((elder/older sibling))

EX. I have a brother three years older than myself.
私には三つ年上の兄がいる。
Watashi ni wa mittsu toshi-ue no ani ga iru.

3. o⌈tooto⌉ 弟 **[a younger male related to one by having the same parent(s)]** ((younger/kid sibling))

EX. My brother was only ten years old when I graduated from the university.
私が大学を卒業したとき弟はまだ十歳でした。
Watashi ga daigaku o sotsugyoo-shita toki otooto wa mada jus-sai deshita.

brow n. **[eyebrow, the ridge over the eye]**
ma⌉yu まゆ

EX. Father knitted his brows upon hearing that.
父はそれを聞くとまゆをひそめた。
Chichi wa sore o kiku to mayu o hisometa.

brown adj. **[having the color of chocolate, a mixture of red, black, and yellow]**
cha-⌈iro no N 茶色のN [of the color of blackish red and yellow]

EX. Lisa has brown hair.
リサは茶色の髪をしている。
Risa wa cha-iro no kami o shite iru.

—— n. **[the color of chocolate, a mixture of red, black, and yellow]**
cha-⌈iro 茶色 [blackish red and yellow]

EX. Tom is always dressed in brown.
トムはいつも茶色を着ている。
Tomu wa itsu-mo cha-iro o kite iru.

brush n. **[a device for cleaning, painting, etc. having bristles, wires, etc. fastened into a back]**
bu⌈rashi ブラシ •f, ha⌈ke⌉ はけ [a tool having bristles implanted in the base.]

EX. Please use a brush to clean it.
{ブラシ/はけ}を使ってきれいにして下さい。
{Burashi/Hake} o tsukatte kireini shite kudasai.

—— vt. **[for s.o. to clean, paint, etc. with a brush]**
⟨-ni⟩ bu⌈rashi o ka⌈ke⌉ru ⟨〜に⟩ブラシをかける ② [for s.o. to apply a brush to], ⟨-o⟩ mi⌈gaku ⟨〜を⟩磨く ① [for s.o. to rub a hard, rough surface and make it smooth and shiny ⟪fig. "make constant efforts to improve one's skill"⟫]

EX. He should brush his shoes before going out.
彼は出掛ける前に靴{にブラシをかける/を磨く}べきだ。
Kare wa dekakeru mae ni kutsu {ni burashi o kakeru/o migaku}-beki da.

bubble n. **[a tiny ball of air/gas in a liquid/solid]**
a⌈wa⌉ 泡 [a form of liquid where air or other gas is mixed in in such a way as to create swollen spheres] ⟪foam, lather⟫

EX. There are lots of bubbles in this beer.
このビールには泡がたくさん入っている。
Kono biiru ni wa awa ga takusan haitte iru.

bucket n. **[a cylindrical container with a curved handle used for carrying water, etc.]**
ba⌈ketsu バケツ •f [a watertight cylindrical metal/plastic container with a fitted handle] ⟪pail⟫

EX. Let's use this bucket to get some water from the well.
このバケツを使って井戸から水をくみましょう。
Kono baketsu o tsukatte ido kara mizu o kumimashoo.

buckwheat n. **[a grain plant with beechnut-shaped seeds or a dark flour made from such seeds]**
so⌈ba そば [a plant with beechnut-shaped seeds or a dark flour made from such seeds or a strip of dough made from this flour]

soba

EX. Buckwheat is a plant popularly grown in Japan.
そばは日本で広く栽培されている植物です。
Soba wa Nihon de hiroku saibai-sarete iru shokubutsu desu.

bud n. **[a small swelling on a plant, from which a shoot, leaf, or flower develops]**
me⌉ 芽 [a swelling from which a leaf develops ⟪fig. "beginning of s.t."⟫], tsu⌈bomi⌉ つぼみ [a swelling from which a flower develops ⟪fig. "beginning of s.t."⟫]

EX. In Japan, buds of most plants come out from March to May.

日本では、ほとんどの植物の{芽/つぼみ}が三月から五月に出てくる。
Nihon de wa, hotondo no shokubutsu no {me/tsubomi} ga san-gatsu kara go-gatsu ni dete-kuru.

Buddha n.
Bu⌉dda 仏だ **•c**, **Sha⌈ka-mu⌉ni** しゃか牟尼 **•c**, **ho⌈toke⌉** 仏

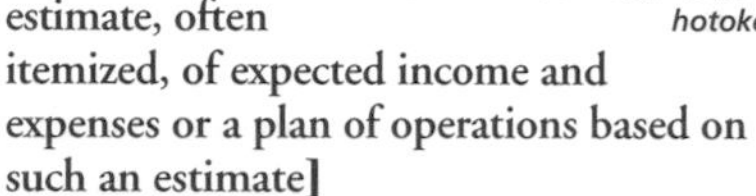

hotoke

Buddhism n.
Bu⌉kkyoo 仏教 **•c**

budget n. **[an estimate, often itemized, of expected income and expenses or a plan of operations based on such an estimate]**
yo⌈san 予算 **•c [an estimating in advance of necessary expenses or these expenses themselves]** ⟪**estimate**⟫
EX. The budget for next year was approved.
来年度の予算が承認された。
Rainen-do no yosan ga shoonin-sareta.

buffalo n. **[any of a variety of wild oxen]**
su⌈igyuu 水牛 **•c [water buffalo of India/South East Asia]**, **ya⌈gyuu** 野牛 **•c [the American/European bison]**

bug n. **[an insect, often with sucking mouth parts]**
mu⌈shi 虫 **[a small organism which comes into being through hatching and crawls on the ground or flies about]** ⟪**insect**⟫
EX. There are bugs and there are bugs, you know.
虫にもいろいろありますからね。
Mushi ni mo iro-iro arimasu kara ne.

build vt. **[for s.o./s.a. to make s.t. by putting together materials, parts, etc.]**
1. ⟨**-o**⟩ **ta⌈te⌉ru** ⟨〜を⟩たてる ② **[to cause s.o./s.t./s.a. to take an upright position** ⟪**fig. "build s.t."**⟫**]** ⟪**erect, make, set up, put up, raise**⟫
㊥ "build"▷建てる, otherwise ▷立てる
EX. Our neighbor built a ferro-concrete house.
うちの隣の人は鉄筋の家を建てた。
Uchi no tonari no hito wa tekkin no ie o tateta.

2. ⟨**-o**⟩ **tsu⌈ku⌉ru** ⟨〜を⟩つくる ① **[for s.o./s.a. to cause s.t./s.o./s.a. to come into existence which did not exist previously]** ⟪**make**⟫
㊥ "build/manufacture"▷造る, otherwise ▷作る
EX. Japan used to build many ships.
日本は昔は多くの船を造ったものだ。
Nihon wa mukashi wa ooku no fune o tsukutta mono da.

— n. **[physique]**
ta⌈ikaku 体格 **•c [the physical form of a person's body, esp. with regard to how well it has been nourished and grown]** ⟪**physical constitution, physique**⟫
EX. Musashi has a strong build.
武蔵はがっちりとした体格をしている。
Musashi wa gatchiri-to-shita taikaku o shite iru.

building n. **[anything that is built]**
ta⌈te⌉-mono 建物 **[s.t. constructed for people to live or work in or for storing things]** ⟪**structure**⟫, **bi⌉rudingu** ビルディング **•f**, **bi⌉ru** ビル **•f [short for building]**
EX. There are more and more tall buildings in Tokyo today.
現在東京ではますます背の高い{建物/ビルディング/ビル}が増えている。
Genzai Tookyoo de wa masu-masu se no takai {tate-mono/birudingu/biru} ga fuete iru.

bulb n. **[an underground bud with roots and a short, scaly stem, as in a lily/onion, or an incandescent electric lamp]**
1. kyu⌈ukon 球根 **•c [an underground spherically-shaped root with stems]**
EX. Kaori planted a dahlia bulb in her backyard.
香は裏庭にダリアの球根を植えた。
Kaori wa ura-niwa ni daria no kyuukon o ueta.

2. de⌈nkyuu 電球 **•c [a vacuum glass ball housing the light source for electric lamps]**
EX. The bulb has burned out.
電球が切れた。
Denkyuu ga kireta.

bullet n. **[a small, shaped piece of lead, steel, etc. to be shot from a firearm]**
ta⌈ma⌉ たま [a spherical or almost spherical object] ((**ball, bowl, globe, sphere, bead, drop**)), **da⌈ngan 弾丸 •c [a ball to be fired from a gun]** ((**shot, shell**))
㊥ "ball"▷球, "gem"▷玉, "bullet"▷たま
EX. The soldier ran out of bullets.
兵隊は{たま/弾丸}がなくなった。
Heitai wa {tama/dangan} ga nakunatta.
PHRASE: bullet train *shinkansen* 新幹線 •c

bulletin n. **[a brief public statement as of late news or a regular publication of an organization]**
1. ke⌈iji 掲示 •c [an act of posting written material at some public place or the written material itself] ((**public notice**))
EX. We request that you look at the bulletin board at least once every day.
少なくとも一日一回は掲示板を見るようお願いします。
Sukunaku-tomo ichi-nichi ik-kai wa keiji-ban o miru yoo o-negai-shimasu.
2. ka⌈ihoo 会報 •c [a magazine or other form of printed matter by which reports are submitted to members of an organization such as a learned society] ((**report**))
EX. The bulletin of this society is published four times a year.
この学会の会報は年四回発行されます。
Kono gakkai no kaihoo wa nen yon-kai hakkoo-saremasu.

bully n. **[one who hurts/browbeats those who are weaker]**
i⌈jimekko いじめっ子 [a naughty child who enjoys inflicting pain on weaker children]
— vt. **[for s.o./s.a. to hurt/browbeat those who are weaker]**
⟨-o⟩ i⌈jimeru ⟨～を⟩いじめる ② [for s.o./s.a. to deliberately inflict pain on those in a weaker position and thereby derive pleasure]
EX. It's a crime to bully weaker people.
弱い人をいじめるのは罪である。
Yowai hito o ijimeru no wa tsumi dearu.

bump vt. **[to hit against]**
⟨-ni⟩ ⟨-o⟩ bu⌈tsukeru ⟨～に⟩⟨～を⟩ぶつける ② [for s.o. to cause s.t. to come together forcefully against s.t. else]
EX. John bumped his head against the lintel.
ジョンはかもいに頭をぶつけた。
Jon wa kamoi ni atama o butsuketa.

bunch n. **[a cluster of similar things growing/grouped together]**
ta⌉ba 束 [a group of oblong/flat things bound by a string/paper] ((**bundle, sheaf**)), **fu⌈sa⌉ 房 [a string of twisted threads/hairs ending with untwisted ones** ((**fig. "bunch"**))**]** ((**tassel, turf, fringe, cluster**))
EX. (**a**) My sister brought me a bunch of flowers.
妹は僕に一束の花をもってきてくれた。
Imooto wa boku ni hito-taba no hana o motte-kite kureta.
(**b**) Grapes grow in bunches.
ぶどうは房になってできる。
Budoo wa fusa ni natte dekiru.

bundle n. **[a number of things bound together; a bunch]**
ta⌉ba 束 [a group of oblong/flat things bound by a string/paper] ((**bunch, sheaf**))
EX. The Christmas cards were delivered in a bundle.
クリスマス・カードが束になって配達された。
Kurisumasu-kaado ga taba ni natte haitatsu-sareta.

burden n. **[heavy load, as of work, care, etc.]**
o⌈mo-ni 重荷 [a heavy load ((**fig. "hardship"**))**]** ((**heavy load**))
EX. I'm prepared to bear the burden.
重荷を背負う覚悟はできています。
Omo-ni o se-ou kakugo wa dekite imasu.
— vt. **[for s.o. to put a heavy load or heavy responsibility or obligation upon s.o.]**
⟨-ni⟩ o⌈mo-ni o o⌈wa-seru ⟨～に⟩重荷を負わせる ② /⟨causative of *ou* ① bear/ [to cause s.o. to bear or shoulder a heavy load] ((**to tax**))

EX. We burdened him too much and he became ill.
彼に重荷を負わせ過ぎて病気になられてしまった。
Kare ni omo-ni o owa-se-sugite byooki ni nara-rete shimatta.

B

bureau n. **[a government department or agency]**
kyo˥ku 局 •c

EX. Yamada works at the Treaty Bureau of the Foreign Office.
山田は外務省の条約局に務めている。
Yamada wa Gaimu-shoo no jooyaku-kyoku ni tsutomete iru.

burn vi. **[to be on fire or be destroyed or injured by fire/heat]**
1. mo˥eru 燃える ② [to catch fire and glow or be in flames] ⟪blaze, glow⟫

EX. The house is burning.
家が燃えている。
Ie ga moete iru.

2. ya˥keru 焼ける ② [to be transformed into a state different from the original state through exposure to heat/fire/sunlight] ⟪be destroyed by fire⟫

EX. A warehouse near my house burned to the ground yesterday.
家のそばの倉庫が昨日火事で焼けてしまった。
Ie no soba no sooko ga kinoo kaji de yakete shimatta.

3. ko˥ge˥ru 焦げる ② [for that part of s.t. solid which is strongly heated by fire, etc. to turn into a charcoal-like state, one stage prior to being completely burned] ⟪be scorched⟫

EX. My steak is burning on the grill.
僕のステーキが網の上で焦げている。
Boku no suteeki ga ami no ue de kogete iru.

—— vt. **[for s.o./s.t. to set on fire/destroy by fire/scorch]**
1. ⟨-o⟩ mo˥yasu ⟨〜を⟩燃やす ① [for s.o. to cause s.t. relatively small such as paper, wood, or trash to catch on fire] ⟪light, kindle⟫, ⟨-o⟩ ya˥ku ⟨〜を⟩焼く ① [to cause a change in s.t. through exposure to heat/fire/sunlight] ⟪destroy by fire, bake, toast, broil, grill, roast, tan⟫

EX. (**a**) She burned the love letters from her ex-boyfriend.
彼女は前のボーイフレンドからのラブレターを{燃やした/?焼いた}。
Kanojo wa mae no booi-furendo kara no rabu-retaa o {moyashita/?yaita}.
(**b**) We had to burn all waste.
ごみは全部{焼かねば/燃やさねば}ならなかった。
Gomi wa zenbu {yakaneba/moyasaneba} naranakatta.

2. ⟨-o⟩ ko˥ga˥su ⟨〜を⟩焦がす ① [to cause s.t. to be scorched] ⟪scorch⟫

EX. Please don't burn my steak, but make it well done.
僕のステーキはウエルダンにして欲しいのですが、焦がさないで下さい。
Boku no suteeki wa uerudan ni shite hoshii no desu ga, kogasanaide kudasai.

burrow n. **[a hole dug in the ground by an animal]**
su 巣 [a nest], a˥na˥ 穴 [a hole]

burst vi. **[to come apart suddenly and violently ⟪fig. "do s.t. suddenly"⟫]**
1. ha˥retsu-suru 破裂する ③ •c [for s.t. to break, revealing the contents] ⟪explode, erupt, rupture, blow out⟫

EX. One of the tires on his car burst.
彼の車のタイヤが一つ破裂した。
Kare no kuruma no taiya ga hitotsu haretsu-shita.

2. kyu˥uni V*masu* hajimeru 急にV*masu*始める ② [for s.t. to start suddenly]

EX. His opponent burst into laughter.
彼の相手は急に笑い始めた。
Kare no aite wa kyuuni warai-hajimeta.

bury vt. **[to put s.t. into the earth/ground]**
⟨-o⟩ u˥meru ⟨〜を⟩埋める ② [to put s.t. into a hole, blank, etc. so that it becomes full or for people to crowd into some space until it becomes full]

EX. Harumi buried the dead dog.

治美は死んだ犬を埋めた。
Harumi wa shinda inu o umeta.

bus n. **[a large motor coach for many passengers, usually following a regular route]**
ba˥su バス •f
EX. This bus is always crowded.
このバスはいつも込んでいる。
Kono basu wa itsu-mo konde iru.

bush n. **[a low woody plant with spreading branches]**
shi┌gemi˥ 茂み **[a place where low trees/grasses grow], ka┌nboku** 潅木 •c **[a tree which does not grow tall], ya┌bu** やぶ **[a thicket]**

business n. **[what one does for an occupation; commerce/trade]**
1. shi┌goto 仕事 **[an activity performed for a particular purpose other than amusement and on which one expends time and effort]** ⟪**work, labor, toil, task, job**⟫, **sho┌ku˥gyoo** 職業 •c **[work as a means of supporting one's life]** ⟪**job, occupation**⟫
EX. What is your father's business?
お父さんの{仕事/職業}は何ですか。
O-too-san no {shigoto/shokugyoo} wa nan desu ka.
2. sho˥ogyoo 商業 •c **[the work of selling for profit goods that one makes or buys wholesale from s.o. else]** ⟪**commerce**⟫, **sho˥obai** 商売 •c **[the activity of buying and selling goods]** ⟪**trade**⟫
EX. (**a**) How is your business?
{商売/*商業}はいかがですか。
*{Shoobai/*Shoogyoo} wa ikaga desu ka.*
(**b**) I am teaching business English.
{商業/*商売}英語を教えています。
*{Shoogyoo/*Shoobai}-eigo o oshiete imasu.*
3. yo┌oji 用事 •c **[s.t. done for a personal/business purpose]** ⟪**a thing to do**⟫, **yo┌oke˥n** 用件 •c **[a matter which has been planned for sometime]** ⟪**engagement, errand**⟫
EX. What business brought you here?
どんな{用事/用件}でこちらへ来られましたか。
Donna {yooji/yooken} de kochira e koraremashita ka.

businessman n. **[a man who engages in commerce]**
ji┌tsugyoo-ka 実業家 •c **[one who operates an economic enterprise ⟨fml⟩], bi┌jinesu˥-man** ビジネスマン •f ⟪**a salaried person**⟫

bustling adj. **[busy, hurried and noisy]**
ni┌gi˥yakana にぎやかな adj(*na*). **[full of vigor and cheerful sounds]** ⟪**thronged, animated, cheerful, flourishing, lively**⟫
EX. Young people seem to prefer bustling cities to the quiet countryside.
若い人は静かな田舎よりにぎやかな都会を好むようだ。
Wakai hito wa shizukana inaka yori nigiyakana tokai o konomu yooda.

busy adj. **[for a person or place to be active or full of activity]**
1. i┌sogashi˥i 忙しい adj(*i*). **[be pressed by urgent matters and not having time for leisure/relaxation]** ⟪**engaged**⟫ ↔ **himana** 暇な adj(*na*). ⟪**free**⟫
EX. A. Are you busy right now?
今忙しいですか。
Ima isogashii desu ka.
B: No, come right in.
いや、どうぞ入って下さい。
Iya, doozo haitte kudasai.
2. ni┌gi˥yakana にぎやかな adj(*na*). **[full of vigor and cheerful sounds]** ⟪**bustling**⟫
EX. This is the busiest section of town.
ここが町で一番にぎやかな場所です。
Koko ga machi de ichiban nigiyakana basho desu.
3. ha┌nashi-chuu 話し中 **[for a telephone line to be engaged]**
EX. The line is busy now.
今、電話は話し中です。
Ima, denwa wa hanashi-chuu desu.
NOTE: "Busy" with regard to an airport is *richakuriku ga ooi,* literally meaning "there are many landings and take-offs."

but conj.
shi┌ka˥shi しかし **[the most general conjunction, negating the content of the**

preceeding discourse or stating s.t. which is contrary to expectation based on the preceding discourse, used in sentence-initial position], ke⌉(re)do(mo) け(れ)ど(も) [a disjunctive subordinate conjunction that combines two sentences] , de⌉mo でも [a disjunctive coordinate conjunction used in sentence-initial position], ga が [a disjunctive coordinate conjunction that combines two sentences]

EX. (**a**) John came, but Mary didn't.
ジョンは来た{が/け(れ)ど(も)/*でも/*しかし}メアリーは来なかった。
*Jon wa kita {ga/ke(re)do(mo)/*demo/*shikashi} Mearii wa konakatta.*
(**b**) I want to travel but I don't have any money.
私は旅行をしたい{が/け(れ)ど(も)/*でも/*しかし}お金がない。
*Watashi wa ryokoo o shitai {ga/ke(re)do(mo)/*demo/*shikashi} o-kane ga nai.*
(**c**) Richard stayed in Japan for two years, but he didn't study Japanese.
リチャードは日本に二年間いた。{しかし/でも/が/けれども}日本語を勉強しなかった。
Richaado wa Nihon ni ni-nenkan ita. {Shikashi/Demo/Ga/Keredomo} Nihon-go o benkyoo-shinakatta.

NOTE: 1. Similar to "but," *ga* combines two sentences which express contrastive ideas. However, the contrastive meaning of *ga* is much weaker than "but," in that it is sometimes used simply to combine two sentences even if they do not represent contrastive ideas. In other words, *ga* may be used simply as a transition word to connect two sentences, often where the first sentence creates a setting for or background to the second sentence. For example, *Paatii o shimasu ga, kimasen ka.* "We're having a party. Won't you come?"
2. S_1 and S_2 in "S_1 *ga* S_2" must be at the same level of formality because each is an independent clause.
3. There are other expressions in Japanese which correspond semantically to "but" in English: for example, *daga*, *dakedo*, *demo*, *shikashi*, and *keredomo*. These express the same idea as *ga*. However, the first four cannot conjoin sentences, unlike *ga*. They occur at the beginning of a sentence, as shown below.
a. S_1 *ga* S_2.
b. *S_1 *{daga/dakedo/demo/shikashi}* S_2.
c. S_1. *{Daga/Dakedo/Demo/Shikashi}* S_2.
Keredomo differs from *ga* in that it is a subordinate conjunction meaning "although." That is, in "S_1 *keredomo* S_2," S_2 is the main clause, and S_1 *keredomo* is a subordinate clause. In "S_1 *ga* S_2," on the other hand, both S_1 and S_2 are independent (=coordinate) clauses. *Keredomo* is often shortened to *keredo*. *Kedo* is a colloquial version of *keredomo*.

butcher n. **[one who cuts meat to sell]**
ni⌈ku⌉-ya 肉屋 [a store which sells meat] ⟪meat shop⟫

EX. Go to the butcher across the street and get me some bacon.
向かいの肉屋へ行ってベーコンを買ってきて下さい。
Mukai no niku-ya e itte beekon o katte-kite kudasai.

butter n. **[a thick, yellowish product made from churning cream]**
ba⌉taa バター •f

EX. I'd like some butter on my toast.
トーストにバターを少しつけてほしい。
Toosuto ni bataa o sukoshi tsukete hoshii.

butterfly n. **[an insect with a slender body and four broad, usually brightly colored wings]**
cho⌉ocho ちょうちょ, cho⌉o ちょう

NOTE: *Choocho* is a more colloquial version of *choo*.

EX. I used to collect butterflies when I was a kid.
子供のころはよく{ちょうちょ/ちょう}を採集したものだ。
Kodomo no koro wa yoku {choocho/choo} o saishuu-shita mono da.

button n. **[any small disk or knob used as a fastening, ornament, etc., as on a garment]**

bo⌈tan ボタン •f

EX. A button came off my suit.
洋服のボタンが取れてしまった。
Yoofuku no botan ga torete shimatta.

buy vt. **[for s.o. to acquire s.t. by paying money]**
⟨-o⟩ ka⌈u ⟨～を⟩買う ① [for s.o. to acquire s.t. in exchange for money] ⟪purchase⟫ ↔ ⟨-o⟩ uru ⟨～を⟩売る ① ⟪sell⟫

EX. I intend to buy a CD player in Japan.
私は日本でCDプレーヤーを買うつもりです。
Watashi wa Nihon de shii-dii-pureeyaa o kau tsumori desu.

buyer n. **[one who buys, sometimes for retail]**
ka⌈i-te 買い手 ↔ uri-te 売り手; ba⌉iyaa バイヤー •f [one whose work is to buy merchandise for a retail store]

EX. Our buyer in Singapore is coming to Japan tomorrow.
我々のシンガポールの{買い手/バイヤー}が明日来日する。
Ware-ware no Shingapooru no {kai-te/baiyaa} ga asu rai-Nichi-suru.

buzz n. **[a sound like the humming of a bee]**
bu⌉n-bun iu o⌈to⌉ ブンブンいう音

by prep. **[a preposition which forms a phrase with the following noun phrase to modify a sentence or verb phrase, indicaing spatial/temporal proximity, instrumentality, or source or standard]**

1. ⟨-no⟩ so⌉ba {ni/de/o} ⟨～の⟩そば{に/で/を} n.+prt. **[near, at]**

EX. Who is the lady standing by the car?
車のそばに立っている女の人はだれですか。
Kuruma no soba ni tatte iru onna no hito wa dare desu ka.

2. made-ni までに prt. **[not later than]**

EX. You have to turn in your paper by Friday.
論文は金曜日までに出しなさい。
Ronbun wa kinyoo-bi made-ni dashinasai.

3. de で prt. **[using s.t.]**

EX. I commuted to my high school by train.
僕は電車で高校へ通学した。
Boku wa densha de kookoo e tsuugaku-shita.

4. ni に [indicating agent in a passive sentence], ni-yo⌈tte によって

EX. Kennedy was killed by an assassin.
ケネディーは暗殺者{に/によって}殺された。
Kenedii wa ansatsu-sha {ni/ni-yotte} korosa-reta.

5. ⟨-o⟩ toot⌉te ⟨～を⟩通って /⟨V *te* of *tooru* ① pass through/ [going from one end to another (of a certain spatial area)**], ⟨-o⟩ ke⌈iyu-shite ⟨～を⟩経由して •c /⟨V *te* of *keiyu-suru* ③ go by way of/ [by way of]**

EX. We came to San Francisco by Seattle.
私たちはシアトルを{通って/経由して}サンフランシスコに来た。
Watashi-tachi wa Shiatoru o {tootte/keiyu-shite} Sanfuranshisuko ni kita.

6. de で prt. **[indicating rate, quantity, degree, price, speed, etc.]**

EX. (**a**) We rented our apartment by the month.
私たちはアパートを月決めで借りました。
Watashi-tachi wa apaato o tsuki-gime de karimashita.
(**b**) It was twelve o'clock by his watch.
彼の時計で十二時だった。
Kare no tokei de juu-ni-ji datta.

7. ⟨-no⟩ a⌈ida ⟨～の⟩間 n. **[the space between two temporal, spatial points], ⟨-no⟩ u⌈chi ni ⟨～の⟩うちに** n.+prt. **[in the course of, during]**

EX. Some young people sleep by day and play by night.
昼の{間/うちに}寝て夜遊ぶ若者もいる。
Hiru no {aida/uchi ni} nete yoru asobu waka-mono mo iru.

C

cabbage n. **[a vegetable with thick leaves forming a round compact head]**
kya⌉betsu キャベツ •f

cabin n. **[a small, crudely/simply built house ⟪fig. "a room or space for passengers, etc. on a ship/in an aircraft"⟫]**
1. ko⌈ya 小屋 [a small simply- or roughly-made building] ⟪hut⟫

EX. My uncle built a cabin in the woods.
伯父は森に小屋を建てた。
Oji wa mori ni koya o tateta.

2. se⌈nshitsu 船室 •c [a compartment in a ship] ⟪space for passengers⟫, kya⌈kushitsu 客室 •c [a room for passengers in general] ⟪passengers' room⟫

EX. No smoking in the cabin.
{船室/客室}では禁煙です。
{Senshitsu/Kyakushitsu} de wa kin'en desu.

cabinet n. **[a case with drawers/shelves or one holding a TV, radio, etc. or a body of advisers to a chief executive]**
1. kya⌉binetto キャビネット •f

EX. This cabinet is made of teak wood.
このキャビネットはチーク材で出来ている。
Kono kyabinetto wa chiiku-zai de dekite iru.

2. na⌉ikaku 内閣 •c [the supreme organ of a country composed of state ministers] ⟪council, government⟫

EX. The new Japanese prime minister named his choices for his cabinet.
新しい日本の総理大臣は、内閣の顔ぶれを指名した。
Atarashii Nihon no Soori-daijin wa, naikaku no kao-bure o shimei-shita.

cable n. **[a thick, heavy rope, often made of wire strands or a bundle of insulated wires for carrying an electric current or a cablegram]**
1. fu⌈to⌉i tsu⌈na⌉ 太い綱 [thick rope] ⟪heavy rope⟫

EX. A suspension bridge is one suspended from cables attached to supports at both ends.
つり橋とは両端の支柱に取り付けられた太い綱からつり下げられた橋のことだ。
Tsuri-bashi to wa ryootan no shichuu ni tori-tsuke-rareta futoi tsuna kara tsuri-sage-rareta hashi no koto da.

2. ke⌈eburu-sen ケーブル線 •f+c ⟪insulated wires⟫
3. de⌈npoo 電報 •c [telegram], ka⌈igai-de⌉npoo 海外電報 •c [overseas telegram]

EX. Due to improved telephone service, we send less cables overseas nowadays than we used to.
国際電話が便利になったため昔ほど(海外)電報を打たなくなった。
Kokusai-denwa ga benrini natta tame mukashi hodo (kaigai-)denpoo o utanaku natta.

Cadillac n. **[an American luxury passenger car]**
Kya⌉derakku キャデラック •f

Caesar n. **[a Roman general and dictator who lived ca.100B.C.–44B.C.]**
Shi⌉izaa シーザー •f

cafeteria n. **[a self-service dining hall or restaurant]**
ka⌈fete⌉ria カフェテリア •f, sho⌈kudoo 食堂 •c [a room/store where meals are served] ⟪dining room, restaurant⟫

cage n. **[a structure of wires, bars, etc. for keeping animals]**
o⌈ri⌉ おり [a container for animals in general], to⌈ri-kago 鳥かご [a container in which to keep birds]

EX. (a) I feel like a bird cooped up in a cage.
私は{鳥かご/*おり}のなかにとじ込められた鳥みたいな気がします。
*Watakushi wa {tori-kago/*ori} no naka ni toji-kome-rareta tori mitaina ki ga shimasu.*
(b) Our cats don't like to be put in the cage.
うちの猫は{おり/*鳥かご}の中に入れられるのが好きじゃない。
*Uchi no neko wa {ori/*tori-kago} no naka ni ire-rareru no ga suki janai.*

cake n. **[a sweet, baked, bread-like food, often covered with frosting]**
ke⌉eki ケーキ •f [western sweets], ka⌉shi 菓子 •c [a generic term for small-sized food, usually sweet, eaten between meals as a snack]

EX. (a) Our daughter baked a delicious cake for us.
娘がおいしい{ケーキ/菓子}を焼いてくれた。
Musume ga oishii {keeki/kashi} o yaite kureta.
(b) The cake they sell in that store is delicious.
あの店で売っている{ケーキ/菓子}はおいしい。
Ano mise de utte iru {keeki/kashi} wa oishii.
(c) A Japanese cake goes well with green tea.
和{菓子/*ケーキ}は緑茶と合う。
*Wa-{gashi/*keeki} wa ryokucha to au.*

calcium n.
ka⌈rushiu⌉mu カルシウム •f

calculate vt. **[for s.o./s.t. to find out s.t. by using mathematics]**
⟨-o⟩ ke⌈isan-suru ⟨〜を⟩計算する ③ •c [for s.o. to find out a number/quantity by means of mathematical operations] ⟪count, reckon, compute, estimate⟫

EX. (a) Let's calculate the number of months we need to complete the project.
プロジェクト完成まで何か月かかるかを計算しよう。
Purojekuto-kansei made nan-kagetsu kakaru ka o keisan-shiyoo.
(b) I'm calculating my income for my tax return.
税金の申告のために自分の収入を計算しています。
Zei-kin no shinkoku no tame ni jibun no shuunyuu o keisan-shite imasu.

calculation n. **[determination of s.t. by means of mathematical computation]**
ke⌈isan 計算 •c [finding numbers/quantities by means of mathematical operations] ⟪computation⟫

EX. By my calculation, we should arrive in another thirty minutes.
私の計算では、あと三十分で着くはずだ。
Watashi no keisan de wa, ato san-jip-pun de tsuku hazu da.

PHRASE: mental calculation *anzan* 暗算 •c

EX. George is strong at mental calculation.
ジョージは暗算が得意だ。
Jooji wa anzan ga tokui da.

calendar n. **[a table that shows the days, weeks and months of a given year or a schedule]**
ka⌈re⌉ndaa カレンダー •f, ko⌈yomi⌉ 暦 [a table, usu. of traditional Japanese style, showing the days, months, and holidays over a period of a year], yo⌈tei-hyoo 予定表 •c [schedule]

EX. We'll mark the event on the calendar.
その行事を{カレンダー/暦/予定表}に書き込んでおきます。
Sono gyooji o {karendaa/koyomi/yotei-hyoo} ni kaki-konde okimasu.

calf n. **[a young cow/bull]**
ko-⌈ushi 子牛

California n. **[a state on the Pacific Coast of the southwestern United States]**
Ka⌈riforunia カリフォルニア •f

calisthenics n. **[athletic exercises]**
ta⌈isoo 体操 •c [the art or practice of training the body, including such training with special apparatus such as parallel bars and rings] ⟪physical exercises, gymnastics⟫

EX. Calisthenics help keep one in good health.
体操は健康を保つのに役立つ。

Taisoo wa kenkoo o tamotsu no ni yakudatsu.

call vt. **[for s.o. to say s.t. in a loud tone or to give a name to s.t. or to phone s.o.]**

1. ⟨-o⟩ yo⌈bu ⟨～を⟩呼ぶ ① [for s.o. to speak aloud to s.o. in order to get his/her attention or to ask s.o. to come] ((**cry out in a loud voice**))

C

EX. (**a**) Someone called my name.
だれかが私の名前を呼んだ。
Dare-ka ga watakushi no namae o yonda.
(**b**) I was called into the professor's office.
私は教授の研究室に呼ばれた。
Watashi wa kyooju no kenkyuu-shitsu ni yoba-reta.

2. ⟨-o⟩ ⟨-to⟩ yo⌈bu ⟨～を⟩⟨～と⟩呼ぶ ① [for s.o. to give a name to s.o./s.t. or to designate s.o./s.t. as s.t.] ((**name**))

EX. In Japanese, a husband often calls his wife "O-kaa-san."
日本語では夫が妻を「お母さん」と呼ぶことがある。
Nihon-go de wa otto ga tsuma o 'o-kaa-san' to yobu koto ga aru.

3. ⟨-ni⟩ de⌈nwa-suru ⟨～に⟩電話する ③ •c [for s.o. to make a telephone call to s.o.] ((**ring, phone**))

EX. (**a**) I called my mother and said that I'd be home late.
母に電話して帰宅が遅くなることを伝えた。
Haha ni denwa-shite kitaku ga osoku naru koto o tsutaeta.
(**b**) I make it a rule to call my mother on Sundays.
日曜日には母に電話することにしています。
Nichiyoo-bi ni wa haha ni denwa-suru koto ni shite imasu.

— n. **[a loud utterance]**

1. yo⌈bi-goe 呼び声 [s.t. said in a loud voice to get the attention of s.o./s.a.], sa⌈kebi-go⌉e 叫び声 [a raised voice, usu. with a tone of urgency] ((**shout, cry**))

EX. (**a**) We heard a call for help.
我々は助けを求める{叫び声/*呼び声}を聞いた。
*Ware-ware wa tasuke o motomeru {sakebi-goe/*yobi-goe} o kiita.*
(**b**) You rarely hear the calls of street peddlers any more these days.
最近は物売りの{呼び声/*叫び声}を聞くことも少なくなった。
*Saikin wa mono-uri no {yobi-goe/*sakebi-goe} o kiku koto mo sukunaku natta.*

2. de⌈nwa 電話 •c [an apparatus for transmitting speech to a distant hearer or an act of using such to communicate with s.o.]

EX. Taro, there's a phone call for you from Hanako.
太郎、花子から電話ですよ。
Taroo, Hanako kara denwa desu yo.

calligraphy n. **[the art of beautiful handwriting]**

shu⌈uji 習字 •c [the study of producing esthetically pleasing written characters], sho⌉doo 書道 •c [the art of writing characters with a brush]

EX. I'm taking lessons in calligraphy from an expert.
私は専門家から{習字/書道}を習っている。
Watakushi wa senmon-ka kara {shuuji/shodoo} o naratte iru.

calm adj. **[for weather/emotions to be tranquil]**

1. o⌈chitsuita N 落ち着いたN /⟨Vpast of *ochitsuku* ① settle down/ [having composure] ((**self-possessed, settled**)), **o⌈chitsuite iru (N) 落ち着いている(N) /⟨V *te iru* of *ochitsuku* ① settle down/**

EX. (**a**) No matter what the circumstances, my father was always calm.
どのような状況にあっても、父はいつも落ち着いていた。
Dono yoona jookyoo ni atte mo chichi wa itsu-mo ochitsuite ita.
(**b**) The winner was calm as she went to the platform to receive her prize.

優勝者は落ち着いた態度で表彰台に上った。
Yuushoo-sha wa ochitsuita taido de hyooshoo-dai ni agatta.
(**c**) He answered the interviewer in a calm voice.
彼は落ち着いた声でインタビューを受けた。
Kare wa ochitsuita koe de intabyuu o uketa.

2. he⌈ikina 平気な adj(*na*). **•c [having the appearance of s.o. who is unmoved by external circumstances] ⟪cool, composed, nonchalant⟫**

EX. (**a**) She wore a calm face as she heard the news.
彼女はそのニュースを聞いたとき平気な顔をしていた。
Kanojo wa sono nyuusu o kiita toki heikina kao o shite ita.
(**b**) How can he always have such a calm expression on his face?
彼がいつも平気な顔をしていられるのはどうしてだろうか。
Kare ga itsu-mo heikina kao o shite i-rareru no wa dooshite daroo ka.

3. shi⌉zukana 静かな adj(*na*). **[comfortably quiet/peaceful] ⟪quiet, still⟫**

EX. (**a**) I enjoy having a leisurely cup of coffee on a calm afternoon.
静かな午後の一時ゆっくりコーヒーを楽しむのが好きです。
Shizukana gogo no hito-toki yukkuri koohii o tanoshimu no ga suki desu.
(**b**) The wind stopped, and it finally became calm outside.
風がやんで外はやっと静かになった。
Kaze ga yande soto wa yatto shizukani natta.
(**c**) My fondest memories of childhood are of fishing with my father on a calm lake.
子供の時の最も楽しい思い出というと、父と一緒に静かな湖で釣りをしたことだ。
Kodomo no toki no mottomo tanoshii omoi-de to iu to, chichi to issho ni shizukana mizuumi de tsuri o shita koto da.

—— vi. **[to become tranquil]**
o⌈chitsuku 落ち着く ① **⟪be composed⟫**

EX. (**a**) Calm down! Everything is going to be okay.
落ち着きなさい。すべてうまくいくから。
Ochitsukinasai. Subete umaku iku kara.
(**b**) If you don't calm down, you may cause an accident.
落ち着かないと事故を起こしますよ。
Ochitsukanai to jiko o okoshimasu yo.

calmly adv. **[in a quiet manner] ⟪peacefully⟫**
o⌈chitsuite 落ち着いて /(V*te* of *ochitsuku* ① settle down/

EX. He took the news of the accident calmly.
彼はその事故のニュースを落ち着いて聞いた。
Kare wa sono jiko no nyuusu o ochitsuite kiita.

camel n. **[a large, domesticated mammal with a humped back and long neck]**
ra⌈kuda らくだ

camera n. **[a device for taking photographs]**
ka⌉mera カメラ •f, sha⌈shi⌉n-ki 写真機 •c

EX. I bought a new camera yesterday.
昨日新しい{カメラ/写真機}を買った。
Kinoo atarashii {kamera/shashin-ki} o katta.

NOTE: *Shashin-ki* is almost archaic.

camp n. **[a place where tents, huts, etc. are put up temporarily or a group of such tents or a recreational place in the country for vacationers]**
kya⌉npu キャンプ •f [putting up a group of tents]

EX. (**a**) Many youngsters go camping in the woods around here in the summer.
多くの若者が夏、この辺の森の中でキャンプをする。
Ooku no waka-mono ga natsu, kono hen no mori no naka de kyanpu o suru.
(**b**) We set up camp near the lake.
私たちは湖の近くでキャンプをしました。

Watashi-tachi wa mizuumi no chikaku de kyanpu o shimashita.

PHRASE: camp grounds *kyanpu-joo* キャンプ場 •f+c

EX. Let's try and keep our camp grounds clean.
キャンプ場をきれいにするよう心がけましょう。
Kyanpu-joo o kireini suru yoo kokoro-gakemashoo.

C

— vi. **[to live/stay in a recreational tent]**
kya⌉npu-suru キャンプする ③ •f **[for s.o. to do camping]**

EX. I went camping by the lake with friends.
友達と湖畔でキャンプした。
Tomodachi to ko-han de kyanpu-shita.

campaign n. **[a series of activities planned for a particular purpose, esp. commercial/political]**
u⌈ndoo 運動 •c **[an act/instance of changing one's location/position with the passage of time or the act of moving one's body to develop it and maintain good health or the act of aggressively and systematically approaching various people/institutions in order to achieve an objective]** **⟪movement, motion, exercise, drive, crusade⟫**, **kya⌈npe⌉en** キャンペーン •f **[an active and systematic group effort of approaching a variety of people/institutions with a view to achieving some objective]** **⟪effort, movement, drive⟫**

EX. (**a**) The university conducted a campaign to raise funds for a new research center.
大学は新しい研究所の資金集めのために{運動/キャンペーン}を行った。
Daigaku wa atarashii kenkyuu-jo no shikin-atsume no tame ni {undoo/kyanpeen} o okonatta.
(**b**) He began his campaign for the presidency with a speech in front of the state capitol.
州会議事堂前での演説をもって彼は大統領選挙のための{運動/キャンペーン}を開始した。
Shuukai-giji-doo-mae de no enzetsu o motte kare wa daitooryoo-senkyo no tame no {undoo/kyanpeen} o kaishi-shita.

camping n. **[the activity of living temporarily in a tent or other outdoor recreational facility]**
kya⌈npu-seika⌉tsu キャンプ生活 •f+c **[life in a camp]**

EX. Children like camping.
子供たちはキャンプ生活が好きだ。
Kodomo-tachi wa kyanpu-seikatsu ga suki da.

can[1] aux. **[an auxiliary verb that expresses the ability to do s.t. or the possibility of s.t. happening or permission to do s.t.]**
1. Vinf. nonpast ko⌈to⌉ ga de⌈ki⌉ru Vinf. nonpastことが出来る ② **[for s.o./s.a. to have the ability or skill to do s.t.]** **⟪be able to, be capable of Ving⟫**

EX. (**a**) There are now many foreigners who can speak Japanese fluently.
今では日本語を上手に話すことが出来る外国人が多くなった。
Ima de wa Nihon-go o joozuni hanasu koto ga dekiru gaikoku-jin ga ooku natta.
(**b**) Can you read and write kanji?
漢字を読んだり書いたりすることができますか。
Kanji o yondari kaitari suru koto ga dekimasu ka.

2. ⟨-ga⟩ **de⌈ki⌉ru** ⟨～が⟩出来る ② **[for s.t. to come into existence spontanesouly ⟪fig. "be able to"⟫]**

EX. Can you play golf?
ゴルフが出来ますか。
Gorufu ga dekimasu ka.

3. Potential form of verbs

EX. (**a**) I can read Japanese novels.
私は日本語の小説が読める。
Watashi wa Nihon-go no shoosetsu ga yome-ru.
(**b**) I cannot eat natto.
僕はなっとうは食べられない。
Boku wa nattoo wa tabe-rarenai.

4. {**V/adj./cop.**} ***te*** **mo** {**i⌉i/ka⌈mawa⌉nai**} {**V/adj./cop.**} ***te***も{いい/構わない} **[for an action or situation to be acceptable]**

EX. (**a**) Can I use your phone?
電話を借りてもいいですか。
Denwa o karite mo ii desu ka.
(**b**) The color can be blue or pink.
色はブルーでもピンクでも{構いません/いいです}。
Iro wa buruu de mo pinku de mo {kamaimasen/ii desu}.

5. {⟨-no⟩/adj(*na*). stem na/{adj(*i*)./V}inf.} **ha⌈zu ga na⌉i** {⟨〜の⟩/adj(*na*). stemな/{adj(*i*)./V}inf.}はずがない **[a modal pattern that expresses the strong expectation that s.t. is not the case]** ⟪**be expected not to**⟫

EX. (**a**) He cannot be the one who committed the crime.
あの人が犯人のはずがない。
Ano hito ga hannin no hazu ga nai.
(**b**) She could not have done such a foolish thing.
彼女がそんなばかなことをするはずがない。
Kanojo ga sonna bakana koto o suru hazu ga nai.

can[2] n. **[a metal container, usu. tin-plated, in which foods, etc. are sealed for preservation]**

1. ka⌉n 缶 •f [a metallic container]

EX. This fruit will never go bad as long as the can is not opened.
この果物は缶を開けない限り、いつまでたっても腐ることはない。
Kono kudamono wa kan o akenai kagiri, itsu made tatte mo kusaru koto wa nai.

2. ka⌈nzume⌉ 缶詰 •c [the contents of a metal container, usu. food]

EX. (**a**) Get me a can of pineapples at the supermarket.
スーパーでパイナップルの缶詰を買って来て下さい。
Suupaa de painappuru no kanzume o katte-kite kudasai.
(**b**) Our cats eat their catfood right out of the can.
うちの猫は缶詰のキャットフードをそのまま食べる。
Uchi no neko wa kanzume no kyatto-fuudo o sono mama taberu.

Canada n.
Ka⌉nada カナダ •f

Canadian adj./n. **[of Canada]**
Ka⌉nada no N カナダのN •f [of/belonging to Canada], Ka⌈nada⌉-jin カナダ人 •f+c [a Canadian person or the people of Canada]

canal n. **[an artificial waterway for transportation/irrigation]**
u⌉nga 運河 •c [a river for transporting s.t.]

EX. (**a**) There have been many problems in the past surrounding the right of use of the Panama Canal.
パナマ運河の使用権を巡って過去様々な問題が起きている。
Panama-unga no shiyoo-ken o megutte kako samazamana mondai ga okite iru.
(**b**) Things are more convenient now that the canal has been built.
運河が出来て便利になった。
Unga ga dekite benrini natta.

cancel vt. **[for s.o. to make s.t. invalid or call s.t. off]**

1. ⟨-o⟩ **to⌈ri-kesu** ⟨〜を⟩**取り消す** ① **[for s.o. to call s.t. off]** ⟪**annul, call off**⟫, ⟨-o⟩ **kya⌉nseru-suru** ⟨〜を⟩**キャンセルする** ③ **•f [for s.o. to declare that s.t. already decided upon or arranged will not take place or be done]** ⟪**nullify**⟫, ⟨-o⟩ **chu⌈ushi-suru** ⟨〜を⟩**中止する** ③ **•c [for s.o. to call off an event which is planned or to discontinue an event which is already underway]** ⟪**discontinue, suspend, break off**⟫

EX. (**a**) They canceled the baseball game due to rain.
雨のため野球の試合を{中止した/*取り消した/*キャンセルした}。
*Ame no tame yakyuu no shiai o {chuushi-shita/*tori-keshita/*kyanseru-shita}.*
(**b**) I canceled my plane reservation due to urgent business.
急用で飛行機の予約を{取り消した/キャンセルした/*中止した}。
Kyuuyoo de hikoo-ki no yoyaku o {tori-

| *keshita/kyanseru-shita/*chuushi-shita}.*

2. ⟨-o⟩ mu⌈koo ni suru ⟨～を⟩無効にする ③ •c [to make s.t. ineffectual or invalid] **《annul, nullify》**

EX. The police canceled Jiro's driver's license.
警察は次郎の運転免許証を無効にした。
Keisatsu wa Jiroo no unten-menkyo-shoo o mukoo ni shita.

C

PHRASE: cancel one's class *kyuukoo ni suru* 休講にする ③ •c

EX. The professor cancels his class so often that his students are complaining.
その教授はよく休講にするので、学生たちは文句を言っている。
Sono kyooju wa yoku kyuukoo ni suru node, gakusei-tachi wa monku o itte iru.

cancer n. **[a malignant growth or tumor that tends to spread 《fig. "s.t. like cancer"》]**
ga⌉n がん

EX. Smoking is linked with lung cancer.
喫煙は肺がんと関係がある。
Kitsuen wa hai-gan to kankei ga aru.

candidate n. **[a person who seeks or is nominated for an office, award, honor, etc.]**
ko⌈oho⌉-sha 候補者 •c [a person who is recommended by others as suitable for an office, award, honor, etc. and who is regarded by people in general as such] **《applicant, nominee》**

EX. (**a**) Mr. Sato was considered as a candidate for a Nobel prize.
佐藤氏がノーベル賞の候補者として考慮された。
Satoo-shi ga Nooberu-shoo no kooho-sha to-shite kooryo-sareta.
(**b**) The Republican candidate for the presidency delivered a speech.
共和党の大統領候補者が演説をした。
Kyoowa-too no daitooryoo-kooho-sha ga enzetsu o shita.

candle n. **[a long, usually slender piece of tallow or wax with an embedded wick, burned to give light]**
ro⌈oso⌉ku ろうそく

EX. (**a**) Let's light the candles on the birthday cake.
バースデーケーキのろうそくに火をつけましょう。
Baasudee-keeki no roosoku ni hi o tsukemashoo.
(**b**) He blew out the candles in one breath.
彼はろうそくの火を一気に吹き消した。
Kare wa roosoku no hi o ikki ni fuki-keshita.

candy n. **[a confection made from sugar, syrup, etc., often combined with other ingredients]**
kya⌉ndee キャンデー •f, a⌈me あめ [a sweet confection which one sucks inside the mouth before eventually swallowing]

EX. Won't you have some of this candy?
この{キャンデー/あめ}少しいかがですか。
Kono {kyandee/ame} sukoshi ikaga desu ka.

cane n. **[a stem of rattan or a walking stick]**

1. to⌉o とう [rattan]

EX. This chair is made of cane.
このいすはとうでできている。
Kono isu wa too de dekite iru.

2. tsu⌉e つえ [a stick to assist in walking], su⌈te⌉kki ステッキ •f 《stick》

EX. Who is that gentleman with the cane?
あの{つえ/ステッキ}をついている男の人はだれですか。
Ano {tsue/sutekki} o tsuite iru otoko no hito wa dare desu ka.

canned food n. **[food kept in a can for preservation]**
ka⌈nzume⌉ 缶詰 [the contents of a metal container, usu. food]

EX. (**a**) Our cats love canned food.
うちの猫は缶詰が大好物だ。
Uchi no neko wa kanzume ga dai-koobutsu da.
(**b**) Canned food comes in handy in an emergency.
缶詰は非常食として便利です。
Kanzume wa hijoo-shoku to-shite benri desu.

cannon n. **[a large, mounted gun for firing heavy projectiles]**
ta⌈ihoo 大砲 •c [big gun]

canoe n. **[a narrow, light boat propelled by paddles]**
ka⌉nuu カヌー •f, ma⌈ruki-bu⌉ne 丸木舟 [a boat made from a log]

canvas n. **[a coarse cloth of hemp, cotton, etc. used for tents, sails, etc. or an oil painting on such a material]**
1. ho⌉-nuno 帆布 [cloth used for the sail of a sailboat] ((sail cloth)), zu⌉kku ズック •f
2. ka⌉nbasu カンバス •f [a rough cloth used for oil painting]

canyon n. **[a long, narrow valley between high cliffs]**
kyo⌈okoku 峡谷 •c [a narrow, V-shaped valley with steep cliffs on both sides]

cap n. **[any cloth head covering, visored or brimless, or a covering for the end/top of s.t. or the top of s.t.]**
1. bo⌈oshi 帽子 •c [a covering for the head], fu⌈chi-nashi-bo⌉oshi 縁なし帽子 •c [a brimless covering for the head], kya⌉ppu キャップ [headgear, usu. brimless] ((hat))

EX. Take your cap off when you enter the room.
部屋に入ったら帽子を取りなさい。
Heya ni haittara booshi o torinasai.

2. kya⌉ppu キャップ •f [a protective cover for a pen, bottle, etc.], fu⌉ta ふた [lid] ((cover))

EX. (**a**) I lost the cap for this fountain pen.
この万年筆の{キャップ/*ふた}をなくしてしまった。
*Kono mannen-hitsu no {kyappu/*futa} o nakushite shimatta.*
(**b**) She took the cap off the jar.
彼女はびんの{ふた/キャップ}をとった。
Kanojo wa bin no {futa/kyappu} o totta.

capable adj. **[having ability, skilled, competent]**
1. {Vinf. nonpast/N no} no⌉oryoku ga a⌉ru (N) {Vinf. nonpast/Nの}能力がある(N) [have the ability to do s.t.] ((able to do s.t., capable)), Potential form of verbs

EX. We're looking for someone capable of teaching Japanese.
日本語を{教える能力がある/教えられる}人を探しています。
Nihon-go o {oshieru nooryoku ga aru/ oshie-rareru} hito o sagashite imasu.

2. yu⌈unoona 有能な adj(*na*) **•c ((competent, able))**

EX. I need a capable secretary.
私は有能な秘書が必要だ。
Watakushi wa yuunoona hisho ga hitsuyoo da.

capacity n. **[the ability to contain, absorb, or receive or the amount of s.t. that can be contained or ability]**
1. shu⌈uyoo-no⌉oryoku 収容能力 •c [the ability to contain/accommodate people/ things]

EX. What is the capacity of this prison?
この刑務所の収容能力はどのくらいですか。
Kono keimu-sho no shuuyoo-nooryoku wa dono-kurai desu ka.

2. no⌉oryoku 能力 •c [the capability to be able to perform a given task] ((ability)), sa⌈inoo 才能 •c [innate intellectual or artistic capability, esp. of an outstanding kind] ((talent))

EX. Taro is a musician of outstanding capacity.
太郎は抜群の{才能/能力}を持った音楽家だ。
Taroo wa batsugun no {sainoo/ nooryoku} o motta ongaku-ka da.

cape n. **[a piece of land projecting into the sea or other body of water]**
mi⌈saki 岬

EX. There is a lighthouse at the tip of the cape.
岬の先に灯台があります。
Misaki no saki ni toodai ga arimasu.

capital n. **[a city that is the seat of government of a state/nation or an upper-case letter or money/property owned by s.o. or used in business]**
1. shu⌉to 首都 •c [the seat of national government]

EX. Washington, D.C., is the capital of the United States.

ワシントンはアメリカ合衆国の首都である。
Washinton wa Amerika-gasshuukoku no shuto dearu.

2. o⌈o-moji 大文字 [upper-case, large characters]

EX. Please write your name in capitals.
名前は大文字で書いて下さい。
Namae wa oo-moji de kaite kudasai.

3. shi⌈hon(-kin) 資本(金) •c [money and material forming the basis of a business]

EX. (**a**) In order to start a business, one has to raise capital first.
企業を興そうと思ったら、まず資本(金)を調達しなければならない。
Kigyoo o okosoo to omottara, mazu shihon(-kin) o chootatsu-shinakereba naranai.
(**b**) How much capital does this company have?
この会社には資本(金)がどのぐらいありますか。
Kono kaisha ni wa shihon(-kin) ga dono-gurai arimasu ka.

Capitol n. **[a building in Washington, D.C. housing the U.S. Congress]**
Ko⌈kkai-giji-doo 国会議事堂 •c [a building housing the Japanese Diet]

Kokkai-gijidoo

EX. (**a**) The journalist reported the news from the Capitol building.
ジャーナリストは国会議事堂からニュースを報道した。
Jaanarisuto wa Kokkai-giji-doo kara nyuusu o hoodoo-shita.
(**b**) We took a commemorative picture with the Capitol building in the background.
国会議事堂をバックに記念写真を撮った。
Kokkai-giji-doo o bakku ni kinen-shashin o totta.

capsule n. **[a soluble gelatinous container enclosing a dose of medicine or a detachable compartment to hold men, instruments, etc. in a rocket]**
ka⌉puseru カプセル •f

captain n. **[a chief/leader or the master of a ship]**

1. shu⌈shoo 主将 •c [the leader or head of a team], kya⌉puten キャプテン •f

EX. He was chosen captain of the varsity team.
彼は大学チームの{主将/キャプテン}に選ばれた。
Kare wa daigaku-chiimu no {shushoo/kyaputen} ni eraba-reta.

2. se⌉nchoo 船長 •c [the master of a ship], ka⌈nchoo 艦長 •c [the master of a warship]

EX. (**a**) The captain gave the order to fire.
{船長/艦長}は攻撃を命令した。
{Senchoo/Kanchoo} wa koogeki o meirei-shita.
(**b**) The captain perished along with his ship.
{船長/艦長}は船と命を共にした。
{Senchoo/Kanchoo} wa fune to inochi o tomo ni shita.

capture vt. **[to take or seize]**
⟨-o⟩ to⌈rae⌉ru ⟨〜を⟩捕らえる ② 《catch, seize》, ⟨-o⟩ tsu⌈kamaeru ⟨〜を⟩捕まえる ② 《catch》

NOTE: *Toraeru* is more formal than *tsukamaeru.*

EX. (**a**) They captured the escaping lion.
彼らは逃げるライオンを{捕らえた/捕まえた}。
Kare-ra wa nigeru raion o {toraeta/tsukamaeta}.
(**b**) The children were absorbed in capturing insects.
子供たちは虫を{捕らえる/捕まえる}のに夢中だった。
Kodomo-tachi wa mushi o {toraeru/tsukamaeru} no ni muchuu datta.

car n. **[an automobile or a vehicle that moves on rails]**

1. ji⌈do⌉osha 自動車 •c [a vehicle driven by a motor and used on the road for transportation], ku⌈ruma 車 [wheel 《fig. "car"》]

EX. (**a**) Do you want to go by car or by train?

{車/?自動車}で行きますか、電車にしますか。
{Kuruma/?Jidoosha} de ikimasu ka, densha ni shimasu ka.
(**b**) They make cars in that factory.
あそこの工場では{自動車/車}を作っています。
Asoko no koojoo dewa {jidoosha/kuruma} o tsukutte imasu.

2. -sha ～車 •c [a vehicle that moves on rails]

EX. Let's go to the dining car for lunch.
食堂車へ行って昼食にしよう。
Shokudoo-sha e itte chuushoku ni shiyoo.

carbon n. **[a chemical element present in all living matter or a sheet of paper coated with a pigmented material]**
1. ta˥nso 炭素 •c [a chemical element present in all living matter]
2. ka˥abo˥n-shi カーボン紙 •f+c [a sheet of paper coated with a pigmented material used between two sheets of plain paper to reproduce on the lower sheet that which is written on the upper]

carburetor n. **[a device for mixing air with gasoline spray in an internal-combustion engine]**
ki˥ka˥-ki 気化器 •c, kya˥bure˥etaa キャブレーター •f

card n. **[a piece of stiff paper or thin pasteboard]**
ka˥ado カード •f

PHRASE: Christmas card *Kurisumasu-kaado* クリスマスカード **•f**, invitation card *shootai-joo* 招待状 **•c**, calling card *meishi* 名刺 **•c**, playing cards *toranpu* トランプ **•f**, picture postcard *e-hagaki* 絵葉書

EX. They gave my son a deck of playing cards on the plane.
息子は飛行機の中でトランプをもらった。
Musuko wa hikoo-ki no naka de toranpu o moratta.

cardboard n. **[stiff, thick paper or pasteboard used in making cards, boxes, etc.]**
bo˥oru-gami ボール紙, a˥tsugami 厚紙 [thick paper]

EX. We need lots of cardboard boxes because we're moving.
引っ越しのため{ボール紙/厚紙}の箱がたくさん必要だ。
Hikkoshi no tame {booru-gami/atsugami} no hako ga takusan hitsuyoo da.

PHRASE: corrugated cardboard *dan-booru* 段ボール **•c+f**

cardinal adj. **[principal/chief]**
ki˥hon-tekina 基本的な adj(*na*). **•c [pertaining to basics] ⟪fundamental, basic⟫**

EX. It is a cardinal rule in the academic community that credit be given to those whose ideas you borrow.
人の考えを借りた場合、その人の名前を明記するのが学問の世界の基本的なルールです。
Hito no kangae o karita baai, sono hito no namae o meiki-suru no ga gakumon no sekai no kihon-tekina ruuru desu.

care n. **[serious attention]**
1. shi˥npai 心配 •c [an uncomfortable feeling caused by uncertainty or by the expectation of danger/evil/s.t. troublesome] ⟪anxiety, uneasiness, fear, apprehension, trouble, concern, worry⟫

EX. Her many cares kept her awake nights.
彼女はいろいろな心配があって、夜寝られなかった。
Kanojo wa iroirona shinpai ga atte, yoru ne-rarenakatta.

2. yo˥ojin 用心 •c [taking measures ahead of time for an unexpected eventuality and being mentally prepared for such] ⟪heed, caution, precaution⟫, chu˥ui 注意 •c [an act of fixing the mind on s.t. ⟪fig. "warning," "advice"⟫] ⟪caution, precaution, heed⟫

EX. (**a**) Handle with care.
取り扱い{注意/*用心}。
*Tori-atsukai {chuui/*yoojin}.*
(**b**) Take care not to expose yourself too much to the sun at the beach.
海岸では日焼けに{注意/用心}して下さい。

Kaigan de wa hi-yake ni {chuui/yoojin}-shite kudasai.

3. se⸢wa⸣ 世話 •c [extending assistance to s.o. to enable him/her to do s.t. he/she could not accomplish alone] ⟪protection, charge, help, assistance, good offices, service⟫

EX. The mother cat was totally absorbed in the care of her kittens.
母猫は子猫の世話に余念がなかった。
Haha-neko wa ko-neko no sewa ni yonen ga nakatta.

PHRASE: take care of **[**to attend to, to provide for**]** ⟨*-o*⟩ *daijini suru* ⟨〜を⟩大事にする ③ **•c [**to attend to**]**, ⟨*-o*⟩ *sewa-suru* ⟨〜を⟩世話する ③ **•c [**to provide for**]** ⟪treasure, cherish⟫

EX. (**a**) Please take care of yourself.
{お大事に/*世話}なさってください。
*{O-daijini/*Sewa} nasatte kudasai.*
(**b**) We took care of the neighbor's dog at our home over the weekend.
週末の間うちで隣の家の犬を{世話して/*大事にして}いた。
*Shuumatsu no aida uchi de tonari no ie no inu o {sewa-shite/*daijini shite} ita.*

— vi. **[for s.o. to feel concern about s.t.] ⟨-o⟩ ki-⸢ni-suru ⟨〜を⟩気にする ③ [for s.o./s.a. to worry about s.t.], ⟨-o⟩ ka⸢ma⸣u ⟨〜を⟩構う ① [for s.o. to pay attention to s.t./s.o./s.a.]**

EX. I don't care if my parents disagree.
親が反対でも僕は{気にしない/構わない}。
Oya ga hantai de mo boku wa {ki-ni-shinai/kamawanai}.

PHRASE: care for ⟨*-o*⟩ *konomu* ⟨〜を⟩好む ① ⟪want⟫

EX. I don't care for milk very much.
牛乳はあまり好みません。
Gyuunyuu wa amari konomimasen.

career n. **[one's progress through life or a profession or occupation]**

1. sho⸣ogai 生涯 •c [the period during which a person lives, usually as an adult] ⟪one's life, lifetime⟫

EX. He chose the career of a pastor.
彼は牧師としての生涯を選んだ。
Kare wa bokushi to-shite no shoogai o eranda.

2. ke⸢ireki 経歴 •c [a record of schools and jobs one has attended/done up through a specified time] ⟪profession, personal history, background⟫, kya⸣ria キャリア •f

EX. He had an incredible career as an actor.
彼は役者としてすばらしい{経歴/キャリア}を持っていた。
Kare wa yakusha to-shite subarashii {keireki/kyaria} o motte ita.

careful adj. **[giving serious attention to s.t./s.o./s.a.]**

chu⸢ui-buka⸣i 注意深い adj(*i*). **[generally cautious] ⟪circumspect, prudent, wary⟫ ↔ fu-chuuina 不注意な** adj(*na*). **•c; ⟨-ni⟩ ki-⸢o-tsuke⸣ru ⟨〜に⟩気を付ける ② [for s.o. to pay attention to s.t/s.o./s.a.] ⟪mindful of⟫**

EX. (**a**) John is always careful.
ジョンはいつも注意深い。
Jon wa itsu-mo chuui-bukai.
(**b**) Takashi is extremely careful about what he eats.
孝は食べるものに特に気を付けている。
Takashi wa taberu mono ni tokuni ki-o-tsukete iru.

carefully adv. **[with serious attention paid to s.t./s.o./s.a.]**

chu⸣ui-shite 注意して /⟨V*te* of *chuui-suru* ③ pay attention/ •c [with caution]

EX. (**a**) Now listen carefully to what I'm going to say.
さあ、これから私が言うことを注意して聞いて下さい。
Saa, kore-kara watakushi ga iu koto o chuui-shite kiite kudasai.
(**b**) Drive carefully, especially on rainy days.
雨の日は特に注意して運転して下さい。
Ame no hi wa tokuni chuui-shite unten-shite kudasai.

careless adj. **[not paying enough attention]**

fu-⸢chu⸣uina 不注意な adj(*na*). **•c [lacking careful attention] ⟪neglectful⟫ ↔ chuui-bukai 注意深い** adj(*i*).

EX. (**a**) Mr. Johnson hardly ever makes careless mistakes.

ジョンソンさんはほとんど不注意な誤りは犯さない。
Jonson-san wa hotondo fu-chuuina ayamari wa okasanai.
(**b**) Everyone please be sure not to display any careless behavior in public.
皆さん、公の場で不注意な言動はしないように。
Minasan, ooyake no ba de fu-chuuina gendoo wa shinai yooni.

carelessly adv. **[without paying serious attention to s.t./s.o./s.a.]**
fu-⌈chu⌉uini-mo 不注意にも •c **[without exercising proper care], u⌈kka⌉ri** うっかり **[absent-mindedly/inattentively]**

EX. (**a**) He carelessly parked the car on a slope without setting the emergency brake.
彼は{不注意にも/うっかり}サイドブレーキをかけずに坂道に車を止めた。
Kare wa {fu-chuuini-mo/ukkari} saido-bureeki o kakezu saka-michi ni kuruma o tometa.
(**b**) I carelessly forgot to lock the door.
私は{不注意にも/うっかり}かぎをかけ忘れた。
Watashi wa {fu-chuuini-mo/ukkari} kagi o kake-wasureta.

cargo n. **[the load carried by a ship, truck, airplane, etc.]**
ka⌉motsu 貨物 •c **[the load carried by a truck, etc.]** 《**freight**》, **tsu⌉mi-ni** 積み荷 **[s.t. carried on a truck, etc.]** 《**load**》

EX. (**a**) The plane had to leave part of its cargo behind.
飛行機は{貨物/積み荷}の一部を残して飛び立たなければならなかった。
Hikoo-ki wa {kamotsu/tsumi-ni} no ichibu o nokoshite tobi-tatanakereba naranakatta.
(**b**) Due to overweight, we had to unload part of the cargo.
重量オーバーのため{貨物/積み荷}の一部を降ろさなければならなかった。
Juuryoo-oobaa no tame {kamotsu/tsumi-ni} no ichibu o orosanakereba naranakatta.
(**c**) For safety, please check the weight of the cargo.
安全のため{貨物/積み荷}の重量をチェックして下さい。
Anzen no tame {kamotsu/tsumi-ni} no juuryoo o chekku-shite kudasai.

caribou n.
to⌈na⌉kai トナカイ

carnival n.
ka⌉anibaru カーニバル •f, **sha⌈niku⌉-sai** 謝肉祭 •c

carpenter n. **[one who builds and repairs wooden things, esp. buildings]**
da⌉iku 大工 •c

carpet n. **[a heavy fabric for covering a floor]**
ka⌉apetto カーペット •f 《**rug**》, **ju⌉utan** じゅうたん •c 《**rug**》

carriage n. **[a wheeled vehicle for passengers, esp. one drawn by horses' or a moving part of a machine]**
1. ba⌉sha 馬車 •c **[a vehicle drawn by horses]**
2. kya⌉rijji キャリッジ •f **[the part of a typewriter, etc. which moves from left to right as one types]**

carrier n. **[one who carries s.t.]**
u⌈npan-nin 運搬人 •c **[one who carries s.t. to s.o. as a business], ha⌈itatsu-nin** 配達人 •c **[one who delivers things]**

carrot n.
ni⌈njin にんじん •c

carry vt. **[to take s.o./s.t./s.a. from one place to another** 《**fig. "transmit," "contain"**》**]**
1. 〈**-o**〉 **ha⌈kobu** 〈～を〉運ぶ ① **[to move s.o./s.t./s.a. from one place to another by hand or by means of a vehicle, etc.]** 《**move**》

EX. I'd like to have this desk carried to the next room.
この机を隣の部屋まで運んでもらいたい。
Kono tsukue o tonari no heya made hakonde morai-tai.

2. 〈**-ni**〉 〈**-o**〉 **tsu⌈taeru** 〈～に〉〈～を〉伝える ② **[for s.o./s.a. to pass along some message to s.o.]** 《**transmit, convey**》

EX. The pigeon carried the message to army headquarters.

伝書ばとがメッセージを陸軍の本部に伝えた。
Densho-bato ga messeeji o riku-gun no honbu ni tsutaeta.

3. ⟨-ni⟩ no⌈ru ⟨〜に⟩のる [to get onto s.t. that can support one's weight ⟪fig. "be recorded"⟫]

㊦ "be on/appear"▷載る, "ride"▷乗る

EX. Newspapers carry obituaries almost daily.
毎日のように死亡記事が新聞に載る。
Mai-nichi no yooni shiboo-kiji ga shinbun ni noru.

—— vi. **[for sound to reach a place]**

{⟨-ni⟩/⟨-made⟩} to⌈do⌉ku {⟨〜に⟩/⟨〜まで⟩}届く ① [for s.t. one has sent/extended to get to a place] ⟪arrive⟫

EX. His voice carries far.
彼の声は遠くまで届く。
Kare no koe wa tooku made todoku.

cart n. **[a small wagon]**

kaa⌉to カート •f

EX. (**a**) The use of a golf cart is free at that golf course.
あのゴルフ場はカートの使用が無料だ。
Ano gorufu-joo wa kaato no shiyoo ga muryoo da.
(**b**) At the supermarket, I always use a cart.
スーパーマーケットではいつもカートを使う。
Suupaa-maaketto de wa itsu-mo kaato o tsukau.

carton n. **[a cardboard box or container]**

ka⌉aton カートン •f, da⌈n-bo⌉oru 段ボール •c+f [a box made from cardboard] ⟪corrugated cardboard⟫, da⌈n-booru⌉-bako 段ボール箱

cartoon n. **[a drawing caricaturing a person or event or a comic strip]**

ma⌈nga 漫画 •c

EX. (**a**) Our children enjoy reading the cartoons in the Sunday newspaper.
うちの子供は日曜日の新聞の漫画を読むのが好きです。
Uchi no kodomo wa nichiyoo-bi no shinbun no manga o yomu no ga suki desu.
(**b**) The satire in this political cartoon hits the mark.
この政治漫画は風刺が効いている。
Kono seiji-manga wa fuushi ga kiite iru.

carve vt. **[for s.o. to make or shape by or as by cutting or to divide by cutting or to slice]**

1. ⟨-o⟩ cho⌈okoku-suru ⟨〜を⟩彫刻する ③ •c [for s.o. to make a sculpture out of wood/stone/metal]

EX. I'm going to carve a rose on this box.
この箱にはばらの花を彫刻するつもりです。
Kono hako ni wa bara no hana o chookoku-suru tsumori desu.

2. ⟨-o⟩ ki⌉tte wa⌈ke⌉ru ⟨〜を⟩切って分ける ② [for s.o. to cut s.t. and divide it], ⟨-o⟩ ki⌈ri-wakeru ⟨〜を⟩切り分ける ② [for s.o. to divide by cutting]

EX. Would you carve the turkey for me?
七面鳥を{切って/切り}分けて下さいませんか。
Shichimen-choo o {kitte/kiri-} wakete kudasaimasen ka.

case[1] n. **[a protective container]**

ha⌈ko 箱 ⟪box⟫, ke⌉esu ケース •f

case[2] n. **[a particular circumstance, specific instance, or example requiring discussion/decision/investigation]**

1. ba⌈ai 場合 [the time at which s.t. has come about or a situation in which s.t./s.o./s.a. finds itself/himself/herself] ⟪instance, example⟫

EX. (**a**) In their case, it was love at first sight.
彼らの場合はお互いに一目ぼれだった。
Kare-ra no baai wa o-tagai ni hito-me-bore datta.
(**b**) Do not use the elevator in case of fire.
火事の場合、エレベーターは使わないでください。
Kaji no baai, erebeetaa wa tsukawanaide kudasai.

2. ji⌈joo 事情 •c [the conditions or facts surrounding an event or situation] ⟪conditions, state of affairs, reason⟫

EX. Such being the case, I cannot accept your offer.
そういう事情なので申し出はお受け出来ません。
Sooiu jijoo na node mooshi-de wa o-uke-dekimasen.

3. ji⌉ken 事件 •c [an incident which is out of the ordinary and attracts attention, esp. of a criminal nature] ⟪event, incident, affair, matter⟫

EX. The Charles Manson case got much publicity in the press.
チャールズ・マンソン事件は世間を騒がせた。
Chaaruzu Manson-jiken wa seken o sawaga-seta.

PHRASE: in case Sinf. nonpast *to ikenai kara* Sinf. nonpastといけないから

EX. (a) I've also packed a raincoat for you in case you need it.
必要になるといけないからレインコートも入れました。
Hitsuyoo ni naru to ikenai kara rein-kooto mo iremashita.
(b) I'm going to take an umbrella in case it rains.
雨が降るといけないから傘をもって行く。
Ame ga furu to ikenai kara kasa o motte-iku.

cash n. **[money in coin or notes]**
ge⌈nki⌉n 現金 •c [money in actual coin or notes, as opposed to checks, bank drafts, etc. ⟪actual money⟫, kya⌉sshu キャッシュ •f

EX. (a) I paid for the car in cash.
車は現金で払った。
Kuruma wa genkin de haratta.
(b) We buy all our inventory in cash.
仕入れは全部{現金/キャッシュ}でします。
Shi-ire wa zenbu {genkin/kyasshu} de shimasu.

—— vt. **[to give/get cash for]**
⟨-o⟩ ge⌈nkin ni {kaeru/suru} ⟨〜を⟩現金に{替える②/する③} [for s.o. to change into money]

EX. I want to cash this check.
この小切手を現金に{替えたい/したい}のですが。
Kono kogitte o genkin ni {kae-tai/shi-tai} no desu ga.

cassette n.
ka⌈se⌉tto カセット •f

cast vt. **[for s.o. to throw s.t. with force ⟪fig. "deposit a ballot/vote," "shape molten metal, etc., by pouring into a mold," "select an actor for a dramatic role"⟫]**

1. (⟨-ni⟩) ⟨-o⟩ na⌈ge⌉ru (⟨〜に⟩)⟨〜を⟩投げる ② [for s.o. to cause s.t. in one's hand to move through the air by means of a quick forward motion of the arm] ⟪toss, hurl, fling, throw⟫

EX. The fishermen cast a net.
漁師たちは網を投げた。
Ryooshi-tachi wa ami o nageta.

2. ⟨-ni⟩ ⟨-o⟩ i⌈reru ⟨〜に⟩⟨〜を⟩入れる ② [for s.o./s.a. to cause s.t./s.o./s.a. to move into an enclosed space] ⟪enter, put in, admit, insert, employ, include⟫

EX. The delegate cast a negative vote.
代表は「否」の票を入れた。
Daihyoo wa 'ina' no hyoo o ireta.

3. ⟨-o⟩ chu⌈uzoo-suru ⟨〜を⟩鋳造する ③ •c [for s.o. to shape s.t. by pouring metal into a mold and letting it harden]

EX. The priests cast a bronze image of Buddha.
僧侶たちは仏像を鋳造した。
Sooryo-tachi wa butsuzoo o chuuzoo-shita.

4. ⟨-ni⟩ ⟨-no⟩ ya⌈ku⌉ o a⌈teru ⟨〜に⟩⟨〜の⟩役を当てる ② [to assign s.o. the part of] ⟪select an actor⟫

EX. The director cast Maria as the queen.
監督はマリアに女王の役を当てた。
Kantoku wa Maria ni jooo no yaku o ateta.

—— n. **[the set of actors in a play]**
ha⌈iyaku 配役 •c, kya⌉suto キャスト •f

castle n. **[a large fortified building or residence of a noble in feudal times]**
shi⌈ro 城

EX. (a) An Englishman's house is his castle.

英国人の家は城だ。
Eikoku-jin no ie wa shiro da.
(**b**) This castle is designated as a national treasure.
この城は国宝の一つに指定されている。
Kono shiro wa kokuhoo no hitotsu ni shitei-sarete iru.

C

cat n.
ne˥ko 猫

EX. (**a**) Ernest Hemingway kept lots of cats.
ヘミングウエイは猫をたくさん飼っていた。
Heminguuei wa neko o takusan katte ita.
(**b**) Nothing in the world is more darling than a cat.
世の中で猫ほどかわいいものはない。
Yo-no-naka de neko hodo kawaii mono wa nai.
(**c**) In Ancient Egypt, the cat was a sacred animal.
古代エジプトでは猫は神聖な動物だった。
Kodai Ejiputo de wa neko wa shinseina doobutsu datta.

catch vt. **[for s.o./s.a. to seize and hold s.t./s.o./s.a. 《fig. "get to in time for boarding," "receive," "incur/contract"》]**
1. 〈-o〉 tsu⌈kamaeru 〈〜を〉捕まえる ② [for s.o./s.a. to take hold of s.t./s.o./s.a. that is trying to flee/leave and try to prevent it/him/her from doing so] 《seize, grab, clutch, arrest, capture》, 〈-o〉 to⌈rae˥ru 〈〜を〉捕らえる ② [for s.o. to capture s.a. or a criminal 《fig. "deeply understand"》 〈fml〉]

EX. (**a**) I caught a rare bird on the island.
その島で珍しい鳥を{捕まえた/?捕らえた}。
Sono shima de mezurashii tori o {tsukamaeta/?toraeta}.
(**b**) Bears are good at catching salmon.
くまはさけを{捕まえる/捕らえる}のが上手だ。
Kuma wa sake o {tsukamaeru/toraeru} no ga joozu da.
(**c**) The monkey that escaped from the zoo was caught by a group of policemen.
動物園から逃げた猿は警官に{捕まえられた/捕らえられた}。
Doobutsu-en kara nigeta saru wa keikan ni {tsukamae-rareta/torae-rareta}.

2. 〈-ni〉 ma-⌈ni-a˥u 〈〜に〉間に合う ① [for s.o./s.t. to get to/be somewhere in time for s.t.] 《make it, be in time for》

EX. (**a**) Ed caught the plane for Oklahoma.
エドはオクラホマ行きの飛行機に間に合った。
Edo wa Okurahoma-yuki no hikoo-ki ni ma-ni-atta.
(**b**) You can still catch the last bus.
今からでも最終バスに間に合うでしょう。
Ima kara demo saishuu-basu ni ma-ni-au deshoo.

3. 〈-ni〉 ka⌈ka˥ru 〈〜に〉かかる ① [for s.t. to extend to and come in contact with s.t./s.o./s.a. else 《fig. "cover," "begin," "be engaged in," "become splashed with," "be built," "require"》]

EX. Take care not to catch the flu.
インフルエンザにかからないよう気を付けて下さい。
Infuruenza ni kakaranai yoo ki-o-tsukete kudasai.

4. V*te* iru tokoro o mi⌈tsukeru V*te*いるところを見付ける ② [for s.o. to find s.o. just as he/she is doing s.t.]

EX. (**a**) The store manager caught the woman shoplifting.
店長はその女性が万引きしているところを見付けた。
Tenchoo wa sono josei ga manbiki-shite iru tokoro o mitsuketa.
(**b**) The teacher caught a student cheating on the test.
先生は生徒が試験でカンニングをしているところを見付けた.
Sensei wa seito ga shiken de kanningu o shite iru tokoro o mitsuketa.

—— vi. **[for s.t. to become held, fastened, etc.]**

⟨-ni⟩ ha⌈sama⌉ru ⟨～に⟩挟まる ① [for s.t. to be pressed in on both sides and unable to move freely]

EX. (**a**) I got the end of my coat caught in the car door.
コートのすそが車のドアに挟まった。
Kooto no suso ga kuruma no doa ni hasamatta.
(**b**) Eating corn can be troublesome as the kernels get caught between your teeth.
とうもろこしは粒が歯に挟まるので困る。
Toomorokoshi wa tsubu ga ha ni hasamaru node komaru.

cathedral n. **[the principal church of a bishop's see or any large, imposing church]**
da⌈i-se⌉idoo 大聖堂 •c

cattle n. **[cows/bulls/steers/oxen]**
u⌈shi 牛 ⟪cow, ox⟫

EX. Jack raises cattle on his farm.
ジャックは農場で牛を飼育している。
Jakku wa noojoo de ushi o shiiku-shite iru.

causative n. **[a grammatical construction expressing causation]**
shi⌈eki 使役 •c

EX. "Watashi wa Taroo o otsukai ni ikaseta" is an example of a causative sentence.
「私は太郎をおつかいに行かせた」は使役文の例である。
'Watashi wa Taroo o otsukai ni ikaseta' wa shieki-bun no rei dearu.

cause n. **[anything producing an effect/result or a reason/motive for producing an effect or an objective which one believes in and actively supports]**
1. ge⌈n'in 原因 •c [a source from which an event or situation originates] ⟪reason⟫, ri⌈yuu 理由 •c [a fact/event/statement that provides an explanation/excuse for s.t. else] ⟪reason⟫

EX. What is the cause of his dissatisfaction?
彼の不満の{原因/理由}は何ですか
Kare no fuman no {gen'in/riyuu} wa nan desu ka.

2. shu⌉gi 主義 •c [a principle acting as a standard for one's thought and behavior] ⟪ism, doctrine⟫, mo⌈kuteki 目的 •c [the intended result of a particular action/behavior] ⟪objective⟫

EX. He will do anything for a cause he considers right.
彼は正しいと思う{主義/目的}のためには手段を選ばない。
Kare wa tadashii to omou {shugi/mokuteki} no tame ni wa shudan o erabanai.

— vt. **[for s.t. to make s.t. else happen or result in s.t. else]**
1. ⟨-no⟩ ge⌈n'in to na⌉ru ⟨～の⟩原因となる ① [for s.t. to act as the source from which an event or situation originates] ⟪be the reason, bring about⟫

EX. (**a**) Road repairs are causing traffic jams at many places.
道路の補修工事が交通渋滞の原因となっているところがたくさんある。
Dooro no hoshuu-kooji ga kootsuu-juutai no gen'in to natte iru tokoro ga takusan aru.
(**b**) A failure in economic policy caused the Premier's downfall.
経済政策の失敗が首相失脚の原因となった。
Keizai-seisaku no shippai ga shushoo-shikkyaku no gen'in to natta.

2. {⟨-ni⟩/⟨-o⟩} {Vneg. + seru/Vstem + saseru/ko-⌈sase⌉ru/sa⌈seru} {⟨～に⟩/⟨～を⟩}{Vneg.+せる/Vstem+させる/来させる/させる} ⟪make⟫

EX. (**a**) What caused him to quit his job?
何が彼に仕事をやめさせたのか。
Nani ga kare ni shigoto o yame-saseta no ka.
(**b**) What caused them to get a divorce?
二人に離婚を決意させたのは何だったのだろうか。
Futari ni rikon o ketsui-saseta no wa nan datta no daroo ka.

caution n. **[a warning or wariness/prudence]**
1. ke⌈ikoku 警告 •c [an act/instance of calling s.o.'s attention to imminent danger/evil] ⟪warning⟫

C

EX. (**a**) The weather bureau sent a caution out to all residents of the area to guard against possible flooding.
気象庁はその地区の住民に洪水が起きるかもしれないので気を付けるよう警告を出した。
Kishoo-choo wa sono chiku no juumin ni koozui ga okiru kamoshirenai node ki-o-tsukeru yoo keikoku o dashita.
(**b**) Lisa was given a caution for speeding.
リサはスピード違反で警告を受けた。
Risa wa supiido ihan de keikoku o uketa.

2. yo˥ojin 用心 •c [taking measures ahead of time for an unexpected eventuality and being mentally prepared for such] ⟪**prudence, carefulness, precaution**⟫, **chu˥ui 注意 •c [the act of fixing the mind on s.t. ⟪fig. "warning," "advice"⟫]** ⟪**attention, care**⟫

EX. Proceed with caution on this hazardous road.
危険な道路なので{用心/注意}して進むように。
Kikenna dooro na node {yoojin/chuui}-shite susumu yooni.

—— vt. **[to warn]**
⟨-ni⟩ {ke┌ikoku/chu˥ui}-suru ⟨〜に⟩{警告/注意}する ③ •c [for s.o. to cause s.o. to pay attention to s.t.] ⟪**warn**⟫

EX. (**a**) I must caution you that this is a new medicine, one that I have not yet tried myself.
これは新しい薬で、私自身まだ飲んだことがないということをあなたに{警告/注意}しておきます。
Kore wa atarashii kusuri de, watakushi-jishin mada nonda koto ga nai to iu koto o anata ni {keikoku/chuui}-shite okimasu.
(**b**) The doctor cautioned the patient about the dangers of smoking.
医者はタバコの害について患者に{警告/注意}した。
Isha wa tabako no gai ni-tsuite kanja ni {keikoku/chuui}-shita.
(**c**) I cautioned people to watch out for poisonous mushrooms.
毒きのこに注意するよう{警告/注意}しておきました。
Doku-kinoko ni chuui-suru yoo {keikoku/chuui}-shite okimashita.
(**d**) We were cautioned to be on the lookout for bears in the mountains.
山ではくまに注意するよう{警告/注意}された。
Yama de wa kuma ni chuui-suru yoo {keikoku/chuui}-sareta.

cautiously adv. **[with caution]**
chu┌ui-bu˥kaku 注意深く /⟨adj(*i*). ***ku*** of ***chuui-bukai*** careful/ ⟪**attentively**⟫, **yoojin-bu˥kaku 用心深く** /⟨adj(*i*). ***ku*** of ***yoojin-bukai*** careful/ **[with great care]** ⟪**carefully**⟫

cave n. **[a natural hollow under the ground or in the side of a hill or mountain]**
ho┌raana 洞穴, do┌okutsu 洞くつ •c

cavity n. **[a hollow place, as in a tooth]**
ku┌udoo 空洞 •c [an open empty area], a┌na 穴 [a hole], mu┌shi-ba 虫歯 [a hollow or soft place on a tooth caused by decay]

cease vt. **[to stop doing s.t. ⟨fml⟩]**
⟨-o⟩ ya┌meru ⟨〜を⟩やめる ② [for s.o. to discontinue s.t. that he/she has been doing, including a plan to do s.t.] ⟪**quit, give up**⟫
㊇ "quit a job"▷辞める, otherwise▷やめる

EX. The company has ceased producing weapons.
その会社は武器の生産をやめた。
Sono kaisha wa buki no seisan o yameta.

—— vi. **[for s.t. to stop]**
ya┌mu やむ ① [for a phenomenon, usually a natural one such as rain/snow/wind/thunder, to come to a halt]

EX. The rain ceased.
雨がやんだ。
Ame ga yanda.

cedar n. **[a cone-bearing, pine-like evergreen tree with aromatic durable wood or its wood]**
hi┌maraya˥-sugi ヒマラヤ杉

ceiling n. **[the inside overhead surface of a room, opposite the floor]**
te┌njoo 天井 •c

celebrate vt. **[for s.o. to commemorate s.t. with festivity]**
⟨-o⟩ i⌈wa⌉u ⟨～を⟩祝う ① **[for s.o. to express in words/deeds a feeling of joy on an auspicious occasion]**

EX. We celebrated Mr. Reed's 85th birthday with a dinner party at our home.
我々はうちで夕食会を開いて、リード氏の八十五歳の誕生日を祝った。
Ware-ware wa uchi de yuushoku-kai o hiraite, Riido-shi no hachi-juu-go-sai no tanjoo-bi o iwatta.

celebration n. **[a commemoration of s.t. joyous with ceremonies/festivities]**
i⌈wa⌉i 祝い, **o-⌈iwai** お祝い, **shu⌈ku⌉ga** 祝賀 **•c**, **shu⌈kuga⌉-kai** 祝賀会 **•c [a ceremony to celebrate s.t./s.o.]** ⟪**congratulation, felicitous ceremony**⟫

EX. We had a big celebration to commemorate the publication of his book.
彼の本の出版を記念して盛大な{お祝い/祝賀会}をした。
Kare no hon no shuppan o kinen-shite seidaina {o-iwai/shukuga-kai} o shita.

celery n. **[a plant with crisp leaf stalks that are eaten as a vegetable]**
se⌉rori セロリ **•f**

cell n. **[the basic structural unit of plant and animal life or a receptacle for generating electricity by means of chemical reactions]**
1. **sa⌈iboo** 細胞 **•c [the basic structural unit of plant and animal life]**
2. **de⌉nchi** 電池 **•c [a device for generating electricity by means of chemical reactions]** ⟪**dry battery**⟫

cellar n. **[a room or group of rooms below ground, usually under a building]**
chi⌈ka-chozo⌉o-{ko/shitsu} 地下貯蔵{庫/室} **•c [basement storage room]**

EX. Do you have a wine cellar in your home?
ご自宅にワイン保存用の地下貯蔵{庫/室}をお持ちですか。
Go-jitaku ni wain-hozon-yoo no chika-chozoo-{ko/shitsu} o o-mochi desu ka.

cement n. **[a powdered substance made of lime and clay which is mixed with water to make mortar or concrete]**
se⌈mento セメント **•f**

cent n. **[a 100th part of a dollar]**
se⌉nto セント **•f**

center n. **[the middle point of a circle or other area ⟪fig. "a pivot, axis," "a principal point, place, or object," "the core or middle of anything"⟫]**
chu⌈ushin 中心 **•c [a point equidistant from all points on the circumference of a circle or surface of a sphere]** ⟪**middle**⟫, **chu⌈uoo** 中央 **•c [the central part of s.t.]** ⟪**middle**⟫, **ma⌈nnaka** 真ん中 **[a point equidistant from all points on the outer perimeter of an area]** ⟪**middle, heart**⟫, **se⌉ntaa** センター **•f [the middle point or the central one of the three players in the outfield in baseball]**

EX. (**a**) He works in the center of Tokyo.
彼は東京の{中心/?中央/?真ん中/?センター}で働いている。
Kare wa Tookyoo no {chuushin/?chuuoo/?mannaka/?sentaa} de hataraite iru.
(**b**) Tokyo is located just about in the center of Japan.
東京は日本のほぼ{中心/中央/真ん中/*センター}にある。
*Tookyoo wa Nihon no hobo {chuushin/chuuoo/mannaka/*sentaa} ni aru.*
(**c**) Central Park is located in the center of New York.
セントラルパークはニューヨークの{中心/中央/真ん中/?センター}にある。
Sentoraru Paaku wa Nyuuyooku no {chuushin/chuuoo/mannaka/?sentaa} ni aru.
(**d**) There is a big shopping center nearby.
近くに大きなショッピング{センター/*中央/*中心/*真ん中}がある。
*Chikaku ni ookina shoppingu-{sentaa/*chuuoo/*chuushin/*mannaka} ga aru.*

centimeter n. **[a unit of measure equivalent to 1/100 of a meter]**
se⌈nchi-{me⌉etoru/me⌉etaa} センチ{メートル/メーター} **•f**, **se⌉nchi** センチ **•f**

central adj. **[in/near/of the center ⟪fig. "basic," "chief"⟫]**

chu⌈ushin no N 中心のN •c, chu⌈uo⌉o no N 中央のN •c

EX. (**a**) Integrated circuits are the central element of a computer.
集積回路はコンピューターの{中心/*中央}の要素です。
*Shuuseki-kairo wa konpyuutaa no {chuushin/*chuuoo} no yooso desu.*
(**b**) We have to get instructions from the central committee.
{中央/*中心}の委員会から指示を受けねばならない。
*{Chuuoo/*Chuushin} no iin-kai kara shiji o ukeneba naranai.*
(**c**) Focus the light on the central figure on stage.
ライトは舞台の{中央/中心}の人物に当ててください。
Raito wa butai no {chuuoo/chuushin} no jinbutsu ni atete kudasai.

century n. **[a period of 100 years esp. as calculated from 1 A.D.]**
se⌉iki 世紀 •c

EX. The 21st century will soon be here.
間もなく二十一世紀になる。
Ma-mo-naku ni-juu-is-seiki ni naru.

cereal n. **[any grain used for food, as wheat, oats, etc.; food made from grain, as oatmeal]**
ko⌈ku⌉motsu 穀物 •c [agricultural food staples such as rice, wheat, beans, etc.], o⌈otomi⌉iru オートミール •f [oatmeal], shi⌉riaru シリアル •f [a breakfast food made from grains]

EX. (**a**) Few Japanese have cereal for breakfast.
朝食に{シリアル/オートミール/*穀物}を食べる日本人は少ない。
*Chooshoku ni {shiriaru/ootomiiru/*kokumotsu} o taberu Nihon-jin wa sukunai.*
(**b**) Wheat, barley, and rye are examples of cereal.
小麦、大麦、ライ麦は{穀物/*シリアル/*オートミール}の例です。
*Komugi, oomugi, raimugi wa {kokumotsu/*shiriaru/*ootomiiru} no rei desu.*

ceremony n. **[a set of formal acts proper to a special occasion, as a religious rite]**
shi⌈ki⌉ 式 •c [a formal event conducted in a fixed sequence and according to certain rules of protocol]

EX. We had our wedding ceremony in Hawaii.
我々はハワイで結婚式を挙げた。
Ware-ware wa Hawai de kekkon-shiki o ageta.

certain adj. **[definite but unnamed or sure, positive]**

1. a⌉ru N あるN [an unspecified N] ⟪**some**⟫

EX. (**a**) A certain lady came to see me.
ある女の人が僕に会いに来た。
Aru onna no hito ga boku ni ai ni kita.
(**b**) I can speak Korean to a certain extent.
ある程度は韓国語が話せます。
Aru teido wa Kankoku-go ga hanase-masu.

2. ka⌈kujitsuna 確実な adj(*na*). **•c [not subject to doubt]**

EX. It is certain that she did it.
彼女がそれをしたことは確実だ。
Kanojo ga sore o shita koto wa kakujitsu da.

certainly adj. **[without doubt/by all means]**

1. ta⌉shikani 確かに /⟨adj(*na*). *ni* of *tashikana* certain/ [with certainty] ⟪**without doubt, surely**⟫

EX. I certainly did see a UFO.
私は確かにUFOを見た。
Watakushi wa tashikani Yuu-efu-oo o mita.

2. Ka⌈shikomarima⌉shita かしこまりました [by all means ⟨fml⟩], Sho⌈ochi-shima⌉shita 承知しました [an affirmative reply to an order, request, etc. ⟨fml⟩]

EX. (**a**) A: Would you take a message if there are any phone calls while I am gone?
留守中に電話があったら伝言を聞いておいて下さいませんか。
Rusu-chuu ni denwa ga attara dengon o kiite oite kudasaimasen ka.
B: Certainly.
{かしこまりました/承知しました}。

{Kashikomarimashita/Shoochi-shimashita}.
(**b**) A: Would you put your answer to this in writing?
この件は手紙でお返事をお願いします。
Kono ken wa tegami de o-henji o o-negai-shimasu.
B: Yes, certainly.
はい、{かしこまりました/承知しました}。
Hai, {kashikomarimashita/shoochi-shimashita}.

chain n. **[a flexible series of joined links]**
ku⌈sari 鎖, {**che⌉in/che⌉en**} {チェイン/チェーン} **•f**
EX. John fastened a chain around the front wheel of his bicycle.
ジョンは自分の自転車の前輪に{鎖/チェイン/チェーン}を巻き付けた。
Jon wa jibun no jitensha no zenrin ni {kusari/chein/cheen} o maki-tsuketa.

chair n. **[a seat, esp. for one person, usually having a back to rest against《fig. "a position of authority"》]**
1. i⌈su いす, **ko⌈shi-kake⌉** 腰掛け /〈V*masu* of *koshi-kakeru* ② sit/ **[s.t. for sitting on]**《**seat**》
EX. (**a**) Uncle Tom sat down in the chair.
トムおじさんは{いす/腰掛け}に座った。
Tomu-oji-san wa {isu/koshi-kake} ni suwatta.
(**b**) This is the chair that my father always loved to use.
これは父の愛用した{いす/腰掛け}です。
Kore wa chichi no aiyoo-shita {isu/koshi-kake} desu.
2. -choo ~長 **•c [a position/person of authority]**
EX. He is the chair of our department.
彼は私たちの学科長です。
Kare wa watakushi-tachi no gakka-choo desu.

chairman n. **[a person in charge of a meeting, committee, etc.]**
gi⌉choo 議長 **•c [s.o. who presides over a meeting], ga⌈kka⌉-choo** 学科長 **•c [s.o. who heads a department of a college]**
EX. Dr. Smith was chosen as chairman by a unanimous vote.
全員一致でスミス博士が{議長/学科長}に選ばれた。
Zen'in-itchi de Sumisu-hakase ga {gichoo/gakka-choo} ni eraba-reta.

chalk n. **[a piece of soft, whitish limestone used for writing on a blackboard]**
cho⌉oku チョーク **•f, ha⌈kuboku** 白墨 **•c**

chalkboard n. **[a board on which to write s.t. with chalk]**
ko⌈kuban 黒板 **•c [blackboard], cho⌈oku-bo⌉odo** チョークボード **•f**

challenge n. **[a call to a duel, contest, etc., or anything that calls for special effort]**
cho⌈osen 挑戦 **•c, cha⌈re⌉nji** チャレンジ **•f [the act of initiating or proposing a fight or contest with s.o.《fig. "attempting a new record or task with determination"》], ka⌈dai** 課題 **•c [a difficult task assigned to one]**《**problem**》
EX. (**a**) It is a tremendous challenge to learn to use a computer at age 80.
八十歳になってコンピューターの操作を覚えるのは大きな{挑戦/チャレンジ/?課題}である。
Hachi-jus-sai ni natte konpyuutaa no soosa o oboeru no wa ookina {choosen/charenji/?kadai} dearu.
(**b**) Constructing a space center will be one of the challenges of the 21st century.
宇宙センターの建設は二十一世紀の大きな{挑戦/チャレンジ/課題}の一つだろう。
Uchuu-sentaa no kensetsu wa ni-juu-is-seiki no ookina {choosen/charenji/kadai} no hitotsu daroo.
(**c**) The most urgent challenge facing us today is protecting the earth's natural environment.
今日我々が直面している最も緊急の{課題/*挑戦/*チャレンジ}は地球の自然環境を守ることだ。
*Konnichi ware-ware ga chokumen-shite iru mottomo kinkyuu no {kadai/*choosen/*charenji} wa chikyuu no*

C

shizen-kankyoo o mamoru koto da.

— vt. **[to call s.o. to a fight, contest, duel etc.]**

⟨-ni⟩ cho⌈osen-suru ⟨〜に⟩挑戦する •c ③ **[for s.o. to initiate or propose a fight or contest with s.o.]**

EX. He is constantly challenging the world record.
彼は常に世界記録に挑戦し続けている。
Kare wa tsune ni sekai-kiroku ni choosen-shi-tsuzukete iru.

challenging adj. **[arousing competitive interest]**

cha⌉renjinguna チャレンジングな adj(*na*). •f **[having the quality to stimulate s.o.]**, **ya⌈ri-gai ga a⌉ru (N)** やりがいがある(N) **[N worth doing]**

EX. An astronaut's job is a challenging task.
宇宙飛行士は{やりがいがある/チャレンジングな}仕事です。
Uchuu-hikoo-shi wa {yari-gai ga aru/charenjinguna} shigoto desu.

chamber n. **[a room, esp. a bedroom, or a meeting hall or a council/board, esp. for business purposes]**

1. he⌈ya⌉ 部屋 **[a partitioned space in a building]** **⟪room⟫**, **shi⌈nshitsu** 寝室 •c **[a room in which to sleep]** **⟪bedroom⟫**

2. ka⌈igi⌉-shitsu 会議室 •c **[a room in which to hold meetings]** **⟪conference room⟫**

3. ka⌈igi-sho 会議所 •c **[a council]** **⟪board⟫**

EX. In Japan, we have a Chamber of Commerce and Industry.
日本には、商工会議所がある。
Nihon ni wa, shookoo-kaigi-sho ga aru.

champion n. **[a person who takes first place in a competition]**

cha⌉npion チャンピオン •f

chance n. **[an opportunity or an accidental circumstance or a possibility/probability]**

1. ki⌈ka⌉i 機会 •c **[a suitable time for doing s.t.]**, **cha⌉nsu** チャンス •f **[a good time to do s.t.]** **⟪opportunity⟫**

EX. Take advantage of every chance to study languages.
あらゆる{機会/チャンス}を利用して語学を勉強しなさい。
Arayuru {kikai/chansu} o riyoo-shite gogaku o benkyoo-shinasai.

2. gu⌈uzen 偶然 •c **[s.t. that happens unexpectedly for no apparent reason]** **⟪accident, happen-stance⟫**

EX. I met an old friend in New York quite by chance the other day.
先日ニューヨークで全く偶然に昔の友だちに会った。
Senjitsu Nyuuyooku de mattaku guuzen ni mukashi no tomodachi ni atta.

3. mi⌈komi 見込み **[an anticipation/expectation/prediction that s.t. is very likely to occur]** **⟪possibility, probability, odds, prospects⟫**

EX. I don't believe that horse has any chance of winning.
あの馬が勝てる見込みはないと思います。
Ano uma ga kate-ru mikomi wa nai to omoimasu.

change vt. **[to make s.t./s.o./s.a. different or to exchange s.t. for s.t. else]**

1. ⟨-o⟩ ⟨-ni⟩ ka⌈eru ⟨〜を⟩⟨〜に⟩かえる ② **[to make s.t./s.o./s.a. different from what it/he/she was before]** **⟪alter, transform⟫**

㊥ "replace"▷代える, "exchange"▷換える, otherwise ▷変える

EX. (**a**) We cannot change our plans at this late stage.
今更計画を変えられません。
Imasara keikaku o kae-raremasen.
(**b**) It's difficult to change one's living habits as one gets older.
年をとるにつれて生活様式を変えるのが難しくなる。
Toshi o toru ni tsurete seikatsu-yooshiki o kaeru no ga muzukashiku naru.

2. ⟨-o⟩ ⟨-to⟩ to⌈ri-kaeru ⟨〜を⟩⟨〜と⟩取り替える ② **[for s.o. to replace s.t. with s.t. else]** **⟪exchange, replace⟫**, **⟨-o⟩ ⟨-to⟩ kookan-suru** ⟨〜を⟩⟨〜と⟩交換する ③ •c **[for s.o. to receive s.t. in exchange for s.t. else]** **⟪to exchange⟫**

EX. She changed the flat tire all by herself.

彼女はパンクしたタイヤを自分で取り替えた。
Kanojo wa panku-shita taiya o jibun de tori-kaeta.

3. ⟨-o⟩ ki-{⌈gae⌉ru/⌈kae⌉ru} ⟨〜を⟩着替える ② [for s.o. to put on other clothes than those worn previously]

EX. Lucy changes clothes two times a day.
ルーシーは一日二回服を着替える。
Ruushii wa ichi-nichi ni-kai fuku o ki-{gaeru/kaeru}.

4. ⟨-o⟩ no⌈ri-kae⌉ru ⟨〜を⟩乗り換える ② [for s.o. to leave one train, bus, etc. and board another]

EX. You have to change planes in London.
ロンドンで飛行機を乗り換えなくてはならない。
Rondon de hikoo-ki o nori-kaenakute wa naranai.

5. ⟨-o⟩ ⟨-ni⟩ ryo⌈ogae-suru ⟨〜を⟩⟨〜に⟩両替する ③ [for s.o. to give or receive a certain sum of money in exchange for an equivalent sum of money of a different type]

EX. (**a**) I would like to have $100 changed into yen.
百ドルを円に両替してもらいたい。
Hyaku-doru o en ni ryoogae-shite morai-tai.
(**b**) You can change money at the airport too.
お金は空港でも両替出来ます。
O-kane wa kuukoo de mo ryoogae-dekimasu.

6. ⟨-o⟩ ku⌈zu⌉su ⟨〜を⟩くずす ① [for s.o. to give or receive a certain sum of money in smaller denominations in exchange for an equivalent sum in larger denominations], ⟨-o⟩ ko⌈ma⌉kaku suru ⟨〜を⟩細かくする [for s.o. to make s.t. small]

EX. Could you change this ¥10,000 bill into thousand yen bills?
この一万円札を千円札に{くずして/細かくして}もらえますか。
Kono ichi-man-en-satsu o sen-en-satsu ni {kuzushite/komakaku shite} moraemasu ka.

— vi. **[to alter, vary]**

1. ka⌈waru かわる ① [to become different from what it/one was before] ((alter)), **he⌉nka-suru 変化する ③ •c [for s.t. to alter its shape, form, etc.]** ((alter, transform))
㊥ "change"▷変わる, "take the place of"▷代わる, "be replaced"▷替わる/換わる

EX. The life style of young Japanese has changed greatly in recent years.
最近、日本の若い人たちのライフスタイルは大変{変わった/変化した}。
Saikin, Nihon no wakai hito-tachi no raifu-sutairu wa taihen {kawatta/henka-shita}.

2. ki-{⌈gae⌉ru/⌈kae⌉ru} 着替える ② [for s.o. to put on other clothes than those worn previously]

3. no⌈ri-kae⌉ru 乗り換える ② [for s.o. to leave one train, bus, etc. and board another]

— n. **[alteration or variation or money returned when an amount paid for an item is greater than the amount owed or loose coins]**

1. he⌉nka 変化 •c [the emergence of a different quality/state in s.t. as it moves through space or time] ((alteration)), **he⌈nkoo 変更 •c [alteration of s.t. scheduled due to new circumstances]** ((alteration, modification))

EX. (**a**) He recognized a slight change in her attitude.
彼は彼女の態度の小さな{変化/*変更}に気が付いた。
*Kare wa kanojo no taido no chiisana {henka/*henkoo} ni ki-ga-tsuita.*
(**b**) There is no change in our schedule.
我々の予定に{変化/変更}はありません。
Ware-ware no yotei ni {henka/henkoo} wa arimasen.

2. tsu⌈ri-sen 釣銭 [money returned when an amount paid for an item is greater than the amount owed], o-⌈tsuri お釣り

EX. Keep the change.
{釣銭/お釣り}はとっておきなさい。

{Tsuri-sen/O-tsuri} wa totte-okinasai.

3. ko-⌈zeni 小銭 [loose coins]

EX. Do you have some small change?
小銭をお持ちですか。
Ko-zeni o o-mochi desu ka.

channel n. **[a wide strait, as between a continent and an island, or a navigable route between two bodies of water or a means of passage or a frequency band assigned to a radio/television station]**

C

1. ka⌈ikyoo 海峡 •c [an area of ocean which is long and slender (narrow) due to the presence of land on either side] ⟪a wide strait⟫

EX. (**a**) England and France are separated by the famous Dover Channel.
イギリスとフランスの間にドーバー海峡という有名な海峡がある。
Igirisu to Furansu no aida ni Doobaa-kaikyoo to iu yuumeina kaikyoo ga aru.
(**b**) The Tsugaru Straits are an ocean channel with beautiful scenery in the winter.
津軽海峡は冬景色が美しい海峡です。
Tsugaru-kaiyoo wa fuyu-geshiki ga utsukushii kaikyoo desu.

2. su⌉iro 水路 •c [that part of the water surface of a river, lake, ocean, etc. which is designated as a passage for ships] ⟪a navigable route, waterway, watercourse⟫

EX. There is a channel for freight ships between Lake Erie and Lake Ontario.
エリー湖とオンタリオ湖の間には貨物船のための水路がある。
Erii-ko to Ontario-ko no aida ni wa kamotsu-sen no tame no suiro ga aru.

3. ke⌈iro 経路 •c [a route which s.t. follows in reaching some place] ⟪a means of passage, course, route⟫

EX. The channel by which this information was acquired is a secret.
この情報の入手経路は秘密です。
Kono joohoo no nyuushu-keiro wa himitsu desu.

4. cha⌉nneru チャンネル •f [a television frequency band]

EX. How many TV channels are there in all in this area?
この辺ではテレビのチャンネルは全部でいくつありますか。
Kono hen de wa terebi no channeru wa zenbu de ikutsu arimasu ka.

chapter n. **[a main division, as of a book] sho⌉o 章 •c**

EX. This book has eight chapters.
この本は八章から成っている。
Kono hon wa has-shoo kara natte iru.

character n. **[a person, esp. with reference to behavior/personality, or a person in a play, novel, etc., or a letter/symbol used in writing/printing]**

1. se⌈ikaku 性格 •c [the characteristics/nature of s.o./s.t./s.a.] ⟪personality⟫

EX. (**a**) That actor can play the role of any character.
あの俳優はどんな性格の役でも出来る。
Ano haiyuu wa donna seikaku no yaku demo dekiru.
(**b**) Sylvia has a cheerful character and is loved by everybody.
シルビアは性格が明るくみんなに好かれる。
Shirubia wa seikaku ga akaruku minna ni suka-reru.

2. ya⌈ku⌉ 役 •c [the responsiblities assumed by s.o. or the role played by s.o. in a dramatic production] ⟪part, role, post, office, position, duty, use, a person in a play⟫

EX. He always plays the evil characters in Shakespeare's plays.
彼はシェークスピアの芝居ではいつも悪役を演じる。
Kare wa Sheekusupia no shibai de wa itsu-mo aku-yaku o enjiru.

3. ji⌉ 字 •c [a written symbol or handwriting] ⟪letter, symbol, word, hand, handwriting⟫

EX. (**a**) I'm poor at writing characters.
僕は字が下手です。
Boku wa ji ga heta desu.
(**b**) A: How many Chinese characters do the Japanese use?

日本人は漢字をいくつぐらい使っていますか。
Nihon-jin wa kanji o ikutsu-gurai tsukatte imasu ka.
B: There are some 2000 basic characters used for everyday purposes.
日常使う基本的なものは二千ぐらいです。
Nichijoo tsukau kihon-tekina mono wa ni-sen-gurai desu.

PHRASE: main character *shujinkoo* 主人公 •c

EX. The main character of this story is Cinderella.
このお話の主人公はシンデレラです。
Kono o-hanashi no shujinkoo wa Shinderera desu.

characteristic n. **[a distinguishing trait/quality]**
to⌈kuchoo 特徴 •c [s.t. which stands out about s.t./s.o./s.a. and which distinguishes him/her/it from others] ⟪special feature, individuality, peculiarity⟫, to⌈kushoku 特色 •c [a feature peculiar to s.t.] ⟪features⟫

EX. (**a**) Do you remember any characteristics of the criminal's face?
犯人の顔の{特徴/*特色}を覚えていますか。
*Hannin no kao no {tokuchoo/ *tokushoku} o oboete imasu ka.*
(**b**) A tendency to borrow and improve on elements from other cultures is one of the characteristics of Japanese civilization.
他の文化のものを借用し、それを改良するのが日本文明の{特色/特徴}の一つである。
Ta no bunka no mono o shakuyoo-shi, sore o kairyoo-suru no ga Nihon-bunmei no {tokushoku/tokuchoo} no hitotsu desu.

— adj. **[typical, distinctive]**
⟨-no⟩ to⌈kuchoo {to ⌈natte i⌉ru/de⌈a⌉ru} (N) ⟨～の⟩特徴{となっている/である}(N) /⟨V*te iru* of *naru* ① become/ [be a feature of s.t./s.o.]

EX. (**a**) Long hair is characteristic of Persian cats.
ペルシャ猫は毛の長いのが特徴{となっている/である}。
Perusha-neko wa ke no nagai no ga tokuchoo {to natte iru/dearu}.
(**b**) Sharpness of smell is highly characteristic of dogs.
きゅう覚が鋭いのは犬の大きな特徴{となっている/である}。
Kyuukaku ga surudoi no wa inu no ookina tokuchoo {to natte iru/dearu}.

characterize vt. **[for s.o. to describe the particular traits of, for s.t. to be a characteristic of]**
⟨-no⟩ to⌈kuchoo o a⌈rawa⌉su ⟨～の⟩特徴を表す ① [to represent the character or quality of s.o./s.t./s.a.], ⟨-o⟩ to⌈kuchoo-zukeru ⟨～を⟩特徴づける ② [for s.o. to describe the character or quality of s.t./s.o./s.a.] ⟪be special features of⟫

EX. This school is characterized by its unique traditional spirit.
独特の校風がこの学校{の特徴を表して/を特徴づけて}いる。
Dokutoku no koofuu ga kono gakkoo {no tokuchoo o arawashite/o tokuchoo-zukete} iru.

charcoal n. **[a black form of carbon made by partially burning wood, etc., in an airless kiln]**
su⌈mi⌉ 炭

charge n. **[s.t. that places a burden on s.o. (such as a monetary fee/care/responsibility)]**
1. ryo⌉okin 料金 •c [money paid for the use of s.t. or for services performed] ⟪cost, fee⟫, -dai ～代 [money required to buy or use s.t.] ⟪expense⟫

EX. What was the charge for the taxi?
タクシー{料金/代}はいくらでしたか。
Takushii-{ryookin/dai} wa ikura deshita ka.

2. se⌈wa⌉ 世話 •c [extending assistance to s.o. to enable him/her to do s.t. he/she could not accomplish alone] ⟪care⟫

EX. (**a**) I had charge of my niece and nephew while my sister and her husband were away on a trip to Europe.

妹夫婦がヨーロッパへ旅行に行っている間、私がおいとめいの世話をしていた。
Imooto-fuufu ga Yooroppa e ryokoo ni itte iru aida, watashi ga oi to mei no sewa o shite ita.
(**b**) Who is in charge of the campers in the junior high school group?
中学生グループのキャンパーの世話係はだれですか。
Chuugaku-sei guruupu no kyanpaa no sewa-gakari wa dare desu ka.

3. ka⌈ntoku 監督 •c [an act of directing some activity or s.o. who directs some activity] ((superintendent, manager, foreman, director; overseeing))

EX. He was in charge of 20 volunteers helping in the cleanup of the street after the parade.
彼はパレードの後の通りの清掃を手伝うボランティア二十人の監督をした。
Kare wa pareedo no ato no toori no seisoo o tetsudau borantia ni-juu-nin no kantoku o shita.

4. se⌈kini⌉n-sha 責任者 •c [a person responsible for s.t.]

—— vt. **[for s.o. to place a burden on s.o. (such as to demand a monetary fee or to accuse of doing wrong) or to supply s.t. with a quantity of electrical energy]**

1. ⟨-ni⟩ ⟨-o⟩ se⌈ikyuu-suru ⟨～に⟩⟨～を⟩請求する ③ •c [for s.o. to demand a monetary fee for s.t. or to demand that s.o. return/pay/lend s.t. to him] ((ask for, request, demand, apply for))

EX. How much did the garage charge you for the repair of your car?
修理工場は車の修理代をいくら請求しましたか。
Shuuri-koojoo wa kuruma no shuuri-dai o ikura seikyuu-shimashita ka.

2. ⟨-o⟩ se⌈me⌉ru ⟨～を⟩責める ② [for s.o. to state that s.o. has done s.t. wrong or illegal] ((accuse, call s.o. to account, hold s.o. accountable, blame, censure, reproach, torture, persecute))

EX. He was charged with carelessness in the matter.
彼はその件での不注意を責められた。
Kare wa sono ken de no fu-chuui o seme-rareta.

3. ⟨-o⟩ ju⌈uden-suru ⟨～を⟩充電する ③ •c [for s.o. to fill s.t. such as a battery with electrical energy]

EX. We need to charge the battery in our car.
うちの車はバッテリーを充電しなければならない。
Uchi no kuruma wa batterii o juuden-shinakereba naranai.

PHRASE: a person in charge *kakari* 係 [a person such as a clerk on duty or responsible for s.t.], *sekinin-sha* 責任者 •c [a person responsible for s.t.]

EX. Who is the person in charge of collecting dues?
会費を集める{係/責任者}はだれですか。
Kaihi o atsumeru {kakari/sekinin-sha} wa dare desu ka.

charm n. **[the power to attract or delight]**
mi⌈ryoku 魅力 •c [s.t. beautiful, excellent, or superb that captivates the heart and mind of s.o. who comes in contact with it] ((fascination))

EX. Her charm is irresistible.
彼女の魅力は抗しがたい。
Kanojo no miryoku wa kooshi-gatai.

charming adj. **[attractive or delightful]**
mi⌈ryoku-tekina 魅力的な adj(*na*). **•c [(usually said of a person) having charm] ((attractive, fascinating)), cha⌉aminguna チャーミングな** adj(*na*). **•f [for a woman to have charm]**

EX. I've never seen such a charming person.
あんなに{魅力的な/チャーミングな}人は今まで見たことがない。
Annani {miryoku-tekina/chaaminguna} hito wa ima made mita koto ga nai.

chart n. **[a sheet that provides information in the form of tables, graphs, etc.]**
hyo⌈o 表 •c [a set of facts or figures presented in an orderly written form for quick and easy comprehension] ((table, graph)), zu⌈hyoo 図表 •c [a drawing

presenting a graphic representation of facts and figures] ((graph)), cha⌉ato チャート •f

EX. The professor used lots of charts in his lecture.
教授は{表/図表/チャート}をたくさん使って講義をした。
Kyooju wa {hyoo/zuhyoo/chaato} o takusan tsukatte koogi o shita.

chase vt. **[for s.o./s.a. to run after s.o./s.a./s.t. in order to catch him/her/it]**
⟨-o⟩ o⌈i-kake⌉ru ⟨～を⟩追いかける ② [for s.o./s.a. to follow s.t./s.o./s.a. moving quickly in order to reach it/him/her] ((run after, follow, pursue))

EX. The cat chased the mouse.
猫はねずみを追いかけた。
Neko wa nezumi o oi-kaketa.

chat vi. **[for s.o. to talk in a light, informal manner]**
o-⌈sha⌉beri (o) suru おしゃべり(を)する ③ [for s.o. to talk informally with people about non-serious topics] ((chatter, gossip, talk))

EX. They chatted on the phone for half an hour.
彼らは三十分電話でおしゃべりをした。
Kare-ra wa san-jip-pun denwa de o-shaberi o shita.

— n. **[light informal talk]**
o-⌈sha⌉beri おしゃべり, za⌈tsudan 雑談 •c [informal talk about non-serious matters] ((chatter))

EX. I've come by for a little chat with you. Do you mind?
ちょっと{おしゃべり/雑談}に来たんですが、構いませんか。
Chotto {o-shaberi/zatsudan} ni kita n desu ga, kamaimasen ka.

chatter vi. **[for s.o. to talk quickly and continually without serious thought or purpose]**
pe⌉cha-kucha sha⌈be⌉ru ぺちゃくちゃしゃべる ② [for s.o. to talk continually and noisily] ((prattle, jabber, gabble))

EX. The children on the schoolbus were chattering noisily.
スクールバスに乗っている子どもたちはぺちゃくちゃしゃべってうるさかった。
Sukuuru-basu ni notte iru kodomo-tachi wa pecha-kucha shabette urusakatta.

— n. **[foolish talk]**
o-⌈sha⌉beri おしゃべり [informal talk about non-serious matters] ((chat)), ba⌈ka-ba⌉nashi ばか話 [informal, non-serious talk about unimportant topics] ((chat))

cheap adj. **[low in price, of little value]**
1. ya⌈su⌉i 安い adj(*i*). **[low in price or requiring less money than anticipated] ((inexpensive, low-priced, low, economical))**
↔ takai 高い adj(*i*).

EX. (**a**) This car was cheap considering all the options that came with it.
色々なオプションがついていることを考えると、この車は安かった。
Iro-irona opushon ga tsuite iru koto o kangaeru to, kono kuruma wa yasukatta.
(**b**) Things are often cheaper at supermarkets than at department stores.
デパートよりスーパーマーケットの方が値段が安いことが多い。
Depaato yori suupaa-maaketto no hoo ga nedan ga yasui koto ga ooi.

2. ya⌈su-ppo⌉i 安っぽい adj(*i*). **[of little value, blatantly inferior in quality] ((cheapish, flashy, tawdry))**

EX. My sister always buys cheap jewelry.
うちの妹はいつも安っぽい宝石を買う。
Uchi no imooto wa itsu-mo yasu-ppoi hooseki o kau.

cheat vt. **[for s.o. to defraud/swindle s.o.]**
1. ⟨-o⟩ da⌈ma⌉su ⟨～を⟩だます ① [for s.o. to cause s.o. to believe s.t. which is not ture], ⟨-o⟩ go⌈makasu ⟨～を⟩ごまかす ① [for s.o. to do s.t. in such a way as to deliberately cause others not to notice s.t. which would be to his/her disadvantage if revealed]

EX. (**a**) The stockbroker cheated the customer.
株屋は客を{だました/*ごまかした}。
*Kabu-ya wa kyaku o {damashita/ *gomakashita}.*
(**b**) The passenger cheated on his fare.

その乗客は運賃を{ごまかした/*だました}。
*Sono jookyaku wa unchin o {gomakashita/*damashita}.*

2. ka⌈nningu-suru カンニングする ③ •f [for s.o. to look at books or notes while taking a test or otherwise give/receive illegitimate aid on a test]

C

EX. If you cheat on this test, you will be asked to leave the room.
この試験でカンニングしたら、部屋を出てもらいます。
Kono shiken de kanningu-shitara, heya o dete moraimasu.

check n. **[a test/inspection that ascertains performance or an inquiry/examination or a mark (✔) to indicate approval/verification or a written order directing a bank to pay money or a bill at a restaurant or a ticket/token verifying ownership of an item left in the care of s.o. else or a pattern of squares]**

1. shi⌈rabe⌉ 調べ [an act of investigating or a musical tune], ke⌉nsa 検査 •c [looking at s.t./s.o./s.a. carefully to see if it/he/she meets a standard or if there is anything wrong with it/him/her, often in an official capacity] ⟪investigation, inquiry, examination, inspection, search⟫, che⌉kku チェック •f

EX. (**a**) The suspicious man received a thorough check at customs.
不審な男は、税関で厳しい{調べ/検査/チェック}を受けた。
Fushinna otoko wa, zeikan de kibishii {shirabe/kensa/chekku} o uketa.
(**b**) Everyone undergoes a check of their belongings when they board a plane.
だれでも飛行機に乗るときは所持品の{調べ/検査/チェック}を受ける。
Dare-demo hikoo-ki ni noru toki wa shoji-hin no {shirabe/kensa/chekku} o ukeru.
(**c**) I had them do an engine check at the gas station.
ガソリンスタンドでエンジンの{検査/チェック/*調べ}をしてもらった。
*Gasorin-sutando de enjin no {kensa/chekku/*shirabe} o shite moratta.*

2. che⌉kku no shi⌈rushi チェックの印 [a check mark] (✔)

EX. Put a check by the languages you can speak.
あなたが話せる言葉の所にチェックの印をして下さい。
Anata ga hanase-ru kotoba no tokoro ni chekku no shirushi o shite kudasai.

3. ko⌈gi⌉tte 小切手 [a written order directing a bank to pay money], che⌉kku チェック •f [an instrument of payment]

EX. Please write a check for $100.
百ドルの{小切手/チェック}を切って下さい。
Hyaku-doru no {kogitte/chekku} o kitte kudasai.

4. se⌈ikyuu-sho 請求書 •c [a written document requesting payment or a bill in general], ka⌈njoo-gaki 勘定書 [a bill for food eaten or drinks consumed], o-⌈kanjoo お勘定 •c [a bill for food eaten or drinks consumed ⟨s⟩]

EX. The check, please?
{請求書/勘定書/お勘定}お願いします。
{Seikyuu-sho/Kanjoo-gaki/O-kanjoo} o-negai-shimasu.

5. a⌈i-fuda 合い札 [a ticket handed over to s.o. as proof of having stored/deposited s.t.], ha⌈nken 半券 •c [the stub of a ticket] ⟪ticket, token⟫

EX. I lost my baggage check for the suitcase.
スーツケースの{合い札/半券}を無くしてしまった。
Suutsukeesu no {ai-fuda/hanken} o nakushite shimatta.

6. ko⌈oshi-jima 格子じま [a grid pattern], che⌉kku チェック •f

EX. She likes to wear skirts with a check pattern.
彼女は{格子じま/チェック}のスカートをはくのが好きだ。
Kanojo wa {kooshi-jima/chekku} no sukaato o haku no ga suki da.

kooshi-jima

— vt. **[to restrain, curb, block or for s.o. to test, verify, etc. by examination/comparison or for s.o. to deposit temporarily]**
1. 〈-o〉 **so⌉shi-suru** 〈～を〉阻止する ③ **•c [for s.o. to get in the way of s.o./s.t. and stop his/her/its action]** **《restrain, block, stop, hold back, obstruct》**

EX. The authorities are trying to check the flow of illegal aliens.
当局は不法入国外国人の潜入を阻止しようとしている。
Tookyoku wa fuhoo-nyuukoku-gaikoku-jin no sennyuu o soshi-shiyoo to shite iru.

2. 〈-o〉 **shi⌈rabe⌉ru** 〈～を〉調べる ② **[for s.o. to observe directly or inquire/read about s.t./s.o./s.a. in order to determine or ascertain s.t. unknown or uncertain about it/him/her], 《investigate, examine, study, inspect》**, 〈-o〉 **ta⌈shikame⌉ru** 〈～を〉確かめる ② **[for s.o. to ascertain s.t.], 《ascertain, make sure, confirm, verify》**, 〈-o〉 **che⌉kku-suru** 〈～を〉チェックする ③ **•f [for s.o. to find out if s.t. is really so or not] 《ascertain, make sure, see, confirm, verify》**

EX. Would you check to see if that information is correct?
その情報が正しいかどうかを{調べて/確かめて/チェックして}下さいませんか。
Sono joohoo ga tadashii ka doo ka o {shirabete/tashikamete/chekku-shite} kudasaimasen ka.

3. 〈-o〉 **(i⌈chi⌉ji) a⌈zuke⌉ru** 〈～を〉(一時)預ける ② **[for s.o. to ask s.o. else to take care of s.o./s.t./s.a. for a while] 《leave, trust, entrust》**

EX. Please check your bag at the counter before entering the store.
店へ入る前にかばんをカウンターに一時預けて下さい。
Mise e hairu mae ni kaban o kauntaa ni ichiji azukete kudasai.

cheek n. **[either side of the face below the eye]**
ho⌉o ほお, **ho⌉ho** ほほ 〈w〉, **ho⌈ppe⌉ta** ほっぺた 〈s〉

cheer n. **[happiness or a shout of happiness, encouragement, or praise]**
ka⌈ssai 喝さい **•c [an excited shout of approval, etc. (after s.t. has been done)] 《applause》**, **ge⌈kirei** 激励 **•c [encouragement (before s.t. is done)]**

EX. The spectators showered the players with cheers.
観客は選手{に喝さいを与えた/を歓声をあげて激励した}。
Kankyaku wa senshu {ni kassai o ataeta/o kansei o agete gekirei-shita}.

— vt. **[to comfort or gladden]**
〈-o〉 **ge⌈nki-zuke⌉ru** 〈～を〉元気づける ② **[for s.o. to give s.o. the spirit, energy, vigor to do s.t. of his/her own volition] 《encourage》**

EX. Dick seems depressed these days, so why don't we try and cheer him up?
ディックは最近落ち込んでいるみたいだから元気づけてやろうよ。
Dikku wa saikin ochikonde iru mitaida kara genki-zukete yaroo yo.

cheerful adj. **[full of cheer]**
yo⌈okina 陽気な adj(*na*). **•c [for s.o. to have a happy disposition and behave pleasantly] 《happy, merry》**, **yu⌉kaina** 愉快な adj(*na*). **•c [experiencing happiness or merriment deriving from a sense of satisfaction with s.t. or causing such a feeling in one] 《pleasant, delightful, merry, joyful》**

EX. Our new secretary is a very cheerful woman.
今度の秘書はとても{陽気な/愉快な}人です。
Kondo no hisho wa totemo {yookina/yukaina} hito desu.

cheerfully adv. **[in a gay or bright maner]**
yo⌈okini 陽気に /〈adj(*na*). *ni* of *yookina* cheerful/ **•c [in a happy a or merry manner]**, **yu⌉kaini** 愉快に /〈adj(*na*). *ni* of *yukaina* delightful/ **•c [in a happy, pleasant satisfying way]**

cheese n. **[a solid food made from milk curds]**
chi⌉izu チーズ **•f**

chemical adj. **[of, made by, or used in chemistry]**

ka⌉gaku no N 化学のN •c [of chemistry], ka⌈gaku-tekina 化学的な adj(*na*). **•c [related to chemistry]**

EX. Dad is conducting some kind of chemical experiment in his laboratory.
父は実験室で何か{化学の/化学的な}実験を行っている。
Chichi wa jikken-shitsu de nani-ka {kagaku no/kagaku-tekina} jikken o okonatte iru.

C

—— n. **[any substance used in or obtained by a process related to chemistry]**
ka⌈gaku-ya⌉kuhin 化学薬品 •c [a chemical substance/medicine]

chemist n. **[a specialist in chemistry]**
ka⌈gaku⌉-sha 化学者 •c [a specialist in chemistry], ya⌈kuza⌉i-shi 薬剤師 •c [a pharmacist, druggist]

chemistry n. **[the science dealing with the composition and properties of substances and with the reactions by which substances are produced from or converted into other substances]**
ka⌉gaku 化学 •c

EX. Dr. Johnson won a Nobel Prize in chemistry.
ジョンソン博士は化学の分野でノーベル賞を授与された。
Jonson-hakase wa kagaku no bun'ya de Nooberu-shoo o juyo-sareta.

NOTE: *Kagaku* in this sense is often referred to as *bake-gaku* to distinguish it in spoken Japanese from the homophonous word *kagaku* "science."

cherish vt. **[to hold s.o./s.t. dear]**
⟨-o⟩ da⌈iji⌉ni suru ⟨〜を⟩大事にする ③ [for s.o. to see to it that s.t. precious and irreplaceable is not harmed/marred/lost] ((**take good care of, be careful of, value**))

EX. She cherishes the cat as if it were her own child.
彼女は猫を我が子のように大事にしている。
Kanojo wa neko o waga-ko no yooni daijini shite iru.

cherry n. **[a small, fleshy fruit with a smooth, hard pit]**
sa⌈kuranbo さくらんぼ

cherry blossom n. **[the flower of a cherry tree]**
sa⌈kura (no ha⌈na⌉) 桜(の花)

EX. The cherry blossoms are in full bloom.
桜(の花)が満開だ。
Sakura (no hana) ga mankai da.

PHRASE: cherry blossom viewing *hana-mi* 花見, cherry tree *sakura no ki* 桜の木

sakura (no hana)

chess n. **[a game played on a checkerboard by two players, each using sixteen pieces]**
che⌉su チェス •f

NOTE: *Shoogi* is a Japanese game which resembles chess.

EX. I like to play chess.
私はチェスをするのが好きだ。
Watakushi wa chesu o suru no ga suki da.

chest n. **[the part of the body enclosed by the ribs and breastbone or a cabinet with drawers, esp. one for storing clothes]**
1. mu⌈ne⌉ 胸 [the part of the body enclosed by the ribs and breastbone, also used as a euphemism for "breast"] ((**breast, bosom, bust**))

EX. He said he had a pain in his chest.
彼は胸に痛みがあると言った。
Kare wa mune ni itami ga aru to itta.

2. ta⌈nsu たんす [a piece of furniture with drawers for storing clothes, etc.] ((**a cabinet**))

EX. We need to get a big chest for the bedroom.
寝室用に大きなたんすが必要だ。
Shinshitsu-yoo ni ookina tansu ga hitsuyoo da.

chew vt. **[for s.o./s.a. to bite and crush with the teeth]**
⟨-o⟩ ka⌉mu ⟨〜を⟩かむ ① [for s.o./s.a. to pinch s.t. between the upper and lower teeth and cut/crush it] ((**bite, gnaw, masticate**))

EX. The more you chew dried cuttlefish, the tastier it becomes.

するめはかめばかむほど味が出る。
Surume wa kameba kamu hodo aji ga deru.

Chicago n.
Shi⌈ka⌉go シカゴ •f

chicken n. **[a common farm bird raised for its edible eggs and flesh, esp. a young one, or its flesh]**
ni⌈watori 鶏 [hen/cock], to⌈ri-niku とり肉 [the meat of a bird]
EX. (a) When I was little, we raised chickens.
私が小さいときうちでは鶏を飼っていた。
Watakushi ga chiisai toki uchi de wa niwatori o katte ita.
(b) Which do you like better, chicken or beef?
とり肉と牛肉とどちらが好きですか。
Tori-niku to gyuuniku to dochira ga suki desu ka.

chief n. **[the head of a group of persons or organization]**
-choo ～長 •c [a position/person of authority], chi⌉ifu チーフ •f
EX. He is our section chief.
彼が我々の課の{課長/チーフ}だ。
Kare ga ware-ware no ka no {kachoo/chiifu} da.
adj. **[most important]**
o⌉mona 主な adj(*na*). **[the most prominent/significant of a group of entities under consideration] ⟪principal, main⟫**
EX. The chief points of the article are as follows.
記事の主なポイントは次のとおりです。
Kiji no omona pointo wa tsugi no toori desu.

chiefly adv. **[most importantly, mainly]**
o⌉moni 主に /⟨adj(*na*). *ni* of *omona* main/, shu-⌈to⌉-shite 主として ⟪principally, mainly⟫
EX. I'm reading mainly books on Chinese history.
私は{主に/主として}中国史の本を読んでいます。
Watakushi wa {omoni/shu-to-shite} Chuugoku-shi no hon o yonde imasu.

child n. **[an infant or a boy/girl before puberty or a son/daughter]**
ko⌈domo 子供 ↔ otona 大人; ko 子 [a person born from the sexual union of a man and woman or a still immature person/animal] ↔ oya 親
EX. (a) I am no longer a child.
私はもう{子供/*子}ではない。
*Watakushi wa moo {kodomo/*ko} dewanai.*
(b) Their child is a boy.
彼らの{子供/子}は男の子ですよ。
Kare-ra no {kodomo/ko} wa otoko-no-ko desu yo.
(c) This is my own child.
この子は私の{子供/子}です。
Kono ko wa watashi no {kodomo/ko} desu.

childhood n. **[the state/period of being a child]**
yo⌈onen-ji⌉dai 幼年時代 •c [the period during which one is a small child], yo⌈onen⌉-ki 幼年期 •c [the period of time from a child's first memories up to entering grade school] ⟪infancy⟫, ko⌈domo no ko⌉ro 子供のころ [a period during which one is a child]
EX. I experienced war during my childhood.
私は{幼年時代/幼年期/子供のころ}に戦争を体験した。
Watakushi wa {yoonen-jidai/yoonen-ki/kodomo no koro} ni sensoo o taiken-shita.

childish adj. **[of/like a child, immature, foolish]**
ko⌈domo-jimi⌉ta N 子供じみたN /⟨Vinf. past of *kodomo-jimiru* ② appear to have the undesirable properties of a child/ [looking/appearing to have the undesirable properties of a child] ⟪immature⟫, ko⌈domo-ppo⌉i 子供っぽい adj(*i*).
EX. He often displays a childish attitude.
彼はよく{子供じみた/子供っぽい}態度をとる。
Kare wa yoku {kodomo-jimita/kodomo-ppoi} taido o toru.

chill n. **[mild but unpleasant coldness, often accompanied by shivers]**

tsu⌈meta-sa 冷たさ /⟨adj(*i*). stem of *tsumetai* cold + suf. *sa* ness/ [having a low temperature physically perceptible to the touch] **《coldness》, sa⌈mu-ke⌉ 寒気 [a feeling of coldness in the body, often accompanied by fever and shivering] 《feverish, shivering》, ka⌉nki 寒気 •c [the state of the air being cold]**

EX. (**a**) I had the chills last night, but I'm okay now.
昨夜{寒気/*寒気/*冷たさ}がしましたが、今は大丈夫です。
*Sakuya {samu-ke/*kanki/*tsumeta-sa} ga shimashita ga, ima wa daijoobu desu.*
(**b**) I felt the morning chill throughout my entire body.
朝の空気の{冷たさ/寒気/*寒気}が身にしみた。
*Asa no kuuki no {tsumeta-sa/kanki/*samu-ke} ga mi ni shimita.*

chilly adj. **[mildly or moderately cold]**
u⌈sura-samu⌉i 薄ら寒い adj(*i*). **[causing a slight sensation of coldness], hi⌈e-bi⌉e-suru 冷え冷えする ③ [for wind/air to be cold] 《cold》**

EX. Mornings in the mountains are chilly even in summer.
山の朝は夏でも{薄ら寒いです/冷え冷えします}。
Yama no asa wa natsu demo {usura-samui desu/hie-bie-shimasu}.

chimney n. **[the passage/structure through which smoke escapes from a fire place, often extending above the roof]**
e⌈ntotsu 煙突 •c

EX. The factory had three chimneys.
その工場には三本の煙突が立っていた。
Sono koojoo ni wa san-bon no entotsu ga tatte ita.

chin n. **[the part of the face below the lower lip]**
a⌈go⌉ あご [the bony parts of the face to which the teeth are attached] 《jaw》

China n. **[a large country in East Asia]**
Chu⌉ugoku 中国 •c

china n. **[any porcelain ware]**
se⌈to-mono 瀬戸物 [porcelain ware] 《crockery》, ji⌉ki 磁器 •c 《porcelain》, to⌉oki 陶器 •c, ya⌈ki-mono 焼き物

EX. (**a**) The tourists bought lots of china in Japan as souvenirs.
旅行者はお土産に日本で{瀬戸物/磁器/焼き物/陶器}をたくさん買った。
Ryokoo-sha wa o-miyage ni Nihon de {seto-mono/jiki/yaki-mono/tooki} o takusan katta.

seto-mono

(**b**) My hobby is to collect old chinaware.
私の趣味は古い{瀬戸物/磁器/焼き物/陶器}を集めることだ。
Watakushi no shumi wa furui {seto-mono/jiki/yaki-mono/tooki} o atsumeru koto da.

Chinese n. **[a person from China or the people of China or the language principally spoken in China]**
1. Chu⌈ugoku⌉-jin 中国人 •c [a person from China or the people of China]
2. Chu⌈ugoku-go 中国語 •c [the principal language of China]

EX. He is Chinese and so he speaks Chinese as his mother tongue.
彼は中国人だから中国語を母語として話す。
Kare wa Chuugoku-jin da kara Chuugoku-go o bogo to-shite hanasu.

— adj. **[of China, its people, language, etc.]**
1. Chu⌉ugoku no 中国のN •c [of China as a country]
2. Chu⌈ugoku⌉-jin no 中国人のN •c [of a person or people from China]
3. Chu⌈ugoku-go no 中国語のN •c [of the language of China]

PHRASE: Chinese character *kanji* 漢字 •c, Chinese cuisine *chuuka-ryoori* 中華料理 •c

chip n. **[a small piece of wood, etc., cut/broken off from a larger whole]**
ki⌈re-hashi 切れ端 [a small piece of s.t. cut/broken off from a larger whole]

EX. Small chips of wood were scattered all over the place.
その辺り一帯に木の切れ端が散らばっていた。
Sono atari ittai ni ki no kire-hashi ga chirabatte ita.

PHRASE: potato chips *poteto-chippu* ポテトチップ •f

chocolate n. **[a drink or candy made from roasted and ground cacao seeds]**
cho⌈kore⌉eto チョコレート •f

choice n. **[the act of choosing or s.t./s.o. chosen]**
1. se⌈ntaku 選択 •c **[the act of choosing what one believes to be the best from among two/more options]** ((selection))

EX. The choice of one's occupation is a serious matter.
職業の選択は重大問題です。
Shokugyoo no sentaku wa juudai-mondai desu.

2. e⌈ra⌉nda {mo⌈no⌉/hi⌈to/tokoro} 選んだ{物/人/ところ} **[thing/person chosen]** ((selected thing))

EX. My parents didn't concur in my choice of a job.
私が就職先として選んだところには両親が反対した。
Watashi ga shuushoku-saki to shite eranda tokoro ni wa ryooshin ga hantai-shita.

choose vt. **[for s.o./s.a. to decide on s.o./s.t./s.a. for a particular purpose from among all that are available]**
⟨-o⟩ e⌈ra⌉bu ⟨～を⟩選ぶ ① **[for s.o./s.a. to single out s.t./s.o./s.a. out of several as being the most desirable for a particular purpose]** ((select, make a choice of, prefer)), **⟨-o⟩ se⌈ntaku-suru** ⟨～を⟩選択する ③ •c **[for s.o. to decide on s.t. out of several as being the most desirable for a particular purpose]** ((select, make choice of, prefer))

EX. (**a**) I chose Korean for my second foreign language.
第二外国語に韓国語を{選びました/選択しました}。
Dai-ni-gaikoku-go ni Kankoku-go o {erabimashita/sentaku-shimashita}.
(**b**) She was chosen as the flagbearer.
彼女が旗手に{選ばれた/*選択された}。
*Kanojo ga kishu ni {eraba-reta/*sentaku-sareta}.*

chop vt. **[for s.o. to cut s.t. by blows with a sharp tool]**
⟨-o⟩ ta⌈taki-ki⌉ru ⟨～を⟩たたき切る ① **[for s.o. to hit s.t. repeatedly and cut it]** ((hack, mangle, cut by blows)), **⟨-o⟩ ki⌈ri-kizamu** ⟨～を⟩切り刻む ① **[for s.o. to cut s.t. into small pieces with a sharp instrument]** ((cut into pieces, hack)), **⟨-o⟩ ki⌉zamu** ⟨～を⟩刻む ① **[for s.o. to cut s.t. into small pieces]**, **⟨-o⟩ mi⌈jin-giri ni suru** ⟨～を⟩みじん切りにする ③ **[for s.o. to cut up vegetables into as fine/small pieces as possible]**

EX. (**a**) The butcher chopped the meat.
肉屋は肉を{たたき切った/切り刻んだ/刻んだ/*みじん切りにした}。
*Niku-ya wa niku o {tataki-kitta/kiri-kizanda/kizanda/*mijin-giri ni shita}.*
(**b**) Mother chopped the onions finely.
母はたまねぎを{細かく刻んだ/細かく切り刻んだ/みじん切りにした/*細かくたたき切った}。
*Haha wa tamanegi o {komakaku kizanda/komakaku kiri-kizanda/mijin-giri ni shita/*komakaku tataki-kitta}.*

—— n. **[a short, sharp stroke or a cut of meat and bone]**
1. cho⌉ppu チョップ •f **[a short, sharp stroke]**

EX. Rikidoozan, a pro wrestler, was noted for his karate chops.
プロレスラーの力道山は空手チョップで有名だった。
Puroresuraa no Rikidoozan wa karate-choppu de yuumei datta.

2. cho⌉ppu チョップ •f **[a cut of meat]**

EX. I ordered pork chops for dinner.
夕食にポークチョップを注文した。
Yuushoku ni pooku-choppu o chuumon-shita.

chopsticks n. **[two small sticks held together in one hand and used in Japan and certain other Asian countries for eating]**
ha˥shi はし

EX. Many Westerners are now pretty good at using chopsticks.
今でははしを上手に使う西洋人が多い。
Ima de wa hashi o joozuni tsukau seiyoo-jin ga ooi.

C

chord n. **[a straight line connecting two points ⟪fig. "a feeling/emotion"⟫]**
1. ki˥nsen 琴線 •c [heartstrings] ⟪emotion, empathy⟫

EX. His speech touched a chord in me.
彼の演説は私の心の琴線に触れた。
Kare no enzetsu wa watashi no kokoro no kinsen ni fureta.

2. wa˥on 和音 •c, ko˥odo コード •f [combination of two/more musical notes sounded at the same time]

chore n. **[a routine task]**
za˥tsuji 雑事 •c [miscellaneous work other than one's job proper] ⟪routine work, miscellaneous personal affairs⟫, shi˥goto 仕事 [an activity performed for a particular purpose other than amusement and on which one expends time and effort]

EX. Housewives are busy all day long with chores.
主婦は一日中{雑事/仕事}が絶えない。
Shufu wa ichi-nichi-juu {zatsuji/shigoto} ga taenai.

chorus n. **[a group of people who sing together]**
ga˥sshoo 合唱 •c, ko˥orasu コーラス •f

Christ n. **[Jesus of Nazareth, regarded by Christans as the Messiah]**
Ki˥risuto キリスト •f

Christian n. **[a believer in Jesus as the Christ or in the religion based on the teachings of Jesus]**
Ki˥risuto-kyoo˥to キリスト教徒 •f+c, Ku˥ri˥suchan クリスチャン •f

EX. Christians make up less than two percent of Japan's population.
{クリスチャン/キリスト教徒}は日本の人口の二パーセント以下である。
{Kurisuchan/Kirisuto-kyooto} wa Nihon no jinkoo no ni-paasento-ika dearu.

—— adj. [of Jesus Christ, his followers, or Christianity]
Ki˥risuto-kyoo no N キリスト教のN •f+c [of the religion of Christ], Ki˥risuto-kyoo˥to no N キリスト教徒のN •f+c [relating to the followers of Christ], Ku˥risu˥chan no N クリスチャンのN •f

EX. (a) Our daughter attends a Christian school.
うちの娘は{キリスト教/クリスチャン/*キリスト教徒}の学校へ通っている。
*Uchi no musume wa {Kirisuto-kyoo/Kurisuchan/*Kirisuto-kyooto} no gakkoo e kayotte iru.*
(b) I have several Christian friends at school.
学校の友達の中に{キリスト教徒/クリスチャン/*キリスト教}の友達が何人かいる。
*Gakkoo no tomodachi no naka ni {Kirisuto-kyooto/Kurisuchan/*Kirisuto-kyoo} no tomodachi ga nan-nin-ka iru.*

Christianity n. **[the Christian religion]**
Ki˥risuto-kyoo キリスト教 •f+c

Christmas n. **[a holiday on December 25 celebrating the birth of Jesus Christ]**
Ku˥risu˥masu クリスマス •f, Ko˥ota˥n-setsu 降誕節 •c

NOTE: *Kootan-setsu* is archaic and rarely used in modern Japanese.

chromosome n. **[any of the microscopic rod-shaped bodies in animal and plant cells bearing genes]**
se˥nshoku-tai 染色体 •c

chrysanthemum n. **[a late-blooming plant of the composite family having brightly-colored flowers]**
ki˥ku˥ 菊 •c ⟪mum⟫, ki˥ku˥ no ha˥na˥ 菊の花 ⟪mum flower⟫

kiku no hana

EX. The crest of Japan's royal family employs a pattern of chrysanthemums.
日本の皇室の紋章は菊の花の模様を用いている。

Nihon no kooshitsu no monshoo wa kiku no hana no moyoo o mochiite iru.

chuckle vi. **[to laugh softly in a low tone]**
ku⌈su⌉-kusu wa⌈rau くすくす笑う ① [for s.o. to laugh softly]
— n. **[a soft, low-toned laugh]**
ku⌈su-kusu-wa⌉rai くすくす笑い /⟨V*masu* of *kusu-kusu warau* ① giggle/ [soft laugh]

chunk n. **[a thick piece of s.t.]**
ka⌈tamari 塊 [a piece of solid substance]
EX. Mother bought a chunk of beef for making stew.
母はシチュー用に牛肉の塊を買った。
Haha wa shichuu-yoo ni gyuuniku no katamari o katta.

church n. **[a building for Christian worship]**
kyo⌈okai 教会 •c

cigar n. **[a compact roll of tobacco leaves for smoking]**
ha-⌈maki 葉巻, shi⌉gaa シガー •f

cigarette n. **[a small roll of finely cut tobacco wrapped in thin paper for smoking]**
shi⌉garetto シガレット •f, ta⌈bako たばこ [tobacco]

circle n. **[a round plane figure made up of points which are at an equal distance from the center or any circular object, formation, or arrangement such as a ring ⟪fig. "a group of people with common interests"⟫]**
1. e⌉n 円 •c [the state of being round] ⟪**curve**⟫
2. ma⌉ru 丸 [s.t. round/spherical] ⟪**a circular object**⟫, **wa⌉ 輪 [that which results from s.t. linear such as a string or wire connected at both ends into a ring]** ⟪**ring**⟫
EX. A boy drew a circle in the sand with his finger.
少年は指で砂に{円/丸/輪}をかいた。
Shoonen wa yubi de suna ni {en/maru/wa} o kaita.
3. na⌈kama⌉ 仲間 [a person in one's in-group with whom one frequently spends time, excluding one's relatives, spouse, and offspring ⟪fig. "the same kind"⟫] ⟪**fellow**⟫, **sa⌉akuru サークル •f [a group of people with common interests]**
EX. He is the youngest of our circle.
彼は私たちの{仲間/サークル}では一番若い。
Kare wa watashi-tachi no {nakama/saakuru} de wa ichiban wakai.
— vt. **[to move in a circular motion with s.t. as its/one's center]**
⟨-o⟩ ma⌈waru ⟨〜を⟩回る ① [to describe a round path of motion about s.t. as its/one's center] ⟪**turn, go around, rotate, revolve**⟫
EX. The earth circles the sun.
地球は太陽の回りを回っている。
Chikyuu wa taiyoo no mawari o mawatte iru.

circular adj. **[in the shape of a circle]**
e⌈nkei no N 円形のN •c [having the shape of a circle], ma⌈rui 丸い adj(*i*). **[having the shape of a circle, ring, or ball]**
EX. There is a circular theater in the center of the park.
公園の中心に{円形の/丸い}劇場がある。
Kooen no chuushin ni {enkei no/marui} gekijoo ga aru.
— n. **[a letter or advertisement for general circulation]**
a⌈nna⌉i-joo 案内状 •c [notice]

circulation n. **[an act/instance of moving around from place to place or person to person ⟪fig "the number of copies distributed or sold"⟫]**
1. ju⌈nkan 循環 •c [an act/instance of repeatedly making a round and return to the original point] ⟪**rotation, cycling**⟫
EX. His blood circulation is bad.
彼は血液の循環が悪い。
Kare wa ketsueki no junkan ga warui.
2. ha⌈kkoo-busu⌉u 発行部数 •c [the number of copies distributed of a newspaper, magazine, etc.]
EX. What magazine has the largest circulation in the world?
世界一発行部数の多い雑誌は何ですか。
Sekai-ichi hakkoo-busuu no ooi zasshi wa nan desu ka.

circumstance n. **[a fact/event accompanying another; (pl.) conditions affecting one]**
ji⌈joo 事情 •c [the conditions of facts surrounding an event or situation] ⟪conditions, reasons, situation, state of things⟫, jo⌈okyoo 状況 •c [state of affairs] ⟪situation, condition⟫

EX. (**a**) Under these circumstances, we are unable to comply with your request.
このような{事情/状況}ですから、ご要望に応じかねます。
Kono yoona {jijoo/jookyoo} desu kara, go-yooboo ni ooji-kanemasu.
(**b**) Do you remember the circumstances under which the incident occurred?
その事件が起きた時の{状況/*事情}を覚えていますか。
*Sono jiken ga okita toki no {jookyoo/ *jijoo} o oboete imasu ka.*
(**c**) She quit her job due to family circumstances.
彼女は家庭の{事情/*状況}で仕事をやめた。
*Kanojo wa katei no {jijoo/*jookyoo} de shigoto o yameta.*

C

citizen n. **[a native/naturalized member of a nation owing allegiance to its government and entitled to its protection]**
shi⌉min 市民 •c [a person who has the right to vote in a nation, city, etc.], ko⌈kumin 国民 •c [a group of persons belonging to the same country or a person who has citizenship in a particular country]

EX. (**a**) Citizens have duties as well as privileges.
{市民/国民}には権利も義務もある。
{Shimin/Kokumin} ni wa kenri mo gimu mo aru.
(**b**) The citizens of New York City chose a new mayor.
ニューヨーク{市民/*国民}は新しい市長を選んだ。
*Nyuuyooku-{shimin/*kokumin} wa atarashii shichoo o eranda.*

citrus n. **[any of a group of trees bearing fruits such as oranges, lemons, limes, etc.]**
ka⌈nkitsu⌉-rui かんきつ類 •c

EX. Winter is the season in which citrus fruit tastes best.
冬はかんきつ類の一番おいしい季節です。
Fuyu wa kankitsu-rui no ichiban oishii kisetsu desu.

city n. **[a large/important population center or an incorporated municipality, usually governed by a mayor]**
shi⌉ 市 •c [a geopolitical unit consisting of a population larger than 50,000 and meeting certain conditions qualifying it as an urban municipality], to⌉shi 都市 •c [the center of politics, economy, and culture of a region having a large population] ⟪urban center⟫, to⌈kai 都会 •c [a highly populated urban area having a central government and commercial/industrial centers as distinct from the countryside] ↔ inaka 田舎

EX. (**a**) The population of cities worldwide has been increasing steadily.
世界中の{都市/都会/*市}の人口がどんどん増えている。
*Sekai-juu no {toshi/tokai/*shi} no jinkoo ga don-don fuete iru.*
(**b**) In accordance with the policy of the city, all first-grade pupils were inoculated against small pox.
{市/*都市/*都会}の方針に従って、小学一年生全員に天然痘の予防注射が実施された。
*{Shi/*Toshi/*Tokai} no hooshin ni shitagatte, shoogaku-ichi-nensei zen'in ni tennentoo no yoboo-chuusha ga jisshi-sareta.*
(**c**) Tired of life in the city, he decided to move to the country.
{都会/?都市/*市}の生活に疲れた彼は田舎に引っ越すことにした。
*{Tokai/?Toshi/*Shi} no seikatsu ni tsukareta kare wa inaka ni hikkosu koto ni shita.*
(**d**) Many young people long for life in the city.
{都会/?都市/*市}の生活にあこがれる若者が多い。

*{Tokai/?Toshi/*Shi} no seikatsu ni akogareru waka-mono ga ooi.*

civil adj. **[having to do with a citizen/citizens or polite]**

1. shi˥min no N 市民のN •c [having to do with a citizen/citizens]

EX. The government is obligated to protect civil rights.
政府は市民の権利を守らなければならない義務がある。
Seifu wa shimin no kenri o mamoranakereba naranai gimu ga aru.

2. re┌igi-tadashi˥i 礼儀正しい adj(*i*). **[well mannered]** **《good mannered, courteous》** ↔ **shitsureina 失礼な** adj(*na*).

EX. The clerk was very civil to us.
係の人はとても礼儀正しい対応をしてくれた。
Kakari no hito wa totemo reigi-tadashii taioo o shite kureta.

civilized adj. **[for a person/country to have advanced out of a primitive/uneducated state《fig. "enlightened," "refined"》]**

1. bu˥nmei-ka-shita N 文明化したN /(Vinf. past of *bunmei-ka-suru* ③ civilize/ [for a country/society to have been changed from a primitive to an advanced stage of civilization] 《no longer primitive》

EX. It is one of the marks of a civilized society to have a written language.
文字を持っていることが文明化した社会の特徴の一つである。
Moji o motte iru koto ga bunmei-ka-shita shakai no tokuchoo no hitotsu dearu.

2. kyo┌oyoo no a˥ru N 教養のあるN [having a wide range of knowledge] 《enlightened, cultured, refined》

EX. Civilization presupposes the existence of a civilized populace.
文明は教養のある民衆の存在が前提だ。
Bunmei wa kyooyoo no aru minshuu no sonzai ga zentei da.

claim vt. **[for s.o. to demand as rightfully belonging to oneself, 《fig. "assert"》]**

1. 《〈-ni〉》〈-o〉 yo┌okyuu-suru 《〈〜に〉》〈〜を〉 要求する ③ •c [for s.o. to ask s.t of s.o. as necessary or as one's right] 《ask, call upon, demand, require》

EX. The victim claimed $1 million in damages.
被害者は百万ドルの損害賠償を要求した。
Higai-sha wa hyaku-man-doru no songai-baishoo o yookyuu-shita.

2. {〈-to〉/〈-o〉} shu┌choo-suru {〈〜と〉/〈〜を〉} 主張する ③ •c [for s.o. to state one's opinion firmly with a view to making others agree with it or accept it] 《assert, insist, allege, maintain》

EX. He always claims that he's right.
彼はいつも自分の意見が正しいと主張する。
Kare wa itsu-mo jibun no iken ga tadashii to shuchoo-suru.

—— n. **[a demand for s.t. as due or as one's right 《fig. "an assertion of s.t. as a fact"》]**

1. yo┌okyuu 要求 •c [asking s.t. of s.o. as necessary or as one's right] 《demand, request, requirement》

EX. John filed a claim for damages.
ジョンは損害賠償の要求をした。
Jon wa songai-baishoo no yookyuu o shita.

2. ke˥nri 権利 •c [a qualification one has to do s.t. freely] 《right, privilege, authority》

EX. She has legal claim to the property.
彼女はその不動産に法的な権利がある。
Kanojo wa sono fu-doosan ni hoo-tekina kenri ga aru.

3. shu┌choo 主張 •c [insistence on one's opinion with a view to making others accept it] 《insistence, assertion》

EX. His claim is based upon fact.
彼の主張は事実に立脚している。
Kare no shuchoo wa jijitsu ni rikkyaku-shite iru.

clam n. **[a hard-shelled bivalve mollusk]**
ha┌ma˥guri はまぐり

clap vi./vt. **[for s.o. to strike the hands together, as in applause]**
ha˥kushu-suru 拍手する ③ •c [for s.o. to strike one's hands together when praying

to a god or expressing approval/ encouragement/blessing] ((applaud))

EX. The audience continued clapping in hopes of a curtain call.
聴衆はアンコールを求めて拍手する手を止めなかった。
Chooshuu wa ankooru o motomete hakushu-suru te o tomenakatta.

C

class n. **[social rank/order ((fig. "a group of students," "instruction"))]**

1. ka⌈ikyuu 階級 •c [a classification of society into groups of persons regarded as having the same social status or living standards] ((a social rank, grade))

EX. The purchasing power of the middle class holds sway over a country's economy.
中産階級の購買力は国の経済を左右する。
Chuusan-kaikyuu no koobai-ryoku wa kuni no keizai o sayuu-suru.

2. ju⌉gyoo 授業 •c [the teaching of s.t. to a group of students at school] ((school, lesson, teaching, instruction))

EX. Professor Tanaka is in class now.
田中先生は今授業中です。
Tanaka-sensei wa ima jugyoo-chuu desu.

3. ku⌉rasu クラス •f, -too 〜等 •c [a counter for order or degree of quality] ((rank, quality, rate, grade, degree, prize))

EX. My father always travels first class.
父はいつも{一等/ファーストクラス}で旅行します。
Chichi wa itsu-mo {it-too/faasuto-kurasu} de ryokoo-shimasu.

4. ku⌉rasu クラス •f, ku⌈mi⌉ 組 [a group of people, such as students, divided on the basis of similarity in behavior, character, academic level, etc.] ((group, party, company, squad))

EX. Tom and Jill were in the same class.
トムとジルは同じ{クラス/組}だった。
Tomu to Jiru wa onaji {kurasu/kumi} datta.

classic n. **[a literary/artistic work recognized as being of excellent quality]**

ko⌈ten 古典 •c [a book written in olden times but still highly regarded in the present day]

EX. *The Tale of Genji* is a classic of Japanese literature.
『源氏物語』は日本文学の古典です。
"Genji-monogatari" wa Nihon-bungaku no koten desu.

classical adj. **[standard and traditional; designating or of music conforming to certain standards of form, complexity, etc.]**

ko⌈ten-tekina 古典的な adj(*na*). **•c [respecting and following the tradition of the classics or worthy of being recognized as a classic] ((traditional))**

EX. Ed is studying classical architecture.
エドは古典的な建築物を研究している。
Edo wa koten-tekina kenchiku-butsu o kenkyuu-shite iru.

PHRASE: classical music *kurashikku(-ongaku)* クラシック(音楽) •f(+c)

EX. My wife loves classical music.
妻はクラシック(音楽)が好きです。
Tsuma wa kurashikku(-ongaku) ga suki desu.

PHRASE: classical ballet *{koten/kurashikku}-baree* {古典/クラシック}バレエ

EX. My daughter is taking classical ballet lessons.
娘は{古典/クラシック}バレエを習っています。
Musume wa {koten/kurashikku}-baree o naratte imasu.

classification n. **[arranging/organizing s.o./s.t./s.a. systematically into classes]**

bu⌈nrui 分類 •c ((division, assortment, arrangement))

EX. What sort of classification system do they use in this library?
この図書館ではどんな分類を使っていますか。
Kono tosho-kan de wa donna bunrui o tsukatte imasu ka.

classify vt. **[for s.o. to arrange s.t. systematically into classes or to put s.t. in a particular class]**

⟨-o⟩ bu⌈nrui-suru ⟨〜を⟩分類する ③ •c

《divide, assort, arrange》

EX. (**a**) It is difficult to find a good standard by which to classify all languages.
全世界の言語を分類するためのよい基準を見つけるのは難しいことだ。
Zen-sekai no gengo o bunrui-suru tame no yoi kijun o mitsukeru no wa muzukashii koto da.
(**b**) We used a computer to classify the data.
コンピューターでデータを分類しましたよ。
Konpyuutaa de deeta o bunrui-shimashita yo.

classmate n. **[a member of the same class at a school or college]**
do⌈okyu⌉u-sei 同級生 •c **[one/all of a group belonging past or present to the same class in an academic institution], ku⌈rasu-me⌉eto** クラスメート •f

classroom n. **[a room where a class is taught at a school or college]**
kyo⌈oshitsu 教室 •c

clause n. **[a particular article/provision in a document or, in grammar, a sequence of words consisting of subject and predicate and constituting a part of a sentence]**
1. **jo⌈okoo** 条項 •c **[one of the sections of a legal document, such as a contract]** 《article, provision, stipulation》

EX. The contract has an escape clause.
契約には免責条項が入っている。
Keiyaku ni wa menseki-jookoo ga haitte iru.

2. **se⌉tsu** 節 •c **[a node 《fig. "time/season," "a paragraph of a thesis," "a part of a sentence"》]**

EX. A clause is also sometimes called an embedded sentence.
節は埋め込み文と呼ばれることもある。
Setsu wa ume-komi-bun to yoba-reru koto mo aru.

claw n. **[a sharp, hooked nail on the foot of an animal or bird]**
tsu⌈me つめ **[the thin, hard protective layer at the end of a finger/toe]** 《nail》

EX. Our cat never uses her claws.
うちの猫は決して爪を立てない。
Uchi no neko wa kesshite tsume o tatenai.

clay n. **[a firm, pliable earth that becomes hard when baked, used in making bricks, etc.]**
ne⌉ndo 粘土 •c

clean adj. **[free from dirt and impurities]**
ki⌉reina きれいな adj(*na*). **[pleasantly attractive due to having beauty or orderliness or due to being free from dirt]** 《beautiful, lovely, pretty, fine, nice, clear, pure, neat, tidy, fair》

EX. (**a**) My sister always keeps her room clean.
妹はいつも部屋をきれいにしている。
Imooto wa itsu-mo heya o kireini shite iru.
(**b**) Let's try to make this a clean election.
これをきれいな選挙にするように努めましょう。
Kore o kireina senkyo ni suru yooni tsutomemashoo.
(**c**) The mountain air is very clean.
山の空気はとてもきれいだ。
Yama no kuuki wa totemo kirei da.

— vt. **[to make s.t. free from dirt and impurities]**
⟨-o⟩ ki⌉reini suru ⟨〜を⟩きれいにする ③ **[for s.o./s.a. to make s.t. clean]** 《put in order, tidy up》, **⟨-o⟩ so⌈oji-suru** ⟨〜を⟩掃除する ⑦ •c **[for s.o. to get rid of dirt and dust by sweeping, etc.]** 《sweep, scrub, dust》

EX. We cleaned the apartment before moving out.
引っ越す前にアパートを{きれいに/掃除}した。
Hikkosu mae ni apaato o {kireini/sooji-} shita.

PHRASE: cleaning rag *zookin* 雑きん •c 《floor cloths, duster, mop, swab》

cleaner n. **[s.o./s.t. that cleans]**
se⌈ntaku-ya 洗濯屋 **[s.o. who cleans dirty clothes professionally]**, 《laundry operator》

EX. Please take these trousers to the cleaners.
このズボンを洗濯屋に出して下さい。
Kono zubon o sentaku-ya ni dashite kudasai.

PHRASE: a cleaner *sooji-ki* 掃除機 •c, *kuriinaa* クリーナー •f

EX. Our vacuum cleaner needs repair.
我が家の{掃除機/クリーナー}は修理が必要だ。
Waga-ya no {sooji-ki/kuriinaa} wa shuuri ga hitsuyoo da.

C

clear adj. **[free from clouds/impurity《fig. "transparent," "obvious," "free from guilt"》]**

1. a⌈karui 明るい adj(*i*). **[for there to be enough light to do s.t. or for s.t. to be not dark in color《fig. "cheerful," "be versed in"》]《light, bright》, hareta N** 晴れたN **/〈Vinf. past of *hareru* ② clear up/ [free from clouds]《fine》, sunda N** 澄んだN **/〈Vinf. past of *sumu* ① become transparent/ [free from impurities]**

EX. (**a**) The sky is clear on most autumn days in Japan.
日本の秋は{明るい/晴れた/澄んだ}空の日が多い。
Nihon no aki wa {akarui/hareta/sunda} sora no hi ga ooi.
(**b**) The water in Lake Mashuu is very clear.
摩周湖の水はとても{澄んだ/*明るい/*晴れた}水です。
*Mashuu-ko no mizu wa totemo {sunda/ *akarui/*hareta} mizu desu.*

2. a⌈ki⌉rakana 明らかな adj(*na*). **[readily seen so that there is no doubt or ambiguity]《obvious, evident, plain, apparent》, ha⌈kki⌉ri-shita N** はっきりしたN **/〈Vinf. past of *hakkiri-suru* ③ become well articulated/ [be well articulated]《distinct, plain, vivid, obvious》, ha⌈kki⌉ri-shite iru (N)** はっきりしている(N) **/〈V*te iru* of *hakkiri-suru* ③ become well articulated/ ② [for s.t. to be well articulated]**

EX. His next move is clear.
彼の次の動きは{明らかだ/はっきりしている}。
Kare no tsugi no ugoki wa {akiraka da/ hakkiri-shite iru}.

—— vt. **[to make s.t. free from s.t. undesirable]**

〈-o〉 ka⌈ta-zuke⌉ru 〈～を〉片付ける ② **[for s.o. to put away s.t./s.o. in its proper place《fig. "marry one's daughter off"》]《tidy, clean》, 〈-o〉 ki⌉reini suru** 〈～を〉きれいにする ③ **[for s.o./s.a. to make s.t. clean]《clean》**

EX. Our son helped clear the room of clutter.
息子が部屋のがらくたを{片付ける/きれいにする}のを手伝ってくれた。
Musuko ga heya no garakuta o {kata-zukeru/kireini suru} no o tetsudatte kureta.

—— vt. **[to pass/leap over without touching]**
〈-o〉 to⌈bi-koe⌉ru 〈～を〉飛び越える ② **[to fly/ jump over s.t.]**

EX. The athlete easily cleared the hurdle.
その選手はやすやすとハードルを飛び越えた。
Sono senshu wa yasu-yasu to haadoru o tobi-koeta.

—— vi. **[to become free from clouds/ impurity]**
ha⌈re⌉ru 晴れる ② **[for the sky to begin to turn blue after clouds, fog, etc., have disappeared]**

EX. (**a**) As the fog cleared, the beautiful shape of Mt. Fuji became visible.
霧が晴れると富士がその美しい姿を現した。
Kiri ga hareru to Fuji ga sono utsukushii sugata o arawashita.
(**b**) The sky cleared quickly after the storm passed.
嵐が過ぎるとすぐに晴れてきた。
Arashi ga sugiru to sugu ni harete kita.

clearing n. **[an area of land cleared of trees]**
a⌈kichi 空き地 **[an empty piece of land available for use]《vacant lot, plot of land》**

clearly adv. **[in a clear manner]**
ha⌈kki⌉ri to はっきりと **《distinctly》, a⌈ki⌉rakani** 明らかに **/〈adj(*na*). *ni* of *akirakana* clear/ [without any doubt]《manifestly》**

EX. (**a**) Mt. Fuji is clearly visible.
富士山が{はっきりと/*明らかに}見える。
*Fuji-san ga {hakkiri to/*akirakani} mieru.*

(**b**) He is clearly wrong.
彼は{明らかに/?はっきりと}間違っている。
Kare wa {akirakani/?hakkiri to} machigatte iru.

clerk n. **[an office worker who keeps records/accounts or a salesperson in a store]**
ji⌈mu⌉-in 事務員 •c [s.o. who does clerical work in an office] ⟪**office worker**⟫, **te⌈n'in 店員 •c [a store employee]** ⟪**salesperson**⟫

EX. My daughter is working as a clerk.
娘は{事務員/店員}として働いている。
Musume wa {jimu-in/ten'in} to-shite hataraite iru.

clever adj. **[intelligent, smart]**
ri⌈koona 利口な adj(*na*). **•c [quick in thinking and understanding]** ⟪**smart, wise, bright, intelligent**⟫, **ka⌈shiko⌉i 賢い** adj(*i*). **[smart, wise]**, **ki⌉yoona 器用な** adj(*na*). **•c [skillful, dextrous]** ⟪**skillful, handy, dextrous**⟫

EX. (**a**) Hachikoo was a most clever dog.
ハチ公は非常に{利口な/賢い/*器用な}犬だった。
*Hachikoo wa hijooni {rikoona/kashikoi/ *kiyoona} inu datta.*
(**b**) The cat is an extremely clever animal.
猫は非常に{利口な/賢い/?器用な}動物です。
Neko wa hijooni {rikoona/kashikoi/ ?kiyoona} doobutsu desu.
(**c**) Yosaku is a clever craftsman.
与作は{器用な/利口な/賢い}職人だ。
Yosaku wa {kiyoona/rikoona/kashikoi} shokunin da.

click n. **[a slight, sharp sound like that of a door latch snapping into place]**
ka⌈chi⌉tto iu o⌈to⌉ カチッという音

EX. The door closed with a click.
ドアはカチッという音で閉まった。
Doa wa kachitto iu oto de shimatta.

cliff n. **[a high, steep face of rock, esp. on a coast]**
ga⌈ke がけ [a section of a mountain or a coast that towers up steeply] ⟪**precipice**⟫, **ze⌈ppeki 絶壁 •c [a towering, well-like precipice]** ⟪**precipice**⟫

EX. When I look down from the top of a cliff, I get dizzy.
{がけ/絶壁}の上から下を見ると目がくらむ。
{Gake/Zeppeki} no ue kara shita o miru to me ga kuramu.

climate n. **[the prevailing weather conditions of a region]**
ki⌈koo 気候 •c [conditions of temperature, weather, etc. which are predominant in a region over an extended period of time] ⟪**weather, season**⟫, **fu⌉udo 風土 •c [the natural or cultural environment of a country, etc.]** ⟪**environment**⟫

EX. (**a**) The climate of Japan is mild.
日本の{気候/*風土}は穏やかだ。
*Nihon no {kikoo/*fuudo} wa odayaka da.*
(**b**) The cultivation of rice fits the climate of Japan.
米の栽培は日本の{気候/風土}によく合っている。
Kome no saibai wa Nihon no {kikoo/ fuudo} ni yoku atte iru.

climax n. **[the final, culminating element in a series, the highest point of s.t.]**
sa⌈i-ko⌉ochoo 最高潮 •c [the highest point of emotion or tension], **ku⌈raima⌉kkusu クライマックス •f**

EX. The festival reached its climax with a grand display of fireworks.
盛大な花火で祭りは{最高潮/クライマックス}に達した。
Seidaina hana-bi de matsuri wa {sai-koochoo/kuraimakkusu} ni tasshita.

climb vi./vt. **[to go/move upward]**
{⟨-ni⟩/⟨-o⟩} no⌈boru {⟨〜に⟩/⟨〜を⟩}のぼる ① [to move to a higher position] ⟪**rise, go up, ascend, mount, reach, add up to, be elevated to, be brought up, be placed before**⟫ ↔ **⟨-o⟩ oriru ⟨〜を⟩降りる ②**
㊅ "climb"▷登る, "for the sun/moon/smoke to rise"▷昇る, otherwise▷上る

EX. Have you ever climbed Mt. Fuji?
富士山に登ったことがありますか。

| *Fuji-san ni nobotta koto ga arimasu ka.*

cling vi. **[to hold on tightly to s.t./s.o./s.a.]** ⟨-ni⟩ **ku⌈ttsu⌉ku** ⟨～に⟩くっつく ① **[to hold fast to s.t./s.o./s.a. and be unable to separate from it/him/her]** ⟪stick, adhere, side with⟫, ⟨-ni⟩ **shi⌈gami-tsu⌉ku** ⟨～に⟩しがみつく ① **[for s.o./s.a. to hold fast to s.t./s.o./s.a. and not let go]** ⟪hold tight⟫

EX. (a) A dead leaf clung to the windshield and wouldn't come off.
フロントガラスに枯れ葉が{くっついて/*しがみついて}なかなか取れなかった。
*Furonto-garasu ni kare-ha ga {kuttsuite/*shigami-tsuite} naka-naka tore-nakatta.*
(b) A baby monkey is carried about clinging to its mother.
赤ちゃん猿は母猿に{しがみついて/くっついて}あちこち移動する。
Aka-chan-zaru wa haha-zaru ni {shigami-tsuite/kuttsuite} achi-kochi idoo-suru.

clip vt. **[for s.o. to cut the outer portion of s.t. long such as hair with shears/scissors]** ⟨-o⟩ **ka⌈ru** ⟨～を⟩刈る ① **[for s.o. to cut short s.t. growing thick from the root with a sharp blade using a shearing action]** ⟪cut, reap, mow, trim, prune, shear⟫, ⟨-o⟩ **ki⌉ru** ⟨～を⟩切る ① **[for s.o. to render s.t. connected/continuous into parts or apart from its main body with a sharp-edged implement ⟪fig. "perform a cutting motion in the air," "put an end to s.t," "turn off a switch"⟫]** ⟪cut, chop, hash, carve, slash, sever, pause, disconnect⟫, ⟨-o⟩ **ki⌈ri-nuku** ⟨～を⟩切り抜く ① **[for s.o. to separate or carve out s.t. from s.t. else using a sharp object]**

EX. (a) It's not easy to clip the hair off sheep.
羊の毛を{刈る/?切る/*切り抜く}のは簡単ではない。
*Hitsuji no ke o {karu/?kiru/*kiri-nuku} no wa kantan dewanai.*
(b) There is an art form in Japan in which paper is clipped to make a picture.
日本には紙を{切って/切り抜いて/*刈って}絵を作る芸がある。
*Nihon ni wa kami o {kitte/kiri-nuite/*katte} e o tsukuru gei ga aru.*
(c) Please clip the article and save it.
その記事を{切り抜いて/?切って/*刈って}おいてください。
*Sono kiji o {kiri-nuite/?kitte/*katte} oite kudasai.*

—— n. **[a plastic/metal object for holding things together tightly]**
ku⌈ri⌉ppu クリップ •f

cloak n. **[a loose, usually sleeveless outer garment]**
ma⌉nto マント •f
PHRASE: cloak room *kurooku* クローク •f

clock n. **[a device for measuring and indicating time, usually by means of pointers moving over a dial]**
to⌈kei 時計 •c **[a device for measuring and indicating time by means of springs, electricity, etc.]** ⟪timepiece, watch⟫, **o⌈ki-do⌉kei** 置き時計 **[a timepiece placed on a desk etc.]**, **ka⌈ke-do⌉kei** 掛け時計 **[a timepiece hung from the wall]**

EX. This clock is a little fast.
この{時計/置き時計/掛け時計}は少し進んでいる。
Kono {tokei/oki-dokei/kake-dokei} wa sukoshi susunde iru.

clog n. **[a shoe with a thick, usually wooden, sole]**
ge⌈ta げた **[wooden clog]**

geta

close[1] vt. **[for s.o. to cause s.t. not to be open ⟪fig. "conclude s.t."⟫]**
⟨-o⟩ **shi⌈me⌉ru** ⟨～を⟩しめる ② **[for s.o. to apply pressure to s.t. so as to leave no opening in it ⟪fig. "economize"⟫]** ⟪tighten, wring, strangle, shut, total, sum up⟫, ⟨-o⟩ **to⌈ji⌉ru** ⟨～を⟩閉じる ② **[for s.o. to render s.t. incapable of performing its proper function or to cause s.t. to lose contact with the outside by removing an opening in it, or to terminate s.t. that has continued**

until that point] ⟪**shut**⟫ ↔ ⟨**-o**⟩ **akeru** ⟨～を⟩ 開ける ②
㊥ "close"▷閉める, "tighten"▷締める, "wring" ▷絞める

EX. (**a**) It's cold, so please close the window.
寒いから窓を{閉めて/*閉じて}下さい。
*Samui kara mado o {shimete/*tojite} kudasai.*
(**b**) Close your eyes, sit back, and relax.
目を{閉じて/*閉めて}体を楽にして下さい。
*Me o {tojite/*shimete} karada o raku ni shite kudasai.*
(**c**) The teacher told the students to close their books.
先生は本を{閉じる/*閉める}よう生徒に言った。
*Sensei wa hon o {tojiru/*shimeru} yoo seito ni itta.*
(**d**) They sold all their merchandise and closed the store for good.
彼らはすべての商品を売って、永久に店を{閉めた/閉じた}。
Kare-ra wa subete no shoohin o utte, eikyuu ni mise o {shimeta/tojita}.

—— vi. **[for s.t. to move spontaneously to a position of being shut** ⟪**fig. "come to an end"**⟫**]**
shi⌉ma⌉ru しまる ① **[for s.t. to be left with no opening as a result of pressure applied to it from all sides]** ⟪**come to an end**⟫
㊥ "close"▷閉まる, "be tightened"▷締まる

EX. The library closes at 10:00 P.M.
図書館は午後十時に閉まります。
Tosho-kan wa gogo juu-ji ni shimarimasu.

—— n. **[an end]**
o⌈wari 終わり /⟨**V*masu* of *owaru*** ① **end**/ **[the point at which s.t. continues no further of the last part of s.t.]** ↔ **hajimari** 始まり

EX. (**a**) Everyone thanked the outgoing chairman at the close of the meeting.
会の終わりに全員が任期満了の学科長に感謝した。
Kai no owari ni zen'in ga ninki-manryoo no gakka-choo ni kansha-shita.
(**b**) At the close of the concert, a big bouquet of flowers was presented to the group.
演奏会の終わりに大きな花束が贈呈された。
Ensoo-kai no owari ni ookina hana-taba ga zootei-sareta.
(**c**) The close of the ceremony was announced by the minister.
式の終わりが牧師によってアナウンスされた。
Shiki no owari ga bokushi ni-yotte anaunsu-sareta.

close[2] adj. **[with little space between** ⟪**fig. "intimate," "familiar," "careful"**⟫**]**

1. chi⌈ka⌉i 近い adj(*i*). **[having little spatial or temporal distance separating s.t. from s.t. else]** ⟪**near**⟫ ↔ **tooi** 遠い adj(*i*).

EX. Our house is close to the train station, so it's convenient.
我が家は駅に近いので便利です。
Waga-ya wa eki ni chikai node benri desu.

2. shi⌈tashi⌉i 親しい adj(*i*). **[feeling little psychological distance between oneself and s.o. else]** ⟪**familiar, dear, intimate**⟫

EX. (**a**) Jim and Beth are close friends.
ジムとベスは親しい友達だ。
Jimu to Besu wa shitashii tomodachi da.
(**b**) Jack and Betty are on close terms.
ジャックとベティは親しい間柄です。
Jakku to Betii wa shitashii aidagara desu.

PHRASE: close friend *shin'yuu* 親友 •c

3. me⌈nmitsuna 綿密な adj(*na*). •c **[taking into account fine details without defect or oversight]** ⟪**minute, detailed, thorough, careful, attentive, scrupulous**⟫ ↔ **sozatsuna** 粗雑な adj(*na*). •c; **sa⌈ishin no N** 細心のN •c **[concentrating one's attention on even minute details]** ⟪**careful, scrupulous**⟫

EX. You should pay close attention to the matter.
その件については{綿密な/細心の}注意を払うべきだ。

Sono ken ni-tsuite wa {menmitsuna/ saishin no} chuui o harau-beki da.

—— adv. **[in a close manner]**
su⌉gu so⌉ba ni すぐそばに **[with no spatio-temporal space in between]** **⟪near⟫**

EX. (**a**) Stay close to me.
僕のすぐそばにいなさい。
Boku no sugu soba ni inasai.
(**b**) There is a fire station close to the police box.
交番のすぐそばに消防署があります。
Kooban no sugu soba ni shooboo-sho ga arimasu.

closely adv. **[in a close manner]**
1. mi⌈ssetsuni 密接に **/⟨adj(*na*). *ni* of *missetsuna* close/ •c [in a mutual position or relationship where no intervening distance exists]** **⟪intimately⟫**

EX. Japan's economy is closely related to the U.S. economy.
日本経済は米国経済と密接に結びついている。
Nihon-keizai wa Beikoku-keizai to missetsuni musubi-tsuite iru.

2 me⌈nmitsuni 綿密に **/⟨adj(*na*). *ni* of *menmitsuna* attentive/ •c [in a manner which takes into account fine details without defect or oversight]** **⟪carefully, attentively⟫**

EX. I have closely examined the financial report.
私は会計報告書を綿密にチェックした。
Watashi wa kaikei-hookoku-sho o menmitsuni chekku-shita.

closet n. **[a small room for storing clothes, supplies, etc.]**
o⌈shiire 押し入れ **[a space with doors in a Japanese-style room for storing items such as bedding], ku⌈ro⌉ozetto** クローゼット **•f**

closing n. **[end of a letter, etc.]**
mu⌈subi 結び **/⟨V*masu* of *musubu* ① tie/ [a conclusion], o⌈wari** 終わり **/⟨V*masu* of *owaru* ① end/ [the point at which s.t. continues no further or the last part of s.t.]** **⟪end, conclusion⟫**

EX. (**a**) In closing, I wish to thank you again.
{結び/終わり}にもう一度お礼を申し上げます。
{Musubi/Owari} ni moo ichi-do o-rei o mooshi-agemasu.
(**b**) Whether in a speech or a letter, the closing tends to be difficult.
スピーチでも手紙でも大抵{結び/終わり}が難しい。
Supiichi demo tegami demo taitei {musubi/owari} ga muzukashii.

cloth n. **[a woven/knitted/pressed fabric made of fibrous material such as cotton, wool, silk, synthetic fibers, etc., or a tablecloth, ashcloth, dustcloth]**
1. nu⌈no 布 **[textile fabrics], ki⌈re⌉** きれ **[textile material], o⌈ri-mono** 織物 **[a woven fabric], fu⌈kuji** 服地 **•c [material for making western suits and dresses, etc.]**

EX. That company specializes in importing cloth.
その会社は{布/服地/織物}の輸入を専門としている。
Sono kaisha wa {nuno/fukuji/ori-mono} no yunyuu o senmon to shite iru.

4. te⌈eburu-ku⌉rosu テーブルクロス **•f [tablecloth]**
5. fu⌈ki⌉n ふきん **•c [a piece of fabric for washing/drying dishes]**
6. zo⌈okin 雑きん **•c [a piece of fabric for wiping things, usually used wet]**

clothes n. **[wearing apparel]**
fu⌈ku⌉ 服 **•c [a generic term for dresses and suits], yo⌈ofuku** 洋服 **•c [western apparel] ↔ wafuku** 和服 **•c**

EX. Tom put on his best clothes.
トムは自分の一番良い{服/洋服}を着た。
Tomu wa jibun no ichiban ii {fuku/ yoofuku} o kita.

clothing n. **[wearing apparel ⟨fml⟩]**
i⌉rui 衣類 **•c [items for wearing such as dresses, trousers, socks, etc.]**

EX. We sent clothing to the earthquake disaster area.
私たちは地震被災地に衣類を送った。
Watashi-tachi wa jishin-hisai-chi ni irui o okutta.

cloud n. **[a visible mass of vapor in the sky]**
ku⌉mo 雲

EX. We can see the mountain top above the clouds.
雲の上に山頂が見える。
Kumo no ue ni sanchoo ga mieru.

cloudy adj. **[covered with clouds]**
ku⌈mo⌉tte iru (N) 曇っている(N) /⟨V *te iru* of *kumoru* ① become cloudy/ [for the sky or a clear surface such as glass to lack transparency due to being covered by clouds, condensed vapor, etc.]

EX. The skies have been cloudy all day.
空は一日中曇っている。
Sora wa ichi-nichi-juu kumotte iru.

clover n. **[any of various herbs with leaves made up of three leaflets and small flowers in dense heads]**
ku⌈ro⌉obaa クローバー •f

clown n. **[one who entertains, as in a circus, by playing tricks or doing stunts]**
do⌈oke(-ya⌉kusha) 道化(役者) •c, pi⌉ero ピエロ •f

club n. **[a group of people associated around a common purpose/interest or a stick used as a weapon or as an instrument in a game such as golf]**
1. ku⌉rabu クラブ •f [a group of people associated around a common purpose/interest], bu⌉ 部 •c [a group of people associated around a common purpose/interest, esp. in a school]

NOTE: *Bu* has a more professional connotation than *kurabu*.

EX. (**a**) I belonged to the table tennis club in high school.
私は高校時代、卓球{部/クラブ}に入っていました。
Watakushi wa kookoo-jidai, takkyuu-{bu/kurabu} ni haitte imashita.
(**b**) My brother is a member of the tennis club.
兄はテニス{部/クラブ}のメンバーです。
Ani wa tenisu-{bu/kurabu} no menbaa desu.

2. ko⌈nboo こん棒 •c [a stick used as a weapon], ku⌉rabu クラブ •f [a stick used as an instrument in golf]

clue n. **[a fact, object, etc. that helps to solve a mystery or problem]**
te-⌈ga⌉kari 手掛かり ⟨⟨key, scent, track, trail, trace, hold⟩⟩

EX. We cannot find any clues to help us solve this mystery.
このなぞを解く手掛かりが全く見つからない。
Kono nazo o toku te-gakari ga mattaku mitsukaranai.

clumsy adj. **[lacking grace or skill]**
bu-⌈ki⌉yoona 不器用な adj(*na*). **•c [not being able to handle things skillfully] ⟨⟨maladroit⟩⟩ ↔ kiyoona 器用な** adj(*na*). **•c**

EX. Mike is clumsy when it comes to sports.
マイクはスポーツとなると不器用だ。
Maiku wa supootsu to naru to bu-kiyoo da.

cluster n. **[a number of things (or persons) grouped together]**
fu⌈sa⌉ 房 [a string of twisted threads/hairs ending with untwisted ones ⟨⟨fig. "bunch"⟩⟩], hi⌉to⌊-katamari 一塊 [a number of things/people/animals closely grouped together]

EX. (**a**) We saw huge clusters of grapes at the vineyard.
ぶどう園で大きなぶどうの{房/* 一塊}を見ました。
*Budoo-en de ookina budoo no {fusa/ *hito-katamari} o mimashita.*
(**b**) A cluster of students was talking excitedly in the hallway.
廊下で{一塊/*房}の学生がわいわいがやがや話していた。
*Rooka de {hito-katamari/*fusa} no gakusei ga wai-wai gaya-gaya hanashite ita.*

clutch n. **[a device for engaging and disengaging a motor or engine]**
ku⌈ra⌉tchi クラッチ •f

coach n. **[a railroad passenger car or an instructor/trainer, as of athletes, actors, singers, etc.]**
1. kya⌈kusha 客車 •c [a passenger car]
2. ko⌉ochi コーチ •f [s.o. who trains s.o. in sports, etc.]

C

—— vt. [to instruct/train]
⟨-ni⟩ ⟨-o⟩ ko˥ochi-suru ⟨〜に⟩⟨〜を⟩コーチする ③ [for s.o. to give instruction in sports], ⟨-ni⟩ ⟨-o⟩ shi˥doo-suru ⟨〜に⟩⟨〜を⟩指導する •c ③ [for s.o. to teach and guide s.o.] 《**guide, lead, direct**》

EX. Would you coach me in golf?
私にゴルフを{コーチ/指導}してくださいませんか。
Watashi ni gorufu o {koochi/shidoo}-shite kudasaimasen ka.

C

coal n. **[a black, combustible mineral used as fuel]**
se˥kita˥n 石炭 •c

coarse adj. **[consisting of rather large particles or rough in texture 《fig. "of poor quality," "vulgar," "crude"》]**
1. a˥rai 粗い adj(*i*). **[made up of large particles 《fig. "not fine," "rough"》]** 《**rough, rugged**》 ↔ **komakai 細かい** adj(*i*). 《**fine**》

EX. The texture of this fabric is coarse.
この生地は布目が粗い。
Kono kiji wa nuno-me ga arai.

2. so˥akuna 粗悪な adj(*na*). **•c [of crude/poor quality]** 《**crude, inferior**》

EX. That store sells nothing but coarse goods.
あの店は粗悪な商品ばかり売っている。
Ano mise wa soakuna shoohin bakari utte iru.

3. so˥yana 粗野な adj(*na*). **•c [of a person whose language and behavior are rough and disregard the feelings of others; vulgar in character]** 《**rough, rude, vulgar**》

EX. (**a**) His language is coarse, but he has a warm heart.
彼の言葉は粗野だが、心は暖かい。
Kare no kotoba wa soya da ga, kokoro wa atatakai.
(**b**) People whose language and attitude are coarse are disliked by others.
言葉や態度が粗野な人は嫌われる。
Kotoba ya taido ga soyana hito wa kirawa-reru.

coast n. **[land alongside the sea]**
ka˥igan 海岸 •c [the land next to the ocean] 《**beach**》

EX. (**a**) All of the Ivy League Schools are on the East Coast of the U.S.
アイビースクールはすべてアメリカの東海岸にある。
Aibii-sukuuru wa subete Amerika no higashi-kaigan ni aru.
(**b**) How long does it take to fly from the East Coast to the West Coast?
東海岸から西海岸まで飛行機で何時間かかりますか。
Higashi-kaigan kara nishi-kaigan made hikoo-ki de nan-jikan kakarimasu ka.

coastal n. **[of a coast]**
ka˥igan-zoi no N 海岸沿いのN [along a coast]

EX. Jack was born in a little coastal town.
ジャックは海岸沿いの小さい町で生まれた。
Jakku wa kaigan-zoi no chiisai machi de umareta.

coat n. **[a sleeved outer garment opening down the front]**
ko˥oto コート •f [the upper part of a suit; raincoat/overcoat], ga˥itoo 外とう •c [a garment worn over a suit to protect against cold weather or for a ceremony] 《**overcoat**》, **o˥obaa オーバー •f, o˥obaa-ko˥oto オーバーコート •f, u˥wa-gi 上着 [a garment worn for formal occasions such as a suit or the upper half of a garment separated into upper and lower parts]**

EX. The man took off his coat and hung it on a hanger.
男は{コート/外とう/オーバー/上着}をぬいでハンガーにかけた。
Otoko wa {kooto/gaitoo/oobaa/uwa-gi} o nuide hangaa ni kaketa.

NOTE: *Gaitoo* is a bit archaic.

coating n. **[a surface coat/layer]**
u˥wa-nuri 上塗り [the last or final layer of paint], to˥soo 塗装 •c [an act/instance of applying paint]

cocoa n. **[powder made from roasted cacao seeds; a drink made of this and hot milk]**
ko˥koa ココア •f

coconut n. **[the fruit of a tropical tree]**
ko˥konatsu ココナツ •f, ko˹ko-ya˥shi (no mi) ココやし(の実) [(the fruit of) the palm tree]

coeducation n. **[an educational system in which students of both sexes attend classes together]**
da˥njo-kyoogaku 男女共学 •c

EX. Not all schools practice coeducation.
すべての学校が男女共学とは限らない。
Subete no gakkoo ga danjo-kyoogaku to wa kagiranai.

coffee n. **[a drink made from the roasted, ground, bean-like seed of a tropical shrub of the maddler family]**
ko˹ohi˥i コーヒー •f

PHRASE: coffee shop *koohii-shoppu* コーヒーショップ •f, *kissa-ten* 喫茶店 •c

coil n. **[a series of rings/a spiral, or anything having this form]**
ko˥iru コイル •f, gu˥ru-guru maita mo˹no˥ ぐるぐる巻いた物 [s.t. that is wound into circular or spiral form]

coin n. **[a piece of stamped metal, issued by a government as money]**
ko˥oka 硬貨 •c [metal currency], ko˥in コイン •f

EX. You need coins to feed the parking meter.
駐車用メーターには{硬貨/コイン}が必要です。
Chuusha-yoo-meetaa ni wa {kooka/koin} ga hitsuyoo desu.

coke n. **[an abbreviation for CocaCola]**
ko˥oku コーク •f, Ko˹kako˥ora コカコーラ •f

cola n. **[a carbonated soft drink made with a syrup from the seeds of kola nuts]**
ko˥ora コーラ •f, se˹iryoo-inryo˥o-sui 清涼飲料水 •c [a cold beverage that refreshes]

cold adj. **[feeling an uncomfortable lack of warmth/heat or having a temperature significantly lower than that of the human body《fig. "not affectionate or cordial"》]**
1. sa˹mu˥i 寒い adj(*i*). **[sensing discomfort due to a low temperature throughout one's body]《too cool, chilly》↔ atsui 暑い** adj(*i*).

EX. (**a**) I forgot to bring a sweater with me and felt very cold.
セーターを持って来るのを忘れて、とても寒かった。
Seetaa o motte-kuru no o wasurete, totemo samukatta.
(**b**) It is very cold out.
外はとても寒いですよ。
Soto wa totemo samui desu yo.

2. tsu˹metai 冷たい adj(*i*). **[for s.t. to have a low temperature physically perceptible to the touch《fig. "lacking a warm heart"》]《chilly, icy, dead》**

EX. (**a**) I jumped into the sea, but it was cold.
海に飛び込んだが、冷たかった。
Umi ni tobi-konda ga, tsumetakatta.
(**b**) Gee, your hands are cold!
まあ、なんて冷たい手なんでしょう。
Maa, nante tsumetai te na n deshoo.
(**c**) I wonder why Catherine was so cold to me.
キャサリンはどうしてあんなに冷たかったのだろう。
Kyasarin wa dooshite annani tsumetakatta no daroo.

—— n. **[lack of heat/warmth or chilly weather or a virus infection of the respiratory tract, causing sneezing, coughing, etc.]**
1. sa˥mu-sa 寒さ /〈adj(*i*). stem of *samui* cold + suf. *sa* ness/ [lack of heat/warmth, chilliness]

EX. (**a**) The people of New England seem to enjoy the severe cold.
ニューイングランドの人々は厳しい寒さを楽しむかのように見える。
Nyuuingurando no hito-bito wa kibishii samu-sa o tanoshimu ka no yooni mieru.
(**b**) The cold weather here has gotten worse.
こちらも寒さが厳しくなって来ました。
Kochira mo samu-sa ga kibishiku natte kimashita.

2. ka˥ze かぜ [a natural movement of air《fig. "a virus infection caused by a cold wind drawn into the body"》]
㊉ "wind"▷風, "a virus infection"▷風邪

EX. (a) Many students caught colds and did not come to class.
風邪を引いてクラスを休んだ学生が大勢いた。
Kaze o hiite kurasu o yasunda gakusei ga oozei ita.
(b) Don't catch a cold, OK?
風邪をひかないようにね。
Kaze o hikanai yooni ne.

C

collar n. **[the part of a garment encircling the neck or a band of leather, etc., for putting around the neck of an animal]**
1. e⌈ri⌉ 襟 [the part of a garment encircling the neck], ka⌉raa カラー •f

EX. (a) The button came off the collar.
{襟/カラー}のボタンが取れてしまった。
{Eri/Karaa} no botan ga torete shimatta.
(b) It is easy to dirty the collar of a dress shirt.
ワイシャツの{襟/カラー}は汚れやすい。
Waishatsu no {eri/karaa} wa yogore-yasui.

2. ku⌈bi-wa 首輪 [a band for putting around the neck of an animal]

EX. Our cat's collar has a bell attached to it.
うちの猫の首輪には鈴がついている。
Uchi no neko no kubi-wa ni wa suzu ga tsuite iru.

collect vt. **[for s.o./s.a. to gather things together]**
⟨-o⟩ a⌈tsume⌉ru ⟨〜を⟩集める ② [for s.o. to cause things or people that are scattered in various places to come to one and the same place], ⟨-o⟩ shu⌈ushuu-suru ⟨〜を⟩収集する ③ •c [for s.o. to gather things for the purpose of interest or research] ((gather))

EX. My hobby is collecting stamps.
私の趣味は切手を{集める/収集する}ことです。
Watashi no shumi wa kitte o {atsumeru/shuushuu-suru} koto desu.

collection n. **[an act/instance of gathering s.t. together]**
shu⌈ushuu 収集 •c [gathering s.t. together for the purpose of interest or research] ((gathering)), a⌈tsume⌉ru ko⌈to⌉ 集めること [an act of gathering together s.t./s.o./s.a.] ((gathering)), ko⌈re⌉kushon コレクション •f [an act of gathering s.t. or s.t. gathered] ((gathering))

EX. (a) Jim has a large stamp collection.
ジムはたくさんの切手の{コレクション/*収集}を持っている。
*Jimu wa takusan no kitte no {korekushon/*shuushuu} o motte iru.*
(b) Mr. Aoki went to the United States for the purposes of data collection.
青木さんはデータ{収集の/を集める/?コレクションの}ためアメリカへ行った。
Aoki-san wa deeta {-shuushuu no/o atsumeru/?-korekushon no} tame Amerika e itta.

college n. **[an institution of higher education that grants baccalaureate degree]**
da⌈igaku 大学 •c [an institution of higher education that grants baccalaureate degrees or baccalaureate and graduate degrees] ((university))

EX. (a) Jim studied Japanese in college.
ジムは大学で日本語を勉強した。
Jimu wa daigaku de Nihon-go o benkyoo-shita.
(b) In Japan, 70% of high school graduates go to college.
日本では高校卒業生の七割が大学に行く。
Nihon de wa kookoo-sotsugyoo-sei no nana-wari ga daigaku ni iku.

color n. **[the visual quality of an object/substance created by the particular wavelengths of light reflected from it]**
i⌈ro⌉ 色 ((hue, tint))

EX. What is the color of your car?
あなたの車は何色ですか。
Anata no kuruma wa nani-iro desu ka.

Columbia n.
Ko⌈ro⌉nbia コロンビア •f

Columbus n.
Ko⌈ro⌉nbusu コロンブス •f

column n. **[a slender round upright structure, usually used to support part of a**

building 《fig. "a vertical section of page"》]
1. e⌈nchuu 円柱 •c [a slender upright cylindrical structure, usually used to support part of a building] 《cylinder》

EX. That building utilizes Corinthian style columns.
あの建物はコリント式の円柱を用いています。
Ano tate-mono wa Korinto-shiki no enchuu o mochiite imasu.

2. ra⌉n 欄 •c [a part of a newspaper devoted to a specific theme] 《space, section》

EX. A: Where did you find your car?
どこで車を見つけましたか。
Doko de kuruma o mitsukemashita ka.
B: I found it in the advertisement column of the newspaper.
新聞の広告欄で見付けました。
Shinbun no kookoku-ran de mitsukemashita.

combination n. **[the act of combining or the state of being combined]**
ku⌈mi-awase 組み合わせ [the act of joining several things into one or the state resulting from such joining] 《joining together, assortment》, **ko⌈nbine⌉eshon コンビネーション •f**

EX. She is good at color combination.
彼女は色の{組み合わせ/コンビネーション}が上手だ。
Kanojo wa iro no {kumi-awase/konbineeshon} ga joozu da.

combine vt. **[to join into one by blending or to unite]**
⟨-o⟩ ku⌈mi-awa-seru ⟨〜を⟩組み合わせる /⟨causative of *kumi-au* ① become combined/ ② **[to join closely several things into a single whole or set]** 《join, unite》, **⟨-o⟩ ke⌈tsugoo-suru ⟨〜を⟩結合する ③ •c [for s.o. to put two things together so as to form one entity]** 《unite, amalgamate, merge》, **⟨-o⟩(⟨-to⟩) mu⌈subi-tsuke⌉ru ⟨〜を⟩(⟨〜と⟩) 結び付ける ② [to tie s.t. together to s.t. else and cause them to adhere together]** 《tie》

EX. (**a**) Ed is good at combining work and pleasure in his daily schedule.
エドは毎日のスケジュールに仕事と遊びを{組み合わせる/結び付ける/?結合する}のがうまい。
Edo wa mai-nichi no sukejuuru ni shigoto to asobi o {kumi-awa-seru/musubi tsukeru/?ketsugoo-suru} no ga umai.
(**b**) It is best to wear kimono and obi patterns which skillfully combine in them an element of the season.
着物や帯の柄は季節と上手に{組み合わせて/結び付けて/*結合して}着るとよい。
*Ki-mono ya obi no gara wa kisetsu to joozuni {kumi-awa-sete/musubi-tsukete/*ketsugoo-shite} kiru to yoi.*
(**c**) Water is formed by combining hydrogen with oxygen.
水素が酸素と{結合して/*組み合わせて/*結び付けて}水ができる。
*Suiso ga sanso to {ketsugoo-shite/*kumi-awa-sete/*musubi-tsukete} mizu ga dekiru.*

come vi. **[to move from somewhere else to the place where the speaker is located or a place with which the speaker identifies** 《fig. "happen," "be available," "become"》**]**
1. {⟨-e⟩/⟨-ni⟩} ku⌉ru {⟨〜へ⟩/⟨〜に⟩}来る ③ [to move to where the speaker is or his/her in-group members is/belongs to] 《arrive》, **{⟨-e⟩/⟨-ni⟩} i⌈rassha⌉ru {⟨〜へ⟩/⟨〜に⟩}いらっしゃる ① [for s.o. to whom the speaker shows deference to move to/stay in a certain place], {⟨-e⟩/⟨-ni⟩} ma⌉iru {⟨〜へ⟩/⟨〜に⟩}参る ① [for s.o./s.t. to move to a certain place, an expression used in humble or very formal contexts]**

EX. (**a**) Spring has come.
春が来た。
Haru ga kita.
(**b**) A: When did you come to Japan?
いつ日本へ{来ました/いらっしゃいました/*参りました}か。
*Itsu Nihon e {kimashita/irasshaimashita/*mairimashita} ka.*
B: I came here in May of last year.

昨年の五月に{来ました/参りました/*いらっしゃいました}。
*Sakunen no go-gatsu ni {kimashita/mairimashita/*irasshaimashita}.*

NOTE: V*masu* of *irassharu* is not *irassharimasu* but *irasshaimasu. Mairu* is mostly used in its *masu* form, i.e. *mairimasu.*

2. {⟨-e⟩/⟨-ni⟩} **iˈku** {⟨〜へ⟩/⟨〜に⟩}行く ① **[to move in a direction or towards a goal away from the speaker]** ⟪**go**⟫, {⟨-e⟩/⟨-ni⟩} **maˈiru** {⟨〜へ⟩/⟨〜に⟩}参る ① **[for s.o./s.t. to move to a certain place, an expression used in humble or very formal contexts],** {⟨-e⟩/⟨-ni⟩} **uˈkagau** {⟨〜へ⟩/⟨〜に⟩}伺う ① **[for the speaker or s.o. the speaker identifies with to visit s.o. else who is older/higher in social status]**

EX. (**a**) A: When may I come to see you then?
では、いつ{行きましたら/参りましたら/伺いましたら}よろしいでしょうか。
Dewa, itsu {ikimashitara/mairimashitara/ukagaimashitara} yoroshii deshoo ka.
B: Why don't you come tomorrow?
明日、{来ません/いらっしゃいません}か。
Ashita, {kimasen/irasshaimasen} ka.
(**b**) A: Mary, dinner is ready.
メアリー、食事の支度ができたよ。
Mearii, shokuji no shitaku ga dekita yo.
B: Yes, Father, I'm coming.
はい、お父さん、今{行きます/?参ります/*伺います}。
*Hai, o-too-san, ima {ikimasu/?mairimasu/*ukagaimasu}.*

3. Vinf. yoˈoni naˈru Vinf.ようになる **[to come to do s.t. regularly or reach the point where s.t. occurs regularly or some state obtains]** ⟪**become**⟫

EX. How did you come to know the secret?
なぜあなたが秘密を知るようになったのですか。
Naze anata ga himitsu o shiru yooni natta no desu ka.

PHRASE: come off *toreru* 取れる ② [for s.t. that is attached to s.t. else to become detached and separated from it] ⟪be separated, removed⟫, *hazureru* はずれる ② [for s.t. to deviate from what is expected or to become disengaged from s.t. else] ⟪miss the mark, be removed⟫

EX. (**a**) A button came off my jacket.
上着のボタンがひとつ{取れた/?はずれた}。
Uwa-gi no botan ga hitotsu {toreta/?hazureta}.
(**b**) The safety pin just won't come off.
安全装置の留め金がなかなか{取れない/外れない}。
Anzen-soochi no tome-gane ga naka-naka {torenai/hazurenai}.

PHRASE: come on *genki o dashite* 元気を出して /⟨V*te* of *genki o dasu* ① cheer up/ [get one's spirits up], *saa* さあ inf. [interjection encouraging the hearer to take action]

EX. Come on!
{元気を出して/さあ}。
{Genki o dashite/Saa}.

PHRASE: come out *dete-kuru* 出て来る ③ ⟪emerge, appear⟫

EX. The stars came out in the evening sky.
夜空に星が出て来た。
Yozora ni hoshi ga dete-kita.

PHRASE: come true *jitsugen-suru* 実現する ③ •c

EX. My dream came true.
夢が実現した。
Yume ga jitsugen-shita.

PHRASE: come up *agaru* あがる ① ⟪arise, rise, ascend, progress⟫ ↔ *sagaru* さがる
㊥ "rise"▷上がる, "(for a kite/flag) to fly/(for carge) to be unloaded/(for food) to be deep-fried"▷揚がる, "(for a hand) to be raised"▷挙がる, otherwise ▷あがる

EX. I saw smoke coming up in the distance.
遠くに煙が上がるのが見えた。
Tooku ni kemuri ga agaru no ga mieta.

PHRASE: come up *okoru* 起こる ① ⟪happen, originate in⟫

EX. (**a**) Something came up and I couldn't attend the party.
ちょっとしたことが起こって、パーティーに出席出来なかった。
Chotto-shita koto ga okotte, paatii ni

shusseki-dekinakatta.
(**b**) I'll let you know if anything comes up.
何か起こったらお知らせします。
Nani-ka okottara o-shira-se-shimasu.

comfort n. **[s.t.that soothes s.o. in distress/sorrow]**
na[gusame 慰め /⟨V*masu* of *nagusameru* ② comfort/ [s.t. which consoles s.o.] ((consolation, solace))

EX. Not even words of comfort can help him at this time.
慰めの言葉も今の彼には役に立たないだろう。
Nagusame no kotoba mo ima no kare ni wa yaku ni tatanai daroo.

—— vt. **[to soothe s.o. in distress/sorrow]**
⟨-o⟩ na[gusame]ru ⟨〜を⟩慰める ② [to cause s.o. to forget his/her sorrow, sadness, loneliness, uneasiness, boredom, etc. temporarily by giving him/her words of encouragement or doing s.t. for him/her] ((console, solace, cheer up))

EX. (**a**) A: I hear that Ed lost his only son.
エドは一人息子を亡くしたそうですよ。
Edo wa hitori-musuko o nakushita soo desu yo.
B: Let's go and comfort him, shall we?
行って慰めてやりませんか。
Itte nagusamete yarimasen ka.
(**b**) She often comforts herself with music when she is lonely.
彼女は寂しいときよく音楽を聴いて自分を慰めます。
Kanojo wa sabishii toki yoku ongaku o kiite jibun o nagusamemasu.

comfortable adj. **[giving physical comfort or ease]**
ki[mochi ga i]i 気持ちがいい adj(*i*). **[giving one a good feeling] ((pleasant, agreeable)), ka[itekina 快適な** adj(*na*). **•c [for s.t. to be in good condition or going well so that there is no room for complaint] ((pleasant, delightful, agreeable))**

EX. (**a**) This apartment is very comfortable.
このアパートはとても{気持ちがいい/快適}です。
Kono apaato wa totemo {kimochi ga ii/kaiteki} desu.
(**b**) The climate of Hawaii is quite comfortable.
ハワイの気候はとても{気持ちがいい/快適}です。
Hawai no kikoo wa totemo {kimochi ga ii/kaiteki} desu.
(**c**) In order to lead a comfortable life, one must work hard.
人は{快適な/?気持ちがいい}生活を送るため、一生懸命働かねばならない.
Hito wa {kaitekina/?kimochi ga ii} seikatsu o okuru tame, isshoo-kenmei hatarakaneba naranai.
(**d**) Our new car is really comfortable to ride in.
今度の車はまことに{快適な/*気持ちがいい}乗り心地ですよ。
*Kondo no kuruma wa makoto ni {kaitekina/*kimochi ga ii} nori-gokochi desu yo.*

command vt. **[to give an order to s.o.]**
⟨-ni⟩ Vinf. yo]oni me[ijiru ⟨〜に⟩Vinf.ように命じる ② [for s.o. in an official position of authority to tell s.o. else to do s.t.]

EX. The captain commanded his men to change the course of the ship.
キャプテンは船の針路を変えるように部下に命じた。
Kyaputen wa fune no shinro o kaeru yooni buka ni meijita.

—— n. **[an act/instance of giving an order to s.o. ((fig. "mastery of a technique"))]**
1. me[irei 命令 •c [an instruction to act issued by a military superior or other person in a position of authority] ((direction, instructions))

EX. (**a**) The captain issued a command that the crew return to the ship by one o'clock.
キャプテンは乗組員が一時までに船に戻るように命令を出した。
Kyaputen wa norikumi-in ga ichi-ji made ni fune ni modoru yooni meirei o dashita.
(**b**) In the military, a command by a

C

superior is to be obeyed absolutely.
軍隊では上官の命令には絶対に従わなければならない。
Guntai de wa jookan no meirei ni wa zettai ni shitagawanakereba naranai.

2. ji⌈yu⌉uni ku⌉shi-suru chi⌈kara⌉ 自由に駆使する力 [the ability to use s.t. freely] ((mastery))

EX. Not many Japanese have a good command of English.
英語を自由に駆使する力を持っている日本人は少ない。
Eigo o jiyuuni kushi-suru chikara o motte iru Nihon-jin wa sukunai.

commemorate vt. **[to serve as a memory of s.t./s.o.]**
⟨-o⟩ ki⌈nen-suru ⟨～を⟩記念する ③ •c [for s.o. to maintain the memory of s.t. by means of some object or ceremony] ((mark))

EX. (**a**) This tower was built to commemorate the 100th anniversary of the founding of the university.
この塔は大学の創立百年を記念して建てられたものです。
Kono too wa daigaku no sooritsu hyaku-nen o kinen-shite tate-rareta mono desu.
(**b**) We had lots of events to commemorate the Olympic Games.
オリンピックを記念する行事がたくさんあった。
Orinpikku o kinen-suru gyooji ga takusan atta.

comment n. **[an explanatory/critical note]**
ro⌈npyoo 論評 •c [critical discussion/analysis of the content of a creative work or of an event], ko⌉mento コメント •f [a supplememtary explanation or critical review] ((opinion, view))

EX. (**a**) Would you care to make some comment on the matter?
本件に関して何か{論評/コメント}なさりたいことがありますか。
Honken ni kanshite nani-ka {ronpyoo/komento} nasari-tai koto ga arimasu ka.
(**b**) I would appreciate your comments on my paper.
論文に{論評/コメント}を頂ければ有り難いのですが。
Ronbun ni {ronpyoo/komento} o itadake-reba arigatai no desu ga.

— vi. **[for s.o. to make a remark by way of explanation or observation]**
i⌉ken o no⌈be⌉ru 意見を述べる ② [for s.o. to state an opinion] ((opine)), **ko⌉mento-suru コメントする ③ •f [for s.o. to make a critical observation regarding s.t.]** ((give a view))

EX. (**a**) Would you please comment on that?
それについて{意見を述べて/コメントして}下さい。
Sore ni-tsuite {iken o nobete/komento-shite} kudasai.
(**b**) The book review commented favorably on your recent book.
書評はあなたの最近の本に好意的な{意見を述べて/コメントをして}いました。
Shohyoo wa anata no saikin no hon ni kooi-tekina {iken o nobete/komento o shite} imashita.

commerce n. **[an interchange of goods, esp. among people in one area]**
sho⌉ogyoo 商業 •c [the work of selling for profit goods that one makes or buys wholesale from s.o. else] ((trade, buying and selling, business))

EX. My uncle majored in commerce in college.
叔父は大学で商業を専攻した。
Oji wa daigaku de shoogyoo o senkoo-shita.

commercial adj. **[of commerce/business]**
sho⌉ogyoo no N 商業のN •c [pertaining to selling goods for profit]

EX. This town has lost its influence as a commercial center in recent years.
この町は近年、商業の中心としての影響力を無くしてしまった。
Kono machi wa kinnen, shoogyoo no chuushin to-shite no eikyoo-ryoku o nakushite shimatta.

— n. **[a paid advertisement on radio or TV]**
ko⌈ma⌉asharu コマーシャル •f

EX. (**a**) There are some interesting differences

between American and Japanese TV commercials.
日本とアメリカのテレビコマーシャルには興味深い相違点がある。
Nihon to Amerika no terebi-komaasharu ni wa kyoomi-bukai sooi-ten ga aru.
(**b**) I like commercials featuring animals.
私は動物が出てくるテレビのコマーシャルが好きだ。
Watashi wa doobutsu ga dete kuru terebi no komaasharu ga suki da.
(**c**) Many countries prohibit cigarette commericals.
タバコのコマーシャルを禁止している国は多い。
Tabako no komaasharu o kinshi-shite iru kuni wa ooi.

commit vt. **[for s.o. to do s.t. wrong/illegal or to promise to a certain position/course of action]**
1. ⟨-o⟩ **o⌈ka⌉su** ⟨～を⟩おかす ① **[for s.o. to fail to observe s.t. sacred or a legal code or a property/right belonging to another]** **⟪violate, err⟫**
㊅ "commit/violate"▷犯す, "risk"▷冒す, "invade"▷侵す
EX. He committed many crimes.
彼は多くの犯罪を犯した。
Kare wa ooku no hanzai o okashita.
2. ⟨-to⟩ **ya⌈kusoku-suru** ⟨～と⟩約束する ③ •c **[for s.o. to make a promise]**
EX. The school committed itself to improving its language teaching.
学校は言語教育を改善すると約束した。
Gakkoo wa gengo-kyooiku o kaizen-suru to yakusoku-shita.

committee n. **[a group of people chosen to report or act upon a certain matter or to perform some service/function]**
i⌈i⌉n-kai 委員会 •c **⟪commission, board⟫**
EX. When is the next meeting of the curriculum committee?
次のカリキュラム委員会の会合はいつですか。
Tsugi no karikyuramu-iin-kai no kaigoo wa itsu desu ka.

common adj. **[belonging to or shared by each/all ⟪fig. "usual," "general"⟫]**
1. fu⌈tsuu no N 普通のN •c **[conforming to a standard/norm ⟪fig. "commonly found"⟫]** **⟪ordinary, normal, usual⟫** ↔ **tokubetsu no N** 特別のN •c
EX. (**a**) This kind of bird is quite common in the area.
この種類の鳥はこの地方ではごく普通です。
Kono shurui no tori wa kono chihoo de wa goku futsuu desu.
(**b**) It is quite common for Japanese children to go to cram school.
日本の子供が学習塾に通うのはごく普通のことです。
Nihon no kodomo ga gakushuu-juku ni kayou no wa goku futsuu no koto desu.
(**c**) It's just a common cold, not the flu.
普通の風邪ですよ。流感じゃない。
Futsuu no kaze desu yo. Ryuukan janai.
2. kyo⌈otsuu no N 共通のN •c **[applying to all of two/more things]** **⟪mutual, similar⟫**
EX. (**a**) All human beings share a common interest in protecting nature.
全人類は自然を保護する上で共通の利害を有する。
Zen-jinrui wa shizen o hogo-suru ue de kyootsuu no rigai o yuusuru.
(**b**) World peace is a hope common to all people.
世界平和は人々の共通の願いだ。
Sekai-heiwa wa hito-bito no kyootsuu no negai da.
PHRASE: common sense *jooshiki* 常識 •c

commonly adv. **[usually, generally]**
i⌈ppan ni 一般に •c **[in a general manner]** **⟪generally, at large⟫**, **fu⌈tsuu** 普通 •c **[in an ordinary manner]** **⟪normally⟫**
EX. (**a**) President Eisenhower was commonly referred to as Ike.
アイゼンハワー大統領は{一般に/普通}アイクと呼ばれた。
Aizenhawaa-daitooryoo wa {ippan ni/futsuu} Aiku to yoba-reta.

C

(**b**) It is commonly believed that a child masters his mother tongue by age five.
{一般に/普通}子供は五歳までに母語をマスターすると思われている。
{Ippan ni/Futsuu} kodomo wa go-sai made ni bogo o masutaa-suru to omowa-rete iru.

communicate vt. **[to impart, transmit or give information]**
⟨-ni⟩ ⟨-o⟩ tsu⌈taeru ⟨～に⟩⟨～を⟩伝える ② [for s.o./s.a. to pass along some message to s.o.], ⟨-ni⟩ ⟨-o⟩ de⌈ntatsu-suru ⟨～に⟩⟨～を⟩伝達する ③ •c [for s.o. to transmit s.t. such as an order, instruction, information, etc., to others] ⦅transmit, tell⦆, ⟨-ni⟩ ⟨-o⟩ shi⌈ra-seru ⟨～に⟩⟨～を⟩知らせる ② [for s.o. to cause s.o. to become aware of s.t.] ⦅inform⦆

EX. (**a**) We will communicate your message to our head office in Tokyo by fax.
あなたのメッセージを東京本社へファックスで{伝えます/伝達します/知らせます}。
Anata no messeeji o Tookyoo-honsha e fakkusu de {tsutaemasu/dentatsu-shimasu/shira-semasu}.
(**b**) Please communicate to us promptly any information you may obtain.
入手出来た情報は何でもすぐに我々に{伝えて/知らせて/?伝達して}下さい。
Nyuushu-dekita joohoo wa nan-demo sugu ni ware-ware ni {tsutaete/shira-sete/?dentatsu-shite} kudasai.
(**c**) It is the duty of the media to communicate the news to the people without error.
ニュースを人々に正確に{伝える/伝達する/知らせる}のが報道の義務です。
Nyuusu o hito-bito ni seikakuni {tsutaeru/dentatsu-suru/shira-seru} no ga hoodoo no gimu desu.
(**d**) The military is set up in such a way that orders are communicated to all personnel instantly.
軍隊では命令を全員に瞬時に{伝える/伝達する/知らせる}体制になっている。
Guntai de wa meirei o zen'in ni shunji ni {tsutaeru/dentatsu-suru/shira-seru} taisei ni natte iru.

— vi. **[to give or exchange information]**
⟨-ni⟩ re⌈nraku-suru ⟨～に⟩連絡する ③ •c [for s.o. to inform people concerned of s.t.] ⦅contact⦆, ⟨-to⟩ i⌉shi no so⌈tsuu o ha⌈ka⌉ru ⟨～と⟩意志の疎通をはかる ① [for s.o. to attempt to convey one's will/intention to s.o. to obtain the understanding of that person]

EX. (**a**) He had a hard time communicating with her father.
彼は彼女の父親{と意志の疎通をはかる/?に連絡する}のに苦労した。
Kare wa kanojo no chichi-oya {to ishi no sotsuu o hakaru/?ni renraku-suru} no ni kuroo-shita.
(**b**) The ambassador lost no time in communicating to the Foreign Minister the extent of the crisis.
大使は直ちに災害の程度を外務大臣{に連絡した/*と意志の疎通をはかった}。
*Taishi wa tadachini saigai no teido o gaimu-daijin {ni renraku-shita/*to ishi no sotsuu o hakatta}.*

communication n. **[a giving/exchanging of information]**
de⌈ntatsu 伝達 •c [transmitting an order/instructions/information to s.o.] ⦅transmission, conveyance⦆, tsu⌈ushin 通信 •c [making contact with s.o. by mail, phone, etc., to provide information about s.t.] ⦅correspondence, intelligence, dispatch⦆, ko⌈myunike⌉eshon コミュニケーション •f, re⌈nraku 連絡 •c [the existence or creation of a connection between two things or people, esp. one involving the transfer of information from one individual to another] ⦅contact⦆

EX. (**a**) We have established communication with the base.
基地と{通信/コミュニケーション/連絡/*伝達}が出来た。
*Kichi to {tsuushin/komyunikeeshon/renraku/*dentatsu} ga dekita.*
(**b**) All communication with the country

ceased after the coup d'état.
クーデターの後その国とのすべての{通信/コミュニケーション/連絡/*伝達}が途絶えた。
*Kuudetaa no ato sono kuni to no subete no {tsuushin/komyunikeeshon/renraku/ *dentatsu} ga todaeta.*
(**c**) Data communication is the business of that corporation.
情報の{伝達/通信/コミュニケーション/*連絡}がその会社の仕事です。
*Joohoo no {dentatsu/tsuushin/ komyunikeeshon/*renraku} ga sono kaisha no shigoto desu.*

communism n. **[socialism as formulated by Marx, Lenin, etc.; a system of social organization in which all economic and social activity is controlled by the state]**
kyo⌈osan-shu⌉gi 共産主義 •c

community n. **[a social group whose members live in a specific locality, share a common government, and have a common heritage]**
chi⌉iki-kyo⌈odoo-tai 地域共同体 •c [family/village ⟨fml⟩], chi⌈iki-sha⌉kai 地域社会 •c [a social group constituted in a given area and having common interests, such as cities, towns, and villages], ko⌈myu⌉nitii コミュニティー •f

EX. (**a**) Mr. Tanaka was given a decoration for his service to the community.
田中氏は{地域共同体/地域社会/コミュニティー}に対する貢献により勲章を授けられた。
Tanaka-shi wa {chiiki-kyoodoo-tai/ chiiki-shakai/komyunitii} ni taisuru kooken ni yori kunshoo o sazuke-rareta.
(**b**) This community is putting great effort into environmental protection.
この{地域共同体/地域社会/コミュニティー}では環境保全に力を入れている。
Kono {chiiki-kyoodoo-tai/chiiki-shakai/ komyunitii} de wa kankyoo-hozen ni chikara o irete iru.

commute vi. **[for s.o. to travel regularly over some distance between one's home and place of work]**
⟨-ni⟩ ka⌈you ⟨〜に⟩通う ① [for a person/vehicle/blood to go to and return from the same place regularly or for s.t. to be exchanged smoothly between two entities] ⟪go to the office/school, attend, circulate⟫, ⟨-ni⟩ tsu⌈ukin-suru ⟨〜に⟩通勤する ③ •c [for s.o. to go to and return from one's place of work regularly] ⟪go, attend⟫, ⟨-ni⟩ tsu⌈ugaku-suru ⟨〜に⟩通学する ③ •c [for s.o. to go to and return from school]

EX. (**a**) It's hard to commute to one's office in the congestion of a large city.
大都会の混雑の中で会社に{通う/通勤する/*通学する}のは大変だ。
*Dai-tokai no konzatsu no naka de kaisha ni {kayou/tsuukin-suru/ *tsuugaku-suru} no wa taihen da.*
(**b**) Many students chose to live in the dorm rather than commute.
多くの学生は{通う/通学する/*通勤する}よりは寮に住むことを選んだ。
*Ooku no gakusei wa {kayou/tsuugaku-suru/*tsuukin-suru} yori wa ryoo ni sumu koto o eranda.*
(**c**) It takes two hours for me to commute to my office.
会社へ{通う/通勤する/*通学する}のに二時間かかります。
*Kaisha e {kayou/tsuukin-suru/ *tsuugaku-suru} no ni ni-jikan kakarimasu.*
(**d**) The bus was full of people commuting to work or school.
バスは会社や学校へ{通勤する/通学する/通う}人たちで満員だった。
Basu wa kaisha ya gakkoo e {tsuukin-suru/tsuugaku-suru/kayou} hito-tachi de man'in datta.

NOTE: *Tsuukin-suru* may not be used in the case of students commuting to school. Instead, *tsuugaku-suru* is used for that meaning, where *gaku* indicates "school."

companion n. **[a person who frequently accompanies another/others]**
na⌈kama⌉ 仲間 [a person in one's in-group

with whom one frequently spends time, excluding one's relatives, spouse, and offspring 《fig. "the same kind"》] 《colleague, fellow worker, comrade, partner》, tsu⌈re 連れ /〈V*masu* of *tsureru* ② take s.o. along/ [person(s) with whom s.o. goes somewhere together] 《company, follow, partner》

C

EX. (**a**) It would be more fun to have a companion on the trip.
旅は{仲間/連れ}がいたほうが楽しい。
Tabi wa {nakama/tsure} ga ita hoo ga tanoshii.
(**b**) Cats and dogs make excellent companions for humans.
犬や猫は人間にとって素晴らしい{仲間/*連れ}である。
*Inu ya neko wa ningen ni-totte subarashii {nakama/*tsure} dearu.*

company n. **[a number of persons associating together, especially for joint action, as in business 《fig. "corporation," "a military subdivision"》]**

1. ko⌈osai 交際 •c [the act of associating with persons other than your family/relatives] 《associate》

EX. John had always enjoyed the company of women.
ジョンはいつも女性との交際を楽しんでいた。
Jon wa itsu-mo josei to no koosai o tanoshinde ita.

2. na⌈kama⌉ 仲間 [a person in one's in-group with whom one frequently spends time, excluding one's relatives, spouse, and offspring 《fig. "the same kind"》] 《companion, fellow, colleague》

EX. A man is known by the company he keeps.
付き合う仲間を見ればその人間の人柄が分かる。
Tsuki-au nakama o mireba sono ningen no hito-gara ga wakaru.

3. kya⌈ku 客 •c [s.o. who visits or is invited to a place or s.o. who comes to buy/see things for a fee] 《guest, customer》

EX. We're having company at our house this evening.
今晩はうちにお客があります。
Konban wa uchi ni o-kyaku ga arimasu.

NOTE: *O-kyaku* or sometimes *o-kyaku-san* is the honorific version of *kyaku*.

4. ka⌈isha 会社 •c [a corporate legal entity established for the purpose of engaging in business for profit] 《firm, corporation》

EX. (**a**) In the field of computers, there are a lot of young companies.
コンピューターの分野には若い会社がたくさんある。
Konpyuutaa no bun'ya ni wa wakai kaisha ga takusan aru.
(**b**) Mr. Yano is the president of a machine company.
矢野さんは機械会社の社長です。
Yano-san wa kikai-gaisha no shachoo desu.
(**c**) The company pays the expenses.
費用は会社持ちです。
Hiyoo wa kaisha-mochi desu.

5. da⌉n 団 •c [a group of people having some specific objective] 《body, corps, group, party, team》

EX. (**a**) A theater company from London is performing in town now.
今、町ではロンドンの劇団が興行している。
Ima, machi de wa Rondon no gekidan ga koogyoo-shite iru.
(**b**) The Shakespeare Company came from the United Kingdom to perform a series of plays.
一連の劇を上演するため英国からシェークスピア劇団が来た。
Ichi-ren no geki o jooen-suru tame Eikoku kara Sheekusupia-gekidan ga kita.

company employee n. **[s.o. who works in a firm]**

ka⌈isha⌉-in 会社員 •c [s.o. who is employed in a firm] 《salaried man》, sa⌈rari⌉i-man サラリーマン •f

NOTE: *Sararii-man* is a word coined in Japan.

EX. (**a**) Japanese company employees often go drinking together after work.
日本の{会社員/サラリーマン}は仕事の後よく一緒に飲みに行く。
Nihon no {kaishya-in/sararii-man} wa shigoto no ato yoku issho ni nomi ni iku.
(**b**) American company employees take longer vacations than their Japanese counterparts.
アメリカの{会社員/サラリーマン}は日本の会社員より長い休みを取る。
Amerika no {kaisha-in/sararii-man} wa Nihon no kaisha-in yori nagai yasumi o toru.
(**c**) My father is a company employee.
私の父は{会社員/サラリーマン}です。
Watashi no chichi wa {kaisha-in/sararii-man} desu.

comparative adj. **[of/pertaining to/proceeding by comparison]**
1. hi⌈kaku no N 比較のN •c [of comparison] ⟪**contrastive**⟫
EX. (**a**) Comparative literature has become a popular discipline recently.
比較文学は最近人気のある学問になった。
Hikaku-bungaku wa saikin ninki no aru gakumon ni natta.
(**b**) I'm doing a comparative study of the educational systems of Japan and America.
私は日米の教育制度の比較研究をしています。
Watashi wa Nichi-Bei no kyooiku-seido no hikaku-kenkyuu o shite imasu.
NOTE: The *no* of *hikaku no* often drops when *hikaku* and the following noun (in this example *bungaku* "literature") form a compound word with a set meaning.
2. ka⌉nari no N かなりのN [of a degree exceeding the extent normally expected] ⟪**relative**⟫
EX. John lived a life of comparative luxury after he got his first job.
最初の仕事を得たあと、ジョンはかなりのぜいたくをして暮らしていた。
Saisho no shigoto o eta ato, Jon wa kanari no zeitaku o shite kurashite ita.

comparatively adj. **[not in absolute terms] wa⌈riai(ni) 割合(に) [to a degree greater than expected]** ⟪**rather, relatively**⟫, **hi⌈kaku-teki 比較的 •c [when compared with the general standard]** ⟪**relatively**⟫, **ka⌉nari かなり [to a degree exceeding the extent normally expected]** ⟪**considerably**⟫
EX. (**a**) To the Japanese, Italian is a comparatively easy language to pronounce.
日本人にとってイタリア語の発音は{割合(に)/比較的/かなり}易しい。
Nihon-jin ni-totte Itaria-go no hatsuon wa {wariai(ni)/hikaku-teki/kanari} yasashii.
(**b**) Some parts of Kyushu can be comparatively cold in winter.
九州は冬{割合(に)/比較的/かなり}寒くなる所がある。
Kyuushuu wa fuyu {wariai(ni)/hikaku-teki/kanari} samuku naru tokoro ga aru.
(**c**) It is comparatively warm today.
今日は{割合(に)/比較的/かなり}暖かい。
Kyoo wa {wariai(ni)/hikaku-teki/kanari} atatakai.
NOTE: Neither English 'comparatively' nor Japanese '*hikaku-teki*' sound natural with an adjective which is itself comparative form, as shown in the following examples. ?It is comparatively warmer today than yesterday. *?Kyoo wa kinoo yori hikaku-teki atatakai.*

compare vt. **[for s.o. to examine two or more things for similarities and differences or to liken one thing to another]**
1. ⟨-o⟩ {⟨-to⟩/⟨-ni⟩} ku⌈raberu ⟨〜を⟩{⟨〜と⟩/⟨〜に⟩}比べる ② [for s.o. to check two/more things against each other for similarities/differences or relative strength/weaknesses] ⟪**contrast**⟫, **⟨-o⟩ ⟨-to⟩ hi⌈kaku-suru ⟨〜を⟩⟨〜と⟩比較する ③ •c**
EX. (**a**) Teachers of Japanese often compare Japanese with English when they explain grammar.
日本語教師は文法説明の際よく日本語を英語と{比べる/比較する}。

Nihon-go-kyooshi wa bunpoo-setsumei no sai yoku Nihon-go o eigo to {kuraberu/hikaku-suru}.
(**b**) It is interesting to compare the grammars of Japanese and English.
日本語と英語の文法を{比べる/比較する}と面白い。
Nihon-go to eigo no bunpoo o {kuraberu/hikaku-suru} to omoshiroi.
(**c**) The first step in cross-cultural understanding is to compare one's native culture with the other.
異文化に対する理解は自分の文化と他の文化を{比べる/比較する}ことから始まる。
I-bunka ni-taisuru rikai wa jibun no bunka to ta no bunka o {kuraberu/hikaku-suru} koto kara hajimaru.

2. **⟨-o⟩ ⟨-ni⟩ ta⌈toe⌉ru ⟨〜を⟩⟨〜に⟩たとえる ② [for s.o. to cite s.t. familiar and similar to the thing/event to be explained in order to make it easier to understand]** ⟪**liken**⟫

EX. I like to compare life to a voyage.
私は人生を航海にたとえるのが好きだ。
Watashi wa jinsei o kookai ni tatoeru no ga suki da.

— vi. **[for s.o./s.t./s.a. to be considered of a caliber equal to s.t./s.o./s.a. else]**
⟨-to⟩ na⌈rabu ⟨〜と⟩並ぶ ① [to be positioned closely to s.t./s.o./s.a. else in an orderly arrangement] ⟪**line up, queue up, rank with**⟫, **⟨-ni⟩ hi⌈tteki-suru ⟨〜に⟩匹敵する ③ •c [to be equal to]** ⟪**rival, match, equal**⟫

EX. No one can compare with Bob in dancing.
踊り(のうまさ)ではボブ{と並ぶ/に匹敵する}ものはいない。
Odori (no uma-sa) de wa Bobu {to narabu/ni hitteki-suru} mono wa inai.

PHRASE: compare favorably with… *⟨-to⟩ kurabete otoranai* ⟨〜と⟩比べて劣らない /⟨Vneg. of *otoru* ① be inferior + *nai* not/

EX. This grammar book compares favorably with any published so far.
この文法書は従来のと比べても劣らない。
Kono bunpoo-sho wa juurai no to kurabete mo otoranai.

comparison n. **[an act or instance of comparing]**
hi⌈kaku 比較 •c [the act of checking one thing against another for similarities/differences or relative strengths/weaknesses], ta⌈ishoo 対照 •c [a juxtaposing of two things in such a way that their similarities or differences are readily apparent; a checking of s.t. against its original to see if there are any differences] ⟪**contrast, antithesis**⟫

EX. (**a**) A comparison of different languages can lead to the discovery of linguistic universals.
いろいろ異なった言語の{比較/対照}は言語の普遍性の発見につながるかもしれない。
Iro-iro kotonatta gengo no {hikaku/taishoo} wa gengo no fuhen-sei no hakken ni tsunagaru kamoshirenai.
(**b**) Let's think about this problem through a comparison with foreign countries.
この問題は外国の例と{比較/対照}して考えてみましょう。
Kono mondai wa gaikoku no rei to {hikaku/taishoo}-shite kangaete mimashoo.

compete vi. **[to strive to do better than another]**
⟨-to⟩ kyo⌈osoo-suru ⟨〜と⟩競争する ③ •c [for s.o. to strive to achieve victory or superiority over another] ⟪**contend, vie**⟫, **⟨-to⟩ ki⌈so⌉u ⟨〜と⟩競う ① [for s.o. to make vigorous efforts not to lose to another]** ⟪**vie, rival**⟫, **⟨-to⟩ a⌈raso⌉u ⟨〜と⟩争う ① [for s.o. to strive to win over another]** ⟪**contest**⟫

EX. (**a**) The two men competed for Meg's heart.
その二人の男はメグの心を勝ち取ろうと{競争した/競った/争った}。
Sono futari no otoko wa Megu no kokoro o kachi-toroo to {kyoosoo-shita/kisotta/arasotta}.
(**b**) America and the Soviet Union were competing during the 1960's to be the first to send a manned rocket to the moon.

アメリカとソビエトは1960年代に有人ロケットで月に一番乗りしようと{競争して/競って/争って}いた。
Amerika to Sobieto wa sen-kyuu-hyaku-roku-juu-nendai ni yuujin-roketto de tsuki ni ichiban-nori-shiyoo to {kyoosoo-shite/kisotte/arasotte} ita.
(**c**) The students are competing to be No. 1 in their class.
学生たちはお互いにクラスで一番になろうと{競争して/競って/争って}いる。
Gakusei-tachi wa o-tagai ni kurasu de ichi-ban ni naroo to {kyoosoo-shite/kisotte/arasotte} iru.

competence n. **[the quality of having the suitable skills, experience, etc. for some purpose]**
no˥oryoku 能力 •c [the capability to be able to perform a given task] ⟪**ability, capability**⟫
EX. (**a**) He did not have the competence to manage the affairs of the department.
彼は学部の業務を管理する能力がなかった。
Kare wa gakubu no gyoomu o kanri-suru nooryoku ga nakatta.
(**b**) He lacks competence as a manager.
彼は管理者としての能力に欠けている。
Kare wa kanri sha to-shite no nooryoku ni kakete iru.
(**c**) While you are young, try to develop the competence to work independently.
若いうちに独立して仕事ができる能力を培うように努めなさい。
Wakai uchi ni dokuritsu-shite shigoto ga dekiru nooryoku o tsuchikau yooni tsutomenasai.
(**d**) It was then that I realized the limits of my competence.
自分の能力の限界を悟ったのはその時だった。
Jibun no nooryoku no genkai o satotta no wa sono toki datta.

competition n. **[an act/instance of competing]**
kyo˥osoo 競争 •c [a contest to achieve victory or superiority over another] ⟪**contest, rivalry, struggle**⟫, **shi˥ai 試合 [a planned event, usu. in sports, where individuals/teams match their skills in an attempt to gain superiority over each other according to rules mutually agreed upon]** ⟪**game, match, fight, tournament**⟫, **kyo˥ogi 競技 •c [an instance of competing in sports]** ⟪**game, match**⟫
EX. (**a**) The competetion for entrance to this university is keen.
この大学へ入学するための{競争/*競技/*試合}は激しい。
*Kono daigaku e nyuugaku-suru tame no {kyoosoo/*kyoogi/*shiai} wa hageshii.*
(**b**) The wrestling competition was well attended.
レスリングの{試合/競技/*競争}は人が大勢入った。
*Resuringu no {shiai/kyoogi/*kyoosoo} wa hito ga oozei haitta.*
(**c**) Skiing competitions are popular.
スキーの{試合/競技/*競争}は人気がある。
*Sukii no {shiai/kyoogi/*kyoosoo} wa ninki ga aru.*

complain vi. **[for s.o. to say that one is discontent or suffering from pain]**
1. fu˥hei o i˥u 不平を言う ① [for s.o. to express a feeling of dissatisfaction with s.o./s.t] ⟪**grumble**⟫
EX. He is always complaining about work.
彼はいつも仕事のことで不平を言っている。
Kare wa itsu-mo shigoto no koto de fuhei o itte iru.
2. (⟨-ni⟩) ⟨-o⟩ **u˥ttae˥ru** (⟨〜に⟩)⟨〜を⟩**訴える ② [for s.o. to communicate s.t. very strongly using verbal or nonverbal means]** ⟪**sue, have recourse to, appeal to**⟫
EX. Sally complained of a stomachache.
サリーは腹痛を訴えた。
Sarii wa fukutsuu o uttaeta.

complaint n. **[an expression of discontent or pain]**
ku˥joo 苦情 •c [dissatisfaction with damage or unfair treatment inflicted by others]

C

《grievance》), **fu⌈hei 不平 •c [a feeling of dissatisfaction] 《discontent, dissatisfaction, grievance》**

EX. (**a**) These days we often hear complaints about the consumption tax.
最近、消費税に対する{苦情/不平}をよく聞く。
Saikin shoohi-zei ni-taisuru {kujoo/fuhei} o yoku kiku.
(**b**) Recently there have been lots of complaints about politics.
最近政治に対する{苦情/不平}が多い。
Saikin seiji ni-taisuru {kujoo/fuhei} ga ooi.
(**c**) If you have any complaints about the matter, let me know.
もし本件に関して{苦情/不平}があれば知らせて欲しい。
Moshi honken ni-kanshite {kujoo/fuhei} ga areba shirasete hoshii.

C

complete vt. **[to make whole/perfect or bring to completion]**
⟨-o⟩ ka⌈nsei-suru ⟨〜を⟩完成する ③ •c [for s.o. to bring s.t. to a finished/perfect state] 《perfect, finish, accomplish》, shi-⌈age⌉ru 仕上げる ②

EX. We completed the project last year.
我々はそのプロジェクトを昨年{完成した/仕上げた}。
Ware-ware wa sono purojekuto o sakunen {kansei-shita/shi-ageta}.

—— adj. **[thorough/perfect]**
ka⌈nzenna 完全な adj(*na*). **•c [lacking no parts and having no faults] 《perfect, whole, entire》 ↔ fu-kanzenna 不完全な** adj(*na*). **•c; ma⌈ttaku no N 全くのN [an expression indicating that s.t. cannot be described other than as N] 《utter, entire, thorough, sheer, downright》**

EX. (**a**) That plan ended in complete failure.
その計画は{完全な/全くの}失敗に終わった。
Sono keikaku wa {kanzenna/mattaku no} shippai ni owatta.
(**b**) We won complete freedom.
私たちは{完全な/*全くの}自由を手にした。
*Watashi-tachi wa {kanzenna/*mattaku no} jiyuu o te ni shita.*

completely adv. **[in a complete manner]**
ma⌈ttaku 全く [in a manner so strongly that it cannot be expressed in any other way] 《exactly, entirely》, kan⌈zenni 完全に /⟨adj(*na*). *ni* of *kanzenna* complete/ •c [in a manner absolutely free from any lack or imperfection], su⌈kka⌉ri すっかり [an expression indicating that some condition is pervasive or exhaustively present] 《perfectly, utterly, thoroughly》

EX. (**a**) I completely forgot about the meeting.
会のことは{全く/完全に/すっかり}忘れていた。
Kai no koto wa {mattaku/kanzenni/sukkari} wasurete ita.
(**b**) The old station building was completely demolished.
古い駅舎は{完全に/すっかり/*全く}取り壊されてしまった。
*Furui ekisha wa {kanzenni/sukkari/*mattaku} tori-kowasa-rete shimatta.*

completion n. **[the act of thoroughly finishing s.t. or the state of s.t. being thoroughly finished]**
ka⌈nsei 完成 •c [the act of bringing s.t. to a perfectly finished state or the state of being perfectly finished] ↔ mi-kansei 未完成 •c

EX. (**a**) The dictionary is nearing completion.
辞書は完成に近づいている。
Jisho wa kansei ni chikazuite iru.
(**b**) Completion of the building is scheduled for May.
ビルの完成は五月に予定されている。
Biru no kansei wa go-gatsu ni yotei-sarete iru.

complex adj. **[complicated/involved]**
fu⌈kuzatsuna 複雑な adj(*na*). **•c [involving circumstances and relationships of various types that are interconnected in such a way as to be difficult to comprehend] 《complicated, intricate》 ↔ tanjunna 単純な** adj(*na*). **•c**

EX. (**a**) This structure is too complex to explain.

この構造は複雑過ぎて説明できない。
Kono koozoo wa fukuzatsu-sugite setsumei-dekinai.
(**b**) International politics are complex.
国際政治は複雑だ。
Kokusai-seiji wa fukuzatsu da.
(**c**) Computers can do complex calculations instantly.
コンピューターは複雑な計算を一瞬にしてしまう。
Konpyuutaa wa fukuzatsuna keisan o isshun ni shite shimau.

complicated adj. **[composed of elaborately connected parts and difficult to analyze/understand]**
fu⌈kuzatsuna 複雑な adj(*na*). **•c [involving circumstances and relationships of various types that are interconnected in such a way as to be difficult to comprehend], ko⌈mi-itta N 込み入ったN /⟨Vinf. past of *komi-iru* ① be intricate/ [intricately involved and convoluted] ⟪complex, intricate⟫, ko⌈mi-itte iru (N) 込み入っている(N) /⟨V *te iru* of *komi-iru* ① be intricate/**

EX. (**a**) The mechanism of this device is complicated.
この装置のメカニズムは{複雑だ/込み入っている}。
Kono soochi no mekanizumu wa {fukuzatsu da/komi-itte iru}.
(**b**) Within minutes he had figured out the complicated wiring of the stereo system.
彼はステレオシステムの{複雑な/込み入った}配線がどうなっているのかが二、三分で分かった。
Kare wa sutereo-shisutemu no {fukuzatsuna/komi-itta} haisen ga doo natte iru no ka ga ni-san-pun de wakatta.
(**c**) We got involved in a series of complicated events.
我々は一連の{複雑な/込み入った}事件に巻き込まれた。
Ware-ware wa ichiren no {fukuzatsuna/komi-itta} jiken ni maki-koma-reta.
(**d**) It's quite a complicated story, isn't it?
随分{複雑な/込み入った}話ですね。
Zuibun {fukuzatsuna/komi-itta} hanashi desu ne.

compose vt. **[for s.o. to create s.t. (artistic) by combining various things together]**
1. ⟨-o⟩ ko⌈osei-suru ⟨〜を⟩構成する ③ •c [for s.o. to assemble various things into an orderly integrated whole; for various things together to make up an orderly integrated whole] ⟪constitute, organize, form⟫

EX. (**a**) In this school, a single class is composed of 15 students.
この学校では一クラスは十五人の学生で構成されている。
Kono gakkoo de wa hito-kurasu wa juu-go-nin no gakusei de koosei-sarete iru.
(**b**) The most basic elements composing a sentence are the subject and the predicate.
文を構成する最も基本的な要素は主語と述語である。
Bun o koosei-suru mottomo kihon-tekina yooso wa shugo to jutsugo dearu.
(**c**) How many musical instruments ordinarily compose an orchestra?
オーケストラを構成している楽器は普通いくつぐらいですか。
Ookesutora o koosei-shite iru gakki wa futsuu ikutsu-gurai desu ka.

2. ⟨-o⟩ tsu⌈ku⌉ru ⟨〜を⟩つくる ① [for s.o./s.a. to cause s.t./s.o./s.a. to come into existence which did not exist previously] ⟪fabricate, make, create⟫, ⟨-o⟩ sa⌈kkyoku-suru ⟨〜を⟩作曲する ③ •c [for s.o. to create music]
㊥ "build/manufacture"▷造る, otherwise ▷作る

EX. (**a**) Schubert composed this symphony.
シューベルトがこの交響曲を{作った/作曲した}。
Shuuberuto ga kono kookyoo-kyoku o {tsukutta/sakkyoku-shita}.
(**b**) Who composed this poem?
だれがこの詩を{作った/*作曲した}んですか。
*Dare ga kono shi o {tsukutta/*sakkyoku-shita} n desu ka.*

C

composition n. **[s.t. composed]**

1. sa⌈kubun 作文 •c [a piece of writing composed on a particular topic] ⟪**writing**⟫

EX. (**a**) In Japanese class we are assigned to write one composition a day.
日本語の授業では毎日一つ作文を書くことが宿題です。
Nihon-go no jugyoo de wa mai-nichi hitotsu sakubun o kaku koto ga shukudai desu.
(**b**) Bob's Japanese composition is better than ones written by Japanese.
ボブの書いた日本語の作文は日本人が書いたものよりも立派だ。
Bobu no kaita Nihon-go no sakubun wa Nihon-jin ga kaita mono yori mo rippa da.
(**c**) I am good at composition.
私は作文が得意です。
Watashi wa sakubun ga tokui desu.

2. sa⌈kkyoku 作曲 •c [composing music or a piece of music that has been composed by s.o.]

EX. (**a**) He specializes in the composition of music for films.
彼の専門は映画音楽の作曲です。
Kare no senmon wa eiga-ongaku no sakkyoku desu.
(**b**) He was asked to write a musical composition commemorating the building of a new concert hall.
彼は新しいコンサートホールの落成を記念する音楽の作曲を依頼された。
Kare wa atarashii konsaato-hooru no rakusei o kinen-suru ongaku no sakkyoku o irai-sareta.

3. ko⌈osei 構成 •c [the assembly of various things into an orderly integrated whole] ⟪**constitution, organization, make-up, construction, formation**⟫

EX. (**a**) The composition in this photograph is excellent.
この写真は構成がすばらしい。
Kono shashin wa koosei ga subarashii.
(**b**) Careful initial attention to planning the overall composition is essential to writing a good book.
いい本を書くには初めの段階で全体の構成について慎重な計画をたてることが必要だ。
Ii hon o kaku ni wa hajime no dankai de zentai no koosei ni-tsuite shinchoona keikaku o tateru koto ga hitsuyoo da.

compromise n. **[a settlement of differences through mutual concessions or the result of such a settlement]**
da⌈kyoo 妥協 •c ⟪**mutual concession, understanding, meeting halfway**⟫

EX. (**a**) Japan and the U.S. finally reached a compromise on the trade issue.
日米は貿易問題でやっと妥協に達した。
Nichi-Bei wa booeki-mondai de yatto dakyoo ni tasshita.
(**b**) He never makes compromises.
彼は決して妥協をしない。
Kare wa kesshite dakyoo o shinai.

— vi. **[to arrive at a settlement of differences through mutual concessions]**
da⌈kyoo-suru 妥協する ③ •c ⟪**make concessions, meet halfway**⟫

EX. (**a**) Both parties compromised in order to reach an agreement.
双方の当事者は同意に達するために妥協した。
Soohoo no tooji-sha wa dooi ni tassuru tame ni dakyoo-shita.
(**b**) Let's compromise on the matter, shall we?
その件は妥協しましょう。
Sono ken wa dakyoo-shimashoo.

— vt. **[for s.o. to expose one's character, reputation, or morals to suspicion or disrepute by unwise action]**
⟨-o⟩ ki⌈zu-tsuke⌉ru ⟨〜を⟩傷つける ② [to inflict physical or mental harm on s.o./s.t./s.a.] ⟪**injure, wound, hurt, disgrace, impair**⟫, **⟨-o⟩ ke⌈ga⌉su ⟨〜を⟩汚す ① [to cause s.t. to become unclean ⟪fig. "desecrate," "disgrace"⟫]** ⟪**defile, disgrace, dishonor**⟫

EX. (**a**) He compromised his reputation by taking a bribe.
彼はわいろを受け取ったことで自分の

評判を{傷つけた/汚した}。
Kare wa wairo o uke-totta koto de jibun no hyooban o {kizu-tsuketa/kegashita}.
(**b**) Don't do anything to compromise your credit.
自分の信用を{傷つける/汚す}ような事をするな。
Jibun no shin'yoo o {kizu-tsukeru/kegasu} yoona koto o suru na.
(**c**) You should not use language that might compromise the honor of the deceased.
故人の名誉を{傷つける/汚す}ような言葉は慎むべきだ。
Kojin no meiyo o {kizu-tsukeru/kegasu} yoona kotoba wa tsutsushimu-beki da.

computer n.
ko⌈npyu⌉utaa コンピューター •f, de⌈nshi-keesa⌉n-ki 電子計算機 •c [electronic computing machine]
PHRASE: personal computer *pasokon* パソコン •f

concentrate vt. **[for s.o. to draw together all one's attention or effort to s.t.]**
⟨-ni⟩ ⟨-o⟩ shu⌈uchuu-suru ⟨〜に⟩⟨〜を⟩集中する ③ •c [for s.o. to cause several things to gather together at one point] ⟪focus on⟫
EX. (**a**) The player concentrated his attention on the ball.
選手はボールに注意を集中した。
Senshu wa booru ni chuui o shuuchuu-shita.
(**b**) The students concentrated all their energy on their college entrance exams.
学生たちは全精力を大学の入学試験に集中した。
Gakusei-tachi wa zen-seiryoku o daigaku no nyuugaku-shiken ni shuuchuu-shita.

—— vi. **[for s.o. to bring all one's attention or effort to bear on one thing or for several things to gather together at one point]**
⟨-ni⟩ shu⌈uchuu-suru ⟨〜に⟩集中する ③ •c [for s.o. to fix one's attention on s.t. or for several things to gather together at one point] ⟪focus on become centered on⟫, ⟨-ni⟩ se⌈nnen-suru ⟨〜に⟩専念する ③ •c [for s.o. to pay exclusive attention to s.t.] ⟪focus on⟫
EX. (**a**) I can't concentrate on studying because it's too noisy.
うるさくて勉強に{集中/専念}できない。
Urusakute benkyoo ni {shuuchuu/sennen}-dekinai.
(**b**) He concentrated for a month on curing the patient's disease.
彼は一か月の間患者の病気の治療に{集中/専念}した。
Kare wa ik-kagetsu no aida kanja no byooki no chiryoo ni {shuuchuu/sennen}-shita.
(**c**) The population in this state tends to concentrate around the lakes.
この州の人口は湖の周囲に{集中/*専念}する傾向がある。
*Kono shuu no jinkoo wa mizuumi no shuui ni {shuuchuu/*sennen}-suru keikoo ga aru.*
(**d**) Everyone's eyes concentrated on him.
みんなの目が彼に{集中/*専念}した。
*Minna no me ga kare ni {shuuchuu/*sennen}-shita.*

concentration n. **[the fixing of one's attention on s.t.]**
shu⌈uchuu 集中 •c [the gathering together of several things at one point] ⟪focus, convergence, centralization⟫
EX. Simultaneous interpretation requires strong powers of concentration.
同時通訳は強じんな集中力が要求される。
Dooji-tsuuyaku wa kyoojinna shuuchuu-ryoku ga yookyuu-sareru.

concept n. **[a general notion/idea]**
ga⌉inen 概念 •c [an idea representing how s.t. is conceived to be] ⟪general idea, notion⟫
EX. (**a**) Ordinary people have a very different concept of grammar from that held by linguists.
一般の人は言語学者とは随分異なった文法の概念をもっている。
Ippan no hito wa gengo-gakusha to wa

C

zuibun kotonatta bunpoo no gainen o motte iru.
(**b**) Please explain to us the concept of culture.
文化の概念について説明してください。
Bunka no gainen ni-tsuite setsumei-shite kudasai.

concern vt. **[to relate to or be connected with s.o./s.t. or to trouble, worry or disquiet s.o.]**
1. ⟨-ni⟩ ka⌈nsu⌉ru ⟨〜に⟩関する ③ •c **[for s.t. to have a relationship to s.t. else]** ⟪**relate to**⟫, **⟨-ni⟩ ka⌈kawa⌉ru** ⟨〜に⟩かかわる ① **[for s.t. to have a (vital) bearing on s.t. else]** ⟪**bear on**⟫
NOTE: 関する appears prenominally.
EX. (**a**) What I wish to discuss with you is a problem that concerns the very survival of our company.
ご相談したいことはうちの会社の存続そのものに{かかわる/関する}問題です。
Go-soodan-shi-tai koto wa uchi no kaisha no sonzoku sono mono ni {kakawaru/kansuru} mondai desu.
(**b**) Clip and file all information that concerns Japan.
日本に{関する/かかわる}すべての情報を切り取ってファイルしなさい。
Nihon ni {kansuru/kakawaru} subete no joohoo o kiri-totte fairu-shinasai.
(**c**) This book discusses Japan's economic policy as it concerns trade issues.
この本では貿易問題に{関する/かかわる}日本の経済政策が取り上げられている。
Kono hon de wa booeki-mondai ni {kansuru/kakawaru} Nihon no keizai-seisaku ga tori-age-rarete iru.
(**d**) Problems that concern security issues between the two countries need to be resolved.
両国の安全保障に{かかわる/関する}問題は解決される必要がある。
Ryookoku no anzen-hoshoo ni {kakawaru/kansuru} mondai wa kaiketsu-sareru hitsuyoo ga aru.

2. ⟨-o⟩ shi⌈npai-saseru ⟨〜を⟩心配させる /⟨**causative of *shinpai-suru*** ③ **worry**/ ② •c **[to cause s.o. to become worried]** ⟪**worry about s.t.**⟫
NOTE: Often this meaning is expressed in English in the passive voice as "be concerned with/over/about…," which is expressed in Japanese as ⟨*-o*⟩ *shinpai-shite iru*, or ⟨*-ga*⟩ *shinpai da*.
EX. (**a**) I am concerned over her health.
私は彼女の健康{を心配しています/が心配です}。
Watakushi wa kanojo no kenkoo {o shinpai-shite imasu/ga shinpai desu}.
(**b**) The President was concerned over the safety of the hostage.
大統領は人質の安全{を心配していた/が心配だった}。
Daitooryoo wa hitojichi no anzen {o shinpai-shite ita/ga shinpai datta}.

— n. **[s.t. that relates to s.o./s.t./s.a. or worry, anxiety or a commercial company]**
1. kan⌈kei 関係 •c **[a quality by which two or more things are considered to be connected or joined together]** ⟪**relation, connection, effect**⟫
EX. This matter is no concern of John's.
この件はジョンと全然関係がない。
Kono ken wa Jon to zenzen kankei ga nai.
2. shi⌈npai 心配 •c **[an uncomfortable feeling caused by uncertainty or by the expectation of danger/evil/s.t. troublesome]** ⟪**worry, anxiety, uneasiness, fear, supense, apprehension**⟫
EX. (**a**) The economist declared that there was no concern of a recession occurring in the near future.
その経済学者は近い将来には不況になる心配はないと言明した。
Sono keizai-gakusha wa chikai shoorai ni wa fukyoo ni naru shinpai wa nai to genmei-shita.
(**b**) The rise in prices recently is a source of grave concern to us.
最近の物価の上昇は我々にとって大きな心配の種だ。

Saikin no bukka no jooshoo wa ware-ware ni-totte ookina shinpai no tane da.

3. ka⌈isha 会社 •c [a corporate legal entity established for the purpose of engaging in business for profit] ⟪company, firm, corporation⟫

EX. His is an up-and-coming concern in the field of computers.
彼の会社はコンピューターの分野では有望な会社だ。
Kare no kaisha wa konpyuutaa no bun'ya de wa yuuboona kaisha da.

4. ka⌈nshi⌉n-ji 関心事 •c [a matter one is interested in] ⟪interest⟫

EX. Money is his greatest concern.
金が彼の最大の関心事だ。
Kane ga kare no saidai no kanshin-ji da.

concerning prep. **[in relation to/regarding]**
ni-tsuite (no N) について(のN) comp. prt. **[relating to]** ⟪**about**⟫, **ni-kanshite** (no N) に関して(のN) comp. prt. **[relating to]** ⟪**regarding**⟫, **ni-ka⌈nsu⌉ru** N に関するN comp. prt. ⟪**regarding**⟫

EX. (**a**) There are a number of theories concerning the origin of the Japanese language.
日本語の起源{について/に関して/*に関する}はいくつかの説がある。
*Nihon-go no kigen {ni-tsuite/ni-kanshite/*ni-kansuru} wa ikutsu-ka no setsu ga aru.*
(**b**) I am doing research concerning the origins of man.
人類の起源{について/に関して/に関する}研究をしています。
Jinrui no kigen {ni-tsuite/ni-kanshite/ni-kansuru} kenkyuu o shite imasu.
(**c**) Many books have been written concerning Japan's modernization.
日本の近代化{について(の)/に関して(の)/に関する}本が沢山書かれている。
Nihon no kindai-ka {ni-tsuite (no)/ni-kanshite (no)/ni-kansuru} hon ga takusan kaka-rete iru.
(**d**) Do you have any books concerning kabuki?
歌舞伎{についての/に関しての/に関する}本をお持ちですか。
Kabuki {ni-tsuite no/ni-kanshite no/ni-kansuru} hon o o-mochi desu ka.
(**e**) I have no comment concerning this incident.
この事件{について/に関して/*に関する}はノーコメントです。
*Kono jiken {ni-tsuite/ni-kanshite/*ni-kansuru} wa noo-komento desu.*

conclude vt. **[to bring s.t. (verbal) to its end ⟪fig. "deduce," "infer," "decide"⟫]**

1. ⟨**-o**⟩ **o⌈eru** ⟨〜を⟩終える ② **[for s.o. to cause s.t. to come to an end]** ⟪**finish, end**⟫ ↔ ⟨**-o**⟩ **hajimeru** ⟨〜を⟩始める ②; ⟨**-o**⟩ **shi⌈me-kuku⌉ru,** ⟨〜を⟩締めくくる ① **[for s.o. to bind things together ⟪fig. "bring to a finish"⟫]**

EX. (**a**) I concluded my letter by wishing him a quick recovery.
早く回復されるように祈って手紙を{終えた/締めくくった}。
Hayaku kaifuku-sareru yooni inotte tegami o {oeta/shime-kukutta}.
(**b**) We concluded the reunion with a song.
同窓会を歌で{終えた/締めくくった}。
Doosoo-kai o uta de {oeta/shime-kukutta}.

2. ⟨**-to**⟩ **ke⌈tsuron-zuke⌉ru** ⟨〜と⟩結論づける ② •c **[for s.o. to judge and determine s.t. to be the case after much thought/discussion]** ⟪**determine, decide**⟫

EX. (**a**) From this evidence I concluded that she was telling the truth.
この証拠から、彼女が本当の事を言っていると結論づけた。
Kono shooko kara, kanojo ga hontoo no koto o itte iru to ketsuron-zuketa.
(**b**) The judge concluded that the man was innocent.
裁判官は男が無実であると結論づけた。
Saiban-kan wa otoko ga mujitsu dearu to ketsuron-zuketa.

3. ⟨**-o**⟩ **mu⌈subu** ⟨〜を⟩結ぶ ① **[for s.o. to tie things together ⟪fig. "create a coherent state**

which did not exist previously by following certain procedures to bring about a result"》] 《tie, bind, join, ally》, ⟨-o⟩ te⌈iketsu-suru ⟨〜を⟩締結する ③ •c [for a nation/company/organization to enter into a treaty/agreement] 《enter into, close》

EX. (**a**) We concluded an agency contract with an American company.
我々はアメリカの会社と代理店契約を{結んだ/締結した}。
Ware-ware wa Amerika no kaisha to dairi-ten-keiyaku o {musunda/teiketsu-shita}.
(**b**) Japan concluded a cultural treaty with the EC.
日本はECと文化条約を{結んだ/締結した}。
Nihon wa Ii-shii to bunka-jooyaku o {musunda/teiketsu-shita}.

conclusion n. **[an act/instance of concluding]**
1. ke⌈tsuron 結論 •c [judging and determining s.t. to be the case after much thought/discussion]

EX. (**a**) We have finally come to the conclusion that we ought to take this matter to court.
とうとうこの問題を裁判にかけるべきだとの結論に達した。
Tootoo kono mondai o saiban ni kakeru-beki da to no ketsuron ni tasshita.
(**b**) His conclusion proved to be untenable.
彼の結論は支持できないものと分かった。
Kare no ketsuron wa shiji-dekinai mono to wakatta.
(**c**) We do not need to be in a hurry to reach a conclusion.
急いで結論を出すことはない。
Isoide ketsuron o dasu koto wa nai.

2. o⌈wari 終わり /⟨V*masu* of *owaru* ① come to an end/ [the point at which s.t. continues no further or the last part of s.t.] 《termination, close, finish》 ↔ hajimari 始まり

EX. (**a**) We will collect the headsets at the conclusion of this flight.
このフライトの終わりにイヤホーンを回収します。
Kono furaito no owari ni iyahoon o kaishuu-shimasu.
(**b**) Make the conclusion of the story a happy one.
話の終わりはハッピーなものにして下さい。
Hanashi no owari wa happiina mono ni shite kudasai.
(**c**) That which has a good beginning has a good conclusion.
始め良ければ終わり良し。
Hajime yokereba owari yoshi.

concrete adj. **[actually existing or able to be seen and felt]**
gu⌈tai-tekina 具体的な adj(*na*). **•c [having a visible form] 《definite》 ↔ chuushoo-tekina 抽象的な** adj(*na*). **•c**

EX. (**a**) Please show us some concrete plans.
具体的な計画を示してください。
Gutai-tekina keikaku o shimeshite kudasai.
(**b**) We need to take concrete measures to cope with this problem.
この問題に対処するため具体的な処置を講じる必要がある。
Kono mondai ni taisho-suru tame gutai-tekina shochi o koojiru hitsuyoo ga aru.

—— n. **[a stonelike building material, made by mixing cement and sand/gravel]**
ko⌈nkuri⌉ito コンクリート •f

condition n. **[a particular state/situation in which s.o./s.t./s.a. exists or anything required for the performance/completion/existence of s.t. else]**
jo⌈otai 状態 •c [the situation in which s.t. exists] 《state, status》, cho⌈oshi 調子 •c [the musical contour formed by a series of sounds of varying pitch and their timing 《fig. "an impression created by s.o.'s way of speaking or writing," "the degree of progress of s.t. that is moving," "the momentum which accompanies s.t. which advances"》] 《tone, tune, key, pitch, time,

rhythm, tempo; manner, way, state; momentum》), jo⌈okyoo 状況 •c [state of affairs] 《state of affairs, circumstances, situation》

EX. (a) The patient is in good condition today.
今日は患者の{状態/調子/*状況}がいい。
*Kyoo wa kanja no {jootai/chooshi/ *jookyoo} ga ii.*
(b) The nation's economy is in a very bad condition.
国の経済は非常に悪い{状態/状況/*調子}にある。
*Kuni no keizai wa hijooni warui {jootai/jookyoo/*chooshi} ni aru.*

NOTE: *Jookyoo* 状況 is sometimes written as 情況 with the same meaning.

2. jo⌈oke⌉n 条件 •c [s.t. which is necessary for and places a limit upon s.t. coming into being] 《terms, requirement, stipulation, proviso》

EX. (a) What are the conditions under which you will accept the job?
どんな条件でこの仕事を引き受けてくれますか。
Donna jooken de kono shigoto o hiki-ukete kuremasu ka.
(b) The conditions for the lease of the apartment are as follows.
アパートの賃貸の条件は次の通りです。
Apaato no chintai no jooken wa tsugi no toori desu.

conduct n. **[personal behavior]**
o⌈konai 行い /〈V*masu* of *okonau* ① do/ [putting an idea or thought into action or the way an action is as seen from the point of view of ethics or common sense] 《act, action, deed, doings, behavior》, fu⌈ruma⌉i 振るまい /〈V*masu* of *furumau* ① behave/ [the way one acts in front of others or the entertainment of a guest with drinks and/ or food etc.] 《behavior, action, manners, entertainment》

EX. (a) The student's conduct was praiseworthy.
その学生の{行い/振るまい}は称賛に値するものだった。
Sono gakusei no {okonai/furumai} wa shoosan ni atai-suru mono datta.
(b) You should be careful about your conduct when you travel.
旅行中は自分の{行い/振るまい}に気を付けなさいよ。
Ryokoo-chuu wa jibun no {okonai/ furumai} ni ki-o-tsukenasai yo.

— vt. **[for s.o to behave oneself or to manage/carry on an activity or to direct a group activity such as an orchestra]**

1. fu⌈ruma⌉u 振るまう ① [for s.o. to act in a certain way in front of others or to entertain s.o. with food or drink] 《behave, entertain》

EX. The child conducted himself admirably.
子供は立派に振るまった。
Kodomo wa rippa ni furumatta.

2. 〈-o〉 o⌈konau 〈〜を〉行う ① •c [for s.o. to put a thought or plan into action or to do s.t. according to an established procedure 〈fml〉]

EX. We conducted our conversation in Chinese.
我々は中国語で会話を行った。
Ware-ware wa Chuugoku-go de kaiwa o okonatta.

3. 〈-o〉 shi⌈ki⌉-suru 〈〜を〉指揮する ③ •c [for s.o. to give directions to a group of people in order to coordinate their actions toward a set goal] 《command, lead, direct, preside over》

EX. A. Who conducted Beethoven's *Ninth Symphony* at this season's opening concert?
今年度最初のコンサートでベートーベンの『第九』を指揮したのはだれですか。
Kon-nendo saisho no konsaato de Beetooben no "dai-ku" o shiki-shita no wa dare desu ka.
B: Ozawa conducted it.
小沢が指揮しました。
Ozawa ga shiki-shimashita.

conference n. **[a meeting for discussion]**
ka⌉igi 会議 •c [a gathering of persons concerned to discuss and come to a decision on an issue] 《meeting, party, confab》, so⌈odan 相談 •c [an act of seeking the advice of another regarding a problem

one is uncertain of being able to solve on one's own] ((meeting, discussion))

EX. (**a**) Japan and the U.S. hold frequent conferences on trade matters.
日米は貿易問題に関して頻繁に{会議/*相談}を開く。
*Nichi-Bei wa booeki-mondai ni-kanshite hinpanni {kaigi/*soodan} o hiraku.*
(**b**) The conference begins at 10:00 A.M.
{会議/*相談}は午前十時から始まります。
*{Kaigi/*Soodan} wa gozen juu-ji kara hajimarimasu.*
(**c**) The conference was a big success.
{会議/*相談}は大成功であった。
*{Kaigi/*Soodan} wa dai-seikoo deatta.*
(**d**) Let's have a family conference to decide on this matter.
この問題は家族で{会議/相談}をして決めましょう。
Kono mondai wa kazoku de {kaigi/soodan} o shite kimemashoo.

confidence n. **[full of trust in s.o/s.t./oneself]**
1. shi⌈n'yoo 信用 •c [the act of believing that s.t./s.o. is certain or reliable enough to act in accordance with it/him/her or a reputation/worth sufficient to cause others to believe in one's financial reliability] ((trust, credit, reputation)), shi⌈nrai 信頼 •c [trusting s.o. completely enough to leave everything to that person] ((trust, dependence, reliance))

EX. (**a**) Taro won the confidence of his boss through his hard work.
太郎は一生懸命働いて上役の{信用/信頼}を得た。
Taroo wa isshoo-kenmei hataraite uwa-yaku no {shin'yoo/shinrai} o eta.
(**b**) Don't do anything to betray the confidence of your friend.
友達の{信用/信頼}を裏切るようなことをするな。
Tomodachi no {shin'yoo/shinrai} o uragiru yoona koto wa suru na.

2. ji⌈shin 自信 •c [a belief that one's own strength or abilities are sufficient to ensure that one will be able to do s.t. well or that one has done s.t. well] ((self-assurance))

EX. (**a**) John was full of confidence during the test.
試験を受けたときジョンは自信満々だった。
Shiken o uketa toki Jon wa jishin-manman datta.
(**b**) I have confidence in my ability to pass the foreign service exam.
外交官試験に受かる(能力に)自信がある。
Gaikoo-kan-shiken ni ukaru (nooryoku ni) jishin ga aru.
(**c**) He had the confidence that he could become President.
彼は大統領になれる自信があった。
Kare wa daitooryoo ni nare-ru jishin ga atta.
(**d**) He had confidence in his speech.
彼は自分の演説に自信があった。
Kare wa jibun no enzetsu ni jishin ga atta.
(**e**) I recommend this method of dieting with full confidence.
ダイエットには自信をもってこの方法を薦めます。
Daietto ni wa jishin o motte kono hoohoo o susumemasu.

confident adj. **[feeling certain or self-assured]**
ka⌈kushin-shite iru (N) 確信している(N) /⟨V*te iru* of *kakushin-suru* ③ be certain of/ •c [for s.o. to be certain] ((be convinced)), ji⌈shin ni mi⌉chita N 自信に満ちたN /⟨*jishin* confidence + prt. *ni* + Vinf. past of *michiru* ② become filled/ [be filled with confidence] ((sure, certain)), ji⌈shin ni mi⌉chite iru (N) 自信に満ちている(N) /⟨*jishin* confidence + prt. *ni* + V*te iru* of *michiru* ② become filled/

EX. (**a**) We were confident that he would win.
私たちは彼の勝利を{確信していた/*自信に満ちていた}。

*Watashi-tachi wa kare no shoori o {kakushin-shite ita/*jishin ni michite ita}.*
(**b**) The doctor is confident that the patient will get better soon.
医者は患者がすぐよくなる事を{確信している/*自信に満ちている}。
*Isha wa kanja ga sugu yoku naru koto o {kakushin-shite iru/*jishin ni michite iru}.*
(**c**) The parents are confident of the child's innocence.
親は子供の無実を{確信して/*自信に満ちて}います。
*Oya wa kodomo no mujitsu o {kakushin-shite/*jishin ni michite} imasu.*
(**d**) The athlete was absolutely confident that he would win.
選手は絶対に自分が勝つと{自信に満ちていた/確信していた}。
Senshu wa zettai ni jibun ga katsu to {jishin ni michite ita/kakushin-shite ita}.
(**e**) The actors seemed confident in the success of their performance.
役者たちは公演の成功{を確信している/に自信に満ちた}顔をしていた。
Yakusha-tachi wa kooen no seikoo {o kakushin-shite iru/ni jishin ni michita} kao o shite ita.

confuse vt. **[to throw s.t. into disorder or to mistake s.t. for s.t. else]**
1. ⟨-o⟩ ko⌈nran-saseru ⟨〜を⟩混乱させる /⟨causative of *konran-suru* ③ become confused/ ② •c [to throw s.o./s.t. into a state of bewilderment or disorder] ⟪put into disorder⟫

EX. (**a**) Her contradictory explanation confused him.
彼女の矛盾だらけの説明は彼を混乱させた。
Kanojo no mujun-darake no setsumei wa kare o konran-saseta.
(**b**) His attempt to settle the dispute between his colleagues confused the situation even more.
けんかをしている同僚に仲直りをさせようとする彼の試みが事態を一層混乱させてしまった。
Kenka o shite iru dooryoo ni naka-naori o saseyoo to suru kare no kokoromi ga jitai o issoo konran-sasete shimatta.

2. ⟨-o⟩ ⟨-to⟩ to⌈ri-chigaeru ⟨〜を⟩⟨〜と⟩取り違える ② [for s.o. to take s.t. to be s.t. else by mistake] ⟪misread, mistake, misinterpret, misconstrue⟫

EX. (**a**) Hanako confused a nickel with a dime.
花子は五セントと十セント硬貨を取り違えた。
Hanako wa go-sento to jis-sento-kooka o tori-chigaeta.
(**b**) I confused the professor with his elder brother.
私は教授とそのお兄さんとを取り違えた。
Watashi wa kyooju to sono o-nii-san to o tori-chigaeta.
(**c**) Even parents sometimes confuse their twin children.
親でも双子の子供は取り違える事がある。
Oya demo futa-go no kodomo wa tori-chigaeru koto ga aru.

confusing adj. **[bewildering, causing confusion]**
ko⌈nran-shi-yasu⌉i 混乱しやすい [causing confusion] ⟪bewildering, mind-boggling⟫, ya⌈yakoshi⌉i ややこしい adj(i). **[complicated and entangled] ⟪bewildering, troublesome⟫**

EX. (**a**) It's confusing because two Tanakas live in the same apartment house.
アパートに田中さんが二人いるので{混乱しやすい/ややこしい}。
Apaato ni Tanaka-san ga futari iru node {konran-shi-yasui/yayakoshii}.
(**b**) It's confusing because the name of the street suddenly changes for no reason at all.
通りの名前が理由もなく急に変わるのは{混乱しやすい/ややこしい}。
Toori no namae ga riyuu mo naku kyuu ni kawaru no wa {konran-shi-yasui/yayakoshii}.
(**c**) Chinese characters can be confusing

because of their various readings.
漢字はいろいろな読み方があって{ややこしい/混乱しやすい}。
Kanji wa iro-irona yomi-kata ga atte {yayakoshii/konran-shi-yasui}.

confusion n. **[the act of confusing or state of being confused]**
ko⌈nran 混乱 •c [the state of being in disorder or at a loss what to do or the act of throwing s.t./s.o. into such a state] ⟪disorder, chaos⟫

EX. (**a**) There was a lot of confusion in Japan right after the war.
日本は戦争直後に大きな混乱があった。
Nihon wa sensoo-chokugo ni ookina konran ga atta.
(**b**) Confusion marked the beginning of the festival.
祭りは混乱から始まった。
Matsuri wa konran kara hajimatta.

congratulation n. **[expression of one's joy as on a happy occasion]**
i⌈wa⌉i 祝い [celebration; an event/gift in celebration of s.t.] ⟪celebration, felicitation, commemoration⟫, o-⌈iwai お祝い
PHRASE: Congratulations! *Omedetoo(-gozaimasu).* おめでとう(ございます)。

connect vt. **[to link/join together]**
⟨-o⟩ ({⟨-to⟩/⟨-ni⟩}) mu⌈subu ⟨〜を⟩({⟨〜と⟩/⟨〜に⟩})結ぶ ① [to unite separate entities or individuals together (by means of s.t.)] ⟪tie, knot, bind, link; conclude, finish, close⟫, ⟨-o⟩ (⟨-ni⟩) tsu⌈nagu ⟨〜を⟩(⟨〜に⟩) つなぐ ① [for s.o. to link or attach s.t./s.o./s.a. onto s.t. else, usu. by means of a cord-like object ⟪fig. "sustain"⟫] ⟪tie, fasten, chain, lash, leash⟫

EX. (**a**) It took several hours to connect a high-voltage wire that had become severed in the storm.
嵐で切れた高圧線を{つなぐ/*結ぶ}のに何時間もかかった。
*Arashi de kireta kooatsu-sen o {tsunagu/*musubu} no ni nan-jikan mo kakatta.*
(**b**) The destinies of the two were to be forever connected by the events of that day.
二人の運命はその日の出来事によって永遠に{結ばれよう/*つながれよう}としていた。
*Futari no unmei wa sono hi no deki-goto ni-yotte eien ni {musuba-reyoo/*tsunaga-reyoo} to shite ita.*
(**d**) Please connect me with Mr. Anderson.
アンダーソンさんに{つないで/*結んで}下さい。
*Andaason-san ni {tsunaide/*musunde} kudasai.*

PHRASE: be connected with ⟨-*to*⟩ *kankei ga aru* ⟨〜と⟩関係がある
EX. Mr. Tanaka is connected with that real estate agent.
田中氏はあの不動産屋と関係がある。
Tanaka-shi wa ano fu-doosan-ya to kankei ga aru.

Connecticut n.
Ko⌈ne⌉chikatto コネチカット •f

connection n.
[link/association/relationship ⟪fig. "associates," "family relation," "friends having some influence or power," "the meeting of trains, planes, etc. for transfer of passengers"⟫]
1. ka⌈nkei 関係 •c [a respect in which two or more things are considered to be related or joined together] ⟪relationship, relation, bearing⟫

EX. (**a**) I had no connection at all with the case.
私は事件とは全く関係がなかった。
Watashi wa jiken to wa mattaku kankei ga nakatta.
(**b**) He must have had some connection with this matter.
彼は本件と何らかの関係があったに違いない。
Kare wa honken to nanra-ka no kankei ga atta ni chigainai.

2. ko⌉ne コネ •f [a relationship/bond with a person or group of persons through which one can expect to derive benefit] ⟪pull⟫
NOTE: *Kone* is derived from an English word "connection."

EX. (**a**) Jiro had a connection with the company and was hired.
次郎はその会社にコネがあって就職した。
Jiroo wa sono kaisha ni kone ga atte shuushoku-shita.
(**b**) Making connections is part of getting ahead in life.
コネも(成功するための)実力のうちだ。
Kone mo (seikoo-suru tame no) jitsuryoku no uchi da.

3. se⌈tsuzoku 接続 •c [a joining of two entities in such a way as to form a continuity; the coordination in schedule of two trains or other forms of transportation so as to permit convenient transfer between them] ⟪joining, linking, junction⟫

EX. (**a**) If you take this train, you will make the best connections when you transfer.
この列車に乗れば乗り換え駅で接続が一番いい。
Kono ressha ni noreba nori-kae-eki de setsuzoku ga ichiban ii.
(**b**) This train makes a connection with the last bus.
この列車は最終バスとの接続がある。
Kono ressha wa saishuu basu to no setsuzoku ga aru.

conscious adj. **[having an awareness of one's own existence, surroundings, etc.]**

1. i⌉shiki-shite iru (N) **意識している**(N) **/**⟨**V** ***te*** **of** ***ishiki-suru*** ③ **be aware of/ [being in a mental condition of clearly knowing what situation one is in] ⟪aware⟫ ↔ ishiki-shite inai 意識していない**

EX. (**a**) Ed was conscious of Nancy's presence.
エドはナンシーが来ているのを意識していた。
Edo wa Nanshii ga kite iru no o ishiki-shite ita.
(**b**) We should all be conscious of our health as we lead our daily lives.
人は健康を意識して生活した方がよい。
Hito wa kenkoo o ishiki-shite seikatsu-shita hoo ga yoi.

2. i⌉shiki ga a⌉ru (N) **意識がある**(N) **[being in a state of consciousness]**

EX. The injured person was conscious when he was taken to the hospital.
けが人は病院に運ばれた時は意識があった。
Kega-nin wa byooin ni hakoba-reta toki wa ishiki ga atta.

consciousness n. **[the state of being aware of one's own existence, surroundings, etc.] i⌉shiki 意識 •c [the mental condition of clearly knowing what one is doing or what situation one is in] ⟪awareness, one's senses⟫**

EX. (**a**) The child caught shoplifting apparently had no consciousness that what he was doing was wrong.
万引をしているところをつかまった子供には、してはいけないことをしていたという意識は全くないようだった。
Manbiki o shite iru tokoro o tsukamatta kodomo ni wa, shite wa ikenai koto o shite iru to iu ishiki wa mattaku nai yoodatta.
(**b**) The boxer immediately lost consciousness upon receiving a heavy blow on the side of his head.
ボクシングの選手は頭の横を強く殴られるとすぐ意識を失った。
Bokushingu no senshu wa atama no yoko o tsuyoku nagura-reru to sugu ishiki o ushinatta.

consent vi. **[for s.o. to agree to or comply with what s.o. else wishes]**
⟨-ni⟩ do⌈oi-suru ⟨〜に⟩同意する ③ •c [for s.o. to have the same opinion as] ⟪agree⟫, ⟨-o⟩ sho⌈odaku-suru ⟨〜を⟩承諾する ③ •c [for s.o. to express a willingness to do s.t. requested by another] ⟪agree, accept⟫

EX. (**a**) The president consented to our proposal.
社長は我々の申し出{に同意した/を承諾した}。
Shachoo wa ware-ware no mooshi-de {ni dooi-shita/o shoodaku-shita}.
(**b**) My parents finally consented to my going on the trip alone.

C

両親はやっと私が一人で旅行に行くこと{に同意して/*を承諾して}くれた。
*Ryooshin wa yatto watashi ga hitori de ryokoo ni iku koto {ni dooi-shite/*o shoodaku-shite} kureta.*

consequence n. **[the effect/result of an earlier occurrence 《fig. "importance," "significance"》]**

C

1. ke⌈kka 結果 •c [a state of affairs brought about by a cause] 《result, outcome, product, upshot》

EX. (**a**) As a consequence of his carelessness, he had his house broken into.
不注意の結果、彼の家は泥棒に入られた。
Fu-chuui no kekka, kare no ie wa doroboo ni haira-reta.
(**b**) Losing her job was a natural consequence of her consistently bad attitude toward her work.
彼女が解雇になったのは普段の仕事に対する態度が悪かったのだから、当然の結果だ。
Kanojo ga kaiko ni natta no wa fudan no shigoto ni-taisuru taido ga warukatta no da kara, toozen no kekka da.
(**c**) As a consequence of his efforts, he finally won an Olympic medal.
彼は努力の結果ついにオリンピックでメダルを取った。
Kare wa doryoku no kekka tsuini Orinpikku de medaru o totta.

2. ju⌈uyoo-sei 重要性 •c [the quality of being indispensable and irreplaceable]

EX. (**a**) That is not a matter of such high consequence.
あれはそんなに重要性の高い問題ではない。
Are wa sonnani juuyoo-sei no takai mondai dewanai.
(**b**) He is not aware of the consequences of the matter.
彼は事の重要性に気がついていない。
Kare wa koto no juuyoo-sei ni ki-ga-tsuite inai.

consequently adv. **[as a result]**
shi⌈tagatte 従って conj. **/⟨V *te* of *shitagau* ① follow/ [a conjunction that is used to indicate that a result follows necessarily from the foregoing situation ⟨fml⟩] 《accordingly, so, therefore》**

EX. (**a**) The price of land went up. Consequently, the rent also increased.
土地の値段が上がった。従って家賃も上がった。
Tochi no nedan ga agatta. Shitagatte yachin mo agatta.
(**b**) The man did not speak Japanese. Consequenty, he needed an interpreter.
その人は日本語が話せなかった。従って通訳が必要だった。
Sono hito wa Nihon-go ga hanase-nakatta. Shitagatte tsuuyaku ga hitsuyoo datta.

consider vt. **[for s.o. to think carefully about s.t.; to believe or suppose s.t. to be the case, to be thoughtful of s.o.]**

1. ⟨-o⟩ yo⌉ku ka⌈ngae⌉ru ⟨〜を⟩よく考える ② [for s.o. to think deeply about s.t.] 《take time to think about》

EX. (**a**) Please consider this proposal from all the angles.
この提案を全ての角度からよく考えてください。
Kono teian o subete no kakudo kara yoku kangaete kudasai.
(**b**) We considered your offer but, sorry to say, we cannot accept it.
あなたの申し出をよく考えましたが、残念ながら受け入れられません。
Anata no mooshi-de o yoku kangaemashita ga, zannen nagara uke-ire-raremasen.
(**c**) It is important to spend money only after considering one's income carefully.
収入をよく考えて支出をするのが大事だ。
Shuunyuu o yoku kangaete shishutsu o suru no ga daiji da.

2. ⟨-to⟩ o⌈mo⌉u ⟨〜と⟩思う ① [for s.o. to spontaneously perceive s.t. in one's mind or

to have an opinion about s.t.] ((feel, think))

EX. (**a**) I considered it best not to disturb him.
彼をわずらわさないのが一番いいと思った。
Kare o wazurawasanai no ga ichiban ii to omotta.
(**b**) People considered him a genius.
人々は彼を天才だと思った。
Hito-bito wa kare o tensai da to omotta.

3. ⟨-o⟩ o⌈moi-yaru ⟨〜を⟩思いやる ① [for s.o. to put oneself in s.o. else's shoes and empathize with his/her feelings] ((sympathize with, feel for (with), put oneself in the place of others))

EX. (**a**) Try to consider her feelings.
彼女の気持ちを少しは思いやってみたら。
Kanojo no kimochi o sukoshi wa omoi-yatte mitara.
(**b**) It is important to consider others' feelings.
人の気持ちを思いやることは大切です。
Hito no kimochi o omoi-yaru koto wa taisetsu desu.
(**c**) We considered his miserable circumstances and threw him a big party to cheer him up.
彼のみじめな境遇を思いやって、元気づけるために大きなパーティーをしてやった。
Kare no mijimena kyooguu o omoi-yatte, genki-zukeru tame ni ookina paatii o shite yatta.

considerably adv. **[to a great extent]**
da⌈ibu 大分 n. •c **[to an extent which is not extreme but by no means small] ((greatly, much, pretty, quite))**, **na⌈ka-naka** なかなか **[to a degree exceeding expectations and creating a strong impression on one] ((very, highly, quite, pretty))**, **ka⌉nari** かなり **[to a degree exceeding ordinary expectations] ((pretty, very, tolerably, fairly, rather, quite))**, **so⌈otoo 相当** •c **[to a degree exceeding the average/standard] ((fairly, pretty, passably, rather, quite))**

EX. (**a**) Ed is considerably advanced in Japanese.
エドは{大分/なかなか/かなり/相当}日本語が上達している。
Edo wa {daibu/naka-naka/kanari/sootoo} Nihon-go ga jootatsu-shite iru.
(**b**) It looks like it is going to take considerably longer than we first expected to complete this project.
このプロジェクトを完成するのには当初考えていたよりも{大分/かなり/相当/*なかなか}時間がかかりそうだ。
*Kono purojekuto o kansei-suru no ni wa toosho kangaete ita yori mo {daibu/kanari/sootoo/*naka-naka} jikan ga kakari-soo da.*
(**c**) He appeared to be considerably better trained than his opponent.
彼は相手(の選手)より{大分/かなり/相当/*なかなか}トレーニングを積んでいるようだった。
*Kare wa aite (no senshu) yori {daibu/kanari/sootoo/*naka-naka} toreeningu o tsunde iru yoodatta.*

consideration n. **[careful thought or thoughtful concern]**
1. ko⌉oryo 考慮 •c **[thinking carefully about s.t. so that a correct judgment may be made] ((thought, deliberation))**

EX. (**a**) Your proposal is now under consideration.
ご提案は目下考慮中です。
Go-teian wa mokka kooryo-chuu desu.
(**b**) His ideas are worthy of consideration.
彼のアイデアは考慮に値する。
Kare no aidea wa kooryo ni atai-suru.

2. o⌈moi-yari 思いやり [the act of putting oneself in the position of another and empathizing with his/her feelings] ((sympathy, delicacy, thoughtfulness))

EX. (**a**) He has no consideration for older people.
彼には老人に対する思いやりがない。
Kare ni wa roojin ni taisuru omoi-yari ga nai.
(**b**) Proper consideration for pedestrians is an important part of good driving manners.
歩行者に対する思いやりが車を運転す

C

る時の大切なマナーです。
Hokoo-sha ni taisuru omoi-yari ga kuruma o unten-suru toki no taisetsuna manaa desu.
(**c**) Consideration for the weak is necessary for a just society.
公平な社会作りには弱者に対する思いやりが必要だ。
Kooheina shakai-zukuri ni wa jakusha ni taisuru omoi-yari ga hitsuyoo da.

consist vi. **[for s.t. to exist or to be composed of smaller elements]**
1. {⟨**-kara**⟩/⟨**-de**⟩} **na⌉ru** {⟨～から⟩/⟨～で⟩}成る ① **[for a larger entity to be made up of constituent elements]** ⟪**be composed of**⟫, {⟨**-kara**⟩/⟨**-de**⟩} **de⌉kite iru** {⟨～から⟩/⟨～で⟩}できている /⟨**V*te iru*** **of** ***dekiru*** ② **come into being**/ ②, {⟨**-kara**⟩/⟨**-de**⟩} **ko⌈osei-sarete iru** {⟨～から⟩/⟨～で⟩}構成されている /⟨**V*te iru*** **of passive form of** ***koosei-suru*** ③ **compose, constitute**/ ② •**c** ⟨**fml**⟩

EX. (**a**) The committee consists of 12 members.
委員会は十二人{から/で}{成る/構成されている/*できている}。
*Iin-kai wa juu-ni-nin {kara/de} {naru/koosei-sarete iru/*dekite iru}.*
(**b**) Bread consists of flour and yeast among other things.
パンは大体小麦粉とイースト{から/で}{できて/*成って/*構成されて}いる。
*Pan wa daitai komugi-ko to iisuto {kara/de} {dekite/*natte/*koosei-sarete} iru.*
(**c**) A symphony orchestra usually consists of string instruments, wind instruments, and percussion instruments.
交響楽団は大抵弦楽器と管楽器と打楽器{から/で}{成って/出来て/構成されて}いる。
Kookyoo-gakudan wa taitei gen-gakki to kan-gakki to da-gakki {kara/de} {natte/dekite/koosei-sarete} iru.

2. ⟨**-ni**⟩ **a⌉ru** ⟨～に⟩ある ① **[for s.t. to exist]** ⟪**lie, exist**⟫

EX. The worth of human beings does not consist merely in their usefulness to society.
人間の価値というのは単にその人が社会にとって有用かどうかにあるのではない。
Ningen no kachi to iu no wa tan ni sono hito ga shakai ni-totte yuuyoo ka doo ka ni aru no dewanai.

constant adj. **[regularly recurrent or not changing or varying]**
1. ta⌈ema-na⌉i 絶え間ない adj(*i*). **[having no break]**

EX. (**a**) Constant laughter could be heard coming from the party.
パーティー会場から絶え間ない笑い声が聞こえていた。
Paatii-kaijoo kara taema-nai warai-goe ga kikoete ita.
(**b**) Her constant efforts led to her ultimate success.
彼女は絶え間ない努力でついに成功した。
Kanojo wa taema-nai doryoku de tsuini seikoo-shita.

2. fu⌈hen no N 不変のN •**c [not changing ⟨w⟩]** ⟪**unchangeable, immutable, permanent, everlasting**⟫, **i⌈ttei no N** 一定のN •**c [for a quantity/condition to be fixed]**

EX. (**a**) His love for her was constant.
彼の彼女への愛は{不変/*一定}だった。
*Kare no kanojo e no ai wa {fuhen/*ittei} datta.*
(**b**) We must strive to maintain constant peace in the world.
我々は世界における{不変/*一定}の平和を守るよう努力しなければならない。
*Ware-ware wa sekai ni okeru {fuhen/*ittei} no heiwa o mamoru yoo doryoku-shinakereba naranai.*
(**c**) Fuel economy can be obtained by maintaining a constant speed.
{一定の/*不変の}速度で走るとガソリンの節約になる。
*{Ittei no/*Fuhen no} sokudo de hashiru to gasorin no setsuyaku ni naru.*
(**d**) I have regular work and a constant income each month.
仕事が順調で毎月{一定/*不変}の収入がある。

*Shigoto ga junchoo de mai-tsuki {ittei/ *fuhen} no shuunyuu ga aru.*

constantly adv. **[without break]**
sho˥tchuu しょっちゅう **[from beginning to end** 《**fig. "always"**》 〈s〉**], i˥tsu-mo** いつも **[no matter when]** 《**always**》, **tsu˥ne ni** 常に **[without break or not changing** 〈w〉**]** 《**always, continually**》, **ta˥ezu** 絶えず **[without interruption]**

EX. (**a**) Those people are constantly complaining.
あの人たちは{しょっちゅう/いつも/常に/絶えず}文句を言っている。
Ano hito-tachi wa {shotchuu/itsu-mo/tsune ni/taezu} monku o itte iru.
(**b**) We see each other constantly.
我々は{しょっちゅう/いつも/常に/絶えず}会っている。
Ware-ware wa {shotchuu/itsu-mo/tsune ni/taezu} atte iru.

constitution n. **[the system of principles according to which a nation/organization is governed or the document embodying such principles or the general physical character of s.t., especially a person's body]**
1. ke˥npoo 憲法 **•c [the supreme law of the land]**

EX. Japan enacted a new constitution after the war.
日本は戦後新しい憲法を制定した。
Nihon wa sengo atarashii kenpoo o seitei-shita.

2. ta˥ikaku 体格 **•c [the physical form of a person's body, esp. with regard to how well it has been nourished and grown]** 《**physique**》

EX. We are looking for an applicant with a strong constitution.
体格のいい応募者を求めています。
Taikaku no ii oobo-sha o motomete imasu.

construct vt. **[for s.o. to build s.t. systematically]**
〈-o〉 ke˥nsetsu-suru 〈〜を〉建設する ③ **•c [for s.o. to build a physical structure of major proportions such as a building, dam, subway, etc.]** 《**build, establish**》 ↔ **〈-o〉 hakai-suru** 〈〜を〉破壊する ③ **•c**

EX. (**a**) The city constructed a dam to generate hydroelectricity.
市は水力発電のためにダムを建設した。
Shi wa suiryoku-hatsuden no tame ni damu o kensetsu-shita.
(**b**) This building was constructed a hundred years ago.
このビルは百年前に建設された。
Kono biru wa hyaku-nen-mae ni kensetu-sareta.

construction n. **[the act of constructing s.t.]**
ke˥nsetsu 建設 **•c [the building of a major physical structure such as a building, dam, subway, etc.]** 《**building, establishment**》, **ko˥oji** 工事 **•c [a project of civil engineering or architecture, typically requiring heavy equipment and significant manpower, including repair work on an existing structure]** 《**civil engineering work**》

EX. (**a**) A new subway line is currently under construction in that city.
あの町では現在新しい地下鉄{を建設/が工事}中です。
Ano machi de wa genzai atarashii chika-tetsu {o kensetsu/ga kooji}-chuu desu.
(**b**) The construction of a new campus is being planned.
新しいキャンパスの{建設/工事}が計画されている。
Atarashii kyanpasu no {kensetsu/kooji} ga keikaku-sarete iru.
(**c**) The road is under construction.
道路は{工事/建設}中です。
Dooro wa {kooji/kensetsu}-chuu desu.

consulate n. **[the premises officially occupied by a consul]**
ryo˥oji˥-kan 領事館 **•c**

consult vt. **[for s.o. to seek advice/information/instruction from s.o. else]**
1. {〈-ni〉/〈-to〉} so˥odan-suru {〈〜に〉/〈〜と〉}相談する ③ **•c [for s.o. to seek the advice of another regarding a problem one is uncertain of being able to solve on one's**

own] ⟪**seek advice, take counsel, talk over**⟫

EX. You had better consult your lawyer about the fine points in this contract.
この契約の細かい点については弁護士{に/と}相談した方がいいですよ。
Kono keiyaku no komakai ten ni-tsuite wa bengo-shi {ni/to} soodan-shita hoo ga ii desu yo.

C

2. ⟨**-ni**⟩ **mi˥te morau** ⟨〜に⟩見てもらう ① **[for s.o. to have s.t. examined by s.o.]**

EX. The pain in my stomach would not go away, so I consulted a specialist.
胃の痛みがなかなか直らないので専門医に見てもらった。
I no itami ga naka-naka naoranai no de senmon-i ni mite moratta.

3. ⟨**-o**⟩ **shi┌rabe˥ru** ⟨〜を⟩調べる ② **[for s.o. to observe directly or inquire/read about s.t./s.o./s.a. in order to determine or ascertain s.t. unknown or uncertain about it/him/her]** ⟪**check, examine, look up, investigate**⟫

EX. Jim could not read the Chinese character, so he consulted a dictionary.
ジムはその漢字が読めなかったので辞書を調べた。
Jimu wa sono kanji ga yome-nakatta node jisho o shirabeta.

NOTE: "Consult a dictionary" may also be translated as 辞書をひく *jisho o hiku.*

— vi. **[for s.o. to talk things over, confer with s.o. else]**
{⟨**-ni**⟩/⟨**-to**⟩} **so┌odan-suru** {⟨〜に⟩/⟨〜と⟩}相談する ③ •**c** ⟪**to have a consultation with**⟫

EX. (**a**) I consulted with my friend about the project.
プロジェクトについて友達{に/と}相談した。
Purojekuto ni-tsuite tomodachi {ni/to} soodan-shita.
(**b**) I consulted with my parents about marriage.
結婚について両親{に/と}相談した。
Kekkon ni-tsuite ryooshin {ni/to} soodan-shita.
(**c**) Be sure to consult with me before making a decision.
決める前に必ず私{に/と}相談して下さい。
Kimeru mae ni kanarazu watashi {ni/to} soodan-shite kudasai.

consultation n. **[an act of consulting]**
so┌odan 相談 •**c** **[an act of seeking the advice of another regarding a problem one is uncertain of being able to solve on one's own]**

EX. We are in consultation with the division manager about the matter.
私たちはその件につき部長と相談中です。
Watashi-tachi wa sono ken ni-tsuki buchoo to soodan-chuu desu.

contact n. **[a touching or meeting of persons or things or the state of being in association or relationship]**
1. re┌nraku 連絡 •**c** **[the existence or creation of a connection between two things or people, esp. one involving the transfer of information from one individual to another]** ⟪**connection, liaison**⟫, **se┌sshoku** 接触 •**c** **[coming close to and touching]** ⟪**touch**⟫

EX. (**a**) We have been in constant contact with headquarters about that matter.
私たちはその件につき絶えず本部と{連絡/接触}をしています。
Watakushi-tachi wa sono ken ni-tsuki taezu honbu to {renraku/sesshoku} o shite imasu.
(**b**) We have lost contact with the group.
そのグループとの{連絡/接触}ができなくなった。
Sono guruupu to no {renraku/sesshoku} ga dekinaku natta.
(**c**) Have you been able to establish contact with the spacecraft?
宇宙船と{連絡/*接触}が出来ましたか。
*Uchuu-sen to {renraku/*sesshoku} ga dekimashita ka.*

2. ko┌osai 交際 •**c** **[the act of associating with persons other than one's family/relatives]**

EX. I have frequent contact with foreigners.
私は外国人との交際が多い。
Watakushi wa gaikoku-jin to no koosai ga ooi.

— vt. **[to establish communication with s.o.]**
⟨-ni⟩ re⌈nraku-suru ⟨〜に⟩連絡する ③ •c [for s.o. to inform people concerned of s.t.] 《communicate, get in touch with》

EX. Please contact me as soon as you arrive.
到着次第、私に連絡して下さい。
Toochaku-shidai, watashi ni renraku-shite kudasai.

contain vt. **[to hold or include s.t. within a certain volume or area 《fig. "hold s.t. under control"》]**
⟨-o⟩ fu⌈ku⌉mu ⟨〜を⟩含む ① [for s.o. to hold s.t. in one's mouth 《fig. "for s.t. to include s.t. else within itself," "imply"》] 《include, comprise, hold, imply》, ⟨-ni⟩ ha⌉itte iru ⟨〜に⟩入っている /(V*te iru* of *hairu* ① enter/ [for s.t. to exist inside s.t. else] 《be included》

EX. (**a**) This medicine contains poison.
この薬は毒{を含んで/が入って}います。
Kono kusuri wa doku {o fukunde/ga haitte} imasu.
(**b**) Vegetables and fruits contain a wealth of vitamins.
野菜や果物にはビタミンがたくさん{入って/含まれて}いる。
Yasai ya kuda-mono ni wa bitamin ga takusan {haitte/fukuma-rete} iru.
(**c**) This box contains apples.
この箱はリンゴ{が入って/*を含んで}いる。
*Kono hako wa ringo {ga haitte/*o fukunde} iru.*

contemporary adj. **[occurring or existing at the same time]**
1. do⌈o-ji⌉dai no N 同時代のN •c [belonging to the same period]

EX. (**a**) Hibari Misora and Chiemi Eri led contemporary careers as popular singers.
美空ひばりと江利チエミは同時代の流行歌手であった。
Misora Hibari to Eri Chiemi wa doo-jidai no ryuukoo-kashu deatta.
(**b**) William Shakespeare and Tokugawa Ieyasu were historically contemporary figures, though their worlds never met.
ウィリアム・シェークスピアと徳川家康は歴史上同時代の人物だったが、それぞれの世界は全く別のものだった。
Uiriamu Sheekusupia to Tokugawa Ieyasu wa rekishi-joo doo-jidai no jinbutsu datta ga, sore-zore no sekai wa mattaku betsu no mono datta.

2. ge⌉ndai no 現代の •c [of the present time] 《modern》

EX. My sister is majoring in contemporary literature.
姉は現代(の)文学を専攻している。
Ane wa gendai (no) bungaku o senkoo-shite iru.

content n. **[that which is contained in s.t. else]**
na⌈iyoo 内容 •c [s.t. that constitutes the inner part of s.t. and gives value to it, including that which is expressed in a piece of writing or a work of art] 《substance, subject matter, meaning, import, depth》, na⌈ka⌉-mi 中身 [that which is located inside s.t.]

EX. (**a**) What are the contents of this package?
この小包の{内容/中身}は何ですか。
Kono ko-zutsumi no {naiyoo/naka-mi} wa nan desu ka.
(**b**) It was easy to understand the content of his lecture.
彼の講義の{内容/中身}は分かりやすかった。
Kare no koogi no {naiyoo/naka-mi} wa wakari-yasukatta.

contest n. **[a competitive event, such as a game or race, where people attempt to out perform one another, typically for a prize]**
ko⌉ntesuto コンテスト •f, kyo⌈ogi-kai 競技会 •c [an event where participants compete with one another for victory in some activity, esp. sports] 《game, tournament, match, meet, competition》

C

EX. (**a**) She entered a beauty contest at the young age of twelve.
彼女は十二歳という若さで美人{コンテスト/*競技会}に参加した。
*Kanojo wa juu-ni-sai to iu waka-sa de bijin-{kontesuto/*kyoogi-kai} ni sanka-shita.*
(**b**) My friend won first prize in the dance contest.
私の友達はダンス{コンテスト/競技会}で一位になった。
Watashi no tomodachi wa dansu-{kontesuto/kyoogi-kai} de ichi-i ni natta.

continent n. **[any of the large main land areas of the earth]**
ta⌈iriku 大陸 •c
EX. We drove across the Notth American continent.
我々は車で北米大陸を横断した。
Ware-ware wa kuruma de Hokubei-tairiku o oodan-shita.

continue vt. **[to go on with/prolong/extend]**
⟨-o⟩ tsu⌈zukeru ⟨～を⟩続ける ② [for s.o. to cause s.t. to go on without stopping or interruption] ⟪keep up, carry on⟫ ↔ ⟨-o⟩ yameru ⟨～を⟩やめる ②
EX. (**a**) Miki continued studying all night long.
美樹は一晩中勉強を続けた。
Miki wa hito-ban-juu benkyoo o tsuzuketa.
(**b**) I intend to continue my present work for the foreseeable future.
私は現在の仕事を当分の間続けるつもりだ。
Watashi wa genzai no shigoto o toobun no aida tsuzukeru tsumori da.
(**c**) I plan to continue working until I am sixty years old.
六十歳まで仕事を続けるつもりです。
Roku-jus-sai made shigoto o tsuzukeru tsumori desu.

—— vi. **[to go on, keep on, last, or endure]**
tsu⌈zuku 続く ① [for one event/state/movement to follow after another in time or space] ⟪go on, keep on, ensue⟫
EX. (**a**) This highway continues for miles and miles.
この高速道路は何マイルも続いている。
Kono koosoku-dooro wa nan-mairu mo tsuzuite iru.
(**b**) The meeting continued for many hours.
会議は何時間も続いた。
Kaigi wa nan-jikan mo tsuzuita.
(**c**) This program will continue next week.
この番組は次の週に続きます。
Kono bangumi wa tsugi no shuu ni tsuzukimasu.

continuous adj. **[going on without stopping]**
ta⌈ema-na⌉i 絶え間ない adj(*i*). **[having no break] ⟪ceaseless, constant⟫**
EX. (**a**) We had continuous snow for a week.
一週間、絶え間ない雪の日が続いた。
Is-shuukan, taema-nai yuki no hi ga tsuzuita.
(**b**) Glenn was kept busy with a continuous flow of work.
グレンは絶え間ない仕事のために忙しかった。
Guren wa taema-nai shigoto no tame ni isogashikatta.
(**c**) Continuous encouragement saved the child's life.
絶え間ない励ましがその子の命を救った。
Taema-nai hagemashi ga sono ko no inochi o sukutta.
(**d**) Everyone was rescued thanks to the continuous work of the firemen.
消防隊員の絶え間ない活動で全員が助かった。
Shooboo-taiin no taema-nai katsudoo de zen'in ga tasukatta.

contract n. **[a written agreement enforceable by law]**
ke⌈iyaku 契約 •c [entering into a legally-binding commitment with another party or a commitment so made] ⟪agreement, engagement, compact, pact⟫
EX. (**a**) I made a contract with the builder.
その建築業者と契約を結んだ。

Sono kenchiku-gyoosha to keiyaku o musunda.
(**b**) The contract between the two companies was canceled.
その二つの会社の間の契約は解消された。
Sono futatsu no kaisha no aida no keiyaku wa kaishoo-sareta.
(**c**) The contract was scrapped as a result of poor negotiation.
下手な交渉の結果、契約は破棄された。
Hetana kooshoo no kekka, keiyaku wa haki-sareta.

contrast n. **[a prominent difference between things being compared] ko⌈ntora⌉suto コントラスト •f [a juxtaposing of two things in such a way that their similarities or differences are visually apparent], ta⌈ishoo 対照 •c [a juxtaposing of two things in such a way that their similarities or differences are readily apparent; a checking of s.t. against its original to see it there are any differences]** ⟪**antithesis, comparison**⟫

EX. (**a**) English and Japanese exhibit some striking contrasts in sentence structure.
英語と日本語は文構造においてきわだった{対照/?コントラスト}を示している。
Eigo to Nihon-go wa bun-koozoo ni oite kiwa-datta {taishoo/?kontorasuto} o shimeshite iru.
(**b**) There is a great contrast between the housing situations in America and in Japan.
アメリカと日本の住宅事情は大きな{対照/?コントラスト}をなしている。
Amerika to Nihon no juutaku-jijoo wa ookina {taishoo/?kontorasuto} o nashite iru.
(**c**) The contrast between black and yellow is the sharpest among all the colors.
全部の色の中で黄色と黒の{コントラスト/対照}が一番はっきりしている。
Zenbu no iro no naka de ki-iro to kuro no {kontorasuto/taishoo} ga ichiban hakkiri-shite iru.

— vt. **[for s.o. to compare two or more things to make clear the differences between/among them] ⟨-o⟩ ⟨-to⟩ ta⌈ishoo-suru ⟨〜を⟩⟨〜と⟩対照する ③ •c [for s.o. to juxtapose two things in such a way that their similarities or differences are readily apparent], ⟨-o⟩ ⟨-to⟩ ta⌉ihi-suru ⟨〜を⟩⟨〜と⟩対比する ③ •c [for s.o. to compare two things in order to determine the differences between them]** ⟪**compare**⟫, **⟨-o⟩ {⟨-to⟩/⟨-ni⟩} ku⌈raberu ⟨〜を⟩{⟨〜と⟩/⟨〜に⟩}比べる ② [for s.o. to check two/more things against each another for similarities/differences or relative strengths/weaknesses]**

EX. (**a**) The purpose of this paper is to contrast communism with socialism.
この論文の目的は共産主義と社会主義を{対照する/対比する/比べる}ことです。
Kono ronbun no mokuteki wa kyoosan-shugi to shakai-shugi o {taishoo-suru/taihi-suru/kuraberu} koto desu.
(**b**) In our anthropology class we contrasted various world cultures.
我々の人類学の授業では世界のいろいろな文化を{対照した/対比した/比べた}。
Ware-ware no jinrui-gaku no jugyoo de wa sekai no iro-irona bunka o {taishoo-shita/taihi-shita/kurabeta}.

contribute vt. **[for s.o. to give money, etc., to a worthy cause or to write an article for a publication or for s.o./s.t. to help bring s.t. else about]**
1. ⟨-ni⟩⟨-o⟩ ki⌉fu-suru ⟨〜に⟩⟨〜を⟩寄付する ③ •c [for s.o. to provide money or other goods gratis for the purpose of promoting some project or cause] ⟪**donate, chip in**⟫

EX. (**a**) Mr. Matsunaga contributed a huge sum of money to charity.
松永さんは巨額の金を慈善事業に寄付した。
Matsunaga-san wa kyogaku no kane o jizen-jigyoo ni kifu-shita.
(**b**) I decided to contribute the royalties

from the book to my alma mater.
母校に著書の印税を寄付することにした。
Bokoo ni chosho no inzei o kifu-suru koto ni shita.

2. ⟨-ni⟩ ⟨-o⟩ ki⌈koo-suru ⟨〜に⟩⟨〜を⟩寄稿する ③ •c [for s.o. to send a manuscript to a publication upon request]

C

EX. (**a**) Mr. Brown contributed an article to the local newspaper every week.
ブラウン氏は、毎週地元の新聞に記事を寄稿した。
Buraun-shi wa, mai-shuu jimoto no shinbun ni kiji o kikoo-shita.
(**b**) The college president contributed his memoirs to the alumni magazine.
学長は同窓会誌に回顧録を寄稿した。
Gakuchoo wa doosoo-kai-shi ni kaiko-roku o kikoo-shita.

— vi. **[for s.o./s.t. to help bring about s.t. else]**
⟨-ni⟩ ko⌈oken-suru ⟨〜に⟩貢献する ③ •c [for s.o./s.t. to play a role in the furtherance or development of s.t. else] ⟪render services⟫

EX. (**a**) The United Nations has contributed greatly to world peace.
国際連合は世界平和に大きく貢献している。
Kokusai-rengoo wa sekai-heiwa ni ookiku kooken-shite iru.
(**b**) Noam Chomsky contributed immeasurably to the advancement of linguistic science.
ノーム・チョムスキーは言語科学の発展に計り知れない程貢献した。
Noomu Chomusukii wa gengo-kagaku no hatten ni hakari-shirenai hodo kooken-shita.
(**c**) I think overseas performances of *kabuki* contribute much to the understanding of Japanese culture.
海外での歌舞伎の上演は日本文化の理解に貢献していると思います。
Kaigai de no kabuki no jooen wa Nihon-bunka no rikai ni kooken-shite iru to omoimasu.

contribution n. **[an act of giving s.t. to a worthy cause or s.t. so given; s.t. written for a publication; s.t. which helps bring s.t. else about]**

1. ki⌉fu 寄付 •c [money or goods provided gratis for the purpose of promoting some project or cause] ⟪gift, donation, benefaction⟫

EX. (**a**) The contribution of a substantial sum of money to the university by the alumnus was much appreciated.
卒業生の大学に対する多額の寄付は大変感謝された。
Sotsugyoo-sei no daigaku ni-taisuru tagaku no kifu wa taihen kansha-sareta.
(**b**) All contributions are tax-deductable.
寄付はすべて税金控除の対象となる。
Kifu wa subete zeikin-koojo no taishoo to naru.

2. ki⌈koo 寄稿 •c [the sending of a manuscript to a newspaper, magazine, etc. or the manuscript itself] ⟪a piece of writing⟫

EX. Mr. A's contributions appear regularly in the local newspaper.
Aさんの寄稿は地元の新聞に定期的に載る。
Ee-san no kikoo wa jimoto no shinbun ni teiki-tekini noru.

3. ko⌈oken 貢献 •c [an act which helps bring s.t. about or which plays a role in the furtherance or development of s.t.] ⟪services⟫

EX. (**a**) Darwin's contribution to the study of evolution was history making.
ダーウインの進化論研究への貢献は歴史に残るものであった。
Daauin no shinka-ron-kenkyuu e no kooken wa rekishi ni nokoru mono deatta.
(**b**) Pasteur's contributions to medicine were unequaled in history.
パスツールの医学への貢献は歴史上比類のないものであった。
Pasutsuuru no igaku e no kooken wa rekishi-joo hirui no nai mono deatta.

(c) The United Nations has made some very important contributions to political stability in the world.
国連は世界の政治の安定に極めて重要な貢献をしている。
Kokuren wa sekai no seiji no antei ni kiwamete juuyoona kooken o shite iru.

control vt. **[to regulate or direct s.t./s.o.]**

1. ⟨-o⟩ shi⌉hai-suru ⟨〜を⟩支配する ③ •c [for s.o. to exercise power over people or organizations to cause them to act or function in the way one desires] ⟪rule, govern, dominate⟫

EX. (a) That company practically controls the whole industry.
その会社はほとんどその業界全体を支配している。
Sono kaisha wa hotondo sono gyookai-zentai o shihai-shite iru.
(b) There are many who believe in the existence of a supreme being that controls the course of world events.
世界情勢の成り行きを支配する神の存在を信じる人が多い。
Sekai-joosei no nari-yuki o shihai-suru kami no sonzai o shinjiru hito ga ooi.
(c) In our household it's my wife who controls the finances.
わが家では財布を支配するのはワイフである。
Waga-ya de wa saifu o shihai-suru no wa waifu dearu.

2. ⟨-o⟩ o⌈sae⌉ru ⟨〜を⟩おさえる ② [to push s.t. down/back ⟪fig. "restrain," "suppress," "arrest," "govern," "cover," "grasp"⟫; for s.o. to prevent s.o./s.a./s.t. from escaping or otherwise acting freely; for s.o. to prevent s.t. undesirable from occurring which would otherwise occur; for s.o. to pay due attention to s.t. as being important] ⟪check, restrain, keep down⟫, ⟨-o⟩ ko⌈ntoro⌉oru-suru ⟨〜を⟩コントロールする ③ •f

EX. (a) The government had to take strong measures to control inflation.
政府はインフレを{抑える/?コントロールする}ため強硬な措置を講じなければならなかった。
Seifu wa infure o {osaeru/?kontorooru-suru} tame kyookoona sochi o koojinakereba naranakatta.
(b) She could not control her feelings.
彼女は感情を{抑えられなかった/コントロールできなかった}。
Kanojo wa kanjoo o {osae-rarenakatta/kontorooru-dekinakatta}.

3. ⟨-o⟩ ki⌈sei-suru ⟨〜を⟩規制する ③ •c [for s.o. to limit s.t. so as to prevent the development of an undesirable situation which may otherwise be foreseen to occur] ⟪restrict, regulate⟫, ⟨-o⟩ ko⌈ntoro⌉oru-suru ⟨〜を⟩コントロールする ③ •f

EX. (a) The police department controlled traffic in the vicinity of the stadium during the Olympic Games.
警察はオリンピックの期間中スタジアム近くの交通を{規制/?コントロール}した。
Keisatsu wa Orinpikku no kikan-chuu sutajiamu chikaku no kootsuu o {kisei/?kontorooru}-shita.
(b) Air fares were controlled for a long time.
航空運賃は長い間{規制されて/コントロールされて}いた。
Kookuu-unchin wa nagai aida {kisei-sarete/kontorooru-sarete} ita.
(c) The Ministry of Education controls the size of enrollments in colleges and universities.
文部省は大学の定員を{規制/コントロール}している。
Monbu-shoo wa daigaku no teiin o {kisei/kontorooru}-shite iru.

—— n. **[the power to direct or regulate s.t./s.o.; a means of directing or regulating s.t./s.o.; a restraint placed on s.t./s.o.]**

1. shi⌈ha⌉i-ken 支配権 •c [the authority to direct s.o. as one wills] ⟪management, supremacy⟫

EX. (a) The investor took control of the company overnight.

その投資家は一夜にしてその会社の支配権を握った。
Sono tooshi-ka wa ichi-ya ni shite sono kaisha no shihai-ken o nigitta.
(**b**) The three brothers are in full control of the business.
三人の兄弟がその事業の完全な支配権を有している。
San-nin no kyoodai ga sono jigyoo no kanzenna shihai-ken o yuushite iru.
(**c**) After much effort, he finally took control of the corporation.
努力の末、彼はついにその会社の支配権を得た。
Doryoku no sue, kare wa tsuini sono kaisha no shihai-ken o eta.

C

2. ka˥nri 管理 •c [the act of directly overseeing an organization or an operation to make sure that it functions properly] ⟪management, administration, charge, care, supervision⟫

EX. (**a**) The American auto industry has in recent years adopted a Japanese-style system of quality control.
アメリカの自動車産業は近年日本式の品質管理制度を採用している。
Amerika no jidoosha-sangyoo wa kinnen Nihon-shiki no hinshitsu-kanri-seido o saiyoo-shite iru.
(**b**) Japan's trade control laws have been simplified recently.
日本の貿易管理法が最近簡素化された。
Nihon no booeki-kanri-hoo ga saikin kanso-ka-sareta.
(**c**) America's policy of immigration control is a very strict one.
アメリカの出入国管理政策はとても厳しいものだ。
Amerika no shutsu-nyuu-koku-kanri-seisaku wa totemo kibishii mono da.

convenience n. **[ease and comfort; s.t. that provides ease and comfort]**

1. tsu˥goo 都合 •c [a set of circumstances having a bearing on the case with which one is able to undertake a particular course of action; the act of somehow making available the time or money necessary for s.t. within the limits of one's resources] ⟪circumstances, reasons⟫

EX. (**a**) Please come and see me at your convenience.
都合のつく時に、私に会いに来てください。
Tsugoo no tsuku toki ni, watashi ni ai ni kite kudasai.
(**b**) If it meets your convenience, I would like to stop by this afternoon.
ご都合がよければ今日の午後お伺いしたいんですが。
Go-tugoo ga yokereba kyoo no gogo o-ukagai-shi-tai n desu ga.

2. be˥nrina 便利な adj(*na*). **•c [the quality of being readily available for or making it easy to achieve some purpose] ⟪easy⟫**

EX. (**a**) I often carry a portable telephone for the convenience it offers in keeping in contact with my customers.
取り引き先と連絡を取り合うのに便利なのでよく携帯電話を持ち歩く。
Torihiki-saki to renraku o tori-au no ni benrina node yoku keitai-denwa o mochi-aruku.
(**b**) Having so many stores nearby is a definite convenience.
近くに商店が多く生活が便利だ。
Chikaku ni shooten ga ooku seikatsu ga benri da.

convenient adj. **[easy to do/use/get to]**

1. be˥nrina 便利な adj(*na*). **[readily available for or making it easy to achieve some purpose] ⟪handy⟫**

EX. (**a**) The telephone answering machine is a convenient device.
留守番電話は便利な装置だ。
Rusu-ban-denwa wa benrina soochi da.
(**b**) I'm trying to find an apartment more convenient to shopping than my current place.
今のところよりもっと買い物に便利なアパートを探しています。
Ima no tokoro yori motto kai-mono ni benrina apaato o sagashite imasu.

2. tsu⌈goo ga i⌉i 都合がいい adj(*i*). **[for a circumstance/situation/condition to be favorable for s.o.]** ((**favorable, fortunate**))

EX. (**a**) Please pay whenever it's convenient.
いつでも都合がいい時にお支払いください。
Itsu demo tsugoo ga ii toki ni o-shiharai kudasai.
(**b**) Would it be convenient for me to drop something off for you now?
今からちょっとお届けしたいものがあるんですが、ご都合はよろしいでしょうか。
Ima kara chotto o-todoke-shi-tai mono ga aru n desu ga, go-tsugoo wa yoroshii deshoo ka.
(**c**) Sunday would be convenient.
日曜日なら都合がいいんですが。
Nichiyoo-bi nara tsugoo ga ii n desu ga.

convention n. **[an assembly, often periodical, of the members of an organization; a custom]**

1. ta⌈ikai 大会 •**c [the largest and most important gathering of an organization]** ((**conference**))

EX. (**a**) The Association for Asian Studies holds its annual convention in different cities each year.
アジア研究学会は毎年違う都市で年次大会を開く。
Ajia-kenkyuu-gakkai wa mai-toshi chigau toshi de nenji-taikai o hiraku.
(**b**) When will the next convention be held?
次の大会はいつごろになりますか。
Tsugi no taikai wa itsu-goro ni narimasu ka.
(**c**) The hotel is full of convention participants.
ホテルは大会参加者でいっぱいだ。
Hoteru wa taikai-sanka-sha de ippai da.

2. ka⌈nshuu 慣習 •**c [a customary practice of a certain community/society]** ((**custom**))

EX. (**a**) It is not easy to break established conventions.
古くからの慣習を破るのは容易ではない。
Furuku kara no kanshuu o yaburu no wa yooi dewanai.
(**b**) It is safest to follow the social conventions of the country in which one lives.
自分が住んでいる国の社会慣習に従うのが一番安全です。
Jibun ga sunde iru kuni no shakai-kanshuu ni shitagau no ga ichiban anzen desu.

conversation n. **[an informal oral exchange between two or more persons]**
ka⌈iwa 会話 •**c [an act/instance of speaking informally with another person]** ((**talk, chat**))

EX. (**a**) Many Japanese attend English conversation classes.
英会話のクラスに出ている日本人は多い。
Ei-kaiwa no kurasu ni dete iru Nihon-jin wa ooi.
(**b**) I can carry on a simple conversation in English.
簡単な会話なら英語で出来ます。
Kantanna kaiwa nara eigo de dekimasu.
(**c**) I teach English conversation as a part-time job.
アルバイトで英会話を教えています。
Arubaito de ei-kaiwa o oshiete imasu.
(**d**) The conversation between the two was hardly audible.
その二人の会話は、ほとんど聞こえなかった。
Sono futari no kaiwa wa, hotondo kikoenakatta.

convey vt. **[to take s.t. from one place to another; for s.o. to communicate s.t. to s.o.]**
⟨-ni⟩ ⟨-o⟩ tsu⌈taeru ⟨〜に⟩⟨〜を⟩伝える ② **[for s.o./s.a. to pass along some message to s.o.]** ((**transmit, communicate, report, impart, teach**)), **⟨-ni⟩ ⟨-o⟩ de⌈ntatsu-suru** ⟨〜に⟩⟨〜を⟩伝達する ③ •**c [for s.o. to transmit s.t. such as an order, instruction, information, etc., to others]** ((**communicate, transmit**))

C

EX. (**a**) I will certainly convey your message to him.
あなたのメッセージを確かに彼に{伝えます/??伝達します}。
Anata no messeeji o tashikani kare ni {tsutaemasu/??dentatsu-shimasu}.
(**b**) Yes, I will convey your wishes to the company president.
はい、ご希望を社長に{お伝え/伝達}致します。
Hai, go-kiboo o shachoo ni {o-tsutae/dentatsu}-itashimasu.
(**c**) Please tell me how I should convey my feelings to my teacher.
わたしの気持ちを先生にどのように{伝えたら/*伝達したら}いいか教えてください。
*Watashi no kimochi o sensei ni dono yooni {tsutaetara/*dentatsu-shitara} ii ka oshiete kudasai.*

convince vt. **[to persuade s.o. of s.t. by argument/evidence]**
⟨-o⟩ na⌈ttoku-saseru ⟨〜を⟩納得させる /⟨**causative of *nattoku-suru*** ③ **become convinced/** ② **•c [to cause s.o. to understand and accept the words or actions of another]** ⟪**persuade**⟫, **⟨-o⟩ se⌈ttoku-suru** ⟨〜を⟩説得する ③ **•c [for s.o. to talk s.o. into doing s.t.]** ⟪**persuade**⟫

EX. (**a**) I finally convinced her to take the job.
私はその仕事をするよう彼女をやっと{納得させた/説得した}。
Watashi wa sono shigoto o suru yoo kanojo o yatto {nattoku-saseta/settoku-shita}.
(**b**) The government made efforts to convince the people to accept a tax increase.
政府は増税を国民に{納得させる/?説得する}努力をした。
Seifu wa zoozei o kokumin ni {nattoku-saseru/?settoku-suru} doryoku o shita.
(**c**) He convinced me of his ability.
彼は能力があることを私に{納得させた/*説得した}。
*Kare wa nooryoku ga aru koto o watashi ni {nattoku-saseta/*settoku-shita}.*
(**d**) It is difficult to convince her.
彼女を{納得させる/説得する}のは難しい。
Kanojo o {nattoku-saseru/settoku-suru} no wa muzukashii.

cook vt. **[for s.o. to prepare (food) with heat as in boiling, baking, etc.]**
(⟨-o⟩) ryo⌉ori-suru (⟨〜を⟩)料理する ③ **•c [for s.o. to prepare (food) (not necessarily with heat)]** ⟪**prepare, fix**⟫, **⟨-o⟩ ni⌈ru** ⟨〜を⟩煮る ② **[for s.o. to prepare food by heating it until it is soft in a seasoned liquid and retaining the liquid]**

EX. My mother cooked meat for the guests.
母はお客に肉を{料理した/煮た}。
Haha wa o-kyaku ni niku o {ryoori-shita/nita}.

— vi. **[for food to be prepared with heat as in boiling, baking, etc.]**
ryo⌉ori-suru 料理する ③ **•c [for s.o. to prepare (food) (not necessarily with heat)]** ⟪**prepare, fix**⟫, **ni⌈eru** 煮える ② **[for food to be prepared by heating it in liquid inside a container]**

EX. (**a**) I could smell fish cooking.
魚{が煮える/を料理する}においがした。
Sakana {ga nieru/o ryoori-suru} nioi ga shita.
(**b**) My wife is cooking in the kitchen.
家内は台所で{料理して/*煮て}います。
*Kanai wa daidokoro de {ryoori-shite/*nite} imasu.*

— n. **[a person who prepares food]**
ryo⌈ori-nin 料理人 **•c [a person who prepares food, usually professionally]**, **ko⌉kku** コック **•f**, **i⌈tamae** 板前 **[s.o. who prepares food professionally, often in a traditional Japanese restaurant such as a sushi-shop]**

itamae

PHRASE: be a good cook *ryoori ga umai* 料理がうまい adj(*i*).

EX. My grandfather was a good cook.
祖父は料理がうまかった。

Sofu wa ryoori ga umakatta.

cooking n. **[the preparation of food or food which is prepared]**
ryo⌈ori 料理 •c **[the preparation of food or food which is prepared]** ⟪cuisine⟫

EX. (**a**) She is a student at a cooking school.
彼女は料理学校の生徒です。
Kanojo wa ryoori-gakkoo no seito desu.
(**b**) I like cooking.
私は料理が好きだ。
Watashi wa ryoori ga suki da.
(**c**) Nothing can compare to my mother's cooking.
おふくろの料理に並ぶものはない。
Ofukuro no ryoori ni narabu mono wa nai.

cool adj. **[moderately free of heat; not excited, composed]**
1. su⌈zushi⌉i 涼しい adj(*i*). **[of a temperature low enough to be comfortable to the human body ⟪fig. "clear and beautiful"⟫]**
↔ **atatakai** 暖かい adj(*i*).

EX. (**a**) We had a cool summer this year.
今年の夏は涼しかった。
Kotoshi no natsu wa suzushikatta.
(**b**) We took a break from hiking in the cool shade of a large oak tree.
大きなかしの木陰の涼しい所で少し休んだ。
Ookina kashi no ko-kage no suzushii tokoro de sukoshi yasunda.

2. re⌈iseina 冷静な adj(*na*). •c **[composed and not driven or disturbed by emotions]** ⟪composed⟫, **ku⌉uruna** クールな adj(*na*). •f
↔ **hottona** ホットな adj(*na*). •f

EX. (**a**) Everyone kept cool when the earthquake occurred and managed to get out of the building safely.
地震が起きた時みんな冷静だったのでビルから無事出ることができた。
Jishin ga okita toki minna reisei datta node biru kara buji deru koto ga dekita.
(**b**) A cool head is needed in a crisis like this.
このような危機には冷静な頭が必要である。
Kono yoona kiki ni wa reiseina atama ga hitsuyoo dearu.

—— vt. **[to make s.t. cool]**
⟨-o⟩ hi⌈ya⌉su ⟨〜を⟩冷やす ① **[for s.o. to make s.t. cold]** ⟪chill⟫, **⟨-o⟩ sa⌈ma⌉su** ⟨〜を⟩冷ます ① **[for s.o. to let the temperature of s.t. go down as far as room temperature]**

EX. (**a**) Let's cool the beer in the fridge.
ビールを冷蔵庫で{冷やそう/*冷まそう}。
*Biiru o reizoo-ko de {hiyasoo/*samasoo}.*
(**b**) Don't cool the room down too much.
部屋をあまり{冷やさないで/*冷まさないで}下さい。
*Heya o amari {hiyasanaide/*samasanaide} kudasai.*
(**c**) Cool the hot water a bit before pouring it into the teapot.
急須に入れる前にお湯をちょっと{冷まして/*冷やして}下さい。
*Kyuusu ni ireru mae ni o-yu o chotto {samashite/*hiyashite} kudasai.*

—— vi. **[for s.t. to become lower in temperature or level of excitement]**
sa⌈me⌉ru 冷める ②

EX. My enthusiasm for the new project soon cooled down.
新しいプロジェクトに対する情熱はすぐ冷めてしまった。
Atarashii purojekuto ni taisuru joonetsu wa sugu samete shimatta.

cooperate vi. **[to work together willingly with another to achieve a common purpose]**
(⟨-to⟩) kyo⌈oryoku-suru (⟨〜と⟩)協力する ③ •c **[for s.o. to work together with s.o. else in achieving]** ⟪collaborate⟫

EX. (**a**) Three people cooperated on this project.
このプロジェクトには三人の人が協力した。
Kono purojekuto ni wa san-nin no hito ga kyooryoku-shita.
(**b**) We must cooperate with one another for world peace.
我々は世界の平和のためにお互いに協力しなければならない。
Ware-ware wa sekai no heiwa no tame

ni o-tagai ni kyooryoku-shinakereba naranai.
(**c**) We cooperated with the U.N. forces in saving the refugees.
国連軍と協力して難民を救った。
Kokuren-gun to kyooryoku-shite nanmin o sukutta.
(**d**) The passers-by cooperated in helping us catch the thief.
通行人が協力して泥棒を捕まえるのを助けてくれた。
Tsuukoo-nin ga kyooryoku-shite doroboo o tsukamaeru no o tasukete kureta.

cooperation n. **[an act/instance of cooperating]**
kyo⌈oryoku 協力 •c [working together with s.o. in achieving s.t] 《collaboration》

EX. (**a**) International cooperation is essential in preventing global warming.
地球の温暖化を防止するには国際協力が不可欠である。
Chikyuu no ondan-ka o booshi-suru ni wa kokusai-kyooryoku ga fukaketsu dearu.
(**b**) We sought the cooperation of the Ministry of Education in conducting the test.
試験の実施に当たっては文部省の協力を仰いだ。
Shiken no jisshi ni atatte wa Monbu-shoo no kyooryoku o aoida.
(**c**) Your cooperation would be appreciated in this matter.
この件についてぜひご協力をお願いします。
Kono ken ni-tsuite zehi go-kyooryoku o o-negai-shimasu.

copy n. **[s.t. made to look exactly like another 《fig. "any of a number of books, magazines etc. having the same contents"》]**
1. u⌈tsushi⌉ 写し /(V*masu* of *utsusu* ① transfer/ [a duplicated document/art object or a picture painted exactly like the original], ko⌉pii コピー •f

EX. (**a**) Please submit the original of the document, not a photo copy.
{写し/コピー}でなく書類の原本を出してください。
{Utsushi/Kopii} denaku shorui no genpon o dashite kudasai.
(**b**) Would you make a copy of this document for me?
この書類の{写し/コピー}を一部作ってください。
Kono shorui no {utsushi/kopii} o ichi-bu tsukutte kudasai.
(**c**) Would you please send a copy of the letter to Mr. Johnson?
手紙の{写し/コピー}をジョンソンさんに送ってくださいますか。
Tegami no {utsushi/kopii} o Jonson-san ni okutte kudasaimasu ka.

2. -bu ～部 •c [a counter for multiples, of the same thing such as books and magazines]

EX. (**a**) This dictionary sold a million copies.
この辞書は百万部売れた。
Kono jisho wa hyaku-man-bu ure-ta.
(**b**) I made two copies of the article.
記事のコピーを二部作った。
Kiji no kopii o ni-bu tsukutta.

—— vt. **[for s.o. to make a duplicate of s.t. 《fig. "imitate"》]**
⟨-o⟩ ko⌉pii-suru ⟨～を⟩コピーする ③ •f [for s.o. to make a duplicate of a document/art object] 《duplicate》, ma⌈ne-suru まねする ③ [to imitate s.o./s.t./s.a.] 《imitate》

EX. (**a**) I copied some example sentences from the book.
私はその本から例文をいくつか{コピー/*まね}した。
*Watashi wa sono hon kara reibun o ikutsu-ka {kopii/*mane}-shita.*
(**b**) It is wrong to copy the product of another company.
よその会社の製品を{コピー/まね}するのは悪いことだ。
Yoso no kaisha no seihin o {kopii/mane}-suru no wa warui koto da.

corner n. **[the point or place where lines/surfaces join and form an angle]**
1. ka⌉do 角 [the place where a road crosses

with another or where it bends at a sharp angle] ⟪**angle**⟫

EX. (**a**) Turn the next corner and you'll see the post office.
次の角を曲がると郵便局があります。
Tsugi no kado o magaru to yuubin-kyoku ga arimasu.
(**b**) The station is just around the corner.
駅はすぐそこの角を曲がったところです。
Eki wa sugu soko no kado o magatta tokoro desu.

2. su⌉mi 隅 **•c [an area inside a space or surface enclosed by planes or lines where the planes or lines meet to form an angle; an area which does not stand out visually or in importance]** ⟪**nook**⟫

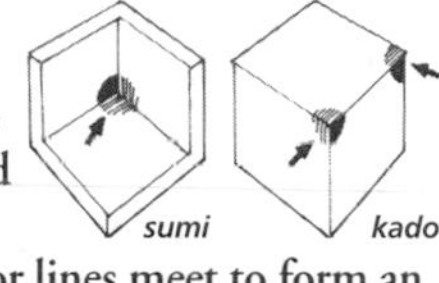

EX. (**a**) Bob has a bust of Beethoven in the corner of his living room.
ボブは居間の隅にベートーベンの胸像を置いている。
Bobu wa ima no sumi ni Beetooben no kyoozoo o oite iru.
(**b**) Dust tends to gather in the corner of the room.
部屋の隅はほこりがたまりやすい。
Heya no sumi wa hokori ga tamari-yasui.

correct adj. **[conforming to an established standard; not mistaken]**
ta⌈dashi⌉i 正しい adj(*i*). **[conforming to an ethical, legal, logical, social, or regulatory standard; free from error]** ⟪**right, just, proper, reasonable, accurate, exact, lawful, legal, legitimate, sound, healthy, straight**⟫

EX. (**a**) Can you tell me the correct way to read this Chinese character?
この漢字の正しい読み方を教えてくれませんか。
Kono kanji no tadashii yomi-kata o oshiete kuremasen ka.
(**b**) There are a number of correct ways to teach a foreign language.
外国語を教える正しい方法はいくつかある。
Gaikoku-go o oshieru tadashii hoohoo wa ikutsu-ka aru.
(**c**) Which is the correct answer, A or B?
AとBのどちらが正しい答えですか。
Ei to bii no dochira ga tadashii kotae desu ka.

— vt. **[for s.o. to set/make s.t. right]**
⟨-o⟩ te⌈isei-suru ⟨〜を⟩訂正する ③ **•c [for s.o. to make right the errors/mistakes in what s.o has said/written]** ⟪**revise, amend**⟫, **⟨-o⟩ na⌈o⌉su** ⟨〜を⟩なおす ① **[for s.o. to restore s.t. damaged to its normal state of functioning ⟪fig. "cure"⟫]** ⟪**rectify, repair, fix**⟫

㊥ "cure"▷治す, otherwise▷直す

EX. (**a**) I would like to correct some mistakes from my lecture last week.
先週の講義の誤りを{訂正し/直し}たいと思います。
Senshuu no koogi no ayamari o {teisei-shi/naoshi}-tai to omoimasu.
(**b**) Please correct any errors in my composition.
作文に間違いがあったら{訂正して/直して}下さい。
Sakubun ni machigai ga attara {teisei-shite/naoshite} kudasai.
(**c**) Would you correct the error in the address book?
住所録の間違いを{訂正して/直して}下さい。
Juusho-roku no machigai o {teisei-shite/naoshite} kudasai.
(**d**) The doctor corrected the child's nearsightedness by means of an operation.
医者は子供の近視を手術で{治した/*訂正した}。
*Isha wa kodomo no kinshi o shujutsu de {naoshita/*teisei-shita}.*

correction n. **[the act of correcting s.t.; s.t. substituted for what is wrong]**
te⌈isei 訂正 **•c [making right the errors/mistakes in what s.o. has said/written]** ⟪**revision, amendment**⟫

EX. (**a**) There are corrections in the handout that you will want to take note of.

プリントには訂正がありますので気をつけて下さい。
Purinto ni wa teisei ga arimasu node ki-o-tsukete kudasai.
(**b**) I had carefully checked my manuscript, and so no corrections were necessary.
注意深く読み直してあったので、自分の原稿は訂正の必要がありませんでした。
Chuui-bukaku yomi-naoshite atta node, jibun no genkoo wa teisei no hitsuyoo ga arimasen deshita.

correctly adv. **[in a correct manner]**
ta⌈dashi⌉ku 正しく /⟨adj(*i*). *ku* of *tadashii* correct/ [in such a way as to conform to an ethical, legal, logical, social, or regulatory standard; in such a way as to be free of error] ⟪**rightly**⟫, **se⌈ikakuni 正確に /⟨adj(*na*). *ni* of *seikakuna* accurate/ •c** ⟪**accurately**⟫

EX. (**a**) Yes, the form is correctly filled out.
ええ、用紙は{正しく/正確に}記入されていますよ。
Ee, yooshi wa {tadashiku/seikakuni} kinyuu-sarete imasu yo.
(**b**) Please make sure the data has been input correctly.
データが{正しく/正確に}入力してあることをご確認下さい。
Deeta ga {tadashiku/seikakuni} nyuuryoku-shite aru koto o go-kakunin kudasai.

correspondence n. **[the state of being in harmony or agreement with s.t.; communication with s.o. by exchange of letters]**
1. tsu⌈ushin 通信 •c [making contact with s.o. by mail, phone, etc., to provide information about s.t.] ⟪**communications**⟫, **bu⌈ntsuu 文通 •c [exchange of letters]**

EX. (**a**) He studied by correspondence.
彼は{通信/*文通}による教育を受けた。
*Kare wa {tsuushin/*buntsuu} ni yoru kyooiku o uketa.*
(**b**) I have had correspondence with him for the past two years.
彼とは過去二年間{文通/?通信}をしています。
Kare to wa kako ni-nenkan {buntsuu/?tsuushin} o shite imasu.

2. i⌈tchi 一致 •c [for two or more things to match or be in harmony] ⟪**unity**⟫

EX. There is perfect correspondence between his words and actions.
彼のことばと行動には完全な一致が見られる。
Kare no kotoba to koodoo ni wa kanzenna itchi ga mi-rareru.

cost vt. **[for s.t. to be obtainable for some sum of money]**
⟨-ni⟩ ka⌈ka⌉ru ⟨〜に⟩かかる ① [for s.t. to extend to and come in contact with s.t./s.o./s.a. else ⟪fig. "cover," "begin," "be engaged in," "become splashed with," "be built," "require"⟫] ⟪**hang, be built, take, need, require, fight against, be imposed on**⟫, **su⌈ru する ③ [for s.o./s.a. to perform a willful action; for s.o./s.a./s.t. to cause s.t. to take on a different state; for s.t. to happen in such a way as to be perceptible to s.o./s.a.; for s.t. to be in a certain state or possess a certain attribute; for an amount of time/money to pass/be required; for some proposition to be posited as true ⟪fig. "put on a somewhat small, ornametal object"⟫]** ⟪**do, make, elapse, be valued, have**⟫

EX. (**a**) How much did it cost you to get to New York?
ニューヨークへ行くのにいくらくらい{かかりました/しました}か。
Nyuuyooku e iku no ni ikura-kurai {kakarimashita/shimashita} ka.
(**b**) The car repair cost $12,000.
車の修理は一万二千ドル{かかった/した}。
Kuruma no shuuri wa ichi-man-ni-sen-doru {kakatta/shita}.

—— n. **[the amount of money, effort, etc. asked/paid for s.t.]**
hi⌉yoo 費用 •c [the money necessary for doing s.t.] ⟪**price**⟫

EX. (**a**) What were the repair costs for the broken window?

割れた窓の修理の費用はいくらでしたか。
Wareta mado no shuuri no hiyoo wa ikura deshita ka.
(**b**) A group tour will enable you to travel overseas at a relatively low cost.
団体旅行なら比較的安い費用で旅行ができます。
Dantai-ryokoo nara hikaku-teki yasui hiyoo de ryokoo ga dekimasu.
(**c**) I want to publish a book, but the cost worries me.
本を出版したいが費用のことが心配だ。
Hon o shuppan-shi-tai ga hiyoo no koto ga shinpai da.

costly adj. **[costing much]**
ta⌈ka⌉i 高い adj(*i*). **[for s.t. or the top of s.t. to be at a point well above the ground or for s.t. to be above the expected level/amount/rate/degree]** ⟪**dear, expensive, raised, loud, exalted, widely-known**⟫ ↔ **yasui** 安い adj(*i*).

EX. (**a**) The house was too costly for us to buy.
その家は高くて手が出なかった。
Sono ie wa takakute te ga denakatta.
(**b**) A new car would be very costly.
新車はとても高いでしょう。
Shinsha wa totemo takai deshoo.

council n. **[a group of people called together for discussion, advice, etc., esp. an administative/legislative body]**
kyo⌈ogi⌉-kai 協議会 •c **[a group of people gathered together for consultation on a particular issue]** ⟪**conference**⟫

EX. (**a**) The university council holds its regular meetings on Wednesdays.
大学協議会は水曜日に定例会議を開きます。
Daigaku-kyoogi-kai wa suiyoo-bi ni teirei-kaigi o hirakimasu.
(**b**) A cooperative council of the parties concerned was established to deal with the problem.
問題処理のため関係者の協力協議会が設置された。
Mondai-shori no tame kankei-sha no kyooryoku-kyoogi-kai ga setchi-sareta.

count vt. **[for s.o. to add up one by one to determine the total number of a group of things/people;** ⟪**fig. "take account of," "include," "believe to be"**⟫
⟨**-o**⟩ **ka⌈zoe⌉ru** ⟨〜を⟩数える ② **[for s.o. to determine clearly the total number of a group of things/people]** ⟪**reckon, calculate, number, take account of**⟫

EX. (**a**) Don't count your chickens before they're hatched.
生まれる前に自分のひよこを数えるな。
Umareru mae ni jibun no hiyoko o kazoeruna.

NOTE: A similar Japanese proverb is *Toranu tanuki no kawa-zan'yoo.*

(**b**) We always count the number of students on the first day of a semester.
学期の最初の日に必ず学生の数を数えます。
Gakki no saisho no hi ni kanarazu gakusei no kazu o kazoemasu.
(**c**) Listing the sorrows in my life would be like counting the number of stars in the sky.
我が人生の不幸を一つ一つ挙げるとなると空の星の数を数えるようなものだ。
Waga jinsei no fukoo o hitotsu hitotsu kazoeru to naru to, sora no hoshi no kazu o kazoeru yoona mono da.

2. (**-o**) {**ka⌈zu/ka⌈njo⌉o**} **ni i⌈reru** (〜を){数/勘定}に入れる ② **[for s.o. to include s.t. in a number]** ⟪**reckon, take account of, include**⟫

EX. (**a**) I hope you will count me in.
私を{数/勘定}に入れていただきたいんですが。
Watakushi o {kazu/kanjoo} ni irete itadaki-tai n desu ga.
(**b**) We forgot to count the children when ordering tickets.
子供たちの切符を{数/勘定}に入れ忘れてしまった。
Kodomo-tachi no kippu o {kazu/kanjoo} ni ire-wasurete shimatta.

3. ⟨**-o**⟩ ⟨**-to**⟩ **mi-⌈nasu** ⟨〜を⟩⟨〜と⟩見なす ① **[for s.o. to regard s.t./s.o./s.a. as s.t./s.o./s.a.]** ⟪**regard**⟫

C

EX. (**a**) They refused to count her among their friends.
彼らは彼女を友達と見なすことを拒否した。
Kare-ra wa kanojo o tomodachi to mi-nasu koto o kyohi-shita.
(**b**) We count our chinchillas as members of our family.
我々はうちのチンチラを家族と見なしています。
Ware-ware wa uchi no chinchira o kazoku to mi-nashite imasu.

counter n. **[a long table on which goods are displayed, business transacted, food served, etc.]**
u⌈ri-ba 売り場 [a place where goods, tickets, etc., are sold], ka⌈untaa カウンター •f

country n. **[a nation or the territory it occupies or a rural district]**
1. ku⌈ni 国 [a nation or one's hometown] ⟪nation⟫
EX. (**a**) We have few natural resources in this country.
我が国には天然資源があまりない。
Waga-kuni ni wa tennen-shigen ga amari nai.
(**b**) The countries along the Pacific rim need to cooperate more with one another.
環太平洋諸国はお互いにもっと協力する必要がある。
Kan-Taiheiyoo-shokoku wa o-tagai ni motto kyooryoku-suru hitsuyoo ga aru.
2. i⌈naka 田舎 [a rural area removed from large cities, esp. an area with many farms or few houses, or one's rural place of up bringing] ⟪countryside⟫ ↔ tokai 都会 ⟪city⟫
EX. (**a**) Our grandparents live out in the country in Nagano Prefecture.
うちの祖父母は長野の田舎に住んでいます。
Uchi no sofubo wa Nagano no inaka ni sunde imasu.
(**b**) After I retire, I want to lead a leisurely life in the country.
退職したら田舎でのんびりした生活をしたいです。
Taishoku-shitara inaka de nonbiri-shita seikatsu o shi-tai desu.

countryside n. **[a rural area]**
i⌈naka 田舎 [a rural area removed from large cities, esp. an area with many farms or few houses, or one's rural place of up bringing] ⟪the country⟫

couple n. **[two persons or things considered to belong together]**
fu⌉ufu 夫婦 [man and wife] •c, fu⌈tari⌉ 二人 [two persons]
EX. That couple gets along well.
あの{夫婦/二人}は仲がいい。
Ano {fuufu/futari} wa naka ga ii.

courage n. **[the ability to overcome fear in the face of difficulty or danger]**
yu⌉uki 勇気 •c [the spirit/strength enabling one to undertake action which ordinary people are not capable of due to anxiety/fear] ⟪bravery⟫
EX. (**a**) I did not have the courage to ask her to marry me.
彼女に結婚を申し込む勇気がなかった。
Kanojo ni kekkon o mooshi-komu yuuki ga nakatta.
(**b**) Have courage. Everything is going to be all right.
勇気を出しなさい。万事うまく行くから。
Yuuki o dashinasai. Banji umaku iku kara.
(**c**) He is a man of courage.
彼は勇気のある男だ。
Kare wa yuuki no aru otoko da.

course n. **[a direction/route taken or a regular/natural order of events ⟪fig. "a program of instruction, as in a university," "a part of a meal served at one time"⟫]**
1. shi⌉nro 進路 •c [the direction or route which s.o./s.t. intends to or is expected to take ⟪fig. "direction in life"⟫] ⟪way, track, path⟫, ho⌈okoo 方向 •c [the direction in which s.o./s.a./s.t. proceeds or a policy/goal dictating which way s.o./s.t. should proceed] ⟪direction⟫
EX. (**a**) The sudden death of his wife brought

about an unexpected change in the course of his life.
奥さんが急になくなったことで、彼の人生の{進路/方向}に思わぬ転換が生じた。
Okusan ga kyuuni nakunatta koto de, kare no jinsei no {shinro/hookoo} ni omowanu tenkan ga shoojita.
(**b**) Young people benefit from guidance as to the course they should pursue in life.
若者には人生においてたどるべき{進路/方向}に関するガイダンスが役に立つ。
Waka-mono ni wa jinsei ni oite tadoru-beki {shinro/hookoo} ni-kansuru gaidansu ga yaku ni tatsu.
(**c**) The airplane suddenly changed course.
飛行機は突然{針路/方向}を変えた。
Hikoo-ki wa totsuzen {shinro/hookoo} o kaeta.

2. na⌈ri-yuki 成り行き [the natural progression of events independently of human will of the result of such progression] ⟪progress, outcome, turn⟫

EX. (**a**) Let matters take their own course for the time being.
現在のところは成り行きに任せよう。
Genzai no tokoro wa nari-yuki ni makaseyoo.
(**b**) The outcome of the next election will probably be largely determined by the course of world events.
次回の選挙の結果は世界情勢の成り行きに大きく左右されるだろう。
Jikai no senkyo no kekka wa sekai-joosei no nari-yuki ni ookiku sayuu-sareru daroo.

3. ko⌉osu コース •f, ko⌈oza 講座 •c [subjects on which instruction is given as in college]

EX. (**a**) John took a course in beginning Japanese in college.
ジョンは大学で初級日本語の{コース/講座}を取った。
Jon wa daigaku de shokyuu-Nihon-go no {koosu/kooza} o totta.
(**b**) This culture center offers many courses in foreign languages.
このカルチャーセンターは外国語の{コース/講座}をたくさん用意しています。
Kono karuchaa-sentaa wa gaikoku-go no {koosu/kooza} o takusan yooi-shite imasu.

4. ko⌉osu コース •f [a part of a meal]

EX. I had a full-course dinner at the Hotel Ritz.
私はリッツホテルでフルコースのディナーを食べた。
Watashi wa Rittsu-hoteru de furu-koosu no dinaa o tabeta.

PHRASE: of course *mochiron* もちろん

EX. A: Do you like cats?
猫はお好きですか。
Neko wa o-suki desu ka.
B: Of course we do!
もちろん好きですよ。
Mochiron suki desu yo.

court n. **[a judicial body duly constituted for the hearing and determination of cases or a session of such a body; a playing space as for tennis; a palace; the family, attendants, and advisors, of a sovereign; an open area surrounded by buildings and walls]**

1. sa⌈iban-sho 裁判所 •c [a legally-constituted assembly for conducting trials]

EX. (**a**) There was a trial at the court house yesterday.
昨日裁判所で裁判があった。
Kinoo saiban-sho de saiban ga atta.
(**b**) The court will hear the case tomorrow.
裁判所は明日その事件の審理を行う。
Saiban-sho wa asu sono jiken no shinri o okonau.
(**c**) I went to court yesterday.
昨日は裁判所に出頭して来た。
Kinoo wa saiban-sho ni shuttoo-shite-kita.

2. ko⌉oto コート •c [a place to play tennis, etc.]

EX. The Hasegawas have a tennis court on their property.
長谷川家では敷地内にテニスコートがある。
Hasegawa-ke de wa shikichi-nai ni tenisu-kooto ga aru.

3. kyu⌈utei 宮廷 •c [the palace]
4. na⌈ka-niwa 中庭 [a space between buildings on an estate] 《courtyard》

EX. A full moon could be seen from the court of the old mansion.
その古い邸宅の中庭から満月が見られた。
Sono furui teitaku no naka-niwa kara mangetsu ga mi-rareta.

C

courtesy n. **[an act or way of behaving that is polite and considerate]**
re⌈igi⌉ 礼儀 •c

EX. (**a**) Diplomats place a high value on courtesy.
外交官は礼儀を重んじる。
Gaikoo-kan wa reigi o omonjiru.
(**b**) It is common courtesy for young people to give up their seat on a train or bus to the elderly.
電車やバスの中で若者がお年寄りに席を譲るのが礼儀です。
Densha ya basu no naka de waka-mono ga o-toshiyori ni seki o yuzuru no ga reigi desu.
(**c**) Courtesy demands that before calling on someone you check with them to see if it would be convenient.
人を訪ねる時相手の都合を聞くのが礼儀ですよ。
Hito o tazuneru toki aite no tsugoo o kiku no ga reigi desu yo.

cousin n. **[the child of one's uncle/aunt]**
i⌈to⌉ko いとこ [the child of a brother or sister of one's parents]

EX. I have many cousins.
私にはいとこが多い。
Watakushi ni wa itoko ga ooi.

cover vt. **[for s.o./s.a. to place s.t. over/upon s.t. else 《fig. "hide from view," "extend over"》]**
⟨-o⟩ o⌈o⌉u ⟨〜を⟩覆う ① [to cause a thin and extensive object to lie completely over the surface of s.t. and protect or hide it from the outside] 《veil, hide, conceal, shield, shelter》

EX. (**a**) When I leave the office, I cover my computer with a plastic sheet.
オフィスを出るときビニールシートでコンピューターを覆います。
Ofisu o deru toki biniiru-shiito de konpyuutaa o ooimasu.
(**b**) We covered the hole with a wooden board.
板で穴を覆った。
Ita de ana o ootta.

2. ⟨-o⟩ ka⌈ku⌉su ⟨〜を⟩隠す ① [for s.o. to put or keep s.t./s.o./s.a. out of sight intentionally] 《conceal, hide》

EX. (**a**) They tried to cover (up) his mistakes.
彼の間違いを隠そうとした。
Kare no machigai o kakusoo to shita.
(**b**) He laughed to cover his embarrassment.
恥かしさを隠すために彼は笑った。
Hazukashi-sa o kakusu tame ni kare wa waratta.

3. ⟨-o⟩ ka⌉baa-suru ⟨〜を⟩カバーする ③ •f [for s.t. to extend over a certain area or for s.o. to cause s.t. to extend in such a way]

EX. (**a**) His research covers a wide range of linguistic topics.
彼の研究は言語学の広い範囲のテーマをカバーしている。
Kare no kenkyuu wa gengo-gaku no hiroi han'i no teema o kabaa-shite iru.
(**b**) What territory does this branch office cover?
この支店はどの地区をカバーしているのですか。
Kono shiten wa dono chiku o kabaa-shite iru no desu ka.

—— n. **[s.t. that covers s.t. else]**
1. hyo⌈oshi 表紙 •c [a thick sheet of paper, cloth, leather, plastic, etc., which forms the outside of a book, notebook, etc.]

EX. (**a**) The cover of this book is beautiful, isn't it?
この本の表紙はきれいですね。
Kono hon no hyooshi wa kirei desu ne.
(**b**) The cover of this old dictionary has come off.
この古い辞書は表紙が取れてしまった。
Kono furui jisho wa hyooshi ga torete shimatta.

2. ka⌉baa カバー •f [s.t. which lies over s.t. else to protect or hide it]

EX. (**a**) You should put a cover over the typewriter.
タイプライターにカバーをかけたほうがよい。
Taipu-raitaa ni kabaa o kaketa hoo ga yoi.
(**b**) This cushion cover needs replacing.
このクッションのカバーは取り替える時期が来ている。
Kono kusshon no kabaa wa tori-kaeru jiki ga kite iru.

cow n.
u⌈shi 牛 [cattle] ⟪ox, bull⟫

crack vi. **[for s.t. to break with a sudden sharp sound or to break without completely coming apart]**
⟨-ni⟩ hi⌈bi⌉ ga hairu ⟨〜に⟩ひびが入る ① [for a rigid object such as glass, china, or plaster to develop a small breakage/flaw without complete separation of parts], ⟨-ni⟩ wa⌈re-me ga deki⌉ru ⟨〜に⟩割れ目ができる ① [for s.t. to develop a crevice/opening]

EX. (**a**) The tea cup cracked a bit when it fell.
茶わんは落ちたとき少し{ひびが入った/割れ目ができた}。
Chawan wa ochita toki sukoshi {hibi ga haitta/ware-me ga dekita}.
(**b**) The ice cracked when I pounded it.
たたいたら氷に{ひびが入った/割れ目ができた}。
Tataitara koori ni {hibi ga haitta/ware-me ga dekita}.

—— vt. [for s.o. to cause s.t. to break without completely coming apart]
⟨-o⟩ wa⌈ru ⟨〜を⟩割る ① [for s.o./s.a. to apply force to a hard substance and render it into two or more pieces ⟪fig. "(in mathematics) find how many times a given number is contained in another"⟫]

EX. (**a**) Mrs. Downs cracked the nut with a little hammer.
ダウンズ夫人は小さなつちで木の実を割った。
Daunzu-fujin wa chiisana tsuchi de ko-no-mi o watta.
(**b**) Mother cracked the egg against the rim of the bowl.
母は茶わんの縁で卵を割った。
Haha wa chawan no fuchi de tamago o watta.

—— n. **[a partial break or fracture]**
hi⌈bi⌉ ひび [a partial breakage without complete separation] ⟪fissure⟫, wa⌈re-me 割れ目 [a small breakage] ⟪crevice, chasm, split⟫

EX. (**a**) We found a crack in the window.
窓に{ひび/割れ目}があるのを見つけた。
Mado ni {hibi/ware-me} ga aru no o mitsuketa.
(**b**) Check to make sure there are no cracks in the engine block.
エンジンブロックに{ひび/割れ目}がないか調べなさい。
Enjin-burokku ni {hibi/ware-me} ga nai ka shirabenasai.

craft n. **[a special manual skill or art or an occupation in which such is required]**
gi⌉noo 技能 •c [the technical proficiency/ability required to perform a task/job] ⟪ability, capacity⟫, ko⌈ogei 工芸 •c [the making of artistic products, chiefly by hand] ⟪technical art⟫

EX. (**a**) This museum specializes in arts and crafts.
この博物館は美術と{工芸/*技能}を専門にしている。
*Kono hakubutsu-kan wa bijutsu to {koogei/*ginoo} o senmon ni shite iru.*
(**b**) Few young people are interested in learning the craft of carpentry.
大工の{技能/*工芸}を学びたいと思っている若者は少ない。
*Daiku no {ginoo/*koogei} o manabi-tai to omotte iru waka-mono wa sukunai.*

craftsman n. **[s.o. who practices a craft]**
sho⌈kunin 職人 •c [a person who makes things manually as a profession] ⟪artisan⟫, me⌈ikoo 名工 •c [a skilled artist]

EX. These days, there are fewer and fewer craftsmen in any of the traditional professions.

最近どの伝統的職業でも{職人/名工}はますます少なくなっている。
Saikin dono dentoo-teki shokugyoo de mo {shokunin/meikoo} wa masu-masu sukunaku natte iru.

crash vi. **[for s.t. to fall, collide, break, etc., with a loud noise]**
{⟨-ni⟩/⟨-to⟩} sho⌈ototsu-suru {⟨〜に⟩/⟨〜と⟩} 衝突する ③ •c [for s.t. to collide with s.t. else or for s.o. to disagree with s.o. else] ⟪**run against, smash**⟫, **{⟨-ni⟩/⟨-to⟩} bu⌈tsukaru {⟨〜に⟩/⟨〜と⟩}ぶつかる ① [to come against s.o./s.t./s.a. by accident forcing a change in the direction of its movement]** ⟪**strike, hit, collide**⟫, **tsu⌈iraku-suru 墜落する ③ •c [for s.t./s.o. to fall from a high place]**

EX. (**a**) The car crashed into the lamp post.
車が電柱{に/*と}{衝突した/ぶつかった/*墜落した}。
*Kuruma ga denchuu {ni/*to} {shoototsu-shita/butsukatta/*tsuiraku-shita}.*
(**b**) The plane crashed but everyone survived.
飛行機が{墜落した/*ぶつかった/*衝突した}が全員助かった。
*Hikoo-ki ga {tsuiraku-shita/*butsukatta/*shoototsu-shita} ga zen'in tasukatta.*

—— n. **[a falling, colliding, breaking, etc. with a loud noise]**
sho⌈ototsu 衝突 •c [a collision of s.t. against s.t. else or a disagreement of s.o. with s.o. else], **tsu⌈iraku 墜落 •c [a falling to the ground (or sea) from a high place]**

EX. (**a**) Fortunately no one was killed in the car crash.
幸いなことに車の{衝突/*墜落}で犠牲者は出なかった。
*Saiwaina koto ni kuruma no {shoototsu/*tsuiraku} de gisei-sha wa denakatta.*
(**b**) It's unusual for all the passengers to survive in the plane crash.
飛行機の{墜落/*衝突}で乗客全員が助かるのは珍しい。
*Hikoo-ki no {tsuiraku/*shoototsu} de jookyaku zen'in ga tasukaru no wa mezurashii.*

crazy adj. **[insane or very enthusiastic/eager]**
1. (ki-ga-)ku⌈ru⌉tte iru (N) (気が)狂っている(N) /⟨V *te iru* of *kuruu* ① go mad or stop functioning properly/ [mad or not functioning properly] ⟪**mad, insane**⟫

EX. (**a**) John is crazy to have given up his job.
仕事をやめてしまうなんてジョンは(気が)狂っている。
Shigoto o yamete shimau nante Jon wa (ki-ga-)kurutte iru.
(**b**) Don't go near him because he's crazy.
彼は(気が)狂っているから近づくな。
Kare wa (ki-ga-)kurutte iru kara chikazuku na.

2. ⟨-ni⟩ mu⌈chuu no N ⟨〜に⟩夢中のN •c [for s.o./s.a. to be exclusively peroccupied with one thing] ⟪**be absorbed in**⟫

EX. (**a**) He is crazy about that woman.
彼はあの女性に夢中だ。
Kare wa ano josei ni muchuu da.
(**b**) I was crazy about *kabuki* when I was young.
若いころは歌舞伎に夢中でした。
Wakai koro wa kabuki ni muchuu deshita.
(**c**) My daughter is crazy about knitting.
うちの娘は編み物に夢中です。
Uchi no musume wa ami-mono ni muchuu desu.

cream n. **[the oily, yellowish part of milk or a creamlike cosmetic ointment]**
ku⌈ri⌉imu クリーム •f

create vt. **[to cause to exist]**
1. ⟨-o⟩ so⌈ozoo-suru ⟨〜を⟩創造する ③ •c [(for God) to cause the universe and the ancestors of man and animals to exist, ⟪fig. "make s.t. new by means of one's original thinking"⟫] ⟪**make**⟫, **⟨-o⟩ so⌈osaku-suru ⟨〜を⟩創作する ③ •c [for s.o. to cause s.t. to exist which did not exist before]** ⟪**make**⟫

EX. (**a**) God created the world.
神が天地を{創造/*創作}した。
*Kami ga tenchi o {soozoo/*soosaku}-shita.*

(**b**) Who created E.T.?
E.T.を{創造/創作}したのはだれですか。
Ii-tii o {soozoo/soosaku}-shita no wa dare desu ka.

2. ⟨-o⟩ so⌈osetsu-suru ⟨〜を⟩創設する ③ •c [for s.o. to bring into existence a new organization/institution] ⟪establish, organize, institute⟫

EX. (**a**) The government created a new agency to deal with the problem.
政府はその問題に対処する新しい省庁を創設した。
Seifu wa sono mondai ni taisho-suru atarashii shoochoo o soosetsu-shita.
(**b**) The university created a new research institute exclusively for the study of U.S.-Japan relations.
大学は日米関係をもっぱら研究の対象とする新しい研究所を創設した。
Daigaku wa Nichi-Bei-kankei o moppara kenkyuu no taishoo to suru atarashii kenkyuu-jo o soosetsu-shita.

creation n. **[the act/result of creating s.t.]**
so⌈ozoo 創造 •c [God's creation of the universe], so⌈ozo⌉o-butsu 創造物 •c [s.t. created ⟨fml⟩], so⌉osaku 創作 •c [an act of creating], so⌈osaku⌉-butsu 創作物 •c [s.t. that is created, esp. of an artistic nature]

EX. (**a**) This work is the creation of a famous architect.
この作品は有名な建築家の{創造物/創作物/創作/?創造}です。
Kono sakuhin wa yuumeina kenchiku-ka no {soozoo-butsu/soosaku-butsu/soosaku/?soozoo} desu.
(**b**) The creation of a work of art is time-consuming.
芸術品の{創造/創作/*創造物/*創作物}は時間がかかる。
*Geijutsu-hin no {soozoo/soosaku/*soozoo-butsu/*soosaku-butsu} wa jikan ga kakaru.*

creative adj. **[having the power of creating or resulting from originality of thought/expression]**
so⌈ozoo-tekina 創造的な adj(*na*). **•c [characterized by the ability to think up s.t. new on one's own]**

EX. (**a**) What sets man apart from the other animals is his creative ability to use language.
人間を他の動物と区別するものは言語を創造的に使う能力である。
Ningen o ta no doobutsu to kubetsu-suru mono wa gengo o soozoo-tekini tsukau nooryoku dearu.
(**b**) Picasso was engaged in creative work throughout his life.
ピカソは生涯を通じて創造的な仕事をした。
Pikaso wa shoogai o tsuujite soozoo-tekina shigoto o shita.
(**c**) Education in Japan should put more emphasis on the formation of creative minds than on rote memorization.
日本の教育は暗記よりもっと創造的精神の養成に力を入れるべきだ。
Nihon no kyooiku wa anki yori motto soozoo-teki-seishin no yoosei ni chikara o ireru-beki da.
(**d**) Is it true that it is the right brain where creative functions are performed?
右の脳が創造的なことに働くって本当ですか。
Migi no noo ga soozoo-tekina koto ni hatarakutte hontoo desu ka.

creature n. **[a living being (including a human being viewed as the object of contempt/pity)]**
i⌈ki⌉-mono 生き物 [a living thing] /⟨V*masu* of *ikiru* ② live + *mono* thing/, do⌈obutsu 動物 •c [living things other than plants], ya⌉tsu やつ [s.o./s.t./s.a. referred to in a derogatory or endearing manner ⟨s⟩]

EX. (**a**) Birds are creatures with wings and an ability to fly.
鳥は羽根を持ち、飛ぶことの出来る{生き物/動物/?やつ}です。
Tori wa hane o mochi, tobu koto no dekiru {iki-mono/doobutsu/?yatsu} desu.
(**b**) The life of any creature is a thing of value.

C

どんな{生き物/動物/?やつ}でも命は貴いものだ。
Donna {iki-mono/doobutsu/?yatsu} demo inochi wa tootoi mono da.
(**c**) There are no creatures more adorable than cats.
猫ほど可愛らしい{生き物/動物/やつ}はいない。
Neko hodo kawairashii {iki-mono/doobutsu/yatsu} wa inai.
(**d**) He is a disgusting creature.
彼はいやな{やつ/*生き物/*動物}だ。
*Kare wa iyana {yatsu/*iki-mono/*doobutsu} da.*

C

credit n. **[trust or favorable reputation or a system of conducting business involving deferred payments or a completed unit of study in a school]**

1. shi⌈n'yoo 信用 •c [the act of believing that s.t./s.o. is certain or reliable enough to act in accordance with it/him/her or a reputation/worth sufficient to cause others to believe in one's financial reliablity] **《trust, confidence》**

EX. No one places any credit in the government's report.
政府の発表は信用がおけない。
Seifu no happyoo wa shin'yoo ga oke-nai.

2. hyo⌈oban 評判 •c [the way s.o./s.t./s.a. is thought of/talked about by people in general]

EX. His credit as a scholar rests completely on his research on superconductors.
彼の学者としての評判はもっぱら超伝導体についての研究に基づくものだ。
Kare no gakusha to-shite no hyooban wa moppara choo-dendoo-tai ni-tsuite no kenkyuu ni motozuku mono da.

3. ku⌈re⌉jitto クレジット •f [a system of conducting business involving deferred payments]

EX. (**a**) He bought a set of golf clubs on credit.
彼はゴルフクラブのセットをクレジットで買った。
Kare wa gorufu-kurabu no setto o kurejitto de katta.
(**b**) That couple depends too much on credit.
あの夫婦はクレジットに頼り過ぎる。
Ano fuufu wa kurejitto ni tayori-sugiru.

4. ta⌉n'i 単位 •c [a quantity chosen as a standard for measuring length/weight/quantity/size]

EX. (**a**) Jim received two credits for the course in advanced Japanese.
ジムは上級日本語のコースで二単位取った。
Jimu wa jookyuu-Nihon-go no koosu de ni-tan'i totta.
(**b**) I have one more credit to earn before graduation.
卒業までにあと一単位取ればいい。
Sotsugyoo made ni ato ichi-tan'i toreba ii.
(**c**) There are a minimum number of credits that a student must take before advancing to the next grade.
学生が進級するためには取らねばならない最低単位数がある。
Gakusei ga shinkyuu-suru tame ni wa toraneba naranai saitei-tan'i-suu ga aru.

creep vi. **[to move with the body close to the ground]**

《(-o)》 ha⌉u 《〜を》はう ① [for a plant to extend over the ground/a wall or for s.o./s.a. to move with one's stomach close to the ground]

EX. (**a**) The cat crept up behind us silently.
猫が後ろから静かにはって近づいて来た。
Neko ga ushiro kara shizukani hatte chikazuite-kita.
(**b**) The alpinists crept up the mountain slope step by step.
アルピニストは山の斜面を一歩一歩はうように登っていった。
Arupinisuto wa yama no shamen o ippo-ippo hau yooni nobotte itta.

crew n. **[a group of persons working together, including those working a ship or aircraft]**

jo⌈omu⌉-in 乗務員 •c [s.o. who either operates a vehicle of public transportation or takes care of passengers on board such a vehicle], no⌈ri-kumi⌉-in 乗組員 [the seaman working on board a ship]

EX. (**a**) This new airplane makes do with a smaller crew.
この新型の飛行機は{乗務員/*乗組員}の数が少なくていい。
*Kono shin-gata no hikoo-ki wa {joomu-in/*norikumi-in} no kazu ga sukunakute ii.*
(**b**) All crew members of the ship were saved.
その船の{乗務員/乗組員}は全員助けられた。
Sono fune no {joomu-in/nori-kumi-in} wa zen'in tasuke-rareta.

crime n. **[an act committed in violation of a law]**
tsu⌉mi 罪 [an act which violates religious/legal codes] ((**sin, vice**)), **ha⌈nzai 犯罪 •c [a criminal offense]**

EX. (**a**) The man committed a serious crime.
その男は重大な{罪/犯罪}を犯した。
Sono otoko wa juudaina {tsumi/hanzai} o okashita.
(**b**) Behind every crime there is a woman.
{犯罪/*罪}の陰に女あり。
*{Hanzai/*Tsumi} no kage ni onna ari.*
(**c**) Dostoevsky's *Crime and Punishment* is a celebrated novel.
ドストエスキーの『罪と罰』は有名な小説である。
Dosutoefusukii no "Tsumi to batsu" wa yuumeina shoosetsu dearu.

crisp adj. **[brittle and easily crumbled; fresh and firm]**
1. pa⌉ri-pari-shita N パリパリしたN /⟨Vinf. past of *pari-pari-suru* ③ be crunchy/ ((**crunchy**)), **pa⌉ri-pari-shite iru (N) パリパリしている(N) /⟨V *te iru* of *pari-pari-suru* ③ be crunchy/**

EX. (**a**) Rice crackers are crisp.
せんべいはパリパリしている。
Senbei wa pari-pari-shite iru.
(**b**) I like my toast thin and crisp.
トーストは薄くて{パリパリした/パリパリしている}のがいいです。
Toosuto wa usukute {pari-pari-shita/pari-pari-shiteiru} no ga ii desu.

2. sa⌈wa⌉yakana さわやかな adj(*na*). **[for the atmosphere or weather to be pleasantly fresh, cool, and bracing]** ((**fresh, refreshing**))

EX. (**a**) A crisp breeze marked the beginning of fall.
さわやかな風が秋の始まりを告げた。
Sawayakana kaze ga aki no hajimari o tsugeta.
(**b**) Summer in New England is crisp and can even be chilly.
ニューイングランドの夏はさわやかで肌寒いことさえある。
Nyuu-ingurando no natsu wa sawayakade hada-samui koto sae aru.

critic n. **[s.o. who writes judgments of books, plays, music, etc., as a profession professionally]**
hyo⌈oron-ka 評論家 •c [s.o. who writes analyses, commentary, or opinions on specialized artistic or literary topics or on general social trends as a profession] ((**commentator**)), **hi⌈hyoo-ka 批評家 •c [s.o. who provides commentary on literary, artistic, and other topics]**

EX. (**a**) He is a literary critic who enjoys finding fault with others.
あいつは他人のあら捜しを楽しむ文芸{評論家/批評家}だ。
Aitsu wa hito no ara-sagashi o tanoshimu bungei-{hyooron-ka/hihyoo-ka} da.
(**b**) He is an extremely insightful critic.
彼は非常に洞察力のある{評論家/批評家}だ。
Kare wa hijooni doosatsu-ryoku no aru {hyooron-ka/hihyoo-ka} da.

critical adj. **[tending to find fault or existing in a state of crisis or so important as to affect the very existence of s.t.]**
hi⌈han-tekina 批判的な adj(*na*). **•c [tending to criticize or view s.t. negatively]**

C

EX. (**a**) He takes a critical attitude toward his father.
彼は父親に批判的な態度を取る。
Kare wa chichi-oya ni hihan-tekina taido o toru.
(**b**) This paper presents a critical analysis of Freudian theory.
この論文はフロイトの理論に対する批判的な分析を提示している。
Kono ronbun wa Furoito no riron ni-tsuite hihan-tekina bunseki o teiji-shite iru.
(**c**) I am critical of so-called cultured persons.
私はいわゆる文化人には批判的なんです。
Watashi wa iwayuru bunka-jin ni wa hihan-tekina n desu.

C

2. ki⌈ki-tekina 危機的な adj(*na*). **•c [characterized by danger]** (**(dangerous, crucial)**), **ki⌈toku no N 危篤のN •c [for s.o. to be near death due to an illness, etc.]** (**(dangerous, serious)**)

EX. (**a**) The nation's economy is in a critical situation.
国の経済は{危機的な/*危篤の}状況にある。
*Kuni no keizai wa {kiki-tekina/*kitoku no} jookyoo ni aru.*
(**b**) The patient is in critical condition.
患者は{危篤の/危機的な}状況にある。
Kanja wa {kitoku no/kiki-tekina} jookyoo ni aru.

criticism n. **[the act/art of judging the quality of a literary/artistic work or fault-finding or censure]**
hi⌈hyoo 批評 •c [discussion of the value of s.t. by considering its merits and demerits, etc.] (**(comment, review, remark)**), **hi⌈han 批判 •c [the act of rendering a judgment, esp. a negative one, as to the relative merits of s.t./s.o./s.a.]** (**(censure)**)

EX. (**a**) His criticism of the novel is quite wide of the mark.
彼のその小説の{批評/批判}は全く見当違いだ。
Kare no sono shoosetsu no {hihyoo/hihan} wa mattaku kentoo-chigai da.
(**b**) The country in question received strong criticism for its recent actions.
問題の国は、最近の行動に関して強い{批判/*批評}を浴びた。
*Mondai no kuni wa, saikin no koodoo ni kanshite tsuyoi {hihan/*hihyoo} o abita.*
(**c**) His action received severe criticism from everyone.
彼の行動はみんなの厳しい{批判/*批評}を浴びた。
*Kare no koodoo wa minna no kibishii {hihan/*hihyoo} o abita.*
(**d**) How one goes about giving criticism varies greatly from person to person.
人によって{批判/批評}の仕方はさまざまだ。
Hito ni-yotte {hihan/hihyoo} no shikata wa sama-zama da.

crop n. **[any agricultural product or the yield of any product in a given season or place]**
sa⌈ku⌉motsu 作物 •c [a generic term for grains, vegetables, etc. grown on a farm] (**(farm products)**)

EX. (**a**) A: What are some of the main crops grown in the United States?
アメリカの主要作物にはどんなものがありますか。
Amerika no shuyoo-sakumotsu ni wa donna mono ga arimasu ka.
B: Wheat, corn, and cotton.
小麦やとうもろこし、それに綿などです。
Komugi ya toomorokoshi, sore ni wata nado desu.
(**b**) Farmers in this area still harvest their crops by hand.
この地方では農家の人々はいまだに手で作物を収穫している。
Kono chihoo de wa nooka no hito-bito wa imada-ni sakumotsu o te de shuukaku-shite iru.
(**c**) Whether we get a good crop or not depends on the weather.
作物の出来、不出来は天候に左右される。

Sakumotsu no deki, fu-deki wa tenkoo ni sayuu-sareru.

2. shu⌈ukaku 収穫 •c [the act of cutting down and gathering in agricultural products] ⟪harvest, yield⟫

EX. I hear they had an exceptionally fine crop of grapes in California this year.
今年カリフォルニアではぶどうの収穫が特に素晴らしかったそうだ。
Kotoshi Kariforunia de wa budoo no shuukaku ga tokuni subarashikatta sooda.

cross n. **[an upright post with another across it on which the ancient Romans executed people or its representation as a symbol of the crucifixion of Jesus ⟪fig. "any mark or design made by two intersecting lines, bars, etc."⟫]**

1. ju⌈uji-ka 十字架 •c

EX. (**a**) Francis was wearing a pendant in the shape of a cross.
フランシスは十字架の形をしたペンダントをしていた。
Furanshisu wa juuji-ka no katachi o shita pendanto o shite ita.
(**b**) The dogwood flower is shaped like a cross.
はなみずきの花は十字架の形をしている。
Hana-mizuki no hana wa juuji-ka no katachi o shite iru.

2. ba⌈tsu-ji⌉rushi ×印 [the mark of an X]

EX. The place is marked on the map with a cross.
場所は地図に×印で示してあります。
Basho wa chizu ni batsu-jirushi de shimeshite arimasu.

— vt. **[to move s.t. so as to form a cross shape ⟪fig. "pass across so as to intersect," "move/extend from one side to the other side of s.t.," "meet and pass (each other)"⟫]**

1. ⟨-o⟩ ku⌉mu ⟨〜を⟩組む ① [for s.o. to pass s.t. across s.t. else so as to intersect and not be separated ⟪fig. "make a whole out of parts by assembling them according to fixed procedures," "create an organization, setup, or structure"⟫] ⟪construct, put together, fold⟫

EX. People often cross their arms when they're thinking.
考えるとき、人はよく腕を組む。
Kangaeru toki, hito wa yoku ude o kumu.

2. ⟨-o⟩ wa⌈taru ⟨〜を⟩渡る ① [for s.o. to go on/over s.t. in order to reach the other side ⟪fig. "go on living, associating with other people," "change hands," "go around to the last person"⟫] ⟪go over, pass over⟫

EX. (**a**) Raise your hand when you cross the street.
道を渡るときは手をあげて。
Michi o wataru toki wa te o agete.
(**b**) I crossed the river by boat.
ボートで川を渡った。
Booto de kawa o watatta.

— vi. **[to move from one side to the other]**

1. ⟨-e⟩ wa⌈taru ⟨〜へ⟩渡る ① [to go over to the other side] ⟪go over, pass over⟫

EX. The child crossed over to the other side of the street.
子供は道の向こう側へ渡った。
Kodomo wa michi no mukoo-gawa e watatta.

2. ⟨-to⟩ su⌈re-chiga⌉u ⟨〜と⟩すれ違う ① [for two people/things/animals to pass very closely by each other and continue on in the opposite direction] ⟪pass, pass by, miss⟫

EX. We crossed right by each other on Ginza street.
我々は銀座通りですれ違った。
Ware-ware wa Ginza-doori de sure-chigatta.

crowd n. **[a large number of persons gathered closely together]**

1. gu⌈nshuu 群衆 •c ⟪multitude⟫, hi⌈to-gomi 人ごみ [the state of many people having gathered together or a place where they are so gathered] ⟪throng of people⟫, o⌈oze⌉i no hi⌈to 大勢の人 [a large number of people]

EX. (**a**) The child was lost in the holiday crowd.
子供は休日の{群衆/人込み/大勢の人}

C

の中で迷子になった。
Kodomo wa kyuujitsu no {gunshuu/hito-gomi/oozei no hito} no naka de maigo ni natta.
(**b**) In the square, there was a large crowd of people shouting something.
広場には何かを叫んでいる{群衆/大勢の人/*人込み}がいた。
*Hiro-ba niwa nani-ka o sakende iru {gunshuu/oozei no hito/*hito-gomi} ga ita.*
(**c**) The crowd appeared to be very excited.
{群衆/*人込み/*大勢の人}は大変興奮しているようであった。
*{Gunshuu/*Hito-gomi/*Oozei no hito} wa taihen koofun-shite iru yoo deatta.*
(**d**) The criminal fled into the crowd.
犯人は{群衆/人込み/大勢の人}の中へ逃げ込んだ。
Hannin wa {gunshuu/hito-gomi/oozei no hito} no naka e nige-konda.

— vi. **[to throng, gather in large numbers]** **⟨-o⟩ to⌈ri-maku ⟨～を⟩取り巻く ① [to encircle s.t./s.o./s.a.] ⟪surround⟫, ⟨-ni⟩ mu⌈raga⌉ru ⟨～に⟩群がる ① [for insects/people to gather in a large number in one place] ⟪flock together, swarm⟫**

EX. A large group of students crowded around the teacher.
多くの学生が先生{を取り巻いた/の回りに群がった}。
Ooku no gakusei ga sensei {o tori-maita/no mawari ni muragatta}.

— vt./vi. **[for s.o. to cause a large number of objects/people to enter s.t. so that it is filled beyond its normal capacity; for people to press into a place in large numbers]**
1. ⟨-o⟩ ⟨-ni⟩ tsu⌈me-komu ⟨～を⟩⟨～に⟩詰め込む ① [for s.o. to fill tightly the inside of s.t. (including the brain) with material] ⟪cram, jam, pack⟫

EX. The driver crowded the children onto the school bus.
運転手は子供たちをスクールバスに詰め込んだ。
Unten-shu wa kodomo-tachi o sukuuru-basu ni tsume-konda.

2. ⟨-ni⟩ tsu⌈me-kake⌉ru ⟨～に⟩詰め掛ける ② [for people to press into a place in large numbers all at once] ⟪throng to⟫

EX. Housewives crowded into the bargain basement.
主婦が特売場に詰め掛けた。
Shufu ga tokubai-joo ni tsume-kaketa.

crowded adj. **[filled to excess]**
ko⌉nde iru 込んでいる ② /⟨V*te iru* of *komu* ① congest/ [filled to capacity so that it is difficult to move] ⟪packed, jammed⟫

EX. (**a**) The subway was terribly crowded during rush hour.
地下鉄は、ラッシュ時に非常に込んでいた。
Chika-tetsu wa, rasshu-ji ni hijooni konde ita.
(**b**) I hate getting on crowded trains.
込んでいる電車に乗るのは嫌いです。
Konde iru densha ni noru no wa kirai desu.

cruel adj. **[causing pain/distress to others]**
za⌈nkokuna 残酷な adj(*na*). **•c [giving pain to s.o./s.a. without reason and feeling no remorse for it] ⟪pitiless, brutal, heartless⟫**

EX. (**a**) Don't be cruel to animals.
動物に残酷なことをしてはいけない。
Doobutsu ni zankokuna koto o shite wa ikenai.
(**b**) His father was a cruel man.
彼の父親は残酷な男だった。
Kare no chichi-oya wa zankokuna otoko datta.

cry vi. **[for s.o. to call out loudly or shed tears or for s.a. to utter its characteristic call]**
1. sa⌈ke⌉bu 叫ぶ ① [for s.o. to utter in a loud voice (spontaneously) in order to bring attention to s.t] ⟪shout, exclaim⟫

EX. (**a**) "Watch out!" he cried.
彼は「気をつけろ」と叫んだ。
Kare wa 'ki-o-tsukero' to sakenda.
(**b**) She cried out with pain.
彼女は痛さのあまり叫んだ。

| *Kanojo wa ita-sa no amari sakenda.*

2. na⌈ku なく ① [for s.o./s.a. to utter sounds spontaneously out of grief/sadness, usually accompanied by tears, or for s.a. to utter its characteristic sound] ⟪weep, bark, etc.⟫

㊥ "for an animal to utter its sound"▷鳴く, otherwise ▷泣く

EX. (**a**) The baby cried because he was hungry.
赤ちゃんは空腹で泣いた。
Aka-chan wa kuufuku de naita.
(**b**) The boy cried himself to sleep.
男の子は泣きながら寝てしまった。
Otoko-no-ko wa naki-nagara nete shimatta.

crystal n. **[a clear, transparent mineral or glass resembling ice]**
su⌉ishoo 水晶 •c, ku⌈ri⌉sutaru クリスタル •f ⟪quartz⟫

EX. (**a**) The water was as clear as crystal.
水は{水晶/クリスタル}のようにきれいでした。
Mizu wa {suishoo/kurisutaru} no yooni kirei deshita.
(**b**) I'd like to buy a crystal rosary.
{水晶/*クリスタル}の数珠を買いたいのですが。
*{Suishoo/*Kurisutaru} no juzu o kai-tai no desu ga.*

cube n. **[a solid bounded by six equal squares]**
ri⌈ppoo-tai 立方体 •c

cuisine n. **[a style of cooking or preparing food or the food prepared, as at a restaurant]**
ryo⌉ori 料理 •c [the preparation of food or food which is prepared] ⟪cooking, cookery, dish⟫

EX. (**a**) You can eat Chinese cuisine almost anywhere these days.
今日では中華料理はほとんど、どこででも食べられます。
Konnichi de wa Chuuka-ryoori wa hotondo, doko de demo tabe-raremasu.
(**b**) That restaurant specializes in French cuisine.
あのレストランはフランス料理が専門だ。
Ano resutoran wa Furansu-ryoori ga senmon da.

cultivate vt. **[for s.o. to prepare land for growing crops ⟪fig. "develop s.t. through education or training"⟫]**

1. ⟨-o⟩ ta⌈gaya⌉su ⟨～を⟩耕す ① [for s.o. to improve soil by tilling so as to make it easier for crops to grow] ⟪till, plow⟫

EX. (**a**) Taro has just finished cultivating his rice field.
太郎はたんぼを耕し終わったところだ。
Taroo wa tanbo o tagayashi-owatta tokoro da.
(**b**) I spent all day cultivating the fields today.
今日は一日中畑を耕しました。
Kyoo wa ichi-nichi-juu hatake o tagayashimashita.

2. ⟨-o⟩ sa⌈ibai suru ⟨～を⟩栽培する ③ •c [for s.o. to grow plants and tend them] ⟪grow, raise⟫

EX. (**a**) Kate is cultivating blueberries in her backyard.
ケイトは裏庭でブルーベリーを栽培している。
Keito wa ura-niwa de buruuberii o saibai-shite iru.
(**b**) Some vegetables can be cultivated in water.
水の中で栽培される野菜もある。
Mizu no naka de saibai-sareru yasai mo aru.

3. ⟨-o⟩ ya⌈shina⌉u ⟨～を⟩養う ① [for s.o. to bring up/feed s.o., esp. one's dependent, or to develop and maintain good health or habits] ⟪support, feed, keep, maintain, bring up, rear⟫

EX. She cultivated a sophisticated sense of language through extensive reading.
彼女は多読を通して洗練された言葉のセンスを養った。
Kanojo wa tadoku o-tooshite senren-sareta kotoba no sensu o yashinatta.

cultural adj. **[of/pertaining to culture]**
bu⌈nka-tekina 文化的な adj(*na*). **•c [relating**

to or befitting culture], bu⌉nka no N 文化のN

EX. (**a**) The two cities are engaged in a cultural exchange with each other.
ふたつの都市はお互いに{文化(の)/?文化的な}交流を行っています。
Futatsu no toshi wa o-tagai ni {bunka (no)/?bunka-tekina} kooryuu o okonatte imasu.
(**b**) The cultural heritage of our country was destroyed in the war.
我が国の{文化的な/文化(の)}遺産は戦争で破壊された。
Waga-kuni no {bunka-tekina/bunka (no)} isan wa sensoo de hakai-sareta.
(**c**) Cultural differences between two countries can sometimes give rise to misunderstanding.
二国間の{文化の/文化的な}違いが誤解を生むことがある。
Ni-koku-kan no {bunka no/bunka-tekina} chigai ga gokai o umu koto ga aru.

culture n. **[the skills, arts, thought patterns, customs, etc., of a given people in a given period or improvement/richness of the mind, manners, etc.]**

1. bu⌉nka 文化 •c [advancement of civilization so that life becomes more convenient or the skills, arts, thought patterns, customs, etc., of a given people in a given period]

EX. The culture of a foreign country is often a source of many surprises to one who first encounters it.
外国の文化に初めて出くわすと驚くことがやたらと多いものだ。
Gaikoku no bunka ni hajimete dekuwasu to odoroku koto ga yatara to ooi mono da.

2. kyo⌈oyoo 教養 •c [a refined mindset acquired through exposure to a wide range of knowledge and ways of thinking] ⟪education, refinement⟫

EX. (**a**) Yamada Taro was a man of culture.
山田太郎は教養のある人だった。
Yamada Taroo wa kyooyoo no aru hito datta.
(**b**) The instillation of culture ought to be one of the primary purposes of a university education.
教養を高めることが大学教育の主な目的の一部であるべきだ。
Kyooyoo o takameru koto ga daigaku-kyooiku no omona mokuteki no ichibu dearu-beki da.

cunning adj. **[crafty or sly]**

zu⌈ru⌉i ずるい adj(*i*). **[skilled in cheating and playing one's part well or having the tendency to feign ignorance of one's duties and thereby neglect them] ⟪tricky, crafty, foxy⟫**

EX. (**a**) She is as cunning as a fox.
彼女はきつねのようにずるい。
Kanojo wa kitsune no yooni zurui.
(**b**) He may appear to be cunning at first sight, but he is really a sincere man.
彼は一見ずるそうに見えるかもしれないが本当は誠実な男だ。
Kare wa ikken zuru-sooni mieru kamoshirenai ga hontoo wa seijitsuna otoko da.

cup n. **[a small, bowl-shaped container of china, metal, etc., for holding beverages, usually with a handle, or a measure of volume used in cooking]**

1. cha⌈wan 茶わん [a container without a handle for tea or cooked rice, usually made of china]

chawan, koohii-jawan

EX. (**a**) I bought some nice coffee cups today.
今日はいいコーヒー茶わんを買った。
Kyoo wa ii koohii-jawan o katta.
(**b**) Chie dropped her tea cup and broke it.
千絵は紅茶茶わんを落として割ってしまった。
Chie wa koocha-jawan o otoshite watte shimatta.
(**c**) I poured myself a generous cup of sake and then gulped it down.

大きな茶わんに並々と酒を注いで一気に飲んだ。
Ookina chawan ni nami-nami to sake o sosoide ikkini nonda.

2. {**-hai/-pai/-bai**} ～杯 **[a counter for liquid, etc., measured in a small bowl-shaped container]**

EX. (**a**) I usually drink two cups of coffee for breakfast.
いつも朝食にコーヒーを二杯飲みます。
Itsu-mo chooshoku ni koohii o ni-hai nomimasu.
(**b**) Would you like a cup of tea?
お茶を一杯いかがですか
O-cha o ip-pai ikaga desu ka.
(**c**) Ed had three cups of soup.
エドはスープを三杯お代わりした。
Edo wa suupu o san-bai o-kawari-shita.

cupboard n. **[a closet/cabinet with shelves for storing cups, plates, food, etc.]**
sho⌈kki⌉-dana 食器棚 **•c [a shelf for storing eating utensils]**

cure n. **[a method/course of remedial treatment, esp. for disease]**
ryo⌈ohoo 療法 **•c [a method of remedial treatment]** **《remedy》**, **chi⌈ryoo** 治療 **•c [the treatment of illness or injury for the purpose of bringing about recovery/healing]** **《treatment, remedy》**

EX. (**a**) Rest is the best cure for you now.
今はあなたにとって安静{療法/??治療}が一番ですよ。
Ima wa anata ni-totte ansei-{ryoohoo/??chiryoo} ga ichiban desu yo.
(**b**) This oriental cure should be effective for your disease.
あなたの病気にはこの東洋の{療法/治療}が効くはずですよ。
Anata no byooki niwa kono tooyoo no {ryoohoo/chiryoo} ga kiku hazu desu yo.
(**c**) The sooner you find a cure, the better.
{治療/*療法}は早ければ早いほどよい。
*{Chiryoo/*Ryoohoo} wa hayakereba hayai hodo yoi.*

curio n. **[an unusual/rare article]**
ko⌈ttoo-hin 骨とう品 **•c [a tool, household article, or artistic object valued more for its age and sentimental character than for its utility in daily life]**

EX. Steve collects Japanese curios.
スティーブは日本の骨董品を収集している。
Sutiibu wa Nihon no kottoo-hin o shuushuu-shite iru.

curiosity n. **[the inquisitiveness to learn about something]**
ko⌈oki⌉-shin 好奇心 **•c [the mental proclivity to feel an interest in or desire to know about things which are out of the ordinary]**

EX. (**a**) I started aikido just out of curiosity, but now I'm completely hooked on it.
私は単なる好奇心から合気道を始めたんですが、今はもう夢中です。
Watashi wa tannaru kooki-shin kara aikidoo o hajimeta n desu ga, ima wa moo muchuu desu.
(**b**) Manjiro satisfied his curiosity for the unknown by going overseas.
万次郎は未知の世界への好奇心を外国へ行くことで満足させた。
Manjiroo wa michi no sekai e no kooki-shin o gaikoku e iku koto de manzoku-saseta.
(**c**) Children are always full of curiosity.
子供は常に好奇心でいっぱいだ。
Kodomo wa tsune ni kooki-shin de ippai da.

curious adj. **[eager to learn or know 《fig. "unusual," "strange"》]**

1. ko⌈oki⌉-shin ga tsu⌈yo⌉i 好奇心が強い adj(*i*). **[having an intense level of curiosity]**

EX. (**a**) The cat is a curious animal.
猫は好奇心が強い動物だ。
Neko wa kooki-shin ga tsuyoi doobutsu da.
(**b**) Curious people are said to live longer.
好奇心が強い人ほど長生きするそうだ。
Kooki-shin ga tsuyoi hito hodo naga-iki-suru sooda.

2. V*masu* ta⌉i V*masu*たい adj(*i*). **[for the speaker (addressee in the case of a question)**

to want to do s.t.], V*masu* ta⌈ga⌉ru V*masu* たがる ① [for a third person to exhibit a desire to do s.t.]

EX. (a) Daniel is curious to learn about Japanese customs.
ダニエルは日本の習慣を知りたがっている。
Danieru wa Nihon no shuukan o shiri-tagatte iru.
(b) I am curious about the content of that package.
その包みの中身が知りたい。
Sono tsutsumi no naka-mi ga shiri-tai.

3. ki⌉myoona 奇妙な adj(*na*). •c **[unusual and mysterious in character/reason]** 《**strange, queer, singular**》

EX. (a) What a curious coincidence!
それは奇妙な偶然ですね。
Sore wa kimyoona guuzen desu ne.
(b) Taro found a curious stone in the river.
太郎は川で奇妙な石をみつけた。
Taroo wa kawa de kimyoona ishi o mitsuketa.

currency n. **[the money in circulation in a given country]**
tsu⌉uka 通貨 •c

EX. (a) What is the currency of Brazil?
ブラジルの通貨は何ですか。
Buraziru no tsuuka wa nan desu ka.
(b) The Japanese currency is the yen.
日本の通貨は円です。
Nihon no tsuuka wa en desu.

current n. **[a flow of water/air/electricity 《fig. "a general tendency"》]**

1. na⌈gare⌉ 流れ /〈V*masu* of *nagareru* ② flow/ [a flow of water/people/cars/events 《fig. "school," "descent"》] 《flow, river, stream, passage》

EX. (a) The current of this river is swift.
この川は流れが速い。
Kono kawa wa nagare ga hayai.
(b) I felt a current of cold air.
冷たい空気の流れを感じた。
Tsumetai kuuki no nagare o kanjita.

2. ke⌈ikoo 傾向 •c [a natural propensity to develop or act in a certain way] 《trend, tendency》, fu⌈uchoo 風潮 •c [a pattern of behavior common to a society or a trend in a public opinion] 《stream, tide, tendency, climate》

EX. (a) The current of public opinion is for a more permissive society.
世論はより寛大な社会へと向かう{傾向/風潮}にある。
Yoron wa yori kandaina shakai e to mukau {keikoo/fuuchoo} ni aru.
(b) We see an anti-war current among certain segments of society.
一部の人に反戦的な{傾向/風潮}がみられる。
Ichibu no hito ni hansen-tekina {keikoo/fuuchoo} ga mi-rareru.
(c) This novel portrays well postwar social currents.
この小説は戦後の社会{風潮/?傾向}をよく表している。
Kono shoosetsu wa sengo no shakai-{fuuchoo/?keikoo} o yoku arawashite iru.

— adj. **[of the present time]**
ge⌉ndai no N 現代のN •c [of the present time] 《modern》, i⌉ma no N 今のN [of now] 《present》, ko⌈nnichi-tekina 今日的な adj(*na*). **•c [of today]**

EX. (a) Yumi is studying the current political climate in South America.
由美は南米での{現代の/今の/*今日的な}政治情勢を研究している。
*Yumi wa Nanbei de no {gendai no/ima no/*konnichi-tekina} seiji-joosei o kenkyuu-shite iru.*
(b) That radio station exclusively broadcasts news commentary on current social topics.
あのラジオ局はもっぱら{現代の/今の/今日的な}社会問題の解説を放送している。
Ano rajio-kyoku wa moppara {gendai no/ima no/konnichi-tekina} shakai-mondai no kaisetsu o hoosoo-shite iru.

curry n. **[a powder prepared from various spices, or a sauce made with this]**
ka⌈ree カレー •f

EX. I want my curry very hot.

僕のカレーはうんと辛くして下さい。
Boku no karee wa unto karaku shite kudasai.

PHRASE: chicken curry *chikin-karee* チキンカレー •f, curry with rice *karee-raisu* カレーライス •f, *raisu-karee* ライスカレー •f

curtain n. **[a piece of cloth, etc. hung at a window, in front of a stage, etc., for decoration or privacy]**

1. ka˥aten カーテン •f [a drapery that is hung at a window]

EX. (**a**) My wife bought new curtains for the kitchen.
妻は台所用に新しいカーテンを買って来た。
Tsuma wa daidokoro-yoo ni atarashii kaaten o katte-kita.
(**b**) We always draw the curtains at night in our home.
うちでは夜になると必ずカーテンを引く。
Uchi de wa yoru ni naru to kanarazu kaaten o hiku.

2. ma┌ku˥ 幕 •c [a drapery concealing the stage, etc., from the audience 《fig. "part of a play that comes between curtains"》] 《drapery》, do┌nchoo どんちょう •c

EX. (**a**) The curtain rises at 7:00 tonight at the opera theater.
オペラ座では今晩七時に{幕/どんちょう}が上がる。
Opera-za de wa konban shichi-ji ni {maku/donchoo} ga agaru.
(**b**) The curtain in that theater has a unique color.
あの劇場の{幕/どんちょう}は独特の色をしている。
Ano gekijoo no {maku/donchoo} wa dokutoku no iro o shite iru.

curve n. **[a line which bends continuously in one direction, without angles 《fig. "a pitched ball that curves as it approches the batter"》]**

ka˥abu カーブ •f, kyo┌kusen 曲線 •c [a line which bends slightly and smoothly throughout its entire length]

EX. (**a**) The graph shows a moderate upward curve.
グラフはなだらかな上昇{カーブ/曲線}を示している。
Gurafu wa nadarakana jooshoo-{kaabu/kyokusen} o shimeshite iru.
(**b**) The pitcher threw a curve.
ピッチャーは{カーブ/*曲線}を投げた。
*Pitchaa wa {kaabu/*kyokusen} o nageta.*

cushion n.

ku˥sshon クッション •f, za-┌bu˥ton ざぶとん [a soft, square pad used for sitting on in Japan]

custom n. **[a usual way of behaving or doing s.t. accepted in a social community]**

shu┌ukan 習慣 •c [the usual way of acting for an individual or members of a social community] 《habit, convention》

EX. (**a**) It is the custom in Japan to take off one's shoes when entering a house.
日本では家に入る時、靴を脱ぐのが習慣です。
Nihon de wa ie ni hairu toki, kutsu o nugu no ga shuukan desu.
(**b**) It's the custom of people in Hawaii to get up early.
早起きはハワイの人の習慣です。
Haya-oki wa Hawai no hito no shuukan desu.
(**c**) Manners and customs differ from country to country.
国によって風俗習慣はかなり違うものだ。
Kuni ni yotte fuuzoku shuukan wa kanari chigau mono da.

customer n. **[s.o. who uses a store/service regularly]**

(o-)kya┌ku (お)客 •c [s.o. who visits or is invited to a place or s.o. who comes to buy/see things for a fee] 《guest, client》

EX. (**a**) That store is always full of customers.
あの店はいつも(お)客でいっぱいだ。
Ano mise wa itsu-mo (o-)kyaku de ippai da.
(**b**) The customer is king
お客さまは王様です。

C

| *O-kyaku-sama wa oo-sama desu.*

cut vt. **[to penetrate/divide with a sharp instrument 《fig. "abridge/shorten," "reduce/curtail," "absent oneself from"》]**

1. 〈-o〉 ki˥ru 〈～を〉切る ① [for s.o. to render s.t. connected/continuous into parts or apart from its main body with a sharp-edged implement 《fig. "perform a cutting motion in the air," "put an end to s.t.," "turn off a switch"》] 《sever, chop, break off, carve, stop, turn off》

EX.| (**a**) She cut the apple in half.
彼女はりんごを半分に切った。
Kanojo wa ringo o hanbun ni kitta.
(**b**) He carelessly cut his finger with a razor.
彼は不注意にもかみそりで指を切った。
Kare wa fu-chuuini-mo kamisori de yubi o kitta.

2. 〈-o〉 sa┌ge˥ru 〈～を〉下げる ② [for s.o. to cause s.t./s.o./s.a. to move to a lower place or to decrease in amount/degree/strength] 《decrease》, 〈-o〉 ki┌ri-tsume˥ru 〈～を〉切り詰める ② [for s.o. to cut back on s.t. to the minimum necessary] 《curtail, make do with less, reduce》, 〈-o〉 ka˥tto-suru 〈～を〉カットする •f ③ [for s.o. to sever or dispense with s.t.] 《sever, reduce, dispense with》

EX.| (**a**) We have cut the prices on all our cars.
当店のクルマの値段はすべて{下げました/?カットしました/*切り詰めました}。
*Tooten no kuruma no nedan wa subete {sagemashita/?katto-shimashita/*kiri-tsumemashita}.*
(**b**) We have to cut the budget in a major way.
予算を大幅に{切り詰めなければ/カットしなければ/*下げなければ}ならない。
*Yosan o oo-habani {kiri-tsumenakereba/katto-shinakereba/*sagenakereba} naranai.*

3. 〈-o〉 sa┌bo˥ru 〈～を〉サボる ① •f [for s.o. to absent oneself from class] 《play hooky》

EX.| Tom cut class yesterday.
トムはきのう学校をサボった。
Tomu wa kinoo gakkoo o sabotta.

NOTE: *Saboru*, which comes from the French word "sabotage," is a slang expression used mostly by students.

— vi. **[for s.t. to be easily divided with a sharp instrument or to act as an instrument effective in making possible such dividing]**

ki┌re˥ru 切れる ② [for s.t. connected/continuous to be rendered into parts or apart from its main body with a sharp-edged implement 《fig. "be able to handle everything well," "be out of stock"》] 《break, collapse, run out》

EX.| This knife cuts well.
このナイフはよく切れる。
Kono naifu wa yoku kireru.

— n. **[the result of cutting, such as an incision, wound, etc. 《fig. "reduction," "a printed picture or illustration"》]**

1. ki┌ri˥-kizu 切り傷 [a wound/injury resulting from a sharp instrument] 《wound, injury, hurt》

EX.| She got a bad cut on her arm.
彼女は腕に深い切り傷を負った。
Kanojo wa ude ni fukai kiri-kizu o otta.

2. sa┌kugen 削減 •c [the act of reducing/decreasing], ka˥tto カット •f [dispensing with s.t.]

EX.| (**a**) All the executives of the company took a salary cut.
会社の重役は全員給与の{削減/カット}を受けた。
Kaisha no jyuuyaku wa zen'in kyuuyo no {sakugen/katto} o uketa.
(**b**) Due to the recession, the budget was subjected to a major cut.
不景気なので予算の大幅な{削減/カット}にあった。
Fu-keikina node yosan no oohabana {sakugen/katto} ni atta.

cute adj. **[pretty/attractive, esp. in a dainty way]**

ka┌wai˥i かわいい adj(*i*). **[having a fragile charm evoking in one the desire to protect and aid it/him/her] 《dear, loving, darling, charming, lovely, sweet, pretty》**

EX.| Azusa is a cute girl.

あずさはかわいい女の子だ。
Azusa wa kawaii onna-no-ko da.

cycle n. **[a recurring period of time, esp. one in which certain events repeat themselves in the same order and intervals]**
shu˥uki 周期 •c [the time neccessary for a phenomenon or motion which repeats itself to complete one full occurrence《fig. "alternation of electric curent"》]《period》, sa˥ikuru サイクル •f

EX. (**a**) The dominant methodology in language teaching seems to change in twenty-year cycles.
言語教育の主流を成す方法論は二十年の{周期/サイクル}で変わるようだ。
Gengo-kyooiku no shuryuu o nasu hoohoo-ron wa ni-juu-nen no {shuuki/saikuru} de kawaru yoo da.
(**b**) Fashion repeats itself in ten-year cycles.
流行は十年{周期/サイクル}で繰り返される。
Ryuukoo wa juu-nen-{shuuki/saikuru} de kurikaesa-reru.
(**c**) Some have argued that the universe expands and contracts in cycles of set length.
宇宙は一定の{周期/サイクル}で伸びたり縮んだりするものだと主張した人がいる。
Uchuu wa ittei no {shuuki/saikuru} de nobitari chijindari suru mono da to shuchoo-shita hito ga iru.

D

daily adj. **[done/occurring every day]**
ma˥i-nichi no N 毎日のN •c [of every day], ni˥chijoo no N 日常のN •c [of every day]《usual, ordinary》

EX. This work is a portrayal of the author's own daily life.
この作品は、作家自身の{毎日の/日常(の)}生活を描いたものです。
Kono sakuhin wa, sakka-jishin no {mai-nichi no/nichijoo (no)} seikatsu o egaita mono desu.

—— adv. **[every day]**
ma˥i-nichi 毎日

EX. (**a**) I swim daily.
私は毎日{泳ぎます/泳いでいます}。
Watakushi wa mai-nichi {oyogimasu/oyoide imasu}.
(**b**) She uses her word processor almost daily.
彼女はほとんど毎日ワープロを使う。
Kanojo wa hotondo mai-nichi waapuro o tsukau.

dairy n. **[a place making or selling milk, cheese, butter, etc.]**
gyu˥unyuu-kakoo-jo 牛乳加工所 •c [a place where milk is processed], nyu˥u-se˥ihin-ha˥nbai-jo 乳製品販売所 •c [a shop where milk products are sold]

EX. Mr. Sasaki runs a small dairy near his home.
佐々木さんは自分の家の近くで小さな{牛乳加工所/乳製品販売所}を経営している。

Sasaki-san wa jibun no ie no chikaku de chiisana {gyuunyuu-kakoo-jo/nyuuseihin-hanbai-jo} o keiei-shite iru.

PHRASE: dairy farm *rakunoo-joo* 酪農場 •c

EX. There are many dairy farms in Hokkaido.
北海道には酪農場がたくさんある。
Hokkaidoo ni wa rakunoo-joo ga takusan aru.

dam n. **[a barrier to hold back the flow of water to create a supply of water, generate hydroelectric power, etc.]**
da͞mu ダム •f

EX. (**a**) Beavers build dams by stopping the flow of water in rivers with logs and branches.
ビーバーは丸太や木の枝などで川をせき止めてダムを作ります。
Biibaa wa maruta ya ki no eda nado de kawa o seki-tomete damu o tsukurimasu.
(**b**) The dam dried up because of the drought.
干ばつでダムが干上がった。
Kanbatsu de damu ga hi-agatta.

damage n. **[harm or injury that reduces the value or usefulness of s.t.]**
so͞ngai 損害 •c [the harm inflicted on s.t. as measured in terms of money] ⟪**injury, harm, loss, casualties**⟫**, hi͞gai 被害 •c [undergoing serious harm or injury or the loss created by this]** ⟪**injury, harm, casualties**⟫ ↔ **kagai 加害 •c**

EX. (**a**) The earthquake which occurred recently in the Philippines caused a lot of damage.
フィリピンで最近起きた地震は大きな{損害/被害}をもたらした。
Firipin de saikin okita jishin wa ookina {songai/higai} o motarashita.
(**b**) The car fell into a ditch, but miraculously there was no damage.
車は溝に落ちたが、奇跡的に何の{損害/被害}もなかった。
Kuruma wa mizo ni ochita ga, kiseki-tekini nan no {songai/higai} mo nakatta.

—— vt. **[to inflict harm or injury on s.t.]**
1. ⟨**-o**⟩ **ki͞zu-tsuke͞ru** ⟨～を⟩**傷つける ② [to inflict physical or mental harm on s.o./s.t./s.a.]** ⟪**injure, harm, mar, hurt**⟫

EX. If you do such a thing, you will damage your reputation.
そんなことをすれば、あなたの名誉を傷つける事になる。
Sonna koto o sureba, anata no meiyo o kizu-tsukeru koto ni naru.

2 ⟨**-ni**⟩ {**so͞ngai/hi͞gai**} **o a͞taeru** ⟨～に⟩{**損害/被害**}**を与える ② [to give harm to s.t.]** ⟪**mar, injure, harm**⟫

EX. (**a**) The drought severely damaged the crops.
干ばつが作物に大きな{損害/被害}を与えた。
Kanbatsu ga sakumotsu ni ookina {songai/higai} o ataeta.
(**b**) The president's loose management policies greatly damaged the company.
社長の放漫経営が会社に大きな{損害/被害}を与えた。
Shachoo no hooman-keiei ga kaisha ni ookina {songai/higai} o ataeta.

dance vi. **[for s.o. to move rhythmically to music]**
da͞nsu o suru ダンスをする ③ •f [for s.o. to move one's body rhythmically to (usually non-Japanese) music], o͞doru 踊る ① [for s.o. to move one's body rhythmically to music or to jump or leap vigorously]

EX. Hanako dances very well.
花子はとても上手に{ダンスをする/踊る}。
Hanako wa totemo joozuni {dansu o suru/odoru}.

—— n. **[rhythmic movement to music]**
da͞nsu ダンス •f [non-Japanese style rhythmic movement to music], o͞dori 踊り /(**V*masu* of *odoru* ① dance/ [**(**Japanese style**) **rhythmic movement to music]**

EX. (**a**) I had the last dance with her.
最後の{ダンス/?踊り}は彼女と踊った。
Saigo no {dansu/?odori} wa kanojo to odotta.
(**b**) I went to see a performance of Japanese dance while in Japan.
日本滞在中に日本の{踊り(日本舞踊)/?ダンス}を見に行った。
Nihon-taizai-chuu ni Nihon no {odori

| (nihon-buyoo)/?dansu} o mi ni itta.

NOTE: *Nihon-buyoo* is a word for traditional Japanese dance.

danger n. **[liability to damage/injury/loss]**
ki⌈ken 危険 •c [the possibility that s.t. harmful/undesirable will happen] ⟪**peril**⟫ ↔ **anzen 安全 •c**

EX. (**a**) He narrowly escaped from danger.
彼はかろうじて危険から逃れた。
Kare wa karoojite kiken kara nogareta.
(**b**) Danger! Keep Out.
危険、立ち入り禁止。
Kiken, tachi-iri kinshi.
(**c**) He was totally unaware of the imminent danger he was in.
彼は自分の身に危険が迫っていることに全く気が付いていなかった。
Kare wa jibun no mi ni kiken ga sematte iru koto ni mattaku ki ga tsuite inakatta.
(**d**) The freighter was in danger of sinking.
貨物船は沈没の危険があった。
Kamotsu-sen wa chinbotsu no kiken ga atta.

dangerous adj. **[full of danger]**
ki⌈kenna 危険な adj(*na*). **•c [not safe]** ⟪**unsafe, perilous, hazardous, risky**⟫, **a⌈bunai 危ない** adj(*i*). **[not safe]** ⟪**unsafe, perilous, hazardous**⟫

EX. (**a**) It appears that space flight is still a dangerous undertaking.
宇宙飛行はまだ{危険な/危ない}仕事だと思う。
Uchuu-hikoo wa mada {kikenna/abunai} shigoto da to omou.
(**b**) It is dangerous to swim in this lake.
この湖で泳ぐのは{危険/危ない}です。
Kono mizuumi de oyogu no wa {kiken/abunai} desu.

Danish adj. **[of Denmark, the Danes, or their language]**
De⌈nma⌉aku no N デンマークのN •f [of Denmark], De⌈nmaaku⌉-jin no N デンマーク人のN •f+c [of the Danes or a Danish person], De⌈nmaaku-go no N デンマーク語のN •f+c [of the Danish language]

—— n. **[the Danish language]**
De⌈nmaaku-go デンマーク語 •f+c

dark adj. **[entirely/partly without light** ⟪**fig. "not light in color"**⟫**]**
1. ku⌈rai 暗い adj(*i*). **[the state of there not being enough light to do s.t.** ⟪**fig. "ignorant of," "gloomy"**⟫**]** ↔ **akarui 明るい** adj(*i*).

EX. (**a**) Be careful when you walk on a dark street.
暗い通りを歩く時は気を付けなさい。
Kurai toori o aruku toki wa ki o tsukenasai.
(**b**) It's already dark outside.
外はもう暗い。
Soto wa moo kurai.

2. ko⌉i 濃い adj(*i*). **[filled with fibrous, gaseous, or liquid matter to the extent light is obstructed, making it impossible to see through, or intense in degree of color or taste]** ⟪**deep, thick, heavy, strong, dense**⟫ ↔ **usui 薄い** adj(*i*).

EX. (**a**) Masako's skirt is dark green.
正子のスカートは濃い緑色です。
Masako no sukaato wa koi midori-iro desu.
(**b**) The color of my school uniform is dark blue.
私の学校の制服の色は濃い青です。
Watashi no gakkoo no seifuku no iro wa koi ao desu.
(**c**) Our pony has dark chestnut hair.
うちの子馬は濃い栗毛色をしている。
Uchi no ko-uma wa koi kuri-ge-iro o shite iru.

3. ku⌈ro⌉i 黒い adj(*i*). **[black or almost so]** ⟪**black**⟫

EX. (**a**) Japanese have dark hair.
日本人は髪が黒い。
Nihon-jin wa kami ga kuroi.
(**b**) Masako has big dark eyes.
正子は大きな黒い目をしている。
Masako wa ookina kuroi me o shite iru.

—— n. **[the absence of light]**
ku⌈ra-yami 暗やみ [the state of being without light and not visible to sight or such a place], ku⌈ragari 暗がり [a dark place]

D

EX. (**a**) Children are afraid of the dark.
子供は{暗やみ/暗がり}を怖がる。
Kodomo wa {kura-yami/kuragari} o kowa-garu.
(**b**) A cat's eyes glitter in the dark.
猫の目は{暗やみ/暗がり}で光る。
Neko no me wa {kura-yami/kuragari} de hikaru.
(**c**) What are you doing here in the dark?
こんな{暗がり/*暗やみ}で何をしているんですか。
*Konna {kuragari/*kura-yami} de nani o shite iru n desu ka.*

D

darkness n. **[the quality of being without light ⟪fig. "iniquity"⟫]**
ku⌈ra-sa 暗さ /⟨adj(*i*). stem of *kurai* dark + suf. *sa* ness/ [the state/degree of being without light], ku⌈ra-yami 暗やみ [the state of being without light and not visible to sight or such a place], ja⌈aku 邪悪 •c [evil] ⟪wickedness, vice, evil⟫

EX. (**a**) This darkness bothers me.
この{暗さ/暗やみ/*邪悪}が気になる。
*Kono {kura-sa/kura-yami/*jaaku} ga ki-ni-naru.*
(**b**) Does what they call hell perhaps refer to darkness that feels like this?
地獄と言うのはこのような{暗やみ/暗さ/邪悪}の感じを言うのだろうか。
Jigoku to iu no wa kono yoona {kura-yami/kura-sa/jaaku} no kanji o iu no daroo ka.

data n. **[facts/figures from which conclusions can be drawn]**
shi⌉ryoo 資料 •c [information used for writing, research, etc.] ⟪materials, documents⟫, de⌉eta データ •f [facts/figures or materials used in research] ⟪materials⟫

EX. (**a**) We've gathered enough data on the case.
この件については十分な{資料/データ}を集めた。
Kono ken ni-tsuite wa juubunna {shiryoo/deeta} o atsumeta.
(**b**) Let's proceed with our research on the basis of this data.
この{資料/データ}に基づいて研究を進めよう。
Kono {shiryoo/deeta} ni motozuite kenkyuu o susumeyoo.

date n. **[the day of the month or the time at which some event happened or will happen or an appointment, often with a person of the opposite sex]**

1. hi-⌈zuke 日付 n. **[the day of the month on which s.t. is done, such as writing a letter]**

EX. What is the date on the letter?
その手紙の日付はいつですか。
Sono tegami no hi-zuke wa itsu desu ka.

2. hi 日 [a period of 24 hours or a particular time/period]

EX. What is your date of birth?
あなたの生まれた日はいつですか。
Anata no umareta hi wa itsu desu ka.

3. ⟨-to⟩ a⌉u ya⌈kusoku ⟨〜と⟩会う約束 •c [a promise to meet s.o.]

EX. I made a business date with him.
彼と仕事のことで会う約束をした。
Kare to shigoto no koto de au yakusoku o shita.

4. de⌉eto デート •f [an appointment to see a person of the opposite sex]

EX. Taro had a date with Hanako.
太郎は花子とデートをした。
Taroo wa Hanako to deeto o shita.

5 de⌉eto no a⌈ite⌉ デートの相手 [a person of the opposite sex with whom one has social engagement]

EX. Who is your date today?
今日のデートの相手はだれなの。
Kyoo no deeto no aite wa dare na no.

—— vt. **[for s.o. to meet s.o. of the opposite sex, usu. on a regular basis, for social companionship]**
⟨-to⟩ de⌉eto-suru ⟨〜と⟩デートする ③ •f [for s.o. to meet s.o. of the opposite sex to go out together], ⟨-to⟩ tsu⌈ki-a⌉u ⟨〜と⟩つきあう ① [for s.o. to meet s.o. (esp. of the opposite sex), for social companionship, usu. on a regular basis]

EX. Taro has been dating Hanako for some time now.
太郎はかなり長いこと花子と{つきあっ

て/*デートして}いる。
*Taroo wa kanari nagai koto Hanako to {tsuki-atte/*deeto-shite} iru.*

daughter n. **[a female child of s.o.]**
mu⌈sume⌉ 娘 [a humble form referring to one's own female child or a young unmarried woman] ((girl)) ↔ musuko 息子; o-⌈jo⌉o-san お嬢さん [a polite term used to refer to s.o. else's daughter or a young unmarried woman] ((young lady))
NOTE: *Musume* refers to one's own daughter, while *musume-san* or *ojoo-san* refers to someone else's daughter.
EX. (**a**) Could you please give this book to your daughter?
この本を{お嬢さん/娘さん/*娘}に渡していただけますか。
*Kono hon o {o-joo-san/musume-san/*musume} ni watashite itadake-masu ka.*
(**b**) I have four daughters.
私には{娘/*娘さん/*お嬢さん}が四人おります。
*Watakushi ni wa {musume/*musume-san/*o-joo-san} ga yo-nin orimasu.*

dawn n. **[daybreak]**
yo-⌈ake⌉ 夜明け [the beginning of the day]
EX. Dawn is the most beautiful time of the day.
一日のうちで夜明けがもっとも美しい。
Ichi-nichi no uchi de yo-ake ga mottomo utsukushii.

day n. **[the time (24 hours) that it takes the earth to revolve once on its axis or the interval of light between two successive nights or a particular time/period]**
1. i⌈chi-nichi⌉ 一日 [24 hours]
EX. (**a**) John wrote the paper in one day.
ジョンはその論文を一日で書き上げた。
Jon wa sono ronbun o ichi-nichi de kaki-ageta.
(**b**) A day consists of 24 hours.
一日は二十四時間からなる。
Ichi-nichi wa ni-juu-yo-jikan kara naru.
2. hi⌈ru-ma⌉ 昼間, hi⌈ru⌉ 昼 [12 o'clock at midday or the time between dawn and sunset or the meal taken at midday] ((daytime)), ni⌈tchuu 日中 •c [the period of time from sunrise to sunset] ↔ yoru 夜
EX. (**a**) Mr. Tanaka sleeps during the day and works at night.
田中さんは{昼間/昼/日中}寝て、夜仕事をする。
Tanaka-san wa {hiru-ma/hiru/nitchuu} nete, yoru shigoto o suru.
(**b**) This room gets lots of sunshine during the day.
この部屋は{昼間/昼/日中}よく日が入る。
Kono heya wa {hiru-ma/hiru/nitchuu} yoku hi ga hairu.
3. hi 日 [a period of 24 hours or a particular time/period]
EX. (**a**) Mother's Day is observed in many countries.
母の日は多くの国にあります。
Haha-no-hi wa ooku no kuni ni arimasu.
(**b**) The U.S. does not celebrate Children's Day.
アメリカでは子供の日は祝わない。
Amerika de wa Kodomo-no-hi wa iwawanai.
PHRASE: the day after tomorrow *asatte* あさって, *myoogo-nichi* 明後日 •c ⟨fml⟩
EX. We have our final exam the day after tomorrow.
学期末試験は{あさって/明後日}です。
Gakki-matsu-shiken wa {asatte/myoogo-nichi} desu.
PHRASE: the day before yesterday *ototoi* おととい, *ototsui* おとつい ⟨s⟩, *issaku-jitsu* 一昨日 •c ⟨fml⟩
EX. All classes were canceled the day before yesterday.
{おととい/おとつい/一昨日}の授業は全部休講でした。
{Ototoi/Ototsui/Issaku-jitsu} no jugyoo wa zenbu kyuukoo deshita.
PHRASE: the first day of the month *tsuitachi* 一日, second *futsuka* 二日, third *mikka* 三日, fourth *yokka* 四日, fifth *itsuka* 五日, sixth *muika* 六日, seventh {*nanoka*/*nanuka*} 七日, eighth *yooka* 八日, ninth *kokonoka* 九日, tenth *tooka* 十日, twentieth *hatsuka* 二十日

NOTE: The Japanese expressions for two days, three days, etc., are the same as the expressions for the second, third, etc., day of the month.

PHRASE: the other day *kono-aida* この間, *senjitsu* 先日 •c

EX. Thank you for the nice gift the other day.
{この間/先日}は結構なものをありがとうございました。
{Kono-aida/Senjitsu} wa kekkoona mono o arigatoo gozaimashita.

PHRASE: the old days *mukashi* 昔

EX. In the old days, there were no pollution problems.
昔は公害問題などはなかった。
Mukashi wa koogai-mondai nado wa nakatta.

PHRASE: these days *kono-goro* このごろ

EX. Everything has gone up in price these days.
このごろは何でも高くなりました。
Kono-goro wa nan-demo takaku narimashita.

daytime n. **[the time between dawn and sunset]**
hi⌈ru-ma⌉ 昼間, hi⌈ru⌉ 昼 [12 o'clock at midday or the time between dawn and sunset or the meal taken at midday] ↔ yoru 夜

EX. (**a**) Please turn off the lights during the daytime.
{昼間/昼}は電気を消して下さい。
{Hiru-ma/Hiru} wa denki o keshite kudasai.
(**b**) The daytime population in the Marunouchi area of Tokyo is very large.
東京の丸の内地区の{昼間/昼}の人口は大変多い。
Tookyoo no Marunouchi-chiku no {hiru-ma/hiru} no jinkoo wa taihen ooi.
(**c**) The roads are terribly crowded during the daytime.
{昼間/昼}は道が込んで大変だ。
{Hiru-ma/Hiru} wa michi ga konde taihen da.

dead adj. **[no longer living ⟪fig. "no longer in use"⟫]**

1. shi⌈nde iru (N) 死んでいる(N) /⟨V*te iru* of *shinu* ① die/ [no longer alive] ↔ ikite iru (N) 生きている(N) ; shi⌈nda N 死んだN /⟨Vinf. past of *shinu* ① die/ [s.o./s.a. that has died]

EX. (**a**) This dog is already dead.
この犬はもう死んでいる。
Kono inu wa moo shinde iru.
(**b**) We don't know whether he is dead or alive.
あの人は死んでいるか生きているか分かりません。
Ano hito wa shinde iru ka ikite iru ka wakarimasen.

2. mo⌉o tsu⌈kawa-rete inai (N) もう使われていない(N) /⟨neg. of V*te iru* of the passive of *tsukau* ① use/ [no longer in use] ⟪old, obsolete, unused⟫ ↔ mada tsukawa-rete iru (N) まだ使われている(N)

EX. Latin is a dead language.
ラテン語はもう使われていない言語です。
Raten-go wa moo tsukawa-rete inai gengo desu.

PHRASE: the dead *shisha* 死者 •c

deaf adj. **[unable to hear]**
mi⌈mi⌉ ga ki⌈koe-nai 耳が聞こえない [for the ear to be unable to hear]

EX. (**a**) She is deaf in one ear.
彼女は片方の耳が聞こえない。
Kanojo wa katahoo no mimi ga kikoe-nai.
(**b**) Helen Keller was deaf all her life.
ヘレン・ケラーは一生耳が聞こえなかった。
Heren Keraa wa isshoo mimi ga kikoe-nakatta.

deal vi./vt. **[to have to do (with)]**

PHRASE: deal with ⟨*-o*⟩ *atsukau* ⟨〜を⟩扱う ① ⟪handle, treat, manage⟫

EX. (**a**) This department deals with imported goods.
この部では輸入品を扱います。
Kono bu de wa yunyuu-hin o atsukaimasu.
(**b**) Japanese banks are having difficulty dealing with the problem of bad debt.

日本の銀行は不良債権の問題で四苦八苦している。
Nihon no ginkoo wa furyoo-saiken no mondai de shiku-hakku-shite iru.

— n. **[a political/business arrangement]**
to⌈ri⌉-hiki 取引 [a business transaction] **((transaction, dealing))**

dealer n. **[one who deals]**
ha⌈nbai-gyo⌉osha 販売業者 •c, di⌉iraa ディーラー •f [s.o./a firm dealing in particular merchandise] **((agent, seller))**

EX. Frank is an automobile dealer.
フランクは自動車の{販売業者/ディーラー}です。
Furanku wa jidoosha no {hanbai-gyoosha/diiraa} desu.

dear adj. **[much loved or high-priced]**
1. shi⌈tashi⌉i 親しい [for s.o. outside one's in-group to arouse in one a feeling of closeness] **((intimate, familar, close, friendly))**, **i⌈toshi⌉i いとしい** adj(*i*). **[to arouse in one a desire to be loving to him/her/it]** **((lovely))**

EX. (**a**) She is a dear friend of ours.
彼女は我々の{親しい/*いとしい}友である。
*Kanojo wa ware-ware no {shitashii/*itoshii} tomo dearu.*
(**b**) No one is as dear to one as one's own child.
自分の子ほど{いとしい/*親しい}者はいない。
*Jibun no ko hodo {itoshii/*shitashii} mono wa inai.*

NOTE: *Shin'ai naru* 親愛なる is used only in formal salutations.

2. ta⌈ka⌉i 高い adj(*i*). **[for s.t. or the top of s.t. to be at a point well above the ground or for s.t. to be above the expected level/amount/rate/degree]** **((expensive, costly))** ↔ **hikui 低い** adj(*i*).

EX. (**a**) Land in Tokyo is too dear for the average person to be able to buy.
東京の土地は高過ぎて一般の人にはとても買えない。
Tookyoo no tochi wa taka-sugite ippan no hito ni wa totemo kae-nai.
(**b**) Works by that artist sell at a very dear price.
あの画家の作品は非常に高い値段で売れる。
Ano gaka no sakuhin wa hijooni takai nedan de ureru.

— interj. **[an exclamation of surprise, distress, etc.]**
o⌉ya-maa おやまあ, a⌉ra-maa あらまあ, ta⌈ihen da 大変だ [it's awful] **((my goodness))**

NOTE: The interjections *oya-maa* and *ara-maa* are usually used by female speakers.

EX. (**a**) Oh dear, I forgot my passport.
{おやまあ/あらまあ/大変だ}パスポートを忘れちゃった。
{Oya-maa/Ara-maa/Taihen da} pasupooto o wasurechatta.
(**b**) Oh dear! Our cat climbed into a tree again.
{おやまあ/あらまあ/大変だ}猫がまた木に上っちゃった。
{Oya-maa/Ara-maa/Taihen da} neko ga mata ki ni nobotchatta.

death n. **[the end of life]**
shi⌉ 死 •c [the end of life]

EX. (**a**) Everybody fears death.
人はだれでも死を怖れる。
Hito wa dare-demo shi o osoreru.
(**b**) The composer became famous after his death.
その作曲家は死後有名になった。
Sono sakkyoku-ka wa shigo yuumeini natta.

debate n. **[(parliamentary) discussion of a given issue]**
to⌉oron 討論 •c, di⌈be⌉eto ディベート •f

EX. (**a**) The panel began a debate on environmental problems.
パネルは環境問題に関しての{討論/ディベート}を始めた。
Paneru wa kankyoo-mondai ni-kanshite no {tooron/dibeeto} o hajimeta.
(**b**) College students often hold debates on campus matters.
大学生はよく学園の事柄について{討

論/ディベート}をする。
Daigaku-sei wa yoku gakuen no kotogara ni-tsuite {tooron/dibeeto} o suru.
(**c**) In America, students learn the art of debate beginning in grade school.
アメリカでは小学生のころから{ディベート/討論}の練習をする。
Amerika de wa shoogaku-sei no koro kara {dibeeto/tooron} no renshuu o suru.
(**d**) The debate between Kennedy and Nixon is well-known.
ケネディーとニクソンの{ディベート/討論}は有名だ。
Kenedii to Nikuson no {dibeeto/tooron} wa yuumei da.

D

—— vt. **[for people to discuss an issue, considering reasons for and against a particular viewpoint]**
{⟨-o⟩/⟨-ni-tsuite⟩} gi⌉ron-suru {⟨〜を⟩/⟨〜について⟩}議論する ③ •c [for people to exchange opinions on some topic], {⟨-o⟩/⟨-ni-tsuite⟩} to⌉oron-suru {⟨〜を⟩/⟨〜について⟩}討論する ③ •c [for people to discuss s.t. thoroughly] ⟪discuss, talk about, argue⟫

EX. (**a**) The participants debated the question of the membership of Eastern European countries in NATO.
参加者は東欧諸国の北大西洋条約機構への加盟の問題{を/について}{議論/討論}した。
Sanka-sha wa Too-Oo-shokoku no kita-taiseiyoo-jooyaku-kikoo e no kamei no mondai {o/ni-tsuite} {giron/tooron}-shita.
(**b**) The faculty debated the proposed revision in the curriculum.
教授たちはカリキュラム変更案{を/について}{議論/討論}した。
Kyooju-tachi wa karikyuramu-henkoo-an {o/ni-tsuite} {giron/tooron}-shita.
(**c**) That issue ought to be thoroughly debated in the U.N.
その問題は国連で徹底的に{討論/議論}されるべきだ。
Sono mondai wa Kokuren de tetteitekini {tooron/giron}-sareru-beki da.

debt n. **[s.t. owed to another or the condition of owing s.t. to another ⟪fig. "a sense of indebtedness"⟫]**

1. sha⌈kki⌉n 借金 •c [money s.o. borrows from s.o. else], fu⌈sai 負債 •c [money, often a large amount, which s.o. owes to a financial institution such as a bank ⟨fml⟩]

EX. (**a**) Some countries bear major debts to other countries.
他の国への多額の{借金/負債}を抱えている国がある。
Ta no kuni e no tagaku no {shakkin/fusai} o kakaete iru kuni ga aru.
(**b**) Although her uncle was poor, he did not leave behind any debt when he passed away.
彼女の伯父は貧乏だったが死んだ後に{借金/負債}は一切なかった。
Kanojo no oji wa binboo datta ga shinda ato ni {shakkin/fusai} wa issai nakatta.
(**c**) His company went bankrupt due to heavy debts.
彼の会社は多額の{借金/負債}を抱えて倒産した。
Kare no kaisha wa tagaku no {shakkin/fusai} o kakaete toosan-shita.

2. o⌉ngi 恩義 •c [indebtedness to s.o. for their kindness] ⟪owing, a sense of gratitude⟫

EX. (**a**) I owe a great debt to you for your kindness.
あなたのご親切に対して大きな恩義を感じています。
Anata no go-shinsetsu ni taishite ookina ongi o kanjite imasu.
(**b**) In Japanese culture, a debt of gratitude is something to be repaid just as if it were a monetary debt.
日本の文化では恩義は借金と同じように返さなければならないものである。
Nihon no bunka de wa ongi wa shakkin to onaji yooni kaesanakereba naranai mono dearu.

deceive vt. **[to make s.o. believe what is not true]**

⟨-o⟩ da⌈ma⌉su ⟨〜を⟩だます ① [for s.o. to tell a lie and make s.o. believe that it is true] **((cheat, fool, take in, trick))**

EX. (**a**) Jack deceived Jill and went out with another woman.
ジャックはジルをだまして、別の女性とデートをした。
Jakku wa Jiru o damashite betsu no josei to deeto o shita.
(**b**) The car salesman deceived him into buying a lemon.
その車のセールスマンは彼をだまして悪い車をつかませた。
Sono kuruma no seerusu-man wa kare o damashite warui kuruma o tsukama-seta.
(**c**) It's wrong to deceive a person like that.
人をだますなんてとんでもないことだ。
Hito o damasu nante tondemo-nai koto da.

December n.
ju⌈u-ni-gatsu 十二月 •c

decide vt. **[for s.o. to make a choice or decision regarding an object/course of action after considering the alternatives] {⟨-to⟩/⟨-o⟩/⟨-ni⟩} ki⌈meru {⟨〜と⟩/⟨〜を⟩/⟨〜に⟩}決める ② [for s.o. to make a judgment as to which of a number of alternatives is best in a given situation and resolve to act accordingly] ((fix, settle, agree upon, choose, resolve))**, **⟨-ni⟩ suru ⟨〜に⟩する ③ {⟨-to⟩/⟨-o⟩} ke⌉sshin-suru {⟨〜と⟩/⟨〜を⟩}決心する ③ •c [for s.o. to resolve to take a particular course of action with regard to s.t. of importance] ((determine, resolve))**

NOTE: Note that Vvol. is often used before ⟨*-to*⟩ as in examples (a) and (b). Also note that when *kimeru* is preceded by an interrogative sentence, as in examples (c) and (d), neither particle *to* nor *o* is used.

EX. (**a**) I decided to become a politician when I was in college.
私は大学の時政治家に{なろうと決めた/なろうと決心した/なることに{決めた/した}}。
Watakushi wa daigaku no toki seiji-ka ni {naroo to kimeta/naroo to kesshin-shita/naru koto ni {kimeta/shita}}.
(**b**) When I was still in grade school my father decided quite on his own that I should become a medical doctor.
私がまだ小学生のころ父は勝手に私を医者に{しようと決めた/しようと決心した/することに{決めた/した}}。
Watashi ga mada shoogaku-sei no koro chichi wa katteni watashi o isha ni {shiyoo to kimeta/shiyoo to kesshin-shita/suru koto ni {kimeta/shita}}.
(**c**) Have you decided where you will go for the holidays?
休みにどこへ行くかもう{決めました/*決心しました}か。
*Yasumi ni doko e iku ka moo {kimemashita/*kesshin-shimashita} ka.*
(**d**) Let's decide first where to eat.
まずどこで食事をするか{決めましょう/*決心しましょう}。
*Mazu doko de shokuji o suru ka {kimemashoo/*kesshin-shimashoo}.*
(**e**) I decided to go abroad to study.
留学することを{決めました/決心しました}。
Ryuugaku-suru koto o {kimemashita/kesshin-shimashita}.

PHRASE: decide on ⟨*-ni*⟩ *kimeru* ⟨〜に⟩決める ②

EX. I have decided on this computer.
このコンピューターに決めた。
Kono konpyuutaa ni kimeta.

PHRASE: be decided *kimaru* 決まる ①, Vinf non-past *koto ni naru* Vinf non-past ことになる ①

EX. It was decided that we should postpone our departure.
出発を延期すること{が決まった/になった}。
Shuppatsu o enki-suru koto {ga kimatta/ninatta}.

decision n. **[the act or result of deciding]**
1. ke⌈ttei 決定 •c [an act/result of deciding to do s.t.] ((determination, conclusion, settlement))

EX. (**a**) He disagreed with the decision of the committee.

彼は委員会の決定に反対だった。
Kare wa iin-kai no kettei ni hantai datta.
(**b**) The decision of the president was final.
社長の決定は最終的なものであった。
Shachoo no kettei wa saishuu-tekina mono deatta.

2. ke⌉sshin 決心 •c [resolving to take a particular course of action with regard to s.t. of importance] ⟪resolve, determination⟫

EX. (**a**) Having made the decision to marry Taro, Reiko would listen to no contrary opinion on the matter.
太郎と結婚する決心をしてから玲子は周囲の反対意見を聞こうともしなかった。
Taroo to kekkon-suru kesshin o shite kara Reiko wa shuui no hantai-iken o kikoo to mo shinakatta.
(**b**) His decision to quit the company is not going to change.
会社を辞める彼の決心はもう変わらない。
Kaisha o yameru kare no kesshin wa moo kawaranai.

declaration n. **[a formal announcement/statement]**

1. se⌈nge⌉n 宣言 •c [the act by an individual/organization of officially announcing to the public one's opinion/policy] ⟪proclamation, statement, pronouncement⟫

EX. Thomas Jefferson drafted America's Declaration of Independence.
トーマス・ジェファーソンはアメリカの独立宣言を起草した。
Toomasu Jefaason wa Amerika no Dokuritsu-sengen o kisoo-shita.

2. shi⌈nkoku 申告 •c [a reporting of s.t. in accordance with regulations] ⟪report, return, statement⟫

EX. You have to fill out this declaration form for customs.
税関に出すためにこの申告書を作成しなければならない。
Zeikan ni dasu tame ni kono shinkoku-sho o sakusei-shinakereba naranai.

declare vt. **[for s.o. to make a public or formal statement on a significant issue]**

1. {⟨-o⟩/⟨-to⟩} **se⌈nge⌉n-suru** {⟨〜を⟩/⟨〜と⟩} **宣言する ③ •c [for s.o. to announce officially to the public one's opinion/policy] ⟪profess, announce⟫**

EX. (**a**) The Crown Prince officially declared the exposition opened at last night's ceremony.
皇太子は昨晩の式で博覧会の開会を宣言した。
Kootaishi wa sakuban no shiki de hakuran-kai no kaikai o sengen-shita.
(**b**) The President declared an end to the economic sanctions against China.
大統領は中国に対する経済制裁の終結を宣言した。
Daitooryoo wa Chuugoku ni-taisuru keizai-seisai no shuuketsu o sengen-shita.
(**c**) Mr. Fujinami declared that he would run in the next gubernatorial election.
藤波氏は次の知事選挙に出馬すると宣言した。
Fujinami-shi wa tsugi no chiji-senkyo ni shutsuba-suru to sengen-shita.

2. ⟨**-to**⟩ **ge⌈nmei-suru** ⟨〜と⟩**言明する ③ •c [for s.o. to clearly affirm s.t. significant ⟨w⟩] ⟪assert, affirm, proclaim, avow⟫**

EX. The minister declared his firm belief in the neccessity of a free market.
大臣は自由市場が必要だと固く信じていると言明した。
Daijin wa jiyuu-shijoo ga hitsuyoo da to kataku shinjite iru to genmei-shita.

3. ⟨**-o**⟩ **shi⌈nkoku-suru** ⟨〜を⟩**申告する ③ •c [for s.o. to make a formal statement to a government office]**

EX. (**a**) Please declare all purchases over $160.
百六十ドル以上の買い物はすべて申告してください。
Hyaku-roku-juu-doru-ijoo no kai-mono wa subete shinkoku-shite kudasai.
(**b**) I have nothing to declare.
何も申告するものはありません。
Nani-mo shinkoku-suru mono wa arimasen.

decline vt. **[for s.o. to refuse (to do) s.t. politely]**

1. ⟨-o⟩ ko⌈towa⌉ru ⟨〜を⟩断る ① [for s.o. to inform s.o. that one cannot accept his/her demand/request/invitation/offer] ⟪refuse, reject, turn down, give notice, tell⟫, ⟨-o⟩ ji⌉tai-suru ⟨〜を⟩辞退する ③ •c [for s.o. to refuse s.t. politely ⟨fml⟩] ⟪refuse, excuse oneself from⟫

EX. (**a**) John declined his neighbor's offer to help.
ジョンは隣人の手伝いの申し出を{断った/辞退した}。
Jon wa rinjin no tetsudai no mooshi-de o {kotowatta/jitai-shita}.
(**b**) She declined my invitation to dinner.
彼女は私の食事への招待を{断った/辞退した}。
Kanojo wa watakushi no shokuji e no shootai o {kotowatta/jitai-shita}.

—— vi. **[to become worse/weaker]**

o⌈toroe⌉ru おとろえる ② [for s.o./s.t./s.a. to lose his/her/its original vigor/prosperity/beauty/strength] ⟪grow weak, lose vigor, fall off, wither, decay, wane⟫, ka⌈tamu⌉ku 傾く ① [to become inclined away from the vertical line ⟪fig. "lose vigor"⟫] ⟪lean, slant, tilt, slope⟫

EX. (**a**) Her popularity as a singer is beginning to decline.
彼女の歌手としての人気は{おとろえ/傾き}はじめている。
Kanojo no kashu to-shite no ninki wa {otoroe/katamuki}-hajimete iru.
(**b**) The wrestler's strength declined with age.
力士は年とともに体力が{おとろえた/*傾いた}。
*Rikishi wa toshi to tomo ni tairyoku ga {otoroeta/*katamuita}.*

decorate vt. **[to furnish s.t. with s.t. beautiful ⟪fig. "to give a medal to"⟫]**

1. ⟨-o⟩ ka⌈zaru ⟨〜を⟩飾る ① [for s.o. to arrange s.t. effectively so as to make it appear beautiful ⟪fig. "embellish," "exhibit"⟫] ⟪ornament, adorn, deck⟫

EX. (**a**) She decorated her room with red roses.
彼女は部屋を赤いばらで飾った。
Kanojo wa heya o akai bara de kazatta.
(**b**) We decorated her birthday cake with candles.
私たちは彼女のバースデーケーキをろうそくで飾った。
Watashi-tachi wa kanojo no baasudee-keeki o roosoku de kazatta.

2. ⟨-ni⟩ ku⌈nshoo o sa⌈zuke⌉ru ⟨〜に⟩勲章を授ける ② [for s.o. to give a medal of honor to s.o.]

EX. The Queen decorated the soldiers for their bravery.
女王陛下は勇敢な兵士たちに勲章を授けた。
Jooo-heika wa yuukanna heishi-tachi ni kunshoo o sazuketa.

decoration n. **[an act/instance of decorating or s.t. used to decorate or a medal conferred]**

1. so⌈oshoku 装飾 •c [an act/instance of decorating or s.t. used to decorate], ⟪ornament, embellishment, trimmings⟫ ka⌈zari 飾り /⟨Vmasu of *kazaru* ① decorate/ ⟪ornament, adornment⟫

EX. (**a**) She specializes in interior decoration.
彼女は室内{装飾/*飾り}を専門にしている。
*Kanojo wa shitsunai-{sooshoku/*kazari} o senmon ni shite iru.*
(**b**) We're thinking about what decorations we need for the Christmas party.
クリスマスパーティーのためどんな{装飾/飾り}が要るか考えています。
Kurisumasu-paatii no tame donna {sooshoku/kazari} ga iru ka kangaete imasu.

2. ku⌈nshoo 勲章 •c [a medal of honor conferred on s.o. by a government]

EX. He received a decoration for his service to his country.
彼は国家に対する貢献により勲章を授与された。
Kare wa kokka ni taisuru kooken ni yori kunshoo o juyo-sareta.

D

decrease vt. **[to make less/smaller]**
⟨-o⟩ he⌈rasu ⟨〜を⟩減らす ① [to cause s.t./s.o./s.a. to become smaller in quantity] **⟪diminish, reduce⟫ ↔ ⟨-o⟩ fuyasu ⟨〜を⟩増やす ①**

EX. Due to the drought, the city office decreased the citizens' water allotment.
雨不足のため役所は市民への水の供給を減らした。
Ame-busoku no tame yakusho wa shimin e no mizu no kyookyuu o herashita.

D

— vi. **[to become less/smaller]**
he⌈ru 減る ① [to become less] ⟪diminish, lessen⟫ ↔ fueru 増える ②

EX. (**a**) The number of smokers has decreased in recent years.
近年たばこを吸う人が減った。
Kinnen tabako o suu hito ga hetta.
(**b**) Our dependence on imported energy sources has decreased somewhat.
我々の輸入エネルギー源に対する依存度は若干減った。
Ware-ware no yunyuu-enerugii-gen ni taisuru izon-do wa jakkan hetta.
(**c**) The birth rate in our country is decreasing year by year.
我が国の出生率は年々減る一方である。
Waga kuni no shusshoo-ritsu wa nen-nen heru ippoo dearu.

— n. **[becoming less or making s.t. less]**
ge⌈nshoo 減少 •c ⟪falling-off, reduction, diminution⟫ ↔ zooka 増加 •c

EX. (**a**) Young laborers are showing a marked decrease in the construction industry.
建設業界では若年労働者が顕著な減少を示している。
Kensetsu-gyookai de wa jakunen-roodoo-sha ga kenchona genshoo o shimeshite iru.
(**b**) After the war, we saw a significant decrease in the rate of death among children.
戦後、子供の死亡率は大幅な減少を見せた。
Sengo, kodomo no shiboo-ritsu wa oo-habana genshoo o miseta.

deep adj. **[extending far downward/inward/backward]**
fu⌈ka⌉i 深い adj(*i*). **[extending far downward from the surface or far toward the back from the front ⟪fig. "profound," "hard to fathom," "dark (color/sound)," "secret," "dense," "intimate"⟫] ⟪profound⟫ ↔ asai 浅い** adj(*i*).

EX. (**a**) We had to walk for many kilometers in the deep snow.
深い雪の中を何キロも歩かなければならなかった。
Fukai yuki no naka o nan-kiro mo arukanakereba naranakatta.
(**b**) This river is deep around there.
この川はあの辺りが深いです。
Kono kawa wa ano atari ga fukai desu.
(**c**) In order to be able to translate effectively, one needs a deep knowledge of the two languages concerned.
きちんと翻訳するには当該の二つの言語の深い知識が必要だ。
Kichinto hon'yaku-suru ni wa toogai no futatsu no gengo no fukai chishiki ga hitsuyoo da.
(**d**) There is no deeper sorrow than that of losing one's child.
自分の子供をなくすほど深い悲しみはありません。
Jibun no kodomo o nakusu hodo fukai kanashimi wa arimasen.

deer n.
shi⌈ka 鹿

defeat vt. **[to win a victory over s.o./a country]**
⟨-o⟩ ma⌈kasu ⟨〜を⟩負かす ① [for s.o. to cause s.o. to lose] ⟪beat, overcome, conquer, vanquish⟫, ⟨-o⟩ ya⌈bu⌉ru ⟨〜を⟩破る ① [to apply force to a part of s.t. thin and flat that has tension such as paper/cloth/a wall/an enemy line/silence and thereby damage it ⟪fig. "break a promise/the law," "beat"⟫] ⟪crush, tear, rip, break⟫

EX. (**a**) Michigan defeated Ohio State ten to zero.
ミシガン大は10対0でオハイオ州立大

を{負かした/破った}。
Mishigan-dai wa jut-tai-zero de Ohaio-shuuritsu-dai o {makashita/yabutta}.
(**b**) Waseda defeated Keio for the second straight time.
早稲田は二度続けて慶応を{負かした/破った}。
Waseda wa ni-do tsuzukete Keioo o {makashita/yabutta}.

—— n. **[the fact/condition of losing victory in a contest]**
ha⌈iboku 敗北 •c [losing a war, match, game, etc.] ↔ shoori 勝利 •c

EX. (**a**) Sam experienced his first defeat in life at the kindergarten Sports Day.
サムは幼稚園の運動会で人生で初めての敗北を経験した。
Samu wa yoochien no undoo-kai de jinsei de hajimete no haiboku o keiken-shita.
(**b**) Men are not made for defeat.
人間は敗北するようには出来ていない。
Ningen wa haiboku-suru yooni wa dekite inai.
(**c**) It was obvious to everyone that defeat was inevitable for the team.
そのチームの敗北が避けられないことはだれの目にも明らかだった。
Sono chiimu no haiboku ga sake-rarenai koto wa dare no me ni mo akiraka datta.

defend vt. **[for s.o. to guard s.t./s.o. from attack]**
⟨-o⟩ (⟨-kara⟩) ma⌈mo⌉ru ⟨～を⟩(⟨～から⟩)守る ① [(to watch s.t./s.o./s.a. in order) to cause s.t./s.o./s.a. not to be harmed/injured/violated] ⟪protect, guard, shield, shelter⟫, ⟨-o⟩ bo⌉ogyo-suru ⟨～を⟩防御する ③ •c [for s.o. to stop/prevent an enemy attack] ⟪protect, shield⟫, ⟨-o⟩ be⌉ngo-suru ⟨～を⟩弁護する ③ •c [for s.o. to speak on behalf of s.o. in a court of law, etc.]

EX. (**a**) We must defend our country against our enemies.
自分の国を敵から{守らなければ/防御しなければ/*弁護しなければ}ならない。
*Jibun no kuni o teki kara {mamoranakereba/boogyo-shinakereba/*bengo-shinakereba} naranai.*
(**b**) She defended her financial interests with the help of a lawyer.
彼女は弁護士の助けをかりて財産を{守った/*防御した/*弁護した}。
*Kanojo wa bengo-shi no tasuke o karite zaisan o {mamotta/*boogyo-shita/*bengo-shita}.*
(**c**) The lawyer defended the accused.
弁護士は被告を{弁護した/守った/*防御した}。
*Bengo-shi wa hikoku o {bengo-shita/mamotta/*boogyo-shita}.*

defense n. **[the act of guarding against or resisting attack or danger]**
1. bo⌈oei 防衛 •c [the act of protecting oneself/one's country] ⟪protection, safeguard⟫ ↔ koogeki 攻撃 •c, bo⌉ogyo 防御 •c [protection from an enemy attack] ⟪protection, shelter⟫

EX. (**a**) The Self-Defense Forces were established for the defense of our land.
自衛隊は国土の{防衛/防御}のために設立されたものである。
Jiei-tai wa kokudo no {booei/boogyo} no tame ni setsuritsu-sareta mono dearu.
(**b**) The champion succeeded in the defense of his title.
チャンピオンはタイトルの{防衛/*防御}に成功した。
*Chanpion wa taitoru no {booei/*boogyo} ni seikoo-shita.*

2. di⌈fensu ディフェンス •f [in sports, the side defending its goal, etc., against scoring]

EX. This football team has a good defense.
このフットボールのチームはディフェンスが固い。
Kono futto-booru no chiimu wa difensu ga katai.

define vt. **[to fix the boundaries of or to state the meaning of s.t.]**
1. ⟨-o⟩ te⌉igi-suru ⟨～を⟩定義する ③ •c [for

D

s.o. to explain explicitly the meaning or contents of concepts or words] ((describe exactly))

EX. (**a**) A dictionary defines the meanings of words.
辞書は単語の意味を定義する。
Jisho wa tango no imi o teigi-suru.
(**b**) What is meant by the "period of maturity" is not defined anywhere in the contract.
「満期」とは何を指すのか、契約のどこにも定義されていない。
"Manki" to wa nani o sasu no ka, keiyaku no doko ni mo teigi-sarete inai.

2. ⟨**-no**⟩ **kyo⌈okai o sa⌈dame⌉ru** ⟨〜の⟩境界を定める ② **[for s.o. to determine the boundaries of s.t.] ((delimit, delineate))**

EX. The boundary between Kentucky and Indiana is clearly defined by the Ohio River.
ケンタッキー州とインディアナ州の境界はオハイオ川によってはっきりと定められている。
Kentakkii-shuu to Indiana-shuu no kyookai wa Ohaio-gawa ni-yotte hakkiri to sadame-rarete iru.

definite adj. **[clearly stated/known]**
me⌈ikakuna 明確な adj(*na*). **•c [be clearly distinguished from others] ((clear, precise, distinct))**

EX. (**a**) She gave no definite answer.
彼女は明確な答えを出さなかった。
Kanojo wa meikakuna kotae o dasanakatta.
(**b**) She has a definite plan for her future.
彼女は自分の将来について明確な青写真をもっている。
Kanojo wa jibun no shoorai ni-tsuite meikakuna aojashin o motte iru.

definition n. **[the exact description of the meaning of a word/concept]**
te⌉igi 定義 **•c ((specification, delineation))**

EX. (**a**) What is the definition of grammar?
文法の定義は何ですか。
Bunpoo no teigi wa nan desu ka.
(**b**) The definition of sexual harassment is very difficult.
セクハラの定義は大変難しい。
Sekuhara no teigi wa taihen muzukashii.

degree n. **[extent; an academic title; a unit of measure for angles/temperature]**
1. te⌉ido 程度 **•c [the extent of a property, quantity, etc., as compared with that of others] ((grade, measure, proportions, rate, standard, level, limit))**

EX. (**a**) Everyone experiences some degree of failure in their life.
人生においてはだれもがある程度のざせつ感を味わうものだ。
Jinsei ni oite wa dare-mo ga aru teido no zasetsu-kan o ajiwau mono da.
(**b**) Whether or not cancer can be cured is largely a matter of to what degree it has advanced when it is discovered.
がんが治るかどうかはほとんどの場合それが発見された時点でどの程度進んでいるかによる。
Gan ga naoru ka doo ka wa hotondo no baai sore ga hakken-sareta jiten de dono teido susunde iru ka ni yoru.

2. ga⌉kui 学位 **•c [an academic title conferred by a college]**

EX. (**a**) My father got his degree from the University of Tokyo.
父は東京大学から学位を得た。
Chichi wa Tookyoo-daigaku kara gakui o eta.
(**b**) I've finally finished writing the thesis for my degree.
やっと学位論文を書き上げた。
Yatto gakui-ronbun o kaki-ageta.

3. do 度 **•c [unit of measure for angles, temperature, eye-glasses, etc.]**

EX. (**a**) Water boils at 100 degrees centigrade.
水は摂氏百度で沸騰する。
Mizu wa sesshi hyaku-do de futtoo-suru.
(**b**) At what degree is the Tower of Pisa leaning?
ピサの斜塔は何度ぐらい傾いていますか。
Pisa no shatoo wa nan-do-gurai

katamuite imasu ka.

delay vt. **[to cause s.t. to occur at a later time than expected or planned]**
⟨-o⟩ e⌈nki-suru ⟨〜を⟩延期する ③ **•c [for s.o. to postpone s.t. to a later time than planned] ⟪postpone, put off, defer⟫, ⟨-o⟩ no⌈ba⌉su ⟨〜を⟩のばす** ① **[for s.o. to cause s.t. to become longer, usu. vertically ⟪fig. "straighten," "hold out," "postpone," "cultivate (abilities)"⟫] ⟪defer, prolong, stretch, extend, lengthen⟫**
㊅ "put off s.t."▷延ばす, otherwise ▷伸ばす

EX. (**a**) The conference was delayed by one day due to the railroad strike.
鉄道のストのため会議が一日{延期された/延ばされた}。
Tetsudoo no suto no tame kaigi ga ichi-nichi {enki-sareta/nobasa-reta}.
(**b**) The control tower delayed departure of the plane due to a storm.
嵐のため管制塔は飛行機の出発を{延期した/延ばした}。
Arashi no tame kansei-too wa hikoo-ki no shuppatsu o {enki-shita/nobashita}.

—— n. **[an act/instance of causing s.t. to occur at a later time than expected or planned or the result of such]**
o⌈kure 遅れ /⟨V*masu* of *okureru* ② become delayed/ [the state of being late] ⟪lateness⟫

EX. There'll be a few minutes' delay in the opening of the meeting.
会の開始に多少の遅れがあります。
Kai no kaishi ni tashoo no okure ga arimasu.

PHRASE: be delayed *okureru* 遅れる ②

EX. The arrival of the shinkansen was delayed by an earthquake.
地震のため新幹線の到着が遅れた。
Jishin no tame shinkansen no toochaku ga okureta.

PHRASE: without delay *sugu (ni)* すぐ(に), *guzu-guzu-shinaide* ぐずぐずしないで

EX. Start without delay.
{すぐ(に)/ぐずぐずしないで}始めなさい。
{Sugu (ni)/Guzu-guzu-shinaide} hajimenasai.

deliberate adj. **[carefully considered ⟪fig. "intentional"⟫]**
shi⌈nchoona 慎重な adj(*na*). **•c [careful and discreet] ⟪cautious, prudent, discreet⟫**

EX. (**a**) She is always deliberate in how she acts.
彼女はいつも慎重な行動をする人だ。
Kanojo wa itsu-mo shinchoona koodoo o suru hito da.
(**b**) His decision was based on careful and deliberate judgment.
彼の決定は慎重な判断に基づくものだった。
Kare no kettei wa shinchoona handan ni motozuku mono datta.

deliberately adj. **[in a deliberate manner]**
1. shi⌈nchooni 慎重に •c ⟪carefully, prudently, cautiously⟫

EX. The carriage bearing the Pope moved slowly and deliberately.
ローマ法王を乗せた馬車はゆっくり慎重に走った。
Rooma Hoooo o noseta basha wa yukkuri shinchooni hashitta.

2. wa⌉za-to わざと [for s.o. to do s.t. with a conscious intention] ⟪purposely, intentionally, knowingly⟫, ko⌉i ni 故意に •c [for s.o. to do s.t. with a conscious intention or knowingly] ⟪intentionally, designedly, wittingly, voluntarily, on purpose⟫

EX. He deliberately crashed the car.
彼は{わざと/故意に}車をぶつけた。
Kare wa {waza-to/koi ni} kuruma o butsuketa.

delicate adj. **[fine in texture, quality, character or requiring great care]**
1. se⌈nsaina 繊細な adj(*na*). **•c [fine and graceful] ⟪nice, fine, subtle⟫, de⌈rike⌉etona デリケートな** adj(*na*). **•f [fine and sensitive or requiring great care]**

EX. (**a**) She has delicate skin.
彼女は{繊細な/デリケートな}肌をしている。
Kanojo wa {sensaina/derikeetona} hada o shite iru.
(**b**) A delicate sense of color is required in

designing textile goods.
織物を作るには{繊細な/デリケートな}色彩感覚が要求される。
Ori-mono o tsukuru ni wa {sensaina/derikeetona} shikisai-kankaku ga yookyuu-sareru.
(**c**) Linguists usually have delicate intuitions about language.
言語学者は普通{繊細な/デリケートな}語感をもっている。
Gengo-gakusha wa futsuu {sensaina/derikeetona} gokan o motte iru.

D

2. bi⌈myoona 微妙な adj(*na*). **•c [so fine and complex as to be difficult to describe], de⌈rike⌉etona デリケートな** adj(*na*). **•f**

EX. (**a**) The negotiations have entered a delicate stage.
交渉は{微妙な/デリケートな}段階に入った。
Kooshoo wa {bimyoona/derikeetona} dankai ni haitta.
(**b**) He is the sort of person who can understand delicate differences.
彼は{微妙な/デリケートな}違いが分かる男だ。
Kare wa {bimyoona/derikeetona} chigai ga wakaru otoko da.

delicious adj. **[very pleasing to the taste/smell]**
o⌈ishii おいしい adj(*i*)., **u⌈ma⌉i うまい** adj(*i*). **[for s.t. to be very pleasant to taste or for s.o./s.a. to be skillful at s.t.]** **⟪nice, good⟫** ↔ **mazui まずい** adj(*i*).

EX. (**a**) Thank you very much for the delicious dinner.
{おいしい/*うまい}食事をありがとうございました。
*{Oishii/*Umai} shokuji o arigatoo gozaimashita.*
(**b**) Let's go out and have something delicious to eat.
何か{おいしい/うまい}ものを食べに行きましょう。
Nani-ka {oishii/umai} mono o tabe ni ikimashoo.

NOTE: The use of *umai* in the meaning of *oishii* is a characteristic of male speech. For example, *Kono mise no sushi wa umai.* "The sushi in this shop is delicious."

delight vt. **[to give great pleasure to s.o.]**
⟨-o⟩ yo⌈rokoba-se⌉ru ⟨～を⟩喜ばせる ② /⟨causative of *yorokobu* ① rejoice/ [to cause s.o. to be satisfied/happy] ⟪please⟫

EX. (**a**) The news delighted everyone.
そのニュースは皆を喜ばせた。
Sono nyuusu wa mina o yorokoba-seta.
(**b**) The birth of their grandchild delighted the grandparents immeasurably.
孫の誕生は祖父母を大変喜ばせた。
Mago no tanjoo wa sofubo o taihen yorokoba-seta.

—— n. **[great pleasure/enjoyment]**
yo⌈rokobi⌉ 喜び /⟨V*masu* of *yorokobu* ① rejoice/ [a feeling of happiness or gladness] ⟪joy, gladness, rejoicing, rapture⟫, ta⌈noshimi 楽しみ /⟨V*masu* of *tanoshimu* ① enjoy/ [feeling pleasant in a certain circumstance or s.t. that causes such a feeling] ⟪pleasure, enjoyment, amusement, comfort⟫

EX. (**a**) Ethel took delight in her weaving.
エセルは織物に{喜び/楽しみ}を見いだした。
Eseru wa ori-mono ni {yorokobi/tanoshimi} o mi-idashita.
(**b**) The vacation brought great delight to the entire family.
休暇は家族全員にとって大きな{楽しみ/喜び}だった。
Kyuuka wa kazoku zen'in ni-totte ookina {tanoshimi/yorokobi} datta.

delighted adj. **[to feel highly pleased]**
(⟨-o⟩) yo⌈roko⌉bu (⟨～を⟩)喜ぶ ① [for s.o. to experience satisfaction and happiness over s.t. pleasant] ⟪rejoice, be glad/pleased⟫

EX. (**a**) The Prince was delighted to meet Cinderella.
王子様はシンデレラに会って大変喜びました。
Ooji-sama wa Shinderera ni atte taihen yorokobimashita.
(**b**) She was very delighted with the gift.

彼女は贈り物をもらって非常に喜びました。
Kanojo wa okuri-mono o moratte hijooni yorokobimashita.
(**c**) I would be delighted to come.
喜んでお伺い致します。
Yorokonde o-ukagai itashimasu.

delightful adj. **[very pleasing]**
ta⌈noshi⌉i 楽しい adj(*i*). **[experiencing intense enjoyment and satisfaction from s.t. and thus being drawn to it or causing such a feeling in one]** **《pleasant, cheerful, enjoyable》**

EX. (**a**) Thank you for the delightful evening.
楽しい夕べをありがとうございました。
Tanoshii yuube o arigatoo gozaimashita.
(**b**) She is a very delightful person.
彼女は大変楽しい人だ。
Kanojo wa taihen tanoshii hito da.

deliver vt. **[to carry or take s.t. to an intended recipient 《fig. "utter," "pronounce"》]**
1. ({〈-e〉/〈-ni〉}) 〈-o〉 **ha⌈itatsu-suru** ({〈〜へ〉/〈〜に〉})〈〜を〉**配達する** ③ •c **[for s.o. to carry and distribute mail, merchandise, etc., to its intended destination]**, ({〈-e〉/〈-ni〉}) 〈-o〉 **to⌈doke⌉ru** ({〈〜へ〉/〈〜に〉})〈〜を〉**届ける** ② **[to cause s.t. to get to s.o. or to report s.t. officially to a superior/government office]** **《send, forward, report, notify, give notice to》**

EX. (**a**) The mailman delivered a package.
郵便屋が小包を{配達した/届けた}。
Yuubin-ya ga ko-zutsumi o {haitatsu-shita/todoketa}.
(**b**) In Japan, there are stores which deliver sushi to your home.
日本には家へすしを{配達して/届けて}くれる店がある。
Nihon ni wa ie e sushi o {haitatsu-shite/todokete} kureru mise ga aru.

2. 〈-o〉 **su⌈ru** 〈〜を〉**する** ③ **[for s.o./s.a. to perform a willful action; for s.o./s.a./s.t. to cause s.t. to take on a different state; for s.t. to happen in such a way as to be perceptible to s.o./s.a.; for s.t. to be in a certain state or possess a certain attribute; for an amount of time/money to pass/be required; for some proposition to be posited as true 《fig. "put on a somewhat small, ornamental object"》]**

NOTE: *Suru* can be combined with various Sino-Japanese compounds to express the meaning of delivering a speech, lecture, etc.

EX. (**a**) John delivered a lecture in Japanese.
ジョンは日本語で講演をした。
Jon wa Nihon-go de kooen o shita.
(**b**) The prime minister delivered a speech in English at the opening ceremony.
首相は開会式で英語で演説をした。
Shushoo wa kaikai-shiki de eigo de enzetsu o shita.

delivery n. **[the act of taking or carrying s.t. to its intended recipient]**
ha⌈itatsu 配達 •c **[distribution of mail, merchandise, etc. to a destination]**, **de⌈mae 出前** **[the act of taking/bringing food to a house from a restaurant, etc.]**

EX. (**a**) There is only one mail delivery on Saturdays.
土曜日には郵便の{配達/*出前}が一度しかない。
*Doyoo-bi ni wa yuubin no {haitatsu/*demae} ga ichi-do shika nai.*
(**b**) We have a pizza delivery service.
ピザの{配達/出前}のサービスを致します。
Piza no {haitatsu/demae} no saabisu o itashimasu.

demand vt. **[for s.o. to ask for s.t. forcefully as if it were one's right]**
1. 〈-ni〉 〈-o〉 **yo⌈okyuu-suru** 〈〜に〉〈〜を〉**要求する** ③ •c **[for s.o. to ask s.o. for s.t. or to do s.t. as if it were one's natural right]** **《require, claim, request, beg, appeal, petition》**

EX. (**a**) The workers demanded a pay raise.
労働者は賃上げを要求した。
Roodoo-sha wa chin'age o yookyuu-shita.
(**b**) The kidnappers demanded a get-away car.
誘拐犯は逃走用の車を要求した。

D

Yuukai-han wa toosoo-yoo no kuruma o yookyuu-shita.

2. ⟨-o⟩ hi⌈tsuyoo to suru ⟨〜を⟩必要とする ③ •c [for s.t./s.o./s.a. to require s.t./s.o./s.a.] ⟪necessitate, need⟫, ⟨-ga⟩ i⌈ru ⟨〜が⟩要る ① [to be necessary/desirable]

EX. (**a**) Operations like this demand the highest degree of care.
このような手術は最大限の注意{を必要とする/が要る}。
Kono yoona shujutsu wa saidai-gen no chuui {o hitsuyoo to suru/ga iru}.
(**b**) Learning a language demands hard work.
語学を学ぶには懸命な努力{を必要とする/が要る}。
Gogaku o manabu ni wa kenmeina doryoku {o hitsuyoo to suru/ga iru}.

— n. **[an act/instance of asking for s.t. forcefully, as if it were one's right]**

1. yo⌈okyuu 要求 •c [asking s.o. for s.t. or to do s.t. as if it were one's natural right] ⟪request, requirement⟫

EX. (**a**) There was strong demand among the people for the resignation of the prime minister.
国民の間で首相の辞任に対する強い要求があった。
Kokumin no aida de shushoo no jinin ni taisuru tsuyoi yookyuu ga atta.
(**b**) The U.S. made repeated demands that the market be opened.
米国は市場を開放するよう繰り返し要求をした。
Beikoku wa shijoo o kaihoo-suru yoo kuri-kaeshi yookyuu o shita.

2. ju⌈yoo 需要 •c [desire for s.t. by people who wish to buy or possess it] ⟪request, want⟫ ↔ kyookyuu 供給 •c

EX. The demand for electric power exceeds the supply.
電力は需要が供給を上回っている。
Denryoku wa juyoo ga kyookyuu o uwa-mawatte iru.

democracy n. **[government by the people, directly or through representatives]**
mi⌈nshu-shu⌉gi 民主主義 •c

EX. That country won its democracy the hard way.
その国は苦労して民主主義を手に入れた。
Sono kuni wa kuroo-shite minshu-shugi o te ni ireta.

democratic adj. **[of/for democracy]**
mi⌈nshu-tekina 民主的な adj(*na*). **•c [of democracy] ↔ dokusai-tekina 独裁的な** adj(*na*). **•c**

EX. (**a**) The company president believes in democratic decision-making.
社長は民主的な意思決定がいいと信じている。
Shachoo wa minshu-tekina ishi-kettei ga ii to shinjite iru.
(**b**) I don't think our procedure for selecting committee members is a very democratic one.
委員会の委員を選考する手続きはあまり民主的だとは思えない。
Iin-kai no iin o senkoo-suru te-tsuzuki wa amari minshu-teki da to wa omoe-nai.

demonstrate vt. **[for s.o. to show the truth of s.t. by reasoning or to describe and explain s.t. (esp. a machine) by using samples or examples]**

1. ⟨-o⟩ ri⌈sshoo-suru ⟨〜を⟩立証する ③ •c [for s.o. to establish the truth of s.t., esp. legally, by using evidence] ⟪prove, substantiate⟫, ⟨-o⟩ sho⌈omei-suru ⟨〜を⟩証明する ③ •c [for s.o. to establish the truth of s.t. on the basis of logic and evidence] ⟪prove, testify, verify⟫

EX. Newton mathematically demonstrated the law of universal gravity.
ニュートンは万有引力の法則を数学的に{立証/証明}した。
Nyuuton wa ban'yuu-inryoku no hoosoku o suugaku-tekini {risshoo/shoomei}-shita.

2. ⟨-o⟩ (jissai ni) V*te* mi⌈se⌉ru ⟨〜を⟩(実際に)V*te*みせる ② [for s.o. to show how s.t. is done or that s.t. is possible by actually doing it]

EX. (**a**) We demonstrated the tea ceremony in front of a group of foreign tourists.
外国人の観光客の前で茶道を実際に行ってみせた。
Gaikoku-jin no kankoo-kyaku no mae de sadoo o jissai ni okonatte miseta.
(**b**) The salesman demonstrated how to operate the new car.
セールスマンは新しい車を実際に運転してみせた。
Seerusu-man wa atarashii kuruma o jissai ni unten-shite miseta.
(**c**) Would you demonstrate how that machine works?
その機械を実際に動かしてみせて下さいませんか。
Sono kikai o jissai ni ugokashite misete kudasaimasen ka.

— vi. **[for s.o. to show one's feelings/views publicly such as in a meeting, etc.] de˥mo o suru デモをする ③ •f [for s.o. to engage in a public display of power or unity in order to press for a demand]**

EX. The workers demonstrated for higher wages.
労働者は賃金の値上げを要求してデモをした。
Roodoo-sha wa chingin no ne-age o yookyuu-shite demo o shita.

demonstration n. **[showing the truth of s.t. by reasoning or describing/explaining by using samples/examples or a public display of support for a cause]**

1. ri⌈sshoo 立証 •c [an act/instance of establishing the truth of s.t. (esp. guilt or innocence)] 《proof, substantiation》, sho⌈omei 証明 •c [an act/instance of proving or authenticating s.t.] 《proof, evidence, substantiation, authentification》

EX. Demonstration of the principles relevant to this theory is difficult.
この理論に関する法則の{立証/証明}は難しい。
Kono riron ni kansuru hoosoku no {risshoo/shoomei} wa muzukashii.

2. ji⌈tsuen 実演 •c [an actual performance of s.t. on stage 《fig. "explanation of s.t. by showing how it actually works"》] 《stage performance》, de⌈monsutore˥eshon デモンストレーション •f [an explanation of s.t by showing how it is actually done]

EX. We will give a demonstration of the new machine tomorrow.
あした、新しい機械の{実演/デモンストレーション}を行います。
Ashita, atarashii kikai no {jitsuen/demonsutoreeshon} o okonaimasu.

3. de˥mo デモ •f [a public display of power or unity in order to press for a demand]

EX. There was a big demonstration yesterday in front of the Parliament building against the new tax law.
きのう国会議事堂前で新しい税法反対の大きなデモがあった。
Kinoo kokkai-gijidoo-mae de atarashii zeihoo hantai no ookina demo ga atta.

dense adj. **[for a group of objects or people to be packed tightly together or for s.t. gaseous such as smoke or fog to be thick]**

1. ko⌈i 濃い adj(*i*). **[filled with fibrous, gaseous, or liquid matter to the extent light is obstructed, making it impossible to see through, or intense in degree of color or taste] 《deep, dark, thick, heavy, strong》 ↔ usui 薄い** adj(*i*).

EX. The airplane was delayed by the dense fog.
飛行機は濃い霧のために遅れた。
Hikoo-ki wa koi kiri no tame ni okureta.

2. mi⌈sshuu-shita N 密集したN •c /〈Vinf. past of *misshuu-suru* ③ crowd/, mi⌈sshuu-shite iru (N) 密集している(N) /〈V*te iru* of *misshuu-suru* ③ crowd/ [be packed together without any room]

EX. Jakarta has a dense population.
ジャカルタは人口が密集している。
Jakaruta wa jinkoo ga misshuu-shite iru.

density n. **[the degree of being dense]**
mi˥tsudo 密度 •c

EX. Japan has a high population density.
日本は人口密度が高い。
Nihon wa jinkoo-mitsudo ga takai.

D

dentist n.
ha⌉-isha 歯医者, shi⌈ka⌉-i⌉ 歯科医 •c ⟨fml⟩

deny vt. **[for s.o. to state that s.t. is not true]**
⟨-o⟩ hi⌈tei-suru ⟨〜を⟩否定する ③ •c ⟪negate, contradict⟫

EX. (**a**) The president denied the rumor.
大統領はうわさを否定した。
Daitooryoo wa uwasa o hitei-shita.
(**b**) There is no denying that Mozart was a genius.
モーツァルトが天才であったことは否定出来ない。
Mootsaruto ga tensai de atta koto wa hitei-dekinai.

depart vi. **[for s.o./s.a./a vehicle to leave a place]**
{⟨-o⟩/⟨-kara⟩} shu⌈ppatsu-suru {⟨〜を⟩/⟨〜から⟩}出発する ③ •c [for s.o./some vehicle to move away from some place at the beginning of a journey] ↔ toochaku-suru 到着する ③ •c; ha⌈ssha-suru 発車する ③ •c [for a train/bus to leave a station, etc.]

EX. (**a**) The airplane departs from Narita.
飛行機は成田から{出発/*発車}する。
*Hikoo-ki wa Narita kara {shuppatsu/ *hassha}-suru.*
(**b**) Hikari 65 will depart from Track No. 14.
ひかり65号は14番線から{出発/発車}します。
Hikari roku-juu-go-goo wa juu-yon-ban-sen kara {shuppatsu/hassha}-shimasu.

department store n. **[a large retail store organized into departments according to merchandise]**
de⌈pa⌉ato デパート •f

departure n. **[an act/instance of leaving]**
shu⌈ppatsu 出発 •c [an act of leaving for a destination/goal] ↔ toochaku 到着 •c; ha⌈ssha 発車 •c [an act/instance of a train/bus leaving], shu⌈kkoo 出港 •c [an act/instance of a ship leaving]

EX. (**a**) The departure of the plane was postponed four hours.
飛行機の{出発/*発車/*出港}は四時間延期された。
*Hikoo-ki no {shuppatsu/*hassha/ *shukkoo} wa yo-jikan enki-sareta.*
(**b**) They blocked the departure of the ship by forceful means.
彼らは船の{出発/出港/*発車}を力づくで阻止した。
*Kare-ra wa fune no {shuppatsu/ shukkoo/*hassha} o chikara-zuku de soshi-shita.*
(**c**) We awaited the departure of the bus for more than an hour.
バスの{出発/発車/*出港}を一時間以上待った。
*Basu no {shuppatsu/hassha/*shukkoo} o ichi-jikan-ijoo matta.*

depend vi. **[to rely on s.o./s.t. for support/ aid or to be determined by s.t. else]**
1. ⟨-ni⟩ ta⌈yo⌉ru ⟨〜に⟩頼る ① [to entrust oneself to s.o./s.t. in the belief that one will receive aid or support from him/her/it] ⟪rely on, count on, fall back on, trust⟫, ⟨-o⟩ a⌈te-ni-suru ⟨〜を⟩当てにする ③ [for s.o. to expect s.t. of s.o./s.t.] ⟪count on, reckon upon, bank on⟫

EX. (**a**) He still depends on his father for money.
彼は金の面でまだ父親{に頼って/を当てにして}いる。
Kare wa kane no men de mada chichi-oya {ni tayotte/o ate-ni-shite} iru.
(**b**) You have only yourself to depend on.
自分しか{頼る/?当てにする}人はいない。
Jibun shika {tayoru/?ate-ni-suru} hito wa inai.
(**c**) The advanced nations now depend on one another for survival.
先進国は現在生き残りのためお互い{に頼って/?を当てにして}いる。
Senshin-koku wa genzai iki-nokori no tame o-tagai {ni tayotte/?o ate-ni-shite} iru.

2. -shidai da 〜次第だ •c [for s.t. to be contingent on s.t. else] ⟪hinge on⟫, ⟨-ni⟩ yo⌈ru ⟨〜に⟩よる ① [for s.t. to be up to s.o./ s.t.], ⟨-ni⟩ ka⌈ka⌉tte iru ⟨〜に⟩かかっている /⟨V *te iru* of *kakaru* ① hang/ ② [for s.t. to hinge on s.t. else], ⟨-ni⟩ yo⌈tte chi⌈gau

〈〜に〉よって違う ① **[for s.t. to differ according to s.o./s.t.]**

EX. (**a**) A: Are we having a picnic tomorrow?
あしたピクニックに行きますか。
Ashita pikunikku ni ikimasu ka.
B: That depends on the weather.
それはお天気{次第です/にかかっています/によります/*によって違います}。
*Sore wa o-tenki {-shidai desu/ni kakatte imasu/ni yorimasu/*ni yotte chigaimasu}.*
(**b**) How one looks at the problem depends on the person.
その問題をどう見るかは人{による/によって違う/次第だ/*にかかっている}。
*Sono mondai o doo miru ka wa hito {ni yoru/ni yotte chigau/-shidai da/*ni kakatte iru}.*

dependable adj. **[to be able to be depended on]**
shi⌈nrai-deki⌉ru (N) **信頼出来る**(N) **[to be able to be trusted]** ⟪**trustworthy**⟫, **ta⌉yori ni naru** (N) **頼りになる**(N) **[can be depended on]**

EX. (**a**) We have dependable information on the matter.
その件については{信頼出来る/?頼りになる}情報を持っている。
Sono ken ni-tsuite wa {shinrai-dekiru/?tayori ni naru} joohoo o motte iru.
(**b**) My new car is not very dependable.
今度の車はあまり{頼りにならない/?信頼出来ない}。
Kondo no kuruma wa amari {tayori ni naranai/?shinrai-dekinai}.

dependent adj. **[relying on s.o./s.t. for support or determined by s.t. else]**
1. 〈**-ni**〉 **ta⌈yo⌉tte iru** (N) 〈〜に〉**頼っている** (N) /〈V *te iru* of *tayoru* ① rely/ **[relying on s.o./s.t.]**

EX. (**a**) He is still dependent on his parents.
彼はまだ両親に頼っている。
Kare wa mada ryooshin ni tayotte iru.
(**b**) Very few students are dependent on their parents for tuition at this college.
この大学では親に学費を頼っている学生は少ない。
Kono daigaku de wa oya ni gakuhi o tayotte iru gakusei wa sukunai.

2. -shidai da 〜次第だ •c [for s.t. to be contingent on s.t. else] ⟪**hinge on**⟫

EX. Success is dependent on one's efforts.
成功は努力次第です。
Seikoo wa doryoku-shidai desu.

—— n. **[a person who depends on s.o. for support]**
fu⌈yoo-ka⌉zoku 扶養家族 •c [a member of a family whom one must support]

EX. I claim two dependents.
私には扶養家族が二人いる。
Watakushi ni wa fuyoo-kazoku ga futari iru.

deposit vt. **[for s.o. to place s.t. in a place for safekeeping]**
〈**-ni**〉 〈**-o**〉 **a⌈zuke⌉ru** 〈〜に〉〈〜を〉**預ける** ② **[for s.o. to ask s.o. else to take care of s.o./s.t./s.a. or to allow a part of one's body to lean against s.t.]** ⟪**leave, trust, entrust**⟫, **yo⌈kin-suru 預金する** ③ **•c [for s.o. to leave money in a bank for interest]**

EX. (**a**) I deposited one million yen in the bank.
私は銀行に百万円{預けた/預金した}。
Watakushi wa ginkoo ni hyaku-man-en {azuketa/yokin-shita}.
(**b**) Please deposit the key in the box at the reception desk when you go out.
お出かけの際は鍵をフロントに{預けて/*預金して}下さい。
*O-dekake no sai wa kagi o furonto ni {azukete/*yokin-shite} kudasai.*

depression n. **[an instance of going to a lower level or a state/place reached as a result of such** ⟪**fig. "a period of low spirits or slow business activity"**⟫**]**
1. te⌈ika 低下 •c [an instance of becoming lower]
2. fu-⌈ke⌉iki 不景気 •c [slow business] ↔ **koo-keiki 好景気 •c**

EX. (**a**) Due to the recent depression, many are out of work.
最近は不景気で失業者が多い。
Saikin wa fu-keiki de shitsugyoo-sha ga ooi.

D

(**b**) A: How's business?
景気はどうですか。
Keiki wa doo desu ka.
B: Not good. We're in a depression, you know.
いや、不景気でね。
Iya, fu-keiki de ne.

3. u⌈tsubyoo うつ病 •c [the state of being in low spirits] ⟪**dejection**⟫

depth n. **[degree of deepness]**
fu⌈ka⌉-sa 深さ /⟨adj(*i*). stem of *fukai* deep + suf. *sa* ness/

D

EX. The depth of the lake is sixty feet.
湖の深さは六十フィートです。
Mizuumi no fuka-sa wa roku-juu-fiito desu.

descendant n. **[an offspring of s.o.]**
shi⌉son 子孫 •c [offspring] ↔ sosen 祖先 •c

EX. Mr. Tokugawa seems to be a descendant of Tokugawa Ieyasu.
徳川さんは徳川家康の子孫らしい。
Tokugawa-san wa Tokugawa Ieyasu no shison rashii.

describe vt. **[to verbally express esp. that which one has seen]**
{⟨-o⟩/⟨-ni-tsuite⟩} **no⌈be⌉ru** {⟨〜を⟩/⟨〜について⟩}**述べる ② [for s.o. to speak/write s.t. in a formal way ⟨w⟩]**, {⟨-o⟩/⟨-ni-tsuite⟩} **ki⌈jutsu-suru** {⟨〜を⟩/⟨について⟩}**記述する ③ •c [to state facts in writing according to the way they have been observed/investigated/experienced]** ⟪**give an account of, make/give a description of**⟫, ⟨-ni⟩ {⟨-o⟩/⟨-ni-tsuite⟩} **se⌈tsumei-suru** ⟨〜に⟩{⟨〜を⟩/⟨〜について⟩}**説明する ③ •c [for s.o. to give an explanation of s.t. to s.o.]** ⟪**explain**⟫, ⟨-o⟩ **byo⌈osha-suru** ⟨〜を⟩**描写する ③ •c [for s.o./a painting/writing/music to objectively express s.t./s.o./s.a. nonverbally]** ⟪**depict, represent, portray**⟫

EX. (**a**) Please describe the facts as they are.
事実をありのままに{述べて/記述して/説明して/描写して}下さい。
Jijitsu o ari-no-mama ni {nobete/kijutsu-shite/setsumei-shite/byoosha-shite} kudasai.
(**b**) He described the new project in his report to the planning committee.
彼は企画委員会への報告書の中で新しいプロジェクトについて{述べた/記述した/説明した/?描写した}。
Kare wa kikaku-iin-kai e no hookoku-sho no naka de atarashii purojekuto ni-tsuite {nobeta/kijutsu-shita/setsumei-shita/?byoosha-shita}.
(**c**) Would you describe the scene of accident?
事故の状況を{述べて/記述して/説明して/描写して}下さい。
Jiko no jookyoo o {nobete/kijutsu-shite/setsumei-shite/byoosha-shite} kudasai.
(**d**) The writer described the psychological state of the girl in detail.
作家は少女の心理状態を細かく{描写した/述べた/説明した/記述した}。
Sakka wa shoojo no shinri-jootai o komakaku {byoosha-shita/nobeta/setsumei-shita/kijutsu-shita}.

description n. **[an act/instance of describing s.t.]**
ki⌈jutsu 記述 •c [a statement of s.t. as a result of observation, investigation or experience] ⟪**account, depiction**⟫, **setsumei 説明 •c [an act/instance of explaining the content of/ reason for/significance of s.t.]** ⟪**account**⟫

EX. (**a**) There is a detailed description of the history of the town in the guide booklet.
案内書に町の歴史の詳しい{記述/説明}があります。
Annai-sho ni machi no rekishi no kuwashii {kijutsu/setsumei} ga arimasu.
(**b**) A concise style is preferred in scientific description.
科学的な{記述/説明}には簡潔なスタイルが好まれる。
Kagaku-tekina {kijutsu/setsumei} ni wa kanketsuna sutairu ga konoma-reru.

desert n. **[a dry, barren sandy area]**
sa⌈baku 砂漠 •c

EX. For days the travelers searched for an oasis in the desert.

旅人は何日間も砂漠の中でオアシスを探した。
Tabi-bito wa nan-nichi-kan mo sabaku no naka de oashisu o sagashita.

—— vt. **[to make a place like a desert《fig. "abandon"》]**
〈-o〉 su⌈teru 〈〜を〉捨てる ② **[for s.o. to let go of s.t. that has become unnecessary or to sever a relationship]《throw away, dump, abandon, discard, give up》↔ 〈-o〉 hirou** 〈〜を〉拾う ①; **〈-o〉 mi-⌈suteru** 〈〜を〉見捨てる ② **[for s.o. to give up s.t./s.o./s.a.]**

EX. I will never desert you.
あなたを{捨てる/見捨てる}ようなことは絶対にしません。
Anata o {suteru/mi-suteru} yoona koto wa zettai ni shimasen.

design n. **[the organization/arrangement of elements in a work]**

1. mo⌉yoo 模様 **•c [an ornamental figure/picture《fig. "the situation as it exists," "appearance"》], de⌈za⌉in** デザイン **•f [ornamental pattern]《pattern》**

EX. (**a**) She chose a butterfly design for her new dress.
彼女は新しいドレスにちょうの{模様/デザイン}を選んだ。
Kanojo wa atarashii doresu ni choo no {moyoo/dezain} o eranda.
(**b**) Many of Japan's traditional designs can be seen on kimono.
着物には日本の伝統的な{模様/デザイン}が多い。
Ki-mono ni wa Nihon no dentoo-tekina {moyoo/dezain} ga ooi.

2. se⌈kkei 設計 **•c [an outline/sketch/plan for an engineering or construction project]**

EX. (**a**) The design of this air terminal is really superb.
この空港の設計は本当にすばらしいですね。
Kono kuukoo no sekkei wa hontoo ni subarashii desu ne.
(**b**) We had to redo the design of the machine.
機械の設計をやり直さなければならなかった。
Kikai no sekkei o yari-naosanakereba naranakatta.

—— vt. **[for s.o. to prepare the plans for s.t.] 〈-o〉 se⌈kkei-suru** 〈〜を〉設計する ③ **•c [for s.o. to make the plans for s.t. to be constructed/made], 〈-o〉 de⌈za⌉in-suru** 〈〜を〉デザインする ③ **•f**

EX. (**a**) My grandfather designed that bridge.
私の祖父があの橋を{設計/デザイン}しました。
Watakushi no sofu ga ano hashi o {sekkei/dezain}-shimashita.
(**b**) Frank Lloyd Wright designed the old Imperial Hotel.
フランク・ロイド・ライトが昔の帝国ホテルを{設計/デザイン}した。
Furanku Roido Raito ga mukashi no Teikoku Hoteru o {sekkei/dezain}-shita.
(**c**) Who designed the new uniform?
新しいユニフォームはだれが{デザイン/*設計}したんですか。
*Atarashii yunifoomu wa dare ga {dezain/*sekkei}-shita n desu ka.*

desirable adj. **[worth having or pleasing] no⌈zomashii** 望ましい adj(*i*). **[having the quality of evoking in one the desire to possess it or for it to be realized]《advisable, preferable》**

EX. (**a**) He married a most desirable woman.
彼は最も望ましい女性と結婚した。
Kare wa mottomo nozomashii josei to kekkon-shita.
(**b**) It is desirable that applicants be able to use a word processor.
応募者はワープロができることが望ましい。
Oobo-sha wa waapuro ga dekiru koto ga nozomashii.
(**c**) It would be desirable for us to be able to settle the matter through negotiation.
その件は話し合いで解決することが望ましい。
Sono ken wa hanashi-ai de kaiketsu-suru koto ga nozomashii.

desire n. **[the mental state of wanting s.t. very badly]**
yo⌈ku⌉ 欲 •c [a strong hope/wish to have/do s.t.] ((**avarice, greed, craving, passion**)), **yo⌈kuboo 欲望 •c [a strong wish to have s.t. one does not have or to do s.t. one cannot presently do]** ((**craving, ambition, appetite**))

EX. (**a**) He has no desire for money.
彼は金銭に対する{欲/欲望}はない。
Kare wa kinsen ni-taisuru {yoku/yokuboo} wa nai.
(**b**) There is no end to man's desire.
人間の{欲/欲望}は果てしないものだ。
Ningen no {yoku/yokuboo} wa hateshinai mono da.

— vt. **[for s.o./s.a. to long for or crave s.t.]**
⟨-o⟩ no⌈zomu ⟨～を⟩望む ① [for s.o. to view a distant place or to want/expect s.t. to happen] ((**want, aspire, hope**))

EX. (**a**) We all desire peace.
我々は皆平和を望んでいる。
Ware-ware wa mina heiwa o nozonde iru.
(**b**) He desired a woman who was beyond his means.
彼は身分不相応な女性を望んだ。
Kare wa mibun-fu-soooona josei o nozonda.

desk n. **[a piece of furniture with a flat top, often with drawers, where one can read, write, etc.]**
tsu⌈kue 机 [an article of furniture for writing, reading, or drawing], de⌉suku デスク •f [an article of furniture used in an office for writing, reading, or drawing]

PHRASE: reception desk *furonto* フロント •f, *uketsuke* 受付; information desk *annai-jo* 案内所 •c

despair n. **[loss or lack of hope]**
ze⌈tsuboo 絶望 •c [loss of hope] ((**hopelessness**))

EX. (**a**) She has been in the depths of despair since the breakup of her marriage.
彼女は結婚に失敗してから絶望のどん底にいる。
Kanojo wa kekkon ni shippai-shite kara zetsuboo no donzoko ni iru.
(**b**) He committed suicide out of despair.
彼は絶望の末自殺してしまった。
Kare wa zetsuboo no sue jisatsu-shite shimatta.

desperate adj. **[reckless due to having little or no hope]**
1. hi⌈sshi no N 必死のN •c [doing one's best] ((**frantic**))

EX. (**a**) The student made a desperate effort to pass the entrance exam.
学生は入学試験に受かるように必死の努力をした。
Gakusei wa nyuugaku-shiken ni ukaru yooni hisshi no doryoku o shita.
(**b**) The soldiers went to the battlefield with a desperate determination.
兵士は必死の覚悟で戦場へ向かった。
Heishi wa hisshi no kakugo de senjoo e mukatta.

2. ze⌈tsuboo-tekina 絶望的な adj(*na*). **•c [for a situation to show no possibility of s.t. good happening]** ((**hopeless**))

EX. The economy of that country is in a desperate state.
あの国の経済は絶望的な状態だ。
Ano kuni no keizai wa zetsuboo-tekina jootai da.

desperately adv. **[most seriously or recklessly due to having little or no hope]**
hi⌈sshi de 必死で •c [for one's life]

EX. (**a**) The escaped prisoner ran desperately to escape the prison guards in pursuit of him.
追い掛けてくる看守から逃れようと脱獄した囚人は必死で走った。
Oi-kakete kuru kanshu kara nogareyoo to datsugoku-shita shuujin wa hisshi de hashitta.
(**b**) The boy swam desperately to save his life.
少年はおぼれまいと必死で泳いだ。
Shoonen wa oboremai to hisshi de oyoida.

dessert n. **[the final course of a meal, usually sweet and consisting of fruit, cake, etc.]**
de⌈za⌉ato デザート •f

EX. (**a**) I'll have ice cream for dessert.

デザートはアイスクリームにします。
Dezaato wa aisu-kuriimu ni shimasu.
(**b**) Sweets are best saved for dessert.
甘いものはデザートに食べるのがいいですね。
Amai mono wa dezaato ni taberu no ga ii desu ne.

destroy vt. **[to reduce s.t. to useless form by violent means, esp. by tearing down or demolishing]**
⟨-o⟩ ha⌈kai-suru ⟨〜を⟩破壊する ③ •c [to render s.t. major, such as a building/system/nature, devoid of its original function and/or into a disintegrated form by forceful means] ⟪break, ruin, wreck, demolish, tear down⟫, ⟨-o⟩ ko⌈wa⌉su ⟨〜を⟩壊す ① [to forcibly change the shape of s.t. and thereby render it useless; to separate s.t. into pieces forcibly and suddenly], ⟨-o⟩ ya⌈ki-sute⌉ru ⟨〜を⟩焼き捨てる ② [for s.o. to burn s.t. down]

EX. (**a**) The earthquake destroyed the entire city.
地震は都市全体を{破壊した/??壊した/*焼き捨てた}。
*Jishin wa toshi-zentai o {hakai-shita/??kowashita/*yaki-suteta}.*
(**b**) They destroyed the old building with dynamite.
ダイナマイトで古い建物を{壊した/?破壊した/*焼き捨てた}。
*Dainamaito de furui tate-mono o {kowashita/?hakai-shita/*yaki-suteta}.*
(**c**) She destroyed the letter from her old boyfriend.
彼女は昔の男友達からの手紙を{焼き捨てた/*破壊した/*壊した}。
*Kanojo wa mukashi no otoko-tomodachi kara no tegami o {yaki-suteta/*hakai-shita/*kowashita}.*

detail n. **[an individual/minute part(s) of s.t.]**
sho⌈osai 詳細 •c [minor points of s.t.] ⟪particulars⟫, ku⌈washi⌉i koto 詳しいこと [s.t. which is detailed] ⟪particulars⟫

EX. (**a**) The news report did not give details of the incident.
ニュースは事件の{詳細/詳しいこと}を報じなかった。
Nyuusu wa jiken no {shoosai/kuwashii koto} o hoojinakatta.
(**b**) I will give you the details in a letter.
{詳細/詳しいこと}は手紙に書きます。
{Shoosai/kuwashii koto} wa tegami ni kakimasu.

detailed adj. **[giving or showing minute particulars of s.t.]**
ku⌈washi⌉i 詳しい adj(*i*). **[(capable of) going into detail]**

EX. Please obtain as much detailed information as possible.
出来るだけ多くの詳しい情報を集めて下さい。
Dekiru dake ooku no kuwashii joohoo o atsumete kudasai.

PHRASE: in detail *kuwashiku* 詳しく, *shoosaini* 詳細に •c

EX. (**a**) He explained the rules in detail.
彼は規則を{詳しく/詳細に}説明した。
Kare wa kisoku o {kuwashiku/shoosaini} setsumei-shita.
(**b**) He narrated the story in great detail.
彼は非常に{詳しく/詳細に}その話をした。
Kare wa hijooni {kuwashiku/shoosaini} sono hanashi o shita.

detect vt. **[to discover s.t. hidden/unclear]**
⟨-o⟩ mi⌈tsukeru ⟨〜を⟩見つける ② [for s.o. to cause s.o./s.t./s.a. hidden/lost/unknown to come to light or be seen], ⟨-o⟩ ha⌈kken-suru ⟨〜を⟩発見する ③ •c [for s.o. to find out for the first time the existence, value, effect, etc., of s.t. not yet known to the world] ⟪discover⟫

EX. (**a**) She detected small flaws in the jewel.
彼女は宝石に小さなきずを{見つけた/発見した}。
Kanojo wa hooseki ni chiisana kizu o {mitsuketa/hakken-shita}.
(**b**) The police dog detected where the drugs were hidden.
警察犬は麻薬の隠し場所を{見つけた/発見した}。
Keisatsu-ken wa mayaku no kakushi-basho o {mitsuketa/hakken-shita}.

D

(c) Illegal laborers are difficult to detect.
不法労働者は{見つける/?発見する}のが難しい。
Fuhoo-roodoo-sha wa {mitsukeru/ ?hakken-suru} no ga muzukashii.

detective n. **[a person who investigates crimes]**
ta⌈ntei 探偵 •c

EX. (a) When I was a child, I read many detective stories.
子供のころ探偵小説をたくさん読みました。
Kodomo no koro tantei-shoosetsu o takusan yomimashita.
(b) She had her husband followed by a detective.
彼女は夫を探偵につけさせた。
Kanojo wa otto o tantei ni tsuke-saseta.

determination n. **[a firm intention]**
ke⌉tsui 決意 •c, [knowing what one must do and making up one's mind to carry it out] ((**resolution**)), **ke⌉sshin 決心 •c [resolving to take a particular course of action with regard to s.t. of importance]** ((**resolution**))

EX. (a) His determination to study abroad was absolutely firm.
彼の留学しようという{決意/決心}は非常に堅かった。
Kare no ryuugaku-shiyoo to iu {ketsui/ kesshin} wa hijooni katakatta.
(b) No one can influence his strong determination to run for office.
だれも彼の立候補しようという強い{決意/決心}を変えられない。
Dare-mo kare no rikkooho-shiyoo to iu tsuyoi {ketsui/kesshin} o kae-rarenai.

determine vt. **[for s.o. to settle or decide s.t. definitely or for s.t. to be a decisive factor influencing s.t.]**
⟨-o⟩ ki⌈meru ⟨〜を⟩決める ② [for s.o. to make a judgment as to which of a number of alternatives is best in a given situation and resolve to act accordingly] ((**decide, fix, settle, resolve**)), **⟨-o⟩ ke⌈ttei-suru ⟨〜を⟩決定する ③ •c [for s.o. to decide s.t.]**

EX. (a) We have to determine a date for the wedding.
結婚式の日取りを{決めなければ/決定しなければ}ならない。
Kekkon-shiki no hi-dori o {kimenakereba/kettei-shinakereba} naranai.
(b) The economic policy of the current administration will undoubtedly determine the future of the country.
現政権の経済政策が国の将来を{決める/決定する}だろう。
Gen-seikin no keizai-seisaku ga kuni no shoorai o {kimeru/kettei-suru} daroo.
(c) Let's determine what to do first.
まず何をするべきかを{決めましょう/?決定しましょう}。
Mazu nani o suru-beki ka o {kimemashoo/?kettei-shimashoo}.

—— vi. **[for s.o. to make a decision]**
⟨-ni⟩ ki⌈meru ⟨〜に⟩決める ② [for s.o. to settle on one of a number of alternatives], ke⌉sshin (o) suru 決心(を)する ③ •c [for s.o. to resolve to take a particular course of action with regard to s.t. of importance], ⟨-ni⟩ suru ⟨〜に⟩する ③ [to decide on one of a number of alternatives or on a particular course of action to be taken]

EX. (a) We determined that the wedding would best be held in May.
五月に挙式する{ことに決めた/ことにした/*決心をした}。
*Go-gatsu ni kyoshiki-suru {koto ni kimeta/koto ni shita/*kesshin o shita}.*
(b) I determined to go abroad to study.
僕は留学する{ことに決めた/ことにした/決心をした}。
Boku wa ryuugaku-suru {koto ni kimeta/koto ni shita/kesshin o shita}.

detour n. **[a roundabout way, especially one used temporarily in place of the main one]**
ma⌈wari⌉-michi 回り道 [a roundabout way], u⌈kai⌉-ro 迂回路 •c

EX. There's a detour ahead on this road.
この道はこの先に{回り道/迂回路}がある。
Kono michi wa kono saki ni {mawari-

| *michi/ukai-ro} ga aru.*

Detroit n.
De⸢toro⸣ito デトロイト •f

develop vt. **[to bring s.t./s.o. to a more advanced/effective state ⟪fig. "cause to grow/expand," "cause to come into being," "put film into chemicals to cause photographs to become visible"⟫]**

1. ⟨-o⟩ ha⸢ttatsu-saseru ⟨～を⟩発達させる /⟨causative of *hattatsu-suru* ③ develop/ ② •c [to cause s.t./s.o. to reach a more mature, advanced stage]

EX. | Japanese ingenuity played a major role in developing the semiconductor industry in Japan.
日本人の器用さが半導体産業を発達させるのに大事な役割を果たした。
Nihon-jin no kiyoo-sa ga han-dootai-sangyoo o hattatsu-saseru no ni daijina yakuwari o hatashita.

2. ⟨-o⟩ ka⸢ihatsu-suru ⟨～を⟩開発する ③ •c [for s.o. to convert land or natural resources into a form beneficial for human life and enterprise ⟪fig. "make s.t. practical through research, etc."⟫] ⟪exploit, cultivate⟫

EX. | (**a**) We must develop alternative sources of energy quickly.
我々は早急に代替エネルギー源を開発しなければならない。
Ware-ware wa sookyuu ni daitai-enerugii gen o kaihatsu shinakereba naranai.
(**b**) Scientists are trying to develop a new theory of gravitation.
科学者は引力に関する新しい理論を開発しようとしています。
Kagaku-sha wa inryoku ni-kansuru atarashii riron o kaihatsu-shiyoo to shite imasu.

3. ⟨-o⟩ ge⸢nzoo-suru ⟨～を⟩現像する ③ •c [for s.o. to make photographs in a film visible by chemical means]

EX. | Please develop this film as soon as possible.
このフィルムをできるだけ早く現像して下さい。
Kono fuirumu o dekiru dake hayaku genzoo-shite kudasai.

— vi. **[to grow into a more advanced/effective state ⟪fig. "to grow or expand," "to come into being," "for a role of film to be turned into a set of photos"⟫]**
ha⸢ttatsu-suru 発達する ③ •c [for s.t. to reach a more mature, advanced stage], ⟪grow, progress, advance⟫, ha⸢tten-suru 発展する ③ •c [for s.t. to move into a more advanced stage and spread over a wider area] ⟪grow, expand extend, prosper⟫

EX. | (**a**) Modern Tokyo developed out of a castle town called Edo.
現代の東京は江戸と呼ばれた城下町から{発展/?発達}した。
Gendai no Tookyoo wa Edo to yoba-reta jooka-machi kara {hatten/?hattatsu}-shita.
(**b**) Most major electronic producers developed from small companies.
多くの大手電子機器メーカーは小さな会社から{発展/*発達}した。
*Ooku no oote-denshi-kiki-meekaa wa chiisana kaisha kara {hatten/*hattatsu}-shita.*
(**c**) In Tokyo, the public transportation system is highly developed.
東京は公共の交通機関が{発達/*発展}している。
*Tookyoo wa kookyoo no kootsuu-kikan ga {hattatsu/*hatten}-shite iru.*
(**d**) Let's see how the situation develops.
事態がどう{発展/*発達}するか見守ってみよう。
*Jitai ga doo {hatten/*hattatsu}-suru ka mi-mamotte miyoo.*

development n. **[an act/instance of developing]**

1. ha⸢ttatsu 発達 •c [an instance of s.t. reaching a mature, advanced stage] ⟪growth, progress, advance⟫, ha⸢tten 発展 •c [an instance of moving into a more advanced stage accompanied by a spreading over a wider area] ⟪growth, expansion, enlargement⟫

EX. | (**a**) The rapid development of the

D

information sector of the economy is a relatively recent phenomenon.
情報産業の急速な{発達/発展}は比較的最近の現象です。
Joohoo-sangyoo no kyuusokuna {hattatsu/hatten} wa hikaku-teki saikin no genshoo desu.
(**b**) The topic of his research was the history of urban development.
彼の研究の題目は都市の{発展/?発達}の歴史についてです。
Kare no kenkyuu no daimoku wa toshi no {hatten/?hattatsu} no rekishi ni-tsuite desu.
(**c**) I am studying the development of transportation systems in large cities.
私は大都市交通機関の{発達/発展}について研究をしています。
Watakushi wa dai-toshi-kootsuu-kikan no {hattatsu/hatten} ni-tsuite kenkyuu o shite imasu.
(**d**) The development of child intelligence cannot be accurately measured.
子供の知能の{発達/*発展}は正確には測れない。
*Kodomo no chinoo no {hattatsu/*hatten} wa seikakuni wa hakare-nai.*

2. ka⌈ihatsu 開発 •c [an act/instance of converting land or natural resources into a form beneficial for human life and enterprise 《fig "making s.t. practical through research, etc."》] 《exploitation, cultivation》

EX. (**a**) The development of new medicines is very costly.
新しい薬の開発は大変金がかかる。
Atarashii kusuri no kaihatsu wa taihen kane ga kakaru.
(**b**) The development of new energy resources is something to be greatly desired.
新しいエネルギー資源の開発が大いに望まれる。
Atarashii enerugii-shigen no kaihatsu ga ooi ni nozoma-reru.

3. ge⌈nzoo 現像 •c [putting film into chemicals to make photographs visible]

EX. This store handles film development, printing, and enlargement.
この店ではフイルムの現像、焼きつけ、引き伸ばしを扱っている。
Kono mise de wa fuirumu no genzoo, yaki-tsuke, hiki-nobashi o atsukatte iru.

device n. **[s.t. made for a particular purpose, usu. mechanical]**
so⌉ochi 装置 •c [a piece of apparatus installed for some purpose] 《equipment, apparatus》

EX. (**a**) The safety device failed to work.
安全装置が作動しなかった。
Anzen-soochi ga sadoo-shinakatta.
(**b**) Human beings come into this world with a so-called language acquisition device.
人間はいわゆる言語獲得装置をもってこの世の中に生まれて来る。
Ningen wa iwayuru gengo-kakutoku-soochi o motte kono yo-no-naka ni umarete kuru.
(**c**) A thermostat is a device which automatically regulates the temperature of a certain spatial area.
サーモスタットとはある空間の温度を自動的に調節するための装置である。
Saamosutatto to wa aru kuukan no ondo o jidoo-tekini choosetsu-suru tame no soochi dearu.

devil n. **[any evil spirit, esp. Satan]**
a⌉kuma 悪魔 •c ↔ tenshi 天使 •c

devote vt. **[for s.o. to set s.t. apart for, or appropriate to, some purpose/cause/activity]**

1. ⟨-ni⟩ ⟨-o⟩ sa⌈sageru ⟨～に⟩⟨～を⟩捧げる ② [for s.o. to give s.t. to a deity or s.o. in the position of nobility 《fig. "give up everything one has to s.o. one respects from the heart"》]

EX. (**a**) Peter devoted his life to scholarship.
ピーターは学問に一生を捧げた。
Piitaa wa gakumon ni isshoo o sasageta.
(**b**) She devoted her career to welfare work.
彼女は自分のキャリアを福祉事業に捧げた。
Kanojo wa jibun no kyaria o fukushi-

jigyoo ni sasageta.

2. ⟨**-ni**⟩ ⟨**-o**⟩ **a⌈teru** ⟨〜に⟩⟨〜を⟩あてる ② **[for s.o. to cause s.t. to make sudden and direct contact with s.t. forming a narrow target area《fig. "apply," "place," "succeed," "expose," "assign," "allocate," "appropriate"》]**

㊅ "appropriate"▷充てる, otherwise ▷当てる

EX. He devotes much time to church work.
彼は教会の仕事に多くの時間を充てている。
Kare wa kyookai no shigoto ni ooku no jikan o atete iru.

diagram n. **[a drawing/plan that outlines and explains the parts, operation, etc., of s.t.]**
zu⌈hyoo 図表 **•c [a drawing presenting a graphic representation of facts and figures]**《**chart, table**》, **zu** 図 **•c**《**drawing**》

EX. (**a**) Let me illustrate the point with a diagram.
この点を{図表/図}を使って説明しましょう。
Kono ten o {zuhyoo/zu} o tsukatte setsumei-shimashoo.
(**b**) I have to look at the wiring diagram before attempting to fix this.
修理に取り掛かる前に配線{図/*図表}を見る必要がある。
*Shuuri ni tori-kakaru mae ni haisen-{zu/*zuhyoo} o miru hitsuyoo ga aru.*

dial n. **[a graduated disk on a radio for tuning in to stations or a rotatable disk on a telephone]**
da⌈iyaru ダイヤル **•f**

EX. (**a**) The dial on the radio was set for FEN.
ラジオのダイヤルはFENにセットしてあった。
Rajio no daiyaru wa efu-ii-enu ni setto-shite atta.
(**b**) The dial telephone is being fast replaced by the push button phone.
ダイヤル電話は急速にプッシュボタン方式に代わりつつある。
Daiyaru denwa wa kyuusokuni pusshu-botan-hooshiki ni kawari-tsutsu aru.

— vt. **[for s.o. to call s.o. on the phone]** ⟨**-ni**⟩ **de⌈nwa-suru** ⟨〜に⟩電話する ③ **•c [for s.o. to make a contact with s.o. by telephone]**, ⟨**-ni**⟩ **de⌈nwa o ka⌈ke⌉ru** ⟨〜に⟩電話をかける ② **[for s.o. to call s.o. by telephone]**

EX. To call the police, dial 110.
警察を呼ぶには110番に{電話する/電話をかける}ことです。
Keisatsu o yobu ni wa hyaku-too-ban ni {denwa-suru/denwa o kakeru} koto desu.

dialect n. **[the form of a language peculiar to a particular region, social group, etc.]**
ho⌈oge⌉n 方言 **•c**

EX. (**a**) How many dialects are there of English?
英語にはいくつの方言がありますか。
Eigo ni wa ikutsu no hoogen ga arimasu ka.
(**b**) Some Japanese are fluent in many Chinese dialects.
多くの中国語の方言に堪能な日本人がいる。
Ooku no Chuugoku-go no hoogen ni tannoona Nihon-jin ga iru.
(**c**) There are a number of dialects in Japan.
日本には方言がたくさんある。
Nihon ni wa hoogen ga takusan aru.

dialogue n. **[a conversation between two or more persons in a play/novel/lesson]**
ta⌈iwa 対話 **•c [the act of two persons talking face to face]**《**conversation**》, **da⌉iaroogu** ダイアローグ **•f**

EX. (**a**) The dialogue in 'Lesson One' is too long.
第一課の{対話/ダイアローグ}は長すぎる。
Dai-ik-ka no {taiwa/daiaroogu} wa naga-sugiru.
(**b**) There's hardly any dialogue between the couple in the play.
その劇では夫婦の間にほとんど{対話/*ダイアローグ}がない。
*Sono geki de wa fuufu no aida ni hotondo {taiwa/*daiaroogu} ga nai.*

diamond n. **[brilliant, crystalline carbon of extreme hardness or a gem made from this《fig. "lozenge figure," "baseball infield"》]**

1. da⌈iyamo⌉ndo ダイヤモンド •f, da⌉iya ダイヤ •f [mineral or gem]
2. hi⌈shi-gata 菱形 [lozenge]
3. na⌈iya 内野 •c [baseball infield], da⌈iyamo⌉ndo ダイヤモンド •f

diary n. [a daily writing of one's experiences]
ni⌈kki 日記 •c ((journal))

EX. (a) Anne Frank kept a detailed diary of her experiences.
アンネ・フランクは自分の経験を詳しく日記に残した。
Anne Furanku wa jibun no keiken o kuwashiku nikki ni nokoshita.
(b) Keeping a diary will help with your language study.
日記を書き続けると言葉の勉強の役に立つ。
Nikki o kaki-tsuzukeru to kotoba no benkyoo no yaku ni tatsu.

D

dictionary n. [a book containing words of a language with their pronunciation, meanings, etc.]
ji⌉sho 辞書 •c [a book which arranges words of a language in an easy-to-find fashion with their pronunciation, meaning, usage, etc.] ((lexicon)), ji⌈ten 辞典 •c ⟨fml⟩ ((lexicon)), ji⌈biki 字引

NOTE: *Jiten* is typically used in compounds. *Jibiki* sounds rather old-fashioned today although it is very much active in expressions like *iki-jibiki* "a walking dictionary."

EX. (a) This is an English-Japanese dictionary.
これは英和{辞典/*辞書/*字引}です。
*Kore wa Ei-Wa-{jiten/*jisho/*jibiki} desu.*
(b) Before class, look up all difficult words in your dictionary.
授業の前に難しい単語を全部{辞書/辞典/字引}で調べていらっしゃい。
Jugyoo no mae ni muzukashii tango o zenbu {jisho/jiten/jibiki} de shirabete irasshai.
(c) It takes time to compile a dictionary.
どんな{辞書/辞典/字引}でも編集に時間がかかる。
Donna {jisho/jiten/jibiki} demo henshuu ni jikan ga kakaru.
(d) I received a dictionary from my father as a going-to-school present.
父から入学祝いに{辞書/辞典/字引}をもらった。
Chichi kara nyuugaku-iwai ni {jisho/jiten/jibiki} o moratta.

PHRASE: walking dictionary *iki-jibiki* 生き字引

die vi. [to stop living]
shi⌈nu 死ぬ ① ↔ ikiru 生きる ②

EX. (a) My father died rather young.
父は若くして死んだ。
Chichi wa wakaku-shite shinda.
(b) Her pet dog died in a traffic accident.
彼女が飼っていた犬は交通事故で死んだ。
Kanojo ga katte ita inu wa kootsuu-jiko de shinda.

diet[1] n. [what one usually eats or a selection of food prescribed to lose weight]
1. sho⌈ku 食 •c [eating a meal, food] ((food, meal)), sho⌈kuji 食事 •c [the act of a person's eating in order to sustain oneself] ((meal))

EX. (a) A low-salt diet is strongly recommended for hypertension patients.
高血圧の患者には減塩{食/*食事}を強く勧める。
*Koo-ketsuatsu no kanja ni wa gen'en-{shoku/*shokuji} o tsuyoku susumeru.*
(b) You'd better get on a high-protein diet.
高たん白の{食事/*食}をとった方がいいですよ。
*Koo-tanpaku no {shokuji/*shoku} o totta hoo ga ii desu yo.*
(c) A balanced diet is necessary for one's health.
健康のためにはバランスのとれた{食事/*食}が大切だ。
*Kenkoo no tame ni wa baransu no toreta {shokuji/*shoku} ga taisetsu da.*

2. sho⌈kuji-se⌉igen 食事制限 •c [a plan of restricted food intake for medical reasons or to lose weight], da⌉ietto ダイエット •f [a plan of restricted food intake to lose weight]

EX. (a) She has diabetes so she is on a diet.

彼女は糖尿病のため{食事制限/?ダイエット}中です。
Kanojo wa toonyoo-byoo no tame {shokuji-seigen/?daietto}-chuu desu.
(**b**) To lose weight you must go on a stricter diet.
体重を減らすにはもっと厳しい{食事制限/ダイエット}をしなくてはならない。
Taijuu o herasu ni wa motto kibishii {shokuji-seigen/daietto} o shinakute wa naranai.

diet[2] n. **[the legislative body of Japan]**
ko⌈kkai 国会 •c [a constitutionally established legislative body comprised of representatives elected by the people]

EX. (**a**) The Diet is now in session.
国会は今会期中です。
Kokkai wa ima kaiki-chuu desu.
(**b**) There was a demonstration yesterday near the Diet building.
きのう国会議事堂の近くでデモがあった。
Kinoo kokkai-gijidoo no chikaku de demo ga atta.

differ vi. **[to be different]**
(⟨-to⟩) chi⌈gau (⟨〜と⟩)違う ① [to be not the same as s.t./s.o./s.a. ⟪fig. "be mistaken," "disagree with," "wrong"⟫] ⟪unlike, run counter to, wrong, no⟫, ⟨-to⟩ ko⌈tona⌉ru ⟨〜と⟩異なる ① [to have some property which is not the same as another] ⟪different⟫ ↔ ⟨-to⟩ onaji ⟨〜と⟩同じ

EX. (**a**) Her idea differed from his.
彼女の考えは彼のとは{違った/異なった}。
Kanojo no kangae wa kare no to wa {chigatta/kotonatta}.
(**b**) My interpretation of the problem differs from the standard view.
その問題に対する私の解釈は標準的な見解とは{違う/異なる}。
Sono mondai ni taisuru watakushi no kaishaku wa hyoojun-tekina kenkai to wa {chigau/kotonaru}.

difference n. **[the state of being different or a respect in which s.t./s.o./s.a. is different from another]**
chi⌈gai 違い /⟨V*masu* of *chigau* ① differ/ [the state of being different or a respect in which s.t./s.o./s.a. is different from another], so⌈oi⌉-ten 相違点 •c [a point in which two/more things are mutually different] ⟪disparity⟫

EX. (**a**) There are many differences between Japanese and English, but there are some similarities, too.
日本語と英語では{違い/相違点}も多いが類似点もある。
Nihon-go to eigo de wa {chigai/sooi-ten} mo ooi ga ruiji-ten mo aru.
(**b**) Let's now turn to some of the cultural differences between the two countries.
今度は二国間の文化の{違い/相違点}をいくつか取り上げてみましょう。
Kondo wa ni-koku-kan no bunka no {chigai/sooi-ten} o ikutsu-ka tori-agete mimashoo.

different adj. **[not the same, or various]**
1. ⟨-to⟩ chi⌈gau N ⟨〜と⟩違うN [to be dissimilar from another or to be mistaken], ⟨-to⟩ chi⌈gatta N ⟨〜と⟩違ったN /⟨Vinf. past of *chigau* ① differ/ ⟪dissimilar⟫, ⟨-to⟩ chi⌈gatte iru (N) ⟨〜と⟩違っている(N) /⟨V*te iru* of *chigau* ① differ/ ②, ⟨-to⟩ ko⌈tona⌉ru N ⟨〜と⟩異なるN [not to be the same as] ⟪non-identical⟫, ⟨-to⟩ ko⌈tonatta N ⟨〜と⟩異なったN /⟨Vinf. past of *kotonaru* ① differ/, ⟨-to⟩ ko⌈tona⌉tte iru (N) ⟨〜と⟩異なっている(N) /⟨V*te iru* of *kotonaru* ① differ/ ②

EX. (**a**) The other party had a different idea about the issue.
相手側はそれについて{違う/違った/異なる/異なった/*違っている/*異なっている}意見を持っていた。
*Aite-gawa wa sore ni-tsuite {chigau/chigatta/kotonaru/kotonatta/*chigatte iru/*kotonatte iru} iken o motte ita.*
(**b**) Their culture is different from ours.
彼らの文化は我々のとは{違って/異なって}いる。
Kare-ra no bunka wa ware-ware no to wa {chigatte/kotonatte} iru.

D

2. i⌈ro-irona 色々な adj(*na*). **[of many kinds]** **《various, diverse, a variety of》, sa⌈ma⌉-zamana 様々な** adj(*na*). **[of various qualities/kinds]**

EX. (**a**) This store has many different kinds of stationery.
この店には{色々な/様々な}文房具が置いてある。
Kono mise ni wa {iro-irona/sama-zamana} bunboo-gu ga oite aru.
(**b**) There are people of many different nationalities living together in the dormitory.
寮には{色々な/様々な}国の人が一緒に住んでいる。
Ryoo ni wa {iro-irona/sama-zamana} kuni no hito ga issho ni sunde iru.

D

differently adv. **[not in the same way]**
be⌈tsu no ho⌈ohoo de 別の方法で n.+prt. **[by other means], chi⌈gau ho⌈ohoo de 違う方法で** n.+prt. **[by means of a dissimilar method]**

EX. I'd do it differently.
僕なら{別の/違う}方法でやるよ。
Boku nara {betsu no/chigau} hoohoo de yaru yo.

difficult adj. **[hard to do or requiring much labor or skill]**
mu⌈zukashii 難しい adj(*i*). **[requiring much time and effort to understand/solve/complete, fussy, particular]** **《hard》, ko⌉nnanna 困難な** adj(*na*). **•c [hard to solve and annoying]** ↔ **yasashii 易しい** adj(*i*)., **yooina 容易な** adj(*na*). **•c**

EX. (**a**) The Japanese language is not that difficult to learn.
日本語を習うのはそんなに{難しく/困難では}ありません。
Nihon-go o narau no wa sonnani {muzukashiku/konnan dewa} arimasen.
(**b**) Compiling a dictionary is a difficult task.
辞書の編集は{難しい/困難な}仕事だ。
Jisho no henshuu wa {muzukashii/konnanna} shigoto da.
(**c**) It was a difficult decision to make.
それは{難しい/困難な}決定だった。
Sore wa {muzukashii/konnanna} kettei datta.
(**d**) That teacher's exams are always difficult.
あの先生の試験はいつも{難しい/*困難だ}。
*Ano sensei no shiken wa itsu-mo {muzukashii/*konnan da}.*

difficulty n. **[the fact/condition of being difficult]**
mu⌈zukashi⌉-sa 難しさ /〈adj(*i*). stem of *muzukashii* difficult + suf. *sa* ness/ [the state of being difficult or the degree to which s.t. is difficult], ko⌉nnan 困難 •c [the state of being hard to solve and annoying or troublesome] 《trouble, hardship, suffering, distress, adversity》

EX. (**a**) She had no difficulty learning how to drive.
彼女は車の運転を覚えるのに{難しさ/困難}を感じなかった。
Kanojo wa kuruma no unten o oboeru no ni {muzukashi-sa/konnan} o kanjinakatta.
(**b**) The company overcame many difficulties and grew into a major corporation.
その会社は多くの{困難/*難しさ}に打ち勝って大企業に成長した。
*Sono kaisha wa ooku no {konnan/*muzukashi-sa} ni uchi-katte dai-kigyoo ni seichoo-shita.*

PHRASE: without difficulty *kantanni* 簡単に **•c** 《with ease》

dig vt. **[for s.o./s.a. to make a hole, tunnel, etc., by removing ground 《fig. "thrust a sharp object into s.t.," "search"》]**
〈-o〉 ho⌉ru 〈〜を〉掘る ① [for s.o./s.a. to create a hole in s.t. hard in order to find s.t.] 《excavate, drive, bore, drill, scoop out》

EX. (**a**) They dug a tunnel between Honshu and Hokkaido.
本州と北海道の間にトンネルを掘った。
Honshuu to Hokkaidoo no aida ni tonneru o hotta.
(**b**) Workers were digging holes in the road.
作業員たちが道に穴を掘っていた。

Sagyoo-in-tachi ga michi ni ana o hotte ita.

digestion n. **[the process of changing food taken into the body into an absorbable form]**
sho⌈oka 消化 •c
EX. Digestion takes place in stages from the mouth to the intestines.
消化は口から腸まで段階を経て行われる。
Shooka wa kuchi kara choo made dankai o hete okonawa-reru.

dignity n. **[an honorable manner, behavior, or quality]**
i⌈gen 威厳 •c [the impression one receives of s.o.'s power and majesty] ⟪**majesty, stateliness**⟫, **so⌈ngen 尊厳 •c [possession of inviolable authority]** ⟪**majesty, sanctity**⟫
EX. (**a**) He was a man of dignity.
彼は{威厳/*尊厳}のある男だった。
*Kare wa {igen/*songen} no aru otoko datta.*
(**b**) The dignity of a human being must be respected.
人は人間としての{尊厳/*威厳}を尊重されるべきだ。
*Hito wa ningen to-shite no {songen/*igen} o sonchoo-sareru-beki da.*
(**c**) He was able to face death with dignity.
彼は{尊厳/??威厳}をもって死を迎えることが出来た。
Kare wa {songen/??igen} o motte shi o mukaeru koto ga dekita.

diligent adj. **[hard-working]**
ki⌈nbenna 勤勉な adj(*na*). **•c** ⟪**industrious, hardworking, laborious**⟫ ↔ **taidana 怠惰な** adj(*na*). **•c**
EX. (**a**) The Japanese are said to be a diligent people.
日本人は勤勉な国民だと言われている。
Nihon-jin wa kinbenna kokumin da to iwa-rete iru.
(**b**) In general, American college students are diligent.
一般にアメリカ人の大学生は勤勉です。
Ippan ni Amerika-jin no daigaku-sei wa kinben desu.

dimension n. **[any measurable extent, such as the length, width, or depth of s.t. or, in the plural, the measurements of s.t. in length, width, and depth** ⟪**fig. "plane"**⟫**]**
1. su⌈npoo 寸法 •c [a quantity found by measuring] ⟪**measurements, size**⟫
EX. I'd like to know the dimensions of that box.
あの箱の寸法が知りたいのですが。
Ano hako no sunpoo ga shiri-tai no desu ga.
2. ji⌈gen 次元 •c [an aspect of a situation, problem, physical object, etc.]
EX. Time is treated as a fourth dimension in theoretical physics.
理論物理学では時間は第四次元として扱われる。
Riron-butsuri-gaku de wa jikan wa dai-yo-jigen to-shite atsukawa-reru.

dine vi. **[to eat dinner]**
sho⌈kuji o suru 食事をする ③ •c [for s.o. to have a meal]
EX. Will you dine with me tonight?
今晩一緒に食事をしませんか。
Konban issho ni shokuji o shimasen ka.

dining n. **[eating dinner]**
sho⌈kuji 食事 •c [the act of a person's eating in order to sustain oneself]
PHRASE: dining car *shokudoo-sha* 食堂車 •c, dining hall *shokudoo* 食堂 •c

dinner n. **[the main meal of the day, often in the evening]**
yu⌈ushoku 夕食 •c [the evening meal ⟨fml⟩], **ba⌈n-go⌉han 晩御飯 [the evening meal]**
EX. (**a**) We had steak for dinner.
{夕食/晩御飯}にステーキを食べた。
{Yuushoku/Ban-gohan} ni suteeki o tabeta.
(**b**) We invited some friends over for dinner.
友達を{夕食/晩御飯}に招待した。
Tomodachi o {yuushoku/ban-gohan} ni shootai-shita.

diplomacy n. **[the conduct of foreign relations]**
ga⌈ikoo 外交 •c ⟪**foreign policy**⟫

EX. (**a**) We should settle the issue through diplomacy.
我々はその問題を外交で解決すべきだ。
Ware-ware wa sono mondai o gaikoo de kaiketsu-su-beki da.
(**b**) Diplomacy is one of his areas of strength.
外交は彼の得意の分野だ。
Gaikoo wa kare no tokui no bun'ya da.

diplomat n. **[a government official representative engaged in international diplomacy]**
ga⌈iko⌉o-kan 外交官 **•c**

EX. (**a**) When I was young, I wanted to be a diplomat.
若いころは外交官になりたいと思っていた。
Wakai koro wa gaikoo-kan ni nari-tai to omotte ita.
(**b**) My grandfather was Japan's first diplomat.
私の祖父は日本で最初の外交官でした。
Watakushi no sofu wa Nihon de saisho no gaikoo-kan deshita.

direct adj. **[not roundabout/interrupted 《fig. "frank"》]**
1. cho⌈kusetsu no N 直接のN **•c [not indirect, straight]** 《**straight, immediate**》

EX. (**a**) Is there a direct flight from Detroit to Tokyo?
デトロイトから東京まで直接の便がありますか。
Detoroito kara Tookyoo made chokusetsu no bin ga arimasu ka.

NOTE: The above is more naturally expressed as follows: *Detoroito kara Tookyoo made no chokkoo-bin ga arimasu ka.*

(**b**) We have no direct connection with the matter.
その事件とは直接の関係はありません。
Sono jiken to wa chokusetsu no kankei wa arimasen.

2. so⌈tchokuna 率直な adj(*na*). **•c [for s.o. to be straightforward about the truth and for one's actions to be typical of that person]**

EX. Thank you for being direct in your advice to me.
率直なご忠告をありがとうございます。
Sotchokuna go-chuukoku o arigatoo gozaimasu.

— vt. **[to enable s.o. to go directly to a goal by pointing to it or giving him/her instructions]**
1. (⟨**-ni**⟩) ⟨**-o**⟩ **shi⌈doo-suru** (⟨〜に⟩)⟨〜を⟩指導する ③ **•c [for s.o. to teach and guide s.o.]** 《**guide, lead, instruct**》

EX. (**a**) The President directed the nation through a difficult time.
大統領は国民を指導して困難な時期を乗り切った。
Daitooryoo wa kokumin o shidoo-shite konnanna jiki o nori-kitta.
(**b**) The professor directed the student's senior thesis.
教授はその学生の卒業論文を指導した。
Kyooju wa sono gakusei no sotsugyoo-ronbun o shidoo-shita.

2. ⟨**-ni**⟩ ⟨**-yoo**(**ni**)⟩ **shi⌉ji-suru** ⟨〜に⟩⟨〜よう(に)⟩指示する ③ **•c [for s.o. in a position of responsibility to give directions to s.o. to do s.t.]** 《**indicate, show, point to, instruct**》, ⟨**-ni**⟩ ⟨**-yoo**(**ni**)⟩ **sa⌉shizu-suru** ⟨〜に⟩⟨〜よう(に)⟩指図する ③ **[for a superior to instruct s.o. to do s.t. in a non-military context]** 《**order, instruct, command**》

EX. (**a**) The teacher directed the students to do their homework.
先生は生徒に宿題をするよう(に){指示/指図}した。
Sensei wa seito ni shukudai o suru yoo(ni) {shiji/sashizu}-shita.
(**b**) The policeman directed the man to stop.
警官は男に止まるよう(に){指示/指図}した。
Keikan wa otoko ni tomaru yoo(ni) {shiji/sashizu}-shita.

3. ⟨**-o**⟩{⟨**-ni**⟩/⟨**-e**⟩} **a⌈nna⌉i-suru** ⟨〜を⟩{⟨〜に⟩/⟨〜へ⟩}案内する ③ **•c [for s.o. to take s.o. to a place]** 《**guide, notify**》

EX. (**a**) The tour conductor directed us to the hotel.
旅行社の人が我々をホテルへ案内してくれた。

Ryokoo-sha no hito ga ware-ware o hoteru e annai-shite kureta.
(**b**) The bell boy directed me to the restroom.
ボーイがトイレに案内してくれた。
Booi ga toire ni annai-shite kureta.

4. 〈-ni〉 **m⌈ichi o o⌈shieru** 〈～に〉道を教える ② **[for s.o. to tell s.o. how to get to a place]** 《**show**》

EX. (**a**) Will you direct me to the station?
駅までの道を教えて下さい。
Eki made no michi o oshiete kudasai.
(**b**) I directed him to the entrance of the freeway.
彼に高速道路の入口までの道を教えて上げた。
Kare ni koosoku-dooro no iriguchi made no michi o oshiete ageta.

5. 〈-o〉 〈-ni〉 **mu⌈keru** 〈～を〉〈～に〉向ける ② **[for s.o. to aim s.t. in a certain direction** 《**fig. "use s.t. for a certain purpose"**》**]** 《**turn**》

EX. (**a**) They directed their attention to the problem at hand.
彼らは当面の問題に注意を向けた。
Kare-ra wa toomen no mondai ni chuui o muketa.
(**b**) I tried to direct my thoughts to my work, but it was no use.
自分の思いを仕事に向けようと努力したが、無理だった。
Jibun no omoi o shigoto ni mukeyoo to doryoku-shita ga, muri datta.

direction n. **[the line along which s.t. lies, faces, moves, etc.** 《**fig. "guidance," "instruction"**》**]**

1. ho⌈okoo 方向 •c **[the direction in which s.o./s.a./s.t. proceeds or a policy/goal dictating which way s.o./s.t. should proceed]** 《**bearing, course, line, aim**》, **ho⌈ogaku** 方角 •c **[the line or course on which s.t. exists as relative to some reference point, esp. the location of the speaker]**

EX. (**a**) My wife has a very good sense of direction.
妻は{方向/*方角}感覚が大変良い。
*Tsuma wa {hookoo/*hoogaku}-kankaku ga taihen yoi.*
(**b**) The cat ran in the direction of the food.
その猫は食べ物の{方向/?方角}へ走って行った。
Sono neko wa tabe-mono no {hookoo/?hoogaku} e hashitte-itta.
(**c**) I lost my direction in the forest.
私は森の中で{方向/方角}が分からなくなった。
Watakushi wa mori no naka de {hookoo/hoogaku} ga wakaranaku natta.

2. shi⌉ji 指示 •c **[an act/instance of indicating s.t. or of instructing s.o. to do s.t.]** 《**indication, pointing out, instructions**》, **sa⌉shizu** 指図 **[an act/instance of ordering/instructing s.o. to do s.t.]** 《**instructions, orders, commands**》, **se⌈tsumei** 説明 •c **[an act/instance of explaining the content of/reason for/significance of s.t.]** 《**explanation, exposition, instructions**》

EX. (**a**) The directions for use were written in Japanese.
使い方の{指示/説明/?指図}は日本語で書いてあった。
Tsukai-kata no {shiji/setsumei/?sashizu} wa Nihon-go de kaite atta.
(**b**) Follow the doctor's directions in taking the medicine.
薬の服用は医者の{指示/指図/説明}に従ってください。
Kusuri no fukuyoo wa isha no {shiji/sashizu/setsumei} ni shitagatte kudasai.

PHRASE: in all directions *hoo-boo ni* 方々に

EX. Chinese restaurants can be found in all directions.
中華料理の店は方々にあります。
Chuuka-ryoori no mise wa hoo-boo ni arimasu.

directly adv. **[in a direct way or instantly]**

1. ma⌈ssu⌉gu(ni) 真っすぐ(に) **[going from one point to another without any curvature/angularity]** 《**straight**》

EX. (**a**) My father came directly home.

父は真っすぐに家へ帰って来た。
Chichi wa massuguni ie e kaette-kita.
(**b**) This road leads directly to the border.
この道は真っすぐ(に)国境へ通じている。
Kono michi wa massugu(ni) kokkyoo e tsuujite iru.

2. cho⌈kusetsu 直接 •c [with nothing coming in between] ⟪immediately, firsthand⟫

EX. (**a**) The war directly affected the supply of oil.
戦争は石油の供給に直接影響を及ぼした。
Sensoo wa sekiyu no kyookyuu ni chokusetsu eikyoo o oyoboshita.
(**b**) The two sides confronted each other directly in the courtroom.
両者は法廷で直接対決した。
Ryoosha wa hootei de chokusetsu-taiketsu-shita.

3. su⌉gu (ni) すぐ(に) [at once/without delay] ⟪instantly, immediately⟫, ya⌈gate やがて [before long ⟨fml⟩]

EX. (**a**) The package will be delivered directly.
小包は{すぐに/やがて}届きます。
Ko-zutsumi wa {sugu ni/yagate} todokimasu.
(**b**) The chairman went to the airport directly after the meeting.
議長は会議の後{すぐ/?やがて}空港に向かった。
Gichoo wa kaigi no ato {sugu/?yagate} kuukoo ni mukatta.

4. so⌈tchokuni 率直に •c [without hiding what one really thinks/feels]

EX. John always talks to me directly.
ジョンはいつも率直に話してくれる。
Jon wa itsu-mo sotchokuni hanashite kureru.

director n. **[s.o. who directs s.t.]**
shi⌈do⌉o-sha 指導者 •c [s.o. who leads/guides/instructs s.o.] ⟪leader, guide, mentor⟫, shi⌈ki⌉-sha 指揮者 •c [s.o. who leads/conducts an orchestra, chorus, etc.] ⟪conductor, commander⟫, ka⌈ntoku 監督 •c [an act of directing some activity or s.o. who directs some activity] ⟪coach⟫, ju⌈uyaku 重役 •c [s.o. who has an important managerial post in a bank or at a business corporation], ri⌉ji 理事 •c [one who directs a school/other public corporation] ⟪trustee⟫, di⌈re⌉kutaa ディレクター •f [one who directs s.t., esp. a movie or artistic project]

dirty adj. **[not clean ⟪fig. "obscene," "despicable"⟫]**
ki⌈tana⌉i 汚い adj(*i*). **[not clean/tidy ⟪fig. "obscene," "despicable," "unfair"⟫] ⟪filthy, unclean, indecent, obscene, despicable, mean, stingy, unfair⟫ ↔ kireina** きれいな adj(*na*).; **yo⌈goreta N 汚れたN /⟨Vinf. past of *yogoreru* ② become soiled/ [soiled], yogorete iru (N) 汚れている(N) /⟨Vinf. past of *yogoreru* ② become soiled/**

EX. (**a**) John's room is always dirty.
ジョンの部屋はいつも{汚い/汚れている}。
Jon no heya wa itsu-mo {kitanai/yogorete iru}.
(**b**) I washed my dirty hands after changing the tires on my car.
自分の車のタイヤを交換したあと{汚れた/?汚い}手を洗った。
*Jibun no kuruma no taiya o kookan-shita ato {yogoreta/*kitanai} te o aratta.*

disagree vt. **[for s.o. to differ in opinion with s.o. else or for s.t. to cause ill effect when eaten]**

1. ⟨-to⟩ i⌉ken ga a⌈wa⌉nai ⟨〜と⟩意見が合わない /⟨*iken* opinion + prt. *ga* + neg. of *au* ① fit, suit/ [for opinions to fail to match] ⟪differ⟫, i⌈tchi-shinai 一致しない /⟨neg. of *itchi-suru* ③ agree/ [not agree]

EX. (**a**) She disagreed with me on practically every issue.
彼女はほとんどの問題について私と意見が{合わなかった/一致しなかった}。
Kanojo wa hotondo no mondai ni-tsuite watakushi to iken ga {awanakatta/itchi-shinakatta}.
(**b**) I disagreed with my colleagues on the matter.

その件に関して私は同僚と意見が{合わなかった/一致しなかった}。
Sono ken ni-kanshite watakushi wa dooryoo to iken ga {awanakatta/itchi-shinakatta}.

2. 〈-ni〉 a⌈wa⌉nai 〈~に〉合わない /〈neg. of *au* ① fit, suit/ [for s.t. not to go well with s.t. else]

EX. Coffee disagrees with him.
コーヒーは彼の体質に合わない。
Koohii wa kare no taishitsu ni awanai.

disappear vi. **[to cease to be seen]**
ki⌈eru 消える ② [for s.t. which has been there to cease to be there] ⟪vanish, fade out, blow out, go out, be extinguished, melt⟫ ↔ arawareru 現れる ②

EX. (**a**) The plane soon disappeared into the sky.
飛行機は間もなく大空に消えた。
Hikoo-ki wa ma-mo-naku oo-zora ni kieta.
(**b**) Before we knew it the crowds had disappeared.
いつの間にか人々の姿が消えていた。
Itsu-no-ma-ni-ka hito-bito no sugata ga kiete ita.

disappoint vt. **[to fail to satisfy the wishes/ expectations of s.o.]**
〈-o〉 shi⌈tsuboo-saseru 〈~を〉失望させる /〈causative of *shitsuboo-suru* ③ be disappointed/ ② [to cause s.o. to lose hope] ⟪discourage⟫

EX. (**a**) The news disappointed him.
そのニュースは彼を失望させた。
Sono nyuusu wa kare o shitsuboo-saseta.
(**b**) The results of the test disappointed the student.
試験の結果はその学生を失望させた。
Shiken no kekka wa sono gakusei o shitsuboo-saseta.

PHRASE: be disappointed 〈*-ni*〉 *gakkari-suru* 〈~に〉がっかりする ③ ⟪be dispirited, be despondent⟫, 〈*-ni*〉 *shitsuboo-suru* 〈~に〉失望する ③ •c ⟪be discouraged, lose one's heart, be disillusioned⟫

EX. (**a**) He was disappointed at the news.
彼はそのニュースに{がっかり/失望}した。
Kare wa sono nyuusu ni {gakkari/shitsuboo}-shita.
(**b**) She was disappointed not to see him there.
彼女は彼がそこにいないことに{がっかり/失望}した。
Kanojo wa kare ga soko ni inai koto ni {gakkari/shitsuboo}-shita.

disappointment n. **[failure to have one's hopes or expectations fulfilled]**
shi⌈tsuboo 失望 •c [losing hope as a result of having one's expectations betrayed] ⟪discouragement, letdown⟫, ra⌈kutan 落胆 •c [loss of spirit] ⟪discouragement, despondency, dismay⟫

EX. (**a**) His disappointment was great after he was rejected for admission to the university.
彼が大学に落ちたときの{失望/落胆}は大きかった。
Kare ga daigaku ni ochita toki no {shitsuboo/rakutan} wa ookikatta.
(**b**) The content of the book was an utter disappointment for me.
あの本の内容には全く{失望/落胆}した。
Ano hon no naiyoo ni wa mattaku {shitsuboo/rakutan}-shita.
(**c**) University life was a great disappointment to him.
彼は大学生活に大いに{失望/落胆}した。
Kare wa daigaku seikatsu ni ooini {shitsuboo/rakutan}-shita.

disaster n. **[an event which causes great damage/harm]**
1. sa⌈igai 災害 •c [damage caused by typhoons, floods, earthquakes, major fires, contagious diseases, etc.] ⟪calamity⟫
2. sa⌈ina⌉n 災難 •c [an unfortunate happening which occurs suddenly, usually to an individual] ⟪misfortune, calamity⟫

EX. (**a**) He narrowly escaped disaster.
彼は辛うじて{災害/災難}を免れた。
Kare wa karoojite {saigai/sainan} o manugareta.
(**b**) They sent relief goods to the disaster area.
{災害/*災難}地域へ救助物資を送った。

D

*{Saigai/*Sainan}-chiiki e kyuujo-busshi o okutta.*
(**c**) This bodes disaster for us.
これは{災難/?災害}の前兆だ。
Kore wa {sainan/?saigai} no zenchoo da.
(**d**) We had an unexpected disaster befall us on the trip.
旅先で思いもよらない{災難/災害}にあった。
Tabi-saki de omoi-mo-yoranai {sainan/saigai} ni atta.

D

discard vt. **[for s.o. to throw away s.t. or stop using s.t. ⟪fig. "dismiss"⟫]**
⟨-o⟩ su⌈teru ⟨～を⟩捨てる ② [for s.o. to let go of s.t. that has become unnecessary or to sever a relationship] ⟪throw away, cast away, dump, abandon, desert, leave, give up⟫ ↔ ⟨-o⟩ hirou ⟨～を⟩拾う ①

EX. (**a**) She discarded all of her old clothes.
彼女は自分の古い服をみんな捨てた。
Kanojo wa jibun no furui fuku o minna suteta.
(**b**) He had to discard any hope of studying abroad.
彼は留学の希望を捨てなければならなかった。
Kare wa ryuugaku no kiboo o sutenakereba naranakatta.

discipline n. **[training that produces skill/character or behavior in accordance with rules of good conduct or a branch of learning]**
1. ku⌉nren 訓練 •c [the act of teaching s.t. to s.o. in order to cause a habit or skill to be internalized in that person] ⟪training, drill⟫

EX. Soldiers are subjected to tough discipline in the military.
軍隊では兵隊に厳しい訓練をする。
Guntai de wa heitai ni kibishii kunren o suru.

2. ki⌈ritsu 規律 •c [a standard of conduct by which an individual lives an orderly life or by which order is maintained in a group] ⟪order⟫, shi⌈tsuke しつけ /⟨V*masu* of *shitsukeru* ② teach manners and etiquette/ [teaching of manners and etiquette] ⟪breeding, training⟫

EX. (**a**) Discipline in the dormitory was very strict.
寮での{規律/?しつけ}は大変厳しかった。
Ryoo de no {kiritsu/?shitsuke} wa taihen kibishikatta.
(**b**) These days, few parents teach their children sufficient discipline.
このごろは子供に十分な{しつけ/*規律}をする親は少ない。
*Kono-goro wa kodomo ni juubunna {shitsuke/*kiritsu} o suru oya wa sukunai.*

3. ga⌈ku⌉mon (no) bu⌉n'ya 学問(の)分野 •c [a field of scholarship]

EX. (**a**) Women's Studies has become an independent discipline in most universities.
大抵の大学で女性学は独立した学問の分野になりました。
Taitei no daigaku de josei-gaku wa dokuritsu-shita gakumon no bun'ya ni narimashita.
(**b**) International Relations is a discipline popular with students.
国際関係論は学生に人気のある学問分野です。
Kokusai-kankei-ron wa gakusei ni ninki no aru gakumon-bun'ya desu.

discourage vt. **[for s.t. to deprive s.o. of courage/confidence or for s.o./s.t. to (try to) persuade s.o. to refrain from doing s.t]**
1. ⟨-o⟩ ga⌈kka⌉ri-saseru ⟨～を⟩がっかりさせる /⟨causative of *gakkari-suru* ③ be discouraged/ ② [to cause s.o.to be disappointed] ⟪disappoint⟫, ⟨-o⟩ ra⌈kutan-saseru ⟨～を⟩落胆させる /⟨causative of *rakutan-suru* ③ be disheartened/ ② [to cause s.o. to lose heart] ⟪disheartened⟫

EX. (**a**) Her attitude discouraged him.
彼女の態度は彼を{がっかり/落胆}させた。
Kanojo no taido wa kare o {gakkari/rakutan}-saseta.
(**b**) The news discouraged his mother.
その知らせは彼の母親を{がっかり/落胆}させた。

Sono shirase wa kare no haha-oya o {gakkari/rakutan}-saseta.

2. ⟨-o⟩ **o⌈moi-todomara-se⌉ru** ⟨〜を⟩**思い止まらせる** /⟨**causative of** ***omoi-todomaru*** ① **refrain from doing s.t./** ② **[for s.o./s.t. to cause s.o. to refrain from doing s.t.]** ⟪**persuade s.o. not to do s.t.**⟫, ⟨-o⟩ **o⌈moi-todomara-seyoo to suru** ⟨〜を⟩**思い止まらせようとする** /⟨**Vvol. of causative of** ***omoi-todomaru*** ① **refrain from doing s.t. +** ***to suru*** **try/** ③ **[for s.o. to try to cause s.o. to refrain from doing s.t.]**

EX. (**a**) The girl's father discouraged her from marrying the boy.
父親は娘がその男と結婚するのを{思い止まらせようとした/思い止まらせた}。
Chichi-oya wa musume ga sono otoko to kekkon-suru no o {omoi-todomara-seyoo to shita/omoi-todomara-seta}.
(**b**) The situation in the region discouraged people from traveling there.
その地域の情勢は人々に旅行を{思い止まらせた/*思い止まらせようとした}。
*Sono chiiki no joosei wa hito bito ni ryokoo o {omoi-todomara-seta/*omoi-todomara-seyoo to shita}.*

PHRASE: be discouraged *gakkari-suru* がっかりする ③

EX. The father was discouraged to hear the news.
父親は知らせを聞いてがっかりした。
Chichi-oya wa shirase o kiite gakkari-shita.

discover vt. **[for s.o. to find out s.t. for the first time]**
⟨-o⟩ **ha⌈kken-suru** ⟨〜を⟩**発見する** ③ •c **[for s.o. to find out for the first time the existence, value, effect, etc., of s.t. not yet known to the world]** ⟪**find out, detect**⟫, ⟨-o⟩ **mi⌈tsukeru** ⟨〜を⟩**見つける** ② **[for s.o. to cause s.o./s.t./s.a. hidden/lost/unknown to come to light or be seen]**, ⟨-ga⟩ **wa⌈ka⌉ru** ⟨〜が⟩**分かる** ① **[for s.o. to be able to figure out the nature, meaning, identity, etc., of s.t./s.o./s.a. which already is/should be in one's mind]** ⟪**see, get, grasp, understand, comprehend, know, realize**⟫

EX. (**a**) A group of mountain climbers has reportedly discovered what appear to be the tracks of the Abominable Snowman in the Himalayas.
ある登山隊がヒマラヤで雪男の足跡らしきもの{を発見した/を見つけた/*が分かった}そうだ。
*Aru tozan-tai ga Himaraya de yuki-otoko no ashi-ato rashiki mono {o hakken-shita/o mitsuketa/*ga wakatta} sooda.*
(**b**) It was the producer at this station who discovered that TV personality.
この局のプロデューサーがあのテレビタレント{を見つけた/?を発見した/*が分かった}のだ。
*Kono kyoku no purodyuusaa ga ano terebi-tarento {o mitsuketa/?o hakken-shita/*ga wakatta} no da.*
(**c**) They discovered his testimony to be false.
彼の証言が偽証であること{が分かった/*を発見した/*を見つけた}。
*Kare no shoogen ga gishoo dearu koto {ga wakatta/*o hakken-shita/*o mitsuketa}.*

discovery n. **[the act of discovering s.t. or s.t. discovered]**
ha⌈kken 発見 •c **[finding out the existence, value, effect, etc., of s.t. not yet known to the world]**

EX. (**a**) Scientists continue their research in quest of new discoveries.
科学者は新しい発見を求めて研究を続けている。
Kagaku-sha wa atarashii hakken o motomete kenkyuu o tsuzukete iru.
(**b**) Who was responsible for the discovery of Treasure Island?
宝島の発見はだれによるものですか。
Takara-jima no hakken wa dare ni yoru mono desu ka.

discuss vt. **[for people to talk together or for s.o. to write about s.t. from various angles to find solutions/points of agreement]**
1. {⟨-o⟩/⟨-ni-tsuite⟩} **gi⌉ron-suru** {⟨〜を⟩/⟨〜について⟩}**議論する** ③ •c **[for people to**

D

exchange opinions on some topic] ⟪argue, dispute debate⟫, {⟨-o⟩/⟨-ni-tsuite⟩} **to˥ogi-suru** {⟨〜を⟩/⟨〜について⟩}討議する ③ •c **[for people to conduct a mutual exchange of opinion and criticism in order to reach agreement or conclusion]** ⟪debate⟫, ⟨-to⟩ {⟨-o⟩/⟨-ni-tsuite⟩} **ha˥nashi-a˥u** ⟨〜と⟩{⟨〜を⟩/⟨〜について⟩}話し合う ① **[for s.o. to talk about s.t. with s.o. else]**

EX. (**a**) The leaders of the world met to discuss trade issues.
世界の指導者たちは貿易問題{を議論する/を討議する/について話し合う}ために集まった。
Sekai no shidoo-sha-tachi wa booeki-mondai {o giron-suru/o toogi-suru/ni-tsuite hanashi-au} tame ni atsumatta.
(**b**) The professor and the students discussed a wide range of issues in the class.
教授と学生はその授業でいろいろな問題について{議論した/討議した/話し合った}。
Kyooju to gakusei wa sono jugyoo de iro-irona mondai ni-tsuite {giron-shita/toogi-shita/hanashi-atta}.

2. {⟨-o⟩/⟨-ni-tsuite⟩} **r˥onjiru** {⟨〜を⟩/⟨〜について⟩}論じる ② •c **[for s.o. to state one's opinion on a matter logically, or for two/more persons to state their opinions on a matter mutually in order to examine their differences]** ⟪argue, debate, dispute⟫

EX. (**a**) The speaker discussed in detail recent changes in U.S. foreign policy.
講師はアメリカの外交政策の最近の動向{を/について}詳しく論じた。
Kooshi wa Amerika no gaikoo-seisaku no saikin no dookoo {o/ni-tsuite} kuwashiku ronjita.
(**b**) Let's discuss Marxism today.
今日はマルクス主義{を/について}論じましょう。
Kyoo wa Marukusu-shugi {o/ni-tsuite} ronjimashoo.

discussion n. **[an act/instance of discussing s.t.]**
ha˥nashi-ai 話し合い **[talking about s.t. with s.o. else]**, **gi˥ron** 議論 •c **[an exchange of opinions on some topic]** ⟪debate⟫, **to˥ogi** 討議 •c **[a mutual exchange of opinion and criticism, often heated]** ⟪argument, dispute, debate⟫, **ro˥ngi** 論議 •c **[a heated exchange of opinions on some issue with a view to achieving a higher level of mutual understanding or implementing some concrete measures]** ⟪argument, debate⟫

EX. (**a**) The Diet conducted a serious discussion on the security of the nation.
国会は国の安全保障について真剣な{議論/討議/論議/話し合い}をした。
Kokkai wa kuni no anzen-hoshoo ni-tsuite shinkenna {giron/toogi/rongi/hanashi-ai} o shita.
(**b**) There was no discussion of the matter at the meeting.
会議ではその問題の{議論/討議/論議/話し合い}は全くなかった。
Kaigi de wa sono mondai no {giron/toogi/rongi/hanashi-ai} wa mattaku nakatta.
(**c**) The problem was solved after a heated discussion.
その問題は活発な{議論/討議/論議/話し合い}の後で決着をみた。
Sono mondai wa kappatsuna {giron/toogi/rongi/hanashi-ai} no ato de ketchaku o mita.

disease n. **[illness in general]**
byo˥oki 病気 •c **[a state/instance of not being in good health]** ⟪sickness, trouble, disorder⟫

EX. (**a**) The cat was cured of its disease.
猫は病気が治った。
Neko wa byooki ga naotta.
(**b**) He is suffering from a mysterious disease.
彼は奇妙な病気にかかっている。
Kare wa kimyoona byooki ni kakatte iru.

dish n. **[a shallow container of pottery, glass, etc., for holding food ⟪fig. "particular kind of food"⟫]**
1. **sa˥ra** 皿 **[a shallow, often round container for holding food]** ⟪plate⟫

EX. (a) The children washed the dishes.
子供たちが皿を洗った。
Kodomo-tachi ga sara o aratta.
(b) We bought a beautiful wooden dish in Vermont.
バーモントで美しい木の皿を買いました。
Baamonto de utsukushii ki no sara o kaimashita.

2. ryo˥ori 料理 •c [the preparation of food or food which is prepared] 《cooking, cuisine, food》

EX. (a) We often enjoy Chinese dishes at home.
家ではよく中華料理を食べます。
Ie de wa yoku chuuka-ryoori o tabemasu.
(b) Shall we order some cold dishes?
何か冷たい料理を注文しましょうか。
Nani-ka tsumetai ryoori o chuumon-shimashoo ka.

disk n. **[any thin, flat, circular thing 《fig. "record"》]**
di˥suku ディスク •f, re⌈ko˥odo レコード •f [a flat, thin circular object on which sounds are recorded for reproduction on a phonograph], e⌈nban 円盤 •c [a round saucer-like object]

dislike vt. **[for s.o./s.a. to have a feeling of not liking s.t./s.o./s.a.]**
⟨-o⟩ ki˥rau ⟨〜を⟩嫌う ① [for s.o./s.a. to have an aversion to seeing/hearing/touching s.t. and want to be away from it] 《hate, abhor, detest》, ⟨-ga⟩ ki⌈raina ⟨〜が⟩嫌いな adj(*na*). **[for s.o./s.a. to not like s.t./s.o./s.a.] 《hate》**

EX. (a) Our children dislike broccoli.
うちの子供はブロッコリー{を嫌っている/が嫌いだ}。
Uchi no kodomo wa burokkorii {o kiratte iru/ga kirai da}.
(b) Many people dislike cigarette smoke.
たばこのけむり{を嫌う/が嫌いな}人が多い。
Tabako no kemuri {o kirau/ga kiraina} hito ga ooi.
(c) Cats dislike taking a bath.
猫は行水{を嫌う/が嫌いだ}。
Neko wa gyoozui {o kirau/ga kirai da}.
(d) I dislike tomato juice.
わたしはトマトジュース{が嫌いです/*を嫌っています}。
*Watashi wa tomato-juusu {ga kirai desu/*o kiratte imasu}.*

NOTE: *Kiratte iru* has a restriction on its subject. As example (a) shows, it can take a third person subject, but it cannot take a first person subject as in example (d).

display vt. **[to show s.t. by spreading it out to view 《fig. "let appear"》]**
1. ⟨-o⟩ te⌈nji-suru ⟨〜を⟩展示する ③ •c [for s.o. to arrange things for public presentation] 《exhibit》, ⟨-o⟩ chi⌈nretsu-suru ⟨〜を⟩陳列する ③ •c [for s.o. to arrange things to show to people] 《exhibit, place on exhibition》

EX. (a) Every merchant displayed his finest wares at the bazaar.
市では商人たちが皆それぞれのすばらしい売り物を{展示/陳列}していた。
Ichi de wa shoonin-tachi ga mina sore-zore no subarashii uri-mono o {tenji/chinretsu}-shite ita.
(b) The artist's newest works were displayed at his recent exhibit.
この間の展示会ではその芸術家の最新作が{展示/陳列}してあった。
Kono aida no tenji-kai de wa sono geijutsu-ka no saishin-saku ga {tenji/chinretsu}-shite atta.

2. ⟨-ni⟩ ⟨-o⟩ shi⌈mesu ⟨〜に⟩⟨〜を⟩示す ① [to cause s.o. to see or be clearly aware of some fact or object by the use of symbols or other indirect means ⟨fml⟩]

EX. The teacher displayed a model of penmanship to the students.
教師は習字のお手本を生徒に示した。
Kyooshi wa shuuji no o-tehon o seito ni shimeshita.

—— n. **[an exhibition]**
te⌈nji 展示 •c [an act/instance of displaying things] 《exhibition, show》, chi⌈nretsu 陳列 •c [an act of arranging things to show to people] 《exhibition, show》

EX. (**a**) Many works of art were on display there.
そこには多くの美術品が{展示/陳列}されていた。
Soko ni wa ooku no bijutsu-hin ga {tenji/chinretsu}-sarete ita.
(**b**) These are for display and not for sale.
これは{展示/陳列}用で、売り物ではありません。
Kore wa {tenji/chinretsu}-yoo de, uri-mono dewaarimasen.

NOTE: 展示 may be used with 会 as in *tenji-kai*, but 陳列 may not be attached to 会 in the same way.

D

dissertation n. **[a formal treatise written as a requirement for the doctor's degree]**
ro⌈nbun 論文 •c [a piece of writing which states the results of one's research] **⟪treatise, thesis, papers⟫**

EX. (**a**) My doctoral dissertation deals with the social behavior of monkeys.
私の博士論文は猿の社会的行動がテーマです。
Watakushi no hakushi-ronbun wa saru no shakai-teki-koodoo ga teema desu.
(**b**) His dissertation was published in both English and Japanese.
彼の論文は日本語と英語で出版されました。
Kare no ronbun wa Nihon-go to eigo de shuppan-saremashita.

dissolve vt. **[to cause s.t. to turn into liquid usu. by means of the action of another liquid 《fig. "make invisible"》]**
⟨-o⟩ to⌈ka⌉su ⟨～を⟩とかす ① [to cause s.t. to turn into liquid 《fig. "comb hair"》] **⟪melt, thaw, fuse⟫** ↔ **⟨-o⟩ katameru ⟨～を⟩固める ②**
㊥ "comb (hair)"▷とかす, otherwise ▷溶かす

EX. (**a**) Water dissolves sugar.
水は砂糖を溶かす。
Mizu wa satoo o tokasu.
(**b**) Take this medicine after dissolving it in warm water.
この薬はお湯に溶かして飲んでください。
Kono kusuri wa o-yu ni tokashite nonde kudasai.

—— vi. **[for s.t. to turn into a liquid, usu. by means of the action of another liquid]**
to⌈ke⌉ru とける ② [for s.t. to turn into liquid due to the presence of heat or to the action of another liquid 《fig. "be solved"》] **⟪melt, get loose, thaw, fuse⟫**
㊥ "be solved"▷解ける, otherwise ▷溶ける

EX. Salt dissolves in water.
塩は水に溶ける。
Shio wa mizu ni tokeru.

distance n. **[the extent of space between two points]**
kyo⌉ri 距離 •c [the space between two points] **⟪range, interval, difference, gap⟫**

EX. (**a**) What is the distance separating Japan and Korea ?
日本と韓国との距離はどのくらいですか。
Nihon to Kankoku to no kyori wa dono-kurai desu ka.
(**b**) The lost cat walked a great distance to get home.
迷子になった猫は長い距離を歩いてうちへ帰った。
Maigo ni natta neko wa nagai kyori o aruite uchi e kaetta.
(**c**) Long-distance calls are expensive.
長距離電話は料金が高い。
Choo-kyori-denwa wa ryookin ga takai.

PHRASE: in the distance *tooku ni* 遠くに

EX. You can see a big tower in the distance, can't you?
遠くに高い塔が見えるでしょう?
Tooku ni takai too ga mieru deshoo?

distant adj. **[far away in time/space]**
to⌈oi 遠い adj(*i*). **[located at a great distance away]** **⟪far⟫** ↔ **chikai 近い** adj(*i*).

EX. (**a**) Nowadays you can send documents to distant places instantly by fax.
今ではファックスを使って直ちに遠い所へ書類が送れる。
Ima de wa fakkusu o tsukatte tadachini tooi tokoro e shorui ga okure-ru.
(**b**) Among the participants in the conference were some who had come from distant lands.

学会の出席者の中には遠い国から来た人もいた。
Gakkai no shusseki-sha no naka ni wa tooi kuni kara kita hito mo ita.
(**c**) In the not-so-distant future we'll have earphone systems capable of simultaneous interpretation.
同時通訳するイヤホーンができるでしょう。それもそんなに遠い将来ではなくね。
Dooji-tsuuyaku-suru iyahoon ga dekiru deshoo. Sore-mo sonnani tooi shoorai dewanaku ne.

distinct adj. **[clearly distinguishable from others]**

1. ((-to)) **chi⌈gau N** ((〜と))**違うN [to be not the same as s.t./s.o./s.a. 《fig. "be mistaken," "disagree with," "wrong"》] ((unlike, different, run counter to, wrong, no, differ)),** ((-to)) **ko⌈tona⌉ru N** ((〜と))**異なるN [to have some property which is not the same as another] ((different, differ))**

EX. (**a**) In English, l's and r's are quite distinct.
英語ではLとRはまったく{違う/異なる}。
Eigo de wa eru to aaru wa mattaku {chigau/kotonaru}.
(**b**) Identical twins may have quite distinct characters.
一卵性双生児でも性格がまったく{違う/異なる}ことがある。
Ichiran-sei-soosei-ji demo seikaku ga mattaku {chigau/kotonaru} koto ga aru.

2. ha⌈kki⌉ri-shita N はっきりしたN **/〈Vinf. past of *hakkiri-suru* ③ become clear/ [be well articulated] ((plain, apparent, conspicuous))**

EX. (**a**) He has a distinct foreign accent.
彼にははっきりした外国語なまりがある。
Kare ni wa hakkiri-shita gaikoku-go-namari ga aru.
(**b**) The house has a distinct tropical character to it.
その家は、はっきりしたトロピカル風の特徴を持っている。
Sono ie wa, hakkiri-shita toropikaru-fuu no tokuchoo o motte iru.
(**c**) Each religion has its own distinct conceptual framework.
それぞれの宗教にははっきりした思想の枠組みがある。
Sore-zore no shuukyoo ni wa hakkiri-shita shisoo no waku-gumi ga aru.

distinction n. **[an act/instance of making s.o./s.t. distinct from others 《fig. "individuality as a merit," "honor"》] ku⌉betsu 区別 •c [a division between two/more things in terms of characteristics] ((difference)), chi⌈gai 違い /〈V*masu* of *chigau* ① differ/ [the state of being different or a respect in which s.t./s.o./s.a. is different from another] ((difference)), so⌈oi⌉-ten 相違点 •c [a point in which two/more things are mutually different] ((points of difference))**

EX. (**a**) Even a child can make a distinction between good and evil.
子供でも良いことと悪いことの{区別がつく/{違い/相違点}がわかる}。
Kodomo demo yoi koto to warui koto no {kubetsu ga tsuku/{chigai/sooi-ten} ga wakaru}.
(**b**) An expert could perhaps make a distinction between these two things, but not me.
専門家ならこの二つの{{違い/相違点}が分かる/区別がつけられる}かもしれないが、私には分からない。
Senmon-ka nara kono futatsu no {{chigai/sooi-ten} ga wakaru/kubetsu ga tsuke-rareru} kamoshirenai ga, watashi ni wa wakaranai.
(**c**) 'Help wanted without gender distinction.'
「男女の{区別/*違い/*相違点}なく人材を募集中。」
*'Danjo no {kubetsu/*chigai/*sooi-ten} naku jinzai o boshuu-chuu.'*
(**d**) Those twins are so alike that they defy any attempt at distinction.
あの双子は区別できないほど似ている。

Ano futago wa kubetsu-dekinai hodo nite iru.

PHRASE: with distinction *yuutoo de* 優等で

EX. Taro graduated from college with distinction.
太郎は大学を優等で卒業した。
Taroo wa daigaku o yuutoo de sotsugyoo-shita.

distinguish vt. **[for s.o./s.a. to recognize s.t./s.o./s.a. as distinct]**
⟨-o⟩ ku⌉betsu-suru ⟨〜を⟩区別する ③ •**c [for s.o. to tell s.t./s.o./s.a. from another]** ⟪**differentiate**⟫

EX. (**a**) Can you always distinguish l's from r's ?
いつもＬとＲを区別することが出来ますか。
Itsu-mo eru to aaru o kubetsu-suru koto ga dekimasu ka.
(**b**) It's difficult for English speakers to distinguish *tsu* from *su* in Japanese.
英語が母語の人には日本語の「つ」と「す」を区別することが難しい。
Eigo ga bogo no hito ni wa Nihon-go no 'tsu' to 'su' o kubetsu-suru koto ga muzukashii.

D

distinguished adj. **[recognized as distinctly eminent]**
yu⌈umeina 有名な adj(*na*). •**c [for a name to be widely known]** ⟪**famous, notorious famed, celebrated**⟫, **cho⌈meina** 著名な adj(*na*). •**c [for s.o. to be well-known in society]** ⟪**prominent, celebrated, well-known, eminent**⟫

EX. Kurosawa is a distinguished movie director.
黒沢は{有名な/著名な}映画監督です。
Kurosawa wa {yuumeina/chomeina} eiga-kantoku desu.

distribute vt. **[for s.o. to divide and give out s.t. in shares]**
⟨-ni⟩ ⟨-o⟩ ku⌈ba⌉ru ⟨〜に⟩⟨〜を⟩配る ① **[for s.o. to give s.t. out as necessary so that it goes around to everybody]** ⟪**deal out, serve out, pass out, deliver, send out all of, apportion**⟫, **⟨-ni⟩ ⟨-o⟩ bu⌈npai-suru** ⟨〜に⟩⟨〜を⟩分配する ③ •**c [for s.o. to apportion s.t. out to s.o.]** ⟪**apportion out**⟫

EX. (**a**) The professor distributed the handout to the students.
教授は学生にプリントを{配った/*分配した}。
*Kyooju wa gakusei ni purinto o {kubatta/*bunpai-shita}.*
(**b**) Oranges were distributed free to the tourists.
観光客にただでオレンジが{配られた/?分配された}。
Kankoo-kyaku ni tada de orenji ga {kubara-reta/?bunpai-sareta}.
(**c**) The clerk in charge distributed the relief goods.
係の人が救援物資を{配った/分配した}。
Kakari no hito ga kyuuen-busshi o {kubatta/bunpai-shita}.

distribution n. **[dividing and giving out or a spread over an area or sales/promotion of merchandise]**
1. ha⌈ibun 配分 •**c [s.t. distributed to one as one's allotment]** ⟪**allotment, apportionment**⟫

EX. (**a**) Excessively unequal distribution of wealth is not good.
富の極端に不平等な配分は好ましくない。
Tomi no kyokutanni fu-byoodoona haibun wa konomashikunai.
(**b**) The distribution of points on an exam is not an easy task.
試験の点数の配分は易しい仕事ではない。
Shiken no tensuu no haibun wa yasashii shigoto dewanai.

2. bu⌈npu 分布 •**c [an act/instance of spreading in various directions over an area]** ⟪**spread**⟫

EX. (**a**) He is doing research on the distribution of bird species in Japan.
彼は日本における鳥類の分布について研究している。
Kare wa Nihon ni-okeru choo-rui no bunpu ni-tsuite kenkyuu-shite iru.
(**b**) This kind of insect has a wide distribution throughout Asia.

この種の昆虫はアジアに広く分布している。
Kono shu no konchuu wa Ajia ni hiroku bunpu-shite iru.

3. ryu⌈utsuu 流通 •c [the flow of air, water, etc., to a different location 《fig. "circulation of money or negotiable instruments," "sound selling and buying of merchandise"》] 《circulation, flow》

EX. (**a**) A revolution in the distribution of goods and services is underway in this country.
この国では物資やサービスの流通革命が進行中である。
Kono kuni de wa busshi ya saabisu no ryuutsuu-kakumei ga shinkoo-chuu dearu.
(**b**) Japan's economic distribution system is often criticized.
日本の流通機構はしばしば批判されている。
Nihon no ryuutsuu-kikoo wa shiba-shiba hihan sarete iru.

district n. **[a region or locality]**

1. chi⌈ho⌉o 地方 •c [a large area which is defined according to some criterion or an area outside major cities] 《locality, region, area, provinces》, chi⌉iki 地域 •c [a geographic division characterizable in terms of climate/culture/natural environment]

EX. (**a**) The typhoon devastated that district.
台風はあの{地方/地域}に大きな被害を与えた。
Taifuu wa ano {chihoo/chiiki} ni ookina higai o ataeta.
(**b**) The district in question is being redeveloped.
問題の{地方/地域}は再開発されている。
Mondai no {chihoo/chiiki} wa sai-kaihatsu-sarete iru.
(**c**) This district is often subject to damage due to cold weather.
この地方はよく冷害に見舞われる。
Kono chihoo wa yoku reigai ni mimawa-reru.

2. chi⌈ku⌉ 地区 •c [an area, specially designated for some purpose] 《zone》

EX. (**a**) In Western cities, commercial districts and residential districts are clearly distinguished.
欧米の都市では商業地区と住宅地区がはっきり区別されている。
Oo-Bei no toshi de wa shoogyoo-chiku to juutaku-chiku ga hakkiri kubetsu-sarete iru.
(**b**) A fire broke out in a densely populated district of the city.
その都市の人口密集地区で火災が発生した。
Sono toshi no jinkoo-misshuu-chiku de kasai ga hassei-shita.

disturb vt. **[to break the calm or settled state of s.t.]**

⟨-no⟩ ja⌈ma o suru ⟨〜の⟩邪魔をする ③ •c [to get in the way of s.o./s.t./s.a. 《fig. "to visit s.o."》] 《obstruct, prevent, disrupt, interrupt》, ⟨-o⟩ bo⌈ogai-suru ⟨〜を⟩妨害する ③ •c [to keep s.t. from occurring or s.o./s.a. from doing s.t., esp. by forcible means], ⟨-o⟩ mi⌈da⌉su ⟨〜を⟩乱す ① [to confuse/interrupt the order and tranquility of s.t.]

EX. (**a**) Regional strife has begun to disturb the international peace.
地域紛争が国際平和を{乱し/?妨害し/*邪魔し}はじめた。
*Chiiki-funsoo ga kokusai-heiwa o {midashi/?boogai-shi/*jama-shi}-hajimeta.*
(**b**) I didn't call you because I didn't want to disturb you.
あなた{の邪魔をしたく/??を妨害したく/*を乱したく}なかったので電話しませんでした。
*Anata {no jama o shi-taku/??o boogai shi-taku/*o midashi-taku} nakatta node denwa-shimasen deshita.*
(**c**) Please don't disturb my sleep.
安眠を{妨害しないで/邪魔しないで/??乱さないで}もらいたい。
Anmin o {boogai-shinaide/jama-shinaide/??midasanaide} morai-tai.

divide vt. **[to separate into parts]**

1. ⟨-o⟩ ⟨-ni⟩ wa⌈ke⌉ru ⟨〜を⟩⟨〜に⟩分ける ②

D

[to part s.t. or a group of things/people/animals into two or more parts/groups (and share them with s.o.)] ⟪part, share, separate, split, distribute⟫, **⟨-ni⟩ ⟨-o⟩ bu⌈npai-suru ⟨〜に⟩⟨〜を⟩分配する ③ •c [for s.o. to apportion s.t. out to s.o.], ⟨-o⟩ ⟨-ni⟩ bu⌈nkatsu-suru ⟨〜を⟩⟨〜に⟩分割する ③ •c [for s.o. to break s.t. into pieces/portions/parts]**

EX. (**a**) In the United States each state is divided into counties.
米国では各州は郡に{分けられて/分割されて/*分配されて}いる。
*Beikoku de wa kaku-shuu wa gun ni {wake-rarete/bunkatsu-sarete/*bunpai-sarete} iru.*
(**b**) The three robbers divided the loot among themselves.
泥棒は盗品を三人で{分けた/分配した/??分割した}。
Doroboo wa toohin o san-nin de {waketa/bunpai-shita/??bunkatsu-shita}.
(**c**) The teacher divided the students into two groups.
先生は生徒たちを二つのグループに{分けた/分割した/*分配した}。
*Sensei wa seito-tachi o futatsu no guruupu ni {waketa/bunkatsu-shita/*bunpai-shita}.*

2. ⟨-o⟩ ⟨-ni⟩ wa⌈ru ⟨〜を⟩⟨〜に⟩割る ① [for s.o./s.a. to apply force to a hard substance and render it into two or more pieces ⟪fig. "(in mathematics) find how many times a given number is contained in another"⟫] ⟪cut, split, crush, separate, do division⟫

EX. Divide twenty by four.
20を4で割りなさい。
Ni-juu o yon de warinasai.

— vi. **[to be separated into parts] ⟨-ni⟩ wa⌈kare⌉ru ⟨〜に⟩分かれる ② [for s.t. to divide spontaneously into parts]**

EX. We divided into three groups and went on a field trip to factories.
我々は三つのグループに分かれて、工場見学をした。
Ware-ware wa mittsu no guruupu ni wakarete, koojoo-kengaku o shita.

division n. **[an act/instance of dividing ⟪fig. "(in mathematics) the process of finding how many times a number is contained in another"⟫]**

1. bu⌈nkatsu 分割 •c [the act of dividing into several parts] ⟪partition⟫

EX. (**a**) The city voted in favor of the division of the school district into three zones.
市は学区を三つに分割することを投票で決めた。
Shi wa gakku o mittsu ni bunkatsu-suru koto o toohyoo de kimeta.
(**b**) The division of the Korean Peninsula is still the source of many problems.
朝鮮半島の分割は依然として色々な問題の原因である。
Choosen-hantoo no bunkatsu wa izen-to-shite iro-irona mondai no gen'in dearu.

2. bu⌉mon 部門 •c [one of a number of subparts within a classification of the whole] ⟪section, department⟫

EX. (**a**) The division of general education in our college is being restructured.
大学の一般教養部門が再編成されている。
Daigaku no ippan-kyooyoo-bumon ga sai-hensei-sarete iru.
(**b**) Fortunately the research division will not be targeted in the current round of personnel cuts.
今回の人員削減では幸い研究部門は対象にならない。
Konkai no jin'in-sakugen de wa saiwai kenkyuu-bumon wa taishoo ni naranai.

3. wa⌈ri⌉-zan 割り算 [the process of finding how many times a number is contained in another]

EX. If you can use an abacus, division is very easy.
もしそろばんが使えたら、割り算はとても簡単です。
Moshi soroban ga tsukae-tara, wari-zan wa totemo kantan desu.

do vt. **[for s.o./s.a. to perform, finish, complete or cause s.t.]**
⟨-o⟩ su⌈ru ⟨〜を⟩する ③ **[for s.o./s.a. to perform a willful action; for s.o./s.a./s.t. to cause s.t. to take on a different state; for s.t. to happen in such a way as to be perceptible to s.o./s.a.; for s.t. to be in a certain state or possess a certain attribute; for an amount of time/money to pass/be required; for some proposition to be posited as true]** ((play, practice, act, make, act as, engage in, wear, feel, cost)), **⟨-o⟩ na⌈sa⌉ru** ⟨〜を⟩なさる ① **[for s.o. to whom the speaker shows deference to perform some action or bring about some state]**, **⟨-o⟩ i⌈tasu** ⟨〜を⟩いたす ① **[for s.o. who is younger and lower in social status than the hearer, typically the speaker or s.o. in the speaker's in-group, to perform some action or bring about some state]**

NOTE: V*masu* of *nasaru* is not *nasari* but *nasai* as in *nasaimasu*. *Itasu* is used usually in its *masu* form when the speaker is speaking very formally to the hearer.

EX. (**a**) A: What are you doing here?
こんな所で何を{している/なさっていらっしゃる}んですか。
Konna tokoro de nani o {shite iru/nasatte irassharu} n desu ka.
B: I was doing my homework, but I must have dozed off.
宿題をしていたんですが、眠ってしまったようです。
Shukudai o shite ita n desu ga, nemutte shimatta yoo desu.
(**b**) I have nothing to do all day today.
今日は一日何もすることがありません。
Kyoo wa ichi-nichi nani-mo suru koto ga arimasen.
(**c**) A: What does your father do?
お父様は何をしていらっしゃいますか。
O-too-sama wa nani o shite irasshaimasu ka.
B: He does business consulting.
経営コンサルタントの仕事を{して/いたして}おります。
Keiei konsarutanto no shigoto o {shite/itashite} orimasu.
(**d**) The professor does research in the evenings in his office.
教授は夜はいつも研究室で仕事を{なさいます/します}。
Kyooju wa yoru wa itsu-mo kenkyuu-shitsu de shigoto o {nasaimasu/shimasu}.
(**e**) I will call you tonight.
今晩お電話を{いたします/します}。
Konban o-denwa o {itashimasu/shimasu}.
(**f**) What are you going to do now?
これからどう{なさいます/します}か。
Kore-kara doo {nasaimasu/shimasu} ka.

PHRASE: do s.o. good *yaku ni tatsu* 役に立つ ①

EX. (**a**) Reading a lot when I was a child did me a lot of good.
子供の時たくさん本を読んだことが役に立った。
Kodomo no toki takusan hon o yonda koto ga yaku ni tatta.
(**b**) It won't do you any good to do that.
そんなことをしても役に立ちませんよ。
Sonna koto o shite mo yaku ni tachimasen yo.

NOTE: A sentence such as "This guide book did me a lot of good when I was in Europe" tends to convey a sarcastic flavor in English. The Japanese version of this sentence "*Kono aida no Yooroppa-ryokoo no toki kono annai-sho ga osoroshiku yaku ni tatta yo*" can also convey a similarly sarcastic meaning with the right use of adverbs such as "*osoroshiku*" and the right intonation.

— vi. **[for s.o./s.a. to behave in a certain way or for s.o. to fare a certain way or for s.t. to be adequate]**
1. ko⌈odoo-suru 行動する ③ •c **[for s.o./s.a. to behave in a certain way]** ((act, behave)), **ya⌈ru** やる ① **[for s.o. to perform an action willfully or to behave or fare in a certain way]**

EX. (**a**) When in Rome, do as the Romans do.
ローマではローマ人のように{行動しなさい/やりなさい}。
Rooma de wa Rooma-jin no yooni

D

{koodoo-shinasai/yarinasai}.

NOTE: A similar Japanese proverb is *Goo ni itte wa goo ni shitagae.*

(**b**) A: How is he doing at school?
彼は学校ではどんな風に{やって/*行動して}いますか。
*Kare wa gakkoo de wa donna fuu ni {yatte/*koodoo-shite} imasu ka.*
B: He is doing very well.
とてもうまく{やって/*行動して}いますよ。
*Totemo umaku {yatte/*koodoo-shite} imasu yo.*

D

2. ⟨-de⟩ ma-⌈ni-a⌉u ⟨〜で⟩間に合う ① [for s.t. to be adequate, serve the purpose] ⟪be of use, serviceable⟫

EX. A: Will this do?
これで間に合いますか。
Kore de ma-ni-aimasu ka.
B: Yes, that will do.
ええ、それで間に合います。
Ee, sore de ma-ni-aimasu.

doctor n. **[a physician or s.o. holding a doctoral degree]**

1. i⌈sha 医者 •c [s.o. whose profession it is to treat sick people], i⌉shi 医師 •c [s.o. whose profession it is to treat sick people ⟨fml⟩]

EX. (**a**) You'd better go and see the doctor.
{医者/*医師}に行って診てもらった方がいい。
*{Isha/*Ishi} ni itte mite moratta hoo ga ii.*
(**b**) I hope to be a doctor in the future.
将来{医者/医師}になるつもりです。
Shoorai {isha/ishi} ni naru tsumori desu.

2. ha⌉kase 博士 •c [a title for a person with an advanced degree or the degree itself granted to s.o. who has done research beyond the standard level in a particular scholarly field of specialization]

EX. (**a**) Dr. Yamada earned his doctoral degree from Tokyo University.
山田博士は東京大学で博士号を取得した。
Yamada-hakase wa Tookyoo-daigaku de hakase-goo o shutoku-shita.

NOTE: This word may also be pronounced *hakushi*, which is more formal sounding. Also, a physician is addressed as *sensei*, and not as *hakase* or *hakushi*.

(**b**) Dr. White is not seeing patients today.
ホワイト{先生/*博士}は今日診察をしていません。
*Howaito-{sensei/*hakase} wa kyoo shinsatsu o shite imasen.*

document n. **[a paper with information written/printed on it]**

sho⌈rui 書類 •c [s.t. written that provides information] ⟪papers⟫

EX. (**a**) Please submit the documents in duplicate.
書類は二部提出して下さい。
Shorui wa ni-bu teishutsu-shite kudasai.
(**b**) These documents should be filled out with care.
この書類は注意して記入しなければならない。
Kono shorui wa chuui-shite kinyuu-shinakereba naranai.

dog n.

i⌈nu⌉ 犬

EX. My sister keeps her dog inside the house.
{妹/姉}は家の中で犬を飼っている。
{Imooto/Ane} wa ie no naka de inu o katte iru.

doll n. **[a child's toy resembling a human being]**

ni⌈ngyoo 人形 •c

EX. My daughter collects *kokeshi* dolls.
娘はこけし人形を集めています。
Musume wa kokeshi-ningyoo o atsumete imasu.

dollar n. **[a monetary unit equal to 100 cents used in the U.S.A., Canada, Australia, etc.]**

do⌉ru ドル •f

EX. (**a**) The dollar is strong again.
ドルはまた強くなった。
Doru wa mata tsuyoku natta.
(**b**) I exchanged my yen for U.S. dollars at the bank.
銀行で円をドルに両替した。

| *Ginkoo de en o doru ni ryoogae-shita.*

domestic adj. **[of the home/family, or of/made in one's country]**

1. ka⌈tei no N 家庭のN •c [of the home/family]

EX. | (**a**) He had to quit his job because of domestic problems.
彼は家庭の問題で仕事を辞めなければならなかった。
Kare wa katei no mondai de shigoto o yamenakereba naranakatta.
(**b**) The movie depicts domestic life in a typical American family.
映画は典型的なアメリカ家庭の生活を描いている。
Eiga wa tenkei-tekina Amerika-katei no seikatsu o egaite iru.

2. ko⌈ku⌉nai no N 国内のN •c [of one's own country]

EX. | (**a**) This is strictly a domestic problem.
これはまったく国内だけの問題です。
Kore wa mattaku kokunai dake no mondai desu.
(**b**) American newspapers carry more domestic news than international news.
アメリカの新聞は国際的なニュースより国内のニュースの方が多い。
Amerika no shinbun wa kokusai-tekina nyuusu yori kokunai no nyuusu no hoo ga ooi.

PHRASE: domestic animal *kachiku* 家畜 •c, domestic line *kokunai-sen* 国内線 •c

dominant adj. **[ruling or prevailing]**

yu⌈useina 優勢な adj(*na*). **•c [stronger or better than s.t./s.o. else] 《super, leading》 ↔ resseina 劣勢な** adj(*na*). **•c**

EX. | (**a**) Japan had the dominant position in the negotiations.
日本は交渉でより優勢な立場にあった。
Nihon wa kooshoo de yori yuuseina tachiba ni atta.
(**b**) It's obvious that he is the dominant candidate.
彼が候補者として優勢なのは明白だ。
Kare ga kooho-sha to-shite yuuseina no wa meihaku da.
(**c**) According to a survey, the opposition view appears to be dominant.
世論調査では野党の意見の方が優勢なようです。
Yoron-choosa de wa ya-too no iken no hoo ga yuuseina yoo desu.

door n. **[a movable barrier for opening and closing an entrance]**

to 戸 [a fixture on a house which can be opened or closed or fitted onto an opening to make a partition], do⌉a ドア •f [a Western-style fixture on a house which can be opened/closed], de-⌈iri⌉-guchi 出入り口 [an opening for exiting or entering an area or space], to⌈bira 扉 [s.t. that opens and closes by swinging around, including a movable barrier for an entrance and the title page of a book/magazine]

EX. | (**a**) The door was closed.
{戸/ドア/出入り口/扉}は閉まっていた。
{To/Doa/De-iri-guchi/Tobira} wa shimatte ita.
(**b**) Please open the door.
{戸/ドア/出入り口/扉}を開けて下さい。
{To/Doa/De-iri-guchi/Tobira} o akete kudasai.

PHRASE: sliding door *hiki-do* 引き戸

dormitory n. **[a building containing many rooms in which students, etc., live and sleep]**

ryo⌉o 寮 •c [a building which people (typically, students) belonging to the same organization use as their living quarters]

EX. | (**a**) Allen Hall is a dormitory for boys.
アレンホールは男子寮です。
Aren-hooru wa danshi-ryoo desu.
(**b**) Japanese students nowadays prefer ordinary apartments to dormitories.
近ごろの日本の学生は寮よりアパートを好む。
Chikagoro no Nihon no gakusei wa ryoo yori apaato o konomu.

dot n. **[a small spot]**

te⌈n 点 •c [a small mark made by the end of a sharp object 《fig. "punctuation," "marks," "respects"》] 《spot, speck, mark,

D

point)), do⌈tto ドット •f

EX. (**a**) Some printers use dots.
{ドット/*点}を使うプリンターもある。
*{Dotto/*Ten} o tsukau purintaa mo aru.*
(**b**) Put three dots after the word.
単語の後に{点/*ドット}を三つ付けなさい。
*Tango no ato ni {ten/*dotto} o mittsu tsukenasai.*

double adj. **[twofold, twice as much]**
(ni-)ba⌈i no N (二)倍のN •c [twice as much/many]

EX. (**a**) Since moving to his new job, he is now earning double his previous salary.
新しい会社に移ってから彼は前の(二)倍の給料を取っている。
Atarashii kaisha ni utsutte kara kare wa mae no (ni-)bai no kyuuryoo o totte iru.
(**b**) Milk costs double what it used to.
牛乳は以前の(二)倍の値段だ。
Gyuunyuu wa izen no (ni-)bai no nedan da.

— vi. **[to become twice as much/many as before]**
1. (ni-)ba⌈i ni na⌉ru (二)倍になる ① [to become twice as much/many]

EX. (**a**) Gasoline prices have recently doubled.
最近ガソリンの値段が(二)倍になった。
Saikin gasorin no nedan ga (ni-)bai ni natta.
(**b**) The population of this area has doubled over the last five years.
過去五年間でこの地区の人口は(二)倍になった。
Kako go-nenkan de kono chiku no jinkoo wa (ni-)bai ni natta.

— vt. **[for s.o. to make s.t. twice as much/many as before]**
⟨-o⟩ (ni-)ba⌈i ni suru ⟨〜を⟩(二)倍にする ③ [for s.o. to make s.t. twice as much/many as before]

EX. (**a**) She doubled her savings by buying stocks.
彼女は株を買って財産を(二)倍にした。
Kanojo wa kabu o katte zaisan o (ni-)bai ni shita.
(**b**) The landlord doubled the rent.
大家は家賃を(二)倍にした。
Ooya wa yachin o (ni-)bai ni shita.

— n. **[a game of ping-pong, tennis, etc., with two players on each side]**
da⌉burusu ダブルス •f

doubt vt. **[for s.o. to distrust or disbelieve s.o./s.t.]**
⟨-o⟩ u⌈tagau ⟨〜を⟩疑う ① [for s.o. to think that s.t. is not true or that s.t. does not exist] ((distrust, disbelieve, suspect)), neg. of Sinf. to o⌈mo⌉u neg. of Sinf. と思う ① [for s.o. to think that S is not true] ((don't think S)), ⟨-ka⟩ do⌉o ka gi⌈mon da ⟨〜か⟩どうか疑問だ [be questionable whether/if]

EX. (**a**) When I heard the rumor, I doubted my ears.
そのうわさを聞いたとき耳を疑った。
Sono uwasa o kiita toki mimi o utagatta.
(**b**) He doubted the truth of what I said.
彼は私の言ったことの信ぴょう性を疑った。
Kare wa watakushi no itta koto no shinpyoo-sei o utagatta.
(**c**) I doubt that she will marry him.
私は彼女は彼と結婚しないと思う。
Watashi wa kanojo wa kare to kekkon-shinai to omou.
(**d**) I doubt whether the yen will continue to appreciate as before.
円高がこのまま続くかどうか疑問だ。
En-daka ga kono-mama tsuzuku ka doo ka gimon da.

— n. **[lack of trust or uncertainty of belief]**
u⌈tagai 疑い /⟨V*masu* of *utagau* ① doubt/[an act of thinking that s.t. is not true or that s.t. does not exist] ((question, suspicion, uncertainty)), gi⌈mon 疑問 •c [an act/instance of doubting] ((question))

EX. (**a**) There are some doubts about her testimony.
彼女の証言には多少の{疑い/疑問}がある。
Kanojo no shoogen ni wa tashoo no {utagai/gimon} ga aru.

(**b**) I have no doubts on the matter.
私はその件について全く{疑い/疑問}を持っていません。
Watakushi wa sono ken ni-tsuite mattaku {utagai/gimon} o motte imasen.

dove n. **[a bird of the pigeon family or a person advocating peace]**
ha˥to はと **[a kind of bird]** ⟪**pigeon**⟫, **ha˹to-ha** (**no hi˹to**) はと派(の人) **[a person advocating peace or a conciliatory national attitude]** ↔ **taka-ha** (**no hi˹to**) たか派(の人)

down adv. **[in/to a low or lower place, condition, amount, etc.]**
shi˹ta e 下へ n.+prt. **[to a low/lower place]**

EX. (**a**) The cat jumped down from the shelf.
猫は棚から下へ飛び下りた。
Neko wa tana kara shita e tobi-orita.
(**b**) She came down from upstairs.
彼女は二階から下へ下りて来た。
Kanojo wa ni-kai kara shita e orite-kita.

— adj. **[going/directed downward]**
1. ku˹dari no N 下りのN **[going downward or outbound]** ↔ **nobori no N** 上りのN

EX. I want a down elevator, not one going up.
上りじゃなくて下りのエレベーターに乗りたいんです。
Nobori janakute kudari no erebeetaa ni nori-tai n desu.

2. sa˹ga˥tte iru 下がっている /⟨V*te iru* of *sagaru* ① become reduced/ **[to be reduced or to be at a low level]**

EX. The price of gasoline is down.
ガソリンの値段が下がっている。
Gasorin no nedan ga sagatte iru.

— prep. **[along/downward]**
⟨-**ni**⟩ **so˹tte** ⟨〜に⟩沿って /⟨V*te* of *sou* ① accompany/ **[on a line parallel to the length of s.t.]**, ⟪**along, on, beside, by**⟫, **o** を prt. **[a particle to indicate space along/in/through which some movement takes place]** ⟪**in, on, across, through, along**⟫

EX. (**a**) Go down this street three blocks and turn left.
この道{に沿って/を}三ブロック行って左へ曲がりなさい。
Kono michi {ni sotte/o} san-burokku itte hidari e magarinasai.
(**b**) He went down the stairs.
彼は階段{を/*に沿って}下りた。
*Kare wa kaidan {o/*ni sotte} orita.*
(**c**) This road follows down the river aways.
この道はしばらく川{に沿って/*を}続きます。
*Kono michi wa shibaraku kawa {ni sotte/*o} tsuzukimasu.*

downtown adv. **[in/toward the main business section of a city]**
sho˹ogyoo-chi˥ku {**e/ni**} 商業地区{へ/に} n.+prt. •c **[to/toward a commercial area ⟨fml⟩]**, **ha˹nka˥-gai** {**e/ni**} 繁華街{へ/に} n.+prt. •c **[to/toward an area where many people gather for shopping, entertainment, etc.]**, **sa˹kari-ba** {**e/ni**} 盛り場{へ/に} n.+prt. **[to/toward an area lined by shops and restaurants where people gather for eating, drinking, shopping, and entertainment]**, **ma˹chi˥** {**e/ni**} 街{へ/に} n.+prt. **[to/toward a town]**

EX. (**a**) We often go downtown on weekends.
私たちは週末によく{繁華街/街/盛り場/*商業地区}へ出掛けます。
*Watakushi-tachi wa shuumatsu ni yoku {hanka-gai/machi/sakari-ba/*shoogyoo-chiku} e dekakemasu.*
(**b**) The trade mission headed downtown.
通商視察団は{商業地区/繁華街/街/盛り場}へ向かった。
Tsuushoo-shisatsu-dan wa {shoogyoo-chiku/hanka-gai/machi/sakari-ba} e mukatta.

— n. **[the main business section of a city]**
sho˹ogyoo-chi˥ku 商業地区 •c **[a commercial area]**, **ha˹nka-ga˥i** 繁華街 •c **[an area where many people gather for shopping, entertainment, etc.]** ⟪**busy quarter, amusement center**⟫, **sa˹kari-ba** 盛り場 **[an area lined by shops and restaurants where people gather for eating, drinking, shopping, and entertainment]**

NOTE: 'Downtown' is often translated as '*shitamachi*' (下町), but the latter now more often than not refers to the merchant and craftsmen quarters located in the Bay area of Tokyo.

EX. (**a**) Ginza is one of Tokyo's downtown areas.
銀座は東京の{商業地区/繁華街/盛り場}の一つです。
Ginza wa Tookyoo no {shoogyoo-chiku/hanka-gai/sakari-ba} no hitotsu desu.
(**b**) Downtown areas often have restaurants that stay open late.
{盛り場/繁華街/*商業地区}には夜遅くまで開いているレストランがあることが多い。
*{Sakari-ba/Hanka-gai/*Shoogyoo-chiku} ni wa yoru osoku made aite iru resutoran ga aru koto ga ooi.*

D

dozen n. **[a set of twelve]**
da˥asu ダース •f

EX. She bought a dozen eggs.
彼女は卵を一ダース買った。
Kanojo wa tamago o ichi-daasu katta.

draft vt. **[for s.o. to compose a preliminary outline of a written document, or to select s.o. for military service]**
1. ⟨-no⟩ {so˥okoo/ge˥nkoo} o ka˥ku ⟨～の⟩{草稿/原稿}を書く ① [for s.o. to make a preliminary outline/manuscript of s.t.] ⸨write a sketch⸩

EX. (**a**) The Prime Minister drafted his speech to the Diet.
首相は国会演説の{草稿/原稿}を書いた。
Shushoo wa kokkai-enzetsu no {sookoo/genkoo} o kaita.
(**b**) A word processor is handy for drafting manuscripts.
ワープロは{草稿/原稿}を書くのに便利だ。
Waapuro wa {sookoo/genkoo} o kaku no ni benri da.

2. ⟨-o⟩ cho˥ohei-suru ⟨～を⟩徴兵する ③ •c [for a government to enlist, conscript s.o.] ⸨enlist, conscript⸩, ⟨-o⟩ sho˥oshuu-suru ⟨～を⟩召集する ③ •c [for an authority to cause people to come to an important function such as for service in the military or as representatives in a legislature]

EX. (**a**) He was drafted into the navy.
彼は海軍に{召集/徴兵}された。
Kare wa kaigun ni {shooshuu/choohei}-sareta.
(**b**) In Japan, there is no system of drafting men into the Self-Defense Forces.
日本には自衛隊に人を{召集/徴兵}する制度はない。
Nihon ni wa jiei-tai ni hito o {shooshuu/choohei}-suru seido wa nai.

— n. **[a preliminary piece of writing or calling of persons for military service]**
1. shi˥ta-gaki 下書き [a preliminary outline in writing] ⸨a rough copy⸩, so˥okoo 草稿 •c, ge˥nkoo 原稿 •c [a piece of writing not yet published or presented before an audience or an incomplete piece of writing still in need of correction] ⸨notes, manuscript⸩

EX. (**a**) He usually doesn't make drafts of his speeches.
彼は大抵演説の{下書き/草稿/原稿}は書かない。
Kare wa taitei enzetsu no {shita-gaki/sookoo/genkoo} wa kakanai.
(**b**) I prepared a draft of my paper on my word processor.
私は論文の{下書き/草稿/原稿}をワープロで作成しました。
Watakushi wa ronbun no {shita-gaki/sookoo/genkoo} o waapuro de sakusei-shimashita.
(**c**) I stayed up all night last night revising the draft of a journal article.
ゆうべは徹夜で雑誌記事の{原稿/下書き/草稿}の手直しをした。
Yuube wa tetsuya de zasshi-kiji no {genkoo/shita-gaki/sookoo} no te-naoshi o shita.

2. cho˥ohei 徴兵 •c [conscription for military service]

EX. The draft system does not exist in our country.
我々の国には徴兵制度はない。
Ware-ware no kuni ni wa choohei-seido wa nai.

3. **do⌈rafuto ドラフト •f [an act of recruiting s.o., especially a baseball player]**

EX. Japanese baseball has a draft system.
日本の野球にはドラフト制度がある。
Nihon no yakyuu ni wa dorafuto-seido ga aru.

drag vt. **[for s.o./s.a. to pull s.t./s.o./s.a. along the ground with effort]**
⟨-o⟩ hi⌈ki-zuru ⟨～を⟩引きずる ① [for s.o./s.a. to pull s.t./s.o./s.a. while it/he/she is in contact with the floor or the ground] ⟪trail⟫

EX. (**a**) I had to walk dragging my suitcases through the airport.
私は空港中スーツケースを引きずって歩かなければならなかった。
Watakushi wa kuukoo-juu suutsukeesu o hiki-zutte arukanakereba naranakatta.
(**b**) She walked slowly, dragging her feet.
彼女は足を引きずってゆっくり歩いた。
Kanojo wa ashi o hiki-zutte yukkuri aruita.

— vi. **[for s.t./s.o. to proceed slowly as if being dragged]**
na⌈ga-bi⌉ku 長引く ① [for s.t. to take more time than expected] ⟪prolong, protract⟫

EX. (**a**) The meeting dragged on till midnight.
会議は深夜まで長引いた。
Kaigi wa shin'ya made naga-biita.
(**b**) The game dragged on and finally had to be called off due to darkness.
試合は長引いてついに日が暮れてコールドゲームとなった。
Shiai wa naga-biite tsuini hi ga kurete koorudo-geemu to natta.

drama n. **[a literary composition in which a story is told in the form of dialogue and acted out on the stage]**
e⌈ngeki 演劇 •c [a general, formal term for theatrical performance] ⟪play⟫, ge⌉ki 劇 •c [a story acted out on stage, esp. in an informal school setting] ⟪play⟫, do⌉rama ドラマ •f [a piece of writing to be performed by actors, esp. on radio/TV]

EX. (**a**) He specializes in Shakespearean drama.
彼はシェークスピアの{演劇/?劇/*ドラマ}を専門にしている。
*Kare wa Sheekusupia no {engeki/?geki/*dorama} o senmon ni shite iru.*
(**b**) That author has written many dramas.
あの作家は多くの{演劇/劇/ドラマ}を書いている。
Ano sakka wa ooku no {engeki/geki/dorama} o kaite iru.

dramatic adj. **[of/like a drama or vivid and striking]**
ge⌈ki-tekina 劇的な adj(*na*). **•c [tense and exciting as if one were watching a drama], do⌈ramachi⌉kkuna ドラマチックな** adj(*na*). **•f**

EX. (**a**) The event came to a dramatic end.
その事件は{劇的な/ドラマチックな}結末をみた。
Sono jiken wa {geki-tekina/doramachikkuna} ketsumatsu o mita.
(**b**) She made a dramatic comeback as a singer.
彼女は歌手として{劇的な/ドラマチックな}カムバックを果たした。
Kanojo wa kashu to shite {geki-tekina/doramachikkuna} kamubakku o hatashita.

draw vt. **[to pull s.o./s.t./s.a. (out) smoothly with constant speed and power ⟪fig. "to sketch s.o./s.t./s.a. in lines, words or by pictures," "elicit," "direct," "get from a source," "infer"⟫]**
1. **hi⌈ku 引く ① [to move s.t./s.o./s.a. concrete or abstract toward the source of a force ⟪fig. "to take out s.t. needed from among many things," "to extend s.t. straight and long further without interrupting or cutting it in midcourse," "for s.t. having the same quality as the essential quality of s.t. existing hitherto to continue uninterrupted," "to withdraw toward oneself s.t. that extended beyond a certain line," "to sever a relationship and create a situation where there is no relationship anymore," "to attract toward oneself"⟫] ⟪pull, tug, tow, haul; make a line; catch (a cold); attract, catch, win, arrest; lead, solicit; admit, install, conduct;**

quote, cite; look up, consult; subtract, deduct, reduce, cut down; oil, wax; be descended from, inherit; continue)) ↔ osu 押す ①

EX. (**a**) The old man drew the chair up to the dining table.
老人は食卓の方にいすを引いた。
Roojin wa shokutaku no hoo ni isu o hiita.
(**b**) It was getting dark, so she drew the curtains.
暗くなってきたので、彼女はカーテンを引いた。
Kuraku natte-kita node, kanojo wa kaaten o hiita.
(**c**) It's hard to draw a line between pity and sympathy.
哀れみと同情の間に線を引くのは難しい。
Awaremi to doojoo no aida ni sen o hiku no wa muzukashii.
(**d**) He draws his stubborn character from his father.
彼は頑固であるという点で父親の血筋を引いている。
Kare wa ganko dearu to iu ten de chichi-oya no chisuji o hiite iru.
(**e**) The farmers drew the water they needed for their paddy fields from a nearby river.
農民は田んぼに必要な水を近くの川から引いた。
Noomin wa tanbo ni hitsuyoona mizu o chikaku no kawa kara hiita.

2. ⟨-o⟩ ka˥ku ⟨〜を⟩かく ① **[for s.o. to create a short line with a pointed object] ((write, paint, scratch)), ⟨-o⟩ e˥ga˥ku** ⟨〜を⟩描く ① **[for s.o. to express s.t./s.o./s.a. using pictures or words or other form of artistic representation] ((paint, sketch, portray, describe, depict))**

㊦ "write"▷書く, "draw a picture/scratch s.t." ▷かく

EX. (**a**) The child drew a picture of her grandmother.
子供は祖母の絵を{描いた/かいた}。
Kodomo wa sobo no e o {egaita/kaita}.
(**b**) Would you draw me a map to your house?
お宅までの地図を{かいて/*描いて}下さいませんか。
*O-taku made no chizu o {kaite/*egaite} kudasaimasen ka.*
(**c**) Please draw a triangle here.
ここに三角形を{かいて/?描いて}下さい。
Koko ni sankak-kei o {kaite/?egaite} kudasai.

—— n. **[a contest ending in a tie]**
hi˥ki-wake 引き分け **[ending a game before the winner or loser has been determined] ((tie))**

EX. The baseball game ended in a draw.
野球の試合は引き分けに終わった。
Yakyuu no shiai wa hiki-wake ni owatta.

drawback n. **[shortcoming or disadvantage]**
ke˥tte˥n 欠点 •c **[s.t. that is insufficient and must be supplemented] ((fault, defect, flaw, weakness)), ta˥nsho** 短所 •c **[weak points in the performance of s.o./s.t.] ((weak point, shortcoming)) ↔ choosho** 長所 •c; **fu˥rina ten** 不利な点 •c **[respects in which one is at a disadvantage] ((demerit))**

EX. (**a**) A quick temper is his only drawback.
短気なことが彼の唯一の{欠点/短所/?不利な点}だ。
Tankina koto ga kare no yuiitsu no {ketten/tansho/?furina ten} da.
(**b**) There are many drawbacks to urban life, too.
都市生活にも多くの{欠点/短所/不利な点}があります。
Toshi-seikatsu ni mo ooku no {ketten/tansho/furina ten} ga arimasu.

drawer n. **[a sliding lidless box used in furniture]**
hi˥ki-dashi 引き出し **/⟨V*masu* of *hiki-dasu* ① pull out/**

EX. My father's desk has four drawers.
父の机には引き出しが四つついている。
Chichi no tsukue ni wa hiki-dashi ga yottsu tsuite iru.

drawing n. **[an act/result of drawing s.t./s.o./s.a. 《fig. "a picture," "sketch," "plan," "lottery"》]**
e⌉ 絵 [a visual representation of s.t./s.o./s.a. drawn on a flat surface] 《**picture, painting**》, **zu⌈men 図面 •c [a plan showing the structure/design of s.t.]** 《**blueprint, sketch, plan**》, **shi⌈ta-e 下絵 [a preliminary sketch for a picture, painting, etc.]**

EX. (**a**) He completed the drawing of the bridge.
彼は橋の{絵/図面/下絵}を完成した。
Kare wa hashi no {e/zumen/shita-e} o kansei-shita.
(**b**) This is only an artist's drawing of the building.
これは画家がかいた建物の{絵/図面/下絵}に過ぎない。
Kore wa gaka ga kaita tate-mono no {e/zumen/shita-e} ni suginai.
(**c**) This is the drawing of the new house.
これが新しい家の{絵/下絵/図面}です。
Kore ga atarashii ie no {e/shita-e/zumen} desu.

dread n. **[strong fear]**
o⌈sore⌉ 恐れ /〈V*masu* of *osoreru* ② fear/ [a feeling of fear] 《**fear, terror, horror**》, **kyo⌉ofu 恐怖 •c [great anxiety caused by the expectation of danger/evil]** 《**fear, terror, horror, panic**》, **kyo⌈ofu⌉-kan 恐怖感 •c [a sense of horror]**
—— vt. **[for s.o./s.a. to fear s.t./s.o./s.a. greatly]**
〈-o〉 o⌈sore⌉ru 〈〜を〉恐れる ② [for s.o./s.a. to be fearful of s.t./s.o./s.a.] 《**fear, be afraid**》, **〈-o〉 ko⌈wa-ga⌉ru 〈〜を〉怖がる ① [for s.o./s.a. to show signs of feeling fright toward s.o./s.t./s.a.]** 《**be frightened, fear, be nervous about**》

EX. (**a**) He dreaded death.
彼は死を{恐れて/怖がって}いた。
Kare wa shi o {osorete/kowa-gatte} ita.
(**b**) It's no use dreading the exams since there's no way of escaping them.
試験は逃れられないんだから{恐れて/怖がって}も仕方がない。
Shiken wa nogare-rarenai n da kara {osorete/kowa-gatte} mo shikata-ga-nai.

dreadful adj. **[inspiring fear, terrible, very bad]**
1. 〈-ga〉 ko⌈wa⌉i 〈〜が〉怖い adj(*i*). [for s.o./s.a. to feel frightened or for s.t. to cause s.o./s.a. to feel frightened] 《**scary, fearful, frightful, horrible**》, **o⌈soroshi⌉i 恐ろしい adj(*i*). [for s.o. to be afraid of s.t./s.o./s.a. which is unusual or mysterious or for s.t./s.o./s.a. to cause such fear]**

EX. (**a**) It was a very dreadful night.
とても{怖い/恐ろしい}夜だった。
Totemo {kowai/osoroshii} yoru datta.
(**b**) I heard the most dreadful story the other day.
この間非常に{怖い/恐ろしい}話を聞いた。
Kono aida hijooni {kowai/osoroshii} hanashi o kiita.

2. hi⌈do⌉i ひどい adj(*i*). [of a frightening kind/degree or cruel] 《**cruel, harsh, severe, terrible**》

EX. (**a**) The food was dreadful there.
あそこの食事はひどかった。
Asoko no shokuji wa hidokatta.
(**b**) We had dreadful weather last Sunday.
先週の日曜日はひどい天気だった。
Senshuu no nichiyoo-bi wa hidoi tenki datta.

dream n. **[images/thoughts/emotions occurring during sleep or a fond hope]**
yu⌈me⌉ 夢

EX. (**a**) I had a strange dream last night.
ゆうべは変な夢を見ました。
Yuube wa henna yume o mimashita.
(**b**) Her dream is to travel around the world by boat.
彼女の夢は船で世界一周をすることだ。
Kanojo no yume wa fune de sekai-isshuu o suru koto da.
(**c**) He fulfilled all his dreams in life.
彼は一生の夢を全部実現させた。
Kare wa isshoo no yume o zenbu jitsugen-saseta.
(**d**) There is nothing like a star-filled night sky to stir up a child's dreams.

D

星でいっぱいの夜空ほど子供の夢をかきたてるものはない。
Hoshi de ippai no yo-zora hodo kodomo no yume o kaki-tateru mono wa nai.

— vt. **[for s.o./s.a. to imagine s.t. in a dream]**
yu⌈me⌉ ni o⌈mo⌉u 夢に思う ① [for s.o./s.a. to imagine s.t./s.o./s.a. in a dream] **《conceive》, 〈-o〉 so⌈ozoo-suru 〈〜を〉想像する ③ •c [for s.o. to form an image of s.t./s.o./s.a. one has never encountered before]** **《imagine, suppose》**

EX. (**a**) I never dreamed that man could travel in space.
人類が宇宙旅行出来るとは{夢にも思わなかった/想像もしなかった}。
Jinrui ga uchuu-ryokoo-dekiru to wa {yume ni mo omowanakatta/soozoo mo shinakatta}.
(**b**) She never dreamed that she would marry him.
彼女は自分が彼と結婚しようとは{夢にも思わなかった/想像もしなかった}。
Kanojo wa jibun ga kare to kekkon-shiyoo to wa {yume ni mo omowanakatta/soozoo mo shinakatta}.

NOTE: *Yume ni omou,* like its literal counterpart in English, is usable only in the negative form, as examples (a) and (b) show. An affirmative sentence such as "I dreamed that I was elected President of the United States" would be rendered as *Amerika no daitooryoo ni natta yume o mita.*

PHRASE: dream of 〈-o〉 *yume-miru* 〈〜を〉夢見る ②

EX. He dreamed of a happy life with Eri.
彼は恵理との幸せな生活を夢見た。
Kare wa Eri to no shiawasena seikatsu o yume mita.

dress n. **[clothing, esp. of the sort worn externally]**
fu⌈kusoo 服装 •c [clothing one wears] **《clothes》, i⌉fuku 衣服 •c [s.t. in which one is clad]** **《clothes》, do⌉resu ドレス •f [a lady's Western-style attire usually consisting of one piece], yo⌈ofuku 洋服 •c [Western apparel], ki⌈ru mono 着るもの [a generic term referring to anything one wears as a garment]**

EX. (**a**) I hear they are very particular about dress at that school.
あの学校では{服装/衣服/洋服/着るもの/*ドレス}にとてもうるさいそうです。
*Ano gakkoo de wa {fukusoo/ifuku/yoofuku/kiru mono/*doresu} ni totemo urusai soodesu.*
(**b**) Miwako wore a beautiful white dress to the party.
美和子はパーティーにきれいな白い{ドレス/洋服/*衣服/*着るもの/*服装}を着て行った。
*Miwako wa paatii ni kireina shiroi {doresu/yoofuku/*ifuku/*kiru mono/*fukusoo} o kite itta.*

— vt. **[for s.o. to put clothes on s.o. else]**
〈-ni〉 fu⌈ku⌉ o ki-⌈seru 〈〜に〉服を着せる ② **《clothe》**

EX. (**a**) The nurse dressed the patient.
看護婦は患者に服を着せた。
Kango-fu wa kanja ni fuku o ki-seta.
(**b**) Will you dress Johnny while I clean the room, honey?
部屋を掃除する間にジョニーに服を着せて下さらない、あなた。
Heya o sooji-suru aida ni Jonii ni fuku o ki-sete kudasaranai, anata.

PHRASE: be dressed in 〈-o〉 *kite iru* 〈〜を〉着ている ② /〈V *te iru* of *kiru* ② wear/ 《wear》

EX. She is dressed in her best today.
彼女は今日よそ行きを着ている。
Kanojo wa kyoo yoso-yuki o kite iru.

drill n. **[a tool for boring holes 《fig. "practice by repetition"》]**
1. do⌉riru ドリル •f, ki⌉ri きり [a tool for boring holes] **《gimlet, awl》**

EX. The carpenter made a hole in the board with a drill.
大工は{きり/ドリル}で板に穴を開けた。
Daiku wa {kiri/doriru} de ita ni ana o aketa.

2. re⌈nshuu 練習 •c [an act of doing s.t. repeatedly to acquire a specific skill]

⟪exercise, training, practice⟫, do˥riru ドリル •f

EX. (a) Drills are an especially important part of language learning.
語学教育では{練習/ドリル}が特に重要です。
Gogaku-kyooiku de wa {renshuu/doriru} ga tokuni juuyoo desu.
(b) In today's class we are going to do some pronunciation drills.
今日の授業では発音の{練習/ドリル}をします。
Kyoo no jugyoo de wa hatsuon no {renshuu/doriru} o shimasu.

— vt. **[to make a hole in s.t. with a drill ⟪fig. "teach by repeated exercises"⟫]**
1. do˥riru de a˥na˥ o a˥keru ドリルで穴を開ける ② [for s.o. to make a hole with a drill]
2. ⟨-ni⟩ re˥nshuu o saseru ⟨〜に⟩練習をさせる ② •c [for s.o. to cause s.o. to do s.t. repeatedly to gain a specific skill] ⟪exercise⟫, ⟨-ni⟩ do˥riru o sa˥seru ⟨〜に⟩ドリルをさせる ② •f [for s.o. to cause s.o. to do drills]

EX. (a) The teacher drilled the students in Chinese characters.
先生は学生に漢字の{練習/ドリル}をさせた。
Sensei wa gakusei ni kanji no {renshuu/doriru} o saseta.
(b) We were drilled in English conversation everyday in high school.
我々は高校の時毎日英会話の{練習/ドリル}をさせられた。
Ware-ware wa kookoo no toki mai-nichi ei-kaiwa no {renshuu/doriru} o sase-rareta.
(c) We drill students for an hour each day in multiplication.
毎日一時間生徒に掛け算の{練習/ドリル}をさせる。
Mai-nichi ichi-jikan seito ni kake-zan no {renshuu/doriru} o saseru.

drink vt. **[to swallow/absorb liquid]**
⟨-o⟩ no˥mu ⟨〜を⟩飲む ① [for s.o./s.a. to put s.t. into one's body through the mouth without chewing it ⟪fig. "to overwhelm," "to suppress," "to acquiesce"⟫]

EX. (a) I drink many cups of green tea in the course of a day.
私は日に何杯も緑茶を飲みます。
Watashi wa hi ni nan-bai mo ryoku-cha o nomimasu.
(b) She never fails to drink grapefruit juice for breakfast.
彼女は朝食に必ずグレープフルーツジュースを飲む。
Kanojo wa choo-shoku ni kanarazu gureepu-furuutsu-juusu o nomu.

— n. **[any liquid, incl. alcohol, for human consumption]**
1. no˥mi˥-mono 飲物 [s.t. one takes in through one's mouth without chewing] ⟪beverage⟫

EX. (a) He ordered soft drinks for all.
彼はみんなにアルコールの入っていない飲物を注文した。
Kare wa minna ni arukooru no haitte inai nomi-mono o chuumon-shita.
(b) Before we left, we bought enough food and drink for the drive.
ドライブに出かける前に十分な食べ物と飲物を買った。
Doraibu ni dekakeru mae ni juubunna tabe-mono to nomi-mono o katta.

2. sa˥ke 酒 [Japanese rice wine or alcoholic drinks in general] ⟪liquor, sake⟫

EX. (a) He is fond of drink.
彼は酒が好きだ。
Kare wa sake ga suki da.
(b) How about a drink?
酒を一杯いかがですか。
Sake o ip-pai ikaga desu ka.

drive vt. **[to propel or send s.t./s.o. in some direction or into some state by means of a strong force ⟪fig. "to operate a motor vehicle," "to carry s.o. to some destination by means of a motor vehicle"⟫]**
1. ⟨-o⟩ u˥nten-suru ⟨〜を⟩運転する ③ •c [for s.o. to control the functioning and movement of a large vehicle, esp. a car] ⟪operate⟫

EX. (a) He drives a truck for a living.

D

彼は仕事でトラックを運転している。
Kare wa shigoto de torakku o unten-shite iru.
(**b**) Does your mother drive a car?
お母さんは車を運転しますか。
O-kaa-san wa kuruma o unten-shimasu ka.

2. ⟨-o⟩ **ku⌈ruma de o⌈kuru** ⟨〜を⟩車で送る ① **[for s.o. to carry s.o. by car to a destination]** ⟪**transport, take, give a ride**⟫

EX. (**a**) Let me drive you home.
家まで車でお送りしましょう。
Ie made kuruma de o-okuri-shimashoo.
(**b**) I drove her home and then returned to my home.
彼女を車で送ってから家へ帰った。
Kanojo o kuruma de okutte kara ie e kaetta.

D

3. ⟨-o⟩ **o⌈i-hara⌉u** ⟨〜を⟩追い払う ① **[for s.o. to chase away s.t./s.o./s.a. that is obnoxious and bothersome]** ⟪**get rid of, send away, put to rout**⟫

EX. (**a**) A horse drives away flies with its tail.
馬はしっぽでハエを追い払う。
Uma wa shippo de hae o oi-harau.
(**b**) The enemy was driven away by our troops.
敵は我々の軍隊に追い払われた。
Teki wa ware-ware no guntai ni oi-harawa-reta.

4. ⟨-o⟩ {**adj(*i*). *ku*/adj(*na*). *ni*/⟨-ni⟩**} **su⌈ru** ⟨〜を⟩{**adj(*i*). *ku*/adj(*na*). *ni*/⟨〜に⟩**}する ③ **[to cause s.t. to take on some new property or form]**, ⟨-de⟩ {**adj(*i*). *ku*/adj(*na*). *ni*/⟨-ni⟩**} **na⌉ru** ⟨〜で⟩{**adj(*i*). *ku*/adj(*na*). *ni*/⟨〜に⟩**}なる ① **[for s.t. to take on some new property or form due to some cause or instrument]**

EX. (**a**) The pain almost drove me mad.
痛みで気が狂いそうになった
Itami de ki-ga-kurui-sooni natta.
(**b**) The noise drives me crazy.
音がうるさくてノイローゼになりそうだ。
Oto ga urusakute noirooze ni nari-soo da.

5. ⟨-o⟩ **u⌈chi-komu** ⟨〜を⟩打ち込む ① **[for s.o. to cause s.t. to penetrate into s.t. by means of a forceful blow]** ⟪**strike, hit**⟫

EX. (**a**) He drove a nail into the wall.
彼は壁にくぎを打ち込んだ。
Kare wa kabe ni kugi o uchi-konda.
(**b**) The workers were driving spikes into the railroad ties.
作業員は枕木に犬くぎを打ち込んでいました。
Sagyoo-in wa makura-gi ni inu-kugi o uchi-konde imashita.

— vi. **[for s.o. to operate a car, etc.]**
u⌈nten-suru 運転する ③ •**c [for s.o. to operate and direct the course of (a vehicle)]**

EX. Mother likes to drive.
母は運転するのが好きだ。
Haha wa unten-suru no ga suki da.

— n. **[a trip in a car]**
do⌈ra⌉ibu ドライブ •**f**

EX. (**a**) Let's go for a drive.
ドライブに行こう。
Doraibu ni ikoo.
(**b**) The children went out for a drive.
子供たちはドライブに出掛けました。
Kodomo-tachi wa doraibu ni dekakemashita.

driver n. **[one who drives a vehicle]**
u⌈nte⌉n-shu 運転手 •**c [one who operates a vehicle, often as a profession]**, **do⌈ra⌉ibaa** ドライバー •**f [one who drives or a screwdriver or a type of golf club]**

EX. (**a**) The taxi driver was very kind.
タクシーの{運転手/ドライバー}は親切だった。
Takushii no {unten-shu/doraibaa} wa shinsetsu datta.
(**b**) I work as a driver on the side.
アルバイトに{運転手/ドライバー}をしています。
Arubaito ni {unten-shu/doraibaa} o shite imasu.

driveway n. **[a path for cars from the street to a garage, house, etc.]**
ge⌉nkan kara to⌈ori made no mi⌈chi 玄関から通りまでの道 **[a road from the entrance of a house to the street]**

EX. We removed snow from the driveway.
玄関から通りまでの道の雪かきをした。
Genkan kara toori made no michi no yuki-kaki o shita.

driving n. **[the act of operating a car]**
u⌈nten 運転 •c [operation of a vehicle, machine, etc.] ⟪operation⟫

EX. (**a**) She is very fond of driving.
彼女は運転が大好きです。
Kanojo wa unten ga dai-suki desu.
(**b**) His driving is reckless.
彼の運転は乱暴です。
Kare no unten wa ranboo desu.

drop vi. **[to fall down suddenly]**
1. o⌈chi⌉ru 落ちる ② [for s.t. which has lost its support or balance to move rapidly from a higher to a lower position due to gravity ⟪fig. "for s.t. which has been in a place or is expected to be in a place to cease to be seen there," "to deteriorate into an inferior condition," "to reach a final/ultimate state," "to fail in an examination or interview"⟫] ⟪fall, give way, collapse, crumble, come off, wash off, die down, fail, be defeated⟫, ra⌈kka-suru 落下する •c ③ [to move rapidly from a higher to lower position due to gravity]

EX. (**a**) An apple dropped from the tree.
リンゴが木から{落ちた/落下した}。
Ringo ga ki kara {ochita/rakka-shita}.
(**b**) I saw something dropping from the roof.
屋根から何かが{落ちる/落下する}のが見えた。
Yane kara nani-ka ga {ochiru/rakka-suru} no ga mieta.
(**c**) It was so silent one could hear a pin drop.
針が{落ちて/落下して}も聞こえるほど静かだった。
Hari ga {ochite/rakka-shite} mo kikoeru hodo shizuka datta.

2. sa⌈ga⌉ru 下がる ① [to hang/go down/become smaller in amount/degree/strength] ⟪go down, fall, hang down, sink, back up, retire⟫ ↔ agaru 上がる ①

EX. (**a**) The price of gasoline shouldn't drop any further for the time being.
ガソリンの値段はしばらくの間これ以上下がらないでしょう。
Gasorin no nedan wa shibaraku no aida kore ijoo sagaranai deshoo.
(**b**) His temperature has already dropped.
熱はもう下がった。
Netsu wa moo sagatta.

PHRASE: drop by *tachi-yoru* 立ち寄る ①

EX. (**a**) She dropped by just to say hello.
彼女はあいさつをするためちょっと立ち寄った。
Kanojo wa aisatsu o suru tame chotto tachi-yotta.
(**b**) Please drop by when you're in the neighborhood.
お近くへおいでの節はぜひお立ち寄り下さい。
O-chikaku e o-ide no setsu wa zehi o-tachi-yori kudasai.

—— vt. **[to let/make s.t. fall down suddenly]**
1. ⟨-o⟩ o⌈to⌉su ⟨～を⟩落とす ① [for s.o./s.a. to allow/cause s.t. to lose its support/balance and move rapidly from a higher to a lower position due to gravity ⟪fig. "to make s.t. which is expected to be in a place not be seen there anymore," "to cause s.t. to become lower/worse in extent, quality, etc.," "to render s.t. into a decided/settled state of affairs"⟫] ⟪let fall, lose, lower, slow down, tune down, forget, remove, deduct⟫

EX. (**a**) The airplane dropped a bomb.
飛行機は爆弾を落とした。
Hikoo-ki wa bakudan o otoshita.
(**b**) She dropped the tea cup and broke it.
彼女は茶わんを落として割ってしまった。
Kanojo wa chawan o otoshite watte shimatta.

2. ⟨-o⟩ sa⌈ge⌉ru ⟨～を⟩下げる ② [for s.o. to cause s.t./s.o./s.a. to move to a lower place or to decrease in amount/degree/strength] ⟪hang, lower, bring down, reduce, push back, take away, draw, carry⟫ ↔ ⟨-o⟩ ageru ⟨～を⟩上げる ②

EX. The increased competition has forced all

D

computer makers to drop their prices.
競争が激しくなったためコンピューター・メーカーはそろって値段を下げざるを得なくなった。
Kyoosoo ga hageshiku natta tame konpyuutaa-meekaa wa sorotte nedan o sagezaru o enaku natta.

PHRASE: drop s.o. off ⟨*-o*⟩ *orosu* ⟨〜を⟩おろす ① ㊥ "let s.o. off a vehicle"▷降ろす, "sell for wholesale"▷卸す, otherwise ▷下ろす

EX. (**a**) Could you drop me off at that corner?
その角で降ろして下さいませんか。
Sono kado de oroshite kudasaimasen ka.
(**b**) I'll drop you off at the gate.
門のところで降ろしてあげよう。
Mon no tokoro de oroshite ageyoo.

PHRASE: drop a line ⟨*-ni*⟩ *{tayori o suru/tegami o kaku}* ⟨〜に⟩{便りをする/手紙を書く}

EX. Drop me a line from time to time, would you?
時々は{便りをして/手紙を書いて}くれよな。
Toki-doki wa {tayori o shite/tegami o kaite} kure yo na.

PHRASE: drop a course *kamoku no jukoo o {tori-kesu/yameru}* 科目の受講を{取り消す/やめる}

EX. John dropped his Japanese course.
ジョンは日本語の科目の受講を{取り消した/やめた}。
Jon wa Nihon-go no kamoku no jukoo o {tori-keshita/yameta}.

—— n. **[a bit of liquid rounded in shape from falling 《fig. "a small amount," "falling," "steep downhill," "liquid medicine"》]**
shi⌈zuku⌉ しずく [small rounded masses of water/other liquid that drip off s.t. and fall], te⌈ika 低下 •c [an act/instance of s.t. going down] 《plummet》

EX. (**a**) Rain drops are falling on my head.
雨の{しずく/*低下}が頭に当たる。
*Ame no {shizuku/*teika} ga atama ni ataru.*
(**b**) The weather bureau recorded an unusual drop in temperature.
気象庁は気温の異常な{低下/*しずく}を記録した。
*Kishoo-choo wa kion no ijoona {teika/*shizuku} o kiroku-shita.*

drugstore n. **[a store where drugs and other daily necessities are sold]**
ku⌈suri-ya 薬屋 《chemist's》, ya⌈kkyoku 薬局 •c [a place where drugs are sold]

EX. (**a**) I've just been to the corner drugstore.
角の{薬屋/薬局}まで行って来たところです。
Kado no {kusuri-ya/yakkyoku} made itte-kita tokoro desu.
(**b**) He bought this detergent at the drugstore.
彼はこの洗剤を{薬屋/*薬局}で買った。
*Kare wa kono senzai o {kusuri-ya/*yakkyoku} de katta.*

NOTE: In Japanese *kusuri-ya*, drugs, cosmetics, and perhaps detergents are sold but not stationery, newspapers, magazines or other nonmedical supplies.

drunk adj. **[intoxicated]**
yo⌉tte iru (N) 酔っている(N) /⟨V*te iru* of *you* ① get intoxicated/ ②

EX. (**a**) He was terribly drunk last night.
彼はゆうべはひどく酔っていた。
Kare wa yuube wa hidoku yotte ita.
(**b**) One should absolutely never drive when drunk.
酔っていたら絶対運転をしてはいけない。
Yotte itara zettai unten o shite wa ikenai.

dry adj. **[not wet/damp 《fig. "not drinking alcohol," "boring," "showing little emotion"》]**
ka⌈wa⌉ita N 乾いたN /⟨Vinf. past of *kawaku* ① dry/ 《parched》, ka⌈nsoo-shita N 乾燥したN /⟨Vinf. past of *kansoo-suru* ③ dry/ •c [for s.t. to be arid, esp. the air/climate] ↔ nureta N ぬれたN, shimetta N しめったN

EX. (**a**) For someone like me with asthma, the dry air around here is really nice.
私のようなぜんそく持ちには、この辺の{乾いた/乾燥した}空気がとてもいい。
Watashi no yoona zensoku-mochi ni

wa, kono hen no {kawaita/kansoo-shita} kuuki ga totemo ii.
(**b**) Fires tend to occur under dry conditions.
空気が{乾いた/乾燥した}状態では火事が起きやすい。
Kuuki ga {kawaita/kansoo-shita} jootai de wa kaji ga oki-yasui.
(**c**) Get him a dry shirt.
彼に{乾いた/*乾燥した}シャツを出してあげて。
*Kare ni {kawaita/*kansoo-shita} shatsu o dashite agete.*

2. ta⌈ikutsuna 退屈な adj(*na*). •**c [causing s.o. to become bored]** ((**boring, be bored, uninteresting, dull**)), **mu⌉mi-kansoona** 無味乾燥な adj(*na*). •**c [lacking taste/interest]**

EX. (**a**) His lecture was dry.
彼の講演は{退屈/無味乾燥}だった。
Kare no kooen wa {taikutsu/mumi-kansoo} datta.
(**b**) Who would buy a dry and uninteresting book like that ?
あんな{退屈な/無味乾燥な}本、だれが買うんだろう。
Anna {taikutsuna/mumi-kansoona} hon, dare ga kau n daroo.

—— vt. **[to make s.t. not wet]**

1. ⟨**-o**⟩ **ka⌈waka⌉su** ⟨～を⟩乾かす ① **[for s.o. to make s.t. not wet]**, ⟨**-o**⟩ **ho⌉su**, ⟨～を⟩干す ① **[for s.o. to put s.t. in a sunny/well-ventilated place to rid it of moisture]** ((**air clothes, mats**))

EX. (**a**) Mother dried the laundry outside.
母は洗濯物を{外で乾かした/外に干した}。
Haha wa sentaku-mono o {soto de kawakashita/soto ni hoshita}.
(**b**) He dried his wet trousers by the fire.
彼はぬれたズボンをたき火で{乾かした/*干した}。
*Kare wa nureta zubon o taki-bi de {kawakashita/*hoshita}.*
(**c**) I dried my wet handkerchief with an electric fan.
私はハンカチを扇風機で{乾かした/*干した}。
*Watakushi wa hankachi o senpuu-ki de {kawakashita/*hoshita}.*

—— vi. **[for s.t. to become not wet]**

ka⌈wa⌉ku かわく ① **[for the moisture/water contained in s.t. to go away** 《**fig. "for the mouth to become dry and thirsty"**》**]** ((**become parched, become thirsty**))
㊈ "for s.o. to become thirsty" ▷渇く, otherwise ▷乾く

EX. (**a**) The paint on the door should have dried by now.
ドアのペンキはもう乾いたでしょう。
Doa no penki wa moo kawaita deshoo.
(**b**) The road has dried completely.
道はすっかり乾いてしまった。
Michi wa sukkari kawaite shimatta.

dull adj. **[not sharp** 《**fig. "boring," "lacking intelligence"**》**]**

1. ni⌈bu⌉i 鈍い adj(*i*). **[not sharp** 《**fig. "lacking intelligence," "boring," "unclear in sound," "dim"**》**]** ((**blunt, dim, slow-witted, not bright**)) ↔ **surudoi** 鋭い adj(*i*).

EX. (**a**) I heard a dull thud upstairs.
二階でドスンと鈍い音がした。
Ni-kai de dosun to nibui oto ga shita.
(**b**) A dull head like mine is not suited for physics.
私のように頭の鈍い者は物理学には向いていない。
Watashi no yooni atama no nibui mono wa butsuri-gaku ni wa muite inai.

2. ta⌈ikutsuna 退屈な adj(*na*). •**c [causing s.o. to become bored]** ((**boring, be bored, uninteresting, dull**)), **o⌈moshi⌉roku na⌉i** 面白くない /⟨**neg. of adj**(*i*). ***omoshiroi*** **interesting**/ **[not interesting]** ((**boring**))

EX. (**a**) She found the party dull.
彼女にはパーティーは{退屈だった/面白くなかった}。
Kanojo ni wa paatii wa {taikutsu datta/omoshiroku nakatta}.
(**b**) The movie was dull.
映画は{退屈だった/面白くなかった}。
Eiga wa {taikutsu datta/omoshiroku nakatta}.

D

duration n. **[the time s.t. continues]**
ki⌈ka⌉n 期間 •c [a specific time span in which s.t. noteworthy occurs] ((**term, period**)), **-chuu ～中 •c [within the span of time of/among the choices represented by]** ((**in, among, during, in progress**))

EX. (**a**) There will be no smoking for the duration of the flight.
飛行{中/*期間}はずっと禁煙です。
*Hikoo-{chuu/*kikan} wa zutto kin'en desu.*
(**b**) What is the anticipated duration of his stay in this country?
彼がこの国に滞在する{期間/*中}は大体どのぐらいでしょうか。
Kare ga kono kuni ni taizai-suru {kikan/-chuu} wa daitai dono-gurai deshoo ka.*

D

during prep. **[throughout the entire time of s.t. or in the course of s.t.]**
1. 〈**-no**〉 **a⌈ida zu⌈tto** 〈～の〉間ずっと n.+adv. **[throughout the entire period of s.t.]** ((**for the duration of**))

EX. (**a**) The students kept talking during the whole lecture.
学生たちは授業の間ずっと話をしていた。
Gakusei-tachi wa jugyoo no aida zutto hanashi o shite ita.
(**b**) I was sleeping during the entire flight.
飛行機に乗っている間ずっと寝ていました。
Hikoo-ki ni notte iru aida zutto nete imashita.

2. {**Vinf. nonpast/N no**} **a⌈ida ni** {**Vinf. nonpast/Nの**}**間に** n.+prt. **[in the course of s.t.]**

EX. (**a**) A war broke out during his visit to the country.
彼がその国を訪問している間に戦争が始まった。
Kare ga sono kuni o hoomon shite iru aida ni sensoo ga hajimatta.
(**b**) The rain changed to snow during the night.
雨は夜の間に雪に変わった。
Ame wa yoru no aida ni yuki ni kawatta.
(**c**) A package was delivered to my house during my absence.
留守の間に小包みが家に届いていた。
Rusu no aida ni ko-zutsumi ga ie ni todoite ita.

dust n. **[fine particles of earth or other matter]**
chi⌈ri ちり [almost invisible particles of earth, etc., floating in the air], ho⌈kori ほこり [very fine particles of earth, sand, etc., which can easily be stirred up into the air]

EX. (**a**) His desk was covered with dust.
彼の机の上は{ちり/ほこり}だらけだった。
Kare no tsukue no ue wa {chiri/hokori}-darake datta.
(**b**) Let's get rid of this dust.
ここの{ちり/ほこり}を取ろう。
Koko no {chiri/hokori} o toroo.
(**c**) The book was lying on the desk covered with dust.
あの本は机の上で{ほこり/ちり}をかぶっていました。
Ano hon wa tsukue no ue de {hokori/chiri} o kabutte imashita.

Dutch adj. **[of the Netherlands/its people/its language]**
O⌈randa no N オランダのN •f [of the Netherlands], O⌈randa⌉-jin no N オランダ人のN •f+c [of the people/a person of the Netherlands], O⌈randa-go no N オランダ語のN •f+c [of the language of the Netherlands]

—— n. **[the people/language of the Netherlands]**
O⌈randa⌉-jin オランダ人 •f+c [the people/a person of the Netherlands], O⌈randa-go オランダ語 •f+c [the language of the Netherlands]

PHRASE: go Dutch *wari-kan ni suru* 割り勘にする

EX. Let's go Dutch today.
きょうは割り勘にしよう。
Kyoo wa wari-kan ni shiyoo.

duty n. **[s.t. one is required to do by moral/legal obligation or action required by one's position ⟪fig. "tax paid at customs"⟫]**
1. gi⌉mu 義務 •c [s.t. one is required to do by virtue of one's position] ⟪obligation, responsibility⟫ ↔ kenri 権利 •c; gi⌈ri⌉ 義理 •c [a course of action one is morally bound to follow by virtue of one's relationship to others in society] ↔ ninjoo 人情 •c

EX. (**a**) A student's primary duty is to study.
学生の第一の{義務/*義理}は勉強することです。
*Gakusei no dai-ichi no {gimu/*giri} wa benkyoo-suru koto desu.*
(**b**) We have a duty to defend our country.
我々には自分の国を守る{義務/*義理}がある。
*Ware-ware ni wa jibun no kuni o mamoru {gimu/*giri} ga aru.*
(**c**) What are the three greatest duties of a citizen?
国民の三大{義務/*義理}は何ですか。
*Kokumin no san-dai-{gimu/*giri} wa nan desu ka.*
(**d**) Japanese often give gifts out of a sense of duty.
日本人はよく{義理/*義務}で人に贈り物をする。
*Nihon-jin wa yoku {giri/*gimu} de hito ni okuri-mono o suru.*
(**e**) Socializing is often done half out of duty.
社交というのは半分{義理/義務}ですることもあります。
Shakoo to iu no wa hanbun {giri/gimu} de suru koto mo arimasu.

2. ze⌈ikin 税金 •c [a compulsory payment of money to support the government]

PHRASE: customs duty *kanzei* 関税 •c

EX. There are no import duties on books.
本は輸入の際、税金がかからない。
Hon wa yunyuu no sai, zeikin ga kakaranai.

each adj./pron. **[every one of two or more considered separately]**
1. so⌈re⌉-zore no N それぞれのN [every one of], o⌈no⌉-ono no N 各々のN [every one of ⟨fml⟩], hi⌈tori-hito⌉ri no N 一人一人のN [of/related to every person considered singly], ka⌉ku- 各〜 [every one respectively]

EX. (**a**) Each student at this university is assigned an ID number.
この大学の{それぞれの/各々の/一人一人の/各}学生には学生番号が与えられている。
Kono daigaku no {sore-zore no/ono-ono no/hitori-hitori no/kaku-} gakusei ni wa gakusei-bangoo ga atae-rarete iru.
(**b**) Each class has a faculty advisor.
{それぞれの/各々の/各}クラスにはアドバイザーの教師がついている。
{Sore-zore no/Ono-ono no/Kaku-} kurasu ni wa adobaizaa no kyooshi ga tsuite iru.
(**c**) I ask that each department please think about this problem.
この問題は{それぞれの/各々の/各}学部で検討してください。
Kono mondai wa {sore-zore no/ono-ono no/kaku-} gakubu de kentoo-shite kudasai.

2. so⌈re⌉-zore それぞれ n. **[in a way applicable to every one respectively], me⌈i-me⌉i めいめい** n. **[every one of a set of persons], o⌈no⌉-ono 各々** n. **[every one of**

⟨fml⟩], hi⌈tori-hito⌉ri 一人一人 n. [every person considered singly]

EX. (a) Each did it in his or her own way.
{それぞれ/めいめい/各々/一人一人}が{それぞれ/めいめい/各々/*一人一人}自分のやり方でやった。
*{Sore-zore/Mei-mei/Ono-ono/Hitori-hitori} ga {sore-zore/mei-mei/ono-ono/ *hitori-hitori} jibun no yari-kata de yatta.*
(b) The teacher gave a dictionary to each of the students.
先生は学生の{それぞれ/めいめい/各々/一人一人}に辞書を一冊与えた。
Sensei wa gakusei no {sore-zore/mei-mei/ono-ono/hitori-hitori} ni jisho o is-satsu ataeta.
(c) Each must write his or her name on his or her possessions.
自分の持ち物には{それぞれ/めいめい/各々}名前をつけること。
Jibun no mochi-mono ni wa {sore-zore /mei-mei/ono-ono} namae o tsukeru koto.

— adv. [apiece]
so⌈re⌉-zore それぞれ [in a way applicable to every one], o⌈no⌉-ono 各々 [every one of ⟨fml⟩], hi⌈tori-hito⌉ri 一人一人 [every person individually]

EX. (a) The professors in this department each have their own assistant.
この学科の教授には{それぞれ/各々/一人一人}助手がついている。
Kono gakka no kyooju ni wa {sore-zore/ono-ono/hitori-hitori} joshu ga tsuite iru.
(b) My wife and I each have a cat.
家内と私は{それぞれ/各々/*一人一人}猫を一匹ずつ飼っている。
*Kanai to watashi wa {sore-zore/ono-ono/ *hitori-hitori} neko o ip-piki-zutsu katte iru.*

PHRASE: each other *(o-)tagai ni* (お)互いに

EX. (a) They hit each other.
彼らは互いに殴り合った。
Kare-ra wa tagai ni naguri-atta.
(b) They congratulated each other on arriving safely.
彼らは互いに無事に到着したことを喜びあった。
Kare-ra wa tagai ni bujini toochaku-shita koto o yorokobi-atta.

eager adj. [keenly desiring or anxious to do s.t.]

1. ⟨-o⟩ ne⌉sshinni ne⌈ga⌉tte iru ⟨〜を⟩熱心に願っている /⟨V*te iru* of *negau* ① wish/ [wishing with enthusiasm] 《anxious》, ⟨-o⟩ {se⌈tsuboo/ne⌈tsuboo}-shite iru ⟨〜を⟩{切望/熱望}している /⟨V*te iru* of {*setsuboo/ netsuboo*}*-suru* ③ long/ •c [hoping with enthusiasm], to⌈temo V*masu* ta-⌈ga⌉tte iru とてもV*masu*たがっている /⟨V*te iru* of V*masu ta-garu* ① showing signs of wanting to do s.t./ ② [wanting to do s.t. very much]

EX. (a) Many students are eager to come to Japan to study Japanese.
多くの学生が日本へ来て日本語を{{勉強することを{熱心に願って/切望して/熱望して}}/とても勉強したがって}いる。
Ooku no gakusei ga Nihon e kite Nihon-go o {{benkyoo-suru koto o {nesshinni negatte/setsuboo-shite/netsuboo-shite}}/ totemo benkyoo-shi-ta-gatte} iru.
(b) He is eager to buy a new car.
彼は新しい車を{{買うことを{熱心に願って/切望して/熱望して}}/とても買いたがって}いる。
Kare wa atarashii kuruma o {{kau koto o {nesshinni negatte/setsuboo-shite/ netsuboo-shite}}/totemo kai-ta-gatte} iru.
(c) Parents are eager for their children to grow up safely.
親は子が無事に成長するよう{熱心に願って/切望して/?熱望して}いる。
Oya wa ko ga bujini seichoo-suru yoo {nesshinni negatte/setsuboo-shite/ ?netsuboo-shite} iru.

2. ⌈ne⌉sshinna 熱心な adj(*na*). •c [passionately interested in and devoted to one thing] 《keen, diligent, hard-working》

EX. (a) Ed is an eager fan of *sumo*.
エドは相撲の熱心なファンです。
Edo wa sumoo no nesshinna fan desu.
(b) Ethel is an eager student of weaving.

エセルは織物の熱心な学生です。
Eseru wa ori-mono no nesshinna gakusei desu.
(**c**) Georgia's eager attitude toward learning is quite admirable.
ジョージアの熱心な学習態度はなかなか立派です。
Joojia no nesshinna gakushuu-taido wa naka-naka rippa desu.

ear n. **[the hearing organ in humans and certain other animals]**
mi⌈mi⌉ 耳
EX. (**a**) She has trouble hearing in one of her ears.
彼女の片方の耳は難聴です。
Kanojo no kata-hoo no mimi wa nanchoo desu.
(**b**) There was a man named Hoichi who didn't have any ears.
法一という男は耳がなかった。
Hooichi to iu otoko wa mimi ga nakatta.
(**c**) He turned a deaf ear to his wife's advice.
彼は奥さんの忠告に耳を貸さなかった。
Kare wa oku-san no chuukoku ni mimi o kasanakatta.
(**d**) I had a pain in one of my ears and couldn't sleep.
耳が痛くて寝られなかった。
Mimi ga itakute ne-rarenakatta.

early adj. **[in the beginning part of a time period or belonging far back in time or before the expected/usual time]**
1. ha⌈ya⌉i はやい adj(*i*). **[taking less time than is normal or expected or occurring at a point in time prior to what is normal or expected]** ↔ osoi 遅い adj(*i*).; **so⌈okyuuna** 早急な adj(*na*). •**c [quick]** ⟪**swift**⟫
㊥ "early"▷早い, "quick"▷速い
EX. (**a**) We expect an early solution to the problem.
問題の{早急な/?早い}解決を望みます。
Mondai no {sookyuuna/?hayai} kaiketsu o nozomimasu.
(**b**) School in the U.S. starts in the early part of September.
アメリカの学校は九月の{早い/*早急な}時期に始まります。
*Amerika no gakkoo wa ku-gatsu no {hayai/*sookyuuna} jiki ni hajimarimasu.*
(**c**) We had an early supper so that we could go out for the evening.
我々は夕方から出掛けるために{早い/*早急な}夕食を取った。
*Ware-ware wa yuugata kara dekakeru tame ni {hayai/*sookyuuna} yuushoku o totta.*
2. sho⌉ki no N 初期のN •**c [belonging to the beginning period of s.t.]**
EX. (**a**) I am re-reading Soseki's early works.
僕は漱石の初期の作品を読み返しています。
Boku wa Sooseki no shoki no sakuhin o yomi-kaeshite imasu.
(**b**) My grandfather was a diplomat in the early period of the Foreign Office.
祖父は外務省の初期のころの外交官だった。
Sofu wa Gaimu-shoo no shoki no koro no gaikoo-kan datta.
(**c**) Early treatment is important in any illness.
どんな病気も初期の治療が肝心だ。
Donna byooki mo shoki no chiryoo ga kanjin da.

— adv. **[before the expected/usual time]**
ha⌉yaku はやく **[prior to the usual or expected time or quickly]** ⟪**fast, swiftly, soon, immediately**⟫
㊥ "early"▷早く, "quickly"▷速く
EX. (**a**) Hisashi showed up early today.
久士は今日は早く来た。
Hisashi wa kyoo wa hayaku kita.
(**b**) She got up early this morning.
彼女は今朝は早く起きた。
Kanojo wa kesa wa hayaku okita.

earn vt. **[for s.o to receive s.t. for one's work]**
⟨-o⟩ ka⌈se⌉gu ⟨～を⟩稼ぐ ① **[for s.o. to work for pay/reward ⟪fig. "devote one's energy and effort to one's business, etc."⟫]** ⟪**work hard, toil, make money, score a point, gain time**⟫

EX. (**a**) How much money do you earn each week?
一週間に金をいくら稼ぎますか。
Is-shuukan ni kane o ikura kasegimasu ka.
(**b**) The student earned ¥3,000 an hour teaching English.
学生は英語を教えて一時間に三千円稼いだ。
Gakusei wa eigo o oshiete ichi-jikan ni san-zen-en kaseida.
(**c**) If you keep on earning money, poverty won't catch up with you.
稼ぎ続ければ、貧乏は追いつかない。
Kasegi-tsuzukereba, binboo wa oi-tsukanai.

E

NOTE: A similar Japanese proverb is *Kasegu ni oi-tsuku binboo nashi.*

earnest adj. **[serious and intense]**
ma⌈jimena まじめな adj(*na*). **[acting with a strong sense of purpose, not prone to showy display, and expecting the same of others] ⟪honest, serious, sincere, diligent⟫,** **⌈ne⌉sshinna 熱心な** adj(*na*). **•c [passionately interested in and devoted to one thing] ⟪eager, fervent, keen, enthusiastic, diligent, hard-working⟫**

EX. (**a**) John is an earnest student.
ジョンは{まじめな/熱心な}学生です。
Jon wa {majimena/nesshinna} gakusei desu.
(**b**) She is making earnest efforts to pass her exams.
彼女は試験の合格を目指して{まじめな/熱心な}努力をしている。
Kanojo wa shiken no gookaku o mezashite {majimena/nesshinna} doryoku o shite iru.
(**c**) Her earnest efforts were rewarded.
彼女の{まじめな/熱心な}努力が報いられた。
Kanojo no {majimena/nesshinna} doryoku ga mukui-rareta.

PHRASE: in earnest *majimeni* まじめに

EX. (**a**) He desires to go to Japan in earnest.
彼はまじめに日本へ行こうと思っている。
Kare wa majimeni Nihon e ikoo to omotte iru.
(**b**) We need to start thinking in earnest about how to finance our children's college education.
子供が大学に入った時の学費をどうやって払うか、そろそろまじめに考えはじめないといけない。
Kodomo ga daigaku ni haitta toki no gakuhi o doo yatte harau ka, soro-soro majimeni kangae-hajimenai to ikenai.

earth n. **[the planet on which man lives or soil]**
1. chi⌈kyuu 地球 •c [the spherical heavenly body inhabited by human beings] ⟪globe⟫

EX. (**a**) We are fellow travelers on this earth.
我々は地球をともに旅をする者である。
Ware-ware wa chikyuu o tomo ni tabi o suru mono dearu.
(**b**) The earth must be protected from environmental pollution.
地球は環境汚染から守られねばならない。
Chikyuu wa kankyoo-osen kara mamora-reneba naranai.
(**c**) I would like to go around the earth in a satellite.
人工衛星で地球を一回りしてみたい。
Jinkoo-eisei de chikyuu o hito-mawari-shite mitai.

2. tsu⌈chi⌉ 土 [the layer of dirt at the surface of the world in which plants grow] ⟪soil⟫

EX. (**a**) The roots of the tree were covered with earth.
木の根は土に覆われていた。
Ki-no-ne wa tsuchi ni oowa-rete ita.
(**b**) Earth became visible as the snow melted.
雪が溶けて土が見えてきた。
Yuki ga tokete tsuchi ga miete-kita.

PHRASE: on earth *ittai(-zentai)* 一体(全体)

EX. (**a**) Where on earth did you go?
一体(全体)どこへ行ったんですか。
Ittai(-zentai) doko e itta n desu ka.
(**b**) What on earth happened to you?
一体(全体)どうしたんですか。
Ittai(-zentai) doo shita n desu ka.

earthquake n.
ji⌈shin 地震 •c
EX. (**a**) There are frequent earthquakes in Japan.
日本はよく地震がある。
Nihon wa yoku jishin ga aru.
(**b**) An earthquake woke me up at midnight.
夜中に地震で目が覚めた.
Yo-naka ni jishin de me ga sameta.

easily adv. **[with ease]**
ka⌈ntanni 簡単に •c [in such a way that minimal effort is required to understand/ use] ((simply)), **ta⌈ya⌉suku たやすく /**(adj(*i*). *ku* of *tayasui* easy/ **[without difficulty]** ((readily))
EX. (**a**) He solved the problem easily.
彼はその問題を{簡単に/たやすく}解いた。
Kare wa sono mondai o {kantanni/ tayasuku} toita.
(**b**) There is unfortunately no way of learning kanji easily.
残念ながら漢字が{簡単に/たやすく}覚えられる方法はありません。
Zannen nagara kanji ga {kantanni/ tayasuku} oboe-rareru hoohoo wa arimasen.

east n. **[the direction from which the sun rises]**
hi⌈gashi 東 ↔ nishi 西
EX. (**a**) The sun rises in the east.
太陽は東から昇る。
Taiyoo wa higashi kara noboru.
(**b**) The wind is blowing from the east.
風は東から吹いている。
Kaze wa higashi kara fuite iru.

—— adj./adv. **[in/of/toward the direction from which the sun rises]**
1. hi⌈gashi no N 東のN ↔ nishi no N 西のN
EX. (**a**) An east wind is blowing today.
今日は東の風が吹いている。
Kyoo wa higashi no kaze ga fuite iru.
(**b**) There is a golf course on the east side of the lake.
湖の東の方にゴルフコースがあります。
Mizuumi no higashi no hoo ni gorufu-koosu ga arimasu.
2. hi⌈gashi no ho⌉o ni 東の方に n.+prt. **[in the direction from which the sun rises] ↔ nishi no hoo ni 西の方に** n.+prt.; **to⌈ohoo ni 東方に** n.+prt. **•c ↔ seihoo ni 西方に** n.+prt. **•c**
EX. (**a**) The jet plane flew east.
ジェット機は{東の方/東方}に飛んでいった。
Jetto-ki wa {higashi no hoo/toohoo} ni tonde itta.
(**b**) The wind was blowing from the east this morning.
今朝、風は{東の方/?東方}から吹いていた。
Kesa, kaze wa {higashi no hoo/?toohoo} kara fuite ita.

East n. **[the Orient or the eastern part of the U.S.]**
1. To⌉oyoo 東洋 •c [the countries lying on the side of the Mediterranean in the direction of the rising sun] ↔ Seiyoo 西洋 •c
EX. (**a**) Japan is the most technologically advanced country in the East.
日本は東洋で最も技術的に発展した国です。
Nihon wa Tooyoo de mottomo gijutsu-tekini hatten-shita kuni desu.
(**b**) What is meant by the mysteries of the East?
東洋の神秘とは何ですか。
Tooyoo no shinpi to wa nan desu ka.
2. to⌉obu 東部 •c [the eastern part of the U.S.] ↔ seibu 西部 •c

eastern adj. **[in, of, toward, or from the east]**
hi⌈gashi no N 東のN ↔ nishi no N 西のN
EX. (**a**) The geese disappeared into the eastern sky.
がちょうは東の空に消えていった。
Gachoo wa higashi no sora ni kiete-itta.
(**b**) The eastern half of the area was flooded.
その地区の東の半分が洪水に見舞われた。
Sono chiku no higashi no hanbun ga koozui ni mimawa-reta.

E

(c) The eastern sky began to grow light.
東の空が白み始めた.
Higashi no sora ga shirami-hajimeta.

easy adj. **[not difficult; free from trouble, anxiety, pain, etc.]**

1. **ya⌈sashii** やさしい adj(*i*). **[causing little or no trouble (to understand) ⟪fig. "gentle"⟫] ⟪simple, plain⟫ ↔ muzukashii** 難しい adj(*i*). ㊌ "can be done with ease"▷易しい, "kind/gentle"▷優しい

EX. (**a**) This assignment is easy.
この宿題は易しいです。
Kono shukudai wa yasashii desu.
(**b**) Reading Japanese is not easy for a beginner.
初心者にとって日本語を読むことは易しくないです。
Shoshin-sha ni-totte Nihon-go o yomu koto wa yasashikunai desu.

2. **ra⌈ku⌉na** 楽な adj(*na*). **•c [free from trouble, anxiety, pain, etc. physical or psychological] ⟪comfortable⟫ ↔ tsurai** つらい adj(*i*). **⟪hard⟫**

EX. (**a**) She leads an easy life.
彼女は楽な生活をしている。
Kanojo wa rakuna seikatsu o shite iru.
(**b**) He was looking for an easier job.
彼はもっと楽な仕事を探していた。
Kare wa motto rakuna shigoto o sagashite ita.

eat vt. **[to take s.t. into the mouth and swallow it after chewing ⟪fig. "have a meal"⟫]**

⟨-o⟩ ta⌈be⌉ru ⟨〜を⟩食べる ② **[for s.o./s.a. to put s.t. edible into one's mouth, chew, and swallow it] ⟪have, take, feed on⟫, sho⌈kuji-suru** 食事する ③ **•c [for s.o. to have a meal], ⟨-o⟩ me⌈shi-agaru** ⟨〜を⟩召しあがる ① **[for s.o. who is older and higher in social status than the speaker to take s.t. edible, either solid or liquid, into the mouth and swallow it], ⟨-o⟩ i⌈tadaku** ⟨〜を⟩いただく ① **[for the speaker or s.o. within the speaker's in-group to receive s.t. from s.o. whose status is higher than the person who receives it], ⟨-o⟩ cho⌈odai-suru** ⟨〜を⟩ちょうだいする ③ **[for the speaker or s.o. within the speaker's in-group to receive s.t. from s.o. else who is older or higher in social status than the recipient ⟨fml⟩]**

EX. (**a**) What did you eat for breakfast?
朝食には何を{食べました/召しあがりました/*食事しました/*いただきました/*ちょうだいしました}か。
*Chooshoku ni wa nani o {tabemashita/meshi-agarimashita/*shokuji-shimashita/*itadakimashita/*choodai-shimashita} ka.*
(**b**) I haven't eaten anything since this morning.
私は今朝から何も{食べて/?いただいて/??食事して/??ちょうだいして/*召しあがって}いません。
*Watashi wa kesa kara nani-mo {tabete/?itadaite/??shokuji-shite/??choodai-shite/*meshi-agatte} imasen.*
(**c**) Where shall we eat?
どこで{ご飯を食べましょう/食事しましょう/?いただきましょう/*ちょうだいしましょう/*めしあがりましょう}か。
*Doko de {gohan o tabemashoo/shokuji-shimashoo/?itadakimashoo/*choodai-shimashoo/*meshi-agarimashoo} ka.*
(**d**) The teacher ate *sushi.*
先生はすしを{召しあがった/?食べた/*いただいた/*ちょうだいした/*食事した}。
*Sensei wa sushi o {meshi-agatta/?tabeta/*itadaita/*choodai-shita/*shokuji-shita}.*

economic adj. **[pertaining to the production, distribution, and use of wealth or having to do with economics]**

1. **ke⌈izai-joo no N** 経済上のN **•c [having to do with the economy]**

EX. (**a**) That country has economic problems.
あの国は経済上の問題を抱えている。
Ano kuni wa keizai-joo no mondai o kakaete iru.
(**b**) The project was canceled for economic reasons.
経済上の理由から計画は中止された。
Keizai-joo no riyuu kara keikaku wa chuushi-sareta.

PHRASE: economic animal *ekonomikku-animaru* エコノミックアニマル •f

EX. The Japanese are sometimes called economic animals.
日本人はエコノミック・アニマルと呼ばれることがある。
Nihon-jin wa ekonomikku-animaru to yoba-reru koto ga aru.

2. ke⌈iza⌉i-gaku no N 経済学のN •c [having to do with economics]

EX. (**a**) He is doing research on a new economic theory.
彼は新しい経済学の理論を研究している。
Kare wa atarashii keizai-gaku no riron o kenkyuu-shite iru.
(**b**) Paul Samuelson made many contributions to economic theory.
ポール・サムエルソンは経済学の理論に多くの貢献をした。
Pooru Samueruson wa keizai-gaku no riron ni ooku no kooken o shita.

economical adj. **[avoiding waste and less expensive]**
ke⌈izai-tekina 経済的な adj(*na*) **•c [relating to/involving money or costing less]** ⟪**cheap, more reasonable**⟫

EX. Buying the larger box of detergent is more economical.
大きい洗剤の箱を買った方が経済的ですよ。
Ookii senzai no hako o katta hoo ga keizai-teki desu yo.

economy n. **[the system by which wealth is produced, distributed, and used in a society or the management of income and spending in a business, government, etc.]**
ke⌉izai 経済 •c

EX. (**a**) Japan's economy can be characterized as a form of managed capitalism.
日本経済は、一種の管理資本主義の特徴を備えていると言えよう。
Nihon-keizai wa, isshu no kanri-shihon-shugi no tokuchoo o sonaete iru to ieyoo.
(**b**) The economy of a nation influences its politics.
一国の経済はその国の政治に影響を与える。
Ik-koku no keizai wa sono kuni no seiji ni eikyoo o ataeru.
(**c**) Stable growth is best for a country's economy.
国の経済は安定成長が一番だ。
Kuni no keizai wa antei-seichoo ga ichiban da.

edge n. **[a line where s.t. ends ⟪fig. "the thin, sharp cutting part of a blade"⟫]**
1. ha⌈shi 端 [the part of s.t. farthest from the center] ⟪**end, margin corner**⟫, **fu⌈chi⌉ 縁 [the outer part of an extended object/space that is farthest from its center]** ⟪**brink, fringe, rim, brim, frame**⟫, **he⌈ri⌉ へり [the area near/along the outer rim of an object or space which occupies a horizontal area]** ⟪**hem, brim, border**⟫

EX. (**a**) We all took a walk along the edge of the lake.
みんなで湖の{端/縁/へり}を散歩した。
Minna de mizuumi no {hashi/fuchi/heri} o sanpo-shita.
(**b**) The movie was shot on the edge of a cliff.
その映画はがけの{縁/?端/*へり}で撮影された。
*Sono eiga wa gake no {fuchi/?hashi/*heri} de satsuei-sareta.*

NOTE: *Gake no fuchi* is sometimes expressed *gakep-puchi.*

(**c**) I embroidered the edge of a handkerchief.
ハンカチの{端/縁/へり}に刺しゅうした。
Hankachi no {hashi/fuchi/heri} ni shishuu-shita.
(**d**) A big pachinko parlor was opened on the edge of town.
町の{端/*縁/*へり}に大きなパチンコ屋ができた。
*Machi no {hashi/*fuchi/*heri} ni ookina pachinko-ya ga dekita.*

2. ha⌉ 刃 •c [the cutting part of a blade or s.t. that looks like it]

EX. This knife has a sharp edge.

このナイフは鋭い刃がついている。
Kono naifu wa surudoi ha ga tsuite iru.

PHRASE: give s.o. the edge over *yuuri da* 有利だ •c

EX. His knowledge of kanji should give him the edge over other students in his Japanese class.
彼は漢字をよく知っているから日本語のクラスの外の学生より有利だ。
Kare wa kanji o yoku shitte iru kara Nihon-go no kurasu no hoka no gakusei yori yuuri da.

Edison n.
E˥jison エジソン •f

edit vt. **[to prepare and arrange s.t. for publication]**
⟨-o⟩ he┌nshuu-suru ⟨〜を⟩編集する ③ •c [for s.o. to collect manuscripts according to a stated policy for publication in book form, etc.] ⟪compile⟫

EX. (**a**) Professors Kamada and Jacobsen edited this book.
鎌田、ヤコブセン両教授がこの本を編集した。
Kamada, Yakobusen ryoo-kyooju ga kono hon o henshuu-shita.
(**b**) All the manuscripts are in. Now all we have to do is edit them.
原稿が集まり、後は編集するだけだ。
Genkoo ga atsumari, ato wa henshuu-suru dake da.

E

editing n. **[the act of preparing and arranging s.t. for publication]**
he┌nshuu 編集 •c ⟪compilation⟫

EX. We still have a lot of editing to do.
まだたくさん編集をしなければならない。
Mada takusan henshuu o shinakereba naranai.

editor n. **[a person who edits]**
he┌nshu˥u-sha 編集者 •c [s.o. who edits] ⟪compiler⟫

EX. The publisher held a meeting of its textbook editors.
その出版社は教科書編集者の会議を行った。
Sono shuppan-sha wa kyookasho-henshuu-sha no kaigi o okonatta.

educated adj. **[having received an education]**
kyo┌oiku o u˥keta N 教育を受けたN /⟨*kyooiku* education + prt. *o* + Vinf. past of *ukeru* ② receive/ [having received an education] ⟪formally instructed or taught, trained⟫, kyo┌oyoo ga a˥ru N 教養があるN [having a wide range of knowledge] ⟪cultured⟫

EX. The new candidate is a highly educated person.
新しい候補者は{高い教育を受けた/とても教養のある人}です。
Atarashii kooho-sha wa {takai kyooiku o uketa/totemo kyooyoo no aru} hito desu.

education n. **[the process of developing s.o.'s knowledge, mind, and character by formal schooling/study]**
kyo┌oiku 教育 •c ⟪schooling, teaching, instruction⟫

EX. (**a**) Adult education has become popular recently.
最近、成人教育が盛んになってきた。
Saikin, seijin-kyooiku ga sakanni natte-kita.
(**b**) More and more people have come to receive a graduate education these days.
近ごろますます多くの人が大学院教育を受けるようになった。
Chika-goro masu-masu ooku no hito ga daigakuin-kyooiku o ukeru yooni natta.

educational adj. **[relating to/of education]**
kyo┌oiku no N 教育のN •c [of education], kyo┌oiku-tekina 教育的な adj(*na*). **•c [relating to or enhancing education] ⟪instructive, informative⟫**

EX. (**a**) That school has high educational standards.
あの学校は{教育の/*教育的な}水準が高い。
*Ano gakkoo wa {kyooiku no/*kyooiku-tekina} suijun ga takai.*
(**b**) The money will be put to some educational use.

この金は{教育の/教育的な}目的の為に使われる。
Kono kane wa {kyooiku no/kyooiku-tekina} mokuteki no tame ni tsukawareru.

eel n.
u⌈nagi うなぎ

effect n. **[a result brought about by some cause]**
1. ko⌉oka 効果 **•c [a good result achieved toward some objective]** ⟪**result, effectiveness, efficacy**⟫
EX. (**a**) This medicine had no effect on his stomachache.
この薬は彼の腹痛には効果がなかった。
Kono kusuri wa kare no fukutsuu ni wa kooka ga nakatta.
(**b**) The new policy will have a beneficial effect on Japan-U.S. relations.
新しい政策は日米関係によい効果をもたらすであろう。
Atarashii seisaku wa Nichi-Bei-kankei ni yoi kooka o motarasu dearoo.
2. ke⌈kka 結果 **•c [a state of affairs brought about by a cause]** ⟪**result, consequence, outcome, fruits, product, end**⟫
EX. (**a**) The relationship between cause and effect is not always transparent.
原因と結果の関係はいつも透明とは限らない。
Gen'in to kekka no kankei wa itsu-mo toomei to wa kagiranai.
(**b**) The introduction of the new import tariff had the effect of raising retail prices.
新しい輸入関税率の導入は輸入品の小売価格上昇という結果を招いた。
Atarashii yunyuu-kanzei-ritsu no doonyuu wa yunyuu-hin no kouri-kakaku jooshoo to iu kekka o maneita.

effective adj. **[producing an expected/desired effect]**
ko⌈oka-tekina 効果的な adj(*na*). **•c [producing a desired result]** ⟪**efficient**⟫
EX. (**a**) No effective measures have been found to cope with the parking problem in Tokyo.
東京の駐車場問題に対する効果的な対策はいまだに見つかっていない。
Tookyoo no chuusha-joo-mondai ni-taisuru kooka-tekina taisaku wa imada ni mitsukatte inai.
(**b**) Isn't there a more effective way of getting this job done?
この仕事を仕上げるのにもっと効果的なやり方がありませんか。
Kono shigoto o shi-ageru no ni motto kooka-tekina yari-kata ga arimasen ka.

effectively adv. **[in an effective manner]**
ko⌈oka-tekini 効果的に **•c [with the desired result]** ⟪**with efficiency**⟫
EX. I am doing research on how to teach foreign languages more effectively.
外国語をどのようにもっと効果的に教えるかの研究をしている。
Gaikoku-go o dono yooni motto kooka-tekini oshieru ka no kenkyuu o shite iru.

efficiency n. **[the quality of accomplishing an objective with a minimum of wasted time, energy, or resources]**
no⌈oritsu 能率 **•c [the degree to which work progresses within a specified period of time]** ⟪**effectiveness, efficacy**⟫
EX. (**a**) More and more companies are emphasizing efficiency over seniority in promoting employees.
ますます多くの会社が昇進に年功序列より能率を重要視するようになっている。
Masu-masu ooku no kaisha ga shooshin ni nenkoo-joretsu yori nooritsu o juuyoo-shi-suru yooni natte iru.
(**b**) Division of labor improves work efficiency.
分業は仕事の能率を向上させる。
Bungyoo wa shigoto no nooritsu o koojoo-saseru.

efficient adj. **[accomplishing an objective with a minimum of wasted time, energy, or resources]**
no⌈oritsu-tekina 能率的な adj(*na*). **•c [having effectiveness]**
EX. You must find a more efficient way to study.

E

あなたはもっと能率的な勉強の方法を見つけなければならない。
Anata wa motto nooritsu-tekina benkyoo no hoohoo o mitsukenakereba naranai.

effort n. **[the use of physical or mental energy in achieving some objective or the energy so used]**
do⌉ryoku 努力 •c ((endeavor, exertion))

EX. (**a**) Much effort is required to get to the point where one can speak a foreign language fluently.
外国語を流ちょうに話すようになるには精いっぱいの努力をすることが必要である。
Gaikoku-go o ryuuchooni hanasu yooni naru ni wa sei-ippai no doryoku o suru koto ga hitsuyoo dearu.
(**b**) He spared no efforts in reaching his goal of becoming a lawyer.
彼は弁護士になるためにいかなる努力も惜しまなかった。
Kare wa bengo-shi ni naru tame ni ikanaru doryoku mo oshimanakatta.

egg n. **[the oval reproductive body laid by a female bird, fish, etc.]**
ta⌈ma⌉go 卵 ((cooked egg))

EX. (**a**) Our hens lay many eggs.
うちのめんどりはたくさん卵を生みます。
Uchi no mendori wa takusan tamago o umimasu.
(**b**) Many English textbooks include a lesson on how to make a scrambled egg.
いり{玉子/卵}の作り方を扱った課がある英語の教科書が多い。
Iri-tamago no tsukuri-kata o atsukatta ka ga aru eigo no kyooka-sho ga ooi.

NOTE: *Tamago* 卵 is sometimes written as 玉子 with the same meaning.

Egypt n.
E⌈jiputo エジプト •f

Egyptian adj. **[of Egypt, its people, etc.]**
E⌈jiputo no N エジプトの N •f [of Egypt], E⌈jiputo⌉-jin no N エジプト人のN •f+c [of the people/a person of Egypt]

— n. **[the language of (ancient) Egypt]**
E⌈jiputo-go エジプト語 •f+c

eight n./adj. **[one more than seven]**
ya⌈ttsu⌉ (no N) 八つ(のN), ha⌈chi⌉ (+counter) (no N) 八(+counter)のN •c SEE APPENDIX II

eighteen n./adj. **[eight more than ten]**
ju⌈u-hachi⌉ (+counter) (no N) 十八 (+counter)(のN) •c SEE APPENDIX II

eighteenth n./adj. **[preceded by seventeen others in a series]**
da⌉i-ju⌈u-hachi⌉ 第十八 n. **•c, ju⌈u-hachi-ban-me 十八番目** n., **ju⌈u-hachi-ban-me no N 十八番目のN** SEE APPENDIX II

EX. This is his eighteenth book.
これは彼の十八番目の本です。
Kore wa kare no juu-hachi-ban-me no hon desu.

eighth n./adj. **[preceded by seven others in a series]**
da⌉i-ha⌈chi⌉ 第八 n. **•c, ha⌈chi-ban-me 八番目** n., **ha⌈chi-ban-me no N 八番目のN** SEE APPENDIX II

EX. Our house is the eighth one from the intersection.
我が家は交差点から八番目の家です。
Waga-ya wa koosa-ten kara hachi-ban-me no ie desu.

eighty n./adj. **[eight times ten]**
ha⌈chi-ju⌉u (+counter) (no N) 八十 (+counter)(のN) •c SEE APPENDIX II

EX. My mother will be eighty this year.
母は今年八十になります。
Haha wa kotoshi hachi-juu ni narimasu.

Einstein n.
A⌈inshuta⌉in アインシュタイン •f

either adj. **[one or the other of two or each of the two]**
1. {do⌉chira(-ka)/do⌉tchi(-ka)} no N {どちら(か)/どっち(か)}のN [one or the other (of two)]

NOTE: *Dotchi-ka* is the colloquial version of *dochira-ka.*

EX. (**a**) Choose either question.
{どちらか/どっちか}の問題を選びなさい。

{Dochira-ka/Dotchi-ka} no mondai o erabinasai.
(**b**) You will lose nothing in either case.
{どちら/どっち}の場合も損はしない.
{Dochira/Dotchi} no baai mo son wa shinai.
(**c**) You can make it if you take either the 8 or 9 o'clock bus.
八時と九時の{どちら/どっち}のバスに乗っても間に合います。
Hachi-ji to ku-ji no {dochira/dotchi} no basu ni notte mo ma-ni-aimasu.

2. ryoˀohoo no N 両方のN •c [of both of two]

EX. There are banks on either side of the street.
通りの両方の側に銀行がある。
Toori no ryoohoo no gawa ni ginkoo ga aru.

3. {doˀchira/doˀtchi} no N mo…neg. {どちら/どっち}のNも…neg. [neither of two]

EX. My girlfriend didn't like either dish I worked hard to prepare for her.
彼女は僕がせっかく作ったのに、{どちら/どっち}の料理も気に入ってくれなかった。
Kanojo wa boku ga sekkaku tsukutta noni, {dochira/dotchi} no ryoori mo ki ni itte kurenakatta.

— pron. **[one or the other]**

1. {doˀchira-ka/doˀtchi-ka} {どちらか/どっちか} n. **[one or the other (of two)], {doˀchira/doˀtchi} prt. V*te* mo {どちら/どっち} prt. V*te*も [even if…one or the other]**

EX. (**a**) You may use either of the cars.
この車のうち{どちら/どっち}を使ってもいいです。
Kono kuruma no uchi {dochira/dotchi} o tsukatte mo ii desu.
(**b**) You must answer either of the two questions.
この二つの設問のうち{どちらか/どっちか}答えなければなりません。
Kono futatsu no setsumon no uchi {dochira-ka/dotchi-ka} kotaenakereba narimsen.

2. {doˀchira-mo/doˀtchi-mo}…neg. {どちらも/どっちも}…neg. [neither of two]

EX. You seem to have plenty of time and money, but I don't have either.
あなたは時間もお金もたくさんあるようだけど僕は{どちらも/どっちも}ないんだ。
Anata wa jikan mo o-kane mo takusan aru yooda kedo, boku wa {dochira-mo/dotchi-mo} nai n da.

— conj. **[used with or, denoting a choice of alternatives]**

1. …ka…ka {doˀchira-ka/doˀtchi-ka} …か…か{どちらか/どっちか} [a choice between…or…], {doˀchira/doˀtchi} prt. V*te* mo {どちら/どっち} prt. V*te*も [even if…one or the other]

EX. (**a**) John wants to major in either Japanese or Korean.
ジョンは日本語か韓国語か{どちらか/どっちか}を専攻したいと思っている。
Jon wa Nihon-go ka Kankoku-go ka {dochira-ka/dotchi-ka} o senkoo-shi-tai to omotte iru.
(**b**) Father is either in his study or in the bedroom.
お父さんは書斎か寝室か{どちらか/どっちか}にいます。
O-too-san wa shosai ka shinshitsu ka {dochira-ka/dotchi-ka} ni imasu.
(**c**) You may choose either A or B.
AとBの{どちら/どっち}を選んでも結構です
Ei to bii no {dochira/dotchi} o erande mo kekkoo desu.

2. …mo…neg. …も…neg. [not…also]

EX. I might be able to stand a life with money and no love, but I could never stand a life without either love or money.
金さえあれば愛のない生活も何とか我慢できるかもしれないが、愛も金もない生活なんてまっぴらだ。
Kane sae areba ai no nai seikatsu mo nan-toka gaman-dekiru kamoshirenai ga, ai mo kane mo nai seikatsu nante mappira da.

— adv. **[also or too]**

…mo…neg. …も…neg. [not…too]

EX. No, I don't like natto, either.
いいえ、私も納豆は好きじゃありません。
Iie, watashi mo natto wa sukija arimasen.

elaborate adj. **[carefully worked out]** **nyu⌈unenna 入念な •c [carefully made/done], ne⌈n-irini tsuku⌈rare⌉ta N 念入りに作られたN /⟨Vinf. past of passive of *tsukuru* ① make/ [made carefully with attention to details] ⟪careful⟫**

EX. He presented an elaborate plan for the project.
彼はプロジェクトの{念入りに作られた/入念な}計画を提出した。
Kare wa purojekuto no {nen-irini tsukura-reta/nyuunenna} keikaku o teishutsu-shita.

—— vi. **[add more details orally or in writing]** **⟨-o⟩ sa⌉rani ku⌈wa⌉shiku no⌈be⌉ru ⟨〜を⟩更に詳しく述べる ② [for s.o. to go into greater detail about s.t.] ⟪detail⟫**

EX. Would you elaborate on that statement?
今言ったことを更に詳しく述べて下さいませんか。
Ima itta koto o sarani kuwashiku nobete kudasaimasen ka.

elbow n. **[the bend/joint of the arm between the upper arm and forearm]** **hi⌈ji⌉ ひじ**

eldest adj. **[superlative of old]** **i⌈chi-ban toshi-ue no N 一番年上のN [the most aged of a group of people]**

EX. Ichiro is our eldest son.
一郎は私たちの一番年上の息子です。
Ichiroo wa watashi-tachi no ichi-ban toshi-ue no musuko desu.

elect vt. **[for people to select s.o. by vote or otherwise]** **⟨-o⟩ e⌈ra⌉bu ⟨〜を⟩選ぶ ① [for s.o./s.a. to single out s.t./s.o./s.a. out of several as being the most desirable for a particular purpose] ⟪choose, select⟫**

EX. (**a**) The party elected a woman as its chairperson.
その党は長として女性を選んだ。
Sono too wa choo to-shite josei o eranda.
(**b**) The people elected a hawkish president.
国民は鷹派の大統領を選んだ。
Kokumin wa taka-ha no daitooryoo o eranda.

election n. **[the act of choosing s.o. to perform an official role from among those having the qualifications for such an office]** **se⌉nkyo 選挙 •c ⟪voting⟫**

EX. (**a**) The election was very close.
その選挙は非常に接戦だった。
Sono senkyo wa hijooni sessen datta.
(**b**) Mrs. Miyagawa decided to run in the mayoral election.
宮川夫人は市長選挙に出ることにした。
Miyagawa-fujin wa shichoo-senkyo ni deru koto ni shita.

electric adj. **[of/charged with electricity]** **de⌉nki no N 電気のN •c [of electricity]**

EX. (**a**) Would you prefer an electric blanket to a regular one?
普通の毛布より電気(の)毛布の方がいいですか。
Futsuu no moofu yori denki (no) moofu no hoo ga ii desu ka.
(**b**) This engine is operated by electric power.
このエンジンは電気の力で動くんです。
Kono enjin wa denki no chikara de ugoku n desu.
(**c**) The presence of electric lights would spoil the atmosphere of the ceremony.
電気の明かりを使うと式の雰囲気を損なうだろう。
Denki no akari o tsukau to shiki no fun'iki o sokonau daroo.

PHRASE: electric heater *denki-sutoobu* 電気ストーブ •c+f

electrical adj. **[operated by electricity]** **de⌉nki no N 電気のN •c [of electricity]**

EX. Lightning is an electrical phenomenon.
稲妻は電気の現象です。
Inazuma wa denki no genshoo desu.

PHRASE: electrical appliance {*katei-yoo-denki-seihin/kaden*} {家庭用電気製品/家電} •c

EX. The refrigerator is a type of electrical appliance.
冷蔵庫は{家庭用電気製品/家電}の一種です。
Reizoo-ko wa {katei-yoo-denki-seihin/kaden} no is shu desu.

electricity n. **[a basic form of energy occurring in certain subatomic particles or a supply of this as a public utility]**
de⌉nki 電気 •c [a basic form of energy occurring in certain subatomic particles or a device powered by such energy which takes away darkness ⟪fig. "light"⟫] ⟪electricity, electric light⟫

EX. Cars driven by electricity have become more common in recent years.
電気で動く車が最近多くなってきた。
Denki de ugoku kuruma ga saikin ooku natte kita.

electronic adj. **[of electronics]**
de⌉nshi no N 電子のN •c
PHRASE: electronic music *denshi-ongaku* 電子音楽

electronics n. **[the science dealing with the flow of electrons in a vacuum, in conductors, and in semiconductors or the electronic industry]**
e⌈rekutoroni⌉kusu エレクトロニクス •f, de⌈nshi-ko⌉ogyoo 電子工業 •c [the industry dealing with electronic engineering], de⌈nshi-ko⌉ogaku 電子工学 •c [the science of electrons] ⟪electronic engineering⟫

elegant adj. **[gracefully refined]**
e⌉regantona エレガントな adj(*na*). **•f, jo⌈ohi⌉nna 上品な** adj(*na*). **•c [sophisticated and pleasing in quality, speech, or behavior] ↔ gehinna 下品な** adj(*na*). **•c; hi⌈n ga i⌉i 品がいい** adj(*i*). **⟪graceful, refined, polished⟫**

EX. She is wearing an elegant dress.
彼女は{エレガントな/上品な/品がいい}ドレスを着ている。
Kanojo wa {eregantona/joohinna/hin ga ii} doresu o kite iru.

element n. **[a component/constituent of a whole or, in chemistry, any substance that cannot be further separated into different substances]**
1. yo⌉oso 要素 •c [a component/condition necessary to the formation of s.t.] ⟪factor⟫

EX. Language is the most important element of culture.
言語は文化の最も重要な要素である。
Gengo wa bunka no mottomo juuyoona yooso dearu.

2. se⌉ibun 成分 •c [a part or constituent of s.t.] ⟪ingredient⟫

EX. Oxygen and hydrogen are the elements making up water.
酸素と水素は水を構成する成分である。
Sanso to suiso wa mizu o koosei-suru seibun dearu.

3. ge⌉nso 元素 •c [one of a number of basic substances constituting the material universe which cannot be further analyzed into more basic substances]

EX. At present, 107 chemical elements are recognized.
現在、107の元素が認められている。
Genzai, hyaku-nana no genso ga mitome-rarete iru.

elementary adj. **[dealing with the simple or beginning part of s.t.]**
sho⌉ho no N 初歩のN •c [of a beginning stage]

EX. This is a textbook of elementary Japanese.
これは初歩の日本語の教科書です。
Kore wa shoho no Nihon-go no kyooka-sho desu.

PHRASE: elementary school *shoo-gakkoo* 小学校 •c ⟪grade school⟫

elephant n.
zo⌉o 象 •c

EX. The elephant has a long trunk.
象は鼻が長い。
Zoo wa hana ga nagai.

elevator n. **[a platform or cage used to hoist or lower things]**
e⌈rebe⌉etaa エレベーター •f

eleven n./adj.
ju⌈u-ichi⌉ (+counter) (no N) 十一(+counter)(のN) •c SEE APPENDIX II

eliminate vt. **[to get rid of s.t. not wanted/needed]**

E

⟨-o⟩ no⌈zoku ⟨～を⟩除く ① **[to exclude s.t. from a list or group]** ⟪get rid of, remove⟫ ⟨-o⟩ ha⌈bu⌉ku ⟨～を⟩省く ① **[for s.o. to intentionally leave out s.t.]** ⟪save, avoid, omit⟫

EX. (**a**) We eliminated his name from the list of candidates.
彼の名前を候補者のリストから{除いた/*省いた}。
*Kare no namae o kooho-sha no risuto kara {nozoita/*habuita}.*
(**b**) We must work to eliminate waste.
むだを{省く/*除く}ように努力しなければならない。
*Muda o {habuku/*nozoku} yooni doryoku shinakereba naranai.*

E

else adv. **[besides or otherwise or if not]** **ho⌈ka no N 外のN, be⌈tsu no N 別のN •c [other, different], ho⌈ka ni 外に [excepting the thing/topic mentioned]**

EX. (**a**) Please find someone else.
だれか{外/別}の人を探して下さい。
Dare-ka {hoka/betsu} no hito o sagashite kudasai.
(**b**) I have nothing else to say.
外に何も言うことはない。
Hoka ni nani-mo iu koto wa nai.

NOTE: *Betsu ni nani-mo iu koto wa nai.* is also grammatical, but means "I have nothing particular/special to say."

(**c**) Where else can I find this?
外にどこでこれを見付けることができますか。
Hoka ni doko de kore o mitsukeru koto ga dekimasu ka.

PHRASE: or else {*samo-nai-to/soo shinai to/denakereba*} {さもないと/そうしないと/でなければ}

EX. You'd better get going, or else you won't make it.
もう行った方がいい。{さもないと/そうしないと/でなければ}遅れるよ。
Moo itta hoo ga ii. {Samo-nai-to/Soo shinai to/Denakereba} okureru yo.

elsewhere adv. **[somewhere else]** **do⌉ko-ka yo⌈so⌉ {de/ni/e} どこかよそ{で/に/へ}** n.+prt. **[at/in/to some other place], do⌉ko-ka ho⌈ka no to⌈koro {de/ni/e} どこかほかの所{で/に/へ}** n.+prt.

EX. (**a**) If you don't like this restaurant, we can go elsewhere.
このレストランがいやならどこか{ほかの所/?よそ}へ行ってもいいよ。
Kono resutoran ga iya nara doko-ka {hoka no tokoro/?yoso} e itte mo ii yo.
(**b**) If you have to fight, do it elsewhere.
けんかするんなら、どこか{よそ/ほかの所}でやってくれ。
Kenka-suru n nara, doko-ka {yoso/hoka no tokoro} de yatte kure.

embarrass vt. **[to cause s.o. to feel self-conscious]**
⟨-o⟩ ko⌈mara-se⌉ru ⟨～を⟩困らせる /⟨causative of *komaru* ① be in trouble/ ② [to cause s.o. to be in an unpleasant or troubled situation] ⟪annoy, bother⟫, **⟨-o⟩ ma⌈go-tsuka-se⌉ru ⟨～を⟩まごつかせる /⟨causative of *mago-tsuku* ① feel at a loss/ ② [to cause s.o. to feel at a loss]** ⟪confuse⟫, **⟨-o⟩ do⌉gi-magi-saseru ⟨～を⟩どぎまぎさせる /⟨causative of *dogi-magi-suru* ③ feel confused/ [to cause s.o. to feel confused]** ⟪annoy⟫

EX. (**a**) The child's impolite question embarrassed her.
子供の不しつけな質問は彼女を{困らせた/まごつかせた/どぎまぎさせた}。
Kodomo no bu-shitsukena shitsumon wa kanojo o {komara-seta/mago-tsuka-seta/dogi-magi-saseta}.
(**b**) The sudden appearance of his wife embarrassed Jim.
奥さんの突然の出現がジムを{困らせた/まごつかせた/どぎまぎさせた}。
Okusan no totsuzen no shutsugen ga Jimu o {komara-seta/mago-tsuka-seta/dogi-magi-saseta}.

PHRASE: be embarrassed *hazukashii* 恥ずかしい adj(*i*).

EX. (**a**) I was embarrassed in the presence of so many young girls.
若い女の子がたくさんいて恥ずかしかった。

Wakai onna-no-ko ga takusan ite hazukashikatta.
(**b**) I was really embarrassed by my grandmother lavishing me with praise like that in front of all my friends.
友達がみんないるのに祖母が私をほめちぎるのでほんとに恥ずかしかった。
Tomodachi ga minna iru noni sobo ga watashi o home-chigiru node honto ni hazukashikatta.

embassy n. **[the official headquarters of an ambassador in the country of his assignment]**
ta⌈ishi⌉-kan 大使館 •c

embrace vt. **[for s.o. to hold s.o. in one's arms lovingly]**
⟨-o⟩ da⌈ku ⟨〜を⟩抱く ① **[for s.o. to take and keep s.o./s.a./s.t. in one's arms or to support s.o./s.a./s.t. in such a way], ⟨-o⟩ da⌈ki-shime⌉ru** ⟨〜を⟩抱き締める ② **[for s.o. to hold s.o./s.t./s.a. tightly in one's arms]** ⟪**hug**⟫
EX. Jack embraced Jill tightly.
ジャックはジルを強く{抱いた/抱き締めた}。
Jakku wa Jiru o tsuyoku {daita/daki-shimeta}.

emerge vi. **[to come into view]**
a⌈raware⌉ru 現れる ② **[to become exposed/visible]** ⟪**appear, show up, come out, come into view**⟫, **de⌉te-kuru** 出てくる ③ **[to come out]** ⟪**appear, show up, come out, come into view**⟫
EX. (**a**) The sun finally emerged.
やっと太陽が{現れた/出てきた}。
Yatto taiyoo ga {arawareta/dete-kita}.
(**b**) New facts about the case emerged as a result of the investigation.
取り調べの結果、その事件にかかわる新しい事実が{現れた/出てきた}。
Tori-shirabe no kekka, sono jiken ni kakawaru atarashii jijitsu ga {arawareta/dete-kita}.
(**c**) Insects emerge from their holes in the spring.
虫たちは春になると穴から{現れる/出てくる}。
Mushi-tachi wa haru ni naru to ana kara {arawareru/dete-kuru}.

emergency n. **[a sudden, generally unexpected occurrence demanding immediate attention]**
ki⌈nkyuu(-ji⌉tai) 緊急(事態) •c ⟪**urgency**⟫
EX. Pull the lever toward you in the case of an emergency.
緊急(事態)の際はレバーを手前に引いて下さい。
Kinkyuu(-jitai) no sai wa rebaa o temae ni hiite kudasai.

emotion n. **[any intense feeling, such as love, hate, fear, anger, etc.]**
ka⌈njoo 感情 •c **[s.t. felt in the mind/heart such as comfort, discomfort, joy, anger, sorrow, etc., which changes constantly in response to outside stimuli]** ⟪**feeling**⟫, **ki⌈mochi** 気持ち **[the state of one's mind]**
EX. (**a**) Love and hatred are opposite emotions.
愛と憎しみは反対の{感情/?気持ち}である。
Ai to nikushi-mi wa hantai no {kanjoo/?kimochi} dearu.
(**b**) I could not suppress my emotions.
私は{感情/気持ち}を抑え切れなかった。
Watashi wa {kanjoo/kimochi} o osae-kire-nakatta.

emotional adj. **[easily aroused to emotion]**
ka⌈njoo-tekina 感情的な adj(*na*). •c **[apt to display changeable feelings in one's action and behavior]** ⟪**excited**⟫, **jo⌉ocho-fu-⌈a⌉nteina** 情緒不安定な adj(*na*). •c **[emotionally unstable]** ⟪**not very stable in emotion**⟫
EX. Mary is always emotional in her words and actions.
メリーの言動はいつも{感情的/情緒不安定}だ。
Merii no gendoo wa itsu-mo {kanjoo-teki/joocho-fu-antei} da.

emperor n. **[the supreme ruler of an empire]**
te⌈nno⌉o 天皇 •c ↔ **koogoo** 皇后 •c ⟪**empress**⟫

emphasis n. **[special importance given to s.t.]**

ju˥ushi 重視 •c [the act of attaching importance to s.t.] ⟪taking seriously⟫, ju˥uten 重点 •c [the most important point] ⟪stress, importance⟫

EX. (**a**) That school is noted for its emphasis on foreign language education.
あの学校は外国語教育{重視/に重点を置いていること}で名高い。
Ano gakkoo wa gaikoku-go-kyooiku {juushi/juuten o oite iru koto} de na-dakai.
(**b**) The summit conference placed great emphasis on economic cooperation.
首脳会談は経済協力{に重点を置いた/を重視した}。
Shunoo-kaidan wa keizai-kyooryoku {ni juuten o oita/o juushi-shita}.

emphasize vt. **[for s.o. to give emphasis to s.t.]**
⟨-o⟩ kyo˥ochoo-suru ⟨～を⟩強調する ③ •c [for s.o. to express s.t. forcefully so as to make it conspicuous to others] ⟪stress⟫

EX. (**a**) The Prime Minister emphasized the importance of economic assistance.
首相は経済援助の重要性を強調した。
Shushoo wa keizai-enjo no juuyoo-sei o kyoochoo-shita.
(**b**) The teacher emphasized grammar in his Japanese course.
その先生は日本語のコースで文法を強調した。
Sono sensei wa Nihon-go no koosu de bunpoo o kyoochoo-shita.

empire n. **[government by an emperor/empress, or a group of states/territories under one ruler]**
te˥ikoku 帝国 •c

PHRASE: The Roman Empire *Rooma-teikoku* ローマ帝国 **•f+c**

employ vt. **[for s.o. to hire the services of s.o. or to use s.t.]**
⟨-o⟩ ya˥to˥u ⟨～を⟩雇う ① [for s.o. to use persons/vehicles at his/her discretion for a certain period of time in return for a fee/wages] ⟪engage, hire, charter⟫, ⟨-o⟩ tsu˥kau ⟨～を⟩使う ① [for s.o./s.a. to cause s.t./s.o./s.a. to act or serve for a purpose or as an instrument or as a material for consumption] ⟪use, spend, speak⟫

EX. (**a**) We're going to have to employ a night guard.
夜警を雇う必要がある。
Yakei o yatou hitsuyoo ga aru.
(**b**) The company employs twenty stenographers.
その会社は速記者を二十人雇っている。
Sono kaisha wa sokki-sha o ni-juu-nin yatotte iru.
(**c**) Lisa employs her spare time doing charity work.
リサは暇な時間を慈善事業に使っている。
Risa wa himana jikan o jizen-jigyoo ni tsukatte iru.

employee n. **[a person employed by another for wages/salary]**
ju˥ugyo˥o-in 従業員 •c [one who works for another as a clerk, factory hand, etc.] ⟪worker, the staff, the men⟫

EX. (**a**) The employees of that company do exercises together every morning.
あの会社の従業員は毎朝一緒に体操をする。
Ano kaisha no juugyoo-in wa mai-asa issho ni taisoo o suru.
(**b**) The airline employees went on strike.
航空会社の従業員がストを行った。
Kookuu-gaisha no juugyoo-in ga suto o okonatta.
(**c**) This is the new uniform for our employees.
これがうちの従業員の新しい制服です。
Kore ga uchi no juugyoo-in no atarashii seifuku desu.

employment n. **[an act/instance of employing or being employed]**
1. sho˥ku 職 •c [a duty ⟪fig. "job"⟫] ⟪job, work, occupation⟫, shi˥goto 仕事 [an activity performed for a particular purpose other than amusement and on which one expends time and effort] ⟪work, job, occupation⟫ ↔ asobi 遊び

EX. (**a**) John is seeking employment.
ジョンは{職/仕事}を探している。
Jon wa {shoku/shigoto} o sagashite iru.
(**b**) Mary currently has no employment.
メアリーは今{職/仕事}がない。
Mearii wa ima {shoku/shigoto} ga nai.

2. shi⌈yoo 使用 •c [an act of using s.t./s.o./s.a.] ⟪use⟫

EX. We prohibit the employment of gas on this compound.
構内でのガスの使用は禁止する。
Koonai de no gasu no shiyoo wa kinshi-suru.

3. ko⌈yoo 雇用 •c [the act of employing s.o.]

EX. (**a**) The employment of as many women as possible is encouraged.
なるべく多くの女性の雇用が奨励されている。
Narubeku ooku no josei no koyoo ga shoorei-sarete iru.
(**b**) The government must create new policies to promote employment.
政府は雇用を促進する新しい政策を打ち出さなければならない。
Seifu wa koyoo o sokushin-suru atarashii seisaku o uchi-dasanakereba naranai.

PHRASE: find employment *shuushoku-suru* 就職する ③ •c

EX. Taro found employment in a foreign trading company.
太郎は外国商社に就職した。
Taroo wa gaikoku-shoosha ni shuushoku-shita.

empty adj. **[containing nothing]**
ka⌈ra⌉ no N 空のN, aki- 空き〜 [having nothing contained within or having no substance] ⟪vacant, hollow⟫

EX. (**a**) The box was empty.
箱は空だった。
Hako wa kara datta.
(**b**) Let's recycle our empty bottles.
{空の瓶/空き瓶}をリサイクルしましょう。
{Kara no bin/Aki-bin} o risaikuru-shimashoo.

PHRASE: have an empty stomach *onaka ga suite iru* おなかがすいている /⟨V *te iru* of *onaka ga suku* ① get hungry/

EX. I have an empty stomach.
おなかがすいています。
Onaka ga suite imasu.

enable vt. **[to make s.o. able to do s.t.]**
(⟨-no⟩ o-⌈kage de)…pot. yo⌉oni naru (⟨〜の⟩おかげで)…pot.ようになる [to become able to do s.t. (thanks to…)]

EX. (**a**) Recent advances in drug treatment have enabled even severely depressed people to lead normal lives.
最近の薬剤治療の進歩のおかげで、重いうつ病の人でも普通の生活ができるようになっている。
Saikin no yakuzai-chiryoo no shinpo no o-kage de, omoi utsu-byoo no hito demo futsuu no seikatsu ga dekiru yooni natte iru.
(**b**) Rockets have enabled man to travel to the moon.
ロケットのおかげで人間は月へ行くことができるようになった。
Roketto no o-kage de ningen wa tsuki e iku koto ga dekiru yooni natta.

enclose vt. **[for s.o. to shut s.t. in all around, ⟪fig. "insert in an envelope with a letter"⟫]**
1. ⟨-o⟩ ⟨-de⟩ ka⌈komu ⟨〜を⟩⟨〜で⟩囲む ① [for s.t. two-/three-dimensional such as lines/walls/trees/people to be all around s.t./s.o./s.a.] ⟪surround, encircle⟫

EX. (**a**) My grandparents' house was enclosed by a ring of fruit trees.
祖父母の家は果物の木でぐるりと囲まれていた。
Sofubo no ie wa kudamono no ki de gururi to kakoma-rete ita.
(**b**) The garden was enclosed with a hedge.
庭は生け垣で囲まれていた。
Niwa wa ikegaki de kakoma-rete ita.
(**c**) We enclosed the garden with a fence so the rabbits could't get in.
庭の回りを柵で囲み、うさぎが入れないようにした。
Niwa no mawari o saku de kakomi, usagi ga hairenai yooni shita.

E

2. ⟨-o⟩ ⟨-ni⟩ **do⌈ofuu-suru** ⟨〜を⟩⟨〜に⟩同封する ③ •c **[for s.o. to put s.t. in an envelope with a letter, etc.]**

EX. (**a**) I enclose some pictures of our cats with this letter.
この手紙にうちの猫の写真を同封します。
Kono tegami ni uchi no neko no shashin o doofuu-shimasu.
(**b**) Enclosed is my current resume.
私の最新の履歴書を同封します。
Watakushi no saishin no rireki-sho o doofuu shimasu.

encounter vt. **[to meet s.o./s.t./s.a. unexpectedly]**
⟨-ni⟩ **de-⌈a⌉u** ⟨〜に⟩出会う ① **[for s.o. to meet s.o. unexpectedly while out and about]** 《**meet, come across, run into**》, ⟨-ni⟩ **so⌈oguu-suru** ⟨〜に⟩遭遇する ③ •c **[to meet s.t. unexpected]** 《**run into, come upon**》

EX. (**a**) I encountered an old friend by chance in the store.
店の中で昔からの友達に偶然{出会った/*遭遇した}。
*Mise no naka de mukashi kara no tomodachi ni guuzen {de-atta/*sooguu-shita}.*
(**b**) John encountered many difficulties on his trip.
ジョンは旅行中に多くの困難に{出会った/遭遇した}。
Jon wa ryokoo-chuu ni ooku no konnan ni {de-atta/sooguu-shita}.

—— n. **[an unexpected meeting]**
de-⌈ai 出会い /⟨V*masu* of *de-au* ① come across/ **[an unexpected meeting]**, **so⌈oguu** 遭遇 •c **[meeting s.t. unexpectedly]**

EX. (**a**) Life can be characterized as a series of chance encounters.
人生は偶然の{出会い/?遭遇}の連続と言っていい。
Jinsei wa guuzen no {de-ai/?sooguu} no renzoku to itte ii.
(**b**) The science fiction writer described his encounter with aliens.
SF作家は自分の宇宙人との{遭遇/出会い}について語った。
Esuefu-sakka wa jibun no uchuu-jin to no {sooguu/de-ai} ni-tsuite katatta.

encourage vt. **[to give hope/confidence to s.o.]**
⟨-o⟩ **yu⌈uki-zuke⌉ru** ⟨〜を⟩勇気づける ② •c **[to give s.o. the spirit/strength to enable one to undertake an action which an ordinary person would not be capable of due to anxiety/fear]** 《**inspire with confidence**》, ⟨-o⟩ **ha⌈gema⌉su** ⟨〜を⟩励ます ① **[for s.o. to give confidence to s.o. by urging him/her not to give up]** 《**urge, give courage**》

EX. (**a**) The teacher encouraged the students before the exam.
先生は試験の前に学生を{勇気づけた/励ました}。
Sensei wa shiken no mae ni gakusei o {yuuki-zuketa/hagemashita}.
(**b**) I was encouraged by my professor to go on to graduate school.
先生に大学院に進むように{励まされた/{励まして/*勇気づけて}もらった}。
*Sensei ni daigaku-in ni susumu yooni {hagema-sareta/{hagemashite/*yuuki-zukete} moratta}.*
(**c**) The doctor encouraged her patient not to lose hope.
医者は患者が生きる望みを失わないように{励ました/勇気づけた}。
Isha wa kanja ga ikiru nozomi o ushinawanai yooni {hagemashita/yuuki-zuketa}.
(**d**) I was encouraged by the understanding attitude of my colleagues.
私は同僚の理解ある態度に{勇気づけられた/励まされた}。
Watashi wa dooryoo no rikai aru taido ni {yuuki-zuke-rareta/hagemasa-reta}.

encyclopedia n. **[a book/set of books with alphabetically arranged articles on various branches of knowledge]**
hya⌈kka-ji⌉ten 百科事典 •c

end n. **[the last part of s.t. or a purpose/goal]**
1. **o⌈wari** 終わり /⟨V*masu* of *owaru* ① end/

[the point at which s.t. continues no further or the last part of s.t.] **⟪close, conclusion⟫ ↔ hajimari 始まり**

EX. (**a**) In Japan the end of the school year comes in March.
日本の学校の一年の終わりは三月です。
Nihon no gakkoo no ichi-nen no owari wa san-gatsu desu.
(**b**) We celebrated the end of exams by going out drinking.
我々は試験の終わりを酒を飲んで祝った。
Ware-ware wa shiken no owari o sake o nonde iwatta.
(**c**) The bells are ringing to signal the end of the year.
一年の終わりを告げる鐘が鳴り響いている。
Ichi-nen no owari o tsugeru kane ga nari-hibiite iru.

2. mo|kuteki 目的 •c [the intended result of a particular action/behavior] ⟪purpose, object, goal, aim⟫

EX. (**a**) He is a ruthless dictator whose sole end in life is to achieve absolute domination over others.
彼は血も涙もない独裁者で、他の人間を完全に支配することが人生における唯一の目的なのだ。
Kare wa chi mo namida mo nai dokusai-sha de, ta no ningen o kanzenni shihai-suru koto ga jinsei ni-okeru yuiitsu no mokuteki na no da.
(**b**) To him, money is purely a means, not an end in itself.
彼にとっては、金は手段にすぎず目的ではない。
Kare ni-totte wa, kane wa shudan ni sugizu mokuteki dewanai.

3. sa⌈ki 先 [the end of a stick/stick-like object ⟪fig. "future," "the other party"⟫] ⟪tip⟫

EX. He held one end of the rope.
彼はロープの片方の先を握った。
Kare wa roopu no kata-hoo no saki o nigitta.

— vi. **[come to a finish]**
o⌈waru 終わる ① [for s.t. continuous to come to a point where it continues no further or for s.o. to reach a point in a task/activity where there is nothing left to do] ⟪come to an end, close, be over, finish, be completed⟫, su⌉mu すむ ① [for s.t. murky to become clean ⟪fig. "reside," "be done completely"] ⟪come to a conclusion, be over, become transparent, live⟫ ↔ hajimaru 始まる ①

㊥ "for s.t. to be over"▷済む, "for s.o. to reside"▷住む, "for s.t. to become clear"▷澄む

EX. (**a**) The festival ended without trouble.
祭りは無事に{終わった/済んだ}。
Matsuri wa bujini {owatta/sunda}.
(**b**) The long speech finally ended.
長い演説がやっと{終わった/済んだ}。
Nagai enzetsu ga yatto {owatta/sunda}.
(**c**) The war ended fifty years ago.
戦争は五十年前に{終わった/*済んだ}。
*Sensoo wa go-juu-nen mae ni {owatta/*sunda}.*

— vt. **[for s.o. to finish s.t.]**
⟨-o⟩ o⌈eru ⟨〜を⟩終える ② [for s.o. to cause s.t. to come to an end] ⟪terminate, close⟫

EX. (**a**) Our grandmother ended her life peacefully in the surroundings of her own home.
祖母は自分の家で安らかに生涯を終えた。
Sobo wa jibun no ie de yasurakani shoogai o oeta.
(**b**) The president ended his term on a successful note with the signing of the trade agreement.
通商協定の締結をもって大統領は成功裏に任期を終えた。
Tsuushoo-kyootei no teiketsu o motte daitooryoo wa seikoo-ri ni ninki o oeta.

PHRASE: end of the war *shuusen* 終戦 •c

EX. Japan made a quick recovery after the end of the war.
日本は終戦後急速に復興した。
Nihon wa shuusen-go kyuusokuni fukkoo-shita.

endless adj. **[having no end/termination]**
o⌈wari no na⌉i N 終わりのないN [having

no end] ((interminable))

EX. (**a**) Writing this dictionary seemed an endless job.
この辞書の執筆は終わりのない仕事のように思えた。
Kono jisho no shippitsu wa owari no nai shigoto no yooni omoe-ta.
(**b**) Research is an endless task.
研究とは終わりのない仕事だ。
Kenkyuu to wa owari no nai shigoto da.

enemy n. **[s.o./some nation hostile to another]**
te⌈ki 敵 •c [an opponent in war, competition, etc.] ((**opponent, foe**)) ↔ **mikata 味方**

EX. (**a**) She had many enemies.
彼女は敵が多かった。
Kanojo wa teki ga ookatta.
(**b**) Illiteracy is perhaps the greatest enemy of our nation.
文盲は我が国の最大の敵であろう。
Monmoo wa waga-kuni no saidai no teki dearoo.

energetic adj. **[having/showing energy/vigor]**
se⌈iryoku-tekina 精力的な adj(*na*). **•c [having the vitality to complete one job after another without exhaustion]** ((**vital, vigorous**)), **e⌈nerugi⌉sshuna エネルギッシュな** adj(*na*). **•f, ge⌉nkina 元気な** adj(*na*). **•c [for s.o./s.a. to be in good health or to have lots of energy]** ((**healthy, fine**))

EX. (**a**) We were lucky to have an energetic teacher for our course.
我々は{精力的な/エネルギッシュな/元気な}先生にこの授業を教えてもらってラッキーだった。
Ware-ware wa {seiryoku-tekina/enerugisshuna/genkina} sensei ni kono jugyoo o oshiete moratte rakkii datta.
(**b**) The candidate carried out an energetic election campaign.
候補者は{精力的な/エネルギッシュな/*元気な}選挙運動を展開した。
*Kooho-sha wa {seiryoku-tekina/enerugisshuna/*genkina} senkyo-undoo o tenkai-shita.*

energy n. **[the capacity for vigorous activity or the capacity of matter to do work because of its motion or mass]**
1. se⌉iryoku 精力 •c [the vitality to complete one job after another without exhaustion] ((**vigor, vitality**)), **ge⌉nki 元気 •c [the vigor and willingness to actively do things]** ((**cheerful spirits, vigor, vitality, pep**)), **ka⌈tsu⌉ryoku 活力 •c [the vitality which makes possible action and motion]** ((**vitality**))

EX. (**a**) John is always full of energy.
ジョンはいつも{精力/元気/活力}いっぱいだ。
Jon wa itsu-mo {seiryoku/genki/katsuryoku}-ippai da.
(**b**) Japan's economy is regaining its energy.
日本経済は{活力/元気/*精力}を取り戻しつつある。
*Nihon-keizai wa {katsuryoku/genki/*seiryoku} o tori-modoshi-tsutsu aru.*

2. e⌈ne⌉rugii エネルギー •f [in physics, the capacity of matter to do work because of its motion or mass]

NOTE: *Enerugii* comes from German *Energie.*

EX. We have to find alternative sources of energy to oil.
石油の代替エネルギー源を探さねばならない。
Sekiyu no daitai-enerugii-gen o sagasaneba naranai.

engage vt. **[for s.o. to hire s.o. for a task]**
1. ⟨-o⟩ ya⌈to⌉u ⟨〜を⟩雇う ① [for s.o. to use persons/vehicles at his/her discretion for a certain period of time in return for a fee/wages] ((**hire, employ**))

EX. My father has engaged a new secretary.
父は新しく秘書を雇いました。
Chichi wa atarashiku hisho o yatoimashita.

PHRASE: be engaged *yakusoku ga aru* 約束がある ①

EX. I am sorry, but I am engaged for the afternoon.
残念ですが、午後は約束がありまして。

Zannen desu ga, gogo wa yakusoku ga arimashite.

2. ⟨-ni⟩ juˈuji-shite iru ⟨〜に⟩従事している •c /⟨V*te iru* of *juuji-suru* ③ be engaged in/

EX. Toshio is engaged in computer science research.
年男はコンピューターサイエンスの研究に従事している。
Toshio wa konpyuutaa-saiensu no kenkyuu ni juuji-shite iru.

3. koˈn'yaku-shite iru 婚約している /⟨V*te iru* of *kon'yaku-suru* ③ promise marriage/ •c

EX. Makiko is already engaged.
真紀子はもう婚約しています。
Makiko wa moo kon'yaku-shite imasu.

engine n. **[a machine that utilizes energy to yield mechanical power]**
eˈnjin エンジン •f

PHRASE: fire engine *shooboo-jidoosha* 消防自動車 •c

engineer n. **[s.o. who is an expert in some branch of engineering or s.o. who operates a locomotive]**

1. eˈnjiˈnia エンジニア •f, giˈshi 技師 •c [s.o. whose occupation is in a specialized field of science/technology]

EX. (**a**) My son wants to be a computer engineer.
息子はコンピューター{エンジニア/技師}になりたがっている。
Musuko wa konpyuutaa-{enjinia/gishi} ni nari-ta-gatte iru.
(**b**) You must be good at mathematics in order to become an engineer.
{エンジニア/技師}になるためには数学に強くなければならない。
{Enjinia/Gishi} ni naru tame ni wa suugaku ni tsuyoku nakereba naranai.

2. kiˈkaˈn-shi 機関士 •c [one who operates a locomotive]

EX. The engineer started the train.
機関士は列車を出発させた。
Kikan-shi wa ressha o shuppatsu-saseta.

engineering n. **[a branch of learning dealing with the application of scientific knowledge toward practical ends, esp. in industry and technology]**
koˈogaku 工学 •c

EX. My uncle majored in mechanical engineering.
叔父は機械工学を専攻した。
Oji wa kikai-koogaku o senkoo-shita.

England n. **[the largest division of the United Kingdom, in S. Great Britain]**
Iˈgirisu イギリス •f [Britain], Eˈikoku 英国 •c [the United Kingdom]

English n. **[the language of the people of England, the U.S., Australia, Canada, New Zealand, etc.]**
eˈigo 英語 •c

EX. I majored in English in college.
僕は大学で英語を専攻した。
Boku wa daigaku de eigo o senkoo-shita.

— adj. **[of England, its people, or its language]**

1. Iˈgirisu no N イギリスのN •f, Eˈikoku no N 英国のN •c [of the UK]

EX. It is an English custom to have tea in the afternoon.
午後にお茶を飲むのは{イギリス/英国}の習慣です。
Gogo ni o-cha o nomu no wa {Igirisu/Eikoku} no shuukan desu.

2. Iˈgirisuˈ-jin no N イギリス人のN •f+c [of the people of/a person of the UK]

EX. She lived with an English family for a while.
彼女はしばらくイギリス人の家族と生活した。
Kanojo wa shibaraku Igirisu-jin no kazoku to seikatsu-shita.

3. eˈigo no N 英語のN •c [of the language of England, the U.S., Australia, Canada, New Zealand, etc.]

EX. Mr. Murakami is an excellent English teacher.
村上先生はすばらしい英語の先生です。
Murakami-sensei wa subarashii eigo no sensei desu.

Englishman n. **[a native or inhabitant of England]**
Iˈgirisuˈ-jin イギリス人 •f+c, Eˈikokuˈ-jin 英国人 •c [the people/a person of the UK]

EX. We have some Englishmen on our faculty.
この大学の先生の中に{イギリス/英国}人が何人かいます。
Kono daigaku no sensei no naka ni {Igirisu/Eikoku}-jin ga nan-nin-ka imasu.

enjoy vt. **[for s.o. to have and use s.t. with joy and satisfaction or to have the use/benefit of s.t.]**

1. 〈-o〉 **ta⌈noshi⌉mu** 〈〜を〉楽しむ ① **[for s.o. to appreciate the goodness of s.t. or to do s.t. one likes or to look forward to s.t. materializing]** **《take pleasure, delight in, have a good time》**

EX. (**a**) Each of us is enjoying life in his or her own way.
我々はそれぞれに人生を楽しんでいます。
Ware-ware wa sore-zore ni jinsei o tanoshinde imasu.
(**b**) We want you to enjoy your stay in Japan.
日本での滞在を楽しんでいただきたいと思います。
Nihon de no taizai o tanoshinde itadaki-tai to omoimasu.
(**c**) I enjoyed the concert fully.
私はコンサートを十分楽しみました。
Watashi wa konsaato o juubun tanoshimimashita.

2. 〈-o〉 **kyo⌉oju-suru** 〈〜を〉享受する ③ •c **[for s.o. to be actively in contact with s.t. and receive a direct and personal benefit from it]**

EX. We are able to enjoy high living standards thanks to technological development.
我々は科学技術の発達のおかげで高い生活水準を享受することができる。
Ware-ware wa kagaku-gijutsu no hattatsu no o-kage de takai seikatsu-suijun o kyooju-suru koto ga dekiru.

enjoyable adj. **[giving joy/pleasure]**
ta⌈noshi⌉i 楽しい adj(*i*). **[experiencing intense enjoyment and satisfaction from s.t. and thus being drawn to it or causing such a feeling in one]** **《pleasant, happy, delightful, joyful》**, **yu⌉kaina** 愉快な adj(*na*). **[experiencing happiness or merriment deriving from a sense of satisfaction with s.t. or causing such a feeling in one]** **《pleasant, delightful, joyful, happy》**

EX. (**a**) Thank you for the enjoyable evening.
{楽しい/愉快な}夕べをありがとうございました。
{Tanoshii/Yukaina} yuube o arigatoo gozaimashita.
(**b**) John had a very enjoyable experience in Japan.
ジョンは日本でとても{楽しい/愉快な}経験をした。
Jon wa Nihon de totemo {tanoshii/yukaina} keiken o shita.

enjoyment n. **[having and using with joy and satisfaction]**
ta⌈noshi⌉mi 楽しみ **/〈V*masu* of *tanoshimu* ① enjoy/** **[feeling pleasant in a certain circumstance or s.t. that causes such a feeling]** **《pleasure, delight》**

EX. My grandmother finds enjoyment in reading.
祖母は読書を楽しみとしている。
Sobo wa dokusho o tanoshimi to shite iru.

enlarge vt. **[to make s.t. large or expand s.t.]**

1. 〈-o〉 **ka⌈kudai-suru** 〈〜を〉拡大する ③ •c **[for s.o. to make the shape/scale of s.t. larger]** **《expand, magnify》**, 〈-o〉 **o⌉okiku suru** 〈〜を〉大きくする ③ **[to make s.t. large]**

EX. (**a**) The company enlarged the scale of its business operations.
その会社は事業の規模を{拡大/大きく}した。
Sono kaisha wa jigyoo no kibo o {kakudai-/ookiku} shita.
(**b**) We need to enlarge the scope of our research.
我々は研究の範囲を{拡大/?大きく}しなければならない。
Ware-ware wa kenkyuu no han'i o {kakudai-/?ookiku} shinakereba naranai.

2. (**sha⌈shin o**) **hi⌈ki-noba⌉su** (写真を)引き伸ばす ① **[for s.o. to make a photograph larger]**

EX. The picture of our cats turned out well so we decided to enlarge it.
飼い猫の写真がよく撮れていたので引き伸ばすことにしました。
Kai-neko no shashin ga yoku torete ita node hiki-nobasu koto ni shimashita.

enough adj. **[as much/many as needed]**
ju⌈ubu⌉nna 十分な adj(*na*). **•c [as much as necessary]** ⟪**sufficient**⟫, **ta⌈riru** 足りる ② **[to exist in the quantity needed]** ⟪**sufficient**⟫

EX. (**a**) We have enough food.
{十分な食べ物があります/食べ物は足りています}。
{Juubunna tabe-mono ga arimasu/ Tabe-mono wa tarite imasu}.
(**b**) Machiko didn't have enough money to buy a car.
真知子は車を買うのに{十分なお金がなかった/お金が足りなかった}。
Machiko wa kuruma o kau no ni {juubunna o-kane ga nakatta/o-kane ga tarinakatta}.

—— n. **[the amount needed]**
ju⌈ubu⌉n 十分 **•c [a sufficient amount/ number]**

EX. A: How about another cup of tea?
お茶をもう一杯いかがですか。
O-cha o moo ip-pai ikaga desu ka.
B: I've had enough, thanks.
ありがとうございます。もう十分いただきました。
Arigatoo gozaimasu. Moo juubun itadakimashita.

—— adv. **[sufficiently/fully]**
ju⌈ubu⌉n(ni) 十分(に) **•c [to the extent required]** ⟪**sufficiently**⟫

EX. (**a**) Tom didn't study Japanese hard enough.
トムは日本語の勉強を十分(に)しなかった。
Tomu wa Nihon-go no benkyoo o juubun(ni) shinakatta.
(**b**) It is impossible to thank you enough.
あなたに十分にお礼を言うことは不可能です。
Anata ni juubunni o-rei o iu koto wa fu-kanoo desu.

enter vt. **[to come/go into]**
⟨-ni⟩ ha⌉iru ⟨〜に⟩入る ① **[to go into some place ⟪fig. "join"⟫]** ⟪**go in, come in, get in**⟫

EX. (**a**) The students all entered the classroom and took their seats.
学生は皆教室に入って席についた。
Gakusei wa mina kyooshitsu ni haitte seki ni tsuita.
(**b**) Our daughter entered college this spring.
娘は今春大学に入った。
Musume wa konshun daigaku ni haitta.

enterprise n. **[a business venture or a difficult undertaking]**
1. ki⌉gyoo 企業 **•c [an organization continuously engaged in business operations such as manufacturing, sales, etc. for the purpose of profit]** ⟪**business, industry**⟫

EX. (**a**) The railway companies of Japan are now private enterprises.
日本の鉄道は今は民間企業です。
Nihon no tetsudoo wa ima wa minkan-kigyoo desu.
(**b**) Prof. Tanaka is studying medium- and small-sized enterprises.
田中教授は中小企業の研究をしている。
Tanaka-kyooju wa chuushoo-kigyoo no kenkyuu o shite iru.

2. ji⌉gyoo 事業 **•c [social/economic activity of relatively large scope]** ⟪**work, task, project**⟫

EX. Our company president has embarked on a new enterprise.
うちの社長は新しい事業に乗り出した。
Uchi no shachoo wa atarashii jigyoo ni nori-dashita.

entertain vt. **[for s.o. to hold the interest/ attention of s.o. or to have as a guest or to consider]**
1. ⟨-o⟩ ta⌈noshima-se⌉ru ⟨〜を⟩楽しませる ② **/⟨causative of *tanoshimu* ① enjoy/ [to cause s.o. to have fun]** ⟪**please, delight, amuse, give pleasure to**⟫

EX. (**a**) The children entertained us at the retirement home with their singing.
子供たちは歌を歌って、老人ホームの

E

我々を楽しませてくれた。
Kodomo-tachi wa uta o utatte, roojin-hoomu no ware-ware o tanoshima-sete kureta.
(**b**) Grandfather's funny stories entertained us all.
祖父の笑い話は我々皆を楽しませてくれた。
Sofu no warai-banashi wa ware-ware mina o tanoshima-sete kureta.

2. ⟨**-o**⟩ **mo⌈tenasu** ⟨〜を⟩もてなす ① **[for s.o. to serve tea, drinks, dinner, etc. to a guest]** ⟪**welcome, treat s.o. to s.t.**⟫

EX. (**a**) The dean entertained the visiting scholar.
学部長は訪問中の学者をもてなした。
Gakubu-choo wa hoomon-chuu no gakusha o motenashita.
(**b**) Cal and Lucie entertained us with a steak dinner.
キャルとルーシーは我々をステーキの夕食でもてなしてくれた。
Kyaru to Ruushii wa ware-ware o suteeki no yuushoku de motenashite kureta.
(**c**) In America, people often build a fire in the fireplace when entertaining guests.
アメリカではよく暖炉をたいて客をもてなす。
Amerika de wa yoku danro o taite kyaku o motenasu.

3. (**shi⌈tsumon na⌉do ni**) **ko⌈tae⌉ru** (質問などに)答える ② **[for s.o. to answer questions from an audience, etc.]**

EX. The speaker is now ready to entertain questions from the floor.
これより講師が皆さんのご質問にお答えします。
Kore yori kooshi ga mina-san no go-shitsumon ni o-kotae-shimasu.

entertainment n. **[the act of entertaining or s.t. that entertains]**
go⌈raku 娯楽 •**c** **[s.t. one does for fun during one's free time]** ⟪**amusement, pastime, recreation**⟫

EX. *Karaoke* is a popular form of entertainment in Japan.
日本ではカラオケはポピュラーな娯楽の一つです。
Nihon de wa karaoke wa popyuraana goraku no hitotsu desu.

enthusiasm n. **[keen interest or zeal]**
netsui 熱意 •**c** **[eagerness to do s.t.]** ⟪**zeal**⟫

EX. She didn't show much enthusiasm for the plan.
彼女はその計画にあまり熱意を示さなかった。
Kanojo wa sono keikaku ni amari netsui o shimesanakatta.

enthusiastic adj. **[having enthusiasm]**
⌈nesshi⌉nna 熱心な adj(*na*). •**c** **[passionately interested and devoted to one thing]** ⟪**zealous, fervent, keen, earnest**⟫

EX. (**a**) He was fortunate to have an enthusiastic audience.
彼は熱心な聴衆に恵まれた。
Kare wa nesshinna chooshuu ni megumareta.
(**b**) He lost the election for lack of enthusiastic supporters.
彼は熱心な支持者がいなくて落選した。
Kare wa nesshinna shiji-sha ga inakute rakusen-shita.

entire adj. **[having an unbroken unity and lacking no parts]**
ze⌈ntai no N 全体のN •**c** **[covering the whole extent of s.t.]** ⟪**whole**⟫, **ze⌉nbu no N** 全部のN •**c** **[covering the whole of s.t.]** ⟪**all**⟫

EX. (**a**) The entire student body was absent from school.
{全部/*全体}の学生が学校を欠席した。
*{Zenbu/*Zentai} no gakusei ga gakkoo o kesseki-shita.*
(**b**) The entire bottle of water leaked out.
瓶{全部/?全体}の水が漏れてしまった。
Bin-{zenbu/?zentai} no mizu ga morete shimatta.
(**c**) Individual students are certainly important, but we want you to think more of the entire class.
一人一人の学生も大事だがもっとクラス{全体/?全部}のことを考えてほしい。
Hitori-hitori no gakusei mo daiji da ga

motto kurasu-{zentai/?zenbu} no koto o kangaete hoshii.

entirely adv. **[wholly, completely]**

ma⌈ttaku 全く [in a manner so strongly that it cannot be expressed in any other way] ⟪**wholly, completely**⟫, **su⌈kka⌉ri すっかり [an expression indicating that some condition is pervasive or exhaustively present]** ⟪**completely**⟫

EX. (**a**) Our stock of nails has been entirely exhausted.
くぎの在庫が{全く/すっかり}底をついた。
Kugi no zaiko ga {mattaku/sukkari} soko o tsuita.
(**b**) I entirely forgot about our wedding anniversary.
僕は結婚記念日を{すっかり/全く}忘れていた。
Boku wa kekkon-kinen-bi o {sukkari/mattaku} wasurete ita.
(**c**) I agree entirely with your position.
あなたの意見には{全く/*すっかり}賛成です。
*Anata no iken ni wa {mattaku/*sukkari} sansei desu.*

entitle vt. **[for s.t. to give a right/title to s.o. to do s.t.]**

1. ⟨**-ni**⟩ **shi⌈kaku o a⌈taeru** ⟨〜に⟩**資格を与える** ② **[for s.o./s.t. to give a qualification to s.o. to do s.t.]** ⟪**qualify**⟫

EX. His outstanding career in baseball entitled him to a place in the Baseball Hall of Fame.
野球における優れた経歴により彼は野球殿堂入りの資格を与えられた。
Yakyuu ni-okeru sugureta keireki ni-yori kare wa yakyuu-dendoo-iri no shikaku o atae-rareta.

2. ⟨**-ga**⟩ **⌈a⌉reba…pot.** ⟨〜が⟩**あれば…pot.** ③ **[with…can do s.t.]**

EX. This ticket entitles you to free admission.
この券があればただで入場できます。
Kono ken ga areba tada de nyuujoo-dekimasu.

3. ⟨**-ni**⟩⟨**-to**⟩ **i⌈u hyo⌈odai o tsu⌈ke⌉ru** ⟨〜に⟩⟨〜と⟩**いう表題をつける** ② **[for s.o. to give a title to a written work]**

EX. (**a**) His first book is entitled *Syntactic Structures.*
彼の最初の本は『文法の構造』という表題がつけられている。
Kare no saisho no hon wa "Bunpoo no koozoo" to iu hyoodai ga tsuke-rarete iru.
(**b**) I intend to entitle this book *A Cat's Monologue.*
この本に『猫の独り言』という表題をつけるつもりです。
Kono hon ni "Neko no hitori-goto" to iu hyoodai o tsukeru tsumori desu.

PHRASE: be entitled to ⟨*-no*⟩ *kenri ga aru* ⟨〜の⟩権利がある ①

EX. I am entitled to an explanation.
説明をしてもらう権利がある。
Setsumei o shite morau kenri ga aru.

entrance n. **[a place for entering or permission/right to enter]**

1. i⌈riguchi 入り口 [an opening by which s.o./s.t./s.a. can enter an area/space] ⟪**door**⟫ **↔ deguchi 出口** ⟪**exit**⟫

EX. (**a**) You must show your pass at the entrance.
入り口で通行証を見せなければいけません。
Iriguchi de tsuukoo-shoo o misenakereba ikemasen.
(**b**) Come to the front entrance.
正面の入り口に来て下さい。
Shoomen no iriguchi ni kite kudasai.
(**c**) Let's meet at the theater entrance.
劇場の入り口で待ち合わせましょう。
Gekijoo no iriguchi de machi-awasemashoo.

2. nyu⌈ujoo 入場 •c [entering some place], nyu⌈ugaku 入学 •c [entering a school]

EX. (**a**) Entrance free.
入場無料。
Nyuujoo muryoo.
(**b**) He won entrance to the University of Tokyo.
彼は東大入学を果たした。
Kare wa Toodai-nyuugaku o hatashita.

PHRASE: entrance examination *nyuugaku-shiken*

E

入学試験 •c, take an entrance exam *juken-suru* 受験する ③ •c

envelope n. **[a flat paper container for a letter, etc.]**
fu⌈utoo 封筒 •c [a paper container in which to put letters or documents]

EX. Don't forget to attach a postage stamp to the envelope.
封筒に切手を貼るのを忘れないで下さい。
Fuutoo ni kitte o haru no o wasurenaide kudasai.

envious adj. **[feeling/showing envy]**
u⌈rayamashi⌉ku o⌈mo⌉tte iru うらやましく思っている /⟨adj(*i*). *ku* of *urayamashii* envious + V*te iru* of *omou* ① think/ ② [having a feeling of envy], ⟨-ga⟩ u⌈rayamashi⌉i ⟨〜が⟩うらやましい adj(*i*). **[discontented because s.o. else has possessions, qualities, or achievements which one wishes were one's own], ⟨-o⟩ urayamashi-gatte iru ⟨〜を⟩うらやましがっている /⟨V*te iru* of *urayamashi-garu* ① show envy/ ② [showing signs of feeling envy]**

E

EX. (**a**) I am envious of his talent.
彼の能力{をうらやましく思っている/がうらやましい}。
Kare no nooryoku {o urayamashiku omotte iru/ga urayamashii}.
(**b**) Liz is envious of Jane's success.
リズはジェーンの成功{をうらやましく思っている/をうらやましがっている/??がうらやましい}。
Rizu wa Jeen no seikoo {o urayamashiku omotte iru/o urayamashi-gatte iru/??ga urayamashii}.

NOTE: *Urayamashii* is used with the first person subject in statements and with the second person subject in question. *Urayamashi-gatte iru* is used only with a third person subject.

environment n. **[the conditions surrounding an organism affecting its growth and well-being]**
ka⌈nkyoo 環境 •c [the outside world surrounding s.o./s.t./s.a.] ⟪surroundings, circumstances⟫

EX. Old folks are extremely sensitive to changes in their environment.
老人は環境の変化に敏感である。
Roojin wa kankyoo no henka ni binkan dearu.

PHRASE: one's home environment *katei-kankyoo* 家庭環境 •c

equal adj. **[of the same quantity, size, value, etc. or having the same rights, privileges, etc.]**
1. hi⌈toshi⌉i 等しい adj(*i*). **[for two/more things to be of the same nature, quantity, state, condition, etc.] ⟪equivalent, identical, similar, same⟫, ki⌈ntoona 均等な** adj(*na*). **•c [for two/more things to be virtually the same in amount, condition, etc.]**

EX. (**a**) These two lines are equal in length.
この二本の線は長さが{等しい/*均等だ}。
*Kono ni-hon no sen wa naga-sa ga {hitoshii/*kintoo da}.*
(**b**) Our two countries must accord equal trade opportunities to each other.
我々両国はお互いに{均等な/等しい}貿易の機会を与えなければならない。
Ware-ware ryookoku wa o-tagai ni {kintoona/hitoshii} booeki no kikai o ataenakereba naranai.

2. byo⌈odoo no N 平等のN •c [having the property that all individuals are treated alike and without discrimination] ⟪impartial, even⟫

EX. (**a**) All people enjoy equal rights in this society.
この社会ではすべての人間は平等の権利を享受する。
Kono shakai de wa subete no ningen wa byoodoo no kenri o kyooju-suru.
(**b**) Our company is an equal opportunity employer.
我が社はみんなに平等の機会を与える雇用者である。
Waga-sha wa minna ni byoodoo no kikai o ataeru koyoo-sha dearu.

equality n. **[the condition of having the same quantity, rights, etc.]**

byo⌈odoo 平等 •c [the property of treating all individuals alike and without discrimination] ⟪impartiality⟫

EX. (**a**) South Africa now enjoys racial equality, at least in principle.
少なくとも原則的には今や南アフリカは人種の平等を享受している。
Sukunaku-tomo gensoku-tekini wa imaya Minami-Afurika wa jinshu no byoodoo o kyooju-shite iru.
(**b**) Lincoln strove for the equality of all people.
リンカーンは全人類の平等のために戦った。
Rinkaan wa zen-jinrui no byoodoo no tame ni tatakatta.

equally adv. **[in an equal manner]**
byo⌈odooni 平等に /⟨adj(*na*). *ni* of *byoodoona* equal/ •c [in equal parts and without discrimination], hi⌈to⌉shiku 等しく /⟨adj(*i*). *ku* of *hitoshii* equal/ [in such a way that all concerned are of the same nature, quantity, state, condition, etc.] ⟪similarly⟫

EX. (**a**) John divided his estate equally among his children.
ジョンは子供たちに財産を{平等に/等しく}分けた。
Jon wa kodomo-tachi ni zaisan o {byoodooni/hitoshiku} waketa.
(**b**) The sun shines equally on all human beings.
太陽はすべての人間を{平等に/等しく}照らす。
Taiyoo wa subete no ningen o {byoodooni/hitoshiku} terasu.
(**c**) Parents lavish love equally on their children in bringing them up.
親は子供たちに{平等に/等しく}愛情を注いで育てる。
Oya wa kodomo-tachi ni {byoodooni/hitoshiku} aijoo o sosoide sodateru.

equipment n. **[s.t. kept/furnished/provided for a specific purpose]**
se⌉tsubi 設備 •c [equipment provided to facilitate some task] ⟪facilities, conveniences, accommodations⟫

EX. (**a**) The factory increased its investment in equipment.
工場は設備投資を増やした。
Koojoo wa setsubi-tooshi o fuyashita.
(**b**) This hospital has spent a lot of money on equipment.
この病院は設備に多額のお金をかけている。
Kono byooin wa setsubi ni tagaku no o-kane o kakete iru.

equivalent adj. **[equal in quantity, value, measure, etc., to s.t./s.o. else]**
⟨-ni⟩ so⌈otoo-suru ⟨〜に⟩相当する •c ③ [having roughly the same status/function as] ⟪equal⟫

EX. We will pay you a sum equivalent to your salary.
あなたの給料に相当する金額をお支払いします。
Anata no kyuuryoo ni sootoo-suru kingaku o o-shiharai shimasu.

era n. **[a period of time measured from some important event]**
ji⌈dai 時代 •c [a subinterval on the continuum of past, present, and future designated for some historical purpose] ⟪period, age⟫

EX. (**a**) Many important things happened during the Meiji era.
明治時代には多くの重要なことが起こった。
Meiji-jidai ni wa ooku no juuyoona koto ga okotta.
(**b**) It is said that we are now in the information era.
我々は現在情報の時代にいると言われています。
Ware-ware wa genzai joohoo no jidai ni iru to iwa-rete imasu.

eraser n. **[a rubber device for erasing pencil marks]**
ke⌈shi-gomu 消しゴム [a small piece of rubber used to erase pencil marks], ko⌈kuba⌉n-fuki 黒板拭き [a pad for removing chalk marks from a blackboard]

E

erect vt. **[for s.o. to set s.t. up in an upright position]**
⟨-o⟩ ta⌈te⌉ru ⟨〜を⟩たてる ② **[for s.o. to cause s.o./s.t./s.a. to take an upright position ⟪fig. "build s.t."⟫]** ⟪**set up, put up, stand, raise**⟫
㊉ "build a building"▷建てる, otherwise ▷立てる

EX. (**a**) The town erected a museum in memory of the earliest pioneers to settle there.
町はそこに最初に住みついた開拓者を記念して博物館を建てた。
Machi wa soko ni saisho ni sumi-tsuita kaitaku-sha o kinen-shite hakubutsu-kan o tateta.
(**b**) The broadcasting station erected a huge antenna on the mountain.
放送局は山の上に巨大なアンテナを立てた。
Hoosoo-kyoku wa yama no ue ni kyodaina antena o tateta.
(**c**) The school erected a statue to commemorate the deceased president.
学校は亡くなった学長を追悼して像を立てた。
Gakkoo wa nakunatta gakuchoo o tsuitoo-shite zoo o tateta.

errand n. **[a short or quick trip to do s.t., usually for s.o. else]**
(o-)tsu⌈kai (お)使い **[taking care of business outside one's home or place of work]** ⟪**message**⟫

EX. (**a**) I sent my secretary on an errand.
秘書を(お)使いにやった。
Hisho o (o-)tsukai ni yatta.
(**b**) I have to run some errands.
ちょっとお使いに行かなければなりません。
Chotto o-tsukai ni ikanakereba narimasen.

error n. **[s.t. done incorrectly/wrongly]**
a⌈yamari⌉ あやまり /⟨V*masu* of *ayamaru* ① err/ **[an act/instance of doing s.t. wrongly or an act/instance of apologizing for s.t. done wrongly]** ⟪**mistake, slip, apology**⟫, ma⌈chiga⌉i 間違い **[an act/instance of doing s.t. incorrectly, usu. s.t. of relatively minor consequence such as an identification, calculation, producing an incorrect spelling or grammatical form, etc.]** ⟪**mistake, fault, accident**⟫
㊉ "apology"▷謝り, otherwise ▷誤り

EX. (**a**) There are many grammatical errors in his composition.
彼の作文には文法の{誤り/間違い}がたくさんある。
Kare no sakubun ni wa bunpoo no {ayamari/machigai} ga takusan aru.
(**b**) It is useful for language teachers to analyze errors committed by students.
学生が犯した{誤り/間違い}を分析することは語学教師にとって有益だ。
Gakusei ga okashita {ayamari/machigai} o bunseki-suru koto wa gogaku-kyooshi ni-totte yuueki da.

escape vi./vt. **[to get away and flee from a location/situation]**
⟨-kara⟩ ni⌈ge⌉ru ⟨〜から⟩逃げる ② **[for s.o./s.a. to go far so as not to be caught or to get away from danger/s.t. which restricts one's freedom]** ⟪**run away, flee, get free, break loose**⟫, {⟨-kara⟩/⟨-o⟩} no⌈gare⌉ru {⟨〜から⟩/⟨〜を⟩}逃れる ② **[for s.o./s.a. to gain freedom from a difficult situation/responsibility]** ⟪**get off, evade**⟫

EX. (**a**) The bird escaped from the cage.
鳥がかごから{逃げた/*逃れた}。
*Tori ga kago kara {nigeta/*nogareta}.*
(**b**) The convict could not escape from prison.
囚人は監獄から{逃げられなかった/*逃れられなかった}。
*Shuujin wa kangoku kara {nige-rarenakatta/*nogare-rarenakatta}.*
(**c**) He couldn't escape from this dilemma.
彼はこのジレンマから{逃れる/*逃げる}ことができなかった。
*Kare wa kono jirenma kara {nogareru/*nigeru} koto ga dekinakatta.*
(**d**) Many refugees escaped the war and went abroad.
多くの難民が戦火を{逃れて/*逃げて}海外へ行った。

E

*Ooku no nanmin ga senka o {nogarete/ *nigete} kaigai e itta.*

Eskimo n. **[a member of one of the native peoples inhabiting Greenland, Alaska, etc.]** **E⌈sukimo⌉o-jin** エスキモー人 **•f+c [people/ a person inhabiting Greenland, etc.], E⌈suki⌉moo no N** エスキモーのN **•f [of people/a person inhabiting Greenland, etc.]**

especially adv. **[very specially/particularly] to⌉kuni** 特に **•c [above all]** ⟪**specially, particularly, in particular**⟫

EX. (**a**) We like small animals, especially chinchillas.
私たちは小さな動物が好きです。特にチンチラが好きです。
Watashi-tachi wa chiisana doobutsu ga suki desu. Tokuni chinchira ga suki desu.
(**b**) She loves flowers, especially roses.
彼女は花の中でも特にバラの花が好きです。
Kanojo wa hana no naka de mo tokuni bara no hana ga suki desu.
(**c**) Japanese people like to travel overseas, especially to the United States.
日本人は海外旅行に行きたがっています。特にアメリカに行きたがっています。
Nihon-jin wa kaigai-ryokoo ni iki-tagatte imasu. Tokuni Amerika ni iki-tagatte imasu.

essay n. **[a short literary composition on a certain theme]** **e⌉ssee** エッセー **•f, zu⌈ihitsu** 随筆 **•c [a composition one writes freely as thoughts come to mind, concerning what one has seen/heard or what one thinks/feels]**

EX. (**a**) Terada Torahiko is famous for his essays.
寺田寅彦はその{エッセー/随筆}で有名です。
Terada Torahiko wa sono {essee/ zuihitsu} de yuumei desu.
(**b**) Our assignment over summer vacation was to write an essay on Edgar Allan Poe.
夏休みの宿題はエドガー・アラン・ポーについて{エッセー/随筆}を書くことだった。
Natsu-yasumi no shukudai wa Edogaa Aran Poo ni-tsuite {essee/zuihitsu} o kaku koto datta.

essential adj. **[absolutely necessary and important]** **ho⌈nshitsu-tekina** 本質的な adj(*na*). **•c [of the essence of s.t.]** ⟪**basic**⟫, ⟨**-ni**⟩ **ka⌈ku ko⌈to⌉ ga de⌈ki⌉nai (N)** ⟨〜に⟩欠くことができない(N) **[unable to be dispensed with]** ⟪**indispensable**⟫

EX. (**a**) There are essential differences between being a polyglot and being a linguist.
たくさんの言語が話せることと言語学者であることの間には{本質的な/*欠くことのできない}違いがある。
*Takusan no gengo ga hanase-ru koto to gengo-gakusha dearu koto no aida ni wa {honshitsu-tekina/*kaku koto no dekinai} chigai ga aru.*
(**b**) Sleep is essential to life.
睡眠は生命に{欠くことのできない/*本質的な}ものだ。
*Suimin wa seimei ni {kaku koto no dekinai/*honshitsu-tekina} mono da.*

essentially adv. **[basically/fundamentally] ho⌈nshitsu-tekini** 本質的に **•c [in essence]**

EX. All human beings have essentially the same skeletal structure.
すべての人間は本質的に同じ骨格をもっている。
Subete no ningen wa honshitsu-tekini onaji kokkaku o motte iru.

establish vt. **[for s.o. to bring s.t. into being on a firm basis]** ⟨**-o**⟩ **se⌈tsuritsu-suru** ⟨〜を⟩設立する ③ **•c [for s.o. to bring into being a system, institution, organization, etc., as a concrete, tangible entity that did not exist before]** ⟪**found, institute, set up**⟫, ⟨**-o**⟩ **ka⌈kuritsu-suru** ⟨〜を⟩確立する **•c [for s.o. to bring into being an abstract entity/ system which is firmly founded and carefully planned]** ⟪**set up firmly**⟫

EX. (**a**) The Sano Foundation established a university for foreign studies.

E

佐野財団は外語大学を{設立/*確立}した。
*Sano-zaidan wa gaigo-daigaku o {setsuritsu/*kakuritsu}-shita.*
(**b**) Radford established himself as a leading psychologist.
ラドフォードは一流の心理学者としての名声を{確立/*設立}した。
*Radofoodo wa ichiryuu no shinri-gakusha to-shite no meisei o {kakuritsu/*setsuritsu}-shita.*
(**c**) Professor Shimizu established the foundation of the Japanese program at this university.
清水教授はこの大学で日本語プログラムの基礎を{確立/*設立}した。
*Shimizu-kyooju wa kono daigaku de Nihon-go-puroguramu no kiso o {kakuritsu/*setsuritsu}-shita.*

E

establishment n. **[the act of establishing or the state of being established or a thing established]**
se⌈tsuritsu 設立 •c [the bringing into being of a system, institution, organization, etc., as a concrete, tangible entity that did not exist before] ⟪**founding**⟫, **ka⌈kuritsu 確立 •c [the bringing into being of an abstract entity/system which is firmly founded and carefully planned]** ⟪**setting up**⟫, **ki⌈ka⌉n 機関 •c [a small autonomous organization having a specific function within a larger body]** ⟪**institution, system, organ**⟫

EX. (**a**) The Ministry of Education approved the establishment of a few new colleges.
文部省は若干の新しい大学の{設立/*確立/*機関}を認可した。
*Monbu-shoo wa jakkan no atarashii daigaku no {setsuritsu/*kakuritsu/*kikan} o ninka-shita.*
(**b**) The establishment of a democratic system is an essential condition for political stability in that country.
その国の政治の安定を図る上で民主的な制度の{確立/*設立/*機関}は不可欠の条件である。
*Sono kuni no seiji no antei o hakaru ue de minshu-tekina seido no {kakuritsu/*setsusritsu/*kikan} wa fukaketsu no jooken dearu.*
(**c**) The *juku* system is a major educational establishment in Japan.
日本の塾は今や大きな教育{機関/*設立/*確立}である。
*Nihon no juku wa imaya ookina kyooiku-{kikan/*setsuritsu/*kakuritsu} dearu.*

estimate n. **[an approximate calculation of a quantity, esp. a probable cost]**
mi⌈-tsumori 見積もり /⟨V*masu* of *mi-tsumoru* ① make an estimate/ [a rough calculation done in advance] ⟪**quotation**⟫

EX. Please submit an estimate for the repair work promptly.
早く修理の見積もりを提出して下さい。
Hayaku shuuri no mi-tsumori o teishutsu-shite kudasai.

— vt. **[for s.o. to calculate s.t. approximately or to judge or evaluate s.t.]**
⟨-o⟩ mi-⌈tsumoru ⟨〜を⟩見積もる ① [for s.o. to calculate s.t. roughly in advance] ⟪**quote a price**⟫, **⟨-o⟩ hyo⌉oka-suru ⟨〜を⟩評価する ③ •c [for s.o. to set a value on s.t.]** ⟪**evaluate, assess, judge**⟫

EX. (**a**) I estimate the damage to be roughly one million yen.
損害は約百万円と{見積もる/*評価する}。
*Songai wa yaku hyaku-man-en to {mi-tsumoru/*hyooka-suru}.*
(**b**) He estimated my ability too highly.
彼は僕の能力をあまり高く{評価し/*見積もり}過ぎた。
*Kare wa boku no nooryoku o amari takaku {hyooka-shi/*mi-tsumori}-sugita.*
(**c**) I had a friend estimate the cost of adding a room to the house.
友達に家の建て増しの経費を{見積もらせた/*評価させた}。
*Tomodachi ni ie no tate-mashi no keihi o {mi-tsumora-seta/*hyooka-saseta}.*

etc. [and so forth]
-nado 〜など [not limited to what precedes]

EX. We bought books, notebooks, etc.
本やノートなどを買いました。
Hon ya nooto nado o kaimashita.

eternal adj. **[everlasting]**
e⌈ien no N 永遠のN •c [continuing infinitely into the future, beyond time] ⦅**permanent, immortal**⦆

EX. Most religions claim the existence of eternal life.
ほとんどの宗教は永遠の生命の存在を主張する。
Hotondo no shuukyoo wa eien no seimei no sonzai o shuchoo-suru.

Europe n.
Yo⌈oro⌉ppa ヨーロッパ •f, O⌉oshuu 欧州 •c

European adj. **[of Europe]**
Yo⌈oro⌉ppa no N ヨーロッパのN •f, O⌉oshuu no N 欧州のN •c

even adv. **[an expression suggesting an extreme case or an unlikely instance, however improbable]**
1. sa⌉e さえ [a particle presenting an example obvious to anybody and suggesting that what happens at any point above or below that level goes without saying or indicating that the condition mentioned alone suffices to accomplish s.t.], de⌉mo でも /⟨cop. *te* + prt. *mo*⟩ [a particle presenting an example of s.t. to which the predicate applies where it might be least expected to with the implication that the predicate will therefore naturally apply to less extreme cases or (when attached to a question word) indicating that the predicate applies to all members in the set of things represented by the question word or presenting an example of s.t. as a polite offer or suggestion], mo も [a particle indicating an example of s.t. to which the predicate applies in addition to a previously mentioned example to which it also applies or indicating that a proposition holds in addition to a previously mentioned proposition or (when attached to a question word) indicating that the predicate applies to all members in the set of things represented by the question word or presenting an example of an extreme case to which the predicate applies with the implication that the predicate will perforce hold in less extreme cases] ⦅**also**⦆, **da⌉tte だって [a particle presenting a particular/representative case to which the predicate applies and implying that the predicate will likewise apply to other cases]**

EX. (**a**) Even a child knows that.
子供{でさえ/でも/も/だって}そんなことは知っている。
Kodomo {de sae/demo/mo/datte} sonna koto wa shitte iru.
(**b**) In Hawaii, it's warm even in winter.
ハワイでは冬{でさえ/でも/も/だって}暖かい。
Hawai de wa fuyu {de sae/demo/mo/datte} atatakai.
(**c**) I couldn't even talk to her on the phone.
彼女とは電話で話すこと{さえ/も/だって/*でも}できなかった。
*Kanojo to wa denwa de hanasu koto {sae/mo/datte/*demo} dekinakatta.*
(**d**) He didn't even touch his food.
彼は食事にはしをつけること{さえ/も/*だって/*でも}しなかった。
*Kare wa shokuji ni hashi o tsukeru koto {sae/mo/*datte/*demo} shinakatta.*

2. sa⌉rani さらに [in addition to s.t. or some condition] ⦅**still more, more and more, again, furthermore**⦆, **i⌈ssoo いっそう [to a stronger degree]** ⦅**all the more**⦆, **mo⌉tto もっと [to a greater degree in quantity/quality]** ⦅**more**⦆

EX. (**a**) Bob's younger brother is even taller than him.
ボブの弟はボブより{さらに/いっそう/もっと}背が高い。
Bobu no otooto wa Bobu yori {sarani/issoo/motto} se ga takai.
(**b**) The statue of the Buddha in Kamakura is big, but the one in Nara is even bigger.
鎌倉の大仏は大きいが奈良の大仏は{もっと/さらに/?いっそう}大きい。

E

Kamakura no daibutsu wa ookii ga Nara no daibutsu wa {motto/sarani/ ?issoo} ookii.

—— adj. **[flat or exactly divisible by two]**

1. ta⌈irana 平らな adj(*na*). **[for a surface to be free from obstructions]** ⟪**level**⟫

EX. I need a board with an even surface.
平らな面をしている板が必要です。
Tairana men o shite iru ita ga hitsuyoo desu.

2. gu⌈usu⌉u no N 偶数のN •c [exactly divisible by two] ↔ kisuu no N 奇数のN •c

EX. Eight is an even number.
8は偶数(の数)です。
Hachi wa guusuu (no kazu) desu.

E

PHRASE: even if (*tatoe*) {V/adj(*i*)./adj(*na*)./cop.}*te mo* (たとえ){V/adj(*i*)./adj(*na*)./cop.}*te*も

EX. The game will be played even if it rains.
(たとえ)雨が降っても試合は行います。
(Tatoe) ame ga futte mo shiai wa okonaimasu.

evening n. **[the last part of the day and the early part of the night]**

1. yu⌈ugata 夕方 [the stretch of time from the setting of the sun to darkness]

EX. (**a**) We usually take a walk in the evening.
私たちは大抵夕方(に)散歩します。
Watashi-tachi wa taitei yuugata (ni) sanpo-shimasu.
(**b**) I'll be back by evening.
夕方までには帰ります。
Yuugata made ni wa kaerimasu.

2. ba⌈n 晩 •c [after dark] ⟪**night**⟫

EX. The party is this Friday evening.
パーティーは今週の金曜日の晩です。
Paatii wa konshuu no kin'yoo-bi no ban desu.

evenly adv. **[equally]**

byo⌈odooni 平等に /⟨**adj**(*na*). ***ni* of *byoodoona* equal/ •c [in equal parts and without discrimination]** ⟪**equally, impartially**⟫

EX. The food was evenly distributed among the refugees.
食糧は難民に平等に配られた。
Shokuryoo wa nanmin ni byoodooni kubara-reta.

event n. **[an occurrence, usually of importance, or a particular contest in a program of sports]**

1. de⌈ki⌉-goto 出来事 [an instance of s.t. occurring in the world of human affairs] ⟪**occurrence, happening, incident**⟫**, ji⌉ken 事件 •c [an incident which is out of the ordinary and attracts attention, esp. of a criminal nature]** ⟪**incident, affair, matter, case, accident**⟫**, gyo⌉oji 行事 •c [ceremonies and functions which take place at specified times in accordance with the customs/ conventions of society]** ⟪**function**⟫

EX. (**a**) One of the purposes of a diary is to record the main events of the day.
日記の目的の一つは一日の主な{出来事/?事件/?行事}を記録することである。
Nikki no mokuteki no hitotsu wa ichi-nichi no omona {deki-goto/?jiken/ ?gyooji} o kiroku-suru koto dearu.
(**b**) All business-related events of the day are normally recorded in this business journal.
仕事関係の一日の{出来事/?事件/?行事}は大抵全部この勤務日誌に記録される。
Shigoto-kankei no ichi-nichi no {deki-goto/?jiken/?gyooji} wa taitei zenbu kono kinmu-nisshi ni kiroku-sareru.
(**c**) The athletic meeting is an important annual event in Japanese schools.
運動会は日本の学校の大切な年間{行事/*出来事/*事件}です。
*Undoo-kai wa Nihon no gakkoo no taisetsuna nenkan-{gyooji/*deki-goto/ *jiken} desu.*
(**d**) The reunification of Germany was a great historical event.
ドイツの再統一は歴史上の大きな{出来事/事件/*行事}でした。
*Doitsu no sai-tooitsu wa rekishi-joo no ookina {deki-goto/jiken/*gyooji} deshita.*

2. shu⌈moku 種目 •c [item organized by kind]

EX. Roy won all three events at the swimming meet.

ロイは水泳競技の全三種目で優勝した。
Roi wa suiei-kyoogi no zen-san-shumoku de yuushoo-shita.

PHRASE: in any event *tonikaku* とにかく

EX. In any event, we have to complete the project by Friday.
とにかく計画は金曜日までに完了しなければならない。
Tonikaku keikaku wa kin'yoo-bi made ni kanryoo-shinakereba naranai.

PHRASE: in the event of ⟨*-no*⟩ *baai wa* ⟨〜の⟩場合は

EX. In the event of fire, do not use the elevator.
火災の場合は、エレベーターは使わないで下さい。
Kasai no baai wa, erebeetaa wa tsukawanaide kudasai.

eventually adv. **[finally, in the end]**
ke⌈kkyoku 結局 •c [finally after various developments along the way] ⟪after all, in the end, finally, in the long run⟫, sa⌉igo ni wa 最後には •c [in the end] ⟪finally⟫

EX. The president's proposal was eventually rejected by the faculty council.
学長の提案は{結局/最後には}教授会で却下された。
Gakuchoo no teian wa {kekkyoku/saigo ni wa} kyooju-kai de kyakka-sareta.

ever adv. **[at any time or (always) up to this time or an emphasis marker]**
1. i⌈tsu-mo いつも [no matter when it is] ⟪always⟫, tsu⌉ne ni 常に [without break or not changing ⟨w⟩] ⟪always, at all times⟫

EX. (**a**) Lisa is ever trying to improve her Japanese.
リサは自分の日本語力を向上させようと{いつも/常に}努力している。
Risa wa jibun no Nihon-go-ryoku o koojoo-saseyoo to {itsu-mo/tsune ni} doryoku-shite iru.
(**b**) The student studied harder than ever after that.
学生はその後{いつも/*常に}より一生懸命勉強した。
*Gakusei wa sono ato {itsu-mo/*tsune ni} yori isshoo-kenmei benkyoo-shita.*

2. i⌈ma-ma⌉de ni 今までに [by now], i⌉tsu-ka いつか [at some unknown/unspecified time]

EX. (**a**) Have you ever been to Kyoto?
{今までに/*いつか}京都へ行ったことがありますか。
*{Ima-made ni/*Itsu-ka} Kyooto e itta koto ga arimasu ka.*
(**b**) This is the best paper you've ever written.
これはあなたが{今までに/*いつか}書いた論文の中で一番いい。
*Kore wa anata ga {ima-made ni/*itsu-ka} kaita ronbun no naka de ichiban ii.*
(**c**) If you ever come to Michigan, do look us up.
{いつか/*今までに}ミシガンへいらしたらお立ち寄り下さい。
*{Itsu-ka/*Ima-made ni} Mishigan e irashitara o-tachi-yori kudasai.*

3. i⌈ttai 一体 •c [in the world]

EX. What ever did he spend all his money on?
一体彼は何に有り金全部使ったんだろう。
Ittai kare wa nani ni ari-gane-zenbu tsukatta n daroo.

NOTE: *Ittai* is used only in questions.

Everest n. **[a peak in the Himalaya mountains and the highest mountain in the world]**
E⌈beresuto⌉-san エベレスト山 •f+c [Mt. Everest], Cho⌈mora⌉nma チョモランマ •f [Mt. Everest]

every adj. **[each, individually and separately, or each interval of]**
1. a⌈rayu⌉ru N あらゆるN [all that can be thought of], su⌉bete no N すべてのN [exhaustively inclusive] ⟪all⟫

EX. (**a**) Every word has a history behind it.
{あらゆる/全ての}単語にはその歴史がある。
{Arayuru/Subete no} tango ni wa sono rekishi ga aru.
(**b**) Every professor in this department has a Ph. D.
この学部では、{全ての/?あらゆる}教

E

授が博士号をもっている。
Kono gakubu de wa, {subete no/ ?arayuru} kyooju ga hakase-goo o motte iru.

2. mai- 毎～ •c [each (unit of time) respectively], -goto (ni) ～ごと(に) [at each recurring occurrence of s.t., without exception], ⟨-ni⟩ wa i⌉tsu-mo ⟨～に⟩はいつも [always at the time of]

EX. (**a**) Nancy goes there every week.
ナンシーは{毎週/*週ごとに}そこへ行きます。
*Nanshii wa {mai-shuu/*shuu-goto ni} soko e ikimasu.*
(**b**) We went to Middlebury, Vermont every summer to teach Japanese .
{夏にはいつも/夏ごとに/毎夏}日本語を教えにバーモントのミドルベリーへ行きました。
{Natsu ni wa itsu-mo/Natsu-goto ni/ Mai-natsu} Nihon-go o oshie ni Baamonto no Midoruberii e ikimashita.
(**c**) Ed gives a lecture every day in his history course.
エドは{毎日/*日ごとに}歴史の授業で講義をします。
*Edo wa {mai-nichi/*hi-goto ni} rekishi no jugyoo de koogi o shimasu.*
(**d**) Satomi changed jobs every six months for two years.
里美は二年間{六か月ごとに/*毎六か月}職を変えた。
*Satomi wa ni-nenkan {rok-kagetsu-goto ni/*mai-rok-kagetsu} shoku o kaeta.*
(**e**) Our daughter makes a new kimono every year.
娘は{毎年/年ごとに}着物を新調します。
Musume wa {mai-toshi/toshi-goto ni} kimono o shinchoo-shimasu.

everybody n. **[every person]**
mi⌈nna⌉ みんな [extending to all things/ persons/animals concerned] ((all))

EX. (**a**) Everybody needs love.
みんな愛を必要としている。
Minna ai o hitsuyoo to shite iru.
(**b**) Aya is loved by everybody.
綾はみんなに愛されている。
Aya wa minna ni ai-sarete iru.

everyday adj. **[daily]**
ma⌉i-nichi no N 毎日のN •c [of every day], ni⌈chijoo no N 日常のN •c [usual]

EX. (**a**) Fighting is an everyday event in their home.
彼らの家ではけんかは{{毎日/日常}の出来事だ/日常茶飯事だ}。
Kare-ra no ie dewa kenka wa {{mai-nichi/nichijoo} no deki-goto/nichijoo-sahanji da}.

NOTE: *-wa {mainichi/nichijoo} no dekigoto da* is often expressed idiomatically by *-wa nichijoo-sahanji da.*

(**b**) I'm learning everyday French conversation.
フランス語の{日常/*毎日}(の)会話を習っています。
*Furansu-go no {nichijoo/*mai-nichi} (no)-kaiwa o naratte imasu.*

everyone n. **[every person]**
mi⌈nna⌉ みんな [extending to all things/ persons/animals concerned] ((all))

EX. (**a**) Everyone knows that.
それはみんなが知っていることだ。
Sore wa minna ga shitte iru koto da.
(**b**) Everyone hated the war.
みんなその戦争を憎んだ。
Minna sono sensoo o nikunda.
(**c**) Everyone wants to be healthy.
だれでもみんな健康でありたいと思うものだ。
Dare demo minna kenkoo de ari-tai to omou mono da.

everything n. **[every thing, all]**
su⌉bete すべて [s.t. exhaustive and all-inclusive] ((all)), **na⌉nimo-⌈ka⌉mo 何もかも [all, whatever it is]**

EX. (**a**) Our teacher knows everything about Japanese grammar.
私たちの先生は日本語の文法について{すべて/何もかも}知っている。
Watashi-tachi no sensei wa Nihon-go no bunpoo ni-tsuite {subete/nanimo-kamo} shitte iru.

(**b**) Everything is more expensive in Tokyo than in New York.
東京では{すべてが/何もかも}ニューヨークより高い。
Tookyoo de wa {subete ga/nanimo-kamo} Nyuuyooku yori takai.
(**c**) Thanks to you, everything went well.
おかげさまで{すべて(が)/何もかも}うまく行きました。
O-kage-sama de {subete (ga)/nanimo-kamo} umaku ikimashita.

everywhere adv. **[in or to every place]**
i⌈taru-tokoro⌉ {de/ni} いたるところ{で/に} n.+prt. **[no matter where one goes], so⌈ko(i)ra-juu {de/ni}** そこ(い)ら中{で/に} n.+prt. **[here and there], do⌈ko ({de/ni}) demo** どこ({で/に})でも n.+prt. **[in every place]**

EX. (**a**) Our cats sleep everywhere.
我が家の猫は{どこ({で/に})でも/そこ(い)ら中で/いたるところで}で寝る。
Waga-ya no neko wa {doko ({de/ni}) demo/soko(i)ra-juu de/itaru-tokoro de} neru.
(**b**) Dictionaries are found everywhere in our house.
うちでは辞書が{そこ(い)ら中に/いたるところに/どこにでも}置いてある。
Uchi de wa jisho ga {soko(i)ra-juu ni/itaru-tokoro ni/doko ni demo} oite aru.
(**c**) Pollution problems abound everywhere.
公害問題は{そこ(い)ら中で/いたるところで/どこにでも}起きている。
Koogai-mondai wa {soko(i)ra-juu de/itaru-tokoro de/doko ni demo} okite iru.
(**d**) You can see kangaroos everywhere in this part of the country.
この地方では{どこ(で)でも/そこいら中で/いたるところで}カンガルーを見ることができます。
Kono chihoo de wa {doko (de) demo/sokoira-juu de/itaru-tokoro de} kangaruu o miru koto ga dekimasu.

evidence n. **[s.t. that proves or disproves s.t.]**
sho⌈oko 証拠 •c **[materials that demonstrate the truth or correctness of s.t.]** ((**proof**))

EX. (**a**) We don't have any reliable evidence in this case.
この事件では確かな証拠がない。
Kono jiken de wa tashikana shooko ga nai.
(**b**) What is the evidence for assuming that he is the killer?
彼が殺人犯だと考える証拠は何ですか。
Kare ga satsujin-han da to kangaeru shooko wa nan desu ka.

evident adj. **[clear and easy to see]**
a⌈ki⌉rakana 明らかな adj(*na*). **[readily seen so that there is no doubt or ambiguity]** ((**clear, plain, obvious, manifest, apparent, distinct**)), **me⌈ihakuna** 明白な adj(*na*). •c **[accepted as such without doubt/suspicion by everybody]** ((**clear, plain, obvious, distinct**))

EX. It is evident that he has lost the documents.
彼がその書類をなくしたのは{明らか/明白}だ。
Kare ga sono shorui o nakushita no wa {akiraka/meihaku} da.

evidently adv. **[clearly, plainly]**
Sinf. rashii Sinf.らしい aux. adj(*i*). **[an auxiliary adjective which indicates that the preceding sentence represents the speaker's conjecture based on what he has heard/read/seen]** ((**look like, appear**)), **Sinf. yoona** Sinf.ような aux. adj(*na*). **[an auxiliary adj(*na*). which expresses the likelihood of s.t. or the likeness of s.t./s.o./s.a. to s.t./s.o./s.a.]** ((**appear**)), **Sinf. mitaina** Sinf.みたいな aux. adj(*na*). **[an auxiliary adj(*na*). which expresses the likelihood of s.t. or the likeness of s.t./s.o./s.a. to s.t./s.o./s.a. ⟨s⟩]**

NOTE: Notice the following special patterns that occur when *rashii*, *yoona* or *mitaina* are connected to a preceding sentence in which the final predicate is a nonpast affirmative form of an adj(*na*). or N + cop.: {adj(*na*). stem/N} {*rashii*/*mitaina*} {adj(*na*). stem + *na*/N *no*} *yoona*.

EX. (**a**) Evidently he is telling a lie.
彼はうそをついている{ようだ/らしい/みたいだ}。

E

Kare wa uso o tsuite iru {yooda/rashii/mitaida}.
(**b**) He evidently left town more than two weeks ago.
彼は二週間以上も前にこの町を出て行った{らしい/ようだ/みたいだ}。
Kare wa ni-shuukan-ijoo mo mae ni kono machi o dete itta {rashii/yooda/mitaida}.

evil adj. **[morally wrong or bad/wicked]**
wa⌈ru⌉i 悪い adj(*i*). **[not good]** **⟪bad, wrong, poor⟫** ↔ **ii** いい adj(*i*)., **yoi** よい adj(*i*).

EX. (**a**) He committed an evil deed and is suffering the pangs of conscience for it.
彼は悪い行いをして、良心のかしゃくにさいなまれている。
Kare wa warui okonai o shite, ryooshin no kashaku ni sainama-rete iru.
(**b**) He feels remorse for his evil deeds.
彼は悪いことをしたと反省している。
Kare wa warui koto o shita to hansei-shite iru.

—— n. **[wickedness]**
a⌉ku 悪 •c **[s.t. bad/undesirable]** **⟪vice⟫** ↔ **zen** 善

EX. (**a**) Drugs are a social evil.
麻薬は社会の悪である。
Mayaku wa shakai no aku dearu.
(**b**) Superman is portrayed as a champion of the weak who fights against evil.
スーパーマンは悪と戦う弱者の味方として描かれている。
Suupaaman wa aku to tatakau jakusha no mikata to-shite egaka-rete iru.
(**c**) Good prospers, evil perishes.
善は栄え、悪は滅びる。
Zen wa sakae, aku wa horobiru.

evolve vt. **[for s.o. to develop s.t. gradually]**
⟨-o⟩ jo⌉joni ha⌈tten-saseru ⟨〜を⟩徐々に発展させる /⟨*jojo ni* gradually + causative of *hatten-suru* ③ develop/ ② **[cause s.t. to develop gradually]**

EX. He evolved his simple idea into a complex theory.
彼は単純な思いつきを徐々に複雑な理論にまで発展させた。
Kare wa tanjunna omoi-tsuki o jojoni fukuzatsuna riron ni made hatten-saseta.

—— vi. **[to develop gradually, esp. by biological evolution]**
shi⌉nka-suru 進化する ③ •c **[for an organism to develop and become better adjusted to its environment]**

EX. Apes are thought to have evolved into human beings.
猿が進化して人類になったとされている。
Saru ga shinka-shite jinrui ni natta to sarete iru.

ex- suf. **[former]**
zen- 前〜 •c, **ma⌉e no N** 前のN **[coming/going before in time or located before]**

EX. (**a**) The ex-president of the company is still living.
会社の{前/前の}社長はまだお元気です。
Kaisha no {zen-/mae no} shachoo wa mada o-genki desu.
(**b**) The ex-president of the U.S. lives in California.
アメリカの{前/前の}大統領はカリフォルニアに住んでいる。
Amerika no {zen-/mae no} daitooryoo wa Kariforunia ni sunde iru.

exact adj. **[accurate and in accord with fact]**
se⌈ikakuna 正確な adj(*na*). •c **[in accord with fact and reliable]** **⟪correct, accurate, precise, right⟫** ↔ **fu-seikakuna** 不正確な adj(*na*). •c

EX. (**a**) What is the exact time now?
今の正確な時間は何時ですか。
Ima no seikakuna jikan wa nan-ji desu ka.
(**b**) Let me know the exact time of your plane's arrival.
あなたの飛行機の正確な到着時間を教えて下さい。
Anata no hikoo-ki no seikakuna toochaku-jikan o oshiete kudasai.

exactly adv. **[accurately/precisely]**
1. se⌈ikakuni 正確に /⟨**adj**(*na*). *ni* of *seikakuna* accurate/ •c **[without any**

E

mistake] ((precisely)), cho⌈odo ちょうど [with no variance whatsoever from a given time, quantity, or location] ((precisely, just))

EX. (**a**) He showed up exactly at twelve noon.
彼は{正確に/ちょうど}正午に現れた。
Kare wa {seikakuni/choodo} shoogo ni arawareta.
(**b**) Tell me exactly what she said.
彼女が言ったことを{正確に/*ちょうど}話して下さい。
*Kanojo ga itta koto o {seikakuni/ *choodo} hanashite kudasai.*

2. (mattaku) sono toori da (全く)その通りだ [just as s.o. has said]

EX. A: I think it's about time this committee got a new chair.
この委員会はもうそろそろ新しい委員長に替わるべき時期に来ているようだな。
Kono iin-kai wa moo soro-soro atarashii iin-choo ni kawaru beki jiki ni kite iru yooda na.
B: Exactly.
(全く)その通りだ。
(Mattaku) sono toori da.

PHRASE: not exactly *chotto chigau* ちょっと違う ①

EX. (**a**) A: Do you love him?
彼のこと、愛して(い)るの。
Kare no koto, aishite (i)ru no?
B: Not exactly. I just like him.
ちょっと違うわ。好きなだけなの。
Chotto chigau wa. Sukina dake na no.
(**b**) John isn't exactly a smart man, you know.
ジョンは頭がいいのとちょっと違うな。
Jon wa atama ga ii no to chotto chigau na.

examination n. **[an examining or being examined or a set of questions asked in testing]**

1. shi⌈ke⌉n 試験 •c [an act/instance of examining the ability/proficiency/quality of s.o./a machine] ((test))

EX. (**a**) To enter a university in Japan, you have to take an entrance examination.
日本では大学に入るには入学試験を受けねばならない。
Nihon de wa daigaku ni hairu ni wa nyuugaku-shiken o ukeneba naranai.
(**b**) Joe flunked his math examination.
ジョーは数学の試験に落ちた。
Joo wa suugaku no shiken ni ochita.
(**c**) I still dream about entrance examinations even after graduation.
学校を卒業してもまだ入学試験の夢を見る。
Gakkoo o sotsugyoo-shite mo mada nyuugaku-shiken no yume o miru.

2. ke⌉nsa 検査 •c [careful checking to see if s.t./s.o./s.a. meets the standard or if there is anything wrong with it/him/her, etc.] ((checking, inspection, test))

EX. (**a**) We have a physical examination at school today.
今日学校で身体検査がある。
Kyoo gakkoo de shintai-kensa ga aru.
(**b**) The blood collected by the Red Cross has to go through a thorough examination.
赤十字で集められた血液は厳重な検査を通らなければならない。
Seki-juuji de atsume-rareta ketsueki wa genjuuna kensa o tooranakereba naranai.

examine vt. **[for s.o. to test s.o. by questioning or to inspect/investigate s.t./s.a.]**

1. ⟨-o⟩ shi⌈ke⌉n-suru ⟨～を⟩試験する ③ •c [for s.o. to consider s.o./s.t., esp. a machine, carefully to see if he/she/it meets a given standard of ability/proficiency/quality] ((test))

EX. (**a**) The professor examined the students and divided them into two classes.
教授は試験して学生を二つのクラスに分けた。
Kyooju wa shiken-shite gakusei o futatsu no kurasu ni waketa.
(**b**) The company examined its freshman employees before deciding on their job assignments.
会社は新入社員の任務を決める前に彼らを試験した。
Kaisha wa shinnyuu-shain no ninmu o

E

kimeru mae ni kare-ra o shiken-shita.
(**c**) Doctors are waiting for a chance to examine the new medicine.
医者は新薬を試験してみたいと思ってその機会を待っている。
Isha wa shin'yaku o shiken-shite mitai to omotte sono kikai o matte iru.

2. ⟨-o⟩ ke⌉nsa-suru ⟨〜を⟩検査する ③ •c [for s.o. to carefully check to see if s.t./s.o./s.a. meets the standard or if there is anything wrong with it/him/her, etc.] ⟪check, inspect, test⟫, ⟨-o⟩ shi⌈rabe⌉ru ⟨〜を⟩調べる ② [for s.o. to observe directly or inquire/read about s.t./s.o./s.a. in order to determine or ascertain s.t. unknown or uncertain about it/him/her] ⟪investigate, study, inspect⟫

EX. (**a**) Passenger luggage is examined at the airport.
空港では乗客の荷物を{検査する/調べる}。
Kuukoo de wa jookyaku no nimotsu o {kensa-suru/shiraberu}.
(**b**) We examined the content of the food carefully.
我々はその食品の成分を詳しく{検査した/調べた}。
Ware-ware wa sono shokuhin no seibun o kuwashiku {kensa-shita/shirabeta}.

example n. **[a part chosen to show the character of the whole or a model to be imitated/avoided]**

1. re⌉i 例 •c [a thing similar to s.t. that has happened before or a specific instance used to make clear a more general idea or to support the correctness of one's claim] ⟪instance⟫

EX. (**a**) In linguistics, it is important to support one's claims with lots of good examples.
言語学では良い例をたくさん挙げて自分の主張を裏づけることが重要です。
Gengo-gaku de wa yoi rei o takusan agete jibun no shuchoo o urazukeru koto ga juuyoo desu.
(**b**) Let's consider some examples from Japanese.
日本語での例を少し考えましょう。
Nihon-go de no rei o sukoshi kangaemashoo.
(**c**) I will now explain the problem by citing a few examples.
それではいくつか例を挙げてその問題について説明しましょう。
Sore-dewa ikutsu-ka no rei o agete sono mondai ni-tsuite setsumei-shimashoo.

2. te⌈ho⌉n 手本 [a person or thing (esp. of manual art) considered excellent for its kind and worthy of being imitated] ⟪copybook, copy, model, pattern⟫

EX. (**a**) When writing kanji, I would follow the example set by the teacher.
漢字を書くとき僕は先生の手本にならって書いた。
Kanji o kaku toki boku wa sensei no tehon ni naratte kaita.
(**b**) Tom set a good example for his colleagues.
トムは仲間にいい手本を示した。
Tomu wa nakama ni ii tehon o shimeshita.

PHRASE: for example *tatoeba* 例えば

EX. Masayoshi speaks several foreign languages—for example, Korean and Chinese.
正芳は外国語をいくつか話します。例えば韓国語と中国語です。
Masayoshi wa gaikoku-go o ikutsu-ka hanashimasu. Tatoeba Kankoku-go to Chuugoku-go desu.

excellent adj. **[remarkably good]**
yu⌈ushuuna 優秀な adj(*na*). **•c [superior to any other of the same kind] ⟪superior⟫, su⌈gu⌉reta N 優れたN /⟨Vpast of *sugureru* ② excel/ ⟪superior, distinguished⟫**

EX. (**a**) Sadaharu Oh was an excellent baseball player.
王貞治は{優秀な/優れた}野球選手でした。
Oo Sadaharu wa {yuushuuna/sugureta} yakyuu-senshu deshita.
(**b**) All our students of Japanese are excellent.
我々の日本語の学生はみんな{優秀です/優れています}。

E

Ware-ware no Nihon-go no gakusei wa minna {yuushuu desu/sugurete imasu}.
(**c**) She graduated from college with excellent grades.
彼女は{優秀な/優れた}成績で大学を卒業した。
Kanojo wa {yuushuuna/sugureta} seiseki de daigaku o sotsugyoo-shita.

except prep. **[leaving out]**
-igai (wa) ～以外(は) •c [with the exception of] ((but))

EX. (**a**) Everyone sang karaoke except her.
彼女以外は全員カラオケで歌った。
Kanojo-igai wa zen'in karaoke de utatta.
(**b**) This department store is open every day except Thursday.
このデパートは木曜日以外は毎日開いています。
Kono depaato wa mokuyoo-bi-igai wa mai-nichi aite imasu.

exception n. **[s.t. excepted/different from others of the same kind]**
re⌈igai 例外 •c [s.t. that is recognized as being in a special situation to which general rules do not apply]

EX. (**a**) There is no rule without exceptions.
例外のない規則はない。
Reigai no nai kisoku wa nai.
(**b**) A person who is able to speak fifteen different languages fluently is an exception.
十五もの違ったことばを流ちょうに話せる人は例外だ。
Juu-go mo no chigatta kotoba o ryuuchooni hanase-ru hito wa reigai da.

excess n. **[the amount by which s.t. exceeds another]**
cho⌈oka 超過 •c [the amount/time that exceeds the allowable framework] ((surplus))

EX. (**a**) The U.S. has the problem of an excess of imports over exports.
アメリカは輸入超過の問題を抱えている。
Amerika wa yunyuu-chooka no mondai o kakaete iru.
(**b**) The load on the truck was in excess of one ton over the prescribed limit.
トラックの積み荷は規定重量を一トン超過していた。
Torakku no tsumi-ni wa kitei-juuryoo o it-ton chooka-shite ita.

excessive adj. **[too much]**
ka⌉do no N 過度のN •c [exceeding a desirable level] ((immoderate, too much, inordinate))

EX. (**a**) Excessive drinking affects one's health.
過度の飲酒は健康に害を及ぼす。
Kado no inshu wa kenkoo ni gai o oyobosu.
(**b**) Excessive work leads to death.
過度の労働は死に至る。
Kado no roodoo wa shi ni itaru.

exchange vt. **[give/receive s.t. for another thing]**
⟨-o⟩ ⟨-to⟩ ko⌈okan-suru ⟨～を⟩⟨～と⟩交換する ③ •c [for s.o. to receive s.t. in exchange for s.t. else] ((trade, barter)), ⟨-o⟩ ⟨-to⟩ to⌈ri-kaeru ⟨～を⟩⟨～と⟩取り換える ② [for s.o. to replace s.t. with s.t. else] ((replace, renew))

EX. (**a**) My wife exchanged the shoes for another pair.
家内は靴を別のと{交換した/取り換えた}。
Kanai wa kutsu o betsu no to {kookan-shita/tori-kaeta}.
(**b**) The sisters exchanged their dresses.
姉妹は洋服をお互いに{交換した/取り換えた}。
Shimai wa yoofuku o o-tagai ni {kookan-shita/tori-kaeta}.

—— n. **[the act of exchanging or the value of one currency in terms of another]**
1. ko⌈okan 交換 •c [the act of trading/bartering s.t.] ((trade, barter))

EX. (**a**) There was an exchange of gifts at the party.
パーティーでは贈り物の交換があった。
Paatii de wa okuri-mono no kookan ga atta.
(**b**) They made an exchange of music cassette tapes with each other.

E

彼らはお互いに音楽のカセットテープの交換を行った。
Kare-ra wa o-tagai ni ongaku no kasetto-teepu no kookan o okonatta.

2. ka⌈wase 為替 [a method of settling debts and obligations between distant places by means of drafts, checks, and negotiable instruments]

EX. We handle foreign exchange at our bank.
うちの銀行は外国為替を扱っています。
Uchi no ginkoo wa gaikoku-kawase o atsukatte imasu.

excited adj. **[stimulated/aroused]**
ko⌈ofun-shita N 興奮したN /⟨Vinf. past of *koofun-suru* ③ become excited/ •c [be aroused and unable to control one's emotions] ⟪**stimulated, agitated, aroused**⟫

EX. (**a**) John was excited at the news.
ジョンは知らせを聞いて興奮した。
Jon wa shirase o kiite koofun-shita.
(**b**) The excited spectators surged onto the football field.
興奮した観客がフットボールのフィールドになだれ込んだ。
Koofun-shita kankyaku ga futto-booru no fiirudo ni nadare-konda

excitedly adv. **[in an excited manner]**
ko⌈ofun-shite 興奮して •c /⟨Vte of *koofun-suru* ③ become excited/ [with excitement]

EX. The crowd at the football game shouted excitedly.
フットボールの観衆は興奮して叫んだ。
Futto-booru no kanshuu wa koofun-shite sakenda.

excitement n. **[an act/instance of exciting or being excited]**
ko⌈ofun 興奮 •c [the state of being stimulated or aroused] ⟪**stimulation**⟫

EX. (**a**) We had a hard time suppressing our excitement.
我々は興奮を抑えるのに苦労した。
Ware-ware wa koofun o osaeru no ni kuroo-shita.
(**b**) The table tennis match caused much excitement.
卓球の試合は大きな興奮を呼んだ。
Takkyuu no shiai wa ookina koofun o yonda.

exciting adj. **[causing excitement, stirring, thrilling]**
ko⌈ofun-sase-rareru N 興奮させられるN [a N by which excitement is causd] /⟨causative-passive of *koofun-suru* ③ become excited/ •c, wa⌉ku-waku-suru N わくわくするN [restless due to happiness, expectation, worry, etc.] ⟪**thrilling**⟫

EX. (**a**) It was a most exciting game.
それはとても{興奮させられる/わくわくする}試合だった。
Sore wa totemo {koofun-sase-rareru/waku-waku-suru} shiai datta.
(**b**) I saw an exciting movie.
私は{興奮させられる/わくわくする}映画を見た。
Watashi wa {koofun-sase-rareru/waku-waku-suru} eiga o mita.

excuse vt. **[for s.o. to overlook the offence/fault of another or to release s.o. from an obligation]**
1. ⟨-o⟩ yu⌈ru⌉su ⟨〜を⟩許す ① [for s.o. to allow s.o. else to do s.t. freely ⟪fig. "forgive"⟫] ⟪**permit, allow, forgive**⟫

EX. (**a**) The section chief excused the subordinate for arriving late.
課長は部下の遅刻を許した。
Kachoo wa buka no chikoku o yurushita.
(**b**) The teacher excused John for his rudeness in class.
先生は授業でのジョンの不作法を許した。
Sensei wa jugyoo de no Jon no bu-sahoo o yurushita.

2. ⟨-o⟩ me⌉njo-suru ⟨〜を⟩免除する ③ •c [for s.o. to permit s.o. to not fulfil his/her duty/obligation] ⟪**except, remit**⟫

EX. (**a**) The teacher excused me from cleaning the classroom for today.
先生は今日だけ教室の掃除を免除してくださった。
Sensei wa kyoo dake kyooshitsu no sooji o menjo-shite kudasatta.

(**b**) Nobody is excused from paying parking fines.
駐車違反の罰金を免除される者はいない。
Chuusha-ihan no bakkin o menjo-sareru mono wa inai.

—— n. **[defense of some action]**
i⌈iwake 言い訳 [reason, not necessarily a false one, put forward to justify one's failure, fault, etc.] ⟪**apology**⟫

EX. (**a**) I have no excuse for my action.
あの行為には言い訳はありません。
Ano kooi ni wa iiwake wa arimasen.
(**b**) You have to give me a better excuse than that.
あなたのその言い訳では通らないですよ。
Anata no sono iiwake de wa tooranai desu yo.
(**c**) I don't want to hear excuses.
言い訳なぞ聞きたくありません。
Iiwake nazo kiki-taku arimasen.

PHRASE: Excuse me. *Shitsurei-shimasu.* 失礼します。*Gomennasai.* 御免なさい。

EX. (**a**) Please excuse me for a minute.
ちょっと失礼します。
Chotto shitsurei-shimasu.
(**b**) Oh, excuse me.
あ、御免なさい。
A, gomennasai.

executive n. **[s.o. having managerial and policy-making authority in an organization]** **ju⌈uyaku 重役 •c [s.o. who has an important managerial post in a bank or at a business corporation]** ⟪**director, senior officer, the directorate**⟫, **ka⌉nbu 幹部 •c [the head/one of the heads of an organization or a corporation]** ⟪**the management, leaders, leading members**⟫

EX. (**a**) Mr. Suzuki is now an executive of a big company.
鈴木氏は今や大会社の{重役/幹部}だ。
Suzuki-shi wa imaya dai-gaisha no {juuyaku/kanbu} da.
(**b**) Not every employee nowadays wants to become an executive.
最近のサラリーマンはみんなが{重役/幹部}になりたがっているわけではない。
Saikin no sararii-man wa minna ga {juuyaku/kanbu} ni nari-ta-gatte iru wake dewanai.

exercise n. **[an activity involving physical/mental exertion done for the purpose of training the body or mind or a task performed repeatedly to develop a skill]**
1. u⌈ndoo 運動 •c [an act/instance of changing one's location/position with the passage of time or the act of moving one's body to develop it and maintain good health or the act of aggressively and systematically approaching various people/institutions in order to achieve an objective], ta⌈isoo 体操 •c [the art or practice of training the body, including such training with special apparatus such as parallel bars and rings]

EX. (**a**) Cal does exercises every morning as soon as he gets up.
キャルは毎朝起きると必ず{運動/体操}をする。
Kyaru wa mai-asa okiru to kanarazu {undoo/taisoo} o suru.
(**b**) Lack of exercise can cause a person to gain weight.
{運動/*体操}不足は太る原因になる。
*{Undoo/*Taisoo}-busoku wa futoru gen'in ni naru.*

2. re⌈nshuu 練習 •c [an act of doing s.t. repeatedly to acquire a specific skill] ⟪**practice, training, drill**⟫

EX. (**a**) Peter did kanji exercises in the library.
ピーターは図書館で漢字の練習をした。
Piitaa wa tosho-kan de kanji no renshuu o shita.
(**b**) There is a grammar exercise session this afternoon for those students needing extra help before the test.
試験の前に助けを必要とする学生のために、今日の午後文法練習の授業があります。
Shiken no mae ni tasuke o hitsuyoo to suru gakusei no tame ni, kyoo no gogo

E

bunpoo-renshuu no jugyoo ga arimasu.

— vi. **[to actively use the body for development and training]**
u˹ndoo-suru 運動する ③ •c [for s.o. to move one's body actively to develop it and maintain good health] ((**do exercise**))

EX. (**a**) I exercise for half an hour every morning.
僕は毎朝三十分運動します。
Boku wa mai-asa san-jup-pun undoo-shimasu.
(**b**) The doctor told her to exercise more.
医者は彼女にもっと運動しなさいと言った。
Isha wa kanojo ni motto undoo-shinasai to itta.

E

exhibit vt. **[for s.o. to show/display s.t. for the public to see]**
⟨-o⟩ te˹nji-suru ⟨〜を⟩展示する ③ •c [for s.o. to arrange things for public presentation] ((**display**))

EX. (**a**) Debby exhibited the pieces of pottery she had made.
デビーは自分で作った焼物を展示した。
Debii wa jibun de tsukutta yaki-mono o tenji-shita.
(**b**) The pupils exhibited their paintings at the school festival.
生徒は学園祭で自分たちの絵を展示した。
Seito wa gakuen-sai de jibun-tachi no e o tenji-shita.

— n. **[a display or s.t. displayed]**
te˹nji-hin 展示品 •c [s.t. arranged for public presentation], te˹nji 展示 •c [exhibition] ((**fair**))

EX. (**a**) Part of the exhibit was stolen by a thief.
{展示品/*展示}の一部が泥棒に盗まれた。
*{Tenji-hin/*Tenji} no ichi-bu ga doroboo ni nusuma-reta.*
(**b**) The exhibit came from Korea.
{展示品/*展示}は韓国から来た。
*{Tenji-hin/*Tenji} wa Kankoku kara kita.*
(**c**) There will be a flower exhibit at Mejiro Kaikan tomorrow.
あした目白会館で花の{展示/*展示品}があります。
*Ashita Mejiro-kaikan de hana no {tenji/*tenji-hin} ga arimasu.*

exist vi. **[to have reality and actual being]**
a˥ru ある ① [for s.t. to have being in a form that can be apprehended by means of sight/hearing/touch or through thought], i˹ru いる ② [for s.o./s.a. to have being in a form that can be apprehended by means of sight/hearing/touch or through thought], so˹nzai-suru 存在する ③ •c [for s.t./s.o./s.a. to have reality and actual being] ((**be in existence**))

EX. (**a**) Do you think ghosts really exist?
幽霊は本当に{存在する/いる/*ある}と思いますか。
*Yuurei wa hontoo ni {sonzai-suru/iru/*aru} to omoimasu ka.*
(**b**) I believe UFOs actually exist.
UFOは実際に{存在する/ある/*いる}と信じています。
*Yuufoo wa jissai ni {sonzai-suru/aru/*iru} to shinjite imasu.*

existence n. **[the state/fact of being]**
so˹nzai 存在 •c [the fact of existing or being present in a place] ((**being**))

EX. (**a**) Some children believe in the existence of E.T.
E.T.の存在を信じている子供がいる。
Iitii no sonzai o shinjite iru kodomo ga iru.
(**b**) The existence of chemical weapons in the country was disclosed in a government report.
政府の報告書によりその国の化学兵器の存在が明らかになった。
Seifu no hookoku-sho ni-yori sono kuni no kagaku-heiki no sonzai ga akirakani natta.

existing adj. **[having reality]**
{ge˹nzon/ge˹nson} no N 現存のN •c [present/actual]

EX. This is the world's oldest existing musical instrument.

これは現存の世界の楽器の中で最も古いものです。
Kore wa {genzon/genson} no sekai no gakki no naka de mottomo furui mono desu.

exit n. **[a way out]**
de'guchi 出口 [way out] ↔ **iriguchi 入り口**
EX. (**a**) In an airplane, all exits are clearly marked.
飛行機の中では、出口はすべてはっきり表示されている。
Hikoo-ki no naka de wa, deguchi wa subete hakkiri hyooji-sarete iru.
(**b**) Excuse me, can you tell me where the exit is?
すみませんが、出口はどちらですか。
Sumimasen ga, deguchi wa dochira desu ka.

expand vi. **[to spread out/increase in size, scope, etc.]**
ha'tten-suru 発展する ③ •c [for s.t. to move into a more advanced stage and spread over a wider area] ⟪develop, grow, prosper, flourish⟫
EX. (**a**) Their business soon expanded to foreign countries.
彼らの商売はすぐに外国へと発展した。
Kare-ra no shoobai wa sugu ni gaikoku e to hatten-shita.
(**b**) It will become more and more difficult for colleges to expand in the future given the decrease in number of college applicants as the birth rate declines.
出生率の低下に伴い、これからは入学志願者の数が減少していくから、大学がこれ以上発展するのはますます難しくなるだろう。
Shussei-ritsu no teika ni tomonai, kore kara wa nyuugaku-shigan-sha no kazu ga genshoo-shite iku kara, daigaku ga kore ijoo hatten-suru no wa masu-masu muzukashiku naru daroo.
(**c**) I believe business in this field is going to expand more and more.
この分野のビジネスはどんどん発展すると思います。
Kono bun'ya no bijinesu wa don-don hatten-suru to omoimasu.

—— vt. **[to cause s.t. to spread out/increase in size, scope, etc.]**
⟨-o⟩ ha'tten-saseru ⟨〜を⟩発展させる /⟨causative of *hatten-suru* ③ develop/ ② •c [to cause s.t. to develop] ⟪develop⟫, **⟨-o⟩ ka'kuchoo-suru ⟨〜を⟩拡張する ③ •c [for s.o. to enlarge s.t.]** ⟪enlarge, develop⟫ ↔ **shukushoo-suru 縮小する ③ •c**
EX. (**a**) The corporation is making every effort to expand its international division.
会社は国際部門を{発展させよう/拡張しよう}と努力している。
Kaisha wa kokusai-bumon o {hatten-saseyoo/kakuchoo-shiyoo} to doryoku-shite iru.
(**b**) The auto company expanded its mid-size line.
自動車会社は中型ラインを{発展させた/拡張した}。
Jidoosha-gaisha wa chuugata-rain o {hatten-saseta/kakuchoo-shita}.

expansion n. **[an expanding/enlargement]**
ha'tten 発展 •c [an instance of moving into a more advanced stage accompanied by a spreading over a wider area] ⟪development, growth⟫, **ka'kuchoo 拡張 •c [an enlarging]** ⟪growth⟫ ↔ **shukushoo 縮小 •c**
EX. (**a**) A sudden expansion in the size of that city due to new businesses being attracted has resulted in a serious housing shortage.
企業誘致によるその町の急激な{発展/?拡張}は深刻な住宅難を招いた。
Kigyoo-yuuchi ni yoru sono machi no kyuugekina {hatten/?kakuchoo} wa shinkokuna juutaku-nan o maneita.
(**b**) The development of experts in foreign languages is essential to the overseas expansion of our company.
うちの会社の海外{発展/*拡張}には外国語のエキスパートの育成が必須だ。
*Uchi no kaisha no kaigai-{hatten/ *kakuchoo} ni wa gaikoku-go no ekisupaato no ikusei ga hissu da.*
(**c**) A considerable sum of money is

E

necessary for the expansion of the division.
その部門の{発展/拡張}にはそれなりの資金が必要だ。
Sono bumon no {hatten/kakuchoo} ni wa sore-nari no shikin ga hitsuyoo da.

expect vt. **[for s.o. to look forward to s.t. happening or to wish for and have confidence that s.t. will happen because it is right or necessary]**

1. 〈-o〉 **ki⌈tai-suru** 〈～を〉期待する ③ **•c [for s.o. to anticipate in one's mind that s.t. desirable will happen]** **《anticipate, hope, look forward to》**

EX. (**a**) Lucy expected a gift from her husband for her birthday.
ルーシーは誕生日に夫からの贈り物を期待していた。
Ruushii wa tanjoo-bi ni otto kara no okuri-mono o kitai-shite ita.
(**b**) I am expecting a letter from my sister.
僕は妹からの手紙を期待している。
Boku wa imooto kara no tegami o kitai-shite iru.
(**c**) My wife is expecting a big catch of fish.
妻は魚がたくさん釣れるのを期待している。
Tsuma wa sakana ga takusan tsureru no o kitai-shite iru.

2. 〈-to〉 **o⌈mo⌉u** 〈～と〉思う ① **[for s.o. to spontaneously perceive s.t. in one's mind or to have an opinion about s.t.]** **《guess, think, feel》**

EX. I expect that dad will be home soon.
パパはもうすぐ帰ると思います。
Papa wa moo-sugu kaeru to omoimasu.

PHRASE: as expected *{yahari/yappari}* {やはり/やっぱり} 《indeed, as one thought》

EX. (**a**) They got married, as expected.
彼らは{やはり/やっぱり}結婚した。
Kare-ra wa {yahari/yappari} kekkon-shita.
(**b**) As expected, he received the Nobel Prize.
彼は{やはり/やっぱり}ノーベル賞をもらった。
Kare wa {yahari/yappari} nooberu-shoo o moratta.

expectation n. **[a fact/instance of expecting or s.t. expected]**
ki⌈tai 期待 **•c [the act of anticipating in one's mind that s.t. desirable will happen]** **《anticipation, hope》**, **yo⌈soo** 予想 **•c [an act of predicting s.t.]** **《anticipation, forecast, surmise, conjecture》**

EX. (**a**) I will try and live up to his expectations.
彼の{期待/*予想}にこたえるように努力します。
*Kare no {kitai/*yosoo} ni kotaeru yooni doryoku-shimasu.*
(**b**) Against all expectations, the enemy was weak.
敵は{予想/*期待}に反して弱かった。
*Teki wa {yosoo/*kitai} ni han-shite yowakatta.*
(**c**) The opponent was strong beyond expectations.
相手は{予想/?期待}以上に強かった。
Aite wa {yosoo/?kitai}-ijoo ni tsuyokatta.
(**d**) The total contributions far exceeded our expectations.
寄付金の合計は{期待/予想}をはるかに超えるものだった。
Kifu-kin no gookei wa {kitai/yosoo} o harukani koeru mono datta.
(**e**) Contrary to our expectations, our team lost the first game.
我々のチームは{期待/予想}に反して一回戦で負けてしまった。
Ware-ware no chiimu wa {kitai/yosoo} ni han-shite ik-kai-sen de makete shimatta.

PHRASE: contrary to one's expectations *angai* 案外 **•c**

EX. Contrary to our expectations, the enemy was weak.
敵は案外弱かった。
Teki wa angai yowakatta.

expenditure n. **[an act/instance of spending money/time or money/time spent]**
shi⌈shutsu 支出 **•c [spending of money or resources on s.t.]** **《expenses, outgo》** ↔ **shuunyuu** 収入 **•c**

EX. (**a**) Our total expenditure was large this month.
今月は支出が大きかった。
Kongetsu wa shishutsu ga ookikatta.
(**b**) The school has to cut down on its expenditures.
学校は支出を切り詰めねばならない。
Gakkoo wa shishutsu o kiri-tsumeneba naranai.

expense n. **[money spent on s.t. or s.t. for which money is spent]**
hi⌉yoo 費用 •c [money necessary for doing s.t.] ⟪expenditure, cost, outlay⟫

EX. (**a**) Nagano City had to pay much of the expense for the Winter Olympics.
長野市は冬季オリンピックの費用の多くを支払わなければならなかった。
Nagano-shi wa tooki-Orinpikku no hiyoo no ooku o shiharawanakereba naranakatta.
(**b**) I attended the conference in Washington at my school's expense.
私は学校の費用でワシントンの学会に出席した。
Watashi wa gakkoo no hiyoo de Washinton no gakkai ni shusseki-shita.

PHRASE: traveling expenses *ryokoo no hiyoo* 旅行の費用 •c, *ryohi* 旅費 •c

expensive adj. **[high-priced/costly]**
ta⌈ka⌉i 高い adj(*i*). **[for s.t. or the top of s.t. to be at a point well above the ground or for s.t. to be above the expected level/amount/rate/degree] ⟪dear, costly⟫ ↔ yasui** 安い adj(*i*).

EX. (**a**) To live in Tokyo is very expensive.
東京に住むのはとても高くつく。
Tookyoo ni sumu no wa totemo takaku tsuku.
(**b**) We cannot afford such an expensive car.
我々はそんな高い車は買えません。
Ware-ware wa sonna takai kuruma wa kae-masen.

experience n. **[s.t. one lives through, or knowledge, skill, etc., derived from that]**
ke⌈iken 経験 •c ⟪undergoing⟫

EX. (**a**) Mieko has lots of teaching experience.
美恵子は教えた経験が豊富だ。
Mieko wa oshieta keiken ga hoofu da.
(**b**) Tell me about your experiences in Kyoto.
京都での経験を聞かせて下さい。
Kyooto de no keiken o kika-sete kudasai.
(**c**) Japan learned a great deal from its war experience.
日本は戦争経験から多くを学んだ。
Nihon wa sensoo-keiken kara ooku o mananda.

— vt. **[for s.o. to undergo s.t. or have an experience of s.t.]**
⟨-o⟩ ke⌈iken-suru ⟨〜を⟩経験する ③ •c ⟪go through, undergo⟫

EX. (**a**) I experienced a lot of hardships overseas.
私は海外で多くの困難を経験しました。
Watashi wa kaigai de ooku no konnan o keiken-shimashita.
(**b**) In Japan George experienced a foreign culture for the first time in his life.
ジョージは日本で生まれて初めての異文化を経験した。
Jooji wa Nihon de umarete hajimete no i-bunka o keiken-shita.

experiment n. **[a test or trial to discover/demonstrate s.t.]**
ji⌈kken 実験 •c [the act of trying out a theory or hypothesis under various conditions to see if the predictions it makes are correct] ⟪test, experimentation⟫

EX. (**a**) The students conducted an experiment to see if air temperature affects the speed of sound.
生徒たちは気温が音の速さに影響があるかどうか、実験を行った。
Seito-tachi wa kion ga oto no hayasa ni eikyoo ga aru ka doo ka, jikken o okonatta.
(**b**) The experiment was a success.
実験は成功だった。
Jikken wa seikoo datta.

— vi. **[for s.o. to conduct a test/trial with s.t. in order to discover/demonstrate s.t.]**
ji⌈kken (o) suru 実験(を)する ③ •c [for s.o. to try out a theory or hypothesis under

various conditions to see if the predictions it makes are correct] ((test, undergo a test))

EX. (**a**) The company experimented with a solar car.
会社はソーラー・カーの実験をした。
Kaisha wa sooraa-kaa no jikken o shita.
(**b**) I will try and experiment with your ideas.
あなたのアイデアを入れて実験してみます。
Anata no aidea o irete jikken-shite mimasu.

experimental adj. **[based on/used for experiments]**
ji⌈kken-tekina N 実験的なN adj(*na*). •**c [of the nature of an experiment]** ((**exploratory**)), **shi⌈ken-tekina** 試験的な adj(*na*). •**c [for the purpose of experimenting to see if s.t. works]**

EX. (**a**) This project is still in an experimental stage.
この計画はまだ{実験的な/試験的な}段階にあります。
Kono keikaku wa mada {jikken-tekina/shiken-tekina} dankai ni arimasu.
(**b**) The stealth aircraft is no longer just an experimental plane.
レーダーに映らない飛行機はもはやただの{実験的な/試験的な}飛行機ではない。
Reedaa ni utsuranai hikoo-ki wa mohaya tada no {jikken-tekina/shiken-tekina} hikoo-ki dewanai.

expert n. **[s.o. having special skill/knowledge in some field]**
se⌈nmon-ka 専門家 •**c [a person who specializes in an academic field]**, **e⌈kisupa⌉ato** エキスパート •**f**

EX. (**a**) Ellis is an expert in foreign language education.
エリスは外国語教育の{専門家/エキスパート}です。
Erisu wa gaikoku-go-kyooiku no {senmon-ka/ekisupaato} desu.
(**b**) We are looking for an expert in foreign trade.
我々は外国貿易の{専門家/エキスパート}を探しています。
Ware-ware wa gaikoku-booeki no {senmon-ka/ekisupaato} o sagashite imasu.

explain vt. **[for s.o. to make s.t. plain, clear, and understandable to others]**
⟨-ni⟩ {⟨-o⟩/⟨-ni-tsuite⟩} se⌈tsumei-suru ⟨〜に⟩{⟨〜を⟩/⟨〜について⟩}説明する ③ •**c ((make plain or clear, illustrate, account for))**

EX. (**a**) Would you explain the meaning of "aphasia" in English?
英語のaphasiaの意味{を/?について}説明して下さいませんか。
Eigo no "aphasia" no imi {o/?ni-tsuite} setsumei-shite kudasaimasen ka.
(**b**) I explained the situation to her.
僕は彼女に状況{を/について}説明した。
Boku wa kanojo ni jookyoo {o/ni-tsuite} setsumei-shita.

explanation n. **[an act/instance of making s.t. plain/clear to others or a statement/fact that makes s.t. clear]**
se⌈tsumei 説明 •**c [an act/instance of explaining the content of/reason for/significance of s.t.] ((account, illustration, explication))**

EX. (**a**) That professor's explanations are always easy to follow.
あの教授の説明はいつも分かり易い。
Ano kyooju no setsumei wa itsu-mo wakari-yasui.
(**b**) I demanded an explanation from him for what he had done yesterday.
私は彼に昨日の行動の説明を求めた。
Watashi wa kare ni kinoo no koodoo no setsumei o motometa.

explode vi. **[for s.t. to burst violently with a loud noise]**
ba⌈kuhatsu-suru 爆発する ③ •**c [for s.t. to cause destruction by expanding suddenly and violently with heat, noise, and light] ((blow up, erupt))**

EX. (**a**) The tank exploded.
タンクが爆発した。
Tanku ga bakuhatsu-shita.

(b) An electric spark caused the gas to explode.
電気の火花でガスが爆発した。
Denki no hi-bana de gasu ga bakuhatsu-shita.

exploration n. **[travel in a little-known region for the purpose of discovery]**
ta⌈nken 探険 •c [braving danger to enter an unknown territory and examine it first-hand] ⟪**expedition**⟫

EX. (a) The modern age is one of space exploration.
現代は宇宙探険の時代である。
Gendai wa uchuu-tanken no jidai dearu.
(b) David Livingstone is known for his exploration of Africa.
デービッド・リビングストーンはアフリカ探険でよく知られている。
Deebiddo Ribingusutoon wa Afurika-tanken de yoku shira-rete iru.

explore vt. **[for s.o. to examine s.t. carefully or to traverse an unknown region for the purpose of discovery]**
1. ⟨-o⟩ cho⌉osa-suru ⟨～を⟩調査する ③ •c [for s.o. to try to find more information about s.t. to understand it better] ⟪**investigate, look into**⟫

EX. (a) Peggy came to Japan to explore job possibilities.
ペギーは仕事の可能性を調査するために日本へ来た。
Pegii wa shigoto no kanoo-sei o choosa-suru tame ni Nihon e kita.
(b) We have to explore this lead further.
我々はこの手掛かりをもっと調査しなければならない。
Ware-ware wa kono te-gakari o motto choosa-shinakereba naranai.

2. ⟨-o⟩ ta⌈nken-suru ⟨～を⟩探険する ③ •c [for s.o. to brave danger by entering an unknown territory and examining it first-hand]

EX. We decided to explore an uninhabited island off Maui.
マウイの沖にある無人島を探険することにした。
Maui no oki ni aru mujin-too o tanken-suru koto ni shita.

explosion n. **[a violent bursting accompanied by a loud noise]**
ba⌈kuhatsu 爆発 •c [sudden expansion, often causing destruction, accompanied by heat, light, and noise] ⟪**eruption**⟫

EX. (a) There was a big explosion at the chemical plant.
化学工場で大きな爆発があった。
Kagaku-koojoo de ookina bakuhatsu ga atta.
(b) It was discovered that the explosion was the work of an arsonist.
爆発は放火によって引き起こされたことが分かった。
Bakuhatsu wa hooka ni-yotte hiki-okosa-reta koto ga wakatta.

export vt. **[for a country/business enterprise to send goods to a foreign country for sale]**
⟨-o⟩ yu⌈shutsu-suru ⟨～を⟩輸出する ③ •c ⟪**ship abroad**⟫ **↔ ⟨-o⟩ yunyuu-suru ⟨～を⟩輸入する ③ •c**

EX. (a) Japan exports many computers.
日本はコンピューターをたくさん輸出している。
Nihon wa konpyuutaa o takusan yushutsu-shite iru.
(b) France used to export machines to Japan.
フランスは以前日本に機械を輸出していた。
Furansu wa izen Nihon ni kikai o yushutsu-shite ita.

—— n. **[s.t. sent abroad for sale or the act of exporting]**
yu⌈shutsu 輸出 •c ↔ yunyuu 輸入 •c; yu⌈shutsu-hin 輸出品 •c [products/production technology sent to a foreign country] ↔ yunyuu-hin 輸入品 •c

EX. (a) The export of high-technology commodities to communist countries was banned.
ハイテク製品の共産圏への{輸出/*輸出品}は禁止されていた。
Haiteku-seihin no kyoosan-ken e no

{yushutsu/*yushutsu-hin} wa kinshi-sarete ita.
(**b**) Automobiles are among the main exports of Japan.
自動車は日本の主な{輸出品/*輸出}の一つである。
*Jidoosha wa Nihon no omona {yushutsu-hin/*yushutsu} no hitotsu dearu.*

expose vt. **[to lay s.t./s.o./s.a. open to danger, harm, etc. 《fig. "reveal"》]**
1. 〈-o〉〈-ni〉 sa⌈rasu 〈～を〉〈～に〉さらす ① **[for s.o. to remove s.t. from a protected place and let it be at the mercy of the sun, rain, wind, etc. 《fig. "show without hiding"》]**

E

EX. (**a**) The adventurers were exposed to danger when heavy thunderstorms caused the river by their campsite to rise suddenly.
激しい雷雨のためキャンプ地近くの川の水かさが急に増した時探険家たちは危険にさらされた。
Hageshii raiu no tame kyanpu-chi chikaku no kawa no mizu-kasa ga kyuuni mashita toki tanken-ka-tachi wa kiken ni sarasa-reta.
(**b**) Don't expose this cloth to the sun.
この布は日にさらさないでください。
Kono nuno wa hi ni sarasanaide kudasai.

2. 〈-o〉 ba⌉kuro-suru 〈～を〉暴露する ③ •c **[for s.o. to make known to the public a secret or s.t. which s.o. does not want people to know about]** 《betray, uncover, disclose》
EX. (**a**) The newspaper exposed the scandal.
新聞がスキャンダルを暴露した。
Shinbun ga sukyandaru o bakuro-shita.
(**b**) His secret was finally exposed.
彼の秘密がとうとう暴露された。
Kare no himitsu ga tootoo bakuro-sareta.

express adj./n. **[fast and direct; a fast and direct train, etc.]**
kyu⌈ukoo 急行 •c **[a train, bus, etc. which makes only a limited number of stops and arrives at its destination quickly], kyu⌈ukoo-re⌉ssha** 急行列車 •c **[a train which makes only a limited number of stops and arrives at its destination quickly]**
EX. Sam took the express train to Tokyo.
サムは{急行/急行列車}で東京へ行った。
Samu wa {kyuukoo/kyuukoo-ressha} de Tookyoo e itta.
PHRASE: special express *tokubetsu-kyuukoo* 特別急行 •c, *tokkyuu* 特急 •c; express ticket *kyuukoo-ken* 急行券 •c, express delivery (Br. E) *sokutatsu* 速達 •c

—— vt. **[to communicate s.t. using verbal/nonverbal means]**
〈-o〉 hyo⌈ogen-suru 〈～を〉表現する ③ •c **[to express ideas using gestures, language, music, painting, etc.]** 《represent, manifest》, **〈-o〉 a⌈rawa⌉su** 〈～を〉あらわす ① **[to cause s.t. to become exposed/visible/recognizable], 〈-o〉 no⌈be⌉ru** 〈～を〉述べる ② **[for s.o. to speak/write s.t. in a formal way 〈w〉]**
㊥ "when it has to do with communication"▷表す, "when it refers to the appearance of s.t." ▷現す
EX. (**a**) I can't express my grief in words.
この深い悲しみはことばでは{表せません/表現できません/?述べられません}。
Kono fukai kanashi-mi wa kotoba de wa {arawase-masen/hyoogen-dekimasen/?nobe-raremasen}.
(**b**) The woman expressed her joy using sign language.
その女の人は手話を使って喜びを{表した/表現した/*述べた}。
*Sono onna no hito wa shuwa o tsukatte yorokobi o {arawashita/hyoogen-shita/*nobeta}.*
(**c**) The boy's face expressed happiness.
少年の顔が幸せを{表して/?表現して/*述べて}いた。
*Shoonen no kao ga shiawase o {arawashite/?hyoogen-shite/*nobete} ita.*
(**d**) When pressed, the man reluctantly expressed his true opinion on the matter.

男はせきたてられてしぶしぶその件について自分の本当の意見を{述べた/??表現した/??表した}。
Otoko wa sekitate-rarete shibu-shibu sono ken ni-tsuite jibun no hontoo no iken o {nobeta/??hyoogen-shita/??arawashita}.

expression n. **[an act or instance of communicating one's thoughts verbally or non-verbally or a word/phrase conveying a particular meaning]**
hyo⌈ogen 表現 •c [communication of s.t. internal or subjective by means of external or emotive means or forms] ⟪representation⟫

EX. (**a**) In Japan, everyone is entitled by law to freedom of expression.
日本では、法律上だれでも表現の自由を持っている。
Nihon de wa, hooritsu-joo dare-demo hyoogen no jiyuu o motte iru.
(**b**) The story was moving beyond expression.
その話は表現できないほど感動的であった。
Sono hanashi wa hyoogen-dekinai hodo kandoo-teki deatta.

extend vt. **[for s.o. to make s.t. longer]**
⟨-o⟩ no⌈ba⌉su ⟨〜を⟩のばす ① [for s.o. to cause s.t. to become longer, usu. vertically ⟪fig. "straighten," "hold out," "postpone," "cultivate (abilities)"⟫] ⟪stretch, lengthen, postpone, defer, prolong⟫
㊥ "prolong/postpone"▷延ばす, otherwise ▷伸ばす

EX. (**a**) The delegation extended their stay in Japan for one week.
代表団は日本滞在を一週間延ばした。
Daihyoo-dan wa Nihon-taizai o is-shuukan nobashita.
(**b**) Sachiko ran toward her mother with both arms extended.
幸子は両腕を伸ばして母親のところへ駆け寄った。
Sachiko wa ryoo-ude o nobashite haha-oya no tokoro e kake-yotta.

—— vi. **[for s.t. to reach as far as s.t. else]**
no⌈bi⌉ru のびる ② [for s.t. to increase in length/height/ability/size] ⟪grow, lengthen, stretch, spread, be postponed, collapse, make progress, become smooth⟫, ⟨-ni⟩ o⌉yobu ⟨〜に⟩及ぶ ① [for s.t. to get to a point beyond what is expected ⟨fml⟩] ⟪reach⟫
㊥ "be prolonged/postponed"▷延びる, otherwise ▷伸びる

EX. (**a**) The politician's influence extends to the police.
政治家の影響は警察にまで{及んで/?伸びて}いる。
Seiji-ka no eikyoo wa keisatsu ni made {oyonde/?nobite} iru.
(**b**) The *Shinkansen* extends from Tokyo to Morioka.
新幹線は東京から盛岡まで{伸びて/*及んで}いる。
*Shinkansen wa Tookyoo kara Morioka made {nobite/*oyonde} iru.*

extension n. **[the act of extending or the state of being extended or s.t. extended ⟪fig. "an extra telephone operating on the principal line"⟫]**
1. e⌈nchoo 延長 •c [an act/instance of extending s.t.] ⟪lengthening⟫

EX. (**a**) We need to apply for an extension of our visas.
ビザの延長を申請する必要がある。
Biza no enchoo o shinsei-suru hitsuyoo ga aru.
(**b**) The resolution calling for extension of the Diet session was hotly debated.
国会の会期延長の決議案は激しく議論された。
Kokkai no kaiki-enchoo no ketsugi-an wa hageshiku giron-sareta.

2. na⌈isen 内線 •c [a telephone line for communicating within a single building]

EX. A: What is your extension number?
あなたの内線は何番ですか。
Anata no naisen wa nan-ban desu ka.
B: My extension is 1234.
私の内線は1234です。

E

Watashi no naisen wa ichi-ni-san-yon desu.

extensive adj. **[having great extent]**
ko⌈o-ha⌉n'i ni wa⌈taru N 広範囲にわたるN [extending over a wide scope] **《comprehensive, far-reaching》**

EX. (**a**) The damage from the volcano was quite extensive.
火山の被害はかなり広範囲にわたった。
Kazan no higai wa kanari koo-han'i ni watatta.
(**b**) They carried out extensive repairs on the road.
彼らは広範囲にわたる道路の修理を行った。
Kare-ra wa koo-han'i ni wataru dooro no shuuri o okonatta.

E

extent n. **[length, amount, volume, degree, or scope to which s.t. extends]**
te⌉ido 程度 •c [degree to which s.t. has a certain property, quantitative or qualitative, in comparison with others] **《degree, grade, measure, standard, level, limit》, ha⌉n'i 範囲 •c [an area defined by certain bounds]** **《range, scope》, ho⌈do ほど [the degree to which s.t. extends]**

EX. (**a**) Although the old man was over ninety, his memory was still accurate to an amazing extent.
老人はもう九十歳を越えているが、記憶は驚く{ほど/*程度/*範囲}確かだった。
*Roojin wa moo kyuu-jus-sai o koete iru ga, kioku wa odoroku {hodo/*teido/*han'i} tashika datta.*
(**b**) What was the extent of the damage from the typhoon?
台風の被害の{程度/範囲/ほど}はどのくらいでしたか。
Taifuu no higai no {teido/han'i/hodo} wa dono-kurai deshita ka.
(**c**) What is the extent of his burns?
彼のやけどの{程度/範囲/?ほど}はどのくらいですか。
Kare no yakedo no {teido/han'i/?hodo} wa dono-kurai desu ka.

PHRASE: to that extent *annani* あんなに, *sonnani* そんなに

EX. If he loves you to that extent, you should think seriously about his proposal.
彼があなたを{あんなに/そんなに}愛しているのなら、彼のプロポーズを真剣に考えるべきですよ。
Kare ga anata o {annani/sonnani} aishite iru no nara, kare no puropoozu o shinkenni kangaeru-beki desu yo.

extra adj. **[beyond what is expected, additional]**
ri⌈nji no N 臨時のN •c [for the immediate occasion only] **《temporary, special》, yo⌈bun no N 余分のN •c [of a quantity more than necessary]** **《excess, surplus》**

EX. (**a**) We had a little extra income this month.
今月は{臨時/余分}の収入が少しあった。
Kongetsu wa {rinji/yobun} no shuunyuu ga sukoshi atta.
(**b**) They put an extra train into service during the holidays.
休みには{臨時/*余分}の列車を走らせる。
*Yasumi ni wa {rinji/*yobun} no ressha o hashira-seru.*
(**c**) I have an extra pencil, so please take it.
{余分/*臨時}の鉛筆がありますから、それは上げます。
*{Yobun/*Rinji} no enpitsu ga arimasu kara, sore wa agemasu.*

extraordinary adj. **[going far beyond the ordinary]**
na⌈mi-hazureta N 並外れたN /〈Vinf. past of *nami-hazureru* ② be uncommon/, na⌈mi-hazurete iru (N) 並外れている(N) /〈V *te iru* of *nami-hazureru* ② be uncommon/ [extremely different from the usual in nature or ability] **《out of the ordinary, uncommon, above the average》**

EX. (**a**) He has an extraordinary memory.
彼の記憶力は並外れている。
Kare no kioku-ryoku wa nami-hazurete iru.
(**b**) Her intelligence is extraordinary.
彼女の知能は並外れている。

Kanojo no chinoo wa nami-hazurete iru.

extreme adj. **[farthest away/excessive]**
kyoˈkutaˈnna 極端な adj(*na*). •**c [farthest away from the average level to the extent that it cannot be compared with the latter]** 《**radical, excessive**》

EX. (**a**) He holds extreme opinions.
彼は極端な意見を持っている。
Kare wa kyokutanna iken o motte iru.
(**b**) They had to cope with extreme poverty.
彼らは極端な貧困に対処しなければならなかった。
Kare-ra wa kyokutanna hinkon ni taisho-shinakereba naranakatta.

extremely adv. **[in an extreme fashion]**
kyoˈkutaˈnni 極端に •**c [excessively]** 《**radically**》, **hiˈjooni** 非常に •**c [to an extreme degree]** 《**very**》

EX. The boy was extremely timid.
少年は{極端に/非常に}臆病だった。
Shoonen wa {kyokutanni/hijooni} okubyoo datta.

eye n. **[the organ of sight** 《**fig. "the power of," "judging," "attention"**》**]**

1. meˈ 目 **[the organ with which s.o./s.a. sees]**

EX. (**a**) She has dark eyes.
彼女は黒い目をしている。
Kanojo wa kuroi me o shite iru.
(**b**) Close your eyes and make a wish.
目を閉じて願い事を言いなさい。
Me o tojite negai-goto o iinasai.
(**c**) A cat's eyes are really mysterious.
猫の目は本当に神秘的だ。
Neko no me wa hontoo ni shinpi-teki da.

2. miˈru-me 見る目 **[a good sense of judgment/appreciation]**

EX. (**a**) The scholar had an eye for Japanese paintings.
その学者は日本の絵画を見る目を持っていた。
Sono gakusha wa Nihon no kaiga o miru-me o motte ita.
(**b**) He has a good eye for women.
彼は女を見る目が高い。
Kare wa onna o miru-me ga takai.

3. chuˈui 注意 •**c [the act of fixing the mind on s.t.** 《**fig. "warning," "advice"**》**]**

EX. (**a**) Would you keep an eye on my luggage?
僕の荷物を注意していて下さいませんか。
Boku no nimotsu o chuui-shite ite kudasaimasen ka.
(**b**) The treasures on display were under the watchful eye of a guard.
展示されている宝物はガードマンの注意の下にあった。
Tenji sarete iru hoomotsu wa gaado-man no chuui no moto ni atta.

PHRASE: eye doctor *me-isha* 目医者, *ganka-i* 眼科医 •**c**

EX. (**a**) I have an appointment with my eye doctor today.
今日は{目医者/*眼科医}に行く日だ。
*Kyoo wa {me-isha/*ganka-i} ni iku hi da.*
(**b**) My older sister became an eye doctor.
姉は{眼科医/目医者}になった。
Ane wa {ganka-i/me-isha} ni natta.

eye glasses n. **[spectacles]**
meˈgane めがね

EX. (**a**) I need to buy a new pair of eye glasses.
新しいめがねを買う必要がある。
Atarashii megane o kau hitsuyoo ga aru.
(**b**) She started wearing eye glasses in the first grade.
彼女は小学校の一年生でめがねをかけ始めた。
Kanojo wa shoo-gakkoo no ichi-nen-sei de megane o kake-hajimeta.

F

face n. **[the front part of the head or its expression ⟪fig. "dignity"⟫]**
ka˥o 顔

EX. (**a**) Who is that girl with the lovely face standing over there?
あそこに立っている、かわいい顔の女の子はだれですか。
Asoko ni tatte iru, kawaii kao no onna-no-ko wa dare desu ka.
(**b**) He looked at me with a sad face.
彼は悲しそうな顔で私を見た。
Kare wa kanashi-soona kao de watashi o mita.
(**c**) I was slapped on the face when I talked back to my teacher.
先生に口答えをしたら顔をたたかれました。
Sensei ni kuchi-gotae o shitara kao o tataka-remashita.
(**d**) Don't make me lose face with your embarrassing behavior in public.
人前で恥ずかしいまねをして私の顔をつぶさないでください。
Hito-mae de hazukashii mane o shite watashi no kao o tsubusanaide kudasai.

—— vt. **[to turn one's face/front toward]**

1. {⟨**-o**⟩/⟨**-ni**⟩} **mu˥ku** {⟨〜を⟩/⟨〜に⟩}向く ① **[to turn one's face/front in the stated direction or to be right and suitable for s.o./s.t./s.a.]** ⟪**to look**⟫

EX. (**a**) A: Which way shall I face?
どちら{を/に}向きましょうか。
Dochira {o/ni} mukimashoo ka.
B: Face to your right, please.
右{を/に}向いてください。
Migi {o/ni} muite kudasai.
(**b**) A: Which direction does your house face?
お宅はどちら{を/に}向いていますか。
Otaku wa dochira {o/ni} muite imasu ka.
B: It faces east.
{東{を/に}向いています/東向きです}。
{Higashi {o/ni} muite imasu/Higashi-muki desu}.

NOTE: Direction + *muki* forms a compound that indicates the direction s.t. is facing.

(**c**) Houses facing south are cool in the summer and warm in the winter.
{南に向いている/南向きの}うちは夏は涼しいし、冬は暖かい。
{Minami ni muite iru/Minami-muki no} uchi wa natsu wa suzushii shi, fuyu wa atatakai.

2. ⟨**-ni**⟩ **mu˥kau** ⟨〜に⟩向かう ① **[to move toward or do s.t. with one's front toward s.t./s.o./s.a. ⟪fig. "oppose"⟫]**

EX. He meditated facing the wall.
彼は壁に向かって、座禅を組んだ。
Kare wa kabe ni mukatte, zazen o kunda.

3. ⟨**-ni**⟩ **me˥n-su˥ru** ⟨〜に⟩面する ③ •**c [for s.t. to front on s.t.]**

EX. (**a**) The city hall faces the river.
市役所は川に面している。
Shi-yakusho wa kawa ni men-shite iru.
(**b**) We stayed in a hotel facing the street.
私たちは通りに面したホテルに泊まりました。
Watashi-tachi wa toori ni men-shita hoteru ni tomarimashita.

4. ⟨**-ni**⟩ **ta˥chi-mukau** ⟨〜に⟩立ち向かう ① **[for s.o. to stand up to s.t./s.o./s.a. courageously]**

EX. He faced the enemy without flinching.
彼は少しもひるまず敵に立ち向かった。
Kare wa sukoshi mo hirumazu teki ni tachi-mukatta.

5. ⟨-ni⟩ cho[kumen-suru ⟨～に⟩直面する ③ •c **[for s.o. to encounter a difficult situation, problem, etc.]** ⟪confront⟫

EX. We have to first solve the problems we are presently facing.
今直面している問題を先ず解決しなければならない。
Ima chokumen-shite iru mondai o mazu kaiketsu-shinakereba naranai.

facility n. **[an ability to do s.t. easily or a means used to help accomplish some activity or goal, such as equipment, an (academic) institution, etc.]**

1. sa[inoo 才能 •c **[innate intellectual or artistic capability, esp. of an outstanding kind]** ⟪talent, aptitude⟫

EX. (**a**) He has an impressive facility for learning languages.
彼には相当な語学の才能があります。
Kare ni wa sootoona gogaku no sainoo ga arimasu.
(**b**) He has no facility for music.
彼には音楽の才能はない。
Kare ni wa ongaku no sainoo wa nai.

2. se]tsubi 設備 •c **[equipment provided to facilitate some task]** ⟪facilities, equipment⟫

EX. (**a**) This building doesn't have heating facilities.
この建物には暖房設備がありません。
Kono tate-mono ni wa danboo-setsubi ga arimasen.
(**b**) This factory is equipped with modern facilities.
この工場は設備が近代的だ。
Kono koojoo wa setsubi ga kindai-teki da.

3. shi[se]tsu 施設 •c **[buildings and equipment required for a particular activity]**

EX. (**a**) This city does not have enough recreational facilities.
この町は娯楽施設が足りない。
Kono machi wa goraku-shisetsu ga tarinai.
(**b**) I am against the construction of military facilities in our neighborhood.
この近所に軍事施設を建設することには反対だ。
Kono kinjo ni gunji-shisetsu o kensetsu-suru koto ni wa hantai da.

fact n. **[s.t. that has actually happened or s.t. true or s.t. known/accepted to be true]**
ji]jitsu 事実 •c ⟪actuality⟫

EX. (**a**) He is writing a story based on fact.
彼は事実に基づいて小説を書いている。
Kare wa jijitsu ni moto-zuite shoosetsu o kaite iru.
(**b**) There is a proverb that says that fact is stranger than fiction.
「事実は小説よりも奇なり」ということわざがある。
'Jijitsu wa shoosetsu yori mo ki nari' to iu kotowaza ga aru.
(**c**) What happened? Tell me just the facts.
何があったんですか。事実だけ教えてください。
Nani ga atta n desu ka. Jijitsu dake oshiete kudasai.

PHRASE: {in fact/as a matter of fact} *jitsu-wa* 実は

EX. He presented a very interesting paper, but in fact his girlfriend had written more than half of it for him.
彼はとても面白い論文を発表しましたが、実はその半分以上は彼のガールフレンドが書いたものなんです。
Kare wa totemo omoshiroi ronbun o happyoo-shimashita ga, jitsu-wa sono hanbun-ijoo wa kare no gaaru-furendo ga kaita mono na n desu.

factor n. **[s.t. that contributes to a result in interaction with other things]**
yo[oin 要因 •c ⟪cause⟫

EX. (**a**) The exchange rate varies according to numerous factors.
為替レートはいろいろな要因によって変わる。
Kawase-reeto wa iro-irona yooin ni yotte kawaru.
(**b**) We need to examine carefully the factors that caused our failure.
我々は失敗の要因を細かく検討する必要がある。

Ware-ware wa shippai no yooin o komakaku kentoo-suru hitsuyoo ga aru.

factory n. **[a building/group of buildings in which merchandise is produced]**

1. ko⌈ojo⌉o 工場 •c [a building/group of buildings in which merchandise is produced on a large scale] **《plant, works》**

EX. (**a**) There is a Matsushita factory near the university.
大学の近くに松下の工場がある。
Daigaku no chikaku ni Matsushita no koojoo ga aru.
(**b**) The factory was closed down due to the workers' strike.
労働者のストライキのためその工場は閉鎖された。
Roodoo-sha no sutoraiki no tame sono koojoo wa heisa-sareta.
(**c**) An automobile manufacturing factory is under construction on the outskirts of town.
町の外れに自動車工場が建設中だ。
Machi no hazure ni jidoosha-koojoo ga kensetsu-chuu da.

2. ko⌈oba⌉ 工場 [a building in which merchandise is produced on a relatively small scale]

EX. There are a lot of small factories around here.
この辺には小さな工場がたくさんある。
Kono hen ni wa chiisana kooba ga takusan aru.

PHRASE: factory worker *kooin* 工員 •c

EX. Factory workers go to work early in the morning.
工員の朝は早い。
Kooin no asa wa hayai.

fade vi./vt. **[to lose color/freshness/strength]**

1. i⌈ro⌉ ga a⌈se⌉ru 色があせる ② [to lose color]

EX. (**a**) The sunlight has faded the curtains.
日に当たって、カーテンの色があせてしまった。
Hi ni atatte, kaaten no iro ga asete shimatta.
(**b**) He likes to wear faded sweaters.
彼は色のあせたセーターを着るのが好きだ。
Kare wa iro no aseta seetaa o kiru no ga suki da.

2. shi⌈oreru しおれる ② [for plants to lose freshness 《fig. "fall into low spirits"》] 《droop, wither》

EX. The flowers faded in a day.
花は一日でしおれてしまった。
Hana wa ichi-nichi de shiorete shimatta.

3. u⌈sureru 薄れる ② [for memory or impressions to disappear slowly]

EX. (**a**) My memories of childhood have faded.
子供の時の記憶は薄れてしまった。
Kodomo no toki no kioku wa usurete shimatta.
(**b**) My impressions of the town have faded from my memory over the years.
その町の印象は年とともに薄れていった。
Sono machi no inshoo wa toshi to tomo ni usurete itta.

4. ki⌈eru 消える ② [for s.t. which has been in a place to cease to be there]

EX. (**a**) Her hopes faded.
彼女の望みは消えた。
Kanojo no nozomi wa kieta.
(**b**) The plane faded into the clouds.
飛行機は雲の中に消えていった。
Hikoo-ki wa kumo no naka ni kiete-itta.

Fahrenheit n./adj.

ka⌉shi 華氏 •c

EX. Water freezes at 32° F.
水は華氏32度で凍る。
Mizu wa kashi san-juu-ni-do de kooru.

fail vi. **[not to succeed in s.t.]**

1. (⟨-ni⟩) shi⌈ppai-suru (⟨〜に⟩)失敗する ③ •c [for s.o./s.a. to come up with a different result than what was originally desired owing to errors in approach/method], ⟨-o⟩ shi⌈kuji⌉ru ⟨〜を⟩しくじる ① [for s.o. to be unable to do s.t. successfully or be fired from a company because of a blunder]

EX. (**a**) He failed in business.
彼は事業{に失敗した/*をしくじった}。

*Kare wa jigyoo {ni shippai-shita/*o shikujitta}.*
(**b**) All our attempts to save the beached whale failed.
浜に乗り上げた鯨を助けようといろいろやってみたが、全部{失敗した/しくじった}。
Hama ni nori-ageta kujira o tasukeyoo to iro-iro yatte mita ga, zenbu {shippai-shita/shikujitta}.
(**c**) The experiment failed.
実験は{失敗した/*しくじった}。
*Jikken wa {shippai-shita/*shikujitta}.*

2. ta⌈rinaku na⌉ru 足りなくなる /⟨adj(*i*). *ku* of neg. of *tariru* ② be sufficient + *naru* ① become/ ① [to fall short]

EX. Our supply of electricity may fail someday in the future.
将来は電気の供給が足りなくなるかもしれない。
Shoorai wa denki no kyookyuu ga tarinaku naru kamoshirenai.

3. ko⌈shoo-suru 故障する ③ •c [for a machine/part of a machine to stop functioning properly]

EX. (**a**) The thermostat on the car failed and caused the engine to overheat.
車のサーモスタットが故障したためエンジンが過熱した。
Kuruma no saamosutatto ga koshoo-shita tame enjin ga kanetsu-shita.
(**b**) The printer on our word processor has failed.
ワープロのプリンターが故障した。
Waapuro no purintaa ga koshoo-shita.

4. yo⌈wa⌉ru 弱る ① [to become weak] ⟪languish, be enfeebled⟫

EX. His eyesight is failing.
彼は視力が弱ってきている。
Kare wa shiryoku ga yowatte-kite iru.

PHRASE: never fail to *kanarazu*…V 必ず…V, Vinf. neg. *koto wa nai* Vinf. neg.ことはない

EX. (**a**) He never fails to call his mother by phone every night.
彼は毎晩{必ずお母さんに電話をかけます/お母さんに電話をかけないことはありません}。
Kare wa mai-ban {kanarazu o-kaa-san ni denwa o kakemasu/o-kaa-san ni denwa o kakenai koto wa arimasen}.
(**b**) She never failed to keep her word.
彼女は{必ず約束を守った/約束を守らなかったことはない}。
Kanojo wa {kanarazu yakusoku o mamotta/yakusoku o mamoranakatta koto wa nai}.

— vt. **[for s.o. to disappoint or forsake s.o. else or to not achieve a passing grade on a test or to not give a passing grade to s.o.]**

1. ⟨-o⟩ shi⌈tsuboo-saseru ⟨〜を⟩失望させる /⟨causative of *shitsuboo-suru* ③ be disappointed/ ② •c [to cause s.o. to lose hope] ⟪discourage⟫

EX. I failed my parents miserably by not going to college.
私は大学へ行かないことでひどく両親を失望させてしまった。
Watashi wa daigaku e ikanai koto de hidoku ryooshin o shitsuboo-sasete shimatta.

2. ⟨-o⟩ o⌈to⌉su ⟨〜を⟩落とす ① [for s.o. to cause s.t. to drop ⟪fig. "debase," "give a failing grade to"⟫], ⟨-ni⟩ ra⌈kuda⌉i-ten o tsu⌈ke⌉ru ⟨〜に⟩落第点を付ける ② [for s.o. to give s.o. a grade of not passing]

EX. The economics professor failed many students.
経済学の教授はたくさんの学生{を落とした/に落第点を付けた}。
Keizai-gaku no kyooju wa takusan no gakusei {o otoshita/ni rakudai-ten o tsuketa}.

3. (⟨-ni⟩) shi⌈ppai-suru (⟨〜に⟩)失敗する ③ •c [for s.o./s.a. to come up with a different result than what was originally desired owing to errors in approach/method], (⟨-o⟩) shi⌈kuji⌉ru (⟨〜を⟩)しくじる ① [for s.o. to be unable to do s.t. successfully or be fired from a company because of a blunder], (⟨-ni⟩) o⌈chi⌉ru (⟨〜に⟩)落ちる ② [to come/go down due to the force of gravity or to be unsuccessful in an

examination] ((flunk))

EX. (**a**) He failed the entrance exam to Tokyo University.
彼は東京大学の入学試験{に失敗した/をしくじった/に落ちた}。
Kare wa Tookyoo-daigaku no nyuugaku-shiken {ni shippai-shita/o shikujitta/ni ochita}.
(**b**) John failed his Japanese test.
ジョンは日本語のテストで{失敗した/しくじった/落ちた}。
Jon wa Nihon-go no tesuto de {shippai-shita/shikujitta/ochita}.

NOTE: *Kanarazu*...V and Vinf. neg. *koto wa nai* correspond to "not fail."

PHRASE: without fail *kanarazu* 必ず

EX. I'll be back here by two o'clock without fail.
必ず二時までにここに帰ってきます。
Kanarazu ni-ji made ni koko ni kaette kimasu.

F

failure n. **[an act/instance of failing]**
shi⌈ppai 失敗 •c

EX. (**a**) All our efforts ended in failure.
私たちの努力は全部失敗に終わった。
Watashi-tachi no doryoku wa zenbu shippai ni owatta.
(**b**) Failure teaches success.
失敗は成功の元。
Shippai wa seikoo no moto.

PHRASE: heart failure *shin-fuzen* 心不全 •c, engine failure *ensuto* エンスト •f

NOTE: *Ensuto* comes from "engine stop."

faint vi. **[for s.o./s.a. to lose consciousness]**
ki o u⌈shinau 気を失う ①, ki⌈zetsu-suru 気絶する ③ •c, ki ga to⌈oku na⌉ru 気が遠くなる ① [for s.o. to almost lose consciousness]

EX. (**a**) She fainted from the pain.
彼女は痛みで{気を失った/気絶した/気が遠くなった}。
Kanojo wa itami de {ki o ushinatta/kizetsu-shita/ki ga tooku natta}.
(**b**) I almost fainted from hunger.
私はおなかが空いて{気が遠くなりそうでした/気を失いそうになりました/気絶しそうになりました}。
Watashi wa o-naka ga suite {ki ga tooku nari-soo deshita/ki o ushinai-soo ni narimashita/kizetsu-shi-soo ni narimashita}.

— adj. **[for s.t./s.o./s.a. to be weak/vague]**
1. yo⌈wa-yowa-shi⌉i 弱々しい adj(*i*). **[for s.o./s.a./its bodily functions to be weak]**

EX. (**a**) She called out to Taro in a faint voice.
彼女は弱々しい声で太郎を呼んだ。
Kanojo wa yowa-yowa-shii koe de Taroo o yonda.
(**b**) His breathing became faint.
彼の呼吸は弱々しくなった。
Kare no kokyuu wa yowa-yowa-shiku natta.

2. ka⌉sukana かすかな adj(*na*). **[for an object to be weakly perceived through the senses] ((dim, vague, weak))**

EX. (**a**) I smelled a faint odor of gas.
かすかなガスのにおいがした。
Kasukana gasu no nioi ga shita.
(**b**) There is a faint hope that she may be cured.
彼女が治るかもしれないというかすかな望みがある。
Kanojo ga naoru kamoshirenai to iu kasukana nozomi ga aru.

fair adj. **[dealing with everyone/everything on an equal basis or clear with no clouds/dark spots or relatively large in amount]**
1. ko⌈oheina 公平な adj(*na*). **•c [dealing with everyone/every party concerned equally] ((impartial)) ↔ fu-kooheina 不公平な** adj(*na*). **•c**

EX. (**a**) I think drawing lots would be the fairest way of deciding who goes first.
だれが最初に行くかくじを引いて決めるのが最も公平なやり方だと思います。
Dare ga saisho ni iku ka kuji o hiite kimeru no ga mottomo kooheina yari-kata da to omoimasu.
(**b**) I can't make a fair judgement unless I'm given more information.
もっと情報をくれなければ、公平な判断ができません。
Motto joohoo o kurenakereba, kooheina handan ga dekimasen.

2. se⌈itoona 正当な adj(*na*). **•c [in accordance with the rules or standards of what is right]** **《lawful, legitimate》**

EX. He won the competition by fair means.
彼は正当な方法で競技に勝った。
Kare wa seitoona hoohoo de kyoogi ni katta.

NOTE: *Seitoo* appears in the following compound: *seitoo-booei* "legitimate self-defense."

3. ko⌈oseina 公正な adj(*na*). **•c [in accordance with principles of justice and impartiality]** **《just》, te⌈kiseina 適正な** adj(*na*). **•c [right for the situation considering all relevant factors]** **《appropriate, proper》**

EX. (**a**) I think that is a fair price.
それは{適正な/*公正な}値段だと思う。
*Sore wa {tekiseina/*kooseina} nedan da to omou.*
(**b**) It was a fair business deal.
それは{公正な/適正な}商取引だった。
Sore wa {kooseina/tekiseina} shoo-torihiki datta.

PHRASE: Fair Trade Commission *Koosei-torihiki-iin-kai* 公正取引委員会

4. ha⌈re⌉ 晴れ n. **[for the weather to be good]**

EX. The weather in Tokyo should be fair tomorrow.
東京のあすの天気は晴れでしょう。
Tookyoo no asu no tenki wa hare deshoo.

5. ka⌉nari かなり adv. **[to a degree exceeding the extent normally expected]** **《quite》**

EX. (**a**) She has a fair chance of success.
彼女が成功する確率はかなり高い。
Kanojo ga seikoo-suru kakuritsu wa kanari takai.
(**b**) A fair number of citizens are against the bill.
かなりの住民がその法案に反対している。
Kanari no juumin ga sono hooan ni hantai-shite iru.

6. i⌈rojiro 色白 n. **[the quality of skin being light in color], ki⌈npatsu 金髪** n. **•c [hair which is light in color]** **《blond》**

EX. She is a fair-haired girl with a fair complexion.
彼女は金髪で、色白の女の子だ。
Kanojo wa kinpatsu de, irojiro no onna-no-ko da.

fairly adv. **[moderately]**

1. wa⌈rini 割に [more than expected] **《comparatively, relatively》, wa⌈riai 割合**

EX. (**a**) His Japanese is fairly good.
彼は{割に/割合}日本語が上手です。
Kare wa {warini/wariai} Nihon-go ga joozu desu.
(**b**) His apartment is fairly big.
彼のアパートは{割に/割合}大きい。
Kare no apaato wa {warini/wariai} ookii.

2. ka⌉nari かなり [to a degree exceeding the extent normally expected] **《quite》**

EX. (**a**) We need a fairly big car.
私たちはかなり大きい車を必要としている。
Watashi-tachi wa kanari ookii kuruma o hitsuyoo to shite iru.
(**b**) She speaks Japanese fairly well.
彼女はかなり上手に日本語を話す。
Kanojo wa kanari joozuni Nihon-go o hanasu.

faith n. **[trust or confidence in s.o./s.t. without proof; religious belief]**

1. shi⌈n'yoo 信用 •c [the act of believing that s.t./s.o. is certain or reliable enough to act in accordance with it/him/her or a reputation/worth sufficient to cause others to believe in one's financial reliability] **《trust, confidence, credit, credibility》, shi⌈nrai 信頼 •c [trusting s.o. completely enough to leave everything to that person]** **《trust, confidence》**

EX. (**a**) People don't have much faith in him.
彼はあまりみんなの{信用/*信頼}がない。
*Kare wa amari minna no {shin'yoo/*shinrai} ga nai.*
(**b**) What he did destroyed our faith in the medical profession.
彼のしたことは我々の医者に対する{信

F

頼/*信用}を大きく損ってしまった。
*Kare no shita koto wa ware-ware no isha ni taisuru {shinrai/*shin'yoo} o ookiku sokonatte shimatta.*
(c) I don't have much faith in what he says.
彼の言うことはあまり{信用/信頼}ができない。
Kare no iu koto wa amari {shin'yoo/shinrai} ga dekinai.

2. shi⌈nkoo 信仰 •c [believing in a religion]

EX. (a) He is of the Buddhist faith.
彼は仏教を信仰している。
Kare wa Bukkyoo o shinkoo-shite iru.
(b) He renounced his faith to marry her.
彼は自分の信仰を捨てて、彼女と結婚した。
Kare wa jibun no shinkoo o sutete, kanojo to kekkon-shita.
(c) Faith can be a source of great emotional support in times of difficulty.
信仰は困った時に大きな精神的支えとなってくれるだろう。
Shinkoo wa komatta toki ni ookina seishin-teki sasae to natte kureru daroo.

fall n. **[an act/instance of going down or the season between summer and winter]**

1. ra⌈kka 落下 •c [an act/instance of s.t. going down], te⌈ika 低下 •c [an instance of s.t. becoming lower] ((drop, decline))

EX. (a) The tunnel was blocked due to a huge rock fall.
巨大な岩石の{落下/*低下}でトンネルがふさがってしまった。
*Kyodaina ganseki no {rakka/*teika} de tonneru ga fusagatte shimatta.*
(b) A sudden fall in temperature affected the crops.
気温の急激な{低下/*落下}で農作物に影響が出た。
*Kion no kyuugekina {teika/*rakka} de noosakubutsu ni eikyoo ga deta.*

2. a⌉ki 秋 [the season between summer and winter] ((autumn))

EX. I came to Japan this fall.
今年の秋、日本へ来ました。
Kotoshi no aki, Nihon e kimashita.

— vi. **[to come/go down]**

1. ((-ni)) **o⌈chi⌉ru** ((〜に))**落ちる** ② **[to come/go down by the force of gravity or to be unsuccessful in an examination]**

EX. (a) A book fell from the shelf.
本が棚から落ちました。
Hon ga tana kara ochimashita.
(b) A child fell into the river.
子供が川に落ちました。
Kodomo ga kawa ni ochimashita.

2. fu⌉ru 降る ① [for rain/snow/hail etc. to come down from the sky] ((rain, snow, hail))

EX. (a) The rain fell all day.
一日中雨が降っていた。
Ichi-nichi-juu ame ga futte ita.
(b) Snow began to fall.
雪が降り出した。
Yuki ga furi-dashita.

3. chi⌈ru 散る ① [for things/people that have been clustered together to disperse in all directions] ((scatter, be scattered))

EX. (a) All the cherry blossoms fell in one day.
桜は一日で全部散ってしまった。
Sakura wa ichi-nichi de zenbu chitte shimatta.
(b) In autumn the leaves fall from the trees.
秋には木の葉が散る。
Aki ni wa ko-no-ha ga chiru.

NOTE: *Chiru* is used for flowers. Both *chiru* and *ochiru* can be used for leaves.

PHRASE: fallen leaves *ochiba* 落ち葉, falling leaves *kare-ha* 枯れ葉

4. ta⌈ore⌉ru 倒れる ② [for s.o./s.t./s.a. standing to lose balance and come to the ground ((fig. "collapse because of sickness"))**]** ((collapse))

EX. (a) Many trees fell in the typhoon.
台風で木がたくさん倒れた。
Taifuu de ki ga takusan taoreta.
(b) The drunk man could not keep his balance and fell to the floor.
酔っぱらいはついにバランスを失って床に倒れてしまった。
Yopparai wa tsuini baransu o ushinatte yuka ni taorete shimatta.

5. ko⌈robu 転ぶ ① [for s.o./s.a. moving to

F

lose balance and come to the ground] ((tumble))

EX. (a) He fell and broke his right arm while jogging.
彼はジョギング中に転んで、右手を折ってしまった。
Kare wa jogingu-chuu ni koronde, migi-te o otte shimatta.
(b) My grandfather slipped and fell in the bath.
祖父は風呂ですべって、転んだ。
Sofu wa furo de subette, koronda.

6. sa⌈ga⌉ru 下がる ① [for s.t. to hang/go down/become smaller in amount/degree/strength] ((go down, drop))

EX. (a) Commodity prices have fallen recently.
最近物価が下がった。
Saikin bukka ga sagatta.
(b) My grades have fallen.
成績が下がった。
Seiseki ga sagatta.
(c) The (atmospheric) temperature fell rapidly this morning.
今朝は気温が急激に下がりました。
Kesa wa kion ga kyuugekini sagarimashita.

PHRASE: fall in love ⟨-ga⟩ *suki ni naru* ⟨〜が⟩好きになる ①

EX. He fell in love with Michiko.
彼は道子が好きになった。
Kare wa Michiko ga suki ni natta.

PHRASE: fall behind *okureru* 遅れる ② ((be late for, be behind in))

EX. (a) I've fallen behind in my homework.
宿題を出すのが遅れている。
Shukudai o dasu no ga okurete iru.
(b) She always falls behind when we walk together.
一緒に歩くと、彼女はいつも遅れる。
Issho ni aruku to, kanojo wa itsu-mo okureru.

false adj. **[not real/right/true]**

1. ma⌈chiga⌉tta N 間違ったN /⟨Vinf. past of *machigau* ① make a mistake/ [different from the facts/truth] ((wrong, mistaken)), ma⌈chiga⌉tte iru (N) 間違っている(N) /⟨V*te iru* of *machigau* ① make a mistake/

EX. (a) It was a false alarm.
それは間違った警報だった。
Sore wa machigatta keihoo datta.
(b) This information is false.
この情報は間違っている。
Kono joohoo wa machigatte iru.

2. ni⌈se no N にせのN [not real/genuine] ((fake))

EX. He obtained a false passport.
彼はにせのパスポートを手に入れた。
Kare wa nise no pasupooto o te ni ireta.

PHRASE: false teeth *ire-ba* 入れ歯, false name *gimei* 偽名 •c

fame n. **[the condition of being known to many people]**
me⌈isei 名声 •c

EX. (a) He doesn't seem to be interested in gaining fame.
彼は名声を得ることに興味がないようだ。
Kare wa meisei o eru koto ni kyoomi ga nai yooda.
(b) His fame as a pianist spread throughout the country.
彼のピアニストとしての名声は国中に広まった。
Kare no pianisuto to-shite no meisei wa kuni-juu ni hiromatta.

familiar adj. **[having a good knowledge of and close relationship with s.o./s.t.]**

1. yo⌉ku shi⌈tte iru よく知っている /⟨adv. *yoku* well + V*te iru* of *shiru* ① come to know/ ② [having a good knowledge of s.o./s.t.]

EX. (a) He is familiar with various Japanese customs.
彼はいろいろな日本の習慣をよく知っている。
Kare wa iro-irona Nihon no shuukan o yoku shitte iru.
(b) Are you familiar with this area?
この辺をよく知っていますか。
Kono hen o yoku shitte imasu ka.

2. ⟨-to⟩ shi⌈tashi⌉i ⟨〜と⟩親しい adj(*i*). **[feeling little psychological distance between**

oneself and s.o. else] ((close, friendly))

EX. (**a**) Are you on familiar terms with Miss Matsuda?
松田さんと親しいですか。
Matsuda-san to shitashii desu ka.
(**b**) You'd better not get too familiar with him.
彼とあまり親しくしないほうがいいですよ。
Kare to amari shitashiku shinai hoo ga ii desu yo.

3. mi-⌈nareta N 見慣れたN /⟨Vinf. past of *mi-nareru* become accustomed to seeing/ [accustomed to seeing]

EX. There before my eyes were the scenes so familiar from my childhood.
子供の時の見慣れた景色がすぐ目の前にあった。
Kodomo no toki no mi-nareta keshiki ga sugu me no mae ni atta.

PHRASE: familiar style (of Japanese grammar) *futsuu-tai* 普通体 •c

EX. I use the familiar style when I talk with my friends in Japanese.
友達と日本語で話す時は普通体を使います。
Tomodachi to Nihon-go de hanasu toki wa futsuu-tai o tsukaimasu.

family n. **[parents and their children or one's children]**

1. ka⌉zoku 家族 •c [a group of people closely related to one another and usually living together, such as husband and wife, parents and children, etc.]

EX. (**a**) My whole family loves music.
家族はみんな音楽が大好きです。
Kazoku wa minna ongaku ga dai-suki desu.
(**b**) We have five people in our family.
家族は五人です。
Kazoku wa go-nin desu.
(**c**) Everyone was kind to me and my family.
みんな私にも家族にも親切にしてくれました。
Minna watashi ni mo kazoku ni mo shinsetsuni shite kuremashita.

2. ko⌈domo 子供 [child/children]

EX. I don't think Tokyo is a good place to bring up a family.
東京は子供を育てるのにいい所だとは思いません。
Tookyoo wa kodomo o sodateru no ni ii tokoro da to wa omoimasen.

3. i⌈chi⌉zoku 一族 •c [all those who share a common ancestor] ((clan))

EX. His family has been living in this village for hundreds of years.
彼の一族は何百年もこの村に住んでいる。
Kare no ichizoku wa nan-byaku-nen mo kono mura ni sunde iru.

4. -zoku 〜族 •c, -ka 〜科 •c, -ha 〜派 •c [a suffix to show a group of living things or languages]

NOTE: *-zoku* is a higher level classification than *-ka* or *-ha*. The former is only used for the classification of languages.

EX. (**a**) These are fresh water fish of the carp family.
これは鯉科の淡水魚です。
Kore wa koi-ka no tansui-gyo desu.
(**b**) English is a Germanic language of the Indo-European family.
英語はインド・ヨーロッパ語族、ゲルマン語派の言語だ。
Eigo wa Indo-Yooroppa-go-zoku, Geruman-go-ha no gengo da.

PHRASE: Imperial family *koozoku* 皇族 •c, distinguished family *meimon* 名門 •c, family line *kettoo* 血統 •c, family name *myooji* 名字 •c, *sei* 姓 •c; family man *mai-hoomu-papa* マイホームパパ •f

famous adj. **[known to many people/having fame]**

yu⌈umeina 有名な adj(*na*). •c ((**well-known, notorious**))

EX. (**a**) She is a famous singer.
彼女は有名な歌手です。
Kanojo wa yuumeina kashu desu.
(**b**) Beppu is a resort famous for its hot springs.
別府は温泉で有名な観光地です。

F

Beppu wa onsen de yuumeina kankoo-chi desu.
(**c**) He is famous as a novelist.
彼は小説家として有名です。
Kare wa shoosetsu-ka to-shite yuumei desu.

fan[1] n. **[a device for creating a current of air]**
1. u⌈chi⌉wa うちわ [a device made of paper with a handle that is waved in the hand for creating a current of air to cool s.o./s.t. or to make a fire]
EX. My mother used a paper fan to cool me while I was eating the hot noodles.
母は熱いうどんを食べている私をうちわであおいでくれた。
Haha wa atsui udon o tabete iru watashi o uchiwa de aoide kureta.
2. se⌈nsu 扇子 •c [folding fan]
EX. My grandmother carries a folding fan with her on hot summer days.
祖母は夏の暑い日には扇子を持ち歩きます。
Sobo wa natsu no atsui hi ni wa sensu o mochi-arukimasu.
NOTE: A fan used in Japanese dance is called *mai-oogi.*
3. se⌈npu⌉u-ki 扇風機 •c [electric fan]
EX. Would you please turn on the fan?
すいませんが、扇風機をつけてくださいませんか。
Suimasen ga, senpuu-ki o tsukete kudasaimasen ka.
4. ka⌈nki-sen 換気扇 •c [ventilating fan]
EX. When you broil fish, be sure to turn on the ventilating fan.
魚を焼く時は必ず換気扇をつけてください。
Sakana o yaku toki wa kanarazu kanki-sen o tsukete kudasai.
—— vt. **[to send a current of air toward or on]**
a⌈o⌉gu あおぐ ①
EX. He fanned himself with his fan.
彼は扇子で(自分を)あおいだ。
Kare wa sensu de (jibun o) aoida.

fan[2] n. **[a keen supporter of s.t./s.o.]**
fa⌉n ファン •f
EX. That singer has lots of fans.
あの歌手はファンが多い。
Ano kashu wa fan ga ooi.
NOTE: This word is often pronounced as *faan* or *fuan.*
PHRASE: fan letter *fan-retaa* ファンレター •f, baseball fan *yakyuu-fan* 野球ファン •c+f

fantastic adj. **[wonderful; wild and strange]**
1. su⌈barashi⌉i すばらしい adj(*i*). **[causing great wonder/admiration/pleasure due to being extremely good] ⟪marvellous, splendid, great⟫**
EX. The concert was just fantastic.
コンサートは本当にすばらしかったです。
Konsaato wa hontoo ni subarashikatta desu.
2. ki⌈batsuna 奇抜な adj(*na*). **•c [for ideas/clothes to be wild and strange] ⟪fanciful, unconventional⟫**
EX. She went to a party in a fantastic costume.
彼女は奇抜な格好をしてパーティーへ行った。
Kanojo wa kibatsuna kakkoo o shite paatii e itta.

far adv./adj. **[at a great distance or considerably]**
1. to⌈oi 遠い adj(*i*). **[located at a great distance away] ⟪distant⟫ ↔ chikai 近い** adj(*i*).; **to⌉oku 遠く** adv. / ⟨adj(*i*). ***ku* of *tooi*⟩**
EX. (**a**) A: Is your house far from here?
お宅はここから遠いですか。
O-taku wa koko kara tooi desu ka.
B: No, it's not very far.
いいえ、あまり遠くありません。
Iie, amari tooku arimasen.
(**b**) A: How far did you go?
どの位遠くまで行ったんですか。
Dono-gurai tooku made itta n desu ka.
B: We didn't go too far.
あまり遠くまで行きませんでした。
Amari tooku made ikimasen deshita.
2. zu⌈tto ずっと adv. **[continuously/considerably] ⟪all the time, by far⟫**
EX. (**a**) The hospital is located far beyond the bridge.
病院は橋のずっと向こうです。

Byooin wa hashi no zutto mukoo desu.
(**b**) It's far quicker to get downtown by subway than by car.
町に出るには車で行くより地下鉄で行った方がずっと速い。
Machi ni deru ni wa kuruma de iku yori chikatetsu de itta hoo ga zutto hayai.
(**c**) I find small cars to be far more convenient than big ones.
小さい車の方が大きい車よりずっと便利だと思います。
Chiisai kuruma no hoo ga ookii kuruma yori zutto benri da to omoimasu.

PHRASE: as far as *made* まで

EX. He walked as far as the station.
彼は駅まで歩きました。
Kare wa eki made arukimashita.

PHRASE: as far as I know *watashi ga {kiita hanashi/shitte iru kagiri} de wa* 私が{聞いた話/知っているかぎり}では

EX. As far as I know, he has already left on his trip.
私が{聞いた話/知っているかぎり}では彼はもう旅行に出かけたそうです。
Watashi ga {kiita hanashi/shitte iru kagiri} de wa kare wa moo ryokoo ni dekaketa soodesu.

PHRASE: as far as one is able *dekiru dake* できるだけ

EX. I'll help you as far as I am able.
できるだけお手伝いします。
Dekiru dake o-tetsudai shimasu.

PHRASE: by far *danzen* 断然 •c

EX. He is by far the best student I've ever taught.
私が教えた学生の中で彼が断然一番だ。
Watashi ga oshieta gakusei no naka de kare ga danzen ichi-ban da.

PHRASE: far from {{V/adj(*i*).}inf. nonpast/adj(*na*).stem na/N} *-dokoro ka* {{V/adj(*i*).}inf. nonpast/adj(*na*).stemな/N}どころか

EX. (**a**) Far from apologizing, he blamed me for everything.
彼は謝るどころか、なにもかも私のせいにした。
Kare wa ayamaru-dokoro ka, nani-mo-kamo watashi no sei ni shita.
(**b**) Far from being stupid, she's a genius.
彼女は馬鹿どころか、天才です。
Kanojo wa baka-dokoro ka, tensai desu.
(**c**) Far from being cool, it's like living in a sauna around here.
この辺は涼しいどころか、サウナに入っているようだ。
Kono hen wa suzushii-dokoro ka, sauna ni haitte iru yooda.

PHRASE: So far, so good. *Koko made wa ii.* ここまではいい。

faraway adj. **[distant in time, space, relation, etc.]**
1. to⌈oi 遠い adj(*i*). ⟪**far, distant**⟫ ↔ **chikai** 近い adj(*i*).

EX. (**a**) Since my father lives in such a faraway place, I seldom see him.
父はとても遠い所に住んでいるので、めったに会いません。
Chichi wa totemo tooi tokoro ni sunde iru node, mettani aimasen.

2. yu⌈me-mi⌉ru-yoona 夢見るような adj(*na*). **[with the look of one dreaming]**

EX. She has a faraway look in her eyes.
彼女は夢見るような目付きをしている。
Kanojo wa yume-miru-yoona me-tsuki o shite iru.

fare n. **[money charged for transportation on a bus, train, taxi, etc. or a passenger who pays such money]**
1. u⌉nchin 運賃 •c [money charged to carry s.o./s.t. in a train, truck, taxi, etc.], -dai ~代 •c [money charged for a commodity, service, or the use of s.t.] ⟪charge, expenses, rate, toll, rent⟫, ryo⌉okin 料金 •c [money paid for a service or the use of s.t.] ⟪charge, rate, toll⟫

EX. (**a**) What is the taxi fare from Narita to Tokyo?
成田から東京までのタクシー{代/の料金/の運賃}はいくらですか。
Narita kara Tookyoo made no takushii {-dai/no ryookin/no unchin} wa ikura desu ka.

(b) Please pay the fare when you get off.
降りる時、{運賃/料金}を払ってください。
Oriru toki, {unchin/ryookin} o haratte kudasai.
(c) Bus fares are going up beginning next month.
来月からバス{代/の料金/の運賃}が値上げされます。
Raigetsu kara basu {-dai/no ryookin/no unchin} ga ne-age-saremasu.

2. jo⌈okyaku 乗客 •c [a person who pays for travel in a vehicle]

EX. The cab driver took his fare to the wrong address.
タクシーの運転手は乗客を間違った所へ連れて行ってしまった。
Takushii no unten-shu wa jookyaku o machigatta tokoro e tsurete-itte shimatta.

farewell n. **[a parting or words spoken at a parting]**
wa⌈kare⌉ 別れ [an act of parting] **⟪separation⟫**

EX. (a) We exchanged final farewells with our neighbors.
私たちは近所の人と別れのあいさつを交わした。
Watashi-tachi wa kinjo no hito to wakare no aisatsu o kawashita.
(b) He gave his girlfriend a farewell kiss.
彼はガールフレンドに別れのキスをした。
Kare wa gaaru-furendo ni wakare no kisu o shita.

PHRASE: farewell party *soobetsu-kai* 送別会 •c

farm n. **[an area of land for growing crops, raising stock, etc.]**
no⌈ojoo 農場 •c [an area of land for growing crops]

EX. (a) My uncle has a farm in Ohio.
うちの叔父はオハイオで農場を経営している。
Uchi no oji wa Ohaio de noojoo o keiei-shite iru.
(b) I worked on a farm in Hokkaido during summer vacation.
私は夏休みに北海道の農場で働きました。
Watashi wa natsu-yasumi ni Hokkaidoo no noojoo de hatarakimashita.

PHRASE: pig farm *yooton-joo* 養豚場 •c, chicken farm *yookei-joo* 養鶏場 •c, livestock farm *bokujoo* 牧場 •c, dairy farm *rakunoo-joo* 酪農場 •c, fruit farm *kaju-en* 果樹園 •c ⟪orchard⟫

—— vt. [for s.o. to use land for growing crops, raising stock, etc.]
no⌉ogyoo o suru 農業をする ③ •c [for s.o. to use land for growing crops]

EX. The settlers had to clear away large sections of virgin forest before they could farm the land.
開拓者は農業をするために先ず原生林を広範囲に渡って切り開かねばならなかった。
Kaitaku-sha wa noogyoo o suru tame ni mazu genseirin o koo-han'i ni watatte kiri-hirakaneba naranakatta.

PHRASE: farming *noogyoo* 農業 •c, chicken farming *yookei* 養鶏 •c, dairy farming *rakunoo* 酪農 •c

farmer n. **[a man who has/runs a farm]**
hya⌈kusho⌉o 百姓 •c [a man who grows crops for a living], no⌈omin 農民 •c [a collective term for people engaged in farming], no⌉oka 農家 •c [a farming family]

EX. (a) This is the busiest season of the year for farmers.
今は一年中で{百姓/農民/農家}の一番忙しい時期です。
Ima wa ichi-nen-juu de {hyakushoo/noomin/nooka} no ichiban isogashii jiki desu.
(b) He is the eldest son of a farmer.
彼は{農家/百姓/*農民}の長男です。
*Kare wa {nooka/hyakushoo/*noomin} no choonan desu.*
(c) My grandfather was a farmer.
祖父は{{百姓/?農民/*農家}でした/農業をしていました}。
*Sofu wa {{hyakushoo/?noomin/*nookla} deshita/noogyoo o shite imashita}.*

F

farther adv. **[to/at a greater distance/depth]** **mo˥tto {sa˩ki/mu˩koo} ni** もっと{先/向こう}に n.+prt. **[to/at a greater distance], o˥ku ni** 奥に n.+prt. **[to/at a greater depth]**

EX. (**a**) The Jones's house is farther down the street form here.
ジョーンズさんのお宅はこの通りの{もっと先/もっと向こう/*奥}にあります。
*Joonzu-san no o-taku wa kono toori no {motto saki/motto mukoo/*oku} ni arimasu.*
(**b**) We went farther into the forest.
私たちは森の{奥/??もっと先/??もっと向こう}に入って行った。
Watashi-tachi wa mori no {oku/??motto saki/??motto mukoo} ni haitte-itta.

—— adj. **[more distant]**
mu˩koo-gawa no N 向こう側のN

EX. The farther one of the two buildings you can see from here is the post office.
ここから見える二つのビルのうち、向こう側のが郵便局です。
Koko kara mieru futatsu no biru no uchi, mukoo-gawa no ga yuubin-kyoku desu.

F

fascinate vt. **[to attract and hold the interest of s.o.]**
ko˩ko˥ro o u˩ba˥u 心を奪う ① **[to completely capture and hold one's attention/interest/heart due to its/his/her charm], ⟨-o⟩ mi˩ryoo-suru** ⟨〜を⟩魅了する ③ **•c [to capture one's heart with charm]** ⟪**captivate**⟫

EX. (**a**) Her beauty fascinated him.
彼女の美しさが彼{の心を奪った/を魅了した}。
Kanojo no utsukushi-sa ga kare {no kokoro o ubatta/o miryoo-shita}.
(**b**) The children were fascinated by the toys in the shop.
子供たちは店のおもちゃに{心を奪われて/?魅了されて}いた。
Kodomo-tachi wa mise no omocha ni {kokoro o ubawa-rete/?miryoo-sarete} ita.

fascinating adj. **[having a strong attraction for one]**
su˩barashi˥i すばらしい adj(*i*). **[causing great wonder/admiration/pleasure due to being extremely good], su˩go˥i** すごい adj(*i*). **[impressive/surprising to a fearful degree ⟨s⟩]** ⟪**great, terrific, superb, fabulous**⟫

EX. (**a**) This novel has a fascinating plot.
この小説の筋は{すばらしい/すごい}。
Kono shoosetsu no suji wa {subarashii/sugoi}.
(**b**) Tokyo is a fascinating city.
東京は{すばらしい/すごい}町だ。
Tookyoo wa {subarashii/sugoi} machi da.

fashion n. **[a (currently prevailing) manner of doing/making s.t.]**
1. ryu˩ukoo 流行 **•c [the prevailing custom or style in clothes, thought, behavior, etc. a disease currently affecting many people]** ⟪**fad, vogue**⟫**, fa˥sshon** ファッション **•f [the prevailing custom or style in clothes, hair, etc.]**

EX. (**a**) What colors are in fashion this year?
今年はどんな色が{流行/?ファッション}ですか。
Kotoshi wa donna iro ga {ryuukoo/?fasshon} desu ka.
(**b**) It's difficult to keep up with current fashions.
{流行/ファッション}に遅れないようにするのは大変だ。
{Ryuukoo/Fasshon} ni okurenai yooni suru no wa taihen da.
(**c**) Could you teach me some expression that's in fashion this year?
何か今年の{流行/*ファッション}語を教えてくださいませんか。
*Nani-ka kotoshi no {ryuukoo/*fasshon}-go o oshiete kudasaimasen ka.*

PHRASE: fashion show *fasshon-shoo* ファッションショー **•f**, fashion model *fasshon-moderu* ファッションモデル **•f**, come into fashion *hayari-dasu* はやりだす ①

EX. When did that style of dress come into fashion?
そのスタイルのドレスはいつごろはやりだしたんですか。

Sono sutairu no doresu wa itsu-goro hayari-dashita n desu ka.

PHRASE: go out of fashion *hayaranaku naru* はやらなくなる ①, *sutareru* すたれる ②

2. V*masu* kata V*masu*方 [a method/manner of doing s.t. indicated by the verb of V*masu*] 《way》, **-fuu** ～風 •c **[type/style of]**

EX. (**a**) He walks in a peculiar fashion.
彼は変な歩き{方/*風}をする。
*Kare wa henna aruki-{kata/*fuu} o suru.*
(**b**) I like my rice cooked in the Japanese fashion.
ご飯は日本{風/*方}のたき方がいいと思います。
*Go-han wa Nihon-{fuu/*kata} no taki-kata ga ii to omoimasu.*

fast adj. **[quick, rapid]**
ha⌈ya⌉i はやい adj(*i*). **[taking less time than is normal or expected or occurring at a point in time prior to what is normal or expected]** ↔ **osoi** 遅い adj(*i*). slow; **su⌈sunde iru** (N) 進んでいる(N) /⟨V*te iru* of *susumu* ① advance/ ② **[to be advanced]**
㊊ "quick"▷速い, "early/soon"▷早い

EX. (**a**) He is a fast runner.
彼は走るのが{速い/*進んでいる}。
*Kare wa hashiru no ga {hayai/*susunde iru}.*
(**b**) My watch is three minutes fast.
私の時計は三分{進んでいます/*早いです}。
*Watashi no tokei wa san-pun {susunde imasu/*hayai desu}.*

— adv. **[quickly]**
ha⌉yaku はやく /⟨**adj**(*i*). ***ku* of *hayai* fast or early/ [prior to the usual/expected time or quickly], za⌉a-zaa** ざあざあ **[(to rain) heavily]**
㊊ "quickly"▷速く, "early/soon"▷早く

EX. (**a**) Please don't walk so fast.
そんなに速く歩かないでください。
Sonnani hayaku arukanaide kudasai.
(**b**) The rain is coming down fast.
雨がざあざあ降っています。
Ame ga zaa-zaa futte imasu.

— adj./adv. **[(attached) firmly or tightly]**
shi⌈kka⌉ri しっかり adv. **[strongly so as not to move]**

EX. (**a**) Hold fast to the rope.
ロープにしっかりつかまってください。
Roopu ni shikkari tsukamatte kudasai.
(**b**) The shutters held fast during the fierce tyhoon.
台風が猛威を振るっている間、雨戸はびくともせずしっかり閉まっていた。
Taifuu ga mooi o furutte iru aida, ama-do wa biku-to-mo-sezu shikkari shimatte ita.

PHRASE: be fast asleep *gussuri nemutte iru* ぐっすり眠っている

fasten vt. **[for s.o. to attach s.t. firmly or to tie/join s.t. together]**
1. ⟨**-o**⟩ ⟨**-ni**⟩ **shi⌈bari-tsuke⌉ru** ⟨～を⟩⟨～に⟩縛り付ける ② **[for s.o. to bind s.t./s.o./s.a. firmly with a rope, string, etc. to s.t.]** 《**bind, tie (up)**》

EX. I fastened the lowered sail to the mast with some rope.
下ろした帆をマストにロープで縛り付けた。
Oroshita ho o masuto ni roopu de shibari-tsuketa.

2. ⟨**-o**⟩ **shi⌈ba⌉ru** ⟨～を⟩縛る ① **[for s.o. to fix s.t./s.o./s.a. firmly by putting a string/string-like object around it 《fig. "restrain"》]** 《**restrain, bind, tie down**》

EX. We fastened a strap around the bulging suitcase to keep it from coming open.
はちきれそうなスーツケースが開いてしまわないようにひもで縛った。
Hachikire-soona suutsukeesu ga aite shimawanai yooni himo de shibatta.

3. ⟨**-o**⟩ **shi⌈me⌉ru** ⟨～を⟩しめる ② **[for s.o. to apply pressure to s.t. so as to leave no opening in it 《fig. "economize"》]** 《**tie (up), tighten, bind, strangle, close**》
㊊ "strangle"▷絞める, "close"▷閉める, otherwise ▷締める

EX. Please fasten your seat belt.
シートベルトを締めてください。

F

| *Shiito-beruto o shimete kudasai.*

4. ⟨-o⟩ to⌈meru ⟨～を⟩とめる ② [for s.o. to prevent s.o./s.t./s.a. from moving/doing s.t. ⟪fig. "put s.o. up," "fasten"⟫] ⟪pin, nail, staple⟫

㊅ "stop"▷止める, "lodge/put s.o. up"▷泊める, "fasten"▷留める

EX. | He fastened the two sheets of paper together with a stapler.
彼は二枚の紙をホッチキスで留めた。
Kare wa ni-mai no kami o hotchikisu de tometa.

fat n. **[a white/yellow greasy substance found in animal bodies]**

shi⌈boo 脂肪 •c, a⌈bura あぶら [a whitish slippery substance found in animal bodies or a thick liquid made from plants used in cooking or a thick liquid made from minerals used for lubrication], a⌈bura-mi 脂身 [the greasy whitish part of meat]

㊅ "liquid oil"▷油, "solid animal fat"▷脂

EX. | (**a**) You don't have to eat the fat on your steak.
ステーキの{脂身/*脂/*脂肪}は食べなくてもいいですよ。
*Suteeki no {abura-mi/*abura/*shiboo} wa tabenakute mo ii desu yo.*
(**b**) Fat is beginning to show around his midriff.
あの人はおなかに{脂肪/?脂/*脂身}が付き始めている。
*Ano hito wa o-naka ni {shiboo/?abura/*abura-mi} ga tsuki-hajimete iru.*
(**c**) Fat dripped from the steak as it was being grilled.
網で焼いているステーキから{脂/?脂肪/*脂身}がしたたり落ちた。
*Ami de yaite iru suteeki kara {abura/?shiboo/*abura-mi} ga shitatari-ochita.*

—— adj. **[having much fat]**

1. fu⌈to⌉tta N 太ったN /⟨Vinf. past of *futoru* ① gain weight/, fu⌈to⌉tte iru (N) 太っている(N) /⟨V*te iru* of *futoru* ① gain weight/ ⟪plump⟫

EX. | (**a**) Fat people tend to experience heart problems.
{太った/太っている}人は心臓病にかかりやすい。
{Futotta/Futotte iru} hito wa shinzoo-byoo ni kakari-yasui.
(**b**) I was fat when I was a kid.
私は子供の時、太っていました。
Watashi wa kodomo no toki, futotte imashita.

2. a⌈burakko⌉i 脂っこい adj(*i*). **⟪greasy, oily⟫, a⌈bura ga o⌉oi 脂が多い** adj(*i*)., **shi⌈boo ga o⌉oi 脂肪が多い** adj(*i*). **⟪fatty⟫**

fatal adj. **[causing death or great harm]**

chi⌈mei-tekina 致命的な adj(*na*). **•c**

EX. | (**a**) The surgeon made a fatal mistake during the operation.
外科医は手術中に致命的なミスを犯した。
Geka-i wa shujutsu-chuu ni chimei-tekina misu o okashita.
(**b**) The scandal was fatal to the minister's career.
そのスキャンダルは大臣には致命的だった。
Sono sukyandaru wa daijin ni wa chimei-teki datta.

PHRASE: fatal wound *chimei-shoo* 致命傷 **•c**

fate n. **[a power believed to control all events in a way that cannot be resisted or what is destined to happen]**

u⌉nmei 運命 •c ⟪destiny⟫

EX. | (**a**) It was their fate never to meet again.
彼らはもう二度と会えない運命だったんです。
Kare-ra wa moo ni-do to ae-nai unmei datta n desu.
(**b**) It must have been through a whim of fate that he was elected to be chairman.
彼が会長に選ばれたのは運命のいたずらだったにちがいない。
Kare ga kaichoo ni eraba-reta no wa unmei no itazura datta ni chigainai.

father n. **[a male parent ⟪fig. "founder/first leader"⟫]**

chi⌈chi⌉ 父 [a humble form used to refer to one's own father when talking to s.o.

outside one's family ⟪fig. "founder"⟫], o-ˈtoˈo-san お父さん [an exalting form used to refer to s.o. else's father or to directly address one's own father or to refer to one's own father when talking with other family members], o-ˈtoˈo-sama お父様 ⟨fml⟩, chiˈchi-oya 父親 [a neutral form used to refer to a male parent with no implication of exaltation/humility or to one's own father]

EX. (**a**) A: What does your father do?
{お父さん/お父様/*父/*父親}はどんなお仕事をしていらっしゃるんですか。
*{O-too-san/O-too-sama/*Chichi/*Chichi-oya} wa donna o-shigoto o shite irassharu n desu ka.*
B: My father is a doctor.
{父/?父親/*お父さん/*お父様}は医者をしております。
*{Chichi/?Chichi-oya/*O-too-san/*O-too-sama} wa isha o shite orimasu.*

NOTE: The use of *o-too-san* or *o-too-sama* in B's response in example (a) is incorrect because it is inappropriate to refer to one's own father in an exalting manner in this context. Such expressions might, however, be used by speakers who have not mastered the socio-linguistic rules of the Japanese language, such as small children.

(**b**) Children like to play with their fathers.
子供たちは{父親/お父さん/*父/*お父様}と遊ぶのが好きだ。
*Kodomo-tachi wa {chichi-oya/o-too-san/*chichi/*o-too-sama} to asobu no ga suki da.*
(**c**) He is the father of our country.
彼は我が国の建国の{父/*父親/*お父さん/*お父様}です。
*Kare wa waga-kuni no kenkoku no {chichi/*chichi-oya/*o-too-san/*o-too-sama} desu.*

PHRASE: father-in-law *giri no chichi* 義理の父, *giri no o-too-san* 義理のお父さん

fatigue n. **[the state of being very tired]**
kyoˈkudo no hiˈroo 極度の疲労 •c ⟪exhaustion⟫

EX. (**a**) All the students showed signs of fatigue.
学生はみんな極度の疲労の色を見せていた。
Gakusei wa minna kyokudo no hiroo no iro o misete ita.
(**b**) I couldn't even stand up from the fatigue.
私は極度の疲労で立ち上がることさえできなかった。
Watashi wa kyokudo no hiroo de tachi-agaru koto sae dekinakatta.

fault n. **[s.t. wrong/imperfect or the responsibility for a mistake]**

1. keˈtteˈn 欠点 •c [s.t. that is insufficient and must be supplemented] ⟪weak point⟫

EX. (**a**) She loves me in spite of all my faults.
彼女はこんなに欠点がたくさんある私を愛してくれている。
Kanojo wa konnani ketten ga takusan aru watashi o aishite kurete iru.
(**b**) No one is free from faults.
欠点のない人はいない。
Ketten no nai hito wa inai.

2. keˈkkan 欠陥 •c [a potentially serious functional/structural imperfection] ⟪defect, flaw⟫

EX. (**a**) There appears to be a fault in the electrical system.
電気系統に欠陥があるらしい。
Denki-keitoo ni kekkan ga aru rashii.
(**b**) This car model was targeted for recall due to a fault in its brake system.
この車種はブレーキ系統の欠陥のため、不良品として回収の対象になった。
Kono shashu wa bureeki-keitoo no kekkan no tame, furyoo-hin to-shite kaishuu no taishoo ni natta.

3. kaˈshitsu 過失 •c [an error committed by s.o.] ⟪error, blunder⟫, seˈi せい [s.t./s.o./s.a. responsible for an undesirable consequence] ⟪result, outcome, effect⟫

EX. (**a**) He was reluctant to recognize his own faults.
彼はなかなか自分の{過失/*せい}を認めようとしなかった。
*Kare wa naka-naka jibun no {kashitsu/*sei} o mitomeyoo to shinakatta.*

F

(**b**) My headache must be the fault of the weather.
僕の頭痛は天気の{せい/*過失}に違いない。
*Boku no zutsuu wa tenki no {sei/ *kashitsu} ni chigainai.*
(**c**) A: Whose fault is it that we are late?
私たちが遅れたのはだれの{せい/?過失}ですか。
Watashi-tachi ga okureta no wa dare no {sei/?kashitsu} desu ka.
B: It's my fault. I'm sorry.
私の{せい/?過失}です。すみません。
Watashi no {sei/?kashitsu} desu. Sumimasen.

PHRASE: find fault with *monku o tsukeru* 文句をつける ②

EX. I find no fault with his work.
彼の仕事は文句のつけようがありません。
Kare no shigoto wa monku no tsukeyoo ga arimasen.

F

favor n. **[a kind act one does willingly for others]**
ko˥oi 好意 •c [kind feelings towards s.o. and willingness to do s.t. for him/her] ⟪**goodwill, kindness**⟫

EX. (**a**) He allowed me to use the data he collected as a favor.
彼は好意で自分の集めたデータを使わせてくれた。
Kare wa kooi de jibun no atsumeta deeta o tsukawa-sete kureta.
(**b**) He doesn't understand that what I did for his wife was as a favor to him.
彼は私が彼の奥さんのためにしてあげたことは彼自身に対する好意によるものだということを分かってくれないんです。
Kare wa watashi ga kare no oku-san no tame ni shite ageta koto wa kare-jishin ni-taisuru kooi ni yoru mono da to iu koto o wakatte kurenai n desu.

PHRASE: Would you do me a favor? *Chotto o-negai ga aru n desu ga.* ちょっとお願いがあるんですが。, in favor of *sansei* 賛成 •c

EX. I am in favor of his proposal.
私は彼の提案に賛成です。
Watashi wa kare no teian ni sansei desu.

PHRASE: show s.o. special favor ⟨*-ni*⟩ *me o kakeru* ⟨〜を⟩目にかける ②

EX. The manager liked him from the beginning and showed him special favor.
監督は初めから彼が気に入っていて、目をかけた。
Kantoku wa hajime kara kare ga ki-ni-itte ite, me o kaketa.

— vt. **[for s.o. unfairly to treat one person, group, etc., better than others]**
⟨-o⟩ e˥ko-hi˥iki-suru ⟨〜を⟩えこひいきする ③ [for s.o. to treat one person, group, etc., better than others] ⟪**play favorites, be partial**⟫

EX. A teacher should not favor any particular student over the others.
先生は学生をえこひいきしてはいけません。
Sensei wa gakusei o eko-hiiki-shite wa ikemasen.

favorable adj. **[giving/showing approval or agreeable or helpful]**
1. sa˥nsei 賛成 n. **•c [being in agreement with s.o.'s opinion/idea/suggestion]**

EX. Is he favorable to the proposal?
彼はその案に賛成ですか。
Kare wa sono an ni sansei desu ka.

2. ko˥oi-tekina N 好意的な adj(*na*). **•c [displaying approval of or kindness toward s.t./s.o.]**

EX. His lecture was given a favorable reception by the students.
彼の講義は学生の間で好意的な評価を得た。
Kare no koogi wa gakusei no aida de kooi-tekina hyooka o eta.

3. yu˥urina 有利な adj(*na*). **•c [having an advantage or giving an advantage to s.o.]**

EX. He gave testimony favorable to the accused.
彼は被告に有利な証言をした。
Kare wa hikoku ni yuurina shoogen o shita.

4. i˥i いい adj(*i*). **[morally correct/satisfactory/agreeable]**

EX. He made a favorable impression on Beth's parents.
彼はベスの両親にいい印象を与えた。
Kare wa Besu no ryooshin ni ii inshoo o ataeta.

favorite n. **[s.o./s.t. that one likes more than anybody/anything else]**

1. o-˥ki-ni-iri お気に入り [s.o./s.t./s.a. that one particularly likes]

NOTE: *O-ki-ni-iri* implies some partiality when used in reference to people.

EX. (**a**) He is the teacher's favorite.
彼は先生のお気に入りです。
Kare wa sensei no o-ki-ni-iri desu.
(**b**) This coat is a favorite of my daughter's.
このコートは娘のお気に入りです。
Kono kooto wa musume no o-ki-ni-iri desu.

2. 〈**-ga**〉 **da˥i-sukina** 〈～が〉**大好きな** adj(*na*). **[for s.o./s.a. to like s.o./s.a./s.t. very much]**

EX. This book is a great favorite of mine.
これは私が大好きな本です。
Kore wa watashi ga dai-sukina hon desu.

PHRASE: One's favorite book *aidoku-sho* 愛読書 •c

3. ni˥nki-mono 人気者 [s.o. very popular]

EX. That singer is a favorite among teenagers.
あの歌手はティーンエージャーの人気者です。
Ano kashu wa tiin-eejaa no ninki-mono desu.

—— adj.

i˥chiban su˥ki˥na 一番好きな adj(*na*). **[most liked by one], i˥chiban ki-˥ni-itte iru (N) 一番気に入っている(N)** /〈***ichiban*** **most + V*te iru* of *ki-ni-iru* ① become pleased with/ ② [that which pleases one most]**

EX. A: What is your favorite color?
{一番好きな/一番気に入っている}色は何ですか。
{Ichiban sukina/Ichiban ki-ni-itte iru} iro wa nan desu ka.
B: Red is my favorite color.
{一番好きな/一番気に入っている}色は赤です。
{Ichi-ban sukina/Ichi-ban ki-ni-itte iru} iro wa aka desu.

fear n. **[anxiety caused by the expectation of danger/evil]**

1. kyo˥ofu 恐怖 •c [great anxiety caused by the expectation of danger/evil], o˥soro˥shi-sa 恐ろしさ /〈**adj(*i*). stem of *osoroshii* fearful + suf. *sa* ness/ [anxiety caused by the expectation of danger/evil]**

EX. (**a**) I was unable to speak out of fear.
私は{恐怖/恐ろしさ}で口がきけなかった。
Watashi wa {kyoofu/osoroshi-sa} de kuchi ga kike-nakatta.
(**b**) Hearing gunshots while patrolling the streets on his first day on the job, the rookie policeman was gripped with fear.
新米の警官は勤務初日のパトロール中に銃声を聞き、{恐怖/*恐ろしさ}に襲われた。
*Shinmai no keikan wa kinmu shonichi no patorooru-chuu ni juusei o kiki, {kyoofu/*osoroshisa} ni osowa-reta.*

2. fu˥an 不安 •c [an uncomfortable feeling caused by uncertainty or by expectation of the worst] 《**anxiety, uneasiness**》, **shi˥npai 心配 •c [an uncomfortable feeling caused by uncertainty or by the expectation of danger/evil/s.t. troublesome]** 《**worry**》

EX. (**a**) I have no fear for the future.
{将来に対する不安はありません/将来のことは何も心配していません}。
{Shoorai ni-taisuru fuan wa arimasen/Shoorai no koto wa nani-mo shinpai-shite imasen}.
(**b**) There's no fear of catching the flu once you've had your flu shot.
予防注射をしていれば流感にかかる{心配/*不安}はありません。
*Yoboo-chuusha o shite ireba ryuukan ni kakaru {shinpai/*fuan} wa arimasen.*
(**c**) He always stayed at home for fear of having his money stolen.
彼は金を盗まれるのが{心配/*不安}で、いつも家にいた。

*Kare wa kane o nusuma-reru no ga {shinpai/*fuan} de, itsu-mo uchi ni ita.*
(**d**) She asked us to be quiet for fear of waking up the child.
彼女は子供が目をさますのが{心配/*不安}で、私たちに静かにしてほしいと言った。
*Kanojo wa kodomo ga me o samasu no ga {shinpai/*fuan} de, watashi-tachi ni shizukani shite-hoshii to itta.*

— vt. **[for s.o./s.a. to be afraid of s.o./s.t./s.a.]**

1. **⟨-o⟩ o⌈sore⌉ru** ⟨〜を⟩恐れる ② **[for s.o. to be afraid of s.t./s.o./s.a. unusual or mysterious]** ((**dread, be frightened of, be terrified of**)), **⟨-o⟩ ko⌈wa-ga⌉ru** ⟨〜を⟩怖がる ①, **⟨-ga⟩ ko⌈wa⌉i** ⟨〜が⟩怖い adj(*i*). **[for s.o./s.a. to be afraid that s.t. dangerous/troublesome will happen to s.o. (esp. oneself) or for s.t./s.o./s.a. to cause such fear]** ((**dread, be scared, be nervous**)), **⟨-ga⟩ o⌈soroshi⌉i** ⟨〜が⟩恐ろしい adj(*i*). **[for s.o. to be afraid of s.t./s.o./s.a. unusual or mysterious or for s.t./s.o./s.a. to cause such fear]**

NOTE: *Kowai* and *osoroshii* are used with the first person subject in statements or with the second person subject in questions. *Osoreru* and *kowagaru* are usually used with the third person subject.

EX. (**a**) There's nothing to fear in experiencing new things in life.
人生で新しい体験をするのに何も{恐れる/怖がる}ことはない。
Jinsei de atarashii taiken o suru no ni nani-mo {osoreru/kowa-garu} koto wa nai.
(**b**) He fears death more than anything else.
彼は何よりも死ぬのを{恐れて/怖がって}いる。
Kare wa nani yori mo shinu no o {osorete/kowagatte} iru.
(**c**) A: Do you fear dying?
死ぬのが{恐ろしい/怖い}ですか。
Shinu no ga {osoroshii/kowai} desu ka.
B: It would be a lie to say I don't fear, but it's not really something I think about much.
{恐ろしくない/怖くない}と言えばうそになるけど、それほどくよくよ考えることでもありません。
{Osoroshikunai/Kowakunai} to ieba uso ni naru kedo, sore-hodo kuyo-kuyo kangaeru koto de mo arimasen.

2. **⟨-ga⟩ shi⌈npaina** ⟨〜が⟩心配な adj(*na*). •c **[for s.o. to feel anxiety about s.t./s.o./s.a.]**

EX. We feared for his safety.
彼の安全が心配でした。
Kare no anzen ga shinpai deshita.

3. **{{V/adj(*i*).}inf./{adj(*na*). stem/N}}{na/datta} no janai ka to o⌈mo⌉u, {{V/adj(*i*).}inf./{adj(*na*). stem/N}}{な/だった}のじゃないかと思う** ① **[for s.o. to have an uneasy feeling about s.t.]**

NOTE: *No* in *no janai ka to omou* is often contracted to *n* in conversation.

EX. (**a**) I fear that my mother may have cancer.
母ががんなんじゃないかと思う。
Haha ga gan na n janai ka to omou.
(**b**) A: Do you think he'll get better?
彼は良くなるでしょうか。
Kare wa yoku naru deshoo ka.
B: I fear not.
良くはならないんじゃないかと思います。
Yoku wa naranai n janai ka to omoimasu.

fearful adj. **[causing fear or worried]**

1. **o⌈soroshi⌉i** 恐ろしい adj(*i*). **[for s.o. to be afraid of s.t./s.o./s.a. unusual or mysterious or for s.t./s.o./s.a. to cause such fear]**, **ko⌈wa⌉i** 怖い adj(*i*).

EX. I hear there was a fearful accident at this traffic light yesterday.
きのうこの信号で{恐ろしい/怖い}事故があったそうです。
Kinoo kono shingoo de {osoroshii/kowai} jiko ga atta soo desu.

2. **⟨-o⟩ o⌈so⌉rete iru** ⟨〜を⟩恐れている **/⟨V *te iru* of *osoreru* ② fear/ ②, ⟨-o⟩ ko⌈wa-ga⌉tte iru** ⟨〜を⟩怖がっている **/⟨V *te iru* of *kowagaru* ① show signs of being scared/** ②

[for s.o./s.t. to show signs of being scared of], ⟨-o⟩ shi⌈npai-shite iru ⟨〜を⟩心配している /⟨V *te iru* of *shinpai-suru* ③ worry/ ② •c [for s.o. to be worried about], ⟨-ga⟩ o⌈soroshi⌉i ⟨〜が⟩恐ろしい adj(*i*). **[for s.o. to be afraid of s.t./s.o./s.a. unusual or mysterious or for s.t./s.o./s.a. to cause such fear], ⟨-ga⟩ ko⌈wa⌉i ⟨〜が⟩怖い** adj(*i*). **[for s.o./s.a. to be afraid that s.t. dangerous/ troublesome will happen to s.o. (esp. oneself) or for s.t./s.o./s.a. to cause such fear] ⟪dread, be scared, be nervous⟫, ⟨-ga⟩ shi⌈npaina ⟨〜が⟩心配な** adj(*na*). **•c [for s.o. to feel anxiety about s.t./s.o./s.a.]**

NOTE: *Osoroshii*, *kowai* and *shinpaina* are used with the first person subject in statements or with the second person subject in questions. The other expressions here are used with a third person subject.

EX. (**a**) He is fearful of the consequences.
彼は結果を{恐れて/怖がって/心配して}いる。
Kare wa kekka o {osorete/kowa-gatte/ shinpai-shite} iru.
(**b**) I am fearful of the consequences.
私は結果が{恐ろしい/怖い/心配}です。
Watashi wa kekka ga {osoroshii/kowai/ shinpai} desu.

feast n. **[a large, elaborate meal on a special occasion ⟪fig. "s.t. that pleases the mind or senses"⟫]**
go-⌈chisoo ごちそう [a splendid meal], kyo⌈oen 饗宴 •c [a banquet ⟪fig. "s.t. that pleases the mind or senses"⟫ ⟨fml⟩], ho⌈yoo 保養 •c [becoming strong again after illness or refreshing to the body and mind] ⟪recuperation, recreation⟫

EX. (**a**) Her parents treated us to a feast after we announced our engagement.
婚約発表のあとで、彼女の両親は私たちに{ごちそう/*饗宴/*保養}をしてくれた。
*Kon'yaku-happyoo no ato de, kanojo no ryooshin wa watashi-tachi ni {go-chisoo/ *kyooen/*hoyoo} o shite kureta.*

NOTE: *Go-chisoo o suru* is used to mean "treat s.o. to a feast."

(**b**) The cherry blossoms in full bloom were a real feast for the eyes.
満開の桜は本当に目の{保養/*饗宴/*ごちそう}になった。
*Mankai no sakura wa hontoo ni me no {hoyoo/*kyooen/*go-chisoo} ni natta.*
(**c**) The movie was a feast of color and sound.
その映画は音と色の{饗宴/*保養/*ごちそう}だった。
*Sono eiga wa oto to iro no {kyooen/ *hoyoo/*go-chisoo} datta.*
(**d**) For a poor student like me, dinner at the Johnsons was a real feast.
貧乏な学生の私には、ジョンソンさんのお宅での食事は大変な{ごちそう/*保養/*饗宴}でした。
*Binboona gakusei no watashi ni wa, Jonson-san no o-taku de no shokuji wa taihenna {go-chisoo/*hoyoo/*kyooen} deshita.*

feather n. **[one of the soft, straight structures growing from a bird's skin and covering its body]**
ha⌈ne 羽 [one/all of the coverings that grow from a bird's skin or one/both of a pair of projecting structures by which a bird/ airplane flies] ⟪wing⟫

EX. (**a**) The bird ruffled up its feathers.
鳥は羽を逆立てた。
Tori wa hane o saka-dateta.
(**b**) Birds of a feather flock together.
同じ羽の鳥はいっしょに群れをなす。
Onaji hane no tori wa issho ni mure o nasu.

NOTE: A similar Japanese proverb is *Rui wa tomo o yobu.*

feature n. **[a part/quality of s.t. easily noticed]**
1. te⌈n 点 •c [a small mark made by the end of a sharp object ⟪fig. "punctuation," "marks," "respects"⟫] ⟪point, respect⟫, to⌈kuchoo 特徴 •c [s.t. which stands out about s.t./s.o./s.a. and which distinguishes him/her/it from others] ⟪characteristic⟫, to⌈kushuu 特集 •c [a special article in a

F

newspaper, magazine, etc.]

EX. (**a**) This system has many undesirable features.
このシステムには問題になる{点/??特徴/*特集}がたくさんある。
*Kono shisutemu ni wa mondai ni naru {ten/??tokuchoo/*tokushuu} ga takusan aru.*
(**b**) Did you read the feature article in the *Asahi* newspaper on volcanos?
火山に関する朝日の{特集/*点/*特徴}記事を読みましたか。
*Kazan ni-kansuru Asahi no {tokushuu/*ten/*tokuchoo}-kiji o yomimashita ka.*
(**c**) What are the chief features of the electoral system in Japan?
日本の選挙制度の主な{特徴/*点/*特集}は何ですか。
*Nihon no senkyo-seido no omona {tokuchoo/*ten/*tokushuu} wa nan desu ka.*

F

2. yo⌈oboo 容ぼう •c [the way the parts of the face are arranged], ka⌈o 顔 [the front part of the head] ⟪**face**⟫

EX. For someone born of Japanese parents, she has strikingly Western facial features.
両親が日本人にしては彼女は驚くほど西洋的な{顔/容ぼう}をしている。
Ryooshin ga Nihon-jin ni-shite wa kanojo wa odoroku hodo seiyoo-tekina {kao/yooboo} o shite iru.

PHRASE: geographical features *chikei* 地形 **•c**

EX. Are you familiar with the geographical features of this district?
この辺の地形をよく知っていますか。
Kono hen no chikei o yoku shitte imasu ka.

February n.
ni-⌈gatsu⌉ 二月 •c

EX. (**a**) She was born in February, 1960.
彼女は1960年の二月に生まれた。
Kanojo wa sen-kyuu-hyaku-roku-juu-nen no ni-gatsu ni umareta.
(**b**) February 11th is a national holiday in Japan.
日本では、二月十一日は祭日です。
Nihon de wa, ni-gatsu juu-ichi-nichi wa saijitsu desu.

federal adj. **[having to do with a government formed by separate states uniting under a central authority]**
re⌈npoo no N 連邦のN •c

EX. In the U.S., foreign policy is set at the level of the federal government.
アメリカ合衆国では外交政策は連邦政府によって決められる。
Amerika-gasshuukoku de wa gaikoo-seisaku wa renpoo-seifu ni-yotte kime-rareru.

fee n. **[money paid for professional advice/services]**
ryo⌉okin 料金 •c [money paid for a service or the use of s.t.] ⟪**fare, charge, rate**⟫

EX. Please pay the fee by check.
料金は小切手で払ってください。
Ryookin wa kogitte de haratte kudasai.

PHRASE: tuition fee *jugyoo-ryoo* 授業料 **•c**, admission fee *nyuujoo-ryoo* 入場料 **•c**, monthly lesson fee *gessha* 月謝 **•c**, handling fee *(tori-atsukai-)tesuu-ryoo* (取り扱い)手数料, membership fee *kaihi* 会費 **•c**, initiation fee *nyuukai-{hi/kin}* 入会{費/金} **•c**, the fee charged for a patient's first visit to a doctor *shoshin-ryoo* 初診料 **•c**, lawyer's fee *bengo-ryoo* 弁護料 **•c**

feed vt. **[for s.o. to give food to s.o./s.a.]**
⟨-ni⟩ e⌈sa⌉ o ya⌈ru ⟨〜に⟩えさをやる ① [for s.o. to give food to an animal], ⟨-ni⟩ ⟨-o⟩ ta⌈be-sase⌉ru ⟨〜に⟩⟨〜を⟩食べさせる /⟨causative of *taberu* ② eat/ ② [for s.o. to let/make s.o./s.a. eat s.t.], ⟨-ni⟩ ⟨-o⟩ no⌈ma-se⌉ru ⟨〜に⟩⟨〜を⟩飲ませる /⟨causative of *nomu* ① drink/ ② [for s.o. to let/make s.o./s.a. drink s.t.]

EX. (**a**) Have you fed the chickens yet?
もう鶏にえさを{やりました/?食べさせました/*飲ませました}か。
*Moo niwatori ni esa o {yarimashita/?tabe-sase mashita/*noma-se mashita} ka.*
(**b**) Please feed the children something.
子供たちに何か{食べさせて/飲ませて/

*えさをやって}ください。
*Kodomo-tachi ni nani-ka {tabe-sasete/noma-sete/*esa o yatte} kudasai.*
(**c**) I fed some milk to the baby.
私は赤ん坊に{牛乳を{飲ませた/*食べさせた}/*えささやった}。
*Watashi wa akanboo ni {gyuunyuu o {noma-seta/*tabe-saseta}/*esa o yatta}.*

PHRASE: feed on ⟨-*o*⟩ *taberu* ⟨〜を⟩食べる ② ⟪eat⟫

EX. The giraffe feeds on leaves growing high in trees.
キリンは木の高いところにある葉っぱを食べる。
Kirin wa ki no takai tokoro ni aru happa o taberu.

PHRASE: be fed up with ⟨-*ga*⟩ *iya ni naru* ⟨〜が⟩いやになる, ⟨-*ni*⟩ *unzari-suru* ⟨〜に⟩うんざりする

NOTE: *Unzari-suru* is stronger sounding than *iya ni naru.*

EX. (**a**) I'm fed up with his endless talk.
彼のきりのないおしゃべり{にうんざりする/がいやになる}。
Kare no kiri no nai o-shaberi {ni unzari-suru/ga iya ni naru}.
(**b**) I got fed up with the long hours and low pay at that company and finally quit.
あの会社の残業や安月給{にうんざりして/がいやになって}とうとう辞めてしまった。
Ano kaisha no zangyoo ya yasu-gekkyuu {ni unzari-shite/ga iya ni natte} tootoo yamete shimatta.

feel vt. **[for s.o. to find out s.t. about s.t. by touching it or to sense s.t.]**

1. ⟨-ni⟩ sa⌈watte mi⌉ru ⟨〜に⟩触ってみる /⟨V *te* of *sawaru* ① touch + *miru* ② see/ ② [for s.o./s.a. to touch s.t./s.o. to see how it/he/she is]

EX. (**a**) Feel me to see if there are any bones broken.
骨が折れていないかどうか触ってみてください。
Hone ga orete inai ka doo ka sawatte mite kudasai.
(**b**) I felt the soft fabric with my fingers.
私はその柔らかい生地に指で触ってみました。
Watashi wa sono yawarakai kiji ni yubi de sawatte mimashita.

PHRASE: feel one's pulse *myaku o toru* 脈を取る ①

2. te-⌈sa⌉guri de sa⌈gasu 手探りで捜す ① [for s.o. to grope for s.t.]

EX. (**a**) She felt in her bag for her wallet.
彼女は手探りでバッグの中の財布を捜した。
Kanojo wa te-saguri de baggu no naka no saifu o sagashita.
(**b**) He felt about in the dark for the light switch.
彼は暗闇の中を手探りで電気のスイッチを探した。
Kare wa kura-yami no naka o te-saguri de denki no suitchi o sagashita.

3. ⟨-o⟩ ka⌈njiru ⟨〜を⟩感じる ② [for s.o./s.a. to become aware of s.o. through physical sensation or to sense s.t. spontaneously, apart from reasoning], ⟨-ga⟩ wa⌈ka⌉ru ⟨〜が⟩分かる ① [for s.o./s.a. to be able to figure out the nature, meaning, identity, etc., of s.t./s.o./s.a. which already is/should be in one's mind] ⟪understand, see, get, grasp, comprehend, know, realize⟫

EX. (**a**) I felt something crawling up my back.
何かが背中をはっているの{を感じた/が分かった}。
Nani-ka ga senaka o hatte iru no {o kanjita/ga wakatta}.
(**b**) I felt my heart beating wildly.
私は胸がどきどきするの{を感じました/が分かりました}。
Watashi wa mune ga doki-doki-suru no {o kanjimashita/ga wakarimashita}.
(**c**) I felt a sharp pain in my eyes.
私は目に鋭い痛み{を感じた/*が分かった}。
*Watashi wa me ni surudoi itami {o kanjita/*ga wakatta}.*
(**d**) I feel responsible for the failure of our new project.
私は新しいプロジェクトの失敗に責任

F

{を感じて/*が分かって}いる。
*Watashi wa atarashii purojekuto no shippai ni sekinin {o kanjite/*ga wakatte} iru.*

NOTE: Various sensations with "feel" are expressed with relevant adjectives or verbs as in the following examples.

EX. (**a**) I feel cold.
寒いです。
Samui desu.
(**b**) I feel hungry.
おなかが空きました。
O-naka ga sukimashita.
(**c**) I feel sorry.
お気の毒です。
O-ki-no-doku desu.
(**d**) Your hands feel cold.
あなたの手は冷たいですね。
Anata no te wa tsumetai desu ne.
(**e**) I feel sick.
気分が悪いです。
Kibun ga warui desu.

4. 〈-to〉 o⌈mo⌉u 〈〜と〉思う ① [for s.o. to spontaneously perceive s.t. in one's mind or to have an opinion about s.t.] ((think))

EX. (**a**) I feel that the plan has lots of problems.
その計画には問題が多いんじゃないかと思う。
Sono keikaku ni wa mondai ga ooi n janai ka to omou.
(**b**) I somehow felt that I would pass the exam.
なんとなく試験に受かると思った。
Nan to naku shiken ni ukaru to omotta.

NOTE: *n janai ka to omou* expresses less certainly than *to omou.*

(**c**) I don't feel he'll tell me the truth.
彼が本当のことを話してくれるような気がしない。
Kare ga hontoo no koto o hanashite kureru yoona ki-ga-shinai.

PHRASE: {feel as if/feel like} *yoona ki-ga-suru* ような気がする ③ ((have a feeling that))

(**a**) She felt as if her head was splitting.
彼女は頭が割れるような気がした。
Kanojo wa atama ga wareru yoona ki-ga-shita.
(**b**) I felt cheated.
私はだまされたような気がした。
Watashi wa damasa-reta yoona ki-ga-shita.
(**c**) Tom doesn't feel like a foreigner to me.
私はトムが外国人のような気がしません。
Watashi wa Tomu ga gaikoku-jin no yoona ki-ga-shimasen.

PHRASE: not feel like Ving Vinf. *ki-ga-shinai* Vinf.気がしない

(**a**) I don't feel like studying today.
今日は勉強する気がしません。
Kyoo wa benkyoo-suru ki-ga-shimasen.
(**b**) I don't feel much like going out these days.
このごろはあまり出かける気がしません。
Kono-goro wa amari dekakeru ki-ga-shimasen.

feeling n. **[the ability to sense s.t. by physical touch or through the emotions; a sensation so produced; physical or mental awareness]**

1. ka⌈nkaku 感覚 •c [a perception based on the five senses or a value judgment] ((sense))

EX. He had lost all feeling in his leg.
足の感覚が全く無くなった。
Ashi no kankaku ga mattaku nakunatta.

2. -kan 〜感 •c [physical/mental awareness of a particular kind]

PHRASE: feeling of hunger *kuufuku-kan* 空腹感 **•c**, feeling of security *anshin-kan* 安心感 **•c**, feeling of crisis *kiki-kan* 危機感 **•c**, feeling of satisfaction *manzoku-kan* 満足感 **•c**, feeling of sleepiness *nemu-ke* 眠気, feeling of tension *kinchoo-kan* 緊張感 **•c**

3. ka⌈njoo 感情 •c [s.t. felt in the mind/heart such as comfort, discomfort, joy, anger, sorrow, etc., which changes constantly in response to outside stimuli], ki⌈mochi 気持ち [the state of one's mind]

EX. (**a**) He appealed to the feelings of his audience rather than to their reason.

彼は聴衆の理性より{感情/?気持ち}に訴えた。
Kare wa chooshuu no risei yori {kanjoo/?kimochi} ni uttaeta.
(**b**) I said something that hurt her feelings.
私は彼女の{感情を害する/気持ちを傷つける}ようなことを言ってしまった。
Watashi wa kanojo no {kanjoo o gai-suru/kimochi o kizu-tsukeru} yoona koto o itte shimatta.
(**c**) Public feeling toward the Japanese has not shown any change in that country over the past fifty years.
あの国における一般大衆の日本人に対する{感情/気持ち}は過去五十年間変わっていない。
Ano kuni ni okeru ippan-taishuu no Nihon-jin ni-taisuru {kanjoo/kimochi} wa kako go-juu-nenkan kawatte inai.
(**d**) It is impossible to express in words the feeling that came over me when I heard the news that the war was over.
戦争が終わったというニュースを聞いたときの私の{気持ち/*感情}はとても言葉では言えません。
*Sensoo ga owatta to iu nyuusu o kiita toki no watashi no {kimochi/*kanjoo} wa totemo kotoba de wa ie-masen.*

4. ka⌈nju-sei 感受性 •c [the ability to experience sentiment] ⟪sensibility, susceptibility, receptivity⟫, do⌈ojoo 同情 •c [sensitivity to and understanding of the sufferings of others] ⟪sympathy⟫

EX. (**a**) She is a woman of deep feeling.
彼女は感受性の強い女性だ。
Kanojo wa kanju-sei no tsuyoi josei da.
(**b**) He doesn't show much feeling for the sufferings of others.
あの人は外の人の苦労にあまり同情しない。
Ano hito wa hoka no hito no kuroo ni amari doojoo-shinai.

PHRASE: ill feeling *hankan* 反感 •c

EX. We shouldn't do anything that might incur the ill feeling of others.
人々の反感を買うようなことをしてはいけない。
Hito-bito no hankan o kau yoona koto o shite wa ikenai.

feet n.
a⌈shi⌉ あし SEE foot

fellow n. **[a man/one's companion]**

1. o⌈toko⌉ 男 [a human male], ya⌈tsu やつ [a person/thing (with derogatory or endearing connotation) ⟨s⟩] ⟪guy⟫

NOTE: *Yatsu* is commonly used by men.

EX. (**a**) He is a pleasant fellow.
彼は気持ちがいい{男/やつ}です。
Kare wa kimochi ga ii {otoko/yatsu} desu.
(**b**) He is a clever fellow.
彼は利口な{男/やつ}です。
Kare wa rikoona {otoko/yatsu} desu.

2. na⌈kama⌉ 仲間 [a person in one's in-group with whom one frequently spends time, excluding one's relatives, spouse, and offspring ⟪fig. "the same kind"⟫] ⟪companions⟫, do⌈okyu⌉u-sei 同級生 •c [one/all of a group belonging past or present to the same class in an academic institution] ⟪classmate⟫

EX. (**a**) He said farewell to his fellow students and went home.
彼は{仲間/同級生}にさよならと言ってうちへ帰った。
Kare wa {nakama/dookyuu-sei} ni sayonara to itte uchi e kaetta.
(**b**) There is going to be a gathering of my fellow students at my home next Sunday.
今度の日曜日に{同級生/?仲間}がうちに集まることになっています。
Kondo no nichiyoo-bi ni {dookyuu-sei/?nakama} ga uchi ni atsumaru koto ni natte imasu.

female adj. **[of the sex that gives birth]**
o⌈nna⌉ no N 女のN ↔ otoko no N 男のN; jo⌈sei no N 女性のN •c [of the human sex that gives birth] ↔ dansei no N 男性のN •c; me⌈su⌉ no N 雌のN [of the sex that gives birth in non-human animal species] ↔ osu no N 雄のN

NOTE: *Josei* is more formal sounding than *onna.*

F

EX. (**a**) Our pet dog is female.
うちの飼い犬は{{雌/??女/*女性}の犬/雌犬}です。
*Uchi no kai-inu wa {{mesu/??onna/*josei} no inu/mesu-inu} desu.*
(**b**) In Kabuki, female parts are played by men.
歌舞伎では{女/女性/*雌}の役を男が演じる。
*Kabuki de wa {onna/josei/*mesu} no yaku o otoko ga enjiru.*

— n. **[female person/animal]**
o⌈nna⌉ 女 [an adult female person, often regarded as a dating/marriage/sexual partner ⟨s⟩], jo⌈sei 女性 •c, me⌈su⌉ 雌 [female animal]

fence n. **[a barrier made of wooden/metal posts, rails, wire, etc., dividing two areas of land to keep animals from straying or to keep out intruders]**
ka⌈ki-ne⌉ 垣根 [a structure put around a property to mark its boundaries and consisting variously of bamboo, wood, metal, wire, hedge, etc.], sa⌉ku 柵 [a barrier made of wooden/metal stakes and rails put around a field, garden etc. to keep animals from straying or to keep out intruders] ⟪paling⟫, he⌈i 塀 [an upright structure of stone, concrete, wood, brick etc., put around a house, field, garden, etc., to keep out intruders or to keep prisoners from escaping] ⟪wall⟫

EX. (**a**) I peeped through the fence into the garden.
私は{垣根/*柵/*塀}から庭をのぞきました。
*Watashi wa {kaki-ne/*saku/*hei} kara niwa o nozokimashita.*
(**b**) The dog jumped over the fence.
犬は{垣根/柵/塀}を飛び越えた。
Inu wa {kaki-ne/saku/hei} o tobi-koeta.

ferry n. **[a boat that carries people and goods across a river, channel, etc.]**
wa⌈tashi-bu⌉ne 渡し船 [an old-fashioned, small boat that crosses a river, channel, etc., carrying people and goods], re⌈nraku-sen 連絡船 •c [a boat that carries people and goods across a channel, river, etc., to connect the railroad services on the two sides], fe⌈rii フェリー •f, fe⌈rii-bo⌉oto フェリーボート •f [a boat that carries people and goods across a river, channel, etc.] ⟪ferryboat⟫

EX. (**a**) Back in 1960 I once took the ferry from Uno in Okayama to Takamatsu in Shikoku.
1960年に私は一度岡山の宇野から四国の高松まで{連絡船/フェリー(ボート)/*渡し船}で行ったことがある。
*Sen-kyuu-hyaku-roku-juu-nen ni watashi wa ichi-do Okayama no Uno kara Shikoku no Takamatsu made {renraku-sen/ferii(-booto)/*watashi-bune} de itta koto ga aru.*
(**b**) We used to cross the river in a small ferry before the bridge was built.
橋ができるまで我々は小さな{渡し船/??フェリー(ボート)/*連絡船}で川を渡っていた。
*Hashi ga dekiru made ware-ware wa chiisana {watashi-bune/??ferii(-booto)/*renraku-sen} de kawa o watatte ita.*

fertile adj. **[for land/a living being/a human mind to be capable of producing much]**
1. hi⌈yokuna 肥沃な adj(*na*). **•c, ko⌉eta N 肥えたN /⟨Vinf. past of *koeru* ② grow fertile/ [for land to be capable of producing much]**

EX. The American Midwest is blessed with a wealth of fertile land.
アメリカの中西部は{肥沃な/肥えた}土地に存分に恵まれている。
Amerika no chuu-seibu wa {hiyokuna/koeta} tochi ni zonbunni megumarete iru.

2. ta⌈san no N 多産のN •c [producing many offspring] ⟪prolific, productive⟫

EX. Mice are very fertile animals.
ねずみは大変多産です。
Nezumi wa taihen tasan desu.

3. so⌈ozo⌉o-ryoku-yu⌉takana 創造力豊かな adj(*na*). **[for one's mind to be very creative]**

EX. His fertile mind has contributed many innovative ideas for product development in our company.
彼は創造力豊かな心を持っており、我が社の新製品開発に斬新な案をいろいろ提供してくれている。
Kare wa soozoo-ryoku-yutakana kokoro o motte ori, waga-sha no shin-seihin-kaihatsu ni zanshinna an o iro-iro teikyoo-shite kurete iru.

fertilizer n. **[material to put on/in the soil to improve crop production]**
hi⌉ryoo 肥料 •c [material added to the soil as nutrients to help plants grow and keep healthy], ko⌈yashi⌉ 肥やし

EX. Don't give the flowers too much fertilizer.
花に{肥料/肥やし}をやり過ぎないでください。
Hana ni {hiryoo/koyashi} o yari-suginaide kudasai.

PHRASE: chemical fertilizer *kagaku-hiryoo* 化学肥料 **•c**

festival n. **[a time/day of celebration]**
ma⌈tsuri 祭り

EX. Japan has many festivals.
日本には色々な祭りがあります。
Nihon ni wa iro-irona matsuri ga arimasu.

NOTE: In compounds, the form *-sai* is used, as follows.

PHRASE: school festival *gakuen-sai* 学園祭 **•c**, art festival *geijutsu-sai* 芸術祭 **•c**

EX. An international art festival is going to be held in Kyoto this June.
今年の六月に京都で国際芸術祭が開かれる。
Kotoshi no roku-gatsu ni Kyooto de kokusai-geijutsu-sai ga hiraka-reru.

fetch vt. **[for s.o./s.a. to go for and bring back s.o./s.t.]**
⟨-o⟩ to⌈tte-ku⌉ru ⟨～を⟩取って来る ③ [for s.o./s.a. to go to a certain place, pick up s.t., and come back] ⟨-o⟩ yonde ku⌉ru ⟨～を⟩呼んで来る ③ [for s.o.to go for and bring back s.o.]

EX. (**a**) Would you fetch me a tape recorder from my office?
私のオフィスからテープレコーダーを{取って/*呼んで}来てくれませんか。
*Watashi no ofisu kara teepu-rekoodaa o {totte/*yonde}-kite kuremasen ka.*
(**b**) Hurry up and fetch your father from the garden.
急いで庭からお父さんを{呼んで/*取って}来てちょうだい。
*Isoide niwa kara o-too-san o {yonde/*totte} kite choodai.*

fever n. **[a body temperature that is higher than normal《fig. "excited state"》]**
ne⌈tsu⌉ 熱 •c [a form of energy that causes the temperature of an object or body to increase《fig. "high bodily temperature," "excited state"》]

EX. (**a**) I've caught a cold and have a small fever.
風邪をひいて、ちょっと熱があるんです。
Kaze o hiite, chotto netsu ga aru n desu.
(**b**) He is sick in bed with a fever.
彼は熱を出して寝ている。
Kare wa netsu o dashite nete iru.
(**c**) My fever has gone down.
熱は下がりました。
Netsu wa sagarimashita.

PHRASE: skiing fever *sukii-netsu* スキー熱 **•f+c**, election fever *senkyo-netsu* 選挙熱 **•c**

few adj. **[small in number]**
1. su⌈ko⌉shi 少し adv. **[(in) a small number/quantity or (to) a small degree]**

EX. (**a**) There are a few foreign students in this class.
このクラスには外国人の学生が少しいます。
Kono kurasu ni wa gaikoku-jin no gakusei ga sukoshi imasu.
(**b**) I'd like a few more yellow chrysanthemums.
黄色の菊がもう少し欲しいです。
Ki-iro no kiku ga moo sukoshi hoshii desu.

2. su⌈kuna⌉i 少ない adj(*i*). **[less than usual in number/quantity]**

NOTE: *Sukunai* is used only as a predicate.

F

EX. (**a**) Few women went to college in the past.
以前は大学へ行く女性は少なかった。
Izen wa daigaku e iku josei wa sukunakatta.
(**b**) There are few coffee shops in this area.
この辺は喫茶店が少ない。
Kono hen wa kissa-ten ga sukunai.

3. wa˥zuka わずか adv. **[very small in quantity]**

EX. There are very few people these days who wear a kimono all day long.
一日中着物を着ている人はこのごろはわずかしかいません。
Ichi-nichi-juu ki-mono o kite iru hito wa konogoro wa wazuka shika imasen.

PHRASE: a few days *suujitsu* 数日 •c, a few people *suunin* 数人 •c

EX. (**a**) We are going away for a few days.
数日の間留守にします。
Suujitsu no aida rusu ni shimasu.
(**b**) Few people attended the ceremony.
式に出た人は数人しかいませんでした。
Shiki ni deta hito wa suunin shika imasen deshita.

fiber n. **[one of the slender strands of which animal and vegetable tissue is formed]**
se˥n'i 繊維 •c

EX. (**a**) Seaweed is rich in fiber.
海草は繊維が豊富だ。
Kaisoo wa sen'i ga hoofu da.
(**b**) The quality of synthetic fiber has improved a lot in recent years.
近年合成繊維の質が非常に良くなった。
Kinnen goosei-sen'i no shitsu ga hijooni yoku natta.

fiction n. **[a story written about characters and events that are not real or a kind of literature consisting of such stories 《fig. "an untrue story invented in s.o.'s mind"》]**
tsu˥kuri-ba˥nashi 作り話 [a made-up story], sho˥osetsu 小説 •c [a long/short written story dealing with people and events that are not real]

EX. (**a**) I had believed what he told me, but it turned out to be pure fiction.
私は彼の言ったことを信じていたんですが、実はそれは全くの{作り話/*小説}だったんです。
*Watashi wa kare no itta koto o shinjite ita n desu ga, jitsu-wa sore wa mattaku no {tsukuri-banashi/*shoosetsu} datta n desu.*
(**b**) I like reading fiction.
私は{小説/??作り話}を読むのが好きです。
Watashi wa {shoosetsu/??tsukuri-banasi} o yomu no ga suki desu.

field n. **[a piece of open land, esp. that used for grazing cattle or growing crops]**

1. ha˥take 畑 [a piece of land for growing crops]

EX. He went out and worked in the fields every day, even when it was raining.
彼は雨の日にも毎日畑に出て働いた。
Kare wa ame no hi ni mo mai-nichi hatake ni dete hataraita.

PHRASE: wheat field *mugi-batake* 麦畑, corn field *toomorokoshi-batake* とうもろこし畑

2. ta˥ 田, su˥iden 水田 •c [cultivated land which is flooded with water for growing rice]

EX. There are lots of rice fields in this village.
この村には{水田/田}が多い。
Kono mura ni wa {suiden/ta} ga ooi.

3. ta˥-hata 田畑 [dry and paddy fields]

EX. His father owns a few fields in this area.
彼のお父さんはこの辺に田畑を少し持っている。
Kare no o-too-san wa kono hen ni ta-hata o sukoshi motte iru.

4. bo˥kuso˥o-chi 牧草地 •c [ground on which vegetation grows used for grazing animals]

5. -joo ～場 •c [an enclosed area used for s.t.]

PHRASE: athletic field *undoo-joo* 運動場 •c, baseball field *(ya)kyuu-joo* (野)球場 •c

6. bu˥n'ya 分野 •c [a branch of study], se˥nmon 専門 •c [a branch of study in which one specializes] 《specialty》

EX. (**a**) His work is well-known in the field of forensic medicine.

F

彼の研究は法医学の{分野/*専門}ではよく知られている。
*Kare no kenkyuu wa hooi-gaku no {bun'ya/*senmon} de wa yoku shira-rete iru.*
(**b**) What is your field of research?
{ご専門/ご研究の分野}は何ですか。
{Go-senmon/Go-kenkyuu no bun'ya} wa nan desu ka.

PHRASE: field work *fiirudo-waaku* フィールドワーク •f

fierce adj. **[violent in temperament or unpleasantly severe]**
do⌈omoona どう猛な adj(*na*). **•c [for s.a. to be violent], mo⌈no-sugo⌉i** ものすごい adj(*i*). **[causing great fear]** ⟪**terrible, awful**⟫

EX. (**a**) The neighbors have a fierce dog.
隣の家では{どう猛な/ものすごい}犬を飼っている。
Tonari no ie de wa {doomoona/mono-sugoi} inu o katte iru.
(**b**) A fierce wind was blowing.
{ものすごい/*どう猛な}風が吹いていた。
*{Mono-sugoi/*Doomoona} kaze ga fuite ita.*

fifteen n./adj.
ju⌉u-go (+counter) (no N) 十五(**+counter**)(のN) **•c** SEE APPENDIX II

EX. (**a**) There are fifteen students in my class.
私のクラスには学生が十五人います。
Watashi no kurasu ni wa gakusei ga juu-go-nin imasu.
(**b**) I bought fifteen apples.
りんごを十五買った。
Ringo o juu-go katta.
(**c**) That song was popular when I was fifteen.
その歌は私が十五の時、はやりました。
Sono uta wa watashi ga juu-go no toki, hayarimashita.

fifth adj. **[number five in a series]**
i⌈tsutsu-me⌉ no N 五つ目のN, **go-⌈ban-me⌉ no N,** 五番目のN, **go +⌈counter me⌉ no** 五**+counter**目のN SEE APPENDIX II

EX. (**a**) He has just published his fifth book.
彼は五冊目の本を出版したばかりだ。
Kare wa go-satsu-me no hon o shuppan-shita bakari da.
(**b**) Turn left at the fifth corner.
{五つ目/五番目}の角を左に曲がってください。
{Itsutsu-me/Go-ban-me} no kado o hidari ni magatte kudasai.
(**c**) Tomorrow is our fifth wedding anniversary.
明日は私たちの{五回目/五度目}の結婚記念日です。
Ashita wa watashi-tachi no {go-kai-me/go-do-me} no kekkon-kinen-bi desu.
(**d**) She is our fifth secretary this year.
彼女は今年五人目の秘書です。
Kanojo wa kotoshi go-nin-me no hisho desu.

PHRASE: January 5th *ichi-gatsu itsuka* 一月五日

fifty n./adj.
g⌈o-ju⌉u (+counter) (no N) 五十(**+counter**)(のN) **•c** SEE APPENDIX II

EX. (**a**) He sent out fifty Christmas cards.
彼はクリスマスカードを五十枚出した。
Kare wa Kurisumasu-kaado o go-juu-mai dashita.
(**b**) She is fifty years old.
彼女は{五十/五十歳}です。
Kanojo wa {go-juu/go-jus-sai} desu.

PHRASE: fifty-fifty ⟪chance⟫ *gobu-gobu* 五分五分

fight vi./vt. **[for an individual or group to use force against another in order to defeat him/her/it]**
1. ⟨**-to**⟩ **ta⌈takau** ⟨〜と⟩たたかう ① **[for s.o. to try in a determined way to defeat an opponent or to overcome a difficulty or to achieve s.t.]**
㊉ "fight in war or in a sports event"▷戦う, "fight against disease, poverty, etc."▷闘う

EX. (**a**) They fought for their independence.
彼らは独立のために戦った。
Kare-ra wa dokuritsu no tame ni tatakatta.
(**b**) He is fighting cancer.
彼はがんと闘っている。
Kare wa gan to tatakatte iru.

F

2. ⟨-to⟩ ke⌈nka-suru ⟨〜と⟩けんかする ③ •c [for s.o./s.a. to engage in a struggle with s.o./s.a. else involving mutual physical and/or verbal attacks] ⟪quarrel, argue⟫

EX. | (**a**) Taro fought with Jiro over a girl.
太郎は女の子のことで二郎とけんかした。
Taroo wa onna-no-ko no koto de Jiroo to kenka-shita.
(**b**) That couple is always fighting over money.
あの夫婦はいつも金のことでけんかしている。
Ano fuufu wa itsu-mo kane no koto de kenka-shite iru.

—— n. **[act of fighting]**

1. ta⌈takai たたかい ⟪battle, struggle⟫

㊊ "a fight in war or a sports event"▷戦い, "a fight against disease, poverty, etc."▷闘い

F

EX. | We have a long way to go in this country before we win in the fight against poverty.
我が国では貧困との闘いに勝利するまでの道のりはまだ遠い。
Waga-kuni de wa hinkon to no tatakai ni shoori-suru made no michinori wa mada tooi.

2. ke⌈nka けんか •c [an angry struggle involving mutual verbal and/or physical attacks] ⟪argument, quarrel⟫

EX. | (**a**) I got drunk and had a fight with my boss.
私は酔っぱらって、上司とけんかしてしまった。
Watashi wa yopparatte, jooshi to kenka-shite shimatta.
(**b**) He lost in the fight with his older brother.
彼は兄とのけんかに負けた。
Kare wa ani to no kenka ni maketa.

fighter n. **[a person/airplane that fights]**

1. ma⌈kezu-gi⌉rai 負けず嫌い [s.o. who hates to lose in anything]

EX. | She is a real fighter and has a hard time compromising with others.
彼女は根っからの負けず嫌いで、容易には人と妥協しない。
Kanojo wa nekkara no makezu-girai de, yooini wa hito to dakyoo-shinai.

2. se⌈nto⌉o-ki 戦闘機 •c [an airplane used in a battle] ⟪fighter plane⟫

figure n. **[a symbol/diagram/drawing to illustrate s.t./s.o. ⟪fig. "s.o. who represents s.t."⟫]**

1. su⌈uji 数字 •c [a symbol indicating a quantity]

EX. | Please give me that telephone number again. I'm bad at figures.
さっきの電話番号をもう一度教えてくれませんか。私、数字に弱いんです。
Sakki no denwa-bangoo o moo ichi-do oshiete kuremasen ka. Watashi, suuji ni yowai n desu.

2. ke⌈ta 桁 [the number of places in a numerical expression]

EX. | (**a**) He has a seven-figure monthly income.
彼は七桁の月収がある。
Kare wa nana-keta no gesshuu ga aru.
(**b**) We want inflation brought down into the single-figure range.
インフレを一桁に押さえたい。
Infure o hito-keta ni osae-tai.

3. zu 図 •c [a diagram/drawing to illustrate s.t.]

EX. | See Figure 8 on page seven.
七ページの図8を見てください。
Nana-peeji no zu-hachi o mite kudasai.

4. su⌉gata 姿 [a visual impression of s.o.]

EX. | Everyone was fascinated by her graceful figure dressed in kimono.
みんな彼女の優美な着物姿に見とれた。
Minna kanojo no yuubina kimono-sugata ni mitoreta.

5. su⌈ta⌉iru スタイル •f [a manner in which s.t. is done/made or s.o.'s bodily shape considered from the point of view of attractiveness]

EX. | (**a**) She's got a fabulous figure.
彼女はすばらしいスタイルをしている。
Kanojo wa subarashii sutairu o shite iru.
(**b**) She was always worrying about her figure.

彼女はいつも自分のスタイルを気にしていた。
Kanojo wa itsu-mo jibun no sutairu o ki-ni-shite ita.
(**c**) I'm on a diet to keep up my figure.
私はスタイルを維持するためにダイエットしています。
Watashi wa sutairu o iji-suru tame ni daietto-shite imasu.

6. hi⌈to-kage 人影 [a human form]

EX. I saw a figure approaching in the darkness.
私は暗闇の中を人影が近づいて来るのを見た。
Watashi wa kura-yami no naka o hito-kage ga chikazuite kuru no o mita.

7. ji⌉nbutsu 人物 •c [a person considered from the point of view of his/her importance in society, history, etc.] ((character))

EX. (**a**) He was a key figure in that country's independence movement.
彼はその国の独立運動の中心的人物だった。
Kare wa sono kuni no dokuritsu-undoo no chuushin-teki-jinbutsu datta.
(**b**) He is a well-known figure in the political world.
彼は政界ではよく知られた人物です。
Kare wa seikai de wa yoku shira-reta jinbutsu desu.

— vt./vi. **[for s.o. to think that s.t. is the case after considering a matter carefully] ⟨-to⟩ o⌈mo⌉u ⟨～と⟩思う ① [for s.o. to spontaneously preceive s.t. in one's mind or to have an opinion about s.t.]**

EX. They figured it was better to stay put where they were.
今いる所にいる方がいいと思った。
Ima iru tokoro ni iru hoo ga ii to omotta.

PHRASE: That figures. *Yappari.* やっぱり。

fill vt. **[to put a large amount of a substance or many things into s.t. to make it full] ⟨-o⟩ i⌈ppai ni suru ⟨～を⟩いっぱいにする ③ [for s.o. to make some space full], ⟨-ni⟩ ⟨-o⟩ tsu⌈me⌉ru ⟨～に⟩⟨～を⟩詰める ② [for s.o. to put s.t./s.o./s.a. into a tight, limited space/time or to cause s.t. to become short] ((pack)), ⟨-o⟩ u⌈meru ⟨～を⟩埋める ② [to put s.t. in a hole, blank, etc. so that it becomes full or for people to get into some space until it becomes full]**

EX. (**a**) She is the only singer who ever filled that hall for a whole month.
そのホールを一か月も{いっぱいにした/*詰めた/*埋めた}歌手は彼女だけです。
*Sono hooru o ik-kagetsu mo {ippai ni shita/*tsumeta/*umeta} kashu wa kanojo dake desu.*
(**b**) A large audience filled the hall.
大勢の観客が会場を{埋めた/いっぱいにした/*詰めた}。
*Oozei no kankyaku ga kaijoo o {umeta/ippai ni shita/*tsumeta}.*
(**c**) I had my cavity filled by the dentist.
歯医者に虫歯を{埋めて/詰めて/*いっぱいにして}もらった。
*Ha-isha ni mushi-ba o {umete/tsumete/*ippai ni shite} moratta.*
(**d**) The smoke filled the room.
部屋は煙でいっぱいになった。
Heya wa kemuri de ippai ni natta.
(**e**) Tears filled her eyes.
彼女の目は涙でいっぱいになった。
Kanojo no me wa namida de ippai ni natta.

NOTE: When the subject of filling is not human as in examples (d) and (e), the intransitive verb *ippai ni naru* "become full" is used.

PHRASE: fill out a form *yooshi ni kaki-komu* 用紙に書き込む ①, Fill it up (with gasoline). *Mantan ni shite kudasai.* 満タンにしてください。

— vi. **[for s.t. to become full] ⟨-de⟩ i⌈ppai ni na⌉ru ⟨～で⟩いっぱいになる ①, ⟨-de⟩ u⌈maru ⟨～で⟩埋まる ① [for space to be filled with s.t.] ((be buried))**

EX. (**a**) My heart filled with expectation as I listened to him speak.
彼の話を聞きながら私の胸は期待で{いっぱいになった/*埋まった}。
Kare no hanashi o kiki-nagara watashi

F

*no mune wa kitai de {ippai ni natta/ *umatta}.*
(**b**) The classroom soon filled with students.
教室は間もなく学生で{いっぱいになった/埋まった}。
Kyooshitsu wa ma-mo-naku gakusei de {ippai ni natta/umatta}.

film n. **[a roll/sheet coated with light-sensitive material used in a camera to take pictures《fig. "movie"》]**
1. fi⌉rumu フィルム •f [a roll/sheet coated with light sensitive material used in a camera to take pictures]
NOTE: The word is often pronounced as *fuirumu* in Japanese.
EX. Would you please load some film into the camera?
カメラにフィルムを入れてくださいませんか。
Kamera ni firumu o irete kudasaimasen ka.
2. e⌉iga 映画 •c [a movie]
EX. I like documentary films.
私は記録映画が好きです。
Watashi wa kiroku-eiga ga suki desu.

filthy adj. **[very dirty]**
ki⌈tana⌉i 汚い adj(*i*). **[not clean/tidy《fig. "obscene," "despicable," "unfair"》]《dirty, unclean, untidy》↔ kireina きれいな** adj(*na*).; **yo⌈goreta N 汚れたN /〈Vinf. past of *yogoreru* ② become dirty/, yo⌈gorete iru (N) 汚れている(N) /〈V *te iru* of *yogoreru* ② become dirty/ ② [dirty], fu⌈ketsuna 不潔な** adj(*na*). **•c [not clean]《unsanitary》↔ seiketsuna 清潔な** adj(*na*). **•c**
EX. (**a**) His room is always filthy.
彼の部屋はいつも{汚い/不潔だ/汚れている}。
Kare no heya wa itsu-mo {kitanai/fuketsu da/yogorete iru}.
(**b**) I couldn't help noticing the filthy shirt he was wearing.
彼の{汚い/不潔な/汚れた/汚れている}シャツが目についた。
Kare no {kitanai/fuketsuna/yogoreta/yogorete iru} shatsu ga me ni tsuita.

F

final adj. **[coming at the end]**
1. sa⌉igo no N 最後のN •c [coming at the end]《last》↔ saisho no N 最初のN •c
EX. I am now writing the final chapter of my senior thesis.
今、卒業論文の最後の章を書いているところです。
Ima, sotsugyoo-ronbun no saigo no shoo o kaite iru tokoro desu.
2. sa⌈ishuu-tekina 最終的な adj(*na*). **•c [cannot be changed/questioned]**
EX. The president's decision is final.
社長の決定は最終的なものだ。
Shachoo no kettei wa saishuu-tekina mono da.
PHRASE: the final game *kesshoo-sen* 決勝戦 **•c**

finally adv. **[lastly]**
1. to⌉otoo とうとう [at the end after various stages, often culminating in an undesirable situation which had been expected]《at last, after all》, tsu⌉i ni ついに [at the end after various stages, culminating in either a desirable or undesirable situation]《at last, in the end》
NOTE: *Tootoo* is typically used when s.t. undesirable happens at the end.
EX. (**a**) She finally died after a long battle with cancer.
彼女はがんとの長い戦いの後、{とうとう/ついに}亡くなった。
Kanojo wa gan to no nagai tatakai no ato, {tootoo/tsuini} nakunatta.
(**b**) The management finally gave in and agreed to the proposed compromise.
経営者側が{とうとう/ついに}折れて、妥協案を承諾した。
Keiei-sha-gawa ga {tootoo/tsuini} orete, dakyoo-an o shoodaku-shita.
2. ya⌈tto やっと [at the end after a long wait or struggle], yo⌈oyaku ようやく〈fml〉
EX. (**a**) Spring has finally come to Hokkaido.
北海道にも{やっと/ようやく}春が来た。
Hokkaidoo ni mo {yatto/yooyaku} haru ga kita.
(**b**) I've finally finished my Ph. D. dissertation.

私は{やっと/ようやく}博士論文を仕上げた。
Watashi wa {yatto/yooyaku} hakushi-ronbun o shi-ageta.

3. sa˥igo ni 最後に •c [at the end] ↔ 最初に •c

EX. Finally, let's consider the issue of overtime work in Japanese industry.
最後に日本企業における時間外労働の問題について考えましょう。
Saigo ni Nihon-kigyoo ni-okeru jikan-gai-roodoo no mondai ni-tsuite kangaemashoo.

finance n. **[the management of money, esp. at the public level]**
za˥isei 財政 •c

EX. Our national finances are still in the red.
我が国の国家財政は依然として赤字です。
Waga-kuni no kokka-zaisei wa izen-to-shite akaji desu.

PHRASE: the Minister of Finance *ookura-daijin* 大蔵大臣, the Ministry of Finance *Ookura-shoo* 大蔵省

financial adj. **[relating to/involving money]** **ke˥izai-tekina 経済的な** adj(*na*). **•c [relating to/involving money or costing less]** **((economic, economical))**, **za˥isei-tekina 財政的な** adj(*na*). **•c [relating to/involving public money]**

EX. (**a**) He had to quit school for financial reasons.
彼は{経済的な/*財政的な}理由で学校をやめなければならなかった。
*Kare wa {keizai-tekina/*zaisei-tekina} riyuu de gakkoo o yamenakereba naranakatta.*
(**b**) The country's financial condition is not very good.
国の{経済/財政}状態はあまり良くない。
Kuni no {keizai/zaisei}-jootai wa amari yokunai.

NOTE: Both *keizai* and *zaisei* often appear in compounds, as in example (b). Other examples include financial support *zaisei-enjo*, financial page (of a newspaper) *keizai-men*, financial plan *zaisei-keikaku*.

find vt. **[for s.o. to discover s.o./s.t. or to become aware of s.t. or to have an opinion about s.t.]**

1. 〈-o〉 mi˥tsukeru 〈～を〉見つける ② [for s.o. to cause s.o./s.t./s.a. hidden/lost/unknown to come to light or be seen], mi˥tsukaru 見つかる ① [to be discovered] ((be found))

EX. (**a**) I found the book I was looking for.
さがしていた本を見つけた。
Sagashite ita hon o mitsuketa.
(**b**) I found a good restaurant near my apartment.
アパートの近くにいいレストランを見つけました。
Apaato no chikaku ni ii resutoran o mitsukemashita.
(**c**) The missing child has not yet been found.
迷子はまだ見つかっていない。
Maigo wa mada mitsukatte inai.
(**d**) He cannot find work.
彼は仕事が見つからない。
Kare wa shigoto ga mitsukaranai.

2. 〈-ga〉 wa˥ka˥ru 〈～が〉分かる ① [to be able to figure out the nature, meaning, identity etc., of s.t./s.o./s.a. which already is/should be in one's mind] ① ((realize, understand))

EX. (**a**) I found him to be much younger than I expected.
彼は思ったよりずっと若いことが分かった。
Kare wa omotta yori zutto wakai koto ga wakatta.
(**b**) When I woke up, I found that I could not move my right arm.
目が覚めた時、右手が動かないことが分かった。
Me ga sameta toki, migi-te ga ugokanai koto ga wakatta.

3. 〈-to〉 o˥mo˥u 〈～と〉思う ① [for s.o. to spontaneously perceive s.t. in one's mind or to have an opinion about s.t.] ((think))

EX. (**a**) I find the weather in this part of the country to be very agreeable.

この地方の天候はなかなか快適だと思う。
Kono chihoo no tenkoo wa nakanaka kaiteki da to omou.
(**b**) I don't find this book interesting at all.
この本は全然面白いと思いません。
Kono hon wa zenzen omoshiroi to omoimasen.

fine adj. **[enjoyable/pleasing or consisting of very small particles ⟪fig. "delicate," "subtle"⟫]**

1. ge˥nkina 元気な adj(*na*). **•c [for s.o./s.a. to be in good health or to have lots of energy]** ⟪**healthy**⟫, **i˥i** いい adj(*i*). **[morally correct/satisfactory/agreeable]** ⟪**nice**⟫, **ke˥kkoona** 結構な adj(*na*). **•c [satisfactory]** ⟪**all right**⟫

EX. (**a**) A: How are you?
お元気ですか。
O-genki desu ka.
B: I'm fine, thanks. And you?
ええ、おかげさまで{元気/*いい/*結構}です。そちらは?
*Ee, o-kage-sama de {genki/*ii/*kekkoo} desu. Sochira wa?*

NOTE: *Okagesama de* means "thanks to (you)."

(**b**) It snowed all morning, but the weather was fine in the afternoon.
午前中は雪だったが、午後は{いい/*元気な/*結構な}天気になった。
*Gozen-chuu wa yuki datta ga, gogo wa {ii/*genkina/*kekkoona} tenki ni natta.*
(**c**) A: Do you want your coffee stronger than that?
コーヒーをもっと濃くしましょうか。
Koohii o motto koku shimashoo ka.
B: No, this is fine.
いいえ、これで{結構/いい/*元気}です。
*Iie, kore de {kekkoo/ii/*genki} desu.*

NOTE: *Kekkoo* sounds a little more formal than *ii.*

2. ko˹maka˥i 細かい adj(*i*). **[as small as a particle ⟪fig. "detailed," "stingy"⟫]** ⟪**minute, small, trifling**⟫

EX. (**a**) The rain was falling in a fine mist.
細かい霧のような雨が降っていた。
Komakai kiri no yoona ame ga futte ita.
(**b**) There is a fine dust in the air.
空中には細かいちりがある。
Kuuchuu ni wa komakai chiri ga aru.
(**c**) You don't have to understand the fine points of this argument.
この議論の細かい点は分からなくても構いません。
Kono giron no komakai ten wa wakaranakute mo kamaimasen.

—— n. **[an amount of money s.o. has to pay as a punishment]**
ba˹kkin 罰金 **•c**

EX. How much was your fine for speeding?
スピード違反の罰金はいくら取られましたか。
Supiido-ihan no bakkin wa ikura tora-remashita ka.

PHRASE: the fine arts/art *bijutsu* 美術 **•c**

finger n. **[one of the five movable body parts at the end of the hand]**
yu˹bi˥ 指 **[any/all of the five body parts at the end of the hand or the foot]** ⟪**toe**⟫

EX. (**a**) She wore a wedding ring on her finger.
彼女は指に結婚指輪をはめていた。
Kanojo wa yubi ni kekkon-yubiwa o hamete ita.
(**b**) There are five fingers on each hand.
手には指が五本ずつある。
Te ni wa yubi ga go-hon-zutsu aru.

PHRASE: little finger *ko-yubi* 小指, ring finger *kusuri-yubi* 薬指, middle finger *naka-yubi* 中指, index finger *hitosashi-yubi* 人指し指, thumb *oya-yubi* 親指, lay a finger on 〈*-ni*〉 *sawaru* 〈〜に〉触る ①, keep one's fingers crossed *umaku iku yooni inoru* うまく行くように祈る ①, have a finger in every pie *te-biroku yaru* 手広くやる ①, won't lift a finger *yoko no mono o tate ni mo shinai* 横の物を縦にもしない

finish vt. **[to bring s.t. to an end]**
〈-o〉 o˹waru 〈〜を〉終わる ① **[for s.o. to bring to an end/settle s.t.]**, **〈-o〉 o˹eru** 〈〜を〉終える ②, **〈-o〉 su˹ma-se˥ru** 〈〜を〉すませる /**〈causative of *sumu* ① become done/ ②**, **〈-o〉 V*te* shi˹mau** 〈〜を〉V*te*しまう ① **[for s.o./s.a. to finish doing s.t. or for s.t. to end up happening (to one's joy/regret)]** ⟪**do s.t. completely**⟫

F

㊊ "become clear"▷澄む, "live"▷住む, "become completely done"▷済む

EX.| I've finished my homework.
宿題を{終わりました/終えました/すませました/してしまいました}。
Shukudai o {owarimashita/oemashita/suma-semashita/shite shimaimashita}.

— vi. **[for s.t. to come to an end]**
o⌈waru 終わる ① ⟪end, be over⟫, **su⌉mu すむ** ① **[for s.t. murky to become clear ⟪fig. "live," "become completly done"⟫]**

㊊ "become clear"▷澄む, "live"▷住む, "become completely done"▷済む

EX.| (**a**) The concert finished at 9:00 P.M.
音楽会は午後九時に{終わった/*すんだ}。
*Ongaku-kai wa gogo ku-ji ni {owatta/ *sunda}.*
(**b**) The meeting has just finished.
会議が{終わった/すんだ}ところです。
Kaigi ga {owatta/sunda} tokoro desu.

NOTE: *Sumu* often implies that some effort was involved in bringing s.t. to a conclusion while *owaru* simply means that the end point of some event has been reached.

Finland n.
Fi⌉nrando フィンランド •f

fire n. **[the flame and heat produced by s.t. burning]**

1. hi⌉ 火

EX.| (**a**) Paper catches fire easily.
紙は火が付きやすい。
Kami wa hi ga tsuki-yasui.
(**b**) He gathered some firewood and lit a fire.
彼はたきぎを集めて、火を付けた。
Kare wa takigi o atsumete, hi o tsuketa.
(**c**) Where there's smoke there's fire.
火のない所に煙は立たぬ。
Hi no nai tokoro ni kemuri wa tatanu.

2. ka⌉ji 火事 •c [an occurrence of destructive burning]

EX.| (**a**) The hotel was completely destroyed by fire.
ホテルは火事で全焼した。
Hoteru wa kaji de zenshoo-shita.
(**b**) A fire broke out in my neighborhood last night.
ゆうべ近所で火事がありました。
Yuube kinjo de kaji ga arimashita.

PHRASE: set fire to ⟨*-ni*⟩ *hi o tsukeru* ⟨〜に⟩火を付ける ⟪light⟫, fire insurance *kasai-hoken* 火災保険 **•c**, fire engine *shooboo-jidoosha* 消防自動車 **•c**, fire station *shooboo-sho* 消防署 **•c**

— vt./vi. **[for s.o. to set off a weapon, esp. a gun, or for a weapon to be set off ⟪fig. "dismiss s.o. from a job"⟫]**

1. ⟨**-o**⟩ **u⌉tsu** ⟨〜を⟩**撃つ** ① **[for s.o. to shoot a weapon/s.o. with a weapon]**

EX.| The policeman fired his pistol at the robber.
警官が強盗に向けてピストルを撃った。
Keikan ga gootoo ni mukete pisutoru o utta.

2. ⟨**-o**⟩ **ku⌈bi ni suru** ⟨〜を⟩**首にする** ③ **[for s.o. to dismiss s.o. from a job]**

EX.| I fired him because he was pilfering money from the store.
彼は店の金をごまかしていたので、首にした。
Kare wa mise no kane o gomakashite ita node, kubi ni shita.

fireman n. **[a person whose job is to put out fires]**
sho⌈oboo⌉-shi 消防士 •c

EX.| Three firemen received slight burn injures while fighting the fire.
消防士が三人、消火中に軽いやけどを負った。
Shooboo-shi ga san-nin, shooka-chuu ni karui yakedo o otta.

fireplace n. **[an open recess in the wall of a room where a fire can be lit]**
da⌉nro 暖炉 •c [an open recess in the wall of a room where a fire can be lit], i⌈rori 囲炉裏 •c [an open wood-burning hearth in a traditional Japanese-style house]

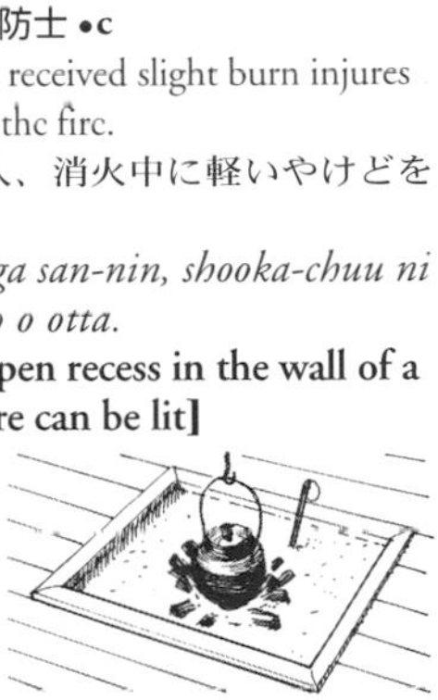

irori

firewood n.
ma⌈ki まき

EX.| John is chopping firewood in the backyard.

F

ジョンは裏庭で薪を割っている。
Jon wa ura-niwa de maki o watte iru.

fireworks n.

ha⌉na-bi 花火

EX. There are fireworks displays at various places throughout Japan during the summer.
夏には日本中いろいろな所で花火大会がある。
Natsu ni wa Nihon-juu iro-irona tokoro de hana-bi-taikai ga aru.

firm adj. **[not yielding when pressed《fig. "for one's mind not to be easily changed or influenced"》]**

1. ka⌈tai かたい adj(*i*). **[not easily changed/broken/influenced]《hard, solid, stiff, tight, tough》**

㊥ "stiff" ▷硬い, "rigid or unyielding (in character)" 堅い, otherwise ▷固い

EX. (**a**) I like a firm mattress.
私は堅いマットレスが好きです。
Watashi wa katai mattoresu ga suki desu.
(**b**) She broke a firm promise she had with me.
彼女は私たちの固い約束を破った。
Kanojo wa watashi-tachi no katai yakusoku o yabutta.

2. ki⌈zen to shita N 毅然としたN /〈***kizen to*** **firmly + Vinf. past of** ***suru*** ③ **do/ •c [for s.o. to have a strong will and not to be easily influenced or tempted]《resolute》, da⌉nko to shita N** 断固としたN /〈***danko*** **flatly + prt.** ***to*** **+ Vinf. past of** ***suru*** ③ **do/ •c [for one's attitude, resolution, etc. not to be moved despite opposition or difficulty]**

EX. (**a**) It's best to take a firm attitude if one doesn't want to be taken advantage of.
弱みにつけこまれたくなかったら、{毅然/断固}とした態度をとることです。
Yowa-mi ni tsuke-koma-re-takunakattara, {kizen/danko} to shita taido o toru koto desu.
(**b**) Father said "No," in a firm voice.
父は{毅然/断固}とした口調で「駄目だ」と言った。
Chichi wa {kizen/danko} to shita kuchoo de 'Dame da' to itta.

3. shi⌈kka⌉ri-shita N しっかりしたN /〈**Vinf. past of** ***shikkari-suru*** ③ **become steady/ [free from weakness/looseness]《steady, sound, tight》, shi⌈kka⌉ri-shite i⌈ru (N)** しっかりしている(N) /〈**V*te iru*** **of** ***shikkari-suru*** ③ **become steady/**

EX. (**a**) Please use a strong, firm ladder.
強い、しっかりしたはしごを使ってください。
Tsuyoi, shikkari-shita hashigo o tsukatte kudasai.
(**b**) Our infant son isn't very firm on his feet yet.
うちの幼い息子はまだ足下がしっかりしていない。
Uchi no osanai musuko wa mada ashi-moto ga shikkari-shite inai.
(**c**) I took firm hold of the rope.
私はロープにしっかりつかまった。
Watashi wa roopu ni shikkari tsukamatta.

NOTE: The literal translation of *shikkari tsukamaru* is "to hold on to s.t. firmly."

firmly adv. **[strongly so as not to move/change]**

shi⌈kka⌉ri しっかり **[strongly so as not to move]《tightly, fast》, ka⌈taku** かたく /〈**adj(*i*).** ***ku*** **of** ***katai*** **firm/ [strongly so as not to change]**

EX. (**a**) He held my arm firmly.
彼は私の腕を{しっかり/*固く}つかんだ。
*Kare wa watashi no ude o {shikkari/*kataku} tsukanda.*
(**b**) His mother was firmly of the belief that he was innocent.
彼の母親は彼が無罪だと{固く/*しっかり}信じていた。
*Kare no haha-oya wa kare ga muzai da to {kataku/*shikkari} shinjite ita.*

first adj. **[coming before the others]**

1. sa⌈isho no N 最初のN •c ↔ **saigo no N** 最後のN •c, **hajime no N** 初めのN ↔ **owari no N** 終わりのN

EX. (**a**) I was very nervous during my first week in Japan.

F

日本での{初め/最初}の一週間は本当に緊張しました。
Nihon de no {hajime/saisho} no is-shuukan wa hontoo ni kinchoo-shimashita.
(**b**) I remember only the first part of this song.
この歌の{初め/最初}の部分しか覚えていない。
Kono uta no {hajime/saisho} no bubun shika oboete inai.

2. ha⌈ji⌉mete no N 初めてのN [not having been seen/heard/experienced by one before]

EX. Is this your first baby?
初めての赤ちゃんですか。
Hajimete no aka-chan desu ka.

— adv. **[coming before the others]**

1. sa⌈isho ni 最初に •c ↔ saigo ni 最後に •c; ha⌈jime ni 初めに ↔ owari ni 終わりに; ma⌉zu (sa⌈isho ni) 先ず(最初に) 《first of all》

EX. (**a**) Who heard the news first?
{最初に/初めに/先ず最初に}そのニュースを聞いたのはだれですか。
{Saisho ni/Hajime ni/Mazu saisho ni} sono nyuusu o kiita no wa dare desu ka.
(**b**) A: What do you want to do while in Japan?
日本にいる間にどんなことをしたいと思いますか。
Nihon ni iru aida ni donna koto o shi-tai to omoimasu ka.
B: First I'd like to master the Japanese language.
{先ず(最初に)/最初に/初めに}日本語を覚えたいと思います。
{Mazu (saisho ni)/Saisho ni/Hajime ni} Nihon-go o oboe-tai to omoimasu.

2. ha⌈ji⌉mete 初めて [for s.t. like this not to have happened before]

EX. (**a**) When I first met Kiko, I never expected that I would marry her.
初めて紀子に会ったとき、彼女と結婚するなんて思いもしなかった。
Hajimete Kiko ni atta toki, kanojo to kekkon-suru nante omoi mo shinakatta.
(**b**) I had squid for the first time in my life the other evening.
この間の晩生まれて初めていかを食べた。
Kono aida no ban umarete hajimete ika o tabeta.

PHRASE: first impression *dai-ichi-inshoo* 第一印象 •c, first of all *mazu* 先ず, for the first time *hajimete* 初めて, at first hand *chokusetsu* 直接 •c, First come, first served. *Senchaku-jun desu.* 先着順です。

— n. **[s.t. coming before the others]**

i⌈chi⌉-ban 一番 •c [number 1 《fig. "the marker of the superlative degree"》] 《top》, sa⌈isho 最初 •c [beginning] ↔ saigo 最後 •c

EX. I was the first in line to get a ticket for the concert.
その音楽会の切符を買うために並んだのは私が{一番/最初}だった。
Sono ongaku-kai no kippu o kau tame ni naranda no wa watashi ga {ichi-ban/saisho} datta.

PHRASE: at first *hajime wa* 初めは, the first day of the month *tsuitachi* 一日

fish n. **[an animal with tail and fins that lives in the water]**

sa⌉kana さかな [an animal with tail and fins that lives in the water 《fig. "food to be eaten with alcoholic beverages"》]

㊥ "fish"▷魚, "food to be eaten with alcoholic beverages"▷さかな

EX. (**a**) We caught many fish.
魚をたくさん釣った。
Sakana o takusan tsutta.
(**b**) We have fish for dinner every Friday.
毎週、金曜日の晩ご飯には魚を食べる。
Mai-shuu, kin'yoo-bi no ban-gohan ni wa sakana o taberu.

PHRASE: fish shop *sakana-ya* 魚屋

EX. There is a good fish shop near my house.
うちの近くにいい魚屋があります。
Uchi no chikaku ni ii sakana-ya ga arimasu.

— vi. **[for s.o. to try to catch fish]**

⟨-o⟩ tsu⌈ru ⟨〜を⟩釣る ① [for s.o. to catch fish using a line and hook] 《catch》, tsu⌈ri o

F

suru 釣りをする ③ [for s.o. to try to catch fish using a line and hook], ryo˥o o suru 漁をする ③ •c [for s.o. to catch fish for a living]

EX. (a) When I'm fishing, I put all thoughts about work out of my mind.
{{釣り/?漁}をして/?釣って}いる間は、仕事のことは全部忘れます。
{{Tsuri/?Ryoo} o shite/?Tsutte} iru aida wa, shigoto no koto wa zenbu wasuremasu.
(b) Is it hard to fish for trout?
{ますを釣る/ますの{?漁をする/*釣りをする}のは難しいですか。
*{Masu o tsuru/masu no {?ryoo o suru/ *tsuri o suru} no wa muzukashii desu ka.*
(c) We can't fish today because a typhoon is coming.
台風が近づいているから、今日は{{漁/釣り}ができない/*釣れない}。
*Taifuu ga chikazuite iru kara, kyoo wa {{ryoo/tsuri} ga dekinai/*tsure-nai}.*

fisherman n. **[a man who catches fish for sport or business]**
ryo˥oshi 漁師 •c [a man who catches fish for a living]

EX. Can you imagine a fisherman who can't swim?
泳げない漁師なんて信じられないでしょう?
Oyoge-nai ryooshi nante shinji-rarenai deshoo?

fishing n. **[an act of trying to catch fish]**
tsu˥ri 釣り

EX. They went fishing and caught a few rainbow trout.
彼らは釣りに行って、にじますを数匹釣ってきた。
Kare-ra wa tsuri ni itte, nijimasu o suu-hiki tsutte-kita.

fit vi. **[for s.t. to be right in size and shape for s.t./s.o.]**
1. {⟨-to⟩/⟨-ni⟩} a˥u {⟨〜と⟩/⟨〜に⟩}あう ① [for two people/objects to come close to each other or to fit each other] ⟪suit⟫
㊈ "meet"▷会う, otherwise ▷合う

NOTE: The particle *to* is used when the relationship or action is seen to be mutual, and the particle *ni* is used when the relationship or action is seen as being directed by one of the entities toward the other rather than being mutual.

EX. (a) I don't think this skirt fits me.
このスカートは私には合わないと思う。
Kono sukaato wa watashi ni wa awanai to omou.
(b) Does this sheet fit a double bed?
このシーツはダブルベッドに合いますか。
Kono shiitsu wa daburu-beddo ni aimasu ka.
(c) The punishment doesn't always fit the crime.
刑罰が犯罪に合わない場合もある。
Keibatsu ga hanzai ni awanai baai mo aru.
(d) The shoes fit me perfectly.
靴は私にぴったり合った。
Kutsu wa watashi ni pittari atta.

2. ⟨-ni⟩ ha˥maru ⟨〜に⟩はまる ① [for s.t. to go into a space tightly and neatly as it is the right size and shape] ⟪fall into, get into⟫

EX. This sliding door doesn't fit well.
このふすまがはまらないんです。
Kono fusuma ga hamaranai n desu.

3. ⟨-ni⟩ ha˥iru ⟨〜に⟩入る ① [to go into some place ⟪fig. "join"⟫] ⟪enter, get in⟫

EX. All my clothes fit into one suitcase.
私の着る物は全部一つのスーツケースに入りました。
Watashi no kiru mono wa zenbu hitotsu no suutsukeesu ni hairimashita.

—— vt. **[to be suitable for s.t./s.o. or to put s.t. into s.t. else]**
1. ⟨-o⟩ tsu˥ke˥ru ⟨〜を⟩付ける ② [for s.o./s.a. to cause s.t./s.o. to adhere to s.t./s.o./s.a. else] ⟪fix, install, put on, mark, spread⟫

EX. Casters can be fitted to this suitcase to make it easier to carry.
このスーツケースは持ち運びを簡単にするためにキャスターが付けられます。
Kono suutsukeesu wa mochi-hakobi o

F

kantanni suru tame ni kyasutaa ga tsuke-raremasu.

2. 〈-o〉 〈-ni〉 i⌈reru 〈～を〉〈～に〉入れる ② [for s.o./s.a. to cause s.t./s.o./s.a. to move into an enclosed space] 《insert, pour, let in, include》

EX. He fitted the photo into the new frame.
彼は写真を新しい額に入れた。
Kare wa shashin o atarashii gaku ni ireta.

3. 〈-ni〉 te⌈ki-su⌉ru 〈～に〉適する ③ [to be suitable for s.t.]

EX. He fits this job well.
彼はこの仕事に適している。
Kare wa kono shigoto ni teki-shite iru.

— adj. **[right and suitable for s.o./s.t./s.a. or physically healthy and strong]**

1. {〈-ni〉/〈-o〉} mu⌈ku {〈～に〉/〈～を〉}向く ① [to turn one's face/front in the stated direction or to be right and suitable for s.o./s.t./s.a.]

EX. (**a**) With her patient character and love for children, she is fit for a career as a teacher.
彼女は辛抱強いし、子供が好きだし、教師の仕事に向いている。
Kanojo wa shinboo-zuyoi shi, kodomo ga suki da shi, kyooshi no shigoto ni muite iru.
(**b**) This dish isn't really fit for children; it's too spicy.
この料理は子供には向かない。香辛料が効きすぎている。
Kono ryoori wa kodomo ni wa mukanai. Kooshin-ryoo ga kiki-sugite iru.

2. ge⌉nkina 元気な adj(*na*). **•c [for s.o./s.a. to be in good health or to have lots of energy] 《fine》**

EX. He swims two kilometers every day; that's why he's so fit.
彼は毎日二キロ泳ぎます。だから元気なんです。
Kare wa mai-nichi ni-kiro oyogimasu. Dakara genkina n desu.

— n. **[a sudden attack of illness/violent seizure]**

ho⌈ssa 発作 •c [a sudden attack of illness] 《attack》

EX. She had an asthmatic fit last night.
彼女はゆうべぜんそくの発作をおこした。
Kanojo wa yuube zensoku no hossa o okoshita.

five n./adj.

i⌈tsu⌉tsu (no N) 五つ(のN), go⌉ (+counter) (no N) 五(+counter)(のN) •c SEE APPENDIX II

NOTE: *Go* is used by itself to express an abstract numeral, as in arithmetic. When used to count concrete things, however, it is used with an appropriate counter. *Itsutsu* cannot be used with a counter, as is the case with all native Japanese (non-Chinese) words for numbers.

EX. (**a**) It's now five o'clock.
今、五時です。
Ima, go-ji desu.
(**b**) My daughter Michiko is five years old.
娘の美智子は{五つ/五歳}です。
Musume no Michiko wa {itsutsu/go-sai} desu.
(**c**) We have five children.
子供が{五人/*五つ}います。
*Kodomo ga {go-nin/*itsutsu} imasu.*

fix vt. **[for s.o. to fasten s.t. onto s.t./s.o. 《fig. "repair," "decide"》]**

1. 〈-ni〉 〈-o〉 to⌈ri-tsukeru 〈～に〉〈～を〉取り付ける ② [for s.o. to set an apparatus into position onto s.t.] 《install, set up》

EX. I had a shelf fixed to the wall of my office.
オフィスの壁に棚を取り付けてもらった。
Ofisu no kabe ni tana o tori-tsukete moratta.

2. 〈-o〉 ki⌈meru 〈～を〉決める ② [for s.o. to make a judgment as to which of a number of alternatives is best in a given situation and resolve to act accordingly] 《determine, settle, set, arrange》

EX. Whose responsibility is it to fix the date of the final exam?
期末試験の日にちを決めるのはだれの仕事ですか。
Kimatsu-shiken no hinichi o kimeru no wa dare no shigoto desu ka.

F

3. ki⌈maru 決まる ① [for s.t. to be decided] ⟪be determined, be settled, be set, be arranged⟫

EX. The wedding is fixed for October 10th.
結婚式は十月十日に決まっています。
Kekkon-shiki wa juu-gatsu tooka ni kimatte imasu.

4. ⟨-o⟩ na⌈o⌉su ⟨〜を⟩なおす ① [for s.o. to restore s.t. damaged to its normal state of functioning ⟪fig. "cure"⟫] ⟪repair, mend⟫
㊥ "fix/correct"▷直す, "cure"▷治す

EX. Would you please fix my word processor?
私のワープロを直してくれませんか。
Watashi no waapuro o naoshite kuremasen ka.

5. ⟨-o⟩ tsu⌈ku⌉ru ⟨〜を⟩つくる ① [for s.o./s.a. to cause s.t./s.o./s.a. to come into existence which did not exist previously] ⟪create, manufacture, build, compose, cast, form, organize⟫
㊥ "build/manufacture"▷造る, otherwise ▷作る

EX. I'll fix the salad.
私がサラダを作ります。
Watashi ga sarada o tsukurimasu.

flag n. **[a piece of cloth used as a sign/signal/symbol of s.t., usu. having a pattern or design on it]**
ha⌈ta⌉ 旗 [a piece of cloth used as a sign/signal/symbol of s.t., usu. having a pattern or design on it], ko⌈kki 国旗 •c [a piece of cloth with a pattern or design on it used as a symbol of a country]

EX. (**a**) The children waved flags and cheered on the Japanese team.
子供たちは{旗/国旗}を振って、日本チームを応援した。
Kodomo-tachi wa {hata/kokki} o futte, Nihon-chiimu o ooen-shita.
(**b**) The national flag was hoisted at the opening ceremony.
開会式で{国旗/*旗}が掲揚された。
*Kaikai-shiki de {kokki/*hata} ga keiyoo-sareta.*

flame n. **[the red or yellow glowing gas that is emitted from something burning ⟪fig. "strong feeling"⟫]**
ho⌉noo 炎

EX. (**a**) My house was in flames.
私の家は炎に包まれていた。
Watashi no uchi wa honoo ni tsutsuma-rete ita.
(**b**) He lit a flame of passion in her soul.
彼は彼女の心の中に情熱の炎を燃え上がらせた。
Kare wa kanojo no kokoro no naka ni joonetsu no honoo o moe-agara-seta.
(**c**) Within seconds the temple went up in flames.
瞬く間に寺は炎に包まれて焼け落ちた。
Matataku ma ni tera wa honoo ni tsutsuma-rete yake-ochita.

flap vi./vt. **[for s.t. to move up and down or from side to side or for s.o./s.a. to cause s.t. to so move]**
ha⌈ta-me⌉ku はためく ① ⟪flutter, wave⟫

EX. The sails were flapping in the wind.
帆が風にはためいていた。
Ho ga kaze ni hata-meite ita.

flash vi. **[to give out a sudden bright light]**
pi⌈ka⌉tto hikaru ぴかっと光る ①

EX. The lightning flashed across the sky.
空に稲妻がぴかっと光った。
Sora ni inazuma ga pikatto hikatta.

NOTE: When the duration of light is a little longer, *pika-pikatto* can be used.

—— vt. **[to cause s.t. (repeatedly) to emit a sudden bright light or cause s.t. to be lit up by such light]**
⟨-o⟩ te⌈nmetsu-saseru ⟨〜を⟩点滅させる /⟨causative of *tenmetsu-suru* ③ blink/ ② •c [for s.o. to make a light shine on and off]

EX. The police were flashing a red signal to stop cars at the intersection where the accident had occurred.
事故が起きた交差点で警察は車を止めるために赤信号を点滅させていた。
Jiko ga okita koosa-ten de keisatsu wa kuruma o tomeru tame ni aka-shingoo o tenmetsu-sasete ita.

flask n. **[a glass bottle with a narrow neck commonly used in laboratories]**

F

fu⌈rasuko フラスコ •f

flat[1] adj. **[level and horizontal]**

1. ta⌈irana 平らな adj(*na*). **[for a surface to be free from obstructions]** ⟪level, smooth, even⟫

EX.| (**a**) People used to think that the earth was flat.
人は以前地球は平らであると思っていた。
Hito wa izen chikyuu wa taira de aru to omotte ita.
(**b**) Do you have a saucepan with a flat bottom?
底が平らな鍋がありますか。
Soko ga tairana nabe ga arimasu ka.

2. he⌈itanna 平たんな adj(*na*). **•c [for a land surface to have no raised/hollow parts]**

EX.| The road across the desert was flat and stretched on endlessly
砂漠を横切る道は平たんでえんえんと続いた。
Sabaku o yoko-giru michi wa heitande en-en to tsuzuita.

PHRASE: be flat on one's back *aomuke ni naru* 仰向けになる ①

EX.| He was lying flat on his back in bed.
彼はベッドに仰向けに横たわっていた。
Kare wa beddo ni aomuke ni yoko-tawatte ita.

PHRASE: be flat on one's face *utsu-buse ni naru* うつ伏せになる ①

EX.| She was lying on the floor flat on her face.
彼女は床にうつ伏せに倒れていた。
Kanojo wa yuka ni utsu-buse ni taorete ita.

PHRASE: have a flat tire *taiya ga panku-suru* タイヤがパンクする ③

flat[2] (Br. E) n. **[a set of rooms in a building for living in]**

a⌈pa⌉ato アパート **•f [a rented room/set of rooms in a building containing rooms for the purpose of being rented out or such a building itself]** ⟪apartment, apartment house⟫, **ma⌉nshon** マンション **•f** ⟪condominium⟫

EX.| I live in a flat in Shinjuku.
新宿の{アパート/マンション}に住んでいる。
Shinjuku no {apaato/manshon} ni sunde iru.

NOTE: A *Manshon* is a better built or more expensive flat than an *apaato.*

flatter vt. **[for s.o. to praise s.o./s.t./s.a. insincerely]**

⟨-ni⟩ o-⌈seji o iu ⟨～に⟩お世辞を言う ① **[for s.o. to try to please s.o. by praising s.o./s.t./s.a. insincerely]**

EX.| (**a**) He's always flattering people, so it's hard to tell when he really means what he says.
彼はいつも人にお世辞を言っているから本気で言っている時とそうでない時の区別が付かない。
Kare wa itsu-mo hito ni o-seji o itte iru kara honki de itte iru toki to soo denai toki no kubetsu ga tsukanai.
(**b**) He flattered her with his compliment on her new dress.
彼は彼女の新しいドレスについてお世辞を言った。
Kare wa kanojo no atarashii doresu ni tsuite o-seji o itta.

PHRASE: be flattered *ureshii* 嬉しい

EX.| I was flattered that Professor Hattori remembered my name.
服部先生が名前を覚えていてくださったのが嬉しかった。
Hattori sensei ga namae o oboete ite kudasatta no ga ureshikatta.

flavor n. **[the distinctive taste that a particular food/drink has ⟪fig. "special quality or characteristic of s.t."⟫]**

1. a⌈ji 味 **[the sensation created by a particular food/drink when put in the mouth]** ⟪savor, taste⟫, **fu⌉umi** 風味 **•c [the distinctive taste and smell of a particular food/drink]** ⟪savor, relish, tang, bouquet⟫

EX.| This tea has a unique flavor.
このお茶は独特の{風味がある/味がする}。
Kono o-cha wa dokutoku no {fuumi ga aru/aji ga suru}.

2. o⌈momuki⌉ 趣 **[a special, attractive**

quality of s.t.] ((taste, elegance, effect, tone, charm, touch))

EX. This theater has that unique flavor of old Japanese architecture.
この劇場は古い日本建築の趣がある。
Kono gekijoo wa furui Nihon-kenchiku no omomuki ga aru.

flee vi./vt. **[for s.o./s.a. to run away from s.t./s.o./some place]**
⟨-kara⟩ ni⌈ge⌉ru ⟨〜から⟩逃げる ② **((run away, escape))**

EX. (**a**) He murdered his wife and fled town.
彼は妻を殺して、町から逃げた。
Kare wa tsuma o koroshite, machi kara nigeta.
(**b**) She tried to flee from her husband with her two children.
彼女は二人の子供を連れて夫から逃げようとした。
Kanojo wa futari no kodomo o tsurete otto kara nigeyoo to shita.

flesh n. **[the soft substance, especially muscle, between the skin and bones in an animal body]**
ni⌈ku⌉ 肉 •c **[the soft part lying under the skin and covering the bones in an animal/human body], ji⌈nniku** 人肉 •c **[the soft substance, especially muscle, between the skin and bones in a human body], ju⌈uniku** 獣肉 •c **[the soft substance, especially muscle, between the skin and bones of four-footed animals]**

EX. Lions are flesh-eating animals.
ライオンは肉食動物だ。
Raion wa nikushoku-doobutsu da.

PHRASE: one's flesh and blood *nikushin* 肉親 •c, flesh of a fruit *kaniku* 果肉 •c

flexible adj. **[for s.t. to be easily bent without breaking ((fig. "for s.o./s.t. to adapt easily to suit new conditions"))]**
ju⌈unanna 柔軟な adj(*na*). •c **[soft and pliable ((fig. "adaptive"))] ((pliable, supple)), yu⌈uzuu ga kiku** (N) 融通が利く(N) **[capable of dealing with each new situation on its own terms] ((elastic, adaptable))** ↔ **yuuzuu ga kikanai** 融通が利かない; **da⌈nryoku-sei ga a⌉ru** (N) 弾力性がある(N) **((elastic))** ↔ **koochoku-shita N** 硬直したN **/⟨Vinf. past of *koochoku-suru* ③ stiffen/ •c**

EX. (**a**) We are hoping for a more flexible policy from the new administration.
我々は新政権に対してより{柔軟な/弾力性のある/?融通が利く}政策を望んでいる。
Ware-ware wa shin-seiken ni-taishite yori {juunanna/danryoku-sei no aru/?yuuzuu ga kiku} seisaku o nozonde iru.
(**b**) Government officials are usually not very flexible.
役人は大抵あまり{融通が利かない/*弾力性がない/*柔軟じゃない}。
*Yakunin wa taitei amari {yuuzuu ga kikanai/*danryoku-sei ga nai/*juunan janai}.*

flight n. **[a journey made by flying]**
hi⌈ko⌉o-ki 飛行機 •c **[an airplane or a journey by an airplane]**

EX. I'm leaving for New York on the 10:00 A.M. flight.
午前十時の飛行機でニューヨークへ発ちます。
Gozen juu-ji no hikoo-ki de Nyuuyooku e tachimasu.

PHRASE: Flight 21 *ni-juu-ichi-bin* 二十一便 •c, non-stop flight *chokkoo-bin* 直行便 •c

fling vt. **[for s.o. to throw s.t. violently]**
1. ⟨-ni⟩ ⟨-o⟩ ra⌈nbooni na⌈ge-tsukeru, ⟨〜に⟩⟨〜を⟩乱暴に投げつける ② **[for s.o. to throw s.t. at s.o./s.t./s.a. violently] ((throw at, hurl at))**

EX. He flung the ball at me.
彼は私にボールを乱暴に投げつけた。
Kare wa watashi ni booru o ranbooni nage-tsuketa.

2. ⟨-ni⟩ ⟨-o⟩ ra⌈nbooni na⌈ge-komu ⟨〜に⟩⟨〜を⟩乱暴に投げ込む ① **[for s.o. to throw s.t. violently/carelessly into a place]**

EX. He flung the book into his bag after he had finished reading it.
彼は本を読み終わると、かばんの中に乱暴に投げ込んだ。
Kare wa hon o yomi-owaru to, kaban

F

no naka ni ranbooni nage-konda.

3. ⟨-o⟩ na⌈ge-da⌉su ⟨〜を⟩投げ出す ① [for s.o. to present s.t. as if throwing it]

EX. (**a**) He flung himself down at Mary's feet.
彼はメアリーの足下に身を投げ出した。
Kare wa Mearii no ashi-moto ni mi o nage-dashita.
(**b**) I flung my bag on the sofa and rushed into the bathroom.
私はかばんをソファーの上に投げ出して、トイレに駆け込んだ。
Watashi wa kaban o sofaa no ue ni nage-dashite, toire ni kake-konda.

float vi. **[to be held up in air/gas/liquid or on the surface of a liquid by the force of buoyancy]**

1. u⌈ku 浮く ① [to be held up in air/gas/liquid or on the surface of a liquid by the force of buoyancy 《fig. "be isolated/separated from"》] 《come to the surface, be buoyed up》, u⌈kabu 浮かぶ ① [for s.t. to be suspended in air, gas, or on the surface of a liquid by the force of buoyancy so that its outline is visible to an observer 《fig. "come across one's mind," "rise in the world"》] 《keep afloat, come up to the surface》

EX. (**a**) What's that floating on the water?
あの水に{浮いて/浮かんで}いるのは何ですか。
Ano mizu ni {uite/ukande} iru no wa nan desu ka.
(**b**) Wood floats on water.
木は水に{浮く/?浮かぶ}。
Ki wa mizu ni {uku/?ukabu}.
(**c**) White clouds were floating in the sky.
空には白い雲が{浮かんで/?浮いて}いた。
Sora ni wa shiroi kumo ga {ukande/?uite} ita.

2. na⌈gare⌉ru 流れる ② [for liquid, electricity, etc., to move steadily and continuously in a stream or stream-like fashion] 《flow, stream》

EX. (**a**) A big peach came floating down the stream.
大きい桃が川を流れてきました。
Ookii momo ga kawa o nagarete kimashita.
(**b**) The boat floated slowly down the middle of the river.
ボートは川の真ん中をゆっくり流れていった。
Booto wa kawa no mannaka o yukkuri nagarete itta.

—— vt. **[for s.o. to cause s.t. to float]**

1. ⟨⟨-ni⟩⟩ ⟨-o⟩ na⌈ga⌉su ⟨⟨〜に⟩⟩⟨〜を⟩流す ① [for s.o. to let liquid flow into some place or to cause s.t. to be carried away by water 《fig. "broadcast"》] 《set afloat》

EX. We made a raft out of logs and floated it down the river.
材木でいかだを作り、川に流しました。
Zaimoku de ikada o tsukuri, kawa ni nagashimashita.

2. ⟨-o⟩ u⌈kaberu ⟨〜を⟩浮かべる ② [for s.o. to cause s.t. to float/surface]

EX. The boy floated a toy duck in the bathtub.
男の子はおもちゃのあひるを浴槽の湯に浮かべた。
Otoko-no-ko wa omocha no ahiru o yokusoo no yu ni ukabeta.

flock n. **[a group of birds and animals of one kind either kept together or feeding and traveling together 《fig. "a large number of people"》]**

mu⌈re⌉ 群れ [a group of people/animals/fish/whales/birds/worms/clouds] 《school, drove, crowd, swarm》

EX. I saw a flock of seagulls from the ship and knew we were near land.
船からかもめの群れが見えたので陸に近づいていることが分かった。
Fune kara kamome no mure ga mieta node riku ni chikazuite iru koto ga wakatta.

flood n. **[a great quantity of water in a place that is usually dry 《fig. "a great quantity of things"》]**

ko⌈ozui 洪水 •c, o⌈omi⌉zu 大水 [a great quantity of water in a place that is usually dry]

EX. Three houses were carried away by the flood.

家が三軒{洪水/大水}で流された。
Ie ga san-gen {koozui/oomizu} de nagasa-reta.

— vt./vi. **[to cover or fill a space with a great quantity of water《fig. "cover or fill with a great number of things"》]**

1. mi⌈zu-bi⌉tashi ni naru 水浸しになる ① [for a place to be covered or filled with a great quantity of water]

EX. Our dishwasher broke and flooded the kitchen.
皿洗い機がこわれて、台所が水浸しになった。
Sara-arai-ki ga kowarete, daidokoro ga mizu-bitashi ni natta.

2. ha⌈nran-suru 氾濫する ③ •c [for a river to overflow《fig. "for a large number of things to spread out over a large area"》]

EX. (**a**) The river flooded the village.
川が氾濫して、村が水浸しになった。
Kawa ga hanran-shite, mura ga mizu-bitashi ni natta.
(**b**) Our cities are being flooded with pornographic literature.
我々の町にはエロ本が氾濫している。
Ware-ware no machi ni wa ero-hon ga hanran-shite iru.

3. sa⌈ttoo-suru 殺到する ③ •c [to come in great quantities/numbers]《rush in, deluge》

EX. Applications flooded in in response to the job advertisement.
求人広告を見て申し込みが殺到した。
Kyuujin-kookoku o mite mooshi-komi ga sattoo-shita.

floor n. **[the lower surface of a room on which one stands and walks《fig. "particular level of a building"》]**

1. yu⌈ka 床

EX. (**a**) The flood water came up to the bedroom floor.
洪水の水が寝室の床まで来た。
Koozui no mizu ga shinshitsu no yuka made kita.
(**b**) Would you sweep the floor, please?
すいませんが、床を掃いてくださいませんか。
Suimasen ga, yuka o haite kudasaimasen ka.

2. ka⌉i 階 •c [different levels/a particular level of a building]《story》

EX. (**a**) My apartment is on the fifth floor.
私のアパートは五階にあります。
Watashi no apaato wa go-kai ni arimasu.
(**b**) Reference books are sold on the next floor up.
参考書はこの上の階で売っています。
Sankoo-sho wa kono ue no kai de utte imasu.

PHRASE: first floor *ik-kai* 一階 •c, second floor *ni-kai* 二階 •c, third floor *san-gai* 三階 •c, which floor *nan-gai* 何階 •c

Florida n.

Fu⌈rorida フロリダ •f

florist n. **[a person/shop that sells flowers and indoor plants]**

ha⌈na⌉-ya 花屋《flower shop, florist's》

EX. I bought a dozen roses at a florist's near my apartment.
僕はアパートの近くの花屋でバラを十二本買った。
Boku wa apaato no chikaku no hana-ya de bara o juu-ni-hon katta.

flour n. **[fine powder made by grinding grain and used for making bread, cakes, pastry, etc.]**

ko⌈na⌉ 粉《powder》

EX. How much flour do we need to make *tenpura*?
てんぷらを作るのに粉がどのくらい要りますか。
Tenpura o tsukuru no ni kona ga dono-kurai irimasu ka.

PHRASE: wheat flour *komugi-ko* 小麦粉, *meriken-ko* メリケン粉, buckwheat flour *soba-ko* そば粉

flourish vi. **[to continue to exist/function and to be successful/active/widespread or to grow in a healthy manner]**

ha⌉njoo-suru 繁盛する ③ •c [for business to go very well]《prosper, thrive》, u⌉maku i⌈ku うまくいく ①, sa⌈kae⌉ru 栄える ② [for a

family/nation to be successful], ha⌈n'ei-suru 繁栄する ③ •c

EX. (**a**) His business is flourishing.
彼の商売は{繁盛して/うまくいって/*栄えて/*繁栄して}いる。
*Kare no shoobai wa {hanjoo-shite/ umaku itte/*sakaete/*han'ei-shite} iru.*
(**b**) England flourished in the eighteenth century.
イギリスは十八世紀に{繁栄した/栄えた/*繁盛した/*うまくいった}。
*Igirisu wa juu-has-seiki ni {han'ei-shita/ sakaeta/*hanjoo-shita/*umaku itta}.*
(**c**) Parliamentary democracy cannot possibly flourish under such circumstances.
このような状態で議会制民主主義が{うまくいく/*繁栄する/*栄える/*繁盛する}はずがない。
*Kono yoona jootai de gikai-sei-minshu-shugi ga {umaku iku/*han'ei-suru/ *sakaeru/*hanjoo-suru} hazu ga nai.*

flourishing adj. **[for nations, religions, etc., to be very active, successful, or widespread] sa⌈kanna 盛んな** adj(*na*). **[for some activity to be popular/widespread]** ((**booming, thriving**))

EX. The automobile industry was flourishing here until ten years ago.
十年前までここでは自動車工業が盛んだった。
Juu-nen-mae made koko de wa jidoosha-koogyoo ga sakan datta.

flow vi. **[for liquid, electricity, etc. to move steadily and continuously (as if) in a stream]**
na⌈gare⌉ru 流れる ② [for liquid, electricity, etc., to move steadily and continuously in a stream or stream-like fashion] ((**run, drift**)), **na⌈gare-ko⌉mu 流れ込む ① [for liquid to move steadily and continuously into a place], na⌈gare-ochi⌉ru 流れ落ちる ② [for liquid to move downward steadily and continuously]**

EX. (**a**) Tears flowed from his eyes.
彼の目から涙が{流れた/流れ落ちた/*流れ込んだ}。
*Kare no me kara namida ga {nagareta/ nagare-ochita/*nagare-konda}.*
(**b**) This river flows into the Inland Sea of Seto around Okayama.
この川は岡山辺りで瀬戸内海に{流れ込む/*流れる/*流れ落ちる}。
*Kono kawa wa Okayama-atari de Seto-naikai ni {nagare-komu/*nagareru/ *nagare-ochiru}.*
(**c**) Traffic was flowing in a steady stream.
車は順調に{流れて/*流れ込んで/*流れ落ちて}いました。
*Kuruma wa junchoo ni {nagarete/ *nagare-konde/*nagare-ochite} imashita.*

PHRASE: let…flow ⟨*-o*⟩ *nagasu* ⟨〜を⟩流す ① ((drain, shed))

—— n. **[a steady continuous movement] na⌈gare⌉ 流れ ((stream, current))**

EX. The flow of traffic is always slow around here.
この辺はいつも車の流れが悪い。
Kono hen wa itsu-mo kuruma no nagare ga warui.

flower n. **[the part of a plant that produces seeds]**
ha⌈na⌉ 花 ((blossom))

EX. (**a**) He gave me flowers on my birthday.
彼は私の誕生日に花をくれました。
Kare wa watashi no tanjoo-hi ni hana o kuremashita.
(**b**) There are always flowers in bloom in his garden.
彼の庭にはいつも何か花が咲いている。
Kare no niwa ni wa itsu-mo nani-ka hana ga saite iru.

PHRASE: flower arrangement *ike-bana* 生け花

fluid n. **[a liquid]**
e⌈kitai 液体 •c

EX. If you heat this fluid, it turns to gas.
この液体を熱すると、気体になる。
Kono ekitai o nessuru to, kitai ni naru.

flush vi. **[for s.o. to become red in the face because of a rush of blood to the skin] (ka⌈o ga) a⌈kaku na⌉ru (顔が)赤くなる**

F

/⟨adj(*i*). *ku* of *akai* red + *naru* ① become/ ① **[(for one's face) to become red], (ka⌈o ga) ma⌈kka⌉ ni naru** (顔が)真っ赤になる /⟨adj(*na*). *ni* of *makkana* scarlet + *naru* ① become/ ① **[(for one's face) to become scarlet], ⟨-o⟩ a⌈karame⌉ru** ⟨〜を⟩赤らめる ② **[for s.o. to become red in the face because of embarrassment/alcoholic drink]** ((**blush**))

EX. (**a**) My face flushed with embarrassment when my stomach rumbled in class.
授業中におなかがなったときは恥ずかしくて{顔が{赤く/真っ赤に}なった/??顔を赤らめた}。
Jugyoo-chuu ni o-naka ga natta toki wa hazukashikute {kao ga {akaku/makka ni} natta/??kao o akarameta}.
(**b**) The girl's cheeks flushed red when I spoke to her.
私が話し掛けると、その女の子は{頰を赤らめた/?頰が{赤く/真っ赤に}なった}。
Watashi ga hanashi-kakeru to, sono onna-no-ko wa {hoo o akarameta/?hoo ga makka ni} natta}.

— vt. **[to clean or drive out s.t. with a sudden rush of water]**
⟨-ni⟩ ⟨-o⟩ na⌈ga⌉su ⟨〜に⟩⟨〜を⟩流す ① **[for s.o. to let liquid flow into some place or to cause s.t. to be carried away by water ⟪fig. "cause a rumor, information, music, etc. to become widespread"⟫]**

EX. (**a**) I tried to flush the toilet, but it wouldn't flush.
トイレに水を流そうとしたんですが、流れないんです。
Toire ni mizu o nagasoo to shita n desu ga, nagarenai n desu.
(**b**) He flushed the medicine down the toilet.
彼は薬をトイレに流した。
Kare wa kusuri o toire ni nagashita.
(**c**) Try flushing the drainpipe in the sink with hot water.
流しの排水管に熱いお湯を流してみてください。
Nagashi no haisui-kan ni atsui o-yu o nagashite mite kudasai.

PHRASE: flush toilet *suisen-benjo* 水洗便所 •c

fly vi. **[to move through the air as a bird does]**
to⌈bu とぶ ① **[for s.o./s.a. to move quickly and suddenly away from a surface by the action of one's leg(s) or to move through the air], hi⌈ko⌉o-ki ni no⌈ru** 飛行機に乗る ① **[for s.o./s.a. to ride an aircraft],** {⟨-e⟩/⟨-ni⟩} **hi⌈ko⌉o-ki de i⌈ku** {⟨〜へ⟩/⟨〜に⟩}飛行機で行く ① **[to go to some place by airplane]**
㊈ "move through the air"▷飛ぶ, "jump through the air"▷跳ぶ

EX. (**a**) I saw a flock of swallows flying over the ocean.
つばめの群れが海の上を飛んでいるのを見ました。
Tsubame no mure ga umi no ue o tonde iru no o mimashita.
(**b**) My mother has never flown in an airplane.
母はまだ飛行機に乗ったことがありません。
Haha wa mada hikoo-ki ni notta koto ga arimasen.
(**c**) I'm going to fly to Hokkaido.
私は飛行機で北海道へ行きます。
Watashi wa hikoo-ki de Hokkaidoo e ikimasu.

— vt. **[for s.o. to control an aircraft or similar vehicle and direct its course]**
⟨-o⟩ so⌈ojuu-suru ⟨〜を⟩操縦する ③ •c **[for s.o. to operate a machine, esp. an airplane ⟪fig. "control"⟫]** ((**control, handle, maneuver, operate**))

EX. Is it difficult to fly a helicopter?
ヘリコプターを操縦するのは難しいですか。
Herikoputaa o soojuu-suru no wa muzukashii desu ka.

— n. **[a small flying insect with two wings]**
ha⌈e はえ

EX. Flies are all over the meat.
肉にはえがたかっていますよ。
Niku ni hae ga takatte imasu yo.

foam n. **[a white mass of small bubbles formed in/on a liquid]**
a⌈wa⌉ 泡 ((**bubble, froth**))

F

EX. He wiped the beer foam off his upper lip with his hand.
彼は手で上唇についたビールの泡をぬぐった。
Kare wa te de uwa-kuchibiru ni tsuita biiru no awa o nugutta.

focus n. **[the point at which rays of light/heat/sound waves meet after passing through a lens or being reflected《fig. "a center of attention/interest, etc."》]**
sho˥oten 焦点 •c [the point at which rays of light meet《fig. "a center of discussion/trouble, etc."》], ma˥to 的 [an object which is aimed at in shooting practice or in a military/verbal attack《fig. "a center of attention/envy, etc."》]《target, mark, object》, pi˥nto ピント •f [the point at which the image of an object is visible in sharpest outline through a lens, on a camera plate, etc.]

EX. (**a**) Our general election is now the focus of world attention.
我が国の総選挙は今、世界の注目の{的/*焦点/*ピント}である。
*Waga-kuni no soo-senkyo wa ima, sekai no chuumoku no {mato/*shooten/*pinto} dearu.*
(**b**) This photo is out of focus.
この写真は{ピント/*焦点/*的}が合っていない。
*Kono shashin wa {pinto/*shooten/*mato} ga atte inai.*
(**c**) What's the focus of the trouble between the two nations?
その二国間の紛争の{焦点/*的/*ピント}は何ですか。
*Sono ni-koku-kan no funsoo no {shooten/*mato/*pinto} wa nan desu ka.*

fog n. **[tiny drops of water suspended in the air at/near the earth's surface and difficult to see through]**
ki˥ri 霧 [very minute waterdrops floating near the surface of the earth]《mist》

EX. (**a**) We often get fog on the lake during autumn.
秋には湖によく霧がかかる。
Aki ni wa mizuumi ni yoku kiri ga kakaru.
(**b**) It's difficult to drive in fog.
霧の中を運転するのは難しい。
Kiri no naka o unten-suru no wa muzukashii.
(**c**) When will the fog clear up?
霧はいつ晴れるでしょうか。
Kiri wa itsu hareru deshoo ka.

PHRASE: dense fog *noomu* 濃霧 •c

foggy adj. **[full of fog]**
ki˥ri ga fu˥ka˥i 霧が深い adj(*i*). **[enveloped in thick fog], ki˥ri ga kakatta N 霧がかかったN /〈*kiri* fog + prt. *ga* + Vinf. past of *kakaru* ① envelope/ [enveloped in fog]**

EX. (**a**) It's best not to go out on a foggy evening like this.
こんなに霧が{深い/かかった}夜は出かけない方がいい。
Konnani kiri ga {fukai/kakatta} yoru wa dekakenai hoo ga ii.
(**b**) Tomorrow will be cold, cloudy and foggy.
明日は曇りで、寒く、霧が{かかる/深い}でしょう。
Ashita wa kumori de, samuku, kiri ga {kakaru/fukai} deshoo.

foil n. **[metal formed into a thin and flexible sheet]**
ho˥iru ホイル •f

EX. Put the cakes in the fridge after wrapping them in foil.
ケーキをホイルで包んでから、冷蔵庫に入れなさい。
Keeki o hoiru de tsutsunde kara, reizoo-ko ni irenasai.

PHRASE: aluminum foil *arumi-hoiru* アルミホイル •f

fold vt. **[for s.o./s.a. to bend one part of s.t. and lay it on the remaining part or to make s.t. smaller by bending parts of it]**
〈-o〉 ta˥tamu 〈〜を〉畳む ① [for s.o. to bend one part of s.t. and lay it on the remaining part《fig. "make s.t. into a smaller shape by closing/bending parts of it"》], 〈-o〉(〈-ni〉) o˥ru 〈〜を〉(〈〜に〉)折る ① [for s.o. to render

F

a long solid object into two or more parts by bending/separating it] ⟪**break, bend**⟫, **⟨-o⟩ (⟨-ni⟩) o⌈ri-tatamu ⟨〜を⟩(⟨〜に⟩)折り畳む** ① **[for s.o. to make s.t. into a smaller shape by bending/closing parts of it]**

EX. (**a**) I folded my kimono and put it in my suitcase.
私は着物を{畳んで/?折り畳んで/*折って}、スーツケースに入れた。
*Watashi wa ki-mono o {tatande/?ori-tatande/*otte}, suutsukeesu ni ireta.*
(**b**) He folded a piece of paper into the figure of a crane.
彼は紙切れで鶴を{折った/*畳んだ/*折り畳んだ}。
*Kare wa kami-kire de tsuru o {otta/*tatanda/*ori-tatanda}.*
(**c**) They folded the tent neatly.
彼らはテントをきちんと{畳んだ/折り畳んだ/*折った}。
*Kare-ra wa tento o kichin-to {tatanda/ori-tatanda/*otta}.*
(**d**) She folded the letter in three and put it into an envelope.
彼女は手紙を三つに{折って/折り畳んで/*畳んで}封筒に入れた。
*Kanojo wa tegami o mittsu ni {otte/ori-tatande/*tatande} fuutoo ni ireta.*

PHRASE: fold one's arms *ude o kumu* 腕を組む ①, *ude-gumi o suru* 腕組みをする ③

—— vi. **[for s.t. to be able to be bent over on itself]**
o⌈ri-tatame-ru 折り畳める /⟨pot. of *ori-tatamu* ① fold/ ②

EX. Does this bed fold up?
このベッドは折り畳めますか。
Kono beddo wa ori-tatame-masu ka.

PHRASE: folding bed *ori-tatami no beddo* 折り畳みのベッド, folding chair *ori-tatami no isu* 折り畳みのいす

folk n. **[people in general or people who share a certain way of life]**
hi⌈to⌉-bito 人々 [a group of persons in the same area ⟨w⟩], hi⌈to⌉-tachi 人たち

NOTE: *Hito-bito* is a little more formal than *hito-tachi.*

EX. (**a**) They are all pleasant folk.
みんな、気のいい{人たち/人々}です。
Minna, ki no ii {hito-tachi/hito-bito} desu.
(**b**) That singer is very popular among young folk.
あの歌手は若い{人たち/人々}の間でとても人気がある。
Ano kashu wa wakai {hito-tachi/hito-bito} no aida de totemo ninki ga aru.
(**c**) Country folk in Japan seldom fail to exercise their right to vote.
日本の田舎の{人たち/人々}はめったに棄権しない。
Nihon no inaka no {hito-tachi/hito-bito} wa mettani kiken-shinai.

PHRASE: folk song *fooku-songu* フォークソング •f, folk dance *fooku-dansu* フォークダンス •f, Hi, folks! *Mina-san, konnichi-wa.* 皆さん、こんにちは。

follow vt. **[to move behind s.o./s.t./s.a. in the same direction or to come directly after s.t. or to go along a river, road, etc. ⟪fig. "accept and act according to advice, rules, orders, etc."⟫]**

1. ⟨-ni⟩ tsu⌉ite-iku ⟨〜に⟩ついて行く /⟨V*te* of *tsuku* ① attach + *iku* ① go/ ① **[to go along with s.o.]**

EX. You go first and I'll follow.
先に行ってください。後について行きますから。
Saki ni itte kudasai. Ato ni tsuite-ikimasu kara.

2. ⟨-ni⟩ tsu⌉ite-kuru ⟨〜に⟩ついて来る /⟨V*te* of *tsuku* ① attach + *kuru* ③ come/ [to come along with s.o.]

EX. A dog followed us home.
犬が一匹家までついて来た。
Inu ga ip-piki uchi made tsuite-kita.

3. ⟨-no⟩ tsu⌈gi⌉ da ⟨〜の⟩次だ [to be/come next to N]

EX. (**a**) Tuesday follows Monday.
火曜日は月曜日の次です。
Kayoo-bi wa getsuyoo-bi no tsugi desu.
(**b**) Answer the questions that follow.
次の質問に答えなさい。

| *Tsugi no shitsumon ni kotaenasai.*

4. 〈-ni〉 shi⌈tagau 〈～に〉従う ① [to accept and act according to advice, rules, orders, etc.] **((obey, conform to, observe, abide by))**

EX. (**a**) Why didn't you follow my advice?
どうして私のアドバイスに従わなかったんですか。
Dooshite watashi no adobaisu ni shitagawanakatta n desu ka.
(**b**) We still follow the old customs around here.
この辺ではまだ古い習慣に従っている。
Kono hen de wa mada furui shuukan ni shitagatte iru.

5. 〈-ni〉 so⌈tte iku 〈～に〉沿って行く /〈V *te* of *sou* ① go along + *iku* ① go/ ① [to move along a river, road, etc.]

NOTE: Verbs like *kuru* "come," *sanpo-suru* "take a walk," etc., can be used after *sotte* instead of *iku* "go," depending on the meaning.

EX. Follow this road till you get to the gate.
門の所まで、この道に沿って行ってください。
Mon no tokoro made, kono michi ni sotte itte kudasai.

6. 〈-ni〉 tsu⌈zuku 〈～に〉続く ① [to move behind s.o./s.t./s.a. in the same direction or to happen after s.t.]

EX. (**a**) I took the entrance exam for Tokyo University following my brother, who had taken it the year before.
前年に受けた兄に続いて、東京大学の入学試験を受けた。
Zennen ni uketa ani ni tsuzuite, Tookyoo-daigaku no nyuugaku-shiken o uketa.
(**b**) Many people were killed by the tsunami that followed the earthquake.
地震に続いて起こった津波でたくさんの人が死んだ。
Jishin ni tsuzuite okotta tsunami de takusan no hito ga shinda.

fond adj. **[for s.o./s.a. to like s.t./s.o./s.a. very much]**

〈-ga〉 da⌉i-sukina 〈～が〉大好きな adj(*na*). **[for s.o./s.a. to like s.o./s.a./s.t. very much] ((love))**

EX. (**a**) I'm very fond of window shopping.
私はウインドーショッピングが大好きです。
Watashi wa uindoo-shoppingu ga dai-suki desu.
(**b**) Tom was very fond of his old aunt.
トムは年取ったおばが大好きだった。
Tomu wa toshi-totta oba ga dai-suki datta.
(**c**) My grandfather is very fond of listening to music.
祖父は音楽を聞くのが大好きです。
Sofu wa ongaku o kiku no ga dai-suki desu.

food n. **[s.t. that can be taken into the body of an animal or plant to keep it alive and to help it grow]**

1. ta⌈be-mono⌉ 食べ物 [s.t. that can be eaten by people/animals to keep them alive and help them grow] ((foodstuffs)), sho⌈ku⌉ryoo 食糧 •c [s.t. that can be eaten by people/animals to keep them alive and help them grow 〈fml〉] ((foodstuffs, provisions))

EX. (**a**) There was little money left for food.
{食べ物/食糧}を買うお金がほとんど残っていなかった。
{Tabe-mono/Shokuryoo} o kau o-kane ga hotondo nokotte inakatta.
(**b**) The country suffers from a serious food shortage.
その国は深刻な{食糧/?食べ物}不足に悩んでいる。
Sono kuni wa shinkokuna {shokuryoo/?tabe-mono}-busoku ni nayande iru.
(**c**) We have lots of food, but not much to drink.
{食べ物/*食糧}はたくさんあるけど、飲み物があまりありません。
*{Tabe-mono/*Shokuryoo} wa takusan aru kedo, nomi-mono ga amari arimasen.*

2. e⌈sa⌉ えさ [food given to s.a. to catch/raise it] ((feed))

3. hi⌉ryoo 肥料 •c [material added to the soil as nutrients to help plants grow and

keep healthy] ⟪**fertilizer**⟫

EX. I bought a new kind of liquid plant food.
私は新しい種類の液体の肥料を買った。
Watashi wa atarashii shurui no ekitai no hiryoo o katta.

PHRASE: frozen foods *reitoo-shokuhin* 冷凍食品 •**c**, food poisoning *shoku-chuudoku* 食中毒 •**c**, baby foods *bebii-fuudo* ベビーフード •**f**, pet food *petto-fuudo* ペットフード •**f**, Japanese style food *washoku* 和食 •**c**, Western style food *yooshoku* 洋食 •**c**

fool n. **[a person of weak judgment or without good sense]**
ba⌉ka ばか •**c**

EX. (**a**) That fool of a secretary has forgotten to book the flight.
あの秘書のばかが飛行機の予約をするのを忘れたんです。
Ano hisho no baka ga hikoo-ki no yoyaku o suru no o wasureta n desu.
(**b**) I was a fool. I should have told her the truth then.
私はばかでした。あの時彼女に本当のことを言えば良かったんです。
Watashi wa baka deshita. Ano toki kanojo ni hontoo no koto o ieba yokatta n desu.
(**c**) There's no cure for a fool.
ばかにつける薬はない。
Baka ni tsukeru kusuri wa nai.

PHRASE: make a fool of s.o. ⟨*-o*⟩ *baka ni suru* ⟨〜を⟩ばかにする ③

EX. He made a fool of me in front of my guests.
彼は客の前で私をばかにした。
Kare wa kyaku no mae de watashi o baka ni shita.

PHRASE: April fool *shi-gatsu-baka* 四月ばか •**c**

F

foolish adj. **[for s.o. to have no good judgment/sense]**
ba⌉kana ばかな adj(*na*). •**c** **[for s.o./s.a. to have no good judgment/sense]** ⟪**stupid, silly**⟫, **ba⌉ka-mitaina** ばかみたいな adj(*na*). **[like a fool]** ⟪**stupid, silly**⟫

EX. (**a**) It was foolish of you to lend him money.
彼にお金を貸すなんて{ばかな/*ばかみたいな}ことをしたものですね。
*Kare ni o-kane o kasu nante {bakana/*baka-mitaina} koto o shita mono desu ne.*
(**b**) I felt foolish after forgetting such an easy kanji.
とてもやさしい漢字を忘れてしまって、{ばかみたいな/*ばかな}気がした。
*Totemo yasashii kanji o wasurete shimatte, {baka-mitaina/*bakana} ki-ga-shita.*
(**c**) It's foolish of you to believe what he says.
彼の言うことを信じるなんて{ばか/ばかみたい}だよ。
Kare no iu koto o shinjiru nante {baka/baka-mitai} da yo.

foot n. **[a part of the body at the end of the leg beginning at the ankle or a measure of length ⟪fig. "lowest part of a mountain/wall/etc."⟫]**
1. a⌈shi⌉ あし **[one of all of the limbs on an animal/human which support the body and are used for walking ⟪fig. "any of the long thin upright supports on which a piece of furniture stands," "walking," "transportation"⟫]** ⟪**leg, foot, paw**⟫
㊞ "for animals/living things"▷足, "for other inanimate objects"▷脚

EX. (**a**) I have small feet.
私は足が小さいです。
Watashi wa ashi ga chiisai desu.
(**b**) He kept on walking in spite of the pain in his foot.
彼は足が痛いのに歩き続けた。
Kare wa ashi ga itai noni aruki-tsuzuketa.

2. fi⌉ito フィート •**f** **[a measure of length]**

EX. She is 5 foot 7 inches tall.
彼女は(背が)五フィート七インチです。
Kanojo wa (se ga) go-fiito-nana-inchi desu.

PHRASE: go on foot *aruite iku* 歩いて行く ①

football n.
sa⌉kkaa サッカー •**f** ⟪**soccer**⟫, {**A⌈merikan-futto-bo⌉oru/A⌈mefu⌉tto**} {アメリカンフットボール/アメフット} •**f** ⟪**American football**⟫

EX. (**a**) I went to see a football game.

私は{サッカー/アメリカンフットボール/アメフット}の試合を見に行った。
Watashi wa {sakkaa/Amerikan-futto-booru/Amefutto} no shiai o mi ni itta.
(**b**) Do you play football?
{サッカー/アメリカンフットボール/アメフット}をしますか。
{Sakkaa/Amerikan-futto-booru/Amefutto} o shimasu ka.

NOTE: In American English, football and soccer are two different games, but they are the same in British English. *Amefutto* in Japanese is often pronounced as *Amefuto.*

footstep n. **[(the sound of) a step made by s.o./s.a. in walking]**
a⌈shi-a⌉to 足跡 [a mark made by the foot of s.o./s.a.] ((footprint, footmark)), a⌈shi-oto⌉ 足音 [the sound of a step made by s.o. in walking] ((step, tread))

EX. (**a**) Her footsteps were clearly marked in the snow in the garden.
庭の雪の上に彼女の足跡がはっきりついていた。
Niwa no yuki no ue ni kanojo no ashi-ato ga hakkiri tsuite ita.
(**b**) She heard soft footsteps passing along the corridor.
彼女は廊下を通るかすかな足音を聞いた。
Kanojo wa rooka o tooru kasukana ashi-oto o kiita.

for prep. **[in place of s.t./s.o./s.a.; directed to or intended to be given to s.o./s.a.; intended as a means toward accomplishing some purpose or goal; because of s.t.; considered by the standards of s.t./s.o./s.a.; in the capacity of s.t.; on the occasion of s.t.; in favor of s.t. by means of paying some amount of money; in the direction of some place; throughout a duration of time or spatial distance]**

1. -kan ～間 •c [duration of time], a⌈ida 間 [the space between two temporal/spatial points] ((interval, midway, time, period, between))

NOTE: *Kan* is optional except for hours and weeks. For example, *ip-pun(-kan)* for one minute, *ichi-jikan* for an hour, *itsuka(-kan)* for five days, *is-shuukan* for one week, *ik-kagetsu (-kan)* for one month, *ichi-nen(-kan)* for a year, etc. Note the exception *ichi-nichi* for one day, where *kan* cannot be used.

EX. (**a**) I was sick in bed for three days.
私は三日(間)、病気で寝ていた。
Watashi wa mikka(-kan), byooki de nete ita.
(**b**) I've been living here for a long time.
私はここに長い間住んでいます。
Watashi wa koko ni nagai aida sunde imasu.

2. Chinese number + a unit for measuring length [indicating distance]

EX. (**a**) I walk for a mile or two every day.
私は毎日一マイルか二マイル散歩します。
Watashi wa mai-nichi ichi-mairu ka ni-mairu sanpo-shimasu.
(**b**) He walked for 10 kilometers.
彼は十キロ歩いた。
Kare wa juk-kiro aruita.

3. ni に prt. [indicating a spatial/temporal point of contact, often construed as a location where s.t./s.o./s.a. exists or a goal or an indirect object] ((to, at, on the occasion of)), {Vinf. nonpast/N no} tame {(ni)/no N} {Vinf. nonpast/Nの}ため{(に)/のN} ((for the sake of))

EX. (**a**) I've got a present for you.
あなた{に/?のために/?のための}プレゼントがあります。
Anata {ni/?no tame ni/?no tame no} purezento ga arimasu.
(**b**) Let's save some of the cake for Yasuko.
靖子さん{に/のために/*のための}ケーキを残しておいてあげましょう。
*Yasuko-san {ni/no tame ni/*no tame no} keeki o nokoshite oite agemashoo.*
(**c**) This is good for your health.
これは健康{に/のために/*のための}いいです。
*Kore wa kenkoo {ni/no tame ni/*no tame no} ii desu.*

(**d**) You are the very man for the job.
あなたはこの仕事{に/*のために/*のための}ぴったりだ。
*Anata wa kono shigoto {ni/*no tame ni/*no tame no} pittari da.*
(**e**) She made some coffee for us.
彼女は私たち{に/のために/*のための}コーヒーを入れてくれた。
*Kanojo wa watashi-tachi {ni/no tame ni/*no tame no} koohii o irete kureta.*
(**f**) I've sent my coat out for cleaning.
私はコートをクリーニング{に/*のために/*のための}出しました。
*Watashi wa kooto o kuriiningu {ni/*no tame ni/*no tame no} dashimashita.*
(**g**) What's this hole in the door for?
このドアの穴は何{のために/*のための/*に}あるのですか。
*Kono doa no ana wa nan {no tame ni/*no tame no/*ni} aru no desu ka.*
(**h**) They went for a walk.
彼らは散歩{に/*のために/*のための}出かけた。
*Kare-ra wa sanpo {ni/*no tame ni/*no tame no} dekaketa.*

NOTE: To express purpose, *ni* can be used alone only with verbs that involve motion from one place to another, such as *iku* "go," *kuru* "come," *dasu* "send out," etc. Otherwise {Vinf. nonpast/N no} *tame ni/no* should be used in expressing purpose.

(**i**) This is a utensil for grating radishes.
これは大根をおろす{ための/*ために/*に}道具です。
*Kore wa daikon o orosu {tame no/*tame ni/*ni} doogu desu.*
(**j**) This is a lounge for students.
ここは学生{のための/*のために/*に}ラウンジです。
*Koko wa gakusei {no tame no/*no tame ni/*ni} raunji desu.*
(**k**) We had a party for the new students.
新入生{のために/のための/*に}パーティーを開いた。
*Shinnyuu-sei {no tame ni/no tame no/*ni} paatii o hiraita.*
(**l**) They chose him for their leader.
彼をリーダー{に/*のために/*のための}選んだ。
*Kare o riidaa {ni/*no tame ni/*no tame no} eranda.*
(**m**) He is not suited for the job.
彼はその仕事{に/*のために/*のための}は向いていない。
*Kare wa sono shigoto {ni/*no tame ni/*no tame no} wa muite inai.*
(**n**) He bought me red roses for my birthday.
彼は私の誕生日{に/?のために/*のための}赤いばらを買ってくれた。
*Kare wa watashi no tanjoo-bi {ni/?no tame ni/*no tame no} akai bara o katte kureta.*
(**o**) Are you coming home for Christmas?
クリスマス{に/*のために/*のための}は家へ帰ってくるの。
*Kurisumasu {ni/*no tame ni/*no tame no} wa uchi e kaette-kuru no.*

4. -yuki no N ～行きのN **[bound for]**

EX. He got on the train for Tokyo.
彼は東京行きの電車に乗った。
Kare wa Tookyoo-yuki no densha ni notta.

5. de で prt. **[indicating a weak causal relationship],** ⟨**-no**⟩ **ta**⌈**me**⌉ (**ni**) ⟨～の⟩ため(に) n.(+prt.) **[indicating cause/purpose]** ⟪**due to**⟫

EX. (**a**) We could hardly see anything for the heavy rain.
大雨{で/のため(に)}ほとんど何も見えなかった。
Oo-ame {de/no tame (ni)} hotondo nani-mo mienakatta.
(**b**) Kyoto is famous for its old temples.
京都は古いお寺{で/*のため}有名です。
*Kyooto wa furui o-tera {de/*no tame} yuumei desu.*

6. {**ni-shite/to-shite**} **wa** {にして/として}は comp. prt. **[indicating a generally agreed upon standard]** ⟪**judging by what is normally expected of**⟫

NOTE: X *ni shite wa* "for an X" normally presupposes that the person/thing referred to by the subject actually is an X, and can be paraphrased as "considering the fact that it is an X" whereas X *to shite wa* "for an X" carries no such presuppositon. In the former case, the judgment made by the speaker sounds more subjective; in the latter case, it sounds more objective and based on conventionally accepted standards.

EX. (**a**) It's quite warm for January.
一月{にして/?として}は割に暖かい。
Ichi-gatsu {ni-shite/?to-shite} wa warini atatakai.
(**b**) He's small for a sumo wrestler.
彼はすもう取り{にして/として}は小さい。
Kare wa sumoo-tori {ni-shite/to-shite} wa chiisai.
(**c**) This package is light for books, isn't it?
この小包は本{にして/*として}は軽いですね。
*Kono ko-zutsumi wa hon {ni-shite/*to-shite} wa karui desu ne.*
(**d**) She knows a lot of kanji for a beginner.
彼女は初心者{にして/?として}は漢字をよく知っている。
Kanojo wa shoshin-sha {ni shite/?to-shite} wa kanji o yoku shitte iru.

7. de で prt. **[expressing rate, quantity, degree, price, speed, etc.]**

EX. Hanako bought this table for 20 dollars.
花子はこのテーブルを二十ドルで買った。
Hanako wa kono teeburu o ni-juu-doru de katta.

8. ga が prt. **[indicating the subject of a sentence]**

EX. (**a**) For a woman to find a decent job is not easy in some countries.
女性がちゃんとした仕事を見つけるのは簡単ではない国もある。
Josei ga chanto-shita shigoto o mitsukeru no wa kantan dewanai kuni mo aru.
(**b**) This suitcase is too heavy for her to carry.
このスーツケースは彼女が持って行くには重過ぎる。
Kono suutsukeesu wa kanojo ga motte-iku ni wa omo-sugiru.
(**c**) The crowd made way for the procession to pass.
群衆は行列が通れるように道を空けた。
Gunshuu wa gyooretsu ga toore-ru yooni michi o aketa.

9. ni-taishite に対して comp. prt. **[directed to]**

EX. I would like to thank you for your cooperation.
御協力に対して感謝いたします。
Go-kyooryoku ni-taishite kansha itashimasu.

10. 〈-ni〉 sa⌈nsei da 〈〜に〉賛成だ **•c [in favor of]** ↔ **〈-ni〉 hantai da** 〈〜に〉反対だ **•c**

EX. Are you for or against the proposal?
あの案に賛成ですか、反対ですか。
Ano an ni sansei desu ka, hantai desu ka.

11. ni(-totte) wa に(とって)は comp. prt. **[from the point of view of]**

EX. (**a**) It was a frightening experience for a child.
それは子供に(とって)はこわい経験だった。
Sore wa kodomo ni(-totte) wa kowai keiken datta.
(**b**) The exam was very difficult for me.
試験は私に(とって)はとても難しかった。
Shiken wa watashi ni(-totte) wa totemo muzukashikatta.

12. 〈-no〉 kawari ni 〈〜の〉代わりに n.+prt. **[in place of s.t./s.o./s.a.]**

EX. He taught my class for me when I was sick.
彼は私が病気だった時代わりに授業をしてくれた。
Kare wa watashi ga byooki datta toki kawari ni jugyoo o shite kureta.

forbid vt. **[to order s.o. not to do s.t.]**
〈-o〉 k⌈inshi-suru 〈〜を〉禁止する ③ **•c, 〈-o〉 ki⌈njiru** 〈〜を〉禁じる ② **•c** **《prohibit》**

EX. (**a**) Students are forbidden to use the word processor in the office.
学生はオフィスにあるワープロを使うのを{禁止されて/禁じられて}いる。

Gakusei wa ofisu ni aru waapuro o tsukau no o {kinshi-sarete/kinji-rarete} iru.
(**b**) The law forbids the use of this food additive.
この食品添加物の使用は法律で{禁止されて/禁じられて}いる。
Kono shokuhin-tenka-butsu no shiyoo wa hooritsu de {kinshi-sarete/kinji-rarete} iru.
(**c**) Japanese law forbids young people under 20 to smoke.
日本の法律は二十歳未満の青少年がたばこを吸うのを{禁止して/禁じて}いる。
Nihon no hooritsu wa ni-jus-sai-miman no sei-shoonen ga tabako o suu no o {kinshi-shite/kinjite} iru.

force n. **[active, outward power]**
chi⌈kara⌉ 力 [a capacity of any kind to do s.t., including physical. intellectual, mental, or spiritual] ((strength, energy, power, ability, authority, vigor, capacity, knowledge))

EX. (**a**) His aim was to unify the country by force.
彼の目的は力でその国を統一することでした。
Kare no mokuteki wa chikara de sono kuni o tooitsu-suru koto deshita.
(**b**) We cannot settle our disputes by force.
私たちは力で紛争を解決することはできない。
Watashi-tachi wa chikara de funsoo o kaiketsu-suru koto wa dekinai.

PHRASE: the armed forces *guntai* 軍隊 •**c**, Air Force *kuugun* 空軍 •**c**, the force of gravity *inryoku* 引力 •**c**

— vt. **[to make s.o./s.a. to do s.t. against his/her will]**
{⟨-ni⟩/⟨-o⟩} {**Vneg. + seru/Vstem + saseru/ko-sase⌉ru/sa⌈seru**} {⟨〜に⟩/⟨〜を⟩}{**Vneg.+せる/Vstem+させる/来させる/させる**} ② **[for s.o./s.a. to cause s.o./s.t./s.a. to do s.t./ to change in state]**

NOTE: Verbs such as *kuru* "come," *iku* "go" and *aruku* "walk" which do not normally take the particle *o* will take this particle when *-seru/-saseru* is attached to indicate the individual which is forced to perform the action.

EX. (**a**) He forced me to drive the whole way.
彼は私に道中ずっと車を運転させた。
Kare wa watashi ni doochuu zutto kuruma o unten-saseta.
(**b**) I doubt she'll do it unless you force her to.
無理にでもさせないと、彼女はしないんじゃないかと思う。
Muri ni demo sasenai to, kanojo wa shinai n janai ka to omou.
(**c**) Her parents forced her to quit her job.
両親は彼女に仕事を辞めさせた。
Ryooshin wa kanojo ni shigoto o yame-saseta.
(**d**) The professor forced his students to buy the book he wrote.
教授は学生に自分の書いた本を買わせた。
Kyooju wa gakusei ni jibun no kaita hon o kawa-seta.

PHRASE: force...on s.o. ⟨*-ni*⟩ ⟨*-o*⟩ *oshi-tsukeru* ⟨〜に⟩⟨〜を⟩押しつける ② ((press...against))

EX. He always forces his ideas on me.
彼はいつも私に自分の考えを押しつける。
Kare wa itsu-mo watashi ni jibun no kangae o oshi-tsukeru.

forecast vt. **[to say what is expected to happen in the future]**
{⟨**-o**⟩/⟨**-to**⟩} **yo⌈soku-suru** {⟨〜を⟩/⟨〜と⟩}**予測する** ③ •**c [for s.o. to foretell what is going to happen on some scientific basis] ((predict))**

EX. Nobody can accurately forecast the future.
だれも未来を正確に予測することはできない。
Dare-mo mirai o seikakuni yosoku-suru koto wa dekinai.

— n. **[a statement about what is expected to happen in the future]**
yo⌈soku 予測 •c [an act/instance of foretelling the future on some scientific basis], yo⌈hoo 予報 •c [an advance report

about what is expected to happen in the future based on scientific data]

PHRASE: weather forecast *tenki-yohoo* 天気予報 •c

forehead n. **[the part of the face above the eyebrows and below the hair]**
hi⌈tai 額

EX. He wiped his forehead with a handkerchief.
彼はハンカチで額をぬぐった。
Kare wa hankachi de hitai o nugutta.

foreign adj. **[living/belonging/relating to countries which are not one's own]**
ga⌈ikoku no N 外国のN •c

EX. I collect foreign stamps.
私は外国の切手を集めている。
Watashi wa gaikoku no kitte o atsumete iru.

PHRASE: foreign language *gaikoku-go* 外国語 •c, the Ministry of Foreign Affairs *Gaimu-shoo* 外務省 •c, foreign policy *gaikoo-seisaku* 外交政策 •c, foreign trade *booeki* 貿易 •c

foreigner n. **[a person living in a country which is not his/her own]**
ga⌈ikoku⌉-jin 外国人 •c, ga⌈ijin 外人 •c

EX. Many foreigners visit Kyoto every year.
毎年、沢山の{外国人/外人}が京都を訪れる。
Mai-toshi, takusan no {gaikoku-jin/gaijin} ga Kyooto o otozureru.

forest n. **[a large area of land covered with trees and bushes]**
mo⌈ri 森 [an area with many old, tall trees, often regarded as a holy place inhabited by Shinto deities] ((woods)), **shi⌈nrin 森林 •c [a large area of land covered with trees and bushes]** ((woods))

EX. We got lost in the forest.
{森林/森}の中で道に迷った。
{Shinrin/Mori} no naka de michi ni mayotta.

PHRASE: forest fire *yama-kaji* 山火事, virgin forest *genseirin* 原生林 •c

forever adv. **[endlessly from now on]**
e⌈ikyuu ni 永久に •c, e⌈ien ni 永遠に •c, i⌉tsu-made-mo いつまでも [as long as one could arbitrarily imagine]

NOTE: *Eikyuu ni* often implies the involvement of one's will in keeping s.t. unchanged indefinitely, while *eien ni* implies eternity.

EX. (**a**) I'm sure I'll remember his name forever.
私は彼の名前を{永久に/永遠に/いつまでも}忘れないだろう。
Watashi wa kare no namae o {eikyuu ni/eien ni/itsu-made-mo} wasurenai daroo.
(**b**) I can't imagine that this peace will last forever.
この平和が{永久に/永遠に/いつまでも}続くとは思えない。
Kono heiwa ga {eikyuu ni/eien ni/itsu-made-mo} tsuzuku to wa omoe-nai.

forget vt. **[to fail to keep s.o./s.t./s.a. in the memory or to fail to remember (to do) s.t.]**
⟨-o⟩ wa⌈sureru ⟨〜を⟩忘れる ②

EX. (**a**) I've forgotten his phone number.
彼の電話番号を忘れてしまいました。
Kare no denwa-bangoo o wasurete shimaimashita.
(**b**) Don't forget to lock the door.
ドアに鍵をかけるのを忘れないでください。
Doa ni kagi o kakeru no o wasurenaide kudasai.
(**c**) I forgot that he was coming this evening.
今晩、彼が来る{の/こと}を忘れていました。
Konban, kare ga kuru {no/koto} o wasurete imashita.
(**d**) I've forgotten where I put my wallet.
どこに財布を置いたか忘れてしまいました。
Doko ni saifu o oita ka wasurete shimaimashita.
(**e**) I've forgotten whether he has a car or not.
彼が車を持っているかどうか忘れてしまった。
Kare ga kuruma o motte iru ka doo ka wasurete shimatta.
(**f**) Let's forget what happened in the past.
過去に起こったことは忘れましょう。
Kako ni okotta koto wa wasuremashoo.

fork n. **[an instrument used for eating food]** **fo˥oku フォーク •f**

EX. It is very strange to eat sushi with a fork.
フォークですしを食べるのはとても変だ。
Fooku de sushi o taberu no wa totemo hen da.

form n. **[outward appearance or an official paper with spaces for answering questions/giving information]**

1. ka˹tachi 形 [the outward appearance of s.t.] ⟪**shape**⟫, **ke˹ishiki 形式 •c [the outward appearance of s.t. as created by human design or convention]** ⟪**formalities**⟫, **su˥gata 姿 [a visual impression of s.o.]** ⟪**figure**⟫

EX. (**a**) The final exam was given in the form of an interview.
期末試験はインタビュー{の形/形式/*姿}で行われた。
*Kimatsu-shiken wa intabyuu {no katachi/-keishiki/*sugata} de okonawareta.*
(**b**) In what form will the book be published?
その本はどんな{形/形式/*姿}で出版されるんですか。
*Sono hon wa donna {katachi/keishiki/*sugata} de shuppan-sareru n desu ka.*
(**c**) Ice is a form of water.
氷は水の一つの{形/*形式/*姿}である。
*Koori wa mizu no hitotsu no {katachi/*keishiki/*sugata} dearu.*
(**d**) The tall graceful form of a woman appeared at the entrance.
玄関に背が高い優美な女の人が{姿/*形/*形式}を現した。
*Genkan ni sei ga takai yuubina onna no hito ga {sugata/*katachi/*keishiki} o arawashita.*

2. yo˹oshi 用紙 •c [paper used for a specific purpose]

EX. Please fill in this application form with the necessary information.
この申し込み用紙に必要事項を記入してください。
Kono mooshi-komi-yooshi ni hitsuyoo-jikoo o kinyuu-shite kudasai.

—— vt. **[to make s.t.]**

⟨-o⟩ tsu˹ku˥ru ⟨〜を⟩つくる [for s.o./s.a. to cause s.t./s.o./s.a. to come into existence which did not exist previously] ⟪**create, manufacture, compose, build, cast, organize, constitute, invent, set up, establish**⟫

㊅ "build a bridge, ship, etc."▷造る, otherwise ▷作る

EX. The "*te* form" of this verb is formed by adding "*te*" to the stem.
この動詞の「て形」は語幹に「て」を付けて作る。
Kono dooshi no 'te-kei' wa gokan ni 'te' o tsukete tsukuru.

formal adj. **[based on accepted rules/customs/conventions or suitable for official occasions, serious writing, etc., but not for ordinary conversation]**

1. se˹ishiki no N 正式のN •c [based on accepted rules/customs/conventions] ⟪**official**⟫, **se˹ishikina 正式な** adj(*na*). **•c**

EX. (**a**) I need a formal receipt.
正式{の/な}領収書が要るんです。
Seishiki {no/na} ryooshuu-sho ga iru n desu.
(**b**) My grandmother had no formal education.
祖母は正式{の/な}教育は全然受けていない。
Sobo wa seishiki {no/na} kyooiku wa zenzen ukete inai.

2. a˹ratama˥tta N 改まったN /⟨Vinf. past of ***aratamaru*** **① be ceremonious/ [used on official occasions, in serious writing, etc., or in accordance with particular conventions]** ⟪**ceremonious**⟫

EX. (**a**) It's best not to use this word in formal situations.
このことばは改まった場所では使わない方がいいです。
Kono kotoba wa aratamatta basho de wa tsukawanai hoo ga ii desu.
(**b**) He asked me in a formal-sounding tone, "Will you marry me?"

彼は非常に改まった口調で「僕と結婚してくれませんか」と言った。
Kare wa hijooni aratamatta kuchoo de 'Boku to kekkon-shite kuremasen ka' to itta.

formation n. **[the process of making/being made or s.t. made]**
ke⌈isei 形成 •c [the process of making/being made]

EX. School life has a great influence on the formation of a child's character.
学校生活は子供の性格形成に大きく影響する。
Gakkoo-seikatsu wa kodomo no seikaku-keisei ni ookiku eikyoo-suru.

former adj. **[of an earlier period]**
ma⌉e no N 前のN [coming/going before in time or located before] ⟪prior⟫

EX. I met her former husband.
彼女の前のご主人に会った。
Kanojo no mae no go-shujin ni atta.

PHRASE: the former *zensha* 前者 •c ↔ *koosha* 後者 •c

EX. Tokyo and Osaka are both big cities but the former has a much larger population.
東京も大阪も大都市だが、前者の方がずっと人口が多い。
Tookyoo mo Oosaka mo dai-toshi da ga, zensha no hoo ga zutto jinkoo ga ooi.

formerly adv. **[in an earlier period]**
i⌉zen (ni) 以前(に) •c [at an earlier time than the time in question] ⟪before⟫, mu⌈kashi 昔 [at a much earlier time than the present] ⟪long, long ago; in old days⟫

EX. (**a**) I formerly lived in Tokyo, but now I live in Osaka.
{以前/昔}東京に住んでいましたが、今は大阪に住んでいます。
{Izen/Mukashi} Tookyoo ni sunde imashita ga, ima wa Oosaka ni sunde imasu.
(**b**) He worked formerly for a trading company.
彼は{以前/昔}貿易会社に勤めていた。
Kare wa {izen/mukashi} booeki-gaisha ni tsutomete ita.

formula n. **[a group of symbols which represent a scientific/mathematical rule]**
ko⌈oshiki 公式 •c

EX. Do you know the formula for converting Celsius to Fahrenheit?
摂氏を華氏に変える公式を知っていますか。
Sesshi o kashi ni kaeru kooshiki o shitte imasu ka.

PHRASE: chemical formula *kagaku-shiki* 化学式 •c

fort n. **[strong building(s) which can be defended against enemy attacks]**
to⌈ride とりで [an edifice built separately from the main castle to defend against enemy attacks], yo⌈osai 要塞 •c [a strong and large edifice used for defense] ⟪fortress⟫

fortunate adj. **[having/bringing good luck]**
u⌉n ga i⌉i 運がいい adj(*i*). **[to be in luck] ⟪lucky⟫, ko⌈ounna 幸運な** adj(*na*). **•c [blessed with luck] ⟪lucky⟫**

EX. It was fortunate for her that a doctor was on board.
医者が乗っていたのは彼女にとって{運が良かった/幸運だった}。
Isha ga notte ita no wa kanojo ni-totte {un ga yokatta/kooun datta}.

fortunately adv. **[by good chance]**
u⌉n-yoku 運よく ⟪luckily⟫ ↔ un-waruku 運悪く, sa⌈iwai(ni⌉ mo) 幸い(にも) ⟪luckily⟫

EX. (**a**) Fortunately, there were not many customers in the store when the fire started.
{運よく/幸い(にも)}火が出たとき、店の中にお客さんはあまりいなかったんです。
{Un-yoku/Saiwai(ni mo)} hi ga deta toki, mise no naka ni o-kyaku-san wa amari inakatta n desu.
(**b**) Fortunately, I was in time for the last train.
{運よく/幸い(にも)}最終電車に間に合った。
{Un-yoku/Saiwai(ni mo)} saishuu-densha ni ma-ni-atta.

NOTE: *Saiwaini mo* is more formal than *saiwai.*

fortune n. **[chance event(s) that have an important influence on s.o./s.t. or a great**

amount of money, possessions, etc.]
1. u˥n 運 •c [the element of chance, particularly as it influences the subsequent course of events for s.o./s.t.] ⟪destiny, one's lot⟫

EX. (**a**) Fortune has begun to smile on Taro.
太郎に運が向いてきた。
Taroo ni un ga muite-kita.
(**b**) As fortune would have it, the stock she bought doubled in value within a year.
運が良いことに、彼女が買った株の価格は一年もしないうちに二倍に跳ね上がった。
Un ga yoi koto ni, kanojo ga katta kabu no kakaku wa ichi-nen mo shinai uchi ni ni-bai ni hane-agatta.

2. za˥isan 財産 •c [the entire amount of money, possessions, etc., one owns] ⟪property⟫, ta˥ikin 大金 •c [a great amount of money]

EX. (**a**) Ken married Hiroko for her fortune.
健は弘子の{財産/*大金}目当てに結婚した。
*Ken wa Hiroko no {zaisan/*taikin}-meate ni kekkon-shita.*
(**b**) She won a fortune in the lottery.
彼女は宝くじで{大金/*財産}を獲得した。
*Kanojo wa takara-kuji de {taikin/*zaisan} o kakutoku-shita.*
(**c**) He made his fortune from the development of a new residential area.
彼は新しい住宅地の開発で{財産/*大金}を築いた。
*Kare wa atarashii juutaku-chi no kaihatsu de {zaisan/*taikin} o kizuita.*

forty n./adj.
{yo˥n-juu/shi-˥ju˥u} (+counter) (no N) 四十(+counter)(のN) •c SEE APPENDIX II

EX. He is still under forty.
彼はまだ{四十/四十歳}になっていない。
Kare wa mada {yon-juu/shi-juu/yon-jus-sai} ni natte inai.

NOTE: *Yon-juu* is now more commonly used than *shi-juu*.

forward adv. **[towards/to the front]**
ma˥e {e/ni} 前{へ/に}

EX. He took a step forward to shake hands with Mr. Yoda.
彼は依田さんと握手するために一歩前{へ/に}出た。
Kare wa Yoda-san to akushu-suru tame ni ip-po mae {e/ni} deta.

PHRASE: go forward *mae {e/ni} susumu* 前{へ/に}進む ① ⟪advance, progress⟫

EX. Their plans are going forward steadily.
彼らの計画は着々と進んでいる。
Kare-ra no keikaku wa chaku-chaku-to susunde iru.

— vt. **[for s.o. to send on letters, parcels, etc. to a new address]**
⟨-o⟩ te˥nsoo-suru ⟨〜を⟩転送する ③ •c [for s.o. to send on letters, parcels, phone calls, etc. to a different place/person] ⟪transfer⟫

EX. I have to forward Yoshiko's mail to her new address in Tokyo.
私は佳子の所へ来た郵便物を東京の引っ越し先に転送しなければならない。
Watashi wa Yoshiko no tokoro e kita yuubin-butsu o Tookyoo no hikkoshi-saki ni tensoo-shinakereba naranai.

foundation n. **[the base upon which a building is built or upon which an idea or belief is formed]**
1. ko˥nkyo 根拠 •c [the facts/conditions that provide a base for a rumor, accusation, etc.] ⟪basis, ground⟫

EX. The rumor was completely without foundation.
そのうわさには何の根拠もなかった。
Sono uwasa ni wa nan no konkyo mo nakatta.

2. ki˥so˥ 基礎 •c [that on which s.t. more complex is built] ⟪basis⟫, do˥dai 土台 •c [the base upon which a building or other structure is built] ⟪base⟫

EX. (**a**) Her early musical training at home gave her a firm foundation for her future career as a professional pianist.
小さい時から家庭で受けていた音楽教育のおかげで、彼女は将来プロのピアニストになるための{基礎/*土台}をしっかり身に付けることができた。

*Chiisai toki kara katei de ukete ita ongaku-kyooiku no o-kage de, kanojo wa shoorai puro no pianisuto ni naru tame no {kiso/*dodai} o shikkari mi ni tsukeru koto ga dekita.*
(**b**) This building is built on a solid foundation.
この建物は{土台/基礎}がしっかりしている。
Kono tate-mono wa {dodai/kiso} ga shikkari-shite iru.

3. so⌈oritsu 創立 •c [the establishment of a school, company, hospital, research institute, etc.]

EX. This university has sent out many talented graduates into society since its foundation.
この大学は創立以来、たくさんの優秀な卒業生を社会に送り出してきた。
Kono daigaku wa sooritsu-irai, takusan no yuushuuna sotsugyoo-sei o shakai ni okuri-dashite-kita.

4. za⌈idan 財団 •c [an organization/institution established by an endowment], ki⌈ki⌉n 基金 •c ((endowment))

EX. (**a**) Our research has been made possible thanks to funding from the Japan Foundation.
私たちの研究は国際交流基金の助成のおかげで可能になりました。
Watashi-tachi no kenkyuu wa Kokusai-kooryuu-kikin no josei no o-kage de kanooni narimashita.
(**b**) He is a trustee of the Rockefeller Foundation.
あの人はロックフェラー財団の理事です。
Ano hito wa Rokkuferaa-zaidan no riji desu.

fountain n. **[a structure that produces a stream of water which rises into the air]**
fu⌈nsui 噴水 •c

EX. This park is famous for its fountain.
この公園は噴水で有名だ。
Kono kooen wa funsui de yuumei da.

PHRASE: fountain pen *mannen-hitsu* 万年筆 •c, drinking fountain *mizu-nomi-ba* 水飲み場

four n./adj.
yo⌈ttsu⌉ (no N) 四つ(のN), {shi⌉/yo⌉n} (+counter) (no N) 四(+counter)(のN) •c
SEE APPENDIX II

EX. (**a**) We have four dogs.
家には犬が{四匹/*四つ}いる。
*Uchi ni wa inu ga {yon-hiki/*yottsu} iru.*
(**b**) He bought four bottles of beer.
彼はビールを{四本/*四つ}買った。
*Kare wa biiru o {yon-hon/*yottsu} katta.*
(**c**) Jim is four years old.
ジムは{四つ/四歳}です。
Jimu wa {yottsu/yon-sai} desu.

fourteen n./adj.
{ju⌈u-shi⌉/ju⌈u-yo⌉n} (+counter) (no N) 十四(+counter)(のN) •c SEE APPENDIX II

EX. (**a**) My brother is fourteen years old.
弟は{十四/十四歳}です。
Otooto wa {juu-shi/juu-yon/juu-yon-sai} desu.
(**b**) I read fourteen books for my paper.
論文のために本を十四冊読んだ。
Ronbun no tame ni hon o juu-yon-satsu yonda.

fourth n./adj.

1. yo⌈kka 四日 [the fourth day of the month]

EX. May 4th is a national holiday in Japan.
五月四日は日本では祝日です。
Go-gatsu yokka wa Nihon de wa shukujitsu desu.

2. yo⌈n-ban-me⌉ no N 四番目のN [the ordinal number 4], yo⌈ttsu-me⌉ no N 四つ目のN [the ordinal number 4], yo⌉n (+counter) no N 四(+counter)のN SEE APPENDIX II

NOTE: *-me no* is preceded by a number with an appropriate counter.

EX. (**a**) She is his fourth wife.
彼女は彼の四人目の奥さんです。
Kanojo wa kare no yo-nin-me no oku-san desu.
(**b**) It's the fourth building from the corner.
角から{四番目/四つ目}の建物です。
Kado kara {yon-ban-me/yottsu-me} no tate-mono desu.

F

(**c**) I can't read the fourth kanji from the top.
上から{四つ目/四番目}の漢字が読めません。
Ue kara {yottsu-me/yon-ban-me} no kanji ga yome-masen.

fox n.
ki⌈tsune きつね
NOTE: In both English and Japanese, the fox is characterized as a crafty, sly animal often compared to a person with such a character.

fragment n. **[a small piece/part of s.t.]**
ha⌈hen 破片 •c [a part of s.t. that has broken off or come off a larger whole] ⟪broken piece⟫, i⌈chi⌉bu 一部 •c [one part of s.t.] ⟪part, portion⟫, da⌈npen 断片 •c [a small piece broken off of s.t.]
EX. (**a**) I tried to scoop up the fragments of the broken vase.
私は割れた花瓶の{破片/*断片/*一部}を集めようとした。
*Watashi wa wareta kabin no {hahen/*danpen/*ichibu} o atsumeyoo to shita.*
(**b**) This is only a fragment of the long conversation I had with Taro.
これは太郎との長い会話のほんの{一部/*破片/*断片}に過ぎない。
*Kore wa Taroo to no nagai kaiwa no hon no {ichibu/*hahen/*danpen} ni suginai.*
(**c**) I accidentally overheard fragments of a conversation in the hallway.
廊下での会話の{断片/一部/*破片}が聞くともなく耳に入ってきた。
*Rooka de no kaiwa no {danpen/ichibu/*hahen} ga kiku to mo naku mimi ni haitte kita.*
PHRASE: break into tiny fragments *warete, kona-gona ni naru* 割れて、粉々になる ①
EX. The bowl she dropped broke into tiny fragments.
彼女が落とした茶わんは割れて、粉々になった。
Kanojo ga otoshita chawan wa warete, kona-gona ni natta.

frame n. **[a border/case into which s.t. is fitted/set]**
wa⌈ku⌉ 枠 [a hollow structure that holds s.t. in place ⟪fig. "limit"⟫] ⟪framework⟫, fu⌈chi⌉ 縁 [the outer part of an extended object/space that is farthest from its center] ⟪rim, border⟫, ga⌈ku-buchi 額縁 [a case into which a picture, certificate, etc. is set] ⟪picture frame⟫, ga⌈ku 額 •c [a case into which a picture, certificate, etc. is set, or a case with a picture, certificate, etc., set in it] ⟪picture frame⟫
EX. (**a**) She wore glasses with plastic frames.
彼女はプラスチックの{縁/??枠/*額/*額縁}の眼鏡をかけていた。
*Kanojo wa purasuchikku no {fuchi/??waku/*gaku/*gaku-buchi} no megane o kakete ita.*
(**b**) Hanako put her painting into a frame.
花子は自分の絵を{額/額縁/*枠/*縁}に入れた。
*Hanako wa jibun no e o {gaku/gaku-buchi/*waku/*fuchi} ni ireta.*
(**c**) The frames on the windows of the prison were all made of steel.
刑務所の窓の{枠/*縁/*額/*額縁}は全部鋼鉄製だった。
*Keimusho no mado no {waku/*fuchi/*gaku/*gaku-buchi} wa zenbu kootetsu-sei datta.*
PHRASE: frame of mind *kibun* 気分 •c ⟪mood⟫
EX. I'm not in the proper frame of mind to tackle this problem.
この問題に取り組むような気分じゃない。
Kono mondai ni tori-kumu yoona kibun janai.

framework n. **[the structure that shapes or supports s.t.]**
wa⌈ku-gumi⌉ 枠組み
EX. I'm still working on the framework for my paper.
まだ論文の枠組みを考えているところだ。
Mada ronbun no waku-gumi o kangaete iru tokoro da.

France n.
Fu⌈ransu フランス •f

frank adj. **[expressing clearly what one thinks/feels]**

F

so⌈tchokuna 率直な adj(*na*). •c ((**candid, straightforward, plain**))

EX. I want to hear your frank opinion.
あなたの率直な意見が聞きたいです。
Anata no sotchokuna iken ga kiki-tai desu.

PHRASE: to be frank with you *sotchokuni itte* 率直に言って, *shoojiki itte* 正直言って⟨s⟩

free adj. **[having no restriction/obstruction]**

1. ji⌈yu⌉una 自由な adj(*na*)./n. •c **[for s.o. to be able to act as one wants]**

EX. Free sex is unsafe sex in the age of AIDS.
エイズの時代に自由なセックスは危険だ。
Eizu no jidai ni jiyuuna sekkusu wa kiken da.

2. hi⌈mana 暇な adj(*na*)./n. **[for s.o. not to be busy]** ((**leisure, spare time**))

EX. (**a**) I am free this afternoon.
今日の午後は暇です。
Kyoo no gogo wa hima desu.
(**b**) I have very little free time during the day.
昼間はほとんど暇な時間がない。
Hiruma wa hotondo himana jikan ga nai.

3. ta⌉da no N ただのN **[for s.t. to cost nothing]** ((**gratis**))

EX. (**a**) My older brother gave me a free ticket to the concert.
兄がコンサートのただの切符をくれた。
Ani ga konsaato no tada no kippu o kureta.
(**b**) The coffee is free.
コーヒーはただです。
Koohii wa tada desu.

4. a⌈ite iru (N) 空いている(N) /⟨V*te iru* of *aku* ① **become empty/** ((**not occupied**))

EX. Is that seat free?
その席、空いていますか。
Sono seki, aite imasu ka.

5. na⌉i 無い adj(*i*). **[for s.t. not to exist]** ↔ **aru** ある ①; **i⌈nai** いない /⟨**neg. of** *iru* ② **exist/ [for s.o./s.a. not to exist]** ↔ **iru** いる ②

EX. (**a**) He is free from worries.
彼には心配事が無い。
Kare ni wa shinpai-goto ga nai.
(**b**) This city is free from thieves.
この町にはどろぼうがいない。
Kono machi ni wa doroboo ga inai.

PHRASE: set s.o. free ⟨*-o*⟩ *kaihoo-suru* ⟨〜を⟩解放する ③ •c ((release, liberate)), ⟨*-o*⟩ *shakuhoo-suru* ⟨〜を⟩釈放する ③ •c

EX. (**a**) All the prisoners of war were set free.
捕虜は全員{釈放/解放}された。
Horyo wa zen'in {shakuhoo/kaihoo}-sareta.
(**b**) The slaves were set free.
奴隷は{解放/?釈放}された。
Dorei wa {kaihoo/?shakuhoo}-sareta.

PHRASE: duty free shop *menzei-ten* 免税店 •c, free translation *iyaku* 意訳 •c, free trade *jiyuu-booeki* 自由貿易 •c, free speech *genron no jiyuu* 言論の自由 •c

freedom n. **[the condition of being free]**

ji⌈yu⌉u 自由 •c

EX. (**a**) I doubt the dictator will give the people the freedom to choose a new leader.
あの独裁者が国民に新しい指導者を選択する自由を与えるとは思わない。
Ano dokusai-sha ga kokumin ni atarashii shidoo-sha o sentaku-suru jiyuu o ataeru to wa omowanai.
(**b**) We have freedom of speech in Japan.
日本には言論の自由がある。
Nihon ni wa genron no jiyuu ga aru.

freely adv. **[openly]**

ji⌈yu⌉uni 自由に /⟨**adj**(*na*). ***ni* of *jiyuuna* free/** •c **[without any limitation]**, **so⌈tchokuni** 率直に /⟨**adj**(*na*). ***ni* of *sotchokuna* frank/** •c **[without hiding what one really thinks/feels]** ((**frankly, plainly, straightforwardly, unreservedly**))

EX. (**a**) You may smoke freely here.
ここでは{自由に/*率直に}たばこを吸っていい。
*Koko de wa {jiyuuni/*sotchokuni} tabako o sutte ii.*
(**b**) I freely admit that what I said was wrong.
私が言ったことは間違っていたということを{率直に/*自由に}認めます。

*Watashi ga itta koto wa machigatte ita to iu koto o {sotchokuni/*jiyuuni} mitomemasu.*

freeze vi./vt. **[for s.t. to become solid/hard due to extreme cold or to make s.t. solid/hard due to extreme cold 《fig. "for s.t./s.o. to be unable to move/work properly due to extreme cold or fear or to hold wages, prices, etc., at a constant level for a set period of time"》]**

1. ko⌈oru 凍る ① [for s.t. to become solid/hard due to extreme cold]

EX. (**a**) Water freezes at the temperature of 0 degrees Celsius.
水は摂氏零度で凍る。
Mizu wa sesshi rei-do de kooru.
(**b**) Last night it was cold enough for milk to freeze.
ゆうべは牛乳が凍るほど寒かった。
Yuube wa gyuunyuu ga kooru hodo samukatta.
(**c**) Watching the horror movie made my blood freeze.
あのホラー映画を見て、怖くて、血が凍るような気がした。
Ano horaa-eiga o mite, kowakute, chi ga kooru yoona ki-ga-shita.

2. 〈-o〉 re⌈itoo-suru 〈〜を〉冷凍する ③ •c [for s.o. to cause s.t. to become solid from extreme cold in order to prevent it from being spoiled]

EX. Let's freeze the rest of the rice.
残りの御飯は冷凍しよう。
Nokori no gohan wa reitoo-shiyoo.

3. ko⌈ori-tsu⌉ku 凍りつく ① [for s.t. to be unable to move/work properly due to the formation of ice]

EX. (**a**) The cold has frozen the lock on the car door.
寒さで車のドアの鍵が凍りついてしまった。
Samu-sa de kuruma no doa no kagi ga koori-tsuite shimatta.
(**b**) The engine is frozen.
エンジンが凍りついた。
Enjin ga koori-tsuita.

4. ku⌈gi-zuke ni na⌉ru 釘付けになる ① [for s.o. to be unable to move because of fear/surprise]

EX. The burglar froze on the spot when he heard footsteps.
泥棒は足音を耳にして、その場に釘付けになった。
Doroboo wa ashi-oto o mimi ni shite, sono ba ni kugi-zuke ni natta.

5. 〈-o〉 to⌈oketsu-suru 〈〜を〉凍結する ③ •c [for s.o. to hold wages or prices at a constant level for a set period of time by official action]

EX. The attempt to freeze wages has failed.
賃金を凍結しようとする試みは失敗した。
Chingin o tooketsu-shiyoo to suru kokoromi wa shippai-shita.

PHRASE: Freeze! *Ugoku na!* 動くな!, freeze to death *tooshi-suru* 凍死する ③ •c, frozen food *reitoo-shokuhin* 冷凍食品 •c

freezing adj. **[for s.o. to feel extremely cold]**
ko⌈ori-tsu⌉ku-yoona 凍りつくような adj(*na*).

EX. It's freezing in this room.
この部屋は寒くて、凍りつくようです。
Kono heya wa samukute, koori-tsuku-yoo desu.

freight n. **[goods carried by truck, ship, airplane, train, etc.]**
ka⌉motsu 貨物 《cargo》

EX. Transportation by freight train is relatively low in cost.
貨物列車による輸送はあまりコストがかからない。
Kamotsu-ressha ni-yoru yusoo wa amari kosuto ga kakaranai.

French adj. **[concerning France]**
Fu⌈ransu no N フランスのN •f

EX. I like French wine.
私はフランスのワインが好きだ。
Watashi wa Furansu no wain ga suki da.

—— n. **[the language/people of France]**

1. Fu⌈ransu-go フランス語 •f+c [the language of France]

EX. Can you speak French?
フランス語が話せますか。

F

| *Furansu-go ga hanase-masu ka.*

2. Fu⌈ransu⌉-jin フランス人 •f+c [the people/a person of France]

EX. | Her husband is French.
彼女の御主人はフランス人だ。
Kanojo no go-shujin wa Furansu-jin da.

Frenchman n. **[a male person from France]**
Fu⌈ransu⌉-jin フランス人 •f+c

frequent adj. **[occurring often]**
o⌉oi 多い adj(*i*). **[large in number/quantity]** **⟪many, a lot, much⟫**, **yo⌉ku よく** adv. **[satisfactorily/carefully/many times]** **⟪often, ably, with care⟫**

EX. | (**a**) Traffic accidents are frequent around here.
この辺は{交通事故が多い/よく交通事故が起こる}。
Kono hen wa {kootsuu-jiko ga ooi/yoku kootsuu-jiko ga okoru}.
(**b**) George's frequent absences from class had an effect on his grade.
ジョージは{欠席が多かった/よく欠席した}ので成績にひびいた。
Jooji wa {kesseki ga ookatta/yoku kesseki-shita} node seiseki ni hibiita.

frequently adv. **[often]**
yo⌉ku よく [satisfactorily/carefully/many times] **⟪well, thoroughly⟫**, **ta⌈bi-tabi たびたび [with high frequency ⟨fml⟩]** **⟪time after time, repeatedly⟫**

EX. | (**a**) He frequently skipped school.
彼は{よく/たびたび}学校をサボった。
Kare wa {yoku/tabi-tabi} gakkoo o sabotta.
(**b**) Earthquakes occur frequently around here.
この辺では{よく/たびたび}地震がある。
Kono hen de wa {yoku/tabi-tabi} jishin ga aru.

fresh adj. **[for s.t. to be newly made or grown and to be in good natural condition]**
1. a⌈tarashi⌉i 新しい adj(*i*). **[to have not existed for long or to have not existed or been seen/heard/experienced before]** **⟪new⟫** ↔ **furui 古い** adj(*i*).; **shi⌈nsenna 新鮮な** adj(*na*). **•c [for meat/fruits/vegetables to be recently harvested/butchered/caught and in good natural condition]**

EX. | (**a**) I don't think this fish is fresh.
この魚は{新しくない/新鮮じゃない}と思う。
Kono sakana wa {atarashikunai/shinsen janai} to omou.
(**b**) Open the window and let some fresh air in.
窓を開けて、{新しい/新鮮な}空気を入れなさい。
Mado o akete, {atarashii/shinsenna} kuuki o irenasai.

2. na⌉ma no N 生のN [for food/data/music/a voice to be in its natural/original condition without having been cooked/processed/recorded] **⟪raw, live⟫**

EX. | I like fresh fruits and vegetables.
私は生の果物や野菜が好きだ。
Watashi wa nama no kudamono ya yasai ga suki da.

PHRASE: fresh water *ma-mizu* 真水, *tansui* 淡水 •c; fresh water fish *tansui-gyo* 淡水魚 •c

freshman n. **[a student in the first year of high school/college/university]**
i⌈chi-ne⌉n-sei 一年生 •c [a student in the first year of any school/college/university]

EX. | He is a freshman at the University of Tokyo.
彼は東京大学の一年生だ。
Kare wa Tookyoo-daigaku no ichi-nen-sei da.

Friday n.
ki⌈n'yo⌉o(-bi) 金曜(日) •c

EX. | (**a**) I have no classes on Friday afternoon.
金曜(日)の午後は授業がない。
Kin'yoo(-bi) no gogo wa jugyoo ga nai.
(**b**) I plan to go to Tokyo next Friday.
来週の金曜(日)に東京へ行く予定です。
Raishuu no kin'yoo(-bi) ni Tookyoo e iku yotei desu.

friend n. **[a person whom one knows and likes well other than a family member]**
1. to⌈modachi 友達, yu⌈ujin 友人 •c

NOTE: *Yuujin* is somewhat more formal than

tomodachi and not used by young children.

EX. | John is an old friend of mine.
ジョンは私の古い{友達/友人}です。
Jon wa watashi no furui {tomodachi/ yuujin} desu.

2. na⌈kama⌉ 仲間 [a person in one's in-group with whom one frequently spends time, excluding one's relatives, spouse, and offspring ⟪fig. "the same kind"⟫] ⟪companion, company, buddy⟫

EX. | (**a**) These are my fishing friends.
この連中は私の釣り仲間です。
Kono renchuu wa watashi no tsuri-nakama desu.
(**b**) He is trusted by his friends.
彼は仲間に信頼されている。
Kare wa nakama ni shinrai-sarete iru.

3. mi⌈kata 味方 [a person/country that sides with one and provides support] ⟪ally, supporter⟫ ↔ teki 敵 •c

EX. | (**a**) He is a good friend of the poor.
彼は貧しい者の味方だ。
Kare wa mazushii mono no mikata da.
(**b**) Don't shoot. We're all friends here.
撃つな。我々はみんな味方だ。
Utsuna. Ware-ware wa minna mikata da.

PHRASE: (one's) good friend *shin'yuu* 親友 •c

friendly adj. **[acting or ready to act as a friend]**
hi⌈to-natsu(k)ko⌉i 人なつ(っ)こい adj(*i*). **[for s.o., esp. a child, to be willing to warm up to a person] ⟪affable⟫, shi⌉nsetsuna 親切な** adj(*na*). **•c [having/showing thoughtfulness for others] ⟪kind⟫**

EX. | (**a**) They're all friendly kids.
みんな{人なつ(っ)こい/?親切な}子供です。
Minna {hito-natsu(k)koi/?shinsetsuna} kodomo desu.
(**b**) My neighbors are all very friendly to me.
近所の人たちはみんなとても{親切に/*人なつ(っ)こく}してくださいます。
*Kinjo no hito-tachi wa minna totemo {shinsetsuni/*hito-natsu(k)koku} shite kudasaimasu.*

friendship n. **[the relationship that exists between friends]**
yu⌈ujoo 友情 •c

EX. | (**a**) Real friendship is more valuable than money.
真の友情は金より貴重だ。
Shin no yuujoo wa kane yori kichoo da.
(**b**) He underestimated the power of friendship.
彼は友情の力を軽く見過ぎた。
Kare wa yuujoo no chikara o karuku mi-sugita.

fright n. **[the feeling of sudden fear]**
kyo⌉ofu 恐怖 •c [great anxiety caused by the expectation of danger/evil] ⟪fear, terror, horror⟫

EX. | (**a**) He was shaking with fright.
彼は恐怖に震えていた。
Kare wa kyoofu ni furuete ita.
(**b**) He was paralyzed with fright.
彼は恐怖で身動きできなかった。
Kare wa kyoofu de mi-ugoki-dekinakatta.

frighten vt. **[to fill an animate being with fear]**
⟨-ni⟩ gyo⌈tto-suru ⟨～に⟩ぎょっとする ③ [for s.o./s.a. to be filled with sudden fear at s.t.], ⟨-ni⟩ o⌈doro⌉ku ⟨～に⟩驚く ① [for s.o./s.a. to be suddenly aroused out of a state of calmness by encountering s.t. unexpected] ⟪be surprised⟫

EX. | (**a**) Did the noise frighten you?
物音に{ぎょっとしました/驚きました}か。
Mono-oto ni {gyotto-shimashita/ odorokimashita} ka.
(**b**) The barking of the dog frightened the burglar away.
犬がほえたので、どろぼうは{ぎょっとして/驚いて}逃げた。
Inu ga hoeta node, doroboo wa {gyotto-shite/odoroite} nigeta.
(**c**) I was frightened by the big dog.
私は大きな犬に{ぎょっとした/驚いた}。
Watashi wa ookina inu ni {gyotto-shita/ odoroita}.

frightening adj. **[causing s.o./s.a. to be afraid]**
ko⌈wa⌉i 怖い adj(*i*). **[for s.o./s.a. to be afraid that s.t. dangerous/troublesome will happen to s.o. (esp. oneself) or for s.t./s.o./s.a. to cause such fear]** ⟪**terrible, fearful, dreadful, scary, afraid, strict**⟫, **o⌈soroshi⌉i** 恐ろしい adj(*i*). **[for s.o. to be afraid of s.t./s.o./s.a. unusual or mysterious or for s.t./s.o./s.a. to cause such fear]** ⟪**terrible, dreadful, fearful, fierce**⟫

EX. (**a**) It is frightening to think of the damage an earthquake might cause.
地震による被害について考えると{怖い/おそろしい}。
Jishin ni yoru higai ni-tsuite kangaeru to {kowai/osoroshii}.
(**b**) It was a frightening experience.
それは{怖い/恐ろしい}経験だった。
Sore wa {kowai/osoroshii} keiken datta.

frog n.
ka⌈eru かえる

from prep. **[indicating a starting point in space/time ⟪fig. "indicating the cause of s.t. or the material out of which s.t. is made"⟫]**
1. kara から prt. **[a particle that indicates a starting point in space/time]**, **de** で prt. **[using s.t.]** ⟪**by, with**⟫

EX. (**a**) This shop is open from 7:00 A.M. to 10:00 P.M.
この店は午前七時{から/*で}午後十時まで開いている。
*Kono mise wa gozen shichi-ji {kara/*de} gogo juu-ji made aite iru.*
(**b**) I usually walk to school from the station.
私はたいてい駅{から/*で}学校まで歩いて来る。
*Watashi wa taitei eki {kara/*de} gakkoo made aruite-kuru.*
(**c**) Please translate this letter from Japanese to English.
この手紙を日本語{から/*で}英語に訳してください。
*Kono tegami o Nihon-go {kara/*de} eigo ni yakushite kudasai.*
(**d**) There were anywhere from 50 to 70 students in the class.
クラスには五十人{から/*で}七十人ぐらいの学生がいた。
*Kurasu ni wa go-juu-nin {kara/*de} nana-juu-nin-gurai no gakusei ga ita.*
(**e**) From the roof of this building you can see Mt. Fuji.
このビルの屋上{から/*で}富士山が見える。
*Kono biru no okujoo {kara/*de} Fuji-san ga mieru.*
(**f**) She took the matches away from her child.
彼女は子供{から/*で}マッチを取り上げた。
*Kanojo wa kodomo {kara/*de} matchi o tori-ageta.*
(**g**) I borrowed money from a stranger.
知らない人{から/*で}お金を借りた。
*Shiranai hito {kara/*de} o-kane o karita.*
(**h**) *Sake* is made from rice.
酒は米{から/で}造られる。
Sake wa kome {kara/de} tsuku-rareru.

2. de で prt. **[indicating a weak causal relationship]** ⟪**because of**⟫

EX. (**a**) My eyes hurt from the wind.
風で目が痛い。
Kaze de me ga itai.
(**b**) Many children died from hunger.
たくさんの子供たちが飢えで死んだ。
Takusan no kodomo-tachi ga ue de shinda.

front n. **[the most forward position; the part of s.t. that faces forward or that is more important]**
1. ma⌉e 前 **[the part of s.t. that faces one]** ↔ **ushiro** 後ろ

EX. (**a**) You have to fasten your seat belt when you sit in the front seat.
前の席に座ったときは、シートベルトを着用しなければいけません。
Mae no seki ni suwatta toki wa, shiito-beruto o chakuyoo-shinakereba ikemasen.

(**b**) This blouse fastens in the front.
このブラウスは前で留めるようになっている。
Kono burausu wa mae de tomeru yooni natte iru.
(**c**) Don't look back. Face the front.
後ろを見ないで、前を向きなさい。
Ushiro o minaide, mae o mukinasai.
(**d**) A tall lady took her seat in the third row from the front.
背の高い女性が前から三列目の席についた。
Sei no takai josei ga mae kara san-retsu-me no seki ni tsuita.

2. i⌈chi-ban ma⌉e 一番前 [the most forward position] ⟪**foremost**⟫

EX. I usually sit at the front of the class.
たいてい教室の一番前に座ります。
Taitei kyooshitsu no ichi-ban mae ni suwarimasu.

F

3. o⌈mote⌉ 表 [the more conspicuous/important side of s.t.] ⟪**face, the right side**⟫ **↔ ura 裏**

EX. (**a**) Don't write your name on the front of the envelope, please.
封筒の表に自分の名前を書かないでください。
Fuutoo no omote ni jibun no namae o kakanaide kudasai.
(**b**) Is this the front of the tablecloth?
このテーブルクロスの表はこちらですか。
Kono teeburu-kurosu no omote wa kochira desu ka.

PHRASE: in front of ⟨*-no*⟩ *mae* ⟨～の⟩前

EX. (**a**) Let's meet in front of the station.
駅の前で会いましょう。
Eki no mae de aimashoo.
(**b**) The teacher stood in front of the class.
先生は学生の前に立った。
Sensei wa gakusei no mae ni tatta.

frost n. **[the white coating of tiny ice crystals which forms on outdoor surfaces when the temperature of the air is below freezing]**
shi⌈mo⌉ 霜

EX. The lawn was covered with frost this morning.
今朝は芝生に霜が下りていた。
Kesa wa shibafu ni shimo ga orite ita.

frosty adj. **[cold enough for frost]**
ko⌈ori-tsu⌉ku-yoona 凍りつくような adj(*na*). **[almost freezing]**

EX. It was a frosty morning.
凍りつくような朝だった。
Koori-tsuku-yoona asa datta.

frown vi. **[for s.o.to draw the eyebrows together causing lines on the forehead when angry/worried/displeased/concentrating]**
⟨-ni⟩ ma⌉yu o hi⌈some⌉ru ⟨～に⟩まゆをひそめる ② [for s.o to draw the eyebrows together causing lines on the forehead when angry/worried/displeased/concentrating], ⟨-ni⟩ ni⌈ga⌉i ka⌈o o suru ⟨～に⟩苦い顔をする ③ [for s.o. to have a look of displeasure/disapproval toward s.o./s.t. on one's face]

EX. He frowned at Miho over her thoughtless behavior.
彼は美穂の無神経なふるまいに{苦い顔をした/眉をひそめた}。
Kare wa Miho no mu-shinkeina furumai ni {nigai kao o shita/mayu o hisometa}.

fruit n.
ku⌈da⌉-mono 果物

EX. (**a**) Is the tomato a fruit or a vegetable?
トマトは果物ですか、野菜ですか。
Tomato wa kuda-mono desu ka, yasai desu ka.
(**b**) Fruit is expensive these days.
このごろは果物が高い。
Kono-goro wa kuda-mono ga takai.

fry vt./vi. **[to cook/be cooked in hot fat/oil]**
1. ⟨-o⟩ a⌈geru ⟨～を⟩あげる ② [to cause s.t./s.o. to rise ⟪fig. "give," "fry," "increase the price"⟫] ⟪**deep fry**⟫
㊅ "raise s.t."▷上げる, "fry/fly (a kite)/raise (a flag)"▷揚げる, "raise one's hand"▷挙げる, otherwise ▷あげる

EX. How about if we deep-fry some pork for dinner?

晩ごはんにトンカツを揚げましょうか。
Ban-gohan ni tonkatsu o agemashoo ka.

2. ⟨**-o**⟩ **i⸢tame⸣ru** ⟨〜を⟩いためる ② **[for s.o. to cook s.t. by stirring it in a small amount of oil]** 《**stir fry**》

EX. I eat lots of stir-fried vegetables.
私はいためた野菜をよく食べます。
Watashi wa itameta yasai o yoku tabemasu.

3. ⟨**-o**⟩ **ya⸢ku** ⟨〜を⟩焼く ① **[for s.o. to cause a change in s.t. through exposure to heat/fire/sunlight]** 《**bake, roast, broil, grill, toast, burn, fire**》

EX. Please fry the fish in butter.
魚をバターで焼いてください。
Sakana o bataa de yaite kudasai.

PHRASE: fried rice *yaki-meshi* 焼き飯, *chaahan* チャーハン •f; eggs fried sunny side up *hanjuku no medama-yaki* 半熟の目玉焼き

fuel n. **[s.t. that is burned to produce heat/energy]**
ne⸢nryo⸣o 燃料 •c

EX. We don't have enough fuel.
燃料が足りない。
Nenryoo ga tarinai.

PHRASE: add fuel to the flames *hi ni abura o sosogu* 火に油を注ぐ ①

full adj. **[for a container/space to hold as much/many of s.t. as it can]**
i⸢ppai no N いっぱいのN

EX (**a**) Professor Inoue's office is full of books.
井上先生の研究室は本でいっぱいだ。
Inoue-sensei no kenkyuu-shitsu wa hon de ippai da.
(**b**) I can't eat any more. I'm full.
もう食べられません。おなかがいっぱいです。
Moo tabe-raremasen. O-naka ga ippai desu.

PHRASE: full of confidence *jishin-manman no* N 自信満々のN •c

EX. He was full of confidence.
彼は自信満々だった。
Kare wa jishin-manman datta.

PHRASE: full moon *mangetsu* 満月 •c, be full of mistakes *machigai-darake no* N 間違いだらけのN, full house *man'in* 満員 •c

EX. It was a full house at the game last night.
ゆうべの試合は満員だった。
Yuube no shiai wa man'in datta.

fully adv. **[completely]**
ju⸢ubu⸣n(ni) 十分(に) •c **[to the extent required]** 《**thoroughly, to one's heart's content**》, **ka⸢nzenni** 完全に /⟨adj(*na*). ***ni*** of ***kanzenna*** complete/ •c **[in a manner absolutely free from any lack or imperfection]** 《**perfectly**》

EX. (**a**) I am fully satisfied with my present life.
現在の生活に{十分に/??完全に}満足しています。
Genzai no seikatsu ni {juubunni/??kanzenni} manzoku-shite imasu.
(**b**) It was weeks before he fully recovered.
彼が{完全に/十分に}良くなるのに何週間もかかった。
Kare ga {kanzenni/juubunni} yoku naru no ni nan-shuukan mo kakatta.
(**c**) Everybody fully enjoyed the party.
みんなパーティーを{十分に/*完全に}楽しんだ。
*Minna paatii o {juubunni/*kanzenni} tanoshinda.*
(**d**) The functions of the brain are still not fully understood.
脳の機能はまだ{完全に/十分に}は分かっていない。
Noo no kinoo wa mada {kanzenni/juubunni} wa wakatte inai.

PHRASE: fully automatic *zen-jidoo no* N 全自動のN •c

fun n. **[amusement/enjoyment/pleasure]**
ta⸢noshi⸣i 楽しい adj(*i*). **[experiencing intense enjoyment and satisfaction from s.t. and thus being drawn to it or causing such a feeling in one]** 《**pleasant, happy, cheerful, delightful, joyous**》, **o⸢moshiro⸣i** 面白い adj(*i*). **[arousing interest]** 《**amusing, entertaining, funny, enjoyable**》

EX. (**a**) It's fun to study kanji.
漢字の勉強は{楽しい/面白い}ですよ。
Kanji no benkyoo wa {tanoshii/omoshiroi} desu yo.

F

(**b**) It's not fun being alone on a Satuday night.
土曜日の夜、一人でいるのは{面白くない/楽しくない}。
Doyoo-bi no yoru, hitori de iru no wa {omoshirokunai/tanoshikunai}.

PHRASE: make fun of ⟨*-o*⟩ *karakau* ⟨〜を⟩からかう ①

EX. He is often made fun of for his Osaka accent.
彼はよく大阪弁をからかわれる。
Kare wa yoku Oosaka-ben o karakawa-reru.

function n. **[the use or purpose of s.t./s.o.]**
ya⌈kuwari⌉ 役割 [the duty assigned to one] ⟪**role, part**⟫, **ki⌉noo 機能 •c [the work s.t. is expected to accomplish as its intended purpose]**

EX. (**a**) The function of the heart is to pump blood through the body.
心臓の{機能/役割}は全身に血液を送り出すことです。
Shinzoo no {kinoo/yakuwari} wa zenshin ni ketsueki o okuri-dasu koto desu.
(**b**) The function of names is to identify individuals.
名前の{機能/役割}は個人を識別することだ。
Namae no {kinoo/yakuwari} wa kojin o shikibetsu-suru koto da.
(**c**) The function of the teacher is not just to teach.
教師の{役割/*機能}は教えることだけではない。
*Kyooshi no {yakuwari/*kinoo} wa oshieru koto dake dewanai.*

— vi. **[to fulfill a function]**
ha⌈taraku 働く ① [for s.t./s.o., esp. a laborer, mechanical device, or biological organ to operate properly or use one's energy productively to accomplish an intended purpose/goal] ⟪**work, operate**⟫

EX. This system is not functioning well.
このシステムはあまりうまく働いていない。
Kono shisutemu wa amari umaku hataraite inai.

fund n. **[a supply of money available for a purpose]**
ki⌈ki⌉n 基金 •c [a substantial sum of money established as capital for a particular project or cause] ⟪**fund, endowment**⟫, **shi⌈ki⌉n 資金 •c [money necessary for a certain activity]** ⟪**capital**⟫

EX. (**a**) We made a contribution to the famine relief fund.
飢餓救済{基金/?資金}に寄付した。
Kiga-kyuusai-{kikin/?shikin} ni kifu-shita.
(**b**) We have no campaign fund.
運動{資金/*基金}がない。
*Undoo-{shikin/*kikin} ga nai.*
(**c**) We held a fund-raising bazaar.
{資金/?基金}集めのバザーをした。
{Shikin/?Kikin}-atsume no bazaa o shita.

funeral n. **[a ceremony held for s.o. who has died before their burial]**
so⌈oshiki 葬式 •c

EX. (**a**) We held my grandfather's funeral at home.
祖父の葬式はうちでしました。
Sofu no sooshiki wa uchi de shimashita.
(**b**) The funeral service is being held at three o'clock.
葬式は三時からです。
Sooshiki wa san-ji kara desu.

funny adj. **[causing amusement/a sense of strangeness]**
o⌈kashi⌉i おかしい adj(*i*). ⟪**amusing, strange, odd, unusual, absurd**⟫, **o⌈ka⌉shina N おかしなN** ⟪**amusing, strange, odd, unusual, absurd**⟫, **he⌉nna 変な** adj(*na*). **•c [exhibiting an unusual characteristic/condition/behavior]** ⟪**strange, weird, odd, queer**⟫

EX. (**a**) What's so funny?
何がそんなに{おかしい/?変な}んですか。
Nani ga sonnani {okashii/?henna} n desu ka.
(**b**) He told funny stories and made everyone laugh.

彼は{おかしな/おかしい/?変な}話をしてみんなを笑わせた。
Kare wa {okashina/okashii/?henna} hanashi o shite minna o warawa-seta.
(**c**) The funny thing is that when I got to the doctor the pain was gone.
{おかしな/?おかしい/?変な}ことに医者に行ったときには、痛みは無くなっていたんです。
{Okashina/?Okashii/?Henna} koto ni isha ni itta toki ni wa, itami wa nakunatte ita n desu.
(**d**) There's something funny about this car.
この車はなんだか{おかしい/変だ}。
Kono kuruma wa nandaka {okashii/hen da}.

fur n. **[the soft thick hair that grows from the skin of animals]**
ke 毛 [a fine threadlike growth that emerges from the skin of humans and certain animals] (**(hair)**), **ke-⌈gawa 毛皮 [an animal skin covered with soft thick hair]**

EX. (a) A lady wearing a fur coat came to the office.
{毛皮/*毛}のコートを着た女の人がオフィスに入ってきた。
*{Ke-gawa/*Ke} no kooto o kita onna no hito ga ofisu ni haitte-kita.*
(**b**) I'm allergic to cat fur.
私は猫の{毛/*毛皮}にアレルギーなんです。
*Watashi wa neko no {ke/*ke-gawa} ni arerugii na n desu.*

furious adj. **[very angry]**
su⌉goku ha⌈ra⌉ {o ta⌈te⌉ru/ga ta⌉tsu} すごく腹{を立てる ②/が立つ ①} [for s.o. to get very angry], ka⌈n-kan ni na⌉tte o⌈ko⌉ru かんかんになって怒る ① [for s.o. to get very angry]

NOTE: When the subject is the first or second person, both *hara ga tatsu* and *hara o tateru* can be used, but with the third person subject *hara ga tatsu* cannot be used.

EX. (a) I think Mary will be furious with us if we don't go to her party.
私たちがパーティーへ行かなかったら、メアリーは{すごく腹を立てる/かんかんになって怒る}と思う。
Watashi-tachi ga paatii e ikanakattara, Mearii wa {sugoku hara o tateru/kan-kanni natte okoru} to omou.
(**b**) I was furious at being kept waiting for many hours.
私は何時間も待たされて、{すごく腹{が立った/を立てた}/かんかんになって怒った}。
Watashi wa nan-jikan mo mata-sarete, {sugoku hara {ga tatta/o tateta}/kan-kan ni natte okotta}.

furnish vt. **[to provide/supply s.t. (esp. furniture)]**
1. ka⌉gu o i⌈reru 家具を入れる ②

EX. It's costly to furnish a new apartment.
新しいアパートに家具を入れるのは金がかかる。
Atarashii apaato ni kagu o ireru no wa kane ga kakaru.

2. ⟨-ni⟩ ⟨-o⟩ so⌈nae-tsuke⌉ru ⟨～に⟩⟨～を⟩備え付ける ② [for s.o. to provide/supply s.t. for some location] (**(equip)**)

EX. Each room is furnished with a television set.
各部屋にテレビが備え付けてある。
Kaku-heya ni terebi ga sonae-tsukete aru.

PHRASE: furnished *kagu-tsuki no* N 家具付きのN

EX. I live in a furnished apartment.
私は家具付きのアパートに住んでいます。
Watashi wa kagu-tsuki no apaato ni sunde imasu.

furniture n. **[large movable objects placed in a room for use in daily living]**
ka⌉gu 家具 •c

EX. The only piece of furniture I bought was a bed.
私が買った家具はベッドだけです。
Watashi ga katta kagu wa beddo dake desu.

further adv. **[to a greater distance or extent]**
1. mo⌉tto sa⌈ki もっと先 [to/at a greater distance]

F

EX. Our school is further along this street.
学校はこの通りに沿ってもっと先です。
Gakkoo wa kono toori ni sotte motto saki desu.

2. mo˥tto もっと [to a greater degree in quantity/quality] ⟪more⟫, ho˥ka ni 外に [excepting that which has been mentioned] ⟪except, in addition, beyond⟫

EX. (**a**) I'll look further into this matter.
この問題を{もっと/*外に}調べてみます。
*Kono mondai o {motto/*hoka ni} shirabete mimasu.*
(**b**) We must get further information.
{もっと/*外に}情報が必要だ。
*{Motto/*Hoka ni} joohoo ga hitsuyoo da.*
(**c**) I have nothing further to say.
{外に/*もっと}言うことはない。
*{Hoka ni/*Motto} iu koto wa nai.*

F

furthermore conj. **[in addition to what has been said ⟨fml⟩]**
S shi, (so˥re ni) Sし、(それに) [in addition to what has been mentioned] ⟪moreover, in addition, what's more⟫, so˥re ni それに [in addition to what has been mentioned in the preceding context] ⟪in addition, moreover, on top of that⟫

EX. This restaurant is not very expensive, and furthermore it is not very crowded.
このレストランはあまり{高くないし、(それに)/高くない。それに}あまり込んでもいない。
Kono resutoran wa amari {takakunaishi, (sore ni)/takakunai. Sore ni} amari konde mo inai.

fury n. **[strong anger]**
i˥kari 怒り [anger ⟨fml⟩] ⟪rage, indignation⟫

EX. He threw the dish at the wall in a fury.
彼は怒りのあまり皿を壁に投げつけた。
Kare wa ikari no amari sara o kabe ni nage-tsuketa.

fuss n. **[an unnecessary, useless expression of excitement about s.t. unimportant]**
o˥o-sa˥wagi 大騒ぎ [a loud expression of excitement] ⟪noise, uproar, clamor⟫

EX. She always creates such a fuss over who gets to sit in the front seat of the car.
だれが車の前の席に座るかで彼女はいつも大騒ぎをする。
Dare ga kuruma no mae no seki ni suwaru ka de kanojo wa itsu-mo oo-sawagi o suru.

future n. **[the period of time after the present]**
sho˥orai 将来 •c [a short period of time after the present], mi˥rai 未来 •c [a long period of time after the present]

EX. (**a**) People may be living on the moon someday in the future.
{未来/*将来}には人間は月に住むようになるかもしれない。
*{Mirai/*Shoorai} ni wa ningen wa tsuki ni sumu yooni naru kamoshirenai.*
(**b**) We're saving as much as we can for our children's future.
子供の{将来/*未来}のためにできるだけ貯金をしている。
*Kodomo no {shoorai/*mirai} no tame ni dekiru-dake chokin o shite iru.*

PHRASE: in the near future *chikai uchi ni* 近いうちに

G

gain vi./vt. **[to get s.t. beneficial/wanted/needed]**
⟨-o⟩ {e˥ru/u˥ru} ⟨〜を⟩得る ② [for s.o. to get s.t. ⟨w⟩] ⟪get, obtain, win, acquire⟫
NOTE: *Uru* is a classical form of *eru* and is used only in this form. That is, it does not have any conjugation.
EX. (**a**) I have nothing to gain by telling a lie.
うそをついて得るものは何もない。
Uso o tsuite {eru/uru} mono wa nani-mo nai.
(**b**) He has gained a reputation for mental sharpness.
彼は頭が切れるという評判を得た。
Kare wa atama ga kireru to iu hyooban o eta.
(**c**) It is important for a salesman to gain the confidence of his customers.
客の信頼を得ることはセールスマンにとって大事なことだ。
Kyaku no shinrai o {eru/uru} koto wa seerusu-man ni-totte daijina koto da.

— n. **[s.t. gained, such as monetary profit] mo˥oke もうけ /⟨V*masu* of *mookeru* ② make money/ ⟪profit, earnings⟫, ri˥eki 利益 •c [an increase in (monetary) wealth generated by an excess of returns over costs] ⟪profit, returns⟫ ↔ sonshitsu 損失 •c**
EX. (**a**) He made substantial gains from his new business.
彼は新しいビジネスで{大もうけをした/多額の利益を得た}。
Kare wa atarashii bijinesu de {oo-mooke o shita/tagaku no rieki o eta}.
(**b**) She invested in the enterprise with the hope of future gain.
彼女は将来の{利益/もうけ}を見込んで、その事業に投資した。
Kanojo wa shoorai no {rieki/mooke} o mi-konde, sono jigyoo ni tooshi-shita.
PHRASE: gain weight *futoru* 太る ①, *taijuu ga fueru* 体重が増える ②, gain confidence *jishin o {tsukeru /motsu}* 自信を{つける ②/持つ ①}

game n. **[a form of play or sport, usu. conducted according to certain rules; wild animals and birds hunted for sport]**
1. a˥sobi 遊び /⟨V*masu* of *asobu* ① have fun/ [s.t. done for amusement instead of study or work ⟪fig. "free motion of a part of machine"⟫] ⟪play, pleasure⟫
EX. What kind of games do Japanese children like to play?
日本の子供たちはどんな遊びが好きですか。
Nihon no kodomo-tachi wa donna asobi ga suki desu ka.
2. shi˥ai 試合 •c [a planned event, usu. in sports, where individuals/teams match their skills in an attempt to gain superiority over each other according to rules mutually agreed upon] ⟪match⟫
EX. (**a**) We went to see a baseball game between the Lions and the Giants.
ライオンズとジャイアンツの野球の試合を見に行った。
Raionzu to Jaiantsu no yakyuu no shiai o mi ni itta.
(**b**) The Lions won the game by a score of 4 to 3.
ライオンズが四対三で試合に勝った。
Raionzu ga yon tai san de shiai ni katta.
(**c**) Our high school soccer team played a soccer game with the team from Brazil.
うちの高校のサッカーチームがブラジルから来たチームとサッカーの試合をした。
Uchi no kookoo no sakkaa-chiimu ga Burajiru kara kita chiimu to sakkaa no shiai o shita.

G

3. ge⌉emu ゲーム •f [a form of play or sport conducted according to certain rules and ending in a win for one of the participants]

EX. (**a**) Computer games are popular among children.
子供たちの間でコンピューターゲームがはやっている。
Kodomo-tachi no aida de konpyuutaa-geemu ga hayatte iru.
(**b**) We played a game in our Japanese class.
日本語の授業でゲームをした。
Nihon-go no jugyoo de geemu o shita.

4. su⌈po⌉otsu スポーツ •f [an activity requiring bodily exertion engaged in for fun]

EX. I find baseball to be a boring game.
野球は退屈なスポーツだと思う。
Yakyuu wa taikutsuna supootsu da to omou.

5. e⌈mono 獲物 [wild animals and birds caught by humans in hunting and fishing]

gang n. **[a group of criminals or a group of friends, esp. young people]**

1. bo⌈oryoku⌉-dan 暴力団 •c [an organized group of people who earn a living by means of violence or illegal activities], gya⌉ngu ギャング •f [a group of criminals], i⌈chi⌉mi 一味 •c [a group of people joined together for a criminal purpose] ⟪**ring**⟫

EX. (**a**) Gangs often make money through gambling.
{暴力団/ギャング/*一味}はとばくで資金を調達することが多い。
*{Booryoku-dan/Gyangu/*Ichimi} wa tobaku de shikin o chootatsu-suru koto ga ooi.*
(**b**) Three policemen were killed by a gang in New York City.
ニューヨークで警官が三人、{ギャング/?暴力団/*一味}に殺された。
*Nyuuyooku de keikan ga san-nin, {gyangu/?booryoku-dan/*ichimi} ni korosa-reta.*
(**c**) He belonged to a gang of terrorists.
彼はテロリストの{一味/*暴力団/*ギャング}だった。
*Kare wa terorisuto no {ichimi/*booryoku-dan/*gyangu} datta.*

2. na⌈kama⌉ 仲間 [a person in one's in-group with whom one frequently spends time, excluding one's relatives, spouse, and offspring ⟪fig. "the same kind"⟫] ⟪**buddy, companion, company**⟫

EX. Have you seen any of the gang lately?
最近だれか我々の仲間に会ったかい。
Saikin dare-ka ware-ware no nakama ni atta kai.

gap n. **[an opening between two objects/two parts of s.t. ⟪fig. "divergence"⟫]**

1. su⌈ki-ma 透き間 ⟪**opening, space**⟫

EX. We peeped inside through a gap in the fence.
私たちは塀の透き間から中をのぞいた。
Watashi-tachi wa hei no suki-ma kara naka o nozoita.

2. nu⌈kete iru bu⌉bun 抜けている部分 [a part which is missing]

EX. There are gaps in my knowledge of Japanese history.
私の日本史の知識には抜けている部分がある。
Watashi no Nihon-shi no chishiki ni wa nukete iru bubun ga aru.

3. gya⌉ppu ギャップ •f [a difference between two things]

EX. There is a big gap between the ideal and reality.
理想と現実の間には大きなギャップがある。
Risoo to genjitsu no aida ni wa ookina gyappu ga aru.

garage n. **[a building in which a car/cars can be kept or a place where one can have a car repaired]**

1. sha⌉ko 車庫 •c [a building in which a car/cars can be kept], ga⌈re⌉eji ガレージ •f

EX. Hiroko put the car in the garage.
弘子は車を{車庫/ガレージ}に入れた。
Hiroko wa kuruma o {shako/gareeji} ni ireta.

2. ga⌈sorin-suta⌉ndo ガソリンスタンド •f [a place where one can buy gasoline] ⟪**gas station**⟫, **(ji⌈do⌉osha-)shu⌈uri-ko⌉ojoo** (自動

車)修理工場 •c **[a place where one can have a car repaired]**

EX. His father runs a garage.
彼のお父さんは{自動車修理工場/ガソリンスタンド}をやっている。
Kare no o-too-san wa {jidoosha-shuuri-koojoo/gasorin-sutando} o yatte iru.

garbage n. **[waste material to be thrown away]**
na⌈ma-gomi 生ごみ [waste material from a kitchen], go⌈mi⌉ ごみ [a general term for waste material] ((**rubbish, litter, trash**))

EX. (**a**) The disposal of garbage is a big problem today.
{ごみ/生ごみ}の処理は今大きな問題だ。
{Gomi/Nama-gomi} no shori wa ima ookina mondai da.
(**b**) How much garbage is produced in this area in a day?
この辺では一日にどのくらい{ごみ/?生ごみ}が出ますか。
Kono hen de wa ichi nichi ni dono-kurai {gomi/?nama-gomi} ga demasu ka.

PHRASE: garbage can *gomi-bako* ごみ箱

garden n. **[a piece of land where flowers or vegetables are grown]**
ni⌈wa 庭 ((**yard**)), **te⌈ien 庭園 •c**

NOTE: *Teien* is larger and more formal than *niwa.*

EX. (**a**) We only have a small garden in our yard.
うちには小さい{庭/*庭園}しかありません。
*Uchi ni wa chiisai {niwa/*teien} shika arimasen.*
(**b**) There are various flowers planted in the garden.
{庭/庭園}にはいろいろな花が植えてあります。
{Niwa/Teien} ni wa iro-irona hana ga uete arimasu.
(**c**) I have to weed out the garden tomorrow.
あしたは{庭/庭園}の草取りをしなければいけません。
Ashita wa {niwa/teien} no kusa-tori o shinakereba ikemasen.

PHRASE: vegetable garden *saien* 菜園 •c, botanical garden *shokubutsu-en* 植物園 •c

gas[1] n. **[a form of matter other than liquid or solid which tends to diffuse evenly throughout a space, esp. that used as a fuel in heating and cooking]**
ga⌉su ガス •f [a gaseous substance used as fuel in heating and cooking], ki⌈tai 気体 •c [a form of matter other than liquid or solid which tends to diffuse evenly throughout a space, such as air]

EX. (**a**) There was a smell of gas so I opened all the windows.
{ガス/*気体}のにおいがしたので、私は窓を全部開けた。
*{Gasu/*Kitai} no nioi ga shita node, watashi wa mado o zenbu aketa.*
(**b**) She turned on the gas to boil water.
彼女は湯をわかすために{ガス/*気体}に火を付けた。
*Kanojo wa yu o wakasu tame ni {gasu/*kitai} ni hi o tsuketa.*
(**c**) The police used tear gas to bring the riot under control.
警察は暴動を鎮めるのに催涙{ガス/*気体}を使った。
*Keisatsu wa boodoo o shizumeru no ni sairui-{gasu/*kitai} o tsukatta.*
(**d**) Oxygen is a gas.
酸素は{気体/*ガス}である。
*Sanso wa {kitai/*gasu} dearu.*

gas[2] n. **[gasoline]**
ga⌈sorin ガソリン ((**petrol** (Br. E)))

EX. We're out of gas.
ガソリンが無くなった。
Gasorin ga nakunatta.

PHRASE: gas station *gasorin-sutando* ガソリンスタンド •f, natural gas *tennen-gasu* 天然ガス •c+f

gasoline n.
ga⌈sorin ガソリン ((**petrol, gas**))

EX. I had gasoline put in the car.
車にガソリンを入れてもらいました。
Kuruma ni gasorin o irete moraimashita.

gate n. **[a movable structure that is used to open or close an opening in a fence/wall]**
mo⌉n 門 •c [a structure at the outer perimeter of a property which one goes through to enter or exit the property]

EX. The school gate was wide open.
学校の門は広く開いていた。
Gakkoo no mon wa hiroku aite ita.

PHRASE: front gate *seimon* 正門 •c, back gate *ura-mon* 裏門

gather vt. **[to bring things/people together or to infer s.t. on the basis of infomation available]**

1. ⟨-o⟩ a⌈tsume⌉ru ⟨〜を⟩集める ② [for s.o. to cause things or people that are scattered in various places to come to one and the same place] 《collect, assemble, attract》

EX. (**a**) He gathered information from various sources for the report.
報告をまとめるためにいろいろなところから情報を集めた。
Hookoku o matomeru tame ni iro-irona tokoro kara joohoo o atsumeta.
(**b**) We saw a rabit while we were gathering wood.
たきぎを集めている時、うさぎを見た。
Takigi o atsumete iru toki, usagi o mita.
(**c**) It took me a year and a half to gather my data.
データを集めるのに一年半かかった。
Deeta o atsumeru no ni ichi-nen-han kakatta.

2. Sinf. to o⌈mo⌉u Sinf.と思う ① [for s.o. to spontaneously perceive s.t. in one's mind or to have an opinion about s.t.] 《think, feel, believe》

EX. I gather he is busy with his paper.
彼は論文で忙しいんだと思う。
Kare wa ronbun de isogashii n da to omou.

— vi. **[to come together]**

1. ⟨-ni⟩ a⌈tsuma⌉ru ⟨〜に⟩集まる ① [for people/things/animals of a similar type scattered apart to come together in the same place] 《assemble, center, crowd》

EX. The children gathered around the teacher.
子供たちは先生の回りに集まった。
Kodomo-tachi wa sensei no mawari ni atsumatta.

2. ta⌈maru たまる ① [for different tokens of a certain kind of thing to come together more and more] 《be saved, be accumulated, be stored, collect》

EX. Dust gathered on the table.
テーブルの上にほこりがたまった。
Teeburu no ue ni hokori ga tamatta.

gay adj. **[happy and full of fun/homosexual]**

1. a⌈karui 明るい adj(*i*). **[for there to be enough light to do s.t. or for s.t. to be not dark in color 《fig. "cheerful," "be versed in"》] 《cheerful, sunny, rosy, light》, yo⌈okina 陽気な** adj(*na*). **•c [for s.o. to have a happy disposition and behave pleasantly] 《lively, merry, jolly》**

EX. She is a gay, carefree girl.
彼女は{明るくて/陽気で}のんきな女の子です。
Kanojo wa {akarukute/yooki de} nonkina onna-no-ko desu.

2. do⌈oseia⌉isha no N 同性愛者のN •c [homosexual]

EX. He is gay.
彼は同性愛者です。
Kare wa dooseiaisha desu.

gaze vi. **[for s.o./s.a. to look long and steadily at s.t./s.o./s.a.]**

⟨-o⟩ ji⌈tto mi⌉ru ⟨〜を⟩じっと見る ② [for s.o./s.a. to look at s.t./s.o./s.a. without averting one's eyes] 《stare》, ⟨-o⟩ mi⌈tsume⌉ru ⟨〜を⟩見つめる ② [for s.o./s.a. to continue watching s.o./s.t./s.a. intently]

EX. (**a**) She sat gazing at the painting on the wall.
彼女は壁の絵を{じっと見ながら/見つめながら}、座っていた。
Kanojo wa kabe no e o {jitto minagara/mi-tsumenagara}, suwatte ita.
(**b**) What are you gazing at?
何を{じっと見て/見つめて}いるんですか。
Nani o {jitto mite/mi-tsumete} iru n desu ka.

NOTE: *Jitto mi-tsumeru* is also possible.

gear n. **[a set of toothed wheels that transmit the power of an engine to an axle and by which adjustments are made in the speed and power of the rotating motion of the axle]**

gi⌉a ギア •f

EX. I put the car into second gear to go down the steep hill.
急な坂を下りるのに車のギアをセカンドに入れた。
Kyuuna saka o oriru no ni kuruma no gia o sekando ni ireta.

gee interj. **[an expression of surprise]**
hee へえ [an interjection to indicate surprise/amazement]

EX. Gee, what a man!
へえ、なんという男だろう。
Hee, nan to iu otoko daroo.

NOTE: *Hee* can be pronounced with a longer vowel as *heee.*

general adj. **[applying to all or most of a class; not limited in applicability; not concerned with details]**
ippan no N 一般のN •c [concerning the ordinary members of a group or set], ippan-tekina 一般的な adj(*na*). **•c [widely applicable to the whole]**

EX. (**a**) Tell me your general opinion on the matter.
この問題に関する{一般の/一般的な}意見を聞かせてください。
Kono mondai ni-kansuru {ippan no/ippan-tekina} iken o kika-sete kudasai.
(**b**) This magazine aims at a general audience.
この雑誌は{一般の/?一般的な}読者を対象にしている。
Kono zasshi wa {ippan no/?ippan-tekina} dokusha o taishoo ni shite iru.
(**c**) The general standard of education in Japan is very high.
日本の{一般的な/一般の}教育水準はたいへん高い。
Nihon no {ippan-tekina/ippan no} kyooiku-suijun wa taihen takai.

PHRASE: general public *ippan-taishuu* 一般大衆 **•c**, general meeting *sookai* 総会 **•c**, general hospital *soogoo-byooin* 総合病院 **•c**, general strike *zenesuto* ゼネスト **•f**, general election *soo-senkyo* 総選挙 **•c**

generally adv. **[usually/not specifically]**
1. taitei 大抵 [in the great majority of cases] ⟪**usually, mostly, for the most part, nearly always**⟫

EX. I generally eat dinner at home.
晩ごはんは大抵うちで食べます。
Ban-gohan wa taitei uchi de tabemasu.

2. ippan ni 一般に •c [in a general manner]

EX. Generally speaking, Japanese college students don't study much.
一般に日本の大学生はあまり勉強しない。
Ippan ni Nihon no daigaku-sei wa amari benkyoo-shinai.

generation n. **[a group of people who are of a similar age]**
sedai 世代 •c

EX. (**a**) Our generation has had no experience of war.
私たちの世代は戦争体験がない。
Watashi-tachi no sedai wa sensoo-taiken ga nai.
(**b**) Four generations of that family live under the same roof.
あの家族は四世代が一軒の家に住んでいます。
Ano kazoku wa yon-sedai ga ik-ken no ie ni sunde imasu.

PHRASE: generation gap *sedai no sooi* 世代の相違, *jenereeshon-gyappu* ジェネレーションギャップ **•f**; from generation to generation *dai-dai* 代々 **•c**

generous adj. **[ready to give money, help, etc., to a needy person or cause ⟪fig. "magnanimous"⟫]**
1. ki-mae ga ii 気前がいい adj(*i*). **[not stingy]**

EX. (**a**) Mrs. Smith's donation to our scholarship fund was a generous one.
スミス夫人の我々の奨学基金に対する寄付は気前がいいものだった。
Sumisu-fujin no ware-ware no shoogaku-kikin ni-taisuru kifu wa ki-mae ga ii mono datta.
(**b**) My grandfather is very generous and gives me pocket money whenever I visit him.
祖父はとても気前がよくて、遊びに行くといつも小遣いをくれる。
Sofu wa totemo ki-mae ga yokute, asobi

| *ni iku to itsu-mo ko-zukai o kureru.*

2. ka⌈ndaina 寛大な adj(*na*). **•c [to be understanding of the faults/failures of others]** **《lenient, tolerant》**

EX. | The teacher was generous in his treatment of the naughty boys.
先生はいたずら坊主たちに対して寛大だった。
Sensei wa itazura-boozu-tachi ni taishite kandai datta.

genius n. **[(a person of) exceptionally great mental or other natural ability]**

1. te⌈nsai 天才 •c

EX. | He is a linguistic genius.
彼は語学の天才だ。
Kare wa gogaku no tensai da.

2. te⌉npu no sa⌉i 天賦の才 [an exceptionally great capacity that one is born with]

EX. | She is a genius at learning languages.
彼女は語学に天賦の才がある。
Kanojo wa gogaku ni tenpu no sai ga aru.

gentle adj. **[kind, mild, not rough]**

G

1. (⟨-ni⟩) ya⌈sashii (⟨〜に⟩)やさしい adj(*i*). **[causing little or no trouble (to understand) 《fig. "gentle"》]** **《easy, tender》** **↔ muzukashii 難しい** adj(*i*)., **kibishii 厳しい** adj(*i*).

㊈ "easy"▷易しい, "tender"▷優しい

EX. | (**a**) He is kind and gentle to women.
彼は女性に親切で優しい。
Kare wa josei ni shinsetsu de yasashii.
(**b**) She said "Good morning" to us in a gentle voice.
彼女は優しい声で「おはようございます」と言った。
Kanojo wa yasashii koe de 'O-hayoo gozaimasu' to itta.

2. o⌈tonashi⌉i おとなしい adj(*i*). **[obedient or reserved in behavior; subdued or inconspicuous in visual effect]** **《well-behaved, good-tempered, mild, quiet, obedient》**

EX. | This horse is very gentle.
この馬はとてもおとなしいです。
Kono uma wa totemo otonashii desu.

gentleman n. **[a man who is well-mannered and who acts honorably]**

shi⌉nshi 紳士 •c ↔ shukujo 淑女 •c

PHRASE: ladies and gentlemen *mina-sama* 皆様, gentleman's agreement *shinshi-kyootei* 紳士協定 **•c**

gently adv. **[in a gentle manner]**

ya⌈sashiku 優しく /⟨adj(*i*). *ku* of *yasashii* gentle/

EX. | (**a**) The old lady smiled gently at Tom.
そのおばあさんはトムに優しくほほえみかけた。
Sono o-baa-san wa Tomu ni yasashiku hohoemi-kaketa.
(**b**) "You have nothing to worry about," he said gently.
彼は「何も心配は要りませんよ」と優しく言った。
Kare wa 'Nani-mo shinpai wa irimasen yo' to yasashiku itta.

geography n. **[(the study of) physical features of the earth's surface, its climate, its population, etc.]**

chi⌉ri 地理 •c

EX. | I don't know much about the geography of Japan.
日本の地理をあまり知りません。
Nihon no chiri o amari shirimasen.

geology n. **[the scientific study of the substances which make up the earth]**

chi⌈shitsu⌉-gaku 地質学 •c

geometry n. **[a field of mathematics that deals with properties and relations of lines, angles, surfaces and solids]**

ki⌈ka⌉(-gaku) 幾何(学) •c

German adj. **[of Germany/its people]**

Do⌉itsu no N ドイツのN •f [of Germany]

EX. | Have you ever tried German bread?
ドイツのパンを食べたことがありますか。
Doitsu no pan o tabeta koto ga arimasu ka.

—— n. **[the language of Germany, Austria, and parts of Switzerland or a person from Germany]**

1. Do⌈itsu-go ドイツ語 •f+c [the language of Germany, Austria, and parts of Switzerland]

EX. Is German difficult to learn?
ドイツ語を習うのは難しいですか。
Doitsu-go o narau no wa muzukashii desu ka.

2. Do⌈itsu⌉-jin ドイツ人 •f+c [the people/a person of Germany]

EX. I have a German friend.
私はドイツ人の友達がいます。
Watashi wa Doitsu-jin no tomodachi ga imasu.

Germany n.
Do⌉itsu ドイツ •f

gesture n. **[a movement of the body, especially the hands, to express a certain meaning]**
ze⌉suchaa ゼスチャー •f, te⌉buri 手振り [a movement of the hands to express a certain meaning], mi⌉buri 身振り [a movement of the body to express a certain meaning]

EX. (**a**) He made an angry gesture.
彼は怒ったような{身振り/ゼスチャー/?手振り}をした。
Kare wa okotta yoona {miburi/zesuchaa/?teburi} o shita.
(**b**) He expressed his satisfaction with a gesture.
彼は{身振り/ゼスチャー/?手振り}で満足したことを表した。
Kare wa {miburi/zesuchaa/?teburi} de manzoku-shita koto o arawashita.
(**c**) We couldn't speak Italian so we had to communicate by gesture.
イタリア語が話せないので、{身振り/手振り/ゼスチャー}でコミュニケーションをしなければなりませんでした。
Itaria-go ga hanase-nai node, {miburi/teburi/zesuchaa} de komyunikeeshon o shinakereba narimasen deshita.

get vt. **[to receive/obtain s.t. or to cause s.o./s.t./s.a. to do s.t. or be a certain way]**
1. {⟨-ni⟩/⟨-kara⟩} ⟨-o⟩ mo⌈rau {⟨〜に⟩/⟨〜から⟩} ⟨〜を⟩もらう ① [for the speaker or s.o. in the speaker's in-group to obtain s.t. from s.o. whose status is equal to or lower than that of the person who receives it] ⟪**receive**⟫, **{⟨-ni⟩/⟨-kara⟩} ⟨-o⟩ i⌈tadaku {⟨〜に⟩/⟨〜から⟩} ⟨〜を⟩いただく ① [for the speaker or s.o. in the speaker's in-group to obtain s.t. from s.o. whose status is higher than that of the person who receives it]** ⟪**receive, accept**⟫
NOTE: *Itadaku* is used to show deference to the giver.

EX. (**a**) I got a small wallet on my birthday from my older sister.
私の誕生日に姉{に/から}小さい財布を{もらいました/*いただきました}。
*Watashi no tanjoo-bi ni ane {ni/kara} chiisai saifu o {moraimashita/*itadakimashita}.*
(**b**) Did you get anything from Mr. Yamada?
山田さん{に/から}何か{もらいました/いただきました}か。
Yamada-san {ni/kara} nani-ka {moraimashita/itadakimashita} ka.
(**c**) I got this book from Prof. Teramura.
寺村先生{に/から}この本を{いただきました/??もらいました}。
Teramura-sensei {ni/kara} kono hon o {itadakimashita/??moraimashita}.

2. ⟨-o⟩ u⌈ke⌉ru ⟨〜を⟩受ける ② [to be exposed to s.t. that has an effect on one and accept it] ⟪**receive, accept, be given, obtain**⟫

EX. (**a**) I got a shock seeing her in that condition.
彼女がそんな状態にあるのを見て、ショックを受けた。
Kanojo ga sonna jootai ni aru no o mite, shokku o uketa.
(**b**) I get the impression that students this year are not working very hard.
今年の学生はあまり一生懸命勉強していないという印象を受ける。
Kotoshi no gakusei wa amari isshoo-kenmei benkyoo-shite inai to iu inshoo o ukeru.

3. ⟨-o⟩ to⌈tte-ku⌉ru ⟨〜を⟩取って来る ③ [for s.o./s.a. to go to a certain place, pick up s.t., and come back] ⟪**go and bring**⟫

EX. Would you get my reading glasses for me, Hanako?
花子、老眼鏡を取って来てくれないか。

Hanako, roogan-kyoo o totte-kite kurenai ka.

4. ⟨-ni⟩ ⟨-o⟩ V*te* mo⌈rau ⟨〜に⟩⟨〜を⟩V*te*もらう [for s.o. to ask for and have s.o. do s.t. for oneself]

EX. (**a**) I have to get this tape recorder repaired.
このテープレコーダーを直してもらわなければなりません。
Kono teepu-rekoodaa o naoshite morawanakereba narimasen.
(**b**) I got my roommate to help me with my homework.
ルームメートに宿題を手伝ってもらいました。
Ruumu-meeto ni shukudai o tetsudatte moraimashita.

5. {⟨-ni⟩/⟨-o⟩} {Vneg. + seru/Vstem + saseru/ko-sase⌉ru/sa⌈seru} {⟨〜に⟩/⟨〜を⟩}{Vneg.+せる/Vstem+させる/来させる/させる} ② [for s.o./s.a. to cause s.o./s.t./s.a. to do s.t./to change in state]

EX. (**a**) I'll get the children ready for school.
子供たちに学校へ行く準備をさせます。
Kodomo-tachi ni gakkoo e iku junbi o sasemasu.
(**b**) I can't get my dog to shake hands.
犬に「お手」をさせることができない。
Inu ni 'ote' o saseru koto ga dekinai.

—— vi. **[to become]**
{adj(*i*). *ku*/adj(*na*). *ni*/⟨-ni⟩} na⌉ru {adj(*i*). *ku*/adj(*na*). *ni*/⟨〜に⟩}なる ①

EX. (**a**) I want to take some pictures before it gets dark.
暗くなる前に写真を撮りたい。
Kuraku naru mae ni shashin o tori-tai.
(**b**) I'm getting worried about my exams.
試験のことがだんだん心配になってきた。
Shiken no koto ga dan-dan shinpai ni natte kita.
(**c**) They must have gotten lost.
迷子になったに違いない。
Maigo ni natta ni chigai-nai.

PHRASE: get along with ⟨*-to*⟩ *tsuki-au* ⟨〜と⟩付き合う ① ⟪be associated with⟫

EX. My classmates are all very easy to get along with.
クラスメートはみんな付き合いやすい人です。
Kurasu-meeto wa minna tsuki-ai-yasui hito desu.

PHRASE: get along with ⟨*-to*⟩ *umaku iku* ⟨〜と⟩うまく行く ① ⟪be on good terms with⟫

EX. Are you getting along with your officemates?
会社の同僚とはうまく行っていますか。
Kaisha no dooryoo to wa umaku itte imasu ka.

PHRASE: get off ⟨*-o*⟩ *oriru* ⟨〜を⟩降りる ②

EX. I got off the bus in front of the station.
駅の前でバスを降りた。
Eki no mae de basu o orita.

PHRASE: get on ⟨*-ni*⟩ *noru* ⟨〜に⟩乗る ① ⟪ride, board, take⟫

EX. I couldn't get on the train because it was packed due to the rush hour.
ラッシュアワーで満員だったので電車に乗れなかった。
Rasshu-awaa de man'in datta node densha ni nore-nakatta.

PHRASE: get sick of ⟨*-ga*⟩ *iyani naru* ⟨〜が⟩いやになる /⟨adj(*na*). *ni* of *iyana* be disgusted + *naru* ① become/ ①

EX. I got sick of studying.
勉強がいやになった。
Benkyoo ga iyani natta.

PHRASE: get to ⟨*-ni*⟩ *tsuku* ⟨〜に⟩着く ① ⟪arrive at, reach⟫

EX. The train got to Perth early in the morning.
列車は朝早くパースに着いた。
Ressha wa asa hayaku Paasu ni tsuita.

PHRASE: get up *okiru* 起きる ②, ⟨*-o*⟩ *okosu* ⟨〜を⟩起こす ① ⟪wake up⟫

EX. (**a**) What time did you get up this morning?
今朝、何時に起きましたか。
Kesa, nan-ji ni okimashita ka.
(**b**) Would you get me up at 6:00 tomorrow?
あした六時に起こしてくれませんか。
Ashita roku-ji ni okoshite kuremasen ka.

PHRASE: get well *naoru* 治る ①, *genkini naru* 元気になる /⟨adj(*na*). *ni* of *genkina* fine + *naru* ① become/ ① ⟪get better, recover, be cured, heal⟫

EX. You'll get well in a few days.

二、三日で{治る/元気になる}でしょう。
Ni-san-nichi de {naoru/genkini naru} desyoo.

ghost n. **[the spirit of a person supposedly seen or felt after the person has died]**
yu⌉urei 幽霊 •c [a person who is believed to have returned from the world of death] **⟪apparition⟫**

EX. (**a**) I don't believe in ghosts.
私は幽霊なんか信じない。
Watashi wa yuurei nanka shinjinai.
(**b**) He looked as if he had seen a ghost.
彼は幽霊でも見たような顔をしていた。
Kare wa yuurei demo mita yoona kao o shite ita.

giant n. **[an imaginary person who is extremely big and strong ⟪fig. "a person of great ability"⟫]**
kyo⌈jin 巨人 •c

gift n. **[s.t. given (by God)]**
1. o⌈kuri-mono 贈り物 ⟪present⟫, pu⌈re⌉zento プレゼント •f ⟪present⟫

EX. (**a**) This scarf is a gift from my friend.
このスカーフは友達からの{贈り物/プレゼント}です。
Kono sukaafu wa tomodachi kara no {okuri-mono/purezento} desu.
(**b**) I gave her a set of handkerchiefs as a gift.
私は彼女に{贈り物/プレゼント}としてハンカチのセットをあげた。
Watashi wa kanojo ni {okuri-mono/purezento} to-shite hankachi no setto o ageta.

2. mi⌈yage 土産 [s.t. one brings home from a trip/visit, usu. to give to those remaining behind, or s.t. one takes to give to one's host(ess) when visiting some place away from home] ⟪present, souvenir⟫

EX. (**a**) I bought some beef while on a trip to Australia as a gift for my colleagues at work.
オーストラリア旅行の土産に会社の同僚には牛肉を買ってきた。
Oosutoraria-ryokoo no miyage ni kaisha no dooryoo ni wa gyuuniku o katte kita.
(**b**) My father would sometimes bring a cake home with him after work as a little gift for his chidren.
父は子供たちへのお土産として仕事の帰りに時々ケーキを買ってきてくれた。
Chichi wa kodomo-tachi e no o-miyage to-shite shigoto no kaeri ni toki-doki keeki o katte-kite kureta.
(**c**) I chose a kokeshi-doll as a gift for my host family.
ホストファミリーへの土産としてこけし人形を選んだ。
Hosuto-famirii e no miyage to-shite kokeshi-ningyoo o eranda.

3. sa⌈inoo 才能 •c [innate intellectual or artistic capability, esp. of an outstanding kind] ⟪talent⟫

EX. He has a gift for music.
彼は音楽の才能がある。
Kare wa ongaku no sainoo ga aru.

ginger n.
sho⌈oga しょうが

giraffe n.
ki⌈rin きりん

girl n. **[a young female]**
1. o⌈nna⌉-no-ko 女の子 [a young female], sho⌉ojo 少女 •c [a female child]

EX. (**a**) Who is that cute girl?
あのかわいい{女の子/少女}はだれですか。
Ano kawaii {onna-no-ko/shoojo} wa dare desu ka.
(**b**) That singer is popular with girls.
あの歌手は{女の子/?少女}に人気がある。
Ano kashu wa {onna-no-ko/?shoojo} ni ninki ga aru.

2. mu⌈sume⌉ 娘 [a humble form referring to one's own female child or a young unmarried woman], mu⌈sume-san 娘さん [a polite term used to refer to s.o. else's daughter or a young woman], o-⌈jo⌉o-san お嬢さん [a polite term used to refer to s.o. else's daughter or a young unmarried woman] ⟪Miss⟫

EX. (**a**) Our girl is going off to college next year.
来年{娘/*娘さん/*お嬢さん}が大学に入ります。

G

*Rainen {musume/*musume-san/*o-joo-san} ga daigaku ni hairimasu.*
(**b**) Mr. Yamada's youngest girl is studying abroad in France.
山田さんの一番下の{娘さん/お嬢さん/?娘}はフランスに留学している。
Yamada-san no ichiban shita no {musume-san/o-joo-san/?musume} wa Furansu ni ryuugaku-shite iru.

PHRASE: girl friend *gaaru-furendo* ガールフレンド •f

give vt. **[to cause/allow s.o. to have s.t.]**

1. 〈**-ni**〉 〈**-o**〉 **a⌈geru** 〈～に〉〈～を〉あげる ② **[for s.o. to cause/allow s.o. else who is not in the speaker's in-group and whose status is equal to/lower than that of the giver to have s.t.]**

EX. (**a**) I gave him a bottle of *sake* to celebrate his promotion.
私は彼に昇進祝いに酒をあげた。
Watashi wa kare ni shooshin-iwai ni sake o ageta.
(**b**) What are you going to give Hanako for Christmas?
クリスマスに花子さんに何をあげますか。
Kurisumasu ni Hanako-san ni nani o agemasu ka.

2. 〈**-ni**〉 〈**-o**〉 **sa⌈shi-ageru** 〈～に〉〈～を〉差し上げる ② **[for s.o. to cause/allow s.o. else who is not in the speaker's in-group and whose status is higher than that of the giver to have s.t.]**

EX. I gave some flowers to my teacher for her birthday.
先生の誕生日に花を差し上げた。
Sensei no tanjoo-bi ni hana o sashi-ageta.

3. 〈**-ni**〉 〈**-o**〉 **ya⌈ru** 〈～に〉〈～を〉やる ① **[for s.o. to cause/allow s.o./s.a./s.t. who is not in the speaker's in-group and whose status is lower than that of the giver to have s.t.]**

EX. (**a**) Hiroshi gives milk to his cat every day.
浩は毎日猫に牛乳をやります。
Hiroshi wa mai-nichi neko ni gyuunyuu o yarimasu.
(**b**) I gave the flowers in the garden some water.
私は庭の花に水をやった。
Watashi wa niwa no hana ni mizu o yatta.

4. 〈**-ni**〉 〈**-o**〉 **ku⌈reru** 〈～に〉〈～を〉くれる ② **[for s.o. whose status is not higher than that of the speaker to cause/allow the speaker or s.o. in the speaker's in-group to have s.t.]**

EX. (**a**) My students gave me a bottle of French wine at the end of the semester.
学期の終わりに学生がフランスのワインをくれました。
Gakki no owari ni gakusei ga Furansu no wain o kuremashita.
(**b**) An old friend of mine gave my son a bicycle.
古い友達が息子に自転車をくれた。
Furui tomodachi ga musuko ni jitensha o kureta.

5. 〈**-ni**〉 〈**-o**〉 **ku⌈dasa⌉ru** 〈～に〉〈～を〉くださる ① **[for s.o. whose status is higher than that of the speaker to cause/allow the speaker or s.o. in the speaker's in-group to have s.t.]**

NOTE: V*masu* of *kudasaru* is *kudasaimasu* rather than *kudasarimasu.*

EX. The manager gave me two tickets to the kabuki performance.
マネージャーが歌舞伎の切符を二枚くださいました。
Maneejaa ga kabuki no kippu o ni-mai kudasaimashita.

NOTE: There is no passive form for *ageru, sashi-ageru, yaru, kureru* or *kudasaru.* That is, "be given" comes out as *itadaku* or *morau* "receive," as in the following example. SEE receive

EX. I was given two tickets to the kabuki performance by the manager.
マネージャーに歌舞伎の切符を二枚いただきました。
Maneejaa ni kabuki no kippu o ni-mai itadakimashita.

6. 〈**-ni**〉 〈**-o**〉 **a⌈taeru** 〈～に〉〈～を〉与える ② **[for s.o. to cause/let s.o. have s.t.]** **《provide, award, allot》**

EX. (**a**) We should give everybody an equal chance.

みんなに公平にチャンスを与えるべきです。
Minna ni kooheini chansu o ataeru-beki desu.
(**b**) I want to make the most of the chance I have been given.
与えられたチャンスを十分に活かしたい。
Atae-rareta chansu o juubunni ikashi-tai.

7. ⟨**-ni**⟩ ⟨**-o**⟩ **yu⌈zuru** ⟨～に⟩⟨～を⟩譲る ① **[for s.o. to hand over one's possession/right/position/status, etc., to s.o. else]** ⟪**transfer, hand over, yield**⟫

EX. I gave my seat to an old woman on the train.
私は電車でおばあさんに席を譲った。
Watashi wa densha de o-baa-san ni seki o yuzutta.

PHRASE: give in ⟨*-ni*⟩ *makeru* ⟨～に⟩負ける ② ⟪be defeated, be overcome, lose⟫

EX. I gave in to temptation and drank beer.
誘惑に負けて、ビールを飲んでしまった。
Yuuwaku ni makete, biiru o nonde shimatta.

PHRASE: give up ⟨*-o*⟩ *yameru* ⟨～を⟩やめる ② ⟪stop⟫

EX. (**a**) I gave up smoking.
たばこをやめました。
Tabako o yamemashita.
(**b**) She had to give up her job.
彼女は仕事をやめなければいけなかった。
Kanojo wa shigoto o yamenakereba ikenakatta.

PHRASE: give up ⟨*-o*⟩ *akirameru* ⟨～を⟩あきらめる ②

EX. (**a**) I have given up on Japanese politics.
日本の政治についてはもうあきらめている。
Nihon no seiji ni-tsuite wa moo akiramete iru.
(**b**) I have given up on going to the United States to study.
私はアメリカに留学するのをあきらめました。
Watashi wa Amerika ni ryuugaku-suru no o akiramemashita.
(**c**) She gave up her son for dead.
彼女は息子は死んだものとあきらめた。
Kanojo wa musuko wa shinda mono to akirameta.

glad adj. **[for s.o. to be pleased/happy about s.t.]**
u⌈reshi⌉i うれしい adj(*i*). **[feeling pleasure or contentment]** ⟪**happy, joyful**⟫ ↔ **kanashii** 悲しい adj(*i*).; ⟨**-o**⟩ **yo⌈roko⌉bu** ⟨～を⟩喜ぶ ① **[for s.o./s.a. to show pleasure/happiness about s.t.]** ⟪**be pleased at, be delighted at**⟫ ↔ ⟨**-o**⟩ **kanashimu** ⟨～を⟩悲しむ ①

NOTE: *Ureshii* is usually used with the first person subject in statements and with the second person subject in questions. But it can be used with the third person subject if some modal (eg. *deshoo*) is used, as in the following example (b). *Ureshii* is also used as a spontaneous expression of pleasure with the first or second person subject.

EX. (**a**) I'm so glad my younger brother passed his entrance exams.
弟が入学試験に通って、{嬉しいです/喜んでいます}。
Otooto ga nyuugaku-shiken ni tootte, {ureshii desu/yorokonde imasu}.
(**b**) He must have been glad to hear that his son won the championship.
息子さんが優勝したと聞いて彼はさぞ{嬉しかった/喜んだ}でしょう。
Musuko-san ga yuushoo-shita to kiite kare wa sazo {ureshikatta/yorokonda} deshoo.
(**c**) Aren't you glad to hear that your parents are coming to Japan?
御両親が日本へいらっしゃると聞いて、{嬉しい/*喜んでいる}んじゃないですか。
*Go-ryooshin ga Nihon e irassharu to kiite, {ureshii/*yorokonde iru} n janai desu ka.*
(**d**) She was glad to hear that her son has gotten engaged.
息子が婚約したと聞いて、彼女は{喜

G

んでいた/*嬉しかった}。
*Musuko ga kon'yaku-shita to kiite, kanojo wa {yorokonde ita/*ureshikatta}.*

NOTE: *Ureshikatta* in example (d) would be possible in a story or novel, even when the subject is the third person, as the writer in such cases has the freedom to take the standpoint of the third person subject.

(**e**) A: I just got a call from the veterinarian saying that our cat can leave the animal hospital today.
うちの猫、今日退院出来るって獣医さんからたった今電話があったよ。
Uchi no neko, kyoo taiin-dekiru tte juui-san kara tatta ima denwa ga atta yo.
B: Oh, I'm so glad!
あら、{嬉しい/*喜んでいる}!
*Ara, {ureshii/*yorokonde iru}!*

(**f**) My classmates were very glad that I won the title.
クラスメートは私の優勝を非常に喜んでくれました。
Kurasu-meeto wa watashi no yuushoo o hijooni yorokonde kuremashita.

(**g**) A: Won't you come to our party tonight?
今晩パーティーへ来ませんか。
Konban paatii e kimasen ka.
B: Sure. I'd be glad to.
ええ、喜んで伺います。
Ee, yorokonde ukagaimasu.

gladly adv. **[willingly]**

yo⌈roko⌉nde 喜んで /⟨V *te* of *yorokobu* ① be pleased/

EX. I'll gladly come and help you.
喜んでお手伝いに伺います。
Yorokonde o-tetsudai ni ukagaimasu.

glance vi. **[to look briefly at s.t./s.o./s.a.]**

1. chi⌈ra⌉tto miru ちらっと見る ②

EX. Hanako glanced at me but showed no sign of recognizing me.
花子は私をちらっと見たけど、全然気がつかないようだった。
Hanako wa watashi o chiratto mita kedo, zen-zen ki-ga-tsukanai yoodatta.

2. |sa⌉tto me⌉ o to⌉osu さっと目を通す ① [for s.o. to read through s.t. briefly] ⟪take a quick look at⟫

EX. She glanced over the list of names I gave her.
彼女は私が渡した名前のリストにさっと目を通した。
Kanojo wa watashi ga watashita namae no risuto ni satto me o tooshita.

—— n. **[a quick short look]**

hi⌈to⌉-me 一目

PHRASE: at a glance *hito-me de* 一目で

EX. I could tell at a glance that she'd been crying.
一目で彼女が泣いていたことが分かった。
Hito-me de kanojo ga naite ita koto ga wakatta.

PHRASE: at first glance *chotto miru to* ちょっと見ると

EX. They look the same at first glance but in fact they are quite different.
ちょっと見ると同じに見えますが、本当は随分違います。
Chotto miru to onaji ni miemasu ga, hontoo wa zuibun chigaimasu.

glass n. **[a usually transparent, hard, easily-broken material used in windows, etc., or a small container made of glass for drinks]**

1. ga⌈rasu ガラス •f [a usually transparent, hard, easily-broken material used in windows, etc.]

EX. (**a**) The kids broke our window glass.
子供がうちの窓ガラスを割ってしまった。
Kodomo ga uchi no mado-garasu o watte shimatta.

(**b**) Be careful of the pieces of glass on the floor.
床の上のガラスの破片に気をつけてください。
Yuka no ue no garasu no hahen ni ki-o-tsukete kudasai.

2. ko⌈ppu コップ •f [a small container usually made of glass from which water, juice, beer, etc., is drunk], gu⌉rasu グラス •f [a small container usually made of glass

from which whiskey, wine, a cocktail, etc., is drunk]

EX. (**a**) I drink a glass of water every morning.
毎朝、{コップ/?グラス}に一杯水を飲みます。
Mai-asa, {koppu/?gurasu} ni ip-pai mizu o nomimasu.
(**b**) I have ordinary glasses but no wine glasses.
普通の{コップ/グラス}はあるけど、ワイン{グラス/*コップ}は持っていないんです。
*Futsuu no {koppu/gurasu} wa aru kedo, wain-{gurasu/*koppu} wa motte inai n desu.*

PHRASE: magnifying glass *mushi-megane* 虫眼鏡, *kakudai-kyoo* 拡大鏡 •c

glasses n. **[two transparent lenses in a frame used by people with bad eyesight to see better]**
me⌉gane めがね **《spectacles》**

EX. (**a**) Our teacher wears thick glasses.
先生は度の強い眼鏡をかけている。
Sensei wa do no tsuyoi megane o kakete iru.
(**b**) My father can't read without his glasses.
父は眼鏡をかけないと、字が読めない。
Chichi wa megane o kakenai to, ji ga yome-nai.

globe n. **[the earth or a model of the earth or an object in the shape of a ball]**
1. chi⌈kyuu 地球 **•c [the spherical heavenly body inhabited by human beings]**
2. chi⌈kyu⌉u-gi 地球儀 **•c [a model of the earth]**
3. kyu⌉u 球 **•c [an object in the shape of a ball]**

glorious adj. **[full of glory or beauty; splendid]**
1. ka⌈gayakashi⌉i 輝かしい adj(*i*). **[blindingly bright 《fig. "brilliant"》] 《bright, brilliant》**

EX. This scandal has left a stain on the glorious history of our team.
このスキャンダルはチームの輝かしい歴史に汚点を残した。
Kono sukyandaru wa chiimu no kagayakashii rekishi ni oten o nokoshita.

2. su⌈barashi⌉i すばらしい adj(*i*). **[causing great wonder/admiration/pleasure due to being extremely good] 《wonderful, great, splendid》**

EX. (**a**) What a glorious color!
すばらしい色ですね。
Subarashii iro desu ne.
(**b**) We enjoyed the glorious glow of the sunset together.
我々はすばらしい夕焼けを一緒に楽しんだ。
Ware-ware wa subarashii yuu-yake o issho ni tanoshinda.

glove n. **[a garment that covers the hand, usually with separated fingers]**
te-⌈bu⌉kuro 手袋

EX. (**a**) Wear rubber gloves to protect your hands when you do the dishes.
お皿を洗うときには、手を守るためにゴムの手袋をはめなさい。
O-sara o arau toki ni wa, te o mamoru tame ni gomu no te-bukuro o hamenasai.
(**b**) She wore black leather gloves.
彼女は黒い革の手袋をしていた。
Kanojo wa kuroi kawa no te-bukuro o shite ita.

glue n. **[a sticky substance used for joining things together]**
no⌈ri⌉ のり **[a sticky substance made from rice/flour or by chemical means for joining things or for stiffening cloth fabrics] 《paste, starch, gum》, se⌈tchaku⌉-zai** 接着剤 **•c [a chemically made substance used for bonding things other than paper together] 《adhesives》**

EX. Can this be fixed with glue?
{のり/接着剤}で直せますか。
{Nori/Setchaku-zai} de naose-masu ka.

—— vt. **[to join/stick s.t. to s.t. else with glue]**
1. 〈-o〉 **(no⌈ri⌉ de) ha⌈ri-tsuke⌉ru** 〈〜を〉(のりで)はりつける ② **[for s.o. to stick s.t. onto s.t. else (with glue)] 《stick, paste, post》**

EX. He glued a poster to the wall.
壁にポスターをのりではり付けた。

G

Kabe ni posutaa o nori de hari-tsuketa.

2. ⟨-o⟩ (⟨-ni⟩) ku⌈ttsuke⌉ru ⟨〜を⟩(⟨〜に⟩)くっつける ② [for s.o. to put things together with no/little space inbetween so that they stay that way] ⟪join, attach, put together, stick⟫

EX. I glued the broken pieces together.
割れたかけらを集めて接着剤でくっつけた。
Wareta kakera o atsumete setchaku-zai de kuttsuketa.

go vi. **[to move in a certain direction or towards a certain goal]**
{⟨-e⟩/⟨-ni⟩} i⌈ku {⟨〜へ⟩/⟨〜に⟩}行く ① [to move in a direction or towards a goal away from the speaker], {⟨-e⟩/⟨-ni⟩} i⌈rassha⌉ru {⟨〜へ⟩/⟨〜に⟩}いらっしゃる ① [for s.o. to whom the speaker shows deference to move to/stay in a certain place], {⟨-e⟩/⟨-ni⟩} ma⌉iru {⟨〜へ⟩/⟨〜に⟩}参る ① [for s.o./s.t. to move to a certain place, an expression used in humble or very formal contexts]

NOTE: V*masu* of *irassharu* is not *irassharimasu* but *irasshaimasu. Mairu* is usually used in its *masu* form, i.e., *mairimasu.*

EX. (**a**) Where are you going?
どこ{へ/に}{行く/いらっしゃる/*参る}んですか。
*Doko {e/ni} {iku/irassharu/*mairu} n desu ka.*
(**b**) Does this bus go to Shinjuku?
このバスは新宿{へ/に}{行きます/*いらっしゃいます/*参ります}か。
*Kono basu wa Shinjuku {e/ni} {ikimasu/*irasshaimasu/*mairimasu} ka.*
(**c**) We're going swimming tomorrow.
あしたは泳ぎに{行きます/参ります/*いらっしゃいます}。
*Ashita wa oyogi ni {ikimasu/mairimasu/*irasshaimasu}.*
(**d**) Mr. Takeshita has gone to Paris.
竹下さんはパリに{行って/いらっしゃって/*参って}います。
*Takeshita-san wa Pari ni {itte/irasshatte/*maitte} imasu.*
(**e**) Did you go to the concert last night?
ゆうべのコンサートに{いらっしゃいました/行きました/*参りました}か。
*Yuube no konsaato ni {irasshaimashita/ikimashita/*mairimashita} ka.*
(**f**) Prof. Yamada is going to Germany this summer.
山田先生は今年の夏、ドイツへ{いらっしゃいます/?行きます/*参ります}。
*Yamada-sensei wa kotoshi no natsu, Doitsu e {irasshaimasu/?ikimasu/*mairimasu}.*
(**g**) We are going to Hawaii for our honeymoon.
新婚旅行でハワイ{へ/に}{参ります/行きます/*いらっしゃいます}。
*Shinkon-ryokoo de Hawai {e/ni} {mairimasu/ikimasu/*irasshaimasu}.*
(**h**) This train goes as far as Tachikawa.
この電車は立川まで{参ります/行きます/*いらっしゃいます}。
*Kono densha wa Tachikawa made {mairimasu/ikimasu/*irasshaimasu}.*

PHRASE: go across ⟨*-o*⟩ *wataru* ⟨〜を⟩渡る ① ⟪cross⟫

EX. There was a lot of traffic on the street so we had to wait a while before we could go across.
交通量が多かったので道を渡るのに大分待たなければならなかった。
Kootsuu-ryoo ga ookatta node michi o wataru no ni daibu matanakereba naranakatta.

PHRASE: go around *hayaru* はやる ① ⟪be in fashion, be popular, spread⟫

EX. The flu is going around the office.
職場でインフルエンザがはやっている。
Shokuba de infuruenza ga hayatte iru.

PHRASE: go around ⟨*-to*⟩ *tsuki-au* ⟨〜と⟩付き合う ① ⟪associate with⟫

EX. You shouldn't go around with such strange people.
ああいう変な人たちと付き合わないほうがいいですよ。
Aa-iu henna hito-tachi to tsuki-awanai hoo ga ii desu yo.

PHRASE: go back *{⟨-e⟩/⟨-ni⟩} kaeru* {⟨〜へ⟩/⟨〜に⟩} 帰る ① ⟪return, go home, come home⟫

EX. Jun is going back to Japan in May.
順さんは五月に日本へ帰ります。
Jun-san wa go-gatsu ni Nihon e kaerimasu.

PHRASE: go down *sagaru* 下がる ① ⟪fall, drop⟫, *ochiru* 落ちる ② ⟪drop⟫

EX. (**a**) The yen has gone down again.
円はまた{下がった/*落ちた}。
*En wa mata {sagatta/*ochita}.*
(**b**) Prices have gone down.
物価が{下がった/*落ちた}。
*Bukka ga {sagatta/*ochita}.*
(**c**) The temperature went down to 10 °C.
気温が摂氏十度に{下がった/*落ちた}。
*Kion ga sesshi juu-do ni {sagatta/*ochita}.*
(**d**) My grades have gone down because I don't study.
勉強しないので、成績が{下がった/落ちた}。
Benkyoo-shinai node, seiseki ga {sagatta/ochita}.
(**e**) The quality of rice has gone down a lot these days.
米は近ごろ非常に質が{落ちた/*下がった}。
*Kome wa chikagoro hijooni shitsu ga {ochita/*sagatta}.*

PHRASE: go into *⟨-ni⟩ hairu* ⟨〜に⟩入る ① ⟪enter, come in, get in, join, participate⟫

EX. He went into the building from the front entrance.
彼は正面玄関から建物の中に入って行った。
Kare wa shoomen-genkan kara tatemono no naka ni haitte itta.

PHRASE: go on *tsuzuku* 続く ① ⟪continue⟫

EX. The party went on until late at night.
パーティーは夜遅くまで続いた。
Paatii wa yoru osoku made tsuzuita.

PHRASE: go on *tsuku* つく ① ⟪stick, arrive, turn on, take, reach⟫

EX. The lights went on.
明かりがついた。
Akari ga tsuita.

PHRASE: go on with *⟨-o⟩ tsuzukeru* ⟨〜を⟩続ける ② ⟪continue⟫

EX. He went on with his story.
彼は話を続けた。
Kare wa hanashi o tsuzuketa.

PHRASE: go out *dekakeru* 出かける ②, *gaishutsu-suru* 外出する ③ •c

EX. (**a**) My mother has gone out shopping.
母は買い物に{出かけました/*外出しました}。
*Haha wa kai-mono ni {dekakemashita/*gaishutsu-shimashita}.*
(**b**) I usually go out on Sundays.
日曜日にはたいてい{外出します/出かけます}。
Nichiyoo-bi ni wa taitei {gaishutsu-shimasu/dekakemasu}.

PHRASE: go out *kieru* 消える ② ⟪disappear, fade away, vanish⟫

EX. The lights in her apartment went out.
彼女のアパートの電気が消えた。
Kanojo no apaato no denki ga kieta.

PHRASE: go up *agaru* あがる ① ⟪rise⟫, *noboru* のぼる ① ⟪climb, rise, mount, amount to⟫
㊦ "climb"▷登る, "rise in the air"▷昇る, otherwise ▷上る

EX. (**a**) We went up to the roof in the elevator.
エレベーターで屋上に{上がった/上った}。
Erebeetaa de okujoo ni {agatta/nobotta}.
(**b**) Prices have gone up again.
物価がまた{上がった/*上った}。
*Bukka ga mata {agatta/*nobotta}.*
(**c**) The temperature went up to 30 °C.
気温が摂氏三十度に{上がった/*上った}。
*Kion ga sesshi san-juu-do ni {agatta/*nobotta}.*
(**d**) We went up the stairs to have a look at the second floor of the house.
私たちは家の二階を見てみようと思って階段を{上った/?上がった}。
Watashi-tachi wa ie no ni-kai o mite miyoo to omotte kaidan o {nobotta/?agatta}.

PHRASE: go with *{⟨-ni⟩/⟨-to⟩} au* {⟨〜に⟩/⟨〜と⟩} あう ① ⟪match, suit, meet⟫

G

㊅ "meet"▷会う, "match/suit"▷合う

EX. I think this color goes very well with your black hair.
この色はあなたの黒い髪とよく合うと思います。
Kono iro wa anata no kuroi kami to yoku au to omoimasu.

goal n. **[s.t. one wishes to achieve ⟪fig. "a place where the ball/puck, etc., must enter for a point to be scored in games such as soccer, hockey, etc."⟫]**

1. mo⌈kuhyoo 目標 •c [s.t. one wishes to achieve] ⟪aim, target⟫

EX. (**a**) The company has achieved all its goals for the year.
会社は今年の目標を全部達成した。
Kaisha wa kotoshi no mokuhyoo o zenbu tassei-shita.
(**b**) We are still far from our goal.
まだまだ目標には届きません。
Mada-mada mokuhyoo ni wa todokimasen.

2. go⌉oru ゴール •f [a place where the ball/puck, etc. must enter for a point to be scored in games such as soccer, hockey, etc., or the finish line in a race]

EX. The ball he kicked missed the goal.
彼のけったボールはゴールを外れた。
Kare no ketta booru wa gooru o hazureta.

PHRASE: goal line *gooru-rain* ゴールライン •f

goat n.

ya⌉gi 山羊

god n. **[a being worshiped as having control over nature and human affairs]**

ka⌉mi 神 ⟪God, deity⟫, ka⌉mi-sama 神様 [an expression of respect for addressing or referring to a deity] ⟪God, deity⟫

EX. I prayed to the gods for help.
{神/神様}に助けてくださいと祈った。
{Kami/Kami-sama} ni tasukete kudasai to inotta.

gold n.

ki⌉n 金 •c

EX. Yoshiko is wearing a gold necklace.
佳子さんは金のネックレスをしている。
Yoshiko-san wa kin no nekkuresu o shite iru.

PHRASE: gold medal *kin-medaru* 金メダル •c+f

golden adj. **[of gold or like gold]**

ki⌉n no N 金のN •c [of gold], ki⌈n-iro no N 金色のN [like gold in color]

EX. She was brushing her golden hair.
彼女は金色の髪にブラシをかけていた。
Kanojo wa kin-iro no kami ni burashi o kakete ita.

PHRASE: golden age *gooruden-eeji* ゴールデンエージ •f

goldfish n.

ki⌉ngyo 金魚 •c

golf n.

go⌉rufu ゴルフ •f

EX. My father plays golf once a month.
父は一か月に一度ゴルフをします。
Chichi wa ik-kagetsu ni ichi-do gorufu o shimasu.

PHRASE: golf course *gorufu-koosu* ゴルフコース •f, golf ball *gorufu-booru* ゴルフボール •f

good adj. **[having the right/desired/satisfactory qualities]**

1. i⌉i いい adj(*i*). [morally correct/satisfactory/agreeable] ⟪nice, fine, adequate, beautiful⟫ ↔ warui 悪い adj(*i*).

NOTE: In conjugating *ii*, the first syllabe *i* changes to *yo* as in *yoku nai* not good, *yokatta* was/were good, etc. *Yoi* is possible in writing or in very formal speech.

EX. (**a**) She is a good mother.
彼女はいい母親だ。
Kanojo wa ii haha-oya da.
(**b**) The exam results for this class were good.
このクラスの試験の結果は良かった。
Kono kurasu no shiken no kekka wa yokatta.
(**c**) That cooking school has a good reputation.
あの料理学校は評判がいい。
Ano ryoori-gakkoo wa hyooban ga ii.
(**d**) This knife is good for cutting vegetables.
この包丁は野菜を切るのにいい。
Kono hoochoo wa yasai o kiru no ni ii.
(**e**) Walking is good for the health.

G

歩くのは健康にいい。
Aruku no wa kenkoo ni ii.

2. o⌈ishii おいしい adj(*i*). **[for the taste of a food/drink to be desirable/satisfactory]** **((delicious, tasty))** ↔ **mazui まずい** adj(*i*).; **u⌈ma⌉i うまい** adj(*i*). **[for s.t. to be very pleasant to taste or for s.o./s.a. to be skillful at s.t.]** **((delicious, tasty, skillful))** ↔ **mazui まずい** adj(*i*)., **hetana 下手な** adj(*na*).

NOTE: The word *umai* in the meaning of "tasty" is usually used by men.

EX. The coffee is very good in that restaurant.
あのレストランのコーヒーはとても{おいしい/うまい}ですよ。
Ano resutoran no koohii wa totemo {oishii/umai} desu yo.

3. jo⌈ozu⌉na 上手な adj(*na*). **[for s.o./s.a. to be able to do s.t. well]** **((skillful))** ↔ **hetana 下手な** adj(*na*).; **u⌈ma⌉i うまい** adj(*i*). **[for s.t. to be very pleasant to taste or for s.o./s.a. to be skillful at s.t.]** **((tasty, delicious, skillful))** ↔ **mazui まずい** adj(*i*)., **hetana 下手な** adj(*na*).

EX. (**a**) I want to marry a man who is good at cooking.
私は料理が{上手な/うまい}男の人と結婚したい。
Watashi wa ryoori ga {joozuna/umai} otoko no hito to kekkon-shi-tai.
(**b**) He is a good skier.
彼はスキーが{上手/うまい}です。
Kare wa sukii ga {joozu/umai} desu.

PHRASE: Good afternoon. *Konnichi-wa.* こんにちは。

NOTE: *Konnichi-wa* is not used among people in the same in-group, such as members of the same family.

PHRASE: Good-bye. *Sayoonara.* さようなら。, *Shitsurei shimasu.* 失礼します。, Good evening. *Konban-wa.* こんばんは。

NOTE: *Konban-wa* is not used among people in the same in-group.

PHRASE: good-looking *kakko ii* かっこいい, *hansamuna* ハンサムな; Good morning. *O-hayoo gozaimasu.* おはようございます。, *O-hayoo.* おはよう。

NOTE: *O-hayoo* is an informal version of *o-hayoo gozaimasu* used among friends and family members, by teachers to students, etc.

PHRASE: Good night. *O-yasuminasai.* お休みなさい。, *O-yasumi.* お休み。

NOTE: *O-yasumi* is an informal version of *O-yasuminasai* used among friends and family members and by someone of higher social position to someone of lower social position in cases where a difference exists in social status.

goods n. **[things for sale]**
sho⌉ohin 商品 •c ((merchandise))

EX. This department store sells a large variety of goods.
このデパートでは実にいろいろな商品を売っている。
Kono depaato de wa jitsuni iro-irona shoohin o utte iru.

PHRASE: leather goods *kawa-seihin* 革製品

goose n.
ga⌈choo が鳥 •c

gossip n. **[talk about other people's private affairs, often including untrue information]** **u⌈wasa-ba⌉nashi うわさ話 [talk about items of news or information the truth of which is uncertain] ((rumor)), go⌈shi⌉ppu ゴシップ •f [talking about other people's private affairs for amusement]**

EX. This magazine is full of gossip about movie stars.
この雑誌は映画スターの{うわさ話/ゴシップ}でいっぱいだ。
Kono zasshi wa eiga-sutaa no {uwasa-banashi/goshippu} de ippai da.

— vi. **[for s.o. to spread gossip]**
u⌈wasa-ba⌉nashi o suru うわさ話をする ③

EX. After work they often go to a bar to gossip about their bosses as a way of relieving stress.
彼らはストレス解消のために仕事が終わってから、しばしばバーに行って上司のうわさ話をする。
Kare-ra wa sutoresu-kaishoo no tame ni shigoto ga owatte kara, shiba-shiba baa ni itte jooshi no uwasa-banashi o suru.

govern vt. **[for s.o. to control and direct s.t., especially the affairs of a country, city, etc.]** **⟨-o⟩ shi˥hai-suru ⟨〜を⟩支配する ③ •c [for s.o. to exercise power over people or organizations to cause them to act or function in the way one desires]** 《**control, rule**》, **⟨-o⟩ sa˥yuu-suru ⟨〜を⟩左右する ③ •c [for s.o./s.t. to have an effect on s.t.]** 《**control, influence**》, **⟨-o⟩ to˥ochi-suru ⟨〜を⟩統治する ③ •c [for s.o. to control the political affairs of a country and its people]**

EX. (**a**) We tend to be too easily governed in our thinking by what others say.
我々の考え方は外の人の言うことにあまりにも{支配/左右/*統治}されやすい。
*Ware-ware no kangae-kata wa hoka no hito no iu koto ni amari-ni mo {shihai/sayuu/*toochi}-sare-yasui.*
(**b**) No human can violate the laws that govern the universe.
人間はだれも宇宙を{支配/*左右/*統治}する法則に逆らうことはできない。
*Ningen wa dare-mo uchuu o {shihai/*sayuu/*toochi}-suru hoosoku ni sakarau koto wa dekinai.*
(**c**) That country has been governed by the military for the last three decades.
その国は過去三十年にわたって軍部によって{統治/支配/*左右}されてきた。
*Sono kuni wa kako san-juu-nen ni watatte gunbu ni-yotte {toochi/shihai/*sayuu}-sarete kita.*

government n. **[the group of people responsible for ruling and managing a country/state/city/town or a particular method of so ruling and managing]**
1. se˥ifu 政府 •c [the group of people responsible for governing a country]

EX. (**a**) The government is considering a bill to lower corporate taxes.
政府は法人税を引き下げる法案を検討中だ。
Seifu wa hoojin-zei o hiki-sageru hooan o kentoo-chuu da.
(**b**) The Japanese government has started negotiations with the United States concerning the importing of rice.
日本政府は米の輸入についてアメリカと交渉を開始した。
Nihon-seifu wa kome no yunyuu ni-tsuite Amerika to kooshoo o kaishi-shita.

2. se˥iken 政権 •c [⟨the particular individuals holding⟩ political power] 《**administrative power, political power, regime**》

EX. How long do you think the present government will last?
現政権はどのぐらいもつと思いますか。
Gen-seiken wa dono-gurai motsu to omoimasu ka.

3. se˥iji 政治 •c [the structures and processes involved in governing a society] 《**politics**》

EX. (**a**) We cannot entrust such a person with the government of our country.
ああいう人にわが国の政治を任すことはできない。
Aa-iu hito ni waga-kuni no seiji o makasu koto wa dekinai.
(**b**) Government by bureaucracy may make for stability but tends to encourage corruption.
官僚政治は安定をもたらす一方汚職を生む土壌ともなりやすい。
Kanryoo-seiji wa antei o motarasu ippoo oshoku o umu dojoo to mo nari-yasui.

PHRASE: government employee *kokka-koomu-in* 国家公務員 •c 《civil servant》

governor n. **[a person who governs a region]** **chi˥ji 知事 •c [a person who governs a prefecture]**

EX. The governor of Okinawa is supposed to make a televised speech tonight.
沖縄県の知事が今晩テレビ演説をするそうだ。
Okinawa-ken no chiji ga konban terebi-enzetsu o suru sooda.

grab vt. **[to take hold of s.o./s.t. with a sudden rough movement]**
⟨-o⟩ tsu˥ka˥mu ⟨〜を⟩つかむ ① [for s.o./s.a. to take hold of s.t./s.o./s.a. tightly, suddenly, and forcibly 《**fig. "understand"**》**]**

G

⟪grasp, seize, catch⟫, ⟨-o⟩ **wa⌈shi-zu⌉kami ni suru** ⟨～を⟩わしづかみにする ③ **[to take hold of s.t. strongly with a rough, clutching motion]**

EX. (**a**) Somebody suddenly grabbed my arm from behind.
だれかが後ろから急に私の腕を{つかんだ/?わしづかみにした}。
Dare-ka ga ushiro kara kyuuni watashi no ude o {tsukanda/?washi-zukami ni shita}.
(**b**) He grabbed the bottle of beer and began guzzling it down.
彼はビールびんを{わしづかみにして/つかんで}がぶがぶ飲みはじめた。
Kare wa biiru-bin o {washi-zukami ni shite/tsukande} gabu-gabu nomi-hajimeta.

graceful adj. **[for a movement to be smooth and attractive]**
yu⌉ugana 優雅な adj(*na*). •c **[for the behavior/life style of s.o. to be elegant and exquisite]** ⟪elegant, refined⟫, **jo⌈ohi⌉nna** 上品な adj(*na*). •c **[sophisticated and pleasing in quality, speech, or behavior]** ⟪refined, polished, tasteful⟫ ↔ **gehinna** 下品な adj(*na*). •c; **shi⌈to⌉yakana** しとやかな adj(*na*). **[for a woman/woman's actions to be gentle, modest, and attractive]** ⟪lady-like⟫

EX. (**a**) I was attracted by her graceful movements.
私は彼女の{優雅な/上品な/しとやかな}立居ふるまいに引きつけられた。
Watashi wa kanojo no {yuugana/joohinna/shitoyakana} tachii-furumai ni hiki-tsuke-rareta.
(**b**) I was impressed by the graceful table manners of the children in that home.
その家庭での子供たちの{上品な/*優雅な/*しとやかな}テーブルマナーに感心した。
*Sono katei de no kodomo-tachi no {joohinna/*yuugana/*shitoyakana} teeburu-manaa ni kanshin-shita.*

grade n. **[a step or degree in value, quality, or rank; a mark given to a student showing how well he/she has done on a test, in a class, etc.]**
1. to⌈okyuu 等級 •c **[rating in quality]**

EX. The price of rice varies depending on its grade.
米の値段は等級によって違う。
Kome no nedan wa tookyuu ni-yotte chigau.

2. te⌈n 点 •c **[a small mark made by the end of a sharp object ⟪fig. "punctuation," "marks," "respects"⟫]** ⟪speck, point, score, dot⟫, **se⌈iseki** 成績 •c **[a mark/rating on an examination, in a school course, etc.]**

EX. (**a**) If you get good grades, you may be able to get a scholarship.
いい{成績/点}をとれば、奨学金がもらえるかもしれません。
Ii {seiseki/ten} o toreba, shoogaku-kin ga morae-ru kamoshiremasen.
(**b**) What was your grade on the last exam?
この前の試験の{点/成績}はどうでしたか。
Kono mae no shiken no {ten/seiseki} wa doo deshita ka.

3. ga⌈kunen 学年 •c **[a division in a school curriculum]** ⟪a school year⟫

PHRASE: grade school *shoo-gakkoo* 小学校 •c ⟪elementary school⟫, first grade *ichi-nen* 一年 •c, second grade *ni-nen* 二年 •c

EX. Ms. Tanaka was my first grade teacher.
田中先生は私が小学校一年の時の先生でした。
Tanaka-sensei wa watashi ga shoo-gakkoo ichi-nen no toki no sensei deshita.

gradual adj. **[happening/changing slowly and little by little]**
da⌈n-dan だんだん adv. **[slowly and little by little]** ⟪gradually⟫

EX. (**a**) There has been a gradual decrease in the number of children in this country.
この国での子供の数はだんだん減ってきている。
Kono kuni de no kodomo no kazu wa dan-dan hette kite iru.
(**b**) His condition is showing gradual improvement.

G

彼の状態はだんだん良くなってきている。
Kare no jootai wa dan-dan yoku natte kite iru.

gradually adv. **[slowly and little by little]**
da⌈n-dan だんだん

graduate vi. **[for s.o. to complete an educational course]**
⟨-o⟩ so⌈tsugyoo-suru ⟨～を⟩卒業する ③ •c ((leave school)) ↔ **⟨-ni⟩ nyuugaku-suru** ⟨～に⟩入学する ③ •c; **⟨-o⟩ de⌉ru** ⟨～を⟩出る ② **[to go away from some place]** ((exit, leave)) ↔ **⟨-ni⟩ hairu** ⟨～に⟩入る ①

EX. He graduated from a university in Tokyo.
彼は東京の大学を{卒業しました/出ました}。
Kare wa Tookyoo no daigaku o {sotsugyoo-shimashita/demashita}.

—— n. **[a person who has completed a course at a university, college, school, etc.]**
so⌈tsugyo⌉o-sei 卒業生 •c

EX. She is a graduate of Tokyo Metropolitan University.
彼女は東京都立大学の卒業生です。
Kanojo wa Tookyoo-toritsu-daigaku no sotsugyoo-sei desu.

PHRASE: a high school graduate *koosotsu* 高卒 •c, graduate school *daigaku-in* 大学院 •c

graduation n. **[the successful completion of a course at a university, college, etc., or a ceremony celebrating such completion]**
1. **so⌈tsugyoo** 卒業 •c **[the successful completion of a course of study at a school]** ↔ **nyuugaku** 入学 •c

EX. Let's celebrate your graduation with a big party.
大きなパーティーをしてあなたの卒業をお祝いしましょう。
Ookina paatii o shite anata no sotsugyoo o o-iwai shimashoo.

2. **so⌈tsugyo⌉o-shiki** 卒業式 •c **[a ceremony to celebrate one's successful completion of a course of study at a school]** ((commencement))

EX. My mother attended my graduation.
母が卒業式に出てくれました。
Haha ga sotsugyoo-shiki ni dete kuremashita.

grain n. **[the seed of a food plant such as rice or wheat or the crop gathered from such plants]**
1. **tsu⌉bu** 粒 **[a small, round object such as the seed of a food plant, a rain drop, or a pearl]**

EX. Eat every grain of rice in your bowl.
お茶わんの御飯は一粒も残さず食べなさい。
O-chawan no gohan wa hito-tsubu mo nokosazu tabenasai.

2. **ko⌈ku⌉motsu** 穀物 •c **[agricultural food staples such as rice, wheat, beans, etc.]**

EX. Grain prices have gone up again.
穀物はまた値上がりした。
Kokumotsu wa mata ne-agari-shita.

gram n.
gu⌉ramu グラム •f

EX. I bought 200 grams of ground beef.
私は牛の挽き肉を二百グラム買った。
Watashi wa gyuu no hiki-niku o ni-hyaku-guramu katta.

grammar n.
bu⌈npoo 文法 •c

EX. We have been taught enough English grammar but we still can't speak the language.
英語の文法は十分教わったけどまだ話せないんです。
Eigo no bunpoo wa juubun osowatta kedo mada hanase-nai n desu.

grand adj. **[splendid in appearance/size]**
su⌈barashi⌉i すばらしい adj(*i*). **[causing great wonder/admiration/pleasure due to being extremely good]** ((wonderful, splendid, magnificent)), **ri⌈ppana** 立派な adj(*na*). •c **[for s.o./some human creation/achievement to cause admiration]** ((splendid, magnificent))

EX. (**a**) We enjoyed a grand view of the ocean from our hotel room.
ホテルの部屋からの海の眺めは{すばらしかった/*立派だった}。
Hoteru no heya kara no umi no nagame

*wa {subarashikatta/*rippa datta}.*
(**b**) She lives in a grand house.
彼女は{すばらしい/立派な}家に住んでいる。
Kanojo wa {subarashii/rippana} ie ni sunde iru.

grandchild n. **[the child of one's son/daughter]**
ma⌈go⌉ 孫, o-⌈mago-san お孫さん [a polite word to refer to the child(ren) of s.o. else's son/daughter]

EX. (**a**) How many grandchildren do you have?
お孫さんは何人いらっしゃいますか。
O-mago-san wa nan-nin irasshaimasu ka.
(**b**) I bought a toy for my grandchild.
孫におもちゃを買ってやった。
Mago ni omocha o katte yatta.

grandfather n. **[the father of one's father/mother]**
o-⌈ji⌉i-san おじいさん [a polite word to refer to the father of s.o. else's father/mother or an old man] ↔ o-baa-san おばあさん; so⌉fu 祖父 •c [the father of one's father/mother] ↔ sobo 祖母 •c

NOTE: To directly address one's own grandfather, *o-jii-san* rather than *sofu* is used.

EX. (**a**) My grandfather is 90 years old.
{祖父/?おじいさん}は九十歳です。
{Sofu/?O-jii-san} wa kyuu-jus-sai desu.
(**b**) Do you often write to your grandfather?
{おじいさん/*祖父}によく手紙を書きますか。
*{O-jii-san/*Sofu} ni yoku tegami o kakimasu ka.*

grandma n. **[an informal form of grandmother]**
o-⌈ba⌉a-chan おばあちゃん [an informal form of o-baa-san with a feeling of intimacy] ↔ o-jii-chan おじいちゃん

grandmother n. **[the mother of one's father/mother]**
o-⌈ba⌉a-san おばあさん [a polite word to refer to the mother of s.o. else's father/mother or an old woman] ↔ o-jii-san おじいさん; so⌉bo 祖母 •c [the mother of one's father/mother] ↔ sofu 祖父 •c

NOTE: To directly address one's own grandmother, *o-baa-san* rather than *sobo* is used.

EX. A: Where does your grandmother live?
{おばあさん/*祖母}はどこに住んでいらっしゃるんですか。
*{O-baa-san/*Sobo} wa doko ni sunde irassharu n desu ka.*
B: She lives in Nara.
{祖母/?おばあさん}は奈良に住んでいます。
{Sobo/?O-baa-san} wa Nara ni sunde imasu.

grandpa n. **[an informal form of grandfather]**
o-⌈ji⌉i-chan おじいちゃん [an informal form of o-jii-san with a feeling of intimacy] ↔ o-baa-chan おばあちゃん

grape n.
bu⌈doo ぶどう

graph n.
gu⌉rafu グラフ •f

EX. I made a graph of the changes in oil prices over the past 10 years.
過去十年間の石油の価格の変動をグラフにした。
Kako juu-nen-kan no sekiyu no kakaku no hendoo o gurafu ni shita.

grasp vt. **[for s.o. to take hold of s.t. firmly 《fig. "understand"》]**
⟨-o⟩ tsu⌈ka⌉mu ⟨〜を⟩つかむ ① 《seize, grip, grab》

EX. (**a**) I think I've grasped the main points of this paper.
この論文の要点はつかんだと思います。
Kono ronbun no yooten wa tsukanda to omoimasu.
(**b**) During the earthquake this morning, I grasped the edge of the table with both hands and sat still.
今朝地震が起きたとき、私は両手でテーブルの端をつかんで、じっと座っていました。
Kesa jishin ga okita toki, watashi wa ryoote de teeburu no hashi o tsukande,

G

jitto suwatte imashita.

grass n. **[a common low-growing plant with blade-shaped green leaves that are eaten by animals]**

1. ku┌sa┐ 草 [a common low-growing plant with blade-shaped green leaves] ⟪**weed**⟫

EX. I walked through the dewy grass early in the morning.
朝早く、露に濡れた草の中を歩いた。
Asa hayaku, tsuyu ni nureta kusa no naka o aruita.

2. shi┌ba-fu 芝生 [an area covered with closely cut grass as in a garden/park] ⟪**lawn**⟫

EX. Keep off the grass.
芝生に入らないでください。
Shiba-fu ni hairanaide kudasai.

grateful adj. **[for s.o. to feel/show thanks to another person]**
⟨-ni⟩ ka┐nsha-suru ⟨〜に⟩感謝する vi. ③ **•c, ⟨-o⟩ a┌rigata┐i to omou** ⟨〜を⟩ありがたいと思う vi. ① **[for s.o. to feel thanks for s.t.]**

EX. (**a**) He was grateful for your help.
彼はあなたに助けていただいたこと{に感謝して/をありがたいと思って}いました。
Kare wa anata ni tasukete itadaita koto {ni kansha-shite/o arigatai to omotte} imashita.
(**b**) I'm grateful to my classmates for coming to see me in the hospital.
同級生が病院へ見舞いに来てくれたこと{をありがたいと思って/に感謝して}います。
Dookyuu-sei ga byooin e mimai ni kite kureta koto {o arigatai to omotte/ni kansha-shite} imasu.
(**c**) He was grateful that he was still alive.
彼は自分がまだ生きていること{をありがたいと思った/に感謝した}。
Kare wa jibun ga mada ikite iru koto {o arigatai to omotta/ni kansha-shita}.

NOTE: To express one's gratitude to another person directly, *arigatoo gozaimasu* is used. For example, *Adobaisu, arigatoo gozaimasu.* "I'm grateful for your advice."

gratitude n. **[a feeling of thankfulness]**
ka┐nsha 感謝 **•c [feeling thankful to s.o. for s.t.]** ⟪**gratefulness, appreciation**⟫

EX. (**a**) In token of his gratitude, he contributed ¥1,000,000 to the scholarship fund.
感謝の印として彼は奨学(金)資金に百万円寄付した。
Kansha no shirushi to-shite kare wa shoogaku(kin)-shikin ni hyaku-man-en kifu-shita.
(**b**) On behalf of the students, I would like to express our gratitude to all of you.
学生を代表して、皆様に感謝のことばを述べたいと思います。
Gakusei o daihyoo-shite, mina-sama ni kansha no kotoba o nobe-tai to omoimasu.

grave adj. **[serious or causing great anxiety]**
ta┌ihenna 大変な adj(*na*). **•c [giving cause for great worry]** ⟪**serious, horrible, terrible**⟫, **ju┌udaina** 重大な adj(*na*). **•c [very important]** ⟪**serious, important, weighty, vital**⟫, **shi┌nkokuna** 深刻な adj(*na*). **•c [requiring urgent attention and causing deep concern]** ⟪**serious, keen, acute**⟫

EX. (**a**) I made a grave mistake in ignoring his advice.
私は彼の忠告を無視することで{大変な/重大な/*深刻な}間違いを犯してしまった。
*Watashi wa kare no chuukoku o mushi-suru koto de {taihenna/juudaina/*shinkokuna} machigai o okashite shimatta.*
(**b**) The situation is even graver than last year.
状況は去年よりも{深刻/大変/重大}だ。
Jookyoo wa kyonen yori mo {shinkoku/taihen/juudai} da.
(**c**) The recent increase in the incidence of traffic accidents is a matter of grave concern.
最近の交通事故の増加は{重大な/深刻な/大変な}問題です。
Saikin no kootsuu-jiko no zooka wa {juudaina/shinkokuna/taihenna} mondai desu.
(**d**) The government announced some grave

economic news this past week.
政府は{重大な/*深刻な/*大変な}経済情報を先週発表した。
*Seifu wa {juudaina/*shinkokuna/ *taihenna} keizai-joohoo o senshuu happyoo-shita.*
(**e**) The country is facing a grave financial crisis.
国は{深刻な/重大な/大変な}経済危機に直面している。
Kuni wa {shinkokuna/juudaina/ taihenna} keizai-kiki ni chokumen shite iru.

—— n. [a burial site]
ha⌈ka⌉ 墓
PHRASE: graveyard *haka-ba* 墓場, *bochi* 墓地 •c

gravel n.
ja⌈ri 砂利 •c

gravity n. **[the force which attracts objects to each other/the center of the earth or seriousness of a matter]**
1. i⌉nryoku 引力 •c [the natural force by which objects are attracted to each other 《fig. "attraction"》] 《magnetism》, ju⌉uryoku 重力 •c [the force which attracts things to the ground, causing them to fall]
EX. (**a**) If you let go of something heavy, gravity causes it to drop to the ground.
何か重い物を手から離すと、{重力/引力}によって地面に落ちる。
Nani-ka omoi mono o te kara hanasu to, {juuryoku/inryoku} ni-yotte jimen ni ochiru.
(**b**) The gravity of the moon causes tides to ebb and flow.
月の{引力/*重力}が潮の満ち干を引き起こす。
*Tsuki no {inryoku/*juuryoku} ga shio no michi-hi o hiki-okosu.*
2. ju⌈udai-sa 重大さ /⟨adj(*na*). stem *juudai* serious + suf. *sa* ness/ •c [seriousness]
EX. He doesn't understand the gravity of the situation.
彼には事態の重大さが分かっていない。
Kare ni wa jitai no juudai-sa ga wakatte inai.

gray adj. **[of the color of ashes or of clouds on a rainy day 《fig. "gloomy"》]**
ne⌈zumi-iro no N ねずみ色のN [of the color of a mouse], gu⌈re⌉e no N グレーのN •f, ha⌈i-iro no N 灰色のN [of the color of ashes 《fig. "for one's life to be gloomy"》]
NOTE: *Guree no* is commonly used in fashion without any negative connotation, while both *nezumi-iro no* and *hai-iro no* often carry such a negative connotation.
EX. (**a**) Japanese businessmen often wear gray suits.
日本のビジネスマンはよく{グレー/ねずみ色/灰色}のスーツを着ている。
Nihon no bijinesu-man wa yoku {guree/ nezumi-iro/hai-iro} no suutsu o kite iru.
(**b**) For someone suffering from depression, every day can be gray and cloudy.
落ち込んでいる人にとっては毎日が{灰色/*ねずみ色/*グレー}で曇りだと言ってよい。
*Ochi-konde iru hito ni-totte wa mai-nichi ga {hai-iro/*nezumi-iro/*guree} de kumori da to itte yoi.*
PHRASE: gray hair *shira-ga* 白髪

graze[1] vt. **[for s.o. to receive a scrape in the skin caused by rubbing against s.t.]**
⟨-o⟩ su⌈ri-mu⌉ku ⟨〜を⟩すりむく ①
EX. Toshiki fell down and grazed his elbow.
俊樹は転んで、ひじをすりむいた。
Toshiki wa koronde, hiji o suri-muita.

graze[2] vi./vt. **[for an animal to eat grass in a field]**
ku⌈sa⌉ o {ku⌉u/ta⌈be⌉ru} 草を{食う ①/食べる ②} [for s.a. to eat grass]
NOTE: *Kuu* is usually used by men.

grease n. **[animal fat melted soft or any thick oily substance]**
a⌈bura あぶら [a whitish slippery substance found in animal bodies or a thick liquid made from plants used in cooking or a thick liquid made from minerals used for lubrication]
㊥ "solid animal fat"▷脂, "liquid oil"▷油
EX. (**a**) You'll need to use lots of hot water to get the grease off the plates.

G

熱いお湯をたくさん使ってお皿の油を落とさないといけない。
Atsui o-yu o takusan tsukatte o-sara no abura o otosanai to ikenai.
(**b**) His hair looked shiny with grease.
彼の髪は油で光っていた。
Kare no kami wa abura de hikatte ita.

great adj. **[to be excellent in quality/ability or to be very large in degree/amount]**
1. e⌈ra⌉i 偉い adj(*i*). **[for s.o. to have been successful and achieved a high position]** **《outstanding, distinguished, excellent》**, **i⌈daina 偉大な** adj(*na*). **•c [for s.o./s.t. to be worthy of high praise]** **《outstanding, distinguished, excellent》**, **su⌈barashi⌉i すばらしい** adj(*i*). **[causing great wonder/admiration/pleasure due to being extremely good]** **《splendid, wonderful, superb》**

EX. (**a**) His father is a great scholar.
彼のお父さんは{偉い/偉大な/すばらしい}学者です。
Kare no o-too-san wa {erai/idaina/subarashii} gakusha desu.
(**b**) She may not be a great scholar, but she is a great teacher.
彼女は{偉い/偉大な/すばらしい}学者ではないかもしれませんが、{すばらしい/偉大な/??偉い}先生です。
Kanojo wa {erai/idaina/subarashii} gakusha dewanai kamoshiremasen ga, {subarashii/idaina/??erai} sensei desu.
(**c**) The party was great.
パーティーは{すばらしかったです/*偉かったです/*偉大でした}。
*Paatii wa {subarashikatta desu/ *erakatta desu/*idai deshita}.*
(**d**) He was presented with an award for his great achievements in the field of language teaching.
彼の語学教育における{偉大な/すばらしい/*偉い}業績に対して賞が贈られた。
*Kare no gogaku-kyooiku ni-okeru {idaina/subarashii/*erai} gyooseki ni-taishite shoo ga okura-reta.*

2. {dai-/tai-} 大〜 pref. **[very large in degree/amount]**

EX. (**a**) The show was a great success.
ショーは大成功だった。
Shoo wa dai-seikoo datta.
(**b**) The plan was supported by a great majority of the people.
その計画には大部分の人が賛成してくれました。
Sono keikaku ni wa dai-bubun no hito ga sansei-shite kuremashita.

PHRASE: the great statue of Buddha *daibutsu* 大仏 **•c**, Great Britain *Dai-ei-teikoku* 大英帝国 **•c**

greatly adv. **[to a large degree]**
hi⌈jooni 非常に •c [to a great degree/extent] **《extremely, tremendously》**

EX. (**a**) His Japanese has improved greatly since he came to know Junko.
順子さんと知り合ってから、彼は日本語が非常に上手になった。
Junko-san to shiri-atte kara, kare wa Nihon-go ga hijooni joozuni natta.
(**b**) He admired his father greatly.
彼は父親を非常に尊敬していた。
Kare wa chichi-oya o hijooni sonkei-shite ita.

Greece n.
Gi⌉risha ギリシア
NOTE: This is usually written as ギリシア but pronounced as *Girisha.*

Greek adj. **[of Greece/its people/the Greek language]**
Gi⌉risha no N ギリシアのN •f [of Greece], **Gi⌈risha⌉-jin no N ギリシア人のN •f+c [of the people/a person of Greece]**, **Gi⌈risha-go no N ギリシア語のN •f+c [of the language of Greece]**

—— n. **[the language/a person of Greece]**
1. Gi⌈risha-go⌉ ギリシア語 •f+c [the language of Greece]
2. Gi⌈risha-jin ギリシア人 •f+c [the people/a person of Greece]

green adj./n. **[(of) the color of newgrown grass and the leaves of most plants and trees]**
mi⌈dori(-iro) (no N) 緑(色)(のN), gu⌈ri⌉in

(no N) グリーン(のN) •f, a˥o (no N) 青(のN) [of the color of the sky on a clear day and also that of newgrown grass and the leaves of most plants and trees] ⟪**blue**⟫, **a˥o˥i 青い** adj(*i*).

NOTE: *Ao/Aoi* are often used to refer to the color of green vegetables and fruits, grass, leaves, and green traffic lights. Otherwise, *midori* or *guriin* is used.

EX. (**a**) Wait till the traffic light turns green before going.
信号が{青/*緑/*グリーン}になるまで待ちなさい。
*Shingoo ga {ao/*midori/*guriin} ni naru made machinasai.*
(**b**) The girl wore a green sweater.
女の子は{緑の/グリーンの/*青い}セーターを着ていた。
*Onna-no-ko wa {midori no/guriin no/*aoi} seetaa o kite ita.*
(**c**) The cherry blossoms looked particularly beautiful surrounded by the green leaves of trees around them.
回りの木の{青い/緑の/?グリーンの}葉に囲まれて桜の花が一際美しく見える。
Mawari no ki no {aoi/midori no/?guriin no} ha ni kakoma-rete sakura no hana ga hitokiwa utsukushiku mieru.

PHRASE: green vegetables *ao-yasai* 青野菜, green tea *Nihon-cha* 日本茶 •c, *ryoku-cha* 緑茶 •c

greenhouse n.
o˥nshitsu 温室 •c

PHRASE: greenhouse effect *onshitsu-kooka* 温室効果 •c

greet vt. **[for s.o. to speak to or welcome s.o. in a friendly and respectful way]**

1. ⟨**-ni**⟩ (⟨**-to**⟩) **a˥isatsu suru** ⟨〜に⟩(⟨〜と⟩)**あいさつする** ③ **•c [for s.o. to address s.o. with courteous words and actions, esp. in meeting and parting]**

EX. (**a**) The pupils greeted their teacher with a cheerful "Good morning."
生徒たちは先生に「おはようございます」と明るくあいさつしました。
Seito-tachi wa sensei ni 'o-hayoo gozaimasu' to akaruku aisatsu-shimashita.
(**b**) The hotel manager came out to greet us.
ホテルのマネージャーがあいさつ(し)に出てきた。
Hoteru no maneejaa ga aisatsu(-shi) ni dete kita.

2. ⟨**-o**⟩ **mu˥kaeru** ⟨〜を⟩**迎える** ② **[for s.o./s.a. to welcome s.o. by being at a certain place at the time of his/her arrival]** ⟪**welcome**⟫

EX. (**a**) Mrs. Tanaka greeted us with a smile.
田中さんは笑顔で私たちを迎えてくださいました。
Tanaka-san wa egao de watashi-tachi o mukaete kudasaimashita.
(**b**) The bride and the groom were greeted with applause.
花嫁と花婿は拍手で迎えられた。
Hana-yome to hana-muko wa hakushu de mukae-rareta.

greeting n. **[words or gestures used upon first meeting s.o. or words used in opening a letter to s.o.]**
a˥isatsu あいさつ •c [words or actions used in meeting, parting with, or opening a letter to s.o. or a brief speech made at a ceremony or party]

EX. (**a**) "Hello," I said in a loud voice, but she didn't return my greeting.
「こんにちは」と大きい声で言ったけど、彼女は私のあいさつに返事をしてくれませんでした。
'Konnichi-wa' to ookii koe de itta kedo, kanojo wa watashi no aisatsu ni henji o shite kuremasen deshita.
(**b**) Mr. Tanaka and Mr. Yamada exchanged greetings at the entrance to the theater.
田中さんと山田さんは劇場の入口でお互いにあいさつを交わした。
Tanaka-san to Yamada-san wa gekijoo no iriguchi de o-tagai ni aisatsu o kawashita.

grief n. **[great sorrow]**
hi˥tan 悲嘆 •c [a state of being sorrowful] ⟪**anguish, lamentation**⟫, **fu˥ka˥i ka˥nashi-mi 深い悲しみ [deep sorrow]**

G

EX. (**a**) She was in deep grief following the death of her only son.
彼女は一人息子に死なれて、{悲嘆にくれていた/深い悲しみに沈んでいた}。
Kanojo wa hitori-musuko ni shina-rete, {hitan ni kurete ita/fukai kanashi-mi ni shizunde ita}.
(**b**) Nothing could ease his grief.
何も彼の{悲嘆/深い悲しみ}を和らげることはできなかった。
Nani-mo kare no {hitan/fukai kanashi-mi} o yawarageru koto wa dekinakatta.

grim adj. **[stern, severe, harsh]**
ki⌈bishi⌉i 厳しい adj(*i*). **[unpleasantly intense to the senses or tending to impose strict rules on others]** ⟪**severe, stern, forbidding, without mercy**⟫ ↔ **yasashii 優しい** adj(*i*)., **rakuna 楽な** adj(*na*).

EX. (**a**) The teacher's expression was grim as she told us that we had all failed the exam.
先生は厳しい表情でみんな試験に落ちたとおっしゃった。
Sensei wa kibishii hyoojoo de minna shiken ni ochita to osshatta.
(**b**) Everyone at some time has to face the grim reality that they must eventually die.
いずれは必ず死ぬという厳しい現実にだれもが直面しなければならない時が来る。
Izure wa kanarazu shinu to iu kibishii genjitsu ni dare-mo ga chokumen-shinakereba naranai toki ga kuru.

G

grind vt. **[to crush s.t. into small pieces/powder between two hard surfaces or to make s.t. smooth/sharp by rubbing it on a rough surface]**
1. ⟨-o⟩ hi⌈ku ⟨〜を⟩ひく ① **[to move s.t./s.o./s.a. concrete or abstract toward the source of a force ⟪fig. "quote," "subtract," "perform music on a stringed instrument, including piano," "grind grain or beans," "consult (a dictionary)," "choose lots," "extend in an uninterrupted fashion," "inherit a characteristic," "remove oneself from a position of public prominence," "catch a cold"⟫], ⟨-o⟩ su⌉ru ⟨〜を⟩する** ① **[for s.o. to rub s.t. hard to the extent that it is crushed]** ⟪**rub, chafe, print**⟫
㊥ "print"▷刷る, "rub"▷擦る

EX. (**a**) When I was in Mexico I learned how to grind corn into flour to make tortillas.
メキシコにいた時、とうもろこしを{ひいて/*すって}できた粉でトルティーヤを作る方法を習った。
*Mekishiko ni ita toki, toomorokoshi o {hiite/*sutte} dekita kona de torutiiya o tsukuru hoohoo o naratta.*
(**b**) I helped my grandmother grind roasted sesame seeds in a mortar.
私はおばあちゃんがすりばちでいりごまを{する/*ひく}のを手伝った。
*Watashi wa o-baa-chan ga suri-bachi de iri-goma o {suru/*hiku} no o tetsudatta.*

PHRASE: ground meat *hiki-niku* ひき肉

2. ⟨-o⟩ to⌉gu ⟨〜を⟩研ぐ ① **[for s.o. to cause a knife to cut better by whetting it on a whetstone or to wash rice in water]** ⟪**sharpen, hone**⟫

EX. He ground all the kitchen knives.
彼は包丁を全部研いだ。
Kare wa hoochoo o zenbu toida.

PHRASE: grind one's teeth *ha-gishiri o suru* 歯ぎしりをする ③

groan vi. **[for s.o./s.a. to make a long, low sound of suffering/unhappiness/disapproval]**
u⌈me⌉ku うめく ① **[for s.o./s.a. to make a low sound due to suffering]** ⟪**moan**⟫

EX. The woman was groaning in pain.
女の人は痛みでうめいていた。
Onna no hito wa ita-mi de umeite ita.

grocery n. **[a shop that sells food and miscellaneous household items]**
sho⌈kuryoo-hi⌉n-ten 食料品店 •c [a shop that sells food], za⌈kka⌉-ten 雑貨店 •c [a shop that sells various small household supplies and some foods], za⌈kka-ya⌉ 雑貨屋
NOTE: *Zakka-ya* is slightly less formal than *zakka-ten.*

EX. I bought some instant coffee at the grocery in the village.

私は村の{食料品店/雑貨屋/雑貨店}でインスタントコーヒーを買いました。
Watashi wa mura no {shokuryoo-hin-ten/zakka-ya/zakka-ten} de insutanto-koohii o kaimashita.

groceries n. **[the goods sold at a grocery/supermarket]**
sho꜀kuryoo(-hin) 食料(品) •c [foodstuffs] ((provisions, eatables)), za꜀kka 雑貨 •c [various small household supplies], ni꜀chiyoo-hin 日用品 •c [things necessary for daily life such as toothpaste, soap, shampoo, etc.] ((daily necessities))

EX. She put the groceries in her car.
彼女は{食料(品)/雑貨/日用品}を自分の車に載せた。
Kanojo wa {shokuryoo(-hin)/zakka/nichiyoo-hin} o jibun no kuruma ni noseta.

ground n. **[the surface of the earth or soil ((fig. "an amount of subject matter or a reason/argument for s.t."))]**

1. ji꜆men 地面 •c [the surface of the earth]

EX. (**a**) Many men were lying on the ground injured.
けがをした人がたくさん地面に倒れていた。
Kega o shita hito ga takusan jimen ni taorete ita.
(**b**) The ground was covered with snow.
地面は雪でおおわれていた。
Jimen wa yuki de oowa-rete ita.

2. tsu꜀chi꜆ 土 [the layer of soil at the earth's surface in which plants grow] ((earth)), to꜀chi 土地 •c [land as property owned by s.o. or utilized for a purpose such as growing crops] ((land))

EX. It is very difficult to determine how much of this ground has been improved.
この{土/土地}がどの程度改良されたかを見極めるのはとても難しい。
Kono {tsuchi/tochi} ga dono teido kairyoo-sareta ka o mi-kiwameru no wa totemo muzukashii.

PHRASE: under ground *chika* 地下 •c, above ground *chijoo* 地上 •c

3. ha꜆n'i 範囲 [an area defined by certain bounds] ((scope, range))

EX. It's impossible to cover so much ground in such a short lecture.
こんなに短い講義でそんなに広い範囲のことをカバーするのは不可能です。
Konnani mijikai koogi de sonnani hiroi han'i no koto o kabaa-suru no wa fu-kanoo desu.

4. ko꜆nkyo 根拠 •c [the facts/conditions that provide a base for a rumor, accusation, etc.] ((basis, foundation)), ri꜀yuu 理由 •c [a fact/event/statement that provides an explanation/excuse for s.t. else] ((reason))

EX. (**a**) Adultery was the grounds for their divorce.
不倫が彼らの離婚の{理由/*根拠}でした。
*Furin ga kare-ra no rikon no {riyuu/*konkyo} deshita.*
(**b**) There are some grounds to the rumor that the school is going to be closed down.
その学校が閉鎖されるといううわさには少しは{根拠/*理由}がある。
*Sono gakkoo ga heisa-sareru to iu uwasa ni wa sukoshi wa {konkyo/*riyuu} ga aru.*
(**c**) There are no grounds to support what he said yesterday.
彼がきのう言ったことには何も{根拠/*理由}がない。
*Kare ga kinoo itta koto ni wa nani-mo {konkyo/*riyuu} ga nai.*

group n. **[a number of people or things considered to belong together because of certain mutual connections or similarities]**
gu꜀ru꜆upu グループ •f [a number of people or things considered to belong together because of certain mutual connections or similarities], da꜀ntai 団体 •c [a relatively large number of people gathered together for a specific purpose] ((organization, party, body)), shu꜀udan 集団 •c [a large number of people or animals considered to belong together because of certain mutual connections or similarities] ((mass))

EX. (**a**) Duty free shops are typically full of

G

Japanese tourists on group tours.
免税店はたいてい{団体/グループ/*集団}旅行の日本人観光客でいっぱいです。
*Menzei-ten wa taitei {dantai/guruupu/*shuudan}-ryokoo no Nihon-jin-kankoo-kyaku de ippai desu.*
(**b**) The Beatles are the best known pop group of the 1960s.
ビートルズは一番よく知られている1960年代のポピュラー音楽の{グループ/*団体/*集団}です。
*Biitoruzu wa ichiban yoku shira-rete iru sen-kyuu-hyaku-roku-juu-nen-dai no popyuraa-ongaku no {guruupu/*dantai/*shuudan} desu.*
(**c**) The Japanese are often said to have a tendency to act in groups rather than as individuals.
日本人は個人としてではなく{集団/グループ/団体}で行動する傾向があるとよく言われている。
Nihon-jin wa kojin to-shite dewanaku {shuudan/guruupu/dantai} de koodoo-suru keikoo ga aru to yoku iwa-rete iru.

PHRASE: a group tour *dantai-ryokoo* 団体旅行 •c, group psychology *shuudan-shinri* 集団心理 •c, pressure group *atsuryoku-dantai* 圧力団体 •c

grove n. **[a group of trees or a small wooded area]**
ko˥-dachi 木立

EX. There was a grove of tall trees on top of the hill.
丘の上に高い木の木立があった。
Oka no ue ni takai ki no ko-dachi ga atta.

grow vi. **[for s.o./s.a. to increase in size by natural development 《fig. "for s.t. to increase in size/degree/amount"》]**
1. no˥bi˥ru のびる ② [for s.t. to become longer, usu. vertically 《fig. "for an ability to improve," "be postponed," "be extended"》] 《make progress, develop, expand》 ↔ chijimu 縮む ①
㊈ "be postponed/extended"▷延びる, "grow" ▷伸びる

EX. (**a**) He's grown seven centimeters this year.
彼はこの一年間で七センチ背が伸びた。
Kare wa kono ichi-nen-kan de nana-senchi se ga nobita.
(**b**) Rain makes the grass grow.
雨が降ると、草が伸びる。
Ame ga furu to, kusa ga nobiru.
(**c**) My hair grows fast.
私の髪は伸びるのが速い。
Watashi no kami wa nobiru no ga hayai.
(**d**) I think Japan's foreign trade surplus will grow even further.
私は日本の貿易黒字はまだ伸びると思う。
Watashi wa Nihon no booeki-kuro-ji wa mada nobiru to omou.

2. se˥ichoo-suru 成長する ③ •c [to increase in size by natural development 《fig. "for an enterprise to grow"》]

EX. (**a**) Children grow up rapidly.
子供は成長するのが速い。
Kodomo wa seichoo-suru no ga hayai.
(**b**) She has grown into a beautiful woman.
彼女は成長して美しい女性になった。
Kanojo wa seichoo-shite utsukushii josei ni natta.
(**c**) The company has grown rapidly in the past five years.
その会社はここ五年で急に成長した。
Sono kaisha wa koko go-nen de kyuuni seichoo-shita.

3. fu˥e˥ru 増える ② [to become greater in amount/number]

EX. The number of women who work part-time is growing.
パートで働く女性が増えている。
Paato de hataraku josei ga fuete iru.

4. ha˥e˥ru 生える ② [for plants to come out of the ground or for a tooth/hair to come out] 《come up, spring up》

EX. The weeds in the garden have grown while we were away.
私たちがいない間に庭に雑草が生えてしまった。
Watashi-tachi ga inai aida ni niwa ni zassoo ga haete shimatta.

5. 〈-ni〉 na˥ru 〈〜に〉なる ① [to change into]

《**become, turn into, turn out**》

EX. (**a**) The noise grew louder.
物音は大きくなった。
Mono-oto wa ookiku natta.
(**b**) I grew to like Japanese food while I was in Japan.
日本にいる間に日本の食べ物がだんだん好きになった。
Nihon ni iru aida ni Nihon no tabe-mono ga dan-dan sukini natta.

PHRASE: grow dark *hi ga kureru* 日が暮れる ②

EX. Around here it grows dark around six.
この辺では六時ごろ日が暮れます。
Kono hen de wa roku-ji-goro hi ga kuremasu.

— vt. **[to cause/allow s.t.to grow]**
⟨-o⟩ no⌈ba⌉su ⟨～を⟩のばす ① [for s.o. to cause s.t. to become longer, usu. vertically 《fig. "straighten," "hold out," "postpone," "cultivate (an ability)"》], ⟨-o⟩ tsu⌈ku⌉ru ⟨～を⟩つくる ① [for s.o./s.a. to cause s.t./s.o./s.a. to come into existence which did not exist previously] 《make, create, manufacture, build》

㊮ "postpone/expand"▷延ばす, "grow"▷伸ばす

㊮ "build/manufacture"▷造る, otherwise ▷作る

EX. (**a**) He has grown a beard.
彼はひげを{伸ばした/*作った}。
*Kare wa hige o {nobashita/*tsukutta}.*
(**b**) We're growing vegetables in our garden.
庭で野菜を{作って/*伸ばして}います。
*Niwa de yasai o {tsukutte/*nobashite} imasu.*

PHRASE: grow up *otona ni naru* 大人になる ①

growth n. **[the process of growing]**

1. se⌈ichoo 成長 •c

EX. (**a**) People were amazed at the rapid growth of Japan's economy.
人々は日本経済の急成長に目をみはった。
Hito-bito wa Nihon-keizai no kyuu-seichoo ni me o mi-hatta.
(**b**) A balanced diet is essential for a child's growth.
バランスのいい食事は子供の成長に不可欠です。
Baransu no ii shokuji wa kodomo no seichoo ni fukaketsu desu.

2. zo⌈oka 増加 •c [increase in number/quantity]

EX. The rapid growth of the population has been a major problem in this country up until now.
急激な人口増加は今までこの国の大きな問題だった。
Kyuugekina jinkoo-zooka wa ima made kono kuni no ookina mondai datta.

guarantee n. **[a formal promise that s.t. will be done]**
ho⌈shoo 保証 •c

EX. (**a**) This refrigerator has a one-year guarantee.
この冷蔵庫は一年の保証付きです。
Kono reizoo-ko wa ichi-nen no hoshoo-tsuki desu.
(**b**) My car is less than a year old so it's still under guarantee.
私の車は買って一年もたたないから、まだ保証期間内です。
Watashi no kuruma wa katte ichi-nen mo tatanai kara, mada hoshoo-kikan-nai desu.
(**c**) Will you give me your guarantee that these goods can be returned if I don't like them?
この商品が気に入らなかったら返してもいいと保証してくれますか。
Kono shoohin ga ki-ni-iranakattara kaeshite mo ii to hoshoo-shite kuremasu ka.
(**d**) There's no guarantee that they're telling the truth.
彼らが本当のことを言っているという保証はない。
Kare-ra ga hontoo no koto o itte iru to iu hoshoo wa nai.

— vt. **[for s.o. to give a firm promise that s.t. will be done]**
{⟨-to⟩/⟨-o⟩} ho⌈shoo-suru {⟨～と⟩/⟨～を⟩}保証する ③ •c [for s.o. to give a formal promise that s.t. will be done]

EX. (**a**) This jam is guaranteed to be free of preservatives.
このジャムには防腐剤が入っていないことを保証します。
Kono jamu ni wa boofu-zai ga haitte inai koto o hoshoo-shimasu.
(**b**) They have guranteed that any faulty parts will be replaced free of charge.
部品に欠陥があれば、ただで取り替えると保証してくれました。
Buhin ni kekkan ga areba, tada de tori-kaeru to hoshoo-shite kuremashita.

guard n. **[s.o. who watches over a place or person to prevent escape or harm; a state of watchful readiness to protect or defend s.o./s.t./s.a.]**

1. mi-ˈhari 見張り [the act of watching over some place/s.o. to prevent escape/harm or s.o. who does this] ((lookout, watch, watchman, lifeguard)), keˈibi 警備 •c [the act of watching over some place to protect it from danger] ((defense, policing))

EX. (**a**) There are policemen on guard at the entrance of the bank.
銀行の入口で警官が{警備/見張り}をしている。
Ginkoo no iriguchi de keikan ga {keibi/mi-hari} o shite iru.
(**b**) There was another guard standing by the fence.
塀のところにも{見張り/*警備}が立っていた。
*Hei no tokoro ni mo {mi-hari/*keibi} ga tatte ita.*

2. goˈei 護衛 •c [a policeman/soldier/warship that accompanies s.o. important to protect them from danger or an act of such accompanying] ((escort, bodyguard))

EX. The police will provide the Prime Minister with an armed guard.
警察が武装して首相の護衛をする。
Keisatsu ga busoo-shite shushoo no goei o suru.

3. shuˈei 守衛 •c [a person hired to watch over some place mainly at the entrance/exit to prevent trouble] ((doorkeeper)), keˈibiˈ-in 警備員 •c [a person hired to watch over some place to prevent theft, attack, danger, etc.] ((security guard))

EX. (**a**) There is a guard on duty at the front gate of the university.
大学の正門のところに{守衛/?警備員}がいます。
Daigaku no seimon no tokoro ni {shuei/?keibi-in} ga imasu.
(**b**) He works for a bank as a night guard.
彼は夜間{警備員/*守衛}として銀行に勤めている。
*Kare wa yakan-{keibi-in/*shuei} to-shite ginkoo ni tsutomete iru.*

PHRASE: prison guard *kanshu* 看守 •c, lower one's guard *yudan-suru* 油断する ③ •c

EX. I was hit in the face the instant I lowered my guard.
一瞬油断したすきに顔をなぐられた。
Isshun yudan-shita suki ni kao o nagura-reta.

—— vt. **[to protect s.t./s.o./s.a.]**

1. ⟨-o⟩ (⟨-kara⟩) maˈmoˈru ⟨～を⟩(⟨～から⟩) 守る ① [(to watch s.t./s.o./s.a. in order) to cause s.t./s.o./s.a. not to be harmed/injured/violated] ((protect, obey, keep)), ⟨-o⟩ keˈibi-suru ⟨～を⟩警備する ③ •c [for s.o. to watch over some place/s.o. to protect it/him/her from danger]

EX. (**a**) Doctors ought to carefully guard the privacy of their patients.
医者は患者の秘密を{守る/*警備する}べきだ。
*Isha wa kanja no himitsu o {mamoru/*keibi-suru}-beki da.*
(**b**) The official residence of the Prime Minister is heavily guarded at all times.
首相官邸は二十四時間厳重に{警備されて/守られて}いる。
Shushoo-kantei wa ni-juu-yo-jikan genjuuni {keibi-sarete/mamora-rete} iru.

2. ⟨-o⟩ mi-ˈharu ⟨～を⟩見張る ① [for s.o. to watch over s.o./s.t./s.a. to prevent escape or harm] ((watch over, look out for))

EX. She was locked in her room and guarded night and day.

G

彼女は自分の部屋にとじこめられて、昼も夜も見張られていた。
Kanojo wa jibun no heya ni toji-kome-rarete, hiru mo yoru mo mi-hara-rete ita.

guess vt./vi. **[for s.o. to form a judgment or to give an opinion without knowing/considering all the facts]**
ke⌈nto⌉o ga tsuku 見当が付く ① [to be able to form a judgment/give an opinion without knowing/considering all the facts], (⟨-ni⟩) a⌈taru (⟨〜に⟩)当たる ① [for s.t. to come into sudden spontaneous contact with s.t. forming a narrow target area ⟪fig. "succeed in giving the correct answer to a problem/question without knowing all the facts/information"⟫], (⟨-ni⟩) ⟨-o⟩ a⌈teru (⟨〜に⟩)⟨〜を⟩あてる ② [for s.o. to make sudden and direct contact with s.t. forming a narrow target area ⟪fig. "(try to) guess the correct answer," "apply," "place," "succeed," "expose," "assign," "allocate," "appropriate"⟫], Sinf. to o⌈mo⌉u Sinf.と思う ① [for s.o. to spontaneously perceive s.t. in one's mind or to have an opinion about s.t.] ⟪suppose⟫
㊅ "appropriate" ▷充てる, otherwise ▷当てる

EX. (**a**) A: Can you guess how old I am?
私が何歳か見当が付きますか。
Watashi ga nan-sai ka kentoo ga tsukimasu ka.
B: I would guess you are about 30.
三十ぐらいだと思います。
San-juu-gurai da to omoimasu.
A: You've guessed right. I'm exactly 30 years old.
当たりましたね。丁度三十です。
Atarimashita ne. Choodo san-juu desu.
(**b**) Mr. Smith guessed my age correctly.
スミスさんは私の年を当てた。
Sumisu-san wa watashi no toshi o ateta.
(**c**) Can you guess how much the price of land is in Tokyo?
東京の土地の値段の見当が付きますか。
Tookyoo no tochi no nedan no kentoo ga tsukimasu ka.
(**d**) Guess what I'm thinking.
私が何を考えているか当ててごらん。
Watashi ga nani o kangaete iru ka atete goran.

— n. **[an attempt to form a judgment without knowing all the facts or an opinion formed without knowing all the facts] so⌈ozoo 想像 •c [s.t. that is imagined] ⟪imagination⟫, su⌈isoku 推測 •c [forming a judgment based on the facts/information available] ⟪conjecture⟫**

EX. My guess is that he didn't come because he didn't want to see Masako.
私の{想像/推測}だけど、彼は正子さんに会いたくなくて、来なかったんだと思う。
Watashi no {soozoo/suisoku} da kedo, kare wa Masako-san ni ai-takunakute, konakatta n da to omou.

PHRASE: wild guess *atezuppoo* あてずっぽう

EX. I made a wild guess, and it turned out to be correct.
あてずっぽうで言ったら、当たったんです。
Atezuppoo de ittara, atatta n desu.

guide vt. **[for s.o. to show s.o. the way by leading]**
1. **⟨-ni⟩ ⟨-o⟩ a⌈nna⌉i-suru ⟨〜に⟩⟨〜を⟩案内する ③ •c [for s.o. to show s.o. around/to a place]**

EX. I guided John around Kyoto for the afternoon.
私は午後ジョンに京都を案内してあげた。
Watashi wa gogo Jon ni Kyooto o annai-shite ageta.

2. **⟨-o⟩ {⟨-e⟩/⟨-ni⟩} a⌈nna⌉i-suru ⟨〜を⟩{⟨〜へ⟩/⟨〜に⟩}案内する ③ •c [for s.o.to take s.o. to a place], ⟨-o⟩ {⟨-e⟩/⟨-ni⟩} tsu⌈rete-iku ⟨〜を⟩{⟨〜へ⟩/⟨〜に⟩}連れて行く /⟨V*te* of *tsureru* ② accompany + *iku* ① go/ ① [for s.o. to go along with s.o./s.a. equal to/lower than oneself in status to a place] ⟪take⟫**

EX. He guided us through the narrow streets to the subway station.
彼は狭い通りを通って、私たちを地下

G

鉄の駅へ{案内して/連れて行って}くれた。
Kare wa semai toori o tootte, watashi-tachi o chika-tetsu no eki e {annai-shite/tsurete-itte} kureta.

— n. **[s.o./s.t. that shows the way to s.o.]**
1. ga⌉ido ガイド •f [s.o. whose job it is to show s.o. around a place]
EX. I'd like a guide to show me the city.
町を案内してくれるガイドが欲しいんですが。
Machi o annai-shite kureru gaido ga hoshii n desu ga.
2. te⌉-biki 手引 [a book which explains the way to do s.t.] ⟪**manual**⟫
EX. This book is a practical guide to teaching English.
この本は英語教育の実用的な手引です。
Kono hon wa eigo-kyooiku no jitsuyoo-tekina te-biki desu.
3. a⌈nnai-sho 案内書 •c [a book which gives information about a place for the sake of visitors] ⟪**guidebook**⟫, **ga⌈ido-bu⌉kku ガイドブック •f**
EX. I bought a guide book to Kyoto at the station.
私は駅で京都の{案内書/ガイドブック}を買いました。
Watashi wa eki de Kyooto no {annai-sho/gaido-bukku} o kaimashita.

G

guidance n. **[the act of directing s.o. or showing s.o. how to do s.t.; advice]**
shi⌈doo 指導 •c [the act of directing s.o. or giving s.o. advice] ⟪**leading, direction, coaching**⟫
EX. (**a**) We give students the guidance they need in selecting their courses.
科目の選択についてはちゃんと学生を指導します。
Kamoku no sentaku ni-tsuite wa chanto gakusei o shidoo-shimasu.
(**b**) The students made rapid progress once they received proper guidance.
学生は適切な指導を得て急速に進歩しました。
Gakusei wa tekisetsuna shidoo o ete kyuusokuni shinpo-shimashita.

guilty adj. **[for s.o. to have broken a law or done s.t. wrong]**
yu⌈uzai no N 有罪のN •c [for s.o. to have committed a crime] ↔ **muzai no N 無罪のN •c**
EX. The defendant was found to be guilty.
被告は有罪の判決を受けた。
Hikoku wa yuuzai no hanketsu o uketa.
PHRASE: feel guilty ⟨*-o*⟩ *warui to omou* ⟨〜を⟩悪いと思う ①
EX. I feel guilty for not writing often to my parents.
めったに両親に手紙を出さないのを悪いと思っている。
Mettani ryooshin ni tegami o dasanai no o warui to omotte iru.

guitar n.
gi⌉taa ギター •f
EX. Do you play the guitar?
ギターを弾きますか。
Gitaa o hikimasu ka.

gulf n.
wa⌉n 湾 •c
PHRASE: the Persian Gulf *Perusha-wan* ペルシャ湾

gun n. **[a firearm containing a metal tube from which shells/bullets are fired]**
ju⌉u 銃 •c [any handheld gun]
EX. (**a**) They have guns and will not hesitate to use them.
彼らは銃を持っていて、使うのをためらわない。
Kare-ra wa juu o motte ite, tsukau no o tamerawanai.
(**b**) A policeman was shot in the stomach with a gun yesterday but is reported to be in good condition after treatment.
きのう警官が銃で腹を撃たれたが、手当てを受けて順調に回復しているそうだ。
Kinoo keikan ga juu de hara o uta-reta ga, te-ate o ukete junchooni kaifuku-shite iru sooda.
PHRASE: a machine gun *kikan-juu* 機関銃 •c

guy n. **[a man ⟨s⟩]**
o⌈toko⌉ 男 [a human male], ya⌉tsu やつ [a person/thing (with derogatory or endearing connotation) ⟨s⟩]
NOTE: *Yatsu* is usually used by men, especially when it means "a person."
EX. He's an interesting guy. I'm sure you'll like him.
彼は面白い{やつ/男}ですよ。きっと気に入りますよ。
Kare wa omoshiroi {yatsu/otoko} desu yo. Kitto ki ni-irimasu yo.
PHRASE: this guy *kono otoko* この男 ⟪this man⟫, *koitsu* こいつ ⟨s⟩

gymnasium n.
ta⌈iiku⌉-kan 体育館 •c
EX. Our school doesn't have a good gymnasium.
私たちの学校にはいい体育館がありません。
Watashi-tachi no gakkoo ni wa ii taiiku-kan ga arimasen.

gymnastics n. **[the art or practice of training the body using special apparatus such as parallel bars and rings]**
ta⌈isoo 体操 •c [the art or practice of training the body, including such training with special apparatus such as parallel bars and rings] ⟪calisthenics, physical education⟫
EX. The world championship games in gymnastics will be held in Tokyo in October.
十月に東京で体操の世界選手権大会が開かれます。
Juu-gatsu ni Tookyoo de taisoo no sekai-senshu ken taikai ga hiraka-remasu.

habit n. **[s.t. one does regularly and repeatedly over a long period of time almost without thinking]**
shu⌈ukan 習慣 •c [the usual way of acting for an individual or members of a social community] ⟪custom⟫, ku⌈se⌉ 癖 [s.t. one does regularly and repeatedly without being conscious of it, usu. s.t. undesirable] ⟪a peculiar way, trait⟫
EX. (**a**) She has a habit of biting her fingernails.
彼女はつめをかむ{癖/*習慣}がある。
*Kanojo wa tsume o kamu {kuse/ *shuukan} ga aru.*
(**b**) I'm in the habit of getting up at five in the morning.
朝は五時に起きるのが{習慣/*癖}です。
*Asa wa go-ji ni okiru no ga {shuukan/ *kuse} desu.*
PHRASE: fall into a habit *kuse ga tsuku* 癖がつく ①, get rid of a habit *kuse o naosu* 癖を直す ①
EX. Bad habits are easy to fall into and hard to get rid of.
悪い癖はつきやすく、直しにくい。
Warui kuse wa tsuki-yasuku, naoshi-nikui.

hail n. **[little balls of ice that fall like snow]**
a⌈rare あられ [tiny balls of ice that fall like snow], hyo⌉o ひょう [small balls of ice that fall like snow in a thunderstorm]
NOTE: *Hyoo* are longer than 5 mm in diameter and can cause damage to crops. *Arare* are smaller than this.

— vi. **[for frozen raindrops to fall]**
{a⌈rare/hyo⌉o} ga fu⌉ru {あられ/ひょう}が降る

EX. It hailed yesterday afternoon.
きのうの午後{あられ/ひょう}が降った。
Kinoo no gogo {arare/hyoo} ga futta.

hair n. **[a fine threadlike growth that emerges from the skin of humans and certain animals]**
ke 毛 [a fine threadlike growth that emerges from the skin of humans and certain animals], ka⌈mi⌉ 髪 [a threadlike growth on the human head]

EX. (**a**) Where did you have your hair cut?
どこで{髪/?毛}を切ってもらったんですか。
Doko de {kami/?ke} o kitte moratta n desu ka.
(**b**) The cat has left white hairs all over the sofa.
猫がソファーに白い{毛/*髪}をいっぱい付けた。
*Neko ga sofaa ni shiroi {ke/*kami} o ippai tsuketa.*
(**c**) I found a woman's hair on my husband's jacket.
主人の上着に女の人の髪(の毛)がついているのに気が付いた。
Shujin no uwa-gi ni onna no hito no kami(-no-ke) ga tsuite iru no ni ki ga tsuita.

PHRASE: gray hair *shira-ga* 白髪, haircut *heaa-katto* ヘアーカット •f, *sanpatsu* 散髪 •c

NOTE: *Heaa-katto* usually refers to a female haircut done at a beauty salon and *sanpatsu* to a male or children's haircut done at a barbershop.

PHRASE: hairdresser *biyoo-shi* 美容師 •c ⟨⟨beautician⟩⟩, hairdresser's *biyoo-in* 美容院 •c ⟨⟨beauty parlour⟩⟩

half n./adj./adv. **[either of the two equal parts into which s.t. is divided]**
ha⌈nbu⌉n 半分 n. **•c, -han ～半 •c**

EX. (**a**) She bought a kilo and a half of rice.
彼女は米を一キロ半買った。
Kanojo wa kome o ichi-kiro-han katta.
(**b**) I got up at half past seven.
私は七時半に起きた。
Watashi wa shichi-ji-han ni okita.
(**c**) Almost half of all traffic accidents are caused by speeding.
交通事故の半分近くはスピードの出し過ぎによるものです。
Kootsuu-jiko no hanbun-chikaku wa supiido no dashi-sugi ni yoru mono desu.
(**d**) I studied for five and a half hours on Sunday for this exam.
私はこの試験のために日曜日に五時間半勉強した。
Watashi wa kono shiken no tame ni nichiyoo-bi ni go-ji-kan-han benkyoo-shita.
(**e**) Half the students were absent today.
今日は学生の半分が欠席だった。
Kyoo wa gakusei no hanbun ga kesseki datta.
(**f**) She filled her half empty glass with more beer.
彼女は半分空になったコップにビールをつぎ足した。
Kanojo wa hanbun kara ni natta koppu ni biiru o tsugi-tashita.

PHRASE: the first half *zenhan* 前半 •c, the latter half *koohan* 後半 •c, half an hour *{san-jip-pun/san-jup-pun}* 三十分 •c, half a day *hannichi* 半日•c, half a year *hantoshi* 半年, half-cooked *nama-nie no* N 生煮えのN

halfway adj./adv. **[at the midpoint between two places]**
to⌈chuu 途中 n. **•c [anywhere between two points in place or time] ⟨⟨middle⟩⟩, ma⌈nnaka 真ん中** n. **[a point equidistant from all points on the outer perimeter of an area] ⟨⟨center⟩⟩**

EX. (**a**) The university is in Shizuoka, halfway between Nagoya and Tokyo.
大学は名古屋と東京の{真ん中/*途中}の静岡にあります。
*Daigaku wa Nagoya to Tookyoo no {mannaka/*tochuu} no Shizuoka ni arimasu.*
(**b**) Halfway to the university my bicycle got a flat tire.

大学へ行く{途中/*真ん中}で自転車のタイヤがパンクしてしまった。
*Daigaku e iku {tochuu/*mannaka} de jitensha no taiya ga panku-shite shimatta.*

hall n. **[the passage/space just inside the front door of a house or a passageway by which other rooms in a building are reached, or (a building with) a large room for conferences, concerts, etc.]**
1. ge⌉nkan 玄関 •c [the front entrance of a building 《fig. "entrance to a nation"》] ((entrance hall, front door)), ro⌈oka 廊下 •c [a passageway in a building leading to various rooms] ((corridor, hallway))

EX. (**a**) Please take your shoes off at the entrance hall.
{玄関/*廊下}で靴を脱いでください。
*{Genkan/*Rooka} de kutsu o nuide kudasai.*
(**b**) Don't run in the hall, please.
{廊下/*玄関}を走らないでください。
*{Rooka/*Genkan} o hashiranaide kudasai.*
(**c**) I waited in the hall at the entrance for Mrs. Yamada to come.
私は{玄関/*廊下}で山田さんが出て来るのを待った。
*Watashi wa {genkan/*rooka} de Yamada-san ga dete kuru no o matta.*

2. ho⌉oru ホール •f [(a building with) a large room for conferences, concerts, etc.]

EX. There were about 2,000 people gathered in the main hall.
ホールには人が二千人ぐらい集まっていた。
Hooru ni wa hito ga ni-sen-nin-gurai atsumatte ita.

PHRASE: city hall *shi-yakusho* 市役所 **•c**, lecture hall *koodoo* 講堂 **•c**, conference hall *kaigi-joo* 会議場 **•c**, concert hall *kansaato-hooru* コンサートホール **•f**

halt vi. **[to stop moving]**
to⌈maru とまる ① [for s.o./s.t./s.a. moving to come to a standstill 《fig. "be fastened"》] ((stop, cease))
㊥ "stay overnight"▷泊まる, "be fastened"▷留まる, "stop moving"▷止まる

EX. He took a step and halted.
彼は一歩進んで、止まった。
Kare wa ip-po susunde, tomatta.

— vt. **[for s.o. to cause s.t./s.o./s.a. to stop]**
⟨-o⟩ to⌈meru ⟨〜を⟩とめる ② ((stop, cease))
㊥ "stop"▷止める, "fasten"▷留める, "give lodging to"▷泊める

EX. The policeman raised his hand to halt the traffic.
警官が車の流れを止めるのに手を挙げた。
Keikan ga kuruma no nagare o tomeru no ni te o ageta.

— n. **[a stop]**
te⌈ishi 停止 •c

PHRASE: come to a halt *teishi-suru* 停止する ③ **•c**

EX. The train came to a halt just in time to avoid an accident.
電車は事故になる寸前に停止した。
Densha wa jiko ni naru sunzen ni teishi-shita.

ham n.
ha⌉mu ハム •f

EX. I had toast, two slices of ham, and coffee for breakfast this morning.
今朝の朝ごはんはトーストにハム二枚にコーヒーでした。
Kesa no asa-gohan wa toosuto ni hamu ni-mai ni koohii deshita.

PHRASE: ham and eggs *hamu-eggu* ハムエッグ

hammer n. **[a tool with a heavy metal head on a handle for striking things with]**
ka⌈na-zu⌉chi 金づち, ha⌉nmaa ハンマー •f

NOTE: *Hanmaa* is a large-sized *kana-zuchi.*

— vt. **[for s.o. to hit s.t. with a tool that has a heavy metal head on a handle]**
({ka⌈na-zu⌉chi/ha⌉nmaa} de) ⟨-o⟩ u⌉tsu ({金づち/ハンマー}で)⟨〜を⟩打つ ①

EX. I hammered a nail into the wall to hang the picture on.
絵をかけるのに壁に(金づちで)釘を打った。
E o kakeru no ni kabe ni (kana-zuchi de) kugi o utta.

PHRASE: hammer throw *hanmaa-nage* ハンマー投げ

hand n. **[the movable part of a person's arm from the wrist down 《fig. "worker"》]**

1. te˥ 手 [the movable part of the body attached to one's shoulder or the movable part of one's arm from the wrist down] **《arm, paw》**

EX. (**a**) She had a pistol in her hand.
彼女は手にピストルを持っていた。
Kanojo wa te ni pisutoru o motte ita.
(**b**) The girl was holding her mother's hand tightly.
女の子は母親の手をしっかり握っていた。
Onna-no-ko wa haha-oya no te o shikkari nigitte ita.
(**c**) Raise your hand, please.
手を上げてください。
Te o agete kudasai.

2. hi˥to-de 人手 [a worker]

EX. We're short on hands for this job. Can you help?
この仕事をするのに人手が足りないんですが、ちょっと手伝ってくれませんか。
Kono shigoto o suru no ni hito-de ga tarinai n desu ga, chotto tetsudatte kuremasen ka.

H

PHRASE: both hands *ryoo-te* 両手, one hand *kata-te* 片手, {give/lend} a hand to *te o kasu* 手を貸す ①, Hands up! *Te o agero.* 手をあげろ, hand in hand *te o tsunaide* 手をつないで, shake hands *akushu-suru* 握手する ③ •c, on the one hand *ippoo de wa* 一方では •c 《on the other hand, meanwhile》, on the other hand *{ippoo de wa/tahoo de wa}* {一方では/他方では} •c, hand on a clock *tokei no hari* 時計の針, the second hand *byooshin* 秒針 •c

EX. The hands on the clock point to three o'clock.
時計の針が三時を指しています。
Tokei no hari ga san-ji o sashite imasu.

—— vt. [for s.o. to give s.t. to s.o. with the hand]

⟨-ni⟩ ⟨-o⟩ wa˥tasu ⟨〜に⟩⟨〜を⟩渡す ① [for s.o. to give s.t. to s.o. with the hand] 《pass over, deliver, give》, ⟨-o⟩ to˥ru ⟨〜を⟩とる ① [for s.o./s.a. to cause s.t./s.o./s.a. to come to one's side] 《take, get, receive, adopt, charge, remove, steal》

㊟ "take a picture"▷撮る, "catch an animal"▷捕る, "employ/adopt"▷採る, "take charge of"▷執る, otherwise ▷取る

EX. (**a**) Could you hand this note to the woman sitting there in the blue dress?
あそこに座っている青いドレスの女性にこのメモを{渡して/*取って}くださいませんか。
*Asoko ni suwatte iru aoi doresu no josei ni kono memo o {watashite/*totte} kudasaimasen ka.*
(**b**) Excuse me, but could you please hand me that book?
すいませんが、その本を{取って/*渡して}くださいませんか。
*Suimasen ga, sono hon o {totte/ *watashite} kudasaimasen ka.*

PHRASE: hand in ⟨-o⟩ *dasu* ⟨〜を⟩出す ① 《turn in》

EX. Did you hand in your homework?
宿題を出しましたか。
Shukudai o dashimashita ka.

PHRASE: hand back ⟨-o⟩ *kaesu* ⟨〜を⟩返す ① 《return, give back》

EX. He handed the room key back to the receptionist.
彼は部屋の鍵を受付の人に返した。
Kare wa heya no kagi o uketsuke no hito ni kaeshita.

PHRASE: hand out ⟨-o⟩ *kubaru* ⟨〜を⟩配る ① 《distribute》

EX. We handed out notices to passersby in front of the station.
駅の前で通行人にビラを配った。
Eki no mae de tsuukoo-nin ni bira o kubatta.

handbag n. **[a small bag used by a woman to carry her wallet and other personal belongings]**

ha˥ndo-ba˥ggu ハンドバッグ •f 《purse》

handful n. **[as much/many of s.t. as can be held in one hand 《fig. "not very many"》]**

hi˥to˥-nigiri 一握り [one grasp]

EX. (**a**) There is only a handful of rice left.

米が一握りしか残っていません。
Kome ga hito-nigiri shika nokotte imasen.
(**b**) Only a handful of students came to the party.
ほんの一握りの学生しかパーティーに来ませんでした。
Hon no hito-nigiri no gakusei shika paatii ni kimasen deshita.

handicap n. **[a condition that causes difficulty or gives one a disadvantage]**
sho⌈ogai 障害 •c [s.t. that prevents movement/action] ⟪trouble, disorder, obstacle⟫, ha⌈ndikya⌉ppu ハンディキャップ •f, fu⌉rina 不利な adj(*na*). **•c [for a condition to be disadvantageous to s.o.] ⟪disadvantageous, unfavorable, bad⟫ ↔ yuurina 有利な** adj(*na*). **•c**
NOTE: *Handikyappu* is sometimes shortened to *handi* or *hande*.
EX. (**a**) Not being able to speak Japanese is a handicap if you want to do business in Japan.
日本でビジネスをしようと思ったら、日本語が話せないのは{不利/ハンディキャップ/?障害}ですよ。
Nihon de bijinesu o shiyoo to omottara, Nihon-go ga hanase-nai no wa {furi/handikyappu/?shoogai} desu yo.
(**b**) He has to live with the difficult handicap of being blind.
彼は目が見えないという大変な{障害/ハンディキャップ/*不利}を背負って生きなければならない。
*Kare wa me ga mienai to iu taihenna {shoogai/handikyappu/*furi} o se-otte ikinakereba naranai.*

handicapped adj. **[having a physical/mental disability]**
ka⌈rada ga fu⌉-jiyuuna 体が不自由な adj(*na*). **[for s.o. to have a disability of the body (euphemism)], sho⌈ogai ga a⌉ru (N) 障害がある(N)**
EX. My friend has a physically handicapped son.
友達には{体が不自由な/体に障害がある}息子がいる。
Tomodachi ni wa {karada ga fu-jiyuuna/karada ni shoogai ga aru} musuko ga iru.
PHRASE: the physically handicapped *shintai-shoogai-sha* **身体障害者 •c**, the mentally handicapped *seishin-shoogai-sha* **精神障害者 •c**

handkerchief n.
ha⌈nkachi ハンカチ •f
EX. She dried her tears with a handkerchief.
彼女はハンカチで涙をふいた。
Kanojo wa hankachi de namida o fuita.

handle n. **[the part of an object by which it is held or controlled]**
to⌈tte 取っ手 [the part of a door, drawer, bucket, teapot, etc., by which it is held] ⟪grip, doorknob, pull⟫, e 柄 [the stick-like part of an umbrella, broom, axe, brush, etc., by which it is held] ⟪grip⟫
EX. (**a**) The handle of this bucket fell off.
このバケツの{取っ手/*柄}が取れた。
*Kono baketsu no {totte/*e} ga toreta.*
(**b**) This broom has a long handle.
このほうきは{柄/*取っ手}が長い。
*Kono hooki wa {e/*totte} ga nagai.*
(**c**) The murderer left his fingerprints on the handle of the knife.
殺人犯はナイフの{柄/*取っ手}に指紋を残していた。
*Satsujin-han wa naifu no {e/*totte} ni shimon o nokoshite ita.*

—— vt. **[for s.o. to touch or hold s.t. with the hand(s) ⟪fig. "for s.o. to deal with s.t./s.o."⟫]**
1. ⟨-ni⟩ sa⌈waru ⟨〜に⟩触る ① [for s.o./s.a. to touch/feel s.t., usually with the hand(s)] ⟪touch⟫
EX. Don't handle my books with your dirty hands.
汚い手で私の本に触らないでください。
Kitanai te de watashi no hon ni sawaranaide kudasai.
2. ⟨-o⟩ a⌈tsukau ⟨〜を⟩扱う ① [for s.o. to deal with s.t./s.o./s.a.] ⟪control, deal with, treat⟫
EX. (**a**) This machine is easy to handle.
この機械は扱いやすい。
Kono kikai wa atsukai-yasui.

(**b**) He wants to become a teacher, but he doesn't know how to handle children.
彼は教師になりたがっているが、子供の扱い方を知らない。
Kare wa kyooshi ni nari-ta-gatte iru ga, kodomo no atsukai-kata o shiranai.
(**c**) He handled the difficult matter carefully.
彼は難しい問題を慎重に扱った。
Kare wa muzukashii mondai o shinchooni atsukatta.

hand-out n. **[s.t. that is handed out]**
1. ho⌈dokoshi-mono 施し物 [s.t. that is handed out to people in need]
2. i⌈nsatsu⌉-butsu 印刷物 •c [printed matter], pu⌈rinto プリント •f

handsome adj. **[for s.o./s.t. to be good-looking, esp. a man]**
ha⌉nsamuna ハンサムな adj(*na*). **•f [for a man to be good-looking]**
EX. Yoshiko has a handsome boyfriend.
佳子さんにはハンサムなボーイフレンドがいる。
Yoshiko-san ni wa hansamuna booi-furendo ga iru.

handy adj. **[to be useful and easy to use]**
be⌉nrina 便利な adj(*na*). **•c [readily available for or making it easy to achieve some purpose]** ⟪convenient⟫ ↔ **fubenna 不便な** adj(*na*). **•c**
EX. (**a**) I bought a small but handy reference book.
私は小さいけど便利な参考書を買った。
Watashi wa chiisai kedo benrina sankoo-sho o katta.
(**b**) A first aid kit is a handy thing to have around the house.
救急箱は家に一つあると便利な物です。
Kyuukyuu-bako wa ie ni hitotsu aru to benrina mono desu.

hang vt. **[for s.o. to fasten s.t. only at the top so that the lower end is free]**
1. ⟨-ni⟩ ⟨-o⟩ ka⌈ke⌉ru ⟨〜に⟩⟨〜を⟩かける ② [for s.o. to cause s.t. to extend to and come in contact with s.t./s.o./s.a. else ⟪fig. "cover," "sit down," "sprinkle," "splash," "bet," "spend," "build (a bridge)"⟫]
㊅ "build a bridge or set a ladder"▷架ける, "hang s.t."▷掛ける, otherwise ▷かける
EX. (**a**) I hung a picture on the living room wall.
居間の壁に絵を掛けた。
Ima no kabe ni e o kaketa.
(**b**) She hung white curtains in the window.
彼女は窓に白いカーテンを掛けた。
Kanojo wa mado ni shiroi kaaten o kaketa.
2. ⟨-o⟩ tsu⌈rusu ⟨〜を⟩つるす ① [for s.o. to fasten s.t. at the top using a string or similar material so that the lower part is free in the air]
EX. A pot of flowers was hung from the ceiling.
天井から花の鉢がつるしてあった。
Tenjoo kara hana no hachi ga tsurushite atta.
PHRASE: hang oneself *kubi o tsuru* 首をつる ①

—— vi. **[for s.t. to be fixed only at the top so that the lower end is free]**
⟨-ni⟩ ka⌈ka⌉ru ⟨〜に⟩かかる ① [for s.t. to extend to and come in contact with s.t./s.o./s.a. else ⟪fig. "cover," "begin," "be engaged in," "become splashed with," "be built," "require"⟫]
㊅ "for a bridge to be built or ladder to be set up"▷架かる, "hang"▷掛かる, otherwise ▷かかる
EX. (**a**) Her coat was hanging on the wall.
彼女のコートが壁に掛かっていた。
Kanojo no kooto ga kabe ni kakatte ita.
(**b**) Blue curtains are hanging in the window.
青いカーテンが窓にかかっている。
Aoi kaaten ga mado ni kakatte iru.

happen vi. **[for s.t. to take place, esp. without being planned]**
1. o⌈ko⌉ru 起こる ① [for an unusual/disturbing event to take place] ⟪occur⟫, **a⌉ru ある ① [for s.t. to exist ⟪fig. "occur"⟫]** ⟪exist⟫
EX. (**a**) What time did the accident happen?
事故が{起こった/あった}のは何時ですか。
Jiko ga {okotta/atta} no wa nan-ji desu ka.

H

(**b**) I pressed the button, but nothing happened.
ボタンを押したけど、何も{起こらなかった/*なかった}。
*Botan o oshita kedo, nani-mo {okoranakatta/*nakatta}.*
(**c**) If anything happens while I am away, please call me.
私が留守の間に何か{起こったら/あったら}電話してください。
Watashi ga rusu no aida ni nani-ka {okottara/attara} denwa-shite kudasai.

2. gu⌈uzen + verb 偶然+verb [for s.o. to do s.t. by chance or for s.t. to take place by chance]

EX. (**a**) I happened to run into her on my way home.
家へ帰る途中で偶然彼女に会った。
Uchi e kaeru tochuu de guuzen kanojo ni atta.
(**b**) A doctor just happened to be there when I fainted on the train.
私が電車の中で気を失ったとき、偶然お医者さんが乗っていたんです。
Watashi ga densha no naka de ki o ushinatta toki, guuzen o-isha-san ga notte ita n desu.

happiness n. **[the state of being pleased and satisfied]**
shi⌈awase しあわせ ↔ **fu-shiawase** ふしあわせ; **ko⌈ofuku** 幸福 •**c** ((**good fortune, blessing**)) ↔ **fukoo** 不幸 •**c**

EX. You can't buy happiness with money.
お金で{しあわせ/幸福}を買うことはできない。
O-kane de {shiawase/koofuku} o kau koto wa dekinai.

happy adj. **[for s.o./s.a. to feel or show pleasure and satisfaction]**
1. shi⌈awasena しあわせな adj(*na*). ↔ **fu-shiawasena** ふしあわせな; **ko⌈ofukuna** 幸福な adj(*na*). •**c** ((**fortunate**)) ↔ **fukoona** 不幸な adj(*na*). •**c**

EX. (**a**) Her marriage has been a happy one.
彼女は{しあわせな/幸福な}結婚生活を送っています。
Kanojo wa {shiawasena/koofukuna} kekkon-seikatsu o okutte imasu.
(**b**) I had a happy childhood.
私は子供の時、{しあわせ/幸福}でした。
Watashi wa kodomo no toki, {shiawase/koofuku} deshita.

2. u⌈reshi⌉i うれしい adj(*i*). **[feeling pleasure or contentment]** ((**glad, pleased, joyful**))

NOTE: *Ureshii* is used with a first person subject in statements and with a second person subject in questions. It can be used with a third person subject if some form is attached which explicitly expresses the speaker's perception or judgment, such as *-soo desu* "appears to be" in example (b).

EX. (**a**) I'm so happy that you could come.
あなたが来てくれて本当に嬉しいです。
Anata ga kite kurete hontoo ni ureshii desu.
(**b**) She looks happy with her grandchildren around her.
彼女は孫に囲まれて、嬉しそうです。
Kanojo wa mago ni kakoma-rete, ureshi-soo desu.

PHRASE: Happy birthday. *O-tanjoo-bi omedetoo gozaimasu.* お誕生日おめでとうございます, Happy New Year. *Shinnen omedetoo gozaimasu.* 新年おめでとうございます, *Akemashite omedetoo gozaimasu.* あけましておめでとうございます。

NOTE: *Shinnen omedetoo gozaimasu.* and *Akemashite omedetoo gozaimasu.* are both used as New Year's greetings. Unlike their English counterparts, these greetings should not be used until after the new year has actually come on January 1.

harbor n.
mi⌈nato 港

EX. We had lunch in a restaurant on the hill overlooking the harbor.
港の見渡せる丘の上のレストランで昼御飯を食べた。
Minato no mi-watase-ru oka no ue no resutoran de hiru-gohan o tabeta.

hard adj. **[for s.t. to be firm and not easily cut/bent** ((**fig. "difficult"**))**]**
1. ka⌈tai かたい adj(*i*). **[not easily changed/**

broken/influenced] ⟪firm, steady, tight, tough, stiff⟫ ↔ yawarakai 柔らかい adj(*i*). ㊅ "stiff and inflexibile"▷硬い, "solid/firm/tight"▷固い, "rigid and unyielding (in character)"▷堅い

EX. (**a**) The cookies I baked were as hard as rock.
私が焼いたクッキーは石のように固かった。
Watashi ga yaita kukkii wa ishi no yooni katakatta.
(**b**) I don't like hard pencils.
私は硬い鉛筆はきらいです。
Watashi wa katai enpitsu wa kirai desu.

2. mu⌈zukashii 難しい adj(*i*). **[requiring much time and effort to understand/solve/complete, fussy, particular] ↔ yasashii 易しい** adj(*i*).

EX. (**a**) The exam was very hard.
試験はすごく難しかったです。
Shiken wa sugoku muzukashikatta desu.
(**b**) It's hard for adults to learn a new language.
大人が新しいことばを習うのは難しい。
Otona ga atarashii kotoba o narau no wa muzukashii.

3. tsu⌈rai つらい adj(*i*). **[full of difficulty/trouble] ⟪trying, tough, bitter⟫**

EX. It was hard to come to Japan and be separated from my girlfriend.
ガールフレンドと別れて日本へ来るのはつらかった。
Gaaru-furendo to wakarete Nihon e kuru no wa tsurakatta.

PHRASE: hard to… V*masu*+*nikui* V*masu*+にくい

EX. This dictionary is hard to use.
この辞書は使いにくい。
Kono jisho wa tsukai-nikui.

—— adv. **[with great energy]**
i⌈sshoo-ke⌉nmei (ni) 一生懸命(に) •c ⟪**with utmost effort**⟫, **yo⌉ku よく [satisfactorily/carefully/many times] ⟪often, a lot⟫**

EX. (**a**) Everyone in the office works hard.
オフィスの人はみんな{一生懸命(に)/よく}仕事をしている。
Ofisu no hito wa minna {isshoo-kenmei (ni)/yoku} shigoto o shite iru.
(**b**) He studies really hard.
彼は本当に{よく/一生懸命(に)}勉強する。
Kare wa hontoo ni {yoku/isshoo-kenmei (ni)} benkyoo-suru.
(**c**) I tried so hard to memorize the kanji, but I couldn't.
私は漢字を{一生懸命(に)/*よく}覚えようとしましたが、覚えられませんでした。
*Watashi wa kanji o {isshoo-kenmei (ni)/*yoku} oboeyoo to shimashita ga, oboe-raremasen deshita.*

hardly adv. **[almost none/not/never]**
ho⌈to⌉ndo…neg. ほとんど…neg. ⟪almost none/not/never, very seldom⟫

EX. (**a**) I hardly have any money left.
お金がほとんど残っていません。
O-kane ga hotondo nokotte imasen.
(**b**) You've hardly eaten anything.
ほとんど何も食べていませんね。
Hotondo nani-mo tabete imasen ne.
(**c**) He's hardly ever late for class.
彼が授業に遅れることはほとんどない。
Kare ga jugyoo ni okureru koto wa hotondo nai.

hardship n. **[a situation causing suffering, difficulty, or pain]**
ku⌉roo 苦労 •c **[painstaking efforts] ⟪trouble, difficulty⟫**

EX. (**a**) My mother has gone through all sorts of hardships since she married my father.
母は父と結婚してからいろいろな苦労をしてきました。
Haha wa chichi to kekkon-shite kara iro-irona kuroo o shite kimashita.
(**b**) Even in life's most difficult moments my wife has always been there to share my hardships with me.
人生で一番大変な時にも妻はいつもそばにいて苦労を共にしてくれた。
Jinsei de ichiban taihenna toki ni mo tsuma wa itsu-mo soba ni ite kuroo o tomo ni shite kureta.

harm n. **[injury, hurt, wrong]**
ga⌉i 害 •c ⟪**damage**⟫ ↔ **eki 益** •c

H

EX. (**a**) What harm is there in smoking once in a while?
たまにたばこを吸うのにどんな害があるというんですか。
Tamani tabako o suu no ni donna gai ga aru to iu n desu ka.
(**b**) A few drinks will do you no harm.
酒を少し飲むだけなら害はありません。
Sake o sukoshi nomu dake nara gai wa arimaen.

PHRASE: mean no harm *waru-gi wa nai* 悪気はない adj(*i*).

EX. He means no harm, but he often offends others.
彼は悪気はないんですが、よく外の人を傷つけます。
Kare wa waru-gi wa nai n desu ga, yoku hoka no hito o kizu-tsukemasu.

— vt. **[to cause s.o. physical injury]**
⟨-ni⟩ ki˥gai o ku˥waeru ⟨〜に⟩危害を加える ②

EX. This kind of snake doesn't harm humans.
こういうへびは人間には危害を加えません。
Kooiu hebi wa ningen ni wa kigai o kuwaemasen.

harmful adj. **[causing injury or damage]**
yu˥ugaina 有害な adj(*na*). •c ↔ **mugaina** 無害な adj(*na*). •c

EX. (**a**) Smoking is harmful to one's health.
たばこは体に有害です。
Tabako wa karada ni yuugai desu.
(**b**) We don't use harmful food additives.
有害な食品添加物は使っていません。
Yuugaina shokuhin-tenka-butsu wa tsukatte imasen.

harmless adj. **[causing no injury or damage]**
mu˥gaina 無害な adj(*na*). •c **[causing no injury or damage]** ↔ **yuugaina** 有害な adj(*na*). •c; **tsu˥mi ga na˥i** (N) 罪がない(N) **[not offending anyone]** ⟪**innocent**⟫

EX. (**a**) I intended it to be a harmless joke, but he got very angry.
私は{罪のない/*無害な}冗談のつもりだったのに、彼はかんかんに怒ってしまった。
*Watashi wa {tsumi no nai/*mugaina} joodan no tsumori datta noni, kare wa kan-kanni okotte shimatta.*
(**b**) This insecticide is harmless to humans.
この殺虫剤は人間には{無害です/*罪がありません}。
*Kono satchuu-zai wa ningen ni wa {mugai desu/*tsumi ga arimasen}.*
(**c**) The police shot at harmless spectators when the riot broke out.
暴動が起きたとき、警察は{罪のない/*無害な}見物人に向けて銃を撃った。
*Boodoo ga okita toki, keisatsu wa {tsumi no nai/*mugaina} kenbutsu-nin ni mukete juu o utta.*

harmony n. **[a state of internal calm and peaceful accord]**
cho˥owa 調和 •c **[a condition of different colors, shapes, or sounds balancing and complementing each other within a larger whole so as to create a sense of esthetic pleasure]** ⟪**accord, agreement**⟫

EX. (**a**) The architecture of this building is in harmony with the surrounding scenery.
この建物は回りの景色と調和がとれている。
Kono tate-mono wa mawari no keshiki to choowa ga torete iru.
(**b**) Perceptions of color harmony can vary between people and cultures.
色の調和に関する感覚は人や文化によって異なることがある。
Iro no choowa ni-kansuru kankaku wa hito ya bunka ni-yotte kotonaru koto ga aru.

PHRASE: be out of harmony *awanai* 合わない ⟪not agree, not match⟫, live in harmony *naka-yoku kurasu* 仲良く暮らす ①

harsh adj. **[unpleasant/rough to the senses]**
i˥ya˥na 嫌な adj(*na*). **[very displeasing to s.o.]** ⟪**disagreeable**⟫, **ki˥bishi˥i** 厳しい adj(*i*). **[unpleasantly intense to the senses or tending to impose strict rules on others]** ⟪**showy, gaudy**⟫ ↔ **jimina** 地味な adj(*na*). •c; **to˥ge-toge-shi˥i** とげとげしい adj(*i*). **[lacking gentleness, stinging]** ⟪**biting, sharp**⟫

EX. (**a**) He has a harsh voice.

H

彼は{嫌な/?とげとげしい/*厳しい}声をしている。
*Kare wa {iyana/?toge-toge-shii/*kibishii} koe o shite iru.*
(**b**) He has a tendency to be a bit too harsh in disciplining his children.
彼は子供のしつけが{厳しすぎる/*嫌な/*とげとげしい}きらいがある。
*Kare wa kodomo no shitsuke ga {kibishi-sugiru/*iyana/*toge-toge-shii} kirai ga aru.*
(**c**) My pride was hurt by their harsh reception.
私は彼らの{とげとげしい/*嫌な/*厳しい}応対にプライドを傷つけられた。
*Watashi wa kare-ra no {toge-toge-shii/*iyana/*kibishii} ootai ni puraido o kizu-tsuke-rareta.*

PHRASE: harsh to the touch *te-zawari ga yokunai* 手ざわりがよくない

harvest n. **[the gathering of a ripe crop or the resulting quantity of crop gathered]** **《crop, yield》**
shu⌈ukaku 収穫 •c [the act of cutting down and gathering in agricultural products], ka⌈ri-ire 刈り入れ [the act of cutting down and gathering in grain crops] 《reaping》

H

EX. (**a**) Even the children had to help with the rice harvest.
子供も米の{刈り入れ/収穫}を手伝わなければならなかった。
Kodomo mo kome no {kari-ire/shuukaku} o tetsudawanakereba naranakatta.
(**b**) This year's wheat harvest was about average.
今年の小麦の{収穫/*刈り入れ}は平年並だった。
*Kotoshi no komugi no {shuukaku/*kari-ire} wa heinen-nami datta.*

PHRASE: good harvest *hoosaku* 豊作 **•c**

EX. We had a good rice harvest this year.
今年は米が豊作だった。
Kotoshi wa kome ga hoosaku datta.

haste n. **[quickness of movement]**
i⌈sogi 急ぎ /〈V*masu* of *isogu* ① hurry, make haste/

PHRASE: in haste *isoide* 急いで

EX. He put the money back into the drawer in haste when he heard the doorbell.
ドアのベルの音がしたとき、彼は急いで金を引き出しに戻した。
Doa no beru no oto ga shita toki, kare wa isoide kane o hiki-dashi ni modoshita.

PHRASE: in great haste *oo-isogi de* 大急ぎで

EX. He left in great haste so as not to miss his train.
彼は電車に遅れないように大急ぎで出ていった。
Kare wa densha ni okurenai yooni oo-isogi de dete itta.

hat n. **[a covering for the head, usu. with a brim round it]**
bo⌈oshi 帽子 •c [a covering for the head with or without a brim] 《cap》

EX. (**a**) She is wearing a nice hat.
彼女はすてきな帽子をかぶっている。
Kanojo wa sutekina booshi o kabutte iru.
(**b**) Please take your hat off.
帽子を脱いでください。
Booshi o nuide kudasai.

hate vt. **[for s.o./s.a. to have a very strong dislike of s.t./s.o./s.a.]**
〈-ga〉 da⌉i-kiraina 〈〜が〉大嫌いな adj(*na*). **[for s.o./s.a. to have a very strong dislike of s.t./s.o./s.a.] ↔ 〈-ga〉 dai-sukina 〈〜が〉大好きな** adj(*na*).; **〈-ga〉 ni⌈ku⌉i 〈〜が〉憎い** adj(*i*). **[for s.o. to bear a grudge against s.o./s.t./s.a.], 〈-o〉 ni⌈ku⌉mu 〈〜を〉憎む ① [for s.o. to bear a grudge against s.o./s.t./s.a.]**

NOTE: *Nikui* is used with first person subjects in statements and with second person subjects in questions.

EX. (**a**) I hate people who smoke in public.
私は人が大勢いる所でたばこを吸う人が大嫌いです。
Watashi wa hito ga oozei iru tokoro de tabako o suu hito ga dai-kirai desu.
(**b**) She hates getting to class late.
彼女は授業に遅れるのが大嫌いです。
Kanojo wa jugyoo ni okureru no ga dai-kirai desu.

(**c**) They hate each other, but they still live together.
彼らはお互いを憎み合っているのに、まだ一緒に暮らしている。
Kare-ra wa o-tagai o nikumi-atte iru noni, mada issho ni kurashite iru.
(**d**) I hate that guy for messing up my life like this.
私の生活をこのようにめちゃくちゃにしたあいつが{憎い/??大嫌いだ}。
Watashi no seikatsu o kono yooni mecha-kucha ni shita aitsu ga {nikui/??dai-kirai da}.

PHRASE: I hate to tell you this, but… *ii-nikui n desu ga…* 言いにくいんですが…

haul vt. **[to pull or drag s.t. with great force]** **⟨-o⟩ hi⌈ppa⌉ru** ⟨〜を⟩引っ張る ① **[to move s.t./s.o./s.a. forcibly towards the source of the force《fig. "entice"》]** **《jerk, drag, stretch》**

EX. (**a**) They hauled the boat up the beach.
彼らは舟を浜に引っ張りあげた。
Kare-ra wa fune o hama ni hippari-ageta.
(**b**) We use horses to haul logs down from the mountain.
山から丸太を引っ張っておろすのに馬を使う。
Yama kara maruta o hippatte orosu no ni uma o tsukau.

haunt vt. **[for s.o., esp. a ghost, to visit some place repeatedly《fig. "be always in one's thoughts"》]**
1. **{⟨-e⟩/⟨-ni⟩} na⌉n-do-mo i⌈ku** {⟨〜へ⟩/⟨〜に⟩}何度も行く ① **[for s.o. to go to some place repeatedly]**, **yu⌉urei ga de⌉ru** 幽霊が出る ② **[for a ghost to appear]**

EX. (**a**) He haunted the art museums while he lived in New York City.
彼はニューヨークに住んでいる時、何度も何度も美術館に行った。
Kare wa Nyuuyooku ni sunde iru toki, nan-do-mo nan-do-mo bijutsu-kan ni itta.
(**b**) That old house is said to be haunted.
あの古い家は幽霊が出るといううわさだ。
Ano furui ie wa yuurei ga deru to iu uwasa da.

2. **⟨-ni⟩ tsu⌈ki-mato⌉u** ⟨〜に⟩つきまとう ① **[for s.t./s.o./s.a. undesirable such as illness, fate, or punishment to stay with s.t./s.o./s.a. no matter what]** **《follow around, hang on, shadow》**

EX. I was haunted constantly by the fear that I would one day encounter my old enemy again.
いつかまた昔の敵に出会うんじゃないかという恐怖感が付きまとって、離れなかった。
Itsu-ka mata mukashi no teki ni de-au n janai ka to iu kyoofu-kan ga tsuki-matotte, hanarenakatta.

have vt. **[to be in possession of some quality or object《fig. "eat," "drink"》]**
1. **⟨-o⟩ mo⌉tsu** ⟨〜を⟩持つ ① **[for s.o. to hold s.t./s.o./s.a. in one's hand《fig. "own"》]** **《possess, hold, carry, keep, endure》**, **⟨-ni⟩ a⌉ru** ⟨〜に⟩ある ① **[for s.t. to exist]**, **⟨-ni⟩ i⌈ru** ⟨〜に⟩いる ② **[for s.o./s.a. to exist]**

EX. (**a**) Do you have a dictionary?
辞書{を持っています/があります/*がいます}か。
*Jisho {o motte imasu/ga arimasu/*ga imasu} ka*
(**b**) Do you have any brothers and sisters?
御兄弟{があります/がいます/*を持っています}か。
*Go-kyoodai {ga arimasu/ga imasu/*o motte imasu} ka.*
(**c**) We have a cat named Tora.
うちにはトラという猫{がいます/*があります/*を持っています}。
*Uchi ni wa tora to iu neko {ga imasu/*ga arimasu/*o motte imasu}.*
(**d**) This skirt has no pockets.
このスカートはポケット{がありません/*がいません/*を持っていません}。
*Kono sukaato wa poketto {ga arimasen/*ga imasen/*o motte imasen}.*
(**e**) She has no imagination.
彼女は想像力{がない/?を持っていない/*がいない}。

H

*Kanojo wa soozoo-ryoku {ga nai/?o motte imnai/*ga inai}.*
(**f**) Do you have a minute to spare now?
今、ちょっと時間{があります/*を持っています/*がいます}か。
*Ima, chotto jikan {ga arimasu/*o motte imasu/*ga imasu} ka.*

2. ⟨-wa⟩ ⟨-ga⟩ adj. **⟨〜は⟩⟨〜が⟩** adj. **[for s.o./s.a./s.t. to be in possession of some mental/physical characteristic]**

EX. (**a**) Our cat has a long tail.
うちの猫はしっぽが長い。
Uchi no neko wa shippo ga nagai.
(**b**) Mary has a good memory.
メアリーは記憶力がいい。
Mearii wa kioku-ryoku ga ii.
(**c**) Tom has big feet.
トムは足が大きい。
Tomu wa ashi ga ookii.
(**d**) He has a lot of experience as a teacher.
あの人は教師としての経験が豊富だ。
Ano hito wa kyooshi to-shite no keiken ga hoofu da.
(**e**) This room has a high ceiling.
この部屋は天井が高い。
Kono heya wa tenjoo ga takai.

3. ⟨-o⟩ ta⌈be⌉ru ⟨〜を⟩食べる ② [for s.o./s.a. to put s.t. edible into one's mouth, chew, and swallow it] ⟪**eat**⟫, **⟨-o⟩ no⌉mu ⟨〜を⟩飲む ① [for s.o./s.a. to put s.t. into one's body through the mouth without chewing it]** ⟪**drink, swallow**⟫

H

EX. I had a bagel and a cup of coffee for breakfast.
朝ご飯にベーグルを食べて、コーヒーを飲んだ。
Asa-gohan ni beeguru o tabete, koohii o nonda.

— aux. **[perfect tenses of verbs]**

1. V*te* shi⌈mau V*te*しまう ① [for s.o. to finish doing s.t. or for s.t. to end up happening to one's regret/joy] ⟪**finish doing s.t.**⟫, **V past [a verb form indicating an event occurring prior to the time when one is speaking or writing or completed by the time when one is speaking or writing]**

EX. (**a**) I've forgotten the time of my exam.
試験の時間を{忘れてしまった/忘れた}。
Shiken no jikan o {wasurete shimatta/wasureta}.
(**b**) Has Mr. Tsutsumi come yet?
堤さんはもう{来ました/*来てしまいました}か。
*Tsutsumi-san wa moo {kimashita/*kite shimaimashita} ka.*

2. Vinf. past ko⌈to⌉ ga a⌉ru Vinf. pastことがある [to have had an experience of doing s.t.]

EX. (**a**) A: Have you ever been to Europe?
ヨーロッパへ行ったことがありますか。
Yooroppa e itta koto ga arimasu ka.
B: No, I haven't.
いいえ、ありません。
Iie, arimasen.
(**b**) I've never told a lie in my life.
私は生まれてから一度もうそをついたことがない。
Watashi wa umarete kara ichi-do mo uso o tsuita koto ga nai.

PHRASE: have a cold *kaze o hiku* 風邪をひく ①

EX. I have a bad cold today.
私は今日ひどい風邪をひいている。
Watashi wa kyoo hidoi kaze o hiite iru.

PHRASE: have to {Vneg./Vstem/*ko*/*shi*/adj(*i*). *ku*/adj(*na*). *te*/cop. *te*}{*nakereba*/*nakute wa*}{*naranai*/*ikenai*}{Vneg./Vstem/来/し/adj(*i*). *ku*/adj(*na*). *te*/cop. *te*}{なければ/なくては}{ならない/いけない}

EX. (**a**) I have to do homework tonight.
今晩は宿題を{しなければ/しなくては}{なりません/いけません}。
Konban wa shukudai o {shinakereba/shinakute wa}{narimasen/ikemasen}.
(**b**) Basketball players have to be tall.
バスケットボールの選手は背が高くなければ{ならない/いけない}。
Basuketto-booru no senshu wa sei ga takakunakereba {naranai/ikenai}.

PHRASE: have s.t. Vpast participle ⟨*-ni*⟩ V*te morau* ⟨〜に⟩V*te*もらう

EX. (**a**) Where did you have your hair cut?.
どこで髪を切ってもらったんですか。

Doko de kami o kitte moratta n desu ka.
(**b**) I need to have these shoes repaired.
この靴を直してもらわなければいけません。
Kono kutsu o naoshite morawanakereba ikemasen.

PHRASE: had better V {Vinf. past aff./Vinf. nonpast. neg.} *hoo ga ii* {Vinf. past aff./Vinf. nonpast. neg.}ほうがいい

EX. (**a**) You'd better apologize.
謝ったほうがいい。
Ayamatta hoo ga ii.
(**b**) You'd better not go outside today.
今日は外に出ないほうがいい。
Kyoo wa soto ni denai hoo ga ii.

Hawaii n.
Ha⌉wai ハワイ **•f**

Hawaiian adj.
Ha⌉wai no N ハワイのN **•f [of Hawaii]**

hawk n.
ta⌈ka たか **[a large predatory bird], ta⌈ka-ha** たか派 **[a person who favors the use of aggression to achieve certain political ends] ↔ hato-ha** はと派

EX. That politician is a hawk.
その政治家はたか派です。
Sono seiji-ka wa taka-ha desu.

hay n.
ho⌉shi-kusa 干し草

PHRASE: hay fever *kafun-shoo* 花粉症 **•c**

he pron. **[the male person/animal previously mentioned]**
ka⌉re 彼 **[the male individual previously mentioned, usu. human but animal also possible ⟪fig. "one's boyfriend"⟫]**

NOTE: *Kare* is not used to refer to one's seniors, family members, or children. "He" is often not expressed at all in Japanese, as in the following examples.

EX. (**a**) A: Where's your roommate, Toshiki?
俊樹さん、ルームメートはどこですか。
Toshiki-san, ruumu-meeto wa doko desu ka.
B: He has gone out with his girlfriend.
{彼は/ø}ガールフレンドと出掛けています。
{Kare wa/ø} gaaru-furendo to dekakete imasu.
(**b**) Noboru got married when he was 25 years old.
昇は{ø/*彼が}二十五歳の時、結婚した。
*Noboru wa {ø/*kare ga} ni-juu-go-sai no toki, kekkon-shita.*

NOTE: The use of *kare* in example (b) would be understood to refer to someone other than Noboru himself. For example, it could mean that Noboru got married when Jiro was 25 years old.

head n. **[that part of the body which contains the eyes, ears, nose, mouth, and brain ⟪fig. "top/front"⟫]**
1. a⌈tama⌉ 頭 **[that part of the body which contains the eyes, ears, nose, mouth, and brain or the ability to learn, reason, and understand] ⟪brain, intelligence⟫**

EX. (**a**) My head hurts.
頭が痛い。
Atama ga itai.
(**b**) Someone hit me on the head.
私はだれかに頭をたたかれた。
Watashi wa dare-ka ni atama o tatakareta.
(**c**) The way that he looked me over from head to toe really embarrassed me.
頭のてっぺんから足の先までじろじろ見られたときはすごく恥ずかしかった。
Atama no teppen kara ashi no saki made jiro-jiro mi-rareta toki wa sugoku hazukashikatta.

2. i⌈chiban ue 一番上 **[top]**

EX. I put the date at the head of the letter.
手紙の一番上に日付を書いた。
Tegami no ichiban ue ni hi-zuke o kaita.

3. se⌈ntoo 先頭 **•c [front]**

EX. I waited at the head of the line for the box office to open.
私は列の先頭で切符売場が開くのを待った。
Watashi wa retsu no sentoo de kippu-uri-ba ga aku no o matta.

PHRASE: nod one's head *kubi o tate ni furu* 首を

縦に振る ①, lose one's head *awateru* あわてる ② «be flustered», the head office *honsha* 本社, the head of a school *koochoo* 校長 «headmaster, headmistress», the head of a department *buchoo* 部長

NOTE: *-choo* "head of" appears in many compounds.

headache n. **[a pain in the head «fig. "difficult problem"»]**

1. zu⌈tsuu 頭痛 •c [a pain in the head]

EX. I couldn't sleep all night because of a bad headache.
私はひどい頭痛で一晩中寝られませんでした。
Watashi wa hidoi zutsuu de hito-ban-juu ne-raremasen deshita.

2. zu⌈tsuu no ta⌉ne 頭痛の種 [a cause of worry]

EX. Trying to get the kids to eat vegetables is one big headache.
どうやったら子供たちが野菜を食べてくれるのか、私の頭痛の種です。
Doo yattara kodomo-tachi ga yasai o tabete kureru no ka, watashi no zutsuu no tane desu.

PHRASE: get a headache *atama ga itaku naru* 頭が痛くなる ①

EX. I always get headaches when I study kanji.
私は漢字を勉強するといつも頭が痛くなります。
Watashi wa kanji o benkyoo-suru to itsu-mo atama ga itaku narimasu.

PHRASE: have a headache *atama ga itai* 頭が痛い adj(*i*)., *zutsuu ga suru* 頭痛がする ③

EX. Do you have any aspirin? I have a bad headache.
アスピリンがありますか。ひどく{頭痛がする/頭が痛い}んです。
Asupirin ga arimasu ka. Hidoku {zutsuu ga suru/atama ga itai} n desu.

headline n. **[the important part of a newspaper article printed in large letters at the beginning]**

mi⌈dashi 見出し

EX. Today's headlines are about the earthquake that struck southern California yesterday.
きのう南カリフォルニアで起きた地震が今日の見出しになっている。
Kinoo Minami-Kariforunia de okita jishin ga kyoo no midashi ni natte iru.

headmaster n. **[the teacher in charge of a school]**

ko⌈ochoo 校長 •c «headmistress, principal»

headquarters n. **[the office that controls the operations of an organization]**

1. ho⌉nbu 本部 •c [the headquarters of an organization, except a private company or the military]

EX. (**a**) The headquarters of UNESCO is in Paris.
ユネスコの本部はパリにある。
Yunesuko no honbu wa Pari ni aru.
(**b**) The union headquarters are in that building.
組合の本部はあの建物の中です。
Kumiai no honbu wa ano tate-mono no naka desu.

2. ho⌉nsha 本社 •c [the headquarters of a private company]

EX. He was transferred to the company headquarters in London.
彼はロンドンの本社に転勤になった。
Kare wa Rondon no honsha ni tenkin ni natta.

3. shi⌈re⌉i-bu 司令部 •c [military headquarters]

EX. Headquarters for the Allied Forces were established in Tokyo.
連合軍の司令部は東京に置かれた。
Rengoo-gun no shirei-bu wa Tookyoo ni oka-reta.

heal vi. **[for a wounded part of the body to become well again]**

na⌈o⌉ru なおる ① [for s.t. in an abnormal and undesirable state such as an illness, injury, mistake, bad habit, or broken machine to return to a normal and desirable state] «recover, get well, be fixed»

㊥ "heal"▷治る, "for s.t. broken to be fixed"▷直る

EX. (**a**) The wound will eventually heal.
傷はやがて治りますよ。

H

Kizu wa yagate naorimasu yo.
(**b**) The cut healed by itself.
切り傷は自然に治った。
Kiri-kizu wa shizen ni naotta.

health n. **[the (good) condition of the body or mind]**
ke⌈nkoo 健康 •c [the state of being physically/mentally well]
EX. (**a**) Too much exercise can damage your health.
運動のしすぎは健康に害になる。
Undoo no shi-sugi wa kenkoo ni gai ni naru.
(**b**) Health is more important to me than money.
私にはお金より健康の方が大事です。
Watashi ni wa o-kane yori kenkoo no hoo ga daiji desu.
(**c**) My father is in good health.
父は健康です。
Chichi wa kenkoo desu.
PHRASE: health food *kenkoo shokuhin* 健康食品 •c, health center *hoken-jo* 保健所 •c

healthy adj. **[for s.o./s.a. to be in good health or for s.t. to be likely to produce good health]**
1. ke⌈nkoona 健康な adj(*na*). **•c [for s.o./s.a. to be in good physical condition], ge⌈nkina 元気な** adj(*na*). **•c [for s.o./s.a. to be in good health or to have lots of energy] ⟪fine, well, energetic⟫**
EX. The children look very healthy.
子供たちはとても{元気/健康}そうだ。
Kodomo-tachi wa totemo {genki/kenkoo}-soo da.
2. ke⌈nkoo-tekina 健康的な adj(*na*). **•c [for s.t. to be likely to produce good health]**
EX. (**a**) We spent our weekend in the healthy mountain air.
健康的な山の空気の中で週末を過ごしました。
Kenkoo-tekina yama no kuuki no naka de shuumatsu o sugoshimashita.
(**b**) He leads a healthy life by getting up at six in the morning and going to bed at ten at night.
彼は朝六時に起きて、夜十時に寝るという健康的な生活をしている。
Kare wa asa roku-ji ni okite, yoru juu-ji ni neru to iu kenkoo-tekina seikatsu o shite iru.
3. ke⌈nzenna 健全な adj(*na*). **•c [for one's mental/economic/financial condition to be in good health or for s.t. to be likely to produce good mental health] ⟪sound⟫**
EX. (**a**) This book is not healthy reading for a child.
この本は子供には健全な読み物ではない。
Kono hon wa kodomo ni wa kenzenna yomi-mono dewanai.
(**b**) The country's economy is healthy at the moment.
国の経済は現在のところ健全です。
Kuni no keizai wa genzai no tokoro kenzen desu.
PHRASE: healthy appetite *ooseina shokuyoku* おう盛な食欲 •c

heap n. **[many things piled up]**
ya⌈ma⌉ 山 [a landmass that rises conspicuously above its surroundings ⟪fig. "large heap," "counter for a pile of merchandise"⟫] ⟪mountain, hill, pile⟫
EX. (**a**) The books were piled in a heap in a corner of the room.
部屋の隅に本が山のように積み上げられていた。
Heya no sumi ni hon ga yama no yooni tsumi-age-rarete ita.
(**b**) I got depressed when I saw the heap of dirty clothes piled in the corner to be washed.
隅に積まれた汚れものの山を見て、いやになった。
Sumi ni tsuma-reta yogore-mono no yama o mite, iyani natta.

hear vt. **[for s.o./s.a. to perceive sounds through the ears or for s.o. to be told s.t.]**
ki⌈koeru 聞こえる ② [for a sound to be passively and spontaneously perceived by the ears], ⟨⟨-ni⟩⟩ ⟨-o⟩ ki⌈ku ⟨⟨~に⟩⟩⟨~を⟩きく ① [for s.o./s.a. to focus one's attention

on a sound so that it is perceived by the ears or to request/receive information from s.o. abot s.t. orally or to take notice and accept s.t. said by another] ⟪**ask, listen**⟫
㊉ "listen to s.t. carefully"▷聴く, otherwise ▷聞く

EX. (**a**) I'm hard of hearing, so I didn't hear him knocking.
私は少し耳が遠いので、彼がノックしているの{が聞こえません/*を聞きません}でした。
*Watashi wa sukoshi mimi ga tooi node, kare ga nokku-shite iru no {ga kikoemasen/*o kikimasen} deshita.*
(**b**) Did you hear the news that he won the election?
彼が当選したというニュース{を聞きました/*が聞こえました}か。
*Kare ga toosen-shita to iu nyuusu {o kikimashita/*ga kikoemashita} ka.*
(**c**) I heard my mother crying in the middle of the night.
夜中に母が泣いているの{が聞こえました/を聞きました}。
Yo-naka ni haha ga naite iru no {ga kikoemashita/o kikimashita}.
(**d**) Can you hear me?
{聞こえます/*聞けます}か。
*{Kikoemasu/*Kike-masu} ka.*

PHRASE: I hear… Sinf. *sooda* Sinf.そうだ

EX. (**a**) I hear Prof. Yamamoto is going to get married.
山本先生が結婚なさるそうです。
Yamamoto-sensei ga kekkon-nasaru soodesu.
(**b**) I hear the cherry blossoms in Yoshino are just beautiful.
吉野の桜はすごくきれいだそうです。
Yoshino no sakura wa sugoku kirei da soodesu.

PHRASE: hear from ⟨*-kara*⟩ *tegami ga kuru* ⟨〜から⟩手紙が来る, ⟨*-kara*⟩ *renraku ga aru* ⟨〜から⟩連絡がある

EX. I heard from my grandmother last week.
先週、祖母から{手紙が来ました/連絡がありました}。
Senshuu, sobo kara {tegami ga kimashita/renraku ga arimashita}.

heart n. **[the organ inside the chest that pumps blood through the body ⟪fig. "the central part of s.t.," "s.t. in the shape of a heart," "the center of one's feelings"⟫]**

1. shi⌈nzoo 心臓 •c [the organ inside the chest that pumps blood through the body]

EX. (**a**) He died suddenly last week of a heart attack.
彼は先週突然心臓麻ひで死んだ。
Kare wa senshuu totsuzen shinzoo-mahi de shinda.
(**b**) It was so quiet that I could hear my heart beating.
心臓の鼓動が聞こえるほど静かだった。
Shinzoo no kodoo ga kikoeru hodo shizuka datta.

2. ka⌈kushin 核心 •c [the central/most important part of a matter] ⟪**core, kernel, point**⟫

EX. This article touches on the heart of the matter.
記事は問題の核心に触れている。
Kiji wa mondai no kakushin ni furete iru.

3. chu⌈ushin 中心 •c [a point equidistant from all points on the circumference of a circle or surface of a sphere]

EX. He has an office in the heart of New York's financial district.
彼はニューヨークの金融街の中心に事務所を持っている。
Kare wa Nyuuyooku no kin'yuu-gai no chuushin ni jimu-sho o motte iru.

4. ha⌈ato ハート •f [s.t. in the shape of a heart]

EX. She sent me a card with a heart on it.
彼女はハートのマークのついたカードを送ってくれた。
Kanojo wa haato no maaku no tsuita kaado o okutte kureta.

5. ko⌈ko⌉ro 心 [the seat of one's thoughts/feelings in the body] ⟪**mind, thought**⟫

EX. (**a**) He is a man with a warm heart.
彼は心が暖かい人です。

H

Kare wa kokoro ga atatakai hito desu.
(**b**) I thanked her from the bottom of my heart.
私は心の底から彼女にお礼を言いました。
Watashi wa kokoro no soko kara kanojo ni o-rei o iimashita.

hearty adj. **[full of warmth and enthusiasm]**
ko⌈ko⌉ro kara no N 心からのN
EX. (**a**) We received a hearty welcome.
私たちは心からの歓迎を受けた。
Watashi-tachi wa kokoro kara no kangei o uketa.
(**b**) The prime minister expressed his hearty welcome to the President.
首相は大統領に心からの歓迎の意を表した。
Shushoo wa daitooryoo ni kokoro kara no kangei no i o hyoo-shita.

heat n. **[a form of energy generated by the movement of molecules or a high temperature]**
a⌉tsu-sa あつさ /⟨adj(*i*). stem of *atsui* hot + suf. *sa* ness/ [the quality of being hot], ne⌈tsu⌉ 熱 •c [a form of energy that causes the temperature of an object or body to increase ⟪fig. "fever," "excited state"⟫]
⟪fever⟫
㊥ "heat one feels with one's entire body"▷暑さ, "heat of a physical object"▷熱さ
EX. (**a**) I can't stand the heat in Osaka in the summer.
私は大阪の夏の{暑さ/*熱}には耐えられません。
*Watashi wa Oosaka no natsu no {atsu-sa/*netsu} ni wa tae-raremasen.*
(**b**) Plastic has a low tolerance to heat.
プラスチックは{熱/??熱さ}に弱いです。
Purasuchikku wa {netsu/??atsu-sa} ni yowai desu.
(**c**) We use solar heat to heat the water in our home.
うちでは水を温めるのに太陽{熱/*熱さ}を使っている。
*Uchi de wa mizu o atatameru no ni taiyoo-{netsu/*atsu-sa} o tsukatte iru.*

PHRASE: heat-resistant *tainetsu-sei no* N 耐熱性のN •c

— vt. **[to make s.t. warm/hot]**
⟨-o⟩ a⌈tatame⌉ru ⟨〜を⟩あたためる ② [for s.o. to cause a physical substance/an environment/one's heart to become warm ⟪fig. "keep s.t. important for a long time"⟫]
㊥ "heat an environment or a part of the body so that one feels warm and comfortable"▷暖める, "heat a physical substance"▷温める
EX. (**a**) I'll heat some milk for the hot chocolate.
ホットチョコレートを作るのに牛乳を温めます。
Hotto-chokoreeto o tsukuru no ni gyuunyuu o atatamemasu.
(**b**) She heated up the cold meat for dinner.
彼女は晩ごはんに冷たくなった肉を温めた。
Kanojo wa ban-gohan ni tsumetaku natta niku o atatameta.

— vi. **[for s.t. to become warm/hot]**
a⌈tatama⌉ru あたたまる ① [to become warm and reach an appropriate temperature]
⟪warm up⟫
㊥ "a physical substance heats up"▷温まる, "the environment or one's body heats up to the point that one feels warm and comfortable"▷暖まる
EX. (**a**) The engine of this car heats up quickly.
この車のエンジンはすぐ温まります。
Kono kuruma no enjin wa sugu atatamarimasu.
(**b**) My room heats up fast because it's small.
私の部屋は小さいので、すぐ暖まります。
Watashi no heya wa chiisai node, sugu atatamarimasu.

PHRASE: heated swimming pool *onsui-puuru* 温水プール •c+f

heater n. **[a piece of equipment used for heating air/water]**
su⌈to⌉obu ストーブ •f
EX. (**a**) Shall I turn off the heater?
ストーブを消しましょうか。
Sutoobu o keshimashoo ka.
(**b**) Is the heater on?
ストーブはついていますか。

H

| *Sutoobu wa tsuite imasu ka.*
PHRASE: electric heater *denki-sutoobu* 電気ストーブ •c+f, gas heater *gasu-sutoobu* ガスストーブ •f, kerosene heater *sekiyu-sutoobu* 石油ストーブ •c+f

heating n. **[a means of providing heat to a building or other environment]**
da⌈nboo 暖房 •c
EX. | (**a**) The heating won't be on until the middle of October.
十月の中旬まで暖房は入りません。
Juu-gatsu no chuujun made danboo wa hairimasen.
(**b**) We had to pay a large heating bill this winter.
今年の冬は暖房費をたくさん払わされました。
Kotoshi no fuyu wa danboo-hi o takusan harawa-saremashita.

heaven n. **[the place where God is believed to live 《fig. "God"》]**
1. te⌉n 天 •c [the space that extends infinitely upward from the earth 《fig. "God"》] ↔ chi 地 •c; ka⌉mi 神 [a deity/God]
EX. | (**a**) I wish this kite could reach as far as heaven.
このたこが{天/*神}に届くといいなあ。
*Kono tako ga {ten/*kami} ni todoku to ii naa.*
(**b**) It was the will of heaven that she should be taken from us at such a tender age.
あんなに若くして天に召されたのは{天/神}のおぼしめしだった。
Anna ni wakaku shite ten ni me-sareta no wa {ten/kami} no oboshimeshi datta.
2. te⌉ngoku 天国 •c [the place where God is believed to live] ↔ jigoku 地獄 •c
EX. | I want to go to heaven after I die.
死んだら、天国へ行きたい。
Shindara, tengoku e iki-tai.

heavy adj. **[having great weight or great in amount/degree/intensity]**
1. o⌈moi 重い adj(*i*). **[having great weight or great in importance/degree] ↔ karui 軽い** adj(*i*).; **o⌈motai 重たい** adj(*i*). ⟨s⟩
EX. | (**a**) This suitcase is too heavy for me to lift.
このスーツケースは{重くて/重たくて}私には持ち上げられません。
Kono suutsu-keesu wa {omokute/omotakute} watashi ni wa mochi-age-raremasen.
(**b**) He dumped the heavy box of books on the desk.
彼は机の上に本の入った{重い/重たい}箱をドスンと置いた。
Kare wa tsukue no ue ni hon no haitta {omoi/omotai} hako o dosun to oita.
(**c**) My responsibilities as head of this section are heavy.
この課の課長としての責任は{重い/?重たい}。
Kono ka no kachoo to-shite no sekinin wa {omoi/?omotai}.
PHRASE: heavy rain *oo-ame* 大雨, heavy work *juu-roodoo* 重労働 •c, heavy food *kotteri-shita tabe-mono* こってりした食べ物, heavy drinker *oo-zake-nomi* 大酒飲み

heel n. **[the back part of the foot or the part of a shoe, boot, sock, etc., supporting it]**
ka⌈kato かかと, hi⌉iru ヒール •f [the raised part on the bottom of a shoe, boot, etc., esp. that of a woman's shoe, supporting the back part of the foot]
EX. | (**a**) I had the heels of my old shoes replaced.
古いくつの{かかと/ヒール}を換えてもらった。
Furui kutsu no {kakato/hiiru} o kaete moratta.
(**b**) I hurt one of my heels while mountain-climbing.
登山の途中で{かかと/*ヒール}を痛めてしまいました。
*Tozan no tochuu de {kakato/*hiiru} o itamete shimaimashita.*
(**c**) There is a big hole in the heel of his sock.
彼の靴下の{かかと/*ヒール}には大きい穴があいている。
*Kare no kutsu-shita no {kakato/*hiiru} ni wa ookii ana ga aite iru.*

height n. **[the measurement from bottom to top of s.t./s.o./s.a.]**
{**se⌉/se⌉i**} **背 [one's back or the measurement**

H

of one's body from bottom to top]《stature》, **shi⌈nchoo 身長 •c [the measurement of the length of an animate body], ta⌉ka-sa 高さ /**〈**adj**(*i*)**. stem of *takai* high + suf. *sa* ness/ [the measurement from bottom to top of s.t.]**

NOTE: *{Se/Sei} no taka-sa* can be used to refer to height in the case of human beings.

EX. (**a**) He is 175 cms in height.
彼は{背(の高さ)/身長/*高さ}が175センチです。
*Kare wa {{se/sei}(no taka sa)/shinchoo/ *taka-sa} ga hyaku-nana-juu-go senchi desu.*
(**b**) I had the height of the chair adjusted.
いすの{高さ/*身長/*背}を調節してもらいました。
*Isu no {taka-sa/*shinchoo/*{se/sei}} o choosetsu-shite moraimashita.*

helicopter n.
he⌈riko⌉putaa ヘリコプター •f

hell n. **[a place where the souls of wicked people are said to be punished after death 《fig. "place/condition of great suffering"》] ji⌈goku⌉ 地獄 •c [a place where wicked people go after death 《fig. "place/condition of great suffering"》] ↔ tengoku 天国 •c**

EX. (**a**) I'm afraid of going to hell when I die.
死んで地獄に行くのがこわい。
Shinde jigoku ni iku no ga kowai.
(**b**) The battlefield was hell on earth.
戦場はこの世の地獄だった。
Senjoo wa kono-yo no jigoku datta.
(**c**) I went through hell when my daughter was kidnapped.
娘が誘拐されたときは、地獄の苦しみを味わった。
Musume ga yuukai-sareta toki wa, jigoku no kurushi-mi o ajiwatta.

PHRASE: what/who/etc. the hell… *ittai*… 一体… •c

EX. What the hell do you want?
一体何が欲しいんですか。
Ittai nani ga hoshii n desu ka.

PHRASE: examination hell *juken-jigoku* 受験地獄 •c

hello int. **[an expression used as a greeting or to call s.o.'s attention to s.t. or as the first word in a telephone conversation] mo⌉shi-moshi もしもし [an expression used to catch s.o.'s attention or as the first word in a telephone conversation], ko⌈nnichi-wa こんにちは [a greeting normally used during the day with people who do not belong to one's in-group]** 《**Good afternoon.**》

EX. (**a**) Hello. Is this Prof. Makino's residence?
{もしもし/*こんにちは}、牧野先生のお宅ですか。
*{Moshi-moshi/*Konnichi-wa}, Makino-sensei no o-taku desu ka.*
(**b**) Hello. How are you?
{こんにちは/*もしもし}。お元気ですか。
*{Konnichi-wa/*Moshi-moshi}. O-genki desu ka.*

helmet n. **[a strong hat worn to protect the head] he⌈rume⌉tto ヘルメット •f [a covering to protect the head worn by motorcyclists, baseball players, construction workers, etc.], ka⌉buto かぶと [a helmet worn by warriors during battle in the old days], te⌈tsu-ka⌉buto 鉄かぶと [an iron helmet worn to protect the head during battle]**

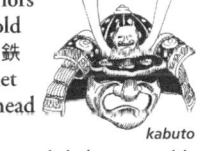

kabuto

NOTE: Both *tetsu-kabuto* and *kabuto* are old-fashioned words.

EX. (**a**) Don't forget to wear a helmet when you ride a motorcycle.
オートバイに乗るときは{ヘルメット/*かぶと}をかぶるのを忘れないでください。
*Ootobai ni noru toki wa {herumetto/ *kabuto} o kaburu no o wasurenaide kudasai.*
(**b**) My mother would often make helmets folded out of newspaper for me when I was a child.
子供の時母がよく新聞紙で{かぶと/*ヘルメット/*鉄かぶと}を折ってくれた。

*Kodomo no toki haha ga yoku shinbun-shi de {kabuto/*herumetto/*tetsu-kabuto} o otte kureta.*
(**c**) My grandfather owns an old steel helmet from World War II
祖父は第二次世界大戦の時使われた古い{鉄かぶと/*かぶと/*ヘルメット}を持っている。
*Sofu wa Dai-ni-ji Sekai-taisen no toki tsukawa-reta furui {tetsu-kabuto/*kabuto/*herumetto} o motte iru.*

help vt. **[to do s.t. for the benefit of s.o. else]** **⟨-o⟩ te⌈tsuda⌉u** ⟨～を⟩手伝う ① **[for s.o. to do part of s.o.'s work for him/her]** ⟪**assist, aid**⟫, **⟨-o⟩ ta⌈suke⌉ru** ⟨～を⟩助ける ② **[for s.o./s.a. to provide resources or one's own time/energy to s.o./s.a. to enable it/him/her to escape danger/death/difficulty or to ensure that s.t. goes well]** ⟪**save**⟫

NOTE: *Tetsudau* usually takes an inanimate object while *tasukeru* takes an animate object.

EX. (**a**) Can you help me with my homework?
宿題を{手伝って/*助けて}くださいませんか。
*Shukudai o {tetsudatte/*tasukete} kudasaimasen ka.*
(**b**) My brother helped the drowning man.
兄はおぼれかかっている人を{助けた/*手伝った}。
*Ani wa obore-kakatte iru hito o {tasuketa/*tetsudatta}.*
(**c**) Mr. Smith helped me write a letter in English.
スミスさんは私が英語で手紙を書くのを{手伝って/*助けて}くれた。
*Sumisu-san wa watashi ga eigo de tegami o kaku no o {tetsudatte/*tasukete} kureta.*
(**d**) "Help me!," she screamed.
「{助けて/*手伝って}!」と彼女は叫んだ。
*'{Tasukete/*Tetsudatte}!' to kanojo wa sakenda.*

— n. **[the act of doing s.t. for the benefit of s.o. else or s.o./s.t./s.a. that provides such a benefit]**
te⌈tsuda⌉i 手伝い **[the act of doing part of the work for another person]** ⟪**aid, assistance**⟫, **ta⌈suke⌉** 助け **[the act of getting s.o./s.o.'s life out of danger/difficulty]** ⟪**rescue**⟫

EX. (**a**) An injured man was asking for help, but nobody paid any attention to him.
けがをした人が{助け/*手伝い}を求めていたけど、だれも見向きもしなかった。
*Kega o shita hito ga {tasuke/*tetsudai} o motomete ita kedo, dare-mo mi-muki mo shinakatta.*
(**b**) I paid $100 for her help.
彼女の{手伝い/*助け}に対して百ドル払った。
*Kanojo no {tetsudai/*tasuke} ni-taishite hyaku-doru haratta.*

PHRASE: be of help *yaku ni tatsu* 役に立つ ① ⟪useful⟫

EX. Is a personal computer of any help in studying kanji?
パソコンは漢字の勉強に役に立ちますか。
Pasokon wa kanji no benkyoo ni yaku ni tachimasu ka.

PHRASE: Help yourself to… *⟨-o⟩ doozo.* ⟨～を⟩どうぞ。

EX. Help yourself to some fruits.
果物をどうぞ。
Kuda-mono o doozo.

PHRASE: It can't be helped. *Shikata ga arimasen.* 仕方がありません。

helpful adj. **[giving help or willing to help]** **(⟨-ni⟩) ya⌈ku⌉ ni tatsu** (⟨～に⟩)役に立つ ① **[to play a role in accomplishing some task/purpose or making some task easier]** ⟪**useful**⟫, **ta⌈suka⌉ru** 助かる ① **[for s.o. to be delivered from danger or harm or to receive some benefit due to a favorable development or to the efforts of another]** ⟪**to be saved**⟫

EX. (**a**) None of the information was very helpful.
情報はどれもあまり{役に立たなかった/*助からなかった}。
*Joohoo wa dore-mo amari {yaku ni tatanakatta/*tasukaranakatta}.*

H

(b) His advice was helpful to me in starting a business in Japan.
彼のアドバイスは日本でビジネスを始めるのに{役に立った/*助かりました}。
*Kare no adobaisu wa Nihon de bijinesu o hajimeru no ni {yaku ni tatta/ *tasukarimashita}.*
(c) It was very helpful of you to give me a ride to the hospital.
病院まで車に乗せていただいて、たいへん{助かりました/*役に立ちました}。
*Byooin made kuruma ni nosete itadaite, taihen {tasukarimashita/ *yaku ni tachimashita}.*

helpless adj. **[unable to look after oneself or to take action in a situation]**
(ji⌈bun de⌉ wa) na⌈ni-mo de⌈ki⌉nai (自分では)何もできない /⟨*nani-mo* anything + neg. of pot. of *suru* ③ do/ **[for s.o. to be unable to do anything without help from another person], mu⌉ryokuna** 無力な adj(*na*). •c **[having no ability/power]** ⟪powerless⟫

EX. I was as helpless as a baby.
私は赤ん坊のように{何もできなかった/無力だった}。
Watashi wa akanboo no yooni {nani-mo dekinakatta/muryoku datta}.

hemisphere n.
ha⌈nkyuu 半球 •c

EX. What is the highest mountain in the southern hemisphere?
南半球で一番高い山は何ですか。
Minami-hankyuu de ichiban takai yama wa nan desu ka.

PHRASE: the northern hemisphere *kita-hankyuu* 北半球

hen n. **[a female chicken]**
me⌈ndori めんどり ↔ **ondori** おんどり
PHRASE: henpecked husband *kyoosai-ka* 恐妻家 •c

her pron. **[of/belonging to a female or the object form of the pronoun she]**
1. ka⌉nojo no N 彼女のN, **ji⌈bun no N** 自分のN •c **[belonging to oneself]**

NOTE: Various nouns corresponding to "she" can be used instead of *kanojo*. It is also often the case that "she" or "her" is not expressed at all when it is clear from the context who is being referred to. Generally speaking, *kanojo* is not used to refer to children or women whose social status is higher than the speaker's.

EX. (a) Is this her book?
これは{彼女の/*自分の/*ø}本ですか。
*Kore wa {kanojo no/*jibun no/*ø} hon desu ka.*
(b) Masako has lost the key to her apartment.
正子は{自分の/彼女の/ø}アパートのかぎをなくしてしまった。
Masako wa {jibun no/kanojo no/ø} apaato no kagi o nakushite shimatta.

NOTE: In example (b), *Jibun no* refers to *Masako* herself. *Kanojo no* or ø can refer either to *Masako* herself or some other person.

(c) Haruko has broken her leg.
春子は{ø/*自分の/*彼女の}足を折った。
*Haruko wa {ø/*jibun no/*kanojo no} ashi o otta.*

NOTE: In reflexive expressions such *ashi o oru* to break one's leg or *te o ageru* to raise one's hand, "her" is not expressed at all.

2. ka⌉nojo + prt. 彼女+prt. SEE the note for her 1

EX. (a) A: Do you know Mrs. Yamamoto?
山本さんの奥さんを知っていますか。
Yamamoto-san no oku-san o shitte imasu ka.
B: No. I haven't met her yet.
いいえ、{ø/??彼女には}まだ会ったことがありません。
Iie, {ø/??kanojo ni wa} mada atta koto ga arimasen.
(b) A: Who should I ask?
だれに聞けばいいですか。
Dare ni kikeba ii desu ka.
B: Please ask her.
{彼女に/あの人に/*ø}聞いてください。
*{Kanojo ni/Ano hito ni/*ø} kiite kudasai.*
(c) Everyone who has talked with Yoshiko likes her.
佳子と話したことがある人はみんな{彼女が/佳子が/*ø}好きだ。

*Yoshiko to hanashita koto ga aru hito wa minna {kanojo ga/Yoshiko ga/*ø} suki da.*
(**d**) I love Rie. I want to marry her.
ぼくは理恵を愛しています。{彼女と/理恵と/ø}結婚したいんです。
Boku wa Rie o aishite imasu. {Kanojo to/Rie to/ø} kekkon-shi-tai n desu.

herd n. **[a group of animals of one kind that live together 《fig. "large group of people who think/behave in a similar manner"》]**
mu⌈re⌉ 群れ [a group of people/animals/fish/whales/birds/worms/clouds] 《flock, school, drove》
EX. We saw a herd of elephants far off in the savannah.
私たちは草原のはるかかなたに象の群れを見た。
Watashi-tachi wa soogen no haruka kanata ni zoo no mure o mita.

here adv. **[at/in/to this place/point]**
ko⌈ko {ni/e/de/o} ここ{に/へ/で/を} n.+prt. **[at/in/to this place/point], ko⌈chira {ni/e/de/o} こちら{に/へ/で/を}** n.+prt. **[at/in/to this way/ this place]**
EX. (**a**) Do you live here?
{ここ/こちら}に住んでいらっしゃるんですか。
{Koko/Kochira} ni sunde irassharu n desu ka.
(**b**) I came here three years ago.
三年前に{ここ/こちら}へ来ました。
San-nen-mae ni {koko/kochira} e kimashita.
(**c**) Let's study here.
{ここ/こちら}で勉強しましょう。
{Koko/Kochira} de benkyoo-shimashoo.
PHRASE: Here you are! *Hora, kore.* ほら、これ。, *Doozo.* どうぞ; Here we are finally. *Saa, yatto tsukimashita yo.* さあ、やっと着きましたよ。

hero n. **[a person respected for his bravery/goodness/great ability or the main male character in a play, story, poem, movie, etc.]**
1. hi⌉iroo ヒーロー •f, e⌈iyuu 英雄 •c [a person respected for his bravery/goodness/great ability, especially a player who has played the most important role in winning a game in team sports]
EX. He is a national hero.
彼は国民的な{英雄/ヒーロー}です。
Kare wa kokumin-tekina {eiyuu/hiiroo} desu.
2. shu⌈ji⌉nkoo 主人公 •c [the main character in a play, story, poem, movie, etc.]
NOTE: *Shujinkoo* can be used for either "hero" or "heroine." *Onna-shujin-koo* is also possible for "heroine."
EX. The hero of the *Tale of Genji* is Hikaru Genji.
『源氏物語』の主人公は光源氏です。
"Genji-monogatari" no shujinkoo wa Hikaru Genji desu.

hers pron. **[the possessive form of the pronoun she]**
ka⌉nojo no 彼女の
NOTE: Other nouns which correspond to "she" such as *ano hito*, can also be used.
EX. This is my umbrella, and hers is over there.
これは私のかさで、彼女のはあそこにあります。
Kore wa watashi no kasa de, kanojo no wa asoko ni arimasu.

herself pron. **[the reflexive/emphatic form of the third person pronoun, she]**
1. ji⌈bun(-ji⌉shin) 自分(自身) •c [a reflexive pronoun that refers (back) to a person with whom the speaker identifies]
NOTE: *-jishin* is used with *jibun* as an emphasizer. "Hurt oneself" is expressed as *kega o suru* in Japanese as in example (b).
EX. (**a**) Amy hates herself for being so indecisive and wants to change.
エイミーは優柔不断な自分が大嫌いで、自分(自身)を変えたいと思っている。
Eimii wa yuujuu-fudanna jibun ga dai-kirai de, jibun(-jishin) o kae-tai to omotte iru.
(**b**) Yuri hurt herself with a kitchen knife.
由里は包丁でけがをした。
Yuri wa hoochoo de kega o shita.

H

2. ji⌈bun de 自分で n.+prt. **[by/for oneself]**

EX. No matter how often she called, her landlord never came, so Judy decided to go ahead and paint the room herself.
いくら電話しても大家さんが来てくれなかったので、ジュディーは自分で部屋にペンキを塗ることにした。
Ikura denwa-shite mo ooya-san ga kite kurenakatta node, Judii wa jibun de heya ni penki o nuru koto ni shita.

hesitate vi. **[for s.o. to pause slightly before doing s.t.]**

1. ⟨-o⟩ **ta⌈mera⌉u** ⟨〜を⟩ためらう ① **⟪waver, pause, vacillate⟫**, ⟨-o⟩ **chu⌉ucho-suru** ⟨〜を⟩ちゅうちょする ③ •c

EX. (**a**) Taro hesitated to show his test paper to his mother.
太郎は答案用紙を母親に見せるのを{ためらった/ちゅうちょした}。
Taroo wa tooan-yooshi o haha-oya ni miseru no o {tameratta/chuucho-shita}.
(**b**) He hesitated to accept Yumi's invitation to the party.
彼は由美のパーティーへの誘いを受けようかどうか{ためらった/ちゅうちょした}。
Kare wa Yumi no paatii e no sasoi o ukeyoo ka doo ka {tameratta/chuucho-shita}.

2. ⟨-o⟩ **e⌈nryo-suru** ⟨〜を⟩遠慮する ③ •c **[for s.o. not to do s.t. out of deference/considerateness] ⟪refrain from⟫**

EX. Don't hesitate to ask if you have any questions.
質問があったら、遠慮しないで聞いてください。
Shitsumon ga attara, enryo shinaide kiite kudasai.

hesitation n. **[a pause or delay in acting due to uncertainty]**

chu⌉ucho ちゅうちょ •c

EX. I accepted his advice without hesitation.
私はちゅうちょなく彼のアドバイスを受け入れた。
Watashi wa chuucho-naku kare no adobaisu o uke-ireta.

hi int. **[an expression used as a greeting]**

ko⌈nnichi-wa こんにちは [a greeting normally used during the day with people who do not belong to one's in-group] ⟪Hello, Good afternoon⟫, ya⌉a やあ [an interjection used by a male speaker to indicate surprise or to address s.o. informally] ⟪hey, ah, hello⟫

NOTE: *Konnichi-wa* cannot be used among members of one's own in-group, such as family members or officemates. It cannot be used to greet one's superiors either.

hide vt. **[to keep s.t./s.o./s.a. out of sight]**

⟨-o⟩ **ka⌈ku⌉su** ⟨〜を⟩隠す ① **[for s.o. to keep s.t./s.o./s.a. out of sight intentionally] ⟪conceal, veil⟫**

EX. (**a**) Naomi hid his shoes under her bed.
直美は彼の靴を自分のベッドの下に隠した。
Naomi wa kare no kutsu o jibun no beddo no shita ni kakushita.
(**b**) I can't find the key. Where did you hide it?
かぎが見つからないんだけど、どこに隠したんですか。
Kagi ga mitsukaranai n da kedo, doko ni kakushita n desu ka.
(**c**) She tried to hide her boyfriend in the closet.
彼女はボーイフレンドを押し入れに隠そうとした。
Kanojo wa booi-furendo o oshiire ni kakusoo to shita.

— vi. **[for s.o./s.a. to keep oneself out of sight]**

ka⌈kure⌉ru 隠れる ② [to place oneself/to be placed so as not to be seen] ⟪to be hidden⟫

EX. Where is he hiding?
彼はどこに隠れているんですか。
Kare wa doko ni kakurete iru n desu ka.

high adj. **[for s.t. or the top of s.t. to be at a point well above the ground or for s.t. to be above the expected level/amount/rate/degree]**

ta⌈ka⌉i 高い adj(*i*). **⟪tall, expensive⟫ ↔ hikui** 低い adj(*i*).

EX. (**a**) Mt. Fuji is the highest mountain in Japan.
富士山は日本で一番高い山です。
Fuji-san wa Nihon de ichiban takai yama desu.
(**b**) My father has high blood pressure.
父は血圧が高いんです。
Chichi wa ketsuatsu ga takai n desu.
(**c**) This city has the highest cost of living in the world.
この町は世界で一番物価が高い。
Kono machi wa sekai de ichiban bukka ga takai.
(**d**) I'd like to get into a university with high academic standards.
私はレベルの高い大学に入りたい。
Watashi wa reberu no takai daigaku ni hairi-tai.

— adv. **[at or to a point well above the ground]**
ta⌉kaku 高く /⟨adj(*i*). *ku* of *takai* high/

EX. (**a**) He hit the ball high into the sky.
彼はボールを空高く打ち上げた。
Kare wa booru o sora-takaku uchi-ageta.
(**b**) I have a high opinion of her teaching.
私は彼女の教え方を高く評価している。
Watashi wa kanojo no oshie-kata o takaku hyooka-shite iru.

NOTE: "High" as an adjective in English is sometimes expressed in an adverbial way with *takaku* in Japanese, as in example (b).

(**c**) You should aim high if you want to become a scientist.
科学者になりたいのなら目標は高くした方がいい。
Kagaku-sha ni nari-tai no nara mokuhyoo wa takaku shita hoo ga ii.

PHRASE: junior high school *chuu-gakkoo* 中学校 •**c**, senior high school *kootoo-gakkoo* 高等学校 •**c**

NOTE: *Chuu-gakkoo* is often shortened to *chuugaku*, and *kootoo-gakkoo* to *kookoo.*

highly adv. **[to a great degree/very well]**
1. hi⌈jooni 非常に •c [to a great degree/extent] ⟪**very, extremely**⟫, **ko⌉odoni 高度に •c [to a high degree]**

EX. We need highly skilled workers.
{非常に/高度に}熟練した労働者が必要です。
{Hijooni/Koodoni} jukuren-shita roodoo-sha ga hitsuyoo desu.

2. ta⌉kaku 高く /⟨adj(*i*). *ku* of *takai* high/ [at/to a point well above the norm]

EX. I think highly of his talent.
私は彼の才能を高く買っている。
Watashi wa kare no sainoo o takaku katte iru.

highway n. **[a broad main road especially one that connects towns/cities]**
ko⌈osoku-do⌉oro 高速道路 •c [a main road for high speed driving used exclusively by motor vehicles] ⟪**freeway**⟫

NOTE: *Koosoku-dooro* is often abbreviated as *koosoku.*

EX. (**a**) There was an accident on the highway between Kyoto and Osaka.
京都と大阪の間の高速道路で事故がありました。
Kyooto to Oosaka no aida no koosoku-dooro de jiko ga arimashita.
(**b**) This highway is always crowded.
この高速道路はいつも込んでいる。
Kono koosoku-dooro wa itsu-mo konde iru.

hike vi. **[to go on a long walk in the country, usu. for pleasure]**
ha⌉ikingu ni i⌈ku ハイキングに行く ①

EX. I like to go hiking.
私はハイキングに行くのが好きです。
Watashi wa haikingu ni iku no ga suki desu.

— n. **[a long walk in the country, usu. for pleasure]**
ha⌉ikingu ハイキング •f

EX. We went for a hike on Mt. Rokko.
六甲山へハイキングに行った。
Rokkoo-san e haikingu ni itta.

hill n. **[a landmass that arises above its surroundings, but not as high as a mountain]**
o⌈ka 丘

EX. Our school stands on a hill.
私たちの学校は丘の上に立っている。

H

Watashi-tachi no gakkoo wa oka no ue ni tatte iru.

hillside n. **[the sloping side of a hill]**
o⌈ka no chu⌈ufuku 丘の中腹

EX. I was born in a small town on a hillside.
私は丘の中腹にある小さな町に生まれた。
Watashi wa oka no chuufuku ni aru chiisana machi ni umareta.

him pron. **[the object form of the pronoun he]**
ka⌉re + prt. 彼+prt.

NOTE: Various nouns corresponding to "he" can be used instead of *kare*. It is also often the case that "he" or "him" is not expressed at all when it is clear from the context who is being referred to.

EX. (**a**) A: Does Ichiro know that he failed the exam?
一郎さんは試験に落ちたのを知っているんですか。
Ichiroo-san wa shiken ni ochita no o shitte iru n desu ka.
B: Yes. I told him so.
ええ。 私が{彼に/ø}そう言いました。
Ee. Watashi ga {kare ni/ø} soo iimashita.
(**b**) A: Where is Jiro?
二郎さんはどこですか。
Jiroo-san wa doko desu ka.
B: I haven't seen him today.
今日は{ø/彼を}見ていませんけど。
Kyoo wa {ø/kare o} mite imasen kedo.
(**c**) A: I understand that Hashimoto has found a job.
橋本さんは就職が決まったそうです。
Hashimoto-san wa shuushoku ga kimatta soo desu.
B: I envy him.
{彼が/ø}うらやましいです。
{Kare ga/ø} urayamashii desu.

himself pron. **[the reflexive/emphatic form of the third person pronoun, he]**
1. ji⌈bun(-ji⌉shin) 自分(自身) •c [a reflexive pronoun that refers (back) to a person with whom the speaker identifies]

NOTE: *-jishin* is used with *jibun* as an emphasizer. "Hurt oneself" is expressed as *kega o suru* in Japanese as in example (b).

EX. (**a**) Tom sacrificed himself to save his drowning son.
トムは自分(自身)を犠牲にしておぼれかけた息子を助けた。
Tomu wa jibun(-jishin) o gisei ni shite obore-kaketa musuko o tasuketa.
(**b**) Bill hurt himself with a lawn mower.
ビルは芝刈り機でけがをした。
Biru wa shiba-kari-ki de kega o shita.

2. ji⌈bun de 自分で n.+prt. **[by/for oneself]**

EX. Do you think that Yamada really wrote this paper himself?
山田さんは本当にこのレポートを自分で書いたのでしょうか。
Yamada-san wa hontoo ni kono repooto o jibun de kaita no deshoo ka.

hinder vt. **[to get in the way of s.t./s.o./s.a. or to delay s.t.]**
1. ⟨-no⟩ ja⌈ma o suru ⟨～の⟩邪魔をする ③ •c [to get in the way of s.o./s.t./s.a. 《fig. "visit s.o."》] 《obstruct, impede》

EX. Don't hinder him in his work.
彼の仕事の邪魔をしないでください。
Kare no shigoto no jama o shinaide kudasai.

2. ⟨-no⟩ ja⌈ma ni na⌉ru ⟨～の⟩邪魔になる ① •c [to get in the way of s.t./s.o./s.a.]

EX. (**a**) Illegally parked cars can hinder traffic.
違法駐車の車は交通の邪魔になる。
Ihoo-chuusha no kuruma wa kootsuu no jama ni naru.
(**b**) The fact that she is married may hinder her career.
彼女が結婚しているということは出世の邪魔になるかもしれない。
Kanojo ga kekkon-shite iru to iu koto wa shusse no jama ni naru kamoshirenai.

3. o⌈kureru 遅れる ② [to move to a later time] 《delay》

EX. The snow hindered me from getting here earlier.
雪でここへ来るのが遅れてしまった。
Yuki de koko e kuru no ga okurete shimatta.

H

hindrance n. **[the act of getting in the way of s.t./s.o./s.a. or s.o./s.t. that gets in the way]**
ja⌈ma 邪魔 •c [an act of keeping s.t. from occurring or s.o./s.a. from doing s.t. or s.t. which has such an effect]

EX. Father tried to help me with the dishes, but he was more of a hindrance than a help.
父は皿洗いを手伝おうとしてくれたが、助けというよりむしろ邪魔だった。
Chichi wa sara-arai o tetsudaoo to shite kureta ga, tasuke to iu yori mushiro jama datta.

hint n. **[a small or indirect sign or suggestion]**
hi⌉nto ヒント •f [s.t. that helps one find an answer to a question] **《clue》**

EX. This question is too difficult for me. Can you give me a hint?
この問題は私には難しすぎます。何かヒントをくださいませんか。
Kono mondai wa watashi ni wa muzukashi-sugimasu. Nani-ka hinto o kudasaimasen ka.

PHRASE: drop a hint *soburi o miseru* そぶりを見せる ②

EX. She dropped a hint that she loved Bill.
彼女はビルを愛しているようなそぶりを見せた。
Kanojo wa Biru o aishite iru yoona soburi o miseta.

— vt./vi. **[for s.o. to suggest s.t. indirectly]**
⟨-ni⟩ ⟨-to⟩ so⌈reto-na⌉ku i⌈u ⟨〜に⟩⟨〜と⟩それとなく言う ① [for s.o. to express s.t. to s.o. only indirectly] 《imply》, ⟨-ni⟩ ⟨-o⟩ ho⌈nomeka⌉su ⟨〜に⟩⟨〜を⟩ほのめかす ① [for s.o. to let s.o. know s.t. indirectly]

EX. I hinted to him that he had very little chance of getting into the University of Kyoto.
私は彼に京都大学に入れる可能性は非常に低い{とそれとなく言った/ことをほのめかした}。
Watashi wa kare ni Kyooto-daigaku ni haire-ru kanoo-sei wa hijooni hikui {to soreto-naku itta/koto o honomekashita}.

hip n. **[the part of either side of the human body just above the legs]**
ko⌈shi 腰 [the narrow part of the human body between the thorax and hips 《fig. "posture," "hardness of paper-thin/stick-like objects"》] 《waist and hips》, shi⌈ri⌉ 尻 [that part of the body on which one sits] 《buttocks》

EX. (**a**) My father was standing in the doorway with his hands on his hips when I got home.
家へ帰ると、父が{腰/*尻}に手をあてて、玄関に立っていた。
*Uchi e kaeru to, chichi ga {koshi/*shiri} ni te o atete, genkan ni tatte ita.*

koshi ni te o ateru

(**b**) The sumo wrestler Konishiki has huge hips.
すもう取りの小錦は{腰/尻}がすごく大きい。
Sumoo-tori no Konishiki wa {koshi/shiri} ga sugoku ookii.

hippopotamus n.
ka⌉ba かば

hire vt. **[for s.o. to have s.o. do a job in return for payment]**
⟨-o⟩ ya⌈to⌉u ⟨〜を⟩雇う ① 《employ》

EX. (**a**) I'd like to hire an assistant who knows how to use a computer.
コンピューターの使える助手を雇いたい。
Konpyuutaa no tsukae-ru joshu o yatoi-tai.
(**b**) She hired a bodyguard to protect her daughter.
彼女は娘を守るためにボディーガードを雇った。
Kanojo wa musume o mamoru tame ni bodii-gaado o yatotta.

his pron. **[of/belonging to him or the possessive form of the pronoun he]**
1. ka⌉re no N 彼のN, ji⌈bun no N 自分のN •c

NOTE: Various nouns corresponding to "he" can be used instead of *kare*. It is also often the case that "he" or "his" may not be expressed at all when it is clear from the context who is being referred to.

EX. (**a**) A: Who is that pretty girl talking with Scott?
スコットと話しているあのきれいな女の子、だれ。
Sukotto to hanashite iru ano kireina onna-no-ko, dare.
B: She's his new girlfriend.
{彼の/ø/*自分の}新しいガールフレンドだよ。
*{Kare no/ø/*Jibun no} atarashii gaaru-furendo da yo.*
(**b**) Mr. Yamada introduced his younger sister to Miss Johnson.
山田さんはジョンソンさんに{自分の/ø/彼の}妹を紹介した。
Yamada-san wa Jonson-san ni {jibun no/ø/kare no} imooto o shookai-shita.

NOTE: The use of *kare* instead of *jibun* or ø in example (b) could also be understood to refer to someone other than *Yamada.*

2. ka⌉re no 彼の [s.t./s.a. belonging to him]

NOTE: Other nouns which correspond to "he" can also be used.

EX. A: Which desk is Mr. Yamashita's?
どの机が山下さんのですか。
Dono tsukue ga Yamashita-san no desu ka.
B: That small one is his.
あの小さいのが{山下さん/彼}のです。
Ano chiisai no ga {Yamashita-san/kare} no desu.

historic adj. **[important in history]**
re⌈kishi-tekina 歴史的な adj(*na*). **•c [of history/important in history]** ((**historical**))

EX. The Emperor's visit to Okinawa was a historic event.
天皇の沖縄訪問は歴史的な出来事であった。
Tennoo no Okinawa-hoomon wa rekishi-tekina deki-goto de atta.

PHRASE: historic spot *shiseki* 史跡 **•c**

historical adj. **[belonging to/pertaining to/having to do with history]**
re⌈kishi-joo no N 歴史上のN •c [belonging/pertaining to history], re⌈kishi-tekina 歴史的な adj(*na*). **•c [of history/important in history]**

EX. (**a**) That novel is based on actual historical events.
あの小説は実際の{歴史上の/?歴史的な}出来事に基づいて書かれたものです。
Ano shoosetsu wa jissai no {rekishi-joo no/?rekishi-tekina} deki-goto ni moto-zuite kaka-reta mono desu.
(**b**) Is Miyamoto Musashi an actual historical figure?
宮本武蔵は実在した{歴史上の/*歴史的な}人物ですか。
*Miyamoto Musashi wa jitsuzai-shita {rekishi-joo no/*rekishi-tekina} jinbutsu desu ka.*
(**c**) I'm interested in the historical aspects of the Japanese language.
私は日本語の{歴史的な/*歴史上の}側面に興味があります。
*Watashi wa Nihon-go no {rekishi-tekina/*rekishi-joo no} sokumen ni kyoomi ga arimasu.*

history n. **[(the study of) the various events in the past of a country/the world/a person/a thing]**
re⌈kishi 歴史 •c

EX. (**a**) I majored in history in college.
私は大学で歴史を専攻しました。
Watashi wa daigaku de rekishi o senkoo-shimashita.
(**b**) This city has many historic spots since it's so old.
この町は歴史が古いので、史跡が多い。
Kono machi wa rekishi ga furui node, shiseki ga ooi.

PHRASE: Japanese history *Nihon-shi* 日本史 **•c**, Oriental history *Tooyoo-shi* 東洋史 **•c**, European history *Yooroppa-shi* ヨーロッパ史 **•f+c**, one's personal history *rireki* 履歴 **•c**

hit vi./vt. **[to come against s.o./s.t./s.a. with force]**
1. 〈**-ni**〉 **a⌈taru** 〈〜に〉当たる ① **[for s.t. to come into sudden spontaneous contact**

with s.t. forming a narrow target area] ⟪strike, beat against, touch⟫, ⟨-ni⟩ bu⌈tsukaru ⟨〜に⟩ぶつかる ① [to come against s.o./s.t./s.a. by accident forcing a change in the direction of its movement] ⟪bump into, run into⟫

EX. (**a**) A bird hit the window.
鳥が窓に{ぶつかった/?当たった}。
Tori ga mado ni {butsukatta/?atatta}.
(**b**) A falling stone hit him on the head.
落ちてきた石が彼の頭に{当たった/ぶつかった}。
Ochite kita ishi ga kare no atama ni {atatta/butsukatta}.
(**c**) The bullet hit the target.
弾丸は的に{当たった/*ぶつかった}。
*Dangan wa mato ni {atatta/*butsukatta}.*

2. ⟨-ni⟩ ⟨-o⟩ a⌈teru ⟨〜に⟩⟨〜を⟩あてる ② [for s.o. to cause s.t. to make sudden and direct contact with s.t. forming a narrow target area] ⟪strike, crash into⟫, ⟨-ni⟩ ⟨-o⟩ bu⌈tsukeru ⟨〜に⟩⟨〜を⟩ぶつける ② [for s.o. to cause s.t. to come hard against s.t. maliciously or by accident] ⟪bump…against, knock…against⟫
㊊ "appropriate"▷充てる, otherwise ▷当てる

H

EX. (**a**) I hit my head against the glass door.
ガラスのドアに頭を{ぶつけて/*当てて}しまった。
*Garasu no doa ni atama o {butsukete/*atete} shimatta.*
(**b**) Jane hit the mark with the bullet.
ジェーンは的に弾丸を{当てた/*ぶつけた}。
*Jeen wa mato ni dangan o {ateta/*butsuketa}.*

3. ⟨-o⟩ u⌉tsu ⟨〜を⟩うつ ① [to bring the hand/s.t. held in the hand forcefully against s.t. or to cause s.t. to come against s.t. forcefully] ⟪strike, beat, slap⟫, ⟨-o⟩ bu⌉tsu ⟨〜を⟩ぶつ ① [for s.o. to bring the hand/s.t. held in the hand forcefully against s.o./s.a. intentionally], ⟨-o⟩ ta⌈ta⌉ku ⟨〜を⟩たたく ① [for s.o. to bring the hand/s.t. held in the hand against s.o./s.t./s.a., usu. repeatedly ⟪fig. "criticize"⟫] ⟪strike, beat, knock, tap, slap, clap, spank, pat⟫, ⟨-o⟩ na⌈gu⌉ru ⟨〜を⟩殴る ① [for s.o. to bring one's fist or to use s.t. against s.o./s.a. hard with the intention of causing harm]
㊊ "shoot s.o./s.a. with a gun"▷撃つ, otherwise ▷打つ

EX. (**a**) She fell down and hit her head against the corner of the table.
彼女は転んで、テーブルの角で頭を{打った/*ぶった/*たたいた/*殴った}。
*Kanojo wa koronde, teeburu no kado de atama o {utta/*butta/*tataita/*nagutta}.*
(**b**) Beth hit Ken on the cheek.
ベスはケンのほっぺたを{打った/ぶった/たたいた/殴った}。
Besu wa Ken no hoppeta o {utta/butta/tataita/nagutta}.
(**c**) He hit a home run over the right field fence.
彼は右翼フェンス越しのホームランを{打った/*ぶった/*たたいた/*殴った}。
*Kare wa uyoku-fensu-goshi no hoomuran o {utta/*butta/*tataita/*nagutta}.*
(**d**) He hit the ball hard.
彼はボールを強く{たたいた/打った/*ぶった/*殴った}。
*Kare wa booru o tsuyoku {tataita/utta/*butta/*nagutta}.*

hive n. **[a place where bees live or a group of bees who live there together]**
ha⌈chi-no-su⌉ はちの巣 [a place bees make to live together and to raise their larvae] ⟪beehive⟫

hobby n. **[an activity that one likes to do in one's free time]**
shu⌉mi 趣味 •c

EX. Painting is my hobby.
絵をかくのが趣味です。
E o kaku no ga shumi desu.

hold vt. **[for s.o. to take and keep s.t./s.o./s.a. in one's hands/arms or to support s.t./s.o./s.a. in one's hands/arms or to cause s.t. to take place]**
1. ⟨-o⟩ da⌈ku ⟨〜を⟩抱く ① [for s.o. to take

and keep s.o./s.a./s.t. in one's arms or to support s.o./s.a./s.t. in such a way] ⟪**hug, embrace**⟫

EX. (**a**) He held the baby in his arms.
彼は両手で赤ん坊を抱いた。
Kare wa ryoo-te de akanboo o daita.
(**b**) Hanako slept holding a teddy bear in her arms.
花子は熊のぬいぐるみを抱いて寝た。
Hanako wa kuma no nui-gurumi o daite neta.

2. ⟨-o⟩ **ni⌈giru** ⟨〜を⟩握る ① **[for s.o. to bend the fingers inward tightly or to take and keep/support s.t. with the hand(s)]** ⟪**clasp, grip, seize, grasp**⟫

EX. (**a**) He was holding a pistol in his hand.
彼は片手にピストルを握っていた。
Kare wa kata-te ni pisutoru o nigitte ita.
(**b**) They sat there quietly holding each other's hands.
彼らは手を握り合って静かにそこに座っていた。
Kare-ra wa te o nigiri-atte shizukani soko ni suwatte ita.
(**c**) She holds his secret in her heart.
彼女は彼の秘密を握っている。
Kanojo wa kare no himitsu o nigitte iru.

3. ⟨-o⟩ **mo⌉tte iru** ⟨〜を⟩持っている /⟨V*te iru* of *motsu* ① have/ ② **[for s.o. to keep s.t. in one's hand(s) or to own s.t.]** ⟪**have**⟫

EX. Could you hold my bag for a minute, please.
ちょっと私のかばんを持っていてください。
Chotto watashi no kaban o motte ite kudasai.

4. ⟨-o⟩ **ka⌈kaeru** ⟨〜を⟩抱える ② **[for s.o. to keep s.t./s.o./s.a. in one's arms** ⟪**fig. "experience (hardship)"**⟫**]**

EX. She left the library holding a stack of books in her arms.
彼女は腕に本をたくさん抱えて図書館を出た。
Kanojo wa ude ni hon o takusan kakaete tosho-kan o deta.

5. ⟨-o⟩ **hi⌈ra⌉ku** ⟨〜を⟩開く ① **[to cause the interior of s.t./s.o./s.a. to become exposed to the outside (often by means of a three-dimensional, symmetrical action)** ⟪**fig. "start"**⟫**]** ⟪**open, start**⟫

EX. An international conference on environmental issues was held in Tokyo last month.
先月東京で環境問題に関する国際会議が開かれた。
Sengetsu Tookyoo de kankyoo-mondai ni-kansuru kokusai-kaigi ga hiraka-reta.

PHRASE: hold on to ⟨*-ni*⟩ *tsukamaru* ⟨〜に⟩つかまる ①

EX. I walked holding on to his shoulders.
私は彼の肩につかまって歩いた。
Watashi wa kare no kata ni tsukamatte aruita.

hole n. **[an empty space inside/going through something solid** ⟪**fig. "fault"**⟫**]**
a⌈na⌉ 穴 ⟪**opening, slit, gap**⟫

EX. (**a**) There is a big hole in my sock.
靴下に大きな穴が開いている。
Kutsu-shita ni ookina ana ga aite iru.
(**b**) We dug a deep hole in the garden.
庭に深い穴を掘った。
Niwa ni fukai ana o hotta.
(**c**) This contract has a few holes in it.
この契約には穴がいくつかある。
Kono keiyaku ni wa ana ga ikutsu-ka aru.
(**d**) I drilled a hole through the wall.
壁にドリルで穴を開けた。
Kabe ni doriru de ana o aketa.

holiday n. **[a time during which one rests from work]**
ya⌈sumi⌉ 休み ⟪**vacation**⟫, **kyu⌈ujitsu** 休日 •c

EX. (**a**) Tomorrow is a holiday.
明日は{休み/休日}です。
Ashita wa {yasumi/kyuujitsu} desu.
(**b**) Many people work even on holidays.
{休み/休日}にも仕事をする人が多い。
{Yasumi/Kyuujitsu} ni mo shigoto o suru hito ga ooi.

PHRASE: national holiday *(kuni no) saijitsu* (国

H

の)祭日 •c, paid holiday *yuukyuu-kyuuka* 有給休暇 •c

Holland n.
O⌈randa オランダ •f

hollow adj. **[having a hole/an empty space inside]**
na⌉ka ga ka⌈rappo no N 中が空っぽのN ((empty, vacant))

EX. The legs on this table are hollow plastic tubes.
このテーブルには中が空っぽのプラスチックのチューブの足がついている。
Kono teeburu ni wa naka ga karappo no purasuchikku no chuubu no ashi ga tsuite iru.

holy adj. **[having to do with God and religion]**
shi⌈nseina 神聖な adj(*na*). **•c ((sacred, sanctified))**

EX. The sumo wrestling ring is traditionally regarded as a holy place.
すもうの土俵は昔から神聖な場所と見なされている。
Sumoo no dohyoo wa mukashi kara shinseina basho to mi-nasa-rete iru.

PHRASE: the Holy Land *seichi* 聖地 •c, the Holy Bible *seisho* 聖書 •c, holy man *seijin* 聖人 •c ((saint))

H

home n. **[the place where one lives, esp. with one's family, or the place where one was born or raised]**
1. ka⌈tei 家庭 •c [a house and the family who live in it], u⌈chi うち [the inside/the place where one lives] ((inside, house))

EX. (**a**) She has never experienced a happy home life.
彼女は幸せな{家庭/*うち}生活を経験したことがない。
*Kanojo wa shiawasena {katei/*uchi}-seikatsu o keiken-shita koto ga nai.*
(**b**) I don't want to destroy his happy home.
彼の幸せな{家庭/*うち}をこわしたくはない。
*Kare no shiawasena {katei/*uchi} o kowashi-taku wa nai.*
(**c**) I left my dictionary at home.
{うち/*家庭}に辞書を置いてきました。
*{Uchi/*Katei} ni jisho o oite kimashita.*
(**d**) I visited my friend's home in Boston.
ボストンの友達の{うち/家庭}を訪ねました。
Bosuton no tomodachi no {uchi/katei} o tazunemashita.

2. ko⌉kyoo 故郷 •c [the place where one was born or raised], fu⌈ru⌉-sato ふるさと ((hometown)), ku⌈ni 国 ((hometown, country))

EX. I'm going home for summer vacation.
夏休みには{国/故郷/ふるさと}へ帰ります。
Natsu-yasumi ni wa {kuni/kokyoo/furu-sato} e kaerimasu.

NOTE: *Kokyoo* and *furu-sato* often carry a nostalgic nuance.

—— adv. **[to/at one's home]**
u⌈chi {e/ni} うち{へ/に} n.+prt.

EX. (**a**) I went home early yesterday.
きのうは早くうち{へ/に}帰りました。
Kinoo wa hayaku uchi {e/ni} kaerimashita.
(**b**) Will you be home tonight?
今晩うち{に/*へ}いますか。
*Konban uchi {ni/*e} imasu ka.*

homemade adj. **[made at home or by hand]**
ji⌈ka-sei no N 自家製のN •c [for foodstuffs to be made at home], te-⌈zu⌉kuri no N 手作りのN [for s.t. to be made by hand] ((handmade)), te-⌈sei no N 手製のN

EX. (**a**) Please try this homemade cake.
この{手作り/手製/自家製}のケーキを食べてみてください。
Kono {te-zukuri/te-sei/jika-sei} no keeki o tabete mite kudasai.
(**b**) Her homemade wine is superb.
彼女の{自家製/手作り/手製}のワインは最高です。
Kanojo no {jika-sei/te-zukuri/te-sei} no wain wa saikoo desu.
(**c**) She came in a homemade dress.
彼女は{手作り/手製/*自家製}のドレスを着て来た。
*Kanojo wa {te-zukuri/te-sei/*jika-sei}*

no doresu o kite kita.

hometown n. **[the place where one was born or raised]**
ko˥kyoo 故郷 •c [the place where one was born or raised], fu┌ru˥-sato ふるさと ⟪home⟫, ku┌ni 国 [one's country/birthplace] ⟪home, country⟫

EX. My hometown has completely changed in the last ten years.
(私の){故郷/ふるさと/国}はこの十年の間にすっかり変わってしまった。
(Watashi no) {kokyoo/furu-sato/kuni} wa kono juu-nen no aida ni sukkari kawatte shimatta.

homework n. **[a school assignment to be done at home]**
shu┌kudai 宿題 •c [school work to be done at home]

EX. (**a**) Please hand in your homework by five o'clock.
五時までに宿題を出してください。
Go-ji made ni shukudai o dashite kudasai.
(**b**) Did you do your homework?
宿題をしましたか。
Shukudai o shimashita ka.

honest adj. **[for s.o. to be not likely to lie/cheat/steal or for one's words or actions to be accurate representations of oneself]**
sho┌ojiki˥na 正直な adj(*na*). **•c [for s.o. to be not likely to lie/cheat/hide the truth or for a person's actions to be typical of that person] ⟪upright, truthful⟫, so┌tchokuna 率直な** adj(*na*). **•c [for s.o. to be straightforward about the truth or for a person's actions to be typical of that person] ⟪frank, open⟫**

EX. (**a**) I want to hear your honest opinion.
あなたの{率直な/正直な}意見が聞きたいです。
Anata no {sotchokuna/shoojikina} iken ga kiki-tai desu.
(**b**) He's an honest man. I can't believe that he told you a lie.
彼は{正直な/*率直な}人です。彼がうそをついたなんて信じられません。
*Kare wa {shoojikina/*sotchokuna} hito desu. Kare ga uso o tsuita nante shinji-raremasen.*

honestly adv. **[in an honest manner or speaking truthfully]**
sho┌ojiki˥ni 正直に /⟨adj(*na*). *ni* of *shoojikina* honest/ [in an honest manner] ⟪truthfully⟫, so┌tchokuni 率直に /⟨adj(*na*). *ni* of *sotchokuna* frank/ [without hiding what one really thinks/feels] ⟪frankly, straightforwardly⟫

EX. (**a**) Answer the questions honestly.
質問に{正直に/率直に}答えてください。
Shitsumon ni {shoojikini/sotchokuni} kotaete kudasai.
(**b**) Honestly speaking, I don't think he has a talent for music.
{正直(に)/率直に}言って、彼に音楽の才能があるとは思いません。
{Shoojiki(ni)/Sotchokuni} itte, kare ni ongaku no sainoo ga aru to wa omoimasen.

honey n. **[a sweet, sticky substance made by bees ⟪fig. "an expression used to address s.o. one loves"⟫]**
ha┌chi-mitsu はちみつ [a sweet, sticky substance made by bees]

PHRASE. honeymoon *hanemuun* ハネムーン •f, *shinkon-ryokoo* 新婚旅行 •c

honor n. **[public respect; high moral standards; s.o./s.t. that brings pride or credit to a person or group]**
1. me˥iyo 名誉 •c [(consciousness of) great respect and admiration given to one] ⟪credit, glory, reputation⟫

EX. (**a**) It's a great honor to be able to sing in front of the Queen.
女王の前で歌うのは大変な名誉だ。
Jooo no mae de utau no wa taihenna meiyo da.
(**b**) Rumors like that can be damaging to the honor of our company.
ああいううわさはわが社の名誉にかかわる。
Aa-iu uwasa wa waga-sha no meiyo ni kakawaru.

H

2. ko⌈oei 光栄 •c **[a feeling of great pride and pleasure]** ((glory, privilege))

EX. It's a great honor to be able to talk to you.
お話できて、大変光栄です。
O-hanashi dekite, taihen kooei desu.

honorific adj./n. **[a linguistic expression showing deference or respect]**
ke⌈igo 敬語 n.

EX. It's difficult to use honorifics appropriately in every situation.
どんな場合にも敬語を正しく使うのはむずかしい。
Donna baai ni mo keigo o tadashiku tsukau no wa muzukashii.

hoof n.
hi⌈zume ひづめ

hook n. **[a curved piece of metal/plastic used for hanging things/catching fish]**
fu⌉kku フック •f **[a curved piece of metal/plastic used for hanging things], bo⌈oshi⌉-kake** 帽子掛け **[a curved piece of metal/plastic for hanging hats and caps], tsu⌈ri-ba⌉ri** 釣り針 **[a curved piece of metal for catching fish]**

EX. (**a**) He hung his hat on the hook.
彼は{帽子掛け/?フック/*釣り針}に帽子を掛けた。
*Kare wa {booshi-kake/?fukku/*tsuri-bari} ni booshi o kaketa.*
(**b**) The bottle opener is on a hook in the kitchen.
栓抜きは台所の{フック/*帽子掛け/*釣り針}に掛けてあります。
*Sen-nuki wa daidokoro no {fukku/*booshi-kake/*tsuri-bari} ni kakete arimasu.*
(**c**) What kind of fishing hooks are suitable for catching sea bream?
たいを釣るにはどんな{釣り針/*フック/*帽子掛け}がいいですか。
*Tai o tsuru ni wa donna {tsuri-bari/*fukku/*booshi-kake} ga ii desu ka.*

hop vi. **[for s.o. to make a short jump on one foot or for a small animal to jump on both or all feet]**
ka⌈ta-ashi de pyon-to to⌈bu 片足でぴょんと跳ぶ ①, **to⌈bi-mawa⌉ru** 飛び回る ① **[for s.o./s.a. to jump around]** ((romp)), **ke⌉nken o suru** けんけんをする ③ **[for s.o. to make a short jump on one foot]**

EX. (**a**) I hurt my left foot and so I had to hop on my right foot.
左足を痛めたので、右足で{けんけんをしなければ/飛び回らなければ/?ぴょんと跳ばなければ}ならなかった。
Hidari-ashi o itameta node, migi-ashi de {kenken o shinakereba/tobi-mawaranakereba/?pyon-to tobanakereba} naranakatta.
(**b**) Sparrows were hopping about on the veranda.
すずめがベランダを{飛び回って/*片足でぴょんと跳んで/*けんけんをして}いた。
*Suzume ga beranda o {tobi-mawatte/*kata-ashi de pyon-to tonde/*kenken o shite} ita.*
(**c**) He hopped across the brook in one jump.
彼は小川を{片足でぴょんと跳んで/けんけんをして/*飛び回って}渡った。
*Kare wa ogawa o {kata-ashi de pyon-to tonde/kenken o shite/*tobi-mawatte} watatta.*

hope n. **[the expectation that s.t. will happen as one desires]**
ki⌈boo 希望 •c **[s.t. which one desires will happen in the future or desiring that s.t. in the future will turn out a certain way]** ((desire, aspiration, wish)), **no⌈zomi** 望み /⟨V*masu* of *nozomu* ① hope/ **[an indication or desire of future success]** ((expectation, chance))

EX. (**a**) There is little hope that they are still alive.
彼らがまだ生きているという{望み/*希望}はほとんどない。
*Kare-ra ga mada ikite iru to iu {nozomi/*kiboo} wa hotondo nai.*
(**b**) Her eyes were gleaming with hope.
彼女の目は{希望/*望み}で輝いていた。
*Kanojo no me wa {kiboo/*nozomi} de kagayaite ita.*

— vi./vt. **[to want s.t. to happen with some belief that it will happen]**

1. Sinf. to i˥i Sinf.といい adj(*i*). **[if…happens, it will be nice]**

NOTE: The sentence before *to ii* must express a situation or event that cannot be directly controlled by the speaker.

EX. (**a**) I hope the weather will be nice tomorrow.
あした天気がいいといいですね。
Ashita tenki ga ii to ii desu ne.
(**b**) I hope that he'll come.
彼が来るといいんですが。
Kare ga kuru to ii n desu ga.
(**c**) She hopes to study in the United States someday.
彼女はいつかアメリカへ留学できるといいと思っている。
Kanojo wa itsu-ka Amerika e ryuugaku-dekiru to ii to omotte iru.

2. V*masu* ta˥i to o┌mo˥u V*masu*たいと思う ① **[for s.o. to want to do s.t.]** ⟪**want**⟫, ⟨**-o**⟩ **ki┌boo-suru** ⟨〜を⟩**希望する** ③ **•c [for s.o. to want to do s.t. in the future]** ⟪**wish, desire, expect**⟫, ⟨**-o**⟩ **no┌zomu** ⟨〜を⟩**望む** ① **[for s.o. to view a distant place or to want/expect s.t. to happen]** ⟪**desire, wish**⟫

EX. (**a**) She hopes to become a journalist someday.
彼女は将来ジャーナリストに{なりたいと思って/?なることを希望して/??なることを望んで}いる。
Kanojo wa shoorai jaanarisuto ni {nari-tai to omotte/?naru koto o kiboo-shite/??naru koto o nozonde} iru.
(**b**) She hopes to go to the United States to study.
彼女は{アメリカに留学したいと思って/アメリカ留学を{希望して/?望んで}}いる。
Kanojo wa {Amerika ni ryuugaku-shi-tai to omotte/Amerika-ryuugaku o {kiboo-shite/?nozonde}} iru.
(**c**) Everybody hopes for a quick settlement of the wage increase negotiations.
みんなが賃上げ交渉の早期妥結を{見たいと思って/望んで/?希望して}いる。
Minna ga chin'age-kooshoo no sooki-daketsu o {mi-tai to omotte/nozonde/?kiboo-shite} iru.

NOTE: *Ryuugaku-shi-tai to omotte iru* shows a stronger desire than *ryuugaku dekiru to ii.* Neither *kiboo-suru* nor *nozomu* is very conversational.

hopeless adj. **[to show no possibility of s.t. good happening]**
ze┌tsuboo-tekina 絶望的な adj(*na*). **•c [for a situation to show no possibility of s.t. good happening]** ⟪**desperate**⟫, **do┌o-shiyoo-mo-na˥i どうしようもない** adj(*i*). **[for there to be nothing which can be done to help or solve a situation]**

EX. (**a**) The situation was hopeless. We had nothing to eat.
状況は{絶望的だった/どうしようもなかった}。食べ物は何もなかった。
Jookyoo wa {zetsuboo-teki datta/doo-shiyoo-mo nakatta}. Tabe-mono wa nani-mo nakatta.
(**b**) He's a hopeless idiot.
彼は{どうしようもない/*絶望的な}馬鹿だ。
*Kare wa {doo-shiyoo-mo-nai/*zetsuboo-tekina} baka da.*

horizon n. **[the faraway line where the sky seems to meet the earth/sea]**
chi┌hei-sen 地平線 •c [the faraway line where the sky seems to meet the earth], su┌ihei-sen 水平線 •c [the faraway line where the sky seems to meet the sea]

EX. (**a**) The sun rose over the horizon on the Pacific Ocean.
太平洋の{水平線/*地平線}から日が上った。
*Taiheiyoo no {suihei-sen/*chihei-sen} kara hi ga nobotta.*
(**b**) I saw the setting sun sink below the horizon on the desert.
砂漠で夕日が{地平線/*水平線}のかなたに沈むのを見た。
*Sabaku de yuuhi ga {chihei-sen/*suihei-sen} no kanata ni shizumu no o mita.*

H

horizontal adj. **[parallel to the horizon]**
yo⌈ko no N 横のN [parallel to a line passing through one's eyes] ↔ tate no N 縦のN

EX. To write the katakana for "na," you first draw a horizontal line.
「ナ」という片仮名を書くときは、横の線を先に引きます。
'Na' to iu kata-kana o kaku toki wa, yoko no sen o saki ni hikimasu.

horn n. **[one of the hard pointed growths on the head of animals such as cattle, sheep, and deer]**
tsu⌈no⌉ 角

EX. In Nara, they cut the horns of the deer every fall.
奈良では毎年秋に鹿の角を切る。
Nara de wa mai-toshi aki ni shika no tsuno o kiru.

horror n. **[a feeling of extreme fear mixed with disgust]**
o⌈soro⌉shi-sa 恐ろしさ /⟨adj(*i*). stem of *osoroshii* scary, fearful + suf. *sa* ness/ [anxiety caused by the expectation of danger/evil] ⟪fear, dreadfulness, terror⟫, kyo⌉ofu 恐怖 •c [great anxiety caused by the expectation of danger/evil] ⟪fear, fright, terror⟫

H

EX. (**a**) I can't describe the horror I experienced on the hijacked plane.
ハイジャックされた機内で経験した{恐怖/恐ろしさ}はことばでは言い表せません。
Hai-jakku-sareta kinai de keiken-shita {kyoofu/osoroshi-sa} wa kotoba de wa ii-arawase-masen.
(**b**) Prof. Smith's class was pure horror for his students.
スミス先生の授業は学生にとって{恐怖/*恐ろしさ}そのものだった。
*Sumisu-sensei no jugyoo wa gakusei ni-totte {kyoofu/*osoroshi-sa} sono mono datta.*
(**c**) I was petrified with horror.
私は{恐怖/恐ろしさ}で身動きできなかった。
Watashi wa {kyoofu/osoroshi-sa} de mi-ugoki-dekinakatta.

horse n.
u⌈ma⌉ 馬

EX. (**a**) I like riding horses.
私は馬に乗るのが好きだ。
Watashi wa uma ni noru no ga suki da.
(**b**) The jockey fell off the horse during the race.
その騎手はレース中に馬から落ちた。
Sono kishu wa reesu-chuu ni uma kara ochita.

PHRASE: horseback riding *jooba* 乗馬 •c, horse racing *keiba* 競馬 •c

hose n. **[a flexible rubber/plastic pipe to direct water onto fires, gardens, etc., or stockings/tights/socks]**
1. ho⌉osu ホース •f

EX. I need to buy a hose to wash my car.
車を洗うのにホースを買いたい。
Kuruma o arau no ni hoosu o kai-tai.

2. ku⌈tsu⌉-shita 靴下 [stockings/socks]

PHRASE: panty hose *pantii-sutokkingu* パンティーストッキング •f

hospital n. **[a place where sick/injured people receive medical treatment and can stay overnight for such treatment if necessary]**
byo⌈oin 病院 •c

EX. (**a**) She was taken to the hospital by ambulance.
彼女は救急車で病院に運ばれた。
Kanojo wa kyuukyuu-sha de byooin ni hakoba-reta.
(**b**) I had an operation for a stomach ulcer at Massachusetts General Hospital.
私はマサチューセッツ総合病院で胃かいようの手術を受けた。
Watashi wa Masachuusettsu-soogoo-byooin de i-kaiyoo no shujutsu o uketa.

PHRASE: hospital ward *byooshitsu* 病室•c, *byootoo* 病棟 •c

hospitalize vt. **[to put s.o. into the hospital]**
⟨-o⟩ nyu⌈uin-saseru ⟨〜を⟩入院させる /⟨causative of *nyuuin-suru* ③ be hospitalized/ ② •c

EX. We'd better hospitalize him. Otherwise he'll never stop drinking.
彼を入院させたほうがいい。そうしなければ彼は酒をやめないと思う。
Kare o nyuuin-saseta hoo ga ii. Soo shinakereba kare wa sake o yamenai to omou.

PHRASE: be hospitalized *nyuuin-suru* 入院する ③ •c

EX. I was hospitalized for a month.
私は一か月入院していた。
Watashi wa ik-kagetsu nyuuin-shite ita.

host n. **[a person who receives guests and looks after them]**
shu˥jin 主人 [a person who receives guests and looks after them or an owner of a shop, restaurant, pet, etc., or a term a woman uses to refer to the man to whom she is married] ((master, owner, husband))

EX. We thanked our host for the party.
私たちはご主人にパーティーのお礼を言った。
Watashi-tachi wa go-shujin ni paatii no o-rei o itta.

PHRASE: host country for the Olympic Games *Orinpikku-kaisai-koku* オリンピック開催国 •f+c

hostile adj. **[showing overt antagonism]**
te˥kii o motta N 敵意を持ったN /⟨*tekii* hostility + prt. *o* + Vinf. past of *motsu* ① have/ [for s.o. to have hatred], te˥kii o motte iru (N) 敵意を持っている(N) /⟨V*te iru* of *tekii o motsu* ① have hostility/

EX. We were surrounded by a hostile crowd.
私たちは敵意を{持った/持っている}群衆に囲まれた。
Watashi-tachi wa tekii o {motta/motte iru} gunshuu ni kakoma-reta.

hot adj. **[having a high temperature]**
a˥tsu˥i あつい adj(*i*). **[having a great amount of heat]**
㊥ "sensing discomfort throughout one's body due to the presence of a great amount of heat" ▷暑い, "for s.t. to have a high temperature physically perceptible to the touch"▷熱い

NOTE: The antonyms for 暑い and 熱い are different as follows. 暑い ↔ *samui* 寒い, 熱い ↔ *tsumetai* 冷たい

EX. (**a**) It was terribly hot this summer.
今年の夏はとても暑かった。
Kotoshi no natsu wa totemo atsukatta.
(**b**) I'd like to have some hot coffee.
熱いコーヒーが飲みたい。
Atsui koohii ga nomi-tai.
(**c**) I can't sleep in such a hot room.
こんな暑い部屋では寝られない。
Konna atsui heya de wa ne-rarenai.
(**d**) This milk is too hot for the baby.
このミルクは赤ちゃんには熱すぎる。
Kono miruku wa aka-chan ni wa atsu-sugiru.

PHRASE: hot water *yu* 湯

EX. Please wash the dishes with hot water.
お皿を(熱い)湯で洗ってください。
O-sara o (atsui) yu de aratte kudasai.

NOTE: The temperature of *yu* can vary, so *atsui yu* "hot hot water" is not necessarily redundant.

PHRASE: hot spring *onsen* 温泉 •c

EX. The Japanese like to bathe in hot springs.
日本人は温泉に入るのが好きです。
Nihon-jin wa onsen ni hairu no ga suki desu.

hotel n. **[a building that provides rooms and meals for travelers in return for payment]**
ho˥teru ホテル •f

EX. (**a**) I checked in at the hotel at about 5:30 p.m.
私はホテルに五時半ごろチェックインした。
Watashi wa hoteru ni go-ji-han-goro chekkuin-shita.
(**b**) I wanted to sleep in a bed, so I stayed at a hotel.
私はベッドで寝たかったので、ホテルに泊まった。
Watashi wa beddo de ne-takatta node, hoteru ni tomatta.

hour n. **[a period of 60 minutes or a fixed period of time for a specific purpose/activity]**
1. -jikan ~時間 •c [the counter for hours]

EX. I waited for her for two hours.

彼女を二時間待った。
Kanojo o ni-jikan matta.

PHRASE: for hours *nan-jikan-mo* 何時間も

2. ji⌈kan 時間 •c [time or a fixed period of time], to⌈ki⌉ 時 [the continuum from past to present into the future or a specific point or subinterval of this at/during which a state, action, or event occurs or continues]

EX. (**a**) The hospital's visiting hours are from four to eight.
病院の面会{時間/*時}は四時から八時までです。
*Byooin no menkai-{jikan/*toki} wa yo-ji kara hachi-ji made desu.*
(**b**) I went shopping during my lunch hour.
昼ごはんの{時間/時}に買い物に行った。
Hiru-gohan no {jikan/toki} ni kai-mono ni itta.
(**c**) My friends were there to help me in my hour of adversity.
友達は私がとても困っている{時/*時間}に助けてくれた。
*Tomodachi wa watashi ga totemo komatte iru {toki/*jikan} ni tasukete kureta.*

house n. **[a building for people to live in]**
u⌈chi うち [the inside/the place where one lives] ⟪home⟫, i⌈e⌉ 家, ⟪home⟫, o-⌈taku お宅 [a term for the house of s.o. to whom one is showing deference ⟪fig. "a term fot the family/husband of s.o. shown deference," "you"⟫ ⟨fml⟩]

EX. (**a**) They live in a big house.
彼らは大きい{家/うち/?お宅}に住んでいます。
Kare-ra wa ookii {ie/uchi/?o-taku} ni sunde imasu.
(**b**) Three houses burnt down in the fire.
火事で{家/うち/*お宅}が三軒焼けてしまった。
*Kaji de {ie/uchi/*o-taku} ga san-gen yakete shimatta.*
(**c**) Do you know where Professor Ootake's house is located?
大竹先生の{お宅/*家/*うち}はどちらにあるかご存じですか。
*Ootake-sensei no {o-taku/*ie/*uchi} wa dochira ni aru ka go-zonji desu ka.*

PHRASE: house for rent *kashi-ya* 貸家

household n. **[all the people living together in a house or everything that is connected with looking after a house and the people who live in it]**
ka⌉zoku 家族 •c [a group of people closely related to one another and usually living together, such as husband and wife, parents and children, etc.], sho⌉tai 所帯 •c [a group of people living together and sharing the attendant costs and responsibilities], se⌉tai 世帯 •c [a group of people living under the same roof as a family and considered as a family unit for legal purposes]

EX. (**a**) Everyone in the household was out at the time.
{家族/*所帯/*世帯}はその時みんな出かけていた。
*{Kazoku/*Shotai/*Setai} wa sono toki minna dekakete ita.*
(**b**) Three households are living in the same apartment unit.
同じアパートに三{所帯/世帯/家族}が住んでいる。
Onaji apaato ni san- {shotai/setai/kazoku} ga sunde iru.
(**c**) I bought a new set of household furnishings to set up house in Tokyo.
東京で暮らすために{所帯/*家族/*世帯}道具を一そろい買った。
*Tookyoo de kurasu tame ni {shotai/*kazoku/*setai}-doogu o hito-soroi katta.*

housewife n. **[a married woman who works for her family, especially one who does not have a full-time job outside the home]**
shu⌉fu 主婦 •c

EX. Many housewives have begun to work part-time.
パートタイムで働いている主婦が多くなった。

H

Paato-taimu de hataraite iru shufu ga ooku natta.

NOTE: *Sengyoo-shufu* 専業主婦 is used for a full-time housewife.

how adv. **[in what way or by what means or in what condition or an exclamation marker]**

1. do˥o どう [in what way or in what condition], i┌ka˥ga いかが [in what condition ⟨fml⟩], do˥o yatte どうやって /⟨*doo* how + V*te* of *yaru* do/ [by what means]

EX. (**a**) Could you tell me how I can get to Kyoto?
京都へは{どう/どうやって/*いかが}行けばいいか教えてくださいませんか。
*Kyooto e wa {doo/doo yatte/*ikaga} ikeba ii ka oshiete kudasaimasen ka.*
(**b**) How do you feel about having to work on Sundays?
日曜日に仕事をしなければいけないことを{どう/*どうやって/*いかが}思いますか。
*Nichiyoo-bi ni shigoto o shinakereba ikenai koto o {doo/*doo yatte/*ikaga} omoimasu ka.*
(**c**) How did you bring so many books here by yourself?
{どうやって/*どう/*いかが}そんなにたくさんの本を一人でここへ運んできたんですか。
*{Doo yatte/*Doo/*Ikaga} sonnani takusan no hon o hitori de koko e hakonde kita n desu ka.*
(**d**) How was life in Japan for you?
日本の生活は{どう/いかが/*どうやって}でしたか。
*Nihon no seikatsu wa {doo/ikaga/*doo yatte} deshita ka.*

PHRASE: how about… ⟨*-wa*⟩ *{ikaga/doo} desu ka.* ⟨〜は⟩{いかが/どう}ですか。

EX. How about some beer?
ビールは{いかが/どう}ですか。
Biiru wa {ikaga/doo} desu ka.

PHRASE: how about… V*masu masen ka.* V*masu* ませんか。

EX. How about sitting over there?
あそこに座りませんか。
Asoko ni suwarimasen ka.

PHRASE: how come *dooshite* どうして ⟪why⟫

EX. How come he failed the exam?
どうして彼が試験に落ちたりしたの?
Dooshite kare ga shiken ni ochitari shita no?

PHRASE: how long *dono-gurai* どのぐらい

EX. How long do you plan to stay in Japan?
日本にどのぐらいいる予定ですか。
Nihon ni dono-gurai iru yotei desu ka.

PHRASE: how many *ikutsu* いくつ

EX. (**a**) How many kanji can you write?
漢字がいくつ書けますか。
Kanji ga ikutsu kake-masu ka.

NOTE: The expression for "how many" usually takes the form *nan* what + counter, where the counter varies depending on the kind of object concerned, as in *nan-satsu* "how many bound objects," *nan-mai* "how many flat objects," etc.

(**b**) I couldn't tell you how many books Prof. Hattori wrote.
服部先生が本を何冊お書きになったか知りません。
Hattori-sensei ga hon o nan-satsu o-kaki ni natta ka shirimasen.

PHRASE: how many times *{nan-do/nan kai}* {何度/何回} •c

EX. How many times have you been to France?
フランスへは{何度/何回}行ったことがありますか。
Furansu e wa {nan-do/nan-kai} itta koto ga arimasu ka.

PHRASE: how much *ikura* いくら

EX. (**a**) How much is this dictionary?
この辞書はいくらですか。
Kono jisho wa ikura desu ka.
(**b**) No matter how much he eats, he doesn't gain weight.
彼はいくら食べても太らない。
Kare wa ikura tabete mo futoranai.

PHRASE: how old *{ikutsu/nan-sai}* {いくつ/何歳} •c

EX. How old is your grandmother?
おばあさんは{おいくつ/何歳}ですか。

O-baa-san wa {o-ikutsu/nan-sai} desu ka.

PHRASE: How are you? *O-genki desu ka.* お元気ですか, How do you do. *Hajimemashite.* はじめまして, how to V V*masu+kata* V*masu*+方

EX. We learned how to write compositions in Japanese in that class.
私たちはその授業で日本語の作文の書き方を習った。
Watashi-tachi wa sono jugyoo de Nihon-go no sakubun no kaki-kata o naratta.

2. **{na⌉nte/na⌉nto}…n daroo** {なんて/なんと}〜んだろう ((**what**))

EX. (**a**) How hot it is!
{なんて/なんと}暑いんだろう。
{Nante/Nanto} atsui n daroo.
(**b**) How kind they all are!
{なんて/?なんと}親切なんでしょう。
{Nante/?Nanto} shinsetsu na n deshoo.

NOTE: *Nante* is a colloquial form of *nanto.* The use of *nante* followed by *deshoo,* as in example (b), is typical of female speech.

however adv. **[to whatever degree]**
{do⌉nna-ni/i⌉kura}…{V/adj./cop.} ***te*****} mo**
{どんなに/いくら}…{V/adj./cop.} ***te*****}も**

EX. (**a**) However cold it is, he never wears socks.
{どんなに/いくら}寒くても、彼は靴下をはかない。
{Donnani/Ikura} samukute mo, kare wa kutsu-shita o hakanai.
(**b**) I'm determined to master Japanese, however long it takes.
{どんなに/いくら}時間がかかっても、絶対に日本語をマスターしたいと思う。
{Donnani/Ikura} jikan ga kakatte mo, zettai ni Nihon-go o masutaa-shi-tai to omou.

— adv. **[in spite of this]**
shi⌈ka⌉shi しかし ((**but**)), **de⌉mo** でも **[a coordinate disjunctive conjunction used in sentence-initial position]** ((**but**))

NOTE: *Demo* is more colloquial than *shikashi.*

EX. They finally got a divorce. However, there still remain many problems.
彼らはついに離婚しました。{しかし/でも}問題はまだたくさん残っています。
Kare-ra wa tsuini rikon-shimashita. {Shikashi/Demo} mondai wa mada takusan nokotte imasu.

howl vi. **[for s.a. such as a dog or wolf to make long a loud wailing cry or for the wind to make a similar sound]**
to⌈o-boe (o) suru 遠ぼえ(を)する ③ **[for s.a. such as a dog or wolf to make a long wailing cry that can be heard far away]**

EX. I couldn't sleep last night because the dogs were howling all night.
ゆうべは一晩じゅう犬が遠ぼえをして寝られなかった。
Yuube wa hito-ban-juu inu ga too-boe o shite ne-rarenakatta.

hug vt. **[for s.o. to hold s.o./s.t./s.a. tightly in one's arms]**
⟨-o⟩ da⌈ki-shime⌉ru ⟨〜を⟩抱き締める ② **[for s.o. to hold s.o./s.t./s.a. tightly in one's arms]** ((**embrace**))

EX. (**a**) My mother hugged me.
母は私を抱き締めた。
Haha wa watashi o daki-shimeta.
(**b**) The girl fell asleep hugging the doll I had given her.
女の子は私があげた人形を抱き締めて、眠ってしまった。
Onna-no-ko wa watashi ga ageta ningyoo o daki-shimete, nemutte shimatta.

huge adj. **[extremely large]**
kyo⌈daina 巨大な adj(*na*). •c **[extremely large in size]** ((**enormous, gigantic**)), **ba⌈kudaina** ばく大な adj(*na*). •c **[extremely large as measured in monetary terms]** ((**enormous**)), **bo⌈odaina** 膨大な adj(*na*). •c **[for data, materials, etc., to be extremely great in amount]**

EX. (**a**) Huge tankers are used to carry oil.
石油を運ぶのに{巨大な/*ばく大な/*膨大な}タンカーが使われる。
*Sekiyu o hakobu no ni {kyodaina/ *bakudaina/*boodaina} tankaa ga tsukawa-reru.*

H

(**b**) He has received a huge inheritance from his uncle.
彼はおじさんから{ばく大な/*巨大な/*膨大な}遺産を相続した。
*Kare wa oji-san kara {bakudaina/*kyodaina/*boodaina} isan o soozoku-shita.*
(**c**) The conclusions he reaches in his book are based on a huge amount of data.
彼があの本の中で達した結論は{膨大な/?ばく大な/*巨大な}量のデータに基づいたものである。
*Kare ga ano hon no naka de tasshita ketsuron wa {boodaina/?bakudaina/*kyodaina} ryoo no deeta ni motozuita mono dearu.*

human adj. **[of/concerning people as opposed to animals or God]**
1. ni⌈ngen no N 人間のN **•c [of/concerning people]**
EX. Is the human brain basically different from that of other animals?
人間の脳は外の動物の脳と基本的に違うんですか。
Ningen no noo wa hoka no doobutsu no noo to kihon-tekini chigau n desu ka.
2. ni⌈ngen-tekina 人間的な **•c [typical of people]**
EX. He's a cold person. I don't think he's capable of showing any human emotion.
彼は冷たい人だ。人間的な感情を見せることができそうもない。
Kare wa tsumetai hito da. Ningen-tekina kanjoo o miseru koto ga dekisoo mo nai.
PHRASE: human being *ningen* 人間 **•c**
EX. Human beings have been entrusted with the duty of protecting the future of this planet.
人間はこの地球の将来を守る任務を託されている。
Ningen wa kono chikyuu no shoorai o mamoru ninmu o takusa-rete iru.
PHRASE: human relations *ningen-kankei* 人間関係 **•c**

humble adj. **[having/showing a modest opinion of oneself, one's position, etc., or to be low in social status/class]**
1. ke⌉nkyona 謙虚な adj(*na*). **•c [underrating oneself, one's achievements, etc.]** ((**modest**)) ↔ **jishin-manman no N** 自信満々のN **•c**
EX. (**a**) I think he's a very humble person.
彼は非常に謙虚な人だと思う。
Kare wa hijooni kenkyona hito da to omou.
(**b**) Humble people are admired in Japanese society.
日本社会では謙虚な人が評価される。
Nihon-shakai de wa kenkyona hito ga hyooka-sareru.
2. i⌈yashii 卑しい adj(*i*). **[to be low in social status/class]** ((**lowly**))
EX. He comes from a humble background.
彼は卑しい家の出だ。
Kare wa iyashii ie no de da.

humid adj. **[for the water content of the air to be high]**
shi⌈kke ga o⌉oi 湿気が多い adj(*i*), **shi⌈tsu⌉do ga ta⌈ka⌉i** 湿度が高い adj(*i*).
EX. My knees hurt on days that are humid.
{湿度が高い/湿気が多い}日にはひざが痛むんです。
{Shitsudo ga takai/Shikke ga ooi} hi ni wa hiza ga itamu n desu.

H

humor n. **[the quality of being amusing or the ability to appreciate what is amusing or to amuse people with one's cleverness or wit]**
yu⌉umoa ユーモア **•f [what is funny in a witty/clever way and makes people laugh]**
EX. (**a**) He has no sense of humor.
彼にはユーモアのセンスがない。
Kare ni wa yuumoa no sensu ga nai.
(**b**) He entertained us with a speech full of humor.
彼はユーモアあふれるスピーチで私たちを楽しませてくれた。
Kare wa yuumoa afureru supiichi de watashi-tachi o tanoshima-sete kureta.

humorous adj. **[having the quality of making people laugh, especailly due to wit or cleverness]**

yu⌉umoa ni to⌉nda N ユーモアに富んだN /⟨*yuumoa* humor + prt. *ni* + Vinf. past of *tomu* ① be rich in/

EX. His humorous way of talking kept everyone in stitches the whole evening.
彼のユーモアに富んだ話しぶりに一晩中皆笑いこけていた。
Kare no yuumoa ni tonda hanashi-buri ni hito-ban-juu mina warai-kokete ita.

hundred n./adj.

hya⌈ku⌉ (+counter) (no N) 百(+counter)(のN) SEE APPENDIX II

EX. (**a**) I need a hundred sheets of white paper.
白い紙が百枚要ります。
Shiroi kami ga hyaku-mai irimasu.
(**b**) We invited about a hundred people to our wedding.
私たちの結婚式に人を百人ぐらい招待した。
Watashi-tachi no kekkon-shiki ni hito o hyaku-nin-gurai shootai-shita.

PHRASE: hundreds of *nan-byaku mo* 何百も •c

EX. That five-year-old boy already knows hundreds of kanji.
あの五歳の男の子はすでに漢字を何百も知っている。
Ano go-sai no otoko-no-ko wa sudeni kanji o nan-byaku mo shitte iru.

NOTE: A counter may come between *nan-byaku* and *mo*, as in *nan-byaku-nin mo* "hundreds of people," *nan-byaku-mai mo* "hundreds of sheets," etc.

H

hungry adj. **[feeling or showing the need or desire for food《fig. "strongly desiring"》]**

1. o-⌈naka ga suku おなかがすく ① [for one's stomach to become empty《fig. "for s.o./s.a. to come to feel the need or desire for food"》]《get hungry》

EX. (**a**) I'm hungry.
おなかがすきました。
O-naka ga sukimashita.
(**b**) You shouldn't drink when you are hungry.
おなかがすいているとき、酒を飲まないほうがいいですよ。
O-naka ga suite iru toki, sake o nomanai hoo ga ii desu yo.
(**c**) I never eat breakfast, so I usually get hungry around 11 o'clock.
朝ごはんを食べないので、大抵十一時ごろになると、おなかがすきます。
Asa-gohan o tabenai node, taitei juu-ichi-ji-goro ni naru to, o-naka ga sukimasu.
(**d**) I was so hungry that I couldn't walk.
おなかがすいて、歩けませんでした。
O-naka ga suite, aruke-masen deshita.

NOTE: *O-naka ga sukimashita* expresses a sense of hunger immediately and spontaneously felt while *o-naka ga suite imasu.* describes a state of hunger more as an objective fact. Both are used with the first person subject in statements and with the second person subject in questions. To describe a state of hunger, in a third person, some form must be attached which explicitly expresses the speaker's perception or judgment, such as *daroo* "probably" or *yooda* "it appears that."

2. (na⌉n-to shi⌈te de⌉mo) V*masu* tai (何としてでも)V*masu*たい adj(*i*). **[want to do s.t. strongly]**

EX. He was hungry to pay back the injustice he had suffered.
彼は何としてでも自分の受けた不当な扱いの仕返しをしたいと思っていた。
Kare wa nan-to shite demo jibun no uketa futoona atsukai no shikaeshi o shi-tai to omotte ita.

hunt vi./vt. **[for s.o./s.a. to go after wild animals to catch or kill them for sport or food《fig. "search diligently"》]**

ka⌉ri o suru 狩りをする ③ [for s.o. to go after wild animals to catch or kill them for sport or food], ⟨-o⟩ o⌈i-kake⌉ru ⟨〜を⟩追いかける ② [for s.o./s.a. to follow s.t./s.o./s.a. moving quickly in order to reach it/him/her], ⟨-o⟩ o⌈u ⟨〜を⟩追う ① [for s.o./s.a. to go after s.o./s.t./s.a.《fig. "search diligently"》]《chase》

NOTE: *Kari* can be used in compounds with the kind of game to be hunted as in *usagi-gari* "rabbit hunting," *kitsune-gari* "fox hunting," etc.

EX. (**a**) We hunted fox in the forest.
森の中で{きつね狩りをした/きつねを{?追いかけた/*追った}}。
*Mori no naka de {kitsune-gari o shita/ kitsune o {?oi-kaketa/*otta}}.*
(**b**) The lion hunted down the zebra.
ライオンは{しま馬を{追いかけた/??追った}/*しま馬狩りをした}。
*Raion wa {shimauma o {oi-kaketa/ ??otta}/*shimauma-gari o shita}.*
(**c**) The police are hunting for a guy who ran away from the scene of the crime.
警察は犯行現場から逃げた{男を{追って/??追いかけて}/*男の狩りをして}いる。
*Keisatsu wa hankoo-genba kara nigeta {otoko o {otte/??oi-kakete}/*otoko no kari o shite} iru.*

hunter n. **[s.o./s.a. that hunts wild animals]**
ryo˥oshi 猟師 **•c [s.o. who professionally hunts wild animals], ryo˥oken** 猟犬 **•c [a dog trained to be used in hunting]** ((a hunting dog))

EX. (**a**) He is a good hunter.
彼は腕のいい{猟師/*猟犬}だ。
*Kare wa ude no ii {ryooshi/*ryooken} da*
(**b**) Our dog is a wonderful hunter.
うちの犬は素晴らしい{猟犬/*猟師}だ。
*Uchi no inu wa subarashii {ryooken/ *ryooshi} da.*

hurl vt. **[to throw s.t. with force]**
1.⟨**-ni**⟩ ⟨**-o**⟩ **na⌈ge-tsuke˥ru** ⟨〜に⟩⟨〜を⟩投げつける ② **[for s.o. to throw s.t. at s.o./s.t./ s.a. on impulse]** ((throw, fling))

EX. He hurled a stone at the dog.
彼は犬に石を投げつけた。
Kare wa inu ni ishi o nage-tsuketa.

2. ⟨**-o**⟩ **ho⌈ori-nage˥ru** ⟨〜を⟩ほうり投げる ② **[for s.o. to throw s.t. with force]** ((fling))

EX. She got so mad that she hurled his bag out the window.
彼女はすごく腹を立てて、彼のかばんを窓からほうり投げた。
Kanojo wa sugoku hara o tatete, kare no kaban o mado kara hoori-nageta.

hurricane
ha⌈rike˥en ハリケーン **•f**

hurriedly adv. **[very quickly]**
i⌈so˥ide 急いで /⟨**V*te* of *isogu*** ① **hurry**/ ((in a hurry))

EX. He brushed his teeth hurriedly.
彼は急いで歯を磨いた。
Kare wa isoide ha o migaita.

hurry vi. **[to move/do s.t. quickly]**
i⌈so˥gu 急ぐ ① **[for s.o. to do s.t. very quickly in order to finish it within a limited amount of time]**

EX. (**a**) There's no need to hurry; they'll wait for us.
急ぐ必要はありません。待ってくれますよ。
Isogu hitsuyoo wa arimasen. Matte kuremasu yo.
(**b**) Hurry up. We don't have much time left.
急いでください。もうあまり時間がありませんから。
Isoide kudasai. Moo amari jikan ga arimasen kara.

—— vt. **[for s.o. to cause s.o. to move/do s.t. quickly]**
i⌈soga-se˥ru 急がせる /⟨**causative of *isogu*** ① **hurry**/ ② **[to cause s.o. to move/do s.t. quickly]**

EX. Don't hurry me. I can't work any faster.
急がせないでください。これ以上速くできません。
Isoga-senaide kudasai. Kore ijoo hayaku dekimasen.

hurt vt. **[to cause physical or mental pain and/or damage to s.t./s.o.]**
⟨**-o**⟩ **i⌈tame˥ru** ⟨〜を⟩いためる ② **[for s.o./ s.a. to cause physical pain and/or damage to s.t.]** ((impair, afflict)), ⟨**-o**⟩ **ki⌈zu-tsuke˥ru** ⟨〜を⟩傷つける ② **[to inflict physical or mental harm on s.o./s.t./s.a.]** ((wound, injure, disfigure, impair, disgrace)), (⟨**-ni**⟩) **ke⌈ga˥ o suru** (⟨〜に⟩)けがをする ③ **[for s.o./s.a. to inflict physical damage to a part of one's body]** ((be wounded))

H

㊥ "damage s.t."▷傷める, "cause physical pain"▷痛める

EX. (**a**) She hurt her foot while trying to escape.
彼女は逃げようとしたとき、足{を{痛めた/*傷つけた}/にけがをした}。
*Kanojo wa nigeyoo to shita toki, ashi {o {itameta/*kizu-tsuketa}/ni kega o shita}.*
(**b**) My criticism seems to have hurt her very much.
私の批判は彼女をひどく{傷つけた/*傷めた}ようだ。
*Watashi no hihan wa kanojo o hidoku {kizu-tsuketa/*itameta} yooda.*

PHRASE: be hurt *kizu-tsuku* 傷つく ①, *kega o suru* けがをする ③

EX. (**a**) I was deeply hurt by the way she talked to me.
私は彼女の私に対する話し方にひどく{傷ついた/*けがをした}。
*Watashi wa kanojo no watashi ni-taisuru hanashi-kata ni hidoku {kizu-tsuita/*kega o shita}.*
(**b**) I was slightly hurt in the traffic accident.
交通事故で{軽いけがをした/*少し傷ついた}。
*Kootsuu-jiko de {karui kega o shita/ *sukoshi kizu-tsuita}.*

H

NOTE: *Kizu-tsukeru* and *kizu-tsuku* can be used to mean "physically wound/be wounded" in written style.

—— vi. **[for s.o. to experience pain or for a part of one's body to produce a feeling of pain]**
i⌈ta⌉i 痛い adj(*i*). **[for s.o./s.a. to experience an unpleasant physical sensation, often in a particular part of the body], i⌈ta⌉mu** いたむ ① **[for a part of one's body to produce a feeling of pain or for s.t. to become damaged]** ⟪**ache**⟫

NOTE: The subject of *itai* and *itamu* is the first person in statements and the second person in questions. *Itai* is used as a spontaneous expression of pain and *itamu* as an objective description of pain. *Itai*!, for example, means "Ouch!"

㊥ "for a part of one's body to produce a feeling of pain"▷痛む, "get damaged"▷傷む

EX. (**a**) My back hurts.
背中が{痛い/痛む}。
Senaka ga {itai/itamu}.
(**b**) Where does it hurt, Mr. Tanaka?
田中さん、どこが{痛い/痛む}んですか。
Tanaka-san, doko ga {itai/itamu} n desu ka.

husband n. **[the man to whom a woman is married]**
o⌈tto 夫 **[the man to whom a woman is married] ↔ tsuma** 妻; **shu⌉jin** 主人 **•c [a person who receives guests and looks after them or an owner of a shop, restaurant, pet, etc., or a term a woman uses to refer to the man to whom she is married] ↔ kanai** 家内 **•c; u⌈chi no hito** うちの人, **ka⌉re** 彼 **[he] ↔ kanojo** 彼女; **go-⌈shu⌉jin** ご主人 **[an honorific form to refer to one's master or to the man to whom another woman is married, i.e., s.o. else's male spouse]**

EX. (**a**) A husband should share the household chores with his wife.
{夫/*主人/*うちの人/*彼/*ご主人}は妻と家事を分担すべきだ。
*{Otto/*Shujin/*Uchi no hito/*Kare/ *Go-shujin} wa tsuma to kaji o buntan-su-beki da.*
(**b**) My husband is a senior high school English teacher.
{主人/うちの人/彼/夫/*ご主人}は高校の英語の教師です。
*{Shujin/Uchi no hito/Kare/Otto/*Go-shujin} wa kookoo no eigo no kyooshi desu.*
(**c**) Do you know Toshiko's husband?
敏子さんの{ご主人/*夫/*主人/*うちの人/*彼}を知っていますか。
*Toshiko-san no {go-shujin/*otto/*shujin/ *uchi no hito/*kare} o shitte imasu ka.*
(**d**) Does your husband smoke?
{ご主人/*夫/*主人/*うちの人/*彼}はたばこを吸われますか。
*{Go-shujin/*Otto/*Shujin/*Uchi no hito/*Kare} wa tabako o suwaremasu ka.*

hut n. **[a small roughly-made house or shelter]**
ko⌈ya 小屋 [a small simply-made or roughly-made building] ((**shed, shanty, cabin**))

EX. They lived in a wooden hut in the forest.
彼らは森の中の木で作った小屋に住んでいた。
Kare-ra wa mori no naka no ki de tsukutta koya ni sunde ita.

hydrogen n.
su⌉iso 水素 •c

EX. Water is a compound of hydrogen and oxygen.
水は水素と酸素の化合物です。
Mizu wa suiso to sanso no kagoo-butsu desu.

hypothesis n. **[an idea which is suggested as a possible explanation for certain facts, as a starting-point for reasoning, etc.]**
ka⌈setsu 仮説 •c

EX. (**a**) He put forward the hypothesis that the ancient country of Yamataikoku was located in Kyushu.
彼は邪馬台国は九州にあったという仮説をたてた。
Kare wa Yamataikoku wa Kyuushuu ni atta to iu kasetsu o tateta.
(**b**) His new hypothesis is drawing public attention.
彼の新しい仮説が世間の注目を浴びている。
Kare no atarashii kasetsu ga seken no chuumoku o abite iru.

I

I pron. **[the person speaking]**
wa⌈tashi わたし [the person speaking], wa⌈takushi 私 [the person speaking ⟨fml⟩], bo⌉ku 僕 [the male person speaking], a⌈tashi あたし [the female person speaking], o⌈re おれ [the male person speaking ⟨s⟩]

NOTE: "I" is often not expressed at all when it can be understood in a given context. 私 can be used to express *watashi* as well as *watakushi.*

EX. (**a**) I want to go to see a movie with my girlfriend.
{僕は/わたしは/私は/ø/?おれは/*あたしは}彼女と一緒に映画を見に行きたいです。
*{Boku wa/Watashi wa/Watakushi wa/ ø/?Ore wa/*Atashi wa} kanojo to issho ni eiga o mi ni iki-tai desu.*
(**b**) I'm waiting for my husband.
{わたしは/私は/あたしは/ø/*僕は/*おれは}主人を待っているんです。
*{Watashi wa/Watakushi wa/Atashi wa/ ø/*Boku wa/*Ore wa} shujin o matte iru n desu.*
(**c**) A: Can you speak French?
フランス語が話せますか。
Furansu-go ga hanase-masu ka.
B: Yes, I can.
ええ、{ø/?私は/?僕は/?わたしは/?あたしは/?おれは}話せます。
Ee, {ø/?watakushi wa/?boku wa/ ?watashi wa/?atashi wa/?ore wa} hanase-masu.

(**d**) A: Would someone return this book to the library?
だれかこの本を図書館に返してくれませんか。
Dare-ka kono hon o tosho-kan ni kaeshite kuremasen ka.
B: I will.
{私が/わたしが/僕が/あたしが/?おれが/*ø}返します。
*{Watakushi ga/Watashi ga/Boku ga/Atashi ga/?Ore ga/*ø} kaeshimasu.*
(**e**) A: Takizawa can speak French. How about you, Ken?
滝沢はフランス語が話せるけど、健、お前は?
Takizawa wa Furansu-go ga hanase-ru kedo, Ken, o-mae wa?
B: I can too.
{おれ/僕/*わたし/*あたし/*私/*ø}も話せるよ。
*{Ore/Boku/*Watashi/*Atashi/*Watakushi/*ø} mo hanase-ru yo.*

ice n. **[water which has frozen into a solid]**
ko⌈ori 氷
NOTE: The long vowel *oo* is usually written with う added to the preceding *hiragana*, but *koori* is an exception written as こおり, not こうり.
EX. (**a**) The ice has melted.
氷が溶けた。
Koori ga toketa.
(**b**) The river was covered with ice.
川に氷が張っていた。
Kawa ni koori ga hatte ita.

ice cream n.
a⌈isu-kuri⌉imu アイスクリーム •f
EX. (**a**) I don't find Japanese ice cream very tasty.
日本のアイスクリームはあまりおいしくないと思う。
Nihon no aisu-kuriimu wa amari oishikunai to omou.
(**b**) We had ice cream for dessert.
デザートにアイスクリームを食べた。
Dezaato ni aisu-kuriimu o tabeta.

Iceland n.
A⌈isura⌉ndo アイスランド •f

icy adj. **[very cold like ice or covered with ice]**
1. ko⌈ori no yo⌉oni tsu⌈metai 氷のように冷たい adj(*i*). **[very cold like ice]**
EX. She gave me an icy look.
彼女は私を氷のように冷たい目で見た。
Kanojo wa watashi o koori no yooni tsumetai me de mita.
2. ko⌈otta N 凍ったN /⟨Vinf. past of ***kooru*** ① **freeze**/ **[in a state of being frozen]** ((**frozen**)), **ko⌈otte iru** (**N**) 凍っている(**N**) /⟨V***te iru*** **of** ***kooru*** ① **freeze**/
EX. I slipped on the icy road and fell.
{凍った/凍っている}道で滑って、転んだ。
{Kootta/Kootte iru} michi de subette, koronda.

Idaho n.
A⌈ida⌉ho アイダホ •f

idea n. **[a plan/thought/suggestion]**
ka⌈nga⌉e 考え /⟨V***masu*** **of** ***kangaeru*** ② **think, consider**/ **[a product of thinking]** ((**a thought, opinion, view**)), **o⌈moitsuki** 思いつき /⟨V***masu*** **of** ***omoi-tsuku*** ① **come up with a thought**/ **[a thought that comes to one's mind spontaneously and instantly]** ((**suggestion, thought**)), **a⌉idea** アイデア •f **[a thought requiring some originality or insight to produce]**
EX. (**a**) I have a good idea.
いい{考え/アイデア/*思いつき}がある。
*Ii {kangae/aidea/*omoitsuki} ga aru.*
(**b**) It was Bill's idea that we should invite some Japanese students to our Japanese class.
日本語の授業に日本人の学生を呼ぼうというのはビルの{考え/アイデア/思いつき}だった。
Nihon-go no jugyoo ni Nihon-jin no gakusei o yoboo to iu no wa Biru no {kangae/aidea/omoitsuki} datta.
NOTE: *Ii kangae desu.* is not used casually as is its English counterpart "That's a good idea."

ideal n. **[a principle/idea/standard that seems perfect]**
ri⌈soo 理想 •c
EX. (**a**) He was a man with high ideals.

彼は理想の高い人だった。
Kare wa risoo no takai hito datta.
(**b**) She can't find a man that measures up to her lofty ideals.
彼女は自分の高い理想にかなう男性が見つけられない。
Kanojo wa jibun no takai risoo ni kanau dansei ga mitsuke-rarenai.
(**c**) There's a big gap between the ideal and reality.
理想と現実の間には大きなギャップがある。
Risoo to genjitsu no aida ni wa ookina gyappu ga aru.

— adj. **[perfect in every way]**
ri⌈soo no N 理想のN •c [the best possible situation one can imagine], ri⌈soo-tekina 理想的な adj(*na*). **•c [perfect in every way]**

EX. (**a**) My husband is an ideal father.
主人は{理想的な/*理想の}父親です。
*Shujin wa {risoo-tekina/*risoo no} chichi-oya desu.*
(**b**) I haven't met the ideal woman yet.
私はまだ自分の{理想の/*理想的な}女性に巡り合えない。
*Watashi wa mada jibun no {risoo no/ *risoo-tekina} josei ni meguri-ae-nai.*
(**c**) He's an ideal teacher.
彼は教師として{理想的/*理想}です。
*Kare wa kyooshi to-shite {risoo-teki/ *risoo} desu.*

identical adj. **[the same]**
⟨-to⟩ o⌈naji N ⟨〜と⟩同じN

EX. (**a**) This car is identical to the one we rented last month.
この車は先月借りたのと同じです。
Kono kuruma wa sengetsu karita no to onaji desu.
(**b**) My suitcase is identical to yours, isn't it?
僕のスーツケースは君のと同じだね。
Boku no suutsukeesu wa kimi no to onaji da ne.

PHRASE: identical twins *ichiran-sei-soosei-ji* 一卵性双生児 •c

identify vt. **[for s.o. to be able to figure out who/what a person/thing is]**

1. ⟨-ga⟩ wa⌈ka⌉ru ⟨〜が⟩分かる ① [to be able to figure out the nature, meaning, identity, etc., of s.t./s.o./s.a. which already is/should be in one's mind] ⟪understand, be comprehensible, can tell, figure out⟫, ⟨-o⟩ ka⌈kunin-suru ⟨〜を⟩確認する ③ •c [for s.o. to make sure who/what a particular person/thing/animal is or whether s.t. is true] ⟪confirm⟫

EX. (**a**) The dead man has not yet been identified.
死んだ人はまだ身元が{わかって/確認されて}いない。
Shinda hito wa mada mimoto ga {wakatte/kakunin-sarete} inai.
(**b**) She identified the man as the criminal.
彼女はその男を犯人だと{確認した/*わかった}。
*Kanojo wa sono otoko o hannin da to {kakunin-shita/*wakatta}.*

2. ⟨-to⟩ na-⌈no⌉ru ⟨〜と⟩名乗る ① [for s.o. to reveal who he/she is] ⟪identify oneself, introduce oneself⟫

EX. She identified herself as Kyoko, a friend of my older brother.
彼女は兄の友達の京子という者だと名乗った。
Kanojo wa ani no tomodachi no Kyooko to iu mono da to na-notta.

3. ⟨-o⟩ mi-⌈wake⌉ru ⟨〜を⟩見分ける ② [for s.o. to tell people/things/animals apart] ⟪distinguish⟫

EX. To identify the sex of chickens is not easy.
ひよこの雌雄を見分けるのは難しい。
Hiyoko no shiyuu o mi-wakeru no wa muzukashii.

identity n. **[who/what a particular person/thing is]**
mi-⌈moto 身元 [who a particular person is] ⟪one's birth and parentage⟫, a⌈ide⌉ntitii アイデンティティー •f [what one thinks he/she is]

EX. (**a**) The identity of the murdered woman has not yet been established.
殺された女性の{身元/*アイデンティティー}はまだはっきりわかっていない。

I

*Korosa-reta josei no {mi-moto/ *aidentitii} wa mada hakkiri wakatte inai.*
(**b**) Many young people suffer from an identity crisis.
{アイデンティティー/*身元}の危機に悩む若者が多い。
*{Aidentitii/*Mi-moto} no kiki ni nayamu waka-mono ga ooi.*

PHRASE: identity card (=ID) *mibun-shoomei-sho* 身分証明書 •c

idle adj. **[for s.o./a machine to be doing nothing when he/she/it could be working] na⌈ni-mo shi⌈nai⌉ de iru 何もしないでいる /⟨*nani-mo* anything + neg. of *suru* ③ do + *de* + *iru* stay/ [for s.o. to exist without doing anything], a⌈sobu 遊ぶ ① [for s.o./s.a. to amuse oneself instead of working or studying] ⟪play, enjoy oneself⟫**

EX. (**a**) I spent many idle hours at the beach during my teenage years.
十代の時、海で何時間も{何もしないで/遊んで}過ごした
Juu-dai no toki, umi de nan-jikan mo {nani-mo shinai de/asonde} sugoshita.
(**b**) We can't afford to be idle for too long.
私たちは長時間{何もしないで/遊んで}いるわけにはいきません。
Watashi-tachi wa choo-jikan {nani-mo shinai de/asonde} iru wake ni wa ikimasen.
(**c**) All this expensive machinery lay idle during the strike.
ストの間、この高い機械は全部{遊んで/*何もしないで}いた。
*Suto no aida, kono takai kikai wa zenbu {asonde/*nani mo shinai de} ita.*

if conj. **[on condition that or supposing that or whenever; an expression indicating a reported question]**
1. {**Vcond. ba/Vstem reba/adj(*i*). stem kereba/{Vneg./Vstem/adj(*i*). *ku*/{adj(*na*). stem/N}{de/ja}}⌈na⌉kereba} {Vcond.ば/Vstemれば/adj(*i*). stemければ/{Vneg./Vstem/adj(*i*). *ku*/{adj(*na*). stem/N}{で/じゃ}}なければ} [a subordinate conjunction indicating that the preceding clause expresses a hypothetical condition], Sinf. past + ra Sinf. past+ら [a subordinate conjunction indicating that the action/state expressed in the main clause takes place after and is dependent on the action/state expressed by the subordinate clause] ⟪when, after, upon⟫, Sinf. nonpast to Sinf. nonpastと [a subordinate conjunction indicating that the action/state in the main clause follows as an immediate, direct, or natural consequence of the action/state in the subordinate clause] ⟪whenever⟫, Sinf. (no) na⌉ra Sinf.(の)なら [a subordinate conjunction indicating that the speaker accepts the truth of the subordinate clause only tentatively, as if it were a statement made by s.o. else, and based on that states his/her own judgment, decision, or opinion in the main clause] ⟪if it is true that, if it is the case that⟫**

NOTE: *No* in Sinf. *(no) nara* is usually shortened to *n* in speaking.

NOTE: When adj(*na*). or N + cop. occurs in the nonpast affirmative form before *nara*, adj(*na*). appears in its stem form and N occurs without the copula.

EX. (**a**) If you're going to that country, you should get a cholera vaccination before you leave.
あの国へ{行くんなら/*行けば/*行ったら/*行くと}、出かける前にコレラの予防注射をしてもらった方がいい。
*Ano kuni e {iku n nara/*ikeba/*ittara/ *iku to}, dekakeru mae ni korera no yoboo-chuusha o shite-moratta hoo ga ii.*
(**b**) If the doctor has come, I'll go home.
お医者さんが{来たのなら/*来れば/*来たら/*来ると}私は帰ります。
*O-isha-san ga {kita no nara/*kureba/ *kitara/*kuru to} watashi wa kaerimasu.*
(**c**) Let me know if I get a letter.
私に手紙が{来たら/*来れば/*来ると/*来るのなら}知らせてください。
*Watashi ni tegami ga {kitara/*kureba/*

*kuru to/*kuru no nara} shirasete kudasai.*
(**d**) I'll buy it if it's cheap.
{安ければ/安かったら/安いのなら/*安いと}買います。
*{Yasukereba/Yasukattara/Yasui no nara/*Yasui to} kaimasu.*
(**e**) If you go to Kyoto, there are lots of temples you've got to see.
京都へ{行けば/行ったら/行くと/*行くのなら}訪れるべきお寺がたくさんあります。
*Kyooto e {ikeba/ittara/iku to/*iku no nara} otozureru-beki o-tera ga takusan arimasu.*
(**f**) A: I think I'll go to Kyoto next week.
来週京都へ行こうと思っているんですよ。
Raishuu Kyooto e ikoo to omotte iru n desu yo.
B: Oh, really? If you're going to Kyoto, you'll be able to see lots of old temples.
そうですか。京都へ{行けば/行ったら/行くんなら/?行くと}古いお寺がたくさん見られますね。
Soo desu ka. Kyooto e {ikeba/ittara/iku n nara/?iku to} furui o-tera ga takusan mi-raremasu ne.
(**g**) If you're free, could you give me a hand with this job?
暇なら、この仕事を手伝って。
Hima nara, kono shigoto o tetsudatte.

2. Sinf. ka do⌉o ka Sinf.かどうか [an expression indicating a reported question with a yes or no answer] ((**whether**))

NOTE: The present affirmative form of the copula *da* is usually deleted before *ka doo ka.*

EX. (**a**) Do you know if she has a boyfriend?
彼女にボーイフレンドがいるかどうか知っていますか。
Kanojo ni booi-furendo ga iru ka doo ka shitte imasu ka.
(**b**) I don't remember if I paid the membership fee or not.
会費を払ったかどうか覚えていません。
Kaihi o haratta ka doo ka oboete imasen.
(**c**) I don't know if Mr. Yamada is free tomorrow or not.
山田さんがあした暇かどうか知りません。
Yamada-san ga ashita hima ka doo ka shirimasen.

PHRASE: even if {{V/adj./cop.}*te*/{Vneg./Vstem/adj(*i*). *ku*/{adj(*na*). stem/N}{*de/ja*} *nakute*}}*mo* {{V/adj./cop.}*te*/{Vneg./Vstem/adj(*i*). *ku*/{adj(*na*). stem/N}{で/じゃ}なくて}}も

EX. (**a**) I'll buy it even if it's expensive.
高くても、買います。
Takakute mo, kaimasu.
(**b**) I'm afraid he won't come even if you invite him.
彼は招待しても来ないんじゃないかと思います。
Kare wa shootai-shite mo konai n janai ka to omoimasu.
(**c**) You should watch your health even if you're healthy.
元気でも体に気をつけたほうがいいですよ。
Genkide mo karada ni ki-o-tsuketa hoo ga ii desu yo.

ignorant adj. **[knowing little or nothing (about s.t.)]**
na⌈ni-mo shiranai N 何も知らないN /⟨*nani mo* anything + neg. of *shiru* ① know/ **[for s.o. to know nothing], mu⌉china 無知な** adj(*na*). •c **[having no knowledge of s.t. (to one's discredit)]**

EX. (**a**) I'm totally ignorant when it comes to computers.
私はコンピューターに関しては{何も知りません/無知です}。
Watashi wa konpyuutaa ni-kanshite wa {nani-mo shirimasen/muchi desu}.
(**b**) I'm ignorant of the reasons for his anger.
彼がどうして怒ったのか私は{何も知りません/*無知です}。
*Kare ga dooshite okotta no ka watashi wa {nani-mo shirimasen/*muchi desu}.*

ignore vt. **[for s.o. to take no notice of s.o./s.t.]**
⟨-o⟩ mu⌉shi-suru ⟨〜を⟩無視する ③ •c

I

EX. (**a**) My opinion was completely ignored.
私の意見は完全に無視された。
Watashi no iken wa kanzenni mushi-sareta.
(**b**) He ignored his doctor's advice and continued to smoke.
彼は医者の忠告を無視して、たばこを吸い続けた。
Kare wa isha no chuukoku o mushi-shite, tabako o sui-tsuzuketa.

ill adj. **[in bad health]**
byo⌈oki no N 病気のN **•c [for s.o./s.a. to be not in good health or pertaining to illness]** ((**sick**))

EX. She fell ill with worry.
彼女は心配のあまり病気になった。
Kanojo wa shinpai no amari byooki ni natta.

Illinois n.
I⌈rinoi イリノイ

illness n. **[a state/instance of the body or mind being in bad health]**
byo⌈oki 病気 **•c [a state/instance of not being in good health]** ((**disease**))

EX. (**a**) Cancer is a very serious illness.
がんは非常に恐ろしい病気だ。
Gan wa hijooni osoroshii byooki da.
(**b**) He died from an unknown illness.
彼は原因不明の病気で死んだ。
Kare wa gen'in-fumei no byooki de shinda.

I

illusion n. **[s.t. one thinks or sees which is not actual or true]**
sa⌈kkaku 錯覚 **•c** ((**imagination**))

EX. Magician makes use of an optical illusion.
魔術師は目の錯覚を利用する。
Majutsu-shi wa me no sakkaku o riyoo-suru.

illustrate vt. **[to make the meaning of s.t. clearer by giving related examples/pictures or for s.o. to supplement a written text with related pictures or drawings]**
1. 〈-o〉 **a⌈rawa⌉su** 〈～を〉あらわす ① **[to cause s.t. to become exposed/visible/recognizable]** ((**exemplify, indicate, point**)), **re⌉i o agete se⌈tsumei-suru** 例を挙げて説明する ③ **[for s.o. to explain by giving related examples]**
㊅ "express s.t."▷表わす, "cause s.t. to appear"▷現わす, "write (a book)"▷著わす

EX. (**a**) That episode illustrates how selfish he is.
あの逸話は彼がいかにわがままであるかを{表わして/*例を挙げて説明して}いる。
*Ano itsuwa wa kare ga ikani wagamama de aru ka o {arawashite/ *rei o agete setsumei-shite} iru.*
(**b**) He tried to illustrate the complex mathematical theorem with concrete examples.
彼は複雑な数学の定理を{具体的な例を挙げて説明しよう/*具体的に表わそう}とした。
*Kare wa fukuzatsuna suugaku no teiri o {gutai-tekina rei o agete setsumei-shiyoo/*gutai-tekini arawasoo} to shita.*

2. sa⌈shi⌉e o ka⌉ku 挿絵をかく ① **[for s.o. to put in pictures to show s.t.]**

EX. He asked his artist friend to illustrate the textbook he wrote.
彼は自分の書いた教科書に挿絵をかいてくれるように画家の友人に頼んだ。
Kare wa jibun no kaita kyooka-sho ni sashie o kaite kureru yooni gaka no yuujin ni tanonda.

illustration n. **[an example or picture which explains/shows/helps to prove s.t.]**
1. re⌉i 例 **•c [a thing similar to s.t. that has happened before or a specific instance used to make clear a more general idea or to support the correctness of one's claim]**

EX. This is a typical illustration of his stinginess.
彼のけちさ加減を示す典型的な例だ。
Kare no kechi-sa-kagen o shimesu tenkei-tekina rei da.

2. sa⌈shi⌉e 挿絵 **[a picture to go with the printed text of a book, magazine, etc.]**

EX. This book has wonderful illustrations.
この本は挿絵がすばらしい。
Kono hon wa sashie ga subarashii.

image n. **[a picture/idea formed in the mind]**
i⌈nshoo 印象 **•c [a picture/effect that is produced in one's mind by a person, event,**

experience, etc.] ((**impression**)), **i⌈me⌉eji イメージ •f [a picture/idea formed in the mind]**

EX. (**a**) That political party is trying to sell an image of being clean.
あの政党は清潔という{イメージ/*印象}を売ろうとしている。
*Ano seitoo wa seiketsu to iu {imeeji/ *inshoo} o uroo to shite iru.*
(**b**) How can we improve our image?
どうすれば{イメージ/*印象}アップができるでしょうか。
*Doo sureba {imeeji/*inshoo}-appu ga dekiru deshoo ka.*
(**c**) What kind of image do you have of Tokyo?
東京についてどんな{印象/イメージ}をお持ちですか。
Tookyoo ni-tsuite donna {inshoo/imeeji} o o-mochi desu ka.

imaginary adj. **[existing only in s.o.'s mind and not real]**
so⌈ozoo-joo no N 想像上のN •c [existing only in s.o.'s mind and not real], ka⌈kuu no N 架空のN •c [fabricated in s.o.'s mind and not real] ((**fictitious**))

EX. (**a**) All the characters in this drama are imaginary.
このドラマに登場するのはみんな{架空/?想像上}の人物です。
*Kono dorama ni toojoo-suru no wa minna {kakuu/*soozoo-joo} no jinbutsu desu.*
(**b**) Godzilla is an imaginary creature.
ゴジラは{想像上/架空}の生き物だ。
Gojira wa {soozoo-joo/kakuu} no iki-mono da.

imagination n. **[the ability to imagine or s.t. which is imagined]**
1. so⌈ozo⌉o-ryoku 想像力 •c [the ability to imagine]

EX. I can't write a novel because I don't have enough imagination.
私は想像力が足りないから、小説は書けません。
Watashi wa soozoo-ryoku ga tarinai kara, shoosetsu wa kake-masen.

2. so⌈ozoo 想像 •c [s.t. which is imagined]

EX. I'll leave it to the imagination of the reader.
読者の想像に任せます。
Dokusha no soozoo ni makasemasu.

imaginative adj. **[showing good use of the imagination or good at forming new ideas in one's mind]**
1. so⌈ozo⌉o-ryoku ni to⌉nda N 想像力に富んだN /⟨*soozoo-ryoku* imagination + prt. *ni* + Vinf. past of *tomu* ① be rich/ [that which is rich in the use of the imagination], so⌈ozo⌉o-ryoku ni to⌉nde iru (N) 想像力に富んでいる(N) /⟨*soozoo-ryoku* imagination + prt. *ni* + V*te iru* of *tomu* ① be rich/

EX. We're looking for someone highly imaginative to develop software for new games.
新しいゲームソフトの開発には想像力に{富んだ/富んでいる}人間が必要だ。
Atarashii geemu-sofuto no kaihatsu ni wa soozoo ryoku ni {tonda/tonde iru} ningen ga hitsuyoo da.

2. so⌉ozo⌉o-ryoku no yu⌉takana 想像力の豊かな adj(*na*). **[rich in one's ability to imagine]**

EX. Children are more imaginative than adults.
子供の方が大人より想像力が豊かだ。
Kodomo no hoo ga otona yori soozoo-ryoku ga yutaka da.

imagine vt. **[for s.o. to form a picture/idea of s.o./s.t./s.a. in one's mind]**
⟨-o⟩ so⌈ozoo-suru ⟨〜を⟩想像する ③ •c [for s.o. to form an image of s.t./s.o./s.a. one has never encountered before] ((**suppose, conjecture, envision**))

EX. (**a**) I can't imagine life without you.
君のいない生活など想像できない。
Kimi no inai seikatsu nado soozoo-dekinai.
(**b**) Can you imagine him skiing?
彼がスキーをしているところなんて想像できますか。
Kare ga sukii o shite iru tokoro nante soozoo-dekimasu ka.
(**c**) You can imagine how pleased I was

when I heard the news.
その知らせを聞いたとき私がどんなに嬉しかったか想像できるでしょう。
Sono shirase o kiita toki watashi ga donnani ureshikatta ka soozoo-dekiru deshoo.
(**d**) Try to imagine yourself singing on stage at Carnegie Hall.
自分がカーネギーホールのステージで歌っているところを想像してごらんなさい。
Jibun ga Kaanegii Hooru no suteeji de utatte iru tokoro o soozoo-shite gorannasai.

imitate vt. **[for s.o./s.a. to try to act, speak, or behave just as another]**
⟨-o⟩ ma⸢neru ⟨〜を⟩まねる ② **⟪mimic⟫**, **⟨-no⟩ ma⸢ne o suru** ⟨〜の⟩まねをする ③ **⟪mimic⟫**

EX. (**a**) He's good at imitating the way the Prime Minister talks.
彼は首相の話し方{をまねる/のまねをする}のがうまい。
Kare wa shushoo no hanashi-kata {o maneru/no mane o suru} no ga umai.
(**b**) Parrots can imitate human speech.
おうむは人間の話し方{をまねる/のまねをする}ことができる。
Oomu wa ningen no hanashi-kata {o maneru/no mane o suru} koto ga dekiru.
(**c**) Children tend to imitate adults.
子供は大人{をまねる/のまねをする}ものだ。
Kodomo wa otona {o maneru/no mane o suru} mono da.

imitation n. **[the act of trying to act, speak, or behave just as another or a copy of the real thing]**
1. ma⸢ne まね **[an act/instance of trying to act, speak, or behave just as another]**

EX. The boy does a good imitation of the President.
その男の子は大統領のまねがうまい。
Sono otoko-no-ko wa daitooryoo no mane ga umai.

2. mo⸢zoo-hin 模造品 **•c [a copy of the real thing] ⟪fake⟫, i⸢mite⸣eshon** イミテーション **•f**

EX. This is not a real diamond; it's an imitation.
これは本物のダイヤモンドではありません。{模造品/イミテーション}です。
Kore wa hon-mono no daiyamondo dewaarimasen. {Mozoo-hin/Imiteeshon} desu.

immediate adj. **[done or happening at once/without delay or nearest in time/space/degree]**
1. su⸣gu すぐ adv. **[at once/without delay] ⟪at once, without delay, instantly⟫, ta⸣dachini** 直ちに adv. **[without any intervening interval of time ⟨fml⟩]**

EX. (**a**) They called for an immediate end to that country's aggression.
その国が侵略行為を{直ちに/?すぐ}停止するように要請した。
Sono kuni ga shinryaku-kooi o {tadachini/?sugu} teishi-suru yooni yoosei-shita.
(**b**) My boss is the type of person who takes immediate action when necessary.
僕の上司は必要な時には{すぐ/直ちに}行動を起こすタイプなんだ。
Boku no jooshi wa hitsuyoona toki ni wa {sugu/tadachini} koodoo o okosu taipu na n da.

2. cho⸢kuzoku no N 直属のN **•c [for s.o. to be under the direct control of s.o. else/an institution], su⸣gu so⸣ba no N** すぐそばのN **[nearest in space]**

EX. (**a**) Mr. Tanaka is my immediate superior.
田中さんは私の{直属/*すぐそば}の上司です。
*Tanaka-san wa watashi no {chokuzoku/*sugu soba} no jooshi desu.*
(**b**) There are no grocery stores in our immediate neighborhood.
うちの{すぐそば/*直属}には食料品店はありません。
*Uchi no {sugu soba/*chokuzoku} ni wa shokuryoo-hin-ten wa arimasen.*

immediately adv. **[without anything intervening between two events in time or two things/people/animals in space]**
su⸣gu すぐ

EX. (**a**) Come to my office immediately, please.
すぐ私のオフィスに来てください。
Sugu watashi no ofisu ni kite kudasai.
(**b**) I'm parked immediately in front of the police station.
私は警察署のすぐ前に駐車した。
Watashi wa keisatsu-sho no sugu mae ni chuusha-shita.
(**c**) I left immediately after the class was over.
授業が終わってからすぐ出ました。
Jugyoo ga owatte kara sugu demashita.

immense adj. **[extremely large in size/degree]**
ha⸢kari-shire⸣-nai 計り知れない adj(*i*). **[so large in degree that it cannot be measured]**

EX. He's made immense contributions to the economic development of this country.
彼はこの国の経済発展に計り知れない貢献をしてきた。
Kare wa kono kuni no keizai-hatten ni hakari-shire-nai kooken o shite kita.

immigrant n. **[s.o. coming into a country from abroad to live permanently]**
i⸢min 移民 **•c [s.o. coming into a country from abroad to live permanently or s.o. leaving one's own country to live permanently in another country or the process of entering another country to live permanently] ⟪emigrant, immigration, emigration⟫**

EX. (**a**) My father is an immigrant from Japan.
父は日本からの移民です。
Chichi wa Nihon kara no imin desu.
(**b**) Does an immigrant have the right to vote in this country?
この国では移民は選挙権がありますか。
Kono kuni de wa imin wa senkyo-ken ga arimasu ka.

immigration n. **[the process of entering another country to live permanently]**
i⸢min 移民 **•c [s.o. coming into a country from abroad to live permanently or s.o. leaving one's own country to live permanently in another country or the process of entering another country to live permanently]**

PHRASE: Immigration Office *nyuukoku-kanri-jimu-sho* 入国管理事務所 **•c**

impact n. **[the force of one object hitting another ⟪fig. "strong/powerful influence caused/produced by an idea, invention, event, etc."⟫]**
sho⸢ogeki 衝撃 **•c ⟪shock, percussion⟫, i⸣npakuto** インパクト **•f**

EX. (**a**) The computer has made a great impact on modern life.
コンピューターは現代生活に大きな{衝撃/インパクト}を与えた。
Konpyuutaa wa gendai-seikatsu ni ookina {shoogeki/inpakuto} o ataeta.
(**b**) He was thrown out of the car upon impact.
彼は衝突の{衝撃/*インパクト}で車の外に投げ出された。
*Kare wa shoototsu no {shoogeki/*inpakuto} de kuruma no soto ni nage-dasa-reta.*
(**c**) His arrest will have a great impact on the financial world.
彼の逮捕は財界に大きな{衝撃/??インパクト}を与えることだろう。
Kare no taiho wa zaikai ni ookina {shoogeki/??inpakuto} o ataeru koto daroo.

impatient adj. **[unable or unwilling to deal calmly with delay, annoyance, or hardship]**
(⟨-ni⟩) **i⸣ra-ira-suru** (⟨〜に⟩)いらいらする ③ **[for s.o./s.a. to be irritated], se⸢kkachina** せっかちな adj(*na*). **[unable or unwilling by nature to accept delay or slowness of action], ki ⸢ga mijika⸣i** 気が短い adj(*i*). **⟪short-tempered⟫**

EX. (**a**) Don't be so impatient when you're teaching your family how to drive.
家族に運転を教えるとき、そんなに{いらいらして/せっかちになって/*気が短くて}はいけません。
*Kazoku ni unten o oshieru toki, sonnani {ira-ira-shite/sekkachini natte/*ki ga mijikakute} wa ikemasen.*
(**b**) Our teacher looked impatient at our being so unprepared.
先生は私たちがあまりにも予習ができ

ていなかったので、{いらいらしている/*せっかちな/*気が短い}ようだった。
*Sensei wa watashi-tachi ga amari ni mo yoshuu ga dekite inakatta node, {ira-ira-shite iru/*sekkachina/*ki ga mijikai} yoo datta.*
(**c**) He is a very impatient teacher.
彼はとても{せっかちな/気が短い/*いらいらしている}先生です。
*Kare wa totemo {sekkachina/ki ga mijikai/*ira-ira-shite iru} sensei desu.*

imply vt. **[for s.o./s.t. to suggest s.t. without stating it directly]**
1. 〈-wa〉 Sinf. to-iu ko⌈to⌉ da 〈～は〉Sinf.ということだ [for a situation or statement to mean that…]
EX. Their absence from the meeting seems to imply a lack of interest in this matter.
彼らが会議に出ないということはこの問題に関心がないということのようだ。
Kare-ra ga kaigi ni denai to-iu koto wa kono mondai ni kanshin ga nai to iu koto no yooda.
2. Sinf. to i⌈u Sinf.と言う ① [for s.o. to express s.t. verbally] ⟪**tell, speak, talk, state, express**⟫
EX. Are you implying that I am wrong?
私が間違っていると言うんですか。
Watashi ga machigatte iru to iu n desu ka.

impolite adj. **[not showing good manners]**
shi⌈tsu⌉reina 失礼な adj(*na*). **•c [for s.o./one's words/one's behavior to lack in politeness]** ⟪**rude, discourteous, impudent**⟫
EX. (**a**) It's impolite to be late for class.
授業に遅れるのは失礼だ。
Jugyoo ni okureru no wa shitsurei da.
(**b**) Chewing gum in class is considered impolite in Japan.
日本では授業中にガムをかむのは失礼だとされている。
Nihon de wa jugyoo-chuu ni gamu o kamu no wa shitsurei da to sarete iru.

import vt. **[to bring in s.t. from another place, esp. another country]**
〈-o〉 yu⌈nyuu-suru 〈～を〉輸入する ③ •c [to bring in s.t. from another country for sale or use]
EX. (**a**) Japan imports a large amount of beef from the United States.
日本はアメリカから牛肉を大量に輸入している。
Nihon wa Amerika kara gyuuniku o tairyoo ni yunyuu-shite iru.
(**b**) We'd like to import wine from Australia.
オーストラリアからワインを輸入したいと思っています。
Oosutoraria kara wain o yunyuu-shitai to omotte imasu.
— n. **[the act of importing or s.t. brought into a country from abroad]**
1. yu⌈nyuu 輸入 •c [the act of importing]
EX. (**a**) Food imports from abroad are increasing.
外国からの食料品の輸入が増えている。
Gaikoku kara no shokuryoo-hin no yunyuu ga fuete iru.
(**b**) The import of some animals is prohibited.
輸入の禁じられている動物がある。
Yunyuu no kinji-rarete iru doobutsu ga aru.
2. yu⌈nyuu-hin 輸入品 •c [s.t. imported from another country]
EX. That store sells imports from Europe.
あの店はヨーロッパからの輸入品を売っている。
Ano mise wa Yooroppa kara no yunyuu-hin o utte iru.

importance n. **[the quality of having great value/effect/influence]**
ju⌈uyoo-sei 重要性 •c [the quality of being indispensable and irreplaceable] ⟪**seriousness**⟫
EX. (**a**) He doesn't understand the importance of this recent series of events.
彼にはごく最近の一連の事件の重要性が分かっていない。
Kare ni wa goku saikin no ichiren no jiken no juuyoo-sei ga wakatte inai.
(**b**) I'd like to stress the importance of foreign language education in a college curriculum.

私は大学のカリキュラムにおける外国語教育の重要性を強調したい。
Watashi wa daigaku no karikyuramu ni-okeru gaikoku-go-kyooiku no juuyoo-sei o kyoochoo-shitai.

PHRASE: attach importance to ⟨-o⟩ *juuyoo-shi-suru* ⟨〜を⟩重要視する ③ •c

important adj. **[having great value/effect/influence]**

da⌈ijina 大事な adj(*na*). •c **[of great consequence]** **⟪precious, valuable, dear⟫**, **ta⌈isetsuna** 大切な adj(*na*). •c **⟪precious, significant, valued, dear⟫**, **ju⌈uyoona** 重要な adj(*na*). •c **[having great effect/influence]** **⟪essential, momentous⟫**

NOTE: It is better to use *taisetsuna* or *daijina* in referring to matters having some personal importance.

EX. (**a**) There's an important meeting tomorrow.
あした{大事な/大切な/重要な}会議があります。
Ashita {daijina/taisetsuna/juuyoona} kaigi ga arimasu.
(**b**) She's a very important person to me.
彼女は私にとってとても{大事な/大切な/*重要な}人です。
*Kanojo wa watashi ni-totte totemo {daijina/taisetsuna/*juuyoona} hito desu.*
(**c**) He's in an important government position.
彼は政府の{重要な/*大事な/*大切な}地位にいる。
*Kare wa seifu no {juuyoona/*daijina/*taisetsuna} chii ni iru.*
(**d**) It's important to get plenty of sleep to stay healthy.
健康でいるには睡眠を十分とることが{大事/大切/重要}です。
Kenkoo de iru ni wa suimin o juubun toru koto ga {daiji/taisetsu/juuyoo} desu.

impossible adj. **[not able to happen, exist, or be done]**

1. **fu-⌈ka⌉noona** 不可能な adj(*na*). •c **[not able to be done or brought about]**

EX. (**a**) It's impossible to sell this kind of junk.
こんながらくたを売るのは不可能です。
Konna garakuta o uru no wa fu-kanoo desu.
(**b**) Don't make impossible demands of your underlings.
部下に不可能な要求をしないでください。
Buka ni fu-kanoona yookyuu o shinaide kudasai.

2. **a⌈ri-e⌉nai** あり得ない /⟨neg. of *arieru* **possible**/ **[not able to happen or exist]**

EX. It would be impossible for my father ever to admit he's wrong.
父が自分の過ちを認めるなんてあり得ません。
Chichi ga jibun no ayamachi o mitomeru nante ari-emasen.

impress vt. **[to influence one deeply, especially so as to create a feeling of admiration]**

⟨**-ni**⟩ **ka⌈nshin-suru** ⟨〜に⟩感心する ③ •c **[for s.o. to feel a sense of admiration for s.t./s.o./s.a.]** **⟪be impressed, be struck with admiration⟫**

EX. (**a**) I was impressed by his knowledge of kanji.
私は彼が漢字をよく知っているのに感心した。
Watashi wa kare ga kanji o yoku shitte iru no ni kanshin-shita.
(**b**) I read his new book but it didn't impress me much.
彼の新しい本を読んだけど、あまり感心しなかった。
Kare no atarashii hon o yonda kedo, amari kanshin-shinakatta.

impression n. **[an image/effect that is produced in the mind by s.o./s.t./s.a.]**

i⌈nshoo 印象 •c

EX. (**a**) What were your first impressions of Japan?
日本の第一印象はどうでしたか。
Nihon no dai-ichi-inshoo wa doo deshita ka.
(**b**) My impression of Japanese students is

that they are not straightforward in expressing their own opinions.
日本の学生ははっきり自分の意見を言わないというのが私の印象です。
Nihon no gakusei wa hakkiri jibun no iken o iwanai to iu no ga watashi no inshoo desu.
(**c**) I had the impression that he was lying.
私は彼がうそをついているような印象を受けた。
Watashi wa kare ga uso o tsuite iru yoona inshoo o uketa.

impressive adj. **[causing admiration or making a deep impression]**
1. fu⌈ka⌉i ka⌈nmei o a⌈taeru (N) 深い感銘を与える(N) ② [making a deep impression], mi⌉gotona 見事な adj(*na*). **[causing admiration due to being visually impressive or skillfully accumplished] ((splendid, admirable))**

EX. It was an impressive speech.
{深い感銘を与える/見事な}スピーチだった。
{Fukai kanmei o ataeru/Migotona} supiichi datta.

2. i⌈nshoo-tekina 印象的な adj(*na*). **•c [which remains clearly in one's mind]**

EX. What was most impressive about the cathedral was the beautiful artwork on its high ceiling.
大聖堂で最も印象的なのはその高い天井にある美しい絵画だった。
Dai-seidoo de mottomo inshoo-tekina no wa sono takai tenjoo ni aru utsukushii kaiga datta.

improve vt. **[to make s.t. better]**
⟨-o⟩ ka⌈iryoo-suru ⟨～を⟩改良する ③ •c [for s.o. to make the quality of s.t. better, such as a machine, soil, a plant or animal variety, etc.] ((reform, better)), ⟨-o⟩ ka⌈izen-suru ⟨～を⟩改善する ③ •c [for s.o. to make living/working conditions better] ((better, ameliorate)), ⟨-o⟩ yo⌉ku suru ⟨～を⟩良くする /⟨adj(*i*). *ku* of *ii* good + *suru* ③ make/ ③ [to make s.t. better]

EX. (**a**) We'll go on strike unless management improves our working conditions.
もし経営者側が労働条件を{改善/良く/*改良}してくれなければ、ストをするつもりだ。
*Moshi keiei-sha-gawa ga roodoo-jooken o {kaizen-/yoku/*kairyoo-} shite kurenakereba, suto o suru tsumori da.*
(**b**) We've got to get computer screens improved for the sake of the health of our office workers.
事務職員の健康のためにもコンピューターの画面を{改良/良く/*改善}してもらわなければ困る。
*Jimu-shokuin no kenkoo no tame ni mo konpyuutaa no gamen o {kairyoo-/yoku/*kaizen-} shite morawanakereba komaru.*

— vi. **[for s.t. to become better]**
yo⌉ku naru 良くなる /⟨adj(*i*). *ku* of *ii* good + *naru* ① become/ ① [to become better] ((recover)), jo⌈ozu⌉ni naru 上手になる /⟨adj(*na*). *ni* of *joozuna* skillful + *naru* ① become/ ① [for s.o./s.a. to come to have better skills]

EX. (**a**) His English pronunciation has greatly improved.
彼の英語の発音は大分{良く/*上手に}なった。
*Kare no eigo no hatsuon wa daibu {yoku/*joozuni} natta.*
(**b**) He has greatly improved in his English pronunciation.
彼は英語の発音が非常に{上手に/良く}なった。
Kare wa eigo no hatsuon ga hijooni {joozuni/yoku} natta.

NOTE: The literal translation of example (b) would be "speaking of him, the English pronunciation has improved." *Joozuna* requires a human subject as shown in the ungrammaticality of example (**a**).

(**c**) Our living conditions have greatly improved.
私たちの生活はずっと{良く/*上手に}なった。
Watashi-tachi no seikatsu wa zutto

| {yoku/*joozuni} natta.

improvement n. **[the act of improving or state of being improved]**
ka⌈iryoo 改良 •c [making the quality of s.t. better, such as a machine, soil, a plant or animal variety, etc.] ⟪**reform**⟫, **ka⌈izen 改善 •c [making living/working conditions better]** ⟪**betterment, amelioration**⟫, **shi⌉npo 進歩 •c [moving ahead in knowledge, ability, social conditions, etc.]** ⟪**progress, advancement**⟫, **jo⌈otatsu 上達 •c [becoming better in a skill]** ⟪**progress, advancement**⟫

EX. (**a**) I see no signs of improvement in his Japanese.
彼の日本語には全然{上達/進歩/*改良/*改善}の跡が見られない。
*Kare no Nihon-go ni wa zen-zen {jootatsu/shinpo/*kairyoo/*kaizen} no ato ga mi-rarenai.*
(**b**) There's still plenty of room for improvement in the design of this word processor.
このワープロの設計にはまだ大いに{改良/*改善/*上達/*進歩}の余地がある。
*Kono waapuro no sekkei ni wa mada ooini {kairyoo/*kaizen/*jootatsu/*shinpo} no yochi ga aru.*
(**c**) She's working hard for the improvement of working conditions in this country.
彼女はこの国の労働条件の{改善/*改良/*上達/*進歩}に力を入れている。
*Kanojo wa kono kuni no roodoo-jooken no {kaizen/*kairyoo/*jootatsu/*shinpo} ni chikara o irete iru.*

impulse n. **[a sudden desire to do s.t.]**
sho⌈odoo 衝動 •c ⟪**urge**⟫

EX. (**a**) He felt a sudden impulse to run away from home.
彼は突然家出したいという衝動に駆られた。
Kare wa totsuzen iede-shi-tai to iu shoodoo ni kara-reta.
(**b**) I had to resist the impulse to give him a slap on the cheek.
私は彼のほおに平手打ちをくらわしてやりたいという衝動を抑えなければならなかった。
Watashi wa kare no hoo ni hirate-uchi o kurawashite yari-tai to iu shoodoo o osaenakereba naranaktta.

PHRASE: on impulse *shoodoo-tekini* 衝動的に •c

EX. I bought an expensive Italian-made handbag on impulse.
私は衝動的にイタリア製の高いバッグを買ってしまった。
Watashi wa shoodoo-tekini Itaria-sei no takai baggu o katte shimatta.

PHRASE: impulse buying *shoodoo-gai* 衝動買い

in prep. **[to/at a place which is surrounded by some space or boundary; at a certain time; within a certain period of time; by means of s.t.]**
1. ((**-no**) **na⌉ka**) {**ni/de/o**} ((〜の)中){に/で/を} n.+prt. **[inside of]** ⟪**inside**⟫

NOTE: When a location can simply be considered as a point in space and the fact that it is "inside" something is either obvious or does not need to be emphasized, then *naka* can be omitted and the particle following it can be used alone, appropriately to the predicate.

EX. (**a**) I put the kitten in a box.
子猫を箱(の中)に入れた。
Ko-neko o hako (no naka) ni ireta.
(**b**) Please don't smoke in this room.
この部屋の中でたばこを吸わないでください。
Kono heya no naka de tabako o suwanaide kudasai.
(**c**) I live in a suburb of Tokyo.
私は東京の郊外に住んでいます。
Watashi wa Tookyoo no koogai ni sunde imasu.
(**d**) The children were running around in the garden.
子供たちは庭を走り回っていた。
Kodomo-tachi wa niwa o hashiri-mawatte ita.
(**e**) I wrote a letter in the library.
図書館で手紙を書いた。
Tosho-kan de tegami o kaita.
(**f**) There is an article on Japan in today's paper.

今日の新聞に日本に関する記事が載っている。
Kyoo no shinbun ni Nihon ni kansuru kiji ga notte iru.

2. ni に prt. **[indicating a spatial/temporal point of contact, often construed as a location where s.t./s.o./s.a. exists, a goal, or an indirect object]**

EX. (**a**) I graduated from senior high school in March of this year.
私は今年、三月に高校を卒業した。
Watashi wa kotoshi, san-gatsu ni kookoo o sotsugyoo-shita.
(**b**) I was born in 1970.
私は1970年に生まれました。
Watashi wa sen-kyuu-hyaku-nana-juu-nen ni umaremashita.

PHRASE: in the morning *asa* 朝, in the afternoon *gogo* 午後 •c

EX. I am usually in my office in the afternoon.
私はたいてい午後オフィスにいます。
Watashi wa taitei gogo ofisu ni imasu.

3. de で prt. **[within the period of time of]**

EX. (**a**) We can get to the station in ten minutes.
駅まで十分で行けますよ。
Eki made jip-pun de ike-masu yo.
(**b**) He learned 500 words in two weeks.
彼は二週間で単語を五百覚えた。
Kare wa ni-shuukan de tango o go-hyaku oboeta.

4. de で prt. **[using s.t.]** ((**by, with**))

EX. (**a**) Please speak in Japanese.
日本語で話してください。
Nihon-go de hanashite kudasai.
(**b**) She sang in a loud voice.
彼女は大きい声で歌を歌った。
Kanojo wa ookii koe de uta o utatta.

inch n. **[a unit for measuring length]**
i˥nchi インチ **•f**

EX. This mattress is 5 feet 8 inches long.
このマットレスは長さが五フィート八インチです。
Kono mattoresu wa naga-sa ga go-fiito hachi-inchi desu.

incident n. **[an event/happening, usually one that is not very important]**
de˥ki˥-goto 出来事 **[an instance of s.t. occurring in the world of human affairs]** ((**occurrence, happening, event**)),
ha˥puningu ハプニング **•f [an event that happens quite unexpectedly and that is not very important]**

EX. (**a**) She told us about some of the amusing incidents that occurred during her trip.
彼女は旅行中の楽しい{出来事/ハプニング}について話してくれた。
Kanojo wa ryokoo-chuu no tanoshii {deki-goto/hapuningu} ni-tsuite hanashite kureta.
(**b**) That kind of incident is not at all unusual.
そのようなことは何も変わった{出来事/??ハプニング}ではない。
Sono yoona koto wa nani-mo kawatta {deki-goto/??hapuningu} dewanai.

include vt. **[to contain/put in s.t./s.o./s.a. as a part of the whole]**

1. ⟨-ni⟩ ha˥iru ⟨〜に⟩入る ① **[to go into some place** ((**fig. "join"**))**]** ((**enter**)) ↔ **{⟨-kara⟩/⟨-o⟩} deru** {⟨〜から⟩/⟨〜を⟩}出る ②

EX. (**a**) My job doesn't include serving tea to the male staff.
私の仕事には男性社員にお茶を出すことは入っていない。
Watashi no shigoto ni wa dansei-shain ni o-cha o dasu koto wa haitte inai.
(**b**) Does this bill include sales tax?
この請求書には消費税が入っていますか。
Kono seikyuu-sho ni wa shoohi-zei ga haitte imasu ka.

2. ⟨-o⟩ ⟨-ni⟩ i˥reru ⟨〜を⟩⟨〜に⟩入れる ② **[for s.o./s.a. to cause s.t./s.o./s.a. to move into an enclosed space]** ((**insert, pour, join**)) ↔ **⟨-o⟩ dasu** ⟨〜を⟩出す ①

EX. (**a**) Could you include me in your study group?
勉強会に私も入れてもらえますか。
Benkyoo-kai ni watashi mo irete morae-masu ka.
(**b**) The students asked the teacher not to include the vocabulary from the previous lesson in the test.

学生は前の課の単語を試験に入れないでほしいと先生に頼んだ
Gakusei wa mae no ka no tango o shiken ni irenaide hoshii to sensei ni tanonda.

income n. **[the amount of money which one receives as salary, interest from investments, etc.]**
shu⌈unyuu 収入 •c ((**revenue, earnings**)) ↔ **shishutsu 支出 •c; sho⌈toku 所得 •c [money/goods one receives]** ((**earnings, profits**))

EX. (**a**) Half of our income goes to pay the mortgage.
{収入/所得}の半分が住宅ローンの支払いに回っている。
{Shuunyuu/Shotoku} no hanbun ga juutaku-roon no shiharai ni mawatte iru.
(**b**) My older brother doesn't have any fixed income.
兄は決まった{収入/所得}がない。
Ani wa kimatta {shuunyuu/shotoku} ga nai.
(**c**) His income is relatively large for his age.
彼は年齢の割に{収入/所得}が多い。
Kare wa nenrei no warini {shuunyuu/shotoku} ga ooi.

PHRASE: income tax *shotoku-zei* 所得税 •c, annual income *nenshuu* 年収 •c

incomplete adj. **[not complete]**
mi-⌈ka⌉nsei no N 未完成のN •c [not completed]

EX. He left many incomplete works after his death.
彼は死後に未完成の作品をたくさん残した。
Kare wa shigo ni mi-kansei no sakuhin o takusan nokoshita.

inconvenient adj. **[causing difficulty/annoyance]**
fu⌉benna 不便な adj(*na*). **•c [for s.t. to cause difficulty]** ↔ **benrina 便利な** adj(*na*). **•c; tsu⌈goo ga waru⌉i 都合が悪い** adj(*i*). **[for s.t. not to suit one's circumstances]** ↔ **tsugoo ga ii 都合がいい** adj(*i*).

EX. (**a**) It's incovenient not to have a car in Los Angeles.
ロサンゼルスで車がないのは{不便だ/*都合が悪い}。
*Rosanzerusu de kuruma ga nai no wa {fuben da/*tsugoo ga warui}.*
(**b**) Is our meeting going to be on Wednesdays? That's an inconvenient day for me.
水曜日にミーティングをするんですか。その日は私には{都合が悪い/*不便な}んですが。
*Suiyoo-bi ni miitingu o suru n desu ka. Sono hi wa watashi ni wa {tsugoo ga warui/*fubenna} n desu ga.*
(**c**) The place where I live now is quiet but inconvenient for getting to work.
今住んでいる所は静かですが、通勤には{不便な/*都合が悪い}んです。
*Ima sunde iru tokoro wa shizuka desu ga, tsuukin ni wa {fubenna/*tsugoo ga warui} n desu.*

incorrect adj. **[not correct]**
ma⌈chiga⌉tta N 間違ったN /⟨Vinf. past of *machigau* ① make a mistake/ [different from the facts/truth] ((**wrong**)), **ma⌈chiga⌉tte iru** (**N**) **間違っている**(**N**) **/⟨V *te iru* of *machigau* ① make a mistake/**

EX. (**a**) Incorrect information is useless.
{間違った/間違っている}情報は役に立たない。
{Machigatta/Machigatte iru} joohoo wa yaku ni tatanai.
(**b**) This answer is incorrect.
この答えは間違っている。
Kono kotae wa machigatte iru.

increase vt. **[to make larger in amount/number/degree]**
⟨-o⟩ fu⌈ya⌉su ⟨〜を⟩増やす ① [for s.o. to make s.t. larger in amount/number] ↔ **⟨-o⟩ herasu ⟨〜を⟩減らす ①; ⟨-o⟩ a⌈geru ⟨〜を⟩あげる ② [to make s.t. higher** ((**fig. "give"**))**]** ((**raise, lift, give**)) ↔ **⟨-o⟩ sageru ⟨〜を⟩下げる ②**
㊥ "raise s.t. to a higher location"▷上げる, "fry/fly (a kite)/raise (a flag)"▷揚げる, "raise one's hand"▷挙げる, otherwise ▷あげる

EX. (**a**) They increased the number of his police bodyguards to protect him.

彼を守るために護衛の警官の数を{増やした/*上げた}。
*Kare o mamoru tame ni goei no keikan no kazu o {fuyashita/*ageta}.*
(**b**) The government has increased the tax on beer by 10%.
政府はビールの税金を10パーセント{上げた/*増やした}。
*Seifu wa biiru no zeikin o jip-paasento {ageta/*fuyashita}.*

—— vi. **[to become larger in amount/number/degree]**
fu⌈e⌉ru 増える ② [to become larger in amount/number] ⟪**multiply**⟫ ↔ **heru 減る ①; a⌈garu あがる ① [to go up in vertical location, temperature, price, status, or level** ⟪**fig. "improve," "stop raining," "get nervous"**⟫**]** ⟪**go up, rise**⟫ ↔ **sagaru 下がる ①**

㊥ "rise to a higher location"▷上がる, "(for a kite/flag) to fly/to be deep-fried"▷揚がる, "(for a hand) to be raised"▷挙がる, otherwise ▷あがる

EX. (**a**) The number of tourists to Kyoto has increased in recent years.
近年京都の観光客の数が{増えた/*上がった}。
*Kinnen Kyooto no kankoo-kyaku no kazu ga {fueta/*agatta}.*
(**b**) The crime rate in Tokyo is increasing every year.
東京の犯罪発生率は毎年{上がって/*増えて}いる。
*Tookyoo no hanzai-hassei-ritsu wa mai-toshi {agatte/*fuete} iru.*
(**c**) My monthly salary has increased by ten thousand yen to two hundred and thirty thousand yen.
月給が一万円{上がって/増えて}二十三万円になった。
Gekkyuu ga ichi-man-en {agatte/fuete} ni-juu-san-man-en ni natta.

NOTE: *Fueru* and *agaru* may be used to express not only "increase" but also "be increased," as would be the case in example (c) if the English were changed to "…has been increased…"

—— n. **[a rise in amount/number/degree]**
zo⌈oka 増加 •c

EX. (**a**) The increase in crime in the big cities has become a serious problem.
大都市における犯罪の増加は深刻な問題になっている。
Dai-toshi ni okeru hanzai no zooka wa shinkokuna mondai ni natte iru.
(**b**) There was a two percent increase in the population of our country last year.
我が国の人口は去年二パーセントの増加だった。
Waga kuni no jinkoo wa kyonen ni-paasento no zooka datta.

incredible adj. **[too amazing to be believed]**
shi⌈nji-rare⌉nai yoona N 信じられないようなN /⟨**neg. of pot. of *shinjiru* ② believe + *yoona* like**/ ⟪**unbelievable**⟫, **bi⌈kku⌉ri-suru yoona N びっくりするようなN** ⟪**surprising**⟫

EX. (**a**) That's an incredible story.
それは{信じられない/びっくりする}ような話です。
Sore wa {shinji-rarenai/bikkuri-suru} yoona hanashi desu.
(**b**) She spends an incredible amount of money every month on clothes.
彼女は毎月服を買うのに{信じられない/びっくりする}ようなお金を使っている。
Kanojo wa mai-tsuki fuku o kau no ni {shinji-rarenai/bikkuri-suru} yoona o-kane o tsukatte iru.

indeed adv. **[without a doubt]**
ho⌈ntoo ni 本当に •c [used for giving force to the expression it modifies ⟪**fig. "an interjection used by a female speaker to indicate incredulousness"**⟫**]** ⟪**really, truly, certainly**⟫, **ji⌈tsu⌉ni 実に •c [used for making a description emphatic]** ⟪**truly, in fact**⟫

EX. (**a**) We enjoyed the concert very much indeed.
コンサートは{本当に/実に}楽しかったです。
Konsaato wa {hontoo ni/jitsuni} tanoshikatta desu.
(**b**) Thank you very much indeed.

{本当に/*実に}ありがとうございました。
*{Hontoo ni/*Jitsuni} arigatoo gozaimashita.*

independence n. **[the state of being independent]**
do˥kuritsu 独立 •c [the state of being independent] ↔ juuzoku 従属 •c; ji˥ritsu 自立 •c [the state of one's not being dependent on others] ((**self-reliance**))

EX. (**a**) Malaysians celebrated their independence from Britain on this day.
マレーシアの人々はこの日にイギリスからの{独立/*自立}を祝った。
*Mareeshia no hito-bito wa kono hi ni Igirisu kara no {dokuritsu/*jiritsu} o iwatta.*
(**b**) I'd like to get a job so I can enjoy economic independence from my parents.
私は就職して、経済的に親から{自立/独立}したい。
Watashi wa shuushoku-shite, keizai-tekini oya kara {jiritsu/dokuritsu}-shi-tai.

PHRASE: The Declaration of Independence *dokuritsu-sengen* 独立宣言 •c, Independence Day *dokuritsu-kinen-bi* 独立記念日 •c

independent adj. **[not governed/controlled/influenced by others or not depending on others]**
1. do˥kuritsu-shita N 独立したN /⟨Vinf. past of *dokuritsu-suru* ③ gain independence/ •c [not being controlled by others or not depending on others] ((**self-supporting**)) **↔ juuzoku-shita N 従属したN •c; do˥kuritsu-shite iru (N) 独立している(N) /⟨V *te iru* of *dokuritsu-suru* ③ gain independence/, ji˥ritsu-shita N 自立したN /⟨Vinf. past of *jiritsu-suru* ③ gain independence/ •c, ji˥ritsu-shite iru (N) 自立している(N) /⟨V *te iru* of *jiritsu-suru* ③ gain independence/ [not depending on others]** ((**self-reliant, self-supporting**))

EX. The number of economically independent women is increasing in that developing country.
あの発展途上国では経済的に{独立した/独立している/自立した/自立している}女性が増えてきている。
Ano hatten-tojoo-koku de wa keizai-tekini {dokuritsu-shita/dokuritsu-shite iru/jiritsu-shita/jiritsu-shite iru} josei ga fuete kite iru.

2. {do˥kuritsu˥/ji˥ritsu˥}-shin ga tsu˥yo˥i {独立/自立}心が強い adj(*i*). **[for s.o. not to want to depend on others]**

EX. She is a very independent woman.
彼女は非常に{独立/自立}心の強い女性です。
Kanojo wa hijooni {dokuritsu/jiritsu}-shin no tsuyoi josei desu.

index n. **[a list of names, subjects, etc., arranged in alphabetical order at the end of a book together with the page numbers where they can be found or a figure indicating the level of prices or wages compared to an eariler time]**
1. sa˥kuin 索引 •c [a list of names, subjects, etc. arranged in order of the Japanese syllabary at the end of a book together with the page numbers where they can be found]

EX. This book has a good index.
この本は索引がいい。
Kono hon wa sakuin ga ii.

2. shi˥su˥u 指数 •c [a figure indicating the level of prices, wages, intelligence, etc., compared to a fixed standard]

EX. Last month's cost of living index showed a two percent rise compared to the year before.
先月の物価指数は前年に比べて二パーセントの上昇を見せた。
Sengetsu no bukka-shisuu wa zennen ni kurabete ni-paasento no jooshoo o miseta.

PHRASE: index finger *hito-sashi-yubi* 人さし指

India n.
I˥ndo インド •f

Indian adj./n. **[of India/its people or s.o. belonging to/connected with any of the indigenous peoples of North, Central, or South America except the Eskimos]**

1. I˥ndo no N インドのN •f [of India], I˥ndo˥-jin インド人 n. •f+c [the people/a person of India]
2. A˥merika-I˥ndian アメリカインディアン •f [s.o. belonging to any of the indigenous peoples of the United States/Canada], I˥ndio インディオ •f [s.o. belonging to any of the original peoples of Central/South America]

indicate vt. **[to point to/show s.t.]**
⟨-o⟩ shi˥mesu ⟨〜を⟩示す ① [to cause s.o. to see or be clearly aware of some fact or object by the use of symbols or other indirect means ⟨fml⟩] ⟪show⟫, ⟨-o⟩ (yu˥bi-)sa˥su ⟨〜を⟩(指)差す ① [for s.o. to draw attention to the presence of s.t./s.o./s.a. using one's finger] ⟪point⟫, ⟨-o⟩ a˥rawa˥su ⟨〜を⟩あらわす ① [to cause s.t. to become exposed/visible/recognizable] ⟪express⟫
㊥ "indicate/express"▷表わす, "write (a book)"▷著わす, "cause s.t. to appear"▷現わす

EX. (**a**) When I asked my son which cake he wanted, he indicated the one in the middle.
息子にどのケーキが欲しいか聞いたら、真ん中のを{(指)差した/?示した/*表した}。
*Musuko ni dono keeki ga hoshii ka kiitara, mannaka no o {(yubi-)sashita/?shimeshita/*arawashita}.*
(**b**) He indicated his approval with a nod.
彼はうなずいて賛意を{表した/示した/*(指)差した}。
Kare wa unazuite san'i o {arawashita/shimeshita/(yubi-)sashita}.*
(**c**) The expression on his face indicated anxiety.
彼の表情は内心の不安を{表して/示して/*(指)差して}いた。
Kare no hyoojoo wa naishin no fuan o {arawashite/shimeshite/(yubi-)sashite} ita.*
(**d**) The thermometer indicates 35 degrees centigrade.
温度計が摂氏三十五度を{示して/差して/*表して}いる。
*Ondo-kei ga sesshi san-juu-go-do o {shimeshite/sashite/*arawashite} iru.*

indirect adj. **[not straight/direct]**
ka˥nsetsu-tekina 間接的な adj(*na*). **•c [not direct], e˥nkyokuna えん曲な** adj(*na*). **•c [for one's way of talking to be not direct] ⟪euphemistic, roundabout⟫**

EX. (**a**) His carelessness was an indirect cause of the accident.
彼の不注意が事故の{間接的な/*えん曲な}原因だ。
*Kare no fu-chuui ga jiko no {kansetsu-tekina/*enkyokuna} gen'in da.*
(**b**) Could you teach me an indirect way of refusing things in Japanese?
日本語での{えん曲な/?間接的な}断り方を教えてもらいたいんですが。
Nihon-go de no {enkyokuna/?kansetsu-tekina} kotowari-kata o oshiete morai-tai n desu ga.

indirectness n. **[the quality of being indirect]**
ka˥nsetsu-sei 間接性 •c

individual n. **[a single person/thing constrasted with the class/group to which he/she/it belongs]**
ko˥jin 個人 •c [a single person contrasted with the class/group to which he/she belongs] ↔ shuudan 集団 •c

EX. (**a**) The rights of the individual are often neglected in this society.
この社会では個人の権利がしばしば無視される。
Kono shakai de wa kojin no kenri ga shiba-shiba mushi-sareru.
(**b**) Every individual should take greater care to prevent accidents.
事故にあわないように個人個人がもっと気をつけるべきだ。
Jiko ni awanai yooni kojin-kojin ga motto ki-o-tsukeru-beki da.

—— adj. **[separate/particular]**
ko˥-ko no N 個々のN •c [of/related to a single animate or inanimate being], hi˥tori-hito˥ri no N 一人一人のN [of/related to a single person]

EX. (**a**) We can't take the individual preferences

of every participant into consideration in organizing a tour.
ツアーを組むのに参加者{一人一人の/個々の}好みを考慮することはできません。
Tsuaa o kumu no ni sanka-sha {hitori-hitori/ko-ko} no konomi o kooryo-suru koto wa dekimasen.
(**b**) Can you identify each individual goldfish in the bowl?
金魚鉢の{個々/*一人一人}の金魚が判別できますか。
*Kingyo-bachi no {ko-ko/*hitori-hitori} no kingyo ga hanbetsu-dekimasu ka.*
(**c**) How to actually use the textbook which has been decided on to teach is left to each individual teacher.
与えられた教科書を実際にどのように使って教えるかは{一人一人/個々}の教師に任されている。
Atae-rareta kyooka-sho o jissai ni dono yooni tsukatte oshieru ka wa {hitori-hitori/ko-ko} no kyooshi ni makasa-rete iru.

indoors adv. **[into/inside a building]**
o⌈ku⌉nai {de/ni/o} 屋内{で/に/を} n.+prt. **•c [inside a building]**, {**u⌈chi/ta⌈te⌉-mono**} **no na⌉ka {de/ni/o}** {うち/建物}の中{で/に/を} n.+prt. **[inside a house/building]**

EX. The ceremony was held indoors due to rain.
雨のため、式は{屋内/{うち/建物}の中}で行われた。
Ame no tame, shiki wa {okunai/{uchi/tate-mono} no naka} de okonawa-reta.

industrial adj. **[of industry and the people who work in it or having highly developed industries]**
1. sa⌈ngyoo no N 産業のN **•c [of industry]**
2. ko⌉ogyoo no N 工業のN **•c [of the manufacturing industry]**

EX. (**a**) Japan is an industrial nation.
日本は{工業/*産業}国だ。
*Nihon wa {koogyoo/*sangyoo}-koku da.*
(**b**) We are destroying our environment through industrial growth.
私たちは{産業/工業}の発展のために環境を破壊しつつある。
Watashi-tachi wa {sangyoo/koogyoo} no hatten no tame ni kankyoo o hakai-shi-tsutsu aru.

PHRASE: industrial revolution *sangyoo-kakumei* 産業革命 **•c**, industrial relations *rooshi-kankei* 労使関係 **•c**

industry n. **[the production of things for sale or a branch of business, trade, or manufacturing]**
1. sa⌈ngyoo 産業 **•c [the production of goods necessary to society or a particular branch of such production]**
2. ko⌉ogyoo 工業 **•c [the production of things by machinery in factories or a particular branch of such production]** **《manufacturing industry》**

EX. (**a**) Agriculture is the principal industry of this country.
農業がこの国の基幹{産業/*工業}です。
*Noogyoo ga kono kuni no kikan-{sangyoo/*koogyoo} desu.*
(**b**) This government does not advocate a policy of nationalizing the manufacturing industry.
現政権は{工業/*産業}の国有化という政策をうたっていない。
*Gen-seiken wa {koogyoo/*sangyoo} no kokuyuu-ka to iu seisaku o utatte inai.*

NOTE: *Seizoo-gyoo* 製造業 is a more specific term for the manufacturing industry. Other industries include *tekkoo-gyoo* 鉄鋼業 "the steel industry," *kagaku-koogyoo* 化学工業 "the chemical industry," *shokuhin-koogyoo* 食品工業 "the food industry" and *sen'i-koogyoo* 繊維工業 "the textile industry."

(**c**) The appearance of television led to the decline of the cinema industry.
テレビの登場は映画{産業/*工業}の衰退を招いた。
*Terebi no toojoo wa eiga-{sangyoo/*koogyoo} no suitai o maneita.*

inevitable adj. **[sure to happen and not able to be avoided]**
sa⌈ke-rare⌉nai 避けられない /〈**neg. of pot. of** ***sakeru*** ② **avoid**/ **《unavoidable, inescapable》**

I

EX. (**a**) Their divorce is probably inevitable given how much they seem to dislike each other.
彼らはお互いをあんなに憎みあっているようだから、多分離婚は避けられないだろう。
Kare-ra wa o-tagai o annani nikumi-atte iru yooda kara, tabun rikon wa sake-rarenai daroo.
(**b**) Death is the inevitable fate of every person.
死はだれにとっても避けられない運命だ。
Shi wa dare ni-totte mo sake-rarenai unmei da.

infant n. **[a very young child]**
nyu⌈uyo⌉o-ji 乳幼児 •c
NOTE: *Nyuuji* is a child still on milk and *yooji* is a child slightly older. *Nyuuyoo-ji* includes both.
EX. The infant mortality rate in Japan is very low.
日本の乳幼児死亡率は非常に低い。
Nihon no nyuuyoo-ji-shiboo-ritsu wa hijooni hikui.

infect vt. **[for s.o./s.t. to cause an animate being to catch a germ-related disease]**
1. ⟨-o⟩ {⟨-ni⟩/⟨-e⟩} **u⌈tsu⌉su** ⟨〜を⟩{⟨〜に⟩/⟨〜へ⟩}うつす ① **[to cause s.o./s.t./s.a. to change to a different location or into a different condition 《fig. "copy," "reflect" "infect" "take a picture"》]**
㊅ "move/transfer"▷移す, "copy/duplicate/take (a picture)"▷写す, "reflect/mirror"▷映す, "infect"▷うつす
EX. Please take care not to infect my child with your cold.
子供にかぜをうつさないように気をつけてください。
Kodomo ni kaze o utsusanai yooni ki o tsukete kudasai.
2. ⟨-ni⟩ **ka⌈nsen-suru** ⟨〜に⟩感染する ③ •c **[for s.o./s.a. to become infected with a disease]**
EX. He is infected with cholera.
彼はコレラに感染している。
Kare wa korera ni kansen-shite iru.

infection n. **[the process or result of infecting]**
ka⌈nsen 感染 •c
EX. (**a**) Washing our hands is one way to prevent flu infection.
手を洗うのはインフルエンザの感染を予防する一つの手段だ。
Te o arau no wa infuruenza no kansen o yoboo-suru hitotsu no shudan da.
(**b**) Is it true that radiation therapy lessens bodily resistance to infection?
放射線治療は病気感染に対する体の抵抗力を弱めるというのは本当ですか。
Hoosha-sen-chiryoo wa byooki-kansen ni taisuru karada no teikoo-ryoku o yowameru to iu no wa hontoo desu ka.

infinite adj. **[without limits 《fig. "extremely large in amount/degree"》]**
1. mu⌈gen no N 無限のN •c **[without limits]** **《limitless, boundless》**
EX. (**a**) The universe is infinite.
宇宙は無限だ。
Uchuu wa mugen da.
(**b**) The number of original sentences a native speaker can generate in his language is infinite.
母語話者がその言語で作ることができる新しい文の数は無限だ。
Bogo-washa ga sono gengo de tsukuru koto ga dekiru atarashii bun no kazu wa mugen da.
2. ka⌈zoe-kire⌉-nai hodo no N 数えきれないほどのN /⟨**neg. of pot. of** ***kazoekiru*** **count the number completely +** ***hodo*** **degree**/ **[to the extent that you can't completely count s.t.]**
EX. The people whose lives that man saved are almost infinite in number.
あの人が命を救った人々の数は数えきれないほどの数になる。
Ano hito ga inochi o sukutta hito-bito no kazu wa kazoe-kire-nai hodo no kazu ni naru.

inflation n.
infure(eshon) インフレ(ーション)
EX. Inflation has gotten worse over the past few months.
インフレーションはここ数か月の間に進んだ。

Infureeshon wa koko suukagetsu no aida ni susunda.

influence n. **[(the power to have) an effect on s.o./s.t./s.a. without the use of direct force or command]**
e⌈ikyoo 影響 •c [effecting a change on s.o./s.t./s.a. without the use of direct force or command] ⟪**effect, repercussions**⟫, **e⌈ikyo⌉o-ryoku 影響力 •c [the power to effect a change on s.o./s.t./s.a. without the use of direct force/command]**

EX. (**a**) You can see the influence of kabuki in his plays.
彼の戯曲には歌舞伎の{影響/*影響力}が見られる。
*Kare no gikyoku ni wa kabuki no {eikyoo/*eikyoo-ryoku} ga mi-rareru.*
(**b**) He still has a lot of influence within the government.
彼はまだ政府内で多大な{影響力/*影響}を持っている。
*Kare wa mada seifu-nai de tadaina {eikyoo-ryoku/*eikyoo} o motte iru.*
(**c**) We are all subject to influence by the mass media.
我々はみんなマスコミから{影響/*影響力}を受けている。
*Ware-ware wa minna masukomi kara {eikyoo/*eikyoo-ryoku} o ukete iru.*

— vt. **[to have an effect on s.o./s.t./s.a.]**
⟨-ni⟩ e⌈ikyoo-suru ⟨〜に⟩影響する ③ •c [to have an effect on s.o./s.t./s.a.] ⟪**affect, have an effect on**⟫, **⟨-ni⟩ e⌈ikyoo o o⌈yobo⌉su ⟨〜に⟩影響を及ぼす ①**

EX. How will public opinion influence the government's decision on this issue?
世論はこの件に関する政府決定に{どのような影響を及ぼす/どのように影響する}でしょうか。
Seron wa kono ken ni-kansuru seifu-kettei ni {dono yoona eikyoo o oyobosu/dono yooni eikyoo-suru} deshoo ka.

PHRASE: be influenced ⟨*-ni*⟩ *eikyoo o ukeru* ⟨〜に⟩影響を受ける ②

EX. Traditional Japanese music seems to have been greatly influenced by Chinese music.
日本の伝統的な音楽は中国の音楽の影響を大きく受けているようです。
Nihon no dentoo-tekina ongaku wa Chuugoku no ongaku no eikyoo o ookiku ukete iru yoo desu.

inform vt. **[for s.o./s.t. to give information/knowledge to s.o.]**
⟨-ni⟩ ⟨-o⟩ shi⌈ra-seru ⟨〜に⟩⟨〜を⟩知らせる /⟨causative of *shiru* ① get to know/ ② [for s.o. to cause s.o. to know s.t.] ⟪**tell, notify, report, pass word to**⟫

EX. (**a**) I informed the office that I would be late for the meeting.
私は会社に会議に遅れることを知らせた。
Watashi wa kaisha ni kaigi ni okureru koto o shira-seta.
(**b**) He informed his friends of his divorce from Hiroko.
彼は友人に弘子との離婚を知らせた。
Kare wa yuujin ni Hiroko to no rikon o shira-seta.
(**c**) I wasn't informed of the date of his arrival.
彼の到着の日を知らされていなかった。
Kare no toochaku no hi o shira-sarete inakatta.

NOTE: *Shira-sareru* rather than *shira-se-rareru* is used as the passive form of *shira-seru.*

informal adj. **[not formal]**
1. hi-⌈ko⌉oshiki no N 非公式のN •c [not following official/established rules, methods, etc.] ⟪**unofficial**⟫ ↔ **kooshiki no N 公式のN •c**

EX. He had informal discussions with the American delegation.
彼はアメリカ代表団と非公式の交渉を行った。
Kare wa Amerika-daihyoo-dan to hi-kooshiki no kooshoo o okonatta.

2. ku⌈da⌉keta N くだけたN /⟨Vinf. past of *kudakeru* ② shatter/ [for a style of writing/speaking, the way one is dressed, etc. not to be formal] ⟪**casual, familiar**⟫

EX. This expression is used only in informal conversation.

この表現はくだけた会話でしか使われない。
Kono hyoogen wa kudaketa kaiwa de shika tsukawa-renai.

information n. **[(something that gives) knowledge in the form of facts, news, etc.]** **jo⌈ohoo 情報 •c, i⌈nfome⌉eshon インフォメーション •f**

EX. (**a**) We've received information that Prof. Eto is moving to another university.
江藤先生が外の大学にお移りになるという{情報/?インフォメーション}を得た。
Etoo-sensei ga hoka no daigaku ni o-utsuri ni naru to iu {joohoo/?infomeeshon} o eta.
(**b**) We have no information yet on the hijacking.
ハイジャックに関してまだ何の{情報/インフォメーション}も入っていない。
Haijakku ni-kanshite mada nan no {joohoo/infomeeshon} mo haitte inai.

PHRASE: information booth *annai-jo* 案内所 •c

inherit vt. **[for s.o. to receive s.t. left by s.o. who has died]**
⟨-o⟩ so⌈ozoku-suru ⟨～を⟩相続する ③ •c [for s.o. to receive s.t. such as property or a title as an heir] ⟪succeed⟫, ⟨-o⟩ u⌈ke-tsugu ⟨～を⟩受け継ぐ ① [for s.o. to receive s.t. such as property or a title as an heir or to receive natural characteristics from one's parents] ⟪succeed⟫

EX. (**a**) My brother inherited my father's liquor shop.
兄が父の酒屋を{相続した/受け継いだ}。
Ani ga chichi no saka-ya o {soozoku-shita/uke-tsuida}.
(**b**) My sister seems to have inherited my father's disposition.
姉は父の気性を{受け継いだ/*相続した}ようだ。
*Ane wa chichi no kishoo o {uke-tsuida/*soozoku-shita} yooda.*

initial adj. **[coming at the beginning]**
sa⌈isho no N 最初のN •c [pertaining to the very first] ⟪the first, the earliest⟫ ↔ saigo no N 最後のN •c; to⌉osho no N 当初のN •c, ha⌈jime no N 初めのN [the first] ↔ owari no N 終わりのN

EX. (**a**) Initial reaction to the announcement of the plan to build a new elementary school was not very favorable.
新小学校建設計画の発表に対する{当初/最初/初め}の反応はあまりよくなかった。
Shin-shoogakkoo-kensetsu-keikaku no happyoo ni-taisuru {toosho/saisho/hajime} no hannoo wa amari yoku nakatta.
(**b**) The cooperation which existed among the various political parties at the initial stages of tax reform seems now to have disappeared.
税制改革の{当初/最初/初め}の段階においては存在していた諸政党間の協力関係が今は消えてしまったようだ。
Zeisei-kaikaku no {toosho/saisho/hajime} no dankai ni-oite wa sonzai-shite ita sho-seitoo-kan no kyooryoku-kankei ga ima wa kiete shimatta yooda.

PHRASE: initial letter *kashira-moji* 頭文字, *inisharu* イニシャル •f

injure vt. **[to cause physical harm to s.o./s.a.]**
1. ⟨-ni⟩ ke⌈ga⌉ o suru ⟨～に⟩けがをする ③ [for s.o./s.a. to inflict physical damage to a part of one's body] ⟪get hurt, be wounded⟫

EX. (**a**) I injured my left leg when I jumped down from the tree.
私は木から飛び下りたとき、左足にけがをした。
Watashi wa ki kara tobi-orita toki, hidari-ashi ni kega o shita.
(**b**) The earthquake injured many people.
地震でたくさんの人がけがをした。
Jishin de takusan no hito ga kega o shita.

2. ⟨-o⟩ ki⌈zu-tsuke⌉ru ⟨～を⟩傷つける ② [to inflict physical or mental harm on s.o./s.t./s.a.] ⟪offend, hurt, damage⟫

EX. The scandal badly injured his reputation.
あのスキャンダルは彼の評判をひどく傷つけた。
Ano sukyandaru wa kare no hyooban o hidoku kizu-tsuketa.

PHRASE: be injured *kega o suru* けがをする ③

EX. Seven people were injured in the accident.
事故で七人がけがをした。
Jiko de shichi-nin ga kega o shita.

injury n. **[harm or damage done to s.o./s.a.]**
ke⌈ga⌉ けが •c [harm or damage done to s.o./s.a.], ki⌈zu 傷 [the part on s.o./s.t that has been harmed or damaged] ⟪**wound, flaw**⟫

EX. (**a**) The child in the back seat received serious injuries to the head in the accident.
その事故で後部座席に座っていた子供が頭に{大怪我をした/ひどい傷を負った}。
Sono jiko de koobu-zaseki ni suwatte ita kodomo ga atama ni {oo-kega o shita/ hidoi kizu o otta}.
(**b**) You should always wear a helmet when riding a bicycle to avoid injury.
自転車に乗る時は{怪我をしない/?傷を負わない}ように必ずヘルメットを着用するようにしなさい。
Jitensha ni noru toki wa {kega o shinai/ ?kizu o owanai} yooni kanarazu herumetto o chakuyoo-suru yooni shinasai.

ink n. **[colored liquid used for writing/ printing/drawing]**
i⌈nku インク •f [colored liquid used for writing/printing/drawing], su⌈mi⌉ 墨 [an ink stick or black liquid prepared from it used in the Japanese/Chinese style of writing/painting with a brush]

EX. (**a**) Would you please fill this fountain pen with black ink?
この万年筆に黒い{インク/*墨}を入れてください。
*Kono mannenhitsu ni kuroi {inku/ *sumi} o irete kudasai.*
(**b**) I need some ink for my calligraphy lesson.
書道のけいこに{墨/*インク}が要る。
*Shodoo no keiko ni {sumi/*inku} ga iru.*

inland adj. **[not near the coast]**
na⌈iriku no N 内陸のN •c [located on land far from the coast]
PHRASE: the Inland Sea of Seto *Seto-naikai* 瀬戸内海 •c

inn n. **[a small, old hotel]**
ryo⌈kan 旅館 •c [a building with Japanese-style rooms and service where travelers can pay to stay]

EX. (**a**) We stayed at a Japanese-style inn in Kyoto.
京都で旅館に泊まりました。
Kyooto de ryokan ni tomarimashita.
(**b**) There are many old inns in this hot-spring resort.
この温泉町には古い旅館がたくさんある。
Kono onsen-machi ni wa furui ryokan ga takusan aru.

inner adj. **[pertaining to the space inside a boundary]**
u⌈chi-gawa no N 内側のN •c ↔ soto-gawa no N 外側のN

EX. He is well versed in the inner workings of Japanese politics.
彼は日本の政治の内側の仕組みをよく知っている。
Kare wa Nihon no seiji no uchi-gawa no shikumi o yoku shitte iru.

innocent adj. **[not guilty of a crime/sin or free from evil/wrong]**
1. mu⌉zai no N 無罪のN •c [not offending anyone] ⟪**not guilty**⟫

EX. (**a**) He insisted that he was innocent.
彼はあくまで無罪だと主張した。
Kare wa akumade muzai da to shuchoo-shita.
(**b**) He was sent to prison although he was innocent.
彼は無罪なのに刑務所に入れられてしまった。
Kare wa muzai na noni keimu-sho ni ire-rarete shimatta.

2. tsu⌉mi ga na⌉i (N) 罪がない(N) [for s.o. not to be guilty of a sin]

EX. Terrorism often makes victims of large numbers of innocent citizens.
テロはしばしば多くの罪のない市民に被害者を出す。
Tero wa shiba-shiba ooku no tsumi no nai shimin ni higai-sha o dasu.

3. mu⌉-jakina 無邪気な adj(*na*). •c **[free from malice]**

EX. I love the innocent smile of a baby.
赤ちゃんの無邪気な笑いが大好きだ。
Aka-chan no mu-jakina warai ga dai-suki da.

inquire vt. **[for s.o. to ask s.o. for information about s.t.]**
(⟨-ni⟩) ⟨-o⟩ ki⌈ku (⟨〜に⟩)⟨〜を⟩きく ① **[for s.o./s.a. to focus one's attention on a sound so that it is perceived by the ears or to request/receive information from s.o. about s.t. orally or to take notice and accept s.t. said by another]** ⟪**hear, listen to, ask**⟫, **(⟨-ni⟩) ⟨-o⟩ ta⌈zune⌉ru** (⟨〜に⟩)⟨〜を⟩ 尋ねる ② **[for s.o. to put a question to s.o.]** ⟪**ask**⟫
㊉ "listen to s.t. carefully" ▷聴く, otherwise ▷聞く

EX. (**a**) I inquired about directions to the museum.
博物館へ行く道を{聞きました/尋ねました}。
Hakubutsu-kan e iku michi o {kikimashita/tazunemashita}.
(**b**) I inquired as to whether the library would be open on Sunday.
日曜日に図書館が開いているかどうか{聞いた/尋ねた}。
Nichiyoo-bi ni tosho-kan ga aite iru ka doo ka {kiita/tazuneta}.

PHRASE: inquire into ⟨*-o*⟩ *shiraberu* ⟨〜を⟩調べる ② ⟪check, investigate⟫

EX. We inquired into the matter.
私たちはその事を調べた。
Watashi-tachi wa sono koto o shirabeta.

insect n. **[a small creature with six legs, a body divided into three parts, and usually with wings, such as an ant/fly/butterfly or any small creature such as a worm or spider]**
ko⌈nchuu 昆虫 •c **[a small creature with six legs, a body divided into three parts, and usually with wings, such as a fly or cicada]**, **mu⌈shi** 虫 **[a small organism which breeds its young by hatching and crawls on the ground or flies about]** ⟪**bug, cricket, worm, caterpillar, moth**⟫

EX. (**a**) Various insects make sounds in our backyard in the autumn.
秋になると、いろいろな{虫/*昆虫}が裏庭で鳴く。
*Aki ni naru to, iro-irona {mushi/*konchuu} ga ura-niwa de naku.*
(**b**) My children like collecting insects.
うちの子供たちは{昆虫/虫}を集めるのが好きです。
Uchi no kodomo-tachi wa {konchuu/mushi} o atsumeru no ga suki desu.
(**c**) My legs were badly bitten by insects.
足を{虫/*昆虫}にひどく刺された。
*Ashi o {mushi/*konchuu} ni hidoku sasa-reta.*

insert vt. **[for s.o. to put s.t. into s.t. else]**
⟨-ni⟩ ⟨-o⟩ i⌈reru ⟨〜に⟩⟨〜を⟩入れる ② **[for s.o./s.a. to cause s.t./s.o./s.a. to move into an enclosed space]** ⟪**put, add, set, admit, include**⟫, **⟨-ni⟩ ⟨-o⟩ sa⌈shi-ko⌉mu** ⟨〜に⟩⟨〜を⟩差し込む ① **[for s.o. to put s.t. in a small opening/gap/crevice]** ⟪**plug, penetrate**⟫

EX. (**a**) He inserted his key into the lock of the door.
彼はドアの鍵穴に鍵を{差し込んだ/入れた}。
Kare wa doa no kagi-ana ni kagi o {sashi-konda/ireta}.
(**b**) I want to insert this paragraph here.
このパラグラフをここに{入れたい/*差し込みたい}。
*Kono paragurafu o koko ni {ire-tai/*sashi-komi-tai}.*

inside n. **[the inner side of s.t.]**
u⌈chi-gawa 内側 **[the inner side of s.t.]** ↔ **soto-gawa** 外側; **u⌈ra** 裏 **[the back/inner side of s.t.]** ↔ **omote** 表; **na⌉ka** 中 **[the inner part/side of s.t.]** ↔ **soto** 外

EX. (**a**) He painted the inside of the house pink.
彼は家の{中/内側/*裏}をピンクに塗った。
*Kare wa ie no {naka/uchi-gawa/*ura} o pinku ni nutta.*
(**b**) This jacket is green on the outside and yellow on the inside.
この上着は表がグリーンで、{裏/内側/中}は黄色です。

Kono uwagi wa omote ga guriin de, {ura/uchi-gawa/naka} wa ki-iro desu.

insist vi./vt. **[for s.o. to state s.t. firmly, esp. in the face of doubt or opposition]**
⟨to⟩ i⌈i-ha⌉ru ⟨と⟩言い張る ① [for s.o. to keep saying s.t. firmly in the face of doubt or opposition] ((assert, maintain)), **⟨to⟩ shu⌈choo-suru ⟨と⟩主張する ③ •c [for s.o. to state one's opinion firmly with a view to making others agree with it or accept it]** ((claim, assert, plead))

EX. (**a**) He insisted on his innocence.
彼は自分は無罪だと{主張した/言い張った}。
Kare wa jibun wa muzai da to {shuchoo-shita/ii-hatta}.

NOTE: *Kare wa muzai o shuchoo-shita* is also possible.

(**b**) She still insists that she wasn't the one who drank the beer.
彼女はまだビールを飲んだのは自分じゃないと{言い張って/主張して}いる。
Kanojo wa mada biiru o nonda no wa jibun janai to {ii-hatte/shuchoo-shite} iru.

inspect vt. **[for s.o./s.a. to examine s.t. carefully/in detail in order to ensure that everything is all right]**
⟨-o⟩ ke⌉nsa-suru ⟨〜を⟩検査する ③ •c [for s.o. to carefully check to see if s.t./s.o./s.a. meets the standard or if there is anything wrong with it/him/her, etc.] ((check, examine)), **⟨-o⟩ shi⌈rabe⌉ru ⟨〜を⟩調べる ② [for s.o. to observe directly or inquire/read about s.t./s.o./s.a. in order to determine or ascertain s.t. unknown or uncertain about it/him/her]** ((check, look up, investigate))

EX. (**a**) The products are thoroughly inspected before they are shipped out.
製品は出荷される前に隅から隅まで{検査される/調べられる}。
Seihin wa shukka-sareru mae ni sumi kara sumi made {kensa-sareru/shirabe-rareru}.
(**b**) Make sure you inspect the car carefully before you buy it.
車を買う前によく{調べた/*検査した}ほうがいい。
*Kuruma o kau mae ni yoku {shirabeta/*kensa-shita} hoo ga ii.*
(**c**) We went to the highway destroyed by the earthquake to inspect the damage.
被害状況を{調べる/*検査する}ために地震で破壊された高速道路へ行った。
*Higai-jookyoo o {shiraberu/*kensa-suru} tame ni jishin de hakai-sareta koosoku-dooro e itta.*

inspire vt. **[to fill s.o. with the desire and confidence to do s.t., esp. a creative act, or with a strong feeling of some positive kind, such as love, hope, or courage]**
⟨-o⟩ fu⌈rui-tata-se⌉ru ⟨〜を⟩奮い立たせる /⟨causative of *furui-tatsu* ① be encouraged/ ②

EX. The President's speech inspired the soldiers in their struggle to defend their homeland.
大統領の演説は自国を守るために戦っている兵隊を奮い立たせた。
Daitooryoo no enzetsu wa jikoku o mamoru tame ni tatakatte iru heitai o furui-tata-seta.

install vt. **[for s.o. to set up an apparatus to make it ready for use]**
⟨-ni⟩ ⟨-o⟩ to⌈ri-tsuke⌉ru ⟨〜に⟩⟨〜を⟩取り付ける ② [for s.o. to set an apparatus into position onto s.t.] ((fit, put up, fix)), **⟨-ni⟩ ⟨-o⟩ so⌈nae-tsuke⌉ru ⟨〜に⟩⟨〜を⟩備え付ける ② [to provide/supply s.t. for some location]** ((provide, furnish, equip))

EX. (**a**) I had a stereo installed in my car.
私は車にステレオを{取り付けて/備え付けて}もらった。
Watashi wa kuruma ni sutereo o {tori-tsukete/sonae-tsukete} moratta.
(**b**) A heater has been installed in each classroom.
各教室にストーブが{備え付けて/取り付けて}ある。
Kaku-kyooshitsu ni sutoobu ga {sonae-tsukete/tori-tsukete} aru.

instant n. **[a moment of time]**
i⌈sshun 一瞬 •c ((moment))

EX. All this happened in an instant.

I

全ては一瞬のうちに起こった。
Subete wa isshun no uchi ni okotta.

PHRASE: instant coffee *insutanto-koohii* インスタントコーヒー •f, for an instant *isshun* 一瞬 •c

EX. I hesitated for an instant.
私は一瞬ちゅうちょした。
Watashi wa isshun chuucho-shita.

instantly adv. **[at once]**
su˥gu すぐ [at once/without delay] ⟪immediately, directly, in an instant, in a moment, right away⟫

EX. (**a**) The security guard came to my help instantly.
守衛がすぐ助けに来てくれた。
Shuei ga sugu tasuke ni kite kureta.
(**b**) I turned down his invitation and instantly regretted it.
私は彼の誘いを断ったが、すぐそれを後悔した。
Watashi wa kare no sasoi o kotowatta ga, sugu sore o kookai-shita.

instead adv. **[in place of s.t./s.o.]**
ka˥wari ni 代わりに

EX. My father was busy, so I went to the meeting instead.
父が忙しかったので、私が代わりにミーティングに行きました。
Chichi ga isogashikatta node, watashi ga kawari ni miitingu ni ikimashita.

PHRASE: instead of ⟨-no⟩ *kawari ni* ⟨〜の⟩代わりに, Vinf. nonpast *kawari ni* Vinf. nonpast 代わりに

EX. (**a**) Did you know that you can reduce a lot of the fat in baking by using apple sauce instead of oil?
パンを焼く時サラダ油の代わりにアップルソースを使うとずいぶん脂肪を減らすことができるのを知っていましたか。
Pan o yaku toki sarada-yu no kawari ni appuru-soosu o tsukau to zuibun shiboo o herasu koto ga dekiru no o shitte imashita ka.
(**b**) Instead of doing his homework, he read comic books all day.
彼は宿題をする代わりに、一日中漫画を読んでいた。
Kare wa shukudai o suru kawari ni, ichi-nichi-juu manga o yonde ita.

instinct n. **[an inborn ability or tendency to behave in a certain way without training or reflection]**
1. ho˥nnoo 本能 •c

EX. (**a**) Everyone is born with an instinct to protect himself from danger.
人には皆、生まれながらに危険から身を守ろうとする本能がある。
Hito ni wa mina, umare-nagara ni kiken kara mi o mamoroo to suru honnoo ga aru.
(**b**) Women are endowed with a maternal instinct.
女性には母性本能がある。
Josei ni wa bosei-honnoo ga aru.

2. cho˥kkan 直観 •c [the ability to understand or know s.t. without conscious reasoning] ⟪intuition⟫

EX. She knew by her woman's instinct that her husband was lying.
彼女には夫がうそをついていることが女の直観で分かった。
Kanojo ni wa otto ga uso o tsuite iru koto ga onna no chokkan de wakatta.

institute n. **[a society/organization set up for a special purpose]**
ke˥nkyuu-jo 研究所 •c [an organization set up to do a particular type of research] ⟪research institute, laboratory⟫

EX. I visited the National Language Research Institute in Tokyo when I was in Japan last year.
私は去年日本へ行った時東京の国立国語研究所を訪ねました。
Watashi wa kyonen Nihon e itta toki Tookyoo no Kokuritu-kokugo-kenkyuu-jo o tazunemashita.

PHRASE: institute of technology *kooka-daigaku* 工科大学 •c

instruct vt. **[for s.o. to give orders/directions/knowledge/information to s.o.]**
1. ⟨-ni⟩ Vinf. nonpast yo˥oni (to) i˥u ⟨〜に⟩ Vinf. nonpastように(と)言う ① [for s.o. to tell s.o. to do s.t.] ⟪say, tell⟫, ⟨-ni⟩ Vinf.

nonpast yo˥oni (to) shi˥ji-suru 〈〜に〉Vinf. nonpastように(と)指示する ③ •c [for s.o. in a position of responsibility to give directions to s.o. to do s.t.] 《direct》

EX. (a) I've been instructed to wait here until everybody arrives.
みんなが着くまでここで待つように(と){言われました/指示されました}。
Minna ga tsuku made koko de matsu yooni (to) {iwa-remashita/shiji-saremashita}.
(b) I'll instruct the children to keep the door locked until we return.
私たちが帰ってくるまでドアに鍵をかけておくように子供に{言いましょう/?指示しましょう}。
Watashi-tachi ga kaette kuru made doa ni kagi o kakete oku yooni kodomo ni {iimashoo/?shiji-shimashoo}.

2. 〈-ni〉 〈-o〉 o˥shieru 〈〜に〉〈〜を〉教える ② [for s.o. to impart knowledge/information/a skill to s.o./s.a.] 《teach》

EX. Yuri instructs children in gymnastics as a part-time job.
由里はアルバイトで子供に体操を教えています。
Yuri wa arubaito de kodomo ni taisoo o oshiete imasu.

instructor n. **[s.o. who teaches or a college teacher ranking below an assistsant professor]**

1. kyo˥oshi 教師 •c [s.o. who teaches academic subjects/a skill/art] 《teacher》, se˥nse˥i 先生 •c [a professional including scholars, instructors, medical doctors, artists, attorneys, politicians, etc., often used as a polite term of address] 《teacher》, insutorakutaa インストラクター •f [s.o. who teaches a sport such as swimming and aerobics]

NOTE: *Sensei* implies respect. Hence, it cannot be used to refer to oneself or one's family members. *Kyooshi,* on the other hand, is neutral in this respect, so it is inappropriate to use it in a situation that requires an expression of respect. Also, *sensei* can be used to address s.o., but not *kyooshi.*

EX. (a) This is my driving instructor.
こちらは私の運転の{先生/?インストラクター/*教師}です。
*Kochira wa watashi no unten no {sensei/?insutorakutaa/*kyooshi} desu.*
(b) My older sister is a swimming instructor.
姉は水泳の{教師/インストラクター/?先生}をしています。
Ane wa suiei no {kyooshi/insutorakutaa/?sensei} o shite imasu.

2. ko˥oshi 講師 •c [s.o. who gives lectures or a college teacher ranked below an assistant professor] 《lecturer》

EX. Mr. Tanaka is an instructor of Japanese at a college in California.
田中さんはカリフォルニアの大学の日本語の講師です。
Tanaka-san wa Kariforunia no daigaku no Nihon-go no kooshi desu.

instrument n. **[a device used for accomplishing a certain kind of work, esp. of a delicate nature, or a device which gives measurements having to do with the operation of a machine, or a device which is used to make musical sounds]**
do˥ogu˥ 道具 •c [a device used for accomplishing a certain kind of work] 《tool, utensil》, ki˥gu 器具 •c [a simple machine or piece of equipment used to accomplish some task, usu. in everyday life] 《appliance, apparatus》, ke˥iki 計器 •c [a device used for giving measurements or readings] 《gauge, meter》

EX. (a) We don't have the medical instruments necessary for the operation.
その手術に必要な医療{器具/*道具/*計器}が足りない。
*Sono shujutsu ni hitsuyoona iryoo-{kigu/*doogu/*keiki} ga tarinai.*
(b) The pilot checked his flight instruments before taking off.
パイロットは離陸する前にいろいろな{計器/器具/*道具}をチェックした。
*Pairotto wa ririku-suru mae ni iro-irona {keiki/kigu/*doogu} o chekku-shita.*

(**c**) A computer is a very useful instrument if you know how to use it.
コンピューターは使い方を知っていれば、非常に便利な{道具/*器具/*計器}です。
*Konpyuutaa wa tsukai-kata o shitte ireba, hijooni benrina {doogu/*kigu/*keiki} desu.*

PHRASE: musical instrument *gakki* 楽器 •c

EX. Can you play any musical instruments?
何か楽器を演奏できますか。
Nani ka gakki o ensoo-dekimasu ka.

insurance n. **[an agreement to pay a fixed amount of money to a company in order to receive payment from them in the case of misfortune]**
ho⌈ken 保険 •c

EX. (**a**) Do you have life insurance?
生命保険に入っていますか。
Seimei-hoken ni haitte imasu ka.
(**b**) Does your health insurance cover dental treatment, too?
あなたの健康保険は歯の治療にも使えますか。
Anata no kenkoo-hoken wa ha no chiryoo ni mo tsukae-masu ka.

PHRASE: fire insurance *kasai-hoken* 火災保険 •c

insure vt. **[for an individual or company to enter into a contract to be paid or pay money in the case of loss of life, property, etc.]**
⟨-ni⟩ ho⌈ken o ka⌈ke⌉ru ⟨〜に⟩保険をかける ② **[for s.o. to enter into a contract to be paid in the case of loss of s.t. such as life or property]**

EX. The fashion model insured her beautiful legs for ten million yen.
そのファッション・モデルは自分の美しい足に一千万円の保険をかけた。
Sono fasshon-moderu wa jibun no utsukushii ashi ni is-sen-man-en no hoken o kaketa.

PHRASE: be insured *⟨-ni⟩ hoken ga kakete aru* ⟨〜に⟩保険がかけてある ①

EX. Is your house insured against fire?
お宅には火災保険がかけてありますか。
O-taku ni wa kasai-hoken ga kakete arimasu ka.

intellectual adj. **[involving the ability to think and understand]**
chi⌈tekina 知的な adj(*na*). •c

EX. (**a**) I need more intellectual stimulation.
私はもっと知的な刺激が欲しい。
Watashi wa motto chitekina shigeki ga hoshii.
(**b**) Frankly, I find the intellectual level of this university disappointing.
正直言ってこの大学の知的なレベル(の低さに)がっかりしている。
Shoojiki itte kono daigaku no chitekina reberu (no hiku-sa) ni gakkari-shite iru.

—— n. **[s.o. who has a well-developed ability to reason and whose tastes reflect this]**
i⌈nteri インテリ •f, **chi⌈shiki⌉-jin** 知識人 •c

NOTE: *Interi* is derived from Russian intjelligencija.

EX. That actress is very popular among intellectuals.
その女優は{インテリ/知識人}に人気がある。
Sono joyuu wa {interi/chishiki-jin} ni ninki ga aru.

intelligence n. **[the ability to learn, understand, and handle new situations well and fast]**
chi⌉noo 知能 •c, **a⌈tama⌉** 頭 **[that part of the body which contains the eyes, ears, nose, mouth, and brain or the ability to learn, reason, and understand]** ((**head**))

EX. (**a**) His theory is too difficult for a man of average intelligence to understand.
彼の理論は難しすぎて、普通の{知能/頭}の人間には分からない。
Kare no riron wa muzukashi-sugite, futsuu no {chinoo/atama} no ningen ni wa wakaranai.
(**b**) Having great intelligence doesn't necessarily make a person socially adept.
{知能/*頭}の高い人がすべて社交性があるとは限らない。
*{Chinoo/*Atama} no takai hito ga subete shakoo-sei ga aru to wa kagiranai.*

PHRASE: intelligence test *chinoo-tesuto* 知能テス

ト •c+f, intelligence quotient *chinoo-shisuu* 知能指数 •c, artificial intelligence *jinkoo-chinoo* 人工知能 •c

intelligent adj. **[for s.o./s.a. to have a well-developed ability to learn, reason, and understand]**
a⌈tama⌉ ga i⌉i 頭がいい adj(*i*). **[for s.o./s.a. to have a well-developed ability to learn, reason, and understand]** ⟪**smart, clever, bright**⟫

EX. (**a**) My seven-year old nephew is an intelligent boy.
私の七歳になるおいは頭のいい男の子です。
Watashi no nana-sai ni naru oi wa atama no ii otoko-no-ko desu.
(**b**) Our dog, Hanako, is very intelligent.
うちの犬の花子はとても頭がいいんです。
Uchi no inu no Hanako wa totemo atama ga ii n desu.

intend vt. **[for s.o. to have s.t. in one's mind as a plan/purpose]**
Sinf. tsu⌈mori da Sinf.つもりだ **[for s.o. to have s.t. in his/her mind as a plan/belief]** ⟪**be convinced, believe, feel sure, mean**⟫

NOTE: Note that when adj(*na*). or N + cop. occurs in the nonpast affirmative form before *tsumori da*, the form used is adj(*na*). stem + *na* or N + *no*, respectively. Note also that the subject has to be s.o. the speaker can identify with, including the speaker himself/herself.

EX. (**a**) A: Do you intend to marry her?
彼女と結婚するつもりですか。
Kanojo to kekkon-suru tsumori desu ka.
B: Yes, I do.
ええ，そのつもりです。
Ee, sono tsumori desu.
(**b**) I intended to study Japanese as no more than a hobby.
日本語の勉強は単なる趣味のつもりでした。
Nihon-go no benkyoo wa tan-naru shumi no tsumori deshita.
(**c**) I didn't intend to hurt her, but it seems that I did.
彼女を傷つけるつもりはなかったんですが、傷つけてしまったようです。
Kanojo o kizu-tsukeru tsumori wa nakatta n desu ga, kizu-tsukete shimatta yoo desu.
(**d**) I don't intend to study during summer vacation.
夏休みには勉強しないつもりだ。
Natsu-yasumi ni wa benkyoo-shinai tsumori da.

intense adj. **[very great or strong in quality, degree, or feeling]**
ha⌈geshi⌉i 激しい adj(*i*). **[of an action/state/character/emotion being extremely strong in force/degree]** ⟪**violent, heated, severe**⟫, **kyo⌈oretsuna** 強烈な adj(*na*). •c **[so strong that one cannot bear or forget it]** ⟪**strong, severe**⟫

EX. (**a**) I was overcome by an intense headache.
私は{激しい/強烈な}頭痛に襲われた。
Watashi wa {hageshii/kyooretsuna} zutsuu ni osowa-reta.
(**b**) Have you ever experienced the intense heat of the desert?
砂漠の{強烈な/激しい}暑さを経験したことがありますか。
Sabaku no {kyooretsuna/hageshii} atsu-sa o keiken-shita koto ga arimasu ka.

NOTE: Note the following collocations. *{hageshii/*kyooretsuna} giron* "heated discussion," *{kyooretsuna/*hageshii} nioi* "strong smell," *{kyooretsuna/*hageshii} inshoo* "strong impression"

intention n. **[a plan of what one is going to do]**
tsu⌈mori つもり **[a plan of what one is going to do], i⌉to** 意図 •c **[what one tries to accomplish in doing s.t.]** ⟪**intent**⟫

NOTE: *Tsumori* indicates a plan in the mind of s.o. the speaker can identify with, including the speaker himself/herself.

EX. (**a**) I have no intention of marrying her.
彼女と結婚する{つもり/意図}はない。
Kanojo to kekkon-suru {tsumori/ito} wa nai.
(**b**) His intentions in asking me for such a large loan of money were not clear.

あれだけの借金を申し込んできた彼の{意図/*つもり}ははっきりしなかった。
*Are dake no shakkin o mooshi-konde kita kare no {ito/*tsumori} wa hakkiri shinakatta.*

interest n. **[a desire to learn more about s.t./s.o./s.a. or to be involved in s.t. or s.t. which creates such a desire or money paid for the use of borrowed money]**

1. kyo⌉omi 興味 **•c [a desire to learn more about s.t./s.o./s.a. or to be involved in s.t.]**

EX. (**a**) I have no interest in baseball.
私は野球には興味がない。
Watashi wa yakyuu ni wa kyoomi ga nai.
(**b**) Our children exhibit a great interest in *kanji.*
うちの子供たちは漢字に大変興味を示している。
Uchi no kodomo-tachi wa kanji ni taihen kyoomi o shimeshite iru.

2. ri⌉shi 利子 **•c [money paid for the use of borrowed money]**

EX. I paid him back the money I borrowed with interest.
借りた金に利子をつけて返した。
Karita kane ni rishi o tsukete kaeshita.

PHRASE: interest rate *riritsu* 利率 **•c**

EX. Where can we borrow money at a low interest rate?
どこへ行けば安い利率で金を借りることができますか。
Doko e ikeba yasui riritsu de kane o kariru koto ga dekimasu ka.

interested adj. **[having interest]**

⟨-ni⟩ kyo⌉omi ga a⌉ru (N) ⟨～に⟩興味がある **(N)** ① **⟪be interested in⟫**

EX. (**a**) Are you interested in sumo wrestling?
すもうに興味がありますか。
Sumoo ni kyoomi ga arimasu ka.
(**b**) He was listening to our conversation with an interested look on his face.
彼は興味がありそうな表情で私たちの会話を聞いていた。
Kare wa kyoomi ga ari-soona hyoojoo de watashi-tachi no kaiwa o kiite ita.

interesting adj. **[attracting one's interest or attention]**

o⌈moshiro⌉i 面白い adj(*i*). **[causing interest] ⟪amusing, entertaining⟫**

EX. (**a**) His new book is very interesting.
彼の新しい本はとても面白い。
Kare no atarashii hon wa totemo omoshiroi.
(**b**) She is an interesting person.
彼女は面白い人だ。
Kanojo wa omoshiroi hito da.
(**c**) A: How was the movie?
映画はどうでしたか。
Eiga wa doo deshita ka.
B: It wasn't interesting at all.
全然面白くありませんでした。
Zen-zen omoshiroku arimasen deshita.

intermediate adj. **[between two levels/stages/degrees/points in time/space]**

1. chu⌈ukyuu no N 中級のN **•c [between high and low in level]**

EX. I've enrolled in an intermediate Japanese course.
中級の日本語コースに登録した。
Chuukyuu no Nihon-go koosu ni tooroku-shita.

2. chu⌈ukan no N 中間のN **•c [between two others] ⟪halfway, middle, neutral⟫**

EX. The radio reported that the epicenter of today's earthquake was at some intermediate point between Yokohama and Odawara.
ラジオによると、今日の地震の震源地は横浜と小田原の中間(の)あたりだそうだ。
Rajio ni yoru to, kyoo no jishin no shingen-chi wa Yokohama to Odawara no chuukan (no) atari da sooda.

internal adj. **[in the inside of s.t./s.o.]**

na⌉ibu no N 内部のN **•c ↔ gaibu no N** 外部のN **•c**

EX. The party leaders are trying to conceal their internal strife.
党の幹部は内部抗争を隠そうとしている。
Too no kanbu wa naibu-koosoo o kakusoo to shite iru.

PHRASE: internal bleeding *nai-shukketsu* 内出血

•c, internal organs *naizoo* 内臓 •c, internal affairs *naisei* 内政 •c ⟪domestic affairs⟫, internal medicine *naika* 内科 •c ↔ *geka* 外科 •c

international adj. **[involving or agreed upon between two or more nations]**
ko⌉kusai-tekina 国際的な adj(*na*). •c

EX. (**a**) She aspires to become an international star.
彼女は国際的なスターになりたいと思っている。
Kanojo wa kokusai-tekina sutaa ni nari-tai to omotte iru.
(**b**) We need to consider this problem from a more international point of view.
この問題はより国際的な見地から考えなくてはいけない。
Kono mondai wa yori kokusai-tekina kenchi kara kangaenakute wa ikenai.

PHRASE: international conference *kokusai-kaigi* 国際会議 •c, international call *kokusai-denwa* 国際電話 •c, international dispute *kokusai-funsoo* 国際紛争 •c, international relations *kokusai-kankei* 国際関係 •c

interpret vt. **[for s.o. to understand the meaning of s.t. in a particular way or to change s.t. from one language to another, esp. in oral communication]**
1. ⟨-o⟩ ⟨-to⟩ ka⌉ishaku-suru ⟨～を⟩⟨～と⟩解釈する ③ •c [for s.o. to understand the meaning of s.t. in a particular way]

EX. I interpreted Mr. Tanaka's "*hai*" as agreement, but it seems I was wrong.
私は田中さんの言った「はい」を同意してくれたものと解釈したけど、間違っていたようだ。
Watashi wa Tanaka-san no itta 'hai' o dooi-shite kureta mono to kaishaku-shita kedo, machigatte ita yooda.

2. ⟨-o⟩ tsu⌉uyaku-suru ⟨～を⟩通訳する ③ •c [for s.o. to put s.t. spoken in one language into the words of another language]

EX. I interpreted what my Japanese friend said for my father, who doesn't speak Japanese at all.
私は日本人の友達の言ったことを日本語を全然知らない父のために通訳した。
Watashi wa Nihon-jin no tomodachi no itta koto o Nihon-go o zenzen shiranai chichi no tame ni tsuuyaku-shita.

interpretation n. **[an explanation of what s.t. means or its oral translation into another language]**
1. ka⌉ishaku 解釈 •c [an explanation of what s.t. means]

EX. (**a**) His interpretation of this rule is different from mine.
彼のこの規則の解釈は私のと違います。
Kare no kono kisoku no kaishaku wa watashi no to chigaimasu.
(**b**) This haiku is open to a variety of interpretations.
この俳句はいろいろな解釈が可能だ。
Kono haiku wa iro-irona kaishaku ga kanoo da.

2. tsu⌉uyaku 通訳 •c [oral translation]

PHRASE: simultaneous interpretation *dooji-tsuuyaku* 同時通訳 •c

interrupt vt./vi. **[to break the continuity of s.t., esp. an action or speech in progress]**
⟨-no⟩ ja⌈ma o suru ⟨～の⟩邪魔をする ③ •c [to get in the way of s.o./s.t./s.a. ⟪fig. "visit s.o."⟫] ⟪interfere, intrude, bother, prevent⟫

EX. Don't interrupt your father. He's working.
お父さんの邪魔をしないでね。お仕事、して(い)るんだから。
O-too-san no jama o shinaide ne. O-shigoto, shite (i)ru n da kara.

PHRASE: be interrupted *chuudan-suru* 中断する ③

EX. The game was temporarily interrupted when some angry fans ran onto the field.
怒ったファンが球場になだれ込んだため、試合は一時中断した。
Okotta fan ga kyuu-joo ni nadare-konda tame, shiai wa ichiji chuudan-shita.

intersection n. **[a point where roads, lines, etc., meet and cross each other]**
ko⌈osa-ten 交差点 •c

EX. There was an accident at the intersection near the university.
大学の近くの交差点で事故があった。
Daigaku no chikaku no koosa-ten de jiko ga atta.

interval n. **[a period of time between two events or actions or the space between two objects or points]**
ka⌈nkaku 間隔 •c 《space》

EX. (**a**) During rush hour, trains arrive at this station at three-minute intervals.
ラッシュアワーにはこの駅に電車が三分間隔で到着する。
Rasshu-awaa ni wa kono eki ni densha ga san-pun-kankaku de toochaku-suru.
(**b**) Policemen were stationed at five-meter intervals along the motorcade route.
自動車の行列が通る通りに沿って警官が五メートル間隔で配置されていた。
Jidoosha no gyooretsu ga tooru toori ni sotte keikan ga go-meetoru-kankaku de haichi-sarete ita.

interview n. **[a formal meeting where one speaks face to face with a person to determine if he/she is suitable for a job, for admission to an academic institution, etc., or to obtain comments or information from him/her]**
1. me⌈nsetsu 面接 •c

EX. I got so nervous at the job interview that I felt sick.
就職の面接で緊張し過ぎて気分が悪くなった。
Shuushoku no mensetsu de kinchoo-shi-sugite kibun ga waruku natta.

2. ka⌈iken 会見 •c [a formal meeting to discuss various problems or a formal meeting with the media to answer various questions], i⌉ntabyuu インタビュー •f [a meeting with the media to answer various questions]

EX. Matsui of the Yomiuri Giants held an interview for the media after the renewal of his contract.
読売ジャイアンツの松井は契約更改の後、{記者会見をした/インタビューに応じた}。
Yomiuri Jaiantsu no Matsui wa keiyaku-kookai no ato, {kisha-kaiken o shita/intabyuu ni oojita}.

into prep. **[to or toward the inside of s.t.; so as to be in contact with s.t. or in a certain state 《fig. "against"》]**
1. (⟨-no⟩ na⌉ka) ni (⟨〜の⟩中)に (n.+)prt.

EX. (**a**) Put all the books into that box.
本は全部あの箱(の中)に入れてください。
Hon wa zenbu ano hako (no naka) ni irete kudasai.
(**b**) The dog jumped into the water.
犬は水の中に飛び込んだ。
Inu wa mizu no naka ni tobi-konda.
(**c**) My father changes into a kimono when he comes home from work.
父は会社から帰ってくると、着物に着替える。
Chichi wa kaisha kara kaette kuru to, ki-mono ni ki-gaeru.

2. ni に prt. [indicating a spatial/temporal point of contact, often construed as a location where s.t./s.o./s.a. exists, a goal, or an indirect object] 《to, at, on, for, against》

EX. (**a**) She translated the novel into English.
彼女はその小説を英語に翻訳した。
Kanojo wa sono shoosetsu o eigo ni hon'yaku-shita.
(**b**) The rain turned into snow.
雨は雪に変わった。
Ame wa yuki ni kawatta.
(**c**) He bumped into the door.
彼はドアにぶつかった。
Kare wa doa ni butsukatta.

introduce vt. **[for s.o. to make s.o. known by name to s.o. else for the first time or to make s.t. known for the first time]**
1. ⟨-ni⟩ ⟨-o⟩ sho⌈okai-suru ⟨〜に⟩⟨〜を⟩紹介する ③ •c [for s.o. to make s.o./s.t. known to s.o. else for the first time]

EX. (**a**) I'm hoping to introduce my girlfriend to my parents over Christmas break.
クリスマス休暇に両親に彼女を紹介したいと思っている。
Kurisumasu-kyuuka ni ryooshin ni kanojo o shookai-shi-tai to omotte iru.
(**b**) Let me introduce my adviser to you. This is Prof. Nakano.
私の指導教授をご紹介します。中野先生です。

Watashi no shidoo-kyooju o go-shookai-shimasu. Nakano-sensei desu.
(c) He was active in introducing Japanese culture to his fellow American high school students.
彼はアメリカの高校の同級生に積極的に日本文化を紹介するようにした。
Kare wa Amerika no kookoo no dookyuu-sei ni sekkyoku-tekini Nihon-bunka o shookai-suru yooni shita.

2. ⟨-o⟩ do⸢onyuu-suru ⟨〜を⟩導入する ③ •c [for s.o. to bring s.t. into use for the first time, often to solve a difficulty]

EX. That company was the first to introduce robots into the production line.
生産ラインに初めてロボットを導入したのはその会社だ。
Seisan-rain ni hajimete robotto o doonyuu-shita no wa sono kaisha da.

PHRASE: be introduced ⟨*-ni*⟩ *hairu* ⟨〜に⟩入る ① ↔ {⟨*-kara*⟩/⟨*-o*⟩} *deru* {⟨〜から⟩/⟨〜を⟩}出る ②

EX. I believe chewing gum was introduced to Japan from the United States.
チューインガムはアメリカから日本へ入ってきたんだと思います。
Chuuingamu wa Amerika kara Nihon e haitte kita n da to omoimasu.

introduction n. **[the act of introducing s.o./s.t.]**

1. sho⸢okai 紹介 •c [the act of introducing s.o./s.t.]

EX. (a) Prof. Nakada wrote a letter of introduction to Prof. Inoue for me.
中田先生が井上先生に紹介状を書いてくださった。
Nakada-sensei ga Inoue-sensei ni shookai joo o kaite kudasatta.
(b) Shall I make the introductions? Prof. Inoue, this is Prof. Jones.
ご紹介します。井上先生、ジョーンズ先生です。
Go-shookai-shimasu. Inoue-sensei, Joonzu-sensei desu.

2. nyu⸢umon 入門 •c [the beginning stage of a study]

EX. I bought a book entitled *An Introduction to Bonsai.*
『盆栽入門』という題の本を買った。
"Bonsai-nyuumon" to iu dai no hon o katta.

invade vt./vi. **[for a group of people to enter a territory by force so as to take control of it]**

⟨-ni⟩ shi⸢nnyuu-suru ⟨〜に⟩侵入する ③ •c [for a group of people to enter the territory of another illegally] ⟪break into, trespass, intrude⟫, ⟨-o⟩ shi⸢nryaku-suru ⟨〜を⟩侵略する ③ •c [for a group of people to enter another country and take control of its land and people by force]

EX. The Japanese army invaded China.
日本軍は中国{に侵入/を侵略}した。
Nihon-gun wa Chuugoku {ni shinnyuu/o shinryaku}-shita.

invader n. **[s.o./s.t. that invades]**

shi⸢nnyu⸣u-sha 侵入者 •c [s.o. who enters illegally into the territory of another], shi⸢nryaku⸣-sha 侵略者 •c [s.o./a group of people that enters another country and takes control of its land and people by force]

EX. (a) We have to repel the invaders.
我々は{侵入者/侵略者}を撃退しなければいけない。
Ware-ware wa {shinnyuu-sha/shinryaku-sha} o gekitai-shinakereba naranai.
(b) Many Chinese still remember Japan as the invader of their homeland.
多くの中国人はいまだに日本を自国の{侵略者/??侵入者}として記憶している。
Ooku no Chuugoku-jin wa imada ni Nihon o jikoku no {shinryaku-sha/??shinnyuu-sha} to-shite kioku-shite iru.

invasion n. **[the act of invading]**

shi⸢nnyuu 侵入 •c [the act of illegally entering the territory of another] ⟪trespass, intrusion⟫, shi⸢nryaku 侵略 •c [the act of entering another country and taking control of its land and people by force] ⟪inroad, aggression⟫

EX. (a) Many Americans in the 1980's were

very concerned over what they saw as an economic invasion by Japan.
1980年代には多くのアメリカ人が日本の経済{侵略/*侵入}と思える事態に非常に敏感になっていた。
*Sen-kyuu-hyaku-hachi-juu-nendai ni wa ooku no Amerika-jin ga Nihon no keizai-{shinryaku/*shinnyuu} to omoeru jitai ni hijooni binkanni natte ita.*
(**b**) Quick action by government forces prevented an invasion of the capital by guerrillas.
政府軍のすばやい対応により、ゲリラの首都への{侵入/*侵略}は食い止められた。
*Seifu-gun no subayai taioo ni-yori, gerira no shuto e no {shinnyuu/ *shinryaku} wa kui-tome-rareta.*

invent vt. **[for s.o. to make or design s.t. for the first time]**
⟨-o⟩ ha⌈tsumei-suru ⟨〜を⟩発明する ③ •c
EX. (**a**) Who was it that invented the telephone?
電話を発明したのはだれですか。
Denwa o hatsumei-shita no wa dare desu ka.
(**b**) When was it that the radio was invented?
ラジオが発明されたのはいつですか。
Rajio ga hatsumei-sareta no wa itsu desu ka.

invention n. **[the act of inventing or s.t. invented]**
ha⌈tsumei 発明 •c [the act of inventing]
EX. (**a**) The telephone was an epoch-making invention.
電話は画期的な発明だった。
Denwa wa kakki-tekina hatsumei datta.
(**b**) It is said that necessity is the mother of invention.
必要は発明の母と言われる。
Hitsuyoo wa hatsumei no haha to iwareru.

inventor n. **[a person who invents s.t. new]**
ha⌈tsumei-ka 発明家 •c
EX. Thomas Edison was a great inventor.
トーマス・エジソンは偉大な発明家だった。
Toomasu Ejison wa idaina hatsumei-ka datta.

invest vt./vi. **[for s.o. to put money/time/energy into s.t. to receive a future benefit from it]**
1. ⟨-ni⟩ ⟨-o⟩ to⌈oshi-suru ⟨〜に⟩⟨〜を⟩投資する ③ •c [for s.o. to put money into a business enterprise to make a profit]
EX. He invested an enormous amount of money in the development of new products.
彼は新製品の開発に莫大な金を投資した。
Kare wa shin-seihin no kaihatsu ni bakudaina kane o tooshi-shita.
2. ⟨-ni⟩ ⟨-o⟩ tsu⌈gi-ko⌉mu ⟨〜に⟩⟨〜を⟩つぎ込む ① [for s.o. to put money/time/energy into s.t.] ⟪put…in⟫
EX. She invested all her time and energy in the project.
彼女はその企画に全時間とエネルギーをつぎ込んだ。
Kanojo wa sono kikaku ni zen-jikan to enerugii o tsugi-konda.

investigate vt./vi. **[for s.o. to look into s.t. carefully to get more information about it]**
⟨-o⟩ shi⌈rabe⌉ru ⟨〜を⟩調べる ② [for s.o. to observe directly or inquire/read about s.t./s.o./s.a. in order to determine or ascertain s.t. unknown or uncertain about it/him/her] ⟪check, study, examine⟫, **⟨-o⟩ cho⌉osa-suru ⟨〜を⟩調査する ③ •c [for s.o. to try to find more information about s.t. to understand it better]** ⟪survey, research, look into⟫, **⟨-o⟩ so⌉osa-suru ⟨〜を⟩捜査する ③ •c [for the authorities concerned to try to ascertain the facts concerning a crime/accident]**
EX. (**a**) The police are investigating the cause of the accident.
警察は事故の原因を{調べて/調査して/捜査して}いる。
Keisatsu wa jiko no gen'in o {shirabete/choosa-shite/soosa-shite} iru.
(**b**) We're investigating foreign markets in which to promote our new product.
新製品の販売のために海外の市場を

{調査して/調べて/*捜査して}いるところだ。
*Shin-seihin no hanbai no tame ni kaigai no shijoo o {choosa-shite/shirabete/*soosa-shite} iru tokoro da.*

investigation n. **[the act of investigating]** **cho˥osa 調査 •c [the act of investigating]** **((survey, examination, inquiry)), so˥osa 捜査 •c [the act of investigating the facts surrounding a crime/accident]**

EX. (**a**) I have to write a report on the investigation.
私は{調査/捜査}の報告書を書かなければなりません。
Watashi wa {choosa/soosa} no hookoku-sho o kakanakereba narimasen.
(**b**) Upon investigation the engine was found to be defective.
{調査/*捜査}の結果、エンジンに欠陥があることが判明した。
*{Choosa/*Soosa} no kekka, enjin ni kekkan ga aru koto ga hanmei-shita.*
(**c**) The police are conducting an investigation into the murder.
警察はその殺人事件の{捜査/*調査}をしている。
*Keisatsu wa sono satsujin-jiken no {soosa/*choosa} o shite iru.*

invisible adj. **[not able to be seen]** **(me˥ ni) mi˥e˥nai (目に)見えない /⟨neg. of *mieru* ② be visible/**

EX. (**a**) We saw many stars that are invisible to the naked eye through the telescope.
私たちは肉眼では見えない多くの星を望遠鏡で見た。
Watashi-tachi wa nikugan de wa mienai ooku no hoshi o booen-kyoo de mita.
(**b**) Sometimes I feel that our lives are being controlled by some invisible force.
私たちの生活は何か(目に)見えない力によって支配されているように感じることがある。
Watashi-tachi no seikatsu wa nani-ka (me ni) mienai chikara ni-yotte shihai-sarete iru yooni kanjiru koto ga aru.

invitation n. **[a request made to s.o. to do s.t. such as to come to a party, meal, etc.]** **sho˥otai 招待 •c**

EX. (**a**) I declined their invitation to a party.
彼らのパーティーへの招待を断った。
Kare-ra no paatii e no shootai o kotowatta.
(**b**) We played golf at the invitation of one of our business clients.
取引先の招待でゴルフをした。
Torihiki-saki no shootai de gorufu o shita.

PHRASE: letter of invitation *shootai-joo* 招待状 •c

invite vt. **[for s.o. to ask s.o. do s.t. such as to come to a party, meal, etc.]**
1. ⟨-o⟩ ⟨-ni⟩ sho˥otai-suru ⟨〜を⟩⟨〜に⟩招待する ③ •c, ⟨-o⟩ ⟨-ni⟩ yo˥bu ⟨〜を⟩⟨〜に⟩呼ぶ ① [for s.o. to speak aloud to s.o. in order to get his/her attention or to ask s.o. to come] ((call, send for, summon))

EX. (**a**) I invited my classmates to my wedding.
私は同級生を結婚式に{呼んだ/招待した}。
Watashi wa dookyuu-sei o kekkon-shiki ni {yonda/shootai-shita}.
(**b**) I've been invited to a party at Prof. Tokugawa's home.
私は徳川先生のお宅のパーティーに{招待されて/呼ばれて}いる。
Watashi wa Tokugawa-sensei no o-taku no paatii ni {shootai-sarete/yoba-rete} iru.

2. ⟨-o⟩ ⟨-ni⟩ sa˥sou ⟨〜を⟩⟨〜に⟩誘う ① [for s.o. to ask s.o. to join in some activity] ((induce, allure))

EX. I invited her to a movie.
私は彼女を映画に誘った。
Watashi wa kanojo o eiga ni sasotta.

involve vt. **[to include s.t./s.o./s.a. as a necessary part or to bring s.o. into difficulty]**
1. ⟨-ni⟩ ⟨-o⟩ ma˥ki-ko˥mu ⟨〜に⟩⟨〜を⟩巻き込む ① [to cause s.o. to become connected with difficulties] ((be caught))

EX. (**a**) Don't involve me in your quarrel with your boyfriend.

恋人との喧嘩に巻き込まないでちょうだい。
Koi-bito to no kenka ni maki-komanaide choodai.
(**b**) He was injured when he became involved in the robbery.
彼は強盗事件に巻き込まれて、怪我をした。
Kare wa gootoo-jiken ni maki-komarete, kega o shita.

2. ⟨-ni⟩ ⟨-ga⟩ hi⌈tsuyoona ⟨〜に⟩⟨〜が⟩必要な adj(*na*). **[essential for s.t./s.o./s.a.]** ((**necessary**))

EX. Success involves cooperation.
成功には協力が必要だ。
Seikoo ni wa kyooryoku ga hitsuyoo da.

Iowa n.
A⌈iowa アイオワ •f

Ireland n.
A⌈irura⌉ndo アイルランド •f

Irish adj.
A⌈irura⌉ndo no N アイルランドのN [of Ireland]

—— n.
1. A⌈irurando⌉-jin アイルランド人 •f+c [the Irish people/an Irish person]
2. A⌈irurando-go アイルランド語 •f+c [the Irish language]

iron n. **[a kind of metal or a device which is heated and used to smooth wrinkles in clothing]**

I

1. te⌈tsu 鉄 •c ((**steel**)), **te⌈tsu⌉bun 鉄分 •c [iron found in food and in blood]**

EX. (**a**) Strike while the iron is hot.
{鉄/*鉄分}は熱いうちに打て。
*{Tetsu/*Tetsubun} wa atsui uchi ni ute.*
(**b**) Liver is a food rich in iron.
レバーは{鉄分/*鉄}の多い食べ物だ。
*Rebaa wa {tetsubun/*tetsu} no ooi tabe-mono da.*

2. a⌈iron アイロン •f [an object which is heated and used to smooth wrinkles in clothing]

—— vt. **[for s.o. to smooth wrinkles in clothing with an iron]**
⟨-ni⟩ a⌈iron o ka⌈ke⌉ru ⟨〜に⟩アイロンをかける ② [for s.o. to smooth wrinkles in clothing using a heated metal device]

EX. She ironed her skirt.
彼女はスカートにアイロンをかけた。
Kanojo wa sukaato ni airon o kaketa.

PHRASE: iron ore *tek-kooseki* 鉄鉱石 **•c**

irregular adj. **[not following a set pattern in shape, arrangement, frequency of occurrence, etc.]**
fu-⌈ki⌉sokuna 不規則な adj(*na*). **•c [not following the accepted pattern] ↔ kisoku-tekina 規則的な** adj(*na*). **•c; fu-⌈zo⌉roi no N 不ぞろいのN [not the same in shape/size or not matched]**

EX. (**a**) These cups are irregular in size.
この湯飲みは大きさが{不ぞろい/*不規則}だ。
*Kono yu-nomi wa ooki-sa ga {fu-zoroi/*fu-kisoku} da.*
(**b**) There are only a few verbs with irregular conjugation in modern Japanese.
現代日本語には活用が{不規則な/*不ぞろいの}動詞は少ない。
*Gendai-Nihon-go ni wa katsuyoo ga {fu-kisokuna/*fu-zoroi no} dooshi wa sukunai.*
(**c**) I don't like working irregular hours.
私は仕事の時間が{不規則な/*不ぞろいな}のはいやです。
*Watashi wa shigoto no jikan ga {fu-kisokuna/*fu-zoroina} no wa iya desu.*

is vi. **[affirmative nonpast tense of the third person singular of the copula and of the existential verb "to be"]**
1. de⌉su です cop. **[formal affirmative nonpast tense of the copula *da*]** ((am, are)), **da だ** cop. **[informal/written style affirmative nonpast tense of the copula]** ((am, are)), **de⌈a⌉ru である** cop. **[written style affirmative nonpast tense of the copula]** ((am, are))

EX. (**a**) He is a well-known opera singer.
彼は有名なオペラ歌手{です/だ/である}。
Kare wa yuumeina opera-kashu {desu/da/dearu}.

(**b**) This book is yours, isn't it?
この本はあなたの{です/?だ/*である}ね。
*Kono hon wa anata no {desu/?da/ *dearu} ne.*

2. a⌉ru ある ① [for s.t. to exist] ((exist)), **i⌈ru いる ② [for s.o./s.a. to exist]** ((exist))

EX. (**a**) There's a kindergarten in our neighborhood.
近所に幼稚園が{ある/*いる}。
*Kinjo ni yoochi-en ga {aru/*iru}.*
(**b**) My father is in San Francisco at the moment.
父は今サンフランシスコに{います/*あります}。
*Chichi wa ima Sanfuranshisuko ni {imasu/*arimasu}.*

— aux. **[an auxiliary verb used in the passive or progressive construction]**

1. V*te* i⌈ru V*te* いる ① [for s.o./s.a./s.t. to be in the middle of doing s.t. or in a state resulting from s.t. that happened earlier]

EX. He is writing a letter.
彼は手紙を書いている。
Kare wa tegami o kaite iru.

2. {Vneg. reru/Vstem rareru/sa⌈re⌉ru} {Vneg.れる/Vstemられる/される} ② [for s.t./s.o./s.a. acting as the subject of the sentence to be affected by the action of the verb of that sentence]

EX. John is constantly being scolded by his teacher.
ジョンはいつも先生にしかられている。
Jon wa itsu-mo sensei ni shikara-rete iru.

island n. **[a piece of land surrounded by water]**

shi⌈ma⌉ 島

EX. Awaji-shima is the largest island in the Inland Sea of Seto.
淡路島は瀬戸内海で一番大きい島です。
Awaji-shima wa Seto-naikai de ichiban ookii shima desu.

-ism suf. **[a suffix denoting a system of belief]**

-shugi 〜主義 •c [a principle acting as a standard for one's thought and behavior]

EX. (**a**) capitalism
資本主義
shihon-shugi
(**b**) socialism
社会主義
shakai-shugi

isn't vi. **[negative nonpast tense of the third person singular of the copula and of the existential verb "to be"]**

1. {dewaa⌈rimase⌉n/jaa⌈rimase⌉n} {ではありません/じゃありません} [formal negative nonpast of the copula *da*] ((aren't, am not)), **{dewa⌈na⌉i/ja⌈na⌉i} {ではない/じゃない} [informal/written style negative nonpast of the copula *da*]** ((aren't, am not))

EX. John isn't a scholar.
ジョンは学者{ではありません/じゃありません/ではない/じゃない}。
Jon wa gakusha {dewaarimasen/ jaarimasen/dewanai/janai}.

2. i⌈nai いない adj(*i*). **[for s.o./s.a. not to exist]** ((aren't, am not, not exist)), **i⌈mase⌉n いません [for s.o./s.a. not to exist ⟨fml⟩], na⌉i ない** adj(*i*). **[for s.t. not to exist], a⌉rimase⌉n ありません [for s.t. not to exist ⟨fml⟩]** ((aren't, not exist))

EX. (**a**) Tom isn't at home now.
トムは今うちに{いない/いません/*ない/*ありません}。
*Tomu wa ima uchi ni {inai/imasen/ *nai/*ariamsen}.*
(**b**) There isn't any comfortable chair in my office.
研究室には座り心地のいいいすが{ない/ありません/*いない/*いません}。
*Kenkyuu-shitsu ni wa suwari-gokochi no ii isu ga {nai/arimasen/*inai/ *iamsen}.*

— aux. **[an auxiliary verb used in the passive or progressive construction]**

1. {Vneg. renai/Vstem rarenai/sarenai} {Vneg.れない/Vstemられない/されない} ② [for s.o./s.a./s.t. acting as the subject of the sentence to be not affected by the action of the verb of that sentence]

EX. This book isn't sold in most bookstores.
この本は一般の書店では売られていない。

Kono hon wa ippan no shoten de wa ura-rete inai.

2. V*te* inai V*te*いない ② [for s.o./s.a./s.t. not to be in the middle of doing s.t. or not to be in a state resulting from s.t. that happened earlier]

EX. He isn't swimming any more.
彼はもう泳いでいない。
Kare wa moo oyoide inai.

isolated adj. **[separated from others and alone]**

ko⌈ritsu-shita N 孤立したN /⟨Vinf. past of *koritsu-suru* ③ become isolated/ •c, ko⌈ritsu-shite iru (N) 孤立している(N) /⟨V*te iru* of *koritsu-suru* ③ become isolated/

EX. He is isolated in the office.
彼は会社で孤立している。
Kare wa kaisha de koritsu-shite iru.

isolation n. **[the condition of being isolated]**

ko⌈ritsu 孤立 •c [the condition of existing alone without the support of others], ka⌉kuri 隔離 •c [the act of keeping s.o. away from others]

EX. (**a**) Its protective trade policy led the nation to international isolation.
その保護主義的貿易政策により国は国際的に{孤立/*隔離}してしまった。
*Sono hogo-shugi-teki booeki-seisaku ni-yori kuni wa kokusai-tekini {koritsu/ *kakuri}-shite shimatta.*
(**b**) We have to keep the patient in isolation.
患者を{隔離/*孤立}しなければならない。
*Kanja o {kakuri/*koritsu}-shinakereba naranai.*

PHRASE: isolation ward *kakuri-byootoo* 隔離病棟 •c

Israel n.

I⌈sura⌉eru イスラエル •f

issue n. **[a problem or subject to be discussed or acted upon or the act of sending/giving out]**

1. mo⌈ndai 問題 •c [a difficult situation or topic that needs attention and thought] ⟪problem, question, matter⟫

EX. (**a**) The opposition party made an issue of the sales tax in last week's session of the Diet.
野党は先週の国会で消費税を問題にした。
Yatoo wa senshuu no kokkai de shoohi-zei o mondai ni shita.
(**b**) They never discuss important issues in that committee.
あの委員会では大事な問題を討議しようとしない。
Ano iin-kai de wa daijina mondai o toogi-shiyoo to shinai.

2. ha⌈kkoo 発行 •c [the act of printed matter being produced and made available to the public] ⟪publication⟫

EX. The Ministry of Posts and Telecommunications announced the issue of a new commemorative stamp.
郵政省は新しい記念切手の発行を発表した。
Yuusei-shoo wa atarashii kinen-kitte no hakkoo o happyoo-shita.

—— vt. **[for an official organ to publish s.t. and make it available to the public]**

⟨-o⟩ ha⌈kkoo-suru ⟨〜を⟩発行する ③ •c [for an official organ to publish s.t. and make it available to the public] ⟪publish⟫, ⟨-o⟩ da⌉su ⟨〜を⟩出す ① [for s.o. to cause s.o./ s.t./s.a. to come out] ⟪put out, take out, send, publish, put up⟫ ↔ ⟨-o⟩ ireru ⟨〜を⟩入れる ②

EX. (**a**) The Bank of Japan plans to issue a newly designed ten thousand yen bill next year.
日本銀行は来年新しいデザインの一万円札を{発行する/出す}予定だ。
Nihon-ginkoo wa rainen atarashii dezain no ichi-man-en-satsu o {hakkoo-suru/dasu} yotei da.
(**b**) The government is expected to issue a statement this morning about the release of the hostages.
政府は人質解放について今朝声明を{出す/*発行する}はずだ。
*Seifu wa hitojichi-kaihoo ni-tsuite kesa seimei o {dasu/*hakkoo-suru} hazu da.*

it pron. **[that thing already mentioned or a word used as grammatical subject to**

indicate the surrounding circumstances or to point to a clause that follows]

1. {so⌈re/ø} {それ/ø}

EX. (**a**) A: Whose calculator is this?
これはだれの電卓ですか。
Kore wa dare no dentaku desu ka.
B: It's mine.
{それは/ø}私のです。
{Sore wa/ø} watashi no desu.
(**b**) I bought a ticket and handed it to Yoko.
私は切符を買って、{それを/ø}洋子さんに渡した。
Watashi wa kippu o katte, {sore o/ø} Yooko-san ni watashita.

2. ø **[a form used as grammatical subject to indicate the surrounding circumstances or to point to a clause that follows]**

EX. (**a**) It's raining.
雨が降っている。
Ame ga futte iru.
(**b**) Gosh, it's a wonderful day.
わあ、素晴らしい天気だ。
Waa, subarashii tenki da.
(**c**) It must be difficult to eat peas with chopsticks.
はしで豆を食べるのは難しいでしょう。
Hashi de mame o taberu no wa muzukashii deshoo.
(**d**) It was Toshiko that drank the beer.
ビールを飲んだのは敏子です。
Biiru o nonda no wa Toshiko desu.
(**e**) It seems that Miho has a key to Ryota's apartment.
美穂は良太のアパートのかぎを持っているようだ。
Miho wa Ryoota no apaato no kagi o motte iru yooda.

Italian n. **[a person from Italy or the language of Italy]**

1. **I⌈taria⌉-jin** イタリア人 **•f+c [the people of/a person from Italy]**
2. **I⌈taria-go** イタリア語 **•f+c [the language of Italy]**

—— adj. **[of Italy/people in Italy/the language of Italy]**

1. **I⌈taria no N** イタリアのN **•f [of Italy]**
2. **I⌈taria⌉-jin no N** イタリア人のN **•f+c [of the people of/a person from Italy]**
3. **I⌈taria-go no N** イタリア語のN **•f+c [of the language of Italy]**

Italy n.

I⌈taria イタリア **•f**

itchy adj. **[feeling or creating an irritating sensation on the skin that makes one want to scratch]**

ka⌈yu⌉i かゆい adj(*i*).

EX. My back feels itchy.
背中がかゆい。
Senaka ga kayui.

NOTE: The subject of *kayui* is usually the first person in statements and the second person in questions. If the subject is a third person, *kayugatte iru* should be used.

item n. **[a single thing on a list or among a set]**

ko⌈omoku 項目 **•c [a matter on a list to be discussed/dealt with] ((heading))**

EX. This is the most important item on today's agenda.
これは今日の議題の中で一番大事な項目だ。
Kore wa kyoo no gidai no naka de ichiban daijina koomoku da.

its pron. **[of/belonging to it]**

{**so⌈no/ø**} {その/ø}

EX. (**a**) I like this pan, but its handle is broken.
私はこのお鍋が好きなんですが、{ø/*その}取っ手がこわれているんです。
*Watashi wa kono o-nabe ga suki na n desu ga, {ø/*sono} totte ga kowarete iru n desu.*
(**b**) Not far from our house is a little park with a statue of George Washington at its center.
うちの近くに小さな公園があり、{その/?ø}中心にジョージ・ワシントンの銅像が立っている。
Uchi no chikaku ni chiisana kooen ga ari, {sono/?ø} chuushin ni Jooji Washinton no doozoo ga tatte iru.

J

jacket n. **[a short coat with sleeves]**
u⌈wa-gi 上着, ja⌉ketto ジャケット •f

EX. (**a**) He took off his jacket.
彼は{上着/ジャケット}を脱いだ。
Kare wa {uwa-gi/jaketto} o nuida.
(**b**) He always wears the same jacket.
彼はいつも同じ{上着/ジャケット}を着ている。
Kare wa itsu-mo onaji {uwa-gi/jaketto} o kite iru.

jail n. **[a place where people are confined after being convicted of a crime or while waiting to be tried for a crime]**
ke⌈imu⌉-sho 刑務所 •c [an institution where people convicted (or accused) of crimes are forced to stay] ((**prison**)), **ko⌈ochi-sho 拘置所 •c [a place where people are confined while waiting to be tried for a crime]** ((**prison**))

EX. (**a**) I went to the jail to see him.
私は{刑務所/拘置所}へ彼に会いに行った。
Watashi wa {keimu-sho/koochi-sho} e kare ni ai ni itta.
(**b**) He is in jail.
彼は{刑務所/拘置所}に入っている。
Kare wa {keimu-sho/koochi-sho} ni haitte iru.
(**c**) He left jail after serving 30 years.
彼は三十年服役して、{刑務所/*拘置所}を出た。
*Kare wa san-juu-nen fukueki-shite, {keimu-sho/*koochi-sho} o deta.*

jam[1] vi./vt. **[for s.o. to pack things or people tightly into a small place]**
⟨-o⟩ ⟨-ni⟩ tsu⌈me-komu ⟨～を⟩⟨～に⟩詰め込む ① [for s.o. to fill tightly the inside of s.t. (including the brain) with material] ((**cram, stuff**)), **⟨-o⟩ ⟨-ni⟩ o⌈shi-{ko⌉mu/komeru} ⟨～を⟩⟨～に⟩押し{込む ①/込める ②} [for s.o. to force s.t./s.o./s.a. in a small space by pushing]** ((**push in, thrust in**))

EX. (**a**) The passengers were jammed into the packed train and couldn't move.
乗客は満員電車の中に{押し{込まれて/込められて}/*詰め込まれて}、動きがとれなかった。
*Jookyaku wa man'in-densha no naka ni {oshi-{koma-rete/kome-rarete}/*tsume-koma-rete}, ugoki ga tore-nakatta.*
(**b**) I jammed all my personal things into two suitcases and left home.
身の回りの物を全部二つのスーツケースに{詰め込んで/押し込んで/*押し込めて}家を出た。
*Mi-no-mawari no mono o zenbu futatsu no suutsukeesu ni {tsume-konde/oshi-konde/*oshi-komete} uchi o deta.*

—— n. **[a mass of people/things pressed so close together that they can hardly move]**
za⌈ttoo 雑踏 •c [a mass of people and vehicles so close together that they can hardly move] ((**congestion**))

PHRASE: traffic jam *kootsuu-juutai* 交通渋滞 •c

jam[2] n. **[a spread made from boiled fruit sweetened with sugar]**
ja⌉mu ジャム •f ((**preserve**))

EX. She spread some strawberry jam generously on a slice of bread.
彼女はパンにいちごジャムをたっぷりつけた。
Kanojo wa pan ni ichigo-jamu o tappuri tsuketa.

January n.
i⌈chi-gatsu⌉ 一月 •c

EX. I went to Australia this past January.
私は今年の一月にオーストラリアへ行った。

Watashi wa kotoshi no ichi-gatsu ni Oosutoraria e itta.

Japan n.
{**Ni⌈ho⌉n/Ni⌈ppo⌉n**} 日本 •c
PHRASE: *Nippon* is the emphatic version of *Nihon.*
EX. (**a**) I taught English in Japan for a year.
私は日本で一年間、英語を教えていた。
Watashi wa {Nihon/Nippon} de ichi-nenkan, eigo o oshiete ita.
(**b**) Mt. Fuji is the highest mountain in Japan.
富士山は日本で一番高い山だ。
Fuji-san wa {Nihon/Nippon} de ichiban takai yama da.
PHRASE: made in Japan *Nihon-sei no* N 日本製のN •c

Japanese n. **[the people of Japan/a person from Japan/the language of Japan]**
1. Ni⌈hon-ji⌉n 日本人 •c **[the people of/a person from Japan]**
EX. He isn't Japanese.
彼は日本人じゃありません。
Kare wa Nihon-jin jaarimasen.
2. Ni⌈hon-go 日本語 •c **[the language of Japan]**
EX. Can you speak Japanese?
日本語が話せますか。
Nihon-go ga hanase-masu ka.

—— adj. **[of Japan/a person from Japan/the people of Japan/the language of Japan]**
1. Ni⌈hon no N 日本のN •c **[of Japan]**
EX. Many Japanese men are workaholics.
日本の男性には仕事中毒の人が多い。
Nihon no dansei ni wa shigoto-chuudoku no hito ga ooi.
2. Ni⌈hon-ji⌉n no N 日本人のN **[of the people of/a person from Japan]**
EX. I'm interested in Japanese opinions on this matter.
この事に関する日本人の意見に興味がある。
Kono koto ni-kansuru Nihon-jin no iken ni kyoomi ga aru.
3. Ni⌈hon-go no N 日本語のN **[of the Japanese language]**
EX. Japanese grammar is very different from English grammar.
日本語の文法は英語の文法と非常に違う。
Nihon-go no bunpoo wa eigo no bunpoo to hijooni chigau.
PHRASE: Japanese style *wafuu* 和風 •c ↔ *yoofuu* 洋風 •c; Japanese-style food *washoku* 和食 •c ↔ *yooshoku* 洋食 •c; Japanese-style clothes *wafuku* 和服 •c ↔ *yoofuku* 洋服 •c; Japanese-style room *Nihon-ma* 日本間 •c ↔ *yooma* 洋間 •c; Japanese history *Nihon-shi* 日本史 •c, Japanese archipelago *Nihon-rettoo* 日本列島 •c, Japanese sash *obi* 帯
EX. I bought an old *kimono* and a Japanese sash at a market in Kyoto.
私は京都の市で古い着物と帯を買った。
Watashi wa Kyooto no ichi de furui ki-mono to obi o katta.

jar n. **[a container with a wide mouth made of glass, stone, clay, etc., and used for storing food]**
bi⌉n 瓶 **[a slender, glass container with a narrow mouth normally used for holding liquids]** ⟨⟨**bottle**⟩⟩, **tsu⌈bo** つぼ **[a round, earthen container with a narrow mouth]** ⟨⟨**pot**⟩⟩
EX. (**a**) Unscrew the cap on this jar, please.
この{瓶/*つぼ}のふたを開けてください。
*Kono {bin/*tsubo} no futa o akete kudasai.*
(**b**) She kept a jar of cookies in the cupboard.
彼女はクッキーの入った{つぼ/瓶}を戸だなにしまっていた。
Kanojo wa kukkii no haitta {tsubo/bin} o to-dana ni shimatte ita.

jaw n. **[either of the two bony parts of the face to which teeth are attached]**
a⌈go⌉ あご ⟨⟨**chin**⟩⟩
EX. I was hit in the jaw.
私はあごを殴られた。
Watashi wa ago o nagura-reta.
PHRASE: the upper jaw *uwa-ago* 上あご, the lower jaw *shita-ago* 下あご

jazz n. **[a kind of music originated by African-Americans]**
ja⌉zu ジャズ •f

J

EX. (**a**) They're playing jazz at a night club.
彼らはナイトクラブでジャズを演奏している。
Kare-ra wa naito-kurabu de jazu o ensoo-shite iru.
(**b**) Is jazz popular among young people these days?
ジャズは近ごろ若者の間で人気がありますか。
Jazu wa chikagoro waka-mono no aida de ninki ga arimasu ka.

jealous adj. **[fearful of or unhappy at losing one's rights or the love of s.o. to another person or discontented because s.o. else has possessions, qualities, or achievements which one wishes were one's own]**
1. **⟨-ni⟩ shi⌈tto⌉-suru** ⟨〜に⟩しっとする ③ **[unhappy or bitter toward s.o. for being better at s.t., having more, or being happier than one]**

EX. (**a**) Taro felt jealous when he saw his wife dancing with a tall, handsome man.
太郎は妻が背の高い、ハンサムな男と踊っているのを見て、しっとした。
Taroo wa tsuma ga se no takai, hansamuna otoko to odotte iru no o mite, shitto-shita.
(**b**) Tomoko was jealous of her baby sister because she always attracted everybody's attention.
智子はいつもみんなの注目を集める赤ん坊の妹にしっとしていた。
Tomoko wa itsu-mo minna no chuumoku o atsumeru akanboo no imooto ni shitto-shite ita.

2. **⟨-ga⟩ u⌈rayamashi⌉i** ⟨〜が⟩うらやましい adj(*i*). **[discontented because s.o. else has possessions, qualities, or achievements which one wishes were one's own]** ⟪**envious**⟫, **⟨-o⟩ ne⌈ta⌉mu** ⟨〜を⟩ねたむ ① **[for s.o. to feel discontented or bitter toward s.o. else for having possessions, qualities, or achievements which one wishes were one's own]** ⟪**envy**⟫

NOTE: *Netamu* implies hostility while *urayamashii* does not. *Urayamashii* changes to *urayamashi-garu* when the subject is a third person.

EX. (**a**) He may feel jealous of your success.
彼はあなたの成功を{うらやましがる/ねたむ}かもしれない。
Kare wa anata no seikoo o {urayamashi-garu/netamu} kamoshirenai.
(**b**) He's jealous of me for passing the entrance exam to Tokyo University.
彼は私が東京大学の入学試験に通ったのを{ねたんで/うらやましがって}いる。
Kare wa watashi ga Tookyoo-daigaku no nyuugaku-shiken ni tootta no o {netande/urayamashi-gatte} iru.
(**c**) I was jealous of Rie's beauty.
私は理恵の美しさ{がうらやましかった/をねたんだ}。
Watashi wa Rie no utsukushi-sa {ga urayamashikatta/o netanda}.

jeans n. **[trousers made of denim]**
ji⌈ipan ジーパン •**f**, **ji⌉inzu** ジーンズ •**f**

NOTE: The word *jiinzu* was introduced into Japanese after *jiipan*, hence sounds more fashionable.

EX. My mother always wears jeans at home.
母は家ではいつも{ジーパン/ジーンズ}をはいている。
Haha wa uchi de wa itsu-mo {jiipan/jiinzu} o haite iru.

jello n. **[a soft semi-solid food made with sweetened fruit juice and gelatin]**
ze⌉rii ゼリー •**f**

EX. I had orange jello for dessert.
私はデザートにオレンジのゼリーを食べた。
Watashi wa dezaato ni orenji no zerii o tabeta.

Jerusalem n.
E⌈rusa⌉remu エルサレム •**f**

jet n. **[an aircraft powered by a stream of hot gas ejected from its engines]**
je⌈tto⌉-ki ジェット機 •**f+c**

EX. It takes about an hour to fly by jet from Haneda to Osaka.
羽田から大阪までジェット機で一時間ぐらいかかる。

Haneda kara Oosaka made jetto-ki de ichi-jikan-gurai kakaru.

PHRASE: jet lag *jisa-boke* 時差ぼけ

Jew n. **[s.o. who believes in and practices Judaism or is a descendant of the ancient Hebrews]**
Yu⌈daya⌉-jin ユダヤ人 •f+c

jewel n. **[a precious stone or an ornament made from such]**
ho⌈oseki 宝石 •c ⟪gem, jewelry⟫

EX. (**a**) She doesn't own any authentic jewels.
彼女は本物の宝石は一つも持っていない。
Kanojo wa hon-mono no hooseki wa hitotsu mo motte inai.
(**b**) She locked her jewels in the safe.
彼女は宝石を金庫にしまって、かぎをかけた。
Kanojo wa hooseki o kinko ni shimatte, kagi o kaketa.

Jewish adj. **[having to do with the Jews or their religion or culture]**
Yu⌈daya⌉-jin no N ユダヤ人のN •f+c

EX. (**a**) My husband is Jewish.
主人はユダヤ人だ。
Shujin wa Yudaya-jin da.
(**b**) I was invited to a Jewish wedding.
私はユダヤ人の結婚式に招待された。
Watashi wa Yudaya-jin no kekkon-shiki ni shootai-sareta.

job n. **[regular paid employment or a piece of work]**
shi⌈goto 仕事 [an activity performed for a particular purpose other than amusement and on which one expends time and effort] ⟪work, business⟫

EX. (**a**) I have to look for a job.
私は仕事をさがさなければなりません。
Watashi wa shigoto o sagasanakereba narimasen.
(**b**) I think I'm not suited for an ordinary nine-to-five job.
私は九時から五時までの普通の仕事には向いていないと思う。
Watashi wa ku-ji kara go-ji made no futsuu no shigoto ni wa muite inai to omou.

PHRASE: part-time job *arubaito* アルバイト •f

EX. Lots of students have part-time jobs.
アルバイトをしている学生が多い。
Arubaito o shite iru gakusei ga ooi.

jog vi. **[to run slowly and steadily, esp. for exercise]**
jo⌉gingu (o) suru ジョギング(を)する ③ •f

EX. I jog along the river every morning.
毎朝川のそばをジョギングします。
Mai-asa kawa no soba o jogingu-shimasu.

join vt. **[to come together or to put s.t./s.o./s.a. together with s.t./s.o./s.a. else so as to become one]**

1. ⟨-o⟩ tsu⌈nagu ⟨〜を⟩つなぐ ① [for s.o. to link or attach s.t./s.o./s.a. onto s.t. else, usu. by means of a cord-like object] ⟪connect, tie, fasten, unite⟫

EX. This highway joins the two cities.
この高速道路が二つの町をつないでいる。
Kono koosoku-dooro ga futatsu no machi o tsunaide iru.

PHRASE: be joined *tsunagaru* つながる ① ⟪be fastened⟫

EX. These two buildings are joined by a passageway.
この二つの建物は廊下でつながっています。
Kono futatsu no tate-mono wa rooka de tsunagatte imasu.

2. ⟨-ni⟩ ha⌉iru ⟨〜に⟩入る ① [to go into some place ⟪fig. "join"⟫] ⟪enter, be included⟫, ⟨-ni⟩ ku⌈wawaru ⟨〜に⟩加わる ① [for s.o. to take part in some group or activity] ⟪participate⟫

EX. (**a**) I joined the Linguistic Society of America last year.
私は去年アメリカ言語学会に{入った/*加わった}。
*Watashi wa kyonen Amerika-gengo-gakkai ni {haitta/*kuwawatta}.*
(**b**) The Japanese students joined in the discussion with the foreign students.
日本人の学生が外国人の学生の議論に{加わった/入った}。

J

Nihon-jin no gakusei ga gaikoku-jin no gakusei no giron ni {kuwawatta/haitta}.

joint adj. **[shared by two/more people] go⌈odoo no N 合同のN •c [done together by a number of people at the same time]** ⟪**combined, united**⟫**, kyo⌈odoo no N 共同のN •c [shared by two/more people on an equal footing]** ⟪**common**⟫

EX. (**a**) The three universities held a joint concert.
三つの大学が{合同/共同}で音楽会を開いた。
Mittsu no daigaku ga {goodoo/kyoodoo} de ongaku-kai o hiraita.
(**b**) Japan and the United States issued a joint statement.
日本とアメリカは{共同/*合同}声明を発表した。
*Nihon to Amerika wa {kyoodoo/ *goodoo}-seimei o happyoo-shita.*
(**c**) My husband and I are joint owners of the restaurant.
主人と私はレストランの{共同/*合同}経営者です。
*Shujin to watashi wa resutoran no {kyoodoo/*goodoo}-keiei-sha desu.*
(**d**) The Self-Defense Forces of Japan held joint maneuvers with the U.S. Army at the foot of Mt. Fuji.
日本の自衛隊はアメリカ軍と富士山ろくで{合同/*共同}演習を行った。
*Nihon no Jiei-tai wa Amerika-gun to Fuji-sanroku de {goodoo/*kyoodoo}-enshuu o okonatta.*

joke n. **[s.t. said/done to make people laugh] jo⌈oda⌉n 冗談 •c [s.t. said to make people laugh]**

EX. (**a**) John took my joke seriously and got angry.
ジョンは私の冗談を真に受けて、怒ってしまった。
Jon wa watashi no joodan o ma-ni-ukete, okotte shimatta.
(**b**) Prof. Yamada does nothing but crack jokes in class.
山田先生は授業中に冗談ばかり言う。
Yamada-sensei wa jugyoo-chuu ni joodan bakari iu.
(**c**) He cracks very funny jokes with a straight face.
彼は真面目な顔をしてすごくおかしな冗談を言う。
Kare wa majimena kao o shite sugoku okashina joodan o iu.

jolly adj. **[happy/pleasant/merry] yu⌉kaina 愉快な** adj(*na*). **•c [experiencing happiness or merriment deriving from a sense of satisfaction with s.t. or causing such a feeling in one]** ⟪**cheerful, amusing, pleasant**⟫, ↔ **fu-yukaina 不愉快な** adj(*na*). **•c; ta⌈noshi⌉i 楽しい** adj(*i*). **[experiencing intense enjoyment and satisfaction from s.t. and thus being drawn to it or causing such a feeling in one]** ⟪**cheerful, pleasant, fun, enjoyable, delightful, happy**⟫

EX. (**a**) He's a jolly guy, always smiling.
彼は{愉快な/楽しい}人で、いつも笑っている。
Kare wa {yukaina/tanoshii} hito de, itsu-mo waratte iru.
(**b**) Santa Claus is a jolly old man.
サンタ・クロースは{愉快な/楽しい}老人だ。
Santa-kuroosu wa {yukaina/tanoshii} roojin da.

journey n. **[the course covered in traveling from one place to another, often over a long distance]**
ryo⌈koo 旅行 •c ⟪**trip, travel, tour**⟫**, ta⌈bi⌉ 旅** ⟪**trip, travel, tour**⟫

EX. (**a**) I went on a long journey across the continental United States.
私はアメリカ横断の長い{旅行/旅}に出た。
Watashi wa Amerika-oodan no nagai {ryokoo/tabi} ni deta.
(**b**) When I was a college student, I made a journey by train to Hokkaido.
大学生の時、北海道へ{汽車の旅/汽車旅行}をした。
Daigaku-sei no toki, Hokkaidoo e {kisha no tabi/kisha-ryokoo} o shita.

(c) Life can be compared to a long journey.
人生は長い{旅/*旅行}のようなものだ。
*Jinsei wa nagai {tabi/*ryokoo} no yoona mono da.*

NOTE: *Tabi* carries a literary, romantic flavor.

joy n. **[a deep feeling of happiness]**
yo⌈rokobi⌉ 喜び /⟨V*masu* of *yorokobu* ① be pleased/ ⟪delight, rejoicing, pleasure⟫, u⌈re⌉shi-sa うれしさ /⟨adj(*i*). stem of *ureshii* happy, glad + suf. *sa* ness/ [a temporary, feeling of happiness tied to the immediate situation] ⟪delight, gladness⟫

EX. (a) She jumped for joy when she heard the news.
彼女はそのニュースを聞いたとき、{喜び/嬉しさ}のあまり、飛び上がった。
Kanojo wa sono nyuusu o kiita toki, {yorokobi/ureshi-sa} no amari, tobi-agatta.
(b) I've experienced both the joys and sorrows of life in this one week.
私はこの一週間の間に人生の{喜び/*嬉しさ}と悲しみの両方を味わった。
*Watashi wa kono is-shuukan no aida ni jinsei no {yorokobi/*ureshi-sa} to kanashi-mi no ryoohoo o ajiwatta.*

judge vt./vi. **[for s.o. to form an opinion about s.t./s.o., esp. one based on careful consideration of all relevant information]**
1. {⟨-o⟩/⟨-to⟩/Sinf. ka do⌉o ka} ha⌉ndan-suru {⟨〜を⟩/⟨〜と⟩/Sinf.かどうか}判断する ③ •c [for s.o. to form an opinion about s.t.]

EX. (a) You shouldn't judge people by their outward appearance.
人を外見で判断してはいけない。
Hito o gaiken de handan-shite wa ikenai.
(b) I can't judge whether or not it's a good school based on this limited information.
これだけの情報ではいい学校かどうか判断できません。
Kore dake no joohoo de wa ii gakkoo ka doo ka handan-dekimasen.

NOTE: The copula *da* is often omitted before *ka doo ka*, as in example (b).

(c) He was judged to be the most suitable person for the post.
彼がその職には最も適任だと判断された。
Kare ga sono shoku ni wa mottomo tekinin da to handan-sareta.

2. ⟨-o⟩ shi⌉nsa-suru ⟨〜を⟩審査する ③ •c [for s.o. to evaluate the performance of s.o. or the quality of s.t., esp. as part of a competition or a ranking relative to others]

EX. I was asked to judge speeches at an English speech contest.
英語の弁論大会でスピーチを審査するよう頼まれた。
Eigo no benron-taikai de supiichi o shinsa-suru yoo tanoma-reta.

— n. **[s.o. who decides issues brought before a court of law or who decides the winner in a competition or who knows enough about a subject to offer an informed opinion on it]**
1. sa⌈iba⌉n-kan 裁判官 •c [s.o. who decides issues brought before a court of law]

EX. The judge sentenced the criminal to death.
裁判官は犯人に死刑の判決を下した。
Saiban-kan wa hannin ni shikei no hanketsu o kudashita.

2. shi⌈nsa⌉-in 審査員 •c [s.o. who evaluates the performance of s.o. or the quality of s.t., esp. as part of a competition or a ranking relative to others]

EX. I acted as a judge at a speech contest.
弁論大会で審査員を務めた。
Benron-taikai de shinsa-in o tsutometa.

judgment n. **[an opinion formed about s.t., esp. as a result of careful consideration of all relevant information, or the ability to form such an opinion competently]**
1. ha⌈nda⌉n-ryoku 判断力 •c [the ability to form an opinion about s.t. competently]

EX. (a) He is a man of sound judgment.
彼はしっかりした判断力の持ち主だ。
Kare wa shikkari-shita handan-ryoku no mochi-nushi da.
(b) I became upset and lost my sense of judgment.

私は気が動転して、判断力を失ってしまった。
Watashi wa ki ga dooten-shite, handan-ryoku o ushinatte shimatta.

2. ha⌉ndan 判断 •c [an opinion formed as a result of considering the relevant information]

EX. My judgment was wrong.
私の判断は間違っていた。
Watashi no handan wa machigatte ita.

juice n. **[the liquid from fruits/vegetables/meats]**

1. shi⌉ru 汁 [the liquid from fruits/vegetables/meats or soup] 《**soup**》

EX. She squeezed juice from the lemon.
彼女はレモンの汁を絞った。
Kanojo wa remon no shiru o shibotta.

2. ju⌉usu ジュース •f [a beverage for drinking made from the liquid from fruits/vegetables]

EX. (**a**) I drink a glass of orange juice every morning.
私は毎朝オレンジジュースを一杯飲みます。
Watashi wa mai-asa orenji-juusu o ip-pai nomimasu.
(**b**) Is this grapefruit juice sweetened?
このグレープフルーツジュースには砂糖が入っていますか。
Kono gureepufuruutsu-juusu ni wa satoo ga haitte imasu ka.

July n.

shi⌈chi-gatsu⌉ 七月 •c

EX. (**a**) He graduated from college last July.
彼は去年の七月に大学を卒業した。
Kare wa kyonen no shichi-gatsu ni daigaku o sotsugyoo-shita.
(**b**) We saw the fireworks this July 4th in Washington, D.C.
今年の七月四日にワシントンで花火を見ました。
Kotoshi no shichi-gatsu yokka ni Washinton de hanabi o mimashita.

jump vi. **[for s.o./s.a. to move quickly and suddenly away from a surface by the action of one's legs]**

1. to⌈bu とぶ ① [for s.o./s.a. to move quickly and suddenly away from a surface by the action of one's leg(s) or to move through the air] 《**leap, hop**》

㊅ "jump"▷跳ぶ, "fly"▷飛ぶ, "in compounds such as *tobi-agaru, tobi-oriru,* etc."▷飛ぶ

NOTE: *Tobu* appears in many compounds, such as *tobi-agaru* "jump up," *tobi-oriru* "jump down," *tobi-komu* "jump into" and *tobi-dasu* "jump out."

EX. How high can you jump?
どのぐらい高く跳べますか。
Dono-gurai takaku tobe-masu ka.

2. to⌈bi-aga⌉ru 飛び上がる /〈V*masu* of *tobu* ① fly, jump + *agaru* ① go up/ ① [to rise into the air suddenly and rapidly] 《**jump up**》

EX. He jumped up to get it.
彼はそれを取るために飛び上がった。
Kare wa sore o toru tame ni tobi-agatta.

3. to⌈bi-ori⌉ru 飛び降りる /〈V*masu* of *tobu* ① fly, jump + *oriru* ② go down/ ② [for s.o./s.a. to move quickly and suddenly down from one place to another by the action of one's leg(s)] 《**jump down**》

EX. (**a**) She jumped down from the speeding train.
彼女は走っている汽車から飛び降りた。
Kanojo wa hashitte iru kisha kara tobi-orita.
(**b**) I managed to jump clear of the car just before it fell into the sea.
私は車が海に落ちる寸前になんとか車から飛び降りた。
Watashi wa kuruma ga umi ni ochiru sunzen ni nan-toka kuruma kara tobi-orita.

4. 〈-ni〉 to⌈bi-ko⌉mu 〈〜に〉飛び込む ① [for s.o./s.a. to move quickly and suddenly into a place] 《**jump into, plunge into, dive into**》

EX. He jumped into the river to save the drowning child.
彼はおぼれかかっている子供を助けるために川に飛び込んだ。
Kare wa obore-kakatte iru kodomo o tasukeru tame ni kawa ni tobi-konda.

5. ⟨-o⟩ to⌈bi-da⌉su ⟨～を⟩飛び出す /⟨V*masu* of *tobu* ① fly, jump + *dasu* ① go out/ ① [for s.o./s.a. to move quickly and suddenly out into an open space by the action of one's leg(s)] ⟪**jump out of, run out of, rush out of**⟫

EX.| I was startled out of my wits when a frog jumped out of my pocket.
かえるがポケットから飛び出したときは、すごくびっくりした。
Kaeru ga poketto kara tobi-dashita toki wa, sugoku bikkuri-shita.

June n.

ro⌈ku-gatsu⌉ 六月 •c

EX.| We got married in June.
私たちは六月に結婚しました。
Watashi-tachi wa roku-gatsu ni kekkon-shimashita.

jungle n. **[land covered with a thick, tangled growth of trees, vines, and other plants, esp. in tropical areas]**

ja⌉nguru ジャングル •f, mi⌈tsurin 密林 •c

EX.| I saw a tiger once in the Malaysian jungle.
私はマレーシアの{ジャングル/密林}でとらを見たことがある。
Watashi wa Mareeshia no {janguru/mitsurin} de tora o mita koto ga aru.

junior n./adj. **[s.o. who is younger or lower in status than s.o. else or a student in the third year at a four-year high school/college/university in the United States]**

1. to⌈shi-shita 年下 n. **[s.o. younger than oneself] ↔ toshi-ue 年上** n.

EX.| He is my junior by five years.
彼は私より五歳年下です。
Kare wa watashi yori go-sai toshi-shita desu.

2. wa⌈ka-te 若手 n. **[a younger member in a group]**

EX.| The junior politicians have organized a study group.
若手の政治家が勉強会を作った。
Waka-te no seiji-ka ga benkyoo-kai o tsukutta.

3. sa⌈n-ne⌉n-sei 三年生 n. **•c [a third-year student/pupil], sa⌈n-nen 三年 •c**

EX.| My son is a junior at Hokkaido University.
息子は北海道大学の三年です。
Musuko wa Hokkaidoo daigaku no san-nen desu.

junk n. **[old/useless/unwanted things]**

ga⌈rakuta がらくた [things of little use/value]

EX.| My tiny apartment is full of junk.
私のちっぽけなアパートはがらくたでいっぱいだ。
Watashi no chippokena apaato wa garakuta de ippai da.

jury n. **[a group of people chosen to hear the facts of a case in a court of law and give their decision as to whether the person is guilty or innocent]**

ba⌈ishi⌉n-in 陪審員 •c

EX.| The jury has rendered a verdict of not guilty.
陪審員は無罪の評決を下した。
Baishin-in wa muzai no hyooketsu o kudashita.

just adv. **[exactly/no more than]**

1. cho⌈odo ちょうど adv. **[with no variance whatsoever from a given time, quantity, or location]**

EX.| (**a**) It started to rain just as I was going out.
ちょうど出かけようとしたとき、雨が降り出した。
Choodo dekakeyoo to shita toki, ame ga furi-dashita.
(**b**) The crown prince passed just by here.
皇太子はちょうどここを通られました。
Koo-taishi wa choodo koko o toora-remashita.

2. dake だけ prt. **[no more/less than or limited only to s.t./s.o./s.a.]** ⟪**only, merely, alone**⟫

EX.| (**a**) I don't want to eat anything; just some water please.
何も食べたくありませんから、水だけお願いします。
Nani-mo tabe-taku arimasen kara, mizu dake o-negai-shimasu.
(**b**) He just stood in the entrance staring at me.

彼は入口に立って、じっと私を見ているだけだった。
Kare wa iri-guchi ni tatte, jitto watashi o mite iru dake datta.

3. to⌈koro ところ [a particular part of space occupied by s.t. or a building occupying a particular part of space《fig. "status," "situation," "occasion," "moment," "passage"》]

EX. (**a**) I have just talked to him over the phone.
彼と電話で話したところです。
Kare to denwa de hanashita tokoro desu.
(**b**) I had just gotten into bed when the fire broke out.
火事になったとき私はちょうど床についたところでした。
Kaji ni natta toki watashi wa choodo toko ni tsuita tokoro deshita.
(**c**) It just turned 9 o'clock.
ちょうど九時を回ったところです。
Choodo ku-ji o mawatta tokoro desu.
(**d**) The class is just about to begin.
授業が始まるところです。
Jugyoo ga hajimaru tokoro desu.

K

kangaroo n.
ka⌈nga⌉ruu カンガルー •f
EX. Are there kangaroos in this zoo?
この動物園にはカンガルーがいますか。
Kono doobutsu-en ni wa kangaruu ga imasu ka.

Kansas n.
Ka⌉nzasu カンザス •f

keen adj. **[very interested in or eager to do s.t.]**
⟨-ni⟩ ne⌉sshinna ⟨〜に⟩熱心な adj(*na*). •c **《eager, enthusiastic》**
EX. (**a**) She's keen on studying Japanese.
彼女は日本語の勉強に熱心だ。
Kanojo wa Nihon-go no benkyoo ni nesshin da.
(**b**) He's a keen golfer.
彼は熱心なゴルファーだ。
Kare wa nesshinna gorufaa da.

keep vt. **[to continue to have s.t., do s.t., or be a certain way without stopping or changing; to do s.t. repeatedly and persistently; to cause s.t./s.o./s.a. to continue in a particular state or situation; to hold s.o./s.t./s.a. back from doing s.t. or changing; for s.o./s.a. to put or store s.t. in a particular place《fig. "honor (a promise, custom, rule, etc.)"》]**
1. ⟨-o⟩ to⌉tte-oku ⟨〜を⟩取っておく **/⟨V*te* of *toru* ① take + *oku* ① to do s.t. in advance for future convenience/ ① 《save, set aside》**
EX. (**a**) I'll keep these old textbooks in case I need them later.

後で要るかもしれないから、この古い教科書を取っておきます。
Ato de iru kamoshirenai kara, kono furui kyooka-sho o totte-okimasu.
(**b**) Would you keep this seat for me while I go to the rest room?
お手洗いに行ってくるから、この席を取っておいてくれませんか。
O-tearai ni itte kuru kara, kono seki o totte-oite kuremasen ka.

2. {⟨-ni⟩/⟨-o⟩} {**Vneg. + seru/Vstem + saseru/saseru**} {⟨〜に⟩/⟨〜を⟩}{**Vneg.+せる/Vstem+させる/させる**} **[for s.o./s.a. to cause s.o./s.t./s.a. to do s.t./to change in state]** ⟪**make, cause, let, have, allow**⟫

EX. (**a**) I'm sorry to keep you waiting for so long.
長い間お待たせしてすみません。
Nagai aida o-mata-se-shite sumimasen.
(**b**) She did a good job of keeping the children amused.
彼女は上手に子供たちを楽しませた。
Kanojo wa joozuni kodomo-tachi o tanoshima-seta.

3. ⟨-o⟩ (⟨-kara⟩) **ma⌈mo⌉ru** ⟨〜を⟩(⟨〜から⟩) 守る ① **[**(**to watch s.t./s.o./s.a. in order**) **to cause s.t./s.o./s.a. not to be harmed/injured/violated]** ⟪**observe**⟫

EX. (**a**) He always keeps his promises.
彼はいつも約束を守る。
Kare wa itsu-mo yakusoku o mamoru.
(**b**) One doesn't necessarily have to know the law in order to keep it.
法律を守るためには必ずしも法律を知っている必要はない。
Hooritsu o mamoru tame ni wa kanarazu-shimo hooritsu o shitte iru hitsuyoo wa nai.

— vi. **[to continue in an activity]**
V*masu* + tsu⌈zukeru V*masu*+続ける ② ⟪**go on, continue**⟫

EX. (**a**) We kept on drinking until 3 o'clock in the morning.
朝三時まで飲み続けた。
Asa san-ji made nomi-tsuzuketa.
(**b**) The population will probably keep on increasing well into the 21st century.
人口は21世紀に入ってもしばらく増え続けるだろう。
Jinkoo wa ni-juu-is-seiki ni haitte mo shibaraku fue-tsuzukeru daroo.

Kentucky n.
Ke⌈nta⌉kkii ケンタッキー •f

Kenya n.
Ke⌉nia ケニア •f

kettle n. **[a metal container used for boiling water]**
ya⌈kan やかん

EX. Please put the kettle on.
やかんを火にかけてください。
Yakan o hi ni kakete kudasai.

key n. **[a small metal instrument for locking/unlocking a door or other opening or s.t. that helps one to understand s.t.** ⟪**fig. "an important role"**⟫**]**
ka⌈gi⌉ かぎ **[a device used to fasten a door, window, lid, or other opening or an instrument used to lock/unlock such a device or s.t. that helps one to understand s.t.** ⟪**fig. "an important role"**⟫**]** ⟪**lock**⟫, **ki⌉i** キー •f **[a small metal instrument for locking/unlocking a door or other opening, esp. that on a car or in a room, or s.t. that helps one to understand s.t.** ⟪**fig. "an important role"**⟫**]**

EX. (**a**) I forgot to bring the key.
{かぎ/キー}を持ってくるのを忘れた。
{Kagi/Kii} o motte-kuru no o wasureta.
(**b**) The weather holds the key to his winning the marathon.
このマラソンで彼が勝つかどうか天候が{かぎ/キー}だ。
Kono marason de kare ga katsu ka doo ka tenkoo ga {kagi/kii} da.

PHRASE: master key *masutaa-kii* マスターキー •f, key ring *kii-horudaa* キーホルダー •f, duplicate key *ai-kagi* 合いかぎ, key word *kii-waado* キーワード •f

kick vt. **[for s.o./s.a. to hit s.o./s.t./s.a. forcefully with the foot]**
⟨-o⟩ **ke⌉ru** ⟨〜を⟩ける ① **[for s.o./s.a. to hit s.o./s.t./s.a. forcefully with the foot** ⟪**fig. "refuse"**⟫**]**

K

EX. (**a**) He kicked the ball with his left foot.
彼は左足でボールをけった。
Kare wa hidari-ashi de booru o ketta.
(**b**) The policeman kicked open the door.
警官はドアをけって開けた。
Keikan wa doa o kette aketa.

kid n. **[a child ⟨s⟩]**
ko⌈domo 子供 **⟪child⟫**

EX. (**a**) I took my kid to the movies on Sunday.
日曜日に子供を映画に連れていった。
Nichiyoo-bi ni kodomo o eiga ni tsurete itta.
(**b**) Don't disturb the kids; they're doing their homework.
子供たちの邪魔をしないでください。宿題をしているんですから。
Kodomo-tachi no jama o shinaide kudasai. Shukudai o shite iru n desu kara.

kill vt. **[to cause to die]**
⟨-o⟩ ko⌈rosu ⟨～を⟩殺す ① **[for s.o./s.a. to cause s.o./s.a. to die] ⟪murder⟫**

EX. (**a**) The hungry lion killed a zebra for food.
腹の減ったライオンはしま馬を殺して食べた。
Hara no hetta raion wa shima-uma o koroshite tabeta.
(**b**) I can't believe he committed suicide. He must have been killed by someone.
彼が自殺をしたなんて信じられない。だれかに殺されたに違いない。
Kare ga jisatsu o shita nante shinji-rarenai. Dare-ka ni korosa-reta ni chigainai.

NOTE: In English, "kill" can be used even when the cause of death is not human or animate, but not so with *korosu* in Japanese. If the cause of death is something non-animate, it is normal to use the verb *shinu* "die" and attach the particle *de* to the cause, as in example (a) below. Note also that a different verb for "die" must be used in the case of a plant dying, as in example (b).

EX. (**a**) He was killed in the war.
彼は戦争で死んだ。
Kare wa sensoo de shinda.
(**b**) The drought killed the rice.
かんばつで稲が枯れた。
Kanbatsu de ine ga kareta.

kilogram n.
ki⌈ro-gu⌉ramu キログラム **•f, ki⌉ro** キロ **•f**

EX. I weigh about 45 kilograms.
私は体重が45キロ(グラム)ぐらいです。
Watashi wa taijuu ga yon-juu-go kiro(-guramu)-gurai desu.

kilometer n.
ki⌈ro-{me⌉etoru/me⌉etaa} キロ{メートル/メーター} **•f, ki⌉ro** キロ **•f**

EX. This tunnel is two kilometers long.
このトンネルは長さが二キロ({メートル/メーター})です。
Kono tonneru wa naga-sa ga ni-kiro (-{meetoru/meetaa}) desu.

kimono n. **[traditional Japanese robe-like clothing]**
ki-⌈mono 着物

kind n. **[a group of individuals whose members share common qualities]**
shu⌉rui 種類 **•c ⟪sort, type⟫**

EX. (**a**) I subscribe to several kinds of magazines.
私は数種類の雑誌をとっています。
Watashi wa suu-shurui no zasshi o totte imasu.
(**b**) What kind of wine do you like?
どんな(種類の)ワインが好きですか。
Donna (shurui no) wain ga suki desu ka.

PHRASE: this kind of *konna* こんな

EX. I don't like this kind of color.
こんな色はきらいです。
Konna iro wa kirai desu.

PHRASE: that kind of *sonna* そんな

EX. Where can I get that kind of bag?
そんなバッグはどこで買えますか。
Sonna baggu wa doko de kae-masu ka.

PHRASE: various kinds of *iro-irona* いろいろな

EX. I met various kinds of people at the party.
私はパーティーでいろいろな人に会った。
Watashi wa paatii de iro-irona hito ni atta.

—— adj. **[gentle and caring towards others]**
⟨-ni⟩ shi⌉nsetsuna ⟨～に⟩親切な adj(*na*). **•c**

[for s.o. to be thoughtful of the needs of other people] **《friendly》**, **〈-ni〉 ya⌈sashii** 〈～に〉やさしい adj(*i*). **[causing little or no trouble (to understand) 《fig. "gentle"》]** **《tender, gentle》**

㊈ "tender"▷優しい, "easy"▷易しい

EX. (**a**) Everyone in the international office is very kind to foreign students.
国際交流課の人はみんな留学生にとても{親切だ/優しい}。
Kokusai-kooryuu-ka no hito wa minna ryuugaku-sei ni totemo {shinsetsu da/yasashii}.
(**b**) She has been very kind about letting us stay at her place.
彼女はとても{親切に/*優しく}私たちを自分の所に泊めてくれました。
*Kanojo wa totemo {shinsetsuni/*yasashiku} watashi-tachi o jibun no tokoro ni tomete kuremashita.*
(**c**) Let's try to be kind to animals.
動物にはなるべく{優しく/*親切に}してあげましょう。
*Doobutsu ni wa narubeku {yasashiku/*shinsetsuni} shite agemashoo.*
(**d**) The nurse that took care of me had a very kind voice.
面倒を見てくれた看護婦は声がとても{優しかった/*親切だった}。
*Mendoo o mite kureta kango-fu wa koe ga totemo {yasashikatta/*shinsetsu datta}.*
(**e**) The drowning kitten was saved by a kind girl.
おぼれかけていた子猫は{親切な/優しい}女の子に助けられた。
Obore-kakete ita ko-neko wa {shinsetsuna/yasashii} onna-no-ko ni tasuke-rareta.

PHRASE: Would you be kind enough to…? *Osoreirimasu ga,* V*te {itadakemasen/kudasaimasen} ka.* 恐れいりますが、V*te*{いただけません/くださいません}か。

kindergarten n. **[a school for young children before they enter elementary school]**
yo⌈ochi⌉-en 幼稚園 **•c**

EX. (**a**) My two kids went to the same kindergarten.
うちの二人の子供は同じ幼稚園へ行きました。
Uchi no futari no kodomo wa onaji yoochi-en e ikimashita.
(**b**) I'd like to become a kindergarten teacher.
私は幼稚園の先生になりたいです。
Watashi wa yoochi-en no sensei ni naritai desu.

kindness n. **[the quality of being gentle and caring/a gentle and caring action]** **shi⌉nsetsu** 親切 **•c** **[thoughtfulness of the needs of other people and actions taken out of such thoughtfulness]**, **ya⌈sa⌉shi-sa** 優しさ **/〈adj(*i*). stem of *yasashii* gentle + suf. *sa* ness/** **[gentleness]** **《tenderness》**

EX. (**a**) I'll never forget your kindness to me during my stay in Japan.
日本滞在中の{ご親切/*優しさ}を忘れません。
*Nihon-taizai-chuu no {go-shinsetsu/*yasashi-sa} o wasuremasen.*

NOTE: The prefix *go* of *go-shinsetsu* shows deference to the person who is/was kind.

(**b**) Her pets seem to sense intuitively her kindness toward animals.
彼女のペットは彼女の動物に対する{優しさ/*親切}を本能的に感じるようだ。
*Kanojo no petto wa kanojo no doobutsu ni taisuru {yasashi-sa/*shinsetsu} o honnoo-tekini kanjiru yooda.*

king n. **[a male ruler of a country 《fig. "the most important man/male animal in a group"》]**
o⌉o 王 **•c**, **ko⌈kuo⌉o** 国王 **•c** **[a male ruler of a country]**

EX. (**a**) The lion is the king of beasts.
ライオンは百獣の{王/*国王}だ。
*Raion wa hyaku-juu no {oo/*kokuoo} da.*
(**b**) The King of Sweden visited Japan last year.
スエーデン{国王/?王}が去年日本を訪問された。

K

Sueeden-{kokuoo/?oo} ga kyonen Nihon o hoomon-sareta.
(**c**) He's been the home run king many times.
彼は何度もホームラン{王/*国王}になったことがある。
*Kare wa nan-do-mo hoomuran-{oo/*kokuoo} ni natta koto ga aru.*
(**d**) The king at the time was killed in the revolution.
当時の{国王/王}は革命で殺された。
Tooji no {kokuoo/oo} wa kakumei de korosa-reta.

kingdom n. **[a country governed by a king/queen]**
o⌈okoku 王国 •c
EX. Is Spain a kingdom?
スペインは王国ですか。
Supein wa ookoku desu ka.

kiss vt./vi. **[to touch with the lips to show love or as a greeting]**
⟨-ni⟩ ki⌉su (o) suru ⟨〜に⟩キス(を)する ③ •f
EX. (**a**) Beth kissed her father goodbye.
ベスは父親にさようならのキスをした。
Besu wa chichi-oya ni sayoonara no kisu o shita.
(**b**) He kissed her on the forehead.
彼は彼女の額にキス(を)した。
Kare wa kanojo no hitai ni kisu (o) shita.
(**c**) He hugged me and kissed me.
彼は私を抱きしめて、キス(を)した。
Kare wa watashi o daki-shimete, kisu (o) shita.

—— n. **[an act of kissing]**
ki⌉su キス •f
EX. I miss my mother's goodnight kiss.
母の「お休み」のキスがなつかしい。
Haha no 'O-yasumi' no kisu ga natsukashii.

kitchen n. **[a room where cooking is done]**
da⌈idokoro 台所, ki⌉tchin キッチン •f
EX. (**a**) My apartment has a tiny kitchen.
私のアパートにはごく小さい{台所/キッチン}がついている。
Watashi no apaato ni wa goku chiisai {daidokoro/kitchin} ga tsuite iru.
(**b**) Mother is in the kitchen.
お母さんは{台所/キッチン}にいます。
O-kaa-san wa {daidokoro/kitchin} ni imasu.

kitten n. **[a young cat]**
ko-⌈ne⌉ko 子猫
EX. (**a**) A kitten is mewing.
子猫がニャーニャー鳴いている。
Ko-neko ga nyaa-nyaa naite iru.
(**b**) She gave milk to the kittens.
彼女は子猫に牛乳をやった。
Kanojo wa ko-neko ni gyuunyuu o yatta.

knee n. **[the middle joint of the leg, where it bends]**
hi⌈za ひざ [the middle joint of the leg, where it bends, and the front part of the thigh] ((**lap**))
EX. (**a**) The jeans he's wearing are worn out at the knees.
彼がはいているジーンズはひざがすり切れている。
Kare ga haite iru jiinzu wa hiza ga suri-kirete iru.
(**b**) I hurt my left knee and can't bend it.
私は左のひざを傷めて、曲げることができません。
Watashi wa hidari no hiza o itamete, mageru koto ga dekimasen.

knife n.
na⌉ifu ナイフ •f
EX. (**a**) She stabbed him with a knife.
彼女は彼をナイフで刺した。
Kanojo wa kare o naifu de sashita.
(**b**) Do you eat this with chopsticks or with a knife and fork?
これはおはしで召し上がりますか、それともナイフとフォークで召し上がりますか。
Kore wa o-hashi de meshi-agarimasu ka, sore-tomo naifu to fooku de meshi-agarimasu ka.
PHRASE: kitchen knife *hoochoo* 包丁 **•c**
EX. This kitchen knife cuts very well.
この包丁はすごくよく切れる。

K

| *Kono hoochoo wa sugoku yoku kireru.*

knit vt. **[to make cloth or clothing by joining yarn into a close network with long needles or by machine]**
⟨-o⟩ a⌉mu ⟨〜を⟩編む ① [for s.o. to make s.t. by joining threads of fabric, hair, bamboo, etc., into a network 《fig. "edit"》] ⟪weave, braid, crochet⟫

EX. (**a**) I knitted my father a sweater.
私は父にセーターを編んであげた。
Watashi wa chichi ni seetaa o ande ageta.
(**b**) I'm knitting a scarf out of red wool.
私は赤い毛糸でマフラーを編んでいます。
Watashi wa akai keito de mafuraa o ande imasu.

—— vi. **[to make cloth or clothing by joining yarn into a close network with long needles]**
a⌈mi⌉-mono o suru 編み物をする ③ ⟪crochet⟫

EX. I usually listen to music while I knit.
私はたいてい音楽を聞きながら、編み物をします。
Watashi wa taitei ongaku o kiki nagara, ami-mono o shimasu.

knock vi. **[to hit s.t./s.o./s.a. hard]**
1. ⟨-o⟩ ta⌈ta⌉ku ⟨〜を⟩たたく ① [for s.o. to bring the hand/s.t. held in the hand against s.o./s.t./s.a., usu. repeatedly 《fig. "criticize"》] ⟪strike, tap, slap⟫, ⟨-o⟩ no⌉kku-suru ⟨〜を⟩ノックする ③ •f [to hit a door with one's hand in order to inform the people inside of one's presence]

EX. (**a**) Please knock before entering.
入る前に{ノックして/*たたいて}ください。
*Hairu mae ni {nokku-shite/*tataite} kudasai.*
(**b**) I knocked on the door but nobody answered.
私はドアを{ノックした/たたいた}けど、だれも答えなかった。
Watashi wa doa o {nokku-shita/tataita} kedo, dare-mo kotaenakatta.
(**c**) I heard a branch knocking against the window.
木の枝が窓を{たたく/*ノックする}のが聞こえた。
*Ki no eda ga mado o {tataku/*nokku-suru} no ga kikoeta.*

2. ⟨-ni⟩ ta⌈taki-tsuke⌉ru ⟨〜に⟩たたきつける ② [to hit s.t./s.o./s.a. against s.t. hard] ⟪bump into⟫

EX. He was knocked against the door.
彼はドアにたたきつけられた。
Kare wa doa ni tataki-tsuke-rareta.

—— vt. **[to hit s.t./s.o./s.a. hard]**
⟨-o⟩ na⌈gu⌉ru ⟨〜を⟩殴る [for s.o. to bring one's fist or to use s.t. against s.o./s.a. hard with the intention of causing harm] ⟪strike, hit, beat⟫, ⟨-o⟩ ta⌈ta⌉ku ⟨〜を⟩たたく ① [for s.o. to bring the hand/s.t. held in the hand against s.o./s.t./s.a., usu. repeatedly 《fig. "criticize"》] ⟪strike, tap, slap⟫

EX. (**a**) He knocked the unruly student on the head.
彼は言うことを聞かない学生の頭を{なぐった/たたいた}。
Kare wa iu koto o kikanai gakusei no atama o {nagutta/tataita}.
(**b**) He got knocked hard on the shoulder with a baseball bat.
彼は野球のバットで肩を強く{たたかれた/*なぐられた}。
*Kare wa yakyuu no batto de kata o tsuyoku {tataka-reta/*nagura-reta}.*

know vt./vi. **[for s.o./s.a. to have s.t. in one's mind from having learned or experienced or deduced it]**
1. {⟨-o⟩/Sinf. ka do⌉o ka} shi⌈ru {⟨〜を⟩/Sinf.かどうか}知る

NOTE: When Sinf. includes a WH-word such as *dare* "who," *doko* "where," *itsu* "when," etc. *doo ka* in the above is deleted and the resulting form is Sinf. *ka shiru*, as in (g) below.

EX. (**a**) Do you know his phone number?
彼の電話番号を知っていますか。
Kare no denwa-bangoo o shitte imasu ka.

K

(**b**) I don't know if he is married or not.
彼が結婚しているかどうか知りません。
Kare ga kekkon-shite iru ka doo ka shirimasen.

NOTE: The negative form of *shitte iru* is usually *shiranai* rather than *shitte inai*.

(**c**) I didn't know that he lives in Kyoto.
彼が京都に住んでいるのを知らなかった。
Kare ga Kyooto ni sunde iru no o shiranakatta.
(**d**) It is impossible to know everything.
何もかもすべてを知ることは不可能だ。
Nani-mo-kamo subete o shiru koto wa fu-kanoo da.
(**e**) Do you know Kyoto well?
京都をよく知っていますか。
Kyooto o yoku shitte imasu ka.
(**f**) She knows a lot about computers.
彼女はコンピューターのことをよく知っている。
Kanojo wa konpyuutaa no koto o yoku shitte iru.
(**g**) Do you know when he's coming back from Japan?
彼がいつ日本から帰ってくるか知っていますか。
Kare ga itsu Nihon kara kaette-kuru ka shitte imasu ka.

2. ⟨**-ga**⟩ **wa⌈ka⌉ru** ⟨〜が⟩ 分かる ① **[to be able to figure out the nature, meaning, identity, etc. of s.t./s.o./s.a. which already is/should be in one's mind]** ⟪**understand, recognize, find**⟫

EX. (**a**) A: What are you going to do this weekend?
今週の週末は何をする予定ですか。
Konshuu no shuumatsu wa nani o suru yotei desu ka.
B: I don't know yet.
まだわかりません。
Mada wakarimasen.
(**b**) I don't know what to do.
どうしたらいいか分かりません。
Doo shitara ii ka wakarimasen.
(**c**) I knew it was her by her voice.
声で彼女だと分かった。
Koe de kanojo da to wakatta.

knowledge n. **[what s.o. has in one's mind as a result of learning or experience]**
chi⌉shiki 知識 •c

EX. (**a**) He always wants to show off his knowledge of Japanese.
彼はいつも日本語についての知識をひけらかしたがる。
Kare wa itsu-mo Nihon-go ni-tsuite no chishiki o hikerakashi-ta-garu.
(**b**) My knowledge of Japanese history is poor.
私の日本史に関する知識は乏しい。
Watashi no Nihon-shi ni kansuru chishiki wa toboshii.

Korea n.
Cho⌈ose⌉n 朝鮮 •c
PHRASE: the Republic of Korea *Daikan-minkoku* 大韓民国 •c, South Korea *Kankoku* 韓国 •c, the Democratic People's Republic of Korea *Choosen-minshu-shugi-jinmin-kyoowakoku* 朝鮮民主主義人民共和国 •c, North Korea *Kita-choosen* 北朝鮮

K

L

label n. **[a piece of paper/other material fixed to s.t. to give information about it] ra˥beru ラベル •f [a piece of paper/other material fixed to s.t. to describe what it is], ni˥-fuda 荷札 [a piece of paper/other material fixed to a package giving the names and addresses of the sender and the addressee]** ((**tag**))

EX. (**a**) The toy had a label saying "Made in Japan."
おもちゃには「日本製」という{ラベル/*荷札}が付いていた。
*Omocha ni wa 'Nihon-sei' to iu {raberu/*ni-fuda} ga tsuite ita.*
(**b**) Please don't take the labels off the library books.
図書館の本の{ラベル/*荷札}を取らないでください。
*Tosho-kan no hon no {raberu/*ni-fuda} o toranaide kudasai.*
(**c**) I put an address label on the parcel which I was sending to Africa.
アフリカに送る小包に{荷札/*ラベル}をつけた。
*Afurika ni okuru ko-zutsumi ni {ni-fuda/*raberu} o tsuketa.*

labor n. **[hard work] ro˹odoo 労働 •c [work done in order to earn wages]**

EX. (**a**) Young people these days seem to be averse to hard physical labor.
近ごろの若い人はきつい肉体労働をいやがる。
Chikagoro no wakai hito wa kitsui nikutai-roodoo o iya-garu.
(**b**) He is involved in a labor movement.
彼は労働運動に関わっている。
Kare wa roodoo-undoo ni kakawatte iru.
(**c**) I'm a member of a labor union.
私は労働組合の組合員です。
Watashi wa roodoo-kumiai no kumiai-in desu.

laboratory n. **[a building/room used for scientific experimentation/research] ji˹kke˥n-shitsu 実験室 •c [a room used for scientific experimentation], ke˹nkyuu-jo 研究所 •c [an organization set up to do a particular type of research]** ((**research institute**))

EX. (**a**) Our school has a large chemistry laboratory.
私たちの学校には大きな化学の{実験室/*研究所}がある。
*Watashi-tachi no gakkoo ni wa ookina kagaku no {jikken-shitsu/*kenkyuu-jo} ga aru.*
(**b**) My father is a physicist and works at a physics laboratory.
父は物理学者で、物理{研究所/*実験室}に勤めている。
*Chichi wa butsuri-gakusha de, butsuri-{kenkyuu-jo/*jikken-shitsu} ni tsutomete iru.*

laborer n. **[s.o. whose job involves hard, physical work] ro˹odo˥o-sha 労働者 •c [s.o. who works to earn wages]** ((**worker**))

EX. (**a**) Many farmers in this area go to Tokyo in the winter to work as seasonal laborers.
この地域の農民の多くは冬になると、東京へ季節労働者として出稼ぎに行く。
Kono chiiki no noomin no ooku wa fuyu ni naru to, Tookyoo e kisetsu-roodoo-sha to-shite de-kasegi ni iku.
(**b**) Laborers are quite well paid these days because of the shortage in the work force.
労働力の不足で最近の労働者の賃金はかなりいい。

Roodoo-ryoku no fusoku de saikin no roodoo-sha no chingin wa kanari ii.

lace n. **[a delicate net-like decorative cloth]**
re⌉esu レース •f

EX. She came in a dress of white lace.
彼女は白いレースの洋服を着てきた。
Kanojo wa shiroi reesu no yoofuku o kite kita.

lack vt. **[not to exist or for there not to be enough of s.t.]**

1. na⌉i 無い adj(*i*). **[for s.t. not to exist]** **⟪there isn't, there aren't⟫ ↔ aru ある ①**

EX. (**a**) He lacks the confidence to achieve his goals.
彼には目標を達成する自信が無い。
Kare ni wa mokuhyoo o tassei-suru jishin ga nai.
(**b**) She lacks the ability to do it.
彼女にはそれをする能力が無い。
Kanojo ni wa sore o suru nooryoku ga nai.

2. ⟨-ga⟩ ta⌈rinai ⟨〜が⟩足りない /⟨neg. of *tariru* ② be sufficient/ [not have enough of s.t.] ⟪not enough, not sufficient, short of⟫

EX. (**a**) That school lacks enough teaching staff.
あの学校は教員が足りない。
Ano gakkoo wa kyooin ga tarinai.
(**b**) She's a nice person but lacks in common sense.
彼女はいい人だけど、常識が足りない。
Kanojo wa ii hito da kedo, jooshiki ga tarinai.

ladder n. **[a structure consisting of two long pieces of wood/rope/metal with steps inbetween for climbing up or down]**
ha⌈shigo はしご

EX. (**a**) We used a ladder to save the child from the burning building.
はしごを使って燃えている建物から子供を助けだした。
Hashigo o tsukatte moete iru tate-mono kara kodomo o tasuke-dashita.
(**b**) I climbed up the ladder to the roof.
私ははしごを伝って屋根に上った。
Watashi wa hashigo o tsutatte yane ni nobotta.
(**c**) He leaned a ladder against the side of the house for use in cleaning the gutters.
彼はといを掃除するために家の横にはしごを立てかけた。
Kare wa toi o sooji-suru tame ni ie no yoko ni hashigo o tate-kaketa.

lady n. **[a woman of polite, dignified and graceful manners and behavior ⟪fig. "a polite word for a woman"⟫]**
fu⌈jin 婦人 •c [an adult, often married female person] ⟪woman⟫, jo⌈sei 女性 •c [the human sex which gives birth] ⟪woman⟫ ↔ dansei 男性 •c; o⌈nna no hito 女の人 [a woman] ↔ otoko no hito 男の人

NOTE: *Fujin* sounds rather old-fashioned, but is used in many compounds, such as *fujin-gutsu* ladies' shoes, *fujin-fuku* ladies' wear, *fujin-keikan* policewoman, etc.

EX. (**a**) Where can I find ladies' shoes?
{婦人/*女性/*女の人}靴はどこですか。
*{Fujin/*Josei/*Onna no hito}-gutsu wa doko desu ka.*
(**b**) Who is that lady?
あの{ご婦人/女性/女の人}はどなたですか。
Ano {go-fujin/josei/onna no hito} wa donata desu ka.

NOTE: The prefix *go* adds politeness to the word *fujin*.

lake n. **[a large body of water, usually fresh, surrounded by land]**
mi⌈zuu⌉mi 湖

EX. (**a**) Can we swim in this lake?
この湖で泳いでもいいですか。
Kono mizuumi de oyoide mo ii desu ka.
(**b**) This lake serves as a reservoir for the people in this area.
この湖はこの地域の人々の貯水池です。
Kono mizuumi wa kono chiiki no hito-bito no chosui-chi desu.
(**c**) The water in this lake is very polluted.
この湖の水は非常に汚染されている。
Kono mizuumi no mizu wa hijooni osen-sarete iru.

lamb n. **[a young sheep or the meat from a young sheep]**

1. ko-ˈhitsuˈji 子羊 [a young sheep]

EX. I bought a stuffed toy lamb in Australia.
私はオーストラリアで子羊のぬいぐるみを買った。
Watashi wa Oosutoraria de ko-hitsuji no nuigurumi o katta.

2. raˈmu ラム [the meat of a young sheep]

EX. I don't like lamb very much.
私はラムはあまり好きじゃありません。
Watashi wa ramu wa amari suki jaarimasen.

lame adj. **[not able to walk properly because of an injury to or defect in one's leg/foot]**
biˈkko no N びっこのN

EX. Our dog is lame from being hit by a car.
うちの犬は車にはねられて今はびっこです。
Uchi no inu wa kuruma ni hane-rarete ima wa bikko desu.

NOTE: *Ashi ga fu-jiyuuna* N is a euphemism for *bikko no* N.

lamp n. **[an apparatus for giving light]**
(deˈnki-)sutaˈndo (電気)スタンド •c+f [a movable electrical apparatus for giving light] ⟪table lamp, floor lamp⟫

EX. (**a**) I turned on the bedside lamp to read.
本を読もうと思ってベッドのそばの(電気)スタンドをつけた。
Hon o yomoo to omotte beddo no soba no (denki-)sutando o tsuketa.
(**b**) I turned off the lamp on the desk.
私は机の上の(電気)スタンドを消した。
Watashi wa tsukue no ue no (denki-) sutando o keshita.

land n. **[the solid dry part of the earth's surface or ground used for farming, building, etc.]**

1. riˈku 陸 •c [the solid dry part of the earth's surface] ↔ umi 海

EX. (**a**) I'm a fisherman; I can't make a living on land.
おれは漁師だ。陸での仕事はできない。
Ore wa ryooshi da. Riku de no shigoto wa dekinai.
(**b**) We were excited when we sighted land after the long voyage.
長い航海のあとで陸を目にしたときは、興奮した。
Nagai kookai no ato de riku o me ni shita toki wa, koofun-shita.

2. toˈchi 土地 •c [the surface of the earth as property owned by s.o. or utilized for a purpose such as growing crops] ⟪soil, lot⟫

EX. (**a**) My father owns some land in the Ginza.
父は銀座に土地を持っている。
Chichi wa ginza ni tochi o motte iru.
(**b**) The price of land in Tokyo is unbelievably high.
東京の土地の値段は信じられないほど高い。
Tookyoo no tochi no nedan wa shinji-rarenai hodo takai.
(**c**) This land is excellent for growing rice.
ここは稲作には最高の土地だ。
Koko wa inasaku ni wa saikoo no tochi da.

— vi. **[to come down from the air to the ground or a water surface or to come ashore from out at sea]**
⟨-ni⟩ chaˈkuriku-suru ⟨〜に⟩着陸する ③ •c [for an airplane to come down to the ground from the air], ⟨-ni⟩ joˈoriku-suru ⟨〜に⟩上陸する ③ •c [for s.o./typhoon to come ashore from the sea]

EX. (**a**) The plane landed on schedule.
飛行機は予定どおり{着陸/*上陸}した。
*Hikoo-ki wa yotei-doori {chakuriku/ *jooriku}-shita.*
(**b**) The allied forces landed on the shores of Normandy on June 6, 1944.
連合軍は1944年6月6日にノルマンディーの海岸に{上陸/*着陸}した。
*Rengoo-gun wa sen-kyuu-hyaku-yon-juu-yo-nen roku-gatsu muika ni Norumandii no kaigan ni {jooriku/ *chakuriku}-shita.*

— vt. **[for s.o. to bring s.t. to land from the sea or air]**
⟨-o⟩ riˈku-age-suru ⟨〜を⟩陸揚げする ③ [for s.o. to bring s.t. to land from water]

EX. The ship landed the cargo at Kobe.
船は神戸で荷物を陸揚げした。

Fune wa Koobe de nimotsu o riku-age-shita.

landlady n. **[a woman from whom one rents a room, building, land, etc.]**
ya˥nushi 家主 [a man or woman from whom one rents a room or building] (**(landlord)**), **o˥oya 大家**

EX. (**a**) I asked my landlady to put in a new ventilation fan in the kitchen.
私は{大家/家主}に台所の換気扇を換えてくれるように頼んだ。
Watashi wa {ooya/yanushi} ni daidokoro no kanki-sen o kaete kureru yooni tanonda.
(**b**) My landlady is a kind woman.
{大家/家主}は親切な女の人です。
{Ooya/Yanushi} wa shinsetsuna onna no hito desu.

landlord n. **[a man from whom one rents a room, building, land, etc.]**
ya˥nushi 家主 [a man or woman from whom one rents a room or building] (**(landlady)**), **o˥oya 大家**

landscape n. **[a wide view of natural scenery or a picture of such scenery]**
ke˥shiki 景色 •c [a view of nature worthy of enjoyment] (**(scenery, view)**), **fu˥ukei 風景 •c [the appearance of a place or a situation in terms of its natural features, people, architecture, etc.]** (**(scenery, view, scene)**), **fu˥ukei-ga 風景画 •c [a picture of a scene from nature]**

EX. (**a**) The landscape of the valley as seen from the top of the hill was breathtaking.
丘の上から見渡せる谷の{景色/風景/*風景画}は何とも言えず美しかった。
*Oka no ue kara mi-watase-ru tani no {keshiki/fuukei/*fuukei-ga} wa nan-tomo iezu utsukushikatta.*
(**b**) He took many pictures of the landscape around his hometown.
彼はふるさとの{景色/風景/*風景画}の写真を何枚も撮った。
*Kare wa furusato no {keshiki/fuukei/*fuukei-ga} no shashin o nan-mai-mo totta.*
(**c**) I love the landscapes by Cezanne.
私はセゼンヌの{風景画/*風景/*景色}が大好きです。
*Watashi wa Sezannu no {fuukei-ga/*fuukei/*keshiki} ga dai-suki desu.*

NOTE: Note the following usages of *keshiki* and *fuukei*. *{Keshiki/*Fuukei} ga ii tokoro* "a scenic spot," *ikka-danran no {fuukei/*keshiki}* "a happy scene of a family gathered together."

language n. **[the system or one of a number of systems used for communicating among humans whereby meaning is expressed in vocal sounds or written letters or a system or symbols used in programming computers]**
1. ko˥toba˥ 言葉 [the system or one of a number of systems used for communicating among humans whereby meaning is expressed in vocal sounds or written letters or a sequence of linguistic sounds forming a unit of meaning in human communication] (**(word)**), **ge˥ngo 言語 •c [the system or one of a number of systems used for communicating among humans whereby meaning is expressed in vocal sounds or written letters or a system of symbols used in programming computers]**

EX. (**a**) A marked difference can be seen in the spoken and written style of most languages.
大抵の{言葉/言語}では話し言葉と書き言葉にはっきりした文体の差が見られる。
Taitei no {kotoba/gengo} de wa hanashi-kotoba to kaki-kotoba ni hakkiri-shita buntai no sa ga mi-rareru.
(**b**) Human language is a fascinating subject to study.
人間の{言葉/言語}は非常に魅力的な研究課題だ。
Ningen no {kotoba/gengo} wa hijooni miryoku-tekina kenkyuu-kadai da.

2. -go 〜語 •c [a particular system of human communication through vocal sounds used by a particular people or nation]

EX. (**a**) How many languages can you speak?
何か国語ぐらい話せるんですか。
Nan-ka-koku-go-gurai hanase-ru n desu ka.
(**b**) Japanese is not my native language.
日本語は私の母語ではありません。
Nihon-go wa watashi no bogo dewaarimasen.
(**c**) It takes time to acquire a foreign language.
外国語を習得するのには時間がかかる。
Gaikoku-go o shuutoku-suru no ni wa jikan ga kakaru.

large adj. **[greater than usual in size/number/amount]**
o⌈oki⌉i 大きい adj(*i*). **[greater than usual in size or degree]** **⟨⟨big, great⟩⟩ ↔ chiisai 小さい** adj(*i*).; **o⌉okina N 大きなN ↔ chiisana N 小さなN**
NOTE: *Ookii* is an ordinary adj(*i*). *Ookina* sounds more subjective and impressionistic than *ookii* and can be used only as a noun modifier.

EX. (**a**) He lives alone in a large house.
彼は{大きい/大きな}うちに一人で住んでいる。
Kare wa {ookii/ookina} uchi ni hitori de sunde iru.
(**b**) This T-shirt is too large for me.
このTシャツは私には大きすぎる。
Kono tii-shatsu wa watashi ni wa ooki-sugiru.
(**c**) This temple isn't very large, is it?
このお寺はあまり大きくないですね。
Kono o-tera wa amari ookiku nai desu ne.

PHRASE: a large number of *takusan no* N たくさんのN ⟨⟨many, much, lots of, plenty of⟩⟩
EX. A large number of people participated in the demonstration.
たくさんの人がデモに参加した。
Takusan no hito ga demo ni sanka-shita.

PHRASE: a large sum of *takusan no* N たくさんのN ⟨⟨many, much, lots of, plenty of⟩⟩
EX. He contributed a large sum of money to the fund.
彼はたくさんのお金を基金に寄付した。
Kare wa takusan no o-kane o kikin ni kifu-shita.

last adj./adv. **[after everything/everybody else or the most recent]**
1. sa⌉igo no N 最後のN •c ⟨⟨final⟩⟩ ↔ saisho no N 最初のN •c
EX. (**a**) I did all my homework on the last day of summer vacation.
夏休みの最後の日に宿題を全部した。
Natsu-yasumi no saigo no hi ni shukudai o zenbu shita.
(**b**) That was the last time I talked to her.
それが彼女と話をした最後だった。
Sore ga kanojo to hanashi o shita saigo datta.

2. ko⌈no ma⌉e no N この前のN [most recent], ko⌈no ma⌉e この前 adv. **[most recently]**
EX. (**a**) When did you last see him?
この前彼に会ったのはいつですか。
Kono mae kare ni atta no wa itsu desu ka.
(**b**) I went shopping with my wife last Sunday.
この前の日曜日に家内と買い物に行った。
Kono mae no nichiyoo-bi ni kanai to kai-mono ni itta.

PHRASE: last week *senshuu* 先週 **•c**, last month *sengetsu* 先月 **•c**, last year *kyonen* 去年 **•c**, last night *yuube* ゆうべ, last January *kyonen no ichi-gatsu* 去年の一月

—— n. **[s.o./s.t./s.a. after all the others]**
sa⌉igo 最後 •c ↔ saisho 最初 •c
EX. He was the last to turn in his exam.
試験を出したのは彼が最後だった。
Shiken o dashita no wa kare ga saigo datta.

late adj. **[coming, happening, etc. after the usual or expected time]**
1. o⌈soi 遅い adj(*i*). **[taking more time than is normal or occurring at a point in time after that which is normal or expected]** **⟨⟨slow⟩⟩ ↔ hayai はやい** adj(*i*).
EX. (**a**) Spring is late in coming this year.

今年は春が来るのが遅い。
Kotoshi wa haru ga kuru no ga osoi.
(**b**) Last Sunday we ate a late breakfast around 10 o'clock.
この前の日曜日には十時ごろ遅い朝食をとった。
Kono mae no nichiyoo-bi ni wa juu-ji-goro osoi chooshoku o totta.

2. ⟨⟨**-ni**⟩⟩ **o⌈kureru** ⟨⟨〜に⟩⟩**遅れる** ② **[arriving, happening, etc., after the arranged time]**

EX. (**a**) I was late for class.
私は授業に遅れた。
Watashi wa jugyoo ni okureta.
(**b**) The bus was twenty minutes late.
バスが二十分遅れた。
Basu ga ni-jup-pun okureta.

— adv. **[after the usual or expected time]**
o⌈soku 遅く /**adj**(*i*). ***ku* of *osoi* late, slow**/ ⟪**slowly**⟫ ↔ **hayaku はやく**

EX. (**a**) I stayed up late last night to type my paper.
私はゆうべ論文のタイプをするために遅くまで起きていた。
Watashi wa yuube ronbun no taipu o suru tame ni osoku made okite ita.
(**b**) I came to school late today.
今日は遅く学校へ来ました。
Kyoo wa osoku gakkoo e kimashita.

lately adv. **[at a recent time]**
sa⌈ikin 最近 •**c** ⟪**recently**⟫

EX. (**a**) I haven't seen her lately.
最近、彼女に会っていません。
Saikin, kanojo ni atte imasen.
(**b**) Have you seen any good movies lately?
最近何かいい映画を見ましたか。
Saikin nani-ka ii eiga o mimashita ka.

later adv. **[at a time after the present time or after some other time mentioned]**
1. a⌉to de 後で n.+prt. ⟪**afterwards**⟫

EX. (**a**) See you later.
また後で。
Mata ato de.
(**b**) At first she denied that the rumor was true, but later she admitted it to be true.
彼女は初めそのうわさを否定したけど、後で本当だと認めた。
Kanojo wa hajime sono uwasa o hitei-shita kedo, ato de hontoo da to mitometa.

2. -go ni 〜後に [at a time later than the time in question by the amount of time indicated]

EX. I met him again three years later.
三年後に彼と再会した。
San-nen-go ni kare to saikai-shita.

PHRASE: sooner or later *osokare hayakare* 遅かれ早かれ

latitude n.
i⌉do 緯度 •**c**

EX. Milwaukee is at about the same latitude as Sapporo.
ミルウォーキーは札幌とだいたい同じ緯度のところにある。
Miruwookii wa Sapporo to daitai onaji ido no tokoro ni aru.

PHRASE: north latitude *hokui* 北緯 •**c**, south latitude *nan'i* 南緯 •**c**

EX. The latitude of that city is 30 degrees south.
その町の緯度は南緯三十度だ。
Sono machi no ido wa nan'i san-juu-do da.

latter adj./n. **[the second of two things or people just mentioned ⟨fml⟩]**
ko⌉osha 後者 n. •**c** ↔ **zensha 前者** n. •**c**

EX. (**a**) Of these two plans, I'd choose the latter.
この二つのプランの中では、私は後者をとる。
Kono futatsu no puran no naka de wa, watashi wa koosha o toru.
(**b**) Of these two albums, the former sold well, but the latter didn't sell at all.
この二つのアルバムの中で、前者はよく売れたが、後者は全然売れなかった。
Kono futatsu no arubamu no naka de, zensha wa yoku ureta ga, koosha wa zen-zen ure-nakatta.

PHRASE: the latter half *koohan* 後半 •**c** ↔ *zenhan/zenpan* 前半 •**c**

laugh vi. **[for s.o. to make vocal sounds expressing amusement, happiness, or ridicule, usu. accompanied by a facial expression such as smiling]**

L

wa⌈rau 笑う ① [for s.o. to make vocal sounds expressing amusement, happiness, or ridicule or to turn up the corners of the mouth, usu. exposing the teeth, in an expression of the same] ⦅smile, grin, giggle, chuckle⦆

EX. (**a**) He just laughed when he saw me fall down.
私が転ぶのを見て、彼はただ笑っただけです。
Watashi ga korobu no o mite, kare wa tada waratta dake desu.
(**b**) Nobody laughs at my jokes.
私が冗談を言っても、だれも笑ってくれない。
Watashi ga joodan o itte mo, dare-mo waratte kurenai.
(**c**) Everybody laughed at me when I dozed off in class.
授業中にいねむりをした時は、みんなに笑われました。
Jugyoo-chuu ni inemuri o shita toki wa, minna ni warawa-remashita.

laundry n. **[the act of washing, drying, and ironing fabric materials such as clothes or a business establishment which does this or fabric materials such as clothes which need to be or have been washed, dried, and/or ironed]**

1. se⌈ntaku 洗濯 •c [the act of washing, drying, and/or ironing fabric materials such as clothes]

EX. I do the laundry every Saturday.
私は毎週土曜日に洗濯をする。
Watashi wa mai-shuu doyoo-bi ni sentaku o suru.

2. se⌈ntaku-ya 洗濯屋 [a business establishment where fabric materials such as clothes are washed, dried, and ironed], ku⌈riiningu-ya クリーニング屋

EX. I took my sweater to the laundry.
私はセーターを{洗濯屋/クリーニング屋}に持っていった。
Watashi wa seetaa o {sentaku-ya/kuriiningu-ya} ni motte itta.

3. se⌈ntaku-mono 洗濯物 [fabric materials such as clothes which need to be or have been washed, dried, and/or ironed]

EX. (**a**) There's a lot of laundry to do.
洗濯物がたくさんたまっている。
Sentaku-mono ga takusan tamatte iru.
(**b**) Please don't hang the laundry out to dry on the veranda.
ベランダに洗濯物を干さないでください。
Beranda ni sentaku-mono o hosanaide kudasai.

lavatory n. **[a room used for ridding oneself of one's urine and feces]**

(o-)⌈tea⌉rai (お)手洗い, to⌉ire トイレ •f ⦅bathroom, rest room, washroom, toilet⦆, be⌈njo 便所 •c

NOTE: Both *o-tearai* and *toire* are polite expressions, while *benjo* is straightforward and lacking in any tone of politeness.

EX. (**a**) Where's the lavatory?
{お手洗い/トイレ/便所}はどこですか。
{O-tearai/Toire/Benjo} wa doko desu ka.
(**b**) I lost my ring in the lavatory.
私は{お手洗い/トイレ/便所}で指輪をなくしてしまった。
Watashi wa {o-tearai/toire/benjo} de yubiwa o nakushite shimatta.

law n. **[a rule or set of rules made and enforced in a society by authority or convention or a statement of what always happens under certain conditions, esp. one based on scientific observation]**

1. ho⌈oritsu 法律 •c [a rule or set of rules made and enforced in a society by a recognized authority in that society]

EX. (**a**) The law forbids driving under the influence of alcohol.
飲酒運転は法律で禁じられている。
Inshu-unten wa hooritsu de kinji-rarete iru.
(**b**) Even foreigners must obey the Japanese law while in Japan.
外国人でも日本にいるあいだは日本の法律を守らなければならない。
Gaikoku-jin de mo Nihon ni iru aida wa Nihon no hooritsu o mamoranakereba naranai.

(c) It's a ridiculous law.
それはばかばかしい法律だ。
Sore wa bakabakashii hooritsu da.

PHRASE: practice law *bengoshi o suru* 弁護士をする ③

2. hoˈosoku 法則 •c [a statement of what always happens under certain conditions, esp. one based on scientific observation]

EX. (a) Newton was the one who formulated the law of universal gravity.
ニュートンが万有引力の法則を発見した。
Nyuuton ga ban'yuu-inryoku no hoosoku o hakken-shita.
(b) We all live subject to the laws of nature.
我々は皆自然の法則の下に生きている。
Ware-ware wa mina shizen no hoosoku no moto ni ikite iru.

lawn n. **[an area of closely cut grass, esp. next to a house]**
shiˈba-fu 芝生 [an area covered with closely cut grass as in a garden/park] 《grass》

EX. (a) I took a nap on the lawn.
芝生の上で昼寝をした。
Shiba-fu no ue de hiru-ne o shita.
(b) If you mow the lawn, I'll give you 5,000 yen.
芝生を刈ってくれたら、五千円あげますよ。
Shiba-fu o katte kuretara, go-sen-en agemasu yo.

lawyer n. **[a person whose profession it is to advise people about matters of law and to represent them in court]**
beˈngoˈ-shi 弁護士 •c 《counselor, attorney, solicitor, barrister》

EX. (a) Why don't you consult a lawyer?
弁護士に相談したらどうですか。
Bengo-shi ni soodan-shitara doo desu ka.
(b) She's a very competent lawyer.
彼女はとても有能な弁護士です。
Kanojo wa totemo yuunoona bengo-shi desu.

lay vt. **[for s.o. to cause s.t. to lie somewhere or for s.a. to produce an egg/eggs]**

1. ⟨-ni⟩ ⟨-o⟩ oˈku ⟨〜に⟩⟨〜を⟩置く ① [for s.o./s.a. to cause s.o./s.t./s.a. to be at/in/on a certain place] 《put, set, place》, ⟨-ni⟩ ⟨-o⟩ yoˈkotaeˈru ⟨〜に⟩⟨〜を⟩横たえる ② [to put s.o./one's body in a lying position], ⟨-ni⟩ ⟨-o⟩ shiˈku ⟨〜に⟩⟨〜を⟩敷く ① [for s.o. to put s.t. flat on the floor/ground] 《spread, cover》

EX. (a) They gently laid the injured child on the grass.
彼らはけがをした子供を草の上にそっと{横たえた/置いた/*敷いた}。
*Kare-ra wa kega o shita kodomo o kusa no ue ni sotto {yokotaeta/oita/*shiita}.*
(b) He laid his hat on the table.
彼はテーブルの上に帽子を{置いた/*横たえた/*敷いた}。
*Kare wa teeburu no ue ni booshi o {oita/ *yokotaeta/*shiita}.*
(c) We are having a new carpet laid in the living room.
居間に新しいじゅうたんを{敷いて/*置いて/*横たえて}もらう予定です。
*Ima ni atarashii juutan o {shiite/*oite/ *yokotaete} morau yotei desu.*

2. ⟨-o⟩ uˈmu ⟨〜を⟩うむ ① [to give birth to s.t./s.o./s.a.]
㊅ "give birth to eggs/babies"▷産む, otherwise ▷生む

EX. Last week our hens laid thirty eggs.
先週、うちのにわとりは卵を三十産んだ。
Senshuu, uchi no niwatori wa tamago o san-juu unda.

layer n. **[a thickness of some substance, often one of several, each extending horizontally and occurring one on top of another]**
soˈo 層 •c [a thickness of some substance, each extending horizontally and occurring one on top of another 《fig. "a group fixed according to certain upper and lower limits"》] 《stratum, bracket》

EX. (a) The jello had three layers of different colors and looked delicious.
ゼリーは三つの違う色が層になっていて、おいしそうだった。

Zerii wa mittsu no chigau iro ga soo ni natte ite oishi-soo datta.
(**b**) There was a thick layer of coal between the two layers of rock.
岩の層の間に石炭の厚い層があった。
Iwa no soo no aida ni sekitan no atsui soo ga atta.

PHRASE: wear several layers of clothing *kasane-gi-suru* 重ね着する ③

lazy adj. **[not willing to work or to make an effort to do s.t.]**
na⌈make-mono no N 怠け者のN ⟪idle⟫

EX. (**a**) Don't be lazy.
怠け者になってはいけません。
Namake-mono ni natte wa ikemasen.
(**b**) He's really a lazy guy.
彼は本当に怠け者だ。
Kare wa hontoo ni namake-mono da.
(**c**) Hitoshi is a lazy student and often plays hooky.
均は怠け者の学生でよく学校をサボる。
Hitoshi wa namake-mono no gakusei de yoku gakkoo o saboru.

lead vt. **[to go in front of or alongside s.o./s.a. so as to take him/her to a place or to show s.o. the way]**
⟨-o⟩ {⟨-e⟩/⟨-ni⟩} mi⌈chibi⌉ku ⟨〜を⟩{⟨〜へ⟩/⟨〜に⟩}導く ① [for s.o. to make s.o./s.t. go in a certain direction/place ⟪fig. "guide," "lead"⟫] ⟪guide⟫, ⟨-o⟩ {⟨-e⟩/⟨-ni⟩} tsu⌈rete-{iku/ku⌉ru} ⟨〜を⟩{⟨〜へ⟩/⟨〜に⟩}連れて{行く/来る} /⟨V *te* of *tsureru* ② accompany + *iku* ① go/ *kuru* ③ come/ [for s.o. to go along with s.o./s.a. equal to/lower than oneself in status to a place] ⟪take, bring⟫, ⟨-o⟩ {⟨-e⟩/⟨-ni⟩} a⌈nna⌉i-suru ⟨〜を⟩{⟨〜へ⟩/⟨〜に⟩} 案内する ③ •c [for s.o. to take s.o. to a place] ⟪guide⟫

EX. (**a**) She led the guests to the drawing room.
彼女は客を応接間に{導いた/案内した/*連れて行った}。
*Kanojo wa kyaku o oosetsu-ma ni {michibiita/annai-shita/*tsurete-itta}.*
(**b**) I'm afraid that he's going to lead the country to economic disaster.
彼が国を経済的な破滅に{導く/*連れて行く/*案内する}んじゃないかと心配だ。
*Kare ga kuni o keizei-tekina hametsu ni {michibiku/*tsurete-iku/*annai-suru} n janai ka to shinpai da.*
(**c**) The teacher led the children to a safe place.
先生は子供たちを安全な場所に{導いた/連れて行った/*案内した}。
*Sensei wa kodomo-tachi o anzenna basho ni {michibiita/tsurete-itta/*annai-shita}.*

—— vi. **[for s.t. to be the means of reaching or going through a place]**
⟨-ni⟩ tsu⌈ujiru ⟨〜に⟩通じる ② [for a street or communication to get through to the other end ⟪fig. "be well versed in," "be understood"⟫] ⟪be understood⟫, ⟨-o⟩ to⌉oru ⟨〜を⟩通る ① [to go along or through s.t. (from one side to the other)] ⟪pass⟫

EX. (**a**) This road leads to the central post office.
この道は中央郵便局に{通じて/*通って}いる。
*Kono michi wa chuuoo-yuubin-kyoku ni {tsuujite/*tootte} iru.*
(**b**) A footpath led through the paddy fields.
あぜ道が田んぼの中を{通って/*通じて}いた。
*Aze-michi ga tanbo no naka o {tootte/*tsuujite} ita.*

leader n. **[s.o. who has the responsibility for directing a group, team, organization, etc.]**
shi⌈do⌉o-sha 指導者 •c ⟪teacher, coach⟫, ri⌉idaa リーダー •f

EX. (**a**) He's one of the leaders of the labor union.
彼は労働組合の{指導者/リーダー}の一人だ。
Kare wa roodoo-kumiai no {shidoo-sha/riidaa} no hitori da.
(**b**) He's a born leader.
彼は{指導者/リーダー}になるべくしてなった人だ。
Kare wa {shidoo-sha/riidaa} ni naru-beku-shite natta hito da.

leadership n. **[the position of being a leader or the qualities necessary to be a leader]**

L

1. shi⌈do⌉o-ken 指導権 •c [the power to lead]

EX. A right-wing fringe group has taken over leadership of that party.
右翼の非主流派がその党の指導権を握った。
Uyoku no hi-shuryuu-ha ga sono too no shidoo-ken o nigitta.

2. shi⌈do⌉o-ryoku 指導力 •c [the ability to be a leader]

EX. He lacks leadership.
彼には指導力がない。
Kare ni wa shidoo-ryoku ga nai.

leaf n. **[any of the usually flat green parts of a plant which grow from its stem or branches]**
ha 葉, happa 葉っぱ ⟨s⟩

EX. (**a**) The trees in the garden are now completely bare of leaves.
庭の木はもうすっかり{葉/葉っぱ}が落ちてしまっている。
Niwa no ki wa moo sukkari {ha/happa} ga ochite shimatte iru.
(**b**) We rested in the shade of the lush green leaves of an enormous maple tree.
私たちは大きなかえでの木の、青々と茂った{葉/葉っぱ}の陰で休んだ。
Watashi-tachi wa ookina kaede no ki no, ao-ao-to shigetta {ha/happa} no kage de yasunda.
(**c**) I bent down to pick up a pretty maple leaf.
私は身をかがめてきれいなかえでの{葉/葉っぱ}を拾った。
Watashi wa mi o kagamete kireina kaede no {ha/happa} o hirotta.

PHRASE: autumn leaves *kooyoo* 紅葉 •c

EX. The Arashiyama district of Kyoto is well-known for its colorful autumn leaves.
京都の嵐山は色鮮やかな紅葉でよく知られている。
Kyooto no Arashiyama wa iro-azayakana kooyoo de yoku shira-rete iru.

league n. **[a group of sports clubs that compete among themselves to be champion or a group of people, countries, etc., who have joined together for their common welfare]**

1. ri⌉igu リーグ •f [a group of sports clubs]

EX. The Hanshin Tigers are a team in the Central League.
阪神タイガースはセントラル・リーグのチームです。
Hanshin-taigaasu wa Sentoraru-riigu no chiimu desu.

2. re⌈nmei 連盟 •c [a group of people, countries, etc., who have joined together for their common welfare] ⟪**federation**⟫

EX. (**a**) Japan left the League of Nations in 1933.
日本は1933年に国際連盟を脱退した。
Nihon wa sen-kyuu-hyaku-san-juu-san-nen ni Kokusai-renmei o dattai-shita.
(**b**) An economic league was formed among several oil-producing states in the Middle East.
中東の産油国数か国の間に経済連盟ができた。
Chuutoo no san'yu-koku suu-kakoku no aida ni keizai-renmei ga dekita.
(**c**) Our team belongs to the Japan High School Baseball League.
私たちのチームは日本高校野球連盟に属している。
Watashi-tachi no chiimu wa Nihon-kookoo-yakyuu-renmei ni zokushite iru.

leak vi./vt. **[for liquid or gas to escape through a small opening in a container or to accidentally allow this to happen]**
mo⌈re⌉ru 漏れる ② [for liquid or gas to enter in or escape from a small opening in a container accidentally ⟪fig. "some hidden information/a secret comes to be known with unwelcome consequences"⟫] ⟪leak out, escape⟫, mo⌉ru 漏る ① [for s.t. to allow liquid or gas to enter in or escape through a small opening in itself]

EX. (**a**) Something smells in here. Gas must be leaking.
くさい。ガスが{漏れて/?漏って}いるにちがいない。
Kusai. Gasu ga {morete/?motte} iru ni chigainai.

(**b**) The roof on this building leaks.
この建物は屋根が{漏る/*漏れる}。
*Kono tate-mono wa yane ga {moru/ *moreru}.*
(**c**) The bathtub seems to be leaking.
ふろおけが{漏って/*漏れて}いるようだ。
*Furo-oke ga {motte/*morete} iru yooda.*
(**d**) This tank is leaking gas.
このタンクからガソリンが{漏れて/漏って}いる。
Kono tanku kara gasorin ga {morete/ motte} iru.

— vt. **[for s.o. to make s.t. known that should be secret]**
⟨-o⟩ mo⌈ra⌉su ⟨〜を⟩漏らす ①

EX. (**a**) Who leaked that information to the press?
新聞記者にその情報を漏らしたのはだれですか。
Shinbun-kisha ni sono joohoo o morashita no wa dare desu ka.
(**b**) Someone in the office leaked our secret plans to our competitor.
会社のだれかが商売敵に秘密の青写真を漏らしてしまった。
Kaisha no dare-ka ga shoobai-gataki ni himitsu no ao-jashin o morashite shimatta.

lean vi. **[to slope or bend away from an upright position or for s.o./s.a. to rest one's body against s.t. or s.o./s.a. else]**
1. ka⌈tamu⌉ku 傾く ① **[to become inclined away from a vertical line ⟪fig. "lose vigor"⟫]** **⟪slant, incline⟫**

EX. (**a**) The trees leaned in the wind.
木が風で傾いた。
Ki ga kaze de katamuita.
(**b**) The five-storied pagoda of that temple is leaning a little toward the east.
あの寺の五重の塔は少し東に傾いている。
Ano tera no go-juu no too wa sukoshi higashi ni katamuite iru.

2. ⟨-ni⟩ mo⌈tare⌉ru ⟨〜に⟩もたれる ② **[for s.o. to rest the weight of one's body against s.t.]**

EX. (**a**) She leaned on his shoulder.
彼女は彼の肩にもたれた。
Kanojo wa kare no kata ni motareta.
(**b**) She was leaning against the tree.
彼女は木にもたれていた。
Kanojo wa ki ni motarete ita.

— vt. **[for s.o. to place s.t. so that it partly rests against s.t.]**
⟨-ni⟩ ⟨-o⟩ mo⌈tase-kake⌉ru ⟨〜に⟩⟨〜を⟩もたせかける ②

EX. She leaned a ladder against the wall.
彼女は壁にはしごをもたせかけた。
Kanojo wa kabe ni hashigo o motase-kaketa.

leap vi. **[for s.o./s.a. to jump]**
⟨-o⟩ to⌈bi-koe⌉ru ⟨〜を⟩飛び越える **/⟨V*masu* of *tobu* ① jump + *koeru* ② go over/ ② [for s.o./s.a. to jump over s.t.], ⟨-ni⟩ to⌈bi-no⌉ru** ⟨〜に⟩飛び乗る **/⟨V*masu* of *tobu* ① jump + *noru* ① ride/ ① [for s.o./s.a. to jump onto/ into s.t.]**

EX. (**a**) The dog leaped over the stream.
犬は小川を飛び越えた。
Inu wa ogawa o tobi-koeta.
(**b**) The cat leaped onto the kitchen table.
猫は台所のテーブルの上に飛び乗った。
Neko wa daidokoro no teeburu no ue ni tobi-notta.

learn vt./vi. **[for s.o./s.a. to come to know s.t. or to come to be able to do s.t.]**
1. ⟨-o⟩ na⌈ra⌉u ⟨〜を⟩習う ① **[for s.o. to gain skill in/knowledge of s.t. through being taught] ⟪take lessons⟫**

EX. (**a**) When did you learn how to drive?
いつ運転を習いましたか。
Itsu unten o naraimashita ka.
(**b**) I'm learning Chinese at school.
私は学校で中国語を習っている。
Watashi wa gakkoo de Chuugoku-go o naratte iru.

2. ⟨-o⟩ shi⌉ru ⟨〜を⟩知る ① **[for s.o./s.a. to come to know s.t.] ⟪know⟫**

EX. (**a**) We learned of their marriage from the newspaper.
新聞で彼らが結婚したことを知った。
Shinbun de kare-ra ga kekkon-shita koto o shitta.

(**b**) When did you learn this news?
このニュースを知ったのはいつですか。
Kono nyuusu o shitta no wa itsu desu ka.

3. ⟨-o⟩ o⌈boe⌉ru ⟨～を⟩覚える ② [for s.o./s.a. to sense s.t. in one's body or mind and as a result come to have it in one's mind] ⟪memorize, remember⟫

EX. (**a**) We have to learn all these new kanji by tomorrow.
私たちはあしたまでにこれだけの新しい漢字を全部覚えなければならない。
Watashi-tatchi wa ashita made ni kore dake no atarashii kanji o zenbu oboenakereba naranai.
(**b**) I just can't seem to learn this word.
どうしてもこの単語が覚えられないんです。
Doo-shite-mo kono tango ga oboe-rarenai n desu.

learning n. **[wide-ranging knowledge acquired through careful study]**
ga⌈ku⌉mon 学問 •c ⟪scholarship⟫

EX. (**a**) She looks down on people without learning.
彼女は学問がない人を軽べつする。
Kanojo wa gakumon ga nai hito o keibetsu-suru.
(**b**) Learning for learning's sake is useless.
学問のための学問は何の役にも立たない。
Gakumon no tame no gakumon wa nan no yaku ni mo tatanai.

least adj./pron. **[smallest in number, size, etc.]**
i⌈chiban {sukuna⌉i, chi⌉isana, etc.} N 一番{少ない, 小さな, etc.}N

EX. (**a**) Learning *kanji* is the least of my problems.
漢字を覚えるのは私には一番小さな問題です。
Kanji o oboeru no wa watashi ni wa ichiban chiisana mondai desu.
(**b**) I bought the coat that cost the least.
私は一番安いコートを買った。
Watashi wa ichiban yasui kooto o katta.

PHRASE: at least *sukunaku-tomo* 少なくとも

EX. (**a**) It will cost at least five thousand yen.
少なくとも五千円はかかる。
Sukunaku-tomo go-sen-en wa kakaru.
(**b**) She is at least 30 years old, I think.
彼女は少なくとも三十にはなっていると思う。
Kanojo wa sukunaku-tomo san-juu ni wa natte iru to omou.

PHRASE: not…in the least *zenzen*…neg. 全然…neg.

EX. She is not in the least worried.
彼女は全然心配していない。
Kanojo wa zenzen shinpai-shite inai.

leather n. **[animal skin specially treated to be used in making shoes, clothes, bags, etc.]**
ka⌈wa⌉ 革

EX. (**a**) She's wearing a leather skirt.
彼女は革のスカートをはいている。
Kanojo wa kawa no sukaato o haite iru.
(**b**) Is this bag made of leather?
このバッグは革(製)ですか。
Kono baggu wa kawa(-sei) desu ka.

leave vi./vt. **[to go away from a place or for s.o. to withdraw from an organization]**
1. ⟨-o⟩ de⌉ru ⟨～を⟩出る ② [to go away from some place] ⟪go out⟫, ⟨-o⟩ shu⌈ppatsu-suru ⟨～を⟩出発する ③ •c [for s.o./some vehicle to move away from some place at the beginning of a journey] ⟪start, depart⟫

EX. (**a**) I left home around seven this morning.
今朝、七時ごろ家を{出た/出発した}。
Kesa, shichi-ji-goro uchi o {deta/shuppatsu-shita}.
(**b**) May I leave the room?
部屋を{出て/*出発して}もいいですか。
*Heya o {dete/*shuppatsu-shite} mo ii desu ka.*
(**c**) I left my hometown 3 years ago to study in Tokyo.
東京で勉強するために三年前に故郷を{出た/*出発した}。
*Tookyoo de benkyoo-suru tame ni san-nen-mae ni kokyoo o {deta/*shuppatsu-shita}.*

L

(**d**) We left Osaka Airport for New York on December 19.
私たちは十二月十九日にニューヨークに向けて大阪空港を{出発した/出た}。
Watashi-tachi wa juu-ni-gatsu juu-ku-nichi ni Nyuuyooku ni mukete Oosaka-kuukoo o {shuppatsu-shita/deta}.

2. ⟨-o⟩ ha⌈nare⌉ru ⟨〜を⟩離れる ② [to become removed from a place/organization/person] ⟪**separate, part from, quit**⟫, **⟨-to⟩ wa⌈kare⌉ru ⟨〜と⟩別れる ② [for s.o. to part with a person]** ⟪**part, break up, get divorced**⟫

NOTE: *Hanareru* takes *o* when s.o./s.a./s.t. intentionally leaves a place to head for another place (including metaphorical uses where a vehicle is the subject), as in the following examples: *Ressha wa eki o hanarete Tookyoo e mukattta* 'The train left the station for Tokyo,' *Fune ga hatoba o hanarete ichiro Beppu ni mukatta* 'The boat left the pier straight for Beppu,' *Hikoo-ki ga kassooro o hanareru* 'The plane leaves the runway,' *Kare wa shoku o hanareta* 'He left his job.' Otherwise *hanareru* takes *kara*, including cases where a person is left rather than a place or where the process of leaving is not intentional, as in the following examples: *Kanojo wa kare kara hanareta* 'She left him,' *Kanojo wa retsu kara hanareta* 'She got out of line,' *Boku no kimochi wa kanojo kara hanareta* 'My feeling for her has now gone.' However, when two people or animate beings part mutually, the particle *to* is used, as in *Jon wa Mearii to hanarete kurashite iru* 'John is living separately from (having separated from) Mary.'

EX. (**a**) I'm leaving Japan for a while.
しばらく日本{を離れる/*と別れる}つもりです。
*Shibaraku Nihon {o hanareru/*to wakareru} tsumori desu.*
(**b**) I left my boyfriend at the station.
私は駅でボーイフレンド{と別れた/*を離れた}。
*Watashi wa eki de booi-furendo {to wakareta/*o hanareta}.*

— vt. **[to allow/cause s.t., s.o. to remain untaken, unused, unchanged, uneaten, etc. in a particular state/position or to allow s.t. to be the responsibility of s.o.]**

1. ⟨-o⟩ no⌈ko⌉su ⟨〜を⟩残す ① [for s.o./s.a. to cause or allow s.t./s.o./s.a. to remain in a particular place or condition without being used, consumed, or otherwise changed] ⟪**keep back, reserve, save**⟫

EX. (**a**) Don't leave any carrots on your plate.
人参を残してはいけませんよ。
Ninjin o nokoshite wa ikemasen yo.
(**b**) I've left some bones for the dog.
犬に骨を残しておいた。
Inu ni hone o nokoshite oita.
(**c**) He's worried about the child he left behind in his hometown.
彼はふるさとに残してきた子供のことを心配している。
Kare wa furusato ni nokoshite kita kodomo no koto o shinpai-shite iru.

2. no⌈ko⌉ru 残る ① [to remain in a particular place or condition without being used, consumed, or otherwise changed] ⟪**remain, survive, linger, stay**⟫

EX. (**a**) He drained what was left of his drink in one gulp.
彼は残っていた飲み物を一気に飲み干した。
Kare wa nokotte ita nomi-mono o ikki ni nomi-hoshita.
(**b**) Nothing was left for us to eat.
食べ物は何も残っていなかった。
Tabe-mono wa nani-mo nokotte inakatta.

3. ⟨-ni⟩ ⟨-o⟩ o⌈ku ⟨〜に⟩⟨〜を⟩置く ① [for s.o./s.a. to cause s.o./s.t./s.a. to be at/in/on a certain place] ⟪**place, lay**⟫

EX. They left their baggage at the hotel and went out.
彼らはホテルに荷物を置いて出かけた。
Kare-ra wa hoteru ni nimotsu o oite dekaketa.

4. ⟨-o⟩ V*masu* ppanashi ni suru ⟨〜を⟩ V*masu*っぱなしにする ③ [to cause s.t./s.o. to remain in an undesirable state/position]

EX. He left his bicycle out in the rain.
彼は自転車を雨の中に置きっぱなしにした。
Kare wa jitensha o ame no naka ni oki-ppanashi ni shita.

5. V*te* + o⸢ku V*te*+おく [to cause to remain in a particular state/position for future convenience] ((**keep**))

EX. Don't close the door, please leave it open.
ドアを閉めないで、開けておいてくださいませんか。
Doa o shimenaide, akete oite kudasaimasen ka.

6. ⟨-o⟩ ⟨-ni⟩ ma⸢kase⸣ru ⟨～を⟩⟨～に⟩任せる ② [for s.o. to allow s.o. to do s.t. as he/she likes] ((**entrust**)), **⟨-ni⟩ ⟨-o⟩ a⸢zuke⸣ru ⟨～に⟩⟨～を⟩預ける ② [for s.o. to ask s.o. else to take care of s.o./s.t./s.a. or to allow a part of one's body to lean against s.t.]** ((**deposit**))

EX. (**a**) She left the children with me while she went to see a movie.
彼女は子供たちを私に{任せて/預けて}、映画を見に行った。
Kanojo wa kodomo-tachi o watashi ni {makasete/azukete}, eiga o mi ni itta.
(**b**) I'll leave it to you to book the hotel.
ホテルの予約はあなたに{任せます/*預けます}。
*Hoteru no yoyaku wa anata ni {makasemasu/*azukemasu}.*
(**c**) I left my baggage in the cloakroom.
私は荷物をクロークに{預けた/*任せた}。
*Watashi wa nimotsu o kurooku ni {azuketa/*makaseta}.*

leaves n. **[pl. of leaf]**
ha 葉, happa 葉っぱ ⟨**s**⟩ SEE leaf

Lebanon n.
Re⸢ba⸣non レバノン •f

lecture n. **[a talk given to a group of people on a particular subject for the purpose of teaching, esp. at a college or university]**
ko⸢ogi⸣ 講義 •c, ko⸢oen 講演 •c [a long informative talk given to a group of people on a particular subject, but not as part of a curriculum] ((**public lecture**))

EX. (**a**) Prof. Ishida gave a lecture on the *Tale of Genji*.
石田先生が『源氏物語』について{講義/講演}をなさった。
Ishida-sensei ga "Genji-monogatari" ni-tsuite {koogi/kooen} o nasatta.
(**b**) I'm enrolled in Prof. Shibata's "Religion in Japan" class, but I can't understand his lectures at all.
私は柴田先生の「日本の宗教」に登録したけど、先生の{講義/*講演}が全然分からないんです。
*Watashi wa Shibata-sensei no 'Nihon no shuukyoo' ni tooroku-shita kedo, sensei no {koogi/*kooen} ga zenzen wakaranai n desu.*

left adj./n. **[on the side of the body where the heart is located]**
hi⸢dari (**no N**) 左(のN) ↔ **migi** (**no N**) 右(のN)

EX. (**a**) Can you write with your left hand?
左(の)手で字が書けますか。
Hidari (no) te de ji ga kake-masu ka.
(**b**) Who is the woman sitting on your left in the picture?
写真であなたの左に座っている女の人はだれですか。
Shashin de anata no hidari ni suwatte iru onna no hito wa dare desu ka.

—— adv. **[towards/in favor of the left]**
hi⸢dari ni 左に n.+prt.

EX. Turn left at the next corner, please.
次の角を左に曲がってください。
Tsugi no kado o hidari ni magatte kudasai.

left-hand adj. **[on/to the left side]**
hi⸢dari-gawa no N 左側のN

EX. (**a**) The picture was on one of the left-hand pages of the book.
その写真は本の左側のページにあった。
Sono shashin wa hon no hidari-gawa no peeji ni atta.
(**b**) The hotel is on the left-hand side of the street.
ホテルは通りの左側にある。
Hoteru wa toori no hidari-gawa ni aru.

NOTE: *Gawa* in *hidari-gawa* literally means "side." So *hidari-gawa* in example (b) corresponds to "the left-hand side."

leg n. **[one of the limbs on a human or animal body ending in a foot which support the body and are used for walking or the part of this limb above the foot《fig. "any of the long thin upright supports on which a piece of furniture stands"》]**
a⌈shi⌉ あし [one or all of the limbs on an animal/human which support the body and are used for walking《fig. "any of the long thin upright supports on which a piece of furniture stands," "walking," "transportation"》]
㊅ "legs of a piece of furniture"▷脚, otherwise ▷足

EX. (**a**) She has beautiful long legs.
彼女は長い、きれいな足をしている。
Kanojo wa nagai, kireina ashi o shite iru.
(**b**) He sat with his legs crossed.
彼は足を組んで腰掛けていた。
Kare wa ashi o kunde koshi-kakete ita.
(**c**) The horse seems to have hurt its left hind leg.
馬は左の後ろ足を傷めたようだ。
Uma wa hidari no ushiro-ashi o itameta yooda.
(**d**) Don't sit on that chair. Its legs are a bit shaky.
そのいすにかけないでください。脚がぐらぐらしていますから。
Sono isu ni kakenaide kudasai. Ashi ga gura-gura-shite imasu kara.
(**e**) He fell off a ladder and broke his leg.
彼ははしごから落ちて、足を折った。
Kare wa hashigo kara ochite, ashi o otta.

legal adj. **[having to do with/allowed by/established by law]**
1. go⌈ohoo-tekina 合法的な adj(*na*). •c **[allowed by law]《lawful》**

EX. (**a**) They organized a legal demonstration.
彼らは合法的なデモを計画した。
Kare-ra wa goohoo-tekina demo o keikaku-shita.
(**b**) Did you acquire this property by legal means?
この土地は合法的な手段で手に入れたんですか。
Kono tochi wa goohoo-tekina shudan de te ni ireta n desu ka.

2. ho⌈o-tekina 法的な adj(*na*). •c **[involving the law]**

EX. (**a**) We have to take some sort of legal action against the rising number of parking violations.
増える一方の駐車違反に対して何らかの法的な措置をとる必要がある。
Fueru ippoo no chuusha-ihan ni-taishite nan-ra-ka no hoo-tekina sochi o toru hitsuyoo ga aru.
(**b**) His remarks have no legal basis. He's just threatening us.
彼の発言にはなんら法的な根拠はない。彼は我々をおどしているだけだ。
Kare no hatsugen ni wa nan-ra hoo-tekina konkyo wa nai. Kare wa ware-ware o odoshite iru dake da.

legend n. **[an old story about great events and people in ancient times, not necessarily based on fact]**
de⌈nsetsu 伝説 •c

EX. (**a**) I am interested in old Japanese legends.
私は日本の古い伝説に興味がある。
Watashi wa Nihon no furui densetsu ni kyoomi ga aru.
(**b**) Paul Bunyan is one of America's great legends.
ポール・バニヤンはアメリカの伝説上の偉大な人物の一人です。
Pooru Baniyan wa Amerika no densetsu-joo no idaina jinbutsu no hitori desu.

leisure n. **[time when one is free from work and can relax]**
yo⌉ka 余暇 •c [time free from work set aside for relaxation]《spare time》, hi⌈ma 暇 [free time]《time, spare time》

EX. (**a**) Being wealthy doesn't necessarily mean being able to lead a life of leisure.
金持ちだからといって{余暇/暇}の多い

生活が送れるとは限らない。
Kane-mochi da kara to itte {yoka/hima} no ooi seikatsu ga okure-ru to wa kagiranai.
(**b**) I spend my leisure (time) playing tennis and listening to music.
私はテニスをしたり、音楽を聞いたりして{余暇/*暇}を過ごします。
*Watashi wa tenisu o shitari, ongaku o kiitari shite {yoka/*hima} o sugoshimasu.*
(**c**) I don't have much leisure (time).
私は{余暇/暇}はあまりありません。
Watashi wa {yoka/hima} wa amari arimasen.

PHRASE: leisure activity *rejaa* レジャー •f ((recreation))

EX. They spend a lot of money on leisure activities.
彼らはレジャーにお金をたくさん使う。
Kare-ra wa rejaa ni o-kane o takusan tsukau.

lemon n.
re⌈mon レモン •f
EX. (**a**) She served me a cup of tea with a slice of lemon.
紅茶にレモンの輪切りを添えて出してくれた。
Koocha ni remon no wa-giri o soete dashite kureta.
(**b**) California exports lemons in large quantities.
カリフォルニアはレモンを大量に輸出している。
Kariforunia wa remon o tairyoo ni yushutsu-shite iru.

lemonade n.
re⌈mone⌉edo レモネード •f
EX. She ordered lemonade.
彼女はレモネードを注文した。
Kanojo wa remoneedo o chuumon-shita.

lend vt. **[for s.o. to allow s.o. to have or use s.t. temporarily on the condition that it or s.t. like it will be returned later]**
⟨-ni⟩ ⟨-o⟩ ka⌈su ⟨〜に⟩⟨〜を⟩貸す ① **[for s.o. to allow s.o. to have or use s.t. temporarily on the condition that it or s.t. like it will be returned later]** ((rent)) ↔ **⟨-ni⟩ ⟨-o⟩ kariru** ⟨〜に⟩⟨〜を⟩借りる ②
EX. (**a**) Tom lent me his word processor.
トムは私にワープロを貸してくれた。
Tomu wa watashi ni waapuro o kashite kureta.
(**b**) Can you lend me 100 yen?
百円貸してくれませんか。
Hyaku-en kashite kuremasen ka.
(**c**) I would never lend my car to my younger brother.
私は弟に車を貸すようなことは絶対しない。
Watashi wa otooto ni kuruma o kasu yoona koto wa zettai shinai.

length n. **[the measurement of s.t. from one end to the other, esp. along its greatest dimension]**
na⌉ga-sa 長さ **/⟨adj(*i*). stem of *nagai* long + suf. *sa* ness/ [the physical extension of s.t. from one end to the other in space or time], ta⌉te** 縦 **[the measurement of the side of s.t. running in a direction perpendicular to a line passing through one's eyes]** ((width)), **yo⌈ko** 横 **[the measurement of the side of s.t. parallel to a line passing through one's eyes]** ((width))
EX. (**a**) I measured the length of the cord.
私はコードの{長さ/*縦/*横}を測った。
*Watashi wa koodo no {naga-sa/*tate/*yoko} o hakatta.*
(**b**) The window is two meters in length and one meter in width.
窓は{縦/横/*長さ}二メートル、{横/縦/*長さ}一メートルです。
*Mado wa {tate/yoko/*naga-sa} ni-meetoru, {yoko/tate/*naga-sa} ichi-meetoru desu.*
(**c**) I bought a table one meter in width, and three meters in length.
私は{縦/*長さ}一メートル、{横/*長さ}三メートルのテーブルを買った。
*Watashi wa {tate/*naga-sa} ichi-meetoru, {yoko/*naga-sa} san-meetoru no teeburu o katta.*

lens n.
re˥nzu レンズ •f
EX. (**a**) I scratched the lens of my glasses.
私は眼鏡のレンズに傷をつけてしまった。
Watashi wa megane no renzu ni kizu o tsukete shimatta.
(**b**) This camera has a very good lens.
このカメラはレンズがとてもいい。
Kono kamera wa renzu ga totemo ii.
PHRASE: contact lens *kontakuto-renzu* コンタクトレンズ •f

leopard n.
hyo˥o ひょう

less adv. **[to a smaller extent (than) or in a smaller amount (than)]**
1. N yo˥ri + adj. Nより+ adj. [adj. to a greater/smaller extent than]
EX. (**a**) The first bus was less crowded than the second one.
初めのバスの方が次のよりすいていた。
Hajime no basu no hoo ga tsugi no yori suite ita.
(**b**) This hotel is less expensive than the one we booked last time.
このホテルは私たちがこの前予約したのより安い。
Kono hoteru wa watashi-tachi ga kono mae yoyaku-shita no yori yasui.
2. ho˥do…neg. ほど…neg. [not so…as]
EX. (**a**) Japanese eat less rice nowadays than they used to.
日本人は前ほど米を食べなくなった。
Nihon-jin wa mae hodo kome o tabenaku natta.
(**b**) A shower uses less water than a bath.
シャワーはおふろほど水を使わなくてすむ。
Shawaa wa ofuro hodo mizu o tsukawanakute sumu.
(**c**) I have less money than you.
私はあなたほどお金を持っていない。
Watashi wa anata hodo o-kane o motte inai.
3. ⟨-o⟩ he˥rasu ⟨〜を⟩減らす ① [to cause s.t./s.o./s.a. to become smaller in quantity] **⟪reduce, decrease, cut down⟫ ↔ ⟨-o⟩ fuyasu ⟨〜を⟩ふやす ①**
EX. (**a**) You should smoke less.
たばこを減らした方がいい。
Tabako o herashita hoo ga ii.
(**b**) Eat less, drink less, and sleep more.
食べる量もアルコールの量も減らして、睡眠を増やしなさい。
Taberu ryoo mo arukooru no ryoo mo herashite, suimin o fuyashinasai.

lesson n. **[s.t. to be learned or taught or a period of time scheduled for teaching or learning s.t.]**
1. ju˥gyoo 授業 •c [the teaching of s.t. to a group of students at school] ⟪class⟫, re˥ssun レッスン •f [private instruction on a regular basis, esp. in music or dance]
EX. (**a**) Today's Japanese lesson was easy.
今日の日本語の{授業/*レッスン}はやさしかったです。
*Kyoo no Nihon-go no {jugyoo/*ressun} wa yasashikatta desu.*
(**b**) We had a lesson on the use of the particles "*wa*" and "*ga*" yesterday.
きのう助詞の「は」と「が」について{授業/*レッスン}を受けた。
*Kinoo joshi no 'wa' to 'ga' ni-tsuite {jugyoo/*ressun} o uketa.*
(**c**) I have a piano lesson today.
今日はピアノの{レッスン/?授業}がある。
Kyoo wa piano no {ressun/?jugyoo} ga aru.
PHRASE: Lesson 1 *Dai-ik-ka* 第一課 •c, give lessons in ⟨*-o*⟩ *oshieru* ⟨〜を⟩教える ② ⟪teach⟫, take lessons in ⟨*-o*⟩ *narau* ⟨〜を⟩習う ① ⟪learn⟫
2. kyo˥okun 教訓 •c [an example or experience which serves as a warning]
EX. That accident taught me a lesson.
あの事故は私にとってはいい教訓だった。
Ano jiko wa watashi ni-totte wa ii kyookun datta.

lest conj. **[so that the situation or event in question does not occur ⟨fml⟩]**
neg. of Vinf. nonpast yo˥oni neg. of Vinf. nonpastように

L

EX. Lest you forget, keep this memo attached to your bathroom mirror.
忘れないようにこのメモを洗面所の鏡にはっておきなさい。
Wasurenai yooni kono memo o senmen-jo no kagami ni hatte okinasai.

let vt. **[for s.o. to allow s.o./s.a. to do s.t./s.t. to happen]**
{⟨-ni⟩/⟨-o⟩} {**Vneg. + seru/Vstem + saseru/ko-saseˈru/saˈseru**} {⟨〜に⟩/⟨〜を⟩}{**Vneg.+せる/Vstem+させる/来させる/させる**} ②
[for s.o./s.a. to cause s.o./s.t./s.a. to do s.t./to change in state] ⟪**make**⟫

EX. (**a**) Please let me treat you to lunch.
お昼ごはんをごちそうさせてください。
O-hiru-gohan o go-chisoo-sasete kudasai.
(**b**) I would never let my younger brother use my car.
弟には私の車は絶対使わせません。
Otooto ni wa watashi no kuruma wa zettai tsukawa-semasen.
(**c**) She lets her children play in the park by themselves.
彼女は公園で子供を自分たちだけで遊ばせます。
Kanojo wa kooen de kodomo o jibun-tachi dake de asoba-semasu.

PHRASE: let's V*masu* + *mashoo* V*masu*+ましょう, Vvol. ⟨s⟩

EX. Let's go see a movie.
映画を見に{行きましょう/行こう}。
Eiga o mi ni {ikimashoo/ikoo}.

PHRASE: let go of ⟨*-o*⟩ *hanasu* ⟨〜を⟩放す ①

EX. Don't let go of the rope.
ロープを放すな。
Roopu o hanasu na.

PHRASE: let me see *soo desu nee* そうですねえ, *eeto* ええと ⟪well, er⟫

letter n. **[a written/printed message usually sent by mail in an envelope or any written linguistic symbol]**
1. teˈgami 手紙 [a written/printed message usually sent by mail in an envelope]

EX. (**a**) I wrote my mother a letter last night.
私はゆうべ母に手紙を書きました。
Watashi wa yuube haha ni tegami o kakimashita.
(**b**) How many letters did you get today?
今日は手紙が何通来ましたか。
Kyoo wa tegami ga nan-tsuu kimashita ka.
(**c**) I stopped by the post office on my way home to mail a letter.
家へ帰る途中で郵便局に寄って手紙を出した。
Uchi e kaeru tochuu de yuubin-kyoku ni yotte tegami o dashita.

PHRASE: letter paper *binsen* 便せん •c

2. moˈji 文字 •c [a written/printed symbol of a sound or other linguistic unit in human language] ⟪**character**⟫, **jiˈ 字 •c**

EX. (**a**) How do you pronounce this letter?
この{字/文字}はどう発音しますか。
Kono {ji/moji} wa doo hatsuon-shimasu ka.
(**b**) He takes notes in very small letters.
彼は非常に小さい{字/?文字}でノートをとる。
Kare wa hijooni chiisai {ji/?moji} de nooto o toru.

PHRASE: capital letter *oo-moji* 大文字, small letter *ko-moji* 小文字

lettuce n.
reˈtasu レタス •f

EX. I fixed a lettuce and cucumber salad.
私はレタスときゅうりのサラダを作った。
Watashi wa retasu to kyuuri no sarada o tsukutta.

level adj. **[having a surface which is flat and smooth, not sloping]**
taˈirana 平らな adj(*na*). **[for a surface to be free from obstructions]** ⟪**even, flat, smooth**⟫, **suˈiheina 水平な** adj(*na*). •c **[not sloping]** ⟪**horizontal**⟫

EX. The washing machine has to be placed on a level floor.
洗濯機は{水平な/平らな}床の上に置かなければいけない。
Sentaku-ki wa {suiheina/tairana} yuka no ue ni okanakereba ikenai.

—— vt. **[to make s.t. flat and even]**
⟨**-o**⟩ **taˈirani suru** ⟨〜を⟩**平らにする** /⟨**adj**(*na*).

***ni* of *tairana* level + *suru* ③ make/**

EX. They used tractors to level the ground.
トラクターを使って地面を平らにした。
Torakutaa o tsukatte jimen o tairani shita.

—— n. [a line/surface parallel to the ground 《fig. "a general standard of quality/quantity"》]

1. da⌉n 段 [a raised surface parallel to the ground] 《step, tier, grade》

PHRASE: above sea level *kaibatsu* 海抜 •c

EX. I climbed a mountain 1,000 meters above sea level.
私は海抜千メートルの山に登った。
Watashi wa kaibatsu sen-meetoru no yama ni nobotta.

2. re⌉beru レベル •f [a general standard of quality/quantity]

EX. (a) The level of rugby playing in this country is not very high.
この国のラグビーのレベルはあまり高くない。
Kono kuni no ragubii no reberu wa amari takakunai.
(b) We must somehow raise the academic level of this university.
この大学の学問的なレベルを何とかしてあげなければならない。
Kono daigaku no gakumon-tekina reberu o nan-toka-shite agenakereba naranai.

liberal adj. **[having progressive views or policies]**
ri⌉beraruna リベラルな adj(*na*). **•f, ji⌈yuu-shugi-tekina** 自由主義的な adj(*na*). **•c, ji⌈yu⌉una** 自由な adj(*na*). **•c**

EX. (a) This school has a liberal atmosphere to it.
この学校には{リベラルな/自由な}雰囲気がある。
Kono gakkoo ni wa {riberaruna/jiyuuna} fun'iki ga aru.
(b) My father has a liberal mind.
父は考え方が{リベラル/自由主義的}だ。
Chichi wa kangae-kata ga {riberaru/jiyuu-shugi-teki} da.

liberty n. **[the state of being free from conditions that limit one's actions]**
ji⌈yu⌉u 自由 **•c 《freedom》**

EX. (a) They fought for liberty.
彼らは自由のために戦った。
Kare-ra wa jiyuu no tame ni tatakatta.
(b) Individual liberties are often neglected in this country.
この国では個人の自由はしばしば無視される。
Kono kuni de wa kojin no jiyuu wa shiba-shiba mushi-sareru.

librarian n. **[a person who works in a library to tend to its collection and to help its users]**
shi⌉sho 司書 **•c [a person who is professionally trained to work in a library], to⌈sho-kan⌉-in** 図書館員 **•c [a person who works in a library]**

library n. **[a room/building where a collection of books is kept for reading and reference]**
to⌈sho⌉-kan 図書館 **•c [a building where a collection of books is kept for reading and reference], to⌈sho⌉-shitsu** 図書室 **•c [a room where a collection of books is kept for reading and reference]**

EX. (a) I borrowed this book from the library.
この本を{図書館/図書室}で借りた。
Kono hon o {tosho-kan/tosho-shitsu} de karita.
(b) This isn't a library book.
これは{図書館/図書室}の本じゃありません。
Kore wa {tosho-kan/tosho-shitsu} no hon jaarimasen.

license n. **[official permission to do s.t. or a document showing that such permission has been given]**
me⌉nkyo 免許 **•c [official permission to do s.t.], me⌈nkyo⌉-shoo** 免許証 **•c [a document showing that official permission has been given to do s.t.], kyo⌉ka** 許可 **•c [an act of allowing s.o. to do s.t. he/she wants to do] 《permission》**

EX. (a) The policeman asked to see my driver's license.

警官に(運転){免許証/*免許/*許可}を見せるようにと言われた。
*Keikan ni (unten-){menkyo-shoo/ *menkyo/*kyoka} o miseru yooni to iwareta.*
(**b**) Is it difficult to get a license to sell alcohol?
酒類の販売{許可/?免許/?免許証}をもらうのは難しいですか。
Shurui no hanbai-{kyoka/?menkyo/ ?menkyo-shoo} o morau no wa muzukashii desu ka.
(**c**) Don't forget to renew your driver's license.
運転{免許/免許証/*許可}を更新するのを忘れないでください。
*Unten-{menkyo/menkyo-shoo/*kyoka} o kooshin-suru no o wasurenaide kudasai.*

lick vt. **[for s.o./s.a. to pass the tongue across the surface of s.t.]**
⟨-o⟩ na⌈me⌉ru ⟨〜を⟩なめる ② [for s.o./s.a. to pass the tongue across the surface of s.t. 《fig. "experience," "despise"》]
EX. (**a**) The cat licked the dish clean.
猫は皿をきれいになめた。
Neko wa sara o kireini nameta.
(**b**) The dog licked the ice cream off the girl's face.
犬は女の子の顔についたアイスクリームをなめてとった。
Inu wa onna-no-ko no kao ni tsuita aisu-kuriimu o namete totta.
(**c**) It's impolite to lick one's plate after eating.
食べ終わって食器をなめるのは行儀が悪い。
Tabe-owatte shokki o nameru no wa gyoogi ga warui.

lid n. **[a movable cover for an open top of a container such as a pot or box]**
fu⌈ta ふた 《cap, cover》
EX. (**a**) My mother caught me taking the lid off the box of cookies.
クッキーの箱のふたを開けようとしているところを母に見つかってしまった。
Kukkii no hako no futa o akeyoo to shite iru tokoro o haha ni mitsukatte shimatta.
(**b**) Put the lid back on the pot. It smells.
におうから、なべにふたをしてください。
Niou kara, nabe ni futa o shite kudasai.

lie[1] vi. **[to put oneself in or be in a flat position on a surface 《fig. "exist"》]**
1. yo⌈ko ni na⌉ru 横になる ①, ne-⌈sobe⌉ru 寝そべる ② [for s.o./s.a. to enter into a flat position with one's body stretched out]
EX. (**a**) He usually lies down for a while after lunch.
彼は昼ごはんの後、たいてい少し{横になる/*寝そべる}。
*Kare wa hiru-gohan no ato, taitei sukoshi {yoko ni naru/*ne-soberu}.*
(**b**) We lay on the floor in front of the fireplace and talked for hours.
暖炉の前の床(の上)に{横になって/寝そべって}何時間も話をした。
Danro no mae no yuka (no ue) ni {yoko ni natte/ne-sobette} nan-jikan-mo hanashi o shita.
(**c**) I lay sunning myself on the beach all day.
一日中ビーチに{寝そべって/?横になって}日光浴をしていた。
Ichi-nichi-juu biichi ni {ne-sobette/ ?yoko ni natte} nikkoo-yoku o shite ita.
2. ⟨-ni⟩ a⌉ru ⟨〜に⟩ある ① [for s.t. to exist] 《be located, be situated, exist》
EX. The islands of Matsushima lie just off the Pacific coast near Sendai.
松島は仙台の近くの太平洋岸沖にある。
Matsushima wa Sendai no chikaku no Taiheiyoo-gan-oki ni aru.

lie[2] vi. **[for s.o. to make an untrue statement]**
u⌉so o tsuku うそをつく ① 《tell a lie》
EX. She lied to me in order to avoid being scolded.
彼女はしかられないようにうそをついた。
Kanojo wa shikara-renai yooni uso o tsuita.
—— n. [an untrue statement]
u⌉so うそ

L

EX. (**a**) She said that she hadn't even seen him, but it was all a lie.
彼女は彼を見たこともないと言ったが、全部うそだった。
Kanojo wa kare o mita koto mo nai to itta ga, zenbu uso datta.
(**b**) Don't tell a lie.
うそをつくな。
Uso o tsuku na.

life n. **[the quality that allows plants and animals to grow and reproduce, distinguishing them from inert matter, or the period of time between the birth and death of a living being]**

1. i˥nochi 命 [the quality that allows plants and animals to grow and reproduce, distinguishing them from inert matter], se˥imei 生命 •c

EX. (**a**) His life can only be saved by a heart transplant.
彼の{命/生命}を救うには心臓移植しかない。
Kare no {inochi/seimei} o sukuu ni wa shinzoo-ishoku shika nai.
(**b**) Many lives were lost in the war.
たくさんの{命/生命}が戦争で失われた。
Takusan no {inochi/seimei} ga sensoo de ushinawa-reta.
(**c**) He saved the drowning child at the risk of his own life.
彼は{命/*生命}がけでおぼれかけている子供を助けた。
*Kare wa {inochi/*seimei}-gake de obore-kakete iru kodomo o tasuketa.*

PHRASE: a matter of life and death *ikiru ka shinu ka no mondai* 生きるか死ぬかの問題, life insurance *seimei-hoken* 生命保険 •c

2. ji˥nsei 人生 •c [(the typical qualities of) human existence]

EX. (**a**) Life is full of surprises.
人生には驚くことがたくさんある。
Jinsei ni wa odoroku koto ga takusan aru.
(**b**) I want to enjoy my life.
私は人生を楽しみたい。
Watashi wa jinsei o tanoshimi-tai.

3. i┌sshoo 一生 •c [the period between one's birth and death or between the present time and one's death] ⟪lifetime, one's whole life⟫

EX. (**a**) My grandfather lived a life full of ups and downs.
祖父の一生は波乱に満ちていた。
Sofu no isshoo wa haran ni michite ita.
(**b**) I'd like to continue studying my whole life.
私は一生勉強を続けたい。
Watashi wa isshoo benkyoo o tsuzuke-tai.

PHRASE: life sentence *shuushin-kei* 終身刑 •c

4. se┌ikatsu 生活 •c [one's activities as a living being] ⟪living⟫

EX. (**a**) I don't want anyone prying into my private life.
私生活はだれにものぞかれたくない。
Shi-seikatsu wa dare-ni-mo nozoka-re-takunai.
(**b**) Married life isn't all fun.
結婚生活は楽しいことばかりではない。
Kekkon-seikatsu wa tanoshii koto bakari dewanai.
(**c**) I lead a busy life in Japan.
私は日本で忙しい生活を送っています。
Watashi wa Nihon de isogashii seikatsu o okutte imasu.

lift vt. **[to bring s.t./s.o. up to a higher level]**
⟨-o⟩ mo┌chi-ageru ⟨～を⟩持ち上げる
/⟨V *masu* of *motsu* ① hold + *ageru* ② raise/ ② ⟪raise, heave, hold up⟫

EX. (**a**) This suitcase is too heavy for me to lift.
このスーツケースは重すぎて、私には持ち上げられません。
Kono suutsukeesu wa omo-sugite, watashi ni wa mochi-age-raremasen.
(**b**) If you could lift up your books, I'll wipe your desk clean for you.
本を持ち上げてくれたら、机をきれいにふいてあげますよ。
Hon o mochi-agete kuretara, tsukue o kirei ni fuite agemasu yo.

light[1] n. **[the natural or artificial form of energy that takes away darkness, so that objects can be seen]**

1. hi⌈kari⌉ 光 /⟨V*masu* of *hikaru* ① shine/ [a natural form of energy that takes away darkness] ⟪**ray, glare, gleam**⟫

EX. (**a**) Sometimes he had to study by the light of the moon.
彼は月の光で勉強しなければならないこともあった。
Kare wa tsuki no hikari de benkyoo-shinakereba naranai koto mo atta.
(**b**) A soft light shone into my room through the *shoji.*
障子を通して、やわらかい光が部屋の中に差し込んだ。
Shooji o tooshite, yawarakai hikari ga heya no naka ni sashi-konda.

2. a⌈kari 明かり [s.t. that produces a radiant energy that illuminates other things] ⟪**lamp**⟫**, de⌈ntoo 電灯 •c [an electric device that removes darkness], de⌉nki 電気 •c [a basic form of energy occurring in certain subatomic particles or a device powered by such energy which takes away darkness]** ⟪**electricity, electric light**⟫

EX. (**a**) Let's turn off the lights and look at the moon.
{明かり/電灯/電気}を消して、月を見ましょう。
{Akari/Dentoo/Denki} o keshite, tsuki o mimashoo.
(**b**) The light is still on in his room.
彼の部屋は{明かり/電灯/電気}がまだついている。
Kare no heya wa {akari/dentoo/denki} ga mada tsuite iru.
(**c**) The first thing I do when I get home is turn on all the lights.
家に帰ると先ず、{明かり/電灯/電気}を全部つける。
Uchi ni kaeru to mazu, {akari/dentoo/denki} o zenbu tsukeru.
(**d**) Please don't forget to switch off the lights when you go out.
出かける時、{明かり/電灯/電気}を消すのを忘れないでください。
Dekakeru toki, {akari/dentoo/denki} o kesu no o wasurenaide kudasai.

L

—— vt. **[for s.o. to cause s.t. to start to burn] ⟨-ni⟩ hi⌉ o tsu⌈ke⌉ru ⟨〜に⟩火をつける ②** ⟪**ignite**⟫

EX. He lit a cigarette.
彼はたばこに火をつけた。
Kare wa tabako ni hi o tsuketa.

—— adj. **[having light or not dark in color] a⌈karui 明るい** adj(*i*). **[for there to be enough light to do s.t. or for s.t. to be not dark in color** ⟪**fig. "cheerful," "be versed in"**⟫**]** ⟪**bright, cheerful**⟫ **↔ kurai 暗い** adj(*i*).

EX. (**a**) I like a light room.
私は明るい部屋が好きです。
Watashi wa akarui heya ga suki desu.
(**b**) I'd better go home while it's still light outside.
外がまだ明るいうちに帰ったほうがいい。
Soto ga mada akarui uchi ni kaetta hoo ga ii.
(**c**) She was wearing a light green blouse.
彼女は明るいグリーンのブラウスを着ていた。
Kanojo wa akarui guriin no burausu o kite ita.

light[2] adj. **[having little weight or small in amount or easy to bear/do]**
ka⌈rui 軽い adj(*i*). **[having little weight or for food to be small in amount and easy to digest] ↔ omoi 重い** adj(*i*).

EX. (**a**) I'm looking for a briefcase that's light and easy to carry around.
軽くて持ち運びに便利なブリーフケースを探しています。
Karukute mochi-hakobi ni benrina buriifukeesu o sagashite imasu.
(**b**) I had a light lunch.
私は軽い昼食をとった。
Watashi wa karui chuushoku o totta.
(**c**) He recovered enough to be able to do some light work.
彼は軽い仕事ができるまで回復した。
Kare wa karui shigoto ga dekiru made kaifuku-shita.

lighter n.
ra⌉itaa ライター •f

EX. Minoru lit a cigarette with a lighter.
実はライターでたばこに火をつけた。
Minoru wa raitaa de tabako ni hi o tsuketa.

lighthouse n.
to⌈odai 灯台 •c

EX. There's a lighthouse on that island.
あの島には灯台がある。
Ano shima ni wa toodai ga aru.

lightning n.
i⌈nabi⌉kari 稲光, **i⌈nazuma** 稲妻

EX. There was a flash of lightning in the sky.
空を{稲光/稲妻}が走った。
Sora o {inabikari/inazuma} ga hashitta.

like[1] vt. **[for s.o./s.a. to have good feelings about s.t./s.o./s.a.]**
⟨-ga⟩ su⌈ki⌉na ⟨～が⟩好きな adj(*na*). **[for s.o./s.a. to have good feelings about s.o. or about a general category of things/animals/activities]** **⟪be fond of, love⟫** ↔ **⟨-ga⟩ kiraina** ⟨～が⟩嫌いな adj(*na*).

EX. (**a**) I like ice cream
私はアイスクリームが好きです。
Watashi wa aisu-kuriimu ga suki desu.
(**b**) She likes eating popcorn while watching movies.
彼女はポップコーンを食べながら映画を見るのが好きだ。
Kanojo wa poppukoon o tabe-nagara eiga o miru no ga suki da.
(**c**) Which do you like better, coffee or tea?
コーヒーとお茶と、どちらの方が好きですか。
Koohii to ocha to, dochira no hoo ga suki desu ka.
(**d**) I've come to like *kanji.*
私は漢字が好きになってきた。
Watashi wa kanji ga sukini natte kita.
(**e**) A: How was the movie last night?
ゆうべの映画、どうだった。
Yuube no eiga, doo datta.
B: I liked it very much.
すごく{良かった/*好きだった}よ。
*Sugoku {yokatta/*suki datta} yo.*

NOTE: *Sukina* cannot be used in reference to a particular object. *Ii* "good," *oishii* "delicious," etc., may be used depending on the object in question.

2. {⟨-ga⟩/⟨-o⟩} **V*masu* ta⌉i** {⟨～が⟩/⟨～を⟩} **V*masu*たい** adj(*i*). **[for the speaker/listener to desire to do s.t.]**

NOTE: V*masu tai* is used with a first person subject in statements and with a second person subject in questions. It can be used with a third person subject only if some form is attached which explicitly expresses the speaker's perception or judgment, such as *daroo* "probably."

EX. (**a**) I'd like to buy a new bicycle.
新しい自転車を買いたいと思います。
Atarashii jitensha o kai-tai to omoimasu.
(**b**) I'd like Ms. Smith to teach me English.
スミスさんに英語を教えていただきたいんですが。
Sumisu-san ni eigo o oshiete itadaki-tai n desu ga.

PHRASE: How do you like…? ⟨-*o*⟩ *doo omoimasu ka.* ⟨～を⟩どう思いますか。

EX. How do you like our new textbook?
新しい教科書をどう思いますか。
Atarashii kyooka-sho o doo omoimasu ka.

like[2] prep. **[in the same way as or with the same qualities as or in a way that shows the probability of or typical of]**
1. N mi⌉taina Nみたいな aux. adj(*na*). **[in the same way as or with the same qualities as or in a way that shows the probability of ⟨s⟩], N no yo⌉ona** Nのような aux. adj(*na*). **[in the same way as or with the same qualities as or in a way that shows the probability of]** **⟪look like, look as if, appear, seem⟫**

EX. (**a**) I don't like women like her.
彼女{のような/みたいな}女性はきらいだ。
Kanojo {no yoona/mitaina} josei wa kirai da.
(**b**) She smiled like an angel.
彼女は天使{のように/みたいに}ほほえんだ。

Kanojo wa tenshi {no yooni/mitaini} hohoenda.
(**c**) He is like a father to me.
彼は私にはお父さん{のよう/みたい}です。
Kare wa watashi ni wa o-too-san {no yoo/mitai} desu.
(**d**) She sounds like the right person for you.
彼女はあなたにお似合いの人{のよう/みたい}ですね。
Kanojo wa anata ni o-niai no hito {no yoo/mitai} desu ne.

2. N rashii Nらしい adj(*i*). **[typical of]** ((**characteristic of**))

EX. (**a**) It's not like him to break his promise.
約束を破るなんて彼らしくない。
Yakusoku o yaburu nante kare-rashikunai.
(**b**) It is just like her to stay up all night to type her friend's paper.
徹夜して友達の論文をタイプしてあげるなんていかにも彼女らしい。
Tetsuya-shite tomodachi no ronbun o taipu-shite ageru nante ikanimo kanojo-rashii.

likely adj. **[having a high probability of occurring]**
{V*masu*/adj(*i*/*na*). stem} + soona {V*masu*/adj(*i*/*na*). stem}+そうな adj(*na*). **[having the appearance of being about to occur or of having a certain quality or of being in a certain state based on what the speaker sees/hears/senses]** ((**look like, seem**))

EX. (**a**) He's likely to pass the exam.
彼は試験に通りそうだ。
Kare wa shiken ni toori-soo da.
(**b**) That is the likely response of the president.
それは社長の見せそうな反応だ。
Sore wa shachoo no mise-soona hannoo da.

lily n.
yu⌈ri ゆり

EX. He sent me some white lilies on my birthday.
彼は私の誕生日に白いゆり(の花)を送ってくれた。
Kare wa watashi no tanjoo-bi ni shiroi yuri (no hana) o okutte kureta.

lime n.
ra⌉imu ライム •f

limit n. **[the point/line/degree beyond which s.t. does not or should not continue]**
1. ge⌈nkai 限界 •c [the point/line/degree beyond which s.t. does not continue]

EX. (**a**) There's a limit to how much we can do in a day.
一日でできることには限界がある。
Ichi-nichi de dekiru koto ni wa genkai ga aru.
(**b**) I'm not even considering applying to Tokyo University; I know my limits.
東大に願書を出そうなんて思っていません。自分の限界は知っていますから。
Toodai ni gansho o dasoo nante omotte imasen. Jibun no genkai wa shitte imasu kara.

2. se⌈ige⌉n 制限 •c [a quantity set by law or convention as being the maximum which cannot be exceeded] ((**restriction**))

EX. (**a**) The speed limit in the city is usually 40 kilometers per hour.
市街地の制限速度は大抵時速四十キロです。
Shigai-chi no seigen-sokudo wa taitei jisoku yon-juk-kiro desu.
(**b**) I was not able to answer all the questions within the time limit.
私は制限時間内にすべての質問に答えることができませんでした。
Watashi wa seigen-jikan-nai ni subete no shitsumon ni kotaeru koto ga dekimasen deshita.

—— vt. **[to keep s.t./s.o./s.a. within a certain scope, bound, or quantity]**
⟨-o⟩ ⟨-ni⟩ se⌈ige⌉n-suru ⟨〜を⟩⟨〜に⟩制限する ③ •c [for s.o. to intentionally keep s.t./s.o./s.a. within a certain scope, bound, or quantity] ((**restrict**)), **⟨-o⟩ ⟨-ni⟩ ka⌈gi⌉ru ⟨〜を⟩⟨〜に⟩限る ① [to keep s.t./s.o./s.a. within or to be within a certain scope, bound, or quantity]** ((**restrict, confine**))
NOTE: *Kagiru* is usually used in the passive.

L

EX. (a) I was told by my doctor to limit myself to 900 calories a day.
私は一日900カロリーに{制限する/*限る}ように医者に言われた。
*Watashi wa ichi-nichi kyuu-hyaku-karorii ni {seigen-suru/*kagiru} yooni isha ni iwa-reta.*
(b) We have to limit our production of oil.
石油の生産を{制限しなければ/*限らなければ}いけない。
*Sekiyu no seisan o {seigen-shinakereba/*kagiranakereba} ikenai.*
(c) Carry-on baggage is limited to one piece per person.
手荷物は一人一個に{限られて/制限されて}います。
Te-nimotsu wa hitori ik-ko ni {kagira-rete/seigen-sarete} imasu.
(d) Our knowledge of the functioning of the brain is still rather limited.
我々の脳の機能に関する知識はまだかなり{限られて/*制限されて}いる。
*Ware-ware no noo no kinoo ni-kansuru chishiki wa mada kanari {kagira-rete/*seigen-sarete} iru.*

limp vi. **[to walk with an uneven step, favoring one leg]**
bi⌉kko o hi⌈ku びっこを引く ①
NOTE: *Bikko* carries with it a discriminatory nuance and should be used with care.
EX. He limped along the street.
彼は通りをびっこを引いて歩いた。
Kare wa toori o bikko o hiite aruita.

Lincoln n.
Ri⌈nkaa⌉n リンカーン •f

line n. **[a long narrow mark on a surface 《fig. "a number of people side by side/one behind the other," "a row of words"》]**
1. se⌉n 線 •c [a long narrow mark on a surface 《fig. "a train track," "an electric cable"》] 《track, lane, route》
EX. Draw a line under the most important word in the sentence.
文中の一番大事な単語の下に線を引きなさい。
Bun-chuu no ichiban daijina tango no shita ni sen o hikinasai.
2. re⌉tsu 列 •c [a procession or row of people or cars] 《queue》
EX. (a) People are waiting in line for the office to open.
人が列を作ってオフィスが開くのを待っている。
Hito ga retsu o tsukutte ofisu ga aku no o matte iru.
(b) Form a line please.
列を作ってください。
Retsu o tsukutte kudasai.
PHRASE: stand in line *narabu* 並ぶ ①
EX. Stand in line please.
並んでください。
Narande kudasai.
3. gyo⌉o 行 •c [a row of words on a printed page]
EX. (a) Please read beginning at the fifth line from the bottom.
下から五行目から読んでください。
Shita kara go-gyoo-me kara yonde kudasai.
(b) What is this *kanji* here on the first line?
一行目のこの漢字は何ですか。
Ichi-gyoo-me no kono kanji wa nan desu ka.

linen n. **[cloth made from the flax plant]**
a⌈sa⌉ 麻
EX. I ironed my linen jacket.
麻の上着にアイロンをかけた。
Asa no uwa-gi ni airon o kaketa.

link n. **[s.t. which connects two things or parts of a thing]**
1. tsu⌈nagari つながり /(V*masu* of *tsunagaru* ① be connected/ 《connection, relation》
EX. (a) Is there any link between stress and cancer?
ストレスとがんの間には何かつながりがありますか。
Sutoresu to gan no aida ni wa nani-ka tsunagari ga arimasu ka.
(b) She tried to cut off all her links with the past.
彼女は過去とのつながりを全部切ろうとした。

Kanojo wa kako to no tsunagari o zenbu kiroo to shita.

2. wa˥ 輪 [that which results from s.t. linear such as a string or wire connected at both ends into a ring] ((loop))

lion n.

ra˥ion ライオン •f ((lioness))

EX. We could hear the roar of a lion in the distance.
遠くでライオンがほえる声が聞こえた。
Tooku de raion ga hoeru koe ga kikoeta.

lip n. **[either of the two reddish edges of the opening of the mouth or the ordinary skin around them]**

ku˥chibiru 唇 [either or both of the two reddish edges of the opening of the mouth]

EX. (**a**) She kissed him on the lips.
彼女は彼の唇にキスした。
Kanojo wa kare no kuchibiru ni kisu-shita.
(**b**) She has a habit of licking her upper lip.
彼女は上唇をなめる癖がある。
Kanojo wa uwa-kuchibiru o nameru kuse ga aru.

liquid n./adj.

e˥kitai (**no N**) 液体(のN) **•c ↔ kitai** (**no N**) 気体(のN) **•c gas, kotai** (**no N**) 固体(のN) **•c solid**

EX. (**a**) There was green liquid in the bottle.
びんの中に緑色の液体が入っていた。
Bin no naka ni midori-iro no ekitai ga haitte ita.
(**b**) She poured the liquid into a glass.
彼女はコップにその液体を注いだ。
Kanojo wa koppu ni sono ekitai o sosoida.
(**c**) We use a liquid detergent at home.
うちでは液体の洗剤を使っている。
Uchi de wa ekitai no senzai o tsukatte iru.

list n. **[a set of things written in an orderly fashion so that one can remember them or check them easily]**

ri˥suto リスト •f

EX. (**a**) I can't find your name on the list.
あなたの名前がリストに見つかりません。
Anata no namae ga risuto ni mitsukarimasen.
(**b**) Do you have a list of things to buy?
買う物のリストを持っていますか。
Kau mono no risuto o motte imasu ka.

— vt. **[for s.o. to put s.t. into a list]**

⟨-o⟩ ri˥suto-a˥ppu-suru ⟨〜を⟩リストアップする ③ **•f**

EX. I listed all the places I wanted to visit.
行ってみたい場所を全部リストアップした。
Itte mitai basho o zenbu risuto-appu-shita.

listen vi. **[for s.o./s.a. to pay attention to s.t. in order to hear it]**

⟨⟨-ni⟩⟩ ⟨-o⟩ ki˥ku ⟨⟨〜に⟩⟩⟨〜を⟩きく ① **[for s.o./s.a. to focus one's attention on a sound so that it is perceived by the ears or to request/receive information from s.o. about s.t. orally or to take notice and accept s.t. said by another]** ((hear, ask))

㊅ "listen to s.t. carefully"▷聴く, otherwise ▷聞く

EX. (**a**) I listened to the tape for two hours.
そのテープを二時間聞いた。
Sono teepu o ni-jikan kiita.
(**b**) He likes listening to classical music.
彼はクラシックを聞くのが好きだ。
Kare wa kurashikku o kiku no ga sukida.
(**c**) She never listens to me.
彼女は私の言うことを聞こうとしない。
Kanojo wa watashi no iu koto o kikoo to shinai.

listener n. **[a person who listens/is listening]**

ki˥ki-te 聞き手 [a person who listens/is listening/asks a question] ((hearer, audience))

EX. (**a**) His talk moved his listeners.
彼の話は聞き手を感動させた。
Kare no hanashi wa kiki-te o kandoo-saseta.
(**b**) A good speaker maintains eye contact with her listeners while talking.

話の上手な人は聞き手の目を見て話す。
Hanashi no joozuna hito wa kiki-te no me o mite hanasu.

liter n.
ri⌈ttoru リットル •f
EX. (**a**) He drinks a liter of water every day.
彼は毎日水を一リットル飲む。
Kare wa mai-nichi mizu o ichi-rittoru nomu.
(**b**) She bought three one-liter cartons of milk.
彼女は一リットル入りの牛乳パックを三つ買った。
Kanojo wa ichi-rittoru-iri no gyuunyuu-pakku o mittsu katta.

literal adj. **[according to the primary meaning of a word or expression]**
mo⌈ji-do⌉ori no N 文字通りのN
EX. Is this word used here in its literal sense?
ここでこのことばはその文字通りの意味で使われていますか。
Koko de kono kotoba wa sono moji-doori no imi de tsukawa-rete imasu ka.
PHRASE: literal translation *chikugo-yaku* 逐語訳 •c

literary adj. **[of literature]**
1. bu⌈ngaku-tekina 文学的な adj(*na*). •c **[concerned with the writing or appreciation of literature]**
EX. (**a**) I have no literary talent.
私は文学的な才能がない。
Watashi wa bungaku-tekina sainoo ga nai.
(**b**) He was awarded a famous literary prize.
彼は有名な文学賞を受賞した。
Kare wa yuumeina bungaku-shoo o jushoo-shita.
2. bungei- 文芸〜 •c **[concerned with poems, novels, plays, etc.]**
EX. (**a**) She is a literary critic.
彼女は文芸評論家だ。
Kanojo wa bungei-hyooron-ka da.
(**b**) I read the literary column of this newspaper every day.
私は毎日この新聞の文芸欄を読んでいます。
Watashi wa mai-nichi kono shinbun no bungei-ran o yonde imasu.

literature n. **[creatively written works which have lasting artistic value or all the written works on a particular subject]**
1. bu⌉ngaku 文学 •c **[creatively written works which have lasting artistic value]**
EX. (**a**) I'm interested in Japanese literature.
私は日本文学に興味がある。
Watashi wa Nihon-bungaku ni kyoomi ga aru.
(**b**) In my college days I used to discuss literature and art until late at night with my friends.
学生時代には友だちと夜遅くまで文学や美術の話をしたものだ。
Gakusei-jidai ni wa tomodachi to yoru osoku made bungaku ya bijutsu no hanashi o shita mono da.
2. bu⌈nken 文献 •c **[all the written works on a particular subject]**
EX. There is a vast literature on World War II.
第二次世界大戦に関してはぼう大な文献がある。
Dai-ni-ji-sekai-taisen ni-kanshite wa boodaina bunken ga aru.

little adj. **[small in size or amount; short in time or distance]**
1. chi⌉isana N 小さなN **[small in size]** ↔ **ookina N** 大きなN
EX. Two little girls came running up to me.
二人の小さな女の子が私の方へ走ってきた。
Futari no chiisana onna-no-ko ga watashi no hoo e hashitte kita.
2. su⌈ko⌉shi 少し n./adv. **[(in) a small number/quantity or (to) a small degree], cho⌉tto** ちょっと **[for a short time or in a small quantity or to a small degree]**
NOTE: *Chotto* is more casual than *sukoshi.*
EX. (**a**) We have only a little water left.
水が{少し/ちょっと}しか残っていない。
Mizu ga {sukoshi/chotto} shika nokotte inai.
(**b**) Give me a little more rice, please.
ご飯をもう{少し/ちょっと}ください。
Gohan o moo {sukoshi/chotto} kudasai.

(c) She knows a little Japanese.
彼女は日本語を{少し/ちょっと}知っている。
Kanojo wa Nihon-go o {sukoshi/chotto} shitte iru.
(d) Can't you stay a little longer?
もう{少し/ちょっと}いられませんか。
Moo {sukoshi/chotto} i-raremasen ka.

3. su⌈kuna⌉i 少ない adj(*i*). **[less than usual in number/quantity] ↔ ooi 多い** adj(*i*).

EX. (a) Little is known about this writer.
この作家について知られていることは少ない。
Kono sakka ni-tsuite shira-rete iru koto wa sukunai.
(b) We had little snow last year.
去年は雪が少なかった。
Kyonen wa yuki ga sukunakatta.

NOTE: *Sukunai* can only be used in predicate position, as shown in the examples (a) and (b).

live vi. **[for s.o./s.a. to be alive (and stay in a certain place)]**

1. i⌈ki⌉ru 生きる ② [for s.o./s.a. to be alive]

EX. (a) Everyone has a right to live in freedom.
みんな、自由に生きる権利がある。
Minna, jiyuuni ikiru kenri ga aru.
(b) He has lost his will to live.
彼は生きる気力をなくした。
Kare wa ikiru kiryoku o nakushita.
(c) Sheep live on grass.
羊は草を食べて生きている。
Hitsuji wa kusa o tabete ikite iru.

2. 〈-ni〉 su⌉mu 〈〜に〉住む ① [for s.o./s.a. to make one's dwelling in a certain place] ⟪reside⟫

EX. (a) I live in Kyoto.
私は京都に住んでいる。
Watashi wa Kyooto ni sunde iru.
(b) Where do you hope to live after you get married?
結婚したらどこに住みたいと思っていますか。
Kekkon-shitara doko ni sumi-tai to omotte imasu ka.

L

—— vi./vt. **[to pass/spend one's life]**
ku⌈rasu 暮らす ① [for s.o. to lead one's daily life], se⌈ikatsu-suru 生活する ③ •c [for s.o. to lead one's normal life, actively engaged in some work]

EX. (a) I hear he's living happily in his hometown.
彼は故郷の町で幸せに{暮らして/?生活して}いるそうです。
Kare wa kokyoo no machi de shiawaseni {kurashite/?seikatsu-shite} iru soo desu.
(b) Can one live on 100,000 yen a month in Japan?
日本では一か月十万円で{暮らせます/生活できます}か。
Nihon de wa ik-kagetsu juu-man-en de {kurase-masu/seikatsu-dekimasu} ka.
(c) They live a life of luxury.
彼らは{ぜいたくな生活をして/ぜいたくに暮らして}いる。
Kare-ra wa {zeitakuna seikatsu o shite/zeitakuni kurashite} iru.

PHRASE: live for 〈*-ga*〉 *ikigai da* 〈〜が〉生きがいだ

EX. She lives only for her children.
彼女は子供だけが生きがいだ。
Kanojo wa kodomo dake ga ikigai da.

PHRASE: live with s.o. 〈*-to*〉 *doosei-suru* 〈〜と〉同棲する ③

EX. Do Hanako's parents know that she's living with an American man?
花子さんがアメリカ人の男性と同棲しているのをご両親はご存じなんですか。
Hanako-san ga Amerika-jin no dansei to doosei-shite iru no o go-ryooshin wa go-zonji na n desu ka.

lively adj. **[active/cheerful/enthusiastic]**
ni⌈gi⌉yakana にぎやかな adj(*na*). **[full of vigor and cheerful sounds] ⟪cheerful, busy, noisy⟫, i⌈ki-i⌉ki-shita N 生き生きしたN /〈Vinf. past of *iki-iki-suru* ③ become lively/ [very alive], i⌈ki-i⌉ki-shite iru (N) 生き生きしている(N) /〈V *te iru* of *iki-iki-suru* ③ become lively/, ka⌈kki ga a⌉ru (N) 活気がある(N) •c [for a place or a verbal exchange to be full of energy] ⟪spirited⟫**

EX. (a) It was a lively party.
{にぎやかな/?活気がある/*生き生きした/*生き生きしている}パーティーだった。

*{Nigiyakana/?Kakki ga aru/*Iki-iki-shita/*Iki-iki-shite iru} paatii datta.*
(**b**) Tokyo is a lively city.
東京は{活気がある/にぎやかな/生き生きした/?生き生きしている}町だ。
Tookyoo wa {kakki ga aru/nigiyakana/iki-iki-shita/?iki-iki-shite iru} machi da.
(**c**) I like teaching a lively class.
私は{にぎやかな/活気がある/生き生きした/?生き生きしている}クラスを教えるのが好きだ。
Watashi wa {nigiyakana/kakki ga aru/iki-iki-shita/?iki-iki-shite iru} kurasu o oshieru no ga suki da.
(**d**) She is always lively.
彼女はいつも{生き生きしている/にぎやかだ/*活気がある}。
*Kanojo wa itsu-mo {iki-iki-shite iru/nigiyaka da/*kakki ga aru}.*
(**e**) We had a lively debate on the subject.
その事について{活気がある/*にぎやかな/*生き生きした/*生き生きしている}議論をした。
*Sono koto ni-tsuite {kakki ga aru/*nigiyakana/*iki-iki-shita/*iki-iki-shite iru} giron o shita.*

liver n. **[an organ in the body that produces bile and cleans the blood]**
ka⌈nzoo 肝臓 •**c**, **re⌉baa レバー** •**f [the liver of an animal used for food]**

EX. (**a**) Children usually don't like liver.
子供たちはたいてい{レバー/*肝臓}がきらいだ。
*Kodomo-tachi wa taitei {rebaa/*kanzoo} ga kirai da.*
(**b**) She's in the hospital to have a liver transplant.
彼女は{肝臓/*レバー}移植手術を受けるために入院している。
*Kanojo wa {kanzoo/*rebaa}-ishoku-shujutsu o ukeru tame ni nyuuin-shite iru.*

living adj. **[alive now]**
i⌉kite iru (N) 生きている(N) / ⟨V *te iru* of *ikiru* ② live/ ⟨⟨alive⟩⟩

EX. (**a**) He has no living relatives.
彼には生きている親せきはいない。
Kare ni wa ikite iru shinseki wa inai.
(**b**) The coelacanth was once thought to be extinct but is now known to still be living.
シーラカンスは一時絶滅したと考えられていたが、今ではまだ生きていることが分かっている。
Siirakansu wa ichiji zetsumetsu-shita to kangae-rarete ita ga, ima de wa mada ikite iru koto ga wakatte iru.

—— n. **[a means of earning money to buy things necessary for one's daily life]**
se⌈ikei 生計 •**c**

EX. (**a**) He makes a living as a fashion model.
彼はファッションモデルをして生計をたてている。
Kare wa fasshon-moderu o shite seikei o tatete iru.
(**b**) She earns her living by teaching English to children.
彼女は子供たちに英語を教えて生計をたてている。
Kanojo wa kodomo-tachi ni eigo o oshiete seikei o tatete iru.

PHRASE: living standards *seikatsu-suijun* 生活水準 •**c**

EX. The living standards in our country have declined in recent years.
我が国の生活水準は近年下がっている。
Waga-kuni no seikatsu-suijun wa kinnen sagatte iru.

living room n. **[a room in a house for general family use or for entertaining guests]**
i⌈ma⌉ 居間

EX. (**a**) We had coffee in the living room after dinner.
晩ごはんの後、居間でコーヒーを飲んだ。
Ban-gohan no ato, ima de koohii o nonda.
(**b**) Our living room is very small.
うちの居間はとても小さい。
Uchi no ima wa totemo chiisai.

lizard n.
to⌈kage とかげ

load n. **[s.t. that is carried or to be carried to esp. s.t. heavy]**
ni˥-motsu 荷物 [s.t. that is carried or to be carried to some place] ⟪baggage⟫

EX. Trucks carrying heavy loads are supposed to use this highway.
荷物をたくさん積んだトラックがこの高速道路を使うことになっている。
Ni-motsu o takusan tsunda torakku ga kono koosoku-dooro o tsukau koto ni natte iru.

—— vt./vi. **[to put s.t. on/in a vehicle, structure, etc.]**
⟨-ni⟩ ⟨-o⟩ tsu⌈mu ⟨〜に⟩⟨〜を⟩積む ① [to stack objects in a heap (on a vehicle) ⟪fig. "acquire," "accumulate"⟫] ⟪pile up⟫

EX. (**a**) Have you finished loading up the truck?
トラックに荷物を積み終わりましたか。
Torakku ni nimotsu o tsumi-owarimashita ka.
(**b**) The ship was loaded with oranges.
その船はオレンジをいっぱい積んでいた。
Sono fune wa orenji o ippai tsunde ita.
(**c**) Please load the furniture onto the truck.
トラックに家具を積んでください。
Torakku ni kagu o tsunde kudasai.

loaf n. **[a mass of bread shaped and baked in one piece]**
hi⌈to˥tsu 一つ [one], i˥k-ko 一個 •c [one piece] SEE APPENDIX II

EX. I bought a loaf of bread.
食パンを{一つ/一個}買った。
Shoku-pan o {hitotsu/ik-ko} katta.

loan vt. **[for s.o. to let s.o. have or use s.t. temporarily]**
⟨-ni⟩ ⟨-o⟩ ka⌈su ⟨〜に⟩⟨〜を⟩貸す ① [for s.o. to allow s.o. to have or use s.t. temporarily on the condition that it or s.t. like it will be returned later] ⟪lend⟫

EX. (**a**) Can you loan me your bicycle?
自転車を貸してくださいませんか。
Jitensha o kashite kudasaimasen ka.
(**b**) How much will you loan me for this ring as security?
この指輪を担保にいくら貸してもらえますか。
Kono yubiwa o tanpo ni ikura kashite morae-masu ka.
(**c**) I loaned my pearl necklace to Akiko.
秋子にパールのネックレスを貸した。
Akiko ni paaru no nekkuresu o kashita.

—— n. **[s.t. which is lent, esp. money]**
ro˥on ローン •f

EX. About how much is interest on mortgages these days?
最近の住宅ローンの金利はどのぐらいですか。
Saikin no juutaku-roon no kinri wa dono-gurai desu ka.

PHRASE: take out a loan *kane o kariru* 金を借りる ②

lobby n. **[a wide hall or passage in a hotel or large building which leads from the main entrance to the rooms]**
ro˥bii ロビー •f

EX. (**a**) I met Mr. Smith in the lobby of the Hilton Hotel.
ヒルトンホテルのロビーでスミスさんに会いました。
Hiruton-hoteru no robii de Sumisu-san ni aimashita.
(**b**) Prof. Arai is waiting for you in the lobby.
新井先生がロビーでお待ちです。
Arai-sensei ga robii de o-machi desu.

lobster n.
i⌈se˥-ebi いせえび, ro˥busutaa ロブスター •f

local adj. **[belonging to or concerned with a particular place or a small area]**
so⌈no to⌈chi no N その土地のN [of/in a certain place or area], chi⌈ho˥o no N 地方のN [of/in a rural area]

EX. (**a**) He is a local government employee.
彼は{地方/*その土地の}公務員だ。
*Kare wa {chihoo-/*sono tochi no} koomu-in da.*
(**b**) Wherever I live, I try to respect the local customs.
住む所がどこであれ、{その土地/*地方}の習慣を大事にするようにしている。
*Sumu tokoro ga doko deare, {sono tochi/*chihoo} no shuukan o daiji ni suru yooni shite iru.*

L

locate vt. **[for s.o. to find where s.o./s.t./s.a. is or to put or settle s.o./s.t. in a certain place]**

1. ⟨-no⟩ i˥chi o mi˥tsukeru ⟨〜の⟩位置を見つける ② [for s.o. to find the position of s.t./s.o./s.a.]

EX. We've located the plane that crashed.
私たちは墜落した飛行機の位置を見つけた。
Watashi-tachi wa tsuiraku-shita hikoo-ki no ichi o mitsuketa.

2. ⟨-ni⟩ a˥ru ⟨〜に⟩ある ① [for s.t. to exist] ⟪be situated, exist⟫

EX. (**a**) Our school is located in Tokyo.
私たちの学校は東京にある。
Watashi-tachi no gakkoo wa Tookyoo ni aru.
(**b**) The hospital is located on the outskirts of town.
病院は町の外れにある。
Byooin wa machi no hazure ni aru.

location n. **[the place or position where s.t./s.o./s.a. is]**

ba˥sho 場所 •c [a point or area in space where s.o./s.t./s.a. exists or where s.t. happens] •c ⟪place, position⟫

EX. (**a**) We have to find a suitable location for the camp.
キャンプにちょうどいい場所を見つけなければならない。
Kyanpu ni choodo ii basho o mitsukenakereba naranai.
(**b**) This is a good location to open a coffee shop.
ここは喫茶店を開くにはいい場所だ。
Koko wa kissa-ten o hiraku ni wa ii basho da.

lock n. **[a device for closing and fastening a door, window, lid, or other opening]**

ka˥gi˥ かぎ [a device used to fasten a door, window, lid, or other opening or an instrument used to lock/unlock such a device or s.t. that helps one to understand s.t. ⟪fig. "an important role"⟫] ⟪key⟫

EX. I had the lock on the front door changed.
玄関のかぎを替えてもらった。
Genkan no kagi o kaete moratta.

—— vt./vi. **[for s.o. to fasten s.t. with a lock]**

⟨-ni⟩ ka˥gi˥ o ka˥ke˥ru ⟨〜に⟩かぎをかける ②, ⟨-ni⟩ ka˥gi˥ ga ka˥ka˥ru ⟨〜に⟩かぎがかかる ① [for s.t. to become fastened or to be able to be fastened with a lock]

EX. (**a**) Please don't forget to lock the car doors.
車のドアにかぎをかけるのを忘れないでください。
Kuruma no doa ni kagi o kakeru no o wasurenaide kudasai.
(**b**) The door is locked.
ドアにかぎがかかっている。
Doa ni kagi ga kakatte iru.
(**c**) This door won't lock.
このドアはかぎがかからない。
Kono doa wa kagi ga kakaranai.

lodge vi. **[to stay, usually for a short time in return for payment]**

⟨-ni⟩ to˥maru ⟨〜に⟩とまる ① •c [for s.o./s.t./s.a. moving to come to a standstill ⟪fig. "lodge," "be fastened"⟫]

㊥ "stay overnight"▷泊まる, "be fastened"▷留まる, "stop moving"▷止まる

EX. We lodged overnight at a motel on the outskirts of town.
私たちは町の外れにあるモーテルに一晩泊まった。
Watashi-tachi wa machi no hazure ni aru mooteru ni hito-ban tomatta.

lodging n.

shu˥kuhaku 宿泊 •c

log n. **[part of the trunk of a tree that has fallen or been cut down]**

ma˥ruta 丸太, ma˥ru-ki 丸木 [a tree that has been felled and has had the branches and bark removed but has otherwise not been processed into lumber]

EX. (**a**) They built a cabin with logs.
{丸太/*丸木}で小屋を建てた。
*{Maruta/*Maru-ki} de koya o tateta.*
(**b**) We crossed over a log bridge.
{丸太/丸木}の橋を渡った。
{Maruta/Maru-ki} no hashi o watatta.

London n.

Ro˥ndon ロンドン •f

lonely adj. **[unhappy because one is alone]**
sa⌈bishi⌉i 寂しい adj(*i*).

EX. (**a**) She looks lonely.
彼女は寂しそうだ。
Kanojo wa sabishi-soo da.
(**b**) Please call me if you feel lonely.
寂しくなったら、電話してください。
Sabishiku nattara, denwa-shite kudasai.
(**c**) My brother has been lonely since I left home.
私が家を出てから、弟は寂しがっている。
Watashi ga uchi o dete kara, otooto wa sabishi-gatte iru.

NOTE: *Sabishii* takes the first person subject in statements and the second person subject in questions. When the subject is a third person, some form should be attached which explicitly expresses the speaker's perception or judgment, such as *-soo da* "appears," as in (a), or the form *sabishi-garu* should be used, as in (c).

long adj. **[having great extension from one end to the other either in spatial measurement or in time]**
na⌈ga⌉i 長い adj(*i*).

EX. (**a**) She has long legs.
彼女は足が長い。
Kanojo wa ashi ga nagai.
(**b**) I have been living here for a long time.
長い間ここに住んでいる。
Nagai aida koko ni sunde iru.
(**c**) It was a long journey.
長い旅だった。
Nagai tabi datta.

2. na⌉ga-sa 長さ n. /⟨adj(*i*). **stem of** ***nagai*** **long + suf.** ***sa*** **ness/ [the physical extension of s.t. from one end to the other in space or time]** **⟪length⟫**

EX. (**a**) How long is this rope?
このロープの長さはどのぐらいですか。
Kono roopu no naga-sa wa dono-gurai desu ka.
(**b**) Do you have a ribbon about one meter long?
長さが一メートルぐらいのリボンがありますか。
Naga-sa ga ichi-meerotu-gurai no ribon ga arimasu ka.

—— adv. **[to a great extent in time]**
na⌉gaku 長く

EX. It won't take long to type this letter.
この手紙をタイプするのに長くはかからない。
Kono tegami o taipu-suru no ni nagaku wa kakaranai.

PHRASE: long and narrow *hoso-nagai* 細長い ⟪slender⟫

EX. His office is in that long and narrow building.
彼のオフィスはあの細長い建物の中にある。
Kare no ofisu wa ano hoso-nagai tatemono no naka ni aru.

look vi. **[for s.o./s.a. to direct one's eyes in order to see s.t./s.o./s.a. ⟪fig. "face in the stated direction"⟫ or having the appearance or expression of doing s.t. or being a certain way]**

1. ⟨**-o**⟩ **mi⌉ru** ⟨〜を⟩みる ② **[for s.o./s.a. to direct one's attention to s.t./s.o./s.a. in order to visually perceive its outward shape or its content]** **⟪see, watch⟫**, ⟨**-o**⟩ **na⌈game⌉ru** ⟨〜を⟩眺める ② **[for s.o. to direct one's eyes in order to visually perceive s.t./s.o./s.a. for an extended period of time]** **⟪watch, get a view of⟫**

㊞ "for a doctor to see his patient"▷診る, otherwise ▷見る

EX. (**a**) What are they looking at?
何を{見て/眺めて}いるんですか。
Nani o {mite/nagamete} iru n desu ka.
(**b**) The child stood looking at the toys displayed in the show window for close to an hour.
子供はショーウィンドウの前に立ってそこに飾ってあるおもちゃを一時間近く{見て/眺めて}いた。
Kodomo wa shoo-uindoo no mae ni tatte soko ni kazatte aru omocha o ichi-jikan-chikaku {mite/nagamete} ita.

2. {⟨**-o**⟩/⟨**-ni**⟩} **mu⌈ku** {⟨〜を⟩/⟨〜に⟩}向く ① **[to turn one's face/front in the stated**

direction or to be right and suitable for s.o./s.t./s.a.] ⟪face⟫, ⟨-ni⟩ **me⌈n-su⌉ru** ⟨〜に⟩面する ③ **•c [for s.t. to front on s.t.]** ⟪face⟫

EX. (**a**) Our house looks south.
うちは南に{向いて/面して}いる。
Uchi wa minami ni {muite/men-shite} iru.
(**b**) The hotel looks out over the river.
ホテルは川に{面して/*向いて}いる。
*Hoteru wa kawa ni {men-shite/*muite} iru.*

3. {**V***masu*/**adj**(*i*/*na*)**. stem**}**-soona** {**V***masu*/**adj**(*i*/*na*)**. stem**}そうな aux. adj(*na*). **[having the appearance of being about to occur or of having a certain quality or of being in a certain state based on what the speaker sees/hears/senses]** ⟪**appear, seem**⟫

NOTE: The adjective *ii* "good" and the negative form *nai* "not exist" change to *yosa-sooda* and *nasa-sooda*, respectively, with this *sooda*.

EX. (**a**) It looks like it will snow.
雪が降りそうだ。
Yuki ga furi-soo da.
(**b**) That suitcase looks heavy.
あのスーツケースは重そうだ。
Ano suutsukessu wa omo-soo da.
(**c**) This book doesn't look so difficult.
この本はあまり難しくなさそうだ。
Kono hon wa amari muzukashikunasa-soo da.
(**d**) That person looks nice. Let's ask him for directions.
あの人が親切そうだ。あの人に道を聞いてみよう。
Ano hito ga shinsetsu-soo da. Ano hito ni michi o kiite miyoo.
(**e**) He's eating a delicious looking piece of cake.
彼はおいしそうなケーキを食べている。
Kare wa oishi-soona keeki o tabete iru.

PHRASE: look down on ⟨-o⟩ *keibetsu-suru* ⟨〜を⟩軽べつする ③ **•c** ⟪despise⟫

EX. She tends to look down on people with less education than herself.
彼女は自分より学歴の低い人を軽べつしがちだ。
Kanojo wa jibun yori gakureki no hikui hito o keibetsu-shi-gachi da.

PHRASE: look for ⟨-o⟩ *sagasu* ⟨〜を⟩さがす ① ㊥ "look for s.t./s.o./s.a. that a person needs"▷探す, "look for s.t./s.o./s.a. that one has lost (sight of)"▷捜す

EX. I am looking for an apartment.
私はアパートを探している。
Watashi wa apaato o sagashite iru.

PHRASE: look forward to ⟨-o⟩ *tanoshi-mi ni suru* ⟨〜を⟩楽しみにする ③

EX. I am looking forward to going to Kyushu.
九州へ行くのを楽しみにしています。
Kyuushuu e iku no o tanoshi-mi ni shite imasu.

PHRASE: look up to ⟨-o⟩ *sonkei-suru* ⟨〜を⟩尊敬する ③ **•c** ⟪respect⟫

EX. I look up to my father.
私は父を尊敬している。
Watashi wa chichi o sonkei-shite iru.

loop n. **[a round shape formed by a piece of string, wire, rope, etc. that crosses itself]** **wa⌉** 輪 ⟪**circle, ring, link**⟫

EX. Form the piece of string into a loop.
ひもで輪を作ってください。
Himo de wa o tsukutte kudasai.

loose adj. **[not firmly fixed/fitted/held in place]**
gu⌉ra-gura-shita N ぐらぐらしたN /⟨**Vinf. past of *gura-gura-suru*** ③ **shake/ [s.t. moving because it is not firmly/tightly fixed in place], gu⌉ra-gura-shite iru** (**N**) ぐらぐらしている(**N**) /⟨**V*te iru* of *gura-gura-suru*** ③ **shake/** ②, **yu⌈tta⌉ri-shita N** ゆったりしたN **[for clothes to be not tightly fitted ⟪fig. "relaxed"⟫], yu⌈tta⌉ri-shite iru** (**N**) ゆったりしている(**N**) /⟨**V*te iru* of *yuttari-suru*** ③ **feel relaxed/** ②

EX. (**a**) One of his front teeth is loose.
彼は前歯が一本{ぐらぐら/*ゆったり}している。
*Kare wa mae-ba ga ip-pon {gura-gura/*yuttari}-shite iru.*
(**b**) A woman in a loose dress came to the door.
{ゆったりした/ゆったりしている/*ぐら

ぐらした/*ぐらぐらしている}ドレスを着た女の人が玄関に出てきた。
*{Yuttari-shita/Yuttari-shite iru/*Gura-gura-shita/*Gura-gura-shite iru} doresu o kita onna no hito ga genkan ni dete kita.*

PHRASE: come loose ⟨*-ga*⟩ *yurumu* ⟨〜が⟩緩む ①

EX. His shoelace came loose while running.
走っている途中で、靴ひもが緩んだ。
Hashitte iru tochuu de, kutsu-himo ga yurunda.

Los Angeles n.
Ro⌈sanze⌉rusu ロサンゼルス •f

lose vt. **[to no longer have s.t./s.o./s.a., esp. as a result of carelessness/accident/death ⟪fig. "fail to win"⟫]**

1. ⟨**-o**⟩ **na⌈kusu** ⟨〜を⟩なくす ① **[for s.o. to no longer have s.t./s.o./s.a. as a result of carelessness/accident/death]**, ⟨**-o**⟩ **u⌈shinau** ⟨〜を⟩失う ① **[to no longer have s.t. intangible/a part of one's body/s.o.]**

㊌ "lose s.t./s.a."▷無くす, "lose s.o."▷亡くす

EX. (**a**) I've lost my dictionary.
辞書を{無くして/*失って}しまった。
*Jisho o {nakushite/*ushinatte} shimatta.*
(**b**) Please don't lose your passport.
パスポートを{無くさないで/*失わないで}ください。
*Pasupooto o {nakusanaide/*ushinawanaide} kudasai.*
(**c**) I lost my son in the war.
戦争で息子を{亡くした/失った}。
Sensoo de musuko o {nakushita/ushinatta}.
(**d**) He lost interest in studying Japanese.
彼は日本語の勉強に興味を{無くした/失った}。
Kare wa Nihon-go no benkyoo ni kyoomi o {nakushita/ushinatta}.
(**e**) He'll lose face if he fails again.
もう一度失敗したら、彼は面目を{失う/*無くす}。
*Moo ichi-do shippai-shitara, kare wa menboku o {ushinau/*nakusu}.*
(**f**) He lost a leg in the battle.
彼は戦闘で片足を{失った/*無くした}。
*Kare wa sentoo de kata-ashi o {ushinatta/*nakushita}.*

2. ⟨**-ni**⟩ **ma⌈keru** ⟨〜に⟩負ける ② **[to be defeated by some concrete or intangible force]** ⟪**be defeated, be beaten**⟫ ↔ ⟨**-ni**⟩ **katsu** ⟨〜に⟩勝つ ①

EX. (**a**) The Giants lost to the Lions in the 1990 Japan Series.
1990年の日本シリーズでジャイアンツはライオンズに負けた。
Sen-kyuu-hyaku-kyuu-juu-nen no Nihon-shiriizu de Jaiantsu wa Raionzu ni maketa.
(**b**) He lost the match to the champion.
彼はチャンピオンとの試合に負けた。
Kare wa chanpion to no shiai ni maketa.

loss n. **[an act/instance of losing s.t./s.o./s.a. or the amount by which one's costs exceed one's income resulting in debt]**

1. fu⌈nshitsu 紛失 **•c [an act/instance of losing s.t.], so⌈nshitsu** 損失 **•c [an act/instance of losing s.t./s.o. which results in disadvantage for one]** ↔ **rieki** 利益 **•c**

EX. (**a**) Did you report the loss of your passport to the embassy?
大使館にパスポートの{紛失/*損失}を届け出ましたか。
*Taishi-kan ni pasupooto no {funshitsu/*sonshitsu} o todoke-demashita ka.*
(**b**) She was an excellent teacher. It's a great loss to our school to see her go.
彼女は非常に優秀な教師だ。彼女を失うのは学校にとって大きな{損失/*紛失}だ。
*Kanojo wa hijooni yuushuuna kyooshi da. Kanojo o ushinau no wa gakkoo ni-totte ookina {sonshitsu/*funshitsu} da.*

2. so⌉n 損 **•c [the amount by which one's costs are greater than one's income]** ⟪**disadvantage**⟫ ↔ **toku** 得 **•c; so⌈ngai** 損害 **•c [the harm inflicted on s.t. as measured in terms of money]** ⟪**damage**⟫

EX. (**a**) He has suffered big losses in the market.
彼は株式市場で大きな{損/*損害}をした。

*Kare wa kabushiki-shijoo de ookina {son/*songai} o shita.*
(**b**) The loss amounted to ¥10,000,000.
{損害/*損}は一千万円に達した。
*{Songai/*Son} wa is-sen-man-en ni tasshita.*

PHRASE: be at a loss *komaru* 困る ①

EX. I was at a loss to explain why I was late for class.
どうして授業に遅れたか説明に困った。
Dooshite jugyoo ni okureta ka setsumei ni komatta.

lost adj. **[not able to be found or not knowing where one is]**
1. na⌈kushita N 無くしたN /⟨Vinf. past of ***nakusu*** ① lose/ **[no longer owned by or able to be found by the person who once owned it]**
2. mi⌈chi ni mayo⌉tta N 道に迷ったN /⟨***michi*** way, road + prt. ***ni*** + Vinf. past of ***mayou*** ① get lost/ **[unable to find one's way]**

EX. I got lost on the way to his house.
彼の家へ行く途中で道に迷ってしまった。
Kare no ie e iku tochuu de michi ni mayotte shimatta.

lot n. **[a large number/amount]**
ta⌈kusa⌉n たくさん n./adv. **((many, much, plenty))**, **o⌉oi** 多い adj(*i*). **[large in number/quantity]** **((many, much, plenty))**

NOTE: *Ooi* is usually used as a predicate.

EX. (**a**) A lot of people travel abroad these days.
このごろは{たくさんの人が海外旅行をする/海外旅行をする人が多い}。
Kono-goro wa {takusan no hito ga kaigai-ryokoo o suru/kaigai-ryokoo o suru hito ga ooi}.
(**b**) I drink a lot of milk every day.
私は毎日牛乳をたくさん飲みます。
Watashi wa mai-nichi gyuunyuu o takusan nomimasu.
(**c**) There are lots of bookstores around here.
この辺には本屋が{たくさんある/多い}。
Kono hen ni wa hon-ya ga {takusan aru/ooi}.

NOTE: *Takusan* usually follows the noun it refers to, as in examples (b) and (c).

loud adj. **[having/producing a large amount of sound]**
o⌈oki⌉i 大きい adj(*i*). **[greater than usual in size or degree]** **((big, large, great))**

EX. He greeted us with a loud "Good morning!"
彼は大きい声で「おはようございます」と言った。
Kare wa ookii koe de 'O-hayoo gozaimasu' to itta.

lounge n. **[a room for sitting and relaxing]**
kyu⌈uke⌉i-shitsu 休憩室 **•c [a room for people to sit and relax in]**, **ra⌉unji** ラウンジ **•f [a room in a public building such as a hotel for people to sit and relax in]**

EX. We had a chat in the lounge.
{休憩室/ラウンジ}でおしゃべりをした。
{Kyuukei-shitsu/Raunji} de o-shaberi o shita.

love n. **[a strong feeling of affection, including sexual attraction]**
1. a⌉i 愛 **•c [a strong feeling of fondness for another person]** **((affection))**

EX. (**a**) The girl was starved for love.
女の子は愛に飢えていた。
Onna-no-ko wa ai ni uete ita.
(**b**) His love for me seems to have cooled down.
彼の私に対する愛は冷めてしまったようだ。
Kare no watashi ni-taisuru ai wa samete shimatta yooda.

2. ko⌉i 恋 **[a feeling of fondness combined with sexual attraction]**, **re⌈n'ai** 恋愛 **•c**

EX. (**a**) He is in love with Kiko.
彼は紀子に{恋/*恋愛}をしている。
*Kare wa Kiko ni {koi/*ren'ai} o shite iru.*
(**b**) He wrote a love story.
彼は{恋愛小説/恋物語}を書いた。
Kare wa {ren'ai-shoosetsu/koi-monogatari} o kaita.

PHRASE: fall in love with ⟨*-ga*⟩ *suki ni naru* ⟨〜が⟩好きになる /⟨adj(*na*). *ni* of *sukina* like + *naru*

L

① become/ ①, ⟨*-to*⟩ *koi ni ochiru* ⟨～と⟩恋におちる ②

EX. She fell in love with Yoshio.
彼女は良雄{が好きになった/と恋におちた}。
Kanojo wa Yoshio {ga suki ni natta/to koi ni ochita}.

— vt. **[to feel a strong feeling of affection or desire for s.o./s.a./s.t. or a strong feeling of friendship with s.o.]**
⟨-o⟩ a˹isu˺ru ⟨～を⟩愛する ③ **•c [for s.o. to feel a strong feeling of affection for s.o.], ⟨-ga⟩ dai˺-sukina** ⟨～が⟩大好きな adj(*na*). **[for s.o./s.a. to like s.o./s.a./s.t. very much]** ((**like very much**)), **⟨-o⟩ ka˹wai-ga˺ru** ⟨～を⟩かわいがる ① **[for s.o. to have a tender feeling of affection for children, pets, etc.]** ((**cherish**))

EX. (**a**) I love my husband.
私は主人{を愛している/が大好きだ/*をかわいがっている}。
*Watashi wa shujin {o aishite iru/ga dai-suki da/*o kawai-gatte iru}.*
(**b**) I love my grandfather.
私は祖父{が大好きだ/?を愛している/?をかわいがっている}。
*Watashi wa sofu {ga dai-suki da/*o aishite iru/*o kawai-gatte iru}.*
(**c**) My grandfather loved me.
祖父は私を{かわいがって/?愛して}くれた。
Sofu wa watashi o {kawai-gatte/?aishite} kureta.

lovely adj. **[beautiful, attractive, pleasant]**
su˹tekina すてきな adj(*na*). **•c [giving a favorable impression to the observer on the basis of outward appearance such as dress, color, pattern, etc.]**

EX. (**a**) A lovely girl walked into the room.
すてきな女の子が部屋に入ってきた。
Sutekina onna-no-ko ga heya ni haitte kita.
(**b**) They live in a lovely little house.
彼らはすてきな小さな家に住んでいる。
Kare-ra wa sutekina chiisana ie ni sunde iru.

lover n. **[s.o., esp. a man, who is in love with s.o. else or s.o., esp. a married person, involved in an illicit love affair]**
ko˹i-bito 恋人, **a˹ijin** 愛人 **[s.o. with whom a married man/woman has illicit sexual relations] •c**

EX. He is her lover.
彼は彼女の{恋人/愛人}だ。
Kare wa kanojo no {koi-bito/aijin} da.

low adj. **[measuring a short distance from the ground/floor/base/bottom or small in degree/amount/value]**
hi˹ku˺i 低い adj(*i*). **[having little vertical length as measured from a horizontal base line, esp. of physical objects such as mountains/buildings but also of temperature/status/(length of) nose]**

EX. (**a**) The garden is surrounded by a low wall.
庭は低い塀に囲まれている。
Niwa wa hikui hei ni kakoma-rete iru.
(**b**) His house is located on a low hill.
彼の家は低い丘の上にある。
Kare no uchi wa hikui oka no ue ni aru.
(**c**) Their standard of living is quite low.
彼らの生活水準はかなり低い。
Kare-ra no seikatsu-suijun wa kanari hikui.
(**d**) This plant doesn't grow well in low temperatures.
この植物は気温が低いと育たない。
Kono shokubutsu wa kion ga hikui to sodatanai.
(**e**) The soldiers' morale was low.
兵士の士気は低かった。
Heishi no shiki wa hikukatta.

lower vt./vi. **[to let/bring s.t. down]**
⟨-o⟩ sa˹ge˺ru ⟨～を⟩下げる ② **[for s.o. to cause s.t./s.o./s.a. to move to a lower place or to decrease in amount/degree/strength]** ((**let down, drop**)) ↔ **⟨-o⟩ ageru** ⟨～を⟩上げる ②; **sa˹ga˺ru** 下がる ① **[for s.t. to hang/go down/become smaller in amount/degree/strength]** ((**fall, decline, drop, go down**)) ↔ **agaru** 上がる ①

EX. (**a**) They've lowered the price of the coat to 10,000 yen.

コートの値段を一万円に下げた。
Kooto no nedan o ichi-man-en ni sageta.
(**b**) The presence of an arctic air mass has lowered temperatures over the upper midwest region.
北極圏に発生した寒気団の影響で中西部の北の方では気温が下がっている。
Hokkyoku-ken ni hassei-shita kanki-dan no eikyoo de chuusei-bu no kita no hoo de wa kion ga sagatte iru.
(**c**) They lowered the room temperature to save electricity.
電力を節約するために室温を下げた。
Denryoku o setsuyaku-suru tame ni shitsuon o sageta.

loyal adj. **[true and faithful to one's friends, principles, country, etc.]**
chu⌈ujitsuna 忠実な adj(*na*). •**c [faithful to one's boss, employer, etc.]**

EX. (**a**) Mr. Yamada has many loyal subordinates.
山田さんには忠実な部下がたくさんいる。
Yamada-san ni wa chuujitsuna buka ga takusan iru.
(**b**) She wants a boyfriend who will be loyal to her.
彼女は忠実な恋人を欲しがっている。
Kanojo wa chuujitsuna koibito o hoshigatte iru.

luck n. **[good or bad things that happen to s.o. without any apparent reason or purpose]**
u⌉n 運 •**c** ⟪**fortune**⟫

EX. (**a**) I may fail, but I want to at least try my luck.
失敗するかもしれませんが、私の運を試すだけ試してみたいんです。
Shippai-suru kamoshiremasen ga, watashi no un o tamesu dake tameshite mi-tai n desu.
(**b**) With luck, you could get a ticket.
運が良ければ、切符が手に入るでしょう。
Un ga yokereba, kippu ga te ni hairu deshoo.
(**c**) I have no luck with men.
私は男運が悪いんです。
Watashi wa otoko-un ga warui n desu.

PHRASE: Good luck. *Ganbatte kudasai.* 頑張ってください。

NOTE: The literal translation of *Ganbatte kudasai.* is "Try hard./Do your best." It would typically be said, for example, to a person who is about to take an exam, compete in a match, etc.

lucky adj. **[having or resulting from or bringing good luck]**
u⌉n ga i⌉i 運がいい adj(*i*). ⟪**fortunate**⟫ ↔ **un ga warui** 運が悪い

NOTE: The *kanji* 良い is pronounced as *yoi*. The dictionary form *ii* is written in *hiragana*, but its conjugated forms *yokatta*, *yokute*, etc. can be written as 良かった, 良くて, etc.

EX. (**a**) You were lucky not to get caught in the rain.
雨に降られなかったなんて運が良かったですね。
Ame ni fura-renakatta nante un ga yokatta desu ne.
(**b**) I was really lucky that a doctor was on board when I got sick on the plane.
飛行機の中で病気になったとき、お医者さんが乗っていてくれたなんて、本当に運が良かったです。
Hikoo-ki no naka de byooki ni natta toki, o-isha-san ga notte ite kureta nante hontoo ni un ga yokatta desu.

lukewarm adj. **[neither hot nor cold as desired, but only slightly warm, esp. of liquid]**
nu⌈ru⌉i ぬるい adj(*i*). **[for liquid to be not hot or cold enough]** ⟪**tepid**⟫, **na⌈ma-nuru⌉i** 生ぬるい adj(*i*). **[not hot or cold enough and thus unpleasant ⟪fig. "not strict enough"⟫]** ⟪**halfway**⟫

EX. (**a**) I hate lukewarm coffee.
私は{ぬるい/生ぬるい}コーヒーは大きらいです。
Watashi wa {nurui/nama-nurui} koohii wa dai-kirai desu.
(**b**) They served me lukewarm water at the restaurant.

L

レストランで{ぬるい/生ぬるい}水を出された。
Resutoran de {nurui/nama-nurui} mizu o dasa-reta.

lumber n.
za⌈imoku 材木 •c

lump n. **[a piece of a solid substance with no special size or shape]**
ka⌈tamari 塊 [a piece of solid substance], shi⌈kori しこり [a hard swelling on the body 《fig. "a hard feeling left among/between people after s.t. unpleasant has happened"》]

EX. (**a**) He threw some lumps of coal into the fire.
彼は火の中に石炭の{塊/*しこり}を投げ込んだ。
*Kare wa hi no naka ni sekitan no {katamari/*shikori} o nage-konda.*
(**b**) The doctor found a lump in his stomach.
医者が彼の腹に{しこり/*塊}を見つけた。
*Isha ga kare no hara ni {shikori/*katamari} o mitsuketa.*

lunar adj. **[having to do with the moon]**
tsu⌈ki⌉ no N 月のN
PHRASE: the lunar calendar *inreki* 陰暦 •c ↔ *taiyoo-reki* 太陽暦 •c; *kyuureki* 旧暦 •c ↔ *shinreki* 新暦 •c; lunar eclipse *gesshoku* 月食 •c

lunch n. **[a meal eaten in the middle of the day]**
hi⌈ru-go⌉han 昼御飯, chu⌈ushoku 昼食 •c

EX. (**a**) What time do you usually have lunch?
大抵何時ごろ{昼御飯/?昼食}を食べますか。
Taitei nan-ji-goro {hiru-gohan/?chuushoku} o tabemasu ka.
(**b**) I had a late lunch today.
私は今日遅い{昼食/?昼御飯}をとった。
Watashi wa kyoo osoi {chuushoku/?hiru-gohan} o totta.
(**c**) I had a sandwich for lunch.
{昼御飯/昼食}にサンドイッチを食べた。
{Hiru-gohan/Chuushoku} ni sandoitchi o tabeta.

PHRASE: {box lunch/packed lunch} *bentoo* 弁当 •c
EX. He takes a box lunch to school.
彼は学校へ弁当を持って行く。
Kare wa gakkoo e bentoo o motte iku.

lung n.
ha⌈i 肺 •c

EX. (**a**) My father died of lung cancer.
父は肺がんで死んだ。
Chichi wa hai-gan de shinda.
(**b**) Smoking is not good for the lungs.
たばこは肺に良くない。
Tabako wa hai ni yokunai.

luxury n. **[a state of great comfort and pleasure or s.t. which brings great comfort and pleasure though perhaps not essential]**
ze⌈itaku⌉(na) ぜいたく(な) n./adj(*na*). •c **((extravagance))**

EX. (**a**) I'd love to lead a life of luxury.
私はぜいたくな生活ができたらいいなと思う。
Watashi wa zeitakuna seikatsu ga dekitara ii na to omou.
(**b**) Having champagne with every dinner may be a luxury, but it's a pleasure I just can't do without.
毎日夕食にシャンペンを飲むのはぜいたくかもしれないが、私には欠かすことのできない楽しみだ。
Mai-nichi yuushoku ni shanpen o nomu no wa zeitaku kamo shirenai ga, watshi ni wa kakasu koto no dekinai tanoshimi da.

M

macaroni n.
ma⌈karoni マカロニ •f

machine n. **[a piece of equipment that transmits and modifies force, power, and motion in such a way as to perform some task]**
ki⌈ka⌉i 機械 •c

EX. (**a**) A new machine was installed in the factory.
新しい機械が工場に備えつけられた。
Atarashii kikai ga koojoo ni sonae-tsuke-rareta.
(**b**) He repaired a machine which had been out of order for a long time.
彼は長い間故障していた機械を修理した。
Kare wa nagai aida koshoo-shite ita kikai o shuuri-shita.
(**c**) Do you know how to operate this machine?
この機械の動かし方を知っていますか。
Kono kikai no ugokashi-kata o shitte imasu ka.

PHRASE: sewing machine *mishin* ミシン, vending machine *jidoo-hanbai-ki* 自動販売機 •c, washing machine *sentaku-ki* 洗濯機 •c

mad adj. **[mentally disturbed or angry]**
1. ki-⌈chiga⌉i (no N) 気違い(のN) **[of a disordered mind]** ((**insane**))

NOTE: *Ki-chigai* by itself means a mad person.

EX. He worked like a madman.
彼は気違いのように仕事をした。
Kare wa ki-chigai no yooni shigoto o shita.

PHRASE: go mad *ki-ga-kuruu* 気が狂う ①

EX. He went mad and was put into a mental hospital.
彼は気が狂って、精神病院に入れられた。
Kare wa ki-ga-kurutte, seishin-byooin ni ire-rareta.

2. o⌈ko⌉tta N 怒ったN /⟨Vinf. past of *okoru* ① **get mad**/

PHRASE: get mad *okoru* 怒る ①

EX. He got mad because nobody listened to him.
だれも彼の言うことを聞こうとしなかったので、彼は怒った。
Dare-mo kare no iu koto o kikoo to shinakatta node, kare wa okotta.

PHRASE: make…mad ⟨*-o*⟩ *okora-seru* ⟨〜を⟩怒らせる ②

EX. I made my father mad because I used his car without permission.
父に無断で車を使って、父を怒らせてしまった。
Chichi ni mudan de kuruma o tsukatte, chichi o okora-sete shimatta.

made adj. **[formed]**
⟨-de⟩ de⌉kita N ⟨〜で⟩できたN **[formed of]**, **-sei no N** 〜製のN •c

EX. (**a**) We bought a table made of wood.
{木でできた/木製の}テーブルを買った。
{Ki de dekita/Moku-sei no} teeburu o katta.
(**b**) She gave me a bag made of leather.
彼女は{革でできた/革製の}バッグをくれた。
Kanojo wa {kawa de dekita/kawa-sei no} baggu o kureta.

PHRASE: made in Japan *Nihon-sei no* N 日本製のN •c

magazine n. **[a paper-covered periodical containing articles, photos, and advertisements]**
za⌈sshi 雑誌 •c ((**journal**))

EX. (**a**) I bought a magazine at the station.
私は駅で雑誌を買った。
Watashi wa eki de zasshi o katta.

M

(**b**) His picture was in the January issue of that magazine.
あの雑誌の一月号に彼の写真が載っていた。
Ano zasshi no ichi-gatsu-goo ni kare no shashin ga notte ita.
(**c**) That magazine has lots of good articles.
あの雑誌にはいい記事が多い。
Ano zasshi ni wa ii kiji ga ooi.

PHRASE: weekly magazine *shuukan-shi* 週刊誌 •c, monthly magazine *gekkan-shi* 月刊誌 •c

magic n. **[the art of using supernatural forces to control events and people]**
ma⌈hoo 魔法 •c

EX. (**a**) I don't believe in magic.
私は魔法を信じない。
Watashi wa mahoo o shinjinai.
(**b**) He uses magic to cure diseases.
彼は病気を治すのに魔法を使う。
Kare wa byooki o naosu no ni mahoo o tsukau.

magician n. **[s.o. who can make supernatural things happen by magic or an entertainer who performs tricks that seem to involve magic]**
1. ma⌈hoo-tsu⌉kai 魔法使い ⟪wizard⟫

EX. I wanted to be a magician when I was small.
私は小さいとき、魔法使いになりたかった。
Watashi wa chiisai toki, mahoo-tsukai ni nari-takatta.

2. ma⌈jutsu⌉-shi 魔術師 •c [an entertainer who performs tricks that seem to involve magic]

EX. He is a great magician.
彼は偉大な魔術師だ。
Kare wa idaina majutsu-shi da.

magnet n. **[a piece of iron which attracts other iron towards it]**
ji⌉shaku 磁石 •c

EX. I used a magnet to collect the nails spilled on the floor.
私は磁石を使って、床にこぼれた釘を集めた。
Watashi wa jishaku o tsukatte, yuka ni koboreta kugi o atsumeta.

magnificent adj. **[splendid in appearance or outstanding in quality]**
su⌈barashi⌉i すばらしい adj(*i*). **[causing great wonder/admiration/pleasure due to being extremely good] ⟪wonderful, splendid, beautiful, great⟫, mi⌉gotona 見事な** adj(*na*). **[causing admiration due to being visually appealing or skillfully accomplished] ⟪wonderful, splendid⟫**

EX. (**a**) He gave me a magnificent *kimono* for my college graduation.
彼は大学の卒業祝いに{すばらしい/見事な}着物をくれた。
Kare wa daigaku no sotsugyoo-iwai ni {subarashii/migotona} ki-mono o kureta.
(**b**) We enjoyed a magnificent view of Mt. Fuji from the hotel.
私たちはホテルから富士山の{すばらしい/見事な}眺めを楽しんだ。
Watashi-tachi wa hoteru kara Fuji-san no {subarashii/migotona} nagame o tanoshinda.
(**c**) This is a magnificent thesis!
これは{すばらしい/?見事な}論文ですね。
Kore wa {subarashii/?migotona} ronbun desu ne.

maid n. **[a female servant at a hotel or private home]**
o-⌈te⌉tsudai-san お手伝いさん [a female servant at a private home], me⌉ido メイド •f [a female servant at a hotel or private home]

EX. (**a**) The maid cleaned the room.
{お手伝いさん/メイド}が部屋を掃除した。
{O-tetsudai-san/Meido} ga heya o sooji-shita.
(**b**) He had the maid polish his shoes.
{お手伝いさん/メイド}に靴を磨かせた。
{O-tetsudai-san/Meido} ni kutsu o migaka-seta.

mail n. **[the postal system or items delivered by post such as letters and parcels]**
yu⌈ubin 郵便 •c ⟪letters, parcels⟫

EX. (**a**) My mother sent me Japanese magazines by mail.
母が郵便で日本の雑誌を送ってくれた。
Haha ga yuubin de Nihon no zasshi o okutte kureta.
(**b**) The mail is delivered around ten every morning.
郵便は毎朝十時ごろ配達される。
Yuubin wa mai-asa juu-ji-goro haitatsu-sareru.
(**c**) The mail hasn't come yet.
郵便はまだ来ない。
Yuubin wa mada konai.

PHRASE: sea mail *funa-bin* 船便

mailbox n. **[a place for putting letters, postcards, etc., in to send out by post or a box used to receive items delivered by post]**

1. po˥suto ポスト •f [a place for putting letters, postcards, etc., in to send out by post]

EX. Is there a mailbox around here?
この辺にポストがありますか。
Kono hen ni posuto ga arimasu ka.

2. yu˥ubi˥n-uke 郵便受け [a box used to receive items delivered by post]

EX. This mailbox is too small.
この郵便受けは小さ過ぎる。
Kono yuubin uke wa chiisa-sugiru.

main adj. **[greatest in size, extent, or importance]**

o˥mona 主な adj(*na*). **[the most prominent/significant of a group of entities under consideration] ⟪principal, chief, leading⟫**

EX. (**a**) What are the main causes of divorce in Japan?
日本における離婚の主な原因は何ですか。
Nihon ni okeru rikon no omona gen'in wa nan desu ka.
(**b**) The main purpose of his visit to the United States is sightseeing.
彼の訪米の主な目的は観光です。
Kare no hoo-Bei no omona mokuteki wa kankoo desu.

PHRASE: main entrance *shoomen-genkan* 正面玄関 **•c**, main gate *seimon* 正門 **•c**, main road *kansen-dooro* 幹線道路 **•c**

mainly adv. **[in most cases/to a large extent]**

o˥moni 主に /⟨adj⟨*na*⟩. *ni* of *omona* main/

EX. (**a**) We talked mainly about work.
私たちは主に仕事の話をした。
Watashi-tachi wa omoni shigoto no hanashi o shita.
(**b**) I want to study mainly spoken Japanese.
主に日本語の話しことばを勉強したいんです。
Omoni Nihon-go no hanashi-kotoba o benkyoo-shi-tai n desu.

maintain vt. **[for s.o./s.t. to cause s.t. to continue to exist or for s.o. to keep s.t. in good repair]**

⟨-o⟩ i˥ji-suru ⟨～を⟩維持する ③ •c ⟪keep, retain⟫

EX. (**a**) It will be difficult to maintain the present rate of economic growth.
現在の経済成長率を維持するのは難しい。
Genzai no keizai-seichoo-ritsu o iji-suru no wa muzukashii.
(**b**) Japan has to maintain friendly relations with the other Asian countries.
日本は他のアジア諸国と友好関係を維持していかなければならない。
Nihon wa ta no Ajia-shokoku to yuukoo-kankei o iji-shite ikanakereba naranai.
(**c**) The military is maintaining law and order in that country.
あの国では軍部が法秩序を維持している。
Ano kuni de wa gunbu ga hoo-chitsujo o iji-shite iru.

major adj. **[greater or more important than others]**

dai- 大～ •c [great in size/number/degree of severity] ⟪big, vast, serious, terrible⟫, shu˥yoona 主要な adj(*na*). **•c [of greatest importance] ⟪main, chief, principal⟫**

EX. (**a**) Nagoya is one of the major cities of Japan.
名古屋は日本の{主要/大}都市の一つです。

M

Nagoya wa Nihon no {shuyoo/dai}-toshi no hitotsu desu.
(**b**) He had a major operation last year.
彼は去年{大/*主要な}手術を受けた。
*Kare wa kyonen {dai-/*shuyoona} shujutsu o uketa.*

— n. **[the main subject that a university/college student is studying or a student studying the subject concerned]**
se⌈nkoo 専攻 •c [the chief subject a student studies at a university], se⌈nmon 専門 •c [a branch of study in which one specializes] ⟪**specialty**⟫

EX. (**a**) What is your major?
{専攻/専門}は何ですか。
{Senkoo/Senmon} wa nan desu ka.
(**b**) She is a history major.
彼女は歴史{専攻/*専門}の学生です。
*Kanojo wa rekishi {senkoo/*senmon} no gakusei desu.*

— vi. **[to study as a chief subject(s) at a university/college]**
⟨-o⟩ se⌈nkoo-suru ⟨〜を⟩専攻する ③ •c

EX. I majored in Chinese literature at Kyoto University.
私は京都大学で中国文学を専攻しました。
Watashi wa Kyooto-daigaku de Chuugoku-bungaku o senkoo-shimashita.

majority n. **[a subpart of a larger whole which is greater in size or amount than the remaining part(s)]**
da⌈i-bu⌉bun 大部分 •c [the greater part of s.t./s.o./s.a.] ⟪**most**⟫, **da⌈i-ta⌉suu 大多数 •c [the greater number of s.t./s.o./s.a.]**

EX. (**a**) The majority of the students in my class failed the exam.
私のクラスの学生の{大部分/大多数}が試験に落ちた。
Watashi no kurasu no gakusei no {dai-bubun/dai-tasuu} ga shiken ni ochita.
(**b**) The majority of people are against war.
{大部分/大多数}の人が戦争に反対だ。
{Dai-bubun/Dai-tasuu} no hito ga sensoo ni hantai da.

make vt. **[to cause s.t./s.o./s.a. to exist/be/do]**

1. ⟨-o⟩ tsu⌈ku⌉ru ⟨〜を⟩つくる ① [for s.o./s.a. to cause s.t./s.o./s.a. to come into existence which did not exist previously] ⟪**manufacture, build**⟫
㊥ "build/manufacture"▷造る, otherwise ▷作る

EX. (**a**) Did you make this cake?
このケーキはあなたが作ったんですか。
Kono keeki wa anata ga tsukutta n desu ka.
(**b**) She made her daughter a doll.
彼女は娘に人形を作ってやった。
Kanojo wa musume ni ningyoo o tsukutte yatta.
(**c**) *Sake* is made from rice.
酒は米で作る。
Sake wa kome de tsukuru.
(**d**) This is the new rule we made.
これは私たちが作った新しい規則です。
Kore wa watashi-tachi ga tsukutta atarashii kisoku desu.

PHRASE: make tea *o-cha o ireru* お茶を入れる ②, make coffee *koohii o ireru* コーヒーを入れる ②, make a mistake ⟨*-o*⟩ *machigaeru* ⟨〜を⟩間違える ②

EX. I made some spelling mistakes.
つづりをいくつか間違えた。
Tsuzuri o ikutsu-ka machigaeta.

2. {⟨-ni⟩/⟨-o⟩} {Vneg. + seru/Vstem + saseru/ko-saseru/saseru} {⟨〜に⟩/⟨〜を⟩}{Vneg.+せる/Vstem+させる/来させる/させる} [for s.o./s.a. to cause s.o./s.t./s.a. to do s.t./to change in state] ⟪**let**⟫

NOTE: Prt. *ni* is used with transitive verbs and either *ni* or *o* can be used with intransitive verbs. *O* is used with actions that do not involve the will of the causes (the person being made to do the action).

EX. (**a**) My mother made me eat liver.
母は私{に/*を}レバーを食べさせた。
*Haha wa watashi {ni/*o} rebaa o tabe-saseta.*
(**b**) I was made to wait for an hour.
私は一時間待たされた。

Watashi wa ichi-jikan mata-sareta.
(c) I made my younger sister cry.
私は妹{を/*に}泣かせてしまった。
*Watashi wa imooto {o/*ni} naka-sete shimatta.*

3. ⟨**-o**⟩ {⟨**-ni**⟩/**adj**(*i*). ***ku***/**adj**(*na*). ***ni***} **su⌈ru** ⟨～を⟩{⟨～に⟩/**adj**(*i*). ***ku***/**adj**(*na*). ***ni***}する ③ **[to cause s.o./s.t./s.a. to take on a certain quality or property or enter into some state]** ⟨⟨**shape**⟩⟩

EX. (a) The king made Esther his queen.
王はエステルをきさきにした。
Oo wa Esuteru o kisaki ni shita.
(b) He made me happy.
彼は私を幸せにしてくれた。
Kare wa watashi o shiawaseni shite kureta.

make-up n. **[powder, paint, etc. applied to the face to improve one's appearance]**
ke⌈sho⌉o 化粧 •**c**

EX. (a) She doesn't wear any make-up.
彼女は全然化粧をしない。
Kanojo wa zenzen keshoo o shinai.
(b) She's wearing heavy stage make-up.
彼女は厚い舞台化粧をしている。
Kanojo wa atsui butai-geshoo o shite iru.

male adj. **[of the sex that cannot give birth]**
o⌈toko no N 男のN **[of the human sex that cannot give birth]** ↔ **onna no N** 女のN; **da⌈nsei no N** 男性のN •**c** ↔ **josei no N** 女性のN •**c**; **o⌈su no N** 雄のN **[of the sex, usually of animals other than humans, that cannot give birth]** ↔ **mesu no N** 雌のN

EX. (a) There are about fifty male members in the club.
そのクラブには五十人ぐらいの{男/男性/*雄}の会員がいる。
*Sono kurabu ni wa go-juu-nin-gurai no {otoko/dansei/*osu} no kaiin ga iru.*
(b) There are few male students at this college.
この大学は{男/男性/*雄}の学生が少ないです。
*Kono daigaku wa {otoko/dansei/*osu} no gakusei ga sukunai desu.*

NOTE: *Danshi-gakusei* is also a common compound for "male students."

(c) We have a male monkey at home.
うちに{雄/*男/*男性}の猿がいる。
*Uchi ni {osu/*otoko/*dansei} no saru ga iru.*

mammal n.
ho⌈nyu⌉urui ほ乳類 •**c**

man n. **[a human being or an adult human male]**

1. o⌈toko⌉ 男 **[a human male]** ⟨⟨**male, guy**⟩⟩ ↔ **onna** 女; **o⌈toko no hito** 男の人 **[an adult human male]** ↔ **onna no hito** 女の人; **da⌈nsei** 男性 •**c** **[an adult human male]** ↔ **josei** 女性 •**c**

EX. (a) A tall man came into the office.
背の高い{男/男の人/男性}がオフィスに入ってきた。
Se no takai {otoko/otoko no hito/dansei} ga ofisu ni haitte kita.
(b) Who is that man talking to Mr. Oda?
小田さんと話しているあの{男/男の人/男性}はだれですか。
Oda-san to hanashite iru ano {otoko/otoko no hito/dansei} wa dare desu ka.

NOTE: The use of *otoko* in example (b) sounds rather rough and is usually used by men.

2. hi⌉to 人 **[a generic term for homo sapiens or a collective noun for people other than oneself or an individual's characteristics]** ⟨⟨**person, woman**⟩⟩, **ni⌉ngen** 人間 •**c** **[a human being as opposed to an animal]** ⟨⟨**human race, mankind, human beings**⟩⟩

EX. (a) All men are mortal.
{人/人間}は皆死ぬものだ。
{Hito/Ningen} wa mina shinu mono da.
(b) Man doesn't live by bread alone.
{人/人間}はパンだけで生きるのではない。
{Hito/Ningen} wa pan dake de ikiru no dewanai.

manage vt. **[for s.o. to be in control of an organization, business, etc.]**
⟨**-o**⟩ **ke⌈iei-suru** ⟨～を⟩経営する ③ •**c** **[for s.o. to be in control of the business affairs of a company, factory, hotel, etc.]** ⟨⟨**run**⟩⟩

M

EX. (**a**) My father manages a small factory.
父は小さい工場を経営している。
Chichi wa chiisai koojoo o keiei-shite iru.
(**b**) It's not easy to manage a hotel.
ホテルを経営するのは簡単ではない。
Hoteru o keiei-suru no wa kantan dewanai.

— vi./vt. **[for s.o./s.a. to succeed in accomplishing s.t. difficult]**
na˥n-toka...verb なんとか…verb

EX. (**a**) I managed to write three papers in a week.
なんとか一週間で論文を三つ書きあげた。
Nan-toka is-shuukan de ronbun o mittsu kaki-ageta.
(**b**) I think I can manage to carry everything by myself.
一人でなんとか全部運べると思います。
Hitori de nan-toka zenbu hakobe-ru to omoimasu.

management n. **[the art/practice of managing or the people in charge of managing]**

1. ke˥iei 経営 •c [the practice of managing a business]

EX. (**a**) I am interested in Japanese-style management.
私は日本式の経営に興味がある。
Watashi wa Nihon-shiki no keiei ni kyoomi ga aru.
(**b**) The company has gone bankrupt due to bad management.
あの会社はまずい経営で、倒産した。
Ano kaisha wa mazui keiei de, toosan-shita.

2. ke˥ie˥i-jin 経営陣 •c [the people who manage a company, industry, etc.]

EX. The management has taken responsibility for the failure and resigned.
経営陣は失敗の責任をとって、辞職した。
Keiei-jin wa shippai no sekinin o totte, jishoku-shita.

manager n. **[s.o. who is responsible for the management of a business or other activity]**
shi˥ha˥i-nin 支配人 •c [s.o. who is in charge of the business affairs of a hotel, restaurant, theater, etc.], ke˥ie˥i-sha 経営者 •c [s.o. who is in control of the business affairs of an enterprise], ma˥ne˥ejaa マネージャー •f [s.o. who manages the business affairs of an entertainer or the training and other activites of an athlete or of a team], ka˥ntoku 監督 •c [an act of directing some activity or s.o. who directs some activity] ((director, supervisor))

EX. (**a**) When we got to the hotel, the manager welcomed us in person.
我々がホテルに着いたとき、{支配人/マネージャー/*経営者/*監督}が直々に迎えてくれた。
*Ware-ware ga hoteru ni tsuita toki, {shihai-nin/maneejaa/*keiei-sha/*kantoku} ga jiki-jiki ni mukaete kureta.*
(**b**) I was once the manager of a professional baseball team.
私はプロ野球のチームの{監督/*マネージャー/*支配人/*経営者}をしていたことがある。
*Watashi wa puro-yakyuu no chiimu no {kantoku/*maneejaa/*shihai-nin/*keiei-sha} o shite ita koto ga aru.*
(**c**) You can't be a good manager if you don't have managerial ability.
経営の才能がなければ、いい{経営者/*支配人/*マネージャー/*監督}にはなれない。
*Keiei no sainoo ga nakereba, ii {keiei-sha/*shihai-nin/*maneejaa/*kantoku} ni wa nare-nai.*
(**d**) The singer married her manager.
あの歌手は自分の{マネージャー/*経営者/*支配人/*監督}と結婚した。
*Ano kashu wa jibun no {maneejaa/*keiei-sha/*shihai-nin/*kantoku} to kekkon-shita.*

mandarin orange n.
mi˥kan みかん

EX. At our home we eat lots of mandarin oranges in the winter.

うちでは冬、みかんをたくさん食べます。
Uchi de wa fuyu, mikan o takusan tabemasu.

Manhattan n.
Ma⌈nha⌉ttan マンハッタン

mankind n. **[the human race]**
ji⌉nrui 人類 •c

EX. (**a**) Mankind will perish if we continue to destroy our environment.
環境を破壊し続ければ、人類は滅亡するだろう。
Kankyoo o hakai-shi-tsuzukereba, jinrui wa metsuboo-suru daroo.
(**b**) Mankind has to coexist with other creatures on this earth.
人類はこの地球上で他の生物と共存しなければならない。
Jinrui wa kono chikyuu-joo de ta no seibutsu to kyoozon-shinakereba naranai.

manner n. **[the way in which s.t. is done/happens ⟨fml⟩]**
fu⌉u 風 •c [the way in which s.t. is done/happens] ⟪way, style, type⟫

EX. (**a**) Please cut it in this manner.
こういう風に切ってください。
Kooiu fuu ni kitte kudasai.
(**b**) We slept on *futon* in the Japanese manner.
日本風にふとんに寝た。
Nihon-fuu ni futon ni neta.

manners n. **[(polite) ways of behaving]**
gyo⌈ogi 行儀 •c [ways of behaving from the point of view of acceptability in a social context], ma⌉naa マナー •f [polite ways of behaving]

EX. (**a**) It's bad manners to sniffle in the middle of a concert.
コンサートの最中に鼻をすするのは{行儀が悪い/マナーに反する}。
Konsaato no saichuu ni hana o susuru no wa {gyoogi ga warui/manaa ni han-suru}.
(**b**) Mrs. Yoshida has impeccable manners.
吉田さんの奥さんは非常に{マナーをわきまえている/行儀がいい}。
Yoshida-san no oku-san wa hijooni {manaa o wakimaete iru/gyoogi ga ii}.

NOTE: *Gyoogi ga ii* can be said of children, but not *manaa o wakimaete iru.*

manufacture vt. **[to produce s.t. in a factory, usually in large quantities]**
⟨-o⟩ se⌈izoo-suru ⟨〜を⟩製造する ③ •c

EX. This factory manufactures auto parts.
この工場は車の部品を製造している。
Kono koojoo wa kuruma no buhin o seizoo-shite iru.

PHRASE: manufactured goods *seihin* 製品 •c

EX. We export manufactured goods to various countries.
我々は製品をいろいろな国へ輸出している。
Ware-ware wa seihin o iro-irona kuni e yushutsu-shite iru.

PHRASE: manufacturing industry *koogyoo* 工業 •c, *seizoo-gyoo* 製造業 •c

manufacturer n. **[a company/s.o. that manufactures s.t.]**
me⌉ekaa メーカー •f

EX. (**a**) Complaints about its products poured into the manufacturer from consumers.
消費者から製品に関する苦情がメーカーに殺到した。
Shoohi-sha kara seihin ni-kansuru kujoo ga meekaa ni sattoo-shita.
(**b**) He works for a leading manufacturer of cameras.
彼はカメラのトップメーカーに勤めている。
Kare wa kamera no toppu-meekaa ni tsutomete iru.

manuscript n. **[a handwritten/typed piece of writing submitted before being published]**
ge⌈nkoo 原稿 •c [a piece of writing not yet published or presented before an audience or an incomplete piece of writing still in need of correction] ⟪draft⟫

EX. (**a**) His new book is still in manuscript form.
彼の新しい本はまだ原稿のままです。
Kare no atarashii hon wa mada genkoo no mama desu.

M

(**b**) He sent the manuscipt of his novel to a publisher.
彼は小説の原稿を出版社に送った。
Kare wa shoosetsu no genkoo o shuppan-sha ni okutta.

many adj. **[a large number of]**
ta⌈kusa⌉n たくさん n./adv. **[(in) a large quantity]** **((much, plenty of, a lot of))**, **o⌉oi** 多い adj(*i*). **[large in number/quantity]** **((much, plenty of, a lot of))**, **o⌈oze⌉i** 大勢 n. **[a large number of people]**

NOTE: *Ooi* is almost always used as a predicate and only rarely as a noun modifier. *Ooku no* may be used as a rather formal noun modifier.

EX. (**a**) Many students were absent today.
今日は{学生が{たくさん/大勢}欠席していた/欠席の学生が多かった}。
Kyoo wa {gakusei ga {takusan/oozei} kesseki-shite ita/kesseki no gakusei ga ookatta}.
(**b**) There are many things that I want to do.
したいことが{{たくさん/*大勢}ある/多い}。
*Shi-tai koto ga {{takusan/*oozei} aru/ooi}.*
(**c**) Not many students get an A in his class.
あの先生の授業でAを取る学生はそんなに{{たくさん/大勢}はいない/多くはない}。
Ano sensei no jugyoo de ei o toru gakusei wa sonnani {{takusan/oozei} wa inai/ooku wa nai}.
(**d**) I have many questions.
質問が{{たくさん/*大勢}あります/*多いです}。
*Shitsumon ga {{takusan/*oozei} arimasu/*ooi desu}.*

map n.
chi⌉zu 地図 **•c** **[a drawing that shows features of an area of the earth's surface]**

EX. (**a**) Could you please draw a map of your neighborhood?
あなたの近所の地図をかいてください。
Anata no kinjo no chizu o kaite kudasai.
(**b**) We looked for the location of the village on the map.
地図で村の位置を調べた。
Chizu de mura no ichi o shirabeta.
(**c**) I bought a big map of Japan.
大きい日本地図を買った。
Ookii Nihon-chizu o katta.

maple n. **[a deciduous tree with many pointed leaves which turn color in the autumn]**
ka⌈ede かえで, **mo⌉miji** もみじ **[a deciduous tree with many pointed leaves which turn color in the autumn or colored leaves in the autumn]**

EX. We're waiting for the maple trees to turn red.
{かえで/もみじ}が紅葉するのを待っている。
{Kaede/Momiji} ga kooyoo-suru no o matte iru.

PHRASE: maple syrup *meepuru-shiroppu* メープルシロップ **•f**

march vi. **[for s.o. or a group of people to walk with regular steps like a soldier]**
ko⌈oshin-suru 行進する ③ **•c** **[for a group of people to walk in formation]**

EX. I saw soldiers marching in the street from the window.
兵隊が通りを行進するのを窓から見た。
Heitai ga toori o kooshin-suru no o mado kara mita.

March n.
sa⌉n-gatsu 三月 **•c**

EX. (**a**) Graduation is usually held in March in Japan.
日本では卒業式は大抵三月にある。
Nihon de wa sotsugyoo-shiki wa taitei san-gatsu ni aru.
(**b**) We're going to move to Tokyo in March.
三月に東京に引っ越します。
San-gatsu ni Tookyoo ni hikkoshimasu.

margarine n.
ma⌉agarin マーガリン **•f**

EX. The taste of margarine has gotten much better recently, I think.

M

マーガリンの味は最近非常に良くなったと思う。
Maagarin no aji wa saikin hijooni yoku natta to omou.

margin n. **[the blank space at the side of a page along the edge]**
ra⌈ngai 欄外 •c [an area along the edge of a page where there is no writing/printing], yo⌈haku 余白 •c [an area of paper where there is no writing/printing/painting/drawing] ⟪blank, space⟫

EX. Don't write anything in the margins of library books.
図書館の本の{欄外/余白}に何も書き込まないでください。
Tosho-kan no hon no {rangai/yohaku} ni nani-mo kaki-komanaide kudasai.

marine adj. **[related to/obtained from the sea]**
kaiyoo- 海洋〜 •c [related to the sea], suisan- 水産〜 •c [obtained from the water], kaisan- 海産〜 •c [obtained from the sea]

EX. (**a**) The Japanese eat lots of marine products.
日本人は{海産/水産/*海洋}物をたくさん食べる。
*Nihon-jin wa {kaisan/suisan/*kaiyoo}-butsu o takusan taberu.*
(**b**) He majored in marine biology in college.
彼は大学で{海洋/*水産/*海産}生物学を専攻した。
*Kare wa daigaku de {kaiyoo/*suisan/*kaisan}-seibutsu-gaku o senkoo-shita.*
(**c**) We visited a marine laboratory.
私たちは{水産/?海産/*海洋}試験場を訪ねた。
*Watashi-tachi wa {suisan/?kaisan/*kaiyoo}-shiken-joo o tazuneta.*

— n. **[a soldier who serves on a ship/in the American Marine Corps]**
ka⌈ihei 海兵 •c

EX. The Marine Corps landed in Haiti.
海兵隊はハイチに上陸した。
Kaihei-tai wa Haichi ni jooriku-shita.

mark n. **[s.t. such as a spot or cut on a surface that spoils its appearance or a symbol of s.t.]**
shi⌈rushi 印 [s.t. visual that serves to distinguish s.t. from other things or to signify s.t.] ⟪sign⟫, **a⌉to あと [a mark created by some event or entity earlier in time ⟪fig. "space behind s.o.," "immediately after s.t. has occurred"⟫]** ⟪trace, track⟫
㊥ "after"▷後, "mark"▷跡

EX. (**a**) Tom's fingers left dirty marks on the wall.
壁にトムの指のきたない{跡/*印}が付いた。
*Kabe ni Tomu no yubi no kitanai {ato/*shirushi} ga tsuita.*
(**b**) What does this mark mean?
この{印/*跡}はどういう意味ですか。
*Kono {shirushi/*ato} wa doo iu imi desu ka.*

— vt. **[to leave a visible imprint, esp. one that is not desired, or to indicate the position of s.t.]**
1. a⌉to ga tsuku 跡が付く ① [for a visible imprint to be left on s.t.]

EX. (**a**) The rubber soles on my boots marked up the kitchen floor.
台所の床に私の長靴のゴム底の跡が付いてしまった。
Daidokoro no yuka ni watashi no naga-gutsu no gomu-zoko no ato ga tsuite shimatta.
(**b**) This wallpaper marks very easily.
この壁紙は跡が付きやすい。
Kono kabe-gami wa ato ga tsuki-yasui.

2. ⟨-ni⟩ shi⌈rushi o tsu⌈ke⌉ru ⟨〜に⟩印を付ける ② [for s.o./s.a. to put a mark on s.t. to identify it]

EX. He marked the mistake in red.
彼は間違いに赤で印を付けた。
Kare wa machigai ni aka de shirushi o tsuketa.

market n. **[a place where people meet to buy and sell goods or a gathering of people to buy and sell goods on certain days at such a place ⟪fig. "an area where there is a demand for goods"⟫]**
1. i⌉chiba 市場 [a designated place where merchants meet regularly to buy and sell

M

things], i˥chi 市 [the activity of gathering on a specified day to buy and sell goods or a place where such activity takes place]

EX. (a) Wherever I travel, I make a point of visiting a market in that distinct.
どこへ旅行に行っても必ずその土地の{市/市場}を訪ねることにしている。
Doko e ryokoo ni itte mo kanarazu sono tochi no {ichi/ichiba} o tazuneru koto ni shite iru.
(b) There is a good market near my house.
家の近くにいい{市場/?市}がある。
Uchi no chikaku ni ii {ichiba/?ichi} ga aru.
(c) Once a month they set up a market in this area where they sell garden plants.
この辺で一か月に一度、植木の{市/*市場}がたつ。
*Kono hen de ik-kagetsu ni ichi-do, ueki no {ichi/*ichiba} ga tatsu.*

PHRASE: fish market *uo-ichiba* 魚市場, vegetable market *aomono-ichiba* 青物市場, flea market *nomi no ichi* のみの市, open-air market *aozora-ichiba* 青空市場

2. shi˥joo 市場 •c [an area where there is a demand for goods]

EX. (a) We want to open up new markets for our industries in China.
我が国の企業のために中国に新しい市場を作り出したいと思っている。
Waga-kuni no kigyoo no tame ni Chuugoku ni atarashii shijoo o tsukuri-dashi-tai to omotte iru.
(b) Our products are mainly exported to overseas markets.
我々の製品は主に海外市場に輸出されている。
Ware-ware no seihin wa omoni kaigai-shijoo ni yushutsu-sarete iru.

PHRASE: buyer's market *kaite-shijoo* 買い手市場, seller's market *urite-shijoo* 売り手市場

marriage n. **[the union of a man and a woman as husband and wife]**
ke˥kkon 結婚 •c ((**matrimony**))

EX. (a) Their marriage didn't last long.
彼らの結婚は長続きしなかった。
Kare-ra no kekkon wa naga-tsuzuki-shinakatta.
(b) Her first marriage was a complete failure.
彼女の最初の結婚は完全な失敗だった。
Kanojo no saisho no kekkon wa kanzenna shippai datta.

PHRASE: arranged marriage *miai-kekkon* 見合い結婚 ↔ *ren'ai-kekkon* 恋愛結婚

married adj. **[being in a state of legal union with s.o., as husband/wife]**
ke˥kkon-shite iru 結婚している /⟨V *te iru* of *kekkon-suru* ③ marry/ ②

EX. (a) Is she married?
彼女は結婚しているんですか。
Kanojo wa kekkon-shite iru n desu ka.
(b) He is married to a Japanese actress.
彼は日本の女優と結婚している。
Kare wa Nihon no joyuu to kekkon-shite iru.
(c) He is dating a married woman.
彼は結婚している女性とつきあっている。
Kare wa kekkon-shite iru josei to tsuki-atte iru.

marry vt./vi. **[for s.o. to enter into a relationship with s.o. as a husband/wife]**
⟨⟨**-to**⟩⟩ **ke˥kkon-suru** ⟨⟨〜と⟩⟩結婚する ③ **•c** ((**get married**))

EX. (a) Will you marry me?
私と結婚してくれませんか。
Watashi to kekkon-shite kuremasen ka.
(b) I don't think he will ever marry.
彼はずっと結婚しないと思う。
Kare wa zutto kekkon-shinai to omou.
(c) I've heard that they're getting married in October.
彼らは十月に結婚するそうだ。
Kare-ra wa juu-gatsu ni kekkon-suru sooda.

marvel n. **[s.t./s.o. that arouses great surprise and admiration]**
kyo˥oi 驚異 •c ((**wonder**))

EX. (a) He's a marvel; he's over 90 and still jogging five miles a day.
九十歳を越しているのにまだ一日に五

マイルもジョギングしているなんて驚異だ。
Kyuu-jus-sai o koshite iru noni mada ichi-nichi ni go-mairu mo jogingu-shite iru nante kyooi da.
(**b**) Our life is full of the marvels of modern technology.
我々の生活は現代技術の驚異に満ちている。
Ware-ware no seikatsu wa gendai-gijutsu no kyooi ni michite iru.

marvelous adj. **[arousing great wonder/admiration/pleasure]**
kyo⌈oi-tekina 驚異的な adj(*na*). **•c [causing great wonder and admiration due to being unbelievably good]** **⟪wonderful⟫,**
su⌈barashi⌉i すばらしい adj(*i*). **[causing great wonder/admiration/pleasure due to being extremely good]** **⟪splendid, wonderful⟫**

EX. (**a**) Japan has achieved marvelous economic progress since World War II.
日本は第二次世界大戦後、{驚異的な/すばらしい}経済発展を遂げた。
Nihon wa Dai-ni-ji-sekai-taisen-go, {kyooi-tekina/subarashii} keizai-hatten o togeta.
(**b**) It's marvelous weather, isn't it!
{すばらしい/*驚異的な}お天気ですね。
*{Subarashii/*Kyooi-tekina} o-tenki desu ne.*

Maryland n.
Me⌈riira⌉ndo メリーランド •f

mask n. **[a covering for all or part of the face]**
ma⌉suku マスク •f [a covering for all or part of the face to protect the wearer from dangerous substances or to protect others from an infection borne by the wearer],
ka⌈men 仮面 •c [a covering for all or part of the face so as to avoid being recognized],
me⌈n 面 •c [any of the flat surfaces of an object ⟪fig. "a covering for the face used in fencing, theater, etc.," "a page of a newspaper"⟫] ⟪aspect⟫

EX. (**a**) Japanese dentists wear masks when they treat patients.
日本の歯医者は患者の治療にあたるとき、{マスク/*仮面/*面}をかける。
*Nihon no ha-isha wa kanja no chiryoo ni ataru toki, {masuku/*kamen/*men} o kakeru.*
(**b**) I went to a fancy dress ball wearing a funny mask.
変な{仮面/面/*マスク}をつけて仮装舞踏会へ行った。
*Henna {kamen/men/*masuku} o tsukete kasoo-butoo-kai e itta.*

PHRASE: *Noh* mask *noomen* 能面 **•c**

mass n. **[a large solid lump or heap, usually without a definite shape]**
ka⌈tamari 塊 [a piece of solid substance] ⟪lump⟫

EX. A huge mass of clouds blocked the sunshine.
大きな雲の塊が日の光を遮った。
Ookina kumo no katamari ga hi no hikari o saegitta.

—— adj. **[in a large number or amount]**
ta⌈iryoo no N 大量のN •c [in large quantities]

EX. (**a**) The new policy produced mass unemployment.
新しい政策により大量の失業者が出た。
Atarashii seisaku ni-yori tairyoo no shitsugyoo-sha ga deta.
(**b**) The price of many things has been lowered by mass production.
大量生産により多くの製品の価格が下がった。
Tairyoo-seisan ni-yori ooku no seihin no kakaku ga sagatta.

massive adj. **[extremely large, solid, and heavy]**
kyo⌈daina 巨大な adj(*na*). **•c [extremely large in size] ⟪huge, enormous, gigantic⟫**

EX. The bank's safe is protected by a massive door.
銀行の金庫は巨大なドアに守られている。
Ginkoo no kinko wa kyodaina doa ni mamora-rete iru.

mast n. **[an upright pole of wood/metal for supporting a flag or the sails on a ship]**

M

ma˥suto マスト •f

EX. All of a sudden, the mast snapped.
マストが急に折れた。
Matuto ga kyuuni oreta.

master n. **[s.o./s.t. in control of s.o./s.t. else]**

1. shu˥jin 主人 [a person who receives guests and looks after them or an owner of a shop, restaurant, pet, etc., or a term a woman uses to refer to the man to whom she is married] ⟪**employer, owner, husband**⟫

EX. (**a**) Don't forget that your father is the master of this house.
お父さんがこの家の主人だということを忘れるな。
O-too-san ga kono uchi no shujin da to iu koto o wasureru na.
(**b**) The dog went to the station every day to meet its master.
犬は毎日、主人を迎えに駅へ行った。
Inu wa mai-nichi, shujin o mukae ni eki e itta.

2. me˥iji˥n 名人 •c [s.o. with outstanding skills in an art or in a particular field or a champion in the game of *shoogi* or *igo*] ⟪**expert**⟫

EX. This vase is the work of a master.
この花瓶は名人の作品だ。
Kono kabin wa meijin no sakuhin da.

3. ma˥sutaa マスター •f [s.t. from which copies are made]

EX. Be careful not to lose the master key.
マスターキーを無くさないように気をつけてください。
Masutaa-kii o nakusanai yooni ki-o-tsukete kudasai.

— vt. **[for s.o. to learn s.t. thoroughly]** **⟨-o⟩ shu˥utoku-suru ⟨〜を⟩習得する ③ •c [for s.o. to learn and internalize s.t.], ⟨-o⟩ ma˥sutaa-suru ⟨〜を⟩マスターする ③ •f**

EX. (**a**) It takes years to master a new language.
新しいことばを{習得/マスター}するのには何年もかかる。
Atarashii kotoba o {shuutoku/masutaa}-suru no ni wa nan-nen mo kakaru.
(**b**) He has mastered computer programming.
彼はコンピューターのプログラミングを{習得/マスター}した。
Kare wa konpyuutaa no puroguramingu o {shuutoku/masutaa}-shita.

PHRASE: master's degree *shuushi(-goo)* 修士(号) •c

mat n. **[a piece of material for covering part of a floor or for putting under objects on a table for protection/decoration]**

1. ma˥tto マット •f [a piece of material for covering part of a floor]

EX. I washed the bath mat since it had gotten very dirty.
大分汚れていたからバスマットを洗濯した。
Daibu yogorete ita kara basu-matto o sentaku-shita.

2. na˥be˥-shiki なべ敷 [s.t. put under a pot/pan on a table so as to protect the surface of the table], ka˥bi˥n-shiki 花瓶敷 [a small piece of material for putting under vases]

EX. (**a**) Put the hot kettle on the mat.
熱いやかんは{なべ敷/*花瓶敷}の上に置きなさい。
*Atsui yakan wa {nabe-shiki/*kabin-shiki} no ue ni okinasai.*
(**b**) Jill crocheted a lace mat for my glass vase.
ジルがガラスの花瓶用にレース編みの{花瓶敷/*なべ敷}を作ってくれた。
*Jiru ga garasu no kabin-yoo ni reesu-ami no {kabin-shiki/*nabe-shiki} o tsukutte kureta.*

match[1] n. **[a competitive game or sports event]**

shi˥ai 試合 ⟪**game**⟫

EX. (**a**) I bought a ticket for the volleyball match on Saturday.
私は土曜日のバレーボールの試合の切符を買った。
Watashi wa doyoo-bi no baree-booru no shiai no kippu o katta.
(**b**) The Japanese team played a match against the Chinese team.
日本チームは中国チームと試合をした。
Nihon-chiimu wa Chuugoku-chiimu to shiai o shita.

—— vi./vt. **[to be compatible because of similarity in some relevant respect such as color, shape, quality, or quantity]**
{⟨-to⟩/⟨-ni⟩} a⌉u {⟨〜と⟩/⟨〜に⟩}あう ① **[for two people/objects to come close to each other or to fit each other]** **⟪suit, go with, meet, fit⟫**

NOTE: The particle *to* is used when the relationship or action is seen to be mutual, and the particle *ni* is used when the relationship or action is seen as being directed by one of the entities toward the other rather than being mutual.

㊥ "meet/see"▷会う, "match/suit"▷合う

EX. (**a**) Does this tie match my gray jacket?
このネクタイはグレーの上着に合いますか。
Kono nekutai wa guree no uwa-gi ni aimasu ka.
(**b**) This skirt and blouse don't match.
このスカートとブラウスは合わない。
Kono sukaato to burausu wa awanai.

match[2] n. **[a short thin stick, usu. of wood, covered at one end with a special substance that burns when the end is rubbed on a rough surface]**
ma⌉tchi マッチ **•f**

EX. (**a**) She lit the candles with a match.
彼女はマッチでろうそくに火をつけた。
Kanojo wa matchi de roosoku ni hi o tsuketa.
(**b**) He collects matchboxes.
彼はマッチ箱を集めている。
Kare wa matchi-bako o atsumete iru.

mate n. **[a friend or a person one works with]**
to⌈modachi 友達 **[a friend], do⌈oryoo** 同僚 **•c [a person of the same status in a place of work]** **⟪colleague, fellow worker⟫**

EX. (**a**) My officemates are all very nice people.
私の職場の{同僚/*友達}はみんなとてもいい人です。
*Watashi no shokuba no {dooryoo/ *tomodachi} wa minna totemo ii hito desu.*
(**b**) He's one of my schoolmates.
彼は学校{友達/*同僚}の一人です。
*Kare wa gakkoo-{tomodachi/*dooryoo} no hitori desu.*

material n. **[s.t. from which s.t. else is/can be made, esp. cloth]**
1. za⌈iryo⌉o 材料 **•c [things from which s.t. is/can be made]** **⟪ingredient⟫**, **shi⌉ryoo** 資料 **•c [information used for writing, research, etc.]** **⟪data⟫**

EX. (**a**) I'm collecting material for a novel.
私は小説の{材料/資料}を集めている。
Watashi wa shoosetsu no {zairyoo/ shiryoo} o atsumete iru.
(**b**) What kind of material is this paper made of?
この紙はどんな{材料/*資料}でできているんですか。
*Kono kami wa donna {zairyoo/*shiryoo} de dekite iru n desu ka.*

2. ki⌉-ji 生地 **[cloth]**

EX. (**a**) I bought three meters of dress material.
私はドレスの生地を三メートル買った。
Watashi wa doresu no ki-ji o san-meetoru katta.
(**b**) What material is your skirt made from?
あなたのスカートの生地は何ですか。
Anata no sukaato no ki-ji wa nan desu ka.

—— adj. **[consisting of physical matter]**
bu⌈sshitsu-tekina 物質的な adj(*na*). **•c [having to do with physical matter]** **⟪physical⟫** ↔ **seishin-tekina** 精神的な adj(*na*). **•c; bu⌈ttekina** 物的な adj(*na*). **•c**

EX. (**a**) My parents have given me a lot of support, both material and emotional.
両親は{物質的に/物的に}も精神的にも大いに助けてくれた。
Ryooshin wa {busshitsu-tekini/ buttekini} mo seishin-tekini mo ooini tasukete kureta.
(**b**) There is no material evidence for the crime.
その犯罪に関しては{物的/*物質的}証拠は何もない。
*Sono hanzai ni-kanshite wa {butteki/ *busshitsu-teki}-shooko wa nani-mo nai.*

M

mathematics n. **[the science of numbers, quantities, and shapes]**
su⌈ugaku 数学 •c, sa⌈nsu⌉u 算数 •c [arithmetic]

EX. (**a**) He is good at mathematics.
彼は{数学/算数}が得意だ。
Kare wa {suugaku/sansuu} ga tokui da.
(**b**) He majored in mathematics in college.
彼は大学で{数学/*算数}を専攻した。
*Kare wa daigaku de {suugaku/*sansuu} o senkoo-shita.*

matter n. **[a subject/event/situation to which attention is given]**
mo⌈ndai 問題 •c [a difficult situation or topic that needs attention and thought] ⟪problem, question⟫, ko⌈to⌉ こと [s.t. intangible or a nominalizer forming a noun clause expressing s.t. perceived indirectly by means of one's rational faculties rather than directly through the five senses]

EX. (**a**) Don't get involved in her private matters.
彼女の個人的な{問題/こと}に巻き込まれてはいけない。
Kanojo no kojin-tekina {mondai/koto} ni maki-koma-rete wa ikenai.
(**b**) There are a few matters we have to discuss.
話し合わなければいけない{問題/こと}がいくつかある。
Hanashi-awanakereba ikenai {mondai/koto} ga ikutsu-ka aru.

PHRASE: a matter of life and death *ikiru ka shinu ka no mondai* 生きるか死ぬかの問題, a matter of time *jikan no mondai* 時間の問題

EX. He will eventually forget everything. It's just a matter of time.
彼はいつかは全部忘れてしまいますよ。時間の問題です。
Kare wa itsu-ka wa zenbu wasurete shimaimasu yo. Jikan no mondai desu.

PHRASE: What's the matter? *Doo shita n desu ka.* どうしたんですか, a matter of course *toozen* 当然 •c, as a matter of fact *jitsu wa* 実は •c

mature adj. **[fully grown or completely developed]**
o⌈tona no N 大人のN [for s.o. to be fully grown and developed] ↔ kodomo-ppoi 子供っぽい

EX. She is mature for her age.
彼女は年の割りに大人だ。
Kanojo wa toshi no wari ni otona da.

maximum adj./n. **[the greatest possible number, amount, degree, etc.]**
saikoo- 最高～ •c [the best/the highest] ↔ saitei- 最低～ •c

EX. (**a**) The maximum we can pay you is ¥50,000.
私たちがお支払いできる最高額は五万円です。
Watashi-tachi ga o-shiharai-dekiru saikoo-gaku wa go-man-en desu.
(**b**) The maximum speed of the Shinkansen is 270km per hour.
新幹線の最高速度は時速270キロだ。
Shinkansen no saikoo-sokudo wa jisoku ni-hyaku-nana-juk-kiro da.

may aux. **[an auxiliary verb indicating possibility of an event happening or of s.t. being the case, permission for s.o. to do s.t., or wish for s.t. to become true]**
1. {{**V/adj(*i*).**}**inf./**{**adj(*na*). stem/N**} {**ø/datta**}} **ka⌉moshirenai** {{**V/adj(*i*).**}**inf./**{**adj(*na*). stem/N**}{**ø/だった**}}**かもしれない** aux. adj(*i*). ⟪**maybe**⟫

EX. (**a**) He may have gained weight.
彼は太ったかもしれない。
Kare wa futotta kamoshirenai.
(**b**) He may be late for the meeting.
会議に遅れるかもしれない。
Kaigi ni okureru kamoshirenai.
(**c**) He may be busy now.
彼は今忙しいかもしれない。
Kare wa ima isogashii kamoshirenai.
(**d**) That department store may be closed today.
あのデパートは今日は休みかもしれません。
Ano depaato wa kyoo wa yasumi kamoshiremasen.
(**e**) He may not be able to speak English.
彼は英語が話せないかもしれません。

Kare wa eigo ga hanase-nai kamoshiremasen.
(**f**) She may have been an actress before.
彼女は以前女優だったかもしれない。
Kanojo wa izen joyuu datta kamoshirenai.
(**g**) He may like cooking.
彼は料理が好きかもしれない。
Kare wa ryoori ga suki kamoshirenai.

2. {V/adj./cop.}*te* mo {i˥i/ka˥mawa˥nai} {V/adj./cop.}*te*も{いい/構わない} [for an action or situation to be acceptable] ((can, be allowed))

EX. (**a**) May I borrow your dictionary?
辞書を借りても{いいです/構いません}か。
Jisho o karite mo {ii desu/kamaimasen} ka.
(**b**) May I come in?
入っても{いいです/構いません}か。
Haitte mo {ii desu/kamaimasen} ka.
(**c**) You may smoke outside.
外でたばこをすっても{いいです/構いません}よ。
Soto de tabako o sutte mo {ii desu/kamaimasen} yo.

May n.
go˥-gatsu 五月 •c

EX. (**a**) May is a good month for hiking.
五月はハイキングにいい月だ。
Go-gatsu wa haikingu ni ii tsuki da.
(**b**) May 5th is a public holiday in Japan.
日本では五月五日は祭日です。
Nihon de wa go-gatsu itsuka wa saijitsu desu.

maybe adv. **[possibly but not certainly]**
{{V/adj(*i*).}inf./{adj(*na*). stem/N} {ø/datta}} ka˥moshirenai {{V/adj(*i*).}inf./{adj(*na*). stem/N}{ø/だった}}かもしれない aux. adj(*i*).

EX. (**a**) Maybe he doesn't like me.
彼は私が嫌いなのかもしれません。
Kare wa watashi ga kiraina no kamoshiremasen.
(**b**) Maybe she won't come to the party.
彼女はパーティーに来ないかもしれません。
Kanojo wa paatii ni konai kamoshiremasen.

mayor n. **[the elected head of a city/town/village]**
shi˹cho˥o 市長 •c [the elected head of a city], cho˥ochoo 町長 •c [the elected head of a town], so˥nchoo 村長 •c [the elected head of a village]

NOTE: A municipal area is called *shi, choo, machi,* or *son(mura)*, depending on the size of its population, from highest to lowest in that order.

EX. (**a**) I met the mayor of Kyoto at an international conference.
国際会議で京都市長にお会いした。
Kokusai-kaigi de Kyooto-shichoo ni o-ai-shita.
(**b**) He has been elected mayor of this town.
彼はこの町の町長に当選した。
Kare wa kono machi no choochoo ni toosen-shita.

me pron. **[object form of I]**
wa˹tashi + prt. 私+prt.

NOTE: The choice of the particle following *watashi* depends on the predicate. Other nouns meaning "I", such as *boku, watakushi*, etc., may be used instead of *watashi*, depending on the speaker and context. "Me" is often not expressed at all when its existence is understood in a given context.

EX. (**a**) He gave me a photo of his children.
彼は{私に/ø}お子さんの写真をくれた。
Kare wa {watashi ni/ø} o-ko-san no shashin o kureta.
(**b**) She wants to marry me.
彼女は{ぼくと/*ø}結婚したがっている。
*Kanojo wa {boku to/*ø} kekkon-shi-tagatte iru.*
(**c**) She seems to hate me.
彼女は{私が/*ø}きらいなようだ。
*Kanojo wa {watashi ga/*ø} kiraina yoo da.*
(**d**) Mr. Yamada invited me to dinner.
山田さんが{私を/ø}晩ごはんに呼んでくれた。
Yamada-san ga {watashi o/ø} ban-gohan ni yonde kureta.

M

meadow n. **[a field of grass, esp. one used for grazing animals]**
bo⌈kuso⌉o-chi 牧草地 •c [ground on which vegetation grows used for grazing animals]

EX. Sheep were feeding on the grass in the meadow.
牧草地で羊が草を食べていた。
Bokusoo-chi de hitsuji ga kusa o tabete ita.

meal n. **[an occasion when food is eaten, such as breakfast, lunch, or dinner]**
sho⌈kuji 食事 •c [the act of a person's eating in order to sustain oneself], go⌉han 御飯 •c [food consumed by people for sustenance or steamed rice]

EX. (**a**) I don't even have time to eat proper meals.
私はまともに{食事をする/御飯を食べる}時間もない。
Watashi wa matomoni {shokuji o suru/gohan o taberu} jikan mo nai.
(**b**) Do you eat three meals a day?
一日に三回{食事をして/御飯を食べて}いますか。
Ichi-nichi ni san-kai {shokuji o shite/gohan o tabete} imasu ka.
(**c**) How are the meals in the dormitory?
寮の{食事/御飯}はどうですか。
Ryoo no {shokuji/gohan} wa doo desu ka.

mean[1] adj. **[stingy; ill-tempered and unkind]**
1. ke⌉china けちな adj(*na*). **[unwilling to give or share what one has with others]** ⟪**stingy**⟫

EX. He owns a huge financial empire but is famous for being mean in the way he pays his workers.
彼は莫大な財産を持っているにもかかわらず労働者に支払う賃金に関してはけちで有名だ。
Kare wa bakudaina zaisan o motte iru nimo-kakawarazu roodoo-sha ni shiharau chingin ni-kanshite wa kechi de yuumei da.

2. hi⌈do⌉i ひどい adj(*i*). **[of a frightening kind/degree or cruel]** ⟪**awful, terrible**⟫, **i⌈ji-wa⌉runa 意地悪な** adj(*na*). **[ill-tempered and deriving a perverse pleasure from doing unkind things to others, esp. ones weaker than oneself]** ⟪**nasty**⟫

EX. (**a**) It's mean of you not to let your younger sister use your car.
妹さんに車を使わせてあげないなんて、{意地悪/ひどい}ですね。
Imooto-san ni kuruma o tsukawa-sete agenai nante, {iji-waru/hidoi} desu ne.
(**b**) Don't be so mean to her.
彼女にそんな{意地悪な/ひどい}ことをしてはいけません。
Kanojo ni sonna {iji-waruna/hidoi} koto o shite wa ikemasen.

mean[2] vt. **[for a symbol or a linguistic expression or a situation to convey a certain meaning or for s.o. to have s.t. in mind as a purpose or intention]**
1. {word/phrase/sentence} wa…to-iu ko⌈to⌉ da {word/phrase/sentence}は…ということだ [a word/phrase/sentence expresses the meaning that…], {word/phrase/sentence} wa…to-iu i⌉mi da {word/phrase/sentence}は…という意味だ

EX. (**a**) What do you mean by that?
それはどういう{意味/こと}ですか。
Sore wa doo iu {imi/koto} desu ka.
(**b**) What does this word mean?
この単語はどういう{意味/*こと}ですか。
*Kono tango wa doo iu {imi/*koto} desu ka.*
(**c**) "Big Apple" means New York City.
「ビッグアップル」というのはニューヨーク{のこと/という意味}です。
'Biggu-appuru' to-iu no wa Nyuuyooku {no koto/to-iu imi} desu.
(**d**) The fact that no one is here must mean class has been cancelled.
だれも来ていないということは休講になったという{こと/*意味}にちがいない。
*Dare-mo kite inai to-iu koto wa kyuukoo ni natta to-iu {koto/*imi} ni chigainai.*

2. {{V/adj(*i*).}inf./adj(*na*). stem {na/datta}/N {no/datta}} tsu⌈mori da {{V/adj(*i*).}inf./

adj(*na*). stem{な/だった}/N{の/だった}}つもりだ [to have in one's mind as a plan/purpose/belief] ⟪**intend, be convinced, believe, feel sure**⟫

EX. (**a**) I'm sorry, I didn't mean to hurt you.
すみません。あなたを傷つけるつもりはなかったんです。
Sumimasen. Anata o kizu-tsukeru tsumori wa nakatta n desu.
(**b**) I meant to give him back the money yesterday.
私はきのう彼にお金を返すつもりだった。
Watashi wa kinoo kare ni o-kane o kaesu tsumori datta.

meaning n. **[that which a word/expression refers to or what is intended to be expressed by a word/expression/person]**
i˥mi 意味 •c [that which s.t. signifies]

EX. (**a**) What is the meaning of this verb?
この動詞はどういう意味ですか。
Kono dooshi wa doo iu imi desu ka.
(**b**) This word has two meanings.
この単語には意味が二つある。
Kono tango ni wa imi ga futatsu aru.

meaningful adj. **[for s.t. to have significant meaning]**
i˥mi no a˥ru N 意味のあるN ⟪**significant**⟫

EX. It's going to take a while before any meaningful conclusions emerge from our research.
我々の研究から意味のある結果が得られるにはまだまだ時間がかかりそうだ。
Ware-ware no kenkyuu kara imi no aru kekka ga e-rareru ni wa mada-mada jikan ga kakari-sooda.

means n. **[a method/way of doing s.t.]**
shu˥dan 手段 •c ⟪**measure**⟫

EX. (**a**) We have no means of getting in touch with him.
彼と連絡をとる手段はない。
Kare to renraku o toru shudan wa nai.
(**b**) Use whatever means available to get it.
どんな手段を使ってもいいから、それを手に入れろ。
Donna shudan o tsukatte mo ii kara, sore o te ni irero.

PHRASE: by all means *zehi* 是非 •c, *doo-shite-mo* どうしても, *zettai* 絶対 •c

meanwhile adv. **[during the time between two events]**
so˥re-ma˥de それまで [until then]

EX. The meeting will be over soon. Meanwhile let's have coffee over there.
会議はもうすぐ終わると思うから、それまであそこでコーヒーでも飲んでいましょう。
Kaigi wa moo sugu owaru to omou kara, sore-made asoko de koohii demo nonde imashoo.

measure vt./vi. **[to determine the size, length, amount, degree, etc., of s.t.]**
⟨-o⟩ ha˥ka˥ru ⟨〜を⟩はかる ①
㊥ "measure amount/weight"▷量る, "measure value/time"▷計る, otherwise ▷測る

EX. (**a**) She measured the length of the curtain.
彼女はカーテンの長さを測った。
Kanojo wa kaaten no naga-sa o hakatta.
(**b**) We measured the distance from our school to the station.
学校から駅までの距離を測った。
Gakkoo kara eki made no kyori o hakatta.
(**c**) She measured the sugar with a measuring cup.
彼女は計量カップで砂糖を量った。
Kanojo wa keiryoo-kappu de satoo o hakatta.
(**d**) The extent of his contributions cannot be measured in terms of money.
彼の貢献度はお金では計れない。
Kare no kooken-do wa o-kane de wa hakare-nai.

measurement n. **[the act of measuring or a result found by measuring]**
1. so˥kutei 測定 •c [the act of measuring]
2. su˥npoo 寸法 •c [a result found by measuring]

EX. The tailor took my measurements.
洋服屋は私の寸法を採った。
Yoofuku-ya wa watashi no sunpoo o totta.

M

meat n. **[the flesh of an animal used as food] ni⌈ku⌉ 肉 •c [the soft part lying under the skin and covering the bones in an animal/human body] ((flesh))**

EX. (**a**) I don't eat meat. I'm a vegetarian.
私は肉を食べません。菜食主義なんです。
Watashi wa niku o tabemasen. Saishoku-shugi na n desu.
(**b**) The meat they serve in the school cafeteria is always tough.
学校の食堂で出る肉はいつも固い。
Gakkoo no shokudoo de deru niku wa itsu-mo katai.

mechanic n. **[a person whose job it is to repair and maintain machinery] shu⌈uri-koo 修理工 •c [a person who repairs machinery as an occupation], ki⌈kai-koo 機械工 •c [a person who handles machinery as an occupation]**

EX. (**a**) Do you know a good garage mechanic?
だれかいい自動車{修理工/*機械工}を知っていますか。
*Dare-ka ii jidoosha-{shuuri-koo/*kikai-koo} o shitte imasu ka.*
(**b**) He got a job in the factory as a mechanic.
彼はその工場に{機械工/修理工}として就職した。
Kare wa sono koojoo ni {kikai-koo/shuuri-koo} to-shite shuushoku-shita.

mechanical adj. **[related to machinery or done from habit rather than will]**

1. ki⌈ka⌉i no N 機械のN •c [related to machinery]

EX. The flight was cancelled due to mechanical trouble.
機械の故障でその便はキャンセルされた。
Kikai no koshoo de sono bin wa kyanseru-sareta.

2. ki⌈kai-tekina 機械的な adj(*na*). **•c [done from habit rather than will]**

EX. After his initial enthusiasm left him, his teaching began to get mechanical.
最初の情熱を失ってから、彼の教え方は機械的になった。
Saisho no joonetsu o ushinatte kara, kare no oshie-kata wa kikai-tekini natta.

mechanism n. **[the way the various parts of a machine or system are arranged and work] shi-⌈kumi 仕組み ((structure)), me⌈kani⌉zumu メカニズム •f, ki⌈koo 機構 •c [the arrangement of the parts of a social system] ((machinery, organization, framework))**

EX. (**a**) Little is known about the mechanisms of the brain.
脳の{仕組み/メカニズム/*機構}については知られていないことがまだたくさんある。
*Noo no {shi-kumi/mekanizumu/*kikoo} ni-tsuite wa shira-rete inai koto ga mada takusan aru.*
(**b**) Are you familiar with the mechanisms of the Japanese judicial system?
日本の裁判制度の{仕組み/?機構/?メカニズム}をよくご存じですか。
Nihon no saiban-seido no {shi-kumi/?kikoo/?mekanizumu} o yoku go-zonji desu ka.
(**c**) It's difficult to bring about change in a highly complex mechanism like the United Nations.
国連のようなきわめて複雑な{機構/?仕組み/*メカニズム}を変えるのは難しい。
*Kokuren no yoona kiwamete fukuzatsuna {kikoo/?shi-kumi/*mekanizumu} o kaeru no wa muzukashii.*

medical adj. **[related to medicine] i⌉gaku no N 医学のN •c**

EX. (**a**) Medical books are expensive.
医学書は高い。
Igaku-sho wa takai.
(**b**) I hope to get into medical school next fall.
来年の秋に医学部に入りたいと思っています。
Rainen no aki ni igaku-bu ni hairi-tai to omotte imasu.

PHRASE: medical treatment *chiryoo* 治療 •c, medical examination *shinsatsu* 診察 •c

EX. Dr. Abe gave me a medical examination.
阿部先生が私を診察してくださった。
Abe-sensei ga watashi o shinsatsu-shite kudasatta.

medicine n. **[a substance used for treating bodily disorders or the science of the treatment and prevention of illness and injury]**

1. ku⌈suri 薬 [a substance used for treating (bodily disorders)]

EX. (**a**) Take this medicine and go to bed.
この薬を飲んで、寝なさい。
Kono kusuri o nonde, nenasai.
(**b**) He is working on the development of new medicine.
彼は新しい薬の開発に取り組んでいる。
Kare wa atarashii kusuri no kaihatsu ni tori-kunde iru.

2. i⌉gaku 医学 •c [the science of the treatment and prevention of illness and injury]

EX. (**a**) Sam is interested in preventive medicine.
サムは予防医学に興味がある。
Samu wa yoboo-igaku ni kyoomi ga aru.
(**b**) He's an authority on oriental medicine.
彼は東洋医学の権威です。
Kare wa Tooyoo-igaku no ken'i desu.

medieval adj. **[of the period between about 1100 and 1500 A.D.]**

chu⌉usei no N 中世のN •c

EX. (**a**) He received his Ph. D. in medieval history.
彼は中世史で博士号を取得した。
Kare wa chuusei-shi de hakushi-goo o shutoku-shita.
(**b**) I'd like to study medieval art.
私は中世の美術を勉強したい。
Watashi wa chuusei no bijutsu o benkyoo-shi-tai.

medium adj. **[having a middle position between extremes in size, degree, amount, quality, etc.]**

chu⌈u-gurai no N 中ぐらいのN [at an intermediate point/level on a range of size, force, etc.]

EX. (**a**) I bought a fish of medium size.
中ぐらいの大きさの魚を買った。
Chuu-gurai no ooki-sa no sakana o katta.
(**b**) Her lunch usually consists of only one medium-sized apple.
彼女の昼ごはんは大抵中ぐらいの大きさのりんごだけです。
Kanojo no hiru-gohan wa taitei chuu-gurai no ooki-sa no ringo dake desu.

PHRASE: of medium height *chuuzei no* N 中背のN

EX. A pretty woman of medium height walked into the room.
中背のきれいな女の人が部屋に入ってきた。
Chuuzei no kireina onna no hito ga heya ni haitte kita.

meet vt./vi. **[for s.o. to come face to face with s.o. else 《fig. "satisfy (the claims of s.o./s.t.)"》]**

1. {⟨-to⟩/⟨-ni⟩} a⌉u {⟨〜と⟩/〜に⟩}あう ① [for two people/objects to come close to each other or to fit each other] 《see》

NOTE: The particle *to* is used when the relationship or action is seen to be mutual, and the particle *ni* is used when the relationship or action is seen as being directed by one of the entities toward the other rather than being mutual.

㊥ "meet"▷会う, "match/fit"▷合う

EX. (**a**) I met a Japanese businessman at the party last night.
ゆうべのパーティーで日本のビジネスマンに会った。
Yuube no paatii de Nihon no bijinesu-man ni atta.
(**b**) I haven't met Yoshiko since we graduated from high school.
佳子には高校を卒業してから、会っていない。
Yoshiko ni wa kookoo o sotsugyoo-shite kara, atte inai.
(**c**) Let's meet this evening for dinner.
今晩会って、一緒に晩ごはんを食べよう。

M

Konban atte, issho ni ban-gohan o tabeyoo.

2. ⟨-o⟩ **mu˹kaeru** ⟨〜を⟩迎える ② **[for s.o./s.a. to welcome s.o. by being at a certain place at the time of his/her arrival]**

EX. (**a**) I went to the airport to meet a guest.
空港へお客さんを迎えに行った。
Kuukoo e o-kyaku-san o mukae ni itta.
(**b**) We were met by Mr. Jones at the entrance of the hotel.
私たちはホテルの玄関でジョーンズさんに迎えられた。
Watashi-tachi wa hoteru no genkan de Joonzu-san ni mukae-rareta.

PHRASE: meet with ⟨*-ni*⟩ *au* ⟨〜に⟩あう ①

EX. The mountaineers met with misfortune in their attempt to scale the summit.
登山家たちは頂上に登ろうとした時不幸な事故にあった。
Tozan-ka-tachi wa choojoo ni noboroo to shita toki fukoona jiko ni atta.

meeting n. **[a gathering of people in order to discuss s.t., make a decision, etc.]**
ka˥igi 会議 **•c [a gathering of persons concerned to discuss and come to a decision on an issue]** ⟪**conference**⟫, **mi˥itingu** ミーティング **•f, u˹chiawase** 打ち合わせ **[an informal gathering to make preliminary arrangements for s.t.]** ⟪**consultation**⟫

EX. (**a**) I have to attend a meeting this afternoon.
私は今日の午後{会議/ミーティング/打ち合わせ}に出なければいけない。
Watashi wa kyoo no gogo {kaigi/miitingu/uchiawase} ni denakereba ikenai.
(**b**) The meeting was over around 5 o'clock.
{会議/ミーティング/打ち合わせ}は五時ごろ終わった。
{Kaigi/Miitingu/Uchiawase} wa go-ji-goro owatta.

melancholy n. **[sadness and depression of spirits ⟨fml⟩]**
yu˹uutsu 憂うつ **•c [the state of being depressed]** ⟪**gloom, low spirits**⟫

— adj. **[sad and depressed ⟨fml⟩]**
yu˹uutsuna 憂うつな adj(*na*). **•c [showing sadness and depression of spirits]** ⟪**gloomy, blue**⟫

EX. I feel melancholy on cold, rainy winter days.
私は冬の寒い雨の日には憂うつになる。
Watashi wa fuyu no samui ame no hi ni wa yuuutsu ni naru.

melody n. **[a succession of sounds that form a tune]**
me˥rodii メロディー **•f [tune]**

EX. (**a**) This song has a beautiful melody.
この歌はメロディーが美しい。
Kono uta wa merodii ga utsukushii.
(**b**) I've heard that melody somewhere before.
そのメロディーは以前どこかで聞いたことがある。
Sono merodii wa izen doko-ka de kiita koto ga aru.

melon n.
me˥ron メロン **•f**

EX. Melons are very expensive in Japan.
メロンは日本ではとても高い。
Meron wa Nihon de wa totemo takai.

melt vt./vi. **[for a solid to become liquid, usu. by the application of heat, or to cause this]**
⟨-o⟩ **to˹ka˥su** ⟨〜を⟩とかす ① **[to cause s.t. to turn into liquid ⟪fig. "comb hair"⟫]** ⟪**dissolve**⟫, **to˹ke˥ru** とける ② **[for s.t. to turn into liquid due to the presence of heat or to the action of another liquid ⟪fig. "be solved"⟫]**

㊌ "melt"▷{溶かす/溶ける}, otherwise ▷{解かす/解ける}

EX. (**a**) I melted the butter in the skillet.
フライパンにバターを溶かした。
Furaipan ni bataa o tokashita.
(**b**) The sun melted the snow.
日光で雪が溶けた。
Nikkoo de yuki ga toketa.
(**c**) The ice on the lake started to melt.
湖の氷が溶け始めた。
Mizuumi no koori ga toke-hajimeta.

member n. **[a person belonging to a club, group, society, etc.]**

M

me⌉nbaa メンバー •f, ka⌈iin 会員 •c [a person belonging to a club or academic society]

EX. (**a**) He is a member of the budget committee.
彼は予算委員会の{メンバー/*会員}だ。
*Kare wa yosan-iin-kai no {menbaa/ *kaiin} da.*
(**b**) I've recently become a member of the golf club.
私は最近あのゴルフクラブの{会員/メンバー}になった。
Watashi wa saikin ano gorufu-kurabu no {kaiin/menbaa} ni natta.
(**c**) All the members of the group are coming to the party.
グループの{メンバー/*会員}は全員パーティーに来ることになっている。
*Guruupu no {menbaa/*kaiin} wa zen'in paatii ni kuru koto ni natte iru.*

memorize vt. **[for s.o. to learn s.t. thoroughly for future use]**
⟨-o⟩ o⌈boe⌉ru ⟨〜を⟩覚える ② ⟪learn, remember⟫, ⟨-o⟩ a⌈nki-suru ⟨〜を⟩暗記する ③ •c

EX. Did you memorize all the new words in this lesson?
この課の新しいことばを全部{覚えました/暗記しました}か。
Kono ka no atarashii kotoba o zenbu {oboemashita/anki-shimashita} ka.

memory n. **[the ability to retain and recall information in one's mind or s.t. that is so retained]**
1. ki⌈oku⌉-ryoku 記憶力 •c [the ability to remember events and experiences]

EX. (**a**) She has a good memory.
彼女は記憶力がいい。
Kanojo wa kioku-ryoku ga ii.
(**b**) My memory has been failing these days.
最近記憶力が落ちてきた。
Saikin kioku-ryoku ga ochite kita.

2. ki⌈oku 記憶 •c [the act of remembering], o⌈moi-de 思い出 [s.t. about the past that is retained in one's mind, esp. a pleasant event] ⟪reminiscence, recollection⟫

EX. (**a**) The accident is still fresh in my memory.
その事故のことはまだ{記憶/*思い出}に新しい。
*Sono jiko no koto wa mada {kioku/ *omoi-de} ni atarashii.*
(**b**) I have a clear memory of the air raids.
空襲のはっきりした{記憶/*思い出}が残っている。
*Kuushuu no hakkiri-shita {kioku/*omoi-de} ga nokotte iru.*
(**c**) My visit to the park brought back many childhood memories.
公園を訪ねると子供のころのたくさんの{思い出/記憶}がよみがえった。
Kooen o tazuneru to kodomo no koro no takusan no {omoi-de/kioku} ga yomigaetta.

PHRASE: if my memory serves me right *tashika* 確か, *watashi no kioku ni machigai ga nakereba* 私の記憶に間違いがなければ

EX. If my memory serves me right, I met you at Yoko's place.
{確か/私の記憶に間違いがなければ}、洋子さんのところでお目にかかりましたね。
{Tashika/Watashi no kioku ni machigai ga nakereba}, Yooko-san no tokoro de o-me-ni-kakarimashita ne.

men n. **[plural of man]**
SEE man

mend vt. **[for s.o. to repair s.t. broken or torn]**
⟨-o⟩ na⌈o⌉su ⟨〜を⟩なおす ① [for s.o. to restore s.t. damaged to its normal state of functioning] ⟪repair, fix, correct, cure⟫, ⟨-o⟩ shu⌉uri-suru ⟨〜を⟩修理する ③ •c [for s.o. to fix machinery, hardware, etc.] ⟪fix⟫
㊅ "cure"▷治す, otherwise ▷直す

EX. (**a**) He mended my bicycle. (Br.E)
彼は私の自転車を{直して/修理して}くれた。
Kare wa watashi no jitensha o {naoshite/shuuri-shite} kureta.
(**b**) My mother mended my jeans.
母は私のジーンズを{直して/*修理して}くれた。

M

*Haha wa watashi no jiinzu o {naoshite/ *shuuri-shite} kureta.*

mental adj. **[related to the activity of the mind]**
se⌈ishin-tekina 精神的な adj(*na*). •c **[of mind as opposed to body]** «spiritual» ↔ **nikutai-tekina** 肉体的な adj(*na*). •c

EX. (**a**) Playing is necessary for a child's mental development.
遊びは子供の精神的な発育に必要だ。
Asobi wa kodomo no seishin-tekina hatsuiku ni hitsuyoo da.
(**b**) His problem is a mental one.
彼の問題は精神的なものだ。
Kare no mondai wa seishin-tekina mono da.

PHRASE: mental hospital *seishin-byooin* 精神病院 •c, mental age *seishin-nenrei* 精神年齢 •c, mental powers *seishin-ryoku* 精神力 •c

mention vt. **[for s.o./s.t. to briefly speak about or refer to s.t.]**
⟨-ni⟩ fu⌈reru ⟨〜に⟩触れる ② **[for s.o. to cause s.t. to come close to and make light contact with s.t./s.o./s.a. or for s.t. to spontaneously come close to and make light contact with s.t. else** «**fig. "mention s.t.," "violate the law"**»**]**, **⟨-to⟩ i⌈u** ⟨〜と⟩言う ① **[for s.o. to express s.t. verbally]**

EX. (**a**) He didn't even mention his retirement at the press conference.
彼は記者会見で引退については{触れ/ *言い}さえしなかった。
*Kare wa kisha-kaiken de intai ni-tsuite wa {fure/*ii} sae shinakatta.*
(**b**) He mentioned that he was planning to quit his job.
彼は仕事を辞めるつもりだと{言った/ *触れた}。
*Kare wa shigoto o yameru tsumori da to {itta/*fureta}.*

menu n. **[a list of the foods that can be ordered in a restaurant]**
me⌉nyuu メニュー •f **[a list of the foods that can be ordered in a restaurant]**, **ko⌈n-date** 献立 **[a list of dishes to be served in a meal]**

EX. (**a**) Can I see the menu, please?
{メニュー/献立}を見せてくださいませんか。
{Menyuu/Kon-date} o misete kudasaimasen ka.
(**b**) Hamburgers are not on the menu at this restaurant.
ハンバーガーはこのレストランの{メニュー/*献立}に載っていない。
*Hanbaagaa wa kono resutoran no {menyuu/*kon-date} ni notte inai.*
(**c**) I have to think about the menu for tonight's dinner.
今晩の晩ごはんの{献立/*メニュー}を考えなければならない。
*Konban no ban-gohan no {kon-date/ *menyuu} o kangaenakereba naranai.*

merchant n. **[a person whose job it is to buy and sell goods]**
sho⌉onin 商人 •c

EX. (**a**) Osaka is a city of merchants.
大阪は商人の町だ。
Oosaka wa shoonin no machi da.
(**b**) He is a notorious merchant of weapons.
彼は悪名高き武器の商人だ。
Kare wa akumei-takaki buki no shoonin da.

mercury n.
su⌈igin 水銀 •c

EX. Some insecticides contain mercury.
殺虫剤には水銀の入っているものがある。
Satchuu-zai ni wa suigin no haitte iru mono ga aru.

mercy n. **[kind and considerate treatment of s.o. above what is expected or deserved]**
na⌉sake 情け **[kindness and compassion to s.o. weak or in trouble]** «**pity, charity, benevolence**»

EX. I desperately wanted to save my son, but I could do nothing but throw myself at the judge's mercy.
私はなんとしてでも息子を救いたかったが、裁判官の情けにすがるしかなかった。
Watashi wa nan-to-shite-demo musuko o sukui-takatta ga, saiban-kan no

nasake ni sugaru shika nakatta.

PHRASE: without mercy *nasake-yoosha-naku* 情け容赦なく

EX. They killed everybody in the royal family without mercy.
彼らは情け容赦なく王族を皆殺しにした。
Kare-ra wa nasake-yoosha-naku oozoku o mina-goroshi ni shita.

mere adj. **[nothing more than]**
ta⌉n-naru N 単なるN •c ⟪simple⟫ , ⟨-ni⟩ su⌈gi⌉nai ⟨〜に⟩過ぎない ⟪only, no more than, nothing but⟫

EX. (**a**) He's a mere child.
彼は(*単なる)子供に過ぎない。
*Kare wa (*tan-naru) kodomo ni suginai.*
(**b**) Buying a house in Tokyo is no more than a mere dream to most people working there.
東京で家を買うなんてそこで働いているほとんどの人にとっては{単なる夢に過ぎない/単なる夢だ/夢に過ぎない}。
Tookyoo de uchi o kau nante soko de hataraite iru hotondo no hito ni-totte wa {tan-naru yume ni suginai/tan-naru yume da/yume ni suginai}.
(**c**) I started karate out of mere curiosity, but now I'm totally hooked on it.
私は単なる好奇心から空手を始めたが、今はその魅力のとりこになっている。
Watashi wa tan-naru kooki-shin kara karate o hajimeta ga, ima wa sono miryoku no toriko ni natte iru.

NOTE: "*Tan-naru*" can be used with "*ni suginai*" to reinforce the meanig of "nothing more than," as in example (b).

merely adv. **[only, simply]**
⟨-ni⟩ su⌈gi⌉nai ⟨〜に⟩過ぎない, -da⌈ke⌉ da 〜だけだ [what is described is all that happened/s.o. did]

EX. (**a**) He's merely an assistant.
彼は助手{に過ぎない/*だけだ}。
*Kare wa joshu {ni suginai/*dake da}.*
(**b**) I merely suggested that he should go home a little earlier. I don't know why he is so angry.
私は彼にもう少し早く家へ帰った方がいいんじゃないかと言った{だけだ/*に過ぎない}。どうしてあんなに怒っているのかわからない。
*Watashi wa kare ni moo sukoshi hayaku uchi e kaetta hoo ga ii n janai ka to itta {dake da/*ni suginai}. Dooshite annani okotte iru no ka wakaranai.*
(**c**) He merely stated what he believed was right.
彼は自分で正しいと思ったことを言った{に過ぎない/だけだ}。
Kare wa jibun de tadashii to omotta koto o itta {ni suginai/dake da}.

merit n. **[the quality of deserving praise or reward or s.t. good/worthwhile]**
cho⌉osho 長所 •c ⟪strong point⟫ ↔ tansho 短所 •c

EX. (**a**) This candidate has few merits.
この候補者には長所があまりない。
Kono kooho-sha ni wa choosho ga amari nai.
(**b**) One of her merits is a strong sense of responsibility.
彼女の長所の一つは責任感が強いことだ。
Kanojo no choosho no hitotsu wa sekinin-kan ga tsuyoi koto da.
(**c**) This proposal has both merits and demerits.
この案には長所も短所もある。
Kono an ni wa choosho mo tansho mo aru.

merry adj. **[lively and cheerful]**
yo⌈okina 陽気な adj(*na*). **•c ⟪cheerful⟫**

EX. There was a merry spirit among all at the Christmas party.
クリスマス・パーティーに来ていた人は皆陽気な気分だった。
Kurisumasu paatii ni kite ita hito wa mina yookina kibun datta.

PHRASE: Merry Christmas! *Merii Kurisumasu!* メリークリスマス!

mess n. **[a dirty or untidy condition ⟪fig. "trouble"⟫]**

M

me⌈cha-kucha めちゃくちゃ [an untidy or terrible situation]

EX. (**a**) My room is a mess.
私の部屋はめちゃくちゃです。
Watashi no heya wa mecha-kucha desu.
(**b**) Her hair was a mess.
彼女の髪はめちゃくちゃだった。
Kanojo no kami wa mecha-kucha datta.

PHRASE: mess up *mecha-kucha ni suru* めちゃくちゃにする

EX. The kids got a little too rowdy and messed up the living room.
子供たちはちょっと暴れ過ぎて居間をめちゃくちゃにしてしまった。
Kodomo-tachi wa chotto abare-sugite ima o mecha-kucha ni shite shimatta.

message n. **[s.t. communicated or intended to be communicated from one person to another, often through an intermediary]**
de⌈ngon 伝言 •c, ko⌈to-zuke⌉ 言付け

EX. (**a**) Did you get a message from Mr. Yoshida?
吉田さんからの{伝言/言付け}を受け取りましたか。
Yoshida-san kara no {dengon/koto-zuke} o uke-torimashita ka.
(**b**) Can I leave a message for Prof. Hirai?
平井先生に{伝言/お言付け}をお願いできますか。
Hirai-sensei ni {dengon/o-koto-zuke} o o-negai dekimasu ka.

metal n. **[a solid mineral substance such as iron, copper, lead, etc.]**
ki⌉nzoku 金属 •c

EX. (**a**) Metal fatigue can lead to serious accidents.
金属疲労が重大な事故の原因になることがある。
Kinzoku-hiroo ga juudaina jiko no gen'in ni naru koto ga aru.
(**b**) Is this bracelet made of metal?
このブレスレットは金属製ですか。
Kono buresuretto wa kinzoku-sei desu ka.

meter n. **[unit of length]**
me⌈etoru メートル •f

NOTE: 1 meter=1.09 yards

EX. (**a**) I need 3 meters of cloth.
布が三メートル要る。
Nuno ga san-meetoru iru.
(**b**) We bought 200 square meters of land.
私たちは二百平方メートルの土地を買った。
Watashi-tachi wa ni-hyaku-heihoo-meetoru no tochi o katta.

method n. **[a way of doing s.t.]**
ho⌈ohoo 方法 •c [the means to achieve a goal] ((**way**)), **-hoo ～法 •c**

EX. (**a**) I've studied various methods of teaching foreign languages.
私はいろいろな外国語の教授法を勉強した。
Watashi wa iro-irona gaikoku-go no kyooju-hoo o benkyoo-shita.
(**b**) I'd like to try a different method of teaching English.
英語を教えるのに違う方法を試してみたい。
Eigo o oshieru no ni chigau hoohoo o tameshite mitai.
(**c**) You can't expect to obtain significant results if you conduct research using improper methods.
間違った方法で研究して有益な結果が得られるはずがない。
Machigatta hoohoo de kenkyuu-shite yuuekina kekka ga e-rareru hazu ga nai.

Mexico n.
Me⌈kishiko メキシコ •f

Miami n.
Ma⌈iami マイアミ •f

mice n. **[plural of mouse]**
ne⌈zumi ねずみ

Michigan n.
Mi⌉shigan ミシガン •f

microbe n.
bi-⌈se⌉ibutsu 微生物 •c ((**microorganism**))

microcomputer n.
ma⌈ikurokonpyu⌉utaa マイクロコンピューター •f

microphone n.
ma⌉iku マイク •f, ma⌈ikuro⌉fon マイクロフォン •f

EX. (**a**) Opera singers perform without using a microphone.
オペラ歌手はマイク(ロフォン)を使わないで歌う。
Opera-kashu wa maiku(rofon) o tsukawanaide utau.
(**b**) This microphone doesn't seem to be working properly.
このマイク(ロフォン)は調子が良くないみたいだ。
Kono maiku(rofon) wa chooshi ga yokunai mitaida.

microscope n.
ke⌈nbi-kyoo 顕微鏡 •c

EX. (**a**) She examined the tissue of the plant under a microscope.
彼女はその植物の組織を顕微鏡で調べた。
Kanojo wa sono shokubutsu no soshiki o kenbi-kyoo de shirabeta.
(**b**) They purchased a new electron microscope.
新しい電子顕微鏡を購入した。
Atarashii denshi-kenbi-kyoo o koonyuu-shita.

middle n. **[at or near a point equidistant from all points on the outer perimeter of an area or between two extremes in space, time, or quantity 《fig. "busy with"》]**
1. ma⌈nnaka 真ん中 [a point equidistant from all points on the outer perimeter of an area] 《center, heart》, na⌈kaba⌉ 半ば [the central point in time]

EX. (**a**) There's a big cherry tree in the middle of the garden.
庭の{真ん中/*半ば}に大きな桜の木がある。
*Niwa no {mannaka/*nakaba} ni ookina sakura no ki ga aru.*
(**b**) I was jogging in the middle of the road.
私は道の{真ん中/*半ば}をジョギングしていた。
*Watashi wa michi no {mannaka/*nakaba} o jogingu-shite ita.*
(**c**) School starts in the middle of April in Japan.
日本では学校は四月の{半ば/*真ん中}に始まる。
*Nihon de wa gakkoo wa shi-gatsu no {nakaba/*mannaka} ni hajimaru.*

2. -chuu ～中 •c [within the span of time of/among the choices represented by], sa⌉ichuu 最中 •c [in the middle of some activity]

NOTE: *-chuu* is preceded by a noun which indicates an activity. It is usually the type of noun which can be made into a verb by adding *suru*, "do."

EX. (**a**) A phone call came for me when I was in the middle of a meeting.
{会議中/会議の最中}に電話がかかってきた。
{Kaigi-chuu/Kaigi no saichuu} ni denwa ga kakatte kita.
(**b**) We had an earthquake right in the middle of the party.
{パーティーの最中/*パーティー中}に地震があった。
*{Paatii no saichuu/*Paatii-chuu} ni jishin ga atta.*
(**c**) Dr. Yoshida is in the middle of an operation at the moment.
吉田先生はただ今{手術の最中/手術中}です。
Yoshida-sensei wa tadaima {shujutsu no saichuu/shujutsu-chuu} desu.

PHRASE: middle school *chuu-gakkoo* 中学校 •c 《junior high school》

midnight n. **[the middle of the night]**
ma-⌈yo⌉naka 真夜中 [12 o'clock at night/very late at night], yo⌉ru ju⌈u-ni⌉-ji 夜十二時 [12 o'clock at night]

EX. (**a**) At midnight the ghosts gather in the museum for a ball.
幽霊は{真夜中/*夜十二時}に舞踏会を開くために博物館に集まってくる。
*Yuurei wa {ma-yonaka/*yoru juu-ni-ji} ni butoo-kai o hiraku tame ni hakubutsu-kan ni atsumatte kuru.*
(**b**) That coffee shop is open until midnight.
あの喫茶店は{真夜中/夜十二時}まで開いている。

Ano kissa-ten wa {ma-yonaka/yoru juu-ni-ji} made aite iru.

Midwest n.

Chu⌈use⌉ibu 中西部 •c

might aux. **[an auxiliary verb indicating the slight possibility of an event happening or of s.t. being the case]**
{V/adj(*i*).}inf. ka⌉moshirenai {V/adj(*i*).}inf. かもしれない, {adj(*na*). stem/N} {ø/datta} ka⌉moshirenai {adj(*na*). stem/N}{ø/datta} かもしれない

EX. (**a**) It might snow tonight.
今晩は雪が降るかもしれない。
Konban wa yuki ga furu kamoshirenai.
(**b**) She might have left the office already.
彼女はもうオフィスを出たかもしれません。
Kanojo wa moo ofisu o deta kamoshiremasen.
(**c**) You might not be able to buy it in Japan.
日本では買えないかもしれない。
Nihon de wa kae-nai kamoshirenai.
(**d**) It might be difficult to find an apartment in this area.
この辺でアパートを見つけるのは難しいかもしれません。
Kono hen de apaato o mitsukeru no wa muzukashii kamoshiremasen.
(**e**) She might be Ichiro's new girlfriend.
彼女は一郎の新しいガールフレンドかもしれない。
Kanojo wa Ichiroo no atarashii gaaru-furendo kamoshirenai.
(**f**) He might be free tomorrow.
彼はあした暇かもしれない。
Kare wa ashita hima kamoshirenai.
(**g**) I might have failed the exam.
試験はだめだったかもしれない。
Shiken wa dame datta kamoshirenai.

migrate vi. **[to move from one place to settle in another, esp. for a limited period of time]**
1. wa⌈tatte {ku⌉ru/i⌈ku} 渡って{来る/行く} /⟨V *te* of *wataru* ① migrate, cross + *kuru* ③ come/ *iku* ① go/ **[for birds or fish to move from one part of the world to another with the change in seasons]**

EX. Swallows migrate to Japan in the early summer and to the south in the fall.
つばめは初夏になると日本へ渡って来て、秋になると南へ渡って行く。
Tsubame wa shoka ni naru to Nihon e watatte kite, aki ni naru to minami e watatte iku.

2. i⌈doo-suru 移動する ③ •c [for s.o./s.a. to (cause s.t. to) change in location from one place to another] ⟪move⟫, **i⌈juu-suru 移住する ③ •c [for s.o. to move to a different country to settle there]**

EX. (**a**) They migrated from Hong Kong to Canada.
彼らはホンコンからカナダへ{移住/*移動}した。
*Kare-ra wa Honkon kara Kanada e {ijuu/*idoo}-shita.*
(**b**) Nomadic tribes migrate with their cattle.
遊牧民は家畜を連れて{移動/*移住}する。
*Yuuboku-min wa kachiku o tsurete {idoo/*ijuu}-suru.*

migration n. **[an act/instance of migrating]**
i⌈doo 移動 •c [the act of moving from one place to another], i⌈juu 移住 •c [the act of moving to a different country to settle there]

EX. (**a**) Migratory birds begin their migration at the turn of the seasons.
渡り鳥は季節の変わり目に{移動/*移住}を始める。
*Watari-dori wa kisetsu no kawari-me ni {idoo/*ijuu} o hajimeru.*
(**b**) The migration of so many people to the cities has become a social problem in this country.
たくさんの人々の都会への{移住/*移動}がこの国では社会問題になった。
*Takusan no hito-bito no tokai e no {ijuu/*idoo} ga kono kuni de wa shakai-mondai ni natta.*

mild adj. **[not harsh or strong in intensity or character]**
1. o⌈nkoona 温厚な adj(*na*). **•c [not violent**

in character] ((gentle)), **o⌈da⌉yakana 穏やかな** adj(*na*). **[gentle and calm]** ((calm, peaceful, quiet))

EX. (**a**) He has a mild nature. I've never seen him angry.
彼は{温厚な/穏やかな}人柄だ。彼が怒るのを見たことがない。
Kare wa {onkoona/odayakana} hito-gara da. Kare ga okoru no o mita koto ga nai.
(**b**) The climate here is mild.
ここは気候が{穏やか/*温厚}です。
*Koko wa kikoo ga {odayaka/*onkoo} desu.*

2. ku⌈se⌉ ga na⌉i (N) くせがない(N) [for food or drink not to be strong in smell or taste], a⌈ssari⌉-shita N あっさりしたN [simple with minimal decoration or not persistent in one's demands or light in taste and easily digested] ((plain, light)) ↔ **shitsuk(k)oi しつ(っ)こい** adj(*i*).; **a⌈ssari⌉-shite iru (N) あっさりしている(N), ka⌈rui 軽い** adj(*i*). **[having little weight or for food to be small in amount and easy to digest]** ((light)) ↔ **omoi 重い** adj(*i*).

EX. (**a**) I like mild cheeses.
私は{くせのない/あっさりした/あっさりしている/*軽い}チーズが好きだ。
*Watashi wa {kuse no nai/assari-shita/assari-shite iru/*karui} chiizu ga sukida.*
(**b**) This cigarette is very mild.
このたばこはとても{軽いです/*あっさりしています/*くせがありません}。
*Kono tabako wa totemo {karui desu/*assari-shite imasu/*kuse ga arimasen}.*

mildew n. **[a soft, usually white, fungus that grows on plants, food, leather, etc., under warm and damp conditions]**
ka⌈bi かび [a soft, white-green fungus that grows on plants, food, leather, etc., under warm and damp conditions] ((mold))

EX. (**a**) There's mildew all over my old books.
私の古い本は全部かびだらけだ。
Watashi no furui hon wa zenbu kabi-darake da.
(**b**) Don't eat food with mildew on it.
かびの生えた食べ物を食べてはいけない。
Kabi no haeta tabe-mono o tabete wa ikenai.

mile n. **[a unit for measuring length]**
ma⌉iru マイル •f

NOTE: 1 mile=1609.35 meters

EX. (**a**) The speed limit on this highway is 70 miles per hour.
この高速道路の制限速度は時速七十マイルです。
Kono koosoku-dooro no seigen-sokudo wa jisoku nana-juu-mairu desu.
(**b**) We walked for miles looking for a telephone.
電話をさがして、何マイルも歩いた。
Denwa o sagashite, nan-mairu mo aruita.

military adj. **[having to do with armed forces/soldiers/war]**
gunji- 軍事～ •c [having to do with armed forces/war]

EX. (**a**) We don't have to provide military aid to other countries.
外の国に軍事援助をする必要はない。
Hoka no kuni ni gunji-enjo o suru hitsuyoo wa nai.
(**b**) Some countries are afraid of the military strength of Japan.
日本の軍事力を恐れている国もある。
Nihon no gunji-ryoku o osorete iru kuni mo aru.

—— n. **[the armed forces]**
gu⌉nbu 軍部 •c ((the military authorities)), **gu⌉ntai 軍隊 •c** ((the troops, the forces))

EX. (**a**) The military has put the city under martial law.
{軍部/?軍隊}がその町に戒厳令をしいた。
{Gunbu/?Guntai} ga sono machi ni kaigen-rei o shiita.
(**b**) The military is keeping order in the city.
{軍部/軍隊}が町の治安を維持している。
{Gunbu/Guntai} ga machi no chian o iji-shite iru.

PHRASE: military officer *shookoo* 将校 **•c**, military uniform *gunpuku* 軍服 **•c**

M

milk n. **[a white liquid produced by female mammals for the feeding of their young] gyu⌈unyuu 牛乳 •c [a white liquid produced by cows], bo⌈nyuu 母乳 •c [a white liquid produced by female mammals for the feeding of their babies], chi⌈chi⌉ 乳 [a white liquid produced by female mammals for the feeding of their young], mi⌉ruku ミルク •f [the white liquid produced by cows, esp. that processed for human consumption, usu. by drying and reconstituting]**

EX. (**a**) I don't like milk but I love yogurt.
{牛乳/?牛の乳}はきらいですが、ヨーグルトは大好きです。
{Gyuunyuu/?Ushi no chichi} wa kirai desu ga, yooguruto wa dai-suki desu.
(**b**) The baby is crying for its milk.
赤ん坊が{お乳/?母乳/?牛乳}を欲しがって、泣いています。
Akanboo ga {o-chichi/?bonyuu/?gyuunyuu} o hoshi-gatte, naite imasu.
(**c**) A mother's milk contains what is indispensable for a baby's growth.
{母乳/お乳/*牛乳}には赤ん坊の成長に不可欠なものが含まれている。
*{Bonyuu/O-chichi/*Gyuunyuu} ni wa akanboo no seichoo ni fukaketsuna mono ga fukuma-rete iru.*

PHRASE: condensed milk *kondensu-miruku* コンデンスミルク, dried milk *kona-miruku* 粉ミルク, skimmed milk *dasshinyuu* 脱脂乳 •c

— vt. **[to take the white liquid from a cow, goat, etc.]**
{chi⌈chi⌉/gyu⌈unyuu} o shi⌈bo⌉ru {乳/牛乳}をしぼる ①

millimeter n. **[a measure of length]**
mi⌉ri ミリ **•f, mi⌈ri-me⌉etoru** ミリメートル **•f**

NOTE: 1 millimeter=0.03937 inch

EX. This board is three millimeters thick.
この板は厚さ三ミリ(メートル)です。
Kono ita wa atsu-sa san-miri(-meetoru) desu.

million adj./n. **[the number 1,000,000]**
hya⌈ku-ma⌉n (+counter) (**no N**) 百万 (+counter)(のN) •c SEE APPENDIX II

EX. The population of this city is about three million.
この市の人口は約三百万人です。
Kono shi no jinkoo wa yaku san-byaku-man-nin desu.

PHRASE: ten million *is-sen-man* 一千万 •c, a hundred million *ichi-oku* 一億 •c

EX. (**a**) She bought a condominium in Kyoto for 100 million yen.
彼女は京都に一億円のマンションを買った。
Kanojo wa Kyooto ni ichi-oku-en no manshon o katta.
(**b**) My house cost 100 million yen.
私の家は一億円しました。
Watashi no ie wa ichi-oku-en shimashita.

mind n. **[the human faculty, originating in the brain, to think, reason, feel, and be aware of one's surroundings]**

1. ko⌈ko⌉ro 心 [the seat of one's thoughts/feelings in the body] ⟪**heart**⟫

EX. (**a**) Her last words still remain fresh in my mind.
彼女の最後の言葉はまだぼくの心にはっきりと残っている。
Kanojo no saigo no kotoba wa mada boku no kokoro ni hakkiri to nokotte iru.
(**b**) She has a narrow mind.
彼女は心が狭い。
Kanojo wa kokoro ga semai.

2. a⌈tama⌉ 頭 [that part of the body which contains the eyes, ears, nose, mouth, and brain or the ability to learn, reason, and understand] ⟪**head, brain**⟫

EX. (**a**) She has a very sharp mind.
彼女はすごく頭の回転が速い。
Kanojo wa sugoku atama no kaiten ga hayai.
(**b**) He must be out of his mind.
彼は頭がおかしくなったにちがいない。
Kare wa atama ga okashiku natta ni chigainai.

PHRASE: be on one's mind ⟨*-ga*⟩ *ki-ni-naru* ⟨〜が⟩気になる①, ⟨*-o*⟩ *ki-ni-suru* ⟨〜を⟩気にする ③

EX. (**a**) I couldn't fall asleep because the test the next day was so much on my mind
翌日のテストが気になって、寝られなかった。
Yokujitsu no tesuto ga ki-ni-natte, nerarenakatta.
(**b**) I wonder what's on his mind.
彼は何を気にしているんだろう。
Kare wa nani o ki-ni-shite iru n daroo.

PHRASE: be unable to get s.t. out of one's mind
⟨*-ga*⟩ *atama kara hanarenai* ⟨〜が⟩頭から離れない

EX. I can't get that mistake out of my mind.
あのミスが頭から離れない。
Ano misu ga atama kara hanarenai.

— vt. **[for s.o. to be troubled by or to dislike s.t.]**
V*te* mo {ka⌈mawa⌉nai/i⌉i} V*te*も{構わない/いい} [for an action or situation to be acceptable] ⟪may, can⟫

EX. (**a**) Do you mind if I smoke?
たばこを吸っても{構いません/いいです}か。
Tabako o sutte mo {kamaimasen/ii desu} ka.
(**b**) A: Which would you like, tea or coffee?
お茶とコーヒーとどちらがよろしいですか。
O-cha to koohii to dochira ga yoroshii desu ka.
B: I don't mind; either will do.
どちらでも{構いません/いいです}。
Dochira demo {kamaimasen/ii desu}.
(**c**) I don't mind if your parents visit our class.
御両親が授業にいらっしゃっても{構いません/いいです}よ。
Go-ryooshin ga jugyoo ni irasshatte mo {kamaimasen/ii desu} yo.
(**d**) I don't mind however much it costs.
お金はいくらかかっても{構いません/いいです}。
O-kane wa ikura kakatte mo {kamaimasen/ii desu}.

PHRASE: Would you mind...? V*te kudasaimasen ka* V*te*くださいませんか

EX. Would you mind turning off the radio?
ラジオを消してくださいませんか。
Rajio o keshite kudasaimasen ka?

mine[1] pron. **[possessive form of I]**
wa⌈tashi no 私の

NOTE: Various nouns meaning "I", such as *boku*, *watakushi*, and *ore* can be used instead of *watashi* depending on the speaker and the context.

EX. (**a**) That beer is mine.
そのビールは私のです。
Sono biiru wa watashi no desu.
(**b**) If Tom is using your dictionary, you can use mine.
トムさんがあなたの辞書を使っているのなら、私のを使ってもいいですよ。
Tomu-san ga anata no jisho o tsukatte iru no nara, watashi no o tsukatte mo ii desu yo.

mine[2] n. **[a deep hole or system of holes dug into the ground from which minerals are extracted]**
ko⌉ozan 鉱山 •c

EX. There was an accident at the mine.
鉱山で事故があった。
Koozan de jiko ga atta.

PHRASE: coal mine *tankoo* 炭鉱 **•c**, gold mine *kinzan* 金山 **•c**

mineral n. **[inorganic substances that occur naturally in the earth such as iron, uranium, and coal]**
ko⌉obutsu 鉱物 •c, mi⌉neraru ミネラル •f [inorganic substances such as calcium, iron, etc., necessary for healthy functioning of the human body]

EX. (**a**) Australia is rich in mineral resources.
オーストラリアは{鉱物/*ミネラル}資源が豊富だ。
*Oosutoraria wa {koobutsu/*mineraru}-shigen ga hoofu da.*
(**b**) Milk is a good source of minerals.
牛乳は{ミネラル/*鉱物}のいい供給源だ。
*Gyuunyuu wa {mineraru/*koobutsu} no ii kyookyuu-gen da.*

PHRASE: mineral water *mineraru-uootaa* ミネラルウオーター

M

minimum adj./n. **[the smallest possible number, amount, degree, etc.]**
sa⌈isho⌉o-gen no N 最小限のN •c [the smallest in amount] ↔ saidai-gen no N 最大限のN •c; sa⌈itei no N 最低のN •c [the lowest] ↔ saikoo no N 最高のN •c

EX. (**a**) She took only the minimum amount of money necessary with her.
彼女は{最小限/*最低}のお金しか持って行かなかった。
*Kanojo wa {saishoo-gen/*saitei} no o-kane shika motte ikanakatta.*
(**b**) She passed the exam with a minimum of effort.
彼女は{最小限/*最低}の努力で試験に通った。
*Kanojo wa {saishoo-gen/*saitei} no doryoku de shiken ni tootta.*
(**c**) He gets only the minimum wage.
彼は{最低/?最小限の}賃金しかもらっていない。
Kare wa {saitei-/?saishoo-gen no} chingin shika moratte inai.
(**d**) This candidate doesn't even satisfy the minimum requirements for this job.
この候補者はこの仕事に必要な{最低/?最小限の}条件も満たしていない。
Kono kooho-sha wa kono shigoto ni hitsuyoona {saitei-/?saishoo-gen no} jooken mo mitashite inai.

minister n. **[a person at the head of a particular governmental department or a member of the Christian clergy, esp. Protestant]**
1. da⌉ijin 大臣 •c [a person at the head of a particular governmental department]

EX. (**a**) Who is the new minister of foreign affairs?
新しい外務大臣はだれですか。
Atarashii gaimu-daijin wa dare desu ka.
(**b**) Shigeru Yoshida left behind many interesting anecdotes from his career as prime minister.
吉田茂は総理大臣として面白い逸話をたくさん残した。
Yoshida Shigeru wa soori-daijin to-shite omoshiroi itsuwa o takusan nokoshita.

2. bo⌈kushi 牧師 •c [a member of the Christian clergy, esp. Protestant] ⟪**clergyman, pastor**⟫

ministry n. **[a governmental department headed by a minister]**
sho⌉o 省 •c

EX. (**a**) He works for the Ministry of Education.
彼は文部省に勤めている。
Kare wa Monbu-shoo ni tsutomete iru.
(**b**) The Ministry of International Trade and Industry has played an important role in Japan's economic development.
通産省は日本の経済発展に重要な役目を果たしてきた。
Tsuusan-shoo wa Nihon no keizai-hatten ni juuyoona yakume o hatashite kita.

PHRASE: the Ministry of Finance *Ookura-shoo* 大蔵省 •**c**, the Ministry of Foreign Affairs *Gaimu-shoo* 外務省 •**c**, the Ministry of Agriculture, Forestry and Fisheries *Noorin-suisan-shoo* 農林水産省 •**c**, the Ministry of Posts and Telecommunications *Yuusei-shoo* 郵政省 •**c**

minor adj. **[lesser in size/number/importance than others]**
ka⌈ntanna 簡単な adj(*na*). **•c [of a tool/task/broblem, etc., requiring minimal effort to understand or use], cho⌉tto ちょっと** adv. **[for a short time or in a small quantity or to a small degree]**

EX. (**a**) He had a minor operation.
彼は簡単な手術を受けた。
Kare wa kantanna shujutsu o uketa.
(**b**) This is a good thesis. It needs only minor alterations.
これはいい論文だ。ちょっと直せばいいだけだ。
Kore wa ii ronbun da. Chotto naoseba ii dake da.

—— n. **[a person below the full legal age]**
mi-⌈seine⌉n-sha 未成年者 •c

EX. (**a**) You're not allowed to sell alcohol to minors.
未成年者に酒を売ってはいけない。
Mi-seinen-sha ni sake o utte wa ikenai.

(**b**) Minors under 18 are prohibited from working after midnight.
十八歳未満の未成年者は夜十二時以降働くことを禁止されている。
Juu-has-sai-miman no mi-seinen-sha wa yoru juu-ni-ji ikoo hataraku koto o kinshi-sarete iru.

minus prep. **[reduced by the stated quantity]**
ma⌈inasu マイナス **•f**

EX. Five minus two equals three.
5マイナス2は3だ。
Go mainasu ni wa san da.

minute n. **[any of the 60 parts that an hour is divided into]**
-{fun/pun} 〜分

NOTE: *Fun* and *pun* are used as follows: *ip-pun* "one minute," *ni-fun* "two minutes," *san-pun* "three minutes," *yon-pun* "four minutes," *go-fun* "five minutes," *rop-pun* "six minutes," *{nana/shichi}-fun* "seven minutes," *hap-pun* "eight minutes," *kyuu-fun* "nine minutes," *{jip/jup}-pun* "ten minutes."

EX. (**a**) The bus leaves every three minutes.
バスは三分置きに出る。
Basu wa san-pun-oki ni deru.
(**b**) It took me twenty minutes to find his phone number.
彼の電話番号を見つけるのに二十分かかった。
Kare no denwa-bangoo o mitsukeru no ni ni-jup-pun kakatta.
(**c**) Please come here at ten minutes to eleven.
十一時十分前にここへ来てください。
Juu-ichi-ji jup-pun-mae ni koko e kite kudasai.
(**d**) It's now fifteen minutes past three.
今、三時十五分です。
Ima, san-ji juu-go-fun desu.

miracle n. **[an action/event thought to be due to supernatural causes 《fig. "a wonderful unexpected event"》]**
ki⌈se⌉ki 奇跡 **•c**

EX. (**a**) It's a miracle that the kid wasn't killed in the accident.
子供が事故で死ななかったなんて奇跡だ。
Kodomo ga jiko de shinanakatta nante kiseki da.
(**b**) It'll take a miracle for my son to pass the entrance exam.
奇跡でも起こらない限り、息子は入学試験に通らないだろう。
Kiseki demo okoranai kagiri, musuko wa nyuugaku-shiken ni tooranai daroo.

mirror n.
ka⌈gami⌉ 鏡

EX. (**a**) She checked herself in the mirror to make sure the *obi* on her *kimono* was properly tied.
彼女は着物の帯がちゃんと結べたかどうか、鏡に映してみた。
Kanojo wa kimono no obi ga chanto musube-ta ka doo ka, kagami ni utsushite mita.
(**b**) I sometimes get confused in my sense of direction when I'm in a room full of mirrors.
鏡の多い部屋にいると方向が分からなくなることがある。
Kagami no ooi heya ni iru to hookoo ga wakaranaku naru koto ga aru.

PHRASE: rearview mirror *bakku-miraa* バックミラー **•f**

EX. I saw a police car in my rearview mirror.
バックミラーにパトカーが映っていた。
Bakku-miraa ni patokaa ga utsutte ita.

mischief n. **[playful behavior, esp. of children, that is intended to cause trouble for s.o.]**
i⌈tazura いたずら **[improper behavior, esp. of children, done in fun to kill time/energy]**

EX. (**a**) It's difficult to keep little boys out of mischief.
小さい男の子にいたずらをさせないようにするのは難しい。
Chiisai otoko-no-ko ni itazura o sasenai yooni suru no wa muzukashii.
(**b**) I often got into mischief when I was a kid.
私は子供の時、よくいたずらをした。
Watashi wa kodomo no toki, yoku itazura o shita.

M

miserable adj. **[causing or feeling great unhappiness or discomfort]**
mi⌉jimena 惨めな adj(*na*). **[so pitiful in condition as to be difficult to look at]** ((wretched)), **hi⌈sanna** 悲惨な adj(*na*). •c **[too painful or sad to observe]** ((wretched, tragic, pathetic)), **na⌈sake-na⌉i** 情けない adj(*i*). **[feeling unhappy and disgusted]** ((shameful, deplorable))

EX. (**a**) Many people lived in miserable conditions during the war.
戦争中はたくさんの人が{惨めな/悲惨な/?情けない}状況の中で生活していた。
Sensoo-chuu wa takusan no hito ga {mijimena/hisanna/?nasake-nai} jookyoo no naka de seikatsu-shite ita.
(**b**) Study hard now if you don't want to feel miserable afterwards.
後で{惨めな/情けない/*悲惨な}思いをしたくなかったら、一生懸命勉強しなさい。
*Ato de {mijimena/nasake-nai/*hisanna} omoi o shi-takunakattara, ishoo-kenmei benkyoo-shinasai.*
(**c**) I felt really miserable after the stupid quarrel I had with my husband.
主人とつまらないけんかをした後、私は本当に{惨めだった/情けなかった/*悲惨だった}。
*Shujin to tsumaranai kenka o shita ato, watashi wa hontoo ni {mijime datta/nasake-nakatta/*hisan datta}.*

misery n. **[a condition of great unhappiness]**
hi⌈san 悲惨 •c **[a condition of wretchedness]**, **fu⌈ko⌉o** 不幸 •c **[a condition of unhappiness]** ((unhappiness, misfortune))

EX. The life that pet dogs have to lead in downtown Tokyo is one of pure misery.
東京の都心の飼い犬の生活は{悲惨/不幸}としか言いようがない。
Tookyoo no toshin no kai-inu no seikatsu wa {hisan/fukoo} to shika ii-yoo ga nai.

miss vi./vt. **[to fail to hit, notice, find, meet, touch, hear, see, etc.]**
1. ⟨-o⟩ **ha⌈zureru** ⟨〜を⟩外れる ② **[to fail to hit s.t.]**

EX. The bullet missed the target.
弾丸は的を外れた。
Dangan wa mato o hazureta.

2. ⟨-ni⟩ **no⌈ri-okure⌉ru** ⟨〜に⟩乗り遅れる ② **[for s.o. to fail to catch a vehicle of public transportation]**

EX. (**a**) I got up late and missed the bus.
朝寝坊して、バスに乗り遅れた。
Asa-neboo-shite, basu ni nori-okureta.
(**b**) I almost missed the 9 o'clock train.
九時の列車にもう少しで乗り遅れるところだった。
Ku-ji no ressha ni moo sukoshi de nori-okureru tokoro datta.

3. ⟨-o⟩ **mi-⌈nogasu** ⟨〜を⟩見逃す ① **[for s.o. to fail to see s.t.]**

EX. I don't want to miss that movie.
あの映画は見逃したくない。
Ano eiga wa mi-nogashi-takunai.

4. ⟨-o⟩ **ki⌈ki-mora⌉su** ⟨〜を⟩聞き漏らす ① **[for s.o. to fail to hear s.t.]**

EX. I appear to have missed an important piece of information.
大事な情報を聞き漏らしたようだ。
Daijina joohoo o kiki-morashita yoo da.

— vt. **[for s.o./s.a. to feel/regret the absence/loss of s.o./s.t./s.a.]**
⟨-ga⟩ **na⌈tsukashi⌉i** ⟨〜が⟩なつかしい adj(*i*). **[for s.o. to feel nostalgia for s.t.]** ((good old)), **sa⌈bishi⌉i** 寂しい adj(*i*). **[for s.o./s.a. to feel lonely]**

NOTE: "*Natsukashi*" and "*sabishii*" are used with a first person subject in statements and with a second person subject in questions. It can be used with a third person subject if some form is attached which explicitly expresses the speaker's perception or judgment, such as "*sooda*" appears to be and "*rashii*" seems to be.

EX. (**a**) My son is now studying at a university in California. I miss him very much.
息子は今カリフォルニアの大学で勉強しています。あの子がいなくて、とても{寂しい/*なつかしい}です。
Musuko wa ima Kariforunia no daigaku de benkyoo-shite imasu. Ano

*ko ga inakute, totemo {sabishii/ *natsukashii} desu.*
(**b**) I miss my childhood friends.
幼なじみが{なつかしい/*寂しい}。
*Osana-najimi ga {natsukashii/*sabishii}.*
(**c**) I miss the friendly smile of our teacher, Miss Tanaka.
田中先生の暖かいほほえみが{なつかしい/*寂しい}。
*Tanaka-sensei no atatakai hohoemi ga {natsukashii/*sabishii}.*

Miss n. **[a title placed before the name of an unmarried woman/girl or before the name of a place to designate the young woman representing it in a contest or activity such as a beauty pageant]**

1. -san 〜さん [a suffix attached to the name of a person or the name of his/her occupation to indicate politeness] ⟪**Mr., Mrs.**⟫

EX. Miss Yoshimura is teaching English to the children.
吉村さんは子供たちに英語を教えている。
Yoshimura-san wa kodomo-tachi ni eigo o oshiete iru.

2. mi⌉su ミス •f [a title placed before the name of a place to designate the young woman representing it in a contest or activity such as a beauty pageant]

EX. If you're chosen to be Miss Japan, you get to travel all around the world.
ミス日本に選ばれると、世界じゅう旅行ができる。
Misu-Nippon ni eraba-reru to, sekai-juu ryokoo ga dekiru.

missile n.

mi⌈sa⌉iru ミサイル •f

EX. Two missiles were launched at the city.
その町に向けてミサイルが二発発射された。
Sono machi ni mukete misairu ga ni-hatsu hassha-sareta.

missing adj. **[lost, not in its usual place]**
na⌈kunatte iru (N) なくなっている(N) /⟨V *te iru* of *nakunaru* ① be gone/ ② [for s.t. to be gone or s.o. to be dead], nu⌈kete iru (N) 抜けている(N) /⟨V *te iru* of *nukeru* ② be left out/ [to be left out], yu⌈kue-fu⌉mei no N 行方不明のN [for s.o.'s whereabouts to be unknown] ⟪**unaccounted for**⟫

NOTE: When referring to a person, *nakunaru* or *nakunatte iru* is a euphemism meaning to die or be dead.

EX. (**a**) I wanted to borrow that book from the library, but it was missing.
図書館からその本を借りたかったけど、{{なくなって/*抜けて}いた}/*行方不明だった}。
*Tosho-kan kara sono hon o kari-takatta kedo, {{nakunatte/*nukete} ita}/*yukue-fumei datta}.*
(**b**) His name is missing from this list.
彼の名前がこのリストから{{抜けて/*なくなって}いる/*行方不明だ}。
*Kare no namae ga kono risuto kara {{nukete/*nakunatte} iru/*yukue-fumei da}.*
(**c**) Hundreds of people are missing due to the earthquake.
その地震で何百人もの人が{行方不明になって/*なくなって/*抜けて}いる。
*Sono jishin de nan-byaku-nin-mo no hito ga {yukue-fumei ni natte/ *nakunatte/*nukete} iru.*

NOTE: The subject of *yukue-fumei no* N can be something inanimate if it is something owned by the speaker or by someone in the speaker's in-group.

EX. Oh, no! My recipe book is missing!
あ、どうしよう。料理の本が{無くなってる/行方不明だ}わ。
A, doo shiyoo. Ryoori no hon ga {nakunatte-ru/yukue-fumei da} wa.

mission n. **[an important task for which a person is sent to a place ⟪fig. "the particular work for which one is destined in life," "a group of people sent abroad to carry out an official task"⟫]**

1. ni⌉nmu 任務 •c [one's duties] ⟪**task, function**⟫

EX. Their mission was to save the hostages.

M

彼らの任務は人質を救出することだった。
Kare-ra no ninmu wa hitojichi o kyuushutsu-suru koto datta.

2. shi⌉mei 使命 •c [the particular work for which one is destined in life]

EX. I feel that my mission in life is to work for children in developing countries.
発展途上国の子供のために働くことが私の使命だと思っている。
Hatten-tojoo-koku no kodomo no tame ni hataraku koto ga watashi no shimei da to omotte iru.

3. shi⌈setsu⌉-dan 使節団 •c [a group of people sent abroad to carry out an official task]

EX. He's been to the United States before as a member of the Japanese trade mission.
彼は以前日本貿易使節団のメンバーとしてアメリカへ行ったことがある。
Kare wa izen Nihon-booeki-shisetsu-dan no menbaa to-shite Amerika e itta koto ga aru.

missionary n.

se⌈nkyo⌉o-shi 宣教師 •c

EX. I learned English from a British missionary.
私はイギリス人の宣教師に英語を教わった。
Watashi wa Igirisu-jin no senkyoo-shi ni eigo o osowatta.

Mississippi

Mi⌈shishi⌉ppii ミシシッピー •f

mist n. **[a large mass of tiny drops of water in the air near ground level]**

ki⌈ri 霧 [very minute waterdrops floating near the surface of the earth] ((fog)), **ka⌈sumi かすみ [a mass of tiny drops of water in the air, occurring in the spring esp. around the bases of mountains and appearing in the distance like clouds]** ((haze)), **mo⌉ya もや [a mass of tiny drops of water in the air near ground level, not as thick as *kiri*]**

EX. A girl was standing in the mist.
女の子が{霧/かすみ/もや}の中に立っていた。
Onna-no-ko ga {kiri/kasumi/moya} no naka ni tatte ita.

mistake n. **[s.t. that is not correctly done, said, or thought]**

ma⌈chiga⌉i 間違い /⟨V*masu* of *machigau* ① err/ [an act/instance of doing s.t. incorrectly, usu. s.t. of relatively minor consequence such as an identification, calculation, producing an incorrect spelling or grammatical form, etc.] ((error)), **a⌈yamari⌉ あやまり /⟨V*masu* of *ayamaru* ① err/ [an act/instance of doing s.t. wrongly or an act/instance of apologizing for s.t. done wrongly]** ((error, slip, apology))

㊌ "apology"▷謝り, otherwise ▷誤り

EX. (**a**) It was a mistake to give him money.
彼にお金をやったのは{間違い/誤り}だった。
Kare ni o-kane o yatta no wa {machigai/ayamari} datta.
(**b**) She never admits her mistakes.
彼女は自分の{間違い/誤り}を認めようとしない。
Kanojo wa jibun no {machigai/ayamari} o mitomeyoo to shinai.
(**c**) There are several mistakes in this report.
このレポートには{間違い/誤り}がいくつかある。
Kono repooto ni wa {machigai/ayamari} ga ikutsu-ka aru.

PHRASE: by mistake *machigatte* 間違って, *ayamatte* 誤って

EX. I used salt instead of sugar by mistake.
私は{間違って/誤って}砂糖の代わりに塩を使ってしまった。
Watashi wa {machigatte/ayamatte} satoo no kawari ni shio o tsukatte shimatta.

PHRASE: make a mistake *machigau* 間違う ①

EX. I made a lot of mistakes on yesterday's exam.
きのうの試験でたくさん間違った。
Kinoo no shiken de takusan machigatta.

—— vt. **[for s.o./s.a. to have an incorrect idea about s.t./s.o.]**

⟨-o⟩ ma⌈chigae⌉ru ⟨〜を⟩間違える ② ((make a mistake, make an error, err, blunder)), ⟨-o⟩ go⌈kai-suru ⟨〜を⟩誤解する ③ •c [for s.o. to

understand incorrectly what s.o. says/ writes]

EX. (**a**) I mistook the time of the bus, and had to wait a whole hour for the next one to come.
私はバスの時間を{間違えて/?誤解して}、次のが来るまで一時間も待たなければいけなかった。
Watashi wa basu no jikan o {machigaete/?gokai-shite}, tsugi no ga kuru made ichi-jikan mo matanakereba ikenakatta.
(**b**) She has completely mistaken what I said.
彼女は私が言ったことを完全に{誤解して/*間違えて}いる。
*Kanojo wa watashi ga itta koto o kanzenni {gokai-shite/*machigaete} iru.*
(**c**) He mistook me for my twin brother.
彼はぼくを双子の{弟/兄}と{間違えた/*誤解した}。
*Kare wa boku o futa-go no {otooto/ani} to {machigaeta/*gokai-shita}.*

mistaken adj. **[having a wrong belief or an incorrect understanding about s.t.]**
ma⌈chiga⌉tta N 間違ったN /⟨Vinf. past of *machigau* ① make a mistake/ [different from the facts/truth], ma⌈chiga⌉tte iru (N) 間違っている(N) /⟨V *te iru* of *machigau* ① make a mistake/

EX. (**a**) You're mistaken in thinking that you can master Japanese in one year.
日本語を一年で習得できると思うなんて間違っている。
Nihon-go o ichi-nen de shuutoku-dekiru to omou nante machigatte iru.
(**b**) You don't have to listen to mistaken opinions.
{間違った/?間違っている}意見を聞く必要はない。
{Machigatta/?Machigatte iru} iken o kiku hitsuyoo wa nai.

misunderstand vi./vt. **[for s.o. to understand s.t. incorrectly]**
⟨-o⟩ go⌈kai-suru ⟨〜を⟩誤解する ③ •c [for s.o. to understand incorrectly what s.o. says/writes]

EX. (**a**) He misunderstood my kindness as romantic interest.
彼は私の好意を誤解して、私が彼に気があると思い込んでしまった。
Kare wa watashi no kooi o gokai-shite, watashi ga kare ni ki ga aru to omoi-konde shimatta.
(**b**) My boss seems to have misunderstood what I said.
上司はぼくの言ったことを誤解したようだ。
Jooshi wa boku no itta koto o gokai-shita yooda.

misunderstanding n. **[an incorrect understanding of s.t. or s.o.'s intentions]**
go⌈kai 誤解 •c

EX. (**a**) I think there's been some misunderstanding. I said I would lend you my computer, but I didn't say that I would give it to you.
ちょっと誤解があったようですね。私はコンピューターを貸してあげるとは言ったけど、あげるとは言いませんでしたよ。
Chotto gokai ga atta yoo desu ne. Watashi wa konpyuutaa o kashite ageru to wa itta kedo, ageru to wa iimasen deshita yo.
(**b**) We have to work harder to avoid misunderstandings stemming from language.
ことばから誤解が生じないように更に努力しなければならない。
Kotoba kara gokai ga shoojinai yooni sarani doryoku-shinakereba naranai.

mix vt./vi. **[to put two or more different things together and combine them so they are not separated]**
1. ⟨-o⟩ ma⌈ze⌉ru ⟨〜を⟩混ぜる ② [for s.o. to cause two or more objects to be combined] ((**mingle, blend**))

EX. (**a**) First you mix the vinegar, sugar and salt.
まず酢と砂糖と塩を混ぜてください。
Mazu su to satoo to shio o mazete kudasai.

M

(**b**) Don't mix these two kinds of bleach together.
この二つの漂白剤を混ぜないでください。
Kono futatsu no hyoohaku-zai o mazenaide kudasai.

2. ma⌈ji⌉ru 混じる ② [for two or more things to be blended together or for s.t. heterogeneous to be introduced into a substance] ⟪be mingled, be blended, join⟫, ma⌈za⌉ru 混ざる ① [for two or more things to be blended together or for s.t. heterogeneous to be introduced into a substance]

EX. (**a**) The dress she's wearing has a bit of red mixed in with the brown.
彼女の着ている茶色のドレスには赤が少し{混じって/混ざって}いる。
Kanojo no kite iru cha-iro no doresu ni wa aka ga sukoshi {majitte/mazatte} iru.
(**b**) Mixed in with his sorrow was a feeling of relief.
彼の悲しみにはほっとした気持ちが{混じって/混ざって}いた。
Kare no kanashi-mi ni wa hotto shita kimochi ga {majitte/mazatte} ita.
(**c**) Mix some thinly sliced cucumbers, finely chopped onions and a small can of corn. When they are mixed thoroughly, put them over a bowl of hot steamed rice.
きゅうりの薄切りとみじん切りの玉ねぎとかんづめのとうもろこしの小さいのを一かんよく混ぜてください。よく{混ざったら/*混じったら}、それを熱い御飯の入ったボールに入れてください。
*Kyuuri no usu-giri to mijin-giri no tamanegi to kanzume no toomorokoshi no chiisai no o hito-kan yoku mazete kudasai. Yoku {mazattara/*majittara}, sore o atsui gohan no haitta booru ni irete kudasai.*

PHRASE: mix up *machigaeru* 間違える ② ⟪make a mistake⟫

EX. He's bad with names. He even mixes up the names of his own children from time to time.
彼は人の名前を覚えるのが苦手だ。時には自分の子供の名前を間違えることさえある。
Kare wa hito no namae o oboeru no ga nigate da. Toki ni wa jibun no kodomo no namae o machigaeru koto sae aru.

NOTE: 交ぜる, 交じる and 交ざる can be used instead of 混ぜる, 混じる and 混ざる.

mixture n. **[s.t. made by mixing two or more things]**

1. ma⌈ze-awa⌉seta mono 混ぜ合わせたもの /⟨Vinf. past of *maze-awaseru* ② mix + *mono* thing/ [s.t. made by mixing two or more things]

EX. (**a**) This wine is a mixture of Japanese and Australian wines.
このワインは日本とオーストラリアのワインを混ぜ合わせたものです。
Kono wain wa Nihon to Oosutoraria no wain o maze-awaseta mono desu.
(**b**) When you have a cold, it's good to drink a mixture of hot *sake* and egg yolk.
風邪を引いたときは熱い酒と卵黄を混ぜ合わせたものを飲むといい。
Kaze o hiita toki wa atsui sake to ran'oo o maze-awaseta mono o nomu to ii.

2. i⌈ri-maji⌉tta N 入り混じったN /⟨Vinf. past of *iri-majiru* ① be mixed in with each other/ [a combination of things, feelings, or people of different kinds]

EX. The feelings I had when I attended my daughter's wedding were a mixture of pleasure and loneliness.
私は喜びと寂しさの入り混じった気持ちで娘の結婚式に出た。
Watashi wa yorokobi to sabishi-sa no iri-majitta kimochi de musume no kekkon-shiki ni deta.

NOTE: 混ぜ合わせる and 入り混じるcan also be represented as 交ぜ合わせる and 入り交じる, respectively.

moan n. **[a low mournful sound indicating pain or sorrow]**

u⌈meki-go⌉e うめき声 [a soft low sound emitted out of pain] ⟪groan⟫

EX. I couldn't sleep at all because of the moans of my wounded friend.

私はけがをした友達のうめき声で全然寝られなかった。
Watashi wa kega o shita tomodachi no umeki-goe de zenzen ne-rarenakatta.

—— vi. **[for s.o. to emit a low sound out of pain]**
u⌈me⌉ku うめく ① **⟪groan⟫**

EX. He moaned all night in pain.
彼は痛みで一晩中うめいていた。
Kare wa ita-mi de hito-ban-juu umeite ita.

mode n. **[a way of doing s.t. or a currently popular fashion ⟨fml⟩]**
yo⌈oshiki 様式 **•c [a way of doing s.t. following a form that has become standard over time]⟪style⟫, mo⌉odo** モード **•f [fashion]**

EX. (**a**) *Tatami* doesn't match the new Japanese mode of living.
畳は日本人の新しい生活{様式/*モード}に合わない。
*Tatami wa Nihon-jin no atarashii seikatsu-{yooshiki/*moodo} ni awanai.*
(**b**) We may have to change our mode of thinking in this age of computers.
このコンピューター時代に我々は思考{様式/*モード}を変えなければいけないかもしれない。
*Kono konpyuutaa-jidai ni ware-ware wa shikoo-{yooshiki/*moodo} o kaenakereba ikenai kamoshirenai.*
(**c**) Are those leather pants the new fashion mode this year?
あの皮のパンツは今年のニュー{モード/*様式}ですか。
*Ano kawa no pantsu wa kotoshi no nyuu-{moodo/*yooshiki} desu ka.*

model n. **[a small-sized copy of an actual or designed object; a person employed to display clothes by wearing them or to pose for a photographer or painter; a person or thing considered excellent for its kind and worthy of being imitated]**
1. mo⌈kei 模型 **•c [a small-sized copy of s.t. to show what it looks like or how it works]**

EX. I bought a model airplane for my son.
私は息子に模型飛行機を買ってやった。
Watashi wa musuko ni mokei-hikoo-ki o katte yatta.

2. mo⌉deru モデル **•f [a person employed to display clothes by wearing them or to pose for a painter or photographer]**

EX. (**a**) She is too short to be a fashion model.
彼女はファッションモデルになるには背が低過ぎる。
Kanojo wa fasshon-moderu ni naru ni wa se ga hiku-sugiru.
(**b**) I know the person who was the model for that painting.
私はあの絵のモデルを知っている。
Watashi wa ano e no moderu o shitte iru.

3. te⌈ho⌉n 手本 **[a person or thing** (**esp. of manual art**) **considered excellent for its kind and worthy of being imitated] ⟪a good example⟫, mo⌈han** 模範 **•c [a person or thing** (**such as a solution to a problem**) **that is a perfect example of its kind to be followed or imitated], mo⌈han-tekina** 模範的な adj(*na*). **•c**

EX. (**a**) She is a model student.
彼女は{{模範/*手本}生/模範的な学生}だ。
*Kanojo wa {{mohan/*tehon}-sei/mohan-tekina gakusei} da.*
(**b**) This country is looked to as a model by many other developing countries.
この国は他の多くの発展途上国から{模範/手本}と見なされている。
Kono kuni wa ta no ooku no hatten-tojoo-koku kara {mohan/tehon} to minasa-rete iru.

moderate adj. **[within reasonable limits or not extreme in size, force, etc.]**
1. chu⌈u-gurai no N 中ぐらいのN **[at an intermediate point/level on a range of size, force, etc.]**

EX. We're looking for a house with a yard of moderate size.
中ぐらいの大きさの庭が付いた家が欲しい。
Chuu-gurai no ooki-sa no niwa ga tsuita uchi ga hoshii.

M

2. te⌉kido no N 適度のN •c **[not excessive but of the desired degree]**

EX. (**a**) Moderate drinking is not harmful.
適度の酒は害にはならない。
Tekido no sake wa gai ni wa naranai.
(**b**) Don't drive too fast. Keep your speed at a moderate level in the city.
スピードを出しすぎてはいけません。市内では適度のスピードで走りなさい。
Supiido o dashi-sugite wa ikemasen. Shinai de wa tekido no supiido de hashirinasai.

3. o⌈nkenna 穏健な adj(*na*). •c **[avoiding ideas that are very different from those of most people]** ⟪**temperate, sound**⟫

EX. Politicians with moderate opinions are often not very popular.
穏健な意見の政治家はあまり人気がないことが多い。
Onkenna iken no seiji-ka wa amari ninki ga nai koto ga ooi.

modern adj. **[of the present or recent times]**

1. ge⌉ndai no N 現代のN •c **[of the present time]** ⟪**the present day, today**⟫

EX. (**a**) I don't like modern music very much.
私は現代音楽はあまり好きじゃない。
Watashi wa gendai-ongaku wa amari suki janai.
(**b**) Our everyday life greatly benefits from modern technology.
我々の毎日の生活は大いに現代の科学技術の恩恵を受けている。
Ware-ware no mai-nichi no seikatsu wa ooini gendai no kagaku-gijutsu no onkei o ukete iru.

2. ki⌉ndai no N 近代のN •c **[of recent times]**, ki⌈ndai-tekina 近代的な adj(*na*). •c **[characteristic of recent times]**

EX. (**a**) The history of modern Japan dates from 1868.
日本の近代史は1868年から始まる。
Nihon no kindai-shi wa sen-hap-pyaku-roku-juu-hachi-nen kara hajimaru.
(**b**) There are many modern buildings on this street.
この通りには{近代的な/*近代の}ビルが多い。
*Kono toori ni wa {kindai-tekina/ *kindai no} biru ga ooi.*

modernization n. **[an act/instance of modernizing]**
ki⌈ndai-ka 近代化 •c

EX. The modernization of Japan progressed rapidly in the latter half of the nineteenth century.
日本の近代化は十九世紀の後半に急速に進んだ。
Nihon no kindai-ka wa juu-kyuu-seiki no koohan ni kyuusokuni susunda.

modernize vt. **[for s.o. to make s.t. modern or suitable to modern times]**
⟨-o⟩ ki⌈ndai-ka-suru ⟨〜を⟩近代化する ③ •c

EX. This library needs to be modernized.
この図書館は近代化する必要がある。
Kono tosho-kan wa kindai-ka-suru hitsuyoo ga aru.

modest adj. **[having or expressing a moderate opinion of one's own abilities, achievements, etc.]**
hi⌈kae-mena 控え目な adj(*na*). **[behaving in a subdued manner so as not to attract the attention of others]** ⟪**reserved**⟫, ke⌉nkyona 謙虚な adj(*na*). •c **[underrating oneself, one's achievements, etc.]** ⟪**humble**⟫

EX. Her modest way of conducting herself has been well received by her colleagues.
彼女の{控え目な/謙虚な}ふるまいは同僚に好意的に受けとめられている。
Kanojo no {hikae-mena/kenkyona} furumai wa dooryoo ni kooi-tekini uke-tome-rarete iru.

modesty n. **[the quality of being modest]**
e⌈nryo 遠慮 •c **[the act of holding oneself back in speech or action out of deference to or consideration of others]** ⟪**hesitation, reserve**⟫

EX. Her modesty prevented Takako from demanding the salary she deserved.
孝子は遠慮して、もらって当然の給料を要求しなかった。
Takako wa enryo-shite, moratte toozen no kyuuryoo o yookyuu-shinakatta.

moisture n. **[the presense of water or other liquid in small quantities causing dampness]**
{shiˈkke/shiˈkki} 湿気 •c [water contained in the air] ⟪humidity⟫

EX. (**a**) During the rainy season the air contains large amounts of moisture.
梅雨時の空気は湿気をたくさん含んでいる。
Tsuyu-doki no kuuki wa {shikke/shikki} o takusan fukunde iru.
(**b**) Keep the medicine in a place with little moisture.
薬はなるべく湿気の少ないところに保管してください。
Kusuri wa narubeku {shikke/shikki} no sukunai tokoro ni hokan-shite kudasai.

mold[1] n. **[a soft green growth caused by fungi that occurs on bread, cheese, etc., as time passes]**
kaˈbi かび [a soft, white-green fungus that grows on plants, food, leather, etc., under warm and damp conditions] ⟪mildew⟫

EX. (**a**) Mold started to grow on the cheese that had been left in the refrigerator.
冷蔵庫の中に残っていたチーズにかびが生え始めた。
Reizoo-ko no naka ni nokotte ita chiizu ni kabi ga hae-hajimeta.
(**b**) You shouldn't eat food with mold on it as it can cause cancer.
かびでがんになることがあるから、かびの生えた物は食べないほうがいい。
Kabi de gan ni naru koto ga aru kara, kabi no haeta mono wa tabenai hoo ga ii.

mold[2] n. **[a hollow container of a particular shape used to make s.t. into that shape]**
kaˈtaˀ 型 [an outward form (to be followed) ⟪fig. "mold"⟫] ⟪type, pattern, form⟫

EX. She poured the jello into a doughnut-shaped mold.
彼女はドーナツの形をした型にゼリーを流し込んだ。
Kanojo wa doonatsu no katachi o shita kata ni zerii o nagashi-konda.

mole[1] n. **[a small furry animal with small eyes and ears that mainly lives underground]**
moˈgura もぐら

mole[2] n. **[a small, dark-colored, slightly raised mark on the human skin]**
hoˈkuro ほくろ

EX. She has a small mole on her chin.
彼女はあごに小さいほくろがある。
Kanojo wa ago ni chiisai hokuro ga aru.

moment n. **[a point of time]**
shuˈnkan 瞬間 •c [a very brief period of time] ⟪second, instant⟫

EX. (**a**) The cameraman caught the critical moment of the accident.
カメラマンは事故の決定的な瞬間を捕えた。
Kamera-man wa jiko no kettei-tekina shunkan o toraeta.
(**b**) The moment he read the letter his face turned pale.
その手紙を読んだ瞬間、彼の顔は青くなった。
Sono tegami o yonda shunkan, kare no kao wa aoku natta.

NOTE: The English word "moment" in example (b) is being used as a conjunction. *Shunkan* in Japanese can also be used in this way, in which case it occurs in a construction of form Vinf. past + *shunkan.*

Monday n.
geˈtsuyoˀo(-bi) 月曜(日) •c

EX. (**a**) Let's meet next Monday.
来週の月曜に会いましょう。
Raishuu no getsuyoo ni aimashoo.
(**b**) We have a *kanji* quiz every Monday.
毎週月曜日に漢字の小テストがあります。
Mai-shuu getsuyoo-bi ni kanji no shoo-tesuto ga arimasu.

money n. **[coins or banknotes used as a medium of exchange]**
kaˈne 金 [a metal; coins or banknotes used as a medium of exchange] ⟪metal⟫, kaˀhei 貨幣 •c [coins or banknotes used as a

M

medium of exchange ⟨fml⟩] ⟪currency⟫

EX. (**a**) Do you have enough money for the trip?
旅行のために十分{お金/*貨幣}がありますか。
*Ryokoo no tame ni juubun {o-kane/ *kahei} ga arimasu ka.*
(**b**) I can't go see the movie, since I don't have the money.
{お金/*貨幣}がないから、映画を見に行けません。
*{O-kane/*Kahei} ga nai kara, eiga o mi ni ike-masen.*
(**c**) If you were given all the money you wanted, what would you do with it?
もし{お金/*貨幣}が欲しいだけあったら、何に使いますか。
*Moshi {o-kane/*kahei} ga hoshii dake attara, nani ni tsukaimasu ka.*
(**d**) He is a collector of old money.
彼は古い{貨幣/お金}の収集家です。
Kare wa furui {kahei/o-kane} no shuushuu-ka desu.

NOTE: *Kane* usually takes the prefix *o-* to avoid any connotation of vulgarity. This is often done with nouns referring to common items of daily life, such as *o-sakana, o-misoshiru, o-niku*, etc., and does not necessarily imply that the item in question belongs to someone other than the speaker, as is the case with other uses of the *o-* prefix.

monkey n.
sa˥ru 猿

EX. Even monkeys sometimes fall from trees.
猿も木から落ちる。
Saru mo ki kara ochiru.

monster n. **[a big, ugly imaginary creature or s.o./s.t./s.a. like it]**
1. ka˹ibutsu 怪物 •c [a big, ugly imaginary creature ⟪fig. "a person of abnormal ability"⟫] ⟪goblin, sphinx⟫

EX. I like monster movies.
僕は怪物の映画が好きだ。
Boku wa kaibutsu no eiga ga suki da.

2. ki˹kei no {do˹obutsu/sho˹ku˥butsu} 奇形の{動物/植物} •c [an animal/plant of abnormal form/shape/size]

month n. **[any of the twelve periods into which the year is divided or a period of time equivalent in duration to one of these]**
tsu˹ki˥ 月 [the largest natural satellite of the earth or any of the twelve periods into which the year is divided or a period of time having a duration of 28 to 31 days] ⟪moon⟫, -kagetsu ～か月 [a counter for a period of time equivalent to one of the twelve periods into which the year is divided]

EX. (**a**) January is the coldest month of the year here.
ここでは一年で一番寒い月は一月です。
Koko de wa ichi-nen de ichiban samui tsuki wa ichi-gatsu desu.
(**b**) I studied Japanese for 3 months.
私は日本語を{三か月/三月}勉強しました。
Watashi wa Nihon-go o {san-kagetsu/ mi-tsuki} benkyoo-shimashita.

NOTE: When *tsuki* is used in the sense of a duration of time of about 30 days, the number preceding it can only be up to 3, i.e., *hito, futa, mi.* Beyond 3, the counter *-kagetsu* must be used.

PHRASE: every month *mai-{tsuki/getsu}* 毎月, last month *sengetsu* 先月 **•c**, next month *raigetsu* 来月 **•c**, this month *kongetsu* 今月 **•c**

monthly adj. **[occurring once a month]**
tsu˹ki˥ i˹chi-do˥ no N 月一度のN, ma˹i-tsuki no N 毎月のN [occurring every month]

EX. Our monthly committee meeting always takes place on the first Monday of the month.
{月一度/毎月}の委員会は第一月曜日にあります。
{Tsuki ichi-do/Mai-tsuki} no iin-kai wa dai-ichi getsuyoo-bi ni arimasu.

PHRASE: monthly magazine *gekkan-shi* 月刊誌 **•c**

mood n. **[a temporary state of mind (evoked by an artistic work)]**
1. ki˥bun 気分 •c [a temporary state of mind or physical feeling] ⟪feeling, sentiment, state of mind⟫, ki˹gen 機嫌 •c [a temporary state of mind as manifested

in one's outward expression or attitude] **((humor))**

EX. (**a**) The boss seems to be in a good mood today.
ボスは今日は{機嫌/?気分}がいいようだ。
Bosu wa kyoo wa {kigen/?kibun} ga ii yooda.
(**b**) I'm tired and not in the mood to dine out today.
今日は疲れて外で食事をする{気分/*機嫌}じゃない。
*Kyoo wa tsukarete soto de shokuji o suru {kibun/*kigen} janai.*

2. fu⌈n'i⌉ki 雰囲気 **•c [a temporary state of mind evoked by an artistic work or an environment] ((atmosphere))**

EX. I like the mood of this coffee house.
私はこの喫茶店の雰囲気が好きだ。
Watashi wa kono kissa-ten no fun'iki ga suki da.

moon n. **[the largest natural satellite of the earth]**

tsu⌈ki⌉ 月 **[the largest natural satellite of the earth or any of the twelve periods into which the year is divided or a period of time having a duration of 28 to 31 days] ((month))**

EX. (**a**) The moon came out.
月が出た。
Tsuki ga deta.
(**b**) I like to watch the moon.
私は月を眺めるのが好きだ。
Watashi wa tsuki o nagameru no ga suki da.

moonlight n.

tsu⌈ki no hikari⌉ 月の光, **ge⌈kkoo** 月光 **•c**

EX. Which do you like better, Debussy's *Claire de Lune* or Beethoven's *Moonlight Sonata*?
ドビュッシーの「月の光」とベートーベンの「月光の曲」と、どちらがお好きですか。
Dobyusshii no 'Tsuki no hikari' to Beetooben no 'Gekkoo no kyoku' to, dochira ga o-suki desu ka.

more adj. **[the comparative form of "many/ much"]**

mo⌉tto もっと adv. **[to a greater degree in quantity/quality] ((further, longer))**

EX. (**a**) Would you care for some more coffee?
コーヒー、もっといかがですか。
Koohii, motto ikaga desu ka.
(**b**) Please add some more sugar to the tea.
紅茶にもっと砂糖を入れてください。
Koocha ni motto satoo o irete kudasai.
(**c**) Please have some more to eat.
もっと食べてください。
Motto tabete kudasai.
(**d**) Tonight I have to study my Japanese some more.
今晩日本語をもっと勉強しなければなりません。
Konban Nihon-go o motto benkyoo-shinakereba narimasen.

PHRASE: once more *moo ichi-do* もう一度, two more days *moo futsuka* もう二日

moreover adv. **[in addition to what has been said]**

(shi) so⌈re ni (し)それに conj. **[in addition to what has been mentioned in the preceding context] ((in addition to that, what is more, besides))**, **(shi) so⌈no ue** (し)その上 conj. **[on top of that] ((on top of that, what is more, besides))**

EX. (**a**) Nancy is bright, and moreover, she's beautiful.
ナンシーは頭もいい{し、/。}{その上/それに}、美人だ。
Nanshii wa atama mo ii {shi,/.} {sono ue/sore ni}, bijin da.
(**b**) I'm busy this weekend; moreover, I don't have the money to go on the trip.
僕は今週の週末は忙しい{し、/。}{それに/??その上}お金もないから、旅行には行けません。
Boku wa konshuu no shuumatsu wa isogashii {shi,/.} {sore ni/??sono ue} o-kane mo nai kara, ryokoo ni wa ike-masen.

morning n. **[the early part of the day beginning at sunrise (and extending until noon)]**

a⌉sa 朝 n./adv.

M

EX. (**a**) About what time do you get up in the morning?
朝何時ごろ起きますか。
Asa nan-ji-goro okimasu ka.
(**b**) For me morning is the worst time of the day.
私には朝が一日のうちで最低の時だ。
Watashi ni wa asa ga ichi-nichi no uchi de saitei no toki da.

PHRASE: from morning till night *asa kara ban made* 朝から晩まで

EX. I work from morning till night.
私は朝から晩まで働きます。
Watashi wa asa kara ban made hatarakimasu.

PHRASE: this morning *kesa* 今朝

EX. What time did you get up this morning?
今朝何時に起きましたか。
Kesa nan-ji ni okimashita ka.

NOTE: Just like English "this morning," Japanese *kesa* does not take a particle, so it is incorrect to say **kesa ni*. In general, the particle *ni* cannot be used with expressions of time that do not include a numerical figure, as in the following: **ashita ni*, **kyoo ni*, **ototoi ni*, etc. Days of the week ending in *-yoobi* are an exception to this and can be followed by *ni*.

Moscow n.
Mo⌈sukuwa モスクワ •f

moss n.
ko⌈ke⌉ こけ

EX. A rolling stone gathers no moss.
転石こけをむさず。
Tenseki koke o musazu.

NOTE: In England and Japan, the above proverb carries a negative connotation, meaning that if one changes jobs too often, one cannot save money. But in the U.S., the same proverb may carry a positive connotation, meaning that a person who is always on the go does not become hampered by undesirable burdens.

most adj. **[the superlative form of "many/much"]**
1. i⌈chiban takusa⌉n no N 一番たくさんのN [greatest in amount/number]

EX. Do you know who has the most money of anyone in the world?
世界で一番たくさんのお金を持っているのはだれなのか知っていますか。
Sekai de ichiban takusan no o-kane o motte iru no wa dare na no ka shitte imasu ka.

2. ta⌈itei no N 大抵のN [the greatest majority of] 《general, usual》, ho⌈to⌉ndo no N ほとんどのN [virtually all of] 《general, usual》

EX. (**a**) Most children like eggs.
{大抵/ほとんど}の子供は卵が好きだ。
{Taitei/Hotondo} no kodomo wa tamago ga suki da.
(**b**) Most people in this town go to church on Sundays.
この町の{大抵/ほとんど}の人は日曜日に教会に行く。
Kono machi no {taitei/hotondo} no hito wa nichiyoo-bi ni kyookai ni iku.

— adv. **[to the greatest extent in quantity/quality/intensity]**
i⌈chiban 一番 •c [number 1 《fig. "the marker of the superlative degree"》]

EX. (**a**) John is the student who studies the most in this class.
ジョンがこのクラスで一番勉強する学生だ。
Jon ga kono kurasu de ichiban benkyoo-suru gakusei da.
(**b**) Among my friends, Taro drinks the most.
友達の中では太郎が一番酒を飲む。
Tomodachi no naka de wa Taroo ga ichiban sake o nomu.

— n. **[the greatest quantity/quality/intensity]**
da⌈i-bu⌉bun 大部分 •c [the greater part of s.t./s.o./s.a.]

EX. Most of the wines in this store are imported from Australia.
この店のワインの大部分はオーストラリアから輸入されたものです。
Kono mise no wain no dai-bubun wa Oosutoraria kara yunyuu-sareta mono desu.

mostly adv. **[for the most part]**
ta⌈itei 大抵 [in the great majority of cases] **⟪usually, generally⟫, o⌉moni 主に [for the most part] ⟪mainly, generally⟫, da⌈i-bu⌉bun wa 大部分は** n.+prt. •c **[for the majority of] ⟪largely, in large part⟫**

EX. (**a**) I spend my weekends mostly reading books.
週末は{大抵/主に/*大部分は}本を読んで過ごします。
*Shuumatsu wa {taitei/omoni/*dai-bubun wa} hon o yonde sugoshimasu.*
(**b**) The students of this high school mostly go to college after graduation.
ここの高校生は卒業をすると、{大抵/大部分は/主に}大学へ進みます。
Koko no kookoo-sei wa sotsugyoo-suru to, {taitei/dai-bubun wa/omoni} daigaku e susumimasu.

motel n.
mo⌉oteru モーテル •f

mother n. **[a female parent ⟪fig. "s.o. like a mother"⟫]**
ha⌉ha 母 [a humble form used to refer to one's own female parent when talking to s.o. outside one's family], o-⌈ka⌉a-san お母さん [an exalting form used to refer to s.o. else's female parent or to directly address one's own female parent or to refer to one's own female parent when talking with other family members], o-⌈ka⌉a-sama お母様 ⟨fml⟩, **ha⌈ha-oya 母親 [a neutral form used to refer to a female parent with no implication of exaltation/humility or to one's own female parent], o-⌈fukuro お袋 [one's own female parent** ⟨s⟩**]**

NOTE: *O-kaa-sama* is a very polite form of *o-kaa-san. O-fukuro* is an informal word used by male speakers in talking about their mother to others.

EX. (**a**) My mother is 91 and still healthy.
{母/お袋/母親/*お母さん/*お母様}は九十一で、まだ元気です。
*{Haha/O-fukuro/Haha-oya/*O-kaa-san/*O-kaa-sama} wa kyuu-juu-ichi de, mada genki desu.*
(**b**) Mother, are you going shopping?
{お母さん、買い物に行くの。/お母様、買い物にいらっしゃるの。}
{O-kaa-san, kai-mono ni iku no./O-kaa-sama, kai-mono ni irassharu no.}
(**c**) How old is your mother?
{お母さん/お母様/*母/*お袋/*母親}はおいくつですか。
*{O-kaa-san/O-kaa-sama/*Haha/*O-fukuro/*Haha-oya} wa o-ikutsu desu ka.*
(**d**) There is a growing number of unwed mothers these days.
このごろ未婚の{母親/母/?お母さん/*お母様/*お袋}が増えている。
*Kono goro mikon no {haha-oya/haha/?o-kaa-san/*o-kaa-sama/*o-fukuro} ga fuete iru.*

motion n. **[the act of changing place/position or a manner doing so ⟪fig. "formal proposal"⟫]**
1. u⌈goki⌉ 動き /⟨V*masu* of *ugoku* ① move/ ⟪movement, trend, drift⟫, u⌈ndoo 運動 •c **[an act/instance of changing one's location/position with the passage of time or the act of moving one's body to develop it and maintain good health or the act of aggressively and systematically approaching various people/institutions in order to achieve an objective] ⟪movement, exercise, campaign, drive, crusade⟫, ka⌈tsudoo 活動** •c **[active movement] ⟪activity, action, operation, working⟫, u⌈nkoo 運行** •c **[the regular progression of trains/celestial bodies along a set course] ⟪revolution, movement⟫**

EX. (**a**) As you grow older, your motions become slower.
年を取ると、{動き/活動/*運行/*運動}が鈍くなる。
*Toshi o toru to, {ugoki/katsudoo/*unkoo/*undoo} ga nibuku naru.*
(**b**) The motion of the pendulum was recorded by a high-speed camera.
振り子の{運動/動き/*活動/*運行}を高速度カメラで撮った。
*Furiko no {undoo/ugoki/*katsudoo/*unkoo} o koosokudo-kamera de totta.*
(**c**) If the motion of the heavenly bodies

M

were to become irregular, the earth would be destroyed.
天体の{運行/??動き/*活動/*運動}が不規則になったら、地球は滅びるだろう。
*Tentai no {unkoo/??ugoki/*katsudoo/*undoo} ga fu-kisoku ni nattara, chikyuu wa horobiru daroo.*

motor n. **[a machine that provides power to a vehicle, boat, or other device with moving parts]**
ha⌈tsudo⌉o-ki 発動機 •c, mo⌉otaa モーター •f

motorcycle n.
mo⌈otaa-sa⌉ikuru モーターサイクル •f, ba⌉iku バイク •f, o⌈oto⌉bai オートバイ •f
NOTE: *Baiku* is used in Japanese to mean "motorbike," not bicycle. *Ootobai* (auto-bike) is a word which was coined in Japan.
EX. Young people like to ride motorcycles.
若い人は{モーターサイクル/バイク/オートバイ}に乗るのが好きだ。
Wakai hito wa {mootaa-saikuru/baiku/ootobai} ni noru no ga suki da.

mountain n. **[a landmass that rises conspicuously above its surroundings 《fig. "a large heap"》]**
ya⌈ma⌉ 山 [a landmass that rises conspicuously above its surroundings 《fig. "a large heap," "a counter for a pile of merchandise"》], -san 〜山 •c [a suffix that is attached to the name of such a landmass] 《Mt.》

yama

EX. (**a**) This summer I intend to climb Mt. Fuji.
今年の夏、富士山に登るつもりです。
Kotoshi no natsu, Fuji-san ni noboru tsumori desu.
(**b**) Mt. Fuji is the highest mountain in Japan.
富士山は日本で一番高い山です。
Fuji-san wa Nihon de ichiban takai yama desu.

mourn vt. **[for s.o. to feel or express sorrow for a deceased person or s.t. which has been lost]**
⟨-o⟩ ka⌈nashi⌉mu ⟨〜を⟩悲しむ ① [for s.o. to feel or express sorrow for s.t.] 《grieve, sorrow, deplore, lament》 ↔ ⟨-o⟩ yorokobu ⟨〜を⟩喜ぶ ①
EX. The people of the land mourned the death of their Emperor.
国民は天皇陛下の死を悲しんだ。
Kokumin wa tennoo-heika no shi o kanashinda.

mouse n. **[a small, furry, long-tailed animal commonly found in fields and in human residences or a device resembling this with which to operate a computer]**
ha⌈tsuka-ne⌉zumi はつかねずみ, ne⌈zumi ねずみ 《rat》, ma⌉usu マウス •f [a device resembling this animal with which to operate a computer]

mouth n. **[the opening in the face of humans and animals through which food and liquid is taken into the body 《fig. "opening in s.t.," "the place where a river enters the sea"》]**
ku⌈chi 口 [the opening in the face of humans and animals through which food and liquid is taken into the body 《fig. "entrance," "opening of s.t.," "job position," "beginning"》], -koo 〜口 •c [an opening in s.t.]
EX. (**a**) Open your mouth wide, please.
口を大きく開けて下さい。
Kuchi o ookiku akete kudasai.
(**b**) I like to fish at the mouth of the river.
{河口/*川の口}で釣りをするのが好きだ。
*{Kakoo/*Kawa no kuchi} de tsuri o suru no ga suki da.*

move vi. **[to change in location or position]**
u⌈go⌉ku 動く ① [to change in location or position 《fig. "shake," "be affected," "change," "be transferred"》] 《stir, shift, swing, go, work, be moved, vary, be transferred》, u⌈tsu⌉ru うつる ① [to change to another place or condition 《fig. "be reflected," "be infected"》] 《remove, shift, be reflected》, hi⌈kko⌉su 引っ越す ① [for s.o. to go to another place to live], yu⌈reru 揺れる ② [for an object/mind to move up

M

and down or from side to side 《fig. "be disturbed"》] ((shake, tremble))
㊥ "be reflected"▷映る, "be taken in a picture/film"▷写る, otherwise ▷移る

EX. (**a**) When he talks his hands move a lot.
彼が話す時、手がよく{動く/?揺れる/*移る/*引っ越す}。
*Kare ga hanasu toki, te ga yoku {ugoku/?yureru/*utsuru/*hikkosu}.*
(**b**) I was so weak with hunger that I couldn't even move.
空腹で体が弱って{動く/*揺れる/*移る/*引っ越す}こともできなかった。
*Kuufuku de karada ga yowatte {ugoku/*yureru/*utsuru/*hikkosu} koto mo dekinakatta.*
(**c**) When are you moving into your new house?
いつ新しい家に{移ります/引っ越します/*揺れます/*動きます}か。
*Itsu atarashii ie ni {utsurimasu/hikkoshimasu/*yuremasu/*ugokimasu} ka.*
(**d**) The tops of the trees moved gently back and forth in the breeze.
木々のこずえがそよ風に優しく{揺れて/?動いて/*引っ越して/*移って}いた。
*Ki-gi no kozue ga soyo-kaze ni yasashiku {yurete/?ugoite/*hikkoshite/*utsutte} ita.*

—— vt. **[to cause s.o./s.t./s.a. to change in location or position]**
⟨-o⟩ u⌈goka⌉su ⟨～を⟩動かす /⟨the shorter causative of *ugoku* ① move/ ① ((stir, set in motion, touch, mobilize)), ⟨-o⟩ {⟨-ni⟩/⟨-e⟩} u⌈tsu⌉su ⟨～を⟩{⟨～に⟩/⟨～へ⟩}うつす ① [to cause s.o./s.t./s.a. to change to a different location or into a different condition 《fig. "copy," "reflect" "infect" "take a picture"》] ((transfer, shift, divert, copy, photograph)), ⟨-o⟩ {⟨-ni⟩/⟨-e⟩} i⌈doo-suru ⟨～を⟩{⟨～に⟩/⟨～へ⟩}移動する ③ •c [for s.o. to (cause s.t. to) change in location from one place to another] ((transfer))

NOTE: Unlike other short causatives, *ugokasu* does not have a longer causative version. *Ugokaseru* means not "to cause s.o./s.a./s.t. to move" but "can move s.t./s.o./s.a."
㊥ "photograph"▷写す, "reflect"▷映す, otherwise ▷移す

EX. Let's move this desk into another room.
この机を別の部屋に{動かしましょう/移しましょう/移動しましょう}。
Kono tsukue o betsu no heya ni {ugokashimashoo/utsushimashoo/idoo-shimashoo}.

movement n. **[an act/instance of moving 《fig. "principal division of a musical work," "campaign"》]**
1. u⌈goki⌉ 動き /⟨V*masu* of *ugoku* ① move/ ((motion, activity)), u⌈ndoo 運動 •c [an act/instance of changing one's location/position with the passage of time or the act of moving one's body to develop it and maintain good health or the act of aggressively and systematically approaching various people/institutions in order to achieve an objective] ((motion, exercise, campaign, drive, crusade)), u⌈nkoo 運行 •c [the regular progression of trains/celestial bodies along a set course]

EX. (**a**) As you grow older your bodily movements become slower.
年を取るにつれて、体の{動き/?運動/*運行}が鈍くなる。
*Toshi o toru ni tsurete, karada no {ugoki/?undoo/*unkoo} ga nibuku naru.*
(**b**) We can follow the movement of the satellite at night by telescope.
夜、人工衛星の{運行/動き/*運動}を望遠鏡で見ることが出来る。
*Yoru, jinkoo-eisei no {unkoo/ugoki/*undoo} o booen-kyoo de miru koto ga dekiru.*
(**c**) He's involved in the movement against nuclear weapons.
彼は反核{運動/*動き/*運行}に関わっている。
*Kare wa hankaku-{undoo/*ugoki/*unkoo} ni kakawatte iru.*

2. he⌈ndoo 変動 •c [the changing of a condition or situation] ((change, fluctuation))

M

EX. I can't keep up on a daily basis with movements in the stock market.
毎日の株価の変動についていけない。
Mai-nichi no kabu-ka no hendoo ni tsuite ikenai.

3. gaˈkushoo 楽章 •c [a principal division in a musical work]

EX. I like the 2nd movement of that symphony.
僕はそのシンフォニーの第二楽章が好きだ。
Boku wa sono shinfonii no dai-ni-gakushoo ga suki da.

movie n.

eˈiga 映画 •c ⟪motion picture, film⟫

EX. (**a**) Have you seen the movie *Seven Samurai*?
「七人の侍」という映画を見たことがありますか。
'Shichi-nin no Samurai' to iu eiga o mita koto ga arimasu ka.
(**b**) Shall we go see a movie tonight?
今晩映画を見に行きましょうか。
Konban eiga o mi ni ikimashoo ka.
(**c**) Where is the movie theater?
映画館はどこですか。
Eiga-kan wa doko desu ka.

mow vt. **[to cut down grass or grain]**

⟨-o⟩ kaˈru ⟨～を⟩刈る ① [for s.o. to cut short s.t. growing thick from the root with a sharp blade using a shearing action]

EX. I have to mow the lawn today.
今日は芝を刈らなければならない。
Kyoo wa shiba o karanakereba naranai.

Mr. n. **[a title prefixed to a the name of an adult male or to the name of the office he holds]**

-san ～さん [a suffix attached to the name of a person or the name of his/her occupation to indicate politeness], -sama ～様 [a suffix attached to the name of an adult person or to a kinship term ⟨fml⟩], -shi ～氏 •c [a suffix attached to the name of an adult person in a formal situation], seˈnseˈi 先生 •c [a professional, including scholars, instructors, medical doctors, artists, attorneys, politicians, etc., often used as a polite term of address] ⟪teacher, master, instructor⟫

NOTE: *Shi* can also be used a pronoun, mainly for a male adult. *San* can be added to occupations such as in the following: *o-isha-san* (*isha*=medical doctor), *ha-isha-san* (*ha-isha*=dentist), *kokku-san* (*kokku*=cook), *daiku-san* (*daiku*=carpenter). It can also be added to the names of various kinds of stores, such as in *hon-ya-san* (*hon-ya*=bookstore), *pan-ya-san* (*pan-ya*=bakery), *hana-ya-san* (*hana-ya*=florist's)

NOTE: In formal and official letters *dono* is often used in place of *sama*, as in *Yoshida Shigeru Dono.*

EX. (**a**) Mr. Yoshida, your friend is waiting at Gate 12.
吉田様、お友達が12番ゲートでお待ちでいらっしゃいます。
Yoshida-sama, o-tomodachi ga juu-ni-ban-geeto de o-machi de irasshaimasu.
(**b**) Today I went to see a movie with Mr. Yonezawa.
今日、米沢さんと映画を見に行った。
Kyoo, Yonezawa-san to eiga o mi ni itta.
(**c**) Mr. Smith seems to like golf a lot.
スミス{さん/氏/先生}はゴルフがお好きのようだ。
Smisu-{san/shi/sensei} wa gorufu ga o-suki no yooda.
(**d**) Mr. Ogawa teaches physics at Kyoto University.
小川先生は京都大学で物理を教えていらっしゃいます。
Ogawa-sensei wa Kyooto-Daigaku de butsuri o oshiete irasshaimasu.

Mrs. n. **[a title prefixed to the last name of a married woman]**

-san ～さん, N no oˈku-{san/sama} Nの奥{さん/様}, fuˈjin 夫人 •c [(a polite title attached to the name of) s.o.'s wife]

EX. Mrs. Kanazawa is working at a department store.
金沢{さん/さんの奥さん/さんの奥様/夫人}はデパートで働いていらっしゃる。
Kanazawa-{san/san no oku-san/san no oku-sama/fujin} wa depaato de hataraite irassharu.

Ms. n. **[a title prefixed to the last or full name of an adult female]**
-san ～さん [a suffix attached to the name of a person or the name of his/her occupation to indicate politeness]

EX. Ms. Hartman used to be a TV anchorwoman.
ハートマンさんはテレビキャスターだったことがある。
Haatoman-san wa terebi-kyasutaa datta koto ga aru.

much adj. **[in a great amount]**
ta⌈kusa⌉n (no) N たくさん(の)N [large in quantity] ⟪a lot of, plenty of, abundant⟫

EX. I've spent much time and money on this project.
このプロジェクトにはたくさん(の)お金と時間をかけてきた。
Kono purojekuto ni wa takusan (no) o-kane to jikan o kakete kita.

—— adv. **[to a great(er) degree or approximately]**
1. to⌈temo とても [to a great extent (in affirmative contexts) or no matter what one does (in negative contexts)] ⟪very, extremely⟫, ta⌈ihen 大変 •c [to a great extent] ⟪very, exceedingly, remarkably⟫

EX. Much to my surpise, Susie married a person from Japan.
{とても/大変}驚いたことに、スージーは日本人と結婚した。
{Totemo/Taihen} odoroita koto ni, Suujii wa Nihon-jin to kekkon-shita.

2. da⌈itai 大体 •c [for the most part ⟪fig. "nearly"⟫] ⟪generally, on the whole, by and large, approximately, almost⟫

EX. This week's test was much the same as last week's.
今週のテストは先週のと大体同じだった。
Konshuu no tesuto wa senshuu no to daitai onaji datta.

murder n. **[an act of willfully killing another person]**
sa⌈tsujin 殺人 •c [an act of killing another person] ⟪homicide⟫

EX. (**a**) There was a murder yesterday in this small college town.
この小さな大学町で昨日殺人があった。
Kono chiisana daigaku-machi de kinoo satsujin ga atta.
(**b**) The murder case is still unsolved.
その殺人事件はまだ未解決だ。
Sono satsujin-jiken wa mada mi-kaiketsu da.

—— vt. **[for s.o. to willfully kill another person]**
⟨-o⟩ sa⌈tsugai-suru ⟨～を⟩殺害する ③ •c ⟪kill, put to death⟫, ⟨-o⟩ ko⌈rosu ⟨～を⟩殺す ① [for s.o./s.a. to cause s.o./s.a. to die] ⟪kill, slay⟫

EX. A student murdered three co-eds living in the same dorm.
学生が同じ寮の女子学生を三人{殺した/殺害した}。
Gakusei ga onaji ryoo no joshi-gakusei o san-nin {koroshita/satsugai-shita}.

muscle n.
ki⌉nniku 筋肉 •c

EX. I developed my arm and leg muscles through weightlifting.
重量上げをして手足に筋肉をつけた。
Juuryoo-age o shite te-ashi ni kinniku o tsuketa.

museum n. **[a building in which objects of lasting interest are displayed and preserved]**
1. ha⌈kubutsu⌉-kan 博物館 •c [a building in which historical, artistic, anthropological, industrial, and scientific objects are displayed and preserved]

EX. On Sunday we went to the National Museum in Ueno.
日曜日に上野の国立博物館に行って来ました。
Nichiyoo-bi ni Ueno no kokuritsu-hakubutsu-kan ni itte kimashita.

2. bi⌈jutsu⌉-kan 美術館 •c [a building in which artistic objects, such as paintings, sculpture, photographs, etc., are displayed and preserved]

EX. I went to the art museum to see an exhibit of Renoir's paintings.

M

美術館にルノワールの絵の展覧会を見に行った。
Bijutsu-kan ni Runowaaru no e no tenran-kai o mi ni itta.

mushroom n.
ki˥noko きのこ, **ma˥sshuru˥umu** マッシュルーム •f

music n. **[an arrangement of sounds in an esthetically pleasing pattern or the art of so arranging sounds or the written/printed form of symbols representing such sounds]**
1. o˥ngaku 音楽 **•c [an arrangement of sounds in an esthetically pleasing pattern or the art of so arranging sounds]**
EX. (**a**) Every day I listen to classical music on FM radio.
私は毎日FMラジオでクラシック音楽を聞きます。
Watashi wa mai-nichi efu-emu rajio de kurashikku-ongaku o kikimasu.
(**b**) I like live music much better than recorded music.
僕はレコードで聞く音楽より生の音楽の方がずっと好きだ。
Boku wa rekoodo de kiku ongaku yori nama no ongaku no hoo ga zutto suki da.
2. ga˥kufu 楽譜 **•c [the written/printed form of symbols representing sounds arranged in an esthetically pleasing pattern]** ((**score**))
EX. I like singing, but I can't read music.
私は歌うのが好きですが、楽譜が読めないんです。
Watashi wa utau no ga suki desu ga, gakufu ga yome-nai n desu.

musical adj. **[of/skilled in/fond of/accompanied by music]**
1. o˥ngaku no N 音楽のN **•c [of music]**
2. o˥ngaku no sa˥inoo ga a˥ru (N) 音楽の才能がある(N) **[talented in music]**
EX. Everyone in Kumiko's family is very musical.
久美子の家族はみんなとても音楽の才能がある。
Kumiko no kazoku wa minna totemo ongaku no sainoo ga aru.
3. o˥ngaku ga su˥ki˥na 音楽が好きな adj(*na*). **[fond of music]**
4. o˥ngaku o to˥mona˥u (N) 音楽を伴う(N) **[accompanied by music]**
—— n. **[a theatrical production with songs and dancing]**
myu˥ujikaru ミュージカル **•f**
EX. Every time I go to New York, I take in a Broadway musical.
ニューヨークへ行く度に、ブロードウエイのミュージカルを見に行く。
Nyuuyooku e iku tabi ni, Buroodouei no myuujikaru o mi ni iku.

musician n. **[a person who is skilled at music or who performs music as a profession]**
{**o˥ngaku-ka/o˥ngak-ka**} 音楽家 **•c**

must aux. **[an auxiliary verb indicating obligation for s.o. to do s.t. or likelihood based on what one knows of s.t. having happened in the past or of s.t. being the case at the present]**
1. {**Vneg./Vstem/shi/ko/adj(*i*). *ku***}{**nakute wa/nakereba**} {**i˥kenai/na˥ra˥nai**}, {**adj(*na*). stem/N**} {**de/ja**}{**na˥kute wa/na˥kereba**} {**i˥kenai/na˥ra˥nai**} {**Vneg./Vstem/**し/来/**adj(*i*). *ku***}{なくては/なければ}{いけない/ならない}, {**adj(*na*). stem/N**}{で/じゃ}{なくては/なければ}{いけない/ならない} **[it won't do if s.o. does not take some action or if s.o./s.t./s.a. is not in a certain state]** ((**have to, need**)), {**V/adj./cop.**}***te* wa i˥kenai** {**V/adj./cop.**}***te***はいけない **[s.o./s.t. is not allowed to do s.t. or be in a certain state]** ((**mustn't**))
EX. (**a**) I absolutely must finish writing my paper by tomorrow.
私はどうしてもレポートをあしたまでに書き終わらなければならない。
Watashi wa doo-shite-mo repooto o ashita made ni kaki-owaranakereba naranai.
(**b**) You must be here by eight o'clock every morning.
あなたはここに毎朝八時までに来なければなりません。
Anata wa koko ni mai-asa hachi-ji made ni konakereba narimasen.

(c) You mustn't smoke in this room.
この部屋でたばこを吸ってはいけません。
Kono heya de tabako o sutte wa ikemasen.

2. {**V/adj(*i*).**}**inf. ni chi⌈gai-na⌉i** {**V/adj(*i*).**}**inf.にちがいない,** {**adj(*na*). stem/N**} {**ø/datta**} **ni chi⌈gai-na⌉i** {**adj(*na*). stem/N**}{**ø/だった**}**にちがいない** adj(*i*). **[a predicate-final form that indicates a speaker's conviction that s.t. is or was the case based on what he/she knows]** 《**there is no doubt that**》

EX. (a) He hasn't come yet? Something must have happened.
彼がまだ来ていない。何かあったにちがいない。
Kare ga mada kite inai. Nani-ka atta ni chigai-nai.
(b) By now the happy couple must be enjoying themselves on Waikiki beach.
幸せな二人は今ごろワイキキのビーチで楽しんでいるにちがいない。
Shiawasena futari wa ima-goro Waikiki no biichi de tanoshinde iru ni chigai-nai.

mustache n.
ku⌈chi-hige 口ひげ

EX. My father has started to grow a mustache.
父は口ひげを伸ばし始めた。
Chichi wa kuchi-hige o nobashi-hajimeta.

mutual adj. **[felt/done by each toward the other** 《**fig. "common/shared"**》**]**
1. (o-)⌈tagai no N (お)互いのN [felt/done by each toward the other] 《**reciprocal, each other's**》

EX. Married life depends on mutual trust.
結婚生活はお互いの信頼次第です。
Kekkon-seikatsu wa o-tagai no shinrai-shidai desu.

2. kyo⌈otsuu no N 共通のN •c [applying to all of two/more things] 《**common**》

EX. I've discovered that Cindy and I share many mutual friends.
シンディーと私に共通の友達が大勢いることが分かった。
Shindii to watashi ni kyootsuu no tomodachi ga oozei iru koto ga wakatta.

my pron. **[the possessive form of the first person singular pronoun I]**
wa⌈tashi no N 私のN [the formal possessive form of the first person singular pronoun *watashi*], bo⌉ku no N 僕のN [the informal possessive form of the singular pronoun *boku* used by male speakers], a⌈tashi no N あたしのN [the informal possessive form of the first person pronoun *atashi* used by female speakers], o⌈re no N おれのN [the very informal possessive form of the first person singular pronoun *ore* used by male speakers]

NOTE: "My" is often not expressed at all when its existence is understood in a given context.

EX. (a) This is my watch.
これは{{私/僕/あたし/?おれ}の/*ø}時計です。
*Kore wa {{watashi/boku/atashi/?ore} no/*ø} tokei desu.*
(b) My book is selling well.
{{私/僕/あたし/おれ}の/*ø}本はよく売れている。
*{{Watashi/Boku/Atashi/Ore} no/*ø} hon wa yoku urete iru.*
(c) My knowledge about Japan is very limited.
{{私/*僕/*あたし/*おれ}の/*ø}日本についての知識はほんのわずかでございます。
*{{Watashi/*Boku/*Atashi/*Ore} no/*ø} Nihon ni-tsuite no chishiki wa hon-no wazuka de gozaimasu.*
(d) Would you like to come over to my place on Saturday?
土曜日に{ø/私の/僕の/あたしの/*おれの}うちへいらっしゃいませんか。
*Doyoo-bi ni {ø/watashi no/boku no/atashi no/*ore no} uchi e irassahimasen ka.*

—— int. **[an interjection used by female speakers to indicate surprise]**
a⌉ra あら [an interjection to indicate surprise or emotional movement (typically

used by female speakers)] 《Good gracious!, Dear me!, My goodness!》

EX. Oh, my! I forgot to mail the letter.
あら、この手紙を出すのを忘れていたわ。
Ara, kono tegami o dasu no o wasurete ita wa.

myself pron. **[the reflexive/emphatic form of the first person pronoun]**

1. ji⌈bun(-ji⌉shin) 自分(自身) •c [a reflexive pronoun that refers (back) to a person with whom the speaker identifies, including himself/herself]

EX. (**a**) I consider myself to be independent.
私は自分(自身)を独立心があると思っている。
Watashi wa jibun(-jishin) o dokuritsu-shin ga aru to omotte iru.
(**b**) It wasn't easy to deceive myself.
自分(自身)をあざむくことは易しくなかった。
Jibun(-jishin) o azamuku koto wa yasashiku nakatta.

2. (wa⌈tashi ga) ji⌈bun de (私が)自分で n.+prt. **[by/for oneself]**

EX. (**a**) I did it myself.
私が自分でやりました。
Watashi ga jibun de yarimashita.
(**b**) I'll go there myself.
私が自分で行きます。
Watashi ga jibun de ikimasu.

mysterious adj. **[full of mystery]**
shi⌈npi-tekina 神秘的な adj(*na*). **•c [incapable of being understood by the human intellect] 《mystic, enigmatic, esoteric》, fu⌈shigina 不思議な** adj(*na*). **•c [going beyond human comprehension] 《wonderful, marvelous, strange, uncanny》**

EX. (**a**) Mona Lisa wears a mysterious smile.
モナリザは{神秘的な/不思議な}微笑を浮かべている。
Mona Riza wa {shinpi-tekina/fushigina} bishoo o ukabete iru.
(**b**) Life is mysterious.
人生は{不思議/??神秘的}だ。
Jinsei wa {fushigi/??shinpi-teki} da.

mystery n. **[s.t. that remains unexplained or is puzzling 《fig. "a story of a puzzling crime," "secret"》]**

1. shi⌈npi 神秘 •c [a secret that cannot be explained by human intellect], fu⌈shigi 不思議 •c [s.t. that goes beyond human comprehension] 《wonderfulness, marvelousness, strangeness》

EX. How the four seasons change is a mystery to me.
四季の変化は僕には{神秘/不思議}だ。
Shiki no henka wa boku ni wa {shinpi/fushigi} da.

2. hi⌈ketsu 秘けつ •c [an effective method of doing s.t. still unknown to s.o.] 《secret》

EX. The mystery behind his good health is swimming.
彼の健康の秘けつは水泳だ。
Kare no kenkoo no hiketsu wa suiei da.

3. su⌈iri-sho⌉osetsu 推理小説 •c [a story of a puzzling crime] 《detective story》, mi⌉suterii ミステリー •f

EX. I love to read mysteries right before going to sleep.
寝る直前に{推理小説/ミステリー}を読むのが大好きだ。
Neru chokuzen ni {suiri-shoosetsu/misuterii} o yomu no ga dai-suki da.

myth n. **[a traditional story about ancient times, esp. about gods and heroes 《fig. "a fictitious story"》]**
shi⌈nwa 神話 •c

EX. (**a**) Do you know the myth of King Oedipus?
エディプス王の神話を知っていますか。
Edipusu-oo no shinwa o shitte imasu ka.
(**b**) It's a myth that he can speak 30 languages.
彼が言語を三十も話せるというのは神話だ。
Kare ga gengo o san-juu mo hanase-ru to iu no wa shinwa da.

N

nail n. **[the thin, hard protective layer at the end of a finger/toe or a small metal spike driven into things with a hammer]**
1. tsu⌈me つめ [the thin, hard protective layer at the end of a finger/toe]

EX. My nails have grown long so I need to clip them.
つめが伸びたから、切らなければいけない。
Tsume ga nobita kara, kiranakereba ikenai.

2. ku⌈gi 釘 [a small metal spike driven into things with a hammer]

EX. It took some practice for me to get to the point where I could hammer a nail straight into wood without bending it.
釘を曲げないでまっすぐ板に打ち込めるようになるにはかなり練習が必要でした。
Kugi o magenai de massugu ita ni uchi-kome-ru yooni naru ni wa kanari renshuu ga hitsuyoo deshita.

PHRASE: nail clippers *tsume-kiri* つめ切り

name n. **[a word/words by which to designate a particular person, place, animal, or thing]**
na⌈mae 名前

EX. (a) May I ask your name?
お名前は何でしょうか。
O-namae wa nan deshoo ka.
(b) Do you know the name of the Japanese restaurant near the university?
大学の近くの日本のレストランの名前を知っていますか。
Daigaku no chikaku no Nihon no resutoran no namae o shitte imasu ka.

PHRASE: name card *meishi* 名刺 •c ⟪business card, calling card⟫

EX. The Japanese businessmen exchange name cards when they meet someone for the first time.
日本のビジネスマンは初めて人に会う時に名刺を交換する。
Nihon no bijinesu-man wa hajimete hito ni au toki ni meishi o kookan-suru.

—— vt. **[for s.o. to give a name to s.o./s.a./s.t.]** **⟨-ni⟩ na(⌈mae) o tsu⌈ke⌉ru ⟨〜に⟩名(前)を付ける ② [for s.o. to attach a name to s.o./s.a./s.t.]**

EX. I named my cat Mini.
私は猫にミニという名(前)を付けた。
Watashi wa neko ni Mini to iu na(mae) o tsuketa.

nap n. **[a short sleep usu. during the day]**
hi⌈ru-ne 昼寝 [a short sleep in the daytime], u⌈tata-ne うたた寝 [a short sleep] ⟪**catnap, doze**⟫

EX. I usually take about a 30-minute nap every afternoon.
私は毎日午後大抵三十分位{昼寝/うたた寝}をします。
Watashi wa mai-nichi gogo taitei san-jup-pun-gurai {hiru ne/utata ne} o shimasu.

napkin n. **[piece of cloth/paper used at meals for protecting one's clothes and wiping one's fingers and lips]**
na⌉pukin ナプキン •f

narrow adj. **[having a small width in proportion to length ⟪fig. "limited"⟫]**
se⌈ma⌉i 狭い adj(*i*). **[occupying a small space or having a small width in proportion to length ⟪fig. "limited"⟫]** ⟪**small, limited, close, tight**⟫ ↔ **hiroi 広い** adj(*i*).; **ho⌈so⌉i 細い** adj(*i*). **[for a cylindrical object to have a small diameter or for a space to have a small width in proportion to length ⟪fig. "(of voice) high and weak"⟫]** ↔ **futoi 太い** adj(*i*).

N

EX. (**a**) The streets are too narrow for cars to get through.
道がとても{狭くて/*細くて}、車は全然通れない。
*Michi ga totemo {semakute/*hosokute}, kuruma wa zenzen toore-nai.*
(**b**) He is very narrow-minded.
あの人はとても心が{狭い/*細い}。
*Ano hito wa totemo kokoro ga {semai/*hosoi}.*
(**c**) A narrow path winds along the ravine.
{細い/狭い}道が渓谷にそって曲がりくねっている。
{Hosoi/Semai} michi ga keikoku ni sotte magari-kunette iru.

nation n. **[a large community of people with political/territorial unity]**
ko⌉kka 国家 •c ⟪**state, country**⟫

EX. Our country is a democratic nation.
我が国は民主国家である。
Waga-kuni wa minshu-kokka dearu.

national adj. **[of/belonging to a nation]**
ku⌈ni no N 国のN [of a country], k⌉okka no N 国家の N •c [of a nation], ku⌈ni ze⌈ntai no N 国全体の N [of the entire country], ko⌈kuritsu no N 国立の N •c [founded and controlled by the central government of a nation] ↔ shiritsu no N 私立のN •c [founded and controlled by a private institute]

EX. (**a**) The national debt must be reduced to spur economic growth.
経済成長を促進するためには{国/国家/国全体/*国立}の負債を軽減しなければならない。
*Keizai-seichoo o sokushin-suru tame ni wa {kuni/kokka/kuni zentai/*kokuritsu} no fusai o keigen-shinakereba naranai.*
(**b**) I'd like to get into a national university.
私は{国立(の)/*国の/*国家の/*国全体の}大学に入りたい。
*Watashi wa {kokuritsu (no)/*kuni no/*kokka no/*kuni zentai no} daigaku ni hairi-tai.*

nationality n. **[the fact/condition of belonging to a particular nation]**
ko⌈kuseki 国籍 •c

EX. A: What is your nationality?
国籍はどこですか。
Kokuseki wa doko desu ka.
B: I'm Korean.
韓国です。
Kankoku desu.

native adj. **[naturally belonging to s.o./s.t.]**
1. u⌈mareta N 生まれたN /⟨Vinf. past of *umareru* + N (a place)⟩/ [(a place) where s.o./s.a. was born]

EX. Hakodate is her native town.
函館が彼女の生まれた町です。
Hakodate ga kanojo no umareta machi desu.

2. ji⌈koku no N 自国のN •c [of one's own country]

EX. It's interesting to study one's native culture.
自国の文化を学ぶことは面白い。
Jikoku no bunka o manabu koto wa omoshiroi.

3. ⟨-ni⟩ sei⌉rai no N ⟨〜に⟩生来のN •c [belonging to s.o. since birth] ⟪**innate, born, congenital**⟫

EX. One's native disposition never goes away completely.
生来の性格は決してなくならない。
Seirai no seikaku wa kesshite nakunaranai.

PHRASE: native language *bogo* 母語 **•c**, native speaker *bogo-washa* 母語話者 **•c**

natural adj. **[of/found in/caused by nature** ⟪**fig. "be expected"**⟫**]**
1. shi⌈zen no N 自然のN •c [pertaining to nature] ↔ jinkoo no N 人工のN •c

EX. I prefer natural beauty to artificial beauty.
私は人工の美しさより自然の美しさの方が好きだ。
Watashi wa jinkoo no utsukushi-sa yori shizen no utsukushi-sa no hoo ga suki da.

2. u⌈maretsuki no N 生まれつきのN [belonging to s.o. since birth] ⟪**innate**⟫

EX. He put his natural gift for languages to good use in becoming a diplomat.
彼は生まれつきの語学の才能を活かして、外交官になった。

Kare wa umaretsuki no gogaku no sainoo o ikashite, gaikoo-kan ni natta.

3. a⌈tarimae no N 当たり前のN [to be expected] 《expected, proper, of matter of course》

EX. It's natural that one should return what one borrows.
借りたものを返すのは当たり前だ。
Karita mono o kaesu no wa atarimae da.

naturally adv. **[according to nature 《fig. "as one would expect"》]**

1. shi⌈zen ni 自然に •c [according to nature] 《spontaneously》

EX. Music seemed to flow naturally from the pianist's fingers.
ピアニストの指から音楽が自然に流れ出るようだった。
Pianisuto no yubi kara ongaku ga shizen ni nagare-deru yoodatta.

2. u⌈maretsuki 生まれつき [since the time of birth] 《innately, congenitally》

EX. No one is naturally evil.
だれも生まれつき悪人ではない。
Dare-mo umaretsuki akunin dewanai.

3. to⌈ozen 当然 •c [to be expected as a matter of course in a given situation] 《as a matter of course, deservedly, rightfully, necessarily》

EX. (**a**) Naturally you get tired after running 10 miles.
十マイルも走れば、当然、疲れますよ。
Juu-mairu mo hashireba, toozen, tsukaremasu yo.
(**b**) Naturally you should return the borrowed money.
当然、借りた金は返さなければいけない。
Toozen, karita kane wa kaesanakereba ikenai.

nature n. **[the physical universe and all that it contains which is not made by man or the inherent character and qualities of s.o./s.t./s.a.]**

1. shi⌈zen 自然 •c [the physical universe and all that it contains which is not made by man] ↔ jinkoo 人工 •c

EX. (**a**) I love living in the midst of nature.
自然の中で暮らすのが大好きです。
Shizen no naka de kurasu no ga daisuki desu.
(**b**) It's important to protect nature.
自然を保護するのは大事だ。
Shizen o hogo-suru no wa daiji da.

2. se⌈ishitsu 性質 •c [the inherent character and properties of s.o./s.t./s.a.]

EX. (**a**) No two dogs have the same nature.
どの二匹の犬をとっても、性質が違う。
Dono ni-hiki no inu o totte mo, seishitsu ga chigau.
(**b**) Gold and silver are quite different in nature.
金と銀では性質がかなり違う。
Kin to gin de wa seishitsu ga kanari chigau.

naval adj. **[having to do with a navy]**
ka⌉igun no N 海軍のN •c

navy n. **[the warships of a country and the men and officers assigned to them]**

1. ka⌉igun 海軍 •c [the men and officers assigned to the warships of a country]

2. ze⌉n-se⌉nkan 全戦艦 •c [an entire fleet of warships]

PHRASE: navy blue *kon* 紺 •c

near prep. **[within a short spatial or temporal distance]**
{⟨-ni⟩/⟨-kara⟩} chi⌈ka⌉i {⟨〜に⟩/⟨〜から⟩}近い adj(*i*). **[having little spatial or temporal distance separating s.t. from s.t. else] 《close》, ⟨-no⟩ chi⌈ka⌉ku no N ⟨〜の⟩近くのN [within a short spatial distance from s.t.]**

EX. (**a**) My home is near the college I am attending.
私の家は通っている大学{の近く/に近い}です。
Watashi no ie wa kayotte iru daigau {no chikaku/ni chikai} desu.
(**b**) Christmas is near.
クリスマスが近い。
Kurisumasu ga chikai.
(**c**) The park is near here.
公園はここ{{に/から}近い/の近くだ}。
Kooen wa koko {{ni/kara} chikai/no chikaku da}.

NOTE: N *{ni/kara} chikai* cannot be used when

N is a temporal expression, so a sentence such as the following is ungrammatical. *Kurisumasu {?ni/*kara} chikai.* The meaning intended here should be expressed as in example (b).

N

nearly adv. **[almost but not quite or in a close manner]**
ho⌈to⌉ndo ほとんど [not entirely but very close to so] ⟪almost, about, practically⟫, mo⌈o suko⌉shi de もう少しで n.+prt. **[very close to s.t. in time but not quite there] ⟪almost, closely⟫**

EX. (**a**) I've nearly finished writing my term paper.
期末レポートを{ほとんど/*もう少しで}書いてしまいました。
*Kimatsu-repooto o {hotondo/*moo sukoshi de} kaite shimaimashita.*
(**b**) I nearly passed out when that happened.
私はその時{ほとんど/もう少しで}気を失いそうになった。
Watashi wa sono toki {hotondo/moo sukoshi de} ki o ushinai-sooni natta.

neat adj. **[clean and tidy]**
ki⌈chi⌉n-to shita N きちんとしたN /⟨Vinf. past of *kichin-to suru* ③ make things tidy/ [in perfect order ⟪fig. "exact"⟫] ⟪tidy, in good order, trim, dandy, well-groomed, exact⟫, ki⌈chi⌉n-to shite iru (N) きちんとしている(N) /⟨V*te iru* of *kichin-to suru* ③ make things tidy/, yo⌉ku ka⌈ta-zu⌉ita N よく片付いたN /⟨Vinf. past of *yoku kata-zuku* ① be straightened up nicely/ [for a place to be tidy] ⟪tidy, in good order⟫, yo⌉ku ka⌈ta-zu⌉ite iru (N) よく片付いている(N) /⟨V*te iru* of *yoku kata-zuku* ① be straightened up nicely/

EX. (**a**) My secretary's table is always neat.
私の秘書の机はいつでも{きちんとして/よく片付いて}いる。
Watashi no hisho no tsukue wa itsu-demo {kichin-to shite/yoku kata-zuite} iru.
(**b**) Mrs. Tanaka's hair-do always looks neat.
田中夫人の髪はいつも{きちんとして/*よく片付いて}いる。
*Tanaka-fujin no kami wa itsu-mo {kichin-to shite/*yoku kata-zuite} iru.*

neatly adv. **[in a neat manner]**
ki⌈chi⌉n-to きちんと [appropriately in terms of the way one arranges things, dresses oneself, or behaves] ⟪exactly, accurately, tidily⟫

EX. (**a**) Mr. Yoshida is neatly dressed today because he has a date tonight.
吉田さんは今晩デートがあるので、今日は服装がきちんとしている。
Yoshida-san wa konban deeto ga aru node, kyoo wa fukusoo ga kichin-to shite iru.
(**b**) You really write *kanji* neatly.
本当に漢字をきちんと書きますね。
Hontoo ni kanji o kichin-to kakimasu ne.

necessarily adv. **[as a necessary result]**
ka⌈narazu-shi⌉mo…neg. 必ずしも…neg., Sinf. to wa ka⌈gira⌉nai Sinf.とは限らない [not always]

EX. (**a**) Regular exercise does not necessarily lead to good health.
定期的に運動すれば健康になるとは限らない。
Teiki-tekini undoo-sureba kenkoo ni naru to wa kagiranai.
(**b**) People who exercise do not necessarily live longer.
必ずしも運動をする人の方がしない人より長生きするとは限らない。
Kanarazu-shimo undoo o suru hito no hoo ga shinai hito yori naga-iki suru to wa kagiranai.

necessary adj. **[s.t. needed in order to accomplish s.t. or unavoidable]**
1. hi⌈tsuyoona 必要な adj(*na*). **•c [essential for s.t./s.o./s.a.] ⟪need, essential⟫ ↔ fuyoona 不要な** adj(*na*). **•c**

EX. (**a**) A knowledge of Japanese is necessary in my business.
私の仕事には日本語の知識が必要なんです。
Watashi no shigoto ni wa Nihon-go no chishiki ga hitsuyoona n desu.
(**b**) More rest is necessary for him to fully regain his health.
彼が完全に健康を取り戻すにはもっと静養が必要です。

Kare ga kanzenni kenkoo o tori-modosu ni wa motto seiyoo ga hitsuyoo desu.

2. ya⌈mu-o-e⌉nai 止むを得ない adj(*i*). **[beyond one's control]** 《**inevitable, unavoidable**》

EX. Failures are a necessary part of achieving great successes.
大成功のためには失敗も止むを得ない。
Dai-seikoo no tame ni wa shippai mo yamu-o-enai.

necessity n. **[the state or fact of being necessary/a necessary thing]**

1. hi⌈tsuyoo 必要 •c [the state or fact of being necessary/required] 《**need, requirement, indispensability**》

EX. (**a**) There is no necessity for anyone to work more than 40 hours per week.
週に四十時間以上働く必要はだれにもない。
Shuu ni yon-juu-jikan-ijoo hataraku hitsuyoo wa dare-nimo nai.
(**b**) Necessity is the mother of invention.
必要は発明の母である。
Hitsuyoo wa hatsumei no haha dearu.

2. hi⌈tsuzen-sei 必然性 •c [the quality of being inevitable] 《**inevitability**》

EX. The view of management was that there was no necessity for strikes.
経営陣から見ると、ストライキの必然性はなかった。
Keiei-jin kara miru to, sutoraiki no hitsuzen-sei wa nakatta.

3. hi⌈tsuyoona mono 必要なもの [a necessary thing]

EX. We had to carry all our daily necessities to the campsite by backpack.
私たちは日常必要なものを全部リュックサックに入れてキャンプ場に運ばなければならなかった。
Watashi-tachi wa nichijoo hitsuyoona mono o zenbu ryukkusakku ni irete kyanpu-joo ni hakobanakereba naranakatta.

neck n. **[the narrow part of the body that connects the head and the torso** 《**fig. "the narrow part of s.t."**》**]**

ku⌈bi 首

EX. The giraffe has a very long neck.
キリンはとても首が長い。
Kirin wa totemo kubi ga nagai.

NOTE: In Japanese *kubi o kiru* "to cut s.o.'s neck" means either literally "to cut off s.o.'s head" or "to fire s.o."

necklace n.

ku⌈bi-ka⌉zari 首飾り, ne⌉kkuresu ネックレス •f

EX. Who is that lady wearing the pearl necklace?
真珠の{首飾り/ネックレス}をしているあの女性はだれですか。
Shinju no {kubi-kazari/nekkuresu} o shite iru ano josei wa dare desu ka.

necktie n.

ne⌉kutai ネクタイ •f

EX. (**a**) This necktie is hard to tie.
このネクタイは締めにくいです。
Kono nekutai wa shime-nikui desu.
(**b**) Please take off your necktie.
ネクタイを外してください。
Nekutai o hazushite kudasai.
(**c**) I like your necktie.
いいネクタイですね。
Ii nekutai desu ne.

need n. **[the state of lacking s.t. necessary/useful or s.t. necessary/useful which is lacking** 《**fig. "poverty," "time of great difficulty"**》**]**

1. hi⌈tsuyoo 必要 •c [the state or fact of being necessary/required] 《**necessity, requirement, indispensability**》

EX. There is a pressing need to improve our educational system.
我々は教育制度を改善する必要に迫られている。
Ware-ware wa kyooiku-seido o kaizen suru hitsuyoo ni semara-rete iru.

2. hi⌈tsuyoona mono 必要なもの [a necessary thing]

3. ma⌉saka-no-toki まさかの時 [time of difficulty]

EX. A friend in need is a friend indeed.
まさかの時の友達が本当の友達だ。
Masaka-no-toki no tomodachi ga hontoo no tomodachi da.

N

—— vt. **[to require s.t.]**
⟨-ga⟩ i⌈ru ⟨〜が⟩要る ① [to be necessary/desirable] ⟪necessary⟫, hi⌈tsuyoona 必要な adj(*na*). **•c [essential for s.t./s.o./s.a.] ⟪necessary, required, indispensable, essential⟫, Vinf. nonpast hi⌈tsuyoo ga a⌉ru Vinf. nonpast必要がある ③ [to have to do s.t.], {Vneg./Vstem/shi/ko/adj(*i*). *ku*} {nakute wa/nakereba} {i⌈kenai/na⌈ra⌉nai}, {adj(*na*). stem/N} {de/ja}{na⌉kute wa/na⌉kereba} {i⌈kenai/na⌈ra⌉nai} {Vneg./Vstem/し/来/adj(*i*). *ku*}{なくては/なければ}{いけない/ならない}, {adj(*na*). stem/N}{で/じゃ}{なくては/なければ}{いけない/ならない} [it won't do if s.o. does not take some action or if s.o./s.t./s.a. is not in a certain state]**

EX. (**a**) We need a lot of money to carry out this project.
この計画を実行するにはお金がたくさん{要ります/必要です}。
Kono keikaku o jikkoo-suru ni wa o-kane ga takusan {irimasu/hitsuyoo desu}.
(**b**) I don't need this desk any longer.
この机はもう{要りません/必要じゃありません}。
Kono tsukue wa moo {irimasen/hitsuyoo jaarimasen}.
(**c**) This car needs washing.
この車は{洗う必要がある/洗わなければならない}。
Kono kuruma wa {arau hitsuyoo ga aru/arawanakereba naranai}.

NOTE: "Don't need to" is expressed by {Vneg./Vstem/*shi*/*ko*/adj(*i*). *ku*} *nakute mo ii* or {adj(*na*). stem/N} {*de*/*ja*} *nakute ii.* More formally it is expressed by {Vinf. nonpast/adj(*i*). inf. nonpast/{adj(*na*)./N} *dearu*} *hitsuyoo wa nai,* as in the following examples:

(**d**) You don't need to go there.
君はそこに{行く必要はない/行かなくてもいい}よ。
Kimi wa soko ni {iku hitsuyoo wa nai/ikanakute mo ii} yo.
(**e**) You don't need to turn in your homework today.
今日は宿題を{出さなくてもいいです/出す必要はありません}。
Kyoo wa shukudai o {dasanakute mo ii desu/dasu hitsuyoo wa arimasen}.
(**f**) Your paper doesn't need to be long.
レポートは{長くなくてもいいです/長い必要はありません}。
Repooto wa {nagakunakute mo ii desu/nagai hitsuyoo wa arimasen}.
(**g**) Your level of proficiency in Japanese doesn't need to be that high.
日本語はそんなに{上手でなくてもいいです/上手である必要はありません}。
Nihon-go wa sonnani {joozu denakute mo ii desu/joozu dearu hitsuyoo wa arimasen}.

needle n. **[a small thin piece of metal for sewing or s.t. of the same shape]**
ha⌉ri 針

EX. I'm far-sighted, so it's very hard for me to thread needles.
遠視なので、針に糸を通すのがとても難しい。
Enshi na node, hari ni ito o toosu no ga totemo muzukashii.

negative adj. **[expressing or implying "no" ⟪fig. "less than zero," "lacking positive qualities"⟫]**

1. hi⌈tei no N 否定のN •c [expressing or implying "no"]

EX. The negative form of *tabemasu* is *tabemasen.*
「食べます」の否定の形は「食べません」です。
'Tabemasu' no hitei no katachi wa 'tabemasen' desu.

2. hi⌈tei-tekina 否定的な adj(*na*). **•c [having an attitude or outlook which is not positive]**

EX. He has a very negative view of life.
彼はとても否定的な人生観を持っている。
Kare wa totemo hitei-tekina jinsei-kan o motte iru.

3. i⌈nsei no N 陰性のN •c [lacking positive qualities]

EX. The result of the test was negative.
検査の結果は陰性だった。
Kensa no kekka wa insei datta.

neglect vt. **[to fail to do s.t. or take care of s.t./s.o.]**

1. ⟨-o⟩ **o⌈kota⌉ru** ⟨〜を⟩怠る ① **[for s.o. to fail to do s.t. one is required to do]** ⟪**fail to attend to, be unmindful of**⟫, ⟨-o⟩ **o⌈ro⌉sokani suru** ⟨〜を⟩おろそかにする ③ **[for s.o. to fail to take proper care of s.t.]** ⟪**be negligent, slight, trifle with**⟫

EX. (**a**) Last semester I neglected my studies and received bad grades.
先学期は勉強を{怠って/おろそかにして}悪い成績をもらった。
Sen-gakki wa benkyoo o {okotatte/orosokani shite} warui seiseki o moratta.
(**b**) I neglected to close the window in my study and all the papers on the desk were blown away.
書斎の窓を閉めるのを{怠った/*おろそかにした}ので、机の上の書類が皆吹き飛ばされてしまった。
*Shosai no mado o shimeru no o {okotatta/*orosokani shita} node, tsukue no ue no shorui ga minna fuki-tobasa-rete shimatta.*

2. ⟨-o⟩ **mu⌉shi-suru** ⟨〜を⟩無視する ③ •c **[for s.o. to treat s.t./s.o./s.a. present as if it/he/she were not present]** ⟪**ignore, disregard, bypass**⟫, ⟨-o⟩ **ke⌈ishi suru** ⟨〜を⟩軽視する ③ •c **[for s.o. to think light of s.t. and not recognize its value]** ⟪**despise, make light of**⟫

EX. (**a**) My husband has been neglecting me for the past two or three years.
主人は過去二、三年、私のことを{無視して/?軽視して}きました。
Shujin wa kako ni, san-nen, watashi no koto o {mushi-shite/?keishi-shite} kimashita.
(**b**) Most colleges have neglected the study of foreign languages.
大抵の大学は語学を{軽視して/無視して}きた。
Taitei no daigaku wa gogaku o {keishi-shite/mushi-shie} kita.

neighbor n. **[a person/country who is located next to/near one]**

1. to⌈nari no hito 隣の人 **[a person located next to one], ki⌉njo no hito** 近所の人 **[a person who lives near one]**

EX. (**a**) Our next-door neighbor appears to be a college professor.
{隣/*近所}の人は大学の先生のようだ。
*{Tonari/*Kinjo} no hito wa daigaku no sensei no yooda.*
(**b**) Our neighbors are very friendly.
{近所/隣}の人たちはとても親切です。
{Kinjo/Tonari} no hito-tachi wa totemo shinsetsu desu.

neighborhood n. **[a district (close to where one lives)]**

1. a⌉tari 辺り **[a district close to a certain place ⟪fig. "roughly"⟫]** ⟪**vicinity, environs, direction, about**⟫, **ki⌉njo** 近所 •c **[the area close to one's home or to the place where one currently finds oneself]** ⟪**vicinity**⟫, **chi⌈ka⌉ku** 近く /⟨adj(*i*). ***ku*** of ***chikai*** close/ **[a place close to a certain place]** ⟪**nearby**⟫, **he⌈n** 辺 •c **[a side or district]** ⟪**side, locality, about**⟫, **fu⌈ki⌉n** 付近 •c **[a place close to a certain place]** ⟪**vicinity, environs, district**⟫

EX. Is there a post office in this neighborhood?
この{辺り/近所/近く/辺/付近}に郵便局がありますか。
Kono {atari/kinjo/chikaku/hen/fukin} ni yuubin-kyoku ga arimasu ka.

2. chi⌉ku⌉ 地区 •c **[an area, specially designated for some purpose]** ⟪**area, region, district**⟫, **chi⌉iki** 地域 •c **[a geographic division characterizable in terms of climate/culture/natural environment]** ⟪**region, area, zone**⟫

EX. This neighborhood is terribly polluted.
この{地区/地域}はひどく汚染されている。
Kono {chiku/chiiki} wa hidoku osen-sarete iru.

neither adv./conj. **[not either]**

{N/adj(*na*). stem} de mo naku {N/adj(*na*). stem} **de⌉ mo na⌉i** {N/adj(*na*). stem}でもなく{N/adj(*na*). stem}でもない **[to be not N/adj(*na*). and not N/adj(*na*). either]**, adj(*i*). ***ku*** mo naku, adj(*i*). ***ku*** mo na⌉i adj(*i*). ***ku***もなく、adj(*i*). ***ku***もない **[to be not adj(*i*). and**

N

not adj(*i*). either], V*masu* mo se⌉zu, V*masu* mo shi⌈nai V*masu*もせず、V*masu*もしない [not to do s.t. and not do s.t. else either], N_1 mo N_2 mo…neg. N_1もN_2も…neg. [for both N_1 and N_2 not to be/do s.t.]

EX. (**a**) What I want is neither money nor fame, just a happy family life.
私が欲しいのは金でもなく名声でもない。幸福な家庭生活、ただそれだけだ。
Watashi ga hoshii no wa kane de mo naku meisei de mo nai. Koofukuna katei-seikatsu, tada sore dake da.
(**b**) My tennis is neither good nor bad.
私のテニスは上手でもなく、下手でもない。
Watashi no tenisu wa joozu de mo naku, heta de mo nai.
(**c**) Our house is neither too large nor too small. It's just about right.
私たちの家は大きくもなく、小さくもない。丁度いい。
Watashi-tachi no ie wa ookiku mo naku, chiisaku mo nai. Choodo ii.
(**d**) I neither studied nor played that semester, just sat in my room depressed.
その学期は勉強もせず、遊びもしなかった。落ち込んでただ部屋に閉じこもっていただけだ。
Sono gakki wa benkyoo mo sezu, asobi mo shinakatta. Ochi-konde tada heya ni toji-komotte ita dake datta.
(**e**) Neither Yamada nor Yamashita came to the party.
山田も山下もパーティーに来なかった。
Yamada mo Yamashita mo paatii ni konakatta.

nephew n.
o⌈i おい ↔ **mei** めい

nerve n.
shi⌉nkei 神経 **•c**

EX. (**a**) I had a nerve extracted and now my toothache is gone.
神経を抜いてもらったら、歯の痛みはなくなった。
Shinkei o nuite morattara, ha no ita-mi wa nakunatta.
(**b**) My current work is wearing down my nerves.
私は今の仕事で神経を擦り減らしています。
Watashi wa ima no shigoto de shinkei o suri-herashite imasu.
(**c**) That guy has a lot of nerve.
あいつは神経がずぶとい。
Aitsu wa shinkei ga zubutoi.

nervous adj. **[of the nerves or temporarily unable to relax]**

1. shi⌉nkei no N 神経のN **•c [of the nerves]**

EX. She is suffering from a nervous breakdown.
彼女は神経(の)衰弱にかかっている。
Kanojo wa shinkei (no) suijaku ni kakatte iru.

2. ki⌈nchoo-shita N 緊張したN **/〈Vinf. past of *kinchoo-suru* ③ become tense/ •c [showing strain] 《tense, strained, high-strung》**

EX. I got very nervous at the interview.
私はその面接でとても緊張した。
Watashi wa sono mensetsu de totemo kinchoo-shita.

3. shi⌈npai de ta⌈maranai 心配でたまらない **[unbearably worried]**

EX. Tomorrow I have a big exam that I'm really nervous about.
あした大きな試験があるんだ。それで、心配でたまらないんだ。
Ashita ookina shiken ga aru n da. Sore de, shinpai de tamaranai n da.

nest n. **[a place where a bird lays its eggs and shelters its young 《fig. "hiding place," "snug place," "hangout"》]**

1. su 巣 **[a place where a bird lays its eggs and shelters its young 《fig. "a place where similar people get together"》] 《hangout, den, haunt》**

EX. A bird built a nest in the tree outside my window.
鳥が部屋の窓から見える木に巣を作った。
Tori ga haya no mado kara mieru ki ni su o tsukutta.

2. ka⌈kure-basho 隠れ場所 **[a place for hiding]**

3. so⌈okutsu 巣くつ •c [a place where criminals live together] ⟪**den, hangout, haunt**⟫

EX. This apartment seems to have been a nest for drug traffickers.
このアパートは麻薬密売者の巣くつだったようだ。
Kono apaato wa mayaku-mitsubai-sha no sookutsu datta yooda.

net n. **[an open, meshed material made out of thread, cord, rope, wire, etc.]**

1. a⌈mi⌉ 網 [an open, meshed material made out of thread, cord, rope, wire, etc.] ⟪**casting net**⟫

EX. (**a**) Fish were caught in the net.
魚が網にかかった。
Sakana ga ami ni kakatta.
(**b**) It looks easier to catch fish in a net than with a fishing pole.
魚は釣るより網で取るほうが易しそうだ。
Sakana wa tsuru yori ami de toru hoo ga yasashi-soo da.

2. ne⌉tto ネット •f [an open, meshed material used in ball games such as tennis, pingpong, volleyball, etc.]

EX. My first serve always hits the net.
僕の最初のサーブはいつもネットに引っかかってしまう。
Boku no saisho no saabu wa itsu-mo netto ni hikkakatte shimau.

Netherlands n.

O⌈randa オランダ •f

network n. **[a net-like pattern or arrangement** ⟪**fig. "a net-like interconnection of people/broadcasting stations/operations"**⟫**]**

1. a⌈mi(-no)-me⌉ 網(の)目 [a net-like pattern] ⟪**meshes in a net**⟫

2. mo⌈ojoo-so⌉shiki 網状組織 •c [a net-like interconnection of operations]

3. ne⌈tto-wa⌉aku ネットワーク •f [a group of broadcasting stations that cooperate together], ho⌈oso⌉o-moo 放送網 •c

EX. In America there are three major TV networks: CBS, NBC and ABC.
アメリカにはCBS、NBC、ABCという三大{ネットワーク/放送網}がある。
Amerika ni wa CBS, NBC, ABC to iu san-dai-{netto-waaku/hoosoo-moo} ga aru.

neutral adj. **[siding with neither of two opposing sides** ⟪**fig. "gray," "neither positive nor negative"**⟫**]**

1. chu⌈uritsu no N 中立のN •c [siding with neither of two opposing sides]

EX. He took a neutral position on that issue.
彼はその問題に関して中立だった。
Kare wa sono mondai ni-kanshite chuuritsu datta.

2. ha⌈i-iro no N 灰色のN [of the color of ashes ⟪**fig. "for one's life to be gloomy"**⟫**]**

3. chu⌈usei no N 中性のN •c [having a character belonging to neither of two opposing categories, esp. neither male nor female]

Nevada n.

Ne⌉bada ネバダ •f

never adv. **[not ever** ⟪**fig. "not at all"**⟫**]**

1. i⌈chi-do mo Vinf. past ko⌈to⌉ ga na⌉i 一度もVinf. pastことがない [for s.o. to have not experienced doing s.t. even once]

EX. (**a**) I have never been to Japan.
私は一度も日本へ行ったことがない。
Watashi wa ichi-do mo Nihon e itta koto ga nai.
(**b**) Dan has never eaten *sushi*.
ダンはすしを一度も食べたことがない。
Dan wa sushi o ichi-do mo tabeta koto ga nai.

2. ni⌈-do⌉ to ...neg. 二度と…neg. [one strongly intends not to do s.t. again], ze⌈ttai ni ...neg. 絶対に…neg. [one will absolutely not do s.t.]

EX. (**a**) I will never speak to him again.
彼とは{二度と/絶対に}口をきかない(つもりだ)。
Kare to wa {ni-do to/zettai ni} kuchi o kikanai (tsumori da).
(**b**) History never repeats itself.
歴史は{二度と/絶対に}繰り返さない。
Rekishi wa {ni-do to/zettai ni} kuri-kaesanai.

PHRASE: never mind *ki-ni-{shinai de kudasai/suru na}* 気に{しないでください/するな}

nevertheless adv. **[in spite of that]** (so⌈re) ni⌉mo-ka⌈kawara⌉zu (それ)にもかかわらず **[regardless of that]** ⟪in spite of, notwithstanding⟫, so⌈re de⌉mo ya⌈ha⌉ri それでもやはり **[in spite of that, as expected]**

EX. (**a**) Tadao studied like mad, but he failed the entrance examination nevertheless.
忠男は気違いのように勉強した。{(それ)にもかかわらず/それでもやはり}、入学試験に失敗した。
Tadao wa ki-chigai no yooni benkyoo-shita. {(Sore) nimo-kakawarazu/Sore demo yahari}, nyuugaku-shiken ni shippai-shita.
(**b**) For two years John received the most advanced medical care available for his cancer, but he died nevertheless.
ジョンは二年間がんに対する最先端の治療を受けた。{(それ)にもかかわらず/それでもやはり}死んでしまった。
Jon wa ni-nenkan gan ni-taisuru sai-sentan no chiryoo o uketa. {(Sore) nimo-kakawarazu/Sore demo yahari} shinde shimatta.

new adj. **[not having existed for long or not having existed or been heard/seen/experienced before]**

1. a⌈tarashi⌉i 新しい adj(*i*). **[for s.t./s.o./s.a. to have not existed for long or to have not existed or been seen/heard/experienced before]** ⟪**fresh**⟫ ↔ **furui 古い** adj(*i*).; **ha⌈ji⌉mete no N 初めてのN [not having been seen/heard/experienced by one before]** ⟪**first**⟫

EX. (**a**) This is my new car.
これが私の{新しい/*初めての}車です。
*Kore ga watashi no {atarashii/ *hajimete no} kuruma desu.*
(**b**) Today a new teacher came to our Japanese class.
今日、日本語の授業に{新しい/初めての}先生が来た。
Kyoo, Nihon-go no jugyoo ni {atarashii/ hajimete no} sensei ga kita.
(**c**) Dining at a Japanese restaurant was a new experience for me.
日本料理屋での食事は僕には{新しい/初めての}経験だった。
Nihon-ryoori-ya de no shokuji wa boku ni wa {atarashii/hajimete no} keiken datta.

2. V*masu* na⌈re⌉nai N V*masu*慣れないN [not used to doing s.t.] ⟪**unaccumstomed to**⟫, **ha⌈ji⌉mete no N 初めてのN [not having been seen/heard/experienced by one before]** ⟪**first**⟫

EX. (**a**) There's a new person over there. I wonder who it is.
あそこに{見慣れない/初めての}人がいますね。だれでしょうか。
Asoko ni {mi-narenai/hajimete no} hito ga imasu ne. Dare deshoo ka.
(**b**) This music is new to me.
この音楽は僕には{初めてだ/?聞き慣れない}。
Kono ongaku wa boku ni wa {hajimete da/?kiki-narenai}.
(**c**) This machine is new to me.
この機械は{使い慣れない/初めてだ}。
Kono kikai wa {tsukai-narenai/hajimete da}.

news n. **[information about a recent event/events or a report of such information in the media]**

1. ha⌈nashi⌉ 話 [an act/instance of speaking ⟪fig. "rumor"⟫] ⟪**story, talk, speech**⟫, **ta⌉yori たより [s.t. one can depend on ⟪fig. "letter"⟫]** ⟪**tidings, words, information, reliance**⟫
㊟ "letter"▷便り, "reliance"▷頼り

EX. (**a**) Did you hear the news about Mr. Kida?
木田さんの{話/*便り}を聞きましたか。
*Kida-san no {hanashi/*tayori} o kikimashita ka.*
(**b**) No news is good news.
便りがないのはいい{便り/*話}だ。
*Tayori ga nai no wa ii {tayori/ *hanashi} da.*

2. nyu⌉usu ニュース •f [a report of information about recent events in the media]

EX. (**a**) I watch the news on TV every morning.
私は毎朝テレビのニュースを見ます。
Watashi wa mai-asa terebi no nyuusu o mimasu.
(**b**) Did you hear the news? Kaori is getting married to Shigeru.
ニュースを聞きましたか。香織が茂と結婚するんです。
Nyuusu o kikimashita ka. Kaori ga Shigeru to kekkon-suru n desu.

PHRASE: news to someone *hatsu-mimi* 初耳

EX. That's news to me.
それは初耳です。
Sore wa hatsu-mimi desu.

newspaper n. **[a publication, usu. issued daily or weekly, printed on sheets of paper and containing news, advertisements, opinion pieces, etc., or the paper on which this is printed]**
1. shi⌈nbun 新聞 •c [a publication printed on sheets of paper containing news, advertisements, opinion pieces, etc. and usually delivered to people's homes once or more a day]

EX. I don't subscribe to any newspaper.
僕は新聞を取っていません。
Boku wa shinbun o totte imasen.

2. shi⌈nbu⌉n(-shi) 新聞(紙) •c [paper on which news, advertisements, etc. are printed]

EX. We recycle newspapers in our town.
私たちの町では新聞(紙)をリサイクルしています。
Watashi-tachi no machi de wa shinbun(-shi) o risaikuru-shite imasu.

New Year('s) n. **[the first few days of a year]**
sho⌈ogatsu 正月 •c [the first 3-7 days of the year]

EX. In Japan, New Year('s) is as important as Christmas is in America.
日本では正月はアメリカのクリスマスと同じぐらい大事だ。
Nihon de wa shoogatsu wa Amerika no Kurisumasu to onaji-gurai daiji da.

New Year's Day n.
ga⌈njitsu 元日 •c

EX. On New Year's Day most Japanese make their first visit to a Shinto shrine to worship.
元日には日本人は大抵神社に初もうでをする。
Ganjitsu ni wa Nihon-jin wa taitei jinja ni hatsu-moode o suru.

New York n.
Nyu⌈uyo⌉oku ニューヨーク •f

next adj. **[nearest to s.t./s.o./s.a. in location or following s.t./s.o./s.a. in time or order]**
tsu⌈gi⌉ no N 次のN [occurring/located/sequenced exactly after s.t./s.o.] ⟪following, coming, ensuing, adjoining⟫

EX. (**a**) Shinbashi is the next station.
新橋は次の駅です。
Shinbashi wa tsugi no eki desu.
(**b**) I'll call you again next Tuesday.
次の火曜日にまたお電話します。
Tsugi no kayoo-bi ni mata o-denwa-shimasu.
(**c**) Who's next?
次の方はどなたですか。
Tsugi no kata wa donata desu ka.

—— adv. **[in the nearest place to s.t./s.o./s.a. or in the temporal order that follows s.t./s.o./s.a.]**
1. tsu⌈gi⌉ ni 次に n.+prt. **[in the temporal order that follows s.t./s.o./s.a.]**

EX. He sang next.
彼が次に歌った。
Kare ga tsugi ni utatta.

2. to⌈nari ni 隣に [in the nearest place to s.t./s.o./s.a.]

EX. Mary sat next to John.
メアリーはジョンの隣に坐った。
Mearii wa jon no tonari ni suwatta.

nice adj. **[pleasant/agreeable to s.o. or involving fine distinctions]**
1. i⌉i いい adj(*i*). **[morally correct/satisfactory/agreeable] ⟪good, right, fine, all right⟫ ↔ warui 悪い** adj(*i*).; **mi⌉gotona 見事な** adj(*na*). **[causing admiration due to being visually appealing or skillfully accomplished] ⟪brilliant, splendid, admirable, superb⟫**

EX. (**a**) Nice serve, John.

ジョン、{いい/見事な}サーブだ。
Jon, {ii/migotona} saabu da.
(**b**) It's a nice day, isn't it?
{いい/?見事な}天気ですね。
{Ii/?Migotona} tenki desu ne.
(**c**) He's really a nice guy.
あの人は本当に{いい/*見事な}人よ。
*Ano hito wa hontoo ni {ii/*migotona} hito yo.*

2. ko⌈maka⌉i 細かい adj(*i*). **[as small as a particle ⟪fig. "detailed," "stingy"⟫], ko⌈ma⌉kana N 細かなN [minute/fine] ⟪small, fine, minute, detailed⟫**

EX. I am not interested in such nice distinctions.
私はそんな{細かい/細かな}区別に興味がありません。
Watashi wa sonna {komakai/komakana} kubetsu ni kyoomi ga arimasen.

nickname n.
a⌈dana あだ名, ni⌈kkune⌉emu ニックネーム •f

EX. Our high school English teacher's nickname was "fire-engine" because he always came to class on time.
私たちの高校の英語の先生の{あだ名/ニックネーム}は消防自動車でした。必ず、授業に遅れずに来たからです。
Watashi-tachi no kookoo no eigo no sensei no {adana/nikkuneemu} wa shooboo-jidoosha deshita. Kanarazu, jugyoo ni okurezu ni kita kara desu.

niece n.
me⌈i めい •c ↔ oi おい

night n. **[the dark hours between sunset and sunrise]**
yo⌉ru 夜 ↔ hiru 昼

EX. (**a**) I studied until late Sunday night.
日曜の夜は遅くまで勉強しました。
Nichiyoo no yoru wa osoku made benkyoo-shimashita.
(**b**) About what time do you go to bed at night?
夜は何時ごろ寝ますか。
Yoru wa nan-ji-goro nemasu ka.

PHRASE: last night *{yuube/kinoo no yoru}* {ゆうべ/昨日の夜}

nine n./adj.
ko⌈ko⌉notsu (no N) 九つ(のN), {kyu⌉u/ku} (+counter) (no N) 九(+counter)(のN) •c SEE APPENDIX II

EX. (**a**) There are nine apples on the table.
テーブルの上にりんごが九つあります。
Teeburu no ue ni ringo ga kokonotsu arimasu.
(**b**) I'm leaving from Narita for New York on the 9:34 flight.
九時三十四分の便で成田を出てニューヨークへ行きます。
*{Ku/*Kyuu}-ji san-juu-yon-pun no bin de Narita o dete Nyuuyooku e ikimasu.*
(**c**) I have nine tickets for the concert.
コンサートの切符が九枚あります。
*Konsaato no kippu ga {kyuu/*ku}-mai arimasu.*
(**d**) I was in Hong Kong for nine days.
僕は香港に九日いた。
Boku wa Honkon ni kokonoka ita.

nineteen adj./n.
ju⌉u-{ku/kyuu} (+counter) (no N) 十九 (+counter)(のN) •c SEE APPENDIX II

ninety adj./n.
kyu⌉u-juu (+counter) (no N) 九十 (+counter)(のN) •c SEE APPENDIX II

ninth n./adj. **[next after eighth or one of nine equally divided parts]**
1. {kyu⌈u-ban-me/ku-⌈ban-me} (no N) 九番目(のN) [next after eighth], da⌈i-ku 第九 •c [next after eighth] SEE APPENDIX II

EX. (**a**) I am the ninth child.
私は{九番目の/*第九}子供です。
*Watashi wa {kyuu-ban-me no/*dai-ku} kodomo desu.*
(**b**) In Japan, Beethoven's Ninth Symphony is traditionally played at the end of the year.
日本では年末にベートーベンの{第九/?九番目の}シンフォニーを演奏する習慣がある。
Nihon de wa nen-matsu ni Beetooben no {dai-ku/?kyuu-ban-me no} shinfonii o ensoo-suru shuukan ga aru.

2. kyu⌈u-bun no i⌈chi⌉ 九分の一 •c [one of nine equally divided parts]

EX. My salary is one-ninth of his.
僕の給料は彼の九分の一だ。
Boku no kyuuryoo wa kare no kyuu-bun no ichi da.

nitrogen n.
chi˥sso 窒素 •c

no adj. **[not any/far from being]**
1. {ze˥nzen/hi˥to˥tsu mo/i˥chi˥ + counter mo}…neg. {全然/一つも/一+counterも}…neg. [not even one N (inanimate)], {ze˥nzen/hi˥tori mo/i˥chi + animal counter mo}…neg. {全然/一人も/一+animal counterも}…neg. [not even one person/animal]
EX. (**a**) There were no dogs in the town.
町には犬が{一匹も/全然}いなかった。
Machi ni wa inu ga {ip-piki mo/zenzen} inakatta.
(**b**) No students showed up for class.
学生は{一人も/全然}授業に出て来なかった。
Gakusei wa {hitori mo/zenzen} jugyoo ni dete konakatta.
(**c**) There was no money in my purse.
私の財布には金は{全然/一円も}なかった。
Watashi no saifu ni wa kane wa {zenzen/ichi-en mo} nakatta.
(**d**) Poor Jenny. She has no friends.
かわいそうに、ジェニーは友達が{一人も/全然}いない。
Kawai-sooni, Jenii wa tomodachi ga {hitori mo/zenzen} inai.
2. ke˥sshite…(na˥nka ja) na˥i 決して…(なんかじゃ)ない [far from being]
EX. He's no scholar, just an instructor.
あの人は決して学者なんかじゃない。ただの教師だ。
Ano hito wa kesshite gakusha nanka janai. Tada no kyooshi da.

— adv. **[a negative marker used to express denial/disagreement/surprise/emphasis]**
1. i˥ie いいえ [a slightly polite negative marker used to express denial or emphasis] ↔ hai はい, ee ええ; u˥u˥n ううん [a very informal negative marker] ⟪nope⟫, i˥ya˥ いや [a negative marker that is used to express denial of what s.o. (including the speaker) has said] ⟪or rather⟫
EX. (**a**) A: Do you like *tofu*?
豆腐が好きですか。
Toofu ga suki desu ka.
B: No, I hate it.
{いいえ/いや/*ううん}、大嫌いです。
*{Iie/Iya/*Uun}, dai-kirai desu.*
(**b**) A: Have you done your homework yet?
宿題(を)もうやった?
Shukudai (o) moo yatta?
B: No, not yet.
{ううん/いや/*いいえ}、まだだよ。
*{Uun/Iya/*Iie}, mada da yo.*
2. ma˥saka まさか adv. **[an adverb that indicates strong incredulousness in the face of an unexpected situation/event] ⟪never, impossible⟫**
EX. A: My boss fired me.
ボスに首(を)切られちゃった。
Bosu ni kubi (o) kira-rechatta.
B: No!
まさか。
Masaka.

nobody pron. **[no person]**
da˥re-mo…neg. だれも…neg. [for what is being described not to apply to any person mentioned]
EX. (**a**) Nobody came to the meeting.
会議にはだれも来なかった。
Kaigi ni wa dare-mo konakatta.
(**b**) Nobody knew of the incident.
だれもその事件を知らなかった。
Dare-mo sono jiken o shiranakatta.

nod vi. **[for s.o. to move one's head up and down repeatedly to express agreement or down and up once as a greeting ⟪fig. "drowse"⟫]**
1. u˥nazuku うなずく ① [for s.o. to bend one's head forward to express agreement or comprehension] ⟪bow one's head in assent⟫, e˥shaku-suru 会釈する ③ •c [for s.o. to make a shallow bow] ⟪salute, bow⟫
EX. (**a**) I asked the girl if she liked the ice cream and she nodded with a smile.
女の子に「アイスクリーム、おいしい?

N

と聞いたら、彼女はにっこりと{うなずいた/*会釈した}。
*Onna-no-ko ni 'Aisu-kuriimu, oishii?' to kiitara, kanojo wa nikkori to {unazuita/*eshaku-shita}.*
(**b**) Whenever I see that lady she nods to me.
その女性は会う度に私に{会釈する/*うなずく}。
*Sono josei wa au tabi ni watashi ni {eshaku-suru/*unazuku}.*

2. i-⌈nemu⌉ri-suru 居眠りする ③ [for s.o./s.a. to sleep while sitting/standing] ⟪doze, catnap⟫, u⌉to-uto-suru うとうとする ③ [for s.o./s.a. to fall into a very shallow sleep] ⟪drowse⟫

EX. Some students were nodding off during the lecture.
講義中に、{居眠りして/うとうとして}いる学生もいた。
Koogi-chuu ni, {i-nemuri-shite/uto-uto-shite} iru gakusei mo ita.

noise n. **[an undesired sound]**
so⌈oon 騒音 •c [loud/harsh sounds] ⟪din⟫, za⌈tsuon 雑音 •c [extraneous sounds], no⌉izu ノイズ •f [undesired extraneous sounds mixed in with the audio signal of a radio, TV, or other sound equipment]

EX. (**a**) I couldn't hear the speech because of the noise.
{騒音/雑音/?ノイズ}のため演説が聞こえなかった。
{Sooon/Zatsuon/?Noizu} no tame enzetsu ga kikoenakatta.
(**b**) There was a lot of noise in the recording.
録音には{雑音/ノイズ/?騒音}がたくさん入っていた。
Rokuon ni wa {zatsuon/noizu/?sooon} ga takusan haitte ita.

noisy adj. **[making a lot of noise]**
ya⌈kamashi⌉i やかましい adj(*i*). **[unpleasantly noisy or constantly making an issue of details] ⟪boisterous, clamorous⟫, u⌈rusa⌉i うるさい** adj(*i*). **[making a lot of noise ⟪fig. "annoying," "particular about s.t."⟫] ⟪bothering, clamorous, particular, fastidious⟫ ↔ shizukana 静かな** adj(*na*).

EX. The neighbor's piano was so noisy that I couldn't study.
隣のピアノが{うるさくて/やかましくて}勉強が出来なかった。
Tonari no piano ga {urusakute/yakamashikute} benkyoo ga dekinakatta.

none pron. **[no person/thing]**
na⌈ni-mo…neg. 何も…neg. [for what is being described not to apply to anything mentioned], da⌈re-mo…neg. だれも…neg. [for what is being described not to apply to any person mentioned], do⌈re-mo…neg. どれも…neg. [for what is being described to not apply to any of the things mentioned]

EX. (**a**) None of my friends are studying Japanese.
私の友達は{だれも/*何も/*どれも}日本語を勉強していない。
*Watashi no tomodachi wa {dare-mo/*nani-mo/*dore-mo} Nihon-go o benkyoo-shite inai.*
(**b**) I went to class having read none of the assigned readings.
宿題の読み物は{何も/どれも/*だれも}読まないで授業に出た。
*Shukudai no yomi-mono wa {nani-mo/dore-mo/*dare-mo} yomanai de jugyoo ni deta.*
(**c**) I got none of these problems right.
この問題は{どれも/*何も/*だれも}分からなかった。
*Kono mondai wa {dore-mo/*nani-mo/*dare-mo} wakaranakatta.*

nonsense n. **[a string of words that makes no sense ⟪fig. "foolish behavior"⟫]**
1. mu-⌈i⌉mina koto 無意味なこと [s.t. meaningless], na⌉nsensuna koto ナンセンスなこと

EX. He's always talking nonsense.
彼はいつも{無意味な/ナンセンスな}ことばかりを言っている。
Kare wa itsu-mo {mu-imina/nansensuna} koto bakari o itte iru.

2. ba⌈ka-geta koto ばかげたこと [s.t. foolish]

EX. What nonsense!

なんてばかげたことだ。
Nante baka-geta koto da.

noodle n. **[a thin strip of dough made from flour and eggs]**
u⌈don うどん [a strip of dough made from flour], so⌉ba そば [a plant with beechnut-shaped seeds or a dark flour made from such seeds or a strip of dough made from this flour] ⟪**buckwheat**⟫, **me⌉n(-rui) めん(類) •c [a general term for food consisting of strips of dough made from flour of various types]**

EX. *Udon* and *soba* are two traditional noodle dishes in Japan.
「うどん」と「そば」は日本の二つの伝統的なめん(類)だ。
'Udon' to 'soba' wa Nihon no futatsu no dentoo-tekina men(-rui) da.

noon n. **[12 o'clock in the day]**
sho⌉ogo 正午 •c [12 o'clock in the day], hi⌈ru⌉ 昼 [12 o'clock in the day/the time between dawn and sunset/lunch] ↔ yoru 夜

EX. There will be a political rally at noon in the quadrangle.
{昼/正午}に中庭で政治集会がある。
{Hiru/Shoogo} ni naka-niwa de seiji-shuukai ga aru.

nor adv./conj. **[and not]**
…mo(…mo)…neg. …も(…も)…neg., …mo…neg. shi, …mo…neg. …も…neg. し、…も…neg.

EX. (**a**) I have neither a TV nor a radio.
私はテレビもラジオもない。
Watashi wa terebi mo rajio mo nai.
(**b**) My father neither drinks nor smokes.
父は酒も飲まないし、たばこも吸わない。
Chichi wa sake mo nomanai shi, tabako mo suwanai.
(**c**) This dish is neither sweet nor salty.
この料理は甘くもないし、辛くもない。
Kono ryoori wa amaku mo nai shi, karaku mo nai.

normal adj. **[conforming to a norm]**
fu⌈tsuu no N 普通のN •c [conforming to a standard/norm ⟪fig. "commonly found"⟫] ⟪ordinary, regular, usual, common, conventional⟫ ↔ tokushuna 特殊な •c, tokubetsu no N 特別のN •c; se⌈ijoona 正常な adj(*na*). **•c [conforming to the usual standard] ⟪regular⟫ ↔ ijoona 異常な** adj(*na*). **•c; no⌉omaruna ノーマルな** adj(*na*). **•f [conforming to the usual standard]**

EX. (**a**) I was brought up in a normal American family.
私はアメリカの{普通の/*正常な/*ノーマルな}家庭で育てられた。
*Watashi wa Amerika no {futsuu no/ *seijoona/*noomaruna} katei de sodate-rareta.*
(**b**) The doctor told me that my cholesterol level was normal.
医者は私のコレステロール値は{正常/ノーマル/?普通}だと言った。
Isha wa watashi no koresuterooru-chi wa {seijoo/noomaru/?futsuu} da to itta.

north n./adj.
ki⌈ta⌉ 北 ↔ minami 南; ki⌈ta no N 北のN ↔ minami no N 南のN

EX. It has started to snow in the north.
北では雪が降り始めた。
Kita de wa yuki ga furi-hajimeta.

northeast n./adj.
ho⌈ku-too 北東 •c; ho⌈ku-too no N 北東のN •c

northern adj. **[of/in the north]**
ki⌉ta no N 北のN [of/in the north] ↔ minami no N 南のN; ki⌈ta kara⌉ no N 北からのN [coming from the north] ↔ minami kara no N 南からのN; {hoku/kita}- 北〜 [of/in the north] ↔ {nan/minami}- 南〜

NOTE: Either *hoku-* or *kita-* may be used as a prefix, depending upon the particular compound it appears in. See the following examples.

EX. (**a**) I come from the northern part of California.
私はカリフォルニアの{北部/北の方}から来ました。
Watashi wa Kariforunia no {hoku-bu/ kita no hoo} kara kimashita.
(**b**) The northern winds here are terribly cold.

N

この辺では北({の/からの})風は恐ろしく冷たいです。
Kono hen de wa kita ({no/kara no}) kaze wa osoroshiku tsumetai desu.
(**c**) When it's summer in the northern hemisphere, it's winter in the southern hemisphere.
北半球が夏の時、南半球は冬だ。
Kita-hankyuu ga natsu no toki, minami-hankyuu wa fuyu da.

northwest n./adj.
ho⌈ku-sei 北西 **•c, ho⌈ku-sei no N** 北西のN **•c**

Norway n.
No⌈ruue⌉e ノルウエー **•f**

nose n. **[the organ at the front of the head in mammals that is used for breathing and smelling 《fig. "sense of smell," "s.t. like a nose"》]**

1. ha⌈na 鼻 **[the organ at the front of the head in mammals that is used for breathing and smelling 《fig. "nasal mucus"》] 《nose, snout, trunk, muzzle》**

EX. (**a**) Your nose is running. You'd better wipe it.
鼻が{出て/垂れて}いるよ。鼻をかみなさい。
Hana ga {dete/tarete} iru yo. Hana o kaminasai.
(**b**) He has a flat nose.
彼は鼻が低い。
Kare wa hana ga hikui.

2. kyu⌈ukaku きゅう覚 **•c [the olfactory sense], ka⌈n** 勘 **[the sixth sense] 《intuition》**

EX. My wife has the nose of a newspaper reporter.
妻には新聞記者の{きゅう覚/勘}がある。
Tsuma ni wa shinbun-kisha no {kyuukaku/kan} ga aru.

3. ki⌉shu 機首 **•c [the nose of an airplane]**

nostril n. **[an opening in the nose]**
ha⌈na no ana⌉ 鼻の穴 **[the holes in the nose], bi⌈koo** 鼻孔 **•c**

not adv. **[an adverb that is used to express a negative or denial or refusal]**
{Vneg./Vstem/shi/ko/adj(*i*). *ku*} nai
{Vneg./Vstem/し/来/adj(*i*). *ku*}ない,
{adj(*na*). stem/N} {dewa⌈na⌉i/ja⌈na⌉i}
{adj(*na*). stem/N}{ではない/じゃない}

EX. (**a**) The movie I saw today was not interesting.
今日見た映画は面白くなかった。
Kyoo mita eiga wa omoshiroku nakatta.
(**b**) My parents are not as healthy as they used to be.
両親は昔のように元気じゃありません。
Ryooshin wa mukashi no yooni genki jaarimasen.
(**c**) I am not going to Japan this year.
今年は日本へ行かない。
Kotoshi wa Nihon e ikanai.
(**d**) Please do not call me at home.
自宅へ電話をしないでください。
Jitaku e denwa o shinai de kudasai.
(**e**) I cannot read a Japanese newspaper unless I have my dictionary with me.
辞書がなければ日本の新聞が読めない。
Jisho ga nakereba Nihon no shinbun ga yome-nai.
(**f**) I do not have the time to take on the duties of chair of this committee.
この委員会の委員長を引き受けるだけの時間の余裕がありません。
Kono iin-kai no iin-choo o hiki-ukeru dake no jikan no yoyuu ga arimasen.

PHRASE: not…at all *{zenzen/mattaku}*…neg. {全然/まったく}…neg.

EX. I cannot eat sushi at all.
すしは{全然/まったく}食べられません。
Sushi wa {zenzen/mattaku} tabe-raremasen.

PHRASE: not only…but also *dake {dewanakute/janakute}…mo* だけ{ではなくて/じゃなくて}…も

EX. He works not only on Saturdays but also on Sundays.
彼は土曜だけ{ではなくて/じゃなくて}、日曜も働きます。
Kare wa doyoo dake {dewanakute/janakute}, nichiyoo mo hatarakimasu.

PHRASE: not…but *{dewanakute/janakute}…da* {ではなくて/じゃなくて}…だ

EX. Taro is not my son, but my nephew.

太郎は僕の息子{じゃなくて/ではなくて}、おいだ。
Taroo wa boku no musuko {janakute/dewanakute}, oi da.

PHRASE: not very… *amari*…neg. あまり…neg.

EX. It's not very hot here in the summer.
ここは夏あまり暑くない。
Koko wa natsu amari atsukunai.

note n. **[**⟨a symbol for⟩ **a single sound in music or s.t. briefly written to aid one's memory or to draw s.o.'s attention to s.t., including a short letter** ⟪**fig. "attention," "distinction"**⟫**]**

1. o⌈boe-gaki 覚書 [s.t. written briefly to aid one's memory] ⟪**memorandum, memo, minute**⟫

EX. The chairperson circulated the note among the committee members.
議長は委員に覚書を回した。
Gichoo wa iin ni oboe-gaki o mawashita.

2. chu⌈u 注 •c [a comment attached to a text to explain its meaning or to provide a reference] ⟪**annotation, comment**⟫

EX. This Japanese textbook has good grammar notes.
この日本語の教科書はいい文法の注が付いている。
Kono Nihon-go no kyooka-sho wa ii bunpoo no chuu ga tsuite iru.

3. chu⌉ui 注意 •c [the act of fixing the mind on s.t. ⟪**fig. "warning," "advice"**⟫**]** ⟪**attention, heed, care**⟫

EX. Please take note of this point.
この点に注意をしてください。
Kono ten ni chuui o shite kudasai.

4. ju⌈uyoo-sei 重要性 •c [the quality of being indispensable and irreplaceable] ⟪**importance**⟫

5. o⌈n 音 •c [a single sound in music]

EX. Her voice can reach very high notes.
彼女の声は非常に高音まで出る。
Kanojo no koe wa hijooni koo-on made deru.

—— vt. **[to write s.t. down as a record or comment or to pay attention to s.t.]**

1. ⟨**-o**⟩ **ka⌈ki-tomeru** ⟨～を⟩**書き留める ② [for s.o. to put s.t. down in writing]** ⟪**jot down, record**⟫

EX. The students noted every word of the professor's lecture.
学生は教授が講義したことを全部書き留めた。
Gakusei wa kyooju ga koogi-shita koto o zenbu kaki-tometa.

2. ⟨**-ni**⟩ **chu⌉ui-suru** ⟨～に⟩**注意する ③ •c [for s.o. to pay/cause s.o. to pay close attention to s.t. or to tell s.o. to be careful so that s.t. undesirable does not occur]**

EX. Please note carefully what I have said.
私が言ったことによく注意してください。
Watashi ga itta koto ni yoku chuui-shite kudasai.

3. ⟨**-ni**⟩ **chu⌈u o tsu⌈ke⌉ru** ⟨～に⟩**注を付ける ② [for s.o. to add notes to a text]**

notebook n. **[a book containing blank pages in which to write s.t.]**

no⌉oto ノート •f [a book containing blank pages in which to write s.t.], te⌈choo 手帳 [a booklet containing blank pages in which to write one's schedule, etc.] ⟪**memo-book**⟫

EX. (**a**) I forgot my notebook, so I just listened to the lecture.
{ノート/*手帳}を忘れたので、講義をただ聞いた。
*{Nooto/*Techoo} o wasureta node, koogi o tada kiita.*
(**b**) I wrote down her address in my notebook.
彼女の住所を{手帳/ノート}に書いた。
Kanojo no juusho o {techoo/nooto} ni kaita.

nothing n. **[no thing** ⟪**fig. "zero," "s.o./s.t. of no importance"**⟫**]**

1. na⌈ni-mo…neg. 何も…neg. [for what is being described not to apply to anything mentioned]

EX. (**a**) I know nothing about the incident.
その事件については何も知らない。
Sono jiken ni-tsuite wa nani-mo shiranai.
(**b**) I tried to pour some wine, but nothing came out of the bottle.

N

ワインをつごうとしたけれど、瓶からは何も出て来なかった。
Wain o tsugoo to shita keredo, bin kara wa nani-mo dete konakatta.

N

2. ze˥ro ゼロ •f
3. tsu˥mara˥nai mono つまらないもの [s.t. uninteresting]
PHRASE: nothing but *-bakari* 〜ばかり
EX. He eats nothing but meat.
彼は肉ばかり食べる。
Kare wa niku bakari taberu.

notice n. **[information conveyed or displayed in written or printed form ⟪fig. "observation"⟫]**
1. shi˥rase 知らせ /⟨V*masu* of *shiraseru* ② inform/ [an act/instance of informing s.o. about s.t. or the content of this, esp. in written/printed form] ⟪information, report, news, word⟫, tsu˥uchi 通知 •c [a communication containing information, usually official or formal] ⟪information, communication⟫, tsu˥ukoku 通告 •c [an official communication instructing s.o. to do s.t.] ⟪notification, announcement, warning⟫, ke˥ikoku 警告 •c [an act/instance of calling s.o.'s attention to imminent danger/evil] ⟪warning, caution⟫, yo˥koku 予告 •c [an act/instance of informing s.o. of an important matter ahead of time] ⟪preliminary announcement⟫, ko˥kuji 告示 •c [governmental information] ⟪bulletin⟫
EX. (**a**) I received a notice from our affiliate office in Japan saying that they were soon moving to a new location.
日本の提携先からじきに移転するという{知らせ/通知/*通告/*警告/*予告/*告示}を受け取った。
*Nihon no teikei-saki kara jikini iten-suru to iu {shirase/tsuuchi/*tsuukoku/*keikoku/*yokoku/*kokuji} o uke-totta.*
(**b**) The IRS sent me a notice asking me to appear at its office.
税務署は事務所に出頭せよという{知らせ/通知/通告/*警告/*予告/*告示}をよこした。
*Zeimu-sho wa jimu-sho ni shuttoo-seyo to iu {shirase/tsuuchi/tsuukoku/*keikoku/*yokoku/*kokuji} o yokoshita.*
(**c**) The parking fee was raised without any notice.
駐車料金が何の{予告/知らせ/通知/?通告/?警告/*告示}もなく上げられた。
*Chuusha-ryookin ga nan no {yokoku/shirase/tsuuchi/?tsuukoku/?keikoku/*kokuji} mo naku age-rareta.*
(**d**) My professor e-mailed me a notice telling me that I was in danger of failing his course.
教授が電子メールで僕が彼の授業で落第するかもしれないという{通知/警告/*通告/*知らせ/*告示/*予告}をしてきた。
*Kyooju ga denshi-meeru de boku ga kare no jugyoo de rakudai-suru kamoshirenai to iu {tsuuchi/keikoku/*tsuukoku/*shirase/*kokuji/*yokoku} o shite kita.*
(**e**) I read a notice from city hall telling everyone to register for the upcoming election.
今度の選挙のために登録をすべしという市役所からの{告示/知らせ/通知/*警告/*通告/*予告}を読んだ。
*Kondo no senkyo no tame ni tooroku o su-beshi to iu shiyaku-sho kara no {kokuji/shirase/tsuuchi/*keikoku/*tsuukoku/*yokoku} o yonda.*

— vt. **[for s.o. to perceive s.t.]**
⟨-ni⟩ ki-˥ga-tsu˥ku ⟨〜に⟩気がつく ① [for s.o./s.a. to become aware of s.t./s.o./s.a.] ⟪become aware of, perceive, realize⟫
EX. After I got off the bus, I noticed that my purse was gone.
バスを降りてから、財布がなくなっていることに気がつきました。
Basu o orite kara, saifu ga nakunatte iru koto ni ki-ga-tsukimashita.

noun n.
me˥ishi 名詞 •c

novel n.
sho˥osetsu 小説 •c
EX. (**a**) Have you ever read the Japanese novel *Snow Country*?

『雪国』という日本の小説を読んだことがありますか。
"Yuki-guni" to iu Nihon no shoosetsu o yonda koto ga arimasu ka.
(**b**) I'd like to write a novel based on my experiences in China.
中国での体験をもとにした小説が書きたいです。
Chuugoku de no taiken o moto ni shita shoosetsu ga kaki-tai desu.

November n.
ju⌈u-ichi-gatsu⌉ 十一月
EX. In Tokyo, November is still autumn.
東京では十一月はまだ秋です。
Tookyoo de wa juu-ichi-gatsu wa mada aki desu.

now adv. **[at the time when or of which one is speaking or writing ⟪fig. "by this time"⟫]**
1. i⌉ma 今 [at the time when one is speaking or writing] ⟪at present, right now⟫, mo⌉kka 目下 •c [at the time when one is speaking or writing ⟨fml⟩] ⟪at present, as of the moment⟫, ge⌉nzai 現在 •c [at the present time as opposed to the past/future] ⟪presently⟫
EX. (**a**) Can you come see me now?
{今/*目下/*現在}会いに来られますか。
*{Ima/*Mokka/*Genzai} ai ni ko-raremasu ka.*
(**b**) I'm now living in Kyoto.
私は{今/現在/?目下}京都に住んでいます。
Watashi wa {ima/genzai/?mokka} Kyooto ni sunde imasu.
(**c**) The incident is now under investigation.
その事件は{今/目下/現在}調査中だ。
Sono jiken wa {ima/mokka/genzai} choosa-chuu da.
2. i⌈magoro wa 今ごろは [by this time], mo⌉o もう [to be no longer in the same state as at some previous time] ⟪(not)...any longer, (not)...any more, yet, already⟫
EX. My father should be in London by now.
父は{今ごろは/もう}ロンドンに着いているはずです。
Chichi wa {imagoro wa/moo} Rondon ni tsuite iru hazu desu.

PHRASE: now that... Vinf. past *kara ni wa* Vinf. pastからには
EX. Now that you've studied Japanese, you should get a job where you can make use of that knowledge.
日本語を勉強したからにはその知識が活かせる仕事がいいでしょうね。
Nihon-go o benkyoo-shita kara ni wa sono chishiki ga ika-seru shigoto ga ii deshoo ne.

—— n. **[the present time at which or of which one is speaking or writing]**
i⌉ma 今 [at the time when one is speaking or writing], ge⌉nzai 現在 •c [at the present time as opposed to the past/future] ↔ kako 過去 •c [the past time/tense], mirai 未来 •c [the period of time after the present]
EX. (**a**) Now is the time to start saving energy.
{今/現在}はまさにエネルギー節約に取りかかるべき時期です。
{Ima/Genzai} wa masa ni enerugii-setsuyaku ni tori-kakaru-beki jiki desu.
(**b**) From now on I'll exercise three times a week.
{今/*現在}からは週三回運動をします。
*{Ima/*Genzai} kara wa shuu san-kai undoo o shimasu.*

nowadays adv. **[at the present time in contrast to a past time]**
ko⌉nnichi de wa 今日では •c [in recent days as opposed to days of the past], to⌈osetsu wa 当節は •c [these days ⟨fml⟩] ⟪these days⟫
EX. Nowadays college students seldom wear uniforms in Japan.
{今日で/当節}は日本の大学生は制服を滅多に着ない。
{Konnichi de/Toosetsu} wa Nihon no daigaku-sei wa seifuku o metta ni kinai.

nowhere adv. **[not at any place]**
do⌈ko ni mo...neg. どこにも…neg. [not to exist at any place], do⌈ko de mo...neg. どこでも…neg. [not to do s.t. at any place], do⌈ko {ni/e} mo {ikanai/ko⌉nai} どこ{に/へ}も{行かない/来ない} [not to go/come to any place]
EX. (**a**) My purse was nowhere to be found.

N

僕の財布はどこ{に/*で}もなかった。
*Boku no saifu wa doko {ni/*de} mo nakatta.*
(**b**) Last weekend I went nowhere.
先週の週末はどこ{へ/に/*で}も行かなかった。
*Senshuu no shuumatsu wa doko {e/ni/*de} mo ikanakatta.*
(**c**) A car like that which is both inexpensive and top quality is nowhere to be found.
そんな安くて上等な車はどこ{に/で}も売っていない。
Sonna yasukute jootoona kuruma wa doko {ni/de} mo utte inai.

nuclear adj. **[having to do with the nucleus of an atom 《fig. "of nuclear energy"》]**
1. ka⌉ku no N 核のN •c [having to do with the small ball-like object in the center of an organic cell 《fig. "of a core," "of the atomic nucleus"》]
2. ge⌈nshi⌉-kaku no N 原子核のN •c [of the atomic nucleus]
3. ge⌈nshi⌉-ryoku no N 原子力のN •c [of atomic energy]
EX. (**a**) We need more nuclear power plants in our country.
我が国は原子力(の)発電所がもっと要る。
Waga-kuni wa genshi-ryoku (no) hatsuden-sho ga motto iru.
(**b**) We should promote the peaceful use of nuclear energy.
私たちは原子力の平和利用を進めなければならない。
Watashi-tachi wa genshi-ryoku no heiwa-riyoo o susumenakereba naranai.

nuisance n. **[an unpleasant/annoying person/thing/action]**
1. me⌉iwakuna hito 迷惑な人 [an unpleasant person who causes one inconvenience and even monetary loss]
EX. She's such a nuisance. She always calls me when I'm busiest.
あの人は迷惑な人だ。一番忙しい時に、いつも電話して来るんだから。
Ano hito wa meiwakuna hito da. Ichiban isogashii toki ni, itsu-mo denwa-shite kuru n da kara.
2. me⌉iwaku 迷惑 •c [an act/instance of causing s.o. a feeling of unpleasantness/loss of profit]
EX. (**a**) The new building next door is a nuisance. Thanks to it we don't get nearly as much sunshine as before.
隣の新しい建物は迷惑だ。おかげで前よりずっと日当たりが悪くなってしまった。
Tonari no atarashii tate-mono wa meiwaku da. Okage de mae yori zutto hi-atari ga waruku natte shimatta.
(**b**) Our neighbor's stereo is a big nuisance.
隣のステレオは大変迷惑だ。
Tonari no sutereo wa taihen meiwaku da.

number n. **[a symbol or word indicating the quantity of s.t. 《fig. "numeral identifying a telephone/house, etc.," "a single issue of a magazine," "total"》]**
1. ka⌉zu 数 《numeral》, su⌉u 数 •c 《numeral》, su⌈uji 数字 •c [a symbol indicating a quantity], su⌈ushi 数詞 •c [a numeral which functions as a part of speech] 《numeral》
EX. (**a**) That three-year old boy already knows all his numbers up to 10,000.
その三歳の男の子はもう一万まで{数/数字/?数/*数詞}を全部知っている。
*Sono san-sai no otoko-no-ko wa moo ichi-man made {kazu/suuji/?suu/*suushi} o zenbu shitte iru.*
(**b**) He is very good with numbers.
彼は{数/数字/?数/*数詞}に強い。
*Kare wa {kazu/suuji/?suu/*suushi} ni tsuyoi.*
(**c**) The number of students taking Japanese is increasing rapidly.
日本語の授業の登録者{の数/数/*数字/*数詞}が急に増えている。
*Nihon-go no jugyoo no tooroku-sha {no kazu/-suu/*suuji/*suushi} ga kyuuni fuete iru.*
(**d**) The Japanese number system consists of both Chinese and Japanese readings.

日本語の{数詞/数/?数/*数字}の体系は音と訓の{数詞/数/?数/*数字}からなっている。
*Nihon-go no {suushi/suu/?kazu/*suuji} no taikei wa on to kun no {suushi/suu/?kazu/*suuji} kara natte iru.*

2. ba⌈ngo⌉o 番号 •c [a numeral that identifies a telephone, house, etc.]

EX. (**a**) A: May I have your telephone number?
電話番号は何番でしょうか。
Denwa-bangoo wa nan-ban deshoo ka.
B: It's 344-8619.
344の8619です。
San-yon-yon no hachi-roku-ichi-kyuu desu.
(**b**) A: May I have your apartment number?
アパートの番号は何番ですか。
Apaato no bangoo wa nan-ban desu ka.
B: It's 358.
358番です。
San-byaku-go-juu-hachi-ban desu.

3. -goo 〜号 •c [a suffix indicating the order in which issues of a magazine appear or an artist's given name] ⟪issue, title, pen name⟫

EX. This is issue number one of the journal.
これは雑誌の(第)一号です。
Kore wa zasshi no (dai-)ichi-goo desu.

PHRASE: a number of *kanari no kazu no* N かなりの数のN

EX. A number of people came to listen to his speech.
彼の演説を聞きに、かなりの数の人が来た。
Kare no enzetsu o kiki-ni, kanari no kazu no hito ga kita.

— vt. **[to give a number to s.t. ⟪fig. "count"⟫]**

1. ⟨-ni⟩ ba⌈ngo⌉o o tsu⌈ke⌉ru ⟨〜に⟩番号を付ける ② [to give a number to s.t.]

EX. Please number each page of your paper.
レポートのページに番号を付けてください。
Repooto no peeji ni bangoo o tsukete kudasai.

2. (⟨-no⟩ na⌉ka) ni i⌈reru (⟨〜の⟩中)に入れる ② [for s.o. to include s.t./s.o./s.a. in s.t.] ⟪count⟫

EX. I would number this song among the best of the decade.
この歌をこの十年間の最もいい歌に入れたい。
Kono uta o kono juu-nenkan no mottomo ii uta ni ire-tai.

PHRASE: be numbered *majikai.* 〜間近い adj(*i*).

EX. His days are numbered.
彼は死期が間近い。
Kare wa shiki ga majikai.

— vi. **[to amount to a certain quantity] ⟨-ni⟩ na⌉ru ⟨〜に⟩なる ① [to turn into s.t.] ⟪become, change, turn, amount to⟫**

EX. The participants in the workshop numbered 200.
講習会の参加者は二百人になった。
Kooshuu-kai no sanka-sha wa ni-hyaku-nin ni natta.

numerous adj. **[very many ⟨fml⟩]**
ta⌈su⌉u no N 多数のN •c [very many] ⟪of a large number, a multitude of⟫

EX. (**a**) There were numerous victims in that plane accident.
その飛行機事故は多数の犠牲者を出した。
Sono hikoo-ki-jiko wa tasuu no gisei-sha o dashita.
(**b**) That professor has written numerous papers in his field.
その教授は専門の分野で多数の論文を書いている。
Sono kyooju wa senmon no bun'ya de tasuu no ronbun o kaite iru.

nurse n. **[a person who takes care of a sick or injured person or a young child]**
ka⌈ngo⌉-fu 看護婦 •c [a female person who takes care of a sick or injured person]

EX. (**a**) My younger sister is a nurse.
妹は看護婦をしています。
Imooto wa kango-fu o shite imasu.
(**b**) Nurse, give me my pain killer, please.
看護婦さん、痛み止めの薬を下さい。
Kango-fu-san, ita-mi-dome no kusuri o kudasai.

nursery n. **[a place where young children are taken care of, esp. during the day]**
1. ta⌈kuji-sho 託児所 •c [a place where young children are taken care of while their mothers are working] ⟪day-care center⟫, ho⌈iku-jo 保育所 •c [a place where pre-schoolers are taken care of during the week while their parents are working], ho⌈iku⌉-en 保育園 •c ⟪day-care center⟫
NOTE: *Hoiku-jo* is also commonly referred to as *hoiku-en.*

EX. I take my child to a nursery near my home at 7:30 every morning.
私は毎朝七時半に子供をうちの近くの{託児所/保育所/保育園}に連れて行きます。
Watashi wa mai-asa shichi-ji-han ni kodomo o uchi no chikaku no {takuji-sho/hoiku-jo/hoiku-en} ni tsurete ikimasu.

2. na⌈e-doko 苗床 [a place where young plants are grown] ⟪seedbed, seed-plot⟫
3. yo⌈osei-jo 養成所 •c [an institution where young people are trained for a special skill] ⟪training school⟫

nut n. **[a kind of fruit with a hard shell ⟪fig. "an eccentric person"⟫]**
1. na⌉ttsu ナッツ •f

EX. Walnuts are my favorite kind of nut.
ナッツの中では、くるみが一番好きだ。
Nattsu no naka de wa, kurumi ga ichiban suki da.

2. ki-⌈chiga⌉i 気違い [a person whose mind is deranged ⟪fig. "a person who is crazy about s.t."⟫] ⟪insanity, lunatic, insane⟫

EX. Don't go near him. He's nuts.
あいつは気違いだから、近づくなよ。
Aitsu wa ki-chigai da kara, chikazuku na yo.

nylon n.
na⌉iron ナイロン •f

EX. Nylon socks are stronger than cotton socks.
ナイロンの靴下は木綿の靴下より強い。
Nairon no kutsu-shita wa momen no kutsu-shita yori tsuyoi.

oak n.
ka⌉shi かし

oar n. **[a wooden stick with a blade at one end used for rowing a boat]**
ka⌉i かい [a wooden stick with a blade on one/both ends with/without an oarlock to propel a canoe/small boat], o⌈oru オール •f [oars for a Western boat]

oath n. **[a promise made by calling on God or s.t. sacred as witness]**
chi⌈kai 誓い /⟨V*masu* of ① *chikau* take a pledge/ [a solemn promise formally made to God, Buddha, or a person] ⟪pledge, vow⟫

EX. (**a**) Bob took an oath stating that he would never break his promise.
ボブは約束を絶対に破らないという誓いを立てた。
Bobu wa yakusoku o zettai ni yaburanai to iu chikai o tateta.
(**b**) The President took his oath of office before the public.
大統領は就任の誓いを公衆の前で行った。
Daitooryoo wa shuunin no chikai o kooshuu no mae de okonatta.

oatmeal n.
o⌈otomi⌉iru オートミール •f

oats n.
ka⌈rasu-mu⌉gi からす麦

obedient adj. **[willing to accept and act according to the dictates of some authority]**

〈-ni〉 ju⌈ujunna 〈〜に〉従順な adj(*na*). •c **[for one's personality/attitude to be gentle and submissive]** **⟪submissive, docile⟫**

EX. The children in that family are obedient and always do as they are told by their parents.
あのうちの子供たちは従順でいつも両親の言うことを聞きます。
Ano uchi no kodomo-tachi wa juujun de itsu-mo ryooshin no iu koto o kikimasu.

obey vt. **[to accept and act according to the dictates of some authority]**

1. 〈-ni〉 shi⌈tagau 〈〜に〉従う ① **[to accept and act according to advice, rules, orders, etc.]** **⟪submit oneself to, comply with⟫** ↔ **〈-ni〉 sakarau** 〈〜に〉逆らう ①

EX. A: Did you always obey your parents?
両親にいつも従いましたか。
Ryooshin ni itsu-mo shitagaimashita ka.
B: No, in fact I disobeyed them more often than I obeyed them.
いや、実は従うことより逆らうことの方が多かったです。
Iya, jitsu wa shitagau koto yori sakarau koto no hoo ga ookatta desu.

object n. **[s.t. that can be perceived to exist by one or more of the five senses]**

1. mo⌈no⌉ 物 **[s.t. tangible or s.t. abstract grasped as if it were tangible]** **⟪thing, substance, matter⟫**, **bu⌈ttai** 物体 •c **[a tangible thing (used in scientific discourse)]**

EX. Can you see that tiny object on the table?
つくえの上の小さな{物/物体}が見えますか。
Tsukue no ue no chiisana {mono/buttai} ga miemasu ka.

2. mo⌈kuteki 目的 •c **[the intended result of a particular action/behavior]** **⟪purpose, aim, end⟫**, **mo⌈kuhyoo** 目標 •c **[s.t. one wishes to achieve]** **⟪mark, sign, goal, objective, target⟫**

EX. (**a**) A: What is the object of this meeting?
この会の{目的/??目標}は何ですか。
Kono kai no {mokuteki/??mokuhyoo} wa nan desu ka.
B: It's to elect a new chair.
新しい委員長を選ぶことです。
Atarashii iin-choo o erabu koto desu.
(**b**) Let's set up the object of this project first.
先ずこのプロジェクトの{目標/*目的}を設定しよう。
*Mazu kono purojekuto no {mokuhyoo/*mokuteki} o settei-shiyoo.*

3. ta⌈ishoo 対象 •c **[s.t. concrete that is mentally under focus]**

EX. The object of our research is solar energy.
私たちの研究の対象は太陽エネルギーです。
Watashi-tachi no kenkyuu no taishoo wa taiyoo-enerugii desu.

4. mo⌈kuteki-go 目的語 •c **[direct/indirect object of a verb (a grammatical term)]**

EX. What is the direct object in the sentence "I love you?"
「私はあなたを愛しています」という文の直接目的語は何ですか。
'Watashi wa anata o aishite imasu' to iu bun no chokusetsu-mokuteki-go wa nan desu ka.

— vi. **[for s.o. to express one's dissatisfaction with and opposition to s.t.]** **〈-ni〉 ha⌈ntai-suru** 〈〜に〉反対する ③ •c **[for s.o. to be in serious conflict with s.o. else's opinion, plan, idea, proposal, etc.]** **⟪oppose, take a stand against⟫** ↔ **〈-ni〉 sansei suru** 〈〜に〉賛成する ③ •c; **〈-ni〉 ha⌈ntai da** 〈〜に〉反対だ •c **[for s.o. to be opposed to s.o. else's opinion]** **⟪be opposed to, be against⟫** ↔ **〈-ni〉 sansei da** 〈〜に〉賛成だ •c

EX. (**a**) A: Do you object to this plan?
この計画に反対{します/です}か。
Kono keikaku ni hantai {-shimasu/desu} ka.
B: No, I agree with it.
いいえ、それには賛成{します/です}。
Iie, sore ni wa sansei {-shimasu/desu}.
(**b**) Some people objected to the plan as not being well thought out.
計画がよく練られていないと言って、反対した人もいた。
Keikaku ga yoku nera-rete inai to itte, hantai-shita hito mo ita.

O

objection n. **[expression of dissatisfaction with and opposition to s.t.]**
ha⌈ntai 反対 •c [(of two opinions) the state of being opposed] ((the inverse, the opposite, opposition, antagonism)) ↔ sansei 賛成 •c; i⌉gi 異議 •c [a different opinion/argument (used in group decision-making contexts)] ((complaint, protest, dissent)), i⌈ron 異論 •c [a different opinion (used in academic discourse)] ((a divergent view, objection, protest, dissent))

NOTE: There are no such *suru*-verbs as **igi-suru* or **iron-suru*. Instead, the following patterns should be used: *igi ga aru/nai* "have/not have an objection," *iron ga aru/nai* "have/not have an objection."

objective n. **[a purpose one is attempting to achieve]**
1. **mo⌈kuteki 目的 •c [the intended result of a particular action/behavior] ((purpose, aim, object))**
2. **mo⌈kuhyoo 目標 •c [s.t. one wishes to achieve] ((mark, landmark, target, goal))**
—— adj. **[not influenced by personal feelings or opinions]**
kya⌈kkan-tekina 客観的な adj(*na*). **•c [looking at s.t from the point of view of a disinterested observer]**

EX. It is an objective fact that the earth is round.
地球が丸いのは客観的な事実だ。
Chikyuu ga marui no wa kyakkan-tekina jijitsu da.

obligation n. **[a course of action which one is morally or legally bound to follow]**
1. **gi⌉mu 義務 •c [s.t. one is required to do by virtue of one's position] ((duty, obligation, liability))**

EX. As citizens we have an obligation to pay taxes.
市民として税金を払う義務があります。
Shimin to-shite zeikin o harau gimu ga arimasu.

2. **gi⌈ri⌉ 義理 •c [a course of action one is morally bound to follow by virtue of one's relationship to others in society] ((duty, debt of gratitude, decency, respectability))**

EX. Even though I don't want to go, I have an obligation to attend the wedding today.
たとえ行きたくなくても今日の結婚式は義理で、出なければなりません。
Tatoe iki-takunakute mo kyoo no kekkon-shiki wa giri de, denakereba narimasen.

obligatory adj. **[morally/legally/socially incumbent on one to perform]**
1. **gi⌈mu-tekina 義務的な** adj(*na*). **•c [having the character of a legal obligation] ((binding, compulsory))**
2. **gi⌈ri no N 義理のN •c [having the character of a social/moral obligation] ((of decency, of respectability))**

oblique adj. **[slanting rather than straight ((fig. "indirect," "devious"))]**
1. **na⌈na⌉me no 斜めの [neither perpendicular nor parallel] ((slanting, diagonal))**

EX. I drew an oblique line across the page.
ページに斜めの線を引いた。
Peeji ni naname no sen o hiita.

2. **to⌈o-ma⌉washi no N 遠回しのN [indirectly circling around s.t.] ((not straight, roundabout, indirect))**

EX. Japanese often use oblique expressions.
日本人はよく遠回しの表現をする。
Nihon-jin wa yoku too-mawashi no hyoogen o suru.

obnoxious adj. **[very unpleasant and objectionable]**
1. **i⌈ya⌉na 嫌な** adj(*na*). **[very displeasing to s.o.] ((unpleasant, disgusting, unwilling, reluctant)), fu-⌈yu⌉kaina 不愉快な** adj(*na*). **•c [causing a feeling not pleasant/enjoyable] ((unpleasant, disagreeable))**

EX. (**a**) He is being obnoxious.
彼は{嫌な/不愉快な}ことをしている。
Kare wa {iyana/fu-yukaina} koto o shite iru.
(**b**) Rock music is really obnoxious.
ロック音楽は本当に{嫌/不愉快}だ。
Rokku ongaku wa hontoo ni {iya/fu-yukai} da.

NOTE: In Japanese, *iya* can mean "reluctant to do s.t.," as in *Benkyoo-suru no ga iya desu* "I am reluctant to study", whereas in English "obnoxious" never carries the meaning of "unwilling" or "reluctant."

observation n. **[an act of noting s.t. with the intent of acquiring evidence or a statement made on the basis of evidence]**

1. ka⌈nsatsu 観察 •c [an act of noting s.t. with the intent of acquiring evidence] ((**view, survey, investigation, probe**))

EX. That comedian makes some interesting observations on human life.
あのコメディアンは人生について面白い観察をする。
Ano komedian wa jinsei ni-tsuite omoshiroi kansatsu o suru.

2. ka⌈nsoku 観測 •c [an act of noting s.t. with the intent of acquiring quantitative evidence] ((**survey**))

EX. As a meteorologist, I make daily observations of the rainfall.
気象学者として毎日の降雨量の観測をしている。
Kishoo-gakusha to-shite mai-nichi no koou-ryoo no kansoku o shite iru.

observe vt. **[for s.o. to note s.t. with the intent of acquiring evidence or to state s.t. on the basis of evidence]**

1. 〈-o〉 ka⌈nsatsu-suru 〈～を〉観察する ③ •c [for s.o. to note s.t. with the intent of acquiring evidence] ((**look at, watch**))

EX. I used to have an interest in observing the behavior of ants.
私は昔ありの行動を観察することに興味を持っていた。
Watashi wa mukashi ari no koodoo o kansatsu-suru koto ni kyoomi o motte ita.

2. 〈-o〉 ka⌈nsoku-suru 〈～を〉観測する ③ •c [for s.o. to note s.t. with the intent of acquiring quantitative evidence] ((**survey**))

EX. As a meteorologist, I have been observing snowfall for the past twenty years.
私は気象学者として過去二十年の降雪量を観測している。
Watashi wa kishoo-gakusha to-shite kako ni-juu-nen no koosetsu-ryoo o kansoku-shite iru.

3. 〈-to〉 no⌈be⌉ru 〈～と〉述べる ② [for s.o. to speak/write s.t. in a formal way 〈w〉] ((**state, express, mention**))

EX. In his lecture, the professor observed that U.S.-Japan relations stand at a critical juncture.
教授は講演の中で日米関係が重大な時期に来ていると述べた。
Kyooju wa kooen no naka de Nichi-Bei-kankei ga juudaina jiki ni kite iru to nobeta.

obtain vt. **[to succeed in getting hold of s.t. valued with effort]**

1. 〈-o〉 ka⌈kutoku-suru 〈～を〉獲得する ③ •c [for s.o. to succeed in getting hold of s.t. valued and abstract with effort] ((**get, gain, acquire**)), **〈-o〉 e⌉ru 〈～を〉得る ② [for s.o. to get s.t. 〈w〉]** ((**get, acquire**)), **〈-o〉 te⌉ ni i⌈reru 〈～を〉手に入れる ② [for s.o. to get hold of s.t.]** ((**get**))

EX. (**a**) Following years of effort Bob obtained a high position in his company.
長年の努力の結果ボブは会社で高い地位を{獲得した/得た/?手に入れた}。
Naga-nen no doryoku o kekka Bobu wa kaisha de takai chii o {kakutoku-shita/eta/?te ni ireta}.
(**b**) I was able to obtain two tickets to the Super Bowl through various connections.
コネでスーパーボールの切符を二枚{手に入れる/*獲得する/*得る}ことができた。
*Kone de suupaa-booru no kippu o ni-mai {te ni ireru/*kakutoku-suru/*eru} koto ga dekita.*

obvious adj. **[s.t. that is easy to see or understand]**

1. a⌈ki⌉rakana 明らかな adj(*na*). **[readily seen so that there is no doubt or ambiguity]** ((**clear, evident**)), **me⌈ihakuna 明白な** adj(*na*). **•c [accepted as such without doubt/suspicion by everybody]** ((**clear, evident**))

EX. It was obvious that someone had been in the room.
部屋にだれかがいたのは{明らか/明白}だった。

Heya ni dare-ka ga ita no wa {akiraka/meihaku} datta.

2. mi⌈e-suita N 見え透いたN /⟨Vinf. past of *mie-suku* ① become transparent/ [for a lie/s.o.'s true feelings to be easily seen through] ⟪transparent⟫

EX. A: Jack said that he didn't spend the money.
ジャックはあの金を使わなかったと言っているよ。
Jakku wa ano kane o tsukawanakatta to itte iru yo.
B: What! That's an obvious lie!
えっ、そいつは見え透いたうそだ。
E!, soitsu wa mie-suita uso da.

occasion n. **[the time at which s.t. occurs or the appropriate time for s.t. to occur] to⌈ki⌉ 時 [the continuum from past to present into the future or a specific point or subinterval or time at/during which a state, action, or event occurs or continues] ⟪time, when⟫, o⌈ri⌉ 折 [a special time distinct from other times] ⟪time, season, juncture, opportunity⟫, ki⌈ka⌉i 機会 •c [a suitable time for doing s.t.] ⟪chance, opportunity⟫, cha⌉nsu チャンス •f [a good time to do s.t.] ⟪chance⟫, ba⌈ai 場合 [the time at which s.t. has come about or a situation in which s.t./s.o./s.a. finds itself/himself/herself] ⟪time, moment, situation, circumstances⟫**

EX. (**a**) On the occasion of my first visit to Japan, I was granted an audience with His Majesty the Emperor.
日本を初めて訪問した{時/折/*機会/*チャンス/*場合}に天皇陛下に拝謁を賜った。
*Nihon o hajimete hoomon-shita {toki/ori/*kikai/*chansu/*baai} ni tennoo-heika ni haietsu o tamawatta.*
(**b**) There was a grand party given to mark the occasion of the President's visit.
大統領訪問の{機会/?チャンス/?時/*折/*場合}を記念して、盛大なパーティーが開かれた。
*Daitooryoo-hoomon no {kikai/?chansu/?toki/*ori/*baai} o kinen-shite, seidaina paatii ga hiraka-reta.*
(**c**) American parties are a wonderful occasion for people to get to know one another.
アメリカのパーティーはお互いが知り合ういい{機会/時/チャンス/*場合/*折}です。
*Amerika no paatii wa o-tagai ga shiri-au ii {kikai/toki/chansu/*baai/*ori} desu.*
(**d**) What would you do on such an occasion?
こんな{時/場合/*折り/*チャンス/*機会}、あなただったらどうしますか。
*Konna {toki/baai/*ori/*chansu/*kikai}, anata dattara doo shimasu ka.*

occasional adj. **[occurring irregularly ⟨w⟩]**

1. to⌈ki-ori no N 時折のN [occurring every now and then ⟨fml⟩]

EX. The baseball game was interrupted by occasional showers.
野球の試合は時折の雨で中断した。
Yakyuu no shiai wa toki-ori no ame de chuudan-shita.

2. fu-⌈te⌉iki no N 不定期のN •c [appearing irregularly] ⟪irregular⟫

EX. A: Does this journal come out regularly?
この雑誌は定期的に出ているんですか。
Kono zasshi wa teiki-tekini dete iru n desu ka.
B: No, it's an occasional publication.
いいえ、不定期(の)刊行物です。
Iie, fu-teiki (no) kankoo-butsu desu.

occasionally adv. **[now and then] to⌈ki-doki 時々 ⟪sometimes⟫, to⌈ki-ori 時折 [now and then ⟨fml⟩] ⟪sometimes⟫**

EX. A: Do you often go to the movies?
よく映画に行きますか。
Yoku eiga ni ikimasu ka.
B: No, I only go occasionally.
いいえ、{時々/時折}見るだけです。
Iie, {toki-doki/toki-ori} miru dake desu.

Occident n. **[Europe and America ⟨fml⟩] se⌉iyoo 西洋 •c [Europe and America as viewed from the Far Eastern countries] ⟪the West⟫ ↔ tooyoo 東洋 •c**

occupant n. **[a person who uses a space ⟪fig. "a job holder"⟫]**

kyo⌈ju⌉u-sha 居住者 •c [a person who lives in a space] ((resident, inhabitant, dweller))

occupation n. **[an act/instance of holding a position (to sustain one's life) or a territory]**

1. shi⌈goto 仕事 [an activity performed for a particular purpose other than amusement and on which one expends time and effort] ((work, labor, business)), **sho⌈ku⌉gyoo 職業 •c [work as a means of supporting one's life]** ((profession, vocation))

EX. A: May I ask your occupation?
失礼ですが、{お仕事/ご職業}は何ですか。
Shitsurei desu ga, {o-shigoto/go-shokugyoo} wa nan desu ka.
B: I'm a high school teacher.
高校の教師です。
Kookoo no kyooshi desu.

2. se⌈nryoo 占領 •c [an act/instance of conquering and controlling a nation or a territory] ((capture, possession))

EX. I'm currently studying the postwar occupation of Japan by the Allied Forces.
私は現在、戦後日本の連合軍による占領について研究しています。
Watashi wa genzai, sengo-Nihon no rengoo-gun ni-yoru senryoo ni-tsuite kenkyuu-shite imasu.

occupy vt. **[to hold and possess space]**

1. ⟨-o⟩ shi⌈me⌉ru ⟨〜を⟩占める ② [to fill a space/position/rank as one's own] ((hold, get))

EX. My TV and stereo occupy about half the space of my room.
ステレオとテレビが部屋の半分ぐらいを占めている。
Sutereo to terebi ga heya no hanbun-gurai o shimete iru.

2. ⟨-o⟩ tsu⌈kau ⟨〜を⟩使う ① [for s.o./s.a. to cause s.t./s.o./s.a. to act or serve for a purpose or as an instrument or as a material for consumption] ((use, employ))

EX. The toilet is now occupied.
お手洗いは今使っています。
O-tearai wa ima tsukatte imasu.

3. ⟨-o⟩ se⌈nryoo-suru ⟨〜を⟩占領する ③ •c [for s.o. to conquer and control a nation/territory ((fig. "monopolize"))**]** ((capture, seize, hold))

EX. Some historians say that if the United States had not occupied Japan, Russia would have.
もしアメリカが日本を占領しなかったら、ロシアが占領しただろうという歴史家もいる。
Moshi Amerika ga Nihon o senryoo-shinakattara, Roshia ga senryoo-shita daroo to iu rekishi-ka mo iru.

occur vi. **[for an event to take place spontaneously** ((fig. "for an idea to enter one's mind"))**]**

1. o⌈ki⌉ru 起きる ② [for s.o./s.a./s.t. that has been lying horizontally dormant to stand up vertically ((fig. "wake up," "occur"))**]** ((get up, rise, wake up, take place, begin to burn)), **o⌈ko⌉ru 起こる ① [for an unusual/disturbing event to take place]** ((happen, take place, spring up, be generated)), **ha⌈ssei-suru 発生する ③ •c [to happen or to come into being suddenly]** ((happen, break out, spring up))

EX. When the earthquake occurred, Mr. Wood was in his office.
地震が{起きた/起こった/発生した}時、ウッド氏は研究室にいた。
Jishin ga {okita/okotta/hassei-shita} toki, Uddo-shi wa kenkyuu-shitsu ni ita.

2. ⟨-ni⟩ u⌈kabu ⟨〜に⟩浮かぶ ① [for s.t. to be suspended in air, gas, or on the surface of a liquid by the force of buoyancy so that its outline is visible to an observer ((fig. "come across one's mind," "rise in the world"))**]** ((float, surface, come across one's mind)) ↔ **⟨-ni⟩ shizumu ⟨〜に⟩沈む ①; ⟨-ni⟩ ki-⌈ga-tsu⌉ku ⟨〜に⟩気がつく ① [for s.o./s.a. to become aware of s.t./s.o./s.a.]** ((notice, note))

EX. (a) A: Where'd you get that idea?
どこからそんな考えが出て来たんだい。
Doko kara sonna kangae ga dete-kita n dai.

O

B: It simply occurred to me.
ただ頭に{浮かんだ/*気がついた}んだよ。
*Tada atama ni {ukanda/*ki-ga-tsuita} n da yo.*
(**b**) It never occurred to me that Mary might dislike me.
メアリーが僕を嫌っていたとは{気がつかなかった/*浮かばなかった}。
*Mearii ga boku o kiratte ita to wa {ki-ga-tsukanakatta/*ukabanakatta}.*

O

occurrence n. **[an instance of occurring]**
1. o⌈ko⌉ru koto 起こること [the fact of occurring], ha⌈ssei 発生 •c [an instance of occurring ⟨fml⟩] ⟪outbreak, genesis, birth, creation, growth⟫
EX. The occurrence of AIDS in Japan is no longer a rare thing.
日本でエイズ{が起こること/の発生}はもう珍しくない。
Nihon de eizu {ga okoru koto/no hassei} wa moo mezurashikunai.
2. de⌈ki⌉-goto 出来事 [an instance of s.t. occurring in the world of human affairs] ⟪event, incident⟫, ji⌉ken 事件 •c [an incident which is out of the ordinary and attracts attention, esp. of a criminal nature] ⟪incident, affair⟫
EX. I met a Japanese person for the first time when I was in high school. That occurrence led me to study the Japanese language.
私は高校の時初めて日本人と出会った。その{出来事/*事件}がきっかけとなり、私は日本語を勉強することになった。
*Watashi wa kookoo no toki hajimete Nihon-jin to de-atta. Sono {deki-goto/*jiken} ga kikkake to nari, watashi wa Nihon-go o benkyoo-suru koto ni natta.*

ocean n. **[the body of salt water that covers most of the earth's surface]**
u⌉mi 海 [the body of salt water that covers most of the earth's surface ⟪fig. "a large amount of liquid/fire"] ⟪sea⟫ ↔ riku 陸; ka⌈iyoo 海洋 •c [the seas ⟨w⟩]
EX. (**a**) A: Which do you like better, swimming in the ocean or in a pool?
{海/*海洋}で泳ぐのとプールで泳ぐのとどっちが好きですか。
*{Umi/*Kaiyoo} de oyogu no to puuru de oyogu no to dotchi ga suki desu ka.*
B: Swimming in the ocean.
{海/*海洋}で泳ぐ方です。
*{Umi/*Kaiyoo} de oyogu hoo desu.*
(**b**) Hawaii is surrounded by ocean, so it's natural that Hawaiian people should like fish.
ハワイは{海/海洋}に囲まれているのだから、ハワイの人が魚を食べるのが好きなのは当たり前です。
Hawai wa {umi/kaiyoo} ni kakomarete iru no da kara, Hawai no hito ga sakana o taberu no ga sukina no wa atarimae desu.
PHRASE: the Atlantic Ocean *Taisei-yoo* 大西洋 •c, the Pacific Ocean *Taihei-yoo* 太平洋 •c

o'clock adv.
-ji ～時 •c [a point at which one of the 24 equal periods into which the day is divided begins]
EX. A: What time does your Japanese class begin?
日本語の授業は何時に始まりますか。
Nihon-go no jugyoo wa nan-ji ni hajimarimasu ka.
B: It begins at 9 o'clock in the morning.
朝九時に始まります。
Asa ku-ji ni hajimarimasu.

October n.
ju⌈u-gatsu⌉ 十月 •c

octopus n.
ta⌉ko たこ
EX. Japanese are not the only people who eat octopus.
たこを食べるのは日本人だけではない。
Tako o taberu no wa Nihon-jin dake dewanai.

odd adj. **[not in accordance with what is usual or normal]**
he⌉nna 変な adj(*na*). **•c [exhibiting an unusual characteristic/condition/behavior] ⟪strange, queer, funny, suspicious⟫, ki⌉myoona 奇妙な** adj(*na*). **•c [unusual and mysterious in character] ⟪strange, odd,**

queer, singular》), **fu[u-ga]warina 風変わりな** adj(*na*). **[strange in the way one looks]** 《**strange, weird**》

EX. (**a**) Look at that lady! Isn't she wearing an odd dress!
あの女の人を見てごらん。{変な/奇妙な/風変わりな}服を着ているなあ。
Ano onna no hito o mite goran. {Henna/Kimyoona/Fuu-gawarina} fuku o kite iru naa.
(**b**) This fish has an odd taste.
この魚は{変な/奇妙な/??風変わりな}味がする。
Kono sakana wa {henna/kimyoona/??fuu-gawarina} aji ga suru.

PHRASE: odd number *kisuu* 奇数 •c ↔ *guusuu* 偶数 •c

EX. The numbers 1, 3, 5, etc., are called odd numbers and the numbers 2, 4, 6, etc. are called even numbers.
1、3、5などの数を奇数と言い、2、4、6などの数を偶数と言う。
Ichi, san, go nado no kazu o kisuu to ii, ni, yon, roku nado no kazu o guusuu to iu.

odor n. **[a smell** ⟨fml⟩**]**
ni[o]i におい [a sensation created in the olfactory organs 《fig, "smack," "flavor"》] 《**smell, scent, smack, flavor**》, **shu]uki 臭気** •c **[bad smell]** 《**stench, stink**》

EX. (**a**) What's that strange odor?
あの変な{におい/??臭気}は何だ。
Ano henna {nioi/??shuuki} wa nan da.
(**b**) There was odor of rotten meat in the kitchen.
台所には腐った肉の{臭気/におい}が漂っていた。
Daidokoro ni wa kusatta niku no {shuuki/nioi} ga tadayotte ita.

of prep. **[a preposition which, followed by a noun phrase, forms a phrase to modify a preceding noun phrase]**
1. no の prt. **[a particle which, preceded by a noun phrase, forms a phrase to modify the noun phrase that follows indicating variously "possession," "location," "belonging," "material from which s.t. is made," "specialized area or occupation," "creation," "an inalienable part of the body," "subject of a subordinate or noun clause," "direct object of a subordinate or noun clause"]**

EX. (**a**) The home of my parents is in Sapporo.
両親のうちは札幌です。
Ryooshin no uchi wa Sapporo desu.
(**b**) Among the temples of Kyoto I like Ryoanji best.
京都のお寺の中で竜安寺が一番好きです。
Kyooto no o-tera no naka de Ryooanji ga ichiban suki desu.
(**c**) When I was a student of Waseda University, I majored in political science.
私は早稲田大学の学生だった時、政治学を専攻していた。
Watashi wa Waseda-daigaku no gakusei datta toki, seiji-gaku o senkoo-shite ita.
(**d**) I love a meal of meat and potatoes.
私は肉とじゃがいもの食事が大好きです。
Watashi wa niku to jagaimo no shokuji ga dai-suki desu.
(**e**) Just being a native speaker of Japanese doesn't mean you can become a teacher of Japanese.
日本人だからといって、それだけでは日本語の先生にはなれません。
Nihon-jin da kara to itte, sore dake de wa Nihon-go no sensei ni wa nare-masen.
(**f**) A: How come you like the music of Mozart so much?
どうしてそんなにモーツァルトの音楽が好きなんですか。
Dooshite sonna ni Mootsuaruto no ongaku ga sukina n desu ka.
B: Because it flows so naturally, like a river.
川のように自然に流れるからです。
Kawa no yooni shizen ni nagareru kara desu.
(**g**) The trunk of an elephant is very long.
象の鼻はとても長い。

O

O

Zoo no hana wa totemo nagai.
(**h**) We celebrated the fourth birthday of our grandchild yesterday.
昨日私たちは孫の四歳の誕生日を祝った。
Kinoo watashi-tachi wa mago no yon-sai no tanjoo-bi o iwatta.
(**i**) The study of Japanese was much easier than I had expected.
日本語の勉強は思っていたよりずっと易しかった。
Nihon-go no benkyoo wa omotte ita yori zutto yasashikatta.

2. ⟨**-to**⟩ **i⌈u** ⟨〜と⟩いう **[a form marking a phrase that provides the name or other identifying information about the noun that follows]**

EX. (**a**) I live in the city of Champaign.
私はシャンペインという町に住んでいます。
Watashi wa Shanpein to iu machi ni sunde imasu.
(**b**) The rumor of Mr. Smith's resignation was completely untrue.
スミスさんが辞めるといううわさは全くのうそだった。
Sumisu-san ga yameru to iu uwasa wa mattaku no uso datta.

PHRASE: be made of ⟨*-de*⟩ *dekite iru* ⟨〜で⟩出来ている ②, die of ⟨*-de*⟩ *shinu* ⟨〜で⟩死ぬ ①, know of *{⟨-no⟩ koto o/ni-tsuite} shitte iru* {⟨〜の⟩ことを/について}知っている ②, speak of *{⟨-no⟩ koto o/ni-tsuite} hanasu* {⟨〜の⟩ことを/について}話す ①

off prep./adv./adj. **[for s.o./s.t. to be separated from a particular space or to be out of its normal or functional state]**

NOTE: There is no corresponding Japanese word for English "off," primarily because "off" is used together with particular verbs to form idiomatic phrases, such as in "get off" (example (a)), "go off" (example (b)), "take off" (example (d)), and "turn off" (example (f)).

EX. (**a**) I got off the bus at the corner of the street.
私は通りの角でバスを降りた。
Watashi wa toori no kado de basu o orita.
(**b**) My girlfriend went off to Paris.
私のガールフレンドはパリに行ってしまった。
Watashi no gaaru-furendo wa Pari ni itte shimatta.
(**c**) You can often see whales off the coast of California.
カリフォルニア沖でよく鯨が見られます。
Kariforunia-oki de yoku kujira ga mi-raremasu.
(**d**) It's hot in here, so please feel free to take off your coat.
ここは暑いですから、どうぞ上着を脱いでください。
Koko wa atsui desu kara, doozo uwa-gi o nuide kudasai.
(**e**) Everything in this store is 10% off.
この店の品物は全部一割引です。
Kono mise no shina-mono wa zenbu ichi-wari-biki desu.
(**f**) Can I turn off the radio?
ラジオを消してもいいですか。
Rajio o keshite mo ii desu ka.
(**g**) I'm off today.
私は今日は休みです。
Watashi wa kyoo wa yasumi desu.
(**h**) The rain fell on and off throughout the day.
雨は一日中降ったり止んだりでした。
Ame wa ichi-nichi-juu futtari yandari deshita.

offend vt. **[for s.o./s.t. to negatively affect s.o.'s sensibilities]**
((-**no**)) **ki⌈o wa⌉ruku-suru** ((〜の))気を悪くする ③ **[to cause bad feeling in s.o.'s mind]**, ⟨**-no**⟩ **ki-⌈ni-sawaru** ⟨〜の⟩気に障る ① **[for s.t. to inadvertently hurt s.o.'s feeling]**, ⟨**-o**⟩ **o⌈kora-se⌉ru** ⟨〜を⟩怒らせる /⟨**causative of *okoru*** ① **get mad/** ② **[to cause s.o. to get angry]** ((**make s.o. angry**))

EX. (**a**) I'm sorry if I offended you.
{気を悪くした/気に障った/??怒らせた}んなら、ごめんなさい。
{Ki o waruku-shita/Ki-ni-sawatta/

??Okora-seta}} n nara, gomennasai.
(**b**) Yoshio didn't realize that his words offended Kazuko that badly.
良雄は自分の言葉{でそんなに和子が気を悪くした/がそんなに和子{の気に障った/を怒らせた}}とは気がつかなかった。
Yoshio wa jibun no kotoba {de sonnani Kazuko ga ki o waruku-shita/ga sonnani Kazuko {no ki-ni-sawatta/o okora-seta}} to wa ki-ga-tsukanakatta.

offer vt. **[to present s.t. to s.o. for acceptance or consideration; for s.o. to say or indicate that one will do s.t. for s.o. else]**

1. ⟨-ni⟩ ⟨-o⟩ su⌈sumeru ⟨〜に⟩⟨〜を⟩勧める ② [for s.o. to present s.o. with some advice/encouragement to do s.t. or to present s.o. with s.t. for him/her to have, such as food or drink]

EX. Betty offered some wine to John.
ベティはジョンにワインを勧めました。
Betii wa Jon ni wain o susumemashita.

2. a⌉ru ある ① [for s.t. to exist] **⟪have, possess, exist⟫**

EX. A: Does this college offer Japanese language courses?
この大学には日本語の科目がありますか。
Kono daigaku ni wa Nihon-go no kamoku ga arimasu ka.
B: Yes, it does.
ええ、ありますよ。
Ee, arimasu yo.

3. V*te* a⌈geru to iu V*te*あげると言う ① [for s.o. to say that she/he will do s.t. for s.o. else who is not in his/her in-group], V*te* ku⌈reru to iu V*te*くれると言う ① [for s.o. to say that she/he will do s.t. for s.o. else who is in the in-group of the person reporting what was said (i.e., the speaker or s.o. in her/his in-group)]

EX. (**a**) I offered to help Tom with his Japanese lesson.
私はトムに日本語の勉強を手伝ってあげると言った。
Watashi wa Tomu ni Nihon-go no benkyoo o tetsudatte ageru to itta.
(**b**) Jane offered me a ride home.
ジェーンは私をうちまで車で送って{くれる/?あげる}と言った。
Jeen wa watashi o uchi made kuruma de okutte {kureru/?ageru} to itta.

— n. **[s.t./some action presented (as a favor) by s.o. to s.o. else]**

1. ⟨-de⟩ wa do⌉o ka to ki⌈ku ⟨〜で⟩はどうかと聞く ① [for s.o. to ask if s.t. (or a favor) presented by him/her is accepable]

EX. The company has made me an offer of $50,000 in salary.
会社は五万ドルの給料ではどうかと聞いてきた。
Kaisha wa go-man-doru no kyuuryoo de wa doo ka to kiite kita.

2. mo⌈oshi-de 申し出 [s.t. proposed by s.o. for s.o. else's acceptance] **⟪proposal, request⟫**

EX. She rejected my offer of financial assistance.
彼女は私の経済的援助の申し出を断った。
Kanojo wa watashi no keizai-teki-enjo no mooshi-de o kotowatta.

office n. **[a place (esp. a room) in which professional duties are carried out ⟪fig. "the duties themselves"⟫]**

1. ji⌈mu⌉-sho 事務所 •c [a place where professional duties (primarily administrative) are carried out], ji⌈mu⌉-shitsu 事務室 •c [a room where professional duties (primarily clerical) are carried out], o⌈fisu オフィス •f [a Western style place where professional duties carried out]

ofisu

EX. (**a**) A: Where is your company's office?
会社の{事務所/オフィス/*事務室}はどこですか。
*Kaisha no {jimu-sho/ofisu/*jimu-shitsu} wa doko desu ka.*
B: It's in Shinbashi.
新橋にあります。
Shinbashi ni arimasu.

(**b**) A: Where is the office in this building?
この建物の{事務室/??事務所/*オフィス}はどこですか。
*Kono tate-mono no {jimu-shitsu/??jimu-sho/*ofisu} wa doko desu ka.*
B: It's at the end of the hallway.
廊下の突き当たりです。
Rooka no tsuki-atari desu.

O

2. ke⌈nkyu⌉u-shitsu 研究室 •c [a college professor's room]

EX. A: Professor Smith, may I see you in your office tomorrow?
スミス先生、あした研究室に伺ってもよろしいですか。
Sumisu-sensei, ashita kenkyuu-shitsu ni ukagatte mo yoroshii desu ka.
B: Yes, you can come see me around 3:30.
ええ、三時半ごろに来て下さい。
Ee, san-ji-han-goro ni kite kudasai.

3. -kyoku ～局 •c [a bureau of government or a broadcasting station], -choo ～庁 •c [a branch of government]

PHRASE: post office *yuubin-kyoku* 郵便局 •c, patent office *Tokkyo-choo* 特許庁 •c

officer n. **[a person who holds a commission in the armed forces or a policeman or a person who holds an important position in an institution/organization]**

1. sho⌉okoo 将校 •c [a person who holds a commission in the armed forces]

2. ke⌈ikan 警官 •c [a policeman]

3. ya⌈ku⌉in 役員 •c [a person who holds an important position in an institution/organization]

official adj. **[having to do with one's office/professional duty or properly authorized by an authority]**

o⌈oyake no N 公のN [belonging to the public/governmental domain] ⟪public, open⟫ ↔ watakushi no N 私のN; ko⌈oshiki no N 公式のN •c [based on or characterized by public formality] ⟪formal⟫ ↔ hi-kooshiki no N 非公式のN •c

EX. I thought it was inappropriate of him to bring up a personal subject like that at an official meeting.
{公/公式}の席であのような個人的な話を持ち出すのは不適切だと思いました。
{Ooyake/Kooshiki} no seki de ano yoona kojin-tekina hanashi o mochi-dasu no wa fu-tekisetsu da to omoimashita.

— n. **[a person who holds an office or position]**

ya⌈kunin 役人 •c [a person who is employed at a government office] ⟪officer⟫, ko⌈omu⌉-in 公務員 •c [a person who is employed at a local/national government office] ⟪public service personnel, public servant⟫

EX. My father was an official until he retired.
父は定年まで{役人/公務員}でした。
Chichi wa teinen made {yakunin/koomu-in} deshita.

office work n. **[clerical work carried out in an office]**

ji⌉mu 事務 •c

EX. I don't think I'm suitable for office work.
私は事務に向いていないと思います。
Watashi wa jimu ni muite inai to omoimasu.

officially adv.

o⌈oyake ni 公に ⟪publicly⟫, ko⌈oshiki ni 公式に •c ⟪publicly⟫

often adv. **[with high frequency]**

yo⌉ku よく /⟨adj(*i*). *ku* of *ii* good/ [satisfactorily/carefully/many times] ⟪well, fully⟫, ta⌈bi-tabi たびたび [with high frequency ⟨fml⟩] ⟪frequently, time after time⟫, shi⌉ba-shiba しばしば [with a very high frequency ⟨w⟩] ⟪many times, frequently⟫

EX. (**a**) A: Do you often go to Japan?
{よく/度々/*しばしば}日本へいらっしゃいますか。
*{Yoku/Tabi-tabi/*Shiba-shiba} Nihon e irasshaimasu ka.*
B: No, I've been there only once.
いいえ、一度しか行っておりません。
Iie, ichi-do shika itte orimasen.
(**b**) When she was young, Janet often fell in love.
若い時ジャネットは{よく/度々/しばしば}恋に落ちた。

Wakai toki Janetto wa {yoku/tabi-tabi/shiba-shiba} koi ni ochita.

NOTE: English "How often...?" is *Nan-{kai/do}-gurai...ka* in Japanese.

Oh int. **[an interjection to indicate acknowledgement or strong emotion, such as surprise, disappointment, pain, anger, etc.]**

a⌉! あっ! [an interjection to indicate surprise or an emotional reaction], o⌉ya! おや! [an interjection to indicate surprise], o! おっ! [an interjection to indicate surprise or an emotional reaction (used in male speech)], a⌉ra! あら! [an interjection to indicate surprise or an emotional reaction (used frequently in female speech)]

EX. (**a**) Oh! Aren't you dressed up today!
{おっ/あっ/おや/?あら}! 今日はおしゃれしているね。
{O/A/Oya/?Ara}! Kyoo wa o-share-shite iru ne.
(**b**) Oh, it was you!
{あっ/あら/おや/*おっ}! あなただったの。
*{A/Ara/Oya/*O}! Anata datta no.*

NOTE: Example (b) is an utterance by a female speaker.

Ohio n.

O⌈ha⌉io オハイオ

oil n. **[a combustible liquid that does not dissolve in water]**

1. a⌈bura あぶら [a whitish slippery substance found in animal bodies or a thick liquid made from plants used in cooking or a thick liquid made from minerals used for lubrication], o⌉iru オイル •f [a thick liquid used to lubricate engines or a thick liquid used to season salads]

㊪ "solid animal fat"▷脂, "liquid oil"▷油

EX. (**a**) This car engine needs some oil.
この車はエンジン{オイル/の油}が要る。
Kono kuruma wa enjin {-oiru/no abura} ga iru.
(**b**) Do you have any oil for *tempura*?
天ぷらの{油/*オイル}は、ありますか。
*Tenpura no {abura/*oiru} wa, arimasu ka.*

2. se⌈kiyu 石油 •c [a liquid mineral found underground which is refined into gasoline, kerosene, etc.]

EX. Modern industry is heavily dependent on the availability of oil.
近代の産業は石油の供給に大きく依存している。
Kindai no sangyoo wa sekiyu no kyookyuu ni ookiku izon-shite iru.

OK int. **[an interjection to indicate safety/approval/agreement]**

1. da⌈ijo⌉obu da 大丈夫だ [strong enough to cope with a difficult situation (used only in predicate position)] ((all right, safe))

NOTE: *Daijoobu da* is an adj(*na*)., but it cannot be used before a noun.

EX. A: Are you OK?
大丈夫ですか。
Daijoobu desu ka.
B: Yes. Thank you. I just slipped a little.
ええ、どうも。ちょっと滑っただけです。
Ee, doomo. Chotto subetta dake desu.

2. (i⌉i) ne (いい)ね [don't you agree/approve?]

EX. A: Return the money to me by Monday, OK?
月曜日までにお金を返して{くださいね/ください。いいですね}。
Getsuyoo-bi made ni o-kane o kaeshite {kudasai ne/kudasai. Ii desu ne}.
B: Sure, no problem.
ええ、間違いなく。
Ee, machigainaku.

okay int.

SEE OK

Oklahoma n.

O⌈kuraho⌉ma オクラホマ

old adj. **[having existed for a relatively long time]**

1. to⌈shi-to⌉tta N 年取ったN /⟨Vinf. past of *toshi-toru* ① get old/ [(for an animate being) to have existed for a relatively long time] ↔ wakai 若い adj(*i*).; **to⌈shi⌉ o to⌉tte iru (N) 年を取っている(N) /⟨V*te iru* of *toshi o toru* ① get old/**

EX. There were a lot of old people in the park.
公園には{年取った/年を取っている}人が大勢いた。
Kooen ni wa {toshi-totta/toshi o totte iru} hito ga oozei ita.

NOTE: "An old person" can also be expressed by *toshi-yori* or *roojin*.

2. -sai no N 〜歳のN •c [of…years in age]

EX. A: How old are you?
{何歳/おいくつ/いくつ}ですか。
{Nan-sai/O-ikutsu/Ikutsu} desu ka.
B: I'm 24 years old.
二十四歳です。
Ni-juu-yon-sai desu.

NOTE: In informal conversation *ikutsu desu ka* is more commonly used to ask s.o.'s age.

3. to⌈shi-ue no N 年上のN [for s.o. to be older than s.o. else] ↔ toshi-shita no N 年下のN

EX. My brother is two years older than me.
兄は私よりも二つ年上です。
Ani wa watashi yori mo futatsu toshi-ue desu.

4. fu⌈ru⌉i 古い adj(*i*). **[for s.t. to have existed for a relatively long time or for s.o. to have lived/worked for a long time in one place] ⟪old-fashioned, out of date⟫ ↔ atarashii 新しい** adj(*i*).; **mu⌈kashi kara a⌉ru 昔からある ① [for s.t. to have existed from a long time ago], mu⌈kashi kara i⌈ru 昔からいる ② [for s.o./s.a. to have existed/lived in some place for a long time]**

EX. (**a**) Nancy is still playing that old piano.
ナンシーはまだあの{古い/昔からある/*昔からいる}ピアノを弾いています。
*Nanshii wa mada ano {furui/mukashi kara aru/*mukashi kara iru} piano o hiite imasu.*
(**b**) Evolution is an old idea but not everybody believes it to be true.
進化論は{昔からある/*古い/*昔からいる}考え方だが、だれもが信じているわけではない。
*Shinka-ron wa {mukashi kara aru/*furui/*mukashi kara iru} kangae-kata da ga, dare-mo ga shinjite iru wake dewanai.*
(**c**) He's an old friend of mine.
彼は僕の{古い/*昔からいる/*昔からある}友達だ。
*Kare wa boku no {furui/*mukashi kara iru/*mukashi kara aru} tomodachi da.*

NOTE: "*Mukashi kara iru*" is ungrammatical in example (c), but "*Mukashi kara no*" would be possible there.

(**d**) Is Tom still riding that old horse of his?
トムはあの{昔からいる/*古い/*昔からある}馬にまだ乗っているの?
*Tomu wa ano {mukashi kara iru/*furui/*mukashi kara aru} uma ni mada notte iru no?*

old-fashioned adj. **[formerly popular but currently out of date]**

1. mu⌈kashi haya⌉tta N 昔はやったN /⟨Vinf. past of *mukashi hayaru* ① be formerly popular/, ryu⌈ukoo-o⌉kure no N 流行遅れのN

EX. Midori is wearing an old-fashioned skirt.
緑は{昔はやった/流行遅れの}スカートをはいている。
Midori wa {mukashi hayatta/ryuukoo-okure no} sukaato o haite iru.

2. fu⌈ru⌉i 古い adj(*i*). **[for s.t. to have existed for a relatively long time or for s.o. to have lived/worked for a long time in one place] ⟪out of date⟫ ↔ atarashii 新しい** adj(*i*).; **kyu⌈ushiki no N 旧式のN •c [for an idea/machine to be outdated] ⟪out-of-date, of the old type⟫**

EX. My grandfather still uses an old-fashioned typewriter.
祖父は{旧式の/古い}タイプライターをまだ使っている。
Sofu wa {kyuushiki no/furui} taipuraitaa o mada tsukatte iru.

olive n.

o⌈ri⌉ibu オリーブ •f, o⌈riibu-iro オリーブ色

NOTE: "*Oriibu-iro*" means olive color.

Olympic Games n.

O⌈rinpi⌉kku オリンピック •f, go⌈rin-ta⌉ikai 五輪大会 •c ⟨w⟩

EX. The 1988 Olympic Games were held in Seoul, Korea.
1988年の{オリンピック/五輪大会}は韓国のソウルで開かれた。
Sen-kyuu-hyaku-hachi-juu-hachi-nen no {Orinpikku/gorin-taikai} wa Kankoku no Souru de hiraka-reta.

omelet n.

o⌈muretsu オムレツ •f

EX. Making an omelet is said to be the first lesson in cooking.
オムレツを作るのは料理の第一課だそうだ。
Omuretsu o tsukuru no wa ryoori no dai-ik-ka da sooda.

omit vt. **[to leave out s.t.]**

1. ⟨-o⟩ ha⌈bu⌉ku ⟨〜を⟩省く ① [for s.o. to intentionally leave out s.t.] ⟪exclude, curtail, eliminate, abbreviate⟫, ⟨-o⟩ sho⌈oryaku-suru ⟨〜を⟩省略する •c [for s.o. to leave out s.t. for simplification] ⟪omit, abbreviate, shorten⟫

EX. The editor omitted all the unnecessary words.
編集者は不要な言葉を全部{省いた/省略した}。
Henshuu-sha wa fuyoona kotoba o zenbu {habuita/shooryaku-shita}.

2. ⟨-o⟩ nu⌉kasu ⟨〜を⟩抜かす ① [for s.o. to unintentionally leave out s.t. that should not have been left out] ⟪leave out, miss out, skip⟫

EX. John accidentally omitted a problem on the final exam.
ジョンは期末試験で問題を一つ抜かしてしまった。
Jon wa kimatsu-shiken de mondai o hitotsu nukashite shimatta.

3. ⟨-o⟩ wa⌈sureru ⟨〜を⟩忘れる ② [for s.o./s.a. to fail to remember s.t. or to do s.t.] ⟪forget, accidentally leave out⟫

EX. Mr. Yamada accidentally omitted his name on the application form.
山田さんはうっかりして願書に自分の名前を書くのを忘れた。
Yamada-san wa ukkari-shite gansho ni jibun no namae o kaku no o wasureta.

on prep. **[a preposition indicating that s.t./s.o./s.a. is in a position above and supported by s.t. or is fully in touch with the surface of s.t. ⟪fig. "exactly at or during a time," "concerning," "by means of"⟫]**

1. ⟨-no⟩ u⌈e {ni/de/o} ⟨〜の⟩上{に/で/を} n.+prt. **[a position which is higher than s.t./s.o./s.a. or which is in contact with the surface of s.t.]**

NOTE: When particles follow ⟨*-no*⟩ *ue*, they add a special meaning to the basic meaning of *ue* described above. The particle *ni* indicates a "location where s.t./s.o./s.a. exists or a goal toward which s.t./s.o./s.a. moves"; the particle *de* indicates a "location where s.o. does s.t. or an event takes place"; and the particle *o* indicates a "path along/across/through which s.t./s.o./s.a. moves."

EX. (a) There is a cat on the roof.
屋根の上に猫がいる。
Yane no ue ni neko ga iru.
(b) A boy is crying on the slide.
男の子が滑り台の上で泣いている。
Otoko-no-ko ga suberi-dai no ue de naite iru.
(c) Please don't walk on the grass.
芝生の上を歩かないでください。
Shibafu no ue o arukanaide kudasai.

2. ni に prt. **[indicating a spatial/temporal point of contact, often construed as a location where s.t./s.o./s.a. exists, a goal, or an indirect object] ⟪at, in, to⟫**

EX. (a) There are no houses on this side of the river.
川のこちら側には家がない。
Kawa no kochira-gawa ni wa ie ga nai.
(b) My house is located on the outskirts of the city.
私のうちは郊外にあります。
Watashi no uchi wa koogai ni arimasu.
(c) There's a fly on the ceiling.
天井にはえが止まっている。
Tenjoo ni hae ga tomatte iru.
(d) A child was sitting on his father's shoulders.

O

子供がお父さんの肩に乗っていた。
Kodomo ga o-too-san no kata ni notte ita.
(**e**) I'm getting married on June 6.
私は六月六日に結婚します。
Watashi wa roku-gatsu muika ni kekkon-shimasu.
(**f**) That professor had a great influence on his students.
その教授は学生に大きな影響を与えた。
Sono kyooju wa gakusei ni ookina eikyoo o ataeta.

3. ni-tsuite について comp. prt. **[in regard to s.o./s.t./s.a.]** ⟪**concerning, about, in regard to**⟫, **ni-kanshite** に関して comp. prt. •c **[relating to s.o./s.t./s.a. ⟨fml⟩]** ⟪**regarding, with respect to**⟫, **ni-tsuite no N** についての N **[relating to s.o./s.t./s.a.]** ⟪**concerning, about, in regard to**⟫, {**ni-kansuru/ni-kanshite no**} **N** {に関する/に関しての}**N [relating to s.o./s.t./s.a. ⟨fml⟩]** ⟪**regarding, with respect to**⟫

EX. Dr. Yamada gave a lecture on the Japanese economy.
山田博士は日本経済に{ついて/関して/ついての/関しての/関する}講演をした。
Yamada-hakase wa Nihon-keizai ni-{tsuite/kanshite/tsuite no/kanshite no/kansuru} kooen o shita.

4. de で prt. **[using s.t.]** ⟪**by, with**⟫

EX. (**a**) On Saturdays I watch baseball on TV.
土曜日には野球をテレビで見ます。
Doyoo-bi ni wa yakyuu o terebi de mimasu.
(**b**) I'm listening to music on my CD player.
私はCDプレーヤーで音楽を聞いています。
Watashi wa shii-dii-pureeyaa de ongaku o kiite imasu.

5. {**Vneg. reru/Vstem rareru/sa⌈reru**} {**Vneg.れる/Vstemられる/される**} aux. **[an auxiliary verb that indicates the passive voice (i.e., the speaker states that s.t. happens to him/her or to a person he/she identifies with, usu. s.t. undesirable)]**

EX. (**a**) What! Jane hung up on me again!
あっ！ジェーンに又電話を切られちゃった。
A! Jeen ni mata denwa o kira-rechatta.
(**b**) A: What happened?
どうしたんだ。
Doo shita n da.
B: My wife ran off on me.
妻に出て行かれちゃったんだ。
Tsuma ni dete ika-rechatta n da.

once adv. **[one time at present or in the past]**

1. i⌈chi-do⌉ 一度 •c /⟨***ichi*** + **counter of frequency *do* time**/ **[one time]**, **i⌈k-ka⌉i** 一回 •c /⟨***ichi*** + **counter of frequency *kai* time**/ **[one time (usually in a fixed set of rounds)]**

NOTE: *Ichi-do* and *ik-kai* are interchageable, except that only the latter is used to mean "the first time around in a fixed set of rounds." For example, "the first inning" in baseball is always *ik-kai*, never **ichi-do*.

EX. A: How many times have you been to Japan?
何{度/回}日本へ行きましたか。
Nan-{do/kai} Nihon e ikimashita ka.
B: I've been there once.
一{度/回}行きました。
{Ichi-do/Ik-kai} ikimashita.

2. mu⌈kashi 昔 n./adv. **[at a much earlier time than the present]** ⟪**ancient times, old days, (in) the past, formerly**⟫, **ka⌉tsute** かつて **[at one point in the past ⟨w⟩]** ⟪**before, formerly, at one time**⟫

EX. Once there used to be a river here, but now a highway runs through the area.
{昔/かつて}はここに川がありましたが、今は高速道路が走っています。
{Mukashi/Katsute} wa koko ni kawa ga arimashita ga, ima wa koosoku-dooro ga hashitte imasu.

PHRASE: all at once *tachimachi* たちまち ⟪instantly, in a moment, in a twinkling⟫

EX. All at once the sky clouded up and it began to shower.
たちまち空が曇ってきて雨が降り出した。
Tachimachi sora ga kumotte kite ame ga furi-dashita.

— conj. **[if s.o. does s.t. one time] i⌈chi-do…{Vinf. nonpast to/Vcond. + ba/ Vstem + reba/sureba/kureba} 一度…{Vinf. nonpast to/Vcond.+ば/Vstem+れば/すれば/来れば}**

NOTE: 一度 is sometimes read as *hito-tabi*, but only in formal/written Japanese.

EX. Once you fall in love, you become blind to your lover's pockmarks (=faults).
一度恋を{すると/すれば}、恋人のあばたが見えなくなる。
{Ichi-do/Hito-tabi} koi o {suruto/sureba}, koi-bito no abata ga mienaku naru.

one n./adj. **[a single unit/item (in particular)] hi⌈to⌉tsu (no N) 一つ(のN) [(of) one unit/ item/year old], i⌈chi (+counter) (no N) 一 (+counter)(のN) •c [a single unit]** SEE APPENDIX II

EX. (**a**) Give me one apple please.
りんごを{一つ/一個/*一}下さい。
*Ringo o {hitotsu/ik-ko/*ichi} kudasai.*

NOTE: 1. The most common position for a quantity expression is following a particle such as *ga* or *o*.
2. *-ko* is a counter for stone/ball-like objects.

(**b**) A: How old is your son?
息子さんはおいくつですか。
Musuko-san wa o-ikutsu desu ka.
B: He is one year old.
{一つ/一歳/*一}です。
*{Hitotsu/Is-sai/*Ichi} desu.*
(**c**) One plus one is two.
{一/?一つ}に{一/?一つ}を足すと{二/?二つ}になる。
{Ichi/?Hitotsu} ni {ichi/?hitotsu} o tasu to {ni/?futatsu} ni naru.
(**d**) I can only do one thing at a time.
同時には一つのことしか出来ない。
Dooji ni wa hitotsu no koto shika dekinai.

— pron. **[a pronoun for s.o./s.t./s.a. that has already been mentioned in the preceding context (to be used with a modifier)] {{V/adj(*i*).}inf./adj(*na*). stem na} no {{V/ adj(*i*).}inf./adj(*na*). stemな}の [a dependent indefinite pronoun]**

EX. (**a**) T-shirts? We have blue ones and yellow ones. Which would you prefer?
Tシャツですか。青いのと黄色いのがありますが、どちらがよろしいですか。
Tii-shatsu desu ka. Aoi no to ki-iroi no ga arimasu ga, dochira ga yoroshii desu ka.
(**b**) The movie I saw two weeks ago was boring, but the one I saw today was pretty interesting.
二週間前に見た映画はつまらなかったけど、今日見たのはとても面白かった。
Ni-shuukan mae ni mita eiga wa tsumaranakatta keredo, kyoo mita no wa totemo omoshirokatta.

— pron. **[a generic, personal pronoun]**
ø

EX. To be well-educated, one ought to read Shakespeare.
教養のためにはシェークスピアを読まなければならない。
Kyooyoo no tame ni wa Sheekusupia o yomanakereba naranai.

NOTE: In this meaning, "one" is usually not expressed at all in Japanese, as the example above shows.

oneself pron. **[a pronoun that is used reflexively or to place emphasis on a particular item in a sentence]**
1. ji⌈bun(-ji⌉shin) 自分(自身) •c [a reflexive pronoun that refers (back) to a human subject with whom the speaker identifies, including himself/herself]

EX. (**a**) John sacrificed himself in order to please his parents.
両親を喜ばせるために、ジョンは自分(自身)を犠牲にした。
Ryooshin o yorokoba-seru tame ni, Jon wa jibun(-jishin) o gisei ni shita.
(**b**) Yoshiko was lying to herself when she told herself that she was happy.
自分(自身)に幸福だと言い聞かせた時、好子は自分を偽っていた。
Jibun(-jishin) ni koofuku da to ii-kika-seta toki, Yoshiko wa jibun o itsuwatte ita.

(c) I thought about killing myself after my girlfriend broke up with me.
僕は失恋した時{自殺しよう/*自分を殺そう}と思った。
*Boku wa shitsuren-shita toki {jisatsu-shiyoo/*jibun o korosoo} to omotta.*

NOTE: The reflexive pronoun *jibun* cannot be used in example (c), because the verb is an action verb. However, *jibun o korosu* is acceptable when it means "to sacrifice oneself" metaphorically.

(d) Hanako likes to look at herself in the mirror.
花子は鏡で自分(自身)を見るのが好きだ。
Hanako wa kagami de jibun(-jishin) o miru no ga suki da.

2. -jishin ～自身 •c [a suffix used to emphasize the human subject of a clause]

EX. (a) It was Bill himself who committed the crime.
犯罪を犯したのはビル自身だった。
Hanzai o okashita no wa Biru-jishin datta.
(b) John took the initiative himself.
ジョン自身が進んでやったのだ。
Jon-jishin ga susunde yatta no da.

3. -jitai ～自体 •c [a suffix used to emphasize an inanimate noun]

EX. It wasn't the course itself but the teacher that was the problem.
問題だったのは科目自体ではなくて先生だった。
Mondai datta no wa kamoku-jitai dewanakute sensei datta.

PHRASE: beside onself *muchuu da* 夢中だ •c **[to be exclusively preoccupied with one thing]** ((keen on, wrapped up in, absorbed in)), *uchooten da* 有頂点だ •c **[to feel as if one were on top of the world]**

EX. (a) When Julian found out that he had been selected to receive a scholarship from the Japanese Education Ministry, he was beside himself.
ジュリアンは文部省の奨学金に受かったと分かった時{有頂点/*夢中}になった。
*Jurian wa Monbu-shoo no shoogaku-kin ni ukatta to wakatta toki {uchooten/*muchuu} ni natta.*
(b) I was beside myself as I listened to Yo-Yo Ma play the cello.
私はヨーヨーマのチェロの演奏を聞いているときは{夢中/*有頂点}だった。
*Watashi wa Yoo Yoo Ma no chero no ensoo o kiite iru toki wa {muchuu/*uchooten} datta.*

PHRASE: by oneself *hitori de* 一人で ((alone)), *jibun de* 自分で •c

EX. (a) This past summer I went to China by myself.
この夏{一人/*自分}で中国に行って来ました。
*Kono natsu {hitori/*jibun} de Chuugoku ni itte kimashita.*
(b) A: Dad, can you help me with this math problem?
お父さん、この数学の問題、手伝ってくれる?
O-too-san, kono suugaku no mondai, tetsudatte kureru?
B: Try doing it by yourself.
{自分/?一人}でしてみなさい。
{Jibun/?Hitori} de shite minasai.

one-way adj. **[moving in only one direction]**

1. ka⌈ta-michi no N 片道のN [of a trip in only one direction, either away from or toward the speaker] ↔ oofuku no N 往復のN •c

EX. A one-way ticket to Osaka, please.
大阪まで、片道一枚、お願いします。
Oosaka made, kata-michi ichi-mai, onegaishimasu.

2. i⌈ppoo-tsu⌉ukoo no N 一方通行のN •c [of a street going in only one direction]

EX. In Manhattan there are so many one-way streets.
マンハッタンには一方通行の道が多い。
Manhattan ni wa ippoo-tsuukoo no michi ga ooi.

onion n.

ta⌈mane⌉gi 玉ねぎ

only adj. **[limited to s.t./s.o./s.a.]**

1. {ta⌉da/ta⌈tta}**...no N** {ただ/たった}…**のN** adv. **[small in number or amount]**

NOTE: In the above, ... is filled in by a number (+counter) expression.

EX. I lost my only friend.
{ただ/たった}一人の友達をなくした。
{Tada/Tatta} hitori no tomodachi o nakushita.

NOTE: *Tatta* is a colloquial version of *tada*.

2. Sinf. no wa N da⌈ke⌉ da Sinf.のはNだけだ [it is only N that S applies to]

EX. (**a**) The only place I visited in Japan was Kyoto.
私が日本で行った{の/所}は京都だけだ。
Watashi ga Nihon de itta {no/tokoro} wa Kyooto dake da.
(**b**) The only person I was introduced to was Mr. Ito.
私が紹介してもらった{の/人}は伊藤さんだけです。
Watashi ga shookai-shite moratta {no/hito} wa Itoo-san dake desu.
(**c**) The only difficult thing about the Japanese language is its grammar.
日本語で難しいのは文法だけだ。
Nihon-go de muzukashii no wa bunpoo dake da.
(**d**) The only person in my family who is healthy is my father.
私の家族で今元気なのは父だけだ。
Watashi no kazoku de ima genkina no wa chichi dake da.
(**e**) Of all the people in the tour group, the only one who was single was Hiroshi.
ツアーのグループの中で独身なのは弘だけだった。
Tsuaa no guruupu no naka de dokushin na no wa Hiroshi dake datta.

NOTE: When adj(*na*). or N + cop. occurs before *no wa*, the form changes to adj(*na*). stem + *na* or N + *na* respectively.

—— adv. **[limited to]**

1. ta⌉da...dake ただ…だけ adv.+prt.

EX. Don't take me seriously. I'm only joking.
本気にするなよ。ただ冗談言ってるだけなんだから。
Honki ni suru na yo. Tada joodan itte ru dake na n da kara.

2. shika...neg. しか…**neg.** prt. **[a particle that marks an element X when nothing but X makes the expressed proposition true, usu. implying that the element in question is small or minimal]** ((**nothing but**))

EX. (**a**) After I received the check for dinner, I realized that I had only five dollars in my wallet.
夕食の勘定書きをもらった時に財布に五ドルしかないことに気がついた。
Yuushoku no kanjoo-gaki o moratta toki ni saifu ni go-doru shika nai koto ni ki-ga-tsuita.
(**b**) It takes only 6 minutes to walk to campus.
大学まで歩いて六分しかかからない。
Daigaku made aruite rop-pun shika kakaranai.

3. ...bakari …ばかり prt. **[a particle which indicates that what is mentioned is the sole thing/state that exists or the sole action taken by one]**

EX. (**a**) Jim only talks. He never listens.
ジムは話すばかりで、聞こうとしない。
Jimu wa hanasu bakari de, kikoo to shinai.
(**b**) Doris speaks not only Japanese but Korean as well.
ドリスは日本語ばかりでなく、韓国語も話す。
Dorisu wa Nihon-go bakari de naku, Kankoku-go mo hanasu.

4. Vinf. past ba⌉kari da Vinf. pastばかりだ [s.o. has done s.t. just prior to the present time]

EX. Hiroko came to America only yesterday.
広子はアメリカにきのう来たばかりだ。
Hiroko wa Amerika ni kinoo kita bakari da.

onto prep. **[a preposition that is used to indicate the surface towards which s.t./s.o./s.a. moves and subsequently makes contact with]**

⟨(-no⟩ u⌈e) ni ⟨(〜の⟩上)に prt. **[on top of s.t./s.o./s.a.]**

EX. The cat jumped onto the sofa.
猫がソファー(の上)に飛び乗った。
Neko ga sofaa (no ue) ni tobi-notta.

oops int. **[an interjection which expresses a reaction to a careless action]**
o⌉tto! おっと! [an interjection which expresses a reaction to a careless action, normally used by a male speaker] ⟪oh⟫, shi⌈ma⌉tta! しまった! [an interjection used to indicate that the speaker has irretrievably done s.t. she/he should not have done] ⟪Shoot!, Damn it!⟫, a, i⌈kenai! あっ、いけない! [an interjection used to indicate that the speaker has done (not always irretrievably) s.t. that he/she should not have done] ⟪oh, no!⟫

EX. (**a**) Oops! I almost slipped.
{おっと/*しまった/*あ、いけない}! もうちょっとで滑るところだった。
*{Otto/*Shimatta/*A ikenai}! Moo chotto de suberu tokoro datta.*
(**b**) Oops! I forgot to send a birthday card to my mother.
{しまった/あ、いけない/*おっと}! 母にお誕生日のカードを送るのを忘れていた。
*{Shimatta/A, ikenai/*Otto}! Haha ni o-tanjoo-bi no kaado o okuru no o wasurete ita.*
(**c**) Oops! I dropped my purse on the tracks.
{しまった/?あ、いけない/*おっと}! 財布を線路に落としちゃった。
*{Shimatta/?A, ikenai/*Otto}! Saifu o senro ni otoshi-chatta.*

open adj. **[allowing exposure of the interior of s.t./s.o./s.a. to the outside]**
a⌈ita N あいたN /⟨Vinf. past of *aku* ① open/ [allowing exposure of the interior of s.t. to the outside] ⟪opened, empty⟫, hi⌈ra⌉ita N 開いたN /⟨Vinf. past of *hiraku* ① open/ [allowing exposure of the interior of s.t./s.o./s.a. to the outside (often resulting from a three-dimensional, symmetrical action of opening)] ↔ tojita N 閉じたN, shimatta N 閉まったN

㊥ "empty"▷空いた, otherwise ▷開いた
NOTE: *Hiraita* and *aita* can be both written as 開いた.

EX. (**a**) I heard laughter coming from the open window.
{開いた/開いた}窓から笑い声が聞こえた。
{Aita/Hiraita} mado kara warai-goe ga kikoeta.
(**b**) There was an open umbrella on the floor.
{開いた/*開いた}傘が床に置いてあった。
*{Hiraita/*Aita} kasa ga yuka ni oite atta.*

NOTE: *Aita* is unacceptable in example (b) because an umbrella has parts that move in opposite directions to each other and therefore opens with a three-dimensional, symmetrical kind of motion.

— vt. **[to cause the interior of s.t. to become exposed to the outside ⟪fig. "begin a performance"⟫]**
1. a⌈keru あける ② [to cause the interior of s.t. to become exposed to the outside] ⟪keep open, leave vacant⟫ ↔ tojiru 閉じる ②, shimeru 閉める ②; ⟨-o⟩ hi⌈ra⌉ku ⟨〜を⟩開く ① [to cause the interior of s.t./s.o./s.a. to become exposed to the outside (often by means of a three-dimensional, symmetrical action) ⟪fig. "start"⟫] ⟪uncover, start⟫ ↔ ⟨-o⟩ tojiru ⟨〜を⟩閉じる ②, ⟨-o⟩ shimeru ⟨〜を⟩閉める ②

㊥ "leave space vacant"▷空ける, otherwise▷開ける

EX. (**a**) Dan opened the door without knocking.
ダンはノックもしないでドアを{開けた/?開いた}。
Dan wa nokku mo shinaide doa o {aketa/?hiraita}.
(**b**) Open your textbooks to page 35.
教科書の三十五ページを{開けなさい/開きなさい}。
Kyooka-sho no san-juu-go-peeji o {akenasai/hirakinasai}.
(**c**) We need to open our minds to new ideas.

新しい考えに心を{開かなければ/*開けなければ}なりません。
*Atarashii kangae ni kokoro o {hirakanakereba/*akenakereba} narimasen.*

2. ⟨-o⟩ **ha⌈jimeru** ⟨〜を⟩**始める** ② **[for s.o./s.a. to perform the first part of an activity]** ↔ ⟨-o⟩ **oeru** ⟨〜を⟩**終える** ②

EX. The professor opened his lecture with an anecdote.
教授は講演を逸話で始めた。
Kyooju wa kooen o itsuwa de hajimeta.

— vi. **[for a moving part of a larger whole to shift position spontaneously to allow the interior to become exposed to the outside]**

1. a⌈ku あく ① **[for the interior of s.t. to become exposed to the outside** 《**fig. "start"**》**]** ⟪**become empty, start**⟫, **hi⌈ra⌉ku 開く** ① **[for interior of s.t./s.o./s.a. to become exposed to the outside (often by means of a three-dimensional, symmetrical action)]**

㊈ "become empty" ▷空く, otherwise ▷開く

EX. (**a**) This umbrella doesn't open.
この傘は{開かない/*開かない}。
*Kono kasa wa {hirakanai/*akanai}.*
(**b**) The bud on the flower began to open.
花のつぼみが{開き/*開き}始めた。
*Hana no tsubomi ga {hiraki/*aki}-hajimeta.*
(**c**) This window doesn't open.
この窓は{開かない/?開かない}。
Kono mado wa {akanai/?hirakanai}.

2. ha⌈jimaru 始まる ① **[for the first part of s.t. to take place]** ⟪**begin, start, arise**⟫

EX. A: When does that Broadway show open?
そのブロードウエイのショーはいつ始まるんですか。
Sono Buroodouei no shoo wa itsu hajimaru n desu ka.
B: It opens this Friday.
今週の金曜日ですよ。
Konshuu no kin'yoo-bi desu yo.

opera n.
ka⌉geki 歌劇 •c, **o⌉pera オペラ** •f

operate vi. **[for s.t./s.o. to function properly]**

1. u⌈go⌉ku 動く ① **[to change in location or position** 《**fig. "shake," "be affected," "change," "be transferred"**》**]** ⟪**move, run, go, stir, work**⟫

EX. The escalator in this department store isn't currently operating.
このデパートのエスカレーターは今動いていません。
Kono depaato no esukareetaa wa ima ugoite imasen.

2. ⟨-o⟩ **shu⌉jutsu-suru** ⟨〜を⟩**手術する** ③ •c **[for a surgeon to cut into or remove part of a body as a medical treatment]**, ⟨-no⟩ **shu⌉jutsu o suru** ⟨〜の⟩**手術をする** ③ •c

EX. The surgeons here operate on about five patients a day.
ここの外科医は一日に五人ほどの患者{を手術する/の手術をする}。
Koko no geka-i wa ichi-nichi ni go-nin hodo no kanja {o shujutsu-suru/no shujutsu o suru}.

— vt. **[for s.o. to cause s.t. such as a machine or institution to function properly]**

1. ⟨-o⟩ **u⌈goka⌉su** ⟨〜を⟩**動かす** ① **[for s.o./s.a. to cause s.t./s.o./s.a. to change in position or location or to function properly]** ⟪**move, set in motion, change the position of, run, work**⟫, ⟨-o⟩ **so⌉osa-suru** ⟨〜を⟩**操作する** ③ •c **[for s.o. to cause a relatively complex machine to function** 《**fig. "manipulate"**》**]** ⟪**handle, manipulate**⟫, ⟨-o⟩ **u⌈nten-suru** ⟨〜を⟩**運転する** ③ •c **[for s.o. to control the functioning and movement of a large vehicle, esp. a car]** ⟪**drive, run**⟫

NOTE: Unlike other short causatives, *ugokasu* does not have a longer causative version. *Ugokaseru* means not "to cause s.o./s.a./s.t. to move" but "can move s.t./s.o./s.a."

EX. (**a**) I don't know how to operate this kind of tractor.
私にはこの手のトラクターは{動かせない/操作出来ない/運転出来ない}。
Watashi ni wa kono te no torakutaa wa {ugokase-nai/soosa-dekinai/unten-dekinai}.

(**b**) Do you know how to operate this word processor?
このワープロを{操作出来ます/?動かせます/*運転出来ます}か。
*Kono waapuro o {soosa-dekimasu/ ?ugokase-masu/*unten-dekimasu} ka.*
(**c**) Can you operate a car with a stick shift?
マニュアル車は{運転できます/?動かせます/??操作できます}か。
Manyuaru-sha wa {unten-dekimasu/ ?ugokase-masu/??soosa-dekimasu} ka.

O

operation n. **[the act of operating s.t. or the way s.t. operates]**
so˥osa 操作 •c [the act or method of causing s.t. such as a machine or vehicle to function or move properly], sa˥gyoo 作業 •c [working using physical or bodily energy] ((**work**)), **shu˥jutsu 手術 •c [the cutting of the body for medical treatment]** ((**surgery**))

EX. (**a**) Last week I had an eye operation.
先週、私は目の{手術/*操作/*作業}を受けました。
*Senshuu, watashi wa me no {shujutsu/ *soosa/*sagyoo} o ukemashita.*
(**b**) The logistical operations involved in excavating the ruins took more than 20 years.
その遺跡を発掘する{作業/*操作/*手術}は二十年以上もかかった。
*Sono iseki o hakkutsu-suru {sagyoo/ *soosa/*shujutsu} wa ni-juu-nen-ijoo mo kakatta.*
(**c**) Have you received training in the operation of this cyclotron?
このサイクロトロンの{操作/*作業/*手術}に関する訓練を受けていますか。
*Kono saikurotoron no {soosa/*sagyoo/ *shujutsu} ni-kansuru kunren o ukete imasu ka.*

operator n. **[a person who operates a machine ((fig. "a shrewd person who knows how to manipulate human affairs"))]**
1. (**de┌nwa-**)**kooka˥n-shu** (電話)**交換手 •c [s.o. who makes connections between lines at a telephone exchange], op┌ere˥etaa オペレーター •f [s.o. who operates a machine]**

EX. A: I lost Mr.Tsuda's telephone number.
津田さんの電話番号をなくしちゃったよ。
Tsuda-san no denwa-bangoo o nakushichatta yo.
B: Why don't you call the operator and ask for it?
{交換手/オペレーター}に聞いてみたらどうですか。
{Kookan-shu/Opereetaa} ni kiite mitara doo desu ka.

2. ya┌rite やり手 [a person who is talented in getting what he/she wants by manipulating people] ((**able man, tactician, wheeler-dealer**))

EX. A: He seems to be moving up in the company rather quickly, doesn't he?
あの男は会社での昇進が早いようだねえ。
Ano otoko wa kaisha de no shooshin ga hayai yooda nee.
B: Yes. He's quite an operator, you know.
うん。なかなかのやり手だからね。
Un. Naka-naka no yarite da kara ne.

opinion n. **[a belief or judgment held strongly by one without actual proof]**
1. i˥ken 意見 •c [an idea or judgment one holds about a matter] ((**view, advice, admonition**))

EX. A: Do you have an opinion on this matter?
この問題について何か(御)意見がありますか。
Kono mondai ni-tsuite nani-ka (go-) iken ga arimasu ka.
B: No, none in particular.
いいえ、別にありません。
Iie, betsu ni arimasen.

2. {**se˥ron/yo˥ron**} **世論 •c [the view on a particular social issue held by the public]** ((**consensus of opinion**))

EX. The American public is of the opinion that democracy is the best form of government.
アメリカの世論によると民主主義が一番いい政治形態である。
Amerika no {seron/yoron} ni yoru to minshu-shugi ga ichiban ii seiji-keitai dearu.

opportunity n. **[a time or situation suitable to achieving some purpose]**
ki⌈ka⌉i 機会 •c [a suitable time for doing s.t.] ⟪chance, occasion⟫, cha⌉nsu チャンス •f [a good time to do s.t.] ⟪chance⟫

EX. I'd like to see my friend again if I ever have the opportunity to go to Boston.
ボストンに行く{機会/チャンス}があったら、また友達に会いたいと思います。
Bosuton ni iku {kikai/chansu} ga attara, mata tomodachi ni ai-tai to omoimasu.

oppose vt. **[for s.o. to be against s.o./s.t. or to put s.o./s.t. in contrast to s.o./s.t. else]**
1. ⟨-ni⟩ {ha⌈ntai-suru/ha⌈ntai da} ⟨〜に⟩{反対する ③/反対だ} •c [for s.o. to be in serious conflict with s.o. else's opinion, plan, idea, proposal, etc.] ⟪object, take a stand against⟫ ↔ ⟨-ni⟩ {sansei-suru/sansei da} ⟨〜に⟩{賛成する ③/賛成だ} •c

EX. I oppose the government's policy on nuclear weapons.
私は政府の核兵器政策に{反対します/反対です}。
Watashi wa seifu no kaku-heiki-seisaku ni {hantai-shimasu/hantai desu}.

2. ⟨-o⟩ ⟨-to⟩ hi⌈kaku-ta⌈ishoo-suru ⟨〜を⟩⟨〜と⟩比較対照する ③ •c [for s.o. to put s.t./s.o./s.a. in sharp contrast with s.t./s.o./s.a. else] ⟪contrast A with B⟫

EX. It's often the case that one's own ideas become better clarified when opposed to someone else's ideas.
他の人の考えと比較対照すると自分の考えがはっきりしてくることがよくあります。
Ta no hito no kangae to hikaku-taishoo-suru to jibun no kangae ga hakkiri shite kuru koto ga yoku arimasu.

opposite adj. **[to be located across from or on the other side of or facing s.t./s.o./s.a.; to be totally different in kind from s.t./s.o./s.a.]**
⟨-no⟩ ha⌈ntai no N ⟨〜の⟩反対のN •c [to be in an opposing relation to s.t./s.o./s.a. in position, direction, content, or type] ⟪contrary, reverse⟫, ⟨-no⟩ ha⌈ntai-gawa no N ⟨〜の⟩反対側のN [on a side across from s.t.], ⟨-no⟩ mu⌈kai(-gawa) no N ⟨〜の⟩向かい(側)のN [an area face to face with a building/room/person]

EX. (**a**) There's a big tree on the opposite side of the river.
川の{反対側/*向かい(側)}に大きな木がある。
*Kawa no {hantai-gawa/*mukai(-gawa)} ni ookina ki ga aru.*
(**b**) Please look at the picture on the opposite page.
{反対側/*向かい(側)}のページの絵を見て下さい。
*{Hantai-gawa/*Mukai(-gawa)} no peeji no e o mite kudasai.*
(**c**) A: Where is the bank?
銀行はどこですか。
Ginkoo wa doko desu ka.
B: It's opposite the post office.
郵便局の{向かい(側)/反対側}です。
Yuubin-kyoku no {mukai(-gawa)/hantai-gawa} desu.
(**d**) My father and I hold opposite views on interracial marriage.
父と私は国際結婚について反対の意見を持っています。
Chichi to watashi wa kokusai-kekkon ni-tsuite hantai no iken o motte imasu.

opposition n. **[an act of resisting s.o./s.t. or of placing s.o./s.t. in contrast to s.o./s.t. else]**
ha⌈ntai 反対 •c [(of two opinions) the state of being opposed] ↔ sansei 賛成 •c

EX. This proposal met with the minority party's strong opposition.
この提案は野党の強い反対にあった。
Kono teian wa yatoo no tsuyoi hantai ni atta.

or conj. **[a disjuntive conjunction that combines two or more words or phrases as alternatives]**
ka か prt. **[a particle which marks an alternative], so⌈re-to⌉mo それとも [a particle that precedes a phrase that presents**

an alternative to what has come before] ((or else)), (ka) a⌈ru⌉iwa (か)あるいは conj. **[a conjunction that marks an alternative ⟨fml⟩]**

EX. (**a**) Either Bob or Mark will be there to meet you.
お迎えにはボブ{か/あるいは/*それとも}マークが行きます。
*O-mukae ni wa Bobu {ka/aruiwa/ *sore-tomo} Maaku ga ikimasu.*
(**b**) A: What do you normally have for breakfast?
朝御飯には何を食べますか。
Asa-gohan ni wa nani o tabemasu ka.
B: I usually have either eggs or pancakes.
大抵卵{か/かあるいは/*それとも}パンケーキを食べます。
*Taitei tamago {ka/ka aruiwa/*sore-tomo} pankeeki o tabemasu.*
(**c**) I don't know whether or not I can go to Japan this year.
今年日本へ行ける{か/かあるいは/かそれとも}行けないか分かりません。
Kotoshi Nihon e ike-ru {ka/ka aruiwa/ ka sore-tomo} ike-nai ka wakarimasen.

NOTE: When *ka* is used in the above example, *ike-ru ka doo ka* would be more common than *ike-ru ka ike-nai ka* in colloquial Japanese.

(**d**) Which do you prefer, coffee or tea?
コーヒー{と/*か/*あるいは/*それとも}紅茶では、どっちの方が好きですか。
*Koohii {to/*ka/*aruiwa/*sore-tomo} koocha de wa, dotchi no hoo ga suki desu ka.*

NOTE: In a construction such as in example (d), *to* (literally meaning "and") is used to express the meaning of "or" in English because X *to* Y *de wa* literally means "between X and Y."

(**e**) Shall we go to a movie? Or shall we watch TV at home?
映画に行きましょうか。{それとも/*か/ *あるいは}うちでテレビを見ましょうか。
*Eiga ni ikimashoo ka. {Sore-tomo/*Ka/ *Aruiwa} uchi de terebi o mimashoo ka.*
(**f**) I'm in the process of trying to decide whether I should stay in Japan another year or return home.
来年も日本にいるべきか{それとも/?あるいは/*か}国へ帰るべきか、今考えているところです。
*Rainen mo Nihon ni iru-beki ka {sore-tomo/?aruiwa/*ka} kuni e kaeru-beki ka, ima kangaete iru tokoro desu.*

oral adj. **[pertaining to the mouth/speech]**
ko⌈otoo no N 口頭のN •c [conveyed or conducted by word of mouth]

EX. Tomorrow I have an oral examination in Japanese.
あした日本語の口頭試験があります。
Ashita Nihon-go no kootoo-shiken ga arimasu.

orange n.
o⌈re⌉nji オレンジ •f [a round juicy citrus fruit with reddish-yellow skin grown primarily in the West] ((navel orange))

NOTE: A Japanese orange (=mandarin orange) is referred to as *mikan.*

orbit n.
ki⌈doo 軌道 •c

EX. There are many satellites in orbit around the earth used for purposes of communication.
通信用の人工衛星がたくさん地球の回りの軌道を回っている。
Tsuushin-yoo no jinkoo-eisei ga takusan chikyuu no mawari no kidoo o mawatte iru.

orchard n.
ka⌈ju⌉-en 果樹園 •c

orchestra n.
ka⌈ngen-ga⌉ku-dan 管弦楽団 •c, o⌈oke⌉sutora オーケストラ •f

order n. **[a state in which elements of a group are properly arranged or that which is requested by a superior or customer]**
1. ju⌉njo 順序 •c [the way in which elements of a group are arranged with regard to each other] ((sequence, procedure))

EX. In Japan the order in which people in a family take their baths was strictly defined.
日本の家庭では風呂に入る順序がやかましかった。

Nihon no katei de wa furo ni hairu junjo ga yakamashikatta.

2. chi˥tsujo 秩序 •c [a state in which elements of a group are properly arranged] ⟪discipline, system⟫

EX. Society cannot exist without law and order.
社会は法と秩序がなければやっていけない。
Shakai wa hoo to chitsujo ga nakereba yatte ikenai.

3. me┌irei 命令 •c [an instruction to act issued by a military superior or other person in a position of authority] ⟪command⟫

EX. I received an order from my boss to fly to London this coming Monday.
来週の月曜日にロンドンに飛べという命令を上司から受けた。
Raishuu no getsuyoo-bi ni Rondon ni tobe to iu meirei o jooshi kara uketa.

4. sa˥shizu 指図 [an act/instance of ordering/instructing s.o. to do s.t.] ⟪directions, instructions⟫

EX. I don't like my older brother giving me orders.
兄に指図をされるのは嫌いです。
Ani ni sashizu o sareru no wa kirai desu.

5. chu┌umon 注文 •c [a customer's request to prepare s.t. according to specification or s.t. that has been prepared according to specification]

EX. (**a**) A: May I take your order, sir?
御注文は何になさいますか。
Go-chuumon wa nani ni nasaimasu ka.
B: Yes, I'd like steak, please.
ステーキをお願いします。
Suteeki o o-negaishimasu.
(**b**) A: Is my order ready yet?
私の注文はもう出来ていますか。
Watashi no chuumon wa moo dekite imasu ka.
B: No, not yet. Sorry.
いいえ、まだちょっと…すいません。
Iie, mada chotto...suimasen.

—— vt. **[for a superior to issue instruction to act or for a customer to request s.t. according to specification]**

1. ⟨-ni⟩ ⟨-yooni⟩ me┌irei-suru ⟨〜に⟩⟨〜ように⟩命令する ③ •c [for a superior, esp. in the military, to command s.o. to do s.t. ⟨fml⟩] ⟪command, direct⟫, ⟨-ni⟩ ⟨-yooni⟩ me┌ijiru ⟨〜に⟩⟨〜ように⟩命じる ② •c [for a superior (hereby) to command s.o. to do s.t.] ⟪command, tell a person to do⟫

EX. The president ordered his subordinate not to leak the incident to the press.
大統領は部下にその事件を記者に漏らさないように{命令した/命じた}。
Daitooryoo wa buka ni sono jiken o kisha ni morasanai yooni {meirei-shita/meijita}.

2. ⟨-ni⟩ ⟨-yoo(ni)⟩ sa˥shizu-suru ⟨〜に⟩⟨〜よう(に)⟩指図する ③ [for a superior to instruct s.o. to do s.t. in a non-military context] ⟪direct, instruct⟫

EX. The teacher ordered her students to arrange the chairs neatly.
先生は学生にいすをきちんと並べるように指図した。
Sensei wa gakusei ni isu o kichin-to naraberu yooni sashizu-shita.

3. chu┌umon-suru 注文する ③ •c [for a customer to request preparation of s.t. according to specification] ⟪place an order⟫

EX. We ordered pizza for dinner.
晩御飯にピザを注文した。
Ban-gohan ni piza o chuumon-shita.

orderly adj. **[in a state where elements of a group are properly arranged]**
se┌izen to shita N 整然としたN /⟨Vinf. past of *seizen to suru* ③ well-ordered/ •c, se┌izen to shite iru (N) 整然としている(N) /⟨V*te iru* of *seizen to suru* ③ well-ordered/ •c [in a state where everything is in order], ki˥chi˥n-to shita N きちんとしたN /⟨Vinf. past of *kichin-to suru* ③ make things neat/, ki┌chi˥n-to shite iru (N) きちんとしている(N) /⟨V*te iru* of *kichin-to suru* ③ make things neat/ [to be neat and proper] ⟪neat, tidy⟫

EX. (**a**) Professor Yamashita's office is always orderly.

山下教授の研究室はいつも{整然/きちん}としている。
Yamashita-kyooju no kenkyuu-shitsu wa itsu-mo {seizen/kichin-} to shite iru.
(**b**) The students at the rally were quiet and orderly.
野外集会の学生は静かで{整然/??きちん}としていた。
Yagai-shuukai no gakusei wa shizukade {seizen/??kichin-} to shite ita.

O

ordinary adj. **[commonly encountered]**
fu⌈tsuu no N 普通のN •c **[conforming to a standard/norm ⟪fig. "commonly found"⟫]** ⟪**normal, common, regular**⟫, **he⌈ibonna** 平凡な adj(*na*). •c **[neither unusual nor exciting]** ⟪**commonplace, common, uneventful, mediocre, banal**⟫

EX. (**a**) A: Can you describe in more detail the young girl you saw waiting at the bus stop?
バス停で待っていた若い女性はどんな人だったか、もっと詳しく言ってもらえますか。
Basu-tei de matte ita wakai josei wa donna hito datta ka motto kuwashiku itte morae-masu ka.
B: Just an ordinary high school girl.
{普通の/平凡な}女子高校生で、外には別に何も…。
{Futsuuu no/Heibonna} joshi-kookoosei de, hoka ni wa betsu ni nani-mo…
(**b**) A: What kind of life did your father lead?
お父さんはどんな人生を送られましたか。
O-too-san wa donna jinsei o okura-remashita ka.
B: Well, it was just an ordinary life, I guess.
そうですね。{平凡な/普通の}人生だったと思いますよ。
Soo desu ne. {Heibonna/Futsuu no} jinsei datta to omoimasu yo.

ore n.
ko⌈oseki 鉱石 •c

Oregon n.
O⌉regon オレゴン •f

organ n. **[a musical instrument consisting of keyboards and pipes or a vital part of any organism]**
1. o⌈rugan オルガン •f **[a musical instrument consisting of keyboards and pipes]**, **pa⌈ipu-o⌉rugan** パイプオルガン •f

EX. It must be pretty hard to play the pipe organ.
パイプオルガンを弾くのはとても難しいに違いない。
Paipu-orugan o hiku no wa totemo muzukashii ni chigainai.

2. ki⌈ka⌉n 器官 •c **[a vital part of an organism]**

EX. The doctor told me that my digestive organs were in bad shape due to my drinking.
医者は飲酒のために僕の消化器管はやられていると言った。
Isha wa inshu no tame ni boku no shooka-kikan wa yara-rete iru to itta.

organism n. **[a living being]**
yu⌈uki-tai 有機体 •c

organization n. **[the act or way of arranging things to form an orderly structure or a social structure formed for a particular purpose]**
so⌉shiki 組織 •c **[a group of interconnected humans/cells]** ⟪**formation, construction, system, tissue**⟫, **da⌈ntai** 団体 •c **[a relatively large number of people gathered together for a specific purpose]** ⟪**party, company, team**⟫

EX. (**a**) Do you know if there is any organization in this country for promoting the study of Japanese?
この国に日本語教育振興のための{組織/団体}があるかどうか知っていますか。
Kono kuni ni Nihon-go-kyooiku shinkoo no tame no {soshiki/dantai} ga aru ka doo ka shitte imasu ka.
(**b**) The organization of Japanese companies is quite different from that of American companies.
日本の会社の{組織/*団体}はアメリカのとかなり違う。
*Nihon no kaisha no {soshiki/*dantai} wa Amerika no to kanari chigau.*

organize vt. **[to arrange things/people to form an orderly structure]**
1. ⟨-o⟩ so˥shiki-suru ⟨〜を⟩組織する ③ •c [for a group of elements to form a structural entity] ⟪form, set up, incorporate⟫

EX. This association was organized in 1950.
この会は1950年に組織された。
Kono kai wa sen-kyuu-hyaku-go-juu-nen ni soshiki-sareta.

2. ⟨-o⟩ se˥iri-suru ⟨〜を⟩整理する ③ •c [for s.o. to put things in a state of order, esp. by eliminating unneccessary elements] ⟪put in order, tidy up, straighten, consolidate, control, dispose of⟫, ⟨-o⟩ ki┌chi˥n-to suru ⟨〜を⟩きちんとする ③ [for s.o. to put things in a neat and proper condition] ⟪tidy, straighten, put in order⟫

EX. Why don't you organize your desk better?
机の上をもっと{整理/きちんと}したらどうですか。
Tsukue no ue o motto {seiri-/kichin to} shitara doo desu ka.

Orient n. **[the countries of Asia, esp. those to the east of the Mediterranean Sea]**
to˥oyoo 東洋 •c [the countries lying on the side of the Mediterranean in the direction of the rising sun] ↔ seiyoo 西洋 •c; o˥riento オリエント •f [the countries of Asia, esp. to the east of the Mediterranean Sea]

EX. The fact that the word "Orient" is no longer commonly used shows how much Western views of the Orient have changed in recent years.
「オリエント」ということばがあまり使われなくなったことからも分かるように、近年西洋の{オリエント/東洋}に対する見方は大分変わってきた。
'Oriento' to iu kotoba ga amari tsukawa-renaku natta koto kara mo wakaru yooni, kinnen seiyoo no {oriento/tooyoo} ni-taisuru mikata wa daibu kawatte kita.

oriental adj. **[pertaining to the Orient]**
to˥oyoo no N 東洋のN •c [pertaining to the countries of East and South Asia] ↔ seiyoo no N 西洋のN •c; to┌oyoo-tekina 東洋的な adj(*na*). **•c [characteristic of the countries/cultures of East and South Asia] ↔ seiyoo-tekina 西洋的な** adj(*na*). **•c**

EX. (**a**) A: Why are you studying Japanese?
どうして日本語を勉強しているんですか。
Dooshite Nihon-go o benkyoo-shite iru n desu ka.
B: Because I got interested in oriental philosophy.
{東洋(の)/*東洋的な}哲学に興味を持ったからです。
*{Tooyoo (no)/*Tooyoo-tekina} tetsugaku ni kyoomi o motta kara desu.*
(**b**) That's an oriental way of dealing with the problem, isn't it?
それは問題に対する{東洋的な/?東洋の}対処の仕方ですね。
Sore wa mondai ni-taisuru {tooyoo-tekina/?tooyoo no} taisho no shikata desu ne.

—— n. **[the people of the Orient]**
to┌oyo˥o-jin 東洋人 •c [the people of East and South Asia] ↔ seiyoo-jin 西洋人 •c

EX. More than 10% of the student body of our university are orientals.
私たちの大学の学生の十パーセント以上は東洋人です。
Watashi-tachi no daigaku no gakusei no jup-paasento-ijoo wa tooyoo-jin desu.

origin n. **[a place/time in which s.t. is created]**
ha┌jimari 始まり /⟨V*masu* of *hajimaru* ① begin/ [the point from which a series of actions/incidents start] ⟪beginning, opening, start⟫ ↔ owari 終わり; mo┌to 元 [a root ⟪fig. "origin," "beginning," "foundation," "cause," "materials," "capital," "under (the influence of)"⟫] ⟪source, beginning, cause⟫, mi┌namoto 源 [the starting point (of a river)] ⟪headwaters, beginning, genesis⟫, ki˥gen 起源 •c [the beginning of things] ⟪beginning, rise, genesis, derivation⟫

EX. (**a**) Very little is known yet about the origin of the Japanese language.
日本語の{起源/始まり/元/源}についてはまだごくわずかしか分かっていない。
Nihon-go no {kigen/hajimari/moto/minamoto} ni-tsuite wa mada goku wazuka shika wakatte inai.
(**b**) Buddhism's place of origin is India.
仏教の{起源/始まり/元/源}はインドです。
Bukkyoo no {kigen/hajimari/moto/minamoto} wa Indo desu.

original adj. **[pertaining to a place/time in which s.t. is created]**
1. sa⌈isho no N 最初のN •c [pertaining to the very first] ((the first, initial, maiden)) ↔ saigo no N 最後のN

EX. The original model for DNA was formulated by Drs. Watson and Crick.
最初のDNAのモデルはワトソン博士とクリック博士によって作られた。
Saisho no Dii-enu-ee no moderu wa Watoson-hakase to Kurikku-hakase ni-yotte tsukura-reta.

2. do⌈kusoo-tekina 独創的な adj(*na*). **•c [creating s.t. without relying on imitation] ((creative)), o⌈ri⌉jinaruna オリジナルな** adj(*na*). **•f [creative]**

EX. Original ideas are hard to come by.
{独創的な/オリジナルな}考えはなかなか出て来ない。
{Dokusoo-tekina/Orijinaruna} kangae wa naka-naka dete konai.

—— n. **[s.t. which is not a copy (but from which copies are made)]**
ge⌉npon 原本 •c [the first written version of s.t., from which copies have been made] ((original copy)), ge⌈nsaku 原作 •c [an artistic work from which a translation/a dramatization/a film has been made] ((original work)), o⌈ri⌉jinaru オリジナル •f [the first version of s.t., including an artistic work, from which copies have been made]

EX. (**a**) Please let me see the original of this document.
この文書の{原本/オリジナル/*原作}を見せてください。
*Kono bunsho no {genpon/orijinaru/*gensaku} o misete kudasai.*
(**b**) This art museum has many Rembrandt originals.
この美術館にはレンブラントの{オリジナル/*原本/*原作}がたくさんあります。
*Kono bijutsu-kan ni wa Renburanto no {orijinaru/*genpon/*gensaku} ga takusan arimasu.*

ostrich n.
da⌈choo だちょう •c

other adj. **[different from the one or ones under discussion]**
ho⌈ka no N 外のN ((another))

EX. (**a**) A: Did Mr. Johnson come to the party?
ジョンソンさんはパーティーに来ましたか。
Jonson-san wa paatii ni kimashita ka.
B: Yes, but my other friends didn't show up.
ええ、でも、外の友達は来ませんでした。
Ee, demo, hoka no tomodachi wa kimasen deshita.
(**b**) Do you have any other questions?
外の質問がありますか。
Hoka no shitsumon ga arimasu ka.
(**c**) Let's watch some other program; this one isn't very interesting.
この番組はつまらないから、何か外の番組を見ましょう。
Kono bangumi wa tsumaranai kara, nani-ka hoka no bangumi o mimashoo.

PHRASE: in other words *tsumari* つまり ((in short, briefly)), *ii-kaeru to* 言い換えると

EX. In other words, "*shin-jinrui*" is a new breed of young Japanese who are more individualistic than traditional Japanese.
{つまり/言い換えると}、「新人類」というのは昔からの日本人より個人主義的な、若い日本人のことなのです。
{Tsumari/Ii-kaeru to}, 'shin-jinrui' to iu no wa mukashi kara no Nihon-jin yori kojin-shugi-tekina, wakai Nihon-jin no koto na no desu.

PHRASE: the other day *kono aida* この間, *senjitsu*

先日 •c, *sendatte* 先だって ⟨fml⟩

EX. (**a**) I met Professor Suzuki the other day in Paris.
{この間/先日/先だって}パリで鈴木先生にお目にかかりましたよ。
{Kono aida/Senjitsu/Sendatte} Pari de Suzuki-sensei ni o-me ni kakarimashita yo.
(**b**) I ran into Bill the other day on the bus.
{この間/先日/先だって}バスの中でビルにばったり会いました。
{Kono aida/Senjitsu/Sendatte} basu no naka de Biru ni battari aimashita.

others pron. **[ones that are different from the ones under discussion]**
ho⌈ka no 外の

EX. These shoes are all the wrong size. Do you have any others?
この靴は全部サイズが違うんですが、外のがありますか。
Kono kutsu wa zenbu saizu ga chigau n desu ga, hoka no ga arimasu ka.

otherwise adv. **[differently or in other respects]**
1. so⌉o dewa⌈na⌉i そうではない **[that is not the case], so⌉o ja⌈na⌉i** そうじゃない **[that is not the case ⟨s⟩]**

EX. John considered the idea a splendid one, but Mary thought otherwise.
ジョンはそのアイデアはすばらしいと思ったが、メアリーはそう{ではない/じゃない}と思った。
Jon wa sono aidea wa subarashii to omotta ga, Mearii wa soo {dewanai/janai} to omotta.

2. so⌈re-i⌉gai de wa それ以外では **[in other respects]**

EX. Taro doesn't do any housework; otherwise, he's a good husband.
太郎はうちのことは何も手伝わないが、それ以外ではいい夫だ。
Taroo wa uchi no koto wa nani-mo tetsudawanai ga, sore-igai de wa ii otto da.

3. (mo⌉shi) so⌉o {ja⌈na⌉i/shi⌈nai} to (もし)そう{じゃない/しない}と **[if such is not the case or if one does not do so], (mo⌉shi so⌈o) shi⌈na⌉kattara** (もしそう)しなかったら **[if such were not/had not been the case or if one did not do/had not done so], sa⌉mo-nai-to** さもないと **[if s.o. does not do so]** **⟪or else⟫**

NOTE: *Samo-nai-to* can be used only when the preceding sentence is a command.

EX. (**a**) Do it right now! Otherwise I'll fire you!
すぐやれ! {(もし)そう{しないと/しなかったら}/さもないと}、首だ!
Sugu yare! {(Moshi) soo {shinai to/shinakattara}/Samo-nai-to}, kubi da!
(**b**) Luckily I found a good doctor. Otherwise I wouldn't be alive now.
幸いいい医者を見つけたんです。(もし)そう{しなかったら/*しないと}、今生きていなかったでしょう。
*Saiwai ii isha o mitsuketa n desu. (Moshi) soo {shinakattara/*shinai to}, ima ikite inakatta deshoo.*
(**c**) Master one foreign language while you are a student. Otherwise you may never again have the opportunity to do so.
学生のうちに一つ外国語をマスターしなさい。そう{じゃないと/しないと/しなかったら}二度と機会はないかもしれませんよ。
Gakusei no uchi ni hitotsu gaikoku-go o masutaa-shinasai. Soo {janai to/shinai to/shinakattara} ni-do to kikai wa nai kamoshiremasen yo.

ought aux. **[an auxiliary verb that indicates an obligation for s.o. to do s.t. or an expectation by the speaker that some event or situation will occur or has occurred]**
1. {**Vneg./Vstem/shi/ko/adj**(*i*). *ku*}{**nakute wa/nakereba**} {**i⌈kenai/na⌈ra⌉nai**} {**Vneg./Vstem/**し/来/**adj**(*i*). *ku*}{なくては/なければ}{いけない/ならない}, {**adj**(*na*). **stem/N**}{**de/ja**}{**na⌉kute wa/na⌉kereba**} {**i⌈kenai/na⌈ra⌉nai**} {**adj**(*na*). **stem/N**}{で/じゃ}{なくては/なければ}{いけない/ならない} **[it won't do if s.o. does not take some action or if s.o./s.t./s.a. is not in a certain state ("s.o." is normally a person the speaker**

identifies with, including the listener)]

EX. (**a**) A: Doctor, do I have to quit smoking?
先生、たばこを{やめなくては/やめなければ}なりませんか。
Sensei, tabako o {yamenakute wa/ yamenakereba} narimasen ka.
B: You ought to.
{やめなくては/やめなければ}なりません。
{Yamenakute wa/Yamenakereba} narimasen.
(**b**) One ought to take along a gift when visiting someone's home in Japan.
日本で人の家を訪ねる時は、お土産を持って{行かなくては/行かなければ}いけない。
Nihon de hito no ie o tazuneru toki wa, o-miyage o motte {ikanakute wa/ ikanakereba} ikenai.

2. Vinf. nonpast be˥ki da Vinf. nonpastべきだ [for s.o. other than the speaker to have an obligation/duty to do s.t. ⟨fml⟩]

EX. You ought to speak more politely to your teacher.
先生にはもっと丁寧に話すべきだ。
Sensei ni wa motto teinei ni hanasu-beki da.

NOTE: When the irregular verb *suru* is followed by *beki da*, the form can be either *su-beki da* or *suru-beki da*.

3. Sinf. ha˥zu da Sinf.はずだ [it is expected by the speaker that s.t. will take place/took place or that s.o./s.t./s.a. is/was in some state] ⟪be expected to, I expect that, I am fairly certain that, ought to⟫

EX. (**a**) I just had this VCR fixed, so it ought to work properly.
このビデオデッキは修理してもらったばかりだから、ちゃんと作動するはずです。
Kono bideodekki wa shuuri-shite moratta bakari da kara, chanto sadoo-suru hazu desu.
(**b**) Mr. Smith ought to be arriving in Kyoto about now.
スミスさんはそろそろ京都に着くはずです。
Sumisu-san wa soro-soro Kyooto ni tsuku hazu desu.

ounce n.
o˥nsu オンス •f

our pron. **[the possessive form of "we"]**
wa˥ta(ku)shi-do˥mo no N 私どものN ⟨fml⟩, wa˥ta(ku)shi˥-tachi no N 私たちのN ⟨fml⟩, bo˥ku-tachi no N 僕たちのN [the possessive form of "we" used in male speech ⟨s⟩] a˥tashi˥-tachi no N あたしたちのN [the possessive form of "we" used in female speech ⟨s⟩], o˥re˥-tachi no N おれたちのN [the possessive form of "we" used in male speech ⟨s⟩], wa˥re-ware no N 我々のN [the most inclusive possessive form of "we," conveying a strong sense of belonging ⟨fml⟩]

NOTE: "Our" is often not expressed at all when it can be understood in a given context.

EX. (**a**) Our team is number one in the nation.
{我々/僕たち/あたしたち/おれたち/私たち/??私ども/*ø}のチームが国内で一番強いんです。
*{Ware-ware/Boku-tachi/Atashi-tachi/ Ore-tachi/Watashi-tachi/??Watashi-domo/*ø} no chiimu ga kokunai de ichiban tsuyoi n desu.*
(**b**) Our company is trying its best to market its products as inexpensively as possible.
{私ども/?私たち/?僕たち/*おれたち/*あたしたち/*我々/*ø}の会社では出来るだけ安く製品をお届けしたいと願っております。
*{Wata(ku)shi-domo/?Wata(ku)shi-tachi/?Boku-tachi/*Ore-tachi/*Atashi-tachi/*Ware-ware/*ø} no kaisha de wa dekiru dake yasuku seihin o o-todoke-shi-tai to negatte orimasu.*

ourselves pron. **[the form of the first person plural pronoun used in reflexive and emphatic contexts]**
wa˥ta(ku)shi-tachi-ji˥shin 私たち自身 [an emphatic form of the first person plural pronoun ⟨fml⟩], wa˥re-ware-ji˥shin 我々自身 [an emphatic form of the most inclusive

form of "we," conveying a strong sense of belonging ⟨fml⟩], ji⌈bun(-ji⌉shin) 自分(自身) •c [a reflexive pronoun that refers (back) to a human subject with whom the speaker identifies, including himself/herself] SEE oneself

EX. (**a**) We tend to overestimate ourselves.
私たちは{自分(自身)/*私たち自身/*我々自身}を過大評価しやすい。
*Watashi-tachi wa {jibun(-jishin)/ *watashi-tachi-jishin/*ware-ware-jishin} o kadai-hyooka shi-yasui.*
(**b**) We ourselves were not aware of the fire.
{私たち自身/?我々自身/*自分自身}も火事に気がつかなかった。
*{Watashi-tachi-jishin/?Ware-ware-jisin/*Jibun-jishin} mo kaji ni ki-ga-tsukanakatta.*
(**c**) Nobody will help us. We'll have to solve the problem ourselves.
だれも助けてはくれない。{我々自身/私たち自身/自分(自身)}で問題を解決しなければならない。
Dare-mo tasukete wa kurenai. {Ware-ware-jishin/Wata(ku)shi-tachi-jishin/Jibun(-jishin)} de mondai o kaiketsu-shinakereba naranai.

out adv. **[away from an enclosed space or not in one's usual place or condition]**
so⌉to {ni/e} 外{に/へ} n.+prt. **[to the outside]**

EX. (**a**) We usually take out the garbage on Monday morning.
私たちは大抵月曜の朝ごみを外{に/へ}出します。
Watashi-tachi wa taitei getsuyoo no asa gomi o soto {ni/e} dashimasu.
(**b**) Don't go out! It's too cold, my dear.
外{に/へ}行っちゃだめよ。とても寒いからね。
Soto {ni/e} itcha dame yo. Totemo samui kara ne.

PHRASE: out of *kara* から ⟨⟨from, since⟩⟩

EX. (**a**) A: Who do you think came out of the restaurant?
だれがレストランから出て来たと思う?
Dare ga resutoran kara dete kita to omou?
B: I have no idea, who?
分からない。だれ?
Wakaranai. Dare?
A: Elizabeth Taylor!
エリザベス・テイラーだよ!
Erizabesu Teiraa da yo!
(**b**) A: Why did you go to Japan?
どうして日本に行ったんですか。
Dooshite Nihon ni itta n desu ka.
B: I went out of curiosity.
好奇心から行ったんですよ。
Kooki-shin kara itta n desu yo.

—— n. **[disqualification of a runner in baseball]**
a⌉uto アウト •f

outcome n. **[a general result]**
ke⌈kka 結果 •c [a state of affairs brought about by a cause] ⟨⟨**result, consequence**⟩⟩ ↔ **gen'in 原因 •c**

EX. A: What was the outcome of the meeting?
その会議の結果はどうでしたか。
Sono kaigi no kekka wa doo deshita ka.
B: No decisions were reached.
何も決まりませんでした。
Nani-mo kimarimasen deshita.

outdoor adj. **[pertaining to or used in the open air]**
o⌈ku⌉gai no N 屋外のN •c [outside but in proximity to a building] ⟨⟨**of the open air**⟩⟩ ↔ **okunai no N 屋内のN •c; ya⌉gai no N 野外のN •c [pertaining to or used in the open air]** ⟨⟨**of fields, of the open air**⟩⟩

EX. (**a**) Does the hotel have an indoor or outdoor swimming pool?
ホテルには屋内プールか{屋外/*野外}プールがありますか。
*Hoteru ni wa okunai-puuru ka {okugai/*yagai}-puuru ga arimasu ka.*
(**b**) The park has two outdoor theaters.
公園には{野外/*屋外}劇場が二つある。
*Kooen ni wa {yagai/*okugai}-gekijoo ga futatsu aru.*

outer adj. **[pertaining to the space beyond a boundary]**
so⌉to no N 外のN [pertaining to the

outside] ↔ **naka no N 中のN, uchi no N 内のN; so⌈to-gawa no N 外側のN [of the exterior]** ⟪**of the outside**⟫ ↔ **naka-gawa no N 中側のN, uchi-gawa no N 内側のN**

EX. The public is allowed within the outer moat of the castle, but not within the inner moat.
一般の人は城の{外/外側}の堀の中には入れますが、{内/内側}の堀の中には入れません。
Ippan no hito wa shiro no {soto/soto-gawa} no hori no naka ni wa haire-masu ga, {uchi/uchi-gawa} no hori no naka ni wa haire-masen.

O

outfit n. **[a set of clothing/tools/equipment]**
1. fu⌈ku⌉ i⌈sshiki 服一式 •c [a set of clothing], fu⌈kusoo 服装 •c [clothing one wears] ⟪**dress, clothing, costume, attire**⟫
2. do⌈ogu⌉ i⌈sshiki 道具一式 •c [a set of tools or equipment]

outline n. **[a line that forms the outer shape of s.t. or a summary of the essential points or facts of s.t.]**
ri⌈nkaku 輪郭 •c [a line that forms the outer shape of s.t. ⟪**fig. "facial features," "gist"**⟫**]** ⟪**contours, skyline**⟫**, a⌈ra-suji 荒筋 [the summary of s.t., esp. a story/drama], yo⌈oyaku 要約 •c [a brief statement that summarizes the main points of a s.t. spoken or written]** ⟪**summary, digest**⟫**, a⌈uto-ra⌉in アウトライン •c [a summary, esp. of a thesis]** ⟪**summary, synopsis**⟫

NOTE: 荒筋 can also be written as 粗筋.

EX. (**a**) I could see the faint outline of his body in the distance.
遠くに彼の体のかすかな{輪郭/*荒筋/*要約/*アウトライン}が見えた。
*Tooku ni kare no karada no kasukana {rinkaku/*ara-suji/*yooyaku/*auto-rain} ga mieta.*
(**b**) The teacher required the students to submit an outline of their paper in advance.
先生は学生にレポートの{要約/アウトライン/*荒筋/*輪郭}を前もって出すように言った。
*Sensei wa gakusei ni repooto no {yooyaku/auto-rain/*ara-suji/*rinkaku} o mae-motte dasu yooni itta.*
(**c**) Please give me a rough outline of the novel.
その小説の大体の{荒筋/*要約/*アウトライン/*輪郭}を教えてください。
*Sono shoosetsu no daitai no {ara-suji/*yooyaku/*auto-rain/*rinkaku} o oshiete kudasai.*

— vt. **[to present the salient features that characterize s.t.]**
1. ⟨**-o**⟩ **yo⌈oyaku-suru** ⟨**～を**⟩**要約する ③ •c [for s.o. to present a summary of s.t. spoken or written]** ⟪**summarize, digest, condense**⟫

EX. My friend outlined the plot of the movie for me.
友達が映画の荒筋を要約してくれた。
Tomodachi ga eiga no ara-suji o yooyaku-shite kureta.

2. ⟨**-no**⟩ **ri⌈nkaku o ka⌉ku** ⟨**～の**⟩**輪郭をかく ① [for s.o. to draw the salient features that characterize s.t.]**

EX. The painter outlined the figures on the canvas.
画家はキャンバスの上に人物の輪郭をかいた。
Gaka wa kyanbasu no ue ni jinbutsu no rinkaku o kaita.

output n. **[the amount/level of s.t. produced or the result of a data-processing task done by a computer]**
1. se⌈isa⌉n-daka 生産高 [amount/level of production] ⟪**yield**⟫

EX. The output of this factory is 3,000 units per day.
この工場の生産高は一日に三千個です。
Kono koojoo no seisan-daka wa ichi-nichi ni san-zen-ko desu.

2. a⌈utopu⌉tto アウトプット •f [information produced by a computer]

EX. After feeding the computer with the information we waited three hours for the output.
コンピューターに情報を入れてから三時間アウトプットを待った。
Konpyuutaa ni joohoo o irete kara, san-

jikan autoputto o matta.

outside n. **[space exterior to s.t. or the exterior surface of s.t.]**

1. ⟨-no⟩ so˥to ⟨〜の⟩外 [the space exterior to s.t.] **⟪exterior, outdoors⟫ ↔ ⟨-no⟩ uchi ⟨〜の⟩内, ⟨-no⟩ naka ⟨〜の⟩中**

EX. My house looks great from the outside, but the inside is awful.
僕のうちは外から見ると立派だけど、中はひどいんだ。
Boku no uchi wa soto kara miru to rippa da kedo, naka wa hidoi n da.

2. ⟨-no⟩ so˥to-gawa ⟨〜の⟩外側 [the exterior surface of s.t.] **⟪exterior, outer side⟫ ↔ ⟨-no⟩ naka-gawa ⟨〜の⟩中側, ⟨-no⟩ uchi-gawa ⟨〜の⟩内側**

EX. The outside of this house looks nice, but the inside is awful.
この家の外側はすばらしいけれど、{中/中側/内側}はひどい。
Kono ie no soto-gawa wa subarashii keredo, {naka/naka-gawa/uchi-gawa} wa hidoi.

outskirts n. **[an area on the extreme periphery of a town]**

ha˥zure はずれ /⟨V*masu* of *hazureru* ② go wide/ [missing the target/center ⟪fig. "an area on the extreme periphery of a town"⟫] **⟪verge, extremity, miss, failure⟫, ko˥ogai 郊外 •c [an area on the periphery of a big city]** **⟪suburb⟫**

EX. (**a**) A: Do you live in central Tokyo?
都心に住んでいらっしゃいますか。
Toshin ni sunde irasshaimasu ka.
B: No, I live on the outskirts of Tokyo.
いいえ、{郊外/*はずれ}です。
*Iie, {koogai/*hazure} desu.*
(**b**) There's a gas station on the outskirts of town.
町の{はずれ/*郊外}にガソリンスタンドがあります。
*Machi no {hazure/*koogai} ni gasorin-sutando ga arimasu.*

outstanding adj. **[excellent/superior]**

su˥gu˥reta N 優れたN /⟨Vinf. past of *sugureru* ② excel/ [better than s.t./s.o./s.a. in ability/skill], ba˥tsugun no N 抜群のN •c [markedly superior in performance to others]

EX. (**a**) Mr. Kim graduated from Seoul National University with an outstanding record of achievement.
キムさんはソウル大学を{優れた/抜群の}成績で卒業した。
Kimu-san wa Souru-daigaku o {sugureta/batsugun no} seiseki de sotsugyoo-shita.
(**b**) That company consistently produces outstanding products.
あの会社は一貫して{優れた/抜群の}製品を生産している。
Ano kaisha wa ikkan-shite {sugureta/batsugun no} seihin o seisan-shite iru.

oval adj. **[shaped like an egg or ellipse]**

ta˥mago-gata no N 卵型のN •c

EX. She has an oval face.
彼女は卵型の顔をしている。
Kanojo wa tamago-gata no kao o shite iru.

—— n. **[the shape of an egg or ellipse]**

ta˥mago-gata 卵型 •c [the shape of an egg], da˥en-kei 楕円形 •c [an ellipse]

oven n.

o˥obun オーブン •f, te˥npi 天火 •c

EX. Let's bake some bread in the oven.
{オーブン/天火}でパンを焼きましょう。
{Oobun/Tenpi} de pan o yakimashoo.

over prep. **[existing or moving in a space above s.o./s.t./s.a.; covering the upper surface of s.t.; at/to the other side of s.t.; exceeding s.t. in quantity]**

1. ⟨-no⟩ u˥e {ni/de/o} ⟨〜の⟩上{に/で/を} n.+prt. **[a position which is higher than s.t./s.o./s.a. or which is in contact with the surface of s.t.]**

NOTE: When particles follow ⟨-*no*⟩ *ue*, they add a special meaning to the basic meaning of *ue* described above. The particle *ni* indicates a "location where s.t./s.o./s.a. exists or a goal toward which s.t./s.o./s.a. moves"; the particle *de* indicates a "location where s.o. does s.t. or an event takes place"; and the particle *o* indicates a "path along/across/through which s.t./s.o./s.a. moves."

EX. (**a**) There are a bunch of books all over the desk.
机の上に本が沢山置いてある。
Tsukue no ue ni hon ga takusan oite aru.
(**b**) The plane circled over the airport.
飛行機は空港の上を旋回した。
Hikoo-ki wa kuukoo no ue o senkai-shita.
(**c**) Machiko draped her sweater over her shoulders.
真知子は肩の上にセーターをかけた。
Machiko wa kata no ue ni seetaa o kaketa.

2. 〈**-no**〉 **mu⌈koo**(**-gawa**) **ni** 〈～の〉向こう(側)に n.+prt. **[at/to a point opposite an intervening object]** ⟪**across, beyond**⟫

EX. Somewhere over the rainbow skies are blue.
どこかにじの向こうに青空がある。
Doko-ka niji no mukoo ni ao-zora ga aru.

3. 〈**-o**〉 **ko⌈ete** 〈～を〉越えて /〈**V*te* of *koeru*** ② **go over**/ **[going beyond some obstacle]** ⟪**beyond**⟫

EX. The prisoners escaped over the wall.
囚人たちは塀を越えて逃亡した
Shuu-jin-tachi wa hei o koete tooboo-shita.

4. **-ijoo** ～以上 •c **[more than]** ⟪**more than**⟫

EX. There were over 15 people in the elevator.
エレベーターの乗客は十五人以上だった。
Erebeetaa no jookyaku wa juu-go-nin-ijoo datta.

— adv. **[(irreversibly) beyond a certain point]**

NOTE: The Japanese word that corresponds to "over" depends on the verb that goes with it.

EX. (**a**) A plane flew over about an hour ago.
飛行機が一時間ぐらい前に上を飛んで行った。
Hikoo-ki ga ichi-jikan-gurai mae ni ue o tonde itta.
(**b**) Why don't you come over to my house?
うちにいらっしゃいませんか。
Uchi ni irasshaimasen ka.
(**c**) A: I spent over two hours trying to solve this problem but couldn't get it.
この問題を解くのに二時間以上もかけたのに結局だめでした。
Kono mondai o toku no ni ni-jikan-ijoo mo kaketa no ni kekkyoku dame deshita.
B: Well, I'll give you a hint and you can try to solve it over again.
じゃあ、ヒントをあげるから、もう一度やってみなさい。
Jaa, hinto o ageru kara, moo ichi-do yatte-minasai.

— adj. **[at the end** ⟪**fig. "be finished"**⟫**]**
o⌈waru 終わる ① **[for s.t. to come to an end]** ⟪**close, finish, terminate**⟫

EX. (**a**) My Japanese class will be over at 9:50.
日本語の授業は9時50分に終わります。
Nihon-go no jugyoo wa ku-ji go-jup-pun ni owarimasu.
(**b**) Bill's relationship with Monica has been over for more than a year now.
ビルとモニカの関係はもう一年以上も前に終わっている。
Biru to Monika no kankei wa moo ichi-nen-ijoo mo mae ni owatte iru.

over- prefix. **[do s.t. too much]**
V*masu* sugiru V*masu*すぎる ②

EX. A: I'm afraid I'm gaining weight these days.
このごろ、あたし、太って来たの。
Kono-goro, atashi, futotte kita no.
B: That's because you overeat.
食べすぎるからよ。
Tabe-sugiru kara yo.

overcoat n.
o⌈obaa-ko⌉oto オーバーコート, **ko⌉oto** コート, **o⌉obaa** オーバー •f

EX. It's very cold, so put on your overcoat.
とても寒いから{オーバーコート/コート/オーバー}を着なさい。
Totemo samui kara {oobaa-kooto/kooto/oobaa} o kinasai.

overcome vt. **[to defeat/conquer s.t./s.o. in a figurative sense]**

⟨-ni⟩ ka⌉tsu ⟨～に⟩勝つ ① **[for s.o./s.a. to fight against and gain victory over an enemy/opponent]** ⟪win, beat, defeat⟫, ⟨-ni⟩ u⌈chi-katsu ⟨～に⟩打ち勝つ ① **[for s.o. to conquer s.t in a figurative sense]** ⟪surmount, resist, get over⟫, ⟨-o⟩ ko⌈kufuku-suru ⟨～を⟩克服する ③ •c **[for s.o. to get over a difficulty (not including a temptation)]** ⟪conquer, subjugate⟫, ⟨-o⟩ u⌈chi-nome⌉su ⟨～を⟩打ちのめす ① **[to deliver a serious (psychological) blow to s.o.]** ⟪knock down, beat s.o. to a pulp⟫

EX. (a) With great effort, John overcame his handicap.
ジョンは努力してハンディキャップ{に勝った/に打ち勝った/を克服した/*を打ちのめした}。
*Jon wa doryoku-shite handikyappu {ni katta/ni uchi-katta/o kokufuku-shita/ *o uchi-nomeshita}.*
(b) Mary was overcome with grief over the death of her father.
メアリーは父親の死{に打ちのめされた/*克服された/*勝たれた/*打ち勝たれた}。
*Mearii wa chichi-oya no shi ni {uchi-nome-sareta/*kokufuku-sareta/ *kata-reta/*uchi-katareta}.*

overhead adv. **[above one's head]**
zu⌈joo {ni/o/de} 頭上{に/を/で} •c

EX. As we were walking, a flock of birds flew overhead.
私たちが歩いていると、頭上を鳥の群れが飛んで行った。
Watashi-tachi ga aruite iru to, zujoo o tori no mure ga tonde itta.

overlap vi. **[for s.t. to partially extend over s.t. else]**
{⟨-to⟩/⟨-ni⟩} ka⌈sanaru {⟨～と⟩/⟨～に⟩}重なる ① **[for s.t. to lie on top of s.t. else ⟪fig. "be scheduled at the same time"⟫]** ⟪pile up, be stacked up, fall on⟫

EX. (a) When we drew the curtains they overlapped a little at the center.
カーテンを閉めた時真ん中でちょっと重なった。
Kaaten o shimeta toki mannaka de chotto kasanatta.
(b) My stay in Kyoto overlapped with Tom's.
僕の京都滞在はトムのと重なった。
Boku no Kyooto taizai wa Tomu no to kasanatta.

overnight adv. **[during or through the night]**
hi⌈to⌉-ban 一晩 adv./n. **[one night]**

EX. Yoshio stayed overnight at his uncle's home.
良雄は叔父の家に一晩泊まった。
Yoshio wa oji no ie ni hito-ban tomatta.

—— adj. **[for or during a night]**
i⌈p-paku no N 一泊のN •c **[of one night]**

EX. I made an overnight trip to Paris.
私はパリに一泊(の)旅行をした。
Watashi wa Pari ni ip-paku (no) ryokoo o shita.

overtake vt. **[to catch up and pass s.t./s.o./s.a. ⟨w⟩]**
1. ⟨-ni⟩ o⌈i-tsu⌉ku ⟨～に⟩追いつく ① **[to catch up with s.t./s.o.]**

EX. After a long chase, the policeman finally overtook the thief.
長時間追いかけた後、ついに警官は泥棒に追いついた。
Choo-jikan oi-kaketa ato, tsuini keikan wa doroboo ni oi-tsuita.

2. ⟨-o⟩ o⌈i-ko⌉su ⟨～を⟩追い越す ① **[to catch up and pass s.t./s.o./s.a.]** ⟪outrun, pass⟫

EX. Japan has already overtaken the U.S. in microchip production.
日本はすでにマイクロチップの生産でアメリカを追い越している。
Nihon wa sudeni maikuro-chippu no seisan de Amerika o oi-koshite iru.

overthrow vt. **[for s.o. to cause the downfall of s.o./s.t.]**
⟨-o⟩ ta⌈o⌉su ⟨～を⟩倒す ① **[to cause s.o./s.t./s.a. standing upright to fall over ⟪fig. "defeat"⟫]** ⟪bring down, level, knock down, defeat, subvert⟫, ⟨-o⟩ u⌈chi-tao⌉su ⟨～を⟩打ち倒す ① **[for s.o. to intentionally cause the downfall of s.o./s.t./s.a.]** ⟪strike down, knock down, bring down⟫

EX. The left-wing radicals attempted to

overthrow the government.
左翼の過激派は政府を{倒そう/打ち倒そう}とした。
Sayoku no kageki-ha wa seifu o {taosoo/uchi-taosoo} to shita.

overtime n. **[time beyond an established time limit or an activity conducted during that time]**

1. za⌈ngyoo 残業 •c [work done at a company beyond the established time limit in a day] **⟪overtime work⟫**

EX. I put in a lot of overtime this month, so my paycheck is going to be fatter.
今月は残業をたくさんしたから、収入は多いはずだ。
Kongetsu wa zangyoo o takusan shita kara, shuunyuu wa ooi hazu da.

2. e⌈nchoo-sen 延長戦 •c [the part of a game played beyond the normally established time limit or extra innings of a baseball game]

EX. Our basketball team lost by one point in overtime.
我々のバスケットボールのチームは延長戦で一点の差で負けた。
Ware-ware no basuketto-booru no chiimu wa enchoo-sen de it-ten no sa de maketa.

—— adv. **[beyond an established time limit]**
ji⌈kan-ga⌉i ni 時間外に •c [outside of working hours]

EX. I have to work overtime on Saturday, so I can't go to the baseball game.
土曜日に時間外に仕事をしなければならないので野球の試合に行けません。
Doyoo-bi ni jikan-gai ni shigoto o shinakereba naranai node yakyuu no shiai ni ike-masen.

overwhelm vt. **[to psychologically/physically overpower s.t./s.o./s.a.]**
⟨-o⟩ a⌈ttoo-suru ⟨〜を⟩圧倒する ③ •c [to overcome s.o. with a greatly superior force] **⟪overpower, overcome, crush, outrival⟫**, **⟨-ni⟩ a⌈sshoo-suru ⟨〜に⟩圧勝する ③ •c [to win by a large margin]** **⟪crush, trample, smash⟫**

EX. (**a**) Waseda University overwhelmed Keio University in the baseball game.
野球の試合で早稲田大学は慶応大学{に圧勝した/を圧倒した}。
Yakyuu no shiai de Waseda-daigaku wa Keioo-daigaku {ni asshoo-shita/o attoo-shita}.
(**b**) The students were overwhelmed by the amount of homework they were given.
学生は宿題の量に{圧倒された/*圧勝された}。
*Gakusei wa shukudai no ryoo ni {attoo-sareta/*asshoo-sareta}.*

overwhelming adj. **[psychologically/physically overpowering]**
a⌈ttoo-tekina 圧倒的な adj(*na*). **[vastly overpowering in amount/force]** **⟪overpowering, preponderant⟫**

EX. Last week the New York Yankees won an overwhelming victory against the Boston Red Sox.
先週ニューヨークヤンキーズはボストンレッドソックスに圧倒的な勝利を収めた。
Senshuu Nyuuyooku-yankiizu wa Bosuton-reddo-sokkusu ni attoo-tekina shoori o osameta.

NOTE: *Attoo-tekina shoori o osameru* can be expressed also as simply *asshoo-suru* "to overwhelm."

overwork vt. **[to cause s.o./s.t./s.a. to do more than is usually expected of him/her/it]**
⟨-o⟩ ha⌈taraka-se-sugi⌉ru ⟨〜を⟩働かせ過ぎる /⟨V*masu* of *hataraka-seru* ② cause to work + *sugiru* ② go beyond/ ② [to cause a person to work too much], **⟨-o⟩ ko⌈ki-tsuka⌉u ⟨〜を⟩こき使う ① [for s.o. to cause one's subordinate to do so much that he/she becomes exhausted]** **⟪work a person like a horse, exploit⟫**

EX. We don't like our new boss because he overworks us.
新しい上司は私たち(のこと)を{働かせ過ぎる/こき使う}から嫌いです。
Atarashii jooshi wa watashi-tachi (no

koto) o {hataraka-se-sugiru/koki-tsukau} kara kirai desu.

— vi. **[to work too much]**

ha⌈taraki-sugi⌉ru 働き過ぎる /⟨V*masu* of *hataraku* ① work + *sugiru* ② go beyond/ ②

EX. People in other countries still think that the Japanese tend to overwork.
他の国の人々は今でも日本人は働き過ぎる傾向があると思っています。
Ta no kuni no hito-bito wa ima demo Nihon-jin wa hataraki-sugiru keikoo ga aru to omotte imasu.

owe vt. **[to be obligated to give or pay s.t.]**

1. {⟨-ni⟩/⟨-kara⟩} ⟨-o⟩ ka⌈rite iru {⟨〜に⟩/⟨〜から⟩}⟨〜を⟩借りている /⟨V*te iru* of *kariru* ② borrow/ ② [for s.o. to have borrowed s.t. (and to still have it)]

EX. I owe Mr. Johnson $100.
私はジョンソンさん{に/から}百ドル借りています。
Watashi wa Jonson-san {ni/kara} hyaku-doru karite imasu.

2. ⟨-no⟩ o-⌈kage da ⟨〜の⟩お陰だ [to attribute one's good fortune to s.o. else's support] ⟪**thanks to**⟫

EX. I owe my success to you, Prof. Yoshida.
私が成功出来たのは吉田先生のお陰です。
Watashi ga seikoo-dekita no wa Yoshida-sensei no o-kage desu.

3. {Vneg./Vstem/shi/ko/adj(*i*). *ku*}{nakute wa/nakereba} {i⌈kenai/na⌈ra⌉nai} {Vneg./Vstem/し/来/adj(*i*). *ku*}{なくては/なければ}{いけない/ならない}, {adj(*na*). stem/N}{de/ja}{na⌉kute wa/ na⌉kereba} {i⌈kenai/na⌈ra⌉nai} {adj(*na*). stem/N}{で/じゃ}{なくては/なければ}{いけない/ならない} [it won't do if s.o. does not take some action or if s.o./s.t./s.a. is not in a certain state] ⟪**have to, should, ought to**⟫

EX. (**a**) I owe Mr. Smith an apology because of something rude I said.
失礼なことを言ったから、スミスさんに謝ら{なければ/なくては}{なりません/いけません}。
Shitsureina koto o itta kara, Sumisu-san ni ayamara{nakereba/nakute wa}{narimasen/ikemasen}.
(**b**) You owe respect to your parents.
両親を敬わ{なければ/なくては}{なりません/いけません}。
Ryooshin o uyamawa{nakereba/nakute wa} {narimasen/ikemasen}.

owl n.

fu⌈kuro⌉o ふくろう

own adj. **[belonging not to others but to oneself/itself]**

1. ji⌈bun(-ji⌉shin) no N 自分(自身)のN •c [belonging to oneself]

EX. (**a**) A: I drove to Kobe yesterday.
昨日車で神戸に行って来たよ。
Kinoo kuruma de Koobe ni itte kita yo.
B: Oh, did you take Miyoko's car again?
あ、そう。また美代子の車で行ったんだろ?
A, soo. Mata Miyoko no kuruma de itta n daro?
A: No, I took my own car.
違うよ。自分の車で行ったよ。
Chigau yo. Jibun no kuruma de itta yo.
(**b**) We tend not to think seriously enough about our own future.
私たちは自分(自身)の将来についてあまり真剣に考えようとしない。
Watashi-tachi wa jibun(-jishin) no shoorai ni-tsuite amari shinken ni kangaeyoo to shinai.

NOTE: 1. *Jishin* is used to add emphatic reflexive meaning to a pronoun, but *jibun-jishin* is seldom used in conversation. SEE oneself
2. "Our own" and "their own" are expressed in Japanese as *jibun-tachi no* N.

2. so⌈re⌉-zore no N それぞれのN [every one of]

EX. (**a**) Each state in the U.S. has its own constitution.
アメリカの各州にはそれぞれの州法がある。
Amerika no kaku-shuu ni wa sore-zore no shuu-hoo ga aru.
(**b**) People all have their own opinion about education.

人々は教育について皆それぞれの意見を持っている。
Hito-bito wa kyooiku ni-tsuite mina sore-zore no iken o motte iru.

— vt. **[to possess s.t./s.o./s.a. concrete as one's property]**
⟨-o⟩ mo˥tsu ⟨〜を⟩持つ ① [for s.o. to hold s.t./s.o./s.a. in one's hand ⟪fig. "own"⟫] ⟪have, hold, carry, possess, harbor⟫, **a˥ru ある ① [for s.t. to exist]** ⟪exist, have⟫, **i˥ru いる ② [for s.o./s.a. to exist]** ⟪exist, be, live, stay⟫, **⟨-o⟩ ka˥tte iru ⟨〜を⟩飼っている /⟨V*te iru* of *kau* ① keep/ ② [for s.o. to keep s.a. and raise it]** ⟪raise, keep, feed⟫, **⟨-o⟩ sho˥yuu-suru ⟨〜を⟩所有する ③ •c [for s.o. to have s.t. such as property ⟨fml⟩]** ⟪have, possess, hold⟫

EX. (**a**) Do you own a car?
車{を持っています/があります/?を所有しています/*を飼っています/*がいます}か。
*Kuruma {o motte imasu/ga arimasu/?o shoyuu-shite imasu/*o katte imasu/*ga imasu} ka.*
(**b**) Do you own a cat?
猫{がいます/を飼っています/*があります/*を持っています/*を所有しています}か。
*Neko {ga imasu/o katte imasu/*ga arimasu/*o motte imasu/*o shoyuu-shite imasu} ka.*
(**c**) Mr. Tanaka owns a vast amount of real estate.
田中氏は膨大な不動産{を所有している/を持っている/がある/*がいる/*を飼っている}。
*Tanaka-shi wa boodaina fudoo-san {o shoyuu-shite iru/o motte iru/ga aru/*ga iru/*o katte iru}.*

owner n. **[a person who possesses s.t./s.a./s.o. concrete as property]**
mo˥chi˥-nushi 持ち主 [a person who possesses a pet or s.t. concrete/abstract] ⟪possessor, proprietor⟫, **sho˥yu˥u-sha 所有者 •c [a person who possesses a relatively valuable object]** ⟪proprietor, possessor⟫, **o˥onaa オーナー •f [a person who possesses something Western such as a baseball team, a Western-style boat, or a car]**

EX. (**a**) Who's the owner of this purse?
この財布の{持ち主/??所有者/*オーナー}はだれですか。
*Kono saifu no {mochi-nushi/??shoyuu-sha/*oonaa} wa dare desu ka.*
(**b**) Mr. Matsudaira is the owner of this estate.
松平氏がこの地所の{所有者/持ち主/*オーナー}です。
*Matsudaira-shi ga kono jisho no {shoyuu-sha/mochi-nushi/*oonaa} desu.*
(**c**) The owner of this golf course is John Johnson.
このゴルフコースの{オーナー/持ち主/所有者}はジョン・ジョンソンです。
Kono gorufu-koosu no {oonaa/mochi-nushi/shoyuu-sha} wa Jon Jonson desu.

ownership n. **[the state of possessing s.t. or the right to possess s.t.]**
1. sho˥yuu 所有 •c [the state of possessing s.t. ⟨fml⟩]
2. sho˥yu˥u-ken 所有権 •c [the legal right to possess s.t.]

ox n.
u˥shi 牛 ⟪cattle⟫, **o˥-ushi 雄牛**

oxygen n.
sa˥nso 酸素 •c

EX. A fire-fighter often wears an oxygen mask when entering a burning house.
消防士は燃えている家に入る時よく酸素マスクをする。
Shooboo-shi wa moete iru ie ni hairu toki yoku sanso-masuku o suru.

oyster n.
ka˥ki かき

P

pa n. **[an informal term of address for one's father]**
(o-)to˥o-chan (お)父ちゃん **[a very informal term of address for one's father]**

pace n. **[the distance covered in a single step or the speed with which one does s.t.]**
1. i˥p-po 一歩 •c [a single cycle of raising one's foot and setting it down again in walking or the distance progressed in such a cycle]
EX. He advanced thirty paces.
彼は三十歩進んだ。
Kare wa san-jup-po susunda.

2. ho˥choo 歩調 •c [the timing of one's walking or actions, esp. with respect to that of others in a group] ⟪step, cadence⟫, pe˥esu ペース •f [the speed with which one does s.t.], cho˥oshi 調子 •c [the musical contour formed by a series of sounds of varying pitch and their timing ⟪fig. "an impression created by s.o.'s way of speaking or writing," "the degree of progress of s.t. that is moving," "the momentum which accompanies s.t. which advances"⟫] ⟪tone, pitch, condition⟫, te˥npo テンポ •f [the rate at which s.t. advances, esp. music] ⟪tempo⟫
EX. (**a**) The pace at which people in Tokyo walk is faster than that of people in Kyoto.
東京の人の{歩調/歩く{ペース/テンポ/*調子}}は京都の人のより速い。
*Tookyoo no hito no {hochoo/aruku {peesu/tenpo/*chooshi}} wa Kyooto no hito no yori hayai.*
(**b**) If you keep working at this pace, you're going to make yourself ill.
こんな{調子/ペース/テンポ/*歩調}で仕事をしたら病気になるよ。
*Konna {chooshi/peesu/tenpo/*hochoo} de shigoto o shitara byooki ni naru yo.*

Pacific Ocean n.
Ta˥ihe˥i-yoo 太平洋 •c
EX. Inazo Nitobe once said that he wanted to act as a bridge across the Pacific Ocean.
新渡戸稲造は太平洋のかけ橋になりたいと言った。
Nitobe Inazoo wa Taihei-yoo no kake-hashi ni nari-tai to itta.

pack n. **[a group of animals of a similar kind (esp. wild canines)/things that are grouped together or bound together for ease in carrying]**
1. Japanese Number + hako Japanese Number+箱 [a box, used as a counter for boxed objects]
EX. Could you buy me a pack of cigarettes, please?
たばこを一箱買って来てくださいませんか。
Tabako o hito-hako katte-kite kudasaimasen ka.

2. hi˥to˥-mure no N 一群れのN [a group of similar animals/people/things] ⟪a school, a herd, a flock⟫, i˥chi-gun no N 一群のN •c [a group of animals/people/things]
EX. A pack of wolves attacked the villagers.
{一群れ/一群}の狼が村人を襲った。
{Hito-mure/Ichi-gun} no ookami ga mura-bito o osotta.

—— vt. **[for s.o. to squeeze s.t./s.o./s.a. into a confined space]**
1. ⟨-o⟩ ⟨-ni⟩ tsu˥me-ko˥mu ⟨～を⟩⟨～に⟩詰め込む ① ⟪cram, stuff, jam⟫
EX. Can you pack all of this into the trunk of your car?
これを全部車のトランクに詰め込めますか。
Kore o zenbu kuruma no toranku ni tsume-kome-masu ka.

P

2. ⟨-no⟩ ni-ˈzuˈkuri o suru ⟨〜の⟩荷造りをする ③ **[for s.o. to bundle s.t. together for the purpose of transporting it]** ⟪pack up⟫

EX. The bus is leaving in half an hour, so you need to pack your things immediately.
バスは後一時間で出るから、すぐに所持品の荷造りをしなくてはいけないよ。
Basu wa ato ichi-jikan de deru kara, sugu ni shoji-hin no ni-zukuri o shinakute wa ikenai yo.

package n. **[a group of objects wrapped together and/or their container]**
tsuˈtsumi 包み /⟨V*masu* of *tsutsumu* ① wrap/ [a set of objects wrapped together and/or their container] ⟪**bundle, packet, parcel**⟫, **ko-ˈzuˈtsumi 小包 [a small wrapped object (sent by mail)]** ⟪**parcel, packet**⟫

EX. (**a**) My heart throbbed with excitement as I opened the package.
胸をドキドキさせながら{小包/包み}を開けた。
Mune o doki-doki-sase-nagara {ko-zutsumi/tsutsumi} o aketa.
(**b**) There's a package for you, Mary.
メアリー、{小包/*包み}が来てるわよ。
*Mearii, {ko-zutsumi/*tsutsumi} ga kite ru wa yo.*

packing n. **[the act of wrapping or boxing (a group of) objects or s.t. used to fill space among such objects to protect them]**
ni-ˈzuˈkuri 荷造り [the act of bundling/wrapping (a group of) objects for mailing or transport] ⟪**baling, crating**⟫, **paˈkkingu パッキング •f [the act of bundling/wrapping things for transport], tsuˈmeˈ-mono 詰め物 [s.t. used to fill space among wrapped or boxed objects to protect them]**

EX. (**a**) A: How long did the packing take you?
{荷造り/パッキング/*詰め物}にどのぐらいかかりましたか。
*{Ni-zukuri/Pakkingu/*Tsume-mono} ni dono-gurai kakarimashita ka.*
B: It took me five hours.
五時間かかりました。
Go-jikan kakarimashita.
(**b**) Please throw out the packing in the parcel once you have unpacked it.
小包の中身を出したら{詰め物/*荷造り/*パッキング}は捨てて下さい。
*Ko-zutsumi no naka-mi o dashitara {tsume-mono/*ni-zukuri/*pakkingu} wa sutete kudasai.*

pad n. **[a layer/layers of s.t. to prevent direct impact/injury/damage]**
1. paˈddo パッド •f [a filler in the shoulders of a coat]

EX. This suit has pads in both shoulders.
このスーツは肩にパッドが入っている。
Kono suutsu wa kata ni paddo ga haitte iru.

2. roˈketto-hassha-dai ロケット発射台 •f+c [a flat surface from which rockets and spacecraft are launched]
3. reˈpooto-yoˈoshi レポート用紙 •f+c [sheets of paper on which to write reports], meˈmo-yoˈoshi メモ用紙 •f+c [sheets of paper on which to write memos]

paddle n. **[a wooden stick with a blade on at least one end used without an oarlock to propel a canoe or small boat ⟪fig. "s.t. having a short handle and broad surface, such as the instrument used to propel the ball in ping-pong"⟫]**
1. kaˈi かい •c [a wooden stick with a blade on one/both ends with/without an oarlock to propel a canoe/small boat] ⟪**oar**⟫
2. raˈkeˈtto ラケット •f [an instrument used to propel a ball, such as in ping-pong, tennis, or badminton]

paddy n. **[an irrigated field where rice is grown]**
taˈnbo たんぼ [an area of cultivated land for growing rice] ⟪**rice field**⟫, **suˈiden 水田 •c [cultivated land which is flooded with water for growing rice]** ⟪**irrigated rice field**⟫, **taˈ 田 ⟨w⟩**

EX. (**a**) The rice paddies are ready for planting.
{水田/たんぼ/田}は、田植えの準備が出来た。
{Suiden/Tanbo/Ta} wa, taue no junbi ga dekita.
(**b**) Today we irrigated the paddies.

今日私たちは{田/水田/たんぼ}に水を引いた。
Kyoo watashi-tachi wa {ta/suiden/tanbo} ni mizu o hiita.

page[1] n. **[one side of a sheet of paper that is part of a book, magazine, letter, etc.]**
pe⌈eji ページ •f [(a counter for) one side of a sheet of paper that is part of a book, magazine, letter, etc.]

EX. Open your book to page 35.
本の三十五ページを開いてください。
Hon no san-juu-go-peeji o hiraite kudasai.

page[2] vt. **[for s.o. to call for s.o. by means of a public address system]**
⟨-o⟩ yo⌈bi-da⌉su ⟨〜を⟩呼び出す ① [for s.o. to call for s.o.] ⟪summon, call, subpoena, invoke⟫

EX. Jane had her friend paged at the airport.
ジェーンは空港で友達を呼び出した。
Jeen wa kuukoo de tomodachi o yobi-dashita.

pagoda n. **[a tall, multi-storied building/tower often found in Hindu and Buddhist temples in Asia]**
to⌉o 塔 •c [a building (of several stories) which is high in proportion to its length and width (built over a sacred relic)]

EX. Have you seen the five-storied pagoda of Nara?
奈良の五重の塔を見たことがありますか。
Nara no gojuu-no-too o mita koto ga arimasu ka.

gojuu-no-too

pail n. **[a watertight cylindrical container with a fitted handle]**
ba⌈ketsu バケツ •f [a watertight cylindrical metal/plastic container with a fitted handle] ⟪water bucket⟫, te-⌈oke 手おけ [a watertight cylindrical wooden container with a fixed handle] ⟪wooden bucket⟫, o⌉ke おけ

NOTE: *Baketsu* comes from the English word "bucket."

pain n. **[an unpleasant physical and/or psychological sensation, usu. caused by injury or illness]**
1. i⌈ta-mi⌉ 痛み /⟨adj(*i*). stem of *itai* painful + suf. *mi* ness/ [a primarily physical, unpleasant (often localized) sensation] ⟪ache, sore⟫, i⌉ta-sa 痛さ /⟨adj(*i*). stem of *itai* painful + suf. *sa* ness/ [a (measurable) degree of unpleasant (often localized) physical sensation] ⟪painful sensation, painfulness⟫

EX. (**a**) A: What sort of pain do you have?
どんな{痛み/?痛さ}ですか。
Donna {ita-mi/?ita-sa} desu ka.
B: It's a sharp, piercing pain.
きりきりする{痛み/?痛さ}です。
Kiri-kiri-suru {ita-mi/?ita-sa} desu.
(**b**) This medicine will relieve the pain.
この薬を飲めば{痛み/*痛さ}はおさまるはずです。
*Kono kusuri o nomeba {ita-mi/*ita-sa} wa osamaru hazu desu.*
(**c**) The pain caused by cutting your finger on paper can be worse than when you cut your finger with a knife.
紙で指を切った時の{痛さ/?痛み}はナイフで切った時の{痛さ/?痛み}よりひどいことがある。
Kami de yubi o kitta toki no {ita-sa/?ita-mi} wa naifu de kitta toki no {ita-sa/?ita-mi} yori hidoi koto ga aru.

2. tsu⌈ra-sa つらさ /⟨adj(*i*). stem of *tsurai* tough + suf. *sa* ness/ [a primarily psychological, extremely unpleasant sensation] ⟪painfulness, sorrow, bitterness, strain on the nerves⟫, ku⌈rushi-mi⌉ 苦しみ /⟨adj(*i*). stem of *kurushii* painful + suf. *mi* ness/ [an extremely unpleasant physical and/or psychological sensation] ⟪torment, distress, agony, suffering, anguish⟫, ku⌈ru⌉shi-sa 苦しさ /⟨adj(*i*). stem of *kurushii* painful + suf. *sa* ness/ [a (measurable) degree of unpleasant physical or psychological sensation] ⟪painfulness, suffering⟫, ku⌈tsuu 苦痛 •c [an unbearably unpleasant physical and/or psychological sensation] ⟪agony, anguish, suffering, pang⟫

EX. (**a**) You cannot understand the pain

P

involved in having to work away from your family unless you've experienced it.
単身赴任の{つらさ/苦しみ/苦しさ/苦痛}は経験しないと分からない。
Tanshin-funin no {tsura-sa/kurushi-mi/kurushi-sa/kutsuu} wa keiken-shinai to wakaranai.
(**b**) I experienced for the first time the pain of loneliness when I was in Japan.
私は日本で初めて孤独の{苦しみ/つらさ/苦痛/?苦しさ}を味わいました。
Watashi wa Nihon de hajimete kodoku no {kurushi-mi/tsura-sa/kutsuu/?kurushi-sa} o ajiwaimashita.
(**c**) I'm not afraid of dying but I am afraid of pain.
死ぬのは怖くないが、{苦痛/*苦しみ/*苦しさ/*つらさ}が怖い。
*Shinu no wa kowakunai ga, {kutsuu/*kurushi-mi/*kurushi-sa/*tsura-sa} ga kowai.*
(**d**) I cannot describe the pain I felt in losing my wife.
妻を亡くした時の{苦痛/つらさ/苦しみ/苦しさ}は口では言えません。
Tsuma o nakushita toki no {kutsuu/tsura-sa/kurushi-mi/kurushi-sa} wa kuchi de wa ie-masen.
(**e**) Please try to understand the pain I've had to go through in this divorce.
私が離婚するにあたって味わってきた{苦痛/苦しみ/?つらさ/??苦しさ}をどうか分かってください。
Watashi ga rikon-suru ni atatte ajiwatte kita {kutsuu/kurushi-mi/?tsura-sa/??kurushi-sa} o dooka wakatte kudasai.

painful adj. **[causing an unpleasant physical and/or psychological sensation]**
1. i⌈ta⌉i 痛い adj(*i*). **[experiencing an unpleasant (often localized) physical sensation]** **⟪sore⟫**
EX. (**a**) It was an awfully painful injury.
恐ろしく痛いけがでした。
Osoroshiku itai kega deshita.
(**b**) The cut on my arm is still painful.
腕の切り傷がまだ痛いんです。
Ude no kiri-kizu ga mada itai n desu.
2. tsu⌈rai つらい adj(*i*). **[full of difficulty/trouble]** **⟪tough, afflicting, cruel, heartbreaking⟫**, **ku⌈rushi⌉i 苦しい** adj(*i*). **[experiencing an unpleasant physical and/or psychological sensation]** **⟪trying, taxing, hard, difficult⟫**, **⟨-ga⟩ ku⌈tsuu da** ⟨〜が⟩苦痛だ n.+cop. •**c** **[for s.o. to feel an extremely unpleasant physical and/or psychological sensation]**
EX. (**a**) My first year in Japan was painful because I couldn't speak a word of Japanese.
日本語が一言も話せなかったから、日本での初めの一年は{つらかったです/苦しかったです/苦痛でした}。
Nihon-go ga hito-koto mo hanase-nakatta kara, Nihon de no hajime no ichi-nen wa {tsurakatta desu/kurushikatta desu/kutsuu deshita}.
(**b**) The dental work I had done today was painful.
今日の歯の治療は{苦しかった/苦痛だった/?つらかった}。
Kyoo no ha no chiryoo wa {kurushikatta/kutsuu datta/?tsurakatta}.
(**c**) To do *seiza* on a tatami floor is painful even for someone Japanese.
日本人でも畳の上に正座するのは{苦痛だ/苦しい/つらい}。
Nihon-jin demo tatami no ue ni seiza-suru no wa {kutsuu da/kurushii/tsurai}.
(**d**) It is painful to talk to a person who has just lost a loved one.
身内の人を亡くしたばかりの人と話すのは{苦痛だ/つらい/?苦しい}。
Miuchi no hito o nakushita bakari no hito to hanasu no wa {kutsuu da/tsurai/?kurushii}.

paint n. **[a viscous oil-based or water-soluble liquid pigment used for artistic purposes or for coating s.t. to decorate or protect it]**
1. e⌈nogu 絵の具 [a viscous oil-based or water-soluble liquid pigment used for artistic purposes]
2. pe⌈nki ペンキ •**f** **[an oil-based or water**

soluble pigment used for coating s.t. to decorate or protect it]

— vt. **[for s.o. to create a picture or coat s.t. with a liquid pigment]**

1. ⟨-no⟩ e˥ o ka˥ku ⟨〜の⟩絵をかく ① **[for s.o. to draw a picture of s.t./s.o./s.a.]**

EX. A: What are you painting?
何の絵をかいているんですか。
Nan no e o kaite iru n desu ka.
B: I'm painting a cat.
猫の絵をかいています。
Neko no e o kaite imasu.

2. ⟨-ni⟩ pe┌nki o nuru ⟨〜に⟩ペンキを塗る ① **[for s.o. to coat s.t. with a liquid pigment to decorate or protect it]**

EX. Americans paint the interior walls of their houses but Japanese usually do not.
アメリカ人は家の中の壁にペンキを塗るが、日本人は普通は塗らない。
Amerika-jin wa ie no naka no kabe ni penki o nuru ga, Nihon-jin wa futsuu wa nuranai.

painter n. **[a person who paints pictures or who paints walls, houses, etc., to earn money]**

1. e-┌kaki˥ 絵かき **[a person who draws pictures (professionally)], ga┌ka** 画家 **•c [a person who draws pictures professionally]**

EX. Are you a painter?
{絵かき(さん)/画家(*さん)}ですか。
{E-kaki(-san)/Gaka(-san)} desu ka.*

2. pe┌nki-ya˥ ペンキ屋 **[a person who coats walls, houses, etc., with paint for a living]**

painting n. **[the act of creating a picture or coating s.t. with paint or a picture created in that way]**

1. e˥ o ka˥ku {koto/no} 絵をかく{こと/の} **[the act of drawing a picture]**

EX. Do you like painting?
絵をかく{こと/の}が好きですか。
E o kaku {koto/no} ga suki desu ka.

2. pe┌nki o nu┌ru {koto/no} ペンキを塗る{こと/の} **[the act of coating s.t. with a liquid pigment], to┌soo** 塗装 **•c ((coating with paint))**

3. e˥ 絵 **[a visual representation of s.t./s.o./s.a. drawn on a flat surface] ((picture, drawing)), ka˥iga** 絵画 **•c [a drawn picture or the art of creating such ⟨fml⟩] ((drawing))**

EX. You have to be rich to collect good paintings.
いい{絵/絵画}を集めるのには金がないとだめだ。
Ii {e/kaiga} o atsumeru no ni wa kane ga nai to dame da.

pair n. **[a set of two people/animals/things (not necessarily separate from each other) that make up a functional unit or are considered to belong together]**

1. tsu┌i 対 **•c [a set of two things (separate from each other) that make up a functional unit or are considered to belong together or a counter for such a set] ((couple, set, twin)), pe˥a** ペア **•f [a set of two people/animals/things that are considered to belong together]**

EX. (**a**) These two bookends make up a pair.
この二つのブックエンドは{対/ペア}になっている。
Kono futatsu no bukku-endo wa {tsui/pea} ni natte iru.
(**b**) Ken and Kaori are wearing a pair of matching sweaters.
健と香織は{ペア/*対}のセーターを着ている。
*Ken to Kaori wa {pea/*tsui} no seetaa o kite iru.*
(**c**) John and Mary played as a pair in the tennis doubles.
ジョンとメアリーはテニスのダブルスで{ペア/*対}を組んだ。
*Jon to Mearii wa tenisu no daburusu de {pea/*tsui} o kunda.*

2. N (particle) + number (+counter)

EX. I bought a pair of pants and two pairs of shoes.
ズボンを一本と靴を二足買った。
Zubon o ip-pon to kutsu o ni-soku katta.

PHRASE: a pair of gloves *tebukuro hitotsu* 手袋一つ, a pair of scissors *hasami it-choo* はさみ一丁, a pair of glasses *megane hitotsu* 眼鏡一つ, a pair

P

of horses *uma ni-too* 馬二頭

— vt. **[for s.o. to form two things or beings into a set]**

⟨-to⟩ ⟨-o⟩ ku⌈mi⌉ ni suru ⟨〜と⟩⟨〜を⟩組にする ③, ⟨-to⟩ ⟨-o⟩ ku⌈ma-se⌉ru ⟨〜と⟩⟨〜を⟩組ませる /⟨causative of *kumu* ① pair/ ③, ⟨-to⟩ ⟨-o⟩ pe⌉a ni suru ⟨〜と⟩⟨〜を⟩ペアにする ③

EX. The teacher paired John and Mary together.
先生はジョンとメアリーを{組にした/組ませた/ペアにした}。
Sensei wa Jon to Mearii o {kumi ni shita/kuma-seta/pea ni shita}.

— vi. **[for two things or beings to be formed into a set]**

⟨-to⟩ ⟨-ga⟩ ku⌈mi⌉ ni na⌉ru ⟨〜と⟩⟨〜が⟩組になる ①, ⟨-to⟩ ⟨-ga⟩ pe⌉a ni na⌉ru ⟨〜と⟩⟨〜が⟩ペアになる ①, ⟨-to⟩ ⟨-ga⟩ pe⌉a o ku⌉mu ⟨〜と⟩⟨〜が⟩ペアを組む ①

EX. John and Mary paired together for the three-legged race.
ジョンとメアリーは二人三脚で{組になった/ペアになった/ペアを組んだ}。
Jon to Mearii wa ni-nin-san-kyaku de {kumi ni natta/pea ni natta/pea o kunda}.

pajamas n.

pa⌉jama パジャマ •f

EX. Taro, put on your pajamas and go to bed.
太郎、パジャマを着て寝なさい。
Taroo, pajama o kite nenasai.

palace n. **[the official residence of a sovereign ⟪fig. "magnificent house"⟫]**

1. kyu⌈uden 宮殿 •c [the official residence of a sovereign or a building in which a deity is enshrined]

EX. Cinderella went to the palace in a coach.
シンデレラは馬車に乗って宮殿へ行きました。
Shinderera wa basha ni notte kyuuden e ikimashita.

2. go⌉ten 御殿 •c [a magnificent residence]

EX. Mr. Tanaka's house is a palace, you know.
田中さんの家は御殿だよね。
Tanaka-san no ie wa goten da yo ne.

pale adj. **[not strong in color]**

1. a⌈ojiro⌉i 青白い adj(*i*). **[bluish-white, esp. in complexion] ⟪pallid, waxy⟫**

EX. What happened? You look pale.
どうしましたか。青白い顔をしていますね。
Doo shimashita ka. Aojiroi kao o shite imasu ne.

2. usu- 薄〜 [not strong in color]

EX. The mountains are a beautiful pale green in the spring.
春は山が薄緑できれいだ。
Haru wa yama ga usu-midori de kirei da.

palm n. **[the inner surface of the hand]**

te-⌈no⌉-hira 手のひら

palm tree n.

ya⌉shi (no ki⌉) やし(の木)

panel n. **[a flat, rectangular piece covering the surface of a wall or a group of people prepared to discuss an issue in public]**

pa⌉neru パネル •f

EX. (**a**) The panels on the wall are green and yellow.
壁のパネルは緑と黄色です。
Kabe no paneru wa midori to ki-iro desu.
(**b**) I was one of the members of the Japanese linguistics panel at the conference.
私は学会で日本語学のパネルのメンバーの一人でした。
Watashi wa gakkai de Nihon-go-gaku no paneru no menbaa no hitori deshita.

panic n. **[a sudden strong sense of fright, including one which causes a sudden rush to buy or sell financial securities]**

kyo⌈okoo 恐慌 •c ⟪crisis⟫, pa⌉nikku パニック •f

EX. (**a**) When the fire broke out, the people in the building went into panic.
火事が起きた時、建物にいた人々は{恐慌/パニック}状態になった。
Kaji ga okita toki, tate-mono ni ita hito-bito wa {kyookoo/panikku}-jootai ni natta.
(**b**) I still remember the panic of the 1920's.
私は1920年代の{(経済)恐慌/パニック}をまだ覚えています。

Watashi wa sen-kyuu-hyaku-ni-juu-nen-dai no {(keizai-)kyookoo/panikku} o mada oboete imasu.

pants n. **[trousers/**(Br. E) **men's underpants]**
pa˥ntsu パンツ •f [a two-legged outer garment that extends from the waist to the ankles or underwear with short legs], zu˥bo˥n ズボン [a Western-style piece of clothing that extends from the waist down to the ankle/knee, covering each leg separately] ⟪**trousers**⟫

EX. She always wears checked pants.
彼女はいつもチェックの{パンツ/ズボン}をはいている。
Kanojo wa itsu-mo chekku no {pantsu/zubon} o haite iru.

NOTE: *Zubon* originated from the French word "jupon."

papa n. **[a term of address for ones' father used by infants and children]**
(o-)to˥o-chan (お)父ちゃん [a very informal term of address for one's father], pa˥pa パパ •f

paper n. **[a very thin sheet made of processed pulp (on which one writes or with which one wraps things)** ⟪**fig. "newspaper," "document," "thesis," "report"**⟫**]**

1. ka˥mi˥ 紙 [a very thin sheet made of processed pulp (on which one writes or with which one wraps things)]

EX. Do you have a piece of paper and a pencil?
紙と鉛筆がありますか。
Kami to enpitsu ga arimasu ka.

2. shi˥nbun 新聞 •c [a newspaper]

EX. I haven't received today's paper yet.
今日の新聞をまだ受け取っていません。
Kyoo no shinbun o mada uke totte imasen.

3. ro˥nbun 論文 •c [a piece of writing which states the results of one's research] ⟪**treatise, essay, dissertation, article**⟫

EX. I have to finish writing my paper by May.
私は論文を五月までに書き終わらなければなりません。
Watashi wa ronbun o go-gatsu made ni kaki-owaranakereba narimasen.

4. {re˥po˥oto/ri˥po˥oto} {レポート/リポート} •f [a written or printed description of the results of an investigation or research project]

EX. Did you write your paper for Economics 101 yet?
経済学101のレポート、もう書いた?
Keizai-gaku-ichi-zero-ichi no {repooto/ripooto}, moo kaita?

5. sho˥rui 書類 •c [s.t. written that provides information]

EX. We had to have papers proving our identity to be let out of the occupied city.
軍事占領下の町を出るのには身分を証明する書類が必要でした。
Gunji-senryoo-ka no machi o deru no ni wa mibun o shoomei-suru shorui ga hitsuyoo deshita.

PHRASE: give a paper *kenkyuu-happyoo o suru* 研究発表をする ③ •c

parade n. **[a public procession on a festive/ceremonial occasion]**
ko˥oshin 行進 •c [proceeding in a group formation] ⟪**parade**⟫**, pa˥re˥edo パレード •f [a Western style procession], e˥ppei 閲兵 •c [a military procession performed on a ceremonial occasion]** ⟪**inspection of troops**⟫

paragraph n.
da˥nraku 段落 •c, pa˥ragurafu パラグラフ •f

parallel adj. **[of two lines/two surfaces that are at an identical distance apart at all points** ⟪**fig. "analogous"**⟫**]**

1. ⟨-to⟩ he˥ikoona ⟨〜と⟩平行な adj(*na*). **•c [of two lines/two surfaces that are at an identical distance apart at all points]**

EX. Line A is parallel to Line B.
線Aは線Bと平行だ。
Sen A wa sen B to heikoo da.

2. ⟨-to⟩ o˥naji da ⟨〜と⟩同じだ [similar to s.o./s.t./s.a.] ⟪**the same, alike**⟫**, ⟨-to⟩ do˥oyoona ⟨〜と⟩同様な** adj(*na*). **•c** ⟪**similar, same, identical**⟫

EX. Sam's argument was parallel to Bill's.
サムの議論はビルのと{同じ/同様}だった。
Samu no giron wa Biru no to {onaji/dooyoo} datta.

P

NOTE: *Onaji* is a unique kind of adjective in that it conjugates exactly like an adj(*na*). except when it is in prenominal position, in which case it acts like an adj(*i*)., as in *onaji hito* "the same person."

parcel n. **[a relatively small wrapped object (sent by mail)]**
ko-⌈zu⌉tsumi 小包 [a small wrapped object (sent by mail)] ⟪packet, package⟫, tsu⌈tsumi⌉ 包み /⟨V*masu* of *tsutsumu* ① wrap/ [a set of objects wrapped together and/or their container] ⟪package, bundle, packet⟫

P

EX. (**a**) How much would it cost to send this parcel to London by surface mail?
この{小包/*包み}はロンドンまで船便でいくらですか。
*Kono {ko-zutsumi/*tsutsumi} wa Rondon made funa-bin de ikura desu ka.*
(**b**) A parcel had been left at my door.
{小包/包み}がドアの所に置いてあった。
{Ko-zutsumi/Tsutsumi} ga doa no tokoro ni oite atta.

pardon vt. **[for s.o. to excuse s.o. from a punishment ⟨fml⟩]**
⟨-o⟩ yo⌉osha-suru ⟨～を⟩容赦する ③ •c, ⟨-o⟩ yu⌈ru⌉su ⟨～を⟩許す ① [for s.o. to allow s.o. else to do s.t. freely ⟪fig. "forgive"⟫] ⟪permit, excuse, allow, approve, admit, trust, confide in, forgive⟫, ⟨-o⟩ sha⌈men-suru ⟨～を⟩赦免する ③ •c [for a legal authority to excuse s.o. from punishment ⟨fml⟩]

EX. (**a**) Please pardon me for writing you this letter with no prior introduction.
突然お手紙を差し上げる失礼を{お許し/御容赦/*御赦免}ください。
*Totsuzen o-tegami o sashi-ageru shitsurei o {o-yurushi/go-yoosha/*go-shamen} kudasai.*
(**b**) President Ford pardoned former president Nixon.
フォード大統領はニクソン前大統領を{赦免した/*容赦した/*許した}。
*Foodo-daitooryoo wa Nikuson-zen-daitooryoo o {shamen-shita/*yoosha-shita/*yurushita}.*

PHRASE: Pardon me. *Sumimasen.* すみません。

—— n. [an act of excusing s.o. from punishment]
yo⌉osha 容赦 •c, yu⌈rushi 許し /⟨V*masu* of *yurusu* ① pardon/ [an act of removing a restriction] ⟪permission, leave, approval⟫

PHRASE: I beg your pardon. *Sumimasen.* すみません, I beg your pardon? *E, Nan desu ka.* えっ、何ですか。

parent n. **[a father or mother]**
o⌈ya⌉ 親, ryo⌉oshin 両親 •c [father and mother] ⟪parents⟫

EX. (**a**) I lost my parents when I was ten.
私は十歳の時に{両親/親}をなくしました。
Watashi wa jus-sai no toki ni {ryooshin/oya} o nakushimashita.
(**b**) By the time one wants to show filial respect to one's parents, they are often no longer around.
孝行したい時には{親/両親}はもういないことが多い。
Kookoo-shi-tai toki ni wa {oya/ryooshin} wa moo inai koto ga ooi.

parenthesis n. **[one of the pair of curved symbols ( )]**
ka⌉kko 括弧 •c [one or both of a pair of symbols used to enclose text, such as ( ), [ ],「 」, etc.]

EX. In the following sentences, put the proper particle in the parentheses.
次の文の括弧の中に適当な助詞を入れなさい。
Tsugi no bun no kakko no naka ni tekitoona joshi o irenasai.

Paris n.
Pa⌉ri パリ •f

park n. **[public land set aside primarily for recreational purposes]**
ko⌈oen 公園 •c [a public garden]

EX. Shall we go to Ueno Park to see the cherry blossoms?
上野公園に花見に行きましょうか。
Ueno Kooen ni hana-mi ni ikimashoo ka.

—— vt. [to leave a vehicle in a place for a time]

〈-ni〉 ku⌈ruma o to⌈meru 〈〜に〉車をとめる ② **[for s.o. to stop a vehicle in a place (and leave it there)]**
㊚ "give lodging to s.o."▷泊める, "fasten"▷留める, "bring s.o./s.t./s.a. to a halt"▷止める

EX. A: Where can I park my car?
どこに車を止めたらいいでしょうか。
Doko ni kuruma o tometara ii deshoo ka.
B: Please park it in that parking area.
あそこの駐車場に止めてください。
Asoko no chuusha-joo ni tomete kudasai.

parking n. **[an act of leaving a vehicle in a place for a time]**
chu⌈usha 駐車 •c

EX. Where is the parking lot?
駐車場はどこですか。
Chuusha-joo wa doko desu ka.

PHRASE: No Parking *Chuusha-kinshi* 駐車禁止 •c

parliament n. **[an assembly that makes the laws of a country]**
gi⌉kai 議会 •c

EX. Japan adopted parliamentary politics after the war.
日本は戦後議会政治を採用した。
Nihon wa sengo gikai-seiji o saiyoo-shita.

parrot n.
o⌈omu おうむ
— vt. **[to mindlessly repeat what s.o. else has said]**
〈-o〉 ku⌈ri-ka⌉esu 〈〜を〉繰り返す ① ((repeat)), 〈-no〉 ma⌈ne o suru 〈〜の〉まねをする ③ •c [to mimic s.o's behavior] ((imitate, copy, mimic))

EX. (**a**) Don't parrot me.
私{の真似をしない/*を繰り返さない}でください。
*Watashi {no mane o shinai/*kuri-kaesanai} de kudasai.*
(**b**) The students parroted the teacher's pronunciation.
学生は先生の発音{を繰り返した/の真似をした}。
Gakusei wa sensei no hatsuon {o kuri-kaeshita/no mane o shita}

part n. **[a portion of a whole]**
1. bu⌉bun 部分 •c [any of the divisions of a whole] ((section, portion)) ↔ zentai 全体 •c

EX. (**a**) I didn't understand the last part of the story.
話の最後の部分が分かりませんでした。
Hanashi no saigo no bubun ga wakarimasen deshita.
(**b**) A: Have you done all of your homework?
宿題を全部やりましたか。
Shukudai o zenbu yarimashita ka.
B: No, I've only done part of it.
いいえ、一部分しか出来ていません。
Iie, ichi-bubun shika dekite imasen.

2. bu⌈hin 部品 •c [a component of a machine] ((components))

EX. Do you know a store that sells automobile parts?
車の部品を売っている店を知っていますか。
Kuruma no buhin o utte iru mise o shitte imasu ka.

3. ya⌈ku⌉ 役 •c [the responsibilities assumed by s.o. or the role played by s.o. in a dramatic production] ((position, office, duty, function, use))

EX. Bill played the part of a soldier in the movie.
ビルはその映画で兵隊の役をやった。
Biru wa sono eiga de heitai no yaku o yatta.

4. -bu 〜部 •c [a counter for a portion of a written work]

EX. We are reading Chapter 2, Part 1 of the book.
私たちはその本の第二章、第一部を読んでいます。
Watashi-tachi wa sono hon no dai-ni-shoo, dai-ichi-bu o yonde imasu.

PHRASE: in part *ichi-bu(bun)* 一部(分) •c, a part of speech *hinshi* 品詞 •c, take part in 〈-ni〉 *kuwawaru* 〈〜に〉加わる ① ((add, join, enter, participate)), 〈-ni〉 *sanka-suru* 〈〜に〉参加する ③ •c ((participate, join, enter))

EX. Do you plan to take part in our research project?

私たちの研究プロジェクトに{加わる/参加する}つもりですか。
Watashi-tachi no kenkyuu-purojekuto ni {kuwawaru/sanka-suru} tsumori desu ka.

—— vi. **[for a unit/group to divide itself ⟪fig. "depart"⟫]**
(⟨-to⟩) wa⌈kare⌉ru (⟨～と⟩)わかれる ② ⟪be divided, split, branch off, fork, separate from, depart, break up, part with⟫
㊥ "s.t. divides itself"▷分かれる, "separate from s.o."▷別れる

P

EX. (**a**) Even without a comb, his hair parted naturally at the center.
くしを使わなくても、彼の髪の毛は自然に真ん中で分かれた。
Kushi o tsukawanakute mo, kare no kami-no-ke wa shizenni mannaka de wakareta.
(**b**) Jennifer parted with her lover at Paris Station on a dark, rainy afternoon.
ジェニファーは暗い、雨の午後パリ駅で恋人と別れた。
Jenifaa wa kurai, ame no gogo Pari-eki de koi-bito to wakareta.

—— vt. **[to cause s.t. to divide (and become distributed)]**
⟨-o⟩ wa⌈ke⌉ru ⟨～を⟩分ける ② ⟪divide, sever, split, separate, distribute, distinguish⟫

EX. He likes to part his hair in the middle.
彼は髪を真ん中で分けるのが好きだ。
Kare wa kami o mannaka de wakeru no ga suki da.

participate vi. **[for s.o. to join in an organized event ⟨fml⟩]**
⟨-ni⟩ sa⌈nka-suru ⟨～に⟩参加する ③ •c [for s.o. to join in an event/project] ⟪join, enter, take part in⟫, ⟨-ni⟩ ku⌈wawa⌉ru ⟨～に⟩加わる ① [for s.o. to take part in some group or activity] ⟪add, join, enter⟫

EX. All of us participated in the women's liberation movement.
私たちは皆女性解放運動に{参加した/加わった}。
Watashi-tachi wa mina josei-kaihoo-undoo ni {sanka-shita/kuwawatta}.

participation n. **[an act of joining in an organized event/project]**
sa⌈nka 参加 •c ⟪joining, entry⟫

EX. Participation in the Olympic Games is more important than victory.
オリンピックは勝つことよりも、参加に意義がある。
Orinpikku wa katsu koto yori mo, sanka ni igi ga aru.

particle n. **[a very small piece ⟪fig. "a grammatical term referring to words that do not have inflection, such as prepositions, postpositions, etc."⟫]**
1. ryu⌉ushi 粒子 •c [a tiny speck ⟨w⟩] ⟪grain⟫

EX. Theoretical physics deals with elementary particles.
理論物理学は素粒子を扱う。
Riron-butsuri-gaku wa so-ryuushi o atsukau.

2. jo⌈shi 助詞 •c [a grammatical term referring to words that do not have inflection, such as prepositions, postpositions, etc.]

EX. "*Wa*" and "*ga*" are said to be the most difficult particles to learn in Japanese.
「は」と「が」は日本語で一番習得しにくい助詞だと言われています。
'Wa' to 'ga' wa Nihon-go de ichiban shuutoku-shi-nikui joshi da to iwa-rete imasu.

particular adj. **[singled out from among a group or very careful about details and hard to please]**
1. to⌈kutei no N 特定のN •c [specially designated/determined] ⟪specified, special⟫

EX. Are you thinking of any particular person?
だれか特定の人を考えているんですか。
Dare-ka tokutei no hito o kangaete iru n desu ka.

2. ⟨-ni⟩ do⌈kutokuna ⟨～に⟩独特な adj(*na*). **•c [for a characteristic to belong exclusively to s.o./s.t./s.a.], ⟨-ni⟩ do⌈kutoku no N ⟨～に⟩独特のN •c**

EX. The Japanese melon has a particular flavor that I cannot find anywhere else in the world.

日本のメロンは世界に例のない、{独特の/独特な}味をしている。
Nihon no meron wa sekai ni rei no nai, {dokutoku no/dokutokuna} aji o shite iru.

3. **⟨-ni⟩ ya⌈kamashi⌉i** ⟨〜に⟩やかましい adj(*i*). **[unpleasantly noisy or constantly making an issue of details]** **《noisy, tumultuous, fault-finding, critical, fastidious, fussy》**, **⟨-ni⟩ u⌈rusa⌉i** ⟨〜に⟩うるさい adj(*i*). **[unpleasantly noisy annoyingly vociferous about one's tastes/beliefs]** **《noisy, annoying, pestilent, bothering》**

EX. Beth is very particular about the way her hair is done.
ベスは髪型に大変{やかましい/うるさい}。
Besu wa kami-gata ni taihen {yakamashii/urusai}.

PHRASE: in particular *tokuni* 特に •c 《especially》, *betsu ni* …neg. 別に…neg. •c 《nothing in particular》

EX. A: Is there anything in particular that you want me to buy?
何か{特に/*別に}買ってきて欲しいものがありますか。
*Nani-ka {tokuni/*betsu ni} katte-kite hoshii mono ga arimasu ka.*
B: No, nothing in particular.
いいえ、{別に/特に}ありません。
Iie, {betsu ni/tokuni} arimasen.

particularly adv. **[in a special way or different from others]**
to⌉kuni 特に •c **[above all]**, **be⌈tsu ni** 別に •c **[(not) in particular]**

NOTE: *Betsu ni* is used with a negative predicate.

EX. (**a**) A: Are you interested in fishing?
釣りに興味がありますか。
Tsuri ni kyoomi ga arimasu ka.
B: No, not particularly.
いいえ、{別に/特に}興味はありません。
Iie, {betsu ni/tokuni} kyoomi wa arimasen.
(**b**) There are many problems in American society, but drugs are a particularly serious problem.
アメリカの社会には色々な問題があるが、麻薬は{特に/*別に}深刻な問題だ。
*Amerika no shakai ni wa iro-irona mondai ga aru ga, mayaku wa {tokuni/*betsu ni} shinkokuna mondai da.*

partly adv. **[in part]**
bu⌈bun-tekini 部分的に •c **《partially, locally》**, **hi⌈to⌉tsu ni wa** 一つには **[for one thing]**

EX. (**a**) A: Did you understand everything he said?
彼が言ったことが全部分かったかい?
Kare ga itta koto ga zenbu wakatta kai?
B: No, I only understood partly.
いいえ、{部分的に/*一つには}しか分かりませんでした。
*Iie, {bubun-tekini/*hitotsu ni wa} shika wakarimasendeshita.*
(**b**) A: Why did you study Japanese?
どうして日本語を勉強したんですか。
Dooshite Nihon-go o benkyoo-shita n desu ka.
B: Partly because my girl friend was Japanese.
{一つには/*部分的に}ガールフレンドが日本人だったからです。
*{Hitotsu ni wa/*Bubun-tekini} gaaru-furendo ga Nihon-jin datta kara desu.*

partner n. **[a person with whom one shares in some activity, esp. in business or sports]**
1. na⌈kama⌉ 仲間 **[a person in one's in-group with whom one frequently spends time, excluding one's relatives, spouse, and offspring 《fig. "the same kind"》]** **《company, companion, comrade, colleague, fellow worker, associate》**, **tsu⌈re** 連れ **[person(s) with whom s.o. goes somewhere together]** **《companion》**

EX. (**a**) I often play golf with my business partners.
私はよく仕事の{仲間/*連れ}とゴルフをする。
*Watashi wa yoku shigoto no {nakama/*tsure} to gorufu o suru.*
(**b**) A trip without any partner is no fun.
{連れ/仲間}のいない旅は楽しくない。
{Tsure/Nakama} no inai tabe wa tanoshiku nai.

2. tsu⌈re-ai 連れあい [a spouse] ⟪one's wife, husband, spouse⟫

EX. I lost my life's partner when I was 63.
私は六十三の時連れあいをなくした。
Watashi wa roku-juu-san no toki tsure-ai o nakushita.

3. a⌈ite⌉ 相手 [a person with whom one does s.t. face-to-face] ⟪companion, mate, pal, opponent⟫, pa⌉atonaa パートナー •f [a person with whom one does some activity, esp. dancing or boxing]

EX. (**a**) A: I'm going to play tennis this afternoon.
今日の午後テニスをするんです。
Kyoo no gogo tenisu o suru n desu.
B: Who's your partner?
{お相手/*パートナー}はだれですか。
*{O-aite/*Paatonaa} wa dare desu ka.*
(**b**) Fred's dancing partner was Ginger.
フレッドがダンスをしていた{パートナー/お相手}はジンジャーでした。
Freddo ga dansu o shite ita {paatonaa/o-aite} wa Jinjaa deshita.

4. kyo⌈odoo-keie⌉i-sha 共同経営者 •c [a person with whom one runs a business]

EX. I lost my business partner to another company.
共同経営者を他社に取られた。
Kyoodoo-keiei-sha o tasha ni tora-reta.

part-time adj. **[(working) fewer than the standard number of hours]**
pa⌈ato(-ta⌉imu) no N パート(タイム)のN •f, hi-⌈jo⌉okin no N 非常勤のN •c [for a professional person to work or teach fewer than the standard number of hours, usu. for lower wages] ↔ jookin no N 常勤のN •c

EX. Since my children are in junior high school, I've now taken a part-time job.
子供が中学に行っているので、私は今{パート(タイム)/非常勤}の仕事をしています。
Kodomo ga chuugaku ni itte iru node, watashi wa ima {paato(-taimu)/hi-jookin} no shigoto o shite imasu.

NOTE: *Paatotaimu no shigoto* is often abbreviated as *paato* in conversational Japanese.

PHRASE: part-time instructor *hi-jookin-kooshi* 非常勤講師 •c

party n. **[a gathering of people to have a good time or a group of people united together for a special purpose, esp. political, or a person/group involved in a legal contract]**

1. se⌈itoo 政党 •c [a political group]

EX. The dominant American political parties are the Democratic Party and the Republican Party.
アメリカの主要政党は民主党と共和党です。
Amerika no shuyoo-seitoo wa minshu-too to kyoowa-too desu.

NOTE: The *-too* in *seitoo* "political party" is also used as a suffix to denote a particular political party.

2. to⌈oji-sha 当事者 •c [the person concerned]

EX. The two parties in this contract are the writer of the original work and the translator.
本契約の当事者は、原著者と翻訳者である。
Hon-keiyaku no tooji-sha wa, gen-chosha to hon'yaku-sha dearu.

3. pa⌉atii パーティー •f [a Western-style gathering for social entertainment], e⌈nkai 宴会 •c [a Japanese-style gathering for social entertainment] ⟪dinner party, feast, banquet⟫

EX. (**a**) The semester is finally over. Shall we throw a party?
今学期もやっと終わった。{パーティー/*宴会}をしようか。
*Kon-gakki mo yatto owatta. {Paatii/*Enkai} o shiyoo ka.*
(**b**) They made me sing a song at the party.
{パーティー/宴会}で歌を歌わされた。
{Paatii/Enkai} de uta o utawa-sa-reta.

4. i⌈kkoo 一行 •c [a group of people gathered for the purpose of going to some specific place] ⟪company, troupe⟫

EX. A party of American high school teachers going to Japan was gathered in the lobby of the airport.

日本へ行くアメリカ人の高校の先生の一行が空港のロビーに集まっていた。
Nihon e iku Amerika-jin no kookoo no sensei no ikkoo ga kuukoo no robii ni atsumatte ita.

pass vi. **[to move by/through/past s.t. or to move from one place or condition to another 《fig. "take a test/examination successfully," "be considered as"》]**

1. 〈-o〉 **to⌉oru** 〈〜を〉**通る** ① **[to go along or through s.t. (from one side to the other)]** 《**go along, get through, pass for, come in, reach**》

EX. The parade passed through the main street of our town.
パレードが我々の町の目抜き通りを通った。
Pareedo ga ware-ware no machi no menuki-doori o tootta.

2. 〈-de〉 **to⌉oru** 〈〜で〉**通る** ① **[for s.o. to be considered as s.t. she/he isn't]** 《**to be taken for**》

EX. Although she is 25, Barbara could pass for a high school student.
バーバラは二十五だけれど、高校生で通るだろう。
Baabara wa ni-juu-go da keredo, kookoo-sei de tooru daroo.

3. su⌈gi⌉ru 過ぎる ② **[to move beyond a point in space or time]** 《**elapse, roll by, expire, exceed, be more than**》, **ta⌉tsu たつ** ① **[for s.o./s.a. in a lying or sitting position to rise** 《**fig. "depart"**》 **or for time to elapse]** ㊥ "stand up" ▷ 立つ, "for time to elapse" ▷ 経つ

EX. Two years have passed already since we met for the first time in London.
初めてロンドンで会ってからもう二年(が){過ぎた/経った}。
Hajimete Rondon de atte kara moo ni-nen (ga) {sugita/tatta}.

4. 〈-ni〉 **to⌉oru** 〈〜に〉**通る** ① **[for s.o. to take a test/examination successfully]**, 〈-ni〉 **go⌈okaku-suru** 〈〜に〉**合格する** ③ •c **[to achieve a satisfactory standard, such as on a test or to meet the necessary qualifications for s.t.]** 《**succeed in examination, stand the test**》, 〈-ni〉 **pa⌉su-suru** 〈〜に〉**パスする** ③ •f **[for s.o. to succeed in an examination]**

EX. I took the bar examination and passed.
私は司法試験に{通った/合格した/パスした}。
Watashi wa shihoo-shiken ni {tootta/gookaku-shita/pasu-shita}.

—— vt. **[for s.o. to hand or move s.t. from one person to another** 《**fig. "judge s.t./s.o. to have met some minimum qualification (as on an examination)," "cause s.t. to become law," "render a legal dicision," "use up time"**》**]**

1. 〈-o〉 **to⌉osu** 〈〜を〉**通す** ① **[to cause s.o./s.t./s.a. to go along or through s.t. (from one side to the other) or to give s.o./s.t. a satisfactory rating on a test/examination/inspection]**

EX. The instructor decided to pass John Smith even though he performed very poorly on the exam.
先生は試験のできが悪かったが、ジョン・スミスを通すことにした。
Sensei wa shiken no deki ga warukatta ga, Jon Sumisu o toosu koto ni shita.

2. 〈-o〉 **to⌈ori-sugi⌉ru** 〈〜を〉**通り過ぎる** ② **[to pass (through and) beyond a point in space or time]** 《**go past, go by**》, 〈-o〉 **to⌈ori-ko⌉su** 〈〜を〉**通り越す** ① **[to go beyond a point in space]** 《**go beyond, walk beyond**》

EX. It was such a small restaurant that I almost passed it by.
小さなレストランだったので、もう少しで{通り過ぎる/通り越す}ところでした。
Chiisana resutoran datta node, moo sukoshi de {toori-sugiru/toori-kosu} tokoro deshita.

3. 〈-o〉 **o⌈i-nu⌉ku** 〈〜を〉**追い抜く** ① **[to catch up with s.o./s.t./s.a. and go beyond** 《**fig. "achieve the same level as"**》**]** 《**overtake, catch up with**》, 〈-o〉 **o⌈i-ko⌉su** 〈〜を〉**追い越す** ① 《**outrun, outpace**》

EX. John passed the front runner just before the goal line.
ゴール近くで、ジョンは一位のランナー

を{追い抜いた/追い越した}。
Gooru chikaku de, Jon wa ichi-i no rannaa o {oi-nuita/oi-koshita}.

4. ⟨**-o**⟩ {⟨**-ni**⟩/⟨**-e**⟩} **u**⌈**tsu**⌉**su** ⟨〜を⟩{⟨〜に⟩/⟨〜へ⟩}うつす ① **[to cause s.o./s.t./s.a. to change to a different location or into a different condition《fig. "copy," "reflect" "infect" "take a picture"》]** **《move, remove, transfer, copy, photograph》**

㊇ "physically move s.t./s.o./s.a."▷移す, "show (a film)"▷映す, "take a picture"▷写す, otherwise ▷うつす

P

EX. It is said that one can cure a cold by passing it on to someone else.
風邪は人にうつすと直ると言います。
Kaze wa hito ni utsusu to naoru to iimasu.

5. ⟨**-o**⟩ **ma**⌈**wasu** ⟨〜を⟩回す ① **[for s.o. to cause s.o./s.t./s.a. to move in a circular motion《fig. "send round," "forward"》]** **《turn, rotate, hand round, forward》**

EX. Pass me the glass, please.
コップを回してください。
Koppu o mawashite kudasai.

PHRASE: pass time *hima-tsubushi ni ...suru* 暇つぶしに…する ③

EX. I passed the time reading magazines while waiting my turn at the doctor's office.
診療所で私の番を待つ間、暇つぶしに雑誌を読んでいた。
Shinryoo-jo de watashi no ban o matsu aida, hima-tsubushi ni zasshi o yonde ita.

PHRASE: pass away *nakunaru* 亡くなる ①

EX. My teacher passed away last week.
私の先生が先週亡くなった。
Watashi no sensei ga senshuu nakunatta.

PHRASE: pass out *kizetsu-suru* 気絶する ③ •c 《faint, black out》

EX. When she heard about her friend's death, Cathy passed out.
友達が死んだことを聞いて、キャシーは気絶した。
Tomodachi ga shinda koto o kiite, Kyashii wa kizetsu-shita.

— n. **[a ticket allowing one free access to an event, a means of transportation, etc., or a satisfactory rating on a test, examination, inspection, etc., or a throw of the ball from one player to another in a game such as football or the act of forfeiting an opportunity or turn, as in a card game, or a gap allowing passage through a mountain range]**

1. mu⌈**ryoo-joosha**⌉**-ken** 無料乗車券 **•c [a free ticket for public transportation], mu**⌈**ryoo-nyuujo**⌉**o-ken** 無料入場券 **•c [a free admission ticket], pa**⌉**su** パス **•f [a free ticket to enter some place or a free or prepaid ticket to ride on a means of public transportation]**

EX. (**a**) Do you have a pass to enter the pool?
プールに入る{無料入場券/パス/*無料乗車券}がありますか。
*Puuru ni hairu {muryoo-nyuujoo-ken/pasu/*muryoo-joosha-ken} ga arimasu ka.*
(**b**) I have a pass for the bus.
僕はバスの{無料乗車券/パス/*無料入場券}があります。
*Boku wa basu no {muryoo-joosha-ken/pasu/*muryoo-nyuujoo-ken} ga arimasu.*

2. go⌈**okaku** 合格 **•c [achieving a satisfactory rating on a test, examination, or inspection], pa**⌉**su** パス **•f [successful completion of an examination/test] ↔ fu-gookaku** 不合格 **•c**

EX. On the exam paper was written "pass."
試験の答案に「{合格/パス}」と書かれていた。
Shiken no tooan ni '{gookaku/pasu}' to kaka-rete ita.

3. pa⌉**su** パス **•f [a throw of the ball from one player to another in a game such as football or basketball]**

4. pa⌉**su** パス **•f [the act of forfeiting one's turn in a card game]**

5. to⌈**oge** 峠 **[a gap allowing passage through a mountain range《fig. "crisis," "maximum"》]**

EX. We took a break at a tea house on the mountain pass.

我々は峠の茶屋で休んだ。
Ware-ware wa tooge no chaya de yasunda.

passage n. **[the act/process of moving from one point to another in space or time or a way through s.t., esp. one which is enclosed, or a section of a piece of music or writing 《fig. "change"》]**

1. tsuʳukoo 通行 •c [an act of passing through s.t. or of coming and going] 《passage, transit, traffic》

EX. No passage is permitted beyond this point.
ここから先は通行禁止(です)。
Koko kara saki wa tsuukoo-kinshi (desu).

2. iʳdoo 移動 •c [the act of moving from one place to another] 《movement, transfer, migration》

3. keʳika 経過 •c [the passing of time or a process of s.t. happening] 《progress, lapse》, suˈii 推移 •c [a (natural) change in state accompanying a lapse in time] 《change, transition》

EX. Old enmities can be forgotten with the passage of time.
人に対する過去の恨みは時の{経過/推移}とともに忘れ去られていくことがある。
Hito ni-taisuru kako no urami wa toki no {keika/suii} to tomo ni wasure-sara-rete iku koto ga aru.

4. buˈbun 部分 •c [a part of s.t.] 《part》, iʳs-setsuˈ 一節 •c [a section from s.t. written, esp. a literary work] 《paragraph, stanza》

EX. This passage from Soseki's "Kokoro" depicts the inner pain the main character is feeling.
漱石の「心」のこの{部分/一節}は主人公の心の悩みを描いている。
Sooseki no 'Kokoro' no kono {bubun/is-setsu} wa shujinkoo no kokoro no nayami o egaite iru.

5. tsuˈuro 通路 •c [a pass on which to come or go] 《path, pathway》

EX. The prisoners escaped through an underground passage.
囚人は地下の通路を通って脱獄した。
Shuujin wa chika no tsuuro o tootte datsugoku-shita.

passenger n. **[a person who travels in a vehicle without controlling its operation] joʳokyaku 乗客 •c, seʳnkyaku 船客 •c [a person who travels in a boat without controlling its operation], toʳojoˈo-kyaku 搭乗客 •c [a person who travels on an airplane without controlling its operation]**

EX. (**a**) Passengers wishing to ride in the green car must purchase a special ticket.
グリーン車の{乗客/*船客/*搭乗客}は特別のチケットを買わなければいけません。
*Guriin-sha no {jookyaku/*senkyaku/*toojoo-kyaku} wa tokubetsu no chiketto o kawanakereba ikemasen.*
(**b**) The passengers on the boat enjoyed a beautiful sunset.
{船客/?船の乗客/*搭乗客}はすばらしい夕焼けを楽しんだ。
*{Senkyaku/?Fune no jookyaku/*Toojoo-kyaku} wa subarashii yuu-yake o tanoshinda.*
(**c**) Passengers on transcontinental flights can watch movies during the flight.
大陸横断飛行の{搭乗客/乗客/*船客}は機内で映画が見られる。
*Tairiku-oodan-hikoo no {toojoo-kyaku/jookyaku/*senkyaku} wa kinai de eiga ga mi-rareru.*

passion n. **[a deep, overwhelming emotion]**

1. haʳgeshiˈi kaʳnjoo 激しい感情 [an extremely strong feeling], geʳkijoo 激情 •c [an extremely strong feeling that cannot be controlled by rational means] 《outburst, wild anger》

EX. Once he's overcome by passion, there's no telling what he'll do.
{激しい感情/激情}に捕われると、あの人は何をするか分からない。
{Hageshii kanjoo/Gekijoo} ni torawa-reru to, ano hito wa nani o suru ka wakaranai.

2. haʳgeshiˈi koˈi 激しい恋 [passionate love], neʳtsuretsuna koˈi 熱烈な恋 [ardent love]

P

EX. In his passion for her he was blind to her faults.
彼女に{激しい/熱烈な}恋をしていたため、彼は彼女の欠点が全然目に入らなかった。
Kanojo ni {hageshii/netsuretsuna} koi o shite ita tame, kare wa kanojo no ketten ga zenzen me ni hairanakatta.

3. ne˥tsui 熱意 •c [eagerness to do s.t.] ⟪zeal, enthusiasm, eagerness⟫, jo˥onetsu 情熱 •c [an enthusiastic feeling] ⟪enthusiasm⟫

EX. I was moved by her passion for social welfare.
私は彼女の社会福祉に対する{熱意/情熱}には感心しました。
Watashi wa kanojo no shakai-fukushi ni-taisuru {netsui/joonetsu} ni wa kanshin-shimashita.

4. jo˥oyoku 情欲 •c [sexual desire] ⟪carnal desire, fleshly appetite⟫

passive adj. **[acted upon rather than taking action; submissive and non-assertive ⟪fig. "containing a passive verb form"⟫]**
u˥ke-mi no N 受け身のN

EX. (**a**) You should stop taking such a passive attitude toward life.
あなたは人生に対してそんな受け身の態度を取るのをやめたほうがいいですよ。
Anata wa jinsei ni-taishite sonna ukemi no taido o toru no o yameta hoo ga ii desu yo.
(**b**) Verbs in Japanese such as "*shikarareru*," "*mirareru*," "*nagurareru*," etc., are called passive verbs.
日本語では「しかられる」、「見られる」、「殴られる」などの動詞は受け身形と呼ばれる。
Nihon-go de wa 'shikara-reru,' 'mi-rareru,' 'nagura-reru' nado no dooshi wa ukemi-kei to yoba-reru.

— n. **[a grammatical category of verbs indicating that the subject is acted upon rather than taking action itself]**
u˥ke-mi-kei 受け身形 [a passive form], ju˥doo-tai 受動態 •c [passive voice] ↔ noodoo-tai 能動態 •c

EX. The passive of "John loves Mary" is "Mary is loved by John."
「ジョンはメアリーを愛している」の{受け身形/受動態}は「メアリーはジョンに愛されている」である。
'Jon wa Mearii o aishite iru' no {ukemi-kei/judoo-tai} wa 'Mearii wa Jon ni aisa-rete iru' dearu.

passively adv. **[in a passive manner]**
o˥tona˥shiku おとなしく /⟨adj(*i*). *ku* of *otonashii* gentle/ [in a docile and quiet manner] ⟪obediently, quietly, gently⟫, ju˥ujunni 従順に /⟨adj⟨*na*⟩. *ni* of *juujunna* obedient/ •c [in a gentle and submissive manner] ⟪obediently⟫

EX. (**a**) The student passively followed the teacher's instructions.
学生は先生の指示に{おとなしく/従順に}従った。
Gakusei wa sensei no shiji ni {otonashiku/juujunni} shitagatta.
(**b**) When the boss yelled at him, Peter just stood listening passively.
ボスにどなりつけられた時に、ピーターはそこに立ってただ{おとなしく/*従順に}聞いていただけだ。
*Bosu ni donari-tsuke-rareta toki ni, Piitaa wa soko ni tatte tada {otonashiku/*juujunni} kiite ita dake da.*

passport n.
pa˥supo˥oto パスポート •f, ryo˥ken 旅券 •c ⟨fml⟩

EX. My passport will expire this June.
私の{パスポート/旅券}は今年の六月に切れます。
Watashi no {pasupooto/ryoken} wa kotoshi no roku-gatsu ni kiremasu.

past adj. **[belonging to a time gone by]**
o˥watta N 終わったN /⟨Vinf. past of *owaru* ① end/, ko˥no N このN [a demonstrative pronoun referring to s.o./s.t./s.a. that belongs within the speaker's territory ⟪fig. "this past…"⟫], ka˥ko no N 過去のN •c [belonging to a point in time earlier than now]

EX. (a) I've been studying Korean for the past five years.
私は{この/過去/*終わった}五年間韓国語を勉強してきました。
*Watashi wa {kono/kako/*owatta} go-nenkan Kankoku-go o benkyoo-shite kimashita.*
(b) I'd rather not dwell on past matters.
私は{過去の/終わった/*この}事をくよくよ考えたくありません。
*Watashi wa {kako no/owatta/*kono} koto o kuyo-kuyo kangae-taku arimasen.*

PHRASE: past form *kako-kei* 過去形 •c ↔ *genzai-kei* 現在形 •c

EX. A: What's the past form of "drink"?
「飲む」の過去形は何ですか。
'Nomu' no kako-kei wa nan desu ka.
B: It's "drank."
「飲んだ」です。
'Nonda' desu.

— n. **[a point in time earlier than now ⟪fig. "past tense in grammar"⟫]**
ka⌉ko 過去 •c

EX. Japanese tend to dwell on their past more than Americans.
日本人の方がアメリカ人より過去のことをくよくよ考えがちだ。
Nihon-jin no hoo ga Amerika-jin yori kako no koto o kuyo-kuyo kangae-gachi da.

— prep. **[beyond a certain point in time or space]**
1. -sugi ～過ぎ [beyond a certain age or point in time]

EX. (a) A: What time do you have?
今何時ですか。
Ima nan-ji desu ka.
B: It's 14 minutes past 9.
九時十四分過ぎです。
Ku-ji juu-yon-pun-sugi desu.
(b) You begin to take on a different perspective on life when you get past 40.
四十過ぎになると人生観が変わってきます。
Yon-juu-sugi ni naru to jinsei-kan ga kawatte kimasu.

NOTE: *Ku-ji-sugi* is acceptable, meaning "past 9 o'clock," but *ku-ji-sugi-juu-yon-pun* is not possible. *-sugi* must occur at the end of the entire time expression.

2. ⟨-o⟩ to⌈ori-koshite ⟨～を⟩通り越して /⟨Vte of *toori-kosu* ①⟩ go past/ [going beyond a certain point in space]

EX. I walked right past the post office without knowing it.
気がつかずに郵便局を通り越してしまった。
Ki-ga-tsukazu ni yuubin-kyoku o toori-koshite shimatta.

paste n. **[a smooth, viscous adhesive or dough made of water, flour, etc.]**
1. no⌈ri⌉ のり [a sticky substance made from rice/flour or by chemical means for joining things or for stiffening cloth fabrics] ⟪glue⟫
2. pe⌉esuto ペースト [a dough made of water, flour, etc.]

— vt. **[for s.o. to cause s.t. to adhere to s.t. with paste]**
⟨-ni⟩ ⟨-o⟩ no⌈ri⌉ de ha⌈ru ⟨～に⟩⟨～を⟩のりではる ①

EX. I pasted a poster on the wall.
私は壁にポスターをのりではった。
Watashi wa kabe ni posutaa o nori de hatta.

pastor n. **[a clergyman who serves a local church]**
bo⌉kushi 牧師 •c ⟪clergyman, churchman⟫

EX. I went to the church to see the pastor.
牧師(さん)に会いに教会へ行きました。
Bokushi(-san) ni ai ni kyookai e ikimashita.

pasture n. **[ground on which vegetation is allowed to grow for grazing animals or the vegetation itself on such ground]**
1. bo⌈kuso⌉o-chi 牧草地 •c [ground on which vegetation grows used for grazing animals] ⟪meadow, grassland⟫

EX. In Hokkaido there are vast pasture lands where cows can graze.
北海道には牛が草を食べられる広大な牧草地がある。
Hokkaidoo ni wa ushi ga kusa o tabe-

P

rareru koodaina bokusoo-chi ga aru.
2. bo⌈kusoo 牧草 •c **[vegetation which cattle feed on]** ⟪grass⟫

pat vt. **[for s.o. to tap or stroke s.o./s.t./s.a. very lightly with the palm of the hand or a flat object]**
1. ⟨-o⟩ ka⌈ruku tata⌉ku ⟨〜を⟩軽くたたく ① **[for s.o. to tap s.o./s.t./s.a. lightly]**
EX. The department chief patted me on the shoulder.
部長が私の肩を軽くたたいた。
Buchoo ga watashi no kata o karuku tataita.
2. ⟨-o⟩ na⌈de⌉ru ⟨〜を⟩なでる ② **[for s.o. to caress s.t. softly with the palm of one's hand ⟪fig. "comb one's hair"⟫]** ⟪stroke⟫
EX. My dog loves to be patted on the head like this.
うちの犬はこうして頭をなでてもらうのが大好きです。
Uchi no inu wa kooshite atama o nadete morau no ga dai-suki desu.

—— n. **[an act of patting]**
ka⌈ruku tata⌉ku ko⌈to⌉ 軽くたたくこと **[an act of tapping s.o./s.t./s.a. lightly]**, na⌈de⌉ru ko⌈to⌉ なでること **[an act of stroking the surface of s.o./s.t./s.a. gently with the palm of one's hand or a flat object]**

patch n. **[a small piece of cloth attached to a larger piece of cloth to conceal a hole or worn area ⟪fig. "small piece of land"⟫]**
1. tsu⌈gi つぎ **[a small piece of cloth attached to a larger piece of cloth to conceal a hole or worn area]**
EX. When I was a kid, my family was so poor that I was always wearing clothes covered with patches.
僕が子供の時はうちがとても貧乏だったのでいつもつぎだらけの服を着ていました。
Boku ga kodomo no toki wa uchi ga totemo binboo datta node itsu-mo tsugi darake no fuku o kite imashita.
2. chi⌉isana to⌈chi 小さな土地 **[a small piece of land]**, ha⌈take 畑 **[a piece of land for growing crops]**

—— vt. **[to affix a small piece of cloth to a larger piece of cloth to conceal a hole or worn area ⟪fig. "smooth over"⟫]**
1. ⟨-ni⟩ tsu⌈gi o ateru ⟨〜に⟩つぎをあてる ② **[to affix a small piece of cloth to a larger piece of cloth to conceal a hole or worn area]**
EX. Mom, could you patch this hole in my pants?
お母さん、ズボンのこの穴につぎをあててくれる?
O-kaa-san, zubon no kono ana ni tsugi o atete kureru?
2. ⟨-o⟩ to⌈ri-tsukurou ⟨〜を⟩取り繕う ① **[for s.o. to smooth over the surface of s.t. in order to conceal a mistake/embarrassment/evil deed]** ⟪mend, repair, smooth over⟫
EX. The boss tried to patch up his ill deeds, but it was too late.
上司は自分の悪事を取り繕おうとしたが、もう手遅れだった。
Jooshi wa jibun no akuji o tori-tsukurooo to shita ga, moo te-okure datta.

patent n. **[⟨an official document which guarantees⟩ the exclusive right of an inventor to sell, make, or use an invention for a limited period of time or an invention for which such an exclusive right has been granted]**
1. to⌉kkyo 特許 •c **[the exclusive right of an inventor to sell, make, or use an invention for a limited period of time]**
EX. When did you receive the patent for this invention?
この発明の特許はいつ取りましたか。
Kono hatsumei no tokkyo wa itsu torimashita ka.
2. to⌈kkyo-sho⌉o 特許証 •c **[an official document which guarantees exclusive rights to an inventor]**
3. to⌈kkyo-hin 特許品 •c **[an invention for which the inventor has been granted certain exclusive rights]**

path n. **[a trail for walking along or the course of motion taken by s.t./s.o./s.a. ⟪fig. "way of life"⟫]**

mi⌈chi 道 [a route that connects two points for people or vehicles to pass along《fig. "method," "the proper way of thinking or conducting oneself," "special field"》]

EX. (**a**) This is the path I took to school every day when I was a high school student.
これは私が高校生の時、毎日学校へ行くのに通った道です。
Kore wa watashi ga kookoo-sei no toki, mai-nichi gakkoo ni iku no ni tootta michi desu.
(**b**) Although we took different paths in life, we reached the same goal.
我々は違った人生の道を歩んだのだが、同じゴールに達した。
Ware-ware wa chigatta jinsei no michi o ayunda no da ga, onaji gooru ni tasshita.

patience n. **[the capacity to endure affliction, annoyance, or inconvenience with calmness]**
ga⌉man 我慢 •c [the willing endurance of physical or mental affliction from s.t. for a relatively short period of time]《endurance, perseverance》, shi⌉nboo 辛抱 •c [the willing endurance of physical or mental affliction for a relatively long period of time]《endurance, long-suffering, forbearance》, ni⌉ntai 忍耐 •c [spiritual endurance of physical or mental affliction]《perseverance, fortitude, stoicism》

EX. (**a**) To achieve success one needs both patience and intelligence.
成功するには{忍耐/辛抱/?我慢}も知能も必要だ。
Seikoo-suru ni wa {nintai/shinboo/?gaman} mo chinoo mo hitsuyoo da.
(**b**) I finally ran out of patience with his haughty attitude.
私は彼のえらそうな態度にとうとう{我慢/辛抱/*忍耐}が出来なくなった。
*Watashi wa kare no era-soona taido ni tootoo {gaman/shinboo/*nintai} ga dekinaku natta.*

patient adj. **[to be capable of enduring affliction, annoyance, or inconvenience with calmness]**
shi⌈nboo-zuyo⌉i 辛抱強い adj(*i*). **[to have the character enabling one to endure relatively long-term physical or mental affliction]《enduring》, ni⌈ntai-zuyo⌉i 忍耐強い** adj(*i*). **[to have the spiritual character enabling one to endure physical or mental affliction]《enduring, stoic》, ga⌈man-zuyo⌉i 我慢強い** adj(*i*). **[to have the character enabling one to endure relatively short-term physical or mental affliction]《forbearing, enduring, persevering》, ⟨-o⟩ ga⌉man-suru ⟨〜を⟩我慢する ③ •c [for s.o./s.a. to willingly endure physical or mental affliction from s.t. for a short period of time]《endure, persevere, forbear》, shi⌉nboo-suru 辛抱する ③ •c [for s.o. to willingly endure physical or mental affliction for a relatively long period of time]《endure, persevere, forbear, put up with》**

EX. (**a**) Though he was in pain, John was patient and didn't say anything.
痛みを感じていたのにジョンは{我慢/辛抱/??忍耐}強いから何も言わなかった。
Ita-mi o kanjite ita no ni Jon wa {gaman/shinboo/??nintai}-zuyoi kara nani-mo iwanakatta.
(**b**) Through the six-year ordeal of her husband's imprisonment, Mary was patient and never lost hope that he would be released.
メアリーは{辛抱/忍耐/??我慢}強い人で夫が拘留されていた苦難の六年間も、いずれ釈放されるだろうという希望を一時も捨てなかった。
Mearii wa {shinboo/nintai/??gaman}-zuyoi hito de otto ga kooryuu-sarete ita kunan no roku-nenkan mo, izure shakuhoo-sareru daroo to iu kiboo o it-toki mo sutenakatta.
(**c**) All you can do is be patient when you have such difficult people to work with.
あんなに気むずかしい人たちと一緒に仕事をするには{我慢/辛抱}するしかない。

Anna ni ki-muzukashii hito-tachi to issho ni shigoto o suru ni wa {gaman/shinboo}-suru shika nai.

— n. **[a person who is under medical treatment]**
ka⌈nja 患者 •c [a sick person under the care of a doctor], byo⌈onin 病人 •c [a sick person] ((invalid))

EX. (**a**) Many patients were waiting for treatment at the hospital.
病院では大勢の{患者/?病人}が治療を受けるのを待っていた。
Byooin de wa oozei no {kanja/?byoonin} ga chiryoo o ukeru no o matte ita.
(**b**) It's difficult for a healthy person to understand what it's like to be a patient.
健康な人には{病人/??患者}の気持ちはなかなか分からない。
Kenkoona hito ni wa {byoonin/??kanja} no kimochi wa naka-naka wakaranai.

patrol n. **[the act of traversing an area to make sure all is secure and orderly or a person who performs such a duty]**
pa⌈toro⌉oru パトロール •f

EX. With the summit meeting approaching, numerous police officers are on patrol in the vicinity of the meeting place.
サミットを控えて大勢の警察官が会場付近のパトロールにあたっている。
Samitto o hikaete oozei no keisatsu-kan ga kaijoo-fukin no patorooru ni atatte iru.

— vi. **[for s.o. to perform patrol duty]**
pa⌈toro⌉oru-suru パトロールする ③ •f, ju⌈nkai-suru 巡回する ③ •c [for s.o. to look around an area for a particular purpose]

patron n. **[s.o. who supports/protects a person, group, business, or cause, esp. in a financial way]**
1. ko⌈oe⌉n-sha 後援者 •c [s.o. who supports an institution with money] ((supporter, backer))

EX. Dale Carnegie was one of America's great patrons of the arts.
デール・カーネギーはアメリカの芸術界の偉大な後援者の一人でした。
Deeru Kaanegii wa Amerika no geijutsu-kai no idaina kooen-sha no hitori deshita.

2. hi⌈iki⌉-kyaku ひいき客 [a frequent customer] ((clientele))
3. ri⌈yo⌉o-sha 利用者 •c [a person who uses s.t. for his/her benefit]

EX. About 1,000 patrons use this library every day.
この図書館の利用者は毎日約千人です。
Kono tosho-kan no riyoo-sha wa mai-nichi yaku sen-nin desu.

4. pa⌈toron パトロン •f [a sponsor (esp. of a geisha)]

patronage n. **[the support or protection of a patron]**
1. ho⌉go-i⌈kusei 保護育成 •c [an act of cultivating s.t. and keeping it from being endangered]

EX. Patronage of the arts is a national responsibility.
芸術の保護育成は国の責任だ。
Geijutsu no hogo-ikusei wa kuni no sekinin da.

2. sho⌈orei 奨励 •c [the act of encouraging s.o. to do s.t. truly worthwhile] ((encouragement))

EX. Patronage of the arts is indispensable for their survival.
芸術の存続には奨励がどうしても不可欠だ。
Geijutsu no sonzoku ni wa shoorei ga doo-shite-mo fukaketsu da.

3. hi⌉iki ひいき [an act of favoring s.o. and assisting him/her financially or otherwise, or a person thus favored]

EX. It is quite natural to want to show gratitude for someone's patronage.
自分のひいきに感謝の気持ちを表したいと思うのは当たり前だ。
Jibun no hiiki ni kansha no kimochi o arawashi-tai to omou no wa atarimae da.

pattern n. **[an orderly (repeated) arrangement of lines and colors or a design/model to be followed in making/doing s.t.]**

1. ka⌈ta⌉ 型 [an outward form (to be followed) ⟪fig. "mold"⟫] ⟪model, mold, die⟫, pa⌈ta⌉an パターン •f [a form/type/model/style/design], yo⌈oshiki 様式 •c [a way of doing s.t. following a form that has become standard over time] ⟪mode, manner⟫

EX. (**a**) Japanese and Korean behavioral patterns are quite different.
日本人と韓国人の行動の{型/様式/パターン}はかなり違う。
Nihon-jin to Kankoku-jin no koodoo no {kata/yooshiki/pataan} wa kanari chigau.
(**b**) We were made to do lots of pattern practice in our Japanese class.
日本語の授業では{パターン・プラクティス/文型練習}をよくさせられます。
Nihon-go no jugyoo de wa {pataan-purakutisu/bunkei-renshuu} o yoku sase-raremasu.

2. ka⌈ta-gami 型紙 [a paper cutout design for making a dress]

EX. I made a blouse using this pattern.
私はこの型紙を使ってブラウスを作りました。
Watashi wa kono kata-gami o tsukatte burausu o tsukurimashita.

3. mo⌈yoo 模様 •c [an ornamental figure/picture ⟪fig. "the situation as it exists," "appearance"⟫] ⟪look, appearance, design⟫, zu⌈an 図案 •c [a decorative design (often tentatively prepared)] ⟪design⟫, ga⌈ra 柄 [the way s.o./s.t. looks in terms of physique, social status, or general design] ⟪build, character, design⟫

EX. (**a**) I like the flower patterns on your *kimono.*
あなたの着物の花の{模様/柄/*図案}、とてもいいわ。
*Anata no ki-mono no hana no {moyoo/gara/*zuan}, totemo ii wa.*
(**b**) Could you show me the pattern you've drawn before you print it?
印刷する前におかきになった{図案/??模様/*柄}を見せて下さい。
*Insatsu-suru mae ni o-kaki ni natta {zuan/??moyoo/*gara} o misete kudasai.*
(**c**) Don't you think that the pattern on this material is a bit flashy?
この織物の{模様/柄/*図案}はちょっと派手じゃない?
*Kono ori-mono no {moyoo/gara/*zuan} wa chotto hade janai?*

—— vt. **[to make s.t. according to a design or model]**
⟨-o⟩ ka⌈ta-do⌉tte tsu⌈ku⌉ru ⟨〜を⟩型取って作る ①

EX. This building was patterned after the Golden Pavilion in Kyoto.
この建物は京都の金閣寺を型取って作られた。
Kono tate-mono wa Kyooto no Kinkaku-ji o kata-dotte tsukura-reta.

pause vi. **[to stop doing s.t. for a short time] i⌉ki o tsu⌈gu 息を継ぐ ① [for s.o. to gather one's breath]**

EX. Joanne suddenly paused in the middle of her sentence.
ジョアンは話の途中で急に息を継いだ。
Joan wa hanashi no tochuu de kyuuni iki o tsuida.

—— n. **[a temporary cessation of activity] ya⌈sumi⌉ 休み /⟨V*masu* of *yasumu* ① rest/[(a period of time during which there is a) cessation of activity ⟪fig. "holiday," "vacation"⟫] ⟪recess, intermission, break, holiday, vacation⟫, sho⌈o-kyu⌉ushi 小休止 •c [a very short cessation of activity] ⟪a short halt, a short break⟫, po⌉ozu ポーズ •f [a short cessation of speech/reading/movement]**

pave vt. **[to cover the surface of a street with a hard material]**
(⟨-de⟩) ⟨-o⟩ ho⌈soo-suru (⟨〜で⟩)⟨〜を⟩舗装する ③ •c

EX. They paved the street in front of my house with asphalt.
アスファルトでうちの前の道路を舗装した。
Asufaruto de uchi no mae no dooro o hosoo-shita.

pavement n. **[the surface of a street paved with a hard material]**
ho⌈soo 舗装 •c

paw n. **[the foot of a clawed animal such as a dog or cat]**
a⌈shi⌉ あし [one or all of the limbs on an animal/human which support the body and are used for walking《fig. "any of the long thin upright supports on which a piece of furniture stands," "walking," "transportation"》] 《foot, leg, walking, transportation》

EX. If human feet were as strong and flexible as a cat's paws, we would have less foot injuries.
人間の足が猫の足のように強くて、柔軟性があったら、足のけがは少ないだろう。
Ningen no ashi ga neko no ashi no yooni tsuyokute, juunan-sei ga attara, ashi no kega wa sukunai daroo.

P

pay vt. **[for s.o. to give money to s.o. in return for what one has received]**
⟨-o⟩ ha⌈ra⌉u ⟨～を⟩払う ① [for s.o. to get rid of s.t. one is plagued with or owes to s.o. or to direct one's attention/respect toward s.o./s.t.] 《clear away, drive away, give money for service/merchandise, show (respect)》

EX. (**a**) How much did you pay for this compact disk?
このCDにいくら払いましたか。
Kono Shii-Dii ni ikura haraimashita ka.
(**b**) We are taught in our society to pay due respect to our elders.
我々の社会では年上の人にちゃんと敬意を払うように教え込まれている。
Ware-ware no shakai de wa toshi-ue no hito ni chanto keii o harau yooni oshie-koma-rete iru.

PHRASE: pay back ⟨*-o*⟩ *kaesu* ⟨～を⟩返す ①

EX. He didn't pay back the money he borrowed.
彼は借りた金を返さなかった。
Kare wa karita kane o kaesanakatta.

—— vi. **[to make a payment or to be profitable]**
1. (**da⌈ikin o**) **shi⌈hara⌉u** (代金を)支払う ① **[for s.o. to make payment for s.t.]**

EX. Do we have to pay now?
今代金を支払わなければなりませんか。
Ima daikin o shiharawanakereba narimasen ka.

2. hi⌈ki-a⌉u 引き合う ① [for s.t. to be worth its cost]

EX. When you consider the effects on your health and family life, it doesn't pay to work such long hours.
健康や家庭生活への影響を考えると、そんなに長時間働くのでは引き合わない。
Kenkoo ya katei-seikatsu e no eikyoo o kangaeru to, sonna ni choo-jikan hataraku no de wa hiki-awanai.

payment n. **[an act of paying]**
shi⌈harai 支払い /⟨V*masu* of *shiharau* ① pay/

EX. Today I made the final payment on my car.
私は今日車の支払いを済ませた。
Watashi wa kyoo kuruma no shiharai o sumaseta.

pea n.
e⌈ndo⌉o(-mame) えんどう(豆)

peace n. **[freedom from war/psychological worries/strife]**
1. he⌈iwa 平和 •c [freedom from war/strife/problems] 《harmony》 ↔ sensoo 戦争 •c

EX. (**a**) Those who have experienced war know the true meaning of peace.
戦争を経験した人は平和の本当の意味を知っています。
Sensoo o keiken-shita hito wa heiwa no hontoo no imi o shitte imasu.
(**b**) Peace at home is probably the most important thing of all.
家庭の平和が一番大切でしょう。
Katei no heiwa ga ichiban taisetsu deshoo.

2. a⌈nshin 安心 •c [freedom from anxiety] 《peace of mind, a sense of security, safety》 ↔ fuan 不安 •c

EX. I felt peace of mind when I heard my

mother's voice over the phone.
母の声を電話で聞いた時、私は安心しました。
Haha no koe o denwa de kiita toki, watashi wa anshin-shimashita.

NOTE: *Anshin* is often used as a *suru*-verb *anshin-suru* "feel reassured."

peaceful adj. **[free from war/psychological worries/strife]**

1. he⌈iwana 平和な •c [free from war/strife] ⟪**tranquil, harmonious**⟫

EX. (**a**) Thankfully we now live in a very peaceful world.
有難いことに我々は今とても平和な世の中に暮らしている。
Arigatai koto ni ware-ware wa ima totemo heiwana yo-no-naka ni kurashite iru.
(**b**) My greatest desire is to have a peaceful home life.
私の最大の夢は平和な家庭を持つことです。
Watashi no saidai no yume wa heiwana katei o motsu koto desu.

2. o⌈da⌉yakana 穏やかな adj(*na*). **[gentle and calm]** ⟪**quiet, calm, mild, tranquil**⟫

EX. (**a**) Yesterday the ocean was stormy but today it was peaceful.
昨日は海が荒れていたが、今日は穏やかだった。
Kinoo wa umi ga arete ita ga, kyoo wa odayaka datta.
(**b**) Look at this baby's face! Doesn't it look peaceful?
この赤ちゃんの顔を見てごらん。穏やかだねえ。
Kono aka-chan no kao o mite goran. Odayaka da nee.

3. he⌈iwa-tekina 平和的な adj(*na*). **•c [motivated by peace]** ⟪**amicable, pacific**⟫

EX. Peaceful uses of atomic energy should be promoted.
原子力の平和的な利用が進められなければならない。
Genshi-ryoku no heiwa-tekina riyoo ga susume-rarenakereba naranai.

NOTE: The compound *heiwa-riyoo* is often used for *heiwa-tekina riyoo.*

peach n.

mo⌈mo 桃

EX. Do you know the old Japanese fairy tale, *Peach Boy*?
『桃太郎』という日本の古いおとぎ話を知っていますか。
"Momotaroo" to iu Nihon no furui otogi-banashi o shitte imasu ka.

peacock n.

ku⌈jaku くじゃく

peak n. **[a pointed extremity ⟪fig. "the (pointed) top of a mountain/hill," "the highest level," "visor"⟫]**

1. se⌈ntan 先端 •c [a pointed extremity ⟪fig. "vanguard"⟫] ⟪**point, tip, vanguard**⟫

EX. The peak of the roof is twenty feet high.
屋根の先端は二十フィートの高さだ。
Yane no sentan wa ni-juf-fiito no taka-sa da.

2. sa⌈nchoo 山頂 •c [the (pointed) top of a mountain] ⟪**summit, mountain top**⟫

EX. An amateur mountaineer wouldn't be able to make it to the peak of that mountain.
普通の登山者はその山頂まで登れない。
Futsuu no tozan-sha wa sono sanchoo made nobore-nai.

3. hi⌈sashi ひさし [eaves ⟪fig. "the brim of a hat"⟫]

4. cho⌉oten 頂点 •c [the highest point ⟪fig. "climax"⟫], pi⌉iku ピーク •f

EX. Electric consumption reaches its peak in January and in August.
電気使用量は一月と八月にその{頂点/ピーク}に達する。
Denki-shiyoo-ryoo wa ichi-gatsu to hachi-gatsu ni sono {chooten/piiku} ni tassuru.

peanut n.

{**pi⌉inattsu/pi⌉inatsu**} {ピーナッツ/ピーナツ} **•f**

pear n.

(**se⌈iyo⌉o-)nashi** (西洋)なし

NOTE: The Japanese pear is much rounder than the Western pear.

pearl n.
shi⌈nju 真珠 •c
EX. My boyfriend gave me a pearl necklace.
ボーイフレンドが真珠のネックレスをくれました。
Booi-furendo ga shinju no nekkuresu o kuremashita.

peasant n. **[a person who tills the soil as a small landowner or tenant farmer]**
ko-⌈bya⌉kushoo 小百姓 •c [a small farmer] **《a petty farmer, tenant》**

P

pebble n. **[a small, water-rounded stone]**
ko-⌈ishi 小石
EX. We sat down on the pebble-covered beach and talked to each other.
私たちは小石の多い海岸に坐って、話し合った。
Watashi-tachi wa ko-ishi no ooi kaigan ni suwatte, hanashi-atta.

peculiar adj. **[unusual or belonging exclusively to a certain person, place, thing, or time]**
1. ka⌈watte iru 変わっている / 〈V *te iru* of *kawaru* ① change/ ② 《strange, weird》, he⌉nna 変な adj(*na*). **•c [exhibiting an unusual characteristic/condition/behavior]** **《strange, odd, queer, abnormal, irregular》**
EX. A: Mie is a bit peculiar, isn't she?
美枝はちょっと{変わっている/変だ}ね。
Mie wa chotto {kawatte-iru/hen da} ne.
B: No, she seems normal to me.
いや、僕には普通に見えるよ。
Iya, boku ni wa futsuu ni mieru yo.
2. (〈-ni〉) to⌈kuyuu no N (〈〜に〉)特有のN •c [for a characteristic to belong uniquely to s.o./s.t.] **《characteristic of》, (〈-ni〉) to⌈kuyuuna (〈〜に〉)特有な** adj(*na*). **•c, 〈-ni〉 do⌈kutoku no N 〈〜に〉独特のN •c [for a characteristic to belong exclusively to s.o./s.t./s.a.]** **《special, original, unique》, 〈-ni〉 do⌈kutokuna 〈〜に〉独特な** adj(*na*). **•c**
EX. (**a**) Psychological dependency is not a phenomenon peculiar to Japanese culture.
甘えは日本文化に{特有の/特有な/独特の/独特な}現象ではありません。
Amae wa Nihon-bunka ni {tokuyuu no/tokuyuuna/dokutoku no/dokutokuna} genshoo dewaarimasen.
(**b**) This recording exemplifies the style of piano playing that was peculiar to Horowitz.
この録音はホロウイッツ{独特の/特有の/*独特な/*特有な}ピアノ演奏スタイルを示すものです。
*Kono rokuon wa Horouittsu {dokutoku no/tokuyuu no/*dokutokuna/*tokuyuuna} piano ensoo-sutairu o shimesu mono desu.*
(**c**) Takashi's English has an accent peculiar to Japanese.
隆の英語には日本人(に){独特/特有}のなまりがある。
Takashi no eigo ni wa Nihon-jin (ni) {dokutoku/tokuyuu} no namari ga aru.

pedagogy n. **[(the technique or profession of) teaching]**
1. kyo⌈oiku⌉-gaku 教育学 •c [the science of teaching]
2. kyo⌈oju-hoo 教授法 •c [a teaching method]
3. kyo⌈oshoku 教職 •c [the teaching profession]

pedal n. **[a lever operated by foot]**
pe⌈daru ペダル •f
EX. (**a**) Push the pedals harder so you can go faster.
もっと速く走れるようにペダルをもっと強く踏みなさい。
Motto hayaku hashire-ru yooni pedaru o motto tsuyoku fuminasai.
(**b**) That pianist uses the pedals too much.
あのピアニストはペダルを使い過ぎる。
Ano pianisuto wa pedaru o tsukai-sugiru.

pedestrian n. **[s.o. who is walking (in contrast to s.o. in a vehicle)]**
ho⌈ko⌉o-sha 歩行者 •c 《walker》, tsu⌈ukoo-nin 通行人 •c [s.o. who is passing through/by a place on foot] **《passerby, wayfarer》**
EX. A car ran into a dozen pedestrians killing two of them and seriously injuring the others.
車が十二、三人の{歩行者/通行人}の中

に突っ込んで、二人が死亡、残りが重傷を負った。
Kuruma ga juu-ni-san-nin no {hokoo-sha/tsuukoo-nin} no naka ni tsukkonde, futari ga shiboo, nokori ga juushoo o otta.

peek vi. **[for s.o./s.a. to take a look at s.o./s.t./s.a. furtively, often from a concealed place]**
1. **⟨-o⟩ chi⌈ra⌉tto mi⌉ru** ⟨〜を⟩ちらっと見る ② **[for s.o./s.a. to take a look s.o./s.t./s.a. very quickly]**

EX. Tim peeked at Liz's boyfriend.
ティムはリズのボーイフレンドをちらっと見た。
Timu wa Rizu no booi-furendo o chiratto mita.

2. **⟨-o⟩ no⌈zoku** ⟨〜を⟩のぞく ① **[for s.o. to take a look at s.o./s.t./s.a. furtively, often, through a small hole/a narrow slit]** **⟪peep, snoop⟫**

EX. The boy peeked at the sunbathing girl through a small window.
男の子が小さい窓から日光浴をしている少女をのぞいた。
Otoko-no-ko ga chiisai mado kara nikkoo-yoku o shite iru shoojo o nozoita.

peel vt. **[to strip away the surface layer of s.t.]**
⟨-o⟩ mu⌈ku ⟨〜を⟩むく ① **[for s.o. to strip away the surface layer of s.t. and expose the contents]** **⟪pare, rind, shuck, hull, skin⟫**, **⟨-o⟩ ha⌈ga⌉su** ⟨〜を⟩はがす ① **[for s.o./s.a. to strip away s.t. thin that is firmly attached to the surface of s.t.]** **⟪strip off, rip off⟫**

EX. (**a**) Peel this apple for me, mom.
お母さん、このりんご、{むいて/*はがして}。
*O-kaa-san, kono ringo {muite/*hagashite}.*
(**b**) Oops, I put on the wrong stamp. Could you peel it off for me?
あっ、間違った切手をはっちゃった。{はがして/*むいて}くれる?
*A, machigatta kitte o hatchatta. {Hagashite/*Muite} kureru?*
(**c**) Don't peel the bark off the tree.
木の樹皮を{はがさない/*むかない}で下さい。
*Ki no juhi o {hagasanai/*mukanai} de kudasai.*

NOTE: *Hagasu* focuses on what is peeled off, whereas *muku* focuses on what is exposed after peeling.

peer n. **[one's equal, usu. in age or social standing]**
na⌈kama⌉ 仲間 **[a person in one's in-group with whom one frequently spends time, excluding one's relatives, spouse, and offspring ⟪fig. "the same kind"⟫]** **⟪company, comrade, fellow worker⟫**, **do⌈oryoo** 同僚 •c **[a person of the same status in a place of work]** **⟪colleague, associate, co-worker⟫**

EX. (**a**) Young people may not listen to their parents but they do listen to their peers.
若い人は両親の言うことは聞かないかもしれないが、{仲間/*同僚}の言うことは聞く。
*Wakai hito wa ryooshin no iu koto wa kikanai kamoshirenai ga, {nakama/*dooryoo} no iu koto wa kiku.*
(**b**) In Japan people often go drinking together with their peers from work after working hours.
日本では会社がひけてから{同僚/仲間}同士でよく飲みに行く。
Nihon de wa kaisha ga hikete kara {dooryoo/nakama}-dooshi de yoku nomi ni iku.

pen n.
pe⌉n ペン •f

EX. A: Can I write my answers in pen?
ペンで答えを書いてもいいですか。
Pen de kotae o kaite mo ii desu ka.
B: No, please use a pencil.
いいえ、鉛筆を使ってください。
Iie, enpitsu o tsukatte kudasai.

pencil n.
e⌈npitsu 鉛筆 •c

EX. A: How much are these red pencils?
この赤い鉛筆はいくらですか。

Kono akai enpitsu wa ikura desu ka.
B: They're 150 yen apiece.
一本百五十円です。
Ip-pon hyaku-go-juu-en desu.

penguin n.
pe⌈ngin ペンギン **•f**

peninsula n.
ha⌈ntoo 半島 **•c**

EX. Kawabata's "*The Izu Dancer*" is a story of platonic love that takes place on the Izu Peninsula.
川端の『伊豆の踊り子』は伊豆半島を舞台にした清純な恋の物語です。
Kawabata no "Izu no odori-ko" wa Izu-hantoo o butai ni shita seijunna koi no monogatari desu.

Pennsylvania n.
Pe⌈nshiruba⌉nia ペンシルバニア

penny n.
pe⌉nii ペニー **•f**

pension n. **[a fixed sum of money paid by the government or a former employer to s.o. retired or disabled]**
ne⌈nkin 年金 **•c**

EX. Older people often complain that they cannot live on their pensions alone.
老人たちは年金だけでは生活出来ないとよく文句を言う。
Roojin-tachi wa nenkin dake de wa seikatsu-dekinai to yoku monku o iu.

people n. **[a group of persons (living in the same area/country)]**
1. hi⌈to⌉-bito 人々 **[a group of persons (living in the same area) ⟨w⟩] ⟪men⟫, ⟨-no⟩ hi⌈to⌉-tachi** ⟨～の⟩人たち **[a group of persons (from the same area)]**

EX. The people of the town were waiting in eager anticipation to see the President.
町の{人々/人たち}は大統領を見ようと首を長くして待っていた。
Machi no {hito-bito/hito-tachi} wa daitooryoo o miyoo to kubi o nagaku shite matte ita.

2. ko⌈kumin 国民 **•c [a group of persons belonging to the same country or a person who has citizenship in a particular country] ⟪nation, citizen⟫**

EX. (**a**) The Japanese are said to be a hardworking people.
日本人はよく働く国民だと言われています。
Nihon-jin wa yoku hataraku kokumin da to iwa-rete imasu.
(**b**) All people in this country have the right to vote.
この国の国民はだれでも選挙権がある。
Kono kuni no kokumin wa dare-demo senkyo-ken ga aru.

pepper n.
ko⌈sho⌉o こしょう

EX. Could you pass me the pepper, please?
こしょうを取ってくださいませんか。
Koshoo o totte kudasaimasen ka.

per prep. **[for each]**
ni-tsuki につき comp. prt. **[attaching to s.o./s.t./s.a. ⟪fig. "concerning," "owing to," "per"⟫], mai + counter of time** 毎+counter of time **[for every unit of time]**

EX. (**a**) How about if we pay $5 per person?
一人につき五ドル払うというのはどうでしょうか。
Hitori ni-tsuki go-doru harau to iu no wa doo deshoo ka.
(**b**) This jet flies at a speed of about 500 miles per hour.
このジェット機は毎時五百マイルぐらいの速度で飛ぶ。
Kono jetto-ki wa mai-ji go-hyaku-mairu-gurai no sokudo de tobu.

perceive vt. **[for s.o./s.a. to become aware of s.t. through the senses ⟨fml⟩]**
⟨-ni⟩ ki-⌈ga-tsu⌉ku ⟨～に⟩気がつく ① **[for s.o./s.a. to become aware of s.t./s.o./s.a.] ⟪notice, realize, find⟫**

EX. (**a**) I perceived a subtle change in our daughter's behavior.
私は娘の行動の微妙な変化に気がついた。
Watashi wa musume no koodoo no bimyoona henka ni ki-ga-tsuita.
(**b**) I didn't perceive any difference between the two arguments.

私はその二つの主張の違いに全然気がつかなかった。
Watashi wa sono futatsu no shuchoo no chigai ni zenzen ki-ga-tsukanakatta.

percent n.
pa⌈ase⌉nto パーセント •f
EX. (**a**) One half equals 50 percent.
二分の一は50パーセントです。
Ni-bun no ichi wa go-jup-paasento desu.
(**b**) Airplanes are said to be 99.999 percent safe.
飛行機は99.999パーセント安全だそうです。
Hikoo-ki wa kyuu-juu-kyuu-ten-kyuu-kyuu-kyuu-paasento anzen da soodesu.

percentage n. **[a rate or proportion expressed in terms of number of parts per hundred]**
ri⌉tsu 率 •c **《rate, probability》**
EX. The percentage of unemployed people in Japan is much lower than in Europe and America.
日本の失業率は欧米よりずっと低い。
Nihon no shitsugyoo-ritsu wa Oo-Bei yori zutto hikui.

perch n. **[s.t. on which a bird rests, such as a bar or branch]**
1. to⌈mari⌉-gi 止まり木 **[a bar hanging in a bird cage or aviary for a bird to rest on 《fig. "tall stool at the bar"》] 《roost》**
EX. The canary was asleep on its perch.
カナリアが止まり木で眠っていた。
Kanaria ga tomari-gi de nemutte ita.
2. ya⌈sumi-basho 休み場所 **[a place for s.o./s.a. to rest]**
— vi. **[for s.a. to rest on a perch]**
⟨ni⟩ to⌈maru ⟨〜に⟩とまる ① **[for s.t./s.o./s.a. moving to come to a standstill in a certain place 《fig. "lodge"》] 《stop, halt, stand still》**
㊥ "stay at a place of lodging" ▷泊まる, otherwise ▷止まる
EX. Look at all the birds perched on that tree!
見てごらん。あそこの木に鳥がいっぱい止まっているよ。
Mite goran. Asoko no ki ni tori ga ippai tomatte iru yo.

perfect adj. **[having no faults and/or missing no parts]**
ka⌈nzenna 完全な adj(*na*). •c **[lacking no parts and having no faults] 《complete, whole, consummate》**, **mo⌈oshi-bun (ga) na⌉i** 申し分(が)ない adj(*i*). **[impossible to find fault with] 《faultless, ideal》**, **⟨-ni⟩ mo⌈tte-ko⌉i no N** ⟨〜に⟩持って来いのN **[to be exactly suitable for s.t.] 《ideal, suitable, right》**
EX. (**a**) No one is perfect.
{完全な/申し分のない/??持って来いの}人なんていない。
{Kanzenna/Mooshi-bun-no-nai/??Motte-koi no} hito nante inai.
(**b**) Today's weather is perfect for tennis.
今日はテニスには{申し分のない/持って来いの/*完全な}天気です。
*Kyoo wa tenisu ni wa {mooshi-bun-no-nai/motte-koi no/*kanzenna} tenki desu.*
— vt. **[for s.o. to cause s.t./s.o. to become perfect]**
⟨-o⟩ ka⌈nsei-suru ⟨〜を⟩完成する ③ •c **[for s.o. to bring s.t. to a finished/perfect state] 《accomplish, complete, finish》**, **⟨-o⟩ ka⌈nzenna mono⌉ ni suru** ⟨〜を⟩完全なものにする ③ **[for s.o. to cause s.t. to become perfect]**
EX. (**a**) Kristina went to France for a year of study in order to perfect her French.
クリスティーナは自分のフランス語を{完全なものにする/*完成する}ために一年間フランスへ留学した。
*Kurisutiina wa jibun no Furansu-go o {kannzenna mono ni suru/*kansei-suru} tame ni ichi-nenkan Furansu e ryuugaku-shita.*
(**b**) It took me two years to perfect this computer program.
このコンピューターのプログラムを{完成する/完全なものにする}のに二年かかった。
Kono konpyuutaa no puroguramu o {kansei-suru/kanzenna mono ni suru} no ni ni-nen kakatta.

perfection n. **[the process of making perfect or state of being perfect]**
ka⌈nsei 完成 •c [the act of bringing s.t. to a perfectly finished state or the state of being perfectly finished] ⟪**completion, accomplishment**⟫, **ka⌈npeki 完ぺき •c [the state of being totally free from flaws or blemishes]** ⟪**flawlessness, completeness**⟫, **ju⌈kutatsu 熟達 •c [the state of having acquired mastery in a skill]** ⟪**proficiency, mastery**⟫

P

EX. (**a**) The perfection of this satellite communication system took over twenty years.
この衛星通信網の{完成/*完ぺき/*熟達}に二十年以上かかった。
*Kono eisei-tsuushin-moo no {kansei/*kanpeki/*jukutatsu} ni ni-juu-nen-ijoo kakatta.*
(**b**) A person who cannot accept anything short of perfection is called a perfectionist.
{完ぺき/*完成/*熟達}でなければ何事も認めない人を完ぺき主義者という。
*{Kanpeki/*Kansei/*Jukutatsu} denakereba nani-goto mo mitomenai hito o kanpeki-shugi-sha to iu.*
(**c**) The perfection of one's ability in a foreign language requires actually living in that country.
外国語の{熟達/*完成/*完ぺき}にはその国で実際に生活することが必要だ。
*Gaikoku-go no {jukutatsu/*kansei/*kanpeki} ni wa sono kuni de jissai ni seikatsu-suru koto ga hitsuyoo da.*

perfectionist n.
ka⌈npeki-shugi⌉-sha 完ぺき主義者 •c

perfectly adv. **[in a perfect way]**
ka⌈nzenni 完全に /⟨adj(*na*). *ni* of *kanzenna* perfect/ •c [in a way absolutely free from imperfections/weaknesses] ⟪**thoroughly, completely, entirely**⟫, **ka⌈npekini 完ぺきに /⟨adj(*na*). *ni* of *kanpekina* flawless/ •c [in a way absolutely free from any imperfections/weaknesses]** ⟪**flawlessly, impeccably**⟫

EX. (**a**) The pitcher hasn't perfectly recovered yet from his elbow injury.
ピッチャーの痛めたひじはまだ{完全に/完ぺきに}は直っていない。
Pitchaa no itameta hiji wa mada {kanzenni/kanpekini} wa naotte inai.
(**b**) Whatever she cooks, she does it perfectly.
彼女は何を料理しても{完ぺきに/*完全に}料理します。
*Kanojo wa nani o ryoori-shite mo {kanpekini/*kanzenni} ryoori-shimasu.*

perform vt. **[for s.o. to carry out an action or to do s.t. in public that requires musical or dramatic skill]**
⟨-o⟩ o⌈konau ⟨〜を⟩行う ① [for s.o. to carry out s.t. as a duty/custom/profession (but not as a dramatic presentation) ⟨fml⟩] ⟪**behave, act, do, conduct, practice, hold, carry out**⟫, **⟨-o⟩ su⌈ru ⟨〜を⟩する ③ [for s.o./s.a. to conduct an action willfully; for s.o./s.a./s.t. to cause s.t. to take on a different state; for s.t. to happen in such a way as to be perceptible to s.o./s.a.; for s.t. to be in a certain state or possess a certain attribute; for an amount of time/money to pass/be required; for some proposition to be posited as true ⟪fig. "put on a somewhat small, ornamental object"⟫]** ⟪**do, make, play**⟫, **⟨-o⟩ e⌈njiru ⟨〜を⟩演じる ② •c [for s.o. to make a public presentation requiring professional skill in drama, music, etc.]** ⟪**play, act, render, stage, put on**⟫, **⟨-o⟩ e⌈nsoo-suru ⟨〜を⟩演奏する ③ •c [for s.o. to play a musical instrument ⟨fml⟩]** ⟪**play, give a recital**⟫

EX. (**a**) The college plans to perform this year's graduation ceremonies outdoors weather permitting.
大学は天気さえよければ今年の卒業式を外で{行う/する/*演じる/*演奏する}予定です。
*Daigaku wa tenki sae yokereba kotoshi no sotsugyoo-shiki o soto de {okonau/suru/*enjiru/*ensoo-suru} yotei desu.*
(**b**) Who performed the role of Hamlet in last night's play?
夕べの劇でだれがハムレットの役を{し

ました/演じました/*行いました/*演奏しました}か。
*Yuube no geki de dare ga Hamuretto no yaku o {shimashita/enjimashita/ *okonaimashita/*ensoo-shimashita} ka.*
(c) The doctor performed an operation on the football player's knee.
医者はフットボールの選手のひざの手術を{行った/した/*演じた/*演奏した}。
*Isha wa futto-booru no senshu no hiza no shujutsu o {okonatta/shita/*enjita/ *ensoo-shita}.*
(d)The orchestra performed Beethoven's Ninth Symphony.
オーケストラはベートーベンの第九シンフォニーを{演奏した/*行った/*した/ *演じた}。
*Ookesutora wa Beetooben no dai-ku-shinfonii o {ensoo-shita/*okonatta/ *shita/*enjita}.*

performance n. **[the act of carrying out an action or of doing s.t. in public that requires musical or dramatic skill]**
1. shi⌈goto-buri 仕事ぶり [the way one does one's work]
EX. Bill's performance at his company is good so far.
ビルの会社での仕事ぶりは今のところ上々だ。
Biru no kaisha de no shigoto-buri wa ima no tokoro joojoo da.
2. e⌉ngi 演技 •c [an act of performing by actors, athletes, acrobats, etc.] ((**acting**)), **pa⌈fo⌉omansu パフォーマンス •f [the act of pretending to do s.t. or of making an artistic presentation in public, esp. one that is avant-garde or amateur]**
EX. (a) Toshiro Mifune puts on a very dignified performance in that movie.
三船敏郎のあの映画の{演技/*パフォーマンス}は大変貫ろくがある。
*Mifune Toshiroo no ano eiga no {engi/ *pafoomansu} wa taihen kanroku ga aru.*
(b) I don't like him because he turns everything into a big performance.
あの人は大げさな{パフォーマンス/演技}が多いから嫌いだ。
Ano hito wa oogesana {pafoomansu/ engi} ga ooi kara kirai da.
3. e⌉nsoo 演奏 •c [playing a musical instrument, including conducting and voice] ((**rendition, recital**))
EX. The performance by the violinist enthralled the audience.
バイオリニストの演奏は聴衆を魅了した。
Baiorinisuto no ensoo wa chooshuu o miryoo-shita.

perfume n.
ko⌈osui 香水 •c
EX. A: What kind of perfume are you wearing?
どんな香水をつけているんだい?
Donna koosui o tsukete iru n dai?
B: Chanel No. 5.
シャネルの五番よ。
Shaneru no go-ban yo.

perhaps adv. **[an adverb indicating the speaker's belief that s.t. may possibly be the case or may possibly occur]**
hyo⌈tto shita⌉ra...(ka⌉moshirenai) ひょっとしたら…(かもしれない) [a form indicating the speaker's belief in the possibility of s.t. occurring, with a probability of 5-10%] ((**possibly**)), **ko⌈to-ni-yotta⌉ra... (ka⌉moshirenai) ことによったら…(かもしれない)** ((**possibly, probably**)), **...ka⌉moshirenai …かもしれない [a form indicating the speaker's belief that s.t. will occur, with a probability of 50-50]** ((**might**))
EX. (a) Mr. Yoshida may perhaps become the next company president.
{ひょっとしたら/ことによったら}吉田さんが今度社長になるかもしれない。
{Hyotto shitara/Koto-ni-yottara} Yoshida-san ga kondo shachoo ni naru kamoshirenai.
(b) Edward may perhaps get into Harvard.
エドワードは{ひょっとしたら/ことによったら}ハーバードに入るかもしれない。
Edowaado wa {hyotto shitara/koto-ni-yottara} Haabaado ni hairu kamoshirenai.

P

period n. **[a length of time, esp. one with particular characteristics or a point used as a punctuation mark indicating the end of a sentence or the time during which menstruation occurs]**

1. ki⌈ka⌉n 期間 •c [a specific time span in which s.t. noteworthy occurs] ⟪term⟫

EX. (**a**) This project will require a preparatory period of at least two years.
この計画は少なくとも二年の準備期間がいる。
Kono keikaku wa sukunaku-tomo ni-nen no junbi-kikan ga iru.
(**b**) The final examination period at this school goes on for three weeks.
この学校では期末試験期間は三週間も続きます。
Kono gakkoo de wa kimatsu-shiken-kikan wa san-shuukan mo tsuzukimasu.

2. ji⌈dai 時代 •c [a subinterval on the continuum of past, present, and future designated for some historical purpose] ⟪age⟫

EX. (**a**) The period in which this story takes places is the Edo Period.
この話の時代は江戸時代です。
Kono hanashi no jidai wa Edo-jidai desu.
(**b**) The Vietnam War marks one of the darkest periods of American history.
ベトナム戦争時代はアメリカ史の一番暗い時代の一つだ。
Betonamu-sensoo-jidai wa Amerika-shi no ichiban kurai jidai no hitotsu da.

3. shu⌈ushi⌉-fu 終止符 •c [a point indicating the end of a sentence in romanized Japanese and most Indo-European languages] ⟪a full stop⟫, pi⌉riodo ピリオド •f [a point indicating the end of a sentence in romanized Japanese and most Indo-European languages] ⟪a full stop⟫

4. se⌉iri (no ki⌈ka⌉n) 生理(の期間) •c [the time during which menstruation occurs]

permanent adj. **[lasting indefinitely]**
e⌈ikyuu no N 永久のN •c ⟪eternal, everlasting⟫, fu⌈hen no N 不変のN •c [not changing ⟨w⟩] ⟪unchangeable, invariable⟫

EX. Is anything permanent in this world?
この世に{永久/不変}の物があるだろうか。
Kono yo ni {eikyuu/fuhen} no mono ga aru daroo ka.

PHRASE: permanent address *honseki* 本籍 •c, permanent residence *eijuu* 永住 •c

EX. Do you desire permanent residence in the U.S.A.?
アメリカ永住を希望しますか。
Amerika-eijuu o kiboo-shimasu ka.

PHRASE: permanent (wave) *paama(nento)* パーマ(ネント)

EX. Sally's blonde hair looks gorgeous with the permanent.
サリーの金髪はパーマがかかってすばらしくきれいだ。
Sarii no kinpatsu wa paama ga kakatte subarashiku kirei da.

permanently adv. **[in an indefinitely lasting way]**
e⌈ikyuu ni 永久に n.+prt. **⟪eternally, perpetually⟫**

EX. Nothing remains permanently the same.
永久に変わらないものはない。
Eikyuu ni kawaranai mono wa nai.

permission n. **[consent to do s.t. from s.o. in a position of authority]**
yu⌈rushi⌉ 許し /⟨V*masu* of *yurusu* ① permit/ [an act of removing a restriction] ⟪leave, sanction, approval, pardon, forgiveness⟫, kyo⌉ka 許可 •c [an act of allowing s.o. to do s.t. he/she wants to do] ⟪leave, approval, sanction, license⟫

EX. Professor Suzuki gave me permission to take the final examination two days earlier than the scheduled date.
鈴木先生は期末試験を予定より二日早く受ける{許可/許し}を下さった。
Suzuki-sensei wa kimatsu-shiken o yotei yori futsuka hayaku ukeru {kyoka/yurushi} o kudasatta.

permit vt. **[for s.o. to allow s.o. to do s.t or some situation to take place]**
(⟨-ni⟩) ⟨-o⟩ **yu⌈ru⌉su** (⟨〜に⟩)⟨〜を⟩許す ①

[for s.o. to allow s.o. else to do s.t. freely《fig. "forgive"》]《**permit, allow, approve, trust, confide in, forgive**》, (⟨-ni⟩) ⟨-o⟩ **kyo˥ka-suru** (⟨～に⟩)⟨～を⟩許可する ③ •c **[for s.o. in authority to formally allow s.o. to do s.t. he/she wants to do]**《**sanction, approve, license, admit**》, {**Vneg. + seru/Vcond. + saseru/ko-˥sase˥ru/sa˥seru**} {**Vneg.+せる/Vcond.+させる/来させる/させる**}《**to let s.o. do s.t.**》

EX.| The university administrators would not permit the students to participate in the demonstration.
大学当局は学生{にデモに参加させなかった/がデモに参加することを{許可しなかった/許さなかった}}。
Daigaku-tookyoku wa gakusei {ni demo ni sanka-sasenakatta/ga demo ni sanka-suru koto o {kyoka-shinakatta/yurusanakatta}}.

— n. **[a document showing that permission has been given to do s.t.]** **kyo˥ka˥-shoo** 許可証 •c **[a document showing that permission has been given to do s.t.]**《**license**》

EX.| Do you have a permit for parking your car here?
駐車の許可証を持っていますか。
Chuusha no kyoka-shoo o motte imasu ka.

perpendicular adj. **[intersecting with s.t. at a right angle or standing vertically]** **su˥ichoku no N** 垂直のN •c

Persia n.
Pe˥rusha ペルシア •f
NOTE: Persia is usually written as ペルシア but pronounced as *Perusha.*

persimmon n.
ka˥ki かき

persist vi. **[for s.o. to continue to do s.t. firmly or obstinately or for s.t. to continue to exist longer than expected]**
1. V*masu* tsuzukeru V*masu*続ける ② [to coninue to do s.t.]《**continue, keep up, go on**》

EX.| Yamamoto persisted in smoking despite his doctor's warning.
山本は医者の警告にもかかわらずたばこを吸い続けた。
Yamamoto wa isha no keikoku nimo-kakawarazu tabako o sui-tsuzuketa.

2. ⟨-to⟩ **i˥i-ha˥ru** ⟨～と⟩言い張る ① **[for s.o. to keep saying s.t. firmly in the face of doubt or opposition]**《**insist, assert, maintain, claim**》, {⟨-to⟩/⟨-o⟩} **shu˥choo-suru** {⟨～と⟩/⟨～を⟩}主張する ③ •c **[for s.o. to state one's opinion firmly with a view to making others agree with it or accept it]**《**insist on, assert, maintain, claim, contend**》

EX.| The man persisted in his claim that he knew nothing of the incident.
男はその事件について何も知らないと{言い張った/主張した}。
Otoko wa sono jiken ni-tsuite nani-mo shiranai to {ii-hatta/shuchoo-shita}.

3. i˥jooni na˥gaku tsu˥zuku 異常に長く続く ① **[for s.t to continue for an unusually long time]**

EX.| If your cough persists, you'd better see a doctor.
せきが異常に長く続くようだったら、医者に見てもらった方がいいですよ。
Seki ga ijooni nagaku tsuzuku yoo dattara, isha ni mite moratta hoo ga ii desu yo.

persistent adj. **[continuing firmly or obstinately or lasting longer than expected]** **ko˥nki-zuyo˥i** 根気強い adj(*i*). **[continuing at s.t. with a strong, unflagging spirit]**《**indomitable, unfailing**》, **ga˥nkona** 頑固な adj(*na*). •c **[firmly refusing to change one's ideas/attitudes《fig. "for a disease to continue longer than expected"》]**《**obstinate, stubborn, hard-nosed**》, **shi˥tsuko˥i** しつこい adj(*i*). **[for s.t. undesirable such as an illness, taste, or way of behaving to continue longer than expected or desired]**《**tenacious, obstinate, importunate, heavy, oily**》

EX.| (**a**) A: What kind of person was your father?
お父さんはどんな人でしたか。

O-too-san wa donna hito deshita ka.
B: My father was a persistent man.
父は{根気強い/頑固な/*しつこい}人でした。
*Chichi wa {konki-zuyoi/gankona/ *shitsukoi} hito deshita.*
(**b**) I had a persistent headache and went to see the doctor.
{しつこい/*頑固な/*根気強い}頭痛のため、医者に行った。
*{Shitsukoi/*Gankona/*Konki-zuyoi} zutsuu no tame, isha ni itta.*
(**c**) I don't like him because he's so persistent.
彼はあまりにも{しつこい/頑固だ/*根気強い}から嫌いだ。
*Kare wa amari-ni mo {shitsukoi/ ganko da/*konki-zuyoi} kara kirai da.*

person n. **[an individual human being or a living body of the same or a grammatical category for disinguishing the speaker hearer, and s.o. spoken about]**
1. hi⌈to 人 [a generic term for homo sapiens or a collective noun for people other than oneself or an individual's characteristics] ⟪people, other people, others⟫, hi⌈to-gara 人柄 [an individual's good characteristics] ⟪personal character, personality⟫
EX. (**a**) At the time of the incident there were about fifty persons in the restaurant.
事故の時レストランには五十人ぐらいの{人/*人柄}がいた。
*Jiko no toki resutoran ni wa go-juu-nin-gurai no {hito/*hito-gara} ga ita.*
(**b**) I like a cheerful person.
明るい{人/人柄}が好きです。
Akarui {hito/hito-gara} ga suki desu.
2. ni⌈nshoo 人称 •c [a grammatical category for distinguishing the speaker, hearer and s.o. spoken about]
EX. In Japanese there are many first and second person pronouns.
日本語には一人称と二人称の代名詞がたくさんある。
Nihon-go ni wa ichi-ninshoo to ni-ninshoo no dai-meishi ga takusan aru.

personal adj. **[relating to a particular individual]**
1. ko⌉jin no N 個人のN •c [of an individual]
EX. In Japan it is sometimes difficult to express one's personal views.
日本では個人の意見が言いにくい場合がある。
Nihon de wa kojin no iken ga ii-nikui baai ga aru.
2. mi⌈jikana 身近な adj(*na*). **[close to oneself] ⟪familiar, near oneself⟫, ko⌈jin-tekina 個人的な** adj(*na*). **•c [relating to an individual] ⟪individual, private⟫**
EX. The Japanese seem to love to write about personal matters.
日本人は{身近な/個人的な}ことを書くのが好きなようだ。
Nihon-jin wa {mijikana/kojin-tekina} koto o kaku no ga sukina yoo da.
3. ta⌈chi-itta N 立ち入ったN /⟨Vinf. past of *tachi-iru* ① enter/ [entering s.o. else's territory ⟪fig. "prying into s.o.'s intimate affairs"⟫]
EX. May I ask you something personal?
立ち入ったことをお聞きしたいんですが。
Tachi-itta koto o o-kiki-shi-tai n desu ga.
PHRASE: personal history *rireki* 履歴 **•c**
EX. My personal history proved unfavorable in finding a new job.
私の履歴は新しい仕事を探すのに不利だった。
Watashi no rireki wa atarashii shigoto o sagasu no ni furi datta.

personality n. **[an individual's characteristics or a celebrity]**
1. hi⌈to-gara 人柄 [an individual's good characteristics] ⟪personal chararacter⟫, se⌈ikaku 性格 •c [the characteristics/nature of s.o./s.t./s.a.] ⟪characteristics, nature⟫, pa⌈asona⌉ritii パーソナリティ •f [one's personal characteristics or a celebrity]
EX. Personality has a lot to do with one's success in society.
{人柄/性格/パーソナリティ}は社会で

の成功と大いに関係がある。
{Hito-gara/Seikaku/Paasonaritii} wa shakai de no seikoo to ooi-ni kankei ga aru.

2. me˥ishi 名士 •c [a famous person noted for having certain talents] ⟪a man of distinction, a noted person, celebrity⟫, pa˥asona˥ritii パーソナリティ •f [one's personal characteristics or celebrity]

EX. This is a restaurant frequented by show business personalities.
ここは芸能界の{名士/パーソナリティ}がよく来るレストランです。
Koko wa geinoo-kai no {meishi/paasonaritii} ga yoku kuru resutoran desu.

personnel n. **[the group of people employed at a company/office]**
sho˥ku˥in 職員 •c [a person employed at an office/school/company to assist in administrative work] ⟪the staff⟫

EX. All personnel have to show their ID cards to enter this building.
この建物に入るには職員は全員、身分証明書を見せなければならない。
Kono tatemono ni hairu ni wa shokuin wa zen'in, mibun-shoomei-sho o misenakereba naranai.

PHRASE: personnel office *jinji-ka* 人事課 •c

EX. If you're looking for job openings, please go to the personnel office.
仕事の空きを探していらっしゃるんでしたら、人事課へいらして下さい。
Shigoto no aki o sagashite irassharu n deshitara, jinji-ka e irashite kudasai.

perspiration n. **[moisture given off through the pores of the skin]**
1. a˥se 汗 [moisture given off through the pores of the skin]

EX. Genius is said to be 99% perspiration and 1% inspiration.
天才は99パーセントの汗と1パーセントのひらめきだと言われる。
Tensai wa kyuu-juu-kyuu-paasento no ase to ichi-paasento no hirameki da to iwa-reru.

2. ha˥kkan 発汗 •c [the process of moisture being given off through the pores of the skin ⟨fml⟩]

EX. Medical treatment is sometimes required to stop abnormal perspiration during sleep.
睡眠中の異常な発汗を止めるには医者に診てもらう必要がある場合もある。
Suimin-chuu no ijoona hakkan o tomeru ni wa isha ni mite morau hitsuyoo ga aru baai mo aru.

perspire vi. **[for s.o./s.a. to give off moisture throuth the pores of the skin ⟨fml⟩]**
a˥se o ka˥ku 汗をかく ① [for s.o./s.a. to give off (salty) moisture through the pores of the skin], a˥se ga de˥ru 汗が出る ② [for moisture to exude spontaneously from pores in the skin], ha˥kkan-suru 発汗する •c [for moisture to exude spontaneously from pores in the skin ⟨fml⟩]

EX. (**a**) The old man perspired greatly as he labored up the mountain.
老人は汗をたらたらかきながら懸命に山を登った。
Roojin wa ase o tara-tara kaki nagara kenmeini yama o nobotta.
(**b**) Taking aspirin can cause one to perspire.
アスピリンを飲むと、{汗をかく/汗が出る/発汗する}ことがある。
Asupirin o nomu to, {ase o kaku/ase ga deru/hakkan suru} koto ga aru.
(**c**) He's never known what it is to perspire from hard work.
彼は{汗をかいて/*汗が出て/*発汗して}働いたことがない。
*Kare wa {ase o kaite/*ase ga dete/*hakkan-shite} hataraita koto ga nai.*

persuade vt. **[for s.o. to cause s.o. to believe or do s.t. by means of argument or entreaty]**
⟨-o⟩ se˥ttoku-suru ⟨～を⟩説得する ③ •c [for s.o. to prevail upon s.o. to do s.t.] ⟪prevail on, talk a person into compliance⟫ ⟨-o⟩ se˥ttoku-shite causative of V ⟨～を⟩説得して causative of V ② [for s.o. to cause s.o. to agree to do s.t.]

EX. (**a**) Mary persuaded Bill to study Japanese.

P

メアリーはビルを説得して日本語を勉強させた。
Mearii wa Biru o settoku-shite Nihon-go o benkyoo-saseta.
(**b**) I was persuaded by my boss to accept a transfer to our London office.
私は上司に説得されてロンドンに転勤した。
Watashi wa jooshi ni settoku-sarete Rondon ni tenkin-shita.

pet n. **[an animal kept for companionship]**
pe˥tto ペット **•f, a˹igan-do˥obutsu** 愛がん動物 **•c**
EX. I keep a dog for a pet.
私は{ペット/愛玩動物}として犬を飼っています。
Watashi wa {petto/aigan-doobutsu} to-shite inu o katte imasu.

petal n.
ha˹nabira˥ 花びら
EX. The cherry blossom petals scattered on the ground looked almost like snow.
地面に散っている桜の花びらはまるで雪のようだった。
Jimen ni chitte iru sakura no hanabira wa marude yuki no yoodatta.

petition n. **[a formal request made to an authority or a document bearing such a request, esp. one signed by many people]**
1. mo˹oshi-tate 申し立て **/⟨V*masu* of *mooshi-tateru* ② state/ [the act of imploring s.o. in authority to give s.o. special consideration or treatment] ⟪statement, declaration⟫, kyo˹ka-ne˥gai** 許可願い **[an act of asking persmission], se˹igan** 請願 **•c [the act of making a formal request to a public authority ⟨fml⟩] ⟪application⟫, ta˹ngan** 嘆願 **•c [the act of strongly imploring s.o. in authority to do s.t. special for one] ⟪entreaty, supplication, appeal⟫**
EX. (**a**) The petition to the governor to stay the execution has been denied.
知事への、死刑執行中止の{申し立て/請願/嘆願/*許可願い}は却下された。
*Chiji e no, shikei-shikkoo-chuushi no {mooshi-tate/seigan/tangan/*kyoka-negai} wa kyakka-sareta.*
(**b**) I made a petition to be allowed to drop the course after the deadline had passed.
締め切りの後で科目を取り消す{{申し立て/*請願/*嘆願}をした/許可願いを出した}。
*Shime-kiri no ato de kamoku o tori-kesu {{mooshi-tate/*seigan/*tangan} o shita/kyoka-negai o dashita}.*
2. mo˹oshi-tate-sho 申し立て書 **[a written request to an authority that special consideration or treatment be given to one], kyo˹ka-negai(-sho)** 許可願い(書) **[a form by which a request for permission is made in writing], se˹igan-sho** 請願書 **•c [a form by which a request is made in writing to a public authority], ta˹ngan-sho** 嘆願書 **•c [a written document strongly imploring s.o. in authority to do s.t. special for one]**
— vt. **[for s.o. to make a formal request to an authority]**
⟨-ni⟩ ⟨-o⟩ mo˹oshi-de˥ru ⟨〜に⟩⟨〜を⟩申し出る ② **[for s.o. to propose s.t. to s.o.] ⟪suggest, offer, apply for⟫, ⟨-ni⟩ ⟨-o⟩ mo˹oshi-tateru** ⟨〜に⟩⟨〜を⟩申し立てる ② **[for s.o. to formally ask some authority to give s.o. special consideration or treatment] ⟪state, declare⟫, ⟨-ni⟩ ⟨-o⟩ se˹igan-suru** ⟨〜に⟩⟨〜を⟩請願する ③ **•c [for a citizen to make a formal request to a public authority ⟨fml⟩] ⟪submit a petition to⟫, ⟨-ni⟩ ⟨-o⟩ ta˹ngan-suru** ⟨〜に⟩⟨〜を⟩嘆願する ③ **•c [for s.o. to strongly implore s.o. in authority to do s.t. special for one] ⟪entreat, supplicate⟫**
EX. (**a**) I have petitioned the department to waive my foreign language requirement.
私は学科に外国語必修の免除を{申し出た/??申し立てた/*請願した/*嘆願した}。
*Watashi wa gakka ni gaikoku-go-hisshuu no menjo o {mooshi-deta/??mooshi-tateta/*seigan-shita/*tangan-shita}.*
(**b**) The condemned criminal petitioned the Ministry of Justice for postponement of his execution.
死刑囚は法務省に死刑執行の延期を{申

し立てた/請願した/嘆願した/?申し出た}。
Shikei-shuu wa Hoomu-shoo ni shikei-shikkoo no enki o {mooshi-tateta/seigan-shita/tangan-shita/?mooshi-deta}.

petrol (Br. E) n.
ga⌈sorin ガソリン •f ((gasoline))

petroleum n.
se⌈kiyu 石油 •c ((kerosene, oil))

EX. Whenever the price of petroleum rises, inflation rises as well.
石油の値段が上がれば、インフレもひどくなる。
Sekiyu no nedan ga agareba, infure mo hidoku naru.

pharmacist n.
ya⌈kuza⌉i-shi 薬剤師 •c ((chemist))

pharmacy n. **[the art or practice of preparing drugs or a place where prescribed drugs are sold]**
1. cho⌉ozai 調剤 •c [the art or practice of preparing drugs]
2. ku⌈suri-ya 薬屋 [a place where drugs are sold] ((drugstore, chemist's)), ya⌈kkyoku 薬局 •c [a place where drugs are sold] ((drugstore, chemist's))

EX. (**a**) Is there a pharmacy around here?
この辺に{薬局/薬屋}はありますか。
Kono hen ni {yakkyoku/kusuri-ya} wa arimasu ka.
(**b**) At a Japanese pharmacy you can buy many kinds of drug without a prescription.
日本の{薬局/薬屋}ではいろいろな薬が処方せんなしに買える。
Nihon no {yakkyoku/kusuri-ya} de wa iroirona kusuri ga shohoo-sen-nashi ni kae-ru.

phase n. **[a stage in the change or development of s.t.]**
me⌉n 面 •c [any of the flat surfaces of an object ((fig. "a covering for the face used in fencing, theater, etc.," "a page of a newspaper"))] ((face, mask, facet, aspect)), kyo⌈kume⌉n 局面 •c [one of a number of different appearances to a situation depending on one's vantage point in space or time] ((aspect, situation))

EX. (**a**) I believe we're seeing only one phase of the problem.
我々はこの問題の一{面/?局面}しか見ていないように思う。
Ware-ware wa kono mondai no ichi-{men/?kyokumen} shika mite inai yooni omou.
(**b**) Japan's economy has reached a critical phase of development.
日本経済の発展は重要な{局面/*面}に達した。
*Nihon-keizai no hatten wa juuyoona {kyokumen/*men} ni tasshita.*

phenomenon n. **[a fact or event that can be perceived by any of the senses or by the mind]**
ge⌈nshoo 現象 •c ((appearance, happening)), ji⌈shoo 事象 •c [things and events] ((matter, event))

EX. (**a**) Political conservatism seems to be a worldwide phenomenon these days.
政治的保守性は近ごろ世界的な{現象/*事象}のようだ。
*Seiji-teki-hoshu-sei wa chikagoro sekai-tekina {genshoo/*jishoo} no yooda.*
(**b**) Among all the phenomena that we experience as human beings the most mysterious is the birth of a new life.
人間が体験するすべての{現象/事象}の中で新しい生命の誕生が一番神秘的だ。
Ningen ga taiken-suru subete no {genshoo/jishoo} no naka de atarashii seimei no tanjoo ga ichiban shinpi-teki da.

Philadelphia n.
Fi⌈raderufi⌉a フィラデルフィア •f

philosophy n. **[the study by means of logical reasoning of the fundamental nature of knowledge, reality, and morality or one's personal views or beliefs on life and the world]**
1. te⌈tsu⌉gaku 哲学 •c [the branch of learning concerned with logical inquiry into fundamental issues of reality and human existence or one's personal views on life and the world deriving from experience],

P

se⌈ka⌉i-kan 世界観 •c **[one's view of the world]** ((Weltanshauung)), ji⌈nse⌉i-kan 人生観 •c **[one's view on life]** ((outlook on life))

EX. (**a**) A: What are you majoring in?
専攻は何ですか。
Senkoo wa nan desu ka.
B: I'm majoring in Western philosophy.
西洋{哲学/*世界観/*人生観}を専攻しています。
*Seiyoo-{tetsugaku/*sekai-kan/*jinsei-kan} o senkoo-shite imasu.*
(**b**) He has a fascinating philosophy of life.
あの人は面白い{人生観/世界観/*哲学}を持っています。
*Ano hito wa omoshiroi {jinsei-kan/sekai-kan/*tetsugaku} o motte imasu.*

2. ka⌈ngae-kata⌉ 考え方 /(V*masu* of *kangaeru* ② think + suf. *kata* way/ [the way one thinks/believes] ((one's point of view)), **mi-⌈kata⌉ 見方 /(V*masu* of *miru* ② + suf. *kata* way/ [a way/manner of looking at s.t.]** ((outlook, viewpoint))

EX. (**a**) My philosophy on issues like this is clearly different from yours.
このような問題に関する私の{考え方/見方}はあなたのと明らかに違います。
Kono yoona mondai ni-kansuru watashi no {kangae-kata/mi-kata} wa anata no to akirakani chigaimasu.
(**b**) I like a philosophy that emphasizes the brighter side of things.
私は物事の明るい面を強調する{考え方/見方}が好きだ。
Watashi wa mono-goto no akarui men o kyoochoo-suru {kangae-kata/mi-kata} ga suki da.

phone n. **[an abbreviated form for telephone or earphone]**
de⌈nwa 電話 •c [an apparatus for transmitting speech to a distant hearer or an act of making contact with s.o. by means of such an apparatus]

EX. (**a**) Is there a phone around here?
この辺に電話がありますか。
Kono hen ni denwa ga arimasu ka.
(**c**) A: What is your office phone number?
勤め先の電話番号は何番ですか。
Tsutome-saki no denwa-bangoo wa nan-ban desu ka.
B: It's 495-5380.
495の5380です。
Yon-kyuu-go(o) no go(o)-san-hachi-zero desu.

NOTE: In pronouncing a telephone number, the numerals 2 and 5, both of which normally have a short vowel, are pronounced with a long vowel as *nii* and *goo*.

— vt.
⟨-ni⟩ de⌈nwa o ka⌈ke⌉ru ⟨〜に⟩電話をかける ② [for s.o. to call s.o. by telephone], ⟨-ni⟩ de⌈nwa-suru ⟨〜に⟩電話する ③ •c [for s.o. to make a contact with s.o. by telephone] ((call, ring, telephone))

EX. (**a**) Can I phone you at home tonight?
今晩ご自宅に{電話して/電話をかけて}もいいですか。
Konban go-jitaku ni {denwa-shite/denwa o kakete} mo ii desu ka.
(**b**) I tried phoning him but he wasn't there.
彼に電話{してみました/をかけてみました}が、いませんでした。
Kare ni denwa {-shite mimashita/o kakete mimashita} ga, imasendeshita.

phonetic adj. **[having to do with the physical properties of human speech or the study of the same]**
1. o⌉nsei no N 音声のN •c [of speech sounds]

EX. *Hiragana* is a phonetic alphabet.
平仮名は一種の音声(の)記号です。
Hira-gana wa isshu no onsei (no) kigoo desu.

2. o⌈nse⌉i-gaku no N 音声学のN •c [having to do with the study of the physical properties of human speech]

phonetics n. **[the study of the physical properties of human speech]**
o⌈nse⌉i-gaku 音声学 •c

photo n. **[an abbreviated form for photograph]**
sha⌈shin 写真 •c ((picture))

EX. (**a**) Where did you take this photo?

この写真はどこで撮りましたか。
Kono shashin wa doko de torimashita ka.
(**b**) The Japanese seem to like group photos, don't they?
日本人はグループ写真が好きなようですね。
Nihon-jin wa guruupu-shashin ga sukina yoo desu ne.

photograph n. **[a picture taken with a camera]**
SEE photo

— vt. **[for s.o. to take a picture with a camera]**
⟨-no⟩ sha⌈shin o to⌉ru ⟨〜の⟩写真を撮る ①

EX. I photographed many temples in Kyoto when I was there.
私は京都にいた時お寺の写真をたくさん撮りました。
Watashi wa Kyooto ni ita toki o-tera no shashin o takusan torimashita.

phrase n. **[a meaningful sequence of words]**
1. ku⌉ 句 •c [a grammatical unit consisting of two or more words《fig. "a poetic unit of 5 or 7 syllables," "haiku"》]《line, stanza, haiku》
2. mo⌉nku 文句 •c [what one says or writes (as a complaint)]《words, expression, wording, complaint》, i⌉i-kata 言い方 /⟨V*masu* of *iu* ① say + *kata* way/《way of speaking》

EX. I wasn't able to come up with the right phrase to express what I meant.
言いたいことを表現するのにちょうどいい{文句/言い方}が出て来ませんでした。
Ii-tai koto o hyoogen-suru no ni choodo ii {monku/ii-kata} ga dete kimasendeshita.

physical adj. **[pertaining to nature, the body, or the material world]**
1. shi⌈zen no N 自然のN •c [pertaining to nature]《natural》↔ jin'i no N 人為のN •c

EX. In general I like this university very much, but I don't like its physical environment.
全体的に見れば私はこの大学が好きですが、それをとりまく自然の環境は好きじゃありません。
Zentai-tekini mireba watashi wa kono daigaku ga suki desu ga, sore o tori-maku shizen no kankyoo wa suki jaarimasen.

2. ka⌈rada no N 体のN [pertaining to the body] ↔ seishin no N 精神のN •c, ni⌈kutai no N 肉体のN •c [pertaining to the body as opposed to the spirit]

EX. (**a**) A: How has your physical condition been recently?
最近は{{体/*肉体}の調子/体調}はどうですか。
*Saikin wa {{karada/*nikutai} no chooshi/taichoo} wa doo desu ka.*
B: It couldn't be better.
上々です。
Joojoo desu.
(**b**) Physical beauty is as important as spiritual beauty.
{肉体/?体}の美しさは精神の美しさと同じように大切だ。
{Nikutai/?Karada} no utsukushi-sa wa seishin no utsukushi-sa to onaji yooni taisetsu da.

3. bu⌈tsuri-tekina 物理的な •c [pertaining to a (scientific) notion of substance]

EX. Much still remains a mystery about the physical properties of light.
光の物理的な性質にはまだ分からないことが多い。
Hikari no butsuri-tekina seishitsu ni wa mada wakaranai koto ga ooi.

physical science n.
shi⌈zen-ka⌉gaku 自然科学 •c《natural science》

physician n. **[a medical doctor, esp. a doctor of internal medicine ⟨fml⟩]**
1. i⌉shi 医師 •c [s.o. whose profession it is to treat sick people ⟨fml⟩]《medical doctor》, i⌈sha 医者 •c [s.o. whose profession it is to treat sick people]《medical doctor》

EX. (**a**) Since my father is a physician, I always assumed I would become one too.
父が{医者/医師}なので私も{医者/医師}になるものとずっと思っていたんです。

Chichi ga {isha/ishi} na node watashi mo {isha/ishi} ni naru mono to zutto omotte ita n desu.
(**b**) You look so tired. You ought to see your physician.
とても疲れた顔をしていますね。{医者/*医師}に見てもらった方がいいですよ。
*Totemo tsukareta kao o shite imasu ne. {Isha/*Ishi} ni mite moratta hoo ga ii desu yo.*

2. na⌈ika⌉-i 内科医 •c [a doctor of internal medicine] ↔ geka-i 外科医 •c

P

physicist n. **[a specialist in physics]**
bu⌈tsuri-ga⌉kusha 物理学者 •c

physics n. **[the science of matter and energy; the properties of matter and energy]**

1. bu⌈tsuri⌉(-gaku) 物理(学) •c [the science of matter and energy]

EX. A: What are you majoring in?
専攻は何ですか。
Senkoo wa nan desu ka.
B: Physics.
物理(学)です。
Butsuri(-gaku) desu.

2. bu⌈ssei 物性 •c [the properties of matter] 《physical properties》

piano n.
pi⌈ano ピアノ •f

EX. (**a**) Do you play the piano?
ピアノを弾きますか。
Piano o hikimasu ka.
(**b**) You play the piano very well.
ピアノがとてもお上手ですね。
Piano ga totemo o-joozu desu ne.

pick vt. **[to remove s.t. from an object to which it is firmly attached using the fingers or s.t. pointed 《fig. "choose"》]**

1. ⟨-o⟩ tsu⌈(t)tsu⌉ku ⟨〜を⟩突(っ)つく ① [for s.o./s.a. to push at s.t. lightly or repeatedly with a pointed object] 《poke, peck》

EX. Don't pick at the cake with your fingers.
指でケーキを突(っ)ついちゃいけませんよ。
Yubi de keeki o tsu(t)tsuicha ikemasen yo.

NOTE: *Tsuttsuku* is more emphatic and colloquial than *tsutsuku.*

2. ⟨-o⟩ ho⌈ji⌉ru ⟨〜を⟩ほじる ① [for s.o. to dig up s.t. with a pointed object 《fig. "pry into"》 ⟨s⟩] 《dig up, grub, pick at s.o.'s faults》, ⟨-o⟩ ho⌈jiku⌉ru ⟨〜を⟩ほじくる ①

EX. Don't pick your nose.
鼻をほじ(く)ってはいけません。
Hana o hoji(ku)tte wa ikemasen.

NOTE: *Hojikuru* is more emphatic and colloquial than *hojiru.*

3. ⟨-o⟩ nu⌈ku ⟨〜を⟩抜く ① [to remove s.t. (usually a stick- or hair-like object) from a place in which it is embedded 《fig. "outpace," "excel"》] 《remove, pull out, extract, omit, outpace》

EX. Could you pick this thorn out of my finger?
この指のとげを抜いてくれませんか。
Kono yubi no toge o nuite kuremasen ka.

4. ⟨-o⟩ tsu⌈mu ⟨〜を⟩摘む ① [for s.o. to remove s.t. such as a bud or tea leaf from a plant before it grows large, usu. with a squeezing motion of the fingers] 《pluck, pull out, trim, clip》, ⟨-o⟩ mo⌉gu ⟨〜を⟩もぐ ① [for s.o. to detach s.t. from s.t. else using a twisting motion, esp. fruit from a plant, usu. with one's fingers]

EX. (**a**) We picked apples and ate them in the orchard.
私たちは果樹園でりんごを{もいで/*摘んで}、食べた。
*Watashi-tachi wa kaju-en de ringo o {moide/*tsunde}, tabeta.*
(**b**) Tea leaves are picked in May in Japan.
五月に日本ではお茶の葉を{摘む/*もぐ}。
*Go-gatsu ni Nihon de wa o-cha no ha o {tsumu/*mogu}.*

5. ⟨-o⟩ e⌈ra⌉bu ⟨〜を⟩選ぶ ① [for s.o./s.a. to single out s.t./s.o./s.a. out of several as being the most desirable for a particular purpose] 《choose, select》

EX. (**a**) Please pick something to eat from the menu.
メニューから何か食べたいものを選んでください。

Menyuu kara nani-ka tabe-tai mono o erande kudasai.
(**b**) In 1960 the American people picked John F. Kennedy for the U.S. Presidency.
1960年にアメリカ国民はジョンF.ケネディを大統領に選んだ。
Sen-kyuu-hyaku-roku-juu-nen ni Amerika-kokumin wa Jon Efu Kenedii o daitooryoo ni eranda.

PHRASE: pick up ⟨-o⟩ *hiroi-ageru* ⟨〜を⟩拾い上げる /⟨V*masu* of *hirou* ① pick + *ageru* ② raise/ ②

EX. John bent down to pick up the coin.
ジョンはかがんでコインを拾い上げた。
Jon wa kagande koin o hiroi-ageta.

PHRASE: pick up ⟨-o⟩ *mukae ni kuru* ⟨〜を⟩迎えに来る ③, ⟨-o⟩ *mukae ni iku* ⟨〜を⟩迎えに行く ①

EX. I'll pick you up at 8 o'clock in the morning.
朝八時に迎えに{来ます/行きます}。
Asa hachi-ji ni mukae ni {kimasu/ikimasu}.

PHRASE: pick up ⟨-o⟩ *tori ni kuru* ⟨〜を⟩取りに来る ③, ⟨-o⟩ *tori ni iku* ⟨〜を⟩取りに行く ①

EX. When can I pick up the dress shirts?
ワイシャツはいつ取りに{来たら/行ったら}いいですか。
Waishatsu wa itsu tori ni {kitara/ittara} ii desu ka.

PHRASE: pick up ⟨-o⟩ *(shizenni) oboeru* ⟨〜を⟩(自然に)覚える ②

EX. A: Where did you pick up your Japanese?
どこで日本語を覚えたんですか。
Doko de Nihon-go o oboeta n desu ka.
B: I picked it up while I was in Japan.
日本にいる間に自然に覚えました。
Nihon ni iru aida ni shizenni oboemashita.

PHRASE: pick up (speed) *sokudo o ageru* 速度を上げる ② ↔ *sokudo o otosu* 速度を落とす ①

EX. The train picked up speed.
汽車は速度を上げた。
Kisha wa sokudo o ageta.

pickle n. **[a vegetable preserved and flavored in brine or vinegar]**
pi˥kurusu ピクルス •f, tsu˥ke-mono 漬物 [vegetables preserved and flavored in salt, rice-bran, etc.]

EX. A meal of rice and good-quality pickles is good enough to satisfy me.
御飯とおいしい漬物があれば、満足です。
Gohan to oishii tsuke-mono ga areba, manzoku desu.

tsuke-mono

picnic n. **[an outing with food taken along and eaten outside]**
pi˥kunikku ピクニック •f, e˥nsoku 遠足 •c [an outing to a distant place usually with lunch and snacks] ⟪**excursion, long walk, trip, outing**⟫

EX. Last weekend we went on a picnic.
先週末、私たちは{ピクニック/遠足}に出かけた。
Senshuu-matsu, watashi-tachi wa {pikunikku/ensoku} ni dekaketa.

picture n. **[a visual image made by drawing, painting, or photography** ⟪**fig. "situation"**⟫**]**
1. e˥ 絵 •c [a visual representation of s.t./s.o./s.a. drawn on a flat surface] ⟪**drawing, painting**⟫

EX. (**a**) My daughter showed me the pictures she had drawn in art class at school.
娘は学校で図画の時間にかいた絵を見せてくれた。
Musume wa gakkoo de zuga no jikan ni kaita e o misete kureta.
(**b**) Can you draw a picture of a horse?
馬の絵がかけますか。
Uma no e ga kake-masu ka.

2. sha˥shin 写真 •c [a photograph]

EX. (**a**) This picture was taken when I was a college freshman.
この写真は大学一年の時に撮ったものです。
Kono shashin wa daigaku ichi-nen no toki ni totta mono desu.
(**b**) You look beautiful in this picture.
この写真のあなたはきれいですね。
Kono shashin no anata wa kirei desu ne.

3. e˥iga 映画 •c [a movie] ⟪**film, cinema, motion picture**⟫

EX. A: What picture is showing now at the town theater?
町の映画館では今どの映画をやっていますか。
Machi no eiga-kan de wa ima dono eiga o yatte imasu ka.
B: Kurosawa's "Ran."
黒沢の「乱」です。
Kurosawa no 'Ran' desu.

4. e⌈izoo 映像 •c [a projected image] ⟪image⟫

EX. This TV has a clear picture.
このテレビは鮮明な映像が写る。
Kono terebi wa senmeina eizoo ga utsuru.

5. ga⌈zoo 画像 •c [a drawn image or an image on an electronic screen] ⟪portrait⟫

6. jo⌈okyoo 状況 •c [state of affairs] ⟪conditions, situation, circumstances⟫

EX. The economic picture in Japan these days is not very bright.
最近の日本の経済状況はあまり明るくない。
Saikin no Nihon no keizai-jookyoo wa amari akaruku nai.

pie n.

pa⌉i パイ •f

EX. I baked an apple pie. Won't you try some?
アップルパイを焼きましたが、ちょっと食べてみませんか。
Appuru-pai o yakimashita ga, chotto tabete mimasen ka.

piece n. **[one of the parts making up a whole, esp. one that has broken or torn off, or an artistic/literary work]**

1. ha⌈hen 破片 •c [a part of s.t. that has broken off or come off] ⟪fragment, splinter⟫

EX. Pieces of the expensive vase were scattered all over the floor.
高価な花瓶の破片が床に散らばっていた。
Kookana kabin no hahen ga yuka ni chirabatte ita.

2. i⌈chi⌉-bu 一部 •c [one part of s.t.] ⟪part, section, portion⟫, bu⌉bun 部分 •c [any of the divisions of a whole] ⟪part, section, section, division⟫

EX. It's impossible to picture the whole just from this one piece.
この{一部/部分}だけから全体を推し量ることは出来ない。
Kono {ichi-bu/bubun} dake kara zentai o oshi-hakaru koto wa dekinai.

3. sa⌈kuhin 作品 •c [an artistic creation by s.o.] ⟪work, product, opus⟫, kyo⌈ku 曲 •c [the state of being crooked or curved ⟪fig. "fun," "a piece of music"⟫] ⟪musical composition⟫

EX. (**a**) Could you play this piano piece by Bach for me?
このバッハのピアノ{曲/??作品}を弾いてくれませんか。
Kono Bahha no piano-{kyoku/??sakuhin} o hiite kuremasen ka.
(**b**) I like this piece by Picasso.
私はピカソのこの{作品/*曲}が好きです。
*Watashi wa Pikaso no kono {sakuhin/*kyoku} ga suki desu.*

PHRASE: piece of N

NOTE: The English "piece" in "piece of" is normally expressed using a Japanese numeral for numbers up to 10 and using a Chinese numeral for numbers beyond 10. However, a specific counter is required depending on the shape of the object, as shown in example (a).

EX. (**a**) Would you care for a piece of bread?
パンを一切れ、いかがですか。
Pan o hito-kire, ikaga desu ka.
(**b**) We're still missing two pieces of luggage we sent from the airport.
空港から送った荷物がまだ二つほど届いていない。
Kuukoo kara okutta nimotsu ga mada futatsu hodo todoite inai.

— vt. **[for s.o. to join together the parts of a whole]**

⟨-o⟩ tsu⌈nagi-awase⌉ru ⟨〜を⟩つなぎ合わせる ② [to join separate objects together] ⟪connect together, join together⟫

EX. Can you piece the fragments together and recreate the original vase?

かけらをつなぎ合わせて、元の花瓶に作り直せますか。
Kakera o tsunagi-awasete, moto no kabin ni tsukuri-naose-masu ka.

pier n. **[a structure to support a bridge or to protect a harbor]**
1. kyo⌈okyaku 橋脚 •c [a pillar supporting a bridge]
2. sa⌈n-bashi 桟橋 [a structure for protecting a harbor or landing ships] ⟪jetty, wharf, quay⟫, fu⌈too ふ頭 •c [a place along which ships dock to receive or discharge cargo or passengers] ⟪wharf, quay⟫, ha⌈to-ba 波止場 [a place along which ships dock] ⟪wharf, quay, jetty⟫

EX. The two kissed and parted at the pier on a rainy autumn night.
二人は{桟橋/ふ頭/波止場}で秋の雨の降る夜にキスして別れた。
Futari wa {san-bashi/futoo/hato-ba} de aki no ame no furu yoru ni kisu-shite wakareta.

pig n.
bu⌈ta 豚 ⟪hog, swine⟫

pigeon n.
ha⌉to はと ⟪dove⟫

EX. It seems like there are always pigeons at Japanese temples.
日本のお寺にはいつもはとがいるようだ。
Nihon no o-tera ni wa itsu-mo hato ga iru yooda.

pile n. **[many objects stacked in a heap]**
ya⌈ma⌉ 山 [a landmass that rises conspicuously above its surroundings ⟪fig. "a large heap," "counter for a pile of merchandise"⟫]

EX. Boy! What a pile of books you have on your desk!
これは驚いた。机の上は本の山ですねえ！
Kore wa odoroita. Tsukue no ue wa hon no yama desu nee!

—— vt. **[to stack objects in a heap]**
⟨-ni⟩ ⟨-o⟩ tsu⌈mu ⟨〜に⟩⟨〜を⟩積む ① [to stack objects in a heap (on a vehicle) ⟪fig. "acquire," "accumulate"⟫] ⟪stack, load⟫, ⟨-o⟩ ka⌈saneru ⟨〜を⟩重ねる ② [for s.o. to stack two or more relatively flat objects of similar size and shape on top of one another ⟪fig. "repeat"⟫] ⟪heap up, repeat⟫

EX. (**a**) Why don't you just pile the books on top of the desk for now?
取りあえず机の上に本を{積んだら/重ねたら}どうですか。
Toriaezu tsukue no ue ni hon o {tsundara/kasanetara} doo desu ka.
(**b**) Let's pile the apples right here.
ここにりんごを{積もう/*重ねよう}。
*Koko ni ringo o {tsumoo/*kasaneyoo}.*

—— vi. **[for things to spontaneously accumulate on top of one another into a heap]**
tsu⌈moru 積もる ① [for things such as dust, snow, items to discuss, grudges, time, etc., to accumulate into a larger and higher mass] ⟪accumulate⟫

EX. (**a**) Even dust can turn into a mountain if it piles up.
ちりも積もれば山となる。
Chiri mo tsumoreba yama to naru.

NOTE: Example (a) is a proverb that means "Every little bit counts."

(**b**) The snow piled up to almost five feet.
雪が五フィート近く積もった。
Yuki ga go-fiito chikaku tsumotta.

PHRASE: be piled up *kasanaru* 重なる ①

EX. A bunch of books were piled up on the desk.
たくさんの本が机の上に重なっていた。
Takusan no hon ga tsukue no ue ni kasanatte ita.

pilgrim n.
ju⌈nre⌉i-sha 巡礼者 •c

pill n. **[a small tablet of medicine, including an oral contraceptive]**
ga⌈n'yaku 丸薬 •c [a tablet of medicine] ⟪pellet, globule⟫, pi⌉ru ピル •f [an oral contraceptive]

EX. (**a**) Taking this pill can help you lose weight.
この{丸薬/*ピル}を飲めば体重を減らせますよ。
*Kono {gan'yaku/*piru} o nomeba*

P

taijuu o herase-masu yo.
(**b**) Are you on the pill these days?
このごろ、{ピル/?丸薬}飲んでいるの?
Kono-goro, {piru/?gan'yaku} nonde iru no?

pillow n. **[a support for the head when reclining]**
ma⌉kura まくら
EX. I prefer a thin pillow to a thick one.
私は高いまくらより低いまくらの方が好きです。
Watashi wa takai makura yori hikui makura no hoo ga suki desu.

P

pilot n. **[a person who operates an airplane or who guides ships in and out of a port]**
1. pa⌈iro⌉tto パイロット •f [a person who operates an airplane], so⌈oju⌉u-shi 操縦士 •c [a person who operates a machine, esp. an airplane]
EX. (**a**) I'd like to become a pilot flying international routes someday.
将来私は国際線の{パイロット/?操縦士}になりたいです。
Shoorai watashi wa kokusai-sen no {pairotto/?soojuu-shi} ni nari-tai desu.
(**b**) My father was once the pilot of a space rocket.
父は宇宙ロケットの{操縦士/*パイロット}をしたことがあります。
*Chichi wa uchuu-roketto no {soojuu-shi/*pairotto} o shita koto ga arimasu.*
2. mi⌈zusaki-annai-nin 水先案内人 •c [a person who guides ships in and out of port]

pin n. **[a short, thin, pointed piece of metal for fastening separate objects together《fig. "brooch"》]**
1. pi⌉n ピン •f [a short, thin, pointed piece of metal for fastening separate objects together]
EX. When I got to work I noticed that the hem of my skirt had come undone so I hurriedly fastened it with a safety pin.
会社に着いてからスカートのすそがほつれているのに気がつき、あわてて安全ピンで留めた。
Kaisha ni tsuite kara sukaato no suso ga hotsurete iru no ni ki ga tsuki, awatete anzen-pin de tometa.
2. bu⌈ro⌉ochi ブローチ •f《brooch》
EX. The woman over there wearing a silver pin on her dress is Mrs. Nakada.
ドレスに銀のブローチを付けているあの女性が中田先生の奥さんです。
Doresu ni gin no buroochi o tsukete iru ano josei ga Nakada-sensei no oku-san desu.

— vt. **[for s.o. to fasten s.t. with a pin or a pin-like object《fig. "cause s.o./s.t. to be unable to move"》]**
1. ⟨-o⟩ (pi⌉n de) to⌈meru ⟨〜を⟩(ピンで)留める ② [for s.o. to fasten s.t. to s.t. else with a pin]
EX. How about pinning this flower to your blouse?
この花をブラウスに留めたらどうですか。
Kono hana o burausu ni tometara doo desu ka.
2. ⟨-o⟩ o⌈sae-tsuke⌉ru ⟨〜を⟩押さえ付ける ② [to press s.o./s.t./s.a. down to keep it/him/her from moving]《press down, hold down》
EX. I was pinned down by the two villains.
私は二人の悪漢に押さえ付けられた。
Watashi wa futari no akkan ni osae-tsuke-rareta.

pinch vt. **[for s.o. to squeeze s.t. between the finger and thumb or between other surfaces, esp. in such a way as to cause pain]**
1. ⟨-o⟩ ⟨-de⟩ ha⌈sa⌉mu ⟨〜を⟩⟨〜で⟩挟む ① [to put s.t. in a narrow space between two objects so that it is held fast from both sides]《put between, insert》
EX. Little Johnny pinched his finger in the door and came screaming to his mother.
ドアに指を挟んでしまったジョニーちゃんは泣きながら母親のところにやってきた。
Doa ni yubi o hasande shimatta Jonii-chan wa naki-nagara haha-oya no tokoro ni yatte kita.
2. ⟨-o⟩ tsu⌈mu ⟨〜を⟩摘む ① [for s.o. to remove s.t. such as a bud or tea leaf from

a plant before it grows large, usu. with a squeezing motion of the fingers] 《pick, pluck, trim, clip》

EX. Tea leaves are harvested by pinching them off by hand.
茶の葉は手で摘んで収穫する。
Cha no ha wa te de tsunde shuukaku-suru.

3. ⟨-o⟩ tsu⌈ne⌉ru ⟨〜を⟩つねる ② [for s.o. to hold s.o.'s skin tightly between one's fingers or fingernails and twist it] 《nip》

EX. Mom, Jimmy pinched me.
お母さん、ジミーが僕をつねった。
O-kaa-san, Jimii ga boku o tsunetta.

4. i⌈ta⌉i 痛い adj(*i*). [for s.o./s.a. to experience an unpleasant physical sensation, often in a particular part of the body]

EX. The small shoes pinched my feet.
靴が小さくて足が痛かった。
Kutsu ga chiisakute ashi ga itakatta.

— n. [an act or result of pinching]

1. hi⌈to⌉-tsumami 一つまみ [a small amount of s.t. (esp. salt) that can be held between two fingers]

EX. Put a pinch of salt in the soup.
スープに一つまみの塩を入れます。
Suupu ni hito-tsumami no shio o iremasu.

2. ki⌈kyuu 危急 •c [a critical moment] 《crisis, emergency, critical moment》, pi⌉nchi ピンチ •f [a critical moment, esp. in a game]

EX. My friend Tom comes to the rescue whenever I'm in a pinch.
友人のトムは{危急/ピンチ}の時には必ず助けに来てくれる。
Yuujin no Tomu wa {kikyuu/pinchi} no toki ni wa kanarazu tasuke ni kite kureru.

PHRASE: give s.o. a pinch ⟨-o⟩ *tsuneru* ⟨〜を⟩つねる ①

pine n.

ma⌉tsu 松

EX. Pine trees have been a central theme in traditional Chinese, Korean and Japanese painting.
中国、韓国、日本の伝統的な絵画では松の木が主要なテーマだ。
Chuugoku, Kankoku, Nihon no dentoo-tekina kaiga de wa matsu no ki ga shuyoona teema da.

pineapple n.

pa⌈ina⌉ppuru パイナップル •f

pink n. [a pale red color]

mo⌈mo-iro 桃色 [the color of peach flowers 《fig. "eroticism"》], pi⌉nku ピンク •f [a pale bluish red color 《fig. "eroticism"》]

— adj. [pale red in color]

mo⌈mo-iro no N 桃色のN [having the color of peach flowers], pi⌉nku no N ピンクのN [pale bluish red in color]

EX. The girl wearing a pink sweater and pink lipstick is my sister.
{桃色/ピンク}のセーターを着て、{ピンク/*桃色}の口紅を付けている女の子が妹です。
*{Momo-iro/Pinku} no seetaa o kite, {pinku/*momo-iro} no kuchi-beni o tsukete iru onna-no-ko ga imooto desu.*

pint n.

pa⌉into パイント •f

NOTE: 1 pint≒0.47 liter (U.S.A.) 1 pint≒0.57 liter (Br.)

pioneer n. [a person who is among the first to settle in a territory 《fig. "a person who is among the first to advance an idea, method, etc."》]

ka⌈itaku⌉-sha 開拓者 •c [a person who develops new land for farming 《fig. "a person who starts a new field of study or research"》] 《settler, pathfinder》, se⌈nku⌉-sha 先駆者 •c [a person who advances a new idea, method, etc., ahead of others] 《herald, forerunner, precursor》, pa⌈ioni⌉a パイオニア •f [a person who is among the first to advance an idea, method, etc.]

EX. (a) What I like about America is its pioneer spirit.
アメリカの好きなところはその{開拓者/パイオニア/*先駆者}精神です。
Amerika no sukina tokoro wa sono

*{kaitaku-sha/paionia/*senku-sha}-seishin desu.*
(**b**) Noam Chomsky is one of the pioneers of modern linguistics.
ノーム・チョムスキーは現代言語学の{開拓者/先駆者/パイオニア}の一人です。
Noomu Chomusukii wa gendai gengo-gaku no {kaitaku-sha/senku-sha/paionia} no hitori desu.

pipe n. **[a long tube for conducting liquid, gas, sound, etc. 《fig. "a tube used for smoking tabacco"》]**
ku˥da 管 [a hollow elongated cylinder with a relatively small diameter] 《tube》, -kan ～管 •c [a suffix indicating a tube], pa˥ipu パイプ •f [a long, hollow tube of metal or a tube used for smoking tabacco]
EX. (**a**) It seems that a broken gas pipe is the cause of the odor.
{ガス管/ガスの管/*ガスのパイプ}が壊れているのがにおいの原因らしい。
*{Gasu-kan/Gasu no kuda/*Gasu no paipu} ga kowarete iru no ga nioi no gen'in rashii.*
(**b**) It's not allowed to smoke a pipe on the plane.
飛行機ではパイプを吸ってはいけない。
Hikoo-ki de wa paipu o sutte wa ikenai.

pirate n. **[a person who attacks and robs ships at sea]**
ka┌izoku 海賊 •c [a person who roams the oceans attacking and robbing ships or plundering coastal settlements] 《sea robber》

pistol n.
pi┌sutoru ピストル •f, ke┌njuu 拳銃 •c [a handgun]
EX. (**a**) Can an ordinary citizen buy a pistol in this country?
この国では普通の市民が{ピストル/拳銃}を買えますか。
Kono kuni de wa futsuu no shimin ga {pisutoru/kenjuu} o kae-masu ka.
(**b**) He shot his wife with a pistol.
彼は{ピストル/拳銃}で妻を撃った。
Kare wa {pisutoru/kenjuu} de tsuma o utta.

piston n.
pi˥suton ピストン •f

pit n. **[a deep vertical hole in the ground 《fig. "a sunken area"》]**
1. ta┌te-ana たて穴 [a vertical hole]
2. ta┌nkoo 炭坑 •c [a coal mine]

pitch vt. **[for s.o. to throw ot toss s.t. or to put up a tent]**
1. (⟨-ni⟩) ⟨-o⟩ na┌ge˥ru (⟨～に⟩)⟨～を⟩投げる ② [for s.o. to cause s.t. in one's hand to move through the air by means of a quick forward motion of the arm] 《throw, hurl, fling, abandon》
EX. The quarterback pitched the football to the halfback.
クオーターバックはフットボールをハーフバックに投げた。
Kuootaa-bakku wa futto-booru o haafu-bakku ni nageta.
2. (te˥nto o) ha┌ru (テントを)張る ① [for s.o. to put up a tent]
EX. Shall we pitch the tent about here?
この辺にテントを張りましょうか。
Kono hen ni tento o harimashoo ka.

pitcher[1] n. **[a baseball player who throws the ball to the batter]**
pi˥tchaa ピッチャー •f
EX. A: What position do you play ?
ポジションはどこですか。
Pojishon wa doko desu ka.
B: I'm the pitcher.
ピッチャーです。
Pitchaa desu.

pitcher[2] n. **[a container with a spout for holding and pouring liquids]**
mi┌zu-sa˥shi 水差し [a container with a spout for holding and pouring water]

pitiful adj. **[arousing sympathy or arousing contempt]**
1. ka┌wai-so˥ona かわいそうな adj(*na*). **[for s.o./s.a. to deserve sympathy due to the adverse situation he/she/it is in] 《poor, pitiable, wretched, pathetic》, ki-┌no-doku˥na 気の毒な** adj(*na*). **[deserving of sympathy for the pain or sorrow one is**

suffering] ⟪**pitiable, miserable, wretched, regrettable**⟫

EX. (**a**) Tom was in a really pitiful state after not only losing his job but his girlfriend too.
トムは会社を首になっただけでなくガールフレンドにもふられて本当に{かわいそうな/気の毒な}状態だった。
Tomu wa kaisha o kubi ni natta dake de naku gaarufurendo ni mo fura-rete hontoo ni {kawai-soona/ki-no-dokuna} jootai datta.
(**b**) The child begging for money had such a pitiful look on her face that I couldn't just pass her by.
金をせびっている子供があまりにも{かわいそうな/*気の毒な}顔をしていたからどうしても素通りすることができなかった。
*Kane o sebitte iru kodomo ga amari-ni mo {kawai-soona/*ki-no-dokuna} kao o shite ita kara dooshite-mo su-doori-suru koto ga dekinakatta.*

2. i⌈yashi⌉mu-beki N 卑しむべきN **[worthy of contempt ⟨w⟩]** ⟪**contemptible, despicable, base**⟫

EX. What a pitiful father to steal his child's savings and gamble them away like that.
子供の貯金を盗んでかけ事に使ってしまうとは何と卑しむべき父親なんだろう。
Kodomo no chokin o nusunde kake goto ni tsukatte shimau to wa nanto iyashimu-beki chichi-oya na n daroo.

Pittsburgh n.
Pi⌈ttsuba⌉agu ピッツバーグ •f

pity n. **[a feeling of sorrow, sympathy, or regret caused by s.o. else's misfortune]**

1. do⌈ojoo 同情 •c **[sensitivity to and understanding of the sufferings of others]** ⟪**sympathy, compassion**⟫

EX. The AIDS patient said that he didn't want pity.
エイズの患者は同情は無用だと言った。
Eizu no kanja wa doojoo wa muyoo da to itta.

2. za⌈nne⌉nna 残念な adj(*na*). •c **[for s.o. to feel dissatisfied and disappointed about s.t. that s.o. has done or s.t. that has happened]** ⟪**disappointing, regrettable**⟫

EX. It's a pity you couldn't come to the party last night. It was a lot of fun.
きのうはパーティーに来られなくて残念でしたね。とても楽しいパーティーだったのに。
Kinoo wa paatii ni ko-rarenakute zannen deshita ne. Totemo tanoshii paatii datta noni.

place n. **[a particular part of space occupied by s.t.; a town, building, district, etc., occupying a particular part of space; a position in a ranking or series** ⟪**fig. "passage"**⟫**]**

1. to⌈koro 所 **[a particular part of space occupied by s.t. or a building occupying a particular part of space** ⟪**fig. "status," "situation," "occasion," "moment," "passage"**⟫**]** ⟪**place, spot, locality, region, room, one's home, point, passage, moment**⟫, **ba⌈sho** 場所 •c **[a point or area in space where s.o./s.t./s.a. exists or where s.t. happens]** ⟪**spot, position, location, room**⟫, **se⌉ki** 席 •c **[s.t. on which one sits** ⟪**fig. "the place where a meeting/ceremony takes place"**⟫**]** ⟪**seat**⟫

EX. (**a**) A: What sort of place would you like to go to?
どんな{所/?場所/*席}へ行きたいですか。
*Donna {tokoro/?basho/*seki} e iki-tai desu ka.*
B: I'd like to go to some kind of place where I can relax.
リラックス出来るような{所/?場所/*席}へ行きたいです。
*Rirakkusu dekiru yoona {tokoro/?basho/*seki} e iki-tai desu.*
(**b**) A: What sort of place would you like to live in?
どんな{所/?場所/*席}に住みたいですか。
*Donna {tokoro/?basho/*seki} ni sumi-tai desu ka.*
B: I'd like to live in a small apartment.
小さなアパートに住みたいです。
Chiisana apaato ni sumi-tai desu.

P

(c) Why don't you come over to my place for a cup of tea?
お茶を飲みに私の{所/*場所/*席}にいらっしゃいませんか。
*O-cha o nomi ni watashi no {tokoro/*basho/*seki} ni irasshaimasen ka.*
(d) There were many places in this book I couldn't understand.
この本には分からない{所/*場所/*席}が沢山あった。
*Kono hon ni wa wakaranai {tokoro/*basho/*seki} ga takusan atta.*
(e) The train was so crowded that there wasn't any place for us to sit down.
電車はとても込んでいて、座る{席/所/場所}がありませんでした。
Densha wa totemo konde ite, suwaru {seki/tokoro/basho} ga arimasendeshita.

2. mi˥bun 身分 [an individual's standing in society relative to others/one's circumstances] ⟪social status, rank, means⟫, chi˥i 地位 •c [the standing which one has acquired in a social group or society] ⟪position, status, post⟫

EX. Despite the important place he occupies in the company, he is a humble person.
あの人は会社で重要な{地位/*身分}にいるのに、とても謙虚だ。
*Ano hito wa kaisha de juuyoona {chii/*mibun} ni iru noni, totemo kenkyo da.*

3. -i ～位 •c [a counter for ranking] ⟪rank⟫, -ban ～番 •c [a counter for ordinal numbers], -chaku ～着 •c [a counter for the order of arrival, usually at the goal in a race], -too ～等 •c [a counter for order or degree of quality]

EX. Who took first place in the marathon?
マラソンではだれが{一位/一番/一着/一等}でしたか。
Marason de wa dare ga {ichi-i/ichi-ban/it-chaku/it-too} deshita ka.

PHRASE: in place of N N *no kawari ni* Nの代わりに

EX. I attended the wedding in place of my father.
父の代わりに私が結婚式に出た。
Chichi no kawari ni watashi ga kekkon-shiki ni deta.

PHRASE: in the first place *mazu dai-ichi ni* まず第一に

EX. In the first place, I don't like to travel by airplane.
まず第一に、私は飛行機で旅するのが好きではない。
Mazu dai-ichi ni, watashi wa hikoo-ki de tabi-suru no ga suki dewanai.

PHRASE: take place *hiraka-reru* 開かれる /⟨passive of *hiraku* ① open/ ②, *okonawa-reru* 行なわれる /⟨passive of *okonau* ① do/ ② ⟪be done, be put into practice, be held⟫

EX. (a) The presidential election took place last week and the Republican candidate was elected.
大統領選挙が先週{行なわれて/*開かれて}共和党の候補が選ばれた。
*Daitooryoo-senkyo ga senshuu {okonawa-rete/*hiraka-rete} kyoowa-too no kooho ga eraba-reta.*
(b) The Summer Olympic Games of 1988 took place in Seoul, Korea.
1988年の夏のオリンピックは韓国のソウルで{開かれた/行なわれた}。
Sen-kyuu-hyaku-hachi-juu-hachi-nen no natsu no Orinpikku wa Kankoku no Souru de {hiraka-reta/okonawa-reta}.

— vt. **[to put s.t./s.o. in a particular location, order, or position]**
⟨-ni⟩ ⟨-o⟩ o˥ku ⟨～に⟩⟨～を⟩置く ① [for s.o./s.a. to cause s.o./s.t./s.a. to be at/in/on a certain place] ⟪put, position, leave⟫

EX. (a) Would you place this bottle on the shelf, my dear?
あなた、この瓶を棚において下さらない?
Anata, kono bin o tana ni oite kudasaranai?
(b) I'm placing my trust in you, you know. Don't disappoint me
私はあなたに信頼を置いているんですよ。がっかりさせるようなことをしないでください。
Watashi wa anata ni shinrai o oite iru n desu yo. Gakkari-saseru yoona koto o shinai de kudasai.

plain adj. **[easy to see, hear, or understand; not showy or attractive in appearance; free from admixture]**

1. wa⌈kari-yasu⌉i 分かりやすい /⟨V*masu* of *wakaru* ① understand + *yasui* easy/ adj(*i*). **[to be easy to figure out]** ↔ **wakari-nikui** 分かりにくい adj(*i*).; **he⌈iina** 平易な adj(*na*). •c **[easy to comprehend]** ⟪easy, simple⟫ ↔ **nankaina** 難解な adj(*na*). •c

EX. Please explain that concept to me in plain Japanese.
{分かりやすい/平易な}日本語でその概念を説明して下さい。
{Wakari-yasui/Heiina} Nihon-go de sono gainen o setsumei-shite kudasai.

2. ji⌈mi⌉na 地味な adj(*na*). •c **[quiet and subdued in color/personality/appearance]** ⟪simple, quiet, sober, unpretentious⟫ ↔ **hadena** 派手な adj(*na*).

EX. (**a**) This tie is too plain for you.
このネクタイはあなたには地味すぎますよ。
Kono nekutai wa anata ni wa jimi-sugimasu yo.
(**b**) She is a plain but very capable woman.
彼女は地味な女だが、とても有能だ。
Kanojo wa jimina onna da ga, totemo yuunoo da.

3. mu⌉ji no N 無地のN •c **[for a fabric to be free from patterns or ornaments]** ⟪of solid color⟫

EX. John wore a plain gray suit to the dinner party.
ジョンは夕食会に無地のグレーのスーツを着ていった。
Jon wa yuushoku-kai ni muji no guree no suutsu o kite itta.

4. ma⌈zari-mono no na⌉i N 混ざり物のないN **[free from admixture of foreign substances]**

—— n. **[an extensive area of flat land]**
he⌈ichi 平地 •c **[flat land]** ⟪flatland, level land⟫ ↔ **sanchi** 山地 •c; **he⌈iya** 平野 •c **[a relatively extensive area of flat land]** ⟪open field⟫

EX. (**a**) I could see a vast plain stretching towards the distant mountains.
遠くの山に向かって広大な{平地/平野}が広がっているのが見えた。
Tooku no yama ni mukatte koodaina {heichi/heiya} ga hirogatte iru no ga mieta.
(**b**) The Kanto Plain is the largest area of flat land in Japan.
関東{平野/*平地}は日本で一番大きい平野だ。
*Kantoo-{heiya/*heichi} wa Nihon de ichiban ookii heiya da.*

plan n. **[a method or procedure for doing s.t. thought out in advance or a drawing showing how s.t. is to be built]**

1. ke⌈ikaku 計画 •c **[a method or procedure for doing s.t. thought out in advance]** ⟪project, scheme⟫, **pu⌉ran** プラン •f

EX. (**a**) It's usually easier to come up with a plan than to put it into practice.
{計画/プラン}を立てるより、それを実行する方が難しいことが多い。
{Keikaku/Puran} o tateru yori, sore o jikkoo-suru koto no hoo ga muzukashii koto ga ooi.
(**b**) What are your plans after graduation?
卒業後の{計画/プラン}は何ですか。
Sotsugyoo-go no {keikaku/puran} wa nan desu ka.
(**c**) The bank robbery went according to plan.
銀行強盗は{計画/?プラン}の通りに進んだ。
Ginkoo-gootoo wa {keikaku/?puran} no toori ni susunda.

2. se⌈kke⌉i-zu 設計図 •c **[a drawing showing how s.t. is to be built]**

EX. The architect has shown us a plan of our new gymnasium.
建築家は新しい体育館の設計図を見せてくれた。
Kenchiku-ka wa atarashii taiiku-kan no sekkei-zu o misete kureta.

—— vt. **[for s.o. to think out a method or procedure for doing s.t. in advance]**
Vvol. to o⌈mo⌉u Vvol.と思う ① **[for s.o. to**

P

determine in his/her mind to do s.t.], Vinf. nonpast ke⌈ikaku da Vinf. nonpast 計画だ •c [for an arrangement to exist to do s.t.], Vinf. nonpast tsu⌈mori da Vinf. nonpast つもりだ [for s.o. to propose in his/her mind ahead of time to do s.t.] 《intend to》

EX. (a) I plan to go to Africa this summer.
私は今年の夏アフリカへ{行こうと思っている/行く計画だ/行くつもりだ}。
Watashi wa kotoshi no natsu Afurika e {ikoo to omotte iru/iku keikaku da/iku tsumori da}.
(b) I wonder if the U.S. plans to take definitive measures to decrease its deficit spending.
アメリカは財政赤字を削減する明確な手段を{取る計画な/取ろうと思っている/取るつもりな}のだろうか。
Amerika wa zaisei-akaji o sakugen-suru meikakuna shudan o {toru keikaku na/toroo to omotte iru/toru tsumori na} no daroo ka.

P

plane n. **[abbreviated form for airplane]**
hi⌈ko⌉o-ki 飛行機 •c 《**aircraft**》

EX. A: How did you get here?
ここへは何で来ましたか。
Koko e wa {nani/nan} de kimashita ka.
B: By plane.
飛行機で来ました。
Hikoo-ki de kimashita.

plant n. **[a living organism which, unlike animals, makes its own food and is not capable of movement or sensation** 《**fig. "manufacturing institution"**》**]**

1. sho⌈ku⌉butsu 植物 •c [a living organism which, unlike animals, makes its own food and is not capable of movement or sensation], ha⌈chi-ue⌉ 鉢植え [flowers, small trees, etc., planted in pots, usu. for keeping indoors]

EX. Sally keeps lots of plants in her apartment.
サリーはアパートに{鉢植え/植物}を沢山置いています。
Sarii wa apaato ni {hachi-ue/shokubutsu} o takusan oite imasu.

2. pu⌈ranto プラント •f [a manufacturing institution]

— vt. **[for s.o. to place s.t. such as seeds or the roots of a flower, tree, bush, etc., in the soil to grow** 《**fig. "place forcibly," "indoctrinate"**》**]**

1. ⟨-o⟩ u⌈eru ⟨～を⟩植える ② [for s.o. to place the roots of a partially grown flower, tree, bush, etc., in the soil to grow] 《**grow, raise**》

EX. Cherry trees were planted on the banks of the Potomac River in Washington as a gift from the Japanese government.
日本政府からの贈り物としてワシントンのポトマック川の岸に桜が植えられた。
Nihon-seifu kara no okuri-mono toshite Washinton no Potomakku-gawa no kishi ni sakura ga ue-rareta.

2. ⟨-ni⟩ ⟨-o⟩ ma⌉ku ⟨～に⟩⟨～を⟩まく ① [for s.o. to distribute liquid or granular-shaped objects such as seeds over a wide area (using a throwing motion)] 《**sow**》

EX. Every spring we plant vegetable seeds in our garden.
毎年春に庭に野菜の種をまきます。
Mai-toshi haru ni niwa ni yasai no tane o makimasu.

3. ⟨-ni⟩ ⟨-o⟩ su⌈eru ⟨～に⟩⟨～を⟩据える ② [for s.o. to place s.t. firmly in such a way that it doesn't move] 《**set, lay, install**》

plastic n.
pu⌈rasuchi⌉kku プラスチック •f

EX. Nowadays toys are mostly made from plastic.
このごろのおもちゃは大抵プラスチックで出来ている。
Kono-goro no omocha wa taitei purasuchikku de dekite iru.

NOTE: "Plastic bag" used for garbage is *biniiru-bukuro* ビニール袋 (lit. vinyl bag).

plate n. **[a flat, hard, and uniformly thick object, esp. metal** 《**fig. "dish"**》**]**

1. i⌈tagane 板金 [a flat, hard, and uniformly thick piece of metal] 《**metal plate**》**, pu⌈reeto プレート •f [a flat piece of metal displaying the license number on a car or a flat piece of white rubber by which the**

batter stands in baseball]

2. sa⌈ra 皿 [a shallow often round container for holding food] ⟪dish, saucer, platter⟫

EX. Would you please set another plate on the table?
食卓にお皿をもう一枚出して下さいませんか。
Shokutaku ni o-sara o moo ichi-mai dashite kudasaimasen ka.

platform n. **[a level surface raised above the adjacent area]**

1. e⌈ndan 演壇 •c [a raised stage for lecturing] ⟪rostrum⟫

EX. A politician whom I didn't know was giving a speech on the platform.
演壇では私の知らない政治家が演説をしていた。
Endan de wa watashi no shiranai seiji-ka ga enzetsu o shite ita.

2. (pu⌈ratto)ho⌉omu (プラット)ホーム •f [a raised area for loading or discharging passengers from trains]

EX. The express train for Osaka leaves from platform #4.
大阪行きの急行は四番のプラットホームから出ます。
Oosaka-yuki no kyuukoo wa yon-ban no purattohoomu kara demasu.

play vi. **[for s.o./s.a. to do s.t. for fun or pleasure or to perform in a musical or dramatic presentation]**

1. a⌈sobu 遊ぶ ① [for s.o./s.a. to amuse oneself instead of working or studying] ⟪amuse oneself⟫

EX. (**a**) A child was playing alone in the yard.
子供が庭で一人で遊んでいた。
Kodomo ga niwa de hitori de asonde ita.
(**b**) In our home we had to study first before playing.
うちでは遊ぶ前に勉強しなければならなかった。
Uchi de wa asobu mae ni benkyoo-shinakereba naranakatta.
(**c**) It's often said the Japanese know how to work, but not how to play.
日本人は働き方は知っているが、遊び方を知らないとよく言われる。
Nihon-jin wa hataraki-kata wa shitte iru ga, asobi-kata o shiranai to yoku iwa-reru.

2. e⌈nsoo ga adj. 演奏がadj. [a musical performance is adj.], e⌉ngi ga adj. 演技がadj. [a dramatic performance is adj.]

EX. (**a**) The pianist in last night's concert played superbly.
ゆうべのコンサートのピアニストの{演奏/*演技}はすばらしかった。
*Yuube no konsaato no pianisuto no {ensoo/*engi} wa subarashikatta.*
(**b**) Meryl Streep plays superbly in that movie.
メリル・ストリープのその映画での{演技/*演奏}は絶妙だ。
*Meriru Sutoriipu no sono eiga de no {engi/*ensoo} wa zetsumyoo da.*

—— vt. **[for s.o./s.a. to do s.t. for fun or pleasure; to take part in a game; to perform a dramatic role; to cause a musical instrument or electronic device to produce sound]**

1. ⟨-o⟩ su⌈ru ⟨〜を⟩する ③ [for s.o./s.a. to conduct an action willfully; for s.o./s.a./s.t. to cause s.t. to take on a different state; for s.t. to happen in such a way as to be perceptible to s.o./s.a.; for s.t. to be in a certain state or possess a certain attribute; for an amount of time/money to pass/be required; for some proposition to be posited as true ⟪fig. "put on a somewhat small, ornamental object"⟫] ⟪do, make, wear⟫, ⟨-o⟩ ya⌈ru ⟨〜を⟩やる ① [for s.o. to perform an action willfully or to behave or fare in a certain way], ⟨-o⟩ e⌈njiru ⟨〜を⟩演じる ② •c [for s.o. to make a public presentation requiring professional skill in drama, music, etc.] ⟪perform⟫

EX. (**a**) Harvard plays Yale next week in basketball.
ハーバードは来週エールと(バスケットボールの試合を){します/やります/*演じます}。
Haabaado wa raishuu Eeru to

P

*(basuketto-booru no shiai o) {shimasu/yarimasu/*enjimasu}.*
(**b**) Which movie are they playing now at the local theater?
地元の映画館では今、どの映画を{やって/*して/*演じて}いますか。
*Jimoto no eiga-kan de wa ima, dono eiga o {yatte/*shite/*enjite} imasu ka.*
(**c**) Shall we play tennis this afternoon?
今日の午後テニスを{しましょう/やりましょう/*演じましょう}か。
*Kyoo no gogo tenisu o {shimashoo/yarimashoo/*enjimashoo} ka.*
(**d**) He has played Hamlet many times.
あの人はハムレットを何回も{した/やった/演じた}ことがあります。
Ano hito wa Hamuretto o nan-kai mo {shita/yatta/enjita} koto ga arimasu.

2. ⟨-o⟩ hi⌈ku ⟨〜を⟩ひく ① [to move s.t./s.o./s.a. concrete or abstract toward the source of a force ⟪fig. "quote," "subtract," "perform music on a stringed instrument, including piano," "grind grain or beans," "consult (a dictionary)," "choose lots," "extend in an uninterrupted fashion," "inherit a characteristic," "remove oneself from a position of public prominence," "catch a cold"⟫], ⟨-o⟩ fu⌈ku⌉ ⟨〜を⟩吹く ① [for s.o. to cause air to come out of one's mouth ⟪fig. "perform music on a wind instrument"⟫] ⟪blow⟫

㊥ "play a stringed instrument" ▷弾く, otherwise ▷引く

EX. (**a**) I can play the piano but not the violin.
私はピアノは{弾けます/*吹けます}が、バイオリンは弾けません。
*Watashi wa piano wa {hike-masu/*fuke-masu} ga, baiorin wa hike-masen.*
(**b**) I used to play the flute.
私は前はフルートを{吹いて/*弾いて}いました。
*Watashi wa mae wa furuuto o {fuite/*hiite} imashita.*

3. ⟨-o⟩ ka⌈ke⌉ru ⟨〜を⟩かける ② [for s.o. to cause s.t. to extend to and come in contact with s.t. else ⟪fig. "cover," "hang," "call s.o. by phone," "bet," "spend," "sprinkle," "splash," "sit down," "build (a bridge)"⟫] ⟪hang⟫

EX. What kind of CD would you like me to play for you?
どんなCDをかけましょうか。
Donna shiidii o kakemashoo ka.

—— n. [s.t. done for amusement; a move or action in a game or sport; a story which is written to be performed on stage]

1. a⌈sobi 遊び /⟨V*masu* of *asobu* ① play/[s.t. done for amusement instead of study or work ⟪fig. "free motion of a part of machine"⟫] ⟪game, pastime, diversion, merrymaking⟫

EX. Play has a crucial role in the healthy development of a child.
幼児が健康に育つのに遊びは非常に大事な役割を果たす。
Yooji ga kenkooni sodatsu no ni asobi wa hijooni daijina yakuwari o hatasu.

2. pu⌈re⌉e プレー •f [a move or action in a game or sport]

EX. The third baseman made several fine plays.
三塁手はいくつかのファインプレーをした。
San-rui-shu wa ikutsu-ka no fain-puree o shita.

3. shi⌈bai 芝居 [traditional Japanese theater, esp. kabuki ⟪fig. "deceitful or insincere behavior"⟫], ge⌉ki 劇 •c [a story acted out on stage, esp. in an informal school setting] ⟪drama⟫, e⌈ngeki 演劇 •c [a general, formal term for theatrical performance] ⟪drama⟫

EX. (**a**) Last night I went to see a play performed by the students in the drama club.
きのうの晩演劇部の学生の演じる{劇/?芝居/??演劇}を見に行きました。
Kinoo no ban engeki-bu no gakusei no enjiru {geki/?shibai/??engeki} o mi ni ikimashita.
(**b**) Do you know the traditional Japanese play called *kabuki*?
歌舞伎という日本の伝統的な{芝居/演劇/?劇}をご存じですか。

Kabuki to iu Nihon no dentoo-tekina {shibai/engeki/?geki} o go-zonji desu ka.

player n. **[a person who plays a sport or performs on a musical instrument or acts in a dramatic performance]**

1. se˥nshu 選手 •c [a person chosen as a representative to participate in a (sports) game], pu˥re˥eyaa プレーヤー •f [a participant in a sport or a phonograph]

EX. (a) When I was small I wanted to become a baseball player.
小さい時、私は野球の{選手/*プレーヤー}になりたいと思っていました。
*Chiisai toki, watashi wa yakyuu no {senshu/*pureeyaa} ni nari-tai to omotte imashita.*
(b) Who do you think is the best player on this year's Brazilian soccer team?
今年のブラジルのサッカーチームでだれが一番いい{選手/プレーヤー}だと思いますか。
Kotoshi no Burajiru no sakkaa-chiimu de dare ga ichiban ii {senshu/pureeyaa} da to omoimasu ka.

2. e˥nso˥o-sha 演奏者 •c [a musical performer on a particular occasion], e˥nsoo-ka 演奏家 •c [an established, professional music performer] ⟪performer⟫

EX. (a) Vladimir Horowitz is one of the greatest piano players of our time.
ウラジミール・ホロウイッツは現代の偉大なピアノ{演奏家/*演奏者}の一人だ。
*Urajimiiru Horouittsu wa gendai no idaina piano-{ensoo-ka/*ensoo-sha} no hitori da.*
(b) Who are the players in today's concert?
今日のコンサートにはどの{演奏者/演奏家}が出るんですか。
Kyoo no konsaato ni wa dono {ensoo-sha/ensoo-ka} ga deru n desu ka.

3. ya˥kusha 役者 •c [a person who plays a role in a dramatic performance ⟪fig. "a person who can pretend to be s.o. else"⟫] ⟪actor, actress⟫, **ha˥iyuu 俳優 •c [a person who acts in dramatic performances as a profession]** ⟪actor, actress⟫

EX. In order to become a *kabuki* player, you have to be born into the family of a *kabuki* player.
歌舞伎{役者/俳優}になるには歌舞伎{役者/俳優}の家に生まれていなければならない。
Kabuki-{yakusha/haiyuu} ni naru ni wa kabuki-{yakusha/haiyuu} no ie ni umarete inakereba naranai.

playground n. **[an outdoor area for children to play in]**

1. a˥sobi-ba 遊び場 /⟨V*masu* of *asobu* ① play + *ba* place/ [an outdoor space for children to play in] ⟪play-yard, recreation ground⟫

EX. Japanese children need more playgrounds.
日本の子供たちはもっと遊び場がいる。
Nihon no kodomo-tachi wa motto asobi-ba ga iru.

2. u˥ndoo-joo 運動場 •c [an outdoor area for play and sports, usu. part of a school campus] ⟪sports field⟫

EX. During physical education class, we play different kinds of sports on the playground.
体育の時間には運動場でいろいろなスポーツをします。
Taiiku no jikan ni wa undoo-joo de iro-irona supootsu o shimasu.

plead vt. **[for s.o. to request s.t. sincerely or desperately or to make a formal statement in answer to a charge in a court of law]**

⟨-ni⟩ ⟨-o⟩ mo˥oshi-tate˥ru ⟨〜に⟩⟨〜を⟩申し立てる ② [for s.o. to formally ask some authority to give s.o. special consideration or treatment] ⟪make a statement, declare⟫, **{⟨-to⟩/⟨-o⟩} shu˥choo-suru {⟨〜と⟩/⟨〜を⟩}主張する ③ •c [for s.o. to state one's opinion firmly with a view to making others agree with it or accept it]** ⟪maintain, contend, lay claim, insist⟫

EX. The defendant pleaded not guilty.
被告は無罪を{申し立てた/主張した}。
Hikoku wa muzai o {mooshi-tateta/shuchoo-shita}.

pleasant adj. **[producing a good feeling to the mind or senses or behaving in a friendly or agreeable manner]**

P

1. **ki⌈mochi (ga) i⌉i 気持ち(が)いい** adj(*i*). **[giving one a good feeling] ((comfortable, agreeable, nice))**

EX. (**a**) What a pleasant day it is today, almost like spring.
今日は春みたいで、気持ち(が)いいですね。
Kyoo wa haru mitai de, kimochi (ga) ii desu ne.
(**b**) I like him because he has such a pleasant voice.
あたし、あの人、とても気持ち(の)いい声をしているから好きよ。
Atashi, ano hito, totemo kimochi (no) ii koe o shite iru kara suki yo.

2. **ta⌈noshi⌉i 楽しい** adj(*i*). **[experiencing intense enjoyment and satisfaction from s.t. and thus being drawn to it or causing such a feeling in one] ((fun, delightful, enjoyable))**

EX. (**a**) We had a very pleasant life in Japan.
私たちの日本での生活はとても楽しかったです。
Watashi-tachi no Nihon de no seikatsu wa totemo tanoshikatta desu.
(**b**) Have a pleasant trip!
どうぞ楽しい御旅行を。
Doozo tanoshii go-ryokoo o.

please vt. **[to cause s.o. to feel satisfied or glad]**
⟨-o⟩ {yo⌈rokoba⌉-su/yo⌈rokoba-se⌉ru} ⟨〜を⟩ {喜ばす①/喜ばせる②} /⟨causative of *yorokobu* ① rejoice/ [to cause s.o. to feel satisfied or happy], ⟨-o⟩ {ta⌈noshima⌉-su/ta⌈noshima-se⌉ru} ⟨〜を⟩{楽します①/楽しませる②} /⟨causative of *tanoshimu* ① enjoy/ [to cause s.o. to have fun], ⟨-o⟩ ma⌉nzoku-saseru ⟨〜を⟩満足させる /⟨causative of *manzoku-suru* ③ be satisfied/ ② [to cause s.o. to feel contented]

EX. (**a**) My father is very hard to please.
父を{喜ばす/喜ばせる/楽します/楽しませる/満足させる}のはとても難しいです。
Chichi o {yorokoba-su/yorokoba-seru/tanoshima-su/tanoshima-seru/manzoku-saseru} no wa totemo muzukashii desu.
(**b**) No matter how hard I try to please my wife by buying her nice presents on her birthday, I never seem to succeed.
誕生日にどんないいプレゼントをして妻を{喜ばそう/?満足させよう/*楽しまそう/*楽しませよう}としてもうまく行ったためしが無い。
*Tanjoo-bi ni donna ii purezento o shite tsuma o {yorokoba-soo/?manzoku-saseyoo/*tanoshima-soo/*tanoshima-seyoo} to shite mo umaku itta tameshi ga nai.*

— adv. **[an adverb to indicate politeness or emphasis in a request]**
do⌉ozo どうぞ [an adverb to indicate politeness in making an invitation or in giving permission] ((kindly)), do⌉oka どうか [an adverb to indicate a polite yet very strong request or pleading] ((kindly, I beg, by all means))

EX. (**a**) A: Can I come in?
入ってもよろしいですか。
Haitte mo yoroshii desu ka.
B: Yes, please do.
ええ、{どうぞ/*どうか}。
*Ee, {doozo/*dooka}.*
(**b**) Please go ahead.
{どうぞ/*どうか}、お先に。
*{Doozo/*Dooka} o-saki ni.*
(**c**) Please take care of yourself.
{どうぞ/どうか}お体をお大事に。
{Doozo/Dooka} o-karada o o-daijini.
(**d**) Please tell me the truth.
{どうか/*どうぞ}本当のことを話してください。
*{Dooka/*Doozo} hontoo no koto o hanashite kudasai.*
(**e**) A: Would you like some cream in your coffee?
コーヒーにクリームをお入れしましょうか。
Koohii ni kuriimu o o-ire-shimashoo ka.
B: Yes, please.
ええ、{お願いします/*どうぞ/*どうか}。
*Ee, {o-negai-shimasu/*doozo/*dooka}.*

NOTE: *O-negai-shimasu* in example (e) is used as an affirmative, polite answer to an offer. *Doozo/dooka* cannot be used in such a context. However, either can be used before *o-negai-shimasu*; thus, *doozo/dooka o-negai-shimasu* is acceptable, although in the context of example (e) *dooka* does not sound right due to its begging overtone.

pleased adj. **[feeling or showing pleasure or satisfaction]**
⟨-o⟩ yo⌈roko⌉nde iru ⟨～を⟩喜んでいる /⟨V*te iru* of *yorokobu* ① rejoice/ ② [for s.o. to feel satisfied or happy] ⟪**be glad, rejoice, be delighted**⟫, **⟨-ni⟩ ma⌉nzoku-shite iru ⟨～に⟩満足している /⟨V*te iru* of *manzoku-suru* ③ be satisfied/ ② [for s.o./s.a. to be satisfied with s.o./s.t./s.a.], ⟨-ga⟩ u⌈reshi⌉i ⟨～が⟩うれしい** adj(*i*). **[feeling pleasure or contentment]** ⟪**glad, happy**⟫

EX. (**a**) I'm very pleased that my book seems to have been so well received.
本が好評のようで、大変{{喜んで/満足して}おります/うれしいです}。
Hon ga koohyoo no yoode, taihen {{yorokonde/manzoku-shite} orimasu/ureshii desu}.

NOTE: *Yorokonde iru* normally takes a third person subject but in written or formal contexts such as example (a) may take a first person subject.

(**b**) My teacher seems to be pleased with my progress in Japanese.
私の先生は私の日本語の進歩{{を喜んで/に満足して}いるようです/*がうれしいようです}。
*Watashi no sensei wa watashi no Nihon-go no shinpo {{o yorokonde/ni manzoku-shite} iru yoodesu/*ga ureshii yoodesu}.*
(**c**) I'm pleased with the result of the experiment.
私は実験の結果{{に満足して/*を喜んで}います/*がうれしいです}。
*Watashi wa jikken no kekka {{ni manzoku-shite/*o yorokonde} imasu/*ga ureshii desu}.*
(**d**) I was pleased to hear that my friend had been released from the hospital.
友達が退院したと聞いて、{うれしかった/{*喜んで/*満足して}いた}。
*Tomodachi ga taiin-shita to kiite, {ureshikatta/{*yorokonde/*manzoku-shite} ita}.*

pleasing adj. **[causing one to feel satisfied or glad]**
ki⌈mochi ga i⌉i 気持ちがいい adj(*i*). **[giving one a good feeling]** ↔ **kimochi ga warui 気持ちが悪い** adj(*i*).; **ka⌈nji ga i⌉i 感じがいい** adj(*i*). **[impressing one in an agreeable way]** ⟪**agreeable, nice**⟫ ↔ **kanji ga warui 感じが悪い** adj(*i*).

EX. (**a**) I find the mountainous setting of Nagano City very pleasing.
山に囲まれた長野市はとても{気持ちがいい/感じがいい}所だと思う。
Yama ni kakoma-reta Nagano-shi wa totemo {kimochi ga ii/kanji ga ii} tokoro da to omou.
(**b**) The new secretary has a very pleasing personality.
今度の秘書は大変{気持ち/感じ}のいい人だ}。
Kondo no hisho wa taihen {kimochi/kanji} no ii hito da.

pleasure n. **[a psychological and/or physical feeling of satisfaction or enjoyment]**
1. yo⌈rokobi⌉ 喜び /⟨V*masu* of *yorokobu* ① rejoice/ [a feeling of happiness or gladness] ⟪**joy, delight, gladness**⟫, **ta⌈no⌉shi-sa 楽しさ /⟨adj(*i*). stem of *tanoshii* enjoyable + suf. *sa* ness/ [an intense feeling of satisfaction or enjoyment]** ⟪**enjoyment, delight, happiness**⟫

EX. (**a**) After studying piano for a year I can now appreciate the pleasure of music as never before.
一年間ピアノを習って、以前よりずっと音楽の{楽しさ/*喜び}が分かるようになりました。
*Ichi-nenkan piano o naratte, izen yori zutto ongaku no {tanoshi-sa/*yorokobi} ga wakaru yooni narimashita.*
(**b**) It gives me great pleasure to be able to introduce our guest to you today.

今日このようにして皆様にお客様を御紹介できますことは私の大きな{喜び/*楽しさ}とするところです。
*Kyoo kono yooni shite mina-sama ni o-kyaku-sama o go-shookai-dekimasu koto wa watashi no ookina {yorokobi/*tanoshi-sa} to suru tokoro desu.*

2. ka⌈iraku 快楽 •c [sensual gratification]

EX. There is no end to the pursuit of pleasure.
快楽の追求に終わりはない。
Kairaku no tsuikyuu ni owari wa nai.

P

plentiful adj. **[more than enough in number or quantity]**

ta⌈kusan 沢山 adv. **[in a large number or quantity《fig. "enough"》]《a great many, much, enough, sufficient》↔ sukoshi 少し** adv.

EX. Food was plentiful at the potluck party.
持ち寄りパーティーには食べ物が沢山あった。
Mochi-yori paatii ni wa tabe-mono ga takusan atta.

plenty n. **[a large number or quantity]**

ta⌈kusan 沢山 adv. SEE plentiful

EX. No need to hurry; we have plenty of time.
時間は沢山あるから、急がなくても大丈夫だよ。
Jikan wa takusan aru kara, isoganakute mo daijoobu da yo.

pliers n.

ya⌈ttoko やっとこ, pe⌉nchi ペンチ •f

NOTE: *Penchi* is a word borrowed from the English "pinchers."

plot n. **[a secret plan or the main story line of a novel/play/film or a small piece of ground]**

1. sa⌈kuryaku 策略 •c [a secret plan to achieve some goal favorable to oneself through deceiving or using others]《trick, scheme, strategy, intrigue》, ta⌈kurami たくらみ /⟨V*masu* of *takuramu* ① play a trick/ [an act/instance of devising a systematic plan, usu. underhanded or secret]《trick, scheme, intrigue》

EX. A plot to overthrow the government was uncovered by the secret police.
政府転覆の{策略/たくらみ}が秘密警察によって暴露された。
Seifu-tenpuku no {sakuryaku/takurami} ga himitsu-keisatsu ni-yotte bakuro-sareta.

2. su⌉ji 筋 [a long fiber or fiber-like object《fig. "story line," "muscle," "streak," "vein"》]《muscle, sinew, vein, stripe》, pu⌈ro⌉tto プロット •f [a cohesive series of events forming the core of a drama]

EX. I can't remember the exact plot of the movie, but I do recall that it was really interesting.
映画の{筋/プロット}を詳しくは覚えていませんけど、面白かったことは確かです。
Eiga no {suji/purotto} o kuwashiku wa oboete imasen kedo, omoshirokatta koto wa tashika desu.

3. chi⌈isa⌉i to⌈chi 小さい土地 [a small piece of land], ji⌉sho 地所 •c [a piece of ground to build on]《land, ground, lot》, shi⌈kichi 敷地 [the land on which a building or street is constructed]《site, ground, lot》

EX. I'm planning to build a house on the plot next to my parents' house.
私は両親の家の隣の{地所/敷地/小さい土地}に家を建てるつもりです。
Watashi wa ryooshin no ie no tonari no {jisho/shikichi/chiisai tochi} ni ie o tateru tsumori desu.

plow n.

su⌈ki すき

—— vt. **[to cultivate soil with a plow]**

su⌈ki de ⟨-o⟩ ta⌈gaya⌉su すきで⟨〜を⟩耕す ①

pluck vt. **[for s.o. to detach s.t. abruptly with a picking motion]**

⟨-o⟩ mu⌈shiru ⟨〜を⟩むしる ① [for s.o. to detach s.t. little by little with a pulling motion of the fingers]《pick off, pull off》, ⟨-o⟩ mo⌉gu ⟨〜を⟩もぐ ① [for s.o. to detach s.t. from s.t. else using a twisting motion, esp. fruit from a plant, usu. with one's fingers]《tear off, wrest away from, snatch away》, ⟨-o⟩ tsu⌈mu ⟨〜を⟩摘む ① [for s.o. to remove s.t. such as a bud or tea leaf from a

plant before it grows large, usu. with a squeezing motion of the fingers] ⟪pick, pull out, trim⟫, ⟨-o⟩ hi⌈ki-nu⌉ku ⟨〜を⟩引き抜く ① [for s.o. to forcibly extract a stick-like object out of a place in which it is embedded ⟪fig. "select"⟫]

EX. (**a**) I plucked some dandelions from the backyard and arranged them in a cup on the table.
裏庭のたんぽぽを{摘んで/*むしって/*もいで/*引き抜いて}きてテーブルの上のカップに飾った。
*Ura-niwa no tanpopo o {tsunde/*mushitte/*moide/*hiki-nuite} kite teeburu no ue no kappu ni kazatta.*
(**b**) I spent the morning plucking ripe apples from the trees in the orchard.
午前中はずっと果樹園の木から熟したりんごを{もいで/*むしって/*摘んで/*引き抜いて}いた。
*Gozen-chuu wa zutto kaju-en no ki kara jukushita ringo o {moide/*mushitte/*tsunde/*hiki-nuite} ita.*
(**c**) I helped my mother pluck feathers from the chicken for supper that night.
母が夕食用のとりの毛を{むしる/*引き抜く/*もぐ/*摘む}のを手伝った。
*Haha ga yuushoku-yoo no tori no ke o {mushiru/*hiki-nuku/*mogu/*tsumu} no o tetsudatta.*
(**d**) The farmer plucked a huge Japanese radish from the field.
お百姓さんは畑から大きな大根を{引き抜いた/*むしった/*もいだ/*摘んだ}。
*O-hyakushoo-san wa hatake kara ookina daikon o {hiki-nuita/*mushitta/*moida/*tsunda}.*

plug n. **[s.t. used to stop up a hole]**
se⌈n 栓 •c

EX. You'd better use ear plugs when you swim.
泳ぐ時は耳栓を使った方がいいですよ。
Oyogu toki wa mimi-sen o tsukatta hoo ga ii desu yo.

plum n.
se⌈iyoo-su⌉momo 西洋すもも, pu⌉ramu プラム •f

plump adj. **[full and round in shape]**
ma⌈ru-ma⌉ru to shita N 丸々としたN [for s.o./s.a. to be full and round] ⟪chubby⟫, fu⌈ku⌉yokana ふくよかな adj(*na*). **[round and soft] ⟪fleshy, round⟫**

EX. Being skinny myself, I'm envious of her plump physique.
自分がやせているので{丸々とした/ふくよかな}彼女の体つきがうらやましい。
Jibun ga yasete iru node {maru-maru to shita/fukuyokana} kanojo no karada-tsuki ga urayamashii.

plunge vi. **[to move suddenly down or into s.t.]**
⟨-ni⟩ to⌈bi-ko⌉mu ⟨〜に⟩飛び込む ① [for s.o./s.a. to move quickly and suddenly into a place] ⟪dive into, jump into⟫, ⟨-ni⟩ mo⌈gu⌉ru ⟨〜に⟩潜る ① [for s.o./s.a. to go under or into s.t., esp. to hide oneself], ⟨-ni⟩ tsu⌈kko⌉mu ⟨〜に⟩突っ込む ① •c [to enter a space forcibly] ⟪thrust, ram, dive⟫

EX. (**a**) Hearing the cry of the drowning child, the young man plunged into the river to rescue her.
おぼれかけている子供の叫び声を聞いて青年は助けようと川に{飛び込んだ/*潜った/*突っ込んだ}。
*Obore-kakete iru kodomo no sakebi-goe o kiite seinen wa tasukeyoo to kawa ni {tobi-konda/*mogutta/*tsukkonda}.*
(**b**) A female diver plunged into the ocean in search of abalones.
海女はあわびをさがしに海に{飛び込んだ/潜った/*突っ込んだ}。
*Ama wa awabi o sagasi ni umi ni {tobi-konda/mogutta/*tsukkonda}.*
(**c**) The motorbike careened out of control and plunged into the roadside hedge.
オートバイは制御がきかなくなって道端の生け垣に{突っ込んだ/*飛び込んだ/*潜った}。
*Ootobai wa seigyo ga kikanaku natte michi-bata no ike-gaki ni {tsukkonda/*tobi-konda/*mogutta}.*

—— vt. **[for s.o. to cause s.t. to move suddenly down or into s.t.]**

P

⟨-o⟩ ⟨-ni⟩ tsu⌈kko⌉mu ⟨〜を⟩⟨〜に⟩突っ込む ① **[for s.o./s.a. to forcibly thrust s.t. into s.t.]** ⟪thrust into, poke into⟫, {⟨-o⟩ ⟨-ni⟩/ ⟨-de⟩ ⟨-o⟩} tsu⌈ki-sa⌉su {⟨〜を⟩⟨〜に⟩/⟨〜で⟩ ⟨〜を⟩}突き刺す ① **[for s.o. to forcibly thrust s.t. sharp into s.t.]** ⟪thrust, pierce, penetrate⟫

EX. (**a**) I plunged my hand into the water to grab the fish.
魚をつかまえようと手を水中に{突っ込んだ/*突き刺した}。
*Sakana o tsukamaeyoo to te o suichuu ni {tsukkonda/*tsuki-sashita}.*
(**b**) Taking careful aim, he plunged his knife deep into the throat of the attacking bear.
彼は十分にねらいを定めて、襲いかかってきた熊ののどに深くナイフを{突き刺した/?突っ込んだ}。
*Kare wa juubunni nerai o sadamete, osoi-kakatte kita kuma no nodo ni fukaku naifu o {tsuki-sashita/ *tsukkonda}.*

plural adj. **[of or having to do with a grammatical form that refers to more than one person or thing]**
fu⌈kusu⌉u no N 複数のN •c ↔ tansuu no N 単数のN •c

EX. The plural form of "table" is "tables."
"Table"の複数形は"tables"だ。
"Table" no fukusuu-kei wa "tables" da.

plus prep. **[in addition to]**
⟨-ni⟩ ku⌈waete ⟨〜に⟩加えて / ⟨V *te* of *kuwaeru* ② add/ **[in addition to]**, **⟨-o⟩ ta⌈su ⟨〜を⟩足す** ① **[for s.o. to join s.t. to s.t. else so as to increase the total amount or as a supplement]** ⟪add, make good⟫, **pu⌈rasu プラス •f ↔ mainasu マイナス •f**

EX. (**a**) Two plus two equals four.
2{プラス/足す/*に加えて}2は4だ。
*Ni {purasu/tasu/*ni kuwaete} ni wa yon da.*
(**b**) Success requires talent plus luck.
成功は才能{プラス/に加えて/*足す}運だ。
*Seikoo wa sainoo {purasu/ni kuwaete/ *tasu} un da.*

— n. **[a symbol for addition ⟪fig. "profit," "asset"⟫]**
pu⌈rasu プラス •f, ri⌉eki 利益 •c [an increase in (monetary) wealth generated by an excess of returns over costs]

EX. It's a big plus for us to have a person like him on our project team.
彼のような人をプロジェクトチームに入れておくのは大きな{プラス/利益}だ。
Kare no yoona hito o purojekuto-chiimu ni irete oku no wa ookina {purasu/rieki} da.

p.m. (=post meridiem)
go⌉go 午後 •c [the time between noon and midnight] ↔ gozen 午前 •c

EX. A: What time does the plane leave?
飛行機は何時に出ますか。
Hikoo-ki wa nan-ji ni demasu ka.
B: It leaves at 4:15 P.M.
午後四時十五分に出ます。
Gogo yo-ji juu-go-fun ni demasu.

pocket n. **[a small pouch, usu. sewn onto or into a piece of clothing]**
po⌈ke⌉tto ポケット •f

EX. (**a**) Don't talk to your superior with your hands in your pockets.
目上の人とはポケットに手を突っ込んだまま話してはいけません。
Me-ue no hito to wa poketto ni te o tsukkonda mama hanashite wa ikemasen.
(**b**) I had a lot of change in my pocket.
私はポケットに小銭を沢山持っていた。
Watashi wa poketto ni ko-zeni o takusan motte ita.

poem n. **[a literary form composed in verse, typically expressing deep feeling or imaginative thought]**
shi 詩

EX. (**a**) I've never written a poem in my life.
私は今まで一度も詩を書いたことがありません。
Watashi wa ima made ichi-do mo shi o kaita koto ga arimasen.
(**b**) The *haiku* is the shortest kind of poem there is in the world.

俳句は世界で一番短い詩です。
Haiku wa sekai de ichiban mijikai shi desu.

poet n. **[a person who writes poems]**
shi⌈jin 詩人 •c [a person who writes poems as a profession]
EX. I am a scientist and not a poet.
私は科学者で、詩人ではない。
Watashi wa kagaku-sha de, shijin dewanai.

poetic adj. **[of or like poetry]**
1. shi ⌈no N 詩のN •c [pertaining to poetry]
EX. What poetic forms do you like?
どんな詩の形が好きですか。
Donna shi no katachi ga suki desu ka.
2. shi-⌈tekina 詩的な adj(*na*). **•c [resembling poetry]**
EX. Even a stone takes on a poetic character in such an idyllic place as this.
こんな牧歌的なところでは石でも詩的な気持ちになるでしょう。
Konna bokka-tekina tokoro de wa ishi demo shi-tekina kimochi ni naru deshoo.

poetry n. **[a collective term for poems]**
shi 詩 •c ↔ sanbun 散文 •c

point n. **[the end of a sharp object or a mark made by such an end; a piece of land projecting into a body of water; a geometric entity having position but no extension in space; a particular location in space or time; the essential idea or purpose of s.t. said or done]**
1. sa⌈ki 先 [the end of a stick/stick-like object《fig. "future," "the other party"》]《end, tip, head》
EX. The burglar held the point of his knife up against my throat.
強盗はナイフの先を私ののどに突き付けた。
Gootoo wa naifu no saki o watashi no nodo ni tsuki-tsuketa.
2. mi⌈saki 岬 [a piece of land projecting into a body of water]《cape》
EX. A lighthouse stood on the point.
岬には灯台が立っていた。
Misaki ni wa toodai ga tatte ita.
3. te⌈n 点 •c [a small mark made by the end of a sharp object《fig. "punctuation," "marks," "respects"》]《spot, dot, mark》
EX. (**a**) A line consists of an infinite sequence of points.
線は無数の点の続いたものだ。
Sen wa musuu no ten no tsuzuita mono da.
(**b**) A: How many points did you get on the *kanji* quiz?
漢字の小テストで何点取りましたか。
Kanji no shoo-tesuto de nan-ten torimashita ka.
B: I got 90 points out of 100.
百点満点で九十点取りました。
Hyaku-ten manten de kyuu-jut-ten torimashita.
4. to⌈koro 所 [a particular part of space occupied by s.t. or a building occupying a particular part of space《fig. "status," "situation," "occasion," "moment," "passage"》]《place, spot, address, home, time, moment》, chi⌈te⌉n 地点 •c [a particular location on the surface of the earth]《spot, place, position》
EX. (**a**) What are some of the points of interest in this town?
この町の面白い{所/*地点}はどこですか。
*Kono machi no omoshiroi {tokoro/ *chiten} wa doko desu ka.*
(**b**) This is the point where the accident occurred.
ここが事故の起きた{所/地点}だ。
Koko ga jiko no okita {tokoro/chiten} da.
5. ji⌉ten 時点 •c [a particular time in focus within a stretch of time], shu⌈nkan 瞬間 •c [a very brief period of time]
EX. (**a**) At that point in his life he was at the peak of his creative activity.
彼は人生のその{時点で/*瞬間に}創造活動の頂点にあった。
*Kare wa jinsei no sono {jiten de/ *shunkan ni} soozoo-katsudoo no chooten ni atta.*

P

(**b**) At the very point we arrived it started to rain.
到着したちょうどその{瞬間に/?時点で}雨が降り出した。
*Toochaku-shita choodo sono {shunkan ni/*jiten de} ame ga furi-dashita.*

6. yo⌈ote⌉n 要点 •c [the essential part of an argument] ⟪**gist, essential**⟫, **po⌈into ポイント •f [the essential idea of s.t. said or a unit of scoring in sports or a size of printing type]**

EX. What is the point of your argument?
あなたの議論の{要点/ポイント}は何ですか。
Anata no giron no {yooten/pointo} wa nan desu ka.

7. mo⌈kuteki 目的 •c [the intended result of a particular action/behavior] ⟪**purpose, objective, aim, goal**⟫, **ta⌈me⌉ ため [s.t. useful/profitable for s.o./s.t./s.a. ⟪fig. "purpose," "cause," "reason"⟫]** ⟪**advantage, benefit, profit, sake, due to, result**⟫

EX. What's the point of learning Japanese?
{何のために/どういう目的で}日本語を勉強しているんですか。
{Nan no tame ni/Doo-iu mokuteki de} Nihon-go o benkyoo-shite iru n desu ka.

PHRASE: a point of view *mi-kata* 見方 ⟪viewpoint, outlook⟫, *kenchi* 見地 **•c** ⟪standpoint⟫, *kangae-kata* 考え方 ⟪way of thinking⟫, *kenkai* 見解 **•c** ⟪opinion, view, outlook⟫, *iken* 意見 **•c** ⟪opinion, idea, suggestion⟫

EX. (**a**) One of the marks of an advanced student in a foreign language is the ability to express varying points of view on a particular issue.
上級に達した外国語学習者の特徴の一つはある問題に関する様々な{見方/考え方/見解/意見/*見地}を表現することができるということだ。
*Jookyuu ni tasshita gaikoku-go gakushuu-sha no tokuchoo no hitotsu wa aru mondai ni-kansuru sama-zamana {mi-kata/kangae-kata/kenkai/iken/*kenchi} o hyoogen-suru koto ga dekiru to iu koto da.*

(**b**) My political point of view is very different from his.
私の政治的{見方/見地/考え方/見解/意見}は彼のと非常に違う。
Watashi no seiji-teki-{mi-kata/kenchi/kangae-kata/kenkai/iken} wa kare no to hijooni chigau.

— vt. **[to direct s.t. in a particular direction]**

1. ⟨-o⟩ ⟨-ni⟩ mu⌈keru ⟨〜を⟩⟨〜に⟩向ける ① [for s.o. to aim s.t. in a certain direction ⟪fig. "use s.t. for a certain purpose"⟫] ⟪**turn, direct, aim**⟫

EX. The soldier approached me with his gun pointed at me.
兵隊は私に銃を向けて近付いてきた。
Heitai wa watashi ni juu o mukete chikazuite kita.

2. ⟨-o⟩ shi⌈mesu ⟨〜を⟩示す ① [to cause s.o. to see or be clearly aware of some fact or object by the use of symbols or other indirect means ⟨fml⟩] ⟪**show, indicate**⟫

EX. The sign points the way to the college.
標識は大学へ行く道を示している。
Hyooshiki wa daigaku e iku michi o shimeshite iru.

— vi. **[to indicate an object or direction using one's finger or a finger-like object] ⟨-o⟩ yu⌈bi-sa⌉su ⟨〜を⟩指差す ① [for s.o. to draw attention to the presence of s.t./s.o./s.a. using one's finger], ⟨-o⟩ shi⌈mesu ⟨〜を⟩示す ① [for s.o./s.t. to cause s.o. to see or be clearly aware of some fact or object by the use of symbols or other indirect means ⟨fml⟩]** ⟪**show, indicate**⟫

EX. (**a**) It's impolite to point at a person with your finger.
人を{指差す/*指で示す}のは失礼です。
*Hito o {yubi-sasu/*yubi de shimesu} no wa shitsurei desu.*

(**b**) This piece of evidence points to the correctness of our claim.
この証拠は私たちの主張の正しさを{示して/*指差して}いる。
*Kono shooko wa watashi-tachi no shuchoo no tadashi-sa o {shimeshite/*yubi-sashite} iru.*

poison n. **[a substance that can harm or kill a living animal or plant by chemical action ⟪fig. "s.t. that can spiritually harm s.o."⟫]**
do⌈ku⌉ 毒 •c ⟪venom, harm⟫

EX. (**a**) The young man killed himself by taking poison.
青年は毒を飲んで自殺した。
Seinen wa doku o nonde jisatsu-shita.
(**b**) Although I know tobacco is a kind of poison, I just can't quit smoking.
たばこを吸うのが毒だとは分かっているけど、どうしてもやめられないんです。
Tabako o suu no ga doku da to wa wakatte iru kedo, doo-shite-mo yame-rarenai n desu.
(**c**) Violence on television is poison to the minds of young children.
テレビの中の暴力は子供の心には毒だ。
Terebi no naka no booryoku wa kodomo no kokoro ni wa doku da.

poisonous adj. **[containing poison capable of harming or killing a living animal or plant]**
⟨-ni⟩ do⌈ku⌉ no N ⟨〜に⟩毒のN **•c, ⟨-ni⟩ yu⌈ugaina** ⟨〜に⟩有害な adj(*na*). **•c [harmful to living animals or plants] ⟪harmful, injurious⟫**

EX. (**a**) Cigarettes are poisonous to one's body.
たばこは体に{毒/有害}だ。
Tabako wa karada ni {doku/yuugai} da.
(**b**) Some people say that comic books have a poisonous influence on children.
漫画は子供に{有害な/*毒の}影響を与えるという人がいる。
*Manga wa kodomo ni {yuugaina/*doku no} eikyoo o ataeru to iu hito ga iru.*

poke vt. **[to push at s.t. with a narrow or stick-like object]**
⟨-o⟩ tsu⌈ku ⟨〜を⟩突く ① **[for s.o./s.a. to make impact with or penetrate s.t./s.o./s.a. with a sharp or stick-like object ⟪fig. "attack sharply"⟫] ⟪prick, stab⟫, ⟨-o⟩ tsu⌈(t)tsu⌉ku** ⟨〜を⟩突(っ)つく ① **[for s.o./s.a. to push at s.t. lightly and repeatedly with a pointed object] ⟪pick, peck at, nudge⟫**

NOTE: *Tsuttsuku* is more colloquial sounding than *tsutsuku*.

EX. (**a**) A man poked my shoulder from behind.
男が後ろから僕の肩を{突いた/突(っ)ついた}。
Otoko ga ushiro kara boku no kata o {tsuita/tsu(t)tsuita}.
(**b**) The burglar apparently poked a hole in the wooden door with an iron bar or something sharp.
泥棒は鉄の棒か何かとがったもので木のドアを{突いて/突(っ)ついて}、穴を開けたらしい。
Doroboo wa tetsu no boo ka nan-ka togatta mono de ki no doa o {tsuite/tsu(t)tsuite}, ana o aketa rashii.

PHRASE: poke one's nose (into someone's business) *o-sekkai o yaku* おせっかいをやく ③, ⟨*-no*⟩ *koto ni kubi o tsukkomu* ⟨〜の⟩ことに首をつっこむ ①

EX. I don't like her because she's always poking her nose into my business.
彼女はいつも{おせっかいをやく/人のことに首を突っ込む}から嫌いだ。
Kanojo wa itsu-mo {osekkai o yaku/hito no koto ni kubi o tsukkomu} kara kirai da.

— vi **[to push at s.t. with a narrow or stick-like object, often repeatedly ⟪fig. "meddle with"⟫]**
⟨-o⟩ tsu⌈(t)tsu⌉ku ⟨〜を⟩突(っ)つく ① **[for s.o./s.a. to push at s.t. lightly and repeatedly with a pointed object] ⟪pick, peck at, nudge⟫**

NOTE: *Tsuttsuku* is more colloquial sounding than *tsutsuku*.

EX. A bird was poking at a worm on the lawn.
鳥が芝生で虫を突(っ)ついていた。
Tori ga shibafu de mushi o tsu(t)tsuite ita.

Poland n.
Po⌈ora⌉ndo ポーランド •f

pole[1] n. **[a long narrow cylindrical object made of wood, metal, or hard material]**
1. **bo⌈o 棒 •c [a long, slim object made of wood/bamboo/metal] ⟪rod⟫**

EX. Don't swing the pole around like that.
棒をそんな風に振り回してはいけないよ。
Boo o sonna fuu ni furi-mawashite wa ikenai yo.

2. ha⌈shira 柱 [a thick vertical structure that supports the weight of the upper part of a building 《fig. "support"》] 《pillar, post》

PHRASE: a telephone pole *denchuu* 電柱 •c

EX. Despite the danger they pose in earthquakes, telephone poles are still a common sight in Japan.
地震が起こると危険であるにもかかわらず日本ではまだ電柱をよく見かける。
Jishin ga okoru to kiken dearu ni-mo-kakawarazu Nihon de wa mada denchuu o yoku mikakeru.

pole² n. **[either extreme of the earth's axis]**
kyo⌉ku 極 •c [an extremity] 《limit, extremeness》

EX. Many countries are sending expeditions to the South Pole these days.
このごろは多くの国が南極へ探検隊を送っている。
Konogoro wa ooku no kuni ga Nankyoku e tanken-tai o okutte iru.

PHRASE: the North Pole *Hokkyoku* 北極 •c

police n.
ke⌈isatsu 警察 •c

EX. (**a**) A: There's a suspicious-looking man loitering outside the house, honey.
あなた、怪しい人がうちの外をぶらぶらしているわよ。
Anata, ayashii hito ga uchi no soto o bura-bura-shite iru wa yo.
B: We'd better call the police.
警察に電話したほうがいいな。
Keisatsu ni denwa-shita hoo ga ii na.
(**b**) The police are investigating the banker to see if he embezzled any money.
警察はその銀行家が金を使い込んだかどうか調べている。
Keisatsu wa sono ginkoo-ka ga kane o tsukai-konda ka doo ka shirabete iru.

police box n.
ko⌈oban 交番 •c [a small structure where one or two policemen are stationed to help prevent crime and to provide assistance to people such as giving them directions] 《police station》

EX. When you get lost in Japan, the best thing to do is to go to a nearby police box.
日本で道に迷ったら、近くの交番へ行くのが一番いい。
Nihon de michi ni mayottara, chikaku no kooban e iku no ga ichiban ii.

policeman n. **[a member of a police force]**
ke⌈ikan 警官 •c ⟨fml⟩ 《police officer》, o-⌈ma⌉wari(-san) お巡り(さん) [a familiar term for referring to a member of the police force] 《police officer, officer》

NOTE: *O-mawari-san* can be used as a form of address, unlike *keikan* or *o-mawari.*

EX. (**a**) I was stopped by a policeman on the highway for speeding.
高速道路でスピードを出し過ぎて、{警官/??お巡り(さん)}に止められた。
Koosoku-dooro de supiido o dashi-sugite, {keikan/??o-mawari(-san)} ni tome-rareta.
(**b**) Japanese policemen often ride around on bicycles.
日本の{警官/お巡り(さん)}はよく自転車に乗って巡回する。
Nihon no {keikan/o-mawari(-san)} wa yoku jitensha ni notte junkai-suru.

policy n. **[a guiding principle used in making decisions by a government, party, or individual]**
se⌈isaku 政策 •c [a guiding principle used in making decisions by a government or party], ho⌈oshin 方針 •c [a guiding principle used in making decisions by an institution] 《principle》, ya⌈ri-kata やり方 /⟨V *masu* of *yaru* ① do + suf. *kata* way/ [a method/manner of doing s.t.]

EX. (**a**) What kind of educational policy does the Liberal Democratic Party support?
自民党はどのような教育{政策/?方針/?のやり方}を支持しているのでしょうか。
Jimin-too wa dono yoona kyooiku {-seisaku/?-hooshin/?no yari-kata} o shiji-shite iru no deshoo ka.

(**b**) The policy of our company is to recruit young people with an international perspective.
この会社の{方針/*政策/*やり方}は国際的な視野を持った若い人を雇うことです。
*Kono kaisha no {hooshin/*seisaku/*yari-kata} wa kokusai-tekina shiya o motta wakai hito o yatou koto desu.*
(**c**) In Japan it's a good policy not to assert yourself too strongly.
日本ではあまり自分を強く出さないのが好ましい{やり方/*政策/*方針}だ。
*Nihon de wa amari jibun o tsuyoku dasanai no ga konomashii {yari-kata/*seisaku/*hooshin} da.*

polio n.
sho⌈oni-ma⌉hi 小児まひ •c, **po⌉rio** ポリオ •f

polish vt. **[for s.o. to make s.t. shiny through rubbing ⟪fig. "refine s.t. through constant effort"⟫]**
⟨**-o**⟩ **mi⌈gaku** ⟨〜を⟩磨く ① **[for s.o. to rub a hard, rough surface and make it smooth and shiny ⟪fig. "make constant efforts to improve one's skill"⟫] ⟪burnish, brush, scour, shine⟫**
EX. (**a**) Do you polish your shoes every day?
毎日靴を磨きますか。
Mai-nichi kutsu o migakimasu ka.
(**b**) During his two years in Japan, Bill polished his ability in Japanese to the point that he could conduct business freely in it.
ビルは日本滞在中の二年間にビジネスの場で使いこなせるところまで日本語の腕を磨いた。
Biru wa Nihon-taizai-chuu no ni-nenkan ni bijinesu no ba de tsukai-konase-ru tokoro made Nihon-go no ude o migaita.

polite adj. **[following social norms of good manners and consideration for others ⟪fig. "refined"⟫]**
1. te⌉ineina 丁寧な adj(*na*). **•c [careful and considerate in giving attention to details, esp. as they relate to one's verbal and nonverbal interactions with others] ⟪courteous, kind, careful, thorough⟫, re⌈igi-tadashi⌉i** 礼儀正しい adj(*i*). **[well mannered] ⟪courteous, proper⟫**
EX. (**a**) You should always use polite speech with your teacher.
先生には必ず{丁寧な/?礼儀正しい}言葉を使いなさい。
Sensei ni wa kanarazu {teineina/?reigi-tadashii} kotoba o tsukainasai.
(**b**) Professor Smith is polite even to his students.
スミス先生は学生にも{丁寧だ/*礼儀正しい}。
*Sumisu-sensei wa gakusei ni mo {teineida/*reigi-tadashii}.*
(**c**) Mr. Yamada's children are very polite, aren't they?
山田さんのうちの子供たちはとても{礼儀正しい/*丁寧だ}ね。
*Yamada san no uchi no kodomo-tachi wa totemo {reigi-tadashii/*teinei da} ne.*
(**d**) Thank you very much for your polite letter of December 15.
十二月十五日の{ご丁寧な/*礼儀正しい}お手紙、ありがとうございました。
*Juu-ni-gatsu juu-go-nichi no {go-teineina/*reigi-tadashii} o-tegami, arigatoo gozaimashita.*
2. jo⌈ohi⌉nna 上品な adj(*na*). **•c [sophisticated and pleasing in quality, speech, or behavior] ⟪graceful, elegant, refined⟫ ⟷ gehinna** 下品な adj(*na*). **•c**
EX. The polite company at the dinner party was a welcome change to the roughness of my usual workaday colleagues.
夕食会に来ていた上品な人たちは普段会社でつきあっているがさつな連中とは対照的でいい気分転換になった。
Yuushoku-kai ni kite ita joohinna hito-tachi wa fudan kaisha de tsuki-atte iru gasatsuna renchuu to wa taishoo-teki de ii kibun-tenkan ni natta.

political adj. **[pertaining to politics]**
se⌈iji no N 政治のN **•c [pertaining to local or national governmental politics], se⌈iji-tekina** 政治的な adj(*na*). **•c [inclined to (non-)governmental politics]**

P

EX. (**a**) Nowadays college students don't show much interest in political issues.
このごろの大学生は{政治の/政治的な}ことに関心を示さない。
Kono-goro no daigaku-sei wa {seiji no/seiji-tekina} koto ni kanshin o shimesanai.
(**b**) He's a bit too political in his dealings with other people for my taste.
彼は他人との接し方があまりにも政治的で私にはなじめない。
Kare wa tanin to no sesshi-kata ga amarini-mo seiji-teki de watashi ni wa najime-nai.
(**c**) It took five years to find a political solution to the border dispute.
国境をめぐる紛争に{政治的な/?政治の}決着をはかるのに五年かかった。
Kokkyoo o meguru funsoo ni {seiji-tekina/?seiji no} ketchaku o hakaru no ni go-nen kakatta.

PHRASE: political party *seitoo* 政党 •**c**, political system *seiji-seido* 政治制度 •**c**

EX. In America there are two major political parties, the Republican and the Democratic parties.
アメリカには共和党と民主党の二大政党がある。
Amerika ni wa Kyoowa-too to Minshu-too no ni-dai-seitoo ga aru.

PHRASE: political science *seiji-gaku* 政治学 •**c** ⟪politics⟫

EX. Do many students major in political science at this university?
この大学では政治学を専攻する学生は多いですか。
Kono daigaku de wa seiji-gaku o senkoo-suru gakusei wa ooi desu ka.

politician n. **[a person who holds or seeks to hold a governmental office]**
1. se⌈iji-ka 政治家 •c [a person involved in government/politics as a profession] ⟪**statesman**⟫

EX. To succeed as a politician one must be skilled in the art of compromise.
政治家として成功するには妥協の術にたけていなければならない。
Seiji-ka to-shite seikoo-suru ni wa dakyoo no jutsu ni takete inakereba naranai.

2. se⌈iji-ya 政治屋 [a person involved in non-governmental politics, usually used in a derogatory sense]

politics n. **[the science or art of governing a community of people, esp. a country]**
1. se⌈iji 政治 •c [the structures and processes involved in governing a society] ⟪**government**⟫, **u⌈n'ei 運営 •c [the act of running or governing an institution]** ⟪**administration, management**⟫

EX. (**a**) Japanese politics went through some remarkable changes in the early 1990's.
日本の{政治/*運営}は1990年代初期に顕著な変化を遂げた。
*Nihon no {seiji/*un'ei} wa sen-kyuu-hyaku-kyuu-juu-nen-dai shoki ni kenchona henka o togeta.*
(**b**) The politics of a large company is very similar to that of a nation.
大会社の{運営/*政治}は国の{政治/*運営}によく似ている。
*Dai-gaisha no {un'ei/*seiji} wa kuni no {seiji/*un'ei} ni yoku nite iru.*

2. se⌈iji⌉-gaku 政治学 •c [the science of governing a country] ⟪**political science**⟫

EX. I'm majoring in politics at Princeton University.
私はプリンストン大学で政治学を専攻しています。
Watashi wa Purinsuton daigaku de seiji-gaku o senkoo-shite imasu.

pollution n. **[a state of impurity in the environment caused by substances harmful to it or such substances themselves]**
o⌈sen 汚染 •c [the process of causing the environment to become impure or unclean by introducing substances harmful to it] ⟪**contamination**⟫

EX. (**a**) The extent of the air pollution in Tokyo has decreased greatly from what it used to be.
東京の大気汚染は昔よりずっと少なくなった。

Tookyoo no taiki-osen wa mukashi yori zutto sukunaku natta.
(**b**) Environmentalists are working hard to solve the problem of pollution.
環境保護に力を入れている人たちは汚染の問題の解決に一生懸命取り組んでいる。
Kankyoo-hogo ni chikara o irete iru hito-tachi wa osen no mondai no kaiketsu ni isshoo-kenmei tori-kunde iru.

pond n. **[a small area of still water surrounded by land]**
i⌈ke⌉ 池 [a small reservoir of still water, either natural or man made] ⟪pool⟫, nu⌈ma⌉ 沼 [a natural reservoir of unclear, still water with a muddy bottom] ⟪marsh, swamp⟫
EX. The children were skating on the frozen pond.
子供たちは氷の張った{池/沼}でスケートをしていた。
Kodomo-tachi wa koori no hatta {ike/numa} de sukeeto o shite ita.

pool n. **[a small body of still water or an artificial enclosure filled with water for swimming ⟪fig. "shared supply of money/vehicles"⟫]**
1. mi⌈zu-tamari 水たまり [a small body of water] ⟪puddle⟫
EX. After the rain there were pools of water here and there on the street.
雨が降ったら、道のあちこちに水たまりが出来た。
Ame ga futtara, michi no achi-kochi ni mizu-tamari ga dekita.
2. pu⌉uru プール •f [an artificial enclosure filled with water for swimming]
EX. Every day for about 30 minutes I swim in the pool.
毎日三十分ぐらいプールで泳ぎます。
Mai-nichi san-jup-pun-gurai puuru de oyogimasu.
3. kyo⌈odoo-to⌉oshi 共同投資 •c [joint investment], kyo⌈odoo-shiki⌉n 共同資金 •c [joint capital]

poor adj. **[having little money or resources or not skilled at s.t. ⟪fig. "deserving sympathy or pity"⟫]**
1. bi⌉nboona 貧乏な adj(*na*). **•c [having little money or resources] ⟪needy⟫ ↔ kane-mochi no N 金持ちのN; ma⌈zushi⌉i 貧しい** adj(*i*). **•c [having little money or resources ⟪fig. "scanty," "small"⟫] ⟪needy⟫ ↔ yutakana 豊かな** adj(*na*).; **to⌈boshi⌉i 乏しい** adj(*i*). **[lacking in money, resources, or experience] ⟪scanty, meager, short, deficient⟫ ↔ hoofuna 豊富な** adj(*na*). **•c**
EX. (**a**) When I was a child we were very poor.
私が子供の時うちは大変{貧乏だった/貧しかった/*乏しかった}。
*Watashi ga kodomo no toki uchi wa taihen {binboo datta/mazushikatta/*toboshikatta}.*
(**b**) This county is poor in water resources.
この国は水資源が{乏しい/*貧乏だ/*貧しい}。
*Kono kuni wa mizu-shigen ga {toboshii/*binboo da/*mazushii}.*
(**c**) He was born into a very poor family.
彼は大変{貧乏な/貧しい/*乏しい}うちに生まれた。
*Kare wa taihen {binboona/mazushii/*toboshii} uchi ni umareta.*
2. ka⌉wai-so⌉ona かわいそうな adj(*na*). **[for s.o./s.a. to deserve sympathy due to the adverse situation he/she/it is in] ⟪pitiful, sad⟫, ki-⌈no-doku⌉na 気の毒な** adj(*na*). **[deserving of sympathy for the pain or sorrow one is suffering] ⟪wretched, pitiable⟫**
EX. (**a**) Poor Angelica had nowhere to turn after she lost her father.
{かわいそうな/気の毒な}アンジェリカはお父さんを亡くしてからだれも頼りにできる人がいなかった。
{Kawai-soona/Ki-no-dokuna} Anjerika wa o-too-san o nakushite kara dare-mo tayori ni dekiru hito ga inakatta.
(**b**) Our poor dog has limped ever since he got run over by a car.
うちの犬は{かわいそうに/*気の毒に}車に

ひかれてからずっとびっこをひいている。
*Uchi no inu wa {kawai-sooni/*ki-no-dokuni} kuruma ni hika-rete kara zutto bikko o hiite iru.*

3. ⟨-ga⟩ he⌈ta⌉na ⟨〜が⟩下手な adj(*na*). **[not skilled at doing s.t.]** ⟪**unskillful, bad**⟫ ↔ **⟨-ga⟩ joozuna** ⟨〜が⟩上手な adj(*na*).

EX. (**a**) I tried to explain American football to my Japanese friend using my poor Japanese.
私は下手な日本語でフットボールのことを日本人の友達に説明しようとした。
Watashi wa hetana Nihon-go de futto-booru no koto o Nihon-jin no tomodachi ni setsumei-shiyoo to shita.
(**b**) Despite all my practice, I'm still poor at tennis.
私は一生懸命練習してきたのにまだテニスが下手です。
Watashi wa isshookenmei renshuu-shite kita no ni mada tenisu ga heta desu.
(**c**) Tom has poor handwriting.
トムは字が下手だ。
Tomu wa ji ga heta da.

popcorn n.
po⌈ppuko⌉on ポップコーン •**f**

EX. Americans love to eat popcorn while watching movies.
アメリカ人はポップコーンを食べながら映画を見るのが好きだ。
Amerika-jin wa poppukoon o tabe-nagara eiga o miru no ga suki da.

popular adj. **[belonging to/oriented toward/liked by the general public]**

1. ta⌈ishuu no N 大衆のN •**c [belonging to the general public]**

EX. It's interesting to study popular culture.
大衆(の)文化を研究するのは面白い。
Taishuu (no) bunka o kenkyuu-suru no wa omoshiroi.

2. ta⌈ishuu-muki no N 大衆向きのN **[oriented toward the general public]**

EX. In Japan, bars for the general public are called "popular bars."
日本では大衆向きのバーを「大衆酒場」という。
Nihon de wa taishuu-muki no baa o 'taishuu-sakaba' to iu.

3. ⟨-ni⟩ ni⌈nki ga a⌉ru (N) ⟨〜に⟩人気がある(N) •**c [to be well liked by a group of people]**

EX. (**a**) That singer is very popular among young people.
あの歌手は若い人にとても人気がある。
Ano kashu wa wakai hito ni totemo ninki ga aru.
(**b**) *Sushi* is very popular among Americans these days.
すしは近ごろアメリカ人にとても人気がある。
Sushi wa chikagoro Amerika-jin ni totemo ninki ga aru.

popularity n. **[the state of being popular]**
ta⌈ishuu-sei 大衆性 •**c [the quality of belonging to the general public], ni⌈nki** 人気 •**c [the state of being well liked by a group of people]**

EX. (**a**) In Japan the portable video recorder is gaining popularity.
日本ではポータブルのビデオレコーダーに{人気/*大衆性}が出てきている。
*Nihon de wa pootaburu no bideo rekoodaa ni {ninki/*taishuu-sei} ga dete kite iru.*
(**b**) The popularity of blue jeans in America is probably due to their informality.
アメリカでジーンズが{大衆性/人気}があるのは格式張らないからだろう。
Amerika de jiinzu ga {taishuu-sei/ninki} ga aru no wa kakushiki-baranai kara daroo.

population n. **[the inhabitants of a certain locality or the total number of these]**

1. ze⌉n-ju⌈umin 全住民 •**c [the entire group of inhabitants in a certain locality]**

EX. The entire population of that small island was against the construction of the airport.
その小さい島の全住民が空港を作ることに反対した。
Sono chiisai shima no zen-juumin ga kuukoo o tsukuru koto ni hantai-shita.

2. ji⌈nkoo 人口 •**c [the total number of inhabitants of a certain locality]**

EX. A: Do you know what the population of Japan is?
日本の人口を知っていますか。
Nihon no jinkoo o shitte imasu ka.
B: Yes, I believe it's approximately 120 million.
ええ、約一億二千万だと思います。
Ee, yaku ichi-oku-ni-sen-man da to omoimasu.

porch n. **[an area with a floor and roof built onto the outside of a house, usu. around a door]**
po˥ochi ポーチ •f

EX. There's nothing like cooling off on the porch on a summer evening with a glass of lemonade or beer.
夏の晩にポーチでレモネードやビールを飲みながら夕涼みをする。これほど気持ちのいいことはない。
Natsu no ban ni poochi de remoneedo ya biiru o nomi-nagara yuu-suzumi o suru. Kore hodo kimochi no ii koto wa nai.

pork n. **[pig meat used as food]**
bu˥ta-niku 豚肉

EX. A: Which do you prefer, pork or beef?
豚肉と牛肉と、どちらがお好きですか。
Buta-niku to gyuuniku to, dochira ga o-suki desu ka.
B: I like pork better.
豚肉の方が好きです。
Buta-niku no hoo ga suki desu.

port n. **[a coastal location where ships can dock or anchor and where goods pass into or out of a country; a town built around such a location]**
1. mi˥nato 港 [a coastal location where ships can dock or anchor to load or unload goods] ((**harbor**))

EX. (**a**) A huge ship is anchored in the port.
大きな船が港に泊まっています。
Ookina fune ga minato ni tomatte imasu.
(**b**) Look! A big tanker is coming into port.
見てご覧。大きなタンカーが港に入って来ているよ。
Mite goran. Ookina tankaa ga minato ni haitte kite iru yo.

2. mi˥nato˥-machi 港町 [a harbor town] ((**port town**))

EX. A port always seems to have a cosmopolitan air to it.
港町にはいつも何かコスモポリタンのようなところがある。
Minato-machi ni wa itsu-mo nani-ka kosumoporitan no yoona tokoro ga aru.

portable adj. **[capable of being carried or moved]**
mo˥chi-hakobi ga de˥ki˥ru (N) 持ち運びが出来る(N) [capable of being held and carried], ke˥itai-yoo no N 携帯用のN •c [capable of being held in the hand or carried in a pocket], po˥ota˥buru no N ポータブルのN •f

EX. This portable color TV is nice to have on long car trips.
この{持ち運びが出来る/携帯用の/ポータブルの}カラーテレビは車で長距離旅行をする時に便利です。
Kono {mochi-hakobi ga dekiru/keitai-yoo no/pootaburu no} karaa-terebi wa kuruma de choo-kyori-ryokoo o suru toki ni benri desu.

portion n. **[a part/share of s.t.]**
1. i˥chi˥-bu 一部 •c [one part of s.t.] ((**part, copy**))

EX. (**a**) We read a portion of the *Tale of Genji* in class.
『源氏物語』の一部を授業で読みました。
"Genji Monogatari" no ichi-bu o jugyoo de yomimashita.
(**b**) We were only able to see a portion of the large campus because of the time constraint we were under.
時間が足りなくて広いキャンパスの一部しか見ることができませんでした。
Jikan ga tarinakute hiroi kyanpasu no ichi-bu shika miru koto ga dekimasen deshita.

2. wa˥ke˥-mae 分け前 [a part of a larger entity, esp. a sum of money, distributed to s.o.] ((**share, cut**))

EX. I haven't yet received my portion of the profits.
僕はまだもうけの分け前をもらっていない。
Boku wa mada mooke no wake-mae o moratte inai.

Portugal n.
Po⌈rutogaru ポルトガル •f

Portuguese adj. **[of Portugal/its people/its language]**
Po⌈rutogaru no N ポルトガルのN •f [of Portugal], Po⌈rutogaru⌉-jin no N ポルトガル人のN •f+c [of the people/a person of Portugal], Po⌈rutogaru-go no N ポルトガル語のN •f+c [of the language of Portugal]
—— n. **[the people/language of Portugal]**
1. Po⌈rutogaru⌉-jin ポルトガル人 •f+c [the people/a person of Portugal]

EX. It was the Portuguese who first brought guns to Japan in 1543.
1543年に初めて日本に鉄砲を持って来たのはポルトガル人だった。
Sen-go-hyaku-yon-juu-san-nen ni hajimete Nihon ni teppoo o motte-kita no wa Porutogaru-jin datta.

2. Po⌈rutogaru-go ポルトガル語 •f+c [the language of Portugal/Brazil]

position n. **[the place occupied by s.t./s.o. or the proper place for s.t./s.o. 《fig. "social status," "view point," "paid job"》]**
1. i⌉chi 位置 •c [the place occupied by s.t./s.o./s.a.] 《location》, po⌈ji⌉shon ポジション •f [the place occupied by a player on the playing field in a ball game]

EX. (**a**) I can't find our position on this map.
私たちの位置がこの地図では分かりません。
Watashi-tachi no ichi ga kono chizu de wa wakarimasen.
(**b**) Is this the right position for the knife and fork?
ナイフとフォークの位置はこれでいいですか。
Naifu to fooku no ichi wa kore de ii desu ka.
(**c**) A: My son plays on his high school's baseball team.
息子は高校の野球チームに入っているんです。
Musuko wa kookoo no yakyuu-chiimu ni haitte iru n desu.
B: What's his position?
ポジションはどこですか?
Pojishon wa doko desu ka?
A: Shortstop.
ショートです。
Shooto desu.

2. chi⌉i 地位 •c [the standing which one has acquired in a social group or society] 《status, rank》, mi⌉bun 身分 [an individual's standing in society relative to others/one's circumstances] 《status》

EX. (**a**) In less than 8 years he advanced to the second highest position in the company.
八年も経たないうちに、彼は会社で二番目に高い{地位/*身分}についた。
*Hachi-nen mo tatanai uchi ni, kare wa kaisha de ni-ban-me ni takai {chii/*mibun} ni tsuita.*
(**b**) All are welcome in this church, no matter what their social position.
この教会は社会的{地位/身分}を問わずだれでも歓迎します。
Kono kyookai wa shakai-teki {chii/mibun} o towazu dare-demo kangei-shimasu.

3. tsu⌈tome⌉-guchi 勤め口 [a job opening sought by one] 《job》, sho⌈ku 職 •c [a duty 《fig. "job"》] 《job, work, post》

EX. I'm looking for a position in the computer industry. Do you know of any?
コンピューター会社の{勤め口/職}を探しているんですが、何かご存じですか。
Konpyuutaa-gaisha no {tsutome-guchi/shoku} o sagashite iru n desu ga, nani-ka go-zonji desu ka.

4. ta⌈chiba⌉ 立場 [a social or physical circumstance in which one finds oneself or one's viewpoint] 《viewpoint, stance, situation》, mi 身 [s.o./s.a.'s body or flesh 《fig. "self," "viewpoint"》] 《body, meat, flesh, one's place》

EX. (**a**) Try putting yourself in my position.
私の{身/立場}になってみてください。
Watashi no {mi/tachiba} ni natte mite kudasai.
(**b**) My friend took a noncommittal position on the proposal.
友達はその提案に対してどっちつかずの{立場/*身}を取った。
*Tomodachi wa sono teian ni-taishite dotchi-tsukazu no {tachiba/*mi} o totta.*

positive adj. **[having no doubt or leaving no room for doubt; exhibiting a favorable attitude toward s.o./s.t.; having a mathematical quantity greater than zero; having an electric charge which is opposite of negative]**

1. (Sinf. no wa) ma⌈chiga⌉i na⌉i to o⌈mo⌉u (Sinf.のは)間違いないと思う ① [to believe for certain that]

EX. (**a**) A: Are you sure we're on the right train?
今乗っている電車で本当にいいと思う?
Ima notte iru densha de hontooni ii to omou?
B: Yes, I'm positive!
うん、間違いないと思うよ。
Un, machigainai to omou yo.
(**b**) I'm positive that our approach is the right one.
僕たちのやり方が正しいのは間違いないと思うよ。
Boku-tachi no yari-kata ga tadashii no wa machigai nai to omou yo.

2. (⟨-ni⟩) se⌈kkyoku-tekina (⟨〜に⟩)積極的な adj(*na*). **•c [inclined to act on one's own initiative ⟪fig. "agreeable"⟫]**

EX. (**a**) I like your positive attitude.
私はあなたの積極的な態度が好きです。
Watashi wa anata no sekkyoku-tekina taido ga suki desu.
(**b**) Japanese politicians try to act at least outwardly positive toward the idea of making Japan a more internationalized society.
日本の政治家は少なくとも表面上は日本の国際化に対して積極的なところをみせようとしている。
Nihon no seiji-ka wa sukunakutomo hyoomen-joo wa Nihon no kokusai-ka ni-taishite sekkyoku-tekina tokoro o miseyoo to shite iru.

3. yo⌈o(-kyoku) no N 陽(極)のN •c [having an electric charge which is opposite of negative] ↔ in(-kyoku) no N 陰(極)のN •c; pu⌈rasu no N プラスのN •f ↔ mainasu no N マイナスのN •f

4. se⌉i no N 正のN •c [having a quantity greater than zero] ↔ fu no N 負のN •c

possess vt. **[for s.o./s.a. to have s.t./s.o./s.a. as one's own property ⟪fig. "gain control over"⟫]**

1. ⟨-o⟩ mo⌉tsu ⟨〜を⟩持つ ① [for s.o. to hold s.t./s.o./s.a. in one's hand ⟪fig. "own"⟫] ⟪have, hold, own, carry, bear⟫, ⟨-ni⟩ ⟨-ga⟩ a⌉ru ⟨〜に⟩⟨〜が⟩ある ① [for s.t. to exist], ⟨-o⟩ sho⌈yuu-suru ⟨〜を⟩所有する ③ •c [for s.o. to have s.t. such as property ⟨fml⟩] ⟪own⟫

EX. (**a**) Mr. Yamashita possesses property in both Japan and the U.S.
山下氏は日本にもアメリカにも土地{を持っている/を所有している/がある}。
Yamashita-shi wa Nihon ni mo Amerika ni mo tochi {o motte iru/o shoyuu-shite iru/ga aru}.
(**b**) It's illegal for common citizens to possess handguns in Japan.
日本では一般の市民が拳銃{を持つ/を所有する/*がある}ことは違法である。
*Nihon de wa ippan no shimin ga kenjuu {o motsu/o shoyuu-suru/*ga aru} koto wa ihoo dearu.*
(**c**) Japanese mothers often think that they possess their children.
日本の母親は、子供{を所有している/*を持っている/*がある}と思っていることがよくある。
*Nihon no haha-oya wa, kodomo {o shoyuu-shite iru/*o motte iru/*ga aru} to omotte iru koto ga yoku aru.*

2. ⟨-ni⟩ to⌈ritsuku ⟨〜に⟩取り付く ① [for a spiritual being or unusual emotional state to take control of s.o.'s mind] ⟪cling to, haunt, obsess⟫

P

EX. The child was possessed by demons.
その子は悪霊に取り付かれていた。
Sono ko wa akurei ni toritsuka-rete ita.

possession n. **[the act or state of possessing or s.t. which is possessed]**
1. sho⌈yuu 所有 •c [the state of possessing s.t. ⟨fml⟩] **⟪ownership⟫**, **sho⌉ji 所持 •c [the act of holding s.t. on one's person]** **⟪own, bear, carry⟫**

EX. (**a**) Possession of a computer is a necessity in modern life.
コンピューターの{所有/*所持}は現代生活に必須だ。
*Konpyuutaa no {shoyuu/*shoji} wa gendai-seikatsu ni hissu da.*
(**b**) Possession of pistols and guns is prohibited in Japan.
日本では拳銃の{所持/?所有}は禁じられている。
Nihon de wa kenjuu no {shoji/?shoyuu} wa kinji-rarete iru.

2. sho⌈yu⌉u-butsu 所有物 •c [s.t. one possesses] **⟪one's property⟫**

EX. Stealing someone else's possessions is considered wrong in any human society.
どこの社会でも人の所有物を盗むことは罪とされている。
Doko no shakai de mo hito no shoyuu-butsu o nusumu koto wa tsumi to sarete iru.

possibility n. **[the fact of being possible or s.t. that may happen or exist]**
1. ka⌈noo-sei 可能性 •c [the likelihood that s.t. will occur] **⟪likelihood, chances, potentiality⟫**

EX. (**a**) The possibility of a nuclear war occurring has not yet disappeared completely.
核戦争が起きる可能性が完全に無くなったわけではない。
Kaku-sensoo ga okiru kanoo-sei ga kanzenni nakunatta wake dewanai.
(**b**) A: Is there any possibility that I might get into Kyoto University?
僕が京大に入れる可能性はありますか。
Boku ga Kyoodai ni haire-ru kanoo-sei wa arimasu ka.
B: I strongly doubt it.
まずないでしょうね。
Mazu nai deshoo ne.

2. a⌈ri-{u⌉ru/e⌉ru} koto あり得る事 [s.t. that is possible]

EX. World War III is an ever-present possibility.
第三次世界大戦は常に有り得る事だ。
Dai-san-ji-sekai-taisen wa tsuneni ari-{uru/eru} koto da.

possible adj. **[capable of being done, existing, or happening]**
1. ⟨-ga⟩ de⌈ki⌉ru ⟨〜が⟩出来る ② [for s.t. to come into existence spontaneously ⟪fig. "be able to"⟫] **⟪can, be able to, be skilled, be capable of Ving⟫**, **ka⌈noona 可能な** adj(*na*). **•c [having some likelihood of happening or existing]** **⟪potential, practicable, feasible⟫** ↔ **fu-kanoona 不可能な** adj(*na*).

EX. (**a**) Is it possible for students of Japanese to read a Japanese newspaper by the end of their third year of study?
三年目の学習が終わるまでに日本語学習者が日本語の新聞を読むことは{可能です/出来ます}か。
San-nen-me no gakushuu ga owaru made ni Nihon-go-gakushuu-sha ga Nihon-go no shinbun o yomu koto wa {kanoo desu/dekimasu} ka.
(**b**) When you are young you think that anything is possible.
若い時は何でも{出来る/可能だ}と思うものだ。
Wakai toki wa nan-demo {dekiru/kanoo da} to omou mono da.

2. a⌈ri-{e⌉ru/u⌉ru} あり得る ② [to have some likelihood of happening or existing ⟨fml⟩] **⟪probable, likely⟫**, **o⌈kori-{e⌉ru/u⌉ru} 起こり得る ② [to have some likelihood of occurring ⟨fml⟩]**

EX. An earthquake is possible even in the midwest part of the United States.
地震はアメリカ中西部でも{有り得る/起こり得る}。
Jishin wa Amerika chuusei-bu de mo

| {ari-{eru/uru}/okori-{eru/uru}}.

NOTE: The negative form of *ari-eru/ari-uru* is *ari-enai.*

PHRASE: as…as possible *dekiru dake…* 出来るだけ…, *narubeku* なるべく ⟪wherever practicable⟫

EX. (**a**) Please use as little salt as possible.
{出来るだけ/なるべく}塩を使わないで下さい。
{Dekiru dake/Narubeku} shio o tsukawanai de kudasai.
(**b**) I know you are busy, but call me as often as possible.
忙しいでしょうけど、{なるべく/*出来るだけ}電話してね。
*Isogashii deshoo kedo, {narubeku/ *dekiru dake} denwa-shite ne.*

possibly adv. **[perhaps; not out of the range of what is possible ⟪fig. "in any way possible"⟫]**

1. {**V/adj**(*i*).}**inf. ka**ˈ**moshirenai** {**V/adj**(*i*).} **inf.**かもしれない, {**adj**(*na*). **stem/N**} {**ø/ datta**} **ka**ˈ**moshirenai** {**adj**(*na*). **stem/N**} {**ø/datta**}かもしれない

EX. (**a**) John could possibly make it into Harvard Law School.
ジョンはハーバードの法学部に入れるかもしれない。
Jon wa Haabaado no hoogaku-bu ni haire-ru kamoshirenai.
(**b**) It could possibly be a nice day tomorrow.
あしたはいい天気になるかもしれない。
Ashita wa ii tenki ni naru kamoshirenai.

2. deˈ**kiru-dake** 出来るだけ **[as much as one can]**

EX. I'll write the paper as quickly as I possibly can.
出来るだけ早く論文を書きます。
Dekiru dake hayaku ronbun o kakimasu.

3. toˈ**temo…neg.** とても…**neg. [not by any possibility]** ⟪**no way**⟫

EX. I cannot possibly read this thick book in a week.
こんな厚い本、一週間ではとても読めないよ。
Konna atsui hon, is-shuu-kan de wa totemo yome-nai yo.

post[1] n. **[a piece of wood or metal fixed firmly upright in the ground to support or mark s.t.]**

haˈ**shira** 柱 **[a thick vertical structure that supports the weight of the upper part of a building ⟪fig. "support"⟫]** ⟪**pillar, column, support**⟫, **ku**ˈ**i** くい **[a stick that is driven into the ground as a mark or for supporting s.t.]** ⟪**stake, picket**⟫

EX. (**a**) The *tokobashira* is an ornamental post located in the *tokonoma* alcove in the drawing room of traditional Japanese homes.
床柱というのは伝統的な日本の家の座敷の床の間にある飾りの{柱/*杭}のことだ。
*Toko-bashira to iu no wa dentoo-tekina Nihon no ie no zashiki no toko-no-ma ni aru kazari no {hashira/*kui} no koto da.*
(**b**) In preparation for building the new fence, we first put up posts all around the perimeter of the pasture.
新しい塀を作る準備として、まず牧場の回りに{杭/*柱}をうった。
*Atarashii hei o tsukuru junbi to shite, mazu bokujoo no mawari ni {kui/ *hashira} o utta.*

—— vt. **[for s.o. to put up an announcement or notice in a place it can be seen publicly]** ⟨**-o**⟩ ⟨**-ni**⟩ **ha**ˈ**ru** ⟨～を⟩⟨～に⟩はる ① **[for s.o. to cause s.t. to become spread out on a surface ⟪fig. "put up a notice/ advertisement on a post/wall"⟫]** ⟪**put up**⟫
㊥ "spread out"▷張る, otherwise ▷はる

EX. The professor posted the grades on his office door.
教授は成績を研究室のドアにはった。
Kyooju wa seiseki o kenkyuu-shitsu no doa ni hatta.

post[2] n. **[a place to which s.o. is assigned ⟪fig. "a place where a soldier is stationed,"**

"rank," "a position in an institution"》]
1. bu⌉sho 部署 •c [the place or duty to which one is assigned within an organized structure such as the police or military]
2. chi⌉i 地位 •c [the standing one has acquired in a social group or society] 《**status, rank**》
EX. Richard was an ambitious man who was desirous of a higher post in the government bureaucracy.
リチャードは官僚機構の中でより高い地位を求めている、野心家だった。
Richaado wa kanryoo-kikoo no naka de yori takai chii o motomete iru, yashin-ka datta.
3. sho⌈ku 職 •c [a duty 《fig. "job"》] 《**position, opening, work**》
EX. A dozen people applied for the post.
十二人の人がその職に応募した。
Juu-ni-nin no hito ga sono shoku ni oobo-shita.

postage n. **[the fee charged for sending s.t. by mail]**
yu⌈ubin-ryo⌉okin 郵便料金 •c
EX. I heard that they're going to raise postage rates again.
郵便料金を又値上げするそうだよ。
Yuubin-ryookin o mata ne-age-suru soo da yo.

postcard n. **[a card which can be sent by mail without an envelope]**
ha⌈gaki はがき
EX. (**a**) Ten postcards, please.
はがきを十枚下さい。
Hagaki o juu-mai kudasai.
hagaki
(**b**) I sent a postcard to my friend in the Philippines.
フィリピンの友達にはがきを出した。
Firipin no tomodachi ni hagaki o dashita.

poster n. **[a large printed sign for announcing or advertising s.t. publicly]**
po⌉sutaa ポスター •f, bi⌈ra ビラ [a sheet of paper advertising s.t.] 《**bill, placard**》
EX. Let's make a poster for the concert.
コンサートの{ポスター/ビラ}を作ろう。
Konsaato no {posutaa/bira} o tsukuroo.
NOTE: *Bira* comes from the English "bill."

post office n.
yu⌈ubi⌉n-kyoku 郵便局 •c
EX. I went to the post office to mail a small package to Japan.
私は郵便局へ行って、小包を日本に送りました。
Watashi wa yuubin-kyoku e itte, ko-zutsumi o Nihon ni okurimashita.
yuubin-kyoku

posture n. **[the way one holds his/her body when sitting, standing, walking, etc. 《fig. "attitude"》]**
shi⌈sei 姿勢 •c 《**position, pose, stance**》
EX. (**a**) A person's bodily posture can tell you much about how that person is feeling inside.
姿勢を見ると人の本音がよく分かる。
Shisei o miru to hito no honne ga yoku wakaru.
(**b**) Good posture is essential to safe driving.
良い姿勢は安全運転に不可欠だ。
Yoi shisei wa anzen-unten ni fukaketsu da.

postwar adj. **[pertaining to the period after a war]**
se⌈ngo no N 戦後のN •c ↔ senzen no N 戦前のN •c
EX. Japan's postwar educational system is quite different from that of prewar times.
日本の戦後の教育制度は戦前のとはとても違います。
Nihon no sengo no kyooiku-seido wa senzen no to wa totemo chigaimasu.

pot n. **[a deep, round metallic or earthen container used for cooking or storage]**
tsu⌈bo つぼ [a round, earthen container with a narrow mouth] 《**crock**》, **bi⌉n 瓶 [a slender, glass container with a narrow mouth normally used for holding liquids]** 《**bottle**》, **ka⌈me⌉ かめ [deep, round earthen or metallic container with a relatively large mouth]** 《**jar, vase**》, **po⌉tto ポット •f [a round ceramic or metallic container or a teapot]**

potato n.
ja⌈gaimo じゃがいも, po⌉teto ポテト •f

potential adj. **[capable of existing but not yet in existence]**
1. **sho⌉orai ⟨-ni⟩ na⌉ru kamoshirenai 将来⟨〜に⟩なるかもしれない** aux. adj(*i*). **[capable of occurring in the future]**

EX. There are a number of potential problems with this plan.
この計画には(将来)問題になるかもしれない点がいくつかあります。
Kono keikaku ni wa (shoorai) mondai ni naru kamoshirenai ten ga ikutsu-ka arimasu.

2. **se⌈nzai-tekina 潜在的な •c [for some unseen possibility or quality such as talent, danger, or feeling to lie hidden inside s.t.]** ⟪**latent**⟫

EX. Every cigarette smoker is a potential lung cancer patient.
たばこを吸う人は、だれでも潜在的な肺がん患者だ。
Tabako o suu hito wa, dare-demo senzai-tekina haigan-kanja da.

pottery n. **[vessels made of baked clay or the art of making these or a workshop where these are made]**
1. **ya⌈ki-mono 焼き物 /⟨V *masu* of *yaku* ① burn + *mono* thing/ [a general term for earthenware/porcelain/ceramics]** ⟪**porcelain, earthenware, ceramics**⟫, **to⌉oki 陶器 •c [glazed china], to⌈o-ji⌉ki 陶磁器 •c [ceramic ware]** ⟪**porcelain**⟫

EX. My hobby is collecting pottery.
私の趣味は{焼き物/陶器/陶磁器}を集めることです。
Watashi no shumi wa {yaki-mono/tooki/too-jiki} o atsumeru koto desu.

2. **to⌈o(-ji)⌉ki-sei⌉zoo 陶(磁)器製造 •c [the craft of producing glazed china and porcelain]**
3. **to⌈o(-ji)⌉ki-se⌈izoo-sho 陶(磁)器製造所 •c [a factory where glazed china and porcelain are produced]**

pound[1] n. **[a measure of weight or the British monetary unit]**
po⌉ndo ポンド •f
NOTE: 1 pound (of weight)=0.454 kilograms

EX. (**a**) A: How much do you weigh?
体重はどれぐらいですか。
Taijuu wa dore-gurai desu ka.
B: About 140 pounds.
140ポンドぐらいです。
Hyaku-yon-jup-pondo-gurai desu.
(**b**) What is the current exchange rate between the British pound and the U.S. dollar?
現在、ポンドと米ドルの為替レートはどうなっていますか。
Genzai, pondo to bei-doru no kawase-reeto wa doo natte imasu ka.

pound[2] vt. **[to strike s.t. repeatedly with vigorous blows]**
⟨-o⟩ u⌈chi-kuda⌉ku ⟨〜を⟩打ち砕く ① [to break s.t. to pieces by striking it forcefully] ⟪**break to pieces**⟫, **⟨-o⟩ do⌉n-don to ta⌈ta⌉ku ⟨〜を⟩どんどんとたたく ① [to knock s.t. repeatedly with a banging sound]**

EX. (**a**) Someone is pounding on the door.
だれかがドアを{どんどんたたいて/*打ち砕いて}いる。
*Dare-ka ga doa o {don-don tataite/ *uchi-kudaite} iru.*
(**b**) Last night someone pounded through the windshield of my car.
昨晩だれかが僕の車のフロントガラスを{打ち砕いた/*どんどんたたいた}。
*Sakuban dare-ka ga boku no kuruma no furonto-garasu o {uchi-kudaita/ *don-don tataita}.*

pour vt. **[to cause s.t. liquid or granular to flow in a stream]**
⟨-ni⟩ ⟨-o⟩ tsu⌈gu ⟨〜に⟩⟨〜を⟩つぐ ① [for s.o. to connect s.t. with s.t. else ⟪**fig. "fill with a liquid"**⟫**]** ⟪**fill, join**⟫, **⟨-ni⟩ ⟨-o⟩ i⌈reru ⟨〜に⟩⟨〜を⟩入れる ② [for s.o. to cause s.t./s.o./s.a. to move into an enclosed space]** ⟪**enter, place**⟫, **⟨-ni⟩ ⟨-o⟩ ka⌈ke⌉ru ⟨〜に⟩⟨〜を⟩かける ② [for s.o. to cause s.t. to extend to and come in contact with s.t. else** ⟪**fig. "cover," "hang," "call s.o. by phone," "bet," "spend," "sprinkle," "splash," "sit**

down," "build (a bridge)"》] ⟪hang, sit down, sprinkle, splash, spend, build⟫, ⟨-ni⟩ ⟨-o⟩ so⌈sogu ⟨〜に⟩⟨〜を⟩注ぐ ① [for s.o. to cause s.t. liquid to flow into/onto s.t. in a stream or shower 《fig. "devote attention/ energy to s.t./s.o."》] ⟪sprinkle, devote⟫
㊅ "hang"▷掛ける, "build (a bridge)"▷架ける, otherwise ▷かける

EX. (**a**) Please pour me a cup of coffee.
コーヒーを一杯{ついで/入れて/*注いで/*かけて}下さい。
*Koohii o ippai {tsuide/irete/*sosoide/ *kakete} kudasai.*
(**b**) We poured water on the coals in the campfire before breaking camp.
キャンプ場を去る前にたき火の燃えさしに水を{かけた/*注いだ/*ついだ/*入れた}。
*Kyanpu-joo o saru mae ni taki-gi no moe-sashi ni mizu o {kaketa/*sosoida/ *tsuida/*ireta}.*
(**c**) The bartender poured another cocktail into my empty glass.
バーテンダーはカクテルをもう一杯私の空になったグラスに{ついだ/注いだ/入れた/*かけた}。
*Baatendaa wa kakuteru o moo ippai watashi no kara ni natta gurasu ni {tsuida/sosoida/ireta/*kaketa}.*

—— vi. **[for s.t. liquid or granular to flow into s.t. in large quantities]**
⟨-ni⟩ do⌈tto nagare-ko⌉mu ⟨〜に⟩どっと流れ込む ① [for s.t. liquid, gaseous, or consisting in a mass to flow into s.t. in large quantities], (a⌉me ga) do⌈sha-buri da (雨が)どしゃ降りだ [for rain to fall in torrents], ⟨-ni⟩ ta⌈kusan ha⌉iru ⟨〜に⟩たくさん入る ① [to enter in large numbers into a place] ↔ ⟨-kara⟩ takusan deru ⟨〜から⟩たくさん出る ②

EX. (**a**) Massive quantites of water poured into Tokyo Bay from the Sumida River following the typhoon.
台風の後、隅田川の水が東京湾に{どっと流れ込んだ/*たくさん入った}。
*Taifuu no ato, Sumida-gawa no mizu ga Tookyoo-wan ni {dotto nagare-konda/*takusan haitta}.*
(**b**) You should wear your raincoat if you're going out. It's really pouring outside.
出かけるんなら、レインコートを着たほうがいいですよ。外は本当にどしゃ降りですから。
Dekakeru n nara, rein-kooto o kita hoo ga ii desu yo. Soto wa hontoo ni dosha-buri desu kara.
(**c**) The traffic coming off the freeway pours into this intersection during rush hour.
ラッシュアワーには高速道路を降りてくる車がこの交差点に{どっと流れ込む/たくさん入って来る}。
Rasshu-awaa ni wa koosoku-dooro o orite kuru kuruma ga kono koosa-ten ni {dotto nagare-komu/takusan haitte-kuru}.

poverty n. **[the state of being poor]**
bi⌉nboo 貧乏 •c [the state of being economically poor] ⟪want, destitution⟫ ↔ kane-mochi 金持ち; hi⌈nkon 貧困 •c [the state of being so poor as to barely be able to go on living 《fig. "lack of important things"》] ⟪pauperism, destitution, need, paucity⟫

EX. Poverty can make people strong.
{貧乏/貧困}は人を強くすることもある。
{Binboo/Hinkon} wa hito o tsuyoku suru koto mo aru.

powder n. **[a mass of small fine particles, often created by grinding or crushing 《fig. "an explosive substance used in guns"》]**
1. ko⌈na⌉ 粉 [a mass of fine particles or grains] ⟪flour, dust⟫, fu⌈nmatsu 粉末 •c
2. ka⌈yaku 火薬 •c [gunpowder]

power n. [the capacity or authority to do s.t. or bring s.t. about]
1. chi⌈kara⌉ 力 [a capacity of any kind to do s.t., including physical, intellectual, mental, or spiritual] ⟪ability, strength, proficiency, force⟫, ta⌉iryoku 体力 •c [the extent to which one has the physical capacity to undertake s.t. or withstand s.t., including disease] ⟪stamina, physical

strength)), pa⌉waa パワー •f [horsepower or the impact of a group on society], i⌈kio⌉i 勢い [the momentum with which s.o./s.t./s.a. moves] ((force, vigor, energy))

EX. Although he's over sixty, he still has a lot of power in him.
あの人は六十を越しているのにまだかなり{力/体力/勢い/パワー}がある。
Ano hito wa roku-juu o koshite iru noni mada kanari {chikara/tairyoku/ikioi/pawaa} ga aru.

2. no⌉oryoku 能力 •c [the capability to be able to perform a given task] ((ability, capacity, competence)), sa⌈inoo 才能 •c [innate intellectual or artistic capability, esp. of an outstanding kind] ((talent, gift)), chi⌈kara⌉ 力 SEE power 1

EX. I believe that John has the power to achieve anything he sets out to do.
ジョンには何でもやり遂げる{能力/才能/力}があると思う。
Jon ni wa nan-demo yari-togeru {nooryoku/sainoo/chikara} ga aru to omou.

3. ke⌉nryoku 権力 •c [the (political) right to command one's subordinates] ((authority, influence)), chi⌈kara⌉ 力 SEE power 1

EX. Everybody seems to want the power to control others.
人はだれでも他人を操る{権力/力}を欲しがるようだ。
Hito wa dare-demo tanin o ayatsuru {kenryoku/chikara} o hoshi-garu yooda.

powerful adj. **[having great power or influence]**

1. tsu⌈yo⌉i 強い adj(*i*). **[having the power to act or perform in an effective way or to resist external force, esp. physically, but also mentally or emotionally] ((strong, violent, stout, healthy, be good at, resistant)) ↔ yowai 弱い** adj(*i*).; **kyo⌈oryokuna 強力な** adj(*na*). **•c [having great power or strength] ((mighty, strong, potent)), chi⌈kara-zuyo⌉i 力強い** adj(*i*). **[commanding in tone or exhibiting such strength or ability as to reassure one of its/his/her dependability] ((vigorous, forceful, forcible))**

EX. (**a**) That sumo wrestler really cuts a powerful figure, doesn't he?
あの相撲取りはとても{強/*力強/*強力}そうですね。
*Ano sumoo-tori wa totemo {tsuyo/*chikara-zuyo/*kyooryoku}-soo desu ne.*
(**b**) This car has a very powerful engine.
この車のエンジンはとても{強い/強力だ/*力強い}。
*Kono kuruma no enjin wa totemo {tsuyoi/kyooryoku da/*chikara-zuyoi}.*
(**c**) The politician delivered a powerful speech.
その政治家は{力強い/*強い/*強力な}演説をした。
*Sono seiji-ka wa {chikara-zuyoi/*tsuyoi/*kyooryokuna} enzetsu o shita.*

2. ke⌉nryoku ga aru (N) 権力がある(N) [having the authority to command one's subordinates], se⌉iryoku ga aru (N) 勢力がある(N) [having strong influence over other people]

EX. Our department chair is unfortunately not one of the more powerful personages in campus politics.
うちの学科主任は残念ながら学内政治でそんなに{権力/勢力}のある者ではない。
Uchi no gakka-shunin wa zannen-nagara gakunai-seiji de sonnani {kenryoku/seiryoku} no aru mono dewanai.

practical adj. **[relating to real life as opposed to theory or suitable for putting to actual use]**

ya⌈ku⌉ ni tatsu (N) 役に立つ(N) [to play a role in accomplishing some task/purpose or making some task easier], ji⌈tsuyoo-tekina 実用的な adj(*na*). **•c [suitable to be readily put to use in actual situations], ji⌈ssen-tekina 実践的な** adj(*na*). **•c [relating to application in real life as opposed to theory or study]**

EX. (**a**) I'd like to be introduced to a practical book on grammar, if there is one.

{役に立つ/実用的な/*実践的な}文法書があったら、教えてください。
*{Yaku ni tatsu/Jitsuyoo-tekina/*Jissen-tekina} bunpoo-sho ga attara, oshiete kudasai.*
(**b**) This language school is popular because its classes are so practical in emphasis.
この日本語学校は授業がとても{実践的な/役に立つ/?実用的な}ので人気がある。
Kono Nihon-go-gakkoo wa jugyoo ga totemo {jissen-tekina/yaku ni tatsu/?jitsuyoo-tekina} node ninki ga aru.

P

practice n. **[the usual or habitual way s.t. is done; the carrying out of a plan or idea as opposed to abstractly conceiving it; the repeated doing of s.t. in order to improve at it]**
1. na⌈rawashi 習わし [a current or traditional custom ⟨fml⟩] ⟪habit, custom, tradition⟫, shu⌈ukan 習慣 •c [the usual way of acting for an individual or members of a social community] ⟪habit, custom, convention⟫, ka⌈nshuu 慣習 •c [the customary practice or a certain community or society] ⟪custom, convention, observance⟫, fu⌈ushuu 風習 •c [the styles and customs traditionally followed in a culture] ⟪custom, ways⟫
EX. In Japan there is a practice of exchanging gifts twice a year, in August and December.
日本には年に二回八月と十二月に贈り物をする{習わし/習慣/慣習/風習}がある。
Nihon ni wa nen ni ni-kai hachi-gatsu to juu-ni-gatsu ni okuri-mono o suru {narawashi/shuukan/kanshuu/fuushuu} ga aru.
2. ji⌈kkoo 実行 •c [the act of carrying out in action s.t. abstract such as a contract, plan, promise] ⟪action, deed, performance, enforcement⟫, ji⌈ssen 実践 •c [the act of applying an idea or belief to an actual situation]
EX. (**a**) What I admire about him is that with him promise and practice go hand in hand.
彼について感心するのは約束と{実行/*実践}がうまくかみ合っていることだ。
*Kare ni-tsuite kanshin-suru no wa yakusoku to {jikkoo/*jissen} ga umaku kami-atte iru koto da.*
(**b**) Religious belief is one thing, practice is another.
宗教の信仰とその教えの{実践/*実行}は別の問題だ。
*Shuukyoo no shinkoo to sono oshie no {jissen/*jikkoo} wa betsu no mondai da.*
3. re⌈nshuu 練習 •c [an act of doing s.t. repeatedly to acquire a specific skill] ⟪training, drill, exercise⟫
EX. (**a**) You need to put in some more practice on this piece by Bach.
あなたにはバッハのこの曲の練習がもっと要りますよ。
Anata ni wa Bahha no kono kyoku no renshuu ga motto irimasu yo.
(**b**) If you neglect practice you'll never become good.
練習を怠けていてはけっして上手になれない。
Renshuu o namakete ite wa kesshite joozuni nare-nai.

— vt. **[for s.o. to actually carry out in action s.t. thought about or talked about or to do s.t. repeatedly in order to improve at it]**
1. ⟨-o⟩ o⌈konau ⟨〜を⟩行う ① [for s.o. to carry out s.t. as a duty/custom/profession (but not as a dramatic presentation) ⟨fml⟩] ⟪do, act, conduct, perform, celebrate⟫, ⟨-o⟩ ji⌈kkoo-suru ⟨〜を⟩実行する ③ •c [for s.o. to actually carry s.t. out in action] ⟪carry out, fulfill, execute⟫, ⟨-o⟩ ji⌈ssen-suru ⟨〜を⟩実践する ③ •c [for s.o. to apply one's ideas or beliefs to actual situations] ⟪put theory into practice, implement⟫
EX. (**a**) Mother Theresa is a true example of what it means to practice Christ's teachings.
マザー・テレサはキリストの教えを{実践する/*行う/*実行する}とはどういうことかを身をもって示している。
*Mazaa Teresa wa Kirisuto no oshie o {jissen-suru/*okonau/*jikkoo-suru} to*

wa doo iu koto ka o mi o motte shimeshite iru.
(**b**) Bill always makes it a habit to practice what he preaches.
ビルは自分が人に勧めることは必ず{実行する/??行う/*実践する}ようにしている。
*Biru wa jibun ga hito ni susumeru koto wa kanarazu {jikkoo-suru/??okonau/*jissen-suru} yooni shite iru.*
(**c**) Japanese still practice the custom of exchanging gifts at mid-year and year's end.
日本ではお中元とお歳暮を贈ることは今でも{行なわれて/*実行されて/*実践されて}いる。
*Nihon de wa o-chuugen to o-seibo o okuru koto wa ima demo {okonawa-rete/*jikkoo-sarete/*jissen-sarete} iru.*

2. ⟨-o⟩ re⌈nshuu-suru ⟨〜を⟩練習する ③ •c [for s.o./s.a. to do s.t. repeatedly to acquire a skill] ⟪**train, drill, rehearse**⟫

EX. I practice the violin for two hours every day.
私はバイオリンを毎日二時間練習します。
Watashi wa baiorin o mai-nichi ni-jikan renshuu-shimasu.

praise vt. **[for s.o. to express high regard or approval of s.o./s.t./s.a. or to glorify a god/saint]**

1. ⟨-o⟩ ho⌈me⌉ru ⟨〜を⟩ほめる ② [for s.o., usu. a superior or equal, to express high regard or approval of s.o's behavior/characteristics/possessions] ⟪**commend, admire, applaude**⟫

EX. (**a**) That teacher makes it a point to praise his students often.
あの先生は学生のことをよくほめることにしています。
Ano sensei wa gakusei no koto o yoku homeru koto ni shite imasu.
(**b**) I often hear foreigners praise the Japanese spirit of harmony.
私は外国人が日本の和の精神をほめるのをよく聞く。
Watashi wa gaikoku-jin ga Nihon no wa no seishin o homeru no o yoku kiku.

2. ⟨-o⟩ ho⌈me-tatae⌉ru ⟨〜を⟩ほめたたえる ② [to express admiration for s.o. superior, esp. a god/saint as an act of worship] ⟪**admire, applaud**⟫

EX. Hymns are songs that praise God.
賛美歌は神をほめたたえる歌だ。
Sanbi-ka wa kami o home-tataeru uta da.

—— n. **[an act/instance of expressing high regard or approval of s.o./s.t./s.a.]**

1. ho⌈me⌉ru koto ほめること [an act/instance of s.o., usu. a superior or equal, to express high regard or approval of s.o.'s behavior/characteristics/possessions], sho⌈osan 賞賛 •c [an act/instance of expressing high regard or approval of s.o./s.t.] ⟪**applause, admiration, commendation**⟫

NOTE: *Shoosan* 賞賛 is sometimes written as 称賛, with the same meaning.

2. ho⌈me-tataeru koto ほめたたえること [an act/instance of expressing admiration for s.o. superior, esp. a god/saint as an act of worship]

pray vi. **[for s.o. to speak to God or some deity to give thanks or make a request ⟪fig. "plead"⟫]**

1. Sinf. yo⌉oni ⟨-ni⟩ i⌈no⌉ru Sinf.ように⟨〜に⟩祈る ① [for s.o. to ask of a deity that something good will happen] ⟪**say grace, wish**⟫

EX. (**a**) I prayed that God would help me pass my entrance examination.
私は入学試験に通るように神様に祈りました。
Watashi wa nyuugaku-shiken ni tooru yooni kami-sama ni inorimashita.
(**b**) I pray (to God) every day that you will get well soon.
すぐ良くなるように毎日(神様に)お祈りします。
Sugu yoku naru yooni mai-nichi (kami-sama ni) o-inori-shimasu.

2. ⟨-ni⟩ ⟨-o⟩ i⌈no⌉ru ⟨〜に⟩⟨〜を⟩祈る ① [for s.o. to ask of a deity that something good will happen] ⟪**say grace, wish**⟫

EX. I prayed to God for world peace.

P

私は世界の平和のために神に祈った。
Watashi wa sekai no heiwa no tame ni kami ni inotta.

3. Sinf. yo⌉oni ⟨-ni⟩ ne⌈ga⌉u Sinf.ように⟨〜に⟩願う ① [for s.o. to request a favor from a deity or a superior] ⟪**desire, wish for, request, hope for**⟫, **Sinf. yo⌉oni ⟨-ni⟩ ko⌈ngan-suru Sinf.ように⟨〜に⟩懇願する ③ •c [for s.o. to make a fervent request to s.o. to do s.t.]** ⟪**entreat, beseech, implore, petition**⟫

EX. I prayed to God for his help.
私は助けてくれるように神様に{お願い/懇願}した。
Watashi wa tasukete kureru yooni kami-sama ni {o-negai/kongan}-shita.

4. (⟨-ni⟩) ⟨-o⟩ ne⌈ga⌉u (⟨〜に⟩)⟨〜を⟩願う ① [for s.o. to ask a favor of a deity or a superior] ⟪**wish, desire, hope for**⟫

EX. I prayed for the success of the project.
私はその計画の成功を願った。
Watashi wa sono keikaku no seikoo o negatta.

prayer n. **[an act/instance of addressing God or some deity to give thanks or to make a request]**

1. i⌈nori⌉ 祈り /⟨V*masu* of *inoru* ① pray/ [an act/instance of asking of a deity that something good will happen] ⟪**supplication, grace, invocation**⟫

EX. (**a**) Some Americans say a prayer before each meal.
アメリカ人の中には食べる前にお祈りをする人がいる。
Amerika-jin no naka ni wa taberu mae ni o-inori o suru hito ga iru.
(**b**) The prayers Japanese say at shrines are directed to Shinto deities.
神社での日本人の祈りは神道の神への祈りだ。
Jinja de no Nihon-jin no inori wa Shintoo no kami e no inori da.

2. ko⌈ngan 懇願 •c [a fervent petition to s.o. to do s.t.] ⟪**entreaty, appeal**⟫

EX. Maria finally acquiesced to the earnest prayers of her parents and decided to pursue a medical career.
マリアはとうとう両親の懇願に負けて、医学の道に進むことにした。
Maria wa tootoo ryooshin no kongan ni makete, igaku no michi ni susumu koto ni shita.

precede vt. **[to come or go before s.t. in time or space]**

⟨-no⟩ ma⌉e ni ku⌉ru ⟨〜の⟩前に来る ③ [to come before s.t. in time or space], **⟨-ni⟩ se⌈nkoo-suru ⟨〜に⟩先行する ③ •c [to go before s.t. in time or space]** ⟪**go ahead of**⟫

EX. (**a**) Winter precedes spring.
冬は春{の前に来る/に先行する}。
Fuyu wa haru {no mae ni kuru/ni senkoo-suru}.
(**b**) The preface precedes the main text of a book but usually follows the table of contents.
序文は本文{の前に来る/に先行する}が、大抵目次の後に来る。
Jobun wa honbun {no mae ni kuru/ni senkoo-suru} ga, taitei mokuji no ato ni kuru.

precious adj. **[having great value or greatly loved]**

1. ki⌈choona 貴重な adj(*na*). **•c [having great value]** ⟪**valuable**⟫

EX. (**a**) I very much appreciate your precious time.
貴重なお時間、ありがとうございました。
Kichoona o-jikan, arigatoo gozaimashita.
(**b**) I gained precious experience for my medical career during my summer internship at the hospital.
病院での夏の研修は医者になろうとしている私にとって貴重な経験になりました。
Byooin de no natsu no kenshuu wa isha ni naroo to shite iru watashi ni-totte kichoona keiken ni narimashita.

2. ko⌉okana 高価な adj(*na*). **•c [very high in price or value]** ⟪**expensive, priceless**⟫ ↔ **renkana 廉価な** adj(*na*). **•c**

EX. I can't accept such a precious gift as this.

こんな高価なものをいただくわけには行きません。
Konna kookana mono o itadaku wake ni wa ikimasen.

3. i⌈toshi⌉i いとしい adj(*i*). **•c [for s.o./s.t./s.a. to arouse in one a desire to be loving to him/her/it]**

EX. She lost her one and only precious son in the war.
彼女はいとしい一人息子を戦争で亡くした。
Kanojo wa itoshii hitori-musuko o sensoo de nakushita.

precise adj. **[exact or clearly and correctly expressed]**
se⌈ikakuna 正確な adj(*na*). **•c [in accord with fact and reliable]** **⟪accurate, correct, exact⟫**, **se⌈imitsuna 精密な** adj(*na*). **•c [detailed and correct]** **⟪minute, detailed, thorough⟫**

EX. (**a**) Stanley's pronunciation of Japanese is so precise as to be almost indistinguishable from that of a native.
スタンレーは日本語の発音が{正確/*精密}で日本人とほとんど区別がつかない。
*Sutanree wa Nihon-go no hatsuon ga {seikaku/*seimitsu} de Nihon-jin to hotondo kubetsu ga tsukanai.*
(**b**) To build a house we'll need a precise blueprint.
家を建てるには{精密な/正確な}設計図が要る。
Ie o tateru ni wa {seimitsuna/seikakuna} sekkei-zu ga iru.

precision n. **[accuracy or exactness]**
se⌈ikaku-sa 正確さ **/adj(*na*). stem of *seikakuna* precise + suf. *sa* ness/ •c [the degree to which s.t. is correct and free from error]**, **se⌈imitsu-sa 精密さ /adj(*na*). stem of *seimitsuna* + suf. *sa* ness/ •c [the degree to which s.t. is accurate to the minutest detail]**, **se⌉ido 精度 •c [the degree of accuracy, esp. of an instrument of measurement]** **⟪accuracy⟫**

EX. (**a**) The precision with which Mimi speaks Japanese is awesome.
ミミが日本語を話す{正確さ/*精密さ/*精度}には感銘を覚える。
*Mimi ga Nihon-go o hanasu {seikaku-sa/*seimitsu-sa/*seido} ni wa kanmei o oboeru.*
(**b**) The precision of this machine is incredible.
この機械の{精密さ/精度/*正確さ}は信じられないぐらいだ。
*Kono kikai no {seimitsu-sa/seido/*seikaku-sa} wa sinji-rarenai-gurai da.*

predicate n. **[the part of a sentence that expresses s.t. about the subject]**
ju⌉tsubu 述部 •c

EX. The predicate of the sentence "I read Japanese newspapers" is "read Japanese newspapers."
「私は日本語の新聞を読む」の述部は「日本語の新聞を読む」である。
'Watashi wa Nihon-go no shinbun o yomu' no jutsubu wa 'Nihon-go no shinbun o yomu' dearu.

predict vt. **[for s.o. to foretell s.t., usu. on the basis of objective evidence]**
⟨-o⟩ yo⌈gen-suru ⟨〜を⟩予言する ③ •c [for s.o. to foretell what is going to happen on the basis of some intuitive faculty] **⟪foretell, prophesy⟫**, **{⟨-o⟩/⟨-to⟩} yo⌉soku-suru {⟨〜を⟩/⟨〜と⟩}予測する ③ •c [for s.o. to foretell what is going to happen on some scientific basis]** **⟪estimate, forecast⟫**

EX. (**a**) The biblical prophets predicted the birth of Christ.
聖書の予言者はキリストの生誕を{予言/*予測}した。
*Seisho no yogen-sha wa Kirisuto no seitan o {yogen/*yosoku}-shita.*
(**b**) It is still very difficult to predict earthquakes in advance.
地震を{予測/*予言}することは今でも難しい。
*Jishin o {yosoku/*yogen}-suru koto wa ima demo muzukashii.*

prediction n. **[an act/instance of foretelling what will happen in the future]**
yo⌈gen 予言 •c [an act/instance of

foretelling what will happen in the future on the basis of some intuitive faculty] **《prophesy, forecast》, yo⌈soku 予測 •c [an act/instance of foretelling the future on some scientific basis] 《forecast, estimate》**

EX. (**a**) Predictions by fortune-tellers very seldom hit the mark.
占い師の{予言/*予測}はめったに当たらない。
*Uranai-shi no {yogen/*yosoku} wa mettani ataranai.*
(**b**) Prediction of future economic trends is now possible to some degree thanks to computers.
コンピューターのおかげで、これからの経済動向の{予測/*予言}が少しは出来るようになった。
*Konpyuutaa no o-kage de, kore-kara no keizai-dookoo no {yosoku/*yogen} ga sukoshi wa dekiru yooni natta.*

prefecture n. **[a political unit that comprises cities, towns, and villages in Japan]**
ke⌉n 県

EX. A: Where do you live?
どこに住んでいますか。
Doko ni sunde imasu ka.
B: I live in Shizuoka Prefecture.
静岡県に住んでいます。
Shizuoka-ken ni sunde imasu.

prefer vt. **[for s.o. to like s.t./s.o./s.a. better than others]**
⟨-yori⟩ ⟨-no ho⌉o ga⟩ su⌈ki⌉ da ⟨～より⟩ ⟨～の方が⟩好きだ 《like…better》

EX. (**a**) I prefer Mozart to Beethoven.
僕はベートーベンよりモーツァルトの方が好きだ。
Boku wa Beetooben yori Mootsaruto no hoo ga suki da.
(**b**) I prefer reading books to watching television.
私はテレビを見るよりも本を読む方が好きだ。
Watashi wa terebi o miru yori mo hon o yomu hoo ga suki da.

prefix n. **[a word-initial affix]**
se⌈tto⌉o-ji 接頭辞 •c ↔ setsubi-ji 接尾辞 •c

EX. The "*o*" of "*o-satoo,*" "*o-shio,*" "*o-shooyu*" is a prefix, and the "*sa*" of "*ooki-sa,*" "*atsu-sa,*" "*taka-sa*" is a suffix.
「お砂糖」、「お塩」、「おしょうゆ」の「お」は接頭辞で、「大きさ」、「暑さ」、「高さ」の「さ」は接尾辞だ。
'O-satoo,' 'o-shio,' 'o-shooyu' no 'o' wa settoo-ji de, 'ooki-sa,' 'atsu-sa,' 'taka-sa' no 'sa' wa setsubi-ji da.

pregnant adj. **[having an unborn baby in the womb 《fig. "full of s.t.," "rich in significance"》]**
1. ni⌈nshin-shite iru (N) 妊娠している(N) /⟨V*te iru* of *ninshin-suru* ③ become pregnant/ •c [for a female animal/human to hold an unborn baby in the womb]

EX. (**a**) That girl looks pregnant, doesn't she?
あの女の子は妊娠しているようですね。
Ano onna-no-ko wa ninshin-shite iru yoo desu ne.
(**b**) When you're pregnant you have to eat a lot.
妊娠している時は沢山食べなくてはいけません。
Ninshin-shite iru toki wa takusan tabenakute wa ikemasen.

2. ⟨-o⟩ ha⌈ra⌉nde iru (N) ⟨～を⟩はらんでいる(N) /⟨V*te iru* of *haramu* ① conceive/ [for a female animal/person to hold an unborn baby in the womb 《fig. "having s.t. hidden inside"》]

EX. Little did they know it, but the situation they were in was pregnant with danger.
彼らは自分たちが危険をはらんだ情況に置かれていることに気づいていなかった。
Kare-ra wa jibun-tachi ga kiken o haranda jookyoo ni oka-rete iru koto ni ki-zuite inakatta.

3. ga⌈nchiku ga a⌉ru (N) 含蓄がある(N) •c [having hidden significance] 《significant》

EX. Even the most minor phrases in Shakespeare's plays are often pregnant with meaning.
シェークスピアの劇に出てくるちょっ

としたた語句にも含蓄があることが多い。
Sheekusupia no geki ni dete kuru chotto-shita goku ni mo ganchiku ga aru koto ga ooi.

prejudice n. **[an opinion of s.o./s.t. formed beforehand without taking into account all relevant facts]**
se⌈nnyu⌉u-kan 先入観 •c [a preconceived idea about s.t./s.o./s.a.] ⟪preconception⟫, he⌈nken 偏見 •c [a one-sided, slanted view of s.t./s.o./s.a.] ⟪bias⟫

EX. People tend to exhibit prejudice toward foreigners.
人々は外国人に{偏見/先入観}を持ちがちだ。
Hito-bito wa gaikoku-jin ni {henken/sennyuu-kan} o mochi-gachi da.

preliminary adj. **[coming before the main part and in preparation for it]**
yo⌉bi no N 予備のN •c ⟪preparatory, introductory⟫, yo⌈bi-tekina 予備的な adj(*na*). **•c [preparatory in character] ⟪preparatory, introductory⟫**

EX. The legislature is conducting preliminary hearings on the desirability of a national health plan.
議会では国民健康保険制度を導入すべきかどうか{予備の/予備的な}ヒアリングを開いて検討している。
Gikai de wa kokumin-kenkoo-hoken-seido o doonyuu-su-beki ka doo ka {yobi no/yobi-tekina} hiaringu o hiraite kentoo-shite iru.

preparation n. **[the act of getting ready or making s.t. ready for some purpose]**
ju⌉nbi 準備 •c [an act of carefully making s.t. ready for some purpose well ahead of time] ⟪provision, preliminary arrangement⟫, shi⌈taku 支度 [an act of making ready s.t. that is necessary for some purpose, esp. a meal/outing/trip] ⟪arrangements⟫, yo⌉oi 用意 •c [an act of preparing for s.t. that will take place fairly soon] ⟪readiness, arrangements⟫

EX. (**a**) My friend attempted to climb the mountain without making proper preparations and narrowly escaped losing his life.
友達はちゃんと{準備/支度/用意}をしないで山に登ろうとしたためあやうく命を落とすところだった。
Tomodachi wa chanto {junbi/shitaku/yooi} o shinaide yama ni noboroo to shita tame ayauku inochi o otosu tokoro datta.
(**b**) Japanese high school seniors are usually so busy with preparations for college entrance examinations that they have no time for anything else.
日本の高校三年生は大抵大学入学試験の{準備/*用意/*支度}で忙しく、外のことをする時間は一切ない。
*Nihon no kookoo san-nen-sei wa taitei daigaku-nyuugaku-shiken no {junbi/*yooi/*shitaku} de isogashiku, hoka no koto o suru jikan wa issai nai.*

prepare vi./vt. **[to get ready or make s.t. ready for some purpose]**
⟨-o⟩ ju⌉nbi-suru ⟨〜を⟩準備する ③ •c [for s.o. to carefully make s.t. ready for some purpose well ahead of time] ⟪arrange, get ready⟫, ⟨-o⟩ shi⌈taku-suru ⟨〜を⟩支度する ③ •c [for s.o. to make ready s.t. that is necessary for some purpose, esp. a meal/outing/trip] ⟪make arrangements⟫, ⟨-o⟩ yo⌉oi suru ⟨〜を⟩用意する ③ •c [for s.o. to make s.t. or oneself ready for some purpose, either physically or mentally] ⟪ready oneself⟫

EX. (**a**) How long did it take you to prepare this meal?
この食事を{準備/支度/用意}するのにどのぐらいかかりましたか。
Kono shokuji o {junbi/shitaku/yooi}-suru no ni dono-gurai kakarimashita ka.
(**b**) It's important to begin to prepare for retirement well in advance.
定年に備えてあらかじめ{準備/用意/*支度}しておくことが大事だ。
*Teinen ni sonaete arakajime {junbi/yooi/*shitaku}-shite oku koto ga daiji da.*

P

preposition n. **[a part of speech which combines with a following noun to form a phrase that expresses when, where, how, etc., s.t. happens or exists]**
ze⌈nchi⌉-shi 前置詞 •c

EX. Japanese has postpositions instead of prepositions.
日本語には前置詞の代わりに後置詞がある。
Nihon-go ni wa zenchi-shi no kawari ni koochi-shi ga aru.

P

presence n. **[the fact of being in a place at a certain time]**
1. 〈-ga〉 i⌈ru koto 〈〜が〉いること [the fact that s.o./s.a. is present in a place], 〈-ga〉 a⌉ru koto 〈〜が〉あること [the fact that s.t. is present in a place], so⌈nzai 存在 •c [the fact of existing or being present in a place] **《existence, subsistence》**

EX. (**a**) The presence of Japanese companies is now strongly felt in the U.S.
日本の会社{の存在/があること/*がいること}がアメリカでは現在強く感じられている。
*Nihon no kaisha {no sonzai/ga aru koto/*ga iru koto} ga Amerika de wa genzai tsuyoku kanji-rarete iru.*
(**b**) One can no longer ignore the presence of homeless people these days.
今日ではホームレスの人々{の存在/がいること/*があること}を無視することは出来なくなった。
*Konnichi de wa hoomu-resu no hito-bito {no sonzai/ga iru koto/*ga aru koto} o mushi-suru koto wa dekinaku natta.*

2. shu⌈sseki 出席 •c [an act of attending a class/meeting] **《attendance, appearance》**
↔ kesseki 欠席 •c

EX. Your presence at this meeting is greatly appreciated.
この会への御出席、深く感謝いたします。
Kono kai e no go-shusseki, fukaku kansha-itashimasu.

3. 〈-ga〉 i⌈ru tokoro 〈〜が〉いる所 [a place where s.o. is present]

EX. John always behaved himself in the presence of the teacher.
先生がいる所では、ジョンはいつもおとなしくしていた。
Sensei ga iru tokoro de wa, Jon wa itsu-mo otonashiku shite ita.

present[1] adj. **[now existing or in progress 《fig. "attending," "under consideration"》]**
1. i⌉ma no N 今のN [of now], ge⌉nzai no N 現在のN •c [pertaining to the current time] **《existing, current》**

EX. (**a**) The present economic condition of our country is the worst I have ever seen.
{今/現在}の我が国の経済状態は最低だ。
{Ima/Genzai} no waga-kuni no keizai-jootai wa saitei da.
(**b**) The present Emperor of Japan studied American democracy when he was young.
{今/現在}の天皇陛下はアメリカの民主主義をお小さい時に学ばれた。
{Ima/Genzai} no tennoo-heika wa Amerika no minshu-shugi o o-chiisai toki ni manaba-reta.

2. shu⌈sseki-shite iru (N) 出席している(N) /〈V *te iru* of *shusseki-suru* ③ attend/ •c [in attendance at a meeting]

EX. All of the local politicians were present at the meeting.
会にはその土地の政治家がみんな出席していた。
Kai ni wa sono tochi no seiji-ka ga minna shusseki-shite ita.

3. to⌈omen no N 当面のN •c [s.t. that one is immediately faced with] **《urgent, pressing, immediate》**

EX. Our present task is to find a way out of this bad situation brought on by poor fiscal management.
ずさんな財政運営の結果生じたこの危機的状況をなんとか打開するのが当面の課題だ。
Zusanna zaisei-un'ei no kekka shoojita kono kiki-teki-jookyoo o nantoka dakai-suru no ga toomen no kadai da.

—— n. **[the time now passing or the grammatical tense referring to that]**
i⌉ma 今 n./adv. **[at the time when one is**

speaking or writing] ((**this time, now**)), **ge|nzai** 現在 n./adv. •**c**

NOTE: *Ima* as an adverb can be used with the past tense marker *-ta/da*, but *genzai* as an adverb cannot. For example, *{Ima/*Genzai} kita tokoro desu* I've just come.

EX. (**a**) Among the past, present, and future, the present is the most important because it is the closest to oneself.
過去、現在、未来の中では現在が自分に一番近いから一番大事だ。
Kako, genzai, mirai no naka de wa genzai ga jibun ni ichiban chikai kara ichiban daiji da.
(**b**) What kind of work are you doing at present?
{今/現在}どんな仕事をしていますか。
{Ima/Genzai} donna shigoto o shite imasu ka.

present[2] vt. **[for s.o. to place s.t. before s.o. else (as a gift) or to introduce s.o. to s.o. else]**

1. 〈**-ni**〉 〈**-o**〉 **o|kuru** 〈～に〉〈～を〉おくる ① **[for s.o. to cause s.t./s.o./s.a. to get to a certain place either by indirectly providing the means to do so (as in mailing or shipping) or by directly accompanying it/him/her]** ((**send, see off, escort, give a person a gift**))
㊥ "send"▷送る, "give a gift"▷贈る

EX. (**a**) Keith presented a diamond ring to his girlfriend.
キースはガールフレンドにダイアモンドの指輪を贈った。
Kiisu wa gaaru-furendo ni daiamondo no yubiwa o okutta.
(**b**) The college presented a gold watch to the retiring president.
大学は退職する学長に金の時計を贈った。
Daigaku wa taishoku-suru gakuchoo ni kin no tokei o okutta.

2. 〈**-ni**〉 〈**-o**〉 **sho|okai-suru** 〈～に〉〈～を〉紹介する ③ •**c [for s.o. to make s.o./s.t. known to s.o. else for the first time]** ((**introduce**))

EX. May I present to you Dr. Yamashita?
山下博士を御紹介いたします。
Yamashita-hakase o go-shookai-itashimasu.

—— n. **[s.t. given as a gift]**
o|kuri-mono 贈り物 ((**gift**)), **pu|re|zento** プレゼント •**c [a gift for s.o. on a special occasion]**, ((**gift**)), **i|wa|i** 祝い **[an expression of congratulations, either verbal or in the form of a gift]**, **o-|iwai** お祝い

EX. (**a**) What kind of present did you give your parents for Christmas?
クリスマスにどんな{贈り物/プレゼント/*お祝い}を両親にしましたか。
*Kurisumasu ni donna {okuri-mono/purezento/*o-iwai} o ryooshin ni shimashita ka.*
(**b**) I received a computer as a graduation present from my parents.
私は卒業の{お祝い/贈り物/?プレゼント}に両親からコンピューターをもらった。
Watashi wa sotsugyoo no {o-iwai/okuri-mono/?purezento} ni ryooshin kara konpyuutaa o moratta.

presently adv. **[after a little while** 〈w〉 **or currently]**
mo|kka 目下 •**c [at the time when one is speaking or writing** 〈fml〉**]** ((**at present, currently**)), **ge|nzai** 現在 n./adv. •**c [at the present time as opposed to the past/future]** ((**now, currently**))

EX. A: Where do you live?
お住まいはどちらですか。
O-sumai wa dochira desu ka.
B: Presently I'm living in Cambridge, Massachusetts.
{目下/現在}マサチューセッツ州のケンブリッジに住んでいます。
{Mokka/Genzai} Masachuusettsu-shuu no Kenburijji ni sunde imasu.

preservation n. **[the act of keeping s.t. safe from loss, damage, or deterioration or the condition of being so kept]**
ho|zon 保存 •**c [the act of keeping s.t. in its original state by artificial means or the state of being so kept]** ((**conservation, maintenance**)), **ho|kan** 保管 •**c [the act of**

P

protecting s.t. from loss or deterioration] ⟪custody, keeping⟫, cho⌈zoo 貯蔵 •c [the act of storing s.t., esp. food] ⟪storage, storing⟫, ho⌉go 保護 •c [the act of keeping s.o./s.t./s.a. from being endangered] ⟪protection⟫

EX. (**a**) The preservation of nature has become a critical issue in the modern industrialized world.
工業化が進んだ現代では自然の{保護/*保存/*保管/*貯蔵}が重大な問題となってきた。
*Koogyoo-ka ga susunda gendai de wa shizen no {hogo/*hozon/*hokan/*chozoo} ga juudaina mondai to natte kita.*
(**b**) Salt is widely used across the world for the preservation of food.
食べ物の{保存/貯蔵/*保管/*保護}には塩が世界中で広く使われている。
*Tabe-mono no {hozon/chozoo/*hokan/*hogo} ni wa shio ga sekai-juu de hiroku tsukawa-rete iru.*
(**c**) This library spends a lot of money on the preservation of rare books.
この図書館はきこう本の{保存/保管/*貯蔵/*保護}にお金を沢山使っている。
*Kono tosho-kan wa kikoo-bon no {hozon/hokan/*chozoo/*hogo} ni o-kane o takusan tsukatte iru.*

preserve vt. **[to keep s.t. safe from loss, damage, or deterioration]**
⟨-o⟩ (⟨-kara⟩) ma⌈mo⌉ru ⟨〜を⟩(⟨〜から⟩)守る ① [(to watch s.t./s.o./s.a. in order) to cause s.t./s.o./s.a. not to be harmed/injured/violated] ⟪protect, defend, guard, observe, keep⟫, ⟨-o⟩ ho⌉go-suru ⟨〜を⟩保護する ③ •c [for s.o. to keep s.t./s.o./s.a. from being endangered] ⟪protect⟫, ⟨-o⟩ ho⌈zon-suru ⟨〜を⟩保存する ③ •c [to keep s.t. in its original state by artificial means] ⟪conserve, keep, maintain⟫, ⟨-o⟩ cho⌈zoo-suru ⟨〜を⟩貯蔵する ③ •c [to store s.t. to keep it from rotting or deterioration] ⟪store, lay up, conserve⟫, ⟨-o⟩ ho⌈kan-suru ⟨〜を⟩保管する ③ •c [for s.o. to protect s.t. from loss or deterioration] ⟪keep in custody⟫

EX. (**a**) It's our responsibility to preserve our cultural heritage.
文化遺産を{守る/保存する/保護する/*貯蔵する/*保管する}のは私たちの責任だ。
*Bunka-isan o {mamoru/hozon-suru/hogo-suru/*chozoo-suru/*hokan-suru} no wa watashi-tachi no sekinin da.*
(**b**) Freezers are the most commonly used means for preserving meats.
肉を{保存する/貯蔵する/*守る/*保護する/*保管する}ために冷凍庫が最も広く使われている。
*Niku o {hozon-suru/chozoo-suru/*mamoru/*hogo-suru/*hokan-suru} tame ni reitoo-ko ga mottomo hiroku tsukawa-rete iru.*
(**c**) The temperature and moisture in the art museum are controlled to preserve the old paintings.
美術館は温度と湿度を調節して、古い絵画を{保存して/保管して/?保護して/*守って/*貯蔵して}いる。
*Bijutsu-kan wa ondo to shitsudo o choosetsu-shite, furui kaiga o {hozon-shite/hokan-shite/?hogo-shite/*mamotte/*chozoo-shite} iru.*

president n. **[a person elected or appointed to be the head of an institution/organization/country]**
1. da⌈ito⌉oryoo 大統領 •c [a person elected or appointed as leader of a country]

EX. George Bush was elected the 41st President of the U.S. in 1988.
ジョージ・ブッシュは1988年に第41代の米大統領に選ばれた。
Jooji Busshu wa sen-kyuu-hyaku-hachi-juu-hachi-nen ni dai-yon-juu-ichi-dai no Bei-daitooryoo ni eraba-reta.

2. sha⌈choo 社長 •c [a person elected or appointed as leader of a company, often also the chief executive officer of the company]

EX. Who is the president of your company?
お宅の会社の社長さんはどなたですか。

O-taku no kaisha no shachoo-san wa donata desu ka.

3. ka⌈ichoo 会長 •c [a person elected or appointed as leader of an organization or association or as a chairman of the board]

EX. Dr. John Smith has been elected the new president of the International Association of Psychologists.
ジョン・スミス博士は国際心理学会の新会長に選ばれた。
Jon Sumisu-hakase wa kokusai-shinri-gakkai no shin-kaichoo ni eraba-reta.

4. ga⌈kuchoo 学長 •c [a person elected or appointed as leader of a college or university], so⌉ochoo 総長 •c [a person elected or appointed as leader of a university]

EX. Usually, public university presidents in Japan are elected by their colleagues.
大抵、日本の公立大学の{学長/総長}は同僚によって選出される。
Taitei, Nihon no kooritsu-daigaku no {gakuchoo/soochoo} wa dooryoo ni-yotte senshutsu-sareru.

press vt. **[to exert steady physical or psycholological force against s.t./s.o./s.a. 《fig. "try hard to persuade"》]**

1. ⟨-o⟩ o⌈su ⟨〜を⟩おす ① [for s.o. to cause s.t./s.o./s.a. to move away from oneself 《fig. "stamp," "recommend"》] 《push, shove》 ↔ ⟨-o⟩ hiku ⟨〜を⟩引く ①

㊥ "recommend"▷推す, otherwise ▷押す

EX. (**a**) The doctor pressed the patient's knee to see if it hurt.
医者は患者のひざが痛むか押してみた。
Isha wa kanja no hiza ga itamu ka oshite mita.
(**b**) Please press the button at the entrance when you arrive.
着いたら入り口のボタンを押してください。
Tsuitara iri-guchi no botan o oshite kudasai.

2. ⟨-o⟩ ⟨-ni⟩ o⌈shi-tsuke⌉ru ⟨〜を⟩⟨〜に⟩押しつける ② [to apply steady force against s.t. (by putting s.t. else in contact with it) 《fig. "force s.o. to do s.t."》]

EX. (**a**) The cat pressed her body against my cheek.
猫が体を私のほおに押しつけてきた。
Neko ga karada o watashi no hoo ni oshi-tsukete kita.
(**b**) If you're not interested in listening, please say so. I won't press my views on you.
聞きたくないならそうおっしゃってください。私は自分の考えを押しつけたりしませんから。
Kiki-takunai nara soo osshatte kudasai. Watashi wa jibun no kangae o oshi-tsuketari shimasen kara.

3. ⟨-o⟩ da⌈ki-shime⌉ru ⟨〜を⟩抱き締める ② [for s.o. to hold s.o./s.t./s.a. tightly in one's arms]

EX. The mother pressed her baby to her bosom.
母親は赤ちゃんを胸に抱きしめた。
Haha-oya wa aka-chan o mune ni daki-shimeta.

4. ⟨-o⟩ o⌈shite no⌈ba⌉su ⟨〜を⟩押してのばす ① [for s.o. to exert pressure on s.t. to flatten it out], ⟨-o⟩ pu⌈re⌉su-suru ⟨〜を⟩プレスする ③ •f, ⟨-ni⟩ a⌈iron o ka⌈ke⌉ru ⟨〜に⟩アイロンをかける ② [for s.o. to smooth wrinkles in clothing using a heated metal device]

5. ⟨-ni⟩ Vinf. nonpast yo⌉oni se⌈ga⌉mu ⟨〜に⟩Vinf. nonpastようにせがむ ① [for s.o. to ask s.o. for s.t. persistently] 《badger, importune》, {⟨-o⟩/⟨-ni⟩} mu⌉ri ni {Vneg. + seyoo/Vstem + saseyoo/ko-⌈saseyo⌉o/sa⌈seyoo} to suru {⟨〜を⟩/⟨〜に⟩}無理に{Vneg.+せよう/Vcond.+させよう/来させよう/させよう}とする ② [to try to forcibly cause s.o. to do s.t.] 《compel》

EX. (**a**) The child pressed his parents to buy him a computer.
子供は両親にコンピューターを{買ってくれるようにせがんだ/*無理に買わせようとした}。
*Kodomo wa ryooshin ni konpyuutaa o {katte kureru yooni segandal/*muri ni kawa-seyoo to shita}.*
(**b**)The parents pressed their son to take the

P

entrance exam to Tokyo University.
両親は息子に{無理に東大を受験させようとした/*東大を受験するようにせがんだ}。
*Ryooshin wa musuko ni {muri ni Toodai o juken-saseyoo to shita/ *Toodai wo juken-suru yooni seganda}.

— n. **[the act of exerting pressure on s.t.; a machine or tool that exerts pressure, esp. for printing; newspapers and periodicals and the institutions that print them]**
1. o⌈su koto 押すこと [the act of causing s.t./s.o./s.a. to move away from oneself]
2. o⌈shi-tsuke⌉ru koto 押しつけること [the act of applying steady force against s.o./s.t./ s.a. 《fig. "force"》]
3. pu⌈re⌉su プレス •f [a machine or tool that exerts pressure; an iron; newspapers and periodicals and the institutions that print them]
4. i⌈nsatsu⌉-ki 印刷機 •c [a printing machine]
5. shu⌈ppa⌉n-butsu 出版物 •c [printed material such as books, articles, and magazines] 《publications》
6. ja⌈anari⌉zumu ジャーナリズム •f [journalism] 《mass media》

pressure n. **[an application of physical or psychological force/power or the result of such]**
a⌈tsu⌉ryoku 圧力 •c [physical or psychological force pressing on s.t./s.o./ s.a.] 《stress》, pu⌈re⌉sshaa プレッシャー •f [psychological stress], juuatsu 重圧 •c

EX. (**a**) The weight of one's body can put tremendous pressure on the legs when jogging.
体重によってはジョギングの時に足にすごい{圧力/??プレッシャー/*重圧}がかかることがある。
*Taijuu ni-yotte wa jogingu no toki ni ashi ni sugoi {atsuryoku/??puresshaa/ *juuatsu} ga kakaru koto ga aru.*
(**b**) The truth seems to have been covered up as a result of pressure from politicians.
政治家の{プレッシャー/圧力/*重圧}でその事実はもみ消されたらしい。
*Seiji-ka no {puresshaa/atsuryoku/ *juuatsu} de sono jijitsu wa momi-kesa-reta rashii.*
(**c**) Air traffic controllers must experience tremendous pressure in their work.
管制塔で働く人たちは恐ろしい{プレッシャー/重圧/*圧力}を経験するはずだ。
*Kansei-too de hataraku hito-tachi wa osoroshii {puresshaa/juuatsu/*atsuryoku} o keiken-suru hazu da.*

— vt. **[to exert pressure on s.t./s.o./s.a.]**
⟨-ni⟩ a⌈tsu⌉ryoku o kakeru ⟨〜に⟩圧力をかける ②

pretend vi./vt. **[for s.o. to act as if s.t. is the case which in reality is not, either to deceive or in play, or to claim s.t.]**
1. Sinf. fu⌈ri⌉ o suru Sinf.ふりをする ③
NOTE: Note the following exceptions where the nonpast form of adj(*na*). or N + cop. occurs before *furi o suru*: adj(*na*). stem + *na furi o suru* N + *no (yoona) furi o suru.*

EX. (**a**) Jim pretended to be asleep.
ジムは{寝ている(ような)/寝た}ふりをした。
Jimu wa {nete iru (yoona)/neta} furi o shita.
(**b**) Pretending to be ill, Carol took the day off.
病気の(ような)ふりをして、キャロルは一日休んだ。
Byooki no (yoona) furi o shite, Kyaroru wa ichi-nichi yasunda.
(**c**) The man had been attending classes at the University of Tokyo, pretending as if he were a student there.
その男は東大生のふりをして、授業に出ていた。
Sono otoko wa Toodai-sei no furi o shite, jugyoo ni dete ita.
(**d**) The lady pretended to be single.
その女は独身の(ような)ふりをした。
Sono onna wa dokushin no (yoona) furi o shita.
(**e**) Mr. Kim pretended to be healthy, not wanting his parents to know that he was ill.

キムさんは両親に自分が病気だということを知られたくないので、元気なふりをした。
Kimu-san wa ryooshin ni jibun ga byooki da to iu koto o shira-re-takunai node, genkina furi o shita.
(**f**) Ichiro isn't really busy; he's just pretending to be.
一郎は忙しいわけではなく、忙しいふりをしているだけです。
Ichiroo wa isogashii wake dewanaku, isogashii furi o shite iru dake desu.

2. Sinf. na˥do to wa o˥mo˥tte mo inai Sinf. **などとは思ってもいない [for s.o. to in no way think that s.t. is the case] ⟪don't claim to⟫**

EX. I don't pretend to have mastered Russian.
ロシア語をマスターしたなどとは思ってもいません。
Roshia-go o masutaa-shita nado to wa omotte mo imasen.

pretense n. **[a false impression that s.o. tries to create]**

1. fu˥ri˥ ふり [an actor's movement on stage ⟪fig. "behavior," "an act of pretending"⟫]

EX. Bob took the day off to go golfing under the pretense that he was calling on clients.
ボブは取り引き先を訪問するふりをして一日中仕事を休んでゴルフをしていた。
Bobu wa tori-hiki-saki o hoomon-suru furi o shite ichi-nichi-juu shigoto o yasunde gorufu o shite ita.

2. ko˥ojitsu 口実 •c [a reason s.o. gives to justify one's behavior] ⟪excuse, pretext⟫

EX. He rarely shows up for class, under the pretense that he is suffering from an illness.
彼は病気を口実にめったに授業に出ない。
Kare wa byooki o koojitsu ni mettani jugyoo ni denai.

pretext n. **[a reason one gives to hide one's true intentions]**

ko˥ojitsu 口実 •c [a reason one gives to justify one's behavior] ⟪excuse⟫

EX. (**a**) I wonder under what pretext he got the key to her apartment?
あの男はどんな口実であの女の人のアパートのかぎを手に入れたのだろう。
Ano otoko wa donna koojitsu de ano onna no hito no apaato no kagi o te ni ireta no daroo.
(**b**) He went home from work early under the pretext that his wife had suddenly been taken ill.
あいつは奥さんの急病を口実に早退したよ。
Aitsu wa oku-san no kyuubyoo o koojitsu ni sootai-shita yo.

pretty adj. **[producing a pleasant sensation to the sight or hearing due to a delicate beauty]**

ki˥reina きれいな adj(*na*). **[pleasantly attractive due to having beauty or orderliness or due to being free from dirt] ⟪beautiful, clean, neat, tidy, good-looking⟫, u˥tsukushi˥i 美しい** adj(*i*). **[aesthetically very pleasing to the eye, ear, mind, etc.] ⟪beautiful, lovely⟫**

EX. (**a**) Tom's younger sister is very pretty.
トムの妹はとても{きれいだ/美しい}。
Tomu no imooto wa totemo {kirei da/utsukushii}.
(**b**) You have pretty eyes.
あなたは目が{きれいだ/?美しい}。
Anata wa me ga {kirei da/?utsukushii}.
(**c**) My little daughter looked as pretty as a rose dressed up in her new dress.
新しいドレスでお目かししたうちの小さい娘はバラのように{きれいだった/美しかった}。
Atarashii doresu de omekashi-shita uchi no chiisai musume wa bara no yooni {kirei datta/utsukushikatta}.

—— adv. **[to a considerable degree]**

ka˥nari かなり [to a degree exceeding the extent normally expected] ⟪quite, considerably, fairly⟫

EX. (**a**) Mr. Shields is pretty good at Japanese.
シールズさんはかなり日本語が上手だ。
Shiiruzu-san wa kanari Nihon-go ga joozu da.
(**b**) After shopping all afternoon, Ms. Wada

P

seemed to be pretty tired.
和田さんは午後ずっと買い物をしてかなり疲れているようだった。
Wada-san wa gogo zutto kai-mono o shite kanari tsukarete iru yoodatta.
(**c**) Today's Japanese quiz was pretty difficult.
今日の日本語のテストはかなり難しかった。
Kyoo no Nihon-go no tesuto wa kanari muzukashikatta.

P

PHRASE: pretty soon *sugu* (*ni*) すぐ(に) ⟪right away, at once, immediately, in a moment⟫

EX. A: When is Mr. Yamada coming back?
山田さんはいつお帰りですか。
Yamada-san wa itsu o-kaeri desu ka.
B: He'll be back pretty soon.
すぐ(に)帰ります。
Sugu (ni) kaerimasu.

prevalent adj. **[occurring commonly, widespread]**
i⌈ppan-tekina 一般的な adj(*na*). •**c [holding true of all or nearly all cases]** ⟪**general**⟫

EX. (**a**) The practice of arranging in advance for the future spouse of a child is still prevalent in parts of South Asia.
南アジアの一部では子供の時にその結婚相手を決める風習がまだ一般的だ。
Minami-Ajia no ichi-bu de wa kodomo no toki ni sono kekkon-aite o kimeru fuushuu ga mada ippan-teki da.
(**b**) The attitude that personal advancement comes before service to society appears to be prevalent among college students these days.
近ごろの大学生の間では社会への奉仕より立身出世を重んじる考え方が一般的なようだ。
Chika-goro no daigaku-sei no aida de wa shakai e no hooshi yori risshin-shusse o omonjiru kangae-kata ga ippan-tekina yooda.

prevent vt. **[to keep s.t. from occurring or s.o./s.a. from doing s.t.]**
1. {**Vinf. nonpast no/N**} **o sa⌈matage⌉ru** {**Vinf. nonpast の/N**}**を妨げる** ② **[to keep s.t. from occurring or s.o./s.a. from doing s.t., esp. with malicious intent]** ⟪**hinder, obstruct, intrude, impede, block**⟫, {**Vinf. nonpast no/N**} **o ja⌈ma-suru** {**Vinf. nonpast の/N**}**を邪魔する** ③ •**c [to keep s.t. from occurring or s.o./s.a. from doing s.t.]** ⟪**hinder, obstruct, hamper, block**⟫, {**Vinf. nonpast no/N**} **o bo⌈ogai-suru** {**Vinf. nonpast の/N**}**を妨害する** ③ •**c [to keep s.t. from occurring or s.o./s.a. from doing s.t., esp. by forcible means]** ⟪**disturb, interrupt, obstruct, interfere**⟫

EX. (**a**) We prevented the enemy forces from advancing further by blowing up all the bridges over the river.
川にかかっている橋を全部爆破して敵軍の前進を{妨げた/妨害した/?邪魔した}。
Kawa ni kakatte iru hashi o zenbu bakuha-shite teki-gun no zenshin o {samatageta/boogai-shita/?jama-shita}.
(**b**) The protest by the radical students prevented the conservative politician from giving his speech as scheduled.
急進的な学生たちのデモが保守的政治家の演説が予定通り行われるのを{さまたげた/邪魔した/妨害した}。
Kyuushin-tekina gakusei-tachi no demo ga hoshu-tekina seiji-ka no enzetsu ga yotei-doori okonawa-reru no o {samatageta/jama-shita/boogai-shita}.

2. {**Vinf. nonpast no/N**} **o fu⌈se⌉gu** {**Vinf. nonpast の/N**}**を防ぐ** ① **[to keep s.t. undesirable or harmful from occurring or s.o./s.a. from doing s.t. undesirable or harmful]** ⟪**defend, protest, keep off**⟫, {**Vinf. nonpast no/N**} **o yo⌈boo-suru** {**Vinf. nonpastの/N**}**を予防する** ③ •**c [to keep s.t. such as a disaster or disease from occurring through aggressive measures taken in advance]** ⟪**protect, ward off, take preventive measures**⟫

EX. (**a**) I'm taking lots of vitamin C to try to prevent catching a cold.
私はかぜを{防ぐ/予防する}ためにビタミンCをたくさんとるようにしています。
Watashi wa kaze o {fusegu/yoboo-suru}

tame ni bitamin-shii o takusan toru yooni shite imasu.

(**b**) In winter they sprinkle salt on the streets to prevent them from freezing.

冬には道路が凍るのを{防ぐ/*予防する}ために道路に塩をまきます。

*Fuyu ni wa dooro ga kooru no o {fusegu/*yoboo-suru} tame ni dooro ni shio o makimasu.*

3. Sinf. ta⌈me⌉ (ni) de⌈ki⌉nai Sinf.ため(に)出来ない [to be unable to do s.t. due to some cause]

NOTE: When the nonpast form of adj(*na*). or cop. occurs before *tame ni*, the form used is {adj(*na*). stem + *na* /N + *no*} *tame ni*.

EX. (**a**) The rain prevented us from going on a picnic.

雨のためにピクニックに行けなかった。

Ame no tame ni pikunikku ni ikenakatta.

(**b**) My poor eyesight prevents me from being able to read the newspaper normally.

視力が弱いため(に)、普通に新聞を読むことが出来ません。

Shiryoku ga yowai tame (ni), futsuu ni shinbun o yomu koto ga dekimasen.

(**c**) Her mother's overprotective childrearing methods prevented Nancy from developing into an independent child.

母親が過保護に育てたため(に)、ナンシーは独立心のある大人になることが出来なかった。

Haha-oya ga ka-hogoni sodateta tame (ni), Nanshii wa dokuritsu-shin no aru otona ni naru koto ga dekinakatta.

prevention n. **[the act of keeping s.t. from occurring or s.o./s.a. from doing s.t.]**
bo⌈oshi 防止 •c [the act of keeping s.t. undesirable from occurring or s.o./s.a. from doing s.t. undesirable] ⟪check, preclusion⟫, yo⌈boo 予防 •c [an act/instance of keeping s.t. such as illness or disaster from occurring through aggressive measures taken in advance] ⟪precaution⟫

EX. Prevention of the further spread of AIDS is probably the most urgent public health issue currently facing the world.

エイズの更なるまん延の{防止/予防}が世界が目下直面している最も重大な公衆衛生上の問題だろう。

Eizu no sara-naru man'en no {booshi/yoboo} ga sekai ga mokka chokumen-shite iru mottomo juudaina kooshuu-eisei-joo no mondai daroo.

previous adj. **[coming before in time]**
ma⌉e no N 前のN [coming/going before in time or located before] ⟪last, late, ex-, front⟫

EX. (**a**) I had been up until three in the morning the previous night.

前の晩は三時まで起きていた。

Mae no ban wa san-ji made okite ita.

(**b**) My previous trips to Japan had been mainly for business.

前の日本への旅行はほとんど出張でした。

Mae no Nihon e no ryokoo wa hotondo shutchoo deshita.

previously adv. **[at a time before the time in question]**

1. ma⌉e ni 前に [at an earlier time or in front of] ⟪before, in front⟫, i⌉zen (ni) 以前(に) •c [at an earlier time than the time in question] ⟪before, formerly⟫

EX. I had read that novel previously.

私はその小説を{前に/以前(に)}読んだことがありました。

Watashi wa sono shoosetsu o {mae ni/izen (ni)} yonda koto ga arimashita.

2. ma⌈e-mo⌉tte 前もって [before doing s.t.] ⟪beforehand, in advance, ahead of time, in anticipation⟫, a⌈rakajime あらかじめ [before doing s.t. ⟨fml⟩] ⟪beforehand, in advance, ahead of time, in anticipation⟫

EX. I had called previously but no one was home.

{前もって/あらかじめ}電話をしておいたが、家にはだれもいなかった。

{Mae-motte/Arakajime} denwa o shite oita ga ie ni wa dare-mo inakatta.

prewar adj. **[before the war]**
se⌈nzen no N 戦前のN •c ↔ sengo no N 戦後のN •c

EX. I received my education under the prewar system.
私は戦前の教育を受けました。
Watashi wa senzen no kyooiku o ukemashita.

price n. **[the sum of money for which s.t. is bought or sold ⟪fig. "sacrifice," "reward"⟫] ne⌈dan 値段 •c [the amount of money for which s.t. is bought or sold] ⟪price, cost⟫, ka⌈kaku 価格 •c [the amount of money for which s.t. is bought or sold ⟨fml⟩] ⟪cost, value⟫, da⌈ika 代価 •c [an amount of money paid in exchange for goods ⟪fig. "sacrifice"⟫ ⟨w⟩] ⟪cost⟫, bu⌈kka 物価 •c [the overall level of expense required for obtaining goods in general (in a particular location)] ⟪cost of living⟫, da⌈ishoo 代償 •c [a payment of money, goods, or labor made in return for damage inflicted] ⟪compensation, reparation, sacrifice⟫**

EX. (**a**) What is the price of this word processor?
このワープロの{値段/価格/?代価/*物価/*代償}はいくらですか。
*Kono waapuro no {nedan/kakaku/?daika/*bukka/*daishoo} wa ikura desu ka.*
(**b**) In Japan the goverment controls the price of rice.
日本では政府が米の{価格/値段/*代価/*物価/*代償}の統制をしている。
*Nihon de wa seifu ga kome no {kakaku/nedan/*daika/*bukka/*daishoo} no toosei o shite iru.*
(**c**) The price one has to pay to become a successful businessman is high.
ビジネスマンとして成功するための{代価/*値段/*価格/*物価/*代償}は高い。
*Bijinesu-man to-shite seikoo-suru tame no {daika/*nedan/*kakaku/*bukka/*daishoo} wa takai.*
(**d**) Prices have gone up this year by about 3.5%.
{物価/*値段/*価格/*代価/*代償}は今年3.5%上がりました。
*{Bukka/*Nedan/*Kakaku/*Daika/*Daishoo} wa kotoshi san-ten-go-paasento agarimashita.*
(**e**) Sexual freedom comes at a price.
性的自由はその{代償/代価/*値段/*価格/*物価}を伴う。
*Sei-teki-jiyuu wa sono {daishoo/daika/*nedan/*kakaku/*bukka} o tomonau.*

pride n. **[a feeling of pleasure or satisfaction in one's own abilities, accomplishments, possessions, or other attributes, or s.t. which creates such a feeling in one]**

1. ji⌈so⌉n-shin 自尊心 •c [a sense of self-respect], pu⌈ra⌉ido プライド •f

EX. Yoshio's pride was badly hurt when he was teased by his classmates for his Tohoku accent.
良雄は同級生に東北なまりをからかわれて、{自尊心/プライド}をひどく傷つけられた。
Yoshio wa dookyuu-sei ni Toohoku-namari o karakawa-rete, {jison-shin/puraido} o hidoku kizutsuke-rareta.

2. u⌈nu-bore うぬぼれ /⟨V*masu* of *unu-boreru* ② be conceited/ [self-conceit] ⟪overconfidence, vanity⟫

EX. He's so full of pride he can't even admit the smallest mistake.
彼はうぬぼれが強くて、どんなに小さなことでも絶対に自分の間違いを認めようとしない。
Kare wa unubore ga tsuyokute, donna ni chiisana koto de mo zettai ni jibun no machigai o mitomeyoo to shinai.

3. ji⌈man 自慢 •c [the act of outwardly exhibiting a sense of pleasure or satisfaction in one's own abilities, accomplishments, possessions, or other attributes] ⟪boasting, conceit, vanity⟫

EX. Their grandchildren were a source of unspeakable pride to the old couple.
その老夫婦にとって孫たちは何よりの自慢の種だった。
Sono roo-fuufu ni-totte mago-tachi wa nani-yori no jiman no tane datta.

PHRASE: take pride in ⟨*-o*⟩ *hokori ni omou* ⟨〜を⟩ 誇りに思う ①

EX. Ian takes pride in his Irish heritage.

イアンは自分がアイルランド系であることを誇りに思っている。
Ian wa jibun ga Airurando-kei dearu koto o hokori ni omotte iru.

— vt. **[for s.o. to indulge oneself in a feeling of pleasure or satisfaction for one's own abilities, accomplishments, possessions, or other attributes]**
⟨-o⟩ ho⌈kori⌉ ni shite iru ⟨〜を⟩誇りにしている /⟨V*te iru* of *hokori ni suru* ③ boast/ ② **[for s.o. to derive a sense of pleasure or satisfaction from some ability, accomplishment, possession, or other attribute of one's own or of s.o. in one's in-group]** ⟪boast of, take pride in⟫, **⟨-(no ko⌈to⌉) o⟩ ji⌈man-suru** ⟨〜(のこと)を⟩自慢する ③ •c **[for s.o. to outwardly exhibit an (unjustified) sense of pleasure or satisfaction in some ability, accomplishment, possession, or other attribute of one's own or of s.o. in one's in-group]** ⟪boast of, speak boastingly of⟫, **u⫰nu-borete iru** うぬぼれている /⟨V*te iru* of *unuboreru* ② be conceited/ ② **[for s.o. to derive a sense of conceit from s.t.]** ⟪be conceited, be puffed up⟫

EX. (**a**) Yukio secretly prides himself on his English ability.
ひそかに幸雄は自分の英語力を{誇りに/*自慢}している。
*Hisokani Yukio wa jibun no eigo-ryoku o {hokori ni/*jiman-} shite iru.*
(**b**) The people in this town pride themselves on the town's cleanliness and safety.
この町の住民は町がきれいで治安がいいことを{自慢/誇りに}している。
Kono machi no juumin wa machi ga kirei de chian ga ii koto o {jiman-/hokori ni} shite iru.
(**c**) Daisy prides herself a little too much on her beauty.
デイジーは自分は美人だとうぬぼれている。
Deijii wa jibun wa bijin da to unuborete iru.

priest n. **[a person who performs the sacred rites of a religion]**
shi⌉sai 司祭 •c **[a member of the Catholic clergy]**, **so⌉oryo** 僧りょ •c **[a person who has devoted his life to teaching and practicing Buddhism]** ⟪monk⟫
NOTE: A Shinto priest is referred to as a *kannushi* 神主.

primarily adv. **[mainly]**
shu-⌈to⌉-shite 主として **[chiefly]** ⟪mainly, for the most part⟫

EX. The Japanese language class I'm teaching is made up primarily of students in business-related fields.
私が教えている日本語クラスの学生は主としてビジネス関係の人たちだ。
Watashi ga oshiete iru Nihon-go kurasu no gakusei wa shu-to-shite bijinesu-kankei no hito-tachi da.

primary adj. **[first in importance]**
da⌉i-ichi no N 第一のN •c **[of the first]** ⟪first⟫, **shu⌈yoona** 主要な adj(*na*). •c **[of greatest importance]** ⟪main, chief, principal⟫

EX. (**a**) My primary concern is health.
私の{第一の/?主要な}関心事は健康だ。
Watashi no {dai-ichi no/?shuyoona} kanshin-ji wa kenkoo da.
(**b**) The primary objective of this research is to clarify how quality control is achieved in Japanese corporations.
この研究の{第一の/主要な}目的は日本企業の品質管理がどう行われているかを明らかにすることだ。
Kono kenkyuu no {dai-ichi no/shuyoona} mokuteki wa Nihon-kigyoo no hinshitsu-kanri ga doo okonawa-rete iru ka o akirakani suru koto da.

prime adj. **[first in importance or quality]**
da⌉i-ichi(-i) no N 第一(位)のN •c **[of the first (rank)]**, **i⌈chiban juuyoona** 一番重要な adj(*na*). •c **[of the greatest importance]**, **sa⌈iko⌉o-kyuu no N** 最高級のN •c **[of the highest quality]** ⟪of the top grade⟫

EX. (**a**) Our prime task as teachers is to offer quality education.

P

我々教師の{第一の/一番重要な/*最高級の}課題はいい教育をすることだ。
*Ware-ware kyooshi no {dai-ichi no/ichiban juuyoona/*saikoo-kyuu no} kadai wa ii kyooiku o suru koto da.*
(**b**) We bought prime rib and had steak for dinner.
私たちは{最高級の/*第一の/*一番重要な}肉を買ってきて、晩ご飯にステーキを食べた。
*Watashi-tachi wa {saikoo-kyuu no/*dai-ichi no/*ichiban juuyoona} niku o katte kite, ban-gohan ni suteeki o tabeta.*

P

primitive adj. **[pertaining to an early stage of civilization 《fig. "crude"》]**
ge⌉nshi no N 原始のN •c [pertaining to the beginnings of s.t. or existing in a natural unchanged state] 《primeval, original》, ge⌈nshi-tekina 原始的な adj(*na*). **•c [characteristic of an early stage of development] 《crude, primitive》**

EX. (**a**) Archaeologists have come to understand much about primitive human life.
考古学者は人間の{原始の/原始的な}生活についてかなり分かるようになった。
Kooko-gaku-sha wa ningen no {genshi no/genshi-tekina} seikatsu ni-tsuite kanari wakaru yooni natta.
(**b**) Why are you still using such a primitive typewriter?
どうしてこんな{原始的な/*原始の}タイプライターをまだ使っているんですか。
*Dooshite konna {genshi-tekina/*genshi no} taipuraitaa o mada tsukatte iru n desu ka.*

prince n. **[the son of a king or emperor 《fig. "a nobleman"》]**
o⌉oji 王子 •c [the son of a king], o⌉oji 皇子 •c [the son of an emperor]

EX. (**a**) Cinderella danced with the prince until midnight.
シンデレラは夜の十二時まで王子様と踊りました。
Shinderera wa yoru no juu-ni-ji made ooji-sama to odorimashita.
(**b**) A prince was born into the emperor's family.
皇子が天皇家にお生まれになった。
Ooji ga tennoo-ke ni o-umare ni natta.

princess n. **[the daughter or daughter-in-law of a king or emperor]**
o⌉ojo 王女 •c [the daughter of a king], ko⌉ojo 皇女 •c [the daughter of an emperor]

principal n. **[a person with controlling authority in an organization, esp. at a secondary educational institution, or a capital sum of money on which interest is earned or charged]**
1. ko⌈ochoo 校長 •c [the person with the highest authority in an elementary or secondary educational institution] 《schoolmaster》

EX. A: What does your father do?
お父さんは何をなさっていらっしゃいますか。
O-too-san wa nani o nasatte irasshaimasu ka.
B: He's an elementary school principal.
父は小学校の校長をしています。
Chichi wa shoo-gakkoo no koochoo o shite imasu.

2. ga⌉nkin 元金 •c [a capital sum of money on which interest is earned or charged]

—— adj. **[most important or having to do with the capital sum of money on which interest is earned or charged]**
1. o⌉mona 主な adj(*na*). **[the most prominent/significant of a group of entities under consideration] 《chief, main, major, prime》, shu⌈yoona 主要な •c [of greatest importance] 《chief, main, major, leading》**

EX. My principal duty here is to plan the budget.
ここでの私の{主な/主要な}仕事は予算を組むことです。
Koko de no watashi no {omona/shuyoona} shigoto wa yosan o kumu koto desu.

2. ga⌉nkin no N 元金のN •c

principle n. **[a basic truth or law that provides a basis for reasoning, summarizes**

a natural tendency, or serves as a guide to behavior]

1. ge⌉nri 原理 •c [a basic scientific law that underlies and provides an explanation for some phenomenon] ⟪theory, fundamentals⟫, **ge⌈nsoku 原則 •c [a basic rule or law that explains or governs all cases to which it applies]** ⟪general rule⟫

EX. (**a**) Are you familiar with Archimedes's principle?
アルキメデスの{原理/*原則}を知っていますか。
*Arukimedesu no {genri/*gensoku} o shitte imasu ka.*
(**b**) In principle I agree with your proposal.
{原則/*原理}としてあなたの提案に賛成です。
*{Gensoku/*Genri} to-shite, anata no teian ni sansei desu.*

2. do⌉ogi 道義 •c [an assumption or belief serving as a guide for human conduct] ⟪morality, morals, ethics⟫

EX. One finds a surprising degree of consistency in principles governing human conduct in cultures across the world.
人間の行動を律する道義は世界のどの文化においても驚くほど共通している。
Ningen no koodoo o rissuru doogi wa sekai no dono bunka ni-oite mo odoroku hodo kyootsuu-shite iru.

print vt. **[to press letters or pictures onto a flat surface, esp. paper ⟪fig. "write letters as if by printing"⟫]**

1. ⟨-o⟩ i⌈nsatsu-suru ⟨～を⟩印刷する ③ •c [for s.o. to press letters or pictures onto paper or a paper-like surface]

EX. (**a**) A: Where was this book printed?
この本はどこで印刷されましたか。
Kono hon wa doko de insatsu-saremashita ka.
B: I believe in Korea.
韓国で印刷されたのだと思います。
Kankoku de insatsu-sareta no da to omoimasu.
(**b**) It took about three months to print this book.
この本を印刷するのに約三か月かかりました。
Kono hon o insatsu-suru no ni yaku san-kagetsu kakarimashita.

2. ⟨-ni⟩ mo⌈yoo o tsu⌉ke⌉ru ⟨～に⟩模様を付ける ② [for s.o. to impress a design onto paper or cloth]

3. ⟨-o⟩ ka⌈tsuji-tai de ka⌉ku ⟨～を⟩活字体で書く ① [for s.o. to write s.t. in the same style as if produced by a mechanical press]

EX. Please print your name here.
ここにお名前を(アルファベットの)活字体で書いて下さい。
Koko ni o-namae o (arufabetto no) katsuji-tai de kaite kudasai.

printing n. **[the process or business of producing printed material such as books, magazines, etc.]**

1. i⌈nsatsu 印刷 •c [the act or process of pressing letters or pictures onto paper or paper-like surfaces] ⟪presswork⟫

EX. The printing business has had to undergo a major adjustment with the advent of word processing.
印刷業はワープロの出現によって大きく転換することを余儀なくされた。
Insatsu-gyoo wa waapuro no shutsugen ni-yotte ookiku tenkan-suru koto o yogi-naku-sareta.

2. i⌈nsatsu⌉-jutsu 印刷術 •c [the art of producing printed material such as books, magazines, etc.]

prism n.

pu⌈ri⌉zumu プリズム •f

prison n. **[a building or other facility where people convicted (or accused) of crimes are forced to stay]**

ke⌈imu⌉-sho 刑務所 •c [an institution where people convicted (or accused) of crimes are forced to stay] ⟪jail⟫

EX. Tom served five years in prison for burglary.
トムは強盗の罪で刑務所に五年入っていた。
Tomu wa gootoo no tsumi de keimu-sho ni go-nen haitte ita.

P

prisoner n. **[a person kept in prison or kept in confinement by another]**
shu⌈ujin 囚人 •c [a person kept in prison] ((**convict**)), **ho⌉ryo 捕虜 •c [a soldier who has been captured by the enemy]** ((**POW**))

EX. (**a**) I hear that a prisoner escaped from the prison last night.
{囚人/*捕虜}が刑務所からゆうべ逃げたそうだ。
*{Shuujin/*Horyo} ga keimu-sho kara yuube nigeta sooda.*
(**b**) For most Japanese soldiers it was a great shame to become a prisoner of war.
大部分の日本人兵士にとって、{捕虜/*囚人}になることは大きな恥だった。
*Dai-bubun no Nihon-jin-heishi ni-totte, {horyo/*shuujin} ni naru koto wa ookina haji datta.*

P

private adj. **[pertaining to a particular individual or non-public institution; not meant to be publicly known, used, etc.]**
1. shi-⌈tekina 私的な adj(*na*). **•c [pertaining to facts about a particular individual not meant to be shared publicly]** ((**personal**)) **↔ koo-tekina 公的な •c; pu⌈raibe⌉etona プライベートな •f**

EX. Jane was a quiet person who never talked much about her private life.
ジェーンは無口な人で{私(的な)/プライベートな}生活についてはあまり話さなかった。
Jeen wa mukuchina hito de {shi-(tekina)/puraibeetona} seikatsu ni-tsuite wa amari hanasanakatta.

2. shi⌈yoo no N 私用のN •c [pertaining to the use by an individual of s.t. that belongs to the public] ↔ kooyoo no N 公用のN •c

EX. He makes a lot of private telephone calls during work hours.
彼は勤務中に私用の電話を沢山掛けます。
Kare wa kinmu-chuu ni shiyoo no denwa o takusan kakemasu.

3. shi⌉ritsu no N 私立のN •c [pertaining to a non-public institution] ↔ kooritsu no N 公立のN •c

EX. (**a**) Tuition is generally much higher at private schools than at public ones.
大抵私立の学校の授業料の方が公立よりずっと高い。
Taitei shiritsu no gakkoo no jugyoo-ryoo no hoo ga kooritsu yori zutto takai.
(**b**) Waseda and Keio are the best known private universities in Japan.
早稲田と慶応は日本で一番良く知られている私立(の)大学だ。
Waseda to Keioo wa Nihon de ichiban yoku shira-rete iru shiritsu (no) daigaku da.

prize n. **[an award that is won in a game, contest, or lottery or that is given to one in recognition of an accomplishment]**
1. sho⌉o 賞 •c [s.t. officially given to one in recognition of an accomplishment] ((**award**)), **ho⌈obi 褒美 •c [money or things given to s.o. to reward good behavior]**

EX. (**a**) Henry received first prize in the speech contest.
ヘンリーはスピーチコンテストで一等賞をもらった。
Henrii wa supiichi-kontesuto de ittoo-shoo o moratta.
(**b**) The teacher gave Tom a prize for his good grades.
先生はトムの成績がよかったので{褒美/*賞}をやった。
*Sensei wa Tomu no seiseki ga yokatta node {hoobi/*shoo} o yatta.*

PHRASE: Nobel prize *Nooberu-shoo* ノーベル賞 **•f+c**

EX. Yasunari Kawabata received the Nobel prize for literature in 1968.
川端康成は1968年に文学の分野でノーベル賞を受賞した。
Kawabata Yasunari wa sen-kyuu-hyaku-roku-juu-hachi-nen ni bungaku no bunya de Nooberu-shoo o jushoo-shita.

2. ke⌈nshoo-kin 懸賞金 •c [money given as an award to s.o. for solving a problem or submitting the best work in a contest] ((**award**))

EX. The winner in this literary competition will

receive a prize of $100,000.
この文学コンクールに優勝した人には、十万ドルの懸賞金が贈られるんです。
Kono bungaku-konkuuru ni yuushoo-shita hito ni wa, juu-man-doru no kenshoo-kin ga okura-reru n desu.

probability n. **[the chances of s.t. taking place, esp. as expressed in a statistical ratio]**
1. mi⌈komi 見込み /⟨**V*masu* of *mi-komu*** ① **expect/ [an anticipation/expectation/prediction that s.t. is very likely to occur]** ⟪**hope, prospects, likelihood, chance, possibility**⟫, **ko⌈osan 公算 •c [the degree of likelihood that s.t. will occur]** ⟪**likelihood**⟫, **ka⌈noo-sei 可能性 •c [the likelihood that s.t. will occur]** ⟪**possibility, likelihood, potentiality**⟫, **ka⌈kuritsu 確率 •c [the mathematical likelihood of s.t. taking place]**

EX. (**a**) What is the probability that he will be able to graduate this spring?
彼がこの春大学を卒業出来る{見込み/公算/可能性/*確率}はどれぐらいあるでしょうか。
*Kare ga kono haru daigaku o sotsugyoo-dekiru {mikomi/koosan/kanoo-sei/*kakuritsu} wa dore-gurai aru deshoo ka.*
(**b**) The probability is quite high that Japan's export surplus will continue for another decade or so.
日本の輸出超過が後十年ぐらい続く{見込み/公算/可能性/*確率}はかなり大きい。
*Nihon no yushutsu-chooka ga ato juu-nen-gurai tsuzuku {mikomi/koosan/kanoo-sei/*kakuritsu} wa kanari ookii.*
(**c**) The probability of a coin landing heads up or tails up is 50% each.
コインが表になるか、裏になるかの{確率/*見込み/*公算/*可能性}はどちらも50%だ。
*Koin ga omote ni naru ka, ura ni naru ka no {kakuritsu/*mikomi/*koosan/*kanoo-sei} wa dochira-mo go-jup-paasento da.*

probable adj. **[likely to be true or to happen]**
1. a⌈ri-{e⌉ru/u⌉ru} あり得る ② [to have some likelihood of happening or existing ⟨fml⟩], o⌈kori-{e⌉ru/u⌉ru} 起こり得る ② [to have some likelihood of occurring ⟨fml⟩], V*masu* soona V*masu* そうな adj(*na*). **[for s.t. to have the appearance of being in a certain state or being about to occur based on what the speaker sees/hears/senses]** ⟪**look like, appear, seem, feel like**⟫

EX. (**a**) A big earthquake is probable in Japan in the near future.
日本では近い将来に大地震が{起こり得る/起こることは有り得る/起こりそうだ}。
Nihon de wa chikai shoorai ni dai-jishin ga {okori-{eru/uru}/okoru koto wa ari-{eru/uru}/okori-sooda}.
(**b**) Judging from the way the sky looks rain is probable.
空模様からすると、雨が{降りそうだ/*あり得る/*起こり得る}。
*Sora-moyoo kara suru to, ame ga {furi-sooda/*ari-{eru/uru}/*okori-{eru/uru}}.*

2. ho⌈ntoo-rashi⌉i 本当らしい adj(*i*). **•c [appearing to be true], yu⌈uboona 有望な** adj(*na*). **•c [having great promise]** ⟪**promising, hopeful**⟫

EX. (**a**) His story sounds probable, doesn't it?
彼の話は{本当らしい/*有望だ}ね。
*Kare no hanashi wa {hontoo-rashii/*yuuboo da} ne.*
(**b**) Dr. Smith is a probable candidate for college president.
スミス博士は{有望な/*本当らしい}学長候補だ。
*Sumisu-hakase wa {yuuboona/*hontoo-rashii} gakuchoo kooho da.*

probably adv. **[with a high likelihood of occurrence; almost certainly]**
ta⌉bun 多分 •c ⟪**most likely**⟫, **o⌈so⌉raku 恐らく [with a high likelihood of occurrence ⟨fml⟩]** ⟪**perhaps, possibly, maybe, as likely as not**⟫

EX. (**a**) A: Do you think Mr. Ogawa will be at the party?
小川さんはパーティーに来ると思いますか。

Ogawa-san wa paatii ni kuru to omoimasu ka.
B: Probably not.
{多分/恐らく}来ないでしょう。
{Tabun/Osoraku} konai deshoo.
(**b**) A: Can I get to the airport in 20 minutes?
空港へ二十分で行けるでしょうか。
Kuukoo e ni-jup-pun de ike-ru deshoo ka.
B: You probably can if you take a taxi.
タクシーに乗っていけば{多分/恐らく}大丈夫でしょう。
Takushii ni notte ikeba {tabun/osoraku} daijoobu deshoo.

problem n. **[a question to solve or s.t./s.o./s.a. that presents a difficulty]**
mo⌈ndai 問題 •c ⟪question, issue⟫

EX. (**a**) A: I have to write this report by tomorrow.
このレポートをあしたまでに書かなければならないんだ。
Kono repooto o ashita made ni kakanakereba naranai n da.
B: Considering that our computer isn't working, that's going to be a problem, isn't it?
コンピューターが故障している時に、それは大問題だね。
Konpyuutaa ga koshoo-shite iru toki ni, sore wa dai-mondai da ne.
(**b**) This was the only problem on the test I couldn't get.
テストの問題で出来なかったのはこれだけだ。
Tesuto no mondai de dekinakatta no wa kore dake da.
(**c**) Housing is one of the greatest problems facing modern Japanese society.
住宅問題は現代の日本社会が抱えている最も大きな問題の一つです。
Juutaku-mondai wa gendai no Nihon-shakai ga kakaete iru mottomo ookina mondai no hitotsu desu.
(**d**) Frank has been a problem ever since he was a small child.
フランクは小さい時からずっと問題児でした。
Furanku wa chiisai toki kara zutto mondai-ji deshita.

procedure n. **[a series of actions followed in properly achieving some goal]**
te-⌈tsu⌉zuki 手続き [a set of formal steps necessary to accomplish s.t.] ⟪process, formalities, steps⟫, te-⌈jun 手順 [the order in which s.t. is done] ⟪process, routine⟫, ju⌉njo 順序 •c [the order in which elements of a group are arranged with regard to each other] ⟪order, sequence⟫

EX. (**a**) What procedure do I need to follow to apply for a visa?
ビザを申請するためにはどんな{手続き/*手順/*順序}をとらなければなりませんか。
*Biza o shinsei-suru tame ni wa donna {te-tsuzuki/*te-jun/*junjo} o toranakereba narimasen ka.*
(**b**) Could you show me the procedure for operating this machine.
この機械を動かす{手順/順序/*手続き}を教えてくださいませんか。
*Kono kikai o ugokasu {te-jun/junjo/*te-tsuzuki} o oshiete kudasaimasen ka.*

proceed vi. **[to go forward or continue ⟪fig. "start s.t.," "come forth from a source"⟫]**
1. su⌈sumu 進む ① [to go forward spontaneously ⟪fig. "make progress," "be advanced," "feel inclined"⟫] ⟪advance, progress⟫, shi⌈nkoo-suru 進行する ③ •c [for s.t. to move forward toward a goal in time (such as a meeting or project) or in space (such as a vehicle) or for a condition such as a disease to become more advanced] ⟪advance, progress, be in motion, go along⟫

EX. (**a**) The line of people proceeded slowly towards the entrance.
人々は列になってゆっくり入り口へ{進んだ/*進行した}。
*Hito-bito wa retsu ni natte yukkuri iri-guchi e {susunda/*shinkoo-shita}.*
(**b**) My research proceeded as scheduled.

私の研究は計画通り{進んだ/進行した}。
Watashi no kenkyuu wa keikaku-doori {susunda/shinkoo-shita}.

process n. **[a series of actions done to make or accomplish s.t. or the course followed by a series of events or natural developments culminating in a goal]**
ka⌈tei 過程 •c [the course followed by a series of events or natural developments culminating in a goal ⟪fig. "curriculum"⟫**]** ⟪course, stage⟫, **pu⌈ro⌉sesu プロセス •f [a method or series of steps followed in accomplishing a task], ko⌈otei 工程 •c [a series of actions performed in producing s.t.]** ⟪stages of work⟫

EX. The process followed in manufacturing cars is basically the same in Japan and the U.S.
車の生産の{過程/工程/プロセス}は日米で基本的には同じだ。
Kuruma no seisan no {katei/kootei/purosesu} wa Nichi-Bei de kihon-tekini wa onaji da.

— vt. **[to treat s.t. in a series of steps to change it into a finished product]**
⟨-o⟩ **sho⌉ri-ka⌈koo-suru** ⟨〜を⟩**処理加工する** ③ **•c [to treat raw materials in a series of steps leading to a finished product]**

produce vt. **[to make or create s.t.; to bring s.t. out so it can be seen; to prepare a play or film for presentation to the public]**
1. ⟨-o⟩ **u⌈mu** ⟨〜を⟩**うむ** ① **[to give birth to s.t./s.o./s.a.]** ⟪bear, give birth to⟫
㊥ "deliver a baby"▷産む, 生む, "yield"▷生む

EX. My cat produced three kittens.
うちの猫は子猫を三匹{産/生}んだ。
Uchi no neko wa ko-neko o san-biki unda.

2. ⟨-o⟩ **se⌈isan-suru** ⟨〜を⟩**生産する** ③ **•c [to bring s.t. into existence, esp. in quantity using machines]** ⟪turn out, put out⟫, ⟨-o⟩ **se⌈izoo-suru** ⟨〜を⟩**製造する** ③ **•c [for s.o. to bring s.t. into existence, esp. in quantity using machines]** ⟪manufacture, turn out, prepare⟫

EX. A: What does this factory produce?
この工場は何を{生産/製造}しているんですか。
Kono koojoo wa nani o {seisan/seizoo}-shite iru n desu ka.
B: TV sets.
テレビを{生産/製造}しています。
Terebi o {seisan/seizoo}-shite imasu.

3. ⟨-o⟩ **da⌉su** ⟨〜を⟩**出す** ① **[for s.o. to cause s.o/s.t./s.a. to come out]** ⟪bring out, pull out, send, take out, give⟫

EX. He produced some change from his pocket.
彼はポケットから小銭を出した。
Kare wa poketto kara ko-zeni o dashita.

4. ⟨-o⟩ **jo⌈oen-suru** ⟨〜を⟩**上演する** ③ **•c [for s.o. to publicly present a play at a theater]** ⟪put on a play⟫

EX. The theater department in our university produced a *Kabuki* version of *Othello* this past spring.
うちの大学の演劇科はこの春歌舞伎版の『オセロ』を上演した。
Uchi no daigaku no engeki-ka wa kono haru Kabuki-ban no "Osero" o jooen-shita.

product n. **[s.t. which is created, either in nature or by human effort]**
se⌈ihin 製品 •c [manufactured goods] ⟪finished goods⟫, **sa⌈nbutsu 産物 •c [s.t. produced agriculturally in a particular region** ⟪fig. "outgrowth"⟫**]** ⟪production, result⟫

EX. (a) Electronic products are sold on the 5th floor.
電子{製品/*産物}は五階で売っています。
*Denshi-{seihin/*sanbutsu} wa go-kai de utte imasu.*
(b) The principal agricultural product of Illinois is corn.
イリノイ州の主な{産物/*製品}はとうもろこしです。
*Irinoi-shuu no omona {sanbutsu/*seihin} wa toomorokoshi desu.*

PHRASE: gross national product *kokumin-soo-seisan* 国民総生産 •c

production n. **[the act of making or creating s.t. or s.t. made or created]**

1. se⌈isan 生産 •c **[an act of bringing s.t. into existence, esp. in quantity using machines]**

EX. The production of cars at this plant has slowed down lately.
この工場の車の生産は最近低下した。
Kono koojoo no kuruma no seisan wa saikin teika-shita.

2. jo⌈oen 上演 •c **[the public presentation of a play at a theater]** **⟪dramatic presentation⟫**

EX. The Broadway production of "*Cats*" was a smashing success.
ブロードウエイでの『キャッツ』の上演は大成功だった。
Buroodouei de no "Kyattsu" no jooen wa dai-seikoo datta.

productive adj. **[capable of producing things, esp. in great amounts]**
se⌈isan-tekina 生産的な adj(*na*). •c, **ta⌈san no N 多産のN** •c **[producing many offspring]** **⟪fecund, prolific, fruitful⟫**, **ta⌈saku no N 多作のN** •c **[producing many literary or artistic works]** **⟪fecund, prolific⟫**, **mi⌈nori ga o⌉oi 実りが多い** adj(*i*). **[producing much in the way of result]** **⟪fruitful⟫**

EX. (**a**) Mozart was an extremely productive composer.
モーツァルトは実に{多作の/*実りが多い/*生産的な/*多産の}作曲家だった。
*Mootsaruto wa jitsuni {tasaku no/ *minori ga ooi/*seisan-tekina/*tasan no} sakkyoku-ka datta.*
(**b**) This has been my most productive year so far.
私にとって今年は今までで最も{生産的な/実りの多い/??多作の/*多産の}年だった。
*Watashi ni-totte kotoshi wa ima made de mottomo {seisan-tekina/minori no ooi/??tasaku no/*tasan no} toshi datta.*
(**c**) The most recent round of discussions between the U.S. and Japan on trade issues was not very productive.
貿易問題に関する最近の日米協議はあまり{生産的では/実りが多く/*多作では/*多産では}なかった。
*Booeki-mondai ni-kansuru saikin no Nichi-Bei-kyoogi wa amari {seisan-teki dewa/minori ga ooku/*tasaku de/*tasan dewa} nakatta.*

profession n. **[an occupation requiring special education and training, such as lawyer, doctor, priest, professor, writer, actor, etc.]**
sho⌈ku⌉gyoo 職業 •c **[work as a means of supporting one's life]** **⟪occupation, calling, vocation, trade, business⟫**

EX. A: What's your profession?
御職業は何でしょうか。
Go-shokugyoo wa nan deshoo ka.
B: I'm a writer.
作家です。
Sakka desu.

professional adj. **[having to do with an occupation requiring special education and training]**
se⌈nmon-tekina 専門的な adj(*na*). •c **[related to a special field of study]** **⟪expert, technical⟫**, **sho⌈kugyoo-joo no N 職業上のN** •c **[relating to one's work as a means of supporting one's life]**, **pu⌉ro no N プロのN** •f **[having to do with a person who makes an occupation out of an activity which is for most people recreational, esp. sports]** ↔ **ama no N アマのN** •f

EX. (**a**) My friend, who is a lawyer, gave me some professional advice.
弁護士をしている友達が{専門的な/職業上の/*プロの}アドバイスをしてくれた。
*Bengo-shi o shite iru tomodachi ga {senmon-tekina/shokugyoo-joo no/ *puro no} adobaisu o shite kureta.*
(**b**) When I was a boy I wanted to become a professional baseball player.
少年のころ、僕は{プロの/*専門的な/*職業上の}野球選手になりたかった。
*Shoonen no koro, boku wa {puro no/ *senmon-tekina/*shokugyoo-joo no} yakyuu-senshu ni nari-takatta.*

—— n. **[a person who has an occupation requiring special education and training or**

s.o. with the attributes of such a person] **se⌈nmon-ka 専門家 •c** **⟪specialist, expert⟫, ku⌉rooto 玄人 [an expert, esp. in arts and crafts ⟪fig. "a woman of pleasure"⟫] ⟪expert, specialist⟫ ↔ shirooto 素人; pu⌉ro プロ •f ↔ ama アマ •f**

EX. (**a**) A: Did you beat Bill in your tennis match?
ビルをテニスで負かしたかい?
Biru o tenisu de makashita kai?
B: No way. He's a professional, you know.
いや、とんでもない。彼は{プロ/*専門家/*玄人}だからね。
*Iya, tondemo nai. Kare wa {puro/ *senmon-ka/*kurouto} da kara ne.*
(**b**) Janet is a professional in Japanese calligraphy.
ジャネットは書道の{専門家/?玄人/*プロ}だ。
*Janetto wa shodoo no {senmon-ka/ ?kurooto/*puro} da.*
(**c**) She can sing like a professional.
彼女の歌は{玄人/*専門家/*プロ}はだしだ。
*Kanojo no uta wa {kurooto/*senmon-ka/*puro}-hadashi da.*

professor n. **[a teacher in a college or university, esp. (in America) one of the highest rank]**

1. da⌈igaku no kyo⌈oin 大学の教員 •c [a teacher in a college or university]

EX. My uncle is a university professor.
うちのおじは大学の教員です。
Uchi no oji wa daigaku no kyooin desu.

2. (se⌈i-)kyo⌉oju (正)教授 •c [a college or university teacher of the highest rank]

EX. Dan was promoted from assistant professor to full professor in just three years.
ダンは専任講師から(正)教授にたった三年で昇進した。
Dan wa sennin-kooshi kara (sei-)kyooju ni tatta san-nen de shooshin-shita.

NOTE: "Assistant professor," "associate professor" and "(full) professor" in the American academic world correspond functionally to *sennin-kooshi, jo-kyooju* and *kyooju*, respectively, in Japan, but are directly translated as *jo-kyooju, jun-kyooju* and *(sei-)kyooju*, respectively.

proficiency n. **[being skilled at s.t. or the degree to which one is skilled at s.t.]** **ju⌈kutatsu 熟達 •c [the state of having acquired mastery in a skill] ⟪mastery⟫, ju⌈kutatsu⌉-do 熟達度 •c [the degree to which one is skilled at s.t.]**

EX. All the students in the Japanese class were required to take a proficiency test in Japanese.
日本語のクラスの学生は皆日本語の熟達度を計るテストを受けなければならなかった。
Nihon-go no kurasu no gakusei wa mina Nihon-go no jukutatsu-do o hakaru tesuto o ukenakereba naranakatta.

proficient adj. **[manifesting an advanced level in a skill]**
{⟨-ga⟩/⟨-ni⟩} ta⌈nnoona {⟨〜が⟩/⟨〜に⟩}たんのうな adj(*na*). **•c [excelling in a skill] ⟪skillful⟫, ⟨-ni⟩ ju⌈kutatsu-shita N** ⟨〜に⟩熟達したN **/⟨Vinf. past of *jukutatsu-suru* ③ master/ •c, ⟨-ni⟩ ju⌈kutatsu-shite iru (N)** ⟨〜に⟩熟達している(N) **/⟨V*te iru* of *jukutatsu-suru* ③ master/ •c [having acquired mastery in a skill] ⟪having attained proficiency⟫, ⟨-ga⟩ ta⌈sshana** ⟨〜が⟩達者な adj(*na*). **•c [excelling in a field or in a state of good health] ⟪skillful, healthy⟫**

EX. (**a**) Ms. Suzuki is highly proficient in English.
鈴木さんは英語{がたんのうだ/が達者だ/に熟達している}。
Suzuki-san wa eigo {ga tannoo da/ga tassha da/ni jukutatsu-shite iru}.
(**b**) I'm glad to have a wife who's proficient in cooking.
料理に{たんのうな/熟達した/*達者な}妻をもって幸せだ。
*Ryoori ni {tannoona/jukutatsu-shita/ *tasshana} tsuma o motte shiawase da.*

profit n. **[the amount by which the returns of a business enterprise exceed its costs or that which is gained by doing s.t.]**

P

ri⌉eki 利益 •c [an increase in (monetary) wealth generated by an excess of returns over costs] ⟪gains, returns, benefit, advantage⟫ ↔ **sonshitsu 損失 •c; e⌉ki 益 •c [s.t. that is useful and profitable]** ⟪gain, profit, benefit⟫ ↔ **son 損 •c, gai 害 •c; to⌈ku 得 •c [s.t. which is gained]** ⟪interest, advantage⟫ ↔ **son 損 •c; mo⌈oke もうけ /⟨V*masu* of *mookeru* ② make a profit/ [monetary gains]** ⟪gains, earnings⟫

EX. (**a**) We realized a sizable profit from the sale of our home.
家を売るとかなりの{利益/もうけ/*益/*得}が出た。
*Ie o uru to kanari no {rieki/mooke/*eki/*toku} ga deta.*
(**b**) I profited in many ways from my year of teaching English in Japan.
日本で一年間英語を教えて私にはいろいろな意味で{得/益/*利益/*もうけ}になった。
*Nihon de ichi-nenkan eigo o oshiete watashi ni wa iro-irona imi de {toku/eki/*rieki/*mooke} ni natta.*

NOTE: Example (b) can also be expressed as *Nihon de no ichi-nen wa iro-irona imi de watashi ni wa yuueki datta.*

— vi. **[for s.o. to gain or benefit in some way from s.t.]**
(⟨-de⟩) mo⌈oke⌉ru (⟨～で⟩)もうける ② [for s.o. to realize a monetary gain by doing s.t.] ⟪cash in⟫, **(⟨-de⟩) to⌈ku o suru (⟨～で⟩)得をする ③ [for s.o. to obtain some benefit (in return for little or no investment)]** ⟪make a profit⟫ ↔ **(⟨-de⟩) son o suru (⟨～で⟩)損をする ③; (⟨-de⟩) ri⌉eki o e⌉ru (⟨～で⟩)利益を得る ② [for s.o. to realize a monetary gain]**

EX. He seems to have profited greatly from dealing in stocks.
あの人は株の売買で随分{もうけた/得をした/利益を得た}らしい。
Ano hito wa kabu no bai-bai de zuibun {mooketa/toku o shita/rieki o eta} rashii.

profound adj. **[exhibiting great understanding and wisdom or deep and intense in degree]**
fu⌈ka⌉i 深い adj(*i*). **[extending far downward from the surface or far toward the back from the front ⟪fig. "profound," "hard to fathom," "dark (color/sound)," "secret," "dense," "intimate"⟫]** ⟪deep, intense, intimate⟫ ↔ **asai 浅い** adj(*i*).; **shi⌈n'enna 深遠な** adj(*na*). **•c [figuratively very deep]** ⟪unfathomable⟫

EX. I was very much impressed by the professor's profound knowledge of eastern philosophy.
私は東洋哲学に関する教授の{深い/深遠な}知識に感銘を受けた。
Watashi wa tooyoo-tetsugaku ni-kansuru kyooju no {fukai/shin'enna} chishiki ni kanmei o uketa.

program n. **[an ordered list of events showing a plan of how to proceed (as in a curriculum of study) or of what will be presented (as in a concert); one of the parts of a schedule for broadcast on radio or television]**
1. ba⌈ngumi⌉ 番組 [one of the parts of an organized schedule of presentations broadcast on radio or television], pu⌈rogu⌉ramu プログラム •f [an ordered list of events to be publicly presented on a particular occasion, esp. in printed form, or a precise list of commands for a computer]

EX. (**a**) On Sunday afternoon there are usually lots of sports programs on TV.
日曜の午後のテレビには大抵スポーツの{番組/*プログラム}が多い。
*Nichi-yoo no gogo no terebi ni wa taitei supootsu no {bangumi/*puroguramu} ga ooi.*
(**b**) Could I have a concert program please?
コンサートの{プログラム/*番組}を下さいませんか。
*Konsaato no {puroguramu/*bangumi} o kudasaimasen ka.*

2. {ko⌈ogi-/ga⌈kka-}na⌉iyoo {講義/学科}内容 •c [the lecture or course offerings of an academic unit], na⌈iyoo 内容 •c [s.t. that constitutes the inner part of s.t. and gives value to it]

EX. Could you give me an idea of what kind of program of courses is offered in the mathematics department?
数学科の{講義内容/学科内容/内容}を教えてくださいませんか。
Suugak(u)-ka no {koogi-naiyoo/gakka-naiyoo/naiyoo} o oshiete kudasaimasen ka.

3. ka⌈tei 課程 •c [the course followed by a series of events or natural developments culminating in a goal ⟪fig. "curriculum"⟫]

EX. I plan to enter a master's program in Japanese literature at the University of Michigan next fall.
この秋にミシガン大学の日本文学の修士課程に入る予定です。
Kono aki ni Mishigan-daigaku no Nihon-bungaku no shuushi-katei ni hairu yotei desu.

progress n. **[forward movement (toward a goal)]**

1. ze⌈nshin 前進 •c [movement forward, esp. by means of walking or running] ⟪advance, drive⟫, shi⌈nkoo 進行 •c [movement toward a goal] ⟪advance, march⟫

EX. (**a**) On the third day out of port our ship made hardly any progress due to bad weather.
港を出て三日目には悪天候のため船はほとんど{前進/*進行}しなかった。
*Minato o dete mikka-me ni wa aku-tenkoo no tame fune wa hotondo {zenshin/*shinkoo} shinakatta.*
(**b**) The meeting is currently in progress.
会議は今{進行/*前進}中です。
*Kaigai wa ima {shinkoo/*zenshin} chuu desu.*

NOTE: Example (b) can also be expressed as *Ima kaigi-chuu desu.*

2. shi⌈npo 進歩 •c [moving ahead in knowledge, ability, social conditions, etc.] ⟪advance, improvement, evolution⟫, ha⌈tten 発展 •c [an instance of moving into a more advanced stage accompanied by a spreading over a wider area] ⟪expansion, enlargement, development⟫, ha⌈ttatsu 発達 •c [an instance of s.t. reaching a mature, advanced stage] ⟪development, growth, progress, advancement⟫

EX. (**a**) The progress my students have made in Japanese is very impressive.
私の学生の日本語の{進歩/*発展/*発達}はすばらしいですよ。
*Watashi no gakusei no Nihon-go no {shinpo/*hatten/*hattatsu} wa subarashii desu yo.*
(**b**) The rate of scientific progress during and after World War II has been amazing.
第二次世界大戦中と戦後の科学の{進歩/発達/?発展}には目覚ましいものがある。
Dai-ni-ji-sekai-taisen-chuu to sengo no kagaku no {shinpo/hattatsu/?hatten} ni wa mezamashii mono ga aru.
(**c**) The rapid progress made by the Japanese economy after the war was largely due to increased exports.
戦後の日本経済の急速な{発展/*進歩/*発達}は輸出の増加に負うところが多かった。
*Sengo no Nihon-keizai no kyuusokuna {hatten/*shinpo/*hattatsu} wa yushutsu no zooka ni ou tokoro ga ookatta.*

—— vi. **[to move forward (toward a goal)]**

1. ze⌈nshin-suru 前進する ③ •c [to move forward] ⟪advance, march forward⟫, shi⌈nkoo-suru 進行する ③ •c [for s.t. to move forward toward a goal in time (such as a meeting or project) or in space (such as a vehicle) or for a condition such as a disease to become more advanced] ⟪advance, proceed, make headway⟫

EX. (**a**) Our football team progressed as far as the ten yard line.
我々のフットボールのチームは十ヤードまで{前進/*進行}した。
*Ware-ware no futto-booru no chiimu wa juu-yaado made {zenshin/*shinkoo}-shita.*
(**b**) Construction on the new building is progressing as scheduled.

新しい建物の建設は予定通り{進行/*前進}している。
*Atarashii tate-mono no kensetsu wa yotei-doori {shinkoo/*zenshin}-shite iru.*

2. shi⌈npo-suru 進歩する ③ •c [to make steady improvement] ⟪advance, improve, evolve⟫, ha⌈tten-suru 発展する ③ •c [for s.t. to move into a more advanced stage and spread over a wider area] ⟪develop, expand, grow, extend⟫

EX. (**a**) My Japanese is progressing very slowly.
僕の日本語はゆっくり{進歩/*発展}しています。
*Boku no Nihon-go wa yukkuri {shinpo/*hatten}-shite imasu.*
(**b**) The Korean economy has progressed through expansion of exports.
韓国の経済は輸出の伸びと共に{発展/*進歩}した。
*Kankoku no keizai wa yushutsu no nobi to-tomoni {hatten/*shinpo}-shita.*

progressive adj. **[moving forward** (**toward a goal**) **⟪fig. "enlightened"⟫]**

1. ze⌈nshin-suru N 前進するN •c [moving forward]

2. shi⌈npo-tekina 進歩的な adj(*na*). **•c [favoring improvement and reform in political structure, social conditions, etc.] ⟪advanced, enlightened, forward-looking⟫ ↔ hoshu-tekina 保守的な** adj(*na*). **•c**

EX. Even in his seventies he is still progressive in his thinking.
七十代でなお、彼の考えは進歩的だ。
Nana-juu-dai de nao, kare no kangae wa shinpo-teki da.

3. shi⌈nkookei no N 進行形のN •c [consisting of a verb form which expresses continuation of an action]

EX. In Japanese the progressive form of the verb is "*te* form + *iru*."
日本語の動詞の進行形は「て形+いる」によって表わされる。
Nihon-go no dooshi no shinkoo-kei wa 'te kei + iru' ni-yotte arawasa-reru.

prohibit vt. **[for s.o to not allow s.o. to do s.t.]**

1. {⟨-ni/-ga⟩} ⟨-o⟩ ki⌈njiru {⟨〜に/〜が⟩}⟨〜を⟩禁じる ② •c [for s.o. not to allow s.o. to do s.t.] ⟪forbid, proscribe, ban, taboo, debar⟫, {⟨-ni/-ga⟩} ⟨-{no/ko⌈to⌉} o⟩ ki⌈nshi-suru {⟨〜に/〜が⟩}⟨-{の/こと}を⟩禁止する ③ •c [for s.o. to not allow s.o. to do s.t.] ⟪forbid, suppress, inhibit, proscribe, ban, taboo]

EX. (**a**) State law prohibits smoking in public places.
州の法律は市民{に/が}公共の場所でたばこを吸う{の/こと}を{禁じて/禁止して}いる。
Shuu no hooritsu wa shimin {ni/ga} kookyoo no basho de tabako o suu {no/koto} o {kinjite/kinshi-shite} iru.
(**b**) All high schools in Japan used to prohibit their students from getting permanents.
日本の高校では以前はどこでも生徒はパーマをかける{の/こと}を{禁じられて/禁止されて}いた。
Nihon no kookoo de wa izen wa doko-demo seito wa paama o kakeru {no/koto} o {kinji-rarete/kinshi-sarete} ita.

2. …V*te*, neg. of pot. [because…, one cannot do s.t.]

EX. A: Can you come to the meeting tomorrow?
あしたの会議に出られますか。
Ashita no kaigi ni de-raremasu ka.
B: No, a prior engagement prohibits me from attending.
いいえ、先約があって、出られません。
Iie, sen'yaku ga atte, de-raremasen.

prohibition n. **[the act of not allowing s.t.]**

1. ki⌈nshi 禁止 •c [the act of not allowing s.o. to do s.t.] ⟪interdiction, taboo, ban, embargo, suppression⟫

EX. The college is trying to enforce its prohibition of alcohol, but students appear to be drinking anyway.
大学はアルコール禁止を徹底させようと努めているのだが、学生たちはお構いなく飲んでいるようだ。
Daigaku wa arukooru-kinshi o tettei-saseyoo to tsutomete iru no da ga,

gakusei-tachi wa o-kamainaku nonde iru yooda.

2. ki⌈nrei 禁令 •c [a decree not allowing s.t.] **⟪interdictory decree⟫**

project n. **[a planned undertaking]**

ke⌉ikaku 計画 •c [a method or procedure for doing s.t. thought out in advance] ⟪plan, scheme⟫, ji⌈gyoo(-ke⌉ikaku) 事業(計画) •c [a social or business undertaking on a relatively large scale] ⟪undertaking, scheme, operation⟫, pu⌈roje⌉kuto プロジェクト •f [a research or business undertaking]

EX. (**a**) The construction firm I work for has bid on a huge project to construct more office buildings downtown.
僕が勤めている建設会社は市の中心部にオフィス・ビルを増設するという巨大な{プロジェクト/計画/事業(計画)}に入札した。
Boku ga tsutomete iru kensetsu-gaisha wa shi no chuushin-bu ni ofisu-biru o zoosetsu-suru to iu kyodaina {purojekuto/keikaku/jigyoo(-keikaku)} ni nyuusatsu-shita.
(**b**) Do you think this project is feasible?
この{計画/プロジェクト/事業(計画)}は実現出来そうですか。
Kono {keikaku/purojekuto/jigyoo (-keikaku)} wa jitsugen deki-soo desu ka.

— vt. **[to cast or throw s.t. outward ⟪fig. "estimate," "cause light/an image to fall on a surface," "cause to protrude"⟫]**

1. ⟨-o⟩ ⟨-ni⟩ to⌈oei-suru ⟨〜を⟩⟨〜に⟩投影する ③ •c [to cast light/an image onto a surface] ⟪cast a shadow⟫, ⟨-o⟩ {⟨-ni⟩/⟨-e⟩} u⌈tsu⌉su ⟨〜を⟩{⟨〜に⟩/⟨〜へ⟩}うつす ① [to cause s.o./s.t./s.a. to change to a different location or into a different condition ⟪fig. "copy," "reflect" "infect" "take a picture"⟫]

㊅ "physically move s.t. from one place to another"▷移す, "copy/describe/take a picture"▷写す, "project an image on a surface"▷映す

EX. We don't have a screen, so let's just project the slides onto the wall.
スクリーンがないから、壁にスライドを映しましょうか。
Sukuriin ga nai kara, kabe ni suraido o utsushimashoo ka.

2. ⟨-o⟩ mi-⌈tsumoru ⟨〜を⟩見積もる ① [for s.o. to calculate s.t. roughly in advance] ⟪estimate value, assess⟫

EX. We projected the construction costs for the new building to be about one million dollars.
新しいビルの建設費を大体100万ドルと見積もった。
Atarashii biru no kensetsu-hi o daitai hyaku-man-doru to mi-tsumotta.

— vi. **[for s.t. to protrude outward from a surface]**

tsu⌈ki-de⌉ru 突き出る ② [for s.t. such as a nail, promontory, or forehead to protrude out from its surroundings] ⟪stick out, stand out ⟫

EX. The cape projects into the ocean.
岬は海に突き出ている。
Misaki wa umi ni tsuki-dete iru.

prolong vt. **[to lengthen s.t. in space or time]**

⟨-o⟩ na⌈gabika-se⌉ru ⟨〜を⟩長引かせる /⟨causative of *nagabiku* ① drag on/ ② [to cause s.t. to unnecessarily take more time than expected or planned] ⟪protract, delay⟫, ⟨-o⟩ (hi⌈ki-)noba⌉su ⟨〜を⟩(引き)のばす ① [to stretch s.t. out in space or time] ⟪draw out, stretch out, elongate, enlarge⟫, ⟨-o⟩ e⌈nchoo-suru ⟨〜を⟩延長する ③ •c [for s.o. to stretch s.t. out in time] ⟪extend⟫

㊅ "pull s.t. and elongate it"▷引き伸ばす, "cause s.t. to take more time"▷引き延ばす

EX. (**a**) The professor prolonged his office hours during the week before the final examination to give time to students needing help.
その教授は期末試験前の一週間、助けの必要な学生に時間を与えるため研究室での質問時間を{延長した/(引き)延ばした/*長引かせた}。
Sono kyooju wa kimatsu-shiken mae no is-shuukan, tasuke no hitsuyoona gakusei ni jikan o ataeru tame kenkyuu-shitsu de no shitsumon-jikan o {enchoo-

*shita/(hiki-)nobashita/*nagabika-seta}.*
(**b**) Modern medicine has been able to prolong life using all sorts of mechanical means.
現代医学は命を{延ばす/*長引かせる/*延長する}ために色々な機械を使います。
*Gendai-igaku wa inochi o {nobasu/*nagabika-seru/*enchoo-suru} tame ni iro-irona kikai o tsukaimasu.*
(**c**) The manager prolonged the game time by his persistent protests to the umpire.
監督は審判員にしつこく抗議をして、試合時間を{長引かせた/引き延ばした/延長した}。
Kantoku wa shinpan-in ni shitsukoku koogi o shite, shiai jikan o {naga-bika-seta/hiki-nobashita/enchoo-shita}.

prominent adj. **[noticeably projecting outward 《fig. "widely known"》]**
1. tsu⌈ki-de⌉ta N 突き出たN /〈Vinf. past of *tsuki-deru* ② jut out/, tsu⌈ki-de⌉te iru (N) 突き出ている(N) /V *te iru* of *tsuki-deru* ② jut out/ [protruding]
EX. In Hokusai's famous woodblock print, the shape of Mt. Fuji is prominent above the waves.
有名な北斎の版画では富士山が波間から突き出ている。
Yuumeina Hokusai no hanga de wa Fuji-san ga namima kara tsuki-dete iru.
2. cho⌈meina 著名な adj(*na*). **•c [for s.o. to be well-known in society]** **《eminent, famous》**
EX. Professor Yamada is a prominent scholar in the field of sociology.
山田教授は社会学の著名な学者だ。
Yamada-kyooju wa shakai-gaku no chomeina gakusha da.

promise n. **[an explicit statement that s.o. will or will not do s.t. or that s.t. will or will not happen or an indication of future success]**
1. ya⌈kusoku 約束 •c [an explicit statement that one will or will not do s.t. or s.t. that one has explicitly said one will or will not do (including a date, engagement, or appointment)]
EX. (**a**) I admire Mike for always keeping his promises.
マイクが約束を必ず守るのには感心します。
Maiku ga yakusoku o kanarazu mamoru no ni wa kanshin-shimasu.
(**b**) A: I'll take you to a nice restaurant this weekend.
今度の週末にいいレストランに連れて行ってやるよ。
Kondo no shuumatsu ni ii resutoran ni tsurete itte yaru yo.
B: Is that a promise?
それ、約束?
Sore, yakusoku?
2. mi⌈komi 見込み /〈V*masu* of *mikomu* ① anticipate/ [an anticipation/expectation/prediction that s.t. is very likely to occur] **《hope, possibility, chance》**, **no⌈zomi 望み /〈V*masu* of *nozomu* ① hope/ [an indication or desire of future success]** **《hope, expectation, ambition, desire, wish》**, **sho⌈orai-sei 将来性 •c [prospects that one's future will be bright]** **《prospect, possibility, bright future》**
EX. (**a**) He's a young scholar of great promise.
彼は大変{将来性/見込み/??望み}のある若い学者だ。
Kare wa taihen {shoorai-sei/mikomi/??nozomi} no aru wakai gakusha da.
(**b**) Is there any promise of a vaccine for AIDS in the near future?
近い将来にエイズのワクチンができる{見込み/望み/??将来性}がありますか。
Chikai shoorai ni eizu no wakuchin ga dekiru {mikomi/nozomi/??shoorai-sei} ga arimasu ka.

— vt. **[for s.o. to make an explicit statement that one will or will not do s.t. or that s.t. will or will not happen]**
1. ka⌈narazu…V 必ず…V adv. **[for s.t. to happen or for s.o. to do s.t. without fail]**
EX. A: Can you promise that you'll find me a job?
必ず仕事を見つけてくれますか。

Kanarazu shigoto o mitsukete kuremasu ka.
B: Yes, I can promise.
ええ、必ず。
Ee, kanarazu.

2. 〈-ni〉 **{Vinf. nonpast to ya⌈kusoku-suru/Vinf. nonpast ya⌈kusoku o suru}** 〈〜に〉 **{Vinf. nonpastと約束する/Vinf. nonpast約束をする}** ③ **•c [for s.o. to give s.o. one's word that one will or will not do s.t.]**

EX. (**a**) I promised to take Mary to a movie on Friday evening.
僕はメアリーに金曜の晩映画に{連れて行く約束をした/連れて行くと約束した}。
Boku wa Mearii ni kin'yoo no ban eiga ni {tsurete-iku yakusoku o shita/tsurete-iku to yakusoku-shita}.
(**b**) Didn't you promise that you would write me?
手紙を{書いてくれるって約束した/書いてくれる約束(を)した}んじゃなかったっけ?
Tegami o {kaite kurerutte yakusoku-shita/kaite kureru yakusoku (o) shita} n janakattakke?

NOTE: *Tte* in example (b) is a colloquial form of *to* used in spoken Japanese.

promptly adv. **[without loss of time]**
su⌉gu (ni) すぐ(に) **[at once/without delay] ⟪right away, immediately, instantly, at once⟫, su⌈ba⌉yaku** すばやく **/adj(*i*). *ku* of *subayai* quick/ [in a manner of acting or thinking which is extremely quick or agile] ⟪quickly, nimbly, agilely⟫, so⌉kuza ni** 即座に n.+prt. **•c [there and then] ⟪right away, immediately, instantly, at once⟫**

EX. (**a**) With the arrival of March the weather promptly turned warm.
三月になると、{すぐに/*すばやく/*即座に}暖かくなった。
*San-gatsu ni naru to, {sugu ni/*subayaku/*sokuza ni} atatakaku natta.*
(**b**) Bill answered the teacher's questions promptly.
ビルは先生の質問に{すぐに/すばやく/即座に}答えた。
Biru wa sensei no shitsumon ni {sugu ni/subayaku/sokuza ni} kotaeta.

pronoun n. **[a grammatical term for a word that stands for a noun or noun phrase]**
da⌈i-me⌉ishi 代名詞 **•c [a word that acts as a substitute for a noun or noun phrase ⟪fig. "personification"⟫]**

EX. In Japanese, third person singular pronouns are usually not expressed.
日本語では三人称単数の代名詞は大抵省略される。
Nihon-go de wa san-nin-shoo tansuu no dai-meishi wa taitei shooryaku-sareru.

pronounce vt. **[for s.o. to articulate a sound in human speech ⟪fig. "declare"⟫]**
1. 〈-o〉 **ha⌈tsuon-suru** 〈〜を〉発音する ③ **•c [for s.o. to articulate a sound in human speech] ⟪enunciate, articulate⟫**

EX. Could you pronounce "*tsu*" again please?
「つ」をもう一度発音してくださいませんか。
'Tsu' o moo ichi-do hatsuon-shite kudasaimasen ka.

2. 〈-to〉 **ha⌈kki⌉ri iu** 〈〜と〉はっきり言う ① **[for s.o. to say clearly that],** 〈-to〉 **i⌈i-ki⌉ru** 〈〜と〉言い切る ① **[for s.o. to say definitely that or to tell everything] ⟪declare, affirm, assert, tell all⟫,** 〈-to〉 **da⌈nge⌉n-suru** 〈〜と〉断言する ③ **•c [for s.o. to declare decisively on the basis of evidence that s.t. is true] ⟪affirm, declare, swear⟫**

EX. The expert pronounced the new procedure to be ineffective in detecting cancer.
専門家はその新しい方法はがんを発見するのに役に立たないと{はっきり言った/言い切った/断言した}。
Senmon-ka wa sono atarashii hoohoo wa gan o hakken-suru no ni yaku ni tatanai to {hakkiri itta/ii-kitta/dangen-shita}.

pronunciation n. **[the way of articulating a sound or group of sounds in human speech]**
ha⌈tsuon 発音 **•c**

EX. He has very good English pronunciation.

彼の英語の発音はとてもいい。
Kare no eigo no hatsuon wa totemo ii.

proof n. **[evidence that demonstrates that s.t. is true or correct ⟪fig. "a trial sheet of printed material"⟫]**

1. sho⌈oko 証拠 •c [materials that demonstrate the truth or correctness of s.t.] ⟪evidence, witness, testimony⟫

EX. (**a**) Is there any proof that he stole the watch?
彼が時計を盗んだという証拠がありますか。
Kare ga tokei o nusunda to iu shooko ga arimasu ka.
(**b**) It's proof of your good health that you don't feel tired after such a hard day's work.
一日のきつい仕事の後疲れを感じないのはあなたが健康な証拠です。
Ichi-nichi no kitsui shigoto no ato tsukare o kanjinai no wa anata ga kenkoona shooko desu.

2. ko⌈osei-zuri 校正刷り [a trial sheet of printed material] ⟪proofs⟫

propeller n. **[a device made of blades that rotate to drive s.t. forward such as a ship or airplane]**

pu⌈ropera プロペラ •f

EX. When I first came to America in 1958 it was by propeller plane.
1958年に初めてアメリカへ来た時はプロペラ機で来ました。
Sen-kyuu-hyaku-go-juu-hachi-nen ni hajimete Amerika e kita toki wa puropera-ki de kimashita.

proper adj. **[appropriate for or characteristic of s.o./s.t./s.a.]**

1. ⟨-ni⟩ fu⌈sawashi⌉i ⟨〜に⟩ふさわしい adj(*i*). **[suitable for a person or situation] ⟪suitable, fitting, becoming, appropriate, congruous⟫, ⟨-ni⟩ te⌈kitoona ⟨〜に⟩適当な** adj(*na*). **•c [right for a given situation/purpose/requirement] ⟪suitable, appropriate, fit⟫**

EX. (**a**) What is the proper dress for a cocktail party?
カクテルパーティーに{ふさわしい/適当な}のはどんな服装でしょうか。
Kakuteru-paatii ni {fusawashii/tekitoona} no wa donna fukusoo deshoo ka.
(**b**) I couldn't come up with the proper thing to say for the occasion.
私はその折に{ふさわしい/適当な}言葉が見つからなかった。
Watashi wa sono ori ni {fusawashii/tekitoona} kotoba ga mitsukaranakatta.

2. ta⌈dashi⌉i 正しい adj(*i*). **[conforming to an ethical, legal, logical, social, or regulatory standard; free from error] ⟪right, correct, righteous, accurate, legal, just⟫**

EX. (**a**) Please teach me the proper way to sit on a *tatami* floor.
畳の上での正しい座り方を教えてください。
Tatami no ue de no tadashii suwari-kata o oshiete kudasai.
(**b**) Put the proper particle in each blank.
空欄に正しい助詞を入れなさい。
Kuuran ni tadashii joshi o irenasai.
(**c**) It isn't proper for a politician to receive kickbacks from private companies.
政治家が民間の会社からリベートをもらうのは正しくない。
Seiji-ka ga minkan no kaisha kara ribeeto o morau no wa tadashikunai.

3. ⟨-ni⟩ ko⌈yuu no N ⟨〜に⟩固有のN •c [uniquely and originally belonging to s.t.] ⟪inherent, native, indigenous⟫, ⟨-ni⟩ do⌈kutoku no N ⟨〜に⟩独特のN •c [for a characteristic to belong exclusively to s.o./s.t./s.a.] ⟪peculiar, characteristic of, unique⟫, ⟨-ni⟩ do⌈kutokuna ⟨〜に⟩独特な adj(*na*). **•c**

EX. Psychological dependency may not be a characteristic proper to the Japanese.
甘えは日本文化に{固有の/独特の/独特な}ものではないかもしれない。
Amae wa Nihon-bunka ni {koyuu no/dokutoku no/dokutokuna} mono de wa nai kamoshirenai.

properly adv. **[in an appropriate manner]**

te⌈kisetsuni 適切に /⟨adj(*na*). *ni* of *tekisetsuna* appropriate/ •c [in an

appropriate manner] ⟪suitably, fitly, appropriately, relevantly⟫, **ki⌈chi⌉n-to きちんと [appropriately in terms of the way one arranges things, dresses oneself, or behaves]** ⟪neatly, tidily, exactly, carefully⟫, **ta⌈dashi⌉ku 正しく /⟨adj(*i*). *ku* of *tadashii* correct/ [in such a way as to conform to an ethical, legal, logical, social, or regulatory standard; in such a way as to be free of error]** ⟪correctly, rightly⟫

EX. (**a**) He's one who knows how to write business correspondence properly.
あの人は{適切に/きちんと/正しく}ビジネスレターが書ける人だ。
Ano hito wa {tekisetsuni/kichin-to/tadashiku} bijinesu-retaa ga kake-ru hito da.
(**b**) It's very hard to translate poems properly.
詩を{正しく/適切に/?きちんと}翻訳するのは大変難しい。
Shi o {tadashiku/tekisetsuni/?kichin-to} hon'yaku-suru no wa taihen muzukashii.

property n. **[s.t. which is owned by s.o., esp. real estate, or a characteristic or s.t.]**

1. sho⌈yu⌉u-butsu 所有物 •c [s.t. which is possessed by s.o. ⟨fml⟩] ⟪possession⟫

EX. The grand piano is Mr. Okada's property.
このグランドピアノは岡田氏の所有物だ。
Kono gurando-piano wa Okada-shi no shoyuu-butsu da.

2. to⌈chi 土地 •c ⟪land, lot⟫

EX. My uncle owns some property along the Pacific seashore.
おじは太平洋沿いに土地を持っている。
Oji wa Taiheiyoo-zoi ni tochi o motte iru.

3. to⌈kusei 特性 •c [a special characteristic inherent in s.t.] ⟪land, lot⟫

EX. Aluminum has the property of being both light and strong.
アルミニウムには軽くてじょうぶであるという特性がある。
Aruminiumu ni wa karukute joobu dearu to iu tokusei ga aru.

proportion n. **[the relation of one thing to another or of a part to a whole in terms of quantity or size; a balanced relationship of parts within the whole]**

1. wa⌈riai 割合 [the relation of one thing to another or of a part to a whole in terms of quantity or size] ⟪rate, ratio, percentage⟫, **hi⌈ritsu 比率 •c [a ratio between two objects being compared]** ⟪ratio, percentage⟫

EX. What is the proportion of female to male students on this campus?
この大学の女子学生と男子学生の{割合/比率}はどうなっていますか。
Kono daigaku no joshi-gakusei to danshi-gakusei no {wariai/hiritsu} wa doo natte imasu ka.

2. tsu⌈ri-ai 釣り合い /⟨V*masu* of *tsuriau* ① balance/ [a balanced relationship of parts within the whole] ⟪balance, equilibrium⟫, **cho⌈owa 調和 •c [a condition of different colors, shapes, or sounds balancing and complementing each other within a larger whole so as to create a sense of esthetic pleasure]** ⟪harmony, accord, agreement⟫, **ki⌈nsei 均整 •c [a state of beautiful symmetry]** ⟪symmetry⟫, **pu⌈ropo⌉oshon プロポーション •f [ratio/balance]**

EX. (**a**) She had the fine bodily proportions of a model.
彼女はモデルのような{釣り合い/均整/?調和/*プロポーション}の取れた体をしていた。
*Kanojo wa moderu no yoona {tsuri-ai/kinsei/?choowa/*puropooshon} no toreta karada o shite ita.*
(**b**) A sense of balanced vertical and horizontal proportions gives this architecture its unique character.
縦と横の{釣り合い/均整/プロポーション/調和}のよさがこの建築の特徴だ。
Tate to yoko no {tsuri-ai/kinsei/puropooshon/choowa} no yo-sa ga kono kenchiku no tokuchoo da.

propose vt. **[for s.o. to put s.t. forward for consideration or discussion]**

1. ⟨-o⟩ te⌈ian-suru ⟨〜を⟩提案する ③ •c [for

P

s.o. to put s.t. forward for discussion or adoption] ⟪**suggest**⟫

EX. Mr. Ogawa proposed that a committee be formed to discuss the matter.
小川氏はその問題を審議するため委員会を作ることを提案した。
Ogawa-shi wa sono mondai o shingi-suru tame iin-kai o tsukuru koto o teian-shita.

2. ⟨-ni⟩ {⟨-o⟩/V*masu* tai to} mo⌜oshi-komu ⟨〜に⟩{⟨〜を⟩/V*masu*たいと}申し込む ① [for s.o. to (formally) convey a request or desire to s.o. else or to an institution in the hopes of having it granted] ⟪**offer, file a protest/application, enter a contest, ask for, request, apply**⟫

EX. (**a**) David proposed marriage to Jill on their second date.
デービッドはジルと二回目のデートの時にジルに結婚を申し込んだ。
Deebiddo wa Jiru to ni-kai-me no deeto no toki ni Jiru ni kekkon o mooshi-konda.
(**b**) I proposed to my college president that we meet directly to discuss the matter further, but was turned down.
私は学長にその問題について更に話し合うため直接お会いしたいと申し込んだが、断られてしまった。
Watashi wa gakuchoo ni sono mondai ni-tsuite sarani hanashi-au tame chokusetsu o-ai-shi-tai to mooshi-konda ga, kotowara-rete shimatta.

prose n. **[writing which is like ordinary language and not poetry]**
sa⌜nbun 散文 •c ↔ inbun 韻文 •c

EX. Poetry is usually harder to read than prose in a foreign language.
韻文は大抵散文より外国語で読むのが難しい。
Inbun wa taitei sanbun yori gaikoku-go de yomu no ga muzukashii.

prospect n. **[an extensive view of a landscape or the possibility/anticipation that s.t. will happen]**
1. na⌜game⌝ 眺め /⟨V*masu* of *nagameru* ② watch/ [a scene worthy of lingering attention, esp. one from a high point and encompassing a large area] ⟪**view, scene**⟫, **cho⌜oboo 眺望 •c [an act of looking far and in a wide circle or a view that one can get by doing so]** ⟪**view**⟫

EX. The mountain commands a fine prospect of the town.
山からの町の{眺め/眺望}はすばらしい。
Yama kara no machi no {nagame/chooboo} wa subarashii.

2. mi⌜komi 見込み /⟨V*masu* of *mikomu* ① anticipate/ [an anticipation/expectation/prediction that s.t. is very likely to occur] ⟪**hope, promise, possibility, likelihood, chance**⟫, **mi-⌜tooshi 見通し /⟨V*masu* of *mi-toosu* ① see through/ [an act of seeing through (into the future) or the outlook one can get by doing so]** ⟪**perspective, unobstructed view, vista, visibility**⟫, **yo⌜soo 予想 •c [an act of predicting s.t.]** ⟪**prediction, prognosis**⟫, **te⌜nboo 展望 •c [an act of looking far away (into the future)]** ⟪**view, outlook, vista**⟫

EX. (**a**) What are the economic prospects for the coming year?
来年の経済の{見通し/予想/展望/?見込み}はどうですか。
Rainen no keizai no {mi-tooshi/yosoo/tenboo/?mikomi} wa doo desu ka.
(**b**) Doctor, is there any prospect of my father recovering?
先生、父は治る{見込み/??見通し/*予想/*展望}がありますか。
*Sensei, chichi wa naoru {mikomi/??mi-tooshi/*yosoo/*tenboo} ga arimasu ka.*

prosperity n. **[a state of economic well-being]**
ha⌜n'ei 繁栄 •c

EX. Japan's economic prosperity began approximately at the time of the Tokyo Olympic Games in 1964.
日本の経済的繁栄は1964年の東京オリンピックのころ始まった。
Nihon no keizai-teki-han'ei wa sen-kyuu-hyaku-roku-juu-yo-nen no

| *Tookyoo-Orinpikku no koro hajimatta.*

prosperous adj. **[enjoying economic well-being and growth]**
ha⌈n'ei shite iru (N) 繁栄している(N) /⟨V*te iru* form of *han'ei-suru* ③ prosper/ •c [for a country/enterprise to be flourishing] ⟪flourishing, thriving, successful⟫**

EX. | Osaka was a very prosperous town during the Edo period.
江戸時代に大阪は大変繁栄している町だった。
Edo-jidai ni Oosaka wa taihen han'ei-shite iru machi datta.

protect vt. **[to keep s.t./s.o./s.a. from danger or harm]**
⟨-o⟩ ⟨⟨-kara⟩⟩ ma⌈mo⌉ru ⟨〜を⟩⟨⟨〜から⟩⟩守る ① [(to watch s.t./s.o./s.a. in order) to cause s.t./s.o./s.a. not to be harmed/injured/violated] ⟪defend, obey, observe⟫ ↔ ⟨-o⟩ semeru ⟨〜を⟩攻める ②; ⟨-o⟩ ka⌈ba⌉u ⟨〜を⟩かばう ① [for s.o. to keep s.o. who is weak from being harmed or injured] ⟪cover, defend, shield, screen⟫, ⟨-o⟩ ⟨⟨-kara⟩⟩ ho⌉go-suru ⟨〜を⟩⟨⟨〜から⟩⟩保護する ③ •c [for s.o. to keep s.t./s.o./s.a. from being endangered] ⟪safeguard, shelter, shield, take care of⟫

EX. | (**a**) It's our duty to protect our country from enemy attack.
自分の国を敵から{守る/*保護する/*かばう}のは我々の義務だ。
*Jibun no kuni o teki kara {mamoru/ *hogo-suru/*kabau} no wa ware-ware no gimu da.*
(**b**) My older brother protected me from being bullied by my classmates.
クラスメートにいじめられないように兄は私を{かばって/守って/*保護して}くれた。
*Kurasu-meeto ni ijime-rarenai yooni ani wa watashi o {kabatte/mamotte/ *hogo-shite} kureta.*
(**c**) In a modernized society special efforts have to be made to protect the natural environment.
近代化した社会では自然環境を{保護する/守る/*かばう}ためには特別の努力が必要だ。
*Kindai-ka-shita shakai de wa shizen-kankyoo o {hogo-suru/mamoru/*kabau} tame ni wa tokubetsu no doryoku ga hitsuyoo da.*

protection n. **[an act/instance of keeping s.t./s.o./s.a. from danger or harm or s.o./s.a. that does so]**
ho⌉go 保護 •c [the act of keeping s.o./s.t./s.a. from being endangered] ⟪shelter, safeguard, care, patronage⟫, yo⌈boo 予防 •c [an act/instance of keeping s.t. such as illness or disaster from occurring through aggressive measures taken in advance] ⟪prevention, precaution⟫, -yoke 〜よけ [s.t. that keeps off a harmful or evil being or object] ⟪shelter against⟫

EX. | (**a**) Regular exercise provides a good protection against disease.
規則的な運動は病気のいい{予防/*保護}になる。
*Kisoku-tekina undoo wa byooki no ii {yoboo/*hogo} ni naru.*
(**b**) Animal protection has in recent years become a popular cause among celebrities.
動物{保護/*予防/*よけ}は近年有名人の間で運動として盛んになった。
*Doobutsu-{hogo/*yoboo/*yoke} wa kinnen yuumei-jin no aida de undoo to-shite sakanni natta.*
(**c**) A dog can provide good protection against burglars.
犬は泥棒{よけ/*の保護/*の予防}になる。
*Inu wa doroboo {-yoke/*no hogo/*no yoboo} ni naru.*

protective adj. **[tending to or desirous of keeping s.o./s.t./s.a. from danger or harm]**
hogo- 保護〜 •c [pertaining to the act of keeping s.t./s.o./s.a. from being endangered]

EX. | Protective trade policies are not good for the world economy.
保護貿易政策は世界の経済に良くない。
Hogo-booeki-seisaku wa sekai no keizai ni yokunai.

P

PHRASE: protective instinct *hogo-honnoo* 保護本能 •c, protective color *hogo-shoku* 保護色 •c

protein n.
ta⌈npaku⌉-shitsu 蛋白質 •c
EX. Eggs are a good source of protein.
卵はいい蛋白質源だ。
Tamago wa ii tanpaku-shitsu-gen da.

protest n. **[a statement or action showing strong disapproval of s.t., often made or done publicly]**
se⌈imei 声明 •c [an act of publicly announcing one's view/opinion on a particular issue] ((**statement, declaration, proclamation**)), **ko⌉ogi 抗議 •c [an oral or written statement of objection]** ((**objection, remonstrance**))
EX. The people of the town submitted a protest against the proposed tax increase.
町の人々は増税に反対する{声明を出した/抗議をした}。
Machi no hito-bito wa zoozei ni hantai-suru {seimei o dashita/koogi o shita}.

—— vt. **[for s.o. to show one's strong disapproval of s.t. either in words or by action, often in a public manner]**
{⟨-o⟩/⟨-to⟩} ge⌈nmei-suru {⟨〜を⟩/⟨〜と⟩}言明する ③ •c [for s.o. to clearly affirm s.t. significant ⟨w⟩] ((**declare, affirm**)), **⟨-to⟩ ko⌉ogi-suru ⟨〜と⟩抗議する ③ •c [for s.o. to express one's strong objection of s.t.]** ((**object, complain**))
EX. Steve protested that he was innocent.
スチーブは自分は無実だと{言明した/抗議した}。
Suchiibu wa jibun wa mujitsu da to {genmei-shita/koogi-shita}.

proud adj. **[feeling pleasure or satisfaction in one's own abilities, accomplishments, possessions, or other attributes]**
⟨-o⟩ ho⌈kori⌉ ni shite iru ⟨〜を⟩誇りにしている /⟨V *te iru* of *hokori ni suru* ③ pride oneself on/ [for s.o. to derive a sense of pleasure or satisfaction from some ability, accomplishment, possession, or other attribute of one's own or of s.o. in one's in-group], ⟨-(no ko⌈to⌉) o⟩ ji⌈man-suru ⟨〜(のこと)を⟩自慢する ③ •c [for s.o. to outwardly exhibit an (unjustified) sense of pleasure or satisfaction in some ability, accomplishment, possession, or other attribute of one's own or of s.o. in one's in-group] ((**boast of, brag about, be boastful of**)), **⟨-ga⟩ ji⌈man no N ⟨〜が⟩自慢のN •c [feeling an (unjustifiable) sense of pleasure or satisfaction from some attribute of oneself or of s.o. in one's in-group], ⟨-ga⟩ to⌈ku⌉ina ⟨〜が⟩得意な** adj(*na*). **•c [feeling pleasure or satisfaction in an accomplishment or attribute of oneself and wanting others to see this]** ((**one's strong point, one's forte**)), **⟨-ga⟩ to⌈ku⌉i no N ⟨〜が⟩得意のN •c, ⟨-de⟩ to⌈ku⌉i ni natte iru ⟨〜で⟩得意になっている /⟨V *te iru* of *tokuini naru* ① become puffed up/ [for s.o./s.a. to derive a visible sense of satisfaction or pleasure in one's performance or some possession or ability one has]** ((**feel triumphant over, glorify, feel elated**))
EX. (**a**) Jill seems to be very proud of her husband and children.
ジルは夫と子供{を大変誇りにしている/が大変自慢/*が大変得意}らしい。
*Jiru wa otto to kodomo {o taihen hokori ni shite iru/ga taihen jiman/ *ga taihen tokui} rashii.*
(**b**) Mr. Smith was obviously proud of the fact that he had married such a beautiful woman.
スミスさんは明らかに美人と結婚したこと{を誇りにしていた/を自慢していた/で得意になっていた}。
Sumisu-san wa akirakani bijin to kekkon-shita koto {o hokori ni shite ita/ o jiman-shite ita/de tokui ni natte ita}.
(**c**) He showed his friends the collection of paintings he was so proud of.
彼は{自慢の/?得意の/?得意になっている/*自慢する}絵のコレクションを友達に見せた。
*Kare wa {jiman no/?tokui no/?tokui ni natte iru/*jiman-suru} e no korekushon*

o tomodachi ni miseta.

prove vt. **[for s.o. to establish the truth of s.t. on the basis of arguments or evidence]** ⟨-o⟩ **sho⌈omei-suru** ⟨〜を⟩証明する ③ •c **[for s.o. to establish the truth of s.t. on the basis of logic and evidence]** ⟪**testify to, attest to, demonstrate**⟫, ⟨-o⟩ **ri⌈sshoo-suru** ⟨〜を⟩立証する ③ •c **[for s.o. to establish the truth of s.t., esp. legally, by using evidence]** ⟪**give proof, substantiate, testify**⟫

EX. (**a**) I can't prove this theorem.
この定理は{証明/*立証}出来ない。
*Kono teiri wa {shoomei/*risshoo} dekinai.*
(**b**) The prosecutor tried hard to prove the man's guilt but was not able to convince the jury.
検事は男の有罪を{立証/*証明}しようとしたが、とうとう陪審員を納得させることができなかった。
*Kenji wa otoko no yuuzai o {risshoo/*shoomei} shiyoo to shita ga, tootoo baishin-in o nattoku-saseru koto ga dekinakatta.*

—— vi. **[for s.t. to turn out to be the case]** ⟨-ko⌈to⌉ ga⟩ **wa⌈ka⌉ru** ⟨〜ことが⟩分かる ① **[for s.o./s.a. to be able to figure out the nature, meaning, identity, etc., of s.t./s.o./s.a. which already is/should be in one's mind]**

EX. (**a**) The alarm proved to be false.
警報は間違いだったことが分かった。
Keihoo wa machigai datta koto ga wakatta.
(**b**) My worry proved to be unfounded.
私の心配は根拠のないことが分かった。
Watashi no shinpai wa konkyo no nai koto ga wakatta.

proverb n. **[a short epigram or maxim that has been long used in a culture]** **ko⌈towaza⌉** ことわざ ⟪**saying, adage**⟫

EX. A: Do you know any Japanese proverbs?
日本語のことわざを何か知っていますか。
Nihon-go no kotowaza o nani-ka shitte imasu ka.
B: Yes, the one I like is "A nail that sticks out is struck down."
ええ、私が好きなのは「出るくいは打たれる」ということわざです。
Ee, watashi ga sukina no wa 'Deru kui wa uta-reru' to iu kotowaza desu.

provide vt. **[to make available s.t. needed or wanted to s.o.]** ⟨-ni⟩ ⟨-o⟩ **te⌈ikyoo-suru** ⟨〜に⟩⟨〜を⟩提供する ③ •c **[for s.o. to make available for use by s.o. s.t. that will benefit that person, such as money, goods, facilities, skills, or information]** ⟪**offer, furnish**⟫, ⟨-ni⟩ ⟨-o⟩ **a⌈taeru** ⟨〜に⟩⟨〜を⟩与える ② **[for s.o. to cause/let s.o. have s.t.]** ⟪**give, present, award**⟫, ⟨-ni⟩ ⟨-o⟩ **kyo⌈okyuu-suru** ⟨〜に⟩⟨〜を⟩供給する ③ •c **[for an authority to furnish s.o. with s.t./s.o./s.a. to meet a certain need]** ⟪**supply, furnish**⟫, ⟨-ni⟩ ⟨-o⟩ **shi⌈kyuu-suru** ⟨〜に⟩⟨〜を⟩支給する ③ •c **[for an institution to give out s.t. to s.o. such as salary or fringe benefits]** ⟪**give, grant, issue**⟫

EX. (**a**) That company provides its employees with housing.
その会社は従業員に住宅を{提供する/与える/*支給する/*供給する}。
*Sono kaisha wa juugyoo-in ni juutaku o {teikyoo-suru/ataeru/*shikyuu-suru/*kyookyuu-suru}.*
(**b**) Farmers provide food such as rice and vegetables for people living in the city.
農民は都会に住んでいる人に米や野菜のような食物を{供給する/*与える/*提供する/*支給する}。
*Noomin wa tokai ni sunde iru hito ni kome ya yasai no yoona shokumotsu o {kyookyuu-suru/*ataeru/*teikyoo-suru/*shikyuu-suru}.*
(**c**) Our company provides us with a commuting, housing, and dependent allowance in addition to our basic salary.
うちの会社は基本給以外に通勤手当、住宅手当、扶養家族手当も{支給して/*与えて/*提供して/*供給して}くれます。
Uchi no kaisha wa kihon-kyuu igai ni

P

*tsuukin-teate, juutaku-teate, fuyoo-kazoku-teate mo {shikyuu-shite/ *ataete/*teikyoo-shite/*kyookyuu-shite} kuremasu.*

provision n. **[the act of making available s.t. needed or wanted to s.o. or a supply of things needed esp. food]** ⟪proviso⟫
1. yo˥oi 用意 •c [an act of preparing for s.t. that will take place fairly soon] ⟪**preparations, readiness, preparedness**⟫, **ju˥nbi 準備 •c [an act of carefully making s.t. ready for some purpose well ahead of time]** ⟪**preparations, arrangement**⟫, **shi˹kyuu 支給 •c [the act of an institution giving out s.t. such as salary or needed supplies]** ⟪**supply, allowance, furnishing**⟫

EX. (**a**) Have provisions been made for a quick evacuation of the school building in case of fire?
火事の時直ちに校舎から避難できるような{準備/用意/*支給}ができていますか。
*Kaji no toki tadachi ni koosha kara hinan-dekiru yoona {junbi/yooi/ *shikyuu} ga dekite imasu ka.*
(**b**) Insufficient provisions of medical equipment had been made for the voyage, and several crew members were lost to disease as a result.
長い航海に備えての医療器具の{準備/用意/*支給}が十分でなかったため、数人の乗組員が病気で命を落とすことになった。
*Nagai kookai ni sonaete no iryoo-kigu no {junbi/yooi/*shikyuu} ga juubun denakatta tame, suu-nin no nori-kumi-in ga byooki de inochi o otosu koto ni natta.*
(**c**) Thanks to the speedy provision of supplies by the government, there was a minimal loss of life following the earthquake.
政府による速やかな必需品の{支給/??準備/??用意}により地震の後の死亡者数は最小限にとどまった。
Seifu ni-yoru sumiyakana hitsuju-hin no {shikyuu/??junbi/??yooi} ni-yori jishin no ato no shiboo-sha-suu wa saishoogen ni todomatta.

2. cho˹zo˥o-butsu 貯蔵物 •c [things stored for future use] ⟪**stored goods, stockpiles**⟫
3. jo˹okoo 条項 •c [one of the sections of a document such as a contract]

psychology n. **[the study of the human mind and behavior]**
1. shi˥nri 心理 •c [a mental process or state] ⟪**state of mind, mental state**⟫

EX. Understanding adolescent psychology is essential to being an effective high school teacher.
高校の教師としてうまくやっていくにはティーン・エイジャーの心理を理解することが不可欠だ。
Kookoo no kyooshi to-shite umaku yatte iku ni wa tiin'eijaa no shinri o rikai-suru koto ga fukaketsu da.

2. shi˹nri˥-gaku 心理学 [the study of the human brain and behavior]

EX. Prof. Saito is a world-famous authority on educational psychology.
斉藤教授は教育心理学の世界的権威だ。
Saitoo-kyooju wa kyooiku-shinri-gaku no sekai-teki-ken'i da.

public adj. **[pertaining to or belonging to or known to people in general as opposed to a private individual]**
1. o˹oyake no N 公のN [pertaining to or belonging to or representing a non-private organization or institution] ⟪**official, governmental, formal**⟫, **ko˹okyoo no N 公共のN •c [pertaining to or belonging to the people in general]** ⟪**common, communal**⟫

EX. (**a**) We should spend more tax money on public facilities.
{公共/?公}の施設にもっと税金を使うべきだ。
{Kookyoo/?Ooyake} no shisetsu ni motto zeikin o tsukau-beki da.
(**b**) Politicians often have defficulty drawing the line between public and private matters.
政治家にとっては{公/*公共}のこととプライベートなことをはっきり分けるのが難しい場合がある。

*Seiji-ka ni-totte wa {ooyake/*kookyoo} no koto to puraibeetona koto o hakkiri wakeru no ga muzukashii baai ga aru.*

2. ko⌈oritsu no N 公立のN •c [established by a local government body] ↔ shiritsu no N 私立のN •c

EX. Our daughter is attending a public junior high school.
うちの娘は公立の中学に行っています。
Uchi no musume wa kooritsu no chuugaku ni itte imasu.

3. shu⌉uchi no N 周知のN •c [known to the people in general]

EX. That scandal is now public knowledge.
あのスキャンダルはもう周知の事実だ。
Ano sukyandaru wa moo shuuchi no jijitsu da.

publication n. **[the act of printing materials, usu. for public consumption or s.t. which is printed such as a book, article, magazine, newspaper, etc.]**

1. shu⌈ppan 出版 •c [the act of printing s.t. such as a book or magazine for public consumption] 《publishing》, ka⌈nkoo 刊行 •c [the act of printing s.t. such as a book, magazine, or newspaper]

EX. (**a**) What's the year of publication of this book?
この本の{出版/刊行}の年はいつですか。
Kono hon no {shuppan/kankoo} no toshi wa itsu desu ka.
(**b**) The publication of the newspaper has continued in spite of decreasing readership.
その新聞の{刊行/?出版}は購読者が減っても続いている。
Sono shinbun no {kankoo/?shuppan} wa koodoku-sha ga hette mo tsuzuite iru.

2. shu⌈ppa⌉n-butsu 出版物 •c [printed material such as books, articles, and magazines], ka⌈nko⌉o-butsu 刊行物 •c [printed material such as books, magazines, and newspapers]

EX. Publications by university presses tend to be in scientific fields.
大学出版会の{出版物/刊行物}は主に科学関係だ。
Daigaku-shuppan-kai no {shuppan-butsu/kankoo-butsu} wa omoni kagaku-kankei da.

publish vt. **[to print books, magazines, articles, etc., for public consumption] 〈-o〉 shu⌈ppan-suru 〈～を〉出版する ③ •c [for s.o. to print books or magazines for public consumption], 〈-o〉 ka⌈nkoo-suru 〈～を〉刊行する ③ •c [for s.o. to publish books, magazines, articles, etc.]**

EX. Professor Ishida has published at least a dozen books on Japanese history.
石田教授は日本史の本を少なくとも十二冊は{出版/刊行}しておられる。
Ishida-kyooju wa Nihon-shi no hon o sukunaku-tomo juu-ni-satsu wa {shuppan/kankoo}-shite ora-reru.

publisher n. **[a person or company in the publishing business]**

1. shu⌈ppan-gyo⌉osha 出版業者 •c [a person in the publishing business], ha⌈kko⌉o-sha 発行者 •c [a person who prints and publishes books, magazines, newspapers, etc.]

EX. (**a**) My father is a publisher of art books.
父は美術書の{出版業者/*発行者}です。
*Chichi wa bijutsu-sho no {shuppan-gyoosha/*hakkoo-sha} desu.*
(**b**) Who is the publisher of this book?
この本の{発行者/*出版業者}はだれですか。
*Kono hon no {hakkoo-sha/*shuppan-gyoosha} wa dare desu ka.*

2. shu⌈ppa⌉n-sha 出版社 •c [a company that publishes books, magazines, newspapers, etc.]

EX. I'm looking for a publisher to publish my new book.
私は最近書き終えた本を出してくれる出版社を探しています。
Watashi wa saikin kaki-oeta hon o dashite kureru shuppan-sha o sagashite imasu.

puff n. **[a short, gentle burst of air or smoke; the sound created by this being exhaled from the mouth 《fig. "a cream puff"》]**

1. pu⌈(u)⌉tto ぷ(う)っと adv. **[in the manner of a sudden, short, small exhalation of air from the mouth]**

EX. (**a**) He gave out a puff of air after finishing his run.
彼は走り終わってから息をぷうっと吐いた。
Kare wa hashiri-owatte kara iki o puutto haita.
(**b**) The place where the mosquito bit me turned into a reddish puff.
蚊に食われた所がぷうっと赤くはれた。
Ka ni kuwa-reta tokoro ga puutto akaku hareta.

2. **shu⌈ukuri⌉imu** シュークリーム •f **[a cream puff in the shape of small cabbage]**
NOTE: *Shuukuriimu* comes from the French word "chou à la crème."

pull vt. **[to hold s.t./s.o./s.a. and cause this to move toward oneself or to remove s.t. in this way]**

1. ⟨-o⟩ **hi⌈ku** ⟨〜を⟩ひく ① **[to move s.t./s.o./s.a. concrete or abstract toward the source of a force《fig. "quote," "subtract," "perform music on a stringed instrument, including piano," "grind grain or beans," "consult (a dictionary)," "choose lots," "extend in an uninterrupted fashion," "inherit a characteristic," "remove oneself from a position of public prominence," "catch a cold"》]**《draw, haul, drag, quote, subtract》, ⟨-o⟩ **hi⌈ppa⌉ru** ⟨〜を⟩引っ張る ① **[to move s.t./s.o./s.a. forcibly towards the source of the force《fig. "entice"》]**《draw, jerk, stretch, entice》
㊥ "play a stringed instrument"▷弾く, otherwise ▷引く

EX. (**a**) If you pull this knob hard the door will open.
この取っ手をぐっと{引けば/引っ張れば}、ドアは開きます。
Kono totte o gutto {hikeba/hippareba}, doa wa akimasu.
(**b**) Don't pull my hand so hard.
私の手をそんなに強く{引っ張らないで/?引かないで}ください。
Watashi no te o sonnani tsuyoku {hipparanaide/?hikanaide} kudasai.
(**c**) The sun is blinding me. Could you pull the curtains shut?
日が当たってまぶしいから、そのカーテンを{引いて/??引っ張って}もらえますか。
Hi ga atatte mabushii kara, sono kaaten o {hiite/??hippatte} morae-masu ka.

2. ⟨-o⟩ **mu⌈shiru** ⟨〜を⟩むしる ① **[for s.o. to detach s.t. little by little with a pulling motion of the fingers]**《pluck off》

EX. My father loves to pull weeds in the backyard.
父は裏庭の雑草をむしるのが好きだ。
Chichi wa ura-niwa no zassoo o mushiru no ga suki da.

3. ⟨-o⟩ **nu⌈ku** ⟨〜を⟩抜く ① **[to remove s.t. (usu. a stick- or hair-like object) from a place in which it is embedded《fig. "outpace," "excel"》]**《extract, remove》, ⟨-o⟩ **hi⌈ki-nu⌉ku** ⟨〜を⟩引き抜く ① **[for s.o. to forcibly extract a stick-like object out of a place in which it is embedded《fig. "select"》]**《extract, select》

EX. (**a**) I had a bad tooth pulled yesterday.
私はきのう虫歯を{抜いて/*引き抜いて}もらった。
*Watashi wa kinoo mushi-ba o {nuite/*hiki-nuite} moratta.*
(**b**) The sheriff pulled his pistol out of his holster and fired it in the air to quiet the crowd.
保安官は群衆を静めるために、ホルスターからピストルを(引き)抜いて空に向けて発砲した。
Hoan-kan wa gunshuu o shizumeru tame ni, horusutaa kara pisutoru o (hiki-)nuite sora ni mukete happoo-shita.

pulp n. **[processed wood fiber for making paper]**
pa⌉rupu パルプ •f

pulse n. **[a regular throbbing caused in the arteries by the contractions of the heart]**
mya⌈ku(-haku) 脈(拍) •c

EX. The doctor took my pulse.
医者は{脈を取った/脈拍を計った}。
Isha wa {myaku o totta/myaku-haku o hakatta}.

pump n.
po⌉npu ポンプ **•f**
EX. The firemen drew water with a pump to extinguish the fire.
消防士たちはポンプで水を汲み上げて消火に努めた。
Shooboo-shi-tachi wa ponpu de mizu o kumi-agete shooka ni tsutometa.

pumpkin n.
ka⌈bocha かぼちゃ
EX. The fairy godmother changed the pumpkin into a carriage.
魔法使いのおばあさんはかぼちゃを馬車に変えました。
Mahoo-tsukai no o-baa-san wa kabocha o basha ni kaemashita.

punch[1] vt. **[for s.o. to strike s.o./s.t. with the fist]**
⟨-o⟩ **na⌈gu⌉ru** ⟨〜を⟩殴る ① **[for s.o. to bring one's fist or to use s.t. against s.o./s.a. hard with the intention of causing harm]** ⟪**beat, strike, knock, hit**⟫
EX. I once got punched in the nose for accidentally bumping into someone on the street.
道でぶつかってしまった人に鼻を殴られたことがある。
Michi de butsukatte shimatta hito ni hana o nagura-reta koto ga aru.

—— n. **[a blow/strike with the fist]**
ko⌈bushi de na⌈gu⌉ru koto こぶしで殴ること **[an act of striking with the fist]**, **pa⌉nchi** パンチ **•f [the act of striking one's opponent in boxing]**

punch[2] n. **[a device for making holes in paper]**
a⌈naake⌉-ki 穴開け器
—— vt. **[to make a hole with a punch]**
(**a⌈naake⌉-ki de**) **a⌈na⌉ o a⌈keru** (穴開け器で)穴を開ける ②

punch[3] n. **[a beverage made from fruit juices with or without alcohol]**
{**pa⌉nchi/po⌉nchi**} {パンチ/ポンチ} **•f**
EX. Punch is often served at receptions.
歓迎パーティーではよく{パンチ/ポンチ}が出る。
Kangei-paatii de wa yoku {panchi/ponchi} ga deru.

punctuation n. **[the use or marks such as commas, periods, etc., to clarify the structure of a sentence or the marks themselves]**
ku⌈too 句読 **•c**, **ku⌈to⌉o-ten** 句読点 **•c [a mark used to clarify the structure of a sentence]**
EX. If you don't use punctuation marks properly, the meaning you intend in a sentence may be misunderstood.
句読点を正しく使わないと、文の意味を誤解されることがある。
Kutoo-ten o tadashiku tsukawanai to, bun no imi o gokai-sareru koto ga aru.

punish vt. **[for s.o. to cause s.o. to suffer or pay a penalty for s.t. wrong that person has done]**
⟨-o⟩ **ba⌈ssuru** ⟨〜を⟩罰する ③ **•c [for s.o. to subject s.o. to loss of money, forfeiture of a privilege, or to physical/psychological pain for his/her wrongdoing]** ⟪**penalize, chastise, discipline**⟫
EX. (**a**) The driver who injured the pedestrian was severely punished.
歩行者にけがをさせた運転手は厳しく罰せられた。
Hokoo-sha ni kega o saseta unten-shu wa kibishiku basse-rareta.
(**b**) People should be punished more severely for the illegal possession of narcotics.
麻薬の不法所有はもっと厳しく罰しなくてはならない。
Mayaku no fuhoo-shoyuu wa motto kibishiku basshinakute wa naranai.

punishment n. **[the act of causing a wrongdoer to suffer or pay a penalty for the wrongdoing or the suffering or penalty itself]**
ke⌉ibatsu 刑罰 **•c [the act of causing a criminal to pay for a crime]** ⟪**penalty**⟫,

ba˥tsu 罰 •c [the act of causing a wrongdoer to suffer or pay a penalty for the wrongdoing or the suffering or penalty itself] ⟪penalty⟫

EX. (**a**) No one would dispute that a murderer should receive punishment for his crime.
殺人者が{刑罰/罰}を受けるのは当たり前だ。
Satsujin-sha ga {keibatsu/batsu} o ukeru no wa atarimae da.
(**b**) High school students in Japan who don't follow school rules normally receive some kind of punishment.
校則を守らない日本の高校生は大抵なんらかの{罰/*刑罰}を受ける。
*Koosoku o mamoranai Nihon no kookoo-sei wa taitei nanra-ka no {batsu/*keibatsu} o ukeru.*

P

pupil n. **[a student in an elementary school/ (Br. E) a student who has not yet completed high school]**
se˥ito 生徒 [a person who studies at a junior/senior high school] ⟪student, school boy, school girl⟫

NOTE: Elementary school students are referred to as *jidoo*.

EX. Pupils in Japanese junior and senior high schools are usually required to wear uniforms.
日本の中学、高校の生徒は大抵制服を着なければならない。
Nihon no chuugaku, kookoo no seito wa taitei seifuku o kinakereba naranai.

puppet n. **[a doll that has movable parts that can be manipulated by hand or string ⟪fig. "a person controlled by the will of other people"⟫]**
1. a˥yatsuri-ni˥ngyoo 操り人形 [a doll that is manipulated by strings] ⟪marionette⟫
2. ni˥ngyoo 人形 •c [a doll made in the form of a human being ⟪fig. "a beautiful girl," "a person controlled by the will of others"⟫] ⟪doll⟫

bunraku

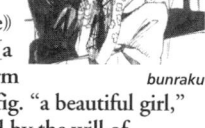

3. ka˥irai かいらい •c [a person or political regime controlled by the will of others] ⟪dummy, robot⟫

puppy n. **[a young dog]**
i˥nu no ko 犬の子 [the offspring of a dog], ko-˥inu 子犬 [a little dog]

EX. The child was happily playing with the puppy.
子供が{犬の子/子犬}と楽しそうに遊んでいた。
Kodomo ga {inu no ko/ko-inu} to tanoshi-sooni asonde ita.

purchase vt. **[for s.o. to receive s.t. in exchange for money ⟨fml⟩]**
⟨-o⟩ ko˥onyuu-suru ⟨〜を⟩購入する ③ •c [for an institution (less commonly, an individual) to receive s.t. relatively major in quantity or importance in exchange for money] ⟪procure⟫, ⟨-o⟩ ka˥u ⟨〜を⟩買う ① [for s.o. to get s.t. in exchange for money] ⟪buy⟫

EX. (**a**) The college purchased a dozen new computers this year.
大学は今年新しいコンピューターを十二台{購入した/買った}。
Daigaku wa kotoshi atarashii konpyuutaa o juu-ni-dai {koonyuu-shita/katta}.
(**b**) I'd like to purchase a three-bedroom house, if I can find one to my liking.
いいのがあれば寝室が三つある家を{購入したい/買いたい}んですが。
Ii no ga areba shinsitsu ga mittsu aru ie o {koonyuu-shi-tai/kai-tai} n desu ga.

— n. **[the act of receiving s.t. in exchange for money or s.t. so received]**
1. ko˥onyuu 購入 •c [the act of receiving s.t. in exchange for money] ⟪buying⟫
2. ko˥onyuu-hin 購入品 •c [s.t. received in exchange for money]

pure adj. **[not mixed with other substances ⟪fig. "not defiled," "complete"⟫]**
1. ju˥nsuina 純粋な adj(*na*). •c [not mixed with alien objects or substances ⟪fig. "not corrupted"⟫] ⟪genuine, real, unalloyed, authentic⟫, ju˥nsui no N 純粋のN •c

EX. (**a**) There are apparently fewer and fewer people these days who can speak the pure Osaka dialect.
純粋{の/な}大阪弁が話せる人は年々少なくなってきているようだ。
Junsui {no/na} Oosaka-ben ga hanase-ru hito wa nen-nen sukunaku natte kite iru yooda.
(**b**) Is this pure aspirin?
これは純粋{の/な}アスピリンですか。
Kore wa junsui {no/na} asupirin desu ka.

2. ki˥ssui no N 生粋のN [born and bred] ⟪to the core, dyed in the wool⟫

EX. Jacqueline is a pure Parisienne.
ジャックリーヌは生粋のパリジェンヌだ。
Jakkuriinu wa kissui no Parijennu da.

3. ki˥reina きれいな adj(*na*). **[pleasantly attractive due to having beauty or orderliness or due to being free from dirt] ⟪clean, beautiful, pretty⟫**

EX. The air in the mountains is purer than that in the city.
山の空気は町のよりきれいです。
Yama no kuuki wa machi no yori kirei desu.

purple n.
mu┌rasaki(-iro) 紫(色)
—— adj.
mu┌rasaki-iro no N 紫色のN, mu┌ra˥saki no N 紫のN

EX. (**a**) Wisteria flowers are usually purple.
藤の花はたいてい紫(色)です。
Fuji no hana wa taitei murasaki(-iro) desu.
(**b**) A purple robe has the air of royalty.
紫(色)の服は高貴に見える。
Murasaki(-iro) no fuku wa kookini mieru.

purpose n. **[the intended result of or reason for one's doing s.t.]**
mo┌kuteki 目的 •c [the intended result of a particular action/behavior] ⟪aim, end, intention⟫, ta┌me˥ ため [s.t. useful/profitable for s.o./s.t./s.a. ⟪fig. "purpose," "cause," "reason"⟫] ⟪advantage, benefit, profit, sake, due to, result, goal⟫

EX. A: What was your purpose in coming to Japan?
何の{目的で/ために}日本に来ましたか。
Nan no {mokuteki de/tame ni} Nihon ni kimashita ka.
B: To teach English at a senior high school.
高校で英語を教えるために日本に来ました。
Kookoo de eigo o oshieru tame ni Nihon ni kimashita.

PHRASE: on purpose *waza-to* わざと ⟪purposely, intentionally, deliberately⟫

EX. (**a**) A: Don't you have your sweater on inside our?
そのセーター、裏表じゃない?
Sono seetaa, ura-omode janai?
B: That's all right. I'm wearing it this way on purpose.
いいの。わざと裏表に着てるの。
Ii no. Waza-to ura-omote ni kite-ru no.
(**b**) Don't be upset. I didn't bump into you on purpose.
怒らないでよ。わざとぶつかったわけじゃないんだから。
Okoranai de yo. Waza-to butsukatta wake janai n da kara.

purse n. **[a small bag, esp. one carried by a woman or a pouch for carrying change]**
ba˥ggu バッグ •f, ko-┌zeni˥-ire 小銭入れ [a pouch for carrying change] ⟪pouch⟫

EX. I forgot my purse at the office today.
今日{バッグ/小銭入れ}を会社に忘れてきてしまった。
Kyoo {baggu/ko-zeni-ire} o kaisha ni wasurete kite shimatta.

NOTE: A bill fold for holding paper money is called *saifu*.

pursue vt. **[to follow s.o./s.t./s.a. persistently in order to catch him/her/it]**
1. ⟨-o⟩ o┌u ⟨~を⟩追う ① [for s.o./s.a. to go after s.o./s.t./s.a. ⟪fig. "search diligently"⟫] ⟪chase, drive away⟫, ⟨-o⟩ tsu┌iseki-suru ⟨~を⟩追跡する ③ •c [to follow s.t./s.o. closely in order to to catch him/her/it or to follow up on a survey] ⟪chase, track⟫

P

EX. The policeman pursued the fleeing burglar.
警官は逃げて行く強盗を{追った/追跡した}。
Keikan wa nigete-iku gootoo o {otta/tsuiseki-shita}.

2. 〈-ni〉 tsu⌈ki-mato⌉u 〈～に〉つきまとう ① [for s.t./s.o./s.a. undesirable such as illness, fate, punishment etc. never to leave one] 《follow about, shadow, tail》

EX. (**a**) I seem to be pursued by allergies no matter where I go.
どこに行っても、アレルギーにつきまとわれるみたいだ。
Doko ni itte mo, arerugii ni tsuki-matowa-reru mitaida.
(**b**) My ex-boyfriend is still pursuing me.
別れたボーイフレンドはまだ私につきまとっている。
Wakareta booi-furendo wa mada watashi ni tsuki-matotte iru.

3. 〈-o〉 mo⌈tome⌉ru 〈～を〉求める ② [for s.o. to desire s.t. and persistently seek to find and obtain it] 《want, request, demand, search for》, 〈-o〉 tsu⌈ikyuu-suru 〈～を〉追求する ③ •c [for s.o. to make every effort to obtain s.t. relatively abstract, such as truth, beauty, pleasure, freedom, etc.] 《seek after, chase》

EX. (**a**) Most of the students in the Japanese language class are pursuing some career related to Japan.
日本語クラスの学生のほとんどは日本関係の仕事を{求めて/*追求して}いる。
*Nihon-go-kurasu no gakusei no hotondo wa Nihon-kankei no shigoto o {motomete/*tsuikyuu-shite} iru.*
(**b**) For many the primary purpose of life is to pursue pleasure.
多くの人にとって人生の主な目的は快楽を{追求する/求める}ことにある。
Ooku no hito ni-totte jinsei no omona mokuteki wa kairaku o {tsuikyuu-suru/motomeru} koto ni aru.

pursuit n. **[the act of pursuing]**

1. tsu⌈iseki 追跡 •c [the act of closely following s.t./s.o. that is fleeing in order to catch him/her/it] 《chase, tracking》

EX. The pursuit of the criminal ended in failure.
犯人の追跡は失敗に終わった。
Hannin no tsuiseki wa shippai ni owatta.

2. tsu⌈ikyuu ついきゅう •c [the act of striving to obtain s.t. relatively abstract, such as truth, beauty, pleasure, freedom, etc.] 《chase, search》

㊥ "pursuit of ideal/happiness/pleasure/profit" ▷追求, "pursuit of truth"▷追究

EX. (**a**) The ultimate goal of a university is the pursuit of truth.
大学の究極の目的は真理の{追究/*追求}にある。
Daigaku no kyuukyoku no mokuteki wa shinri no tsuikyuu ni aru.
(**b**) The pursuit of profit is the ultimate goal of business.
利潤の{追求/*追究}が企業の至上命題である。
Rijun no tsuikyuu ga kigyoo no shijoo-meidai dearu.

push vt. **[to exert force on s.t./s.o./s.a. so that this moves away from oneself 《fig. "exert oneself hard to achieve a goal"》]**

1. 〈-o〉 o⌈su 〈～を〉おす ① [for s.o. to cause s.t./s.o./s.a. to move away from oneself 《fig. "stamp," "recommend"》] 《thrust, shove, press, impress, stamp》 ↔ 〈-o〉 hiku 〈～を〉引く ①

㊥ "recommend"▷推す, otherwise ▷押す

EX. (**a**) If you push this button, the car will cruise at a constant speed.
このボタンを押せば、車は一定のスピードで走ります。
Kono botan o oseba, kuruma wa ittei no supiido de hashirimasu.
(**b**) Don't pull the door. Push it.
ドアは引かないで、押してください。
Doa wa hikanaide, oshite kudasai.

2. 〈-ni〉 〈-o〉 se⌈ma⌉ru 〈～に〉〈～を〉迫る ① [for s.o. to approach s.o. and strongly urge him/her to do s.t.] 《approach, press, urge》

EX. I don't have what it takes to push my boss for a raise.

私はボスに昇給を迫ることは出来ない。
Watashi wa bosu ni shookyuu o semaru koto wa dekinai.

pushy adj. **[unpleasantly aggressive and presumptuous]**
o⌈shi ga tsu⌉yoi 押しが強い adj(*i*)., **go⌈oinna 強引な** adj(*na*). •c **[coercive in manner]** **⟪high-handed, forcing⟫**

EX. I don't like him, because he's so pushy.
あの人はとても{押しが強い/強引だ}から、嫌いだ。
Ano hito wa totemo {oshi ga tsuyoi/gooin da} kara, kirai da.

put vt. **[to cause s.t./s.o./s.a. to occupy a place ⟪fig. "cause s.t./s.o./s.a. to undergo s.t."⟫]**

1. ⟨-ni⟩ ⟨-o⟩ o⌈ku ⟨〜に⟩⟨〜を⟩置く ① [for s.o./s.a. to cause s.o./s.t./s.a. to be at/in/on a certain place] ⟪place, lay, leave⟫

NOTE: When s.t./s.o./s.a. is put "in" a place, do not use *oku* but use *ireru*. SEE put 2

EX. (**a**) A: Where did you put the camera?
カメラをどこに置きましたか。
Kamera o doko ni okimashita ka.
B: I put it on the desk.
机の上に置きましたよ。
Tsukue no ue ni okimashita yo.
(**b**) Please put your suitcase here.
スーツケースはここに置いて下さい。
Suutsukeesu wa koko ni oite kudasai.

2. ⟨-ni⟩ ⟨-o⟩ i⌈reru ⟨〜に⟩⟨〜を⟩入れる ② [for s.o. to cause s.t./s.o./s.a. to move into an enclosed space] ⟪add, insert, admit⟫, ⟨-ni⟩ ⟨-o⟩ a⌈zuke⌉ru ⟨〜に⟩⟨〜を⟩預ける ② [for s.o. to ask s.o. else to take care of s.o./s.t./s.a. or to allow a part of one's body to lean against s.t.] ⟪deposit, entrust, commit…to s.o.'s care⟫

EX. (**a**) Please put some hot water in the pot.
ポットにお湯を{入れて/*預けて}ください。
*Potto ni o-yu o {irete/*azukete} kudasai.*
(**b**) I usually put any money I receive in the bank.
私は大抵お金をもらうと銀行に{入れます/預けます}。
Watashi wa taitei o-kane o morau to ginkoo ni {iremasu/azukemasu}.

3. ⟨-ni⟩ ⟨-o⟩ tsu⌈ke⌉ru ⟨〜に⟩⟨〜を⟩つける ② [for s.o./s.a. to cause s.t./s.o. to adhere to s.t./s.o./s.a. else] ⟪attach, join, stick, apply, light, follow⟫

EX. Thinking about how many children to have before finding someone to marry is like putting the cart before the horse, isn't it?
結婚相手を見つける前に何人子供をつくるか考えるのは荷馬車を馬の前につけるようなものですね。
Kekkon-aite o mi-tsukeru mae ni nan-nin kodomo o tsukuru ka kangaeru no wa ni-basha o uma no mae ni tsukeru yoona mono desu ne.

NOTE: The above is more naturally expressed in Japanese as follows: *Hon-matsu tentoo desu ne.*

PHRASE: put away ⟨*-o*⟩ *katazukeru* ⟨〜を⟩片付ける ② ⟪tidy up, put straight⟫, ⟨*-o*⟩ *shimau* ⟨〜を⟩仕舞う ① ⟪stow away, store, hide away⟫

EX. Put the books on the table away.
テーブルの上の本を{片付けなさい/仕舞いなさい}。
Teeburu no ue no hon o {katazukenasai/shimainasai}.

PHRASE: put off ⟨*-o*⟩ *nobasu* ⟨〜を⟩のばす ① ⟪postpone, stretch, elongate, let grow⟫, ⟨*-o*⟩ *enki-suru* ⟨〜を⟩延期する ③ •c ⟪postpone⟫ ㊥ "postpone"▷延ばす, otherwise ▷伸ばす

EX. Don't put off until tomorrow what you can do today.
今日出来ることは明日まで延ばすな。
Kyoo dekiru koto wa asu made nobasu na.

PHRASE: put on (the torso) ⟨*-o*⟩ *kiru* ⟨〜を⟩着る ② ⟪get on, throw on, have on⟫ ↔ ⟨*-o*⟩ *nugu* ⟨〜を⟩脱ぐ ①

EX. (**a**) Which dress should I put on for the party?
パーティーには何を着て行ったらいいでしょうか。
Paatii ni wa nani o kite ittara ii deshoo ka.
(**b**) Johnny, put on your overcoat. It's very cold outside.

P

ジョニー、外はとても寒いからオーバーを着なさいよ。
Jonii, soto wa totemo samui kara oobaa o kinasai yo.

PHRASE: put on (below the belt) ⟨*-o*⟩ *haku* ⟨〜を⟩はく ① ⟪get on, have on⟫ ↔ ⟨*-o*⟩ *nugu* ⟨〜を⟩脱ぐ ①

㊥ "put on footwear"▷履く, otherwise ▷はく

EX. (**a**) Japanese usually put on slippers when they enter a Western style room.
日本人は洋式の部屋に入る時大抵スリッパを履く。
Nihon-jin wa yooshiki no heya ni hairu toki taitei surippa o haku.
(**b**) You should put on rubber boots when going out in the snow.
雪の時に外に出るならゴム長を履いた方がいい。
Yuki no toki ni soto ni deru nara gomu-naga o haita hoo ga ii.

PHRASE: put on (the head) ⟨*-o*⟩ *kaburu* ⟨〜を⟩かぶる ① ⟪cover, be covered with⟫

EX. My son likes to put on his Chicago Cubs cap when he goes to school.
うちの息子はシカゴ・カブスの野球帽をかぶって学校へ行くのが好きだ。
Uchi no musuko wa Shikago-kabusu no yakyuu-boo o kabutte gakkoo e iku no ga suki da.

PHRASE: put on (gloves) ⟨*-o*⟩ *hameru* ⟨〜を⟩はめる ② ⟪slip on, get in, fit, insert⟫ ↔ ⟨*-o*⟩ *hazusu* ⟨〜を⟩はずす ①

EX. My mother usually puts on rubber gloves when she washes the dishes.
母は大抵ゴム手袋をはめて、お皿を洗います。
Haha wa taitei gomu-te-bukuro o hamete, o-sara o araimasu.

PHRASE: put on (a mask or accessory) ⟨*-o*⟩ *tsukeru* ⟨〜を⟩つける ② ↔ ⟨*-o*⟩ *toru* ⟨〜を⟩取る ①

EX. At the masquerade party everybody put on a mask.
仮装舞踏会ではみんなが仮面をつけた。
Kasoo-butoo-kai de wa minna ga kamen o tsuketa.

PHRASE: put on (an accessory) ⟨*-o*⟩ *suru* ⟨〜を⟩する ③ ⟪do, play, make, perform, wear⟫

EX. Cheryl puts rings on practically all of her fingers.
シェリルはほとんど全部の指に指輪をしている。
Sheriru wa hotondo zenbu no yubi ni yubiwa o shite iru.

PHRASE: put on (glasses) ⟨*-o*⟩ *kakeru* ⟨〜を⟩かける ② ⟪sit down, lock, wear, sprinkle, spend⟫ ↔ ⟨*-o*⟩ *hazusu* ⟨〜を⟩はずす ①, ⟨*-o*⟩ *toru* ⟨〜を⟩取る ①

EX. I have to put on my glasses to see distant objects.
私は遠くのものを見るのに眼鏡を掛けなければならない。
Watashi wa tooku no mono o miru no ni megane o kakenakereba naranai.

PHRASE: put out ⟨*-o*⟩ *kesu* ⟨〜を⟩消す ① ⟪extinguish, turn off, erase, disappear⟫ ↔ ⟨*-o*⟩ *tsukeru* ⟨〜を⟩つける ②

EX. The firefighters couldn't put out the fire even after five hours.
消防士たちはその火事を五時間たっても消せなかった。
Shooboo-shi-tachi wa sono kaji o go-jikan tatte mo kese-nakatta.

PHRASE: put up with ⟨*-o*⟩ *gaman-suru* ⟨〜を⟩我慢する ③ •c ⟪endure, persevere, be patient⟫

EX. I can't put up with his selfish attitude any longer.
あいつのわがままな態度にはもう我慢出来ない。
Aitsu no wagamamana taido ni wa moo gaman-dekinai.

puzzle n. **[a problem that is hard to solve or a toy or game presenting such a problem] 1. na⌈nmon 難問 •c [a question that is very difficult to solve]** ⟪**a Gordian knot**⟫, **na⌈ndai 難題 •c [a difficult theme to handle in a literary work or a difficult problem], na⌈zo なぞ [s.t. that defies one's understanding]** ⟪**riddle, mystery**⟫

EX. (**a**) Our math teacher seems to enjoy giving us puzzles.
私たちの数学の先生は{難問/難題/*なぞ}を出すのが好きなようだ。

*Watashi-tachi no suugaku no sensei wa {nanmon/nandai/*nazo} o dasu no ga sukina yooda.*
(**b**) John's personality is still a puzzle to me.
ジョンの性格は私には今でも{なぞ/*難問/*難題}だ。
*Jon no seikaku wa watashi ni wa ima demo {nazo/*nanmon/*nandai} da.*

2. pa⌉zuru パズル •f [a general term for a problem or game meant to test one's ingenuity]

EX. Americans seem to like crossword puzzles.
アメリカ人はクロスワードパズルが好きなようだ。
Amerika-jin wa kurosuwaado-pazuru ga sukina yooda.

— vt. **[to cause s.o. great difficulty in comprehending]**
⟨-o⟩ {ko⌈mara⌉-su/ko⌈mara-se⌉ru} ⟨～を⟩{困らす①/困らせる②} /⟨causative of *komaru* ① be in distress/ [to cause s.o. to be placed in a difficult situation/plight], **⟨-o⟩ to⌈owaku-saseru ⟨～を⟩当惑させる /⟨causative of *toowaku-suru* ③ be perplexed/ ② •c [to cause s.o. to be perplexed]**

EX. I was puzzled by his sudden kindnesses.
私はあの人が急に親切になったので{困った/当惑した}。
Watashi wa ano hito ga kyuuni shinsetsuni natta node {komatta/toowaku-shita}.

NOTE: The English "to be puzzled" corresponds to *komaru, toowaku-suru.*

pyramid n.
pi⌈rami⌉ddo ピラミッド •f

quality n. **[a characteristic that distinguishes s.t./s.o./s.a. from others or the degree of excellence of s.t./s.o./s.a.]**
shi⌈tsu 質 •c [a set of inherent characteristics determining the degree to which s.t./s.o. is or is not excellent] ((**nature, disposition**)), **se⌈ishitsu 性質 •c [the inherent character and properties of s.o./s.t./s.a.]** ((**nature, disposition, temperament, character, property**)), **hi⌈nshitsu 品質 •c [a set of features determining the degree of excellence of a product]**

EX. (**a**) A: What is the level of quality of students you have at this school?
この学校の学生の{質/*性質/*品質}はどうですか。
*Kono gakkoo no gakusei no {shitsu/*seishitsu/*hinshitsu} wa doo desu ka.*
B: Excellent.
優秀ですよ。
Yuushuu desu yo.
(**b**) Japanese companies are known for their quality control.
日本の会社は{品質/*質/*性質}管理で有名だ。
*Nihon no kaisha wa {hinshitsu/*shitsu/*seishitsu} kanri de yuumei da.*
(**c**) Iron and copper have very different qualities.
鉄と銅は{性質/*質/*品質}が違う。
*Tetsu to doo wa {seishitsu/*shitsu/*hinshitsu} ga chigau.*

Q

(**d**) Americans often talk about the need to improve the quality of their educational system.
アメリカ人はよく教育制度の{質/*性質/*品質}を向上させる必要があることを話題にする。
*Amerika-jin wa yoku kyooiku-seido no {shitsu/*seishitsu/*hinshitsu} o koojoo-saseru hitsuyoo ga aru koto o wadai ni suru.*

quantity n. **[an amount or quantity]**
ryo⌉o 量 •c ((**amount, volume, magnitude**)), **bu⌈nryo⌉o 分量 •c [the extent to which the amount of s.t., such as its weight, volume, number, or ratio with respect to s.t. else, is large or small]** ((**measure, amount, dose**))

EX. (**a**) He is a good teacher but the quantity of homework he assigns us is too much.
いい先生なんですが、出す宿題の{量/分量}が多すぎます。
Ii sensei na n desu ga, dasu shukudai no {ryoo/bunryoo} ga oo-sugimasu.
(**b**) Quality is more important than quantity.
{量/?分量}より質だ。
{Ryoo/?Bunryoo} yori shitsu da.

quarrel n. **[an angry dispute]**
ke⌈nka けんか •c [an angry struggle involving mutual verbal and/or physical attacks] ((**argument, fight, coming to blows**))

EX. There were constant quarrels in my house between me and my brothers.
僕たち兄弟は、うちでよくけんかをした。
Boku-tachi kyoodai wa, uchi de yoku kenka o shita.

—— vi. **[to engage in an angry dispute with s.o.]**
⟨-to⟩ ke⌈nka-suru ⟨〜と⟩けんかする ③ •c [for s.o./s.a. to engage in a struggle with s.o./s.a. else involving mutual physical and/or verbal attacks] ((**argue, disagree, fight, scuffle, come to blows**))

EX. (**a**) My parents constantly quarreled over money matters.
うちの両親は金のことでけんかばかりしていた。
Uchi no ryooshin wa kane no koto de kenka bakari shite ita.
(**b**) The two boys who quarreled during recess were made to clean up the playground after school as a punishment.
休憩時間にけんかした二人の男の子は罰として放課後運動場の掃除をさせられた。
Kyuukei-jikan ni kenka-shita futari no otoko-no-ko wa batsu to-shite hooka-go undoo-joo no sooji o sase-rareta.

quart n. **[one quarter of a gallon]**
ku⌈o⌉oto クォート •f
NOTE: 1 quart=0.946 litre (US)/1.137 litre (UK)

quarter n. **[one of four equal parts into which s.t. is divided or a section of a town or (in plural form) housing, esp. for military personnel]**

1. yo⌈n-bun-no-i⌈chi⌉ 四分の一 [one fourth]

EX. (**a**) What is a quarter of 24?
二十四の四分の一は何ですか。
Ni-juu-yon no yon-bun-no-ichi wa nan desu ka.
(**b**) A: What time is it?
何時ですか。
Nan-ji desu ka.
B: It's quarter to seven.
七時十五分前です。
Shichi-ji juu-go-fun mae desu.

NOTE: Quarter can mean fifteen minutes, *juu-go-fun* because it is one-forth of an hour.

2. ni⌉-juu-⌈go se⌉nto 二十五セント •c+f [one fourth of a dollar] ((**25 cents**))

EX. Do you have a quarter?
二十五セント、ありますか。
Ni-juu-go-sento, arimasu ka.

3. chi⌉iki 地域 •c [a geographic division characterizable in terms of climate/culture/natural environment] ((**district, region, area, zone**)), **-gai 〜街 •c [an area formed by a major street with buildings clustered on either side]** ((**street, avenue, town**))

EX. The area we're walking through now is the residential quarter of town.
今歩いている所はこの町の住宅{地域/街}です。
Ima aruite iru tokoro wa kono machi

| *no juutaku-{chiiki/gai} desu.*
4. he⌉isha 兵舎 •c **[army barracks]**

quarterback n.
ku⌈ootaa-ba⌉kku クォーターバック **•f**

queen n. **[the wife or widow of a king or the female sovereign of a kingdom** «**fig. "an eminent woman"**»**]**
jo⌈o⌉o 女王 **•c ↔ oo** 王 **•c**
EX. | Britain has a long history of famous queens.
イギリスは名高い女王の長い歴史がある。
Igirisu wa na-dakai jooo no nagai rekishi ga aru.

queer adj. **[odd to the extent of being abnormal]**
he⌉nna 変な adj(*na*). **•c [exhibiting an unusual characteristic/condition/behavior]** «**odd, strange, eccentric, suspicious**», **ki⌉myoona** 奇妙な adj(*na*). **•c [unusual and mysterious in character]** «**strange, curious, odd, bizarre**», **o⌈kashi⌉i** おかしい adj(*i*). **[(funny due to being) not normal]** «**funny, side-splitting, strange, unusual, odd**», **o⌈ka⌉shina N** おかしなN adj(*na*).
EX. | (**a**) Look at that guy! What a queer hairdo!
あいつを見ろよ。{変な/奇妙な/おかしな/??おかしい}髪をしているな。
Aitsu o miro yo. {Henna/Kimyoona/Okashina/??Okashii} kami o shite iru na.
(**b**) His behavior is a little queer these days.
彼の行動は最近ちょっと{変だ/おかしい/奇妙だ}。
Kare no koodoo wa saikin chotto {hen da/okashii/kimyoo da}.

question n. **[a type of sentence used to request information or to get an answer]**
1. **shi⌈tsumon** 質問 **•c [the act of asking for an answer or of requesting information or a type of sentence used to do this]** «**query, interrogation, inquiry, quiz**»
EX. | A: Do you have any questions?
質問がありますか。
Shitsumon ga arimasu ka.
B: No, I don't.
いいえ、ありません。
Iie, arimasen.
2. **mo⌈ndai** 問題 **•c [a difficult situation or topic that needs attention and thought]** «**problem, issue, subject**»
EX. | (**a**) Professor, I don't understand the meaning of this question.
先生、この問題の意味が分かりません。
Sensei, kono mondai no imi ga wakarimasen.
(**b**) To be or not to be, that is the question.
生きるか、死ぬか、それが問題だ。
Ikiru ka, shinu ka, sore ga mondai da.
(**c**) A: By the year 2000, 30-40% of the Japanese population will be 60 years old or older.
2000年までに日本人の人口の30から40%が六十歳かそれ以上になります。
Ni-sen-nen made ni Nihon-jin no jinkoo no sanjuu kara yon-jup-paasento ga roku-jus-sai ka sore-ijoo ni narimasu.
B: That's going to raise some difficult questions about how to finance care for the elderly, isn't it?
そうすると老人介護に必要な財源をめぐる難しい問題が色々と出てきますね。
Soo-suru-to roojin-kaigo ni hitsuyoona zaigen o meguru muzukashii mondai ga iro-iro to dete kimasu ne.
PHRASE: out of the question *mondai-gai da* 問題外だ **•c**
EX. | Buying a house in Tokyo is out of the question.
東京で家を買うのは問題外だ。
Tookyoo de ie o kau no wa mondai-gai da.

—— vt. **[for s.o. to ask s.o. for information about s.t. or to express doubt about s.t.]**
1. **⟨-ni⟩ {⟨-no⟩ ko⌈to⌉ o/⟨-ni-tsuite⟩} ki⌈ku** ⟨〜に⟩{⟨〜の⟩ことを/⟨〜について⟩}聞く ① **[for s.o. to request or receive information about s.t. from s.o.]** «**ask, inquire**», **⟨-ni⟩ {⟨-no⟩ ko⌈to⌉ o/⟨-ni-tsuite⟩} ta⌈zune⌉ru** ⟨〜に⟩{⟨〜の⟩ことを/⟨〜について⟩}尋ねる ② **[for s.o. to seek information about s.t. from s.o.]** «**ask, inquire**», **⟨-ni⟩ {⟨-no⟩ ko⌈to⌉ o/⟨-ni-tsuite⟩} shi⌈tsumon-suru** ⟨〜に⟩{⟨〜の⟩ことを/⟨〜について⟩}質問する ③ **•c [for s.o. to ask for information about s.t. from**

s.o.] ((**ask a question**))

EX. I questioned my professor about his theory of the origins of the Japanese people.
私は先生に日本民族の起源に関する先生の説{のことを/について}{聞きました/尋ねました/質問しました}。
Watashi wa sensei ni Nihon-minzoku no kigen ni-kansuru sensei no setsu {no koto o/ni-tsuite} {kikimashita/ tazunemashita/shitsumon-shimashita}.

2. Sinf. (no/n) {dewana˥i/janai} ka to o˥mo˥u Sinf.(の/ん){ではない/じゃない}かと思う ① [to wonder if…is not really the case], ⟨-o⟩ u˥tagau ⟨〜を⟩疑う ① [for s.o. to think that s.t. is not true or that s.t. does not exist] ((**doubt**))

Q

NOTE: When the nonpast affirmative form of adj(*na*). or N + cop. appears before {*no*/ *n*} {*dewanai*/*janai*} *ka to omou*, the form {adj(*na*). stem/N} *na* is used.

EX. I question his integrity.
私は{彼は信頼できないんじゃないかと思います/彼の誠実さを疑います}。
Watashi wa {kare wa shinrai-dekinai n janai ka to omoimasu/kare no seijitsu-sa o utagaimasu}.

quick adj. **[taking less time than is normal or expected; able to think, learn, or react in a short time]**
ha˥ya˥i はやい adj(*i*). **[taking less time than is normal or expected or occurring at a point in time prior to what is normally expected]** ((**fast, speedy, early**)) ↔ **osoi** 遅い adj(*i*).
㊨ "fast"▷速い, "early"▷早い

EX. (**a**) Have you finished lunch already? That was quick.
昼御飯をもう食べたんですか。速かったですね。
Hiru-gohan o moo tabeta n desu ka. Hayakatta desu ne.
(**b**) A: What is the quickest way to memorize *kanji*?
漢字を覚える一番速い方法は何ですか。
Kanji o oboeru ichiban hayai hoohoo wa nan desu ka.
B: To use associations, I guess.
連想を使うことでしょうね。
Rensoo o tsukau koto deshoo ne.
(**c**) He has a quick mind, doesn't he?
あの人は頭の回転が速いですね。
Ano hito wa atama no kaiten ga hayai desu ne.

quickly adv. **[with speed]**
ha˥yaku はやく /⟨**adj**(*i*). ***ku* of *hayai* fast**/ ((**speedily, fast**)), **i˥so˥ide** 急いで /⟨**V*te* of *isogu* ① hurry**/ ((**hurriedly**))
㊨ "quickly"▷速く, "early"▷早く

EX. Quickly, Miki, everybody is waiting for you.
美紀、{急いで/速く}。みんなが待ってるんだから。
Miki, {isoide/hayaku}. Minna ga matteru n da kara.

quiet adj. **[making little or no sound or movement]**
1. shi˥zukana 静かな adj(*na*). ((**calm, still, tranquil**)) ↔ **urusai** うるさい adj(*i*).

EX. (**a**) During Christmas vacation the campus was quiet.
クリスマスの休み中はキャンパスは静かだった。
Kurisumasu no yasumi-chuu wa kyanpasu wa shizuka datta.
(**b**) The ocean was very quiet today.
今日は海がとても静かだった。
Kyoo wa umi ga totemo shizuka datta.
(**c**) Be quiet, please.
静かにして下さい。
Shizukani shite kudasai.
(**d**) Carol speaks with a quiet voice.
キャロルは静かな声で話す。
Kyaroru wa shizukana koe de hanasu.

2. o˥tonashi˥i おとなしい adj(*i*). **[obedient or reserved in behavior; subdued or inconspicuous in visual effect]** ((**gentle, mild, meek, dove-like, obedient**))

EX. Kazuo is a quiet but bright boy.
一男はおとなしいけど、頭のいい子だ。
Kazuo wa otonashii kedo, atama no ii ko da.

quietly adv. **[in such a way as to make little or no sound or movement]**
shi˥zukani 静かに /⟨**adj**(*na*). ***ni* of *shizukana***

quiet/ [in such a way as to make little or no sound or movement], o⌈da⌉yakani 穏やかに /⟨adj(*na*). *ni* of *odayakana* calm/ [in a gentle and calm manner] ⟪calmly⟫, o⌈tona⌉shiku おとなしく /⟨adj(*i*). *ku* of *otonashii* obedient/ ⟪gently, meekly, like a sheep⟫

EX. (**a**) Can't you talk more quietly?
もっと{穏やかに/静かに/*おとなしく}話したらどうですか。
*Motto {odayakani/shizukani/ *otonashiku} hanashitara doo desu ka.*
(**b**) A child was playing quietly by himself in the playground.
子供が遊び場で一人で{静かに/おとなしく/*穏やかに}遊んでいた。
*Kodomo ga asobi-ba de hitori de {shizukani/otonashiku/*odayakani} asonde ita.*

quit vt. **[for s.o./s.a. to stop doing s.t. or to leave a place of employment] ⟨-o⟩ ya⌈meru ⟨～を⟩やめる ② [for s.o. to discontinue s.t. that he/she has been doing, including a plan to do s.t.] ⟪discontinue, stop, give up, terminate⟫, ⟨-o⟩ yo⌉su ⟨～を⟩よす ① [for s.o. to stop doing s.t. that he/she has been doing for a brief time or to give up the idea of doing s.t. of a brief nature ⟨s⟩] ⟪discontinue, stop, give up⟫**

㊟ "quit a job/resign" ▷辞める, otherwise ▷ やめる

EX. (**a**) A: You should quit smoking, you know.
たばこを吸うのは{やめた/よした}方がいいよ。
Tabako o suu no wa {yameta/yoshita} hoo ga ii yo.
B: I know, but I can't.
分かっているけど、{やめられない/*よせない}んだよ。
*Wakatte iru kedo, {yame-rarenai/ *yose-nai} n da yo.*
(**b**) Quit biting your fingernails like that.
そんな風に爪をかむのを{やめろ/よせ}よ。
Sonna fuu ni tsume o kamu no o {yamero/yose} yo.
(**c**) We quit going to the annual picnic because of the long distance we had to travel each time.
例年のピクニックは毎回遠い所まで行かなければならないので行くのを{やめた/よした}。
Reinen no pikunikku wa mai-kai tooi tokoro made ikanakereba naranai node iku no o {yameta/yoshita}.
(**d**) I've decided to quit my job.
私は会社を{辞める/*よす}ことにしました。
*Watashi wa kaisha o {yameru/*yosu} koto ni shimashita.*

quite adv. **[completely or to some extent]**
1. ma⌈ttaku 全く [in a manner so strongly that it cannot be/unable to be expressed in any other way] ⟪entirely, utterly, completely, totally⟫, ze⌈nzen 全然 •c [not at all (used with a negative predicate)] ⟪wholly, utterly, entirely, completely⟫, su⌈kka⌉ri すっかり [an expression indicating that some condition is pervasive or exhaustively present] ⟪utterly, completely, wholly, perfectly⟫

NOTE: *Zenzen* must be used with a negative predicate, whereas *sukkari* must be used with an affirmative predicate.

EX. (**a**) It was quite hot today, wasn't it?
今日は{全く/*全然/*すっかり}暑かったですね。
*Kyoo wa {mattaku/*zenzen/*sukkari} atsukatta desu ne.*
(**b**) His lecture was quite incomprehensible to me.
あの人の講演は{全然/全く/*すっかり}分かりませんでした。
*Ano hito no kooen wa {zenzen/mattaku/ *sukkari} wakarimasendeshita.*
(**c**) Pam has become quite beautiful since entering college.
パムは大学に入ってから{すっかり/?全く/*全然}きれいになった。
*Pamu wa daigaku ni haitte kara {sukkari/?mattaku/*zenzen} kirei ni natta.*

Q

2. to⌈temo とても **[to a great extent (in affirmative contexts) or no matter what one does (in negative contexts)]** **⟪very, exceedingly, awfully, cannot possibly⟫**, **ta⌈ihen 大変 •c [to a great extent]** **⟪exceedingly, awfully, extraordinarily⟫**

EX. I'm quite tired today.
今日は{とても/大変}疲れている。
Kyoo wa {totemo/taihen} tsukarete iru.

quotation n. **[an act/instance of repeating exactly what s.o. else has said or written or the content of what is so repeated]**
i⌈n'yoo 引用 •c

EX. (**a**) Quotations from Shakespeare are quite common in English literature.
シェークスピアの引用は英文学には多い。
Sheekusupia no in'yoo wa ei-bungaku ni wa ooi.
(**b**) Is this sentence a quotation from the Bible?
この文はバイブルからの引用ですか。
Kono bun wa baiburu kara no in'yoo desu ka.

PHRASE: quotation mark *in'yoo-fu* 引用符

EX. Japanese quotation marks are not written as " " but as「 」.
日本語の引用符は" "ではなくて「 」と書く。
Nihon-go no in'yoo-fu wa " " dewanakute 「 」 *to kaku.*

quote vt. **[for s.o. to repeat exactly what s.o. else has said or written ⟪fig. "to name the current price"⟫]**
{⟨-o⟩/⟨-kara⟩} i⌈n'yoo-suru {⟨～を⟩/⟨～から⟩} 引用する ③ •c

EX. (**a**) My professor often quotes Plato.
私の先生はプラトン{を/から}よく引用します。
Watashi no sensei wa Puraton {o/kara} yoku in'yoo-shimasu.
(**b**) Let me quote a passage from *the Tale of Genji.*
『源氏物語』の一節{を/*から}引用させていただきます。
*"Genji monogatari" no is-setsu {o/*kara} in'yoo-sasete itadakimasu.*

R

rabbit n.
u⌈sagi うさぎ

raccoon n.
a⌈ra⌉i-guma あらいぐま

race n. **[a contest of speed to reach a certain point or complete s.t. before one's competitors]**
1. kyo⌈osoo 競走 •c [a running contest] **⟪running, dash, sprint⟫**, **re⌉esu レース •f [a contest of running, swimming, driving etc.]**

EX. (**a**) I took part in the 100-meter race and came in second.
僕は百メートル{競走/レース}に出場して二位になった。
Boku wa hyaku-meetoru-{kyoosoo/reesu} ni shutsujoo-shite ni-i ni natta.
(**b**) What time do the swim races start?
今日の水泳の{レース/*競走}は何時からですか。
*Kyoo no suiei no {reesu/*kyoosoo} wa nan-ji kara desu ka.*

2. kyo⌈osoo 競争 •c [a contest to achieve victory or superiority over another] **⟪competition, contest, rivalry, struggle⟫**

EX. There are many races one must compete in in life.
人生には避けて通ることのできない競争が沢山ある。
Jinsei ni wa sakete tooru koto no dekinai kyoosoo ga takusan aru.

—— vi. **[for s.o./s.a. to compete in a contest of speed]**

1. kyo⌈osoo-suru 競走する ③ •c [for s.o. to compete in a contest of running] ⟪**run a race**⟫

EX. Shall we race to the other side of the park?
公園の向こうまで競走しようか。
Kooen no mukoo made kyoosoo-shiyoo ka.

2. kyo⌈osoo-suru 競争する ③ •c [for s.o. to strive to achieve victory or superiority over another] ⟪**rival, vie with, contest**⟫

EX. Those two companies are racing with each other to develop and market a new anti-cancer drug.
その二社はどちらが先に新しい抗がん剤を開発して発売できるか競争している。
Sono ni-sha wa dochira ga saki ni atarashii kooganzai o kaihatsu-shite hatsubai-dekiru ka kyoosoo-shite iru.

rack n. **[a framework for hanging things on or holding things in]**

ta⌈na 棚 •c [a flat, rectangular board fixed at right angles to a vertical surface] ⟪**ledge, hob**⟫**, -kake ～掛け [a framework for hanging things on]** ⟪**peg**⟫

EX. (**a**) Could you put this luggage up on the rack for me?
この荷物を{棚/*掛け}の上に載せてもらえますか。
*Kono nimotsu o {tana/*kake} no ue ni nosete morae-masu ka.*
(**b**) Is there a hat rack around here?
ここには帽子{掛け/*棚}がありますか。
*Koko ni wa booshi-{kake/*dana} ga arimasu ka.*

NOTE: A "magazine rack" is called *magajin rakku*. Neither *tana* nor *-kake* can be used in this case.

radar n.

re⌉edaa レーダー •f

EX. The airplane suddenly disappeared from the radar screen.
飛行機は急にレーダーのスクリーンから姿を消した。
Hikoo-ki wa kyuuni reedaa no sukuriin kara sugata o keshita.

radiant adj. **[giving out heat or light** ⟪**fig. "beaming"**⟫**]**

1. a⌈karui 明るい adj(*i*). **[having enough light to do s.t. or not dark in color** ⟪**fig. "cheerful," "be versed in"**⟫**] ↔ kurai 暗い** adj(*i*).; ((⟨-de⟩)) **ka⌈gaya⌉ite iru** (N) ((⟨～で⟩))輝いている(N) /⟨V *te iru* of *kagayaku* ① shine/②, ⟨-de⟩ **ka⌈gaya⌉ku** (N) ⟨～で⟩輝く(N) /⟨Vinf. nonpast of *kagayaku* ① shine/ **[shining with s.t.]** ⟪**shining, sparkling, gleaming**⟫

EX. (**a**) We walked along the mountain path in the radiant light of the full moon.
{明るい/*輝く/*輝いている}満月の光の中、山道を歩いていた。
*{Akarui/*Kagayaku/*Kagayaite iru} mangetsu no hikari no naka, yama-michi o aruite ita.*
(**b**) The room was radiant in the light of the gorgeous chandelier.
部屋は豪華なシャンデリアの光で{明るかった/輝いていた}。
Heya wa gookana shanderia no hikari de {akarukatta/kagayaite ita}.
(**c**) A cat approached me in the dark with radiant eyes.
猫が{輝く/??輝いている/*明るい}目をして暗闇の中を私に近づいて来た。
*Neko ga {kagayaku/??kagayaite iru/ *akarui} me o shite kura-yami no naka o watashi ni chikazuite kita.*
(**d**) She is well-liked for her radiant personality.
彼女はその{明るい/*輝く/*輝いている}性格のためにみんなに好かれている。
*Kanojo wa sono {akarui/*kagayaku/ *kagayaite iru} seikaku no tame ni minna ni suka-rete iru.*

2. ni⌈ko⌉yakana にこやかな adj(*na*). **[softly smiling]** ⟪**beaming, smiling**⟫

EX. Chris always has a radiant face.
クリスはいつもにこやかな顔をしている。
Kurisu wa itsu-mo nikoyakana kao o shite iru.

radiation n.

ho⌈osha-sen 放射線 •c

R

EX. Jill is undergoing radiation therapy.
ジルは放射線治療を受けている。
Jiru wa hoosha-sen-chiryoo o ukete iru.

radio n.

ra⌉jio ラジオ **•f**

EX. (**a**) Please turn off the radio.
ラジオを消して下さい。
Rajio o keshite kudasai.
(**b**) I watch the news on television; I seldom listen to the news on the radio.
私はテレビのニュースを見るから、ラジオのニュースはめったに聴きません。
Watashi wa terebi no nyuusu o miru kara, rajio no nyuusu wa mettani kikimasen.

radius n.

ha⌉nkei 半径 **•c**

EX. There are as many as three supermarkets within a radius of two miles of my house.
家から半径二マイル以内に三つもスーパーがある。
Ie kara hankei ni-mairu inai ni mittsu mo suupaa ga aru.

raft n.

i⌈kada いかだ

EX. They went down the river on a raft.
彼らはいかだで川を下った。
Kare-ra wa ikada de kawa o kudatta.

rag n. **[a scrap of cloth or a worn-out piece of clothing]**

1. bo⌉ro ぼろ **[a scrap of cloth《fig. "defect"》]《shred, scrap, defect》, bo⌈ro⌉kire** ぼろきれ

EX. I need a rag to polish my car.
車を磨くのにぼろ(きれ)が要ります。
Kuruma o migaku no ni boro(-kire) ga irimasu.

2. bo⌉ro ぼろ **[a worn-out piece of clothing], bo⌈ro⌉-fuku** ぼろ服

EX. Cinderella wore rags.
シンデレラはぼろ(服)を着ていた。
Shinderera wa boro(-fuku) o kite ita.

rage n. **[violent anger or rough wind/seas]**

1. ge⌉kido 激怒 **•c [violent anger]《wrath, fury, blowup》**

EX. My father's rage was beyond description after learning that I married the girl he disliked.
私が父の嫌いな女の子と結婚したと分かったときの父の激怒は表現できないくらいだった。
Watashi ga chichi no kiraina onna-no-ko to kekkon-shita to wakatta toki no chichi no gekido wa hyoogen-dekinai kurai datta.

2. do⌈too 怒涛 **•c [violently rough seas]《rough waves, angry waves, raging billows》**

EX. The boat managed to reach the island despite the billowing rage of the seas.
船は怒涛の中を、どうにか島に着くことが出来た。
Fune wa dotoo no naka o, doo-nika shima ni tsuku koto ga dekita.

raid n. **[a sudden attack or invasion by a military or police force]**

1. shu⌈ugeki 襲撃 **•c [a sudden attack]《assault, attack》**

EX. The raid upon us took place at dawn.
我々に対する襲撃は早朝に起きた。
Ware-ware ni-taisuru shuugeki wa soochoo ni okita.

2. te⌈ire⌉ 手入れ **[the act of putting one's hands into s.t.《fig. "mending," "trimming," "round-up"》]《repairs, mending, trimming, care, round-up》**

EX. The raid by the police on the apartment uncovered a large stash of cocaine.
警察によるアパートの手入れで、大量のコカインが発見された。
Keisatsu ni yoru apaato no teire de, tairyoo no kokain ga hakken-sareta.

—— vt. **[for s.o. to launch a sudden attack on s.o., esp. an enemy, or to invade a place suddenly]**

1.〈-ni〉se⌈me-ko⌉mu〈〜に〉攻め込む ① **[for s.o. to invade a place]**

EX. The enemy raided our base from behind.
敵は後ろから我々の基地に攻め込んだ。
Teki wa ushiro kara ware-ware no kichi ni seme-konda.

2.〈-o〉kyu⌈ushuu-suru〈〜を〉急襲する ③ **•c [for s.o. to attack an enemy suddenly]**

EX. An air squadron of the Japanese Navy raided Pearl Harbor on the morning of December 7, 1941.
1941年12月7日の朝、日本海軍の飛行編隊がパールハーバーを急襲した。
Sen-kyuu-hyaku-yon-juu-ichi-nen juu-ni-gatsu nanoka no asa, Nihon-kaigun no hikoo-hentai ga Paaruhaabaa o kyuushuu-shita.

3. 〈-ni〉 te⌈ire⌉ (o) suru 〈〜に〉手入れ(を)する ③ [to put one's hands into s.t. 《fig. "repair," "trim," "make a raid on"》]

EX. The police raided the red-light district last night.
警察はゆうべ赤線地区に手入れ(を)した。
Keisatsu wa yuube akasen-chiku ni teire (o) shita.

rail n. **[a long wooden/metal bar supported by vertical posts or a bar of steel forming a track on which a train or streetcar runs]**

1. yo⌈ko-boo 横棒 [a horizontal (wooden) barrier] 《bar》, yo⌈ko-gi 横木 [a horizontal wooden bar] 《bar, crosspiece, crossbar》

2. re⌈eru レール •f [a single bar or parallel bars on which s.t. such as a train runs]

EX. Trains run on rails.
電車はレールの上を走る。
Densha wa reeru no ue o hashiru.

3. te⌈tsudoo 鉄道 •c [a track for trains] 《railroad, railway》

EX. The trip will cost much less by rail than by air.
今度の旅行は飛行機より鉄道の方がずっと安くあがる。
Kondo no ryokoo wa hikoo-ki yori tetsudoo no hoo ga zutto yasuku agaru.

railroad n. **[a road with rails for trains]**
te⌈tsudoo 鉄道 •c [a track for trains]

EX. In Japan you can go practically anywhere by railroad.
日本では鉄道を使って、ほとんどどこへでも行ける。
Nihon de wa tetsudoo o tsukatte, hotondo doko e demo ike-ru.

PHRASE: railroad station *eki* 駅 •c

railway (Br. E) n.
SEE railroad

rain n. **[drops of water that fall from the sky due to the cooling of atmospheric moisture 《fig. "s.t. like rain"》]**
a⌉me 雨

EX. (**a**) It's been so dry lately. We need some rain.
最近乾燥しているから、雨が欲しいな。
Saikin kansoo-shite iru kara, ame ga hoshii na.
(**b**) A rain of ash fell from the volcano.
火山から雨のように灰が降って来た。
Kazan kara ame no yooni hai ga futte-kita.

—— vi. **[for drops of water condensed from atmospheric moisture to fall from the sky]**
a⌉me ga fu⌉ru 雨が降る ①

EX. (**a**) According to the radio weather forecast it's going to rain today.
ラジオの天気予報によると、今日は雨が降るそうです。
Rajio no tenki-yohoo ni yoru to, kyoo wa ame ga furu soodesu.
(**b**) It started to rain two days ago, and it's still coming down hard today.
二日前に雨が降り始めましたが、今日もまだ激しく降っています。
Futsuka-mae ni ame ga furi-hajimemashita ga, kyoo mo mada hageshiku futte imasu.

rainbow n.
ni⌈ji⌉ にじ

EX. After the rain, a beautiful rainbow appeared over the mountains.
雨の後、美しいにじが山の向こうにかかった。
Ame no ato, utsukushii niji ga yama no mukoo ni kakatta.

raincoat n.
re⌈in-ko⌉oto レインコート •f

EX. I prefer wearing a raincoat to using an umbrella when walking in the rain.
雨の中を歩く時、私は傘をさすよりもレインコートを着るほうが好きだ。
Ame no naka o aruku toki, watashi wa

R

kasa o sasu yori mo rein-kooto o kiru hoo ga suki da.

rainfall n.

(ko⌈o)u⌉-ryoo (降)雨量 •c

EX.| In Japan June is the month with the most rainfall.
日本では(降)雨量が最大なのは六月です。
Nihon de wa (koo)u-ryoo ga saidai na no wa roku-gatsu desu.

rainy adj. **[having or bringing rain, esp. in large amounts]**

1. a⌉me no N 雨のN [marked by the occurrence of rain]

EX.| I walked for hours with her in the woods on a rainy spring day.
春の雨の日に、僕は彼女と何時間も林の中を歩いた。
Haru no ame no hi ni, boku wa kanojo to nan-jikan mo hayashi no naka o aruita.

2. a⌉me ga o⌉oi 雨が多い adj(*i*). **[having a lot of rain]**

EX.| In Japan, the rainy season is from June to mid-July.
日本では雨の多い季節は六月から七月の半ばまでだ。
Nihon de wa ame no ooi kisetsu wa roku-gatsu kara shichi-gatsu no nakaba made da.

raise vt. **[to cause s.t./s.o./s.a. to move to an upright position or to a higher place or level or to care for s.o. until the age of maturity or to collect s.t. such as money for a purpose]**

1. ⟨-o⟩ ta⌈ta-se⌉ru ⟨〜を⟩立たせる /⟨causative of *tatsu* ① stand/ ②, ⟨-o⟩ o⌈ko⌉su ⟨〜を⟩起こす ① [to cause s.o./s.t./s.a. that is dormant or lying down to become more active or to stand/wake up] ⟪raise up, wake up, begin, bring about⟫, ⟨-o⟩ ta⌈te⌉ru ⟨〜を⟩たてる ② [to cause s.o./s.t./s.a. to take an upright position ⟪fig. "build s.t."⟫] ⟪erect, set up, put up, hoist, build⟫

㊇ "build"▷建てる, otherwise ▷立てる

EX.| (**a**) The work crew used a crane to raise up the telephone poles that had fallen over in the earthquake.
作業員がクレーンを使って地震で倒れた電柱を{起こした/立てた/*立たせた}。
*Sagyoo-in ga kureen o tsukatte jishin de taoreta denchuu o {okoshita/tateta/ *tata-seta}.*
(**b**) The large truck raised a cloud of dust as it went by.
大きなトラックがほこりをいっぱい{立てて/*起こして/*立たせて}通り過ぎた。
*Ookina torakku ga hokori o ippai {tatete/*okoshite/*tata-sete} toori-sugita.*
(**c**) The man claims to be able to raise people from the dead.
あの男は死人を{立たせる/起こす/?立てる}ことができると言う。
Ano otoko wa shinin o {tata-seru/okosu/ ?tateru} koto ga dekiru to iu.

2. ⟨-o⟩ a⌈geru ⟨〜を⟩あげる ② [to make s.t. higher ⟪fig. "give"⟫] ⟪elevate, lift, increase, usher in, throw up, give⟫, ⟨-o⟩ ta⌉kaku suru ⟨〜を⟩高くする ③ [to make s.t. higher (in price)]

㊇ "raise s.t."▷上げる, "deepfry/fly (a kite)/ raise (a flag)"▷揚げる, "raise one's hand"▷挙げる, otherwise ▷あげる

EX.| The government raised the tax on beer.
政府はビールの税金を{上げた/高くした}。
Seifu wa biiru no zeikin o {ageta/ takaku shita}.

3. ⟨-o⟩ so⌈date⌉ru ⟨〜を⟩育てる ② [for s.o. to cause or help a plant, animal, or human to grow] ⟪bring up, rear, breed⟫

EX.| I was raised by my grandmother.
私は祖母に育てられました。
Watashi wa sobo ni sodate-raremashita.

4. ⟨-o⟩ a⌈tsume⌉ru ⟨〜を⟩集める ② [for s.o. to cause things or people that are scattered in various places to come to one and the same place] ⟪gather, collect⟫

EX.| He's very good at raising money.
彼はお金を集めるのがとても上手だ。
Kare wa o-kane o atsumeru no ga totemo joozu da.

rake n. **[a tool with a long handle and a comb-like cross-bar at one end used for gathering things such as leaves and for smoothing loose soil or gravel]**
ku⌈ma-de⌉ 熊手 **[a bamboo stick with comb-like bamboo teeth at one end used for gathering fallen leaves]**
— vt. **[to gather things such as fallen leaves with a rake]**
⟨-o⟩ ku⌈ma-de⌉ de ka⌈ki-atsume⌉ru ⟨〜を⟩熊手でかき集める ②
EX. The people in the village were raking the fallen leaves and burning them.
村の人々は落ち葉を熊手でかき集めて、燃やしていた。
Mura no hito-bito wa ochiba o kuma-de de kaki-atsumete, moyashite ita.

rally vt. **[for s.o. to bring together members of a group for a common purpose or to revive one's will or strength to do s.t.]**
1. ⟨-o⟩ yo⌈bi-atsume⌉ru ⟨〜を⟩呼び集める ② **[to call together the members of a group]** **《call together, assemble, convene》**
EX. The departmental chief rallied his subordinates before the campaign.
キャンペーンの前に部長は部下を呼び集めた。
Kyanpeen no mae ni buchoo wa buka o yobi-atsumeta.
2. ⟨-o⟩ to⌈ri-modosu ⟨〜を⟩取り戻す ① **[to take s.t./s.o./s.a. back which had been given away or lost, including mental states such as consciousness or composure]** **《get back, retake, recover, recapture》**
EX. Becky rallied her strength in the fourth set to win the match.
ベッキーは第四セットで力を取り戻して、その試合に勝った。
Bekkii wa dai-yon-setto de chikara o tori-modoshite, sono shiai ni katta.
— vi. **[for members of a group to come together for a common purpose for one's will or strength to be revived]**
1. ⟨-ni⟩ a⌈tsuma⌉ru ⟨〜に⟩集まる ① **[for people/things/animals of a similar type scattered apart to come together in the same place]** **《gather, assemble, be collected》**
EX. The students rallied in front of the administration building to protest the tuition hike.
学生は授業料値上げ反対のために本部の前に集まった。
Gakusei wa jugyoo-ryoo-ne-age hantai no tame ni honbu no mae ni atsumatta.
2. ka⌈ifuku-suru 回復する ③ •c **[for s.o./s.t./s.a. to return to the original state he/she/it was in]** **《recover, regain》**, **mo⌈do⌉ru** 戻る ① **[to go back to the place or condition one was at/in originally]** **《return, revert》**
EX. Jill's strength rallied enough for her to be able to go back to school.
ジルの体力は学校に戻れるぐらいに{回復した/戻った}。
Jiru no tairyoku wa gakkoo ni modore-ru gurai ni {kaifuku-shita/modotta}.
— n. **[an act/instance of coming together or bringing together the members of a group for a common purpose or of reviving one's will or strength to do s.t.; a large gathering of people for a common interest or purpose]**
1. ke⌈kki-ta⌉ikai 決起大会 •c **[a mass meeting called in protest of s.t.]**
EX. A farmers' rally was held to protest the importing of rice.
農民の米の輸入反対の決起大会があった。
Noomin no kome no yunyuu hantai no kekki-taikai ga atta.
2. ka⌈ifuku 回復 •c **[recovery from an undesirable condition]** **《recovery, restoration, rehabilitation》**
3. ra⌉rii ラリー •f **[an exchange of several strokes in tennis/ping-pong or a car race]**

ram n.
o-⌈hitsu⌉ji 雄羊

ranch n.
da⌈i-bo⌉kujoo 大牧場 •c **[a huge farmland]**

rancher n.
da⌈i-bokujoo-keie⌉i-sha 大牧場経営者 •c

random adj. **[lacking a pattern or causal/logical relationship]**
de⌈taramena でたらめな adj(*na*)., **[lacking any pattern or system or logic]** ((**haphazard, wild**)), **de⌈tarame no N でたらめのN, ni⌈n'i no N 任意のN •c [chosen arbitrarily]** ((**optional, voluntary**)), **mu-⌈sa⌉kui no N 無作為のN •c [not manipulated in any artificial way]**

EX. (**a**) Your random approach to research will lead you nowhere.
君のような{でたらめな/でたらめの/*任意の/*無作為の}研究法ではどうにもらならないよ。
*Kimi no yoona {detaramena/detarame no/*nin'i no/*mu-sakui no} kenkyuu-hoo de wa doo ni mo naranai yo.*
(**b**) In this experiment it's necessary to make a random choice of subjects.
この実験では被験者の{無作為の/任意(の)/*でたらめの/*でたらめな}抽出をしなければいけない。
*Kono jikken de wa hiken-sha no {mu-sakui no/nin'i (no)/*detarame no/*detaramena} chuushutsu o shinakereba ikenai.*

—— n. [the condition of lacking any pattern or causal/logical relationship]
de⌈tarame でたらめ [the condition of lacking any pattern or system or logic]

PHRASE: at random *detarameni* でたらめに, *tekitooni* 適当に •c

EX. I arranged the cards at random, but he was still able to pick out the correct one.
私はトランプのカードを{でたらめに/適当に}並べたが、それでも彼は正しいカードを当てることができた。
Watashi wa toranpu no kaado o {detarameni/tekitooni} narabeta ga, soredemo kare wa tadashii kaado o ateru koto ga dekita.

PHRASE: at random *te-atari-shidai ni* 手当たりしだいに

EX. During summer vacation, I read book after book at random.
夏休みには手当たりしだいにたくさん本を読んだ。
Natsu-yasumi ni wa te-atari-shidai ni takusan hon o yonda.

range n. **[the space defined by the limits to which s.t. extends or a large stove having burners and an oven or a series of mountains]**

1. ha⌉n'i 範囲 •c [an area defined by certain bounds] ((**extent, scope, sphere, limits, bounds, confines**)), **ryo⌈oiki 領域 •c [the territory making up a country or the area comprised by a field of specialty]** ((**territory, domain, field**))

EX. (**a**) There isn't a gas station anywhere within a range of 50 miles from here.
ここから五十マイルの{範囲/??領域}にはガソリンスタンドはありません。
Koko kara go-juu-mairu no {han'i/??ryooiki} ni wa gasorin-sutando wa arimasen.
(**b**) May I ask what the range of material to be covered on the final examination will be?
期末試験の{範囲/*領域}を教えていただけますか。
*Kimatsu-shiken no {han'i/*ryooiki} o oshiete itadake-masu ka.*
(**c**) Professor Nakatani's range of knowledge is very wide.
中谷教授の知識の{範囲/領域}はとても広い。
Nakatani-kyooju no chishiki no {han'i/ryooiki} wa totemo hiroi.

2. sha⌈tei-kyo⌉ri 射程距離 •c [the maximum distance reached by a projectile]

EX. This missile has a 1,500-mile range.
このミサイルは千五百マイルの射程距離がある。
Kono misairu wa sen-go-hyaku-mairu no shatei-kyori ga aru.

3. re⌉nji レンジ •f [a cooking stove with oven and burners]

4. -nami ～並 [a series or chain of things]

EX. The mountain ranges in Vermont are beautiful all year round.
バーモントの山並みは一年中きれいだ。

Baamonto no yama-nami wa ichi-nen-juu kirei da.

rank n. **[a row or one's relative position in a group/institution/society]**
chi|i 地位 **•c [the standing which one has acquired in a social group or society]**

EX. (**a**) What rank does Mr. Johnson have in his company?
ジョンソンさんの会社での地位はなんですか。
Jonson-san no kaisha de no chii wa nan desu ka.
(**b**) The rank of "*jo-kyooju*" in Japanese universities corresponds to that of "associate professor" in American universities.
日本の「助教授」の地位はアメリカの「アソシエートプロフェッサー」に相当する。
Nihon no 'jo-kyooju' no chii wa Amerika no 'asoshieeto-purofessaa' ni sootoo-suru.

— vt. **[to arrange things or people in a row/rows or to determine the relative position of s.t./s.o./s.a. in a group/institution/society]**
1. ⟨-o⟩ **re|tsu ni na⌈raberu** ⟨～を⟩列に並べる ② **[to cause things or people to form a row/rows]**

EX. He ranked the kids by height in two rows.
彼は背の高さで子供たちを二列に並べた。
Kare wa se no taka-sa de kodomo-tachi o ni-retsu ni narabeta.

2. ⟨-ni⟩ **ju|n'i o tsu⌈ke|ru** ⟨～に⟩順位を付ける ② **[for s.o. to assign a position to s.o./s.t./s.a.]**, ⟨-ni⟩ **to⌈okyuu o tsuke|ru** ⟨～に⟩等級を付ける ② **[to assign a position to s.t./s.a.]**

EX. (**a**) We have ranked the top five applicants.
我々は上位五人の応募者に{順位/*等級}を付けた。
*Ware-ware wa jooi go-nin no oobo-sha ni {jun'i/*tookyuu} o tsuketa.*
(**b**) Can you rank Japanese beers according to taste?
日本のビールに味による{等級/順位}が付けられますか。
Nihon no biiru ni aji ni yoru {tookyuu/jun'i} ga tsuke-raremasu ka.

rapid adj. **[very fast in movement or occurrence]**
ha|ya|i はやい adj(*i*). **[taking less time than is normal or expected or occurring at a point in time prior to what is normal or expected]** ⟪**quick, speedy, swift, brisk, prompt, early, premature**⟫, **ji⌈nsokuna** 迅速な adj(*na*). **•c [very quick to act or move]** ⟪**quick, swift, prompt, speedy**⟫, **kyu⌈usokuna** 急速な adj(*na*). **•c [very quick to develop, progress, or become realized]** ⟪**prompt, expeditious**⟫, **su⌈baya|i** すばやい adj(*i*). **[very quick to act, move, or think]** ⟪**quick, agile, nimble**⟫
㊉ "early"▷早い, "fast"▷速い

EX. (**a**) The flow of the river was too rapid for us to be able to cross.
川の流れはあまりにも{速くて/*迅速で/*急速で/*すばやくて}渡れなかった。
*Kawa no nagare wa amari-ni mo {hayakute/*jinsoku de/*kyuusoku de/*subayakute} watare-nakatta.*
(**b**) Japan made rapid economic progress after World War II.
日本は第二次大戦後{急速な/*速い/*迅速な/*すばやい}経済発展をとげた。
*Nihon wa dai-ni-ji-taisen-go {kyuusokuna/*hayai/*jinsokuna/*subayai} keizai-hatten o togeta.*
(**c**) They have a really rapid delivery service at that pizza place.
あのピザ屋の出前はとても{速い/迅速だ/?すばやい/*急速だ}。
*Ano piza-ya no demae wa totemo {hayai/jinsoku da/?subayai/*kyuusoku da}.*
(**d**) I was really impressed by the rapid movements of the workers bagging the groceries in that store.
あの店の食料品を袋に詰める店員の{すばやい/?速い/*迅速な/*急速な}手さばきに感心した。
Ano mise no shokuryoo-hin o fukuro ni tsumeru ten'in no {subayai/?hayai/

R

**jinsokuna/*kyuusokuna} te-sabaki ni kanshin-shita.*

rapidly adv. **[with great speed in movement or occurrence]**
ha˥yaku はやく /⟨adj(*i*). *ku* of *hayai* early/ fast/ **[prior to the usual or expected time or quickly]** ⟪quickly, speedily, swiftly, briskly, promptly, early, prematurely⟫, **ji┌nsokuni** 迅速に /⟨adj(*na*). *ni* of *jinsokuna* speedy/ •c **[with great speed in acting or moving]**, **kyu┌usokuni** 急速に /⟨adj(*na*). *ni* of *kyuusokuna* speedy/ •c **[with great speed in developing, progressing, or becoming realized]** ⟪promptly, expeditiously⟫, **su┌ba˥yaku** すばやく /⟨adj(*i*). *ku* of *subayai* speedy/ **[with great speed in acting, moving, or thinking]** ⟪quickly, agilely, nimbly⟫
㊅ "early"▷早く, "fast"▷速く

EX. (**a**) He spoke Chinese so rapidly that I couldn't understand a word.
彼が中国語をあまりに{速く/*迅速に/*急速に/*すばやく}話したので、一言も分からなかった。
*Kare ga Chuugoku-go o amarini {hayaku/*jinsokuni/*kyuusokuni/*subayaku} hanashita node, hito-koto mo wakaranakatta.*
(**b**) Big cities are rapidly turning into slums.
大都会のスラム化が{急速に/*速く/*迅速に/*すばやく}進んでいる。
*Dai-tokai no suramu-ka ga {kyuusokuni/*hayaku/*jinsokuni/*subayaku} susunde iru.*
(**c**) A student needs to be able to read books rapidly.
学生は本を{速く/迅速に/すばやく/*急速に}読む必要がある。
*Gakusei wa hon o {hayaku/jinsokuni/subayaku/*kyuusokuni} yomu hitsuyoo ga aru.*

rare adj. **[uncommon (and highly valued)]**
1. **me┌zurashi˥i** 珍しい adj(*i*). **[seldom occurring ⟪fig. "unusual," "nice"⟫]** ⟪infrequent, unusual, novel⟫, **ma┌rena** まれな adj(*na*). **[very infrequently occurring or found, esp. of an event or person]** ⟪uncommon, unusual, scarce⟫

EX. (**a**) It's rare to see snow in Florida.
フロリダで雪を見るのは{珍しい/まれだ}。
Furorida de yuki o miru no wa {mezurashii/mare da}.
(**b**) They showed us their collection of rare books.
{珍しい/?まれな}本のコレクションを見せてくれた。
{Mezurashii/?Marena} hon no korekushon o misete kureta.

2. **su┌barashi˥i** すばらしい adj(*i*). **[causing great wonder/admiration/pleasure due to being extremely good]** ⟪splendid, glorious, superb, wonderful⟫

EX. Toru Takemitsu has a rare talent as a composer.
武満徹は作曲家としてすばらしい才能を持っている。
Takemitsu Tooru wa sakkyoku-ka to-shite subarashii sainoo o motte iru.

rat n. **[a rodent similar to but larger than a mouse]**
ne┌zumi ねずみ **[a generic term for a small rodent]** ⟪mouse⟫

EX. The rat was eaten by the cat.
ねずみが猫に食べられた。
Nezumi ga neko ni tabe-rareta.

rate n. **[the number or quantity of one thing expressed in relation to that of another; a price or charge for s.t.]**
1. **ri˥tsu** 率 •c **[the number or quantity of one thing expressed in relation to the total number or quantity]** ⟪proportion, percentage⟫

EX. Approximately what are the current rates of birth, marriage, divorce, and death in Japan?
現在の日本人の出生率、結婚率、離婚率、死亡率はおよそどの位ですか。
Genzai no Nihon-jin no shussei-ritsu, kekkon-ritsu, rikon-ritsu, shiboo-ritsu wa oyoso dono-kurai desu ka.

2. **ryo˥okin** 料金 •c **[money paid for a service or the use of s.t.]** ⟪charge, fee, fare⟫

EX. A: What is your rate for a single room?
シングルの料金はいくらですか。
Shinguru no ryookin wa ikura desu ka.
B: It is 20,000 yen per night.
一泊二万円です。
Ip-paku ni-man-en desu.

PHRASE: at any rate *tonikaku* とにかく

EX. I don't know if I can write a novel, but, at any rate, I'll give it a try.
私に小説が書けるかどうか分かりませんが、とにかく書いてみます。
Watashi ni shoosetsu ga kake-ru ka doo ka wakarimasen ga, tonikaku kaite mimasu.

PHRASE: at this rate *kono bun da to* この分だと

EX. At this rate I can finish writing my thesis by the end of this month.
この分だと、今月の終わりまでに論文を書き終わることができます。
Kono bun da to, kongetsu no owari made ni ronbun o kaki-owaru koto ga dekimasu.

— vt. **[for s.o. to assign a value or ranking to s.t./s.o.]**
⟨-o⟩ hyo˥oka-suru ⟨〜を⟩評価する ③ •c [for s.o. to set a value on s.t.] ⟪appraise, value, assess, estimate, appreciate, evaluate⟫

EX. It's pretty hard to rate the proficiency level of a student's ability in Japanese.
学生の日本語の熟達度を評価するのはとても難しいんです。
Gakusei no Nihon-go no jukutatsu-do o hyooka-suru no wa totemo muzukashii n desu.

rather adv. **[an adverb indicating the choice of the speaker/writer of one alternative over another]**
1. mu˥shiro むしろ [an adverb indicating the choice of the speaker/writer of one alternative over another] ⟪better than, preferably⟫, do˥chira ka to ieba どちらかと言えば [an adverbial phrase indicating the choice of the speaker/writer of one alternative over another in a tentative, uncertain fashion]

EX. (**a**) I'd like to have *sake* rather than beer.
ビールより{むしろ/どちらかと言えば}酒が飲みたいです。
Biiru yori {mushiro/dochira ka to ieba} sake ga nomi-tai desu.
(**b**) I'd rather die than marry him.
あの人と結婚するぐらいなら、{むしろ/*どちらかと言えば}死んだ方がいい。
*Ano hito to kekkon-suru gurai nara, {mushiro/*dochira ka to ieba} shinda hoo ga ii.*
(**c**) A: What kind of a person is she?
彼女はどんなタイプの人ですか。
Kanojo wa donna taipu no hito desu ka.
B: Well, she's a rather shy person.
そうですね。{どちらかと言えば/*むしろ}内気な人です。
*Soo desu ne. {Dochira ka to ieba/*Mushiro} uchikina hito desu.*

2. ...to iu yo˥ri wa mu˥shiro …と言うよりはむしろ [an adverbial phrase used to correct, rephrase, or clarify s.t. said or written earlier]

EX. Although I'm a teacher, it would be more correct to say that I'm learning rather than teaching when I'm in the classroom.
私は教師ではあるが、教室にいる時、教えていると言うよりはむしろ学んでいると言った方が正しいだろう。
Watashi wa kyooshi de wa aru ga, kyooshitsu ni iru toki, oshiete iru to iu yori wa mushiro manande iru to itta hoo ga tadashii daroo.

ratio n.
hi˥ritsu 比率 •c ⟪percentage⟫

EX. The ratio of male to female students at this college is about six to four.
このキャンパスの男女学生の比率は六対四です。
Kono kyanpasu no danjo-gakusei no hiritsu wa roku tai yon desu.

rational adj. **[having the ability to reason or based on reason]**
ri˥sei-tekina 理性的な adj(*na*). **•c [having the ability to reason or based on reason] ⟪reasonable⟫ ↔ ka˥njoo-tekina 感情的な** adj(*na*). **•c; go˥ori-tekina 合理的な** adj(*na*).

R

•c **[conforming to reason]** **⟪logical, reasonable⟫ ↔ hi-goori-tekina 非合理的な** adj(*na*). •c

EX. (**a**) Human nature is a mixture of the rational and the irrational.
{理性的な/?合理的な}面と非理性的な面を合わせ持つのが人間性だ。
{Risei-tekina/?Goori-tekina} men to hi-risei-tekina men o awase-motsu no ga ningen-sei da.
(**b**) What would be a rational way to solve this problem?
この問題を解決する{合理的な/*理性的な}方法は何だろうか。
*Kono mondai o kaiketsu-suru {goori-tekina/*risei-tekina} hoohoo wa nan daroo ka.*

raw adj. **[being (nearly) in a natural state without having been cooked or processed ⟪fig. "lacking in experience"⟫]**

1. na⌉ma no N 生のN [for food/data/music/a voice to be in its natural/original condition without having been cooked/processed/recorded] ⟪uncooked, half-boiled, green, fresh⟫

EX. (**a**) *Sashimi* refers to raw fish sliced thinly.
「刺身」というのは生の魚を薄く切ったものです。
'Sashimi' to iu no wa nama no sakana o usuku kitta mono desu.

NOTE: "Raw fish" is *nama-zakana*, but if it is sliced into small pieces in preparation for eating, it is called *sashimi.*

(**b**) I'm afraid that it will take time to analyze these raw data.
これらの生のデータを分析するのには時間がかかると思います。
Kore-ra no nama no deeta o bunseki-suru no ni wa jikan ga kakaru to omoimasu.

NOTE: In Japanese "draft beer" and "live music" are *nama-biiru* and *nama-ensoo*, respectively.

ray n. **[a line of light radiating from a bright object]**

ko⌈osen 光線 •c **⟪light, beam⟫**

EX. Rays of sunshine streamed in through the window.
太陽の光線が窓から差し込んでいた。
Taiyoo no koosen ga mado kara sashi-konde ita.

rayon n.

re⌉eyon レーヨン •f

razor n.

ka⌈mi-sori⌉ かみそり

EX. I finally got tired of shaving with a razor every morning and decided to grow a beard.
毎朝かみそりでひげをそるのがとうとう嫌になって、ひげを伸ばすことにした。
Mai-asa kami-sori de hige o soru no ga tootoo iya ni natte, hige o nobasu koto ni shita.

reach vt. **[to arrive at a place or for s.o. to extend part of one's body such as an arm to grasp/touch s.t. or to make contact with s.o., esp. by telephone]**

1. ⟨-ni⟩ tsu⌈ku⌉ ⟨〜に⟩つく ① [to become attached to s.t./s.o./s.a. ⟪fig. "get to (a place)," "come/turn on"⟫] ⟪arrive, get to, occupy, stick to, become attached to, accompany, become lit⟫, {⟨-ni⟩/⟨-made⟩} to⌈do⌉ku {⟨〜に⟩/⟨〜まで⟩}届く ① [for s.t. one has sent/extended to get to a place] ⟪get to, attain to, arrive, be received⟫

㊥ "arrive"▷着く, "stick to"▷付く, "go to bed/take a job/study under"▷就く

EX. (**a**) We reached the summit of Mt. Fuji at about 3:30 P.M.
私たちは富士山の頂上に午後三時半ごろ{着いた/*届いた}。
*Watashi-tachi wa Fuji-san no choojoo ni gogo san-ji-han-goro {tsuita/*todoita}.*
(**b**) Can you reach that picture frame up there?
あそこの額ぶちに{届きます/*着きます}か?
*Asoko no gaku-buchi ni {todokimasu/*tsukimasu} ka?*
(**c**) The letter reached me on Sunday.
手紙は日曜に{着いた/届いた}。
Tegami wa nichiyoo ni {tsuita/todoita}.

2. {⟨-ni⟩/⟨-to⟩} re⌈nraku-suru {⟨〜に⟩/⟨〜と⟩}

連絡する ③ •c [for s.o. to make a connection with s.o./s.t., esp. for the purpose of transferring information] ⟪communicate, inform, contact, get in touch with⟫

EX. A: How can I reach you?
どうやってあなた{に/と}連絡したらいいですか。
Doo yatte anata {ni/to} renraku-shitara ii desu ka.
B: You can reach me by phone.
電話で連絡して下さい。
Denwa de renraku-shite kudasai.

3. ⟨-ni⟩ hi⌈rogaru ⟨〜に⟩広がる ① [for s.t. closed/folded/localized to open/unfold/expand] ⟪spread, expand, extend, stretch⟫, ⟨-ni⟩ ta⌈ssuru ⟨〜に⟩達する ③ •c [for s.t. to get to a certain level or point in space] ⟪arrive at, get to, amount to⟫, ⟨-ni⟩ o⌈yobu ⟨〜に⟩及ぶ ① [for s.t. to get beyond an expected point ⟨fml⟩] ⟪attain to, amount to, come up to, match⟫

EX. (**a**) The forest fire has reached the residential area.
山火事は住宅地にまで{広がった/達した/?及んだ}。
Yama-kaji wa juutaku-chi ni made {hirogatta/tasshita/?oyonda}.
(**b**) The rumor reached every corner of the town.
そのうわさは町中に{広がった/??達した/??及んだ}。
Sono uwasa wa machi-juu ni {hirogatta/??tasshita/??oyonda}.
(**c**) Damages from the typhoon have reached the level of one hundred million dollars.
台風の被害は一億ドルに{達した/及んだ/*広がった}。
*Taifuu no higai wa ichi-oku-doru ni {tasshita/oyonda/*hirogatta}.*

—— vi. **[for s.o. to extend part of one's body such as an arm to grasp/touch s.t. ⟪fig. "try to attain s.t."⟫]**

1. te⌉ o no⌈ba⌉su 手を伸ばす ① [for s.o. to extend one's hand]

EX. The bartender reached for a bottle of whiskey on the shelf.
バーテンは棚のウイスキーに手を伸ばした。
Baaten wa tana no uisukii ni te o nobashita.

2. ⟨-o⟩ e⌈yo⌉o to tsu⌈tome⌉ru ⟨〜を⟩得ようと努める ② [for s.o. to try to get or attain s.t.]

react vi. **[to act in response to a stimulus] ⟨-ni⟩ ha⌈nnoo-suru ⟨〜に⟩反応する ③ •c [for s.t. to act or change under the direct effect of a stimulus] ⟪act upon, respond to⟫, ta⌉ido ni de⌉ru 態度に出る ② [for s.o. to assume a certain attitude]**

EX. (**a**) A: I told Tom that if he doesn't behave I'll kick him out.
トムにちゃんとしなければ、追い出すと言ってやったの。
Tomu ni chan-to shinakereba, oi-dasu to itte yatta no.
B: How did he react to that?
彼は{それにどう反応した/どんな態度に出た}?
Kare wa {sore ni doo hannoo-shita/donna taido ni deta}?
(**b**) If you mix carbon with oxygen, how do you think it will react?
炭素に酸素を混ぜたら、{どう反応する/*どんな態度に出る}と思いますか。
*Tanso ni sanso o mazetara, {doo hannoo-suru/*donna taido ni deru} to omoimasu ka.*

reaction n. **[an action, event, or change brought about in response to a stimulus] ha⌈nnoo 反応 •c [an event or change brought on by a stimulus] ⟪response, effect⟫, ta⌉ido 態度 •c [a verbal or non-verbal manifestation of what one is thinking or feeling] ⟪attitude, posture, bearing, behavior⟫**

EX. (**a**) If you mix these two substances an interesting chemical reaction takes place.
この二つの物質を混ぜると、おもしろい化学{反応/*態度}が起きます。
*Kono futatsu no busshitsu o mazeru to, omoshiroi kagaku-{hannoo/*taido} ga okimasu.*

R

(**b**) What was Bob's reaction when he was told that story?
その話を聞いた時のボブの{反応/態度}はどうでしたか。
Sono hanashi o kiita toki no Bobu no {hannoo/taido} wa doo deshita ka.

read vt. **[for s.o. to look at and understand the meaning of s.t. that is written 《fig. "to interpret the meaning of s.t. based on its outward appearance," "indicate"》]**
1. 〈**-o**〉 **yo⌉mu** 〈〜を〉よむ ① **[for s.o. to look at and understand the meaning of s.t. written 《fig. "count," "compose haiku or waka," "say aloud what is written," "try to figure out the meaning of s.t. based on its outward appearance"》]** 《**count, peruse, recite, chant, guess, compose haiku/waka**》
㊞ "compose *haiku* or *waka*"▷詠む, otherwise ▷読む

R

EX. (**a**) A: What's that you're reading?
今何を読んでいるんですか。
Ima nani o yonde iru n desu ka.
B: A novel by Camus.
カミュの小説です。
Kamyu no shoosetsu desu.
(**b**) George couldn't read her thoughts.
ジョージは彼女の心が読めなかった。
Jooji wa kanojo no kokoro ga yome-nakatta.

—— vi. **[for an instrument to indicate s.t., esp. a physical quantity, or for s.t. written to be recognized as consisting of certain words]**
1. 〈**-o**〉 **hyo⌈oji-suru** 〈〜を〉表示する ③ **•c [for s.t./s.o. to indicate s.t. clearly]** 《**indicate, show, express**》

EX. The thermometer read 100°F today.
今日寒暖計は華氏で百度を表示した。
Kyoo kandan-kei wa kashi de hyaku-do o hyooji-shita.

2. 〈**-to**〉 **ka⌉ite aru** 〈〜と〉書いてある /〈V ***te*** of ***kaku*** ① write + ***aru*** ① exist/ ① **[for s.t. to be written to the effect that]**

EX. It reads, "Cigarette smoking is hazardous to your health."
たばこを吸うのは健康に害があると書いてある。
Tabako o suu no wa kenkoo ni gai ga aru to kaite aru.

reader n. **[a person who reads s.t.]**
yo⌉mu hito 読む人, **do⌉kusha** 読者 **•c [a person who reads a particular book, magazine, article, etc.]** 《**subscriber, the reading public**》

EX. This magazine must be for teenage readers.
この雑誌{を読む人/の読者}はティーンエイジャーに違いない。
Kono zasshi {o yomu hito/no dokusha} wa tiin-eijaa ni chigainai.

readily adv. **[right away, without any reluctance or difficulty]**
su⌉gu (ni) すぐ(に) **[at once/without delay]** 《**at once, immediately, promptly, instantly**》, **ta⌉dachini** 直ちに **[without any intervening interval of time 〈fml〉]** 《**at once, immediately, directly**》, **ka⌈nntan ni** 簡単に /〈adj(***na***). ***ni*** of ***kantanna*** simple/ **[in such a way that minimal effort is required]** 《**easily, briefly**》

EX. (**a**) Is this merchandise readily available?
この商品は{すぐに/直ちに/簡単に}手に入りますか。
Kono shoohin wa {sugu ni/tadachini/kantanni} te ni hairimasu ka.
(**b**) Bob readily solved the problem.
ボブはその問題を{すぐに/直ちに/簡単に}解いた。
Bobu wa sono mondai o {sugu ni/tadachini/kantanni} toita.

reading n. **[the act of looking at and understanding the meaning of s.t. which is written]**
do⌉kusho 読書 **•c [the act of looking at and understanding the meaning of what is written in a book]**

EX. In Japan people say that autumn is the best season for reading.
日本では秋は読書の季節だと言われる。
Nihon de wa aki wa dokusho no kisetsu da to iwa-reru.

ready adj. **[in a suitable condition to do s.t. or to be used or consumed; willing to do s.t.]**

1. ⟨-no⟩ ju˥nbi ga de˥kita N ⟨～の⟩準備が出来たN /⟨Vinf. past of *junbi ga dekiru* ② become prepared/ [physically or mentally prepared to do s.t. or prepared to be used or consumed], ⟨-no⟩ yo˥oi ga de˥kita N ⟨～の⟩用意が出来たN /⟨Vinf. past of *yooi ga dekiru* ② become prepared/ [prepared for use or action on some occasion soon to occur, either physically or mentally]

EX. (**a**) Is dinner ready yet?
晩御飯の{準備/用意}は出来ましたか。
Ban-gohan no {junbi/yooi} wa dekimashita ka.
(**b**) Are you ready for Monday's final exam?
月曜日の期末試験の{準備/用意}は出来ましたか。
Getsuyoo-bi no kimatsu-shiken no {junbi/yooi} wa dekimashita ka.

2. i˥tsu-demo yo˥roko˥nde V いつでも喜んでV [to be willing to do s.t. at any time]

EX. He is always ready to help other people.
彼はいつでも喜んで人を助ける。
Kare wa itsu-demo yorokonde hito o tasukeru.

3. ka˥ku˥go ga dekite iru (N) 覚悟が出来ている(N) /⟨V*te iru* of *kakugo ga dekiru* ② mentally become prepared/ [mentally prepared for s.t.]

EX. Even before being told so by the doctor, Dad seemed ready to face the fact that he had terminal cancer.
医者に末期がんだと言われる前から、父はその覚悟が出来ているらしかった。
Isha ni makki-gan da to iwa-reru mae kara, chichi wa sono kakugo ga dekite iru rashikatta.

PHRASE: get ready for ⟨ *no*⟩ *{junbi/yooi} o suru* ⟨～の⟩{準備/用意}をする ③

EX. I have to get ready for my trip to Japan.
日本旅行の{準備/用意}をしなければならない。
Nihon-ryokoo no {junbi/yooi} o shinakereba naranai.

real adj. **[actually existing as a substantive entity or occurring as a fact ⟪fig. "consisting of immovable property"⟫]**

ho˥ntoo no N 本当のN •c [not a fiction or a lie] ⟪true, actual⟫ ↔ uso no N うそのN; ho˥n-mono no N 本物のN [not imitation or fake] ⟪genuine, true, natural⟫ ↔ nise no N にせのN; ji˥tsuzai no N 実在のN •c [actually existing] ⟪actual, existent, substantive⟫ ↔ kakuu no N 架空のN •c

EX. (**a**) What's the real reason that you stayed in the classroom?
あなたが教室に残った{本当/*本物/*実在}の理由は何ですか。
*Anata ga kyooshitsu ni nokotta {hontoo/ *hon-mono/*jitsuzai} no riyuu wa nan desu ka.*
(**b**) I saw a real live musical in New York.
ニューヨークで{本物/本当/*実在}のミュージカルを見た。
*Nyuuyooku de {hon-mono/hontoo/ *jitsuzai} no myuujikaru o mita.*
(**c**) Hamlet seems to have been a real person.
ハムレットは{実在/*本当/*本物}の人物だったらしい。
*Hamuretto wa {jitsuzai/*hontoo/*hon-mono} no jinbutsu datta rashii.*

reality n. **[the state or quality of being real]**

1. ge˥njitsu 現実 •c [that which actually exists or occurs before one's eyes] ⟪actuality⟫ ↔ risoo 理想 •c; ji˥tsuzai 実在 •c [actual existence] ⟪actuality⟫ ↔ kakuu 架空 •c

EX. (**a**) It's fine to have ideals, but reality can be harsh, you know.
理想を持つのもいいけど、{現実/*実在}は甘くないからね。
*Risoo o motsu no mo ii kedo, {genjitsu/ *jitsuzai} wa amakunai kara ne.*
(**b**) I cannot believe in the reality of God.
私は神の{実在/*現実}を信じない。
*Watashi wa kami no {jitsuzai/ *genjitsu} o shinjinai.*

2. ge˥njitsu˥-mi 現実味 •c [a sense of actually existing], ri˥a˥ritii リアリティー •f

EX. This painting lacks reality.
この絵には{現実味/リアリティー}がない。
Kono e ni wa {genjitsu-mi/riaritii} ga nai.

PHRASE: in reality *jissai ni wa* 実際には •c

EX. Nick talks a lot, but in reality he doesn't do much of anything.
ニックは口では色々言うが、実際にはほとんど何もしない。
Nikku wa kuchi de wa iro-iro iu ga, jissai ni wa hotondo nani-mo shinai.

realize vt. **[for s.o. to be fully aware of s.t. as a fact or to turn an idea or plan into s.t. actual]**

1. ⟨**-o**⟩ **shi⌈tte iru** ⟨〜を⟩知っている /⟨V*te iru* of *shiru* ① **come to know**/ ② **[for s.o. to have s.t. in one's mind from having learned, experienced, or deduced it]** ⟪**know, be aware of**⟫, ⟨**-ga**⟩ **wa⌈ka⌉tte iru** ⟨〜が⟩分かっている /⟨V*te iru* of *wakaru* ① **figure out**/ ② **[for s.o. to be already fully aware of s.t.]**

EX. (**a**) A: You need to do more exercise.
もっと運動をしなければいけないね。
Motto undoo o shinakereba ikenai ne.
B: I realize that, but I simply don't have the time.
そんなこと{分かっている/?知っている}けど、暇がないんだ。
Sonna koto {wakatte iru/?shitte iru} kedo, hima ga nai n da.
(**b**) I realize that smoking is bad for my health, but I'm just not able to quit.
たばこを吸うのが体に悪いことは{知っている/分かっている}けど、やめられないんだよ。
Tabako o suu no ga karada ni warui koto wa {shitte iru/wakatte iru} kedo, yame-rarenai n da yo.

2. ⟨⟨**-o**⟩⟩ **ji⌈tsugen-suru** ⟨⟨〜を⟩⟩実現する ③ **•c [for s.o. to turn s.t. such as a plan or idea into s.t. actual]** ⟪**actualize, materialize, bring to fruition**⟫

EX. When he sent his son off to Harvard, Stewart felt as if he had realized a dream.
スチュワートは息子をハーバードにやった時、自分の夢を実現したと思った。
Suchuwaato wa musuko o Haabaado ni yatta toki, jibun no yume o jitsugen-shita to omotta.

really adv. **[actually, in fact ⟪fig. "very," "incredible"⟫]**

1. ho⌈ntoo ni 本当に **•c [used for giving force to the expression it modifies ⟪fig. "an interjection used by a female speaker to indicate incredulousness"⟫]**

EX. (**a**) Do you really want to marry me?
本当に私と結婚したいの?
Hontoo ni watashi to kekkon-shi-tai no?
(**b**) A: It's really cold today, isn't it?
今日は本当に寒いですねえ。
Kyoo wa hontoo ni samui desu nee.
B: It sure is!
本当にそうですねえ。
Hontoo ni soo desu nee.

2. ho⌈ntoo wa 本当は **•c [in actuality, although things may appear otherwise]**

EX. He looks stupid, but he's really quite bright.
彼はばかに見えるけど、本当はなかなか頭がいいんです。
Kare wa baka ni mieru kedo, hontoo wa nakanaka atama ga ii n desu.

3. ho⌈ntoo ni 本当に **•c [used for giving force to the expression it modifies ⟪fig. "an interjection used by a female speaker to indicate incredulousness"⟫], ho⌈o** ほう int. **[an interjection used in male speech to indicate slight surprise or incredulouslness]** ⟪**is that right?**⟫, **he⌈e, so⌉o desu ka** へえ、そうですか **[an interjection used to indicate surprise or incredulousness], ma⌉saka** まさか adv. **[an adverb that indicates strong incredulousness in the face of an unexpected situation/event]** ⟪**surely…not, you don't say so, impossible, never, not at all likely, incredible, no kidding**⟫

EX. A: Sue told me that she's getting married to Tom.
スーはトムと結婚するんだって。
Suu wa Tomu to kekkon-suru n datte.
B: What! Really?
{本当に/ほう/へえ、そうですか/まさか}。
{Hontoo ni/Hoo/Hee, soo desu ka/Masaka}.

rear n. **[the part or area which is farthest from the front part of s.t.]**

R

1. uꜛshiro 後ろ [the area opposite to or farthest from the front] ⟪back, hind⟫ ↔ mae 前

EX. (**a**) I was aware that someone was approaching me from the rear.
私は後ろからだれかが近づいてくるのに気がついていた。
Watashi wa ushiro kara dare-ka ga chikazuite kuru no ni ki-ga-tsuite ita.
(**b**) In the rear of the house was a beautiful rose garden.
家の後ろにはきれいなバラ園があった。
Ie no ushiro ni wa kireina bara-en ga atta.

2. oꜜku 奥 [the area farthest to the back or to the interior as viewed from the front part of an enclosure] ⟪interior, inner part, innermost recess⟫

EX. In the rear of the room was standing a child in a kimono.
部屋の奥には着物を着た子供が立っていた。
Heya no oku ni wa ki-mono o kita kodomo ga tatte ita.

— adj. **[at or in the area which is farthest from the front part of s.t.]**

1. ⟨-no⟩ uꜛshiro no N ⟨〜の⟩後ろのN [at or in the area opposite to or farthest from the front] ⟪at the back, behind⟫

EX. In Japan, guests usually sit in the rear seat of a car.
日本ではお客さんは大抵車の後ろの座席に座る。
Nihon de wa o-kyaku-san wa taitei kuruma no ushiro no zaseki ni suwaru.

2. ⟨-no⟩ oꜜku no N ⟨〜の⟩奥のN [at or in the area farthest to the back or to the interior as viewed from the front part of an enclosure]

EX. Could you squeeze more toward the rear of the bus, sir?
お客様、もっとバスの奥につめてくださいませんか。
O-kyaku-sama, motto basu no oku ni tsumete kudasaimasen ka.

reason n. **[(the faculty of) rational thought; the motive, cause, or explanation for s.t. happening or for thinking or acting in a certain way]**

waꜜke 訳 [the grounds or circumstances providing an explanation for a fact or situation ⟪fig. "meaning," "cause," "circumstances"⟫], riꜛyuu 理由 •c [a fact/event/statement that provides an explanation/excuse for s.t. else] ⟪cause, grounds⟫

EX. (**a**) I don't know the reason why those two separated.
二人が別れた{訳/理由}は知りません。
Futari ga wakareta {wake/riyuu} wa shirimasen.
(**b**) Do you know the reason why Japanese people live so long?
日本人がこんなに長生きする{訳/理由}を知っていますか。
Nihon-jin ga konna-ni naga-iki-suru {wake/riyuu} o shitte imasu ka.

reasonable adj. **[in accordance with rational thinking or good sense; willing to act in accordance with this ⟪fig. "moderate," "inexpensive"⟫]**

1. moꜛttoꜜmona もっともな adj(*na*). **[in accordance with good sense] ⟪understandable, rational, justifiable⟫**

EX. What you have just said is very reasonable.
今あなたがおっしゃったことは本当にもっともなことです。
Ima anata ga osshatta koto wa hontoo ni mottomona koto desu.

2. kiꜛki-wake ga iꜜi 聞き分けがいい adj(*i*). **[listening to what s.o. says and accepting and acting in accordance with the logic in it]**

EX. A: Ken, will you stay home while mom and dad go to a party?
けんちゃん、お母さんとお父さんがパーティーに行っている間留守番頼むわよ。
Ken-chan, o-kaa-san to o-too-san ga paatii ni itte iru aida rusu-ban tanomu wa yo.
B: Sure.
うん、いいよ。
Un, ii yo.

R

A: Thanks for being so reasonable, dear.
随分聞き分けがいいのね。ありがとう。
Zuibun kiki-wake ga ii no ne. Arigatoo.

3. te⌈gorona 手ごろな adj(*na*). **[neither too big/expensive nor too small/inexpensive] ⟪handy, handy-sized, suitable, moderate⟫**

EX. Are there any apartments for rent at a reasonable price in this neighborhood?
手ごろな家賃のアパートがこの辺にありますか。
Tegorona yachin no apaato ga kono hen ni arimasu ka.

reasoning n. **[the process of drawing a logical inference or the arguments for drawing such an inference]**

1. su⌈iron 推論 •c [(the process of drawing) a logical inference] ⟪deduction, inference⟫

EX. Mathematical reasoning has many applications in daily life.
数学的な推論は日常生活にも大いに役に立ちます。
Suugaku-tekina suiron wa nichijoo-seikatsu ni mo ooini yaku ni tachimasu.

2. ro⌈npoo 論法 •c [a method of argumentation] ⟪argument, logic⟫

EX. I can't follow your reasoning.
あなたの論法について行けません。
Anata no ronpoo ni tsuite ike-masen.

recall vt. **[to call back s.t./s.o./s.a. ⟪fig. "recollect"⟫]**

1. ⟨-o⟩ ⟨-kara⟩ yo⌈bi-{ka⌉esu/modo⌉su} ⟨〜を⟩⟨〜から⟩呼び{返す/戻す} ① [for s.o. to call s.o. back] ⟪call back⟫

EX. The ambassador to the U.S. was suddenly recalled to Japan to report to the Ministry of Foreign Affairs.
駐米大使は外務省へ報告のため急きょ日本に呼び{返された/戻された}。
Chuu-Bei-taishi wa Gaimu-shoo e hookoku no tame kyuukyo Nihon ni yobi-{kaesa-reta/modosa-reta}.

2. ⟨-o⟩ o⌈moi-da⌉su ⟨〜を⟩思い出す ① [for s.o./s.a. to bring s.t./s.o./s.a. to one's memory] ⟪remember⟫

EX. (**a**) I can't recall the name of that Japanese restaurant.
その日本料理店の名前を思い出せません。
Sono Nihon-ryoori-ten no namae o omoi-dase-masen.
(**b**) Can you recall where you were on the afternoon of August 31, 1957?
1957年8月31日の午後どこにいたか思い出せますか。
Sen-kyuu-hyaku-go-juu-shichi-nen hachi-gatsu san-juu-ichi-nichi no gogo doko-ni ita ka omoi-dase-masu ka.

3. ⟨-o⟩ ka⌈ishuu-suru ⟨〜を⟩回収する ③ •c [for s.o. to take back items that have previously been distributed, esp. defective merchandise, used items, or responses to a questionnaire] ⟪withdraw, recycle, collect⟫

NOTE: *Kaishuu-suru* can take garbage as its direct object, meaning "to collect garbage," even though "recall" cannot be used in this way in English.

EX. The automobile company had to recall its 1975 models due to engine problems.
その自動車会社は1975年型の車をエンジンに問題があって回収しなければならなかった。
Sono jidoosha-gaisha wa sen-kyuu-hyaku-nana-juu-go-nen-gata no kuruma o enjin ni mondai ga atte kaishuu-shinakereba naranakatta.

4. ⟨-o⟩ ka⌈inin-suru ⟨〜を⟩解任する ③ •c [for s.o. to dismiss s.o. from an official appointment] ⟪release from office⟫, ⟨-o⟩ ri⌈ko⌉oru-suru ⟨〜を⟩リコールする ③ •f [for an electorate to suspend s.o. from elected office by popular vote]

EX. The mayor was recalled from his office because of the scandal.
市長はスキャンダルのせいで{解任/リコール}された。
Shichoo wa sukyandaru no sei de {kainin/rikooru}-sareta.

—— n. **[the act of calling back s.o./s.t./s.a.]**

1. o⌈moi-de 思い出 [s.t. about the past that is retained in one's mind, esp. a pleasant event] ⟪memory, remembrance⟫

2. ka⌈ishuu 回収 •c [the act of taking back

items that have previously been distributed, esp. defective merchandise, used items, or responses to a questionnaire] ((withdrawal, recycling, collection))

3. ka[inin 解任 •c [the act of dismissing s.o. from an official appointment], ri[ko]oru リコール •f [the act of suspending s.o. from elected office by popular vote]

receipt n. [an act/instance of receiving s.t. or a written statement showing that s.t. has been received or that a sum of money has been paid]

1. u[ke-toru koto 受け取ること [the act of receiving s.t.], ju[ryoo 受領 •c [the act of receiving s.t. important or official ⟨w⟩] ((acceptance))

2. ryo[oshuu-sho 領収書 •c [a written acknowledgement that s.t. has been received, esp. money], re[shi]ito レシート •f [a statement showing that a sum of money has been paid, printed out by a cash register in a store]

EX. I need a receipt for tax purposes.
税金の申告のために{領収書/レシート}が要るんですが。
Zeikin no shinkoku no tame ni {ryooshuu-sho/reshiito} ga iru n desu ga.

receive vt. [to take s.t. into one's possession or to be subjected to or affected by some force or action]

1. ⟨-o⟩ u[ke-toru ⟨～を⟩受け取る ① [for s.o. to take s.t. that is offered into one's possession] ((get, take, accept))

EX. When did you receive the letter?
その手紙をいつ受け取りましたか。
Sono tegami o itsu uke-torimashita ka.

2. ⟨-o⟩ u[ke]ru ⟨～を⟩受ける ② [to allow s.t. to come into one's possession or to be exposed to the effect of some force or action] ((accept, be given, have, take, get, catch, inherit))

EX. (a) He received a prestigious award for his many scholarly contributions to his professional field.
彼は自分の専門分野での様々な学問的貢献により権威ある賞を受けた。
Kare wa jibun no senmon-bun'ya de no sama-zamana gakumon-teki kooken ni-yori ken'i aru shoo o uketa.
(b) A: Where did you receive your college education?
大学教育はどこで受けましたか。
Daigaku-kyooiku wa doko de ukemashita ka.
B: At Hokkaido University.
北海道大学で受けました。
Hokkaidoo-daigaku de ukemashita.
(c) I received a severe injury to my leg in the accident.
事故で足にひどい傷を受けた。
Jiko de ashi ni hidoi kizu o uketa.
(d) Mr. Okada received harsh criticism for his actions.
岡田氏の行動は厳しい批判を受けた。
Okada-shi no koodoo wa kibishii hihan o uketa.
(e) The yacht sped along, receiving the full force of the wind in its sails.
ヨットは帆に風をいっぱい受けて、滑るように進んで行った。
Yotto wa ho ni kaze o ippai ukete, suberu yooni susunde itta.

3. ⟨-o⟩ u[ke-ireru ⟨～を⟩受け入れる ② [to admit s.o. into one's social network or sphere of influence or to agree to a request, proposal, or idea] ((accept, comply with))

EX. We're looking for host families to receive five Japanese high school students this fall.
今年の秋から五人の日本人高校生を受け入れてくれるホストファミリーを捜しています。
Kotoshi no aki kara go-nin no Nihon-jin kookoo sei o uke-irete kureru hosuto-famirii o sagashite imasu.

4. {⟨-ni⟩/⟨-kara⟩} ⟨-o⟩ mo[rau {⟨～に⟩/⟨～から⟩}⟨～を⟩もらう ① [for the speaker or s.o. in the speaker's in-group to obtain s.t. from s.o. whose status is equal to or lower than oneself] ((get, be given, accept)), {⟨-ni⟩/⟨-kara⟩} ⟨-o⟩ i[tadaku {⟨～に⟩/⟨～から⟩}⟨～を⟩いただく ① [for the speaker or s.o. in the speaker's in-group to obtain s.t. from

R

s.o. whose status is higher than oneself] **⟪get, be given, accept⟫**

EX. (**a**) I received a Christmas card from my younger brother.
僕は弟{に/から}クリスマスカードを{もらった/*いただいた}。
*Boku wa otooto {ni/kara} kurisumasu-kaado o {moratta/*itadaita}.*
(**b**) I received an English-Japanese dictionary from my teacher.
私は先生{に/から}英和辞典を{いただいた/?もらった}。
Watashi wa sensei {ni/kara} ei-wa-jiten o {itadaita/?moratta}.

NOTE: 1. In example (b) *moratta* can be used when the teacher is not felt to be physically or psychologically present.
2. The particle *ni* can be used only when something is received from a person. When something is received from an institution, *kara* must be used, as in *Watashi wa Monbu-shoo {kara/*ni} shoogaku-kin o moratta.* "I received a scholarship from the Ministry of Education."

R

receiver n. **[a person who receives s.t. or an electronic device that receives signals and converts them into sound or pictures]**
1. u⌈ketori-nin 受取人 [a person who takes s.t. that is offered into his/her possession] ⟪recipient, payee, remittee, beneficiary⟫

EX. Please guard this package carefully until it is securely in the hands of its receiver.
受取人の手に無事に届くまでこの小包をよく見ていて下さい。
Uketori-nin no te ni bujini todoku made kono ko-zutsumi o yoku mite ite kudasai.

2. re⌈shi⌉ibaa レシーバー •f [a person who returns a ball that is served in a game such as (table) tennis, volleyball, or badminton, or an apparatus that receives electronic signals and converts them into sounds or pictures], ju⌈wa⌉-ki 受話器 •c [the part of a telephone or radio that converts electronic signals into sounds]

EX. (**a**) The receiver wasn't able to return his fast serves.
レシーバーは彼の速いサーブを打ち返せなかった。
Reshiibaa wa kare no hayai saabu o uchi-kaese-nakatta.
(**b**) Even though I held the receiver right up to my ear, I still couldn't hear well.
{受話器/レシーバー}を耳に付けても、まだよく聞こえなかった。
{Juwa-ki/Reshiibaa} o mimi ni tsukete mo, mada yoku kikoenakatta.

recent adj. **[done, existing, or occurring at a time not long ago]**
ko⌈no-goro no N このごろのN [done, existing, or occurring at a time not long ago, typically within several days to a week of the present] ⟪at present, now⟫, chi⌈ka⌉goro no N 近ごろのN [done, existing, or occurring at a time not long ago, typically within several weeks to a year of the present] ⟪late, these days⟫, sa⌈ikin no N 最近のN •c [done, existing, or occurring within or over a period of time from the near past up to the present] ⟪latest⟫

EX. (**a**) A recent survey shows that the percentage of people who attend church has not changed over the past five years.
{最近/*このごろ/*近ごろ}の調査によるとこの五年間教会に行く人の率は変わっていないそうだ。
*{Saikin/*Kono-goro/*Chikagoro} no choosa ni yoru to kono go-nenkan kyookai ni iku hito no ritsu wa kawatte inai sooda.*
(**b**) I make no attempt to follow recent fashion in what I wear.
服装に関しては{最近/このごろ/近ごろ}の流行を追おうなどとは思っていない。
Fukusoo ni-kanshite wa {saikin/kono-goro/chikagoro} no ryuukoo o ooo nado to wa omotte inai.
(**c**) The recent trend among college students seems to be toward greater political conservatism.
政治に関してかなり保守寄りなのが{最近/このごろ/近ごろ}の大学生の傾向のようだ。

Seiji ni-kanshite kanari hoshu-yori na no ga {saikin/kono-goro/chikagoro} no daigaku-sei no keikoo no yooda.

recently adv. **[at a time not long ago]**
ko⌈no-goro このごろ [at a time not long ago, typically within several days to a week of the present] ⟪now, present, in these days⟫, ko⌈no-aida この間 [at a point in time in the near past, approximately several days to weeks ago] ⟪the other day, some time ago, not long ago, lately⟫, chi⌈ka⌉goro 近ごろ [at a time not long ago, typically within several weeks to a year of the present] ⟪lately, nowadays, now⟫, sa⌈ikin 最近 •c [during or over a period of time from the near past up to the present] ⟪lately, of late⟫

EX. (**a**) A: How have you been?
どうですか。
Doo desu ka.
B: I've been pretty busy recently.
{このごろ/近ごろ/最近/*この間}忙しくてね。
*{Kono-goro/Chikagoro/Saikin/*Kono-aida} isogashikute ne.*
(**b**) Dr. Kobayashi hasn't been attending conferences recently as he has been ill.
小林博士はご病気だったので{最近/このごろ/近ごろ/*この間}学会に出席していらっしゃらない。
*Kobayashi-hakase wa go-byooki datta node {saikin/kono-goro/chikagoro/*kono-aida} gakkai ni shusseki-shite irassharanai.*
(**c**) I bumped into Ayako recently at Ginza.
私は{この間/最近/*このごろ/*近ごろ}綾子に銀座で偶然会った。
*Watashi wa {kono-aida/saikin/*kono-goro/*chikagoro} Ayako ni Ginza de guuzen atta.*
(**d**) June hasn't been to see me recently.
ジューンは{このごろ/近ごろ/最近/*この間}僕に会いに来ない。
*Juun wa {kono-goro/chikagoro/saikin/*kono-aida} boku ni ai ni konai.*

NOTE: *Kono-aida* can only be used with a momentary action verb, but *kono-goro* and *chikagoro* are used with verbs that express situations having some duration, especially stative and negative verbs. *Saikin* can be used with either an action or a stative verb.

reception n. **[the act of receiving s.t./s.o. or the way in which s.t./s.o. is received or a gathering held to welcome guests or the quality of the broadcast signals received by a radio/television]**
1. u⌈ke-toru koto 受け取ること [the act of receiving s.t.]
2. u⌈ketsuke 受付 [the act of taking applications/subscriptions or of receiving a visitor; a person who performs such an act]

EX. The reception of applications begins on February 1.
願書の受付は二月一日に始まります。
Gansho no uketsuke wa ni-gatsu tsuitachi ni hajimarimasu.

3. ka⌈ngei 歓迎 •c [the act of welcoming s.o.] ⟪welcome⟫

EX. The reception of the Olympic athletes by the citizens of Seoul was an enthusiastic one.
ソウル市民によるオリンピック選手の歓迎は熱がこもっていた。
Souru-shimin ni yoru Orinpikku-senshu no kangei wa netsu ga komotte ita

4. hi⌈ro⌉o-en 披露宴 •c [a social function, esp. a dinner party, for welcoming people attending a marriage ceremony] ⟪wedding banquet⟫, ka⌈nge⌉i-kai 歓迎会 •c [a social function for welcoming s.o.] ⟪welcome party⟫, re⌈se⌉pushon レセプション •f [a Western style social function for welcoming s.o.]

EX. (**a**) The wedding ceremony was followed by a reception.
結婚式に続いて{披露宴/レセプション/*歓迎会}があった。
*Kekkon-shiki ni tsuzuite {hiroo-en/resepushon/*kangei-kai} ga atta.*
(**b**) The college held a reception for the Japanese *kabuki* troupe.
大学で日本の歌舞伎の一行のために{レセプション/歓迎会/*披露宴}があった。

*Daigaku de Nihon no kabuki no ikkoo no tame ni {resepushon/kangei-kai/ *hiroo-en} ga atta.*

5. **ju⌈shin 受信 •c [the receiving of radio or TV signals]**

EX. TV reception is poor in this building.
この建物の中ではテレビの受信はよくない。
Kono tate-mono no naka de wa terebi no jushin wa yokunai.

reception desk n. **[a front desk at a hotel]**
fu⌈ronto フロント •f

recess n. **[the cessation of an activity in which one has been engaged, esp. at a school or legislature, or the period of such a cessation]**

1. **ya⌈sumi⌉ 休み /⟨V*masu* of *yasumu* ① take rest/ [(a period of time during which there is a) cessation of activity《fig. "holiday," "vacation"》]**

EX. We have a week-long spring recess at the end of March.
三月の末に一週間の春休みがある。
San-gatsu no sue ni is-shuukan no haru-yasumi ga aru.

2. **kyu⌈ukei 休憩 •c [a short, temporary cessation of activity]《rest, break, intermission》**

EX. We will now take a 10-minute recess.
ここで十分間の休憩を取ります。
Koko de jup-pun-kan no kyuukei o torimasu.

3. **kyu⌈ukai 休会 •c [a cessation of activity at a legislature]**

EX. The Diet goes into recess on December 22.
国会は十二月二十二日に休会に入る。
Kokkai wa juu-ni-gatsu ni-juu-ni-nichi ni kyuukai ni hairu.

recipe n. **[a set of directions for preparing a dish]**
ryo⌈ori-hoo 料理法 •c《how to cook, cookery, culinary art》

EX. This is really good! Would you mind giving me the recipe for it?
これはおいしいわ! 料理法を教えてくださらない?
Kore wa oishii wa! Ryoori-hoo o oshiete kudasaranai?

recite vt. **[for s.o. to repeat s.t. one has memorized or heard]**

1. **⟨-o⟩ a⌈nshoo-suru ⟨～を⟩暗唱する ③ •c [for s.o. to say s.t. by rote memory]《repeat from memory》**

EX. When I was a high school student, my French teacher always had us recite French poems in class.
高校生の時フランス語の先生が授業中にフランスの詩を必ず暗唱させた。
Kookoo-sei no toki Furansu-go no sensei ga jugyoo-chuu ni Furansu no shi o kanarazu anshoo-saseta.

2. **⟨-no⟩ ko⌈to⌉ o ku⌈wa⌉shiku ha⌈na⌉su ⟨～の⟩ことを詳しく話す ① [for s.o. to talk about s.t./s.o./s.a. in detail]**

EX. Taro recited to his friends everything that happened on his trip to Hawaii.
太郎はハワイへの旅行中に起こったことを何もかも友達に詳しく話した。
Taroo wa Hawai e no ryokoo-chuu ni okotta koto o nani-mo-kamo tomodachi ni kuwashiku hanashita.

reckon vt. **[for s.o. to count or calculate s.t.《fig. "consider"》]**

1. **⟨-o⟩ ke⌈isan-suru ⟨～を⟩計算する ③ •c [for s.o. to find out a number/quantity by means of mathematical operations], ⟨-o⟩ sa⌈nshutsu-suru ⟨～を⟩算出する ③ •c**

EX. The taxes one pays to the government are reckoned on the basis of one's income.
国に納める税金は所得に比例して{算出/計算}される。
Kuni ni osameru zeikin wa shotoku ni hirei-shite {sanshutsu/keisan}-sareru.

2. **⟨-o⟩ ha⌈ka⌉ru ⟨～を⟩はかる ① [for s.o. to determine the size, weight, length, amount, etc., of s.t.《fig. "scheme," "deceive"》]《measure, gauge, weigh, fathom, sound》**

㊮ "compute numbers/quantity"▷計る, "measure distance/speed/ability"▷測る, "measure weight"▷量る, "scheme"▷図る, "deceive"▷謀る, "consult"▷諮る

EX. We tried to reckon the distance of the

thunderstorm by counting the number of seconds between the flashes of lightning and the sound of the thunder.
稲妻が光ってから雷が鳴るまでの秒数を数えて雷の距離を測ってみた。
Inazuma ga hikatte kara kaminari ga naru made no byoosuu o kazoete kaminari no kyori o hakatte mita.

3. ⟨⟨-o⟩⟩ ⟨-to⟩ o⌈mo⌉u ⟨⟨〜を⟩⟩⟨〜と⟩思う ① [for s.o. to spontaneously perceive s.t. in one's mind or to have an opinion about s.t.] ⟪think, suppose, guess, imagine, believe, consider⟫

EX. I reckon Jim to be the smartest person in our class.
僕はジムをクラスで一番頭のいい人だと思う。
Boku wa Jimu o kurasu de ichiban atama no ii hito da to omou.

recognition n. **[the act of identifying s.t./s.o./s.a. from previous experience ⟪fig. "appreciation"⟫]**

1. ⟨-o⟩ mi⌈tomeru koto ⟨〜を⟩認めること [the act of seeing and comprehending the value of s.t./s.o./s.a. ⟪fig. "approval"⟫] ⟪approval⟫, ⟨-o⟩ mite so⌈re to wa⌈ka⌉ru koto ⟨〜を⟩見てそれと分かること [the act of seeing and being able to tell what s.t./s.o./s.a. is]

EX. Recognition of one's own weaknesses is a sign of strength.
自分の弱さを{認める/見てそれと分かる}ことは強さの印だ。
Jibun no yowa-sa o {mitomeru/mite sore to wakaru} koto wa tsuyo-sa no shirushi da.

2. ka⌉nsha 感謝 •c [the state of feeling thankfulness to s.o. for s.t. or the act of expressing this] ⟪appreciation, gratitude, gratefulness, acknowledgment⟫

EX. Mr. Wood deserves recognition for his contributions to our community.
ウッド氏は私たちの町に貢献してくださったのですから、感謝をされて当たり前です。
Uddo-shi wa watashi-tachi no machi ni kooken-shite kudasatta no desu kara, kansha o sarete atarimae desu.

recognize vt. **[for s.o. to identify s.t./s.o./s.a. from previous experience ⟪fig. "approve"⟫]**

1. ⟨-ga⟩ wa⌈ka⌉ru ⟨〜が⟩分かる ① [for s.o. to be able to figure out the nature, meaning, identity, etc., of s.t./s.o./s.a. which already is/should be in one's mind]

EX. A: How did you recognize me?
どうして私のことが分かりましたか。
Dooshite watashi no koto ga wakarimashita ka.
B: Because I had seen your picture.
あなたの写真を見たからですよ。
Anata no shashin o mita kara desu yo.

2. ⟨-o⟩ mi⌈tomeru ⟨〜を⟩認める ② [for s.o. to see and comprehend the value or significance of s.o./s.t./s.a.] ⟪find, admit, acknowledge, accept, allow, permit⟫

EX. Christianity teaches that if one recognizes his sins he will be forgiven.
キリスト教では罪を認めれば許されると教えられている。
Kirisuto-kyoo de wa tsumi o mitomereba yurusa-reru to oshie-rarete iru.

3. ⟨-o⟩ ⟨-to-⌈shite⟩ mi⌈tomeru ⟨〜を⟩⟨〜として⟩認める ② [for s.o. to accept s.o./s.t./s.a. as] ⟪acknowledge, accept⟫

EX. In Japan one is recognized as a novelist of professional standing once one has been awarded the Akutagawa Prize.
日本では芥川賞をもらうと一人前の小説家として認められる。
Nihon de wa Akutagawa-shoo o morau to ichi-nin-mae no shoosetsu-ka to-shite mitome-rareru.

recollect vt. **[for s.o. to bring s.t. back to one's mind]**

⟨-o⟩ o⌈moi-da⌉su ⟨〜を⟩思い出す ① [for s.o./s.a. to bring s.t./s.o./s.a. to one's memory] ⟪call to mind, recall⟫

EX. A: Do you remember where you were on the night of the incident?
その事件の晩、どこにいたか覚えていますか。

R

Sono jiken no ban, doko ni ita ka oboete imasu ka.
B: No, I can't recollect where I was on that night.
いいえ、その晩どこにいたか思い出せません。
Iie, sono ban doko ni ita ka omoi-dase-masen.

recommend vt. **[for s.o. to advise s.o. to do s.t. or to speak favorably of s.t./s.o., esp. as a candidate worthy of employment, advancement, or admission to an academic program]**
⟨-ni⟩ ⟨-o⟩ su⌈isen-suru ⟨～に⟩⟨～を⟩推薦する ③ **•c [for s.o. to speak favorably to s.o. of s.o./s.t. (other than food) as worthy of being employed, admitted to a program, tried, etc.]** ⟪say a good word for⟫, **⟨-ni⟩ {⟨-o⟩/Sinf. nonpast yo⌉oni} su⌈sumeru ⟨～に⟩{⟨～を⟩/Sinf. nonpastように}勧める** ② **[for s.o. to speak favorably to s.o. of s.o./s.t. as worthy or qualified for a particular purpose or to advise s.o. to do s.t.]** ⟪advise, urge, encourage⟫

R

EX. (**a**) I recommended Mr. Hayashi for the position.
私は林氏をその職に{勧めた/推薦した}。
Watashi wa Hayashi-shi o sono shoku ni {susumeta/suisen-shita}.
(**b**) I recommend that you go to Japan at the earliest possible opportunity.
私はあなたに出来るだけ早く日本にいらっしゃる{ことを/ように}{勧めます/*推薦します}。
*Watashi wa anata ni dekiru dake hayaku Nihon ni irassharu {koto o/yooni} {susumemasu/*suisen-shimasu}.*
(**c**) A: Which beer would you recommend?
どのビールを{勧めます/*推薦します}か。
*Dono biiru o {susumemasu/*suisen-shimasu} ka.*
B: Let's see… I'd recommend this Japanese beer.
そうですね。この日本のビールを{お勧めします/*ご推薦します}。
*Soo desu ne. Kono Nihon no biiru o {o-susume-shimasu/*go-suisen-shimasu}.*

recommendation n. **[the act of recommending s.t. or s.t. which is recommended]**
1. su⌈isen 推薦 •c [the act of speaking favorably of s.o./s.t. (other than food) as worthy of being employed admitted to a program, tried, etc.]

EX. (**a**) Could I ask you to write me a letter of recommendation?
推薦状を書いて下さいませんか。
Suisen-joo o kaite kudasaimasen ka.
(**b**) Mr. Ikeda was admitted to the research institute on the recommendation of Dr. Johnson.
池田氏はジョンソン博士の推薦で研究所に入った。
Ikeda-shi wa Jonson-hakase no suisen de kenkyuu-jo ni haitta.

2. su⌈sume 勧め /⟨V*masu* of *susumeru* ② advise/ [the act of speaking favorably of s.o./s.t. or of advising s.o. to do s.t.], ka⌈nkoku 勧告 •c [the act of advising s.o. to take a particular course of action ⟨w⟩] ⟪**advice**⟫

EX. (**a**) The recommendation of this committee is to build another freeway crossing the state.
この委員会の{勧告/*勧め}は州を横断する高速道路をもう一つ作ることです。
*Kono iin-kai no {kankoku/*susume} wa shuu o oodan-suru koosoku-dooro o moo hitotsu tsukuru koto desu.*
(**b**) I bought this dictionary on my teacher's recommendation.
私の先生の{勧め/*勧告}でこの辞書を買いました。
*Watashi no sensei no {susume/*kankoku} de kono jisho o kaimashita.*

record vt. **[for s.o. to set s.t. down in writing or other permanent form; to preserve sound on tape, disk, or other medium, esp. by electronic means]**
1. ⟨-o⟩ ki⌈roku-suru ⟨～を⟩記録する ③ **•c** ⟪**register**⟫, **⟨-o⟩ ka⌈ki-tomeru ⟨～を⟩書き留める** ② **[for s.o. to put s.t. down in writing]** ⟪**make a note**⟫

EX. The Japanese seem to love to record their thoughts in diary form.
日本人は自分の考えを日記に{記録する/書き留める}のが大好きなようだ。
Nihon-jin wa jibun no kangae o nikki ni {kiroku-suru/kaki-tomeru} no ga dai-sukina yoo da.

2. ⟨-o⟩ **shi⌈mesu** ⟨〜を⟩示す ② **[for s.o./s.t. to cause s.o. to see or be clearly aware of some fact or object by the use of symbols or other indirect means ⟨fml⟩]** ⟪show, indicate, express, display⟫, ⟨-o⟩ **hyo⌈oji-suru** ⟨〜を⟩表示する ③ •c **[for s.t./s.o. to indicate s.t. clearly]** ⟪indicate, express, designate⟫

EX. The thermometer recorded a temperature of 5°C this morning.
今朝、寒暖計は摂氏五度を{示して/表示して}いた。
Kesa, kandan-kei wa sesshi go-do o {shimeshite/hyooji-shite} ita.

3. ⟨-o⟩ **ro⌈kuon-suru** ⟨〜を⟩録音する ③ •c **[for s.o. to preserve sound by electronic means]** ⟪make a recording of⟫, ⟨-o⟩ **ro⌈kuga-suru** ⟨〜を⟩録画する ③ •c **[for s.o. to preserve images by electronic means]** ⟪videotape⟫

EX. (**a**) Did you record the interview?
インタビューを録音しておきましたか。
Intabyuu o rokuon-shite okimashita ka.
(**b**) Let's record the wedding ceremony on videotape.
結婚式をビデオ・テープに録画しよう。
Kekkon-shiki o bideo-teepu ni rokuga-shiyoo.

— n. **[information preserved in writing or other permanent form; all the facts making up the past history of s.o./s.t.; a disk on which sounds are encoded ⟪fig. "the best known performance up to this point in time"⟫]**

1. ki⌈roku 記録 •c ⟪documents, minutes, proceedings⟫

EX. (**a**) Do we have a record of the meeting?
会議の記録がありますか。
Kaigi no kiroku ga arimasu ka.
(**b**) Mr. Furuhashi set a world record last year in the 1000-meter freestyle swim event.
古橋氏は1000メートルの自由形水泳で去年世界記録を作った。
Furuhashi-shi wa sen-meetoru no jiyuu-gata-suiei de kyonen sekai kiroku o tsukutta.

2. se⌈iseki 成績 •c **[a mark/rating on an examination, in a school course, etc.]** ⟪result, showing, score, grades, mark⟫

EX. Ann's school records are superb.
アンの学校の成績は上々だ。
An no gakkoo no seiseki wa joojoo da.

3. re⌈ko⌉odo レコード •f **[a flat, thin circular object on which sounds are recorded for reproduction on a phonogragh]**

EX. People are not buying as many records as they used to now that compact disks have become available.
コンパクトディスクが出てからはレコードを前のように買わなくなった。
Konpakuto-disuku ga dete kara wa rekoodo o mae no yooni kawanaku natta.

PHRASE: off the record *hi-kooshiki ni* 非公式に •c, *ofureko de* オフレコで •f

EX. The politician spoke off the record on the current trade friction between the U.S. and Japan.
政治家は日米間の貿易摩擦のことを{オフレコで/非公式に}話した。
Seiji-ka wa Nichi-Bei-kan no booeki-masatsu no koto o {ofureko de/hi-kooshiki ni} hanashita.

— adj. **[the best or worst of its kind of to occur so far]**
ki⌈roku-tekina 記録的な adj(*na*). •c **[surpassing all other previous occurrences of its kind]** ⟪record-breaking⟫

EX. We had a record crop of rice last year.
去年は記録的な米の収穫があった。
Kyonen wa kiroku-tekina kome no shuukaku ga atta.

recorder n. **[a person who sets down information in writing or keeping track of**

R

such information; a machine that encodes sounds by electronic means; a musical instrument similar to a flute]

1. ki⌈roku⌉-sha 記録者 •c [a person who registers information in writing or by electronic or other means]

2. te⌈epu-reko⌉odaa テープレコーダー •f [a machine for encoding sound on tape]

EX. I recorded our interview on a tape recorder.
インタビューをテープレコーダーで録音しました。
Intabyuu o teepu-rekoodaa de rokuon-shimashita.

3. re⌈ko⌉odaa レコーダー •f [a machine which encodes sounds or a flute with eight finger holes]

recording n. **[the sound or image preserved on tape, disk, or other medium by mechanical means]**

R

1. ro⌈kuon 録音 •c [an act/instance of preserving sounds by mechanical means]

EX. What is the date of recording of this concert?
このコンサートの録音はいつでしたか。
Kono konsaato no rokuon wa itsu deshita ka.

2. ro⌈kuga 録画 •c [an act/instance of preserving images by mechanical means] ⟪**videotaping**⟫

EX. The quality of the recording on this videotape is poor.
このビデオ・テープは録画の質が悪い。
Kono bideo-teepu wa rokuga no shitsu ga warui.

recover vt. **[to get s.t. back]**

⟨-o⟩ to⌈ri-modosu ⟨〜を⟩取り戻す ① [to take s.t./s.o./s.a. back which had been given away or lost, including mental states such as consciousness or composure] ⟪**take back, regain, resume, restore, redeem, retrieve, recapture**⟫**, ⟨-o⟩ to⌈ri-kaesu ⟨〜を⟩取り返す ① [for s.o. to get s.t./s.o./s.a. back which had been taken away other than a mental or physiological state]** ⟪**get back, regain, retrieve, recall, redeem**⟫**, ⟨-o⟩ ka⌈ifuku-suru ⟨〜を⟩回復する ③ •c [for s.o. to regain the original state one was in, esp. consciousness or health]**

EX. (**a**) I was able to recover my stolen car.
盗まれた車を{取り戻す/取り返す/*回復する}ことが出来た。
*Nusuma-reta kuruma o {tori-modosu/tori-kaesu/*kaifuku-suru} koto ga dekita.*
(**b**) It took me about two years to fully recover my health.
健康を完全に{取り戻す/回復する/*取り返す}のに二年もかかった。
*Kenkoo o kanzenni {tori-modosu/kaifuku-suru/*tori-kaesu} no ni ni-nen mo kakatta.*
(**c**) Japan is making efforts to recover its northern islands from Russia.
日本はロシアから北方領土を{取り戻そう/取り返そう/*回復しよう}と努力している。
*Nihon wa Roshia kara hoppoo-ryoodo o {tori-modosoo/tori-kaesoo/*kaifuku-shiyoo} to doryoku-shite iru.*
(**d**) My mother didn't recover consciousness for two hours after the operation.
母は手術後二時間も意識を{取り戻さなかった/回復しなかった/*取り返さなかった}。
*Haha wa shujutsu-go ni-jikan mo ishiki o {tori-modosanakatta/kaifuku-shinakatta/*tori-kaesanakatta}.*

—— vi. **[to regain normalcy]**

na⌈o⌉ru なおる ① [for s.t. in an abnormal and undesirable state such as illness, injury, mistake, bad habit, or mechanical disorder to return to a normal and desirable state] ⟪**be fixed, be cured, be corrected, improve**⟫**, ⟨-kara⟩ ta⌈chi-naoru ⟨〜から⟩立ち直る ① [for an individual or economic condition to regain health and/or vitality]** ⟪**improve, firm up, rally**⟫

㊥ "be repaired"▷直る, "be cured"▷治る

EX. (**a**) Has your father recovered from his illness yet?
お父さんの病気はもう{治りました/*立ち直りました}か。

*O-too-san no byooki wa moo {naorimashita/*tachi-naorimashita} ka.*
(**b**) It took about 20 years for Japan to recover from her defeat in the war.
日本は敗戦から{立ち直る/*直る}のに約二十年かかった。
*Nihon wa haisen kara {tachi-naoru/*naoru} no ni yaku ni-juu-nen kakatta.*

recreation n. **[an act/instance of refreshing oneself through pleasurable activity]**
go⌈raku 娯楽 •c [s.t. one does for fun during one's free time] **《amusement, pleasure, pastime》, re⌈kurie⌉eshon レクリエーション •f [an act of refreshing one's body through exercise or pleasurable activity]**

EX. What sort of recreation do you enjoy?
どんな{娯楽/レクリエーション}が好きですか。
Donna {goraku/rekurieeshon} ga suki desu ka.

NOTE: *Rekurieeshon* can also be pronounced as *rikurieeshon.*

recruit vt. **[for s.o. to seek to add new members to an organization, group, military force, etc.]**
⟨-o⟩ bo⌈shuu-suru ⟨〜を⟩募集する ③ •c [for s.o. to seek publicly and to add new members to one's organization or group] **《levy, enlist, enroll, raise》, ⟨-o⟩ tsu⌈no⌉ru ⟨〜を⟩募る ① [for s.o. to call on people to join together for a particular purpose]** **《raise, call for, advertise for》**

EX. (**a**) The Japanese Ministry of Education is recruiting applicants for its scholarship.
日本の文部省は奨学金の応募者を{募って/募集して}いる。
Nihon no Monbu-shoo wa shoogaku-kin no oobo-sha o {tsunotte/boshuu-shite} iru.
(**b**) The English Speaking Society of the college is currently recruiting new members.
今、大学のESSは新会員を{募って/募集して}いる。
Ima, daigaku no ii-esu-esu wa shin-kaiin o {tsunotte/boshuu-shite} iru.

—— n. **[a member who has newly joined an organization, group, military force, etc.]**
1. shi⌉npei 新兵 •c [a newly enlisted member of the military services] **《a new conscript, rookie》**
2. shi⌈n-ka⌉iin 新会員 •c [a newly enrolled member of a non-military organization]

rectangle n.
cho⌈o-hookei 長方形 •c [a geometric figure with four sides and four right angles] **《oblong》**

EX. College quadrangles are typically laid out in the shape of a rectangle.
大学の中庭は大抵長方形に作られている。
Daigaku no naka-niwa wa taitei choo-hookei ni tsukura-rete iru.

rectangular adj. **[having the shape of a rectangle]**
cho⌈o-hookei no N 長方形のN •c [shaped like a geometric figure with four sides and four right angles]

EX. Most churches have a rectangular chapel, but this church has a square one.
大抵の教会は長方形の礼拝堂を持っているのに、この教会のは正方形だ。
Taitei no kyookai wa choo-hookei no reihai-doo o motte iru noni, kono kyookai no wa seihoo-kei da.

red adj. **[having the color of blood 《fig. "pertaining to a deficit," "related to communism"》]**
a⌈kai 赤い adj(*i*).

EX. A: Your face is red. What happened?
顔が赤いね。どうしたの?
Kao ga akai ne. Doo shita no?
B: I'm afraid I had a little too much to drink.
酒をちょっと飲み過ぎたんです。
Sake o chotto nomi-sugita n desu.

—— n. **[the color of blood]**
a⌉ka 赤

reduce vt. **[to cause s.t./s.o./s.a. to become less in size, degree, quantity, or strength]**
1. ⟨-o⟩ he⌈rasu ⟨〜を⟩減らす ① [to cause s.t./s.o./s.a. to become smaller in quantity]

R

⟪decrease, lessen, diminish⟫ ↔ ⟨-o⟩ fuyasu ⟨〜を⟩増やす ①

EX. The company reduced the number of its employees due to the economic slump.
その会社は不景気のため、従業員の数を減らした。
Sono kaisha wa fu-keiki no tame, juugyoo-in no kazu o herashita.

2. ⟨-o⟩ sa⌈ge⌉ru ⟨〜を⟩下げる ② [for s.o. to cause s.t./s.o./s.a. to move to a lower place or to decrease in amount/degree/strength] ⟪lower, hang, drop⟫ ↔ ⟨-o⟩ ageru ⟨〜を⟩上げる ②; ⟨-o⟩ o⌈to⌉su ⟨〜を⟩落とす ① [for s.o./s.a. to allow/cause s.t. to lose its support/balance and move rapidly from a higher to a lower position due to gravity ⟪fig. "give a failing grade to," "make s.t. which is expected to be in a place not be seen there anymore," "cause s.t. to become lower/worse in extent, quality, etc.," "render s.t. into a decided/settled state of affairs"⟫] ⟪drop, lower, remove, degrade⟫

EX. (**a**) You have to reduce your speed as you leave the freeway and get on the exit ramp.
高速道路を出て一般道に入る所ではスピードを{落とさなければ/?下げなければ}ならない。
Koosoku-dooro o dete ippan-doo ni hairu tokoro de wa supiido o {otosanakereba/?sagenakereba} naranai.
(**b**) Mr. Spencer's position was reduced from that of department chief to section chief.
スペンサー氏の地位は部長から課長へ{下げられた/落とされた}。
Supensaa-shi no chii wa buchoo kara kachoo e {sage-rareta/otosa-reta}.

3. ⟨-o⟩ ⟨-ni⟩ ka⌈ngen-suru ⟨〜を⟩⟨〜に⟩還元する ③ •c [to return s.t. to its original state or component parts]

EX. Professor Tanaka is good at reducing a complex theory to its simplest components.
田中教授は複雑な理論を単純な構成要素に還元するのが上手だ。
Tanaka-kyooju wa fukuzatsuna riron o tanjunna koosei-yooso ni kangen-suru no ga joozu da.

reed n.

a⌉shi あし

EX. Pascal said that man is a thinking reed.
パスカルは人間は考えるあしだと言った。
Pasukaru wa ningen wa kangaeru ashi da to itta.

refer vi. **[to point to s.t. using words or turn one's attention to s.t. as an intended meaning, a source of information, an authority, or an antecedent in discourse]**

1. ⟨-no⟩ ko⌈to⌉ o sa⌉shite iu ⟨〜の⟩ことを指して言う ① [for s.o. to point to s.t. in the act of speaking as an intended meaning, source of information, authority, or discourse antecedent], ⟨-no⟩ ko⌈to⌉ o sa⌉su ⟨〜の⟩ことを指す ① [to point to s.t. as an intended meaning, source of information, authority, or discourse antecedent] ⟪point to, indicate⟫

EX. When Jim said "incident," he was referring to the Watergate Incident.
ジムが「事件」と言った時、ウォーターゲート事件のことを{指して/指して言って}いたのだ。
Jimu ga 'jiken' to itta toki, Uootaageeto-jiken no koto o {sashite/sashite itte} ita no da.

2. ⟨-o⟩ sa⌈nshoo-suru ⟨〜を⟩参照する ③ •c [for s.o. to look at and compare s.t., esp. a separate passage or text, for informational purposes] ⟪consult, see, compare⟫

EX. Please refer to chapter three, section four of this book.
この本の第三章、第四節を御参照ください。
Kono hon no dai-san-shoo, dai-yon-setsu o go-sanshoo kudasai.

—— vt. **[for s.o. to direct s.t./s.o./s.a. to a proper source of information or assistance]**

1. ⟨-ni⟩ ⟨-o⟩ sho⌈okai-suru ⟨〜に⟩⟨〜を⟩紹介する ③ •c [for s.o. to make s.o./s.t. known for the first time] ⟪carry in, bring in⟫

EX. The doctor referred the patient to a specialist for treatment.

治療のために医者はその患者を専門医に紹介した。
Chiryoo no tame ni isha wa sono kanja o senmon-i ni shookai-shita.

2. ⟨**-o**⟩ **sa⌈nshoo-suru** ⟨〜を⟩参照する SEE refer vi. 2

EX. For the details I would refer you to Dr. Yamamoto's book.
詳細は山本博士の本を御参照下さい。
Shoosai wa Yamamoto-hakase no hon o go-sanshoo kudasai.

reference n. **[the act of directing the attention of s.o. to s.t., esp. a source of information, or s.t. that provides such information]**

1. ge⌈nkyuu-suru koto 言及すること **[the act of touching on s.t. verbally], fu⌈reru-koto** 触れること **[an act/instance of coming close to and making light contact with s.t./s.o./s.a. ⟪fig. "the act of referring to s.o./s.t./s.a."⟫]**

EX. In evaluating the senator's record he was careful to avoid any reference to the senator's personal life.
上院議員の業績を評価する際、その私生活に{触れる/言及する}ことを注意深く避けた。
Jooin-giin no gyooseki o hyooka-suru sai, sono shi-seikatsu ni {fureru/genkyuu-suru} koto o chuui-bukaku saketa.

2. sa⌈nkoo 参考 **•c [the act of consulting s.t. as a source of information]**

EX. For your reference I have enclosed the relevant documents with this letter.
御参考までに関連書類を同封しました。
Go-sankoo made ni kanren-shorui o doofuu-shimashita.

3. sa⌈nkoo-bu⌉nken 参考文献 **•c [books or publications providing background or relevant information to an article, research, report, etc.]**

EX. A list of references is provided at the end of the book.
参考文献のリストは巻末に出ています。
Sankoo-bunken no risuto wa kanmatsu ni dete imasu.

refined adj. **[free from impurities or vulgarity]**

1. se⌈isei-shita N 精製したN /⟨Vinf. past of *seisei-suru* ③ refine/ **•c [carefully manufactured]**

EX. They say that refined sugar is not good for your health.
精製した砂糖は体に良くないそうだ。
Seisei-shita satoo wa karada ni yokunai sooda.

2. jo⌈ohi⌉nna 上品な adj(*na*). **•c [sophisticated and pleasing in quality, speech, or behavior] ⟪elegant, polished, tasteful, graceful, genteel, delicate, decent⟫ ↔ gehinna** 下品な adj(*na*). **•c; yu⌉ugana** 優雅な adj(*na*). **•c [exquisitely elegant in behavior or style] ⟪graceful, urbane, exquisite⟫ ↔ soyana** 粗野な adj(*na*). **•c**

EX. (**a**) Mrs. Doi has very refined tastes in fashion.
土井さんの奥さんは服装の趣味が{上品/*優雅}だ。
*Doi-san no oku-san wa fukusoo no shumi ga {joohin/*yuuga} da.*
(**b**) You lead quite a refined life, I must say.
{優雅な/*上品な}生活をしているね。
*{Yuugana/*Joohinna} seikatsu o shite iru ne.*

reflect vt. **[for a surface to throw back light, heat, or sound, or for a mirror/mirror-like object to show an image]**

1. ⟨**-o**⟩ **ha⌈nsha-suru** ⟨〜を⟩反射する ③ **•c ⟪throw back, reverberate, mirror⟫,** ⟨**-o**⟩ **ha⌈ne-kaesu** ⟨〜を⟩跳ね返す ① **[for a surface to throw s.t. back from itself] ⟪repel, recoil⟫**

EX. The asphalt street reflected the bright summer sunshine.
アスファルトの道は夏のギラギラする日の光を{跳ね返した/反射した}。
Asufaruto no michi wa natsu no gira-gira-suru hi no hikari o {hane-kaeshita/hansha-shita}.

2. ⟨**-o**⟩ {⟨**-ni**⟩/⟨**-e**⟩} **u⌈tsu⌉su** ⟨〜を⟩{⟨〜に⟩/⟨〜へ⟩}うつす ① **[to cause s.o./s.t./s.a. to change to a different location or into a**

different condition《fig. "copy," "reflect" "infect" "take a picture"》]《copy, imitate, reproduce, describe, photograph, mirror, remove, transfer》

㊅ "photograph/copy"▷写す, "project an image on the surface of a screen/water"▷映す, "remove"▷移す

EX. The lake reflected the scenic mountains on its surface.
湖は水面にきれいな山を映していた。
Mizuumi wa minamo ni kireina yama o utsushite ita.

3. ⟨-o⟩ a⌈rawa⌉su ⟨〜を⟩あらわす ① [to cause s.t. to become exposed/visible/recognizable]《show, indicate, display, express, represent》, ⟨-o⟩ ha⌈n'ei-suru ⟨〜を⟩反映する ③ [to mirror s.t. figuratively]

㊅ "make s.t. hidden visible to others by means of action"▷現わす, "make s.t. hidden visible to others by linguistic or expressive means"▷表す

R

EX. The expressions on people's faces these days reflect the economic condition of the country.
近ごろの人々の顔は国の経済状態を{反映して/表して}いる。
Chika-goro no hito-bito no kao wa kuni no keizai-jootai o {han'ei-shite/arawashite} iru.

— vi. **[for light, heat, or sound to be thrown back from a surface or for an image to be shown on s.t.]**

1. ha⌈nsha-suru 反射する ③ •c [for s.t. to be thrown back from a surface]《reverberate, mirror》

EX. The lights of the city were reflected on the river.
川に都市の明かりが反射していた。
Kawa ni toshi no akari ga hansha-shite ita.

2. u⌈tsu⌉ru うつる ① [to change to a different place or condition《fig. "be reflected," "be infected"》]《remove, be imaged, be mirrored》

㊅ "be reflected"▷映る, "be photographed"▷写る, otherwise ▷移る

EX. Mt. Fuji was reflected beautifully on the lake.
富士山が湖に美しく映っていた。
Fuji-san ga mizuumi ni utsukushiku utsutte ita.

reflection n. **[light or an image which is thrown back from a surface《fig. "meditation"》]**

1. ha⌈nsha 反射 •c《reverberation》, ha⌈ne-kaeri 跳ね返り /⟨V*masu* of *hanekaeru* ② rebound/ [a sudden rebounding]《recoil, backlash, rebound》

2. ka⌉ge かげ [an image created when light is intercepted by an object]《shadow, shade, back, behind》, su⌉gata 姿 [a visual impression of s.o.]《shape, figure, form, appearance, dress, posture》

㊅ "shade"▷陰, "image/shadow"▷影

EX. Narcissus fell in love with his own reflection in the pool of water.
ナルキッソスは泉の中の自分の{姿/影}に恋をした。
Narukissosu wa izumi no naka no jibun no {sugata/kage} ni koi o shita.

3. ju⌈kkoo 熟考 •c [the act of thinking very carefully]《deliberation》, ju⌉kuryo 熟慮 •c [the act of thinking very deliberately]《mature deliberation》

EX. Upon reflection I've decided to participate in the project even though there is some lack of clarity in its goals at this point.
{熟考/熟慮}の結果、現段階では海のものとも山のものとも分からないプロジェクトに参加することにした。
{Jukkoo/Jukuryo} no kekka, gen-dankai de wa umi no mono to mo yama no mono to mo wakaranai purojekuto ni sanka-suru koto ni shita.

reform vt. **[for s.o. to make s.t. better, esp. an institution or s.o.'s behavior]**

1. ⟨-o⟩ ka⌈izen-suru ⟨〜を⟩改善する ③ •c [for s.o. to make s.t. better, esp. living or working conditions]《improve, better》, ⟨-o⟩ ka⌈ikaku-suru ⟨〜を⟩改革する ③ •c [for s.o. to improve a system of organization which has become old or ineffective]《reorganize》

EX. We need to reform our entrance

EX. examination system.
我々は入学試験制度を{改善/改革}しなければならない。
Ware-ware wa nyuugaku-shiken-seido o {kaizen/kaikaku}-shinakereba naranai.

2. o⌈konai o a⌈ratame-sase⌉ru 行いを改めさせる /⟨causative of *okonai o aratameru* ② mend one's behavior/ ② [to cause s.o. to mend his/her behavior]

EX. It's very difficult to reform an adult.
大人に行いを改めさせるのはとても難しい。
Otona ni okonai o aratame-saseru no wa totemo muzukashii.

—— n. [the act of improving s.t., esp. an institution or s.o.'s behavior; a change which has been made for the better in this]
1. ka⌈izen 改善 •c [the act of making s.t. better, esp. living or working conditions] ⟪improvement, betterment⟫, ka⌈ikaku 改革 •c [the act of improving a system or organization which has become old or ineffective] ⟪reorganization, reformation⟫
2. kyo⌈osei 矯正 •c [the act of correcting an evil, esp. undesirable human behavior] ⟪correction, rectification, remedy⟫

refrigerator n.
re⌈izo⌉o-ko 冷蔵庫 •c

EX. You'd better put the meat in the refrigerator right away so it won't spoil.
腐るといけないから、肉は冷蔵庫にすぐ入れたほうがいいですよ。
Kusaru to ikenai kara, niku wa reizoo-ko ni sugu ireta hoo ga ii desu yo.

refuge n. **[(a place of) protection from danger, trouble, or pursuers]**
1. hi⌉nan 避難 •c [the act of escaping from danger/hardship] ⟪shelter, harborage, evacuation⟫

EX. We took refuge in the park after the earthquake.
私たちは地震の後、公園に避難をした。
Watashi-tachi wa jishin no ato, kooen ni hinan o shita.

2. hi⌉nan-jo 避難所 •c [a place where one escapes from danger]

EX. There are several places of refuge in that national park.
その国立公園には避難所が数か所ある。
Sono kokuritsu-kooen ni wa hinan-jo ga suu-kasho aru.

3. ta⌈ikutsu-shi⌉nogi 退屈しのぎ [an escape from boredom] ⟪kill-time⟫

EX. As a refuge from my boredom, I would often watch movies all through the night.
退屈しのぎに夜どおし映画を見ることが多かった。
Taikutsu-shinogi ni yo-dooshi eiga o miru koto ga ookatta.

refuse vt. **[for s.o. to decline to do/accept/give/allow s.t.]**
⟨-o⟩ ko⌈towa⌉ru ⟨〜を⟩断る ① [for s.o. to inform s.o. that one cannot accept his/her demand/request/invitation/offer] ⟪decline, ask to be excused⟫, ⟨-o⟩ kyo⌉hi-suru ⟨〜を⟩拒否する ③ •c [for s.o. to inform s.o. that one cannot accept his/her demand/request ⟨fml⟩] ⟪deny, disapprove, turn down⟫, ⟨-o⟩ kyo⌉zetsu-suru ⟨〜を⟩拒絶する ③ •c [for s.o. to decline firmly to accept s.o.'s demand/request ⟨fml⟩] ⟪reject, disclaim, rebuff, turn down⟫

EX. (**a**) Despite the desperate financial situation he was in, Tom refused all offers of help from his friends.
トムは金銭的にどうしようもない状況にあるにもかかわらず、友人からの援助の申し出をすべて{断った/拒否した/?拒絶した}。
Tomu wa kinsen-tekini doo shiyoo mo nai jookyoo ni aru ni mo kakawarazu, yuujin kara no enjo no mooshide o subete {kotowatta/kyohi-shita/?kyozetsu-shita}.
(**b**) The union refused the alternative proposal made by the company's management.
組合は会社の経営側の代案を{拒否した/拒絶した/?断った}。
Kumiai wa kaisha no keiei-gawa no daian o {kyohi-shita/kyozetsu-shita/?kotowatta}.

R

regard vt. **[for s.o./s.a. to look at s.t./s.o./s.a. steadily or to consider s.t./s.o./s.a. to be a certain way]**

1. ⟨-o⟩ **ji⌈tto mi⌉ru** ⟨〜を⟩じっと見る ② **[for s.o./s.a. to look at s.t./s.o./s.a. without averting one's eyes],** ⟨-o⟩ **mi-⌈tsumeru** ⟨〜を⟩見つめる ② **[for s.o./s.a. to watch s.o./s.t./s.a. continuously and intently]** ⟪**gaze at, stare at**⟫, ⟨-o⟩ **gyo⌉oshi-suru** ⟨〜を⟩凝視する ③ •c **[for s.o. to strain one's eyes to see s.o./s.t./s.a.]** ⟪**fix one's eyes on, stare at, gaze at**⟫

EX. The stranger regarded me with curiosity for a few moments.
その見知らぬ人は物珍しそうにしばらく私を{じっと見た/見つめた/凝視した}。
Sono mi-shiranu hito wa mono-mezurashi-sooni shibaraku watashi o {jitto mita/mi-tsumeta/gyooshi-shita}.

2. ⟨-o⟩ ⟨-to⟩ **ka⌈ngae⌉ru** ⟨〜を⟩⟨〜と⟩考える ② **[for s.o. to consider s.o./s.t./s.a. to be a certain way],** ⟨-o⟩ ⟨-to⟩ **mi-⌈nasu** ⟨〜を⟩⟨〜と⟩見なす ① **[for s.o. to view s.o./s.t. as being a certain way]** ⟪**consider, reckon**⟫

EX. (**a**) I regard my students as outstanding.
私は自分の学生を優秀だと{考えて/見なして}いる。
Watashi wa jibun no gakusei o yuushuu da to {kangaete/mi-nashite} iru.
(**b**) My husband appears to regard me as his servant.
主人は私のことを召し使いと{考えて/見なして}いるようです。
Shujin wa watashi no koto o meshitsukai to {kangaete/mi-nashite} iru yoodesu.

—— n. **[a feeling of respect]**

ke⌉ii 敬意 •c **[a feeling of respect]** ⟪**respect, homage**⟫, **so⌈nkei** 尊敬 •c **[the act of showing deference to a person]** ⟪**respect, esteem, reverence, deference**⟫

EX. The students hold the college president in high regard for not succumbing to governmental pressure.
学生は政府の圧力に負けなかった学長に対して{敬意/尊敬}の念を抱いている。
Gakusei wa seifu no atsuryoku ni makenakatta gakuchoo ni-taishite {keii/sonkei} no nen o idaite iru.

PHRASE: Give my regards to… ⟨-ni⟩ *doozo yoroshiku (o-tsutae kudasai).* ⟨〜に⟩どうぞよろしく(お伝えください)。

regarding prep. **[with respect to s.t./s.o./s.a.]**

ni-kanshite に関して comp. prt. /⟨V*te* of *kansuru* ③ **relate to**/ •c **[relating to s.o./s.t./s.a. ⟨fml⟩]** ⟪**pertaining to, concerning, about**⟫, **ni-tsuite** について comp. prt. **[in regard to s.o./s.t./s.a.]** ⟪**concerning, about**⟫

EX. (**a**) Do you have any information regarding John's whereabouts?
ジョンの居所{について/に関して}何か情報はありませんか。
Jon no i-dokoro {ni-tsuite/ni-kanshite} nani-ka joohoo wa arimasen ka.
(**b**) I wrote an article regarding the current banking crisis in Japan.
私は現在の日本の金融危機{について/に関して}記事を書きました。
Watashi wa genzai no Nihon no kin'yuu-kiki {ni-tsuite/ni-kanshite} kiji o kakimashita.

regardless adj. **[paying no attention to s.t.]**

⟨-o⟩ **mu⌉shi-suru** ⟨〜を⟩無視する ③ •c **[for s.o. to treat s.t./s.o./s.a. present as if it/he/she were not present]** ⟪**ignore, disregard**⟫

EX. He continues to smoke regardless of his doctor's warnings.
彼は医者の警告を無視してたばこを吸い続けている。
Kare wa isha no keikoku o mushi-shite tabako o sui-tsuzukete iru.

PHRASE: regardless of… *{⟨-ni⟩/⟨-to⟩} kankei naku* {⟨〜に⟩/⟨〜と⟩}関係なく

EX. Everyone can excercise regardless of age or sex.
運動は年や性別{に/と}関係なくだれにでも出来ます。
Undoo wa toshi ya seibetsu {ni/to} kankei naku dare ni demo dekimasu.

region n. **[any large area with certain defining characteristics]**

chi⌉iki 地域 •c [a geographic division characterizable in terms of climate/culture/natural environment] ⟪area, zone, territory⟫, chi⌈ho⌉o 地方 •c [a large area which is defined according to some criterion or an area outside major cities] ⟪locality, district, area, section⟫

EX. (**a**) There are a lot of mountainous regions in Japan.
日本には山の多い{地域/地方}が沢山ある。
Nihon ni wa yama no ooi {chiiki/chihoo} ga takusan aru.
(**b**) It snows heavily in this region in the winter.
この{地域/地方}は冬雪が多い。
Kono {chiiki/chihoo} wa fuyu yuki ga ooi.

register n. **[an official record of important items such as names, births, marriages, deaths, etc., or a machine that counts and records figures]**
to⌈oroku⌉-bo 登録簿 •c [an official document in which important items of information are recorded], re⌉ji(sutaa) レジ(スター) •f [a machine that counts and records sales figures in a store]

EX. A: Where can I pay for this?
これ、どこで払ったらいいですか。
Kore, doko de harattara ii desu ka.
B: Please go to the cash register and pay there.
レジに行ってお払い下さい。
Reji ni itte o-harai kudasai.

— vt. **[for s.o. to enter important items of information into an official record, such as names, births, marriages, deaths, etc.] ⟨-o⟩ to⌈oroku-suru ⟨〜を⟩登録する ③ •c [for s.o. to make an official record of important items of information such as names, births, marriages, deaths, etc.] ⟪enter, enrol⟫**

EX. The names of all the new members in the club have been registered.
クラブの新会員の名前はすべて登録されている。
Kurabu no shin-kaiin no namae wa subete tooroku-sarete iru.

PHRASE: registered mail *kakitome* 書留

EX. I'd like to send this letter by registered mail.
この手紙を書留で送りたいんですが。
Kono tegami o kakitome de okuri-tai n desu ga.

registration n. **[an act/instance of making an official record of important information]**
to⌈oroku 登録 •c [the act of making an official record of important items of information such as names, births, marriages, deaths, etc., esp. at a public office] ⟪registration, entry, record⟫

EX. Registration for fall courses was held in the large gymnasium.
秋学期の科目の登録は大きな体育館であった。
Aki-gakki no kamoku no tooroku wa ookina taiiku-kan de atta.

regret vt. **[for s.o. to feel sorry about for s.t.]**
1. ⟨-o⟩ ku⌈ya⌉mu ⟨〜を⟩悔やむ ① [for s.o. to feel sorry for having done s.t. or s.t. having happened to s.o., esp. oneself] ⟪regret, repent⟫, ⟨-o⟩ ko⌉okai-suru ⟨〜を⟩後悔する ③ •c [for s.o. to feel sorry for what one has done] ⟪repent, do penitence for, suffer remorse⟫

EX. I regret that I didn't marry my high school sweetheart.
高校の時の恋人と結婚しなかったことを{悔やんで/後悔して}いる。
Kookoo no toki no koi-bito to kekkon-shinakatta koto o {kuyande/kookai-shite} iru.

2. {⟨-o⟩/Vstem of pot. na⌉kute} za⌈nne⌉n ni omou {⟨〜を⟩/Vstem of pot.なくて}残念に思う ① [for s.o. to feel sorry for s.t. having happened to s.o., esp. oneself]

EX. I regret that I wasn't able to attend his wedding.
彼の結婚式に出席出来なくて残念に思います。
Kare no kekkon-shiki ni shusseki-dekinakute zannen ni omoimasu.

R

— n. **[a feeling of sadness or sorrow about s.t.]**
1. **ko˥okai** 後悔 •c **[a state of feeling sorry for what one has done]** ⟪repentance, penitence, remorse, contrition⟫
2. **ka˹nashi-mi** 悲しみ /⟨adj(*i*). stem of *kanashii* sad + suf. *mi* ness/ **[psychological pain brought on by circumstances difficult to endure]** ⟪sorrow, sadness, grief, distress⟫

regrettable adj. **[unfortunate and causing sorrow]**
1. **za˹nne˥nna** 残念な adj(*na*). •c **[causing disappointment and dissatisfaction over s.t. that s.o. has done or s.t. that has happened]** ⟪disappointing⟫, **o˹shi˥i** 惜しい adj(*i*). **[feeling that one cannot let go of s.t. because it is s.t. indispensable to oneself]** ⟪disappointing, pitiful⟫

EX. (**a**) It's regrettable that you can't make it to our party this weekend.
今週末うちのパーティーへいらっしゃれないのは{残念/*惜しい}です。
*Konshuu-matsu uchi no paatii e irasshare-nai no wa {zannen/*oshii} desu.*
(**b**) It's regrettable that you had to sell the land given to you by your grandfather.
おじいさんからもらった土地を売らなければいけなくなったのは{残念/惜しい}ですね。
O-jii-san kara moratta tochi o uranakereba ikenaku natta no wa {zannen/oshii} desu ne.

2. **ki-˹no-doku˥na** 気の毒な adj(*na*). **[deserving of sympathy for the pain or sorrow one is suffering]** ⟪pitiable, unfortunate, miserable⟫

EX. It's regrettable that her husband had to lose his job while their children are still in their teens.
子供がまだ十代なのに、御主人が失職なさったとはお気の毒ですね。
Kodomo ga mada juudai na noni, go-shujin ga shisshoku-nasatta to wa o-ki-no-doku desu ne.

regular adj. **[occurring or spaced in a uniform manner; having characteristics usual or normal for its kind]**
1. **ki˹soku-tekina** 規則的な adj(*na*). •c **[having an orderly character consistent with some rule or principle]** ⟪orderly, systematic, methodical⟫, **ki˹soku-tadashi˥i** 規則正しい adj(*i*). **[following a rule-governed schedule]** ⟪systematic, methodical, orderly⟫

EX. John keeps to a regular daily schedule.
ジョンは毎日の生活が{規則正しい/規則的だ}。
Jon wa mai-nichi no seikatsu ga {kisoku-tadashii/kisoku-teki da}.

2. **i˥tsu-mo no N** いつものN **[the usually occurring]** ⟪usual⟫, **te˹iki-tekina** 定期的な adj(*na*). •c **[held, conducted, or published at fixed intervals]** ⟪periodical⟫

EX. (**a**) Regular concerts are held ten times during the year.
{定期的な/*いつもの}コンサートは年に十回ある。
*{Teiki-tekina/*Itsu-mo no} konsaato wa nen ni juk-kai aru.*
(**b**) The regular staff meeting was canceled this week.
{いつもの/定期的な}職員会議は今週は中止になった。
{Itsu-mo no/Teiki-tekina} shokuin-kaigi wa konshuu wa chuushi ni natta.

— n. **[a person who visits a place (of business) or participates in an organization or function on a consistent basis]**
1. **re˥gyuraa** レギュラー •f **[sports players in a starting line-up]**
2. **jo˹oren** 常連 •c **[customers or patrons who frequent a place of business or an organizational function; an adult peer]** ⟪hangers-on, frequenters⟫

EX. Dan is a regular at that bar.
ダンはそのバーの常連だ。
Dan wa sono baa no jooren da.

regularly adv. **[at uniformly-spaced intervals of time]**
1. **ki˹soku-tekini** 規則的に /⟨adj(*na*). *ni* of *kisoku-tekina* regular/ •c ⟪methodically,

systematically)), **ki**｢**soku-tadashi**｣**ku 規則正しく** /⟨adj(*i*). ***ku*** **of** ***kisoku-tadashii*** **regular/ ((methodically, systematically))**

EX.| (**a**) You can stay healthy if you exercise regularly.
運動を{規則的に/規則正しく}やれば丈夫でいられる。
Undoo o {kisoku-tekini/kisoku-tadashiku} yareba joobude i-rareru.
(**b**) They say your chances of gaining weight are lower if you regularly eat three meals a day.
一日三回{規則的に/規則正しく}食事をとった方が太りにくいそうだ。
Ichi-nichi san-kai {kisoku-tekini/kisoku-tadashiku} shokuji o totta hoo ga futori-nikui sooda.

2. te｢**iki-tekini 定期的に** /⟨adj(*na*). ***ni*** **of** ***teiki-tekina*** **regular/ •c [at fixed intervals of occurrence]**

EX.| We regularly hold brown bag seminars during the lunch hour.
我々は定期的にお弁当持参のゼミをしています。
Ware-ware wa teiki-tekini o-bentoo jisan no zemi o shite imasu.

regulation n. **[a rule or law which restricts how people may act]**

1. ki｢**so**｣**ku 規則 •c [a principle or standard governing how one is to act or behave in a situation] ((rule))**

EX.| Japanese schools have strict regulations on what students may wear.
日本の学校には学生の着るものについての厳しい規則がある。
Nihon no gakkoo ni wa gakusei no kiru mono ni-tsuite no kibishii kisoku ga aru.

2. ki｢**sei 規制 •c [a control imposed by an official authority] ((control))**

EX.| The number of foreign automobiles that can be imported into the U.S. is currently limited by governmental regulation.
アメリカに輸入される外車の数は現在政府の規制によって制限されている。
Amerika ni yunyuu-sareru gaisha no kazu wa genzai seifu no kisei ni-yotte seigen-sarete iru.

reign n. **[(the duration of) rule by a monarch]**

1. to｣**ochi 統治 •c [the act of governing a society or country by means of established political processes] ((rule, government)), chi**｢**sei 治世 •c [(the duration of) rule of a country usually by a monarch or peaceful times] ((rule))**

EX.| The reign of Czar Nikolai II in Russia lasted for 23 years, from 1894 until the Bolshevik Revolution.
ニコライ二世によるロシアの{統治/治世}は1894年からボルシェビキ革命まで23年間続いた。
Nikorai-ni-sei ni-yoru Roshia no {toochi/chisei} wa sen-hap-pyaku-kyuu-juu-yo-nen kara Borushebiki-kakumei made ni-juu-san-nenkan tsuzuita.

2. to｢**ochi-ki**｣**kan 統治期間 •c [the period of time s.o. rules a society or country], mi**｣**yo 御世 [the period of time an emperor rules over a country, esp. Japan]**

EX.| During the reign of Emperor Meiji, Japan developed into a modern society.
明治天皇の{御世/統治期間}に日本は近代化を遂げた。
Meiji tennoo no {miyo/toochi-kikan} ni Nihon wa kindai-ka o togeta.

—— vi. **[for a monarch to rule a country ((fig. "be predominant"))]**

1. ⟨**-o**⟩ **to**｣**ochi-suru** ⟨**〜を**⟩**統治する ③ •c ((rule, govern, administer))**

EX.| The current Japanese emperor does not technically reign; he is nothing more than a symbol of Japan.
日本の今の天皇は専門的に言えば統治はしていない。日本の象徴に過ぎない。
Nihon no ima no tennoo wa senmon-tekini ieba toochi wa shite inai. Nihon no shoochoo ni suginai.

2. ⟨**-o**⟩ **shi**｣**hai-suru** ⟨**〜を**⟩**支配する ③ •c [for s.o. to exercise power over people or organizations to cause them to act or function in the way one desires] ((control, govern, rule))**

EX. Fidel Castro has reigned over Cuba for almost 40 years.
フィデル・カストロはキューバを40年近くも支配している。
Fideru Kasutoro wa Kyuuba o yon-juu-nen chikaku mo shihai-shite iru.

3. se⌉iryoku o fu⌈ruu 勢力をふるう ① [to wield influence] ⸨**dominate, sway**⸩

EX. The Democrats have long reigned in the United States House of Representatives.
アメリカの下院では長年民主党が勢力をふるっている。
Amerika no kain de wa naga-nen Minshu-too ga seiryoku o furutte iru.

rein(s) n.
ta⌈zuna 手綱 •c

reindeer n.
to⌈na⌉kai トナカイ

relate vt. **[for s.o. to bring s.t. into a natural or logical connection with s.t. else; for s.o. to tell s.t. in detail ⟨fml⟩]**

1. ⟨-o⟩ ⟨-to⟩ ka⌈nkei-zuke⌉ru ⟨〜を⟩⟨〜と⟩関係付ける ② [for s.o. to bring s.t. into a natural or logical connection with s.t. else]

EX. It would be premature to relate this murder case with the one that occurred last year.
この殺人事件を去年の事件と関係付けるのは時期尚早だ。
Kono satsujin-jiken o kyonen no jiken to kankei-zukeru no wa jiki-shoosoo da.

2. {⟨-o⟩/⟨-ni-tsuite⟩}ha⌈na⌉su {⟨〜を⟩/⟨〜について⟩}話す ① [for s.o. to convey orally information on some topic] ⸨**talk, speak, discuss, tell**⸩, **{(⟨-no⟩ ko⌈to⌉) ⟨-o⟩/⟨-ni-tsuite⟩} no⌈be⌉ru {(⟨〜の⟩こと)⟨〜を⟩/⟨〜について⟩} 述べる ② [for s.o. to speak/write s.t. in a formal way ⟨w⟩]** ⸨**state, speak, observe, mention**⸩

EX. It's always intriguing to hear a person relate his or her own unique personal experiences.
人が珍しい個人的体験{を/について}{述べる/話す}のを聞くのはいつも面白い。
Hito ga mezurashii kojin-teki taiken {o/ni-tsuite} {noberu/hanasu} no o kiku no wa itsu-mo omoshiroi.

—— vi. [to have a natural or logical connection with another or for s.o. to interact with other people, esp. in a positive way]

1. {⟨-to⟩/⟨-ni⟩} ka⌈nkei-suru {⟨〜と⟩/⟨〜に⟩} 関係する ③ •c [to have a relationship with s.t./s.o./s.a.] ⸨**have to do with, take part in**⸩

EX. He only shows interest in things that relate directly to himself.
あの人は自分{と/に}直接関係することにしか興味を示さない。
Ano hito wa jibun {to/ni} chokusetsu kankei-suru koto ni shika kyoomi o shimesanai.

2. ⟨-to⟩ u⌉maku iku ⟨〜と⟩うまくいく ① [for s.o. to get along well with s.o. else]

EX. Professor Yoshida relates very well to his students.
吉田先生は学生と大変うまくいっている。
Yoshida-sensei wa gakusei to taihen umaku itte iru.

relation n. **[a natural, logical, or social connection]**
ka⌈nkei 関係 •c ⸨**relationship, connection, bearing**⸩, **a⌈idagara 間柄 [a connection between two people]** ⸨**relationship, terms**⸩

EX. (**a**) Is there any historical relation between the Japanese and Korean languages?
日本語と韓国語の間に歴史的{関係/*間柄}がありますか。
*Nihon-go to Kankoku-go no aida ni rekishi-teki {kankei/*aidagara} ga arimasu ka.*
(**b**) A: What relation is Jane to Bob?
ジェーンとボブはどういう{関係/間柄}ですか。
Jeen to Bobu wa doo-iu {kankei/aidagara} desu ka.
B: They are husband and wife.
夫婦です。
Fuufu desu.

relationship n. **[the state or fact of being related]**
1. ka⌈nkei 関係 •c ⸨**relation, connection, bearing**⸩

EX. There isn't much of a relationship between money and happiness.
お金と幸福の関係はたいしてない。
O-kane to koofuku no kankei wa taishite nai.

2. shi⌈nzoku-ka⌉nkei 親族関係 •c [the state or fact of being related historically or as kin] **《kinship》**

EX. No clear relationship has yet been established between the Korean and Japanese languages.
韓国語と日本語の間には明らかな親族関係はいまだに立証されていない。
Kankoku-go to Nihon-go no aida ni wa akirakana shinzoku-kankei wa imadani risshoo-sarete inai.

relative adj. **[(considered) in connection with s.o./s.t. else]**

1. {⟨-to⟩/⟨-ni⟩} ka⌈nkei ga a⌉ru N {⟨〜と⟩/⟨〜に⟩}関係があるN ① •c [having a connection with s.t./s.o./s.a. else]

EX. There is no evidence relative to the crime.
犯罪{に/と}関係のある証拠は一つもない。
Hanzai {ni/to} kankei no aru shooko wa hitotsu mo nai.

2. so⌈otai-tekina 相対的な adj(*na*). **•c [considered in connection with s.t. else]** **《correlative, reciprocal》 ↔ zettai-tekina 絶対的な** adj(*na*). **•c**

EX. Happiness is a purely relative matter.
幸福感は全く相対的なものだ。
Koofuku-kan wa mattaku sootai-tekina mono da.

—— n. **[s.o. related by kinship]**

shi⌈nrui 親類 •c [people related by blood or by marriage] **《kinsfolk》, shi⌈nseki 親せき •c** **《kinsman》, mi-⌈uchi 身内 [people related by core kinship bonds, esp. parents and siblings]** **《relations》**

EX. (**a**) On Thanksgiving Day I'm having a group of relatives over for a reunion at my house.
感謝祭の日に私の{親類/親せき/身内}が私のうちに集まる予定になっています。
Kansha-sai no hi ni watashi no {shinrui/shinseki/mi-uchi} ga watashi no uchi ni atsumaru yotei ni natte imasu.
(**b**) I have many relatives living in Taipei.
私は台北に{親類/親せき/身内}が大勢います。
Watashi wa Taipei ni {shinrui/shinseki/mi-uchi} ga oozei imasu.

relatively adv. **[in a relative manner]**

hi⌈kaku-teki 比較的 •c [when compared with the general standard], wa⌈riai (ni) 割合(に) [to a greater degree than expected] **《comparatively, in comparison》**

EX. A: How was the summer in Tokyo?
東京の夏はどうでしたか。
Tookyoo no natsu wa doo deshita ka.
B: It was relatively cool.
{比較的/割合}涼しかったです。
{Hikaku-teki/Wariai} suzushikatta desu.

relax vi. **[to become less tense, tight, or strict 《fig. "rest"》]**

ku⌈tsuro⌉gu くつろぐ ① [for s.o. to feel free of physical or psychological tension] **《make oneself comfortable, feel at ease》, ri⌈ra⌉kkusu-suru リラックスする ③ •f, o⌈chitsuku 落ち着く ① [to become less stiff physically or psychologically 《fig. "fix one's residence"》]** **《fix one's residence, recover one's composure, calm down, be steady》 ↔ kinchoo-suru 緊張する ③ •c**

EX. (**a**) A: Can't you relax even on Sunday?
日曜日にも{くつろげない/リラックスできない/*落ち着けない}んですか。
*Nichiyoo-bi ni mo {kutsuroge-nai/rirakkusu-dekinai/*ochitsuke-nai} n desu ka.*
B: Businessmen can't afford to relax, you know.
ビジネスマンは{リラックスする/くつろぐ/*落ち着く}余裕なんかないんだよ。
*Bijinesu-man wa {rirakkusu-suru/kutsurogu/*ochitsuku} yoyuu nanka nai n da yo.*
(**b**) Just relax, Yuriko.
百合子さん、{落ち着いて/?リラックスして/*くつろいで}。

*Yuriko-san, {ochitsuite/?rirakkusu-shite/ *kutsuroide}.*

— vt. **[to make s.t./s.o./s.a. less tense, tight, or strict]**

1. **⟨-o⟩ yu⌈rume⌉ru ⟨～を⟩緩める ② [to cause s.t. to become lax or loose] ⟪loosen, mitigate, relieve⟫ ↔ ⟨-o⟩ shimeru ⟨～を⟩締める ②**

EX. We relaxed the pace of our work over the summer months.
私たちは夏の間仕事のペースを緩めた。
Watashi-tachi wa natsu no aida shigoto no peesu o yurumeta.

2. **⟨-o⟩ ku⌈tsuroga-se⌉ru ⟨～を⟩くつろがせる /⟨causative of *kutsurogu* ① take things easy/ [to cause s.o. to feel free from physical or psychological tension]**

EX. Taking a bath after a day's work will relax you a great deal.
一日の仕事が終わってからの一風呂は人をくつろがせる。
Ichi-nichi no shigoto ga owatte kara no hito-furo wa hito o kutsuroga-seru.

relaxation n. **[the act of relaxing or state of being relaxed]**

kyu⌈uyoo 休養 •c [a relatively long rest] ⟪rest, repose, recreation, recuperation⟫, i⌈kinuki⌉ 息抜き [a relatively short rest or break] ⟪diversion, recreation, respite⟫

EX. Golf is a great source of relaxation for me.
ゴルフは私にはとてもいい{休養/息抜き}になる。
Gorufu wa watashi ni wa totemo ii {kyuuyoo/ikinuki} ni naru.

relay n. **[a fresh group of individuals replacing a prior group, esp. in a race; a race conducted in this way; a device that receives and passes on broadcast signals]**

1. **ri⌈ree リレー •f [a race where different members of a term successively take over from one another]**

2. **chu⌈ukei 中継 •c [passing on broadcast signals from one station to another] ⟪relay broadcasting⟫**

release vt. **[to set s.o./s.a./s.t. free]**

1. **⟨-o⟩ ha⌈na⌉su ⟨～を⟩放す ① [for s.o. to let s.t./s.o./s.a. go] ⟪let go, unloose, disengage⟫ ↔ ⟨-o⟩ tsukamaeru ⟨～を⟩捕まえる ②**

EX. Alex released his grasp on Mary's hand.
アレックスはつかんでいたメアリーの手を放した。
Arekkusu wa tsukande ita Mearii no te o hanashita.

2. **⟨-o⟩ ⟨-kara⟩ ka⌈ihoo-suru ⟨～を⟩⟨～から⟩解放する ③ •c [for s.o. to free s.o./s.t./s.a. from bondage or restrictions] ⟪set free, discharge, parole⟫**

EX. I was very glad when I was released from my duties as committee chairman.
委員長の仕事から解放された時にはとても嬉しかった。
Iin-choo no shigoto kara kaihoo-sareta toki ni wa totemo ureshikatta.

3. **⟨-o⟩ ⟨-kara⟩ sha⌈kuhoo-suru ⟨～を⟩⟨～から⟩釈放する ③ •c [for s.o. to set s.o. free from prison] ⟪set free, discharge, parole⟫**

EX. A lot of people objected to the criminal being released from prison.
犯罪者が刑務所から釈放されることに大勢の人が反対した。
Hanzai-sha ga keimu-sho kara shakuhoo-sareru koto ni oozei no hito ga hantai-shita.

4. **⟨-o⟩ fu⌈u-gi⌉ru ⟨～を⟩封切る ① [to allow a film to be seen by the public for the first time], ⟨-o⟩ ha⌈tsubai-suru ⟨～を⟩発売する ③ •c [to put s.t. on the market for the first time] ⟪sell, put on the market⟫, ⟨-o⟩ ha⌈ppyoo-suru ⟨～を⟩発表する ③ •c [for s.o. to make s.t. known or available to the public, such as factual information, an opinion, a literary/artistic work, or a piece of technology] ⟪announce, publish, issue⟫**

EX. (**a**) When are they going to release Kurosawa's new film?
黒沢の新しい映画はいつ{封切られます/*発売されます/*発表されます}か。
*Kurosawa no atarashii eiga wa itsu {fuu-gira-remasu/*hatsubai-saremasu/ *happyoo-saremasu} ka.*
(**b**) A new CD of the Beatles' best-loved songs has recently been released.

ビートルズの最も親しまれている曲の入った新しいCDが最近{発売された/*封切られた/*発表された}。
*Biitoruzu no mottomo shitashima-rete iru kyoku no haitta atarashii shii-dii ga saikin {hatsubai-sareta/*fuu-gira-reta/*happyoo-sareta}.*
(c) A White House spokesman released the details of the President's plan to visit Japan.
ホワイトハウスのスポークスマンが大統領の日本訪問の予定の詳細を{発表した/*封切った/*発売した}。
*Howaito Hausu no supookusu-man ga daitooryoo no Nihon-hoomon no yotei no shoosai o {happyoo-shita/*fuu-gitta/*hatsubai-shita}.*

— n. **[the act of setting s.o./s.a./s.t. free or s.t. which has recently been made available to the public]**

1. ka⌈ihoo 解放 •c [the act of freeing s.o./s.t./s.a. from bondage or restrictions] ⦅**liberation, disengagement**⦆, **sha⌈kuhoo 釈放 •c [the act of setting s.o. free from prison]** ⦅**discharge, liberation**⦆

EX. The release of prisoners of war took place yesterday as agreed upon.
きのう予定通り捕虜の{釈放/解放}があった。
Kinoo yotei-doori horyo no {shakuhoo/kaihoo} ga atta.

2. fu⌉u-giri 封切り [the first public showing of a new film]

EX. When is the public release of the film scheduled?
その映画の封切りはいつの予定ですか。
Sono eiga no fuu-giri wa itsu no yotei desu ka.

3. ha⌈tsubai 発売 •c [the act of putting s.t. on the market for the first time]

EX. March 1 is the date set for the release of the author's new book.
その著者の新しい本の発売は三月一日になっている。
Sono chosha no atarashii hon no hatsubai wa san-gatsu tsuitachi ni natte iru.

4. ha⌈ppyoo 発表 •c [the act of making s.t. known or available to the public, esp. factual information] ⦅**announcement, publication, statement**⦆

EX. The release of the news of the Emperor's death was made by the Imperial Household Agency.
天皇陛下の崩御の発表は宮内庁によってなされた。
Tennoo-heika no hoogyo no happyoo wa Kunai-choo ni-yotte nasa-reta.

relief n. **[the easing of physical or psychological pain or s.t. that eases this]**

1. ⟨-o⟩ ka⌈ruku suru koto ⟨〜を⟩軽くすること [the act of making s.t. less heavy], ⟨-o⟩ ya⌈warage⌉ru koto ⟨〜を⟩和らげること [the act of easing s.t., esp. pain]

EX. The relief of pain is critical in treating cancer patients.
がん患者の治療では苦痛を{軽くする/和らげる}ことが大事だ。
Gan-kanja no chiryoo de wa kutsuu o {karuku suru/yawarageru} koto ga daiji da.

2. ho⌈tto-shita kimochi ほっとした気持ち [the feeling of being relieved]

EX. When the doctor told me that nothing was wrong with me, I felt a great sense of relief.
医者が何でもないと言った時に私は本当にほっとした気持でした。
Isha ga nan-demo nai to itta toki ni watashi wa hontoo ni hotto-shita kimochi deshita.

3. kyu⌉ujo 救助 •c [the act of saving s.o. from disaster or poverty] ⦅**rescue, assistance, aid**⦆

EX. They extended a hand of relief to the earthquake victims.
地震の被害者に救助の手を差し伸べた。
Jishin no higai-sha ni kyuujo no te o sashi-nobeta.

religion n.

shu⌉ukyoo 宗教 •c

EX. A: What is your religion?
あなたの宗教は何ですか。
Anata no shuukyoo wa nan desu ka.

R

B: I believe in Christianity.
キリスト教を信じています。
Kirisuto-kyoo o shinjite imasu.

religious adj. **[pertaining to religion ⟪fig. "extremely faithful or scrupulous"⟫]**

1. shu˥ukyoo no N 宗教のN •c [pertaining to religion]

EX. Most Japanese do not take religious matters very seriously.
大抵の日本人は宗教のことをあまり真剣に考えない。
Taitei no Nihon-jin wa shuukyoo no koto o amari shinkenni kangaenai.

2. shi˹njin-buka˥i 信心深い adj(*i*). **[very devout] ⟪devout, pious, faithful⟫**

EX. My grandmother was a very religious person.
私の祖母は大変信心深い人でした。
Watashi no sobo wa taihen shinjin-bukai hito deshita.

3. ryo˹oshin-tekina 良心的な adj(*na*). **•c [conforming to one's conscience] ⟪scrupulous, conscientious⟫, shu˹ukyoo-tekina 宗教的な** adj(*na*). **•c [having the characteristics of religious faith]**

EX. The mayor rebuilt the city with a religious fervor.
市長は{良心的な/宗教的な}熱意で町を建て直した。
Shichoo wa {ryooshin-tekina/shuukyoo-tekina} netsui de machi o tate-naoshita.

reluctant adj. **[unwilling to do s.t.]**
⟨-ni⟩ ki˹nori ga shinai ⟨〜に⟩気乗りがしない [for the speaker or s.o. the speaker identifies with to feel disinclined to do s.t.], ki ga hi˹keru 気が引ける ② [for s.o. to feel bad about imposing in some way on others] ⟪feel embarrassed⟫

EX. (**a**) I'm reluctant to take on a part-time job while taking a full load of college courses.
大学で科目を目一杯とっているからアルバイトはあまり{気乗りがしません/*気が引けます}。
*Daigaku de kamoku o me-ippai totte iru kara arubaito wa amari {kinori ga shimasen/*ki ga hikemasu}.*
(**b**) I don't know why, but David is reluctant to study Japanese.
どうしてか分かりませんが、デビッドは日本語の勉強に{気乗りがしない/*気が引ける}ようです。
*Dooshite ka wakarimasen ga, Debiddo wa Nihon-go no benkyoo ni {kinori ga shinai/*ki ga hikeru} yoodesu.*
(**c**) I was reluctant to let him pay for my lunch, but he insisted.
彼に昼をおごってもらうのは{気が引けた/気乗りがしなかった}のだが、彼はおごると言って聞かなかった。
Kare ni hiru o ogotte morau no wa {ki ga hiketa/kinori ga shinakatta} no da ga, kare wa ogoru to itte kikanakatta.

reluctantly adv. **[against one's will]**
shi˹bu-shibu(-nagara) 渋々(ながら) ↔ susunde 進んで

EX. My teacher reluctantly agreed to extend the deadline on my paper for another week.
先生は渋々(ながら)私の論文の締切をあと一週間延ばすことを承諾してくださった。
Sensei wa shibu-shibu(-nagara) watashi no ronbun no shimekiri o ato is-shuukan nobasu koto o shoodaku-shite kudasatta.

rely vi. **[for s.o. to have complete confidence in s.o./s.t./s.a.]**

1. ⟨-o⟩ ta˥yori ni suru ⟨〜を⟩頼りにする ③ [for s.o./s.a. to trust and depend on s.o.] ⟪depend on, count on, lean on, reckon on⟫, ⟨-o⟩ shi˹nrai-suru ⟨〜を⟩信頼する ③ •c [for s.o. to believe s.o./s.t. to be truthful, reliable, or strong and able to be depended on] ⟪depend on, confide in, trust⟫

EX. Your boss seems to rely on you a great deal.
君の上司は君をとても{頼りに/信頼}しているようだね。
Kimi no jooshi wa kimi o totemo {tayori ni/shinrai-} shite iru yooda ne.

2. ⟨-ni⟩ ta˹yo˥ru ⟨〜に⟩頼る ① [for s.o. to entrust oneself to s.o./s.t. in the belief that one will receive aid or support from him/her/it] ⟪depend on, count on, lean on, trust⟫

EX. (a) Stop relying on others and rely more on yourself.
人に頼るのはやめて、もっと自分自身を信頼しなさい。
Hito ni tayoru no wa yamete, motto jibun-jishin o shinrai-shinasai.
(b) That old man has to rely on his cane to get around.
あの老人は歩くのにつえに頼らなければならない。
Ano roojin wa aruku no ni tsue ni tayoranakereba naranai.

NOTE: In Japanese, *tayoru* carries a negative implication of "leaning on others" which is absent in the English "rely on."

remain vi. **[to be left over or left behind or to be in the same situation or condition as before]**
1. no⌈ko⌉ru 残る ① [to remain untaken, unused, unchanged, uneaten, etc., in a particular condition or position] ((**be left, stay**))

EX. We've eaten our fill, but there still remains lots of food.
おなかいっぱい食べたのに、まだ沢山食べ物が残っています。
Onaka ippai tabeta noni, mada takusan tabe-mono ga nokotte imasu.

2. 〈-no〉 ma⌈ma⌉ de iru 〈〜の〉ままでいる ② [for an already existing situation or condition to stay the same], ma⌉da まだ [in a manner unchanged from before] ((**still, (not) yet**))

EX. (a) Dorothy remained unmarried until she was 43 years old.
ドロシーは四十三歳になるまで独身のままでいた。
Doroshii wa yon-juu-san-sai ni naru made dokushin no mama de ita.
(b) It's April, but the weather here still remains cold.
四月なのに、ここの気候はまだ寒い。
Shi-gatsu na noni, koko no kikoo wa mada samui.

PHRASE: It remains to be seen if Sinf. *ka doo ka wa ato ni natte minai to wakaranai.* Sinf.かどうかは後になってみないと分からない。

EX. It remains to be seen if my theory proves to be correct.
私の理論が正しいかどうかは後になってみないと分からない。
Watashi no riron ga tadashii ka doo ka wa ato ni natte minai to wakaranai.

—— n. **[s.t. which is left or a dead body]**
1. no⌈kori-mono⌉ 残り物 [s.t. which is left over] ((**leftovers, scraps**))
2. i⌈tai 遺体 •c [a polite word for corpse] ((**dead body, corpse**)), **shi⌈tai 死体 •c [dead body]** ((**corpse**))

remainder n. **[the part of a whole or of a group that is left behind]**
1. no⌈kori⌉ 残り /〈V*masu* of *nokoru* ① remain/ ((**leftovers, leavings**))

EX. We spent the remainder of the summer in Manila.
私たちは夏の残りをマニラで過ごした。
Watashi-tachi wa natsu no nokori o Manira de sugoshita.

remark vt./vi. **[for s.o. to make a brief comment about s.t. in speaking or writing]**
1. 〈-to〉 i⌈u 〈〜と〉言う ① [for s.o. to express s.t. verbally] ((**say, observe, tell, mention, talk, speak**))

EX. When I showed him my son's painting, Mr. Smith remarked what a splendid picture it was.
息子の絵を見せたら、スミス氏はすばらしい絵だと言ってくれた。
Musuko no e o misetara, Sumisu-shi wa subarashii e da to itte kureta.

2. 〈-to〉 ka⌉ku 〈〜と〉かく ① [for s.o. to make a short line on a surface with a pointed object] ((**write, draw a picture, scratch**))
㊅ "write"▷書く, "scratch/draw a picture,"▷かく

EX. Rosa remarked in her diary how beautiful the college campus was in the spring.
ローザは春の大学のキャンパスがいかにきれいか日記に書いた。
Rooza wa haru no daigaku no kyanpasu ga ikani kirei ka nikki ni kaita.

R

— n. **[a brief comment made in speaking or writing]**
i⌉ken 意見 •c [an idea or judgment one holds about a matter] ⟪opinion, view, idea, suggestion⟫

EX. I was intrigued by the remarks of my guests from Russia on the world financial situation.
ロシアからのお客さんの世界の金融情勢に関する意見は非常におもしろいと思った。
Roshia kara no o-kyaku-san no sekai no kin'yuu-joosei ni-kansuru iken wa hijooni omoshiroi to omotta.

remarkable adj. **[worthy of notice ⟪fig. "wonderful"⟫]**
1. chu⌈umoku-sube⌉ki N 注目すべきN •c [worthy of notice ⟨w⟩]

EX. The most remarkable invention of this century is no doubt the computer.
今世紀の最も注目すべき発明はコンピューターにちがいない。
Kon-seiki no mottomo chuumoku-subeki hatsumei wa konpyuutaa ni chigai-nai.

2. su⌈barashi⌉i すばらしい adj(*i*). **[causing great wonder/admiration/pleasure due to being extremely good] ⟪wonderful, splendid, grand, excellent⟫, su⌈gu⌉reta N 優れたN /⟨Vinf. past of *sugureru* ② excell/ [better than s.t./s.o./s.a. in ability/skill] ⟪superior, surpassing, excellent, superb⟫**

EX. Chomsky has made some remarkable contributions to the field of psychology as well as that of linguistics.
チョムスキーは言語学だけでなく心理学の分野でも{すばらしい/優れた}貢献をしている。
Chomusukii wa gengo-gaku dake denaku shinri-gaku no bun'ya demo {subarashii/sugureta} kooken o shite iru.

remedy n. **[s.t. that cures disease or corrects an evil]**
1. chi⌈ryoo(-hoo) 治療(法) •c [(a method of) caring for an illness or injury for the purpose of bringing about recovery or healing] ⟪treatment⟫

EX. A: What is the best remedy for colds?
風邪の一番いい治療(法)は何ですか。
Kaze no ichiban ii chiryoo(-hoo) wa nan desu ka.
B: The best remedy is to get plenty of rest.
一番いい治療(法)は十分休むことです。
Ichi-ban ii chiryoo(-hoo) wa juubun yasumu koto desu.

2. ka⌈iketsu⌉-saku 解決策 •c [a method or means for dealing with an undesirable situation]

EX. Is there any effective remedy for the economic slump Japan is in now?
日本の現在の経済不況に有効な解決策はありますか。
Nihon no genzai no keizai-fukyoo ni yuukoona kaiketsu-saku wa arimasu ka.

— vt. **[to cure disease or to correct an evil]**
1. ⟨-o⟩ i⌈ya⌉su ⟨〜を⟩いやす ① •c [to cure disease or pain] ⟪heal, cure⟫

EX. Two weeks' vacation in the Bahamas was enough to remedy the extreme stress I was experiencing.
バハマでの二週間の休暇はたまっていた強度のストレスをいやすのに十分だった。
Bahama de no ni-shuukan no kyuuka wa tamatte ita kyoodo no sutoresu o iyasu no ni juubun datta.

2. ⟨-o⟩ ka⌈izen-suru ⟨〜を⟩改善する ③ •c [for s.o. to make living/working conditions better] ⟪correct, rectify, redress⟫

EX. It is very difficult to remedy a bad social system.
悪い社会制度を改善することは難しい。
Warui shakai-seido o kaizen-suru koto wa muzukashii.

remember vt. **[for s.o. to keep s.t. in one's mind or bring back s.t. to mind]**
1. ⟨-o⟩ o⌈moi-da⌉su ⟨〜を⟩思い出す ① [for s.o./s.a. to bring s.t./s.o./s.a. to one's memory] ⟪recollect, recall⟫

EX. (a) A: Do you remember where you left your umbrella?
傘をどこに置いてきたか覚えてる?

Kasa o doko ni oite kita ka oboete-ru?
B: No, I can't remember.
いや、思い出せないんだ。
Iya, omoi-dase-nai n da.
(b) I can't remember the name of the store.
店の名前が思い出せません。
Mise no namae ga omoi-dase-masen.

2. ⟨-o⟩ o⌈boe⌉ru ⟨〜を⟩覚える ② [for s.o./s.a. to sense s.t. in one's body or mind and as a result come to have it in one's mind] ⟪memorize, learn, feel⟫

EX. Japanese names are easy to remember.
日本人の名前は覚えやすい。
Nihon-jin no namae wa oboe-yasui.

3. ⟨-o⟩ oboete iru ⟨〜を⟩覚えている /⟨V*te iru* of *oboeru* ② memorize/ ② [for s.o./s.a. to keep s.o./s.t./s.a. in one's mind]

EX. Do you still remember me?
私のことをまだ覚えていますか。
Watashi no koto o mada oboete imasu ka.

PHRASE: Remember me to s.o. *⟨-ni⟩ yoroshiku (o-tsutae kudasai).* ⟨〜に⟩よろしく(お伝え下さい)。

PHRASE: If I remember correctly, *Watashi no kioku ni machigai ga nakereba* 私の記憶に間違いがなければ, *Tashika* 確か

EX. If I remember correctly, Hanako's birthday is April 1.
花子さんの誕生日は{私の記憶に間違いがなければ/確か}四月一日です。
Hanako-san no tanjoo-bi wa {watashi no kioku ni machigai ga nakereba/tashika} shi-gatsu tsuitachi desu.

remembrance n. **[an instance of remembering or being remembered or s.t. that causes one to remember s.t./s.o./s.a.]**

1. o⌈moi-de 思い出 [s.t. about the past that is retained in one's mind, esp. a pleasant event] ⟪memory, recollection⟫

EX. The fondest remembrance of my college years is dancing with you that winter evening.
学生時代の一番楽しい思い出はあの冬の晩、君と踊ったことだ。
Gakusei-jidai no ichiban tanoshii omoi-de wa ano fuyu no ban, kimi to odotta koto da.

2. ki⌈nen 記念 •c [s.t. that one retains in order to remember s.t. by or the act of renewing one's memory of an event] ⟪commemoration, memory⟫

EX. Please accept this as a remembrance of your stay in Kyoto.
京都にいらした記念にこれを差し上げます。
Kyooto ni irashita kinen ni kore o sashi-agemasu.

remind vt. **[to cause s.o. to bring s.t./s.o./s.a. to mind]**

1. ⟨-o⟩{mi⌉ru/ki⌈ku} to ⟨-o⟩ o⌈moi-da⌉su ⟨〜を⟩{見る/聞く}と⟨〜を⟩思い出す ① [for s.o. to think of s.t./s.o./s.a. when one sees/hears s.t./s.o./s.a.]

EX. (a) Mary reminds me of my cat.
メアリーを見ると私の猫を思い出します。
Mearii o miru to watashi no neko o omoi-dashimasu.
(b) Hearing this Brahms symphony reminds me of the summer of 1980 when I first dated Rosetta.
このブラームスのシンフォニーを聞くとロゼッタと初めてデートした1980年の夏を思い出す。
Kono Buraamusu no shinfonii o kiku to Rozetta to hajimete deeto-shita sen-kyuu-hyaku-hachi-juu-nen no natsu o omoi-dasu.

2. ⟨-no⟩ ko⌈to⌉ o chu⌉ui-suru ⟨〜の⟩ことを注意する ③ •c [for s.o. to see to it that no danger, negligence, excessiveness, or failure occurs with regard to s.t.] ⟪pay attention, be careful, guard against, counsel, warn, admonish⟫

EX. I'm very forgetful, so could you remind me later of the deadline?
私は忘れっぽいですから、後で締切のことを注意して下さいませんか。
Watashi wa wasure-ppoi desu kara, ato de shime-kiri no koto o chuui-shite kudasaimasen ka.

remote adj. **[distant in place/time/ connection ⟨fml⟩]**
to⌈oi 遠い adj(*i*). **⟪far, distant⟫ ↔ chikai 近い** adj(*i*).

EX. (**a**) Why do you live in such a remote place?
どうしてこんな遠いところに住んでいらっしゃるんですか。
Dooshite konna tooi tokoro ni sunde irassharu n desu ka.
(**b**) A: You should think more about your future, you know.
将来のことをもっと考えなくっちゃ駄目だよ。
Shoorai no koto o motto kangaenakutcha dame da yo.
B: I don't have time to think about things that remote.
そんな遠い将来のことなど考える暇がないんですよ。
Sonna tooi shoorai no koto nado kangaeru hima ga nai n desu yo.
(**c**) Tom is a remote relation of mine.
トムは僕の遠い親せきなんです。
Tomu wa boku no tooi shinseki na n desu.

remove vt. **[to take s.o./s.a./s.t. away from or off of some place or to get rid of s.t.]**
1. **⟨-o⟩ {⟨-ni⟩/⟨-e⟩} u⌈tsu⌉su ⟨〜を⟩{⟨〜に⟩/⟨〜へ⟩}うつす** ① **[to cause s.o./s.t./s.a. to change to a different location or into a different condition ⟪fig. "copy," "reflect," "infect," "take a picture"⟫] ⟪transfer, pour, carry⟫**
㊅ "remove physically"▷移す, "photograph/copy"▷写す, "project an image on the surface of a screen/water"▷映す

EX. Let's remove this sofa from the family room.
このソファーを居間から移しましょう。
Kono sofaa o ima kara utsushimashoo.

2. **⟨-o⟩ to⌈ri-nozoku ⟨〜を⟩取り除く** ① **[to eliminate s.t. undesirable from a place] ⟪set apart, get rid of⟫, ⟨-o⟩ ha⌈zusu ⟨〜を⟩外す** ① **[for s.o. to take s.t. off from s.t. on which it is hung or to which it is attached (and where it normally belongs)] ⟪take off, unfasten, detach⟫**

EX. (**a**) The doctor removed an egg-sized tumor from the neck of the patient.
医者は卵大のしゅようを患者の首から{取り除いた/*外した}。
*Isha wa tamago-dai no shuyoo o kanja no kubi kara {tori-nozoita/*hazushita}.*
(**b**) Can you remove this lid for me, Bill?
ビル、このふた、{外して/*取り除いて}くれる?
*Biru, kono futa, {hazushite/*tori-nozoite} kureru?*

renaissance n.
bu⌈ngei-fu⌉kkoo 文芸復興 •c, ru⌈ne⌉s(s)ansu ルネ(ッ)サンス •f

render vt. **[to cause s.t. to be changed into a different form or condition or for s.o. to give or present s.t. to s.o., esp. s.t. that is owed]**
1. **⟨-o⟩ {⟨-ni⟩/adj(*i*). *ku*/adj(*na*). *ni*} su⌈ru ⟨〜を⟩{⟨〜に⟩/adj(*i*). *ku*/adj(*na*). *ni*}する** ③ **[to cause s.t./s.o./s.a. to change into a different form or state]**

EX. Render the following Japanese into English.
次の日本語を英語にしなさい。
Tsugi no Nihon-go o eigo ni shinasai.

2. **⟨-no⟩ ta⌈me⌉ ni {Vinf. nonpast yo⌉o ni/adj(*i*). *ku*/adj(*na*). *ni*} na⌉ru ⟨〜の⟩ために{Vinf. nonpastように/adj(*i*). *ku*/adj(*na*). *ni*}なる [for s.t./s.o./s.a. to change into a different form or state owing to some cause]**

EX. The illness rendered Kazuko incapable of moving about on her own.
病気のために和子は自分では動けなくなった。
Byooki no tame ni Kazuko wa jibun de wa ugoke-naku natta.

3. **⟨-ni⟩ ⟨-o⟩ a⌈taeru ⟨〜に⟩⟨〜を⟩与える** ② **[for s.o. to cause/let s.o. have s.t.]**

EX. The church rendered assistance to the victims of the earthquake.
教会は地震の被害者に援助を与えた。
Kyookai wa jishin no higai-sha ni enjo o ataeta.

renew vt. **[for s.o. to restore s.t. to its original state or amount or to cause s.t. to**

continue (to be valid) for a period of time]
1. ⟨-o⟩ ko┌oshin-suru ⟨〜を⟩更新する ③ •c [for s.o. to turn s.t. already existing into a new state, such as a record (in sports, etc.) or institution, or to extend the period for which s.t. is valid, such as a contract or subscription] ⟪renovate, innovate, break a record⟫

EX. Since my visa has expired, I have to renew it.
ビザが切れたので更新しなければならない。
Biza ga kireta node kooshin-shinakereba naranai.

2. ⟨-o⟩ shi┌npin no yo┐o ni suru ⟨〜を⟩新品のようにする ③ [for s.o. to make s.t. appear brand new]

EX. Polishing the rusty kettle renewed its luster.
さびのついたやかんを磨いて、そのつやを新品のようにした。
Sabi no tsuita yakan o migaite, sono tsuya o shinpin no yooni shita.

renovate vt. **[for s.o. to repair s.t. major or restore it to a new or original state]**
1. ⟨-o⟩ a┌tara┐shiku-suru ⟨〜を⟩新しくする ③ [for s.o. to make s.t. new]

EX. The old equipment in this factory is in dire need of being renovated.
この工場のどうしようもない古い設備を一日も早く新しくしなければならない。
Kono koojoo no doo shiyoo mo nai furui setsubi o ichi-nichi mo hayaku atarashiku shinakereba naranai.

2. ⟨-o⟩ shu┐uri-suru ⟨〜を⟩修理する ③ •c [for s.o. to fix s.t. which is out of order, such as machinery, hardware, etc.] ⟪repair, mend⟫ ⟨-o⟩ ka┌ichiku-suru ⟨〜を⟩改築する ③ •c [for s.o. to remodel a building] ⟪rebuild, reconstruct, remodel⟫, ⟨-o⟩ ka┌izoo-suru ⟨〜を⟩改造する ③ •c [for s.o. to rebuild the defective parts of a machine, building, or organization] ⟪remodel, reconstruct, restructure⟫

EX. (**a**) We are currently renovating our dormitories.
現在、寮を{修理/改築/改造}しているところです。
Genzai, ryoo o {shuuri/kaichiku/kaizoo}-shite iru tokoro desu.
(**b**) The prime minister announced at the press conference his intention of renovating his cabinet in the fall.
総理大臣は記者会見で秋には内閣を{改造/*修理/*改築}するつもりだと述べた。
*Soori-daijin wa kisha-kaiken de aki ni wa naikaku o {kaizoo/*shuuri/*kaichiku}-suru tsumori da to nobeta.*

renovation n. **[the act of repairing s.t. major or of restoring it to a new or original state]**
1. sa┌sshin 刷新 •c [the act of making an organization entirely new] ⟪reform, innovation⟫

EX. The scandal eventually led to the renovation of the party's leadership structure.
スキャンダルは最終的にその政党の指導部の刷新につながった。
Sukyandaru wa saishuu-tekini sono seitoo no shidoo-bu no sasshin ni tsunagatta.

2. shu┐uri 修理 •c [the act of fixing s.t. which is out of order, such as machinery, hardware, etc.] ⟪repair, mending⟫, ka┌ichiku 改築 •c [the act of remodeling a building] ⟪reconstruction, remodeling⟫, ka┌izoo 改造 •c [the act of rebuilding the defective parts of a machine, building, or organization] ⟪remodeling, reconstruction, rebuilding⟫

EX. (**a**) The renovation of the dorms took five years.
寮の{修理/改築/改造}に五年かかった。
Ryoo no {shuuri/kaichiku/kaizoo} ni go-nen kakatta.
(**b**) The government seems to be considering a renovation of its cabinet.
政府は内閣の{改造/*修理/*改築}を考えているようだ。
*Seifu wa naikaku no {kaizoo/*shuuri/*kaichiku} o kangaete iru yooda.*

rent n. **[the amount paid by s.o. for the use of s.t., esp. living quarters]**
ya┐chin 家賃 •c [the amount paid by s.o.

R

for use of a living space, normally larger than one room], he⌈ya-dai 部屋代 [the amount paid by s.o. for use of a room, usu. to live in], a⌈paato-dai アパート代 •f+c [the amount paid by s.o. for use of an apartment to live in]

EX. A: How much is the rent for this place?
ここの{家賃/部屋代/アパート代}はいくらですか。
Koko no {yachin/heya-dai/apaato-dai} wa ikura desu ka.
B: It's 50,000 yen a month.
一か月五万円です。
Ik-kagetsu go-man-en desu.

PHRASE: house for rent *kashi-ya* 貸家

— vt. **[for s.o. to obtain or give the right to occupy or use s.t. in return for regular payments]**

1. ka⌈ne o ha⌈ra⌉tte ⟨-o⟩ ka⌈riru 金を払って⟨〜を⟩借りる ② [for s.o. to obtain the right to occupy or use s.t. in return for regular payments] ⟪lease⟫

R

EX. (**a**) I rented a TV over the summer.
夏の間、金を払ってテレビを借りた。
Natsu no aida, kane o haratte terebi o karita.
(**b**) In America you can rent practically anything.
アメリカでは全く何でも金を払って借りることが出来る。
Amerika de wa mattaku nan-demo kane o haratte kariru koto ga dekiru.

rent-a-car n.
re⌈nta⌉-kaa レンタカー •f

EX. Last weekend I took a trip to Osaka in a rent-a-car.
先週末レンタカーで大阪に行ってきました。
Senshuu-matsu renta-kaa de Oosaka ni itte kimashita.

repair vt. **[for s.o. to put s.t. into good condition again after it has been damaged, injured, or worn down]**

1. ⟨-o⟩ na⌈o⌉su ⟨〜を⟩なおす ① [for s.o. to make the damaged part of s.t. right ⟪fig. "cure"⟫] ⟪mend, fix, correct⟫ ↔ ⟨-o⟩ kowasu ⟨〜を⟩壊す ①; ⟨-o⟩ shu⌈uzen-suru ⟨〜を⟩修繕する ③ •c [for s.o. to fix s.t. small and simple, esp. an item of daily household use] ⟪mend, doctor, refit⟫, ⟨-o⟩ shu⌉uri-suru ⟨〜を⟩修理する ③ [for s.o. to fix s.t. which is out of order, such as machinery, hardware, etc.]

㊥ "cure disease/injury"▷治す, "mend s.t."▷直す

EX. (**a**) Mr. Jones next door kindly repaired our broken door for us.
隣のジョーンズさんが親切にうちの壊れたドアを{直して/修繕して/修理して}くれました。
Tonari no Joonzu-san ga shinsetsuni uchi no kowareta doa o {naoshite/shuuzen-shite/shuuri-shite} kuremashita.
(**b**) The doctor repaired my broken bone.
医者は骨折した所を{治して/*修理して/*修繕して}くれました。
*Isha wa kossetsu-shita tokoro o {naoshite/*shuuri-shite/*shuuzen-shite} kuremashita.*

NOTE: Unlike English "repair," Japanese *naosu* can be used in the medical sense to cover both the meaning of "repair an injury" and "cure a disease."

— n. **[the act of putting s.t. into good condition again after it has been damaged, injured, or worn down]**

shu⌈uzen 修繕 •c [the act of fixing s.t. small and simple, esp. an item of daily household use] ⟪mending, refit⟫, shu⌉uri 修理 •c [the act of fixing s.t. which is out of order, such as machinery, hardware, etc.] ⟪mending, refit⟫

EX. (**a**) Car repairs have cost us a lot of money this year.
今年は車の{修理/?修繕}にお金が沢山かかった。
Kotoshi wa kuruma no {shuuri/?shuuzen} ni o-kane ga takusan kakatta.
(**b**) This sewing machine needs repair.
このミシンは{修繕/修理}が必要だ。

Kono mishin wa {shuuzen/shuuri} ga hitsuyoo da.

repeat vt. **[for s.o. to say or do the same thing more than once]**
⟨-o⟩ ku⌈ri-kaesu ⟨～を⟩繰り返す ① [for s.o. to do the same thing more than once], ⟨-o⟩ ku⌈ri-kaeshite iu ⟨～を⟩繰り返して言う ① [for s.o. to say the same thing more than once]

EX. (**a**) Our Japanese teacher asked us to repeat the word.
日本語の先生は私たちに同じ言葉を{繰り返す/繰り返して言う}ようにおっしゃった。
Nihon-go no sensei wa watashi-tachi ni onaji kotoba o {kuri-kaesu/kuri-kaeshite iu} yooni osshatta.
(**b**) History repeats itself.
歴史は繰り返す。
Rekishi wa kuri-kaesu.

repetition n. **[the act of repeating s.t.]**
ku⌈ri-kaeshi 繰り返し /⟨V*masu* of *kuri-kaesu* ① repeat/, ha⌈npuku 反復 •c [the act of doing the same thing again and again] ⟪reiteration⟫

EX. Human life is full of repetition.
人生には{繰り返し/反復}が多い。
Jinsei ni wa {kuri-kaeshi/hanpuku} ga ooi.

replace vt. **[for s.o. to put s.t. back in its original place or to take or fill a position s.t./s.o./s.a. else used to occupy]**
1. ⟨-ni⟩ to⌉tte-kawaru ⟨～に⟩取って代わる ① [to take a position s.t./s.o./s.a. else used to occupy] ⟪take another's place, supplant, supersede⟫, ⟨-no⟩ ko⌈oke⌉i-sha ni na⌉ru ⟨～の⟩後継者になる ① [for s.o. to become s.o.'s successor] ⟪succeed⟫

EX. (**a**) Compact discs have almost completely replaced traditional records.
コンパクトディスクは百パーセント近く昔からのレコード{に取って代わった/*の後継者になった}。
*Konpakuto-disuku wa hyaku-paasento chikaku mukashi kara no rekoodo {ni totte-kawatta/*no kookei-sha ni natta}.*
(**b**) I wonder who's going to replace the president of the company.
だれが社長{に取って代わる/の後継者になる}のだろう。
Dare ga shachoo {ni totte-kawaru/no kookeisha ni naru} no daroo.

2. ⟨-o⟩ ⟨-to⟩ to⌈ri-kaeru ⟨～を⟩⟨～と⟩取り替える ② [for s.o. to put or obtain s.t. in the place of or in return for s.t. else] ⟪exchange, swap⟫

EX. Can you replace the broken window here with a new one?
この壊れた窓を新しいのと取り替えてくれませんか。
Kono kowareta mado o atarashii no to tori-kaete kuremasen ka.

replacement n. **[an act/instance of replacing s.t./s.o. or s.o./s.t. that replaces s.o./s.t. else]**
1. mo⌉to e mo⌉do⌉su koto 元へ戻すこと [an act of putting s.t. back in its original place]
2. ko⌈ota⌉i-sha 交代者 •c [a person who replaces s.o. else], ka⌈wari no hi⌉to 代わりの人 [a person who replaces s.o. else]
3. to⌈ri-kae 取り替え /⟨V*masu* of *tori-kaeru* ② exchange/ [the act of exchanging]

reply vi. **[for s.o. to answer s.o./s.t. in speech, writing, or action, or to say s.t. in answer to s.o. ⟨fml⟩]**
⟨-ni⟩ ko⌈tae⌉ru ⟨～に⟩こたえる ② [for s.o. to say or do s.t. to fulfill a request from s.o. else for information or action; for s.o. to meet a demand or expectation placed on one; to react, usu. in a negative way, to a physical or psychological stimulus such as temperature or stress] ⟪answer, respond, solve⟫, (⟨-ni⟩) ka⌈itoo-suru (⟨～に⟩)回答する ③ •c [to respond formally to a question] ⟪answer, respond⟫, (⟨-ni⟩) he⌈nji⌉ o suru (⟨～に⟩)返事をする ③ •c [for s.o. to respond in speech or writing to some auditory or written stimulus, such as a letter, written question, or oral greeting] ⟪respond⟫
㊫ "respond verbally"▷答える, otherwise ▷こたえる

EX. (**a**) I asked her his name but she didn't reply.

R

彼女に彼の名前を聞いたが、{答えなかった/*返事をしなかった/*回答しなかった}。
*Kanojo ni kare no namae o kiita ga, {kotaenakatta/*henji o shinakatta/ *kaitoo-shinakatta}.*
(**b**) I knocked on the door but nobody replied.
ドアをノックしたが、だれも{返事をしなかった/?答えなかった/*回答しなかった}。
*Doa o nokku-shita ga, dare-mo {henji o shinakatta/?kotaenakatta/*kaitoo-shinakatta}.*
(**c**) The president asked me to reply to the letter from our client.
社長は取引先からの手紙に{返事をする/?回答する/*答える}よう私に頼んだ。
*Shachoo wa torihiki-saki kara no tegami ni {henji o suru/?kaitoo-suru/ *kotaeru} yoo watashi ni tanonda.*
(**d**) The president hasn't replied yet to the union's demand for a pay raise.
社長は組合の賃上げ要求にまだ{回答して/こたえて/返事をして}いない。
Shachoo wa kumiai no chin'age yookyuu ni mada {kaitoo-shite/kotaete/henji o shite} inai.

—— n. **[s.t. which is said, written, or done in answer to s.o./s.t.]**
ko⌈ta⌉e 答え /⟨V*masu* of *kotaeru* ② answer/ [s.t. which is said or written in response to a question or an oral stimulus such as a greeting] ⟪answer⟫, he⌈nji⌉ 返事 •c [an act/ instance of responding in speech or writing to some auditory or written stimulus, such as a letter, written question, or oral greeting] ⟪response, answer⟫, ka⌈itoo 回答 •c [the act of responding formally to a question or letter or s.t. said or written in response to such] ⟪response, answer⟫

EX. (**a**) I received a reply from Mr. Dodge on April 23.
私はドッジ氏から四月二十三日に{返事/回答/?答え}を受け取った。
Watashi wa Dojji-shi kara shi-gatsu ni-juu-san-nichi ni {henji/kaitoo/?kotae} o uke-totta.
(**b**) The replies to my question about whether the pace of the class was too slow were all in the negative.
その授業の進度が遅すぎないかという私の質問への{答え/回答/?返事}はみんな否定的だった。
Sono jugyoo no shindo ga oso-suginai ka to iu watashi no shitsumon e no {kotae/kaitoo/?henji} wa minna hitei-teki datta.

report vt. **[for s.o. to present a formal account of s.t. in speech or writing]**
{⟨-o⟩/⟨-ni-tsuite⟩/⟨-to⟩} ho⌈okoku-suru {⟨～を⟩/⟨～について⟩/⟨～と⟩}報告する ③ •c ⟪inform, give an account of⟫, {⟨-o⟩/⟨-to⟩} ho⌈ojiru {⟨～を⟩/⟨～と⟩}報じる ② •c [to present a formal journalistic account of s.t. ⟨w⟩] ⟪inform, acquaint, communicate, repay⟫

EX. (**a**) Did you report the budget situation to the president?
予算の状況{について/を}社長に{報告しました/*報じました}か。
*Yosan no jookyoo {ni-tsuite/o} shachoo ni {hookoku-shimashita/*hoojimashita} ka.*
(**b**) Every major newspaper reported on its front page the news of the dollar's sharp fall against the yen.
主な新聞はみんなドルが円に対して暴落した{ことを/と}一面で{報じて/*報告して}いた。
*Omona shinbun wa minna doru ga en ni-taishite booraku-shita {koto o/to} ichi-men de {hoojite/*hookoku-shite} ita.*

—— vi. **[for s.o. to present a formal account of s.t. in speech or writing or to present oneself to an authority]**
1. ⟨-ni⟩ ⟨-o⟩ ho⌈okoku-suru ⟨～に⟩⟨～を⟩報告する ③ •c [for s.o. to present a formal account of s.t. to s.o. in speech or writing]

EX. The committee chair has not yet reported to us on the problem of declining applications for admission.

委員長は入学志願者数の減少の問題について我々にまだ報告していない。
Iin-choo wa nyuugaku-shigan-sha-suu no genshoo no mondai ni-tsuite ware-ware ni mada hookoku-shite inai.

2. ⟨**-ni**⟩ **shu⌈ttoo-suru** ⟨〜に⟩出頭する ③ **•c [for s.o. to present oneself to an authority at a designated time and place]**

EX. Please report to the police station by 8:00 A.M. tomorrow.
あした午前八時までに警察署に出頭して下さい。
Ashita gozen hachi-ji made-ni keisatsu sho ni shuttoo-shite kudasai.

—— n. **[a formal account of s.t. presented in speech or writing]**
ho⌈okoku(-sho) 報告(書) **•c ⟪account, statement⟫**, {**re⌈po⌉oto/ri⌈po⌉oto**} {レポート/リポート} **•f [an account, usu. written, of the results of an investigation or research study]**, **ho⌈odoo** 報道 **•c [a journalistic account of s.t.] ⟪information, intelligence, news⟫**

EX. (**a**) I have to finish my report by Monday.
月曜までに{報告(書)/レポート/リポート/*報道}を書かなければならない。
*Getsuyoo made ni {hookoku(-sho)/repooto/ripooto/*hoodoo} o kakanakereba naranai.*
(**b**) Did you read the report in today's paper on the new drug for cancer treatment?
がん治療の新薬に関する今日の新聞の{報道/レポート/リポート/?報告}を読みましたか。
Gan-chiryoo no shin'yaku ni-kansuru kyoo no shinbun no {hoodoo/repooto/ripooto/?hookoku} o yomimashita ka.

reporter n. **[a person who gathers and reports news for publication or broadcast]**
(**shu⌈zai-)kisha⌉** (取材)記者 **•c [a person who gathers and reports news and information for the printed media] ⟪journalist, newspaperman, pressman⟫**, {**re⌈po⌉otaa/ri⌈po⌉otaa**} {レポーター/リポーター} **•f [a person who gathers and reports news and information for publication or broadcast, esp. one who reports directly from the scene of a news event]**

EX. I'm presently working as a reporter for NHK.
私は現在、NHKの{記者/レポーター/リポーター}として働いている。
Watashi wa genzai, Enu-eichi-kei no {kisha/repootaa/ripootaa} to-shite hataraite iru.

NOTE: "NHK" is *Nihon Hoosoo Kyookai* (Japan Broadcasting Corporation).

PHRASE: newspaper reporter *shinbun-kisha* 新聞記者 •c

represent vt. **[to stand for s.t. objectively as a sign, symbol, or picture; for s.o. to portray s.t./s.o./s.a. in symbolic, artistic, or verbal form; for s.o. to act in place of or for a group, esp. in an officially elected capacity]**
1. ⟨**-o**⟩ **a⌈rawa⌉su** ⟨〜を⟩あらわす ① **[to cause s.t. to become exposed/visible/recognizable] ⟪show, indicate, manifest, dispay, exhibit, expose, express, distinguish⟫**, ⟨**-o**⟩ **hyo⌈oge⌉n-suru** ⟨〜を⟩表現する ③ **•c [to make an inward thought or feeling known or perceptible to others in some external symbolic form such as gesture, language, music, painting, etc.] ⟪express, manifest⟫**, ⟨**-o**⟩ **e⌈ga⌉ku** ⟨〜を⟩描く ① **[for s.o. to express s.t./s.o./s.a. using pictures or words or other artistic medium] ⟪draw, picture, paint, express⟫**, ⟨**-o**⟩ **byo⌈osha-suru** ⟨〜を⟩描写する ③ **•c [for s.o./a painting/writing/music to express s.t./s.o./s.a. in an objectively perceptible way] ⟪depict, describe, portray⟫**, ⟨**-o**⟩ **i⌉mi-suru** ⟨〜を⟩意味する ③ **•c [to signify s.t., usu. by linguistic means] ⟪mean, stand for⟫**, ⟨**-o**⟩ **sho⌈ochoo-suru** ⟨〜を⟩象徴する ③ **•c [for s.t. concrete to stand for s.t. abstract] ⟪symbolize⟫**

㊅ "represent/express"▷表わす, "show, display, manifest, expose"▷現わす

EX. (**a**) I don't understand what this painting by Picasso represents.
このピカソの絵が何を{表わして/表現

して/描いて/描写して/意味して/象徴して}いるか分かりません。
Kono pikaso no e ga nani o {arawashite/hyoogen-shite/egaite/byoosha-shite/imi-shite/shoochoo-shite} iru ka wakarimasen.
(**b**) For Christians, the cross represents Christ's death and resurrection.
クリスチャンにとって、十字架はキリストの死と復活を{表わします/象徴します/意味します/??表現します/*描きます/*描写します}。
*Kurisuchan ni-totte, juujika wa Kirisuto no shi to fukkatsu o {arawashimasu/shoochoo-shimasu/imi-shimasu/??hyoogen-shimasu/*egakimasu/*byoosha-shimasu}.*

NOTE: Unlike English "represent," Japanese *arawasu* and *hyoogen-suru*, can be used to mean to "express a subjective feeling such as appreciation, anxiety, joy, etc."

EX. (**c**) I don't know how I can {express/*represent} my feeling of appreciation to you.
感謝の気持ちをどう{表わしたら/表現したら/*描いたら/*描写したら/*意味したら/*象徴したら}いいか分かりません。
*Kansha no kimochi o doo {arawashitara/hyoogen-shitara/*egaitara/*byoosha-shitara/*imi-shitara/*shoochoo-shitara} ii ka wakarimasen.*

2. ⟨-o⟩ da⌈ihyoo-suru ⟨～を⟩代表する ③ •c [for an individual to serve as an example of a class or group of individuals or for s.o. to act or speak on behalf of a group of people as its official delegate] ⟪act for, be a representative of⟫

EX. I will be representing IBM at the White House dinner next week.
来週ホワイトハウスの晩さん会に、私がIBMを代表して出席することになっています。
Raishuu Howaito Hausu no bansan-kai ni, watashi ga Ai-bii-emu o daihyoo-shite shusseki-suru koto ni natte imasu.

representative adj. **[characteristic of a group or kind]**
da⌈ihyoo-tekina N 代表的なN [serving as a typical instance of a group or class of things]

EX. *Ikebana* is representative of Japanese art in its simplicilty and use of materials from nature.
生け花は簡素で自然の材料を使用している点で日本の代表的な芸術である。
Ikebana wa kansode shizen no zairyoo o shiyoo-shite iru ten de Nihon no daihyoo-tekina geijutsu dearu.

— n. **[a person who speaks or acts on behalf of a group of people as its delegate]**
da⌈ihyo⌉o(-sha) 代表(者) •c [s.o. that serves as an official delegate for a group of people]

EX. Representatives of the company will be visiting our campus tomorrow.
会社の代表(者)が明日キャンパスに来る。
Kaisha no daihyoo(-sha) ga asu kyanpasu ni kuru.

reproduce vt. **[for s.o. to produce a copy of s.t. or to translate recorded signals into live sound or images or for s.o./s.a./s.t. to produce offspring]**
1. ⟨-o⟩ fu⌈kusha-suru ⟨～を⟩複写する ③ •c [for s.o. to produce a copy of s.t., esp. written documents] ⟪duplicate, mimeograph⟫, ⟨-o⟩ fu⌈kusei-suru ⟨～を⟩複製する ③ •c [for s.o. to make a replica of s.t., esp. literary documents or a work of art] ⟪reprint⟫, ⟨-o⟩ ko⌉pii-suru ⟨～を⟩コピーする ③ •f [for s.o. to make a duplicate of a document or an object of art] ⟪copy, duplicate⟫

EX. (**a**) Reproducing CDs without permission is against the law.
許可なくCDを{コピー/複製/*複写}することは違法です。
*Kyoka naku shii-dii o {kopii/fukusei/*fukusha}-suru koto wa ihoo desu.*
(**b**) A copy machine can reproduce an original any number of times.
コピー機はオリジナルを何度も{複製/コピー/複写}することができる。

Kopii-ki wa orijinaru o nan-do-mo {fukusei/kopii/fukusha}-suru koto ga dekiru.

2. ⟨-o⟩ **sa⌈isei-suru** ⟨〜を⟩**再生する** ③ **•c [to cause s.t./s.o./s.a. to come back to life** 《**fig. "translate recorded signals into live sound"**》**]** 《**regenerate, play back**》

EX. (**a**) This paper is reproduced from old newspapers.
この紙は古新聞から再生されたものです。
Kono kami wa furu-shinbun kara saisei-sareta mono desu.
(**b**) The sound reproduced by this stereo system is virtually indistinguishable from live sound.
このステレオで再生される音は生の音とほとんど区別がつかない。
Kono sutereo de saisei-sareru oto wa nama no oto to hotondo kubetsu ga tsukanai.

3. ⟨-o⟩ **u⌈mu** ⟨〜を⟩**うむ** ① **[to give birth to s.t./s.o./s.a.]** 《**engender, breed, yield**》
㊥ "give birth to an offspring"▷産む, "give birth to an offspring/artistic work or give rise to an accident, rumor, interest etc."▷生む

reproduction n. **[the act of producing a copy of s.t., producing offspring, or translating recorded signals into live sound or images; s.t. that is made in imitation or an original]**
1. fu⌈kusha 複写 •c [the act of producing a copy of s.t.] 《**duplication, reprint, copy**》
2. sa⌈isei 再生 •c [the act of causing s.t./s.o./s.a. to come back to life, including translating recorded signals into live sound or images] 《**regeneration, playback**》
3. se⌈ishoku 生殖 •c [the sexual process by which offspring are regenerated] 《**procreation, generation**》

reptile n.
ha⌈chu⌉u-rui はちゅう類 •c

republic n. **[a country governed by popularly elected representatives or a president]**
kyo⌈owa⌉-koku 共和国 •c

reputation n. **[**(**high**) **estimation by the general public]**
1. hyo⌈oban 評判 •c [the way s.o./s.t./s.a. is thought of or talked about by people in general] 《**world opinion, popularity, fame, notoriety**》

EX. (**a**) That doctor has a very good reputation in this town.
あの医者はこの町でとても評判がいいです。
Ano isha wa kono machi de totemo hyooban ga ii desu.
(**b**) He has a reputation for always speaking well of others.
彼はいつも人をほめるという評判だ。
Kare wa itsu-mo hito o homeru to iu hyooban da.

2. ko⌈ohyoo 好評 •c [a good estimation by the general public] 《**favorable criticism**》

EX. The young pianist's performance gained her an instantaneous reputation.
若いピアニストの演奏はたちまち好評を博した。
Wakai pianisuto no ensoo wa tachimachi koohyoo o hakushita.

request vt. **[for s.o. to ask s.o. for s.t. or to ask s.o. to do s.t.]**
1. ⟨-o⟩ **ne⌈ga⌉u** ⟨〜を⟩**願う** ① **[for s.o. to verbally express a strong desire or hope for s.t. to a superior** (**including God**)**]** 《**desire, wish, hope, beg, implore**》, ⟨-o⟩ **mo⌈tome⌉ru** ⟨〜を⟩**求める** ② **[for s.o. to desire s.t. and persistently seek to find and obtain it** ⟨**fml**⟩**]** 《**want, wish for, demand, search for, seek**》

EX. (**a**) We request the pleasure of your company at a dinner to be held on the 20th day of January, 2000.
2000年1月20日の晩さん会に御臨席のほど(を)お願い申し上げます。
Ni-sen-nen ichi-gatsu hatsuka no bansan-kai ni go-rinseki no hodo (o) o-negai mooshi-agemasu.
(**b**) I was requested to attend the meeting, but my busy schedule prevented me from doing so.
会に出席を{求められた/*願われた}の

R

ですが、予定が詰まっていて出席できませんでした。
*Kai ni shusseki o {motome-rareta/ *negawa-reta} no desu ga, yotei ga tsumatte ite shusseki-dekimasen deshita.*

2. ⟨-ni⟩ Vinf. nonpast yo˥o (ni) ne┌ga˥u ⟨〜に⟩Vinf. nonpastよう(に)願う ① [for s.o. to express a desire to a superior or a deity that he/she do s.t.], ⟨-ni⟩ Vinf. nonpast yo˥o (ni) ta┌no˥mu ⟨〜に⟩Vinf. nonpastよう(に)頼む ① [for s.o. to express a desire to s.o. that he/she do s.t.] ((ask, beg, entrust, employ, depend on))

EX. I earnestly request that you reply to my letter at your earliest convenience.
ご都合つき次第(私の手紙に)ご返事をくださいますよう、切にお{願い/頼み}申し上げます。
Go-tsugoo tsuki-shidai (watakushi no tegami ni) go-henji o kudasaimasu yoo, setsuni o-{negai/tanomi} mooshi-agemasu.

NOTE: *O-{negai/tanomi} mooshi-agemasu* is a very polite formal form of *negau/tanomu.*

— n. **[the act of asking s.o. for s.t. or asking s.o. to do s.t. or s.t. that is asked for]**
1. ne┌ga˥i 願い /⟨V*masu* of *negau* ① beg/ [an act/instance of asking s.o. or God for s.t. or asking s.o. or God to do s.t.] ((desire, wish, entreaty, solicitation)), ta┌nomi 頼み /⟨V*masu* of *tanomu* ① ask/ [the act of depending on s.o. or asking s.o. for s.t.] ((favor, reliance, dependence)), yo┌osei 要請 •c [an act/instance of asking s.o. for s.t. or asking s.o. to do s.t. as required from an authoritative standpoint]

EX. (**a**) The king agreed to the request of his field commanders that he increase the strength of their army.
国王は軍隊を増強せよという陸軍司令官たちの{要請/願い/??頼み}を聞き入れた。
Kokuoo wa guntai o zookyoo-seyo to iu riku-gun shirei-kan-tachi no {yoosei/ negai/??tanomi} o kiki-ireta.
(**b**) I have a request for you. Can you come to my office right away?
ちょっと君に{頼み/*願い/*要請}があるんだ。すぐ僕の部屋に来てくれないか。
*Chotto kimi ni {tanomi/*negai/*yoosei} ga aru n da. Sugu boku no heya ni kite kurenai ka.*

NOTE: *Negai* in example (b) would be acceptable if prefixed by *o-*.

2. ne┌gai-goto˥ 願い事 [s.t. that one asks of a superior], ta┌nomi-goto 頼み事 [s.t. that one asks of s.o., usu. an equal or inferior]

EX. (**a**) You said you had a request for me.
{頼み事/*願い事}があるって言ったね。
*{Tanomi-goto/*Negai-goto} ga arutte itta ne.*
(**b**) On the day of Tanabata, the Japanese traditionally offer requests to the stars.
日本には古くから七夕の日に星に{願い事/*頼み事}をする習慣がある。
*Nihon ni wa furuku kara tanabata no hi ni hoshi ni {negai-goto/*tanomi-goto} o suru shuukan ga aru.*

NOTE: "Tanabata" is the Star Festival held on July 7. People write their wishes on strips of colored paper and decorate bamboo cuttings with them.

require vt. **[to have a need for s.t. or for s.o. to put an obligation on s.o. to do s.t.] ⟨-ni⟩ ⟨-o⟩ yo┌okyuu-suru ⟨〜に⟩⟨〜を⟩要求する ③ •c [for s.o. to ask s.o. for s.t. or ask s.o. to do s.t. as if it were one's natural right to so ask] ((claim, demand)), ⟨-ni⟩ {⟨-o⟩/Vinf. nonpast yo˥o ni} {me┌ijiru/ me┌izu˥ru} ⟨〜に⟩{⟨〜を⟩/Vinf. nonpastように}{命じる ②/命ずる} •c [for s.o. in an official position of authority to tell s.o. to do s.t.] ((order, command, direct)), ⟨-o⟩ yo┌osuru ⟨〜を⟩要する ③ •c [for s.o. to have need of s.t. in order to accomplish s.t. ⟨w⟩], yo┌okyuu-sareru 要求される /⟨passive of *yookyuu-suru* ③ demand/ ②**

NOTE: *Meijiru* conjugates freely like any other Group 2 verb, but *meizuru* is used only in the Vinf. nonpast form.

EX. (**a**) Our boss required us to finish the work by the end of this month.
上司は我々にその仕事を今月末までに

R

終える{ことを要求した/ように命じた}。
Jooshi wa ware-ware ni sono shigoto o kongetsu sue made ni oeru {koto o yookyuu-shita/yooni meijita}.
(**b**) The study of a foreign language requires patience and effort.
外国語の勉強は忍耐と努力{を要する/が要求される}。
Gaikoku-go no benkyoo wa nintai to doryoku {o yoosuru/ga yookyuu-sareru}.

PHRASE: required course *hissu-kamoku* 必須科目 •c ↔ *sentaku-kamoku* 選択科目 •c

NOTE: 科 can also be written here as 課.

requirement n. **[s.t. that is necessary or demanded of one as an obligation or duty] hi⌈tsuyoo-jo⌉oken 必要条件 •c [a necessary condition], shi⌈kaku 資格 •c [a set of conditions one must meet to qualify for a task or a position]** ⟪**qualification, capability**⟫

EX. Good health is the most important requirement for this job.
この仕事に最も大切な{必要条件/資格}は健康であることです。
Kono shigoto ni mottomo taisetsuna {hitsuyoo-jooken/shikaku} wa kenkoo dearu koto desu.

rescue vt. **[for s.o. to save s.o. from immediate or impending danger or disaster or to free s.o. from captivity] ⟨-o⟩ ⟨-kara⟩ su⌈kui-da⌉su ⟨～を⟩⟨～から⟩救い出す ① [for s.o. to deliver s.o./s.a. from immediate danger]** ⟪**help, extricate, deliver**⟫, **⟨-o⟩ ⟨-kara⟩ kyu⌈ushutsu-suru ⟨～を⟩⟨～から⟩救出する ③ •c [for s.o. to deliver s.o./s.a. from danger], ⟨-o⟩ su⌈kuu ⟨～を⟩すくう ① [for s.o. to pull s.o./s.t./s.a. up and out of a place or set of circumstances that is undesirable or dangerous** ⟪**fig. "help," "save"**⟫**]**
㊈ "help/save/deliver"▷救う, "scoop up"▷すくう

EX. (**a**)The police attempted to rescue the hostages from the plane, but failed.
警察は機内の人質を{救おう/救い出そう/救出しよう}としたが、失敗した。
Keisatsu wa kinai no hitojichi o {sukuoo/sukui-dasoo/kyuushutsu-shiyoo} to shita ga, shippai-shita.
(**b**) A firefighter rescued the baby from the burning house.
消防士が燃えている家から赤ん坊を{救った/救い出した/救出した}。
Shooboo-shi ga moete iru ie kara akanboo o {sukutta/sukui-dashita/kyuushutsu-shita}.

— n. **[the act of saving s.o. from immediate or impending danger or disaster or of freeing s.o. from captivity] kyu⌉ujo 救助 •c [the act of saving s.o. from disaster or poverty]** ⟪**relief, deliverance, aid, assistance**⟫, **kyu⌈ushutsu 救出 •c [the act of saving s.o. who is in danger]** ⟪**relief, saving, deliverance**⟫

EX. The rescue of the girl who had fallen into the well took about four hours.
井戸の中に落ちた女の子の{救助/救出}作業は四時間ぐらいかかった。
Ido no naka ni ochita onna-no-ko no {kyuujo/kyuushutsu} sagyoo wa yo-jikan-gurai kakatta.

research n. **[careful study or inquiry, esp. for the purpose of uncovering new facts or information] ke⌉nkyuu 研究 •c [careful inquiry into facts/theory]** ⟪**study, investigation, inquiry**⟫

EX. A: What sort of research are you doing?
どんな研究をしていますか。
Donna kenkyuu o shite imasu ka.
B: I'm doing research on semiconductors.
半導体の研究をしています。
Handootai no kenkyuu o shite imasu.

NOTE: "Research" in English is sometimes casually used by students to mean "reading books to search for information relevant to writing a paper." In this case, the appropriate Japanese expression would be *benkyoo-suru* "study" or *shiraberu* "survey."

resemble vt. **[to be similar to s.t./s.o./s.a.] {⟨-to⟩/⟨-ni⟩} ni⌈te iru {⟨～と⟩/⟨～に⟩}似ている /⟨V*te iru* of *niru* ② resemble/ ② [to look like s.t./s.o./s.a.]**

R

EX. (**a**) You sure resemble your father.
お父さんによく似ていますね。
O-too-san ni yoku nite imasu ne.
(**b**) My friends say that my face resembles that of a cat.
友達は私の顔が猫に似ていると言っています。
Tomodachi wa watashi no kao ga neko ni nite iru to itte imasu.

resentment n. **[a deep, bitter feeling about the wrong one has endured from s.o.]**
i⌈kidoori 憤り /⟨V*masu* of *ikidooru* ① feel anger/ [a bitter feeling of anger] ⟪indignation⟫

EX. I felt resentment over the way my boss treated Bill.
上司のビルの扱い方に憤りを感じた。
Jooshi no Biru no atsukai-kata ni ikidoori o kanjita.

R

reservation n. **[an arrangement to have s.t. kept aside for future use by a particular individual or group or s.t. which causes one to hold back from fully accepting an idea or proposal]**
1. jo⌈oke⌉n 条件 •c [s.t. which is necessary for and/or places a limit upon s.t. coming into being] ⟪stipulation, proviso, condition⟫

EX. I recommended Mr. Yamaguchi with some reservation.
私は山口氏を条件つきで推薦した。
Watashi wa Yamaguchi-shi o jooken-tsuki de suisen-shita.

2. yo⌈yaku 予約 •c [an arrangement by which one secures s.t. such as a hotel room, seat in a restaurant, theater, etc., for one's future use] ⟪booking⟫

EX. (**a**) Do we need a reservation at the restaurant?
そのレストランは予約が要りますか。
Sono resutoran wa yoyaku ga irimasu ka.
(**b**) You'd better make hotel reservations right away if you're going to visit Kyoto during Golden Week.
ゴールデンウイークに京都に行くんなら、すぐ旅館の予約をした方がいいですよ。
Gooruden-uiiku ni Kyooto ni iku n nara, sugu ryokan no yoyaku o shita hoo ga ii desu yo.

reserve vt. **[for s.o. to keep s.t. back for a future purpose or to have s.t. kept aside for future use by a particular individual or party]**
1. ⟨-o⟩ ho⌈ryuu-suru ⟨～を⟩保留する ③ •c [for s.o. to postpone a decision on a matter] ⟪defer⟫

EX. The student chose to reserve the right to read his instructor's recommendation letter.
学生は先生が書いた推薦状を読む権利を保留した。
Gakusei wa sensei ga kaita suisen-joo o yomu kenri o horyuu-shita.

2. ⟨-o⟩ yo⌈yaku-suru ⟨～を⟩予約する ③ •c [for s.o. to make an arrangement by which one secures s.t. in advance]

EX. Have you reserved a ticket yet for the next concert?
次のコンサートの切符はもう予約しましたか。
Tsugi no konsaato no kippu wa moo yoyaku-shimashita ka.

—— n. **[s.t. kept back for future use or a tendency to keep one's thoughts or feelings to oneself]**
1. ho⌈zo⌉n-butsu 保存物 •c [s.t. kept in a state where it does not spoil or deteriorate]
2. tsu⌈tsushimi-bu⌉ka-sa 慎み深さ /⟨adj(*i*). stem of *tsutsushimi-bukai* modest + suf. *sa* ness/ [the act of holding oneself back in speech or action out of deference to or consideration of others] ⟪reservation, diffidence, hesitation, modesty⟫

EX. Mrs. Yano has an air of reserve shared by many Japanese women of her generation.
矢野夫人には同世代の日本女性の多くに共通の慎み深さがある。
Yano-fujin ni wa doo-sedai no Nihon-josei no ooku ni kyootsuu no tsutsushimi-buka-sa ga aru.

reside vi. **[for s.o. to make one's permanent home in a place ⟪fig. "exist"⟫ ⟨fml⟩]**

1. ⟨**-ni**⟩ **su**ˡ**mu** ⟨〜に⟩住む ① **[for s.o./s.a. to make one's dwelling in a certain place]** ((**live, dwell**))

EX. A: Where do your parents reside?
御両親はどこに住んでいらっしゃいますか。
Go-ryooshin wa doko ni sunde irasshaimasu ka.
B: In Thailand.
タイに住んでいます。
Tai ni sunde imasu.

2. ⟨**-ni**⟩ **zo**ˡ**kusu**ˡ**ru** ⟨〜に⟩属する ③ •**c** **[to be a member of an institution/group/genre]** ((**belong**))

EX. According to the U.S. Constitution, the power to declare war resides in Congress.
アメリカの憲法によると宣戦布告権は議会に属する。
Amerika no kenpoo ni yoru to sensen-fukoku-ken wa gikai ni zokusuru.

residence n. **[the act or period of making one's home in a place or the place which one has made one's permanent home]** **te**ˡ**itaku** 邸宅 •**c** **[a mansion-like house]** ((**mansion**)), **o-**ˡ**taku** お宅 •**c** **[a term for the house of s.o. to whom one is showing deference** ((**fig. "a term for the family/husband of s.o. shown deference"**))**]**

EX. (**a**) This is Elizabeth Taylor's residence.
これがエリザベス・テーラーの{邸宅/?お宅}です。
Kore ga Erizabesu Teeraa no {teitaku/?o-taku} desu.
(**b**) Is this Mr. Ishikawa's residence?
石川さんの{お宅/*邸宅}でしょうか。
*Ishikawa-san no {o-taku/*teitaku} deshoo ka.*

PHRASE: be in residence in ⟨*-ni*⟩ *sunde iru* ⟨〜⟩に住んでいる

EX. I have been in residence here in the U.S. for two years.
私はここアメリカに二年住んでいます。
Watashi wa koko Amerika ni ni-nen sunde imasu.

resist vt. **[to strive to keep from being overcome by s.o./s.a./s.t. such as an assailant, disease, or temptation by means of force or inherent strength; for s.o. to strive to keep s.t. from happening]** ⟨**-ni**⟩ **te**ˡ**ikoo-suru** ⟨〜に⟩抵抗する ③ •**c** **[to strive to work against a force that encroaches on one from the outside]** ((**struggle, oppose, defy, fight**)), ⟨**-ni**⟩ **ha**ˡ**ntai-suru** ⟨〜に⟩反対する ③ •**c** **[for s.o. to be against an opinion, idea, or proposal of another]** ((**oppose, object**))

EX. The college president firmly resisted the movement by the faculty to unionize.
学長は教員の組合結成の動きに強く{抵抗/反対}した。
Gakuchoo wa kyooin no kumiai-kessei no ugoki ni tsuyoku {teikoo/hantai}-shita.

resistance n. **[the act of striving to keep from being overcome or keep s.t. from happening or the power to do so]**

1. teˡ**ikoo** 抵抗 •**c** **[the act of striving to work against a force that encroaches on one from the outside]**

EX. The invading army encountered virtually no armed resistance from the inhabitants of the small country.
侵攻した軍はその小国の住民から武器による抵抗はほとんど受けなかった。
Shinkoo-shita gun wa sono shookoku no juumin kara buki ni-yoru teikoo wa hotondo ukenakatta.

2. teˡ**iko**ˡ**o-ryoku** 抵抗力 •**c** **[the ability to work against a force that encroaches on one from the outside]**

EX. I was told that if you take lots of vitamin C you can develop a resistance to colds.
ビタミンCを沢山取っていると、風邪に対する抵抗力がつくそうです。
Bitamin-shii o takusan totte iru to, kaze ni-taisuru teikoo-ryoku ga tsuku soodesu.

resolution n. **[the quality of being firm in one's decision or s.t. decided upon or the act/process of settling or solving a problem]**

1. keˡ**sshin** 決心 •**c** **[the act of making up**

one's mind firmly to take a particular course of action] ((determination))

EX. My resolution to quit smoking surprised everybody .
私のたばこをやめる決心にみんなが驚いた。
Watashi no tabako o yameru kesshin ni minna ga odoroita.

2. ke⌉tsugi 決議 •c [an act/instance of voting or deciding on an issue in an official meeting] ((decision, vote))

EX. The union reached a resolution to go on strike.
組合はストライキに入るという決議をした。
Kumiai wa sutoraiki ni hairu to iu ketsugi o shita.

resolve vt. **[for s.o. to make up one's mind firmly or to settle or solve a problem]**

R

1. Vvol. to ke⌉sshin-suru Vvol.と決心する ③ •c [for s.o. to firmly make up one's mind to take a particular course of action] ((determine, make up one's mind))

EX. I resolved to quit smoking on New Year's Day, 1997.
1997年の元日にたばこをやめようと決心した。
Sen-kyuu-hyaku-kyuu-juu-nana-nen no ganjitsu ni tabako o yameyoo to kesshin-shita.

2. ⟨-o⟩ ka⌈iketsu-suru ⟨～を⟩解決する ③ •c [for s.o. to find an answer or terms of mutual agreement to a difficult problem or legal case] ((solve, settle, fix))

EX. Japan and the U.S. have still not resolved some of their long-standing trade disputes.
日米間の長年の貿易紛争はまだ完全には解決していない。
Nichi-Bei-kan no naga-nen no booeki-funsoo wa mada kanzenni wa kaiketsu-shite inai.

resource n. **[a source of materials or energy which one can rely on to provide support or assistance as needed]**

1. kyo⌈okyu⌉u-gen 供給源 •c [a source which supplies s.t. needed]

EX. Japan has practially no oil resources of its own.
日本は自国に石油の供給源がないと言ってよい。
Nihon wa jikoku ni sekiyu no kyookyuu-gen ga nai to itte yoi.

2. za⌉igen 財源 •c [a source of finances] ((a source of revenue, funds))

EX. This small college has enormous financial resources.
この小さな大学は巨大な財源を持っている。
Kono chiisana daigaku wa kyodaina zaigen o motte iru.

3. shi⌉gen 資源 •c [natural products such as minerals, crude oil, woods, aquatic products, etc., necessary for industrial production]

EX. The U.S. is rich in natural resources.
アメリカは天然資源が豊富だ。
Amerika wa tennen-shigen ga hoofu da.

respect vt. **[for s.o. to hold s.o./s.t. in high regard or honor]**

1. ⟨-o⟩ so⌈nkei-suru ⟨～を⟩尊敬する ③ •c [for s.o. to hold s.o. in high regard] ((esteem, revere, honor))

EX. A: Who do you respect most of all the people you know?
あなたが知っている人で一番尊敬する人はだれですか。
Anata ga shitte iru hito de ichiban sonkei-suru hito wa dare desu ka.
B: My parents.
両親です。
Ryooshin desu.

2. ⟨-o⟩ (⟨-kara⟩) ma⌈mo⌉ru ⟨～を⟩(⟨～から⟩)守る ① [(to watch s.t./s.o./s.a. in order) to cause s.t./s.o./s.a. not to be harmed/injured/violated] ((defend, protect, guard, keep, observe)), **⟨-o⟩ so⌈nchoo-suru ⟨～を⟩尊重する ③ •c [for s.o. to think very highly of s.o./s.t., including the law, human life, and the rights or opinions of others]** ((value, esteem))

EX. (a) In order for a democracy to succeed, citizens must respect the laws of the land.

民主主義を定着させるためには市民は国の法律を{守らなければ/尊重しなければ}ならない。
Minshu-shugi o teichaku-saseru tame ni wa shimin wa kuni no hooritsu o {mamoranakereba/sonchoo-shinakereba} naranai.
(**b**) It's hard to get along with a person who doesn't respect opinions different from his own.
自分と違う意見を{尊重しない/*守らない}人と仲良くするのは難しい。
*Jibun to chigau iken o {sonchoo-shinai/ *mamoranai} hito to naka-yoku suru no wa muzukashii.*

—— n. **[high regard or honor shown to s.o./s.t. either out of a sense of admiration or a sense of duty 《fig. "particular point," "relation"》]**

1. so⌈nkei 尊敬 •c [the act of holding s.o. in high regard] 《esteem, honor, reverence, deference》

EX. I would like to be considered a person worthy of respect.
私は尊敬に値する人間だと思われたい。
Watashi wa sonkei ni atai-suru ningen da to omowa-re-tai.

2. so⌈nchoo 尊重 •c [the act of placing a high value on s.o./s.t., including the law, human life, and the rights and opinions of others] 《esteem, regard》

EX. Respect for the law is an essential part of living together in society.
法律の尊重は社会でみんなが一緒に生活していく上で大事なことだ。
Hooritsu no sonchoo wa shakai de minna ga issho ni seikatsu-shite iku ue de daijina koto da.

3. te⌈n 点 •c [a small mark made by the end of a sharp object 《fig. "punctuation," "marks," "detail"》] 《dot, spot, speck, point, score, detail》

EX. (**a**) Emily is beautiful in every respect.
エミリーはどの点から見ても美しい。
Emirii wa dono ten kara mite mo utsukushii.
(**b**) Japan and England are similar in the respects that they are both island nations and are both constitutional monarchies.
日本とイギリスは島国で立憲君主国であるという点で似ている。
Nihon to Igirisu wa shima-guni de rikken-kunshu-koku dearu to iu ten de nite iru.

PHRASE: with respect to... ⟨-*ni*⟩ *kanshite* ⟨〜に⟩関して

EX. I have nothing further to say with respect to this matter.
この件に関してはこれ以上申し上げることはありません。
Kono ken ni-kanshite wa kore ijoo mooshi-ageru koto wa arimasen.

respectively adv. **[in the order stated]** **so⌈re⌉-zore それぞれ [in a way applicable to every one] 《each》**

EX. John and Bob are married to Cindy and Nancy, respectively.
ジョンはシンディーと、ボブはナンシーとそれぞれ結婚している。
Jon wa Shindii to, Bobu wa Nanshii to sore-zore kekkon-shite iru.

respond vi. **[for s.o. to give an answer to s.o./s.t. or to act or change in reaction to a stimulus, including medical treatment]**

1. ⟨-ni⟩ ko⌈tae⌉ru ⟨〜に⟩こたえる ② [for s.o. to say or do s.t. to fulfill a request from s.o. else for information or action; for s.o. to meet a demand or expectation placed on one; to react, usu. in a negative way, to a physical or psychological stimulus such as temperature or stress] 《answer, reply, come home to, tell on》, ⟨-ni⟩ o⌈otoo-suru ⟨〜に⟩応答する ③ •c [for s.o. to give a verbal answer; to reply to s.t.] 《answer, reply》, ⟨-ni⟩ ha⌈nnoo-suru ⟨〜に⟩反応する ③ •c [for s.t. to act or change under the direct effect of a stimulus] 《react》

㊥ "respond verbally"▷答える, "respond non-verbally"▷こたえる

EX. (**a**) When a Japanese person is asked if he has a religion, he is most likely to respond "No, I don't."

日本人に宗教があるかと聞けば、まず、「ない」と{答える/??応答する/*反応する}だろう。
*Nihon-jin ni shuukyoo ga aru ka to kikeba, mazu, 'nai' to {kotaeru/??ootoo-suru/*hannoo-suru} daroo.*
(**b**) Japanese industries seem to know how to respond to the demands of consumers.
日本の企業は消費者の要求にどう{こたえる/*反応する/*応答する}かを知っているようだ。
*Nihon no kigyoo wa shoohi-sha no yookyuu ni doo {kotaeru/*hannoo-suru/*ootoo-suru} ka o shitte iru yooda.*
(**c**) Blood pressure in the body reponds to changes in the outside temperature.
血圧は気温の変化に{反応する/*答える/*応答する}。
*Ketsuatsu wa kion no henka ni {hannoo-suru/*kotaeru/*ootoo-suru}.*
(**d**) Nobody responded when we knocked so we went in.
ノックしてもだれも{応答しなかった/*答えなかった/*反応しなかった}から中に入った。
*Nokku-shite mo dare-mo {ootoo-shinakatta/*kotaenakatta/*hannoo-shinakatta} kara naka ni haitta.*

R

response n. **[s.t. said or done in answer to s.o./s.t.; an event or change brought about by a stimulus]**
1. o⌈otoo 応答 •c [an answer given verbally in reply to s.o./s.t. such as a question, sound of a knock or doorbell, etc.] **⟪answer, reply⟫**
EX. The policeman knocked on the door several times, but there was no response.
警官はドアを四、五回ノックしたが、応答がなかった。
Keikan wa doa o shi, go-kai nokku-shita ga, ootoo ga nakatta.
2. ha⌈nnoo 反応 •c [an event or change brought on by a stimulus] **⟪reaction, effect⟫**
EX. The response of the audience to the pianist's performance was enthusiastic.
聴衆はピアニストの演奏に熱狂的な反応を示した。
Chooshuu wa pianisuto no ensoo ni nekkyoo-tekina hannoo o shimeshita.

responsible adj. **[having as one's duty to do s.t.; being the main cause of s.t. happening; trustworthy and reliable]**
1. {⟨**-ni**⟩ **se⌈kinin ga a⌉ru**/⟨**-no**⟩ **se⌈kinin da**} {⟨〜に⟩責任がある ①/⟨〜の⟩責任だ} **[for s.o. to be accountable for s.t.]** **⟪take responsibility for⟫**
EX. I am responsible for the failure of this project.
このプロジェクトが失敗したのは私{に責任がある/の責任だ}。
Kono purojekuto ga shippai-shita no wa watashi {ni sekinin ga aru/no sekinin da}.
2. se⌈kinin ga a⌉ru (N) 責任がある(N) ① **[involving important duties], se⌈kinin ga o⌈moi** 責任が重い adj(*i*). **[involving heavy duties]**
EX. A responsible position generally carries with it a better salary, but can also carry more stress.
責任の{ある/重い}仕事につけば、大抵給料は上がるが、ストレスも多くなる可能性がある。
Sekinin no {aru/omoi} shigoto ni tsukeba, taitei kyuuryoo wa agaru ga, sutoresu mo ooku naru kanoo-sei ga aru.
3. ⟨**-no**⟩ **ge⌈n'in to na⌉ru** (N) ⟨〜の⟩原因となる(N) **[acting as the source from which an event or situation originates]**
EX. Cigarette smoking is responsible for much of the incidence of lung cancer.
喫煙は肺がんの原因となっていることが多い。
Kitsuen wa haigan no gen'in to natte iru koto ga ooi.

rest[1] n. **[the act of stopping activity, motion, or work, esp. to regain one's strength, or the state of being inactive or asleep]**
1. ya⌈sumi⌉ 休み / ⟨V*masu* of *yasumu* ① take rest/ **[⟨a period of time during which there is a) cessation of activity ⟪fig. "holiday,"**

"vacation")] ((recess, intermission, break, pause, holiday, vacation, absence)), **kyu⌈ukei 休憩 •c [a short, temporary cessation of activity] ((recess, interval))**

EX. I think we're tired. Let's take a ten-minute rest.
疲れましたね。十分{休み/休憩}をとりましょう。
Tsukaremashita ne. Jup-pun {yasumi/kyuukei} o torimashoo.

NOTE: Unlike English "rest," *yasumi* can be used in compounds, such as *haru-yasumi* "spring break," *natsu-yasumi* "summer vacation," etc.

2. se⌈iyoo 静養 •c [the act of recuperating from illness or exhaustion] ((recuperation, convalescence))

EX. Recovering from this illness requires plenty of rest.
この病気は全治するのに十分な静養が必要です。
Kono byooki wa zenchi-suru no ni juubunna seiyoo ga hitsuyoo desu.

PHRASE: rest room (*kooshuu-*)*benjo* (公衆)便所 •c, *o-tearai* お手洗い ((washroom, toilet)), *toire* トイレ •f

EX. There are rest areas along this highway, but there are no public rest rooms.
この高速道路には休む所はあるけど、{公衆便所/お手洗い/トイレ}はない。
Kono koosoku-dooro ni wa yasumu tokoro wa aru kedo, {kooshuu-benjo/o-tearai/toire} wa nai.

— vi. **[for s.o./s.a. to stop activity, motion, or work, esp. to regain one's strength]**

1. ya⌈su⌉mu 休む ① [for s.o./s.a. to stop activity, motion, or work for a set period of time, esp. to regain one's strength ((fig. "take a day off"))] ((repose, take a day off, pause, discontinue)), kyu⌈ukei-suru 休憩する ③ •c [for s.o. to take a short break from some activity] ((take time off, take a rest, take a respite))

NOTE: Unlike English "rest," *yasumu* is often used to mean "go to bed."

rest² n. **[that which remains; the others]**

no⌈kori⌉ 残り /⟨V*masu* of *nokoru* ① remain/ [s.t./s.o./s.a. that is left over or remains behind]

EX. (**a**) My older brother ate about a quarter of the pizza and gave me the rest.
兄はピザを四分の一ぐらい食べて、残りを僕にくれた。
Ani wa piza o yon-bun no ichi gurai tabete, nokori o boku ni kureta.
(**b**) About half of my high school classmates went to college and the rest got jobs.
高校のクラスメートの半数は大学に行ったが、残りは就職した。
Kookoo no kurasu-meeto no hansuu wa daigaku ni itta ga, nokori wa shuushoku-shita.

restaurant n.

re⌉sutoran レストラン •f, ryo⌈ori⌉-ya 料理屋 [a relatively formal Japanese-style eatery] ((eating house, cookshop))

EX. Let's eat at the restaurant by the river.
川のほとりの{レストラン/料理屋}で食べましょう。
Kawa no hotori no {resutoran/ryoori-ya} de tabemashoo.

restless adj. **[unable to cease activity]**

1. ya⌈sume⌉-nai (N) 休めない(N) /⟨the neg. potential of *yasumu* ① take rest/ [unable to take a rest]

EX. I spent two weeks of restless nights leading up to the exam but somehow managed to survive.
試験当日まで二週間ばかり夜も休めない日が続いたが、なんとかがんばった。
Shiken toojitsu made ni-shuukan bakari yoru mo yasume-nai hi ga, tsuzuita ga, nan-toka ganbatta.

2. o⌈chitsuki ga na⌉i (N) 落ち着きがない(N) [unable to settle down physically or psychologically] ((nervous, uneasy, fidgety, hurried))

EX. At that time I was a young and restless student.
そのころ私は若い、落ち着きのない学生だった。
Sono koro watashi wa wakai, ochitsuki no nai gakusei datta.

R

restoration n. **[the act of bringing s.o./s.t./s.a. back to its original condition or place]**
1. fu⌈kkoo 復興 •c [the process of a once weakened country or organization regaining strength and prosperity] ⟪**revival, resuscitation, resurgence**⟫

EX. The postwar restoration of Japanese society was accomplished at an amazing speed.
戦後の日本社会の復興は目覚ましい早さで成し遂げられた。
Sengo no Nihon-shakai no fukkoo wa mezamashii haya-sa de nashi-toge-rareta.

2. fu⌈kugen 復{元/原} •c [the process of bringing old buildings, objects of art, documents, etc. back to their original condition or form] ⟪**rehabilitation, reconstruction**⟫

EX. How long did the restoration of this old church take?
この古い教会の復{元/原}にどのぐらいかかりましたか。
Kono furui kyookai no fukugen ni dono-gurai kakarimashita ka.

3. i⌉shin 維新 •c [the renewal of a political system, esp. that of the Meiji era (1868–1912)]

EX. The Meiji Restoration was a bloodless revolution.
明治維新は無血革命だった。
Meiji-ishin wa muketsu-kakumei datta.

restore vt. **[for s.o. to bring s.o./s.t./s.a. back to its original condition or place]**
1. ⟨-o⟩ fu⌈kugen-suru ⟨〜を⟩復{元/原}する ③ •c [to bring old buildings, objects of art, documents etc. back to their original condition or form] ⟪**reconstruct**⟫

EX. It took years to restore Michelangelo's frescoes.
ミケランジェロの壁画を復{元/原}するのに何年もかかった。
Mikeranjero no hekiga o fukugen-suru no ni nan-nen-mo kakatta.

2. ⟨-o⟩ to⌈ri-modosu ⟨〜を⟩取り戻す ① [to take s.t./s.o./s.a. back which had been given away or lost, including mental states such as consciousness or composure] ⟪**take back, regain, resume, redeem**⟫

EX. Jane's health was restored within a month or so of her falling ill.
病気になってから一か月かそこいらで、ジェーンは健康を取り戻した。
Byooki ni natte kara ik-kagetsu ka sokoira de, Jeen wa kenkoo o tori-modoshita.

3. ⟨-o⟩ sa⌈iken-suru ⟨〜を⟩再建する ③ •c [for s.o. to rebuild s.t.] ⟪**reconstruct**⟫, **⟨-o⟩ fu⌈kkoo-suru ⟨〜を⟩復興する ③ •c [for s.o. to revitalize a country once weakened]** ⟪**build up, revive, resuscitate**⟫

EX. The U.S. helped post-war Japan restore its economy.
アメリカは戦後の日本が経済を{再建/復興}するのを助けた。
Amerika wa sengo no Nihon ga keizai o {saiken/fukkoo}-suru no o tasuketa.

restrain vt. **[for s.o. to hold s.o./s.t. back from moving or acting or to keep s.t. under control by physical or legal means]**
1. ⟨-o⟩ ha⌈ba⌉mu ⟨〜を⟩阻む ① [to obstruct s.t./s.o. from proceeding ⟨fml⟩] ⟪**obstruct, impede, deter, hinder**⟫, **⟨-o⟩ se⌈ishi-suru ⟨〜を⟩制止する ③ •c [for s.o. to control or stop the movement or action of s.o./s.t.]** ⟪**control, check, stop**⟫, **⟨-o⟩ to⌈meru ⟨〜を⟩とめる ② [for s.o. to cause s.o./s.t./s.a. to cease moving or acting or to keep s.o./s.t./s.a. from moving or acting ⟪fig. "put s.o. up," "fasten"⟫]** ⟪**stop, fasten, check, forbid, lodge**⟫

㊥ "cause s.t. to stop"▷止める, "fasten"▷留める, "give a person lodging"▷泊める

EX. When the Beatles appeared on stage, the excited crowd tried to rush toward them but were restrained by the police.
ビートルズが舞台に現れた時熱狂した聴衆が彼らに向かって突進しようとしたが、警官に{阻まれた/制止された/止められた}。
Biitoruzu ga butai ni arawareta toki nekkyoo-shita chooshuu ga kare-ra ni mukatte tosshin-shiyoo to shita ga,

keikan ni {habama-reta/seishi-sareta/ tome-rareta}.

2. 〈-o〉 o⌈sae⌉ru 〈〜を〉おさえる ② [to push s.t. down/back 《fig. "restrain," "suppress," "arrest," "govern," "cover," "grasp"》; for s.o. to prevent s.o./s.a./s.t. from escaping or otherwise acting freely; for s.o. to prevent s.t. undesirable from occurring which would otherwise occur; for s.o. to pay due attention to s.t. as being important] 《press down, stop, suppress, control》

㊥ "press down physically"▷押さえる, "control"▷抑える

EX. (**a**) Jessica couldn't restrain her anger at Tom's insensitive remarks.
ジェシカはトムの無礼な発言に怒りを抑えられなかった。
Jeshika wa Tomu no bureina hatsugen ni ikari o osae-rarenakatta.
(**b**) The U.S. is making efforts to restrain its burgeoning trade deficit with Japan.
アメリカは膨れる一方の対日貿易赤字を抑えようと努力している。
Amerika wa fukureru ippoo no tai-Nichi booeki-akaji o osaeyoo to doryoku-shite iru.

restrict vt. **[for s.o. to keep some quantity or activity within certain limits]**
〈-o〉 se⌈ige⌉n-suru 〈〜を〉制限する ③ •c [for s.o. to intentionally keep s.t./s.o./s.a. within a certain scope, bound, or quantity] 《limit, confine》

EX. (**a**) I've had to restrict my eating habits since I've begun gaining weight.
太ってきているから食事を制限しなければならなくなった。
Futotte kite iru kara shokuji o seigen-shinakereba naranaku natta.
(**b**) The doctor told me to restrict my working hours.
医者は私に仕事の時間を制限するように言った。
Isha wa watashi ni shigoto no jikan o seigen-suru yooni itta.

result n. **[s.t. brought about by an action or event]**
ke⌈kka 結果 •c [a state or affairs brought about by a cause] 《outcome》

EX. (**a**) Professor, when will you be able to let us know the results of the exam?
先生、この試験の結果はいつ教えていただけますか。
Sensei, kono shiken no kekka wa itsu oshiete itadake-masu ka.
(**b**) Most traffic accidents are the result of carelessness.
大抵の交通事故は不注意の結果だ。
Taitei no kootsuu-jiko wa fu-chuui no kekka da.

PHRASE: as a result *sono kekka* その結果

EX. Tom was ill and unable to study properly for his final exams. As a result, he failed two of his classes.
トムは病気で期末試験のために十分勉強出来なかった。その結果、二科目で落第点をとった。
Tomu wa byooki de kimatsu-shiken no tame ni juubun benkyoo-dekinakatta. Sono kekka, ni-kamoku de rakudai-ten o totta.

— vi. **[for s.t. to occur as an outcome of some action or event or to lead to some action or event which it causes]**
〈-ni〉 o⌈waru 〈〜に〉終わる ① [for some action or event to end in s.t. as an outcome], 〈kara〉 {sho⌈ojiru/sho⌈ozuru} 〈〜から〉{生じる ②/生ずる} [for s.t. to originate from s.t. as its cause] 《happen, come about, take place, derive》

NOTE: *Shoozuru* is used only in the Vinf. nonpast form.

EX. (**a**) Japan's first try for the soccer World Cup resulted in defeat.
日本のワールドカップサッカー初挑戦は完敗{に終わった/*から生じた}。
*Nihon no Waarudo Kappu sakkaa hatsu-choosen wa kanpai {ni owatta/ *kara shoojita}.*
(**b**) The whole situation resulted from a simple misunderstanding.
事態はすべてちょっとした誤解{から生じた/*に終わった}。

R

*Jitai wa subete chotto-shita gokai {kara shoojita/*ni owatta}.*

retail vt. **[to sell s.t. in small quantities directly to]**
⟨-o⟩ ⟨-ni⟩ ko-⌈uri-suru ⟨〜を⟩⟨〜に⟩小売りする ③

EX. Is there any store around here that retails furniture?
家具を小売りしている店がこの辺にありますか。
Kagu o ko-uri-shite iru mise ga kono hen ni arimasu ka.

—— n. **[the sale of goods in small quantities directly to consumers]**
ko-⌈uri 小売り

EX. What is the retail price of this merchandise?
この商品の小売り価格はいくらですか。
Kono shoohin no ko-uri-kakaku wa ikura desu ka.

retain vt. **[to continue to have or possess s.o./s.t./s.a. ⟪fig. "employ the services of"⟫]**
1. ⟨-o⟩ mo⌈chi-tsuzukeru ⟨〜を⟩持ち続ける **/⟨V*masu* of *motsu* ① hold + *tsuzukeru* ② continue/ ② [for s.o. to continue to have or hold s.o./s.t./s.a.], ⟨-o⟩ ho⌉ji-suru** ⟨〜を⟩保持する ③ **[for s.o. to cause s.t. to be maintained in its current state, such as political power, a tradition, etc.] ⟪maintain, preserve, sustain, keep⟫**

EX. (**a**) It becomes difficult to retain your youthful drive as you get older.
年をとると若い時の根気を{持ち続ける/保持する}のが難しくなる。
Toshi o toru to wakai toki no konki o {mochi-tsuzukeru/hoji-suru} no ga muzukashiku naru.
(**b**) The city of Kyoto retains many of Japan's old traditions.
京都の町は日本の古い伝統の多くを{保持して/持ち続けて}いる。
Kyooto no machi wa Nihon no furui dentoo no ooku o {hoji-shite/mochi-tsuzukete} iru.

2. ⟨-o⟩ ya⌈to⌉tte iru ⟨〜を⟩雇っている **/⟨V*te iru* of *yatou* ① employ/ ② [to keep s.o. in one's employ] ⟪employ⟫**

EX. Our corporation has retained three lawyers in the civil suit currently being brought against it.
うちの会社は会社に対して起こされている民事訴訟に弁護士を三人雇っている。
Uchi no kaisha wa kaisha ni-taishite okosa-rete iru minji-soshoo ni bengo-shi o san-nin yattote iru.

NOTE: Unlike English "retain," *mochi-tsuzukeru* can be used to mean "continue to hold s.t. concrete, such as a book, pen, etc." English "retain" typically requires something abstract as its object, such as a value, spirit, composure, right, respect, etc., so that it is strange to say, for example, "John retained a book in his hand."

retire vi. **[for s.o. to withdraw from a public space, esp. from one's regular work because of advancing age]**
te⌈inen-ta⌉ishoku-suru 定年退職する ③ **•c, ta⌈ishoku-suru** 退職する ③ **•c, i⌉ntai-suru** 引退する ③ **•c [for s.o. to withdraw from business or public life, esp. s.o. important]**

EX. (**a**) President Okamoto of Okamoto Electric retired this March after being with the company for more than 40 years.
岡本電機の岡本社長は四十年以上働いて、今年の三月に{引退/退職}した。
Okamoto Denki no Okamoto-shachoo wa yon-juu-nen ijoo hataraite, kotoshi no san-gatsu ni {intai/taishoku}-shita.
(**b**) I plan to retire from my company this year.
私は今年会社を{定年退職/?引退}する予定です。
Watashi wa kotoshi kaisha o {teinen-taishoku/?intai}-suru yotei desu.

retired adj. **[having withdrawn from one's regular work, esp. because of advancing age]**
te⌈inen-ta⌉ishoku-shita N 定年退職したN **/⟨Vinf. past of *taishoku-suru* ③ retire/ •c, ta⌈ishoku-shita N** 退職したN **•c, i⌉ntai-shita N** 引退したN **/⟨Vinf. past of *intai-suru* ③ retire/ •c [for s.o. to have withdrawn from business or public life, esp. because of advancing age]**

EX. He is a retired politician.
あの人は{退職/引退}した政治家だ。
Ano hito wa {taishoku/intai}-shita seiji-ka da.

retreat vi. **[for s.o./s.t. to withdraw or move back, esp. a military force]**
⟨-ni⟩ shi⌈rizo⌉ku ⟨〜に⟩退く ① [for s.o. to withdraw, esp. from an exposed or dangerous position] ⟪recede, move backward⟫ ↔ ⟨-ni⟩ susumu ⟨〜に⟩進む ①; ⟨-ni⟩ ko⌈otai-suru ⟨〜に⟩後退する ③ •c [for s.o./s.t. to move backward or decrease in vigor] ⟪go back, retrocede, recede⟫ ↔ ⟨-ni⟩ zenshin-suru ⟨〜に⟩前進する ③ •c

EX. As our army pushed forward, the enemy retreated.
我々の軍が前進すると、敵は{退いた/後退した}。
Ware-ware no gun ga zenshin-suru to, teki wa {shirizoita/kootai-shita}.

— n. **[the act of withdrawing or a place to which one withdraws]**
1. ko⌈otai 後退 •c [an act/instance of withdrawing or decreasing in vigor] ⟪retrocession, recession, retrogression⟫

EX. Today's agreement with management signals a retreat on the part of the union.
今日の会社側との合意は組合側の後退を意味する。
Kyoo no kaisha-gawa to no gooi wa kumiai-gawa no kootai o imi-suru.

2. intai 隠退 •c [the act of withdrawing from business or public life to a life of leisure]

EX. A retreat from public life into retirement proves to be a difficult emotional adjustment for many people.
隠退後の生活に適応していくのは多くの人にとって精神的に大変なことのようだ。
Intai-go no seikatsu ni tekioo-shite iku no wa ooku no hito ni-totte seishin-tekini taihenna koto no yooda.

3. hi⌈ki-komo⌉ru {i⌈e⌉/to⌈koro} 引きこもる{家/所} [a house/place to which one withdraws]

return vi. **[to come or go back to a place or condition one was in before ⟨fml⟩]**
⟨-ni⟩ ka⌉eru ⟨〜に⟩かえる ② [to come or go back to a place or condition one was in before, esp. one's home or a place one belongs ⟪fig. "be returned to the owner"⟫] ⟪go/come back, leave, come again⟫, ⟨-ni⟩ mo⌈do⌉ru ⟨〜に⟩戻る ① [to come or go back to a place or condition one was in before] ⟪come/go back, revert, be sent back⟫
㊵ "come/go back to a place one was at before" ▷帰る, "come back to the owner or a condition one was in before" ▷返る

EX. (**a**) What time did you return home yesterday?
きのうは何時に家に{帰りました/戻りました}か。
Kinoo wa nan-ji ni ie ni {kaerimashita/modorimashita} ka.
(**b**) The lost camera returned to its rightful owner.
なくなったカメラは持ち主に{返って/戻って}きた。
Nakunatta kamera wa mochi-nushi ni {kaette/modotte}-kita.

— vt. **[to cause s.o./s.t./s.a. to come or go back to a place or condition it/he/she was in before ⟨fml⟩]**
⟨-o⟩ ⟨-ni⟩ ka⌉esu ⟨〜を⟩⟨〜に⟩かえす ② [for s.o. to cause s.o./s.t./s.a. to come or go back to a place or condition it/he/she was in before, esp. the home or place it/he/she belongs in] ⟪let…go back, put…back in its place, give back⟫, ⟨-o⟩ ⟨-ni⟩ mo⌈do⌉su ⟨〜を⟩⟨〜に⟩戻す ① [for s.o. to cause s.o./s.t./s.a. to come or go back to a place or condition it/he/she was in before] ⟪give back, restore, put back⟫, ⟨-o⟩ ⟨-ni⟩ he⌈nkyaku-suru ⟨〜を⟩⟨〜に⟩返却する ③ •c [for s.o. to cause s.t. to come or go back to its original owner] ⟪give back, repay⟫
㊵ "cause s.t./s.o./s.a. to come/go back to a place it/he/she was at before" ▷帰す, "cause s.t./s.o./s.a. to come/go back to its owner or a condition it/he/she was in before" ▷返す

R

EX. (**a**) Could you return the book I lent you about a month ago?
一か月ばかり前にお貸しした本を{返して/返却して/*戻して}下さいませんか。
*Ik-kagetsu bakari mae ni o-kashi-shita hon o {kaeshite/henkyaku-shite/ *modoshite} kudasaimasen ka.*
(**b**) Please return the book to the bookshelf after using it.
本は使ったら本棚に{戻して/返して/*返却して}下さい。
*Hon wa tsukattara hon-dana ni {modoshite/kaeshite/*henkyaku-shite} kudasai.*

reunion n. **[a gathering together again of members of a group or family who have been apart]**

1. shi⌈nseki no a⌈tsumari⌉ 親せきの集まり •c [a gathering of family members who have been apart]

EX. We have a family reunion every Thanksgiving.
私たちは毎年感謝祭に親戚の集まりをもちます。
Watashi-tachi wa mai-toshi kansha-sai ni shinseki no atsumari o mochimasu.

2. do⌈oso⌉o-kai 同窓会 •c [a gathering of graduates of the same school], ku⌈rasu⌉-kai クラス会 •f+c [a gathering of members of the same class]

EX. (**a**) At the school reunion I met old friends I hadn't seen in 30 years.
同窓会で私は三十年ぶりに昔の友達に会った。
Doosoo-kai de watakushi wa san-juu-nen-buri ni mukashi no tomodachi ni atta.
(**b**) We held a reunion in Tokyo of our sixth grade class from Chikusa Elementary School.
千草小学校六年の時の{クラス会/同窓会}を東京で開いた。
Chikusa-shoo-gakkoo roku-nen no toki no {kurasu-kai/doosoo-kai} o Tookyoo de hiraita.

reveal vt. **[to make visible or known s.t. that was hidden or unknown]**

1. a⌈raware⌉ru あらわれる ② [to become exposed/visible] ⟪come out, appear, emerge⟫ ↔ kakureru 隠れる ②

㊬ "be expressed"▷表れる, "appear, come into view"▷現れる

EX. The morning sun revealed the beautiful mountain scenery surrounding the hotel.
朝の太陽の光でホテルの回りの美しい山の風景が現われた。
Asa no taiyoo no hikari de hoteru no mawari no utsukushii yama no fuukei ga arawareta.

2. ⟨-de⟩ ⟨-ga⟩ wa⌈ka⌉ru ⟨〜で⟩⟨〜が⟩分かる ① [for s.o. to be able to figure out the nature, meaning, identity, etc., of s.t./s.o./s.a. (by some means)] ⟪understand, comprehend, see⟫

EX. The eyes often reveal what is in the mind.
目で人の考えが分かることが多い。
Me de hito no kangae ga wakaru koto ga ooi.

3. ⟨-o⟩ ba⌉kuro-suru ⟨〜を⟩暴露する ③ •c [for s.o. to make known to the public a secret or s.t. which s.o. does not want people to know about] ⟪disclose, divulge, expose⟫

EX. The clergyman's love affair was revealed in an article in the local newspaper.
牧師の情事は地元の新聞の記事で暴露された。
Bokushi no jooji wa jimoto no shinbun no kiji de bakuro-sareta.

reverse vt. **[to turn s.t. in the opposite direction, upside down, or inside out or to reorder s.t. in the opposite way]**
⟨-o⟩ gya⌈ku ni suru ⟨〜を⟩逆にする ③ •c [for s.o. to direct or order s.t. in the opposite way from the way it was or from what is normal or expected], ⟨-o⟩ ha⌈ntai ni suru ⟨〜を⟩反対にする ③ •c [for s.o. to make the left-right, front-back, or up-down orientation of s.t. opposite of what it is normally or should be]

EX. Someone reversed the order of lunch and the president's speech on the printed program.

だれかがプログラムのプリントで昼食と会長のスピーチの順序を{逆/反対}にした。
Dare-ka ga puroguramu no purinto de chuushoku to kaichoo no supiichi no junjo o {gyaku/hantai} ni shita.

— adj. **[opposite or contrary to s.t. else or to what is normal or expected]**
gya⌈ku no N 逆のN •c [opposite in order or direction to s.t. else or to what is normal or expected] ⟪the inverse⟫, ha⌈ntai no N 反対のN •c [in an opposing relation in position, direction, content, or type to s.t. else or to what is normal or expected] ⟪opposite, contrary, reverse⟫

EX. (**a**) The husband's salary used to be higher than that of the wife, but he number of the reverse case is gradually increasing.
以前は夫の方が妻より給料が多いのが普通だったが、今では{逆/反対}のケースが徐々に増えてきている。
Izen wa otto no hoo ga tsuma yori kyuuryoo ga ooi no ga futsuu datta ga, ima de wa {gyaku/hantai} no keesu ga jojoni fuete kite iru.
(**b**) We are unable to see the reverse side of the moon from earth.
地球からは月の{反対/*逆}側は見えない。
*Chikyuu kara wa tsuki no {hantai/ *gyaku}-gawa wa mienai.*

— n. **[a state of being opposite or contrary to s.t. else or to what is normal or expected]**
gya⌈ku 逆 •c [a state of being opposite in order or direction to s.t. else or to what is normal or expected] ⟪the inverse⟫, ha⌈ntai 反対 •c [a state of being in an opposing relation in position, direction, content, or type to s.t. else or to what is normal or expected] ⟪opposite⟫

EX. (**a**) I think it should be the reverse, but in the U.S. a customer thanks the clerk at the store.
私は{逆/反対}だと思いますが、アメリカの店では客が店の人に「ありがとう」と言っていますね。
Watashi wa {gyaku/hantai} da to omoimasu ga, Amerika no mise de wa kyaku ga mise no hito ni "arigatoo" to itte imasu ne.
(**b**) It's relatively easy for Japanese to translate English into Japanese, but for Americans the reverse is the case.
日本人には、英語を日本語に訳す方がどちらかというと易しいけれど、アメリカ人は、その{逆/?反対}だ。
Nihon-jin ni wa, eigo o Nihon-go ni yakusu hoo ga dochira ka to iu to yasashii keredo, Amerika-jin wa, sono {gyaku/?hantai} da.

review vt. **[for s.o. to look over, study, or consider s.t. again ⟪fig. "write a critical report on a book"⟫]**

1. ⟨-o⟩ mi-⌈naosu ⟨〜を⟩見直す ① [for s.o. to look over or examine s.t. again or to come to think better of s.o./s.t. than before], ⟨-o⟩ sa⌈i-cho⌉osa-suru ⟨〜を⟩再調査する ③ •c [for s.o. to examine or investigate s.t./s.o. again carefully]

EX. The district attorney's office is currently reviewing the case.
地方検察庁では現在その事件を{見直して/再調査して}いる。
Chihoo-kensatsu-choo de wa genzai sono jiken o {mi-naoshite/sai-choosa-shite} iru.

2. ⟨-no⟩ hi⌈hyoo o ka⌉ku ⟨〜の⟩批評を書く ① [for s.o. to write a report discussing the merits and demerits of s.t.], ⟨-no⟩ sho⌈hyoo o ka⌉ku ⟨〜の⟩書評を書く ① [for s.o. to write a critical report on a book]

EX. I was asked to review Prof. Nojima's new book.
私は野島教授の新しい本の{批評/書評}を書くように頼まれた。
Watashi wa Nojima-kyooju no atarashii hon no {hihyoo/shohyoo} o kaku yooni tanoma-reta.

3. ⟨-o⟩ fu⌈kushuu-suru ⟨〜を⟩復習する ③ •c [for s.o. to study again what one has studied earlier] ⟪go over one's lesson⟫

R

EX. I have to review lessons one to twenty for the final examination.
私は期末試験のために第一課から第二十課まで復習しなければなりません。
Watashi wa kimatsu-shiken no tame ni dai-ik-ka kara dai-ni-juk-ka made fukushuu-shinakereba narimasen.

— n. **[the act of looking over, studying, or considering s.t. again or a critical evaluation in writing of the merits of a book or artistic/dramatic performance]**

1. sa⌈i-cho⌉osa 再調査 •c [the act of examining or investigating s.t./s.o. again carefully]

EX. A review of the police's handling of the murder investigation is in progress.
警察のその殺人事件の捜査に関する再調査が進行中だ。
Keisatsu no sono satsujin-jiken no soosa ni-kansuru sai-choosa ga shinkoo-chuu da.

2. hi⌈hyoo 批評 •c [discussion of the value of s.t. by considering its merits and demerits, etc.] ⟪**criticism, critique**⟫, **sho⌈hyoo 書評 •c [a critical report on a book]**

EX. (**a**) That pianist told me that she never reads reviews of her performances.
そのピアニストは自分の演奏の{批評/*書評}は決して読まないと私に言った。
*Sono pianisuto wa jibun no ensoo no {hihyoo/*shohyoo} wa kesshite yomanai to watashi ni itta.*
(**b**) I usually buy a book only after reading a review of it.
私は大抵{書評/?批評}を読んでからでないと、本を買わない。
Watashi wa taitei {shohyoo/?hihyoo} o yonde kara denai to, hon o kawanai.

revolt vi./vt. **[for s.o. to rebel against a government or authority or to feel disgust at s.o./s.t.]**

1. ha⌈nran o okosu 反乱を起こす ① •c [for s.o. to rebel against authority] ⟪**oppose, resist, disobey, rebel against**⟫

EX. The oppressed peasants revolted against their landlord.
しいたげられていた小作人たちは地主に対して反乱を起こした。
Shiitage-rarete ita kosaku-nin-tachi wa jinushi ni-taishite hanran o okoshita.

2. ⟨-ni⟩ mu⌈tto-suru ⟨〜に⟩むっとする ③ [for s.o. to feel disgusted at s.t./s.o.]

EX. His rude joke revolted me.
彼の下品な冗談にむっとした。
Kare no gehinna joodan ni mutto-shita.

revolution n. **[a rotating motion, esp. that of one complete orbit ⟪fig. "a sudden radical change, esp. in a political system"⟫]**

1. ka⌈iten 回転 •c [a rotating motion, esp. that of one complete orbit]

EX. The rate at which this wheel is rotating is 200 revolutions per minute.
この車輪の回転速度は一分に二百回です。
Kono sharin no kaiten-sokudo wa ip-pun ni ni-hyak-kai desu.

2. ka⌈kumei 革命 •c [a sudden radical change in political system]

EX. Do you know when the French Revolution took place?
フランス革命がいつ起きたか知っていますか。
Furansu-kakumei ga itsu okita ka shitte imasu ka.

revolutionary adj. **[pertaining to or having the characteristics of a revolution]**

1. ka⌈kumei no N 革命のN •c [pertaining to a revolution]

EX. The twentieth century can be called a revolutionary period in the field of science.
二十世紀は科学の分野での革命の時期だと言える。
Ni-jus-seiki wa kagaku no bun'ya de no kakumei no jiki da to ie-ru.

2. ka⌈kumei-tekina 革命的な adj(*na*). **•c [having the characteristics of a revolution]**

EX. The computer brought many revolutionary changes to our daily life.
コンピューターは様々な革命的な変化を我々の日常生活にもたらした。
Konpyuutaa wa sama-zamana

kakumei-tekina henka o ware-ware no nichijoo-seikatsu ni motarashita.

reward n. **[s.t. given or received, esp. money, in return for s.t. done, esp. for some extraordinary achievement or service]**
1. ho⌈oshuu 報酬 •c [s.t. given, esp. money, in compensation for s.o.'s work or efforts] **《remuneration, compensation》**

EX. What did you receive as a reward for your efforts?
その労力に対する報酬として何を受け取りましたか。
Sono rooryoku ni-taisuru hooshuu to shite nani o uke-torimashita ka.

2. ho⌈oshoo-kin 報奨金 •c [money given or received in compensation for worthy behavior (esp. for the return of a lost article or the capture of a criminal)] **《indemnity, compensation》**

EX. A reward of $10,000 will be given to anyone providing us information leading to the arrest of the killer.
殺人者の逮捕につながる情報を提供した人に一万ドルの報奨金を出す。
Satsujin-sha no taiho ni tsunagaru joohoo o teikyoo-shita hito ni ichi-man-doru no hooshoo-kin o dasu.

— vt. **[for s.o. to give s.t., esp. money, to s.o. in return for doing s.t., esp. some extraordinary achievement or service]**
〈-ni〉 ho⌈oshoo(-kin) o a⌈taeru 〈〜に〉報奨(金)を与える ②

EX. The company will reward the group which achieves the best quality control.
会社は品質管理を一番よくやるグループに報奨(金)を与えるそうだ。
Kaisha wa hinshitsu-kanri o ichiban yoku yaru guruupu ni hooshoo(-kin) o ataeru sooda.

rewrite vt. **[to write s.t. again, esp. in order to improve its content or style]**
〈-o〉 ka⌈ki-nao⌉su 〈〜を〉書き直す /〈V*masu* of *kaku* ① write + *naosu* ① repair/ ①

EX. I'm thinking of rewriting this paper and submitting it to an essay contest.
この作文を書き直して作文コンクールに出そうと思っています。
Kono sakubun o kaki-naoshite sakubun-konkuuru ni dasoo to omotte imasu.

Rhode Island n.
Ro⌈odo-a⌉irando ロードアイランド **•f**

rhyme n.
(o⌈o)in (押)韻 •c

EX. Japanese traditional poems like *haiku* and *waka* do not typically use rhyme.
俳句や和歌のような伝統的な日本の詩歌には大抵(押)韻はない。
Haiku ya waka no yoona dentoo-tekina Nihon no shiika ni wa taitei (oo)in wa nai.

— vi.
〈-to〉 i⌈n o fumu 〈〜と〉韻を踏む ①

EX. "Pride" rhymes with "bride."
「プライド」は「ブライド」と韻を踏む。
'Puraido' wa 'buraido' to in o fumu.

rhythm n.
ri⌉zumu リズム **•f**

EX. I like the rhythm of tango.
タンゴのリズムが好きだ。
Tango no rizumu ga suki da.

rhythmical adj. **[having rhythm]**
ri⌈zumi⌉karuna リズミカルな adj(*na*). **•f**

EX. I like music that's fast and rhythmical.
私はテンポの速いリズミカルな音楽が好きです。
Watashi wa tenpo no hayai rizumikaruna ongaku ga suki desu.

rib n. **[one of the bones covering the lungs and heart 《fig. "a cut of meat including a rib"》]**
a⌈bara-bone あばら骨, ro⌈kkotsu ろっ骨 •c

EX. I broke one of my ribs while playing football.
フットボールをしている時に、私は{あばら骨/ろっ骨}を折った。
Futto-booru o shite iru toki ni, watashi wa {abara-bone/rokkotsu} o otta.

ribbon n.
ri⌉bon リボン **•f**

EX. Who's that little girl with the pretty ribbon in her hair?
きれいなリボンを髪に付けている、あ

R

の小さな女の子はだれですか。
Kireina ribon o kami ni tsukete iru, ano chiisana onna-no-ko wa dare desu ka.

rice n. **[a variety of grass plant (Oryza sativa) grown in warm climates that produces seeds used for food or the seeds of this] ko⌈me⌉ 米 [uncooked seeds of the Oryza sativa plant after the chaff has been removed], ra⌉isu ライス •f [the seeds of the Oryza sativa plant cooked to be served with Western-style cuisine], go⌉han 御飯 •c [food consumed by people for sustenance or the seeds of the Oryza sativa (rice) plant steamed for human consumption]**

EX. (**a**) You have to wash rice before cooking it.
{米/*ライス/*御飯}は炊く前にとがなければならない。
*{Kome/*Raisu/*Gohan} wa taku mae ni toganakereba naranai.*
(**b**) Cooked rice is called "gohan" in Japanese.
炊いた{米/*ライス/*御飯}は日本語で「御飯」と言います。
*Taita {kome/*raisu/*gohan} wa Nihon-go de 'gohan' to iimasu.*
(**c**) Which would you like, rice or bread?
{ライス/御飯/*米}になさいますか。パンになさいますか。
*{Raisu/Gohan/*Kome} ni nasaimasu ka. Pan ni nasaimasu ka.*

PHRASE: rice bowl *gohan-jawan* 御飯茶わん •c

EX. In Japan it's okay to hold your rice bowl close to your mouth while you eat.
日本では食べる時、御飯茶わんを口に持って行っても構いません。
Nihon de wa taberu toki, go-han-jawan o kuchi ni motte itte mo kamaimasen.

PHRASE: rice field *tanbo* たんぼ, *ta* 田, *suiden* 水田 •c; rice plant *ine* 稲

EX. Rice plants were swaying in the autumn wind.
稲が秋風に揺れていました。
Ine ga aki-kaze ni yurete imashita.

rich adj. **[having much of s.t., esp. money or wealth]**

1. ka⌈ne-mochi⌉ no N 金持ちのN [having much money or wealth] ((wealthy, affluent)), yu⌉ufukuna 裕福な adj(*na*). **•c [having financial resources sufficient to lead a comfortable life] ((wealthy, affluent, well-off))**

EX. (**a**) This is a school for children who come from rich families.
ここは{金持ちの/裕福な}家庭の子供が通う学校です。
Koko wa {kane-mochi no/yuufukuna} katei no kodomo ga kayou gakkoo desu.
(**b**) That man drives a Porsche. He must be rich.
あの男はポルシェを運転している。{金持ち/裕福}に違いない。
Ano otoko wa Porushe o unten-shite iru. {Kane-mochi/Yuufuku} ni chigai-nai.

2. yu⌉takana 豊かな adj(*na*). **[existing in more than sufficient quantities and to spare] ((abundant, plentiful, affluent, opulent)), ⟨-ni⟩ to⌉nda N ⟨~に⟩富んだN /⟨Vinf. past of *tomu* ① abound/ [abounding in s.t. such as nutrition, natural resources, experiences, ideas, wit, etc. ⟨fml⟩], ⟨-ni⟩ to⌉nde iru (N) ⟨~に⟩富んでいる(N) /⟨V*te iru* of *tomu* ① abound/**

EX. (**a**) Japan is not rich in natural resources.
日本は天然資源{が豊かではない/に富んでいない}。
Nihon wa tennen-shigen {ga yutaka dewanai/ni tonde inai}.
(**b**) That singer has a rich voice.
あの歌手は声量{が豊かだ/??に富んでいる}。
Ano kashu wa seiryoo {ga yutaka da/??ni tonde iru}.
(**c**) Potatoes are rich in vitamin C.
じゃがいもはビタミンC{が豊かだ/に富んでいる}。
Jagaimo wa bitamin-shii {ga yutaka da/ni tonde iru}.
(**d**) Mr. Noda has rich experience as a music instructor.
野田氏は音楽の教師として経験{が豊かだ/?に富んでいる}。

Noda-shi wa ongaku no kyooshi to shite keiken {ga yutaka da/?ni tonde iru}.

riches n. **[abundant wealth]**

za⌈isan 財産 •c [the entire amount of money, possessions, etc., one owns] **《estate, fortune, means, property》**, **to⌉mi 富 [an abundant supply of property/money/resources ⟨w⟩] 《wealth, fortune, opulence, affluence》**

EX. (**a**) Janet has riches beyond belief; she has nothing to worry about in her future.
ジャネットは信じられない程{財産/??富}があるから、将来を心配する必要は何もない。
Janetto wa shinji-rarenai hodo {zaisan/??tomi} ga aru kara, shoorai o shinpai-suru hitsuyoo wa nani-mo nai.
(**b**) My grandfather accumulated his riches single-handedly through hard work.
祖父は苦労に苦労を重ねてたった一人で{富/財産}を築いた。
Sofu wa kuroo ni kuroo o kasanete tatta hitori de {tomi/zaisan} o kizuita.

rid vt. **[to eliminate s.t. undesirable or objectionable from s.t.]**

⟨-kara⟩ ⟨-o⟩ to⌈ri-nozoku ⟨～から⟩⟨～を⟩取り除く ① [to eliminate s.t. undesirable from a place] 《remove, set aside》

PHRASE: get rid of ⟨*-o*⟩ *tori-nozoku* ⟨～を⟩取り除く ①

EX. Please get rid of the weeds in the backyard.
裏庭の雑草を取り除いてください。
Ura-niwa no zassoo o tori-nozoite kudasai.

riddle n.

na⌈zo-nazo なぞなぞ

EX. Can you figure out this riddle? No matter how much of it you eat, you don't gain weight. What is it?
このなぞなぞ分かる？　食べても食べても太らないもの、なあに。
Kono nazo-nazo wakaru? Tabete mo tabete mo futoranai mono, naani.

ride vt. **[to sit on s.t. mobile such as an animal or vehicle and control its movement]**

1. ⟨-ni⟩ no⌈ru ⟨～に⟩のる ① [to get onto s.t./s.o./s.a. that is able to support one's weight 《fig. "appear in a publication"》] 《get on, board, take a vehicle, lie on, be on top of, be recorded》 ↔ {⟨-kara⟩/⟨-o⟩} oriru {⟨～から⟩/⟨～を⟩}降りる ②

㊅ "get onto s.t./s.o./s.a. that is perceived to be mobile"▷乗る, "get onto s.t./s.o./s.a. that is immobile"▷載る

EX. Do you like to ride horses?
馬に乗るのが好きですか。
Uma ni noru no ga suki desu ka.

2. ⟨-ni⟩ no⌈tte-iku ⟨～に⟩乗って行く ① [for s.o./s.a. to get to some place on a vehicle]

EX. I ride the bus to work every morning.
毎朝会社へバスに乗って行きます。
Mai-asa kaisha e basu ni notte-ikimasu.

rider n. **[a person who is carried on s.t. mobile such as an animal or vehicle]**

1. no⌈ru hito 乗る人

2. ki⌉shu 騎手 •c [a person who rides a horse] 《horseman》

ridge n. **[a narrow, raised part of s.t., such as the line formed by a series of mountain crests]**

o⌉ne 尾根 [the line formed by a series of mountain crests]

EX. I walked about 10 kilometers along the mountain ridge.
私は山の尾根を十キロぐらい歩いた。
Watashi wa yama no one o juk-kiro-gurai aruita.

ridiculous adj. **[deserving of laughter or contempt]**

ko⌈kke⌉ina こっけいな adj(*na*). **•c [deserving of (contemptuous) laughter] 《comic, funny, humorous, ludicrous》**, **ba⌈ka⌉-geta N ばかげたN**, **ba⌈ka⌉-gete iru (N) ばかげている(N) [looking foolish] 《absurd, foolish, idiotic》**

EX. (**a**) I got mad at him for saying such ridiculous things.
私は彼があんまり{ばかげた/*こっけいな}事を言うのでおこった。
Watashi wa kare ga anmari {baka-geta/

**kokkeina} koto o iu node okotta.*
(**b**) His funny stories are more ridiculous than comic.
あの人の笑い話はおかしいというより{こっけいだ/ばかげている}。
Ano hito no warai-banashi wa okashii to iu yori {kokkei da/baka-gete iru}.

riding n. **[the act of being carried on an animal or vehicle]**
1. jo⌈oba 乗馬 •c [the act of sitting on and controlling the movement of a horse]
2. jo⌈osha 乗車 •c [the act of being carried on a vehicle]

rifle n.
ra⌈ifuru⌉-juu ライフル銃 •f+c, ra⌉ifuru ライフル •f
EX. The robber pointed a rifle at the bank teller and demanded $10,000 in cash.
強盗は銀行員にライフル(銃)を向けて現金で一万ドル出せと言った。
Gootoo wa ginkoo-in ni raifuru(-juu) o mukete genkin de ichi-man-doru dase to itta.

R

right adj. **[conforming to what is just, morally good, true, correct, or proper or on the side of the body away from the heart]**
1. ta⌈dashi⌉i 正しい adj(*i*). **[conforming to an ethical, legal, logical, social, or regulatory standard; free from error] 《just, righteous, proper, correct, lawful, legal》 ↔ chigau 違う ①**
EX. (**a**) What Mr. Harada said is right.
原田さんが言ったことは正しい。
Harada-san ga itta koto wa tadashii.
(**b**) Is this the right way to hold chopsticks?
おはしの持ち方はこれで正しいですか。
O-hashi no mochi-kata wa kore de tadashii desu ka.
(**c**) Bill's spoken Japanese is always grammatically right, but somehow it doesn't sound quite natural.
ビルの話す日本語は文法的にはいつも正しいんだけど、どうも自然じゃないんです。
Biru no hanasu Nihon-go wa bunpoo-tekini wa itsu-mo tadashii n da kedo, doomo shizen janai n desu.
2. mi⌈gi(-gawa) no N 右(側)のN [on the side of the body away from the heart] ↔ hidari(-gawa) no N 左(側)のN
EX. You should hold your rice bowl with your left hand and your chopsticks with your right hand.
御飯茶わんは左(の)手で、はしは右(の)手で持ちます。
Gohan-jawan wa hidari (no) te de, hashi wa migi (no) te de mochimasu.
PHRASE: right hand *migi-te* 右手 ↔ *hidari-te* 左手
PHRASE: right hand man *kata-ude* 片腕 **[**one arm 《fig. "highly dependable person"》**]**
EX. Mr. Tani is my right hand man.
谷さんは私の片腕です。
Tani-san wa watashi no kata-ude desu.

—— n. **[that which is just, morally good, true, correct, or proper; s.t. to which one is justly entitled; the side of the body away from the heart]**
1. ta⌈dashi⌉i koto 正しいこと [that which comforms to an ethical, legal, logical, social, or regulatory standard or is free from error]
2. ke⌉nri 権利 •c [a qualifications one has to do s.t. freely] 《claim》 ↔ gimu 義務 •c
EX. (**a**) Men and women are granted the same rights under the law.
法律の下では男性と女性は同じ権利を与えられている。
Hooritsu no moto de wa dansei to josei wa onaji kenri o atae-rarete iru.
(**b**) It's not proper to insist solely on one's rights without at the same time fulfilling one's obligations.
権利だけ主張して義務を果たさないのはよくない。
Kenri dake shuchoo-shite gimu o hatasanai no wa yokunai.
PHRASE: human rights *jinken* 人権 **•c**
3. mi⌈gi(-gawa) 右(側) [the side of the body opposite to the heart] ↔ hidari(-gawa) 左(側)
EX. Please turn right at the next corner.

次の角を右に曲がって下さい。
Tsugi no kado o migi ni magatte kudasai.

—— adv. [in a just, morally good, true, correct, or proper manner]

1. ta⌈da⌉shiku 正しく /⟨adj(*i*). *ku* of *tadashii* right/ ⟪properly, correctly, lawfully, legally⟫, cha⌈n-to ちゃんと [in a proper or accurate way ⟨s⟩] ⟪perfectly, properly, correctly⟫

EX. If you don't use it right, it won't work.
{正しく/ちゃんと}使わないとうまく行きませんよ。
{Tadashiku/Chan-to} tsukawanai to umaku ikimasen yo.

2. cho⌈odo ちょうど [with no variance whatsoever from a given time, quantity, or location] ⟪just, exactly, precisely⟫

EX. (**a**) A statue of the founder of the university stands right in the center of the campus.
大学の創立者の銅像がキャンパスのちょうど真ん中に立っている。
Daigaku no sooritsu-sha no doozoo ga kyanpasu no choodo mannaka ni tatte iru.
(**b**) The train arrived right on time.
汽車はちょうど時間通りに着いた。
Kisha wa choodo jikan-doori ni tsuita.

right-handed adj. **[using the hand on the side of the body away from the heart habitually and with greater ease]**
mi⌈gi-kiki no N 右利きのN ↔ hidari-kiki no N 左利きのN

EX. A: Are you right-handed?
右利きですか。
Migi-kiki desu ka.
B: No, I'm left handed.
いいえ、左利きです。
Iie, hidari-kiki desu.

rigid adj. **[not easily bending or flexible to change]**

1. ka⌈tai かたい adj(*i*). **[not easily changed/broken/influenced] ⟪hard, solid, stiff, tough, tight, strict, safe, obstinate⟫**
㊊ "solid, as opposed to liquid" ▷固い, "figuratively stiff" ▷堅い, otherwise ▷硬い

EX. This bamboo feels unusually rigid.
この竹は異常に{固/硬}そうですね。
Kono take wa ijooni kata-soo desu ne.

2. yu⌈uzuu ga kikanai (N) 融通がきかない (N) [for s.o. to be unwilling or unable to accommodate to new conditions] ⟪thickheaded⟫, ga⌉nkona 頑固な adj(*na*). **•c [firmly refusing to change one's ideas/attitudes ⟪fig. "for a disease to continue longer than expected"⟫] ⟪stubborn, inflexible, obstinate, stiff-headed, bigoted⟫**

EX. My father is totally rigid; he won't listen to anything I say.
父は全く{融通がきかない/頑固な}ので何を言っても聞いてくれません。
Chichi wa mattaku {yuuzuu ga kikanai/gankona} node nani o itte mo kiite kuremasen.

3. ge⌈nkakuna 厳格な adj(*na*). **•c [so strict as to allow no mistake or sloppiness] ⟪strict, stern, rigorous, severe⟫**

EX. That teacher's rigid way of dealing with students has made him unpopular.
あの先生は学生の扱い方が厳格過ぎて人気がない。
Ano sensei wa gakusei no atsukai-kata ga genkaku-sugite ninki ga nai.

rim n. **[the outer border of an object, esp. a circular one ⟨fml⟩]**

1. fu⌈chi⌉ 縁 [the outer part surrounding a two-demensional object or area] ⟪edge, verge, shore, brink, margin⟫

EX. I don't like the rims on these eyeglasses.
この眼鏡の縁が気に入らないんです。
Kono megane no fuchi ga ki ni iranai n desu.

2. shu⌈uhen 周辺 •c [an area on the periphery of s.t.] ⟪circumference, environs, outskirts⟫

EX. A hotel stands on the rim of the volcano.
火山の周辺にホテルがある。
Kazan no shuuhen ni hoteru ga aru.

PHRASE: the Pacific rim *kan-taihei-yoo* 環太平洋

ring[1] n. **[a circular object with an empty circular area at the center]**

1. wa⌉ 輪 ⟪circle, link, wheel⟫

R

EX. "*Wanage*" is a game where you toss rings onto a peg.
「輪投げ」は輪を棒に投げ入れる遊びだ。
'Wa-nage' wa wa o boo ni nage-ireru asobi da.

2. yu⌈bi-wa 指輪 [a circular ornament worn on the finger]

EX. He must be married because he's wearing a ring.
彼は指輪をはめているから、きっと結婚しているんでしょう。
Kare wa yubi-wa o hamete iru kara, kitto kekkon-shite iru n deshoo.

ring² vi. **[for s.t. to give off a clear bell-like sound]**
na⌈ru 鳴る ① [for s.t. such as a bell, telephone, or musical instrument to give off a clear, sonorous sound] 《sound, jangle, roar》

R

EX. I woke up to the telephone ringing at three o'clock in the morning.
朝の三時に電話が鳴った時に目が覚めてしまった。
Asa no san-ji ni denwa ga natta toki ni me ga samete shimatta.

—— n. **[a clear bell-like sound or a telephone call]**

1. (na⌈ru) o⌈to (鳴る)音 [a clear, sonorous sound such as produced by a bell, telephone, or musical instrument]

EX. I can always hear the ring of the telephone in the neighbor's apartment.
隣のアパートの電話の鳴る音がいつも聞こえてくる。
Tonari no apaato no denwa no naru oto ga itsu-mo kikoete kuru.

2. de⌈nwa 電話 •c [an apparatus for transmitting speech to a distant hearer or an act of making contact with s.o. by means of such an apparatus]

EX. I'll give you a ring tonight, OK?
今晩電話をかけるからね。
Konban denwa o kakeru kara ne.

ripe adj. **[fully developed or matured and ready to be harvested or eaten; ready to undergo s.t.]**
ju⌈ku⌉shita N 熟したN /⟨Vinf. past of *jukusu* ① become ripe/ [fully developed or grown and ready to be eaten; timely in opportunity] 《mature, mellow》

EX. Ripe persimmons hanging from a tree against the blue sky in late autumn make a beautiful scene.
晩秋の青空を背に熟した柿が木になっているのは、美しい風景だ。
Banshuu no ao-zora o se ni jukushita kaki ga ki ni natte iru no wa, utsukushii fuukei da.

rise vi. **[to move from a lower to higher position or for s.o./s.a. to get up from a lying or sitting position]**

1. a⌈garu あがる ① [to go up in vertical position, temperature, price, status, or level 《fig. "improve," "stop raining," "get nervous"》] 《go up, be advanced, progress》 ↔ sagaru 下がる ①
㊥ "rise to a higher location"▷上がる, "(for a kite/flag) to fly/be deep-fried"▷揚がる, "(for a hand) to be raised"▷挙がる, otherwise ▷あがる

EX. (**a**) The temperature rose to 100°F this afternoon.
今日の午後温度は華氏百度に上がった。
Kyoo no gogo ondo wa kashi hyaku-do ni agatta.
(**b**) The prices of Japanese cars have risen more than 10% over the past year.
日本の車の値段はこの一年で10%以上上がっている。
Nihon no kuruma no nedan wa kono ichi-nen de jup-paasento-ijoo agatte iru.
(**c**) Each time Yamashita rose in rank in the company his work load also increased, and he would come home from work later and later.
山下さんは会社での地位が上がるたびに仕事も増え、帰宅時間が遅くなった。
Yamashita-san wa kaisha de no chii ga agaru tabi ni shigoto mo fue, kitaku-jikan ga osoku natta.

2. no⌈boru のぼる ① [to move to a higher position] 《ascend, climb, mount, amount

up to》↔ oriru 下りる ②
㊥ "for the sun/moon/smoke to rise"▷昇る, "climb"▷登る, otherwise ▷上る

EX. (**a**) The sun rose above the horizon.
太陽が水平線の上に昇った。
Taiyoo ga suihei-sen no ue ni nobotta.
(**b**) Smoke is rising from the chimney.
煙が煙突から上っている。
Kemuri ga entotsu kara nobotte iru.

3. o⌈ki⌉ru 起きる ② [for s.o./s.a./s.t. that has been lying horizontally dormant to stand up vertically《fig. "wake up," "occur"》]《wake up, happen, come to pass, occur, take place, break out, crop up, begin to burn》

EX. When I was a boy I had to rise every day at dawn to milk the cows.
子供の時毎朝牛の乳をしぼるために夜明けと共に起きなければならなかった。
Kodomo no toki mai-asa ushi no chichi o shiboru tame ni yo-ake to tomo ni okinakereba naranakatta.

4. ta⌈chi-agaru 立ち上がる ① [for s.o./s.a. to get into an upright position《fig."take action"》]《stand up, get up》

EX. After the performance the audience rose from their seats and applauded.
聴衆は演奏が終わると立ち上がって、拍手した。
Chooshuu wa ensoo ga owaru to tachi-agatte, hakushu-shita.

risk n. **[the possibility of suffering loss, harm, or failure]**
ki⌈ken 危険 •c [the possibility that s.t. harmful/undesirable will happen]《danger, peril, jeopardy》, bo⌈oken 冒険 •c [the act of doing s.t. dangerous or s.t. that may not be successful]《adventure, hazard》

EX. (**a**) You can never really succeed unless you take risks.
{危険を冒さなければ/冒険をしなければ}、本当には成功しない。
{Kiken o okasanakereba/Booken o shinakereba}, hontoo ni wa seikoo-shinai.
(**b**) If you smoke, your risk of getting lung cancer increases greatly.
たばこを吸えば、肺がんになる{危険/*冒険}はずっと大きい。
*Tabako o sueba, haigan ni naru {kiken/ *booken} wa zutto ookii.*

—— vt. **[to expose s.o./s.t./s.a. to the possibility of suffering loss, harm, or failure]**
⟨-o⟩ ki⌈ken ni sa⌈rasu ⟨～を⟩危険にさらす ① [to expose s.o./s.t./s.a. to s.t. harmful/ undesirable]

EX. I wouldn't risk my life by swimming in such a swift river.
こんな流れの速い川を泳いで命を危険にさらしたくありません。
Konna nagare no hayai kawa o oyoide inochi o kiken ni sarashi-taku arimasen.

rival n. **[s.o./s.t. that competes with s.o./s.t. else]**
kyo⌈osoo-a⌉ite 競争相手 [a person one competes with]《competitor》, ra⌉ibaru ライバル •f [a person one competes with (in a love affair)], ko⌈i-ga⌉taki 恋敵 [a person one competes with in a love affair]《corrival》

EX. (**a**) Korea is no doubt a rival of Japan economically.
韓国は日本にとって経済上の{競争相手/ライバル/*恋敵}だ。
*Kankoku wa Nihon ni-totte keizai-joo no {kyoosoo-aite/raibaru/*koi-gataki} da.*
(**b**) Both he and I loved Jane. In other words, we were rivals.
彼も僕もジェーンが好きだった。つまり、私たちはお互いに{競争相手/ライバル/恋敵}だったのだ。
Kare mo boku mo Jeen ga sukidatta. Tsumari, watashi-tachi wa o-tagai ni {kyoosoo-aite/raibaru/koi-gataki} datta no da.

—— vt. **[for s.o./s.t. to be or try to be as good as s.o./s.t. else]**
⟨-to⟩ kyo⌈osoo-suru ⟨～と⟩競争する ③ •c [for s.o. to strive to achieve victory or superiority over another]《compete with, vie with》, ⟨-to⟩ ha⌈ri-a⌉u ⟨～と⟩張り合う ①

R

[for people of equal strength or ability to compete to attain a common object] **《compete with, vie with》**

EX. I can't rival Bob in math.
数学で僕はボブと{競争できない/張り合えない}。
Suugaku de boku wa Bobu to {kyoosoo-dekinai/hari-ae-nai}.

river n.
ka⌈wa⌉ 川

EX. The Mississippi River is the longest river in the United States.
ミシシッピ川は米国で一番長い川です。
Mishishippi-gawa wa Beikoku de ichiban nagai kawa desu.

road n. **[a man-made way by which people or vehicles may pass from one place to another]**
mi⌈chi 道 **[a strip of paved or cleared ground for getting from one place to another or the distance covered in a journey 《fig. "method," "the proper way of thinking or conducting oneself," "special field"》] 《way, street, path, journey, morality》, do⌉oro** 道路 **•c [a way for people or vehicles to pass along] 《way, street, thoroughfare》**

EX. Since it's a holiday, the roads are very crowded.
休日で、{道/道路}が大変込んでいる。
Kyuujitsu de, {michi/dooro} ga taihen konde iru.

R

roadside n. **[an area along the side of a road]**
do⌈oro-waki 道路わき, **mi⌈chibata** 道端

EX. I bought a can of coffee at a vending machine by the roadside.
{道端/道路わき}の自動販売機で缶コーヒーを買った。
{Michibata/Dooro-waki} no jidoo-hanbai-ki de kan-koohii o katta.

roam vi. **[to wander about without any particular purpose]**
1. ⟨-o⟩ a⌈ruki-mawa⌉ru ⟨〜を⟩歩き回る ① **[for s.o./s.a. to walk around] 《walk about, wander》**

EX. We roamed through the woods yesterday for almost three hours.
昨日は森を三時間近く歩き回りました。
Kinoo wa mori o san-jikan chikaku aruki-mawarimashita.

2. ⟨-o⟩ hyo⌈ohaku-suru ⟨〜を⟩漂泊する ③ **•c [to wander from one place to another without any particular purpose ⟨w⟩] 《drift》**

roar vi. **[for a lion to utter a deep, loud sound 《fig. "make a sound like a lion," "laugh loudly"》]**
ho⌈e⌉ru ほえる ② **[for a dog, wolf, etc., to utter a sharp, loud sound] 《bark, yelp, howl》**

EX. A lion seldom roars in the zoo.
動物園でライオンはめったにほえない。
Doobutsu-en de raion wa metta ni hoenai.

PHRASE: roar with laughter *oo-warai-suru* 大笑いする ③

EX. The audience roared with laughter at the comedian's antics.
聴衆はコメディアンのしぐさに大笑いした。
Chooshuu wa komedian no shigusa ni oo-warai-shita.

roast vt. **[to cook meat in an oven or over an open fire or to dry and brown s.t. with heat, such as coffee beans or chestnuts]**
1. ⟨-o⟩ ya⌈ku ⟨〜を⟩焼く ① **[for s.o. to cause a change in s.t. through exposure to heat/fire/sunlight] 《burn, fire, broil, grill, bake, toast, char, cremate, print》**

EX. It can take up to six hours to roast a large turkey in the oven.
大きな七面鳥をオーブンで焼くのに六時間もかかる場合がある。
Ookina shichimen-choo o oobun de yaku no ni roku-jikan mo kakaru baai ga aru.

2. ⟨-o⟩ i⌉ru ⟨〜を⟩いる ① **[for s.o. to heat beans/rice/raw egg] 《parch》**

EX. I used to love the smell when my mother would roast coffee beans when I was small.
小さい時母がコーヒーの豆をいるにおいは最高だった。

Chiisai toki haha ga koohii no mame o iru nioi wa saikoo datta.

— n. **[a piece of meat cooked or to be cooked in an oven or open fire]**
1. ro⌈osuto-bi⌉ifu ローストビーフ •f [a piece of beef cooked in an oven or open fire]
2. ro⌈osuto⌉-niku ロースト肉 [a piece of meat cooked or to be cooked in an oven or open fire], ro⌉osuto ロースト •f

rob vt. **[for s.o. to take property away from s.o. by force or illegal means]**
1. ⟨⟨-kara⟩⟩ ⟨-o⟩ nu⌈su⌉mu ⟨⟨〜から⟩⟩⟨〜を⟩盗む ① ⟪steal, take, purloin, plagiarize⟫, ⟨⟨-kara⟩⟩ ⟨-o⟩ to⌉ru ⟨⟨〜から⟩⟩⟨〜を⟩取る ① [for s.o./s.a. to cause s.t. to come into one's possession from s.o./s.a. else] ⟪take, receive⟫, ⟨-no⟩ na⌉ka no mo⌈no⌉ o nu⌈su⌉mu ⟨〜の⟩中の物を盗む ① [for s.o. to steal s.t. out of a container (such as a safe, house, box, etc.)], ⟨-no⟩ na⌉ka no mono o to⌉ru ⟨〜の⟩中の物を取る ① [for s.o. to take s.t. out of a container]

EX. (**a**) Someone robbed me of my gold watch at the office.
事務所で誰かが私の金時計{を盗んだ/を取った/*の中の物を盗んだ/*の中の物を取った}。
*Jimu-sho de dare-ka ga watashi no kin-dokei {o nusunda/o totta/*no naka no mono o nusunda/*no naka no mono o totta}.*
(**b**) A burglar robbed my uncle's house during broad daylight.
泥棒が白昼に私の叔父の家{の中の物を盗んだ/の中の物を取った/*を盗んだ/*を取った}。
*Doroboo ga hakuchuu ni watashi no oji no ie {no naka no mono o nusunda/no naka no mono o totta/*o nusunda/*o totta}.*

robber n. **[a person who takes property away from s.o. by force or illegal means]**
do⌈roboo 泥棒 [a person who takes property away from s.o. by stealth in an illegal manner] ⟪thief⟫, go⌈otoo 強盗 •c [a person who takes property away from s.o. by illegal means, esp. using threat or violence]

EX. A robber entered my house while I was out yesterday and took my money and jewelry.
きのう留守の間に僕の家に{泥棒/強盗}が入って、金と宝石を取って行った。
Kinoo rusu no aida ni boku no ie ni {doroboo/gootoo} ga haitte, kane to hooseki o totte itta.

robe n. **[a long, loose-fitting garment]**
ro⌉obu ローブ •f

robot n.
ro⌈bo⌉tto ロボット •f

EX. "Industrial robots" are replacing workers more and more in automobile factories.
自動車工場では、いわゆる「産業ロボット」がますます労働者に取って代わっている。
Jidoosha-koojoo de wa, iwayuru 'sangyoo robotto' ga masu-masu roodoosha ni totte-kawatte iru.

rock n. **[a mass of hard mineral matter of the sort naturally occurring in the earth's crust]**
1. i⌈wa⌉ 岩 [a large mass of naturally-occurring hard mineral matter, usually attached to the earth's surface]

EX. I love to climb rocks.
僕は岩に登るのが好きです。
Boku wa iwa ni noboru no ga suki desu.

2. i⌈shi⌉ 石 [a relatively small mass of naturally-occurring hard mineral matter] ⟪stone⟫

EX. The student demonstrators threw rocks at the policemen.
デモをしている学生は警官に石を投げつけていた。
Demo o shite iru gakusei wa keikan ni ishi o nage-tsukete ita.

rocket n.
ro⌈ke⌉tto ロケット •f

EX. I still remember the thrill I felt when I saw the first manned rocket launch on TV.
私はテレビで最初の有人ロケットの打ち上げを見た時の感激をまだ覚えています。

Watashi wa terebi de saisho no yuujin-roketto no uchi-age o mita toki no kangeki o mada oboete imasu.

rocky adj. **[abounding in or consisting of rock; like rock]**

1. i⌈wa⌉ no o⌉oi N 岩の多いN [abounding in rocks]

EX. We slowly climbed up the rocky mountain path.
私たちは岩の多い山道をゆっくりと登った。
Watashi-tachi wa iwa no ooi yama-michi o yukkuri to nobotta.

2. i⌈wa⌉ de de⌉kita N 岩で出来たN [made of rock]

3. i⌈wa no yoo⌉na 岩のような adj(*na*). **[like rock]**

rod n. **[a straight, thin stick or metal bar, esp. one used for punishing]**

1. ho⌈so-naga⌉i bo⌈o 細長い棒 [a straight, slender stick]

2. mu⌉chi むち ⟪whip, cane⟫

EX. Spare the rod and spoil the child.
むちを惜しむと、だめな子になる。
Muchi o oshimu to, damena ko ni naru.

PHRASE: fishing rod *tsuri-zao* 釣りざお

role n. **[the part or duty performed by s.o. such as an actor or an individual in a group]**

ya⌈ku⌉ 役 •c [the responsibilites assumed by s.o. or the person represented by an actor in a dramatic production] ⟪office, post, position, duty, function, part⟫, ya⌈kume⌉ 役目 [the part or duty one is expected to play, esp. as an individual of a certain social rank] ⟪duty, office, function, mission⟫, ya⌈kuwari⌉ 役割 [the duty assigned to one] ⟪duty, function, part, position⟫

EX. (**a**) What role did Meryl Streep play in that movie?
その映画ではメリル・ストリープの{役/*役目/*役割}は何でしたか。
*Sono eiga de wa Meriru Sutoriipu no {yaku/*yakume/*yakuwari} wa nan deshita ka.*
(**b**) It seems to me that a wife's role is not just that of raising children.
妻の{役/役目/役割}は子供を育てるだけではないと思います。
Tsuma no {yaku/yakume/yakuwari} wa kodomo o sodateru dake dewanai to omoimasu.

roll vi. **[to move along a surface by turning over and over or on wheels]**

ko⌈rogaru 転がる ① [to move along a surface by turning over and over or for s.t./s.o./s.a. standing to fall over] ⟪trundle, fall⟫

EX. The ball rolled down the stairs.
ボールが階段を転がっていった。
Booru ga kaidan o korogatte itta.

—— vt. **[to cause s.t./s.o./s.a. to move along a surface on wheels or by turning over and over]**

1. ⟨-o⟩ ko⌈roga-su ⟨〜を⟩転がす ① [for s.o. to cause s.t./s.o./s.a. to move along a surface by turning over and over or to cause s.t./s.o./s.a. standing to fall over]

EX. The children rolled the snowball down the hill.
子供たちは丘の上から雪の玉を転がした。
Kodomo-tachi wa oka no ue kara yuki no tama o korogashita.

2. ⟨-o⟩ ma⌈ku ⟨〜を⟩巻く ① [to twist or wrap s.t. (around s.t. else)] ⟪coil⟫

EX. *Makizushi* is made by rolling cooked rice in seaweed.
巻きずしは御飯をのりで巻いて作るものだ。
Maki-zushi wa gohan o nori de maite tsukuru mono da.

—— n. **[s.t. made by turning s.t. over and over on itself into a cylindrical shape or a back and forth swaying motion]**

1. ma⌈ite a⌉ru mono 巻いてある物 [s.t. that has been turned over and over around itself or s.t. else]

2. -hon 〜本 [a counter for a cylindrical object] SEE APPENDIX II

EX. I have three rolls of film on me now.
今フイルムを三本持っています。
Ima fuirumu o san-bon motte imasu.

3. yo⌈ko-yure 横揺れ [a sideways swaying motion]

EX. The constant pitches and rolls of the ship made me seasick.
船の絶え間ない縦揺れと横揺れに船酔いした。
Fune no taema-nai tate-yure to yoko-yure ni funa-yoi-shita.

Roman n. **[a person of or the people of ancient Rome]**
ko⌈dai Rooma⌉-jin 古代ローマ人 •c+f+c
— adj. **[of ancient Rome or the people of ancient Rome]**
ko⌈dai Ro⌉oma no N 古代ローマのN •c+f, ko⌈dai Rooma⌉-jin no N 古代ローマ人のN •c+f+c

romantic adj.
ro⌈manchi⌉kkuna ロマンチックな adj(*na*). **•f**

EX. A: My wife and I often go for walks along the beach of sunset.
家内とよく日が沈むころ海岸を散歩します。
Kanai to yoku hi ga shizumu koro kaigan o sanpo-shimasu.
B: How romantic!
ロマンチックですねえ。
Romanchikku desu nee.

Rome n.
Ro⌉oma ローマ •f

roof n.
ya⌉ne 屋根

EX. The house over there with a blue roof is my house.
あの青い屋根の家が私の家です。
Ano aoi yane no ie ga watashi no ie desu.

room n. **[space which is available for being used or a partitioned space in a building]**
1. he⌈ya⌉ 部屋 [a partitioned space in a building] ⟪**chamber**⟫

EX. A: How many rooms are there in this house?
この家には部屋がいくつありますか。
Kono ie ni wa heya ga ikutsu arimasu ka.
B: There are six rooms.
六部屋あります。
Roku-heya arimasu.

2. yo⌉chi 余地 •c [a space in which more people or things can be accommodated than currently exist there] ⟪**margin, scope, place, blank**⟫, **yo⌈yuu 余裕 •c [an amount of s.t. such as space, time, or money beyond that which is needed]** ⟪**surplus, elbowroom, margin**⟫, **yu⌈tori ゆとり [physical, temporal, or psychological space which is uncrowded and allows freedom of movement]** ⟪**elbowroom, latitude, margin**⟫

EX. (**a**) Is there room in your trunk for this package?
トランクにこの荷物が入る{余地/ゆとり/余裕}がありますか。
Toranku ni kono nimotsu ga hairu {yochi/yutori/yoyuu} ga arimasu ka.
(**b**) His firm tone of voice left no room for discussion on the matter.
彼の強固な口調からするとその問題に関しては議論の{余地/*ゆとり/*余裕}はないようだった。
*Kare no kyookona kuchoo kara suru to sono mondai ni-kanshite wa giron no {yochi/*yutori/*yoyuu} wa nai yoodatta.*

roommate n.
do⌈oshitsu⌉-sha 同室者 •c, ru⌈umu-me⌉ito ルームメイト •f

EX. I'm renting an apartment with two roommates.
{ルームメイト/同室者}二人とアパートを借りています。
{Ruumu-meito/Dooshitsu-sha} futari to apaato o karite imasu.

rooster n.
o⌉ndori おんどり

root n. **[the part of a plant that grows into and attaches to the soil** ⟪**fig. "source," "foundation" "origin"**⟫**]**
1. ne⌉ 根 [the part of a plant that grows into and attaches to the soil ⟪**fig. "real nature"**⟫**]** ⟪**nature**⟫, **ne⌈kko⌉ 根っ子 [the part of a plant that grows into and attaches to the soil ⟨s⟩]** ⟪**stump**⟫

EX. The root of a bamboo tree grows very deeply.

竹の{根/根っ子}はとても深くまで伸びる。
Take no {ne/nekko} wa totemo fukaku made nobiru.

2. ko⌈npon 根本 •c [the most fundamental part of s.t. forming the basis or source of the rest] ⟪source, origin, foundation, cause⟫, **ko⌈ngen 根源 •c [the ultimate source of s.t.]** ⟪origin, source, basis⟫

EX. A lack of sense of individual responsibility lies at the root of many of today's social ills.
今日の社会悪の多くの{根本/根源}には個人の責任感が薄れてきているという問題がある。
Konnichi no shakai-aku no ooku no {konpon/kongen} ni wa kojin no sekinin-kan ga usurete kite iru to iu monndai ga aru.

rope n. **[a stout thick cord]**

na⌈wa⌉ 縄 [a stout cord made of twisted strands of straw, hemp, or palm], tsu⌈na⌉ 綱 [a stout cord made of twisted strands of natural or chemical fibers or wire], ro⌉opu ロープ •f

PHRASE: {skip rope/jump rope (Br. E)} *nawa-tobi* 縄跳び

rose n.

ba⌈ra ばら

EX. He sent me some red roses on my birthday.
彼は私の誕生日に赤いばらを贈ってくれた。
Kare wa watashi no tanjoo-bi ni akai bara o okutte kureta.

rot vi. **[for s.t. organic to lose its original form or function due to the decaying action of microorganisms or oxidation over time]**

ku⌈sa⌉ru 腐る ① [for a substance, esp. meat or vegetable, to lose its original form or function due to the chemical action caused by bacteria, fungi, oxidation, etc. ⟪fig. "be very much discouraged"⟫]

EX. If you don't keep meat in the refrigerator it rots quickly.
肉は冷蔵庫の中に入れておかないと、すぐ腐りますよ。
Niku wa reizoo-ko no naka ni irete okanai to, sugu kusarimasu yo.

rotate vi. **[for s.t. to revolve around an axis or for people to do s.t. by turns]**

1. ka⌈iten-suru 回転する ③ •c [for s.t. to move in a circular motion around an axis/center] ⟪revolve, gyrate⟫

EX. Copernicus was the first to argue that the earth rotates on its own axis once a day.
地球が一日に一度その軸を中心に回転するということを初めて主張したのはコペルニクスだった。
Chikyuu ga ichi-nichi ni ichi-do sono jiku o chuushin ni kaiten-suru to iu koto o hajimete shuchoo-shita no wa Koperunikusu datta.

2. ko⌈otai-suru 交替する ③ •c [for people to do s.t. in turns] ⟪take turns, alternate, rotate⟫

EX. In American football all the players rotate depending on whether the team is on the offensive or defensive.
アメリカンフットボールでは攻めるか、守るかによって選手が完全に交替する。
Amerikan-futto-booru de wa semeru ka, mamoru ka ni-yotte senshu ga kanzenni kootai-suru.

rough adj. **[having an uneven or coarse surface; involving or exhibiting force or violence; lacking grace or politeness in manners or temperament]**

1. za⌉ra-zara-shita N ざらざらしたN /⟨Vinf. past of *zara-zara-suru* ③ feel coarse/, za⌉ra-zara-shite iru (N) ざらざらしている(N) /⟨V *te iru* of *zara-zara-suru* ③ feel coarse/ [for the surface of s.t. such as cloth, skin, or a face to be coarse to the touch] ⟪sandy, granular⟫

EX. This cloth feels rough.
この布は{ざらざらした感じがする/ざらざらしている}。
Kono nuno wa {zara-zara-shita kanji ga suru/zara-zara-shite iru}.

2. de⌈ko-boko no N 凸凹のN [having a surface with uneven highs and lows] ⟪uneven, rugged⟫

EX. The country road was very rough.
田舎道は凸凹だらけだった。
Inaka-michi wa deko-boko darake datta.

3. a⌈reta N 荒れたN /〈Vinf. past of *areru* ② become wild/, a⌈rete iru (N) 荒れている(N) /〈V*te iru* of *areru* ② become wild/ [for the weather or ocean to be turbulent/wild]

EX. The weather was rough throughout the entire trip.
旅行中天気はずっと荒れていた。
Ryokoo-chuu tenki wa zutto arete ita.

4. ha⌈geshi⌉i 激しい adj(*i*). **[involving an excessively high degree of force or strength, either physical or emotional] 《violent, strong, vehement, fierce, furious, intense, acute, severe, ardent, passionate, strong》**

EX. He has a very rough temperament.
彼の気性はとても激しい。
Kare no kishoo wa totemo hageshii.

5. a⌈ra-ara-shi⌉i 荒々しい adj(*i*). **[violent or harsh in temperament or physical or verbal behavior] 《rude, wild, violent, harsh》**

EX. Yukie was upset when her boyfriend talked to her in such a rough way.
雪江は恋人が荒々しい言い方をした時にびっくりした。
Yukie wa koi-bito ga ara-ara-shii ii-kata o shita toki ni bikkuri-shita.

6. da⌈itai no N 大体のN •c [making up or involving the larger part of s.t.] 《general, main》, o⌈omakana 大まかな adj(*na*). **[involving the general outline of s.t. without concern for details]**

EX. (**a**) Can you give me a rough account of what happened?
事件の{大体の/大まかな}話をして下さいませんか。
Jiken no {daitai no/oomakana} hanashi o shite kudasaimasen ka.
(**b**) I've only completed a rough draft of my paper.
論文の{大体の/大まかな}下書きしかできていません。
Ronbun no {daitai no/oomakana} shita-gaki shika dekite imasen.

roughly adv. **[in a rough manner or approximately]**

1. te-⌈araku 手荒く /〈adj(*i*). *ku* of *te-arai* rough/ [handling s.t. in a rough manner] 《violently, rudely》, te-⌈arani 手荒に /〈adj(*na*). *ni* of *te-arana* rough/

EX. Don't treat your kids so roughly.
子供たちをそんなに{手荒く/手荒に}扱ってはいけない。
Kodomo-tachi o sonna-ni {te-araku/te-arani} atsukatte wa ikenai.

2. da⌈itai 大体 •c [for the most part 《fig. "nearly"》] 《generally, by and large, more or less》

EX. A: How many students are there in this university?
この大学に学生は何人いますか。
Kono daigaku ni gakusei wa nan-nin imasu ka.
B: There are roughly 20,000.
大体二万人ぐらいいます。
Daitai ni-man-nin-gurai imasu.

round adj. **[shaped like a ball or circle or having a curved shape or exact only to a specific decimal]**

1. ma⌈rui 丸い adj. **[having the shape of a circle, ring, or ball] 《circular, spherical》**

EX. See that girl with the round face? She's my daughter.
あそこに丸い顔をした女の子がいるでしょう。あれが私の娘です。
Asoko ni marui kao o shita onna-no-ko ga iru deshoo. Are ga watashi no musume desu.

2. ha⌈su⌉u no na⌉i N 端数のないN [expressed as a numeral with no fractions]

PHRASE: go round *mawaru* 回る ① 《revolve, patrol, make a detour》

— n. **[s.t. shaped like a circle or a circular, often repetitive, movement or routine]**

1. ma⌈rui mo⌈no⌉ 丸いもの [s.t. shaped like a circle]

2. i⌈chi-jun 一巡 •c [one complete cycle of a circular movement] 《patrol》

3. ku⌈ri-kaeshi 繰り返し /〈V*masu* of *kuri-kaesu* ① repeat/ [the act of doing the same

R

thing again and again] **《repetition》**
4. ra⌉undo ラウンド •f [one section of a boxing match]

round-trip n.
o⌈ofuku(-ryo⌉koo) 往復(旅行) •c
EX. One round-trip (ticket) to New York City, please.
ニューヨークまで往復一枚、お願いします。
Nyuuyooku made oofuku ichi-mai o-negai-shimasu.

route n. **[the course followed in traveling from one place to another or an assigned territory covered by s.o. who delivers s.t., esp. mail]**
1. mi⌈chi 道 [a strip of paved or cleared ground for getting from one place to another or the distance covered in a journey 《fig. "method," "the proper way of thinking or conducting oneself," "special field"》] 《way, street, road, course》, -goo-sen 〜号線 •c [a counter for highways]
EX. A: Which route did you take here?
どの道を通ってきましたか。
Dono michi o tootte kimashita ka.
B: I took Route 7.
七号線を通ってきました。
{Shichi/Nana}-goo-sen o tootte kimashita.
2. ha⌈itatsu-ku⌉iki 配達区域 •c [an assigned territory covered by s.o. who delivers s.t.]
EX. Is my house on your delivery route?
私の家は配達区域に入っていますか。
Watashi no ie wa haitatsu-kuiki ni haitte imasu ka.

row[1] n. **[a series of people or things arranged in a line or a unit used for counting such a series]**
re⌉tsu 列 •c 《line, file, rank, queue》
EX. (**a**) The students were lined up in a row.
学生たちは一列に並んでいた。
Gakusei-tachi wa ichi-retsu ni narande ita.
(**b**) Jane was sitting in the third row at the concert.
コンサートでジェーンは第三列目に座っていた。
Konsaato de Jeen wa dai-san-retsu-me ni suwatte ita.

row[2] vt. **[for s.o. to propel a boat with oars]**
⟨-o⟩ ko⌉gu ⟨〜を⟩こぐ ① [for s.o. to propel a boat with oars or to move a swing or bicycle by bending and stretching the knees]
EX. After rowing the boat for an hour I was too exhausted to go on.
一時間ボートをこいだ後、疲れて続けられなくなった。
Ichi-jikan booto o koida ato, tsukarete tsuzuke-rarenaku natta.

rowboat n.
bo⌉oto ボート •f

royal adj. **[pertaining to or suitable for a monarch 《fig. "magnificent"》]**
1. ko⌈kuo⌉o no N 国王のN •c [pertaining to the king of a country]
EX. The royal funeral was held yesterday.
きのう国王の葬式があった。
Kinoo kokuoo no sooshiki ga atta.
2. o⌈oshitsu no N 王室のN •c [pertaining to the family of a king or queen]
EX. Interest in the affairs of the royal family runs high among the general populace.
一般の市民の間では王室のことに興味のある人が多い。
Ippan no shimin no aida de wa ooshitsu no koto ni kyoomi no aru hito ga ooi.
3. ri⌈ppana 立派な adj(*na*). **•c [for s.o./some human creation/achievement to cause admiration] 《wonderful, splendid, good, fine》, su⌈barashi⌉i すばらしい** adj(*i*). **[causing great wonder/admiration/pleasure due to being extremely good] 《wonderful, splendid, great》**
EX. We were treated to a royal feast at our friends' home.
友達の家で{立派な/すばらしい}ご馳走をいただいた。
Tomodachi no ie de {rippana/subarashii} gochisoo o itadaita.

rub vt. **[to move s.t. back and forth over the surface of s.t. while applying pressure to it]**

《polish, erase, create heat, alleviate itch/pain》
〈-o〉 ko⌈su⌉ru 〈～を〉こする ① **[to press one object against another while moving it back and forth]** 《scrub, scrape》, 〈-o〉 ma⌈satsu-suru 〈～を〉摩擦する ③ •c **[to apply friction to s.t.]** 《chafe》

EX. (a) Don't rub your eyes so much.
目をそんなに{こすって/*摩擦して}はいけません。
*Me o sonnani {kosutte/*masatsu-shite} wa ikemasen.*
(b) When you're cold, you can warm yourself by rubbing your skin with a dry towel.
寒い時は、乾いたタオルで皮膚を{こする/摩擦する}と、暖かくなります。
Samui toki wa, kawaita taoru de hifu o {kosuru/masatsu-suru} to, atatakaku narimasu.

rubber n. **[a tough elastic substance made from the sap of certain tropical trees]**
1. go⌉mu ゴム •f 《gum》
EX. I always wear rubber shoes when it's rainy.
雨の日にはいつもゴム靴を履きます。
Ame no hi ni wa itsu-mo gomu-gutsu o hakimasu.

2. go⌈mu-se⌉ihin ゴム製品 **[a product made out of a tough elastic substance made from the sap of certain tropical trees]**

rubbish n. **[useless waste material or s.t. having no value]**
1. ga⌈rakuta がらくた **[things of little use or value]** 《trash, junk》, go⌈mi⌉ ごみ **[a general term for waste material]** 《dust, litter, trash》
2. da⌈saku 駄作 •c **[a worthless creation]** 《poor stuff, trash》 ↔ kessaku 傑作 •c
EX. That writer's work is nothing but rubbish.
あの作家の作品は駄作以外の何物でもない。
Ano sakka no sakuhin wa dasaku-igai no nani-mono demonai.

3. ba⌈ka⌉-geta koto ばかげたこと **[s.t. that is foolish]**, ku⌈daranai koto くだらないこと **[s.t. that is worthless]**

rude adj. **[lacking politeness, sophistication, or refinement in one's manners or personal character]**
1. shi⌈tsu⌉reina 失礼な adj(*na*). •c **[lacking politeness in one's words or behavior]** 《impolite, impudent, discourteous》, bu⌈re⌉ina 無礼な adj(*na*). •c **[totally lacking politeness in one's words, behavior, or personal character]** 《impolite, discourteous, disrespectful》
EX. (a) A: He left the dinner party without even saying good-bye to his host.
あの人ね、招待してくれた人にさよならも言わないで夕食会から帰ったのよ。
Ano hito ne, shootai-shite kureta hito ni sayonara mo iwanai de yuushoku-kai kara kaetta no yo.
B: Really? How rude!
そう？ {失礼/??無礼}ねえ。
Soo? {Shitsurei/??Burei} nee.
(b) How rude of him to cut across our back yard without our permission.
断りもなしにうちの裏庭を横切るなんて{失礼な/無礼な}奴だな。
Kotowari mo nashi ni uchi no ura-niwa o yoko-giru nante {shitsureina/bureina} yatsu da na.

NOTE: *Bureina* is not commonly used by a female speaker. If person B in example (a) were a male speaker he could have said: *Soo kai. Burei da nee.*

2. ra⌈nboona 乱暴な adj(*na*). •c **[rough and careless in one's words, actions, or behavior]** 《rough, violent, wild, careless》
EX. (a) Please don't use rude language like that around the children.
子供の回りでそんな乱暴な言葉を使わないで下さい。
Kodomo no mawari de sonna ranboona kotoba o tsukawanaide kudasai.
(b) My son is being bullied by some rude kids at school.
息子は学校で乱暴な子供たちにいじめられています。
Musuko wa gakkoo de ranboona kodomo-tachi ni ijime-rarete imasu.

rug n. **[a partial floor covering made of a thick, heavy fabric]**
shi⌈ki-mono 敷物

EX. There was a beautiful rug on the floor in front of the fireplace.
暖炉の前の床にきれいな敷物が敷かれていた。
Danro no mae no yuka ni kireina shiki-mono ga shika-rete ita.

rugged adj. **[having a rough uneven surface or outline; strong and unyielding in build, constitution, or character]**

1. de⌈ko-boko no N 凸凹のN [having a surface with uneven highs and low] **⟪uneven, rough, jagged⟫**

EX. The roads around here are a bit rugged, aren't they?
この辺の道はちょっと凸凹だね。
Kono hen no michi wa chotto deko-boko da ne.

2. za⌉ra-zara-shita N ざらざらしたN /⟨Vinf. past of *zara-zara-suru* ③ feel coarse/ [for the surface of s.t. such as cloth, skin, or a face to be coarse to the touch] ⟪rough, coarse, sandy⟫, za⌉ra-zara-shite iru (N) ざらざらしている(N) /⟨V *te iru* form of *zara-zara-suru* ③ feel coarse/

EX. This paper feels kind of rugged, doesn't it?
この紙は何かざらざらしているね。
Kono kami wa nanka zara-zara-shite iru ne.

3. ga⌈sshi⌉ri-shita N がっしりしたN /⟨Vinf. past of *gasshiri-suru* ③ look firm/ [strong and firm in build or structure] ⟪substantial, massive, stout, sturdy⟫, ga⌈sshi⌉ri-shite iru (N) がっしりしている(N) /⟨V *te iru* of *gasshiri-suru* ③ look firm/

EX. The football players were a rugged looking bunch of fellows.
フットボールの選手たちはがっしりした体をしている連中だった。
Futto-booru no senshu-tachi wa gasshiri-shita karada o shite iru renchuu datta.

ruin n. **[the severe damage, destruction, or demise of a thing, person, or place]**
ha⌈kai 破壊 •c [the act of rendering s.t. major, such as a building/system/nature, devoid of its original function and/or into a disintegrated form of forceful means] ⟪destruction, wreck, collapse, downfall⟫, ha⌈metsu 破滅 •c [the total destruction of s.o.] ⟪destruction, wreck, collapse, downfall⟫, bo⌈tsuraku 没落 •c [the downfall of a person of high social standing] ⟪fall, collapse, downfall, wreck⟫

EX. (**a**) The war brought about the ruin of entire cities.
戦争はあらゆる町の完全な{破壊/*破滅/*没落}をもたらした。
*Sensoo wa arayuru machi no kanzenna {hakai/*hametsu/*botsuraku} o motarashita.*
(**b**) Alcohol led the young man to ruin.
酒が若い男の身を{破滅/?没落/*破壊}に追いやった。
*Sake ga wakai otoko no mi o {hametsu/?botsuraku/*hakai} ni oi-yatta.*
(**c**) The world war brought about the ruin of many aristocratic families.
世界大戦は多くの華族の{没落/?破滅/*破壊}をもたらした。
*Sekai-taisen wa ooku no kazoku no {botsuraku/?hametsu/*hakai} o motarashita.*

— vt. **[to cause s.t. to be severely damaged or destroyed, esp. s.t. major such as a building or city, or to cause the demise of s.o.]**
⟨-o⟩ ha⌈kai-suru ⟨〜を⟩破壊する ③ •c [to render s.t. major, such as a building/system/nature, devoid of its original function and/or into a disintegrated form by forceful means] ⟪destroy, break, wreck, demolish⟫, ⟨-o⟩ ha⌈metsu-saseru ⟨〜を⟩破滅させる /⟨causative of *hametsu-suru* ③ become disintegrated/ ② •c [to cause s.t. to be totally destroyed, esp. the social life of s.o.], ⟨-o⟩ bo⌈tsuraku-saseru ⟨〜を⟩没落させる /⟨causative of *botsuraku-suru* ③ downfall/ ② •c [to cause the downfall of a person of high social standing]

EX. (a) There are many industries that are ruining our natural environment.
自然環境を{破壊して/*破滅させて/*没落させて}いる産業が多い。
*Shizen-kankyoo o {hakai-shite/*hametsu-sasete/*botsuraku-sasete} iru sangyoo ga ooi.*
(b) A love affair can ruin your life.
情事は身を{破滅させる/*破壊する/*没落させる}ことがある。
*Jooji wa mi o {hametsu-saseru/*hakai-suru/*botsuraku-saseru} koto ga aru.*
(c) Yamada plotted to ruin the count's family.
山田はその伯爵家を{没落させよう/破滅させよう/*破壊しよう}とたくらんだ。
*Yamada wa sono hakushaku-ke o {botsuraku-saseyoo/hametsu-saseyoo/*hakai-shiyoo} to takuranda.*

rule n. **[the exercise of authority, esp. by a monarch or other political power; a principle or standard governing how one is to act or behave in a situation, esp. in a game]**
1. to˥ochi 統治 •c [the act of governing a society or country by means of established political processes] ((**rule, reign, government**))
EX. The rule of the Tokugawa Shogunate lasted over 200 years.
徳川幕府の統治は二百年以上続いた。
Tokugawa-bakufu no toochi wa ni-hyaku-nen ijoo tsuzuita.
2. ki˥so˥ku 規則 •c [a principle or standard governing how one is to act or behave in a situation] ((**regulations**)), **ru˥uru ルール •f [principles according to which a game is played or a social system is maintained]**
EX. (a) Everyone has to obey traffic rules.
だれでも交通{規則/ルール}に従わなければなりません。
Dare de mo kootsuu-{kisoku/ruuru} ni shitagawanakereba narimasen.
(b) I don't find grammatical rules very helpful in language study.
私は言語の勉強に文法の{規則/*ルール}はあまり役に立たないと思います。
*Watashi wa gengo no benkyoo ni bunpoo no {kisoku/*ruuru} wa amari yaku ni tatanai to omoimasu.*
(c)The rules in American football are pretty complicated.
アメリカンフットボールの{ルール/規則}はかなり複雑だ。
Amerikan-futto-booru no {ruuru/kisoku} wa kanari fukuzatsu da.

— vt. **[for s.o. to govern s.o./s.t. by means of established political processes]**
⟨-o⟩ shi˥hai-suru ⟨～を⟩支配する ③ •c [for s.o. to exercise power over people or organizations to cause them to act or function in the way one desires] ((**manage, control, govern, dominate**)), **⟨-o⟩ to˥ochi-suru ⟨～を⟩統治する ③ •c [for s.o. to control the political affairs of a country and its people]** ((**govern, administer**))
EX. (a) Some people are afraid that the Japanese will come to rule the world economically.
日本が経済的に世界を{支配する/*統治する}ようになるのではないかと恐れている人がいる。
*Nihon ga keizai-tekini sekai o {shihai-suru/*toochi-suru} yooni naru no dewanai ka to osorete iru hito ga iru.*
(b) Japan ruled Korea for 35 years, until the end of World War II.
日本は第二次大戦が終わるまで三十五年間韓国を{統治/支配}した。
Nihon wa dai-ni-ji-taisen ga owaru made san-juu-go-nenkan Kankoku o {toochi/shihai}-shita.

ruler n. **[a person who governs a country or society; an instrument with which to measure length or draw straight lines]**
1. shi˥ha˥i-sha 支配者 •c [a person who controls a society, organization, or other people] ((**master, dominator**)), **to˥ochi˥-sha 統治者 •c [a person who governs a country or people]** ((**the sovereign**))
EX. Hitler was not a mere ruler; he was a dictator.
ヒットラーはただの{支配者/統治者}で

R

はなかった。独裁者だった。
Hittoraa wa tada no {shihai-sha/toochi-sha} dewanakatta. Dokusai-sha datta.

2. mo⌈no-sashi⌉ 物差し [a wooden/metal/plastic strip used to draw straight lines or measure length《fig. "standard"》]《measure, scale》, jo⌉ogi 定規 •c [a wooden/metal strip used to draw straight lines or measure length]《yardstick》

EX. Why don't you measure the length of the parcel with this ruler?
この{物差し/定規}で小包の長さを測ったらどうですか。
Kono {mono-sashi/joogi} de ko-zutsumi no naga-sa o hakattara doo desu ka.

rumor n. **[information passed by word of mouth which has not been verified by any reliable source]**
u⌈wasa うわさ《report, gossip, hearsay》

R

EX. (**a**) Rumor has it that Mr. Kato will be the next president of the company.
うわさによると、加藤さんが次の社長になるそうだ。
Uwasa ni yoru to, Katoo-san ga tsugi no shachoo ni naru sooda.
(**b**) Is the rumor that Mr. Jackson is getting divorced true?
ジャクソンさんが離婚するってうわさ、本当ですか。
Jakuson-san ga rikon-surutte uwasa, hontoo desu ka.

run vi. **[for s.o./s.a. to move quickly by foot in such a way that not all feet are on the ground at any given time; for s.t. to flow or spread, esp. beyond the bounds intended; for s.t. to continue or extend as far as a certain point in space or time; for s.t. mechanical to be in operation; for s.o. to enter a contest, esp. for political office]**

1. ha⌈shi⌉ru 走る ① [for s.o./s.a./a vehicle to go along a surface in a set direction at a pace faster than walking《fig. "go to excess," "for s.t. long and narrow to extend far," "appear momentarily"》]《rush, dash, dart, sail》

EX. I ran to the bus stop but the bus had already left.
バス停まで走って行ったのにバスは出てしまった後だった。
Basu-tei made hashitte itta noni basu wa dete shimatta ato datta.

2. na⌈gare⌉ru 流れる ② [for liquid, electricity, etc., to move steadily and continuously in a stream or stream-like fashion]《stream, flow, trickle, ooze》

EX. A river runs behind the school.
学校の裏を川が流れている。
Gakkoo no ura o kawa ga nagarete iru.

3. 〈-ni〉 tsu⌈ujiru 〈〜に〉通じる ② •c [for a street or communication to get through to the other end《fig. "be well versed in," "be understood"》]《pass, be opened, end, be well versed in, be understood》

EX. This highway runs all the way to Boston.
この高速道路はボストンまで通じている。
Kono koosoku-dooro wa Bosuton made tsuujite iru.

4. 〈-ni〉 hi⌈romaru 〈〜に〉広まる ① [for s.t. such as a rumor, fad, reputation, or idea to spread widely]《spread, be diffused, pervade, be circulated》

EX. There is a rumor running around that Midori and Yoshio are planning to get married.
緑と良夫は結婚するといううわさが広まっている。
Midori to Yoshio wa kekkon-suru to iu uwasa ga hiromatte iru.

5. u⌈go⌉ku 動く ① [to change in location or position《fig. "shake," "be affected," "change," "be transferred"》]《move, stir, shake, work, change, be affected》

EX. The engine is running, but the car won't move.
エンジンは動いていますが、車が動かないんです。
Enjin wa ugoite imasu ga, kuruma ga ugokanai n desu.

6. tsu⌈zuku 続く ① [for one event/state/movement to follow after another in time or space]《continue, follow, be contiguous》

EX. The summer Japanese language course runs for nine weeks.
夏期日本語コースは九週間続きます。
Kaki-Nihongo-koosu wa kyuu-shuukan tsuzukimasu.

7. ⟨-ni⟩ ri⌈kko⌉oho-suru ⟨〜に⟩立候補する ③ •c [for s.o. to become a candidate for a public office] ⟪**come forward as a candidate**⟫

EX. Bob Dole ran for President of the U.S. in 1996.
ボブ・ドールは1996年にアメリカ大統領に立候補した。
Bobu Dooru wa sen-kyuu-hyaku-kyuu-juu-roku-nen ni Amerika daitooryoo ni rikkooho-shita.

— vt. **[for s.o. to cause s.o./s.a. to move quickly by foot in such a way that not all feet are on the ground at any given time; for s.o. to operate a machine or manage an organization]**

1. ⟨-o⟩ ha⌈shira-se⌉ru ⟨〜を⟩走らせる /⟨causative form of *hashiru* ① run/ ② [for s.o. to cause s.o./s.a./a vehicle to go along a surface in a set direction at a pace faster than walking]

EX. I ran my horse around the inside of the corral for a while to warm her up.
私は準備運動のためしばらく囲いの中で馬を走らせた。
Watashi wa junbi-undoo no tame shibaraku kakoi no naka de uma o hashira-seta.

2. ⟨-o⟩ u⌈goka⌉su ⟨〜を⟩動かす ① [for s.o. to cause s.t./s.o./s.a. to change in position or location or to function properly] ⟪**move, shift, remove, impress**⟫

NOTE: Unlike other short causatives, *ugokasu* does not have a longer causative version. *Ugokaseru* means not "to cause s.o./s.a./s.t. to move" but "can move s.t./s.o./s.a."

EX. It's not that hard to run this machine.
この機械を動かすのはそんなに難しくない。
Kono kikai o ugokasu no wa sonnani muzukashiku nai.

3. ⟨-o⟩ ke⌈iei-suru ⟨〜を⟩経営する ③ •c [for s.o. to be in control of the business affairs of a company, factory, hotel, etc.] ⟪**manage a firm, operate, administrate**⟫

EX. I'm currently running a supermarket.
私は今スーパーを経営しています。
Watashi wa ima suupaa o keiei-shite imasu.

PHRASE: run after ⟨*-no*⟩ *ato o {oi-kakeru/okkakeru}* ⟨〜の⟩後を{追いかける/追っかける} ②

EX. A dog was running after a cat in the park.
公園で犬が猫を{追いかけて/追っかけて}いた。
Kooen de inu ga neko o {oi-kakete/okkakete} ita.

runaway n. **[a person who has run away]**
to⌈obo⌉o-sha 逃亡者 •c **[a criminal who has run away from prison]** ⟪**escapee**⟫

runner n. **[a person who runs]**
so⌉osha 走者 •c, ra⌉nnaa ランナー •f **[a person who runs or a baseball player who gets to a base]**

running n. **[the act of moving quickly on one's feet, esp. for sport or exercise]**
ra⌈nningu ランニング •f

runway n. **[a long, narrow surface on which aircraft take off and land]**
ka⌈sso⌉o-ro 滑走路 •c ⟪**airstrip**⟫

EX. The plane overran the runway.
飛行機は滑走路を越えてしまった。
Hikoo-ki wa kussoo-ro o koete shimatta.

rural adj. **[pertaining to or similar to the countryside]**
i⌈naka no N 田舎のN ↔ tokai no N 都会のN •c**

EX. I much prefer rural life to urban life.
私は都会の生活より田舎の生活の方がずっと好きです。
Watashi wa tokai no seikatsu yori inaka no seikatsu no hoo ga zutto suki desu.

rush vi. **[to move or act with speed]**

1. to⌈sshin-suru 突進する③ •c [to move with intensity and speed toward a goal] ⟪**dash, charge**⟫

R

EX. A wild boar suddenly rushed at us out of the thicket.
やぶの中から突然いのししが我々目がけて突進して来た。
Yabu no naka kara totsuzen inoshishi ga ware-ware me-gakete tosshin-shite kita.

2. i⌈so⌉gu 急ぐ ① [for s.o. to do s.t. very quickly in order to finish it within a limited amount of time] ((make haste, hurry, be in a hurry))

EX. (**a**) The plane leaves in five minutes. We've got to rush.
飛行機が後五分で出るから、急がなきゃ。
Hikoo-ki ga ato go-fun de deru kara, isoganakya.
(**b**) If you don't rush you'll be late for school.
急がないと、学校に遅れますよ。
Isoganai to, gakkoo ni okuremasu yo.

R

— n. **[an act/instance of moving or acting with speed]**
to⌈sshin 突進 •c [the act of moving with intensity and speed toward a goal] ((onrush, dash, charge))

PHRASE: in a rush *isogashii* 忙しい adj(*i*).

EX. I was in a rush to finish my paper by the next day.
私は次の日までに論文を仕上げようとしていて、忙しかった。
Watashi wa tsugi no hi made ni ronbun o shiageyoo to shite ite, isogashikatta.

PHRASE: rush hour *rasshu awaa* ラッシュアワー •f

EX. The peak of rush hour occurs at this station between 7:00 and 8:30 a.m.
この駅のラッシュアワーのピークは午前七時から八時半までです。
Kono eki no rasshu awaa no piiku wa gozen shichi-ji kara hachi-ji-han made desu.

Russia n.
Ro⌉shia ロシア •f

Russian adj. **[pertaining to Russia]**
Ro⌉shia no N ロシアのN •f

— n. **[a person of or the people of Russia or the language of Russia]**

1. Ro⌈shia⌉-jin ロシア人 •f+c [a person of or the people of Russia]

EX. I am a Russian born in Moscow.
私はモスクワ生まれのロシア人です。
Watashi wa Mosukuwa-umare no Roshia-jin desu.

2. Ro⌈shia-go ロシア語 •f+c [the language of Russia]

EX. Can you speak Russian?
ロシア語が話せますか。
Roshia-go ga hanase-masu ka.

rust n.
sa⌈bi⌉ さび

EX. The knife had not been used for a long time and was covered with rust.
ナイフを長い間使っていなかったので、すっかりさびがついてしまった。
Naifu o nagai aida tsukatte inakatta node, sukkari sabi ga tsuite shimatta.

— vi.
sa⌈bi⌉ru さびる ②

EX. Wipe off the pots and pans carefully. They will rust if you don't.
なべはちゃんとふいて。そうしないとさびるからね。
Nabe wa chan-to fuite. Soo shinai to sabiru kara ne.

rustle vi. **[to make or cause a soft sound like foliage moving in the wind]**
sa⌉ya-saya to o⌈to⌉ o tateru さやさやと音を立てる ② [for s.t. such as leaves to make a soft sound], ka⌉sa-kasa to o⌈to⌉ o tateru かさかさと音を立てる ② [for a dry object to make a dry, whispering sound], sa⌉ra-sara to o⌈to⌉ o tateru さらさらと音を立てる ② [for s.t. such as silk or a flowing river to make a soft, flowing sound]

EX. (**a**) The bamboo leaves rustled in the breeze.
竹の葉がそよ風で{さやさや/?かさかさ/?さらさら}と音を立てた。
Take no ha ga soyo-kaze de {saya-saya/?kasa-kasa/?sara-sara} to oto o tateta.
(**b**) The dead leaves rustled under our feet with each step we took.
歩く度に足の下で落ち葉が{かさかさ/*さらさら/*さやさや}と音を立てた。

*Aruku tabi ni ashi no shita de ochiba ga {kasa-kasa/*sara-sara/*saya-saya} to oto o tateta.*
(**c**) Rosemary's silken dress rustled as she danced.
踊っている時にローズマリーの絹のドレスが{さらさら/*かさかさ/*さやさや}と音を立てた。
*Odotte iru toki ni Roozumarii no kinu no doresu ga {sara-sara/*kasa-kasa/ *saya-saya} to oto o tateta.*

rusty adj. **[covered with rust《fig. "not functioning properly due to lack of practice or old age"》]**
1. sa˥bi-tsuku さびつく ① [to become covered with rust《fig. "not functioning properly due to lack of practice or old age"》]
EX. (**a**) This knife is terribly rusty.
このナイフはひどくさびついています。
Kono naifu wa hidoku sabi-tsuite imasu.
(**b**) My Japanese has gotten rusty since I haven't used it for so many years.
私の日本語は何年も使っていないから、今はさびついています。
Watashi no Nihon-go wa nan-nen mo tsukatte inai kara, ima wa sabi-tsuite imasu.
2. sa˥bita N さびたN /〈Vinf. past of *sabiru* ② rust/, sa˥bite iru (N) さびている(N) /〈V *te iru* of *sabiru* ② rust/ ②
EX. Be careful not to step on the rusty nails.
{さびた/さびている}くぎを踏まないように気をつけなさい。
{Sabita/Sabite iru} kugi o fumanai yooni ki o tsukenasai.

rye n.
ra˥i-mu˥gi ライ麦

S

's suf. **[a possessive marker]**
no の SEE of
EX. A: Whose camera is this?
これはだれのカメラですか。
Kore wa dare no kamera desu ka.
B: That's Bob's.
それはボブのです。
Sore wa Bobu no desu.

sack n. **[a large bag made of coarse cloth/paper for holding grains and other bulk items]**
o˥o-bu˥kuro 大袋 [a big bag], fu˥kuro˥ 袋 [a non-rigid container made out of paper, plastic, etc.]《paper, cloth, plastic container》

sacred adj. **[judged to be worthy of religious veneration]**
shi˥nseina 神聖な adj(*na*). **•c [set apart from the secular world and inspiring religious awe]《holy, sanctified, consecrated, divine》**
EX. A wedding is a sacred ceremony.
結婚式は神聖な儀式です。
Kekkon-shiki wa shinseina gishiki desu.

sacrifice n. **[the act of offering s.a./s.o. to a deity or s.a./s.o. so offered《fig. "giving up of s.t. valuable for the sake of another," "selling s.t. much cheaper than it is actually worth, or s.t. sold that way"》]**
1. i˥kenie o sa˥sageru koto いけにえを捧げること [an act of offering s.a./s.o. to a deity]
2. i˥kenie いけにえ [s.a./s.o. offered to a deity]

S

3. gi⌈sei 犠牲 •c [giving up s.t. valuable (including one's life) for the sake of another] ⟪**self-sacrifice, self-immolation**⟫

EX. Many people working in Japanese companies make a sacrifice of their personal lives.
日本の企業で働く多くの人々は私生活を犠牲にしている。
Nihon no kigyoo de hataraku ooku no hito-bito wa shi-seikatsu o gisei ni shite iru.

4. na⌈ge-uri 投げ売り /⟨Vmasu of *nageru* ② throw + Vmasu of *uru* ① sell/ [the act of selling s.t. much cheaper than it is actually worth] ⟪**sacrifice sale, clearance sale**⟫, **mi⌈kiri-hin 見切り品 [merchandise sold at a much lower price than it is actually worth]** ⟪**bargain**⟫

—— vt. **[for s.o./s.a. to offer s.a./s.o. as a sacrifice to a deity ⟪fig. "give up s.t. valuable for the sake of another"⟫]**

1. ⟨-o⟩ i⌈kenie ni suru ⟨～を⟩いけにえにする ③ [for s.o. to offer s.a./s.o. as a sacrifice to a deity]

S

2. ⟨-o⟩ gi⌈sei ni suru ⟨～を⟩犠牲にする ③ [for s.o./s.a. to offer/give up one's life or s.t. precious for the sake of another]

EX. The mother sacrificed her life to save her child from drowning in the river.
母親は川でおぼれかけていた我が子を助けるために自分の命を犠牲にした。
Haha-oya wa kawa de obore-kakete ita waga-ko o tasukeru tame ni jibun no inochi o gisei ni shita.

sad adj. **[causing/expressing sorrow or unhappiness]**
ka⌈nashii 悲しい adj(*i*). **[experiencing sorrow or unhappiness (subject limited to the first person)]** ⟪**sorrowful, mournful, doleful**⟫ ↔ **ureshii 嬉しい** adj(*i*).

EX. (**a**) I was very sad when my dog died.
私は犬が死んだ時とても悲しかった。
Watashi wa inu ga shinda toki totemo kanashikatta.
(**b**) Why are Japanese movies so sad?
日本の映画はどうしてあんなに悲しいんですか。
Nihon no eiga wa dooshite annani kanashii n desu ka.

sadly adv. **[in such a way as to cause or express sorrow]**
ka⌈nashi-{geni/so⌉oni} 悲し{げに/そうに} [looking sad] ⟪**sorrowfully, mournfully, dolefully, plaintively**⟫

EX. Francesca looked at me sadly when I told her goodbye.
僕が「さよなら」を告げると、フランチェスカは悲し{そうに/げに}私の顔を見た。
Boku ga 'sayonara' o tsugeru to, Furanchesuka wa kanashi-{sooni/geni} watashi no kao o mita.

NOTE: *kanashi-geni* is normally used in written Japanese, whereas *kanashi-sooni* is used in both spoken and written Japanese.

sadness n. **[the state of feeling/causing sorrow]**
ka⌈nashi-mi 悲しみ /⟨adj(*i*). stem of *kanashii* sad + suf. *mi* ness/ [psychological pain brought on by circumstances difficult to endure] ⟪**sorrow, grief**⟫, **ka⌈na⌉shi-sa 悲しさ /⟨adj(*i*). stem of *kanashii* sad + suf. *sa* ness/** ⟪**sorrowfulness, mournfulness**⟫

EX. I have never felt such sadness before.
こんな悲し{み/さ}を感じたことはない。
Konna kanashi-{mi/sa} o kanjita koto wa nai.

safe adj. **[free from danger/harm/injury/evil/loss]**
a⌈nzenna 安全な adj(*na*). **•c [free from danger/harm/injury/theft]** ⟪**secure**⟫ ↔ **kikenna 危険な** adj(*na*). **•c**

EX. (**a**) Let's put this money in a safe place.
この金を安全な所に置いておこう。
Kono kane o anzenna tokoro ni oite okoo.
(**b**) Is it safe to drink this water?
この水は飲んでも安全ですか。
Kono mizu wa nonde mo anzen desu ka.
(**c**) Which company's stock is the safest?
どの会社の株が一番安全ですか。

Dono kaisha no kabu ga ichiban anzen desu ka.
(**d**) Due to AIDS, safe sex has become necessary.
エイズのために、安全なセックスが必要になった。
Eizu no tame ni, anzenna sekkusu ga hitsuyoo ni natta.

— n. **[a metal container in which valuables are kept]**
ki⌉nko 金庫 •c
EX. I have put the jewels in the safe.
宝石は金庫に入れました。
Hooseki wa kinko ni iremashita.

safely adv. **[without incurring danger/harm/injury/evil/loss]**
a⌈nzenni 安全に /⟨adj⟨*na*⟩. *ni* of *anzenna* safe/ •c [without incurring danger/harm/injury/theft] ⟪securely⟫, **bu⌈jini 無事に /⟨adj⟨*na*⟩. *ni* of *bujina* safe/ •c [achieving s.t. without any problem/trouble in the process]** ⟪without incident, without any trouble, successfully⟫
EX. (**a**) I arrived home safely at about 11:00 P.M. last night.
昨晩十一時ごろ{無事に/*安全に}帰宅した。
*Sakuban juu-ichi ji goro {bujini/ *anzenni} kitaku-shita.*
(**b**) Please teach me how to invest safely.
{安全に/*無事に}投資する方法を教えてください。
*{Anzenni/*Bujini} tooshi-suru hoohoo o oshiete kudasai.*

safety n. **[freedom from danger/harm/injury/evil/loss]**
a⌈nzen 安全 •c [freedom from danger/harm/injury/theft] ⟪security, freedom from danger⟫, **bu⌈ji 無事 •c [freedom from any trouble in the process of achieving s.t.]** ⟪security⟫

sail n. **[a length of fabric attached to a ship to catch the wind and propel it]**
ho⌉ 帆
— vi. **[for a boat/person to go across the surface of water (as if) propelled by a sail]**
1. ha⌈nsoo-suru 帆走する ③ •c [to move over water by means of a sail]
2. fu⌉ne de i⌈ku 船で行く ① [for s.o. to go by boat]
3. (ha⌈nsen no yo⌉o ni) {su⌈sumu/i⌈ku} (帆船のように){進む/行く} ① [to proceed/go like a sail boat]
— vt. **[for a boat/person to travel over an area of water by sail]**
⟨-o⟩ fu⌉ne de wa⌈taru ⟨〜を⟩船で渡る ① [for s.o. to travel over an area of water surface by boat]
EX. I sailed the Pacific a couple of times before the war began.
私は戦前に二、三回、太平洋を船で渡った。
Watashi wa senzen ni ni, san-kai, Taihei-yoo o fune de watatta.

sailboat n.
ha⌈nsen 帆船 •c

sailor n.
se⌈n'in 船員 •c [s.o. who works on board a ship], **se⌉eraa セーラー •f**

saint n.
se⌈ijin 聖人 •c

sake[1] n. **[purpose/profit]**
ta⌈me⌉ ため [s.t. useful/profitable for s.o./s.t./s.a. ⟪fig. "purpose," "cause," "reason"⟫] ⟪advantage, benefit, profit, welfare⟫
EX. (**a**) For the sake of my health I usually eat only vegetables.
健康のため、大抵野菜しか食べません。
Kenkoo no tame, taitei yasai shika tabemasen.
(**b**) For the sake of appearance Mary acts as if she were happily married.
世間体のためにメアリーは結婚がうまく行っているふりをしている。
Seken-tei no tame ni Mearii wa kekkon ga umaku itte iru furi o shite iru.

PHRASE: for God's sake *goshoo da kara* 後生だから
EX. For God's sake please forgive me.
後生だから、許してください。
Goshoo da kara, yurushite kudasai.

S

sake² n. **[Japanese rice wine]**
sa⌈ke 酒 [Japanese rice wine or alcoholic drinks in general]

EX. (**a**) *Sake* is made from rice.
酒は米から作る。
Sake wa kome kara tsukuru.
(**b**) When Japanese people say "I drink *sake*" it means they drink either rice wine or alcohol in general.
日本人が「私は酒を飲みます」という時は、酒またはほかのアルコール飲料を飲むという意味だ。
Nihon-jin ga 'Watashi wa sake o nomimasu' to iu toki wa, sake mata wa hoka no arukooru-inryoo o nomu to iu imi da.

salad n.
sa⌉rada サラダ •f

EX. Alex usually has salad for breakfast.
アレックスは大抵朝御飯にサラダを食べる。
Arekkusu wa taitei asa-gohan ni sarada o taberu.

S

salaried adj. **[earning a regular salary]**
ge⌈kkyu⌉u-tori no N 月給取りのN [earning a monthly salary]

PHRASE: salaried man *sararii-man* サラリーマン **•f**

EX. A Japanese salaried man often works on Saturdays.
日本のサラリーマンは土曜日でも働くことが多い。
Nihon no sararii-man wa doyoo-bi demo hataraku koto ga ooi.

salary n. **[a fixed monetary compensation for services paid on a regular basis]**
kyu⌉uryoo 給料 •c [monetary compensation paid on a regular basis], ho⌈okyuu 俸給 •c [a fixed monetary compensation for bureaucrats/white collar workers ⟨fml⟩], sa⌉rarii サラリー •f [a fixed monetary compensation, (esp. for white collar workers)]

EX. A: Your salary must be pretty good.
君の{給料/俸給/サラリー}はいいだろうね。
Kimi no {kyuuryoo/hookyuu/sararii} wa ii daroo ne.
B: No, not at all.
いいえ、とんでもないですよ。
Iie, tonde-mo-nai desu yo.

sale n. **[an act of selling s.t. (for a cheap price)/extent to which s.t. sells]**
1. ha⌈nbai 販売 •c [an act of selling] ⟪selling, marketing⟫

EX. Because of the high yen, the sale of Japanese goods in the U.S. decreased.
円高のためにアメリカでの日本製品の販売が落ちた。
En-daka no tame ni Amerika de no Nihon-seihin no hanbai ga ochita.

2. u⌈re-yuki 売れ行き /⟨V*masu* of *ureru* ② sell + V*masu* of *yuku* ① go/ [extent to which s.t. sells] ⟪demand, run⟫

EX. This book has been enjoying a high volume of sales.
この本の売れ行きはとてもいいです。
Kono hon no ure-yuki wa totemo ii desu.

3. ya⌈su-uri 安売り /⟨adj(*i*). stem of *yasui* cheap + V*masu* of *uru* ① sell/ [the act of selling s.t. at a very low price] ⟪selling cheaply, bargain sale⟫, o⌈o-yasu⌉-uri 大安売り, ba⌉agen バーゲン •f

EX. I bought this stereo at a sale.
このステレオは{安売り/バーゲン}で買いました。
Kono sutereo wa {yasu-uri/baagen} de kaimashita.

PHRASE: for sale *uri-mono no* N 売り物のN

EX. This computer is not for sale.
このコンピューターは売り物ではありません。
Kono konpyuutaa wa uri-mono dewaarimasen.

PHRASE: on sale *tokka de* 特価で **•c**, *seeru de* セールで **•f** ⟪at a special price, at a bargain price⟫

EX. I bought this bicycle on sale.
この自転車を{特価/セール}で買いました。
Kono jitensha o {tokka/seeru} de kaimashita.

salesgirl n.
jo-⌈te⌉n'in 女店員 •c
salesperson n. **[a person employed to sell goods/services]**
te⌈n'in 店員 •c **[a store employee]** ⟪**clerk, shopboy, shopgirl**⟫, **se⌈erusu⌉-man** セールスマン •f **[a man employed to sell goods/services by visiting homes]**

EX. (**a**) I am a salesperson at this store.
私はこの店の{店員/セールスマン}です。
Watashi wa kono mise no {ten'in/seerusu-man} desu.
(**b**) Someone told me that Yamamoto visits more than twenty houses a day as an encyclopedia salesperson.
山本さんは百科事典の{セールスマン/*店員}として一日に二十軒以上のお宅を訪問するそうです。
*Yamamoto-san wa hyakka-jiten no {seerusu-man/*ten'in} to-shite ichi-nichi ni ni-juk-ken ijoo no o-taku o hoomon-suru soodesu.*

salmon n.
{**sa⌉ke/sha⌉ke**} {さけ/しゃけ}
salt n.
shi⌈o⌉ 塩

EX. Could you pass me the salt, please.
お塩を取ってくださいませんか。
O-shio o totte kudasaimasen ka.

saltwater adj. **[of water containing salt]**
shi⌈o⌉-mizu no N 塩水のN, **e⌈nsui no N** 塩水のN •c **[of water containing salt]** ⟪**brine**⟫, **ka⌈isui no N** 海水のN •c **[ocean water]**
salty adj. **[having the taste of salt ⟪fig. "spicy"⟫]**
ka⌈ra⌉i からい adj(*i*). **[having the tongue-piercing taste of salt/spice ⟪fig. "strict," "painful"⟫]** ⟪**briny, hot, pungent**⟫, **shi⌈o-kara⌉i** 塩からい adj(*i*). **[having the tongue-piercing taste of salt]** ↔ **amai** 甘い adj(*i*).; **shop⌈pa⌉i** しょっぱい adj(*i*). **[having the taste of salt]**

EX. (**a**) Japanese often eat salty pickles.
日本人はよく{からい/塩からい/しょっぱい}漬物を食べる。
Nihon-jin wa yoku {karai/shio-karai/shoppai} tsuke-mono o taberu.
(**b**) If you eat salty foods too much, you can get high blood pressure.
{からい/塩からい/しょっぱい}物を食べ過ぎると、高血圧になる。
{Karai/Shio-karai/Shoppai} mono o tabe-sugiru to, koo-ketsuatsu ni naru.

salute vt. **[for s.o. to respectfully greet/recognize s.o. with words/specific gestures]**
1. ⟨**-ni**⟩ **a⌉isatsu-suru** ⟨〜に⟩あいさつする ③ •c **[for s.o. to address s.o. with courteous words and actions, esp. in meeting and parting]** ⟪**greet**⟫

EX. The gentleman took off his hat to salute the lady.
紳士は帽子を脱いで婦人にあいさつした。
Shinshi wa booshi o nuide fujin ni aisatsu-shita.

2. ⟨**-ni**⟩ **ke⌈irei-suru** ⟨〜に⟩敬礼する ③ •c **[for s.o. recognize s.o./a deity with specific gestures prescribed by (military or religious) regulations]** ⟪**bow, pay reverence to**⟫

EX. The guard saluted the queen.
衛兵は女王に敬礼した。
Eihei wa jooo ni keirei-shita.

salvage vt. **[for s.o. to save s.t. esp. a ship from total loss/destruction]**
⟨**-o**⟩ **mo⌈chi-dasu** ⟨〜を⟩持ち出す ① **[for s.o. to take s.t. out]** ⟪**save**⟫, ⟨**-o**⟩ **hi⌈ki-age⌉ru** ⟨〜を⟩引き上げる ② **[for s.o. to pull s.t./s.o./s.a. up]** ⟪**recover**⟫

EX. (**a**) He was successful in salvaging most of his valuables from the burning house.
彼は燃えている家から自分の貴重品を{持ち出す/*引き上げる}ことに成功した。
*Kare wa moete iru ie kara jibun no kichoo-hin o {mochi-dasu/*hiki-ageru} koto ni seikoo-shita.*
(**b**) They have salvaged a sunken boat from the ocean.
沈んだ船を海から{引き上げた/*持ち出した}。
*Shizunda fune o umi kara {hiki-ageta/*mochi-dashita}.*

S

— n. **[an act of saving a ship from total loss/destruction]**
sa⌈rube⌉eji サルベージ •f [an act of pulling up a sunken ship from the ocean bottom]

same adj. **[not changing/different 《fig. "previously mentioned"》]**
⟨-to⟩ o⌈naji (N) ⟨〜と⟩同じ(N) [of two/more things identical/equal] 《identical, equal》 ↔ ⟨-to⟩ chigau (N) ⟨〜と⟩違う ①

EX. (**a**) I'm wearing the same T-shirt as my younger brother.
私は弟と同じＴシャツを着ています。
Watashi wa otooto to onaji tii-shatsu o kite imasu.
(**b**) A: Are you two from the same state?
お二人は同じ州からですか。
O-futari wa onaji shuu kara desu ka.
B: No, we are from different states.
いいえ、違う州からです。
Iie, chigau shuu kara desu.
(**c**) My car is the same model as Steve's.
私の車はスティーブのと同じ型です。
Watashi no kuruma wa Sutiibu no to onaji kata desu.

S

— pron. **[(used with "the") s.t./s.o./s.a. identical/equal to another]**
1. o⌈naji hito 同じ人 [s.o. identical/equal to another]

EX. Is this actor the same as the one who appeared in *Seven Samurai*?
この俳優は『七人の侍』に出た人と同じ人ですか。
Kono haiyuu wa "Shichi-nin no Samurai" ni deta hito to onaji hito desu ka.

2. o⌈naji mono 同じ物 [a tangible object identical/equal to another], o⌈naji koto 同じこと [an intangible object identical/equal to another]

EX. (**a**) Is this dish the same as the one you cooked before?
この料理は前に作ってくれた{物/*こと}と同じ{物/*こと}ですか。
*Kono ryoori wa mae ni tsukutte kureta {mono/*koto} to onaji {mono/*koto} desu ka.*
(**b**) The same is true of other cases.
同じ{こと/*物}が外の場合にも言えます。
*Onaji {koto/*mono} ga hoka no baai ni mo ie-masu.*

sample n. **[s.t. representative of an entire class]**
mi⌈hon 見本 [s.t./s.o. representative of an entire class 《fig. "good example"》] 《specimen》, hyo⌈ohon 標本 •c [a zoological/statistical example for exhibition or testing] 《specimen》

EX. (**a**) Could I see a sample of this merchandise?
この商品の{見本/*標本}を見せてください。
*Kono shoohin no {mihon/*hyoohon} o misete kudasai.*
(**b**) I used to collect samples of butterflies.
昔、ちょうの{標本/*見本}を集めていたことがあります。
*Mukashi, choo no {hyoohon/*mihon} o atsumete ita koto ga arimasu.*

sand n. **[a small particle resulting from the breakdown of rock or an expanse of such particles]**
1. su⌈na 砂 [a small particle resulting from the breakdown of rock] 《grit》

EX. (**a**) It was so windy at the beach that sand got in my eyes.
海辺の風が強かったので砂が目に入った。
Umi-be no kaze ga tsuyokatta node suna ga me ni haitta.
(**b**) The children are making a mountain and a tunnel in the sand.
子供たちが砂で山やトンネルを作っています。
Kodomo-tachi ga suna de yama ya tonneru o tsukutte imasu.

2. sa⌈kyuu 砂丘 •c [an expanse of sand] 《dune, down》

sandal n.
sa⌈ndaru サンダル •f

EX. The Japanese *geta* is a kind of sandal.
日本のげたはサンダルのようなものだ。

Nihon no geta wa sandaru no yoona mono da.

sandwich n.
sa⌈ndoi⌉tchi サンドイッチ •f
EX. American children love peanut butter and jelly sandwiches.
アメリカの子供はピーナッツバターとジャムのサンドイッチが大好きだ。
Amerika no kodomo wa piinattsu-bataa to jamu no sandoitchi ga dai-suki da.

—— vt. [for s.o. to insert s.t. between two layer-like objects]
⟨-o⟩ ha⌈sa⌉mu ⟨〜を⟩挟む ① [to put s.t. in a narrow space between two objects so that it is held fast from both sides] ⟪put between, contain, insert⟫
EX. I was sandwiched between the two cars.
私は二台の車に挟まれた。
Watashi wa ni-dai no kuruma ni hasama-reta.

sandy adj. **[of/like/covered with/having the color of sand]**
1. su⌈na no N 砂のN [of sand]
2. su⌈na-da⌉rake no N 砂だらけのN [covered with sand]
EX. The kid's body was sandy from playing at the beach.
砂浜で遊んだので、子供の体は砂だらけだった。
Suna-hama de asonda node, kodomo no karada wa suna-darake datta.
3. su⌈na-iro no N 砂色のN [having the color of sand]
EX. The girl has sandy hair.
女の子は砂色の髪の毛をしている。
Onna-no-ko wa suna-iro no kami-no-ke o shite iru.

San Francisco n.
Sa⌈nfuranshi⌉suko サンフランシスコ •f

sap n. **[the fluid that circulates through a plant or body]**
1. ju⌈eki 樹液 •c [the fluid that circulates through a tree] ⟪milk⟫
EX. Maple syrup is made from the sap of the maple tree.
メープルシロップは楓の木の樹液から作る。
Meepuru-shiroppu wa kaede no ki no jueki kara tsukuru.
2. ta⌉ieki 体液 •c [a bodily fluid such as blood, lymph, semen, etc.] ⟪body fluids, humors⟫

sash[1] n. **[an ornamental band/ribbon worn about the waist or over the shoulder]**
(ka⌈zari-)o⌉bi (飾り)帯, sa⌉sshu サッシュ •f

obi

sash[2] n. **[a window/door frame]**
ma⌈do-waku 窓枠 [a window frame], a⌈rumi-sa⌉sshi アルミサッシ •f [an aluminum sash]

sashimi n. **[small slices of fresh, raw fish]**
sa⌈shimi⌉ 刺身
EX. Japanese eat *sashimi* by dipping it into soy sauce mixed with Japanese horseradish.
日本人は刺身をわさびの入ったしょうゆにつけて食べる。
Nihon-jin wa sashimi o wasabi no haitta shooyu ni tsukete taberu.

satellite n.
e⌈isei 衛星 •c
EX. I don't know exactly how many man-made satellites are circling around the earth now.
現在人工衛星がいくつ地球のまわりを回っているか知らない。
Genzai jinkoo-eisei ga ikutsu chikyuu no mawari o mawatte iru ka shiranai.

satisfaction n. **[fulfillment of a desire/need resulting in positive pleasure]**
ma⌈nzoku⌉-kan 満足感 •c [a feeling of perfect sufficiency] ⟪gratification, complacency, contentent⟫
EX. You have to devote yourself to work in order to get a sense of satisfaction.
満足感を得るためには仕事に打ち込まなければなりません。
Manzoku-kan o eru tame ni wa shigoto ni uchi-komanakereba narimsen.

satisfactory adj. **[causing fulfillment of a desire/need resulting in positive pleasure]**

S

ma˥nzokuna 満足な adj(*na*). **•c [causing a feeling of perfect sufficiency] ⟪gratifying, content⟫, ma˥nzoku ga iku (N) 満足が行く (N) [causing a real feeling of satisfaction], mo┌oshi-bun (ga) na˥i 申し分(が)ない** adj(*i*). **[impossible to find fault with] ⟪perfect, faultless, ideal⟫**

EX. (**a**) My grades of the last semester were all satisfactory.
先学期の成績は皆{満足でした/申し分(が)ありませんでした/満足の行くものでした}。
Sen-gakki no seiseki wa mina {manzoku deshita/mooshi-bun (ga) arimasendeshita/manzoku no iku mono deshita}.
(**b**) There isn't any satisfactory Japanese language textbook.
どこにも{満足な/満足の行く/申し分のない}日本語の教科書はない。
Doko ni mo {manzokuna/manzoku no iku/mooshi-bun no nai} Nihon-go no kyooka-sho wa nai.

S **satisfy** vt. **[to cause fulfillment of a desire/need resulting in positive pleasure]** **⟨-o⟩ ma˥nzoku-saseru ⟨〜を⟩満足させる /⟨causative of *manzoku-suru* ③ be satisfied/ ② •c [to cause s.o. to feel contented], {⟨-ni⟩/⟨-de⟩} ma˥nzoku-suru {⟨〜に⟩/⟨〜で⟩}満足する ③ •c [for s.o. to feel content that s.t. is sufficient] ⟪be satisfied with, be gratified with, be content(ed) with⟫**

EX. (**a**) Betty's work did not satisfy me.
ベティの仕事{に私は満足しなかった/?は私を満足させなかった}。
Betii no shigoto {ni watashi wa manzoku-shinakatta/?wa watashi o manzoku-sasenakatta}.
(**b**) The steak satisfied my taste.
{そのステーキは私の舌を満足させてくれた/私はそのステーキの味に満足した}。
{Sono suteeki wa watashi no shita o manzoku-sasete kureta/Watashi wa sono suteeki no aji ni manzoku-shita}.

Saturday n.
do┌yo˥o(-bi) 土曜(日)

EX. Some Japanese white collar workers now take Saturdays off.
日本のサラリーマンの中には土曜日に休みを取る人も今はいる。
Nihon no sararii-man no naka ni wa doyoo-bi ni yasumi o toru hito mo ima wa iru.

NOTE: In conversational Japanese the *bi* of *doyoo-bi* is often omitted. This is true of all days of the week.

sauce n.
so˥osu ソース •f

EX. What kind of sauce do you use with your spaghetti?
スパゲッティにはどんなソースをかけますか。
Supagetti ni wa donna soosu o kakemasu ka.

saucer n. **[a small dish for holding a cup]**
u┌ke˥-zara 受け皿 [a small dish for holding a cup/drippings], cha┌taku 茶たく •c [a small, wooden dish for holding a traditional tea cup]

PHRASE: flying saucer *sora-tobu-enban* 空飛ぶ円盤, *yuu-foo* UFO •f

savage adj. **[not civilized]**
1. ya┌banna 野蛮な adj(*na*). **•c [having a natural and uncivilized character] ⟪barbarous, unrefined, uncivilized, unenlightened, wild⟫**

EX. I don't enjoy the company of savage men like him.
私は彼のように野蛮な人とつきあうのは嫌いです。
Watashi wa kare no yooni yabanna hito to tsuki-au no wa kirai desu.

2. ya┌sei no N 野生のN •c [of a plant/animal growing in a natural state] ⟪wild⟫

EX. I have never seen a savage lion.
私は野生のライオンを見たことがない。
Watashi wa yasei no raion o mita koto ga nai.

—— n. **[an uncivilized person/an untamed animal]**

1. ya⌈ban-ji⌉n 野蛮人 •c **[an uncivilized person]** ⟪**barbarian, wild man**⟫

EX. He had the air of a savage about him.
彼には野蛮人のような雰囲気がただよっていた。
Kare ni wa yaban-jin no yoona fun'iki ga tadayotte ita.

2. ya⌈sei no do⌈obutsu 野生の動物 •c [an untamed animal] ⟪**a wild animal**⟫

save vt. **[to keep/protect s.o./s.t. from death, loss, damage, disaster or other undesirable events]**

1. ⟨-o⟩ su⌈kuu ⟨～を⟩すくう ① [to pick up s.t./s.o./s.a. out of some (undesirable) place such as water, fire, wreckage] ⟪**scoop, ladle, rescue, deliver, release, redeem**⟫, **⟨-o⟩ ta⌈suke⌉ru ⟨～を⟩助ける ② [for s.o./s.a. to provide resources or one's own time/energy to s.o./s.a. to enable it/him/her to escape danger/death/difficulty or to ensure that s.t. goes well]** ⟪**help, aid, assist, stand by, second, rescue, deliver, spare, promote**⟫, **⟨-o⟩ (⟨-kara⟩) ma⌈mo⌉ru ⟨～を⟩(⟨～から⟩)守る ① [(to watch s.t./s.o./s.a. in order) to cause s.t./s.o./s.a. not to be harmed/injured/violated]** ⟪**protect, defend, cover, guard, obey, observe**⟫ ↔ **⟨-o⟩ semeru ⟨～を⟩攻める ②**

㊥ "scoop/ladle"▷すくう, "rescue"▷救う

EX. (**a**) I was about to drown when I was saved by the young man.
私がおぼれそうなところを、青年が{救って/助けて/*守って}くれました。
*Watashi ga obore-soona tokoro o, seinen ga {sukutte/tasukete/*mamotte} kuremashita.*
(**b**) Japanese often strive to save face.
日本人はよく面子を{守ろう/*救おう/*助けよう}とする。
*Nihon-jin wa yoku mentsu o {mamoroo/*sukuoo/*tasukeyoo} to suru.*

2. ⟨-o⟩ ta⌈meru ⟨～を⟩ためる ② [for s.o./s.a. to accumulate more and more of a certain thing] ⟪**accumulate, amass, collect, gather, store, hoard, lay up**⟫, **⟨-o⟩ ta⌈kuwae⌉ru ⟨～を⟩蓄える ② [for s.o. to keep s.t. esp. money/physical power/mental power]** ⟪**store, lay up, keep**⟫, **⟨-o⟩ cho⌈kin-suru ⟨～を⟩貯金する ③ •c [for s.o. to collect money by depositing it in a financial institution]** ⟪**deposit money, save money**⟫, **⟨-o⟩ to⌉tte-oku ⟨～を⟩取っておく ① [for s.o./s.a. to keep a non-monetary object for emergency purposes]** ⟪**keep, hold, set aside**⟫

EX. (**a**) A: Why are you saving money?
どうしてお金を{ためて/蓄えて/貯金して/*取っておいて}いるんですか。
*Dooshite o-kane o {tamete/takuwaete/chokin-shite/*totte-oite} iru n desu ka.*
B: I plan to get married next June.
来年の六月に結婚するんです。
Rainen no roku-gatsu ni kekkon-suru n desu.
(**b**) I forgot to save my report on the word processor.
私はレポートをワープロに{取って/*ためて/*蓄えて/*貯金して}おくのを忘れた。
*Watashi wa repooto o waapuro ni {totte-/*tamete/*takuwaete/*chokin-shite} oku no o wasureta.*

3. {⟨-no⟩ o-⌈kage de/Sinf. nonpast to}…ha⌈buke⌉-ru {⟨～の⟩おかげで/Sinf. nonpastと}…省ける ② [thanks to s.o./by doing s.t. one can avoid time/labor], {⟨-no⟩ o-⌈kage de/Sinf. nonpast to}…se⌈tsuyaku-deki⌉ru {⟨～の⟩おかげで/Sinf. nonpastと}…節約出来る ② •c [thanks to s.o./by doing s.t. one can avoid spending time/money], (⟨-no⟩) o-⌈kage de…{Vneg. + zu/Vstem + zu/sezu/kozu} ni su⌉mu (⟨～の⟩)おかげで{Vneg.+ず/Vstem+ず/せず/来ず}に済む ① [thanks to s.o./s.t. one does not have to do s.t.]

EX. (**a**) Airplanes save a lot of travel time.
飛行機のおかげで移動時間が大幅に{省ける/節約出来る}。
Hikoo-ki no o-kage de idoo-jikan ga oo-haba ni {habuke-ru/setsuyaku-dekiru}.
(**b**) By buying the plane tickets early you can save $300.
航空券は早く買うと三百ドル{節約出来る/*省ける}。
Kookuu-ken wa hayaku kau to san-

S

*byaku-doru {setsuyaku-dekiru/*habuke-ru}.*
(**c**) A: I'm going to the post office. Do you have any letters to send?
郵便局に行きますが、何か出す手紙がありますか。
Yuubin-kyoku ni ikimasu ga, nani-ka dasu tegami ga arimasu ka.
B: Yes, thank you! You saved me a trip.
ええ、ありがとう。おかげで行かずに済みます。
Ee, arigatoo. O-kage de ikazu ni sumimasu.

saw n.
no⌈kogiri⌉ のこぎり
— vt. **[cut with a saw]**
⟨-o⟩ no⌈kogiri⌉ de ki⌉ru ⟨〜を⟩のこぎりで切る ①

say vt. **[for s.o./s.a. to express s.t. verbally]**
1. {⟨-o⟩/⟨-to⟩} **i⌈u** {⟨〜を⟩/⟨〜と⟩}言う ① **⸨remark, observe, utter, tell, call⸩**

EX. (**a**) Can you say the days of the week in Japanese?
日本語で曜日が言えますか。
Nihon-go de yoo-bi ga ie-masu ka.
(**b**) Say that again, please?
もう一度言ってください。
Moo ichi-do itte kudasai.
(**c**) A: What did Dan say?
ダンは何と言いましたか。
Dan wa nan to iimashita ka.
B: He said he'd like to go there.
行きたいと言っていました。
Iki-tai to itte imashita.
(**d**) A: Why don't you tell him that you want to marry him?
どうしてあの人に結婚したいと言わないの。
Dooshite ano hito ni kekkon-shi-tai to iwanai no?
B: I just cannot say it.
どうしても言えないのよ。
Dooshite mo ie-nai no yo.
(**e**) It goes without saying that Japanese grammar is more difficult than Chinese grammar.
日本語の文法が中国語の文法より難しいのは言うまでもない。
Nihon-go no bunpoo ga Chuugoku-go no bunpoo yori muzukashii no wa iu made mo nai.

PHRASE: that is to say *sunawachi* すなわち, *tsumari* つまり

EX. The UN, that is to say the United Nations, is in New York City.
国連、すなわち国際連合はニューヨーク市にある。
Kokuren, sunawachi Kokusai-rengoo wa Nyuuyooku-shi ni aru.

scale[1] n. **[a small platelike structure that forms the external covering of fish/reptiles]**
u⌈roko うろこ

EX. When I listened to his lecture I felt as if scales fell from my eyes.
彼の講演を聞いた時、目からうろこが落ちるような気持がした。
Kare no kooen o kiita toki, me kara uroko ga ochiru yoona kimochi ga shita.

scale[2] n. **[an instrument for weighing]**
ha⌈kari⌉ はかり /⟨V*masu* of *hakaru* ① measure/ **[any instrument for weighing s.t./s.o./s.a.]** **⸨balance, steelyard, lever scales⸩**, **te⌈nbin** 天びん •c **[any instrument for the exact weighing of s.t./s.o./s.a.]** **⸨balance⸩**

hakari

tenbin

— vt. **[to weigh s.t. with an instrument for weighing]**
⟨-o⟩ te⌈nbin de ha⌈ka⌉ru ⟨〜を⟩天びんで量る ①

scale[3] n. **[a system of ordered marks at fixed intervals indicating gradations/dimensions/ranks/levels/degrees/musical gradations]**
1. me-⌈mori⌉ 目盛 **[a graduation on a ruler/scale]** **⸨division of a scale, graduation(s)⸩**
2. o⌈oki-sa 大きさ /⟨adj(*i*). stem of *ookii* big + suf. *sa* ness/ **[the degree of largeness of an object/person/animal/sound]** **⸨size, magnitude, volume⸩**

EX. This area is reduced to a scale of one-hundredth its actual size on the map.
地図ではこの地域は実際の百分の一の大きさに縮小されている。
Chizu de wa kono chiiki wa jissai no hyaku-bun no ichi no ooki-sa ni shukushoo-sarete iru.

3. ki˥bo 規模 •c [size of a project] ⟪scope⟫, su˥ke˥eru スケール •f [scope of s.t./a person's caliber/musical gradations]

EX. The scale of the project was enormous.
プロジェクトの{規模/スケール}は巨大だった。
Purojekuto no {kibo/sukeeru} wa kyodai datta.

4. o˥nkai 音階 •c [the gradation of musical sounds within an octave]

scalp n.
a˥tama no ji˥hada 頭の地肌

EX. This shampoo will stimulate your scalp.
このシャンプーは頭の地肌を刺激します。
Kono shanpuu wa atama no jihada o shigeki-shimasu.

scandal n. **[an action bringing disgrace or malicious talk damaging to the character]**
shu˥ubun 醜聞 •c [gossip about other people's shameful deeds] ⟪ill fame⟫, su˥kya˥ndaru スキャンダル •f [s.t. disgraceful that one does/hears]

EX. The scandal forced the prime minister to resign.
その{スキャンダル/醜聞}で首相は辞めなければならなかった。
Sono {sukyandaru/shuubun} de shushoo wa yamenakereba naranakatta.

Scandinavia n.
Su˥kanjina˥bia スカンジナビア •f

scarce adj. **[insufficient to meet demand]**
fu˥soku-shite iru (N) 不足している(N) /⟨V *te iru* of *fusoku-suru* ③ lack/ ② [for s.t. to be lacking] ⟪insufficient, fail, be in short supply⟫

EX. When I visited Russia, I noticed that meats and vegetables were very scarce.
私はロシアに行った時、肉と野菜が大変不足しているのに気がついた。
Watashi wa Roshia ni itta toki, niku to yasai ga taihen fusoku-shite iru no ni ki-ga-tsuita.

scarcely adv. **[by a scant margin]**
ho˥to˥ndo (neg.) ほとんど(neg.) [almost (all)] ⟪almost, nearly⟫

EX. A: Do you know Mr. Ito?
伊藤さんをご存じですか。
Itoo-san o go-zonji desu ka.
B: I scarcely remember him.
ほとんど覚えていません。
Hotondo oboete imasen.

scare vt. **[to suddenly cause s.o./s.a. to feel frightened]**
⟨-o⟩ o˥dokasu ⟨〜を⟩おどかす ① [for s.o./s.a. to surprise/threaten s.o.] ⟪threaten, menace, startle, frighten⟫, ko˥wagara-se˥ru 怖がらせる /⟨causative of *kowagaru* ① feel frightened/ ② [to cause s.o./s.a. to feel frightened]

EX. (a) A: (Sneaking up to s.o.) Hi!
こんにちは!
Konnichi-wa!
B: Don't scare me.
{おどかさない/??怖がらせない}でください。
{Odokasanai/??Kowagara-senai} de kudasai.
(b) A: They aren't maintaining their airplanes properly, you know.
飛行機の整備をちゃんとやっていないんだよ。
Hikoo-ki no seibi o chan-to yatte inai n da yo.
B: Don't scare me!
{おどかさない/??怖がらせない}でください。
{Odokasanai/??Kowagara-senai} de kudasai.
(c) A: This place is haunted at night.
ここは夜、幽霊が出るんだよ。
Koko wa yoru, yuurei ga deru n da yo.
B: Don't scare the kids for heaven's sake.
お願いだから、子供たちを{怖がらせない/おどかさない}でちょうだい。

O-negai da kara, kodomo-tachi o {kowagara-senai/odokasanai} de choodai.

scared adj. **[to feel frightened]**
⟨-ga⟩ **ko⌈wa⌉i** ⟨〜が⟩怖い adj(*i*). **[to feel frightened or to cause s.o./s.a. to feel frightened]** ⟪**fearful, dreadful, awful, dreadful**⟫

EX. (**a**) I am scared of dogs.
私は犬が怖い。
Watashi wa inu ga kowai.
(**b**) Last night on my way home I became very scared when a man started to follow me.
昨晩、帰り道で、男につけられ始めた時、とても怖かったです。
Sakuban, kaeri-michi de, otoko ni tsuke-rare-hajimeta toki, totemo kowakatta desu.
(**c**) When the earthquake came, I was scared to death.
地震が起きたとき、私は怖くて死ぬかと思った。
Jishin ga okita toki, watashi wa kowakute shinu ka to omotta.

S

scarf n.
su⌈ka⌉afu スカーフ •f
EX. Who is that lady with the pink scarf?
あのピンクのスカーフをしている女の人はだれですか。
Ano pinku no sukaafu o shite iru onna no hito wa dare desu ka.

scarlet n.
hi(-⌈**iro**⌉) ひ(色)
—— adj.
hi(-⌈**iro**⌉) **no N** ひ(色)のN

scary adj. **[causing s.o./s.a. to feel suddenly frightened]**
⟨-ga⟩ **ko⌈wa⌉i** ⟨〜が⟩怖い adj(*i*). **[for a person or situation to be harsh and unyielding]** ⟪**fearful, dreadful, awful, dreadful**⟫, ⟨-ga⟩ **o⌈soroshi⌉i** ⟨〜が⟩恐ろしい adj(*i*). **[for s.o. to be afraid of s.t./s.o./s.a. unusual or mysterious or for s.t./s.o./s.a. to cause such fear]** ⟪**terrible, dreadful, fearful, fierce**⟫, ⟨-ga⟩ **o⌈kkana⌉i** ⟨〜が⟩おっかない adj(*i*). **[for s.o. to feel threatened by s.t./s.o./s.a. that is powerful/harmful** ⟨s⟩**]** ⟪**dreadful, fearful, frightful**⟫

NOTE: *Okkanai* is quite colloguial.

EX. (**a**) It was so scary when one of the engines on my plane exploded.
乗っていた飛行機のエンジンの一つが爆発した時にはとても{怖かった/恐ろしかった/おっかなかった}。
Notte ita hikoo-ki no enjin no hitotsu ga bakuhatsu-shita toki ni wa totemo {kowakatta/osoroshikatta/okkanakatta}.
(**b**) What has been the most scary experience of your life?
今までで、一番{怖かった/恐ろしかった/おっかなかった}経験は何ですか。
Ima made de, ichiban {kowakatta/ /osoroshikattaokkanakatta} keiken wa nan desu ka.

scatter vt. **[for s.o. to disperse widely in a haphazard way]**
1. ⟨**-ni**⟩ ⟨**-o**⟩ **ma⌉ku** ⟨〜に⟩⟨〜を⟩まく ① **[for s.o. to distribute liquid or granular-shaped objects such as seeds over a wide area (using a throwing motion)]** ⟪**sow, sprinkle, scatter**⟫, ⟨**-ni**⟩ ⟨**-o**⟩ **ma⌈ki-chirasu** ⟨〜に⟩⟨〜を⟩まき散らす ① **[for s.o. to disperse s.t. by throwing in random fashion]** ① ⟪**strew, sprinkle**⟫

EX. (**a**) The farmers were scattering seeds in the fields.
農民たちは畑に種を{まいて/*まきちらして}いた。
*Noomin-tachi wa hatake ni tane o {maite/*maki-chirashite} ita.*
(**b**) The child scattered small pieces of paper on the carpet.
子供がじゅうたんに紙切れを{まき散らした/?まいた}。
Kodomo ga juutan ni kami-kire o {maki-chirashita/?maita}.

2. ⟨**-o**⟩ **o⌈i-hara⌉u** ⟨〜を⟩追い払う ① **[for s.o. to chase away s.t./s.o./s.a. that is obnoxious and bothersome]** ⟪**drive away, dispel**⟫

EX. The police scattered the demonstrators.
警官はデモ隊を追い払った。

Keikan wa demo-tai o oi-haratta.

—— vi. [to break up and disperse in many directions]

1. chiˈru 散る ① [to disperse in all directions]

EX. The demonstrators scattered when they saw the policemen.
デモ隊は警官を見て散った。
Demo-tai wa keikan o mite chitta.

2. 〈-ni〉 saˈnzai-suru 〈〜に〉散在する ③ •c [for buildings/trees to exist in a dispersed way] 《lie scattered, be found here and there》

EX. Farm houses are scattered across the wide prairie.
農家が大草原に散在している。
Nooka ga dai-soogen ni sanzai-shite iru.

scene n. **[the place in which an action/event takes place]**

1. baˈmen 場面 [the dramatic surroundings of an action/event] 《place, spectacle》, shiˈin シーン •f

EX. In that scene the father is talking with his son.
その{場面/シーン}では父親が息子と話している。
Sono {bamen/shiin} de wa chichi-oya ga musuko to hanashite iru.

2. ba 場 [the place/time of an action/event] 《place, spot, site, seat, occasion》

EX. Do you remember Act 1, Scene 1 of Shakespeare's *Hamlet*?
シェークスピアのハムレットの(第)一幕(第)一場を覚えていますか。
Sheekusupia no Hamuretto no (dai-)ichi-maku (dai-)ichi-ba o oboete imasu ka.

3. geˈnba 現場 [the actual site of an incident/construction work] 《spot, locale》

EX. The police hurried to the scene of the crime.
警官は犯行の現場に急行した。
Keikan wa hankoo no genba ni kyuukoo-shita.

4. joˈokei 情景 •c [the emotive surroundings of a (past) action/event] 《sight》

EX. The photos reminded me of scenes from my childhood.
その写真を見て、子供のころの情景を思い出した。
Sono shashin o mite, kodomo no koro no jookei o omoi-dashita.

scenery n. **[the landscape of a district]**

keˈshiki 景色 •c [a view of nature worthy of enjoyment] 《scene, landscape, view》, fuˈukei 風景 •c [the appearance of a place or a situation in terms of its natural features, people, architecture, etc.] 《scene, view, landscape》

EX. **(a)** The scenery of Hokkaido is like that of the American midwest.
北海道の{景色/風景}はアメリカ中西部のそれに似ている。
Hokkaidoo no {keshiki/fuukei} wa Amerika-chuusei-bu no sore ni nite iru.
(b) The scenery seen from the balcony was breathtaking.
バルコニーからの{景色/風景}は息をのむほどだった。
Barukonii kara no {keshiki/fuukei} wa iki o nomu hodo datta.

scent n. **[a faint, distinctive smell emanating from s.t. organic]**

niˈoˈi におい /〈V*masu* of *niou* ① smell/ [a sensation created in the olfactory organs 《fig. "smack," "flavor"》] 《smell, odor》

EX. **(a)** I like the scent of pine trees.
私は松の木のにおいが好きだ。
Watashi wa matsu-no-ki no nioi ga suki da.
(b) My sister is allergic to the scent of cats.
僕の妹は猫のにおいにアレルギーです。
Boku no imooto wa neko no nioi ni arerugii desu.

schedule n. **[a list of s.t. prearranged such as prices or planned events]**

1. hyoˈo 表 •c [a set of facts or figures presented in an orderly written form for quick and easy comprehension] 《table, diagram, chart, list》

EX. Do you have a bus schedule?
バスの時刻表がありますか。

Basu no jikoku-hyoo ga arimasu ka.

2. yo⌈tei 予定 •c [an act of prearranging an event or s.t. prearranged] ⟪prearrangement, program, plan, expectation⟫, su⌈ke⌉juuru スケジュール •f [prearrangement/ prearranged events (of a day)]

EX. Could you give me your schedule for today?
今日の{御予定/スケジュール}を教えていただけますか。
Kyoo no {go-yotei/sukejuuru} o oshiete itadake-masu ka.

3. ji⌈kan-wari 時間割り [a time-table, esp. for classes]

EX. A: Do you know when and where we meet for Japanese 101?
日本語の101はいつ、どこであるか知ってる?
Nihon-go no ichi-{zero/maru}-ichi wa itsu, doko de aru ka shitte ru?
B: I don't know. Why don't you look at the schedule?
知らないよ。 時間割りを見たら?
Shiranai yo. Jikan-wari o mitara?

S

scheme n. **[a systematic (often underhand/ secret) plan of action]**
ke⌈ikaku 計画 •c [a method or procedure for doing s.t. thought out in advance] ⟪plan, project, design, program⟫, ku⌈wadate⌉ 企て /⟨Vmasu of *kuwadateru* ② plan/ [an act/instance of planning s.t. and trying to put it into practice] ⟪plan, plot, project, attempt, venture⟫, mo⌈kuromi⌉ もくろみ /⟨Vmasu of *mokuromu* ① plan/ [the act of making a plan for doing s.t.] ⟪plan, project, frame-up, intention, aim⟫, ta⌈kurami たくらみ /⟨Vmasu of *takuramu* ① plot/ [an act/instance of devising a systematic plan, usually underhand or secret] ⟪design, trick, contrivance, frame-up, plot⟫

EX. (**a**) Our company president had a 10-year scheme to steal the company's fortunes.
社長は会社の財産を奪う十年がかりの{計画/企て/もくろみ/たくらみ}を持っていた。
Shachoo wa kaisha no zaisan o ubau juu-nen-gakari no {keikaku/kuwadate/ mokuromi/takurami} o motte ita.
(**b**) We have an interesting scheme for earning money.
面白い金もうけの{計画/企て/もくろみ/?たくらみ}がある。
Omoshiroi kane-mooke no {keikaku/ kuwadate/mokuromi/?takurami} ga aru.
(**c**) I don't like Jill because she always seems to have some scheme up her sleeve.
ジルはいつも何か{たくらみ/*計画/*企て/*もくろみ}があるみたいで嫌いだ。
*Jiru wa itsu-mo nani-ka {takurami/ *keikaku/*kuwadate/*mokuromi} ga aru mitai de kirai da.*

scholar n. **[a person with in-depth learning on a particular subject]**
ga⌈kusha 学者 •c [a person who pursues scholarship or research ⟪fig. "erudite person"⟫]

EX. (**a**) Scholars shouldn't hole themselves up in their ivory towers.
学者は象げの塔に閉じこもるべきではない。
Gakusha wa zooge no too ni toji-komoru bekidewanai.
(**b**) Many scholars are working on superconductivity.
超伝導を研究している学者は多い。
Choo-dendoo o kenkyuu-shite iru gakusha wa ooi.

scholarship n. **[knowledge resulting from study or research in a field or a financial grant to assist a student]**
1. ga⌈kushiki 学識 •c [a scholar's knowledge in his/her field] ⟪learning, scholarly attainment⟫, ga⌈ku⌉mon 学問 •c [a branch of learning or knowledge resulting from study or research in a branch of learning] ⟪learning, studies, attainments⟫

EX. I was overwhelmed by my professor's degree of scholarship.
私は教授の{学識/学問}に圧倒された。
Watashi wa kyooju no {gakushiki/ gakumon} ni attoo-sareta.

2. sho⌈ogaku-kin 奨学金 •c [a financial

grant to support study by a student]

EX. How can I apply for the Ministry of Education Scholarship?
文部省の奨学金を申し込むにはどうしたらいいでしょうか。
Monbu-shoo no shoogaku-kin o mooshikomu ni wa doo shitara ii deshoo ka.

school[1] n. **[an educational institution or a department (within a college/university) or a group of intellectuals/artists adhering to the same beliefs or styles]**

1. ga⌈kkoo 学校 •c [an educational institution]

EX. (**a**) What time does your school begin in the morning?
学校は朝何時に始まりますか。
Gakkoo wa asa nan-ji ni hajimarimasu ka.
(**b**) I was late for school today.
今日は学校に遅れました。
Kyoo wa gakkoo ni okuremashita.

2. ga⌈kubu 学部 •c [an undergraduate department in a college/university] ⟪department⟫

EX. In America, law schools, business schools and medical schools are all at the graduate level.
アメリカでは法学部，経営学部，医学部は皆大学院だ。
Amerika de wa hoo-gakubu, keiei-gakubu, i-gakubu wa mina daigaku-in da.

3. -ryuu ～流 [a group of intellectuals/artists adhering to the same beliefs or styles] ⟪styles⟫

EX. I am a follower of the Soogetsu school of ikebana .
私は生け花の草月流に属している。
Watashi wa ikebana no Soogetsu-ryuu ni zokushite iru.

school[2] n. **[a group of fish/whales/people]**
mu⌈re⌉ 群れ [a group of people/animals/insects/clouds] ⟪crowd, herd, flock, pack, shoal, swarm⟫

EX. While scuba diving, I saw a school of beautiful fish.
スキューバダイビングをしている時、きれいな魚の群れを見た。
Sukyuuba-daibingu o shite iru toki, kireina sakana no mure o mita.

schoolhouse n.
ko⌉osha 校舎 •c ⟪school building⟫

EX. Since enrollments have increased, they are building a new schoolhouse.
学生数が増えたので、新しい校舎を建てています。
Gakusei-suu ga fueta node, atarashii koosha o tatete imasu.

koosha

schoolroom n. **[a room in a school for holding classes]**
kyo⌈oshitsu 教室 •c [a room in a school for holding classes ⟪fig. "school for skill-oriented instruction"⟫]

EX. When I went to the schoolroom nobody was there.
私が教室に行った時にはだれもいなかった。
Watashi ga kyooshitsu ni itta toki ni wa dare-mo inakatta.

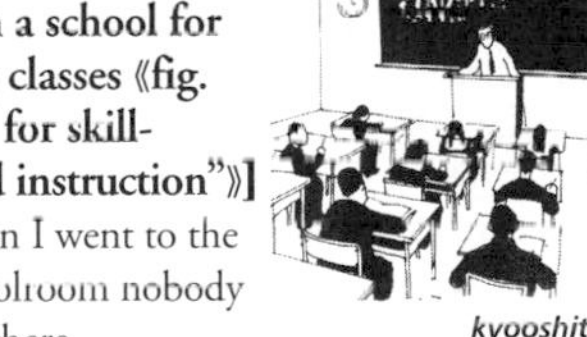
kyooshitsu

schooner n. **[a boat with two masts]**
su⌈ku⌉unaa スクーナー •f

science n.
ka⌉gaku 科学 •c

EX. (**a**) Science has advanced rapidly over the past two decades.
科学は過去二十年の間に急速に進歩した。
Kagaku wa kako ni-juu-nen no aida ni kyuusokuni shinpo-shita.
(**b**) Science can be an enemy of mankind.
科学は人類の敵にもなり得る。
Kagaku wa jinrui no teki ni mo nari-{eru/uru}.

scientific adj. **[of/pertaining to science]**
ka⌈gaku-tekina 科学的な adj(*na*). **•c**

S

[characterized by positivism/rationalism/a systematic approach]

EX. I think that the idea is very scientific.
その考えはとても科学的だと思います。
Sono kangae wa totemo kagaku-teki da to omoimasu.

scientist n. **[an expert in science]**
ka⌈gaku⌉-sha 科学者 •c

EX. Our modern life owes a great deal to scientists.
現代の我々の生活は科学者に負うところが多い。
Gendai no ware-ware no seikatsu wa kagaku-sha ni ou tokoro ga ooi.

scissors n.
ha⌈sami⌉ はさみ

EX. (**a**) These scissors do not cut well.
このはさみはよく切れない。
Kono hasami wa yoku kirenai.
(**b**) Could you trim my hair with these scissors?
このはさみで髪の毛を切ってくださいませんか。
Kono hasami de kami-no-ke o kitte kudasaimasen ka.

scold vt. **[for a superior to reprimand an inferior harshly]**
⟨-o⟩ shi⌈karu ⟨〜を⟩しかる ① [for s.o. to criticize or reprove a child/inferior for his/her wrongdoing/mistake/failure/weakness] ⟪chide, reprove, rebuke⟫, ⟨-o⟩ shi⌈kari-tsuke⌉ru ⟨〜を⟩しかりつける ② [for s.o. to criticize or reprove openly and severely a child/inferior for his/her wrongdoing/mistake/failure/weakness] ⟪chide, rebuke, reprove, reprimand, lecture⟫

EX. (**a**) When I forgot to turn in my homework, my teacher scolded me severely.
宿題を出すのを忘れた時、先生にひどく{しかられた/しかりつけられた}。
Shukudai o dasu no o wasureta toki, sensei ni hidoku {shikara-reta/shikari-tsuke-rareta}.
(**b**) My father never scolded me no matter what I did.
父は私が何をやっても{しかりませんでした/?しかりつけませんでした}。
Chichi wa watashi ga nani o yatte mo {shikarimasendeshita/?shikari-tsukemasen deshita}.

scope n. **[a range/area of perception/activity]**
ha⌉n'i 範囲 •c [an area defined by certain bounds] ⟪extent, sphere, limits, bounds⟫

EX. May I ask about the scope of the exam?
試験の範囲を教えてください。
Shiken no han'i o oshiete kudasai.

score n. **[a notch made to keep a tally ⟪fig. "point," "tally," "a set of twenty," "written music"⟫]**
1. ki⌈zami-me 刻み目 [an incision] ⟪notch, indent, nick⟫
2. te⌉n 点 •c [a small mark made by the end of a sharp object ⟪fig. "punctuation," "marks," "respects"⟫] ⟪dot, speck, mark, point, detail, respect⟫, to⌈kuten 得点 •c [the mark obtained in an exam or sports game] ⟪points, runs⟫, su⌈ko⌉a スコア •f

EX. A: What was the score in the game?
試合の{点/得点/スコア}は何点でしたか。
Shiai no {ten/tokuten/sukoa} wa nan-ten deshita ka.
B: It was 15 to 13.
15対13でした。
Juu-go tai juu-san deshita.

3. ni⌉-juu 二十 •c [twenty]

EX. The school was founded three score and five years ago.
学校は六十五年前に建てられた。
Gakkoo wa roku-juu-go-nen mae ni tate-rareta.

4. ga⌈kufu 楽譜 •c [the written/printed form of symbols representing sounds arranged in an esthetically pleasing pattern] ⟪a sheet of music⟫

EX. Can John read a musical score?
ジョンは楽譜が読めますか。
Jon wa gakufu ga yome-masu ka.

—— vt./vi. **[for s.o. to make a notch for keeping a tally ⟪fig. "gain points," "keep a record of the score"⟫]**
1. ⟨-ni⟩ ki⌈zami-me o tsu⌈ke⌉ru ⟨〜に⟩刻み目

をつける ② **[to make a notch on a surface]**
2. 〈-ni〉 te⌈n o tsuke⌉ru 〈～に〉点をつける ② [for s.o. to assign points esp. in an exam/game]
EX. Last night I was busy scoring my students' exam papers.
昨晩は学生の試験に点をつけるので忙しかった。
Sakuban wa gakusei no shiken ni ten o tsukeru node isogashikatta.
3. te⌈n o to⌉ru 点を取る ① [to obtain points in an exam/game]
EX. I scored 99 points out of 100 on the exam.
私は試験で100点満点中99点を取った。
Watashi wa shiken de hyaku-ten-manten-chuu kyuu-juu-kyuu-ten o totta.

Scotland n.
Su⌈kottora⌉ndo スコットランド •f

scout n. **[a reconnoitering person/aircraft/ship《fig. "a member of the Boy Scouts"》]**
1. se⌈kkoo(-hei) 斥候(兵) •c [a reconnoitering soldier]《patrol, feeler》
2. te⌈isatsu-kan 偵察艦 •c [a reconnoitering ship]
3. te⌈isatsu⌉-ki 偵察機 •c [a reconnaissance plane]《spotter plane》
4. su⌈ka⌉uto スカウト •f [a reconnoitering/recruiting person in sports]
— vi./vt. **[for s.o. to explore an enemy position or other situation to obtain strategic information]**
1. 〈-o〉 te⌈isatsu-suru 〈～を〉偵察する ③ •c [to secretly watch enemy positions and activity]《patrol, feel》
EX. Five soldiers were sent out to scout the enemy.
五人の兵士が敵を偵察するために送り出された。
Go-nin no heishi ga teki o teisatsu-suru tame ni okuri-dasa-reta.
2. 〈-o〉 su⌈ka⌉uto-suru 〈～を〉スカウトする ③ •f [for s.o. to reconnoiter another team (to recruit players)]
EX. College basketball coaches were watching the high school game to scout talented players.
大学のバスケットのコーチたちは有能なプレーヤーをスカウトするためにその高校の試合を見ていた。
Daigaku no basuketto no koochi-tachi wa yuunoona pureeyaa o sukauto-suru tame ni sono kookoo no shiai o mite ita.

scramble vi. **[for s.o./s.a. to move hastily and awkwardly esp. on the hands and knees《fig. "for a fighter plane to take off quickly to attack the enemy"》]**
1. 〈-o〉 ha⌉u 〈～を〉はう ① [for a plant to extend over the ground/a wall or for s.o./s.a. to move with one's stomach close to the ground]《crawl》
EX. The baby was scrambling over the floor.
赤ちゃんが床をはっていた。
Aka-chan ga yuka o hatte ita.
2. ki⌈nkyuu-ha⌉sshin-suru 緊急発進する ③ •c [for a fighter plane to take off quickly to attack the enemy]
— vt. **[for s.o. to mix hastily and haphazardly]**
1. 〈-o〉 ka⌈ki-mazeru 〈～を〉かき混ぜる ② [for s.o./s.a. to move s.t. around so that it becomes mixed together]《stir up, beat up》
EX. The kid scrambled the neatly arranged cards.
子供がそろえたカードをかき混ぜてしまった。
Kodomo ga soroeta kaado o kaki-mazete shimatta.
2. (ta⌈ma⌉go o) i⌈ri-ta⌉mago ni suru (卵を)いり卵にする ③ [for s.o. to cook eggs while stirring]
EX. A: How do you like your eggs?
卵はどうしたのがお好きですか。
Tamago wa doo shita no ga o-suki desu ka.
B: I like them scrambled.
いり卵にしたのが好きです。
Iri-tamago ni shita no ga suki desu.
3. 〈-o〉 go⌈chamaze ni suru 〈～を〉ごちゃ混ぜにする ③ [for s.o. to mix things up]
EX. The words in the following sentence are scrambled. Can you unscramble them?
次の文は単語がごちゃ混ぜにしてあり

S

ますが、元に戻せますか。
Tsugi no bun wa tango ga gochamaze ni shite arimasu ga, moto ni modose-masu ka.

4. ⟨-o⟩ ki⌈nkyuu-ha⌉sshin-saseru ⟨〜を⟩緊急発進させる /⟨causative of *kinkyuu-hasshin-suru* ③ take off quickly to attack the enemy/ •c [for s.o. to cause a fighter plane to take off quickly to attack the enemy]

scrap n. **[a small detached piece of cloth/paper/wood/metal/food/land]**

1. ki⌈re-hashi 切れ端 [a small detached piece of a two-dimensional object, esp. cloth/paper] ⟪odds and ends⟫

EX. The waste basket was full of scraps of paper.
くずかごには紙の切れ端がたくさん入っていた。
Kuzu-kago ni wa kami no kire-hashi ga takusan haitte ita.

NOTE: *Kami no kire-hashi* is usually expressed by *kami-kire.*

2. ku⌈zutetsu くず鉄 [iron pieces discarded as refuse] ⟪scrap iron⟫, su⌈kura⌉ppu スクラップ •f

—— vt. **[for s.o. to break s.t. down into small detached pieces ⟪fig. "discard s.t. as useless"⟫]**

⟨-o⟩ su⌈kura⌉ppu ni suru ⟨〜を⟩スクラップにする ③ [for s.o. to discard s.t. as refuse], ⟨-o⟩ ha⌈iki-suru ⟨〜を⟩廃棄する ③ •c [for s.o. to discard s.t. as useless ⟨fml⟩] ⟪annul, abolish, abandon, discard⟫

EX. (**a**) The president of the company scrapped the original 10-year plan.
社長は当初の十年計画を{廃棄した/*スクラップにした}。
*Shachoo wa toosho no juu-nen-keikaku o {haiki-shita/*sukurappu ni shita}.*
(**b**) They are scrapping junk cars at the factory.
その工場ではぼろ車を{スクラップにして/?廃棄して}いる。
Sono koojoo de wa boro-guruma o {sukurappu ni shite/?haiki-shite} iru.

scrape vt. **[to rub/scratch a surface with strong pressure in order to remove s.t. from it or to make it smooth or to gather s.t. together (figuratively) or to produce a harsh, grating sound]**

1. ⟨-o⟩ ko⌈suri-to⌉ru ⟨〜を⟩こすり取る ① [for s.o. to rub a surface with strong pressure in order to remove s.t. from it]

EX. I scraped the old paint off the wall.
壁の古いペンキをこすり取った。
Kabe no furui penki o kosuri-totta.

2. ⟨-o⟩ ta⌈irani suru ⟨〜を⟩平らにする ③ [for s.o. to make a surface smooth and flat]

EX. They were scraping the street with a road leveler.
地ならし機で道路を平らにしていた。
Ji-narashi-ki de dooro o tairani shite ita.

3. ⟨-o⟩ ka⌈ki-atsume⌉ru ⟨〜を⟩かき集める ② [for s.o. to scratch a surface using strong pressure in order to gather (figuratively) s.t. together]

EX. An old man was scraping the fallen leaves together with a rake.
老人が熊手を使って落ち葉をかき集めていた。
Roojin ga kuma-de o tsukatte ochiba o kaki-atsumete ita.

4. ⟨-o⟩ ki⌈shira-se⌉ru ⟨〜を⟩きしらせる /⟨causative of *kishiru* ① squeak/ ② [to rub/scratch/pull s.t. in such a way as to create a harsh, grating sound]

EX. The child scraped his fingers over the window pane.
子供がガラス窓を指できしらせた。
Kodomo ga garasu-mado o yubi de kishira-seta.

scratch vt. **[to make a short line/shallow cut on a surface with a pointed object such as a nail/thorn/pen/fingernail]**

1. ⟨-o⟩ ka⌉ku ⟨〜を⟩かく ① [for s.o./s.a. to make a short line on a surface with a pointed object such as a nail/thorn/pen/fingernail]

㊮ "scratch/draw a picture"▷かく, "write"▷書く

EX. Japanese men often scratch their head when they make an embarrassing mistake in front of others.

日本人は人前で恥ずかしい間違いをした時よく頭をかく。
Nihon-jin wa hito-mae de hazukashii machigai o shita toki yoku atama o kaku.

2. ⟨-o⟩ **hik˹ka˺ku** ⟨～を⟩引っかく ① **[for s.o./s.a. to make a short line on a surface by pulling a pointed object such as a nail/thorn/pen/fingernail across it]** ⟪claw, maul⟫

EX. (**a**) Don't scratch your rash. It will only make it worse.
発しんは引っかいてはいけませんよ。もっとひどくなるから。
{Hasshin/Hosshin} wa hikkaite wa ikemasen yo. Motto hidoku naru kara.
(**b**) My cat scratched my face.
僕は猫に顔を引っかかれちゃった。
Boku wa neko ni kao o hikkaka-rechatta.

scream vi. **[for s.o./s.a. to utter a loud, piercing, hysterical cry]**
(⟨-to⟩) **ka˹na-kiri-go˺e o {a˹geru/da˺su}** (⟨～と⟩)金切り声を{あげる ②/出す ①} **[for s.o. to utter a piercingly high-pitched cry]** ⟪shout, cry, yell, exclaim, shriek⟫, **kyaa˺ tto i˹u** きゃあっと言う ① **[for s.o. to cry out making the sound kyaa]**

EX. (**a**) I heard a young lady's voice screaming for help.
私は若い女性が「助けて!!」と、{金切り声を{出して/あげて}/*きゃあっと言って}いるのを聞いた。
*Watashi wa wakai josei ga 'Tasukete!!' to, {kana-kiri-goe o {dashite/agete}/*kyaa tto itte} iru no o kiita.*
(**b**) The girl screamed when she saw the snake.
女の子は蛇を見た時{金切り声を{出した/あげた}/きゃあっと言った}。
Onna-no-ko wa hebi o mita toki {kana-kiri-goe o {dashita/ageta}/kyaa tto itta}.

screen n. **[a framed device that is used to compartmentalize space, to conceal/protect s.t. or to project an image on or to filter out s.t.]**
1. tsu˹itate ついたて **[a framed device used to compartmentalize a room]** ⟪a single-leaf screen⟫, **byo˹obu** びょうぶ **[a foldable, framed, esthetic object used to compartmentalize a room]**
2. a˹mi˺do 網戸 **[a framed, net-like object designed to keep out insects]** ⟪window-screen⟫
3. su˹kuri˺in スクリーン •**f [a surface onto which an image (such as a movie) is projected]**

— vt. **[to conceal s.t. from view]**
1. ⟨-o⟩ **sa˹egi˺ru** ⟨～を⟩さえぎる ② **[to interrupt the progress/passage/view of s.t./s.o./s.a.]** ⟪interrupt, block, intercept⟫, ⟨-o⟩ **mi˹e˺naku suru** ⟨～を⟩見えなくする ③ **[to cause s.t./s.o./s.a. to be invisible]**, ⟨-o⟩ **o˹o˺u** ⟨～を⟩覆う ① **[to cause a thin and extensive object to lie completely over the surface of s.t. and protect or hide it from the outside]** ⟪cover, veil, hide, conceal, shield, wrap, shade⟫

EX. (**a**) The trees screened the hot sun.
木が暑い日差しを{さえぎって/*覆って/*見えなくして}いた。
*Ki ga atsui hi-zashi o {saegitte/*ootte/*mienaku shite} ita.*
(**b**) When a Japanese girl laughs, she often screens her mouth with her hand.
日本の女の子は笑う時よく口を手で{覆う/?見えなくする/*さえぎる}。
*Nihon no onna-no-ko wa warau toki yoku kuchi o te de {oou/?mienaku suru/*saegiru}.*
(**c**) The police screened the young suspect from onlookers with a curtain as he got in the police car.
若い容疑者が車に乗る時、警察は幕を張って{見えなくした/さえぎった/覆った}。
Wakai yoogi-sha ga kuruma ni noru toki, keisatsu wa maku o hatte {mienaku shita/saegitta/ootta}.

2. ⟨-o⟩ **shi˹ki˺ru** ⟨～を⟩仕切る ① **[for s.o. to compartmentalize space]** ⟪partition, compart, divide, rail off⟫

EX. We have screened off a room for the party.

S

パーティーのために部屋を仕切った。
Paatii no tame ni heya o shikitta.

screw n.
ne⅃ji ねじ
EX. (**a**) The screw on the door came off.
ドアのねじが外れました。
Doa no neji ga hazuremashita.
(**b**) Please turn the screw tightly.
ねじをきつく締めてください。
Neji o kitsuku shimete kudasai.

—— vt. **[for s.o. to fasten/tighten with a screw]**
⟨-o⟩ ne⅃ji de shi⌈me⅃ru ⟨〜を⟩ねじで締める ②

screwdriver n.
ne⌈ji-ma⅃washi ねじ回し, **do⌈ra⅃ibaa** ドライバー **•f**

scrub vt. **[for s.o./s.a. to rub s.t. hard with a brush/cloth/soap to clean it]**
⟨-o⟩ go⅃shi-goshi ko⌈su⅃ru ⟨〜を⟩ごしごしこする ① **[for s.o. to rub s.t. very hard with s.t.]**, **⟨-o⟩ go⅃shi-goshi a⌈rau** ⟨〜を⟩ごしごし洗う ① **[for s.o. to wash s.t. very hard with s.t.]**
S
EX. (**a**) The stain on the floor didn't come off even after I scrubbed it with soap.
床の染みは石けんでいくらごしごし{こすって/洗って}も落ちなかった。
Yuka no shimi wa sekken de ikura goshi-goshi {kosutte/aratte} mo ochinakatta.
(**b**) This stain on your shirt needs scrubbing.
シャツの染みはごしごし{洗わない/こすらない}と落ちませんよ。
Shatsu no shimi wa goshi-goshi {arawanai/kosuranai} to ochimasen yo.

sea n. **[the body of salt water that covers most of the earth's surface ⟪fig. "a vast expanse of s.t."⟫]**
u⅃mi 海 **[the body of salt water that covers most of the earth's surface ⟪fig. "a large amount of liquid/fire"⟫]** ⟪**ocean**⟫ ↔ **riku** 陸 **•c**
EX. (**a**) I prefer swimming in the sea to swimming in a pool.
私はプールで泳ぐより海で泳ぐ方が好きです。
Watashi wa puuru de oyogu yori umi de oyogu hoo ga suki desu.
(**b**) The massacre left a sea of blood in the street.
虐殺事件で道路は血の海だった。
Gyakusatsu-jiken de dooro wa chi no umi datta.

seafood n. **[edible animals from the sea]**
gyo-⌈ka⅃i-rui 魚介類 **•c [fish and shellfish]** ⟪**fishery products**⟫, **ka⌈isan⅃-butsu** 海産物 **•c [food produced from the sea]**, **u⅃mi-no-sa⅃chi** 海の幸 **[marine products]** ↔ **yama-no-sachi** 山の幸
EX. Japanese cuisine could not exist without seafood.
{魚介類/海産物/海の幸}がなければ日本料理は出来ない。
{Gyo-kai-rui/Kaisan-butsu/Umi-no-sachi} ga nakereba Nihon-ryoori wa dekinai.

seal[1] n. **[an amphibious sea animal with very short limbs]**
a⌈za⅃rashi あざらし ⟪**sea lion, sea cat**⟫

seal[2] n. **[a substance used to close an opening to prevent s.t. from passing through ⟪fig. "a marker of guarantee/rank/end of a contract"⟫]**
1. ha⅃n 判 **•c [a stamp used for validating documents or a size of paper]** ⟪**handstamp, format**⟫, **ha⌈nko⅃** 判子 **[a stamp used for validating documents]** ⟪**stamp**⟫, **i⌈nkan** 印鑑 **•c** ⟨**fml**⟩
EX. Japanese people use a seal instead of a signature on important documents.
日本では重要書類に署名する代わりに{判/判子/印鑑}を使う。
Nihon de wa juuyoo-shorui ni shomei-suru kawari ni {han/hanko/inkan} o tsukau.

hanko

2. ho⌈shoo 保証 **•c [the act of guaranteeing s.t.]** ⟪**guarantee, security, pledge**⟫
3. shi⅃iru シール **•f [a small decorative stamp]**

—— vt. [to affix a seal to s.t. or to close s.t. as if with a seal]

1. ⟨-ni⟩ ha˥n o o┌su ⟨〜に⟩判を押す ① [for s.o. to affix a seal to s.t.]

EX. My duty is to simply seal each document.
私の仕事はただ文書に判を押すだけです。
Watashi no shigoto wa tada bunsho ni han o osu dake desu.

2. ⟨-o⟩ fu┌ujiru ⟨〜を⟩封じる ② [for s.o. to affix a seal to s.t. to prevent anything from entering it or to close s.t. as if with a seal] ((**glue up, fasten, block**))

EX. We sealed the hole in the ceiling to prevent drafts of air from coming in.
すき間風が入って来ないように、天井の穴を封じた。
Sukima-kaze ga haitte konai yooni, tenjoo no ana o fuujita.

seam n. **[a line of junction formed by sewing/joining two parts together]**

1. nu┌i-me˥ 縫い目 [a line of junction formed by sewing two objects together] ((**stitch, suture**))

EX. The seam of my jacket is coming apart.
背広の縫い目がほころんで来ている。
Sebiro no nui-me ga hokoronde kite iru.

2. tsu┌gi-me 継ぎ目 [a line of junction formed by joining two parts together] ((**joint**))

EX. Water leaked from the seam in the bathtub.
浴槽の継ぎ目から水が漏れた。
Yokusoo no tsugi-me kara mizu ga moreta.

seaman n. **[a business term used to refer to a sailor]**

fu┌na˥-nori 船乗り /(*fune* boat + V*masu* of *noru* ① ride/ ((**sailor, crewman**)), **se┌n'in 船員 •c [s.o. who works on board a ship]** ((**mariner, sailor**))

EX. My father was a seaman on a cargo boat.
父は貨物船の{船乗り/船員}でした。
Chichi wa kamotsu-sen no {funa-nori/sen'in} deshita.

search vi. **[for s.o./s.a. to look for s.t./s.o./s.a. that one has lost (sight of)]**

⟨-o⟩ sa┌gasu ⟨〜を⟩さがす ① [for s.o. to make an effort to find s.t./s.o./s.a. that has become lost or to find s.t./s.o./s.a. which satisfies certain criteria] ((**search for, look for, try to locate, trace**))

㊮ "look for s.t./s.o./s.a. that a person needs"▷探す, "look for s.t./s.o./s.a. that one has lost (sight of)"▷捜す

EX. (**a**) I am searching for my purse.
財布を{捜して/*探して}いるんです。
Saifu o sagashite iru n desu.
(**b**) I searched for a good English-Japanese dictionary.
いい英和辞典を{探した/*捜した}。
Ii Ei-Wa-jiten o sagashita.

—— vt. [for s.o./s.a. to examine s.t./s.o./s.a. carefully and thoroughly]

⟨-o⟩ shi┌rabe˥ru ⟨〜を⟩調べる ② [for s.o. to observe directly or inquire/read about s.t./s.o./s.a. in order to determine or ascertain s.t. unknown or uncertain about it/him/her] ((**investigate, examine, survey, check up, test, inspect, consult**)), **⟨-o⟩ so┌osaku-suru ⟨〜を⟩捜索する ③ •c [for s.o. to look for s.t./s.o./s.a. lost or for police to investigate a building/articles]** ((**look for, hunt for, probe**))

EX. (**a**) At the airport the security officers searched the possessions of every passenger.
空港では警備官が乗客一人一人の持ち物を{調べた/*捜索した}。
*Kuukoo de wa keibi-kan ga jookyaku hitori-hitori no mochi-mono o {shirabeta/*soosaku-shita}.*
(**b**) The policemen searched the apartment for drugs.
警官はアパートを{調べて/捜索して}麻薬を捜した。
Keikan wa apaato o {shirabete/soosaku-shite} mayaku o sagashita.

—— n. [the act of looking for s.t./s.o./s.a. or examining s.t./s.o./s.a. very carefully and thoroughly]

1. so˥osa 捜査 •c [the act of investigating the facts surrounding a crime/accident] ((**criminal investigation, manhunt**))

EX. The search for the escapee is expected to

S

continue indefinitely.
脱走犯の捜査はずっと続くはずだ。
Dassoo-han no soosa wa zutto tsuzuku hazu da.

2. ke⌉nsa 検査 •c [looking at s.t./s.o./s.a. carefully to see if it/he/she meets a standard or if there is anything wrong with it/him/her, often in an official capacity] ⟪inspection, examination, test⟫

EX. The search of the man's possessions did not reveal any drugs.
男の所持品検査の結果、麻薬はまったく出て来なかった。
Otoko no shoji-hin-kensa no kekka, mayaku wa mattaku dete-konakatta.

seashore n. **[land near the sea]**
ka⌈igan 海岸 •c [the land next to the ocean], u⌈mi-be⌉ 海辺 [land near the sea (with poetic connotations)]

EX. (**a**) I sunbathed on the seashore.
私は{海岸/海辺}で日光浴をしました。
Watashi wa {kaigan/umi-be} de nikkoo-yoku o shimashita.
(**b**) I used to like to jog along the seashore.
私は昔は{海岸/海辺}をジョギングするのが好きだった。
Watashi wa mukashi wa {kaigan/umi-be} o jogingu-suru no ga suki datta.

seaside n. **[land by the sea esp. that used as a resort area]**
ka⌈igan 海岸 •c [the land next to the ocean], u⌈mi-be⌉ 海辺 [land near the sea (with poetic connotations)]

EX. I plan to stay at a seaside hotel.
{海岸/海辺}のホテルに泊る予定です。
{Kaigan/Umi-be} no hoteru ni tomaru yotei desu.

season n. **[a time of the year with distinct weather characteristics or the prime time in which s.t. takes place]**
ki⌈se⌉tsu 季節 •c, ji⌉ki 時季 •c [the time of the year in which s.t. takes place] ⟪time⟫, shi⌉izun シーズン •f [the prime time in which s.t. takes place]

EX. (**a**) In Japan there are four distinct seasons.
日本にははっきりとした四つの{季節/*時季/*シーズン}があります。
*Nihon ni wa hakkiri to shita yottsu no {kisetsu/*jiki/*shiizun} ga arimasu.*
(**b**) A: When is the best season for a trip to Japan?
日本旅行に一番いい{季節/時季/シーズン}はいつですか。
Nihon-ryokoo ni ichiban ii {kisetsu/jiki/shiizun} wa itsu desu ka.
B: I'd say spring or fall.
春か秋でしょう。
Haru ka aki deshoo.
(**c**) Autumn is the season for reading books.
秋は読書の{季節/時季/シーズン}です。
Aki wa dokusho no {kisetsu/jiki/shiizun} desu.

— vt. **[for s.o. to enhance the flavor of s.t. by adding seasoning]**
⟨-ni⟩ a⌈ji o tsu⌈ke⌉ru ⟨〜に⟩味を付ける ② [for s.o. to add flavor to s.t.] ⟪flavor⟫

EX. A: How should I season this meat?
この肉にどう味を付けたらいいですか。
Kono niku ni doo aji o tsuketara ii desu ka.
B: Why don't you season it with ginger and soy sauce?
しょうがとおしょうゆで味を付けたらどうですか。
Shooga to o-shooyu de aji o tsuketara doo desu ka.

seat n. **[s.t. on which one sits ⟪fig. "position," "place where s.t. exists"⟫]**
1. se⌉ki 席 •c [s.t. on which one sits ⟪fig. "the place where a meeting/ceremony takes place"⟫], za⌈seki 座席 •c [a place where one sits esp. seats in a theater/church/bus/train/plane] ⟪pew⟫

EX. (**a**) How many seats are there in this hall?
このホールには{座席/席}がいくつありますか。
Kono hooru ni wa {zaseki/seki} ga ikutsu arimasu ka.
(**b**) Please take your seat.
{座席/席}に着いてください。
{Zaseki/Seki} ni tsuite kudasai.

S

2. gi⌈seki 議席 •c **[a position in parliament]**

EX. No party was able to get the majority of seats in the Diet.
どの党も過半数の議席を取れなかった。
Dono too mo ka-hansuu no giseki o tore-nakatta.

3. sho⌈za⌉i-chi 所在地 •c [the location of some official building/institution], ba⌈sho 場所 •c [a point or area in space where s.o./s.t./s.a. exists or where s.t. happens] ⟪place⟫

EX. Where is the seat of the prefectural office?
県庁の{所在地/場所}はどこですか。
Kenchoo no {shozai-chi/basho} wa doko desu ka.

PHRASE: seat belt *shiito-beruto* シートベルト •f

EX. Please wear your seat belt when you are driving.
運転しているときはシートベルトをしてください。
Unten-shite iru toki wa shiito-beruto o shite kudasai.

Seattle n.

Shi⌈a⌉toru シアトル •f

seaweed n. **[a plant growing in the sea]**

ka⌈isoo 海藻 •c ⟪marine plants, algae⟫

EX. Japanese eat a lot of seaweed, including *nori, konbu,* and *wakame.*
日本人はのり、こんぶ、わかめなどの海藻をたくさん食べる。

nori, konbu, wakame

Nihon-jin wa nori, konbu, wakame nado no kaisoo o takusan taberu.

second[1] adj. **[coming next after the first]**

1. da⌉i-ni no N 第二のN •c [coming next after the first, esp. in time/quality], ni-⌈ban-me⌉ no N 二番目のN [coming next after the first, esp. in order/place/rank/time/quality]

EX. (**a**) A: Who is the young blond lady sitting in the second row?
{二番目/*第二}の列に座っている金髪の若い女性はだれですか。
*{Ni-ban-me/*Dai-ni} no retsu ni suwatte iru kinpatsu no wakai josei wa dare desu ka.*
B: That's my younger sister.
あれは僕の妹です。
Are wa boku no imooto desu.
(**b**) A: Are your children all boys?
お子さんはみんな男の子ですか。
O-ko-san wa minna otoko-no-ko desu ka.
B: No, the first one is a boy, but the second one is a girl.
いいえ、一番目(の)は男の子ですが、{二番目/*第二}(の)は女の子です。
*Iie, ichi-ban-me (no) wa otoko-no-ko desu ga, {ni-ban-me/*dai-ni} (no) wa onna-no-ko desu.*
(**c**) After surviving the accident I felt as though I was living a second life.
事故で死ななかったので、その後の人生は私にとってまるで{第二/??二番目}の人生のようでした。
Jiko de shinanakatta node, sono go no jinsei wa watashi ni-totte marude {dai-ni/??ni-ban-me} no jinsei no yoodeshita.

2. ni-⌈too no N 二等のN •c [coming next after the first in quality] ⟪second-class⟫

EX. What was the second prize?
{二等の賞品/二等賞}は何でしたか。
{Ni-too no shoohin/Ni-too-shoo} wa nan deshita ka.

PHRASE: the second day (of the month) *futsuka* 二日 SEE APPENDIX II, second(ly) *dai-ni ni* 第二に

— n. **[s.t./s.o./s.a. coming next after the first]**

1. da⌉i-ni 第二 •c [s.t./s.o./s.a. coming next after the first, esp. in time/quality]

2. ni-⌈ban-me⌉ 二番目 [s.t./s.o./s.a. coming next after the first, esp. in order/place/rank/time/quality]

3. ni-⌈kyuu-hin 二級品 •c [merchandise coming next after the first in quality] ⟪second-class goods⟫

4. o-⌈ka⌉wari お代わり [second helping of food]

S

5. ni˥-rui 二塁 •c **[second base (in baseball)], se˥kando セカンド •f**

—— vt. [for s.o. to support/supplement s.o. else's words/deeds]

1. ⟨-o⟩ shi˥ji-suru ⟨〜を⟩支持する ③ •c [for s.o. to agree to s.o.'s opinion and act/speak in favor of it] ⟪support, maintain, back up, espouse⟫

EX. I will second your idea if you propose it in the meeting.
その考えを会議で出したら、僕は支持するよ。
Sono kangae o kaigi de dashitara, boku wa shiji-suru yo.

2. do˥ogi ni sa˥nsei-suru 動議に賛成する ③ [for s.o. to endorse a motion] ⟪agree, approve, support, favor, endorse⟫

EX. Who will second the motion?
動議に賛成する方はいらっしゃいますか。
Doogi ni sansei-suru kata wa irasshaimasu ka.

second[2] n. **[a unit of time equal to one-sixtieth of a minute]**
byo˥o 秒 •c

S

EX. My friend swam 100 meters in one minute and forty-six seconds.
私の友達は百メートルを一分四十六秒で泳いだ。
Watashi no tomodachi wa hyaku-meetoru o ip-pun yon-juu-roku-byoo de oyoida.

secondary adj. **[second in importance/position/competence/value/order]**

1. ni-˥ji-tekina 二次的な adj(*na*). **•c [second in importance]**

EX. Pneumonia was a secondary cause of his death.
肺炎は二次的な死因だった。
Haien wa ni-ji-tekina shiin datta.

2. chu˥utoo-kyo˥oiku no N 中等教育のN •c [of education between elementary school and college]

EX. I'm teaching at a secondary school in the U.S.
私はアメリカの中等教育の学校で教えています。
Watashi wa Amerika no chuutoo-kyooiku no gakkoo de oshiete imasu.

second-class adj. **[belonging to a class lower than the top]**

1. ni-˥too no N 二等のN •c [coming next after the first in quality]

EX. I bought a second-class ticket.
私は二等の切符を買った。
Watashi wa ni-too no kippu o katta.

2. ni-˥ryuu no N 二流のN •c [being of second rate] ⟪second-rate, minor, inferior⟫

EX. It is better to be at the top at a second-class college than to be at the bottom at a first-class college.
一流の大学で最下位になるより二流の大学でトップになる方がいい。
Ichi-ryuu no daigaku de sai-kai ni naru yori ni-ryuu no daigaku de toppu ni naru hoo ga ii.

secondhand adj. **[used (merchandise)/(information) obtained from another]**

1. chu˥uko no N 中古のN •c [of merchandise already used and a little old], se˥ko-han no N セコハンのN •f

EX. (**a**) I bought a secondhand car yesterday.
きのう{中古/*セコハン}車を買いました。
*Kinoo {chuuko/*seko-han}-sha o kaimashita.*
(**b**) My brother got a secondhand TV from his friend.
弟は友達から{中古/セコハン}のテレビをもらいました。
Otooto wa tomodachi kara {chuuko/seko-han} no terebi o moraimashita.

2. u˥keuri no N 受け売りのN [(merchandise/ideas) received from elsewhere and resold/passed on] ⟪ready-made⟫

EX. A: Is that your own idea?
それは自分の考えかい?
Sore wa jibun no kangae kai?
B: Sorry, it's secondhand.
済みません。受け売りです。
Sumimasen. Ukeuri desu.

secret n. **[s.t. that is kept from the knowledge/view of others]**
1. hi⌈mitsu 秘密 •c [s.t. hidden from the knowledge of others] ⟪**private**⟫
EX.| Our marriage is still a secret to my parents.
私たちの結婚は両親にはまだ秘密なんです。
Watashi-tachi no kekkon wa ryooshin ni wa mada himitsu na n desu.
2. hi⌈ke⌉tsu 秘けつ •c [an effective method of doing s.t. still unknown to s.o.] ⟪**mystery, key**⟫**, ko⌈tsu こつ [a special skill or method of doing s.t.]** ⟪**knack, trick**⟫
EX.| What is the secret of becoming proficient in a foreign language?
外国語が上達する{秘けつ/こつ}は何ですか。
Gaikoku-go ga jootatsu-suru {hiketsu/kotsu} wa nan desu ka.
— adj. **[concealed from the knowledge/view of others]**
hi⌈mitsu no N 秘密のN •c [not publicly known and kept to oneself or people closest to s.o.]
EX.| He seems to have a secret job.
あの人には秘密の仕事があるらしい。
Ano hito ni wa himitsu no shigoto ga aru rashii.

secretary n. **[a person who is employed to do various kinds of clerical work or an official who is employed to maintain records/correspondence for an institution or a top official for a governmental department]**
1. hi⌈sho⌉ 秘書 •c [a person who is employed to do various kinds of clerical work]
EX.| Why don't you ask the secretary to fax this document to the Tokyo office?
秘書に頼んでこの文書を東京の事務所にファックスで送ってもらったらどうですか。
Hisho ni tanonde kono bunsho o Tookyoo no jimu-sho ni fakkusu de okutte morattara doo desu ka.
2. sho⌈ki(⌉-choo) 書記(長) •c [an official who is employed to maintain records/correspondence for an institution]
PHRASE: the Secretary of State *kokumu-chookan* 国務長官

secretly adv. **[in a secret way/manner]**
ko⌈sso⌉ri to こっそりと [in a way that no one will notice] ⟪**stealthily, quietly, surreptitiously**⟫**, hi⌈so⌉kani ひそかに ⟨w⟩** ⟪**stealthily, privately**⟫
EX.| The two met secretly at a small coffee shop.
二人は{こっそりと/ひそかに}小さな喫茶店で会った。
Futari wa {kossori to/hisokani} chiisana kissa-ten de atta.

section n. **[the act/result of cutting s.t. (surgically)]**
1. se⌉kkai 切開 •c [the act of cutting a bodily part surgically] ⟪**incision, operation**⟫
EX.| My wife underwent a Caesarian section.
妻は帝王切開を受けた。
Tsuma wa teioo-sekkai o uketa.
2. bu⌉bun 部分 •c [any of the divisions of a whole] ⟪**part, portion**⟫
EX.| I have read only a section of the report.
私はそのレポートの一部分を読んだだけです。
Watashi wa sono repooto no ichi-bubun o yonda dake desu.
3. se⌉tsu 節 •c [a node ⟪**fig. "time/season," "a paragraph of a thesis," "a part of a sentence"**⟫**]** ⟪**occasion, paragraph, part, clause**⟫
EX.| Read section eight of the chapter.
その章の第八節を読みなさい。
Sono shoo no dai-has-setsu o yominasai.
4. ra⌉n 欄 •c [a part of a newspaper devoted to a specific theme]
EX.| The first thing I read in the newspaper is the sports section.
新聞で最初に読むのはスポーツ欄です。
Shinbun de saisho ni yomu no wa supootsu-ran desu.

secure adj. **[free from danger/fear/doubt/weakness/looseness/breakage]**
1. a⌈nzenna 安全な adj(*na*). **•c [free from danger/harm/injury/theft]** ⟪**safe**⟫ ↔ **kikenna 危険な** adj(*na*). **•c**

EX. What would be a secure way to earn money?
お金をもうける安全な方法は何でしょうか。
O-kane o mookeru anzenna hoohoo wa nan deshoo ka.

2. a┌nshinna 安心な adj(*na*). **•c [free from anxiety]** ((**safe, assured**))

EX. I feel secure when I am with you.
あなたと一緒にいると安心なんです。
Anata to issho ni iru to anshin na n desu.

3. shi┌kka┐ri-shita N しっかりしたN /〈Vinf. past of *shikkari-suru* ③ become firm/ [free from weakness/looseness] ((**strong, solid, firm, stable**))

EX. The house is built on a secure foundation.
家はしっかりした土台の上に建てられている。
Ie wa shikkari-shita dodai no ue ni tate-rarete iru.

— vt. **[for s.o. to cause s.t./s.o./s.a. to be secure]**

1. 〈-no〉 a┌nzen o ka┐kuho-suru 〈〜の〉安全を確保する ③ •c [for s.o. to cause s.t./s.o./s.a. to be free from danger]

EX. In order to secure our country we have to strengthen our defense.
我が国の安全を確保するためには国防を強化しなければならない。
Waga kuni no anzen o kakuho-suru tame ni wa kokuboo o kyooka-shinakereba naranai.

2. 〈-o〉 te┐ ni ireru 〈〜を〉手に入れる ② [for s.o. to get hold of s.t.] ((**get, obtain, acquire, get hold of**)), **〈-o〉 ka┐kuho-suru 〈〜を〉確保する ③ •c [for s.o. to maintain s.t. firmly]** ((**ensure**))

EX. In business it is very important to secure a network of human relations.
ビジネスでは人間関係のネットワークを{手に入れる/確保する}のが大事だ。
Bijinesu de wa ningen-kankei no netto-waaku o {te ni ireru/kakuho-suru} no ga daiji da.

3. {〈-to〉/〈-o〉} ho┌shoo-suru {〈〜と〉/〈〜を〉} 保証する ③ •c [for s.o. to give a formal promise that s.t. will be done] ((**guarantee, warrant, assure, ensure, endorse**))

EX. We will secure the rights of the workers.
私たちは労働者の権利を保証する。
Watashi-tachi wa roodoo-sha no kenri o hoshoo-suru.

4. 〈-o〉 shi┌kka┐ri shi┌me┐ru 〈〜を〉しっかりしめる ② [for s.o. to fasten or close s.t. tightly]

㊥ "close"▷閉める, "tighten"▷締める

EX. I thought that I had secured the window, but a burglar managed to break into the room.
窓をしっかり閉めたと思いましたが、泥棒に部屋に入られました。
Mado o shikkari shimeta to omoimashita ga, doroboo ni heya ni haira-remashita.

security n. **[the state of being secure or s.t. that causes s.o./s.t./s.a. to be secure]**

1. a┌nzen 安全 •c [freedom from danger/harm/injury/theft] ((**safety**))

EX. Please put security first.
安全第一にしてください。
Anzen dai-ichi ni shite kudasai.

2. a┌nshi┐n-kan 安心感 •c [a sense of being free from anxiety/worry] ((**safety**))

EX. John gives me security when I am with him.
ジョンと一緒にいると安心感がある。
Jon to issho ni iru to anshin-kan ga aru.

3. bo┌oei 防衛 •c [the act of protecting oneself/one's country] ((**defense, safeguard, protection**)), **a┌nzen-ho┐shoo 安全保障 •c [the act of taking measures to protect s.t./s.o. from danger or disaster]**

EX. Each country should take its security seriously.
どの国も{防衛/安全保障}を真剣に考えなければならない。
Dono kuni mo {booei/anzen-hoshoo} o shinkenni kangaenakereba naranai.

4. yu┌uka-sho┐oken 有価証券 •c [stocks and bonds]

see vt. **[for s.o./s.a. to perceive s.t./s.o./s.a. visually** ((**fig. "understand"**))**]**

1. 〈-o〉 mi┐ru 〈〜を〉みる ② [for s.o./s.a. to

direct one's attention to s.t./s.o./s.a. in order to visually perceive its outward shape or its content] **《look at, witness, observe, read, look over, examine, judge》**

㊝ "for a doctor to see his patient"▷診る, otherwise ▷見る

EX. (**a**) I saw Julie swimming in the pool.
私はジュリーがプールで泳いでいるのを見た。
Watashi wa Jurii ga puuru de oyoide iru no o mita.
(**b**) I saw some shooting stars last night.
私はきのうの晩流れ星を見た。
Watashi wa kinoo no ban nagare-boshi o mita.
(**c**) The doctor kindly came to see my ailing mother.
お医者さんが親切にも病気の母を診に来てくれた。
O-isha-san ga shinsetsu ni mo byooki no haha o mi ni kite kureta.
(**d**) Will you see if the engine works all right?
エンジンが大丈夫か、見てくれませんか。
Enjin ga daijoobu ka, mite kuremasen ka.
(**e**) Did you see my message?
僕の伝言、見ましたか。
Boku no dengon, mimashita ka.

2. {⟨**-to**⟩/⟨**-ni**⟩} **a˥u** {⟨〜と⟩/⟨〜に⟩}あう ① **[for two people/objects to come face to face or in contact with each other or to fit each other]** **《meet, encounter, fit, coincide, match》**

㊝ "fit"▷合う, "meet a person"▷会う, "encounter an accident/opposition"▷あう

NOTE: *Ni* in "X *ga* Y *ni au*" is used when X moves in the direction of Y, whereas *to* in "X *ga* Y *to au*" is used when both X and Y move toward a common location where they meet.

EX. (**a**) Did you see your professor yesterday?
きのう先生{に/?と}会いましたか。
Kinoo sensei {ni/?to} aimashita ka.
(**b**) By chance I saw Mr. Mori in the Ginza.
偶然銀座で森さん{と/?に}会いました。
Guuzen Ginza de Mori-san {to/?ni} aimashita.

3. ⟨**-ga**⟩ **wa˥ka˥ru** ⟨〜が⟩分かる ① **[for s.o. to be able to figure out the nature, meaning, identity, etc., of s.t./s.o./s.a. which already is/should be in one's mind]** **《know, recognize, realize》**

EX. Don't you see that Jill likes Bill?
ジルがビルを好きなことが分からない?
Jiru ga Biru o sukina koto ga wakaranai?

PHRASE: as I see it *watashi no miru tokoro de wa* 私の見るところでは

EX. As I see it, the Japanese economy is still in good shape.
私の見るところでは、日本の経済はまだ調子がいい。
Watashi no miru tokoro de wa, Nihon no keizai wa mada chooshi ga ii.

PHRASE: see someone off ⟨*-o*⟩ *mi-okuru* ⟨〜を⟩見送る ① ↔ ⟨*-o*⟩ *mukaeru* ⟨〜を⟩迎える ②

EX. I saw my American friend off at the airport.
アメリカ人の友達を空港で見送った。
Amerika-jin no tomodachi o kuukoo de mi-okutta.

PHRASE: I see *naruhodo* なるほど

EX. A: You should hold the racket this way.
ラケットはこう握るんですよ。
Raketto wa koo nigiru n desu yo.
B: I see.
なるほど。
Naruhodo.

seed n. **[a small plant ovule capable of germinating into a new plant 《fig. "beginning of s.t."》]**
ta˥ne 種 **[a small plant ovule capable of germinating into a new plant 《fig. "breed," "subject of talk," "cause"》]**

EX. Did you plant the flower seeds yet?
花の種をもうまきましたか。
Hana no tane o moo makimashita ka.

seek vi./vt. **[for s.o./s.a. to make an effort to find s.t./s.o./s.a.]**
⟨**-o**⟩ **sa˥gasu** ⟨〜を⟩さがす ① **[for s.o. to make an effort to find s.t./s.o./s.a. that has become lost or to find s.t./s.o./s.a. which**

satisfies certain criteria] ((search for, look for, hunt, trace)), ⟨-o⟩ **sa⌈gashi-motome⌉ru** ⟨〜を⟩さがし求める ② **[for s.o./s.a. to move about trying to find s.t./s.o./s.a. that is lost/wanted ⟨fml⟩]**

㊐ "look for s.t./s.o./s.a. that is missing"▷捜す, "look for s.t./s.o./s.a. that is desired"▷探す

EX. (**a**) I am seeking a good Japanese grammar book.
私は日本語のいい文法書を{探して/?探し求めて}います。
Watashi wa Nihon-go no ii bunpoo-sho o {sagashite/?sagashi-motomete} imasu.
(**b**) We are seeking the missing child.
いなくなった子供を{捜して/捜し求めて}います。
Inaku natta kodomo o {sagashite/sagashi-motomete} imasu.
(**c**) The college is seeking a new President.
大学は新しい学長を{探して/探し求めて}います。
Daigaku wa atarashii gakuchoo o {sagashite/sagashi-motomete} imasu.

S

seem vi. **[to appear to one's mind]** **Sinf. ra⌈shi⌉i Sinf.**らしい aux. adj(*i*). **[an auxiliary adjective which indicates that the preceding sentence represents the speaker's conjecture based on what he has heard/read/seen]** ((look like, appear)), **Sinf. yo⌉ona Sinf.**ような aux. adj(*na*). **[an auxiliary adj(*na*). which expresses the likelihood of s.t. or the likeness of s.t./s.o./s.a. to s.t./s.o./s.a.]** ((appear)), **Sinf. yo⌉oni o⌈mowa-re⌉ru Sinf.**ように思われる ② **[s.t./s.o./s.a. gives one the impression that ⟨w⟩]** ((appear)), **Sinf. mi⌉taina Sinf.**みたいな aux. adj(*na*). **[an auxiliary adj(*na*). which expresses the likelihood of s.t. or the likeness of s.t./s.o./s.a. to s.t./s.o./s.a. ⟨s⟩]**

NOTE: Notice the following special patterns that occur when *rashii*, *yoona* or *mitaina* are connected to a preceding sentence when the final predicate in that sentence is an adj.(*na*) or N:
{adj(*na*). stem/N} {*rashii/mitaina*}
{adj(*na*). stem + *na*/N *no*} *yoona*

EX. (**a**) A: Do you know any good summer Japanese language programs?
何かいい夏の日本語講座を知っていますか。
Nani-ka ii natsu no Nihon-go-kooza o shitte imasu ka.
B: Middlebury's Japanese School seems to be the best.
ミドルベリー日本語学校が一番いい{らしいです/ようです/みたいです/?ように思われます}。
Midoruberii Nihon-go Gakkoo ga ichiban ii-{rashii desu/yoodesu/mitaidesu/?yooni omowa-remasu}.
(**b**) A: Is Mr. Ito still here?
伊藤さんはまだここにいますか。
Itoo-san wa mada koko ni imasu ka.
B: No, he seems to have gone home.
いいえ、家に帰った{らしいです/ようです/みたいです/??ように思われます}。
Iie, ie ni kaetta {rashii desu/yoodesu/mitaidesu/??yooni omowa-remasu}.
(**c**) According to what I heard from a friend yesterday, Liz seems to be going to Korea next month.
きのう友達に聞いた所ではリズは来月韓国へ行く{らしいです/?ようです/?みたいです/*ように思われます}。
*Kinoo tomodachi ni kiita tokoro de wa Rizu wa raigetsu Kankoku e iku {rashii desu/?yoodesu/?mitaidesu/*yooni omowa-remasu}.*
(**d**) It seems that the current increase in Japanese language enrollment started sometime towards the end of the 70's.
現在の日本語の学生の増加は70年代の終わりごろに始まった{ようだ/らしい/ように思われる/?みたいだ}。
Genzai no Nihon-go no gakusei no zooka wa nana-juu-nen-dai no owari goro ni hajimatta {yooda/rashii/yooni omowa-reru/?mitaida}.
(**e**) Mr. James is coughing all the time. He seems to have a cold.
ジェームズさんはせきばかりしています。風邪を引いている{らしいです/よう

です/みたいです/?ように思われます}。
Jeemuzu-san wa seki bakari shite imasu. Kaze o hiite iru {rashii desu/yoodesu/mitaidesu/?yooni omowa-remasu}.

segment n. **[any of the parts into which something can be divided]**
bu⌉bun 部分 •c [any of the divisions of a whole] **《part, section, portion, percentage》**
↔ zentai 全体 •c
EX. This segment of the discussion is devoted to the topic of energy.
討議のこの部分はエネルギーの問題を扱う。
Toogi no kono bubun wa enerugii no mondai o atsukau.

—— vt. **[for s.o. to divide into parts]**
⟨-o⟩ ⟨-ni⟩ wa⌈ke⌉ru ⟨〜を⟩⟨〜に⟩分ける ② [to part s.t. or a group of things/people/animals into two or more parts/groups (and share them with s.o.)] **《divide, part, sever, split》**
EX. Can you segment this passage into three parts?
この文章を三つに分けられますか。
Kono bunshoo o mittsu ni wake-raremasu ka.

—— vi. **[for s.t. to divide itself into parts]**
⟨-ni⟩ wa⌈kare⌉ru ⟨〜に⟩わかれる ② [for s.t. whole or a group of things/people/animals to come to exist in parts] **《branch off, diverge, split, be divided, part with, break up》**
㊅ "part with/break up"▷別れる, otherwise ▷分かれる

seize vt. **[for s.o./s.a. to grasp s.t./s.o./s.a. quickly, suddenly and forcibly]**
1. ⟨-o⟩ tsu⌈ka⌉mu ⟨〜を⟩つかむ ① [for s.o./s.a. to take hold of s.t./s.o./s.a. tightly, suddenly, and forcibly 《fig. "understand"》] **《catch, grasp, grip, grab》**
EX. (**a**) David seized my hand and said "I love you."
デビッドは私の手をつかんで「君が大好きだ」と言った。
Debiddo wa watashi no te o tsukande 'Kimi ga dai-suki da' to itta.
(**b**) He never fails to seize an opportunity.
あの人はいつもいい機会をつかむ。
Ano hito wa itsu-mo ii kikai o tsukamu.
2. ⟨-o⟩ tsu⌈kamaeru ⟨〜を⟩捕まえる ② [for s.o./s.a. to take hold of s.t./s.o./s.a. that is trying to flee/leave and try not to let it/him/her go] **《catch, take hold of, clutch, hold on to, grasp, grab, arrest, capture》**,
⟨-o⟩ to⌈rae⌉ru ⟨〜を⟩捕らえる ② [for s.o. to capture s.a./a criminal 《fig. "deeply understand"》 ⟨fml⟩] **《catch, capture, arrest》**
EX. The police seized the burglar.
警官が泥棒を{捕まえた/捕えた}。
Keikan ga doroboo o {tsukamaeta/toraeta}.
3. ⟨-o⟩ sa⌈shi-osaeru ⟨〜を⟩差し押さえる ② [for s.o. to distrain s.o.'s goods or to impound documents]
EX. Because he didn't pay his taxes, they seized his house.
税金を払わなかったので、彼の家は差し押さえられた。
Zeikin o harawanakatta node, kare no ie wa sashi-osae-rareta.

seldom adv. **[not often]**
me⌉ttani…neg. めったに…neg.
EX. A: Do you often go to the movies?
よく映画を見に行きますか。
Yoku eiga o mi ni ikimasu ka.
B: No, I seldom go to the movies.
いいえ、めったに見に行きません。
Iie, mettani mi ni ikimasen.

select vt. **[for s.o./s.a. to carefully single out one/more things/people out of many of the same kind]**
⟨-o⟩ e⌈ra⌉bu ⟨〜を⟩選ぶ ① [for s.o./s.a. to single out s.t./s.o./s.a. out of several as being the most desirable for a particular purpose] **《choose, prefer, single out, elect》**
EX. A: May I ask why you selected our product?
どうして私どもの製品をお選びくださったのでしょうか。
Dooshite watakushi-domo no seihin o o-erabi-kudasatta no deshoo ka.
B: I selected it because it lasts so long.
長持ちするから選びました。

| *Naga-mochi-suru kara erabimashita.*

— adj. **[selected (and therefore best)]** **e⌈raba⌉-reta N 選ばれたN /⟨Vinf. past of the passive of *erabu* ① select/, e⌈rinuki no N えり抜きのN [selected as No.1] ⟪well-chosen, best, choice⟫**

EX. | Only select students can enter this college.
{えり抜きの/選ばれた}学生しかこの大学に入れない。
{Erinuki no/Eraba-reta} gakusei shika kono daigaku ni haire-nai.

selection n. **[the act of selecting s.t./s.o./s.a. or s.t./s.o./s.a. selected]**

1. se⌈ntaku 選択 •c [the act of choosing what one believes to be the best from two/more things/people/animals]

EX. | Selection of the right college is very difficult.
自分にいい大学の選択は非常に難しい。
Jibun ni ii daigaku no sentaku wa hijooni muzukashii.

2. ji⌈nsen 人選 •c [the act of selecting a suitable person] ⟪choice of a person⟫

EX. | I think that the president you chose is a fine selection.
社長の人選はよかったと思います。
Shachoo no jinsen wa yokatta to omoimasu.

3. ba⌈ssui 抜粋 •c [a quote/summary/sample of s.t. written or printed] ⟪extraction, quotation, excerpt, abstract⟫

EX. | I'm reading selections from Yukio Mishima.
私は三島由紀夫の抜粋を読んでいます。
Watashi wa Mishima Yukio no bassui o yonde imasu.

selective adj. **[of or marked by selection]**

1. se⌈ntaku no N 選択のN •c

EX. | We need selective eyes to choose friends.
友達を選ぶには選択の眼が必要だ。
Tomodachi o erabu ni wa sentaku no me ga hitsuyoo da.

2. se⌈ntaku ni ya⌈kamashi⌉i 選択にやかましい adj(*i*). **[for s.o. too particular in choosing s.t./s.o./s.a.], ⟨-ni⟩ u⌈rusa⌉i ⟨〜に⟩うるさい** adj(*i*). **[unpleasantly noisy annoyingly vociferous about one's tastes/beliefs ⟪fig. "annoying," "particular about s.t."⟫] ⟪noisy, annoying, fastidious⟫**

EX. | Ed is very selective in choosing neckties.
エドはネクタイ{の選択にとてもやかましい/にとてもうるさい}。
Edo wa nekutai {no sentaku ni totemo yakamashii/ni totemo urusai}.

self[1] n. **[the individual person as distinct from others; the qualities distinguishing one individual from another]**
ji⌈bun 自分 •c [a reflexive pronoun that refers back to a human subject with whom the speaker empathizes or an emphatic pronoun] ⟪self, oneself⟫

EX. | It is hardest to know the self.
自分を知るのが一番難しい。
Jibun o shiru no ga ichiban muzukashii.

self[2] pron./suf. **[a reflexive/emphatic suffix]**

1. ji⌈bun(-ji⌉shin) 自分(自身) •c [a reflexive pronoun that refers (back) to a person with whom the speaker identifies, including himself/herself]

EX. | (**a**) Tamiko seems to be hard on herself.
民子は自分(自身)に厳しいようだ。
Tamiko wa jibun(-jishin) ni kibishii yooda.
(**b**) A person who can criticize herself can make a fine leader.
自分(自身)を批判出来る人はいいリーダーになれる。
Jibun(-jishin) o hihan-dekiru hito wa ii riidaa ni nare-ru.

NOTE: *Jibun-jishin* cannot be used as a direct object of a perceptual verb such as *miru* or *kiku* as in the following.

EX. | Mary saw herself in the mirror.
メアリーは{*自分(自身)/自分の顔/自分の姿}を鏡で見た。
*Mearii wa {*jibun(-jishin)/jibun no kao/jibun no sugata} o kagami de mita.*

2. -jishin 〜自身 •c [a suffix used to emphasize the human subject of a clause]

EX. | I was very surprised that the president himself came to pick me up at the airport.
私は社長自身が空港に迎えに来てくれたので大変驚いた。

Watashi wa shachoo-jishin ga kuukoo ni mukae ni kite kureta node taihen odoroita.

self-defense n.

ji⌈(ko-bo⌉o)ei 自(己防)衛 •c

EX. Japan's de facto army is supposed to be for self-defense only.
日本の事実上の軍隊は自衛のためだけのはずだ。
Nihon no jijitsu-joo no guntai wa jiei no tame dake no hazu da.

Self-Defense Force n.

Ji⌈ei-tai 自衛隊 •c

selfish adj. **[concerned not with others but only with oneself]**

wa⌈gamama⌉na わがままな adj(*na*). **[doing what one likes regardless of what others think]** **《self-centered, egoistic, willful》, ri⌈ko-shu⌉gi no N** 利己主義のN •c **[concerned only with one's own profit]** **《egoistic》 ↔ rita-shugi no N** 利他主義のN •c; **ri⌈ko-tekina** 利己的な •c **[concerned only with one's own profit]** **《egoistic, self-seeking》 ↔ rita-tekina** 利他的な •c

EX. (**a**) I hate him because he's so selfish.
私はあの人はとても{わがまま/利己主義/利己的}だから大嫌いです。
Watashi wa ano hito wa totemo {wagamama/riko-shugi/riko-teki} da kara dai-kirai desu.
(**b**) A selfish person doesn't usually succeed.
{わがままな/利己主義の/利己的な}人は大抵成功しない。
{Wagamamana/Riko-shugi no/Riko-tekina} hito wa taitei seikoo-shinai.

selfishness n. **[the state of being concerned only with oneself]**

wa⌈gamama⌉ わがまま **[the condition of doing what one likes regardless of what others think]** **《egotism》, ri⌈ko-shu⌉gi** 利己主義 •c **[the state of being concerned only with one's own profit]** **《egotism》 ↔ rita-shugi** 利他主義 •c

EX. The "me generation" is a generation of selfishness.
『ミージェネレーション』は{わがまま/利己主義}を通す世代だ。
"Mii Jenereeshon" wa {wagamama/riko-shugi} o toosu sedai da.

sell vt. **[for s.o. to exchange s.t. for money 《fig. "betray"》]**

1. ⟨**-o**⟩ **u⌈ru** ⟨〜を⟩売る ① **《deal in, dispose of, betray》,** ⟨**-o**⟩ **u⌈ri-ko⌉mu** ⟨〜を⟩売り込む ① **[for s.o. to persuade s.o. else to buy s.t. or to adopt an idea]** **《find a market》**

EX. (**a**) I'd like to sell my car but I don't know the best way to do so.
車を{売り/*売り込み}たいんですが、一番いい方法が分からないんです。
*Kuruma o {uri/*uri-komi}-tai n desu ga, ichiban ii hoohoo ga wakaranai n desu.*
(**b**) I sold my stereo to a friend for $500.
ステレオを友達に五百ドルで{売りました/*売り込みました}。
*Sutereo o tomodachi ni go-hyaku-doru de {urimashita/*uri-komimashita}.*
(**c**) Can't you sell me this for a lower price?
これをもっと安く{売って/*売り込んで}くれませんか。
*Kore o motto yasuku {utte/*uri-konde} kuremasen ka.*
(**d**) A: Why did he throw such a big party?
どうしてあの人はこんな大きなパーティーをしたんですか。
Dooshite ano hito wa konna ookina paatii o shita n desu ka.
B: Because he wanted to sell his name to the world.
自分の名前を世間に{売りたかった/売り込みたかった}からだよ。
Jibun no namae o seken ni {uri-takatta/uri-komi-takatta} kara da yo.

2. ⟨**-o**⟩ **u⌈ragi⌉ru** ⟨〜を⟩裏切る ① **[for s.o. to betray s.o./s.o.'s expectation]** **《double-cross, sell out》**

EX. Judas sold Christ to the chief priests for thirty pieces of silver.
ユダはキリストを裏切って銀貨三十枚で祭司長に手渡した。
Yuda wa Kirisuto o uragitte ginka san-juu-mai de saishi-choo ni te-watashita.

—— vi. **[for s.t to be for sale or to attract large number of buyers]**
u⌈reru 売れる ②

EX. Do you think my pictures will sell?
私の絵は売れると思いますか。
Watashi no e wa ureru to omoimasu ka.

PHRASE: sell out ⟨*-o*⟩ *uri-kiru* ⟨〜を⟩売り切る ①, be sold out *uri-kireru* 売り切れる ②

EX. A: Do you have any fresh tuna?
新鮮なまぐろがありますか。
Shinsenna maguro ga arimasu ka.
B: Sorry, we are all sold out.
すみません。売り切れました。
Sumimasen. Uri-kiremashita.

sellout n.
u⌈ri-kire 売り切れ /⟨V*masu* of *uri-kireru* ② be sold out/

EX. The concert was a sellout.
コンサートは売り切れ(の盛況)だった。
Konsaato wa uri-kire (no seikyoo) datta.

seminar n. **[a group of students supervised by a professor or a course for such a group]**
ze⌈mina⌉aru ゼミナール •f, ze⌉mi ゼミ •f, se⌉minaa セミナー •f

NOTE: *Zemi(naaru)* comes from the German *Seminar.*

EX. Prof. Komatsu's economics seminar is said to be the best.
小松教授の経済の{ゼミ/セミナー/ゼミナール}が一番いいそうだ。
Komatsu-kyooju no keizai no {zemi/seminaa/zeminaaru} ga ichiban ii sooda.

senate n. **[a council of people with legislative power]**
1. jo⌈oin 上院 •c [the upper legislative house]
2. hyo⌈ogi-i⌉n-kai 評議員会 •c [a council of faculty members with legislative power]

senator n. **[a member of a council of people with legislative power]**
1. jo⌈oin-gi⌉in 上院議員 •c [a member of an upper legislative house] ↔ kain-giin 下院議員 •c
2. hyo⌈ogi⌉-in 評議員 •c [a member of a council of faculty members with legislative power]

send vt. **[to cause s.t./s.o./s.a. to get to a certain place by mailing/transporting/throwing/delivering/emitting it/him/her or to cause s.t./s.o./s.a. to enter into a certain state of mind]**
1. ⟨-ni⟩ ⟨-o⟩ o⌈kuru ⟨〜に⟩⟨〜を⟩おくる ① [for s.o. to cause s.t./s.o./s.a. to get to a certain place either by indirectly providing the means to do so (as in mailing or shipping) or by directly accompanying it/him/her] ⟪transmit, forward, see off, escort, spend, present⟫

EX. (**a**) My mother sent me rice crackers from Japan.
母が日本からおせんべいを送ってくれました。
Haha ga Nihon kara o-senbei o okutte kuremashita.
(**b**) What would be the most inexpensive way to send this package to England?
この小包をイギリスに一番安く送る方法は何でしょうか。
Kono ko-zutsumi o Igirisu ni ichiban yasuku okuru hoohoo wa nan deshoo ka.

㊅ "s.o. gives s.t./s.a. to s.o. else" ▷贈る, otherwise ▷送る

2. ⟨-o⟩ ⟨-ni⟩ i⌈ka-seru ⟨〜を⟩⟨〜に⟩行かせる /⟨causative of *iku* ① go/ ② [for s.o. to cause s.o./s.a. to get to a certain place], ⟨-o⟩ ⟨-ni⟩ ya⌈ru ⟨〜を⟩⟨〜に⟩やる ① [for s.o. to cause s.o. (inferior)/s.t./s.a. to move from one place to another] ⟪give, dispatch⟫, ⟨-o⟩ ⟨-ni⟩ yo⌈ko⌉su ⟨〜を⟩⟨〜に⟩よこす ① [for s.o. to cause s.t./s.o./s.a. to come to the place where the speaker belongs] ⟪deliver, hand over⟫

EX. (**a**) Nowadays it is very expensive to send a child to college.
近ごろは子供を大学に{行かせる/やる/*よこす}のに大変金がかかる。
*Chikagoro wa kodomo o daigaku ni {ika-seru/yaru/*yokosu} no ni taihen kane ga kakaru.*
(**b**) My younger sister sent me a letter saying that she wants to come to New York.
妹はニューヨークに来たいと言って、

手紙を{よこした/*行かせた/*やった}。
*Imooto wa Nyuuyooku ni ki-tai to itte, tegami o {yokoshita/*ika-seta/*yatta}.*

PHRASE: send for ⟨-o⟩ *yobi ni yaru* ⟨〜を⟩呼びにやる ①

EX. I sent for a doctor because my baby had a fever.
赤ん坊が熱を出したので医者を呼びにやった。
Akanboo ga netsu o dashita node isha o yobi ni yatta.

senior adj. **[the elder of the two bearing an identical name or above others in rank/time of service]**

1. to⌈shi-ue no N 年上のN [for s.o. to be older than s.o. else] ⟪elder⟫ ↔ **toshi-shita no N 年下のN**

EX. Senior students watch over junior ones in this dormitory.
この寮では年上の学生が年下の学生の面倒を見ている。
Kono ryoo de wa toshi-ue no gakusei ga toshi-shita no gakusei no mendoo o mite iru.

NOTE: John Thompson Sr. is rendered *Tonpuson no o-too-san no hoo,* but this sounds awkward due to there not being a practice in Japan of naming one's children after their father.

2. se⌉npai no N 先輩のN •c [of a person of an in-group system who is above others in rank/time of service/experience]

EX. A senior member of the company gave me on-the-job training.
先輩の社員が現場指導をしてくれた。
Senpai no shain ga genba-shidoo o shite kureta.

PHRASE: senior member *kanbu-{shain/shokuin}* 幹部{社員/職員} •c

—— n. **[a person older than s.o. or an older person of two bearing an identical name or s.o. above others in rank/time of service]**

1. to⌈shi-ue 年上 [a person older than others] ↔ **toshi-shita 年下**

2. sa⌈i-jookyu⌉u-sei 最上級生 •c [a high school/college student in the graduating year], yo-⌈ne⌉n-sei 四年生 •c [a student in the fourth year of high school/college], (ko⌈okoo-)sa⌈n-ne⌉n-sei (高校)三年生 •c [a student in the third year of high school/college]

NOTE: In Japanese high schools, students become seniors in their third year.

EX. (**a**) Tamio, who is a senior in high school, has to study hard for college entrance exams.
高校の{最上級生/三年生}の民雄は入学試験をひかえて一生懸命勉強をしなければならない。
Kookoo no {sai-jookyuu-sei/san-nen-sei} no Tamio wa nyuugaku-shiken o hikaete isshoo-kenmei benkyoo o shinakereba naranai.
(**b**) Seniors at this college have to write a senior thesis.
この大学の{四年生/?最上級生}は卒業論文を書かなければならない。
Kono daigaku no {yo-nen-sei/?sai-jookyuu-sei} wa sotsugyoo-ronbun o kakanakereba naranai.

3. se⌈npai 先輩 •c [a person in an in-group system who is above others in time of service/experience] ⟪**superior, elder, progenitor, old-timer**⟫ ↔ **koohai 後輩 •c**

EX. Mr. Ogawa was my senior by two years at Kyoto University.
小川さんは京都大学で二年先輩でした。
Ogawa-san wa Kyooto Daigaku de ni-nen senpai deshita.

seniority n. **[state/status of being senior]**

1. to⌈shi-ue 年上 [a person older than others]

2. ne⌈nkoo-jo⌉retsu 年功序列 •c [status achieved by length of service] ↔ **jitsuryoku-shugi 実力主義 •c**

EX. In Japanese companies promotions usually are decided by seniority.
日本の会社では昇進は大抵年功序列で決まる。
Nihon no kaisha de wa shooshin wa taitei nenkoo-joretsu de kimaru.

sensation n. **[a physical perception of s.t. such as coldness/warmth/sleepiness/**

fatigue/excitement received through one of the five senses]

1. kaˈnkaku 感覚 •c [a perception based on the five senses or a value judgment] ((sense, feeling)), **kaˈnji 感じ •c** /(V*masu* of *kanjiru* ② feel/ **[a physical perception/impression]** ((sense, feeling, impression)), **kiˈmochi 気持ち [the state of one's mind and body]** ((feeling, mood, frame of mind))

EX. (**a**) After my stroke I lost all sensation in my left limbs.
脳卒中を起こしてから左の手足の{感覚/感じ/*気持ち}がなくなりました。
*Noo-sotchuu o okoshite kara hidari no te-ashi no {kankaku/kanji/*kimochi} ga nakunarimashita.*
(**b**) It is a splendid sensation to walk in the crisp air of an autumn morning.
秋の朝のぴりっとした空気の中を歩くと、とてもいい{感じ/気持ち/*感覚}がする。
*Aki no asa no piritto-shita kuuki no naka o aruku to, totemo ii {kanji/kimochi/*kankaku} ga suru.*

S

2. seˈnseˈeshon センセーション •f [a condition of intense public excitement]

EX. The suicide of Yukio Mishima caused a sensation among the public.
三島由紀夫の自殺は大衆にセンセーションをまき起こした。
Mishima Yukio no jisatsu wa taishuu ni senseeshon o maki-okoshita.

sense n. **[any of the perceptual functions of hearing/seeing/smelling/touching/tasting or perception/meaning/proper judgment based on one of these perceptual functions]**

1. -kaku ～覚 •c [any of the perceptual functions of hearing/seeing/smelling/touching/tasting]

EX. The five senses are the senses of touch, sight, hearing, taste and smell.
五感は触覚、視覚、聴覚、味覚、きゅう覚である。
Go-kan wa shokkaku, shikaku, chookaku, mikaku, kyuukaku dearu.

2. kaˈnkaku 感覚 •c [a perception based on the five senses or a value judgment] ((sensation, feeling)), **kaˈnji 感じ •c [a physical perception/impression]** ((feeling, impression)), **kiˈmochi 気持ち [the state of one's mind or a sensation created through touch or sight]** ((feeling, mood, frame of mind)), **-kan ～感 •c [a physical/mental awareness]** ((feeling))

EX. (**a**) I had a sense of imminent danger.
危険が近づいているという{感じ/気持ち/*感覚}がした。
*Kiken ga chikazuite iru to iu {kanji/kimochi/*kankaku} ga shita.*
(**b**) I had a sense of accomplishment after finishing my graduation thesis.
卒業論文を書き終わった時に満足感があった。
Sotsugyoo-ronbun o kaki-owatta toki ni manzoku-kan ga atta.
(**c**) I have a poor sense of direction.
私は方向{感覚/*感じ/*感}が悪い。
*Watashi wa hookoo-{kankaku/*kanji/*kan} ga warui.*
(**d**) The visual sense is the most important of the senses.
視覚は五感の中で一番大事だ。
Shikaku wa go-kan no naka de ichiban daiji da.

3. fuˈnbetsu 分別 •c [a rational judgment made as a responsible adult] ((discretion, judgment, wisdom))

EX. Mrs. Ozawa has enough sense not to do such a thing.
小沢夫人は分別があるから、そんなことはしませんよ。
Ozawa-fujin wa funbetsu ga aru kara, sonna koto wa shimasen yo.

4. iˈmi 意味 •c [that which s.t. signifies] ((meaning, significance, point))

EX. (**a**) I don't understand the sense in which this word is being used.
この言葉がどういう意味で用いられているか分かりません。
Kono kotoba ga doo iu imi de mochii-rarete iru ka wakarimasen.

(b) What you are saying doesn't make any sense to me.
あなたのおっしゃっていることは全然意味をなしません。
Anata no osshatte iru koto wa zenzen imi o nashimasen.

—— vt. [for s.o./s.a. to feel s.t. by means of some perceptual faculty]
⟨-o⟩ ka⌈njiru ⟨〜を⟩感じる ② •c [for s.o./s.a. to perceive s.t. physically or mentally] ⟪feel, be conscious of, respond⟫

EX. Upon entering the room I sensed everybody's eyes turning on me.
部屋に入るとみんなの視線が自分に向けられているのを感じた。
Heya ni hairu to minna no shisen ga jibun ni mukera-rete iru no o kanjita.

sensible adj. **[perceptible or judicious]**
fu⌈nbetsu ga a⌉ru N 分別があるN •c [judicious about world affairs] ⟪discreet, prudent, thoughtful, wise⟫

EX. He is too sensible a person to accept such an offer.
彼はとても分別がある人だからあんな申し出は受けないでしょう。
Kare wa totemo funbetsu ga aru hito da kara anna mooshide wa ukenai deshoo.

sensitive adj. **[highly responsive to outer stimuli]**
1. ⟨-ni⟩ bi⌈nkanna ⟨〜に⟩敏感な adj(*na*). **•c [for s.o./s.a. highly responsive to a weak stimulus] ⟪susceptible, susceptive, impressionable⟫ ↔ ⟨-ni⟩ donkanna ⟨〜に⟩鈍感な** adj(*na*). **•c**

EX. I don't know why but I'm very sensitive to fluorescent lights.
どうしてか分かりませんが、私は蛍光灯にとても敏感なんです。
Dooshite ka wakarimasen ga, watashi wa keikootoo ni totemo binkanna n desu.

2. ki⌈zu-tsuki-yasu⌉i 傷つきやすい adj(*i*). **[easily hurt] ⟪vulnerable⟫**

EX. You have to speak to Yuri carefully because she's a very sensitive person.
ゆりはとても傷つきやすい人だから、よく気をつけて話さなければなりません。
Yuri wa totemo kizu-tsuki-yasui hito da kara, yoku ki-o-tsukete hanasanakereba narimasen.

sentence n. **[a grammatical unit expressing a complete thought, normally consisting of a noun phrase combined with a verb phrase ⟪fig. "a declaration of punishment by a court"⟫]**
1. bu⌉n 文 •c [a grammatical unit expressing a complete thought, normally consisting of a predicate combined with the noun phrases necessary to complete its meaning ⟪fig. "writing"⟫] ⟪text, writing⟫

NOTE: In Japanese linguistics *bun*, meaning a single sentence, is distinguished from *bunshoo*, which refers to an extended written discourse.

EX. (a) What is the subject of the sentence "John loves Mary?"
「ジョンがメリーを愛している」という文の主語は何ですか。
'Jon ga Merii o ai-shite iru' to iu bun no shugo wa nan desu ka.
(b) Make a sentence using "*tsumori da.*"
「つもりだ」を使って文を作りなさい。
'Tsumori da' o tsukatte bun o tsukurinasai.

2. ha⌈nketsu 判決 •c [a declaration of the decision made by a court] ⟪judgment, decision, decree⟫

EX. The defendant received a heavy sentence.
被告は厳しい判決を受けました。
Hikoku wa kibishii hanketsu o ukemashita.

sentiment n. **[a feeling or a view based on feeling]**
1. ki⌈mochi 気持ち [the state of one's mind and body] ⟪feeling, sensation, mood, frame of mind⟫, ka⌈nji 感じ /⟨V*masu* of *kanjiru* ② feel/ •c [a physical perception/impression] ⟪sense, feeling, impression⟫

EX. What sort of sentiment does this picture evoke?
この絵を見るとどんな{気持ち/感じ}がしますか。
Kono e o miru to donna {kimochi/kanji} ga shimasu ka.

S

2. ka⌈nsoo 感想 •c [a view based on feeling] ⟪**thoughts, impressions, feelings**⟫, **i⌉ken 意見 •c [an idea or judgment one holds about a matter]** ⟪**opinion, view, idea, suggestion**⟫

EX. What sentiments are being expressed in this editorial?
この社説にはどんな{意見/感想}が述べられていますか。
Kono shasetsu ni wa donna {iken/kansoo} ga nobe-rarete imasu ka.

separate vt. **[for s.o./s.a. to divide into parts/groups]**

1. ⟨-o⟩ ⟨-ni⟩ wa⌈ke⌉ru ⟨〜を⟩⟨〜に⟩分ける ② [to part s.t. or a group of things/people/animals into two or more parts/groups (and share them with s.o.)] ⟪**divide, part, sever, split, isolate**⟫

EX. (**a**) We separated the Japanese class into beginning and intermediate levels.
日本語のクラスを初級と中級に分けた。
Nihon-go no kurasu o shokyuu to chuukyuu ni waketa.
(**b**) This machine is used to separate the eggs into large ones and small ones.
この機械を使って卵を大きいのと小さいのとに分ける。
Kono kikai o tsukatte tamago o ookii no to chiisai no to ni wakeru.

2. ⟨-o⟩ ⟨-kara⟩ ki⌈ri-hana⌉su ⟨〜を⟩⟨〜から⟩切り離す ① [for s.o. to cut s.t./s.o./s.a. off from s.t./s.o./s.a. else] ⟪**detach, sever, cleave, dismember**⟫, **⟨-o⟩ ⟨-kara⟩ hi⌈ki-hana⌉su ⟨〜を⟩⟨〜から⟩引き離す ① [to pull s.t./s.o./s.a. apart from s.t./s.o./s.a. else]** ⟪**draw apart, cut asunder**⟫

EX. (**a**) For a Japanese white collar worker it is difficult to separate work from play.
日本のホワイトカラーには仕事を遊びから{切り離す/?引き離す}ことが難しい。
Nihon no howaito-karaa ni wa shigoto o asobi kara {kiri-hanasu/?hiki-hanasu} koto ga muzukashii.
(**b**) It is too much for a child to be separated from his or her parents.
子供を両親から{切り離す/引き離す}のは酷だ。
Kodomo o ryooshin kara {kiri-hanasu/hiki-hanasu} no wa koku da.

— vi. **[to become divided into parts/groups]**

1. wa⌈kare⌉ru わかれる ② [to become divided into two/more groups/parts (and be shared with s.o.)] ⟪**part from, say good-bye to, branch off**⟫

㊥ "part with/break up"▷別れる, otherwise ▷分かれる

EX. (**a**) The couple have separated and live in separate homes.
二人は別れて、別居している。
Futari wa wakarete, bekkyo-shite iru.
(**b**) The river separates into two streams at the foot of the mountain.
山のふもとで川は分かれて、二本の川になっている。
Yama no fumoto de kawa wa wakarete, ni-hon no kawa ni natte iru.

2. ⟨-kara⟩ ha⌈nare⌉ru ⟨〜から⟩離れる ② [to become removed from a place/organization/person] ⟪**part from, become disjoined**⟫

EX. The bone won't separate from the meat.
骨が肉から離れない。
Hone ga niku kara hanarenai.

— adj. **[set apart from the rest]**

1. ⟨-kara⟩ ha⌈na⌉reta N ⟨〜から⟩離れたN /⟨Vinf. past of *hanareru* ② become removed from/ [to be physically distant from a place] ⟪**distant from**⟫

EX. That student likes to sit separate from the others.
あの学生は他の学生から離れたところに座りたがる。
Ano gakusei wa ta no gakusei kara hanareta tokoro ni suwari-ta-garu.

2. be⌈tsu-betsu no N 別々のN [different from each other] ⟪**respective**⟫

EX. (**a**) We slept in separate rooms.
私たちは別々の部屋で寝た。
Watashi-tachi wa betsu-betsu no heya de neta.

(**b**) My classmates and I went our separate ways.
級友と私は別々の道を行った。
Kyuuyuu to watashi wa betsu-betsu no michi o itta.

September n.
ku˥-gatsu 九月 **•c**
EX. In the United States the school year usually starts in September.
アメリカでは新学期は大抵九月に始まります。
Amerika de wa shin-gakki wa taitei ku-gatsu ni hajimarimasu.
NOTE: Note that **kyuu-gatsu* is incorrect, just as **yon-gatsu* is incorrect.

sequence n. **[a set of objects or events which follow one after another]**
1. re˥nzoku 連続 **•c [a number of actions/states/similar objects occurring one after another] ((continuity, succession, series, chain))**
EX. A sequence of scandals resulted in the resignation of the prime minister.
不祥事の連続で、首相は辞任に追い込まれた。
Fushooji no renzoku de, shushoo wa jinin ni oi-koma-reta.
2. ju˥njo 順序 **•c [the way in which elements of a group are arranged with regard to each other] ((order, procedure, method))**
EX. When you tell a story, tell it in proper sequence.
話をする時には正しい順序で話しなさい。
Hanashi o suru toki ni wa tadashii junjo de hanashinasai.
—— vt. **[for s.o. to put s.t. in temporal/spatial order]**
{⟨-no⟩/⟨-o⟩} **ju˥n ni naraberu** {⟨〜の⟩/⟨〜を⟩} 順に並べる ②
EX. (**a**) Let's sequence the words in alphabetical order.
単語をアルファベット(の)順に並べよう。
Tango o arufabetto (no) jun ni narabeyoo.
(**b**) Tell me the events by sequencing them chronologically.
出来事を起きた順に(並べて)話してください。
Deki-goto o okita jun ni (narabete) hanashite kudasai.

series n. **[a sequence of two/more objects]**
1. re˥nzoku 連続 **•c [a number of actions/states/similar objects occurring one after another] ((continuity, succession, sequence, chain))**
EX. There was a series of murders in this town last year.
去年この町で連続殺人事件があった。
Kyonen kono machi de renzoku-satsujin-jiken ga atta.
2. shi˥riizu シリーズ **•f [a sequence of books/movies/magazines/sports events which are grouped together]**
EX. (**a**) *Columbo* was a very popular detective series on American TV.
『刑事コロンボ』はアメリカのテレビで大変人気のある探偵もののシリーズでした。
"Keiji Koronbo" wa Amerika no terebi de taihen ninki no aru tantei-mono no shiriizu deshita.
(**b**) I went to Yankee Stadium to see the World Series.
私はヤンキースタジアムにワールドシリーズを見に行きました。
Watashi wa Yankii Sutajiamu ni Waarudo Shiriizu o mi ni ikimashita.

serious adj. **[solemn and thoughtful; sincere; important]**
1. ma˥jimena まじめな adj(*na*). **[acting with a strong sense of purpose, not prone to showy display, and expecting the same of others] ((sober, grave, earnest)), shi˥nkokuna** 深刻な adj(*na*). **•c [requiring urgent attention and causing deep concern] ((grave, keen, poignant))**
EX. A: You look so serious today!
今日はずいぶん{まじめな/深刻な}顔をしているねえ。
Kyoo wa zuibun {majimena/

S

shinkokuna} kao o shite iru nee.
B: Yeah, I'm trying to think of a topic for my paper.
うん、論文のテーマを探しているんだ。
Un, ronbun no teema o sagashite iru n da.

2. ho⌈nki no N 本気のN **•c [expressive of one's real feelings/earnest in intention] ⸨earnest⸩**

EX. A: I'm getting married this June.
今年の六月に結婚するつもりなんだ。
Kotoshi no roku-gatsu ni kekkon-suru tsumori na n da.
B: What? Are you serious?
えっ、本気かい。
E, Honki kai.

3. o⌈moi 重い adj(*i*). **[weighing much or great in importance/degree] ⸨heavy, weighty, grave, critical, important⸩ ↔ karui** 軽い adj(*i*).

EX. A: John was hospitalized yesterday.
ジョンがきのう入院したよ。
Jon ga kinoo nyuuin-shita yo.
B: Oh, is it serious?
えっ、重い病気なんですか。
E, omoi byooki na n desu ka.

S

servant n. **[a person who serves a superior] me⌈shitsu⌉kai** 召し使い **[a person employed to do house chores ⟨w⟩], ke⌉rai** 家来 **•c [a subject to a feudal lord] ⸨subject, retainer, vassal⸩, ho⌈oshi⌉-sha** 奉仕者 **•c [a person who devotes himself/herself to God/the arts/other social causes]**

serve vt./vi. **[to work for or perform useful services for s.o./s.t. or to wait on s.o.]**

1. ⟨-ni⟩ tsu⌈kaeru ⟨〜に⟩仕える ② **[for s.o. to work for a superior/company ⟨w⟩] ⸨work for, work under, attend to⸩**

EX. One of his ancestors was a samurai who served the Tokugawa shogunates.
彼の先祖は徳川幕府に仕える武士だった。
Kare no senzo wa Tokugawa-bakufu ni tsukaeru bushi datta.

2. {⟨-no⟩/⟨-ni⟩} ya⌈ku⌉ ni ta⌉tsu {⟨〜の⟩/⟨〜に⟩}役に立つ ① **[to play a role in accomplishing some task/purpose or making some task easier] ⸨useful, helpful⸩**

EX. (**a**) This English-Japanese dictionary serves me well in my Japanese study.
この英和辞典は日本語の勉強に役に立つ。
Kono ei-wa-jiten wa Nihon-go no benkyoo ni yaku ni tatsu.
(**b**) It's my pleasure to serve you.
あなたのお役に立つことが出来て光栄です。
Anata no o-yaku ni tatsu koto ga dekite kooei desu.

3. kyu⌉uji-suru 給仕する ③ **•c [for s.o. to wait on s.o. else at a table] ⸨wait on⸩**

EX. In an American family the husband often serves his family dinner.
アメリカの家庭では夫がよく家族に夕食を給仕する。
Amerika no katei de wa otto ga yoku kazoku ni yuushoku o kyuuji-suru.

4. ⟨-o⟩ da⌉su ⟨〜を⟩出す ① **[for s.o. to cause s.o/s.t./s.a. to come out] ⸨put out, bring out, reach out, present, send, produce, pay⸩**

EX. At that bed and breakfast they serve you a nice breakfast.
その民宿ではすばらしい朝御飯を出してくれる。
Sono minshuku de wa subarashii asa-gohan o dashite kureru.

service n. **[the act of serving people/God or an institution which serves people]**

1. tsu⌈tome⌉ 勤め **/⟨V*masu* of *tsutomeru* ② be employed/ ⸨duty, work⸩, ki⌉nmu** 勤務 **•c [an act/instance of working for an institution] ⸨duty, work⸩**

EX. I have spent 20 years in the service of this company.
この会社での{勤め/勤務}は二十年になります。
Kono kaisha de no {tsutome/kinmu} wa ni-juu-nen ni narimasu.

2. he⌈ieki 兵役 **•c [military duty] ⸨conscription⸩**

EX. During the Vietnam War many young people refused to enter the military service.

ベトナム戦争の時は兵役を拒否する若者が多かった。
Betonamu-sensoo no toki wa heieki o kyohi-suru waka-mono ga ookatta.

3. ho˥oshi 奉仕 •c [the act of working for a country/community without regard for compensation] ⸨sacrifice⸩, sa˥abisu サービス •f [the act of waiting on a customer at a restaurant/store/hotel or the act of selling s.t. at a discount price]

EX. (**a**) Service for one's community is required of everyone.
社会への{奉仕/サービス}はだれにでも求められている。
Shakai e no {hooshi/saabisu} wa dare ni demo motome-rarete iru.
(**b**) A: Why are you buying a car from this dealer again?
どうしてこの店でまた車を買うんですか。
Dooshite kono mise de mata kuruma o kau n desu ka.
B: Because they give good service.
{サービス/*奉仕}がいいからです。
*{Saabisu/*Hooshi} ga ii kara desu.*

4. ko˥oeki-ji˥gyoo 公益事業 •c [a public business/institution such as a post office/telephone company]

serviceperson n. **[a soldier or a person who repairs equipment]**

1. gu˥njin 軍人 •c [a military person] ⸨soldier, military officer⸩

2. sei˥bi-koo 整備工 •c [a person who repairs equipment] ⸨repairman⸩

session n. **[(the duration of) a meeting of a group of people]**

1. ka˥iki 会期 •c [the duration of a meeting or legislative assembly]

2. ka˥itei-ki˥kan 開廷期間 •c [the duration of a juridical meeting]

3. ga˥kki 学期 •c [a school semester] ⸨school term⸩

EX. We do not offer a Japanese history course during the winter session.
冬学期には日本史は開講されません。
Fuyu-gakki ni wa Nihon-shi wa kaikoo-saremasen.

set vt. **[for s.o./s.t. to put/place/position s.o./s.t./s.a. in a certain place]**

1. ⟨-ni⟩⟨-o⟩ o˥ku ⟨〜に⟩⟨〜を⟩置く ① [for s.o./s.a. to cause s.o./s.t./s.a. to be at/in/on a certain place] ⸨put, place, position, leave, assign⸩

EX. Please set cups and plates on the table.
テーブルの上にカップと皿を置いてください。
Teeburu no ue ni kappu to sara o oite kudasai.

2. ⟨-o⟩ ha˥ichi-suru ⟨〜を⟩配置する ③ •c [for s.o. to arrange s.t./s.o. in a certain position] ⸨arrange, distribute, post⸩

EX. Obstacles were set along the street to keep back the crowds.
群集を抑えるため、障害物が道に添って配置された。
Gunshuu o osaeru tame, shoogai-butsu ga michi ni sotte haichi-sareta.

3. ⟨-ni⟩⟨-o⟩ tsu˥ke˥ru ⟨〜に⟩⟨〜を⟩つける ② [for s.o./s.a. to cause s.t./s.o. to adhere to s.t./s.o./s.a. else] ⸨attach, join, couple, stick, fasten, glue, put on, apply, light, follow, add⸩

㊀ "attach/spread/fix"▷付ける, "wear"▷着ける, otherwise▷つける

EX. (**a**) Who set fire to the house?
だれが家に火をつけたんですか。
Dare ga ie ni hi o tsuketa n desu ka.
(**b**) Billy set his eyes on the pretty girl.
ビリーはそのきれいな女の子に目をつけた。
Birii wa sono kireina onna-no-ko ni me o tsuketa.

4. ⟨-o⟩ ⟨-ni⟩ su˥ru ⟨〜を⟩⟨〜に⟩する ③ [to cause s.o./s.t./s.a. to take on a certain quality or property or enter into some state]

EX. (**a**) President Lincoln set the slaves free.
リンカーン大統領は奴隷を自由にした。
Rinkaan-daitooryoo wa dorei o jiyuu ni shita.
(**b**) Her kind words set my heart at ease.
彼女の優しい言葉が私の心を楽にした。

S

Kanojo no yasashii kotoba ga watashi no kokoro o raku ni shita.

PHRASE: set {apart/aside} ⟨-o⟩ *betsu ni shite oku* ⟨～を⟩別にしておく ①

EX. I set {apart/aside} the caviar for the party.
キャビアをパーティー用に別にしておいた。
Kyabia o paatii-yoo ni betsu ni shite oita.

PHRASE: set in *hajimaru* 始まる ①

EX. Here fall sets in towards the end of September.
ここでは九月の終わりごろ秋が始まります。
Koko de wa ku-gatsu no owari goro aki ga hajimarimasu.

PHRASE: set up ⟨-o⟩ *tateru* ⟨～を⟩たてる ② ⟪stand, erect, raise, build, construct⟫, ⟨-o⟩ *kumi-tateru* ⟨～を⟩組み立てる ② ⟪construct, frame, assemble, erect⟫

㊉ "erect"▷立てる, "build"▷建てる

EX. (**a**) We set up a tent on the camping ground.
キャンプ場でテントを立てた。
Kyanpu-joo de tento o tateta.
(**b**) It took me two hours to set up the computer system.
コンピューターのシステムを組み立てるのに二時間かかった。
Konpyuutaa no shisutemu o kumi-tateru no ni ni-jikan kakatta.

setting n. **[the way/place in which s.t. is set]**

1. ka⌈nkyoo 環境 •c [the outside world surrounding s.o./s.t./s.a.] ⟪environment⟫, ha⌈ikei 背景 •c [s.t. that exists behind a focused item] ⟪background, backdrop⟫

EX. (**a**) The story has its setting in the northeastern region of Japan's main island.
物語の{背景/*環境}は日本の本州の東北地方である。
*Monogatari no {haikei/*kankyoo} wa Nihon no honshuu no toohoku-chihoo dearu.*
(**b**) A quiet suburban setting is the most ideal for life after retirement.
退職後の生活には静かな郊外の{環境/*背景}が理想的だ。
*Taishoku-go no seikatsu ni wa shizukana koogai no {kankyoo/*haikei} ga risoo-teki da.*

2. shi⌈zumu koto 沈むこと [the sinking of sun/moon]

3. gyo⌉oko 凝固 •c [a process of hardening] ⟪solidification, congelation, coagulation⟫

4. zo⌈ogan 象眼 •c [a thing in which s.t. is embedded] ⟪inlay⟫

settle vt. **[for s.o. to cause s.t./s.o./s.a. to be positioned/arranged/resolved in a desired manner]**

1. ⟨-o⟩ o⌈chitsuka-seru ⟨～を⟩落ち着かせる / ⟨causative of *ochitsuku* ① settle down/ ② [to cause s.t./s.o./s.a. to change from a state of agitation/impermanence to a state of calmness/permanence] ⟪calm down⟫

EX. (**a**) I settled my family in the countryside.
私は家族を田舎に落ち着かせた。
Watashi wa kazoku o inaka ni ochitsuka-seta.
(**b**) The teacher's kind words settled my irritated nerves.
先生の優しい言葉は私のいらだった神経を落ち着かせた。
Sensei no yasashii kotoba wa watashi no iradatta shinkei o ochitsuka-seta.

2. ⟨-o⟩ ka⌈iketsu-suru ⟨～を⟩解決する ③ •c [for s.o. to find a solution to a difficult problem or legal case] ⟪solve, fix⟫

EX. It took three months before they could settle the labor dispute.
労働争議を解決するのに三か月かかった。
Roodoo-soogi o kaiketsu-suru no ni san-kagetsu kakatta.

— vi. **[to be positioned/arranged/resolved in a desired manner]**

1. ⟨-ni⟩ kyo⌉ o sa⌈dame⌉ru ⟨～に⟩居を定める ② [for s.o. to decide to live in a certain place ⟨w⟩], te⌈ijuu-suru 定住する ③ •c [for s.o. to live in a certain place as one's permanent residence]

EX. My ancestors seem to have settled in Osaka about a century ago.

私の先祖は一世紀ぐらい前に大阪に{居を定めた/定住した}らしい。
Watashi no senzo wa is-seiki-gurai mae ni Oosaka ni {kyo o sadameta/teijuu-shita} rashii.

2. o⌈chitsuku 落ち着く ① [to become less stiff physically/psychologically ⟪fig. "fix one's residence"⟫] ⟪fix one's residence, keep one's head, become calm, calm down⟫

EX. Takeshi finally got married and settled down.
武はとうとう結婚して落ち着いた。
Takeshi wa tootoo kekkon-shite ochitsuita.

3. ⟨-o⟩ ki⌈meru ⟨〜を⟩決める ② [for s.o. to make a judgment as to which of a number of alternatives is best in a given situation and resolve to act accordingly] ⟪fix, determine, decide, be resolved⟫

EX. I have already settled on the date of our marriage.
私は結婚の日取りをもう決めた。
Watashi wa kekkon no hi-dori o moo kimeta.

4. {⟨-ni⟩/⟨-de⟩} ma⌉nzoku-suru {⟨〜に⟩/⟨〜で⟩}満足する ③ •c [to feel content that s.t. is sufficient] ⟪be satisfied, be gratified, be happy, be content⟫

EX. I wasn't able to settle for that boring job.
僕はあんなつまらない仕事では満足出来ませんでした。
Boku wa anna tsumaranai shigoto de wa manzoku-dekimasendeshita.

5. ⟨-ni⟩ to⌈maru ⟨〜に⟩とまる ① [for s.t./s.o./s.a. to come to a standstill in a certain place ⟪fig. "lodge"⟫] ⟪stop, cease, perch⟫
㊗ "stop"▷止まる, "stay"▷泊まる

EX. A flock of birds settled on the branches of the pine tree.
鳥の群れが松の枝に止まった。
Tori no mure ga matsu no eda ni tomatta.

settlement n. **[the act/process of settling or a place where people have settled]**

1. kyo⌈ju⌉u-chi 居住地 •c [a residential district] ⟪residence, abode, dwelling, habitation⟫

EX. This area became a settlement for immigrants towards the beginning of the 19th century.
この辺は十九世紀の初めごろに移民の居住地になった。
Kono hen wa juu-kyuu-seiki no hajime-goro ni imin no kyojuu-chi ni natta.

2. ka⌈iketsu 解決 •c [an act/process of solving a problem or legal case] ⟪solution, resolution⟫

EX. The settlement of the labor dispute took six years.
労働争議の解決には六年かかった。
Roodoo-soogi no kaiketsu ni wa roku-nen kakatta.

settler n. **[a person who settles (s.t.)]**

1. ka⌈itaku⌉-sha 開拓者 •c [a person who develops new land for farming ⟪fig. "a person who starts a new field of study or research"⟫] ⟪pioneer, cultivator, colonist⟫

EX. Hokkaido used to be a land of settlers.
昔北海道は開拓者の土地だった。
Mukashi Hokkaidoo wa kaitaku-sha no tochi datta.

2. ka⌈iketsu-suru {hi⌈to/mo⌈no⌉} 解決する{人/物} [a person/thing that solves a difficult problem or legal case]

seven n./adj

na⌈na⌉tsu (no N) 七つ(のN), **{shi⌈chi⌉/nana} (+counter) (no N)** 七(+counter)(のN) SEE APPENDIX II

EX. (**a**) It is seven o'clock.
七時です。
*{Shichi/*Nana}-ji desu.*
(**b**) There are seven sheets of paper.
紙が七枚あります。
Kami ga {shichi/nana}-mai arimasu.

NOTE: *Nana* cannot be used with *ji* ("o'clock"), the counter for hours, as shown in example (a) above.

seventeen n./adj.

ju⌈u-shichi⌉ (+counter) (no N) 十七(+counter)(のN) **•c, ju⌈u-na⌉na (+counter) (no N)** 十七(+counter)(のN) SEE APPENDIX II

seventeenth adj.
(dai-)ju⌈u-shichi-ban-me⌉ (no N) (第)十七番目(のN) •c, (dai-)ju⌈u-nana-ban-me⌉ (no N) (第)十七番目(のN) SEE APPENDIX II

seventh n./adj.
(dai-)shi⌈chi-ban-me (no N) (第)七番目(のN) •c, (dai-)na⌈na-ban-me (no N) (第)七番目(のN) SEE APPENDIX II

seventy n./adj.
na⌈na⌉-juu (+counter) (no N) 七十(+counter)(のN), shi⌈chi-ju⌉u (+counter) (no N) 七十(+counter)(のN) •c SEE APPENDIX II

several adj. **[more than two, but not many (usually five or six)]**
i⌉kutsu-ka no N いくつかのN, na⌉n + counter ka no N 何+counterかのN
EX. (**a**) I'd like to visit several cities in France.
フランスのいくつかの町に行ってみたいです。
Furansu no ikutsu-ka no machi ni itte mitai desu.
(**b**) I met several Americans at the party.
パーティーで{何人/*いくつ}かのアメリカ人に会った。
*Paatii de {nan-nin/*ikutsu-} ka no Amerika-jin ni atta.*

severe adj. **[adhering rigidly to a rule/principle or imposing harsh conditions]**
1. ki⌈bishi⌉i 厳しい adj(*i*). **[unpleasantly intense to the senses or tending to impose strict rules on others]** **《strict, stern, rigid, harsh, intense, extreme》**
EX. (**a**) Winter in Hokkaido is very severe.
北海道の冬はとても厳しい。
Hokkaidoo no fuyu wa totemo kibishii.
(**b**) The punishment was very severe.
罰は大変厳しかった。
Batsu wa taihen kibishikatta.
2. hi⌈do⌉i ひどい adj(*i*). **[of a frightening kind/degree or cruel]** **《cruel, hard, rough, merciless, unjust, wrong, violent, bitter》**
EX. I have a severe headache today.
今日はひどい頭痛がしています。
Kyoo wa hidoi zutsuu ga shite imasu.
3. ge⌈njuuna 厳重な adj(*na*). **•c [adhering rigidly to a rule/principle]** **《strict, exact, precise, rigid》**
EX. The customs agent's inspection was severe.
税関職員の検査は厳重だった。
Zeikan-shokuin no kensa wa genjuu datta.

sew vt. **[for s.o. to join cloth/cloth-like objects such as skin with needle and thread]**
⟨-o⟩ nu⌉u ⟨〜を⟩縫う ①, ⟨-o⟩ nu⌈i-awaseru ⟨〜を⟩縫い合わせる ② [for s.o. to join cloth/cloth-like objects together] **《suture》**
EX. (**a**) A: What are you sewing?
何を{縫って/*縫い合わせて}るの?
*Nani o {nutte/*nui-awasete} ru no?*
B: I'm sewing a *kimono*.
着物を{縫って/*縫い合わせて}るのよ。
*Ki-mono o {nutte/*nui-awasete} ru no yo.*
(**b**) The doctor sewed the cut on her finger with several stitches.
医者は彼女の指の傷口を数針{縫った/縫い合わせた}。
Isha wa kanojo no yubi no kizu-guchi o suu-hari {nutta/nui-awaseta}.

sex n. **[the distinction between male and female or sexual urge/intercourse]**
1. se⌈ibetsu 性別 •c [the distinction between human male and female] **《sex distinction》**, **shi⌉yuu no be⌈tsu 雌雄の別 •c [the distinction between animal male and female]**
EX. (**a**) You can tell the sex of your baby before it is born thanks to developments in medical technology.
現代医学のおかげで赤ちゃんの{性別/*雌雄の別}は生まれる前に分かります。
*Gendai-igaku no o-kage de aka-chan no {seibetsu/*shiyuu no betsu} wa umareru mae ni wakarimasu.*
(**b**) Can you tell a chicken's sex?
ひよこの{雌雄の別/性別}が分かりますか。
Hiyoko no {shiyuu no betsu/seibetsu} ga wakarimasu ka.
2. se⌈iyoku 性欲 •c [sexual appetite]

3. se⌉kkusu セックス •f [sexual urge or sexual intercourse], se⌈ikoo 性交 •c [sexual intercourse ⟨w⟩]

EX. AIDS has made us very cautious about sex.
エイズのために{セックス/性交}をする時にとても用心深くなった。
Eizu no tame ni {sekkusu/seikoo} o suru toki ni totemo yoojin-bukaku natta.

shack n. **[a small crudely built hut/cabin]**
ho⌈ttate-goya 掘立小屋 ⟪shanty, a rude cabin⟫

shade n. **[(an area with) light diminished in its intensity due to interception]**
1. ka⌉ge 陰 [an area which light/wind/a person cannot reach because of some intercepting object] ⟪shadow, silhouette, reflection⟫, hi⌈kage 日陰 [an area which sunlight cannot reach because of some intercepting object]

EX. (**a**) I like to read in the shade of a tree.
木の{陰/*日陰}で本を読むのが好きです。
*Ki no {kage/*hikage} de hon o yomu no ga suki desu.*
(**b**) Take a rest in the shade every now and then, or you might get sunstroke.
日射病にならないように、時々、{日陰/陰}で休みなさい。
Nisshubyoo ni naranai yooni, toki-doki {hikage/kage} de yasuminasai.

NOTE: The compound word *ko-kage* 木陰 can also be used for *ki no kage.*

2. i⌈roai 色合い [a tint of color] ⟪hue, tint⟫
3. bi⌈myoona chigai 微妙な違い [subtle difference]

EX. There are always subtle shades of meaning that distinguish synonyms.
同意語にはいつも意味の微妙な違いがある。
Dooi-go ni wa itsu-mo imi no bimyoona chigai ga aru.

shadow n. **[an area where light cannot reach because of some intercepting object or a dark image of the intercepting object]**
ka⌉ge 影 [an image created when light is intercepted by an object] ⟪light, trace, reflection, image⟫

EX. (**a**) The shadow of the large mansion was reflected on the lake.
大きなやかたの影が湖に映っていた。
Ookina yakata no kage ga mizuumi ni utsutte ita.
(**b**) That's like running after your own shadow.
それは自分の影を追っかけるようなものですよ。
Sore wa jibun no kage o okkakeru yoona mono desu yo.

shady adj. **[giving shade ⟪fig. "of secrecy," "of questionable character"⟫]**
1. hi⌈ga ataranai (N) 日が当たらない(N) [not receiving sunlight]

EX. There was a long shady path behind the house.
家の裏に長い、日の当たらない道があった。
Ie no ura ni nagai, hi no ataranai michi ga atta.

2. i⌈kagawashi⌉i いかがわしい adj(*i*). **[of dubious nature/character] ⟪undependable, doubtful, dubious, fishy, suspicious⟫**

EX. Don't associate with shady characters.
いかがわしい人とつきあうなよ。
Ikagawashii hito to tsuki-au na yo.

shaft[1] n. **[an arrow/arrow-like pole]**
1. ji⌈ku⌉ 軸 •c [an axle for wheels] ⟪axis, spindle, pivot⟫, sha⌉futo シャフト •f
2. shi⌉nboo 心棒 •c [a central axle] ⟪stem, axle⟫
3. i⌈chi⌉-joo no hi⌈kari⌉ 一条の光 [a stream of light]

EX. A shaft of light broke through the clouds.
一条の光が雲の間からさした。
Ichi-joo no hikari ga kumo no aida kara sashita.

shaft[2] n. **[a vertical tunnel for mining or an elevator]**
sha⌉futo シャフト •f, ta⌈te-koo 立坑 [a vertical tunnel]

shaggy adj. **[resembling rough hair]**
1. ke⌉ ga na⌈ga⌉i 毛が長い adj(*i*).

EX. I have a cat with a shaggy coat of fur.
私は毛が長い猫を飼っています。

S

Watashi wa ke ga nagai neko o katte imasu.

2. ke-a⌈shi ga naga⌉i 毛足が長い adj(*i*). **[for a cloth/carpet to have a rough nap]** **⟪nappy, plushy, cottony⟫**

EX. The carpet is shaggy.
そのじゅうたんは毛足が長い。
Sono juutan wa ke-ashi ga nagai.

shake vi. **[to move quickly (and violently) back and forth, up and down]**

1. yu⌈reru 揺れる ② [for an object/mind to move up and down or from side to side ⟪fig. "be disturbed"⟫] ⟪quake, rock, sway, tremble, pitch, roll, toss, swing, oscillate⟫

EX. When the earthquake hit, the house shook up and down.
地震が来た時、家は上下に揺れた。
Jishin ga kita toki, ie wa joo-ge ni yureta.

2. fu⌈rueru 震える ② [to move from side to side rapidly and continuously ⟪fig. "shiver due to cold/terror"⟫] ⟪tremble, quiver, quake, shiver, shudder, vibrate⟫

EX. (**a**) It was so cold that my body shook violently.
とても寒くて、私の体はがたがた震えた。
Totemo samukute, watashi no karada wa gata-gata furueta.
(**b**) I was so scared that my knees were shaking.
私はとても怖くてひざががくがく震えていました。
Watashi wa totemo kowakute hiza ga gaku-gaku furuete imashita.

—— vt. **[to cause s.t. to move/tremble quickly (and violently) back and forth, up and down]**

⟨-o⟩ fu⌈ru ⟨〜を⟩振る ① [for s.o./s.a. to cause s.t. to move/tremble quickly back and forth, up and down ⟪fig. "sprinkle"⟫] ⟪wave, swing⟫, ⟨-o⟩ yu⌈suru ⟨〜を⟩揺する ① [for s.o./s.a. to move s.t./s.o./s.a. back and forth with a regular rhythm] ⟪rock, swing, roll, joggle⟫

EX. (**a**) Let's shake him so that he wakes up.
起きるように{揺すって/*振って}見よう。
*Okiru yooni {yusutte/*futte} miyoo.*
(**b**) The ketchup won't come out unless you shake it hard.
よく{振らない/*揺すらない}とケチャップは出て来ませんよ。
*Yoku {furanai/*yusuranai} to kechappu wa dete kimasen yo.*

PHRASE: shake hands with ⟨*-to*⟩ *akushu-suru* ⟨〜と⟩握手する ③

EX. I felt like I was in a dream when I shook hands with the President.
大統領と握手した時、夢のようだった。
Daitooryoo to akushu-shita toki, yume no yoo datta.

Shakespeare n.

She⌈ekusu⌉pia シェークスピア •f

EX. Among Shakespeare's plays I like *Macbeth* best.
シェークスピアの劇の中で、私は『マクベス』が一番好きだ。
Sheekusupia no geki no naka de, watashi wa "Makubesu" ga ichiban suki da.

shall aux. **[an auxiliary verb that indicates the intention of the speaker in a declarative sentence, and in a question indicates ① an offer to do s.t. if the subject is "I" ② an invitation or suggestion if the subject is "we"]**

Sinf. tsu⌈mori da Sinf.つもりだ [for s.o. to have s.t. in one's mind as an intention or belief] ⟪intend to, decide to⟫, Vinf. nonpast sho⌈zonda Vinf. nonpast所存だ •c [one's intention/decision ⟨fml⟩] ⟪intention, plan, thought⟫

NOTE: {Adj(*na*). stem + *na*/N *no*} is used when the nonpast affirmative form of adj(*na*). or cop. occurs before *tsumori da*.

EX. I shall stay in London for two weeks.
私はロンドンに二週間いる{つもり/所存}です。
Watashi wa Rondon ni ni-shuukan iru {tsumori/shozon} desu.

PHRASE: Shall I/we…? V*masu mashoo ka.* V*masu* ましょうか, Vvol. ka. Vvol.か。

S

EX. (**a**) A: Shall I open the window?
窓を開けましょうか。
Mado o akemashoo ka.
B: Yes, please.
ええ、お願いします。
Ee, o-negai-shimasu.
(**b**) A: Shall we go see a movie tonight?
今晩映画を見に行こうか。
Konban eiga o mi ni ikoo ka.
B: Yes. Let's.
うん、そうしよう。
Un, soo shiyoo.

shallow adj. **[measuring little from bottom to surface《fig. "lacking depth in character"》]**
a⌈sai 浅い adj(*i*). **[measuring little from bottom to surface《fig. "superficial," "pale," "not close"》]《superficial, short, light, pale》↔ fukai 深い** adj(*i*).

EX. (**a**) Don't swim where it's deep. Stay in the shallow end of the pool.
深いところで泳がないで、プールの浅いところにいなさい。
Fukai tokoro de oyoganai de, puuru no asai tokoro ni inasai.
(**b**) He talks big, but his mind is very shallow.
あの人は大きいことを言うけれど、考えは浅い。
Ano hito wa ookii koto o iu keredo, kangae wa asai.

shame n. **[a painful feeling due to a sense of guilt/embarrassment/disgrace/unworthiness]**
1. ha⌈zuka⌉shi-sa 恥ずかしさ /〈adj(*i*). stem of *hazukashii* shameful + suf. *sa* ness/ [a feeling of hesitation due to shyness/embarrassment]

EX. I blushed with shame at the big mistake I had made.
大きな間違いをした時、恥ずかしさで顔が赤くなった。
Ookina machigai o shita toki, hazukashi-sa de kao ga akaku natta.

2. ha⌈ji⌉ 恥 [a painful feeling of guilt caused by one's failure/defeat/wrong behavior, esp. due to a consciousness of how one appears to the outside world]《disgrace, dishonor, infamy, ignominy》

EX. (**a**) In Japan, it causes shame to the parents if a child does something evil.
日本では子供が何か悪いことをすれば親の恥です。
Nihon de wa kodomo ga nani-ka warui koto o sureba, oya no haji desu.
(**b**) Japanese culture is often said to be a "culture of shame."
日本の文化はよく「恥の文化」だと言われる。
Nihon no bunka wa yoku 'haji no bunka' da to iwa-reru.

PHRASE: Shame on you! *(Sonna koto o shite) hazukashikunai n desu ka.* (そんなことをして) 恥ずかしくないんですか。

NOTE: Shame on you! can also be expressed much more strongly as *haji o shire.*

shape n. **[an external, concrete form]**
1. ka⌈tachi 形 [the outward appearance of s.t.], ka⌈kkoo 格好 •c [an external form (taken on temporarily)]《appearance, figure, form》

EX. (**a**) *Kanji* have various shapes.
漢字は色々な{形/格好}をしている。
Kanji wa iro-irona {katachi/kakkoo} o shite iru.
(**b**) My house has the shape of the *katakana* character "*ko.*"
私の家は片仮名の「コ」の字の{形/格好}をしています。
Watashi no ie wa katakana no 'ko' no ji no {katachi/kakkoo} o shite imasu.

2. ka⌈rada-tsuki 体つき [the way a body looks]《figure》, su⌉gata 姿 [a total visual image]《figure, form, posture》

EX. (**a**) That ballerina is in beautiful shape.
そのバレリーナはきれいな{体つき/姿}をしている。
Sono Bareriina wa kireina {karada-tsuki/sugata} o shite iru.
(**b**) Masatoshi's face resembles his mother's, but his body shape is just like that of his father.

S

雅俊は顔は母親に似ているが、{体つき/姿}は父親そっくりだ。
Masatoshi wa kao wa haha-oya ni nite iru ga, {karada-tsuki/sugata} wa chichi-oya sokkuri da.
(**c**) The actor left the stage and came back after a few seconds in the shape of a fox.
その役者は舞台の袖に消えると、数秒後にきつねの{姿/?体つき}で舞台に再び現れた。
Sono yakusha wa butai no sode ni kieru to, suu-byoo-go ni kitsune no {sugata/?karada-tsuki} de butai ni futatabi arawareta.

— vt. **[to give s.t. an outward visible, concrete form]**

1. ⟨-o⟩ ka⌈tachi-zuku⌉ru ⟨～を⟩形作る ① [for s.o. to give a concrete/abstract form to s.t. ⟨w⟩] ⟪form, mold, make, construct⟫

EX. Bach was the one who shaped the foundations of classical music as we know it today.
バッハが今日のクラシック音楽の基礎を形作った。
Bahha ga konnichi no kurashikku-ongaku no kiso o katachi-zukutta.

2. ⟨-o⟩ ⟨-ni⟩ su⌈ru ⟨～を⟩⟨～に⟩する ③ [to cause s.o./s.t./s.a. to take on a certain quality or property or enter into some state]

EX. Tom shaped his ideas into a book.
トムは自分のアイデアを本にした。
Tomu wa jibun no aidea o hon ni shita.

share vt. **[for s.o./s.a. to possess/use/experience s.t. with s.o. else]**
⟨-o⟩ ⟨-to⟩ (i⌈ssho ni) V ⟨～を⟩⟨～と⟩(一緒に) V, ⟨-o⟩ kyo⌈oyuu-suru ⟨～を⟩共有する ③ •c [for s.o. to possess s.t. in common with s.o. else] ⟪own jointly, hold in common⟫

EX. (**a**) I shared an apartment with my older brother.
私は兄とアパートで一緒に暮らしていた。
Watashi wa ani to apaato de issho ni kurashite ita.
(**b**) I shared a car with my friend.
私は友達と車を{一緒に使って/共有して}いた。
Watashi wa tomodachi to kuruma o {issho ni tsukatte/kyooyuu-shite} ita.
(**c**) I shared a taxi with a stranger.
私は知らない人とタクシーに{一緒に乗った/*共有した}。
*Watashi wa shiranai hito to takushii ni {issho ni notta/*kyooyuu-shita}.*
(**d**) I have shared both happiness and sorrow with my wife.
私は喜びも悲しみも妻と{一緒に味わった/*共有した}。
*Watashi wa yorokobi mo kanashi-mi mo tsuma to {issho ni ajiwatta/*kyooyuu-shita}.*

— n. **[a portion which an individual is supposed to possess]**

1. wa⌈ke⌉-mae 分け前 [a part of a larger entity, esp. a sum of money, distributed to s.o.] ⟪cut, portion⟫, bu⌉n 分 •c [a part/role] ⟪division, part, segment⟫, bu⌈ntan 分担 •c [a portion of assigned responsibility] ⟪apportionment⟫

EX. (**a**) The child started to cry because his share of the cake was so small.
子供は自分の{分け前/分/*分担}のケーキがすごく少なかったので泣き出した。
*Kodomo wa jibun no {wake-mae/bun/*buntan} no keeki ga sugoku sukunakatta node naki-dashita.*
(**b**) I think I paid my share of the expense.
費用の私の{分担/分/*分け前}は払ったと思います。
*Hiyoo no watashi no {buntan/bun/*wake-mae} wa haratta to omoimasu.*

2. ka⌉n'yo 関与 •c [the act of participating in doing s.t.] ⟪participation, involvement⟫, ko⌈oken 貢献 •c [an act which helps s.t. to develop or prosper] ⟪contribution, service⟫

EX. She had a large share in organizing the political party.
彼女はその政党を組織するのに多大な{関与/貢献}をした。
Kanojo wa sono seitoo o soshiki-suru no ni tadaina {kan'yo/kooken} o shita.

3. ka⌈bu 株 [a counter for stock in a company]

EX. How many shares of stock did you purchase?
何株買いましたか。
Nan-kabu kaimashita ka.

shark n.
sa⌈me さめ

sharp adj. **[having a fine edge or point that is capable of cutting or piercing《fig. "quick to understand," "intense"》]**

1. su⌈rudo⌉i 鋭い adj(*i*). **[for a knife/pen/light/attack/mind/behavior/pain/sound/eyes/ears/observation/words/judgment to be capable of cutting/piercing s.t. (figuratively)]《pointed, violent, strong, biting, scathing, acute, poignant, keen, piercing, quick, smart, shrewd》↔ nibui** 鈍い adj(*i*).

EX. (**a**) A woman was stabbed with a sharp knife.
女性が鋭い刃物で刺された。
Josei ga surudoi ha-mono de sasa-reta.
(**b**) A cameraman has to have sharp eyes.
カメラマンは鋭い目が必要だ。
Kamera-man wa surudoi me ga hitsuyoo da.
(**c**) I heard the sharp cry of a bird.
私は鳥の鋭い鳴き声を聞いた。
Watashi wa tori no surudoi naki-goe o kiita.
(**d**) The student was discouraged by the sharp criticism he received from the professer for his report.
その学生は自分の発表について教授から鋭い批評を受けて気落ちした。
Sono gakusei wa jibun no happyoo ni-tsuite kyooju kara surudoi hihyoo o ukete kiochi-shita.
(**e**) A: What sort of pain is it?
どんな痛みですか。
Donna ita-mi desu ka.
B: It's a sharp pain.
鋭い痛みです。
Surudoi ita-mi desu.
(**f**) A: Is John stupid?
ジョンは鈍いかい?
Jon wa nibui kai?
B: No, he's really sharp.
いや、あいつはとても鋭いよ。
Iya, aitsu wa totemo surudoi yo.

2. mi⌉ o ki⌉ru yoona 身を切るような adj(*na*). **[of coldness as if piercing the skin]**

EX. I've never experienced such a sharp chill.
こんな身を切るような寒さは経験したことがありません。
Konna mi o kiru yoona samu-sa wa keiken-shita koto ga arimasen.

3. tsu⌈yo⌉i 強い adj(*i*). **[having the power to act or perform in an effective way or to resist external force, esp. physically, but also mentally or emotionally]《strong, powerful, mighty, vigorous, stout, healthy, brave, violent, durable, solid》↔ yowai** 弱い adj(*i*).

EX. I don't like this cheese because it has such a sharp smell.
このチーズはにおいが強すぎるから嫌いだ。
Kono chiizu wa nioi ga tsuyo-sugiru kara kirai da.

4. kyuuna 急な adj(*na*). **•c [occurring abruptly/quickly or forming an acute incline or curve]《urgent, pressing, sudden, shift》**

EX. The road makes a sharp curve at the foot of the mountain.
道は山のふもとで急(な)カーブになっている。
Michi wa yama no fumoto de kyuu(na) kaabu ni natte iru.

sharpen vt. **[for s.o./s.a. to cause s.t. to become sharp]**

1. 〈-o〉 to⌉gu 〈～を〉研ぐ ① **[for s.o. to cause a knife to cut better by whetting it on a whetstone or to wash rice in water]《whet, grind, hone》**

EX. This knife doesn't cut well. Will you sharpen it for me?
このナイフはよく切れないから、研いでくれませんか。
Kono naifu wa yoku kire-nai kara,

S

| *toide kuremasen ka.*

2. ⟨-o⟩ to⌈gara⌉su ⟨〜を⟩尖らす ① [for s.o. to cause the tip/end of s.t. to become sharp] ⟪point⟫

EX. | If you sharpen your pencil too much, it will be hard to write with it.
鉛筆を尖らせ過ぎると書きにくいですよ。
Enpitsu o togarase-sugiru to kaki-nikui desu yo.

3. ⟨-o⟩ ke⌈zuru ⟨〜を⟩削る ① [for s.o. to gradually slice off the surface of s.t. ⟪fig. "curtail"⟫] ⟪plane, shave, whittle, chip⟫

EX. | I'd like to sharpen my pencil. Do you have a pencil sharpener?
鉛筆を削りたいんですが、鉛筆削りがありますか。
Enpitsu o kezuri-tai n desu ga, enpitsu-kezuri ga arimasu ka.

4. ⟨-o⟩ su⌈rudo⌉ku suru ⟨〜を⟩鋭くする ③ [for s.o. to cause s.t. esp. perceptions to become sharp]

EX. | Exercise seems to sharpen one's mind.
運動は頭脳を鋭くするようだ。
Undoo wa zunoo o surudoku suru yooda.

S

sharply adv. **[in a sharp manner]**

1. su⌈rudo⌉ku 鋭く /⟨adj(*i*). *ku* of *surudoi* sharp/ [in a sharp manner] ⟪pointedly, acutely, piercingly, strongly⟫

EX. | (**a**) The end of the stick was sharply pointed.
棒の先は鋭くとがっていた。
Boo no saki wa surudoku togatte ita.
(**b**) My mistake was sharply criticized.
私の間違いは鋭く批判された。
Watashi no machigai wa surudoku hihan-sareta.

2. ha⌈ge⌉shiku 激しく /⟨adj(*i*). *ku* of *hageshii* fierce/ [in a fierce manner] ⟪violently, vehemently, strongly, furiously⟫

EX. | Words of anger were exchanged sharply between the two rivals.
怒りの言葉が二人のライバルの間で激しく交わされた。
Ikari no kotoba ga futari no raibaru no aida de hageshiku kawasa-reta.

3. ku⌈kki⌉ri to くっきりと [in bold, clearcut relief] ⟪distinctly, clearly, strikingly, remarkably⟫

EX. | The snow-clad form of Mt. Fuji was sharply outlined against the blue winter sky.
雪を抱いた富士山が冬の青空にくっきりと浮き上がって見えた。
Yuki o idaita Fuji-san ga fuyu no ao-zora ni kukkiri to uki-agatte mieta.

shatter vt. **[for s.o./s.t. to cause s.t. with tension such as glass to suddenly break into pieces]**

1. ⟨-o⟩ ko⌈na-gona ni {waru/suru} ⟨〜を⟩粉々に{割る ①/する ③} [to forcefully cause s.t. to disintegrate into powder]

EX. | Who shattered this vase?
だれがこの花瓶を粉々に{割った/した}んだ?
Dare ga kono kabin o kona-gona ni {watta/shita} n da?

2. ⟨-o⟩ so⌈kona⌉u ⟨〜を⟩損なう ① [for s.o. to cause s.t. to become nonfunctional] ⟪destroy, damage⟫

EX. | Too much drinking shattered his health.
彼は酒の飲み過ぎで健康を損なった。
Kare wa sake no nomi-sugi de kenkoo o sokonatta.

shave vt. **[for s.o. to remove, cut or trim s.t., esp. body hair]**

1. ⟨-o⟩ so⌉ru ⟨〜を⟩そる ① [for s.o. to cut off/remove body hair]

EX. | I got up very late and didn't have time to shave my beard.
遅く起きたので、ひげをそる時間がなかった。
Osoku okita node, hige o soru jikan ga nakatta.

2. ⟨-o⟩ ke⌈zuru ⟨〜を⟩削る ① [for s.o. to gradually slice off the surface of s.t. ⟪fig. "curtail"⟫] ⟪plane, sharpen, whittle, chip⟫

EX. | The carpenter shaved some wood off the edge of the door.
大工はドアの端をちょっと削った。
Daiku wa doa no hashi o chotto kezutta.

— vi. **[to remove/cut/trim s.t., esp. body hair]**
hi⌈ge o so⌉ru ひげをそる ① [for s.o. to cut off one's beard]
EX. Gee, I forgot to shave this morning.
あっ、今朝はひげをそるのを忘れた。
A, kesa wa hige o soru no o wasureta.

shaver n. **[a person who shaves or an electric razor]**
de⌈nki-ka⌉misori 電気かみそり [an electric razor]

shawl n. **[a fabric worn over the shoulders]**
sho⌉oru ショール •f, ka⌈ta⌉-kake 肩掛け /⟨*kata* shoulder + V*masu* of *kakeru* ② hang/

she pron. **[the third person singular pronoun (nominative case) for a female person/animal or s.t. that the speaker feels empathetic with]**
ka⌉nojo 彼女 [the third person singular pronoun for a female person or one's girl friend]
EX. (**a**) A: Is Mary coming to the party?
メアリーはパーティーに来ますか。
Mearii wa paatii ni kimasu ka.
B: No, she isn't.
いいえ、{ø/彼女は}来ません。
Iie, {ø/kanojo wa} kimasen.
(**b**) When she came home, Janet was very tired.
{ø/*彼女が}家に帰った時、ジャネットはとても疲れていた。
*{ø/*Kanojo ga} ie ni kaetta toki, Janetto wa totemo tsukarete ita.*
(**c**) I love this tractor 'cause she does just what I want her to do.
このトラクターはおれの言うことを聞いてくれるから{ø/*彼女が}大好きなんだ。
*Kono torakutaa wa ore no iu koto o kiite kureru kara {ø/*kanojo ga} dai-sukina n da.*

NOTE: The English third person pronoun (i.e. "he," "she," "it," "they") normally becomes ø in Japanese. This phenomenon is a special case of the more general phenomenon of ellipsis in Japanese. *Kanojo* in Japanese acts like a noun, so it can be freely modified by an adjective or a relative clause as in: *kireina kanojo* literally "beautiful she" or *moo sugu kekkon-suru kanojo* literally "she who is going to marry soon."

shed vt. **[to cause s.t. such as liquid/light/heat/smell/leaves/skin to come out/off]**
1. (⟨-ni⟩) ⟨-o⟩ na⌈ga⌉su (⟨〜に⟩)⟨〜を⟩流す ① [for s.o. to let liquid flow into some place or to cause s.t. to be carried away by water 《fig. "broadcast"》] 《dash out, pour, float》
EX. Even when he learned of his mother's death, Daniel didn't shed any tears.
母の死を知った時でさえ、ダニエルは涙を流さなかった。
Haha no shi o shitta toki de sae, Danieru wa namida o nagasanakatta.
2. ⟨-o⟩ o⌈to⌉su ⟨〜を⟩落とす ① [for s.o./s.a. to cause s.t. to fall in a vertically straight line 《fig. "debase," "fail"》] 《drop, let fall, lose, debase》
EX. By early September the trees had already shed their leaves.
九月の初めに、もう木は葉を落としてしまった。
Ku-gatsu no hajime ni, moo ki wa ha o otoshite shimatta.

sheep n.
hi⌈tsuji 羊
EX. Gentle people are often likened to sheep.
おとなしい人はよく羊にたとえられます。
Otonashii hito wa yoku hitsuji ni tatoe-raremasu.

sheer adj. **[transparent and pure 《fig. "utter"》]**
1. to⌈omeina 透明な adj(*na*). **•c [totally clear and free from turbidity 《fig. "clear (voice)"》] 《transparent, limpid, clear》**
2. ju⌈nsuina 純粋な adj(*na*). **•c [not mixed with alien objects or substances 《fig. "not corrupted"》] 《pure, genuine, real》**
3. ma⌉ttaku no N 全くのN [indicating that s.t. cannot be expressed otherwise] 《utter, downright》
EX. A: We spent ¥20,000 at the slot machine.
パチンコに二万円使ったよ。

S

Pachinko ni ni-man-en tsukatta yo.
B: What a sheer waste of money!
やれやれ、それは全くの浪費だ。
Yare-yare, sore wa mattaku no roohi da.

sheet n. **[a thin, wide object esp. of cloth/paper/glass/board/ice]**
1. shi˥itsu シーツ •f [a rectangular piece of linen, etc., used as a basic article of bedding]
2. u˩su-ita 薄板 [a thin board]
3. hi˩rogari 広がり [the result of expanding s.t. to cover more space]
4. i˩chi˥-mai no ka˩mi 一枚の紙 [one piece of paper], -mai ～枚 [a counter for paper/paper-thin objects]
EX. How many sheets of paper do you have?
紙が何枚ありますか。
Kami ga nan-mai arimasu ka.

shelf n. **[a flat, rectangular piece of wood/metal/glass fastened horizontally to a wall]**
ta˩na 棚 ⟪**rack, ledge**⟫
PHRASE: book shelf *hon-dana* 本棚

shell n. **[the hard outer covering of eggs, nuts, and animals such as snails/crabs/tortoises]**
1. ka˩ra˥ 殻 [the hard outer covering of grains/fruits/nuts/eggs] ⟪**husk, hull, shuck, castoff skin**⟫
2. ko˩ora˥ 甲羅 •c [the hard outer covering of a snail/crab/tortoise] ⟪**carapace**⟫
3. ka˩i-gara 貝殻 [the hard outer covering of any mollusk living in (salt) water]
EX. I enjoy looking for beautiful shells at the seashore.
私は海岸できれいな貝殻を拾うのが好きです。
Watashi wa kaigan de kireina kai-gara o hirou no ga suki desu.
4. ka˩wa˥ 皮 [the outer covering of a vegetable, fruit, plant or animal body] ⟪**husk, skin, hide, leather, bark, rind**⟫
5. ya˩kkyoo 薬きょう •c [the hard outer covering of bullets] ⟪**cartridge**⟫
— vt. **[for s.o./s.a. to remove the hard outer covering of grains ⟪fig. "fire explosive shells"⟫]**
1. ⟨-o⟩ ka˩ra˥ kara da˥su ⟨～を⟩殻から出す ① [for s.o. to remove the outer covering of grains/mollusks]
2. ⟨-o⟩ ho˩ogeki-suru ⟨～を⟩砲撃する ③ •c [for s.o. to bombard s.t. with explosive shells] ⟪**fire at, bombard, cannonade**⟫

shellfish n.
ka˥i 貝

shelter n. **[a place where one hides oneself/escapes from danger/weather]**
1. hi˥nan-jo 避難所 •c [a place where one escapes from danger], ko˩ya 小屋 [a small simply- or roughly-made building] ⟪**cottage, hut, shed, shanty, cabin, shack**⟫
EX. When the eruption occurred, the hikers ran to the shelter.
爆発が起きた時、ハイカーは{避難所/小屋}に逃げ込んだ。
Bakuhatsu ga okita toki, haikaa wa {hinan-jo/koya} ni nige-konda.
2. hi˥nan 避難 •c [the act of escaping from danger/hardship] ⟪**evacuation, refuge**⟫
— vt. **[to hide s.o. or to protect s.o./s.t. from danger]**
⟨-o⟩ (⟨-kara⟩) ma˩mo˥ru ⟨～を⟩(⟨～から⟩)守る ① [(to watch s.t./s.o./s.a. in order) to cause s.t./s.o./s.a. not to be harmed/injured/violated] ⟪**protect, guard, obey, observe, fulfill**⟫**, ⟨-o⟩ ka˩ba˥u ⟨～を⟩かばう ① [for s.o. to keep s.o. who is weak from being harmed or injured]** ⟪**protect, cover, defend, shield, take under one's wing, plead for**⟫
EX. It is a mother's instinct to shelter her baby.
赤ん坊を{守る/かばう}のは母親の本能だ。
Akanboo o {mamoru/kabau} no wa haha-oya no honnoo da.

shepherd n.
hi˩tsuji˥-kai 羊飼い

sheriff n.
ho˩a˥n-kan 保安官 •c

sherry n.
she˥rii シェリー •f
EX. Sherry is a strong white wine.
シェリーは強い、白ぶどう酒だ。
Sherii wa tsuyoi, shiro-budoo-shu da.

shield n. **[a metal piece of armor used to protect s.o. from missiles/thrusts《fig. "a trophy shaped like a shield," "a shield-like object that protects s.t."》]**

1. ta⌉te 盾 /〈V*masu* of *tateru* ② erect/ [a piece of armor, usually wooden, used to protect s.o. from arrows/spears]《buckler》

EX.| In the Middle Ages, the shield was a necessary weapon for soldiers.
中世には盾は兵士にとって必要な武具だった。
Chuusei ni wa tate wa heishi ni-totte hitsuyoona bugu datta.

2. sha⌈he⌉i-butsu 遮へい物 •c [an object that protects s.t.]《cover, shelter, screening》

EX.| We need a shield to shut out the noise from the highway traffic.
ハイウエーの車の騒音をなくす遮へい物が必要だ。
Haiuee no kuruma no sooon o nakusu shahei-butsu ga hitsuyoo da.

— vt. **[to protect s.t./s.o./s.a. from danger/discovery]**

〈-o〉《〈-kara〉》ma⌈mo⌉ru〈～を〉《〈～から〉》守る ① [(to watch s.t./s.o./s.a. in order) to cause s.t./s.o./s.a. not to be harmed/injured/violated]《protect, guard, obey, observe, fulfill》, 〈-o〉 ka⌈ba⌉u〈～を〉かばう ① [for s.o. to keep s.o. who is weak from being harmed or injured]《protect, cover, defend, take under one's wing》

EX.| (**a**) The bodyguard shielded the President when he was shot at by the young man.
大統領が青年に撃たれた時、ボディーガードが大統領を{守った/かばった}。
Daitooryoo ga seinen ni uta-reta toki, bodii gaado ga daitooryoo o {mamotta/kabatta}.
(**b**) I worked to shield my house from the flames when the forest fire broke out.
山火事が起きた時、家を火から{守ろう/*かばおう}とした。
*Yama-kaji ga okita toki, ie o hi kara {mamoroo/*kabaoo} to shita.*

shift vt. **[for s.o. to cause s.t. to change place/position/direction within certain limits]**

1. 〈-o〉{〈-ni〉/〈-e〉} u⌈tsu⌉su〈～を〉{〈～に〉/〈～へ〉}うつす ① [to cause s.o./s.t./s.a. to change to a different location or into a different condition《fig. "copy," "reflect," "infect," "take a picture"》]《move, remove, transfer, divert, copy, imitate, infect》

㊅ "transfer s.t./s.o./s.a. from one place to another physically"▷移す, "copying/photograph"▷写す, "reflect"▷映す

NOTE: *Utsusu* takes the particle *ni* "to", when it means "to physically transfer s.t./s.o./s.a. from one place to another."

EX.| Will you help me shift those chairs to the back of the room?
このいすを部屋の奥に移すのを手伝ってくれませんか。
Kono isu o heya no oku ni utsusu no o tetsudatte kuremasen ka.

2. 〈-o〉《〈-ni〉》ka⌈eru〈～を〉《〈～に〉》変える ② [for s.o. to cause s.t./s.o./s.a. to become something else]《change, alter, convert, reform, revise, renew, substitute》

EX.| (**a**) I shifted gears as I drove up the steep mountain.
私はギアを変えて、険しい山道を上って行った。
Watashi wa gia o kaete, kewashii yama-michi o nobotte itta.
(**b**) Before I realized it, the bus had shifted its course to the south.
気がつかないうちにバスは方向を南に変えていた。
Ki-ga-tsukanai uchi ni basu wa hookoo o minami ni kaete ita.

— vi. **[for the location/position/direction of s.t. to change, usu. to a small extent]**

1. u⌈tsu⌉ru うつる ① [to change to another place/condition《fig. "be reflected," "be infected"》]《be reflected, be mirrored, be photographed, move, change, turn, be infected》

㊅ "for the physical location of s.o./s.t./s.a. to change"▷移る, "be photographed"▷写る, "be reflected"▷映る

EX.| The season has shifted from summer to fall.

S

季節は夏から秋に移った。
Kisetsu wa natsu kara aki ni utsutta.

2. ka⌈waru かわる ① [to change spontaneously]

㊥ "take s.o.'s place"▷代わる, "be replaced"▷換わる, otherwise▷変わる

EX. The wind shifted from north to south.
風向きが北から南に変わった。
Kaza-muki ga kita kara minami ni kawatta.

— n. **[a change of place or a change in the work force of a company/factory according to a regular schedule]**

1. i⌈ten 移転 •c [a change of place] 《moving, removal, transfer》

2. he⌉nka 変化 •c [the coming into being of a different quality or state in s.t. through space or time] 《change, variation, alternation, transformation》

3. ko⌈otai(-ji⌉kan) 交替(時間) •c [(the time at which) a worker doing a particular task switches with another] 《alternation, relief, relay》

S

EX. We are working in two shifts.
私たちは二交替で働いています。
Watashi tachi wa ni-kootai de hataraite imasu.

shine vi. **[for s.t. to give out light 《fig. "excel"》]**

1. hi⌈ka⌉ru 光る ① [to give out light 《fig. "excel"》] 《shine, be bright, be brilliant, glitter, twinkle, sparkle》, ka⌈gaya⌉ku 輝く ① [to give off very luminous light 《fig. "look glorious," "glow with hope"》] 《sparkle, gleam, beam, glisten, be radiant, be brilliant》, ki⌈rame⌉ku きらめく ① [for a star/eye/neon-sign/jewel to give off a glittering light] 《glitter, glisten, sparkle, twinkle, flash》, te⌉ru 照る ① [for the sun/moon to give off light]

EX. (**a**) The sun shone very brightly throughout the day.
一日中太陽が明るく{輝いて/*照って/*光って/*きらめいて}いた。
*Ichi-nichi-juu taiyoo ga akaruku {kagayaite/*tette/*hikatte/*kirameite} ita.*
(**b**) The diamond ring on Mariko's finger shone brightly.
万里子のダイヤモンドの指輪がきらきらと{輝いて/きらめいて/光って/*照って}いた。
*Mariko no daiyamondo no yubi-wa ga kira-kira to {kagayaite/kirameite/hikatte/*tette} ita.*
(**c**) The sun seldom shines during the rainy season.
雨季に日が{照る/?輝く/*光る/*きらめく}のはめずらしい。
*Uki ni hi ga {teru/?kagayaku/*hikaru/*kirameku} no wa mezurashii.*
(**d**) She was like a shining star.
彼女は{輝く/きらめく/光る/*照る}星のような存在だった。
*Kanojo wa {kagayaku/kirameku/hikaru/*teru} hoshi no yoona sonzai datta.*

2. i⌈sai o hana⌉tsu 異彩を放つ ① [to radiate a conspicuous color 《fig. "excel"》 ⟨w⟩] 《be conspicuous, cut a conspicuous figure》

EX. Mr. Miyamoto's talent as a painter shone from the time he was in grade school.
宮本氏の画才は小学校の時に既に異彩を放っていた。
Miyamoto-shi no gasai wa shoo-gakkoo no toki ni sude ni isai o hanatte ita.

— vt. **[to cause s.t. to give out light/luster]**

1. ⟨-o⟩ hi⌈kara-se⌉ru ⟨〜を⟩光らせる /⟨causative of *hikaru* ① shine/ ② [to cause s.t. to give out light/luster], ⟨-o⟩ mi⌈gaku ⟨〜を⟩磨く ① [for s.o. to rub a hard, rough surface and make it smooth and shiny 《fig. "make constant efforts to improve one's skill"》] 《polish, brighten, rub》

EX. (**a**) My wife loves to shine the silver.
妻は銀器を{光らせる/磨く}のが大好きだ。
Tsuma wa ginki o {hikara-seru/migaku} no ga dai-suki da.
(**b**) Will you shine my shoes please?
靴を{磨いて/*光らせて}くれませんか。
*Kutsu o {migaite/*hikara-sete} kuremasen ka.*

2. ⟨-o⟩ te⌈ra⌉su ⟨〜を⟩照らす ① [to cause s.t./s.o. to become lit up ⟨w⟩] ⟪shed light on, illuminate⟫

EX. The moon shone on Miki's beautiful profile.
月が美樹の美しい横顔を照らしていた。
Tsuki ga Miki no utsukushii yoko-gao o terashite ita.

—— n. **[light/luster]**

1. hi⌈kari⌉ 光 / ⟨V*masu* of *hikaru* ① shine/ [a natural form of energy that takes away darkness] ⟪light, ray, glare, gleam, luster⟫

2. tsu⌈ya つや [a gloss appearing on a smooth surface] ⟪gloss, luster, glaze⟫

EX. This table has a good shine to it.
このテーブルはつやがいい。
Kono teeburu wa tsuya ga ii.

Shinto n. **[a Japanese aboriginal religion revering nature and ancestors]**
Shi⌉ntoo 神道 ⟪Shintoism⟫

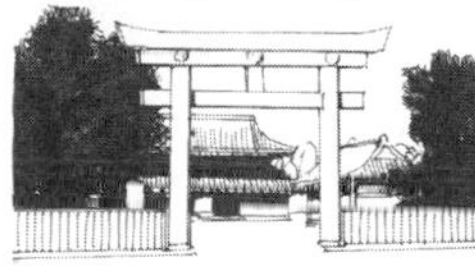

A Shinto shrine

shiny adj. **[giving off light/luster ⟪fig. "fine (weather)"⟫]**

1. pi⌈ka-pika no N ぴかぴかのN [giving off bright light] ⟪glittering, sparkling, flashing, shining⟫

EX. He always wears shiny shoes.
あの人はいつもぴかぴかの靴を履いている。
Ano hito wa itsu-mo pika-pika no kutsu o haite iru.

2. i⌉i te⌉nki no N いい天気のN [for weather to be beautiful]

EX. Today was a shiny day.
今日はいい天気だった。
Kyoo wa ii tenki datta.

ship n. **[any large seagoing vessel, except a boat that is propelled with oars]**
fu⌉ne 船 [a vehicle for transportation on water] ⟪boat, vessel, steamer, liner, barge⟫

EX. I would like to go to Japan by ship.
船で日本へ行ってみたいです。
Fune de Nihon e itte mitai desu.

—— vt. **[to put s.t. on board a ship for conveyance to a destination and/or to send s.t. by ship/other means of transportation]**

1. ⟨-o⟩ fu⌉ne ni tsu⌈mu ⟨〜を⟩船に積む ① [for s.o. to put s.t. on board a ship]

2. ⟨-o⟩ (fu⌉ne de) o⌈kuru ⟨〜を⟩(船で)送る ① [for s.o. to send s.t. (by ship)]

EX. It took three weeks to ship my books from Japan to the U.S.
日本からアメリカまで本を船で送るのに三週間かかった。
Nihon kara Amerika made hon o fune de okuru no ni san-shuukan kakatta.

shipbuilding n. **[the business/technique of building ships]**
zo⌈osen⌉(-jutsu) 造船(術) •c

shirt n. **[a piece of clothing for the upper part of the body, usually with a collar, sleeves and an opening in front]**
sha⌉tsu シャツ •f, wa⌈ishatsu ワイシャツ •f

NOTE: The Japanese word *waishatsu* is derived from the English "white shirt."

EX. (a) I like to wear T-shirts.
私はTシャツを着るのが好きです。
Watashi wa Tii-shatsu o kiru no ga suki desu.
(b) Steve is wearing a blue shirt.
スティーブは青い(ワイ)シャツを着ている。
Sutiibu wa aoi (wai)shatsu o kite iru.

shiver vi. **[for s.o./s.a. to tremble due to coldness/fear/wind/illness/excitement]**
fu⌈rueru 震える ② [for a person/animal/ voice/leaves/strings to tremble due to coldness/fear/illness] ⟪tremble, quiver, quake, shake, shudder, thrill, vibrate⟫, ⟨-de⟩ o⌈nono⌉ku ⟨〜で⟩おののく ① [for s.o. to tremble due to fear ⟨w⟩]

EX. (a) My body shivered after I swam in the cold pool.
冷たいプールで泳いだ後で、体が{震えた/*おののいた}。
*Tsumetai puuru de oyoida ato de, karada ga {furueta/*ononoita}.*
(b) The leaves of the tree were shivering slightly in the wind.

S

木の葉が風でわずかに{震えて/*おののいて}いた。
*{Ki/Ko} no ha ga kaze de wazukani {furuete/*ononoite} ita.*
(**c**) My entire body shivered from fear.
私の全身が恐怖で{おののいた/震えた}。
Watashi no zenshin ga kyoofu de {ononoita/furueta}.

— n. **[an action of trembling due to a cold sensation/illness/excitement/fear/wind]**
1. mi-⌈bu⌉rui 身震い [the trembling of the body due to a cold sensation/fear/illness] ⟪trembling, shuddering, quivering, tremble⟫
2. o⌈nonoki おののき /⟨V*masu* of *ononoku* ① tremble with fear/ [trembling due to fear] ⟪shudder, quiver⟫

shock n. **[a violent physical/psychological impact]**
sho⌈ogeki 衝撃 •c, sho⌉kku ショック •f, da⌈geki 打撃 •c [an act of hitting or the resulting damage] ⟪blow, hit, knock⟫

EX. (**a**) The clock stopped ticking due to the shock of the earthquake.
地震の{衝撃/ショック/*打撃}で時計が止まった。
*Jishin no {shoogeki/shokku/*dageki} de tokei ga tomatta.*
(**b**) My father's sudden death was a great shock to me.
父の急死は私には大きな{打撃/衝撃/ショック}だった。
Chichi no kyuushi ni wa watashi ni ookina {dageki/shoogeki/shokku} datta.
(**c**) Japanese group behavior was a source of culture shock to me.
日本人の集団行動はカルチャー{ショック/*打撃/*衝撃}でした。
*Nihon-jin no shuudan-koodoo wa karuchaa-{shokku/*dageki/*shoogeki} deshita.*

— vt. **[for s.o./s.t. to strike s.o. with great surprise/disgust]**
⟨-ni⟩ ta⌈mage⌉ru ⟨～に⟩たまげる ② [for s.o. to be greatly surprised by s.t. ⟨s⟩] ⟪become astonished, become appalled⟫, ⟨-ni⟩ a⌈kireru ⟨～に⟩あきれる ② [for s.o. to be greatly surprised and disgusted by s.t.] ⟪amazed, dumfounded, astonished, disgusted⟫

NOTE: *Tamageru* is quite colloquial usually used by male speakers.

EX. (**a**) The marriage of Nelly and Ichiro shocked me.
ネリーと一郎の結婚には{たまげて/あきれて}しまった。
Nerii to Ichiroo no kekkon ni wa {tamagete/akirete} shimatta.
(**b**) I was simply shocked by his selfish behavior.
彼の自分勝手なやり方には{あきれて/たまげて}しまった。
Kare no jibun-kattena yari-kata ni wa {akirete/tamagete} shimatta.

shocking adj. **[causing great astonishment/disgust]**
sho⌉kkinguna ショッキングな adj(*na*). **•f, sho⌈ogeki-tekina 衝撃的な** adj(*na*). **•c [causing a very strong physical/psychological impact]**

EX. Mr. Ishida's suicide was the most shocking news of the year.
石田氏の自殺はその年の一番{ショッキングな/衝撃的な}ニュースだった。
Ishida-shi no jisatsu wa sono toshi no ichi-ban {shokkinguna/shoogeki-tekina} nyuusu datta.

shoe n.
ku⌈tsu⌉ 靴

EX. (**a**) In Japan you have to take off your shoes in the entrance hall.
日本では玄関で靴を脱がなければいけません。
Nihon de wa genkan de kutsu o nuganakereba ikemasen.
(**b**) Ed slept with his shoes on.
エドは靴を履いたまま寝てしまった。
Edo wa kutsu o haita mama nete shimatta.
(**c**) I'd like to buy a pair of shoes.
靴を一足買いたいんですが。
Kutsu o is-soku kai-tai n desu ga.

shoot vt. **[for s.o. to discharge s.t. such as a bullet/arrow/net/anchor/tongue/words at a target in a quick, straight line]**

1. ⟨-o⟩ **u⌉tsu** ⟨〜を⟩うつ ① **[to bring the hand/s.t. held in the hand forcefully against s.t. or to cause s.t. to come against s.t. forcefully]** ⟪strike, hit, beat, whack, fire, discharge⟫, ⟨-o⟩ **i⌉ru** ⟨〜を⟩射る ② **[for s.o./s.t. to let off an arrow]** ⟪let off⟫, ⟨-o⟩ **sha⌈satsu-suru** ⟨〜を⟩射殺する ③ •c **[for s.o. to kill s.o./s.a. with a gun/pistol/rifle]**, ⟨-o⟩ **ha⌈ssha-suru** ⟨〜を⟩発射する ③ •c **[for s.o. to shoot a bullet/rocket/missile into the air]** ⟪discharge, launch⟫, ⟨-ni⟩ **ha⌈ppoo-suru** ⟨〜に⟩発砲する ③ •c **[for s.o. to discharge a bullet at s.o.]** ⟪open fire at, discharge a gun⟫

㊥ "hit or strike"▷打つ, "fire a bullet"▷撃つ

EX. (**a**) The police shot at the rioters.
警官は暴徒{に発砲した/を撃った/*を射た/*を射殺した/*に発射した}。
*Keikan wa booto {ni happoo-shita/o utta/*o ita/*o shasatsu-shita/*ni hassha-shita}.*
(**b**) I shot an arrow into the air.
私は空に矢を{射た/*発砲した/*撃った/*射殺した/*発射した}。
*Watashi wa sora ni ya o {ita/*happoo-shita/*utta/*shasatsu-shita/*hassha-shita}.*
(**c**) The fighter shot a missile at the aircraft carrier.
戦闘機が航空母艦にミサイルを{発射した/?撃った/*射た/*射殺した/*発砲した}。
*Sentoo-ki ga kookuu-bokan ni misairu o {hassha-shita/?utta/*ita/*shasatsu-shita/*happoo-shita}.*
(**d**) The pilot shot the hijacker.
パイロットはハイジャック犯{を射殺した/を撃った/?に発砲した/*を射た/*を発射した}。
*Pairotto wa haijakku-han {o shasatsu-shita/o utta/?ni happoo-shita/*o ita/*o hassha-shita}.*

2. ⟨-o⟩ **ya⌈tsugibaya ni a⌈bise-kake⌉ru** ⟨〜を⟩矢継ぎ早やに浴びせ掛ける ② **[for s.o. to shower s.o. with words without rest]**

EX. The teacher shot one question after another at the students.
先生は学生に質問を矢継ぎ早やに浴びせ掛けた。
Sensei wa gakusei ni shitsumon o yatsugibaya ni abise-kaketa.

3. ⟨-o⟩ **da⌉su** ⟨〜を⟩出す ① **[for s.o. to cause s.o/s.t./s.a. to come out]** ⟪take out, reach out, stick out, expose, send, publish, hoist, produce, pay⟫

EX. The bamboo plant shoots out new growth in late March.
竹は三月末に新芽を出す。
Take wa san-gatsu-matsu ni shinme o dasu.

— vi. **[for s.t. such as a bullet/arrow/fire/car/tears/pain/price/bud to discharge itself in a quick, straight line]**

1. ⟨-o⟩ **u⌉tsu** ⟨〜を⟩うつ SEE shoot vt. 1

EX. I heard you have a gun. Can you shoot?
銃を持ってるそうだけど、撃てるんですか。
Juu o motte ru sooda kedo, ute-ru n desu ka.

2. {**su⌈ba⌉yaku/sa⌉tto**} **V** {すばやく/さっと} **V [to do s.t. very quickly]**

EX. (**a**) The car shot through the intersection at about 100 miles per hour.
車は時速百マイルぐらいで交差点を{素早く/さっと}走り抜けた。
Kuruma wa jisoku hyaku-mairu-gurai de koosa-ten o {subayaku/satto} hashiri-nuketa.
(**b**) The flame shot up 100 meters into the air.
炎が百メートル{さっと/*素早く}空に燃え上がった。
*Honoo ga hyaku-meetoru {satto/*subayaku} sora ni moe-agatta.*

3. **ha⌈shi⌉ru** 走る ① **[for s.o./s.a./a vehicle to go along a surface in a set direction at a pace faster than walking ⟪fig. "go to excess," "for s.t. long and narrow to extend far," "appear momentarily"⟫]** ⟪run, rush, dash, sail⟫

S

EX. A sharp pain shot through my right leg.
鋭い痛みが右足を走った。
Surudoi ita-mi ga migi-ashi o hashitta.

4. {⟨-o⟩/⟨-kara⟩/⟨-ni⟩} de⌉ru {⟨～を⟩/⟨～から⟩/⟨～に⟩}出る ② [for s.t./s.o./s.a. invisible/hidden inside of s.t. to come out 《fig. "graduate," "attend," "be published"》] 《appear, emerge, haunt, be found, be brought, go out》

EX. Around here the new bamboo growth begins to shoot out of the ground in late March.
この辺では竹の新芽は三月末に地面から出始める。
Kono hen de wa take no shinme wa san-gatsu-matsu ni jimen kara de-hajimeru.

— n. **[an act of rapidly discharging s.t. such as a bullet/arrow/ball/bud/water/rocket/film images in a straight line or the result of such discharging]**

1. sha⌈geki 射撃 •c [an act of discharging a bullet] 《firing, gunshot》

2. sha⌈geki-ka⌉i 射撃会 •c [a shooting contest]

shop n. **[a small (retail) store or a small place where s.t. is manufactured/customized/repaired]**

1. mi⌈se⌉ 店 [a place where merchandise is displayed and sold] /⟨V*masu* of *miseru* ② display/ 《store, booth, office》, sho⌉oten 商店 •c ⟨fml⟩ 《store》, ko⌈uri⌉-ten 小売店 [a retail store], -ten ～店 •c [a suffix for a store], -ya ～屋 [a suffix for either a merchant specializing in a particular commodity or service or his store]

NOTE: The suffix *-ten* is more formal than the suffix *-ya*. The following chart shows when to use *-ya* and *-ten*.

-ten ～店, *yoohin-{ten/*ya}* 洋品{店/*屋} store dealing with Western goods, *kissa-{ten/*ya}* 喫茶{店/*屋} coffee shop, *rihatsu-{ten/*ya}* 理髪{店/*屋} barber shop, *hyakka-{ten/*ya}* 百貨{店/*屋} department store

-ya ～屋, *kashi-{ya/*ten}* 菓子{屋/*店} confectionery, *saka-{ya/*ten}* 酒{屋/*店} liquor store, *yao-{ya/*ten}* 八百{屋/*店} grocery store, *hon-{ya/*ten}* 本{屋/*店} bookstore, *niku-{ya/*ten}* 肉{屋/*店} butcher, *sakana-{ya/*ten}* 魚{屋/*店} fishmonger, *kusuri-{ya/*ten}* 薬{屋/*店} drugstore

-ya ～屋, *-ten* ～店, *kagu-{ya/ten}* 家具{屋/店} furniture store, *gofuku-{ya/ten}* 呉服{屋/店} dry-goods store

EX. (**a**) What kind of a shop is that?
あれはどんな{店/商店/小売店}ですか。
Are wa donna {mise/shooten/kouri-ten} desu ka.
(**b**) This afternoon I'll go to the barbershop.
今日の午後、床屋に行きます。
Kyoo no gogo, toko-ya ni ikimasu.

PHRASE: doughnut shop *doonatsu-ya* ドーナツ屋, repair shop *shuuri-ya* 修理屋, copy shop *kopii-ya* コピー屋

2. shi⌈goto-ba 仕事場 [a place where one engages in work, esp. manufacturing/repairing] 《workshop, office》

— vi. **[for s.o. to go to a store to buy merchandise]**

ka⌈i-mono o suru 買い物をする ③ [for s.o. to buy merchandise at a store], ka⌈i-mono ni iku 買い物に行く ① [for s.o. to go to a store to buy merchandise]

EX. Where do you usually shop?
大抵どこ{で買い物をします/に買い物に行きます}か。
Taitei doko {de kai-mono o shimasu/ni kai-mono ni ikimasu} ka.

shopping n. **[an act of buying goods]**

ka⌈i-mono 買い物 /⟨V*masu* of *kau* ① buy + *mono* thing/ 《purchase》, sho⌈ppingu ショッピング •f [an act of buying goods]

EX. (**a**) Shopping is great for getting rid of stress.
ストレス解消には{買い物/ショッピング}が一番いい。
Sutoresu-kaishoo ni wa {kai-mono/shoppingu} ga ichiban ii.
(**b**) I did so much shopping yesterday that I had to take a taxi to get everything home.
きのう{買い物/?ショッピング}をしすぎたので、全部持って帰るのにタクシーに乗らなければなりませんでした。

Kinoo {kai-mono/?shoppingu} o shi-sugita no de, zenbu motte kaeru no ni takushii ni noranakereba narimasen deshita.

shore n. **[the land along the edge of an ocean/lake/big river]**

1. ki⌈shi⌉ 岸 ((**shore, coast, beach, border, margin, brink**))

EX. (**a**) I was swimming near the shore.
僕は岸の近くで泳いでいました。
Boku wa kishi no chikaku de oyoide imashita.
(**b**) The boat was approaching the shore.
船が岸に近づいて来ました。
Fune ga kishi ni chika-zuite kimashita.

2. o⌈ka おか [land as against ocean] ((**land**)) ↔ **umi 海**

EX. When the shore came into sight, we hugged each other out of joy.
おかが見えた時に私たちは抱き合って喜びました。
Oka ga mieta toki ni watashi-tachi wa daki-atte yorokobimashita.

short adj. **[having little spatial/temporal length or having insufficient experience/food/money]**

1. mi⌈jika⌉i 短い adj(*i*). **[to have little spatial or temporal length]** ((**brief, short-lived, ephemeral**)) ↔ **nagai 長い** adj(*i*).

NOTE: Japanese *mijikai* cannot be used in regard to human height. "He is short" is not **Kare wa se ga mijikai*, but *Kare wa se ga hikui*.

EX. (**a**) This pencil is very short.
この鉛筆はとても短いです。
Kono enpitsu wa totemo mijikai desu.
(**b**) A: Who is that girl with the short hair?
あの短い髪の毛の女の子はだれですか。
Ano mijikai kami-no-ke no onna-no-ko wa dare desu ka.
B: That's my younger sister.
あれは僕の妹です。
Are wa boku no imooto desu.
(**c**) Winter vacation is much shorter than summer vacation.
冬休みは夏休みよりずっと短いです。
Fuyu-yasumi wa natsu-yasumi yori zutto mijikai desu.
(**d**) He has a short temper.
彼は気が短い。
Kare wa ki ga mijikai.

2. hi⌈ku⌉i 低い adj(*i*). **[having little vertical length as measured from a horizontal base line, esp. of physical objects such as mountains/buildings, but also of temperature/status/(length of) nose]** ((**low, humble, mean**)) ↔ **takai 高い** adj(*i*).

EX. (**a**) The Eiffel Tower is shorter than the Tokyo Tower.
エッフェル塔は東京タワーより低い。
Efferu too wa Tookyoo-tawaa yori hikui.
(**b**) My older brother is shorter than me.
兄は僕より背が低いです。
Ani wa boku yori se ga hikui desu.

3. fu⌈soku-shite iru (N) **不足している**(N) /⟨V *te iru* of *fusoku-suru* ② **lack**/ **[for s.t. to be lacking]**

EX. It hasn't rained for several weeks and we are short of water.
四、五週間雨が降らなかったので、水が不足している。
Shi, go-shuukan ame ga furanakatta node, mizu ga fusoku-shite iru.

—— n.

ha⌈n-zu⌉bon 半ズボン •c+f [a pair of pants that covers one's legs down to the knees] ((**knee-pants, knee breeches**)) ↔ **naga-zubon 長ズボン; sho⌉otsu ショーツ •f**

EX. In summer I wear shorts.
夏は{半ズボン/ショーツ}をはきます。
Natsu wa {han-zubon/shootsu} o hakimasu.

PHRASE: In short *yoosuru ni* 要するに

EX. In short, what are you trying to say?
要するに、何が言いたいんですか。
Yoosuru ni, nani ga ii-tai n desu ka.

shorten vt. **[for s.o. to cause s.t. to become short]**

⟨**-o**⟩ **mi⌈jika⌉ku suru** ⟨～を⟩**短くする** ③, ((⟨**-ni**⟩)) ⟨**-o**⟩ **tsu⌈me⌉ru** ((⟨～に⟩))⟨～を⟩**詰める** ② **[for s.o. to put s.t./s.o./s.a. in a tight, limited space/time or to cause s.t. to**

S

become short] ⟪**cram, pack, put close, cut short, reduce, attend**⟫, ⟨**-o**⟩ **chi⌈jimeru** ⟨〜を⟩ **縮める** ② **[for s.o. to cause s.t. to become small/short]** ⟪**contract, shrink, reduce, lessen**⟫ ↔ ⟨**-o**⟩ **nobasu** ⟨〜を⟩**伸ばす** ①

EX. (**a**) Please have this skirt shortened.
このスカートの丈を{短くして/詰めて/*縮めて}ください。
*Kono sukaato no take o {mijikaku shite/tsumete/*chijimete} kudasai.*
(**b**) My thesis was a bit too long, so I shortened it by about one-third.
論文はちょっと長過ぎたから、三分の一ぐらい{短くしました/詰めました/縮めました}。
Ronbun wa chotto naga-sugita kara, san-bun-no-ichi gurai {mijikaku shimashita/tsumemashita/chijimemashita}.

— vi. **[for s.t. to become short]**
mi⌈jika⌉ku naru 短くなる ①

EX. My commute time has shortened considerably since moving into the city.
市内に引っ越してから、通勤時間がずいぶん短くなりました。
Shinai ni hikkoshite kara, tsuukin-jikan ga zuibun mijikaku narimashita.

shortly adv. **[soon/briefly]**
ma-⌈mo⌉-naku 間もなく [without much temporal space ⟨fml⟩] ⟪**soon, soon after, presently, before long, in a short time**⟫, **su⌉gu すぐ [at once/without delay]** ⟪**at once, immediately, right away, promptly, instantly, in a moment**⟫

EX. The conference will start shortly.
会議は{間もなく/すぐ}始まります。
Kaigi wa {ma-mo-naku/sugu} hajimarimasu.

short-tempered adj. **[having a quick temper]**
ki⌉ ga mi⌈jika⌉i 気が短い adj(*i*). ⟪**hot-tempered**⟫, **ta⌉nkina 短気な** adj(*na*). •c

EX. (**a**) My father is very short-tempered.
父はとても{気が短い/短気だ}。
Chichi wa totemo {ki ga mijikai/tanki da}.
(**b**) A short-tempered person seldom gets along well with others.
{気が短い/短気な}人は滅多に他の人とうまくやっていけない。
{Ki ga mijikai/Tankina} hito wa mettani hoka no hito to umaku yatte ikenai.

shot n. **[an act of shooting a bullet/rocket/ball/photo/film or a bullet to shoot with or its range** ⟪**fig. "injection"**⟫**]**
1. ha⌈ppoo 発砲 •c **[an act of discharging a bullet]** ⟪**firing, discharge**⟫, **ha⌈ssha 発射** •c **[an act of discharging a bullet/rocket/smell/light/heat]** ⟪**discharge, firing, emission**⟫, **sha⌈geki 射撃** •c **[an act of discharging a bullet]** ⟪**firing**⟫

EX. (**a**) Shots occurred around noon in the vicinity of the bank.
昼ごろ銀行の近くで{発砲/*発射/*射撃}事件が起きた。
*Hiru-goro ginkoo no chikaku de {happoo/*hassha/*shageki}-jiken ga okita.*
(**b**) We were allowed to witness the first test shot of the new missile.
新しいミサイルの初の{発射/*発砲/*射撃}実験を見ることを許可された。
*Atarashii misairu no hatsu no {hassha/*happo/*shageki} jikken o miru koto o kyoka-sareta.*
(**c**) As the shots continued long, we were holed up in the basement for hours.
{発砲/射撃/*発射}が長く続いたので、我々は何時間も地下室に隠れていた。
*{Happoo/Shageki/*Hassha} ga nagaku tsuzuita node, ware-ware wa nan-jikan-mo chika-shitsu ni kakurete ita.*

2. ta⌈ma たま [a spherical or almost spherical object] ⟪**ball, bowl, globe, gem**⟫, **da⌈ngan 弾丸** •c **[a ball to be fired from a gun]** ⟪**bullet, cannon ball, shell, shrapnel**⟫
㊥ "bullet"▷たま, "ball"▷球, "jewel"▷玉

EX. A piece of shot has been extracted from his arm.
彼の腕から{たま/弾丸}が一個取り出された。

Kare no ude kara {tama/dangan} ga ik-ko tori-dasa-reta.

3. sha⌈tei(-kyo⌉ri) 射程(距離) •c [the maximum distance reached by a projectile] ((range))

4. sa⌈tsuei 撮影 •c [an act/result of shooting a picture/film] ((photographing))

5. sho⌉tto ショット •f [a shooting of a tennis/pingpong/pool/golf ball]

6. chu⌈usha 注射 •c [an act of injecting medicine (into the vein) with a syringe] ((injection))

EX. I had my doctor give me a flu shot.
医者に流感の注射をしてもらった。
Isha ni ryuukan no chuusha o shite moratta.

should aux. **[an auxiliary verb that indicates an obligation to do s.t. or an expectation by the speaker that some event or situation will occur or has occurred]**

1. {Vneg./Vstem/shi/ko/adj(*i*). *ku*} {nakute wa/nakereba} {i⌈kenai/na⌈ra⌉nai} {Vneg./Vstem/し/来/adj(*i*). *ku*}{なくては/なければ}{いけない/ならない}, {adj(*na*). stem/N} {de/ja}{na⌉kute wa/na⌉kereba} {i⌈kenai/na⌈ra⌉nai} {adj(*na*). stem/N}{で/じゃ}{なくては/なければ}{いけない/ならない} [it won't do if s.o. does not take some action or if s.o./s.t. is not in a certain state] ((have to, must, need)), {V/adj./cop.} *te* wa i⌈kenai {V/adj./cop.}*te*はいけない [s.o./s.t. is not allowed to do s.t. or be in a certain state] ((mustn't)), Vinf. past ra ⌈i⌉i Vinf. pastらいい [it would be good if s.o. did s.t., offered as advice], {Vinf. past affirmative/Vinf. nonpast negative} ho⌉o ga i⌉i {Vinf. past affirmative/Vinf. nonpast negative}方がいい [it would be better to do s.t./one had better do s.t.]

EX. (a) You should read more books.
もっと本を{読まなければ{なりません/いけません}/読んだ方がいいです}。
Motto hon o {yomanakereba {narimasen/ikemasen}/yonda hoo ga ii desu}.
(b) I should exercise more because I'm gaining weight.
太って来たから、もっと運動を{しなければ{なりません/いけません}/した方がいいです/*したらいいです}。
*Futotte kita kara, motto undoo o {shinakereba {narimasen/ikemasen}/shita hoo ga ii desu/*shitara ii desu}.*
(c) I lost my cash card. What should I do?
キャッシュカードを無くしちゃったんですが、どう{したらいい/?しなければ{ならない/いけない}/*した方がいい}でしょうか。
*Kyasshu-kaado o nakushichatta n desu ga, doo {shitara ii/*shinakereba {naranai/ikenai}/*shita hoo ga ii} deshoo ka.*

2. i⌈ttai...ka 一体…か adv. **[an adverb used (in questions) to express an attitude of incredulity]**

EX. I was standing on a street in Seoul and who should I meet but Uncle Ben.
ソウルの通りに立っていたら一体だれに会ったと思いますか。ベンおじさんですよ。
Souru no toori ni tatte itara ittai dare ni atta to omoimasu ka. Ben-ojisan desu yo.

NOTE: The word "should" does not always have a direct counterpart in Japanese. In the following examples it is associated with attitudes of surprise, misfortune, etc., which are expressed in differing ways in Japanese.

EX. (a) It's strange that it should be this cool in August.
八月にこんなに涼しいなんて変だ。
Hachi-gatsu ni konnani suzushii nante hen da.
(b) It's a pity that an intelligent man like Tim should be a drug addict.
ティムのように頭のいい男が麻薬中毒だなんて残念だ。
Timu no yooni atama no ii otoko ga mayaku-chuudoku da nante zannen da.

3. ma⌉n'ichi Sinf. past ⌈ra 万一Sinf. pastら [if s.t. occurs by a chance in ten thousand]

EX. If I should marry Robert, Tom will kill me.
万一私がロバートと結婚したら、トム

S

に殺されるでしょう。
Man'ichi watashi ga Robaato to kekkon-shitara, Tomu ni korosa-reru deshoo.

4. Sinf. ha⌈zu da Sinf.はずだ [it is expected by the speaker that s.t. will take place/took place or that s.o./s.t./s.a. is/was in some state] 《be expected to, I expect that, I am fairly certain that, ought to》

NOTE: When the nonpast affirmative form of adj(*na*). or N+cop. occurs before *hazu da*, the form changes to adj(*na*). stem + *na* or N *no* respectively.

EX. (**a**) A: What time does Miranda arrive at the airport?
ミランダは何時に空港に着くんですか。
Miranda wa nan-ji ni kuukoo ni tsuku n desu ka.
B: Her scheduled arrival time has already passed, so she should be arriving any minute.
到着時間はもう過ぎていますから、もうすぐ着くはずですよ。
Toochaku-jikan wa moo sugite imasu kara, moo sugu tsuku hazu desu yo.
(**b**) It should be easy to get a tourist visa.
観光ビザをもらうのは簡単なはずです。
Kankoo-biza o morau no wa kantanna hazu desu.

shoulder n.
ka⌉ta 肩

EX. I have a stiff shoulder.
僕は肩が凝っている。
Boku wa kata ga kotte iru.

shout vi. **[for s.o. to cry/speak/yell loudly]**

1. sa⌈ke⌉bu 叫ぶ ① [for s.o. to utter in a loud voice (spontaneously) in order to bring attention to s.t] 《cry, exclaim, shriek, scream》, do⌈na⌉ru 怒鳴る ① [for s.o. to utter in a loud voice (to scold s.o.)] 《cry aloud, roar, bawl, growl, bark at》

EX. (**a**) He shouted for joy, when he received an A on the midterm exam.
中間試験でAをもらった時、彼は喜び{叫んだ/*怒鳴った}。
*Chuukan-shiken de ei o moratta toki, kare wa yorokobi {sakenda/*donatta}.*
(**b**) I saw someone moving outside the window, so I shouted "Who's there?"
窓の外でだれかが動くのを見たので、「だれだ」と{怒鳴った/叫んだ}。
Mado no soto de dare-ka ga ugoku no o mita node, 'Dare da' to {donatta/sakenda}.
(**c**) I was shouted at by my boss when I came in late this morning.
今朝遅く出勤したら上役に{怒鳴られた/*叫ばれた}。
*Kesa osoku shukkin-shitara uwa-yaku ni {donara-reta/*sakeba-reta}.*

2. o⌈o-go⌉e de ha⌈na⌉su 大声で話す ① [to talk with a loud voice]

EX. I always have to shout at my grandfather, because he is hard of hearing.
祖父は耳が遠いので、私はいつも大声で話さなければなりません。
Sofu wa mimi ga tooi node, watashi wa itsu-mo oo-goe de hanasanakereba narimasen.

— vt. **[for s.o. to cry/speak/yell s.t. loudly to s.o.]**
《-to》 sa⌈ke⌉bu 《〜と》叫ぶ ① [for s.o. to say s.t. to s.o. in a loud voice] 《cry, exclaim, shriek》, 〈-to〉 do⌈na⌉ru 〈〜と〉怒鳴る ① [for s.o. to say s.t. to s.o. in a loud, scolding voice] 《cry aloud, roar, bawl, growl》

EX. (**a**) Someone shouted "Help!" in the parking lot.
だれかが駐車場で「助けて」と{叫んだ/*怒鳴った}。
*Dare-ka ga chuusha-joo de 'Tasukete' to {sakenda/*donatta}.*
(**b**) "Don't let me ever see you again!" he shouted.
「もう二度と会いに来るな!」と彼は{怒鳴った/叫んだ}。
'Moo ni-do to ai ni kuru na!' to kare wa {donatta/sakenda}.

shove vt. **[for s.o./s.a. to give a rough/rude (thrust/push) to s.o./s.t.]**
〈-o〉 o⌈su 〈〜を〉押す ① [for s.o. to cause s.t./s.o./s.a. to move away from oneself 《fig. "stamp," "recommend"》] 《push, thrust,

press, impress, stamp)), ⟨-o⟩ **tsu⌈ku** ⟨〜を⟩突く ① **[for s.o./s.a. to make impact with or penetrate s.t./s.o./s.a. with a sharp or stick-like object** ⟪**fig. "attack sharply"**⟫**]** ((**thrust, poke, prod, pierce, dab, stab, prick, strike**))

EX. During rush hour in Japan people have to push and shove each other to get onto the trains.
日本ではラッシュアワーには乗客は電車に乗るのにお互いを押したり、突いたりしなければなりません。
Nihon de wa rasshu-awaa ni wa jookyaku wa densha ni noru no ni o-tagai o oshitari tsuitari, shinakereba narimasen.

shovel n.

sha⌉beru シャベル •f

EX. We used the shovel to clear the sidewalk of snow.
シャベルで歩道の雪かきをした。
Shaberu de hodoo no yuki-kaki o shita.

— vt. **[for s.o. to scoop/dig s.t. with a shovel]**
sha⌉beru de su⌈kuu シャベルですくう ① **[for s.o. to scoop s.t. with a shovel]**, **sha⌉beru de ho⌉ru** シャベルで掘る ① **[for s.o. to dig s.t. with a shovel]**

show vt. **[to cause s.o./s.a. to see/figure out s.o./s.t./s.a.** ⟪**fig. "indicate"**⟫**]**

1. ⟨-ni⟩ ⟨-o⟩ **mi⌈se⌉ru** ⟨〜に⟩⟨〜を⟩見せる ② **[for s.o. to cause s.o./s.a. to see s.t./s.a./s.o. such as a tangible object or an emotion]** ((**let a person see, exhibit, display**))

EX. (**a**) Could you show me your new house?
新しい家を見せてくださいませんか。
Atarashii ie o misete kudasaimasen ka.
(**b**) One must never show any emotions when conducting negotiations.
交渉をしている時はいかなる感情も見せてはならない。
Kooshoo o shite iru toki wa ikanaru kanjoo mo misete wa naranai.

2. ⟨-o⟩ **shi⌈mesu** ⟨〜を⟩示す ① **[for s.o./s.t. to cause s.o. to see s.t. so that he/she can understand it well ⟨fml⟩]** ((**point to, indicate, denote, signify, express**))

EX. (**a**) The thermometer showed the temperature to be 37°C.
寒暖計が摂氏三十七度を示していた。
Kandan-kei ga sesshi san-juu-nana-do o shimeshite ita.
(**b**) Don't just say it. Show your love by your actions.
言葉だけではだめです。愛は行為で示しなさい。
Kotoba dake de wa dame desu. Ai wa kooi de shimeshinasai.

3. ⟨-ni⟩⟨-o⟩ **o⌈shieru** ⟨〜に⟩⟨〜を⟩教える ② **[for s.o. to impart knowledge/information/a skill to s.o./s.a.]** ((**teach, tell, inform**))

EX. (**a**) Could you show me the way to Harajuku?
原宿への行き方を教えてくださいませんか。
Harajuku e no iki-kata o oshiete kudasaimasen ka.
(**b**) Would you show me how to swim?
泳ぎ方を教えてくれませんか。
Oyogi-kata o oshiete kuremasen ka.

— vi. **[for s.t. to appear spontaneously]**
mi⌈e⌉ru 見える ② **[(can) be spontaneously seen by the eye or mind]** ((**be seen, visible, be in sight, look (like), seem, appear**)), **a⌈raware⌉ru** あらわれる ② **[to become exposed/visible]** ((**come out, appear, show up, come into sight, reveal itself, be found**)), **wa⌉ka⌉ru** 分かる ① **[for s.o./s.a. to be able to figure s.t. out]** ((**be comprehensible, understand, can tell, figure out**))
㊗ "appear"▷現れる, "be expressed"▷表れる

EX. (**a**) His true self showed through the incident.
この事件を通して、彼の本性が{見えた/現れた/分かった}。
Kono jiken o tooshite, kare no honshoo ga {mieta/arawareta/wakatta}.
(**b**) Sadness showed in her eyes.
悲しみが彼女の目に{現れた/*見えた/*分かった}。
*Kanashi-mi ga kanojo no me ni {arawareta/*mieta/*wakatta}.*

PHRASE: show off ⟨-o⟩ *yoku miseru* ⟨〜を⟩よく見

S

せる ②, 〈-o〉 *mise-birakasu* 〈～を〉見せびらかす ①

EX. (**a**) Yukie went out in her best *kimono* to show herself off at the garden party.
幸江は園遊会で自分を{よく見せる/*見せびらかす}ために晴れ着を着て出かけた。
*Yukie wa en'yuu-kai de jibun o {yoku miseru/*mise-birakasu} tame ni haregi o kite dekaketa.*
(**b**) I can't wait to show off the new car I just bought to my friends.
買ったばかりの新車を友達に{見せびらかしたくて/*よく見せたくて}しょうがない。
*Katta bakari no shinsha o tomodachi ni {mise-birakashi-takute/*yoku mise-takute} shoo ga nai.*

PHRASE: show up 〈-ni〉 *arawareru* 〈～に〉現れる ②

EX. I don't know why, but the boss didn't show up at the party.
どうしてか分からないが、上役はパーティーに現れなかった。
Dooshite ka wakaranai ga, uwa-yaku wa paatii ni arawarenakatta.

S

—— n. **[an act/event of showing or an indication of s.t.]**
1. mi⌈se-birakashi 見せびらかし /〈V*masu* of *mese-birakasu* ① show off/ [an act of showing off s.t.]
2. te⌈nra⌉n-kai 展覧会 •c [an exhibition of one's creative work] ⟪**exhibition, exhibit**⟫, **te⌈nji⌉-kai 展示会 •c [an exhibition of specific items]** ⟪**exhibition**⟫
3. ko⌈ogyoo 興行 •c [a showing or performance of a movie/theatrical arts/ sumo etc. for profit] ⟪**performance, run**⟫, **sho⌉o ショー •f [a showing or performance of a Western-style form of entertainment such as a musical, circus, jazz concert, etc.]**
4. yo⌈osu 様子 •c [the way s.o./s.t./s.a. looks] ⟪**appearance, manner, circumstances, signs, indication**⟫

shower n. **[a (brief) downfall of rain/hail/ sleet/snow/water/shooting stars** ⟪**fig. "a gift-giving party for a bride-to-be/mother-to-be"**⟫**]**
1. ni⌈waka-a⌉me にわか雨 [a sudden, brief rainfall]

EX. (**a**) There are always a couple of rain showers each day during the summer.
夏はいつも一日に、二、三回、にわか雨が降ります。
Natsu wa itsu-mo ichi-nichi ni, ni, san-kai, niwaka-ame ga furimasu.
(**b**) This is just a passing shower, so let's wait here.
これはにわか雨だから、ここで待っていよう。
Kore wa niwaka-ame da kara, koko de matte iyoo.

2. sha⌉waa シャワー •f [a wash using a spray of water]

EX. Americans like to take a shower in the morning.
アメリカ人は朝シャワーを浴びるのが好きです。
Amerika-jin wa asa shawaa o abiru no ga suki desu.

shrill adj. **[piercing and high-pitched in sound]**
ki⌉i-kii i⌈u N きいきい言うN, ka⌈nakiri-go⌉e no N 金切り声のN [having a piercingly high-pitched voice] ⟪**high-pitched**⟫

EX. I'm fed up with my neighbor's shrill voice.
私は隣の人の{金切り声/きいきい言う声}にはうんざりだ。
Watashi wa tonari no hito no {kanakiri-goe/kii-kii iu koe} ni wa unzari da.

shrimp n. **[a sea crustacean between one and two inches in length having ten legs]**
e⌈bi えび [a crustacean with ten legs] ⟪**prawn**⟫

shrine n. **[a container/tomb/site for sacred relics such as the bones of saints]**
1. ji⌉nja 神社 •c [a Shinto shrine], o-mi⌈ya お宮

EX. Early in the morning on New Year's Day, Japanese go to a Shinto shrine to pay their respects.

元日の早朝、日本人は{神社/お宮}に参拝に行く。
Ganjitsu no soochoo, Nihon-jin wa {jinja/o-miya} ni sanpai ni iku.

2. se⌈i-i⌈butsu⌉-ire 聖遺物入れ [a container for sacred relics]
3. se⌈ikotsu⌉-ire 聖骨入れ [a container for the bones of saints]
4. se⌈idoo 聖堂 •c [a tomb/site for sacred relics/bones of saints]

PHRASE: portable shrine *(o-)mikoshi* (お)みこし

shrub n. **[a woody plant smaller than a tree]**
ka⌈nboku かん木 •c ⟪bush⟫

shrug vt. **[for s.o. to raise both shoulders as a gesture of discomfort/despair/surprise/doubt/indifference]**
ka⌉ta o su⌈kume⌉ru 肩をすくめる ②

NOTE: It is not normal in Japanese society to shrug one's shoulders to express resignation or consternation.

shut vt. **[for s.o./s.a. to move s.t. such as a door/window/lid to a closed position ⟪fig. "prevent access to"⟫]**
⟨-o⟩ shi⌈me⌉ru ⟨～を⟩しめる ② [for s.o. to apply pressure to s.t. so as to leave no opening in it ⟪fig. "economize"⟫] ⟪close, tighten, fasten, wring, strangle⟫ ↔ ⟨-o⟩ akeru ⟨～を⟩開ける ②

㊅ "close"▷閉める, "tighten"▷締める

EX. It's getting cold so please shut the window.
寒くなってきましたから、窓を閉めてください。
Samuku natte kimashita kara, mado o shimete kudasai.

PHRASE: shut down ⟨*-o*⟩ *heisa-suru* ⟨～を⟩閉鎖する ③ •c ⟪close, lock, wind up⟫

EX. During the anti-Vietnam War demonstrations, quite a few universities had to shut down their campuses.
ベトナム戦争反対のデモが行われたころは、かなり多くの大学がキャンパスを閉鎖しなければならなかった。
Betonamu-sensoo hantai no demo ga okonawareta koro wa, kanari ooku no daigaku ga kyanpasu o heisa-shinakereba naranakatta.

— vi. **[for s.t. such as a door/window/lid to move spontaneously to a closed position]**
1. shi⌈ma⌉ru しまる ① [for s.t. to be left with no opening as a result of pressure applied to it from all sides] ⟪be closed, close, tighten⟫ ↔ aku 開く ①

㊅ "be closed"▷閉まる, "tighten"▷締まる

EX. The door shut by itself.
ドアがひとりでに閉まった。
Doa ga hitori-de ni shimatta.

2. he⌈isa-suru 閉鎖する ③ •c [for a business/factory/company to close]

shy adj. **[timid or reserved and lacking confidence in the presence of others ⟪fig. "lack"⟫]**
u⌈chikina 内気な adj(*na*). **[having a withdrawn and reserved personality] ⟪bashful, reserved, timid⟫**

EX. My younger sister is so shy that she won't go to parties.
妹はとても内気で、パーティーに行こうとしない。
Imooto wa totemo uchiki de, paatii ni ikoo to shinai.

sick adj. **[not in good health or to feel like vomiting ⟪fig. "be fed up with"⟫]**
1. byo⌈oki no N 病気のN •c [for s.o./s.a. to be not in good health or pertaining to illness]

EX. A: Why didn't you come to class yesterday?
きのうはどうして授業に来なかったんですか。
Kinoo wa dooshite jugyoo ni konakatta n desu ka.
B: Because I was sick.
病気だったんです。
Byooki datta n desu.

2. ha⌈ki-so⌉ona 吐きそうな / (V*masu* of *haku* ① vomit + *soona* adj(*na*). look/feel like/ adj(*na*). **[to feel like vomiting]**

EX. A: Is something the matter?
どうしたんですか。
Doo shita n desu ka.
B: I feel sick.
吐きそうなんです。
Haki-soona n desu.

S

3. ⟨-ni⟩ u⌈nza⌉ri-suru ⟨〜に⟩うんざりする ③ [for s.o. to become fed up with s.t./s.o.] ⟪become disgusted, have enough, become tired⟫

EX. I'm really sick of this boring work.
このつまらない仕事に本当にうんざりしているんだ。
Kono tsumaranai shigoto ni hontoo ni unzari-shite iru n da.

sickness n. **[a state/instance of not being in good health/feeling like vomiting]**

1. byo⌈oki 病気 •c [a state/instance of not being in good health] ⟪illness, disease, malady⟫

EX. Sickness kept me in bed for two weeks.
病気で二週間も寝ていました。
Byooki de ni-shuukan mo nete imashita.

2. ha⌈ki-ke⌉ 吐き気 [a sensation of having to vomit] ⟪nausea, retch⟫

EX. I couldn't eat anything due to the feeling of sickness.
吐き気で何も食べられませんでした。
Haki-ke de nani-mo tabe-raremasen deshita.

S

side n. **[a place, space, or direction with respect to a center or line/plane of division; one of the flat inner or outer surfaces of a three-dimensional object as distinct from the top/bottom or front/back; the right or left part of an animal/human body]**

1. -gawa 〜側 [a place, space, or direction with respect to a center or line/plane of division]

EX. (**a**) Why don't you leave through the door on this side?
こちら側のドアから出たらどうですか。
Kochira-gawa no doa kara detara doo desu ka.
(**b**) Downtown is on the west side of the campus.
街はキャンパスの西側にあります。
Machi wa kyanpasu no nishi-gawa ni arimasu.
(**c**) In Japan you have to drive on the left side of the street.
日本では道の左側を運転しなければいけません。
Nihon de wa michi no hidari-gawa o unten-shinakereba ikemasen.
(**d**) Can I use the other side of the paper?
紙の裏側を使ってもいいですか。
Kami no ura-gawa o tsukatte mo ii desu ka.
(**e**) A: Which side are you on?
あなたはどちら側ですか。
Anata wa dochira-gawa desu ka.
B: I'm on the workers' side.
労働者側です。
Roodoo-sha-gawa desu.

2. me⌉n 面 •c [any of the flat surfaces of an object ⟪fig. "a covering for the face used in fencing, theater, etc.," "a page of a newspaper"⟫] ⟪face, mask, surface, aspect⟫

EX. (**a**) Let's discuss the educational side of TV.
テレビの教育的な面を話し合いましょう。
Terebi no kyooiku-tekina men o hanashi-aimashoo.
(**b**) There are always two sides to a coin.
物事にはいつも両面がある。
Mono-goto ni wa itsu-mo ryoomen ga aru.

3. yo⌈ko-bara 横腹 [the right or left part of the trunk of a body], yo⌈ko-ppara横っ腹 ⟨s⟩

EX. I felt a pain in my side.
{横腹/横っ腹}に痛みを感じた。
{Yoko-bara/Yoko-ppara} ni ita-mi o kanjita.

PHRASE: take one's sides ⟨*-no*⟩ *mikata o suru* ⟨〜の⟩味方をする ③

EX. When the disagreement arose, Tom took my side.
議論が分かれた時、トムは私の味方をしてくれた。
Giron ga wakareta toki, Tomu wa watashi no mikata o shite kureta.

PHRASE: right side *omote* 表, wrong side *ura* 裏

—— vi. **[for s.o. to align oneself with s.o.] ⟨-no⟩ mi⌈kata o suru ⟨〜の⟩味方をする ③**

EX. Please side with me on this.
この件では僕の味方をして欲しい。
Kono ken de wa boku no mikata o shite hoshii.

sidewalk n.
ho⌈doo 歩道 •c [a street on which people walk as opposed to one where vehicles are driven]

EX. A lot of people jog on the sidewalk.
歩道をジョギングしている人が沢山いる。
Hodoo o jogingu-shite iru hito ga takusan iru.

sideways adv. **[from/toward one side]**
yo⌈ko ni 横に n.+prt. **[toward a direction perpendicular to the speaker's line of vision], na⌈na⌉me ni 斜めに** n.+prt. **[toward a direction different from the speaker's line of vision] ((obliquely))**

EX. It's hard to walk sideways like a crab.
かにのように{横/斜め}に歩くのは難しい。
Kani no yooni {yoko/naname} ni aruku no wa muzukashii.

sigh vi. **[for s.o. to exhale a long, deep, audible breath owing to physio-psychological causes such as tiredness/sorrow/despair/regret/relief/yearning]**
ta⌈me-i⌉ki o tsuku ため息をつく ①

EX. (**a**) When Jerry saw the amount of homework he had, he sighed deeply.
ジェリーは宿題の山を見た時、深くため息をついた。
Jerii wa shukudai no yama o mita toki, fukaku tame-iki o tsuita.
(**b**) I sighed with relief when I finally finished my term paper.
期末レポートをやっと終えた時、ほっとしてため息をついた。
Kimatsu-repooto o yatto oeta toki, hotto-shite tame-iki o tsuita.

—— n. **[an act/sound of sighing]**
ta⌈me-i⌉ki ため息

sight n. **[the ability to see or an instance of seeing s.t.]**
1. shi⌈kaku 視覚 •c [the perceptive sense by which things are seen] ((vision, eyesight))

EX. Sight is the most important of the five senses.
視覚は五感の中で一番大事な感覚だ。
Shikaku wa gokan no naka de ichiban daijina kankaku da.

2. shi⌉ryoku 視力 •c [the degree to which one's eyes are able to see objects at a distance] ((eyesight, vision))

EX. As you grow older, your sight gradually weakens.
年を取ると、段々視力が落ちる。
Toshi o toru to, dan-dan shiryoku ga ochiru.

3. mi⌉ru koto 見ること [an instance of seeing s.t.]
4. ko⌈okei 光景 •c [s.t. which is seen to the eyes, esp. that which creates a positive or negative impression] ((spectacle, scene)), ke⌉shiki 景色 [a picturesque view of nature] ((scenery, scene, landscape, view)), na⌈game⌉ 眺め /⟨V*masu* of *nagameru* ② watch/ [a scene worthy of lingering attention, esp. one from a high point and encompassing a large area] ((view, scene, outlook))

EX. (**a**) I will never forget the sights of poverty I encountered in that village.
その村で出会った貧困の{光景/*景色/*眺め}は忘れられません。
*Sono mura de de-atta hinkon no {kookei/*keshiki/*nagame} wa wasure-raremasen.*
(**b**) The sight from the summit of Mt. Everest was breathtaking.
エベレスト山頂からの{景色/眺め/*光景}はすばらしかった。
*Eberesuto-sanchoo kara no {keshiki/nagame/*kookei} wa subarashikatta.*

sightseeing n. **[an act of visiting a place of interest]**
ka⌈nkoo 観光 •c, ke⌈nbutsu 見物 •c [an act of seeing and enjoying a famous place/event] ((visit))

EX. We went to Hawaii on a sightseeing trip.
{ハワイへ観光旅行に行って/ハワイ見物をして}来ました。
{Hawai e kankoo-ryokoo ni itte/Hawai-kenbutsu o shite} kimashita.

sightseer n. **[a person who goes sightseeing]**
ka⌈nko⌉o-kyaku 観光客 •c ((tourist, visitor))

EX. No matter what large city you go to in the

world, there are Japanese sightseers everywhere.
世界のどの大都市へ行っても日本人観光客が大勢いる。
Sekai no dono dai-toshi e itte mo, Nihon-jin kankoo-kyaku ga oozei iru.

sign n. **[s.t. visual that serves to signify s.t. else]**

1. shi⌈rushi 印 /⟨V*masu* of *shirusu* ① mark/ [s.t. visual that serves to distinguish s.t. from other things or to signify s.t.] ⟪mark, symbol, badge, proof, token⟫

EX. A dove is a sign of peace.
はとは平和の印だ。
Hato wa heiwa no shirushi da.

2. shi⌈ngoo 信号 •c [an act/medium of communication using visual/auditory means] ⟪signal, signaling⟫, a⌉izu 合図 [a (secret) method of communication agreed upon between specific people] ⟪signal, sign⟫

EX. (**a**) A word is a sign that conveys meaning.
言葉は意味を伝える{信号/*合図}だ。
*Kotoba wa imi o tsutaeru {shingoo/ *aizu} da.*
(**b**) I made a sign to my friend to run.
私は友達に走れという{合図/*信号}をした。
*Watashi wa tomodachi ni hashire to iu {aizu/*shingoo} o shita.*

3. ka⌈nban 看板 •c [a board/plate bearing the name of a store, merchandise, etc., displayed to attract the attention of customers] ⟪signboard, bill, poster, billboard⟫

EX. A: What does the sign say?
看板に何と書いてありますか。
Kanban ni nan to kaite arimasu ka.
B: It says "Watermelons for sale."
『すいか、安売り』と書いてあります。
"Suika, yasu-uri" to kaite arimasu.

4. hyo⌈oshiki 標識 •c [a visual or other signal, esp. one conveying warning or instructions to automobile drivers on a road] ⟪mark, signal, beacon⟫

EX. You have to be able to recognize road signs in order to drive.
車を運転するには道路標識を知らなければいけない。
Kuruma o unten-suru ni wa dooro-hyooshiki o shiranakereba ikenai.

5. yo⌈osu 様子 •c [the way s.o./s.t./s.a. looks] ⟪appearance, circumstance, air, indication, symptom⟫

EX. Even after jogging twenty miles, John showed no sign of fatigue.
二十マイルジョギングしても、ジョンは疲労の様子を見せなかった。
Ni-juu-mairu jogingu-shite mo, Jon wa hiroo no yoosu o misenakatta.

— vt. **[to give one's signature to s.t.]**
⟨-ni⟩ sho⌈mei-suru ⟨〜に⟩署名する ③ •c ⟪autograph⟫, ⟨-ni⟩ sa⌉in o suru ⟨〜に⟩サインをする ③ •f

EX. Please sign your name here.
ここに{署名して/サインをして}ください。
Koko ni {shomei-shite/sain o shite} kudasai.

signal n. **[an act, event, or object that has been agreed upon as giving specific information or a command]**

1. shi⌈ngoo 信号 •c [an act/medium of communication using visual/auditory means]

EX. It's dangerous to cross the street before the signal turns green.
信号が青になる前に道を渡ると危ないですよ。
Shingoo ga ao ni naru mae ni michi o wataru to abunai desu yo.

2. a⌉izu 合図 •c [a means of communication (secretly) agreed upon in advance]

EX. The marathon runners took off running at the starter's signal.
マラソン走者はスタートの合図で走り出した。
Marason-soosha wa sutaato no aizu de hashiri-dashita.

signboard n. **[a board bearing a sign/ advertisement]**
ka⌈nban 看板 •c [a board/plate bearing the name of a store, merchandise, etc.,

displayed to attract the attention of customers] ((billboard))

significance n. **[meaning/meaningfulness]**

1. i⌉mi 意味 •c [that which s.t. signifies] ((meaning, sense, purport, purpose)), i⌉gi 意義 •c [the meaning/value of s.t.] ((meaning, sense, import))

EX. (**a**) It is sometimes difficult to grasp the significance of life.
人生の{意味/意義}を理解するのが困難な時もある。
Jinsei no {imi/igi} o rikai-suru no ga konnanna toki mo aru.
(**b**) What's the significance of this project?
このプロジェクトの{意味/意義}は何ですか。
Kono purojekuto no {imi/igi} wa nan desu ka.

2. ju⌈uyoo-sei 重要性 •c [the quality of being indispensable and irreplaceable] ((importance, consequence))

EX. It took many years before people became aware of the significance of that scientific discovery.
その科学的発見の重要性を理解するのに何年もかかった。
Sono kagaku-teki hakken no juuyoo-sei o rikai-suru no ni nan-nen mo kakatta.

significant adj. **[having an important meaning]**

1. i⌉mi ga a⌉ru N 意味があるN •c [having meaning/motivation/value], i⌉gi ga a⌉ru N 意義があるN •c [having a deep meaning/reason for existence]

EX. Although he died young, he led a significant life.
彼は若くして死んだけれど、{意味/意義}{の/が}ある人生を送った。
Kare wa wakaku shite shinda keredo, {imi/igi} {no/ga} aru jinsei o okutta.

2. ju⌈uyoona 重要な adj(*na*). **•c [having great effect/influence] ((important, momentous, essential, cardinal]**

EX. He made many significant contributions to computer science.
彼はコンピューター・サイエンスに数多くの重要な貢献をした。
Kare wa konpyuutaa-saiensu ni kazu-ooku no juuyoona kooken o shita.

silence n. **[absence of sound]**

1. chi⌈nmoku 沈黙 •c [an act of refraining from speech] ((taciturnity, reticence)), mu⌈gon 無言 •c [a state of not speaking or of a song, drama, religious training having no words] ((muteness))

EX. (**a**) Do you know the proverb "Silence is golden?"
『{沈黙/*無言}は金なり』ということわざを知っていますか。
*"{Chinmoku/*Mugon} wa kin nari" to iu kotowaza o shitte imasu ka.*
(**b**) I was told to maintain silence no matter what.
何があっても{沈黙/*無言}を守るように言われた。
*Nani ga atte mo {chinmoku/*mugon} o mamoru yooni iwa-reta.*
(**c**) The scolded student demonstrated his protest by silence.
しかられた学生は{無言/*沈黙}で抗議の意を示した。
*Shikara-reta gakusei wa {mugon/*chinmoku} de koogi no i o shimeshita.*

2. shi⌉zuke⌉-sa 静けさ [the state of being quiet] ((stillness, hush, quietness, quietude)), se⌈ijaku(-sa) 静寂(さ) •c [the state of being very quiet ⟨w⟩] ((stillness, quietness, tranquility, hush))

EX. Silence like a graveyard covered the village that evening.
その晩、村は墓地のような{静けさ/静寂(さ)}に包まれていた。
Sono ban, mura wa bochi no yoona {shizuke-sa/seijaku(-sa)} ni tsutsuma-rete ita.

—— vt. **[for s.o. to cause s.o./s.t./s.a. to become silent]**
⟨-o⟩ da⌈mara-se⌉ru ⟨〜を⟩黙らせる /⟨causative of *damaru* ① cease to speak/ [to cause s.o./s.a. to keep his/her/its mouth shut], ⟨-o⟩ chi⌈nmoku-saseru ⟨〜を⟩沈黙させ

S

る /⟨causative of *chinmoku-suru* ③ keep silent/ ② [to cause s.o. to keep silent]

EX. (a) The mother wasn't able to silence her crying baby.
母親は泣く子を{黙らせる/*沈黙させる}ことが出来なかった。
*Haha-oya wa naku ko o {damara-seru/ *chinmoku-saseru} koto ga dekinakatta.*
(b) The government will find it difficult to silence the voices of the people crying out for democracy.
政府は国民の民主化への叫びを{沈黙させる/??黙らせる}ことは出来ないだろう。
Seifu wa kokumin no minshu-ka e no sakebi o {chinmoku-saseru/??damara-seru} koto wa dekinai daroo.

silent adj. **[having no (verbal) sound]**

1. da⌈ma⌉tte iru (N) 黙っている(N) /⟨V*te iru* of *damaru* ① cease to speak/ [for a person who has been speaking to refrain from speaking further/to make no verbal sound] ⟪close one's lips, shut up, stop speaking, say nothing⟫

EX. (a) I cannot help you at all if you are silent.
黙っていたら、何もしてあげられないよ。
Damatte itara, nani-mo shite age-rarenai yo.
(b) Ichiro is always silent in class.
一郎は教室ではいつも黙っている。
Ichiroo wa kyooshitsu de wa itsu-mo damatte iru.

2. shi⌉zukana 静かな adj(*na*). [comfortably quiet/peaceful] ⟪quiet, still, calm, tranquil, peaceful, gentle⟫

EX. (a) Be silent!
静かにしなさい!
Shizukani shinasai!
(b) Everything was silent on the night of Christmas Eve.
クリスマスイブの夜は静かだった。
Kurisumasu-ibu no yoru wa shizuka datta.

silk n.

ki⌉nu 絹

EX. George always wears a silk tie.
ジョージはいつも絹のネクタイをしている。
Jooji wa itsu-mo kinu no nekutai o shite iru.

silly adj. **[lacking common sense/wisdom]**
ba⌉kana ばかな adj(*na*). •c [for s.o./s.a. to completely lack good judgment/sense] ⟪foolish, stupid, dull-witted, idiotic⟫

EX. (a) Don't ask me such a silly question.
そんなばかな質問をするなよ。
Sonna bakana shitsumon o suru na yo.
(b) A: I'll marry you no matter what.
何としても君と結婚するよ。
Nan to shite mo kimi to kekkon-suru yo.
B: Don't be silly, dear.
ばかなことをおっしゃい。
Bakana koto o osshai.
(c) It's silly of you to play golf on such a rainy day.
こんな雨の日にゴルフをするなんて、あなたはばかよ。
Konna ame no hi ni gorufu o suru nante, anata wa baka yo.

silver n. **[a white precious metal or s.t. that is made of it]**

1. gi⌉n 銀 •c [a white precious metal]

EX. Silver is less expensive than gold.
銀は金より安い。
Gin wa kin yori yasui.

2. gi⌉nki 銀器 •c [silverware]

EX. They use real silver at every meal.
彼らは食事のたびに銀器を使っている
Kare-ra wa shokuji no tabi ni ginki o tsukatte iru.

PHRASE: to be born with a silver spoon (in one's mouth) *kane-mochi no ie ni umareru* 金持ちの家に生まれる ②

similar adj. **[resembling s.t./s.o./s.a. but not the same]**
⟨⟨-to⟩⟩ **o⌈naji yo⌉ona** ⟨⟨〜と⟩⟩同じような adj(*na*). **[appearing to be no different from]**, {⟨-to⟩/⟨-ni⟩} **ni⌈te iru** (N) {⟨〜と⟩/⟨〜に⟩}似ている(N) /⟨V*te iru* of *niru* ② resemble/ **[to resemble s.t./s.o./s.a.]**

EX. (a) This car is similar to mine.
この車は僕のと{同じようだ/似ている}。

S

Kono kuruma wa boku no to {onaji yooda/nite iru}.
(**b**) He seems to have ideas similar to mine, doesn't he?
彼は僕と{同じような/似ている}考えを持っているようだね。
Kare wa boku to {onaji yoona/nite iru} kangae o motte iru yooda ne.

similarity n. **[the fact of being similar or the respect in which s.t. is similar]**
1. ru⌈iji 類似 •c [of two or more objects having many common features] ⟪**resemblance, likeness, affinity**⟫ ↔ **sooi 相違 •c**

EX. Similarities in language are more striking than their differences.
言語間の類似は相違より顕著だ。
Gengo-kan no ruiji wa sooi yori kencho da.

2. ru⌈iji⌉-ten 類似点 •c [features common to two or more objects] ⟪**point of resemblance**⟫ ↔ **sooi-ten 相違点 •c**

EX. There are many similarities between the Korean and Japanese cultures, but there are many differences, too.
韓国と日本の文化の間には類似点が多いが、相違点も多い。
Kankoku to Nihon no bunka no aida ni wa ruiji-ten ga ooi ga, sooi-ten mo ooi.

simple adj. **[not complex or elaborate in form, content, or structure/not mentally sophisticated]**
1. ka⌈ntanna 簡単な adj(*na*). **•c [of a tool/task/problem etc. requiring minimal effort to understand or use]** ⟪**brief, short, concise, easy, uncomplicated**⟫ ↔ **fukuzatsuna 複雑な** adj(*na*). **•c; ta⌈njunna 単純な** adj(*na*). **•c [of a structure/form/(brain) function which is not complicated]** ⟪**simple, uncomplicated, plain**⟫ ↔ **fukuzatsuna 複雑な** adj(*na*). **•c**

EX. (**a**) A: This is a complicated problem, isn't it?
これは複雑な問題じゃないですか。
Kore wa fukuzatsuna mondai janai desu ka.
B: No, it's actually a rather simple problem.
いいえ、どちらかと言うと{簡単な/単純な}問題です。
Iie, dochira ka to iu to {kantanna/tanjunna} mondai desu.
(**b**) A: He's a bit on the complex side, isn't he?
あの人はどちらかと言うと複雑な人じゃないですか。
Ano hito wa dochira ka to iu to fukuzatsuna hito janai desu ka.
B: No, he's a very simple person.
いいえ、とても{単純な/*簡単な}人です。
*Iie, totemo {tanjunna/*kantanna} hito desu.*
(**c**) I ate a simple lunch today.
今日は{簡単な/*単純な}昼食を食べました。
*Kyoo wa {kantanna/*tanjunna} chuushoku o tabemashita.*
(**d**) Mozart's music sounds simple at first.
モーツァルトの音楽は初めは{単純に/*簡単に}聞こえる。
*Mootsaruto no ongaku wa hajime wa {tanjunni/*kantanni} kikoeru.*
(**e**) The structure of this machine is very simple.
この機械の構造はとても{簡単/単純}だ。
Kono kikai no koozoo wa totemo {kantan/tanjun} da.

2. ka⌉nsona 簡素な adj(*na*). **•c [eliminating waste and saving money]** ⟪**plain, frugal**⟫, **shi⌉ssona 質素な** adj(*na*). **•c [plain in living accommodations]** ⟪**plain, homely, modest, quiet, unpretentious**⟫ ↔ **zeitakuna ぜい沢な** adj(*na*). **•c; ji⌈mi⌉na 地味な** adj(*na*). **[quiet and subdued in color/personality/appearance]** ⟪**plain, quiet**⟫ ↔ **hadena 派手な** adj(*na*).

EX. (**a**) Although he is rich,Taro lives a simple life.
太郎は金持ちだけど、{簡素な/質素な/地味な}生活をしている。
Taroo wa kane-mochi da kedo, {kansona/shissona/jimina} seikatsu o shite iru.

S

(**b**) Dorothy always wears simple clothes.
ドロシーはいつも{地味な/簡素な/質素な}服を着ている。
Doroshii wa itsu-mo {jimina/kansona/shissona} fuku o kite iru.

simplify vt. **[for s.o./s.t. to make s.t. simple]**
1. ka⌈ntanni suru 簡単にする ③ •c [for s.o. to do s.t. to a tool/task/problem etc. so that it requires minimal effort to understand or use] ↔ fukuzatsuni suru 複雑にする ③ •c; ta⌈njunni suru 単純にする ③ •c [for s.o. to make s.t. such as a structure/form/(brain) function not complicated]

EX. I think we should simplify the decision-making process in this organization.
この機関の意志決定の方法はもっと{簡単に/単純に}した方がいいと思う。
Kono kikan no ishi-kettei no hoohoo wa motto {kantanni/tanjunni} shita hoo ga ii to omou.

2. ⟨-o⟩ ka⌈nso-ka-suru ⟨〜を⟩簡素化する ③ •c [for s.o. to eliminate waste and save money]

S

EX. If we simplified our life style, we could save money for more creative purposes.
生活様式を簡素化すれば、お金をためて、もっと創造的なことが出来る。
Seikatsu-yooshiki o kanso-ka-sureba, o-kane o tamete, motto soozoo-tekina koto ga dekiru.

simply adv. **[without ambiguity/embellishment]**
1. ka⌈ntanni 簡単に /⟨adj⟨*na*⟩. *ni* of *kantanna* simple/ •c [in such a way that minimal effort is required]

EX. This machine is simply constructed.
この機械は簡単に組み立てられている。
Kono kikai wa kantanni kumi-tate-rarete iru.

2. ka⌉nsoni 簡素に /⟨adj⟨*na*⟩. *ni* of *kansona* simple/ •c [in such a way that one eliminates waste and saves money], shi⌉ssoni 質素に /⟨adj⟨*na*⟩. *ni* of *shissona* plain/ •c [in such a way that one requires minimal living accommodations] ↔ zeitakuni ぜい沢に •c; ji⌈mi⌉ni 地味に /⟨adj⟨*na*⟩. *ni* of *jimina* simple/ •c [in a non-showy manner] ↔ hadeni 派手に •c

EX. (**a**) I'd like to live simply.
{簡素に/質素に/地味に}生活したい。
{Kansoni/Shissoni/Jimini} seikatsu-shitai.
(**b**) That office building is designed simply.
あのオフィスビルは{簡素に/地味に/*質素に}できている。
*Ano ofisu-biru wa {kansoni/jimini/*shissoni} dekite iru.*

3. ma⌈ttaku (neg.) 全く(neg.) [in a manner so strongly that it cannot be expressed in any other way] ⟪entirely, utterly, totally, perfectly, truly, really⟫

EX. Why he killed himself is simply a mystery.
どうして彼が自殺したかは全く分からない。
Dooshite kare ga jisatsu-shita ka wa mattaku wakaranai.

4. ta⌉nni 単に •c [just/only] ⟪only, merely, solely, just⟫

EX. John married Mary simply because she is rich.
ジョンは単にメアリーが金持ちだという理由で結婚した。
Jon wa tanni Mearii ga kane-mochi da to iu riyuu de kekkon-shita.

simultaneous adj. **[occurring or being performed at the same time]**
do⌈oji no N 同時のN •c

EX. I can't figure out how people can do simultaneous interpretation between Japanese and English.
日英語の同時通訳をどうやって出来るのか不思議です。
Nichi-eigo no dooji-tsuuyaku o doo yatte dekiru no ka fushigi desu.

sin n. **[violation of a religious or moral law esp. in Judaism and Christianity]**
tsu⌉mi 罪 [an act of violating a religious or legal code] ⟪crime, vice, offense, fault, guilt, blame⟫

EX. (**a**) In Christianity "sin" is any thought or act which violates God's laws.
キリスト教では神のおきてに反する考

えや行為がすべて「罪」である。
Kirisuto-kyoo de wa kami no okite ni hansuru kangae ya kooi ga subete 'tsumi' dearu.
(**b**) In any culture murder is an unpardonable sin.
どの文化でも人を殺すのは許されない罪だ。
Dono bunka demo hito o korosu no wa yurusa-renai tsumi da.

since[1] conj. **[after a certain point of time in the past]**
V*te* kara V*te*から [after a point in time at which s.t. takes place] ((after, having done s.t.)), V*te* i˥rai V*te*以来 •c [after a point in time at which s.t. took place continuously up to the present time ⟨fml⟩]

EX. (**a**) A: Where have you been staying since you came here?
ここへ来て{から/??以来}どこに住んでいるんですか。
Koko e kite {kara/??irai} doko ni sunde iru n desu ka.
B: I have been staying with a friend of mine.
友達の家に住んでいます。
Tomodachi no ie ni sunde imasu.
(**b**) Japan has been striving to catch up with America and the European countries since its defeat in the war.
日本は戦争に負けて{から/以来}欧米に追いつこうと努力して来た。
Nihon wa sensoo ni makete {kara/irai} Oo-Bei ni oi-tsukoo to doryoku shite kita.

since[2] conj. **[a subordinate conjunction indicating reason or cause]**
S kara Sから [a subordinate conjunction expressing a reason or cause] ((because, so)), Sinf. no˥de Sinf.ので [a subordinate conjunction expressing a reason or cause. In S_1 node S_2, the speaker believes that the information he/she provides in "S_1" as cause/reason for "S_2" is valid and is also evident and acceptable to the listener]
NOTE: When the nonpast affirmative form of adj(*na*). or N+cop. occurs before *node*, {adj(*na*). stem/N} *na* is used.

EX. (**a**) I'm studying Japanese now since I'll be going to Japan to teach English next year.
来年日本へ英語を教えに行く{から/ので}、今日本語を勉強しています。
Rainen Nihon e eigo o oshie ni iku {kara/node}, ima Nihon-go o benkyoo-shite imasu.
(**b**) Since it's going to get cold tonight, why don't you stay home?
今晩は冷える{から/*ので}、うちにいたら。
*Konban wa hieru {kara/*node}, uchi ni itara.*
(**c**) Since you've kept your friend waiting for 15 minutes you'd better apologize to him.
友達を十五分も待たせている{んだから/*ので}謝った方がいいですよ。
*Tomodachi o juu-go-fun mo mata-sete iru {n da kara/*node} ayamatta hoo ga ii desu yo.*
(**d**) Since the concert doesn't start for another hour, why don't we go have something to eat?
コンサートが始まるまであと一時間もある{から/*ので}、ちょっと何か食べて来ようか。
*Konsaato ga hajimaru made ato ichi-jikan mo aru {kara/*node}, chotto nani-ka tabete koyoo ka.*
(**e**) Since this paper is very important, you'd better read it.
この論文はすごく重要{だから/??なので}読んだ方がいいよ。
Kono ronbun wa sugoku juuyoo {da kara/??na node} yonda hoo ga ii yo.
(**f**) Since we received all this *sake* as gifts and can't use it all, please take some home with you.
お土産にこんなにお酒をもらって、全部飲みきれない{から/??ので}、少し持って帰って。
O-miyage ni konnani o-sake o moratte, nomi-kirenai {kara/??node}, sukoshi motte kaette.

S

NOTE: It is better to avoid using *node* if S2 is a request, piece of advice, suggestion or invitation as shown in examples (b), (c), (d), (e), (f). Use *kara* instead, but in a formal situation such as a public announcement, *node* may be used even in these cases.

— adv. **[after a certain event or point of time in the past]**

so⌈re i⌉rai それ以来 conj. •c **[after a point in time at which s.t. took place, continuously up to the present time]** **《from that time on》**, **so⌈re i⌉go** それ以後 conj. •c **[after a point in time at which s.t. took place]** **《after this, from this time》**

EX. (**a**) John lost his beloved wife three years ago and has been depressed ever since.
ジョンは三年前に愛妻をなくしてそれ{以来/以後}落ち込んでいる。
Jon wa san-nen-mae ni aisai o nakushite sore {irai/igo} ochi-konde iru.
(**b**) The house burnt down a few years back, but it has since been rebuilt.
家は二、三年前に焼けたが、それ{以後/*以来}建て直した。
*Ie wa ni, san-nen-mae ni yaketa ga, sore {igo/*irai} tate-naoshita.*

sing vt. **[for s.o./s.a. to make a musical sound using one's voice]**

⟨-o⟩ u⌈tau ⟨〜を⟩歌う ① **[for s.o. to utter melodic sounds]** **《chant, recite》**, **sa⌈ezu⌉ru** さえずる ① **[for a bird to chirp melodically]** **《chirp, twitter, warble》**

EX. (**a**) I like to sing while taking a shower.
シャワーを浴びながら{歌う/*さえずる}のが好きです。
*Shawaa o abi-nagara {utau/*saezuru} no ga suki desu.*
(**b**) In spring, I like to listen to the birds singing.
春、鳥が{さえずって/?歌って}いるのを聞くのが好きだ。
Haru, tori ga {saezutte/?utatte} iru no o kiku no ga suki da.

singer n. **[a person who sings]**

1. ka⌉shu 歌手 •c **[a person who sings professionally]** **《vocalist》**

EX. Placido Domingo is one of the greatest singers of our time.
プラシッド・ドミンゴは現代の偉大な歌手の一人だ。
Purashiddo Domingo wa gendai no idaina kashu no hitori da.

2. u⌈ta⌉ ga jo⌈ozu⌉na 歌が上手な adj(*na*). **[for s.o. to be good at singing]**

EX. Mr. Ogawa is a good singer, isn't he?
小川さんは歌が上手ですね。
Ogawa-san wa uta ga joozu desu ne.

single adj. **[only one]**

1. ta⌈tta hi⌈to⌉tsu no N たった一つのN, **tatta no i⌈chi⌉ + counter mo** たったの一+counterも

EX. (**a**) Even a single error can affect one's grade.
たった{一つ/一個}の間違いでも成績に影響する可能性がある。
Tatta {hitotsu/ik-ko} no machigai demo seiseki ni eikyoo-suru kanoo-sei ga aru.
(**b**) I cannot find even a single pencil in this drawer.
この引き出しの中には鉛筆がたったの一本もありません。
Kono hiki-dashi no naka ni wa enpitsu ga tatta no ip-pon mo arimasen.

2. do⌈kushin no N 独身のN •c **[unmarried]**, **hi⌈to⌉ri no N** 一人のN **[of one person]**

EX. A: Are you married?
結婚していますか。
Kekkon-shite imasu ka.
B: No, I'm single.
いいえ、{独身/一人}です。
Iie, {dokushin/hitori} desu.

— n. **[a single one]**

1. hi⌈to⌉ri 一人 **[one person]**

2. i⌉k-ko 一個 •c **[one piece]**

3. shi⌉ngurusu シングルス •f **[a singles game in tennis/ping-pong game]** ↔ **daburusu** ダブルス •f

singular adj. **[of a person/event/phenomenon not comparable to others 《fig. "odd," "eccentric"》 or a noun/verb form used to indicate one person/thing]**

ta⌈nsu⌉u no N 単数のN •c [of a noun/verb form used to indicate one person/thing] ↔ fukusuu no N 複数のN •c

EX. The singular form of "men" is "man."
Menの単数形はmanです。
Men no tansuu-kei wa man desu.

sink vi. **[for s.t./s.o./s.a. (including price/value) to fall slowly downward (and deeply) 《fig. "become deeply absorbed," "become depressed"》]**

1. shi⌈zumu 沈む ① [to go under the surface of s.t. such as water and become invisible 《fig. "become depressed"》] 《be submerged, go down, go under, feel depressed》

EX. (**a**) The boat sank in a matter of a few minutes.
船はものの二、三分で沈んだ。
Fune wa mono-no ni, san-pun de shizunda.
(**b**) The sun sank below the horizon.
太陽は地平線に沈んだ。
Taiyoo wa chihei-sen ni shizunda.

2. sa⌈ga⌉ru 下がる ① [to hang/go down/become smaller in amount/degree/strength] 《hang, dangle, drop, fall, go down》

EX. The value of the dollar started to sink in the mid-1980's.
ドルの価値は80年代半ばから下がり始めた。
Doru no kachi wa hachi-juu-nen-dai nakaba kara sagari-hajimeta.

3. ⟨-ni⟩ fu⌈ke⌉ru ⟨～に⟩ふける ① [for s.o. to become deeply absorbed in one thing] 《be addicted to, indulge in》, ⟨-ni⟩ o⌈chiiru ⟨～に⟩陥る ① [for s.t. to fall into an unfavorable place or situation] 《fall into, get into, slide into》

EX. (**a**) My mother sank into a deep coma after surgery.
母は手術の後、深い昏睡状態に{陥った/*ふけった}。
*Haha wa shujutsu no ato, fukai konsui-jootai ni {ochiitta/*fuketta}.*
(**b**) When I was a girl, I would often sink into reveries after reading good books.
私は少女のころ、おもしろい本を読んだ後、よく空想に{ふけった/*陥った}ものです。
*Watashi wa shoojo no koro, omoshiroi hon o yonda ato, yoku kuusoo ni {fuketta/*ochiitta} mono desu.*

4. o⌈chi-komu 落ち込む ① [for s.o. to become depressed]

EX. My heart sank when my girlfriend told me she didn't want to see me any more.
恋人に別れたいと言われた時、私はひどく落ち込んだ。
Koi-bito ni wakare-tai to iwa-reta toki, watashi wa hidoku ochi-konda.

— vt. **[for s.t./s.a. to cause s.t./s.o./s.a. to sink]**

1. ⟨-o⟩ shi⌈zumeru ⟨～を⟩沈める ② [for s.o. to cause s.t./s.o./s.a. to go under the surface of s.t. such as water and become invisible] 《send to the bottom of the sea, put under water》

EX. The enemy tried to sink our oil tanker.
敵は石油タンカーを沈めようとした。
Teki wa sekiyu-tankaa o shizumeyoo to shita.

2. ⟨-o⟩ bo⌈tsuraku-saseru ⟨～を⟩没落させる /⟨causative of *botsuraku-suru* ③ go to ruin/ ② [for s.o./s.t. to cause the downfall of a person of high social standing] 《ruin》

3. ⟨-o⟩ u⌈shinawasu ⟨～を⟩失わす /⟨the short causative of *ushinau* ① lose/ ① [for s.o./s.t. to cause s.o. to lose s.t.]

— n. **[a fixed basin with a pipe where one washes dishes or one's body]**

na⌈gashi 流し /⟨V*masu* of *nagasu* ① cause to flow/ 《scullery, draining floor》

EX. Dishes are piled up in the sink.
流しに皿が山積みになっている。
Nagashi ni sara ga yama-zumi ni natte iru.

sir n. **[a polite form of address for a male person]**

ø, mo⌈shi-moshi もしもし int. **[an expression used to catch s.o.'s attention or as the first word in a telephone**

S

conversation], **ka⌈shikomarima⌉shita** かしこまりました ⟪yes sir, certainly sir⟫

NOTE: Sir often corresponds to ø in Japanese, as in example (a).

EX. (**a**) May I take your luggage, sir?
荷物をお持ちしましょうか。
Nimotsu o o-mochi-shimashoo ka.
(**b**) Sir, this seat is taken.
{もしもし/ø}、こちらの席は人が来ますが。
{Moshi-moshi/ø}, kochira no seki wa hito ga kimasu ga.
(**c**) A: Come here at eight tomorrow.
明日八時にここへ来なさい。
Asu hachi-ji ni koko e kinasai.
B: Yes, sir.
はい、かしこまりました。
Hai, kashikomarimashita.

PHRASE: Dear Sir *haikei* 拝啓 •c

siren n.

sa⌉iren サイレン •f

EX. I heard the sound of the siren right before the tornado struck.
竜巻の直前にサイレンの音を聞いた。
Tatsumaki no chokuzen ni sairen no oto o kiita.

sister n. **[a daughter of the same parents as s.o. or a fellow woman of a group esp. of nuns]**

1. shi⌉mai 姉妹 •c **[older and younger sisters]**

NOTE: An older sister of the speaker is *ane* and a younger sister is *imooto*. An older sister of others is *o-nee-san* and a younger one is *imooto-san*.

EX. (**a**) A: Where is your (older) sister working?
{お姉さん/*姉/*姉妹/*妹さん/*妹}はどこで仕事をしていらっしゃいますか。
*{O-nee-san/*Ane/*Shimai/*Imooto-san/*Imooto} wa doko de shigoto o shite irasshaimasu ka.*
B: She is working at a securities company.
{姉/*お姉さん/*姉妹/*妹/*妹さん}は証券会社で働いています。
*{Ane/*O-nee-san/*Shimai/*Imooto/*Imooto-san} wa shooken-gaisha de hataraite imasu.*
(**b**) Mr. Nakayama's sisters are like twins, aren't they?
中山さんのところの姉妹は双子のようですね。
Nakayama-san no tokoro no shimai wa futa-go no yoodesu ne.

2. shu⌈udo⌉o-jo 修道女 •c **[a Catholic sister], -shi** 〜姉 **[a form of adderss for a Catholic sister], shi⌉sutaa** シスター •f **[a Catholic sister]**

sit vi. **[for s.o./s.a. to put oneself in a position in which one's body rests upright on one's buttocks]**

1. su⌈waru 座る ① **[for s.o./s.a. to take a seat by bending one's knees and lowering one's bottom]** ⟪squat, take a seat, be seated⟫ ↔ **tatsu** 立つ ①; ⟨-ni⟩ **ko⌈shi** (o) **ka⌈ke⌉ru** ⟨〜に⟩腰(を)掛ける ② **[for s.o./s.a. to take a seat on s.t.]**

EX. (**a**) Please sit down in this chair.
どうぞ、このいすに{座って/腰を掛けて}ください。
Doozo, kono isu ni {suwatte/koshi o kakete} kudasai.
(**b**) He no sooner sat down in the chair than he fell fast asleep.
彼はいすに{座る/腰掛ける}やいなや眠り込んでしまった。
Kare wa isu ni {suwaru/koshi-kakeru} ya-ina-ya nemuri-konde shimatta.

2. ⟨**-ni**⟩ **to⌈maru** ⟨〜に⟩とまる ① **[for s.t./s.o./s.a. moving to come to a standstill at some location ⟪fig. "lodge"⟫]** ⟪stop, halt, park, lodge, stay⟫

㊅ "s.t. comes to a stop"▷止まる, "stay somewhere overnight"▷泊まる

EX. A bird was sitting on the branch of the tree.
鳥が木の枝に止まっていた。
Tori ga ki no eda ni tomatte ita.

PHRASE: sit up *oki-agaru* 起き上がる ①, *nezu ni okite iru* 寝ずに起きている ②

EX. I sat up until late at night writing my paper.
論文を書くために夜遅くまで寝ずに起きていた。
Ronbun o kaku tame ni yoru osoku

S

made nezu ni okite ita.

site n. **[the place where a building stood/stands/is to stand or where some event or activity takes place/took place]**
ba˹sho 場所 •c [a point or area in space where s.o./s.t./s.a. exists or where s.t. happens] ⟪place, spot, locality, position, scene⟫, shi˹kichi 敷地 [the land on which a building or street is constructed] ⟪ground⟫, i˹seki 遺跡 •c [a historical place] ⟪remains, ruins⟫

EX. (**a**) Which site did you choose to build your house on?
どの{場所/敷地/*遺跡}に家を建てることにしたんですか。
*Dono {basho/shikichi/*iseki} ni ie o tateru koto ni shita n desu ka.*
(**b**) I visited many historical sites in Japan.
日本では色々な{遺跡/歴史に残る場所/*歴史に残る敷地}を見て歩きました。
*Nihon de wa iro-irona {iseki/rekishi ni nokoru basho/*rekishi ni nokoru shikichi} o mite arukimashita.*

situation n. **[a physical/psychological surrounding in which one finds oneself]**
1. jo˹okyoo 状況 •c [state of affairs] ⟪state of affairs, conditions, setting, context⟫

EX. The political situation in Japan is basically stable.
日本の政治的状況は基本的には安定している。
Nihon no seiji-teki jookyoo wa kihon-tekini wa antei-shite iru.

2. kyo˹oguu 境遇 •c [the total environment in which one lives] ⟪circumstances, one's lot, station in life⟫

EX. He is doing his best to improve the situation he is in now.
彼は自分が今置かれている境遇を改善しようと頑張っている。
Kare wa jibun ga ima oka-rete iru kyooguu o kaizen-shiyoo to ganbatte iru.

3. ta˹chiba˺ 立場 [a social or physical circumstance in which one finds oneself or one's viewpoint] ⟪footing, standpoint, point of view, position⟫

EX. Please try to understand my situation.
私の立場を分かってください。
Watashi no tachiba o wakatte kudasai.

4. ba˹men 場面 •c [the dramatic surroundings of an action/event] ⟪scene, place, site⟫

EX. What does the heroine do in that situation?
その場面でヒロインは何をするんですか。
Sono bamen de hiroin wa nani o suru n desu ka.

six n./adj.
mu˹ttsu (no N) 六つ(のN), ro˹ku˺ (+counter) (no N) 六(+counter)(のN) •c SEE APPENDIX II

sixteen n./adj.
ju˹u-ro˺ku (+counter) (no N) 十六(+counter)(のN) •c SEE APPENDIX II

sixteenth n./adj.
(dai-)ju˹u-roku-ban-me (no N) (第)十六番目(のN) SEE APPENDIX II

sixth n./adj.
(dai-)ro˹ku-ban-me (no N) (第)六番目(のN) SEE APPENDIX II

sixtieth n./adj.
(dai-)ro˹ku-juu-ban-me (no N) (第)六十番目(のN) SEE APPENDIX II

sixty n./adj.
ro˹ku-ju˺u (+counter) (no N) 六十(+counter)(のN) •c SEE APPENDIX II

size n. **[the measurement/extent of s.t.]**
o˹oki-sa 大きさ /⟨adj(*i*). stem of *ookii* big + suf. *sa* ness/ [the largeness of an object/person/animal/sound] ⟪dimension, magnitude⟫, sa˺izu サイズ •f [the largeness of an item, usu. small and Western in character]

EX. (**a**) What is your shoe size?
靴の{大きさ/サイズ}はいくつですか。
Kutsu no {ooki-sa/saizu} wa ikutsu desu ka.
(**b**) Do you know the size of the school?
学校の{大きさ/*サイズ}を知っていますか。
*Gakkoo no {ooki-sa/*saizu} o shitte imasu ka.*

S

skate n. **[either of a pair of boots with metal blades used to slide on ice]**
su⌈keeto-gutsu スケート靴
—— vi. [for s.o. to move on ice wearing boots with metal blades]
su⌈keeto o suru スケートをする ③ •f

EX. I like to skate on the lake in winter.
冬には湖の上でスケートをするのが好きです。
Fuyu ni wa mizuumi no ue de sukeeto o suru no ga suki desu.

PHRASE: roller skate *rooraa-sukeeto* ローラースケート •f

EX. On American university campuses you sometimes see students going from one class to another on roller skates.
アメリカのキャンパスでは時々学生がローラースケートで教室から教室への移動をしているのを見かける。
Amerika no kyanpasu de wa toki-doki gakusei ga rooraa-sukeeto de kyooshitsu kara kyooshitsu e no idoo o shite iru no o mi-kakeru.

S

skeleton n. **[the supportive bone structure of an animal's body 《fig. "any supporting structure"》]**
1. ga⌉ikotsu がい骨 •c [the bone structure remaining after s.o./s.a. dies]

EX. He's a skeleton compared to fat Albert.
太ったアルバートと比べると彼はがい骨だ。
Futotta Arubaato to kuraberu to kare wa gaikotsu da.

2. ko⌈kkaku 骨格 •c [a bone structure 《fig. "any supporting structure"》] 《bone structure》

EX. Can you draw a human skeleton?
人間の骨格をかくことができますか。
Ningen no kokkaku o kaku koto ga dekimasu ka.

sketch n. **[a rough drawing or written description]**
1. su⌈ke⌉tchi スケッチ •f [a simple, rough drawing], sha⌈sei 写生 •c [a drawing/piece of writing that depicts s.t. realistically]

EX. An artist was making a sketch of the campus.
絵かきがキャンパスの{スケッチ/写生}をしていた。
E-kaki ga kyanpasu no {suketchi/shasei} o shite ita.

2. ga⌈iryaku 概略 •c [an outline] 《summary, outline, résumé, gist》

EX. Could you give me a brief sketch of your plan?
計画の概略を言ってください。
Keikaku no gairyaku o itte kudasai.

3. sho⌈ohin 小品 •c [a short essay/piece of writing or a small object of art]
—— vt. [for s.o. to draw s.t. roughly or describe s.t. roughly in writing]
〈-o〉 byo⌈osha-suru 〈～を〉描写する ③ •c [for s.o. to depict s.t./s.o./s.a. through verbal or nonverbal means such as painting/writing/music/pantomime] 《describe, represent》

EX. Beethoven's *6th Symphony* sketches a pastoral scene.
ベートーベンの交響曲第六番は田園の風景を描写している。
Beetooben no kookyoo-kyoku dai-roku-ban wa den'en no fuukee o byoosha-shite iru.

PHRASE: sketch pictures of 〈-o〉 *suketchi-suru* 〈～を〉スケッチする ③ •f, 〈-o〉 *shasei-suru* 〈～を〉写生する ③ •c

EX. The children are sketching pictures of flowers in a vase.
子供たちは花瓶の花を{スケッチ/写生}している。
Kodomo-tachi wa kabin no hana o {suketch/shasei}-shite iru.

ski vi. **[for s.o. to glide on skis, esp. as a sport]**
su⌈ki⌉i o suru スキーをする ③ •f

EX. During winter vacation I went skiing in Aspen, Colorado.
冬休みにスキーをしにコロラドのアスペンに行きました。
Fuyu-yasumi ni sukii o shi ni Kororado no Asupen ni ikimashita.

skill n. **[an ability to do s.t. well]**
1. ju⌈kuren 熟練 •c [expertness in doing a

task] ⟪**experience, proficiency**⟫

EX. Any type of manual work requires skill.
どんな手仕事も熟練を必要とする。
Donna te-shigoto mo jukuren o hitsuyoo to suru.

2. gi⌉noo 技能 **•c [the technical proficiency/ability required to perform a task/job]**

EX. Mr. Johnson's skill in reading Japanese is very high.
ジョンソンさんの日本語を読む技能はとても高い。
Jonson-san no Nihon-go o yomu ginoo wa totemo takai.

skillful adj. **[having a proficient skill in doing s.t.]**

1. jo⌈ozu⌉na 上手な adj(*na*). **•c [for s.o./s.a. to be able to do s.t. well]** ⟪**dexterous, clever, proficienct, good at**⟫ ↔ **hetana** 下手な adj(*na*).

EX. Females seem to be more skillful at learning foreign languages than males.
女性の方が男性より外国語の習得が上手なようだ。
Josei no hoo ga dansei yori gaikoku-go no shuutoku ga joozuna yooda.

2. ⟨**-ni**⟩ **ju⌈kuren-shite iru (N)** ⟨～に⟩熟練している(N) **/**⟨**V*te iru* of *jukuren-suru*** ③ **become skilled at/ •c [for s.o. to be expert at doing a task]**

EX. Bob is skillful at operating this machine.
ボブはこの機械の操作に熟練している。
Bobu wa kono kikai no soosa ni jukuren-shite iru.

skillfully adv. **[with proficient skill]**

jo⌈ozu⌉ni 上手に **/**⟨**adj(*na*).** ***ni* of *joozuna* skillful/ •c [with a great deal of skill]**

EX. (**a**) He handled the delicate negotiations skillfully.
彼は微妙な交渉を上手に取り仕切った。
Kare wa bimyoona kooshoo o joozuni tori-shikitta.
(**b**) A salesman has to talk skillfully when selling his merchandise.
セールスマンは商品を売り込むときは上手に話さなければなりません。
Seerusu-man wa shoohin o uri-komu toki wa joozuni hanasanakereba narimasen.

skim vt. **[for s.o. to take floating matter from the surface of a liquid ⟪fig. "glide over," "read quickly and roughly"⟫]**

1. ⟨**-kara**⟩ **su⌈kui-to⌉ru** ⟨～から⟩すくい取る ① **[for s.o. to scoop up (floating matter) from liquid]**

EX. I skimmed the oil off the soup.
私はスープから油をすくい取った。
Watashi wa suupu kara abura o sukui-totta.

2. ⟨**-no**⟩ **u⌈e o su⌈be⌉ru yo⌉oni {i⌈ku/to⌈bu}** ⟨～の⟩上を滑るように{行く ①/飛ぶ ①} **[to go over a surface as if skating]**

EX. A butterfly skimmed over the surface of the pond.
ちょうが池の上を滑るように飛んでいった。
Choo ga ike no ue o suberu yooni tonde itta.

3. ⟨**-o**⟩ **za⌈tto yo⌉mu** ⟨～を⟩ざっと読む ① **[for s.o. to read s.t. rapidly for its gist]**

EX. You don't need to read the book in detail. Just skim it.
その本は詳しく読まなくてもいいです。ざっと読むだけでいいですよ。
Sono hon wa kuwashiku yomanakute mo ii desu. Zatto yomu dake de ii desu yo.

skin n. **[the flexible continuous covering of the human or other animal body]**

1. hi⌉fu 皮膚 **•c [the outer covering of the human or other animal body]**

EX. Healthy skin comes with a healthy body.
体が健康だと、皮膚も健康だ。
Karada ga kenkoo da to, hifu mo kenkoo da.

2. ka⌈wa⌉ 皮 **[the outer covering of a vegetable, fruit, plant, or animal body]**
㊥ "tanned skin (=leather)"▷革, otherwise ▷皮

EX. Japanese usually peel off the skin of apples and grapes before eating them.
日本人は大抵りんごやぶどうの皮をむいて食べる。

S

Nihon-jin wa taitei ringo ya budoo no kawa o muite taberu.

— vt. **[for s.o. to strip the skin off an animal, vegetable, or fruit]**

1. ⟨**-no**⟩ **ka⌈wa⌉ o ha⌉gu** ⟨〜の⟩皮をはぐ ① **[for s.o. to tear the skin off an animal]**

EX. The Eskimos were skinning the seals they had just caught.
エスキモーたちは捕らえたばかりのあざらしの皮をはいでいた。
Esukimoo-tachi wa toraeta bakari no azarashi no kawa o haide ita.

2. ⟨**-no**⟩ **ka⌈wa o mu⌉ku** ⟨〜の⟩皮をむく ① **[for s.o. to peel the skin off a vegetable, fruit, or plant]**

EX. Will you skin this apple, please?
このりんごの皮をむいてくれませんか。
Kono ringo no kawa o muite kuremasen ka.

skip vi./vt. **[for s.o. to run taking two steps with each foot in turn ⟪fig. "pass quickly from one place to another"⟫]**

1. su⌈ki⌉ppu-suru スキップする ③ **•f [for s.o. to run taking two steps with each foot in turn]**

EX. The children skipped away down the sidewalk.
子供たちは歩道をスキップして行った。
Kodomo-tachi wa hodoo o sukippu-shite itta.

2. ⟨**-o**⟩ **to⌈basu** ⟨〜を⟩飛ばす ① **[for s.o. to let s.t. go/fly from one place to another, omitting what lies between] ⟪let fly, scatter, spatter, splash, omit⟫**

EX. Don't skip through the book. Read it carefully.
その本を飛ばさないで、よく読みなさい。
Sono hon o tobasanai de, yoku yominasai.

— n. **[an act of skipping]**

1. su⌈ki⌉ppu スキップ **•f [an act of running taking two steps with each foot in turn]**

2. sho⌈oryaku 省略 **•c [an act of omitting/deleting s.t.] ⟪omission, deletion⟫**

PHRASE: skip a grade (in school) *tobi-kyuu-suru* 飛び級する ③

EX. A: How come he's just 16 years old and a sophomore in college?
どうして彼は十六歳なのに大学二年生なんだい。
Dooshite kare wa juu-roku-sai na noni daigaku ni-nen-sei nan dai.
B: He skipped some grades.
飛び級したからだよ。
Tobi-kyuu-shita kara da yo.

skirt n. **[a piece of woman's clothing which hangs down from the waist ⟪fig. "periphery"⟫]**

su⌈ka⌉ato スカート **•f [a woman's garment which hangs down from the waist]**

EX. I have to put on a skirt because I have a cocktail party this evening.
今晩カクテルパーティーがあるから、スカートをはかなくちゃ。
Konban kakuteru-paatii ga aru kara, sukaato o hakanakucha.

— vt. **[to go along the border of a place]**

⟨**-no**⟩ **he⌈ri⌉ o to⌉oru** ⟨〜の⟩へりを通る ① **[to pass through the outer parts of a space]**

EX. The freeway skirts the edge of the city.
高速道路はその町のへりを通っている。
Koosoku-doora wa sono machi no heri o tootte iru.

skull n.

zu⌈ga⌉i-kotsu 頭蓋骨 **•c**

skunk n.

su⌈ka⌉nku スカンク **•f**

EX. I must have run over a skunk. The stench is terrible.
スカンクをひいたにちがいない。ひどくくさい。
Sukanku o hiita ni chigai-nai. Hidoku kusai.

sky n.

so⌉ra 空 **⟪the blue, heavens⟫**

EX. (**a**) It stopped raining and the sky began to clear.
雨がやんで、空が晴れて来ました。
Ame ga yande, sora ga harete kimashita.
(**b**) A beautiful red balloon is flying in the sky.

S

| きれいな赤い風船が空を飛んでいる。
| *Kireina akai fuusen ga sora o tonde iru.*

slack adj. **[loose or sluggish]**

1. yu⌈ru⌉nda N 緩んだN /⟨Vinf. past of *yurumu* ① become loose/, yu⌈ru⌉nde iru (N) 緩んでいる(N) /⟨V*te iru* of *yurumu* ① become loose/

EX.| My bicycle chain was slack, so I took it to a bike shop.
自転車のチェーンが緩んでいたので、自転車屋へ持って行った。
Jitensha no cheen ga yurunde ita node, jitensha-ya e motte itta.

2. no⌈ro⌉i のろい adj(*i*). **[not alert, lively, or moving quickly ⟨s⟩]**

EX.| He is slack in his work.
彼は仕事がのろい。
Kare wa shigoto ga noroi.

3. da⌈ra⌉kete iru (N) だらけている(N) /⟨V*te iru* of *darakeru* ② become loose/ [lacking sufficient care or discipline in doing s.t.] ⟪lacking, languid, listless⟫

EX.| He's been slack in his work habits since being transferred to the personnel division.
人事課に回されてから彼の仕事ぶりはだらけている。
Jinji-ka ni mawasa-rete kara kare no shigoto-buri wa darakete iru.

— n. **[the state of being slack or the slack part of s.t. ⟪fig. "informal trousers"⟫]**

1. yu⌈rumi⌉ 緩み /⟨V*masu* of *yurumu* ① become loose/ [the state of being loose/a loose part]

2. fu⌈kyoo(-ji) 不況(時) •c [a time of little work/trade/business] ⟪recession, depression, lull in business⟫

EX.| The slack in business came unexpectedly.
思いがけず事業の不況がやって来た。
Omoigakezu jigyoo no fukyoo ga yatte kita.

3. su⌈ra⌉kkusu スラックス •f [full-cut trousers for casual wear] ⟪pants⟫

PHRASE: slack off *yurumu* 緩む ① ⟪loosen, abate, lessen, relax⟫ ↔ *shimaru* 締まる ①

EX.| The cold wave finally slacked off.
寒波がやっと緩んだ。
| *Kanpa ga yatto yurunda.*

slam vt. **[for s.o. to shut a door forcefully with a loud sound ⟪fig. "hit s.o. forcefully"⟫] ⟨-o⟩ {pi⌈sha⌉ri/ba⌈ta⌉n} to shi⌈me⌉ru ⟨〜を⟩{ぴしゃり/ばたん}と閉める ② [for s.o. to shut s.t. forcefully and noisily]**

EX.| He slammed the door in anger as he left.
彼は怒って、部屋を出るとドアを{ぴしゃり/ばたん}と閉めた。
Kare wa okotte, heya o deru to doa o {pishari/batan} to shimeta.

— vi. **[for s.t. to hit against s.t. forcefully] ⟨-ni⟩ gekitotsu-suru ⟨〜に⟩激突する ③ •c [to crash into s.t.]**

EX.| The car slammed into the guardrail after skidding out of control on the ice.
車はコントロールが利かなくなって氷の上を滑りながらガードレールに激突した。
Kuruma wa kontorooru ga kikanaku natte koori no ue o suberi nagara gaadreeru ni gekitotsu-shita.

slant vi. **[for s.t.to incline away from a right or level line]**
na⌈na⌉me ni na⌉ru 斜めになる ① [to become inclined away from a straight or level orientation], ka⌈tamu⌉ku 傾く ① [to become inclined away from a vertical line ⟪fig. "lose vigor"⟫] ⟪lean, slope, incline, careen, decline, sink⟫

EX.| (a) The house slanted about 10 degrees after the earthquake.
地震の後、家が十度位{傾いた/?斜めになった}。
Jishin no ato, ie ga juu-do-gurai {katamuita/?naname ni natta}.
(b) My handwriting somehow always ends up slanted.
私の字はどういうわけかいつも{斜めになって/?傾いて}しまう。
Watashi no ji wa doo iu wake ka itsumo {naname ni natte/?katamuite} shimau.

— n. **[an incline/inclined plane ⟪fig. "tendency"⟫]**

1. ke⌈isha 傾斜 •c [a state of being inclined

S

away from the vertical or the degree of such inclination] ⟪**inclination, slope, dip, list, incline, tilt**⟫

EX. The slant of the pillar was about 30 degrees.
柱の傾斜は三十度位でした。
Hashira no keisha wa san-juu-do-gurai deshita.

2. sha⌉men 斜面 **•c [an inclined surface]** ⟪**slope**⟫

EX. They built their house on a slant that commands an ocean view.
彼らは海の見える斜面に家を建てた。
Kare-ra wa umi no mieru shamen ni ie o tateta.

slap vt. **[for s.o. to strike s.o./s.t./s.a. with s.t. flat]**
⟨-o⟩ (⟨-de⟩) pi⌈sha⌉ri to u⌉tsu ⟨～を⟩(⟨～で⟩) ぴしゃりと打つ ①

EX. Dorothy slapped her child in the face when he didn't listen to her.
子供が言うことを聞かなかった時、ドロシーは手で顔をぴしゃりと打った。
Kodomo ga iu koto o kikanakatta toki, Doroshii wa te de kao o pishari to utta.

— n. **[an act of striking s.o./s.t./s.a. with s.t. flat]**
hi⌈ra-te-uchi 平手打ち

sleep n. **[an act/instance of sleeping]**
ne⌈muri 眠り **/⟨V*masu* of *nemuru* ① sleep/** ⟪**slumber, nap, doze**⟫, **su⌈imin** 睡眠 **•c** ⟪**slumber**⟫

EX. It wasn't until Sleeping Beauty was kissed by the prince that she awoke from her deep sleep.
眠れる美女が深い{眠り/??睡眠}から目をさましたのは王子にキスされた時だった。
Nemureru bijo ga fukai {nemuri/??suimin} kara me o samashita no wa ooji ni kisu-sareta toki datta.

— vi. **[for s.o./s.a. to be in a natural and periodically recurring state of rest characterized by inactivity, unconsciousness, and lessened responsiveness to external surroundings]**
ne⌈muru 眠る ①, **ne⌈ru** 寝る ② **[for s.o./s.a. to lie down or to go to bed or to enter into a state of rest where one is inactive, unconsciousness, and has both eyes closed]**

EX. (**a**) A: How many hours do you usually sleep at night?
夜は大抵何時間{寝ます/眠ります}か。
Yoru wa taitei nan-jikan {nemasu/nemurimasu}ka.
B: I usually sleep about six hours.
大抵六時間ぐらい{寝ます/眠ります}。
Taitei roku-jikan gurai {nemasu/nemurimasu}.

NOTE: In example (a) "*nemasu*" sounds more colloquial than "*nemurimasu*".

EX. (**b**) I didn't sleep well last night.
きのうの晩はよく{寝られませんでした/眠れませんでした}。
Kinoo no ban wa yoku {neraremasendeshita/nemuremasendeshita}.

NOTE: "*Nemuru*" has the same basic meaning as English 'sleep' but it has the additional figurative meaning of "for s.t. valuable to remain undiscovered."

sleepy adj. **[feeling a desire to sleep]**
ne⌈mui 眠い adj(*i*). **[to feel like sleeping]** ⟪**drowsy**⟫, **ne⌈mutai** 眠たい adj(*i*). **[to want to sleep]** ⟪**drowsy**⟫

EX. A: You look sleepy, Mike.
マイク、{眠/眠た}そうだね。
Maiku, {nemu/nemuta} soo da ne.
B: Yeah, I was up until three o'clock this morning.
うん、今朝の三時まで起きていたからね。
Un, kesa no san-ji made okite ita kara ne.

sleeve n. **[the part of a shirt that covers the arms]**
so⌈de そで **[the part of a shirt that covers the arms ⟪fig. "wing of a building"⟫]**

EX. I got my shirt sleeves caught on a rose thorn.
僕はシャツのそでをバラのとげに引っ掛けてしまった。
Boku wa shatsu no sode o bara no toge ni hikkakete shimatta.

slender adj. **[gracefully thin]**
ho┌so-naga┐i 細長い adj(*i*). **[long and having little width]** ⟪**long and narrow, lean and tall**⟫, **ho┌sso┐ri-shita N** ほっそりしたN /⟨**Vinf. past of *hossori-suru*** ③ **get slim**/, **ho┌sso┐ri-shite iru** (**N**) ほっそりしている(**N**) /⟨**V*te iru* of *hossori-suru*** ③ **get slim**/ ② **[small in girth in proportion to height usu. of a person's length]** ⟪**slim, slight**⟫, **su┌ra┐tto-shita N** すらっとしたN, **su┌ra┐tto-shite iru** (**N**) すらっとしている(**N**) **[**(**for a body/bodily part**) **to be pleasantly slim and tall]** ⟪**slim, svelte**⟫

EX. (**a**) How did you get to look so slender?
どうやってそんなに{ほっそりした/すらっとした/ほっそりしている/?すらっとしている/*細長い}体になったの?
*Doo-yatte sonnani {hossori-shita/ suratto-shita/hossori-shite iru/?suratto-shite iru/*hoso-nagai} karada ni natta no?*
(**b**) You always manage to stay so slender, Sharon. How do you do it?
シャロンはいつも{ほっそりしている/すらっとしている/*細長い}のね。その秘けつは何なの。
Sharon wa itsu-mo {hossori-shite iru/ suratto-shite iru/hoso-nagai} no ne. Sono hiketsu wa nan na no.
(**c**) The slender river snaked through the forest.
{細長い/*ほっそりした/*ほっそりしている/*すらっとした/*すらっとしている}川が森の中を曲がりくねって流れていた。
*{Hoso-nagai/*Hossori-shita/*Hossori-shite iru/*Suratto-shita/*Suratto-shite iru} kawa ga mori no naka o magari-kunette nagarete ita.*

slice n. **[a thin, broad piece]**
1. hi┌to┐-kire 一切れ **[one thin, broad piece]** ⟪**piece**⟫
EX. I ate only one slice of pizza.
ピザを一切れしか食べませんでした。
Piza o hito-kire shika tabemasen deshita.

—— vt. [to cut/divide s.t. into slices]
⟨**-o**⟩ **u┌suku ki┐ru** ⟨〜を⟩薄く切る ① **[for s.o. to cut s.t. into thin pieces]**
EX. Could you slice this meat?
この肉を薄く切ってくれませんか。
Kono niku o usuku kitte kuremasen ka.
PHRASE: slice off ⟨*-o*⟩ *kiri-toru* ⟨〜を⟩切り取る ⟪cut off, cut out⟫
EX. Can I slice off a small piece of this pie?
このパイから小さいのを一切れ切り取ってもいいですか。
Kono pai kara chiisai no o hito-kire kiri-totte mo ii desu ka.

slide vi. **[to move rapidly and smoothly over a surface with firm, continuous contact]**
su┌be┐ru 滑る ① **[to move quickly and smoothly over a surface]** ⟪**glide, skate, slip**⟫
EX. We slid down the hill on our bottoms.
しりもちをついた格好で丘を滑り下りた。
Shiri-mochi o tsuita kakkoo de oka o suberi-orita.

—— n. [an act/result of sliding or s.t. that slides]
1. su┌raido スライド **•f [a transparency plate bearing a picture or an act of sliding towards a base in baseball]**
EX. I took a lot of slides during my stay in China.
中国にいた時、スライドをたくさん撮りました。
Chuugoku ni ita toki, suraido o takusan torimashita.
2. su┌beri┐-dai 滑り台 **[a chute for children]**
EX. The children are enjoying themselves on the slide.
子供たちは滑り台に乗って楽しんでいる。
Kodomo-tachi wa suberi-dai ni notte tanoshinde iru.
3. na┌dare 雪崩 **[the fall down a slope of a mass of snow]** ⟪**avalanche, snowslide**⟫, **ji-┌su┐beri** 地滑り **[the fall down a slope of a mass of land]**

slight adj. **[small in amount or degree]**
su┌ko┐shi 少し adv. **[**(**in**) **a small number/**

S

quantity or (to) a small degree] ((a little, a few)), cho⌉tto ちょっと adv. [for a short time or in a small quantity or to a small degree] ((for a moment, a little bit))

EX. (**a**) I had a slight headache this morning.
今朝{少し/ちょっと}頭が痛かった。
Kesa {sukoshi/chotto} atama ga itakatta.
(**b**) I have some slight anxiety about my future.
私は自分の将来について{少し/ちょっと}不安があります。
Watashi wa jibun no shoorai ni-tsuite {sukoshi/chotto} fuan ga arimasu.

—— vt. **[for s.o. to treat s.o. as not being worth one's attention]**
⟨-o⟩ na⌈ozari ni suru ⟨～を⟩なおざりにする ③ [for s.o. to do s.t. carelessly/poorly] ((neglect, disregard)), ⟨-o⟩ ba⌈ka-ni-suru ⟨～を⟩ばかにする ③ •c [for s.o. to treat s.o./s.t./s.a. with disrespect] ((hold in contempt, look down on, despise, make fun of))

EX. People who slight their duties like that don't have much hope of advancement in this firm.
この会社では、あんな風に仕事を{なおざりにする/ばかにする}人はほとんど昇進の見込みがない。
Kono kaisha de wa, anna fuu ni shigoto o {naozari ni suru/baka-ni-suru} hito wa hotondo shooshin no mikomi ga nai.

slightly adv. **[to a very small degree]**
su⌈ko⌉shi 少し [(in) a small number/quantity or (to) a small degree] ((a little, a few)), cho⌉tto ちょっと [for a short time or in a small quantity or to a small degree] ((for a moment, a few, a little))

EX. A: How are you feeling today?
今日は具合はどうですか。
Kyoo wa guai wa doo desu ka.
B: I'm feeling slightly better.
{少し/ちょっと}具合がよくなりました。
{Sukoshi/Chotto} guai ga yoku narimashita.

slim adj. **[small in quantity or small in girth/thickness in relation to height/length]**
1. ho⌈sso⌉ri-shita N ほっそりしたN [small in girth in proportion to height, usu. of a person] ((slender)), ho⌈sso⌉ri-shite iru (N) ほっそりしている(N)

EX. Michelle has a slim body.
ミッシェルはほっそりした体をしている。
Missheru wa hossori-shita karada o shite iru.

2. su⌈kuna⌉i 少ない adj(*i*). **[less than usual in number/quantity] ((few, little, rare))**

EX. A: Do you think you can get the scholarship?
奨学金がもらえると思いますか。
Shoogaku-kin ga morae-ru to omoimasu ka.
B: My chances seem very slim.
その可能性はとても少なそうです。
Sono kanoo-sei wa totemo sukuna-soo desu.

slip vi. **[to suddenly and accidentally slide on a surface]**
1. su⌈be⌉ru 滑る ① [to move quickly and smoothly over a surface] ((glide, slide, skate)), (su⌈ru⌉tto) su⌈be⌉tte ko⌈robu (するっと)滑って転ぶ ① [for s.o./s.a. to lose one's footing on a smooth surface and fall down]

EX. Each winter I slip at least a couple of times on icy streets.
冬にはいつも、凍った道で、少なくとも二、三回は{滑る/滑って転ぶ}。
Fuyu ni wa itsu-mo, kootta michi de, sukunaku-tomo ni, san-kai wa {suberu/subette korobu}.

2. (shi⌈ranai uchi ni ji⌈kan ga) ta⌉tsu (知らないうちに時間が)たつ ① [for time to lapse before one becomes aware of it] ((pass, go by, expire))

EX. The time slipped by quickly while I was talking with my friend.
友達と話しているうちに、あっと言う間に時間がたってしまった。
Tomodachi to hanashite iru uchi ni, atto iu ma ni jikan ga tatte shimatta.

3. (ki⌈ka⌉i ga) na⌈ku naru (機会が)なくなる ① [for an opportunity/chance to become

S

lost/gone] ⟪**be lost, be missing, run short, disappear**⟫

EX. During the year I was ill, my chances for promotion gradually slipped away.
一年病気している間に、昇進の機会が次第になくなってしまった。
Ichi-nen byooki shite iru aida ni, shoosin no kikai ga shidai ni nakunatte shimatta.

slipper n. **[footgear that can be easily slipped on and off]**
su⌈ri⌉ppa スリッパ •**f**

EX. Japanese wear slippers in Western style rooms.
日本人は洋間ではスリッパをはきます。
Nihon-jin wa yooma de wa surippa o hakimasu.

slit n. **[a long narrow cut/opening]**
(ho⌈so-naga⌉i) ki⌈ri⌉-kuchi (細長い)切り口, **su⌈ri⌉tto** スリット •**f [a long, narrow cut in a woman's skirt]**

EX. It seems that long skirts with slits are popular this year.
今年はスリットの入った長いスカートがはやっているらしい。
Kotoshi wa suritto no haitta nagai sukaato ga hayatte iru rashii.

slope n. **[an inclined line/plane]**
1. **ke⌈isha** 傾斜 •**c [a state of being inclined away from the vertical or the degree of such inclination]** ⟪**inclination, dip, slant, incline, tilt**⟫, **ko⌈oba⌉i** こう配 •**c [a scientific term for an incline/gradient]** ⟪**incline, grade, gradient**⟫

EX. The slope of the roof is about 20 degrees.
屋根の{傾斜/こう配}は二十度位だ。
Yane no {keisha/koobai} wa ni-juu-do-gurai da.

2. **sa⌈ka⌉** 坂 **[a stretch of road or path that rises or falls]** ⟪**incline, hill**⟫

EX. This slope is steep, so it's hard to climb.
この坂は急だから、上るのが大変です。
Kono saka wa kyuu da kara, noboru no ga taihen desu.

slot n. **[a long, narrow opening/groove]**
1. **(ho⌈so-naga⌉i) a⌈na⌉** (細長い)穴 **[a narrow opening]**, **su⌈ro⌉tto** スロット •**f**

EX. Put your coin in this slot.
この{細長い穴/スロット}にコインを入れなさい。
Kono {hoso-nagai ana/surotto} ni koin o irenasai.

2. **(shi⌈meru-be⌉ki)** {**ba⌈sho/i⌉chi/ji⌈kan(-tai)**} (占めるべき){場所/位置/時間(帯)} •**c [a place/position/time to be occupied by s.o./s.t.]** ⟪**place, position**⟫

EX. There is a slot of time reserved every evening on the news for public announcements.
毎晩のニュースには公共のお知らせのために取ってある時間帯がある。
Mai-ban no nyuusu ni wa kookyoo no o-shirase no tame ni totte aru jikan-tai ga aru.

slow adj. **[moving at a low speed]**
1. **o⌈soi** 遅い adj(*i*). **[taking more time than is normal or occurring at a point in time after that which is normal or expected]** ⟪**late, tardy**⟫ ↔ **hayai** はやい adj(*i*).; **yu⌈kku⌉ri** ゆっくり adv. **[intentionally not hurrying]** ⟪**unhurriedly, leisurely**⟫, **no⌈ro⌉i** のろい adj(*i*). **[not alert, lively, or moving quickly ⟨s⟩]** ⟪**tardy, sluggish, slack, dull**⟫
㊥ "quick"▷速い, "early"▷早い

EX. (**a**) My word processor is very slow.
僕のワープロはとても{遅い/ゆっくりだ/のろい}。
Boku no waapuro wa totemo {osoi/yukkuri da/noroi}.
(**b**) He's really slow. It took him a couple of days to understand my joke.
あいつはとても{のろい/?遅い/*ゆっくりだ}よ。僕の冗談が分かるのに四、五日かかったんだからね。
*Aitsu wa totemo {noroi/?osoi/*yukkuri da} yo. Boku no joodan ga wakaru no ni shi, go-nichi kakatta n da kara ne.*

2. **fu-⌈ke⌉ikina** 不景気な adj(*na*). •**c [(for business) to be sluggish]** ⟪**dull, slack**⟫ ↔ **keiki ga ii** 景気がいい adj(*i*).

EX. The Japanese economy has been slow lately.
最近、日本経済は不景気です。
Saikin, Nihon-keizai wa fu-keiki desu.

S

—— vt. [to cause movement to be slow(er)] ⟨-o⟩ o⌈soku suru ⟨〜を⟩遅くする ③ [for s.o. to cause s.t. to take place late/to be more time-consuming], ⟨-no⟩ so⌉kudo o o⌈to⌉su ⟨〜の⟩速度を落とす ① [for s.o. to lessen the speed of s.t.]

slowly adv. **[in a slow manner]**
o⌈soku 遅く /⟨adj(*i*). *ku* of *osoi* slow/ [for an event or action to require more than the normal or expected amount of time or to occur after the normal or expected point in time], no⌉ro-noro のろのろ [for a physical action to occur in such a way as to lack speed and liveliness], yu⌈kku⌉ri (to) ゆっくり(と) [intentionally not hurrying] ⟪unhurriedly, leisurely⟫ ↔ hayaku {早く/速く}

EX. (**a**) Why is he walking so slowly?
どうしてあの人はあんなに{ゆっくり/のろのろ/?遅く}歩いているんですか。
Dooshite ano hito wa annani {yukkuri/noro-noro/osoku} aruite iru n desu ka.
(**b**) Could you speak more slowly?
もっと{ゆっくり/*遅く/*のろのろ}話してくださいませんか。
*Motto {yukkuri/*osoku/*noro-noro} hanashite kudasaimasen ka.*
(**c**) On this expressway, you are not supposed to travel more slowly than 40 mph.
この高速道路では時速四十マイルより{遅く/ゆっくり/のろのろ}走ってはだめなんです。
Kono koosoku-dooro de wa jisoku yon-juu-mairu yori {osoku/yukkuri/noro-noro} hashitte wa damenan desu.

S

small adj. **[less than average in size/quantity ⟪fig. "trivial"⟫]**
1. chi⌈isa⌉i 小さい adj(*i*). **[less than average in volume/size/area/height/number/quantity/degree/scale] ↔ ookii 大きい** adj(*i*).; **chi⌉isana N 小さなN ↔ ookina N 大きなN**

NOTE: *Chiisai* can be *chiisana* before a noun as in *chiisana hon* (a small book). The difference between *chiisai hon* and *chiisana hon* is that the former is descriptive, objective and measurable while the latter carries an emotive overtone. Note the following example, in which only *chiisana* is acceptable: a small kindness *{chiisana/*chiisai} shinsetsu.*

EX. (**a**) I bought a small word processor.
私は{小さい/小さな}ワープロを買いました。
Watashi wa {chiisai/chiisana} waapuro o kaimashita.
(**b**) When I was small, I lived in a big city.
{小さい/*小さな}時は大きい町に住んでいました。
*{Chiisai/*Chiisana} toki wa ookii machi ni sunde imashita.*

2. su⌈kuna⌉i 少ない adj(*i*). **[less than usual in number/quantity] ⟪few, little, limited, scarce⟫ ↔ ooi 多い** adj(*i*).

EX. There are only a small number of students in this school who can speak Japanese.
この学校では日本語が話せる学生は少ないです。
Kono gakkoo de wa Nihon-go ga hanase-ru gakusei wa sukunai desu.

3. ku⌈daranai くだらない adj(*i*). **[not worthy of discussing/mentioning] ⟪worthless, trashy, trifling, insignificant⟫**

EX. Why are you worried about such a small matter?
どうしてこんなくだらないことにくよくよしているんですか。
Dooshite konna kudaranai koto ni kuyo-kuyo-shite iru n desu ka.

smart adj. **[characterized by sharpness in mind/movement/dress]**
1. ri⌈koona 利口な •c [quick in thinking understanding] ⟪clever, bright, intelligent, shrewd⟫, a⌈ta⌉ma ga i⌉i 頭がいい adj(*i*). **[for s.o./s.a. to have a well-developed ability to learn, reason, and understand] ⟪clever, bright, sharp, intelligent⟫ ↔ atama ga warui 頭が悪い** adj(*i*).

EX. Tom is smart. He knows how to deal with his boss.
トムは{利口だ/頭がいい}ね。上司とのつきあい方を心得ているよ。

Tomu wa {rikoo da/atama ga ii} ne. Jooshi to no tsuki-ai-kata o kokoro-ete iru yo.

2. wa⌈ru-gashiko⌉i 悪賢い adj(*i*). **[to be clever in evil matters]** **⟪cunning, sly, crafty⟫**

EX. Be careful. Dan is very smart.
注意しろよ。ダンはとても悪賢いからね。
Chuui-shiro yo. Dan wa totemo waru-gashikoi kara ne.

smash vt. **[to break s.t. into pieces violently, noisily and abruptly]**

⟨-o⟩ ko⌈na-gona ni ko⌈wa⌉su ⟨〜を⟩粉々に壊す ① [for s.o. to break/shatter s.t. into pieces], ⟨-o⟩ u⌈chi-kuda⌉ku ⟨〜を⟩打ち砕く ① [to break s.t. to pieces by striking it forcefully]

EX. (**a**) All of a sudden Yoshio flared up and began to smash everything within his reach.
突然良男はかっとなって、手当たり次第、物を{粉々に壊し/?打ち砕き}始めた。
Totsuzen Yoshio wa katto natte, te-atari shidai, mono o {kona-gona ni kowashi/?uchi-kudaki}-hajimeta.
(**b**) The accident smashed Ken's hopes of becoming a baseball player.
健はその事故で野球選手になる夢を{打ち砕かれた/*粉々に 壊された}。
*Ken wa sono jiko de yakyuu-senshu ni naru yume o {uchi-kudaka-reta/*kona-gona ni kowasa-reta}.*

— vi. **[for s..t. to be broken/shattered into pieces]**

ko⌈na-gona ni na⌉ru 粉々になる ①

EX. I dropped the glass vase on the floor, and it smashed into pieces.
ガラスの花瓶を床に落としたら、粉々になった。
Garasu no kabin o yuka ni otoshitara, kona-gona ni natta.

— n. **[an act or sound of smashing]**

1. fu⌈nsai 粉砕 •c [an act/result of breaking s.t. into pieces] ⟪pulverization, grinding⟫

2. ha⌈metsu 破滅 •c [the total destruction of s.o.] ⟪destruction, ruin, downfall⟫

3. su⌈ma⌉sshu スマッシュ •f [an overhand (table) tennis/badminton stroke that is difficult to return because of its speed and power]

smell vt. **[for s.o./s.a. to perceive the scent of s.t. by means of the olfactory sense ⟪fig. "detect"⟫]**

1. ⟨-no⟩ ni⌈o⌉i o ka⌉gu ⟨〜の⟩においをかぐ ① [for s.o./s.a. to become aware of s.t. by means of the olfactory sense] ⟪scent, sniff⟫

EX. I love to smell roses.
バラのにおいをかぐのが大好きです。
Bara no nioi o kagu no ga dai-suki desu.

2. ⟨-o⟩ ka⌉gi-tsuke⌉ru ⟨〜を⟩かぎつける ② [for s.o./s.a. to find out s.t. by means of the olfactory sense ⟪fig. "detect"⟫]

EX. The detective smelled something fishy about the old man.
探偵は老人に何か怪しいものをかぎつけた。
Tantei wa roojin ni nani-ka ayashii mono o kagi-tsuketa.

— vi. **[for the scent of s.t. to come to the olfactory sense]**

ni⌈o⌉u におう ① [to have/emit a scent/odor] ⟪give out a smell, reek⟫, ku⌈sa⌉i 臭い adj(*i*). **[having a bad odor] ⟪stinking, smelly⟫, ⟨-no⟩ ni⌈o⌉i ga suru ⟨〜の⟩においがする ③ [for there to be a scent of s.t./s.o./s.a.]**

EX. (**a**) Something smells! Did you turn off the gas?
何か{におう/臭い/?においがする}ね。ガス、とめた?
Nani-ka {niou/kusai/?nioi ga suru} ne. Gasu, tometa?
(**b**) This rose smells lovely!
このバラ、いいにおいがするね。
Kono bara, ii nioi ga suru ne.
(**c**) Your socks smell!
君の靴下、{におう/臭い/?においがする}ね。
Kimi no kutsu-shita, {niou/kusai/?nioi ga suru} ne.
(**d**) Your hands smell of soap.
あなたの手は石けんのにおいがします。
Anata no te wa sekken no nioi ga shimasu.

— n. **[an act or result of smelling or the olfactory sense]**

1. ka⌈gu koto かぐこと [an act of smelling]

2. kyu⌈ukaku きゅう覚 •c [the olfactory sense]

3. ni⌈o⌉i におい [a sensation created in the olfactory organs《fig. "smack," "flavor"》], ka⌈ori 香り [good scent]《smell, scent, aroma, fragrance》

EX. I like the smell of this tea.
このお茶の{香り/におい}が好きです。
Kono o-cha no {kaori/nioi} ga suki desu.

smile vi. **[for s.o. to indicate pleasure or amusement by means of a facial expression with the edges of the mouth curved upward]**

1. ni⌉ko-niko-suru にこにこする ③ [for s.o. to make a facial expression indicating pleasure/affection/friendliness without uttering sounds], ho⌈hoe⌉mu ほほえむ ① [for s.o. to make a faint facial expression indicating pleasure/affection/friendliness without uttering sounds ⟨w⟩], ⟨-ni⟩ ho⌈hoemi-kake⌉ru ⟨～に⟩ほほえみかける ② [for s.o. to make a smiling face to s.o. ⟨w⟩]

EX. (**a**) A: Why are you smiling today?
どうして今日は{にこにこして/?ほほえんで/*ほほえみかけて}いるの。
*Dooshite kyoo wa {niko-niko-shite/?hohoende/*hohoemi-kakete} iru no.*
B: Because it's payday.
給料日だからだよ。
Kyuuryoo-bi da kara da yo.
(**b**) American children smile even at strangers.
アメリカの子供たちは知らない人にも{ほほえみかける/?ほほえむ/?にこにこする}。
Amerika no kodomo-tachi wa shiranai hito ni mo {hohoemi-kakeru/?hohoemu/?niko-niko-suru}.
(**c**) The lady in this picture is smiling ever so slightly.
この絵の女性はいつもかすかに{ほほえんで/?ほほえみかけて/*にこにこして}いる。
*Kono e no josei wa itsu-mo kasukani {hohoende/?hohoemi-kakete/*niko-niko-shite} iru.*

2. {ni⌈ya⌉ri to/ni⌈ya⌉tto} {wa⌈rau/suru} {にやりと/にやっと}{笑う ①/する ③} [for s.o. to make a facial expression showing pride/irony/derision]《grin, simper》

EX. Jimmy smiled when he saw that his tennis partner couldn't return his service.
ジミーはテニスのパートナーがサービスを受け損なったのを見て、{にやりと/にやっと}{笑った/した}。
Jimii wa tenisu no paatonaa ga saabisu o uke-sokonatta no o mite, {niyari to/niyatto} {waratta/shita}.

— n. **[an act/instance of smiling]**

e⌉gao 笑顔 [a facial expression indicating pleasure/affection/friendliness]《radiant look》

EX. When I see the smiles of my children, I feel as if all the hard work has been worth it.
子供の笑顔を見ると、こちらの苦労がすべて報われた気がする。
Kodomo no egao o miru to, kochira no kuroo ga subete mukuwa-reta ki ga suru.

smoke n. **[a visible vapor given off by s.t. burning《fig. "s.t. like smoke"》]**

ke⌈muri 煙

EX. Look, smoke is coming out of the window!
見てご覧、窓から煙が出ているよ。
Mite goran, mado kara kemuri ga dete iru yo.

— vi. **[for smoke to be emitted from a place《fig. "smoke a cigarette/cigar"》]**

1. ke⌈muri ga de⌉ru 煙が出る ② [for smoke to come out]

2. ta⌈bako o suu たばこを吸う ① [for s.o. to smoke a cigarette], ha⌈maki o suu 葉巻を吸う ① [for s.o. to breathe in smoke from a cigar]

EX. A: Do you smoke?
{たばこ/葉巻}を吸いますか。
{Tabako/Hamaki} o suimasu ka.
B: I used to smoke, but I stopped.
前は吸っていましたが、やめました。

S

Mae wa sutte imashita ga, yamemashita.

—— vt. [for s.o. to inhale smoke created by s.t. or to expose s.t. (esp. meat) to smoke for preservation]

1. **⟨-o⟩ i⌈bu⌉su** ⟨〜を⟩いぶす ① **[for s.o. to burn s.t. for the purpose of creating smoke or to give a burnt finish to s.t.]** **⟪fumigate, fume⟫**
2. **⟨-o⟩ ku⌈nsei ni suru** ⟨〜を⟩くん製にする ③ •c **[for s.o. to treat meat with smoke for flavoring and curing]**
3. **⟨-o⟩ su⌈u** ⟨〜を⟩吸う ① **[for s.o./s.a to draw liquid/gas into the body through the mouth/nose]** **⟪inhale, breathe, suck, absorb⟫**

smoky adj. **[producing smoke in large quantity]**
ke⌈mu⌉i けむい adj(*i*)., **ke⌈muta⌉i** けむたい adj(*i*). ⟨s⟩

smooth adj. **[for a surface/words/behavior to be free from roughness/irregularities]**

1. **na⌈me⌉rakana** 滑らかな adj(*na*). **[having an even surface without any roughness/ projections]** **⟪soft, velvety⟫, su⌉be-sube-shita N** すべすべしたN **/⟨Vinf. past of *sube-sube-suru* ③ feel smooth/ [of skin/leather/hair having a slippery, even surface]** **⟪velvety, silky, sleek⟫, su⌉be sube shite iru (N)** すべすべしている(N) **/⟨V*te iru* of *sube-sube-suru* ③ feel smooth/**

EX. (**a**) The surface of this desk isn't very smooth.
この机の表面はあまり{滑らかではない/すべすべしていない}。
Kono tsukue no hyoomen wa amari {nameraka dewanai/sube-sube-shite inai}.
(**b**) Yoko's fair and smooth skin is very attractive.
洋子の白くて{すべすべした/すべすべしている/滑らかな}肌はとても魅力的だ。
Yooko no shirokute {sube-sube-shita/ sube-sube-shite iru/namerakana} hada wa totemo miryoku-teki da.

2. **mo⌈no-yawa⌉rakana** もの柔らかな adj(*na*). **[for words/behavior to be suave and gentle]** **⟪mild, gentle, suave, quiet⟫**

EX. He is a smooth talker all right, but I can never tell what he's really thinking.
あの人はもの柔らかな話し方をしますが、本音は分かりません。
Ano hito wa mono-yawarakana hanashi-kata o shimasu ga, honne wa wakarimasen.

—— vt. [for s.o./s.t. to cause a surface to become smooth]

1. **⟨-o⟩ na⌈me⌉rakani suru** ⟨〜を⟩滑らかにする ③ **[for s.o. to cause an uneven surface to become even]**

EX. I smoothed the rough surface of my desk with a plane.
ざらざらの机の表面をかんなで滑らかにした。
Zara-zara no tsukue no hyoomen o kanna de namerakani shita.

2. **⟨-o⟩ no⌈ba⌉su** ⟨〜を⟩のばす ① **[for s.o. to cause s.t. to become longer, usu. vertically ⟪fig. "straighten," "hold out," "postpone," "cultivate (abilities)"⟫]** **⟪lengthen, extend, prolong, stretch, unbend, postpone, defer⟫, ⟨-o⟩ na⌈de-tsukeru** ⟨〜を⟩なで付ける ② **[for s.o. to comb down one's hair]** **⟪slick down one's hair⟫**

㊥ "spatially extend s.t."▷伸ばす, "temporally extend s.t."▷延ばす

EX. (**a**) Would you smooth out the wrinkles in this suit?
この洋服のしわを{伸ばして/*なで付けて}くれない。
*Kono yoofuku no shiwa o {nobashite/ *nade-tsukete} kurenai.*
(**b**) Before he met his date, Jim smoothed out his hair with a comb.
ジムはデートの相手に会う前にくしで髪を{なで付けた/*伸ばした}。
*Jimu wa deeto no aite ni au mae ni kushi de kami o {nade-tsuketa/ *nobashita}.*

snail n.
ka⌈tatsu⌉muri かたつむり, **de⌈nde⌉n-mushi** でんでんむし

EX. He walks like a snail, doesn't he?
あの人はまるで{かたつむり/でんでんむし}のような歩き方をするね。
Ano hito wa marude {katatsumuri/ denden-mushi} no yoona aruki-kata o suru ne.

snake n.
he⌉bi 蛇

EX. I was bitten by a snake while hiking in the forest.
森の中をハイキングしている時に、蛇にかまれた。
Mori no naka o haikingu-shite iru toki ni, hebi ni kama-reta.

snap vt./vi. **[for s.t. to make or for s.o. to cause s.t. to make a sharp cracking sound/ for s.t. to break or for s.o. to cause s.t. to break with such a sound]**
1. pu⌈tsu⌉n to ki⌈re⌉ru ぷつんと切れる ② [for s.t. to be cut suddenly]

EX. The telephone lines snapped due to the force of the wind.
強風で電話線がぷつんと切れた。
Kyoofuu de denwa-sen ga putsun to kireta.

2. ⟨-o⟩ po⌈ki⌉tto o⌉ru ⟨〜を⟩ぽきっと折る ① [for s.o. to break a stick/stick-like object with a sudden action]

EX. The wrestler snapped a 10-inch stick in two.
レスラーは十インチもの太さの棒をぽきっと折った。
Resuraa wa juu-inchi mo no futo-sa no boo o pokitto otta.

—— n. **[an act/result of snapping s.t. or s.t. that gives a snapping sound or the sound that results]**
1. po⌈ki⌉n to o⌈re⌉ru koto ぽきんと折れること [an instance of a stick/stick-like object breaking suddenly with a sharp sound], pu⌈ttsu⌉ri to ki⌈re⌉ru koto ぷっつりと切れること [an instance of s.t. being suddenly cut]
2. {pa⌈chi⌉n/po⌈ki⌉n/pi⌈shi⌉n/cho⌈ki⌉n} to i⌈u o⌈to⌉ {ぱちん/ぽきん/ぴしん/ちょきん}という音 [the sound "pachin/pokin/pishin/chokin"]
3. su⌈nap⌉pu スナップ •f [a buckle/clasp]

snarl vi. **[for s.a. to growl with the teeth bared]**
u⌈na⌉ru うなる ① [for s.a./s.o. to growl in the manner of a dog baring its teeth] ⟪groan, moan, roar, howl, snarl⟫

EX. The neighbor's dog always snarls at the mailman.
隣の犬はいつも郵便配達員に向かってうなる。
Tonari no inu wa itsu-mo yuubin-haitatsu-in ni mukatte unaru.

sneeze vi.
ku⌈sha⌉mi o suru くしゃみをする ③

EX. In early spring I sneeze a lot because I'm allergic to pollen.
花粉アレルギーなので、春先はよくくしゃみをします。
Kafun-arerugii na node, haru-saki wa yoku kushami o shimasu.

—— n. **[an act/instance of sneezing]**
ku⌈sha⌉mi くしゃみ

sniff vi./vt. **[for s.o./s.a. to inhale a short, audible breath through the nose ⟪fig. "indicate ridicule/contempt"⟫]**
⟨-o⟩ ku⌉n-kun ka⌈gu ⟨〜を⟩くんくんかぐ ① [for s.o./s.a. to to take in short, forceful breaths in order to catch the scent of s.t.]

EX. The dog sniffed at the garbage can.
犬はごみ箱をくんくんかいだ。
Inu wa gomi-bako o kun-kun kaida.

—— n. **[an act of sniffing]**
ku⌉n-kun ka⌈gu koto くんくんかぐこと [an act of taking in short, forceful breaths to catch the scent of s.t.]

snore vi. **[a grunting sound made while sleeping]**
i⌈biki⌉ o ka⌉ku いびきをかく ①

EX. I can't sleep well because my husband snores so much.
主人がすごくいびきをかくので、よく寝られないんです。
Shujin ga sugoku ibiki o kaku node, yoku ne-rarenai n desu.

—— n. **[an act/instance of snoring]**
i⌈biki⌉ いびき

snort vi. **[for s.a./s.o. to exhale forcibly through the nose]**
ha⌈na o narasu 鼻をならす ① [for s.o./s.a. to force breath suddenly and violently through the nostrils, making a harsh sound]

snow n. **[crystals of ice that fall from the sky 《fig. "s.t. like snow"》]**
1. yu⌈ki⌉ 雪
EX. (**a**) Yesterday five inches of snow fell.
きのう雪が五インチも降った。
Kinoo yuki ga go-inchi mo futta.
(**b**) Around here the snow starts to melt in April.
この辺では雪は四月に溶け始める。
Kono hen de wa yuki wa shi-gatsu ni toke-hajimeru.
(**c**) Her skin is as white as snow.
彼女の肌は雪のように白い。
Kanojo no hada wa yuki no yooni shiroi.
2. yu⌈ki⌉ no yo⌉ona mono 雪のようなもの [s.t. white like snow]
—— vi. **[snow falls]**
yu⌈ki⌉ ga fu⌉ru 雪が降る ①
EX. It snowed quite a bit last night.
ゆうべは雪がかなり降った。
Yuube wa yuki ga kanari futta.

snowstorm n. **[a storm with falling snow]**
fu⌉buki 吹雪 /(V*masu* of *fubuku* ① blow hard/
EX. Jim had to go to work in the middle of a snowstorm.
ジムは吹雪の中を出勤しなければならなかった。
Jimu wa fubuki no naka o shukkin-shinakereba naranakatta.

snowy adj. **[currently snowing or potentially abounding in snow or resembling snow]**
1. yu⌈ki⌉ ga fu⌉ru 雪が降る ① [for snow to fall]
EX. Tomorrow it will be snowy.
明日は雪が降るでしょう。
Asu wa yuki ga furu deshoo.
2. yu⌈ki⌉ ga o⌉oi 雪が多い adj(*i*). **[for snow to fall a lot]**
EX. It's very snowy in Hokkaido, the northernmost island of Japan.
日本の最北の島、北海道はとても雪が多い。
Nihon no saihoku no shima, Hokkaidoo wa totemo yuki ga ooi.
3. yu⌈ki no yo⌉ona 雪のような adj(*na*). **[like snow]**
EX. The snowy white of the cherry blossoms formed a breathtaking contrast against the deep blue sky in the background.
桜の雪のような白さが背景の青空と絶妙のコントラストを成していた。
Sakura no yuki no yoona shiro-sa ga haikei no ao-zora to zetsumyoo no kontorasuto o nashite ita.

so pron. **[a pronoun referring to the propositional content of an utterance]**
so⌉o そう adv. **[an adverb referring to the way s.t. has been stated or is believed to be the case by the hearer]** 《like that, that way, all that》
EX. (**a**) A: Do you think Scott loves Liz?
スコットはリズを愛してると思う?
Sukotto wa Rizu o aishite ru to omou?
B: No, I don't think so.
ううん、そうは思わない。
Uun, soo wa omowanai.
(**b**) A: I heard that Mr. Yoshinaga is going to China.
吉永さんは中国に行くそうだね。
Yoshinaga-san wa Chuugoku ni iku sooda ne.
B: Who told you so?
だれがそう言ったんですか。
Dare ga soo itta n desu ka.
(**c**) A: I'm really tired.
本当に疲れちゃった。
Hontoo ni tsukarechatta.
B: So am I.
私もそう。
Watashi mo soo .
—— adv. **[to that extent/very]**
1. so⌈nnani そんなに [to an extent indicated by s.t. said or written earlier,

S

either by another person (esp. the hearer) or by the first person, in either case implying that the information in question is not common knowledge to the first person and the other person]

EX. I didn't intend to stay in Japan for so long.
私は日本にそんなに長くいるつもりではなかったんです。
Watashi wa Nihon ni sonnani nagaku iru tsumori dewanakatta n desu.

2. so⌈re to o⌈naji yo⌉oni それと同じように [like that]

EX. Just as you love Mozart, so I love Bach.
君はモーツァルトが好きですね。それと同じように僕はバッハが好きです。
Kimi wa Mootsaruto ga suki desu ne. Sore to onaji yooni boku wa Bahha ga suki desu.

3. to⌈temo とても [to a great extent (in affirmative contexts) or no matter what one does (in negative contexts)] ((very, extremely, by no means, utterly, at all))

S

EX. I'm so happy when I'm with you.
あなたと一緒にいるととても幸せよ。
Anata to issho ni iru to totemo shiawase yo.

— conj. **[a coordinate conjunction indicating reason/cause/purpose]**

1. da⌉kara だから [a conjunction used to state the result/conclusion of a cause given in the preceeding sentence] ((therefore, consequently, for that reason)), so⌈ko-de そこで [a conjunction that indicates the basis upon or reason for which s.t. else consequentially takes place] ((then, upon this, therefore, thereupon)), shi⌈tagatte 従って /⟨V*te* of *shitagau* ① follow/ [a conjunction indicating that the result stated in the following clause follows necessarily from the foregoing situation ⟨fml⟩] ((therefore, accordingly))

EX. (**a**) The sushi bar was closed so we went out for pizza.
すし屋が閉まっていたんです。{だから/そこで/*従って}ピザを食べに行きました。
*Sushi-ya ga shimatte ita n desu. {Dakara/Soko-de/*Shitagatte} piza o tabe ni ikimashita.*
(**b**) This ends my presentation of computer basics, so let me answer any questions you may have before I go on to the next topic.
以上でコンピューターの基礎についての話を終わります。{そこで/*だから/*従って}先に進む前にご質問がありましたら、お答えしたいと思います。
*Ijoo de konpyuutaa no kiso ni-tsuite no hanashi o owarimasu. {Soko-de/*Dakara/*Shitagatte} saki ni susumu mae ni go-shitsumon ga arimashitara, o-kotae-shi-tai to omoimasu.*
(**c**) In this town you cannot drink if you're under 21. You are 18, so, for you to drink is against the law.
この町では二十一歳未満の者は酒を飲んではいけないんです。あなたは十八ですね。{だから/従って/*そこで}飲酒は法律違反です。
*Kono machi de wa ni-juu-is-sai miman no mono wa sake o nonde wa ikenai n desu. Anata wa juu-hachi desu ne. {Dakara/Shitagatte/*Soko-de} inshu wa hooritsu-ihan desu.*

2. {⟨-no⟩/Sinf.} ta⌈me⌉ (ni) {⟨〜の⟩/Sinf.}ため(に) [for the benefit of s.o./s.a./s.t. or for the purpose/reason/cause indicated in the preceding clause] ((on account of, for the benefit of, for the good of, for the sake of, in order to, because of)), Vinf. yo⌉o(ni) Vinf.よう(に) conj. **[to do s.t. in such a way that] ((so that))**

EX. (**a**) I'm going to Japan so I can learn karate.
空手を習う{ために/*ように}日本へ行きます。
*Karate o narau {tame ni/*yooni} Nihon e ikimasu.*
(**b**) Please speak a bit more loudly so the elderly gentleman can hear you.
おじいさんに聞こえる{ように/*ために}もう少し大きい声で話してください。
*O-jii-san ni kikoeru {yooni/*tame ni}*

moo sukoshi ookii koe de hanashite kudasai.

PHRASE: if so *moshi soo nara(ba)* もしそうなら(ば)

EX. A: Mary seems to love Sunny.
メアリーはサニーが大好きなようだよ。
Mearii wa Sanii ga dai-sukina yooda yo.
B: If so, why won't she marry him?
もしそうなら(ば)、どうして結婚しないんでしょうね。
Moshi soo nara(ba), dooshite kekkon-shinai n deshoo ne.

PHRASE: so…that *amari…{kara/node}* あまり…{から/ので}

EX. It's spring, but it's still so cold that I had to turn on the heater.
春だというのに、まだすごく寒い{ので/から}ストーブをつけなければならなかった。
Haru da to iu noni, mada sugoku samui {node/kara} sutoobu o tsukenakereba naranakatta.

PHRASE: so what? *sore ga doo shita* それがどうした, *dakara doo datte iu n da* だからどうだって言うんだ。

EX. A: You can't speak French very well, can you?
君はフランス語があまり話せないんだろう?
Kimi wa Furansu-go ga amari hanase-nai n daroo?
B: So what?
{それがどうした/だからどうだって言うんだ}。
{Sore ga doo shita/Dakara doo datte iu n da}.

soak vt. **[to make s.t. become fully wet/saturated with liquid]**
1. ⟨-o⟩ bi⌈sho-nure ni suru ⟨〜を⟩びしょぬれにする ③ [for s.o. to make s.t./s.o./s.a. thoroughly wet] ⟪drench⟫
2. ⟨-o⟩ ⟨-ni⟩ tsu⌈keru ⟨〜を⟩⟨〜に⟩つける ② [for s.o. to put s.t. in liquid or to steep foodstuffs in liquid/salt/sugar/soybean paste/rice-bran paste for flavoring] ⟪steep in, pickle⟫
㊅ "steep foodstuffs in liquid/salt/sugar/paste"▷漬ける, otherwise ▷つける

EX. Before you cook rice you have to wash it, soak it in water, and let it sit for 30 minutes or so.
ごはんをたく前に、お米は研いで、水に漬けて、三十分ぐらいそのままにしておきます。
Gohan o taku mae ni, o-kome wa toide, mizu ni tsukete, san-jup-pun-gurai sono mama ni shite okimasu.

—— vi. **[for s.t. to be soaked]**
1. bi⌈sho-nure ni na⌉ru びしょぬれになる ① [for s.o./s.a. to become thoroughly wet] ⟪get drenched⟫
2. ⟨-ni⟩ shi⌈mi-ko⌉mu ⟨〜に⟩しみ込む ① [for liquid/ointment to penetrate into the inside of s.t.] ⟪penetrate, filter into, seep into⟫

EX. The rain soaked through to my underwear.
雨が下着にまでしみ込んだ。
Ame ga shita-gi ni made shimi-konda.

so-and-so n. **[an unspecified person]**
da⌉re-sore だれそれ [an unspecified person]

EX. She's always going around the office spreading rumors that so-and-so is getting divorced or that so-and-so is in trouble with the boss. I'm just fed up with her.
彼女はだれそれが離婚するとか、だれそれが上司とうまく行っていないとか、会社でうわさを言いふらしてばかりいる。もう彼女にはうんざりだ。
Kanojo wa dare-sore ga rikon-suru toka, dare-sore ga jooshi to umaku itte inai toka, kaisha de uwasa o ii-furashite bakari iru. Moo kanojo ni wa unzari da.

soap n.
se⌈kken 石けん •c

EX. Wash your dirty hands with soap.
汚い手を石けんで洗いなさい。
Kitanai te o sekken de arainasai.

soar vi. **[for a bird/plane/price to fly/rise high]**
1. ma⌈i-aga⌉ru 舞い上がる ① [for s.a./s.t. to fly high into the sky] ⟪go up into the sky,

S

fly high》), ta˥kaku a┌garu 高く上がる ① [for s.t. to reach a high point] 《climb, ascend, rise》

EX. I always experience a thrill whenever I see an airplane take off and soar into the sky.
飛行機が離陸して空に{舞い上がる/高く上がる}のを見ると、いつもスリルを感じる。
Hikoo-ki ga ririku-shite sora ni {mai-agaru/takaku agaru} no o miru to itsu-mo suriru o kanjiru.

2. bo┌otoo-suru 暴騰する ③ •c [for prices to suddenly rise very high] 《jump, rise steeply》

EX. Stocks soared in Tokyo at news of the settlement of the trade dispute.
貿易摩擦の解決が報道されると、東京で株が暴騰した。
Booeki-masatsu no kaiketsu ga hoodoo-sareru to, Tookyoo de kabu ga bootoo-shita.

so-called adj. **[known generally by this term]**

S

i┌wa˥yuru N いわゆるN

EX. Mr. Suzuki graduated from one of the so-called "elite" universities.
鈴木さんはいわゆる「エリート」の大学を卒業した。
Suzuki-san wa iwayuru 'eriito' no daigaku o sotsugyoo-shita.

social adj. **[having to do with (high) society 《fig. "sociable"》]**

1. sha˥kai no N 社会のN •c [of society]

EX. Bullying in the elementary and junior high schools is one of Japan's major social problems.
小、中学校でのいじめは日本(の)社会の大きな問題の一つだ。
Shoo-, chuu-gakkoo de no ijime wa Nihon (no) shakai no ookina mondai no hitotsu da.

2. sha┌koo-tekina 社交的な adj(*na*). **•c [having a desire to interact with others] 《sociable》**

EX. A: What kind of a person is she?
彼女はどんな人ですか。
Kanojo wa donna hito desu ka.
B: She's a very sociable person.
実に社交的な人です。
Jitsu ni shakoo-tekina hito desu.

3. sha┌ko˥o-kai no N 社交界のN •c [of high society]

— n. **[an informal get-together]**
ko┌nshi˥n-kai 懇親会 •c [a meeting for the purpose of baving people get to know each other better]

society n. **[an organized community of people/animals/plants living in a similar environment]**

1. sha˥kai 社会 •c [a homogeneous group of people living together in a similar environment] 《world, community》, se˥ken 世間 •c [people who belong to the same community] 《world, public, people》

EX. (**a**) Japanese society is often called a vertical society.
日本の社会はよく縦{社会/*世間}と言われる。
*Nihon no shakai wa yoku tate-{shakai/ *seken} to iwa-reru.*
(**b**) Japanese people seem to be very concerned with how they are viewed by society.
日本人は{世間/*社会}にどう見られるかに非常に気を遣うようだ。
*Nihon-jin wa {seken/*shakai} ni doo mi-rareru ka ni hijooni ki o tsukau yooda.*

2. kyo┌okai 協会 •c [an organization established and maintained by a group of people cooperating together for some public purpose] 《association, league, confraternity》, ga˥kkai 学会 •c [an academic organization or a meeting of such an organization] 《learned society, institute》

EX. (**a**) I am a member of the Anthropological Society of Japan.
私は日本人類学{学会/*協会}の会員です。
*Watashi wa Nihon Jinrui-gaku {Gakkai/*Kyookai} no kaiin desu.*
(**b**) There is a society for the prevention of

cruelty to animals in Japan.
日本には動物愛護{協会/*学会}がある。
*Nihon ni wa doobutsu-aigo-{kyookai/ *gakkai} ga aru.*

3. sha⌈ko⌉o-kai 社交界 •c [the social community of the affluent] ⟪fashionable world, highsociety⟫

sociology n.
sha⌈ka⌉i-gaku 社会学 •c

sock n.
ku⌈tsu⌉-shita 靴下 [a stocking], so⌉kkusu ソックス •f

EX. Put on your socks.
{靴下/ソックス}をはきなさい。
{Kutsu-shita/Sokkusu} o hakinasai.

sod n. **[a layer/piece of turf]**
1. shi⌈ba-fu 芝生 [an area covered with closely cut grass as in a garden/park]
2. shi⌈ba-tsuchi⌉ 芝土 [a piece of turf]

soda n.
so⌉oda ソーダ •f, so⌈oda⌉-sui ソーダ水 •f+c

EX. I'll have soda.
僕はソーダ(水)を注文する。
Boku wa sooda(-sui) o chuumon-suru.

sodium n.
na⌈tori⌉umu ナトリウム •f

sofa n.
so⌉faa ソファ •f

EX. Please have a seat on the sofa.
ソファーにお座りください。
Sofaa ni o-suwari kudasai.

soft adj. **[pleasing to the senses due to a lack of harshness/roughness/intensity]**
1. ya⌈wa⌉rakana 柔らかな adj(*na*). **[for a physical object/food/light/attitude/speech to be pleasing to the tactual/visual/auditory senses due to a lack of hardness/harshness/ intensity] ⟪gentle, tender⟫, ya⌈waraka⌉i 柔らかい** adj(*i*). ↔ **katai かたい** adj(*i*).

NOTE: *Yawarakana* sounds more subjective and emotive than *yawarakai.*

EX. (**a**) The hotel's bed was too soft for me to enjoy a good night's sleep.
ホテルのベッドが柔らかすぎてよく寝られなかった。
Hoteru no beddo ga yawaraka-sugite yoku ne-rarenakatta.
(**b**) The baby's skin is sensitive so you'd better use soft tissues.
赤ちゃんの肌は敏感だから、{柔らかい/柔らかな}ティッシュを使った方がいい。
Aka-chan no hada wa binkan da kara, {yawarakai/yawarakana} tisshu o tsukatta hoo ga ii.
(**c**) Mr. Hirai is a strict teacher though the way he talks is always soft.
平井先生は話し方はいつも{柔らかい/?柔らかだ}けど、厳しい先生です。
Hirai-sensei wa hanashi-kata wa itsu-mo {yawarakai/?yawaraka da} kedo, kibishii sensei desu.
(**d**) The color of the rooms in my apartment is a soft, light green.
私のアパートの部屋の色は{柔らかい/柔らかな}薄緑です。
Watashi no apaato no heya no iro wa {yawarakai/yawarakana} usu-midori desu.

2. shi⌉zukana 静かな adj(*na*). **[comfortably quiet/peaceful] ⟪quiet, silent, calm, still, placid, serene, peaceful, gentle, tranquil⟫, ya⌈wa⌉rakana 柔らかな** adj(*na*). SEE soft 1

EX. The sound of soft baroque music soothes my sprits.
{静かな/柔らかな}バロック音楽の音は私の心を静めてくれます。
{Shizukana/Yawarakana} Barokku-ongaku no oto wa watashi no kokoro o shizumete kuremasu.

softly adv. **[in a soft way/fashion]**
1. ya⌈waraka⌉ku 柔らかく /⟨adj(*i*). *ku* of *yawarakai* soft/ [in such a way that hardness/harshness/intensity is reduced], ya⌈wa⌉rakani 柔らかに /⟨adj(*na*). *ni* of *yawarakana* soft/

EX. My wife massaged my shoulders softly.
妻が私の肩を{柔らかく/柔らかに}もんでくれた。
Tsuma ga watashi no kata o {yawarakaku/yawarakani} monde kureta.

S

2. shi˥zukani 静かに /⟨adj(*na*). *ni* of *shizukana* quiet/ **[making almost no sound or movements]**, {chi˥isa˥i/chi˥isana} ko˥e de {小さい/小さな}声で n.+prt. **[in a low/quiet voice]**

EX. Jane spoke so softly that I couldn't hear her.
ジェーンがあんまり{静かに/{小さい/小さな}声で}話すので聞こえなかった。
Jeen ga anmari {shizuka ni/{chiisai/chiisana} koe de} hanasu node kikoenakatta.

soil n. **[the surface layer of the earth used for growing s.t. ⟪fig. "environment"⟫]**
tsu˥chi˥ 土 [the layer of dirt at the surface of the earth in which plants grow] ⟪earth, ground, clay⟫, do˥joo 土壌 •c [the outermost layer of the earth ⟪fig. "environment"⟫] ⟪earth, ground, environment⟫

EX. The American midwest has fertile soil.
アメリカの中西部は{土/土壌}が肥えている。
Amerika no chuusei-bu wa {tsuchi/dojoo} ga koete iru.

S

solar adj. **[of/coming from/produced by the sun]**
ta˥iyoo no N 太陽のN •c

EX. Solar energy appears to be inexhaustible.
太陽(の)エネルギーは限りないようだ。
Taiyoo (no) enerugii wa kagiri-nai yooda.

soldier n. **[a person (experienced in) serving in an army (as an enlisted person) or a person like a soldier]**
1. ri˥kugun-gu˥njin 陸軍軍人 •c [a man serving in an army]
2. ka˥shi-ka˥n 下士官 •c [a man serving in an army as an enlisted person] ⟪noncommissioned officer, petty officer⟫
3. yu˥ushi 勇士 •c [a man brave in battle] ⟪warrior⟫, to˥oshi 闘士 •c [a person who fights for a cause] ⟪fighter, combatant, champion⟫

sole[1] adj. **[without another/another's help]**
1. ta˥da hi˥to˥tsu no N ただ一つのN [one and only] ⟪only⟫, yu˥iitsu no N 唯一のN •c [one and only] ⟪only⟫

EX. Her sole word to him was "goodbye."
彼女の{ただ一つ/唯一}の言葉は「さようなら」だった。
Kanojo no {tada hitotsu/yuiitsu} no kotoba wa 'Sayoonara' datta.

2. ta˥tta hito˥ri no N たった一人のN [of only one person], ta˥ndoku no N 単独のN •c [without another/another's help] ⟪independent, individual, single, lone, separate, single-handed⟫

EX. (**a**) Sachiko was the sole survivor of the accident.
幸子がその事故の{たった一人/*単独}の生存者だった。
*Sachiko ga sono jiko no {tatta hitori/ *tandoku} no seizon-sha datta.*
(**b**) It turned out that the man was the sole culprit in the murder.
殺人はその男の{単独/??たった一人}の犯行だったことが分かった。
Satsujin wa sono otoko no {tandoku/ ??tatta hitori} no hankoo datta koto ga wakatta.

sole[2] n. **[the bottom surface of the foot or the part of a shoe that corresponds to it]**
1. a˥shi no ura 足の裏 [the bottom surface of the foot]

EX. I walked so much that the soles of my feet became sore.
あまり歩いたので足の裏が痛くなった。
Amari aruita node ashi no ura ga itaku natta.

2. ku˥tsu-zoko 靴底 [the part of a shoe corresponding to the bottom of the foot]

sole[3] n. **[a flatfish resembling a shoe sole]**
shi˥ta-bi˥rame 舌平目

solemn adj. **[awe-inspiringly serious]**
1. i˥kameshi˥i いかめしい adj(*i*). **[so serious that one is afraid of approaching] ⟪stern, grave, dignified⟫, ge˥nshukuna 厳粛な** adj(*na*). **•c [for a ceremony/situation to be stern and awe-inspiring] ⟪grave, serious⟫**

EX. (**a**) The guards at the palace looked solemn.
宮殿の衛兵たちは{いかめしく/*厳粛に}見えた。

*Kyuuden no eihei-tachi wa {ikameshiku/*genshukuni} mieta.*
(**b**) The attendants of the ceremony looked solemn.
儀式の出席者は{厳粛な/*いかめしい}顔をしていた。
*Gishiki no shusseki-sha wa {genshukuna/*ikameshii} kao o shite ita.*

2. shi⌈nseina 神聖な adj(*na*). **•c [set apart from the secular world and inspiring religious awe]** **《holy, consecrated, divine》**

EX. The marriage ceremony is supposed to be a solemn one.
結婚式は神聖なはずだ。
Kekkon-shiki wa shinseina hazu da.

solid adj. **[consisting in its entirety of substantial matter, not liquid or gas]**

1. ko⌈tai no N 固体のN •c [of substance that does not easily change such as stone, metal, wood, etc.] ↔ ekitai no N 液体のN •c [of liquid], kitai no N 気体のN •c [of gas]

EX. The structure of solid matter is still not fully understood.
固体の構造はまだ分からないところがある。
Kotai no koozoo wa mada wakaranai tokoro ga aru.

2. ga⌈sshi⌉ri-shita N がっしりしたN /〈Vinf. past of *gasshiri-suru* ③ become sturdy/ [strong and firm in build or structure] 《sturdy, stout, stalwart》, ga⌈sshi⌉ri-shite iru (N) がっしりしている(N) /〈V *te iru* of *gasshiri-suru* ③ become sturdy/ ②, jo⌈obuna 丈夫な adj(*na*). **•c [not easily broken/prone to illness] 《healthy, hardy, tough, strong》**

EX. Do you have a box solid enough to hold these heavy things?
この重い物を入れたいんですが、{がっしりした/がっしりしている/丈夫な}箱、ありますか。
Kono omoi mono o ire-tai n desu ga, {gasshiri-shita/gasshiri-shite iru/joobuna} hako, arimasu ka.

3. ho⌈n-mono no N 本物のN [not imitation or fake] 《genuine》

EX. This is solid marble.
これは本物の大理石です。
Kore wa hon-mono no dairiseki desu.

4. ka⌈nzenna 完全な adj(*na*). **•c [lacking no parts and having no faults] 《perfect, complete》**

EX. I enjoy solid satisfaction from my work.
私は仕事から完全な満足を得ている。
Watashi wa shigoto kara kanzenna manzoku o ete iru.

—— n. **[a substance that does not easily change under pressure]**
ko⌈tai 固体 •c ↔ ekitai 液体 •c [liquid], kitai 気体 •c [gas]

solo n./adj. **[s.t. one does by oneself (without another's help)]**
so⌉ro ソロ •f [s.t. one does by oneself esp. a musical performance], ta⌈ndoku no N 単独のN •c [without another/another's help] 《independent, single》

EX. (**a**) Rose gave a solo violin recital.
ローズはバイオリンの{ソロ/*単独の}リサイタルをした。
*Roozu wa baiorin no {soro/*tandoku no} risaitaru o shita.*
(**b**) I made a solo flight for the first time this year.
僕は今年初めて{単独(の)/ソロ}飛行をした。
Boku wa kotoshi hajimete {tandoku (no)/soro} hikoo o shita.
(**c**) Nobody has ever succeeded in a solo ascent of Mt. Everest.
だれもエベレストの{単独(の)/*ソロの}登頂を成し遂げてはいない。
*Dare-mo Eberesuto no {tandoku (no)/ *soro no} toochoo o nashi-togete wa inai.*

solution n. **[an act/method/process/result of solving/dissolving s.t.]**

1. ka⌈iketsu 解決 •c [an act/process of solving a problem/case] 《settlement, fixing, resolution》

EX. A solution of the drug problem is going to require enormous time and money.

S

麻薬問題の解決には莫大な時間と金がかかる。
Mayaku-mondai no kaiketsu ni wa bakudaina jikan to kane ga kakaru.

2. ka⌈itoo 解答 •c [the process/result of solving a question in an examination] ⟪**answer**⟫

EX. Do you know the solution to this math problem?
この数学の問題の解答を知っていますか。
Kono suugaku no mondai no kaitoo o shitte imasu ka.

3. ka⌈iketsu-hoo 解決法 •c [a method of solving a relatively large-scale problem/case]

EX. Please tell me what your solution to the land problem would be.
土地問題に対するあなたの解決法を教えてください。
Tochi-mondai ni-taisuru anata no kaiketsu-hoo o oshiete kudasai.

4. yo⌈okai 溶解 •c [an act/process of dissolving s.t.] ⟪**melting, dissolution, fusion**⟫

S

5. yo⌉oeki 溶液 •c [a homogeneous liquid made up of two or more substances mixed together] ⟪**medium**⟫

solve vt. **[for s.o. to find an answer/explanation to a problem]**
⟨-o⟩ to⌉ku ⟨〜を⟩とく ① [for s.o. to cause s.t. tight/entangled/hardened to become loose ⟪fig. "answer a question/problem"⟫] ⟪**untie, undo, unbind, loosen, unfasten, unpack, comb, work out, dispel, remove**⟫, **⟨-o⟩ ka⌈iketsu-suru ⟨〜を⟩解決する ③ •c [for s.o. to find an answer/explanation to a significant problem/case]** ⟪**settle, resolve**⟫
㊥ "figure out the answer to a question/problem"▷解く, "dissolve s.t."▷溶く

EX. (a) Did you solve the puzzle?
パズル、{解きました/*解決しました}か。
*Pazuru, {tokimashita/*kaiketsu-shimashita} ka.*
(b) China is trying hard to solve its population problem.
中国は人口問題を一生懸命{解決しよう/*解こう}としている。
*Chuugoku wa jinkoo-mondai o isshoo-kenmei {kaiketsu-shiyoo/*tokoo} to shite iru.*

somber adj. **[dark and gloomy]**

1. u⌈su-gurai 薄暗い adj(*i*). **[for a place/lighting to be slightly dark]** ⟪**dim, gloomy**⟫

EX. We broke camp in the somber light before dawn and continued on our journey.
未明に薄暗い光の中でキャンプをたたんで、旅を続けた。
Mimei ni usu-gurai hikari no naka de kyanpu o tatande, tabi o tsuzuketa.

2. i⌈nkina 陰気な adj(*na*). **•c [of an atmosphere/person/personality/face with depressed mood]** ⟪**gloomy, dismal, melancholy, cheerless**⟫ **↔ yookina 陽気な** adj(*na*). **•c**

EX. I find the somber atmosphere of the library unappealing.
図書館の陰気な雰囲気は私には気に入らない。
Tosho-kan no inkina fun'iki wa watashi ni wa ki ni iranai.

3. ku⌈ro-zu⌉nda N 黒ずんだN /⟨Vinf. past of *kuro-zumu* ① become blackish/ [to be tinged with dark/blackish color] ⟪**dark, blackish**⟫, **ku⌈roppo⌉i 黒っぽい** adj(*i*). **[close to, but not exactly, black]** ⟪**blackish, dark**⟫, **ji⌈mi⌉na 地味な** adj(*na*). **•c [of a color/personality/appearance which is quiet and subdued]** ⟪**plain, quiet, modest, unpretentious**⟫ **↔ hadena 派手な** adj(*na*).

EX. Yumiko was wearing a somber dress.
由美子は{黒っぽい/黒ずんだ/地味な}ドレスを着ていた。
Yumiko wa {kuroppoi/kuro-zunda/jimina} doresu o kite ita.

some adj. **[an unspecified number/quantity]**

1. i⌉kutsu-ka (no) N いくつか(の)N, na⌉n + counter ka (no) N 何+counterか(の)N [an unspecified number]

EX. (a) There are some apples on the table.
{{いくつか/何個か}のりんごが/りんご

が{いくつか/何個か}机の上にある。
{{Ikutsu-ka/Nan-ko-ka} no ringo ga/ Ringo ga {ikutsu-ka/nan-ko-ka}} tsukue no ue ni aru.
(**b**) There are some Japanese literature books in the library.
図書館には{何冊かの日本文学の本が/日本文学の本が何冊か}ある。
Tosho-kan ni wa {nan-satsu-ka no Nihon-bungaku no hon ga/Nihon-bungaku no hon ga nan-satsu-ka} aru.

NOTE: *Ikutsu-ka* and *nan*-counter-*ka* following the noun they modify are more colloquial and less formal-sounding than *ikutsu-ka no* and *nan*-counter-*ka no* preceding the noun they modify.

2. ø, su⌈ko⌉shi (no) 少し(の) [a little], ta⌈shoo (no) 多少(の) •c [a small amount of s.t. intangible ⟨fml⟩] ⟪somewhat, to some degree, slightly⟫

EX. (**a**) How about some tea?
お茶を{ø/少し/*多少}いかがですか。
*O-cha o {ø/sukoshi/*tashoo} ikaga desu ka.*

NOTE: When *sukoshi* is not used, *wa* instead of *o* is used. The sentence comes out as *O-cha wa ikaga desu ka.*

(**b**) I have some anxiety about my future.
将来について{ø/少し/多少}心配しています。
Shoorai ni-tsuite {ø/sukoshi/tashoo} shinpai-shite imasu.

3. cho⌈tto-shita N ちょっとしたN [worthy of mentioning]

EX. A: Did you see the football game yesterday?
きのうフットボールの試合、見た?
Kinoo futto-booru no shiai, mita?
B: No.
いや。
Iya.
A: That was some game, I'll tell you.
ちょっとした試合だったよ。
Chotto-shita shiai datta yo.

—— pron. **[an unspecified number (of people)/quantity]**

1. Sinf. hi⌈to⌉ mo iru Sinf.人もいる [there are certain people who…]

EX. There are some who go to college; others who don't.
大学に行く人もいれば、行かない人もいる。
Daigaku ni iku hito mo ireba, ikanai hito mo iru.

2. ø, i⌉kutsu-ka いくつか [an unspecified number], i⌉kura-ka いくらか [to some extent in quantity/number/degree], na⌉n + counter ka 何+counterか

EX. (**a**) A: Do you have any money?
お金、ある?
O-kane, aru?
B: Yeah, I have some.
うん、{ø/いくらか/*いくつか/*何円か}持ってる。
*Un, {ø/ikura-ka/*ikutsu-ka/*nan-en-ka} motte ru.*
(**b**) A: Do you have any Japanese-English dictionaries?
和英辞典を持っていますか。
Wa-ei-jiten o motte imasu ka.
B: Yes, I have some.
ええ、{ø/いくつか/何冊か/*いくらか}持っています。
*Ee, {ø/ikutsu-ka/nan-satsu-ka/*ikura-ka} motte imasu.*

3. ø, su⌈ko⌉shi 少し adv. **[(in) a small number/quantity or (to) a small degree] ⟪a little, a dash, a few⟫, ta⌈shoo 多少** adv. •c **[a small amount of s.t. intangible ⟨fml⟩]**

EX. (**a**) A: Do you have some sugar?
砂糖、{ø/少し/??多少}ある?
Satoo, {ø/sukoshi/??tashoo} aru?
B: Yes, I do.
はい、あります。
Hai, arimasu.
(**b**) There is some hope that this disease can be cured.
この病気が治る希望が{ø/少しは/多少は}ある。
Kono byooki ga naoru kiboo ga {ø/sukoshi wa/tashoo wa} aru.

somebody pron. **[an unspecified, unknown person]**

da⌉re-ka だれか [a person whom the speaker/writer cannot specify] ((someone))

EX. (a) Somebody wants to see you.
だれか(が)会いに来ていますよ。
Dare-ka (ga) ai ni kite imasu yo.
(b) I heard from somebody that you're going to get married.
あなたが結婚するって、だれかに聞いたんだけど。
Anata ga kekkon-suru tte, dare-ka ni kiita n da kedo.

— n. **[a person of importance]**
hi⌈to⌉-kado no ni⌈ngen ひとかどの人間 [a respectable person]

EX. He thinks he is a somebody.
あの人は自分がひとかどの人間だと思っている。
Ano hito wa jibun ga hito-kado no ningen da to omotte iru.

someday adv. **[at some future time]**
i⌉tsu-ka いつか [at some unknown/ unspecified time] ((once, before, in the course of time))

S

EX. A: When are you going to France?
いつフランスに行きますか。
Itsu Furansu ni ikimasu ka.
B: Someday I'll go, but I don't know when.
いつか行きますが、いつになるか分かりません。
Itsu-ka ikimasu ga, itsu ni naru ka wakarimasen.

somehow adv. **[in an unspecifiable way]**
do⌉o ni ka (ko⌉o ni ka) どうにか(こうにか) [(accomplished) in some way with effort though not perfectly] ((in some way))

EX. Somehow I was able to survive in Africa.
どうにか(こうにか)アフリカで持ちこたえることが出来ました。
Doo ni ka (koo ni ka) Afurika de mochi-kotaeru koto ga dekimashita.

someone pron. **[an unspecified, unknown person]**
da⌉re-ka だれか [a person whom the speaker/writer cannot specify]

EX. (a) Yumi, someone is waiting for you.
ゆみさん、だれか(が)待っていますよ。
Yumi-san, dare-ka (ga) matte imasu yo.
(b) Is there someone here who can speak Japanese?
だれか日本語が話せる人がここにいますか。
Dare-ka Nihon-go ga hanase-ru hito ga koko ni imasu ka.

something n. **[an unspecified, unknown thing or an important thing/person]**
1. na⌉ni-ka 何か [a thing/situation/animal which the speaker/writer cannot specify] ((anything))

EX. (a) I want something to drink.
何か(が)飲みたいよ。
Nani-ka (ga) nomi-tai yo.
(b) Did you say something?
何か、言った?
Nani-ka, itta?
(c) Something must have happened to him because he's been acting strange lately.
あの人に何かあったにちがいない。このごろ様子がおかしいんだ。
Ano hito ni nani-ka atta ni chigai-nai. Kono-goro yoosu ga okashii n da.

2. cho⌈tto-shita {mono/mo⌉n} ちょっとした{もの/もん} [a thing worthy of admiration or respect ⟨s⟩]

EX. Look at this machine! Isn't it something?
この機械を見てご覧。ちょっとした{もの/もん}だろう。
Kono kikai o mite goran. Chotto-shita {mono/mon} daroo.

sometime adv. **[at some unknown/ unspecified time]**
i⌉tsu-ka いつか [at some unknown/ unspecified time] ((some day, before))

EX. If you have a chance sometime, you should give Bill a call.
いつか暇な時、ビルに電話したらどうだい?
Itsu-ka himana toki, Biru ni denwa-shitara doo dai?

sometimes adv. **[at various times but not always]**
to⌈ki-doki 時々 ((occasionally, once in a while)), **Sinf. nonpast ko⌈to⌉ {ga/mo} aru**

Sinf. nonpast こと{が/も}ある ① [there are times when...]

NOTE: When adj(*na*). or N cop. comes before *koto {ga/mo} aru*, the form changes to adj(*na*). stem + *na* or N *no* respectively.

EX. (**a**) I sometimes watch soap operas on TV.
私は{時々テレビのメロドラマを見ます/テレビのメロドラマを見ること{が/も}あります}。
Watashi wa {toki-doki terebi no merodorama o mimasu/terebi no merodorama o miru koto {ga/mo} arimasu}.
(**b**) I sometimes call my parents in Hokkaido.
私は{時々北海道の両親に電話します/北海道の両親に電話すること{が/も}あります}。
Watashi wa {toki-doki Hokkaidoo no ryooshin ni denwa-shimasu/Hokkaidoo no ryooshin ni denwa-suru koto {ga/mo} arimasu}.
(**c**) I'm poor at *kanji*, but I sometimes find the characters interesting.
漢字は苦手ですが、{時々面白いと思います/面白いと思うこと{が/も}あります}。
Kanji wa niga-te desu ga, {toki-doki omoshiroi to omoimasu/omoshiroi to omou koto {ga/mo} arimasu}.

PHRASE: sometimes…sometimes… Sinf. past *ri*, Sinf. past *ri suru* Sinf. past り、Sinf. past りする ③

EX. A: What do you do on weekends?
週末には何をしますか。
Shuumatsu ni wa nani o shimasu ka.
B: Well, sometimes I play tennis, and sometimes I read books.
そうですね、テニスをしたり、本を読んだりします。
Soo desu ne, tenisu o shitari, hon o yondari shimasu.

somewhat adv. **[to some extent]**
ya˥ya やや [slightly different from the standard in extent/degree] **((a little, to some extent, in a way, slightly))**, **i˥kubun 幾分 [to some extent or degree]** **((partly, more or less))**, **i˥kura-ka いくらか [to some extent in quantity/number/degree]** **((a little, more or less, in some degree))**

EX. (**a**) Tomorrow should be somewhat colder than today.
明日は今日より{やや/幾分/いくらか}寒いでしょう。
Asu wa kyoo yori {yaya/ikubun/ikura-ka} samui deshoo.
(**b**) The quiz was somewhat difficult, but I managed to do well on it.
小テストは{やや/幾分/いくらか}難しかったが、よく出来た。
Shoo-tesuto wa {yaya/ikubun/ikura-ka} muzukashikatta ga, yoku dekita.

somewhere adv. **[at/in/to some unspecified, unknown place/time/degree]**
1. do˥ko-ka ({ni/e/de}) どこか({に/へ/で}) [at/in/to a place which the speaker/writer cannot specify] **((anywhere, some place))**

EX. (**a**) There must be a good restaurant somewhere in this town.
この町のどこか{に/*へ/*で}いいレストランがあるに違いありません。
*Kono machi no doko-ka {ni/*e/*de} ii resutoran ga aru ni chigai-arimasen.*
(**b**) It's such a nice day. Let's go for a picnic somewhere.
すばらしい天気だ。どこか{へ/に/*で}ピクニックに行こう。
*Subarashii tenki da. Doko-ka {e/ni/*de} pikunikku ni ikoo.*

2. -{gurai/ku˥rai} ～{ぐらい/くらい} [of an approximate quantity/extent]

EX. Her age is somewhere between 21 and 25.
彼女の年は二十一と二十五の間{ぐらい/くらい}だ。
Kanojo no toshi wa ni-juu-ichi to ni-juu-go no aida {gurai/kurai} da.

son n. **[a male child (including a son-in-law)]**
1. mu˥suko 息子 [a male child] **((boy))**, **se˥gare せがれ [a humble form usually used by men to refer to a male child]**

EX. My son is in college now.

S

{息子/せがれ}は今大学に行っています。
{Musuko/Segare} wa ima daigaku ni itte imasu.

NOTE: Unlike English, Japanese *musuko/segare* cannot be used as an address form. Its use in the following sentence is therefore inappropriate. **Musuko, hanashi-tai koto ga aru.* "I have something to talk to you about, son.'

2. o-⌈mae お前 [an informal second person singular pronoun usually used by men to address or refer to s.o. equal or inferior to oneself ⟨s⟩] ⟪you⟫

EX. I have something to talk to you about, son.
お前に話したいことがある。
O-mae ni hanashi-tai koto ga aru.

song n. **[an act/instance of singing or a musical composition for singing or poetry]**

1. u⌈ta⌉ 歌 [an act/instance of singing or a musical composition for singing or a traditional 31-syllable waka poem] ⟪ode, poetry, ballad, singing⟫

EX. (**a**) We were taught this Japanese song in class.
授業でこの日本の歌を教わりました。
Jugyoo de kono Nihon no uta o osowarimashita.
(**b**) I usually sing English songs when I go to *karaoke* bars.
カラオケバーに行くとたいてい英語の歌を歌います。
Karaoke-baa ni iku to taitei eigo no uta o utaimasu.

2. ka⌉kyoku 歌曲 •c [a Western-style musical composition for singing]

EX. I like songs by Schubert like "*Winterreise.*"
私は『冬の旅』のようなシューベルトの歌曲が好きです。
Watashi wa "Fuyu no tabi" no yoona Shuuberuto no kakyoku ga suki desu.

3. shi 詩 •c ⟪poetry, verse⟫

soon adv. **[in a (very) short time]**

1. mo⌈o su⌉gu もうすぐ [in a very short time], so⌈no-uchi(-ni) そのうち(に) [in the near future] ⟪before long, one of these days, someday⟫, ma-⌈mo⌉-naku 間もなく [about to occur within a very short time ⟨fml⟩] ⟪presently, shortly⟫, ya⌈gate やがて [before long ⟨fml⟩] ⟪presently, by and by, in a short time⟫

EX. (**a**) It will soon begin getting cold in these parts.
このへんは{もうすぐ/そのうちに/間もなく/やがて}寒くなります。
Kono hen wa {moo sugu/sono-uchi-ni/ma-mo-naku/yagate} samuku narimasu.
(**b**) The next bus will come soon.
次のバスは{もうすぐ/そのうちに/間もなく/やがて}来ます。
Tsugi no basu wa {moo sugu/sono-uchi-ni/ma-mo-naku/yagate} kimasu.
(**c**) The meeting will start soon.
会議は{もうすぐ/間もなく/やがて/??そのうちに}始まります。
Kaigi wa {moo sugu/ma-mo-naku/yagate/?? sono-uchi-ni} hajimarimasu.

2. ha⌉yaku はやく [prior to the usual or expected time or quickly]

㊥ "early"▷早く, "speedily/quickly"▷速く

NOTE: "Early" is always represented by 早く, but "speedily" is sometimes represented by 早く as well.

EX. Please do it as soon as possible.
出来るだけ早くしてください。
Dekiru dake hayaku shite kudasai.

PHRASE: sooner or later *osokare hayakare* 遅かれ早かれ

EX. Her patience with him is bound to run out sooner or later.
彼のことでは、遅かれ早かれ彼女の堪忍袋の緒が切れるでしょう。
Kare no koto de wa, osokare hayakare kanojo no kannin-bukuro no o ga kireru deshoo.

sore adj. **[causing or feeling physical or mental pain, often associated with raw skin or overworked muscles]**

hi⌉ri-hiri-suru N ひりひりするN [for s.o. to feel pain or hotness in the throat or on the skin] ⟪stinging, pungent, hot⟫, i⌈ta⌉i 痛い adj(*i*). **[for s.o./s.a. to experience an unpleasant physical sensation, often in a**

S

particular part of the body] ((painful, hurts))

EX. (a) The wound is still sore.
傷口がまだ{ひりひりする/痛い}。
Kizu-guchi ga mada {hiri-hiri-suru/itai}.
(b) I have a sore throat.
私はのどが{ひりひりする/痛い}。
Watashi wa nodo ga {hiri-hiri-suru/itai}.
(c) My legs are sore from dancing all night.
一晩中踊ったので、足が{痛い/*ひりひりする}んです。
*Hito-ban-juu odotta node, ashi ga {itai/*hiri-hiri-suru} n desu.*

—— n. [a source or location of physical/psychological pain]
i⌈ta⌉i tokoro 痛い所 [a painful or weak spot]

sorrow n. **[a deep, continuing anguish caused by loss/separation/disappointment, etc. or its cause]**
1. ka⌈nashi-mi 悲しみ /⟨adj(*i*). stem of *kanashii* sad + suf. *mi* ness/ [psychological pain brought on by circumstances difficult to endure] ((sadness, unhappiness, grief, distress)), hi⌈tan 悲嘆 •c ((grief, anguish))

EX. (a) Her friend's death caused Jane deep sorrow.
友達の死にジェーンは{悲しみに打ちひしがれた/悲嘆にくれた}。
Tomodachi no shi ni Jeen wa {kanashi-mi ni uchihishiga-reta/hitan ni kureta}.
(b) It's hard to know how to talk to someone overwhelmed by sorrow at the loss of a loved one.
最愛の人を亡くして{悲しみ/悲嘆}にくれている人にどう話せばいいか分からない。
Saiai no hito o nakushite {kanashi-mi/hitan} ni kurete iru hito ni doo hanaseba ii ka wakaranai.

sorry adj. **[feeling sympathy/regret]**
ki-⌈no-doku⌉na 気の毒な adj(*na*). **[deserving of sympathy for the pain or sorrow one is suffering] ((pitiful, miserable, regrettable, unfortunate)), ka⌈wai-so⌉ona かわいそうな** adj(*na*). **[for s.o./s.a. to deserve sympathy due to the adverse situation he/she/it is in] ((poor, pitiful, miserable, wretched))**

EX. (a) I was sorry to hear of my friend's failing his entrance exam to Tokyo University.
友だちが東京大学の入学試験に受からなかったことを聞いて{気の毒/かわいそう}だと思った。
Tomodachi ga Tookyoo-daigaku no nyuugaku-shiken ni ukaranakatta koto o kiite {ki-no-doku/kawai-soo} da to omotta.
(b) I feel sorry for Sally. I heard that her husband was badly injured in a traffic accident.
サリー、{気の毒/かわいそう}ね。御主人が交通事故で大けがをしたんだって。
Sarii, {ki-no-doku/kawai-soo} ne. Go-shujin ga kootsuu-jiko de oo-kega o shita n datte.

2. za⌈nne⌉nna 残念な adj(*na*). **•c [causing disappointment and dissatisfaction over s.t. that s.o. has done or s.t. that has happened] ((unfortunate, regrettable, disappointing))**

EX. I'm sorry now that I didn't study business administration.
今思うと経営学を勉強しなかったのが残念だ。
Ima omou to keiei-gaku o benkyoo-shinakatta no ga zannen da.

PHRASE: Sorry! *Sumimasen.* すみません, *Suimasen.* すいません。⟨s⟩

NOTE: *Sumimasen* is used not only to mean "sorry" but also to mean "thank you (for taking the trouble of doing s.t. for me)."

sort n. **[a natural group with some common characteristics]**
shu⌈rui 種類 •c ((kind, variety, type))

EX. (a) A: What sort of music do you like?
どんな種類の音楽が好きですか。
Donna shurui no ongaku ga suki desu ka.
B: I like opera.
オペラが好きです。
Opera ga suki desu.
(b) There are many different sorts of plants on this mountain.

この山には色々な種類の植物があります。
Kono yama ni wa iro-irona shurui no shokubutsu ga arimasu.

— vt. **[to classify and arrange things]**
⟨-o⟩ buˈnrui-suru ⟨～を⟩分類する ③ •c **⟪classify, group, assort⟫**

EX. Could you please sort these cards for me according to color?
このカードを色別に分類してくれませんか。
Kono kaado o iro-betsu ni bunrui-shite kuremasen ka.

PHRASE: sort out ⟨-o⟩ *seiri-suru* ⟨～を⟩整理する ③ •c

EX. It took me weeks to sort out the mess left by the previous secretary.
前の秘書が色々なものをめちゃくちゃにしたままやめてしまったので、全部整理するのに何週間もかかった。
Mae no hisho ga iro-irona mono o mecha-kucha ni shita mama yamete shimatta node, zenbu seiri-suru no ni nan-shuukan mo kakatta.

S

soul n. **[the immortal spiritual or moral essence of a human being ⟪fig. "essentail part of s.t."⟫]**
1. seˈishin 精神 •c [the mind as opposed to the body] ⟪spirit, mind, will⟫ ↔ nikutai 肉体 •c; taˈmashii 魂 [s.t. supernatural that resides in and gives life to s.o./s.t./s.a.] ⟪spirit⟫

EX. (**a**) Japanese "*ki*" is body and soul rolled into one.
日本語の「気」とは肉体と{魂/精神}を一つにしたものだ。
Nihon-go no 'ki' to wa nikutai to {tamashii/seishin} o hitotsu ni shita mono da.
(**b**) The human soul is said to depart from the body upon death.
人間の{魂/*精神}は死ぬと肉体を離れると言われる。
*Ningen no {tamashii/*seishin} wa shinu to nikutai o hanareru to iwa-reru.*

2. seˈizui 精髄 •c [the essence of s.t.] **⟪essence, quintessence⟫**

EX. Football is said to be the soul of American culture.
フットボールはアメリカ文化の精髄と言われる。
Futto-booru wa Amerika-bunka no seizui to iwa-reru.

sound n. **[acoustic vibrations audible to the ear]**
oˈtoˈ 音 [acoustic vibrations perceived by the ear] ⟪noise⟫, moˈno-otoˈ 物音 [acoustic vibrations made by s.t.] ⟪noise⟫

EX. (**a**) A: Did you hear that sound? I wonder what it was.
あの{音/*物音}、聞いた? 何だろう。
*Ano {oto/*mono-oto}, kiita? Nan daroo.*
B: Oh, that was just the sound of the wind.
ああ、あれはただの風の{音/*物音}だよ。
*Aa, are wa tada no kaze no {oto/*mono-oto} da yo.*
(**b**) When I heard the strange sound downstairs I went to investigate it right away.
下で変な{音/物音}がした時すぐ調べに下りてみた。
Shita de henna {oto/mono-oto} ga shita toki sugu shirabe ni orite mita.

— vi. **[for a sound to be heard (to give a mental impression) ⟪fig. "seem"⟫]**
Sinf. yoˈona kuˈchi-buri da Sinf.ような口ぶりだ [to talk as if]

NOTE: When the nonpast affirmative form of adj(*na*). or N+cop. comes before *yoona*, the form changes to adj(*na*). stem + *na* or N *no*, respectively.

EX. (**a**) She sounded excited about her new job when I talked to her yesterday.
きのう話した時、彼女は新しい仕事のことでわくわくしているような口ぶりだった。
Kinoo hanashita toki, kanojo wa atarashii shigoto no koto de waku-waku-shite iru yoona kuchi-buri datta.
(**b**) My boss sounded as if he couldn't care less about me as a person.
ボスは僕のことなんかどうでもいいよ

うな口ぶりだった。
Bosu wa boku no koto nan ka doodemo ii yoona kuchi-buri datta.

— vt. **[for s.o. to cause s.t. to emit sound (to examine a part of the body by causing it to emit a sound)]**
⟨-no⟩ o⌈to⌉ o da⌉su ⟨〜の⟩音を出す ① **[to emit the sound of s.t.]**, **⟨-o⟩ na⌈rasu** ⟨〜を⟩鳴らす ① **[for s.o. to cause a wind/percussion instrument to emit sound]**

EX. (**a**) It's not easy to sound a gong in the proper way.
ちゃんとどら{の音を出す/を鳴らす}のは易しくない。
Chanto dora {no oto o dasu/o narasu} no wa yasashikunai.
(**b**) The driver sounded the horn to warn the pedestrians.
運転手は歩行者にクラクション{を鳴らして/*の音を出して}注意した。
*Unten-shu wa hokoo-sha ni kurakushon {o narashite/*no oto o dashite} chuui-shita.*

soup n.
su⌉upu スープ •f

EX. Please eat your soup while it's warm.
あったかいうちにスープを飲んでください。
Attakai uchi ni suupu o nonde kudasai.

NOTE: In Japanese "to eat soup" is *suupu o nomu*. **Suupu o taberu* is unacceptable.

sour adj. **[having an unpleasantly sharp acid taste either inherently or due to fermentation ⟪fig. "bad-tempered"⟫]**
1. su⌈ppa⌉i 酸っぱい adj(*i*). **[having a sharp acid taste either inherently or due to fermentation]** ⟪acid, tart⟫

EX. (**a**) This grapefruit is so sour!
このグレープフルーツはすごく酸っぱいなあ。
Kono gureepufuruutsu wa sugoku suppai naa.
(**b**) The milk turned sour overnight.
牛乳が一晩で酸っぱくなった。
Gyuunyuu ga hito-ban de suppaku natta.

2. fu-⌈ki⌉genna 不機嫌な adj(*na*). •c **[in a bad mood/temper, usually temporarily]** ⟪sullen, bad-tempered, cross, displeased⟫

EX. Why do you look so sour today?
どうして今日はそんなに不機嫌なの?
Dooshite kyoo wa sonna ni fu-kigenna no?

source n. **[the starting point (of a river)]**
1. mi⌈namoto 源 **[the starting point (of a river)]** ⟪origin, beginning, root⟫, **su⌈igen** 水源 •c **[the starting point of a river]** ⟪headspring⟫

EX. Where is the source of this river?
この川の{源/水源}はどこですか。
Kono kawa no {minamoto/suigen} wa doko desu ka.

2. mo⌈to 元 **[a root ⟪fig. "origin," "beginning," "foundation," "cause," "materials," "capital," "under (the influence of)"⟫]**, **de-⌈do⌉koro** 出所 **[a place from which s.t. concrete originates]** ⟪origin⟫, **shu⌈tten** 出典 •c **[the origin from which a historical fact/idiom/quote is taken]** ⟪authority⟫, **mi⌈namoto** 源 **[the starting point (of a river)]** ⟪origin, beginning, root⟫

EX. (**a**) Much of Japanese culture finds its source in China.
日本文化の多くは中国が{源/元/??出所/*出典}だ。
*Nihon-bunka no ooku wa Chuugoku ga {minamoto/moto/??de-dokoro/*shutten} da.*
(**b**) You should give the sources of all your quotes.
引用文の{出典/*元/*源/*出所}を全部示すべきだ。
*In'yoo-bun no {shutten/*moto/*minamoato/*de-dokoro} o zenbu shimesu beki da.*
(**c**) The police are investigating the source of the money.
警察はその金の{出所/*元/*源/*出典}を洗っている。
*Keisatsu wa sono kane no {de-dokoro/*moto/*minamoto/*shutten} o aratte iru.*

S

south n. **[the direction opposite of north]**
mi⌈nami 南 ↔ kita 北; na⌉nbu 南部 •c [the southern part] ↔ hokubu 北部

EX. (**a**) My room faces south.
私の部屋は南向きです。
Watashi no heya wa minami-muki desu.
(**b**) Have you ever been to the south?
南部に行ったことがありますか。
Nanbu ni itta koto ga arimasu ka.

— adj.
mi⌈nami no N 南のN [of the south]

EX. The college is located at the south end of town.
大学は町の南の外れにあります。
Daigaku wa machi no minami no hazure ni arimasu.

— adv. **[to the south]**
mi⌈nami {**e/ni**} 南{へ/に}

EX. Swallows fly south when it gets cold.
つばめは寒くなると南{に/へ}飛んで行く。
Tsubame wa samuku naru to minami {ni/e} tonde iku.

PHRASE: South America *Minami-Amerika* 南アメリカ, *Nanbei* 南米 •c

S

South Carolina n.
Sa⌈usu-karora⌉ina サウスカロライナ •f

South Dakota n.
Sa⌈usu-da⌉kota サウスダコタ •f

southeast n.
na⌈n-too 南東 •c, na⌈ntoo chiho⌉o 南東地方 •c [the southeastern district]

southern adj. **[in/of/from/facing south]**

1. mi⌈nami ni a⌉ru (**N**) 南にある(**N**) **[existing in the south]**

EX. We went to a southern island.
我々は南にある島に行った。
Ware-ware wa minami ni aru shima ni itta.

2. mi⌈nami no N 南のN [of the south]

EX. The restaurant stands at the southern end of the mall.
レストランは商店街の南の端に立っている。
Resutoran wa shooten-gai no minami no hashi ni tatte iru.

3. na⌉nbu no N 南部のN •c [of the south district]

EX. The southern and northern states of America have quite different culture.
アメリカでは南部の州と北部の州の文化はかなり違う。
Amerika de wa nanbu no shuu to hokubu no shuu no bunka wa kanari chigau.

4. mi⌈nami kara no N 南からのN [from the south]

EX. There was a steady southern wind.
ひっきりなしに南からの風が吹いていた。
Hikkiri-nashi ni minami kara no kaze ga fuite ita.

NOTE: *Minami kara no kaze* can also be expressed as the compound *minami-kaze*.

5. mi⌈nami-muki no N 南向きのN [facing south]

EX. I like a house with a southern exposure.
南向きの家が好きだ。
Minami-muki no ie ga suki da.

southwest n.
na⌈n-sei 南西 •c, na⌈n-sei chiho⌉o 南西地方 •c [the southwestern district]

— adv.
na⌈n-sei {**e/ni**} 南西{へ/に} **•c [toward the southwest]**

southwestern adj.
na⌈n-sei no N 南西のN •c

souvenir n. **[s.t. kept as a remembrance of a place/occasion/person]**
ki⌈nen-hin 記念品 •c [s.t. given in remembrance of a special occasion] ((**memento, keepsake**)), **ka⌈ta-mi 形見 [s.t. kept in remembrance of a person who has died/gone away]** ((**keepsake, memento**)), (**o-**)**mi⌈yage** (お)**土産 [s.t. one brings home from a trip/visit, usu. to give to those remaining behind, or s.t. one takes to give to one's host**(**ess**) **when visiting some place away from home]** ((**present, gift**))

EX. (**a**) We received a souvenir on the occasion of the centennial anniversary of the university.

大学の創立百年祭の折に{記念品/*形見/*土産}をもらった。
*Daigaku no sooritsu hyaku-nen-sai no ori ni {kinen-hin/*kata-mi/*miyage} o moratta.*
(**b**) My father gave me this watch as a souvenir.
父がこの時計を{形見/土産/*記念品}にくれた。
*Chichi ga kono tokei o {kata-mi/miyage/*kinen-hin} ni kureta.*
(**c**) In Japan it's normal to give souvenirs to friends after returning from a trip.
日本では旅行から戻ると友人に{お土産/*記念品/*形見}をあげるのが普通だ。
*Nihon de wa ryokoo kara modoru to yuujin ni {o-miyage/*kinen-hin/*kata-mi} o ageru no ga futsuu da.*

sow vt. **[for s.o. to plant seeds 《fig. "disseminate"》]**
〈-ni〉 ta⌉ne o ma⌉ku 〈～に〉種をまく ① **[for s.o. to plant a field with seeds 《fig. "begin s.t."》]**
EX. (**a**) It's about time to sow flower seeds in the garden.
もうそろそろ庭に花の種をまくころですよ。
Moo soro-soro niwa ni hana no tane o maku koro desu yo.
(**b**) You reap what you sow.
まいた種は刈らなければなりません。
Maita tane wa karanakereba narimasen.

soy (sauce) n.
sho⌈oyu しょう油 **•c**
EX. We eat *sashimi* by dipping it in soy sauce.
刺身はしょう油をつけて食べます。
Sashimi wa shooyu o tsukete tabemasu.

spa n. **[(a resort having) a mineral spring]**
1. ko⌈osen 鉱泉 **•c [a spring that includes many minerals and gas at a temperature below 25°C]** **《mineral spring》, o⌈nsen** 温泉 **•c [a spring that includes many minerals and gas at a temperature above 25°C]** **《hot spring》**

onsen

EX. There are lots of spas in Japan.
日本には{温泉/鉱泉}がたくさんあります。
Nihon ni wa {onsen/koosen} ga takusan arimasu.
2. o⌈nse⌉n-chi 温泉地 **•c [a resort having a mineral spring]**
EX. Izu Peninsula has many famous spas.
伊豆半島には有名な温泉地がたくさんある。
Izu-hantoo ni wa yuumeina onsen-chi ga takusan aru.

space n. **[an expanse extending in all directions (beyond the earth) or between/within things or a room for some purpose]**
1. ku⌈ukan 空間 **•c [an expanse extending in all directions] 《the infinite, room》**
EX. The way people use space is different from culture to culture.
空間の使い方は文化によって違う。
Kuukan no tsukai-kata wa bunka ni yotte chigau.
2. u⌉chuu 宇宙 **•c [an expanse extending in all directions beyond the earth] 《universe, cosmos》**
EX. (**a**) I would like to take a trip into space.
私は宇宙旅行に行きたいです。
Watashi wa uchuu-ryokoo ni iki tai desu.
(**b**) When one considers space, one cannot help wondering how it was created.
宇宙のことを考えると、どのようにして創造されたのかつい考えてしまう。
Uchuu no koto o kangaeru to, dono yooni shite soozoo-sareta no ka tsui kangaete shimau.
3. me⌉nseki 面積 **•c [a two-demensional expanse extending over a surface] 《size, area, square measure》**
EX. The space taken up by an average American college campus is much larger than that of one in Japan.
普通アメリカの大学のキャンパスの面

積は日本のそれよりはるかに大きい。
Futsuu Amerika no daigaku no kyanpasu no menseki wa Nihon no sore yori harukani ookii.

4. su⌈ki-ma 透き間 [room between things] ⟪crevice, gap, opening, aperture⟫, kuuran 空欄 •c [a blank area that is expected to be filled in] ⟪blank column, blank⟫

EX. (**a**) Write down your answers in the space provided.
{空欄/*透き間}に答えを書きなさい。
*{Kuuran/*Suki-ma} ni kotae o kakinasai.*
(**b**) I cleaned up the space between my bookshelf and the wall.
本棚と壁の{透き間/*空欄}を掃除した。
*Hon-dana to kabe no {suki-ma/ *kuuran} o sooji-shita.*

5. ba⌈sho 場所 •c [a point or area in space where s.o./s.t./s.a. exists or where s.t. happens] ⟪place, spot, locality, area, region⟫, -joo 〜場 •c [a place for some purpose]

EX. (**a**) Where is the parking space for this store?
この店の駐車{場/?の場所}はどこですか。
Kono mise no chuusha {-joo/?no basho} wa doko desu ka.
(**b**) There isn't enough space in our apartment for kids to play in.
私たちのアパートでは子供たちが遊ぶ場所がないんですよ。
Watashi-tachi no apaato de wa kodomo-tachi ga asobu basho ga nai n desu yo.
(**c**) The bus was so crowded that there wasn't even any space to stand.
バスは込んでいて立つ場所もなかった。
Basu wa konde ite tatsu basho mo nakatta.

— vt. **[to arrange s.t. with space between, esp. lines of writing]**
gyo⌈okan o a⌈keru 行間を空ける ②

EX. Why don't you space your lines a bit more widely?
行間をもう少し広く空けたらどうですか。
Gyookan o moo sukoshi hiroku aketara doo desu ka.

spacecraft n.
u⌈chuu-sen 宇宙船 •c

spaceship n.
u⌈chuu-sen 宇宙船 •c

EX. I'd like to take a ride to the moon in spaceship.
宇宙船に乗って月に行きたい。
Uchuu-sen ni notte tsuki ni iki-tai.

spacious adj. **[having much space]**
hi⌈ro-bi⌉ro-to shita N 広々としたN, hi⌈ro-bi⌉ro-to shite iru (N) 広々としている(N) [for the space occupied by s.t. to extend widely] ⟪extensive, open, wide, vast, sweeping⟫

EX. Good heavens! You have such a spacious living room!
わあ。実に広々と{した/している}居間ですねえ。
Waa. Jitsuni hiro-biro-to {shita/shite iru} ima desu nee.

Spain n.
Su⌈pe⌉in スペイン •f

span n. **[a full yet limited spatial/temporal expanse between two endpoints]**
ze⌈nchoo 全長 •c [the total length of s.t.]

EX. The wing span of this bird is about ten inches.
この鳥の羽の全長は十インチだ。
Kono tori no hane no zenchoo wa juu-inchi da.

— vt. **[for s.t. to connect the two sides or ends of s.t.]**
⟨-ni⟩ ka⌈ka⌉ru ⟨〜に⟩かかる ① [for s.t. to extend to and come in contact with s.t./ s.o./s.a. else ⟪fig. "cover," "begin," "be engaged in," "become splashed with," "be built," "require"⟫]
㊅ "for both sides to be connected"▷架かる, "be hung"▷掛かる, otherwise ▷かかる

EX. A long bridge spans the river.
長い橋がその川に架かっている。
Nagai hashi ga sono kawa ni kakatte iru.

Spanish n. **[the Spanish language/the Spanish people]**
1. Su⌈pein-go スペイン語 •f+c [the Spanish language]
2. Su⌈pein-ji⌉n スペイン人 •f+c [a Spanish person or the Spanish people] ⟪**Spaniard**⟫
— adj. **[of Spain/the Spanish language/the Spanish people]**
1. Su⌈pe⌉in no N スペインのN •f [of Spain]
2. Su⌈pein-go no N スペイン語のN •f+c [of the Spanish language]
3. Su⌈pein-ji⌉n no N スペイン人のN •f+c [of a Spanish person or the Spanish people]

spare vt. **[to refrain from doing/letting happen/using/having s.t.]**
1. ⟨-o⟩ ta⌈suke⌉te {ageru/yaru} ⟨〜を⟩助けて{あげる ②/やる ①} [for s.o. to help or refrain from killing/injuring s.t./s.o./s.a.] ⟪**help, assist, save, deliver**⟫
EX. The king spared the man's life.
王様は男の命を助けてやりました。
Oo-sama wa otoko no inochi o tasukete yarimashita.
2. ⟨-ni⟩ ⟨-o⟩ {Vneg./Vstem/shi/ko} nai de su⌉mu yo⌉oni suru ⟨〜に⟩⟨〜を⟩{Vneg./Vstem/し/来}ないで済むようにする ③ [for s.o. to make it possible for s.o. not to have to do s.t.]
EX. I spared her the boring job of cleaning the kitchen floor.
私は彼女が台所のゆかを掃除するというつまらない仕事をしないで済むようにした。
Watashi wa kanojo ga daidokoro no yuka o sooji-suru to iu tsumaranai shigoto o shinai de sumu yooni shita.
3. N na⌉shi de su⌈ma⌉su Nなしで済ます ① [for s.o. to dispense with s.t.] ⟪**do without**⟫
EX. I can't spare my car even for a day.
私は一日でも車なしで済ますことはできません。
Watashi wa ichi-nichi demo kuruma nashi de sumasu koto wa dekimasen.
4. ⟨-o⟩ o⌈shi⌉mu ⟨〜を⟩惜しむ ① [for s.o. to begrudge having to use s.t./throw away s.t./part with s.o.] ⟪**be not generous with, be stingy with, regret**⟫
EX. You shouldn't spare any effort on this project.
この計画に努力を惜しんではいけません。
Kono keikaku ni doryoku o oshinde wa ikemasen.
— adj. **[not in use or over and above what is needed** ⟪**fig. "small/lean amount"**⟫**]**
yo⌉bi no N 予備のN •c [prepared in advance] ⟪**preparatory, preliminary, reserve**⟫, **yo⌈bun no N 余分のN •c [of a quantity more than necessary]** ⟪**excess, extra, surplus**⟫
EX. (**a**) I ended up using my spare money.
{予備/余分}のお金まで使ってしまった。
{Yobi/Yobun} no o-kane made tsukatte shimatta.
(**b**) I don't have any spare time to watch TV.
テレビを見たりする{余分/*予備}の時間はない。
*Terebi o mitari suru {yobun/*yobi} no jikan wa nai.*
— n. **[s.t. extra, esp. auto parts/money/rooms]**
a⌈mari⌉ 余り /⟨V*masu* of *amaru* ① be left over/ **[what is left over]** ⟪**rest, remainder, remnant, surplus, balance**⟫, **su⌈pea-ta⌉iya スペアタイヤ •f [extra tire], yo⌈bi⌉-shitsu 予備室 •c [an extra room]**

spark n. **[a small glowing particle generated by a fire or a similar flash of light caused by an electric discharge]**
1. hi⌉-bana 火花 [a small glowing particle thrown out of a fire]
EX. Sparks flew when we threw the log on the fire.
火にまきをくべると火花が散った。
Hi ni maki o kuberu to hi-bana ga chitta.
2. ki⌈rameki⌉ きらめき /⟨V*masu* of *kirameku* ① sparkle/ **[flash of light]** ⟪**glitter, twinkling**⟫
3. su⌈pa⌉aku スパーク •f [a flash of light

caused by an electric discharge]

EX. The two electric wires touching each other caused sparks.
電線が二本触れ合って、スパークを起こしていた。
Densen ga ni-hon fure-atte, supaaku o okoshite ita.

— vi. **[to produce ignited particles or flashes of light (for an engine to start)]**
1. hi˥-bana ga chi˥ru 火花が散る ① **[for sparks to fly]**
2. ki˥rame˥ku きらめく ① **[for a star/eyes/neon-signs/jewels to give off a glittering light]** ⟪**glitter, glisten, sparkle, gleam, glimmer**⟫

sparkling adj. **[giving off sparks of light]**
ki˥rame˥ku N きらめくN **[shining brightly and beautifully]** ⟪**glittering, glistening, glimmering**⟫

EX. The sparkling beauty of Cinderella caught the prince's eyes.
シンデレラのきらめく美しさが王子様の目に留まった。
Shinderera no kirameku utsukushi-sa ga ooji-sama no me ni tomatta.

sparrow n.
su˥zume すずめ

speak vi. **[for s.o. to communicate by uttering words/sentences]**
1. ha˥na˥su 話す ① **[for s.o. to communicate verbally]** ⟪**talk, discuss, speak**⟫, **sha˥be˥ru** しゃべる ① **[for s.o. to chit-chat with s.o.⟨s⟩]** ⟪**chat, chatter, gabble**⟫

EX. Don't be quiet. You have to speak.
黙っていては駄目だ。{話さなければ/しゃべらなければ}いけないんだ。
Damatte ite wa dame da. {Hanasanakereba/Shaberanakereba} ikenai n da.

2. e˥nzetsu o suru 演説をする ③ **•c [for s.o. to make a speech]** ⟪**deliver a speech**⟫

EX. The president will speak to the nation on TV.
大統領が全国向けにテレビで演説をする。
Daitooryoo ga zenkoku-muke ni terebi de enzetsu o suru.

PHRASE: speak up *hakkiri jibun no iken o iu* はっきり自分の意見を言う ①

EX. I finally gathered up enough courage to speak up on the issue.
やっと勇気を出して、その問題に関してはっきり意見を言うことができた。
Yatto yuuki o dashite, sono mondai ni-kanshite hakkiri iken o iu koto ga dekita.

— vt. **[for s.o. to express one's thoughts/sentiments or to have the ability to communicate orally in a language]**
{⟨-o⟩/⟨-to⟩} **i˥u** {⟨〜を⟩/⟨〜と⟩}言う ① **[for s.o. to express s.t. verbally]** ⟪**say, state, tell, call**⟫, {⟨-o⟩/⟨-ni-tsuite⟩} **ha˥na˥su** {⟨〜を⟩/⟨〜について⟩}話す ① **[for s.o. to convey orally information on some topic]** ⟪**talk**⟫, ⟨-o⟩ **i˥i-arawa˥su** ⟨〜を⟩言い表す ① **[for s.o. to express one's thoughts/sentiments by uttering words/sentences]** ⟪**express**⟫, ⟨-o⟩ **hyo˥oge˥n-suru** ⟨〜を⟩表現する ③ **•c [to express ideas using gestures, language, music, painting, etc.]** ⟪**express, represent**⟫

EX. (**a**) It is important to speak one's opinion in language easily understood by others.
自分の意見を他人に分かりやすい言葉で{言う/話す/言い表す/表現する}のは大事だ。
Jibun no iken o tanin ni wakari-yasui kotoba de {iu/hanasu/ii-arawasu/hyoogen-suru} no wa daiji da.
(**b**) Ms. Johnson speaks Japanese very well.
ジョンソンさんは日本語を大変上手に{話します/*言います/*言い表します/*表現します}。
*Jonson-san wa Nihon-go o taihen joozuni {hanashimasu/*iimasu/*ii-arawashimasu/*hyoogen-shimasu}.*

speaker n. **[a person who speaks]**
ha˥nashi-te 話し手 **[the one speaking as opposed to the one listening]** ↔ **kiki-te** 聞き手; **wa˥sha** 話者 **•c [the one speaking as opposed to the one listening]** ↔ **kiki-te** 聞き手; **e˥nzetsu˥-sha** 演説者 **•c [a person making a public speech]**, **ko˥oe˥n-sha** 講演

者 •c **[a person giving a special lecture on a topic]** ⟪**lecturer**⟫

EX. (**a**) Today we have the honor of welcoming Dr. Brown as our speaker.
今日は{講演者/*演説者/*話し手/*話者}にブラウン博士をお招きしております。
*Kyoo wa {kooen-sha/*enzetsu-sha/*hanashi-te/*washa} ni Buraun-hakase o o-maneki shite orimasu.*
(**b**) The level of politeness of a Japanese sentence depends largely on the social relationship of the speaker to the hearer.
日本語の文の丁寧さはほとんど{話し手/話者/*講演者/*演説者}と聞き手の社会的関係によって決まる。
*Nihon-go no bun no teinei-sa wa hotondo {hanashi-te/washa/*kooen-sha/*enzetsu-sha} to kiki-te no shakai-teki-kankei ni-yotte kimaru.*
(**c**) I have never heard such an eloquent speaker.
こんな説得力のある{演説者/講演者/?話し手/?話者}の話を聞いたことがない。
Konna settoku-ryoku no aru {enzetsu-sha/kooen-sha/?hanashi-te/?washa} no hanashi o kiita koto ga nai.

NOTE. "He is a good speaker of Japanese" is expressed in Japanese as *Ano hito wa Nihon-go ga joozu desu.*

spear n.
ya⌈ri やり

special adj. **[having (unusual/exceptional/unique) features distinct from other members of the same class]**
to⌈kubetsuna 特別な adj(*na*). •c **[to be different in a particular respect from other members of the same class]** ⟪**special, particular, extraordinary**⟫ ↔ **futsuu no N** 普通のN •c; **to⌈kushuna** 特殊な adj(*na*). •c **[out of the ordinary]** ⟪**peculiar, unique**⟫ ↔ **ippan-tekina** 一般的な adj(*na*). •c; **do⌈kutoku no N** 独特のN •c **[for a characteristic to belong exclusively to s.o./s.t./s.a.]** ⟪**unique, peculiar**⟫, **do⌈kutokuna** 独特な adj(*na*). •c

EX. (**a**) His son was put in a special class because his IQ was way above average.
彼の息子はIQが平均よりずっと高いので{特別な/??特殊な/*独特の/*独特な}クラスに入った。
*Kare no musuko wa IQ ga heikin yori zutto takai node {tokubetsuna/??tokushuna/*dokutoku no/*dokutokuna} kurasu ni haitta.*
(**b**) Every culture has its own special characteristics as well as general characteristics it shares with other cultures.
どの文化にも{特殊な/特別な/独特の/独特な}特徴と他の文化と共通の一般的な特徴とがある。
Dono bunka ni mo {tokushuna/tokubetsuna/dokutoku no/dokutokuna} tokuchoo to ta no bunka to kyootsuu no ippan-tekina tokuchoo to ga aru.
(**c**) Japanese tend to think that their culture is special and not like that of any other culture in the world.
日本人は日本の文化は{特殊/特別/独特}で、世界の他の文化と異なると思いがちだ。
Nihon-jin wa Nihon no bunka wa {tokushu/tokubetsu/dokutoku} de sekai no ta no bunka to kotonaru to omoi-gachi da.

specialist n. **[a person who specializes in a specific field]**
se⌈nmon-ka 専門家 •c **[a person who specializes in an academic field]** ⟪**expert**⟫

EX. Mr. Harada is a specialist in Chinese economics.
原田氏は中国経済の専門家です。
Harada-shi wa Chuugoku-keizai no senmon-ka desu.

specialize vi. **[for s.o. to concentrate on a particular area of a subject]**
⟨-o⟩ se⌈nkoo-suru ⟨〜を⟩専攻する ③ •c **[for s.o. to major in a certain field of study]** ⟪**major in**⟫

EX. I am specializing in Japanese sociology.
私は日本の社会学を専攻している。
Watashi wa Nihon no shakai-gaku o senkoo-shite iru.

S

specially adv. **[in a special way]**
1. to⌈kubetsuni 特別に /⟨adj(*na*). *ni* of *tokubetsuna* special/ [in a special and distinct way] ⟪especially, expressly, particularly, exceptionally⟫
EX. His food was specially prepared since he was a vegetarian.
彼は菜食主義なので、食事が特別に用意された。
Kare wa saishoku-shugi na node, shokuji ga tokubetsuni yooi-sareta.

specialty n. **[a special quality/feature/product or a field in which one specializes]**
1. se⌈nmon 専門 •c [a branch of study in which one specializes] ⟪special subject of study, profession⟫
EX. My specialty is computer science.
私の専門はコンピューターサイエンスです。
Watashi no senmon wa konpyuutaa-saiensu desu.
2. to⌈kushoku 特色 •c [such features as are peculiar to s.t.] ⟪characteristic, peculiarity, distinction, individuality⟫
EX. The specialty of this university is its emphasis on undergraduate education.
この大学の特色は学部生の教育に力点を置いていることです。
Kono daigaku no tokushoku wa gakubu-sei no kyooiku ni rikiten o oite iru koto desu.

S

species n. **[a distinct kind or sort]**
1. shu⌉ 種 [a distinct kind] ⟪sort, type, class⟫
EX. Rats and squirrels belong to the same species.
ねずみとりすは同じ種に属する。
Nezumi to risu wa onaji shu ni zokusuru.
2. shu⌉rui 種類 •c [a group of individuals sharing common characteristics] ⟪kind, sort, variety, type⟫
EX. There are many species of butterflies in Japan.
日本には色々な種類のちょうちょがいる。
Nihon ni wa iro-irona shurui no choocho ga iru.

specific adj. **[distinct from others ⟪fig. "expressed in explicit terms"⟫]**
1. to⌈kutei no N 特定のN •c [specially designated/determined] ⟪special, exceptional⟫
EX. The majority of students seem to enter college without any specific goal in mind.
大多数の学生は特定の目的を持たないで大学に入るようだ。
Dai-tasuu no gakusei wa tokutei no mokuteki o motanai de daigaku ni hairu yooda.
2. to⌈kushuna 特殊な adj(*na*). **•c [out of the ordinary] ⟪special, particular, peculiar, distinct⟫ ↔ ippan no N 一般のN •c**
EX. I'm studying a very specific problem.
私はとても特殊な問題の研究をしています。
Watashi wa totemo tokushuna mondai no kenkyuu o shite imasu.

specimen n. **[an item or part typical of a group or a whole]**
mi⌈hon 見本 [s.t./s.o. representative of an entire class ⟪fig. "a good example"⟫] ⟪sample, pattern⟫, hyo⌈ohon 標本 •c [a zoological/statistical item typical of a group used for display or testing]
EX. Do you have a specimen of this butterfly?
このちょうちょの{見本/標本}がありますか。
Kono choocho no {mihon/hyoohon} ga arimasu ka.

spectacle n. **[a striking or impressive sight]**
mi-⌈mono⌉ 見もの [an object worthy of looking at] ⟪sight, attraction⟫, so⌈okan 壮観 •c [a magnificent sight] ⟪grand sight⟫
EX. The finale of the circus was a spectacle worth beholding.
そのサーカスのフィナーレは{見もの/壮観}だった。
Sono saakasu no finaare wa {mi-mono/sookan} datta.

spectacular adj. **[striking, impressive, amazing]**
mi-⌈mono⌉ no N 見もののN [of an object

worthy of being looked at], so⌈okan no N 壮観のN •c [of a magnificent sight], su⌈go⌉i すごい adj(*i*). **[fearful or impressive in degree/extent ⟨s⟩] ⟪horrible, awful, amazing⟫, su⌈barashi⌉i すばらしい** adj(*i*). **[causing great wonder/admiration/pleasure because it/one is extremely good] ⟪splendid, superb, magnificent, astounding⟫**

EX. The Gion festival in Kyoto was spectacular.
祇園祭りは{見ものでした/壮観でした/すごかったです/すばらしかったです}。
Gion-matsuri wa {mi-mono deshita/sookan deshita/sugokatta desu/subarashikatta desu}.

spectator n. **[a person who watches an event/performance]**

1. bo⌈oka⌉n-sha 傍観者 •c [a person who watches an event without becoming involved] ⟪onlooker, bystander, sideliner⟫

EX. Don't just be a spectator. Be a participant too.
ただの傍観者であってはいけない。参加者にもなりなさい。
Tada no bookan-sha de atte wa ikenai. Sanka-sha ni mo narinasai.

2. ke⌈nbutsu-nin 見物人 •c [s.o. watching an entertaining event or a sightseer] ⟪onlooker, sightseer⟫, ka⌈nkyaku 観客 •c [s.o. who watches (usu. seated and having paid) **an event such as the circus/a sports game/a movie] ⟪audience, visitor⟫, ka⌈nshuu 観衆 •c [a mass of people watching a sports game/a festival] ⟪audience⟫**

EX. (**a**) Thousands of spectators lined the roadsides to watch the Olympic marathon.
何千人という{見物人/観衆/*観客}が沿道に並んでオリンピックのマラソンを見ていた。
*Nan-zen-nin to iu {kenbutsu-nin/kanshuu/*kankyaku} ga endoo ni narande Orinpikku no marason o mite ita.*
(**b**) The number of spectators at the baseball game was about 60,000.
その野球の{観衆/観客/?見物人}は約六万人だった。
Sono yakyuu no {kanshuu/kankyaku/?kenbutsu-nin} wa yaku roku-man-nin datta.

spectrum n.

su⌈pe⌉kutoramu スペクトラム •f

speech n. **[the act of speaking or one's manner of speaking or the ability to speak or language used in speaking]**

1. ha⌈na⌉su koto 話すこと [the act of speaking], ha⌈nashi⌉ 話 /⟨V*masu* of *hanasu* ① speak/ [an act/instance of speaking ⟪fig. "rumor"⟫] ⟪talk, conversation, chat, lecture, story, rumor⟫, e⌈nzetsu 演説 •c [an act of orally expressing one's (political) **beliefs/opinions in public] ⟪address, oration, lecture⟫**

EX. (**a**) Although he has many strengths, speech is not one of them.
彼には様々な長所があるが、{話すこと/演説/?話}はその一つではない。
Kare ni wa samazamana choosho ga aru ga {hanasu koto/enzetsu/?hanashi} wa sono hitotsu dewanai.
(**b**) Did you listen to the speech of the presidential candidate?
大統領候補の{演説/話/?話すこと}を聞きましたか。
Daitooryoo-kooho no {enzetsu/hanashi/?hanasu koto} o kikimashita ka.

2. ha⌈nashi-kata⌉ 話し方 /⟨V*masu* of *hanasu* ① speak + *kata* way/ [way/manner of speaking], ha⌈nashi-buri 話し振り [a manner in which one talks], ho⌈oge⌉n 方言 •c [a dialect]

EX. (**a**) From his speech, you can tell that he is not a native of these parts.
彼の{話し方/話し振り/方言}からこの辺の出身ではないとすぐ分かる。
Kare no {hanashi-kata/hanashi-buri/hoogen} kara kono hen no shusshin de wa nai to sugu wakaru.
(**b**) Male speech is quite different from female speech in Japanese.
日本語では男性の{話し方/*方言/*話し

振り}は女性のそれと違う。
*Nihon-go de wa dansei no {hanashi-kata/*hoogen/*hanashi-buri} wa josei no sore to chigau.*
(**c**) I find Judy's speech utterly charming.
ジュディの{話し方/?話し振り/?方言}は私には本当に魅力的だ。
Judii no {hanashi-kata/?hanashi-buri/?hoogen} wa watashi ni wa hontoo ni miryoku-teki da.

3. ha⌈na⌉su chi⌈kara⌉ 話す力 [ability to speak], ha⌈na⌉su no⌉oryoku 話す能力 [ability to speak]

speed n. **[the rate of time at which s.t. moves/operates or rapidity of movement]**
1. ha⌈ya⌉i koto 速いこと [an act/state of moving rapidly]
2. ha⌉ya-sa 速さ /⟨adj(*i*). stem of *hayai* rapid + suf. *sa* ness/ [(degree of) quickness of motion], so⌉kudo 速度 •c [degree of quickness of motion] ⟪rate, pace, velocity⟫, su⌈piido スピード •f

EX. (**a**) This jet flies at a speed of 600 miles per hour.
このジェットは一時間六百マイルの{速度/速さ/スピード}で飛ぶ。
Kono jetto wa ichi-jikan rop-pyaku-mairu no {sokudo/haya-sa/supiido} de tobu.
(**b**) She can type at the incredible speed of 100 words per minute.
彼女は毎分百語という信じられない{速度/速さ/スピード}でタイプが打てます。
Kanojo wa mai-fun hyaku-go to iu shinji-rarenai {sokudo/haya-sa/supiido} de taipu ga ute-masu.

—— vi. **[for s.o./a vehicle to move (more) rapidly (than is safe or lawful), often violating traffic rules]**
su⌈piido o da⌉su スピードを出す ① [for s.o./a vehicle to increase speed], tsu⌈ppashi⌉ru 突っ走る ① [to run very rapidly] ⟪dash, rush, dart⟫, shi⌈ssoo-suru 疾走する ① •c [to run very rapidly] ⟪spank, scuttle, dash⟫

EX. (**a**) The car sped through the red light.
車は赤信号を{突っ走った/*疾走した/*スピードを出した}。
*Kuruma wa aka-shingoo o {tsuppashitta/*shissoo-shita/*supiido o dashita}.*
(**b**) As I was waiting at the bus stop two ambulances sped by with their sirens going.
バス停で待っていると、救急車が二台サイレンを鳴らしながら、そばを{突っ走って/疾走して/*スピードを出して}行った。
*Basu-tei de matte iru to, kyuukyuu-sha ga ni-dai sairen o narashi-nagara, soba o {tsuppashitte/shissoo-shite/*supiido o dashite} itta.*
(**c**) Don't speed. Drive carefully.
{スピードを出す/*疾走する/*突っ走る}な。注意深く運転しろ。
*{Supiido o dasu/*Shissoo-suru/*Tsuppashiru} na. Chuui-bukaku unten-shiro.*

PHRASE: speed up *supiido o ageru* スピードを上げる ②

speedy adj. **[moving/done quickly]**
ha⌈ya⌉i はやい adj(*i*). **[taking less time than is normal or expected or occurring at a point in time prior to what is normal or expected] ⟪early, fast, quick⟫, bi⌈nsokuna 敏速な** adj(*na*). **•c [for motion/work to be very quick] ⟪quick, prompt, brisk, active, alert⟫**
㊥ "quick"▷速い, "early"▷早い
NOTE: 早い is also sometimes used for "quick" or "speedy" as well.

EX. (**a**) Did you finish already? That was speedy!
もう終わったんですか。{速い/*敏速}ですねえ。
*Moo owatta n desu ka. {Hayai/*Binsoku} desu nee.*
(**b**) We look forward to a speedy response from the government.
我々は政府の{敏速な/早い}対応を期待している。
Ware-ware wa seifu no {binsokuna/hayai} taioo o kitai-shite iru.

spell vt. **[for s.o. to write or name in their proper order the letters of the alphabet**

forming a word or words 《fig. "mean"》] ⟨-o⟩ tsu⌈zuru ⟨～を⟩つづる ① [for s.o. to link or connect things together 《fig. "sew," "bind," "write"》] 《write, patch, bind》

EX. Can you spell the name of the longest river in the U.S.?
アメリカで一番長い川の名前をつづれますか。
Amerika de ichiban nagai kawa no namae o tsuzure-masu ka.

spelling n. **[an act/method of writing or naming in their proper order the letters of the alphabet forming a word or words] tsu⌈zuri つづり /⟨V*masu* of *tsuzuru* ① spell/ 《orthography》, se⌈isho⌉-hoo 正書法 •c [the proper way of writing words] 《orthography》**

spend vt. **[for s.o. to use money/time/ energy for some purpose]**

1. ⟨⟨-ni⟩⟩ ⟨-o⟩ tsu⌈kau ⟨⟨～に⟩⟩⟨～を⟩使う ① [for s.o./s.a. to cause s.t./s.o./s.a. to act or serve for a purpose or as an instrument or as a material for consumption] 《use, utilize》, ⟨-ni⟩ ⟨-o⟩ tsu⌈iya⌉su ⟨～に⟩⟨～を⟩費やす ① [for s.o. to use money/time abundantly/wastefully for some purpose ⟨w⟩] 《expend, consume, waste, squander》, ⟨-ni⟩ ⟨-o⟩ ka⌈ke⌉ru ⟨～に⟩⟨～を⟩かける ② [for s.o. to cause s.t. to extend to and come in contact with s.t./s.o./s.a. else 《fig. "sit down," "sprinkle," "splash," "bet," "spend," "build (a bridge)"》]

㊊ "build a bridge or set a ladder"▷架ける, "hang s.t."▷掛ける, otherwise ▷かける

EX. (**a**) We spent five years building the log house.
私たちはログハウスを建てるのに五年{使った/費やした/かけた}。
Watashi-tachi wa roguhausu o tateru no ni go-nen {tsukatta/tsuiyashita/kaketa}.
(**b**) Don't you think that Japanese spend too much money on education?
日本人は教育にお金を{かけすぎる/使いすぎる/費やしすぎる}と思いませんか。
Nihon-jin wa kyooiku ni o-kane o {kake-sugiru/tsukai-sugiru/tsuiyashi-sugiru} to omoimasen ka.

2. ⟨-o⟩ ⟨⟨-de⟩⟩ su⌈go⌉su ⟨～を⟩⟨⟨～で⟩⟩過ごす ① [for s.o. to allow time to go by (in some place)] 《pass, tide over》

EX. We spent the winter together in Hawaii.
私たちは冬を一緒にハワイで過ごしました。
Watashi-tachi wa fuyu o issho ni Hawai de sugoshimashita.

sperm n.
se⌉ishi 精子 •c

sphere n. **[a (celestial) globe or the domain of one's influence/action/existence]**
1. te⌈nkyuu 天球 •c [a celestial globe]
2. ha⌉n'i 範囲 •c [an area defined by certain bounds] 《extent, scope, limits》

EX. The sphere of this research is very much limited.
この研究の範囲は非常に限られている。
Kono kenkyuu no han'i wa hijooni kagira-rete iru.

spice n.
ya⌈kumi 薬味 •c 《condiments, seasoning》, ko⌈oshi⌉n-ryoo 香辛料 •c, su⌈pa⌉isu スパイス •f

spicy adj. **[flavored with spice 《acrid》]**
1. {ya⌈kumi/ko⌈oshi⌉n-ryoo} ga ki⌈ita N {薬味/香辛料}がきいたN, ka⌈ra⌉i からい adj(*i*). **[having the tongue-piercing taste of salt/ spice 《fig. "strict," "painful"》] 《hot, salty》 ↔ amai 甘い** adj(*i*). **《sweet》**

㊊ "spicy"▷辛い, otherwise ▷からい

EX. I like spicy food.
私は{{薬味/香辛料}{の/が}きいた/辛い}食べ物が好きだ。
Watashi wa {{yakumi/kooshin-ryoo} {no/ga} kiita/karai} tabe-mono ga suki da.

2. shi⌈nratsuna 辛らつな adj(*na*). **•c [extremely harsh in one's criticism or satire] 《bitter, sharp, harsh》**

spider n.
ku⌉mo くも

spill vt. **[for s.o./s.a. to cause a liquid/ granular substance to come out of its container and fall]**

S

⟨-o⟩ **ko⌈bo⌉su** ⟨〜を⟩こぼす ① **[for s.o. to cause a liquid/granular substance to come out of its container and fall]** ⟪drop, shed⟫, ⟨⟨-ni⟩⟩ ⟨-o⟩ **na⌈ga⌉su** ⟨⟨〜に⟩⟩⟨〜を⟩流す ① **[for s.o. to let liquid flow into some place or to cause s.t. to be carried away by water** ⟪**fig. "broadcast"**⟫**]**

EX. (**a**) Be careful not to spill the milk when you pour it.
ミルクをつぐ時{こぼさない/*流さない}ように注意しなさい。
*Miruku o tsugu toki {kobosanai/ *nagasanai} yooni chuui-shinasai.*
(**b**) The factory was spilling toxic chemicals into the river.
工場は川に有毒な化学薬品を{流して/*こぼして}いた。
*Koojoo wa kawa ni yuudokuna kagaku-yakuhin o {nagashite/*koboshite} ita.*

— vi. **[for a liquid/granular substance to come out from its container and fall]**
ko⌈bore⌉ru こぼれる ② **[for a granular or liquid substance such as tears to come out of its container and fall]** ⟪**fall, drop, overflow**⟫

S

EX. The coffee spilled when the plane shook.
飛行機が揺れた時、コーヒーがこぼれた。
Hikoo-ki ga yureta toki, koohii ga koboreta.

spin vt. **[for s.o. to draw out and twist fibers into thread** ⟪**fig. "rotate s.t."**⟫**]**
1. ⟨-o⟩ **tsu⌈mu⌉gu** ⟨〜を⟩紡ぐ ① **[for s.o. to make yarn]**
2. ⟨-o⟩ **ma⌈wasu** ⟨〜を⟩回す ① **[for s.o. to cause s.o./s.t./s.a. to move in a circular motion** ⟪**fig. "send round," "forward"**⟫**]** ⟪**turn, revolve, rotate**⟫

EX. When I was small I used to love spinning my top.
子供の時こまを回すのが好きだった。
Kodomo no toki koma o mawasu no ga suki datta.

spinal adj. **[of a spine]**
1. **to⌈ge⌉ no N** とげのN **[of a thorn/prickle]**
2. **se-⌈bone no N** 背骨のN **[of a backbone]**

spine n. **[a thorn/prickle/backbone]**
1. **to⌈ge⌉** とげ **[a thorn/prickle]**
2. **se-⌈bone** 背骨 **[a backbone]**

spiral n. **[a spiral curve or an object shaped in that way]**
1. **ra⌉sen** らせん •c **[a spiral curve]**
2. **ra⌉sen-kei no mono** らせん形の物 **[an object shaped as a spiral curve]**

— adj. **[of a spiral]**
ra⌈sen-(kei) no N らせん(形)のN

EX. The Statue of Liberty has a spiral staircase inside.
「自由の女神」の中にはらせん形の階段がある。
'Jiyuu no me-gami' no naka ni wa rasen-kei no kaidan ga aru.

spirit n. **[s.t. supernatural that animates/possesses the human body]**
1. **se⌉ishin** 精神 •c **[the mind as opposed to the body]** ⟪**soul, mind, will**⟫ ↔ **nikutai** 肉体 •c, **busshitsu** 物質 •c; **ko⌈ko⌉ro** 心 **[the seat of one's thoughts/feelings in the body]** ⟪**mind, heart, thought, mood**⟫, **ta⌉mashii** 魂 **[s.t. supernatural that resides in and gives life to s.o./s.t./s.a.]** ⟪**soul**⟫, **re⌉ikon** 霊魂 •c **[s.t. supernatural that resides in and gives life to the human body]** ⟪**soul**⟫

EX. (**a**) The spirit of a culture can be said to reside in its language.
文化の{精神/心/魂/*霊魂}はその言語に宿っていると言える。
*Bunka no {seishin/kokoro/tamashii/ *reikon} wa sono gengo ni yadotte iru to ie-ru.*
(**b**) Do you believe that the human spirit is immortal?
人間の{魂/霊魂/??精神/*心}は不滅だと思いますか。
*Ningen no {tamashii/reikon/??seishin/ *kokoro} wa fumetsu da to omoimasu ka.*

2. **se⌉irei** 精霊 •c **[the Holy Spirit of the Christian religion]**
3. **yu⌉urei** 幽霊 •c **[a being who is believed to have returned from the world of the dead]**

EX. I hear that the house is haunted by spirits.
その家は幽霊がよく出るそうだ。
Sono ie wa yuurei ga yoku deru sooda.

4. se⌉iki 生気 •c [a positive, lively energy] ⟪animation, vitality, vigor⟫

EX. John seems to be always in good spirits.
ジョンはいつも生気にあふれているようだ。
Jon wa itsu-mo seiki ni afurete iru yooda.

5. tsu⌈yo⌉i sake 強い酒 [strong liquor]

spiritual adj. **[relating to spirit]**

1. se⌉ishin no N 精神のN •c [of mind as opposed to body], ko⌈ko⌉ro no N 心のN [relating to the seat of human intellect/sentiment/knowledge/will], re⌉ikon no N 霊魂のN •c [of s.t. supernatural that resides in and gives life to the human body], se⌈ishin-tekina 精神的な adj(*na*). **•c [of mind as opposed to body] ↔ nikutai-tekina 肉体的な** adj(*na*). **•c, busshitsu-tekina 物質的な** adj(*na*). **•c**

EX. (**a**) We need spiritual as well as physical nourishment.
われわれは肉体の滋養ばかりでなく{精神の/精神的な/?心の/*霊魂の}滋養も必要だ。
*Ware-ware wa nikutai no jiyoo bakari de naku {seishin no/seishin-tekina/?kokoro no/*reikon no} jiyoo mo hitsuyoo da.*
(**b**) Everyone has a longing for some kind of spiritual salvation.
だれでもなんらかの{精神の/精神的な/霊魂の/心の}救いを切望するものだ。
Dare-demo nanra-ka no {seishin no/seishin-tekina/reikon no/kokoro no} sukui o setsuboo-suru mono da.

2. se⌈irei no N 聖霊のN •c [of the Holy Spirit]

spit vi./vt. **[for s.o./s.a. to eject s.t. such as saliva, blood, etc. out of the mouth]**
tsu⌉ba o ha⌉ku つばを吐く ① [for s.o./s.a. to eject saliva out of the mouth]

EX. It's bad manners to spit in public.
人前でつばを吐くのは行儀が悪い。
Hito-mae de tsuba o haku no wa gyoogi ga warui.

spite n. **[an evil feeling towards another person]**
a⌉kui 悪意 •c [evil thought/intention] ⟪malice, hostility, venom⟫, u⌈rami⌉ うらみ /⟨V*masu* of *uramu* ① have a grudge against/ [a grudge held against s.o.] ⟪bitter feeling, hatred, rancor, enmity⟫

EX. I don't feel any spite towards him.
私はあの人に何にも{悪意/恨み}を持っていません。
Watashi wa ano hito ni nan-nimo {akui/urami} o motte imasen.

PHRASE: in spite of Sinf. *noni* Sinf.のに, Sinf. *nimo-kakawarazu* Sinf.にもかかわらず ⟨w⟩

NOTE: When the nonpast affirmative form of adj(*na*). or N+cop. occurs before *noni/nimo-kakawarazu* the following forms are used.
{adj(*na*). stem/N} *na noni*
{adj(*na*). stem/N} *dearu nimo-kakawarazu*

EX. They climbed the mountain in spite of the bad weather.
彼らは天気が悪かった{のに/にもかかわらず}山に登ってしまった。
Kare-ra wa tenki ga warukatta {noni/nimo-kakawarazu} yama ni nobotte shimatta.

splash vt. **[to cause water/mud to scatter** (so as to make s.o./s.a./s.t. wet)**]**
⟨-o⟩ ha⌈ne-ka⌉su ⟨〜を⟩跳ねかす ① [to cause water/mud to scatter] ⟪bespatter, dabble⟫, ⟨-o⟩ ha⌈ne-kake⌉ru ⟨〜を⟩跳ねかける ② [for s.o./a vehicle to cause water/mud to scatter and hit s.o.] ⟪bespatter, dabble⟫

EX. (**a**) The children were splashing water at each other in the pool.
子供たちはプールで水を{跳ねかし/?跳ねかけ}あっていた。
Kodomo-tachi wa puuru de mizu o {hane-kashi/?hane-kake}-atte ita.
(**b**) The car splashed mud on me, staining my skirt.
車に泥を{跳ねかけられて/*跳ねかされて}、スカートにしみがついた。
Kuruma ni doro o {hane-kake-rarete/

**hane-kasa-rete}, sukaato ni shimi ga tsuita.*

— n. **[an act/sound of splashing or splashed water]**

ha⌈ne-ka⌉su koto 跳ねかすこと **[an act of splashing]**

PHRASE: with a splash *zabun to* ザブンと

EX. He dived into the water with a splash.
水にザブンと飛び込んだ。
Mizu ni zabun to tobi-konda.

splendid adj. **[displaying splendor]**

1. ka⌈gayakashi⌉i 輝かしい adj(*i*). **[so bright as to be blinding ⟪fig. "brilliant"⟫] ⟪bright, radiant, brilliant⟫**

2. ri⌈ppana 立派な adj(*na*). **•c [for s.o./some human creation/achievement to cause admiration] ⟪good, fine, gorgeous-looking, magnificent, great, praiseworthy⟫, su⌈barashi⌉i** すばらしい adj(*i*). **[causing great wonder/admiration/pleasure due to being extremely good] ⟪wonderful, marvelous, superb, great, fantastic⟫**

EX. (**a**) He lives in a splendid house.
あの人は{立派な/すばらしい}家に住んでいる。
Ano hito wa {rippana/subarashii} ie ni sunde iru.
(**b**) It's a splendid autumn day, isn't it?
{すばらしい/*立派な}秋の日ですね。
*{Subarashii/*Rippana} aki no hi desu ne.*
(**c**) Professor Yoshida is a splendid teacher.
吉田先生は{立派な/すばらしい}先生ですね。
Yoshida-sensei wa {rippana/subarashii} sensei desu ne.

splendor n. **[brilliance, magnificence, grandeur]**

1. ka⌈gayaki 輝き **/⟨V*masu* of *kagayaku* ① shine/ ⟪brilliance, radiance, brightness, glitter⟫**

2. ka⌈rei-sa 華麗さ **•c [magnificent beauty] ⟪magnificence, gorgeousness, brilliance, glory⟫**

split vt. **[for s.o./s.t. to break/cut/divide s.t. into two or more parts (to share it) ⟪fig. "divide people into hostile groups"⟫]**

1. ⟨-o⟩ (⟨-ni⟩) wa⌈ru ⟨〜を⟩(⟨〜に⟩)割る ① **[for s.o./s.a. to apply force hard to a substance and render it into two or more pieces ⟪fig. "(in mathematics) find how many times a given number is contained in another"⟫] ⟪divide, cut, break, smash⟫, ⟨-o⟩ ⟨-ni⟩ sa⌉ku** ⟨〜を⟩⟨〜に⟩裂く ① **[for s.o. to separate s.t. two-dimensional into two parts] ⟪tear, rend, cut up⟫**

EX. (**a**) In these parts you have to split a lot of firewood to make it through the winter.
この地方では冬を越すのに、まきをたくさん{割らなければ/*裂かなければ}ならない。
*Kono chihoo de wa fuyu o kosu no ni, maki o takusan {waranakereba/*sakanakereba} naranai.*
(**b**) We split a cold watermelon into a dozen pieces and ate it.
冷たいすいかを十二に{割って/*裂いて}食べた。
*Tsumetai suika o juu-ni ni {watte/*saite} tabeta.*
(**c**) The tailor split the material into three parts.
洋服屋は布地を三つに{裂いた/*割った}。
*Yoofuku-ya wa nuno-ji o mittsu ni {saita/*watta}.*

2. ⟨-o⟩ ⟨-ni⟩ wa⌈ke⌉ru ⟨〜を⟩⟨〜に⟩分ける ③ **•c [for s.o. to divide s.o./s.t./s.a. into two or more parts/groups (and share them with s.o.)] ⟪divide, cut up⟫**

EX. Let's split our earnings three ways.
我々の収入を三つに分けよう。
Ware-ware no shuunyuu o mittsu ni wakeyoo.

3. ⟨-no⟩ na⌉ka o sa⌉ku ⟨〜の⟩仲を裂く ① **[for s.o. to cause a relationship between people to break up]**

EX. Tomoko became jealous of their relationship and tried to split them up.
友子は二人の関係をねたんでその仲を裂こうとした。
Tomoko wa futari no kankei o netande sono naka o sakoo to shita.

PHRASE: split personality *nijuu-jinkaku* 二重人格 •c

—— n. **[an act of splitting s.t. or the state of being split]**
wa⌈ru koto 割ること [an act of breaking s.t. into two or more parts without folding], sa⌉ku koto 裂くこと [an act of separating s.t. two-dimensional into two parts], bu⌈nkatsu 分割 •c [an act of dividing s.t. into several parts] ⟪division, partition⟫, bu⌈nretsu 分裂 •c [for s.t. unified to be broken into parts] ⟪dissolution, disunion, breakup, division⟫

spoil vt. **[for s.o./s.t. to cause s.t. to become useless/valueless]**
1. ⟨⟨-de⟩⟩ da⌈me⌉ ni naru ⟨⟨～で⟩⟩駄目になる ① [for s.o./s.t. to become useless/valueless due to some cause], ⟨⟨-de⟩⟩ da⌈i-nashi ni na⌉ru ⟨⟨～で⟩⟩台無しになる ① [for s.t. to become totally useless due to some cause] ⟪ruin, mess up⟫

EX. (**a**) The rain spoiled our tennis match.
雨でテニスの試合が{駄目/台無し}になってしまった。
Ame de tenisu no shiai ga {dame/dai-nashi} ni natte shimatta.

NOTE: *Ame de shiai ga dame ni natta* means "the game was canceled due to rain," whereas *Ame de shiai ga dai-nashi ni natta* means "the game which took place was miserable due to rain."

(**b**) One careless word spoiled their relationship.
二人の関係は不注意な一言で{駄目/台無し}になってしまった。
Futari no kankei wa fu-chuuina hito-koto de {dame/dai-nashi} ni natte shimatta.

2. ⟨-o⟩ ku⌈sara-se⌉ru ⟨～を⟩腐らせる /⟨causative of *kusaru* ① rot/ ② [for s.o./s.t. to cause s.t. to rot]

EX. I forgot to put the eggs in the refrigerator and they were spoiled.
卵を冷蔵庫に入れるのを忘れて、腐らせてしまった。
Tamago o reizoo-ko ni ireru no o wasurete, kusara-sete shimatta.

3. ⟨-o⟩ a⌈mayaka⌉su ⟨～を⟩甘やかす ① [for s.o. to cause/allow s.o. junior to the speaker to depend too much on him/her] ⟪indulge, pamper⟫

EX. Japanese mothers tend to spoil their children.
日本の母親は子供を甘やかしがちだ。
Nihon no haha-oya wa kodomo o amayakashi-gachi da.

—— vi. **[for s.t. to become useless/valueless]**
1. ⟨⟨-de⟩⟩ da⌈me⌉ ni naru ⟨⟨～で⟩⟩駄目になる ①, ⟨⟨-de⟩⟩ da⌈i-nashi ni na⌉ru ⟨⟨～で⟩⟩台無しになる ① SEE spoil vt. 1
2. ku⌉sa⌉ru 腐る ① [for a substance, esp. meat or vegetables, to lose its original form and function due to chemical action caused by bacteria, fungi, oxidation, etc. ⟪fig. "be very much discouraged"⟫] ⟪rot, go bad, decay, corrupt⟫, i⌈ta⌉mu いたむ ① [for s.o. to experience a feeling of pain or for s.t. to get damaged] ⟪feel pain, be spoiled⟫
㊯ "feel pain"▷痛む, "become spoiled"▷傷む, "grieve"▷悼む

EX. This fish could spoil quickly.
この魚はすぐに{腐る/傷む}かも知れないよ。
Kono sakana wa sugu ni {kusaru/itamu} kamoshirenai yo.

sponge n. **[a kind of water animal with a porous structure or its skeletal structure]**
1. ka⌈imen 海綿 •c [a kind of water animal with a porous structure]
2. su⌈ponji スポンジ •f [the skeletal structure of the sponge]

spoon n.
sa⌉ji さじ, su⌈pu⌉un スプーン •f

EX. Koreans often use a spoon to eat with.
韓国人は食べるのに{さじ/スプーン}をよく使う。
Kankoku-jin wa taberu no ni {saji/supuun} o yoku tsukau.

PHRASE: be born with a silver/gold spoon in one's mouth *kane-mochi no ie ni umareru* 金持ちの家に生まれる ②

sport n. **[an activity engaged in for amusement, esp. one requiring bodily exertion, or an object of ridicule]**

S

1. su⌈po⌉otsu スポーツ •f [an activity requiring bodily exertion engaged in for fun]

EX. A: Do you do any sports?
スポーツを何かしますか。
Supootsu o nani-ka shimasu ka.
B: Yes, I swim every day.
ええ、毎日泳いでいます。
Ee, mai-nichi oyoide imasu.

2. go⌈raku 娯楽 •c [s.t. one does for fun during one's free time] ⟪pleasure, amusement, recreation, pastime, entertainment⟫, yu⌉ugi 遊戯 •c [playful exercise, esp. of children] ⟪game, play, pastime, amusement⟫

3. wa⌈rai-mono 笑い物 [an object of ridicule]

spot n. **[a particularly small part of an area that is different from other parts of the same area in terms of color, texture, etc. ⟪fig. "flaw"⟫]**

1. shi⌈mi 染み [a small part of an area distinct from other parts of the same area in terms of color] ⟪blot, smear, smudge⟫

S

EX. (**a**) My new dress has a spot on its sleeve.
私の新しいドレスには袖の所に染みがついている。
Watashi no atarashii doresu ni wa sode no tokoro ni shimi ga tsuite iru.
(**b**) As you grow older you get spots on your face.
年を取ると顔に染みが出来る。
Toshi o toru to kao ni shimi ga dekiru.

2. chi⌉ten 地点 •c [a particular location on the surface of the earth] ⟪place⟫

EX. The accident took place at this spot.
事故はこの地点で起きた。
Jiko wa kono chiten de okita.

PHRASE: weak spot *ketten* 欠点 **•c** ⟪fault, defect, blemish⟫

EX. Everybody has his or her weak spots.
だれでも欠点を持っている。
Dare demo ketten o motte iru.

PHRASE: on the spot *sugu sono ba de* すぐその場で

EX. I accepted the offer on the spot.
すぐその場で申し出を受けた。
Sugu sono ba de mooshi-de o uketa.

— vt. **[to catch sight of or recognize ⟪fig. "discover a spot/spot-like object"⟫]**
⟨-o⟩ mi⌈tsukeru ⟨～を⟩見つける ② [for s.o./s.a. to find s.t./s.o./s.a.]

EX. That policeman is very good at spotting narcotic dealers.
その警官は麻薬の売人を見つけるのがうまい。
Sono keikan wa mayaku no bainin o mitsukeru no ga umai.

spray n. **[a mist/jet of fine liquid particles or a device for creating this]**

1. shi⌈buki⌉ しぶき [a mist of fine liquid particles] ⟪splash⟫

2. fu⌈nmu⌉-ki 噴霧器 •c [a device for creating a jet of fine liquid particles] ⟪sprayer, atomizer⟫, su⌈pu⌉ree スプレー •f, ki⌈ri-fu⌉ki 霧ふき

— vt. **[for s.o./s.a. to direct/shoot spray onto s.t./s.o./s.a.]**
⟨-o⟩ ⟨-ni⟩ fu⌈ki-tsuke⌉ru ⟨～を⟩⟨～に⟩吹きつける ② [for s.o./s.a. to blow/shoot s.t. in fine liquid particle form onto s.t./s.o./s.a.]

EX. John sprayed paint on the wall.
ジョンはペンキを壁に吹きつけた。
Jon wa penki o kabe ni fuki-tsuketa.

spread vt. **[for s.o./s.a. to expand s.t. to cover more space]**

1. ⟨-o⟩ hi⌈rogeru ⟨～を⟩広げる ② [for s.o./s.a. to open/unfold/expand s.t. closed/folded/localized] ⟪extend, expand, enlarge, widen, broaden⟫ ↔ ⟨-o⟩ sebameru ⟨～を⟩狭める ②

EX. (**a**) Please spread your arms.
腕を広げてください。
Ude o hirogete kudasai.
(**b**) The art dealer spread a picture scroll in front of me.
画商は絵巻物を私の前で広げた。
Gashoo wa emaki-mono o watashi no mae de hirogeta.

2. ⟨-ni⟩ ⟨-o⟩ shi⌈ku ⟨～に⟩⟨～を⟩敷く ① [for s.o. to expand s.t. flat over the floor/ground] ⟪lay, stretch, pave⟫

EX. How about spreading a mattress on the floor to sleep on?
床にマットレスを敷いて寝たらどうですか。
Yuka ni mattoresu o shiite netara doo desu ka.

3. ⟨-ni⟩ ⟨-o⟩ nu⌈ru ⟨〜に⟩⟨〜を⟩塗る ① [for s.o. to apply an unctuous substance such as paint/butter/jam to a surface] ⟪paint, plaster, varnish, apply, rub in⟫

EX. Here, why don't you use this knife to spread butter on the toast.
ほら、トーストにバターを塗るのにこのナイフを使ったら。
Hora, toosuto ni bataa o nuru no ni kono naifu o tsukattara.

4. ⟨-o⟩ hi⌈romeru ⟨〜を⟩広める ② [for s.o. to make s.t. more widely influential/known/felt/appreciated] ⟪diffuse, disseminate, propagate, popularize⟫

EX. The early Christians through their zealous evangelism spread the teachings of Christ throughout the entire Mediterranean region.
初期のキリスト教徒たちはその熱心な伝道によってキリストの教えを地中海の全域に広めた。
Shoki no Kirisuto kyooto tachi wa sono nesshinna dendoo ni-yotte Kirisuto no oshie o Chichuukai no zen'iki ni hirometa.

—— vi. **[for s.t. to be expanded to cover more space]**

1. ⟨-ni⟩ hi⌈rogaru ⟨〜に⟩広がる ① [for s.t. closed/folded/localized to open/unfold/expand] ⟪extend, stretch, reach, get around⟫

EX. (**a**) The rumor spread through the town like wildfire.
うわさはまたたく間に町中に広がった。
Uwasa wa matataku ma ni machi-juu ni hirogatta.
(**b**) Before we knew it, the cold had spread to the entire class.
知らないうちに風邪はクラス全体に広がった。
Shiranai uchi ni kaze wa kurasu zentai ni hirogatta.

2. u⌈tsu⌉ru うつる ① [to change to a different place or condition ⟪fig. "be reflected," "be infected"⟫] ⟪move, remove, change, be reflected, be infected⟫

㊞ "move/change"▷移る, "be reflected"▷映る

EX. The fire spread to the neighboring department store.
火は隣のデパートに移った。
Hi wa tonari no depaato ni utsutta.

—— n. **[the process/result of s.t. expanding to cover more space]**

1. hi⌈rogari 広がり /⟨V*masu* of *hirogaru* ①⟩ extend/ [the result of s.t. expanding to cover more space] ⟪extent, stretch, expanse⟫

2. de⌉npa 伝ぱ •c [an act of expanding s.t. to cover more space] ⟪dissemination, popularization⟫

3. mi⌈hiraki 見開き [two pages of a newspaper/magazine facing each other]

spring vi. **[for s.t., esp. water, to burst out from the soil ⟪fig. "rise," "jump," "gush out"⟫]**

1. to⌈bu とぶ ① [for s.o./s.a. to move quickly and suddenly away from a surface by the action of one's leg(s) or to move through the air] ⟪fly, flit, jump, leap⟫, ha⌈ne⌉ru 跳ねる ② [to move rapidly away from the surface/ground into the air] ⟪leap, jump, hop⟫

㊞ "fly/jamp/leap"▷飛ぶ, "jump/leap"▷跳ぶ

EX. A frog sprang out of the pond.
蛙が池から{飛んで/跳んで/跳ねて}出た。
Kaeru ga ike kara {tonde/tonde/hanete} deta.

2. to⌈bi-aga⌉ru 飛び上がる ① [for s.o./s.a. to rise into the air suddenly and rapidly] ⟪fly up, soar up, take off⟫

EX. The lady sprang to her feet when she saw the snake sliding toward her.
その婦人は蛇が自分の方にはって来ているのを見て飛び上がった。
Sono fujin wa hebi ga jibun no hoo ni hatte kite iru no o mite tobi-agatta.

3. ha⌈ne-kaeru 跳ね返る ① [for s.t. to be

S

thrown back from a surface] 《rebound, recoil》

EX. When I released the branch, it sprang back and hit me in the eye.
枝を離したら、跳ね返って目に当たった。
Eda o hanashitara, hane-kaette me ni atatta.

4. ho⌈tobashiri-de⌉ru ほとばしり出る ② [for liquid/passion to gush out with force] 《gush out, spout, spurt》

EX. The water was springing out from a hole in the pipe.
水がパイプの穴からほとばしり出ていた。
Mizu ga paipu no ana kara hotobashiri-dete ita.

5. o⌈ki⌉ru 起きる ② [for s.o./s.a./s.t. that has been lying horizontally dormant to stand up vertically 《fig. "wake up," "occur"》] 《get up, rise, wake up, happen, take place, occur》, ha⌈ssei-suru 発生する ③ •c [to happen or to come into being suddenly] 《occur, happen, break out, come into existence》

S

— n. **[the act of leaping/jumping or the season from March to May in the northern hemisphere or a device that reverts to its original shape after being compressed/ stretched or a natural flow of water out of the ground]**

1. ha⌉ru 春 [the season lasting from March to May in the northern hemisphere]

EX. (**a**) I prefer spring to fall.
私は秋より春の方が好きです。
Watashi wa aki yori haru no hoo ga suki desu.
(**b**) The long winter is gone, and spring has finally come.
長い冬が終わって、やっと春が来ました。
Nagai fuyu ga owatte, yatto haru ga kimashita.

2. cho⌈oyaku 跳躍 •c [an act of leaping/ jumping] 《jump, leap》

3. ba⌉ne ばね [a steel device that reverts to its original shape after being compressed/ stretched 《fig. "bounce"》] 《bounce》

4. i⌈zumi 泉 [a flow of water out of the earth 《fig. "origin"》] 《fountain, source》, ge⌈nsen 源泉 •c [a natural source of water 《fig. "origin"》]

5. ka⌈tsu⌉ryoku 活力 •c [the vitality which makes possible action and motion] 《vitality, vim, sap of life》

sprinkle vt. **[for s.o. to scatter water/ granular objects (on s.t.) in small drops] (⟨-ni⟩) ⟨-o⟩ ma⌉ku (⟨～に⟩)⟨～を⟩まく ① [for s.o. to distribute liquid or granular-shaped objects such as seeds over a wide area (using a throwing motion)] 《sow, scatter, strew》, ⟨-o⟩ (⟨-ni⟩) fu⌈ri-kake⌉ru ⟨～を⟩ (⟨～に⟩)振り掛ける ② [for s.o. to spread liquid/granular objects over s.t./s.o./s.a. in small quantities using a waving motion] 《rain on, spatter, splash》**

EX. (**a**) It tastes good if you sprinkle some sesame seeds on your rice.
御飯にごまを{振り掛ける/*まく}とおいしいですよ。
*Gohan ni goma o {furi-kakeru/*maku} to oishii desu yo.*
(**b**) In some churches they baptize people by sprinkling water on their heads.
教会によっては頭に水を{振り掛けて/ *まいて}洗礼を施す所もある。
*Kyookai ni-yotte wa atama ni mizu o {furi-kakete/*maite} senrei o hodokosu tokoro mo aru.*
(**c**) They sprinkle salt on the icy street in the winter to prevent slipping.
冬にはすべらないように凍った通りに塩を{まく/*振り掛ける}。
*Fuyu ni wa suberanai yooni kootta toori ni shio o {maku/*furi-kakeru}.*

spy n.

su⌉pai スパイ •f

EX. They say that there were many Soviet spies in the United States during the cold war.
冷戦時代にはアメリカにソビエトのスパイがたくさんいたそうだ。
Reisen-jidai ni wa Amerika ni Sobieto no supai ga takusan ita sooda.

square n. **[a two-dimensional figure/space having four equal sides and four right angles《fig. "an old-fashioned, inflexible, formal person"》]**
1. se⌈ihoo-kei 正方形 •c [a two-dimensional figure/space having four equal sides and four right angles ⟨fml⟩], shi⌈kaku⌉ 四角 •c [a two-dimensional figure/space having four equal sides and four right angles]
2. hi⌉ro-ba 広場 [an open area bounded by several streets]《open space, vacant lot, plaza》
EX. I saw a parade in Moscow's Red Square.
私はモスクワの赤の広場でパレードを見た。
Watashi wa Mosukuwa no Aka no Hiro-ba de pareedo o mita.
3. ji-⌈joo 二乗 •c [the number derived by multiplying a number by itself]
EX. The square of 3 is 9.
3の2乗は9だ。
San no ji-joo wa kyuu da.
—— adj. **[(having the characteristic) of a square《fig. "stout," "angular," "proper"》]**
1. se⌈ihoo-kei no N 正方形のN •c, shi⌈kaku⌉ no N 四角のN •c, shi⌈kakui 四角い adj(*i*). **•c**
EX. My friend built a square house.
僕の友達が{正方形の/四角の/四角い}家を建てた。
Boku no tomodachi ga {seihoo-kei no/shikaku no/shikakui} ie o tateta.
2. ka⌈do-ba⌉tta N 角張ったN [having sharp corners]《angular》, ga⌈sshi⌉ri-shita N がっしりしたN [strong and firm in build or structure]《sturdy, stout, massive》
EX. He has square shoulders.
彼は{がっしりした/角張った}肩をしている。
Kare wa {gasshiri-shita/kadobatta} kata o shite iru.
3. cha⌈n-to shita N ちゃんとしたN [to be correct and proper]《correct, proper, regular》
EX. I eat three square meals a day.
毎日三度ちゃんとした食事をとる。
Mai-nichi san-do chan-to shita shokuji o toru.
4. ko⌈oseina 公正な adj(*na*). **•c [in accordance with regulations]《just, fair, righteous, impartial》**
EX. I think they'll give us a square deal.
あの人たちは公正な取引をしてくれると思います。
Ano hito-tachi wa kooseina torihiki o shite kureru to omoimasu.

squash vt. **[for s.o. to press s.t. hard and crush it into pulp《fig. "suppress"》]**
⟨-o⟩ o⌈shi-tsubu⌉su ⟨〜を⟩押しつぶす ① [for s.o./s.a./s.t. heavy and mobile to press and crush s.t.]《crush, smash, quash, squeeze》
EX. They squashed the grapes with their feet for making wine.
ぶどう酒を造るためにぶどうを足で押しつぶした。
Budoo-shu o tsukuru tame ni budoo o ashi de oshi-tsubushita.

squeak vi./vt. **[for s.t./s.a. to make a thin, sharp high-pitched sound]**
ki⌉i-kii iu きいきい言う ① [for s.a./s.t. to make a metallic high-pitched sound]《creak, screech》, chu⌉u-chuu naku ちゅうちゅう鳴く ① [for a mouse/rat to make a sharp, high-pitched sound]
EX. This old chair squeaks a lot.
この古いいすはやたらと{きいきいいう/*ちゅうちゅう鳴く}。
*Kono furui isu wa yatara to {kii-kii iu/*chuu-chuu naku}.*

squeeze vt. **[for s.o./s.t. to press s.t./s.o. hard/tightly (so that it fits into a small space)]**
1. ⟨-o⟩ shi⌈me-tsukeru ⟨〜を⟩締め付ける ② [for s.o. to fasten/tighten s.t.]《fasten, tighten, compress》
EX. I felt as if my throat were being squeezed.
のどを締め付けられているような気がした。
Nodo o shimetsuke-rarete iru yoona ki-ga-shita.
2. ⟨-o⟩ gyu tto nigiru ⟨〜を⟩ぎゅっと握る ① [for s.o. to grasp s.t. very tightly]

S

《crush, smush, squash》

EX. He squeezed the ball in his hand.
彼は手でボールをぎゅっと握った。
Kare wa te de booru o gyu tto nigitta.

3. 〈-ni〉 〈-o〉 o⌈shi-{ko⌉mu/kome⌉ru} 〈～に〉〈～を〉押し{込む ①/込める ②} [for s.o. to force s.t./s.o./s.a. in a small space by pushing] 《push in, crowd into》

EX. I was able to squeeze five big suitcases into the trunk of my car.
車のトランクにスーツケースを五つ{押し込む/押し込める}ことが出来た。
Kuruma no toranku ni suutsukeesu o itsutsu {oshi-komu/oshi-komeru} koto ga dekita.

4. 〈-o〉 da⌈ki-shime⌉ru 〈～を〉抱き締める ② [for s.o. to hold s.o./s.t./s.a. tightly in one's arms] 《embrace, hold s.o. in one's arms》

EX. Upon finding the lost boy, the mother squeezed him tightly in her arms for several minutes, crying softly.
母親は迷子になっていた子供を見つけると、子供をしっかり抱き締めながらしばらく声を殺して泣いていた。。
Haha-oya wa maigo ni natte ita kodomo o mitsukeru to, kodomo o shikkari daki-shime-nagara shibaraku koe o koroshite naite ita.

squirrel n.
ri⌉su りす

EX. On American college campuses one sees many squirrels.
アメリカの大学のキャンパスではりすをよく見かける。
Amerika no daigaku no kyanpasu de wa risu o yoku mikakeru.

St. = Saint
sei- 聖～ **•c**

EX. We visited St. Patrick's cathedral in New York City.
私たちはニューヨークの聖パトリック大聖堂を訪ねた。
Watashi-tachi wa Nyuuyooku no Sei-Patorikku dai-seidoo o tazuneta.

stab vt. **[for s.o. to thrust a pointed object such as a needle/knife/dagger into s.o.'s/s.a.'s flesh (to kill or maim)]**
〈-o〉 (〈-de〉) sa⌉su 〈～を〉(〈～で〉)刺す ① [for s.o. to thrust a pointed object such as a knife/dagger/needle/skewer into s.t./s.o./s.a. (to kill or maim)] 《stick, pierce, thrust, sting》, 〈-o〉 (〈-de〉) tsu⌈ku 〈～を〉(〈～で〉)突く ① [for s.o./s.a. to make impact with or penetrate s.t./s.o./s.a. with a sharp or stick-like object 《fig. "attack sharply"》] 《poke, pierce, prick, butt》

EX. The mugger stabbed the old lady with a knife.
追いはぎは老女をナイフで{刺した/突いた}。
Oihagi wa roojo o naifu de {sashita/tsuita}.

stability n. **[the state/characteristic of being stable]**
a⌈ntei(-sei) 安定(性) **•c [the state of being peaceful and free from radical change] 《steadiness, equilibrium, balance, settlement, composure》**

EX. It's risky to invest in industries in countries that lack political stability.
政治の安定(性)に欠ける国の事業に投資するのは危険だ。
Seiji no antei(-sei) ni kakeru kuni no jigyoo ni tooshi-suru no wa kiken da.

stable adj. **[not easily thrown off balance]**
1. a⌈ntei-shita N 安定したN /〈Vinf. past of *antei-suru* ③ become stable/ **[peaceful and free from radical change] 《firm》 ↔ fu-anteina** 不安定な adj(*na*). **•c**

EX. Japan appears to be a stable society.
日本は安定した社会のようだ。
Nihon wa antei-shita shakai no yooda.

2. shi⌈kka⌉ri-shita N しっかりしたN /〈Vinf. past of *shikkari-suru* ③ become firm/ **[free from weakness/looseness], shi⌈kka⌉ri-shite iru (N)** しっかりしている(N) /〈V *te iru* of *shikkari-suru* ③ become firm/, **mo⌈no⌉ ni do⌈ojinai** ものに動じない adj(*i*). **[not easily shaken/moved] 《composed, unmoved, calm, cool》**

EX. He has a stable personality.
{彼は性格がしっかりしている/彼は{し

っかりした/物に動じない/*しっかりしている}性格をしている}。
*{Kare wa seikaku ga shikkari-shite iru/ Kare wa {shikkari-shita/mono ni doojinai/*shikkari-shite iru} seikaku o shite iru}.*

stable n. **[a shelter for animals]**
u⌈maya うまや, **u⌈ma-goya** 馬小屋

stack n. **[a (symmetrically arranged) pile, esp. of hay, or a vertical pipe to carry off smoke]**
1. ya⌈ma⌉ 山 **[a landmass that rises conspicuously above its surroundings ⟪fig. "a large heap," "a counter for a pile of merchandise"⟫]**
EX. There was a stack of wood in front of the hut.
その小屋の前には薪の山があった。
Sono koya no mae ni wa maki no yama ga atta.
2. e⌈ntotsu 煙突 **•c [a chimney]**
PHRASE: library stack *shoko* 書庫 •c
EX. Only faculty members and graduate students can use the library stacks.
書庫は教員と大学院生しか使えません。
Shoko wa kyooin to daigaku-in-sei shika tsukae-masen.
— vt. **[for s.o. to pile up many things]**
⟨-o⟩ tsu⌈mi-kasane⌉ru ⟨〜を⟩積み重ねる ② **⟪heap up, pile up, accumulate⟫**
EX. I usually end up stacking my books on my desk.
私は大抵本を机の上に積み重ねてしまいます。
Watashi wa taitei hon o tsukue no ue ni tsumi-kasanete shimaimasu.

staff n. **[a stick used as a weapon/support/measuring tool ⟪fig. "a group of people to assist a person in authority"⟫]**
1. sho⌈ku⌉in 職員 **•c [a person employed at an office/school/company to assist in administrative work] ⟪personnel⟫, sha⌉in** 社員 **•c [a company employee] ⟪personnel⟫**
EX. Our company has a staff of about one hundred young employees.
私たちの会社には約百名の若い{職員/社員}がいます。
Watashi-tachi no kaisha ni wa yaku hyaku-mei no wakai {shokuin/shain} ga imasu.
2. bo⌈o 棒 **•c [a long, slim object made of wood/bamboo/metal] ⟪rod, pole, club⟫**
3. tsu⌉e つえ **[a stick to assist in walking] ⟪stick, cane⟫**
4. ha⌈ta-za⌉o 旗竿 **[a pole for supporting a flag] ⟪flagpole, flagstaff⟫**
5. sa⌈sae 支え **/⟨V*masu* of *sasaeru* ② support/ [s.t./s.o. that supports s.o./s.t.] ⟪prop, stay⟫**
— vt. **[for s.o. to provide a place with a staff]**
⟨-ni⟩ sho⌈ku⌉in o i⌈reru ⟨〜に⟩職員を入れる ②
EX. I'm looking for people to staff my new office.
新しい事務所に職員を入れようと、人を探しているところです。
Atarashii jimu-sho ni shokuin o ireyoo to, hito o sagashite iru tokoro desu.

stage n. **[a platform/floor on which speeches/plays are presented ⟪fig. "scene," "theatrical profession," "period," "station"⟫]**
1. bu⌉tai 舞台 **•c [a platform for performing plays/dance ⟪fig. "a place where one displays his/her talents"⟫], su⌈te⌉eji** ステージ **•f [a platform usually for performing Western-style plays/dance]**
EX. Mariko is going to perform a Japanese dance on stage tonight.
真理子は今晩{舞台/ステージ}で日本舞踊を踊ります。
Mariko wa konban {butai/suteeji} de Nihon-buyoo o odorimasu.
2. da⌈nkai 段階 **•c [a period in the course of development of s.t.] ⟪step, phase⟫, -ki⌉** 〜期 **•c [a suffix to indicate a demarcated period of time]**
EX. (a) My son is now going through his rebellious stage.
息子は今反抗期です。
Musuko wa ima hankoo-ki desu.
(b) I am at a stage now where I can manage to survive in Japanese.

S

私の日本語はどうやらやっていける段階です。
Watashi no Nihon-go wa dooyara yatte ike-ru dankai desu.

3. e⌈ngeki 演劇 •c [a general, formal term for theatrical performance] ⟪**play, drama**⟫

EX. My friend has become very well known on stage in these parts.
私の友だちはこの辺では演劇で有名になった。
Watashi no tomodachi wa kono hen de wa engeki de yuumei ni natta.

—— vt. **[for s.o. to present s.t. on a stage ⟪fig. "plan"⟫]**

⟨-o⟩ jo⌈oen-suru ⟨〜を⟩上演する ③ •c [for s.o. to publicly present a play at a theater] ⟪**put on, play**⟫

EX. Mishima sometimes staged his own plays.
三島は自分の戯曲を上演したことがある。
Mishima wa jibun no gikyoku o jooen-shita koto ga aru.

stain vt. **[to spoil s.t. by coloring/soiling it ⟪fig. "blemish"⟫]**

1. ⟨-o⟩ yo⌈gosu ⟨〜を⟩汚す ① [for s.o./s.a. to make s.t. dirty] ⟪**soil, defile, pollute, taint, contaminate**⟫

EX. The child stained his T-shirt with mud.
子供はＴシャツを泥で汚した。
Kodomo wa tii-shatsu o doro de yogoshita.

2. ⟨-o⟩ ke⌈ga⌉su ⟨〜を⟩汚す ① [for s.o. to make s.t. dirty ⟪fig. "desecrate s.t.," "disgrace"⟫] ⟪**foul, pollute, defile**⟫

EX. You have permanently stained the reputation of our company by your evil actions.
あなたはこの悪行で我が社の名を完全に汚してしまったのだ。
Anata wa kono akugyoo de waga-sha no na o kanzenni kegashite shimatta noda.

—— n. **[a spot resulting from staining ⟪fig. "moral blemish"⟫]**

1. yo⌈gore 汚れ /⟨V*masu* of *yogoreru* ② get stained/ [a dirty spot] ⟪**blot, smudge**⟫, **shi⌈mi 染み [a small part of an area distinct from other parts of the same area in terms of color]** ⟪**blot, spot, blob, smear**⟫

2. o⌈ten 汚点 •c [a moral blemish] ⟪**blot, spot, blur, flaw**⟫

stairs n.

ka⌈idan 階段 •c

EX. Prof. Matsuda's office is the first room on your right at the top of the stairs.
松田先生の研究室は階段を上がって右側の最初の部屋です。
Matsuda-sensei no kenkyuu-shitsu wa kaidan o agatte migi-gawa no saisho no heya desu.

stake n. **[a stick or post with a pointed end (used for execution by fire) ⟪fig. "execution by fire," "s.t. risked, esp. money"⟫]**

1. ku⌉i くい [a stick that is driven into the ground as a mark or for supporting s.t.] ⟪**post, pile**⟫

EX. They erected a stake every 100 meters.
彼らは百メートルごとにくいを立てた。
Kare-ra wa hyaku-meetoru goto ni kui o tateta.

2. hi-⌈a⌉buri no ha⌈shira 火あぶりの柱 [a stake used for execution by burning]

3. hi-⌈a⌉buri no ke⌉i 火あぶりの刑 [execution by burning], ka⌈kei 火刑 •c ⟨w⟩

4. ka⌈ke⌉ かけ /⟨V*masu* of *kakeru* ② bet/ [an act of betting] ⟪**gambling**⟫

PHRASE: at stake *kakatte iru* かかっている ②

EX. The future of the company is at stake in this business deal.
会社の将来はこの取引の成立いかんにかかっている。
Kaisha no shoorai wa kono torihiki no seiritsu-ikan ni kakatte iru.

stalk n. **[the stem of a plant ⟪fig. "stem/axis-like object"⟫]**

1. ku⌈ki⌉ 茎 [the long narrow part of a plant]

EX. The corn plant has a long stalk.
とうもろこしは茎が長い。
Toomorokoshi wa kuki ga nagai.

2. ho⌈so-naga⌉i mono 細長いもの [a long, lean object]

S

stall n. **[a booth-like compartment for keeping a domestic animal/displaying items for sale/seating people in a church, theater, etc.]**
1. **ba⌈iten 売店 •c [a small store esp. in a station]** ⟪stand, kiosk, booth⟫, **ya⌉tai 屋台 [a street stand]** ⟪portable stall⟫
2. **kyo⌈okai no se⌉ki 教会の席 •c [a pew in a church]** ⟪pew⟫
3. **ko⌈shitsu 個室 •c [an individual room]** ⟪single room⟫
4. **e⌈njin-te⌉ishi エンジン停止 •f+c [engine stoppage], e⌈nsuto エンスト •f**
NOTE: *Ensuto* is derived from "engine stall."
— vt. **[for s.o. to cause a horse to enter a stable ⟪fig. "cause engine to stop"⟫]**
1. **u⌈ma⌉ o u⌈ma⌉ya ni i⌈reru 馬をうまやに入れる ② [for s.o. to put a horse in a stable]**
2. **e⌉njin o te⌈ishi-saseru エンジンを停止させる /⟨causative of *teishi-suru* ③ stop/ ③ [for s.o./s.t. to cause an engine to stop]**
— vi. **[for s.a. to be kept in a stall ⟪fig. "an engine stops without turning the ignition key"⟫]**
1. **ta⌈chi-o⌉ojoo-suru 立ち往生する ③ [for s.o./s.t. to be brought to a standstill]** ⟪be held up⟫
2. **e⌉njin ga to⌈matte shimau エンジンが止まってしまう ① [for an engine to stop without turning the ignition key], e⌈n-suto-suru エンストする ③ •f** SEE stall n. 4

stallion n.
ta⌈ne⌉-uma 種馬

stamp vt. **[for s.o./s.a. to bring s.t. such as one's foot or a device containing an impression down forcibly upon s.t. else]**
1. **a⌉shi⌉ de fu⌈mi-tsuke⌉ru 足で踏み付ける ② [for s.o./s.a. to trample down with the foot]**
EX. The man stamped out his cigarette.
男はタバコを足で踏み付けた。
Otoko wa tabako o ashi de fumi-tsuketa.
2. **⟨-ni⟩ {i⌉n/ha⌉n} o o⌈su ⟨〜に⟩{印/判}を押す ① [for s.o. to imprint a mark on s.t.], ⟨-ni⟩ su⌈ta⌉npu o o⌈su ⟨〜に⟩スタンプを押す ① •f [for s.o. to imprint s.t. with a seal usually made of rubber]**
EX. (**a**) Please stamp your seal right here.
ここに{印/判/*スタンプ}を押してください。
*Koko ni {in/han/*sutanpu} o oshite kudasai.*
(**b**) I forgot to stamp the date on the document.
書類に日付の{スタンプ/印/*判}を押すのを忘れました。
*Shorui ni hizuke no {sutanpu/in/*han} o osu no o wasuremashita.*
3. **⟨-ni⟩ ki⌈tte o haru ⟨〜に⟩切手をはる ① [for s.o. to paste a postal stamp on an envelope]**
EX. I sent the letter without stamping it.
切手をはらないで手紙を出してしまいました。
Kitte o haranai de tegami o dashite shimaimashita.
— n. **[a device for making an impression or the impression made by such a device or a piece of printed paper affixed in evidence that a tax/fee has been paid]**
ki⌈tte 切手 [a postage stamp]
EX. Two 500-yen stamps and five 100-yen stamps, please.
五百円切手二枚と百円切手五枚ください。
Go-hyaku-en-kitte ni-mai to hyaku-en-kitte go-mai kudasai.

stand vi. **[to stay in/take an upright position ⟪fig. "be located," "remain (unchanged)," "be in a state"⟫]**
1. **ta⌈chi-agaru 立ち上がる ① [for s.o./s.a. to get into an upright position ⟪fig. "take action"⟫]** ⟪rise (up)⟫ ↔ **suwaru 座る ①**
EX. When I entered the room Prof. Smith stood up and greeted me.
私が部屋に入って行くとスミス先生は立ち上がってあいさつをしてくださった。
Watashi ga heya ni haitte iku to Sumisu-sensei wa tachi-agatte aisatsu o shite kudasatta.

S

2. ta˥tte iru 立っている /⟨V *te iru* of *tatsu* ① stand/ ② [to stay in an upright position]
↔ suwatte iru 座っている ②

EX. I got really tired standing in the sun all day.
一日中日なたで立っていたので本当に疲れた。
Ichi-nichi-juu hinata de tatte ita node hontoo ni tsukarareta.

3. ⟨-ni⟩ a˥ru ⟨〜に⟩ある ① [for s.t. to exist in a place] ⟪be, exist, be found, be situated, have, own⟫

EX. The mansion stands on a cliff overlooking the ocean.
そのやかたは海を見渡す岸壁にある。
Sono yakata wa umi o mi-watasu ganpeki ni aru.

4. ø [to remain (unchanged)]

NOTE: There is no corresponding Japanese word for this meaning of "stand." See the following examples.

EX. (**a**) He stood firm over his decision to quit.
彼の辞める決意は堅かった。
Kare no yameru ketsui wa katakatta.
(**b**) His theory stood unchallenged for many years.
彼の理論は長年定説になっていた。
Kare no riron wa naganen teisetsu ni natte ita.
(**c**) The thermometer stood at 32°C all day long.
寒暖計は一日中摂氏三十二度だった。
Kandan-kei wa ich-nichi-juu sesshi san-juu-ni-do datta.
(**d**) Eric stood at the head of his class for four years straight.
エリックは四年間ずっとクラスのトップだった。
Erikku wa yo-nenkan zutto kurasu no toppu datta.

— vt. **[to cause s.t./s.o. to take/stay in an upright position ⟪fig. "endure"⟫]**

1. ⟨-o⟩ ta˥te˥ru ⟨〜を⟩たてる ② [to cause s.o./s.t./s.a. to take an upright position ⟪fig. "build s.t."⟫] ⟪raise, build, erect, establish, lay down⟫, {⟨-o⟩/⟨ni⟩} ta˥ta-se˥ru {⟨〜を⟩/⟨〜に⟩}立たせる /⟨causative of *tatsu* ① stand/ ② [to cause s.o./s.a. to take an upright position]

㊥ "build"▷建てる, otherwise ▷立てる

EX. (**a**) We always stand the Christmas tree by the window so you can see it from the outside.
外から見えるように、いつも窓のそばにクリスマスツリーを{立てる/*立たせる}ことにしている。
*Soto kara mieru yooni, itsu-mo mado no soba ni Kurisumasu-tsurii o {tateru/ *tata-seru} koto ni shite iru.*
(**b**) He stood the little boy on the tall chair so that he could see outside.
外が見えるように彼は小さな男の子を高いいすの上に{立たせた/*立てた}。
*Soto ga mieru yooni kare wa chiisana otoko-no-ko o takai isu no ue ni {tata-seta/*tateta}.*

2. ⟨-o⟩ ga˥man-suru ⟨〜を⟩我慢する ③ •c [for s.o./s.a. to willingly endure physical or mental affliction from s.t. for a relatively short period of time] ⟪bear, put up with⟫, ⟨-ni⟩ ta˥e˥ru ⟨〜に⟩耐える ② [for s.o./s.a. to not succumb to pain/pressure/distress caused by s.t.]

EX. (**a**) Whew, what a stench! I can't stand it!
こいつはひどいにおいだ。{我慢出来ない/耐えられない}。
Koitsu wa hidoi nioi da. {Gaman-dekinai/Tae-rarenai}.
(**b**) My friend was not able to stand the cold winters of Alaska.
私の友達はアラスカの冬の寒さ{に耐えられなかった/が我慢出来なかった}。
Watashi no tomodachi wa Arasuka no fuyu no samu-sa {ni tae-rarenakatta/ ga gaman-dekinakatta}.

— n. **[the action/result of taking an upright position ⟪fig. "endurance," "resistance," "position," "a raised platform," "kiosk"⟫]**

1. ta˥tsu koto 立つこと [an act/state of standing]

2. ba˥sho 場所 •c [a point or area in space where s.o./s.t./s.a. exists or where s.t. happens] ⟪place, location⟫, ta˥chiba˥ 立場

S

[a social or physical circumstance in which one finds oneself or one's viewpoint] **《point of view, standpoint》**

EX. (**a**) What is your stand on this issue?
この問題に関してあなたはどんな{立場/*場所}を取るんですか。
*Kono mondai ni-kanshite anata wa donna {tachiba/*basho} o toru n desu ka.*
(**b**) The soldiers took their stand near the gate.
兵隊たちは門の近くに{場所/*立場}を取った。
*Heitai-tachi wa mon no chikaku ni {basho/*tachiba} o totta.*

3. te⌈ikoo 抵抗 •c [the act of striving to counteract s.t./s.o./s.a.]

EX. He took a firm stand against abortion.
彼は人工妊娠中絶に強い抵抗を見せた。
Kare wa jinkoo-ninshin-chuuzetsu ni tsuyoi teikoo o miseta.

standard n. **[s.t. that is used as a symbol for s.t. or a basis for comparison]**
hyo⌈ojun 標準 •c [an average providing a basis for judgment/comparison/action] **《norm, criterion, measure, level》, ki⌈jun きじゅん •c [a norm used in making a judgment or taking action]** **《criterion, yardstick, basis, point of reference》, su⌈ijun 水準 •c [a (water) level]** **《level》**

㊉ for "the social norms of behavior" ▷規準, for "standard/standards of comparison" ▷基準

EX. (**a**) What standard is there for gauging different levels of foreign language proficiency?
外国語の熟達度のレベルを測る{基準/*標準/*水準}は何ですか。
*Gaikoku-go no jukutatsu-do no reberu o hakaru {kijun/*hyoojun/*suijun} wa nan desu ka.*
(**b**) This country has high standards in education.
この国は教育の{水準/標準/?基準}が高い。
Kono kuni wa kyooiku no {suijun/hyoojun/?kijun} ga takai.

— adj. **[pertaining to a standard]**
hyo⌈ojun-tekina 標準的な adj(*na*). **•c [conforming to a standard],** SEE standard n.

EX. This is standard procedure for this type of trial.
これはこの種の裁判の標準的な手続きである。
Kore wa kono shu no saiban no hyoojun-tekina te-tsuzuki dearu.

PHRASE: standard English *hyoojun-eigo* 標準英語 •c, standard test *hyoojun-tesuto* 標準テスト •c+f

standpoint n. **[a (mental) position from which s.t. is viewed]**
ta⌈chiba⌉ 立場 •c [a social or physical circumstance in which one finds oneself or one's viewpoint] **《position, footing, stand》, ka⌉nten 観点 •c [a mental position from which one observes and thinks about s.t.]** **《a point of view, viewpoint, angle》**

EX. Let's look at this issue from the standpoint of the students.
この問題を学生の{立場/観点}から見てみよう。
Kono mondai o gakusei no {tachiba/kanten} kara mite miyoo.

star n. **[a celestial body visible as a point of light in the sky, esp. at night 《fig. "star-like object," "a brilliant person"》]**

1. ho⌈shi 星 [a celestial body visible as a point of light in the sky, esp. at night 《fig. "bull's eye," "one's fortune"》]

EX. (**a**) The stars are beautiful tonight, aren't they?
今夜は星がきれいですね。
Kon'ya wa hoshi ga kirei desu ne.
(**b**) Look how brightly that star over the mountain is shining.
山の上のあの星、きらきら輝いていますね。
Yama no ue no ano hoshi, kira-kira kagayaite imasu ne.

2. su⌈ta⌉a スター •f [a brilliant person, esp. a prominent actor/actress]

EX. When I was small I dreamed of becoming a movie star.

小さい時、映画スターになるのを夢見ていました。
Chiisai toki, eiga-sutaa ni naru no o yume-mite imashita.

starch n. **[a carbohydrate which is an important ingredient in foods and which is used for stiffening cloth fabrics]**
1. ta⌈nsui-ka⌉butsu 炭水化物 •c [a carbohydrate], ka⌈takuri-ko⌉ かたくり粉 [a starch made from the dog-tooth violet]
2. no⌈ri⌉ のり [a sticky substance made from rice/flour or by chemical means for joining things or for stiffening cloth fabrics]

stare vi. **[for s.o./s.a. to gaze at s.t./s.o./s.a. steadily/intently]**
⟨-o⟩ ji⌈tto mi⌉ru ⟨〜を⟩じっと見る ② [for s.o./s.a. to look at s.t./s.o./s.a. without averting one's eyes] ⟪gaze at, look hard⟫, ⟨-o⟩ mi⌈tsumeru ⟨〜を⟩見つめる ② [for s.o./s.a. to look at s.o./s.t./s.a. continuously and intently]

EX. (**a**) In Japan Caucasian foreigners are often stared at.
日本では白人の外国人はよく{じっと見られる/見つめられる}。
Nihon de wa hakujin no gaikoku-jin wa yoku {jitto mi-rareru/mi-tsume-rareru}.
(**b**) Lovers often stare at each other.
恋人同士はよく{じっと見合う/見つめ合う}。
Koi-bito dooshi wa yoku {jitto mi-au/mi-tsume-au}.

S

starfish n.
hi⌈tode ひとで

start vi. **[for an event, process, or action to begin]**
1. ha⌈jimaru 始まる ① [for the first part of s.t. to take place] ⟪begin, commence⟫, o⌈ki⌉ru 起きる ② [for s.o./s.a./s.t. that has been lying horizontally and dormant to stand up vertically ⟪fig. "wake up," "occur"⟫] ⟪wake up, get up, take place, occur⟫

EX. (**a**) The meeting started at 9:00 A.M.
会議は午前九時に{始まった/*起きた}。
*Kaigi wa gozen ku-ji ni {hajimatta/*okita}.*
(**b**) The fire started at about 4:00 P.M.
火事は午後四時ごろ{起きた/*始まった}。
*Kaji wa gogo yo-ji-goro {okita/*hajimatta}.*

2. u⌈goki⌉-hajime⌉ru 動き始める /⟨V*masu* of *ugoku* ① move + *hajimeru* ② begin/ ② [to begin to move]

EX. The engine finally started.
エンジンがやっと動き始めた。
Enjin ga yatto ugoki-hajimeta.

3. ⟨⟨-o⟩⟩ ha⌈jimeru ⟨⟨〜を⟩⟩始める ② [for s.o./s.a. to perform the first part of an activity] ⟪begin, commence⟫

EX. Let's start!
さあ、始めよう!
Saa, hajimeyoo!

—— vt. **[for s.o./s.a. to cause an event, process, or action to begin]**
⟨-o⟩ ha⌈jimeru ⟨〜を⟩始める ② [for s.o./s.a. to perform the first stage of an activity/event] ⟪begin, commence⟫

EX. A: When did you start your study of Japanese?
日本語の勉強はいつ始めたんですか。
Nihon-go no benkyoo wa itsu hajimeta n desu ka.
B: Two years ago.
二年前です。
Ni-nen mae desu.

PHRASE: start to do V*masu* + *dasu* V*masu*+出す ①, V*masu* + *hajimeru* V*masu*+始める ②

EX. (**a**) I started to study Korean a year ago.
私は一年前に韓国語を勉強{し始めた/?し出した}。
Watashi wa ichi-nen mae ni Kankoku-go o benkyoo-{shi-hajimeta/?shi-dashita}.
(**b**) It started to rain.
雨が{降り出した/降り始めた}。
Ame ga {furi-dashita/furi-hajimeta}.

—— n. **[the event of s.t. starting or a sudden movement due to surprise or pain]**
1. o⌈doro⌉ite to⌈bi-aga⌉ru koto 驚いて飛び

上がること **[making a sudden motion due to surprise]**
2. ha⌈jimari 始まり /⟨V*masu* of *hajimaru* ① begin/ [the point from which a series of actions/incidents originates] ⟪beginning, outset, inception⟫ ↔ owari 終わり; ha⌈jime 初め /⟨V*masu* of *hajimeru* ② begin/ [the origin or starting point of s.t.] ⟪beginning, origin, inception, outset⟫ ↔ owari 終わり; ka⌈ishi 開始 •c [an act of beginning s.t. or an event of s.t. beginning ⟪commencement, beginning, inception, opening⟫ ↔ shuuryoo 終了 •c; shu⌈ppatsu 出発 •c [an act/event of leaving for a destination/goal] ⟪departure⟫ ↔ toochaku 到着 •c; su⌈ta⌉ato スタート •f [the beginning of a race/new life]

EX. (**a**) The sudden drop in stock prices marked the start of a world economic crisis.
株価の暴落は世界恐慌の{始まり/開始/*初め/*出発/*スタート}を示していた。
*Kabu-ka no booraku wa sekai-kyookoo no {hajimari/kaishi/*hajime/*shuppatsu/*sutaato} o shimeshite ita.*
(**b**) Because they got an early start, they were able to reach their destination by noon.
{出発/スタート/*開始/*始まり/*初め}が早かったので、昼までに目的地に到着することができた。
*{Shuppatsu/Sutaato/*kaishi/*hajimari/*hajime} ga hayakatta node, hiru made ni mokuteki-chi ni toochaku-suru koto ga dekita.*
(**c**) It was a thoroughly exciting movie from start to finish.
{初め/*始まり/*開始/*出発/*スタート}から終わりまで、わくわくする映画でした。
*{Hajime/*Hajimari/*Kaishi/*Shuppatsu/*Sutaato} kara owari made waku-waku-suru eiga deshita.*

startle vt. **[to excite or cause s.o./s.a. to move suddenly, esp. out of fear/surprise] ⟨-o⟩ o⌈doroka⌉-su ⟨～を⟩驚かす /⟨short causative of *odoroku* ① be surprised/ ① [to shock s.o./s.a. unawares] ⟪surprise, astonish, amaze, astound⟫, ⟨-o⟩ o⌈doroka⌉-seru ⟨～を⟩驚かせる /⟨causative of *odoroku* ① be surprised/ ②, ⟨-o⟩ bi⌈kku⌉ri-saseru ⟨～を⟩びっくりさせる /⟨causative of *bikkuri-suru* ③ be surprised/ ② [to cause s.o./s.a. to be surprised at a sudden or unexpected event] ⟪surprise, astonish, astound⟫, ⟨-o⟩ gyo⌈oten-saseru ⟨～を⟩仰天させる /⟨causative of *gyooten-suru* ③ be astounded/ ② •c [to cause s.o. to be extremely surprised] ⟪astound, astonish⟫**

EX. Don't startle your grandpa by telling him the sad news.
おじいさんにその悲しいニュースを伝えて{驚かせない/びっくりさせない/仰天させない}でください。
O-jii-san ni sono kanashii nyuusu o tsutaete {odoroka-senaide/bikkuri-sasenaide/gyooten-sasenaide} kudasai.

PHRASE: be startled *odoroku* 驚く ①, *bikkuri-suru* びっくりする ③ ⟪be astonished, be amazed, be frightened⟫

EX. (**a**) I was startled to suddenly discover that my purse was missing.
私は突然財布がないのに気づいて{びっくりした/驚いた}。
*Watashi wa totsuzen saifu ga nai no ni ki-zuite {bikkuri-shita/*hatto odoroita}.*
(**b**) I was startled by the sudden change in her facial expression.
私は彼女の表情がさっと変わったのに{驚いた/びっくりした}。
Watashi wa kanojo no hyoojoo ga satto kawatta no ni {odoroita/bikkuri-shita}.

starve vi. **[to die from lack of food ⟪fig. "become very hungry"⟫]**
1. ga⌉shi-suru 餓死する ③ •c [for s.o./s.a. to die from lack of food] ⟪die of hunger⟫
2. o-⌈naka ga pe⌈ko-peko da おなかがぺこぺこだ [to be very hungry ⟨s⟩]

EX. I'm starving!
おなかがぺこぺこだ!
O-naka ga peko-peko da!

state n. **[a condition of being or one's position in life or a community of people organized under one goverment]**
1. jo⌈otai 状態 •c [the situation in which s.t.

S

exists] ⟪**situation, condition, appearance**⟫, **ji⌈joo 事情 •c [the conditions or facts surrounding an event or situation]** ⟪**circumstance, condition, situation, reason**⟫

EX. (**a**) It is difficult to explain the state of mind of one who has suffered such a psychological shock.
あれほどの精神的な衝撃を受けた人の心の{状態/*事情}は説明しにくい。
*Are hodo no seishin-tekina shoogeki o uketa hito no kokoro no {jootai/*jijoo} wa setsumei-shi-nikui.*
(**b**) I finally began to understand the state of affairs our company was in.
会社の{事情/状態}がやっと分かり始めた。
Kaisha no {jijoo/jootai} ga yatto wakari-hajimeta.

2. mi⌉bun 身分 [an individual's standing in society relative to others/one's circumstances] ⟪**social standing, rank**⟫, **chi⌉i 地位 •c [the standing which one has acquired in a social group or society]** ⟪**position, rank, status**⟫

3. ku⌈ni 国 [one's country/birthplace] ⟪**country, land, native place**⟫, **ko⌉kka 国家 •c [the sovereign governing body of a people living in a given land ⟨w⟩]** ⟪**country, nation**⟫

EX. Many newly independent states have joined the United Nations in recent years.
近年、独立したばかりの{国/国家}が数多く国連に加盟している。
Kinnen, dokuritsu-shita bakari no {kuni/kokka} ga kazu ooku Kokuren ni kamei-shite iru.

4. shu⌉u 州 [a governmental unit in the U.S.]

EX. The state of Vermont is in the upper northeast section of the U.S.
バーモント州はアメリカの東北部にある。
Baamonto-shuu wa Amerika no toohoku-bu ni aru.

—— vt. **[for s.o./s.t. to express/specify s.t. formally and explicitly]**

1.⟨-to⟩ no⌈be⌉ru ⟨〜と⟩述べる ② [for s.o. to speak/write s.t. in a formal way ⟨w⟩] ⟪**express, tell, relate, explain, give one's opinion**⟫, **⟨-to⟩ ge⌈nmei-suru ⟨〜と⟩言明する ③ •c [for s.o. to make s.t. significant clearly known ⟨w⟩]** ⟪**declare**⟫, **⟨-to⟩ chi⌈njutsu-suru ⟨〜と⟩陳述する ③ •c [for s.o. to give one's opinion orally ⟨w⟩]** ⟪**make a statement**⟫

EX. The premier stated that Japan will make efforts to open its market to foreign imports.
首相は輸入品の市場を開放するよう努めると{述べた/言明した/陳述した}。
Shushoo wa yunyuu-hin no shijoo o kaihoo-suru yoo tsutomeru to {nobeta/genmei-shita/chinjutsu-shita}.

2. ⟨-o⟩ ki⌈tei-suru ⟨〜を⟩規定する ③ •c [for s.o./s.t. to specify by law or regulation the way s.t. is to be done] ⟪**specify, appoint**⟫

EX. The period and conditions of employment are stated in the letter of appointment.
雇用期間とその条件は契約書に規定されている。
Koyoo-kikan to sono jooken wa keiyaku-sho ni kitei-sarete iru.

stately adj. **[with a dignified appearance]** **i⌈gen ga a⌉ru N 威厳があるN •c [imposing and majestic]** ⟪**dignified, majestic**⟫, **do⌈o-doo⌉ to shita N 堂々としたN •c [fearless and grand in appearance]** ⟪**grand, magnificent, majestic**⟫, **ri⌈ppana 立派な** adj(*na*). **•c [for s.o./some human creation/achievement to cause admiration]** ⟪**fine, nice, superb, excellent, splendid, magnificent**⟫

EX. Mr. Hunt lives in a stately residence.
ハント氏は{威厳のある/堂々とした/立派な}邸宅に住んでいる。
Hanto-shi wa {igen no aru/doo-doo to shita/rippana} teitaku ni sunde iru.

statement n. **[an act/result of stating s.t.]**

1. chi⌈njutsu 陳述 •c [an act of giving one's opinion orally ⟨w⟩], se⌈imei 声明 •c [an act of publicly announcing one's view/opinion on a particular issue] ⟪**public declaration, proclamation**⟫

EX. (**a**) First there was the prosecution's statement, followed by that of the defense.
最初に検察側の{陳述/*声明}があり、次に弁護側の{陳述/*声明}があった。
*Saisho ni kensatsu-gawa no {chinjutsu/*seimei} ga ari, tsugi ni bengo-gawa no {chinjutsu/*seimei} ga atta.*
(**b**) The senator is soon to make a statement about her candidacy for president.
上院議員は大統領選出馬の{声明/*陳述}を近いうちに発表することになっている。
*Jooin-giin wa daitooryoo-sen-shutsuba no {seimei/*chinjutsu} o chikai uchi ni happyoo-suru koto ni natte iru.*

2. ho⌈okoku 報告 •c [an act of informing s.o. of s.t.] ⟪report, account, information⟫, se⌈imei-sho 声明書 •c [a written public announcement of a view/opinion about a specific issue] ⟪manifesto⟫

EX. The representative of the labor union read a statement about the decision to go on strike.
労働組合の代表者がストライキを決議した{報告/声明書}を読んだ。
Roodoo-kumiai no daihyoo-sha ga sutoraiki o ketsugi-shita {hookoku/seimei-sho} o yonda.

static adj. **[not moving]**
se⌈i-tekina 静的な adj(*na*). **•c ↔ doo-tekina 動的な** adj(*na*). **•c**

station n. **[an assigned post/place where duties are performed or a building where public services are performed or where trains/buses stop]**

1. e⌉ki 駅 •c [a place where railway trains stop]

EX. (**a**) There is a beauty parlor in front of the station.
駅の前に美容院があります。
Eki no mae ni biyoo-in ga arimasu.
(**b**) It takes 10 minutes to get to the station by bike.
駅まで自転車で十分かかります。
Eki made jitensha de jup-pun kakarimasu.

2. ho⌈oso⌉o-kyoku 放送局 •c [a place where broadcasting takes place]

3. -sho ～署 [a place for an assigned duty]

EX. In this town the police station and the fire station are right next to each other.
この町では警察署と消防署が隣り合わせだ。
Kono machi de wa keisatsu-sho to shooboo-sho ga tonari-awase da.

4. mi⌉bun 身分 [an individual's standing in society relative to others/one's circumstances] ⟪one's walk of life, rank, position⟫

stationery n. **[writing materials and related goods]**
bu⌈nbo⌉o-gu 文房具 •c

statue n. **[a life-size or larger sculptured figure of a person/animal]**
cho⌈ozoo 彫像 •c ⟪statuary⟫, zo⌉o 像 •c [a sculptured figure of a deity/person/animal or a projected image] ⟪image, figure, portrait⟫

EX. At the entrance of the building stands a statue of the donor.
建物の入口に寄贈者の{彫像/像}が立っている。
Tate-mono no iriguchi ni kizoo-sha no {choozoo/zoo} ga tatte iru.

status n. **[a person's (high) position/rank]**
mi⌉bun 身分 [an individual's standing in society relative to others/one's circumstances] ⟪one's walk of life, one's station in life⟫, chi⌉i 地位 •c [the standing which one has acquired in a social group or society] ⟪position, situation, rank, social standing⟫

EX. (**a**) The status of women in Japan is still lower than that of men.
日本の女性の{地位/*身分}はまだ男性より低い。
*Nihon no josei no {chii/*mibun} wa mada dansei yori hikui.*
(**b**) My current status is that of assistant professor.
私の今の{身分/*地位}は助教授です。
*Watashi no ima no {mibun/*chii} wa jo-kyooju desu.*

S

stay vi. **[to continue to be in the same place/condition]**

1. **⟨-ni⟩ i⌈ru ⟨〜に⟩いる** ② **[for s.o./s.a. to exist in a certain place]** **⟪be⟫**, **⟨-ni⟩ ta⌈izai-suru ⟨〜に⟩滞在する** ③ **•c [for s.o. to go to some place and remain there for a certain period of time]** **⟪remain, sojourn, stop⟫**, **⟨-ni⟩ to⌈maru ⟨〜に⟩とまる** ① **[for s.t./s.o./s.a. moving to come to a halt at a place ⟪fig. "lodge"⟫]** **⟪stop, halt, perch, lodge⟫** ㊥ "stay at a hotel or s.o.'s home"▷泊まる, "stop"▷止まる

EX. (**a**) Last weekend I didn't go anywhere. I stayed home.
先週末は、私はどこにも行かずに家に{いました/*滞在しました/*泊まりました}。
*Senshuu-matsu wa, watashi wa doko ni mo ikazu ni ie ni {imashita/*taizai-shimashita/*tomarimashita}.*
(**b**) Where are you staying in Tokyo?
東京ではどこに{{滞在して/泊まって}いる/いる}んですか。
Tookyoo de wa doko ni {{taizai-shite/tomatte} iru/iru} n desu ka.

2. **zu⌈tto ずっと** adv. **[continuously/considerably]**

EX. The weather stayed nice during the month of October.
十月はずっと天気がよかった。
Juu-gatsu wa zutto tenki ga yokatta.

3. **(⟨-de⟩) ⟨-o⟩ ma⌉tsu (⟨〜で⟩)⟨〜を⟩待つ** ① **[to wait for s.o. to come/s.t. to happen]** **⟪wait, await⟫**

EX. Stay right here, okay?
ここで待っていなさいよ。
Koko de matte inasai yo.

— n. **[an action/state of continuing to be in the same place/condition for an extended period of time]**

1. **ta⌈izai 滞在** **•c [an act of going to some place and remaining there for a certain period of time]** **⟪sojourn⟫**

EX. My stay in Korea was for just three months.
私の韓国滞在は三か月だけでした。
Watashi no Kankoku taizai wa san-kagetsu dake deshita.

2. **e⌈nki 延期** **•c [an act of postponing s.t.]** **⟪postponement, deferment⟫**

EX. The governor of New York ordered a stay of execution.
ニューヨークの州知事は死刑執行の延期を命じた。
Nyuuyooku no shuu-chiji wa shikei-shikkoo no enki o meijita.

PHRASE: stay young *waka-sa o tamotsu* 若さを保つ ①

EX. What is the secret of staying young?
若さを保つ秘けつは何ですか。
Waka-sa o tamotsu hiketsu wa nan desu ka.

steadily adv. **[in a steady manner]**

shi⌈kka⌉ri(-to) しっかり(と) **[in a firm, dependable manner]** **⟪firmly, securely, tightly, reliably⟫**, **cha⌈ku-chaku-to 着々と** **•c [progressing as scheduled]** **⟪step by step⟫**

EX. (**a**) If you work at your studies steadily, you can enter a good university.
{しっかり(と)/?着々と}勉強すればいい大学に入れますよ。
{Shikkari(-to)/?Chaku-chaku-to} benkyoo-sureba ii daigaku ni haire-masu yo.
(**b**) The construction of the building is progressing steadily.
建物の建築は{着々と/しっかりと}進んでいる。
Tate-mono no kenchiku wa {chaku-chaku-to/shikkari-to} susunde iru.

steady adj. **[firm/stable/consistent]**

1. **shi⌈kka⌉ri-shita N しっかりしたN** /⟨**Vinf. past of *shikkari-suru*** ③ **be firm**/ **[free from weakness/looseness]** **⟪strong, solid, firm, stable, secure⟫**

EX. The 90-year-old man walked with a steady step.
九十歳の老人はしっかりした足取りで歩いた。
Kyuu-jus-sai no roojin wa shikkari-shita ashidori de aruita.

2. **zu⌈tto ずっと** adv. **[continuously/considerably]** **⟪much more, long,**

S

throughout, all along, all the way》

EX. (**a**) My father's steady financial support made it possible for me to complete my graduate work without incurring major debt.
父がずっと金銭的に支えてくれたおかげで、大した借金もせずに大学院の課程を修了することができた。
Chichi ga zutto kinsen-tekini sasaete kureta okage de, taishita shakkin mo sezu ni daigaku-in no katei o shuuryoo-suru koto ga dekita.
(**b**) The man in the corner of the room never averted his steady gaze from Mary.
部屋の隅の男はメアリーから目をそらさずにずっと見つめていた。
Heya no sumi no otoko wa Mearii kara me o sorasazu ni zutto mi-tsumete ita.

—— n. **[one's regular sweetheart ⟨s⟩]**
ko˥i-bito 恋人 [a person one loves] 《lover, boyfriend, girlfriend》

EX. Do you have a steady?
恋人がいるの?
Koi-bito ga iru no?

steak n.
su˥te˥eki ステーキ •f

steal vi./vt. **[to take s.o.'s property/ideas without permission]**
⟨-kara⟩ ⟨-o⟩ nu˥su˥mu ⟨〜から⟩⟨〜を⟩盗む ① [for s.o. to take s.o.'s property/ideas without permission] 《pilfer, purloin》, ⟨-o⟩ to˥ru ⟨〜を⟩とる ① [for s.o./s.a. to cause s.t./s.o./s.a. to come to one's side] 《take, pick up, hold, obtain, choose, keep, reserve》

EX. (**a**) You shouldn't steal someone else's ideas.
人の考えを{盗んで/取って}はいけない。
Hito no kangae o {nusunde/totte} wa ikenai.
(**b**) Someone stole my purse.
私は財布を{盗まれた/取られた}。
Watashi wa saifu o {nusuma-reta/tora-reta}.

—— n. **[stealing (a base in baseball)]**
1. nu˥sumi˥ 盗み /⟨V *masu* of *nusumu* ① steal/ [an act of stealing]
2. to˥orui 盗塁 •c [stealing a base in baseball], su˥chi˥iru スチール •f

steam n. **[vapor that occurs as a result of boiling water 《fig. "power," "energy"》]**
1. jo˥oki 蒸気 •c 《vapor》, yu˥ge 湯気 《vapor》

EX. The steam rising from the hot spring looked white in the cold air.
温泉から出る{蒸気/湯気}が冷たい空気の中で白く見えた。
Onsen kara deru {jooki/yuge} ga tsumetai kuuki no naka de shiroku mieta.

2. chi˥kara˥ 力 [a capacity of any kind to do s.t., including physical, intellectual, mental, or spiritual] 《strength, force, effect, ability》, se˥iryoku 精力 •c [physical/mental energy] 《energy, vigor, vitality, virility》

EX. He worked so hard during the past month that he appeared to be out of steam.
彼は先月働きすぎて、{力/精力}がなくなったようだ。
Kare wa sengetsu hataraki-sugite, {chikara/seiryoku} ga naku natta yooda.

—— vt. **[for s.o. to treat s.t. with steam in cooking]**
⟨-o⟩ mu˥su ⟨〜を⟩蒸す ① [for s.o. to heat s.t. with steam 《fig. "be sultry"》], ⟨-o⟩ fu˥ka˥su ⟨〜を⟩ふかす ① [for s.o. to heat (and cook) food with steam]

EX. Let's steam the sweet potatoes.
さつまいもを{ふかそう/蒸そう}。
Satsumaimo o {fukasoo/musoo}.

steamboat n. **[a boat driven by steam]**
ki˥sen 汽船 •c 《steamer, steamship》

steamer n. **[s.t. operated by steam power]**
1. ki˥sen 汽船 •c 《steamship, steamboat》
2. mu˥shi˥-ki 蒸し器 •c [a pot or device for cooking with steam]

steel n. **[iron alloyed with carbon/other metals or products made of iron]**
1. ha˥gane 鋼 [iron alloyed with carbon/other metals], ko˥otetsu 鋼鉄 •c
2. ko˥otetsu-sei no mono 鋼鉄製のもの [products made of alloyed iron]

steep adj. **[having a sharp slope]**
ke˥washi˥i 険しい adj(*i*). **[for a slope/mountain to rise sharply making it**

S

difficult to climb 《fig. "stern"》] 《precipitous, severe, grim, stern》, kyu⌈u-ko⌉obai no N 急勾配のN •c [having a sharp degree of incline] 《steep slope》

EX. The mountain path was so steep that it took us several hours to reach the summit.
山道が{険しかった/急勾配だった}ので頂上に着くのに四、五時間かかった。
Yama-michi ga {kewashikatta/kyuu-koobai datta} node choojoo ni tsuku no ni shi, go-jikan kakatta.

steer vt. **[for s.o. to direct the course of s.t./s.o./s.a. by means of s.t. 《fig. "direct," "control"》]**

1. ⟨-no⟩ ka⌉ji o to⌉ru ⟨〜の⟩かじを取る ① [for s.o. to guide a boat 《fig. "direct"》], ⟨-o⟩ u⌈nten-suru ⟨〜を⟩運転する ③ •c [for s.o. to control the functioning and movement of a large vehicle, esp. a car] 《work, operate, drive》

EX. (**a**) We steered the boat to the east.
我々は東に{船のかじを取った/*船を運転した}。
*Ware-ware wa higashi ni {fune no kaji o totta/*fune o unten-shita}.*
(**b**) I wanted to steer the truck but wasn't allowed to.
トラック{を運転したかった/*のかじを取りたかった}けどさせてもらえなかった。
*Torakku {o unten-shi-takatta/*no kaji o tori-takatta} kedo, sasete marae-nakatta.*

2. ⟨-o⟩ {⟨-e⟩/⟨-ni⟩} mi⌈chibi⌉ku ⟨〜を⟩{⟨〜へ⟩/⟨〜に⟩}導く ① [for s.o. to make s.o./s.t. go in a certain direction/place 《fig. "guide," "lead"》] 《lead, guide》, ⟨-ni⟩ ⟨-o⟩ shi⌈doo-suru ⟨〜に⟩⟨〜を⟩指導する ③ •c [for s.o. to teach and guide s.o.] 《guide, lead, direct》

EX. My teacher steered me in the right direction.
先生は私を正しい方向に{導いて/指導して}くださった。
Sensei wa watashi o tadashii hookoo ni {michibiite/shidoo-shite} kudasatta.

PHRASE: steering wheel *handoru* ハンドル •f

NOTE: *Handoru* comes from the English "handle."

—— vi. **[for a vehicle to be operated (easily)]**

1. so⌈ojuu-deki⌉ru 操縦出来る ② •c [for an airplane to be (easily) operable], u⌈nten-deki⌉ru 運転出来る ② •c [for a car to be (easily) operable]

EX. (**a**) This car steers very easily.
この車は簡単に{運転/*操縦}出来ます。
*Kono kurum wa kantanni {unten/*soojuu}-dekimasu.*
(**b**) This glider doesn't steer very easily.
このグライダーはそう簡単には{操縦/*運転}出来ない。
*Kono guraidaa wa soo kantanni wa {soojuu/*unten}-dekinai.*

2. su⌈sumu 進む ① [to go forward of one's/its own accord 《fig. "make progress," "be advanced," "feel inclined"》] 《advance, go forward, progress》

EX. The car suddenly steered to the left and hit the on-coming car.
車は急に左に進んで、前から来る車とぶつかった。
Kuruma wa kyuuni hidari ni susunde, mae kara kuru kuruma to butsukatta.

stem n. **[the main central part of a tree or plant 《fig. "stalk-like object," "stem of a word," "bow of a boat," "lineage"》]**

1. mi⌉ki 幹 [the wooden central part of a tree] 《stalk, bole》, ku⌈ki⌉ 茎 [the long narrow part of a plant] 《stalk, pipe》

EX. (**a**) Tulips have long stems.
チューリップは{茎/*幹}が長い。
*Chuurippu wa {kuki/*miki} ga nagai.*
(**b**) The stem of this tree can grow to as high as ten meters.
この木の{幹/*茎}は高さ十メートルにもなり得る。
*Kono ki no {miki/*kuki} wa taka-sa juu-meetoru ni mo nari-{uru/eru}.*

2. go⌈kan 語幹 •c [the part of a word that does not conjugate/decline]

EX. The stem of the adjective *yasui* is *yasu.*
形容詞「安い」の語幹は「やす」である。
Keiyooshi 'yasui' no gokan wa 'yasu' dearu.

S

— vi. **[for s.t. to originate from s.t.] ⟨-kara⟩ o⌈ko⌉ru ⟨〜から⟩起こる ① [for an unusual/disturbing event to take place]** ⟪**happen, come to pass, occur, take place**⟫, **⟨-kara⟩ sho⌈ojiru ⟨〜から⟩生じる ② [for s.t. to come into existence ⟨w⟩]** ⟪**happen, occur, be caused**⟫, **⟨-o⟩ ki⌉gen to suru ⟨〜を⟩起源とする ③ •c [for s.t. to have s.t. as its origin/genesis]**

EX. | (**a**) The dispute stemmed from mutual misunderstanding.
論争はお互いの誤解{から{起こった/生じた}/*を起源とした}。
*Ronsoo wa o-tagai no gokai {kara {okotta/shoojita}/*o kigen to shita}.*
(**b**) The Japanese tea ceremony stems from the medicinal use of tea in China.
日本の茶道は中国の薬用茶{を起源とする/から{起こって/生じて}いる}。
Nihon no sadoo wa Chuugoku no yakuyoo-cha {o kigen to suru/kara {okotte/shoojite} iru}.

step n. **[the action of moving one's foot once or the distance covered by such a motion ⟪fig. "manner of walking," "dancing," "stair," "stage," "means"⟫]**

1. i⌉p-po 一歩 •c [a single cycle of raising one's foot and setting it down again in walking or the distance progressed in such a cycle]

EX. | I couldn't walk even a step.
一歩も歩けませんでした。
Ip-po mo aruke-masen deshita.

2. a⌈ruki-kata 歩き方 /⟨V*masu* of *aruku* ① walk + *kata* manner/ [a manner/way of walking]

EX. | His step is always very brisk.
あの人の歩き方はいつも元気がいい。
Ano hito no aruki-kata wa itsu-mo genki ga ii.

3. su⌈te⌉ppu ステップ •f [a manner of dancing or a footboard], da⌉n 段 [a sequence of board-like objects of different height ⟪fig. "scene," "situation," "paragraph"⟫] ⟪**stair, paragraph, scene, occasion**⟫

EX. | This step is too high for me.
この{段/ステップ}は高すぎます。
Kono {dan/suteppu} wa taka-sugimasu.

4. da⌈nkai 段階 •c [a period in the course of development of s.t.] ⟪**rank, stage**⟫

EX. | There are ten steps involved in mastering this skill.
この技術をマスターするには段階が十あります。
Kono gijutsu o masutaa-suru ni wa dankai ga too arimasu.

— vi. **[for s.o./s.a. to lift and set down the foot in walking ⟪fig. "walk a short distance," "put one's foot down"⟫]**

1. a⌈shi⌉ o fu⌈mi-da⌉su 足を踏み出す ① [for s.o./s.a. to move forward]

2. cho⌉tto a⌈ru⌉ku ちょっと歩く ① [for s.o./s.a. to walk a short distance]

3. su⌈te⌉ppu o fu⌈mu ステップを踏む ① [for s.o. to move with a measured step]

PHRASE: step on ⟨-o⟩ *fumu* ⟨〜を⟩踏む ①

EX. | Someone stepped on my toe.
足の指を踏まれちゃった。
Ashi no yubi o fuma-rechatta.

stern adj. **[for s.o./s.t. to be harsh or strict] ki⌈bishi⌉i 厳しい** adj(*i*). **[unpleasantly intense to the senses or tending to impose strict rules on others]** ⟪**severe, strict, rigid, harsh, relentless**⟫, **ko⌈wa⌉i 怖い** adj(*i*). **[for a person or situation to be harsh and unyielding]** ⟪**frightened, scared, frightening, scary, dreadful**⟫

EX. | (**a**) They took stern measures to punish the drug traffickers.
麻薬密売人を罰するために{厳しい/*怖い}手段を取った。
*Mayaku-mitsubai-nin o bassuru tame ni {kibishii/*kowai} shudan o totta.*
(**b**) The Japanese export industry in the past had to face the stern reality of yen-appreciation.
日本の輸出産業は以前円高の{厳しい/*怖い}現実に直面しなければならなかった。
*Nihon no yushutsu-sangyoo wa izen en-daka no {kibishii/*kowai} genjitsu ni chokumen-shinakereba naranakatta.*

S

(c) Professor Yamashita looks stern.
山下先生は{怖そう/厳しそう}だ。
Yamashita-sensei wa {kowa-soo/kibishi-soo} da.

sternly adv. **[in a stern manner]**
ki⌈bi⌉shiku 厳しく /⟨adj(*i*). *ku* of *kibishii* strict/ [harshly and unyieldingly]

EX. Drunken drivers ought to be sternly punished.
酔っ払い運転は厳しく罰せられるべきだ。
Yopparai-unten wa kibishiku basse-rareru-beki da.

stew n.
shi⌈chu⌉u シチュー •f

stick n. **[a long, slender piece of wood ⟪fig. "a walking staff"⟫]**
1. ko-⌈eda 小枝 [a small branch] ⟪twig, sprig⟫
2. ki-⌈gire⌉ 木切れ [a small piece of wood]
3. ko⌈nboo こん棒 •c [a stick used as a weapon] ⟪club⟫

EX. The policeman hit the student demonstrators with his stick.
警官はデモの学生をこん棒で殴った。
Keikan wa demo no gakusei o konboo de nagutta.

4. shi⌈futo-re⌉baa シフトレバー •f [the shift stick on a car]

— vi. **[to be attached to s.t. or to jut out]**
⟨-ni⟩ tsu⌈ku⌉ ⟨〜に⟩つく ① [for s.o./s.t. to attach himself/herself/itself to s.o./s.t. else] ⟪cling to, adhere to, get to, arrive⟫, ⟨-ni⟩ ku⌈ttsu⌉ku ⟨〜に⟩くっつく ① [to adhere closely to s.t./s.o./s.a. ⟪fig. "become intimate"⟫ ⟨s⟩]
㊟ "arrive"▷着く, "adhere"▷付く

EX. The stamp won't stick to the envelope.
切手が封筒に{付かない/くっつかない}。
Kitte ga fuutoo ni {tsukanai/kuttsukanai}.

PHRASE: stick out *tsuki-deru* 突き出る ② ⟪project, stand out⟫

EX. His nose sticks out like that of Pinocchio.
彼の鼻はピノキオの鼻のように突き出ている。
Kare no hana wa Pinokio no hana no yooni tsuki-dete iru.

— vt. **[for s.o. to cause s.t./s.o./s.a. to attach to s.t./s.o. or to thrust a pointed object at or into s.t.]**
1. ⟨-o⟩ ⟨-ni⟩ ku⌈ttsuke⌉ru ⟨〜を⟩⟨〜に⟩くっつける ② [for s.o. to put things together with no/little space in between so that they stay that way] ⟪join, put together, attach⟫

EX. Stick this sticker on your car, will you?
このステッカーを車にくっつけてくれるね。
Kono sutekkaa o kuruma ni kuttsukete kureru ne.

2. ⟨-o⟩ ⟨-ni⟩ (tsu⌈ki-)sa⌉su ⟨〜を⟩⟨〜に⟩(突き)刺す ① [for s.o. to stab s.t. into s.t. else] ⟪pierce, stab, thrust⟫, ⟨-ni⟩ ⟨-o⟩ sa⌈shi-ko⌉mu ⟨〜に⟩⟨〜を⟩差し込む ① [for s.o. to put s.t. into a small or narrow opening] ⟪insert, put in, thrust in⟫

EX. (a) Don't stick your chopsticks into your rice like that.
そういう風にはしを御飯に{突き刺して/*差し込んで}はいけません。
*Soo-iu fuu ni hashi o gohan ni {tsuki-sashite/*sashi-konde} wa ikemasen.*
(b) Could you please stick this plug in the outlet.
このプラグをコンセントに{差し込んで/*突き刺して}ください。
*Kono puragu o konsento ni {sashi-konde/*tsuki-sashite} kudasai.*

PHRASE: walking stick *sutekki* ステッキ •f

EX. My grandfather uses a walking stick to get around.
うちの祖父はステッキを使って歩く。
Uchi no sofu wa sutekki o tsukatte aruku.

PHRASE: get stuck ⟨*-ni*⟩ *hamari-komu* ⟨〜に⟩はまりこむ ①

EX. My car got stuck in the mud.
車がぬかるみにはまりこんだ。
Kuruma ga nukarumi ni hamari-konda.

sticky adj. **[tending to stick to what is touched ⟪fig. "muggy"⟫]**

1. **be˥ta-beta-suru べたべたする ③ [tending to stick like candy《fig. "dally"》], ne˥ba-neba-suru ねばねばする ③ [tending to stick like *nattoo* (fermented soybean)]**

EX. (**a**) This candy is sticky.
このあめは{べたべた/?ねばねば}する。
Kono ame wa {beta-beta/?neba-neba}-suru.
(**b**) I don't like *nattoo* because it's so sticky.
納豆はやたらと{ねばねば/*べたべた}するから嫌だ。
*Nattoo wa yatarato {nebe-neba/*beta-beta}-suru kara iya da.*

2. **mu┌shi-atsu˥i 蒸し暑い** adj(*i*). **[very hot and humid]《muggy, sultry, stuffy》**

EX. Tokyo summers are very hot and sticky.
東京の夏は蒸し暑い。
Tookyoo no natsu wa mushi-atsui.

stiff adj. **[not easily bent or stirred《fig. "formal," "strict," "strong"》]**

1. **ka┌tai かたい** adj(*i*). **[not easily changed/broken/influenced], ko˥tte iru 凝っている /〈V *te iru* of *koru* ① grow stiff/ [tensed and hard esp. of muscles《fig. "refined"》]**

㊟ "stiff/inflexible"▷硬い, "solid/firm/tight"▷固い, "rigid/strict"▷堅い

EX (**a**) His facial expression looked stiff in front of his boss.
ボスの前で彼の表情は{固かった/*凝っていた}。
*Bosu no mae de kare no hyoojoo wa {katakatta/*kotte ita}.*
(**b**) The gears on this car get very stiff in winter.
この車のギアは冬にはとても{固くなる/*凝る}。
*Kono kuruma no gia wa fuyu ni wa totemo {kataku naru/*koru}.*
(**c**) My shoulders are stiff from typing all day.
一日中タイプを打っていたので、肩が{凝っている/*固い}。
*Ichi-nichi-juu taipu o utte ita node, kata ga {kotte iru/*katai}.*

2. **ka┌ta-kurushi˥i 堅苦しい** adj(*i*). **[painfully formal]《formal, strait-laced》**

EX. The atmosphere of the meeting was very stiff.
会議の雰囲気はとても堅苦しかった。
Kaigi no fun'iki wa totemo kata-kurushikatta.

3. **ki┌bishi˥i 厳しい** adj(*i*). **[unpleasantly intense to the senses or tending to impose strict rules on others]《severe, strict, rigid, hard, relentless》**

EX. There are stiff penalties for traffic violations.
交通違反には厳しい罰則がある。
Kootsuu-ihan ni wa kibishii bassoku ga aru.

still adv. **[continuing unchanged up to the time indicated (and beyond)]**

ma˥da まだ [s.t./s.o./s.a. being in the same state as before]《not yet》

EX. (**a**) I feel as if I'm still young.
私はまだ若いと思っています。
Watashi wa mada wakai to omotte imasu.
(**b**) When I came back late last night my wife was still up.
昨夜私が遅く帰ってきた時妻はまだ起きていました。
Sakuya watashi ga osoku kaette kita toki tsuma wa mada okite imashita.
(**c**) It's been cold up to now, but it'll get still colder.
今までも寒かったですが、これからもまだ寒くなりますよ。
Ima made mo samukatta desu ga, kore kara mo mada samuku narimasu yo.
(**d**) My father is eighty-four years old, but he's still working.
父は八十四歳ですが，まだ働いています。
Chichi wa hachi-juu-yon-sai desu ga, mada hataraite imasu.

— adj. **[motionless and quiet]**

u┌goka˥nai 動かない adj(*i*). **/〈Vneg. of *ugoku* ① move + *nai* not/ [not moving]《stationary》, shi˥zukana 静かな** adj(*na*). **[comfortably quiet/peaceful]《silent, calm》**

EX. (**a**) Please sit still for a minute or so.

S

一分ぐらい{動かないで/静かに}座っていてください。
Ip-pun-gurai {ugokanai de/shizukani} suwatte ite kudasai.
(**b**) It was snowing and everything was still.
雪が降っていて、何もかも{静かだった/*動かなかった}。
*Yuki ga futte ite, nani-mo kamo {shizuka datta/*ugokanakatta}.*

— n. **[a still photograph]**
su⌈chi⌉iru スチール(写真) **•f**(+c)

stimulate vt. **[to make s.t./s.o./s.a. more active or excited]**
⟨-o⟩ shi⌈geki-suru ⟨〜を⟩刺激する ③ **•c**
EX. The adrenal glands secrete adrenalin when stimulated.
副腎は刺激されるとアドレナリンを分泌する。
Fukujin wa shigeki-sareru to adorenarin o bunpitsu-suru.

stimulus n.
shi⌈geki 刺激 **•c**
EX. If there is a stimulus, there is a response.
刺激があれば、反応がある。
Shigeki ga areba, hannoo ga aru.

sting vt. **[to prick or wound s.t. (esp. a bodily part) with a small sharp point causing pain ⟪fig. "cause psychological pain"⟫]**
1. **⟨⟨-de⟩⟩ ⟨-o⟩ sa⌉su** ⟨⟨〜で⟩⟩⟨〜を⟩刺す ① **[for s.o. to thrust a pointed object such as a knife/dagger/needle/skewer into s.t./s.o./s.a. (to kill or maim)] ⟪stick, pierce, stab, thrust⟫**
EX. A bee stung me on the neck.
蜂に首を刺された。
Hachi ni kubi o sasa-reta.
2. **⟨-o⟩ ku⌈rushime⌉ru** ⟨〜を⟩苦しめる ② **[to cause s.o. unbearable mental/physical pain]**
EX. Tom's careless remarks stung her deeply.
トムの不注意な言葉は彼女をひどく苦しめた。
Tomu no fu-chuuina kotoba wa kanojo o hidoku kurushimeta.

— n. **[an act/result of stinging]**
1. **sa⌉su koto** 刺すこと **[an act of stinging]**
2. **sa⌉su yoona i⌈ta-mi⌉** 刺すような痛み **[pain as if one were stung]**
3. **ko⌈ko⌉ro no i⌈ta-mi⌉** 心の痛み **[psychological pain], ku⌈noo** 苦悩 **•c [pain and suffering] ⟪suffering, distress, anguish⟫**

stink vi. **[to emit a very unpleasant smell ⟪fig. "offensive"⟫]**
1. **i⌈ya⌉na ni⌈o⌉i ga suru** 嫌なにおいがする ③ **[to emit a very unpleasant smell], ku⌈sa⌉i** くさい adj(*i*). **[having a bad odor] ⟪ill-smelling, smelly⟫**
EX. This room stinks!
この部屋は{嫌なにおいがする/くさい}。
Kono heya wa {iyana nioi ga suru/kusai}.
2. **fu-⌈yu⌉kaina** 不愉快な adj(*na*). **•c [causing a feeling which is not pleasant/enjoyable] ⟪unpleasant, disagreeable, unhappy⟫**
EX. The bureaucracy stinks!
官僚制度は不愉快だ。
Kanryoo-seido wa fu-yukai da.

stir vi./vt. **[to cause to move slightly or to mix the contents of s.t. by moving it around esp. with an object such as a spoon ⟪fig. "excite," "provoke"⟫]**
1. **⟨-o⟩ u⌈goka⌉su** ⟨〜を⟩動かす /⟨**short causative of *ugoku*** ① **move/** ① **[to cause s.t./s.o./s.a. to move in location/position/mental state] ⟪move, shift, remove, change⟫**
NOTE: Unlike other short causatives *ugokasu* does not have a corresponding longer causative version. *Ugokaseru* means not "to cause s.o./s.a./s.t. to move" but "can move s.t./s.o./s.a."
EX. The sleeping baby stirred its head slightly.
寝ている赤ん坊は首をかすかに動かした。
Nete iru akanboo wa kubi o kasukani ugokashita.
2. **⟨-o⟩ ⟨⟨-de⟩⟩ ka⌈ki-mawasu** ⟨〜を⟩⟨⟨〜で⟩⟩かき回す ① **[for s.o. to move liquid in a circular motion to mix its ingredients] ⟪churn⟫, ⟨-o⟩ ⟨⟨-de⟩⟩ ka⌈ki-mazeru** ⟨〜を⟩⟨⟨〜で⟩⟩かき混ぜる ② **[for s.o./s.a. to move s.t. around so that it becomes mixed together]**

EX. Before you drink the medicine you'd better stir it with a spoon.
薬を飲む前に、スプーンで{かき回して/かき混ぜて}ね。
Kusuri o nomu mae ni, supuun de {kaki-mawashite/kaki-mazete} ne.

3. ⟨-o⟩ ko⌈ofun-saseru ⟨〜を⟩興奮させる /⟨causative of *koofun-suru* ③ get excited/ ② •c [to excite/provoke s.o./s.a.]

EX. His lecture stirred the hearts of the audience.
彼の講義は聴衆の心を興奮させた。
Kare no koogi wa chooshuu no kokoro o koofun-saseta.

NOTE: The above can also be expressed as follows: *Chooshuu wa kare no koogi o kiite koofun-shita.*

—— vi. **[for s.t./s.o./s.a. to move slightly]**
u⌈go⌉ku 動く ① [to change in location or position《fig. "shake," "be affected," "change," "be transferred"》]《move, shift, work》, yu⌈reru 揺れる ② [for an object/ mind to move up and down or from side to side《fig. "be disturbed"》]《shake, sway, quake》

EX. The leaves stirred in the wind.
木の葉が風で{動いた/揺れた}。
Ko-no-ha ga kaze de {ugoita/yureta}.

stitch n. **[one movement of a threaded needle or the result of this]**
-hari 〜針

EX. The injury to my foot required nine stiches.
私は足に九針も縫うけがをした。
Watashi wa ashi ni kyuu-hari mo nuu kega o shita.

—— vt. **[to sew s.t.]**
⟨-o⟩ nu⌉u ⟨〜を⟩縫う ①《sew》

stock n. **[the trunk/stump of a tree《fig. "ancestry," "language family," "store/ supply," "shares of corporate capital," "livestock"》]**

1. mi⌉ki 幹 [the wooden central part of a tree]《trunk, bole》

2. se⌉nzo 先祖 •c [ancestry]《forefather, ancestral》

3. ta⌈kuwae⌉ 蓄え /⟨V*masu* of *takuwaeru* ② store/ [a result of storing s.t.]《store, reserve, supplies》, cho⌈zoo 貯蔵 •c [the act of storing s.t., esp. food]《storage, storing》, su⌈to⌉kku ストック •f [a result of storing]

4. ka⌈bu 株 [shares of corporate capital]

EX. I purchased one thousand shares of IBM stock last year.
私は去年IBMの株を千株買った。
Watashi wa kyonen ai-bii-em no kabu o sen-kabu katta.

5. ka⌈chiku 家畜 •c [a domesticated animal kept for use or profit]《livestock, cattle》

—— vi./vt. **[to store s.t. somewhere]**
(⟨-ni⟩) ⟨-o⟩ ta⌈kuwae⌉ru (⟨〜に⟩)⟨〜を⟩蓄える ② [for s.o. to store objects/money/ knowledge for future use]《store, save》, ⟨-o⟩ shi-⌈ire⌉ru ⟨〜を⟩仕入れる ② [for a merchant to purchase merchandise and store it]《buy in, lay in》

EX. (**a**) Everyone in Japan was stocking up on toilet paper at the time of the oil shock.
オイルショックの時は日本人は皆トイレットペーパーを{蓄えていた/*仕入れた}。
*Oiru-shokku no toki wa Nihon-jin wa mina toiretto-peepaa o {takuwaeteita/ *shi-ireta}.*
(**b**) That record shop stocks a lot of CDs.
あのレコード店はＣＤをたくさん{仕入れて/*蓄えて}いる。
*Ano rekoodo-ten wa shii-dii o takusan {shi-irete/*takuwaete} iru.*

stockings n.
ku⌈tsu-shita⌉ 靴下《socks》, su⌈to⌉kkingu ストッキング •f

EX. It's cold so you'd better wear stockings.
寒いから{靴下/ストッキング}をはいた方がいいよ。
Samui kara {kutsu-shita/sutokkingu} o haita hoo ga ii yo.

stole n.
su⌈to⌉oru ストール •f

EX. Whenever we visited her, my grandma would always be sitting in this chair with a stole on her shoulders.
私たちが遊びに行った時、おばあちゃんはいつもストールを肩にかけてこのいすに座っていたものだ。
Watashi-tachi ga asobi ni itta toki, o-baa-chan wa itsu-mo sutooru o kata ni kakete kono isu ni suwatte ita mono da.

stomach n. **[a bodily organ where initial digestion takes place]**
o-⌈naka おなか [a colloquial, general term for the bodily organs where digestion takes place] ⟪belly, tummy⟫, i 胃 •c [a bodily organ where initial digestion takes place]

EX. I have a pain in my stomach.
私は{おなか/胃}が痛いんです。
Watashi wa {o-naka/i} ga itai n desu.

— vt. **[to be able to eat ⟪fig. "tolerate"⟫]**
1. ta⌈be-rare⌉ru 食べられる /⟨pot. of *taberu* ② eat/ ② [can eat]

EX. How can you stomach this food?
こんな食べ物、食べられないよ。
Konna tabe-mono, tabe-rarenai yo.

2. ⟨-o⟩ ga⌉man-suru ⟨～を⟩我慢する ③ •c [for s.o./s.a. to willingly endure physical or mental affliction from s.t. for a relatively short period of time] ⟪bear, put up with⟫

S

EX. I can't stomach people like that.
そんな人には我慢できない。
Sonna hito ni wa gaman-dekinai.

stomachache n.
fu⌈kutsuu 腹痛 •c [pain in the stomach/intestines], i⌈tsuu 胃痛 •c [pain in the stomach]

stone n. **[a piece of rock (used in building/as a gravestone) ⟪fig. "hailstone," "calculus," "stone-like seed," "gem"⟫]**
1. i⌈shi⌉ 石 [a (usually small) piece of rock] ⟪pebble, small rock⟫

EX. (**a**) This house is made of stone.
この家は石で出来ています。
Kono ie wa ishi de dekite imasu.
(**b**) A kid threw a stone and broke my window.
子供が石を投げて、うちの窓ガラスを割った。
Kodomo ga ishi o nagete, uchi no mado-garasu o watta.

2. se⌈kizai 石材 •c [stone used in building] ⟪building stone⟫
3. bo⌈seki 墓石 •c [a gravestone] ⟪tombstone⟫
4. hyo⌉o ひょう •c [small balls of ice that fall like snow in a thunderstorm]
5. ke⌈sseki 結石 •c [a stone formed in the body] ⟪calculus⟫
6. ta⌉ne 種 [the germ of a plant ⟪fig. "breed," "subject of talk," "cause"⟫]

PHRASE: stone age *sekki-jidai* 石器時代 •c, stone lantern *ishi-dooroo* 石灯ろう

stool n. **[a seat with three/four legs and without a back or a toilet seat or a footrest ⟪fig. "toilet," "a bowel movement"⟫]**
1. i⌈su いす ⟪seat, chair⟫, su⌈tsu⌉uru スツール •f

EX. There's a cat sitting on the stool.
猫が{いす/スツール}に座っている。
Neko ga {isu/sutsuuru} ni suwatte iru.

2. a⌈shi-dai 足台 [a footrest]
3. be⌉nki 便器 •c [a toilet stool]

stoop vi. **[for the upper part of the body to bend forward ⟪fig. "condescend," "sweep down"⟫]**
1. mi⌉ o ka⌈gameru 身をかがめる ② [for s.o. to bend the upper part of the body forward], ko⌈shi o ma⌈geru 腰を曲げる ② [for s.o. to bend over at the hips]

EX. I stooped to pick up a beautiful autumn leaf.
私は{身をかがめて/腰を曲げて}美しい秋の紅葉を拾った。
Watashi wa {mi o kagamete/koshi o magete} utsukushii aki no momiji o hirotta.

2. he⌈rikudaru へり下る ① [to lower oneself figuratively] ⟪condescend, humble oneself, be modest⟫

— n. **[the state of one's back being bent]**
ne⌈ko⌉-ze 猫背

stop vt. **[to prevent s.t./s.o./s.a. from moving/acting/occurring]**
1. ⟨-o⟩ to⌈meru ⟨～を⟩とめる ② [for s.o. to prevent s.o./s.t./s.a. from moving/doing s.t. ⟪fig. "put s.o. up," "fasten"⟫] ⟪bring to a halt, fasten, forbid, dissuade, turn off, put s.o. up⟫

㊦ "put s.o. up"▷泊める, "fasten"▷留める, "bring s.o./s.t./s.a. to a halt"▷止める

EX. The policeman stopped a car which had been speeding at over 80 miles per hour.
警官は時速八十マイル以上のスピードを出していた車を止めた。
Keikan wa jisoku hachi-juu-mairu-ijoo no supiido o dashite ita kuruma o tometa.

2. ⟨-o⟩ ya⌈meru ⟨～を⟩やめる ② [for s.o. to discontinue s.t. that he/she has been doing, including a plan to do s.t.] ⟪cease, end, leave off, give up, quit, resign⟫ ↔ ⟨-o⟩ hajimeru ⟨～を⟩始める ②

㊦ "resign"▷辞める, otherwise ▷やめる

EX. (**a**) When did you stop smoking?
たばこを吸うのをいつやめましたか。
Tabako o suu no o itsu yamemashita ka.
(**b**) I stopped running and started to walk.
走るのをやめて、歩き出した。
Hashiru no o yamete, aruki-dashita.

3. ⟨-o⟩ fu⌈sagu ⟨～を⟩ふさぐ ① [for s.o. to close off an opening] ⟪close, shut, fill up, cover, block, obstruct⟫

EX. I stopped up the hole that the mice were coming in through.
ねずみが入って来る穴をふさいだ。
Nezumi ga haitte kuru ana o fusaida.

4. ⟨-o⟩ sa⌈matage⌉ru ⟨～を⟩妨げる ② •c [for s.o. to create a hindrance to s.t.] ⟪obstruct, hinder, interrupt⟫, {Vneg./Vstem/shi/ko} na⌉i yooni suru {Vneg./Vstem/し/来}ないようにする ③ [to do s.t. so that s.o. does not/cannot do s.t.]

EX. We must not stop our children from attaining their full potential in life.
子供が人生において能力{を十分に発揮するのを妨げては/が十分に発揮できないようにしては}ならない。
Kodomo ga jinsei ni-oite nooryoku {o juubunni hakki-suru no o samatagete wa/ga juubunni hakki-dekinai yoo ni shite wa} naranai.

— vi. **[to cease moving/acting/occurring]**

1. ta⌈chi-domaru 立ち止まる ① [for s.o./s.a. to cease walking/running] ⟪stand still⟫

EX. (**a**) I stopped and looked to see if there was a toilet around.
私は立ち止まって、お手洗いがないかと見回した。
Watashi wa tachi-domatte, o-tearai ga nai ka to mi-mawashita.
(**b**) I stopped to ask a passer-by the time.
私は立ち止まって、通行人に時間を聞いた。
Watashi wa tachi-domatte, tsuukoo-nin ni jikan o kiita.

2. to⌈maru とまる ① [for s.o./s.t./s.a. moving to come to a standstill ⟪fig. "be fastened"⟫] ⟪halt, stand still, cease, stay at⟫

㊦ "stay at"▷泊まる, "halt"▷止まる, "be fastened"▷留まる

EX. (**a**) The engine suddenly stopped while I was driving.
運転中にエンジンが急に止まった。
Unten-chuu ni enjin ga kyuu ni tomatta.
(**b**) We stopped for the night at a small roadside motel.
私たちは道路に面した小さなモーテルに一晩泊まった。
Watashi-tachi wa dooro ni menshita chiisana mooteru ni hito-ban tomatta.

3. ya⌈mu やむ ① [for a phenomenon, usually a natural one such as rain/snow/wind/thunder, to come to a halt] ⟪cease, die down⟫

EX. (**a**) It stopped raining.
雨がやんだ。
Ame ga yanda.
(**b**) The wind stopped.
風がやんだ。
Kaze ga yanda.

— n. **[an act of stopping or a place where s.t./s.o./s.a. stops]**

1. to⌈maru koto 止まること [an act of stopping] ⟪cessation⟫

2. te⌈iryuu-jo 停留所 •c [a bus stop], ba⌈su-tei バス停 •f+c

3. ta⌈izai 滞在 •c [an act of going to some place and remaining there for a certain

S

period of time] ⟪stay⟫, shu⌈kuhaku 宿泊 •c [an act of staying at a place of lodging] ⟪stay⟫
4. bo⌈ogai 妨害 •c [an act of forcibly preventing s.t./s.o. from doing s.t.] ⟪obstruction⟫
5. shu⌈ushi⌉-fu 終止符 •c [a point indicating the end of a sentence in romanized Japanese and most Indo-European languages]
6. he⌈isa⌉-on 閉鎖音 •c [a sound pronounced by an occlusion of the air in the vocal tract, such as "p"/"b"]

storage n. [an act of/place for storing s.t]
1. cho⌈zoo 貯蔵 •c [the act of storing s.t., esp. food]
EX. Food storage was revolutionized by the advent of the refrigerator.
冷蔵庫が発明されて、食品の貯蔵が全く新しいやり方に変わった。
Reizoo-ko ga hatsumei-sarete, shokuhin no chozoo ga mattaku atarashii yari-kata ni kawatta.
2. so⌉oko 倉庫 •c [a building in which one stores s.t.] ⟪warehouse, storehouse⟫
EX. Last summer we put our furniture in storage while we sublet our house.
去年の夏家を貸していた時は、家具を倉庫に入れておいた。
Kyonen no natsu ie o kashite ita toki wa, kagu o sooko ni irete oita.

S

storehouse n. [a place in which one stores s.t.]
so⌉oko 倉庫 •c ⟪warehouse, storage, depot⟫

storekeeper n. [a person who owns or manages a store]
te⌉nshu 店主 •c [a person who owns or manages a store] ⟪owner⟫

storm n. [a severe atmospheric disturbance ⟪fig. "a storm of bullets," "a storm of criticism"⟫]
a⌉rashi 嵐 [a severe atmospheric disturbance characterized by strong winds and rain], bo⌈ofu⌉u-u 暴風雨 •c [violent wind and rain], bo⌈ofu⌉u 暴風 •c [a strong wind of 64-75 miles per hour]
EX. According to the weather forecast, a storm is coming late this afternoon.
天気予報によると、今日の午後遅く{嵐/暴風(雨)}がやってくるそうだ。
Tenki-yohoo ni yoru to, kyoo no gogo osoku {arashi/boofuu(-u)} ga yatte kuru sooda.

— vt. [to attack the enemy violently like a storm]
⟨-o⟩ shu⌈ugeki-suru ⟨～を⟩襲撃する ③ •c [for s.o. to suddenly attack the enemy] ⟪attack, assault, charge⟫, ⟨-o⟩ o⌈so⌉u ⟨～を⟩襲う ① [to initiate harmful action upon s.o./s.a./some place] ⟪assail, assault, make a raid on⟫
EX. We stormed the enemy's castle early in the morning.
われわれは敵の城を早朝{襲撃した/襲った}。
Ware-ware wa teki no shiro o soochoo {shuugeki-shita/osotta}.

— vi. [to behave violently or angrily ⟪fig. "rage," "move like a storm"⟫]
te⌉nki ga a⌈reru 天気が荒れる ② [for weather to be violent]
EX. It stormed throughout the night.
一晩中天気が荒れた。
Hito-ban-juu tenki ga areta.
PHRASE: storm into {*kan-kan ni natte/okotte*} ⟨*-ni*⟩ *hairu* {かんかんになって/怒って}⟨～に⟩入る ①, storm out of {*kan-kan ni natte/okotte*} ⟨*-o*⟩ *deru* {かんかんになって/怒って}⟨～を⟩出る ②
EX. The angry customer stormed out of the bank.
客は{かんかんになって/怒って}銀行を出ていった。
Kyaku wa {kan-kan ni natte/okotte} ginkoo o dete itta.

stormy adj. [of a storm ⟪fig. "violent," "raging"⟫]
1. a⌉rashi no N 嵐のN [of a storm], bo⌈ofu⌉u(-u) no N 暴風(雨)のN •c [of a storm]
EX. We were on the mountain that stormy night.

私たちはあの{嵐/暴風(雨)}の晩、山にいました。
Watashi-tachi wa ano {arashi/boofuu(-u)} no ban, yama ni imashita.

2. a˥rashi no yoona 嵐のような adj(*na*). **[like a storm]**

EX. He lived a stormy life.
あの人は嵐のような人生を送った。
Ano hito wa arashi no yoona jinsei o okutta.

story[1] n. **[an oral/written account of an event/events to inform/entertain people]**
ha˥nashi˥ 話 /⟨V*masu* of *hanasu* ① speak/ [an act/instance of speaking ⟪fig. "rumor"⟫] ⟪talk, conversation, speech⟫, mo˥no-ga˥tari 物語 /⟨V*masu* of *monogataru* ① narrate/ [a legendary story/prose-style literary work] ⟪tale, narrative, legend, fiction⟫, su˥to˥orii ストーリー •f [the plot of a story/movie] ⟪plot, outline, synopsis⟫, su˥ji 筋 [a fiber/long fiber-like object ⟪fig. "a story line," "muscle," "streak," "vein"⟫] ⟪muscle, fiber, vein, plot, stripe, lineage⟫

EX. (**a**) Is that story true?
その{話/*物語/*ストーリー/*筋}、本当かい。
*Sono {hanashi/*mono-gatari/*sutoorii/*suji}, hontoo kai*
(**b**) I like to read old stories.
私は昔の{話/物語/*ストーリー/*筋}を読むのが好きです。
*Watashi wa mukashi no {hanashi/mono-gatari/*sutoorii/*suji} o yomu no ga suki desu.*
(**c**) Do you remember how the story went in that movie?
あの映画の{ストーリー/筋/*話/*物語}を覚えていますか。
*Ano eiga no {sutoorii/suji/*hanashi/*mono-gatari} o oboete imasu ka.*

story[2] n. **[the space between floors of a building]**
ka˥i 階 [different levels/a particular level of a building] ⟪floor⟫

EX. I'm living in a two-story building.
私は二階建ての家に住んでいます。
Watashi wa ni-kai-date no ie ni sunde imasu.

stout adj. **[strong in character/physical build/material composition or bulky in body]**

1. gan˥joona 頑丈な adj(*na*). **•c [for s.t. to be not easily broken or for a body to be not prone to illness] ⟪strong, burly, strongly-built⟫, jo˥obuna 丈夫な** adj(*na*). **•c [not easily broken/prone to illness] ⟪healthy, strong, solid, firm, durable⟫, ga˥sshi˥ri-shita N がっしりしたN [strong and firm in build or structure]**

EX. (**a**) Football players are typically stout in physical build.
フットボールの選手はたいてい{がっしりした/頑丈な/丈夫な}体をしている。
Futto-booru no senshu wa taitei {gasshiri-shita/ganjoona/joobuna} karada o shite iru.
(**b**) This car has a stout frame.
この車は作りが{頑丈だ/がっしりしている/丈夫だ}。
Kono kuruma wa tsukuri ga {ganjoo da/gasshiri-shite iru/joobu da}.

2. fu˥kutsu no N 不屈のN •c [unyielding in the face of difficult circumstances] ⟪sturdy, indomitable, determined⟫

EX. He is stout in character and is not easily swayed by the opinions of others.
彼は不屈の精神を持っており、他人の意見には容易に影響されない。
Kare wa fukutsu no seishin o motte ori, tanin no iken ni wa yooini eikyoo-sarenai.

stove n. **[an apparatus for cooking/heating a living space]**

1. su˥to˥obu ストーブ •f [an apparatus for heating a living space]

EX. Could you turn on the stove please?
ストーブをつけてくださいませんか。
Sutoobu o tsukete kudasaimasen ka.

2. (ga˥su-)re˥nji (ガス)レンジ •f

NOTE: *Gasu-renji* comes from "gas range."

straight adj. **[extending in one direction without any curves or angles ⟪fig. "candid,"**

S

"honest," "methodical," "accurate," "reliable," "outspoken," "unmixed"》]

1. ma⌈ssu⌉guna 真っすぐな adj(*na*). **[direct without any curvature/angularity 《fig. "honest"》] 《upright, erect, honest》**

EX. The teacher drew two straight lines on the blackboard.
先生は黒板に真っすぐな線を二本書いた。
Sensei wa kokuban ni massuguna sen o ni-hon kaita.

2. so⌈tchokuna 率直な adj(*na*). **•c [for s.o. to be straightforward about the truth and for one's actions to be typical of that person] 《straightforward, frank, candid》**

EX. I need your straight opinion about this plan.
この計画について率直な御意見をうかがいたいんですが。
Kono keikaku ni-tsuite sotchokuna go-iken o ukagai-tai n desu ga.

3. sho⌈ojiki⌉na 正直な adj(*na*). **•c [for s.o. to be not likely to lie/cheat/hide the truth or for a person's actions to be typical of that person] 《upright, square》**

EX. You don't need to worry about being cheated by John. He's a thoroughly straight person.
ジョンにだまされる恐れはない。根っから正直な人なんだから。
Jon ni damasa-reru osore wa nai. Nekkara shoojikina hito na n da kara.

4. sei⌈kakuna 正確な adj(*na*). **•c [in accord with fact and reliable] 《exact, precise》**

EX. We expect our news reporters to give us nothing but the straight facts.
報道記者は我々に正確な事実のみを提供するべきだ。
Hoodoo-kisha wa ware-ware ni seikakuna jijitsu nomi o teikyoo-suri-beki da.

5. su⌈tore⌉eto no N ストレートのN •f [for whiskey not to be mixed with water/ice or for a baseball to be thrown directly without curvature or for hair to be without a permanent/natural curls or for jeans to fit very tightly]

—— adv. **[in a straight way]**

1. ma⌈ssu⌉gu(ni) 真っすぐ(に) [going from one point to another without any curvature/angularity] 《directly》, i⌈tchoku⌉sen ni 一直線に •c [in a single straight line]

EX. My husband comes straight home after work since our child was born.
子供が生まれてから夫は仕事が終わると{一直線に/真っすぐ}うちへ帰ってくるようになった。
Kodomo ga umarete kara otto wa shigoto ga owaru to {itchokusen ni/ massugu} uchi e kaette kuru yooni natta.

2. so⌈tchokuni 率直に /〈adj(*na*). *ni* of *sotchokuna* candid/ •c [without hiding what one really thinks/feels] 《candidly, straightforwardly》, su⌈tore⌉etoni ストレートに /〈adj(*na*). *ni* of *sutoreetona* straight/ •f, sho⌈ojiki⌉ni 正直に /〈adj(*na*). *ni* of *shoojikina* honest/ •c [in an honest manner]

EX. I told him straight that if he didn't improve his performance he would be fired.
もっとちゃんと仕事をしないとくびになるぞと彼に{率直に/ストレートに/正直に}言った。
Motto chanto shigoto o shinai to kubi ni naru zo to kare ni {sotchokuni/ sutoreetoni/shoojikini} itta.

3. su⌈tore⌉eto de ストレートで •f [without adding water/ice or direct without any curvature]

EX. (**a**) I would like my whiskey straight.
ウィスキーをストレートでください。
Uisukii o sutoreeto de kudasai.
(**b**) Kazuo got into Tokyo University straight out of high school.
一男は東大に高校からストレートで入った。
Kazuo wa Toodai ni kookoo kara sutoreeto de haitta.

straighten vt. **[for s.o. to cause s.t. to become straight]**

〈-o〉 no⌈ba⌉su 〈〜を〉のばす ① [for s.o. to cause s.t. to become longer, usu. vertically

《fig. "straighten," "hold out," "postpone," "cultivate (abilities)"》]

㊊ "prolong (time)"▷延ばす, otherwise ▷伸ばす

EX. After using my computer for about an hour, I make a point of straightening my back to feel better.
コンピューターを一時間ぐらい使ったあと、気分をよくするために背筋を伸ばすようにしています。
Konpyuutaa o ichi-jikan gurai tsukatta ato, kibun o yoku-suru tame ni se-suji o nobasu-yooni shite imasu.

PHRASE: straighten up ⟨-o⟩ *kichin to-suru* ⟨〜を⟩ きちんとする ③

EX. How about straightening up your room for the guests?
お客さんが来るから部屋をきちんとしたらどうですか。
O-kyaku-san ga kuru kara heya o kichin-to shitara doo desu ka.

PHRASE: straighten out ⟨-o⟩ *kaiketsu-suru* ⟨〜を⟩ 解決する ③

EX. It took a week to straighten out the problem.
その問題を解決するのに一週間かかった。
Sono mondai o kaiketsu-suru noni is-shuukan kakatta.

PHRASE: straighten out ⟨-o⟩ *massuguni suru* ⟨〜を⟩ 真っすぐにする ③

EX. Your tie is crooked. Straighten it out.
ネクタイが曲がっているよ。真っすぐにしなさい。
Nekutai ga magatte iru yo. Massuguni shinasai.

—— vi. **[for s.t. to become straight]**

1. ma⌈ssu⌉gu ni naru 真っすぐになる ① [for a line to become straight]

EX. No matter how hard I pushed the bent iron pole, it wouldn't straighten out.
曲がった鉄の棒はどんなに押しても真っすぐにならなかった。
Magatta tetsu no boo wa donna-ni oshite mo massugu ni naranakatta.

2. ma⌈tomo ni na⌉ru まともになる ① [for a person who used to commit wrong to become an upright person]

strain vt. **[to draw tight or exert s.t. to its limits or to separate solid matter from a liquid by using a sieve, etc.]**

1. ⟨-o⟩ hi⌈ppa⌉ru ⟨〜を⟩引っ張る ① [to move s.t./s.o./s.a. forcibly towards the source of the force 《fig. "entice"》] 《pull, draw, drag, tug》

EX. The rope was strained almost to the breaking point.
ロープは引っ張られて、切れる寸前だった。
Roopu wa hippara-rete, kireru sunzen datta.

2. (⟨-de⟩) ki⌈nchoo-suru (⟨〜で⟩)緊張する ③ •c [for a body/bodily part to become very tense] 《become tense》

EX. Friction over trade strained the relationship between the two countries.
貿易摩擦で二国間の関係は緊張した。
Booeki-masatsu de ni-koku-kan no kankei wa kinchoo-shita.

3. ⟨-de⟩ ⟨-o⟩ tsu⌈kai-sugi⌉ru ⟨〜で⟩⟨〜を⟩使い過ぎる ② [to overuse s.t. such as a body part]

EX. I strained my leg muscles jogging.
ジョギングで足の筋肉を使い過ぎました。
Jogingu de ashi no kinniku o tsukai-sugimashita.

4. ⟨-o⟩ ko⌈su ⟨〜を⟩こす ① [for s.o. to filter out unwanted matter using an instrument with narrow openings] 《filter, percolate, leach》, ⟨-no⟩ mi⌈zu o ki⌉ru ⟨〜の⟩水をきる ① [for s.o. to drain off water from s.t. boiled]

EX. (**a**) Could you please strain the water from the noodles?
うどん{の水を切って/*をこして}ください。
*Udon {no mizu o kitte/*o koshite} kudasai.*
(**b**) Flannel is the best material to use for straining soups.
スープ{をこす/*の水を切る}にはフランネルが一番いい。

S

*Suupu {o kosu/*no mizu o kiru} ni wa furanneru ga ichiban ii.*

PHRASE: strain one's eyes (to see) ⟨-o⟩ *gyooshi-suru* ⟨〜を⟩凝視する ③ •c, strain one's ears (to hear) *mimi o sumashite* ⟨-o⟩ *kiku* 耳を澄まして⟨〜を⟩聞く ①

— n. **[a state of being excessively tight]**

1. ki⌈nchoo 緊張 •c [mental/physical/nervous tenseness] ⟪**stress, tension, anxiety**⟫

EX. College entrance examinations place a lot of strain on high school students.
大学入試は高校生に大変な緊張を強いる。
Daigaku-nyuushi wa kookoo-sei ni taihenna kinchoo o shiiru.

2. tsu⌈kai-sugi 使い過ぎ /⟨V*masu* of *tsukai-sugiru* ② use s.t. too much/ [overuse of s.t.]

strait n. **[a narrow water passage that connects two seas]**

ka⌈ikyoo 海峡 •c

EX. The Tsugaru Straits lie between Honshu and Hokkaido.
津軽海峡は本州と北海道の間にある。
Tsugaru Kaikyoo wa Honshuu to Hokkaidoo no aida ni aru.

S

strand n. **[one of a number of fibers or fiber-like materials twisted into the form of a rope]**

1. yo⌈ri⌉ より [s.t. twisted] ⟪**twist, ply**⟫

2. fu⌈sa⌉ 房 [a string of twisted threads/hairs ending with untwisted ones ⟪fig. "bunch"⟫] ⟪**tuft, fringe, tress**⟫

strange adj. **[unfamiliar or surprising ⟪fig. "queer," "odd"⟫]**

1. shi⌈ranai N 知らないN [of s.t./s.o./s.a. not known to one], mi-⌈narenai N 見慣れないN adj(*i*). **[of seeing s.t./s.o./s.a. which one is not used to seeing]** ⟪**unfamiliar**⟫, **mi-⌈shiranu N 見知らぬN [of s.t./s.o./s.a. unfamiliar to s.o. ⟨w⟩], ki⌈ki-narenai N 聞き慣れないN** adj(*i*). **[of s.t./s.o./s.a. which one is not used to hearing]**

EX. (**a**) I found myself in a strange place.
気がついたら{知らない/見知らぬ/見慣れない/*聞き慣れない}所に来ていた。
*Ki-ga-tsuitara {shiranai/mi-shiranu/mi-narenai/*kiki-narenai} tokoro ni kite ita.*
(**b**) A lot of strange people came to the party.
パーティーには{知らない/見知らぬ/見慣れない/*聞き慣れない}人が大勢来た。
*Paatii ni wa {shiranai/mi-shiranu/mi-narenai/*kiki-narenai} hito ga oozei kita.*
(**c**) A couple next to me was speaking in a strange language.
私の隣の二人は{聞き慣れない/知らない/*見知らぬ/*見慣れない}言葉を話していた。
*Watashi no tonari no futari wa {kiki-narenai/shiranai/*mi-shiranu/*mi-narenai} kotoba o hanashite ita.*

2. na⌈jimi no na⌉i なじみのない adj(*i*). **[not used to s.t.]** ⟪**unfamiliar**⟫

EX. It was difficult to adjust to the strange customs of the local people.
地元の人のなじみのない習慣に慣れるのは大変だった。
Jimoto no hito no najimi no nai shuukan ni nareru no wa taihen datta.

3. he⌉nna 変な adj(*na*). **•c [exhibiting an unusual characteristic/condition/behavior ⟪fig. "suspicious-looking," "queer"⟫]** ⟪**odd, suspicious-looking, weird, funny**⟫, **ki⌉myoona 奇妙な** adj(*na*). **•c [unusual and mysterious in character/reason]** ⟪**curious, odd, queer, singular, weird**⟫, **fushigina 不思議な** adj(*na*). **•c [beyond logical/common-sensical explanation]** ⟪**wonderful, marvelous, mysterious**⟫

EX. (**a**) It's strange that he hasn't called me.
彼が電話をかけて来ないのは{変/奇妙/不思議}だ。
Kare ga denwa o kakete konai no wa {hen/kimyoo/fushigi} da.
(**b**) A strange person was walking with a strange dog.
{変な/奇妙な/不思議な}人が{変な/奇妙な/不思議な}犬を連れて歩いていた。
{Henna/Kimyoona/Fushigina} hito ga

{henna/kimyoona/fushigina} inu o tsurete aruite ita.
(c) Strange as it may sound, he had never ridden in a car before.
{不思議な/*変な/*奇妙な}ことに、車に乗るのは彼にとって初めてのことだった。
*{Fushigina/*Henna/*Kimyoona} koto ni, kuruma ni noru no wa kare ni-totte hajimete no koto datta.*

stranger n. **[a person who is not known to another/who is not familiar with s.t.]**
1. shi⌈ranai hito 知らない人 [a person who one doesn't know]
EX. A stranger was standing in front of the gate.
知らない人が門の前に立っていました。
Shiranai hito ga mon no mae ni tatte imashita.
2. shi⌈nmai 新米 •c [new rice ⟪fig. "a person unaccustomed to s.t. that requires a certain level of skill"⟫] ⟪beginner, novice, greenhorn⟫
EX. As you know, I am a total stranger to computers.
ご存知のように、私はコンピューターは全くの新米です。
Go-zonji no yooni, watashi wa konpyuutaa wa mattaku no shinmai desu.

strap n. **[a narrow band of leather with a fastener for binding]**
ka⌈wa-himo 革ひも [a leather thong] ⟪thong, leash⟫, tsu⌈ri-kawa つり革 [a leather band suspended from above on a train or bus for passengers to hang onto for support]
— vt. **[to fasten/hit with a strap]**
1. ka⌈wa-himo de ku⌈kuru 革ひもでくくる ① [for s.o. to fasten s.t. with a strap]
2. ka⌈wa-himo de ta⌈ta⌉ku 革ひもでたたく ① [for s.o. to hit s.o./s.a. with a strap]

strawberry n.
i⌈chigo いちご

stray vi. **[to wander from a place ⟪fig. "deviate," "digress"⟫]**
1. m⌈ichi ni ma⌈yo⌉u 道に迷う ① [for s.o./s.a. to lose one's way]
EX. The children strayed off the path while walking in the deep forest.
深い森を歩いているうちに子供は道に迷ってしまった。
Fukai mori o aruite iru uchi ni kodomo wa michi ni mayotte shimatta.
2. yo⌈ko-michi ni so⌈re⌉ru 横道にそれる ② [to go off on a tangent] ⟪deviate, digress⟫
EX. He tends to stray off the topic in his lectures.
あの先生は講義の中で横道にそれることが多い。
Ano sensei wa koogi no naka de yoko-michi ni soreru koto ga ooi.
— adj. **[having strayed]**
mi⌈chi ni ma⌈yo⌉tta N 道に迷ったN [unable to find one's way], ma⌉igo no N 迷子のN [having wandered away from familiar territory]
EX. On his first day at the large public school, Mike was like a stray sheep.
大きな公立校に登校した初日は、マイクは{道に迷った/迷子の}羊のようなものだった。
Ookina kooritsu-koo ni tookoo-shita shonichi wa, Maiku wa {michi ni mayotta/maigo no} hitsuji no yoona mono datta.

streak n. **[a long line/stripe usually different from its surroundings in color ⟪fig. "stratum of mineral," "a layer of fat in meat," "a continuous behavioral pattern," "a continuous period of s.t."⟫]**
1. shi⌈ma⌉ しま [(a fabric with) vertical, horizontal, or oblique lines differing in color from their surroundings] ⟪stripe, band⟫
EX. My T-shirt has a pattern of white and red streaks in it.
僕のＴシャツは赤と白のしまが入っている。
Boku no T-shatsu wa aka to shiro no shima ga haitte iru.
2. ko⌈omyaku 鉱脈 •c [a long, narrow vein of ore/mineral]

S

3. so˥o 層 •c [a thickness of some substance, extending horizontally and occurring one on top of another《fig. "a group fixed according to certain upper and lower limits"》]《stratum, seam, class》
4. ki˥shitsu 気質 •c [personal traits]《temperament, disposition》
5. i˥chi-ren no N 一連のN •c [a series of s.t.]《a chain of》

EX. A streak of luck on the stock market made him an instant millionaire.
株式市場における一連の幸運で彼はあっと言う間に億万長者になった。
Kabushiki-shijoo ni-okeru ichi-ren no kooun de kare wa atto-iu-ma-ni okuman-chooja ni natta.

stream n. **[a continuous flow of water or other liquid or of gas, light, or a mass of things in succession, including people《fig. "continuity," "tendency"》]**
1. na˥gare˥ 流れ /〈V*masu* of *nagareru* ② flow/ [a flow of water/people/cars/events《fig. "school," "descent"》]《flowing, flow, descent, school》

EX. I swam against the stream.
僕は流れに逆らって泳いだ。
Boku wa nagare ni sakaratte oyoida.

2. o˥gawa 小川 [small river]《brook》

EX. There is a small stream running behind my house.
うちの裏を小川が流れている。
Uchi no ura o ogawa ga nagarete iru.

3. ke˥ikoo 傾向 •c [a natural propensity to develop or act in a certain way]《tendency, trend, drift, inclination》

—— vi. [for liquid/gas/light to flow]
na˥gare˥ru 流れる ② [for liquid, electricity, etc., to move steadily and continuously in a stream or stream-like fashion]《run, float, be called off, be forfeited》

EX. The sweat streamed from her forehead.
彼女の額から汗が流れた。
Kanojo no hitai kara ase ga nagareta.

PHRASE: stream back *nabiku* なびく ①

EX. Her long hair streamed back as she ran in the wind.
風に向かって走ると、彼女の長い髪がなびいた。
Kaze ni mukatte hashiru to, kanojo no nagai kami ga nabiita.

street n. **[a public road lined with buildings wide enough to accommodate automobile traffic, usu. with sidewalks]**
to˥ori˥ 通り /〈V*masu* of *tooru* ① pass/ [an act of passing or a road along which people and cars can pass]《road, passage》

EX. Lining the streets of the Ginza are many willow trees.
銀座通りには柳の木がたくさん並んでいる。
Ginza-doori ni wa yanagi no ki ga takusan narande iru.

streetcar n.
ro˥men-de˥nsha 路面電車 •c, shi˥den 市電 •c [a municipal street railway], To-˥den 都電 •c [a street railway in Tokyo]

strength n. **[the quality of being strong or the degree of power, force, or intensity of s.o./s.a./s.t.]**
1. tsu˥yo-sa 強さ /〈adj(*i*). stem of *tsuyoi* strong + suf. *sa* ness/ ↔ yowa-sa 弱さ

EX. Her strength lies in her ability to think logically.
彼女の強さは論理的に思考する能力にある。
Kanojo no tsuyo-sa wa ronri-tekini shikoo-suru nooryoku ni aru.

2. ta˥iryoku 体力 •c [the extent to which one has the physical capacity to undertake s.t. or withstand s.t., including disease]《physical stamina》

EX. To build up strength one has to exercise regularly.
体力をつけるためには規則的に運動をしなければなりません。
Tairyoku o tsukeru tame ni wa kisoku-tekini undoo o shinakereba narimasen.

3. tsu˥yo-mi˥ 強み /〈adj(*i*). stem of *tsuyoi* strong + suf. *mi* ness/ [a strong point]《one's forte》↔ yowa-mi 弱み

EX. The strength of that student is his inquisitive mind.

あの学生の強みは探求心です。
Ano gakusei no tsuyo-mi wa tankyuu-shin desu.

4. he⌉iryoku 兵力 •c [military force], gu⌈nji⌉-ryoku 軍事力 •c [military power]

strengthen vt. **[to cause s.t./s.o./s.a. to become stronger]**

⟨-o⟩ tsu⌉yoku suru ⟨〜を⟩強くする ③ [to make s.t. stronger], ⟨-o⟩ kyo⌉oka-suru ⟨〜を⟩強化する ③ •c [for s.o. to fortify s.t.] ⟪**build up, toughen, solidify**⟫

EX. (**a**) Walking is the best way to strengthen your legs.
歩くのが足を{強くする/??強化する}一番いい方法です。
Aruku no ga ashi o {tsuyoku suru/??kyooka-suru} ichiban ii hoohoo desu.
(**b**) The police have strengthened their control over the drug traffic.
警察は麻薬の取り締まりを{強化した/?強くした}。
Keisatsu wa mayaku no tori-shimari o {kyooka-shita/?tsuyoku shita}.

stress vt. **[to place physical/mental pressure on s.o./s.t.** ⟪**fig. "emphasize"**⟫**]**

⟨-ni⟩ o⌈moki⌉ o o⌈ku ⟨〜に⟩重きをおく ① [for s.o. to put emphasis on s.t.], ⟨-o⟩ kyo⌈ochoo-suru ⟨〜を⟩強調する ③ •c [for s.o. to express s.t. forcefully so as to make it conspicuous to others] ⟪**lay emphasis on**⟫

EX. My Japanese instructor stressed the importance of practice.
私の日本語の先生は練習{に重きをおいた/を強調した}。
Watashi no Nihon-go no sensei wa renshuu {ni omoki o oita/o kyoochoo-shita}.

— n. **[a pressure of force exerted on s.o./s.a./s.t. so as to cause strain]**

1. a⌈tsu⌉ryoku 圧力 •c [physical or psychological force pressing on s.t./s.o./s.a.] ⟪**pressure**⟫**, su⌈to⌉resu ストレス •f [psycho-somatic strain induced by physical, chemical, or emotional factors in the environment], ju⌈uatsu 重圧 •c [heavy pressure]**

EX. I cannot stand the stress of my responsibilities as department manager any longer.
私は部長としての責任の{圧力/ストレス/重圧}にもう耐えられない。
Watashi wa buchoo to-shite no senkinin no {atsuryoku/sutoresu/juuatsu} ni moo tae-rarenai.

2. kyo⌈ochoo 強調 •c [expresing s.t. forcefully so as to make it conspicuous to others] ⟪**emphasis**⟫**, tsu⌉yo-sa 強さ**

stretch vt. **[for s.o. to pull s.t. tightly or to cause s.t. to reach/extend to its full extent** ⟪**fig. "bend a law," "twist"**⟫**]**

⟨-o⟩ no⌈ba⌉su ⟨〜を⟩のばす ① [for s.o. to cause s.t. to become longer, usu. vertically ⟪**fig. "straighten," "hold out," "postpone," "cultivate (abilities)"**⟫**]** ⟪**lengthen, extend, elongate, straighten, put off**⟫**, ⟨-o⟩ hi⌈ppa⌉ru ⟨〜を⟩引っ張る ① [to move s.t./s.o./s.a. forcibly towards the source of the force** ⟪**fig. "entice"**⟫**]** ⟪**pull, draw, drag, tug**⟫
㊥ "prolong (in time)"▷延ばす, otherwise ▷伸ばす

EX. (**a**) I stretched my arm as high as I could to catch the fly ball, but it was no use.
フライをとるためにできるだけ高く腕を{伸ばした/*引っ張った}がだめだった。
*Furai o toru tame ni dekiru dake ude o {nobashita/*hippatta} ga dame datta.*
(**b**) You have to stretch out your arms for this exercise.
この運動には腕を{伸ばさなければ/*引っ張らなければ}ならない。
*Kono undoo ni wa ude o {nobasanakereba/*hipparanakereba} naranai.*
(**c**) I stretched the shoe lace until it broke.
靴のひもを切れるまで{引っ張って/*伸ばして}しまった。
*Kutsu no himo o kireru made {hippatte/*nobashite} shimatta.*

— n. **[an act/instance of stretching** ⟪**fig. "continuous space," "bending"**⟫**]**

1. no⌈bi⌉ のび / (V*masu* of *nobiru* ② extend,

S

be postponed/ [an act/instance of s.t. becoming longer] ⟪growth, postponement, extension⟫

㊊ "prolongation"▷延び, otherwise ▷伸び

2. i˥kki 一気 •c [one continuous time-span] ⟪one breath⟫

EX. We finished the work in one stretch.
われわれはその仕事を一気にやってしまった。
Ware-ware wa sono shigoto o ikki ni yatte shimatta.

strict adj. [comforming exactly to standards/ rules]

1. ki┌bishi˥i 厳しい adj(*i*). [unpleasantly intense to the senses or tending to impose strict rules on others] ⟪severe, rigid, harsh, relentless⟫

EX. That teacher is very strict about students' grammatical errors.
あの先生は学生の文法の間違いにとても厳しい。
Ano sensei wa gakusei no bunpoo no machigai ni totemo kibishii.

S

2. se┌ikakuna 正確な adj(*na*). •c [in accord with fact and reliable] ⟪exact, precise, correct⟫

EX. This is a strict replica of the original painting.
これは原画の正確な複製です。
Kore wa genga no seikakuna fukusei desu.

3. ka┌nzenna 完全な adj(*na*). •c [lacking no parts and having no faults] ⟪complete, perfect⟫

EX. He is a strict vegetarian.
あの人は完全な菜食主義者です。
Ano hito wa kanzenna saishoku-shugi-sha desu.

strike vt. [for s.o./s.a./a natural force to hit or suddenly attack s.t./s.o./s.a. ⟪fig. "cause s.o. to feel s.t."⟫]

1. ⟨-o⟩ (⟨-de⟩) u˥tsu ⟨〜を⟩(⟨〜で⟩)うつ ① [to bring the hand/s.t. held in the hand forcefully against s.t. or to cause s.t. to come against s.t. forcefully] ⟪hit, shoot⟫, ⟨-o⟩ (⟨-de⟩) bu˥tsu ⟨〜を⟩(⟨〜で⟩)ぶつ ① [for s.o. to bring the hand/s.t. held in the hand forcefully against s.o./s.a. intentionally] ⟪hit, spank⟫, ⟨-o⟩ (⟨-de⟩) ta┌ta˥ku ⟨〜を⟩(⟨〜で⟩)たたく ① [for s.o. to bring the hand/s.t. held in the hand against s.o./s.t./ s.a., usu. repeatedly ⟪fig. "criticize"⟫] ⟪hit, beat, knock, slap⟫, ⟨-o⟩ na┌gu˥ru ⟨〜を⟩殴る ① [for s.o. to bring one's fist or to use s.t. against s.o./s.a. hard with the intention of causing harm] ⟪hit, beat, thump, punch, knock, slap⟫

㊊ "shoot s.o./s.a. with a gun"▷撃つ, otherwise ▷打つ

EX. (**a**) One of the guards suddenly struck the prisoner on the head with a stick.
監守の一人が突然囚人の頭を棒で{打った/ぶった/たたいた/殴った}。
Kanshu no hitori ga totsuzen shuujin no atama o boo de {utta/butta/tataita/ nagutta}.
(**b**) Have you ever struck your child out of anger?
怒って子供を{たたいた/ぶった/殴った/ *打った}ことがありますか。
*Okotte kodomo o {tataita/butta/ nagutta/*utta} koto ga arimasu ka.*

2. {⟨-ni⟩/⟨-to⟩} bu┌tsukaru {⟨〜に⟩/⟨〜と⟩}ぶつかる ① [to come against s.o./s.t./s.a. by accident forcing a change in the direction of its movement] ⟪hit, bump into, run against, collide with⟫, ⟨-ni⟩ a┌taru ⟨〜に⟩当たる ① [for s.t. to come into sudden spontaneous contact with s.t. forming a narrow target area ⟪fig. "bask," "correspond"⟫] ⟪hit, be exposed to, bask, correspond to, fall on⟫

EX. (**a**) The car struck an electric pole.
車が電柱に{ぶつかった/*当たった}。
*Kuruma ga denchuu ni {butsukatta/ *atatta}.*
(**b**) A ball struck the window.
ボールが窓に{当たった/*ぶつかった}。
*Booru ga mado ni {atatta/ *butsukatta}.*

3. ⟨-o⟩ o┌sou ⟨〜を⟩襲う ① [to initiate harmful action upon s.o./s.a./some place]

EX. The tornado struck a small town in Texas.
竜巻がテキサスの小さな町を襲った。
Tatsumaki ga Tekisasu no chiisana machi o osotta.

4. ((-o)) ⟨-to⟩ **o⌈mo⌉u** ((〜を))⟨〜と⟩思う ① **[for s.o. to spontaneously perceive s.t. in one's mind or to have an opinion about s.t.]** ⟪feel, think⟫

EX. A: How does his thesis strike you?
彼の論文をどう思いますか。
Kare no ronbun o doo omoimasu ka.
B: It strikes me as superb.
すばらしいと思います。
Subarashii to omoimasu.

5. …po⌉ozu o to⌉ru …ポーズを取る ① **[to assume a certain position or attitude for a picture]**

EX. Yukie struck a charming pose in front of the camera.
カメラの前で幸江は魅力的なポーズを取った。
Kamera no mae de Yukie wa miryoku-tekina poozu o totta.

6. to⌈kei ga -ji o u⌉tsu 時計が〜時を打つ ① **[for a clock to give the time by making a sound]**

EX. When the clock struck twelve, Cinderella had to leave the castle.
時計が十二時を打ち、シンデレラはお城を出なければなりませんでした。
Tokei ga juu-ni-ji o uchi, Shinderera wa o-shiro o denakereba narimasen deshita.

— vi. **[for s.o./s.a./a natural force to hit or suddenly attack s.t./s.o./s.a.** ⟪fig. "ignite," "for a clock to give the time," "refuse to work," "feel"⟫**]**

1. ⟨-ni⟩ **tsu⌈ki-sasa⌉ru** ⟨〜に⟩突き刺さる ① **[for s.t. to stick into s.t.]** ⟪pierce, penetrate⟫

EX. The knife struck deep into his arm.
ナイフは彼の腕に深く突き刺さった。
Naifu wa kare no ude ni fukaku tsuki-sasatta.

2. ({⟨-ni⟩/⟨-to⟩}) **bu⌈tsukaru** ({⟨〜に⟩/⟨〜と⟩}) ぶつかる ① **[to come against s.o./s.t./s.a. by accident forcing the direction of its movement to change]**

EX. The two arrows struck in midair.
二本の矢は空中でぶつかった。
Ni-hon no ya wa kuuchuu de butsukatta.

3. ⟨-o⟩ **o⌈sou** ⟨〜を⟩襲う ① SEE strike vt. 3

EX. The tornado struck at midnight when everyone was asleep.
みんなが眠っていた真夜中に竜巻が襲った。
Minna ga nemutte ita ma-yonaka ni tatsumaki ga osotta.

4. su⌈tora⌉iki o suru ストライキをする ③ **[to go on strike]**

EX. The major automobile unions struck in May.
五月に主な自動車会社の労働組合がストライキをした。
Go-gatsu ni omona jidoosha-gaisha no roodoo-kumiai ga sutoraiki o shita.

— n. **[an act of striking]**

1. ko⌈ogeki 攻撃 •c **[a physical/verbal attack]** ⟪attack, assault, raid⟫, **o⌉oda** 殴打 •c **[hitting a person/animal with the intention of causing injury]**

2. su⌈tora⌉iki ストライキ •f **[laborers' refusal to work in order to win concessions from management]**

EX. In Japan there are railroad strikes every spring.
日本では春にはいつも鉄道のストライキがある。
Nihon de wa haru ni wa itsu-mo tetsudoo no sutoraiki ga aru.

3. su⌈tora⌉iku ストライク •f **[an accurately pitched baseball which is not hit by the batter]**

string n. **[a thin line of twisted threads or wire for tying/binding or a series of objects strung together** ⟪fig. "cords stretched on a musical instrument"⟫**]**

1. (hoso-)**hi⌈mo** (細)ひも **[a (small) cord]**

2. i⌈chi-ren 一連 •c **[a series of related objects or events]** ⟪a series of, a chain of⟫

3. ge⌉n 弦 •c **[strings on a stringed instrument]**

S

EX. A Japanese *koto* has 13 strings.
日本の琴には弦が十三本ある。
Nihon no koto ni wa gen ga juu-san-bon aru.

PHRASE: no strings attached *himo-tsuki dewanai* ひもつきではない

— vt. **[to fasten/tie s.t. with a string or to put objects on a string 《fig. "tighten," "excite"》]**

1. 〈-o〉 hi⌈mo de shi⌈ba⌉ru 〈～を〉ひもで縛る ① [for s.o. to fasten/tie s.t. with a string]

2. 〈-ni〉 hi⌈mo o tsu⌈ke⌉ru 〈～に〉ひもを付ける ② [for s.o. to attach string to s.t.]

3. 〈-ni〉 ge⌉n o ha⌈ru 〈～に〉弦を張る ① [to attach strings to a musical instrument]

4. 〈-o〉 hi⌈ki-shime⌉ru 〈～を〉引き締める ② [to pull s.t. tight]

strip vt. **[to remove a covering such as clothing 《fig. "deprive s.o./s.t./s.a. of a title/possessions/attributes"》]**

1. 〈-o〉 ha⌈daka ni suru 〈～を〉裸にする ③ [to make s.o. naked]

EX. The guerrillas stripped the hostages and took all their belongings.
ゲリラ兵は人質を裸にして、所持品を何もかも奪ってしまった。
Gerira-hei wa hitojichi o hadaka ni shite, shoji-hin o nani-mo kamo ubatte shimatta.

2. 〈-kara〉 〈-o〉 u⌈ba⌉u 〈～から〉〈～を〉奪う ① [to deprive s.o. of s.t.]

EX. The military regime stripped the people of their freedom.
軍事政権は人々から自由を奪った。
Gunji-seiken wa hito-bito kara jiyuu o ubatta.

— vi. **[to undress]**

(kite iru mo⌈no⌉ o) nu⌉gu (着ている物を)脱ぐ ① [for s.o. to take off one's clothing]

stripe n. **[a long, narrow band]**

shi⌈ma⌉ しま [(a fabric with) vertical, horizontal, or oblique lines differing in color from their surroundings]

EX. A: What kind of necktie would you like?
どんなネクタイがよろしいですか。
Donna nekutai ga yoroshii desu ka.
B: I'd like one with red and blue stripes.
赤と青のしまの入ったのをお願いします。
Aka to ao no shima no haitta no o o-negai-shimasu.

stroke[1] n. **[an act of striking or a single unbroken movement or a sequence of particular movements]**

1. da⌈geki 打撃 •c [an act of hitting or the resulting damage or shock] 《blow, knock, hit》, **i⌈chi⌉-da 一打 •c [one motion of striking]**

2. hi⌈to⌉-kaki 一かき [a single cycle of motions of the arms in swimming]

3. i⌈p-pitsu 一筆 •c [a single motion of the arms/hands in calligraphy 《fig. "a few lines of letter"》] 《a few lines》

4. u⌉tsu o⌈to⌉ 打つ音 [the sound of s.t. striking esp. a bell or clock]

5. so⌈tchuu 卒中 •c [a sudden attack of illness esp. apoplexy/paralysis]

EX. My father had a stroke when he was in his fifties.
父は五十代の時卒中を起こした。
Chichi wa gojuu-dai no toki sotchuu o okoshita.

PHRASE: stroke order *hitsujun* 筆順 •c

— vt. **[for s.o. to move one's hands/arms to draw a line or to hit a ball]**

1. se⌉n o ka⌉ku 線をかく ① [for s.o. to draw a line]

2. bo⌈oru o u⌉tsu ボールを打つ ① [for s.o. to hit a ball esp. in baseball/tennis]

stroke[2] vt. **[to caress s.o./s.a./s.t. gently with one's hand]**

1. 〈-o〉 na⌈de⌉ru 〈～を〉なでる ② [for s.o. to caress s.t. softly with the palm of one's hand 《fig. "comb one's hair"》]

EX. In Japan parents stroke their children on the head when they do a good job.
日本の親たちは子供がよくやったときに頭をなでる。
Nihon no oya-tachi wa kodomo ga yoku yatta toki ni atama o naderu.

stroll vi. **[for s.o. to walk idly and leisurely]**

bu⌉ra-bura a⌈ru⌉ku ぶらぶら歩く ① [for

s.o./s.a. to walk aimlessly]

EX. I like to stroll in the woods when I feel stressed out.
疲れた時は森の中をぶらぶら歩くのが好きだ。
Tsukareta toki wa mori no naka o bura-bura aruku no ga suki da.

strong adj. **[physically/intellectually/psychologically/structurally/militarily/perceptively powerful]**

1. tsu⌈yo⌉i 強い adj(*i*). **[having the power to act or perform in an effective way or to resist external force, esp. physically, but also mentally or emotionally]** ⟪**powerful, mighty, robust, stout, violent, intense, durable**⟫ ↔ **yowai 弱い** adj(*i*).; **chi⌈kara⌉ ga a⌉ru** (N) **力がある**(N) **[having power]**, **ga⌈njoona 頑丈な** adj(*na*). •c **[for s.t. to be not easily broken or for a body to be not prone to illness]** ⟪**burly, strong-built**⟫, **jo⌈obuna 丈夫な** adj(*na*). •c **[not easily broken/prone to illness]** ⟪**solid, firm, durable, healthy**⟫

EX. (a) *Sumo* wrestlers have to be strong.
相撲取りは{強く/力が/?頑丈で/?丈夫で}なくてはならない。
Sumoo-tori wa {tsuyoku/chikara ga/?ganjoode/?joobude} nakute wa naranai.
(b) He has a strong constitution, so he seldom gets tired.
彼は体質的に{頑丈だ/丈夫だ/強い/*力がある}から滅多に疲れない。
*Kare wa taishitsu-tekini {ganjoo da/joobu da/tsuyoi/*chikara ga aru} kara mettani tsukarenai.*
(c) The Los Angeles Dodgers were for many years America's strongest baseball team.
ロサンゼルスのドジャースは長年アメリカで一番{強い/力がある/*頑丈な/*丈夫な}野球チームでした。
*Rosanzerusu no Dojaasu wa naganen Amerika de ichiban {tsuyoi/chikara ga aru/*ganjoona/*joobuna} yakyuu-chiimu deshita.*
(d) My little brother is strong in math.
弟は数学{が強い/の力がある/*が頑丈だ/*が丈夫だ}。
*Otooto wa suugaku {ga tsuyoi/no chikara ga aru/*ga ganjoo da/*ga joobu da}.*
(e) Asian countries are afraid of a strong Japan.
アジアの国々は{強い/力がある/*頑丈な/*丈夫な}日本を恐れている。
*Ajia no kuni-guni wa {tsuyoi/chikara ga aru/*ganjoona/*joobuna} Nihon o osorete iru.*
(f) This coffee is too strong for me.
このコーヒーは私には{強/*力があり/*頑丈/*丈夫}すぎます。
*Kono koohii wa watashi ni wa {tsuyo/*chikara ga ari/*ganjoo/*joobu}-sugimasu.*
(g) I don't like the strong smell of this cheese.
私はこのチーズの{強い/*力がある/*頑丈な/*丈夫な}においが嫌いだ。
*Watashi wa kono chiizu no {tsuyoi/*chikara ga aru/*ganjoona/*joobuna} nioi ga kirai da.*

2. shi⌈kka⌉ri-shite iru (N) **しっかりしている**(N) /(V *te iru* of *shikkari-suru* ③ become firm/ **[free from weakness/looseness]**

EX. I believe our son is emotionally strong enough to go abroad by himself to study.
うちの息子はしっかりしているから、一人で外国へ留学しても大丈夫だと思う。
Uchi no musuko wa shikkari-shite iru kara, hitori de gaikoku e ryuugaku-shite mo daijoobu da to omou.

structural adj **[pertaining to a structure]**
ko⌈ozoo(-joo) no N 構造(上)のN •c **[pertaining to the internal mechanism of a machine/system]** ⟪**systematic**⟫, **ko⌈ozoo-tekina 構造的な** adj(*na*). •c **[pertaining to the internal mechanism of a machine/system]**, **so⌉shiki(-joo) no N 組織(上)のN** •c **[pertaining to a human organization]** ⟪**organizational**⟫

EX. (a) Traditional Japanese architecture has a

S

structural simplicity which is appealing.
伝統的な日本の建築は{構造(上)の/*組織(上)の/*構造的な}簡潔さがあって魅力的だ。
*Dentoo-tekina Nihon no kenchiku wa {koozoo(-joo) no/*soshiki(-joo) no/*koozoo-tekina} kanketsu-sa ga atte miryoku-teki da.*
(**b**) This company suffers from structural problems.
この会社は{組織(上)の/構造的な/*構造(上)の}問題を抱えている。
*Kono kaisha wa {soshiki(-joo) no/koozoo-tekina/*koozoo(-joo) no} mondai o kakaete iru.*

structure n. **[the manner in which s.t. is built or organized]**

1. ko⌈ozoo 構造 •c [the internal mechanical organization of a machine/system] ⟪**construction, organization, make**⟫

EX. (**a**) No one yet fully understands the chemical structure of the human gene.
人間の遺伝子の化学構造はいまだにだれにも完全には分かっていません。
Ningen no iden-shi no kagaku-koozoo wa imada ni dare ni mo kanzenni wa wakatte imasen.
(**b**) Could you explain the grammatical structure of this sentence?
この文の文法構造を説明してくださいませんか。
Kono bun no bunpoo-koozoo o setsumei-shite kudasaimasen ka.

2. so⌉shiki 組織 •c [a group of interconnected humans/cells] ⟪**organization, formation, system**⟫

EX. (**a**) We came to understand the structure of cells better.
細胞の組織が前よりよく分かるようになった。
Saiboo no soshiki ga mae yori yoku wakaru yooni natta.
(**b**) The societal structure of Japan is different from that of China.
日本の社会の組織は中国とは違う。
Nihon no shakai no soshiki wa Chuugoku to wa chigau.

S

struggle vi. **[for s.o./s.a. to fight vigorously with an opponent or to make a great effort to do s.t.]**

1. ⟨**-to**⟩ **ha⌈ge⌉shiku a⌈raso⌉u** ⟨〜と⟩**激しく争う** ① **[for s.o. to fight fiercely with another]**

EX. (**a**) I struggled with the authorities for many years to win their approval for the building project.
建築計画の許可を得ようと長年当局と激しく争った。
Kenchiku-keikaku no kyoka o eyoo to naganen tookyoku to hageshiku arasotta.
(**b**) There was evidence of struggle at the scene of the murder .
殺人現場には激しく争った跡があった。
Satsujin-genba ni wa hageshiku arasotta ato ga atta.

2. (**Vvol. to shite**) **mo⌈ga⌉ku** (**Vvol.として**) **もがく** ① **[for s.o./s.a. to move one's arms and legs vigorously** (**to escape from pain**)**]** ⟪**writhe, wriggle**⟫, (**Vvol. to shi⌈te**) **a⌈ga⌉ku** (**Vvol.として**)**あがく** ① **[for s.o./s.a. to move one's arms and legs vigorously to escape]** ⟪**flounder**⟫, (**Vvol. to shite**) **fu⌈ntoo-suru** (**Vvol.として**)**奮闘する** ③ **•c [for s.o. to make strenuous efforts to achieve s.t.]** ⟪**strive, exert oneself**⟫

EX. (**a**) The boy was struggling in the water when I jumped in to save him.
私が助けようと飛び込んだ時、男の子は水の中で{もがいて/あがいて/*奮闘して}いた。
*Watashi ga tasukeyoo to tobi-konda toki, otoko-no-ko wa mizu no naka de {mogaite/agaite/*funtoo-shite} ita.*
(**b**) The Japanese marathon runner struggled to take the lead in the race.
日本のマラソン選手はレースで先頭に立とうとして{奮闘した/*もがいた/*あがいた}。
*Nihon no marason-senshu wa reesu de sentoo ni tatoo to shite {funtoo-shita/*mogaita/*agaita}.*

— n. **[an act of struggling]**

mo⌈gaki⌉ もがき /⟨**V*masu* of *mogaku*** ①

struggle/ **[moving one's arms and legs vigorously to escape from pain], fu⌈ntoo 奮闘 •c [strenuous efforts]**

PHRASE: struggle for existence *seizon-kyoosoo* 生存競争 •c

stubborn adj. **[strongly refusing to yield] ga⌉nkona** 頑固な adj(*na*). **•c [firmly refusing to change one's ideas/attitudes ⟪fig. "for a disease to continue longer than expected"⟫] ⟪persistent, tenacious⟫, ga⌈nkyoona** 頑強な adj(*na*). **•c [for one's attitude not to yield or for a body to be stout] ⟪dogged, persistent, die-hard, stout⟫, go⌈ojoona** 強情な adj(*na*). **•c [for s.o. to strongly refuse to change one's ideas/attitudes] ⟪obstinate, headstrong, uncompromising, bullheaded⟫, shi⌈tsuyoona** しつような adj(*na*). **•c [persistently unyielding in behavior or attitude] ⟪persistent, tenacious⟫**

EX. (a) After all is said and done, you're not going to change your views, are you? You're a stubborn one!
結局、まだ考えを変えないのか。君も{頑固/強情/*しつよう/*頑強}だな。
*Kekkyoku, mada kangae o kaenai no ka. Kimi mo {ganko/goojoo/*shitsuyoo/*gankyoo} da na.*
(b) When I tried to convince the others I faced a stubborn opposition.
外の人を説得しようとした時、私は{しつような/頑強な/*頑固な/*強情な}反対にあった。
*Hoka no hito o settoku-shiyoo to shita toki, watashi wa {shitsuyoona/gankyoona/*gankona/*goojoona} hantai ni atta.*

student n. **[a person who attends a school or who is engaged in the study of s.t.]**
1. ga⌈kusei 学生 **•c [a person who studies, esp. at a college or university], se⌉ito** 生徒 **•c [a person who studies at a junior/senior high school], ji⌉doo** 児童 **•c [a child, esp. one studying at an elementary school] ⟪child, juvenile⟫**

NOTE: A student at an elementary school, at a junior high school, at a senior high school, or at a college is referred to formally as *shoogaku-sei, chuugaku-sei, kookoo-sei, daigaku-sei*, respectively.

EX. A: Are you a college student?
大学生ですか。
Daigaku-sei desu ka.
B: No, I'm still in senior high school.
いいえ、まだ高校生です。
Iie, mada kookoo-sei desu.

2. ga⌈kusha 学者 **•c [a person who is engaged in scholarship ⟪fig. "erudite person"⟫] ⟪scholar⟫, ke⌈nkyu⌉u-sha** 研究者 **•c [a person who is professionally engaged in research] ⟪researcher⟫**

EX. My friend is a student of atomic physics.
友人は原子物理学の{研究者/学者}です。
Yuujin wa genshi-butsuri-gaku no {kenkyuu-sha/gakusha} desu.

studio n. **[the working room of an artist or a room from which radio/television programs are broadcast]**
1. a⌈torie アトリエ **•f [the working room of an artist]**

NOTE: *Atorie* comes from the French *atelier.*

2. sha⌈shin-satsue⌉i-shitsu⌉ 写真撮影室 **•c [a room where photographs are taken]**
3. (e⌉iga-)sa⌈tsuei-jo (映画)撮影所 **•c [a place where films are made]**
4. su⌈tajio スタジオ **•f [a room from which radio/television programs are broadcast]**

study vi./vt. **[for s.o. to read/examine/memorize/think about s.t. carefully in order to learn from it]**
(⟨-o⟩) be⌈nkyoo-suru (⟨〜を⟩)勉強する ③ **•c [for s.o. to incorporate as part of oneself knowledge or a skill through careful reading, consideration, or practice] ⟪work⟫, (⟨-o⟩) ke⌈nkyuu-suru** (⟨〜を⟩)研究する ③ **•c [for s.o. to examine/investigate s.t. carefully in order to gain better factual knowledge or theoretical understanding] ⟪research, investigate⟫, (⟨-o⟩) ke⌈ntoo-suru** (⟨〜を⟩)検討する ③ **•c [for s.o. to investigate s.t. carefully] ⟪examine, investigate, inquire into⟫**

S

EX. (a) A: What are you studying in college?
大学で何を{勉強/研究/*検討}していますか。
*Daigaku de nani o {benkyoo/kenkyuu/*kentoo}-shite imasu ka.*
B: I'm studying Japanese.
日本語を{勉強/研究/*検討}しています。
*Nihon-go o {benkyoo/kenkyuu/*kentoo}-shite imasu.*
(b) We're studying Shakespeare now in our English literature class.
英文学のコースでは今シェークスピアを{研究/勉強/*検討}しています。
*Ei-bungaku no koosu de wa ima Sheekusupia o {kenkyuu/benkyoo/*kentoo}-shite imasu.*
(c) The committee is still studying the matter, so it's going to take a little longer before they reach a decision.
委員会はその問題をまだ検討しているので、決着がつくまでにもう少し時間がかかる。
Iin-kai wa sono mondai o mada kentoo-shite iru node, ketchaku ga tsuku made ni moo sukoshi jikan ga kakaru.

S

—— n. [an act/instance of studying or a place for studying]
1. be⌈nkyoo 勉強 •c [an act of studying] **(work)**, **ga⌈kushuu 学習 •c [learning and incorporating knowledge, esp. at school]** **(learning)**, **ke⌈nkyuu 研究 •c [careful inquiry into facts/theory]** **(research, investigation)**
2. ke⌈nkyuu-ro⌉nbun 研究論文 •c [a research paper], ro⌉nbun 論文 •c
EX. Do you know of any studies in English on Chinese influences on Japanese architecture during the Heian period?
平安時代における日本の建築への中国の影響について英語でかかれた(研究)論文を知りませんか。
Heian-jidai ni-okeru Nihon no kenchiku e no Chuugoku no eikyoo ni-tsuite eigo de kaka-reta (kenkyuu-) ronbun o shirimasen ka.
3. sho⌈sai 書斎 •c [a study room]
EX. I usually prepare for my classes in my study.
私は大抵書斎で授業の準備をします。
Watashi wa taitei shosai de jugyoo no junbi o shimasu.

stuff n. **[material necessary for doing/making s.t. or useless matter]**
1. mo⌈no⌉ 物 [s.t.tangible or s.t. abstract grasped as if it were tangible] **(thing, object, matter, substance, article, commodities)**
EX. What kind of stuff is this?
これはどんな物ですか。
Kore wa donna mono desu ka.
2. ga⌈rakuta がらくた [things of little use/value] **(junk, rubbish)**, **ku⌈daranai mo⌈no⌉ くだらない物 [worthless matter/objects]**
EX. (a) How can you read stuff like this?
よくもこんな{くだらない物/*がらくた}が読めるね。
*Yoku mo konnna {kudaranai mono/*garakuta} ga yome-ru ne.*
(b) Where did you pick up all this stuff?
どこでこんな{がらくた/くだらない物}を拾って来たんですか。
Doko de konna {garakuta/kudaranai mono} o hirotte kita n desu ka.

—— vt. [for s.o. to fill the inside of s.t. with material]
1. ⟨-ni⟩ ⟨-no⟩ tsu⌈me⌉-mono o suru ⟨〜に⟩⟨〜の⟩詰め物をする ③ [for s.o. to put stuffing into s.t.], ⟨-ni⟩ ⟨-o⟩ tsu⌈me⌉ru ⟨〜に⟩⟨〜を⟩詰める ② [for s.o. to put s.t./s.o./s.a. in a tight, limited space/time or to cause s.t. to become short] **(fill, sit close, write closely, shorten, curtail, pack)**, **⟨-o⟩ ⟨-ni⟩ tsu⌈me-komu ⟨〜を⟩⟨〜に⟩詰め込む ① [for s.o. to fill tightly the inside of s.t. (including the brain) with material]** **(cram, jam, squeeze, pack)**
EX. (a) We stuffed the chicken with various vegetables.
とりの中に色々な野菜{の詰め物をした/を{詰めた/?詰め込んだ}}。

Tori no naka ni iro-irona yasai {no tsume-mono o shita/o {tsumeta/?tsume-konda}}.
(**b**) They stuffed a lot of people into the small room.
小さな部屋に大勢の人{を{詰めた/詰め込んだ}/*の詰め物をした}。
*Chiisana heya ni oozei no hito {o {tsumeta/tsume-konda}/*no tsume-mono o shita}.*

2. ⟨-o⟩ ha⌈kusei ni suru ⟨〜を⟩はく製にする ③ [for s.o. to fill the skin of an animal to preserve it]

stumble vi. **[for s.o./s.a. to miss one's proper step in walking/running (and fall down) 《fig. "fail to talk/do things properly"》]**

1. ⟨-ni⟩ tsu⌈mazuku ⟨〜に⟩つまずく ① [for s.o./s.a. to hit one's foot against s.t. and almost fall down 《fig. "fail"》] ((trip over, lose one's footing, fail, be balked)), (⟨-ni⟩) tsu⌈mazuite ko⌈robu (⟨〜に⟩)つまずいて転ぶ ① [for s.o./s.a. to hit one's foot against s.t. and fall down]

EX. While I was walking home from the station last night I stumbled over a stone.
ゆうべ、駅からうちへ歩いて帰る時に、石に{つまずいた/つまずいて転んだ}。
Yuube, eki kara uchi ni aruite kaeru toki ni, ishi ni {tsumazuita/tsumazuite koronda}.

2. yo⌈rome⌉ku よろめく ① [for s.o. to walk as if one had tripped over s.t.] ((totter, stagger, falter, reel))

EX. Every Friday night the main street in front of the station is full of drunken salarymen stumbling home from work.
毎週金曜日の晩、駅前の大通りはよろめきながらうちへ帰る酔っぱらったサラリーマンでいっぱいだ。
Mai-shuu kin'yoo-bi no ban, eki-mae no oo-doori wa yoromeki-nagara uchi e kaeru yopparatta sararii-man de ippai da.

3. ku⌈chi-gomo⌉ru 口ごもる ① [for words to stay inside the mouth and not be plainly heard] ((falter, hesitate, mumble)), do⌈mo⌉ru どもる ① [to stutter for pathological reasons] ((stammer, stutter))

EX. Poor Janet, she stumbled and couldn't say a word in front of her teacher.
かわいそうに、ジャネットは先生の前で、{口ごもって/どもって}、一言も言えなかった。
Kawai-sooni, Janetto wa sensei no mae de, {kuchi-gomotte/domotte}, hito-koto mo ie-nakatta.

4. ya⌈ri-sokona⌉u やり損なう ① [for s.o. to fail to do s.t. properly] ((do s.t. badly, slip up, bungle, be unsuccessful)), tsu⌉mi o o⌈ka⌉su 罪を犯す ① [for s.o. to commit a sin]

EX. Everybody stumbles once or twice in their life.
人はだれでも一生に一、二回は{やりそこなう/罪を犯す}。
Hito wa dare demo isshoo ni ichi, ni-kai wa {yari-sokonau/tsumi o okasu}.

—— vt. **[to cause s.o. to stumble]**
⟨-o⟩ tsu⌈mazuka-se⌉ru ⟨〜を⟩つまずかせる /⟨causative of *tsumazuku* ① stumble/ ②

stump n. **[what remains of a tree/plant in the ground after its trunk has been cut off at the lowest point 《fig. "what remains of a limb/tooth after it has been cut/broken off"》]**

1. ki⌈ri⌉-kabu 切り株 [what remains of a tree/plant in the ground after its trunk has been cut off at the lowest point]

2. o⌉reta ha⌉ no ne⌉ 折れた歯の根 [the root of a broken tooth]

stunt n. **[an unusual or difficult feat performed to attract attention]**
myo⌉ogi 妙技 •c [an unusual skill] ((wonderful performance, feat)), ha⌈nare-waza 離れ業 [a daring feat] ((feat))

EX. The spectators were astounded by the pilot's stunts.
見物人は飛行士の{妙技/離れ業}に舌を巻いた。
Kenbutsu-nin wa hikoo-shi no {myoogi/hanare-waza} ni shita o maita.

stupid adj. **[lacking normal intelligence]**
1. ba⌉kana ばかな adj(*na*). **[for s.o./s.a. to**

lack good judgment/sense] ↔ rikoona 利口な adj(*na*). **•c**

NOTE: *Bakana* can be used in the sense of both "stupid" and "silly."

EX. You can't understand something this simple? Are you that stupid?
こんなに簡単なことが分からないのか。そんなにお前はばかか。
Konna ni kantanna koto ga wakaranai no ka. Sonnani omae wa baka ka.

2. ku⌈daranai くだらない adj(*i*). **[not worth discussing/mentioning] ⟪trifling, trivial, worthless, trashy⟫, tsu⌈mara⌉nai** つまらない adj(*i*). **[causing dissatisfaction due to lack of worth or interest] ⟪trifling, trivial, petty, trashy, uninteresting⟫**

EX. A: How was the movie?
映画はどうだった?
Eiga wa doo datta?
B: It was really stupid.
{くだらない/つまらない}ものだったよ。
{Kudaranai/Tsumaranai} mono datta yo.

S

3. ba⌈ka⌉-geta N ばかげたN **[looking foolish] ⟪foolish, idiotic, insane⟫, ba⌈ka⌉-gete iru** ばかげている ②, **ba⌈kabakashi⌉i** ばかばかしい adj(*i*). **[extremely foolish] ⟪absurd, ridiculous⟫**

EX. (**a**) I was thinking of asking my wife's parents to lend me money to start a new business, but soon realized what a stupid idea that was.
新しい事業を始めるために妻の両親にお金を貸してくれるよう頼もうと思ったが、すぐに{ばかげた/ばかばかしい/?ばかげている}考えだということに気が付いた。
Atarashii jigyoo o hajimeru tame ni tsuma no ryooshin ni o-kane o kashite kureru yoo tanomoo to omotta ga, sugu ni {baka-geta/bakabakashii/?baka-gete iru} kangae da to iu koto ni ki ga tsuita.
(**b**) It's stupid to buy such an expensive car for a teenager.
ティーンエージャーにそんなに高い車を買ってやるなんて{ばかげている/ばかばかしい}。
Tiin'eejaa ni sonna ni takai kuruma o katte yaru nante {baka-gete iru/bakabakashii}.

sturdy adj. **[solidly built or hard to overcome]**

1. tsu⌈yo⌉i 強い adj(*i*). **[having the power to act or perform in an effective way or to resist external force, esp. physically, but also mentally or emotionally] ⟪powerful, mighty, robust, stout, violent, intense, durable⟫ ↔ yowai** 弱い adj(*i*).; **shi⌈kka⌉ri-shitaN** しっかりしたN **[free from weakness/looseness], shi⌈kka⌉ri-shite iru (N)** しっかりしている(N) **[free from weakness/looseness] ⟪strong, solid, strong-minded⟫, ga⌈njoona** 頑丈な adj(*na*). **•c [for s.t. to be not easily broken or for a body to be not prone to illness] ⟪solid, firm, rugged, robust, hardy⟫, jo⌈obuna** 丈夫な adj(*na*). **•c [not easily broken/prone to illness] ⟪solid, firm, healthy, durable⟫**

EX. (**a**) He looks sturdy, but he gets sick often.
あの人は{強そう/頑丈そう/丈夫そう/*しっかりしていそう}ですが、よく病気になります。
*Ano hito wa {tsuyo-soo/ganjoo-soo/joobu-soo/*shikkari-shite i-soo} desu ga, yoku byooki ni narimasu.*
(**b**) This toy is sturdy—it won't break easily.
このおもちゃはとても{強い/しっかりしている/頑丈だ/丈夫だ}から簡単には壊れない。
Kono omocha wa totemo {tsuyoi/shikkari-shite iru/ganjoo da/joobu da} kara kantanni wa kowarenai.

2. da⌉nko to shita N 断固としたN **[for one's attitude, resolution, etc. not to be easily changed in the face of opposition or difficulty] ⟪resolute, decisive, strong⟫, tsu⌈yo⌉i** 強い adj(*i*). SEE sturdy 1

EX. We encountered sturdy opposition to our plan.
我々の案に対する{強い/断固とした}反対にあった。

Ware-ware no an ni-taisuru {tsuyoi/ danko to shita} hantai ni atta.

style n. **[the (refined) manner in which s.t. is accomplished/performed]**

1. bu⌈ntai 文体 •c [the manner in which a text is organized], su⌈ta⌉iru スタイル •f [the manner in which s.t. is accomplished/ performed or s.o.'s figure]

EX. His novels are written in a style which is hard to read.
あの作家の小説は読みにくい{文体/スタイル}で書かれている。
Ano sakka no shoosetsu wa yomi-nikui {buntai/sutairu} de kaka-rete iru.

2. ha⌈nashi-buri 話振り /⟨V*masu* of *hanasu* ① talk + suf. *buri* manner/ [the manner in which one talks]

3. hyo⌈ogen-yo⌉oshiki 表現様式 •c [the manner in which s.t. is expressed], su⌈ta⌉iru スタイル •f [the manner in which s.t. is accomplished/performed or s.o.'s shape considered from the point of view of its attractiveness]

4. ya⌈rikata やり方 /⟨V*masu* of *yaru* ① do + suf. *kata* way/ [a method/manner of doing s.t.] ⟪way, method, how to do, measure⟫

EX. I don't like my boss's style.
上司のやり方は好きじゃありません。
Jooshi no yarikata wa suki jaarimasen.

5. sa⌈kufuu 作風 •c [the original manner in which an artistic work is created]

EX. It takes years to develop one's own unique style.
独自の作風を確立するのには何年もかかる。
Dokuji no sakufuu o kakuritsu-suru no ni wa nan-nen mo kakaru.

6. ryu⌈ukoo 流行 •c [the prevailing custom in clothes, thought, behavior, etc. or a rampant disease] ⟪vogue⟫

EX. Japanese girls are very quick to catch on to changes in style.
日本の女の子は流行をつかむのが早い。
Nihon no onna-no ko wa ryuukoo o tsukamu no ga hayai.

7. ki⌈hin 気品 •c [gracefulness in appearance/behavior] ⟪grace, dignity, refinement⟫

EX. That lady has style.
あの女の人には気品がある。
Ano onna no hito ni wa kihin ga aru.

PHRASE: informal style (in Japanese grammar) {*futsuu-tai/jootai*} {普通体/常体} •c, formal style (in Japanese grammar) {*teinei-tai/keitai*} {丁寧体/敬体} •c

EX. The informal style of *yomimasu* is *yomu.*
「読みます」の{普通体/常体}は「読む」です。
'Yomimasu' no {futsuu-tai/jootai} wa 'yomu' desu.

stylish adj. **[conforming to a currently fashionable style of behavior (esp. in dress)]**
ryu⌈ukoo no N 流行のN •c [pertaining to/characterized by current fashion]

EX. I cannot afford to buy stylish dresses.
私には流行のドレスは買えません。
Watashi ni wa ryuukoo no doresu wa kae-masen.

subject adj. **[(easily) controlled by s.t./s.o./ s.a.]**

1. ⟨-ni⟩ fu⌈kujuu-suru ⟨～に⟩服従する ③ •c [for s.o./s.a. to obey the will/order of s.o./ s.a.] ⟪obey, be obedient to, submit to⟫

EX. Japanese wives were traditionally subject to their husbands.
昔は日本の妻は夫に服従していた。
Mukashi wa Nihon no tsuma wa otto ni fukujuu-shite ita.

2. V*masu* ya⌈su⌉i V*masu*やすい adj(*i*). **[easy to do s.t. or for s.t. to happen], V*masu* ga⌈chi da V*masu*がちだ [having a tendency to do s.t. or to happen] ⟪be apt to, be prone to, tend to, be susceptible to⟫**

EX. (**a**) I don't know why, but I'm subject to frequent colds.
どうしてか知らないけれど僕は風邪をひき{やすい/がちだ}。
Dooshite ka shiranai keredo boku wa kaze o hiki-{yasui/gachi da}.
(**b**) A foreigner is subject to discrimination in this country.

S

この国では外国人は差別され{やすい/がちだ}。
Kono kuni de wa gaikoku-jin wa sabetsu-sare-{yasui/gachi da}.

3. -shidai da ～次第だ •c [for s.t. to be contingent on s.t. else] **⟪hang on, depend on⟫**

EX. This research is subject to the director's approval.
この研究は所長の許可次第だ。
Kono kenkyuu wa shochoo no kyoka-shidai da.

PHRASE: be subject to change *kawaru koto ga aru* 変わることがある

EX. The airfare is subject to change.
航空運賃は変わることがございます。
Kookuu-unchin wa kawaru koto ga gozaimasu.

— n. **[s.o./s.t./s.a. one can control ⟪fig. "topic," "grammatical subject," "academic course," "self in philosophy," "a person used in an experiment," "patient"⟫]**

1. shi˥nka 臣下 •c [a person under the control of a ruler] ⟪vassal, retainer⟫

2. shu˥dai 主題 •c [main theme of discussion/an artistic work] ⟪theme, topic⟫, te˥ema テーマ •f [a theme]

EX. The subject of this novel is father-son relationships.
この小説の{主題/テーマ}は父と息子の関係である。
Kono shoosetsu no {shudai/teema} wa chichi to musuko no kankei dearu.

3. shu˥go 主語 •c [a noun/noun phrase about which s.t. is predicated in a sentence]

EX. The subject of the sentence "Taro came here" is "Taro."
「太郎が来ました」という文の主語は「太郎」だ。
'Taroo ga kimashita' to iu bun no shugo wa 'Taroo' da.

4. ka˥moku {科/課}目 •c [an academic course] ⟪course⟫

EX. A: What subjects are you taking this semester?
今学期はどんな{科/課}目を取っていますか。
Kon-gakki wa donna kamoku o totte imasu ka.
B: I'm taking Japanese language and Japanese history.
日本語と日本史を取っています。
Nihon-go to nihon-shi o totte imasu.

5. shu˥tai 主体 •c [self as instigator of action] ↔ kyakutai 客体 •c

6. hi˥ke˥n-sha 被験者 •c [a person used in an experiment]

EX. We need 100 subjects for this psychology experiment.
この心理実験には百名の被験者が必要です。
Kono shinri-jikken ni wa hyaku-mei no hiken-sha ga hitsuyoo desu.

7. ka˥nja 患者 •c [a sick person under the care of a doctor] ⟪patient⟫

— vt. **[to cause/allow s.t./s.o./s.a. to come under the control of s.t./s.o./s.a.]**

1. ⟨-o⟩ ⟨-ni⟩ fu˥kujuu-saseru ⟨～を⟩⟨～に⟩服従させる /⟨causative of *fukujuu-suru* ③ obey/ ② [for s.o. to bring s.t./s.o./s.a. under one's authority] ⟪subjugate⟫

EX. The king subjected the common people to his tyranny.
王は一般市民を圧政に服従させた。
Oo wa ippan-shimin o assei ni fukujuu-saseta.

2. S_1 {no˥de/ka˥ra} S_2 S_1{ので/から}S_2 [because S_1, S_2]

EX. (**a**) Her weakness subjected her to many diseases.
彼女は体が弱かった{ので/から}、色々な病気にかかった。
Kanojo wa karada ga yowakatta {node/kara}, iro-irona byooki ni kakatta.
(**b**) His wealth subjected him to many temptations.
彼は金持ちだった{ので/から}色々な誘惑にあった。
Kare wa kane-mochi datta {node/kara} iro-irona yuuwaku ni atta.

submarine n.
se˥nsui-kan 潜水艦 •c

submit vi. **[for s.o./s.a. to yield to a higher authority]**
⟨-ni⟩ shi⌈tagau ⟨〜に⟩従う ① [for s.o./s.a. to accept and act according to advice, rules, orders, etc.] ⟪obey, yield to, comply with, conform to⟫

EX. The student submitted to his teacher's wishes.
学生は先生の意志に従った。
Gakusei wa sensei no ishi ni shitagatta.

—— vt. **[for s.o. to present s.t. to s.o. else for consideration]**
1. **(⟨-ni⟩) ⟨-o⟩ te⌈ishutsu-suru (⟨〜に⟩)⟨〜を⟩提出する ③ •c [for s.o. to hand in/turn in s.t. to s.o. ⟨fml⟩] ⟪submit⟫**

EX. The application form for this grant has to be submitted by March 1.
この奨学金の願書は三月一日までに提出しなければなりません。
Kono shoogaku-kin no gansho wa san-gatsu tsuitachi made-ni teishutsu-shinakereba narimasen.

2. **i⌉ken o mo⌈oshi-ageru 意見を申し上げる ② [for s.o. to offer one's opinion], ⟨-to⟩ o⌈mo⌉u ⟨〜と⟩思う ① [for s.o. to spontaneously perceive s.t. in one's mind or to have an opinion about s.t.] ⟪feel, think⟫**

EX. (**a**) May I submit my opinion for your consideration?
御参考までに私の意見を申し上げます。
Go-sankoo made ni watashi no iken o mooshi-agemasu.
(**b**) I submit that there is a better way to solve the problem.
問題解決にはもっとよい方法があると思いますが。
Mondai-kaiketsu ni wa motto yoi hoohoo ga aru to omoimasu ga.

subscribe vi./vt. **[for s.o. to express agreement (by signing one's signature) or to contribute money or to pay for a periodical in advance for a set period of time]**
1. **(bu⌉nsho ni) sho⌈mei-suru (文書に)署名する ③ •c [for s.o. to sign one's signature on a form]**
2. **⟨-o⟩ te⌈iki-ko⌉odoku-suru ⟨〜を⟩定期購読する ③ •c [for s.o. to purchase a periodical, etc. for a set period of time ⟨fml⟩], ⟨-o⟩ to⌉ru ⟨〜を⟩とる ① [for s.o./s.a. to cause s.t./s.o./s.a. to come to one's side] ⟪take, pick up, hold, seize, get, obtain, secure, win, receive⟫** ㊅ "adopt"▷採る, "perform one's duties"▷執る, "catch (a fish/ball)"▷捕る, "take a picture"▷撮る, otherwise ▷取る

EX. Do you subscribe to any weekly magazine?
週刊誌を{定期購読して/取って}いますか。
Shuukan-shi o {teiki-koodoku-shite/totte} imasu ka.

3. **ka⌈ne o ki⌉fu-suru 金を寄付する ③ [for s.o. (to sign one's signature to indicate agreement) to contribute money] ⟪endow, donate⟫**

subscription n. **[an act of subscribing]**
1. **ki⌉fu 寄付 •c [an act of contributing s.t. to s.o. or s.t. contributed] ⟪contribution, donation⟫**
2. **yo⌈yaku-ko⌉odoku 予約購読 •c [purchasing a periodical, etc. for a set period of time]**
3. **ko⌈odoku⌉-ryoo 購読料 •c [payment for subscribing to s.t.]**

substance n. **[physical matter or the essence of s.t. ⟪fig. "content," "property"⟫]**
1. **bu⌈sshitsu 物質 •c [physical matter] ⟪matter⟫ ↔ seishin 精神 •c**

EX. According to Einstein's theory, substance can be transformed into energy.
アインシュタインの理論によると、物質をエネルギーに変えることが可能だそうだ。
Ainshutain no riron ni-yoru to, busshitsu o enerugii ni kaeru koto ga kanoo da sooda.

2. **ho⌈nshitsu 本質 •c [the real nature unique to s.t.] ⟪essence, real nature, intrinsic quality⟫**

EX. Nobody knows exactly what the basic substance of the universe is.
だれも宇宙の本質を正確には知らない。
Dare-mo uchuu no honshitsu o seikakuni wa shiranai.

S

3. na⌈iyoo 内容 •c **[s.t. that constitutes the inner part of s.t. and gives value to it]** **《content, matter, import》** ↔ **keishiki** 形式 •c; **na⌈ka⌉-mi** 中身 **[s.t. contained in an enclosed object]** **《contents, interior》**

EX. | This book has little substance to it.
この本は{内容/中身}がほとんどない。
Kono hon wa {naiyoo/naka-mi} ga hotondo nai.

4. ko⌉sshi 骨子 •c **[the main points of a matter]** **《essential part, essence, bones (of a matter)》**

EX. | What was the substance of the ambassador's speech?
大使の演説の骨子は何でしたか。
Taishi no enzetsu no kosshi wa nan deshita ka.

substantial adj. **[consisting of solid material or large in amount 《fig. "real," "ample," "wealthy"》]**

1. bu⌈sshitsu no N 物質のN •c **[material in substance]**

2. ji⌈sshitsu-tekina 実質的な adj(*na*). •c **[having substance as opposed to mere appearance]** **《real, essential, material》** ↔ **keishiki-tekina** 形式的な adj(*na*). •c

EX. | We need more substantial support for this project from the government.
私たちは政府からこの企画へのより実質的な援助が必要だ。
Watashi-tachi wa seifu kara kono kikaku e no yori jisshitsu-tekina enjo ga hitsuyoo da.

3. ji⌈yoo ho⌈ofuna 滋養豊富な adj(*na*). •c **[highly nutritious]**, **cha⌈nto shita N** ちゃんとしたN /〈Vinf. past of *chanto suru* ③ to do s.t. just as it should be done/ **[done just as it should be or having the characteristics it should]** **《perfect, proper, correct》**

EX. | They served us a substantial meal.
{滋養豊富な/ちゃんとした}食事が出た。
{Jiyoo hoofuna/Chanto shita} shokuji ga deta.

substitute vt. **[for s.o. to cause s.t./s.o./s.a. to replace s.t./s.o./s.a. else]**
〈-ni〉〈-no〉 ka⌈wari o saseru 〈～に〉〈～の〉代わりをさせる /〈causative of *kawari o suru* ③ take another's place/ ② **[for s.o. to make/let s.t./s.o./s.a. replace s.t./s.o./s.a. else]**, **〈-no〉 ka⌈wari ni 〈-o〉 tsukau** 〈～の〉代わりに〈～を〉使う ① **[for s.o. to use s.t./s.o./s.a. in place of s.t./s.o./s.a. else]**

EX. | (**a**) The coach substituted a rookie for the injured pitcher.
コーチは{新人選手にけがをした投手の代わりをさせた/けがをした投手の代わりに新人選手を使った}。
Koochi wa {shinjin-seishu ni kega o shita tooshu no kawari o saseta/kega o shita tooshu no kawari ni shinjin-senshu o tsukatta}.
(**b**) We substituted margarine for butter in baking the cake.
ケーキを焼くのに、{バターの代わりにマーガリンを使った/*マーガリンにバターの代わりをさせた}。
*Keeki o yaku no ni, {bataa no kawari ni maagarin o tsukatta/*maagarin ni bataa no kawari o saseta}.*

— vi. **[for s.o. to replace s.o. else temporarily]**
〈-no〉 ka⌈wari o tsutome⌉ru 〈～の〉代わりを務める ② **[for s.o. to serve in place of another]**, **〈-ni〉 to⌉tte-kawaru** 〈～に〉取って代わる ① **[to occupy a position s.t./s.o./s.a. else used to occupy]** **《replace, supplant, supersede》**

EX. | (**a**) I substituted for the injured player.
けがをした選手{の代わりを務めた/*に取って代わった}。
*Kega o shita senshu {no kawari o tsutometa/*ni totte kawatta}.*
(**b**) At the dance, taped music substituted for live music.
ダンスパーティーでテープ演奏が生演奏{に取って代わった/*の代わりを務めた}。
*Dansu paatii de teepu-ensoo ga nama-ensoo {ni totte-kawatta/*no kawari o tsutometa}.*

— n. **[s.t./s.o./s.a. that substitutes for s.t./s.o./s.a. else]**
〈-no〉 ka⌈wari 〈～の〉代わり /〈V*masu* of

kawaru ① **be replaced, change/ 《proxy, deputy, relief》, da⌈iri(-nin) 代理(人) •c [s.o. who takes the place of s.o. else in an official capacity] 《proxy, deputy, agent》, da⌈iyaku 代役 •c [s.o./s.a. who stands in for s.o./s.a. else in a film/drama] 《stand-in》, da⌈iyoo-hin 代用品 •c [s.t. that is used in place of s.t. else]**

EX. (**a**) Margarine is often used as a substitute for butter.
マーガリンはよくバターの{代用品/代わり/*代理/*代役}として使われる。
*Maagarin wa yoku bataa no {daiyoo-hin/kawari/*dairi/*daiyaku} to-shite tsukawa-reru.*
(**b**) My secretary is taking a month off. Can you find me a substitute?
僕の秘書が一か月休暇を取るんです。{代わり/*代用品/*代理/*代役}を探してくれませんか。
*Boku no hisho ga ik-kagetsu kyuuka o toru n desu. {Kawari/*Daiyoohin/*Dairi/*Daiyaku} o sagashite kuremasen ka.*
(**c**) It won't be easy to find a substitute for the chairman.
議長の{代わり/代理/*代用品/*代役}を探すのは簡単じゃないでしょう。
*Gichoo no {kawari/dairi/*daiyoo-hin/*daiyaku} o sagasu no wa kantan janai deshoo.*
(**d**) I was asked to act as a substitute for the actress because she suddenly took ill.
その女優が急に病気になったので彼女の{代わり/代役/*代理/*代用品}を頼まれた。
*Sono joyuu ga kyuuni byooki ni natta node kanojo no {kawari/daiyaku/*dairi/*daiyoo-hin} o tanoma-reta.*

subtle adj. **[slight and difficult to detect 《fig. "thin," "ingenious," "mysterious," "crafty"》]**
1. se⌈nsaina 繊細な adj(*na*). **•c [fine and graceful] 《delicate, fine》, bi⌈myoona 微妙な** adj(*na*). **•c [so fine and complex as to be difficult to describe] 《delicate, nice, fine》**

EX. (**a**) Debussy's piano music has a subtle beauty to it.
ドビュッシーのピアノ音楽には{繊細な/微妙な}美しさがある。
Dobyusshii no piano-ongaku ni wa {sensaina/bimyoona} utsukushi-sa ga aru.
(**b**) Japanese culture is close to Korean culture, but there are some subtle differences between the two.
日本の文化は韓国の文化に近いが、{微妙な/*繊細な}違いもある。
*Nihon no bunka wa Kankoku no bunka ni chikai ga, {bimyoona/*sensaina} chigai mo aru.*

2. u⌈sui 薄い adj(*i*). **[having little depth/intensity 《fig. "(for color/taste) to be weak"》] 《thin, light, pale, faint, weak》 ↔ atsui 厚い** adj(*i*)., **koi 濃い** adj(*i*).

subtract vt. **[for s.o. to deduct s.t. from s.t. else]**
⟨-kara⟩ ⟨-o⟩ (sa⌈shi-)hiku ⟨〜から⟩⟨〜を⟩(差し)引く ①

EX. If you subtract 9 from 20, you get 11.
20から9を(差し)引くと、11になる。
Ni-juu kara kyuu o (sashi-)hiku to, juu-ichi ni naru.

subtraction n.
hi⌈ki⌉-zan 引き算

suburb n. **[a (residential) district on the outskirts of a city]**
ko⌉ogai 郊外 •c [an area on the periphery of a big city] 《environs, outskirts》, ki⌈nkoo 近郊 •c [an area close to a big city] 《environs》

EX. My apartment complex is located in the suburbs of Tokyo.
私の団地は東京の{郊外/近郊}にある。
Watashi no danchi wa Tookyoo no {koogai/kinkoo} ni aru.

subway n.
chi⌈ka-tetsu 地下鉄 •c

EX. I took the subway to Ginza.
地下鉄に乗って銀座へ行った。
Chika-tetsu ni notte Ginza e itta.

succeed vi. **[for s.o. to follow after s.o./s.t./s.a. (into a better position) 《fig. "be able to achieve s.t."》]**

(⟨-ni⟩) se⸢ikoo-suru (⟨〜に⟩)成功する ③ •c **[for s.o. to accomplish s.t. with good results in s.t.]** ((get ahead, prosper)), **shu⸢sse-suru** 出世する ③ •c **[for s.o. to rise in the world]** ((attain distinction))

EX. (**a**) They succeeded in producing the world's smallest computer chip.
世界で一番小さいコンピューターチップの生産に{成功/*出世}した。
*Sekai de ichiban chiisai konpyuutaa-chippu no seisan ni {seikoo/*shusse}-shita.*
(**b**) It's hard to tell who is most likely to succeed in the graduating class.
卒業生の中でだれが一番{成功/出世}する確率が高いかは簡単には言えない。
Sotsugyoo-sei no naka de dare ga ichiban {seikoo/shusse}-suru kakuritsu ga takai ka wa kantanni wa ie-nai.

— vt. **[to follow after s.o./s.t. (into a position/possession)]**

1. ⟨-no⟩ **a⸣to ni tsu⸢zuku** ⟨〜の⟩後に続く ① **[to follow s.t./s.o./s.a.]**

EX. The atomic age has been succeeded by the computer age.
原子力の時代の後にコンピューターの時代が続いている。
Genshi-ryoku no jidai no ato ni konpyuutaa no jidai ga tsuzuite iru.

2. ⟨-no⟩ **a⸣to o tsu⸢gu** ⟨〜の⟩後を継ぐ ① **[for s.o./s.a. to come after and take the place of s.o./s.a.]**, ⟨-no⟩ **ko⸢onin {ni/to} na⸣ru** ⟨〜の⟩後任{に/と}なる ① **[for s.o. to take a post subsequent to s.o. else]**

EX. Mr. Akita succeeded Mr. Kobayashi as president of the company.
秋田氏は小林社長の{後を継いだ/後任になった}。
Akita-shi wa Kobayashi-shachoo no {ato o tsuida/koonin ni natta}.

success n. **[an act/instance of accomplishing s.t. (in the world)]**
se⸢ikoo 成功 •c ((hit)) ↔ **shippai** 失敗 •c; **shu⸢sse** 出世 •c **[an act/instance of rising in the world]** ((distinction, eminence))

EX. (**a**) I want to put my family first. Success in my career is secondary in my mind.
私は家族を第一にしたいです。{出世/*成功}は二の次だと思っています。
*Watashi wa kazoku o dai-ichi ni shitai desu. {Shusse/*Seikoo} wa ni no tsugi da to omotte imasu.*
(**b**) I wish you great success!
大{成功/*出世}をお祈りします。
*Dai-{seikoo/*shusse} o o-inori-shimasu.*
(**c**) This year's college festival was a great success.
今年の大学祭は大{成功/*出世}だった。
*Kotoshi no daigaku-sai wa dai-{seikoo/*shusse} datta.*

successful adj. **[achieving/having achieved an objective]**
se⸢ikoo-shite iru (N) 成功している(N) / (V*te iru* of *seikoo-suru* ③ succeed/ •c **[for s.o. to have success in s.t.]**, **shu⸢sse-suru** 出世する ③ •c **[for s.o. to rise in the world]** ((get ahead))

EX. (**a**) His business has been very successful.
あの人の商売は{成功/*出世}している。
*Ano hito no shoobai wa {seikoo/*shusse}-shite iru.*
(**b**) Hayato was a failure as a businessman, but he was very successful in the political world.
隼人はビジネスマンとしては駄目だったが、政界でとても{出世/成功}した。
Hayato wa bijinesu-man to-shite wa dame datta ga, sei-kai de totemo {shusse/seikoo}-shita.

succession n. **[an act of following another/one after another]**

1. **so⸢ozoku** 相続 •c **[an act of inheriting property]** ((inheritance))

2. **re⸢nzoku** 連続 •c **[a number of actions/states/similar objects occurring one after another]** ((continuity, series, chain))

EX. My life has been a succession of failures.
今までの私の人生は失敗の連続でした。
Ima made no watashi no jinsei wa shippai no renzoku deshita.

successive adj. **[occurring one after another]**
tsu⸢zuite ⟨-ga⟩ **a⸣ru** 続いて⟨〜が⟩ある ①

[for a number of events to occur one after another], aˈi-tsugu N 相次ぐN [occurring one after another ⟨w⟩] ⟪successively occur one after another⟫

EX. There were four successive car accidents on this stretch of freeway this morning.
高速道路のこのあたりでは今朝{続いて/相次ぐ}自動車事故が四つもあった。
Koosoku-dooro no kono atari de wa kesa {tsuzuite/ai-tsugu} jidoosha-jiko ga yottsu mo atta.

such adj. **[of the same/similar kind as one previously mentioned/implied]**
koˈnna N こんなN [of the same/similar kind as this one] ⟪this kind of⟫, soˈnna N そんなN [of the same/similar kind as one close to or mentioned by the hearer] ⟪that kind of⟫, aˈnna N あんなN [of the same/similar kind as one equally removed from both the speaker and hearer or known to both the speaker and hearer from previous experience] ⟪that kind of⟫

EX. (a) I've never read such a book before.
{こんな/あんな/そんな}本は今までに読んだことがない。
{Konna/Anna/Sonna} hon wa ima made ni yonda koto ga nai.
(b) You'd better not marry such a guy.
{こんな/あんな/そんな}男とは結婚しないほうがいいわよ。
{Konna/Anna/Sonna} otoko to wa kekkon-shinai hoo ga ii wa yo.
(c) He's always punctual. I like working with such people.
あの人はいつも時間を守る。僕は{あんな/*こんな/*そんな}人と一緒に仕事をするのが好きだ。
*Ano hito wa itsu-mo jikan o mamoru. Boku wa {anna/*konna/*sonna} hito to issho ni shigoto o suru no ga suki da.*

PHRASE: such as ⟨*-no*⟩ *yoona* ⟨〜の⟩ような

EX. I enjoy reading Japanese authors such as Tanizaki, Kawabata and Mishima.
私は谷崎、川端、三島のような作家の本を読むのが好きだ。
Watashi wa Tanizaki, Kawabata, Mishima no yoona sakka no hon o yomu no ga suki da.

PHRASE: not such a N as to V Vinf. nonpast *hodo no* N {*dewanai/janai*} Vinf. nonpast ほどのN{ではない/じゃない}

EX. I'm not such a fool as to believe that.
私はそれを信じるほどのばかじゃない。
Watashi wa sore o shinjiru hodo no baka janai.

PHRASE: such and such *shika-jika no* N しかじかのN

EX. He told me to wait for him at such and such a place.
彼は私にしかじかのところで待つように言った。
Kare wa watashi ni shika-jika no tokoro de matsu yooni itta.

suck vi./vt. **[for s.o./s.a. to draw liquid into the mouth by using the lip muscles to create suction ⟪fig. "lick"⟫]**
1. ⟨-o⟩ suˈu ⟨〜を⟩吸う ① [for s.o./s.a. to draw liquid/gas into the body through the mouth/nose] ⟪breathe in, inhale, absorb, smoke⟫

EX. A baby was sucking milk from its mother's breast.
赤ん坊が母親の乳房からお乳を吸っていた。
Akanboo ga haha-oya no chibusa kara o-chichi o sutte ita.

2. ⟨-o⟩ naˈmeˈru ⟨〜を⟩なめる ② [for s.o./s.a. to pass the tongue across the surface of s.t. ⟪fig. "experience," "despise"⟫] ⟪lick, taste, experience, treat s.o. with contempt⟫

EX. Don't suck your pencil.
鉛筆をなめてはいけません。
Enpitsu o namete wa ikemasen.

sudden adj. **[happening quickly and unexpectedly]**
toˈtsuzen no N 突然のN •c [occurring quickly and unexpectedly] ⟪abrupt, unexpected⟫, oˈmoigakenaˈi 思いがけない adj(*i*). **[not anticipated] ⟪unexpected, unsuspected, never dreamed of, unprepared for⟫, kyuˈuna 急な** adj(*na*). **•c [steep in slope or without warning]**

EX. We were shocked by her sudden death.
彼女の{突然の/思いがけない/急な}死にひどく驚いた。
Kanojo no {totsuzen no/omoigakenai/kyuuna} shi ni hidoku odoroita.

suddenly adv. **[occurring in a quick and unexpected manner]**
to⌈tsuzen 突然 •c ⟪**abruptly, all at once, without warning, out of the blue**⟫, **o⌈moigakena⌉ku 思いがけなく** /⟨adj(*i*). ***ku*** of ***omoigakenai*** unexpected/ **[of a significant event occurring unexpectedly]** ⟪**unexpectedly**⟫, **kyu⌈uni 急に** /⟨adj(*na*). ***ni*** of ***kyuuna*** sudden/ **•c [sloping steeply or occurring without warning]** ⟪**hastily, all of a sudden**⟫, **fu⌈i ni 不意に •c [very unexpectedly and quickly]** ⟪**abruptly, unexpectedly**⟫, **i⌈kinari いきなり [for s.o./s.a. to do s.t. unexpectedly]** ⟪**all of a sudden, abruptly, without warning**⟫

EX. (**a**) A child suddenly dashed out from a side street in front of my car.
子供が{突然/急に/不意に/いきなり/*思いがけなく}わき道から私の車の前に飛び出して来た。
*Kodomo ga {totsuzen/kyuuni/fui ni/ikinari/*omoigakenaku} waki-michi kara watashi no kuruma no mae ni tobi-dashite kita.*
(**b**) My ex-girlfriend showed up suddenly one day in my office.
ある日{突然/急に/不意に/思いがけなく/いきなり}昔のガールフレンドが事務所に現われた。
Aru hi {totsuzen/kyuuni/fui ni/omoigakenaku/ikinari} mukashi no gaaru-furendo ga jimu-sho ni arawareta.
(**c**) A man suddenly attacked me from behind.
{いきなり/急に/突然/不意に/思いがけなく}後ろから男がおそいかかってきた。
{Ikinari/Kyuuni/Totsuzen/Fui ni/Omoigakenaku} ushiro kara otoko ga osoi-kakatte kita.
(**d**) Suddenly it started to rain.
{急に/突然/不意に/思いがけなく/?いきなり/}雨が降ってきた。
{Kyuuni/Totsuzen/Fui ni/Omoigakenaku/?Ikinari} ame ga futte kita.

sue vt. **[for s.o. to bring civil action against s.o. else in court]**
⟨-o⟩ u⌈ttaeru ⟨〜を⟩訴える ② [for s.o. to bring civil action against s.o. else ⟪**fig. "express one's demand/complaint/grudge," "take recourse in s.t."**⟫**]** ⟪**go to court against s.o., complain, resort to, appeal**⟫

EX. If you don't return my money I'll sue you.
私の金を返さないと訴えますよ。
Watashi no kane o kaesanai to uttaemasu yo.

suffer vt. **[to undergo s.t. painful/unpleasant (and to endure it)]**
⟨-o⟩ ko⌈omuru ⟨〜を⟩被る ① [for s.o./s.t. to receive an action/favor/damage] ⟪**undergo, sustain, receive**⟫, **⟨-o⟩ u⌈ke⌉ru ⟨〜を⟩受ける ② [to allow s.t. to come into one's possession or to be exposed to the effect of some force or action]** ⟪**receive, be given, take, get, obtain, catch, sustain, accept**⟫

EX. The commercial district suffered the greatest damage in the fire.
その火事で商店街が一番被害を{受けた/被った}。
Sono kaji de shooten-gai ga ichiban higai o {uketa/koomutta}.

—— vi. **[to experience s.t. negative such as pain/harm/loss/injury]**
{⟨-de⟩/⟨-ni⟩} ku⌈rushi⌉mu {⟨〜で⟩/⟨〜に⟩}苦しむ ① [for s.o. to experience physical/emotional adversity or pain] ⟪**feel pain, be tormented by, be in trouble**], **{⟨-de⟩/⟨-ni⟩} na⌈ya⌉mu {⟨〜で⟩/⟨〜に⟩}悩む ① [for s.o. to feel physical/psychological pain]** ⟪**be troubled by, be distressed by**⟫, **⟨-ni⟩ na⌈yamasa-re⌉ru ⟨〜に⟩悩まされる** /⟨**passive of *nayamasu* ① cause physical, psychological pain/ ②**

EX. (**a**) A: Have you ever suffered from prolonged illness?
長期の病気{で{苦しんだ/悩んだ}/に悩まされた}ことがありますか。

Chooki no byooki {de {kurushinda/nayanda}/ni nayamasa-reta} koto ga arimasu ka.
B: Yes, I've suffered from insomnia for many years.
ええ、長いこと不眠症{で{苦しんだ/悩んだ}/に悩まされた}ことがあります。
Ee, nagai koto fumin-shoo {de {kurushinda/nayanda}/ni nayamasa-reta} koto ga arimasu.
(**b**) My mother suffers from allergies.
母はアレルギー{{で/に}{苦しんで/悩んで}/に悩まされて}います。
Haha wa arerugii {{de/ni} {kurushinde/nayande}/ni nayamasa-rete} imasu.

sufficient adj. **[as much as is needed/specified]**
ju⌈ubu⌉nna 十分な adj(*na*). **•c [as much as necessary]** **⟪enough, ample, plenty, full⟫**
EX. (**a**) Is there sufficient money for the research?
研究をするのに十分なお金がありますか。
Kenkyuu o suru no ni juubunna o-kane ga arimasu ka.
(**b**) A: How many chairs do you have?
いすはいくつありますか。
Isu wa ikutsu arimasu ka.
B: Two hundred.
二百あります。
Ni-hyaku arimasu.
A: Oh, that should be sufficient.
ああ、それで十分なはずです。
Aa, sore de juubunna hazu desu.

sufficiently adv. **[to a sufficent degree]**
ju⌈ubu⌉n(ni) 十分(に) •c [to the extent required] **⟪enough, fully, thoroughly, in full⟫**
EX. (**a**) I never feel well unless I exercise sufficiently.
私は十分に運動しないと元気が出ません。
Watashi wa juubunni undoo-shinai to genki ga demasen.
(**b**) I learned Japanese sufficiently enough to survive in Japan.
私は日本で生きていけるぐらい十分(に)日本語を勉強しました。
Watashi wa Nihon de ikite ike-ru gurai juubun(ni) Nihon-go o benkyoo-shimashita.

suffix n.
se⌈tsubi⌉-ji 接尾辞 •c
EX. The "*sa*" of "*samusa*" is a suffix.
「寒さ」の「さ」は接尾辞である。
'Samu-sa' no 'sa' wa setsubi-ji dearu.

sugar n.
sa⌈to⌉o 砂糖
EX. Would you like sugar in your coffee?
コーヒーに砂糖を入れましょうか。
Koohii ni satoo o iremashoo ka.

suggest vt. **[for s.o. to bring an idea/problem/feeling/desire indirectly to s.o.'s attention]**
Vinf. past + ra do⌉o ka to {i⌈u/te⌈ian-suru}
Vinf. past+らどうかと{言う ①/提案する ③}
[for s.o. to put s.t. forward for discussion or adoption] **⟪propose⟫**
EX. I suggested that we should all put our heads together to solve the problem.
私は問題を解くためにみんなで考えたらどうかと{言った/提案した}。
Watashi wa mondai o toku tame ni minna de kangaetara doo ka to {itta/teian-shita}.

suit¹ n. **[an act of suing s.o./requesting s.t.]**
1. so⌈shoo 訴訟 •c [an act of suing s.o.] **⟪lawsuit, litigation⟫**
EX. My suit against the company was unsuccessful.
会社に対する訴訟は失敗に終わった。
Kaisha ni taisuru soshoo wa shippai ni owatta.
2. ta⌈ngan 嘆願 •c [an act of strongly imploring an authority to consider some special case] **⟪petition, entreaty, appeal⟫**

suit² n. **[a set of clothes to be worn together]**
su⌉utsu スーツ •f, mi⌈tsu-zo⌉roi 三つ揃い [a three-piece lounge suit]
—— vi./vt. **[to be/make suitable for s.t./s.o.]**
1. tsu⌈goo ga i⌉i 都合がいい adj(*i*). **[for a circumstance/situation/condition to be**

S

favorable for s.o.] ((convenient))

EX. A: Is Monday okay with you?
月曜日はいいですか。
Getsuyoo-bi wa ii desu ka.
B: Yes, it suits me fine.
ええ、都合がいいです。
Ee, tsugoo ga ii desu.

2. ⟨-ni⟩ **ni-⌈a⌉u** ⟨〜に⟩似合う ① **[for s.t./s.o./s.a. to be in perfect harmony with s.t./s.o./s.a. else]** ((**become, befit, match well**))

EX. That sweater suits you nicely, Kazuko.
そのセーター、和子によく似合うね。
Sono seetaa, Kazuko ni yoku ni-au ne.

suitable adj. **[right/proper for s.t./s.o.]**

1. ⟨-ni⟩ **te⌈kitoona** ⟨〜に⟩適当な adj(*na*). •c **[right for a given situation/purpose/requirement]** ((**fitting, apt, adequate, appropriate**))

EX. I cannot find suitable words to express my gratitude.
感謝の気持ちを表す適当な言葉を知りません。
Kansha no kimochi o arawasu tekitoona kotoba o shirimasen.

S

2. {⟨-to⟩/⟨-ni⟩} **a⌉u** {⟨〜と⟩/⟨〜に⟩}あう ① **[for two people/objects to come face to face or in contact with each other or to fit each other]** ((**meet, match well, encounter**))

NOTE: The particle *to* is chosen when the action in question is seen as mutual, and the particle *ni* is chosen when the action in question is seen as non-mutual and occurring in one direction from one party to the other.

㊅ "meet a person"▷会う, "fit"▷合う, "encounter"▷あう

EX. The climate in this area is suitable for producing apples.
この辺の天候はりんごの栽培に合っている。
Kono hen no kikoo wa ringo no saibai ni atte iru.

suitcase n.

su⌈utsuke⌉esu スーツケース •f

EX. A suitcase with wheels is very convenient for moving about in airports.
キャスター付きのスーツケースは空港内を動き回るのにとても便利だ。
Kyasutaa-tsuki no suutsukeesu wa kuukoo-nai o ugoki-mawaru no ni totemo benri da.

sum n. **[the (total) amount resulting from adding two or more numbers together or an amount of money]**

1. ga⌉ku 額 •c **[an amount of money]** ((**amount**))

EX. He received a huge sum of money through his uncle's will.
彼はおじさんの遺言によりばく大なお金をもらった。
Kare wa oji-san no yuigon ni-yori bakudaina o-kane o moratta.

2. so⌈o-gaku 総額 •c **[the whole amount of money]** ((**total, aggregate**))

EX. The sum of the company's profits was ten million dollars.
その会社の利益の総額は一千万ドルだった。
Sono kaisha no rieki no soo-gaku wa is-sen-man-doru datta.

PHRASE: sum total *soo-suu* 総数 •c ((total))

EX. The sum total of the students at that university is 35,000.
その大学の学生の総数は三万五千だ。
Sono daigaku no gakusei no soo-suu wa san-man-go-sen da.

—— vt. **[to determine a total by adding two or more numbers** ((**fig. "summarize"**))**]**

⟨-o⟩ **yo⌈oyaku-suru** ⟨〜を⟩要約する ③ •c **[for s.o. to present a summary of s.t. spoken or written]** ((**summarize**))

EX. Let me sum up what I have discussed so far.
今までお話ししたことを要約してみます。
Ima made o-hanashi-shita koto o yooyaku-shite mimasu.

summary n. **[a brief statement that summarizes main points]**

yo⌈oyaku 要約 •c **[a brief statement that summarizes the main points of s.t. spoken or written]** ((**digest, resume**))

EX. Read the following passage and write a summary of it.

次の文章を読んで、要約を書きなさい。
Tsugi no bunshoo o yonde, yooyaku o kakinasai.

summer n. **[the months of June, July and August in the northern hemisphere and December, January and February in the southern hemisphere]**
na⌈tsu 夏 ↔ fuyu 冬

EX. A: What do you usually do during the summer?
夏は大抵どんなことをしますか。
Natsu wa taitei donna koto o shimasu ka.
B: I go swimming in the ocean a lot.
よく海に泳ぎに行きます。
Yoku umi ni oyogi ni ikimasu.

summit n. **[the uppermost point of a hill/mountain 《fig. "the highest degree," "acme"》]**
cho⌈ojo⌉o 頂上 •c [the highest point of a mountain 《fig. "the highest level"》] 《top, zenith, peak》, cho⌉oten 頂点 •c [the highest point 《fig. "climax"》] 《top, zenith, peak, acme, climax, apex》

EX. (**a**) We finally reached the summit of Mt. Fuji just as the sun was rising.
我々はちょうど日の出の時刻にやっと富士山の{頂上/*頂点}に着いた。
*Ware ware wa choodo hi-no-de no jikoku ni yatto Fuji-san no {choojoo/ *chooten} ni tsuita.*
(**b**) He reached the summit of his scholarly career when he was in his twenties.
彼は二十代で学者としての{頂点/*頂上}に達した。
*Kare wa ni-juu-dai de gakusha to-shite no {chooten/*choojoo} ni tasshita.*

PHRASE: summit meeting *shunoo-kaidan* 首脳会談 **•c**, *samitto* サミット **•f**

EX. The next summit meeting will be held in Malta.
次の{首脳会談/サミット}はマルタで開かれる。
Tsugi no {shunoo-kaidan/samitto} wa Maruta de hiraka-reru.

summon vt. **[for an authority to order s.o. to an important function such as a trial/legislative session/jury duty]**
⟨-o⟩ yo⌈bi-tsuke⌉ru ⟨～を⟩呼びつける ② [for a superior to call for s.o.] 《have s.o. come to one, send for s.o., convene》, ⟨-o⟩ yo⌈bi-da⌉su ⟨～を⟩呼び出す ① [for s.o. to call for s.o.] 《page, subpoena, decoy》, ⟨-o⟩ sho⌈oshuu-suru ⟨～を⟩召集する ③ •c [for an authority to cause people to come to an important function such as for service in the military or as representatives in a legislature] 《call, convene, convoke, muster, draft》, ⟨-o⟩ sho⌈okan-suru ⟨～を⟩召喚する ③ •c [for a court authority to call for a defendant/witness] 《subpoena, issue a summons against》

EX. (**a**) The principal of the school summoned the student who had bullied his classmates.
学校長は同級生をいじめた学生を{呼びつけた/呼び出した/*召集した/*召喚した}。
*Gakuchoo wa dookyuu-sei o ijimeta gakusei o {yobi-tsuketa/yobi-dashita/ *shooshuu-shita/*shookan-shita}.*
(**b**) The President summoned the cabinet members for an emergency meeting.
大統領は緊急会議に閣僚を{召集した/呼び出した/*呼びつけた/*召喚した}。
*Daitooryoo wa kinkyuu-kaigi ni kakuryoo o {shooshuu-shita/yobi dashita/*yobi-tsuketa/*shookan-shita}.*
(**c**) The judge summoned a witness to the court.
裁判長は証人を法廷に{召喚した/呼び出した/*呼びつけた/*召集した}。
*Saiban-choo wa shoonin o hootei ni {shookan-shita/yobi-dashita/*yobi-tsuketa/*shooshuu-shita}.*

sun n. **[the star around which the earth revolves and from which it receives light and warmth or the light or warmth produced by it]**
hi 日 [the fixed star around which the earth travels and from which it receives light and warmth or the period of a day], ta⌉iyoo 太陽 •c [the fixed star around which the earth travels and from which it

S

receives light and warmth], hi ⌈no hikari 日の光 [light from the fixed star that the earth travels around], ni⌉kkoo 日光 •c

EX. (**a**) The sun sets at about 6:00 P.M. at this time of year
この時期には{日/太陽/*日の光/*日光}は六時ごろ沈む。
*Kono jiki ni wa {hi/taiyoo/*hi no hikari/*nikkoo} wa roku-ji-goro shizumu.*
(**b**) The sun was so strong that we had to draw the curtain.
{日の光/日光/?日/*太陽}があまり強いからカーテンを閉めなければならなかった。
*{Hi no hikari/Nikkoo/?Hi/*Taiyoo} ga amari tsuyoi kara kaaten o shimenakereba naranakatta.*
(**c**) You should avoid exposing yourself to the sun's rays directly for that many hours.
そんなに何時間も直射{日光/*日の光/*太陽/*日}に当たるのは避けた方がいい。
*Sonnani nan-jikan mo chokusha-{nikkoo/*hi no hikari/*taiyoo/*hi} ni ataru no wa saketa hoo ga ii.*

S

Sunday n.
ni⌈chiyo⌉o(-bi) 日曜(日) •c

EX. A: What do you usually do on Sundays?
日曜日はどうしていますか。
Nichiyoo-bi wa doo shite imasu ka.
B: I go golfing every Sunday.
毎週、日曜日には、ゴルフをします。
Mai-shuu, nichiyoo-bi ni wa, gorufu o shimasu.

sunlight n.
ni⌉kkoo 日光 [light from the sun] •c, hi no hi⌈kari⌉ 日の光 •c

EX. The sunlight streamed in through the window.
{日光/日の光}が窓から差し込んできた。
{Nikkoo/Hi no hikari} ga mado kara sashi-konde kita.

sunny adj. **[of/like the sun or full of sunshine ⟪fig. "cheerful," "warm"⟫]**
1. ta⌉iyoo no N 太陽のN •c [of the sun]
2. ta⌉iyoo no yoona 太陽のような adj(*na*). **[like the sun]**
3. yo⌈okina 陽気な adj(*na*). **•c [for s.o. to have a happy disposition and behave pleasantly]**

EX. I like Judy because she has such a sunny disposition.
ジュディは(性格が)陽気だから好きだ。
Judii wa (seikaku ga) yooki da kara suki da.

4. hi-⌈atari ga i⌉i 日当たりがいい adj(*i*). **[located in such a way as to receive much sunlight]**

EX. My room faces south and is very sunny.
私の部屋は南向きで、大変日当たりがいい。
Watashi no heya wa minami-muki de, taihen hi-atari ga ii.

5. te⌉nki ga i⌉i 天気がいい adj(*i*). **[for weather to be fine]**

EX. It will be sunny tomorrow.
明日は天気がいいでしょう。
Asu wa tenki ga ii deshoo.

sunrise n. **[the time when the sun makes its appearance]**
hi-⌈no-de 日の出 ↔ hi-no-iri 日の入り; a⌈katsuki 暁 [the (time of) morning glory ⟨w⟩] ⟪dawn⟫

EX. (**a**) Tomorrow's sunrise will be at 6:34 A.M.
明日の{日の出/*暁}は午前六時三十四分です。
*Asu no {hi-no-de/*akatsuki} wa gozen roku-ji san-juu-yon-pun desu.*
(**b**) The vista from the mountain top at sunrise was just splendid.
{日の出/暁}の時の山頂からの景色は本当にすばらしかった。
{Hi-no-de/Akatsuki} no toki no sanchoo kara no keshiki wa hontoo ni subarashikatta.

sunset n. **[the time when the sun goes down]**
hi-⌈no-iri 日の入り, ni⌈chibotsu 日没 •c ↔ hi-no-de 日の出; yu⌈u-yake 夕焼け [evening glow] ⟪the glow of the sunset⟫

EX. (**a**) Tomorrow's sunset will be at 7:08 P.M.

明日の{日の入り/日没/*夕焼け}は七時八分です。
*Asu no {hi-no-iri/nichibotsu/*yuuyake} wa shichi-ji hap-pun desu.*
(**b**) I love to watch the sunset over the mountain.
山の{夕焼け/*日の入り/*日没}を見るのが大好きだ。
*Yama no {yuu-yake/*hi-no-iri/*nichibotsu} o miru no ga dai-suki da.*

sunshine n. **[direct light from the sun or a place on which the sun shines ⟪fig. "cheerfulness"⟫]**

1. ni⌈kkoo 日光 •c [light from the sun]

EX. Sunshine creates vitamin D in our body.
日光は体の中にビタミンDを作る。
Nikkoo wa karada no naka ni bitamin-dii o tsukuru.

2. hi⌈nata 日なた [a place on which the sun shines]

EX. Let's lie down in the sunshine.
日なたで寝ころぼう。
Hinata de ne-koroboo.

3. yo⌈oki 陽気 •c [liveliness and cheerfulness ⟪fig. "weather"⟫]

super adj. **[excellent in quality or skill] sa⌈ikoo no N 最高のN •c [highest in location/quality] ↔ saitei no N 最低のN •c**

EX. A: I was able to get a ticket to the Super Bowl.
スーパーボールの切符を手に入れることが出来たよ。
Suupaa Booru no kippu o te-ni-ireru koto ga dekita yo.
B: Wow! That's super!
わあ、それは最高だ。
Waa, Sore wa saikoo da.

NOTE: The borrowed word *suupaa* in Japanese means only "supermarket," although it closely resembles English "super." It is actually a truncated form of *suupaa-maaketto* "supermarket."

superior adj. **[higher/better than s.t./s.o./s.a. in rank/value/quality/power or proud and self-conceited]**

1. ⟨-yori⟩ ta⌈ka⌉i ⟨〜より⟩高い adj(*i*). **[higher than s.t./s.o./s.a. else in location/rank/degree/ability/price/acoustic frequency], ⟨-yori⟩ u⌈e no N ⟨〜より⟩上のN [above s.t./s.o./s.a. in rank]**

EX. Mr. Takagi's rank in the company is superior to mine.
高木氏の会社での地位は私より{高い/上だ}。
Takagi-shi no kaisha de no chii wa watashi yori {takai/ue da}.

2. su⌈gu⌉reta N 優れたN /⟨Vinf. past of *sugureru* ② excel/ [better than s.t./s.o./s.a. in ability/skill] ⟪excellent, superb, fine, outstanding⟫, su⌈gu⌉rete iru (N) 優れている(N) /⟨V *te iru* of *sugureru* ② excel/, ko⌈okyuuna 高級な adj(*na*). **•c [of high class in content/quality] ⟪advanced, high-class, expensive, deluxe⟫ ↔ teikyuuna 低級な** adj(*na*). **•c; jo⌈oshitsu no N 上質のN •c [excellent in quality] ⟪of fine quality⟫, jo⌈otoo no N 上等のN •c [excellent in rank/quality] ⟪very good, the best⟫, jo⌈otoona 上等な** adj(*na*). **•c**

EX. (**a**) I used all my savings to purchase a leather coat of superior quality at an exclusive department store in New York.
私はニューヨークの高級デパートで{高級な/上等の/上等な/上質の/?優れた/*優れている}革のコートを買うのに貯金を全部使ってしまった。
*Watashi wa Nyuuyooku no kookyuu-depaato de {kookyuuna/jootoo no/jootoona/jooshitsu no/?sugureta/*sugurete iru} kawa no kooto o kau no ni chokin o zenbu tsukatte shimatta.*
(**b**) This is a superior piece of furniture.
これは{優れた/高級な/上質の/上等の/上等な/?優れている}家具だ。
Kore wa {sugureta/kookyuuna/jooshitsu no/jootoo no/jootoona/?sugurete iru} kagu da.
(**c**) The university will award the prize to a senior thesis of superior merit.
大学は{優れた/優れている/?上質の/*高級な/*上等の/*上等な}卒業論文を書いた人に賞を与える。
Daigaku wa {sugureta/sugurete iru/

S

?jooshitsu no/*kookyuuna/*jootoo no/*jootoona} sotsugyoo-ronbun o kaita hito ni shoo o ataeru.

3. ⟨-yori⟩ tsu⌈yo⌉i ⟨〜より⟩強い adj(*i*). **[stronger than s.t./s.o./s.a. in ability/skill/degree/physical power/structural durability]** ⟪strong, powerful, mighty, stout⟫ ↔ ⟨-yori⟩ yowai ⟨〜より⟩弱い adj(*i*).; ⟨-yori⟩ yu⌈useina ⟨〜より⟩優勢な adj(*na*). •c **[stronger or better than s.t./s.o./s.a.]** ⟪leading, predominant, have the edge⟫

EX. The Giants are superior to the other teams in their league this year.
ジャイアンツは今年は同じリーグの外のチームより{強い/優勢だ}。
Jaiantsu wa kotoshi wa onaji riigu no hoka no chiimu yori {tsuyoi/yuusei da}.

— n. **[a person who is superior]**
me-⌈ue 目上 **[a person who is above another in terms of position/class/age]** ⟪one's senior, one's better⟫, **se⌈npai** 先輩 •c **[a person who has entered a school/company before another or a person who is above another in skill/experience/age/position]** ⟪one's senior⟫

EX. In Japan you have to listen attentively to your superiors.
日本では{目上/先輩}の言うことをよく聞かなければならない。
Nihon de wa {me-ue/senpai} no iu koto o yoku kikanakereba naranai.

S

superman n.
su⌈upa⌉aman スーパーマン •f, **cho⌈ojin** 超人 •c

EX. (**a**) Did you see the movie "*Superman*"?
『スーパーマン』という映画を見ましたか。
"Suupaaman" to iu eiga o mimashita ka.
(**b**) He's a superman, I tell you.
あの人は{超人/スーパーマン}ですよ。
Ano hito wa {choojin/suupaaman} desu yo.

supermarket n.
su⌉upaa スーパー •f

EX. I usually buy my groceries at a nearby supermarket.
食料品は大抵近くのスーパーで買います。
Shokuryoo-hin wa taitei chikaku no suupaa de kaimasu.

supervise vt. **[for s.o. to oversee and/or direct the work or activities of others]**
⟨-o⟩ **ka⌈ntoku-suru** ⟨〜を⟩監督する ③ •c **[for s.o. to oversee and direct actors/students/workers/sports players]** ⟪control, oversee, direct, be in charge of⟫, ⟨-ni⟩ ⟨-o⟩ **shi⌈doo-suru** ⟨〜に⟩⟨〜を⟩指導する ③ •c **[for s.o. to teach and guide s.o.]** ⟪guide, lead, direct, coach⟫

EX. (**a**) One man was supervising the thirty workers.
一人の男が三十人の労働者たちを{監督/指導}していた。
Hitori no otoko ga san-juu-nin no roodoo-sha-tachi o {kantoku/shidoo}-shite ita.
(**b**) Professor Hillman supervised my graduation thesis.
ヒルマン先生が私の卒論を{指導/*監督}してくださった。
*Hiruman-sensei ga watshi no sotsuron o {shidoo/*kantoku}-shite kudasatta.*

supervision n. **[an act of supervising or a state of being supervised]**
ka⌈ntoku 監督 •c **[an act of directing some activity or s.o. who directs some activity]** ⟪control, director⟫, **shi⌈doo** 指導 •c **[the act of directing s.o. or giving s.o. advice]** ⟪guidance, leadership⟫

EX. (**a**) We played baseball under the supervision of Mr. Yamada.
山田氏の{監督/指導}の下で野球をやった。
Yamada-shi no {kantoku/shidoo} no moto de yakyuu o yatta.
(**b**) As a graduate student I received excellent supervision from Prof. Richards.
大学院生としてリチャーズ教授からすばらしい{指導/*監督}を受けました。
Daigaku-in-sei to-shite Richaazu-kyooju kara subarashii {shidoo/

| *kantoku} o ukemashita.

supper n. **[the last meal of the day, usu. served in the evening]**
ba⌈n-go⌉han 晩御飯 •c [the evening meal], yu⌈ushoku 夕食 •c [the evening meal ⟨fml⟩]

EX. A: When do you have supper?
{夕食/晩御飯}はいつ召し上がりますか。
{Yuushoku/Ban-gohan} wa itsu meshi-agarimasu ka.
B: Usually around seven o'clock, depending on the day.
日によって違いますが、たいてい七時ごろです。
Hi ni-yotte chigaimasu ga, taitei shichi-ji-goro desu.

supply vt. **[to furnish s.o. with s.t./s.o. needed or lacking]**
1. ⟨-ni⟩ ⟨-o⟩ kyo⌈okyuu-suru ⟨〜に⟩⟨〜を⟩供給する ③ •c [for an authority to furnish s.o. with s.t./s.o./s.a. to meet a certain need]

EX. The government supplied its overseas troops with generous food rations.
政府が海外の軍隊に豊富な食糧を供給した。
Seifu wa kaigai no guntai ni hoofuna shokuryoo o kyookyuu-shita.

2. ⟨-o⟩ u⌈me-awase⌉ru ⟨〜を⟩埋め合わせる ② [to compensate for an insufficiency/deficiency] ⟪make up for, make amends⟫

EX. We had to supply the amount that was lacking.
私たちは不足分を埋め合わせなければなりませんでした。
Watashi-tachi wa fusoku-bun o ume-awasenakereba narimasen deshita.

—— n. **[an act/instance of furnishing s.o. with s.t./s.o. or people/materials available to be used for a particular purpose]**
1. kyo⌈okyuu 供給 •c [an act of furnishing s.o. with s.t./s.o./s.a.] ⟪service⟫ ↔ juyoo 需要 •c

EX. The price of commodities is determined by the law of supply and demand.
商品の価格は需要と供給の法則によって決まる。
Shoohin no kakaku wa juyoo to kyookyuu no hoosoku ni-yotte kimaru.

2. kyo⌈okyu⌉u-butsu 供給物 •c [materials made available for a particular use], za⌈iko 在庫 •c [stocked supplies] ⟪stock, stockpile⟫

support vt. **[to keep s.o./s.t./s.a. from falling ⟪fig. "give approval to s.o.," "encourage s.o.," "provide s.o. with s.t."⟫]**
1. ⟨-o⟩ sa⌈saeru ⟨〜を⟩支える ② [to hold up s.t./s.o./s.a. which has weight] ⟪maintain, hold, prop up⟫

EX. I supported my mother after she stumbled on a stone.
母が石につまずいたので、支えてあげた。
Haha ga ishi ni tsumazuita node, sasaete ageta.

2. ⟨-o⟩ shi⌉ji-suru ⟨〜を⟩支持する ③ •c [for s.o. to agree to s.o.'s opinion and act/speak in favor of it] ⟪back up, espouse⟫, ⟨-ni⟩ sa⌈nsei-suru ⟨〜に⟩賛成する ③ •c [for s.o. to think that s.o.'s opinion is good/right and express that openly] ⟪approve of, second, agree⟫

EX. There are few people who support the president any more.
今は大統領{を支持する/に賛成する}人は少ない。
Ima wa daitooryoo {o shiji-suru/ni sansei-suru} hito wa sukunai.

3. ⟨-o⟩ ha⌈gema⌉su ⟨〜を⟩励ます ① [for s.o. to give confidence to s.o. by urging him/her not to give up] ⟪encourage, cheer up⟫

EX. My parents supported me in whatever I did.
何をしても両親は私を励ましてくれた。
Nani o shite mo ryooshin wa watashi o hagemashite kureta.

4. ⟨-o⟩ ya⌈shinau ⟨〜を⟩養う ① [for s.o. to bring up/feed s.o., esp. one's dependent, or to develop and maintain good health or habits] ⟪bring up, raise, feed, maintain, develop⟫, ⟨-o⟩ fu⌈yoo-suru ⟨〜を⟩扶養する ③ •c [for s.o. to take care of/feed s.o., esp. one's family member(s) ⟨fml⟩] ⟪maintain⟫

EX. I have been supporting my aging parents for several years.

S

私はここ数年間年取った両親を{養って/扶養して}います。
Watashi wa koko suunen-kan toshitotta ryooshin o {yashinatte/fuyoo-shite} imasu.

PHRASE: support oneself *jikatsu-suru* 自活する ③ •c

EX. I supported myself all through my college years.
大学時代はずっと自活していた。
Daigaku-jidai wa zutto jikatsu-shite ita.

— n. **[an act of supporting s.o./s.t.]**
1. shi˥ji 支持 •c [an act of giving approval to s.o./s.o.'s ideas] ((maintenance, espousal))
2. sa˹sae 支え /(V*masu* of *sasaeru* ② support/ [s.t./s.o. that supports s.o./s.t.]
3. yo˹oiku 養育 •c [an act of taking care of and bringing up children] ((upbringing, fostering, nurture)), fu˹yoo 扶養 •c [an act of taking care of and feeding s.o.] ((maintenance))

suppose vt. **[for s.o. to tentatively hold to be true or to imagine to be true/possible]**
1. Sinf. da˹ro˥o to o˹mo˥u Sinf.だろうと思う ①

EX. I suppose we can get there in thirty minutes.
三十分で行けるだろうと思いますが。
San-jup-pun de ike-ru daroo to omoimasu ga.

NOTE: When the nonpast affirmative form of adj(*na*). or N+cop. comes before *daroo to omou*, adj(*na*). stem or N are used alone, without any copula following.

2. (mo˥shi) Sinf. to shi˹ta˥ra (もし)Sinf.としたら [assuming hypothetically that a situation is true/possible]

EX. (**a**) A: Supposing you knew you would die tomorrow, what would you do today?
もしあした死ぬと分かっていたとしたら、今日何をしますか。
Moshi ashita shinu to wakatte ita to shitara, kyoo nani o shimasu ka.
B: I'd call all of my friends to say "good-bye," I guess.
友達全部に電話して「さようなら」と言うでしょうね。
Tomodachi zenbu ni denwa-shite 'Sayoonara' to iu deshoo ne.
(**b**) Supposing you had $100,000, what would you buy?
(もし)十万ドルあったとしたら、何を買いますか。
(Moshi) juu-man-doru atta to shitara, nani o kaimasu ka.
(**c**) Supposing I were you, I wouldn't do that.
(もし)僕が君だったとしたら、そうしないだろうな。
(Moshi) boku ga kimi datta to shitara, soo shinai daroo na.
(**d**) Supposing this house was 50% cheaper, would you buy it?
(もし)この家が五割安かったとしたら、買いますか。
(Moshi) kono ie ga go-wari yasukatta to shitara, kaimasu ka.

PHRASE: be supposed to {Vneg./Vstem/ko/shi/adj(*i*). *ku*} {*nakute wa*/*nakereba*} {*ikenai*/*naranai*} {Vneg./Vstem/来/し/adj(*i*). *ku*}{なくては/なければ}{いけない/ならない}, {adj(*na*). stem/N} {*de*/*ja*}{*nakute wa*/*nakereba*} {*ikenai*/*naranai*} {adj(*na*). stem/N}{で/じゃ}{なくては/なければ}{いけない/ならない}

EX. When you live in a foreign country you're supposed to learn its language and culture.
外国に住んでいる時はその国の言葉と文化を学ばなければ{ならない/いけない}。
Gaikoku ni sunde iru toki wa sono kuni no kotoba to bunka o manabanakereba {naranai/ikenai}.

supreme adj. **[highest in rank/power/quality/achievements]**
sa˹ikoo no N 最高のN •c [highest in location/quality] ↔ saitei no N 最低のN •c; sa˹ijoo no N 最上のN •c [highest in rank/degree/quality, esp. in degree of pleasure/satisfaction produced] ((best, finest, highest))

EX. (**a**) The Olympic athletes put on a supreme performance.
オリンピックの選手たちは{最高/*最上}の技を見せた。

*Orinpikku no senshu-tachi wa {saikoo/ *saijoo} no waza o miseta.*
(**b**) I have married the ideal husband, and am now experiencing supreme happiness.
私は理想的な夫と結婚して、{最上/最高}の幸福を味わっています。
Watashi wa risoo-tekina otto to kekkon-shite, {saijoo/saikoo} no koofuku o ajiwatte imasu.

PHRASE: supreme court *saikoo-saiban-sho* 最高裁判所 •c

sure adj. **[not open to doubt or dispute 《fig. "having no doubt," "destined to do/ happen"》]**
1. ta˥shikana 確かな adj(*na*). **[able to be relied upon with confidence as true] 《certain, positive, undoubted, reliable, authentic, safe, secure》 ↔ fu-tashikana 不確かな** adj(*na*).; **ka┌kujitsuna 確実な** adj(*na*). **•c [not open to doubt], 《certain, reliable, safe》 ↔ fu-kakujitsuna 不確実な** adj(*na*). **•c**

EX. I have sure evidence that Bob is the murderer.
ボブが殺人犯だという{確かな/確実な}証拠を持っている。
Bobu ga satsujin-han da to iu {tashikana/kakujitsuna} shooko o motte iru.

2. ma┌chiga˥inaku 〈-to〉 o┌mo˥u 間違いなく〈〜と〉思う ① [for s.o. to believe without doubt that s.t. is true]

EX. I'm sure that our team will win.
間違いなく我々のチームが勝つと思いますよ。
Machigainaku ware-ware no chiimu ga katsu to omoimasu yo.

3. ma┌chiga˥inaku 間違いなく adv. **[destined to do/happen]**

EX. (**a**) It is sure to rain today.
今日は間違いなく雨が降ります。
Kyoo wa machigainaku ame ga furimasu.
(**b**) He is sure to become a great scholar.
あの人は間違いなく大学者になる。
Ano hito wa machigainaku dai-gakusha ni naru.

PHRASE: Are you sure? *hontoo (desu ka).* 本当(ですか)。, *Daijoobu (desu ka).* 大丈夫(ですか)。

EX. A: Shall I carry your suitcase?
スーツケース、お持ちしましょうか。
Suutsukeesu, o-mochi-shimashoo ka.
B: That's OK. I can carry it.
大丈夫です。持てますから。
Daijoobu desu. Mote-masu kara.
A: Are you sure?
{大丈夫/本当}ですか。
{Daijoobu/Hontoo} desu ka.

— int. **[an interjection used in answering a request in a positive way]**
e˥e ええ [an interjection that indicates an affirmative answer], do˥ozo, do˥ozo どうぞ、どうぞ adv. **[a phrase that indicates a willing granting of permission or an invitation to do s.t. 〈s〉], a˥a, i˥i tomo ああ、いいとも [a phrase that indicates an unreservedly positive answer to a request 〈s〉], mo┌chi˥ron もちろん** adv. **•c [of course]**

EX. A: Is it all right if I borrow ten dollars from you?
十ドル、借りてもいい?
Juu-doru, karite mo ii?
B: Sure.
{ええ/どうぞ、どうぞ/ああ、いいとも/もちろん}。
{Ee/Doozo, doozo/Aa, ii tomo/ Mochiron}.

NOTE: *Aa ii tomo* is usually used by male speakers.

surely adv. **[with assurance or without doubt]**
ta˥shikani 確かに /〈adj(*na*). *ni* of *tashikana* certain/ 《certainly》, ka┌kujitsuni 確実に /〈adj(*na*). *ni* of *kakujitsuna* certain/ •c 《certainly, reliably, safely》, ka┌narazu 必ず [(s.t. happens/s.o. does s.t.) without fail] 《certainly, without fail, always》

EX. (**a**) We've surely made progress in our research on AIDS.
{確かに/確実に/*必ず}エイズの研究は進歩した。
*{Tashikani/Kakujitsuni/*Kanarazu} eizu no kenkyuu wa shinpo-shita.*

S

(**b**) I'll surely be there for the meeting tomorrow.
あしたの会議には{必ず/*確かに/*確実に}出ます。
*Ashita no kaigi ni wa {kanarazu/ *tashikani/*kakujitsuni} demasu.

— int. **[an interjection used in answering a request in a positive way]**
SEE sure int.

surf n. **[the swelling and breaking of waves on the shore/reef]**
u⌈chi-yose⌉ru na⌈mi⌉ 打ち寄せる波

— vi. **[to ride the surf** (as on a surfboard)**]**
na⌈mi-nori⌉ o suru 波乗りをする ③, sa⌉afin o suru サーフィンをする ③ •f

surface n. **[the outer face** (of a solid) **on the top of a body of water** 《**fig. "appearance"**》**]**
1. hyo⌈ome⌉n 表面 •c 《**face, outside, exterior, appearance**》**, ga⌈imen 外面 •c [outer face of a solid** 《**fig. "appearance"**》**]** 《**outside, exterior**》 **↔ naimen 内面 •c**

EX. (**a**) The surface of this paper is very smooth.
この紙の{表面/*外面}はとても滑らかだ。
*Kono kami no {hyoomen/*gaimen} wa totemo nameraka da.*
(**b**) I painted the surface of the old bookcase white.
古い本箱の{表面/外面}をペンキで白く塗った。
Furui hon-bako no {hyoomen/gaimen} o penki de shiroku nutta.

2. u⌈wa-be 上辺 [outward appearance] 《**exterior, outside**》**, mi⌈kake 見かけ [an impression created by outward appearance]** 《**looks, show**》**, ga⌈ikan 外観 •c [the way s.t. appears from the outside]** 《**appearance, exterior, look**》**, hyo⌈ome⌉n 表面 •c** SEE surface 1, **ga⌈imen 外面 •c** SEE surface 1

EX. People always seem to want to put on a false surface.
人はいつも{表面/見かけ/上辺/外観/外面}を取り繕いたがるようだ。
Hito wa itsu-mo {hyoomen/mikake/ uwa-be/gaikan/gaimen} o tori-tsukuroi-ta-garu yooda.

3. su⌈imen 水面 •c [the area forming the top of a body of water]

EX. Colorful, small fish were swimming just below the surface.
水面のすぐ下を色とりどりの小さな魚が泳いでいた。
Suimen no sugu shita o iro-tori-dori no chiisana sakana ga oyoide ita.

— vi. **[to rise to the surface]**
1. u⌈kabi-aga⌉ru 浮かび上がる ① [for s.t. such as a submarine to rise to the surface of the water 《**fig. "emerge from obscurity," "loom up"**》**], a⌈karu-mi ni de⌉ru 明るみに出る ② [for an event/truth to come to light** ⟨**w**⟩**]**

EX. (**a**) While we were watching, a whale suddenly surfaced by the side of the boat.
見ていると、鯨が突然、船のそばに{浮かび上がった/*明るみに出た}。
*Mite iru to, kujira ga totsuzen fune no soba ni {ukabi-agatta/*akaru-mi ni deta}.*
(**b**) The incident surfaced thanks to an astute newspaper reporter.
敏腕の新聞記者のおかげで事件が{明るみに出た/*浮かび上がった}。
*Binwan no shinbun-kisha no o-kage de jiken ga {akaru-mi ni deta/*ukabi-agatta}.*

surgery n. **[**(a branch of medicine dealing with) **the removal and repair of diseased or damaged parts of the body]**
1. shu⌉jutsu 手術 •c [the cutting of the body for medical treatment] 《**operation**》

EX. My mother recently underwent surgery for breast cancer.
うちの母は最近乳がんの手術をした。
Uchi no haha wa saikin nyuu-gan no shujutsu o shita.

2. ge⌈ka 外科 •c [a branch of medicine dealing with operations]
3. shu⌈jutsu⌉-shitsu 手術室 •c [an operation room]
4. ge⌈ka-byo⌉oin 外科病院 •c [a hospital for surgical operations]

surname n.

myo˥oji 名字 **•c** **《family name, last name》**, **se˥i** 姓 **•c** **《family name, last name》**

EX. My surname is Sasaki and my given name is Kumiko.
私の{名字/姓}は佐々木で、名は久美子です。
Watashi no {myooji/sei} wa Sasaki de, na wa Kumiko desu.

surprise vt. **[to cause s.o./s.a. to feel sudden wonder or amazement by an unexpected action]**

1. 〈-o〉 o⌈doroka˥-su 〈~を〉驚かす **/〈short causative of *odoraku* ① be surprised/** ① **[to shock s.o./s.a. unawares]** **《astonish, amaze, shock, startle》**, **〈-o〉 o⌈doroka-se˥ru** 〈~を〉驚かせる **/〈causative of *odoroku* ① be surprised/** ②

EX. **(a)** The news of the collapse of the Berlin Wall surprised the world.
ベルリンの壁崩壊のニュースは世界を{驚かした/驚かせた}。
Berurin no kabe hookai no nyuusu wa sekai o {odoroka-shita/odoraka-seta}.
(b) I don't mean to surprise you, my dear, but I was told that I will be promoted to an executive position in July.
君を{驚かしたく/驚かせたく}はないけど、僕は七月から重役に昇進すると言われたんだ。
Kimi o {odoroka-shi-taku/odoraka-se-taku} wa nai kedo, boku wa shichi-gatsu kara juuyaku ni shooshin-suru to iwa-reta n da.

NOTE: English "be surprised" is expressed in Japanese by the intransitive verbs *odoroku* ① or *bikkuri-suru* ③, as in the following. *Fianse ga shisshin-shita node totemo {odoroita/bikkuri-shita}.* "I was very much surprised when my fiancee fainted."

2. 〈-o〉 ki⌈shuu-suru 〈~を〉奇襲する ③ **•c** **[for s.o. to attack the enemy suddenly and unexpectedly]**

—— n. **[an act of surprising s.o./s.a. or a state of being surprised or s.t. that surprises s.o./s.a.]**

1. o⌈doroka˥-su koto 驚かすこと **[an act of surprising]**

2. o⌈doroki 驚き **/〈V *masu* of *odoroku* ① be surprised/**

EX. Jenny's marrying Taro was a big surprise to me.
ジェニーが太郎と結婚したのは大きな驚きだった。
Jenii ga Taroo to kekkon-shita no wa ookina odoroki datta.

3. ki⌈shuu 奇襲 **•c** **[a surprise attack]**

4. o⌈doroku-be˥ki koto 驚くべきこと **[s.t. that merits astonishment]**

PHRASE: to one's surprise *odoroita koto ni* 驚いたことに

EX. To my surprise my daughter had twins.
驚いたことに娘に双子が生まれたんです。
Odoroita koto ni musume ni futa-go ga umareta n desu.

surrender vt. **[to give up s.t. completely after having striven to keep it 《fig. "yield oneself to an emotion"》]**

1. 〈-o〉 〈-ni〉 hi⌈ki-wata˥su 〈~を〉〈~に〉引き渡す ① **[for s.o. to hand s.t./s.o./s.a. over to s.o./some place]** **《deliver, transfer》**, **〈-o〉 〈-ni〉 yu⌈zuri-wata˥su** 〈~を〉〈~に〉譲り渡す ① **[for s.o. to yield possession of s.t./s.o./s.a. to another]** **《turn over, transfer》**

EX. The farmer finally surrendered the land to the city.
農場主はついにその土地を市に{引き渡した/譲り渡した}。
Noojoo-nushi wa tsuini sono tochi o shi ni {hiki-watashita/yuzuri-watashita}.

2. 〈-o〉 na˥ge-suteru 〈~を〉投げ捨てる ② **[for s.o. to throw s.t. away]**

EX. Having surrendered his position and honors, the man exiled himself.
その男は地位も名誉も投げ捨てて亡命した。
Sono otoko wa chii mo meiyo mo nage-sutete boomei-shita.

3. 〈-ni〉 mi ⌈o makase˥ru 〈~に〉身を任せる ② **[for s.o. to give up one's body and soul to s.t. 〈w〉]**

S

EX. The girl surrendered herself to illicit love.
女の子は不倫の恋に身を任せてしまった。
Onna-no-ko wa furin no koi ni mi o makasete shimatta.

—— vi. **[to yield to s.o.'s power/control]** **⟨-ni⟩ ko⌈ofuku-suru ⟨〜に⟩降伏する** ③ **•c [for s.o. to capitulate to the enemy]** **⟪capitulate⟫**, **⟨-ni⟩ ku⌈ssu⌉ru ⟨〜に⟩屈する** ③ **•c [for s.o. to physically/psychologically bend to s.t./s.o.]** **⟪flinch, submit⟫**, **⟨-ni⟩ ku⌈ppuku-suru ⟨〜に⟩屈服する** ③ **•c [for s.o. to yield to s.o. with power]** **⟪submit, yield⟫**

EX. (**a**) Japan surrendered to the U.S. in 1945.
日本は1945年にアメリカに{{降伏/*屈服}した/*屈した}。
*Nihon wa sen-kyuu-hyaku-yon-juu-go-nen ni Amerika ni {{koofuku/*kuppuku}-shita/*kusshita} .*
(**b**) Refusing to surrender to the pressure of her superiors in the company, she disclosed the scandal to the media.
彼女は会社の上司の圧力に{屈せず/{屈服/*降伏}せず}、その不祥事をマスコミに暴露した。
*Kanojo wa kaisha no jooshi no atsuryoku ni {kussezu/{kuppuku/*koofuku}-sezu}, sono fushooji o masukomi ni bakuro-shita.*

S

surround vi./vt. **[to encircle s.t./s.o./s.a. on all sides ⟪fig. "encircle (one's) enemies"⟫]**
1. ⟨-o⟩ ka⌈komu ⟨〜を⟩囲む ① **•c [for s.t. two-/three-dimensional such as lines/walls/trees/people to be all around s.t./s.o./s.a.]** **⟪encircle⟫**, **⟨-o⟩ to⌈ri-maku ⟨〜を⟩取り巻く** ① **[to encircle s.t./s.o./s.a.]** **⟪encircle, ring s.t. about, gather⟫**, **⟨-o⟩ ⟨-de⟩ ka⌈kou ⟨〜を⟩⟨〜で⟩囲う** ① **[for s.o. to artificially and semi-permanently enclose s.t. (esp. a house)]** **⟪enclose, fence, rope off⟫**

EX. (**a**) The city is surrounded by mountains.
町は山に{囲まれて/*取り巻かれて/*囲われて}いる。
*Machi wa yama ni {kakoma-rete/*tori-maka-rete/*kakowa-rete} iru.*
(**b**) The movie star was surrounded by her fans.
映画スターがファンに{取り巻かれて/囲まれて/*囲われて}いた。
*Eiga-suttaa ga fuan ni {tori-maka-rete/kakoma-rete/*kakowa-rete} ita.*
(**c**) We surrounded our house with a fence.
家を垣根で{囲った/*取り巻いた/*囲んだ}。
*Ie o kakine de {kakotta/*tori-maita/*kakonda}.*

2. te⌈ki o ho⌉oi-suru 敵を包囲する ③ **[to encircle one's enemies]**

surrounding n.
ka⌈nkyoo 環境 •c [the outside world surrounding s.o./s.t./s.a.] **⟪environment⟫**

EX. I'm looking for a house with quiet surroundings.
静かな環境にある家を探しています。
Shizukana kankyoo ni aru ie o sagashite imasu.

—— adj. **[belonging to an area located around s.t.]**
ma⌈wari no N 周りのN [belonging to an area located around s.t./s.o./s.a.], **shu⌉ui no N 周囲のN •c [found in an area located around s.t.]**

EX. The airport and the surrounding area were blanketed in thick fog.
空港とその{周り/周囲}の地域は濃い霧に包まれていた。
Kuukoo to sono {mawari/shuui} no chiiki wa koi kiri ni tsutsuma-rete ita.

survey vt. **[for s.o. to examine s.t. to determine its condition or value ⟪fig. "make an overview of s.t.," "measure land"⟫]**
1. ⟨-o⟩ ga⌈ikan-suru ⟨〜を⟩概観する ③ **•c [for s.o. to take a general view of s.t.]**

EX. This is a course which surveys the current system of education in Japan.
これは現在の日本の教育制度を概観する講義です。
Kore wa genzai no Nihon no kyooiku-seido o gaikan-suru koogi desu.

2. ⟨-o⟩ so⌈kuryoo-suru ⟨〜を⟩測量する ③ **•c**

[for s.o. to measure the height/location/shape/area of a parcel of land] ((measure, sound))
3. ⟨-o⟩ **cho⌉osa-suru** ⟨〜を⟩調査する ③ •c **[for s.o. to try to find more information about s.t. to understand it better]** ((investigate, examine, inquire into))

EX. We surveyed the citizens of the town on their attitudes on gun control.
銃規制に関する町の住民の意見を調査した。
Juu-kisei ni-kansuru machi no juumin no iken o choosa-shita.

— n. **[an act of surveying]**
1. **mi-⌈watasu koto** 見渡すこと **[an act of looking out over s.t.]**
2. **ga⌈ikan** 概観 •c **[a general overview of s.t.]** ((overview))
3. **so⌈kuryoo** 測量 •c **[a measurement of the height/location/shape/area of a parcel of land]**
4. **cho⌉osa** 調査 •c **[an act of investigating]** ((investigation, examination))

survival n. **[an act/state of surviving or s.t./s.o./s.a. that survives]**
1. **i⌈ki-noko⌉ru koto** 生き残ること **[an act of surviving]**, **sa⌈ba⌉ibaru** サバイバル •f, **se⌈izon** 生存 •c **[an act/state of living/surviving a tragedy]** ((existence, being))
2. **se⌈izo⌉n-sha** 生存者 •c **[a person who survives a tragedy]** ((survivor))
3. **za⌈n{so⌉n/zo⌉n}-butsu** 残存物 •c **[s.t. that survives]**

PHRASE: the survival of the fittest *tekisha-seizon* 適者生存 •c

survive vt. **[to live/exist longer than s.o./s.a. else/through a traumatic experience]**
1. ⟨-ni⟩ **sa⌈ki-data-re⌉ru** ⟨〜に⟩先立たれる /⟨passive of *saki-datsu* ① die before/ ② **[for s.o. to suffer from s.o. else dying before oneself ⟨fml⟩]**, ⟨-yori⟩ **na⌈ga-iki⌉-suru** ⟨〜より⟩長生きする ② **[for s.o./s.a. to live longer than s.o./s.a.]** ((outlive)), ⟨-yori⟩ **a⌉to made no⌈ko⌉ru** ⟨〜より⟩後まで残る ① **[to remain after s.t.]**

EX. (a) The husband seldom survives his wife in today's world.
今の世の中では夫が妻{より長生きする/に先立たれる/*より後まで残る}ことは滅多にない。
*Ima no yo-no-naka de wa otto ga tsuma {yori naga-iki-suru/ni saki-data-reru/*yori ato made nokoru} koto wa mettani nai.*
(b) This company should easily survive its competitors because of its innovative ideas.
この会社は新しいアイディアがあるから、難なく競争相手{より後まで残る/*より長生きする/*に先立たれる}はずだ。
*Kono kaisha wa atarashii aidia ga aru kara, nan-naku kyoosoo-aite {yori ato made nokoru/*yori naga-iki-suru/*ni saki-data-reru} hazu da.*

2. ((⟨-de⟩)) **ta⌈suka⌉ru** ((⟨〜で⟩))助かる ① **[for s.o. to be delivered from danger or harm or to receive some benefit due to a favorable development or to the efforts of another]** ((be saved, be rescued, escape)), ⟨-o⟩ **ta⌉e-nu⌈ku** ⟨〜を⟩耐え抜く ① **[for s.o. to endure s.t. all the way through]** ((endure, stick s.t. out))

EX. (a) A girl miraculously survived the airplane crash.
女の子は飛行機事故で奇跡的に{助かった/*耐え抜いた}。
*Onna-no-ko wa hikoo-ki-jiko de kiseki-tekini {tasukatta/*tae-nuita}.*
(b) My students all survived the nine-week intensive Japanese language course.
私の学生はみんな九週間の日本語の集中講座{を耐え抜いた/*で助かった}。
*Watashi no gakusei wa minna kyuu-shuukan no Nihon-go no shuuchuu-kooza {o tae-nuita/*de tasukatta}.*

— vi. **[to live/exist longer than s.o./s.a./through a traumatic experience]**
1. **i⌈ki-noko⌉ru** 生き残る ① **[for s.o./s.a. not to die and remain alive]**, **i⌈ki-nobiru** 生き延びる ① **[for s.o./s.a. to escape from a life-threatening situation and live]** ((live on borrowed time))

EX. (**a**) In that battle John was one of the very few soldiers who survived.
ジョンはその戦いでわずかに生き{残った/*延びた}兵士の一人だった。
*Jon wa sono tatakai de wazukani iki-{nokotta/*nobita} heishi no hitori datta.*
(**b**) She came very close to dying, but she survived.
彼女は死にそうになったが生き{延びた/*残った}。
*Kanojo wa shini-sooni natta ga iki-{nobita/*nokotta}.*

2. ta⌈suka⌉ru 助かる ① SEE survive vt. 2, **ta⌈e-nu⌉ku 耐え抜く** ① SEE survive vt. 2

suspect vt. **[for s.o. to believe it to be likely that s.t. is true, esp. s.t. undesirable, or to believe that s.o. is guilty of s.t. without proof]**
Sinf. no dewanai (daroo) ka to o⌈mo⌉u Sinf.のではない(だろう)かと思う ① **[for s.o. to wonder if it is not the case that], Sinf. no dewanai (daroo) ka to u⌈tagau Sinf.のではない(だろう)かと疑う** ① **[for s.o. to wonder if it is not the case that] ⟪doubt⟫, Sinf. no dewanai (daroo) ka to a⌈yashi⌉mu Sinf.のではない(だろう)かと怪しむ** ① **[for s.o. to feel that something is wrong/strange about s.t./s.o.] ⟪doubt, wonder⟫**

NOTE: When the nonpast affirmative form of adj(*na*). or N+cop. appears before *no dewanai (daroo) ka to omou*, the form {adj(*na*). stem/N} *na* is used. {Adj(*na*). stem/N} *dewanai (daroo) ka to omou* is also possible as in example (b).

EX. (**a**) I suspect that Dorothy likes Jim.
ドロシーはジムが好きなんじゃないかと{思います/*疑います/*怪しみます}。
*Doroshii wa Jimu ga sukina n janai ka to {omoimasu/*utagaimasu/*ayashimimasu}.*
(**b**) People suspect that Hanako is the culprit.
人々は花子が犯人ではないかと{思って/疑って/怪しんで}いる。
Hito-bito wa Hanako ga hannin dewanai ka to {omotte/utagatte/ayashinde} iru.

—— n. **[a person who is suspected of a crime or s.t. of that nature]**
yo⌈ogi⌉-sha 容疑者 •c

EX. The suspect in the murder case was caught by the police today.
殺人の容疑者が今日警察に捕まった。
Satsujin no yoogi-sha ga kyoo keisatsu ni tsukamatta.

suspend vt. **[for s.o. to hang s.t. from above ⟪fig. "cause s.t. to cease for a (specified) time," "keep s.t. undecided"⟫]**
1. ⟨-o⟩ tsu⌈rusu ⟨〜を⟩つるす ① **[for s.o. to fasten s.t. at the top using a string or similar material so that the lower part is free in the air] ⟪hang, sling⟫**

EX. We suspended ropes from the branch of a tree and made a swing.
枝からロープをつるして、ぶらんこを作った。
Eda kara roopu o tsurushite, buranko o tsukutta.

2. ⟨-o⟩ i⌈chi⌉-ji te⌈ishi-saseru ⟨〜を⟩一時停止させる /⟨causative of *teishi-suru* ③ stop/ ② **•c [to cause s.t. to stop temporarily], ⟨-o⟩ te⌈ishoku ni suru ⟨〜を⟩停職にする** ③ **•c [for s.o. to relieve s.o. of his/her duties for a set time], ⟨-o⟩ te⌈igaku ni suru ⟨〜を⟩停学にする** ③ **•c [for s.o. to dismiss a student from school for a set time]**

EX. (**a**) That restaurant's license was suspended after it served alchoholic beverages to a minor.
そのレストランはアルコール飲料を未成年者に出したので業務を{一時停止/*停職に/*停学に}させられた。
*Sono resutoran wa arukooru-inryoo o mi-seinen-sha ni dashita node gyoomu o {ichi-ji teishi-/*teishoku ni/*teigaku ni} sase-rareta.*
(**b**) The man was suspended from the company for wrongdoing.
男は悪いことをしたので{停職/*一時停止/*停学}になった。
*Otoko wa warui koto o shita node {teishoku/*ichi-ji teishi/*teigaku} ni natta.*

(c) The high school student was suspended from school for smoking cigarettes.
その高校生はタバコを吸ったので{停学/*一時停止/*停職}になった。
*Sono kookoo-sei wa tabako o sutta node {teigaku/*ichi-ji teishi/*teishoku} ni natta.*

NOTE: In examples (b) and (c) the Japanese versions are not in the passive forms *teishoku ni sase-rareta* nor *teigaku ni sase-rareta* but *teishoku ni natta* and *teigaku ni natta*, respectively.

3. ⟨-o⟩ mi-ˈawaseru ⟨〜を⟩見合わせる ② [for people/animals to look at each other/ for s.o. to put off doing s.t.] ⟪exchange glances, postpone, defer⟫

EX. The television network is suspending further broadcasts of the commercial until the court rules on its legality.
テレビ局はそのコマーシャルの合法性を巡る裁判で判決が下るまで、その放送を見合わせている。
Terebi-kyoku wa sono komaasharu no goohoo-sei o meguru saiban de hanketsu ga kudaru made, sono hoosoo o mi-awasete iru.

suspense n. **[a state of s.t. hanging in the air or a state of mental uncertainty]**

1. chuˈuburarin 宙ぶらりん [a state of s.t. physically hanging in the air ⟪fig. "indecisiveness"⟫] ⟪pendency⟫

EX. If you don't intend to marry me, please tell me. I can't stand being kept in suspense any longer.
僕と結婚する気がないのならそう言ってください。これ以上宙ぶらりんでほうっておかれるのはたまりませんから。
Boku to kekkon-suru ki ga nai no nara soo itte kudasai. Kore ijoo chuuburarin de hootte-oka-reru no wa tamarimasen kara.

2. saˈsupeˈnsu サスペンス •f [psychological tension and anxiety]

EX. I love to read suspense stories.
サスペンス・ストーリーを読むのが好きだ。
Sasupensu-sutoorii o yomu no ga suki da.

suspicion n. **[an act/instance of suspecting s.t./s.o./s.a.]**

uˈtagai 疑い /⟨V*masu* of *utagau* ① suspect/ [an act of thinking that s.t. is not true or that s.t. does not exist] ⟪doubt, question, uncertainty⟫

EX. The doctor had a suspicion that it was a stomach ulcer that was causing the patient's pain.
医者は胃にできたかいようが患者に痛みを与えている疑いがあると思った。
Isha wa i ni dekita kaiyoo ga kanja ni itami o ataete iru utagai ga aru to omotta.

PHRASE: I have a suspicion that Sinf. *no dewanai ka to omou* Sinf.のではないかと思う ①

NOTE: When expressing a suspicion about whether s.t. is true or not or whether s.t. is authentic or not, *hontoo ka doo ka utagawashii* or *honmono ka doo ka utagawashii* should be used respectively.

EX. I have a suspicion that John will object to this idea.
ジョンはこの考えに反対するのではないかと思います。
Jon wa kono kangae ni hantai-suru no dewanai ka to omoimasu.

suspicious adj. **[arousing/showing/ expressing suspicion]**

1. uˈtagawashiˈi 疑わしい adj(*i*). [arousing a feeling of suspicion] ⟪doubtful, dubious, unreliable⟫, aˈyashii 怪しい adj(*i*). [arousing a feeling of mystery/suspicion] ⟪doubtful, questionable, uncertain, dubious⟫

NOTE: When the nonpast affirmative form of adj(*na*) or N+cop. appears before *no dewanai (daroo) ka to omou*, the form {adj(*na*). stem/N} *na* is used. {Adj(*na*). stem/N} *dewanai (daroo) ka to omou* is also possible as in example (b).

EX. A suspicious person was standing at the front door.
玄関先に{怪しい/疑わしい}男が立っていた。
Genkan-saki ni {ayashii/utagawashii} otoko ga tatte ita.

S

2. u⌈tagawashi-gena 疑わしげな adj(*na*). **[showing signs of feeling suspicion]**

EX. The detective looked at me with suspicious eyes.
刑事は私のことを疑わしげな目で見た。
Keiji wa watashi no koto o utagawashi-gena me de mita.

sustain vt. **[to support s.t./s.o./s.a. from below《fig. "maintain s.t.," "provide s.o. with s.t.," "endure," "suffer"》]**

1. 〈-o〉 sa⌈saeru 〈〜を〉支える ② [to hold up s.t./s.o./s.a. which has weight《fig. "maintain"》]

EX. I don't understand how you can sustain such a heavy object on your head.
どうやって頭であんな重いものを支えられるのか分かりません。
Doo yatte atama de anna omoi mono o sasae-rareru no ka wakarimasen.

2. 〈-o〉 ji⌈zoku-suru 〈〜を〉持続する ③ •c [for s.o. to continue in a certain state without stopping]《continue, carry on》, 〈-o〉 tsu⌈zukeru 〈〜を〉続ける ② [to cause s.t. not to stop or be interrupted]《continue, keep up, go on》

EX. I cannot sustain the traditional Japanese sitting posture of *seiza* for more than one minute.
日本式の正座を一分間以上{続ける/持続する}ことは出来ません。
Nihon-shiki no seiza o ip-punkan-ijoo {tsuzukeru/jizoku-suru} koto wa dekimasen.

3. 〈-o〉 ya⌈shinau 〈〜を〉養う ① [for s.o. to bring up/feed s.o., esp. one's dependent, or to develop and maintain good health or habits]《bring up, raise, feed, maintain, develop》

EX. This amount of food can sustain my family for only a week.
この食べ物の量では私の家族を一週間しか養えません。
Kono tabe-mono no ryoo de wa watashi no kazoku o is-shuukan shika yashinae-masen.

4. 〈-o〉 ko⌈rae⌉ru 〈〜を〉こらえる ② [for s.o. to endure suffering without outwardly showing it]《bear, stand, put up with, control》

EX. She sustained great pain due to the disease for years without complaining.
彼女は病気から来る激しい痛みを不平も言わずに何年もこらえた。
Kanojo wa byooki kara kuru hageshii itami o fuhei mo iwazu ni nan-nen mo koraeta.

5. 〈-o〉 u⌈ke⌉ru 〈〜を〉受ける ② [to allow s.t. to come into one's possession or to be exposed to the effect of some force or action]《receive, be given, have, take, get, catch, suffer, incur, accept》, 〈-o〉 ko⌈omu⌉ru 〈〜を〉被る ① [for s.o./s.t. to receive an action/favor/damage]《undergo, suffer》

EX. The building sustained damage from the typhoon.
建物は台風で被害を{受けた/被った}。
Tate-mono wa taifuu de higai o {uketa/koomutta}.

swallow[1] vt. **[for s.o./s.a. to take s.t. into one's stomach without chewing《fig. "absorb," "put up with," "refrain from expressing," "receive gullibly"》]**

1. 〈-o〉 no⌉mu 〈〜を〉飲む ① [for s.o./s.a. to put s.t. into one's body through the mouth without chewing it《fig. "overwhelm," "suppress," "acquiesce"》]《drink, take, have, guzzle, gulp, accept》, 〈-o〉 no⌈mi-komu 〈〜を〉飲み込む ① [for s.o./s.a. to take s.t. into one's stomach without chewing《fig. "understand, to keep s.t. inside oneself"》], 〈-o〉 mu⌈ne⌉ ni o⌈same⌉ru 〈〜を〉胸に納める ② [for s.o. to keep s.t. inside oneself without expressing it]

EX. (**a**) Mommy, I swallowed a big piece of candy!
お母さん、大きなあめを{飲んじゃった/飲み込んじゃった/*胸に納めちゃった}。
*O-kaa-san, ookina ame o {nonjatta/nomi-konjatta/*mune ni osamechatta}.*
(**b**) I wanted to say "no," but I swallowed my words and kept silent.
嫌だと言いたかったが、その言葉を{飲

み込んで/胸に納めて/*飲んで}沈黙を守った。
*Iya da to ii-takatta ga, sono kotoba o {nomi-konde/mune ni osamete/*nonde} chinmoku o mamotta.*

2. ⟨-o⟩ **so⌈no-mama shi⌈nji⌉ru** ⟨〜を⟩そのまま信じる ② **[for s.o. to take s.o. else's word at face value]**

EX. Not realizing that he was a swindler, she swallowed his story whole.
彼がペテン師だということに気がつかず、彼女は彼の話をそのまま信じた。
Kare ga peten-shi da to iu koto ni ki ga tsukazu, kanojo wa kare no hanashi o sono-mama shinjita.

swallow[2] n. **[a small migratory bird with a forked tail]**
tsu⌈bame つばめ

EX. Swallows are gone for the winter but come back in the spring.
つばめは冬の間いなくなるが、春またここに来る。
Tsubame wa fuyu no aida inaku naru ga, haru mata koko ni kuru.

swamp n. **[an area of wet, spongy land]**
nu⌈ma-chi 沼地 **[an area of wet land covered with deep mud]** ⟪**bogland, marshland, swampland**⟫, **shi⌈tchi** 湿地 •c **[an area of moist/wet land]** ⟪**bog**⟫

swan n.
ha⌈kuchoo 白鳥 •c

EX. Have you ever seen the ballet "*Swan Lake*"?
『白鳥の湖』というバレエを見たことがありますか。
"Hakuchoo no mizuumi" to iu baree o mita koto ga arimasu ka.

swarm n. **[a large (moving) mass of insects (esp. bees)]**
(ko⌈nchuu no) mu⌈re⌉ (昆虫の)群れ **[a large mass (of insects)]**, **(ko⌈nchuu no) ta⌈igun** (昆虫の)大群 •c **[a large moving mass of insects (esp. bees)]**

EX. In the woods I was attacked by a swarm of bees.
林の中で私ははちの{群れ/大群}に襲われた。
Hayashi no naka de watashi wa hachi no {mure/taigun} ni osowa-reta.

— vi. **[for insects (esp. bees) to gather (and fly off) in a large number]**
⟨-ni⟩ **mu⌈raga⌉ru** ⟨〜に⟩群がる ① **[for insects/people to gather in a large number in one place]** ⟪**crowd, throng, flock**⟫

EX. (**a**) Bees were swarming around the flowers.
みつばちが花の周りに群がっていた。
Mitsu-bachi ga hana no mawari ni muragatte ita.
(**b**) Reporters were swarming around the entrance of the hotel.
記者がホテルの入り口に群がっていた。
Kisha ga hoteru no iri-guchi ni muragatte ita.

2. mu⌈raga⌉tte to⌈nde iku 群がって飛んで行く ① **[for insects (esp. bees) to gather in a large number and fly off]**

3. u⌉yo-uyo-shite iru うようよしている /⟨V *te iru* of *uyo-uyo-suru* ③ gather in a large number/ ② **[for insects/worms to gather in a large number and crawl among each other slowly]**

swear vi. **[for s.o. to make a solemn pledge (by invoking God/the Bible) or to curse]**
1. ({**ka⌉mi/se⌉isho**} **ni ka⌉kete**) **chi⌈ka⌉u** ({神/聖書}に掛けて)誓う ① **[for s.o. to make a solemn pledge (by invoking God/the Bible)]**

EX. He swore an oath of loyalty to his company.
彼は会社への忠誠を誓った。
Kare wa kaisha e no chuusei o chikatta.

2. ze⌈ttai ni 絶対に •c **[an adverb that indicates the speaker/writer's strong assertion about s.t.]** ⟪**absolutely, positively, unconditionally**⟫

EX. A: You haven't returned my money to me yet.
まだお金を返してもらっていないよ。
Mada o-kane o kaeshite moratte inai yo.
B: I swear I returned it.
絶対に返したよ。
Zettai ni kaeshita yo.
A: I swear you haven't.
絶対に返してもらっていないよ。

S

| *Zettai ni kaeshite moratte inai yo.*

3. ⟨-o⟩ no⌈noshi⌉ru ⟨～を⟩ののしる ① [for s.o. to criticize or attack s.o. using foul language] ⟪**speak ill of, call names, rail against**⟫, **⟨-ni⟩ a⌈kutai o tsu⌉ku ⟨～に⟩悪態をつく ① [for s.o. to use abusive language against s.o.]** ⟪**call s.o. bad names**⟫

EX. | Daniel swore at his opponent after he lost the tennis game.
ダニエルはテニスの試合に負けて、相手{をののしった/に悪態をついた}。
Danieru wa tenisu no shiai ni makete, aite {o nonoshitta/ni akutai o tsuita}.

sweat n.
a⌉se 汗

— vi. **[for skin/a skin-like surface to give off (salty) moisture in droplets ⟪fig. "work very hard"⟫]**

1. a⌉se o ka⌉ku 汗をかく ① [for s.o./s.a. to give off (salty) moisture through the pores of the skin ⟪fig. "manifest surface moisture"⟫] ⟪**perspire**⟫

EX. | (**a**) I sweat a lot when I exercise.
私は運動をすると、たくさん汗をかく。
Watashi wa undoo o suru to, takusan ase o kaku.
(**b**) The high humidity caused the wall to sweat.
湿気が高くて壁が汗をかいた。
Shikke ga takakute kabe ga ase o kaita.
(**c**) John was sweating with anxiety as he awaited Wendy's answer to his proposal of marriage.
結婚の申し込みに対するウエンディの返事を待ちながら、ジョンは心配で汗をかいていた。
Kekkon no mooshi-komi ni-taisuru Uendii no henji o machi-nagara, Jon wa shinpai de ase o kaite ita.

2. a⌉se-mizu na⌈ga⌉shite ha⌈taraku 汗水流して働く ① [for s.o. to work so hard as to give off sweat], mu⌉ri o suru 無理をする ③ •c [for s.o./s.a. to do s.t. unreasonable/forcibly] ⟪**strain oneself, overwork**⟫

sweater n.
se⌉etaa セーター •f

EX. | Autumn is the season for sweaters.
秋はセーターの季節だ。
Aki wa seetaa no kisetsu da.

Sweden n.
Su⌈e⌉eden スエーデン •f

Swedish adj. **[of Sweden/the Swedish language/the Swedish people]**

1. Su⌈eeden-ji⌉n no N スエーデン人のN •f+c [of a Swedish person or the people of Sweden]

2. Su⌈eeden-go no N スエーデン語のN •f+c [of the language of Sweden]

3. Su⌈e⌉eden no N スエーデンのN •f [of Sweden]

— n. **[the people/language of Sweden]**

1. Su⌈eeden-ji⌉n スエーデン人 •f+c [a Swedish person or the people of Sweden]

2. Su⌈eeden-go スエーデン語 •f+c [the language of Sweden]

sweep vt. **[to clear/clean a place with a broom ⟪fig. "clear s.t. with a sweeping motion," "win overwhelmingly"⟫]**

1. ⟨-o⟩ so⌈oji-suru ⟨～を⟩掃除する ③ •c [for s.o. to rid a place of dirt and dust by sweeping, mopping, dusting, etc.] ⟪**clean, dust**⟫, **⟨-o⟩ ha⌉ku ⟨～を⟩掃く ① [for s.o. to clear/clean an area with a broom]**

EX. | I swept my room before the party.
パーティーの前に部屋を{掃除した/掃いた}。
Paatii no mae ni heya o {sooji-shita/haita}.

2. ⟨-o⟩ i⌈ssoo-suru ⟨～を⟩一掃する ③ •c [for s.o./s.t. to clean s.t. with a sweeping motion] ⟪**clear away, wipe out, get rid of**⟫

EX. | The strong wind swept away the polluted air from over the city.
町の上の汚れた空気を強い風が一掃した。
Machi no ue no yogoreta kuuki o tsuyoi kaze ga issoo-shita.

3. ren⌈shoo-suru 連勝する ③ •c

EX. | Our team swept the three-game series.
我々のチームが三連戦に連勝した。
Ware-ware no chiimu ga san-rensen ni renshoo-shita.

— vi. **[to clear/clean a place with a broom «fig. "pass with speed and gracefulness," "reach/extend in a long graceful curve"»] so⌈oji-suru 掃除する ③ •c, ha⌉ku 掃く ①** SEE sweep vt. 1

PHRASE: sweep down *fuki-orosu* 吹き下ろす ①

EX. A cold wind swept down from the mountain.
冷たい風が山から吹き下ろしてきた。
Tsumetai kaze ga yama kara fuki-oroshite kita.

PHRASE: sweep through *matataku ma ni moe-hirogaru* 瞬く間に燃え広がる ①

EX. The fire swept through the abandoned warehouse.
火事は使われなくなった倉庫全体に瞬く間に燃え広がった。
Kaji wa tsukawa-renaku natta sooko zentai ni matataku mani moe-hirogatta.

sweeping adj. **[that sweeps]**

1. **i⌈ssoo-suru** (N) **一掃する**(N) **[s.t. that cleans s.t. with a sweeping motion]** SEE sweep vt. 2

2. **hi⌈ro⌉i 広い** adj(*i*). **[extensive in terms of two-dimensional space/knowledge/vision//intellect] «wide, broad, spacious»**

3. **te⌈ttei-tekina 徹底的な** adj(*na*). **•c [doing s.t. completely/perfectly] «thorough, exhaustive, complete»**

EX. Our party is in need of sweeping reform.
わが党は徹底的な改革が必要だ。
Waga too wa tettei-tekina kaikaku ga hitsuyoo da.

4. **o⌈oza⌉ppana 大雑把な** adj(*na*). **[not concerned with details] «rough, sketchy»**

EX. He has a tendency to make sweeping generalizations.
あの人は大雑把な一般化をしがちだ。
Ano hito wa oozappana ippan-ka o shi-gachi da.

sweet adj. **[having the taste of sugar «fig. "for a smell/sound/appearance/character/utterance to be pleasant"»]**

1. **a⌈mai 甘い** adj(*i*). **[having the taste of sugar «fig. "too soft," "too optimistic," "lenient," "for a sound/appearance/utterance to be pleasant"»] «soft, indulgent, too optimistic, lenient» ↔ karai 辛い** adj(*i*).

EX. (**a**) This drink is too sweet for me.
この飲み物は私には甘すぎる。
Kono nomi-mono wa watashi ni wa ama-sugiru.
(**b**) I like my coffee sweet.
コーヒーは甘い方がいい。
Koohii wa amai hoo ga ii.
(**c**) I like her because she has such a sweet voice.
あの女の子はとても甘い声をしているので好きだ。
Ano onna-no-ko wa totemo amai koe o shite iru node suki da.
(**d**) The sweet strains of a waltz wafted up to us from the dance hall below.
ワルツの甘い調べが下のフロアから聞こえてきた。
Warutsu no amai shirabe ga shita no furoa kara kikoete kita.

2. **i⌉i いい** adj(*i*). **[morally correct/satisfactory/agreeable] «good, nice, fine, excellent, beautiful, suitable», shi⌉nsetsuna 親切な** adj(*na*). **•c [for s.o. to be thoughtful of the needs of other people] «kind, good, friendly, nice, kindhearted»**

EX. A: I'll give you a ride to your home.
うちまで乗せて行ってあげるよ。
Uchi made nosete itte ageru yo.
B: Oh, how sweet of you!
{いい人ね/親切ね}、あなたって。
{Ii hito ne/Shinsetsu ne}, anata tte.

— n.**[s.t. which has the taste of sugar] a⌈mai-mono 甘い物 «sweets», kya⌉ndee キャンデー «candy»**

EX. Don't eat too many sweets! You'll put on weight!
あんまり{甘い物/キャンデー}を、食べちゃだめよ。太るわよ。
Anmari {amai mono/kyandee} o tabecha dame yo. Futoru wa yo.

sweetheart n. **[a (female) lover (used sometimes as a term of endearment)]**

1. **ko⌈i-bito 恋人 [a person one loves] «lover»**

NOTE: *Koi-bito* is usually an unmarried person whom an unmarried person loves. The English "mistress" is *aijin* in Japanese.

EX. Our son married his high school sweetheart.
息子は高校の時からの恋人と結婚した。
Musuko wa kookoo no toki kara no koi-bito to kekkon-shita.

2. a⌈na⌉ta あなた [the second person singular pronoun used to refer to one's equal, esp. one's husband, or to a conversational partner of inferior social rank or to a general audience such as in a survey]

NOTE: When *anata* is used by a wife to her husband, it typically implies endearment.

EX. Dinner is ready, sweetheart.
あなた、御飯が出来ましたよ。
Anata, gohan ga dekimashita yo.

swell vi. **[to become larger from within 《fig. "bulge," "increase in number/quantity/ acoustic volume/emotion," "puff up"》]**

1. fu⌈kuramu 膨らむ ① [to become round and large due to pressure from within 《fig. "for an idea/plan/hope to increase in size"》] ⟪expand, be inflated, bulge⟫, o⌉okiku naru 大きくなる ① [to become larger in volume/ area/height]

S

EX. If you put a sponge in water, it will swell.
海綿を水に入れると{膨らむ/大きくなる}。
Kaimen o mizu ni ireru to {fukuramu/ ookiku naru}.

2. fu⌈e⌉ru 増える ② [to become greater in amount/number] ⟪increase, gain, multiply, rise, breed⟫

EX. After a week's rain, the river swelled to twice its normal level.
一週間続きの雨で川の水かさがいつもの倍に増えた。
Is-shuukan-tsuzuki no ame de kawa no mizu-kasa ga itsu-mo no bai ni fueta.

3. (⟨-de⟩) mu⌈ne⌉ ga i⌈ppai ni na⌉ru (⟨～で⟩) 胸がいっぱいになる ① [for one's heart to be filled with emotion]

EX. When I met my old grade school teacher after not having seen her for twenty years my heart swelled with emotion.
二十年ぶりに小学校時代の先生に会った時、こみ上げてくる感情で胸がいっぱいになった。
Ni-juu-nen-buri ni shoogakkoo-jidai no sensei ni atta toki, komi-agete kuru kanjoo de mune ga ippai ni natta.

4. u⌈nu-boreru うぬぼれる ② [for s.o. to become proud of oneself, believing that she/he is better than she/he actually is] ⟪have a swelled head, flatter oneself, become puffed up⟫

PHRASE: swell up *fukuramu* 膨らむ ①, *ookiku naru* 大きくなる ①

EX. The bruise swelled up quite a bit.
傷がかなり{膨らんだ/大きくなった}。
Kizu ga kanari {fukuranda/ookiku natta}.

swift adj. **[moving or happening quickly] ha⌈ya⌉i はやい** adj(*i*). **[taking less time than is normal or expected or occurring at a point in time prior to what is normal or expected] ⟪early, speedy, fast, quick⟫**
㊮ "early"▷早い, "fast"▷速い

EX. (**a**) His decisions are always swift.
あの人はいつも決断が速い。
Ano hito wa itsu-mo ketsudan ga hayai.
(**b**) The current in this river is extremely swift.
この川の流れはとても速い。
Kono kawa no nagare wa totemo hayai.

swim vi. **[for s.o./s.a. to move through water by moving the arms/legs/fins 《fig. "move as if by swimming," "float," "be flooded"》]**

1. o⌈yo⌉gu 泳ぐ ① [for s.o./s.a. to move through water by moving the arms/legs/ fins 《fig. "get along," "totter"》] ⟪get along, totter⟫

EX. A: Can you swim?
泳げますか。
Oyoge-masu ka.
B: Yes, in fact I swim every day at the pool.
ええ、実はプールで毎日泳いでいるんです。

Ee, jitsu wa puuru de mai-nichi oyoide iru n desu.

2. u⌈kabu 浮かぶ ① [for s.t. to be suspended in air, gas, or on the surface of a liquid by the force of buoyancy so that its outline is visible to an observer《fig. "come across one's mind," "rise in the world"》]《float》, u⌈ku 浮く ① [to be held up in air/gas/liquid or on the surface of a liquid by the force of buoyancy《fig. "be isolated/separated from"》]《float》↔ shizumu 沈む ①

EX. A tiny object was swimming in the water.
小さい物が水に{浮かんで/浮いて}いた。
Chiisai mono ga mizu ni {ukande/uite} ita.

3. a⌈fure⌉ru あふれる ② [for s.t. to be filled to the extent of spilling over]《overflow, brim over, flood》

EX. Mary's eyes swam with tears.
メアリーの目には涙があふれた。
Mearii no me ni wa namida ga afureta.

swimmer n. **[a person who swims]**

NOTE: There is no Japanese word corresponding to the English "swimmer," which can be translated in many ways using the verb *oyogu* "to swim." See also the following.

PHRASE: to be a good swimmer *oyogu no ga joozu da* 泳ぐのが上手だ

EX. Yukiko is a good swimmer.
由紀子は泳ぐのが上手です。
Yukiko wa oyogu no ga joozu desu.

NOTE: The above example sentence cannot be translated as **Yukiko wa joozuni oyogu hito desu.* The same is true of other sentences with similar meanings such as the following. *Piano ga joozu desu ne.* "You are a good pianist, aren't you?" *Hanashi ga o-joozu desu nee.* "You are a good speaker, aren't you?"

swimming n. **[an act of swimming]**

o⌈yogi 泳ぎ /〈V *masu* of *oyogu* ① swim〉/, su⌈iei 水泳 •c

EX. I like swimming very much.
私は{泳ぎ/水泳/泳ぐ{の/こと}}が大好きです。
Watashi wa {oyogi/suiei/oyogu {no/koto}} ga dai-suki desu.

NOTE: "*Oyogu {no/koto}*" is a verb which has been nominalized.

swing vi. **[to move backward and forward or from side to side in a regular rhythm《fig. "walk as if swinging," "be suspended," "turn on a swivel," "move on a swing"》]**

1. yu⌈reru 揺れる ② [for an object/mind to move up and down or from side to side《fig. "be disturbed"》]《shake, sway, quake, pitch, roll, rock, toss, vibrate, jolt》

EX. The tall building swung back and forth for a minute or so when the earthquake occurred.
その地震が起きた時、高層ビルは一分ぐらい揺れた。
Sono jishin ga okita toki, koosoo-biru wa ip-pun-gurai yureta.

2. i⌈sei yo⌉ku a⌈ru⌉ku 威勢よく歩く ① [for s.o. to walk as if swinging]

EX. The boy walked swinging down the street.
少年が通りを威勢よく歩いていった。
Shoonen ga toori o isei yoku aruite itta.

3. 〈-ni〉 bu⌈ra-sagaru 〈〜に〉ぶら下がる ① [to hang down from s.t.]《hang down from, dangle from》

EX. A cat was swinging from the branch of a tree.
猫が木の枝にぶら下がっていた。
Neko ga ki no eda ni bura-sagatte ita.

4. gu⌈ru⌉tto ma⌈waru ぐるっと回る ①

EX. The door swung open.
ドアがぐるっと回って開いた。
Doa ga gurutto mawatte aita.

— vt. **[to cause s.t./s.o. to swing]**

1. 〈-o〉 fu⌈ru 〈〜を〉振る ① [for s.o./s.a. to cause s.t. to move/tremble quickly back and forth, up and down《fig. "sprinkle"》]《wave, shake》, 〈-o〉 yu⌈suru 〈〜を〉揺する ① [to move s.t./s.o./s.a. backward and forward, with regular rhythm]《rock, roll》

EX. (a) My child likes to be swung from my arms.
うちの子は私の腕で{揺すられる/*振られる}のが好きだ。
Uchi no ko wa watashi no ude de

S

*{yusura-reru/*fura-reru} no ga suki da.*
(**b**) The batter struck out without swinging the bat once.
打者は一度もバットを{振らない/*揺すらない}で三振してしまった。
*Dasha wa ichi-do mo batto o {furanai/ *yusuranai} de sanshin-shite shimatta.*

2. ⟨-o⟩ fu⌈ri-mawa⌉su ⟨～を⟩振り回す ① [for s.o. to hold s.t. on its end and cause it to move around and around] ⟪brandish, throw about, sway⟫

EX. Don't swing your umbrella. It's dangerous.
傘を振り回してはいけません。危ないでしょ。
Kasa o furi-mawashite wa ikemasen. Abunai desho.

3. ⟨-o⟩ tsu⌈rusu ⟨～を⟩つるす ① [for s.o. to fasten s.t. at the top using a string or similar material so that the lower part is free in the air] ⟪suspend, sling, dangle⟫

EX. I swung the laundry over the clothesline to dry.
洗濯物を干すためにひもにつるした。
Sentaku-mono o hosu tame ni himo ni tsurushita.

— n. **[an act of swinging ⟪fig. "manner of striking a ball with a golf club/baseball bat," "walking as if by swinging," "swinging rhythm," "a kind of jazz"⟫]**

1. fu⌈ru koto 振ること [the act of shaking s.t. while holding it on its end], fu⌈ri-mawa⌉su koto 振り回すこと [moving s.t. repeatedly around while holding it on its end]

2. fu⌈ri-kata 振り方 /⟨V*masu* of *furu* ① swing + *kata* manner/ [manner of swinging s.t.], su⌈i⌉ngu スイング •f [the way one swings a baseball bat/golf club or a type of jazz]

EX. The swing of the club was OK, but the ball didn't go far.
クラブの{振り方/スイング}はよかったが、ボールは遠くに飛ばなかった。
Kurabu no {furi-kata/suingu} wa yokatta ga, booru wa tooku ni tobanakatta.

3. cho⌈oshi no i⌉i a⌈ruki-kata 調子のいい歩き方 [walking as if by swinging]

Swiss n. **[the people of Switzerland]**
Su⌈isu⌉-jin スイス人 •f+c [a Swiss person or the people of Switzerland]

— adj. **[of Switzerland/the Swiss people]**
1. Su⌉isu no N スイスのN •f [of Switzerland]
2. Su⌈isu⌉-jin no N スイス人のN •f+c [of a Swiss person or the Swiss people]

swollen adj. **[having become larger due to pressure from within]**
fu⌈kuranda N 膨らんだN /⟨Vinf. past of *fukuramu* ① swell/ [having become round and large due to pressure from within] ⟪blown up, bulging⟫, ha⌈reta N はれたN /⟨Vinf. past of *hareru* ② swell/ [for a part of the skin to have become large due to inflammation or an external blow]

EX. My finger became swollen after being hit by the ball.
ボールが強く当たったので、指が{膨らんだ/はれた}。
Booru ga tsuyoku atatta node, yubi ga {fukuranda/hareta}.

sword n. **[a long, sharp pointed blade with a hilt and a sharp edge on one or both sides]**
1. ka⌈tana⌉ 刀 [a long pointed blade with a hilt and a sharp edge on one side]
2. tsu⌈rugi⌉ 剣 [a long pointed blade with a hilt and a sharp edge on both sides]

syllabary n. **[a set/table of written characters, such as Japanese hiragana, representing syllables in a language]**
o⌈nsetsu-moji-hyo⌉o 音節文字表 •c

syllable n.
o⌈nsetsu 音節 •c

EX. A Japanese *haiku* is made up of three lines of five, seven, and five syllables each, as in *Fu-ru-i-ke-ya, ka-wa-zu to-bi-ko-mu mi-zu-no-o-to* ("An old pond, a frog jumps in, with a splash").
日本の俳句は「古池や、かわず飛び込む、水の音」のように、五ー七ー五の音節から出来ている。
Nihon no haiku wa 'Furuike ya,

kawazu tobi-komu, mizu no oto' no yooni, go-shichi-go no onsetsu kara dekite iru.

symbol n. **[s.t. (concrete) that stands for s.t. (abstract)]**

1. sho⌈ochoo 象徴 •c [s.t. concrete that stands for s.t. abstract] ((emblem)), **shi⌉nboru シンボル •f**

EX. A dove is a symbol of peace.
はとは平和の{象徴/シンボル}だ。
Hato wa heiwa no {shoochoo/shinboru} da.

2. ki⌈goo 記号 [a mark/letter/abbreviation that stands for s.t.] ((mark, sign, emblem))

EX. ¥ is the symbol for the Japanese monetary unit.
¥は日本の貨幣単位を表わす記号だ。
¥ wa Nihon no kahei-tan'i o arawasu kigoo da.

sympathy n. **[the state of having the same feeling as that of another person]**

1. do⌈ojoo 同情 •c [sensitivity to and understanding of the sufferings of others], a⌈waremi 哀れみ /〈Vmasu of *awaremu* ① show pity/ [a feeling of pity for a person who suffers] ((compassion, mercy, pity))

EX. (**a**) Many people sent John letters of sympathy when he lost his wife.
妻を亡くした時、ジョンのところにはたくさんの人から{同情/?哀れみ}の手紙が届いた。
Tsuma o nakushita toki, Jon no tokoro ni wa takusan no hito kara {doojoo/?awaremi} no tegami ga todoita.
(**b**) I don't like people who beg for sympathy.
{同情/哀れみ}を乞う人は嫌いだ。
{Doojoo/Awaremi} o kou hito wa kirai da.

2. kyo⌈okan 共感 •c [the same feeling as that felt by another person] ((empathy)), **sa⌈nsei 賛成 •c [being in agreement with s.o.'s opinion/idea/suggestion]** ((approval, agreement, support))

EX. (**a**) I am in sympathy with those who advocate a policy of increasing domestic consumption.
私は国内消費を増やす政策の主張者に{賛成/*共感}です。
*Watashi wa kokunai-shoohi o fuyasu seisaku no shuchoo-sha ni {sansei/*kyookan} desu.*
(**b**) Ecologists tend to have a strong sense of sympathy with nature.
生態学者は自然に対して強い{共感/*賛成}を持つ傾向がある。
*Seitai-gakusha wa shizen ni-taishite tsuyoi {kyookan/*sansei} o motsu keikoo ga aru.*

symphony n.

ko⌈okyo⌉o-kyoku 交響曲 •c, shi⌉nfonii シンフォニー •f

EX. In Japan, Beethoven's *9th Symphony* is often played towards the end of the year.
日本ではベートーベンの第九{交響曲/シンフォニー}がよく年末に演奏される。
Nihon de wa Beetooben no dai-ku {kookyoo-kyoku/shinfonii} ga yoku nen-matsu ni ensoo-sareru.

symptom n. **[s.t. that indicates the existence/occurrence of s.t. else]**

shi⌈rushi 印 [s.t. visual that serves to distinguish s.t. from other things or to signify s.t.] ((sign, mark, symbol, proof, indicators)), **cho⌈okoo 兆候 •c [s.t. that indicates the occurrence of s.t. else]** ((sign, indicator)), **sho⌉ojo⌉o 症状 •c [conditions accompanying a disease/injury]**

EX. (**a**) Were there any symptoms of recession in the economy at that time?
そのころ不況の{印/兆候/*症状}が何かあったんですか。
*Sono koro fukyoo no {shirushi/chookoo/*shoojoo} ga nani-ka atta n desu ka.*
(**b**) This is a definite symptom of a heart attack.
これは間違いなく心臓発作の{兆候/症状/*印}です。
*Kore wa machigai-naku shinzoo-hossa no {chookoo/shoojoo/*shirushi} desu.*

synagogue n.

Yu⌈daya-kyookaidoo ユダヤ教会堂 •c

S

synonym n. **[a different word with a similar meaning]**
do⌈oi⌉-go 同意語 •c, do⌈ogi⌉-go 同義語 •c ↔ igi-go 異義語 •c

EX. The words "quick" and "speedy" are said to be synonyms.
"quick" と "speedy" は{同義語/同意語}だと言われる。
"Quick" to "speedy" wa {doogi-go/dooi-go} da to iwa-reru

syrup n.
shi⌉roppu シロップ •f

system n. **[an interrelated and interconnected group of things forming a whole《fig. "method underlying a system"》]**
so⌉shiki 組織 •c [group of interconnected humans/cells]《organization, formation, structure》, ta⌈ikei 体系 •c [a group of facts/entities ordered by some principle into a larger whole, esp. that constituting a field of knowledge]《organization》, se⌉ido 制度 •c [a set of rules/regulations that govern a nation/group]《institution, organization》, shi⌉sutemu システム •f

EX. (**a**) The system of labor unions is different in Japan and America.
日米の労働組合の{組織/制度/システム/*体系}は違う。
*Nichi-Bei no roodoo-kumiai no {soshiki/seido/?shisutemu/*taikei} wa chigau.*
(**b**) The grammatical systems of Korean and Japanese are very similar.
日本語と韓国語の文法の{体系/組織/?システム/*制度}は大変似ている。
*Nihon-go to Kankoku-go no bunpoo no {taikei/soshiki/?shisutemu/*seido} wa taihen nite iru.*
(**c**) The post-war educational system of Japan is patterned after the American system.
戦後の日本の教育{制度/システム/*体系/*組織}はアメリカに倣っている。
*Sengo no Nihon no kyooiku-{seido/shisutemu/*taikei/*soshiki} wa Amerika ni naratte iru.*

T

table n. **[a piece of furniture with a flat top supported by one or more legs《fig. "a flat land," "a compact list"》]**
1. sho⌈kutaku 食卓 •c [a piece of furniture for eating on consisting of a flat top with legs], te⌈eburu テーブル •f [a Western-style piece of furniture with a flat top for eating on]

EX. We sat down at the table to eat at about 6:30 P.M.
私たちは食事をするために六時半ごろ{食卓/テーブル}についた。
Watashi-tachi wa shokuji o suru tame ni roku-ji-han-goro {shokutaku/teeburu} ni tsuita.

2. shu⌈jutsu-dai 手術台 •c [a flat slab for surgical operations]
3. hyo⌈o 表 •c [a set of facts or figures presented in an orderly written form for quick and easy comprehension]

EX. Please refer to Table 5 on page 105.
105ページの第五表を参照してください。
Hyaku-go-peeji no dai-go-hyoo o sanshoo-shite kudasai.

PHRASE: table tennis *takkyuu* 卓球 •c, *pinpon* ピンポン •f

EX. A: How about a game of table tennis?
{卓球/ピンポン}をしようか?
{Takkyuu/Pinpon} o shiyoo ka.
B: Yes, let's.
うん、しよう。
Un, shiyoo.

tack n. **[a short nail with a broad, flat head 《fig. "direction of a boat," "policy"》]**
1. byo˥o びょう •c [a short nail or pin]
2. shi˥nro 進路 •c [the direction or route which s.o./s.t. intends to or is expected to take 《fig. "direction in life"》] 《course》
3. se˹isaku 政策 •c [a guiding principle used in making decisions by a government, party, or individual] 《policy》
—— vt. **[for s.o. to attach s.t. with a short nail or pin]**
〈-o〉 byo˥o de to˹meru 〈～を〉びょうで留める ② [for s.o. to attach s.t. with a short nail or pin]

EX. I tacked a note to his door asking him to give me a call.
彼の部屋のドアに私に電話してほしいとのメモをびょうで留めておいた。
Kare no heya no doa ni watashi ni denwa-shite hoshii to no memo o byoo de tomete oita.

tackle n. **[a pulley or pulley-like apparatus used to raise or move heavy weights 《fig. "seizing and forcing to the ground one's opponent in rugby or football"》]**
1. ka˹ssha 滑車 •c [a pulley]
2. tsu˹ri-do˥ogu 釣り道具 [fishing apparatus]
3. ta˥kkuru タックル •f [seizing and forcing to the ground one's opponent in football]
—— vi./vt. **[for s.o. to seize and stop s.o./s.a. by bringing him/her/it to the ground or to undertake a difficult task]**
1. 〈-ni〉 ta˥kkuru-suru 〈～に〉タックルする ③ •f [for a football/rugby player to grasp an opponent around the legs and stop him from advancing further by bringing him to the ground]

EX. The quarterback injured his leg when he was tackled.
クォーターバックはタックルされた時、足にけがをした。
Kuootaabakku wa takkuru-sareta toki, ashi ni kega o shita.

2. 〈-to〉 to˹ri-kumu 〈～と〉取り組む ① [to wrestle with s.o./s.t.] 《wrestle with, come to grips with》

EX. A government panel is currently tackling the issue of how to strengthen the finances of the social security system.
政府の審議会は今社会保障制度の財政をどうやって強化するかという問題に取り組んでいる。
Seifu no shingi-kai wa ima shakai-hoshoo-seido no zaisei o doo yatte kyooka-suru ka to iu mondai ni tori-kunde iru.

tag n. **[a paper or other label attached to s.t. to identify it or give information about it] fu˹da 札 [a piece of wood, paper, or fabric on which information of some kind is displayed] 《card, label, board, ticket》, ni˥-fuda 荷札 [a piece of paper or other material fixed to a package displaying the name and address of the sender and the addressee] 《a tie-on-label》, sho˹o-fuda 正札 [a piece of paper displaying the price of s.t.] 《price-tag》**

EX. (**a**) Please attach this tag to your suitcase.
スーツケースにこの{札/?荷札/*正札}を付けてください。
*Suutsukeesu ni kono {fuda/?ni-fuda/ *shoo-fuda} o tsukete kudasai.*
(**b**) Please write your name and affiliation on your name tag.
{名札/*正札/*荷札}にお名前と所属をお書きください。
*{Na-fuda/*Shoo-fuda/*Ni-fuda} ni o-namae to shozoku o o-kaki kudasai.*
(**c**) There were no price tags attached to the merchandise.
商品には{正札/?札/*荷札}が付いていませんでした。
*Shoohin ni wa {shoo-fuda/?fuda/*ni-fuda} ga tsuite imasen deshita.*

—— vt. **[for s.o. to attach a small label or label-like object to s.t.]**
〈-ni〉 fu˹da o tsuke˥ru 〈～に〉札を付ける ② [for s.o. to attach a piece of wood, paper, or fabric to s.t. which displays some kind of information about it], 〈-ni〉 ni˥-fuda o tsu˹ke˥ru 〈～に〉荷札を付ける ② [for s.o. to attach a tie-on label to s.t.], 〈-ni〉 sho˹o˥-

T

fuda o tsu⌈ke⌉ru 〈～に〉正札を付ける ②[for s.o. to attach a piece of paper to s.t. which displays its price]

tail n. [a flexible appendage at the rear end of an animal's body《fig. "s.t. resembling such an appendage"》]

1. shi⌈ppo⌉ しっぽ [a flexible appendage at the rear end of the body of an animal, fish, or bird]《end》, o⌈ppo⌉ 尾っぽ, o⌉ 尾 [a flexible appendage at the rear end of the body of an animal, fish, or bird 〈w〉]《brush, scut》

EX. (**a**) My cat has a long tail.
うちの猫は{しっぽ/尾っぽ/??尾}が長いよ。
Uchi no neko wa {shippo/oppo/??o} ga nagai yo.
(**b**) Our dog was happily wagging its tail.
うちの犬がうれしそうに{しっぽ/尾っぽ/尾}を振っていた。
Uchi no inu ga ureshi-sooni {shippo/oppo/o} o futte ita.

2. su⌈isei no o⌉ すい星の尾 [a luminous trail behind a comet]

3. bi⌉bu 尾部 •c [the rear part of a plane]

— vt. [for s.o. to follow s.o. closely and secretly]

〈-o〉 bi⌈koo-suru 〈～を〉尾行する ③ •c [for s.o. to follow s.o. stealthily]《shadow, dog》

EX. The private detective tailed Mr. Yoshida at Mrs. Yoshida's request.
吉田さんの奥さんの依頼を受けて、探偵が吉田さんを尾行した。
Yoshida-san no oku-san no irai o ukete, tantei ga Yoshida-san o bikoo-shita.

tailor n. [a maker of men's clothes]

yo⌈ofuku-ya 洋服屋

EX. Today I went to a tailor to order a suit.
今日僕は洋服屋に行って背広を注文した。
Kyoo boku wa yoofuku-ya ni itte sebiro o chuumon-shita.

— vt. [for s.o. to cut, form, produce, or alter s.t. (esp. clothes) to fit s.o.'s body/needs]

1. fu⌈ku⌉ o shi⌈tate⌉ru 服を仕立てる ② [for s.o. to make clothes]

EX. I had my suit tailored at a department store.
私はデパートで背広を仕立ててもらいました。
Watashi wa depaato de sebiro o shitatete moraimashita.

2. 〈-o〉 sa⌈idan-suru 〈～を〉裁断する ③ •c [for s.o. to cut cloth or paper to a prescribed size《fig. "judge"》]

take vt. [for s.o. to grasp s.t. in one's hand; to get possession of s.t., esp. by force or skill; to subscribe to a publication, esp. a newspaper; to eat, drink, or swallow s.t., to choose s.t.; to transfer s.t. from a location or literary passage to another location; to think (wrongly) of s.t./s.o./s.a. as having a certain meaning or identity; to cause s.t./s.o./s.a. to come or go along with oneself to a place; for s.t. to require s.t., esp. time; for s.o. to use s.t. as a means of transportation to get to a place]

1. 〈-o〉 to⌉ru 〈～を〉とる ① [for s.o./s.a. to cause s.t./s.o./s.a. to come into one's possession]《pick up, hold, seize, get, obtain, secure, win, receive, choose, remove, catch, understand》, 〈-o〉 tsu⌈kamaeru 〈～を〉捕まえる ② [for s.o./s.a. to take hold of s.t./s.o./s.a. that is trying to flee/leave and try to prevent it/him/her from doing so]《catch, capture, seize》, 〈-o〉 tsu⌈ka⌉mu 〈～を〉つかむ ① [for s.o./s.a. to take hold of s.t./s.o./s.a. tightly, suddenly, and forcibly《fig. "understand"》]《grasp, seize, catch》, 〈-o〉 to⌈rae⌉ru 〈～を〉捕らえる ② [for s.o. to catch s.o./s.a.《fig. "comprehend"》]《catch, seize, grasp, lay hands on, capture》

㊥ "adopt"▷採る, "take a picture"▷撮る, "attend to"▷執る, "catch"▷捕る, otherwise ▷取る

EX. (**a**) There are some handouts in the back of the room. Please take one.
部屋の後ろの方にプリントがあります。どうぞ一部お{取り/*捕まえ/*つかみ/*捕らえ}ください。
Heya no ushiro no hoo ni purinto ga arimasu. Doozo ichi-bu o-{tori/

**tsukamae/*tsukami/*torae} kudasai.*
(**b**) The public health inspector took several cockroaches from the apartment for analysis in his laboratory.
公衆衛生検査官は実験室で分析するためにそのアパートでゴキブリを数匹{取った/捕まえた/?捕らえた/*つかんだ}。
*Kooshuu-eisei kensa-kan wa jikken-shitsu de bunseki-suru tame ni sono apaato de gokiburi o suu-hiki {totta/tsukamaeta/?toraeta/*tsukanda}.*
(**c**) The policeman took the thief to jail.
警官は泥棒を{捕まえて/捕らえて/*つかんで/*取って}拘置所に入れた。
*Keikan wa doroboo o {tsukamaete/toraete/*tsukande/*totte} koochi-sho ni ireta.*
(**d**) All of a sudden Henry took my arm and began to dance with me.
ヘンリーは突然私の腕を{つかんで/取って/*捕まえて/*捕らえて}踊りだした。
*Henrii wa totsuzen watashi no ude o {tsukande/totte/*tsukamaete/*toraete} odori-dashita.*

2. (⟨-kara⟩) ⟨-o⟩ to˥ru (⟨〜から⟩)⟨〜を⟩とる ① SEE take 1, **(⟨-kara⟩) ⟨-o⟩ nu˥su˥mu (⟨〜から⟩)⟨〜を⟩盗む ① [for s.o. to cause to come into one's possession s.t. that belongs to another without permission or by illegal means] ⟪steal, rob⟫**

EX. (**a**) I wonder who could have taken my purse.
だれが私の財布を{とった/盗んだ}んだろう?
Dare ga watashi no saifu o {totta/nusunda} n daroo?
(**b**) Someone took my stereo set while I was out.
私は留守中にだれかにステレオを{とられた/盗まれた}。
Watashi wa rusu-chuu ni dare-ka ni sutereo o {tora-reta/nusuma-reta}.
(**c**) A thief took from the man all the money he had.
泥棒がその男からあり金を全部{とった/盗んだ}。
Dorobooga sono otoko kara ari-gane o zenbu {totta/nusunda}.

3. ⟨-o⟩ ka˥kutoku-suru ⟨〜を⟩獲得する ③ •c [for s.o. to succeed in getting hold of s.t. valued and abstract with effort] ⟪acquire, obtain, secure, gain, get⟫, ⟨-o⟩ te˥ ni ireru ⟨〜を⟩手に入れる ② [for s.o. to get hold of s.t.] ⟪get, get hold of, obtain, come by, secure, win⟫

EX. Mary took first prize in the literary contest with her short story.
メリーはその短編小説で文学コンクールの一等賞を{獲得した/手に入れた}。
Merii wa sono tanpen-shoosetsu de bungaku-konkuuru no it-too-shoo o {kakutoku-shita/te ni ireta}.

4. ⟨-o⟩ to˥ru ⟨〜を⟩とる ① SEE take 1, **⟨-o⟩ ko˥odoku-suru ⟨〜を⟩購読する ③ •c [for s.o. to pay to receive a newspaper/magazine regularly] ⟪subscribe to⟫**

EX. A: Which newspaper do you take?
どの新聞を{取って/購読して}いますか。
Dono shinbun o {totte/koodoku-shite} imasu ka.
B: I take the *New York Times*.
「ニューヨークタイムズ」を取っています。
"Nyuuyooku-taimuzu" o totte imasu.

5. ⟨-o⟩ ta˥be˥ru ⟨〜を⟩食べる ② [for s.o./s.a. to put s.t. edible into one's mouth, chew, and swallow it] ⟪eat, live on, subsist on, taste⟫, ⟨-o⟩ toru ⟨〜を⟩とる SEE take 1

EX. We recessed briefly at noon to take a light lunch.
昼ごろ少し休憩をして{軽い昼食をとった/簡単なお昼御飯を食べた}。
Hiru-goro sukoshi kyuukei o shite {karui chuushoku o totta/kantanna o-hiru-gohan o tabeta}.

NOTE: *Toru* in the sense of "to eat" is used in formal context.

6. ⟨-o⟩ no˥mu ⟨〜を⟩飲む ① [for s.o./s.a. to put s.t. into one's body through the mouth without chewing it ⟪fig. "overwhelm," "suppress," "acquiesce"⟫] ⟪drink, swallow, gulp down, guzzle, make light of, accept as is⟫

EX. I took an aspirin for my severe headache.
頭がひどく痛かったんで、アスピリンを飲みました。
Atama ga hidoku itakatta n de, asupirin o nomimashita.

7. ⟨**-o**⟩ **e⌈ra⌉bu** ⟨～を⟩選ぶ ① **[for s.o./s.a. to single out s.t./s.o./s.a. out of several as being the most desirable for a particular purpose]** ⟪**choose, opt, elect, select**⟫

EX. Please take whichever flavor of ice cream you like.
どれでもいいですから、好きな種類のアイスクリームを選んでください。
Dore demo ii desu kara, sukina shurui no aisukuriimu o erande kudasai.

8. ⟨**-kara**⟩ ⟨**-o**⟩ **to⌉ru** ⟨～から⟩⟨～を⟩取る ⟪**quote**⟫ SEE take 1

EX. I took this sentence from the Bible.
この文は聖書から取りました。
Kono bun wa seisho kara torimashita.

9. (**sha⌈shin o**) **to⌉ru** (写真を)撮る ① **[for s.o. to photograph s.t./s.o./s.a.]**

EX. Let me take your picture.
写真を撮らせてください。
Shashin o tora-sete kudasai.

10. ⟨**-o**⟩ **u⌈ke⌉ru** ⟨～を⟩受ける ② **[to allow s.t. to come into one's possession or to be exposed to the effect of some force or action]** ⟪**receive, be given, obtain, catch, suffer, incur, sit for**⟫

EX. (**a**) I couldn't take the exam because I had a cold.
かぜをひいたのでその試験が受けられなかった。
Kaze o hiita node sono shiken ga uke-rarenakatta.
(**b**) The boxer took a heavy punch on his jaw.
ボクサーは強いパンチをあごに受けた。
Bokusaa wa tsuyoi panchi o ago ni uketa.
(**c**) I took piano lessons when I was in elementary school.
小学校の時ピアノのレッスンを受けた。
Shoo-gakkoo no toki piano no ressun o uketa.

11. (**-no ko⌈to⌉ o**) (**ma⌈chiga⌉tte**) ⟨**-to**⟩ **o⌈mo⌉u** (～のことを)(間違って)⟨～と⟩思う ① **[for s.o. to (wrongly) assume s.t./s.o./s.a. to have a certain identity or meaning]**

EX. (**a**) I took Jenny to be a decent young woman.
ジェニーを上品な女の子だと思った。
Jenii o joohinna onna-no-ko da to omotta.
(**b**) I mistakenly took Dan for a student.
私はダンを間違って学生だと思った。
Watashi wa Dan o machigatte gakusei da to omotta.

12. ⟨**-o**⟩ {⟨**-e**⟩/⟨**-ni**⟩} **tsu⌈rete-iku** ⟨～を⟩{⟨～へ⟩/⟨～に⟩}連れて行く ① **[for s.o. to go along with s.o./s.a. equal to/lower than oneself in status to a place],** ⟨**-o**⟩ {⟨**-e**⟩/⟨**-ni**⟩} **mo⌈tte-iku** ⟨～を⟩{⟨～へ⟩/⟨～に⟩}持って行く ① **[for s.o. to carry s.t. (with one) to a place]**

EX. (**a**) Last weekend I took my parents to a hot spring.
先週末、両親を温泉へ{連れて/*持って}行きました。
*Senshuu-matsu, ryooshin o onsen e {tsurete/*motte}-ikimashita.*
(**b**) It might rain today, so take your umbrella along with you to school.
今日は雨が降るかも知れないから、学校へ傘を{持って/*連れて}行きなさいよ。
*Kyoo wa ame ga furu kamoshirenai kara, gakkoo e kasa o {motte/*tsurete}-ikinasai yo.*

13. ⟨**-ni**⟩ **ka⌈ka⌉ru** ⟨～に⟩かかる ① **[for s.t. to extend to and come in contact with s.t. else** ⟪**fig. "hang," "cover," "begin," "be engaged in," "become splashed with," "be built," "require"**⟫**]** ⟪**hang, be locked, require, cost**⟫, **hi⌈tsuyoona** 必要な adj(*na*). **•c [essential for s.t./s.o./s.a.]** ⟪**necessary, needed, indispensable, call for**⟫

EX. (**a**) It took me four hours to drive to Osaka.
車で大阪まで四時間{かかった/?必要だった}。
Kuruma de Oosaka made yo-jikan {kakatta/?hitsuyoo datta}.
(**b**) This project is going to take more than

T

the six of us to accomplish.
このプロジェクトを完成するには私たち六人より多くの人が{必要/*かかる}でしょう。
*Kono purojekuto o kansei-suru ni wa watashi-tachi roku-nin yori ooku no hito ga {hitsuyoo/*kakaru} deshoo.*

14. ⟨-ni⟩ no⌈tte-{iku/ku⌉ru} ⟨〜に⟩乗って{行く ①/来る ③} **[for s.o. to use s.t. as a means of transportation to get to a place]**

EX. A: Which train did you take to get here?
ここまで来るのにどの電車に乗ってきましたか。
Koko made kuru no ni dono densha ni notte-kimashita ka.
B: I took the Yamanote Line.
山手線に乗ってきました。
Yamanote-sen ni notte-kimashita.

PHRASE: take a look ⟨*-o*⟩ *miru* ⟨〜を⟩見る ②

EX. Take a look at this. Someone wrote all over my paper.
ちょっとこれを見ろよ。だれかが僕のレポートにいっぱい書き込んでしまった。
Chotto kore o miro yo. Dare-ka ga boku no repooto ni ippai kaki-konde shimatta.

PHRASE: take a nap *hiru-ne o suru* 昼寝をする ③

EX. My father takes a nap every day.
父は毎日昼寝をします。
Chichi wa mai-nichi hiru-ne o shimasu.

PHRASE: take notice ⟨*-ni*⟩ *ki-ga-tsuku* ⟨〜に⟩気がつく ①

EX. He took notice of the fact that she wasn't wearing a wedding ring.
彼は彼女が結婚指輪をしていないことに気がついた。
Kare wa kanojo ga kekkon-yubiwa o shite inai koto ni ki-ga-tsuita.

PHRASE: take notes *nooto o toru* ノートを取る ①

EX. It's hard to take notes in Japanese.
日本語でノートを取るのは難しい。
Nihon-go de nooto o toru no wa muzukashii.

PHRASE: take away ⟨*-o*⟩ *motte iku* ⟨〜を⟩持って行く ① ⟪remove⟫

EX. I need these tools later so please don't take them away from here.
この道具は後で使うから外の所へ持って行かないでね。
Kono doogu wa ato de tsukau kara, hoka no tokoro e motte-ikanai de ne.

PHRASE: take off ⟨*-o*⟩ *nugu* ⟨〜を⟩脱ぐ ① ⟪remove⟫

EX. In Japan and Korea you have to take off your shoes when you enter a house.
日本や韓国では家に入る時に靴を脱がなくてはならない。
Nihon ya Kankoku de wa ie ni hairu toki ni kutsu o nuganakute wa naranai.

PHRASE: take off *dekakeru* 出かける ② ⟪leave the house, start off⟫

EX. I have to take off now, so I'll see you later.
もう出かけなくちゃ。じゃ、後で。
Moo dekakenakucha. Ja, ato de.

PHRASE: take off *ririku-suru* 離陸する ③ •c ↔ *chakuriku-suru* 着陸する ③ •c

EX. The accident occurred seconds after the plane took off.
事故は飛行機が離陸して数秒後に起きた。
Jiko wa hikoo-ki ga ririku-shite suubyoo-go ni okita.

PHRASE: take a rest *yasumu* 休む ①

EX. I'm tired. Let's take a rest.
疲れた。休もうよ。
Tsukareta. Yasumoo yo.

talent n. **[(a person of) (superior) native ability]**

1. sa⌈inoo 才能 **[(superior) innate intellectual or artistic capability]**

EX. Your daughter appears to have an unusual talent for the piano.
お嬢さんにはピアノの並外れた才能があるようです。
O-joo-san ni wa piano no nami-hazureta sainoo ga aru yoodesu.

2. sa⌈ijin 才人 **•c [an adult of superior native ability]** **⟪clever person⟫**

EX. I'd hate to lose a talent like Tanaka from our research team.
田中のような才人をうちの研究チームから失いたくない。

T

Tanaka no yoona saijin o uchi no kenkyuu-chiimu kara ushinai-takunai.

talk vi. **[for s.o. to communicate one's thoughts in words to or with s.o. else ⟪fig. "gossip," "chatter"⟫]**

1. ({⟨-o⟩/⟨-ni-tsuite⟩}) **ha⌈na⌉su** ({⟨〜を⟩/⟨〜について⟩})話す ① **[for s.o. to convey orally information on some topic]** ⟪**tell, narrate**⟫

EX. (**a**) A: Who did you talk with about that?
そのことはだれと話しましたか。
Sono koto wa dare to hanashimashita ka.
B: I talked with my teacher.
先生と話しました。
Sensei to hanashimashita.
(**b**) I talked for some time with Mr. Kim in Korean.
キムさんとしばらくの間韓国語で話した。
Kimu-san to shibaraku no aida Kankoku-go de hanashita.

2. sha⌈be⌉ru しゃべる ① **[for s.o. to informally express or exchange one's thoughts in words to or with s.o. else ⟨s⟩]** ⟪**chit-chat**⟫

EX. My office mates at work like to talk, so I often have to go someplace else to get work done.
会社の同僚が仕事中にしゃべるのが好きなので外の所へ行って仕事をしなければならないことがよくある。
Kaisha no dooryoo ga shigoto-chuu ni shaberu no ga sukina node hoka no tokoro e itte shigoto o shinakereba naranai koto ga yoku aru.

T

— n. **[an exchange of spoken words between two or more people; an informal lecture or speech; rumor or gossip]**

1. ha⌈nashi⌉ 話 /⟨V*masu* of *hanasu* ① speak/ **[an act/instance of speaking ⟪fig. "rumor"⟫]** ⟪**conversation, chat, speech, lecture, story, statement**⟫, **o-⌈sha⌉beri** おしゃべり /⟨V*masu* of *shaberu* ① talk informally/ ⟪**chit-chat**⟫, **ka⌈iwa** 会話 •**c [an act/instance of speaking informally with another person]** ⟪**conversation**⟫

EX. I had a nice talk with your father the other day.
この間あなたのお父さんと{話/おしゃべり/会話}をして楽しかったです。
Kono aida anata no o-too-san to {hanashi/o-shaberi/kaiwa} o shite tanoshikatta desu.

2. ko⌈oen 講演 •**c [a long informative talk given to a group of people on a particular subject, but not as part of a curriculum]** ⟪**lecture, address**⟫, **ha⌈nashi⌉** 話 SEE talk n. 1

EX. Did you hear the talk by Prof. Chomsky yesterday?
チョムスキー教授のきのうの{講演/話}を聞きましたか。
Chomusukii-kyooju no kinoo no {kooen/hanashi} o kikimashita ka.

3. u⌈wasa うわさ **[an act/instance of speaking behind s.o.'s back]** ⟪**rumor, gossip**⟫

EX. A: Is it true that Mr. Koyama is leaving the company soon?
小山さんが会社をもうすぐ辞めるって本当ですか。
Koyama-san ga kaisha o moo-sugu yameru tte hontoo desu ka.
B: No, that's just talk.
いや、ただのうわさだよ。
Iya, tada no uwasa da yo.

tall adj. **[having greater height than average (esp. in stature) or having a certain height]** **(se⌉(i) ga) ta⌈ka⌉i** (背が)高い adj(*i*). **[having greater stature than average]**, **{se⌉(i)/shi⌈nchoo} ga…da** {背/身長}が…だ **[for one's stature to be…]**

EX. (**a**) My son is taller than me.
息子は私より(背が)高い。
Musuko wa watashi yori (se ga) takai.
(**b**) Chicago has many tall buildings.
シカゴには高い建物がたくさんある。
Shikogo ni wa takai tate-mono ga takusan aru.

NOTE: *Se(i) ga takai* can only be used when the subject is animate.

(**c**) That *sumo* wrestler is 1.93 meters tall.
その相撲取りは{背/身長}が一メートル九十三センチだ。

Sono sumoo-tori wa {se(i)/shinchoo} ga ichi-meetoru kyuu-juu-san-senchi da.

NOTE: *Takai* by itself can mean either "high" or "expensive."

tame vt. **[to change s.t./s.a. from a wild state to a domesticated state《fig. "make s.o. obey"》]**

〈-o〉 ka⌈i-nara⌉su 〈〜を〉飼い慣らす ① **[to domesticate an animal]《domesticate》**

EX. It can take several years to tame a wild horse.
野生の馬を飼い慣らすのには数年かかることもある。
Yasei no uma o kai-narasu no ni wa suu-nen kakaru koto mo aru.

— adj. **[having been changed from a wild state to a domesticated state《fig. "submissive," "without spirit," "dull"》]**

1. ka⌈i-narasa⌉-rete iru (N) 飼い慣らされている(N) **/〈V *te iru* of the passive of *kai-narasu* ① domesticate/ [for an animal to have been changed from a wild to a domesticated state]**

EX. The rabbit was so tame it would eat from our hands.
そのうさぎは私たちの手からえさを食べるほどに飼い慣らされていた。
Sono usagi wa watashi-tachi no te kara esa o taberu hodo ni kai-narasa-rete ita.

2. o⌈tonashi⌉i おとなしい adj(*i*). **[obedient or reserved in behavior; subdued or inconspicuous in visual effect]《gentle, mild, meek, obedient, quiet》**

tan n. **[a yellowish-brown color《fig. "a yellowish-brown color of the skin due to sunshine"》]**

1. o⌈o-ka⌉sshoku 黄褐色 **•c [a yellowish-brown color]**

2. hi-⌈yake 日焼け **[a yellowish-brown color of the skin due to sunshine]**

— vt. **[to give a yellowish-brown color to the skin or to change hide into leather by soaking it in tannin extracted from the bark of oak]**

1. hi⌉fu o hi-⌈yake-saseru 皮膚を日焼けさせる **/〈causative of *hi-yake-suru* ③ become dark or burnt from sun/ ②**

EX. Some people like to tan their skin using artificial light.
人工光線で皮膚を日焼けさせるのが好きな人たちもいる。
Jinkoo-koosen de hifu o hi-yake-saseru no ga sukina hito-tachi mo iru.

2. ka⌈wa o na⌈me⌉su 皮をなめす ① **[to change hide into leather by removing the fur and fat and softening it]**

tangerine n.

mi⌉kan みかん

tangible adj. **[able to be touched《fig. "having actual form," "definite"》]**

1. sa⌈ware-ru (N) 触れる(N) **/〈potential of *sawaru* ① touch/ [able to be touched]**

EX. It's easier to believe in that which is visible and tangible.
見えて触れるものの方が信じやすい。
Miete saware-ru mono no hoo ga shinji-yasui.

2. yu⌈ukei no N 有形のN **•c [having actual form] ↔ mukei no N** 無形のN **•c**

3. ka⌈kutei-tekina 確定的な adj(*na*). **•c [firmly decided or settled]**

EX. I won't feel at ease until I get a tangible response.
確定的な返事がもらえないと安心出来ない。
Kakutei-tekina henji ga morae nai to anshin-dekinai.

tangle vt. **[to cause s.t. to become twisted together in a confused mass]**

〈-o〉〈-to〉 mo⌈tsure-sase⌉ru 〈〜を〉〈〜と〉もつれさせる **/〈causative of *motsureru* ② get entangled/ ② [to cause s.t. to become entwined and inseparable with s.t. else],**

〈-o〉{〈-ni〉/〈-to〉} ka⌈rama-se⌉ru 〈〜を〉{〈〜に〉/〈〜と〉}絡ませる **/〈causative of *karamu* ① become entwined/ ② [for s.o. to cause s.t. long and narrow to become entwined with s.t. larger]**

EX. (**a**) The boy flying the kite purposely tangled his kite line with someone else's.
たこを揚げている男は、わざと自分の糸をほかのたこの糸に{もつれさせた/絡ませた}。

T

Tako o agete iru otoko wa, waza-to jibun no ito o hoka no tako no ito ni {motsure-saseta/karama-seta}.
(**b**) The kitten tangled the yarn all up while playing with it.
子猫が毛糸にじゃれているうちにそれを{もつれさせて/?絡ませて}しまった。
Ko-neko ga ke-ito ni jarete iru uchi ni sore o {motsure-sasete/?karama-sete} shimatta.

— vi. **[for s.t. to become twisted together in a confused mass《fig. "become complicated"》]**
1. ⟨-ni⟩ ka⌈ra⌉mu ⟨〜に⟩絡む ① [for s.t. long and narrow to become entwined with s.t. larger]《entwine, get caught in》
EX. The morning glory vines tangled around the branches of the tree.
朝顔のつるが木の枝に絡んだ。
Asagao no tsuru ga ki no eda ni karanda.
2. fu⌈nkyuu-suru 紛糾する ③ •c [for discussions or negotiations on an issue to become entwined in conflict]《be thrown into confusion, fall into disorder》
EX. Labor and management tangled over the issue of pay raises.
賃上げの問題で労使の話し合いは紛糾していた。
Chin-age no mondai de roo-shi no hanashi-ai wa funkyuu-shite ita.
PHRASE: get tangled *motsureru* もつれる ②
EX. My hair got all tangled in the strong wind.
髪の毛が強風でもつれてしまった。
Kami no ke ga kyoofuu de motsurete shimatta.

tank[1] n. **[a large container for holding liquid or gas《fig. "gas tank"》]**
1. ta⌈me-ike ため池 [a natural or artificial reservoir for water], ta⌉nku タンク •f
2. ga⌈su-ta⌉nku ガスタンク •f [a container for holding gas or gasoline]

tank[2] n. **[an armored vehicle used in war]**
se⌉nsha 戦車 •c, ta⌉nku タンク •f

tap vi./vt. **[to strike s.t./s.o./s.a. lightly and rapidly with s.t.]**
⟨-o⟩ ka⌈ruku ta⌈ta⌉ku ⟨〜を⟩軽くたたく ① [for s.o. to hit s.o./s.t./s.a. lightly], ⟨-o⟩ ko⌉tsu-kotsu to ta⌈ta⌉ku ⟨〜を⟩こつこつとたたく ① [for s.o. to strike s.t. forcefully and repeatedly with s.t. hard]
EX. (**a**) Someone tapped my shoulder.
だれかが私の肩を{軽く/*こつこつと}たたいた。
*Dare-ka ga watashi no kata o {karuku/*kotsu-kotsu to} tataita.*
(**b**) I tapped on the door but nobody answered.
ドアを{こつこつと/軽く}たたいたが、だれも答えなかった。
Doa o {kotsu-kotsu to/karuku} tataita ga, dare-mo kotaenakatta.

— n. **[the act or sound of striking s.t./s.o./s.a. lightly and rapidly with s.t.]**
ka⌈ruku ta⌈ta⌉ku koto 軽くたたくこと [the act of striking s.t./s.o./s.a. lightly and rapidly with s.t.], ka⌈ruku ta⌈ta⌉ku oto 軽くたたく音 [the sound of striking s.t. lightly and rapidly with s.t.]

tape n. **[a long narrow strip of material such as cloth, paper, or plastic; a specially treated plastic strip on which sound or images can be recorded]**
1. te⌉epu テープ •f [a long narrow strip of cloth, paper, or plastic]
EX. Rolls of tape were thrown out from the decks as the boat left port.
船が港を出る時、デッキからテープがたくさん投げられた。
Fune ga minato o deru toki, dekki kara teepu ga takusan nage-rareta.
2. ro⌈kuon-te⌉epu 録音テープ •c+f [a long narrow magnetic strip for recording sounds]《audio tape》
3. bi⌈deo-te⌉epu ビデオテープ •f [a long narrow magnetic strip for recording images]《video tape》
4. ma⌈ki-jaku 巻尺 [a long narrow strip of cloth or plastic marked in units for measuring things]《tape measure》

— vt. **[for s.o. to fasten s.t. with a long narrow strip of material or to record**

sounds/images on a specially treated strip of material]
1. ⟨-ni⟩ te⌉epu o tsu⌈ke⌉ru ⟨〜に⟩テープをつける ② [for s.o. to put a long narrow strip of material on s.t.]
2. ⟨-ni⟩ te⌉epu o ma⌈ku ⟨〜に⟩テープを巻く ① [for s.o. to put a long narrow strip of material around s.t.]
3. ⟨-o⟩ ro⌈kuon-suru ⟨〜を⟩録音する ③ •c [for s.o. to preserve sound by electronic means] ⟪record⟫

EX. We plan to tape the speech contest.
スピーチコンテストを録音する予定だ。
Supiichi-kontesuto o rokuon-suru yotei da.

4. ⟨-o⟩ ro⌈kuga-suru ⟨〜を⟩録画する ③ •c [for s.o. to preserve images by electronic means]

EX. I tape my favorite TV program every day.
私は毎日好きなテレビ番組を録画している。
Watashi wa mai-nichi sukina terebi-bangumi o rokuga-shite iru.

tape recorder n.
te⌈epu-reko⌉odaa テープレコーダー •f

EX. I use a tape recorder every day to study Japanese.
私は日本語を習うためにテープレコーダーを毎日使っています。
Watashi wa Nihon-go o narau tame ni teepu-rekoodaa o mai-nichi tsukatte imasu.

tar n. [a thick dark liquid produced from coal or wood]
ta⌉aru タール •f

target n. [a mark or object at which s.t. is aimed ⟪fig. "object of criticism or scorn"⟫]
1. ma⌈to 的 [an object which is aimed at in shooting practice or in a military/verbal attack ⟪fig. "object of envy/interest/ridicule"⟫] ⟪mark, object⟫, hyo⌈oteki 標的 •c [an object which is aimed at in shooting practice or in a military attack] ⟪mark, object⟫

EX. (a) The arrow failed to hit the target.
矢が{的/標的}に当たらなかった。
Ya ga {mato/hyooteki} ni ataranakatta.
(b) The target of the attack was a covert desert military camp.
砂漠にある秘密の軍事基地が攻撃の{標的/的}だった。
Sabaku ni aru himitsu no gunji-kichi ga koogeki no {hyooteki/mato} datta.

2. ko⌈ogeki-mo⌉kuhyoo 攻撃目標 •c [the object of a military attack]
3. mo⌈no-wa⌉rai no ta⌉ne 物笑いの種 [the object of ridicule] ⟪laughingstock, butt of a joke⟫

EX. He became the target of ridicule for the crass things he was always saying.
いつもばかなことを言うので、彼は物笑いの種になった。
Itsu-mo bakana koto o iu node, kare wa mono-warai no tane ni natta.

4. hi⌉nan no ma⌈to 非難の的 [an object of criticism]

EX. The company president became an instant target of criticism when he made his son vice president.
息子を副社長にした時、社長はすぐ非難の的になった。
Musuko o fuku-shachoo ni shita toki, shachoo wa sugu hinan no mato ni natta.

task n. [a piece of (difficult) work one is assigned to do as a duty]
shi⌈goto 仕事 [an activity performed for a particular purpose other than amusement and on which one expends time and effort] ⟪work, business, labor, job, employment, occupation, mission⟫, sho⌉kumu 職務 •c [the duty assigned to each person in an institutional system] ⟪office, function⟫, sa⌉gyoo 作業 •c [work requiring physical or bodily energy] ⟪work, operation⟫

EX. (a) Our task is to find practical and cost-efficient ways to harness solar energy as a source of power.
私たちの{仕事/*職務/*作業}は、太陽をエネルギー源として利用する実用的で、費用に見合った方法を見付けることだ。
*Watashi-tachi no {shigoto/*shokumu/*

T

**sagyoo} wa, taiyoo o enerugii-gen to-shite riyoo-suru jitsuyoo-tekide, hiyoo ni mi-atta hoohoo o mitsukeru koto da.*
(**b**) This task requires patience and intelligence.
この{仕事/職務/作業}は忍耐力と頭脳を要する。
Kono {shigoto/shokumu/sagyoo} wa nintai-ryoku to zunoo o yoosuru.

taste vt. **[for s.o./s.a. to perceive the sensation of a flavor《fig. "taste the flavor of s.t.," "experience s.t."》]**
1. 〈-o〉 **shi⌈shoku-suru** 〈〜を〉**試食する** ③ **•c [for s.o. to sample the flavor of a food]**《**sample**》
2. 〈-o〉 **a⌈jiwa⌉u** 〈〜を〉**味わう** ① **[for s.o. to test or enjoy the taste of s.t.《fig. "appreciate s.t.," "experience s.t."》]**《**savor, relish**》
EX. A: How was the *sushi*?
すし、どうでしたか。
Sushi, doo deshita ka.
B: I've never tasted anything like it before.
こんな物は前に味わったことがありません。
Konna mono wa mae ni ajiwatta koto ga arimasen.
3. 〈-o〉 **a⌈jiwa⌉u** 〈〜を〉**味わう** ① SEE taste 2, 〈-o〉 **ke⌈iken-suru** 〈〜を〉**経験する** ③ **•c [for s.o. to live through, participate in, or be subjected to some event or activity]**《**experience**》
EX. I was able to taste just briefly what life in France is like during a trip I took there as a college student.
学生時代に旅行をした時ほんの少しフランスの生活を{味わう/経験する}ことができた。
Gakusei-jidai ni ryokoo o shita toki hon-no sukoshi Furansu no seikatsu o {ajiwau/keiken-suru} koto ga dekita.

— n. **[the sensation created on the tongue by the flavor of s.t. or the faculty of perceiving such a sensation; a small amount of food eaten or drunk as a sample; a slight experience of s.t.; the ability to appreciate s.t.]**
1. a⌈ji 味 [the sensation created by a particular food/drink when put in the mouth]《**savor, flavor**》
EX. I like the taste of Japanese persimmons.
私は日本の柿の味が好きです。
Watashi wa Nihon no kaki no aji ga suki desu.
2. mi⌈kaku 味覚 •c [the faculty by which flavors are sensed]
EX. If you always eat good food, your sense of taste becomes sharper.
いつもいいものを食べると、味覚が鋭くなる。
Itsu-mo ii mono o taberu to, mikaku ga surudoku naru.
3. shi⌈shoku 試食 •c [eating s.t. as a test to see if its flavor is satisfactory]《**sampling**》, **a⌈ji-mi⌉ 味見 [eating s.t. while cooking it to check if its flavor is satisfactory]**《**sampling**》
4. ke⌈iken 経験 •c [an act/instance of living through, participating in, or being subjected to some event or activity]
5. shu⌉mi 趣味 •c [an ability or inclination to appreciate s.t. or s.t. one enjoys doing in one's free time]《**interest, hobby**》, **ko⌈nomi⌉ 好み /**〈***V masu* of *konomu*** ① **like/ [things one likes]**《**liking, preference, choice**》
EX. You and I have totally different tastes, don't we?
君と僕は{趣味/好み}がぜんぜん違うね。
Kimi to boku wa {shumi/konomi} ga zenzen chigau ne.

tasteless adj. **[lacking flavor《fig. "lacking a sense of what is good, beautiful, or proper," "uninteresting"》]**
1. a⌈ji ga na⌉i 味がない adj(*i*). **[having no flavor], ma⌈zu⌉i まずい** adj(*i*). **[having a bad flavor《fig. "ugly," "unskillful," "awkward"》]**《**unsavory, ugly, unwise, unskillful, bad**》 ↔ **oishii おいしい** adj(*i*).
EX. This meat is tasteless, isn't it?
この肉は{味がない/まずい}ね。
Kono niku wa {aji ga nai/mazui} ne.
2. tsu⌈mara⌉nai つまらない adj(*i*). **[causing dissatisfaction due to lack of worth or interest]**《**trivial, insignificant, valueless,**

useless, unexciting》↔ **omoshiroi おもしろい** adj(*i*).
3. shu˥mi ga wa┌ru˥i 趣味が悪い adj(*i*). **[lacking a sense of what is good, beautiful, or proper] ↔ shumi ga ii 趣味がいい** adj(*i*).

EX. I find the way she dresses herself to be tasteless.
彼女の服の着こなしは趣味が悪いと思う。
Kanojo no fuku no ki-konashi wa shumi ga warui to omou.

tasty adj.
a┌ji ga i˥i 味がいい adj(*i*). **[having a good flavor], o┌ishii おいしい** adj(*i*). **[for the taste of a food/drink to be desirable/satisfactory]** **《delicious, good》↔ mazui まずい** adj(*i*).

EX. This French bread is very tasty. How about trying some?
このフランスパンはとても{味がいい/おいしい}ですよ。少し食べてみたらどうですか。
Kono Furansu-pan wa totemo {aji ga ii/oishii} desu yo. Sukoshi tabete mitara doo desu ka.

tax n. **[a compulsory payment of a certain percentage of one's income, property, consumption costs, etc. to support the government 《fig. "a heavy burden"》]**
1. zei┌kin 税金 •c [a compulsory payment of money to support the government], ze˥i 税 •c

EX. (**a**) Income tax in this country runs as high as 40%.
この国の所得税は40%にもなる。
Kono kuni no shotoku-zei wa yon-jup-paasento ni mo naru.
(**b**) The president promised not to raise taxes.
大統領は税(金)を上げないと公約した。
Daitooryoo wa zei(kin) o agenai to kooyaku-shita.

2. o┌mo-ni 重荷 [a heavy load 《fig. "hardship"》]

taxi n.
ta˥kushii タクシー •f 《cab》

EX. (**a**) Let's go by taxi.
タクシーで行きましょう。
Takushii de ikimashoo
(**b**) It is easy to catch a taxi around here.
この辺ではタクシーをつかまえるのはやさしいです。
Kono hen de wa takushii o tsukamaeru no wa yasashii desu.

tea n. **[a kind of shrub cultivated in China, India, or Japan for its leaves or the dried or fermented leaves of this or the beverage made from these]**
(o-)┌cha (お)茶 •c [a kind of shrub cultivated in China, India, or Japan for its leaves or the (dried or fermented) leaves of this shrub or the beverage made from these 《fig. "tea ceremony"》], ko┌ocha 紅茶 •c [the dried leaves of a special kind of shrub grown mainly in India and treated for making a Western-style beverage or the beverage made from this]

EX. (**a**) Shall I fix some tea for you?
{お茶/紅茶}を入れましょうか。
{O-cha/Koocha} o iremashoo ka.
(**b**) I never drink tea before going to bed.
寝る前は{お茶/紅茶}を飲みません。
Neru mae wa {o-cha/koocha} o nomimasen.
(**c**) Tea is grown in the warmer southern regions of Japan.
{お茶/*紅茶}は日本の比較的暖かな南部に育つ。
*{O-cha/*Koocha} wa Nihon no hikaku-teki atatakana nanbu ni sodatsu.*
(**d**) Tea is said to be rich in vitamin C.
{お茶/?紅茶}にはビタミンCがたくさんあると言われる。
{O-cha/?Koocha} ni wa bitamin-shii ga takusan aru to iwa-reru.
(**e**) I prefer tea to coffee.
僕はコーヒーより{紅茶/お茶}の方がいい。
Boku wa koohii yori {koocha/o-cha} no hoo ga ii.

PHRASE: green tea *ryokucha* 緑茶 **•c**, tea bag *tii-baggu* ティーバッグ **•f**, tea ceremony *o-cha* お茶, *{cha/sa} doo* 茶道 **•c**, *cha-no-yu* 茶の湯

teach vi./vt. **[for s.o./s.t. to cause or help s.o./s.a. to learn s.t. such as knowledge or a skill]**
⟨-ni⟩ ⟨-o⟩ o⌈shieru ⟨〜に⟩⟨〜を⟩教える ② [for s.o. to impart knowledge/information/a skill to s.o./s.a.] ⟪give lessons, tell, instruct, inform, show, point out, explain, guide, coach⟫, (⟨-de⟩) ⟨-ga⟩ wa⌈ka⌉ru (⟨〜で⟩)⟨〜が⟩ 分かる ① [for s.o. to grasp in one's mind the nature, meaning, identity, etc., of s.t./s.o./s.a. (by some means)] ⟪understand, figure out⟫

EX. (**a**) Mr. Yamamoto teaches electrical engineering at a local college.
山本さんは地元の大学で電気工学を教えている。
Yamamoto-san wa jimoto no daigaku de denki-koogaku o oshiete iru.
(**b**) I'm teaching my son how to use a word processor.
息子にワープロの使い方を教えています。
Musuko ni waapuro no tsukai-kata o oshiete imasu.
(**c**) My three-month stay in Korea taught me some of the differences between Japanese and Korean cultures.
三か月の韓国滞在で、日本と韓国の文化の違いが少し分かった。
San-kagetsu no Kankoku-taizai de, Nihon to Kankoku no bunka no chigai ga sukoshi wakatta.

NOTE: The meaning of "give information to others" which is present in *oshieru* is sometimes expressed in English by "show," as in "Please show me the way to the station." This would be expressed in Japanese as *Eki e no iki-kata o oshiete kudasai.*

teacher n. **[a person who teaches as a profession]**
se⌈nse⌉i 先生 •c [a person with professional skill, knowledge, or status, such as a scholar, attorney, politician, or one who helps others learn, often used as a polite form of address] ⟪master, instructor, doctor⟫, kyo⌉oshi 教師 •c [a person who imparts knowledge or skills to students in academic disciplines as a profession] ⟪instructor⟫

EX. (**a**) A: May I ask what your occupation is?
御職業は何でしょうか。
Go-shokugyoo wa nan deshoo ka.
B: I'm a high school teacher.
高校の{教師/*先生}です。
*Kookoo no {kyooshi/*sensei} desu.*
(**b**) My piano teacher is Mr. Suzuki.
私のピアノの{先生/*教師}は鈴木さんです。
*Watashi no piano no {sensei/*kyooshi} wa Suzuki-san desu.*

NOTE: *Sensei* cannot be used in example (a)-B, because *sensei* is an honorific term which cannot be used to refer to oneself. On the other hand, in example (b) *kyooshi* is not appropriate, because *kyooshi* can only be used in a neutral or humble sense. *Sensei* can be used as a term of address, but *kyooshi* cannot. Thus, only *sensei* would be appropriate in the sentence "Teacher, I have a question." *{Sensei/*Kyooshi}, shitsumon ga arimasu.*

teacup n. **[a container with a handle from which tea is drunk, usually made of china]**
cha⌈wan 茶わん •c [a container without a handle for holding tea or cooked rice, usually made of china]

EX. Japanese teacups don't have handles.
日本の茶わんには取っ手がない。
Nihon no chawan ni wa totte ga nai.

team n.
chi⌉imu チーム •f

EX. Our basketball team lost the game.
私たちのバスケットボールのチームは試合に負けた。
Watashi-tachi no basuketto-booru no chiimu wa shiai ni maketa.

—— vi. **[for s.o. to form a group with others to achieve a common purpose or to play together on the same side in a game]**
⟨-to⟩ chi⌉imu o tsu⌈ku⌉ru ⟨〜と⟩チームを作る ①

EX. I teamed up with several of my colleagues to work on the project.
プロジェクトに取り組むのに同僚数人とチームを作った。

T

| *Purojekuto ni tori-kumu no ni dooryoo suu-nin to chiimu o tsukutta.*

tear[1] vt. **[to pull s.t. apart by force or to make a hole or cut in s.t. in this way《fig. "disrupt"》]**
⟨-o⟩ hi⌈ki-sa⌉ku ⟨～を⟩引き裂く ① [to pull s.t. apart suddenly and forcefully《fig. "alienate"》], ⟨-o⟩ ya⌈bu⌉ku ⟨～を⟩破く ① [to pull apart a thin object such as paper or cloth by force ⟨s⟩]《rend, break》, ⟨-o⟩ ya⌈bu⌉ru ⟨～を⟩破る ① [to apply force to s.t. thin and flat which has tension, such as paper, fabric, or the surface of a wall, and thereby damage it《fig. "break the silence," "break a promise/law," "break through a line of resistance," "defeat"》]《rend, break, violate, defeat》

EX. (**a**) After my daughter read the letter from her old boyfriend, she tore it up.
娘は前の彼氏からの手紙を読んだ後それを{引き裂いた/破った/破いた}。
Musume wa mae no kareshi kara no tegami o yonda ato sore o {hiki-saita/yabutta/yabuita}.
(**b**) What are you trying to do, tear apart my relationship with my son?
息子と私の関係を{引き裂こう/*破こう/*破ろう}とでもしているのか。
*Musuko to watashi no kankei o {hiki-sakoo/*yabukoo/*yaburoo} to demo shite iru no ka.*

tear[2] n.
na⌉mida 涙

EX. (**a**) John shed tears when he learned of the death of his old friend.
ジョンは旧友の死を知った時、涙を流した。
Jon wa kyuuyuu no shi o shitta toki, namida o nagashita.
(**b**) Tears rolled down her cheek when she met her father whom she hadn't seen in 15 years.
十五年ぶりに父親に会った時、涙が彼女のほおをつたって流れた。
Juu-go-nen buri ni chichi-oya ni atta toki, namida ga kanojo no hoo o tsutatte nagareta.

tease vi./vt. **[for s.o. to annoy or make fun of s.o./s.a. in a playful or unkind way]**
1. ⟨-o⟩ ka⌈raka⌉u ⟨～を⟩からかう ① [for s.o. to annoy s.o. purposely for amusement]《make fun of, play a joke on, banter》, ⟨-o⟩ hi⌈yaka⌉su ⟨～を⟩冷やかす ① [for s.o. to annoy s.o. verbally《fig. "just look around in a store with no intention of buying anything"》]《poke fun at, just look at the goods》, ⟨-o⟩ i⌈jimeru ⟨～を⟩いじめる ② [for s.o. to deliberately cause pain to s.o. in a weaker position for amusement]《ill-treat, treat s.o. harshly, bully》

EX. (**a**) A: Hey, look at you all dressed up like a princess.
何だい。王女様みたいに着飾っちゃってさ。
Nan dai. Oojo-sama mitaini ki-kazatchatte sa.
B: Stop teasing me.
{からかわない/冷やかさない/??いじめない}で。
{Karakawanai/Hiyakasanai/??Ijimenai} de.
(**b**) In Japanese schools a student who stands out from the others is often teased.
日本の学校では他の学生と違って目立つ学生はよく{いじめられる/からかわれる/*冷やかされる}。
*Nihon no gakkoo de wa ta no gakusei to chigatte medatsu gakusei wa yoku {ijime-rareru/karakawa-reru/*hiyakasa-reru}.*

technical adj. **[having to do with engineering or the mechanical or industrial arts; involving specialized scientific, academic, or artistic knowledge or terminology]**
gi⌈jutsu-tekina 技術的な adj(*na*). **•c [having to do with the methods or actually doing or creating s.t., esp. those involving the application of scientific knowledge]《technological》, se⌈nmon-tekina 専門的な** adj(*na*). **•c [related to a special field of study]《expert》**

T

EX. (**a**) Most young people in the town don't have the necessary technical skills to be employed in the new factory.
この町の若い人たちの大部分は新しい工場で雇われるだけの{技術的な/?専門的な}腕がない。
Kono machi no wakai hito-tachi no dai-bubun wa atarashii koojoo de yatowa-reru dake no {gijutsu-tekina/?senmon-tekina} ude ga nai.
(**b**) Sorry, but I am unable to answer a technical question like that.
済みませんが、そのような{専門的な/?技術的な}御質問にはお答え出来ません。
Sumimasen ga, sono yoona {senmon-tekina/?gijutsu-tekina} go-shitsumon ni wa o-kotae-dekimasen.

technique n. **[a method of doing, performing, or creating s.t., esp. one involving skill or knowledge in a science or an art]**
1. gi˥jutsu 技術 •c [a method of doing or creating s.t., esp. one involving the application of scientific knowledge] 《art, skill, technology》

EX. Modern agricultural techniques have made possible the growth of many crops even in desert regions.
近代的農業技術のおかげで砂漠地帯でも多くの作物の栽培が可能になってきた。
Kindai-teki noogyoo-gijutsu no o-kage de sabaku-chitai de mo ooku no sakumotsu no saibai ga kanooni natte kita.

2. gi˥koo 技巧 •c [the level of skill involved in performing or creating s.t., esp. in the arts 《fig. "trick"》] 《craftsmanship, workmanship, finesse》, te˥kunikku テクニック •f [the degree of expertness]

EX. The pianist demonstrated her superior technique in yesterday's recital.
ピアニストはきのうのリサイタルで最高の{技巧/テクニック}を示した。
Pianisuto wa kinoo no risaitaru de saikoo no {gikoo/tekunikku} o shimeshita.

technology n.
(sa˥ngyoo-)gi˥jutsu (産業)技術 •c, te˥kuno˥rojii テクノロジー •f

EX. Japanese advanced technology has produced many high quality electronic goods.
日本の進んだ{産業技術/テクノロジー}は上質の電子製品を数多く生んだ。
Nihon no susunda {sangyoo-gijutsu/tekunorojii} wa jooshitsu no denshi-seihin o kazu ooku unda.

teenage adj. **[between thirteen and nineteen years old or having to do with a person of that age]**
ju˥u-dai no N 十代のN

EX. Teenage delinquency is up sharply this year.
十代の非行が今年は急に増えている。
Juu-dai no hikoo ga kotoshi wa kyuuni fuete iru.

teenager n. **[a person between thirteen and nineteen years old]**
ti˥in-e˥ejaa ティーンエージャー •f

EX. Most teenagers love rock music.
大抵のティーンエージャーはロック音楽が大好きだ。
Taitei no tiin-eejaa wa rokku-ongaku ga dai-suki da.

telegram n.
de˥npoo 電報 •c

EX. (**a**) I sent a telegram to my younger sister in New York.
私はニューヨークにいる妹に電報を打った。
Watashi wa Nyuuyooku ni iru imooto ni denpoo o utta.
(**b**) Now that the use of telephones, faxes, and e-mail is so common, telegrams will undoubtedly soon become obsolete.
電話やファックスや電子メールがこんなに普及したからには、電報はやがてすたれるだろう。
Denwa ya fakkusu ya denshi-meeru ga konnani fukyuu-shita kara ni wa, denpoo wa yagate sutareru daroo.

telegraph n. **[an apparatus for sending a message by electric impulses or a message sent by such an apparatus]**

1. de⌈nshi⌉n-ki 電信機 •c [an apparatus for sending a message by electric impulses]
2. de⌈npoo 電報 •c [a message sent over cable by electrical impulses using a special apparatus fot that purpose]

telephone n. [an electronic apparatus for transmitting speech to a distant hearer, esp. over wire]
1. ju⌈wa⌉-ki 受話器 •c [an electronic device for transmitting speech to a distant hearer, esp. the part of this that converts electronic signals into sounds or vice versa], de⌈nwa 電話 •c [an apparatus for transmitting speech to a distant hearer or an act of making contact with s.o. by means of such an apparatus]

EX. (a) I had a telephone installed in my room.
部屋に{電話/*受話器}を入れてもらった。
*Heya ni {denwa/*juwa-ki} o irete moratta.*
(b) Just as I hung up the telephone, it rang again.
{受話器/電話}をおいたら、また鳴った。
{Juwa-ki/Denwa} o oitara, mata natta.

2. de⌈nwa 電話 •c SEE telephone 1

EX. I'll talk to you again later by telephone.
後でまた電話で話します。
Ato de mata denwa de hanashimasu.

PHRASE: public telephone *kooshuu-denwa* 公衆電話 •c, telephone book/directory *denwa-choo* 電話帳 •c, telephone operator *kookan-shu* 交換手 •c

telescope n.
bo⌈oen-kyoo 望遠鏡 •c

EX. I enjoy looking at the moon and stars through a telescope.
望遠鏡で月や星を眺めるのが好きだ。
Booen-kyoo de tsuki ya hoshi o nagameru no ga suki da.

television n.
te⌉rebi テレビ •f

EX. I've heard that American children watch an average of two hours of television every day.
アメリカの子供たちは一日に平均して二時間テレビを見るそうです。
America no kodomo-tachi wa ichi-nichi ni heikin-shite ni-jikan terebi o miru soodesu.

tell vt. [for s.o. to make known s.t. to s.o. or direct s.o. to do s.t. using words]
1. {⟨-o⟩/⟨-to⟩/Vinf. nonpast yo⌉oni} i⌈u {⟨～を⟩/⟨～と⟩/Vinf. nonpastように}言う ① [for s.o. to express one's thoughts or feelings verbally or to direct s.o. verbally to do s.t. or to call s.o./s.t./s.a. a certain name] ((say, state, call))

EX. (a) My father always told me that honesty was the best policy.
父はいつも私に正直が一番だと言っていました。
Chichi wa itsu-mo watashi ni shoojiki ga ichiban da to itte imashita.
(b) My professor told me I should go to Japan to study.
私の先生は日本へ留学するように言った。
Watashi no sensei wa Nihon e ryuugaku-suru yooni itta.
(c) I was taught since childhood never to tell a lie.
私は子供の時からうそを言ってはならないと教えられてきた。
Watashi wa kodomo no toki kara uso o itte wa naranai to oshie-rarete kita.
(d) When I was told by the doctor that I had cancer, I had thoughts of taking my own life.
がんだと医者に言われた時、死のうかと思いました。
Gan da to isha ni iwa-reta toki, shinoo ka to omoimashita.

2. {⟨-o⟩/ni-tsuite} ha⌈na⌉su {⟨～を⟩/について}話す ① [for s.o. to convey orally information on some topic] ((narrate))

EX. (a) Please tell me about your experience in Japan.
日本での体験について話してください。
Nihon de no taiken ni-tsuite hanashite kudasai.
(b) My mother is good at telling stories.
母は物語を話すのが上手です。
Haha wa monogatari o hanasu no ga joozu desu.

T

NOTE: Unlike English "tell," in Japanese *hanasu* can take as its direct object the name of a language, such as *Nihon-go* "Japanese." Thus one can say *Nihon-go o sukoshi hanashimasu,* but not "*I tell Japanese a little."

3. 〈-no〉 chi⌈gai ga wa⌈ka⌉ru 〈〜の〉違いが分かる ① [for s.o. to recognize the difference between two things]

EX. I can't tell the difference between Chinese and Japanese people.
私には中国人と日本人との違いが分かりません。
Watashi ni wa Chuugoku-jin to Nihon-jin to no chigai ga wakarimasen.

PHRASE: I tell you what. *Nee, koo shinai?* ねえ、こうしない?

EX. I tell you what. You let me use your car tonight and I'll buy you lunch tomorrow.
ねえ、こうしない? 今晩車を使わせてくれたらあしたお昼をおごってあげる。
Nee, koo shinai? Konban kuruma o tsukawa-sete kuretara, ashita o-hiru o ogotte ageru.

temper n. **[the state of mind one is in, esp. whether one is calm or angry, or the ability to remain calm emotionally or the tendency to become angry]**

1. ki⌈gen 機嫌 •c [a temporary state of mind as manifested in one's outward expression or attitude] ⟪mood, humor⟫

EX. My father is in a bad temper because he had a quarrel with my mother this morning.
父は今朝母とけんかしたので機嫌が悪い。
Chichi wa kesa haha to kenka-shita node kigen ga warui.

2. ta⌉nki 短気 •c [having a tendency to become angry with little provocation] ⟪irritability, touchiness, being short-tempered⟫

EX. My husband has a temper.
主人は短気です。
Shujin wa tanki desu.

PHRASE: lose one's temper *kanshaku o okosu* かんしゃくを起こす ①

T

temperature n. **[the degree of hotness or coldness of s.t.]**

ki⌈on 気温 •c [the degree of hotness or coldness of the atmosphere], ta⌉ion 体温 •c [the degree of hotness or coldness of the body], o⌉ndo 温度 •c [the degree of hotness or coldness of anything other than a body]

EX. (**a**) The lowest temperature of the year comes around January.
一年で{気温/温度/*体温}が一番低くなるのは一月ごろです。
*Ichi-nen de {kion/ondo/*taion} ga ichiban hikuku naru no wa ichi-gatsu-goro desu.*
(**b**) The temperature fell 30 degrees during the night.
{気温/温度/*体温}が夜の間に三十度下がった。
*{Kion/Ondo/*Taion} ga yoru no aida ni san-juu-do sagatta.*
(**c**) A: What is your normal temperature?
普段の{体温/*気温/*温度}はどのぐらいですか。
*Fudan no {taion/*kion/*ondo} wa dono-gurai desu ka.*
B: About 36.5°C.
三十六度五分位です。
San-juu-roku-do go-bu-gurai desu.
(**d**) The oven temperature should be 350°F.
オーブンの{温度/*気温/*体温}は華氏三百五十度でなければならない。
*Oobun no {ondo/*kion/*taion} wa kashi san-byaku-go-juu-do de nakereba naranai.*

PHRASE: have/run a temperature *netsu ga aru* 熱がある ③

EX. My son has a temperature.
息子は熱がある。
Musuko wa netsu ga aru.

temple n. **[a building used for worship of a god, including Buddha]**

(o-)te⌈ra (お)寺 [a building housing an image of Buddha in which Buddhist sacred rites and exercises are performed], ji⌉in 寺院 •c [a building housing an image of Buddha in which Buddhist sacred rites and

exercises are performed ⟨fml⟩], shi⌈nden 神殿 •c [a building in which Greek, Roman, or Shinto gods are worshiped]

EX. (**a**) If you go to Kyoto, be sure to visit the temples there.
京都に行ったら、ぜひ{お寺/寺院/*神殿}へ行ってください。
*Kyooto ni ittara, zehi {o-tera/jiin/*shinden} e itte kudasai.*
(**b**) I'd love to go to Greece and visit some of the ancient Greek temples.
私はギリシャへ行って古代ギリシャの古い{神殿/*お寺/*寺院}を見たい。
*Watashi wa Girisha e itte kodai-Girisha no furui {shinden/*o-tera/*jiin} o mi-tai.*

tempo n.
te⌈npo テンポ •f

EX. (**a**) I like the tempo of Latin American music.
私はラテンアメリカの音楽のテンポが好きだ。
Watashi wa Raten-Amerika no ongaku no tenpo ga suki da.
(**b**) The tempo of life in Tokyo is too fast for me.
東京の生活のテンポは私には速すぎる。
Tookyoo no seikatsu no tenpo wa watashi ni wa haya-sugiru.

temporary adj. **[lasting for a limited time]**
i⌈chiji-tekina 一時的な adj(*na*). **•c [for a certain time only] ↔ eikyuu-tekina 永久的な** adj(*na*). **•c; to⌈oza no N 当座のN •c [for the time being] ⟪immediate, present⟫, ri⌈nji no N 臨時のN •c [for the immediate occasion only] ⟪special, extraordianary, extra⟫**

EX. A: Is your job a permanent one?
仕事はずっと続くんですか。
Shigoto wa zutto tsuzuku n desu ka.
B: No, it's just temporary.
いいえ、{一時的な/臨時の/当座の}仕事に過ぎません。
Iie, {ichiji-tekina/rinji no/tooza no} shigoto ni sugimasen.

tempura n. **[a Japanese dish of deep-fried vegetables and fish]**
te⌈npura てんぷら

EX. I had some really good shrimp tempura at the shop in front of the station yesterday.
私はきのう駅前の店で本当においしいえびのてんぷらを食べました。
Watashi wa kinoo eki-mae no mise de hontoo ni oishii ebi no tenpura o tabemashita.

ten n./adj.
to⌉o (no N) 十(のN), ju⌉u (+counter) (no N) 十(+counter)(のN) •c SEE APPENDIX II

EX. She keeps ten dogs in that small house.
彼女はあの小さな家に犬を十匹も飼っている。
Kanojo wa ano chiisana ie ni inu o jup-piki mo katte iru.

PHRASE: ten thousand *ichi-man* 一万

tend vi. **[to move in a particular direction or to be inclined to act or be a certain way]**
1. ⟨-e to⟩ mu⌈kau ⟨〜へと⟩向かう ① [to move toward or do s.t. with one's front toward s.t./s.o./s.a. ⟪fig. "oppose"⟫] ⟪face, oppose, go to, head for⟫

EX. As Roman society became more affluent it tended toward decadence.
ローマ社会は裕福になるにつれて堕落へと向かった。
Rooma-shakai wa yuufukuni naru ni-tsurete daraku e to mukatta.

2. V*masu* ga⌈chi da V*masu*がちだ [to be inclined to happen or do s.t.] ⟪be apt to, be prone to, be liable to⟫, Vinf. nonpast ke⌈ikoo ga a⌉ru Vinf. nonpast傾向がある ① [to have a natural propensity to develop or act in a certain way ⟨fml⟩]

EX. (**a**) As one becomes older one tends to become more conservative.
人は年を取ると保守的に{なりがちだ/なる傾向がある}。
Hito wa toshi o toru to hoshu-tekini {nari-gachi da/naru keikoo ga aru}.
(**b**) Japanese tend to think that their culture is unique.
日本人は日本文化をユニークだと{考

T

えがちだ/考える傾向がある}。
Nihon-jin wa Nihon-bunka o yuniiku da to {kangae-gachi da/kangaeru keikoo ga aru}.
(**c**) In winter people tend to shut themselves up in their homes.
冬には人々は家の中に{閉じこもりがちだ/閉じこもる傾向がある}。
Fuyu ni wa hito-bito wa ie no naka ni {toji-komori-gachi da/toji-komoru keikoo ga aru}.

tendency n. **[an inclination or disposition to act or be a certain way]**
ke⌈ikoo 傾向 •c [a natural propensity to develop or act in a certain way] ⟪trend, inclination, disposition⟫
EX. (**a**) There is a growing world-wide tendency towards political conservatism.
世界中でますます政治が保守主義に向かう傾向がある。
Sekai-juu de masu-masu seiji ga hoshu-shugi ni mukau keikoo ga aru.
(**b**) Our department chief has a tendency to discount his subordinates' ideas.
部長は部下の考えに耳を貸さない傾向がある。
Buchoo wa buka no kangae ni mimi o kasanai keikoo ga aru.

T

tender adj. **[soft and easy to chew; kind and loving; lacking in strength and vulnerable]**
1. ya⌈waraka⌉i 柔らかい adj(*i*). **[easily shaped due to lacking hardness; gentle and pleasant to the tactile, visual, or auditory senses due to lacking intensity, harshness, or roughness] ⟪soft, gentle, mild⟫**
EX. This steak is really tender, isn't it?
このステーキはとても柔らかいですね。
Kono suteeki wa totemo yawarakai desu ne.
2. ya⌈sashii 優しい adj(*i*). **[mild in effect and lacking in harshness; caring and nondemanding of other people] ⟪gentle-mannered, kind⟫, o⌈moi-yari ga a⌉ru (N) 思いやりがある(N) [sympathetic of the plight of others] ⟪thoughtful, considerate, sympathetic, kind⟫, shi⌉nsetsuna 親切な** adj(*na*). **•c [having or showing thoughtfulness for others] ⟪kind, friendly⟫**
EX. Kayoko became more and more attracted to Tomokazu's tender character.
加代子は友和の{優しい/思いやりのある/親切な}人柄に段々 ひかれていった。
Kayoko wa Tomokazu no {yasashii/omoi-yari no aru/shinsetsuna} hitogara ni dan-dan hika-rete-itta.
3. ka-⌈yowai か弱い adj(*i*). **[fragile and delicate in appearance] ⟪weak, delicate, frail⟫**

Tennessee n.
Te⌉neshii テネシー •f

tennis n.
te⌉nisu テニス •f
EX. I used to play tennis when I was a student.
学生時代にはよくテニスを{しました/やりました}。
Gakusei-jidai ni wa yoku tenisu o {shimashita/yarimashita}.

tense adj. **[stretched or drawn tightly ⟪fig. "showing or causing strain"⟫]**
1. pi⌈n-to hatta N ぴんと張ったN /⟨Vinf. past of *pin-to haru* ① stretch tightly/ [stretched tightly], pi⌈n-to hatte iru (N) ぴんと張っている(N) /⟨V*te iru* of *pin-to haru* ① stretch tightly/ [stretched tightly]
EX. (**a**) The rope between the two pillars was so tense that a man could walk on it.
二本の柱の間のロープはその上を人が歩けるほどぴんと張っていた。
Ni-hon no hashira no aida no roopu wa sono ue o hito ga aruke-ru hodo pin-to hatte ita.
(**b**) The acrobat was doing somersaults on a tense rope.
曲芸師はぴんと{張った/張っている}ロープの上で宙返りをしていた。
Kyokugei-shi wa pin-to {hatta/hatte iru} roopu no ue de chuugaeri o shite ita.
2. ki⌈nchoo-shita N 緊張したN /⟨Vinf. past of *kinchoo-suru* ③ become tight and strained/ •c [showing strain], ki⌈nchoo-shite iru (N) 緊張している(N) /⟨V*te iru* of *kinchoo-suru* ③ become tight and

strained/ •c [showing strain]

EX. (**a**) You look tense. What happened?
緊張しているね。どうしたんだ。
Kinchoo-shite iru ne. Doo-shita n da.
(**b**) There was a tense moment preceding the announcement of the first prize.
一等賞の発表のすぐ前に、{緊張した/?緊張している}瞬間があった。
It-too-shoo no happyoo no sugu mae ni, {kinchoo-shita/?kinchoo-shite iru} shunkan ga atta.

tense n. **[a grammatical category indicating the time of occurrence of an event or situation, as in "present tense," "past tense," or "future tense"]**
ji⌈sei 時制 •c, te⌉nsu テンス •f

EX. His research project deals with tense in Japanese.
彼の研究プロジェクトは日本語の{時制/テンス}についてです。
Kare no kenkyuu purojekuto wa Nihon-go no {jisei/tensu} ni-tsuite desu.

tension n. **[the state of being stretched tightly or the forces at work in such a state 《fig. "mental/nervous strain"》]**
1. ha⌈ru koto 張ること [the state of a physical object such as paper, rope, etc., being stretched tightly]
2. ki⌈nchoo 緊張 •c [mental or physical tautness produced by nervous anxiety] 《strain, stress》 ↔ shikan し緩 •c

EX. (**a**) I felt a lot of tension in my first job interview.
初めて就職のための面接を受けた時はかなり{の緊張を感じた/緊張した}。
Hajimete shuushoku no tame no mensetsu o uketa toki wa kanari {no kinchoo o kanjita/kinchoo-shita}.
(**b**) Tensions between the two countries are subsiding.
両国間の緊張は解けてきている。
Ryookoku-kan no kinchoo wa tokete-kite iru.

tent n.
te⌉nto テント •f

EX. Let's pitch the tent right here.
ここにテントを張りましょう。
Koko ni tento o harimashoo.

tentative adj. **[done on a trial basis; not definite or final]**
ka⌈ri no N 仮のN [provisional and temporary in nature 《fig. "unauthorized"》] 《temporary, interim, provisional》, i⌈chioo no N 一応のN •c [satisfactory for the time being] 《temporary, a sort of》

EX. (**a**) The tentative title of my talk is "Japan in the 21st century."
私の話の{仮の/?一応の}題は「二十一世紀の日本」です。
Watashi no hanashi no {kari no/?ichioo no} dai wa 'Ni-juu-is-seiki no Nihon' desu.
(**b**) Our year-long research project has yielded some tentative results.
我々の一年間の研究プロジェクトは{一応の/*仮の}成果を出すことが出来た。
*Ware-ware no ichi-nenkan no kenkyuu-purojekuto wa {ichioo no/*kari no} seika o dasu koto ga dekita.*

tentatively adv. **[in a temporary or provisional manner]**
ka⌈ri ni 仮に [in a temporary or provisional manner 《fig. "supposedly"》] 《for the time being, temporarily, provisionally》, shi⌈ken-tekini 試験的に •c [on an experimental basis] 《experimentally》, i⌈chioo 一応 •c [satisfactorily for the time being] 《for the time being, for the present》

EX. (**a**) Let's tentatively set our next meeting date for Monday.
会議の日取りを{仮に/一応/*試験的に}来週の月曜日と決めておきましょう。
*Kaigi no hi-dori o {kari ni/ichioo/*shiken-tekini} raishuu no getsuyoo-bi to kimete okimashoo.*
(**b**) I tentatively put Tom in charge of the project.
私は{一応/試験的に/仮に}トムにその仕事を担当させることにした。
Watashi wa {ichioo/shiken-tekini/kari ni} Tomu ni sono shigoto o tantoo-saseru koto ni shita.

T

tenth n./adj. **[next after the ninth or one of ten equal parts]**

1. (da⌉i-)ju⌈u-ban-me⌉ (no N) (第)十番目(のN) **[next after the ninth]** SEE APPENDIX II

2. ju⌈u-bun no ichi⌉ 十分の一 **[one of ten equal parts]**

term n. **[a period of time for which s.t. lasts, esp. one that is set officially 《fig. "a condition stipulated in a contract or legal document," "a word with a specific or technical meaning"》]**

1. ki⌈ka⌉n 期間 **•c [a specific time span over which s.t. noteworthy occurs] 《period, tenure》**

EX. My term as dean will be for four years.
学部長を務める期間は四年です。
Gakubu-choo o tsutomeru kikan wa yo-nen desu.

2. ga⌈kki 学期 **•c [a school semester] 《semester, session》**

EX. During the winter term I'll be taking three courses.
冬学期は三科目取るつもりです。
Fuyu-gakki wa san-kamoku toru tsumori desu.

3. ke⌈iyaku-jo⌉oken 契約条件 **•c [formally stipulated conditions in a contract]**

4. yo⌈ogo 用語 **•c [a word with a technical meaning] 《technical term》**

EX. This article has many terms in it that I don't understand.
この記事には私に分からない用語がたくさんある。
Kono kiji ni wa watashi ni wakaranai yoogo ga takusan aru.

terminal adj. **[at the end of s.t. in time or space]**

1. shu⌈uten no N 終点のN **•c [at the end of a railway line]**

EX. In big Japanese cities there is usually a department store at the terminal station of a train line.
日本の大都市では終点の駅に大抵デパートがある。
Nihon no dai-toshi de wa shuuten no eki ni taitei depaato ga aru.

2. ma⌉kki no N 末期のN **•c [of the final period/stage]**

EX. This hospital has a special ward for terminal patients.
この病院には末期患者の特別病棟があります。
Kono byooin ni wa makki-kanja no tokubetsu-byootoo ga arimasu.

—— n. **[the final part or point of s.t. in space or time 《fig. "a bus, train, or air station which is at the end of a line or which serves a large area," "the monitor of a computer"》]**

1. ma⌈ttan 末端 **•c [the extreme point on a line or stick-like object 《fig. "the smallest subject of an organization"》] 《end, tip》**

2. shu⌈uten 終点 **•c [the end of a railway line], ta⌉aminaru** ターミナル **•f [the end of a railway line or a computer terminal], shu⌈uchaku⌉-eki** 終着駅 **•c [the end of a railway line]**

EX. I fell asleep and didn't wake up until the train reached the terminal.
私は寝てしまって電車が{終点/ターミナル/終着駅}に着くまで目が覚めなかった。
Watashi wa nete shimatte densha ga {shuuten/taaminaru/shuuchaku-eki} ni tsuku made me ga samenakatta.

3. ta⌈nmatsu⌉(-ki) 端末(機) **•c [a computer monitor]**

EX. There are about fifty terminals in the school's computer laboratory.
学校のコンピューター室にはコンピューターの端末(機)が五十台ぐらいあります。
Gakkoo no konpyuutaa-shitsu ni wa konpyuutaa no tanmatsu(-ki) ga go-juu-dai-gurai arimasu.

terrace n. **[a raised flat mound on the slope of a mountain or hillside 《fig. "a paved area adjacent to a house"》]**

1. sha⌉men no he⌈ichi 斜面の平地 **•c**

EX. In Japan even mountain terraces are used for farming.
日本では山の斜面の平地も耕している。

Nihon de wa yama no shamen no heichi mo tagayashite iru.

2. te˥rasu テラス •f **[a paved area adjacent to a house]**

terrain n. **[the natural features of a stretch of land]**

chi˹kei 地形 •c [the shape of a stretch of land] ⟪**configuration of the land, topography**⟫, **chi˹sei 地勢 •c [the appearance of a piece of land]** ⟪**geographical features, topography**⟫

EX. The terrain of this area is ideally suited for a golf course.
この辺の{地形/地勢}はゴルフ場にぴったりだ。
Kono hen no {chikei/chisei} wa gorufu-joo ni pittari da.

terrible adj. **[causing fear ⟪fig. "very bad"⟫]**

1. **o˹soroshi˥i** 恐ろしい adj(*i*). **[feeling afraid of s.t./s.o./s.a. unusual or mysterious or causing such fear or cruel]** ⟪**frightening, terrifying, fearful, dreadful, frightful, awesome**⟫

EX. Today I saw a terrible car accident on my way to work.
今日仕事に来る途中恐ろしい自動車事故を見かけたよ。
Kyoo shigoto ni kuru tochuu osoroshii jidoosha-jiko o mi-kaketa yo.

2. **hi˹do˥i** ひどい adj(*i*). **[of a frightening kind/degree]** ⟪**cruel, merciless, violent, serious, dreadful, awful**⟫

EX. (**a**) The hamburger I had at that place was terrible.
あの店で食べたハンバーガーはひどかった。
Ano mise de tabeta hanbaagaa wa hidokatta.
(**b**) Man! What a terrible wind!
うわあ、ひどい風だ!
Uwaa, hidoi kaze da!
(**c**) I got terrible grades last semester.
先学期はひどい成績をもらった。
Sen-gakki wa hidoi seiseki o moratta.

terribly adv. **[to the extent that s.t. causes fear ⟪fig. "very"⟫]**

o˹soro˥shiku 恐ろしく /⟨adj(*i*). *ku* of *osoroshii* fearful/ [to the extent that s.t./s.o./s.a. causes fear], hi˥doku ひどく /⟨adj(*i*). *ku* of *hidoi* extremely bad/ [to the extent that one feels awful ⟪fig. "very"⟫]

EX. (**a**) I'm terribly tired, so I'm going to bed.
{ひどく/恐ろしく}疲れたので、寝るよ。
{Hidoku/Osoroshiku} tsukareta node, neru yo.
(**b**) When I heard my father's voice over the telephone, I was terribly happy.
父の声を電話で聞いた時には{ひどく/?恐ろしく}うれしかった。
Chichi no koe o denwa de kiita toki ni wa {hidoku/?osoroshiku} ureshikatta.

terrific adj. **[extremely good or great in size/intensity]**

su˹barashi˥i すばらしい adj(*i*). **[causing great wonder/admiration/pleasure due to being extremely good]** ⟪**wonderful, marvelous, magnificent, splendid, superb, fantastic, great, fabulous**⟫

EX. (**a**) I met a terrific girl at the party last night.
ゆうべのパーティーですばらしい女の子に会ったよ。
Yuube no paatii de subarashii onna-no-ko ni atta yo.
(**b**) A: I got a scholarship from the Ministry of Education.
文部省の奨学金をもらったんだ。
Monbu-shoo no shoogaku-kin o moratta n da.
B: That's terrific!
へえ。それはすばらしい!
Hee. Sore wa subarashii!

terrify vt. **[to cause s.o./s.a. to feel intense fear]**

⟨-o⟩ hi˥doku o˹sore˥ru ⟨～を⟩ひどく恐れる ② **[for s.o./s.a. to fear s.o./s.t./s.a. intensely], ⟨-ni⟩ o˹bieru** ⟨～に⟩おびえる ② **[for s.o./s.a. to be scared of s.o./s.t./s.a.]** ⟪**become frightened, become intimidated**⟫

NOTE: "Terrify," which takes an inanimate object as its subject, cannot be literally translated into *osore-saseru* (cause to make s.o. terrified), but is more naturally expressed in Japanese as s.t. *ni*

T

obieru/s.t. *o hidoku osoreru*, as in the following example.

EX. Elevators terrified the child because he had once been trapped in one.
その子は一度とじ込められたことがあるのでエレベーター{におびえた/をひどく恐れた}。
Sono ko wa ichi-do toji-kome-rareta koto ga aru node erebeetaa {ni obieta/o hidoku osoreta}.

territory n. **[land belonging to a nation]**
ryoˈodo 領土 •c ⟪**dominion, domain**⟫

EX. Disputes over territory often lead to war.
領土争いはよく戦争の原因になる。
Ryoodo-arasoi wa yoku sensoo no gen'in ni naru.

terror n. **[extreme fear]**
kyoˈofu 恐怖 •c [great anxiety caused by the expectation of danger/evil] ⟪**fear, fright, scare, horror**⟫

EX. I was stricken with terror when I saw the dead corpse.
死体を見た時に恐怖に襲われた。
Shitai o mita toki ni kyoofu ni osowa-reta.

test n. **[an act/method of determining or evaluating the nature, qualities, or abilities of s.t./s.o./s.a.** ⟪**fig. "an examination in an academic subject"**⟫**]**
1. keˈnsa 検査 •c [looking at s.t./s.o./s.a. carefully to see if it/he/she meets a standard or if there is anything wrong with it/him/her, often in an official capacity] ⟪**inspection, examination, checkup**⟫**, shiˈkeˈn 試験 •c [an act/instance of determining or evaluating the ability/proficiency/quality of s.o./a machine]** ⟪**examination, quiz**⟫**, teˈsuto テスト •f [an examination or experiment]**

EX. (**a**) Blood tests are an essential part of a physical examination.
血液{検査/*試験/*テスト}は健康診断に(とって)絶対に必要だ。
*Ketsueki{-kensa/*shiken/*testuto} wa kenkoo-shindan ni (-totte) zettai ni hitsuyoo da.*
(**b**) I did well on my Japanese language test today.
今日の日本語の{試験/テスト/*検査}はよく出来た。
*Kyoo no Nihon-go no {shiken/tesuto/*kensa} wa yoku dekita.*

2. jiˈkken 実験 •c [the act of trying out a theory or hypothesis under various conditions to see if the predictions it makes are correct] ⟪**experiment**⟫

EX. Any form of nuclear test should be totally banned.
どんな核実験も絶対禁じられなければいけない。
Donna kaku-jikken mo zettai kinji-rarenakereba ikenai.

3. keˈnsa-hoo 検査法 •c [a method of looking at s.o./s.t./s.a. carefully to see if it/he/she meets a standard or if there is anything wrong with it/him/her], shiˈndan-hoo 診断法 •c [a method of medically examining a patient ⟪**fig. "a method of examining s.t. by a professional"**⟫**], shiˈken-hoo 試験法 •c [a method of determining or evaluating the ability/proficiency/quality of s.o./a machine], teˈsuto-hoo テスト法 •f+c [a method for conducting an examination or experiment]**

EX. (**a**) Medical tests rely on computers to a great extent these days.
今日の医学{診断法/?検査法/*試験法/*テスト法}はコンピューターに負う所が大きい。
*Konnichi no igaku {shindan-hoo/?kensa-hoo/*shiken-hoo/*tesuto-hoo} wa konpyuutaa ni ou tokoro ga ookii.*
(**b**) Do you think IQ tests are really reliable?
知能{検査(法)/?テスト(法)/*診断(法)/*試験(法)}は信頼できると思いますか。
*Chinoo {kensa(-hoo)/?tesuto(-hoo)/*shindan(-hoo)/*shiken(-hoo)} wa shinrai dekiru to omoimasu ka.*
(**c**) There are all sorts of tests available for evaluating foreign language competence.

外国語能力を調べる{テスト法/試験法/?診断法/*検査法}は色々ある。
*Gaikoku-go-nooryoku o shiraberu {tesuto-hoo/shiken-hoo/?shindan-hoo/*kensa-hoo} wa iro-iro aru.*

4. shi⌈ken-mo⌉ndai 試験問題 •c [an examination question or set of questions for an examination]

EX. It took us hours to prepare the test.
試験問題を準備するのに何時間もかかった。
Shiken-mondai o junbi-suru no ni nan-jikan mo kakatta.

— vt. **[for s.o. to subject s.o./s.t./s.a. to an examination]**

1. ⟨-ni⟩ ⟨-no⟩ shi⌈ke⌉n o suru ⟨〜に⟩⟨〜の⟩試験をする ③ •c [for s.o. to consider s.o./s.t., esp. a machine, carefully to see if he/she/it meets a given standard of ability/proficiency/quality] ⟪examine⟫, **⟨-ni⟩ ⟨-no⟩ te⌉suto o suru ⟨〜に⟩⟨〜の⟩テストをする ③ •f**

EX. My Japanese instructor tested us on our *kanji* today.
日本語の先生は今日私たちに漢字の{試験/テスト}をした。
Nihon-go no sensei wa kyoo watashi-tachi ni kanji no {shiken/tesuto} o shita.

2. ⟨-no⟩ ji⌈kken o suru ⟨〜の⟩実験をする ③ •c [for s.o. to try out a theory or hypothesis under various conditions to see if the predictions it makes are correct]

EX. All countries should be banned from testing nuclear bombs.
すべての国が核実験をするのを阻止すべきです。
Subete no kuni ga kaku-jikken o suru no o soshi-su-beki desu.

3. ⟨-o⟩ ke⌉nsa-suru ⟨〜を⟩検査する ③ •c [for s.o. to look at s.t./s.o./s.a. carefully to see if it/he/she meets a standard or if there is anything wrong with it/him/her] ⟪inspect, examine, check⟫

EX. The new drug must first be tested to see if it works on other symptoms.
新薬は他の症状にも効くかどうか、まず検査されなければならない。
Shin'yaku wa hoka no shoojoo ni mo kiku ka doo ka, mazu kensa-sarenakereba naranai.

4. ⟨-o⟩ ta⌈me⌉su ⟨〜を⟩試す ① [for s.o. to actually do s.t. or to examine or use s.t. to find out what one wants to know about it] ⟪try, attempt⟫

EX. A: Do you know the Japanese word for "democracy?"
"デモクラシー" に当たる日本語を知っている?
"Demokurashii" ni ataru Nihon-go o shitte iru?
B: Are you testing my Japanese vocabulary?
日本語の単語の知識を試しているのかい?
Nihon-go no tango no chishiki o tameshite iru no kai?

Texas n.
Te⌉kisasu テキサス •f

text n. **[the main body of what is printed, esp. in a book, as distinct from notes, illustrations, etc.; the original or actual words of s.t. written or spoken]**

1. ho⌉nbun 本文 •c [the main body of s.t. written, as distinct from notes, commentary, quotes, etc.] ⟪body⟫

EX. The book consists of text and lots of illustrations.
その本は本文とたくさんの図解とからなっている。
Sono hon wa honbun to takusan no zukai to kara natte iru.

2. ge⌈nbun 原文 •c [the original words of an author, as distinct from their translation] ⟪the original⟫, **te⌉kisuto テキスト •f [the original words of an author or a book used as a source of information in an academic course]**

EX. I can't tell if this is a mistranslation or not unless I check it against the original text.
{原文/テキスト}に当たってみないと、これが誤訳かどうかは分かりません。
{Genbun/Tekisuto} ni atatte minai to, kore ga goyaku ka doo ka wa wakarimasen.

textbook n. **[a book used as a source of information in an academic course]** **kyo⌈oka-sho 教科書 •c, te⌉kisuto テキスト •f [the original words of an author or a book used as a source of information in an academic course]**

EX. Do you know of any good elementary Japanese textbooks?
何かいい初級日本語の{教科書/テキスト}を知っていますか。
Nani-ka ii shokyuu Nihon-go no {kyooka-sho/tekisuto} o shitte imasu ka.

textile n. **[a woven fabric or the raw material used in making this]**

1. o⌈ri-mono 織物 [a woven fabric] **《clothes, fabrics, woven stuff》**

EX. The textile industry in Japan has a long history.
日本の織物産業の歴史は古い。
Nihon no ori-mono-sangyoo no rekishi wa furui.

2. o⌈ri-mono-ge⌉nryoo 織物原料 [the raw materials used in making woven fabrics]

texture n. **[the physical characteristics of a woven fabric 《fig. "the physical characteristics of a flat surface such as skin, wood, a painting, etc."》]**

T

1. ki⌉-ji 生地 [cloth] 《stuff, cloth, material》

2. o⌈ri-gu⌉ai 織り具合 [the physical characteristics of a woven fabric]

EX. I like the texture of this material.
私はこの織物の織り具合が好きなの。
Watashi wa kono ori-mono no ori-guai ga suki na no.

3. ki⌈me⌉ きめ [the grain of a wood 《fig. "the sense produced by touching the flat surface of s.t. such as skin, stone, etc."》] 《grain》

4. ka⌈nshoku 感触 •c [the physical feeling produced by touching s.t.] 《touch, feel》

EX. The texture of this silk is like velvet.
この絹はベルベットのような感触だ。
Kono kinu wa berubetto no yoona kanshoku da.

than conj. **[a conjunction to indicate the second element in a comparison or an exception]**

1. {N/adj(*na*). stem/{V/adj(*i*).} inf. nonpast}} yo⌉ri (mo) {N/adj(*na*). stem/{V/adj(*i*).} inf. nonpast}}より(も) [a particle that indicates the second element in a comparison]

EX. (**a**) A: Who is taller, John or Bill?
ジョンとビルと、どちらが背が高いですか。
Jon to Biru to, dochira ga se ga takai desu ka.
B: John is taller than Bill.
ジョンの方がビルより高いです。
Jon no hoo ga Biru yori takai desu.
(**b**) Do you find Chinese to be easier than Japanese?
中国語は日本語よりやさしいと思いますか。
Chuugoku-go wa Nihon-go yori yasashii to omoimasu ka.
(**c**) Meat is about three times more expensive in Japan than in the U.S.
肉はアメリカよりも日本の方が三倍ぐらい高い。
Niku wa Amerika yori mo Nihon no hoo ga san-bai-gurai takai.
(**d**) Tonight I'd rather stay home and watch TV than go out somewhere.
今晩はどこかへ行くより家でテレビを見ている方がいい。
Konban wa doko-ka e iku yori ie de terebi o mite iru hoo ga ii.

2. ⟨-yori⟩ ho⌈ka ni ⟨〜より⟩外に [other than]

EX. (**a**) A: Can you think of a more suitable person for that position than Mr. Okada?
あのポストに岡田氏より外にいい人がいると思いますか。
Ano posuto ni Okada-shi yori hoka ni ii hito ga iru to omoimasu ka.
B: No, Mr. Okada seems to be the best.
いいえ、岡田氏が一番いいようですよ。
Iie, Okada-shi ga ichiban ii yoodesu yo.
(**b**) A: Did Junko talk a lot about me?
順子は私のことをよく話しましたか。
Junko wa watashi no koto o yoku hanashimashita ka.

B: No, she talked about nothing more than her school life.
いいえ、学校のことより外に何も話しませんでした。
Iie, gakkoo no koto yori hoka ni nanimo hanashimasendeshita.

thank vt. **[for s.o. to express one's appreciation to s.o.]**
⟨-ni⟩ a⌈ri⌉gatoo to i⌈u ⟨〜に⟩ありがとうと言う ① **[for s.o. to literally say "thank you" to s.o.], ⟨-ni⟩ ka⌉nsha-suru ⟨〜に⟩感謝する** ③ **•c [for s.o. to feel or express gratitude to s.o. for s.t.]**

EX. (**a**) I thank you for your kindness from the bottom of my heart.
御親切には心の底から{感謝します/*ありがとうと言います}。
*Go-shinsetsu ni wa kokoro no soko kara {kansha-shimasu/*arigatoo to iimasu}.*
(**b**) Though I gave Tom a ride home, he didn't even thank me. Strange, isn't it?
トムをうちまで車で送ってあげたのに、{ありがとうも言わなかった/??感謝もしなかった}よ。変だね。
Tomu o uchi made kuruma de okutte ageta noni, {arigatoo mo iwanakatta/??kansha mo shinakatta} yo. Hen da ne.

PHRASE: Thank you. *Arigatoo (gozaimasu)* ありがとう(ございます)。

NOTE: When you thank someone who is superior to you, you should use the longer version, i.e., *arigatoo gozaimasu*, no matter how well you know him/her. Japanese usually do not respond with *arigatoo* when complimented by a superior; it is instead common to respond negatively using *iie*.

EX. A: I hear that you speak English very well.
君は英語がとても上手だそうだね。
Kimi wa eigo ga totemo joozu da sooda ne.
B: Thank you.
いいえ(、{それほどでは/まだまだです})。
Iie (, {sore hodo de wa/mada mada desu}).

NOTE: In Japan it is normal to thank someone who is a superior twice for a kindness, first, at the time of receiving the kindness and secondly, on meeting the person the next time, at which time the appropriate phrase to use is *Kono aida wa doomo arigatoo gozaimashita* "Thank for your kindness the last time I met you."

thankful adj. **[expressing or feeling appreciation]**
⟨-ni⟩ ⟨-o⟩ ka⌉nsha-shite iru ⟨〜に⟩⟨〜を⟩感謝している /⟨V*te iru* of *kansha-suru* ③ thank/ ② **•c [for s.o. to be in a state of feeling appreciation], ⟨-o⟩ a⌈rigata⌉i to omou ⟨〜を⟩あり難いと思う** ① **[for s.o. to feel gratitude for s.t.], ⟨-o⟩ a⌈rigata⌉i to o⌈mo⌉tte iru ⟨〜を⟩あり難いと思っている** ②

EX. (**a**) The students were thankful to their teacher for his fine teaching.
学生はいい教育をしてくれた先生に{感謝して/?有り難いと思って}いた。
Gakusei wa ii kyooiku o shite kureta sensei ni {kansha-shite/?arigatai to omotte} ita.
(**b**) I'm thankful that he was willing to recommend a person like me for the job.
私のような者をその仕事に推薦してくださったことを{あり難いと思って/感謝して}いる。
Watashi no yoona mono o sono shigoto ni suisen-shite kudasatta koto o {arigatai to omotte/kansha-shite} iru.

thanks n. **[an expression of appreciation]**
ka⌉nsha 感謝 •c [the state of feeling thankfulness to s.o. for s.t. or the act of expressing this] ⟪gratitude⟫, sha⌉i 謝意 •c [a feeling of appreciation ⟨fml⟩]

EX. (**a**) The newly elected congressman expressed his thanks to his supporters.
初めて当選した議員は支持者に{謝意/?感謝}を表明した。
Hajimete toosen-shita giin wa shiji-sha ni {shai/?kansha} o hyoomei-shita.
(**b**) Words of thanks can help smooth human relationships.
{感謝/*謝意}の言葉は人間関係をスムーズにすることができる。
*{Kansha/*Shai} no kotoba wa ningen-kankei o sumuuzu ni suru koto ga dekiru.*

T

NOTE: "Thanks" is expressed as *arigatoo.*
PHRASE: thanks to ⟨*-no*⟩ *o-kage de* ⟨〜の⟩おかげで, *o-kage-sama de* おかげさまで

EX. A: Thanks to you, Prof. Hirai, I was able to find a good job.
{平井先生のおかげで/おかげさまで}いい仕事が見つかりました。
{Hirai-sensei no o-kage de/O-kage-sama de} ii shigoto ga mitsukarimashita.
B: Oh, I'm glad to hear that.
ああ、そう。それはよかった!
Aa, soo. Sore wa yokatta!

thanksgiving n. **[an expression of appreciation, esp. to God]**
ka˥nsha no hyo˥oge˥n 感謝の表現 •c [an expression of gratitude], ka˥nsha no i˥nori˥ 感謝の祈り [a prayer of gratitude to God]
PHRASE: Thanksgiving Day *kansha-sai* 感謝祭 •c

EX. In the United States, on the fourth Thursday of each November people celebrate Thanksgiving Day by getting together with family members and eating turkey and pumpkin pie.
アメリカでは毎年十一月の第四木曜日に家族が集まって、七面鳥やかぼちゃのパイを食べて、感謝祭を祝う。
Amerika de wa mai-toshi juu-ichi-gatsu no dai-yon mokuyoo-bi ni kazoku ga atsumatte, shichimenchoo ya kabocha no pai o tabete, kansha-sai o iwau.

T

that[1] pron. **[a demonstrative pronoun referring to s.t./s.o./s.a. that has been previously mentioned or s.t. not close to the speaker/writer]**
1. so˥re それ [a demonstrative pronoun that refers to s.t./s.o./s.a. that is physically close to the hearer/reader or to s.t./s.o./s.a. that either the hearer/reader or speaker/writer has mentioned but may not be familiar to the other] ⟪it⟫, a˥re あれ [a demonstrative pronoun that refers to s.t./s.o./s.a. that is physically neither close to the speaker/writer nor to the hearer/reader or to s.t./s.o./s.a. that both the hearer/reader and speaker/writer are familiar with from a common shared experience in the past] ⟪that...over there⟫

EX. (**a**) A: What's that?
{それ/あれ}は何ですか。
{Sore/Are} wa nan desu ka.
B: A Japanese dictionary.
日本語の辞書です。
Nihon-go no jisho desu.
(**b**) A: What's that building over there?
あの建物は何ですか。
Ano tate-mono wa nan desu ka.
B: That's a hospital.
{あれ/*それ}は病院です。
*{Are/*Sore} wa byooin desu.*
(**c**) A: Today my wife and I ate at that Japanese restaurant you recommended the other day.
今日僕と妻は先日君がすすめてくれた日本料理のレストランで食事したよ。
Kyoo boku to tsuma wa senjitsu kimi ga susumete kureta Nihon-ryoori no resutoran de shokuji-shita yo.
B: Oh, yeah? Which one was that?
へえ、{それ/*あれ}はどのレストランだい?
*Hee, {sore/*are} wa dono resutoran dai?*
(**d**) To be or not to be, that is the question.
生きるか死ぬか、{それ/*あれ}が問題だ。
*Ikiru ka shinu ka, {sore/*are} ga mondai da.*
(**e**) The size of the entranceway in the Yamadas' house is much larger than that in the Hashimotos'.
山田家の玄関の大きさは橋本家の({それ/*あれ})よりはるかに大きい。
*Yamada-ke no genkan no ooki-sa wa Hashimoto-ke no ({sore/*are}) yori harukani ookii.*

— adj. **[a demonstrative adjective that refers to s.t. that has been previously mentioned or s.t. not close to the speaker/writer]**
so˥no N そのN [a demonstrative adjective that refers to s.t./s.o./s.a. that is physically close to the hearer/reader or to s.t./s.o./s.a. that either the hearer/reader or speaker/

writer has mentioned but may not be familiar to the other], a⌈no N あのN [a demonstrative adjective that refers to s.t./s.o./s.a. that is physically neither close to the speaker/writer nor to the hearer/reader or to s.t./s.o./s.a. that both the hearer/reader and speaker/writer are familiar with from a common shared experience in the past] ⟪that…over there⟫

EX. (**a**) A: Where'd you buy that book?
{その/*あの}本、どこで買いましたか。
*{Sono/*Ano} hon, doko de kaimashita ka.*
B: This? I bought it at the college bookstore.
これですか。大学の本屋で買いました。
Kore desu ka. Daigaku no honya de kaimashita.
(**b**) A: Did you see that girl over there?
{あの/*その}女の子、見た?
*{Ano/*Sono} onna-no-ko, mita?*
B: You mean the girl wearing a red sweater?
赤いセーターを着た女の子?
Akai seetaa o kita onna-no-ko?
(**c**) A: You remember that restaurant where we had the steak dinner?
晩御飯にステーキを食べた{あの/*その}レストラン、覚えてる?
*Ban-gohan ni suteeki o tabeta {ano/*sono} resutoran, oboete ru?*
B: Yes, the one in Ginza, right?
うん、銀座のだろう?
Un, Ginza no daroo?
(**d**) A: During the summer of my junior year in college I worked at a bank in Saint Louis.
大学三年生の夏、セントルイスにある銀行でアルバイトをしていた。
Daigaku san-nen-sei no natsu, Sentoruisu ni aru ginkoo de arubaito o shite ita.
B: Oh?
そう。
Soo.
A: It was at that bank that I met the woman who is now my wife.
{その/*あの}銀行で今の妻に会ったんだ。
*{Sono/*Ano} ginkoo de ima no tsuma ni atta n da.*

— adv. **[to that extent]**
so⌈nnani そんなに [to an extent indicated by s.t. said or written earlier, either by another person (esp. the hearer) or by the first person, in either case implying that the information in question is not common knowledge to the first person and the other person], a⌈nnani あんなに [to the extent of s.t./s.o./s.a. familiar to both the hearer/reader and speaker/writer from a common shared experience in the past]

EX. (**a**) A: My son is now six feet five inches tall.
息子の身長は今六フィート五インチです。
Musuko no shinchoo wa ima roku-fiito go-inchi desu.
B: Really? That tall?
本当に? {そんなに/*あんなに}高いんですか。
*Hontoo ni? {Sonnani/*Annani} takai n desu ka.*
(**b**) We've never seen a Japanese instructor who can teach that well, have we?
{あんなに/*そんなに}上手に教えられる日本語の先生は見たことがないですね。
*{Annani/*Sonnani} joozuni oshie-rareru Nihon-go no sensei wa mita koto ga nai desu ne.*

PHRASE: That is (to say) *sunawachi* すなわち conj. ⟪namely, or, viz⟫

EX. The capital of Japan, that is to say Tokyo, used to be called Edo.
日本の首都、すなわち東京は昔は江戸と呼ばれていた。
Nihon no shuto, sunawachi Tookyoo wa mukashi wa Edo to yoba-rete ita.

PHRASE: that kind of *sonna* N そんなN ⟪such, that sort of⟫, *anna* N あんなN ⟪such, that sort of⟫

EX. (**a**) A: My daughter wants to get married to a guy who makes his living gambling.
娘がばくちで生活している男と結婚したがっているんだ。

T

Musume ga bakuchi de seikatsu-shite iru otoko to kekkon-shi-ta-gatte iru n da.
B: You'd better talk her out of marrying that kind of guy.
{そんな/*あんな}男と結婚するのはやめさせた方がいいよ。
*{Sonna/*Anna} otoko to kekkon-suru no wa yame-saseta hoo ga ii yo.*
(**b**) Mom, see the sweater Laura's wearing? I want that kind of sweater.
お母さん、ローラが着ているセーターね、{あんな/*そんな}セーターが欲しいよ。
*O-kaa-san, Roora ga kite iru seetaa ne, {anna/*sonna} seetaa ga hoshii yo.*

PHRASE: that way *soo iu fuu ni* そういう風に, *aa iu fuu ni* ああいう風に

EX. (**a**) A: Should I turn the knob this way?
この取っ手はこう回すんですか。
Kono totte wa koo mawasu n desu ka.
B: No, not that way. Turn it counter-clockwise.
いいえ、{そう/*ああ}いう風にじゃなくて、時計と反対方向に回すんです。
*Iie, {soo/*aa} iu fuu ni janakute, tokei to hantai-hookoo ni mawasu n desu.*
(**b**) A: Can you show me how to tie a square knot?
こま結びの結び方、教えてくれる?
Koma-musubi no musubi-kata, oshiete kureru?
B: I can't, but watch him do it.
僕にはできないけど、あの人のやっているのを見てごらん。
Boku ni wa dekinai kedo, ano hito no yatte iru no o mite goran.
A: Oh, that way!
ああ、{ああ/*そう}いう風にか。
*Aa, {aa/*soo} iu fuu ni ka.*

that[2] pron. **[a relative pronoun which introduces a sentence modifying the preceding noun]**
ø

NOTE: The Japanese language has no relative pronouns. A sentence modifying a noun simply precedes that noun.

EX. (**a**) I forgot to return a book that I checked out from the library a month ago.
一か月前に図書館で借りた本を返すのを忘れていた。
Ik-kagetsu mae ni tosho-kan de karita hon o kaesu no o wasurete ita.
(**b**) The building that used to stand here is gone now.
ここに立っていた建物はもうなくなってしまった。
Koko ni tatte ita tate-mono wa moo nakunatte shimatta.

that[3] conj. **[a conjunction introducing a subordinate clause indicating purpose, cause, result, or subject or object of a predicate]**

1. Sinf. (to iu) no Sinf.(という)の [a particle added to a sentence to form a noun clause, usually expressing s.t. relatively concrete and directly apprehended by the speaker/writer] ((to, Ving)), **Sinf. (to iu) koto Sinf.(という)こと [a particle added to a sentence to form a noun clause, usually expressing s.t. relatively abstract and indirectly apprehended by the speaker]** ((to, Ving))

EX. (**a**) Is it true that in Korea you're not supposed to pick up your rice bowl while eating?
韓国では食べる時に御飯茶わんを手で持ってはいけないという{の/??こと}は本当ですか。
Kankoku de wa taberu toki ni gohan-jawan o te de motte wa ikenai to iu {no/??koto} wa hontoo desu ka.
(**b**) Did you know that Gary went to Japan?
ゲリーが日本に行った(という){の/こと}を知っていますか。
Gerii ga Nihon ni itta (to iu) {no/koto} o shitte imasu ka.
(**c**) I wasn't aware until today that you had lost your mother.
お母さんがなくなった{こと/の}を今日まで知りませんでした。
O-kaa-san ga nakunatta {koto/no} o kyoo made shirimasendeshita.

2. S to iˈu N SというN [a noun the

content of which is described by S]

EX. (a) I heard a rumor that John and Mary are going to get divorced.
メアリーとジョンが離婚するといううわさを聞きましたよ。
Mearii to Jon ga rikon-suru to iu uwasa o kikimashita yo.
(b) Is there any clear evidence that he embezzled funds?
彼が金を着服したという確かな証拠はありますか。
Kare ga kane o chakufuku shita to iu tashikana shooko wa arimasu ka.

3. Vinf. nonpast ta⌈me⌉ ni Vinf. nonpastために [a subordinate conjunction expressing purpose or cause] ⟪as a result of, because of, owing to⟫

EX. I worked hard so that my family could be fed.
家族が食べていくために私は一生懸命働いた。
Kazoku ga tabete iku tame ni watashi wa isshoo-kenmei hataraita.

4. Sinf. no⌉de Sinf.ので [a subordinate conjunction expressing reason or cause] ⟪so, since, because⟫, Sinf. kara Sinf.から [a subordinate conjunction expressing reason or cause]

NOTE: When the nonpast affirmative form of adj(*na*). or N+cop. occurs before *node*, it changes to the form {adj(*na*). stem/N} *na node.*

EX. (a) Mozart's piano concerto was so beautifully played that I was moved to tears.
モーツァルトのピアノ協奏曲の演奏があまりにもすばらしかった{から/ので}感動のあまり涙を流した。
Mootsaruto no piano-kyoosoo-kyoku no ensoo ga amari-nimo subarashikatta {kara/node} kandoo no amari namida o nagashita.
(b) I drank so much last night that I slept until noon.
きのうの晩、飲み過ぎた{から/ので}昼まで目が覚めなかった。
Kinoo no ban, nomi-sugita {kara/node} hiru made me ga samenakatta.

5. V*te* V*te* [a conjunction loosely relating two sentences in a temporal or logical sequence] ⟪...and⟫

EX. (a) I'm very glad that you could come.
いらして下さって、とても嬉しいです。
Irashite kudasatte, totemo ureshii desu.
(b) I'm very sorry that you cannot accept my offer.
私の申し出を受けていただけなくて、大変残念です。
Watashi no mooshi-de o ukete itadake-nakute, taihen zannen desu.

theater n. **[a building or other place where plays or movies are presented ⟪fig. "drama"⟫]**

1. ge⌈kijoo 劇場 •c [a building or other place where plays are performed] ⟪playhouse⟫, e⌈iga⌉-kan 映画館 •c [a building or other place where movies are presented]

NOTE: Names of theaters for plays and movies can be followed either by *-gekijoo*, as in *Sakura Gekijoo*, or by *-za* as in *Geijutsu-za.*

EX. (a) A: Is there a theater near the campus?
大学の近くに{映画館/劇場}がありますか。
Daigaku no chikaku ni {eiga-kan/gekijoo} ga arimasu ka.
B: Yes, there's one called Jinsei-za.
ええ、人生座と言うのがあります。
Ee, Jinsei-za to iu no ga arimasu.
(b) "Titanic" is currently showing at the town theater.
町の{映画館/*劇場}で今『タイタニック』をやってるよ。
*Machi no {eiga-kan/*gekijoo} de ima "Taitanikku" o yatte-ru yo.*

2. e⌈ngeki 演劇 •c [a general, formal term for theatrical performance] ⟪play, drama⟫, do⌉rama ドラマ •f [a piece of writing to be performed by actors, esp. on radio or TV]

their pron. **[the possessive form of the third person plural pronoun "they"]**

ø, ka⌉re-ra no N 彼らのN [the possessive form of the human third person plural pronoun *kare-ra* ⟨fml⟩], ka⌉nojo-ra no N 彼

T

女らのN [the possessive form of the female human third person plural pronoun *kanojo-ra* ⟨w⟩], ka˥nojo-tachi no N 彼女たちのN [the possessive form of the female human third person plural pronoun *kanojo-tachi*], so┌re˥-ra no N それらのN [the possessive form of the non-human third person plural pronoun *sore-ra*]

NOTE: "Their" is often not expressed at all in Japanese when it can be understood in a given context.

EX. (**a**) A: What do you think of young people these days?
今の若い人をどう思いますか。
Ima no wakai hito o doo omoimasu ka.
B: I don't understand their life style.
{彼らの/*ø/*彼女らの/*彼女たちの/*それらの}生き方は私には分かりませんね。
*{Kare-ra no/*ø/*Kanojo-ra no/*Kanojo-tachi no/*Sore-ra no} iki-kata wa watashi ni wa wakarimasen ne.*
(**b**) A lot of women are now working as white collar workers and their stress level at work is beginning to approach that of men.
今は多くの女性がホワイトカラーとして働いているが、{彼女たちの/彼女らの/ø/*彼らの/*それらの}職場でのストレス度は男性のそれと似てきている。
*Ima wa ooku no josei ga howaito-karaa to-shite hataraite iru ga, {kanojo-tachi no/kanojo-ra no/ø/*kare ra no/*sore-ra no} shokuba de no sutoresu-do wa dansei no sore to nite-kite iru.*
(**c**) The relationship between sound and meaning in language is generally said to be arbitrary, but there are words where their relationship is not so, such as those that mimic sounds and voices.
言語では一般的に音と意味の関係は恣意的だと言われるが、擬声語のように{それらの/*ø/*彼らの/*彼女らの/*彼女たちの}関係がそうでない言葉もある。
*Gengo de wa ippan-tekini on to imi no kankei wa shii-teki da to iwa-reru ga, gisei-go no yooni {sore-ra no/*ø/*kare-ra no/*kanojo-ra no/*kanojo-tachi no} kankei ga soo denai kotoba mo aru.*

them pron. **[the direct or indirect object form of the third person plural pronoun "they"]**
ka˥re-ra {o/ni} 彼ら{を/に} [the direct or indirect object form of the human third person plural pronoun *kare-ra* ⟨fml⟩], ka˥nojo-ra {o/ni} 彼女ら{を/に} [the direct or indirect object form of the female human third person plural pronoun *kanojo-ra*], ka˥nojo-tachi {o/ni} 彼女たち{を/に} [the direct or indirect object form of the female human third person plural pronoun *kanojo-tachi*], so┌re-ra {o/ni} それら{を/に} [the direct or indirect object form of the non-human third person plural pronoun *sore-ra* ⟨fml⟩], so┌no hito˥-tachi {o/ni} その人たち{を/に} [the direct or indirect object form of a group of people that is physically close to the hearer/reader or that either the hearer/reader or speaker/writer has mentioned but may not be familiar to the other], a┌no hito˥-tachi {o/ni} あの人たち{を/に} [the direct or indirect object form of a group of people that is physically close to the speaker/writer nor to the hearer/reader or that both the speaker/writer and hearer/reader are familiar with from a common shared experience in the past]

NOTE: "Them" is often not expressed at all in Japanese when it can be understood in a given context.

EX. (**a**) A: Have you seen John and Mary?
ジョンとメアリーを見かけましたか。
Jon to Mearii o mi-kakemashita ka.
B: Yes, I saw them in the library a little while ago.
ええ、さっき図書館で{彼らを/ø/その人たちを/あの人たちを/*彼女らを/*彼女たちを/*それらを}見かけましたよ。
*Ee, sakki tosho-kan de {kare-ra o/ø/sono hito-tachi o/ano hito-tachi o/*kanojo-ra o/*kanojo-tachi o/*sore-ra o} mi-kakemashita yo.*

(**b**) A: Have you asked the students if they've purchased the textbook yet?
学生に教科書をもう買ったかどうか聞きましたか。
Gakusei ni kyooka-sho o moo katta ka doo ka kikimashita ka.
B: No, I haven't asked them yet.
いいえ、まだ{ø/*彼らに/*彼女らに/*彼女たちに/*その人たちに/*あの人たちに/*それらに}聞いていません。
*Iie, mada {ø/*kare-ra ni/*kanojo-ra ni/*kanojo-tachi ni/*sono hito-tachi ni/*ano hito-tachi ni/*sore-ra ni} kiite imasen.*
(**c**) A: Did you know everyone at the party last night?
昨夜のパーティーに来ていた人をみんな知っているんですか。
Sakuya no paatii ni kite ita hito o minna shitte iru n desu ka.
B: Yes, I knew them all because I had taught them all English before.
ええ、{ø/*彼らを/*彼女らを/*彼女たちを/*その人たちを/*あの人たちを/*それらを}知っています。{ø/彼らには/あの人たちには/*その人たちには/*彼女らには/*彼女たちには/*それらには}英語を教えましたから。
*Ee, {ø/*kare-ra o/*kanojo-ra o/*kanojo-tachi o/*sono hito-tachi o/*ano hito-tachi o/*sore-ra o} shitte imasu. {ø/Kare-ra ni wa/Ano hito-tachi ni wa/*Sono hito-tachi ni wa/*Kanojo-ra ni wa/*Kanojo-tachi ni wa/*Sore-ra ni wa} eigo o oshiemashita kara.*
(**d**) There are three constellations of stars clustered just over the northern horizon. It's hard to distinguish them with the naked eye, but you can see them clearly with a telescope.
北の地平線の真上に三つの星座が一かたまりになっている。肉眼では{それらを/ø/*彼らを/*彼女らを/*彼女たちを/*その人たちを/*あの人たちを}見分けることがむずかしいが、望遠鏡でははっきり見える。
*Kita no chihei-sen no ma-ue ni mittsu no seiza ga hito-katamari ni natte iru. Nikugan de wa {sore-ra o/ø/*kare-ra o/*kanojo-ra o/*kanojo-tachi o/*sono hito-tachi o/*ano hito-tachi o} mi-wakeru koto ga muzukashii ga, booen-kyoo de wa hakkiri mieru.*

theme n. **[the main subject on which s.t. is written, spoken, or thought 《fig. "the main melody in a piece of music"》]**
1. da⌈imoku 題目 •c [an idea, issue, or matter which is central to a discussion or study; the title of a book; the noun in a sentence which grammatically expresses what the rest of the sentence is about] 《topic, subject》, da⌉i 題 •c [s.t. about which a book is written or a discussion is conducted] 《subject, topic, title》, te⌉ema テーマ •f

EX. I'm writing a paper on the theme of Japanese modernization.
私は日本の近代化という{題目/題/テーマ}で論文を書いています。
Watashi wa Nihon no kindai-ka to iu {daimoku/dai/teema} de ronbun o kaite imasu.

2. e⌈ndai 演題 •c [the subject or title of a lecture or speech] 《subject》

EX. The theme of Dr. Yasui's lecture was "Chinese painting during the Tang Dynasty."
安井博士の講演の演題は「唐代の中国絵画」だった。
Yasui-hakase no kooen no endai wa 'Too-dai no Chuugoku-kaiga' datta.

3. shu⌈dai 主題 •c [the main idea, issue, or matter about which a literary or artistic work is composed or written or about which a discussion is conducted] 《topic, subject》

EX. The main theme of this symphony is stated at the very outset of the first movement.
このシンフォニーの主題は第一楽章の一番初めに出てくる。
Kono shinfonii no shudai wa dai-ichi-gakushoo no ichiban hajime ni dete-kuru.

T

themselves pron. **[the reflexive/emphatic form of the third person plural pronoun]** **ji⌈bu⌉n-tachi 自分たち •c [the plural form of the reflexive pronoun, used also for emphasis]**

EX. (**a**) It's not right to demand that the students work hard when the teachers themselves don't do the same.
先生は学生にはよく勉強するように言いながら、自分たちがそうしないのはおかしい。
Sensei wa gakusei ni wa yoku benkyoo-suru yooni ii-nagara, jibun-tachi ga soo shinai no wa okashii.
(**b**) The students of this university appear to consider themselves the best in the country.
この大学の学生は自分たちが全国一だと思っているらしい。
Kono daigaku no gakusei wa jibun-tachi ga zenkoku-ichi da to omotte iru rashii.

then adv. **[at that time or after that]**

1. so⌈no-toki⌉ その時 [at that time] ⟪at that time⟫

EX. A: It was exactly 30 years ago today that I first met my wife.
妻に初めて会ったのはちょうど三十年前の今日です。
Tsuma ni hajimete atta no wa choodo san-juu-nen mae no kyoo desu.
B: Where were you then?
その時どこにいましたか。
Sono-toki doko ni imashita ka.
A: In Paris.
パリにいました。
Pari ni imashita.

2. so⌈re-kara それから [after that or in addition to that] ⟪after that, and, and also⟫

EX. I went to Chicago and then to Boston.
シカゴへ行って、それから、ボストンへ行きました。
Shikago e itte, sore-kara, Bosuton e ikimashita.

—— conj. **[in that case]**
so⌈re-na⌉ra それなら [if that can be assumed to be true], so⌈nna⌉ra そんなら [if that can be assumed to be true ⟨s⟩], so⌈re-de⌉wa それでは [if that is the case ⟪fig. "a signal to indicate that s.t. is to begin or end or two people are to part"⟫], so⌈re-ja⌉a それじゃあ [if that is the case ⟪fig. "a signal to indicate that s.t. is to begin or end or two people are to part"⟫ ⟨s⟩]

EX. A: It looks like rain.
雨のようですよ。
Ame no yoodesu yo.
B: Then we'll have to postpone our tennis match.
{それなら/そんなら/それでは/それじゃあ}テニスの試合は延ばさなければなりませんね。
{Sore-nara/Sonnara/Sore-dewa/Sore-jaa} tenisu no shiai wa nobasanakereba narimasen ne.

—— n. **[that time]**
so⌈no-toki⌉ その時

EX. By then I was used to life in Brazil.
その時までにはブラジルでの生活に慣れていました。
Sono-toki made ni wa Burajiru de no seikatsu ni narete imashita.

theory n. **[a set of ideas or principles formulated to explain s.t. or an opinion based on speculation]**

1. ri⌉ron 理論 •c [a set of ideas or principles formulated to explain s.t.] ↔ jissen 実践 •c

EX. (**a**) Chomsky first made public his theory of transformational grammar in 1957.
チョムスキーは1957年に初めて変形文法の理論を発表した。
Chomusukii wa sen-kyuu-hyaku-go-juu-shichi-nen ni hajimete henkei-bunpoo no riron o happyoo-shita.
(**b**) Theory without practice is no better than practice without theory.
実践の伴わない理論は理論の伴わない実践と同じように悪い。
Jissen no tomonawanai riron wa riron no tomonawanai jissen to onaji yooni warui.

2. ke⌈nkai 見解 •c [one's evaluation of or

judgment about s.t.] ⟪**guess, conjecture, speculation**⟫

EX. According to the theory put forward by the investigators, the murder was committed by a family member of the victim.
殺害者は被害者の身内だというのが捜査陣の見解だ。
Satsugai-sha wa higai-sha no miuchi da to iu no ga soosa-jin no kenkai da.

there adv. **[at/in/to that place** ⟪**fig. "in that respect"**⟫**]**
so⌈ko {ni/de/e/o/ga} そこ{に/で/へ/を/が} **[at/in/to a place that is physically close to the hearer/reader or that either the hearer/reader or speaker/writer has mentioned but may not be familiar to the other]**, **a⌈soko {ni/de/e/o/ga}** あそこ{に/で/へ/を/が} **[at/in/to a place that is physically neither close to the speaker/writer nor to the hearer/reader or that both the hearer/reader and speaker/writer are familiar with from a common shared experience in the past]** ⟪**over there**⟫

NOTE: "There" is often not expressed at all in Japanese when it can be understood in a given context.

EX. (**a**) A: I've just returned from a year in Madrid, Spain.
スペインのマドリッドへ一年行って来たよ。
Supein no Madoriddo e ichi-nen itte kita yo.
B: What were you doing there?
{ø/そこで/*あそこで}何をしていたの?
*{ø/Soko de/*Asoko de} nani o shite ita no?*
(**b**) Ah, but you're wrong there.
ああ、{そこが/*あそこが/*ø}違うんだよ。
*Aa, {soko ga/*asoko ga/*ø} chigau n da yo.*
(**c**) See that smoke over there? That's a forest fire.
{あそこに/*そこに/*ø}煙が見えるだろ? あれは山火事だよ。
*{Asoko ni/*Soko ni/*ø} kemuri ga mieru daro? Are wa yama-kuji da yo.*

PHRASE: there is/are *{aru/iru}* {ある ①/いる ②}

NOTE: *Aru* takes an inanimate subject and *iru* an animate subject, except plants.

EX. (**a**) There are two books on the desk.
机の上に本が二冊ある。
Tsukue no ue ni hon ga ni-satsu aru.
(**b**) There are 150 students in my Japanese class.
私の日本語のクラスには学生が百五十人いる。
Watashi no Nihon-go no kurasu ni wa gakusei ga hyaku-go-juu-nin iru.

PHRASE: then and there *sugu sono ba de* すぐその場で

EX. I decided to buy a fax machine then and there.
ファックス(の機械)をすぐその場で買うことに決めた。
Fakkusu (no kikai) o sugu sono ba de kau koto ni kimeta.

PHRASE: here and there *achi-kochi* あちこち

EX. Cherry blossoms were beginning to bloom here and there.
あちこちに桜が咲き始めていた。
Achi-kochi ni sakura ga saki-hajimete ita.

— int. **[an interjection to indicate satisfaction, approval, encouragement, sympathy, or dismay]**
ho⌈ra ほら **[an interjection used to draw s.o.'s attention to s.t.]**, **so⌈ra** そら **[an interjection used to draw the hearer's attention to s.t. close to him/her]**

EX. (**a**) (Finally succeeding in opening the door) There!
ほら!
Hora!
(**b**) (After serving an ace in tennis) There!
{そら!/ほら!}行くよ。
{Sora!/Hora!} Iku yo.

— pron. **[that place]**
so⌈ko そこ **[a place that is physically close to the hearer/reader or that either the hearer/reader or speaker/writer has mentioned but may not be familiar to the other]**, **a⌈soko** あそこ **[a place that is physically neither close to the speaker/writer nor to the hearer/**

reader or that both the hearer/reader and speaker/writer are familiar with from a common shared experience in the past]

NOTE: "There" is often not expressed at all in Japanese when it can be understood in a given context.

EX. A: Where were you last night?
きのうの晩、どこにいましたか。
Kinoo no ban, doko ni imashita ka.
B: At a coffee shop.
喫茶店にいました。
Kissaten ni imashita.
A: About what time did you leave there?
何時ごろ{そこを/??ø}出ましたか?
Nan-ji-goro {soko o/??ø} demashita ka.
B: Around 11:30.
十一時半ごろ{ø/??そこを}出ました。
Juu-ichi-ji-han-goro {ø/??soko o} demashita.

thereafter adv. **[from that time on or after that ⟨w⟩]**
so⌈no-go その後 ⟪**subsequently, afterward**⟫

EX. He moved to Osaka in l948 and lived in that city thereafter until he died in 1956.
彼は1948年に大阪に引っ越し、その後1956年に死ぬまでそこで暮らした。
Kare wa sen-kyuu-hyaku-yon-juu-hachi-nen ni Oosaka ni hikkoshi, sono-go sen-kyuu-hyaku-go-juu-roku-nen ni shinu made soko de kurashita.

thereby adv. **[by that means, in that way ⟨w⟩]**
so⌈re ni-yotte それによって [by means of or because of that]

EX. The economy of the country flourished, thereby improving the quality of life of everyone.
国の経済は繁栄し、それによって国民の生活の質が向上した。
Kuni no keizai wa han'ei-shi, sore ni-yotte kokumin no seikatsu no shitsu ga koojoo-shita.

therefore adv. **[for that reason or as a result of that]**
da⌉kara だから [a conjunction used to state the result/conclusion of a cause given in the preceeding sentence] ⟪**so, accordingly**⟫, **de⌉sukara ですから [a formal version of "dakara"], shi⌈tagatte 従って [a conjunction indicating that the result stated in the following clause follows necessarily from the foregoing situation ⟨fml⟩]** ⟪**accordingly, consequently, hence**⟫, **so⌈no kekka (to-shite) その結果(として) •c [as a result of that]**

EX. (**a**) The survey was likely to require a large amount of time. Therefore we decided not to undertake it.
その調査は時間がとてもかかりそうでした。{だから/ですから/??従って/*その結果}しないことにしました。
*Sono choosa wa jikan ga totemo kakari-soo deshita. {Dakara/Desukara/??Shitagatte/*Sono kekka} shinai koto ni shimashita.*
(**b**) The cost was enormous. Therefore we abandoned the project.
費用が莫大だった。{従って/その結果/だから/*ですから} その計画をあきらめた。
*Hiyoo ga bakudai datta. {Shitagatte/Sono kekka/Dakara/*Desukara} sono keikaku o akirameta.*

there's [a contracted form of "there is/has"]
a⌉ru ある ① [for s.t. to exist] ⟪**be, exist, be located**⟫, **i⌈ru いる ② [for s.o./s.a. to exist]** ⟪**be, exist, live, reside**⟫

EX. (**a**) There's a bookstore over there.
あそこに本屋があります。
Asoko ni hon-ya ga arimasu.
(**b**) There's a tiger in the cage.
おりの中にとらがいる。
Ori no naka ni tora ga iru.
(**c**) There's been talk of building a new hotel in front of the station.
駅の前に新しいホテルを建てようという話があった。
Eki no mae ni atarashii hoteru o tateyoo to iu hanashi ga atta.

thermometer n. **[an instrument that measures temperature]**
ka⌉ndan-kei 寒暖計 •c [an instrument that measures atmospheric temperature], o⌈ndo-

T

kei 温度計 •c [an instrument that measures temperature], ta⌈ion-kei 体温計 •c [an instrument that measures bodily temperature]

EX. (a) The thermometer read -5°C.
{寒暖計/温度計/*体温計}は摂氏マイナス五度を示していた。
*{Kandan-kei/Ondo-kei/*Taion-kei} wa sesshi mainasu go-do o shimeshite ita.*
(b) The child's mother put the thermometer in her mouth to take her temperature.
母親は熱を計るために{体温計/*寒暖計/*温度計}を子供の口に入れた。
*Haha-oya wa netsu o hakaru tame ni {taion-kei/*kandan-kei/*ondo-kei} o kodomo no kuchi ni ireta.*

these pron. **[the plural form of the pronoun "this"]**
ko⌈re⌉-ra これら [the plural form of *kore*, a pronoun used to refer to s.t. close to the speaker/writer ⟨w⟩]
NOTE: In conversational Japanese *kore* is normally used instead of *kore-ra*.

EX. (a) A high national deficit, a low savings rate, and high wages—these are some of the causes of weakness in the dollar.
国の赤字、低貯蓄率、高賃金、これらがドルが弱い原因に数えられる。
Kuni no akaji, tei-chochiku-ritsu, koo-chingin, kore-ra ga doru ga yowai gen'in ni kazoe-rareru.
(b) What are these?
{これ/*これら}は何ですか。
*{Kore/*Kore-ra} wa nan desu ka.*

— adj. **[the plural form of the adjective "this"]**
ko⌈re⌉-ra no N これらのN [the plural form of *kono*, a demonstrative adjective used to refer to s.t. close to the speaker/writer ⟨w⟩]
NOTE: In conversational Japanese *kono* is normally used instead of *kore-ra no*.

EX. (a) Visuality and indirectness—these elements seem to be central to Japanese culture.
視覚性と間接性、これらの要素が日本文化の中心をなしているようだ。
Shikaku-sei to kansetsu-sei, kore-ra no yooso ga Nihon-bunka no chuushin o nashite iru yooda.
(b) Whose books are these?
{この/*これらの}本はだれのですか。
*{Kono/*Kore-ra no} hon wa dare no desu ka.*

thesis n. **[a proposition put forward with arguments to support it or a lengthy essay, esp. one submitted to meet a requirement for an academic degree]**
1. me⌈idai 命題 •c [a proposition]
2. ro⌈nbun 論文 •c [a piece of writing presenting the results of one's research]

EX. (a) I am writing an M.A. thesis on Taisho era democratic movements.
私は大正時代における民主主義の運動について修士論文を書いている。
Watashi wa Taishoo-jidai ni-okeru minshu-shugi no undoo ni-tsuite shuushi-ronbun o kaite iru.
(b) Have you read Dr. Doi's thesis on the Japanese psychology of dependency?
土居博士の日本人の甘えに関する論文を読んだことがありますか。
Doi-hakase no Nihon-jin no amae ni kansuru ronbun o yonda koto ga arimasu ka.

they pron. **[the third person plural pronoun, used to refer to a previously mentioned group of things or people or to people in general]**
ka⌉re-ra 彼ら [the third person plural pronoun, used to refer to a previously mentioned group of people], so⌈no hito⌉-tachi その人たち [a group of people that is physically close to the hearer/reader or that either the hearer/reader or speaker/writer has mentioned but may not be familiar to the other] ⟪those people⟫, a⌈no hito⌉-tachi あの人たち [a group of people that is physically neither close to the speaker/writer nor to the hearer/reader or that both the speaker/writer and hearer/reader are familiar with from a common shared experience in the past] ⟪those people⟫,

T

so⌈re⌉-ra それら [the plural of *sore*, a pronoun referring to s.t./s.o./s.a. that is physically close to the hearer/reader or that either the hearer/reader or speaker/writer has mentioned but may not be familiar to the other ⟨w⟩], ka⌉nojo-ra 彼女ら [the female human third person plural pronoun], ka⌉nojo-ra 彼女たち [the female human third person plural pronoun]

NOTE: "They" is often not expressed at all in Japanese when it can be understood in a given context.

EX. (**a**) A: Who are those people?
あの人たちはだれですか。
Ano hito-tachi wa dare desu ka.
B: They're scientists from Japan.
{ø/彼らは/あの人たちは/彼女たちは/彼女らは/*その人たちは/*それらは}日本の科学者です。
*{ø/Kare-ra wa/Ano hito-tachi wa/Kanojo-tachi wa/Kanojo-ra wa/*Sono hito-tachi wa/*Sore-ra wa} Nihon no kagaku-sha desu.*

(**b**) A: A group of Japanese scientists came by to see you yesterday while you were out.
きのうお留守の間に日本の科学者が数人会いに来ましたよ。
Kinoo o-rusu no aida ni Nihon no kagaku-sha ga suu-nin ai ni kimashita yo.
B: Which university were they from?
{その人たちは/彼らは/?彼女たちは/?彼女らは/??ø/*あの人たちは}どこの大学から来たんですか。
*{Sono hito-tachi wa/Kare-ra wa/?Kanojo-tachi wa/?Kanojo-ra wa/??ø/*Ano hito-tachi wa} doko no daigaku kara kita n desu ka.*

(**c**) They're from Quebec so they can speak French as well as English.
{彼らは/その人たちは/あの人たちは/彼女らは/彼女たちは/*ø}ケベック出身だから、英語もフランス語も話すことができる。
*{Kare-ra wa/Sono hito-tachi wa/Ano hito-tachi wa/Kanojo-ra wa/Kanojo-tachi wa/*ø} Kebekku-shusshin da kara, eigo mo Furansu-go mo hanasu koto ga dekiru.*

(**d**) I've lent out books to so many people that I've lost track of where they all are now.
沢山の本を大勢の人に貸したので今{ø/?それらが/*彼らが/*彼女らが/*彼女たちが}どこにあるか分からなくなりました。
*Takusan no hon o oozei no hito ni kashita node ima {ø/?sore-ra ga/*kare-ra ga/*kanojo-ra ga/*kanojo-tachi ga} doko ni aru ka wakaranaku narimashita.*

(**e**) A: I have five cats at home.
僕は猫を五匹飼っているんだ。
Boku wa neko o go-hiki katte iru n da.
B: Are they all the same kind?
{ø/??それらは/*彼らは/*彼女らは/*彼女たちは}皆同じ種類ですか。
*{ø/??Sore-ra wa/*Kare-ra wa/*Kanojo-ra wa/*Kanojo-tachi wa} minna onaji shurui desu ka.*

(**f**) Yesterday they were having a sale on software at the computer store, so I bought three new software programs for my home computer. Altogether they cost me over $1,000.
きのうコンピューターの店でソフトが安くなっていたので、我が家のコンピューター用にソフトを三つ購入した。{それらは/ø/*彼らは/*その人たちは/*あの人たちは/*彼女らは/*彼女たちは}全部で1,000ドル少々だった。
*Kinoo konpyuutaa no mise de sofuto ga yasuku natte ita node, waga-ya no konpyuutaa-yoo ni sofuto o mittsu koonyuu-shita. {Sore-ra wa/ø/*Kare-ra wa/*Sono hito-tachi wa/*Ano hito-tachi wa/*Kanojo-ra wa/*Kanojo-tachi wa} zenbu de sen-doru-shooshoo datta.*

thick adj. **[consisting of two opposite sides or surfaces separated by a large volume of matter; having a special depth between two opposing surfaces; consisting of matter**

T

densely crowded together; not pouring or flowing easily]

1. a⌈tsui 厚い adj(*i*). **[consisting of two opposite surfaces separated by a large volume of matter 《fig. "heartfelt"》] 《heavy, kind, cordial》 ↔ usui 薄い** adj(*i*).; **(Amount) no a⌈tsu-sa no N (Amount)の厚さのN /〈adj(*i*). stem of *atsui* thick + suf. *sa* ness/ [for s.t. to have a specified depth between two opposing surfaces]**

EX. A: How thick is the wall?
壁はどのぐらい厚いんですか。
Kabe wa dono-gurai atsui n desu ka.
B: It's about 10 centimeters thick.
十センチぐらいの厚さです。
Jus-senchi-gurai no atsu-sa desu.

2. fu⌈to⌉i 太い adj(*i*). **[having a large diameter in relation to length 《fig. "deep in voice"》] ↔ hosoi 細い** adj(*i*).

EX. This pencil is ideal for drawing thick lines.
この鉛筆は太い線をかくのにちょうどいい。
Kono enpitsu wa futoi sen o kaku no ni choodo ii.

3. ko⌉i 濃い adj(*i*). **[filled with fibrous, gaseous, or liquid matter to the extent that light is obstructed, making it difficult to see through, or intense in degree of color or taste] 《dark, deep, strong, heavy》 ↔ usui 薄い** adj(*i*).; **fu⌈ka⌉i 深い** adj(*i*). **[extending far downward from the surface or far toward the back from the front 《fig. "profound," "hard to fathom," "dark (color/sound)," "secret," "dense," "intimate"》] 《deep, dense, heavy, fathomless》 ↔ asai 浅い** adj(*i*).

EX. **(a)** This milk shake is really thick, isn't it?
このミルクセーキは本当に{濃い/*深い}ねえ。
*Kono miruku-seeki wa hontoo ni {koi/*fukai} nee.*
(b) He had thick, masculine eyebrows.
彼の眉毛は{濃くて/*深くて}男性的だった。
*Kare no mayu-ge wa {kokute/*fukakute} dansei-teki datta.*
(c) This morning there was a thick mist in the air.
今朝はもやが{濃かった/深かった}。
Kesa wa moya ga {kokatta/fukakatta}.
(d) Japanese girls tend to wear their make-up thicker than American girls.
日本の女の子の化粧は大体アメリカの女の子の化粧より{濃い/*深い}。
*Nihon no onna-no-ko no keshoo wa daitai Amerika no onna-no-ko no keshoo yori {koi/*fukai}.*
(e) The forest is extremely thick around here.
この辺はとても{深い/*濃い}森になっている。
*Kono hen wa totemo {fukai/*koi} mori ni natte iru.*

thicket n. **[a thick growth of shrubs or small trees]**
shi⌈gemi⌉ 茂み [an area of thickly growing trees or tall grass] 《bush》, ya⌈bu やぶ [an area of thickly growing small trees, bamboo, or tall grass] 《grass tussock, bamboo grove》

thickness n. **[the degree to which two opposing sides or surfaces are separated by a large volume of matter or the quality of consisting of two surfaces so separated; the degree of denseness of a substance or the quality of being dense]**
1. a⌈tsu-sa 厚さ /〈adj(*i*). stem of *atsui* thick + suf. *sa* ness/ [the measurable degree to which two opposing sides or surfaces are separated by a large volume of matter or the quality of consisting of two surfaces so separated] ↔ usu-sa 薄さ; a⌈tsu-mi 厚み /〈adj(*i*). stem of *atsui* thick + suf. *mi* ness/ [the quality of consisting of two sides or surfaces separated by matter which is great in volume, though not specified in exact terms]

EX. **(a)** What is the thickness of this wall?
この壁の{厚さ/?厚み}はどのぐらいですか。
Kono kabe no {atsu-sa/?atsu-mi} wa dono-gurai desu ka.

T

(b) Hey, look at the thickness of this steak!
ほら、このステーキの{厚み/厚さ}、すごいね。
Hora, kono suteeki no {atsu-mi/atsu-sa}, sugoi ne.

2. fu⌈to⌉-sa 太さ /⟨adj(*i*). stem of *futoi* thick + suf. *sa* ness/ [the degree to which the diameter of a cylindrical object is large in relation to its length or the quality of having such a shape] ⟪depth⟫ ↔ hoso-sa 細さ

EX. Could you please measure the thickness of this pole?
この柱の太さを測ってください。
Kono hashira no futo-sa o hakatte kudasai.

3. ko⌉-sa 濃さ /⟨adj(*i*). stem of *koi* thick + suf. *sa* ness/ [the degree to which s.t. consists of matter densely crowded together and obstructing light or the quality of consisting of such matter; the degree of intenseness of color or taste or the quality of being so intense] ⟪concentration, depth, density⟫ ↔ usu-sa 薄さ

EX. The thickness of her make-up made it impossible to recognize her.
化粧の濃さのため彼女だということが全く分からなかった。
Keshoo no ko-sa no tame kanojo da to iu koto ga mattaku wakaranakatta.

thief n. **[a person who steals]**
do⌈roboo 泥棒 [a person who takes property away from s.o. by stealth in an illegal manner] ⟪robber⟫, ko⌈so-doro こそ泥 [a person who steals relatively inexpensive small items secretly] ⟪sneak thief, pilferer⟫

EX. I had my camera stolen by a thief.
僕はカメラを{泥棒/こそ泥}に盗まれた。
Boku wa kamera o {doroboo/koso-doro} ni nusuma-reta.

thin adj. **[consisting of two opposite sides or surfaces separated by little volume; pouring or flowing easily; consisting of entities sparsely spaced ⟪fig. "not fat," "weak in voice, color, or taste"⟫]**

1. u⌈sui 薄い adj(*i*). **[having little depth or intensity ⟪fig. "weak in color or taste"⟫] ↔ atsui 厚い** adj(*i*)., **koi 濃い** adj(*i*).

EX. (a) My hair is getting thin as I get older.
年を取るにつれて髪の毛が薄くなってきた。
Toshi o toru ni tsurete kami-no-ke ga usuku natte kita.
(b) This paper is very thin but strong.
この紙はとても薄いのに丈夫だ。
Kono kami wa totemo usui no ni joobu da.
(c) The paint on this car is thin and easily scratched.
この車のペンキは薄くて、傷が付きやすい。
Kono kuruma no penki wa usukute, kizu ga tsuki-yasui.
(d) This soup is too thin for my taste.
このスープは僕には(味が)薄すぎる。
Kono suupu wa boku ni wa (aji ga) usu-sugiru.

2. ho⌈so⌉i 細い adj(*i*). **[having a cylindrical shape small in diameter compared to length or having an area with little width compared to length] ⟪fine, slim, slender, narrow, small⟫ ↔ futoi 太い** adj(*i*).

EX. (a) You look so thin!
ずいぶん(体が)細いねえ!
Zuibun (karada ga) hosoi nee!
(b) The pianist had thin, long fingers.
ピアニストの指は細くて、長かった。
Pianisuto no yubi wa hosokute, nagakatta.

thing n. **[whatever can be objectively perceived by the senses, grasped by the mind, done, or said, except for a human or animal being]**

1. mo⌈no⌉ 物 [whatever is or may be objectively perceived by the senses] ⟪object, matter, substance, goods, material⟫, ya⌉tsu やつ [a person or object (used in a derogatory or endearing sense) ⟨s⟩] ⟪fellow, chap, guy, stuff⟫

EX. (a) A: What kind of things do you plan to buy for Christmas presents?

クリスマスプレゼントにどんな{物/*やつ}を買う予定ですか。
*Kurisumau-purezento ni donna {mono/ *yatsu} o kau yotei desu ka.*
B: I plan to buy practical, inexpensive things.
安くて実用的な{物/*やつ}を買うつもりです。
*Yasukute jitsuyoo-tekina {mono/*yatsu} o kau tsumori desu.*
(**b**) In the ideal world imagined by Taro there would be no such things as tests.
太郎が考えた理想の世界にはテストなどという{物/*やつ}はなかった。
*Taroo ga kangaeta risoo no sekai ni wa tesuto nado to iu {mono/*yatsu} wa nakatta.*
(**c**) Can you see that small thing in the sky?
空の、あの小さな{物/*やつ}が見えますか。
*Sora no, ano chiisana {mono/*yatsu} ga miemasu ka.*
(**d**) Look, a kitten! What a cute little thing!
ほら、子猫だよ。何てかわいい{やつ/ *物}なんだろ。
*Hora, ko-neko da yo. Nan-te kawaii {yatsu/*mono} na n daro.*

2. ko⌈to⌉ こと [whatever is or may be said, done, or conceived of as an event, fact, or situation occurring in time; a nominalizer forming a noun clause expressing what is perceived indirectly by means of one's rational faculties rather than directly through the five senses] ⟪matter, affair, business⟫

EX. (**a**) The best thing about going abroad is the possibility of rediscovering your own country.
外国旅行の一番いいことは、自分の国の再発見が出来ることだろう。
Gaikoku-ryokoo no ichiban ii koto wa, jibun no kuni no sai-hakken ga dekiru koto daroo.
(**b**) It's a good thing I wasn't in Tokyo when the earthquake struck.
幸いなことに、地震が起きた時、私は東京にいなかった。
Saiwaina koto ni, jishin ga okita toki, watashi wa Tookyoo ni inakatta.

think vi./vt. **[for s.o. to exercise one's mind in order to form an idea]**
{⟨-no⟩ **ko⌈to⌉ o**/⟨-to⟩} **ka⌈ngae⌉ru** {⟨～の⟩ことを/⟨～と⟩}考える ② **[for s.o. to exercise one's mind in order to form an idea or arrive at a logical conclusion] ⟪think of/ about/that, believe, judge, conclude⟫**, ⟨-to⟩ **o⌈mo⌉u** ⟨～と⟩思う ① **[for s.o. to spontaneously perceive s.t. in one's mind or to have an opinion about s.t.] ⟪feel, seem⟫**

NOTE: *Kangaeru* typically involves a mental process, whereas *omou* involves an emotional process, much like English "feel."

EX. (**a**) I think it's a pity that so few students these days choose careers as teachers.
最近は教師という職業を選ぶ学生が少なくて残念だと{思う/*考える}。
*Saikin wa kyooshi to iu shokugyoo o erabu gakusei ga sukunakute zannen da to {omou/*kangaeru}.*
(**b**) I thought about that math problem for hours, but couldn't solve it.
その数学の問題を何時間も{考えた/*思った}が、解けなかった。
*Sono suugaku no mondai o nan-jikan mo {kangaeta/*omotta} ga, toke-nakatta.*
(**c**) A: Do you think we should hire a new manager for our New York office?
ニューヨーク支店には新しい支店長を雇った方がいいと{思います/?考えます}か。
Nyuuyooku-shiten ni wa atarashii shiten-choo o yatotta hoo ga ii to {omoimasu/?kangaemasu} ka.
B: Let me think about that for a while.
しばらく{考えさせて/*思わせて}ください。
*Shibaraku {kangae-sasete/*omowa-sete} kudasai.*
(**d**) When you think of it, culture is nothing more than a collection of life styles.
{考えて/*思って}みると、文化とは一

連の生活様式に過ぎない。
*{Kangaete/*Omotte} miru to, bunka to wa ichiren no seikatsu-yooshiki ni suginai.*
(**e**) A: What should I do about this problem?
この問題はどうしたらいいですか。
Kono mondai wa doo shitara ii desu ka.
B: Do as you think fit.
{考えて、いいように/思うように}しなさい。
{Kangaete, ii yooni/Omou yooni} shinasai.
(**f**) He seems to be the type to think carefully before he acts.
彼は行動する前によく{考える/*思う}タイプのようだ。
*Kare wa koodoo-suru mae ni yoku {kangaeru/*omou} taipu no yooda.*
(**g**) Pascal said that man is a thinking reed.
パスカルは人間は{考える/*思う}あしだと言った。
*Pasukaru wa ningen wa {kangaeru/*omou} ashi da to itta.*
(**h**) When I was in Japan, I often thought of my parents back in my homeland.
日本にいた時、僕はよく故郷の両親のことを{考えて/思って}いた。
Nihon ni ita toki, boku wa yoku kokyoo no ryooshin no koto o {kangaete/omotte} ita.

thinking n. **[the act or result of exercising one's mind to form an idea]**
1. ka⌈ngae⌉ru koto 考えること [the act of exercising one's mind in order to form an idea or arrive at a logical conclusion], shi⌈koo 思考 •c [the mental process of forming ideas ⟨w⟩] ⟪thought, consideration⟫
EX. Nothing important can be achieved without thinking.
{考えること/思考}なしでは、有意義なことは何にも出来ない。
{Kangaeru koto/Shikoo}-nashi de wa, yuu-igina koto wa nan-nimo dekinai.
2. ka⌈nga⌉e 考え /⟨V*masu* of *kangaeru* ② think/ [the product of exercising one's mind to arrive at a logical conclusion] ⟪thought, idea, notion, consideration⟫, i⌉ken 意見 •c [an idea or judgment one holds about a matter] ⟪opinion, idea, view, suggestion⟫
EX. My thinking on this is naturally different from yours.
このことについて私の{考え/意見}はもちろんあなたのとは違います。
Kono koto ni-tsuite watashi no {kangae/iken} wa mochiron anata no to wa chigaimasu.

third adj. **[preceded by two others in a series]**
sa⌈n+counter me no N 三+counter目のN •c [preceded by two others in a series], mi⌈ttsu-me⌉ no N 三つ目のN [preceded by two others in a series] SEE APPENDIX II
EX. (**a**) A: Where should I get off the train?
どこで電車を降りたらいいんですか。
Doko de densha o oritara ii n desu ka.
B: At the third station from here.
ここから{三番目/三つ目}の駅です。
Koko kara {san-ban-me/mittsu-me} no eki desu.
(**b**) There was apparently a third man involved in the crime.
その犯罪に加わった{三人目/*三つ目}の男がいたらしい。
*Sono hanzai ni kuwawatta {san-nin-me/*mittsu-me} no otoko ga ita rashii.*
(**c**) My professor is writing his third book.
私の先生は{三冊目/?三つ目}の本を書いていらっしゃいます。
Watashi no sensei wa {san-satsu-me/?mittsu-me} no hon o kaite irasshaimasu.

—— n. **[s.t. preceding two others in a series or one of three equal parts]**
1. da⌉i-sa⌈n no mono 第三のもの [s.t. preceded by two others in a series]
2. sa⌈n-bun no ichi 三分の一 [one of three equal parts]
EX. I'll settle for one-third of the profit.
利益の三分の一をくれればいい。
Rieki no san-bun no ichi o kurereba ii.

thirst n. **[the feeling created by a need or desire to drink liquid ⟪fig. "strong desire"⟫]**
1. no˥do no ka˥waki˥ のどの渇き /⟨*nodo* throat + prt. *no* + V*masu* of *kawaku* ① dry/ [the state of the throat being dry] ⟪dryness⟫

EX. I was nearly fainting from thirst but kept on walking.
のどの渇きのため気を失いそうだったが、歩き続けた。
Nodo no kawaki no tame ki o ushinai-soo datta ga, aruki-tsuzuketa.

2. yo˥ku˥ 欲 •c [a strong hope or wish to have or do s.t.] ⟪desire, avarice, greed⟫, yo˥kkyuu 欲求 •c [a strong desire to do or obtain s.t.] ⟪desire, demand, urge⟫

NOTE: *Yoku* is often used as the second element of a Chinese compound, as in *shoku-yoku* "appetite for food," *sei-yoku* "sexual appetite," *chishiki-yoku* "appetite for knowledge," etc.

thirsty adj. **[feeling a desire to drink liquid or a strong desire to have s.t.]**
1. no˥do ga ka˥wa˥ita N のどが渇いたN /⟨Vinf. past of *kawaku* ① dry/ [feeling a desire to drink liquid], no˥do ga ka˥wa˥ite iru (N) のどが渇いている(N) /⟨V*te iru* of *kawaku* ① dry/ ② [for a third person to feel a desire to drink liquid]

EX. (**a**) Boy, am I thirsty!
ああ、のどが渇いた。
Aa, nodo ga kawaita.

NOTE: In an exclamatory sentence such as (a), only informal forms are acceptable.

(**b**) When I'm thirsty, I usually drink cold water.
のどが{渇いた/渇いている}時は大抵冷たい水を飲む。
Nodo ga {kawaita/kawaite iru} toki wa taitei tsumetai mizu o nomu.
(**c**) This dog looks thirsty.
この犬はのどが渇いているようだ。
Kono inu wa nodo ga kawaite iru yooda.

2. -yo˥ku˥ ga a˥ru (N) 〜欲がある(N) [having a strong desire to do or have s.t.]

EX. He was so thirsty for knowledge he would read every book he could get his hands on from cover to cover.
彼は大変知識欲があって、手当たり次第にありとあらゆる本を読破した。
Kare wa taihen chishiki-yoku ga atte, te-atari shidai ni ari to arayuru hon o dokuha-shita.

thirteen n./adj.
ju˥u-san (+counter) (no N) 十三(+counter)(のN) •c SEE APPENDIX II

thirty n./adj.
sa˥n-juu (+counter) (no N) 三十(+counter)(のN) •c SEE APPENDIX II

this pron. **[a demonstrative pronoun used to refer to s.t. close to the speaker or to s.t. that has just been or is about to be mentioned]**
1. ko˥re これ [a demonstrative pronoun used to refer to s.t. close to the speaker or to s.t. that has been mentioned in the very near past]

EX. (**a**) A: What's this?
これは何ですか。
Kore wa nan desu ka.
B: Japanese *sake.*
日本の酒ですよ。
Nihon no sake desu yo.
(**b**) As I saw her off at the station I had a strange feeling that this was the last time I would ever see her.
駅で見送った時にこれが彼女に会う最後になるという妙な予感がした。
Eki de mi-okutta toki ni kore ga kanojo ni au saigo ni naru to iu myoona yokan ga shita.

2. tsu˥gi˥ no koto 次のこと [s.t. that comes next]

EX. What I told him was this. If he was late one more time to work he'd be looking for a new job.
彼に言ったのは次のことだ。今度会社に遅刻したらくびだぞ。
Kare ni itta no wa tsugi no koto da. Kondo kaisha ni chikoku-shitara kubi da zo.

—— adj. **[a demonstrative adjective that refers to s.t. that is close to the speaker or**

T

s.t. that has just been or is about to be mentioned]

1. ko⌈no N このN [a demonstrative pronoun used to refer to s.o./s.t./s.a. close to the speaker or considered to belong to the speaker's territory or s.o./s.t./s.a. that has been mentioned in the very near past 《fig. "this past..."》]

EX. (**a**) I've found this dictionary very useful in my study of Japanese.
この辞書は日本語を勉強する上で大変役に立っています。
Kono jisho wa Nihon-go o benkyoo-suru ue de taihen yaku ni tatte imasu.
(**b**) I had this student in a class two years ago.
この学生は二年前に私の授業を取っていました。
Kono gakusei wa ni-nen mae ni watashi no jugyoo o totte imashita.
(**c**) This man worked for me at a securities firm ten years ago.
この男は十年前、ある証券会社で私の部下でした。
Kono otoko wa juu-nen mae, aru shooken-gaisha de watashi no buka deshita.

T

2. tsu⌈gi⌉ no yoona N 次のようなN [able to be described or identified in the following way]

EX. I'd like you to take this bit of advice from me. Stay out of debt at all costs.
君に次のような忠告をしたい。借金は絶対するな。
Kimi ni tsugi no yoona chuukoku o shi-tai. Shakkin wa zettai suru na.

PHRASE: this time *kondo wa* 今度は •c

EX. (**a**) Let me pay this time.
今度は僕に払わせてください。
Kondo wa boku ni harawa-sete kudasai.
(**b**) I usually fly economy class but this time I'm going to fly first class.
大抵エコノミークラスに乗るんですが、今度はファーストクラスに乗るつもりです。
Taitei ekonomii-kurasu ni noru n desu ga, kondo wa faasuto-kurasu ni noru tsumori desu.

PHRASE: this way *koo* こう, *koo yatte* こうやって

EX. (**a**) A: How do you open this door?
このドアはどうやって開けるんですか。
Kono doa wa doo yatte akeru n desu ka.
B: This way.
{こうやって/?こう}開けるんですよ。
{Koo yatte/?Koo} akeru n desu yo.
(**b**) This *kanji* is written this way.
この漢字は{こう/*こうやって}書きます。
*Kono kanji wa {koo/*koo yatte} kakimasu.*

—— adv. **[to the extent indicated]**

ko⌈nnani こんなに

EX. (**a**) The snow accumulated this high.
雪がこんなに高く積もったんだ。
Yuki ga konnani takaku tsumotta n da.
(**b**) I didn't know that coffee could taste this good.
コーヒーがこんなにおいしいとは知らなかった。
Koohii ga konnani oishii to wa shiranakatta.

thorn n.

to⌈ge⌉ とげ

EX. I got a rose thorn stuck in my finger.
ばらのとげが指に刺さってしまった。
Bara no toge ga yubi ni sasatte shimatta.

thorough adj. **[careful and complete in every detail]**

ka⌈nzenna 完全な adj(*na*). **•c [lacking no parts and having no faults], te⌈ttei-tekina 徹底的な** adj(*na*). **•c [doing s.t. completely/perfectly] 《perfect, complete》, hi⌉ no u⌈chi-dokoro ga na⌉i 非の打ちどころがない** adj(*i*). **[completely free from any aspect that could be faulted] 《impeccable, unimpeachable》**

EX. (**a**) Following the revolution, the country underwent a thorough change.
革命後その国は{完全な/徹底的な/*非の打ちどころのない}変化を遂げた。
*Kakumei-go sono kuni wa {kanzenna/tettei-tekina/*hi no uchi-dokoro no nai} henka o togeta.*

(**b**) Mr. Okada has a thorough knowledge of Kenzaburo Oe's literature.
岡田氏は大江健三郎の文学について{完全な/*徹底的な/*非の打ちどころがない}知識を持っている。
*Okada-shi wa Ooe Kenzaburoo no bungaku ni-tsuite {kanzenna/*tettei-tekina/*hi no uchi-dokoro ga nai} chishiki o motte iru.*
(**c**) Mr. Smith is a very thorough worker.
スミス氏は{非の打ちどころのない/?完全な/*徹底的な}働きぶりだ。
*Sumisu-shi wa {hi no uchi-dokoro no nai/?kanzenna/*tettei-tekina} hataraki-buri da.*

thoroughly adv. **[in a careful and complete way, leaving out no detail]**
ka⌈nzenni 完全に /⟨adj⟨*na*⟩. *ni* of *kanzenna* complete/ •c [in a way absolutely free from imperfections/weaknesses] ⟪perfectly, quite, entirely, wholly, fully, completely⟫, te⌈ttei-tekini 徹底的に /⟨adj⟨*na*⟩. *ni* of *tettei-tekina* complete/ •c [in such a way as to extend to and affect every part] ⟪completely, through and through, to the hilt⟫, ka⌈npekini 完ぺきに /⟨adj⟨*na*⟩. *ni* of *kanpekina* perfect/ •c [in a way absolutely free from any imperfections/weaknesses] ⟪perfectly, flawlessly, completely⟫

EX. (**a**) He's the type of person who does everything thoroughly.
あの人は物事を{完全に/完ぺきに/徹底的に}するタイプの人だ。
Ano hito wa mono-goto o {kanzenni/kanpekini/tettei-tekini} suru taipu no hito da.
(**b**) The politician was thoroughly criticized by the mass media for his misconduct.
政治家はその悪事のためにマスコミに{徹底的に/*完ぺきに/*完全に}たたかれた。
*Seiji-ka wa sono akuji no tame ni masukomi ni {tettei-tekini/*kanpekini/*kanzenni} tataka-reta.*

those pron. **[the plural form of the pronoun "that"]**
so⌈re⌉-ra それら [the plural of *sore*, a demonstrative pronoun used to refer to s.t./s.o./s.a. that is physically close to the hearer/reader or to s.t./s.o./s.a. that either the hearer/reader or speaker/writer has mentioned but may not be familiar to the other], hi⌈to⌉-bito 人々 [a group of persons (living in the same area) ⟨w⟩] ⟪people⟫

NOTE: In conversation *sore* is normally used instead of *sore-ra.*

EX. (**a**) Prof. Johnson mentions in his article a low savings rate and high national debt as factors contributing to weakness in the dollar. While those are certainly some of the causes, we must also not forget the role played by speculative buying and selling of currencies by large private investors.
ジョンソン教授は論文の中で、ドルの価値の低下の原因として国の膨大な赤字と低貯蓄率を挙げている。確かに{それら/*人々}も原因であるには違いないが、同時に大口の個人投資家による通貨の投機的な売買の影響も忘れてはならない。
*Jonson-kyooju wa ronbun no naka de, doru no kachi no teika no gen'in to-shite kuni no boodaina akaji to tei-chochiku-ritsu o agete iru. Tashikani {sore-ra/*hito-bito} mo gen'in dearu ni wa chigainai ga, dooji ni ooguchi no kojin-tooshi-ka ni-yoru tsuuka no tooki-tekina baibai no eikyoo mo wasurete wa naranai.*
(**b**) Those who want to master a foreign language should go and spend time in the country where it is spoken.
外国語をマスターしたい{人々/*それら}はその言語が話されている国に行ってしばらく滞在するべきだ。
*Gaikoku-go o masutaa-shi-tai {hito-bito/*sore-ra} wa sono gengo ga hanasa-rete iru kuni ni itte shibaraku taizai-suru-beki da.*

— adj. **[the plural form of the adjective "that"]**
so⌈re⌉-ra no N それらのN [the possessive

T

form of the non-human third person pronoun *sore-ra*]

NOTE: In conversation *sono* is normally used instead of *sore-ra no*.

EX. (**a**) An editorial in this morning's paper lists the environment, the economy, political corruption, and educational reform as the four major issues facing our country at the present. Among those issues, however, I believe that the most urgent issue is the environment.
今朝の新聞の社説に現在我が国が直面する四つの主要な問題として環境、経済、政治腐敗、教育改革が挙げられていた。しかし、私はそれらの問題の中で、環境問題が最も急を要する課題だと思う。
Kesa no shinbun no shasetsu ni genzai waga-kuni ga chokumen-suru yottsu no shuyoona mondai to-shite kankyoo, keizai, seiji-fuhai, kyooiku-kaikaku ga agera-rete ita. Shikashi, watashi wa sore-ra no mondai no naka de, kankyoo-mondai ga mottomo kyuu o yoosuru kadai da to omou.
(**b**) Watch it—those apples are mine.
{その/*それらの}りんごは僕のだぞ。
*{Sono/*Sore-ra no} ringo wa boku no da zo.*

T

thou pron. **[an archaic second person singular pronoun ⟨w⟩]**
na⌈nji なんじ [an archaic second person singular pronoun used to refer to s.o. of lesser status than the speaker/writer ⟨w⟩]

EX. Thou shalt not steal.
なんじ、盗むなかれ。
Nanji, nusumu nakare.

though conj. **[in spite of the fact that or even if]**
1. ke⌉(re)do け(れ)ど [a disjunctive subordinate conjunction that combines two sentences] ⟨⟨but, although, however, nevertheless⟩⟩, **ke⌉redomo けれども, ga が [a disjunctive coordinate conjunction that combines two sentences]** ⟨⟨but, and⟩⟩

NOTE: *Kedo* is a colloquial version of *keredo*.

EX. (**a**) Though it was raining we jogged anyway.
雨が降っていた{けれども/けれど/が}、ジョギングをした。
Ame ga futte ita {keredomo/keredo/ga}, jogingu o shita.
(**b**) Bob can speak Japanese very well, even though he can't read it at all.
ボブは日本語が全然読めません{けれど/が/けれども}、話すのは上手です。
Bobu wa Nihon-go ga zenzen yome-masen {keredo/ga/keredomo}, hanasu no wa joozu desu.

2. de⌉mo でも [a coordinate disjunctive conjunction used in sentence-initial position]

EX. Even though Karen and I have been friends for a long time, I have never thought once of getting married to her.
カレンとは長いつきあいだ。でも結婚しようと思ったことは一度もない。
Karen to wa nagai tsuki-ai da. Demo kekkon-shiyoo to omotta koto wa ichi-do mo nai.

PHRASE: as though *marude* Sinf. *ka no yooni* まるでSinf.かのように

NOTE: When the nonpast affirmative form of adj(*na*). or N+cop. occurs before *ka no yooni*, the form used is {adj(*na*). stem/N} *dearu*, as in example (a).

EX. (**a**) Mr. Nelson speaks Japanese as though he were a Japanese.
ネルソンさんはまるで日本人であるかのように日本語を話す。
Neruson-san wa marude Nihon-jin dearu ka no yooni Nihon-go o hanasu.
(**b**) Tom raised his hand as though he was going to hit me.
トムはまるで僕を殴りたいかのように手を上げた。
Tomu wa marude boku o naguri-tai ka no yooni te o ageta.

thought n. **[the act of thinking or an idea that occurs as a product of thinking]**
1. ka⌈ngae⌉ru koto 考えること [the act of exercising one's mind in order to form an

idea or arrive at a logical conclusion], shi⌈koo 思考 •c [the mental process of forming ideas ⟨w⟩] ⟪thinking, consideration⟫

EX. The process of thought differentiates humans from animals.
{考えること/思考}が人を動物から区別する。
{Kangaeru koto/Shikoo} ga hito o doobutsu kara kubetsu-suru.

2. ka⌈nga⌉e 考え /⟨V *masu* of *kangaeru* ② think⟩/ [the act of exercising one's mind to arrive at a logical conclusion] ⟪idea, intention, thinking, notion, consideration⟫, shi⌈soo 思想 •c [a systematic, usu. academic, framework of thinking about the world, life, or the nature of reality] ⟪idea, ideology⟫

EX. (**a**) My colleague came up with an interesting thought about how to teach Japanese.
同僚が日本語の教え方について面白い{考え/*思想}を出した。
*Dooryoo ga Nihon-go no oshie-kata ni-tsuite omoshiroi {kangae/*shisoo} o dashita.*
(**b**) Recently I read a book on the post-war history of thought in Japan.
最近日本の戦後思想史の本を読んだ。
Saikin Nihon no sengo-shisoo-shi no hon o yonda.
(**c**) The priest shared with me some profound thoughts about life.
その神父は人生についての深遠な{思想/考え}を話してくださった。
Sono shinpu wa jinsei ni-tsuite no shin'en na {shisoo/kangae} o hanashite kudasatta.
(**d**) I gave some thought to becoming a novelist when I was a college student.
大学生の時小説家になろうという{考え/*思想}があった。
*Daigaku-sei no toki shoosetsu-ka ni naroo to iu {kangae/*shisoo} ga atta.*

3. tsu⌈mori つもり [a plan of what one is going to do], i⌉to 意図 •c [what one tries to accomplish in doing s.t.] ⟪intent⟫

EX. (**a**) I had no thought of going anywhere for the weekend.
週末はどこへも行く{つもり/*意図}はなかった。
*Shuumatsu wa doko e mo iku {tsumori/*ito} wa nakatta.*
(**b**) It was my thought to give support to your viewpoint by what I said, but apparently it had the opposite effect.
あなたの考えを支持する{つもり/意図}で発言したんですが、逆効果になってしまったようですね。
Anata no kangae o shiji-suru {tsumori/ito} de hatsugen-shita n desu ga, gyaku-kooka ni natte shimatta yoodesu ne.

4. i⌉ken 意見 •c [an idea or judgment one holds about a matter] ⟪idea, view⟫, ka⌈nsoo 感想 •c [the images or feelings remaining with one after experiencing s.t.] ⟪impressions, sentiments⟫, ke⌈nkai 見解 •c [one's evaluation of or judgment about s.t.] ⟪view⟫

EX. Please express your thoughts on the matter freely.
この件に関して御{意見/感想/見解}を自由にお述べください。
Kono ken ni-kanshite go-{iken/kansoo/kenkai} o jiyuu ni o-nobe kudasai.

thoughtful adj. **[involving careful thinking or showing consideration for others] o⌈moi-yari ga a⌉ru (N) 思いやりがある(N) [sympathetic of the plight of others] ⟪considerate, sympathetic, kind, warm-hearted⟫**

EX. I was most attracted to him because he is such a thoughtful person.
彼の思いやりがあるというところに一番ひかれたんです。
Kare no omoi-yari ga aru to iu tokoro ni ichiban hika-reta n desu.

thoughtless adj. **[lacking thought or consideration for others]**

1. shi⌉ryo ga na⌉i (N) 思慮がない(N) [lacking careful thought], fu-⌈chu⌉uina 不注意な adj(*na*). **•c [lacking careful attention]**

⟪careless, heedless, inattentive⟫

EX. It was pretty thoughtless of him to say that straight to his boss.
上役にあんなにずけずけ物を言うなんて彼は{思慮がない/不注意だ}。
Uwa-yaku ni annani zuke-zuke mono o iu nante kare wa {shiryo ga nai/fu-chuui da}.

2. o⌈moi-yari ga na⌉i (N) 思いやりがない(N) [lacking consideration for others] ⟪inconsiderate, unkind⟫

EX. A: My husband often brings his colleagues home from work with him without telling me in advance.
うちの人はね、前もって何にも言わないで、よく会社の同僚を家へ連れてくるのよ。
Uchi no hito wa ne, mae-motte nan-nimo iwanai de, yoku kaisha no dooryoo o uchi e tsurete-kuru no yo.
B: That' pretty thoughtless of him.
思いやりがないのねえ。
Omoi-yari ga nai no nee.

thousand n./adj.
se⌉n (+counter) (no N) 千(+counter)(のN)
•c SEE APPENDIX II

thread n. **[a very fine cord made of spun fiber ⟪fig. "any object like a fine cord," "an idea or thought connecting different parts of s.t. said or written"⟫] ⟪yarn⟫**

1. i⌉to 糸 [a very fine cord made of strands of spun silk or other fiber]

EX. It's difficult for an old person to get a thread through the eye of a needle.
老人には糸を針の穴に通すのが難しい。
Roojin ni wa ito o hari no ana ni toosu no ga muzukashii.

2. su⌉ji 筋 [a long fiber or fiber-like object ⟪fig. "story line," "muscle," "streak," "vein"⟫] ⟪plot, string⟫

EX. I got distracted by a sneeze in the audience and momentarily lost the thread of my speech.
聴衆の中から出たくしゃみに気を取られて一瞬話の筋を忘れてしまった。
Chooshuu no naka kara deta kushami ni ki o tora-rete isshun hanashi no suji o wasurete shimatta.

— vt. **[for s.o. to put a thread through the eye of a needle ⟪fig. "weave"⟫]**

1. ⟨-ni⟩ i⌉to o to⌉osu ⟨〜に⟩糸を通す ① [for s.o. to put a thread through s.t. esp. the eye of a needle]

EX. Can you thread this needle for me?
この針に糸を通してくれませんか。
Kono hari ni ito o tooshite kuremasen ka.

2. ⟨-o⟩ nu⌉tte-iku ⟨〜を⟩縫って行く ① [to move in a winding fashion through an area filled with obstacles]

EX. We threaded our way through the crowd to the other side of the stadium.
人込みの中をスタジアムの向こう側へ縫って行った。
Hito-gomi no naka o sutajiamu no mukoo-gawa e nutte itta.

threat n. **[an expression of intent to cause s.t. undesirable to occur, esp. punishment or harm, or an indication that such will occur]**

1. o⌈doshi 脅し /⟨V*masu* of *odosu* ① threat/ [the act of doing or saying s.t. which causes fear in order to influence s.o. to act the way one wants] ⟪menace, intimidation⟫

EX. A: If you value your life I suggest you never set foot in this town again.
命が惜しいなら二度とこの町に足を踏み入れるな。
Inochi ga oshii nara ni-do to kono machi ni ashi o fumi-ireru na.
B: Is that supposed to be a threat?
それは脅しのつもりか。
Sore wa odoshi no tsumori ka.

2. ⟨-no⟩ o⌈sore⌉ ⟨〜の⟩恐れ /⟨V*masu* of *osoreru* ② fear/ [a sense that s.t. dangerous or undesirable is impending] ⟪fear, dread, awe, danger⟫

EX. (**a**) The threat of economic panic hung over New York in October of 1987.
1987年の十月にはニューヨークで経済恐慌の恐れが感じられた。
Sen-kyuu-hyaku-hachi-juu-shichi-nen

no juu-gatsu ni wa Nyuuyooku de keizai-kyookoo no osore ga kanji-rareta.
(**b**) The threat of a tornado caused us to change our travel plans.
竜巻の恐れがあったので旅行の計画を取りやめた。
Tatsumaki no osore ga atta node ryokoo no keikaku o tori-yameta.

threaten vt. **[for s.o. to express an intent to cause s.t. undesirable to occur, esp. punishment or harm, or for s.t. to show signs of s.t. undesirable occurring]**
1. ((〈-de〉)) 〈-o〉 **o⌈dosu** ((〈～で〉))〈～を〉脅す ① **[for s.o. to say or do s.t. (using an instrument) to cause fear in an attempt to influence s.o. to act the way one wants]** ((**terrify, browbeat, scare**))
EX. While walking alone one night in New York, I was threatened by a young man with a pistol.
ある時、夜ニューヨークの通りを一人で歩いていたら、若い男にピストルで脅された。
Aru toki, yoru Nyuuyooku no toori o hitori de aruite itara, wakai otoko ni pisutoru de odosa-reta.
2. (**i⌉ma-nimo**) 〈**-ni**〉 **na⌈ri-so⌉ona** (今にも)〈～に〉なりそうな adj(na). **[indicating that some change or event is about to take place at any moment]**
EX. The clouds were threatening rain so we had to cut our picnic short and return home.
今にも雨になりそうな空模様だったのでピクニックをやめてうちに帰った。
Ima-nimo ame ni nari-soona sora-moyoo datta node pikunikku o yamete uchi ni kaetta.

three n./adj.
mi⌈ttsu⌉ (**no N**) 三つ(のN), **sa⌈n** (**+counter**) (**no N**) 三(+counter)(のN) •c SEE APPENDIX II
EX. I bought three lottery tickets.
宝くじを三枚買った。
Takara-kuji o san-mai katta.

thrill n. **[a sudden intense sense of pleasure or excitement]**
zo⌉ku-zoku-suru kanji ぞくぞくする感じ **[a shivering sensation]**, **su⌉riru** スリル •f **[a sharp sense of pleasure or excitement created by danger or suspense]**
EX. (**a**) I always get a thrill from roller-coaster rides.
ジェットコースターに乗るといつも{スリルを感じる/ぞくぞくする}。
Jetto-koosutaa ni noru to itsu-mo {suriru o kanjiru/zoku-zoku-suru}.
(**b**) I love the thrill of downhill skiing.
スキーで滑降する時の{ぞくぞくする感じ/スリル}が好きだ。
Sukii de kakkoo-suru toki no {zoku-zoku-suru kanji/suriru} ga suki da.

—— vt. **[to cause s.o. to experience a sudden intense sense of pleasure or excitement]**
〈**-o**〉 **gu⌈tto ka⌈ndoo-sase⌉ru** 〈～を〉ぐっと感動させる /〈**causative of *kandoo-suru* ③ be moved**/ ② **[to cause s.o. to be strongly moved]**, 〈**-o**〉 **zo⌈tto-saseru** 〈～を〉ぞっとさせる /〈**causative of *zotto-suru* ③ shiver**/ ② **[to cause s.o. to shiver with fear or emotional excitement]**
EX. (**a**) During summer camp I would thrill the children with ghost stories around the campfire every night.
夏期キャンプでは毎晩キャンプファイアーを囲んで子供に怪談を聞かせて{ぞっとさせた/*ぐっと感動させた}。
*Kaki-kyanpu de wa mai-ban kyanpu-faiaa o kakonde kodomo ni kaidan o kika-sete {zotto-saseta/*gutto kandoo-saseta}.*
(**b**) The very thought of being able to meet and shake hands with the movie star I had worshiped as a child thrilled me.
子供の時に崇拝していた映画スターに会って握手すると考えただけで{ぐっと感動した/*ぞっとした}。
*Kodomo no toki ni suuhai-shite ita eiga-sutaa ni atte akushu-suru to kangaeta dake de {gutto kandoo-shita/*zotto-shita}.*

NOTE: *Zotto-suru* and *Gutto kandoo-suru* are the intransitive versions of *zotto-saseru* and *gutto kandoo-saseru*, respectively.

throat n. **[the front part of the neck or the passage between the mouth and esophagus through which food and air pass ⟪fig. "a narrow passage"⟫]**
no˥do のど [the front part of the neck or the passage between the mouth and esophagus through which food and air pass ⟪fig. "voice"⟫] ⟪windpipe, voice⟫
EX. (**a**) I have a sore throat.
私はのどが痛い。
Watashi wa nodo ga itai.
(**b**) Some food got stuck in my throat and I couldn't talk.
食べ物がのどに詰まって、話せなかった。
Tabe-mono ga nodo ni tsumatte, hanase-nakatta.
NOTE: "Thirsty" is expressed in Japanese as *nodo ga kawaita* "My throat has become dry."

throne n. **[a chair on which a king, queen, bishop, etc., sits on official occasions ⟪fig. "rank of king"⟫]**
gyo˥kuza 玉座 •c, o˥oi 王位 •c [the rank of king]

through prep. **[from one end to another of some interval in space or from the beginning to end of some interval of time ⟪fig. "by means of," "because of"⟫]**
1. ⟨-o⟩ to˥otte ⟨〜を⟩通って /⟨V*te* of *tooru* ① pass/ [going from one end to another of a specified interval of space], V*masu* ki˥ru V*masu*切る ① [to do s.t. completely] ⟪finish completely, dare to⟫, kara から prt. [a particle that indicates a starting point in space/time] ⟪from⟫, -juu o 〜中を [for the entire time of s.t. or covering the entire space of s.t.] ⟪throughout, everywhere⟫, V*masu* nuku V*masu*抜く ① [to move from one end to another of a specified interval of space], ⟨-no⟩ na˥ka o ⟨〜の⟩中を [going along or covering the inside of s.t.], V*masu* nukeru V*masu*抜ける ② [to move from one end to another of an interval of space]
EX. (**a**) We passed through a vast stretch of desert and finally got to a small town.
広大な砂漠{を通って/を歩き切って/*から/*中を/*を歩き抜いて/*を歩き抜けて}、ようやく小さな町にたどり着いた。
*Koodaina sabaku {o tootte/o aruki-kitte/ *kara/*-juu o/*o aruki-nuite/*o aruki-nukete}, yooyaku chiisana machi ni tadori-tsuita.*
(**b**) I somehow managed to make it through the 25-kilometer marathon.
僕は二十五キロのマラソンをなんとか走り{切った/抜いた/*抜けた}。
*Boku wa ni-juu-go-kiro no marason o nan-toka hashiri-{kitta/nuita/*nuketa}.*
(**c**) The bullet went through his heart.
弾丸は彼の心臓を打ち{抜いた/*抜けた/*切った}。
*Dangan wa kare no shinzoo o uchi-{nuita/*nuketa/*kitta}.*
(**d**) Every day I would gaze at Mt. Fuji through the hospital window.
病院の窓{から/*を通って/*中を/*の中を}、毎日富士山を眺めていた。
*Byooin no mado {kara/*o tootte/*-juu o/ *no naka o}, mai-nichi Fuji-san o nagamete ita.*
(**e**) I could feel the blood surging through my body.
私は血が体{中を/の中を/*を通って}駆け抜けるのを感じた。
*Watashi wa chi ga karada{-juu o/no naka o/*o tootte} kake-nukeru no o kanjita.*
(**f**) In Tokyo you have to wade through crowds of people during rush hour.
東京ではラッシュ時には群衆{の中を/*中を/*を通って}押し分けて歩かなければならない。
Tookyoo de wa rasshu-ji ni wa gunshuu {no naka o/-juu o/*o tootte} oshi-wakete arukanakereba naranai.*
(**g**) The train passed through numerous tunnels before it reached Hakata.
電車は博多に着くまでにトンネルをたくさん通り{抜けた/*抜いた/*切った}。
*Densha wa Hakata ni tsuku made ni tonneru o takusan toori-{nuketa/*nuita/ *kitta}.*

2. ⟨-made⟩ zu˥tto ⟨〜まで⟩ずっと [the whole

T

time until…], -juu zu⌈tto ～中ずっと [throughout the time of…], V*masu* toosu V*masu*通す ① [to do s.t. continuously from beginning to end] ((**keep Ving**))

EX. (**a**) According to the weather report, this bad weather is supposed to continue through Friday.
天気予報によると、この悪天候は金曜日いっぱいまでずっと続くそうです。
Tenki-yohoo ni yoru to, kono aku-tenkoo wa kin'yoo-bi ippai made zutto tsuzuku soo desu.
(**b**) A: Did you get a good rest last night?
ゆうべはよく寝られましたか。
Yuube wa yoku ne-raremashita ka.
B: No, unfortunately I was up all through the night with a cough that wouldn't stop.
いや、あいにく一晩中ずっとせきが止まらなくて寝られなかったんです。
Iya, ainiku hito-ban-juu zutto seki ga tomaranakute ne-rarenakatta n desu.
(**c**) I don't have time to read through the whole novel — can you just tell me roughly what happens?
私は小説を読み通す時間がないから大体の筋を教えてもらえないかな。
Watashi wa shoosetsu o yomi-toosu jikan ga nai kara daitai no suji o oshiete moraenai ka na.

3. ⟨**-o**⟩ **to⌉oshite** ⟨～を⟩**通して /**⟨**V*te* of *toosu* ① pass/ [by means of s.o./s.t. that serves as an intermediary, esp. for providing information], de** で prt. **[using s.t.]** ((**with, by**))

EX. (**a**) We learned about the big earthquake in Japan through radio.
ラジオ{を通して/で}日本の大地震について知った。
Rajio {o tooshite/de} Nihon no dai-jishin ni-tsuite shitta.
(**b**) Nowadays we get information about world events primarily through television.
今日私たちは主にテレビ{を通して/で}世界の出来事を知らされる。
Konnichi watashi-tachi wa omo ni terebi {o tooshite/de} sekai no deki-goto o shira-sareru.

4. ni-yotte によって comp. prt. **[a particle phrase indicating the cause of s.t.; the means by which s.t. is done; a variable factor depending upon which s.t. will or will not happen; the agent in a passive sentence]** ((**by which, because of, with, depending on**)), **de** で prt. SEE through 3

EX. Through consistent effort he was able to rise to the top of his class.
たゆまぬ努力{で/によって}彼はクラスで一番になることができた。
Tayumanu doryoku {de/ni-yotte} kare wa kurasu de ichiban ni naru koto ga dekita.

— adv. **[from one end to another of a spatial interval or from the beginning to end of an interval of time]**
ka⌈nzenni 完全に /⟨**adj.**(***na***) ***ni*** **of *kanzenna* complete/ •c [in a manner absolutely free from any lack or imperfection]** ((**perfectly**))

EX. My clothes were soaked through from the rain.
雨で服が完全にぬれてしまった。
Ame de fuku ga kanzenni nurete shimatta.

PHRASE: let…through ⟨*-o*⟩ *toosu* ⟨～を⟩通す ①

EX. Please move over and let the child through.
ちょっとどいて、子供を通してあげてください。
Chotto doite, kodomo o tooshite agete kudasai.

PHRASE: get through ⟨*-o*⟩ *toori-nukeru* ⟨～を⟩通り抜ける ②

EX. The tunnel was blocked and we couldn't get through.
トンネルがふさがっていたため、通り抜けることができなかった。
Tonneru ga fusagatte ita tame, toori-nukeru koto ga dekinakatta.

— adj. **[finished (with s.t.)]**
o⌈waru 終わる ① [for s.t. continuous to come to a point where it continues no further or for s.o. to reach a point in a task/activity where there is nothing left to do] ((**end, finish**)), **su⌉mu** すむ ① **[for s.t. murky**

T

to become clear《fig. "reside," "become completely done"》] ⟪end, be completed, terminate⟫
㊎ "become clear"▷澄む, "live"▷住む, "become completely done"▷済む

EX. Are you through with this newspaper?
この新聞、{済みました/終わりました}か。
Kono shinbun, {sumimasita/ owarimashita} ka.

throughout prep. **[in every part of a space or during the entire period of an interval of time]**
-juu (ni) ～中(に) •c [in every part of a space or during the entire period of an interval of time], i⌈ttai ni 一帯に •c [in every part of a place] ⟪**in the whole neighborhood**⟫

EX. (**a**) There are hot springs throughout this region.
この辺り{中/一帯}に温泉があります。
Kono atari {-juu/ittai} ni onsen ga arimasu.
(**b**) I was busy making business trips throughout the year.
一年中出張で忙しかったです。
Ichi-nen-juu shutchoo de isogashikatta desu.

T

throw vt. **[to cause s.t. to move through the air by some propulsive means《fig. "do s.t. using an action similar to propelling an object through the air"》]**
1. (⟨-ni⟩) ⟨-o⟩ na⌈ge⌉ru (⟨～に⟩)⟨～を⟩投げる ② [for s.o. to cause s.t. in one's hand to move through the air by means of a quick forward motion of the arm], ⟨-o⟩ ho⌈oru ⟨～を⟩ほうる ① [for s.o. to cause s.t. to fly through the air to a distant location without care for where it lands] ⟪**hurl, fling**⟫

EX. (**a**) The pitcher threw me a curve.
ピッチャーは僕にカーブを{投げた/?ほうった}。
Pitchaa wa boku ni kaabu o {nageta/ ?hootta}.
(**b**) Yoshio, don't throw things around like that.
良男、回りに物をそんな風に{ほうって/投げて}はいけませんよ。
Yoshio, mawari ni mono o sonna fuu ni {hootte/nagete} wa ikemasen yo.

2. ⟨-o⟩ na⌈ge-taosu ⟨～を⟩投げ倒す ① [for s.o. to cause s.o./s.a. to fly through the air and fall] ⟪**throw s.o. down**⟫

EX. The little *sumo* wrestler threw his much larger opponent out of the ring.
小さな相撲取りが自分よりずっと大きな相撲取りを土俵の外へ投げ倒した。
Chiisana sumoo-tori ga jibun yori zutto ookina sumoo-tori o dohyoo no soto e nage-taoshita.

PHRASE: throw a kiss *nage-kisu o suru* 投げキスをする ③, throw a party *paatii o suru* パーティーをする ③, throw away ⟨*-o*⟩ *suteru* ⟨～を⟩捨てる ②, ⟨*-o*⟩ *nage-suteru* ⟨～を⟩投げ捨てる ②, throw a glance at ⟨*-ni*⟩ *shisen o nageru* ⟨～に⟩視線を投げる ②, throw up *haku* 吐く ① ⟪vomit⟫

thrust vi./vt. **[for s.o. to push s.t./s.o. with a sudden force at or into s.t./s.o./s.a. or away from oneself]**
⟨-o⟩ tsu⌈ku ⟨～を⟩突く ① [for s.o./s.a. to make impact with or penetrate s.t./s.o./s.a. with a sharp or stick-like object《fig. "attack sharply"》] ⟪**poke, push, pick, stab, prick, attack**⟫, **⟨-o⟩ tsu⌈ki-sa⌉su ⟨～を⟩突き刺す ① [for s.o. to forcibly cause a sharp or stick-like object to penetrate into s.t./s.o./ s.a.]** ⟪**penetrate**⟫

EX. Watching for just the right moment, the warrior thrust his sword into his enemy's abdomen.
すきを見て戦士は剣で敵の腹を{突いた/突き刺した}。
Suki o mite senshi wa ken de teki no hara o {tsuita/tsuki-sashita}.

PHRASE: be thrust out of ⟨*-kara*⟩ *oshi-dasa-reru* ⟨～から⟩押し出される ②

EX. I was thrust out of the room.
私は部屋から押し出された。
Watashi wa heya kara oshi-dasa-reta.

— n. **[a sudden strong push or the force of this]**
1. o⌈shi 押し /⟨V*masu* of *osu* ① push/ [a sudden, forceful push]

EX. That *sumo* wrestler uses a technique in the ring that consists exclusively of making thrusts at his opponent.
その相撲取りは土俵の上では押しの一手だ。
Sono sumoo-tori wa dohyoo no ue de wa oshi no itte da.

2. tsu⌈ki 突き /〈V*masu* of *tsuku* ① thrust/ [a stab]

EX. One thrust with a knife was enough to kill the bear.
熊はナイフのひと突きで殺された。
Kuma wa naifu no hito-tsuki de korosa-reta.

thumb n. **[the short, thick finger separated from the other four on the hand]**
o⌈ya-yubi 親指 [the short, thick finger or toe separated from the other four fingers or toes on the hand or foot]

thump vt. **[to hit s.t. with a heavy blunt object, causing a dull sound]**
〈-o〉 do⌈shi⌉n to tsu⌈ku 〈～を〉どしんと突く ①

EX. I thumped the wall with my fist to signal the neighbors to quiet down.
隣の人たちに静かにするよう合図するためげんこつで壁をどしんと突いた。
Tonari no hito-tachi ni shizukani suru yoo aizu-suru tame genkotsu de kabe o doshin to tsuita.

— vi. **[to emit a dull sound as a result of hitting s.t., or being hit with a heavy blunt object]**
do⌈shi⌉n-do⌈shi⌉n to V どしんどしんとV [an onomatopoeic sound that describes the manner in which s.t. heavy repeatedly falls or hits against s.t. else]

EX. (**a**) The heavy barrel thumped on each step as it rolled down the stairs.
重いたるが一段ごとにどしんどしんと音を立てながら階段を転がり落ちていった。
Omoi taru ga ichi-dan-goto ni doshin-doshin to oto o tate-nagara kaidan o korogari-ochite itta.
(**b**) Something was thumping in the attic all night long.
一晩中屋根裏で何かがどしんどしんと音を立てていた。
Hito-ban-juu yane-ura de nani-ka ga doshin-doshin to oto o tatete ita.

— n. **[a muffled sound produced by s.t. being hit with a heavy blunt object]**
do⌈sa⌉t to iu oto どさっという音 [a sound describing the manner in which a heavy object or objects fall], do⌈shi⌉n to iu oto どしんという音 [a sound describing the manner in which s.t. heavy falls or hits against s.t. else]

EX. Several volumes of large dictionaries fell to the floor with a thump.
大きな辞書が四、五冊{どさっ/どしん}という音と共に床に落ちた。
Ookina jisho ga shi, go-satsu {dosat/doshin} to iu oto to tomoni yuka ni ochita.

thunder n.
ka⌈minari⌉ 雷

— vi. **[for a sound to occur following lightning《fig. "make a sound like that produced by lightning"》]**

1. ka⌈minari ga na⌈ru 雷が鳴る ①

EX. It started to thunder just as we finished our game of golf.
ゴルフを丁度やり終わった時、雷が鳴り始めた。
Gorufu o choodo yari-owatta toki, kaminari ga nari-hajimeta.

2. ga⌉mi-gami do⌈na⌉ru がみがみどなる ① [for s.o. to scold with a voice like that of the sound produced by lightning]

EX. My father's voice used to thunder, but it has gotten much softer in his old age.
父は昔はがみがみどなったものだが、年をとるにつれて静かになってきた。
Chichi wa mukashi wa gami-gami donatta mono da ga, toshi o toru ni tsurete shizukani natte kita.

Thursday n.
mo⌈kuyo⌉o(-bi) 木曜(日) •c

thus adv. **[in this way or as a result]**

1. {so⌈no/ko⌈no} yo⌉oni {その/この}ように [in that/this way]

T

EX. (**a**) The king decreed thus to his subjects: "All children in the kingdom shall be taught to read and write."
王は臣下に{この/*その}ように宣言した。「我が国のすべての子供に読み書きを教えるべし。」
*Oo wa shinka ni {kono/*sono} yooni sengen-shita. 'Waga-kuni no subete no kodomo ni yomi-kaki o oshieru beshi.'*
(**b**) "Everything has a soul." The philosopher taught his followers thus.
「すべてのものには魂がある。」哲学者は{その/この}ように弟子たちに説いた。
'Subete no mono ni wa tamashii ga aru.' Tetsugaku-sha wa {sono/kono} yooni deshi-tachi ni toita.

2. {**so⌈no/ko⌈no**} **ta⌈me⌉ ni** {その/この}ために **[for that/this reason or purpose]**

EX. The budget was cut. It thus became impossible to continue the project.
予算が削減された。そのためにプロジェクトを続けられなくなった。
Yosan ga sakugen-sareta. Sono tame ni purojekuto o tsuzuke-rarenaku natta.

PHRASE: thus far *ima made no tokoro* 今までのところ

EX. Thus far nobody has objected to the proposal.
今までのところだれもその提案に反対していない。
Ima made no tokoro dare-mo sono teian ni hantai-shite inai.

thy pron. **[the possessive form of the second person singular pronoun "thou" ⟨w⟩]**
na⌈nji no N なんじのN

EX. Thou shalt love thy neighbor as thyself.
なんじの隣人を己のごとく愛せよ。
Nanji no rinjin o onore no gotoku aise yo.

ticket n. **[a written or printed piece of paper which gives its holder a certain right, such as admission to an event, or a notification of a traffic offense]**
1. ki⌈ppu 切符 **•c [a written or printed piece of paper showing that the price has been paid allowing the holder to board a train or other vehicle, be admitted to an event, etc.], chi⌈ke⌉tto** チケット **•f [a piece of written or printed paper that gives its holder the right to board a vehicle, be admitted to a vehicle, in a public place, etc.]**

EX. (**a**) Tickets for the baseball game are all sold out.
野球の{切符/チケット}は売り切れた。
Yakyuu no {kippu/chiketto} wa uri-kireta.
(**b**) I bought a plane ticket to London.
ロンドンまでの飛行機の{切符/チケット}を買いました。
Rondon made no hikoo-ki no {kippu/chiketto} o kaimashita.

2. kyo⌈ka⌉-sho 許可書 **•c [a certificate permitting s.o. to do s.t.]**
3. tsu⌈ke⌉-fuda 付け札 **[a card fastened to goods for identification]** **《tag, tab》**
4. ba⌈kkin-tsu⌉uchi 罰金通知 **•c [an official notification of a fine for a traffic violation]**

PHRASE: get a ticket *-ihan de kippu o kiṛe-reru* ～違反で切符を切られる ②

EX. I got two tickets for parking violations today.
私は今日駐車違反で切符を二枚も切られてしまった。
Watashi wa kyoo chuusha-ihan de kippu o ni-mai mo kira-rete shimatta.

tidal adj. **[relating to or caused by the alternate rise and fall of the water level of the ocean]**
shi⌈o⌉ no N 潮のN

PHRASE: tidal wave *tsunami* 津波

tide n. **[the alternate rise and fall of the water level of the ocean 《fig. "time"》]**
shi⌈o⌉ しお **[salt or the alternate rise and fall of the water level of the ocean]**
㊞ "salt"▷塩, otherwise ▷潮

EX. High and low tides are caused by lunar gravity.
満ち潮と引き潮は月の引力で起きる。
Michi-shio to hiki-shio wa tsuki no inryoku de okiru.

PHRASE: Time and tide wait for no man. *Saigetsu hito o matazu.* 歳月人を待たず。

— vt. **[to cause s.t. to float away with the rise and fall of the water level of the ocean]** **⟨-o⟩ shi⌈o⌉ ni na⌈ga⌉su** ⟨〜を⟩潮に流す ①
PHRASE: tide…over *⟨-de⟩ (nan-toka) yatte ikeru* ⟨〜で⟩(何とか)やって行ける ②

EX. This money should tide me over until my next paycheck.
このお金で今度の給料日まで何とかやって行けるでしょう。
Kono o-kane de kondo no kyuuryoo-bi made nan-toka yatte ikeru deshoo.

tidy adj. **[neat in appearance]** **ki⌈chi⌉n-to shita N** きちんとしたN /⟨Vinf. past of *kichin-to suru* ③ arrange in a well-ordered and pleasing fashion/ **[arranged in a well-ordered and pleasing fashion]** ⟪neat, trim, dandy, scrupulously⟫, **ki⌈chi⌉n-to shite iru (N)** きちんとしている(N) /⟨V*te iru* of *kichin-to suru* ③ arrange in a well-ordered and pleasing fashion/, **se⌈izen to shita N** 整然としたN /⟨Vinf. past of *seizen to suru* ③ well-ordered/ •c **[in a state where everything is in order]** ⟪orderly, systematic, well-organized⟫, **se⌈izen to shite iru (N)** 整然としている(N) /⟨V*te iru* of *seizen to suru* ③ well-ordered/ •c **[in a state where everything is in order]**

EX. (a) He's always tidy in the way he's dressed.
彼はいつも見なりが{きちんと/*整然と}している。
*Kare wa itsu-mo mi-nari ga {kichin-to/*seizen to} shite iru.*
(b) Swiss towns always look so tidy.
スイスの町はどこも{きちんと/整然と}している。
Suisu no machi wa doko mo {kichin-to/seizen to} shite iru.

— vt. **[to make s.t. neat in appearance]** **⟨-o⟩ ki⌈chi⌉n-to suru** ⟨〜を⟩きちんとする ③ **[for s.o. to cause s.t. to be in a neat, proper, ordered condition]**, **⟨-o⟩ ka⌈ta-zuke⌉ru** ⟨〜を⟩片付ける ② **[for s.o. to put s.t./s.o. away in its/his/her proper place ⟪fig. "marry one's daughter off"⟫]** ⟪clear away, remove, get s.t. out of the way, solve⟫

EX. We're having company tonight, so we'd better tidy our rooms.
今晩お客さんがあるから部屋を{きちんとしなくちゃ/片付けなくちゃ}。
Konban o-kyaku-san ga aru kara heya o {kichin-to shinakucha/kata-zukenakucha}.

tie vi./vt. **[for s.o. to fasten s.t. to s.t. else with a string or string-like object or to arrange string or a string-like object so that it forms a knot or bow ⟪fig. "restrict," "equal the score with s.o."⟫]**
1. **(⟨-de⟩) ⟨-o⟩ ⟨-to⟩ mu⌈subu** (⟨〜で⟩)⟨〜を⟩⟨〜と⟩結ぶ ⓪ **[to unite separate entities or individuals together (by means of s.t.)]** ⟪knot, fasten, bind, enter into relationship, conclude, ally, unite⟫, **⟨-de⟩ ⟨-o⟩ shi⌈ba⌉ru** ⟨〜で⟩⟨〜を⟩縛る ① **[for s.o. to fix s.t./s.o./s.a. firmly by putting a string/string-like object around it ⟪fig. "restrain"⟫]** ⟪bind, fasten, truss, lash⟫, **⟨-o⟩ (⟨-ni⟩) tsu⌈nagu** ⟨〜を⟩(⟨〜に⟩)つなぐ ① **[for s.o. to link or attach s.t./s.o./s.a. to s.t. else, usu. by means of a cord-like object ⟪fig. "sustain"⟫]** ⟪fasten, chain, tether, moor, connect, link, join, sustain, hold⟫, **⟨-o⟩ (⟨-de⟩) yu⌈wae⌉ru** ⟨〜を⟩(⟨〜で⟩)結わえる ② **[for s.o. to fasten objects together with a string or string-like object]** ⟪fasten, bind⟫, **⟨-o⟩ shi⌈me⌉ru** ⟨〜を⟩しめる ② **[for s.o. to apply pressure to s.t. so as to leave no opening in it ⟪fig. "economize"⟫]** ⟪bind, tighten, strangle, buckle, shut, close, economize, control⟫
㊅ "tighten"▷締める, "strangle"▷絞める, "close"▷閉める

EX. (a) Could you please tie those old newspapers together with this string?
このひもで古新聞を{結んで/縛って/結わえて/*つないで/*締めて}くれませんか。
*Kono himo de furu-shinbun o {musunde/shibatte/yuwaete/*tsunaide/*shimete} kuremasen ka.*
(b) I tied my dog to a telephone pole.
僕は犬を電柱に{つないだ/*結んだ/*結わえた/*縛った}。
Boku wa inu o denchuu ni {tsunaida/

T

**musunda/*yuwaeta/*shibatta}.*
(c) Our five year old boy still can't tie his shoes.
うちの五歳の男の子はまだ靴のひもが{結べない/締められない/?結わえられない/?縛れない/*つなげない}。
*Uchi no go-sai no otoko-no-ko wa mada kutsu no himo ga {musube-nai/shime-rarenai/?yuwae-rare-nai/?shibare-nai/*tsunage-nai}.*

2. 〈-to〉 hi⌈ki-wake ni na⌉ru 〈～と〉引き分けになる ① [to earn an equal score in a game with s.o.] ⟪**draw**⟫

EX. Waseda University tied Keio University in today's baseball game.
今日の野球の試合で早稲田は慶応と引き分けになった。
Kyoo no yakyuu no shiai de Waseda wa Keioo to hiki-wake ni natta.

—— n. **[a string with which to fasten s.t. or an ornamental piece of clothing that is fastened around the neck or a game ending in an equal score ⟪fig. "restraint"⟫]**

1. mu⌈subu mono 結ぶもの SEE tie vi./vt. 1, **shi⌈ba⌉ru mono 縛るもの** SEE tie vi./vt. 1, **tsu⌈nagu mono つなぐもの** SEE tie vi./vt. 1, **yu⌈wae⌉ru mono 結わえるもの** SEE tie vi./vt. 1

T

2. ne⌉kutai ネクタイ •f [an ornamental piece of clothing that is fastened around the neck] ⟪**necktie**⟫

EX. I still remember the first time I put on a tie with the help of my father.
父に手伝ってもらって、初めてネクタイを締めた時のことをまだ覚えています。
Chichi ni tetsudatte moratte, hajimete nekutai o shimeta toki no koto o mada oboete imasu.

3. hi⌈ki-wake 引き分け [ending a game before the winner or loser has been determined]

EX. The game ended in a tie.
試合は引き分けに終わった。
Shiai wa hiki-wake ni owatta.

tiger n.

to⌈ra とら

EX. The tiger crouched silently, waiting for its prey.
とらは身を低くして静かにえじきを待っていた。
Tora wa mi o hikuku shite shizukani ejiki o matte ita.

tight adj. **[fitting closely, esp. so that penetration by outside elements is resisted; fastened securely and difficult to move; tensely stretched; having little spare time or room]**

1. 〈-o〉 to⌈osa⌉nai 〈～を〉通さない [not allowing s.t. to pass through] ⟪**-proof**⟫

EX. This bucket is water tight.
このバケツは水を通さない。
Kono baketsu wa mizu o toosanai.

2. 〈-ni〉 pi⌈tta⌉ri tsuita N 〈～に〉ぴったり付いたN /〈Vinf. past of *pittari tsuku* ① attach closely to/, 〈-ni〉 pi⌈tta⌉ri tsuite iru (N) 〈～に〉ぴったり付いている(N) /〈V *te iru* of *pittari tsuku* ① attach closely to/ [attached closely to s.t./s.o.]

EX. The lid was on the pan so tight that I couldn't open it.
ふたがなべにぴったり付いていて開けることができなかった。
Futa ga nabe ni pittari tsuite ite akeru koto ga dekinakatta.

3. pi⌈n-to hatta N ぴんと張ったN /〈Vinf. past of *pin to haru* ① become tense/, pi⌈n-to hatte iru (N) ぴんと張っている(N) /〈V *te iru* of *pin to haru* ① become tense/ [having tension along one or more dimensions, such as the length of a string, the surface of a sheet of paper, etc.]

EX. The acrobat crossed the tightrope on a unicycle.
曲芸師は一輪車に乗ってぴんと{張った/張っている}ロープを渡っていった。
Kyokugei-shi wa ichirin-sha ni notte pin-to {hatta/hatte iru} roopu o watatte itta.

4. kyu⌉ukutsuna 窮屈な adj(*na*). **•c [having no spare room to allow free movement ⟪fig. "formal"⟫]** ⟪**narrow, stiff, formal, ill at ease**⟫, **ki⌈tsu⌉i きつい** adj(*i*). **[having little spare time or room ⟪fig. "unbearable," "stern"⟫]** ⟪**hard, stern, harsh**⟫

EX. This jacket is a bit tight for me. Do you have something a bit larger?
この上着はちょっと{きつい/窮屈}です。もう少し大きいのはありませんか。
Kono uwagi wa chotto {kitsui/kyuukutsu} desu. Moo sukoshi ookii no wa arimasen ka.

tightly adv. **[in a closely fitting, securely fastened, or tensely stretched manner; leaving little spare time or room]**
pi⌈tta⌉ri to ぴったりと [leaving no opening or spare room 《fig. "exactly"》] 《closely, exactly》, pi⌈n-to ぴんと [with tension along one or more dimensions or with a quick release of tension 《fig. "quick to understand s.t."》]

EX. (**a**) The child clung tightly to his mother.
子供は母に{ぴったり/*ぴん}と寄り添っていた。
*Kodomo wa haha ni {pittari/*pin-} to yori-sotte ita.*
(**b**) A man was walking along the tightly stretched rope.
男が{ぴん/*ぴったり}と張ったロープの上を歩いていた。
*Otoko ga {pin-/*pittari} to hatta roopu no ue o aruite ita.*

tile n. **[a thin, flat piece of fired clay used in roofing or flooring]**
1. ka⌈wara かわら [a thin, rectangular piece of fired clay used in roofing]

EX. Japanese roofs are usually made of tiles.
日本の屋根は大抵かわらでできている。
Nihon no yane wa taitei kawara de dekite iru.

2. ta⌉iru タイル •f [a thin, flat piece of fired clay used in flooring]

EX. Our kitchen floor is tiled.
うちの台所の床はタイル張りです。
Uchi no daidokoro no yuka wa tairu-bari desu.

till prep. **[up to the time of]**
made まで prt. **[a particle which indicates the extent of an action or motion in time or space or a limit on a quantitative scale or which marks s.t./s.o./s.a. as exceeding the normal bounds of what is expected] 《as far as, up to, until, through, even》**

EX. (**a**) I was up till 3:00 last night studying.
きのうの晩は三時まで勉強していた。
Kinoo no ban wa san-ji made benkyoo-shite ita.
(**b**) I didn't hear about the incident till the following morning.
その事件のことは翌朝まで知りませんでした。
Sono jiken no koto wa yokuchoo made shirimasen deshita.

— conj. **[up to the time when]**
Vinf. nonpast affirmative made Vinf. nonpast affirmative まで SEE till prep.

EX. (**a**) Could you wait till she comes back?
彼女が帰ってくるまでお待ちくださいませんか。
Kanojo ga kaette-kuru made o-machi kudasaimasen ka.
(**b**) He's the type not to decide on anything till he's absolutely sure he can do it.
彼は絶対に出来るということがはっきりするまでやろうと決心しないタイプの人です。
Kare wa zettai ni dekiru to iu koto ga hakkiri suru made yaroo to kesshin-shinai taipu no hito desu.

tilt vi. **[to incline away from a vertical or horizontal position 《fig. "thrust with a lance"》]**
ka⌈tamu⌉ku 傾く ① [to become inclined away from a vertical line 《fig. "lose vigor"》] 《lean, slope, incline, wane》

EX. The building tilted after the earthquake.
その建物は地震の後傾いた。
Sono tate-mono wa jishin no ato katamuita.

— vt. **[to cause s.t. to incline away from a vertical or horizontal position]**
⟨-o⟩ ka⌈tamuke⌉ru ⟨～を⟩傾ける ② [for s.o. to cause s.t. to incline away from a vertical line] 《incline, lean, tip off》

EX. When someone serves you beer in Japan you're supposed to tilt your glass.
日本ではビールをついでもらう時はコ

T

ップを傾けなければならない。
Nihon de wa biiru o tsuide morau toki wa koppu o katamukenakereba naranai.

timber n. **[wood prepared for use in building things such as houses and ships] mo⌈ku⌉zai 木材 •c [trees cut down and processed for use in building things such as homes and furniture] ⟪lumber, wood⟫, za⌈imoku 材木 •c [wood prepared for use in building things such as houses and furniture] ⟪wood, log, lumber⟫**

time n. **[the continuum from past to present into the future or a specific point or subinterval of this at/during which a state, action, or event occurs or continues ⟪fig. "frequency," "multiplication"⟫]**

1. to⌈ki⌉ 時 [the continuum from past to present into the future or a specific point or subinterval of this at/during which a state, action, or event occurs or continues] ⟪moment, case, occasion⟫, ji⌈kan 時間 •c [the continuum from past to present into the future or a subinterval of this during which a state, action, or event occurs or continues] ⟪hour, leisure⟫

EX. Time flies like an arrow.
{時/時間}は矢のように過ぎ去る。
{Toki/Jikan} wa ya no yooni sugi-saru.

PHRASE: The above proverb is more naturally expressed in Japanese as follows: *Kooin ya no gotoshi.*

2. -ji ～時 •c [a point at which one of the 24 equal periods into which the day is divided begins] ⟪o'clock⟫, ji⌈dai 時代 •c [a subinterval on the continuum of past, present, and future designated for some historical purpose] ⟪period, epoch, age, era⟫

EX. (**a**) What time is it?
何時ですか。
Nan-ji desu ka.
(**b**) The time covered by the Showa emperor's reign is one of the longest of any Japanese emperor in history.
昭和天皇の在位した時代は天皇制の歴史において最も長いものの一つだ。
Shoowa-tennoo no zaii-shita jidai wa tennoo-sei no rekishi ni oite mottomo nagai mono no hitotsu da.

3. ji⌈kan 時間 •c SEE time 1, **hi⌈ma 暇 [a period during which one is free from commitments] ⟪free time, spare time, leisure⟫**

EX. A: Do you have time to see a movie tonight?
今晩映画を見に行く{時間/暇}ある?
Konban eiga o mi ni iku {jikan/hima} aru?
B: No, I don't have time for that.
ううん、そんな{時間/暇}ない。
Uun, sonna {jikan/hima} nai.

4. -kai ～回 •c [a counter for s.t. that takes place more than once, such as innings, rounds, and other repeated events] ⟪round, inning⟫, -do ～度 •c [a counter for units on a graded scale, such as temperature or angles, or for frequency of occurrence] ⟪degree, extent⟫

EX. A: How many times have you been to Japan?
何{回/度}日本へ行きましたか。
Nan-{kai/do} Nihon e ikimashita ka.
B: I've been there five times.
五{回/度}行きました。
Go-{kai/do} ikimashita.

5. -bai ～倍 •c [a counter for multiplication]

EX. My friend's house is three times as big as mine.
友達の家は僕の家より三倍大きい。
Tomodachi no ie wa boku no ie yori san-bai ookii.

PHRASE: for the first time in a while *hisashi-buri ni* 久しぶりに

EX. It rained today for the first time in a while.
今日久しぶりに雨が降った。
Kyoo hisashi-buri ni ame ga futta.

PHRASE: all the time *zu(u)tto* ず(う)っと ⟪throughout, all along, by far⟫

EX. A: Where were you?
どこにいたの?
Doko ni ita no?

T

B: I was standing here all the time. Didn't you see me?
ず(う)っとここに立っていた。気がつかなかった?
Zu(u)tto koko ni tatte ita. Ki ga tsukanakatta?

PHRASE: for some time *shibaraku* しばらく

EX. I hadn't talked to my mother for some time so I gave her a call last night.
しばらく母と話をしていなかったのでゆうべ電話をした。
Shibaraku haha to hanashi o shite inakatta node yuube denwa o shita.

PHRASE: for the first time *hajimete* 初めて

EX. I fell immediately in love with Jane when I met her for the first time at John's party.
私はジェーンにジョンのパーティーで初めて会った時にすぐ恋をしてしまった。
Watashi wa Jeen ni Jon no paatii de hajimete atta toki ni sugu koi o shite shimatta.

PHRASE: from time to time *toki-doki* 時々 ⟪sometimes, occasionally⟫

EX. I go to New York from time to time.
私は時々ニューヨークへ行きます。
Watashi wa toki-doki Nyuuyooku e ikimasu.

PHRASE: in time for ⟨-ni⟩ *ma-ni-au* ⟨〜に⟩間に合う ①

EX. If you leave here at 6.30 you'll make it in time for the 8:30 plane.
ここを六時半に出れば、八時半の飛行機に間に合いますよ。
Koko o roku-ji-han ni dereba, hachi-ji-han no hikoo-ki ni ma-ni-aimasu yo.

PHRASE: in no time *ma-mo-naku* 間もなく, *sugu ni* すぐに

EX. Once the Shinkansen left Kyoto we were in Osaka in no time.
新幹線は京都を出ると{間もなく/すぐに}大阪に着いた。
Shinkansen wa Kyooto o deru to {ma-mo-naku/sugu ni} Oosaka ni tsuita.

—— vt. **[for s.o. to set or choose the time to do s.t. or to measure the time required for s.t.]**

1. Vinf. nonpast affirmative to⌈ki⌉ o mi⌈hakarau Vinf. nonpast affirmative 時を見計らう ① [for s.o. to choose the right time to do s.t.]

EX. I timed my visit to Boston so that I could meet Mr. Fox.
フォックス氏に会える時を見計らってボストンを訪ねた。
Fokkusu-shi ni ae-ru toki o mi-hakaratte Bosuton o tazuneta.

2. ji⌈kan o ha⌈ka⌉ru 時間を計る ① [for s.o. to measure the time required for s.t.]

EX. The coach timed the runners.
監督はランナーの時間を計った。
Kantoku wa rannaa no jikan o hakatta.

tin n.
su⌉zu すず

tiny adj. **[very small]**
chi⌉ppo⌉kena ちっぽけな adj(*na*). **[very small (usually in a derogatory sense)], chi⌈tcha⌉i ちっちゃい** adj(*i*). **[very small ⟨s⟩], chi⌈tcha⌉na N ちっちゃなN**

EX. (**a**) Billy is tiny but very strong.
ビリーは{ちっちゃい/?ちっぽけだ}がとても強い。
Birii wa {chitchai/?chippoke da} ga totemo tsuyoi.
(**b**) How can you get your whole family into such a tiny car?
どうやって家族全員でこんな{ちっぽけな/ちっちゃい/ちっちゃな}車に乗れるんだい?
Doo yatte kazoku zen'in de konna {chippokena/chitchai/chitchana} kuruma ni nore-ru n dai?

tip[1] n. **[the very end of a pointed object ⟪fig. "s.t. that is attached to the end of s.t."⟫]**
sa⌈ki 先 [the end of a stick/stick-like object ⟪fig. "future," "the other party"⟫] ⟪point, end, before, ahead⟫, ha⌈shi 端 [the part of s.t. farthest from the center] ⟪end, extremity, edge, border⟫

EX. A bird was perched on the tip of the flagpole.
鳥が旗ざおの{先/端}に止まっていた。

T

Tori ga hata-zao no {saki/hashi} ni tomatte ita.

tip² n. **[a small amount of money given to s.o. in acknowledgment of his/her services]**
ko⌈koro-zuke 心付け [a small amount of money given to s.o. in acknowledgment of his/her (traditional Japanese) services] **《gratuity》, chi⌉ppu チップ •f [a small amount of money given to s.o. in acknowledgment of his/her (Western-style) services]**

EX. (**a**) In Japanese restaurants waiters and waitresses don't expect a tip.
日本のレストランではウエイターやウエイトレスは{チップ/*心付け}を期待しない。
*Nihon no resutoran de wa ueitaa ya ueitoresu wa {chippu/*kokoro-zuke} o kitai-shinai.*
(**b**) We gave our gardener a tip for his services.
植木屋さんに{心付け/*チップ}をあげた。
*Ueki-ya-san ni {kokoro-zuke/*chippu} o ageta.*

— vt. **[for s.o. to give s.o. a small amount of money in acknowledgment of his/her services]**
〈-ni〉 {chi⌉ppu/ko⌈koro-zuke} o {a⌈geru/ ya⌈ru} 〈〜に〉{チップ/心付け}を{あげる ②/ やる ①}

NOTE: *Ageru* is more polite than *yaru* as the latter implies that the receiver of the tip is lower in social status than the giver.

EX. I forgot to tip the waitress.
ウエイトレスにチップを{あげる/やる}のを忘れた。
Ueitoresu ni chippu o {ageru/yaru} no o wasureta.

tire¹ vi./vt. **[for s.o. to become fatigued or bored or to cause s.o. to become fatigued or bored]**
1. {〈-de〉/V*te*} tsu⌈kare⌉ru {〈〜で〉/V*te*}疲れる ② [for (a body part of) s.o./s.a. to become physically or mentally fatigued] **《grow weary, become fatigued》**

EX. (**a**) Using the word processor for too long tires my eyes.
ワープロを長時間使用すると目が疲れる。
Waapuro o choo-jikan shiyoo-suru to me ga tsukareru.
(**b**) The 15-mile walk tired me out.
十五マイル歩いて、とても疲れてしまった。
Juu-go-mairu aruite, totemo tsukarete shimatta.
(**c**) The older members of the hiking party soon tired of the fast pace.
ハイキング・グループの中の年寄り連中はペースが速いので間もなく疲れてきた。
Haikingu-guruupu no naka no toshiyori-renchuu wa peesu ga hayai node ma-mo-naku tsukarete kita.

2. 〈-ni〉 a⌈ki⌉ru 〈〜に〉飽きる ② [for s.o./s.a. to become bored with s.t./s.o./s.a.] **《become weary of, get sick of, lose interest in》**

EX. The children soon tired of the monotonous game.
子供は単調なゲームにすぐ飽きてしまった。
Kodomo wa tanchoona geemu ni sugu akite shimatta.

tire² n. **[a covering encircling a wheel, usu. made of rubber]**
ta⌈iya タイヤ •f

EX. I got a flat tire on the way to work today.
今日は出勤途中でタイヤがパンクしてしまった。
Kyoo wa shukkin-tochuu de taiya ga panku-shite shimatta.

tired adj. **[weary and in need of sleep or rest or bored]**
1. tsu⌈ka⌉reta N 疲れたN /〈Vinf. past of *tsukareru* ② get tired/ [to be in a state of weariness needing rest], tsu⌈ka⌉rete iru (N) 疲れている(N) /〈V*te iru* of *tsukareru* ② get tired/ ②

EX. Aren't you tired after working for five straight hours?
五時間も働き続けて疲れていませんか。

Go-jikan mo hataraki-tsuzukete tsukarete imasen ka.

2. ⟨-ni⟩ a˥kita N ⟨〜に⟩飽きたN /⟨Vinf. past of *akiru* ② get bored/ [for s.o./s.a. to be in the state of being bored with s.t./s.o./s.a.], ⟨-ni⟩ a˥kite iru (N) ⟨〜に⟩飽きている(N) /⟨Vte *iru* of *akiru* ② get bored/ ②, i˥ya˥-ni-naru いやになる ① [for s.o. to become weary of or have had enough of s.t./s.o./s.a.]

EX. Although young, he appeared to be already tired of life.
まだ若いのにあの青年はもう人生{に飽きている/がいやになった}ようだった。
Mada wakai noni ano seinen wa moo jinsei {ni akite iru/ga iya-ni-natta} yoodatta.

tissue n. **[a group of cells in a plant or animal that are similar in shape and function; soft, thin paper, esp. for use in the toilet or as a handkerchief; fine fabric such as gauze]**

1. so˥shiki 組織 •c [a group of interconnected humans/cells] ⟪organization, system, structure⟫

EX. The doctor did a biopsy on the tissue.
医者はその組織の検査をした。
Isha wa sono soshiki no kensa o shita.

2. chi˥rigami ちり紙 [paper used in the toilet or as a handkerchief], ti˥sshu ティッシュ •f [soft absorbent paper, esp. for use as a handkerchief]

EX. I need some tissue to blow my nose.
鼻をかむのに{ちり紙/ティッシュ}が要る。
Hana o kamu no ni {chirigami/tisshu} ga iru.

3. usui o˥ri-mono 薄い織物 [a thin, light fabric]

title n. **[a word or phrase used to show the social or academic rank of s.o. or the name of an artistic or literary work or (a document attesting) legal right of ownership of property]**

1. sho˥ogoo 称号 •c [an appellation indicating social or academic rank] ⟪name, appellation⟫

EX. The title of Doctor of Education was conferred on him at the graduation ceremony yesterday.
彼には昨日の卒業式で教育学博士の称号が与えられた。
Kare ni wa kinoo no sotsugyoo-shiki de kyooiku-gaku-hakase no shoogoo ga atae-rareta.

2. ka˥ta-gaki 肩書き [a word or phrase used to show one's social position, usually indicated on the right side of a business card ⟪fig. "social status"⟫]

EX. She bears the title of professor at Tokyo University.
彼女は東大教授の肩書きがある。
Kanojo wa Toodai kyooju no kata-gaki ga aru.

3. da˥imei 題名 •c [the name of an artistic or literary work] ⟪name⟫

EX. I forgot the title of James Joyce's most famous novel.
ジェームズ・ジョイスの一番有名な小説の題名を忘れてしまった。
Jeemuzu Joisu no ichiban yuumeina shoosetsu no daimei o wasurete shimatta.

4. sho˥yu˥u-ken 所有権 •c [the legal right to possess s.t.] ⟪ownership, dominion⟫

— vt. **[for s.o. to give a name to s.t./s.o.] ⟨-ni⟩ da˥i(mei) o tsu˥ke˥ru ⟨〜に⟩題(名)を付ける ② [for s.o. to give a name to an artistic or literary work]**

EX. Please title your paper before handing it in.
提出する前に論文に題名をつけてください。
Teishutsu-suru mae ni ronbun ni daimei o tsukete kudasai.

to prep. **[in the direction of some place; so as to be at some place or in contact with s.t.; for the purpose of s.t.; so that s.o. owns s.t. or benefits or is affected by one's action; as far as some place; until some time; as compared with s.t.; per s.t.]**

1. ni に prt. **[indicating a spatial/temporal point of contact, often construed as a location where s.t./s.o./s.a. exists, a goal,**

or an indirect object] ⟪**at, in, on, by, from, onto, towards, to do s.t.**⟫, **e** へ prt. **[a particle that indicates the direction toward which a movement or action proceeds]** ⟪**to, towards**⟫

EX. (**a**) I saw Tom walking to the library a minute ago.
さっきトムが図書館{へ/に}歩いていくのを見ました。
Sakki Tomu ga tosho-kan {e/ni} aruite-iku no o mimashita.
(**b**) I went to Thailand last summer.
僕はこの前の夏タイ{に/へ}行きました。
Boku wa kono mae no natsu Tai {ni/e} ikimashita.
(**c**) Cindy came to Japan to study Japanese.
シンディーは日本{へ/に}日本語を勉強しに来ました。
Shindii wa Nihon {e/ni} Nihon-go o benkyoo-shi ni kimashita.
(**d**) I gave some money to my little sister.
私は妹{に/*へ}お金をやりました。
*Watashi wa imooto {ni/*e} o-kane o yarimashita.*

2. made まで prt. **[a particle which indicates the extent of an action or motion in time or space or a limit on a quantitative scale or which marks s.t./s.o./s.a. as exceeding the normal bounds of what is expected]** ⟪**as far as, till, up to, through, even**⟫

EX. (**a**) Mr. Johnston works from 9 A.M. to 5 P.M. Monday through Friday.
ジョンストンさんは月曜から金曜の午前九時から午後五時まで働きます。
Jonsuton-san wa getsuyoo kara kin'yoo no gozen ku-ji kara gogo go-ji made hatarakimasu.
(**b**) The water in the basement came up to our waists.
地下室の水が腰まで来た。
Chika-shitsu no mizu ga koshi made kita.
(**c**) The Queen shook hands with every single person to the very end of the line.
女王は列の最後の一人とまで握手をした。
Jooo wa retsu no saigo no hitori to made akushu o shita.

3. ta͞i 対 •c **[as compared with]** ⟪**opposite, against, toward, vs.**⟫

EX. The final score of the football game was 10 to 3.
フットボールの試合の結果は10対3だった。
Fotto-booru no shiai no kekka wa jut-tai san datta.

4. ni-tsu͞ki につき **[for each** ⟪**fig. "concerning," "owing to"**⟫**]**

EX. I realized a gain on my investment of 50 cents to the dollar.
その投資金から一ドルにつき五十セントという利益を得た。
Sono tooshi-kin kara ichi-doru ni-tsuki go-jus-sento to iu rieki o eta.

PHRASE: to one's… …*koto ni* …ことに

EX. (**a**) To my great surprise it took him only nine weeks to learn to speak Japanese.
大変驚いたことに、彼はたった九週間で日本語が話せるようになった。
Taihen odoroita koto ni, kare wa tatta kyuu-shuukan de Nihon-go ga hanase-ru yooni natta.
(**b**) To my regret I wasn't able to attend my friend's wedding ceremony.
残念なことに僕は友達の結婚式に出られなかった。
Zannenna koto ni boku wa tomodachi no kekkon-shiki ni de-rarenakatta.

PHRASE: it…to Vinf. nonpast *{koto/no} wa* Vinf. nonpast{こと/の}は

EX. (**a**) It's all right to smoke in this room.
この部屋でたばこを吸う{の/こと}は構わない。
Kono heya de tabako o suu {no/koto} wa kamawanai.
(**b**) It's great fun to study *kanji.*
漢字を勉強する{の/こと}は大変面白い。
Kanji o benkyoo-suru {no/koto} wa taihen omoshiroi.

toad n.
hi͞ki-ga͞eru ひきがえる

toast[1] n. **[a sliced piece of bread browned by heat]**
to˥osuto トースト •f
EX. I usually have toast and eggs for breakfast.
私はたいてい朝御飯にトーストと卵を食べる。
Watashi wa taitei asa-gohan ni toosuto to tamago o taberu.

— vt. **[for s.o. to brown the surface of s.t. by heating or to warm s.t. thoroughly]**
⟨-o⟩ to˥osuto ni suru ⟨〜を⟩トーストにする ③ [for s.o. to brown the surface of a slice of bread by heating it], to˥osutaa de pa˥n o ya˥ku トースターでパンを焼く ① [for s.o. to brown the surface of a slice of bread using a toaster], ⟨-o⟩ a˥bu˥ru ⟨〜を⟩あぶる ① [for s.o. to dry, cook, or warm s.t. through exposure to fire, esp. food such as meat, fish, or seaweed] **((roast, broil, grill, warm, dry))**
EX. (**a**) Would you like your bread toasted?
{パンをトーストにしましょう/トースターでパンを焼きましょう/*パンをあぶりましょう}か。
*{Pan o toosuto ni shimashoo/Toosutaa de pan o yakimashoo/*Pan o aburimashoo} ka.*
(**b**) I toasted a sheet of *nori* seaweed over a slow fire.
のりをとろ火で{あぶった/*トーストにした}。
*Nori o toro-bi de {abutta/*toosuto ni shita}.*

toast[2] n. **[the act of drinking in honor of or for the purpose of expressing best wishes to s.o./s.t. or the person or thing honored or wished well in this way]**
1. ka˥npai-sareru hito 乾杯される人 [a person honored or wished well in an act of drinking]
2. ka˥npai 乾杯 •c [the act of drinking in honor of or for the purpose of expressing best wishes to s.o./s.t.]
EX. A toast to your health.
あなたの健康のために乾杯!
Anata no kenkoo no tame ni kanpai!

tobacco n.
ta˥bako たばこ •f [a plant producing leaves from which cigarettes and cigars are made or products made from this such as cigarettes and cigars] **((cigarette, cigar))**
EX. American professional baseball players often chew tobacco during games.
アメリカのプロ野球の選手は試合をしながらよくかみたばこをかむ。
Amerika no puro-yakyuu no senshu wa shiai o shi-nagara yoku kami-tabako o kamu.

today adv. **[on or during the present day or at the present time]**
1. kyo˥o 今日 [on or during the present day]
EX. I'm going to Chicago today.
今日はシカゴへ行きます。
Kyoo wa Shikago e ikimasu.
NOTE: *Kyoo* does not take the particle *ni*. It is ungrammatical to say *kyoo ni*, just as it is ungrammatical to say "on/at today" in English.
2. ko˥nnichi 今日 •c [at the present time ⟨fml⟩] **((these days, nowadays, at present))**
EX. The world is getting smaller today due to the increasingly widespread use of the Internet.
今日インターネット使用の普及により世界はますます小さくなっている。
Konnichi intaanetto shiyoo no fukyuu ni-yori sekai wa masu-masu chiisaku natte iru.

toe n. **[any of the slender extensions on the front part of a human or animal foot]**
(a˥shi no) yu˥bi˥ (足の)指

together adv. **[with another individual or group; in or into one group or mass]**
⟨-to⟩ i˥ssho ni ⟨〜と⟩一緒に [with s.o./s.t./s.a. else] **((in company with, alongside))**
EX. (**a**) A: Did you go to Europe by yourself?
ヨーロッパへ一人で行ったんですか。
Yooroppa e hitori de itta n desu ka.
B: No, I went together with some friends.
いいえ、友達と一緒に行きました。
Iie, tomodachi to issho ni ikimashita.
(**b**) Everyone repeat this word together.
皆さん一緒にこの言葉を繰り返してください。

T

Mina-san issho ni kono kotoba o kuri-kaeshite kudasai.

PHRASE: get together *atte hanasu* 会って話す ①

EX. Let's get together sometime.
いつか会って話しましょう。
Itsu-ka atte hanashimashoo.

toil vi. **[for s.o./s.a. to work hard and long or to move forward with difficulty]**

1. a˥kuseku (to) ha˥taraku あくせく(と)働く ① [for s.o. to work very hard]

EX. I toiled at that job for two years at very low wages.
私は二年間その会社でとても安い給料であくせく(と)働いた。
Watashi wa ni-nenkan sono kaisha de totemo yasui kyuuryoo de akuseku (to) hataraita.

2. ku˥roo-shite su˥sumu 苦労して進む ① [for s.o./s.a. to move forward with difficulty]

EX. We toiled along the mountain path in the rain.
私たちは雨の中の山道を苦労して進んだ。
Watashi-tachi wa ame no naka no yama-michi o kuroo-shite susunda.

— n. **[long, hard work or effort]**

ho˥ne-ori˥ 骨折り [the act of taking pains to do s.t.]

T

toilet n. **[a room containing an apparatus for eliminating human waste, one which is usu. bowl-shaped and connected to plumbing; the act of grooming oneself or a room for this purpose]**

1. (o-)˥tea˥rai (お)手洗い [a place for eliminating human waste] ⟪water closet, restroom, men's room, ladies' room⟫, to˥ire トイレ •f, be˥njo˥ 便所 •c

NOTE: Of the three words *o-tearai, toire,* and *benjo, o-tearai* is the most polite and *benjo* the least polite.

EX. Excuse me, but can you tell me which way the toilet is?
すみませんが、{お手洗い/トイレ/?便所}はどちらでしょうか。
Sumimasen ga, {o-tearai/toire/?benjo} wa dochira deshoo ka.

2. ke˥sho˥o 化粧 •c [the process of dressing or grooming oneself] ⟪makeup, dressing⟫

3. ke˥sho˥o-shitsu 化粧室 •c [a room for dressing or grooming oneself]

PHRASE: toilet paper *toiretto-peepaa* トイレットペーパー •f

token n. **[s.t. which is a sign of s.t. else, esp. s.t. small given as a sign of one's feeling ⟪fig. "a piece of stamped metal used as a substitute for money"⟫]**

shi˥rushi 印 /⟨V *masu* of *shirusu* ① mark/ [s.t. visual that serves to distinguish s.t. from other things or to signify s.t.] ⟪sign, mark, symbol, emblem, evidence, indication, symptom⟫

EX. Please accept this as a token of my appreciation.
どうぞこれを私の感謝の印としてお受け取りください。
Doozo kore o watashi no kansha no shirushi to-shite o-uke-tori kudasai.

Tokyo n. **[the name of the capital of Japan, literally "eastern capital"]**

To˥okyoo 東京 •c

told v. **[the past or past participle form of the verb "tell"]**

PHRASE: all told *zenbu de* 全部で

EX. All told there were about two hundred people at the reception.
レセプションには全部で二百人ぐらいいました。
Resepushon ni wa zenbu de ni-hyaku-nin-gurai imashita.

toll n. **[a tax or charge paid for the right to do s.t. or use s.t.; the damage or death caused by a natural disaster or incurred in attempting to accomplish s.t.]**

1. tsu˥uko˥o-ryoo 通行料 •c [the charge paid for going on a road or other thoroughfare], ryo˥okin 料金 •c [money paid for a service or the use of s.t.] ⟪charge, rate, fee⟫

EX. You have to pay a toll at the toll gate.
料金所で{通行料/料金}を払わなければなりません。

Ryookin-jo de {tsuukoo-ryoo/ryookin} o harawanakereba narimasen.

2. tsu⌈uwa⌉-ryoo 通話料 •c [a charge paid for using a telephone], ryo⌉okin 料金 •c [money paid for a service or the use of s.t.] 《charge, rate, fee》

EX. No tolls are charged for the use of emergency phones along the highway.
道路沿いの非常電話を使うのには{通話料/料金}がかかりません。
Dooro-zoi no hijoo-denwa o tsukau no ni wa {tsuuwa-ryoo/ryookin} ga kakarimasen.

3. shi⌈shoosha⌉-suu 死傷者数 •c [the number of people injured or dead]

PHRASE: death toll *shisha(-suu)* 死者(数) •c

EX. The earthquake took a heavy death toll.
その地震で多数の死者が出た。
Sono jishin de tasuu no shisha ga deta.

tomato n.
to⌉mato トマト •f

tomorrow adv./n. **[(on) the day after today or an indefinite time in the future]**
a⌈shita⌉ あした [(on) the day after today], a⌈su⌉ 明日 [(on) the day after today or an indefinite time in the near future]

NOTE: *Asu* is more formal than *ashita* when used in the sense "the day after today."

EX. (**a**) I'm leaving for Madrid tomorrow.
僕は{あした/明日}マドリッドに出かけるんだ。
Boku wa {ashita/asu} Madoriddo ni dekakeru n da.
(**b**) It is today's youth who will chart the course of tomorrow's Japan.
{明日/*あした}の日本の針路を決めるのは今の若者だ。
*{Asu/*Ashita} no Nihon no shinro o kimeru no wa ima no waka-mono da.*

ton n. **[an unit of weight equal to 907.2 kilograms in the U.S. or 1,016 kilograms in Britain]**
to⌉n トン •f

tone n. **[the quality of a musical or vocal sound or a sound used as a signal, esp. in a telephone answering machine 《fig. "one's manner of speaking," "bodily condition," "a shade of color"》]**

1. cho⌈oshi 調子 •c [the musical contour formed by a series of sounds of varying pitch and their timing 《fig. "an impression created by s.o.'s way of speaking or writing," "the degree of progress of s.t. that is moving," "the momentum which accompanies s.t. which advances"》] 《tune, note, pitch, values, manner》, ne-⌈iro 音色 [the quality of a musical or vocal sound] 《tone quality》

EX. (**a**) Of all the tones produced by musical instruments I like the cello's best.
楽器の{音色/*調子}の中ではチェロのが一番好きだ。
*Gakki no {ne-iro/*chooshi} no naka de wa chero no ga ichiban suki da.*
(**b**) His tone of voice was undeniably accusatory.
彼の声の{調子/*音色}は明らかに相手を責める調子だった。
*Kare no koe no {chooshi/*ne-iro} wa akirakani aite o semeru chooshi datta.*

2. ha⌈sshi⌉n-on 発信音 •c [a sound used as a signal, esp. in a telephone answering machine]

EX. Please record your message after the tone.
発信音の後にメッセージをおっしゃってください。
Hasshin-on no ato ni messeeji o osshatte kudasai.

3. ha⌈nashi-kata⌉ 話し方 /〈V*masu* of *hanasu* ① talk + *kata* way/ [one's way or manner of speaking]

EX. His tone of speech is always gentle and soft.
あの人の話し方はいつも穏やかで、柔らかい。
Ano hito no hanashi-kata wa itsu-mo odayakade, yawarakai.

4. shi⌈kichoo 色調 •c [a shade/quality of color] 《color tone》

EX. The color tone of the interior of the house apparently struck her fancy.
彼女はその家の内部の色調が気に入ったようだ。

T

Kanojo wa sono ie no naibu no shikichoo ga ki-ni-itta yooda.

tongue n. **[a movable muscular organ located at the bottom of the mouth ⟪fig. "language"⟫]**

1. shi⌈ta⌉ 舌 [a movable muscular organ located at the bottom of the mouth]

EX. When you pronounce English "t," the tip of the tongue touches the upper ridge behind the teeth.
英語の「t」を発音する時、舌の先は上の歯茎に触る。
Eigo no 't' o hatsuon-suru toki, shita no saki wa ue no haguki ni sawaru.

2. ko⌈toba⌉ 言葉 [the system or one of a number of systems used for communicating among humans whereby meaning is expressed in vocal sounds or written letters; a sequence of linguistic sounds forming a unit of meaning in human communication] ⟪speech, language, word, phrase, expression, term⟫, ge⌉ngo 言語 •c [the system or one of a number of systems used for communicating among humans whereby meaning is expressed in vocal sounds or written letters; a system of symbols used in programming computers] ⟪language, speech, words⟫

EX. The man was speaking in a tongue I didn't understand.
その男は私には分からない{言語/言葉}で話していた。
Sono otoko wa watashi ni wa wakaranai {gengo/kotoba} de hanashite ita.

NOTE: "Mother tongue" is not **bo-gengo* but *bokoku-go* or *bogo* .

PHRASE: (with) tongue in cheek *hiyakashi-hanbun ni* ひやかし半分に

EX. Don't take him seriously. What he said was just tongue in cheek.
彼の言ったことを本気にしないで。ひやかし半分に言っただけだから。
Kare no itta koto o honki ni shinai de. Hiyakashi-hanbun ni itta dake da kara.

tonight adv. **[on or during the present or coming night]**

ko⌉nban 今晩 •c [the night of today] ⟪this evening⟫, ko⌉n'ya 今夜 •c

NOTE: *Kon'ya* is slightly more formal and sophisticated sounding than *konban.*

EX. (**a**) Where shall we stay tonight?
{今晩/今夜}はどこに泊まりましょうか。
{Konban/Kon'ya} wa doko ni tomarimashoo ka.
(**b**) The moon is so beautiful tonight.
{今晩/今夜}は月がとてもきれいね。
{Konban/Kon'ya} wa tsuki ga totemo kirei ne.
(**c**) Where does tonight's dance take place?
{今晩/今夜}のダンスパーティーはどこであるんですか。
{Konban/Kon'ya} no dansu-paatii wa doko de aru n desu ka.

too adv. **[in addition or also; more than is desired; very]**

1. mo も prt. **[a particle indicating that the same thing is true of s.t. as is true of another noun mentioned previously or implied; a particle indicating emphasis] ⟪also, even⟫**

EX. (**a**) A: I hear Mr. Lee has gone to Japan.
リーさんは日本へ行ったそうですね。
Rii-san wa Nihon e itta soodesu ne.
B: Yes, Mr. Lin has, too.
ええ、リンさんも行きましたよ。
Ee, Rin-san mo ikimashita yo.
(**b**) A: In America, opera has become very popular recently.
アメリカでは最近オペラが好きな人が増えましたよ。
Amerika de wa saikin opera ga sukina hito ga fuemashita yo.
B: It's become popular in Japan, too.
日本でも同じですよ。
Nihon de mo onaji desu yo.

2. {adj(*i/na*). stem/V*masu*} su⌈gi⌉ru {adj(*i/na*). stem/V*masu*}すぎる ② [to do s.t. or be in some state to an excessive degree]

EX. (**a**) A: What do you think of this camera?
このカメラはどう思いますか。
Kono kamera wa doo omoimasu ka.
B: That's too expensive.
それは高すぎます。

Sore wa taka-sugimasu.
(**b**) This Japanese class is too tough for me.
この日本語の授業は私には大変すぎます。
Kono Nihon-go no jugyoo wa watashi ni wa taihen-sugimasu.
(**c**) I have to be careful not to eat too much.
食べすぎないように気をつけなくちゃいけません。
Tabe-suginai yooni ki-o-tsukenakucha ikemasen.

PHRASE: too…to adj. stem *sugite*…neg. of V. adj. stemすぎて…neg. of V.

EX. (**a**) This problem was too hard to solve.
この問題は難しすぎて解けなかった。
Kono mondai wa muzukashi-sugite toke-nakatta.
(**b**) This lid is too tight to open.
このふたは固すぎて開かない。
Kono futa wa kata-sugite akanai.

NOTE: Note that the verb used in the Japanese version of these examples is either potential in form or the intransitive member of an intransitive/transitive verb pair, such as *aku* (vi.) vs. *akeru* (vt.) "open," *shimaru* (vi.) vs. *shimeru* (vt.) "close," *kowareru* (vi.) vs. *kowasu* (vt.) "break," etc.

PHRASE: not too adj. *amari*… あまり

EX. My grandfather hasn't been too well recently.
うちの祖父はこのところあまり元気じゃない。
Uchi no sofu wa kono tokoro amari genki janai.

tool n. **[an object, usu. held in the hand, designed to help accomplish a certain kind of work《fig. "a person or thing used by s.o. to achieve some goal"》]**
do⌈ogu⌉ 道具 •c [a device used for accomplishing a certain kind of work]《utensil, apparatus, instrument》

EX. (**a**) Do you have the tools necessary to repair a TV?
テレビを直すのに必要な道具がありますか。
Terebi o naosu no ni hitsuyoona doogu ga arimasu ka.
(**b**) Language is a tool for communication.
言語はコミュニケーションの道具だ。
Gengo wa komunikeeshon no doogu da.

tooth n. **[a hard, bone-like organ set in the jaws of most vertebrates used for biting and chewing food《fig. "a part or projection shaped like a tooth"》]**
ha⌉ 歯 [a hard, bonelike organ set in the jaws of most vertebrates used for biting and chewing food《fig. "s.t. that resembles a tooth"》]

EX. (**a**) I brush my teeth twice a day.
私は歯を一日に二回磨きます。
Watashi wa ha o ichi-nichi ni ni-kai migakimasu.
(**b**) She has pretty teeth.
彼女は歯がきれいだ。
Kanojo wa ha ga kirei da.

toothache n.
ha-⌈ita 歯痛

EX. My toothache didn't let up for several days.
歯痛が四、五日止らなかった。
Ha-ita ga shi-go-nichi tomaranakatta.

PHRASE: have a toothache *ha ga itai* 歯が痛い

toothbrush n.
ha-⌈bu⌉rashi 歯ブラシ

toothpaste n.
(ne⌈ri-)ha-mi⌉gaki (ねり)歯磨き

toothpick n.
yo⌈oji ようじ, tsu⌈ma-yo⌉oji つまようじ

top n. **[the highest point of s.t.《fig. "(s.o./s.t. of) the highest rank or importance," "the earliest part"》]**
1. te⌈ppe⌉n てっぺん •c [the highest part of s.t. which extends relatively far from the ground, such as a head, mountain, building, etc. ⟨s⟩]《summit, apex, crown, pate, scalp》, i⌈tadaki 頂 [the highest point of a mountain or hill ⟨w⟩]《summit, zenith》, cho⌈ojo⌉o 頂上 •c [the highest point of a mountain《fig. "the highest level"》]《summit, zenith》

EX. (**a**) The view from the top of Mt. Fuji was fantastic.
富士山の{てっぺん/頂上/頂}からの景

T

色はすばらしかった。
Fuji-san no {teppen/choojoo/itadaki} kara no keshiki wa subarashikatta.
(**b**) A bee stung him on the top of his head.
はちが彼の頭の{てっぺん/*頂/*頂上}を刺した。
*Hachi ga kare no atama no {teppen/ *itadaki/*choojoo} o sashita.*
(**c**) We often flew kites from the top of the hill behind our house when we were kids.
僕たちは子供の時よくうちの裏の丘の{てっぺん/頂/??頂上}でたこを揚げた。
Boku-tachi wa kodomo no toki yoku uchi no ura no oka no {teppen/itadaki/ ??choojoo} de tako o ageta.

2. ⟨**-no**⟩ **u⌈e** ⟨〜の⟩上 **[a position which is higher than s.t./s.o./s.a. or which is in contact with the surface of s.t. ⟪fig. "an age older than one's own age"⟫] ⟪upper part, surface, summit, up, older, topmost⟫** ↔ ⟨**-no**⟩ **shita** ⟨〜の⟩下

EX. (**a**) On top of the table was a pile of books.
机の上には本が山ほど置いてあった。
Tsukue no ue ni wa hon ga yama hodo oite atta.
(**b**) Please write your name at the top of each page.
ページごとに上の方に名前を書いてください。
Peeji-goto ni ue no hoo ni namae o kaite kudasai.

T

3. shu⌉i 首位 •**c** **[first place, esp. in sports] ⟪primacy, leading position⟫, to⌉ppu** トップ •**f** **[the first in order or rank ⟪fig. "the right uppermost space on a newspaper page"⟫]**

EX. (**a**) She is the top in her profession.
彼女は自分の仕事の分野では{トップ/*首位}だ。
*Kanojo wa jibun no shigoto no bun'ya de wa {toppu/*shui} da.*
(**b**) The top in the golf competition turned out to be an absolute beginner.
ゴルフコンペでの{首位/トップ}はずぶの素人が取った。
Gorufu-konpe de no {shui/toppu} wa zubu no shirooto ga totta.

4. ha⌈jime 初め **[the starting point, point of origin of s.t.] ⟪beginning, origin, outset⟫**

EX. OK, let's take this piece from the top once more.
よし、この曲の初めからもう一度やろう。
Yoshi, kono kyoku no hajime kara moo ichi-do yaroo.

PHRASE: on top of that *sono ue (ni)* その上(に)

EX. The apartment was very expensive. On top of that it was a long way from the nearest station.
アパートはとても家賃が高かった。その上(に)、一番近くの駅からでもとても遠かった。
Apaato wa totemo yachin ga takakatta. Sono ue (ni), ichiban chikaku no eki kara demo totemo tookatta.

— adj. **[highest in location, position, rank, or degree]**

1. te⌈ppe⌉n no N てっぺんのN •**c** SEE top n. 1, **i⌈tadaki no N** 頂のN SEE top n. 1, **cho⌈ojo⌉o no N** 頂上のN •**c** SEE top n. 1

2. u⌈e no N 上のN SEE top n. 2

EX. Could you get that book on the top shelf for me?
あの上の棚の本を取ってくれませんか。
Ano ue no tana no hon o totte kuremasen ka.

3. to⌉ppu no N トップのN •**f**, **shu⌉i no N** 首位のN •**c** SEE top n. 3

EX. (**a**) She is one of the top biochemists in the country.
彼女は全国で{トップ/*首位}の生化学研究者の一人だ。
*Kanojo wa zenkoku de {toppu/*shui} no sei-kagaku-kenkyuu-sha no hitori da.*
(**b**) This year the New York Yankees were the top baseball team.
今年はニューヨークヤンキースが{首位/?トップ}の野球チームだった。
Kotoshi wa Nyuuyooku-Yankiisu ga {shui/?toppu} no yakyuu-chiimu datta.

topic n. **[that which a speech, discussion, or written work is about]**

wa⌈dai 話題 •**c** **[the subject matter of a conversation or talk], da⌈imoku** 題目 •**c** **[an**

idea, issue, or matter which is central to a discussion or study; the title of a book; the noun in a sentence which grammatically expresses what the rest of the sentence is about] ⟪theme, title⟫, to˥pikku トピック •f **[a matter which is central to interest or discussion, esp. in the current news]**

EX. (**a**) The topic of the talk was the current state of the Japanese economy.
{話題/話の題目/話のトピック}は現在の日本経済の状態についてでした。
{Wadai/Hanashi no daimoku/Hanashi no topikku} wa genzai no Nihon-keizai no jootai ni-tsuite deshita.
(**b**) The big topic in the news that year was the unification of the two Germanies.
その年のニュースの大きな{話題/トピック/*題目}は二つのドイツの統一だった。
*Sono toshi no nyuusu no ookina {wadai/toppiku/*daimoku} wa futatsu no Doitsu no tooitsu datta.*

tornado n.
ta˥tsumaki 竜巻

toss vt./vi. **[for s.o. to throw s.t. lightly or carelessly into or through the air; to move back and forth turbulently or to cause s.t. to move in this way ⟪fig. "to throw a coin in the air to decide s.t. according to which way it falls"⟫]**

1. ⟨-o⟩ yu˥saburu ⟨〜を⟩揺さぶる ① **[to cause s.t./s.o./s.a. to swing up and down or from side to side ⟪fig. "disturb one's mind"⟫]** ⟪shake, jolt, disturb⟫

EX. The wind and waves tossed the little boat about mercilessly.
小さな船は容赦なく波風に揺さぶられた。
Chiisana fune wa yoosha-naku nami-kaze ni yusabura-reta.

2. ⟨-o⟩ ho˥oru ⟨〜を⟩ほうる ① **[to cause s.t. to fly through the air to a distant location without care for where it lands]** ⟪hurl, fling⟫, (⟨-ni⟩) ⟨-o⟩ na˥ge˥ru (⟨〜に⟩)⟨〜を⟩投げる ② **[for s.o. to cause s.t. in one's hand to move through the air by means of a quick forward motion of the arm]** ⟪throw, give up⟫, ⟨-o⟩ to˥su-suru ⟨〜を⟩トスする ③ •f **[for s.o. to throw a baseball to a baseman at close range or to throw up a volley ball so that s.o. can jump up and hit it hard or to throw a coin to decide s.t. in sports, such as which team takes the offensive position first in sports]**

EX. (**a**) The children started tossing stones into the pond.
子供は池に石を{ほうり/投げ/*トスし}始めた。
*Kodomo wa ike ni ishi o {hoori/nage/*tosu-shi}-hajimeta.*
(**b**) We tossed a coin to decide who would go first.
だれが一番先に始めるかを決めるためにコインを{投げた/トスした/*ほうった}。
*Dare ga ichiban saki ni hajimeru ka o kimeru tame ni koin o {nageta/tosu-shita/*hootta}.*

total adj. **[making up the whole or including everyone/everything]**

1. ze˥ntai no N 全体のN •c **[covering the whole extent of s.t.]** ⟪whole, entire, general⟫, zen- 全〜 pref. •c **[including all of or the entire extent of]** ⟪whole, entire, pan-⟫, soo- 総〜 pref. •c **[including all of or having control over all of]** ⟪whole, entire, general, aggregate, combined⟫

EX. (**a**) About one-third of the total number of students in this high school go on to college.
この高校の{全体の/全/*総}学生の約三分の一が大学に進学します。
*Kono kookoo no {zentai no/zen-/*soo-} gakusei no yaku san-bun no ichi ga daigaku ni shingaku-shimasu.*
(**b**) The total population of Japan is about 120 million.
日本の{全/総/??全体の}人口は約一億二千万人だ。
Nihon no {zen-/soo-/??zentai no} jinkoo wa yaku ichi-oku-ni-sen-man-nin da.

2. ka˥nzenna 完全な adj(*na*). •c **[lacking no parts and having no faults]** ⟪perfect, complete⟫

T

EX. Mr. Yamada is a total vegetarian.
山田さんは完全な菜食主義者です。
Yamada-san wa kanzenna saishoku-shugi-sha desu.

— n. **[the whole amount or number]**

1. so͡oryoo 総量 •c [the whole amount or weight] ⟪gross amount/volume⟫, **so͡ogaku 総額 •c [the whole amount of money]** ⟪sum⟫, **go͡okei 合計 •c [the entire amount]** ⟪sum total⟫

EX. (**a**) My total purchase came to around ¥58,000.
買い物の{総額/合計/*総量}は約五万八千円だった。
*Kai-mono no {soogaku/gookei/*sooryoo} wa yaku go-man-has-sen-en datta.*
(**b**) The total number of daily calories required by a person is about 3,000.
一人当たりの毎日の必要カロリーの{総量/合計/*総額}は約三千カロリーです。
*Hitori no hito atari no mai-nichi no hitsuyoo karorii no {sooryoo/gookei/*soogaku} wa yaku san-zen karorii desu.*

2. so͡osu͝u 総数 •c [the whole number] ⟪aggregate⟫

EX. The total number of students in this university is about 35,000.
この大学の学生の総数は約三万五千人です。
Kono daigaku no gakusei no soosuu wa yaku san-man-go-sen-nin desu.

— vt. **[for s.o. to find the sum of s.t.]**
⟨-o⟩ so͡okei-suru ⟨〜を⟩総計する ③

EX. Please total your expenses and submit them to the accounting department.
支出を総計して会計課に提出してください。
Shishutsu o sookei-shite kaikei-ka ni teishutsu-shite kudasai.

— vi. **[to amount as a whole to a certain figure]**
so͡okei (ga) ⟨-ni⟩ na͝ru 総計(が)⟨〜に⟩なる ① [for the entire amount to amount to a certain figure], so͡ogaku (ga) ⟨-ni⟩ na͝ru 総額(が)⟨〜に⟩なる ① [for the entire sum of money to amount to a certain figure], go͡okei (ga) ⟨-ni⟩ na͝ru 合計(が)⟨〜に⟩なる ① [for the entire amount to add up to a certain figure], soosuu (ga) ⟨-ni⟩ naru 総数(が)⟨〜に⟩なる ①

EX. (**a**) Our expenses totaled $25,000.
支出は{総計/総額/合計/*総数}二万五千ドルだった。
*Shishutsu wa {sookei/soogaku/gookei/*soosuu} ni-man-go-sen-doru datta.*
(**b**) The number of votes cast totaled 28,534.
投票{総数/*合計/*総額/*総計}は二万八千五百三十四だった。
*Toohyoo-{soosuu/*gookei/*soogaku/*sookei} wa ni-man-has-sen-go-hyaku-san-juu-yon datta.*

totally adv. **[completely, entirely]**
ma͡ttaku 全く [in a manner so strongly that it cannot be expressed in any other way] ⟪entirely, utterly, truly⟫, **ze͡nzen…neg. 全然…neg. •c [not…at all]**

EX. (**a**) I was totally ignorant of the fact that those two were married.
僕はあの二人が結婚しているなんて{全然/全く}知らなかった。
Boku wa ano futari ga kekkon-shite iru nante {zenzen/mattaku} shiranakatta.
(**b**) I totally agree with your idea.
僕はあなたの考えに{全く/*全然}賛成です。
*Boku wa anata no kangae ni {mattaku/*zenzen} sansei desu.*

NOTE: *Zenzen* has begun to be used even with affirmative predicates in casual speech in modern Japanese.

touch vt. **[for s.o./s.a. to put one's hand or other body part on or against s.t. lightly; to come in physical contact with s.t. else or for s.o. to bring s.t. in physical contact with s.t. else ⟪fig. "arouse emotion or sympathy"⟫]**
1. ⟨-ni⟩ (⟨-de⟩) sa͡waru ⟨〜に⟩(⟨〜で⟩)触る ① [for s.o./s.a. to put one's hand or other body part on or against s.t./s.o./s.a. lightly or for a body part of s.o./s.a. to come in

T

contact with s.t./s.o./s.a. unintentionally], 〈-o〉 sa⌈waru 〈〜を〉触る ① [for s.o./s.a. to put one's hand or other body part on or against s.t./s.o./s.a. intentionally], 〈-ni〉 (〈-de〉) fu⌈reru 〈〜に〉(〈〜で〉)触れる ② [for s.o. to cause s.t. to come close to and make light contact with s.t./s.o./s.a. or for s.t. to spontaneously come close to and make light contact with s.t. else 《fig. "mention s.t.," "violate the law"》] 《feel, refer to, mention, conflict with》, 〈-to〉 se⌈sshoku-suru 〈〜と〉接触する ③ •c [for s.o. to have social contact with s.o. else or for s.t. to make contact spontaneously with s.t. else] 《contact》, 〈-ni〉 se⌈ssuru 〈〜に〉接する ③ •c [to come or be in close or direct contact with s.t. else; for s.o. to have spontaneous social contact with s.o. else; for s.o. to encounter s.t. unexpectedly] 《come in contact with, border on, be adjacent to, receive》

EX. (**a**) As I touched her dark hair gently from behind with my fingers, she turned around and kissed me.
後ろから彼女の黒髪に指でそっと{触る/触れる/*接触する/*接する}と、彼女は振り向いて、私にキスをした。
*Ushiro kara kanojo no kuro-kami ni yubi de sotto {sawaru/fureru/*sesshoku-suru/*sessuru} to, kanojo wa furi-muite, watashi ni kisu o shita.*
(**b**) Don't touch the painting, please.
絵に{触らない/触れない/*接触しない/*接しない}でください。
*E ni {sawaranai/furenai/*sesshoku-shinai/*sesshinai} de kudasai.*
(**c**) Line X touches circle A at point B.
線Xは点Bで円Aに{接して/??接触して/*触って/*触れて}いる。
*Sen ekkusu wa ten bii de en ei ni {sesshite/??sesshoku-shite/*sawatte/*furete} iru.*

2. 〈-o〉 ka⌈ndoo-saseru 〈〜を〉感動させる /〈causative of *kandoo-suru* ③ be moved/ ② •c [to move s.o. emotionally]

EX. Mother Teresa's speech at the United Nations touched many people's hearts deeply.
マザー・テレサの国連での演説は大勢の人を深く感動させた。
Mazaa Teresa no kokuren de no enzetsu wa oozei no hito o fukaku kandoo-saseta.

NOTE: The more natural version of the above translation is *Mazaa Teresa no kokuren de no enzetsu ni oozei no hito ga fukaku kandoo-shita.*

—— n. [an act, intance, or manner of coming in physical contact with s.t./s.o./s.a. or bringing s.t. in physical contact with s.t. else; the faculty of being able to feel things through physical contact; a slight amount of s.t.; a relationship with s.o. requiring continuing communication to be maintained]

1. fu⌈de-zu⌉kai 筆使い [the manner in which a brush is handled in painting], ta⌉tchi タッチ •f [the act of bringing s.t., esp. one's hand, in physical contact with s.t.; the manner in which the keyboard responds to the fingers; the manner in which a brush is handled in painting; involvement with s.t.]

EX. (**a**) I like the touch of this piano.
私はこのピアノの{タッチ/*筆使い}が好きです。
*Watashi wa kono piano no {tatchi/*fude-zukai} ga suki desu.*
(**b**) This painting is drawn with a light touch.
この絵は軽い{タッチ/筆使い}で描かれています。
Kono e wa karui {tatchi/fude-zukai} de egaka-rete imasu.

2. sho⌈kkaku 触覚 •c [the faculty of being able to feel things through physical contact]

EX. A blind person typically has a keener sense of touch than a person with sight.
目の見えない人はたいてい触覚が目の見える人よりも鋭い。
Me no mienai hito wa taitei shokkaku ga me no mieru hito yori mo surudoi.

3. ka⌈nji 感じ /〈V*masu* of *kanjiru* ② feel/ [a

T

physical perception/impression] ((**feeling, sense, feel, impression**)), **te-⌈za⌉wari** 手ざわり **[the sensation produced by putting one's hand on or against s.t.]** ((**feel**))

EX. (**a**) I felt a touch of coldness in the way he spoke to me.
彼の話し方は何か冷たい{感じ/*手ざわり}がした。
*Kare no hanashi-kata wa nani-ka tsumetai {kanji/*te-zawari} ga shita.*
(**b**) This material is silky to the touch.
この生地は絹のような{手ざわり/感じ}だ。
Kono kiji wa kinu no yoona {te-zawari/kanji} da.

4. {**V*masu*/N**} **gimi** {**V*masu*/N**}気味 **•c [to be verging on a certain state]** ((**feeling, dash**))

EX. I have a touch of a cold today.
今日は風邪気味です。
Kyoo wa kaze-gimi desu.

5. se⌈sshoku 接触 **•c** SEE touch vt. 1

PHRASE: get in touch with s.o. ⟨*-to*⟩ *renraku o toru* ⟨～と⟩連絡を取る ①

EX. Can you tell me how I can get in touch with Professor Kunihiro?
国広先生とはどのようにして連絡を取ればいいか教えてもらえますか。
Kunihiro-sensei to wa dono yooni shite renraku o toreba ii ka oshiete morae-masu ka.

tough adj. **[difficult to break, damage, cut, or chew; strong and able to withstand hardship; difficult to do or endure]**

1. tsu⌈yo⌉i 強い adj(*i*). **[having the power to act or perform in an effective way or to resist external force, esp. physically, but also mentally or emotionally]** ((**powerful, mighty, robust, stout, violent, intense, durable**)) ↔ **yowai** 弱い adj(*i*).; **ka⌈tai** かたい adj(*i*). **[not easily changed/broken/influenced]** ((**hard, solid, stiff, strict, rigid, safe**)), **ga⌈nkyoona** 頑強な adj(*na*). **•c [unyielding in attitude or stout in physical constitution]** ((**stout, stubborn**)), **ga⌉nkona** 頑固な adj(*na*). **•c [firmly refusing to change one's ideas/attitudes** ((**fig. "for a disease to continue longer than expected"**))**]** ((**stubborn, obstinate, stiff-necked**))

㊰ "the nature of an object"▷硬い, "a state or attitude"▷堅い, otherwise ▷固い

EX. (**a**) A: How does your meat taste?
その肉はどうですか。
Sono niku wa doo desu ka.
B: It tastes good, but it's a bit tough and hard to chew.
おいしいけど、ちょっと{固くて/*強くて/*頑強で/*頑固で}よくかめません。
*Oishii kedo, chotto {katakute/*tsuyokute/*gankyoode/*gankode} yoku kame-masen.*
(**b**) I'm sure he's tough enough to get through this difficult period just fine.
彼は{強い/頑強だ/*固い/*頑固だ}から問題なくこの困難な時期を乗り切れるよ。
*Kare wa {tsuyoi/gankyoo da/*katai/*ganko da} kara mondai-naku kono konnanna jiki o nori-kire-ru yo.*
(**c**) My father's a tough character. He never changes his opinion on things.
父はとても{頑固な/強い/*頑強な/*固い}人間です。自分の意見を絶対に変えないんですから。
*Chichi wa totemo {gankona/tsuyoi/*gankyoona/*katai} ningen desu. Jibun no iken o zettai ni kaenai n desu kara.*

2. ta⌈ihenna 大変な adj(*na*). **[giving cause for great worry or requiring unusually hard work and effort]** ((**horrible, terrible, awful, immense**)), **mu⌈zukashii** 難しい adj(*i*). **[requiring much time and effort to understand/solve/complete; fussy and particular]** ((**difficult, hard**))

EX. This Japanese course is the toughest course I've had in college.
この日本語の授業は今まで大学で取った科目の中で一番{大変な/難しい}科目だ。
Kono Nihon-go no jugyoo wa ima made daigaku de totta kamoku no naka de ichiban {taihenna/muzukashii} kamoku da.

tour n. **[a trip through an area or through a building in which many places are visited or many things seen]**
1. ryo⌈koo 旅行 •c [the act of leaving one's home to go to a relatively distant place], tsu⌉aa ツアー •f [a group trip for the purpose of sight-seeing]
EX. My parents are presently on a tour in Europe.
両親は今ヨーロッパ{旅行/ツアー}に行っています。
Ryooshin wa ima Yooroppa-{ryokoo/tsuaa} ni itte imasu.
2. ju⌈ngyoo 巡業 •c [a long trip by a theatrical group]
—— vi./vt. **[to take a trip or excursion on which many places are visited or many things seen]**
1. ryo⌈koo o suru 旅行をする ③ [to take a trip on which many different places are visited], tsu⌉aa de ⟨-ni⟩ i⌈ku ツアーで⟨〜に⟩行く ① •f [to go somewhere on a group trip]
EX. I toured Kyushu in May with a group of people from my company.
私は五月に会社の同僚と{ツアーで九州へ行った/九州旅行をした}。
Watashi wa go-gatsu ni kaisha no dooryoo to {tsuaa de Kyuushuu e itta/Kyuushuu-ryokoo o shita}.
2. ju⌈ngyoo-suru 巡業する ③ •c [for a troupe of performers, such as actors or sumo wrestlers, to make a trip through an area to put on a series of performances]

tourist n. **[a person who travels or visits a place for pleasure]**
ryo⌈ko⌉o-sha 旅行者 •c [a person who takes a trip] ⟪traveler⟫, **ka⌈nko⌉o-kyaku 観光客 •c [a person who goes to see a place or places of interest for pleasure]** ⟪sightseer, visitor⟫, **tsu⌈uri⌉suto ツーリスト •f**
EX. I've never visited a foreign country as an exchange student, only as a tourist.
私は留学生としてでなく、{旅行者/観光客/ツーリスト}としてしか外国を訪れたことがない。
Watashi wa ryuugaku-sei to-shite de naku, {ryokoo-sha/kankoo-kyaku/tsuurisuto} to-shite shika gaikoku o otozureta koto ga nai.

tow vt. **[to pull s.t. behind oneself by hand, rope, or a rope-like object]**
1. ⟨-o⟩ hi⌈ppa⌉tte iku ⟨〜を⟩引っ張って行く ① [for s.o. to pull s.o./s.a. behind oneself by hand]
EX. The mother towed the child away.
お母さんが子供を引っ張って行った。
O-kaa-san ga kodomo o hippatte itta.
2. ⟨-o⟩ ke⌈n'in-suru ⟨〜を⟩けん引する ③ •c [to pull s.t. such as a car or other vehicle using a rope or chain]
EX. The illegally parked car was towed away.
違反駐車していた車がけん引されて行った。
Ihan-chuusha-shite ita kuruma ga ken'in-sarete itta.

toward(s) prep. **[in the direction of s.t./s.o./s.a. or in regard to ⟪fig. "close to in time"⟫]**
1. ⟨-no⟩ ho⌉o {ni/e} ⟨〜の⟩方{に/へ} n.+prt., **ni に** prt. **[a particle indicating a spatial/temporal point of contact, often construed as a location where s.t./s.o./s.a. exists, a goal, or an indirect object]** ⟪to⟫, **N e N へ** prt. **[a particle that indicates the direction in which a movement or action proceeds]** ⟪to⟫, **⟨-ni⟩ ta⌈isu⌉ru N ⟨〜に⟩対するN [facing s.t./s.o./s.a ⟪fig. "in relation to"⟫]**
EX. (**a**) I was walking towards the beach when it started to rain.
雨が降り出した時海岸(の方){に/へ}歩いていました。
Ame ga furi-dashita toki kaigan (no hoo) {ni/e} aruite imashita.
(**b**) Yumi's attitude towards me was always friendly and kind.
私に対する由美の態度はいつも優しく、親切でした。
Watashi ni-taisuru Yumi no taido wa itsu-mo yasashiku, shinsetsu deshita.
2. chi⌈ka⌉ku ni 近くに [physically or temporally close to s.t.]
EX. Our baby was born towards the end of December.

T

十二月の終り近くに私たちの赤ん坊が生まれた。
Juu-ni-gatsu no owari chikaku ni watashi-tachi no akanboo ga umareta.

towel n. **[a piece of cloth or paper used to wipe or dry things]**
te⌈nugui 手ぬぐい [a piece of thin cotton cloth used to wipe or dry the hands, face or body] ⟪hand towel, wash-cloth⟫, ta⌉oru タオル •f [a piece of thick, absorbent cloth used to wipe or dry the hands, face or body⟫

EX. You don't need to bring a towel, because they provide you with one at the inn.
{タオル/手ぬぐい}は持って来なくてもいいです。旅館にありますから。
{Taoru/Tenugui} wa motte-konakute mo ii desu. Ryokan ni arimasu kara.

tower n. **[a tall narrow building or structure]**
to⌉o 塔 •c [a building (of several stories) often found in Hindu and Buddhist temples in Asia (built over a sacred relic)] ⟪pagoda, steeple⟫, ta⌉waa タワー •f [a Western-style tall narrow building or structure]

EX. (**a**) From the observation deck of the Tokyo Tower you can see the entire city of Tokyo.
東京{タワー/*塔}の展望台からは東京の町全体が見えます。
*Tookyoo {Tawaa/*Too} no tenboo-dai kara wa Tookyoo no machi zentai ga miemasu.*

Tokyo Tower

(**b**) The tall tower over there is part of the Buddhist temple near the center of town.
向こうの高い{塔/*タワー}は町の中心近くのお寺の一部です。
*Mukoo no takai {too/*tawaa} wa machi no chuushin chikaku no o-tera no ichi-bu desu.*

— vi. **[to rise high above the surroundings or in comparison to others]**
(to⌉o no yooni) ta⌉kaku so⌈bie⌉ru (塔のように)高くそびえる ② [for s.t. such as a mountain or building to rise high]

EX. The mountain towers over the city.
山は町を見下ろすように高くそびえている。
Yama wa machi o mi-orosu yooni takaku sobiete iru.

towering adj. **[rising very high or extreme in intensity of emotion, esp. anger]**
1. ta⌉kaku so⌈bie⌉ru (N) 高くそびえる(N) [for s.t. such as a mountain or building to rise high]

EX. As we climbed the mountain, the fog lifted, revealing the peak towering above us.
山を登っていくうちに霧が晴れて高くそびえる頂上が見えてきた。
Yama o nobotte iku uchi ni kiri ga harete takaku sobieru choojoo ga miete kita.

2. ha⌈geshi⌉i 激しい adj(*i*). **[involving an excessively high degree of force or strength, either physical or emotional] ⟪violent, strong, vehement, fierce, furious, intense⟫**

EX. In a fit of towering rage he ordered his son to leave home.
彼は息子に対して激しい怒りを覚え、家を出て行けと命じた。
Kare wa musuko ni-taishite hageshii ikari o oboe, ie o dete ike to meijita.

town n. **[a populated area larger than a village but smaller than a city]**
ma⌈chi⌉ まち [a populated area or an area formed by a major street with buildings, clustered on either side] ⟪city, street, quarter⟫, to⌈kai 都会 •c [a highly populated urban area having a central government and commercial/industrial centers as distinct from the countryside] ⟪city⟫

NOTE: まち is normally written with the character 町, but can be represented by 街 when it refers to a particular district of a town or city, as in example (c).

EX. (**a**) When I was 17, I moved from the countryside to live in town.
十七の時田舎から{町/都会}に出て来ました。
Juu-shichi no toki inaka kara {machi/tokai} ni dete-kimashita.

(**b**) Today I'm going to town to buy a car.
今日は車を買いに{町/*都会}に行きます。
*Kyoo wa kuruma o kai ni {machi/ *tokai} ni ikimasu.*
(**c**) This part of the city is called "College Town" because of the large number of college students who live here.
町のこの辺りは大学生が大勢住んでいるため「学生街」と呼ばれている。
Machi no kono atari wa daigaku-sei ga oozei sunde iru tame 'gakusei-gai' to yoba-rete iru.

toy n. **[s.t. to play with or intended for amusement rather than serious use]**
o⌈mo⌉cha おもちゃ [s.t. for a child to play with]

EX. Children love to play with toys.
子供はおもちゃで遊ぶのが大好きだ。
Kodomo wa omocha de asobu no ga dai-suki da.

— vi. **[for s.o. to play with s.t.]**
⟨-o⟩ mo⌈te-asobu ⟨～を⟩もてあそぶ ① [for s.o. to play with s.t. in one's hands ⟪fig. "fool around or trifle with"⟫]

EX. (**a**) The cat toyed with the mouse before killing it.
猫はねずみを殺す前にもてあそんだ。
Neko wa nezumi o korosu mae ni mote-asonda.
(**b**) Don't toy around with my feelings like that!
私の気持ちをそんな風にもてあそばないで!
Watashi no kimochi o sonna fuu ni mote-asobanaide!

trace n. **[a small amount or mark of s.t. providing evidence of its (earlier) presence]**
a⌉to あと [a visible alteration in the appearance of s.t. created by some entity or event earlier in time ⟪fig. "space behind s.o.," "immediately after s.t. has occurred"⟫] ⟪mark, print, impression, track, ruins, back, rear, later⟫, {a⌈shi-a⌉to/so⌈kuseki} 足跡 •c [a mark made by the foot of s.o./s.a. ⟪fig. "a visible effect left by s.t."⟫] ⟪footprint, achievement⟫, ko⌈nseki 痕跡 •c [a mark showing the earlier presence of s.t.] ⟪marks, vestiges⟫, sho⌈oko 証拠 •c [materials that demonstrate the truth or correctness of s.t.] ⟪proof, evidence⟫
㊉ "a physical mark showing that s.t. has occurred"▷跡, "time after s.t. has occurred"▷後
NOTE: *Ashi-ato* and *sokuseki* are the Japanese and Chinese readings, respectively, of 足跡.

EX. (**a**) The veteran burglar spared no effort to ensure that no traces remained of his having entered the house.
常習犯の泥棒は自分がその家に入った{跡/足跡/痕跡/証拠/*足跡}が一切残らないように万全の注意をはらった。
*Jooshuu-han no doroboo wa jibun ga sono ie ni haitta {ato/ashi-ato/konseki/ shooko/*sokuseki} ga issai nokoranai yooni banzen no chuui o haratta.*
(**b**) There was no trace whatsoever of a castle having stood there in the past.
城があった{跡/痕跡/証拠/*足跡/*足跡}は何もなかった。
*Shiro ga atta {ato/konseki/shooko/*ashi-ato/*sokuseki} wa nani-mo nakatta.*

— vt. **[for s.o. to follow a trail (of factual evidence) to its origin or cause or to copy a figure by following lines seen through a transparent sheet of paper]**
1. ⟨-o⟩ ta⌈do⌉ru ⟨～を⟩たどる ① [for s.o. to follow a trail (of factual evidence) to its origin or to one's destination] ⟪follow up, pursue⟫

EX. If I trace my family line it goes back as far as the Edo period.
私の家系をたどると江戸時代までさかのぼります。
Watashi no kakei o tadoru to Edo-jidai made sakanoborimasu.

2. shi⌈ki-utsushi o suru 敷き写しをする ③ [to copy s.t. by following lines seen through a transparent sheet of paper], ri⌈nkaku o e⌈ga⌉ku 輪郭を描く ① [to draw an outline]

track n. **[a mark or series of marks left by a human or animal passing ⟪fig. "route," "railways"⟫]**

T

1. ⟨-ga⟩ to⌉otta a⌉to ⟨〜が⟩通った跡 [a trace left by s.o./s.a. having passed], a⌈shi-a⌉to 足跡 [a mark made by the foot of s.o./s.a.] ⟪footprint, footmark⟫

EX. Look! Bear tracks!
見てご覧。熊{が通った跡/の足跡}だ。
Mite go-ran. Kuma {ga tootta ato/no ashi-ato} da.

2. shi⌉nro 進路 •c [the direction or route which s.o./s.t. intends to or is expected to take《fig. "direction in life"》] ⟪course, way, route, path⟫

EX. Fortunately there were no major population centers in the track of the typoon.
台風の進路には幸い大きな人口密集地はなかった。
Taifuu no shinro ni wa saiwai ookina jinkoo-misshuu-chi wa nakatta.

3. se⌉nro 線路 •c [a set of rails on which a train runs], -ban-sen 〜番線 [a number assigned to a platform in a train station]

EX. (**a**) A car was stalled on the tracks.
車が線路で動けなくなっていた。
Kuruma ga senro de ugoke-naku natte ita.
(**b**) The train for Chicago leaves from Track No. 4.
シカゴ行きの列車は四番線から出ます。
Shikago-{i/yu}ki no ressha wa yon-ban-sen kara demasu.

PHRASE: the beaten track *fumi-narasa-reta michi* 踏みならされた道

EX. Even though it may appear to be the easiest to do so, it's not always the most rewarding to follow the beaten track.
たとえそれが一番楽なように見えても踏みならされた道を行くのが一番実りが多いとは限らない。
Tatoe sore ga ichiban rakuna yooni miete mo fumi-narasa-reta michi o iku no ga ichiban minori ga ooi to wa kagiranai.

— vi./vt. **[for s.o./s.a. to follow the marks or trail left by s.o./s.a./s.t. or to leave marks on s.t.]**

1. ⟨-o⟩ tsu⌈iseki-suru ⟨〜を⟩追跡する ③ •c [to follow s.t./s.o. closely in order to to catch him/her/it or to follow up on a survey] ⟪pursue, chase⟫

EX. We were unable to track down the burglar.
私たちは強盗を追跡し損なった。
Watashi-tachi wa gootoo o tsuiseki-shi-sokonatta.

2. ⟨-ni⟩ a⌈shi-a⌉to o tsu⌈ke⌉ru ⟨〜に⟩足跡を付ける ② [for s.o./s.a. to leave marks on s.t.]

EX. The children tracked mud all over the carpet.
子供がじゅうたん一面にどろんこの足跡を付けてしまった。
Kodomo ga juutan ichi-men ni doronko no ashi-ato o tsukete shimatta.

tractor n.
to⌈ra⌉kutaa トラクター •f

trade n. **[an occupation, esp. one requiring manual or mechanical skill; the business of buying and selling goods or exchanging goods for other goods; the people engaged in a particular occupation]**

1. sho⌉obai 商売 •c [the activity of buying and selling goods] ⟪business, commerce, deal⟫, shi⌈goto 仕事 [an activity performed for a particular purpose other than amusement and on which one expends time and effort] ⟪work, job, business, labor⟫, sho⌈ku⌉gyoo 職業 •c [an activity which one pursues in order to make a living] ⟪occupation, calling, vocation, profession⟫

EX. My father was a jeweler by trade.
父の{商売/仕事/職業}は宝石商でした。
Chichi no {shoobai/shigoto/shokugyoo} wa hooseki-shoo deshita.

2. ba⌉i-bai 売買 •c [the activity of buying and selling] ⟪dealing, transaction, bargain⟫, to⌈ri⌉-hiki 取引 [a business transaction] ⟪transactions, dealings, sales, business⟫, bo⌈oeki 貿易 •c [the activity of importing and exporting goods between nations] ⟪commerce⟫

EX. (**a**) Our company engages freely in trade with anyone having an interest in dealing with us.

私どもの会社は当社に関心のある方とならどなたとも自由な{売買/取引/*貿易}をしております。
*Watakushi-domo no kaisha wa toosha ni kanshin no aru kata to nara donata to mo jiyuuna {bai-bai/tori-hiki/ *booeki} o shite orimasu.*
(**b**) Trade friction is undoubtedly the biggest problem in Japan-U.S. relations today.
今日の日米関係で{貿易/*売買/*取引}摩擦が一番大きい問題だろう。
*Konnichi no Nichi-Bei-kankei de {booeki/*bai-bai/*tori-hiki}-masatsu ga ichiban ookii mondai daroo.*

3. do⌈ogyo⌉o-sha 同業者 •c [people engaged in the same occupation]

—— vi./vt. [for s.o. to engage in the buying and selling of s.t. as a business or to exchange s.t. in return for s.t. else]

1. ⟨-o⟩ ⟨-to⟩ ba⌉i-bai-suru ⟨〜を⟩⟨〜と⟩売買する ③ •c [for s.o. to engage in the buying and selling of s.t. with s.o. else] ⟪deal in, traffic⟫, ⟨-o⟩ ⟨-to⟩ to⌈ri⌉-hiki-suru ⟨〜を⟩⟨〜と⟩取引する ③ [for s.o. to engage in business transactions in some commodity with s.o. else] ⟪transact, do business with, deal with⟫, ⟨-to⟩ bo⌈oeki-suru ⟨〜と⟩貿易する ③ •c [for an individual, firm, or nation to engage in the international importing or exporting of commodities with another individual, firm, or nation] ⟪commerce⟫

EX. (**a**) Japan trades heavily with other Asian countries.
日本はアジアの国とさかんに{貿易/??取引/*売買}している。
*Nihon wa Ajia no kuni to sakan ni {booeki/??tori-hiki/*bai-bai}-shite iru.*
(**b**) We trade in jewels as a business.
私たちは宝石を{売買/取引/*貿易}しています。
*Watashi-tachi wa hooseki o {bai-bai/ tori-hiki/*booeki}-shite imasu.*

2. ⟨-o⟩ (⟨-to⟩) ko⌈okan-suru ⟨〜を⟩(⟨〜と⟩)交換する ③ •c [for s.o. to receive s.t. in return for s.t. else] ⟪exchange⟫

EX. If you're done reading that, shall we trade newspapers?
もう読んでしまったんなら新聞を交換しませんか。
Moo yonde shimatta n nara shinbun o kookan-shimasen ka.

trader n. **[a person who is engaged in buying and selling as a business]**
sho⌉onin 商人 •c [a person who is engaged in commercial business] ⟪merchant, tradesman, dealer⟫, bo⌈oeki-gyo⌉osha 貿易業者 •c [a person who is engaged in international importing and exporting as a business]

tradition n. **[the handing down of beliefs or customs from generation to generation or beliefs and customs handed down in this way]**

1. de⌈ntoo 伝統 •c [a custom handed down from one generation to another]

EX. This college has a long tradition of academic excellence.
この大学は優れた学問の長い伝統がある。
Kono daigaku wa sugureta gakumon no nagai dentoo ga aru.

2. de⌈nshoo 伝承 •c [the act of handing down beliefs, customs, and legends from one generation to another] ⟪transmission⟫

EX. The code of ethics in that tribe was handed down by tradition from generations in the distant past.
その民族の道徳律ははるか昔から伝承で代々伝えられてきたものである。
Sono minzoku no dootoku-ritsu wa haruka mukashi kara denshoo de dai-dai tsutae-rarete kita mono dearu.

traditional adj. **[following the beliefs or customs unique to a social group]**
de⌈ntoo-tekina 伝統的な adj(*na*). **•c**

EX. *Sushi* is one of Japan's traditional cuisines.
すしは日本の伝統的な食べ物の一つだ。
Sushi wa Nihon no dentoo-tekina tabe-mono no hitotsu da.

traffic n. **[vehicles, airplanes, ships, or pedestrians moving along a route or the**

T

buying and selling of goods, esp. of an illegal nature]

1. bo⌈oeki 貿易 •c [the activity of importing and exporting goods between nations] ⟪**trade, commerce**⟫, **to⌈ri⌉-hiki 取引 [a business transaction]** ⟪**transactions, dealings, sales, business**⟫

EX. The amount of illegal drug traffic in this city has increased in recent years.
この町では近年不法な麻薬の{取引/*貿易}が増えている。
*Kono machi de wa kinnen fuhoona mayaku no {tori-hiki/*booeki} ga fuete iru.*

2. ko⌈otsuu 交通 •c [vehicles or pedestrians moving along a route] ⟪**transportation**⟫, **o⌈orai 往来 •c [the coming and going of vehicles or pedestrians]** ⟪**coming and going**⟫, **hi⌈to-doori 人通り [the coming and going of people]** ⟪**passing, passage, transit**⟫

EX. There's a lot of traffic on this road, so let's go another way.
この通りは{交通/往来/人通り}が激しいから、外の道を通りましょう。
Kono toori wa {kootsuu/oorai/hito-doori} ga hageshii kara, hoka no michi o toorimashoo.

T

PHRASE: traffic in *fusei-tori-hiki o suru* 不正取引をする ③

EX. They were arrested for trafficking in drugs.
彼らは麻薬の不正取引をしている疑いで逮捕された。
Kare-ra wa mayaku no fusei-tori-hiki o shite iru utagai de taiho-sareta.

tragedy n. **[a serious drama, usu. one with a sorrowful conclusion ⟪fig. "a disastrous event"⟫]**

hi⌉geki 悲劇 •c, sa⌉nji 惨事 •c [a disastrous accident or event] ⟪**disaster, catastrophe**⟫, **sa⌈ina⌉n 災難 •c [a misfortune which occurs suddenly, usu. to an individual]** ⟪**calamity, disaster, fatality, accident**⟫

EX. (**a**) I prefer comedies to tragedies.
私は{悲劇/*惨事/*災難}より喜劇の方が好きです。
*Watashi wa {higeki/*sanji/*sainan} yori kigeki no hoo ga suki desu.*
(**b**) A: Tom lost his wife in a plane crash.
トムは飛行機事故で奥さんを亡くしたんだ。
Tomu wa hikoo-ki-jiko de okusan o nakushita n da.
B: What a tragedy!
何という{悲劇/災難/*惨事}だ!
*Nan to iu {higeki/sainan/*sanji} da!*
(**c**) This afternoon two children were run over by a car at the main town intersection. I happened to be there to witness the tragedy.
今日の午後二人の子供が町の中央の交差点で車にひかれたんです。僕は丁度そこに居合わせてその{惨事/??悲劇/*災難}を見てしまいました。
*Kyoo no gogo futari no kodomo ga machi no chuuoo no koosa-ten de kuruma ni hika-reta n desu. Boku wa choodo soko ni i-awasete sono {sanji/??higeki/*sainan} o mite shimaimashita.*

tragic adj. **[having to do with or in the style of tragedy; extremely sorrowful or causing great sorrow]**

1. hi⌉geki no N 悲劇のN •c [having to do with tragedy]

EX. Hamlet is one of the great tragic heroes of world literature.
ハムレットは世界の文学の有名な悲劇の主人公の一人だ。
Hamuretto wa sekai no bungaku no yuumeina higeki no shujinkoo no hitori da.

2. hi⌈sanna 悲惨な adj(*na*). **•c [so sad or cruel as to be painful to observe]** ⟪**miserable, wretched, sad, pitiable, pathetic, sorrowful**⟫

EX. (**a**) It's tragic for a 90-year-old person to have to live alone and unassisted like that.
九十歳の老人があのように一人で、何の助けもなく暮らさなければならないのは悲惨だ。
Kyuu-jus-sai no roojin ga ano yooni hitori de, nan no tasuke mo naku kurasanakereba naranai no wa hisan da.

(**b**) We must never forget the tragic significance of what happened at Hiroshima and Nagasaki in 1945.
1945年に広島と長崎で起こった出来事の悲惨な意味をいつまでも忘れてはならない。
Sen-kyuu-hyaku-yon-juu-go-nen ni Hiroshima to Nagasaki de okotta dekigoto no hisanna imi o itsu-made-mo wasurete wa naranai.

trail vt. **[for s.o./s.a. to drag s.t. loosely behind one, esp. along the ground; for s.o./s.a. to follow behind s.o./s.a. or to follow the scent or traces left behind by s.o./s.a.]**

1. 〈-o〉 hi⌈ki-zuru 〈～を〉引きずる ① [for s.o./s.a. to pull s.t./s.o./s.a. behind one along the floor or ground] 《drag, prolong》

EX. Johnny went unhappily upstairs to bed, trailing his teddy bear behind him.
ジョニーはふくれっつらをしてぬいぐるみのくまを引きずりながら二階の寝室へ上がって行った。
Jonii wa fukurettsura o shite nuigurumi no kuma o hiki-zuri-nagara ni-kai no shinshitsu e agatte itta.

2. 〈-ni〉 (kut)tsu⌉ite-iku 〈～に〉(くっ)ついて行く ① [for s.o./s.a. to stick closely with s.o.], 〈-ni〉 tsu⌉ite-kuru 〈～に〉ついて来る ③ [to come along with s.o.], 〈-o〉 tsu⌈iseki-suru 〈～を〉追跡する ③ •c [to follow s.t./s.o. closely in order to catch him/her/it or to follow up on a survey] 《pursue, chase, track, run after》

EX. (**a**) My cat trails me to the bus stop every morning.
私の猫は毎朝バス停まで{(くっ)ついて来る/*追跡する}。
*Watashi no neko wa mai-asa basu-tei made {(kut)tsuite-kuru/*tsuiseki-suru}.*
(**b**) The rats trailed the Pied Piper out of town.
ねずみたちは町の外へと笛吹き{に(くっ)ついて行った/*を追跡した}。
*Nezumi-tachi wa machi no soto e to fue-fuki {ni (kut)tsuite-itta/*o tsuiseki shita}.*
(**c**) The police trailed the criminal into the woods.
警官は森の中へと犯人{を追跡した/*に(くっ)ついて行った}。
*Keikan wa mori no naka e to hannin {o tsuiseki-shita/*ni (kut)tsuite-itta}.*

—— vi. **[for s.t. to be dragged loosely behind s.o./s.a./s.t., esp. along the ground 《fig. "extend over a surface," "flow in thin streams," "proceed slowly"》]**

1. 〈-o〉 hi⌈ki-zuru 〈～を〉引きずる ① [for s.o./s.a. to pull s.t./s.o./s.a. behind one along the floor or the ground] 《drag》

EX. Her long skirt trailed along the floor.
彼女の長いスカートが床を引きずった。
Kanojo no nagai sukaato ga yuka o hiki-zutta.

2. 〈-o〉 ha⌉u 〈～を〉はう ① [for a plant to extend over the ground/a wall or for s.o./s.a. to move with one's stomach close to the ground] 《crawl, creep》

EX. The ivy trailed along the ground next to the house.
つたが家のそばの地面をはっていた。
Tsuta ga ie no soba no jimen o hatte ita.

3. ta⌈na-bi⌉ku 棚引く ① [for a cloud or mist to flow sideways in thin streams] 《hang over》, 〈-ni〉 ka⌈ka⌉ru 〈～に〉かかる ① [for s.t. to extend to and come in contact with s.t. else 《fig. "hang," "cover," "begin," "be engaged in," "become splashed with," "be built," "require"》] 《hang, be locked, require, cost》

EX. The early morning mist trailed over the fields and hills.
早朝の霧が野や山に{棚引いて/かかって}いた。
Soochoo no kiri ga no ya yama ni {tana-biite/kakatte} ita.

4. a⌈shi o hikizutte yu⌈kku⌉ri aruku 足を引きずってゆっくり歩く ① [for s.o./s.a. to walk slowly dragging one's limbs]

EX. I was trailing behind the others for most of the hike.
私はハイキングのほとんどを、みんな

の後ろから足を引きずってゆっくり歩いていた。
Watashi wa haikingu no hotondo o, minna no ushiro kara ashi o hiki-zutte yukkuri aruite ita.

— n. **[a small path, esp. in a wilderness region, or a mark or scent left by s.o./s.a. that has passed]**
1. mi⌈chi 道 [a strip of paved or cleared ground for getting from one place to another or the distance covered in a journey 《fig. "method," "the way," "special field"》] 《path, lane》
EX. There are a lot of hiking trails in these mountains.
この山にはハイキングのための(小)道がたくさんある。
Kono yama ni wa haikingu no tame no (ko-)michi ga takusan aru.
2. a⌈shi-a⌉to 足跡 [a mark made by the foot of s.o./s.a.]

trailer n. **[a vehicle pulled by an automobile or truck]**
to⌈re⌉eraa トレーラー •f [a vehicle drawn by an automobile or other engine-powered vehicle]
EX. During the summer many Americans go traveling with camping trailers.
夏はキャンピングトレーラーで旅行するアメリカ人が大勢います。
Natsu wa kyanpingu-toreeraa de ryokoo-suru Amerika-jin ga oozei imasu.

T

train n. **[a line of railroad cars pulled by a locomotive in front; a group of people, animals, or vehicles moving in a line; a sequence of events or thoughts; the retinue following a member of royalty]**
1. re⌈ssha 列車 •c [a set of railroad cars connected in a line], ki⌈sha⌉ 汽車 •c [a line of railroad cars drawn by a steam-powered locomotive], de⌉nsha 電車 •c [a line of railroad cars powered by electricity] 《streetcar》
EX. I went to New York by train.
ニューヨークへ{電車/汽車/列車}で行きました。
Nyuuyooku e {densha/kisha/ressha} de ikimashita.
2. re⌉tsu 列 •c [a procession or row of people or cars] 《row, line, file, rank》, gyo⌈oretsu 行列 •c [people or things lined up in an orderly fashion] 《procession, parade, queue, line》
EX. A camel train was moving slowly across the desert.
ラクダの{列/行列}がゆっくりと砂漠を渡っていた。
Rakuda no {retsu/gyooretsu} ga yukkuri to sabaku o watatte ita.
3. mya⌈kuraku 脈絡 •c [a logical interrelationship connecting a series of entities], tsu⌈nagari つながり [a set of objects or events which are connected to each other] 《connection, link, relation》
EX. A knock on the door interrupted my train of thought.
ドアをたたく音で考えの{脈絡/つながり}を断たれた。
Doa o tataku oto de kangae no {myakuraku/tsunagari} o tata-reta.
4. o-⌈to⌉mo お供 [a person following and acting according to the wishes of s.o. superior] 《follower, attendant, servant, retinue》, ju⌉usha 従者 •c [a person in feudal times following and acting according to the wishes of his master] 《follower, attendant, squire, servant》

— vt. **[for s.o. to teach or discipline s.o./s.a. to act, perform, or think in a certain way or according to a certain standard]**
⟨-o⟩ ki⌈tae⌉ru ⟨～を⟩鍛える ② [for s.o. to cause the body or mind of s.o. to become strong through discipline or practice] 《build up》, ku⌉nren-suru 訓練する ③ •c [for s.o. to teach s.t. to s.o. in order to cause a habit or skill to be internalized in that person] 《drill》
EX. (a) It takes much time and effort to train a good simultaneous interpreter.
優れた同時通訳者を{訓練する/?鍛える}のには時間と労力が要る。

Sugureta dooji-tsuuyaku-sha o {kunren-suru/?kitaeru} no ni wa jikan to rooryoku ga iru.
(**b**) *Judo* is an excellent way to train the mind and body of a young person.
若い人の心身を{鍛える/訓練する}には柔道がとてもいい。
Wakai hito no shinshin o {kitaeru/kunren-suru} ni wa juudoo ga totemo ii.

training n. **[the act of teaching or disciplining the mind or body of s.o./s.a. to act, perform, or think in a certain way or according to a certain standard]**
ku⌉nren 訓練 •c [the act of teaching s.t. to s.o. in order to cause a habit or skill to be internalized in that person] ⟪drill, exercise, discipline⟫, kyo⌈oiku 教育 •c [education], to⌈re⌉eningu トレーニング •f [practice in sports], shi⌈tsuke しつけ [teaching of manners and etiquette] ⟪discipline⟫, yo⌈osei 養成 •c [the act of teaching s.o. so that he/she will acquire certain knowledge or skills] ⟪education, nurture, civilization⟫

EX. (**a**) Baseball training started last week.
野球チームの{トレーニング/訓練/*教育/*養成/*しつけ}が先週始まった。
*Yakyuu-chiimu no {toreeningu/kunren/*kyooiku/*yoosei/*shitsuke} ga senshuu hajimatta.*
(**b**) Training workshops for Japanese teachers have become common recently.
最近日本語教師{養成/*トレーニング/*訓練/*教育/*しつけ}講座が多くなってきた。
*Saikin Nihon-go-kyooshi-{yoosei/*toreeningu/*kunren/*kyooiku/*shitsuke}-kooza ga ooku natte kita.*
(**c**) The training of children at home is the most important part of education.
家庭での子供の{しつけ/教育/*訓練/*トレーニング/*養成}が一番重要な教育の部分だ。
*Katei de no kodomo no {shitsuke/kyooiku/*kunren/*toreeningu/*yoosei} ga ichiban juuyoona kyooiku no bubun da.*
(**d**) Generally speaking, Japanese white collar workers learn their skills through on-the-job training.
一般に日本のサラリーマンは実地{教育/訓練/トレーニング/*しつけ/*養成}によって仕事を身につける。
*Ippan ni Nihon no sararii-man wa jitchi-{kyooiku/kunren/toreeningu/*shitsuke/*yoosei} ni-yotte shigoto o mi ni tsukeru.*

trait n. **[a distinctive characteristic of a person or animal]**
to⌈kuchoo 特徴 •c [s.t. which stands out about s.t./s.o./s.a. and which distinguishes him/her/it from others] ⟪distinguishing mark, distinction, peculiarity, characteristic, idiosyncracy⟫

EX. (**a**) Individualism is often pointed to as an American trait.
個人主義はアメリカ国民の特徴としてよく挙げられる。
Kojin-shugi wa Amerika-kokumin no tokuchoo to-shite yoku age-rareru.
(**b**) Honesty is one of John's most admirable traits.
正直であることがジョンの最も賞賛すべき特徴の一つだ。
Shoojiki dearu koto ga Jon no mottomo shoosan-su-beki tokuchoo no hitotsu da.

tramp vi./vt. **[for s.o. to walk with a heavy, loud step or to travel over an area by foot]**
1. ⟨-o⟩ **a⌈ruki-mawa⌉ru** ⟨～を⟩歩き回る ① **[for s.o./s.a. to walk around]**
2. do⌈shi⌉n-do⌈shi⌉n to a⌈ru⌉ku どしんどしんと歩く ① **[for s.o. to walk with a heavy, loud step], do⌉ta-dota to a⌈ru⌉ku** どたどたと歩く ① **[for s.o. to walk in a noisy way]**

EX. Someone was tramping around all night on the floor above us.
だれかが上の階で一晩中{どしんどしん/どたどた}と歩いていた。
Dare-ka ga ue no kai de hito-ban-juu {doshin-doshin/dota-dota} to aruite ita.

3. ⟨-o⟩ **fu⌈mi-tsuke⌉ru** ⟨～を⟩踏み付ける ② **[for s.o. to tread on s.t.]**

EX. Someone tramped all over my painting with muddy shoes.

だれかが僕の絵を泥だらけの靴で踏み付けた。
Dare-ka ga boku no e o doro-darake no kutsu de fumi-tsuketa.

transfer vi. **[for s.a./s.o./s.t. to move from one place or vehicle to another]**
1. ((-kara))((-ni)) **u⌈tsu⌉ru** ((〜から))((〜に)) うつる **[to change to a different place or condition 《fig. "be reflected," "be infected"》]** **《move, remove, change, be infected with, be reflected》**, ⟨-ni⟩ **te⌈nkin-suru** ⟨〜に⟩転勤する ③ •c **[for s.o. to move to another office of the same company]**
㊥ "be reflected"▷映る, "be photographed"▷写る, otherwise ▷移る

EX. It's been decided that I'll be transfered to the Seoul office next month.
私は来月ソウル支店に{転勤する/移る}ことになった。
Watashi wa raigetsu Souru-shiten ni {tenkin-suru/utsuru} koto ni natta.

2. ⟨-ni⟩ **no⌈ri-kae⌉ru** ⟨〜に⟩乗り換える ② **[for s.o. to leave one train, bus, etc., and board another]**

EX. To get to where you're going you have to transfer at Shinjuku from the Yamanote line to the Odakyu line.
そこへ行くのには新宿で山手線から小田急線に乗り換えなければいけません。
Soko e iku no ni wa Shinjuku de Yamanote-sen kara Odakyuu-sen ni nori-kaenakereba ikemasen.

— vt. **[to cause s.t./s.o./s.a. to move from one place to another 《fig. "hand over a possession of," "copy"》]**
1. ⟨-o⟩ {⟨-ni⟩/⟨-e⟩} **u⌈tsu⌉su** ⟨〜を⟩{⟨〜に⟩/⟨〜へ⟩}うつす ① **[to cause s.o./s.t./s.a. to change to a different location or to a different condition 《fig. "copy," "reflect," "infect," "take a picture"》]** **《move, direct, infect, copy, describe, photograph》**
㊥ "reflect"▷映す, "photograph"▷写す, otherwise ▷移す

EX. (**a**) I've transferred $4,000 from my bank account in the U.S. to my bank account in Japan.
アメリカの銀行の自分の口座から日本の銀行の口座へ四千ドル移した。
Amerika no ginkoo no jibun no kooza kara Nihon no ginkoo no kooza e yon-sen-doru utsushita.
(**b**) The police transferred the image of the fingerprints to a computer file.
警察署ではその指紋の形をコンピューターのファイルに移した。
Keisatsu-sho de wa sono shimon no katachi o konpyuutaa no fairu ni utsushita.

2. ⟨-ni⟩ ⟨-o⟩ **jo⌉oto-suru** ⟨〜に⟩⟨〜を⟩譲渡する ③ •c **[for s.o. to give up the right to do or own s.t. to another ⟨fml⟩]**

EX. The father transferred rights to that property to his eldest son.
父親は長男にその土地の所有権を譲渡した。
Chichi-oya wa choonan ni sono tochi no shoyuu-ken o jooto-shita.

— n. **[an act of transferring]**
1. jo⌉oto 譲渡 •c **[an act/instance of giving up the right to do or own s.t. to another]** **《conveyance, grant, settlement》**
2. i⌈doo 移動 •c **[the act of moving from one place to another]** **《movement, locomotion, shifting》**
3. no⌈ri-kae 乗り換え /⟨V*masu* of *noru* ① ride + V*masu* of *kaeru* ② change/ **[the act of leaving one bus, train, etc., to board another]**

EX. Please keep your ticket if you want to transfer.
お乗り換えの方は切符をそのままお持ちください。
O-nori-kae no kata wa kippu o sono mama o-mochi kudasai.

4. te⌈nsha-ga 転写画 •c **[a picture or design that has been copied from one surface to another]**

transform vt. **[to cause s.t. to change in form or appearance]**
⟨-o⟩ ⟨-ni⟩ **ka⌈eru** ⟨〜を⟩⟨〜に⟩かえる ② **[for s.o. to cause s.t./s.o./s.a. to become s.t. else]** **《change, alter, reverse, reform, revise,**

convert, substitute, replace》, 〈-o〉 he˥nka-saseru 〈〜を〉変化させる /〈causative of *henka-suru* ③ change/ ② •c **[to cause the nature of s.t. or the state which s.t. is in to change to s.t. else]**, 〈-o〉 hen˥kei-suru 〈〜を〉変形する ③ •c **[for s.o. to change the form of s.t.]** 《metamorphose》
㊟ "exchange"▷換える "substitute"▷代える, otherwise ▷変える

EX. (**a**) That country is trying its best to transform itself into a democratic nation.
その国は自国を民主主義の国に{変えよう/変化させよう/*変形しよう}と努めている。
*Sono kuni wa jikoku o minshu-shugi no kuni ni {kaeyoo/henka-saseyoo/*henkei-shiyoo} to tsutomete iru.*
(**b**) It's very difficult to transform one's personality into something different once one has reached adulthood.
大人になると自分の性格を{変える/*変化させる/*変形する}のは難しい。
*Otona ni naru to jibun no seikaku o {kaeru/*henka-saseru/*henkei-suru} no wa muzukashii.*
(**c**) To transform an active sentence into a passive sentence do the following.
能動文を受動文に{変える/変形する/変化させる}には次のようにすればいい。
Noodoo-bun o judoo-bun ni {kaeru/henkei-suru/henka-saseru} ni wa tsugi no yooni sureba ii.

transition n. **[the process of change or movement from one stage or condition to another]**
he˥nka 変化 •c [the coming into being of a different quality or state in s.t. as it moves through space or time] 《change, alteration, mutation》, u˥tsuri-kawari 移り変わり /〈V*masu* of *utsuri-kawaru* ① change/ **[a gradual change]** 《change, mutability》, i˥koo 移行 •c **[the process of change from one state of affairs to another]** 《shift, switch, change》, su˥ii 推移 •c **[a (natural) change in state accompanying a lapse in time]** 《change, progress》, he˥nsen 変遷 •c **[an (artificial) change in state accompanying a lapse in time]** 《change, vicissitude, ups and downs》

EX. (**a**) The Showa era was a period of many transitions.
昭和は{変化/移り変わり/推移/変遷/*移行}の多い時代だった。
*Shoowa wa {henka/utsuri-kawari/suii/hensen/*ikoo} no ooi jidai datta.*
(**b**) The Japanese educational system has undergone numerous transitions over the past three decades.
日本の教育制度は過去三十年の間に様々な{変化/*変遷/*移り変わり/*推移/*移行}を遂げた。
*Nihon no kyooiku-seido wa kako san-juu-nen no aida ni sama-zamana {henka/*hensen/*utsuri-kawari/*suii/*ikoo} o togeta.*
(**c**) The gradual transitions in nature from season to season are celebrated in many forms in Japanese culture.
季節から季節へのゆっくりした自然の{変化/移り変わり/移行/?推移/*変遷}は日本文化の中で様々な形でめでられる。
*Kisetsu kara kisetsu e no yukkuri-shita shizen no {henka/utsuri-kawari/ikoo/?suii/*hensen} wa Nihon-bunka no naka de sama-zamana katachi de mede-rareru.*

transitive adj. **[of a verb taking a direct object]**
ta- 他〜 •c [oriented not to the self but to others 《fig. "of a verb taking a direct object"》] ↔ ji- 自〜 •c
NOTE: Unlike English "transitive" in "transitive verb," Japanese *ta-* is used not only in *ta-dooshi* "transitive verb," but in a variety of words having to do with "other," such as *ta-nin* "other people," *ta-koku* "foreign country," *ta-satsu* "killing of others = murder," etc.

EX. Is "*wakarimasu*" an intransitive verb or a transitive verb?
「分かります」は自動詞ですか、それとも他動詞ですか。
'Wakarimasu' wa ji-dooshi desu ka,

T

| *sore-tomo ta-dooshi desu ka.*

transitory adj. **[lasting only for a limited time]**
hi⌈to⌉-toki no N 一時のN [existing for or having to do with a short period of time], tsu⌈ka-no-ma no N 束の間のN [existing for or having to do with a brief duration] **⟪brief, momentary, ephemeral⟫**

EX.| From the perspective of eternity, our life on earth is but a transitory phenomenon.
永遠の存在から見ると我々の地上での人生は{束の間/一時}の現象でしかない。
Eien no sonzai kara miru to ware-ware no chijoo de no jinsei wa {tsuka-no-ma/hito-toki} no genshoo de shika nai.

translate vt. **[for s.o. to change s.t. into a different form of expression, esp. a different language]**
1. ⟨-o⟩ {⟨-ni⟩/⟨-e⟩} u⌈tsu⌉su ⟨〜を⟩{⟨〜に⟩/⟨〜へ⟩}うつす ① [to cause s.o./s.t./s.a. to change to a different location or to a different condition ⟪fig. "copy," "reflect," "infect," "take a picture"⟫] ⟪move, transfuse, direct, infect, copy, describe, photograph⟫
㊅ "reflect"▷映す, "photograph"▷写す, otherwise ▷移す

EX.| It takes literary talent to skillfully translate a visual image into a verbal expression.
視覚的なイメージをうまく言葉に移すのにはそれ相応の文学的な才能が要る。
Shikaku-tekina imeeji o umaku kotoba ni utsusu no ni wa sore soooo no bungaku-tekina sainoo ga iru.

2. ⟨-o⟩ (⟨-ni⟩) ya⌈ku⌉su ⟨〜を⟩(⟨〜に⟩)訳す ① [for s.o. to change s.t. into one's own or another language], ⟨-o⟩ (⟨-ni⟩) ho⌈n'yaku-suru ⟨〜を⟩(⟨〜に⟩)翻訳する ③ •c

EX.| (**a**) Translate the following Japanese into English.
次の日本語を英語に{翻訳しなさい/訳しなさい}。
Tsugi no Nihon-go o eigo ni {hon'yaku-shinasai/yakushinasai}.
(**b**) It is next to impossible to accurately translate poems.
詩を正確に{翻訳する/訳す}のはほとんど不可能だ。
Shi o seikakuni {hon'yaku-suru/yakusu} no wa hotondo fu-kanoo da.

translation n. **[the act of changing s.t. into a different form of expression, esp. a different language, or a piece of writing which has been changed from another language while preserving the original meaning]**
ho⌈n'yaku 翻訳 •c [an act/instance of changing s.t. expressed in written form in one language to the written form of another language] ⟪rendering⟫, ya⌉ku 訳 •c [an act/instance of changing a piece of writing in one language into that of another with the same meaning or a piece of writing so changed] ⟪rendering⟫, ya⌈ku-bun 訳文 •c [a sentence or passage which has been changed into a different language while preserving the original meaning] ⟪rendering⟫

EX.| (**a**) This translation is full of errors.
この{翻訳/訳/訳文}は間違いだらけだ。
Kono {hon'yaku/yaku/yaku-bun} wa machigai-darake da.
(**b**) Japan is a culture of translations. You name it—it's been translated into Japanese.
日本は{翻訳/*訳/*訳文}文化の国だ。何だって日本語に翻訳されている。
*Nihon wa {hon'yaku/*yaku/*yaku-bun}-bunka no kuni da. Nan-datte Nihon-go ni hon'yaku-sarete iru.*

transmit vt. **[to send or convey s.t. from one person or place to another]**
1. ⟨-o⟩ {⟨-ni⟩/⟨-e⟩} o⌈kuru ⟨〜を⟩{⟨〜に⟩/⟨〜へ⟩}おくる ① [for s.o. to cause s.t./s.o./s.a. to get to a certain place either by indirectly providing the means to do so (as in mailing or shipping) or by directly accompanying it/him/her] ⟪send, ship, see off, escort, spend (time), give s.t. as a present⟫
㊅ "send"▷送る, "present (a gift)"▷贈る

EX.| This is a special device for transmitting secretly encoded messages.

これは暗号文を送る特別な装置だ。
Kore wa angoo-bun o okuru tokubetsuna soochi da.

2. ⟨-ni⟩ ⟨-o⟩ shi⌈raseru ⟨〜に⟩⟨〜を⟩知らせる /⟨causative of *shiru* ① get to know/ ② [for s.o. to cause s.o. to become aware of s.t.] ⟪inform, notify, make matters known⟫, ⟨-ni⟩ ⟨-o⟩ tsu⌈taeru ⟨〜に⟩⟨〜を⟩伝える ② [for s.o. to pass along some message to s.o.] ⟪convey, report, deliver, tell, teach, communicate⟫

EX. (**a**) Our Moscow special correspondent has been transmitting the latest developments in the Russian presidential election to us on the hour.
モスクワ特派員がロシアの大統領選挙に関する最新のニュースを一時間ごとに{伝えて/知らせて}きている。
Mosukuwa-tokuha-in ga Roshia no daitooryoo-senkyo ni-kansuru saishin no nyuusu o ichi-jikan-goto ni {tsutaete/shirasete} kite iru.
(**b**) The oral tradition of that society has been transmitted down through the generations for thousands of years.
あの社会の口承文学は何千年もの昔から代々{伝えられて/*知らせられて}きたものだ。
*Ano shakai no kooshoo-bungaku wa nan-zen-nen mo no mukashi kara dai-dai {tsutae-rarete/*shirase-rarete} kita mono da.*

3. ⟨-o⟩ ⟨-ni⟩ to⌉osu ⟨〜を⟩⟨〜に⟩通す ① [to cause s.t. to go along or through s.t. (from one side to the other)] ⟪pass, run⟫

EX. They succeeded in transmitting heat at a high temperature through the fiberglass.
ガラス繊維に高熱を通すのに成功した。
Garasu-sen'i ni koonetsu o toosu no ni seikoo-shita.

4. za⌈isan o yu⌈zuru 財産を譲る ① [for s.o. to hand down one's estate to another]

5. ⟨-o⟩ de⌉npa-suru ⟨〜を⟩伝ぱする ③ •c [to convey s.t. in a widespread fashion]

EX. Language plays a central role in transmitting culture.
言語は文化を伝ぱするのに中心的な役割を果たす。
Gengo wa bunka o denpa-suru no ni chuushin-tekina yakuwari o hatasu.

transmitter n. **[a person or machine that sends or conveys s.t., esp. a message]**

1. o⌈kuri-te⌉ 送り手 [a person who sends s.t.], de⌈ntatsu⌉-sha 伝達者 •c [a person who communicates a message to s.o.]

2. so⌈oshi⌉n-ki 送信機 •c [a machine which sends out voice or electric waves]

transparent adj. **[allowing light to pass through so that things on the other side can be seen ⟪fig. "frank," "obvious," "easy to understand"⟫]**

1. to⌈omeina 透明な adj(*na*). **•c [totally clear and free from turbidity ⟪fig. "clear (voice)"⟫] ↔ fu-toomeina 不透明な** adj(*na*). **•c; suki-⌈to⌉otta N 透き通ったN /⟨Vinf. past of *suki-tooru* ① be seen through/ [allowing visibility through itself ⟪fig. "clear (voice)"⟫], suki-⌈to⌉otte iru (N) 透き通っている(N) /⟨V *te iru* of *suki-tooru* ① be seen through/**

EX. The ocean there was so transparent that we could see to the bottom.
あそこの海はとても{透明で/透き通っていて}海底が見えた。
Asoko no umi wa totemo {toomei de/suki-tootte ite} kaitei ga mieta.

2. so⌈tchokuna 率直な adj(*na*). **•c [speaking or acting in a way which is straightforward and does not hide or embellish the truth] ⟪candid, frank, honest, straightforward, outspoken⟫**

EX. I like him because he's so transparent and never tries to conceal things.
彼はとても率直で、物事を隠そうとしないから好きだ。
Kare wa totemo sotchoku de, mono-goto o kakusoo to shinai kara suki da.

3. mi⌈e-suita N 見え透いたN /⟨Vinf. past of *mie-suku* ① be easily seen through/ [easily seen through despite one's attempts to hide the truth or one's true feelings] ⟪plain, obvious, blatant⟫, mi⌈e-suite iru (N) 見え透

いている(N) /⟨V *te iru* of *mie-suku* ① be easily seen through/

EX. His lie was totally transparent, so I was able to figure out immediately what had really happened.
彼のうそはひどく{見え透いていた/見え透いたうそだった}ので、真相はすぐ分かった。
Kare no uso wa hidoku {mie-suite ita/mie-suita uso datta} node, shinsoo wa sugu wakatta.

4. me⌈ikaina 明快な adj(*na*). **•c [clear and easy to understand in logical structure] ⟪clear, articulate, precise⟫**

EX. Shiga Naoya's writing is very transparent.
志賀直哉の書いたものはとても明快だ。
Shiga Naoya no kaita mono wa totemo meikai da.

transport vt. **[to move or convey s.t./s.o./s.a. from one place to another ⟪fig. "carry s.o. away emotionally"⟫]**

1. ⟨-o⟩ yu⌈soo-suru ⟨〜を⟩輸送する ③ •c [to move s.t./s.o./s.a. from one place to another by means of a conveyance such as a boat, car, airplane, or train] ⟪carry, convey, deport⟫, ⟨-o⟩ ha⌈kobu ⟨〜を⟩運ぶ ① [to move s.o./s.t./s.a. from one place to another by hand or by means of a vehicle, etc.] ⟪carry, convey, bring, advance, progress⟫

EX. Cargo planes regularly transport fresh fish from the U.S. to Japan.
貨物機が定期的に鮮魚をアメリカから日本へ{輸送して/運んで}いる。
Kamotsu-ki ga teiki-tekini sengyo o Amerika kara Nihon e {yusoo-shite/hakonde} iru.

2. ⟨-de⟩ wa⌉re o wa⌈surete yo⌈roko⌉bu ⟨〜で⟩我を忘れて喜ぶ ① [for s.o. to forget oneself from joy], ⟨-de⟩ u⌈cho⌉oten ni naru ⟨〜で⟩有頂天になる ① [for s.o. to become ecstatic due to s.t.] ⟪be carried away⟫

EX. When Nancy said yes to my marriage proposal I was transported to seventh heaven out of joy.
ナンシーが結婚に同意してくれたとき僕は{我を忘れて喜んだ/有頂天になった}。
Nanshii ga kekkon ni dooi-shite kureta toki boku wa {ware o wasurete yorokonda/uchooten ni natta}.

— n. **[the act or process of moving or conveying s.t./s.o./s.a. from one place to another; a ship or airplane on which people or freight are carried ⟪fig. "state of being carried away by one's emotions"⟫]**
yu⌈soo 輸送 •c [the movement of s.t./s.o./s.a. from one place to another by means of a conveyance such as a boat, car, airplane, or train] ⟪conveyance, carriage⟫, u⌈npan 運搬 •c [the act of carrying s.t./s.a. (by hand) from one place to another] ⟪conveyance, carriage⟫

EX. (**a**) The transport of oil is primarily accomplished by using oil tankers.
石油の{輸送/*運搬}は主にタンカーでする。
*Sekiyu no {yusoo/*unpan} wa omoni tankaa de suru.*
(**b**) For the transport of a piano this size we're going to need the help of at least four people.
これだけ大きなピアノの{運搬/*輸送}には少なくとも四人の手が必要だ。
*Kore dake ookina piano no {unpan/*yusoo} ni wa sukunaku tomo yo-nin no te ga hitsuyoo da.*

transportation n. **[the act or means of moving or conveying s.t./s.o./s.a. from one place to another]**

1. yu⌈soo 輸送 •c SEE transport 1, **u⌈npan 運搬 •c** SEE transport 1

EX. (**a**) In this country we rely primarily on trucks for the domestic transportation of goods.
我が国では貨物の国内{輸送/運搬}は主としてトラックに頼っている。
Waga-kuni de wa kamotsu no kokunai-{yusoo/unpan} wa shu-to-shite torakku ni tayotte iru.
(**b**) The transportation of the injured people to the hospital took about six hours.
けが人の病院への{輸送/?運搬}には約六時間かかった。

T

Kega-nin no byooin e no {yusoo/?unpan} ni wa yaku roku-jikan kakatta.

2. yu⸢soo-hoo 輸送法 •c [a method of moving or conveying s.t. from one place to another], u⸢npan-hoo 運搬法 •c [a method of moving or conveying s.t. from one place to another], no⸢ri-mono 乗り物 /⟨V*masu* of *noru* ① ride + *mono* thing/ [a conveyance such as a train, bus, plane, etc] ⟪vehicle⟫, ko⸢otsuu-kika⸣n 交通機関 •c [a means of travel or carrying freight] ⟪traffic, travel facilities⟫

EX. (**a**) Is there any means of transportation for getting downtown?
町まで行く{乗り物/交通機関/*輸送法/*運搬法}がありますか。
*Machi made iku {nori-mono/kootsuu-kikan/*yusoo-hoo/*unpan-hoo} ga arimasu ka.*
(**b**) This country has developed an efficient transportation system.
この国は効率のよい{交通機関/輸送法/運搬法/乗り物}が発達している。
Kono kuni wa kooritsu no yoi {kootsuu-kikan/yusoo-hoo/unpan-hoo/nori-mono} ga hattatsu-shite iru.

trap n. **[a device for capturing animals ⟪fig. "a clever trick for ensnaring s.o."⟫]**
wa⸣na わな [a device used to capture animals ⟪fig. "a clever trick for ensnaring s.o."⟫] ⟪hook, snare⟫, o⸢toshi⸣-ana 落とし穴 /⟨V*masu* of *otosu* ① drop + *ana* hole/ [a covered pit used for capturing animals ⟪fig. "a clever trick for ensnaring s.o."⟫] ⟪pitfall⟫

EX. The lawyer's question was a trap to get the witness to reveal her true relationship with the defendant.
弁護士の質問は証人に被告人との本当の関係を明らかにさせようとする{わな/落とし穴}だった。
Bengo-shi no shitsumon wa shoonin ni hikoku-nin to no hontoo no kankei o akirakani saseyoo to suru {wana/otoshi-ana} datta.

—— vt. **[for s.o. to catch an animal using a device intended for that purpose ⟪fig. "force s.o. into a position from which he/she cannot escape"⟫]**

1. ⟨-o⟩ wa⸣na ni ka⸢ke⸣ru ⟨〜を⟩わなにかける ② [for s.o. to catch an animal using a device intended for that purpose ⟪fig. "deceive"⟫], o⸣toshiireru 陥れる ② [for s.o. to force s.o. into an undesirable situation or action through cunning means] ⟪entrap, ensnare, beguile⟫

EX. (**a**) We managed to trap the rabbits that had been eating vegetables in our garden.
庭の野菜を食べていたうさぎを{わなにかける/*陥れる}ことができた。
*Niwa no yasai o tabete ita usagi o {wana ni kakeru/*otoshiireru} koto ga dekita.*
(**b**) The defendant was trapped into confessing the crime by the prosecutor's skillful questioning.
被告人は検察官の巧みな尋問によって犯罪を告白せざるを得ない状況に{陥れられた/*わなにかけられた}。
*Hikoku-nin wa kensatsu-kan no takumina jinmon ni-yotte hanzai o kokuhaku-sezaru o enai jookyoo ni {otoshiire-rareta/*wana ni kake-rarete}.*

2. ⟨-ni⟩ ⟨-o⟩ to⸢ji-komeru ⟨〜に⟩⟨〜を⟩閉じ込める ② [for s.o. to confine s.t./s.o./s.a. in a limited space] ⟪shut in, lock in, cage in, confine⟫

EX. Yesterday I was trapped in an elevator for three hours.
きのう三時間もエレベーターの中に閉じ込められた。
Kinoo san-jikan mo erebeetaa no naka ni toji-kome-rareta.

trash n. **[worthless things, esp. ones to be thrown away ⟪fig. "s.o. worthless"⟫]**

1. ha⸢iki⸣-butsu 廃棄物 •c [s.t. in a broken or useless condition to be thrown away] ⟪waste⟫, go⸢mi⸣ ごみ [s.t. very small that dirties a place or s.t. in a broken or useless condition to be thrown away] ⟪dust, rubbish, litter, garbage, refuse⟫, ku⸣zu くず [s.t. in a broken or useless condition to be thrown away ⟪fig. "a worthless person"⟫]

T

《rubbish, refuse, waste, scum, junk, dregs of mankind》

EX. (**a**) The industrial trash created by that factory is threatening to become an environmental hazard.
あの工場から出る{廃棄物/ごみ/くず}は環境汚染の原因になる恐れがある。
Ano koojoo kara deru {haiki-butsu/gomi/kuzu} wa kankyoo-osen no gen'in ni naru osore ga aru.
(**b**) Months' worth of trash had accumulated in the old man's apartment.
老人のアパートには何か月分もの{ごみ/くず/*廃棄物}がたまっていた。
*Roojin no apaato ni wa nan-ka-getsu-bun mo no {gomi/kuzu/*haiki-butsu} ga tamatte ita.*

2. ba⌉kana ha⌈nashi⌉ ばかな話 [empty, silly talk]

EX. How can you listen to such trash!
お前はよくこんな馬鹿な話が聞けるね。
Omae wa yoku konna bakana hanashi ga kike-ru ne.

3. ni⌈ngen no ku⌉zu 人間のくず [a worthless person] 《dregs of humanity》

EX. That brother of mine is nothing but trash.
弟のやつは人間のくずとしか言いようがない。
Otooto no yatsu wa ningen no kuzu to shika ii-yoo ga nai.

PHRASE: trash can *gomi-bako* ごみ箱, trash collector *haihin-kaishuu-gyoosha* 廃品回収業者 •c

travel vi. **[for s.o./s.t. to move from one point to another, esp. for a relatively long distance]**

1. {⟨-ni⟩/⟨-o⟩} ryo⌈koo-suru {⟨〜に⟩/⟨〜を⟩} 旅行する ③ •c [for s.o. to leave one's home and go to or throughout a relatively distant area] 《journey, make a trip》

EX. (**a**) I'm traveling to China this summer.
私は今年の夏中国に旅行します。
Watashi wa kotoshi no natsu Chuugoku ni ryokoo-shimasu.
(**b**) Where in France do you plan to travel?
フランスのどこを旅行する予定ですか。
Furansu no doko o ryokoo-suru yotei desu ka.

2. su⌈sumu 進む ① [to go forward spontaneously 《fig. "make progress," "become advanced," "feel inclined"》] ↔ shirizoku 退く ①; ha⌈shi⌉ru 走る ① [for s.o./s.a./a vehicle to go along a surface in a set direction at a pace faster than walking 《fig. "go to excess," "for s.t. long and narrow to extend far," "appear momentarily"》] 《run, flee》

EX. (**a**) Light travels faster than sound.
光は音より速く{進む/*走る}。
*Hikari wa oto yori hayaku {susumu/*hashiru}.*
(**b**) The car was traveling at the speed of 100 kph when its tire blew.
タイヤがパンクした時、車は時速百キロのスピードで{走って/*進んで}いた。
*Taiya ga panku-shita toki, kuruma wa jisoku hyak-kiro no supiido de {hashitte/*susunde} ita.*

3. ⟨-o⟩ u⌈tte aru⌉ku ⟨〜を⟩売って歩く ① [for s.o. to go from place to place selling things]

EX. My friend travels as a salesman for an encyclopedia company.
友人は百科事典を売って歩いている。
Yuujin wa hyakka-jiten o utte aruite iru.

— vt. **[for s.o. to make a trip covering an area]**

⟨-o⟩ ryo⌈koo-suru ⟨〜を⟩旅行する ③ 《make a trip, journey》

EX. He traveled the length and breadth of the African continent in his career as an anthropologist.
彼は人類学者として活躍中にアフリカ大陸を隅から隅まで旅行した。
Kare wa jinrui-gakusha to-shite katsuyaku-chuu ni Afurika-tairiku o sumi kara sumi made ryokoo-shita.

— n. **[(amount of) movement in a given direction]**

1. ryo⌈koo 旅行 •c [the act of leaving one's home to go to a relatively distant place]

《trip, journey》, ta⌈bi⌉ 旅 [the act of going a relatively long distance from one place to another] 《trip, journey》

EX. (**a**) The airline strike disrupted our travel in Europe.
航空会社のストでヨーロッパ{旅行/の旅}は大変だった。
Kookuu-gaisha no suto de Yooroppa {-ryokoo/no tabi} wa taihen datta.
(**b**) My travels in Japan are full of enjoyable memories.
私の日本での{旅行/旅}は楽しい思い出でいっぱいです。
Watashi no Nihon de no {ryokoo/tabi} wa tanoshii omoide de ippai desu.

2. u⌈ndoo 運動 •c [an act/instance of changing one's location/position with the passage of time or the act of moving one's body to develop it and maintain good health or the act of aggressively and systematically approaching various people/institutions in order to achieve an objective] 《exercise, motion, sports, campaign, drive, crusade》

EX. The travel of light through empty space has been a phenomenon extensively researched by physicists.
何もない空間を進む光の運動は物理学者によって徹底的に研究されてきた現象だ。
Nani-mo nai kuukan o susumu hikari no undoo wa butsuri-gakusha ni-yotte tettei-tekini kenkyuu-sarete kita genshoo da.

traveler n. **[a person who travels]**

1. ryo⌈ko⌉o-sha 旅行者 •c [a person who travels], ta⌈bi-bito 旅人 [a person who travels ⟨w⟩]

EX. (**a**) You find Japanese travelers the world over, but nowhere so many as in Hawaii.
日本人の{旅行者/*旅人}は世界中どこへ行ってもいますが、特に多いのがハワイです。
*Nihon-jin no {ryokoo-sha/*tabi-bito} wa sekai-juu doko e itte mo imasu ga, tokuni ooi no ga Hawai desu.*
(**b**) A lone traveler was walking along the mountain path.
一人の{旅行者/旅人}が山道を歩いていた。
Hitori no {ryokoo-sha/tabi-bito} ga yama-michi o aruite ita.

2. ta⌈bi-sho⌉onin 旅商人 [a person who travels making sales] 《traveling salesman》

traveling adj. **[engaging in or related to travel]**

ryo⌈koo no N 旅行のN •c [related to travel], ta⌈bi no N 旅のN [related to travel ⟨w⟩], ryo⌈koo-yoo no N 旅行用のN •c [used for travel]

EX. (**a**) I need a traveling companion. Why don't you come with me?
私は{旅行の仲間/旅の道連れ}が欲しいんだけど、一緒に来ませんか。
Watashi wa {ryokoo no nakama/tabi no michi-zure} ga hoshii n da kedo, issho ni kimasen ka.
(**b**) Do you have a traveling suitcase?
{旅行用(の)/*旅行の/*旅の}スーツケースがありますか。
*{Ryokoo-yoo (no)/*Ryokoo no/*Tabi no} suutsukeesu ga arimasu ka.*

tray n. **[an open flat utensil with a low rim, esp. for carrying things]**

bo⌈n 盆 •c [an open flat utensil with a low rim used for carrying things, esp. items of food] 《server, platter》

EX. Put your food on a tray and take it to your seat.
食べ物をお盆にのせて自分の席に持って行きなさい。
Tabe-mono o o-bon ni nosete jibun no seki ni motte-ikinasai.

treasure n. **[wealth stored up or hoarded, esp. in the form of money or jewels 《fig. "s.t./s.o./s.a. considered precious"》]**

1. ta⌈kara(-mono⌉) 宝(物) [s.t. of great value such as money, jewels, or precious metals 《fig. "s.t./s.o. priceless"》] 《precious article, riches, wealth, jewels》, za⌈isan 財産 •c [the entire amount of money, possessions, etc., one owns] 《estate, fortune, property》

T

EX. (**a**) My toy collection was my treasure as a child.
子供の時おもちゃは私にとって{宝物/*財産}だった。
*Kodomo no toki omocha wa watashi ni-totte {takara-mono/*zaisan} datta.*
(**b**) Many wealthy people went down on the Titanic with all their earthly treasures.
タイタニックの沈没で多くの金持ちが全{財産/*宝物}とともに沈んでしまった。
*Taitanikku no chinbotsu de ooku no kanemochi ga zen-{zaisan/*takara-mono} to tomo ni shizunde shimatta.*

2. ki⌈choo-hin 貴重品 •c [s.t. having significant worth or importance] ⟪valuables⟫

EX. The family treasures were placed in the care of a bank.
うちの貴重品は銀行に預けられた。
Uchi no kichoo-hin wa ginkoo ni azuke-rareta.

3. me⌉ no naka ni i⌈rete⌉ mo i⌈ta⌉ku⌈na⌉i ko 目の中にいれても痛くない子 [s.o., esp. one's child, who is considered precious] ⟪the apple of one's eye⟫

— vt. **[to keep or think of s.t. as precious ⟪fig. "cherish"⟫]**

T

⟨-o⟩ da⌈iji⌉ni suru ⟨〜を⟩大事にする ③ [for s.o. to see to it that s.t. precious and irreplaceable is not harmed, marred, or lost] ⟪prize, value, esteem, cherish⟫

EX. I treasure my friendship with her very highly.
私は彼女との交友関係をとても大事にしている。
Watashi wa kanojo to no kooyuu-kankei o totemo daijini shite iru.

treat vt. **[to handle, act toward, or deal with s.t./s.o./s.a. in a certain way; to give medical care to s.o./s.a.; to pay for the food or entertainment of s.o. else; to take up as a topic in speech or writing]**

1. ⟨-o⟩ a⌈tsukau ⟨〜を⟩扱う ① [for s.o. to deal with s.t./s.o./s.a.], ⟨-o⟩ to⌈ri-atsukau ⟨〜を⟩取り扱う ① [for s.o. to hold and use s.t. with the hands ⟪fig. "deal with," "take care of"⟫] ⟪deal with, manage, handle⟫

EX. (**a**) The way he treats his subordinates is awful.
あの人は部下の{扱い/*取り扱い}方がひどい。
*Ano hito wa buka no {atsukai/*tori-atsukai}-kata ga hidoi.*
(**b**) I like that store because they treat their customers so nicely.
あの店は客を大事に{扱って/*取り扱って}くれるので好きだ。
*Ano mise wa kyaku o daijini {atsukatte/*tori-atsukatte} kureru node suki da.*
(**c**) You have to treat this machine with care.
この機械は注意して(取り)扱わなければなりません。
Kono kikai wa chuui-shite (tori-) atsukawanakereba narimasen.
(**d**) In this book the author succeeds well in treating all the competing viewpoints on the abortion issue fairly.
この本で著者は妊娠中絶の問題をめぐる相反する様々な立場を公平に{扱う/?取り扱う}ことに見事に成功している。
Kono hon de chosha wa ninshin-chuuzetsu no mondai o meguru ai-hansuru sama-zamana tachiba o kooheini {atsukau/?tori-atsukau} koto ni migotoni seikoo-shite iru.

2. ⟨-o⟩ chi⌈ryoo-suru ⟨〜を⟩治療する ③ •c [for s.o. to care for (s.o. with) an illness or injury in order to bring about recovery or healing] ⟪cure, remedy⟫

EX. Dr. Smith was the one who treated my mother when she had cancer.
母ががんになった時、治療して下さったのはスミス先生でした。
Haha ga gan ni natta toki, chiryoo-shite kudasatta no wa Sumisu-sensei deshita.

3. ⟨-ni⟩ ⟨-o⟩ o⌈goru ⟨〜に⟩⟨〜を⟩おごる ① [for s.o. to pay for the food or drink of s.o. else] ⟪give a treat⟫, ⟨-ni⟩ ⟨-o⟩ go-⌈chisoo-suru ⟨〜に⟩⟨〜を⟩ごちそうする ③ [for s.o. to provide s.o. with s.t. to eat or drink free of charge]

NOTE: *Ogoru* can be used either as a transitive or intransitive verb meaning "pay for the food or drink of s.o. else." When used intransitively, it can also mean "act in a superior way to others."

EX. Let me treat you to a beer.
ビールを{おごって/ごちそうして}あげよう。
Biiru o {ogotte/go-chisoo-shite} ageyoo.

PHRASE: treat oneself to *funpatsu-shite* V 奮発してV •c

EX. I like to treat myself to a steak dinner now and then.
たまには奮発してステーキの夕飯を食べるのが好きだ。
Tama ni wa funpatsu-shite suteeki no yuuhan o taberu no ga suki da.

— n. **[the act of paying for the food or entertainment of s.o. else or an unexpected pleasure]**

1. o⌈gori おごり /⟨V*masu* of *ogoru* ① pay for the food or drink of s.o. else/

EX. It's my treat today.
今日は僕のおごりだよ。
Kyoo wa boku no ogori da yo.

2. u⌈reshi⌉i koto うれしいこと [s.t. that makes one feel happy], ta⌈noshi⌉i koto 楽しいこと [s.t. enjoyable]

treatment n. **[the way of handling, acting toward, or dealing with s.o./s.a./s.t. or s.t. done to care for an illness or injury]**

1. (to⌈ri-)atsukai (取り)扱い /⟨V*masu* of *(tori-)atsukau* ① handle/ SEE treat vt. 1

EX. (a) His treatment of us was most kind.
彼の私たちに対する{扱い/*取り扱い}はとても親切でした。
*Kare no watashi-tachi ni-taisuru {atsukai/*tori-atsukai} wa totemo shinsetsu deshita.*
(b) This object is fragile and requires careful treatment.
これは壊れものだから取り扱いに注意する必要がある。
Kore wa koware-mono da kara tori-atsukai ni chuui-suru hitsuyoo ga aru.

2. ro⌈nji-kata 論じ方 /⟨V*masu* of *ronjiru* ② discuss + *kata* way/ [the manner in which one discusses s.t.], ro⌈njutsu 論述 •c [the act of setting forth one's thinking in a logical fashion ⟨w⟩] ⟪enunciate, state⟫

EX. The author's treatment of that political issue appears to be one-sided.
著者のその政治問題の{論じ方/論述}は一方的のようだ。
Chosha no sono seiji-mondai no {ronji-kata/ronjutsu} wa ippoo-teki no yooda.

3. i⌈ryoo 医療 •c [caring for an illness or injury for the purpose of bringing about recovery or healing] ⟪remedy⟫

EX. The medical treatment I received at that hospital was superb.
あの病院で受けた医療はすばらしかった。
Ano byooin de uketa iryoo wa subarashikatta.

treaty n. **[a formal agreement made between countries]**

jo⌈oyaku 条約 •c [a formal agreement made between countries] ⟪pact, convention, agreement⟫

EX. It was during the Yoshida administration that Japan concluded a peace treaty with the United States.
日本がアメリカと平和条約を結んだのは吉田内閣の時だった。
Nihon ga Amerika to heiwa-jooyaku o musunda no wa Yoshida-naikaku no toki datta.

tree n. **[a perennial plant with a single stem or trunk made of hard, woody tissue ⟪fig. "a branching diagram, esp. one indicating ancestral relationships"⟫]**

1. ki⌉ 木 [a perennial plant with a single stem or trunk made of hard, woody tissue or a piece of wood] ⟪wood, timber, lumber⟫

EX. We have a couple of apple trees in our back yard.
うちの裏庭にりんごの木が二、三本ある。
Uchi no ura-niwa ni ringo no ki ga ni, san-bon aru.

2. za⌈imoku 材木 •c [wood prepared for use in building things such as houses and furniture] ⟪wood, timber, lumber⟫

EX. We used cedar trees to build our house.

私たちは杉の材木を使って家を建てました。
Watashi-tachi wa sugi no zaimoku o tsukatte ie o tatemashita.

treetop n. **[the topmost part of a tree]**
ko⸢zue こずえ

tremble vi. **[to shake or vibrate involuntarily, esp. due to cold, fear, or emotion]**
fu⸢rueru 震える ② [to move from side to side rapidly and continuously, esp. due to cold or fear] ⟪quiver, quake, shake, shiver⟫, (⟨-de⟩) yu⸢reru (⟨〜で⟩)揺れる ② [to shift back and forth or up and down in position or to be unsettled emotionally] ⟪shake, vibrate, sway⟫

EX. (**a**) I was trembling with cold while waiting for the bus to come.
バスを待ちながら、私は寒さで{震えて/*揺れて}いました。
*Basu o machi-nagara, watashi wa samu-sa de {furuete/*yurete} imashita.*
(**b**) The trees were trembling gently in the wind.
木が風で静かに{揺れて/震えて}いました。
Ki ga kaze de shizukani {yurete/furuete} imashita.

NOTE: In example (b) the use of *furuete* involves personification and is thus poetic in tone.

— n. **[a shaking or quivering movement]**
fu⸢rue 震え /⟨V*masu* of *furueru* ② tremble/ [a shaking movement, esp. due to cold, fear, or emotion]

tremendous adj. **[great in size, power, or degree of excellence]**
(mo⸢no-)sugo⸣i (もの)すごい adj(*i*). **[impressive or surprising to an extent evoking awe ⟨s⟩] ⟪horrible, ghastly, superb, wonderful, amazing, terrific⟫, o⸢soroshi⸣i 恐ろしい** adj(*i*). **[feeling afraid of s.t./s.o./s.a. unusual or mysterious or causing such fear] ⟪terrible, fearful, dreadful, grim⟫, o⸢soroshi⸣i hodo no N 恐ろしいほどのN [to an astonishing extent] ⟪astonishingly⟫**

EX. (**a**) Yukio made a tremendous effort to get into Tokyo University.
幸男は東京大学に入るのに{(もの)すごい/恐ろしいほどの/*恐ろしい}努力をした。
*Yukio wa Tookyoo-daigaku ni hairu no ni {(mono-)sugoi/osoroshii hodo no/ *osoroshii} doryoku o shita.*
(**b**) A red Mercedes Benz passed us on the freeway going at a tremendous speed.
高速道路で赤いベンツが{すごい/恐ろしい/恐ろしいほどの}スピードで私たちの車を追い越していった。
Koosoku-dooro de akai Bentsu ga {sugoi/osoroshii/osoroshii hodo no} supiido de watashi-tachi no kuruma o oi-koshite itta.

trial n. **[the process of trying or testing the quality or performance of s.t.; a formal proceeding leading to judgment in a court of law regarding a civil or criminal case; a test of one's strength, patience, or faith]**
1. ta⸢meshi⸣ 試し /⟨V*masu* of *tamesu* ① try/ [the act of actually doing s.t. or of examining or using s.t. to find out what one wants to know about it] ⟪attempt, experiment, test⟫

EX. I have my doubts as to whether this machine will work or not, but I'm willing to give it a month's trial.
この機械がうまく動くかどうか疑問だが、一か月試しに使ってみてもいいと思う。
Kono kikai ga umaku ugoku ka doo ka gimon da ga, ik-ka-getsu tameshi ni tsukatte mite mo ii to omou.

2. sa⸣iban 裁判 •c [a formal legal proceeding before a tribunal leading to judgment on a civil or criminal case] ⟪justice, hearing⟫, ko⸢ohan 公判 •c [a public legal proceeding leading to judgment on a criminal case] ⟪a public hearing⟫

EX. A trial of war criminals took place in Tokyo after the war.
戦争のあと戦争犯罪者の{裁判/公判}が東京であった。
Sensoo no ato sensoo-hanzai-sha no

{saiban/koohan} ga Tookyoo de atta.

3. shi˥ren 試練 •c [a test of human endurance through suffering] **《test, ordeal》**

EX. He withstood every trial he encounterd in life.
彼は人生のあらゆる試練に耐えた。
Kare wa jinsei no arayuru shiren ni taeta.

PHRASE: trial and error *shikoo-sakugo* 試行錯誤

EX. Our most useful lessons in life are probably those learned through trial and error.
人生で最も役に立つ知恵はおそらく試行錯誤によって身につくものだろう。
Jinsei de mottomo yaku ni tatsu chie wa osoraku shikoo-sakugo ni-yotte mi-ni-tsuku mono daroo.

triangle n. **[a polygon having three sides 《fig. "a drafting instrument having this shape," "a percussion instrument having this shape," "a love relationship among three people"》]**

1. sa˥nka˥kkei 三角形 •c [a polygon having three sides]

EX. If you fold a square sheet of paper diagonally, you get a triangle.
四角の紙を斜めに折ると、三角形になります。
Shikaku no kami o naname ni oru to, sankakkei ni narimasu.

2. sa˥nkaku-jo˥ogi 三角定規 •c [a drafting instrument shaped like a polygon with three sides] **《ruler》**

PHRASE: love triangle *sankaku-kankei* 三角関係 •c

EX. A: Both Lisa and I love Richard.
私もリサもリチャードが大好きなの。
Watashi mo Risa mo Richaado ga dai-sukina no.
B: Then it's a love triangle, isn't it!
じゃあ、三角関係じゃないか。
Jaa, sankaku-kankei janai ka.

triangular adj. **[shaped like or having to do with a polygon with three sides 《fig. "having to do with three people or countries," "having to do with a love relationship among three people"》]**

1. sa˥nka˥kkei no N 三角形のN •c [shaped like or having to do with a polygon with three sides]

EX. I bought a triangular lot and built a house on it.
私は三角形の土地を買ってそこに家を建てた。
Watashi wa sankakkei no tochi o katte soko ni ie o tateta.

2. sa˥n-sha-ka˥n no N 三者間のN [having to do with three people or parties], sa˥n-goku-ka˥n no N 三国間のN [having to do with three countries]

EX. A triangular treaty was concluded between Japan, Russia, and the U.S.
日米ロ{三者間/三国間}の条約が結ばれた。
Nichi-Bei-Ro {sansha-kan/san-goku-kan} no jooyaku ga musuba-reta.

tribal adj. **[having to do with a primitive community sharing the same ancestors and culture]**

shu˥zoku no N 種族のN •c [having to do with a primitive community sharing the same ancestors and culture], bu˥zoku no N 部族のN •c [having to do with a primitive community sharing the same culture and political control]

EX. Many American Indians still observe ancient tribal traditions.
アメリカインディアンの中にはまだ{種族/部族}の昔からの伝統を守っている人が多い。
Amerika Indian no naka ni wa mada {shuzoku/buzoku} no mukashi kara no dentoo o mamotte iru hito ga ooi.

tribe n. **[a (primitive) community sharing the same ancestors and culture]**

shu˥zoku 種族 •c [a primitive community sharing the same ancestors and culture] **《race, stock, family》**, **bu˥zoku 部族 •c [a primitive community sharing the same culture and political leadership]** **《genes》**

EX. Which Indian tribe inhabited this area when the white settlers first arrived?
白人の移住者が初めて住みついたころどのインディアンの{部族/種族}がこの

T

辺に住んでいましたか。
Hakujin no ijuu-sha ga hajimete sumi-tsuita koro dono Indian no {buzoku/shuzoku} ga kono hen ni sunde imashita ka.

trick n. **[s.t. done to deceive or cheat s.o.; a clever or skillful act, esp. one done for entertainment; a particular way of doing s.t. that is more effective or efficient than any other way; a practical joke or prank]**
1. sa⌈kuryaku 策略 •c [a secret plan to achieve some goal favorable to oneself through deceiving or using others] ⟪stratagem, ruse, tactics, strategy⟫, a⌈no te ko⌈no te あの手この手 •c [a series of clever or skillful actions, esp. ones done to deceive or cheat s.o. ⟨s⟩] ⟪strategy⟫

EX. He's always devising tricks at work to get credit for things he hasn't actually done.
彼は会社で本当はしていないことをあたかも自分でしたかのように見せかけるためいつも{あの手この手/策略}を使っている。
Kare wa kaisha de hontoo wa shite inai koto o atakamo jibun de shita ka no yooni mise-kakeru tame itsu-mo {ano te kono te/sakuryaku} o tsukatte iru.

T

2. te⌉jina 手品 [a dexterous feat by which to puzzle and entertain people] ⟪juggler's trick, juggling⟫

EX. The magician entertained the children with tricks such as producing a bird from a hat.
奇術師は帽子から鳥を出す手品などで子供を楽しませた。
Kijutsu-shi wa booshi kara tori o dasu tejina nado de kodomo o tanoshima-seta.

3. ko⌈tsu こつ •c [a particular method for doing s.t. that is more effective or efficient than any other way] ⟪knack, ropes⟫, hi⌈ke⌉tsu 秘けつ •c [an effective method of doing s.t. still unknown to s.o.] ⟪secret, key⟫
㊥ "bone"▷骨, otherwise ▷こつ

EX. Let me teach you the trick to getting bread to rise just right.
パンをちょうどいい具合にふくらませる{こつ/秘けつ}を教えてあげましょう。
Pan o choodo ii guai ni fukurama-seru {kotsu/hiketsu} o oshiete agemashoo.

4. i⌈tazura いたずら [improper behavior, esp. of children, done in fun to kill time/energy] ⟪mischief, devilment, practical joke, fun, prank⟫

EX. The neighborhood boys are always playing mean tricks on the old woman next door.
近所の腕白坊主がいつも隣のおばあちゃんに意地悪ないたずらをしている。
Kinjo no wanpaku-boozu ga itsu-mo tonari no o-baa-chan ni ijiwaruna itazura o shite iru.

—— vt. **[to deceive s.o. by cunning]**
⟨-o⟩ da⌈ma⌉su ⟨〜を⟩だます ① [for s.o. to cause s.o. to believe s.o. which is not true]

EX. A: They told me that I can get a free trip to Hawaii just by participating in their survey!
調査に参加するだけでハワイまでただで旅行が出来るんだって。
Choosa ni sanka-suru dake de Hawai made tada de ryokoo ga dekiru n datte.
B: I hope you haven't been tricked.
だまされたんじゃないといいけどね。
Damasa-reta n janai to ii kedo ne.

tricky adj. **[skilled at or given to deceiving others; requiring careful thought or treatment]**
1. zu⌈ru⌉i ずるい adj(*i*). **[skilled in cheating and playing one's part well or having the tendency to feign ignorance of one's duties and thereby neglect them] ⟪cunning, crafty, slick, unfair⟫, sa⌈kuryaku ga u⌈ma⌉i (N) 策略がうまい(N) [skilled at strategizing to achieve one's goals, esp. through deceit or cunning]**

EX. Be careful. He's a tricky character, you know.
注意しろよ。あいつはとても{ずるい/策略がうまい}やつだからね。
Chuui-shiro yo. Aitsu wa totemo {zurui/sakuryaku ga umai} yatsu da kara ne.

2. ki⌈wado⌉i きわどい adj(*i*). **[located on the brink of danger ⟪fig. "verging on indecent"⟫] ⟪dangerous, critical, delicate⟫, te⌈giwa no iru (N) 手際の要る(N)**

[requiring care and skill]

EX. With fluctuating exchange rates, international trade can be a tricky business.
為替レートが変動するから、貿易は{きわどい/手際の要る}仕事だ。
Kawase-reeto ga hendoo-suru kara, booeki wa {kiwadoi/tegiwa no iru} shigoto da.

trim vt. **[to make s.t. neat or orderly by cutting or clipping away parts of it 《fig. "curtail," "arrange things properly," "decorate"》]**

1. 〈-o〉 **ki⌈ri-to⌉ru** 〈～を〉切り取る ① **[for s.o. to cut a piece off of s.t.],** 〈-o〉 **ka⌈ri-ko⌉mu** 〈～を〉刈り込む ① **[for s.o. to clip s.t., esp. plant or hair growth, to make it neat]** 《**cut, crop, prune**》

EX. (**a**) Could you trim my hair a bit?
ちょっと頭を{刈り込んで/*切り取って}くれませんか。
*Chotto atama o {kari-konde/*kiri-totte} kuremasen ka.*
(**b**) The pine tree looks much better since the gardener trimmed it.
植木屋が{刈り込んで/*切り取って}から松の木がずっとよく見える。
*Ueki-ya ga {kari-konde/*kiri-totte} kara matsu-no-ki ga zutto yoku mieru.*
(**c**) Trim the fat off of this piece of meat, please.
この肉の脂身を{切り取って/*刈り込んで}ください。
*Kono niku no abura-mi o {kiri-totte/ *kari-konde} kudasai.*

2. 〈-o〉 **he⌈rasu** 〈～を〉減らす ① **[to cause s.t./s.o./s.a. to become smaller in quantity]** 《**reduce, decrease, lessen**》 ↔ 〈-o〉 **fuyasu** 〈～を〉増やす ①

EX. We have to trim our budget this year.
今年は予算を減らさなければならない。
Kotoshi wa yosan o herasanakereba naranai.

3. 〈-no〉 **te⌈ire⌉ o suru** 〈～の〉手入れをする ③ **[for s.o. to keep s.t. such as plant growth, hair growth, or a machine properly maintained through care and upkeep]**

EX. He's always trimming his mustache.
彼はいつも口ひげの手入れをしている。
Kare wa itsu-mo kuchi-hige no teire o shite iru.

4. 〈-o〉 **ka⌈zaru** 〈～を〉飾る ① **[for s.o. to arrange s.t. effectively so as to make it appear beautiful 《fig. "embellish," "exhibit"》]** 《**ornament, decorate, adorn, deck**》

EX. When I was small we used to trim the Christmas tree with handmade ornaments.
子供の時よく手作りの飾りでクリスマスツリーを飾ったものだ。
Kodomo no toki yoku te-zukuri no kazari de Kurisumasu-tsurii o kazatta mono da.

trip vi. **[for s.o./s.a. to stumble on s.t. (and fall) or to make a mistake]**

1. 〈-ni〉 **tsu⌈mazuku** 〈～に〉つまずく ① **[for s.o./s.a. to hit one's foot against s.t. and almost fall down 《fig. "fail"》]**

EX. I tripped over a rock and fell.
石につまずいて転んでしまった。
Ishi ni tsumazuite koronde shimatta.

2. 〈-ni〉 **shi⌈ppai-suru** 〈～に〉失敗する ③ •c **[for s.o./s.a. to come up with a different result on s.t. than what was originally desired owing to errors in approach/ method]** 《**fail, be unsuccessful**》

EX. We tripped up several times before we finally succeeded in the experiment.
やっと成功するまでにその実験に数回失敗した。
Yatto seikoo-suru made ni sono jikken ni suu-kai shippai-shita.

—— vt. **[to cause s.o. to stumble]**

1. 〈-o〉 **tsu⌈mazuka-seru** 〈～を〉つまずかせる /〈causative of *tsumazuku* ① falter/ ② **[to cause s.o. to hit one's foot against s.t. and almost fall down]**

EX. John stuck out his leg and tripped his little brother.
ジョンは足を出して弟をつまずかせた。
Jon wa ashi o dashite otooto o tsumazuka-seta.

2. (〈-de〉) **shi⌈ppai-suru** (〈～で〉)失敗する ③

•c [for s.o./s.a. to come up with a different result on s.t. than what was originally desired owing to errors in approach/method] ((fail))

EX. The last question on the test was difficult and tripped up several students.
試験の最後の問題が難しくて、それで失敗した学生が数人いる。
Shiken no saigo no mondai ga muzukashikute, sore de shippai-shita gakusei ga suu-nin iru.

— n. **[an act/instance of traveling from one place to another]**

1. ryo⌈koo 旅行 •c [the act of leaving one's home to go to a relatively distant place] ((travel, journey)), ta⌈bi⌉ 旅 [the act of going a relatively long distance from one place to another] ((travel, journey))

EX. (**a**) A: How was your trip to Japan?
日本への{旅行/?旅}はどうでしたか。
Nihon e no {ryokoo/?tabi} wa doo deshita ka.
B: It was most enjoyable.
とても楽しかったです。
Totemo tanoshikatta desu.
(**b**) It's been a long time since I enjoyed a trip alone with my wife.
妻とふたりっきりの{旅/旅行}を楽しんでから久しい。
Tsuma to futarikkiri no {tabi/ryokoo} o tanoshinde kara hisashii.

2. o⌈ofuku 往復 •c [going and returning] ((both ways))

EX. I made two trips to the post office today.
今日は郵便局まで二度往復(を)した。
Kyoo wa yuubin-kyoku made ni-do oofuku (o) shita.

triumph n. **[a great victory or success]**

1. sho⌉ori 勝利 •c [an act/instance of overcoming one's opponent in a game or war] ((victory, conquest, success))

EX. The triumph of Japan in the Russo-Japanese War of 1904–5 was an important milestone in Japan's rise as a world power.
1904年から5年にかけての日露戦争での日本の勝利は日本が世界の大国になる上で大事な一里塚だった。
Sen-kyuu-hyaku-yo-nen kara go-nen ni kakete no Nichi-Ro-sensoo de no Nihon no shoori wa Nihon ga sekai no taikoku ni naru ue de daijina ichi-ri-zuka datta.

2. da⌈i-se⌉ikoo 大成功 •c [a great success]

EX. The discovery of the polio vaccine was one of the early triumphs of modern medicine.
ポリオワクチンの発見は近代医学の初期における大成功の一つである。
Porio-wakuchin no hakken ha kindai-igaku no shoki ni-okeru dai-seikoo no hitotsu dearu.

— vi. **[to obtain success or victory or to celebrate this]**

1. sho⌉ori o o⌈same⌉ru 勝利を収める ② [to obtain success or victory]

2. sho⌉ori o i⌈wa⌉u 勝利を祝う ① [to celebrate success or victory]

troop n. **[a group of people doing s.t. together, esp. soldiers, or a group of animals]**

1. o⌈oze⌉i 大勢 [a large number of people] ((crowd, hot)), mu⌈re⌉ 群れ [a group of people or animals gathered together] ((group, crowd, throng, flock, pack))

EX. (**a**) A troop of demonstrators gathered in front of the embassy.
デモ隊が大使館の前に{群れをなして/大勢}集まった。
Demo-tai ga taishi-kan no mae ni {mure o nashite/oozei} atsumatta.
(**b**) A troop of antelopes was running down the hill.
かもしかの群れが丘を駆け下りていた。
Kamoshika no mure ga oka o kake-orite ita.

2. gu⌉ntai 軍隊 •c [soldiers]

EX. American troops stayed in the region after the end of the war to maintain peace.
アメリカの軍隊は治安を維持するため戦争が終わってもその地域に残った。
Amerika no guntai wa chian o iji-suru tame sensoo ga owatte mo sono chiiki ni nokotta.

tropic n. **[a line of latitude 23°27' north of the equator]**
ka⌈iki-sen 回帰線 •c

tropical adj. **[of or found in the torrid zone]**
ne⌈ttai no N 熱帯のN •c

EX. I'd love to go to a tropical island over the Christmas break.
僕はクリスマス休暇には熱帯の島に行けたらいいと思う。
Boku wa kurisumasu-kyuuka ni wa nettai no shima ni iketara ii to omou.

trot n. **[a moderately fast movement on foot by a horse or person at a pace between walking and running]**
so⌉kuho 速歩 •c [fast walking], i⌈sogi⌉-ashi 急ぎ足 /⟨V*masu* of *isogu* ① hurry + *ashi* foot, leg/ [a quick pace] ⟪a quick pace⟫

—— vi. **[for s.o./s.a. to move on foot at a moderate pace between walking and running]**
ha⌉yaku a⌈ru⌉ku 速く歩く ① [for s.o./s.a. to walk fast], ko-⌈ba⌉shiri ni a⌈ru⌉ku 小走りに歩く ① [for s.o./s.a. to walk fast with short steps] ⟪trip along, go at a trot⟫

trouble vt. **[to cause s.o. mental or physical inconvenience or discomfort]**
⟨-o⟩ ku⌈rushime⌉ru ⟨〜を⟩苦しめる ② [to cause s.o. mental or physical adversity or pain] ⟪torment, distress, worry, annoy⟫, ⟨-o⟩ na⌈yama-se⌉ru ⟨〜を⟩悩ませる /⟨causative of *nayamu* ① worry/ ② [to cause s.o. mental affliction] ⟪afflict, torment, harass, agonize, vex, annoy⟫, ⟨-ni⟩ me⌉iwaku o ka⌈ke⌉ru ⟨〜に⟩迷惑をかける ② [to cause s.o. to feel unpleasant or experience inconvenience] ⟪annoy, bother, worry, be a nuisance, inconvenience⟫, ⟨-o⟩ wa⌈zurawasu ⟨〜を⟩煩わす ① [to cause s.o. inconvenience or worry] ⟪trouble, bother, annoy, pester⟫

EX. (**a**) Something must be troubling him.
何かが彼{を苦しめて/を悩ませて/*に迷惑をかけて/*を煩わして}いるに違いない。
*Nani-ka ga kare {o kurushimete/o nayama-sete/*ni meiwaku o kakete/*o wazurawashite} iru ni chigainai.*
(**b**) Keiko's cold attitude troubled Akira.
恵子の冷たい態度が明{を悩ませた/を苦しめた/*に迷惑をかけた/*を煩わした}。
*Keiko no tsumetai taido ga Akira {o nayama-seta/o kurushimeta/*ni meiwaku o kaketa/*o wazurawashita}.*
(**c**) I'm sorry to have to trouble you again.
またあなた{に迷惑をかけて/を煩わして/*を苦しめて/*を悩ませて}すみません。
*Mata anata {ni meiwaku o kakete/o wazurawashite/*o kurushimete/*o nayama-sete} sumimasen.*

—— n. **[an unpleasant state or situation involving difficulty, danger, inconvenience, or worry or s.t. causing this]**
1. shi⌈npai 心配 •c [an uncomfortable feeling caused by uncertainty or by the expectation of danger/evil/s.t. troublesome] ⟪concern, anxiety, apprehension, uneasiness, fear, worry, care⟫, na⌈yami⌉ 悩み /⟨V*masu* of *nayamu* ① worry/ [mental affliction] ⟪affliction, anguish, worry, distress⟫, ku⌉roo 苦労 •c [painstaking efforts] ⟪hardship, suffering, difficulty⟫

EX. My troubles have made my hair gray.
私は{心配/悩み/苦労}で白髪が増えた。
Watashi wa {shinpai/nayami/kuroo} de shiraga ga fueta.

2. fu⌈nsoo 紛争 •c [entangled dispute] ⟪dispute, conflict⟫

EX. There was a lot of trouble on college campuses during the 60's and early 70's.
60年代と70年代の初めには大学紛争がたくさんあった。
Roku-juu-nen-dai to nana-juu-nen-dai no hajime ni wa daigaku-funsoo ga takusan atta.

3. byo⌈oki 病気 •c [a state/instance of not being in good health]

EX. I've had stomach troubles for many years.
僕は何年も胃の病気に悩まされている。
Boku wa nan-nen mo i no byooki ni nayama-sarete iru.

4. me⌉iwaku 迷惑 •c [an act/instance of causing s.o. a feeling of unpleasantness or

T

inconvenience] ⟨⟨**annoyance, inconvenience, nuisance**⟩⟩

EX. I'm sorry I caused you so much trouble.
大変ご迷惑をかけて申し訳ございません。
Taihen go-meiwaku o kakete mooshi-wake gozaimasen.

5. ko⌈shoo 故障 •c [a malfunction in a machine or body] ⟨⟨**hitch, obstacle, fault, breakdown**⟩⟩

EX. Our plane developed engine trouble right after take-off.
私たちの飛行機は離陸直後にエンジンが故障をおこした。
Watashi-tachi no hikoo-ki wa ririku-chokugo ni enjin ga koshoo o okoshita.

PHRASE: go to all the trouble *sekkaku* せっかく ⟨⟨at great pain⟩⟩

EX. We went to all the trouble of climbing the mountain but couldn't see anything from the top because of the fog.
せっかく山に登ったのに、霧で頂上からは何も見えなかった。
Sekkaku yama ni nobotta noni, kiri de choojoo kara wa nani-mo mienakatta.

troublesome adj. **[causing difficulty, danger, inconvenience, worry, or other unpleasantness]**
me⌈ndo⌉ona 面倒な adj(*na*). **•c [causing trouble for one]** ⟨⟨**worrisome**⟩⟩, **ya⌉kkaina 厄介な** adj(*na*). **•c [causing trouble, difficulty, and annoyance]** ⟨⟨**annoying, burdensome**⟩⟩

EX. Like any job, mine has some troublesome aspects to it, but I'm at least glad to be employed.
どんな仕事でもそうですが、私の仕事にも{面倒な/厄介な}ことがあります。しかし、仕事があるだけでありがたいと思っています。
Donna shigoto demo soo desu ga, watashi no shigoto ni mo {mendoona/yakkaina} koto ga arimasu. Shikashi, shigoto ga aru dake de arigatai to omotte imasu.

trousers n. **[a two-legged outer garment reaching from the waist to the ankles]**
zu⌈bo⌉n ズボン •f, pa⌉ntsu パンツ •f [a two-legged outer garment reaching from the waist to the ankles or underwear with two short legs]

NOTE: *Zubon* comes from the French "*jupon.*"

EX. Mr. Yoshida wears blue trousers almost every day.
吉田さんはほとんど毎日青い{ズボン/パンツ}をはいている。
Yoshida-san wa hotondo mai-nichi aoi {zubon/pantsu} o haite iru.

trout n.
ma⌈su⌉ ます

truck n. **[a large motor vehicle used for carrying heavy loads]**
to⌈ra⌉kku トラック •f

EX. We rented a truck to move into our new house.
新しい家に引越すのにトラックを借りた。
Atarashii ie ni hikkosu no ni torakku o karita.

true adj. **[conforming to reality and free from falsity]**
ho⌈ntoo no N 本当のN •c [not a fiction or a lie] ⟨⟨**real, actual**⟩⟩ ↔ **uso no N うそのN; shi⌉n no N 真のN •c [conforming to reality and free from falsity ⟨w⟩]** ⟨⟨**true, real**⟩⟩ ↔ **uso no N うそのN; ta⌈dashi⌉i 正しい** adj(*i*). **[conforming to an ethical, legal, logical, social, or regulatory standard; free from error]** ⟨⟨**right, righteous, honest, proper, correct, lawful**⟩⟩ ↔ **machigatta N 間違ったN**

EX. (**a**) They say that your true self surfaces when you're faced with danger.
危険に直面すると{本当の/真の/*正しい}性格が出るそうだ。
*Kiken ni chokumen-suru to {hontoo no/shin no/*tadashii} seikaku ga deru sooda.*
(**b**) There is only one true answer to this question.
この問題には{正しい/本当の/真の}答えは一つしかありません。
Kono monda ni wa {tadashii/hontoo

no/shin no} kotae wa hitotsu shika arimasen.
(c) Believe it or not, this is a true story.
信じてもらえないかも知れませんが、これは{本当の/*真の/*正しい}話です。
*Shinjite morae-nai kamoshiremasen ga, kore wa {hontoo no/*shin no/*tadashii} hanashi desu.*

truly adv. **[in a way totally free from falsity, inaccuracy, or insincerity]**
ho⌈ntoo ni 本当に •c [used for giving force to the expression it modifies 《fig. "an interjection used by a female speaker to indicate incredulousness"》] 《really》, ko⌈ko⌉ro kara 心から [from the bottom of one's heart], chu⌈ujitsuni 忠実に /〈adj(*na*). *ni* of *chuujitsuna* faithful/ •c [as exactly or accurately as required] 《loyally, devotedly, faithfully》, ta⌈da⌉shiku 正しく /〈adj(*i*). *ku* of *tadashii* correct/ [in such a way as to conform to an ethical, legal, logical, social, or regulatory standard; in such a way as to be free from error] 《correctly, properly》

EX. (a) I truly loved that girl.
僕はその女の子を{心から/本当に/*忠実に/*正しく}愛していた。
*Boku wa sono onna-no-ko o {kokoro kara/hontoo ni/*chuujitsuni/ *tadashiku} aishite ita.*
(b) The people of this company are truly dedicated to their work.
この会社の人たちは{忠実に/本当に/心から/*正しく}仕事に打ち込んでいる。
*Kono kaisha no hito-tachi wa {chuujitsuni/hontoo ni/kokoro kara/ *tadashiku} shigoto ni uchi-konde iru.*
(c) It takes great skill to produce a translation that truly conveys the meaning of the original text.
原文の意味を{正しく/忠実に/*本当に/*心から}伝える訳文に直すのには相当の技能が要る。
*Genbun no imi o {tadashiku/ chuujitsuni/*hontoo ni/*kokoro kara} tsutaeru yaku-bun ni naosu no ni wa sootoo no ginoo ga iru.*

trumpet n.
to⌈ranpe⌉tto トランペット •f

EX. Bill can play the trumpet.
ビルはトランペットが吹ける。
Biru wa toranpetto ga fuke-ru.

trunk n. **[the main stem of a tree or the main part of a body apart from the head and appendages 《fig. "luggage compartment of a car," "the nose of an elephant"》]**
1. mi⌉ki 幹 [the wooden central part of a tree]

EX. The cat was chased by the dog up the trunk of a tree.
猫が犬に追いかけられて、木の幹に登った。
Neko ga inu ni oikake-rarete, ki no miki ni nobotta.

2. do⌉o 胴 •c [the part of a human or animal body apart from the head and appendages] 《torso》

EX. He has a long trunk and short legs.
彼は胴が長くて、足が短い。
Kare wa doo ga nagakute, ashi ga mijikai.

3. to⌈ra⌉nku トランク •f [the luggage compartment of a car]

EX. The trunk of our car has ample space to hold this luggage.
うちの車のトランクはこの荷物を入れるのに十分スペースがある。
Uchi no kuruma no toranku wa kono nimotsu o ireru no ni juubun supeesu ga aru.

4. zo⌉o no ha⌈na 象の鼻 [the nose of an elephant]

EX. How much water do you think an elephant can hold in its trunk?
象は鼻の中にどれだけ水を吸い込んでおくことができると思う?
Zoo wa hana no naka ni dore-dake mizu o sui-konde oku koto ga dekiru to omou?

trust vt. **[for s.o. to believe s.t./s.o. to be true, reliable, or honest or to place s.t. in s.o.'s care based on this belief]**
1. 〈-o〉 shi⌈nrai-suru 〈～を〉信頼する ③ •c

T

[for s.o. to believe s.o./s.t. to be truthful, reliable, or strong and able to be depended on] ⦅rely on, depend on, put confidence in⦆, ⟨-o⟩ **shi⌈n'yoo-suru** ⟨〜を⟩信用する ③ •c **[for s.o. to believe without doubt in the correctness or honesty of s.o./s.t.]** ⦅place confidence in, give credence to, accept…as true⦆

EX. (**a**) I shouldn't have trusted that salesman's word.
私はそのセールスマンのことばを{信用/??信頼}すべきじゃな かった。
Watashi wa sono seerusu-man no kotoba o {shin'yoo/?? shinrai}-subeki janakatta.
(**b**) I'd like to marry someone I can trust.
{信頼/??信用}出来る人と結婚したいです。
{Shinrai/??Shin'yoo}-dekiru hito to kekkon-shi-tai desu.
(**c**) How can you trust a guy like that?
どうしてあんな奴を{信用/信頼}出来るんだい?
Dooshite anna yatsu o {shin'yoo/ shinrai}-dekiru n dai?

2. ⟨-o⟩ **shi⌈ntaku-suru** ⟨〜を⟩信託する ③ •c **[for s.o. to believe in the honesty and reliability of s.o. enough to put s.t. important, esp. property or money, under the care or management of that person]**

—— n. **[a strong belief in the truth, reliability, or honesty of s.t./s.o.; the care or management of s.t./s.o. on the basis of such belief being placed in one; a group of business firms allied together to reduce competition]**

1. **shi⌈nrai** 信頼 •c **[an attitude of accepting the reliability or honesty of s.o. with such certainty as to leave everything to that person]** ⦅reliance, dependence, confidence⦆

EX. My trust in him was lost when he slandered me like that.
彼が僕のことを中傷した時にあの人への信頼はなくなってしまった。
Kare ga boku no koto o chuushoo-shita toki ni ano hito e no shinrai wa nakunatte shimatta.

2. **ka⌈kushin** 確信 •c **[conviction that s.t. is the case]** ⦅conviction, assurance, confidence⦆

EX. I have full trust that my son will succeed in his business.
私には息子が事業に成功するという確信がある。
Watashi ni wa musuko ga jigyoo ni seikoo-suru to iu kakushin ga aru.

3. **shi⌈ntaku** 信託 •c **[an act of relying on s.o. for the care and management of one's money or property]**

4. **to⌈ra⌉suto** トラスト •f **[an association of businesses to protect a monopoly]**

truth n. **[the property of conforming to reality and being free from falsity or that which has this property]**
shi⌉nri 真理 •c **[that which conforms to reality, viewed as an abstract essence]**, **shi⌉njitsu** 真実 •c **[that which is factual and free from falsity]** ⦅reality, fact⦆ ↔ **uso** うそ; **ho⌈ntoo no koto** 本当のこと **[that which is not a fiction or a lie]**

EX. (**a**) Beauty is truth and truth is beauty.
美は{真理/真実/*本当のこと}で、{真理/真実/*本当のこと}は美だ。
*Bi wa {shinri/shinjitsu/*hontoo no koto} de, {shinri/shinjitsu/*hontoo no koto} wa bi da.*
(**b**) Please tell me the truth.
どうか{本当のこと/真実/*真理}をおっしゃってください。
*Doo-ka {hontoo no koto/shinjitsu/ *shinri} o osshatte kudasai.*

try vt. **[for s.o./s.a. to make an effort to do s.t.; to use or examine s.t. or actually do s.t. to determine if it is useful or good for one's purposes; to put a strain on s.o./s.t.; to examine s.o. in a formal legal proceeding to decide a case brought against him/her]**

1. **Vvol. to suru** Vvol.とする ③ **[for s.o./ s.a. to make an effort to do s.t.]**

EX. (**a**) I tried to lift the big box by myself, but it was too heavy.
大きな箱を一人で持ち上げようとした

が重くて出来なかった。
Ookina hako o hitori de mochi-ageyoo to shita ga, omokute dekinakatta.
(**b**) Surrounded by his pursuers the fugitive tried to escape, but to no avail.
追っ手に取り囲まれてしまった脱走者は、逃げようとしたがだめだった。
Otte ni tori-kakoma-rete shimatta dassoo-sha wa, nigeyoo to shita ga dame datta.

2. ⟨-o⟩ **ko⌈koromi⌉ru** ⟨〜を⟩**試みる** ② **[for s.o. to do s.t. to see if it is possible or if one can be successful at it** ⟨w⟩**]** **⟪make a trial, try one's hand at, have a try at⟫**, ⟨-o⟩ **ta⌈me⌉su** ⟨〜を⟩**試す** ① **[for s.o. to actually do s.t. or to examine or use s.t. to find out what one wants to know about it]** **⟪attempt, put to the test⟫**, **V*te* miru V*te*みる** ② **[for s.o./s.a. to do s.t. to see what it is like or what the result will be]**

EX. (**a**) Sales of this product have been disappointing so far, so we've decided to try a new approach in marketing it.
この製品は今のところ売り上げがもう一つなので、新しい販売のやり方を{試みる/やってみる/してみる/?試す}ことにした。
Kono seihin wa ima no tokoro uri-age ga moo hitotsu na node, atarashii hanbai no yari-kata o {kokoromiru/yatte miru/shite miru/?tamesu} koto ni shita.
(**b**) The doctor tried a new drug on his cancer patient.
医者はがんの患者に新薬{の使用を試みた/?を使ってみた/??を試した}。
Isha wa gan no kanja ni shin'yaku {no shiyoo o kokoromita/?o tsukatte mita/??o tameshita}.
(**c**) We tried a different approach after our first approach failed.
最初のやり方で失敗した後、私たちは違った方法を{試した/使ってみた/試みた}。
Saisho no yari-kata de shippai-shita ato, watashi-tachi wa chigatta hoohoo o {tameshita/tsukatte mita/kokoromita}.
(**d**) The first time I tried Japanese miso soup, I didn't like it.
初めて日本のみそ汁を{飲んでみた/??試した/*試みた}時、おいしいとは思わなかった。
*Hajimete Nihon no miso-shiru o {nonde mita/??tameshita/*kokoromita} ga, oishii to wa omowanakatta.*

3. {⟨**-de**⟩/**V*te***} **tsu⌈kare⌉ru** {⟨〜で⟩/**V*te***}**疲れる** ② **[for (a body part of) s.o./s.a. to become physically or mentally fatigued]** **⟪grow weavy, become fatigued⟫**

EX. Using the computer all day long tried my eyes sorely.
コンピューターを一日中使って非常に目が疲れた
Konpyuutaa o ichi-nichi-juu tsukatte hijooni me ga tsukareta

4. ⟨-o⟩ **sa⌈ba⌉ku** ⟨〜を⟩**さばく** ① **[for s.o. to control s.t. skillfully with one's hands ⟪fig. "deal with a problem," "judge if s.o. is guilty or not guilty"⟫]**, ⟨-o⟩ **sa⌉iban ni ka⌈ke⌉ru** ⟨〜を⟩**裁判にかける** ② **[for s.o. to put s.o. on trial]**
㊥ "control s.t. skillfully with one's hands," "deal with a problem"▷さばく, "judge if s.o. is guilty or not guilty"▷裁く

EX. They tried the former Prime Minister on charges of bribery.
前首相が収賄の容疑で{裁かれた/裁判にかけられた}。
Zen-shushoo ga shuuwai no yoogi de {sabaka-reta/saiban ni kake-rareta}.

tub n. **[an open flat-bottomed, round container, esp. for use in washing or bathing]**
o⌉ke おけ [an open flat-bottomed, round container, usu. made of wood] **⟪kit, pail⟫**, **ta⌈rai たらい [a flat-bottomed container for holding liquid used in washing or bathing]** **⟪washbasin⟫**, **fu⌈ro-o⌉ke ふろおけ ⟪bathtub⟫**

tube n. **[a hollow elongated cylinder ⟪fig. "anything with the structure of a hollow elongated cylinder"⟫]**
1. ku⌉da 管 [a hollow elongated cylinder

T

with a relatively small diameter] ⟪**pipe**⟫, **tsu⌈tsu 筒 [a hollow elongated cylinder shorter than a *kuda*]** ⟪**pipe**⟫

EX. (**a**) In the hospital my father was being fed through a tube.
父は病院で{管/*筒}で栄養を取っていた。
*Chichi wa byooin de {kuda/*tsutsu} de eiyoo o totte ita.*
(**b**) Water flows through a bamboo tube into the pond in the garden.
水が竹の{筒/*管}を通って庭の池に流れ込む。
*Mizu ga take no {tsutsu/*kuda} o tootte niwa no ike ni nagare-komu.*

2. to⌈nneru トンネル •f ⟪**tunnel**⟫

3. ta⌈iya no chu⌉ubu タイヤのチューブ •f [a small cylinder on a tire through which air is pumped]

tuck vt. **[for s.o. to push or fold the edge of s.t. into or under s.t., esp. so that it is covered ⟪fig. "cover snugly"⟫]**

1. ⟨-o⟩ ⟨-ni⟩ o⌈shi-ko⌉mu ⟨〜を⟩⟨〜に⟩押し込む ① [for s.o. to force s.t. into a small space by pushing] ⟪**press in, crowd into, squeeze in, herd into**⟫

EX. Your shirt's hanging out. Tuck it in.
シャツが出ているよ。押し込んだら。
Shatsu ga dete iru yo. Oshi-kondara.

2. ⟨-o⟩ ⟨-de⟩ ku⌈ru⌉mu ⟨〜を⟩⟨〜で⟩くるむ ① [for s.o. to wrap s.t./s.o. completely in s.t. such as cloth or paper] ⟪**wrap in**⟫

EX. The baby looks cold. Let's tuck him in a blanket.
赤ちゃんが寒そうにしているよ。毛布でくるんでやろう。
Aka-chan ga samu-sooni shite iru yo. Moofu de kurunde yaroo.

Tuesday n.

ka⌈yo⌉o(-bi) 火曜(日)

EX. I'm leaving for Japan this coming Tuesday.
今度の火曜日に日本へ発ちます。
Kondo no kayoo-bi ni Nihon e tachimasu.

tug vi. **[to pull hard on s.t./s.o./s.a.]**

⟨-o⟩ tsu⌉yoku hi⌈ppa⌉ru ⟨〜を⟩強く引っ張る ① [to pull hard on s.t./s.o./s.a. ⟨s⟩]

EX. Someone was tugging at my shirt from behind. When I turned around, it was my little brother.
だれかが後ろから私のシャツを強く引っ張ったので、振り返ってみると、弟だった。
Dare-ka ga ushiro kara watashi no shatsu o tsuyoku hippatta node, furi-kaette miru to, otooto datta.

—— n. **[a hard pull]**

tsu⌉yoku hi⌈ppa⌉ru koto 強く引っ張ること [an act of pulling hard on s.t./s.o./s.a.]

PHRASE: tug of war *tsuna-hiki* 綱引き

tumble vi. **[to fall in a helpless or clumsy way or to roll over and over or back and forth]**

1. ko⌈rogaru 転がる ① [to move along a surface by turning over and over or for s.t./s.o./s.a. standing to fall over] ⟪**roll over, fall, lie down**⟫

EX. I tumbled down the icy slope.
凍った坂道を転がり落ちた。
Kootta saka-michi o korogari-ochita.

PHRASE: tumble over *taoreru* 倒れる ② ⟪fall down⟫

EX. The wall tumbled over in the earthquake.
地震で塀が倒れた。
Jishin de hei ga taoreta.

2. chu⌈uga⌉eri o suru 宙返りをする ③ [for s.o./s.a. to do a somersault]

EX. The gymnast tumbled three times on the mat.
体操選手がマットの上で三回宙返りをした。
Taisoo-senshu ga matto no ue de san-kai chuugaeri o shita.

tuna n.

ma⌈guro まぐろ

EX. Tuna is the fish most commonly used in making *sushi.*
まぐろはすしに一番よく使われる魚だ。
Maguro wa sushi ni ichiban yoku tsukawa-reru sakana da.

tundra n. **[a treeless plain found in arctic or subarctic regions]**

tsu⌈ndora ツンドラ •f

tune n. **[a series of musical tones, esp. one which is pleasing or easily remembered; the correct pitch]**
kyo⌉ku 曲 •c [the state of being crooked or curved《fig. "fun," "a piece of music"》]《piece of music, melody, air, interest》, fu⌈shi⌉ 節 [a node or a node-like object《fig. "melody"》]《joint, node, lump, air, melody, point》

EX. Can you name this tune?
この{曲/節}が分かる?
Kono {kyoku/fushi} ga wakaru?

PHRASE: be out of tune *chooshi-{hazure/ppazure}* 調子{はずれ/っぱずれ}

EX. John's singing is always out of tune.
ジョンの歌はいつも調子{はずれ/っぱずれ}だ。
Jon no uta wa itsu-mo chooshi-{hazure/ppazure} da.

— vt. **[for s.o. to adjust a musical instrument to the correct pitch or to set a radio, TV, etc. to receive transmissions of a certain wavelength]**
⟨-no⟩ cho⌉oshi o awase⌉ru ⟨〜の⟩調子を合わせる ②

EX. I love the sound of an orchestra tuning its instruments right before a concert starts.
私はオーケストラが演奏直前に楽器の調子を合わせているのを聞くのが好きだ。
Watashi wa ookesutora ga ensoo-chokuzen ni gakki no chooshi o awasete iru no o kiku no ga suki da.

PHRASE: tune in ⟨-ni⟩ *daiyaru o awaseru* ⟨〜に⟩ダイヤルを合わせる ②

EX. I always tune in to the local classical station when I'm at home.
私はうちにいる時いつも地元のクラシック音楽のラジオ局にダイヤルを合わせている。
Watashi wa uchi ni iru toki itsu-mo jimoto no kurashikku-ongaku no rajio-kyoku ni daiyaru o awasete iru.

tunnel n. **[a passage built underground, under a body of water, or through a hill, etc.]**
1. to⌈nneru トンネル •f [a horizontal passage built underground, under a body of water, or through a hill, etc.]

EX. Everything suddenly became dark as the train entered the tunnel.
汽車がトンネルに入ると急に辺りが暗くなった。
Kisha ga tonneru ni hairu to kyuuni atari ga kuraku natta.

2. chi⌈ka⌉-doo 地下道 •c [an underground passageway]《underpass》

EX. Tunnels connect the buildings on campus so you don't have to go out into the cold during the winter.
冬の寒い時に外に出なくてもいいようにキャンパスの建物が地下道でつながっている。
Fuyu no samui toki ni soto ni denakute mo ii yooni kyanpasu no tatemono ga chika-doo de tsunagatte iru.

3. ko⌈odoo 坑道 •c [a mine shaft]《a mine level》

Turk n.
To⌈ruko⌉-jin トルコ人 •f+c

turkey n.
shi⌈chimen-choo 七面鳥 •c

EX. Americans traditionally eat turkey on Thanksgiving Day.
アメリカには感謝祭の日に七面鳥を食べる伝統がある。
Amerika ni wa kansha-sai no hi ni shichimen-choo o taberu dentoo ga aru.

Turkey n.
To⌉ruko トルコ •f

turn vt. **[to cause s.t./s.o./s.a. to move in a circular motion, change direction or position so as to face a different way, or change to a new state]**
1. ⟨-o⟩ ma⌈wasu ⟨〜を⟩回す ① [for s.o. to cause s.o./s.t./s.a. to move in a circular motion《fig. "send round," "forward"》]《revolve, spin, wheel, send around, forward》, ⟨-o⟩ ka⌈iten-saseru ⟨〜を⟩回転させる /⟨causative of *kaiten-suru* ③ revolve/ ②

EX. (a) In the TV game show *Wheel of Fortune* the contestants turn a wheel to determine

T

how much money they will play for.
『運命の輪』というテレビのゲーム番組では出場者は輪を{回して/回転させて}いくらかけて勝負するかを決める。
"Unmei no wa" to iu terebi no geemu-bangumi de wa shutsujoo-sha wa wa o {mawashite/kaiten-sasete} ikura kakete shoobu-suru ka o kimeru.
(**b**) Should I turn the key clock-wise?
かぎは時計回りに{回せば/?回転させれば}いいんですか。
Kagi wa tokei-mawari ni {mawaseba/ ?kaiten-sasereba} ii n desu ka.

2. ⟨**-o**⟩ **hi⌈kkuri-ka⌉esu** ⟨〜を⟩ひっくり返す ① **[for s.o. to reverse the orientation of s.t. up vs. down or front vs. back; to cause s.t. standing to fall over forcefully; to cause s.t. thought to be certain or firm to become uncertain or changeable]** ⟪**upset, overturn, tip over**⟫, ⟨**-o**⟩ **me⌈kuru** ⟨〜を⟩めくる ② **[for s.o. to use a rolling, peeling motion to cause a different side of s.t. thin and flat such as paper to face up]**

EX. (**a**) Watch out or you're going to turn the boat over.
ボートを{ひっくり返さない/*めくらない}ように気をつけろ。
*Booto o {hikkuri-kaesanai/*mekuranai} yooni ki o tsukero.*
(**b**) Please turn the page when you're ready.
用意ができたらページを{めくって/*ひっくり返して}ください。
*Yooi ga dekitara peeji o {mekutte/ *hikkuri-kaeshite} kudasai.*

3. ⟨**-o**⟩ ⟨**-ni**⟩ **mu⌈keru** ⟨〜を⟩⟨〜に⟩向ける ② **[for s.o. to aim s.t. in a certain direction ⟪fig. "use s.t. for a certain purpose"⟫]** ⟪**face, direct, train, apply**⟫

EX. Turn your face towards me, please.
顔を私の方に向けてください。
Kao o watashi no hoo ni mukete kudasai.

4. ⟨**-o**⟩ ⟨**-ni**⟩ **ka⌈eru** ⟨〜を⟩⟨〜に⟩かえる ② **[for s.o. to cause s.t./s.o./s.a. to become s.t. else]** ⟪**change, alter, vary, renew, replace**⟫
㊐ "replace"▷代える, "exchange"▷換える, otherwise ▷変える

EX. Do you know the story of how Christ turned water into wine?
キリストが水をぶどう酒に変えたという話を知っていますか。
Kirisuto ga mizu o budoo-shu ni kaeta to iu hanashi o shitte imasu ka.

5. ⟨**-o**⟩ (⟨**-ni**⟩) {**ya⌈ku⌉su/ya⌈kusu⌉ru**} ⟨〜を⟩(⟨〜に⟩){訳す ①/訳する} **[for s.o. to change s.t. into one's own or another language]** ⟪**translate, render**⟫, ⟨**-o**⟩ (⟨**-ni**⟩) **ho⌈n'yaku-suru** ⟨〜を⟩(⟨〜に⟩)翻訳する ③ **[for s.o. to change s.t. written in one language into another language]** ⟪**translate, render, put**⟫

NOTE: *Yakusuru* is exceptional in that it can be used only in the informal nonpast form. *Yakusu* is used for other conjugated forms.

EX. I'm having a hard time turning this long Japanese sentence into smooth English.
この長文の日本語を英語らしい英語に{訳す/訳する/翻訳する}のに苦労している。
Kono choobun no Nihon-go o eigo rashii eigo ni {yakusu/yakusuru/ hon'yaku-suru} no ni kuroo-shite iru.

— vi. **[to move in a circular motion; to change direction or position so as to face a different way; to change to a new state]**

1. ma⌈waru 回る ① **[to move in a circular motion]** ⟪**go round, rotate, travel about**⟫

EX. I tried it several times, but the key wouldn't turn.
数回やってみたが、かぎは回らなかった。
Suu-kai yatte mita ga, kagi wa mawaranakatta.

2. fu⌈ri-mu⌉ku 振り向く ① **[for s.o./s.a. to look back]** ⟪**face about**⟫

EX. I called her name, but Dorothy didn't turn around.
名前を呼んだのに、ドロシーは振り向かなかった。
Namae o yonda noni, Doroshii wa furi-mukanakatta.

3. {**adj(*i*). *ku*/adj(*na*). *ni*/⟨-ni⟩**} **na⌉ru** {**adj(*i*). *ku*/adj(*na*). *ni*/**⟨〜に⟩}なる ① **[to change**

T

into] ⟪become, get, make, grow, go, change to⟫

EX. (a) My father turned 85 last month.
父は先月八十五になりました。
Chichi wa sengetsu hachi-juu-go ni narimashita.
(b) Wait till the signal turns green.
信号が青になるまで待ちなさい。
Shingoo ga ao ni naru made machinasai.
(c) My friend suddenly turned pale.
友だちの顔が急に青くなった。
Tomodachi no kao ga kyuuni aoku natta.

PHRASE: turn off ⟨-o⟩ *kesu* ⟨〜を⟩消す ①

EX. Turn off the light before going to sleep, OK?
寝る前に電気を消すんだよ。
Neru mae ni denki o kesu n da yo.

PHRASE: turn in ⟨-o⟩ *dasu* ⟨〜を⟩出す ①

EX. I forgot to turn in my homework today.
今日は宿題を出すのを忘れた。
Kyoo wa shukudai o dasu no o wasureta.

PHRASE: turn on ⟨-o⟩ *tsukeru* ⟨〜を⟩つける ②

EX. Could you turn on the TV, please?
テレビをつけてくれませんか。
Terebi o tsukete kuremasen ka.

PHRASE: be turned upside down *hikkuri-kaeru* ひっくり返る ① ⟪be upset, be overturned, tip over⟫

EX. Due to a printer's error, all the figures in the article were turned upside down.
印刷屋の間違いで論文の中の図が全部ひっくり返っていた。
Insatsu-ya no machigai de ronbun no naka no zu ga zenbu hikkuri-kaette ita.

—— n. [a circular motion; a change in position, direction, or state; a time or opportunity which comes to one in a fixed order relative to others]

1. ka⌈iten 回転 •c [a rotating motion, esp. that of one complete orbit]

EX. The gymnast executed a beautiful turn on the bar.
体操選手は鉄棒ですばらしい回転をやった。
Taisoo-senshu wa tetsuboo de subarashii kaiten o yatta.

2. ho⌈okoo-te⌉nkan 方向転換 •c [a change in direction]

EX. Our bus made a sudden turn to the left at the intersection.
乗っていたバスが交差点で急に左に方向転換をした。
Notte ita basu ga koosa-ten de kyuuni hidari ni hookoo-tenkan o shita.

3. he⌉nka 変化 •c [the coming into being of a different quality or state in s.t. as it moves through space or time] ⟪change, variation, alteration⟫

EX. During my mid forties, my life took an interesting turn for the better.
四十の半ばで人生が好転するという面白い変化が訪れた。
Yon-juu no nakaba de jinsei ga kooten-suru to iu omoshiroi henka ga otozureta.

4. ba⌉n 番 [watching out for s.t. or a fixed order in which s.t. occurs or a counter for ordinal numbers]

EX. It's my turn to wash the dishes.
皿を洗うのは僕の番だ。
Sara o arau no wa boku no ban da.

turnip n.
ka⌈bu かぶ

turtle n.
ka⌉me かめ, u⌈mi-game 海がめ [a turtle living in the ocean]

tusk n.
ki⌉ba きば

EX. The elephant has two long tusks.
象には長いきばが二本ある。
Zoo ni wa nagai kiba ga ni-hon aru.

TV n.
te⌉rebi テレビ •f

EX. My children watch TV three to four hours a day.
うちの子供たちはテレビを一日に三、四時間見ます。
Uchi no kodomo-tachi wa terebi o ichi-nichi ni san, yo-jikan mimasu.

twelve n./adj.
ju⌈u-ni (+counter) (no N) 十二(+counter)

T

(のN) •c SEE APPENDIX II

twentieth n./adj.
(da˥i-)ni˩-juu-ban-me˥ (no N) (第)二十番目(のN) •c SEE APPENDIX II

twenty n./adj.
ni˥-juu (+counter) (no N) 二十(+counter)(のN) •c, **ha˥tachi (no N)** 二十(歳)(のN) **[having an age in years which is one more than nineteen]** SEE APPENDIX II

EX. (**a**) A: What time is it now?
今何時ですか。
Ima nan-ji desu ka.
B: It's twenty past eight.
八時二十分(すぎ)です。
Hachi-ji nijup-pun (sugi) desu.
(**b**) A: How old are you?
おいくつですか。
O-ikutsu desu ka.
B: I'm twenty.
二十(歳)です。
Hatachi desu.

twice adv. **[two times]**
ni-˩do 二度 •c **[two times, implying no cycle], ni-˩kai** 二回 •c **[two times, esp. as part of a cycle], ni-˩bai** 二倍 •c **[two times as large in quantity]**

EX. (**a**) I've been to New York twice this year.
今年私はニューヨークへ{二度/二回/*二倍}行っています。
*Kotoshi watashi wa Nyuuyooku e {ni-do/ni-kai/*ni-bai} itte imasu.*
(**b**) The mailman comes around twice a day in this neighborhood.
郵便配達員はこの辺は一日に{二回/二度/*二倍}回って来る。
*Yuubin-haitatsu-in wa kono hen wa ichi-nichi ni {ni-kai/ni-do/*ni-bai} mawatte kuru.*
(**c**) Houses cost twice as much as they did ten years ago.
家は十年前の{二倍/*二度/*二回}する。
*Ie wa juu-nen mae no {ni-bai/*ni-do/*ni-kai} suru.*

twig n. **[a small branch]**
ko-˩eda 小枝

EX. Look, there's a nightingale singing on a twig in that plum tree.
ほら、あそこの梅の小枝でうぐいすが鳴いているよ。
Hora, asoko no ume no ko-eda de uguisu ga naite iru yo.

twilight n. **[(the time of) hazy light occurring just before sunrise or just after sunset, esp. the latter《fig. "a state not clearly defined," "a period of decline"》]**
ta˩sogare(-doki) たそがれ(時) **[the time of hazy light just after sunset《fig. "period of decline"》]**

EX. (**a**) It's best to turn on your car headlights well before twilight.
たそがれ時にならないうちに車のヘッドライトをつけた方がいい。
Tasogare-doki ni naranai uchi ni kuruma no heddo-raito o tsuketa hoo ga ii.
(**b**) When I turned seventy, I suddenly realized I was in the twilight of my life.
七十になった時、自分が人生のたそがれに入ったことに急に気づいた。
Nana-juu ni natta toki, jibun ga jinsei no tasogare ni haitta koto ni kyuuni ki-zuita.

twin n. **[one of two children born to the same mother at the same time or one of two things that are identical]**
1. fu˩ta-go 双子 **[one of two children born to the same mother at the same time]**

EX. My sister and I are twins.
私と{妹/姉}は双子です。
Watashi to {imooto/ane} wa futa-go desu.

2. tsu˩i no hi˩to˥tsu 対の一つ **[one of two things that belong together]**

— adj. **[being one of two or a pair of children born to the same mother at the same time or being one of two or a pair of things that are identical]**
1. fu˩ta-go no N 双子のN **[being one of two or a pair of children born to the same mother at the same time]**

EX. I have a pair of twin brothers and a pair of twin sisters.

私には双子の兄弟と双子の姉妹があります。
Watashi ni wa futa-go no kyoodai to futa-go no shimai ga arimasu.

2. tsu⌈i no N 対のN [being one of two or a pair of things that belong together]

EX. These are twin cups.
これは対のコップです。
Kore wa tsui no koppu desu.

PHRASE: twin bed *tsuin(-beddo)* ツイン(ベッド) •f

twinkle vi. **[to shine with a flickering light]** **ki⌉ra-kira (to) hi⌈ka⌉ru きらきら(と)光る ① [to shine with a flickering cold, piercing light], pi⌉ka-pika (to) hi⌈ka⌉ru ぴかぴか(と)光る ① [to shine with light/luster]**

EX. Look at the stars twinkling in the sky.
見てご覧。空に星が{きらきら/ぴかぴか}光っているよ。
Mite go-ran. Sora ni hoshi ga {kira-kira/pika-pika} hikatte iru yo.

twist vt. **[for s.o. to wind strand-like objects around each other 《fig. "contort," "distort the meaning of s.t."》]**

1. ⟨-o⟩ yo⌈ru ⟨〜を⟩よる ① [for s.o. to wind strand-like objects around each other to form a single cord] 《twine, entwist》, ⟨-o⟩ ⟨-ni⟩ ma⌈ki-tsuke⌉ru ⟨〜を⟩⟨〜に⟩巻き付ける ② [for s.o. to coil s.t. around s.t. else] 《wind, coil》, ⟨-o⟩ ne⌈ji⌉ru ⟨〜を⟩ねじる ② [for s.o. to apply a rotating force to s.t. straight and narrow which is fixed at one end so that it turns or to turn the opposite ends of s.t. straight and narrow in opposite directions] 《wrench, screw, wring》, ⟨-o⟩ yo⌈ji⌉ru ⟨〜を⟩よじる ① [for s.o. to apply a rotating force to s.t. so as to bend it or change the direction in which it faces] 《wrench, screw, wring》

EX. (**a**) My father used to twist straw together to make rope.
父は昔わらを{よって/*巻き付けて/*ねじって/*よじって}縄を作った。
*Chichi wa mukashi wara o {yotte/*maki-tsukete/*nejitte/*yojitte} nawa o tsukutta.*
(**b**) A policeman caught the young man and twisted his arm behind his back.
警官は青年を捕まえて、腕をうしろに{よじった/ねじった/*よった/*巻き付けた}。
*Keikan wa seinen o tsukamaete, ude o ushiro ni {yojitta/nejitta/*yotta/*maki-tsuketa}.*
(**c**) I somehow twisted my ankle when I came out of the pool.
私はプールから出る時に、どうしてか足首を{よじって/ねじって/*よって/*巻き付けて}しまった。
*Watashi wa puuru kara deru toki ni, dooshite-ka ashi-kubi o {yojitte/nejitte/*yotte/*maki-tsukete} shimatta.*
(**d**) She has a habit of twisting her hair around her finger.
彼女は指に髪の毛を{巻き付ける/*よる/*ねじる/*よじる}くせがある。
*Kanojo wa yubi ni kami no ke o {maki-tsukeru/*yoru/*nejiru/*yojiru} kuse ga aru.*

2. ⟨⟨-de⟩⟩ ⟨-o⟩ yu⌈gameru ⟨⟨〜で⟩⟩⟨〜を⟩ゆがめる ② [to apply force to s.t. so that it loses its original shape 《fig. "distort the facts"》] 《distort, contort, warp》

EX. He twisted his face in pain.
彼は苦痛で顔をゆがめた。
Kare wa kutsuu de kao o yugameta.

— vi. **[for strand-like objects to become wound around each other]**
⟨-ni⟩ ma⌈ki-tsu⌉ku ⟨〜に⟩巻き付く ① [for s.t. to become coiled around s.t. else] 《coil, twine》, ne⌈jire⌉ru ねじれる ② [for s.t. straight and narrow which is fixed at one end to turn under the application of force or for the opposite ends of s.t. straight and narrow to turn in opposite directions under the application of force] 《grow warped, be distorted》, yo⌈jire⌉ru よじれる ② [for s.t. to bend or change in direction under the application of a rotating force] 《grow warped, become distorted》

EX. (**a**) My ankle seems to have twisted when I fell down.
倒れた時、足首が{よじれた/ねじれた/*巻き付いた}らしい。

*Taoreta toki, ashi-kubi ga {yojireta/nejireta/*maki-tsuita} rashii.*
(**b**) Ivy twisted around the trunk of the old tree.
つたが古い木の幹に{巻き付いて/*ねじれて/*よじれて}いた。
*Tsuta ga furui ki no miki ni {maki-tsuite/*nejirete/*yojirete} ita.*

two n./adj.
fu˹tatsu (+counter) (no N) 二つ(+counter)(のN), **ni˺ (+counter) (no N)** 二(+counter)(のN) •c SEE APPENDIX II

type n. **[a class of things, people, or animals sharing certain distinguishing characteristics; a rectangular block or collection of blocks of metal with raised letters or numbers used in printing]**
1. ka˹ta˺ 型 **[an outward form (to be followed) ⟪fig. "mold"⟫], shu˺rui** 種類 •c **[a group of individuals sharing common characteristics] ⟪kind, sort, variety⟫, ta˺ipu** タイプ •f **[an individual exhibiting the characteristics unique to a particular group or class; a typewriter]**
EX. This is a new type of hybrid car with a battery that doesn't require recharging.
この車は充電の要らない新しい{タイプ/型/種類}のハイブリッドカーです。
Kono kuruma wa juuden no iranai atarashii {taipu/kata/shurui} no haiburiddo-kaa desu.
2. ka˹tsuji 活字 •c **[a rectangular block of metal with raised letters or numbers used in printing]**
— vi. **[to write using a typewriter]**
ta˹ipu(ra˺itaa) o u˺tsu タイプ(ライター)を打つ ①
— vt. **[to write s.t. using a typewriter]**
ta˹ipu(ra˺itaa) de u˺tsu タイプ(ライター)で打つ ①

typewriter n.
ta˹ipu(ra˺itaa) タイプ(ライター) •f
EX. Once you have used a word processor, you never feel like using a typewriter again.
一度ワープロを使うと、もうタイプ(ライター)を使いたいとは思いません。
Ichi-do waapuro o tsukau to, moo taipu(raitaa) o tsukai-tai to wa omoimasen.

typhoon n. **[a violent cyclone that forms in the Southern Pacific and moves north, esp. in September and October]**
ta˹ifu˺u 台風 •c
EX. According to the radio, the typhoon is expected to land in Kyushu early tomorrow morning.
ラジオによると、あしたの朝早く、台風が九州に上陸するそうです。
Rajio ni yoru to, ashita no asa hayaku, taifuu ga Kyuushuu ni jooriku-suru soodesu.

typical adj. **[exhibiting characteristics normal for one or common to the members of a particular group]**
1. te˹nkei-tekina 典型的な adj(*na*). •c **[having the characteristics distinct to a particular group of people, things, or animals] ⟪representative, model, ideal⟫**
EX. He's a typical Tokyoite.
あの人は典型的な江戸っ子です。
Ano hito wa tenkei-tekina Edok-ko desu.
2. to˹kuchoo-tekina 特徴的な adj(*na*). •c **[characteristic of s.t./s.o./s.a.] ⟪characteristic, distinctive⟫**
EX. Claudia has a temperament typical of the Harrison family.
クローディアはハリソン家に特徴的な気質を有している。
Kuroodia wa Harison-ke ni tokuchoo-tekina kishitsu o yuushite iru.

U

ugly adj. **[unpleasant, esp. to see or hear]**

1. mi⌈niku⌉i 醜い adj(*i*). **[difficult to look at due to being hideous or repulsive]** **《unlovely, unattractive, unsightly, indecent, disgraceful》**

EX. I had an ugly mole on my nose removed by the doctor.
鼻にある醜いほくろを医者にとってもらった。
Hana ni aru minikui hokuro o isha ni totte moratta.

2. fu-⌈yu⌉kaina 不愉快な adj(*na*). **•c [causing a disagreeable feeling] 《unpleasant, uncomfortable, disagreeable》** ↔ **yukaina** 愉快な adj(*na*). **•c**

EX. The quarrel at the last committee meeting left an ugly taste in everyone's mouth.
この間の委員会での口論はみんなを不愉快にさせた。
Kono aida no iin-kai de no kooron wa minna o fu-yukaini saseta.

ukulele n.

u⌈kurere ウクレレ **•f**

EX. People in Hawaii love to play the ukulele.
ハワイの人はウクレレをひくのが好きだ。
Hawai no hito wa ukurere o hiku no ga suki da.

ultimate adj. **[the very last 《fig. "eventual," "fundamental"》]**

1. sa⌈ishuu-tekina 最終的な **•c [the very last or final]**

EX. The ultimate objective of this research is to shed light on the interrelationship of elementary particles.
この研究の最終的な目標は素粒子間の関係に光を当てることだ。
Kono kenkyuu no saishuu-tekina mokuhyoo wa soryuushi-kan no kankei ni hikari o ateru koto da.

2. kyu⌈ukyoku no N 究極のN **•c [being or located at the farthest point to be reached] 《final, extreme》**

EX. The ultimate goal of our movement is totally abolish nuclear experiments.
核実験の全面的な廃止が我々の運動の究極の目標だ。
Kaku-jikken no zenmen-tekina haishi ga ware-ware no undoo no kyuukyoku no mokuhyoo da.

3. ko⌈npon-tekina 根本的な **•c [having to do with the basic and most important part of s.t.] 《basic, cardinal, radical》**

EX. The ultimate cause of John and Mary's divorce was an irreconcilable personality conflict.
ジョンとメアリーの離婚の根本的な原因はそりの合わない二人の性格の不一致だった。
Jon to Mearii no rikon no konpon-tekina gen'in wa sori no awanai futari no seikaku no fu-itchi datta.

umbrella n. **[a circular piece of fabric mounted on a metal frame which can be folded up so as to be carried about, used as a protection against rain 《fig. "a protecting force serving as a shield against attack from above"》]**

ka⌉sa 傘 **[a circular piece of paper or fabric mounted on a metal or wooden frame which can be folded up so as to be carried about, used as a protection against rain], a⌈ma-ga⌉sa** 雨傘

EX. (**a**) Be careful not to hit anyone when you open your umbrella.
{傘/雨傘}を広げる時は人に当たらないように気を付けなさいよ。
{Kasa/Ama-gasa} o hirogeru toki wa

hito ni ataranai yooni ki-o-tsukenasai yo.
(**b**) It's started to rain. You'd better get out your umbrella.
雨が降り始めましたよ。{傘/雨傘}を出したほうがいいですよ。
Ame ga furi-hajimemashita yo. {Kasa/Ama-gasa} o dashita hoo ga ii desu yo.
(**c**) The so-called "nuclear umbrella" cannot really guarantee world peace.
いわゆる「核の傘」は本当に世界平和を保証することは出来ない。
Iwayuru 'kaku no kasa' wa hontoo ni sekai-heiwa o hoshoo-suru koto wa dekinai.

unable adj. **[lacking the power to do s.t.]**
de⌈ki⌉nai 出来ない /⟨Vstem of *dekiru* ② can + *nai* not/ [be not capable of doing s.t.] ⟪cannot⟫, Vstem of pot. + nai Vstem of pot.+ない

EX. (**a**) A: Were you able to speak Japanese at the time you first went to Japan?
初めて日本へ行った時日本語が話せましたか。
Hajimete Nihon e itta toki Nihon-go ga hanase-mashita ka.
B: No, I was still unable to at the time.
いいえ、そのころはまだ{出来ませんでした/話せませんでした}。
Iie, sono koro wa mada {dekimasen deshita/hanase-masen deshita}.
(**b**) When I asked if he was coming to the meeting, he said he was unable to due to a prior engagement.
その会に出るかと彼に聞いたら、先約があって{出られない/?出来ない}と言った。
Sono kai ni deru ka to kare ni kiitara, sen'yaku ga atte {de-rarenai/?dekinai} to itta.

unaware adj. **[not realizing or knowing s.t.]**
⟨-ni⟩ ki-⌈ga-tsuka⌉nai ⟨〜に⟩気がつかない /⟨Vneg. of *ki-ga-tsuku* ① notice + *nai* not/ [not notice s.t.]

EX. I was unaware of my illness until this last April.
私はこの四月まで自分の病気に気がつかなかった。
Watashi wa kono shi-gatsu made jibun no byooki ni ki-ga-tsukanakatta.

unbelievable adj. **[difficult to believe, amazing]**
shi⌈nji-rare⌉nai 信じられない /⟨Vstem of pot. of *shinjiru* ② believe + *nai* not/

EX. (**a**) My uncle had some unbelievable experiences as a soldier in World War II.
叔父は第二次世界大戦中に兵隊として信じられないような体験をしている。
Oji wa dai-ni-ji-sekai-taisen-chuu ni heitai to-shite shinji-rarenai yoona taiken o shite iru.
(**b**) I got 100 on my math test. Unbelievable, isn't it?
数学のテストで百点を取ったんだ。信じられないだろう?
Suugaku no tesuto de hyaku-ten o totta n da. Shinji-rarenai daroo?

unbroken adj. **[not broken, surpassed, or interrupted]**
1. ya⌈bura⌉-rete inai (N) 破られていない(N) /⟨neg. of V*te iru* of the passive of *yaburu* ① break/ [existing unsurpassed or unviolated]

EX. His world record remains unbroken.
彼の世界記録はまだ破られていません。
Kare no sekai-kiroku wa mada yabura-rete imasen.

2. ko⌈wa⌉rete inai (N) 壊れていない(N) /⟨neg. of V*te iru* of *kowareru* ② be broken/ [not physically broken]

EX. The porcelain my mother sent me by airmail arrived unbroken.
航空便で母が送ってくれた磁器は壊れていなかった。
Kookuu-bin de haha ga okutte kureta jiki wa kowarete inakatta.

3. bu⌈ttsuzuke no N ぶっ続けのN [continuing without a break] ⟪continuous, nonstop⟫, bu⌈ttooshi no N ぶっ通しのN [continuing without a break from beginning to end] ⟪continuous, nonstop⟫

EX. We've had three weeks of unbroken fine weather.

三週間{ぶっ通し/ぶっ続け}の好天だった。
San-shuukan {buttooshi/buttsuzuke} no kooten datta.

4. **ku⌈jikena⌉i** くじけない adj(*i*). •c **[unyielding/untiring]** ⟪**indomitable**⟫

EX. Even after that horrible car accident Peter's spirits remained unbroken.
あの恐ろしい自動車事後の後でもピーターは心がくじけなかった。
Ano osoroshii jidoosha-jiko no ato de mo Piitaa wa kokoro ga kujikenakatta.

uncertain adj. **[not known for sure or not to be depended on]**

1. **ha⌈kki⌉ri-shi⌈te inai (N)** はっきりしていない(N) /⟨neg.of V*te iru* of *hakkiri suru* ③ become clear/distinct/ **[not clear or distinct]**

EX. (**a**) The date of our departure for India is still uncertain.
私たちがインドへいつ出発するかはまだはっきりしていません。
Watashi-tachi ga Indo e itsu shuppatsu-suru ka wa mada hakkiri-shite imasen.
(**b**) A: What do you plan to major in?
何を専攻するつもりですか。
Nani o senkoo-suru tsumori desu ka.
B: I'm still uncertain.
まだはっきりしていないんです。
Mada hakkiri-shite inai n desu.

2. **a⌈te ni nara⌉nai (N)** 当てにならない(N) /⟨Vstem of *ate ni naru* ① depend + *nai* not/ **[unable to be depended on]** ⟪**unreliable, undependable, shaky**⟫

EX. A politician's campaign pledges always remain uncertain.
政治家の公約はいつも当てにならない。
Seiji-ka no kooyaku wa itsu-mo ate ni naranai.

uncle n. **[the brother or brother-in-law of one's father or mother ⟪fig. "a term of address used by a child toward an unrelated male adult friend"⟫]**

o⌈ji おじ **[the brother or brother-in-law of one's father or mother], o⌈ji-san** おじさん **[the brother or brother-in-law of s.o. else's father or mother; a form used in addressing the brother or brother-in-law of one's father or mother or a form used by children in addressing any male adult]**

㊥ "older brother or brother-in-law of a parent" ▷伯父, "younger brother or brother-in-law of a parent"▷叔父, "older male person"▷小父

EX. (**a**) A: What does your uncle do?
叔父さんは何をしていらっしゃいますか。
Oji-san wa nani o shite irasshaimasu ka.
B: He's a lawyer.
叔父は弁護士をしております。
Oji wa bengo-shi o shite orimasu.
(**b**) Will you take me to the zoo today, uncle?
叔父さん、今日動物園に連れて行ってくれる?
Oji-san kyoo doobutsu-en ni tsurete-itte kureru?
(**c**) Uncle George was a frequent guest at our home.
ジョージ小父さんは家によく出入りしていました。
Jooji oji-san wa uchi ni yoku de-iri shite imashita.

uncomfortable adj. **[causing or feeling discomfort]**

fu-⌈yu⌉kaina 不愉快な adj(*na*). •c **[causing a disagreeable feeling]** ↔ **yukaina** 愉快な adj(*na*). •c; **V*masu* gokochi ga yo⌈kuna⌉i (N) V*masu*心地がよくない(N) [not creating a good sensation when some action is taken involving it]** ↔ **V*masu* gokochi ga ii (N) V*masu*心地がいい(N)**

EX. (**a**) A: How does the dress feel?
そのドレスはどう?
Sono doresu wa doo?
B: It's a little uncomfortable.
ちょっと{着心地がよくない/*不愉快だ}わ。
*Chotto {ki-gokochi ga yokunai/*fu-yukai da} wa.*
(**b**) This chair is really uncomfortable.
このいすは全然{座り心地がよくない/*不愉快だ}。

U

*Kono isu wa zenzen {suwari-gokochi ga yokunai/*fu-yukai da}.*
(c) I get uncomfortable in front of him.
あの人の前にいると{不愉快に/*居心地がよくなく}なるんです。
*Ano hito no mae ni iru to {fu-yukai ni/ *i-gokochi ga yokunaku} naru n desu.*

unconditional adj. **[having no conditions or limitations attached]**
mu-⌈jo⌉oken no N 無条件のN •c **⟪unqualified, categorical, without condition⟫**

EX. Japan agreed to unconditional surrender in 1945.
日本は1945年に無条件(の)降伏を受け入れた。
Nihon wa sen-kyuu-hyaku-yon-juu-go-nen ni mu-jooken (no) koofuku o uke-ireta.

unconscious adj. **[not knowing s.t. or not done intentionally or not in a state of mental awareness of one's surroundings]**
1. ⟨-ni⟩ ki-⌈ga-tsu⌉ite i⌈nai (N) ⟨〜に⟩気がついていない(N) **/⟨neg. of V*te iru* of *ki ga tsuku* ① notice/ [not aware of s.t.] ⟪unaware, inattentive⟫**

EX. That man is unconscious of his own arrogance.
その人は自分の横柄さに気がついていない。
Sono hito wa jibun no oohei-sa ni ki-ga-tsuite inai.

2. mu-⌈i⌉shiki no N 無意識のN •c **[lacking intent or awareness] ⟪involuntary, spontaneous⟫**

EX. According to psychoanalytic theory, much of our behavior is governed by unconscious impulses.
精神分析の理論によると、我々の行動の多くは無意識の衝動によって支配されているという。
Seishin-bunseki no riron ni-yoru to, ware-ware no koodoo no ooku wa mu-ishiki no shoodoo ni-yotte shihai-sarete iru to iu.

3. i⌉shiki-fu⌈mei no N 意識不明のN •c **[not in a state of mental awareness of one's surroundings] ⟪senseless, in a coma⟫**

EX. After the stroke my grandfather was unconscious for three days in the hospital.
祖父は卒中の後三日間病院で意識不明だった。
Sofu wa sotchuu no ato mikka-kan byooin de ishiki-fumei datta.

uncovered adj. **[having no cover or not eligible for reimbursement according to the terms of an insurance contract]**
1. o⌈oi no na⌉i (N) 覆いのない(N) **[having no cover]**
2. (ho⌈ken ga) ki⌈kanai N (保険が)きかないN **[not eligible for reimbursement (according to the terms of an insurance contract)]**

under prep. **[to/at/in a place or position lower than s.t./s.o./s.a.; less than some amount; supervised or controlled by s.o.]**
1. ⟨-no⟩ shi⌈ta ({ni/de/o}) ⟨〜の⟩下({に/で/を}) n.+prt. **[to/at/along a place or position lower than s.t./s.o./s.a.; supervised or controlled by s.o.] ↔ ⟨-no⟩ ue ({ni/de/o})** ⟨〜の⟩上({に/で/を}) n.+prt.

EX. (a) A: Have you seen my camera?
僕のカメラ、知りませんか。
Boku no kamera, shirimasen ka.
B: It's under the table.
机の下ですよ。
Tsukue no shita desu yo.
(b) A dog sat under the tree barking up at a cat in the tree.
犬が木の上にいる猫を見上げながら木の下に座ってほえていた。
Inu ga ki no ue ni iru neko o mi-age-nagara ki no shita ni suwatte hoete ita.
(c) There's a bench under the cherry tree. Let's sit there.
桜の木の下にベンチがある。そこに座ろう。
Sakura no ki no shita ni benchi ga aru. Soko ni suwaroo.
(d) We walked under the cherry trees in full blossom.
満開の桜の下を歩いた。

Mankai no sakura no shita o aruita.

2. ⟨-no⟩ na˥ka ({ni/de/o}) ⟨～の⟩中({に/で/を}) n.+prt. **[to/at/along a point or set of points which are part of a space surrounded by s.t.]** **((inside, interior))**

EX. The duck dived under water and came up two minutes later in a different part of the pond.
あひるは水の中にもぐって二分後に池の別の所に出てきた。
Ahiru wa mizu no naka ni mogutte ni-fun-go ni ike no betsu no tokoro ni dete kita.

3. -ika no N ～以下のN •c **[consisting of or having a quantity lower than s.t.], -miman** ～未満 •c **[not reaching a certain number]** **((below, not more than, less than))**

EX. (**a**) People under 20 are not allowed to drink alcohol.
二十歳{未満/以下}の人は酒を飲んではいけない。
{Ni jus-sai/Hatachi}-{miman/ika} no hito wa sake o nonde wa ikenai.
(**b**) On a scale of 4.0, his grade point average was under 2.0.
彼の成績の平均点は4点満点で2点{以下/?未満}だった。
Kare no seiseki no heikin-ten wa yon-ten-manten de ni-ten-{ika/?miman} datta.
(**c**) It's hard to find a new car anymore for under $15,000.
このごろは一万五千ドル{以下/?未満}の新車はなかなか見つからない。
Kono-goro wa ichi-man-go-sen-doru-{ika/?miman} no shinsha wa nakanaka mitsukaranai.

4. ⟨-no⟩ shi˹ta de ⟨～の⟩下で **[supervised or controlled by s.o.], ⟨-no⟩ mo˹to˥ de** ⟨～の⟩もとで **[guided by an eminent person]**

EX. (**a**) I'd hate to work under a guy like that.
あんな男の{下/?もと}では働きたくない。
Anna otoko no {shita/?moto} de wa hataraki-takunai.
(**b**) I studied under Professor Inoue at Tokyo University.
私は東大で井上教授の{もと/下}で勉強しました。
Watashi wa Toodai de Inoue-Kyooju no {moto/shita} de benkyoo-shimashita.

—— adv. **[to/at/in a place or position lower than s.t./s.o./s.a.]**

1. shi˹ta {ni/e} 下{に/へ} n.+prt. **[to/at a place or position lower than s.t./s.o./s.a.]**

EX. I hear some strange sounds in the boat's engine so I'm going under to check it out.
エンジンの音が変だからボートの下{に/へ}もぐって調べて来る。
Enjin no oto ga hen da kara booto no shita {ni/e} mogutte shirabete kuru.

2. ⟨-no⟩ na˥ka {ni/de/o} ⟨～の⟩中{に/で/を} n.+prt. **[to/at/along a point or set of points which are part of a space surrounded by s.t.]**

EX. The rear portion of the Titanic was the last to go under.
タイタニックの後部が最後に水の中に沈んだ。
Taitanikku no koobu ga saigo ni mizu no naka ni shizunda.

—— adj. **[located at a place or position lower than s.t./s.o./s.a.]**

shi˹ta (no) N 下(の)N **[located at a place or position lower than s.t./s.o./s.a.]**

EX. Most car manufacturers nowadays rust-proof the under side of new cars.
最近はほとんどのメーカーが新車の下側にさび止めの加工をする。
Saikin wa hotondo no meekaa ga shinsha no shita-gawa ni sabi-dome no kakoo o suru.

undergo vt. **[for s.o. to endure or be made to experience some circumstance or event]**

1. ⟨-o⟩ ke˹iken-suru ⟨～を⟩経験する ③ •c **[for s.o. to live through, participate in, or be subjected to some event or activity]** **((experience, go through, taste))**, **⟨-o⟩ u˹ke˥ru** ⟨～を⟩受ける ② **[to allow s.t. to come into one's possession or to be exposed to the effect of some force or action]** **((receive, accept, take, get, obtain, catch, go through, suffer, face, inherit))**

U

EX. (**a**) My father underwent excruciating pain after his back injury.
父は背中にけがをしてひどい苦痛を{経験した/*受けた}。
*Chichi wa senaka ni kega o shite hidoi kutsuu o {keiken-shita/*uketa}.*
(**b**) My older brother is scheduled to undergo an operation tomorrow.
兄はあした手術を{受ける/*経験する}ことになっている。
*Ani wa ashita shujutsu o {ukeru/*keiken-suru} koto ni natte iru.*

2. ⟨-ni⟩ ta⌈e⌉ru ⟨～に⟩耐える ② [for s.o./s.a. to not succumb to pain/pressure/distress] ⟪endure, support, withstand, be equal to⟫

EX. We underwent many hardships during the war.
戦争中私たちは色々な困難に耐えた。
Sensoo-chuu watashi-tachi wa iro-irona konnan ni taeta.

underground adj. **[located below the surface of the earth ⟪fig. "secret"⟫] chi⌈ka⌉ no N 地下のN •c [located below the surface of the earth] ⟪subterranean⟫, hi⌈mitsu no N 秘密のN •c [not publicly known and kept to oneself or people closest to s.o.] ⟪secret, confidential, clandestine, hidden, privy⟫**

EX. (**a**) This underground shopping center is very convenient in the winter time.
この{地下/*秘密}のショッピングセンターは冬とても便利だ。
*Kono {chika/*himitsu} no shoppingu-sentaa wa fuyu totemo benri da.*
(**b**) The police are working to expose an underground crime syndicate.
警察は{地下の/秘密の}犯罪組織をあばこうとしている。
Keisatsu wa {chika no/himitsu no} hanzai-soshiki o abakoo to shite iru.

—— adv. **[to/at a place below the surface of the earth ⟪fig. "secretly"⟫]**

1. chi⌈ka⌉ {ni/de/o} 地下{に/で/を} [to/at/along a place or space below the surface of the earth]

EX. (**a**) My father is a miner who works underground all day long.
父は坑夫で、一日中地下で働いています。
Chichi wa koofu de, ichi-nichi-juu chika de hataraite imasu.
(**b**) A capsule containing poisonous gas had been buried underground.
毒ガスの入ったカプセルが地下に埋めてあった。
Doku-gasu no haitta kapuseru ga chika ni umete atta.

2. ko⌈sso⌉ri to こっそりと [in such a way that no one will notice]

EX. The plan was being devised underground.
計画はこっそりとたてられていた。
Keikaku wa kossori to tate-rarete ita.

underline vt. **[for s.o. to draw a line under s.t. written]**
⟨-ni⟩ ka⌈sen o hiku ⟨～に⟩下線を引く ①

EX. Underline any words you don't understand.
分からない言葉に下線を引きなさい。
Wakaranai kotoba ni kasen o hikinasai.

—— n. **[a line drawn under s.t. written] ka⌈sen 下線 •c**

underneath prep. **[beneath or below s.t. ⟪fig. "hidden beneath s.t.," "subjected to s.o."⟫]**

1. ⟨-no⟩ shi⌈ta ni ⟨～の⟩下に [to/at a place or position lower than s.t./s.o./s.a.]

EX. He wasn't wearing anything underneath his sweater.
彼はセーターの下には何も着ていなかった。
Kare wa seetaa no shita ni wa nani-mo kite inakatta.

2. ⟨-o⟩ hi⌈to⌉-kawa mukeba ⟨～を⟩一皮むけば [if one peels off the skin of s.o.]

EX. She has the devil underneath her angelic face.
彼女は天使のような顔をしているが、一皮むけば悪魔だ。
Kanojo wa tenshi no yoona kao o shite iru ga, hito-kawa mukeba akuma da.

understand vt. **[for s.o./s.a. to grasp in one's mind the meaning, significance, or nature of s.t.; to know very well how to**

U

work with or deal with s.t./s.o./s.a.; to be told or assume some information]

1. ((-**ni**)) ⟨-**ga**⟩ **wa**⌈**ka**⌉**ru** ((〜に))⟨〜が⟩分かる ① **[for s.o. to grasp in one's mind the nature, meaning, identity, etc., of s.t./s.o./s.a.]** ((**see, get, grasp, comprehend, know, realize**))

EX. (**a**) Bill understands a little Japanese.
ビルは日本語が少し分かる。
Biru wa Nihon-go ga sukoshi wakaru.
(**b**) He's always so unreasonable. I just don't understand him.
あの人は無理ばかり言うんだ。私には彼のことがさっぱり分からない。
Ano hito wa muri bakari iu n da. Watashi ni wa kare no koto ga sappari wakaranai.
(**c**) I don't understand girls. One minute they act as if they like you and the next minute they act as if they don't even know you.
女の子は分からないよ。好きだと思わせるようなことをしたかと思うと、次の瞬間には会ったこともないようなふるまいをするんだから。
Onna-no-ko wa wakaranai yo. Suki da to omowa-seru yoona koto o shita ka to omou to, tsugi no shunkan ni wa atta koto mo nai yoona furumai o suru n da kara.
(**d**) I don't have the kind of mind it takes to understand economics.
私は経済が分かるような頭をしていません。
Watashi wa keizai ga wakaru yoona atama o shite imasen.

2. Sinf. n {**de**⌉**su/da**} **ne Sinf.**ん{です/だ}ね **[Am I right in assuming…], Sinf.** ⌈**to**⌉ **iu koto** {**de**⌉**su/da**} **ne Sinf.**ということ{です/だ}ね

NOTE: The nonpast affirmative form of adj(*na*). or N+cop. changes to {adj(*na*)., stem/N} *na* when it occurs before *n {desu/da} ne*.

EX. (**a**) A: I understand that you have plans to go to graduate school.
君は大学院に行く{ん/ということ}だね。
Kimi wa daigaku-in ni iku {n/to iu koto} da ne.
B: Yes, that's right.
ええ、そうです。
Ee, soo desu.
(**b**) Are we to understand that there is no room in the budget for our project?
私たちのプロジェクトの予算はない{ん/ということ}ですね。
Watashi-tachi no purojekuto no yosan wa nai {n/to iu koto} desu ne.
(**c**) I understand that you don't like rock music.
ロックは{きらいなん/きらいだということ}ですね。
Rokku wa {kiraina n/kirai da to iu koto} desu ne.

understanding n. **[the act of grasping the meaning, significance, or nature of s.t. or the ability to do this; an opinion or belief one has about s.t.; sympathy for, agreement with, or tolerance of the opinion or feelings of another]**

1. ri⌉**kai** 理解 •**c [the act of grasping in one's mind the meaning or content of s.t. or of sympathizing with the thoughts or feelings of another]** ((**comprehension, appreciation**))

EX. It takes time and effort to achieve a comprehensive understanding of Japanese grammar.
日本語文法に対する総合的な理解に至るには時間がかかるし、努力も要る。
Nihon-go-bunpoo ni tai-suru soogoo-tekina rikai ni itaru ni wa jikan ga kakaru shi, doryoku mo iru.

2. ri⌈**ka**⌉**i-ryoku** 理解力 •**c [the ability to grasp in one's mind the meaning or content of s.t. or to sympathize with the thoughts or feelings of another]**

EX. My friend Jim has a remarkable understanding of scientific technology.
友達のジムは科学技術の理解力がすばらしい。
Tomodachi no Jimu wa kagaku-gijutsu no rikai-ryoku ga subarashii.

3. ta⌈gai no ryo⌈okai 互いの了解 [an agreement of opinion or feeling between two parties] ⟪mutual understanding⟫, kyo⌈otei 協定 •c [an arrangement made between two parties on some matter of mutual interest] ⟪agreement, pact⟫

EX. Labor and management have finally reached an understanding with each other.
労使はついに{互いの了解/協定}に達した。
Rooshi wa tsuini {tagai no ryookai/kyootei} ni tasshita.

undertake vt. **[for s.o. to attempt or start to do s.t.; to agree or promise to do s.t.]**

1. ⟨-o⟩ ku⌈wadate⌉ru ⟨〜を⟩企てる ② [for s.o. to plan s.t. and make an effort to bring it about] ⟪plan, scheme, project, design, aim⟫

EX. Ten years ago the city undertook the project of providing sewage facilities to all residential housing.
十年前に市は全住宅に下水設備を提供するプロジェクトを企てた。
Juu-nen mae ni shi wa zen-juutaku ni gesui-setsubi o teikyoo-suru purojekuto o kuwadateta.

2. ⟨-o⟩ u⌈keo⌉u ⟨〜を⟩請け負う ① [for s.o. to accept to do a job by contractual agreement] ⟪contract, take on⟫, ⟨-o⟩ hi⌈ki-uke⌉ru ⟨〜を⟩引き受ける ② [for s.o. to take on the responsibility for s.t./s.o./s.a.] ⟪answer for, responsible for⟫

EX. Our firm has undertaken the construction of a new bridge across Tokyo Bay.
我が社は東京湾にかかる新しい橋の建設を{請け負いました/引き受けました}。
Waga-sha wa Tookyoo-wan ni kakaru atarashii hashi no kensetsu o {uke-oimashita/hiki-ukemashita}.

3. ⟨-o⟩ ya⌈kusoku-suru ⟨〜を⟩約束する ③ •c [for s.o. to give s.o. one's word that one will or will not do s.t.] ⟪promise, contract, pledge oneself⟫

EX. I undertook the responsibility of overseeing the administration of the department while our chairman was temporarily out of the country.
学科長が短期間外国に行っている間、私は学科運営の責任を負うことを約束した。
Gakka-choo ga tan-kikan gaikoku ni itte iru aida, watashi wa gakka-un'ei no sekinin o ou koto o yakusoku-shita.

undertaking n. **[s.t. one attempts, starts, or agrees to do]**

1. shi⌈goto 仕事 [an activity performed for a particular purpose other than amusement and on which one expends time and effort] ⟪work, job, business⟫, ji⌉gyoo 事業 •c [a social or economic activity planned on a relatively large scale] ⟪activity, project, operation⟫

EX. Renovating the old school building turned out to be a major undertaking.
古い校舎の修理は実際やってみるとなかなかの{大仕事/大事業}だということが分かった。
Furui koosha no shuuri wa jissai yatte miru to nakanaka no {oo-shigoto/dai-jigyoo} da to iu koto ga wakatta.

2. ya⌈kusoku 約束 •c [an explicit statement that one will or will not do s.t. or s.t. that one has explicitly said one will or will not do (including a date, engagement, or appointment)]

underwater adj. **[located or done below the surface of water]**

su⌈ichuu no N 水中のN •c

EX. Last week I went to see a performance of underwater ballet.
先週水中(の)バレエの演技を見に行きました。
Senshuu suichuu (no) baree no engi o mi ni ikimashita.

underwear n. **[clothing worn next to skin]**

shi⌈ta-gi 下着 ⟪undergarments, underclothes, undershirt, lingerie⟫

EX. It's best to put on fresh underwear every day.
下着は毎日取り替えた方がいいですよ。
Shita-gi wa mai-nichi tori-kaeta hoo ga ii desu yo.

U

undoubtedly adv. **[without uncertainty, surely]**
ma⌈chiga⌉inaku 間違いなく, ta⌉shikani 確かに /⟨adj⟨*na*⟩. *ni* of *tashikana* certain/ [with certainty] ⟪certainly, surely, doubtlessly⟫

EX. Mr. Lee is undoubtedly the best student in the class.
{間違いなく/確かに}リーさんはこのクラスで一番の学生だ。
{Machigainaku/Tashikani} Rii-san wa kono kurasu de ichiban no gakusei da.

uneasy adj. **[feeling or showing discomfort or worry]**
1. o⌈chitsukanai 落ち着かない /⟨Vneg. of *ochitsuku* ① settle down + *nai* not/ [to feel unsettled ⟪fig. "awkward"⟫] ⟪awkward, embarrassed⟫, kyu⌉ukutsuna 窮屈な •c [have no spare room to allow free movement] ⟪narrow, confined, limited, stiff, tight⟫

EX. When I'm around him, I feel uneasy.
あの人のそばにいると{落ち着かない/窮屈な}気がします。
Ano hito no soba ni iru to {ochitsukanai/kyuukutsuna} ki-ga-shimasu.

2. fu⌈anna 不安な •c [having an uncomfortable feeling caused by uncertainty or expectation of the worst] ⟪ill at ease, restless, anxious⟫, shi⌈npaina 心配な •c [having an uncomfortable feeling caused by uncertainty or by the expectation of danger/evil/s.t. troublesome] ⟪anxious, jittery, worried⟫

EX. I feel uneasy about my son's future.
息子の将来のことが{不安な/心配な}んです。
Musuko no shoorai no koto ga {fuanna/shinpaina} n desu.

unemployed adj. **[having no paid job]**
1. shi⌈goto ga na⌉i (N) 仕事がない(N) [having no work to do], shi⌈tsugyoo-shita N 失業したN /⟨Vinf. past of *shitsugyoo-suru* ③ lose one's job/ •c [having lost one's job], shi⌈tsugyoo-shite iru (N) 失業している(N) /⟨V*te iru* of *shitsugyoo-suru* ③ lose one's job/ •c

EX. I was fired last week and so I'm now unemployed.
先週首になって、今は{失業しています/仕事がありません}。
Senshuu kubi ni natte, ima wa {shitsugyoo-shite imasu/shigoto ga arimasen}.

2. ka⌈tsuyoo-sarete inai (N) 活用されていない(N) /⟨neg. of V*te iru* of the passive of *katsuyoo-suru* ③ utilize/ ② [not being utilized]

EX. Solar energy is as yet a largely unemployed resource in meeting the energy needs of modern society.
太陽エネルギーは、現代社会のエネルギー需要を満たすのにほとんど活用されていない資源だ。
Taiyoo-enerugii wa, gendai-shakai no enerugii-juyoo o mitasu no ni hotondo katsuyoo-sarete inai shigen da.

unemployment n. **[the condition of being out of work ⟪fig. "number of people out of work"⟫]**
shi⌈tsugyoo 失業 •c [the condition of being out of work] ⟪loss of employment, joblessness⟫

EX. (**a**) Unemployment is a major problem in this town.
この町では失業が大きな問題になっている。
Kono machi de wa shitsugyoo ga ookina mondai ni natte iru.
(**b**) The unemployment rate in this country is about seven percent.
この国の失業者数は労働力の約七%だ。
Kono kuni no shitsugyoo-sha-suu wa roodoo-ryoku no yaku nana-paasento da.

unequal adj. **[not the same in quantity or quality ⟪fig. "unbalanced," "unfair," "inadequate"⟫]**
1. (⟨-to⟩) chi⌈gau (N) (⟨〜と⟩)違う(N) [not the same as another ⟪fig. "be mistaken," "disagree with," "wrong"⟫], (⟨-to⟩) chi⌈gatte iru (N) (⟨〜と⟩)違っている(N)

EX. The two front wheels of the car are

U

unequal in size, making it extremely difficult to drive.
車の二つの前輪の大きさが{違っている/違う}ため運転するのが大変だ。
Kuruma no futatsu no zenrin no ookisa ga {chigatte iru/chigau} tame untensuru no ga taihen da.

2. fu-⌈tsu⌉riai no N 不釣り合いのN [unbalanced]

EX. Coming from such dissimilar economic backgrounds, their marriage was an unequal one but they still loved each other deeply.
彼らの実家は経済的にかなり差があり、不釣り合いの結婚だったが二人は深く愛し合っていた。
Kare-ra no jikka wa keizai-tekini kanari sa ga ari, fu-tsuriai no kekkon datta ga futari wa fukaku aishi-atte ita.

3. fu-⌈ko⌉oheina 不公平な adj(*na*). **•c [not dealing with everyone/every part concerned in the same manner] ⟪unfair, unjust, partial, biased⟫**

EX. In most countries the treatment minority groups receive is unequal to that of the majority.
ほとんどの国で少数民族は多数民族に比べて不公平な扱いを受けている。
Hotondo no kuni de shoosuu-minzoku wa tasuu-minzoku ni kurabete fu-kooheina atsukai o ukete iru.

U

4. ⟨-ni⟩ fu-⌈te⌉kitoona ⟨〜に⟩不適当な adj(*na*). **•c [not right for a given situation, purpose, or requirement] ⟪bad, unsuitable, ill-suited, unfit⟫ ↔ tekitoona 適当な** adj(*na*). **•c**

EX. I think that Kate is unequal to the task of managing others.
ケイトは人を管理する仕事に不適当だと思います。
Keito wa hito o kanri-suru shigoto ni fu-tekitoo da to omoimasu.

uneven adj. **[not smooth or level ⟪fig. "not uniform"⟫]**

1. ta⌈ira dena⌉i (N) 平らでない(N) [not level] ↔ tairana 平らな adj(*na*).; **de⌈ko-boko no N 凸凹のN [having a surface with irregular highs and lows] ⟪rough, jagged, scraggly⟫**

EX. The house was built on uneven land.
家は{平らでない/凸凹の}土地に建てられた。
Ie wa {taira denai/deko-boko no} tochi ni tate-rareta.

2. i⌈chiyoo dena⌉i (N) 一様でない(N) [not uniform], yo⌉kattari, wa⌉rukattari no N 良かったり、悪かったりのN [sometimes good, sometimes bad in quality], ki⌈nshitsu dena⌉i (N) 均質でない(N) •c [not of homogeneous quality] ⟪inconsistent⟫

EX. The pianist gave an uneven performance.
ピアニストの演奏は{良かったり、悪かったりだった/一様でなかった/均質でなかった}。
Pianisuto no ensoo wa {yokattari, warukattari datta/ichiyoo denakatta/kinshitsu denakatta}.

unexpected adj. **[not anticipated, happening without warning]**

o⌈moigakena⌉i 思いがけない adj(*i*). **[not anticipated] ⟪least expected, unsuspected, unthought of⟫, i⌈gaina 意外な** adj(*na*). **•c [different from what was anticipated] ⟪unforeseen, unanticipated⟫ ↔ yosoo-doori no 予想通りのN**

EX. An unexpected tragedy changed her life completely.
{思いがけない/意外な}悲劇で彼女の生活は一変した。
{Omoigakenai/Igaina} higeki de kanojo no seikatsu wa ippen-shita.

unfamiliar adj. **[not known or recognized]**

1. yo⌉ku shi⌈ranai (N) よく知らない(N) [not well known to one]

EX. (**a**) I enjoy visiting unfamiliar places.
よく知らない所へ行くのが大好きだ。
Yoku shiranai tokoro e iku no ga dai-suki da.
(**b**) There were a lot of unfamiliar faces at the party.
そのパーティーにはよく知らない顔が多かった。

Sono paatii ni wa yoku shiranai kao ga ookatta.

2. 〈-ni〉 fu˥-narena 〈～に〉不慣れな adj(*na*). **[not used to s.t.], 〈-ni〉 fu-˥a˥nnai no N** 〈～に〉不案内のN **•c [having no experience with s.t.] 《ignorant》**

EX. (**a**) I'm still largely unfamiliar with how to operate a computer.
私はコンピューターの操作にまだ大分{不慣れ/不案内}です。
Watashi wa konpyuutaa no soosa ni mada daibu {fu-nare/fu-annai} desu.
(**b**) I'm totally unfamiliar with this neighborhood.
私はこの辺は全く{不慣れ/不案内}です。
Watashi wa kono hen wa mattaku {fu-nare/fu-annai} desu

unfortunate adj. **[having bad luck 《fig. "unsuitable"》]**

1. tsu˥ite inai (N) ついていない(N) **/〈neg. of V*te iru* of *tsuku* ① attach/ [not having good fortune attached to oneself] 《unlucky》, fu˥ko˥ona** 不幸な adj(*na*). **•c [not happy] 《unhappy, miserable, wretched》 ↔ koofukuna** 幸福な adj(*na*). **•c; u˥n ga wa˥ru˥i** 運が悪い adj(*i*). **[having temporary bad luck] 《unlucky》 ↔ un ga ii** 運がいい adj(*i*).; **fu˥unna** 不運な adj(*na*). **•c [having bad luck 〈w〉] 《unlucky, luckless, ill-fated》 ↔ koounna** 幸運な adj(*na*). **•c; za˥nne˥nna** 残念な adj(*na*). **•c [causing disappointment and dissatisfaction over s.t. that s.o. has done or s.t. that has happened]**

EX. (**a**) While in Tokyo I had the unfortunate experience of having my wallet stolen on the train by a pickpocket.
東京に行っていた時{運が悪い/不運な/ついていない/*不幸な/*残念な}ことに電車の中で財布をすりにすられてしまった。
*Tookyoo ni itte ita toki {un ga warui/fuunna/tsuite inai/*fukoona/*zannenna} koto ni densha no naka de saifu o suri ni sura-rete shimatta.*
(**b**) Jim has led an unfortunate life ever since childfood.
ジムの人生は子供の時からずっと{ついていなかった/不運だった/不幸だった/??運が悪かった/*残念だった}。
*Jimu no jinsei wa kodomo no toki kara zutto {tsuite inakatta/fuun datta/fukoo datta/??un ga warukatta/*zannen datta}.*
(**c**) She has the unfortunate habit of always being in the wrong place at the wrong time.
彼女は悪い時に悪い所に居合わせるという{ついていない/不運な/運が悪い/*不幸な/*残念な}人だ。
*Kanojo wa warui toki ni warui tokoro ni i-awaseru to iu {tsuite inai/fuunna/un ga warui/*fukoona/*zannenna} hito da.*
(**d**) We had such a good time in Kyoto. It was unfortunate we couldn't stay longer.
京都での滞在は楽しくて、もっと長くいられないのが{残念でした/*ついていませんでした/*不幸でした/*運が悪かったです/*不運でした}。
*Kyooto de no taizai wa tanoshikute, motto nagaku i-rarenai no ga {zannen deshita/*tsuite imasen deshita/*fukoo deshita/*un ga warukatta desu/*fuun deshita}.*

2. ma˥zu˥i まずい adj(*i*). **[having a bad flavor 《fig. "ugly," "unskillful," "awkward"》] 《unsavory, ugly, unskillful, unwise》**

EX. A: Did you tell George to his face that he was senile?
ジョージに面と向かっておいぼれだと言ったのかい。
Jooji ni men to mukatte oibore da to itta no kai.
B. Yeah, that was an unfortunate choice of words.
うん、まずい言葉の選択だったけどね。
Un, mazui kotoba no sentaku datta kedo ne.

unfortunately adv. **[in a manner of occurrence or timing such as to cause disappointment, dissatisfaction, or unhappiness]**

u˥n waruku 運悪く **[in a manner that is**

unlucky for a limited scope of time] ↔ un yoku 運良く; fu⌉unni-mo 不運にも [in an unlucky manner ⟨w⟩] ↔ koounni-mo 幸運にも •c; fu⌈ko⌉oni-mo 不幸にも [in an unhappy manner ⟨w⟩] ↔ saiwaini mo 幸いにも; a⌈iniku あいにく [in such a way as to cause disappointment or inconvenience due to bad timing] ⟪unluckily, as ill luck would have it, to make matters worse, to one's disappointment⟫, za⌈ne⌉nna koto ni 残念なことに [in such a way as to cause disappointment and dissatisfaction over s.t. that s.o. has done or s.t. that has happened]

EX. (**a**) Unfortunately the museum was closed on the day we planned to visit it.
{残念なことに/あいにく/運悪く/?不運にも/*不幸にも}ちょうど見に行こうと思っていた日に博物館は閉まっていた。
*{Zannenna koto ni/Ainiku/Un waruku/?Fuunni-mo/*Fukooni-mo} choodo mi ni ikoo to omotte ita hi ni hakubutsu-kan wa shimatte ita.*
(**b**) Unfortunately my friend's father passed away just as my friend was about to graduate from college.
{不幸にも/不運にも/?運悪く/*残念なことに/*あいにく}友達は大学の卒業直前にお父さんを亡くした。
*{Fukooni-mo/Fuunni-mo/?Un waruku/*Zannenna koto ni/*Ainiku} tomodachi wa daigaku no sotsugyoo-chokuzen ni o-too-san o nakushita.*

U

unfriendly adj. **[not exhibiting warmth, liking, or a desire for closer relations; not favorable in physical setting or conditions]**
1. fu-⌈shi⌉nsetsuna 不親切な adj(*na*). **•c [not having or showing thoughtfulness for others] ⟪unkind, inhospitable⟫ ↔ shinsetsuna 親切な** adj(*na*). **•c; hi⌉-yu⌈ukoo-tekina 非友好的な** adj(*na*). **•c [not exhibiting a desire for closer (diplomatic) relations] ⟪not fraternal⟫ ↔ yuukoo-tekina 友好的な** adj(*na*). **•c**

EX. (**a**) My roommate is an unfriendly kind of person.
私のルームメートは{不親切な/*非友好的な}人です。
*Watashi no ruumu-meeto wa {fu-shinsetsuna/*hi-yuukoo-tekina} hito desu.*
(**b**) Our relations with that country have always been unfriendly.
あの国とはずっと{非友好的な/*不親切な}関係が続いている。
*Ano kuni to wa zutto {hi-yuukoo-tekina/*fu-shinsetsuna} kankei ga tsuzuite iru.*

2. ⟨-ni⟩ mu⌈kanai (N) ⟨〜に⟩向かない(N) /⟨Vneg. of *muku* ① suit + *nai* not/ [not suitable for], -muki dewa⌈na⌉i 〜向きではない

EX. I find the climate in this area unfriendly.
この辺の気候は{私には向かない/私向きではない}。
Kono hen no kikoo wa {watashi ni wa mukanai/watashi-muki dewanai}.

unhappy adj. **[not feeling or exhibiting joy, sad]**
fu⌈ko⌉ona 不幸な adj(*na*). **•c ⟪miserable, wretched⟫ ↔ koofukuna 幸福な** adj(*na*). **•c; mi⌉jimena 惨めな** adj(*na*). **[so pitiful in condition as to be difficult to look at] ⟪pitiful, pitiable, sad, wretched⟫**

EX. Hanako's life since her divorce has been an unhappy one.
離婚してからの花子の生活は{不幸/惨め}だった。
Rikon-shite kara no Hanako no seikatsu wa {fukoo/mijime} datta.

uniform adj. **[consistently the same, not changing or different in any part]**
1. i⌈ttei no N 一定のN •c [fixed in quantity, number, or duration] ⟪definite, certain, established, regular⟫

EX. It is critical to the success of the experiment that the laboratory be kept at a uniform temperature.
実験を成功させるには実験室を一定の温度に保っておくことが重要である。
Jikken o seikoo-saseru ni wa jikken-shitsu o ittei no ondo ni tamotte oku

koto ga juuyoo dearu.

2. ⟨(-to)⟩ **o⌈naji yo⌉ona** ⟨(〜と)⟩同じような **[appearing to be no different from]** ↔ ⟨(-to)⟩ **chigau** ⟨(〜と)⟩違う ①; **ki⌈n'itsu no N** 均一のN **•c [not varying in quantity or quality]** ⟪uniform, equal⟫

EX. The cars you see on the roads in Japan all appear to be uniform in size, at least compared to the U.S.
日本の道路を走っている車は、少なくともアメリカに比べると皆{同じような/均一の}大きさのようだ。
Nihon no dooro o hashitte iru kuruma wa, sukunaku to mo Amerika ni kuraberu to mina {onaji yoona/kin'itsu no} ooki-sa no yooda.

—— n. **[a distinctive kind of clothing worn by members of a particular institution or group]**
se⌈ifuku 制服 **•c, yu⌉nifoomu** ユニフォーム **•f [a distinctive kind of clothing worn by athletes or cheerleaders]**

EX. (**a**) In Japan and Korea all children wear uniforms to school.
日本と韓国では子供がみんな{制服/*ユニフォーム}を着て学校に行く。
*Nihon to Kankoku de wa kodomo ga minna {seifuku/*yunifoomu} o kite gakkoo ni iku.*
(**b**) Mom, could you buy me a baseball uniform?
お母さん、野球の{ユニフォーム/*制服}買ってくれない?
*O-kaa-san, yakyuu no {yunifoomu/*seifuku} katte kurenai?*

unify vt. **[for s.o. to cause people or things to be or feel like one unit]**
⟨-o⟩ **to⌈oitsu-suru** ⟨〜を⟩統一する ③ **•c [for s.o. to cause different people or things to become one in conformity with a certain standard, direction, or purpose]** ⟪consolidate, coordinate⟫

EX. The President succeeded in unifying his party behind him.
大統領は自分の属する政党を自分の方針通りに統一することに成功した。
Daitooryoo wa jibun no zokusuru seitoo o jibun no hooshin-doori ni tooitsu-suru koto ni seikoo-shita.

unimportant adj. **[having no particular value or significance]**
ju⌈uyoo {**dena⌉i/jana⌉i**} (**N**) 重要{でない/じゃない}(N), {**tsu⌈mara⌉nai/tsu⌈ma⌉nnai**} {つまらない/つまんない} adj(*i*). **[causing dissatisfaction due to lack of worth or interest]** ⟪uninteresting, trivial, worthless⟫

NOTE: *Juuyoo janai* and *tsumannai* are informal, colloquial versions of *juuyoo denai* and *tsumaranai*, respectively.

EX. I don't want to waste time on such unimportant matters.
私はそんな{重要{でない/じゃない}/つまらない/つまんない}ことに無駄な時間を使いたくないんです。
Watashi wa sonna {juuyoo {denai/janai}/tsumaranai/tsumannai} koto ni mudana jikan o tsukai-takunai n desu.

unintentionally adv. **[not on purpose, accidentally]**
tsu⌉i つい **[in a manner lacking conscious thought, often resulting from habit or instinct and not serving any desirable purpose]** ⟪carelessly, inadvertently, by mistake⟫, **u⌈kka⌉ri** うっかり **[absent-mindedly/inattentively]** ⟪carelessly, unconsciously, thoughtlessly, heedlessly⟫

EX. (**a**) Even though I quit smoking several months ago I still have the habit of unintentionally bringing my right hand to my mouth when in deep thought.
数か月前にたばこをやめたのに、長年の癖で考え込むと{つい/*うっかり}右手を口に持っていってしまう。
*Suu-kagetsu mae ni tabako o yameta noni, naga-nen no kuse de kangae-komu to {tsui/*ukkari} migi-te o kuchi ni motte-itte shimau.*
(**b**) I unintentionally left out the company president's name from the list of people to be invited to the dinner party.
夕食会の招待者名簿に{うっかり/*つい}社長の名前を抜かしてしまった。

U

*Yuushoku-kai no shootai-sha-meibo ni {ukkari/*tsui} shachoo no namae o nukashite shimatta.*

uninteresting adj. **[not causing or holding interest or attention]**
o⌈moshiro⌉kuna⌉i (N) 面白くない(N) /⟨adj(*i*). ***ku*** **of** ***omoshiroi*** **interesting +** ***nai*** **not/, tsu⌈mara⌉nai** つまらない adj(*i*). **[causing dissatisfaction due to lack of worth or interest]** ⟪**trivial, worthless**⟫

EX. A: Don't you find it uninteresting to memorize long lists of *kanji*?
漢字の長いリストを丸暗記するのは{面白くない/つまらない}と思いませんか。
Kanji no nagai risuto o maru-anki-suru no wa {omoshirokunai/tsumaranai} to omoimasen ka.
B: No, it's fun.
いいえ、面白いですよ。
Iie, omoshiroi desu yo.

union n. **[a joining together of two or more things or people into one; s.t. created by such joining together; a group of laborers organized together for increased bargaining power]**

1. ke⌈tsugoo 結合 **•c [the act or result of putting two things together so as to form one entity]** ⟪**combination, coupling, linkage, bond**⟫

EX. The union of hydrogen and oxygen results in the formation of water.
水素と酸素の結合で水ができる。
Suiso to sanso no ketsugoo de mizu ga dekiru.

2. ga⌈ppei 合併 **•c [the formation of a single unit from two or more smaller units joining together, esp. business firms or political units]** ⟪**combination, consolidation, merger, coalition, affiliation, amalgamation**⟫

EX. The city of Joetsu in Niigata Prefecture came into being from the union of the two towns of Takada and Naoetsu.
新潟県にある上越市は高田と直江津という二つの町の合併で生まれた市です。
Niigata-ken ni aru Jooetsu-shi wa Takada to Naoetsu to iu futatsu no machi no gappei de umareta shi desu.

3. (ro⌈odoo-)ku⌉miai (労働)組合 **•c [a group of laborers organized together for increased bargaining power]**

EX. In Japan each company has its own union.
日本では一つ一つの会社が他とは別の労働組合を持っている。
Nihon de wa hitotsu-hitotsu no kaisha ga ta to wa betsu no roodoo-kumiai o motte iru.

PHRASE: student union *gakusei-kaikan* 学生会館 **•c**

EX. Let's go to the student union for some coffee.
学生会館に行ってコーヒーを飲もう。
Gakusei-kaikan ni itte koohii o nomoo.

unique adj. **[being the only one of its kind or not having an equal]**

1. do⌈kutokuna 独特な adj(*na*). **•c [belonging exclusively to s.o./s.t./s.a. as a characteristic]** ⟪**peculiar to, original, characteristic of**⟫, **do⌈kutoku no N** 独特のN **•c, yu⌈ni⌉ikuna** ユニークな adj(*na*). **•f [having characteristics very different from others]**

EX. Some people believe that Japanese culture is not unique as is often claimed in Japan.
日本文化は日本でよく言われているようには{独特/ユニーク}ではないと思っている人もいる。
Nihon-bunka wa Nihon de yoku iwarete iru yooni wa {dokutoku/yuniiku} dewanai to omotte iru hito mo iru.

2. me⌈zurashi⌉i 珍しい adj(*i*). **[seldom occurring ⟪fig. "unusual," "nice"⟫]** ⟪**new, novel, rare, curious, unusual, nice**⟫, **ma⌈ta⌉-to-nai (N)** またとない(N) adj(*i*). **[never occurring again as an opportunity]**

EX. (**a**) Aren't you going to join the group tour to Japan? It's a unique opportunity you shouldn't miss.
日本への団体旅行に参加しないんですか。{またとない/*珍しい}機会なのに逃しちゃもったいないですよ。
Nihon e no dantai-ryokoo ni sanka-

*shinai n desu ka. {Mata-to-nai/ *Mezurashii} kikai na noni nogashi cha mottainai desu yo.*
(**b**) You have a really unique name. Where does it come from?
あなたの名前はとても{珍しいです/*またとありません}ね。どういう由来の名前なんですか。
*Anata no namae wa totemo {mezurashii desu/*mata-to-arimasen} ne. Doo-iu yurai no namae na n desu ka.*

unit n. **[a single entity forming part of a larger group or a certain quantity designated as a standard for measuring other quantities]**
ta⌉n'i 単位 •c [a quantity chosen as a standard for measuring length/weight/quantity/size]

EX. The basic units for measuring time are seconds, minutes and hours.
時間を計る基本的な単位は秒、分、時間である。
Jikan o hakaru kihon-tekina tan'i wa byoo, fun, jikan dearu.

unite vt. **[to join together into one]**
1. ⟨-o⟩ **ke⌈tsugoo-suru** ⟨〜を⟩結合する ③ •c **[for s.o. to put two things together so as to form one entity]** ⟪**combine, couple, link, bond**⟫, ⟨-o⟩ (⟨-to⟩) **mu⌈subi-tsuke⌉ru** ⟨〜を⟩ (⟨〜と⟩)結び付ける ② **[to cause two or more things to become attached together]** ⟪**tie, join, link, connect**⟫

EX. (**a**) Unite the following two sentences using a conjunction.
次の二つの文を接続詞を使って{結び付けなさい/結合しなさい}。
Tsugi no futatsu no bun o setsuzoku-shi o tsukatte {musubi-tsukenasai/ketsugoo-shinasai}.
(**b**) The threat of attack from outside the country united the two adversaries.
国外からの攻撃の恐れが二人の敵を{結び付けた/*結合した}。
*Kokugai kara no koogeki no osore ga futari no teki o {musubi-tsuketa/ *ketsugoo-shita}.*

2. ⟨-o⟩ **ke⌈kkon-saseru** ⟨〜を⟩結婚させる **/⟨causative of *kekkon-suru* ③ get married/ ② [for s.o. to cause two people to get married]**

united adj. **[joined together into one]**
1. re⌈ngoo-shita N 連合したN /⟨Vinf. past of *rengoo-suru* ③ become united/ •c [combined into a single group]

EX. The united forces of the two nations were able to defeat the invader.
二つの国の連合(した)軍が侵略者を退けることに成功した。
Futatsu no kuni no rengoo(-shita)-gun ga shinryaku-sha o shirizokeru koto ni seikoo-shita.

2. da⌈nketsu-shita N 団結したN /⟨Vinf. past of *danketsu-suru* ③ band together/ •c [banded together] ⟪**combined, leagued, solid**⟫

EX. The united workers negotiated with the management.
団結した労働者が雇用者と交渉に当たった。
Danketsu-shita roodoo-sha ga koyoo-sha to kooshoo ni atatta.

United States of America n.
A⌈merika Gasshuu-koku アメリカ合衆国 •f+c

unity n. **[the state of being one]**
1. ta⌈n'itsu-sei 単一性 •c [the state of being one] ⟪**singleness**⟫

EX. The unity of the Japanese race is a myth.
日本民族の単一性は神話だ。
Nihon-minzoku no tan'itsu-sei wa shinwa da.

2. to⌈oitsu 統一 •c [the state of being one in conformity with a certain standard, direction, or purpose] ⟪**unification, consolidation, coherence**⟫ ↔ **bunretsu 分裂 •c**

EX. A unity among all Christian churches, although it would be ideal, has never been achieved.
全キリスト教会の統一は理想だろうが、実現したことがない。
Zen-Kirisuto-kyookai no tooitsu wa

U

risoo daroo ga, jitsugen-shita koto ga nai.

3. cho⌈owa 調和 •c [a condition of different colors, shapes, or sounds, balancing and complementing each other within a larger whole so as to create a sense of esthetic pleasure] ⟪harmony, accord, agreement⟫

EX. One senses a unity between nature and human beings in New Zealand.
ニュージーランドには自然と人間の調和がある感じがする。
Nyuujiirando ni wa shizen to ningen no choowa ga aru kanji ga suru.

universal adj. **[applying to, belonging to, or participated in by all]**

1. fu⌈hen-tekina 普遍的な adj(*na*). **•c [applying to all cases] ⟪omnipresent, ubiquitous, all-pervasive⟫**

EX. Language is a universal tool for human communication.
言語は人類の普遍的な伝達手段である。
Gengo wa jinrui no fuhen-tekina dentatsu-shudan dearu.

2. i⌈ppan-tekina 一般的な adj(*na*). **•c [holding true of all or nearly all cases] ⟪general⟫**

EX. Some anthropologists argue that there is no moral code universal to all human culture.
人類学者の中には全人類共通の一般的な道徳規準はないと主張する人もいる。
Jinrui-gakusha no naka ni wa zen-jinrui-kyootsuu no ippan-tekina dootoku-kijun wa nai to shuchoo-suru hito mo iru.

—— n. **[a proposition or concept applying to all members of a set or class]**

1. ze⌈nshoo-me⌉idai 全称命題 •c [a proposition applying to all members of a set or class] ⟪universal proposition⟫

2. i⌈ppan-ga⌉inen 一般概念 •c [a general concept]

universe n. **[the entire cosmos containing all existing things]**

1. u⌉chuu 宇宙 •c [the physical expanse containing earth and all that is in it and all heavenly bodies] ⟪cosmos, space⟫

EX. The 21st century will undoubtedly see explorations into the universe on a scale unimaginable to us now.
二十一世紀には今では考えられないほど大規模な宇宙の探検が実現するだろう。
Ni-juu-is-seiki ni wa ima de wa kangae-rarenai hodo dai-kibona uchuu no tanken ga jitsugen-suru daroo.

2. ba⌉nbutsu 万物 •c [all existing things, including living things, inanimate objects, and phenomena]

EX. So far as we know, man is the most intelligent creature in the universe.
我々が知る限り、人間は万物の中で最も聡明な生き物だ。
Ware-ware ga shiru kagiri, ningen wa banbutsu no naka de mottomo soomeina iki-mono da.

university n. **[an institution of higher learning made up of one or more colleges, graduate schools, and professional schools and offering degree programs and research facilities in many areas of advanced learning]**

so⌈ogoo-da⌉igaku 総合大学 •c [an institution of higher education that grants baccalaureate, master's, and doctoral degrees in the humanites and (social) sciences], da⌈igaku 大学 •c [an institution of higher education that grants baccalaureate degrees or baccalaureate and graduate degrees] ⟪college⟫

EX. Nagoya University is a university where one can pursue a degree in practically any field.
名古屋大学はほとんどどの分野でも学位が取れる(総合)大学です。
Nagoya-daigaku wa hotondo dono bun'ya demo gakui ga tore-ru (soogoo-) daigaku desu.

unknown adj. **[not familiar or existing in one's mind ⟪fig. "rare," "inexpressible"⟫]**

1. shi⌈ranai (N) 知らない(N) /⟨Vneg. of *shiru* ① come to know + *nai* not/ [not known or knowing], mi⌉chi no N 未知のN

•c **[not yet known]** ⟪**strange**⟫ ↔ **kichi no N** 既知のN •c

EX. (**a**) While walking through town last night I suddenly found myself in an area unknown to me.
ゆうべ町を歩いているうちに気がついたら{知らない/未知の}土地に出ていた。
Yuube machi o aruite iru uchi ni ki-ga-tsuitara {shiranai/michi no} tochi ni dete ita.
(**b**) The world of international finance is an unknown world to me.
国際金融界は私にとって{知らない/未知の}世界だ。
Kokusai-kin'yuu-kai wa watashi ni-totte {shiranai/michi no} sekai da.

2. me⌈zurashi⌉i 珍しい adj(*i*). **[seldom occurring** ⟪**fig. "unusual," "nice"**⟫**]** ⟪**rare, novel, unique**⟫

EX. The scientist discovered an unknown fish.
その科学者は珍しい魚を発見した。
Sono kagaku-sha wa mezurashii sakana o hakken-shita.

unless conj. **[if…not]**

(**mo⌉shi**) {**Vneg./Vstem/ko/shi/adj**(*i*). ***ku***} {**nakereba/nai to**} (もし){**Vneg./Vstem/来/し/adj**(*i*). ***ku***}{なければ/ないと}, (**mo⌉shi**) {**adj**(*na*). **stem/N**} {**de/ja**}{**na⌉kereba/na⌉i to**} (もし){**adj**(*na*). **stem/N**}{で/じゃ}{なければ/ないと}

EX. (**a**) A: Are you coming to the party?
パーティーに来ますか。
Paatii ni kimasu ka.
B: Yes, I plan to unless some urgent business comes up.
ええ、急用が{なければ/*ないと}行くつもりです。
*Ee, kyuuyoo ga {nakereba/*nai to} iku tsumori desu.*
(**b**) Unless you study harder, you're going to flunk the course.
もっと勉強{しないと/しなければ}、落第するよ。
Motto benkyoo-{shinai to/shinakereba}, rakudai-suru yo.
(**c**) Unless it's an emergency the hospital doesn't accept patients on Sundays.
病院は急患の場合{でなければ/でないと}日曜は患者を受け入れない。
Byooin wa kyuukan no baai {denakereba/denai to} nichiyoo wa kanja o uke-irenai.
(**d**) Unless you call, I'll assume that you're coming, OK?
電話が{なければ/*ないと}、来ると思っているからね。
*Denwa ga {nakereba/*nai to}, kuru to omotte iru kara ne.*
(**e**) Unless it rains soon, our lawn is probably going to die.
そろそろ雨が{降らなければ/降らないと}芝生が枯れちゃうでしょう。
Soro-soro ame ga {furanakereba/furanai to} shibafu ga karechau deshoo.
(**f**) Our son will not get up unless we wake him up.
うちの息子は{起こさなければ/起こさないと}、いつまでも寝ている。
Uchi no musuko wa {okosanakereba/okosanai to}, itsu-made-mo nete iru.

NOTE: *-nai to* can only be used when the verb in the main clause (i.e., the final verb) expresses an event which is not under the control of the subject of the subordinate clause (i.e., the first verb), as in examples (b), (c), (e) and (f).

unlike prep. **[different from]**

1. ⟨**-to**⟩ **chi⌈gatte** ⟨〜と⟩違って /⟨**V*te* of *chigau*** ① **differ/ [different from]**

EX. Unlike most Japanese people, I don't like *sushi.*
普通の日本人と違って、私はすしが好きじゃないんです。
Futsuu no Nihon-jin to chigatte, watashi wa sushi ga suki janai n desu.

2. ra⌈shi⌉ku⌈na⌉i (N) らしくない(N) **[not characteristic of]**

EX. It's unlike you to say something like that.
そんなこと言うなんて君らしくないね。
Sonna koto iu nante kimi-rashikunai ne.

—— adj. **[different from]**

o⌈naji jana⌉i (N) 同じじゃない(N) **[not the same], ni⌈te inai (N)** 似ていない(N) /⟨**neg.**

U

of V*te iru* of *niru* ② resemble/ ② [not resembling]

EX. Those two sisters are as unlike as strangers.
あの二人の姉妹は他人のように似ていない。
Ano futari no shimai wa tanin no yooni nite inai.

unlikely adj. **[not reasonably expected to be, happen, or succeed]**

1. a⌈ri-so⌉oni (mo) na⌉i (N) ありそうに(も)ない(N) [not reasonably expected to be], a⌈ri-so⌉o mo na⌉i (N) ありそうもない(N)

EX. It's unlikely that I'll finish my M.A. thesis by May.
修士論文を五月までに書き終えることは{ありそうに(も)/ありそうも}ない。
Shuushi-ronbun o go-gatsu made ni kaki-oeru koto wa {ari-sooni (mo)/ ari-soo mo} nai.

2. se⌈ikoo-shi-so⌉oni (mo) na⌉i (N) 成功しそうに(も)ない(N) [not reasonably expected to succeed], se⌈ikoo-shi-so⌉o mo na⌉i (N) 成功しそうもない(N)

EX. The committee came up with an unlikely plan to raise one million dollars for the project by year's end.
委員会では年内にその企画のために百万ドル集めるという、{成功しそうに(も)/成功しそうも}ない計画を考え出した。
Iin-kai de wa nennai ni sono kikaku no tame ni hyaku-man-doru atsumeru to iu, {seikoo-shi-sooni (mo)/seikoo-shi-soo mo} nai keikaku o kangae-dashita.

U

unnecessary adj. **[needless]**

i⌈ranai 要らない adj(*i*). **/⟨Vneg. of *iru* ① need + *nai* not/, hi⌈tsuyoo {dena⌉i/jana⌉i} 必要{でない/じゃない} /⟨adj(*na*). stem of *hitsuyoona* necessary + {*denai*/*janai*} not/, fu-⌈hi⌉tsuyoona 不必要な** adj(*na*). **•c ⟪needless, unessential⟫**

EX. (**a**) A: Will we need a map?
地図が要りますか。
Chizu ga irimasu ka.
B: No, that'll be unnecessary.
いいえ、{要りません/必要じゃありません/不必要です}。
Iie, {irimasen/hitsuyoo jaarimasen/fu-hitsuyoo desu}.
(**b**) Try not to take along so many unnecessary things when you travel.
旅行の時{要らない/必要じゃない/不必要な}ものをそんなにたくさん持って行かないようにしてほしい。
Ryokoo no toki {iranai/hitsuyoo janai/fu-hitsuyoona} mono o sonnani takusan motte ikanai yooni shite hoshii.

unnoticed adj. **[not seen or observed by others]**

hi⌈to-me o hikanai (N) 人目を引かない(N) /⟨*hito-me* people's attention + prt. *o* + Vneg. of *hiku* ① draw + *nai* not/ [not drawing people's attention], me⌈data⌉nai (N) 目立たない(N) /⟨Vneg. of *medatsu* ① stand out + *nai* not/ ① [not standing out], ki-⌈zuka-re⌉nai (N) 気づかれない(N) /⟨Vstem of passive of *ki-zuku* ① notice + *nai* not/ [not seen or perceived by others] ⟪not found⟫

EX. (**a**) The famous actress walked along the crowded streets of New York City unnoticed.
有名な女優がニューヨークの雑踏の中を歩いていたが、{人目を引かなかった/目立たなかった/気づかれなかった}。
Yuumeina joyuu ga Nyuuyooku no zattoo no naka o aruite ita ga, {hito-me o hikanakatta/medatanakatta/ki-zuka-renakatta}.
(**b**) I was able to slip out of the house unnoticed.
私は{気づかれないで/??人目を引かないで/??目立たないで}家を出ることが出来た。
Watashi wa {ki-zuka-renai de/??hito-me o hikanai de/??medatanai de} ie o deru koto ga dekita.

NOTE: "Unnoticed" in example (b) is used as a manner adverb and so its Japanese counterpart takes an adverbial ending such as *zu ni* or *nai de*.

unobserved adj. **[not seen or noticed; not kept or obeyed]**

1. ki-⌈zuka-re⌉nai (N) 気づかれない(N) /⟨Vstem of passive of *ki-zuku* ① notice + *nai* not/ [not seen or perceived by others]

EX. His shoplifting went unobserved by the people in the store.
彼は店の人に気づかれないで万引きをした。
Kare wa mise no hito ni ki-zuka-renai de manbiki o shita.

2. ma⌈mora-re⌉nai (N) 守られない(N) /⟨Vstem of passive of *mamoru* ① obey (a law) + *nai* not/ [not kept, obeyed, or protected]

EX. In this town, traffic rules seem to go unobserved.
この町では、交通規則が守られないようだ。
Kono machi de wa, kootsuu-kisoku ga mamora-renai yooda.

unpleasant adj. **[not pleasing or agreeable]** **i⌈ya⌉na** 嫌な adj(*na*). **[very displeasing to one]** **⟪disagreeable, distasteful, disgusting, odious, offensive, rotten⟫ ↔ sukina** 好きな adj(*na*).; **fu-⌈yu⌉kaina** 不愉快な adj(*na*). **•c [causing a disagreeable feeling] ⟪uncomfortable, cheerless, unhappy⟫ ↔ yukaina** 愉快な adj(*na*). **•c**

EX. (**a**) My boss is a really unpleasant kind of guy.
上役が実に{嫌な/不愉快な}奴でね。
Uwa-yaku ga jitsuni {iyana/fu-yukaina} yatsu de ne.
(**b**) It creates such an unpleasant atmosphere when people come into the office in the morning without so much as a word of greeting.
朝出勤した時、お互いに一言のあいさつさえしないと実に{嫌な/不愉快な}雰囲気になる。
Asa shukkin-shita toki, o-tagai ni hito-koto no aisatsu sae shinai to jitsu ni {iyana/fu-yukaina} fun'iki ni naru.

unqualified adj. **[not having the proper qualifications or not restricted]**

1. shi⌈kaku ga na⌉i (N) 資格がない(N) •c [not having the proper qualifications]

EX. Don is unqualified as a French teacher.
ドンはフランス語の先生としての資格がない。
Don wa Furansu-go no sensei to-shite no shikaku ga nai.

2. mu-⌈jo⌉oken no N 無条件のN •c [not having any conditions attached] ⟪unrestricted, unconditional, free⟫

EX. I need unqualified support from my boss before I can start this project.
この仕事を始めるには上役の無条件の承諾が必要なんだ。
Kono shigoto o hajimeru ni wa uwa-yaku no mu-jooken no shoodaku ga hitsuyoona n da.

unreasonable adj. **[not exhibiting or using good sense; exceeding what is normally expected or what is considered fair or just]**

1. ri⌈sei-teki {dena⌉i/jana⌉i} (N) 理性的{でない/じゃない}(N) /⟨adj.(*na*). stem of *risei-tekina* rational + {*denai/janai*} not/ •c [not based on rational thinking]

EX. Even people who are normally very rational can say unreasonable things when they become emotional.
普段は大変理性的な人でも感情的になると理性的{でない/じゃない}ことを言うことがある。
Fudan wa taihen risei-tekina hito demo kanjoo-tekini naru to risei-teki {denai/janai} koto o iu koto ga aru.

2. ri⌈kutsu ni awa⌉nai (N) 理屈に合わない(N) /⟨Vneg. of *rikutsu ni au* ① conform to reason + *nai* not/ [not conforming to reason] ⟪against reason⟫, do⌈ori⌉ ni a⌈wa⌉nai (N) 道理に合わない(N) /⟨Vneg. of *doori ni au* ① conform to reason + *nai* not/

EX. A: He says that if you don't let him do it his way, he's not going to do it at all.
彼は自分のやり方でやらせてくれないんなら、一切やらないって言ってるよ。
Kare wa jibun no yari-kata de yara-sete kurenai n nara, issai yaranai tte itte ru yo.
B: That's being unreasonable.
それは{理屈/道理}に合わないよ。

U

Sore wa {rikutsu/doori} ni awanai yo.

3. mu˥rina 無理な adj(*na*). **•c [going beyond reason] ⟪unjustifiable, unwarranted, unnatural⟫, fu┌toona** 不当な adj(*na*). **•c [not justifiable in manner of treatment or price] ⟪unjust, wrongful, unfair, improper, exorbitant⟫, ho˥ogaina** 法外な adj(*na*). **•c [excessive in degree, esp. with regard to price, demand, or ambition] ⟪exorbitant, extraordinary, absurd, outrageous⟫**

EX. (**a**) I'm afraid this may be asking an unreasonable favor of you.
{無理な/*不当な/*法外な}お願いかもしれませんが。
*{Murina/*Futoona/*Hoogaina} o-negai kamoshiremasen ga.*
(**b**) What? They charge $500 per night? That's unreasonable!
何? 一晩五百ドルだって? それは{法外な/不当な/?無理な}値段だ。
Nani? Hito-ban go-hyaku-doru datte? Sore wa {hoogaina/futoona/?murina} nedan da.

unseen adj. **[not visibly perceived]**

1. ma˥da mi˥te i┌nai (N) まだ見ていない(N) **/⟨Vstem of *mite iru* ② having seen, be watching + *nai* not/ [not having seen yet]**

EX. We tend to be most afraid of dangers still unseen.
私たちはまだ見ていない危険を一番恐れがちだ。
Watashi-tachi wa mada mite inai kiken o ichiban osore-gachi da.

2. mi┌e˥nai (N) 見えない(N) **/⟨Vstem of *mieru* ② visible + *nai* not/ [not able to be seen] ⟪invisible⟫**

EX. I always sensed unseen danger when walking in the alleys of that town.
あの町の路地を歩いていると、いつも見えない危険を感じた。
Ano machi no roji o aruite iru to, itsu-mo mienai kiken o kanjita.

unskillful adj. **[not having an ability in, clumsy]**

he┌ta˥na 下手な adj(*na*). **•c [not skilled at doing s.t.] ⟪unskilled, inexpert, poor at, clumsy, weak in⟫ ↔ joozuna** 上手な adj(*na*). **•c; bu-┌ki˥yoona** 不器用な adj(*na*). **•c [lacking in manual dexterity] ⟪clumsy, awkward, unhandy⟫ ↔ kiyoona** 器用な adj(*na*). **•c**

EX. (**a**) A: Are you good at repairing things?
物を直すのが上手ですか。
Mono o naosu no ga joozu desu ka.
B: No, I'm actually very unskillful at that.
いいえ、実は物を直すのはとても{下手/?不器用}なんです。
Iie, jitsu wa mono o naosu no wa totemo {heta/?bu-kiyoo} na n desu.
(**b**) I'm unskillful at doing anything.
私は何をするにも{不器用/下手}だ。
Watashi wa nani o suru ni mo {bu-kiyoo/heta} da.

untidy adj. **[not neat]**

ra┌nzatsuna 乱雑な adj(*na*). **•c [disordered and confused in spatial arrangement] ⟪disorderly, confused, cluttered⟫, da┌rashi ga na˥i (N)** だらしがない(N) **[loose and slovenly in one's manner of doing things] ⟪slovenly, lax, slack, sloppy⟫**

EX. (**a**) Your room is untidy, John. Clean it up.
ジョン、部屋が{乱雑だ/*だらしがない}よ。きれいにしなさい。
*Jon, heya ga {ranzatsu da/*darashi ga nai} yo. Kireini shinasai.*
(**b**) Don't wear your hair like that. It looks so untidy.
そんな髪をしてはだめよ。とても{だらしなく/*乱雑に}見えるから。
*Sonna kami o shite wa dame yo. Totemo {darashinaku/*ranzatsuni} mieru kara.*

until prep. **[continuing up to the time of]**

made まで prt. **[a particle which indicates the extent of an action or motion in time or space or a limit on a quantitative scale or which marks s.t./s.o./s.a. as exceeding the normal bounds of what is expected] ⟪till, up to, to, as far as, to the extent of, even⟫**

EX. (**a**) A: Until how late do you plan to work today?
今日は何時まで働く予定ですか。

Kyoo wa nan-ji made hataraku yotei desu ka.
B: Just until 5:00 P.M.
きっちり午後五時までです。
Kitchiri gogo go-ji made desu.
(**b**) I didn't know that Mariko had gotten married until yesterday.
万里子が結婚したことをきのうまで知りませんでした。
Mariko ga kekkon-shita koto o kinoo made shirimasendeshita.

—— conj. **[continuing up to the time when] Vinf. nonpast affirmative made Vinf. nonpast affirmative まで [continuing up to the time when] ⟪till⟫**

EX. (**a**) Keep reading the book until you get the gist of its main argument.
その本の中心をなす主張の要点がつかめるまで読み続けなさい。
Sono hon no chuushin o nasu shuchoo no yooten ga tsukame-ru made yomi-tsuzukenasai.
(**b**) I plan to stay in Japan until my Japanese is fluent.
私は日本語が流ちょうに話せるようになるまで日本にいるつもりです。
Watashi wa Nihon-go ga ryuuchooni hanase-ru yooni naru made Nihon ni iru tsumori desu.

unusual adj. **[not ordinary or common] fu⌈tsuu {dena⌉i/jana⌉i} (N) 普通{でない/じゃない}(N) •c, i⌈joona 異常な** adj(*na*). **•c [different from the ordinary state of affairs] ⟪extraordinary, abnormal, uncommon⟫, me⌈zurashi⌉i 珍しい** adj(*i*). **[seldom occurring ⟪fig. "unusual," "nice"⟫] ⟪rare, novel⟫**

EX. (**a**) It's unusual for Mr. Jackson to come to work this late. Something must have happened.
ジャクソンさんがこんなに遅く会社に来るのは{普通でない/普通じゃない/珍しい/?異常}です。何かがあったに違いありません。
Jakuson-san ga konnani osoku kaisha ni kuru no wa {futsuu denai/futsuu janai/mezurashii/?ijoo} desu. Nani-ka ga atta ni chigaiarimasen.
(**b**) I heard an unusual sound coming from the left engine of the plane.
飛行機の左のエンジンから{異常な/??普通でない/??普通じゃない/*珍しい}音がしてくるのを聞いた。
*Hikoo-ki no hidari no enjin kara {ijoona/??futsuu denai/??futsuu janai/*mezurashii} oto ga shite kuru no o kiita.*

unusually adv. **[to an extent which is not ordinary or common] i⌈jooni 異常に** /⟨adj(*na*). *ni* of *ijoona* **uncommon/ •c [in a manner which is different from the ordinary] ⟪extraordinarily, abnormally⟫, hi⌈jooni 非常に •c [to a degree or extent which is much more than average] ⟪exceedingly, excessively, remarkably⟫**

EX. The doctor told me that my blood pressure was unusually high.
医者は私の血圧が{異常に/非常に}高いと言った。
Isha wa watashi no ketsuatsu ga {ijooni/hijooni} takai to itta.

unwillingly adv. **[in a reluctant manner] i⌈ya-iya(-nagara) いやいや(ながら) [against one's will] ⟪grudgingly, reluctantly, as a matter of unpleasant necessity⟫, fu-⌈ho⌉n'i-nagara 不本意ながら •c [against one's true intentions] ⟪reluctantly, to one's regret⟫**

EX. He was unwillingly transferred to Nagoya by his company.
彼は会社に{いやいや(ながら)/不本意ながら}名古屋に転勤させられた。
Kare wa kaisha ni {iya-iya(-nagara)/fu-hon'i-nagara} Nagoya ni tenkin-sase-rareta.

up adv. **[to/at/in a higher level, place, or position; to/in a vertical position ⟪fig. "completely"⟫]**

NOTE: "Up" corresponds to different Japanese expressions depending on the meaning of the accompanying verb, as shown in examples below.

U

EX. (**a**) John brought up the topic of the current elections.
ジョンは現在の選挙のことを話題に取り上げた。
Jon wa genzai no senkyo no koto o wadai ni tori-ageta.
(**b**) Could you speak up a little, please?
もう少し大きい声で話してくださいませんか。
Moo-sukoshi ookii koe de hanashite kudasaimasen ka.
(**c**) Suddenly the man got up and left the room.
突然男は立ち上がって、部屋を出て行った。
Totsuzen otoko wa tachi-agatte, heya o dete-itta.
(**d**) I ran up the stairs as quickly as I could.
僕は全力で階段を駆け上がった。
Boku wa zenryoku de kaidan o kake-agatta.
(**e**) I couldn't easily come up with a good idea.
アイデアはそう簡単には浮かんでこなかった。
Aidea wa soo kantanni wa ukande konakatta.
(**f**) What's up?
どうしてる。
Doo shite ru.

—— prep. **[to/at a point further along or higher on s.t.]**
(⟨**-no**⟩ **u⌈e**) {**ni/e**} (⟨〜の⟩上){に/へ} n.+prt. **[to a position which is higher than s.t./s.o./s.a. or which is in contact with the surface of s.t.]** ⟪**on, onto**⟫, **o** を prt. **[a particle to indicate space along/in/through which some movement takes place]**

EX. (**a**) Frightened by the dog, the cat scampered up a tree.
犬におびえて猫は木{(の上){に/へ}/を}駆け上がった。
Inu ni obiete neko wa ki {(no ue) {ni/e}/o} kake-agatta.
(**b**) I'm going to take a walk up the street for some exercise. Want to come along?
運動のために通り{を/*(の上){に/へ}}ちょっと歩いてくるけど、一緒に行かない?
Undoo no tame ni toori {o/(no ue) {ni/e}} chotto aruite kuru kedo, issho ni ikanai?*

—— adj. **[at/in a higher level, place, or position; above the horizon]**
de⌉ru 出る ② **[for s.t./s.o./s.a. which is invisible or hidden to come out]** ⟪**appear, come out, emerge**⟫, **a⌈garu** あがる ① **[to go higher in vertical position, temperature, price, status, or level]**, **ne-⌈agari-suru** 値上がりする ③ **[to go higher in price]**
㊥ "rise to a higher location"▷上がる, "(for a kite) to fly/(for a flag) to be raised/(for cargo) to be unloaded/(for food) to be deep-fried"▷揚がる, "(for a hand) to be raised"▷挙がる, otherwise ▷あがる

EX. (**a**) The sun was already up.
太陽はもう{出て/上がって/*値上がりして}いた。
*Taiyoo wa moo {dete/agatte/*ne-agari-shite} ita.*
(**b**) The price of lettuce is up this month.
レタスは今月{値上がりして/値段が上がって/*出て}いる。
*Retasu wa kongetsu {ne-agari-shite/nedan ga agatte/*dete} iru.*

upon prep. **[in a position above and in contact with s.t. ⟪fig. "immediately after"⟫]**
1. ⟨**-no**⟩ **u⌈e** {**ni/de**} ⟨〜の⟩上{に/で} n.+prt. **[to/at a position which is higher than s.t./s.o./s.a. or which is in contact with the surface of s.t.]**

EX. Jesus said that Peter was the rock upon which he would build his church.
イエスはペテロは岩であり、その上に教会を建てると宣言された。
Iesu wa Petero wa iwa de ari, sono ue ni kyookai o tateru to sengen-sareta.

2. ⟨**-to**⟩ **su⌉gu** ⟨〜と⟩すぐ adv. **[as soon as s.t. takes place]**

EX. Upon returning to China, Ms. Chen began to teach Japanese.
中国に帰るとすぐ、チェンさんは日本語を教え始めた。

U

Chuugoku ni kaeru to sugu, Chen-san wa Nihon-go o oshie-hajimeta.

PHRASE: Once upon a time *mukashi-mukashi* 昔々

upper adj. **[higher in level, position, or rank]**

1. u⌈e no N 上のN [higher than s.t./s.o./s.a. in level, position, or rank] ↔ shita no N 下のN

EX. Pronouncing "p" requires the use of both the upper and lower lips.
「P」の音を発音するためには上の唇と下の唇の両方を使わなければならない。
'Pii' no on o hatsuon-suru tame ni wa ue no kuchibiru to shita no kuchibiru no ryoohoo o tsukawanakereba naranai.

2. jo⌈oryuu no N 上流のN •c [located closer to or in the direction of the source of a river《fig. "higher in social or economic rank"》] ↔ karyuu no N 下流のN •c

EX. This is an upper class residential area.
この辺は上流階級の人たちの住宅地です。
Kono hen wa jooryuu-kaikyuu no hito-tachi no juutaku-chi desu.

upright adj. **[standing straight up《fig. "strictly honest"》]**

1. ma⌈ssu⌉gu tatta N 真っすぐ立ったN /〈Vinf. past of *massugu tatsu* ① stand straight up/ [standing straight up], ma⌈ssu⌉gu tatte iru (N) 真っすぐ立っている(N) /〈V *te iru* of *massugu tatsu* ① stand straight up/

EX. There aren't many upright trees in this area due to the high winds.
強風のためこの辺には真っすぐ{立った/立っている}木があまりない。
Kyoofuu no tame kono hen ni wa massugu {tatta/tatte iru} ki ga amari nai.

2. sho⌈ojiki⌉na 正直な adj(*na*). **•c [truthful in character and not prone to lying, cheating, or hiding the truth; accurately representing one's true self in words or actions]《honest, square》**

EX. Very few people are as upright as John is.
ジョンほど正直な人は珍しいです。
Jon hodo shoojikina hito wa mezurashii desu.

upset vt. **[to turn or knock s.t. over or set s.t. in a state of disarray; to cause one's digestive processes to be out of order; to cause s.o. to feel worried or angry; for s.o. to defeat s.o. unexpectedly]**

1. 〈-o〉 hi⌈kkuri-ka⌉esu 〈～を〉ひっくり返す ① [for s.o. to reverse the orientation of s.t. up vs. down or front vs. back; to cause s.t. standing to fall over forcefully; to cause s.t. thought to be certain or firm to become uncertain or changeable]《capsize, overturn, tip over》

EX. The puppy upset the flower vase.
小犬が花びんをひっくり返した。
Ko-inu ga kabin o hikkuri-kaeshita.

2. 〈-o〉 ba⌈n-kuru⌉wase de ma⌈kasu 〈～を〉番狂わせで負かす ① [for s.o./s.a. to unexpectedly defeat s.o./s.a. in a game]

EX. Our football team upset the champion team.
我々のフットボールのチームはチャンピオンのチームを番狂わせで負かした。
Ware-ware no futto-booru no chiimu wa chanpion no chiimu o ban-kuruwase de makashita.

3. 〈〈-de〉〉〈-o〉 wa⌈ruku-suru 〈〈～で〉〉〈～を〉悪くする ③ [to harm s.t. by means of s.t.]

EX. Last night's shrimp seems to have upset my stomach.
きのうの晩のえびでおなかを悪くしたようだ。
Kinoo no ban no ebi de o-naka o waruku-shita yooda.

4. 〈-o〉 do⌈oyoo-saseru 〈～を〉動揺させる /〈causative of *dooyoo-suru* ③ become mentally disturbed/ ② •c [to cause s.o. mental disturbance]

EX. I'm sorry if I've said anything to upset you.
あなたを動揺させるようなことを言ったのならすみませんでした。
Anata o dooyoo-saseru yoona koto o itta no nara sumimasendeshita.

upside-down adv. **[in such a way that the upper and the lower parts are reversed]**

sa⌈kasama ni 逆さまに n.+prt. **《bottom up, wrong side up》**

EX. Look, the painting is hanging on the wall upside down.
見てご覧。壁に絵が逆さまにかかっているよ。
Mite go-ran. Kabe ni e ga sakasama ni kakatte iru yo.

upstairs adv. **[to/on a higher floor (usu. the second floor)]**

ni⌈kai + prt. 二階+prt. •c [to/on the second floor]

EX. (**a**) A: Where is the lounge?
ラウンジはどこでしょうか。
Raunji wa doko deshoo ka.
B: It's upstairs.
二階です。
Ni-kai desu.
(**b**) We have two bedrooms upstairs.
二階に{寝室/ベッドルーム}が二つあります。
Ni-kai ni {shinshitu/beddo-ruumu} ga futatsu arimasu.

upward adv. **[(in a direction) from lower to higher]**

1. u⌈e (no ho⌉o) {e/ni} 上(の方){へ/に} n.+prt. **[in a direction toward a point higher than s.t./s.o./s.a.]**

EX. (**a**) After crossing a wide plateau, the mountaineers began climbing slowly upward again.
登山家たちは広い高原を横切るとまたゆっくり上(の方){へ/に}登り始めた。
Tozan-ka-tachi wa hiroi koogen o yoko-giru to mata yukkuri ue (no hoo) {e/ni} nobori-hajimeta.
(**b**) The best strategy for moving upward in the company is to network with the right people.
会社で上(の方){へ/に}上がるには力になってくれそうな人とうまくやって行くのが最も効果的な戦略だ。
Kaisha de ue (no hoo) {e/ni} agaru ni wa chikara ni natte kure-soona hito to umaku yatte iku no ga mottomo kooka-tekina senryaku da.

2. -ijoo 〜以上 •c [more than]

EX. A: How much does it cost to hire a good lawyer?
いい弁護士を雇うにはどのぐらいかかるかな。
Ii bengo-shi o yatou ni wa dono-gurai kakaru ka na.
B: Oh, I'd say upward(s) of $100 an hour.
そうだな。一時間百ドル以上だろうね。
Soo da na. Ichi-jikan hyaku-doru-ijoo daroo ne.

—— adj. **[moving or directed toward a point higher than s.t./s.o./s.a.]**

u⌈wa-muki no N 上向きのN [facing upward] 《rising》, jo⌈oshoo no (N) 上昇の(N) •c [going upward]

EX. Based on all economic indicators, our country's economy appears now to be on an upward swing.
種々の経済指標から見て我が国の経済は現在{上向き/上昇}の方向に転じてきているようだ。
Shuju no keizai-shihyoo kara mite waga kuni no keizai wa genzai {uwa-muki/jooshoo} no hookoo ni tenjite kite iru yooda.

uranium n.

u⌈ranyu⌉umu ウラニウム •f

NOTE: There is a gap between its pronunciation ([uranyuumu]) and *katakana* representation (ウラニウム [uraniumu]).

urban adj. **[having to do with or located in a city]**

1. to⌈kai no N 都会のN •c [having to do with a city] ↔ inaka no N 田舎のN

EX. I prefer urban life to rural life.
私は田舎の生活より都会の生活の方が好きです。
Watashi wa inaka no seikatsu yori tokai no seikatsu no hoo ga suki desu.

2. to⌈kai-tokuyuu no N 都会特有の N •c [characteristic of a city]

EX. Large cities such as Tokyo, New York, London and Paris share many similar urban problems.
東京、ニューヨーク、ロンドン、パリ

U

などの大都市は似たような都会特有の問題をたくさん抱えている。
Tookyoo, Nyuuyooku, Rondon, Pari nado no dai-toshi wa nita yoona tokai-tokuyuu no mondai o takusan kakaete iru.

urge vt. **[for s.o. to drive s.o./s.a. on by force or encouragement; for s.o. to try hard to convince or persuade s.o. to do s.t.]**
1. ⟨-o⟩ **o⌈i-tate⌉ru** ⟨〜を⟩追い立てる ② **[for s.o. to drive s.o./s.a. on or away from a place ⟪fig. "hurry"⟫]** ⟪send away, hurry⟫
EX. The shepherd urged his sheep along the country path.
羊飼いが田舎道で羊を追い立てていた。
Hitsuji-kai ga inaka-michi de hitsuji o oi-tatete ita.
2. ⟨-ni⟩ {⟨-o⟩/Sinf. nonpast yo⌉oni} **su⌈sumeru** ⟨〜に⟩{⟨〜を⟩/Sinf. nonpast ように}勧める ② **[for s.o. to speak favorably to s.o. of s.o./s.t. as worthy or qualified for a particular purpose or to advise s.o. to do s.t.]** ⟪exhort, counsel, persuade, advise⟫
EX. The teacher urged his students to invest in a good word processor.
先生は学生にいいワープロを買うように勧めた。
Sensei wa gakusei ni ii waapuro o kau yooni susumeta.
3. {⟨-o⟩/⟨-to⟩} **ri⌈kisetsu-suru** {⟨〜を⟩/⟨〜と⟩}力説する ③ •c **[for s.o. to insist on s.t. very strongly]** ⟪emphasize, stress⟫
EX. Japanese intellectuals have for years been urging greater efforts toward internationalization in Japan.
日本の知識層は何年も前から{日本の国際化への更なる努力の必要性を/日本は国際化に向けて更に努力すべきだと}力説している。
Nihon no chishiki-soo wa nan-nen-mo mae kara {Nihon no kokusai-ka e no sara-naru doryoku no hitsuyoo-sei o/ Nihon wa kokusai-ka ni mukete sara-ni doryoku-su-beki da to} rikisetsu-shite iru.

— n. **[a strong desire or impulse to do s.t.]** **tsu⌈yo⌉i sho⌈odoo** 強い衝動 **[a strong impulse to do s.t.]**
EX. All of a sudden I felt an urge to hit the guy.
突然僕はその男をなぐりたいという強い衝動にかられた。
Totsuzen boku wa sono otoko o naguri-tai to iu tsuyoi shoodoo ni karereta.

urgent adj. **[requiring immediate attention or action]**
sa⌈shi-sematta N 差し迫ったN /⟨Vinf. past of *sashi-semaru* ① be imminent/ **[for an event or situation to be pressing on one]** ⟪pressing, imminent, exigent⟫, **ki⌈nkyuu no N** 緊急のN •c **[requiring immediate attention or action]** ⟪pressing, emergent⟫
EX. Due to some urgent business that has come up, I will not be able to attend tomorrow's committee meeting.
{差し迫った/緊急の}用事ができて、明日の委員会に出られなくなった。
{Sashi-sematta/Kinkyuu no} yooji ga dekite, asu no iin-kai ni de-rarenaku natta.

us pron. **[the object form of "we"]**
wa⌈tashi⌉-tachi o 私たちを **[the direct object form of the first person plural pronoun]**, **wa⌈tashi⌉-tachi ni** 私たちに **[the indirect object form of the first person plural pronoun]** ⟪to us⟫
NOTE: Various nouns corresponding to "we" can be used instead of *watashi-tachi*. It is also often the case that "we" or "us" is not expressed at all when it is clear from the context who is being referred to.
EX. (**a**) My parents took us to many places when we were kids.
子供の時に両親は{私たち{を/*に}/ø}色々な所へ連れて行ってくれました。
*Kodomo no toki ni ryooshin wa {watashi-tachi {o/*ni}/ø} iro-irona tokoro e tsurete-itte kuremashita.*
(**b**) A Japanese college student taught us Japanese when we were kids.
子供の時日本人の大学生が{私たち{に/*を}/ø}日本語を教えてくれました。

U

*Kodomo no toki Nihon-jin no daigaku-sei ga {watashi-tachi {ni/*o}/ø} Nihon-go o oshiete kuremashita.*

usage n. **[a way of handling s.t. or of putting it into service, esp. a word or phrase in a language]**
tsuˈkai-kata 使い方 /⟨V*masu* of *tsukau* ① use + *kata* method/ [the way in which to handle s.t. or put it to service]

EX. Could you explain to me the usage of this word?
この言葉の使い方を教えてくださいませんか。
Kono kotoba no tsukai-kata o oshiete kudasaimasen ka.

use vt. **[for s.o. to cause s.t./s.o./s.a. to act or serve for a particular purpose, including as an instrument or as material which is consumed]**
1. (⟨-ni⟩) ⟨-o⟩ tsuˈkau (⟨〜に⟩)⟨〜を⟩使う ① [for s.o. to put s.t./s.o./s.a. into service for a particular purpose, including as an instrument or as material which is consumed] ⟪employ, handle, manipulate, spend, speak, practice, take⟫, (⟨-ni⟩)⟨-o⟩ riˈyoo-suru (⟨〜に⟩)⟨〜を⟩利用する ③ •c [for s.o. to put s.t./s.o./s.a. into service for some purpose which brings benefit to one] ⟪utilize, make use of, put to good use, take advantage of, employ profitably⟫, ⟨-o⟩ shiˈyoo-suru ⟨〜を⟩使用する ③ •c [for s.o. to put s.t./s.o./s.a. having concrete or tangible form into service, including as an instrument or as material which is consumed ⟨fml⟩] ⟪employ, apply, consume⟫, ⟨-o⟩ moˈchiˈiru ⟨〜を⟩用いる ② [for s.o. to put s.t./s.o. having concrete or tangible form into service so as to benefit from some capability or function it/that person has ⟨w⟩] ⟪employ, have recourse to⟫

EX. (**a**) I didn't have a can opener so I used a knife to open the can.
缶切りがなかったのでナイフを{使って/用いて/?使用して/?利用して}缶を開けた。
Kan-kiri ga nakatta node naifu o {tsukatte/mochiite/?shiyoo-shite/?riyoo-shite} kan o aketa.
(**b**) I used the money my grandmother sent me to buy a new pair of shoes.
祖母が送ってくれたお金を{使って/*用いて/*使用して/*利用して}新しい靴を買った。
*Sobo ga okutte kureta o-kane o {tsukatte/*mochiite/*shiyoo-shite/*riyoo-shite} atarashii kutsu o katta.*
(**c**) The reason Ann does so well in school is not because she's so smart, but because she uses her time well.
アンが学校での成績がいいのは頭がいいからではなく、うまく時間を{使う/利用する/?使用する/*用いる}からだ。
*An ga gakkoo de no seiseki ga ii no wa atama ga ii kara dewanaku, umaku jikan o {tsukau/riyoo-suru/?shiyoo-suru/*mochiiru} kara da.*
(**d**) One of the solutions to the world's energy needs in the future will be to develop better ways to use solar energy.
将来の世界のエネルギー需要にこたえるためには太陽エネルギーを{使う/利用する/使用する/?用いる}、より良い方法を開発するのも一つの手だ。
Shoorai no sekai no enerugii-juyoo ni kotaeru tame ni wa taiyoo-enerugii o {tsukau/riyoo-suru/shiyoo-suru/?mochiiru}, yori-yoi hoohoo o kaihatsu-suru no mo hitotsu no te da.
(**e**) Jeff has a bad reputation for using people for his own selfish purposes.
ジェフは自分にとって都合のいいように人を{使う/利用する/*使用する/*用いる}という悪評を買っている。
*Jefu wa jibun ni-totte tsugoo no ii yooni hito o {tsukau/riyoo-suru/*shiyoo-suru/*mochiiru} to iu akuhyoo o katte iru.*
(**f**) Bricks were too expensive, so we had to use concrete blocks to build the wall.
れんがは高すぎるので、コンクリートブロックを{使って/使用して/用いて/*利用して}塀を作らなければならなかった。
Renga wa taka-sugiru node, konkuriito-

U

*burokku o {tsukatte/shiyoo-shite/mochiite/*riyoo-shite} hei o tsukuranakereba naranakatta.*

2. 〈-o〉 no⌉mu 〈〜を〉飲む ① [for s.o./s.a. to put s.t. into one's body through the mouth without chewing it 《fig. "overwhelm," "suppress," "acquiesce"》] 《drink, take, swallow》

EX. I use sleeping pills every night to help me get to sleep.
私は眠れるように毎晩睡眠薬を飲んでいる。
Watashi wa nemure-ru yooni mai-ban suimin-yaku o nonde iru.

— n. **[the act or way of causing s.t./s.o./s.a. to act or serve for a particular purpose or the state of being so caused to act or serve; the right or ability to cause s.t./s.o./s.a. to act or serve for a particular purpose; the quality of being helpful or useful; a need for the help or service of s.t./s.o./s.a.]**

1. shi⌈yoo 使用 •c [the act of putting into service s.t./s.o./s.a. having concrete or tangible form, including as an instrument or as material which is consumed] 《employment, application》, ri⌈yoo 利用 •c [the act of putting s.t./s.o./s.a. into service for some purpose which brings benefit to one] 《utilization, profitable employment》

EX. (**a**) The use of electric devices is prohibited on board the plane.
飛行機内での電気製品の{使用/*利用}は禁じられています。
*Hikoo-ki-nai de no denki-seihin no {shiyoo/*riyoo} wa kinji-rarete imasu.*
(**b**) The use of atomic energy is quite widespread in Japan.
原子力の{利用/?使用}は日本ではかなり広がっている。
Genshi-ryoku no {riyoo/?shiyoo} wa Nihon de wa kanari hirogatte iru.

2. tsu⌈kai-kata 使い方 /(V*masu* of *tsukau* ① use + *kata* method/ [the way or manner in which s.t./s.o./s.a. is put into service for a particular purpose. including as an instrument or as material which is consumed] 《how to use》, shi⌈yoo-hoo 使用法 •c [a method of putting into service s.t./s.o./s.a. which is concrete or tangible, including as an instrument or as material which is consumed] 《way to use》, ri⌈yoo-hoo 利用法 •c [a method of putting s.t./s.o./s.a. into service for some purpose which brings benefit to one] 《way to use》

EX. (**a**) He is extremely knowledgeable in the medical uses of laser technology.
彼はレーザー技術の医療における{利用法/使用法/?使い方}を熟知している。
Kare wa reezaa-gijutsu no iryoo ni-okeru {riyoo-hoo/shiyoo-hoo/?tsukai-kata} o jukuchi-shite iru.
(**b**) I began using the machine without having been properly trained in its use.
その機械の{使い方/使用法/?利用法}の訓練を十分受けないで使い始めてしまった。
Sono kikai no {tsukai-kata/shiyoo-hoo/?riyoo-hoo} no kunren o juubun ukenaide tsukai-hajimete shimatta.

3. tsu⌈kai-michi 使い道 [a way in which to use s.t.]

EX. Do you have any use for this old box?
この古い箱は何か使い道がありますか。
Kono furui hako wa nani-ka tsukai-michi ga arimasu ka.

PHRASE: of no use *yaku ni tatanai* (N) 役に立たない(N)

EX. This dictionary is so old that it's of no use to me anymore.
この辞書は古くてもう役に立たない。
Kono jisho wa furukute moo yaku ni tatanai.

PHRASE: there is no use in …ing V*te mo yaku ni tatanai* V*te*も役に立たない, V*te mo shoo ga nai* V*te*もしょうがない

EX. There's no use in discussing this issue any further.
これ以上この問題について長く話し合っても{役に立たない/しょうがない}。
Kore ijoo kono mondai ni-tsuite nagaku hanashi-atte mo {yaku ni tatanai/shoo ga nai}.

U

PHRASE: out of use *tsukawa-rete inai* (N) 使われていない(N)

EX. This expression has long since gone out of use.
この表現は大分前から使われていない。
Kono hyoogen wa daibu mae kara tsukawa-rete inai.

PHRASE: put to use ⟨*-o*⟩ *tsukau* ⟨〜を⟩使う ① ((employ, handle, need)), ⟨*-o*⟩ *shiyoo-suru* ⟨〜を⟩使用する ③ •c ((use, employ, apply)), ⟨*-o*⟩ *riyoo-suru* ⟨〜を⟩利用する ③ •c ((utilize, employ for profit))

EX. Why don't you put all this old furniture to use?
この古い家具を全部{利用したら/使用したら/使ったら}どうですか。
Kono furui kagu o zenbu {riyoo-shitara/shiyoo-shitara/tsukattara} doo desu ka.

used¹ adj. **[accustomed to (doing) s.t.]** **⟨-ni⟩ na˥rete iru (N) ⟨〜に⟩慣れている(N) /⟨V*te iru* of *nareru* ② get used to/ [be accustomed to (doing) s.t.]**

EX. It's taken a while, but I've finally gotten used to life in Tokyo.
ずいぶん時間がかかりましたが、やっと東京の生活に慣れてきました。
Zuibun jikan ga kakarimashita ga, yatto Tookyoo no seikatsu ni narete kimashita.

used² adj. **[secondhand, not new]** **tsu˥kai-furushi no N 使い古しのN [having become old through handling or service over a long period of time (used of portable items)] ((worn-out, well-worn)), chu˥uko no N 中古のN •c [not new because of having been put to service by s.o. else previously] ((secondhand))**

EX. (**a**) We bought a used car because we couldn't afford a new one.
新しいのを買う余裕がなかったので{中古/*使い古し}の車を買いました。
*Atarashii no o kau yoyuu ga nakatta node {chuuko/*tsukai-furushi} no kuruma o kaimashita.*
(**b**) You don't mind buying this used racket?
この{使い古し/中古}のラケットでも買ってくれるんですか。
Kono {tsukai-furushi/chuuko} no raketto demo katte kureru n desu ka.

used³ vi. **[(with the infinitive) indicating a situation that continued for some extended time in the past but that no longer occurs or exists, including a state of being or an action performed regularly or repeatedly]**
ma˥e wa...Vinf. past (mo˥no˥ da) ga i˥ma wa...neg. 前は…Vinf. past(ものだ)が、今は…neg.

EX. (**a**) I used to exercise every day, but not any more.
前は毎日運動したものですが、今はしていません。
Mae wa mai-nichi undoo-shita mono desu ga, ima wa shite imasen.
(**b**) I used to hate raw fish, but now I love it.
前はさしみが大嫌いだったのですが、今は大好きです。
Mae wa sashimi ga dai-kirai datta no desu ga, ima wa dai-suki desu.

useful adj. **[serviceable for some purpose]** **⟨-ni⟩ ya˥ku˥ ni ta˥tsu (N) ⟨〜に⟩役に立つ(N) ① [playing a role in accomplishing some task/purpose or making some task easier] ((helpful, of use, efficient, capable)), yu˥uekina 有益な** adj(*na*). **•c [profitable or beneficial to one] ((beneficial, instructive, edifying, serviceable)) ↔ muekina 無益な** adj(*na*). **•c**

EX. (**a**) This English-Japanese dictionary should be particularly useful to students of elementary Japanese.
この英和辞典は特に初級日本語の学習者に{役に立つ/有益な}はずです。
Kono Ei-Wa-jiten wa toku ni shokyuu Nihon-go no gakushuu-sha ni {yaku ni tatsu/yuuekina} hazu desu.
(**b**) I wouldn't throw these old class notes away. They might come in useful some day.
この古い授業のノートは捨てない方がいいと思う。いつか{役に立つ/*有益になる}かもしれないから。
Kono furui jugyoo no nooto wa sutenai

U

*hoo ga ii to omou. Itsu-ka {yaku ni tatsu/ *yuueki ni naru} kamoshirenai kara.*
(**c**) Thank you very much for your useful advice.
{役に立つ/有益な}アドバイスをありがとうございました。
{Yaku ni tatsu/Yuuekina} adobaisu o arigatoo gozaimashita.

useless adj. **[not serviceable for any purpose]**
{⟨-ni⟩/⟨-no⟩} **ya⌈ku⌉ ni ta⌈ta⌉nai (N)** {⟨〜に⟩/⟨〜の⟩}役に立たない **(N)** /⟨**Vneg. of *yaku ni tatsu*** ① **be useful + *nai* not**/ **[not playing a role in accomplishing some task/purpose or making some task easier], mu⌉ekina** 無益な adj(*na*). **•c [not profitable or beneficial to one]** ⟪**futile**⟫ ↔ **yuuekina** 有益な adj(*na*). **•c**

EX. (**a**) Don't become a person useless to society.
社会に{役に立たない/*無益な}人になるな。
*Shakai ni {yaku ni tatanai/*muekina} hito ni naru na.*
(**b**) This bike is too far gone to be fixed—it's useless.
この自転車はがたがたで直しようがないからもう{何の役にも立たない/*無益だ}。
*Kono jitensha wa gata-gata de naoshi-yoo ga nai kara {nan no yaku ni mo tatanai/*mueki da}.*
(**c**) My husband is useless. He doesn't do a bit of work around the house.
うちの主人は{役に立ちません/*無益です}。家のことを何もしないんですから。
*Uchi no shujin wa {yaku ni tachimasen/ *mueki desu}. Ie no koto o nani-mo shinai n desu kara.*
(**d**) It would be useless for the people in this area to build a dam.
ダムを作ってもこの地域の人々には{無益/役に立たない}だろう。
Damu o tsukutte mo kono chiiki no hito-bito ni wa {mueki/yaku ni tatanai} daroo.

usual adj. **[such as happens, is done, or is used on many or most occasions]**
fu⌈tsuu no N 普通のN **•c [conforming to a standard/norm** ⟪**fig. "commonly found"**⟫**]** ⟪**normal, regular, ordinary, conventional**⟫ ↔ **tokubetsu no N** 特別のN **•c; i⌉tsu-mo no N** いつものN **[consistent with what happens or is done on most occasions]** ⟪**ordinary, habitual, customary**⟫

EX. (**a**) A: What will you have today?
今日は何にする?
Kyoo wa nani ni suru?
B: The usual, a beer.
{いつも/*普通}のビール。
*{Itsu-mo/*Futsuu} no biiru.*
(**b**) On a usual day I leave home at about 7:30 in the morning.
{いつも/普通}の日には朝七時半ごろ家を出ます。
{Itsu-mo/Futsuu} no hi ni wa asa shichi-ji-han-goro ie o demasu.
(**c**) The way he talked today wasn't usual for him.
今日のあの人の話し方は{普通/いつもの話し方}じゃなかった。
Kyoo no ano hito no hanashi-kata wa {futsuu/itsu-mo no hanashi-kata} janakatta.

usually adv. **[on most occasions]**
ta⌈itei 大抵 **•c [in the great majority of cases]** ⟪**generally, mostly, for the most part, largely, nearly always**⟫, **fu⌈tsuu** 普通 **•c [in most ordinary cases]** ⟪**normally, commonly**⟫, **fu⌉dan** 普段 **•c [under normal circumstances]** ⟪**always, in and out of season**⟫

EX. (**a**) On weekends, I usually play golf.
週末は、{大抵/普通/*普段}ゴルフをやります。
*Shuumatsu wa {taitei/futsuu/*fudan} gorufu o yarimasu.*
(**b**) I'm usually in the library studying till eleven in the evening.
{普段/大抵/普通}は夜十一時まで図書館で勉強している。
{Fudan/Taitei/Futsuu} wa yoru juu-ichi-ji made tosho-kan de benkyoo-shite iru.

Utah n.
Yu˥ta ユタ [(State of) Utah]
utensil n. **[an instrument or container, esp. for domestic use in the kitchen]**
1. da˥idokoro-yo˥ohin 台所用品 •c [an instrument or container for use in the kitchen]

EX. We just got married so we still don't have many kitchen utensils.
結婚したばかりなので、まだ台所用品があまりありません。
Kekkon-shita bakari na node, mada daidokoro-yoohin ga amari arimasen.

2. do˥ogu˥ 道具 •c [a device used for accomplishing a certain kind of work] ((appliance, implement, tool, gadget))

EX. We can't start this job without the proper utensils.
適当な道具がなければこの仕事を始めることはできません。
Tekitoona doogu ga nakereba kono shigoto o hajimeru koto wa dekimasen.

utmost adj. **[greatest, farthest, most extreme]**
1. i˥chiban tooi 一番遠い adj(*i*). **[the farthest]**

EX. The king commanded the messengers to carry the news of his victory to the utmost reaches of his kingdom.
王は使者たちに勝利の知らせを国の一番遠い所まで伝えてくるよう命じた。
Oo wa shisha-tachi ni shoori no shirase o kuni no ichiban tooi tokoro made tsutaete kuru yoo meijita.

2. kyo˥kuta˥nna 極端な •c [at a point on a scale farthest from the median point] ((extreme, radical, excessive)), sa˥ida˥i-gen no N 最大限のN •c [the maximum]

EX. (**a**) I put my utmost effort into preparing for the examination.
試験に向けて準備するのに{最大限の/*極端な}努力をした。
*Shiken ni mukete junbi-suru no ni {saidai-gen no/*kyokutanna} doryoku o shita.*
(**b**) The people in the mountain village were living in utmost poverty.
山村の人々は{極端な/*最大限の}貧困のうちに暮らしていた。
*Sanson no hito-bito wa {kyokutanna/*saidai-gen no} hinkon no uchi ni kurashite ita.*

utterly adv. **[completely, absolutely]**
ma˥ttaku 全く [in a manner so strongly that it cannot be expressed in any other way] ((entirely, completely, thoroughly, not at all, not in the least)), su˥kka˥ri すっかり adv. **[an expression indicating that some condition is pervasive or exhaustively present] ((all, quite, entirely, wholly, totally)), ka˥nzenni 完全に /(adj(*na*). *ni* of *kanzenna* complete/ •c [in a way absolutely free from imperfections/weaknesses] ((perfectly, entirely, completely))**

EX. (**a**) I was utterly astounded when I heard about the murder of my colleague at work.
会社の同僚が殺されたと聞いた時は{全く/*すっかり/*完全に}驚いた。
*Kaisha no dooryoo ga korosa-reta to kiita toki wa {mattaku/*sukkari/*kanzenni} odoroita.*
(**b**) I utterly forgot about my wife's birthday.
私は妻の誕生日のことを{全く/すっかり/完全に}忘れてしまった。
Watashi wa tsuma no tanjoo-bi no koto o {mattaku/sukkari/kanzenni} wasurete shimatta.

V

vacant adj. **[empty of content or occupants]**
a⌈ite iru (N) あいている(N) /⟨V*te iru* of *aku* ① open/ ② [for the interior of s.t. to be exposed to the outside ⟪fig. "be empty"]**
㊮ "for a window/door to be open"▷開いている, otherwise ▷空いている
EX. (**a**) Is there a vacant room in this hotel?
このホテルには空いている部屋がありますか。
Kono hoteru ni wa aite iru heya ga arimasu ka.
(**b**) Is this seat vacant?
この席は空いていますか。
Kono seki wa aite imasu ka.

vacation n. **[a period of rest from activity at work or school (often spent away from home)]**
ya⌈sumi⌉ 休み /⟨V*masu* of *yasumu* ① take rest/ **[(a period of time during which there is a) cessation of activity ⟪fig. "holiday," "vacation"⟫]** ⟪rest, respite, repose, recess, holiday⟫, **kyu⌈uka** 休暇 •c **[a leave of absence from work or school]** ⟪holiday, leave of absence, furlough, sabbatical leave⟫
EX. I took a one-month vacation in Hawaii.
私は一か月の{休み/休暇}を取って、ハワイで過ごした。
Watashi wa ik-kagetsu no {yasumi/kyuuka} o totte, Hawai de sugoshita.

vaccine n.
wa⌉kuchin ワクチン •f
EX. Every winter I get a flu vaccine shot.
毎年冬には、インフルエンザのワクチンを注射してもらいます。
Mai-toshi fuyu ni wa, infuruenza no wakuchin o chuusha-shite moraimasu.

vacuum n. **[a space totally devoid of air or other matter ⟪fig. "void"⟫]**
shi⌈nkuu 真空 •c **[a space totally devoid of air or other]**, **ku⌈uhaku** 空白 •c **[a blank space]** ⟪void, blank⟫
EX. (**a**) In a vacuum everything falls at the same speed.
{真空/*空白}では何でも同じスピードで落ちる。
*{Shinkuu/*Kuuhaku} de wa nan-demo onaji supiido de ochiru.*
(**b**) Nobuo felt a huge vacuum in his heart after Yumi was gone.
由美がいなくなって、信男の心に大きな{空白/*真空}が出来た。
*Yumi ga inaku natte, Nobuo no kokoro ni ookina {kuuhaku/*shinkuu} ga dekita.*
PHRASE: vacuum cleaner *denki-sooji-ki* 電気掃除機 •c

— vt. **[for s.o. to clean s.t., esp. an area in a building, using a vacuum cleaner]**
⟨-ni⟩ **so⌈oji⌉-ki o kakeru** ⟨〜に⟩掃除機をかける ②
EX. It takes over an hour to vacuum all the rooms in our house.
うちの全部の部屋に掃除機をかけるのに一時間以上かかります。
Uchi no zenbu no heya ni sooji-ki o kakeru no ni ichi-jikan-ijoo kakarimasu.

vague adj. **[not clearly sensed, expressed, or defined]**
1. **ha⌈kki⌉ri mi⌈e⌉nai** (N) はっきり見えない (N) /⟨Vstem of ***hakkiri mieru*** ② clearly visible + ***nai*** not/ **[not clearly visible]**, **ha⌈kki⌉ri ki⌈koenai** (N) はっきり聞こえない (N) /⟨Vstem of ***hakkiri kikoeru*** clearly audible + ***nai*** not/ **[not clearly audible]**, **bo⌈n'ya⌉ri-shita N** ぼんやりしたN /⟨Vinf. past of ***bon'yari-suru*** ③ be hazy/ **[for a shape or one's state of mind to be hazy]**

⟪blank, absent-minded, dim, obscure⟫, **bo⌈n'ya⌉ri-shite iru (N)** ぼんやりしている(N) /⟨V*te iru* of *bon'yari-suru* ③ to be hazy/ ②

EX. (a) We could only see the vague outline of the bridge due to the thick fog.
濃い霧のため橋の輪郭が{ぼんやりしていた/はっきり見えなかった}。
Koi kiri no tame hashi no rinkaku ga {bon'yari-shite ita/hakkiri mienakatta}.
(b) The recorded voice was too vague to be understood.
録音の声は{はっきり聞こえない/*ぼんやりしている}ので聞き取れなかった。
*Rokuon no koe wa {hakkiri kikoenai/ *bon'yari-shite iru} node kiki-tore-nakatta.*

2. a⌈imaina あいまいな adj(*na*). •c **[unclear in meaning or intent] ⟪ambiguous, obscure, equivocal, dubious⟫, ba⌈kuzen to shita N** 漠然としたN /⟨V*inf. past* of *bakuzen to suru* ③ be obscure/ •c **[too obscure to discern a coherent whole] ⟪obscure, ambiguous, hazy, misty⟫, ba⌈kuzen to shite iru (N)** 漠然としている(N) /⟨V*te iru* of *bakuzen to suru* ③ be obscure/ •c, **fu-⌈me⌉iryoona** 不明瞭な adj(*na*). •c **[unclear in meaning or pronunciation] ⟪indistinct, obscure, opaque, dim, blurred⟫**

EX. (a) The meaning of this sentence is vague, isn't it?
この文の意味は{あいまいだ/漠然としている/不明瞭だ}ね。
Kono bun no imi wa {aimai da/ bakuzen to shite iru/fu-meiryoo da} ne.
(b) It bothers me how his answers to my questions are always so vague.
こちらの質問に対する彼の答えはいつも{あいまいな/漠然としている/不明瞭な}ので、とても不愉快だ。
Kochira no shitsumon ni-taisuru kare no kotae wa itsu-mo {aimaina/bakuzen to shite iru/fu-meiryoona} node, totemo fu-yukai da.

vain adj. **[conceited, esp. about how one looks; having no worth or importance; not successful, futile]**

1. ⟨-ga⟩ ji⌈man no N ⟨〜が⟩自慢のN •c **[outwardly exhibiting a sense of pleasure or satisfaction in one's own abilities, accomplishments, possessions, or other attributes] ⟪plume oneself on⟫**

EX. Anna can be a bit vain about her looks, but other than that she's a very friendly girl.
アンナは美ぼうが自慢のようなところがあるけれど、その点を除けばとても親切な女性だ。
Anna wa biboo ga jiman no yoona tokoro ga aru keredo, sono ten o nozokeba totemo shinsetsuna josei da.

2. mu-⌈i⌉mina 無意味な adj(*na*). •c **[having no meaning] ⟪meaningless⟫**

EX. After losing Mary, life began to look vain and empty to me.
メアリーを亡くしてから人生が無意味で、空しく思えてきた。
Mearii o nakushite kara jinsei ga mu-imi de, munashiku omoete kita.

PHRASE: in vain *mudana* 無駄な adj(*na*). ⟪wasteful⟫

EX. Our efforts to turn the forest into a national park were in vain.
その森林を国立公園にしようとする私たちの努力は無駄だった。
Sono shinrin o kokuritsu-kooen ni shiyoo to suru watashi-tachi no doryoku wa muda datta.

valley n. **[a long low area between hills/ mountains or an area drained by a river]**

1. ta⌈ni⌉ 谷 **[a long low area between mountains ⟪fig. "trough"⟫] ⟪dale, hollow, gorge⟫, ta⌈ni-{ma/ai}** 谷{間/あい} **[space between mountains or tall buildings] ⟪ravine, gorge, chasm⟫**

EX. There was a small village in the valley.
その谷(-{間/あい})に小さな村があった。
Sono tani(-{ma/ai}) ni chiisana mura ga atta.

2. ryu⌈uiki 流域 •c **[an area drained by a river] ⟪basin⟫**

valuable adj. **[having (monetary) worth or importance ⟪fig. "expensive"⟫]**

V

1. ka¹chi ga aru (N) 価値がある(N) [having a quality which makes s.t./s.o./s.a. useful, good, or exchangeable for money], ki⌈choona 貴重な adj(*na*). **•c [having some quality to a rare or unusual degree which makes s.t./s.o./s.a. very useful, good, dear, or expensive] ⟪precious⟫**

EX. (**a**) In Japan land is said to be more valuable than money.
日本では土地の方が金より{価値がある/貴重だ}そうだ。
Nihon de wa tochi no hoo ga kane yori {kachi ga aru/kichoo da} sooda.
(**b**) Thank you very much for taking your valuable time to help me.
私のために{貴重な/*価値がある}お時間を使っていただき、大変ありがとうございました。
*Watashi no tame ni {kichoona/*kachi ga aru} o-jikan o tsukatte itadaki, taihen arigatoo gozaimashita.*

2. ko¹okana 高価な adj(*na*) **•c [very high in price or worth] ⟪expensive, costly, high-priced⟫**

EX. (**a**) This jewel is something extremely valuable.
この宝石はとても高価なものです。
Kono booseki wa totemo kookana mono desu.
(**b**) Thank you very much for such a valuable gift.
高価な贈り物を、どうもありがとうございます。
Kookana okuri-mono o, doomo arigatoo gozaimasu.

— n. **[a personal possession of great monetary worth, usu. s.t. small] ki⌈choo-hin 貴重品 •c**

EX. We cannot take responsibility for loss or theft of valuables.
貴重品の紛失や盗難については責任を追いかねます。
Kichoo-hin no funshitsu ya toonan ni-tsuite wa sekinin o oi-kanemasu.

value n. **[the (monetary) worth or importance of s.t.]**

1. da⌈ika 代価 •c [an amount of money paid in exchange for goods ⟪fig. "sacrifice"⟫ ⟨w⟩] ⟪price, cost⟫, ka⌈kaku 価格 •c [the amount of money for which s.t. is bought or sold ⟨fml⟩] ⟪price, cost⟫

EX. The value of the stolen stereo was around $1,500.
盗まれたステレオの{価格/代価}は千五百ドルぐらいだった。
Nusuma-reta sutereo no {kakaku/daika} wa sen-go-hyaku-doru-gurai datta.

2. ka¹chi 価値 •c [the degree to which s.t./s.o./s.a. is useful, good, or exchangeable for money] ⟪worth, merit⟫

EX. (**a**) I don't think that a child could appreciate the value of this book.
子供にこの本の価値は分からないと思います。
Kodomo ni kono hon no kachi wa wakaranai to omoimasu.
(**b**) The value of the yen has increased again.
円の価値がまた上がった。
En no kachi ga mata agatta.
(**c**) A person's value can't be determined by how much money he makes.
人の価値を収入で決めてはいけない。
Hito no kachi o shuunyuu de kimete wa ikenai.

— vt. **[for s.o. to estimate the (monetary) worth of s.t./s.o./s.a. ⟪fig. "think highly of s.t./s.o./s.a."⟫]**

1. ⟨-ni⟩ (⟨-no⟩) ne¹ o tsu⌈ke¹ru ⟨〜に⟩(⟨〜の⟩) 値を付ける ② [for s.o. to set the price for] ⟪price, appraise⟫

EX. The realtor valued our house at $230,000.
不動産業者は私たちの家に二十三万ドルの値を付けた。
Fudoo-san-gyoosha wa watashi-tachi no ie ni ni-juu-san-man-doru no ne o tsuketa.

2. ⟨-o⟩ so⌈nchoo-suru ⟨〜を⟩尊重する ③ •c [for s.o. to think very highly of s.o./s.t., including the law, human life, and the rights or opinions of others], ⟨-o⟩ ta⌈isetsu ni suru ⟨〜を⟩大切にする ③ [for s.o. to

V

treat s.t./s.o./s.a. as being important or dear to one or with respect] **《cherish, treasure, care much for》**

EX. (**a**) A society that values its older members is a good society.
老人を{尊重する/大切にする}社会はいい社会だ。
Roojin o {sonchoo-suru/taisetsu ni suru} shakai wa ii shakai da.
(**b**) You can tell from the many parks in this town how much the people here value their natural environment.
この町に公園が多いことからここの住民がどんなにその自然環境を{大切にして/*尊重して}いるかが見て取れる。
*Kono machi ni kooen ga ooi koto kara koko no juumin ga donnani sono shizen-kankyoo o {taisetsu ni shite/ *sonchoo-shite} iru ka ga mite tore-ru.*

valve n. **[a movable device that controls the flow of gas or liquid through a pipe or vessel]**
be⌉n 弁 •c [a flower petal 《fig. "a movable device that controls the flow of gas or liquid through a pipe or vessel"》] 《petal》, ba⌈rubu バルブ •f [a mechanical device that controls the flow of gas or liquid through a pipe]

EX. (**a**) The doctor told me that I have a bad heart valve.
医者は私の心臓の{弁/*バルブ}が悪いと言った。
*Isha wa watashi no shinzoo no {ben/ *barubu} ga warui to itta.*
(**b**) Pressure cookers have a valve that releases steam when it builds up.
圧力釜にはたまった蒸気を逃がす{弁/バルブ}がついている。
Atsuryoku-gama ni wa tamatta jooki o nigasu {ben/barubu} ga tsuite iru.

van n. **[a covered vehicle used for transporting goods, animals, or people]**
ba⌉n バン •f

EX. I borrowed a friend's van to move into my new apartment.
私は新しいアパートに引っ越すのに友達のバンを借りた。
Watashi wa atarashii apaato ni hikkosu no ni tomodachi no ban o karita.

vanish vi. **[to disappear suddenly without leaving any trace]**
ki⌈eru 消える ② [for s.t. which has been in a place to cease to be there] 《be extinguished, melt, disappear, wear away, be defaced, die away, evaporate, peter out》
↔ arawareru 現われる ②

EX. When the magician opened his hand the coin had vanished.
手品師が手を開くとコインは消えていた。
Tejina-shi ga te o hiraku to koin wa kiete ita.

vapor n. **[moisture suspended in the air, esp. steam]**
1. jo⌉oki 蒸気 •c [gas formed by the evaporation or sublimation of a liquid or solid] 《steam》, su⌈ijo⌉oki 水蒸気 •c [gas formed by the evaporation of water] 《steam》, yu⌉ge 湯気 [the gas which rises from hot water] 《steam》

EX. (**a**) Vapor was coming out through the valve of the pressure cooker.
{蒸気/水蒸気/?湯気}が圧力釜の弁から出ていた。
{Jooki/Suijooki/?Yuge} ga atsuryoku-gama no ben kara dete ita.
(**b**) The cat was watching the vapor coming out through the mouth of the kettle.
猫が湯わかしの口から{蒸気/水蒸気/湯気}が出てくるのを見ていた。
Neko ga yu-wakashi no kuchi kara {jooki/suijooki/yuge} ga dete-kuru no o mite ita.

2. mo⌉ya もや [a mass of tiny drops of water in the air near ground level, not as thick as *kiri*] 《haze, mist》, ki⌈ri 霧 [a mass of very minute waterdrops floating near the surface of the earth]

EX. There was a thick vapor hanging over the top of the mountain.
山の頂には濃い{霧/もや}がかかっていた。

Yama no itadaki ni wa koi {kiri/moya} ga kakatte ita.

variable adj. **[changing often or able to be changed]**

1. ka⌈wari-yasu⌉i 変わりやすい adj(*i*). **/⟨V*masu* of *kawaru* ① change + *yasui* adj(*i*). easy/ [tending to change] ↔ kawari-nikui** 変わりにくい adj(*i*).

EX. Mountain weather tends to be variable.
山の天気は変わりやすい。
Yama no tenki wa kawari-yasui.

2. ka⌈e-rareru 変えられる **/⟨pot. of *kaeru* ② change s.t./** ②

EX. The color of the chameleon's skin is variable according to its surroundings.
カメレオンはその皮膚の色を環境に合わせて変えられる。
Kamereon wa sono hifu no iro o kankyoo ni awa-sete kae-rareru.

—— n. **[s.t. that changes or can change]**

1. ka⌈wari-yasu⌉i mono 変わりやすいもの **[s.t. that tends to change]**

2. he⌈nsu⌉u 変数 **•c [a quantity that may assume any value] ↔ teisuu** 定数 **•c**

EX. In y=3x, x and y are called variables.
y=3xでxとyは変数と呼ばれる。
Wai ikooru san ekkusu de ekkusu to wai wa hensuu to yoba-reru.

variation n. **[an occurrence of change; the extent to which s.t. changes; a different form of s.t., esp. a musical theme repeated in a different form from before]**

1. he⌉nka 変化 **•c [the coming into being of a different quality or state in s.t. as it moves through space or time] ⟪change, alteration, mutation⟫, he⌈ndoo** 変動 **•c [the changing of a condition or situation] ⟪change, alteration, fluctuation⟫**

EX. (**a**) There has been little variation in public opinion these past few years in the percentages for and against abortion.
ここ数年間妊娠中絶に対する世論の賛否の割合にはあまり{変化/?変動}はない。
Koko suu-nenkan ninshin-chuuzetsu ni-taisuru seron no sanpi no wariai ni wa amari {henka/?hendoo} wa nai.
(**b**) There have been wide variations in the prices of stocks over the past year.
この一年の間に株価に大きな{変動/?変化}があった。
Kono ichi-nen no aida ni kabu-ka ni ookina {hendoo/?henka} ga atta.

2. he⌉nshu 変種 **•c [a member of a group or class exhibiting a difference from the other members in some characteristic such as shape] ⟪mutation, monster⟫**

EX. This must be some variation of a frog.
これはかえるの変種に違いない。
Kore wa kaeru no henshu ni chigainai.

3. he⌈nso⌉o(-kyoku) 変奏(曲) **•c [a musical theme repeated in a different form], ba⌈rie⌉eshon** バリエーション **•f**

varied adj. **[having numerous forms or kinds]**

i⌈ro-irona 色々な adj(*na*). **[of many kinds] ⟪various, diverse, a variety of⟫**

EX. As in any language, there are varied dialects in Japanese as well.
どの言語もそうであるように、日本語にも色々な方言があります。
Dono gengo mo soo dearu yooni, Nihon-go ni mo iro-irona hoogen ga arimasu.

variety n. **[the quality of not being the same (all the time); a number of different things or kinds; an individual or group of individuals which is different in some way from other members of its class]**

shu⌉rui 種類 **•c [a group of individuals sharing common characteristics] ⟪kind, sort, class⟫, he⌉nka** 変化 **•c [the coming into being of a different quality or state in s.t. as it moves through space or time] ⟪change, variation, alteration⟫, ba⌈ra⌉etii** バラエティー **•f [a number of different things or kinds; a show consisting of singing, dancing, and skits]**

EX. (**a**) There is an incredible variety of magazines published in Japan.
日本では驚くほど様々な{種類/*バラエティー/*変化}の雑誌が出ている。

V

*Nihon de wa odoroku hodo sama-zamana {shurui/*baraetii/*henka} no zasshi ga dete iru.*
(**b**) He had a life rich in variety.
彼の人生は{変化/??バラエティー/*種類}に富んでいた。
*Kare no jinsei wa {henka/??baraetii/*shurui} ni tonde ita.*
(**c**) We're planning to have an event rich in variety.
{バラエティー/*種類/*変化}に富んだ催しものを計画しています。
*{Baraetii/*Shurui/*Henka} ni tonda moyooshi-mono o keikaku-shite imasu.*
(**d**) I enjoy watching television variety shows.
テレビで{バラエティー/*種類/*変化}ショーを見るのが好きです。
*Terebi de {baraetii/*shurui/*henka}-shoo o miru no ga suki desu.*

various adj. **[of different kinds or more than one]**
i⌈ro-irona 色々な adj(*na*). **[of many kinds]** ((**diverse, a variety of**)), **i⌈ronna いろんな** adj(*na*). **[of many kinds ⟨s⟩]**
EX. (**a**) I believe there are various solutions to this problem.
この問題には{色々な/いろんな}解決法があると思う。
Kono mondai ni wa {iro-irona/ironna} kaiketsu-hoo ga aru to omou.
(**b**) This restaurant specializes in various sea food dishes.
このレストランは{色々な/いろんな}海鮮料理の専門店です。
Kono resutoran wa {iro-irona/ironna} kaisen-ryoori no senmon-ten desu.
(**c**) This semester I'm taking various courses on Japan.
今学期は{色々な/いろんな}日本学の科目を取っています。
Kon-gakki wa {iro-irona/ironna} Nihon-gaku no kamoku o totte imasu.

V

vary vt. **[to cause s.t. to be or become different]**
⟨**-o**⟩ ((⟨**-ni**⟩)) **ka⌈eru** ⟨〜を⟩((⟨〜に⟩))かえる ② **[for s.o. to cause s.t./s.o./s.a. to become s.t. else]** ((**change, alter, shift, convert, reverse, transform**))
㊥ "cause s.t./s.o./s.a. to change"▷変える, "cause s.t./s.o./s.a. to replace s.t./s.o./s.a. else"▷代える, "exchange s.t. for s.t. else"▷換える
EX. At our restaurant we try to vary the menu from season to season.
当店では季節によってメニューを変えるようにしています。
Tooten de wa kisetsu ni-yotte menyuu o kaeru yooni shite imasu.
— vi. **[to be or become different]**
1. ka⌈waru かわる ① **[for s.t./s.o./s.a. to become different from what it/one was before]** ((**change, alter, shift, convert, reverse, be replaced**))
㊥ "change"▷変わる, "take the place of"▷代わる, "be exchanged"▷換わる
2. sa⌈ma⌉-zamana 様々な adj(*na*). **[of various states or kinds]**
EX. Attitudes on gun control in the U.S. vary widely.
銃の規制に関するアメリカでの意見は様々だ。
Juu no kisei ni-kansuru Amerika de no iken wa sama-zama da.

vase n. **[a vessel, usually tall and round, used as an ornament or for holding flowers]**
ka⌈bin 花瓶 •**c**
EX. Which vase should I put these flowers in?
この花はどの花瓶に生けましょうか。
Kono hana wa dono kabin ni ikemashoo ka.

vast adj. **[very great in size, extent, or amount]**
ko⌈odaina 広大な adj(*na*). •**c [extremely wide and large]** ((**extensive, immense, huge, gigantic, monstrous**)), **kyo⌈daina 巨大な** adj(*na*). •**c [extremely large in size]** ((**gigantic, huge, enormous, colossal, monstrous, gargantuan**)), **ba⌈kudaina ばく大な** adj(*na*). •**c [extremely large as measured in monetary terms]** ((**huge, immense, colossal, enormous, tremendous**))

EX. (**a**) In front of the cathedral was a vast plaza.
大聖堂の前には{巨大な/*広大な/*ばく大な}広場があった。
*Dai-seidoo no mae ni wa {kyodaina/ *koodaina/*bakudaina} hiro-ba ga atta.*
(**b**) He owns a vast fortune.
あの人は{ばく大な/*巨大な/*広大な}財産を持っている。
*Ano hito wa {bakudaina/*kyodaina/ *koodaina} zaisan o motte iru.*
(**c**) We passed through the vast Midwest prairies on our trip accross the U.S.A.
米国横断旅行中に私たちは中西部の{広大な/*巨大な/*ばく大な}草原を通りすぎた。
*Beikoku-oodan-ryokoo-chuu ni watashi-tachi wa Chuuseibu no {koodaina/ *kyodaina/*bakudaina} soogen o toori-sugita.*

vegetable n. **[a herbaceous plant grown as food 《fig. "a person who is physically alive but whose brain has ceased to function, esp. due to illness or injury"》]**

1. ya⌈sai 野菜 •c [a herbaceous plant grown as food]

EX. You should try to eat less meat and more vegetables.
肉を少な目にして、野菜をもっと多目に食べるようにするといいよ。
Niku o sukuna-me ni shite, yasai o motto oo-me ni taberu yooni suru to ii yo.

2. sho⌈kubutsu-ni⌉ngen 植物人間 •c [a person who is physically alive but whose brain has ceased to function, esp. due to illness or injury]

EX. My father has been a vegetable since suffering his stroke.
卒中を起こしてから、父は植物人間になってしまいました。
Sotchuu o okoshite kara, chichi wa shokubutsu-ningen ni natte shimaimashita.

vegetarian n. **[a person who lives on a vegetable diet]**
sai⌈shoku-shugi⌉-sha 菜食主義者 •c

EX. I'm not a vegetarian, but I seldom eat meat.
私は菜食主義者じゃありませんが、肉はめったに食べません。
Watashi wa saishoku-shugi-sha jaarimasen ga, niku wa mettani tabemasen.

vegetation n. **[plants or the growth on plants]**
sho⌈ku⌉butsu 植物 •c [a living organism which, unlike animals, makes its own food and is not capable of movement or sensation] 《plant, botany》 ↔ doobutsu 動物 •c

EX. (**a**) The vegetation of Okinawa is sub-tropical.
沖縄の植物は亜熱帯性だ。
Okinawa no shokubutsu wa a-nettai-sei da.
(**b**) Abundant rain accelerates the growth of vegetation in this area.
豊かな雨がこの地域の植物の成長を速める。
Yutakana ame ga kono chiiki no shokubutsu no seichoo o hayameru.

vehicle n. **[a medium of transportation 《fig. "a means of expressing or accomplishing s.t."》]**

1. no⌈ri-mono 乗り物 /〈V*masu* of *noru* ① ride + *mono* a tangible thing/ [a conveyance such as a train, bus, plane, etc.] 《conveyance, means of transport》

EX. I tend to get sick riding in almost any kind of vehicle—cars, ships, or planes.
私は車、船、飛行機など、どんな乗り物に乗っても酔ってしまう体質なんです。
Watashi wa kuruma, fune, hikoo-ki nado, donna nori-mono ni notte mo yotte shimau taishitsu na n desu.

2. shu⌉dan 手段 •c [a concrete method of achieving some purpose] 《means, way, step, device》, ba⌈itai 媒体 •c [a means by which to express s.t.] 《medium》

EX. Television is a powerful vehicle for mass communication.
テレビはマスコミの強力な{手段/媒体}だ。

Terebi wa masukomi no kyooryokuna {shudan/baitai} da.

vein n. **[a continuous band of mineral found in rock inside the earth; one of the tubes forming a network in a human or animal body through which blood is carried to the heart; a mood or manner, esp. of speaking]**

1. ko⌈omyaku 鉱脈 •c [a long, narrow band of mineral found inside the earth] ⟪**deposit**⟫

2. ke⌈kkan 血管 •c [one of the network of tubes that carry blood in a human or animal body], jo⌈omyaku 静脈 •c [one of the network of tubes that carry blood toward the heart from different parts of the body in animals and humans]

EX. The doctor injected the vitamins directly into my vein.
医者は直接{血管/静脈}にビタミンを注射した。
Isha wa chokusetsu {kekkan/joomyaku} ni bitamin o chuusha-shita.

3. cho⌈oshi 調子 •c [the musical contour moving forward by a series of sounds of varying pitch and their timing ⟪fig. "an impression created by s.o.'s way of speaking or writing," "the degree of progress of s.t. that is moving," "the momentum which accompanies s.t. which advances"⟫]

EX. He delivered his speech in a humorous vein.
彼はユーモラスな調子でスピーチをした。
Kare wa yuumorasuna chooshi de supiichi o shita.

V

velocity n. **[the rate of motion, esp. in a given direction]**

ha⌉ya-sa 速さ /⟨adj(*i*). stem of *hayai* early/quick + suf. *sa* ness/ [(degree of) quickness of motion] ⟪**speed, pace**⟫**, so⌉kudo 速度 •c [degree of quickness of motion]** ⟪**speed, pace, rate**⟫

EX. Can you guess what the velocity of that pitcher's fast ball is?
あのピッチャーの速球の{速度/速さ}はどのぐらいだと思いますか。
Ano pitchaa no sokkyuu no {sokudo/haya-sa} wa dono-gurai da to omoimasu ka.

velvet n.

bi⌈roodo ビロード •f, be⌈rube⌉tto ベルベット •f

NOTE: *Biroodo* comes from Portuguese "veludo" or from Spanish "velludo" and *berubetto* from English "velvet."

EX. When Junko showed up in a purple velvet outfit, I at first didn't recognize her.
順子が紫色の{ビロード/ベルベット}の服を着て現われた時は最初知らない人だと思った。
Junko ga murasaki-iro no {biroodo/berubetto} no fuku o kite arawareta toki wa saisho shiranai hito da to omotta.

— adj.

bi⌈roodo no N ビロードのN •f, be⌈rube⌉tto no N ベルベットのN •f

venture n. **[a risky undertaking]**

1. bo⌈oken 冒険 •c [the act of doing s.t. dangerous or s.t. that may not be successful] ⟪**adventure, hazard, risk**⟫

EX. Solo mountain climbing is a risky venture I would not recommend for the inexperienced.
単独登山は未経験者には勧められない危険な冒険だ。
Tandoku-tozan wa mi-keiken-sha ni wa susume-rarenai kikenna booken da.

2. to⌉oki 投機 •c [an action undertaken against uncertain odds in the hope of realizing significant profit] ⟪**speculative gambling**⟫

EX. My uncle's business venture succeeded beyond all expectations, turning him into a wealthy man.
叔父の事業投機は予想以上の成功を収め、彼は金持ちになった。
Oji no jigyoo tooki wa yosoo-ijoo no seikoo o osame, kare wa kanemochi ni natta.

PHRASE: joint venture *gooben(-gaisha)* 合弁(会社) •c

EX. Joint ventures between Japanese and

American companies have become common these days.
アメリカと日本の会社の合弁の例は最近多くなってきている。
Amerika to Nihon no kaisha no gooben no rei wa saikin ooku natte kite iru.

— vi./vt. **[for s.o. to dare to do s.t.]**
o⌈mo⌉i-kitte V 思い切ってV [to dare to do s.t.], ⟨-ni⟩ ⟨-o⟩ ka⌈ke⌉ru ⟨〜に⟩⟨〜を⟩かける ② [for s.o. to cause s.t. to extend to and come in contact with s.t. else《fig. "cover," "hang," "call s.o. by phone," "bet," "spend," "sprinkle," "splash," "sit down," "build (a bridge)"》] 《hang, put a bridge over, sit down, sprinkle, put on, ring up, spend, bet, risk》
㊊ "physically hang s.t. over s.t. else"▷掛ける, "build a bridge over a river"▷架ける, "bet"▷かける

EX. (**a**) Henry was so shy he just couldn't bring himself to venture a conversation with Sally.
ヘンリーは内気で、思い切ってサリーに話しかける勇気を出すことができなかった。
Henrii wa uchiki de, omoi-kitte Sarii ni hanashi-kakeru yuuki o dasu koto ga dekinakatta.
(**b**) How much capital are you willing to venture for this project?
このプロジェクトにどのぐらいの資本をかけますか。
Kono purojekuto ni dono-gurai no shihon o kakemasu ka.

Venus n.
Bi⌉inasu ビーナス •f

verb n. **[a part of speech that expresses an action, event, or state of being]**
do⌈oshi 動詞 •c

EX. In a Japanese sentence the verb comes at the end.
日本語の文では動詞は終わりに来る。
Nihon-go no bun de wa dooshi wa owari ni kuru.

PHRASE: intransitive verb *ji-dooshi* 自動詞 •c, transitive verb *ta-dooshi* 他動詞 •c, auxiliary verb *jo-dooshi* 助動詞 •c

verse n. **[(a line of) metrical writing that distinguishes poetry from prose]**
i⌈nbun 韻文 •c [metrical writing that distinguishes poetry from prose] 《poetry, composition》 ↔ sanbun 散文 •c; shi 詩 •c [(a piece of) metrical writing] 《poetry, poem》

EX. (**a**) His scientific articles read like verse.
あの人の科学論文は{韻文/?詩}のように読める。
Ano hito no kagaku-ronbun wa {inbun/?shi} no yooni yome-ru.
(**b**) A: Has this author written anything in verse?
この作家が書いたもので、{韻文/詩}によるものはありますか。
Kono sakka ga kaita mono de, {inbun/shi} ni yoru mono wa arimasu ka.
B: Yes, he has, if you call *waka* of verse.
和歌を{詩/韻文}と言うなら、ありますよ。
Waka o {shi/inbun} to iu nara, arimasu yo.

version n. **[a translation of s.t. into another language; an account of s.t. given from a particular point of view; a form of s.t. which is different in some way from the original]**
1. -yaku 〜訳 •c [the form of a written work rendered into another language], -ban 〜版 •c [an edition of s.t.]

EX. Until the mid-twentieth century, the King James Version was the only commonly available English version of the Bible.
二十世紀の半ばまで一般に手に入る聖書の英語{訳/版}はきん定訳しかなかった。
Ni-jus-seiki no nakaba made ippan ni te ni hairu seisho no eigo-{yaku/ban} wa kintei-yaku shika nakatta.

2. se⌈tsumei 説明 •c [an act/instance of making the content of, reason for, or significance of s.t. easily understood by another] 《explanation, exposition, interpretation, illustration》

EX. Can you give me your version of the incident?

V

事件に関するあなたの説明を聞かせてください。
Jiken ni kansuru anata no setsumei o kikasete kudasai.

3. ⟨-o⟩ ⟨-ni⟩ shi⌈ta mono ⟨〜を⟩⟨〜に⟩したもの [s.t. that has been turned into s.t. else]

EX. Have you seen the film version of Yasunari Kawabata's *Snow Country*?
川端康成の『雪国』を映画にしたものを見たことがありますか。
Kawabata Yasunari no "Yuki-guni" o eiga ni shita mono o mita koto ga arimasu ka.

vertical adj. **[situated or moving perpendicular to the horizon]**
su⌈ichoku no N 垂直のN •c [perpendicular to the horizon] ⟪perpendicular⟫

EX. Two climbers were climbing the vertical face of the cliff.
二人の登山家が岸壁の垂直の面を登っていくところだった。
Futari no tozan-ka ga ganpeki no suichoku no men o nobotte iku tokoro datta.

very adv. **[to a high degree]**
to⌈(t)temo と(っ)ても [to a great extent (in affirmative contexts) or no matter what one does (in negative contexts)] ⟪exceedingly, cannot possibly⟫, ta⌈ihen 大変 •c [to a great extent] ⟪awfully, exceedingly, dreadfully⟫, hi⌈jooni 非常に •c [to a degree or extent which is much more than average] ⟪remarkably, considerably, unusually⟫

V

NOTE: *Tottemo* is an emphatic version of *totemo.*

EX. (**a**) It's very hot today, isn't it?
今日は{と(っ)ても/大変/非常に}暑いですね。
Kyoo wa {to(t)temo/taihen/hijooni} atsui desu ne.
(**b**) It would be very difficult to get there in one hour.
あそこまで一時間で行くのは{と(っ)ても/大変/非常に}難しいです。
Asoko made ichi-jikan de iku no wa {to(t)temo/taihen/hijooni} muzukashii desu.

PHRASE: not...very *a(n)mari*...neg. あ(ん)まり…neg.

EX. A: Was the movie interesting?
映画は面白かったですか。
Eiga wa omoshirokatta desu ka.
B: No, not very.
いいえ、あんまり面白くありませんでした。
Iie, anmari omoshiroku arimasen deshita.

— adv. **[absolutely, in the truest sense]**
ho⌈ntoo ni 本当に [used for giving force to the expression it modifies ⟪fig. "an interjection used by a female speaker to indicate incredulousness"⟫]

EX. Yoshio was the very best student in his class.
良男はクラスで本当に一番出来る学生だった。
Yoshio wa kurasu de hontoo ni ichiban dekiru gakusei datta.

— adj. **[exact, none other than]**
1. ma⌉sani...da 正に…だ [exactly (now) ⟨w⟩] ⟪exactly, properly, now⟫

EX. Mr. Yoshida is the very person we have been looking for.
吉田さんは正に我々が探していた人物だ。
Yoshida-san wa masani ware-ware ga sagashite ita jinbutsu da.

2. made mo までも [even so far as s.t./s.o./s.a.]

EX. I studied up until the very last minute.
最後の一分までも勉強した。
Saigo no ip-pun made mo benkyoo-shita.

3. dake だけ prt. **[no more/less than or limited only to s.t./s.o./s.a.] ⟪only, merely⟫**

EX. The very thought of seeing Melissa again filled Jim with excitement.
メリッサにまた会えると考えただけでジムはわくわくした。
Merissa ni mata ae-ru to kangaeta dake de Jim wa waku-waku-shita.

4. N sono mono Nそのもの •c [none

other than, (the thing) itself]

EX. (**a**) The series of setbacks he has experienced recently has weakened his very resolve to live.
このごろ立て続けにざ折を味わい、彼は生きる意欲そのものを失いつつある。
Kono goro tate-tsuzuke ni zasetsu o ajiwai, kare wa ikiru iyoku sono mono o ushinai-tsutsu aru.
(**b**) The Japanese Socialist Party was at that time opposed to the very existence of the Self Defense Force.
日本社会党は当時、自衛隊の存在そのものに異議を唱えていた。
Nihon shakai-too wa tooji, jiei-tai no sonzai sono mono ni igi o tonaete ita.

vessel n. **[a ship or large boat; a hollow container for holding things ⟨fml⟩]**
1. fu˥ne 船 [a vehicle for transportation over water] ⟪boat, ship, steamer, liner⟫

EX. A number of large ocean-going vessels were docked at the pier.
外洋航行の大きな船が数隻桟橋につないであった。
Gaiyoo kookoo no ookina fune ga suu-seki sanbashi ni tsunaide atta.

2. yo˥oki 容器 •c [a container]
3. ke˥kkan 血管 •c [one of the network of tubes that carry blood in a human or animal body]

via prep. **[by way of or by means of]**
1. ⟨-o⟩ to˥otte ⟨～を⟩通って /V *te* of tooru ① pass/ [going from one end to another of a specified interval of space], -ke˥iyu de ～経由で n.+prt. **•c [passing through a place enroute to another place] ⟪going by way of⟫**

EX. We flew to Hong Kong via Seoul.
私たちはソウル{経由で/を通って}香港に飛んだ。
Watashi-tachi wa Souru {keiyu de/o tootte} Honkon ni tonda.

2. de で prt. **[using s.t.] ⟪by, with⟫**

EX. We traveled from London to Venice via The Orient Express.
ロンドンからベニスまでオリエント・エクスプレスで行った。
Rondon kara Benisu made Oriento Ekusupuresu de itta.

vibrate vi. **[to move rapidly and continuously back and forth or up and down ⟪fig. "resound"⟫]**
1. shi˥ndoo-suru 振動する ③ •c [to move back and forth rapidly and continuously at regular intervals] ⟪oscillate, swing⟫, fu˥rueru 震える ② [to move from side to side rapidly and continuously, esp. due to cold or fear] ⟪tremble, quiver, quake, shake, shudder⟫, shi˥ndoo-suru 震動する ③ •c [for s.t. large and fixed such as the earth or a building to tremble] ⟪shake, quake, tremble, quiver⟫, yu˥reru 揺れる ② [to shift back and forth or up and down in position or to be unsettled emotionally] ⟪shake, quake, tremble, pitch, roll⟫

EX. (**a**) My car is very old and often vibrates violently.
僕の車はとても古いので激しく{振動する/揺れる/*震動する/*震える}ことがよくある。
*Boku no kuruma wa totemo furui node hageshiku {shindoo-suru/yureru/*shindoo-suru/*furueru} koto ga yoku aru.*
(**b**) As we were sitting down to eat, an earthquake struck and our house started to vibrate.
食卓につこうとしている時に地震が起きて、家が{震動し/揺れ/*振動し/*震え}始めた。
*Shokutaku ni tsukoo to shite iru toki ni jishin ga okite, ie ga {shindoo-shi/yure/*shindoo-shi/*furue}-hajimeta.*
(**c**) The leaves on the trees were vibrating gently in the wind.
木の葉が風に優しく{震えて/揺れて/*震動して/*振動して}いた。
*Ko no ha ga kaze ni yasashiku {furuete/yurete/*shindoo-shite/*shindoo-shite} ita.*

2. hi˥biki-wataru 響き渡る ① [for a sound to resound throughout a space ⟪fig. "have an impact on"⟫] ⟪resound, affect⟫

EX. The singer's voice vibrated throughout the concert hall.
歌手の声はコンサートホール中に響き渡った。
Kashu no koe wa konsaato-hooru-juu ni hibiki-watatta.

— vt. **[to cause s.t. to move rapidly and continuously back and forth or up and down]**
⟨-o⟩ shi⌈ndoo-saseru ⟨〜を⟩しんどうさせる /⟨causative of *shindoo-suru* ③ vibrate/ ② SEE vibrate vi., **⟨-o⟩ fu⌈rue-saseru ⟨〜を⟩震えさせる /⟨causative of *furueru* ③ tremble/** ② SEE vibrate vi.

NOTE: See vi. for the difference between the two *kanji* representations of *shindoo-saseru*: 振動させる and 震動させる.

vibration n. **[rapid and continuous movement back and forth or up and down]**
shi⌈ndoo 震動 •c [the trembling movement of s.t. large and fixed such as the earth or a building] ⟪**tremor, shock, quake**⟫, **shi⌈ndoo 振動 •c [rapid and continuous movement back and forth at regular intervals]**

EX. (**a**) All of a sudden we felt a strange vibration in the engine.
私たちは急にエンジンの変な{振動/*震動}を感じた。
*Watashi-tachi wa kyuu ni enjin no henna {shindoo/*shindoo} o kanjita.*
(**b**) Vibrations in the earth are called "earthquakes."
大地の{震動/*振動}を「地震」と言う。
*Daichi no {shindoo/*shindoo} o 'jishin' to iu.*

V

vicinity n. **[the area near or surrounding a certain place]**
1. ⟨-ni⟩ chi⌈ka⌉i koto ⟨〜に⟩近いこと [the state of being near to s.t.]

EX. Being in the vicinity of a big city is an asset for our town.
大都会に近いことはこの町の強みだ。
Dai-tokai ni chikai koto wa kono machi no tsuyo-mi da.

2. chi⌈ka⌉ku 近く /⟨adj(*i*). *ku* of *chikai* near/ [a place close to a certain place], ki⌉njo 近所 •c [the area close to one's home or to the place where one currently finds oneself] ⟪**neighborhood**⟫, **fu⌈ki⌉n 付近 •c [a place close to a certain place]** ⟪**neighborhood, environs, district**⟫, **ki⌉nkoo 近郊 •c [an area close to a big city]** ⟪**environs**⟫, **ki⌉npen 近辺 •c [the area near or surrounding a certain place]** ⟪**neighborhood**⟫

EX. (**a**) Is there a post office in this vicinity?
この{近く/近所/付近/近辺/*近郊}に郵便局がありますか。
*Kono {chikaku/kinjo/fukin/kinpen/*kinkoo} ni yuubin-kyoku ga arimasu ka.*
(**b**) Do you have a map showing the used-bookstore districts in the vicinity of Tokyo?
東京{近郊/近辺/*付近/*近く/*近所}の古書店街の地図をお持ちですか。
*Tookyoo-{kinkoo/kinpen/*fukin/*chikaku/*kinjo} no koshoten-gai no chizu o o-mochi desu ka.*

victim n. **[a living being sacrificed to a deity or a person who suffers injury or loss of property or life due to natural disaster or to the actions of another]**
1. i⌈kenie いけにえ [s.a./s.o. offered to a deity] ⟪**sacrificial offering, scapegoat**⟫
2. gi⌈sei⌉-sha 犠牲者 •c [s.o. who gives up his/her life or s.t. of value for the sake of s.o./s.t. else; s.o. who suffers injury or loss in an accident or disaster] ⟪**prey, martyr**⟫, **hi⌈ga⌉i-sha 被害者 •c [s.o. who suffers injury or loss in an accident, disaster, or crime]** ⟪**sufferer, injured person**⟫

EX. (**a**) Three students in our high school were victims in a traffic accident over the weekend.
先週の週末、うちの高校の生徒が三人交通事故の{犠牲者/*被害者}になった。
*Senshuu no shuumatsu, uchi no kookoo no seito ga san-nin kootsuu-jiko no {gisei-sha/*higai-sha} ni natta.*
(**b**) A young coed in my class was the victim in an armed robbery the other day.
先日同級生の若い女子学生が強盗の{被害者/*犠牲者}になった。
Senjitsu dookyuu-sei no wakai joshi-

*gakusei ga gootoo no {higai-sha/*gisei-sha} ni natta.*

PHRASE: fall victim to ⟨-no⟩ *gisei ni naru* ⟨～の⟩犠牲になる ①

EX. Many children seem to fall victim to child abuse.
幼児虐待の犠牲になる子供が大勢いるらしい。
Yooji-gyakutai no gisei ni naru kodomo ga oozei iru-rashii.

victory n. **[an act/instance of overcoming an enemy, opponent, or hardship]**

1. sho⌉ori 勝利 •c [an act/instance of overcoming one's opponent in a game or war] ⟪triumph, conquest, win⟫ ↔ haiboku 敗北 •c

EX. Our team achieved a stunning victory over its rival.
我々のチームは宿敵に対して驚くべき勝利を納めた。
Ware-ware no chiimu wa shukuteki ni-taishite odoroku-beki shoori o osameta.

2. ko⌈kufuku 克服 •c [an act/instance of overcoming a hardship] ⟪conquest, subjugation⟫

EX. The victory over AIDS will probably not come until the 21st century.
エイズの克服は二十一世紀にならないと実現しないだろう。
Eizu no kokufuku wa ni-juu-is-seiki ni naranai to jitsugen-shinai daroo.

video n.

bi⌉deo ビデオ •f

EX. Let's record this program on video.
この番組をビデオに録画しましょう。
Kono bangumi o bideo ni rokuga-shimashoo.

video-disk n.

bi⌈deo-di⌉suku ビデオディスク •f

videotape n.

bi⌈deo-te⌉epu ビデオテープ •f

Vietnam n.

Be⌈tonamu ベトナム •f

EX. The Vietnam War was a turning point in American history.
ベトナム戦争はアメリカ史の一つの転換点だった。
Betonamu-sensoo wa Amerika-shi no hitotsu no tenkan-ten datta.

view n. **[an act/instance of seeing s.t.; (the range of) what can be seen from a particular standpoint ⟪fig. "a personal opinion," "a scenic prospect"⟫]**

1. i⌈kken 一見 •c [one (brief) look at s.t./s.o./s.a.] ⟪a look, a sight, a glance⟫

EX. The view from the plane of the vast cornfields below told me immediately that we were flying over the Great Plains.
飛行機から下の広大なとうもろこし畑を一見して、中西部大平原の上を飛んでいるんだとすぐ分かった。
Hikoo-ki kara shita no koodaina too-morokoshi-batake o ikken-shite, chuusei-bu dai-heigen no ue o tonde iru n da to sugu wakatta.

2. na⌈game⌉ 眺め /⟨V*masu* of *nagameru* ② watch/ [a scene worthy of lingering attention, esp. one from a high point and encompassing a large area] ⟪scene, outlook, prospect⟫, ke⌉shiki 景色 •c [a picturesque view of nature] ⟪scenery, landscape⟫

EX. (**a**) The view of the Golden Gate Bridge from the hotel was spectacular.
ホテルからの金門橋の{眺め/景色}はすばらしかった。
Hoteru kara no Kinmonkyoo no {nagame/keshiki} wa subarashikatta.
(**b**) A: You seem to be a frequent customer at that restaurant on the 12th floor.
あの十二階のレストランへよくいらっしゃるようですね。
Ano juu-ni-kai no resutoran e yoku irassharu yoodesu ne.
B: Yes, I enjoy taking in the view while I dine.
ええ、{眺め/景色}を楽しみながら食事をするのが好きでね。
Ee, {nagame/keshiki} o tanoshimi-nagara shokuji o suru no ga suki de ne.

3. shi⌉ya 視野 •c [one's field of vision ⟪fig. "range of one's knowledge," "one's way of

seeing things"》] 《field of vision, mental horizon》

EX. All of a sudden an airplane came into view overhead.
突然上空の飛行機が視野に入ってきた。
Totsuzen jookuu no hikoo-ki ga shiya ni haitte-kita.

4. i˥ken 意見 •c [an idea or judgment one holds about a matter] 《opinion, idea》, ke⌈nkai 見解 •c [one's evaluation of or judgment about s.t.] 《opinion》

EX. (**a**) In my view the Japanese work too hard.
日本人は働き過ぎるというのが私の{意見/?見解}です。
Nihon-jin wa hataraki-sugiru to iu no ga watashi no {iken/?kenkai} desu.
(**b**) It is the view of the Ministry of Education that Japan's universities should reform their entrance examination system.
文部省の{見解/*意見}では日本の大学は入試制度の改革が必要だ。
*Monbu-shoo no {kenkai/*iken} de wa Nihon no daigaku wa nyuushi-seido no kaikaku ga hitsuyoo da.*

5. mi⌈komi 見込み /〈V*masu* of *mi-komu* ① expect/ [a prediction or anticipation that s.t. is very likely to occur] 《hope, promise, outlook, possibility》, me˥-ate 目当て [a thing, place, or result that one aims for 《fig. "purpose"》]

EX. I'm studying Japanese with a view to eventually using it in business.
将来ビジネスに使える{見込み/目当て}があるので日本語を勉強しています。
Shoorai bijinesu ni tsukae-ru {mikomi/me-ate} ga aru node Nihon-go o benkyoo-shite imasu.

— vt. **[for s.o. to look at s.t. from a particular perspective or to consider s.t. in a certain way]**

1. 〈-o〉 mi˥ru 〈〜を〉見る ② [for s.o. to direct one's attention to s.t./s.o./s.a. in order to visually perceive its outward shape or its content]

EX. We viewed the fireworks from the balcony of my friend's tenth-story apartment.
友達の十階のアパートのバルコニーから花火を見た。
Tomodachi no juk-kai no apaato no barukonii kara hana-bi o mita.

2. 〈-o〉 〈-to〉 mi˥ru 〈〜を〉〈〜と〉見る ② [for s.o. to regard s.t. as being a certain way], 〈-o〉 〈-to〉 ka⌈ngae˥ru 〈〜を〉〈〜と〉考える ② [for s.o. to consider s.o./s.t./s.a. to be a certain way]

EX. Prof. Ito is viewed by many as being the most eminent scholar in his field.
伊藤教授は多くの人にその専門分野において最も優れた学者だと{見られて/考えられて}いる。
Itoo-kyooju wa ooku no hito ni sono senmon-bun'ya ni-oite mottomo sugureta gakusha da to {mi-rarete/kangae-rarete} iru.

viewpoint n. **[the standpoint or perspective one takes on a matter]**
mi-⌈kata˥ 見方 /〈V*masu* of *miru* ② see + *kata* way, manner/ [a way/manner of looking at s.t.] 《view, outlook》, ka⌈nte˥n 観点 •c [a mental position from which one observes and thinks about s.t.] 《standpoint》

EX. A: Why is it that we can't seem to agree on this?
このことについてどうして意見が合わないんだろう。
Kono koto ni-tsuite dooshite iken ga awanai n daroo.
B: We just have different viewpoints.
{見方/観点}が違うんだよ。
{Mi-kata/Kanten} ga chigau n da yo.

vigor n. **[active physical or mental energy or strength; forcefulness of speech or expression]**
ka⌈tsu˥ryoku 活力 •c [the vitality which makes possible action and motion] 《vitality, energy, sap of life》, se˥iryoku 精力 •c [the vitality which makes it possible for one to maintain a continuous output of work without tiring] 《energy, vitality, virility》, e⌈ne˥rugii エネルギー •f [in physics, the capacity of matter to do work because of

V

its motion or mass], i⌈kio⌉i 勢い [the momentum or force with which s.t./s.o. moves or acts] ⟪**force, power, energy, spirit, dash**⟫

NOTE: *Energii* comes from German *Energie.*

EX. (**a**) Exercising every morning gives me the vigor I need for the work facing me that day.
毎朝運動することでその日の仕事に必要な{活力/エネルギー/精力/??勢い}を蓄えることができるんです。
Mai-asa undoo-suru koto de sono hi no shigoto ni hitsuyoona {katsuryoku/ enerugii/seiryoku/??ikioi} o takuwaeru koto ga dekiru n desu.
(**b**) His speech has lost its former vigor with age.
年を取るにつれて、彼の演説には以前の{勢い/エネルギー/?活力/*精力}がなくなってきた。
*Toshi o toru ni-tsurete, kare no enzetsu ni wa izen no {ikioi/enerugii/ ?katsuryoku/*seiryoku} ga nakunatte kita.*

vigorous adj. **[having active energy or strength]**
ge⌉nkina 元気な adj(*na*). •**c [for s.o./s.a. to be in good health or to have lots of energy]** ⟪**high-spirited, lively, healthy, cheerful**⟫, **ka⌈ppatsuna** 活発な adj(*na*). •**c [lively in physical action or verbal expression]** ⟪**lively, sprightly, active, brisk, spirited**⟫, **chi⌈kara-zuyo⌉i** 力強い adj(*i*). **[commanding in tone or exhibiting such strength or ability as to reassure one of its/his/her dependability]** ⟪**forcible, assuring**⟫, **se⌈iryoku-tekina** 精力的な adj(*na*). •**c [having the vitality to maintain a continuous output of work without tiring]** ⟪**energetic, driving, virile**⟫

EX. (**a**) You always look so vigorous. What's your secret?
いつも{元気/活発/精力的/*力強い}ですね。秘けつは何ですか。
*Itsu-mo {genki/kappatsu/seiryoku-teki/ *chikara-zuyoi} desu ne. Hiketsu wa nan desu ka.*
(**b**) I like the vigorous sound of his voice.
あの人の{力強い/元気な/*活発な/*精力的な}声が好きです。
*Ano hito no {chikara-zuyoi/genkina/ *kappatsuna/*seiryoku-tekina} koe ga suki desu.*

Viking n. **[a Scandinavian seagoing explorer and pirate of the 8th to 10th centuries]**
ba⌉ikingu バイキング •**f [a Scandinavian seagoing explorer and pirate of the 8th to 10th centuries or food prepared and served in the Scandinavian smorgasbord style]**

village n. **[a rural community consisting of a small group of houses]**
mu⌈ra⌉ 村 **[a community smaller than a town]**

EX. (**a**) I was born in a small village in Nagano Prefecture.
私は長野県の小さな村で生まれました。
Watashi wa Nagano-ken no chiisana mura de umaremashita.
(**b**) After the war many young people left their villages to go to work in large cities such as Tokyo and Osaka.
戦後若い人が大勢村を出て、東京や大阪のような大都会で働き始めた。
Sengo wakai hito ga oozei mura o dete, Tookyoo ya Oosaka no yoona dai-tokai de hataraki-hajimeta.

villager n. **[an inhabitant of a rural community consisting of a small group of houses]**
mu⌈ra no hito 村の人 **[people belonging to a community smaller than a town], so⌈nmin** 村民 •**c [people living in a community smaller than a town], mu⌈ra-bito** 村人 ⟨**w**⟩

EX. According to the villagers now living there, the village was long ago once destroyed by flood.
今そこに住んでいる{村の人/村民/村人}によると、その村は昔洪水で破壊されたことがあるそうだ。
Ima soko ni sunde iru {mura no hito/ sonmin/mura-bito} ni-yoru to, sono mura wa mukashi koozui de hakai-sareta koto ga aru sooda.

villain n. **[an evil or wicked person]**
wa⌈ru-mono 悪者 /⟨adj(*i*). stem of *warui* bad + *mono* person/ [a bad person] ⟪wicked fellow, rogue, knave, rascal, scoundrel⟫, a⌈kkan 悪漢 •c [a wicked man] ⟪rascal, scoundrel, knave⟫

EX. Watch out for him! He's a villain.
あいつに気をつけろよ。ひどい{悪者/悪漢}だからな。
Aitsu ni ki-o-tsukero yo. Hidoi {warumono/akkan} da kara na.

vine n. **[a plant with a long, thin stem that creeps along the ground or coils around trees and other upright objects]**
1. bu⌈doo no ki⌉ ぶどうの木 [a grape plant]
2. tsu⌈ru⌉ つる [a long, thin plant stem that creeps along the ground or coils around trees and other upright objects]
3. tsu⌈ru no a⌉ru sho⌈ku⌉butsu つるのある植物 [a plant with a long, thin stem that creeps along the ground or coils around trees and other vertical objects]

vinegar n.
su⌉ 酢

EX. To make *sushi* you add vinegar, sugar and salt to cooked rice.
すしを作る時には御飯に酢と砂糖と塩を入れる。
Sushi o tsukuru toki ni wa gohan ni su to satoo to shio o ireru.

vinyl n.
bi⌈ni⌉iru ビニール •f

EX. These shoes are made of vinyl.
この靴はビニール製です。
Kono kutsu wa biniiru-sei desu.

V

violate vt. **[for s.o. to break or fail to keep s.t. such as a law or promise; to desecrate a sacred thing or place; to rape s.o.]**
1. ⟨-o⟩ ya⌈bu⌉ru ⟨〜を⟩破る ① [to apply force to s.t. thin and flat that has tension, such as paper, fabric, or the surface of a wall, and thereby damage it ⟪fig. "break the silence," "break a promise/law," "break through a line of resistance," "defeat"⟫] ⟪tear, rip, break, destroy, trespass, beat⟫, ⟨-o⟩ o⌈ka⌉su ⟨〜を⟩おかす ① [for s.o. to do harm to s.t. considered sacred or an object of respect, such as a law, political territoty, a holy place, s.o.'s rights, s.o.'s chastity, or logic] ⟪sin against, break, commit (crime), transgress, disregard, attack, rape, defy, risk⟫, ⟨-ni⟩ i⌈han-suru ⟨〜に⟩違反する ③ •c [to act in a way that goes against a rule, law, command, or agreement] ⟪infringe, contravene, act contrary to⟫
㊥ "sin against"▷犯す, "transgress"▷侵す, "defy"▷冒す, "illness strikes s.o."▷侵す, "illness strikes a specific part of the body"▷冒す

EX. (**a**) His behavior may have been reprehensible, but he did not violate any law.
彼の行動は非難されるべきかもしれないが、法律{を破った/を犯した/に違反した}わけではない。
Kare no koodoo wa hinan-sareru-beki kamoshirenai ga, hooritsu {o yabutta/o okashita/ni ihan-shita} wake dewanai.
(**b**) Many wars have been started by one country violating the territory of another.
戦争の多くはある国が他の国の領土{を侵す/*を破る/*に違反する}ことから始まっている。
*Sensoo no ooku wa aru-kuni ga ta no kuni no ryoodo {o okasu/*o yaburu/*ni ihan-suru} koto kara hajimatte iru.*

2. ⟨-o⟩ o⌈ka⌉su ⟨〜を⟩おかす ① SEE violate 1, **⟨-o⟩ go⌈okan-suru ⟨〜を⟩強かんする ③ [for s.o. to rape a female person] ⟪rape, assault⟫**

EX. It is a serious crime to violate a woman.
女性を{犯す/強かんする}ことは重大な犯罪だ。
Josei o {okasu/gookan-suru} koto wa juudaina hanzai da.

3. ⟨-o⟩ mi⌈da⌉su ⟨〜を⟩乱す ① [to introduce disorder or confusion into an orderly or tranquil state of affairs] ⟪disturb, disarrange, agitate⟫, ⟨-o⟩ ja⌈ma-suru ⟨〜を⟩邪魔する ③ •c [to get in the way of s.o./s.t./s.a. ⟪fig. "visit s.o."⟫] ⟪interfere, interrupt, disturb, bother⟫

EX. (**a**) The quietness of my time alone reading in the park was violated by a group of noisy kids.
公園で一人で静かに本を読んでいるところをやかましい子供たちに{邪魔された/*乱された}。
*Kooen de hitori de shizukani hon o yonde iru tokoro o yakamashii kodomo-tachi ni {jama-sareta/*midasa-reta}.*
(**b**) There are always discontented elements who seek to violate the order of a society.
社会の秩序を{乱す/*邪魔する}ようにたくらむ不平分子はいつでもいる。
*Shakai no chitsujo o {midasu/*jama-suru} yooni takuramu fuhei-bunshi wa itsu-demo iru.*

4. ⟨-o⟩ ke⌈ga⌉su ⟨～を⟩汚す ① [to cause s.t. to become unclean ⟪fig. "desecrate s.t.," "disgrace"⟫] ((stain, foul, pollute, disgrace, dishonor, desecrate))

EX. Improper words or conduct while in the temple were considered to violate the sanctity of the temple and were subject to punishment.
神殿におけるみだらな言動は神殿の神聖を汚すものとしてそれにより処罰を受けることもあった。
Shinden ni okeru midarana gendoo wa shinden no shinsei o kegasu moto to-shite sore ni-yori shobatsu o ukeru koto mo atta.

violation n. **[an act/instance of breaking or failing to keep s.t. such as a law or promise or of desecrating a sacred thing or place or of raping s.o.]**
1. i⌈han 違反 •c [an action that goes against a law, command, agreement, or rule (except in sports)] ((contravention, infringement, transgression, breach)), ha⌈nsoku 反則 •c [an action that goes against a law or rule, including a rule in a sports game] ((infringement of law, foul play))

EX. (**a**) Look, he double-dribbled. That's a violation!
あ、ダブルドリブルしたよ。あれは{反則/*違反}だ!
*A, daburu-doriburu-shita yo. Are wa {hansoku/*ihan} da!*
(**b**) A: The police searched my pockets without giving me any reason.
理由も告げられずに警官にポケットの中を探られたんだ。
Riyuu mo tsuge-rarezu ni keikan ni poketto no naka o sagura-reta n da.
B: That's a violation of your constitutional rights.
それは憲法{違反/*反則}だ。
*Sore wa kenpoo-{ihan/*hansoku} da.*

2. bo⌈otoku 冒とく •c [the desecration of s.t. considered sacred or an object of respect] ((blasphemy, profanity, sacrilege))
3. go⌈okan 強かん •c [a rape]

violence n. **[the use of strong physical force so as to harm, injure, or abuse s.t./s.o./s.a.]**
1. ha⌈ge⌉shi-sa 激しさ /⟨adj(*i*). stem of *hageshii* vehement + suf. *sa* ness/ [extreme intensity of force or strength, either physical or emotional] ((vehemence, intensity, passion))

EX. The violence of the inner-city gangs has driven most businesses out of the area.
都市中心部のギャングの暴力の激しさのため、ほとんどの企業がその区域から移転せざるを得なかった。
Toshi-chuushin-bu no gyangu no booryoku no hageshi-sa no tame, hotondo no kigyoo ga sono kuiki kara iten-sezaru o enakatta.

2. bo⌈okoo 暴行 •c [an action involving strong physical force intended to harm or injure s.o. ⟪fig. "rape"⟫] ((outrage, attack, assault)), bo⌈oryoku 暴力 •c [strong physical force used to arbitrarily carry out one's intentions] ((brute force))

EX. The policemen were disciplined for inflicting violence on the demonstrators.
警官はデモをしている人たちに{暴行を加えた/暴力をふるった}ということで処罰を受けた。
Keikan wa demo o shite iru hito-tachi ni {bookoo o kuwaeta/booryoku o furutta} to iu koto de shobatsu o uketa.

violent adj. **[marked by extreme intensity of physical force or of emotion]**
ha⌈geshi⌉i 激しい adj(*i*). **[involving an excessively high degree of force or strength, either physical or emotional]** ⟪**vehement, intense, ardent, passionate**⟫, **mo⌈oretsuna** 猛烈な adj(*na*). **•c [extreme in degree]** ⟪**strong, vehement, fierce, intense, awful**⟫, **ra⌈nboona** 乱暴な adj(*na*). **•c [rough and careless in one's words, actions, or behavior]** ⟪**rough, rude, wild, careless, outrageous**⟫

EX. (**a**) We had to walk home in a violent snowstorm.
私たちは{激しい/猛烈な/*乱暴な}吹雪の中を歩いて家に帰らなければならなかった。
*Watashi-tachi wa {hageshii/mooretsuna/*ranboona} fubuki no naka o aruite ie ni kaeranakereba naranakatta.*
(**b**) Jane's husband is sometimes violent towards her.
ジェーンの夫は彼女に対して{乱暴な/*激しい/*猛烈な}振る舞いをすることがあるんです。
*Jeen no otto wa kanojo ni-taishite {ranboona/*hageshii/*mooretsuna} furumai o suru koto ga aru n desu.*

violet n. **[a small, wild plant with purple flowers or the color of the flower of this plant]**
1. su⌈mire すみれ **[a small, wild plant with purple flowers]**
2. su⌈mire-iro すみれ色 **[the purple color of the sumire flower]**

violin n.
ba⌈iorin バイオリン **•f**

EX. Allen can play the violin very well.
アレンはバイオリンが上手に弾ける。
Aren wa baiorin ga joozuni hike-ru.

Virginia n.
Ba⌈ajinia⌉ バージニア **•f**

virtually adv. **[almost entirely ⟪fig. "so in effect"⟫]**
ho⌈to⌉ndo ほとんど **[not entirely but very close to so]** ⟪**almost, nearly, practically**⟫, **ji⌈jitsu-joo** 事実上 **•c [for all practical purposes]** ⟪**for all intents and purposes, practically, de facto**⟫, ⟨**-mo**⟩ **do⌈ozen da** ⟨〜も⟩同然だ **•c [to be essentially the same as if s.t. (else) had happened or been done]**

EX. (**a**) That novelist is virtually unknown even in his own country.
その小説家は自分の国でも{{ほとんど/*事実上}知られていない/*知られていないも同然だ}。
*Sono shoosetsu-ka wa jibun no kuni de mo {{hotondo/*jijitsu-joo} shira-rete inai/*shira-rete inai mo doozen da}.*
(**b**) A: Are those two married?
二人は結婚しているんですか。
Futari wa kekkon-shite iru n desu ka.
B: No, but they virtually are, because they've been living together for five years.
いいえ。でも、五年も一緒に住んでいるんですから、{{事実上/*ほとんど}結婚しているんです/結婚しているも同然です}。
*Iie. Demo, go-nen mo issho ni sunde iru n desu kara, {{jijitsu-joo/*hotondo} kekkon-shite iru n desu/kekkon-shite iru mo doozen desu.}*

virus n.
{**u⌈i⌉rusu/bi⌉irusu**} {ウイルス/ビールス} **•f**

EX. I seem to have a flu virus.
インフルエンザの{ウイルス/ビールス}にやられたみたいです。
Infuruenza no {uirusu/biirusu} ni yarareta mitai desu.

visible adj. **[able to be seen with the eyes]**
1. mi⌈e⌉ru 見える ② **[for s.t. to be spontaneously seen or able to be seen by the eye or mind]** ⟪**be able to see, catch sight of, look (like), seem, appear**⟫

EX. (**a**) Mt. Fuji was visible through the window of our hotel room.
ホテルの部屋の窓から富士山が見えました。
Hoteru no heya no mado kara Fuji-san ga miemashita.
(**b**) Due to the fog, nothing was visible beyond 100 meters in front of us.

霧で百メートル先しか見えなかった。
Kiri de hyaku-meetoru saki shika mienakatta.

2. me⌈da⌉tsu 目立つ ① [to stand out] **((conspicuous, stick out, salient, showy))**

EX. It was hard not to notice the girl standing there in her highly visible mini-skirt.
そこに立っている女性は大変目立つミニスカートをはいていたので、つい彼女に目が行ってしまった。
Soko ni tatte iru josei wa taihen medatsu mini-sukaato o haite ita node, tsui kanojo ni me ga itte shimatta.

3. ⟨-o⟩ a⌈ri-a⌉ri-to mi⌈se⌉ru ⟨～を⟩ありありと見せる ② [for s.o. to make s.t. plainly seen]

EX. When I told my subordinate to work harder, he abruptly left the room with a visible show of dissatisfaction.
部下にもっと働くように言ったら、不満の色をありありと見せて急に部屋を出て行った。
Buka ni motto hataraku yooni ittara, fuman no iro o ari-ari-to misete kyuu ni heya o dete-itta.

vision n. **[the faculty of being able to see things; the ability to imagine what will happen in the future and plan ahead; s.t. seen, esp. in the imagination or a dream]**

1. shi⌉ryoku 視力 •c [the degree to which one's eyes are able to see objects at a distance] ((sight, eyesight)), shi⌈kaku 視覚 •c [the perceptive sense by which things are seen] ((sense of sight, sight))

EX. (**a**) I have 20-20 vision in both eyes.
僕の視力は両方とも2.0です。
Boku no shiryoku wa ryoohoo tomo nii-ten-{rei/zero} desu.

NOTE: Note that the digit 2, which is normally pronounced *ni*, is sometimes pronounced *nii*, especially when it is used alone without a counter following it, as in the above example.

(**b**) Of all the five senses, vision is the one we depend on the most.
五感の中で、我々が一番頼りにしているのは視覚だ。
Gokan no naka de, ware-ware ga ichiban tayori ni shite iru no wa shikaku da.

2. ma⌈boroshi 幻 [s.t. which is seen even though it does not actually exist] ((phantom, illusion, dream)), yu⌈me⌉ 夢 [a series of pictures, thoughts, or sensations one experiences while asleep; an ideal one hopes will be realized eventually], ku⌈usoo 空想 •c [an empty fantasy] ((fancy, daydream, fantasy)), mi⌈rai-zo⌉o 未来像 •c [a sight imagined in the future], bi⌉jon ビジョン •f [a sight imagined in the future]

EX. (**a**) A: I believe that with proper education for all we can achieve a society where prisons don't exist.
社会の人々全員に適切な教育を施せばいずれ刑務所のない社会が実現すると信じているんだ。
Shakai no hito-bito zen'in ni tekisetsuna kyooiku o hodokoseba izure keimu-sho no nai shakai ga jitsugen-suru to shinjite iru n da.
B: Well, that sounds good, but it's nothing more than a vision with no basis in reality.
まあ、響きはいいけど、現実性のない{幻/夢/空想/?未来像/?ビジョン}にすぎないと思うよ。
Maa, hibiki wa ii kedo, genjitsu-sei no nai {maboroshi/yume/kuusoo/?mirai-zoo/?bijon} ni suginai to omou yo.
(**b**) To be a good leader, one has to have vision.
優れた指導者になるには{未来像/ビジョン/夢/*幻/*空想}がなければいけない。
*Sugureta shidoo-sha ni naru ni wa {mirai-zoo/bijon/yume/*maboroshi/*kuusoo} ga nakereba ikenai.*

visit vt. **[for s.o. to come or go to see s.o./s.t./s.a. (and stay with that person or at that place temporarily)]**

1. ⟨-o⟩ ta⌈zune⌉ru ⟨～を⟩たずねる ② [for s.o. to seek out a person or a place or to seek information about s.t.] ((call on, call at, come to see, look for, ask)), ⟨-ni⟩ ai⌉ ni {iku/ku⌉ru} ⟨～に⟩会いに{行く ①/来る ③} [for

V

s.o. to go or come to a place to see s.o.], {⟨-ni⟩/⟨-e⟩} **i⌈ku/ku⌉ru** {⟨〜に⟩/⟨〜へ⟩}{行く ①/来る ③} **[to move to or toward a place away from the speaker/to or toward a place where the speaker is located],** {⟨-e⟩/⟨-ni⟩} **a⌈sobi ni** {**iku/ku⌉ru**} {⟨〜へ⟩/⟨〜に⟩}遊びに{行く ①/来る ③} **[for s.o. to go or come to a place for some social purpose]**
㊈ "ask"▷尋ねる, "visit"▷訪ねる

EX. (**a**) Have you ever visited Japan?
日本{を訪ねた/へ(遊びに)行った/*に会いに行った}ことがありますか。
*Nihon {o tazuneta/e (asobi ni) itta/ *ni ai ni itta} koto ga arimasu ka.*
(**b**) A friend is coming to visit me tonight.
友達が今晩{{会い/遊び}に来ます/訪ねて来ます}。
Tomodachi ga konban {{ai/asobi} ni kimasu/tazunete kimasu}.

2. ⟨**-ni**⟩ ⟨**-o**⟩ **shi⌈satsu ni** {**iku/ku⌉ru**} ⟨〜に⟩⟨〜を⟩視察に{行く ①/来る ③} **[for s.o. to come or go to a place for an inspection of s.t.],** ⟨**-o**⟩ **o⌈oshin-suru** ⟨〜を⟩往診する ③ **•c [for a doctor to come or go to see a patient at the patient's home]**

EX. (**a**) The doctor was kind enough to personally come and visit my wife.
医者は親切にも妻を{往診して/*視察に来て}くれた。
*Isha wa shinsetsuni mo tsuma o {ooshin-shite/*shisatsu ni kite} kureta.*
(**b**) The Minister of Agriculture went to visit the rice fields in the Tohoku district.
農林大臣は東北地方の水田を{視察に行った/*往診した}。
*Noorin-daijin wa Toohoku-chihoo no suiden o {shisatsu ni itta/*ooshin-shita}.*

— vi. **[for s.o. to talk socially with s.o. else]** ⟨**-to**⟩ **ha⌈nashi⌉ o suru** ⟨〜と⟩話をする ③ **[for s.o. to talk with s.o.]**

EX. I visited with my aunt for about a half hour before I had to leave.
三十分ほど叔母と話をしてから帰った。
San-jup-pun hodo oba to hanashi o shite kara kaetta.

— n. **[a short stay]**
tai⌈zai 滞在 **•c [an act of going to some place and staying there for a certain period of time], ho⌈omon** 訪問 **•c [an act of going to call s.o.]** ⟪**call**⟫

EX. (**a**) Our visit to Kyoto was a very pleasant one.
京都{滞在/訪問}はとても楽しかった。
Kyooto {taizai/hoomon} wa totemo tanoshikatta.
(**b**) We paid a courtesy visit to the governor of Ishikawa Prefecture.
私たちは石川県知事を表敬{訪問/*滞在}した。
*Watashi-tachi wa Ishikawa-ken-chiji o hyookei-{hoomon/*taizai}-shita.*

PHRASE: have a visit with ⟨*-to*⟩ *hanashi o suru* ⟨〜と⟩話をする ③

EX. I had a pleasant visit with my high school buddies.
高校の時の仲間と楽しい話をした。
Kookoo no toki no nakama to tanoshii hanashi o shita.

visitor n. **[one who comes to see s.o. or who stays temporarily with s.o. or at a place] ho⌈omo⌉n-{sha/kyaku}** 訪問{者/客} **•c [a person who comes to see s.o. at his/her home** ⟨**fml**⟩**]** ⟪**caller, visitant**⟫, **ra⌈iho⌉o-{sha/kyaku}** 来訪{者/客} **•c [a person who comes to see s.o./some place** ⟨**w**⟩**]** ⟪**caller**⟫, **ra⌈ikyaku** 来客 **•c [a person who comes to see s.o. (esp. the speaker)]** ⟪**caller, guest**⟫, **ka⌈nko⌉o-kyaku** 観光客 **•c [a person who goes to see a place or places of interest for pleasure]** ⟪**sightseer, tourist**⟫, **sa⌈nkan-nin** 参観人 **•c [a person who goes to see a place of interest such as a school, museum, or temple], sa⌈npa⌉i-sha** 参拝者 **•c [a person who comes to see a shrine or temple]**

EX. (**a**) We had visitors last night and were up rather late talking.
きのうの晩{来客/*来訪{者/客}/*訪問{者/客}/*参拝者/*参観人/*観光客}があって遅くまで起きて話をしていた。
*Kinoo no ban {raikyaku/*raihoo-{sha/kyaku}/*hoomon-{sha/kyaku}/*sanpai-*

V

*sha/*sankan-nin/*kankoo-kyaku} ga atte osoku made okite hanashi o shite ita.*
(**b**) Today the President received five foreign visitors.
大統領には今日五人の外国からの{来訪{客/者}/訪問{客/者}/来客/*参拝者/*参観人/*観光客}があった。
*Daitooryoo ni wa kyoo go-nin no gaikoku kara no {raihoo-{kyaku/sha}/hoomon-{kyaku/sha}/raikyaku/*sanpai-sha/*sankan-nin/*kankoo-kyaku} ga atta.*
(**c**) San Francisco is a beautiful city that attracts visitors all year round.
サンフランシスコはとてもきれいな町だから一年中{観光客/*訪問{者/客}/*来訪{者/客}/*来客/*参観人/*参拝者}が来る。
*San Furanshisuko wa totemo kireina machi da kara ichi-nen-juu {kankoo-kyaku/*hoomon-{sha/kyaku}/*raihoo-{sha/kyaku}/*raikyaku/*sankan-nin/*sanpai-sha} ga kuru.*
(**d**) This temple attracts many visitors every day.
この寺には{参拝者/参観人/観光客/*来訪{者/客}/*訪問{者/客}/*来客}が毎日大勢来る。
*Kono tera ni wa {sanpai-sha/sankan-nin/kankoo-kyaku/*raihoo-{sha/kyaku}/*hoomon-{sha/kyaku}/*raikyaku} ga mai-nichi oozei kuru.*

visual adj. **[having to do with or used in seeing]**
shi⌈kaku (no) N 視覚(の)N **•c [having to do with the sense of sight], me⌉ ni mi⌈e⌉ru (N)** 目に見える(N) **[visible to the eye], shi⌈kaku-tekina** 視覚的な adj(*na*). **•c [having to do with or in a form perceptible by sight]**
EX. (**a**) Are you more of a visual or an auditory type person?
あなたは{視覚型/*視覚的}ですか、それとも聴覚型ですか。
*Anata wa {shikaku-gata/*shikaku-teki} desu ka, sore-tomo chookaku-gata desu ka.*
(**b**) My Japanese teacher uses a lot of visual aids.
私の日本語の先生は{視覚/*視覚的な/*目に見える}教材をたくさん使います。
*Watashi no Nihon-go no sensei wa {shikaku-/*shikaku-tekina/*me ni mieru} kyoozai o takusan tsukaimasu.*
(**c**) The Japanese seem to be especially responsive to things visual.
日本人は{目に見える/視覚的な/*視覚の}物に特に敏感なようだ。
*Nihon-jin wa {me ni mieru/shikaku-tekina/*shikaku no} mono ni tokuni binkanna yooda.*

vital adj. **[necessary for or having to do with life《fig. "animated," "most important"》]**
1. i⌉nochi ni ka⌈kawa⌉ru (N) 命にかかわる(N) **[having a bearing on the existence or maintenance of life], se⌉imei ni ka⌈kawa⌉ru (N)** 生命にかかわる(N) **•c**
EX. The heart is a vital organ.
心臓は{命/生命}にかかわる器官だ。
Shinzoo wa {inochi/seimei} ni kakawaru kikan da.
2. i⌈ki-i⌉ki-shita N 生き生きしたN **/〈Vinf. past of *iki-iki-suru* ③ become alive/ [full of life and energy]《lively, sprightly, vivid》, i⌈ki-i⌉ki-shite iru (N)** 生き生きしている(N) **/〈V *te iru* of *iki-iki-suru* ③ become alive/**
EX. Peter's vital style of leadership kept us going even through the worst of times.
ピーターの生き生きした指導によって私たちはどんな困難にもめげずにやってこられた。
Piitaa no iki-iki-shita shidoo ni yotte watashi-tachi wa donna konnan ni mo megezu ni yatte-ko-rareta.
3. ki⌈wa⌉me-te ju⌈uyoona 極めて重要な adj(*na*). **•c [extremely important], ka⌈n'yoona** 肝要な adj(*na*). **•c [pivotally important]《very important, essential, indispensable》**
EX. Further investment in basic research is vital to our future.
我々の将来にとって基礎研究への更なる投資は{極めて重要/肝要}だ。
Ware-ware no shoorai ni-totte kiso-

V

kenkyuu e no sara-naru tooshi wa {kiwame-te juuyoo/kan'yoo} da.

vitamin n.

bi⌈ta⌉min ビタミン •f

EX. A: Are you taking any vitamins?
ビタミンを何か飲んでいますか。
Bitamin o nani-ka nonde imasu ka.
B: Yes, I take vitamin C pills every day.
ええ、ビタミンCの錠剤を毎日飲んでいます。
Ee, bitamin-shii no joozai o mai-nichi nonde imasu.

vivid adj. **[brilliant, clear, or lively in visual appearance, expressiveness, or imagination]**

i⌈ki-i⌉ki-shita N 生き生きしたN /⟨Vinf. past of *iki-iki-suru* ③ become alive/ [full of life and energy] ⟪lively, sprightly, vital⟫, i⌈ki-i⌉ki-shite iru (N) 生き生きしている(N) /⟨V *te iru* of *iki-iki-suru* ③ become alive/, a⌈za⌉yakana 鮮やかな adj(*na*). **[brilliant and distinct in color or shape ⟪fig. "extremely skillful"⟫] ⟪clear, brilliant, neat⟫, na⌈ma-namashi⌉i 生々しい** adj(*i*). **[fresh in appearance ⟪fig. "graphic"⟫] ⟪fresh, graphic, green⟫**

EX. (**a**) Kristen's vivid eyes gave her a striking beauty.
クリスティンは目が{生き生きしていて/*鮮やかで/*生々しくて}圧倒されるほど美しかった。
*Kurisutin wa me ga {iki-iki-shite ite/ *azayaka de/*nama-namashikute} attoo-sareru hodo utsukushikatta.*
(**b**) I still have vivid memories from the war.
私はまだ戦争の{生々しい/鮮やかな/*生き生きした}記憶がある。
*Watashi wa mada sensoo no {nama-namashii/azayakana/*iki-iki-shita} kioku ga aru.*

V

vocabulary n. **[a list of words, esp. to be learned as part of the study of a language; all the words used by a linguistic community or by an individual speaker]**

ta⌈ngo 単語 •c [the smallest linguistic unit which is not bound to another form] ⟪word⟫, ta⌈ngo-hyoo 単語表 •c [a list of linguistic forms, each of which is a minimal unit not bound to another form], go⌉i 語い •c [a collection of words ⟨fml⟩] ⟪glossary⟫, go⌈i-hyoo 語い表 •c [a list of words ⟨fml⟩]

EX. (**a**) This passage has a lot of unfamiliar vocabulary in it.
この読み物には知らない{単語/語い}がたくさんあります。
Kono yomi-mono ni wa shiranai {tango/goi} ga takusan arimasu.
(**b**) My business vocabulary is too weak to allow me to conduct business in Japanese.
ビジネス関係の{単語/語い}を十分知らないので日本語でビジネスの話はできません。
Bijinesu-kankei no {tango/goi} o juubun shiranai node Nihon-go de bijinesu no hanashi wa dekimasen.
(**c**) He has a rich vocabulary for a five-year old child.
五歳の子供にしては{語い/*単語}が豊かだ。
*Go-sai no kodomo ni-shite-wa {goi/ *tango} ga yutaka da.*
(**d**) Professor, could you give us a vocabulary list for this story?
先生、この話の{単語/語い}表を下さいませんか。
Sensei, kono hanashi no {tango/goi}-hyoo o kudasaimasen ka.

vocal adj. **[produced by having to do with the voice ⟪fig. "outspoken," "sung by the human voice"⟫]**

1. ko⌉e no N 声のN [having to do with the voice]

EX. Ted's vocal characteristics are almost identical to those of his father.
テッドの声の質は彼のお父さんのにほとんどそっくりです。
Teddo no koe no shitsu wa kare no o-too-san no ni hotondo sokkuri desu.

2. ka⌈nga⌉e o ha⌈kki⌉ri i⌈u 考えをはっきり言う ① [for s.o. to express one's view clearly and without reservation]

EX. Japanese people have become much more vocal than they used to be.
日本人は前よりずっと考えをはっきり言うようになった。
Nihon-jin wa mae yori zutto kangae o hakkiri iu yooni natta.

3. se⌈igaku no N 声楽のN •c [sung by the human voice]

EX. Mary majored in vocal music when she was at the conservatory.
メアリーは音楽学校にいた時、声楽を専攻していた。
Mearii wa ongaku-gakkoo ni ita toki, seigaku o senkoo-shite ita.

—— n. **[a sound produced by the voice or music sung by the voice]**
1. se⌈ion 声音 •c [a sound produced by the voice]
2. se⌈igaku⌉-kyoku 声楽曲 •c [a piece of music composed for the voice], bo⌈okaru ボーカル •f

voice n. **[sounds produced through special organs in the mouth, esp. by humans in speech or singing; the ability to produce such sounds《fig. "opinion"》]**
1. ko⌉e 声 [sounds produced through special organs in the mouth of humans or birds, the sound produced by a bell; the chirp of an insect《fig. "opinion"》] 《tone, opinion of the masses》

EX. (**a**) I appreciate teachers who speak in a clear voice.
はっきりした声で話す先生が好きです。
Hakkiri-shita koe de hanasu sensei ga suki desu.
(**b**) I love the sweet voices of the birds in spring.
春の鳥の甘い鳴き声が大好きです。
Haru no tori no amai naki-goe ga dai-suki desu.

2. i⌉ken 意見 •c [an idea or judgment one holds about a matter] 《view, idea, suggestion》

EX. The college newspaper provides a medium for students' voices to be heard.
大学新聞は学生に意見を発表する場を提供している。
Daigaku-shinbun wa gakusei ni iken o happyoo-suru ba o teikyoo-shite iru.

volcanic adj. **[of, like, or produced by a volcano《fig. "explosively violent"》]**
ka⌉zan (no) N 火山(の)N •c [of or produced by a volcano], ka⌉zan no yoona 火山のような adj(*na*). **[like a volcano]**

EX. Japan is made up of a series of volcanic islands.
日本は火山列島だ。
Nihon wa kazan-rettoo da.

volcano n.
ka⌉zan 火山 •c

kazan

EX. Mt. Fuji is currently a dormant volcano.
富士山は今は休火山だ。
Fuji-san wa ima wa kyuu-kazan da.

volition n. **[the capacity to decide or act of one's own will]**
ke⌈tsudan 決断 •c [an act/result of making a definite decision] 《decision, determination》, **i⌉shi 意志 •c [the mental faculty by which one determines a course of action for oneself and directs one's efforts toward that end]** 《will》, **i⌉yoku 意欲 •c [a strong desire to follow a certain course of action on which one has decided]** 《will, zest》

EX. (**a**) I joined the army of my own volition.
自分の{決断/意志/*意欲}で軍隊に入った。
*Jibun no {ketsudan/ishi/*iyoku} de guntai ni haitta.*
(**b**) Once my husband decides to do something, his volition never wavers until he accomplishes it.
夫は一度あることをしようと決めたら、成し遂げるまで、{その意志を貫き通す/その決断を曲げない/それに対する意欲を失うことはない}。
Otto wa ichi-do aru koto o shiyoo to kimetara, nashi-togeru made, {sono ishi o tsuranuki-toosu/sono ketsudan o magenai/sore ni-taisuru iyoku o ushinau koto wa nai}.

V

volleyball n.
ba⌈ree-bo⌉oru バレーボール •f

volume n. **[a book, esp. a large one forming part of a set ⟪fig. "a counter for books," "amount of space s.t. occupies," "degree of loudness"⟫]**

1. (o⌉okina) hon (大きな)本 [(a large) book], sho⌉motsu 書物 •c [a book ⟨fml⟩]

EX. The author of this volume was a professor of mine in college.
私の学生時代の先生がこの{本/書物}の著者だ。
Watashi no gakusei-jidai no sensei ga kono {hon/shomotsu} no chosha da.

2. -kan 〜巻 •c [a counter for serialized books], -satsu 〜冊 •c [a counter for books]

EX. (**a**) This encyclopedia consists of 20 volumes.
この百科事典は{二十巻/*二十冊}で構成されている。
*Kono hyakka-jiten wa {ni-juk-kan/*ni-jus-satsu} de koosei-sarete iru.*
(**b**) This library houses about five million volumes.
この図書館には本が約五百万{冊/*巻}ある。
*Kono tosho-kan ni wa hon ga yaku go-hyaku-man-{satsu/*kan} aru.*

3. ryo⌉o 量 •c [quantity] ⟪magnitude, quantity⟫, bo⌈ryuumu ボリューム •f [quantity (of sound)], o⌈nryoo 音量 •c [degree of loudness] ⟪sound volume⟫

EX. (**a**) The volume of food served in American restaurants is usually too much for me.
アメリカのレストランで出てくる食べ物の{量/ボリューム}は大抵私には多すぎる。
Amerika no resutoran de dete kuru tabe-mono no {ryoo/boryuumu} wa taitei watashi ni wa oo-sugiru.
(**b**) Would you please turn down the volume of that radio?
ラジオの{音量/ボリューム}を下げてくれませんか。
Rajio no {onryoo/boryuumu} o sagete kuremasen ka.

V

volunteer n. **[a person who offers to do s.t. of his/her own will, usually without pay; a person who enlists in the military voluntarily, without being drafted]**

1. bo⌈ranti⌉a ボランティア •f [a person who voluntarily offers to perform some service of a non-military nature]

EX. My 80-year-old mother still works as a volunteer at the hospital.
私の八十歳の母はまだ病院でボランティアをしています。
Watashi no hachi-jus-sai no haha wa mada byooin de borantia o shite imasu.

2. shi⌈ga⌉n-hei 志願兵 •c [a person who enlists in the military voluntarily, without being drafted]

vote vi. **[for s.o. to express a choice or opinion on a matter by some formal means designated in a political system]**
⟨-ni⟩ to⌈ohyoo-suru ⟨〜に⟩投票する ③ •c [for s.o. to submit a ballot expressing one's political opinion in response to a poll] ⟪cast a ballot⟫

EX. (**a**) I voted for Mr. Kawamura.
私は川村氏に投票した。
Watashi wa Kawamura-shi ni toohyoo-shita.
(**b**) I voted against the tax hike.
増税反対の方に投票した。
Zoo-zei-hantai no hoo ni toohyoo-shita.

—— vt. **[for a group of people to decide on or decide to do s.t. by an expression of the opinion of the majority through some established political procedure]**
⟨-o⟩ hyo⌈oketsu-suru ⟨〜を⟩票決する ③ •c [for a group of people to decide on s.t. by an expression of the opinion of the majority through some established political procedure] ⟪take a vote on⟫, ⟨-o⟩ to⌈ohyoo de kimeru ⟨〜を⟩投票で決める ②, ⟨-o⟩ gi⌈ketsu-suru ⟨〜を⟩議決する ③ •c [for a group of people to deliberate on an issue and decide on it by an expression of the opinion of the majority through some established political procedure] ⟪decide, resolve⟫

EX. (**a**) Shall we vote on whether or not to accept the tax hike?
増税を容認すべきかどうかを{票決しましょう/投票で決めましょう/*議決しましょう}か。
*Zoozei o yoonin-su-beki ka doo ka o {hyooketsu-shimashoo/toohyoo de kimemashoo/*giketsu-shimashoo} ka.*
(**b**) The congress has voted on an appropriation bill.
議会は政府歳出予算案を{議決した/票決した/?投票で決めた}。
Gikai wa seifu-saishutsu-yosan-an o {giketsu-shita/hyooketsu-shita/?toohyoo de kimeta}.

—— n. **[a formal expression of one's choice or opinion on a matter by some formal means designated in a political system or a decision made by such means or a count of individuals having expressed a choice or opinion by such means]**
1. to⌈ohyoo 投票 •c [an act of submitting a ballot expressing one's political opinion in response to a poll]
EX. Let's decide this matter by a vote.
この問題は投票で決めましょう。
Kono mondai wa toohyoo de kimemashoo.
2. to⌈ohyoo-ho⌉ohoo 投票方法 •c [a method by which individual political opinions or choices are submitted by ballot and counted]
3. to⌈ohyoo-soosu⌉u 投票総数 •c [the total number of individuals having submitted a ballot in response to a poll]

voter n. **[a person who expresses a choice or opinion on a matter by some formal means designated in a political system]**
to⌈ohyoo-suru hito 投票する人 [a person who submits a ballot expressing a political opinion in response to a poll], yu⌈uke⌉n-sha 有権者 •c [a person who possesses the right to cast a ballot expressing a political opinion in response to a poll]
EX. (**a**) Voters should exercise their right to vote.
有権者は投票権を行使すべきだ。
Yuuken-sha wa toohyoo-ken o kooshi-su-beki da.
(**b**) The number of voters turning out for an election is often influenced by the weather.
選挙で{投票する人/*有権者}の数はしばしば天候に左右される。
*Senkyo de {toohyoo-suru hito/*yuuken-sha} no kazu wa shiba-shiba tenkoo ni sayuu-sareru.*

vowel n.
bo⌈in 母音 •c
EX. There are only five vowels in the Japanese language.
日本語には母音が五つしかない。
Nihon-go ni wa boin ga itsutsu shika nai.

voyage n. **[a trip made by sea or air]**
1. fu⌈na⌉-tabi 船旅 [a trip made by sea] ((sea trip))
EX. A voyage by sea from the United States to Japan takes about two weeks.
アメリカから日本への船旅は二週間ぐらいかかる。
Amerika kara Nihon e no funa-tabi wa ni-shuukan-gurai kakaru.
2. so⌈ra no tabi 空の旅 [a trip made by air] ((**air travel, travel by plane**))
EX. A voyage to the moon by rocket has been dreamed of by man for a long time.
ロケットによる月への(空の)旅は長い間人間の夢だった。
Roketto ni yoru tsuki e no (sora no) tabi wa nagai aida ningen no yume datta.

W

wade vi. **[to walk through s.t such as water or mud with difficulty 《fig. "proceed with difficulty"》]**

1. 〈**-o**〉 **a⌈ru⌉ite wataru** 〈～を〉歩いて渡る ① **[for s.o./s.a. to walk across s.t.]**, 〈**-o**〉 **a⌈ru⌉ite** {**i⌈ku/ku⌉ru**} 〈～を〉歩いて{行く ①/来る ③} **[for s.o./s.a. to walk to a place away from the speaker/where the speaker is located]**

EX. (**a**) We had to wade through the deep snow for five kilometers.
深い雪の中を五キロも歩いて{行かなければ/*渡らなければ}ならなかった。
*Fukai yuki no naka o go-kiro mo aruite {ikanakereba/*wataranakereba} naranakatta.*
(**b**) I love the feeling of wading through a shallow river during summer time.
夏、浅い川を歩いて{行く/渡る}のは気持ちがいい。
Natsu, asai kawa o aruite {iku/wataru} no wa kimochi ga ii.

2. ku⌉roo-shite V 苦労してV **[for s.o. to do s.t. with difficulty]**

EX. I somehow managed to wade through the difficult book.
苦労して何とか難しい本を読んだ。
Kuroo-shite nanto ka muzukashii hon o yonda.

wage n. **[a payment of money for labor or services performed]**

chi⌉ngin 賃金 •**c** **[money paid for labor]** 《**pay**》, **kyu⌉uryoo** 給料 •**c** **[monetary compensation paid on a regular basis]** 《**pay, salary, stipend**》

EX. (**a**) The wages of a university professor are not that high in America.
アメリカの大学の先生の{賃金/給料}はそんなに高くない。
Amerika no daigaku no sensei no {chingin/kyuuryoo} wa sonnani takakunai.
(**b**) Wages are always an issue in labor-management negotiations.
{賃金/給料}はいつも労使交渉の問題点になる。
{Chingin/Kyuuryoo} wa itsu-mo roo-shi kooshoo no mondai-ten ni naru.
(**c**) I'm paid a wage of ¥350,000 per month.
僕の月々の{給料/*賃金}は三十五万円です。
*Boku no tsuki-zuki no {kyuuryoo/*chingin} wa san-juu-go-man-en desu.*

wagon n. **[a four-wheeled vehicle for carrying heavy loads, usu. drawn by horses 《fig. "a station wagon"》]**

1. ni-⌈ba⌉sha 荷馬車 •**c**

2. wa⌉gon ワゴン •**c** **[a station wagon]**

PHRASE: hitch one's wagon to a star *kiboo o hoshi ni tsunagu* 希望を星につなぐ ①

waist n. **[the part of the human body between the ribs and hips, usu. narrower than the rest of the body 《fig. "a narrow part of s.t."》]**

1. ko⌈shi 腰 **[the part of the human body between the ribs and pelvis, usu. narrower than the rest of the body 《fig. "posture," "hardness of paper-thin/stick-like objects"》]** 《**lower back, loin**》, **u⌈e⌉suto** ウエスト •**f** **[the part of the human body between the ribs and hips, usu. narrower than the rest of the body (a term used in measuring western clothes)]**

EX. (**a**) The boy was walking with his arm around the girl's waist.
男の子が腕を女の子の{腰/*ウエスト}に回して歩いていた。
*Otoko-no-ko ga ude o onna-no-ko no {koshi/*uesuto} ni mawashite aruite ita.*

(**b**) My waist is about 65 centimeters.
{ウエスト/*腰}は六十五センチぐらいです。
*{Uesuto/*Koshi} wa roku-juu-go senchi gurai desu.*

2. ku⌈bire⌉ (no bu⌉bun) くびれ(の部分) /⟨V*masu* of *kubireru* ② become compressed/ [the narrowed middle part of s.t.] ⟪constricted part, intake⟫

EX. The vase was broken at its waist.
花瓶がくびれの部分で割れていた。
Kahin ga kubire no bubun de warete ita.

wait vi. **[for s.o./s.a. to stay in a place until s.t. happens or s.o. comes ⟪fig. "serve at meals"⟫]**

1. ⟨-o⟩ ma⌉tsu ⟨〜を⟩待つ ① [for s.o./s.a. to let time pass until s.t. happens or s.o./s.t. arrives] ⟪await, abode, watch for⟫

EX. (**a**) Who are you waiting for?
だれを待っているんですか。
Dare o matte iru n desu ka.
(**b**) Wait here until I come back, OK?
私が帰ってくるまで、ここで待っていなさいよ。
Watashi ga kaette kuru made, koko de matte inasai yo.
(**c**) I waited a half hour for a taxi to come along.
僕はタクシーが来るのを三十分も待っていた。
Boku wa takushii ga kuru no o san-jup-pun mo matte ita.

2. kyu⌉uji-suru 給仕する ③ •c [for s.o. to assist s.o. dining at a table by bringing food, clearing away used items, etc.] ⟪serve⟫

EX. Three young women waited on our table.
私たちのテーブルでは三人の女の子が給仕してくれた。
Watashi-tachi no teeburu de wa san-nin no onna-no-ko ga kyuuji-shite kureta.

PHRASE: Thank you for waiting. *o-matase shimashita.* お待たせしました。⟨fml⟩, *o-machi-doo-sama.* お待ちどうさま。

waiter n. **[a male person who serves s.o. at a table]**

u⌈e⌉etaa ウエーター •f, bo⌈oi ボーイ •f

EX. The service we received from the waiter was very good.
{ウエーター/ボーイ}のサービスは上々だった。
{Ueetaa/Booi} no saabisu wa joojoo datta.

waiting room n. **[a room provided in a station, hospital, etc., for people to pass time until the time comes to board, be seen, etc.]**

ma⌈chia⌉i-shitsu 待合室 [a room provided in a station, hospital, etc., for people to pass time until the time comes to board, be seen, etc.]

EX. I waited for a whole hour in the waiting room at the dentist's office.
私は歯医者の待合室で一時間も待った。
Watashi wa ha-isha no machiai-shitsu de ichi-jikan mo matta.

waitress n. **[a female person who serves s.o. at a table]**

u⌈e⌉etoresu ウエートレス •f

EX. I'm working as a waitress at a downtown restaurant.
私は町のレストランでウエートレスをしています。
Watashi wa machi no resutoran de ueetoresu o shite imasu.

wake vi. **[for s.o./s.a. to become conscious again after being asleep]**

o⌈ki⌉ru 起きる ② [for s.o./s.a./s.t. that has been lying horizontally and dormant to stand up vertically ⟪fig. "wake up," "occur"⟫] ⟪get up, rise, wake up, occur, begin to burn⟫, me⌉ ga sa⌈me⌉ru 目が覚める ② [for the first person to become conscious again after being asleep] ⟪wake up, realize⟫, me⌉ o sa⌈ma⌉su 目を覚ます ① [for s.o./s.a. to become conscious again after being asleep] ⟪wake up, realize⟫

EX. I woke up around five o'clock this morning.
今朝は五時ごろに{起きました/目が覚めました/目を覚ましました}。
Kesa wa go-ji goro ni {okimashita/me ga samemashita/me o samashimashita}.

W

— vt. **[to rouse s.o./s.a. from a state of sleep]**
⟨-o⟩ o⌈ko⌉su ⟨～を⟩起こす ① **[to cause s.o./s.t./s.a. that is dormant or lying down to become more active or to stand up]** 《raise up, bring about, wake up, establish, begin》

EX. Could you wake me up at 7:30 tomorrow morning?
あしたの朝七時半に起こしてくれませんか。
Ashita no asa shichi-ji-han ni okoshite kuremasen ka.

— n. **[an act of remaining awake in watch over a dead person]**
(o-)⌈tsu⌉ya (お)通夜 •c

Wales n.
U⌈e⌉eruzu ウエールズ •f

walk vi. **[for s.o./s.a. to move on foot at a normal pace such that at least one foot is on the ground at any given time]**
a⌈ru⌉ku 歩く ① **[for s.o./s.a. to move along at a normal pace on foot or to go around to various places doing s.t., either on foot or in a vehicle]** 《go on foot, pace, trek》, **a⌈yu⌉mu** 歩む ① **[for s.o. to move along at a normal pace on foot** 《fig. "proceed"》 **⟨w⟩]** 《step》, **sa⌈npo-suru** 散歩する ③ •c **[for s.o. to move along at a normal pace on foot for exercise or pleasure]** 《take a walk, stroll, ramble》

EX. **(a)** I walk three times a week for exercise.
運動のために週三回{歩いて/散歩して/*歩んで}います。
*Undoo no tame ni shuu san-kai {aruite/sanpo-shite/*ayunde} imasu.*
(b) A: How do you get to school?
どうやって学校に行きますか。
Doo yatte gakkoo ni ikimasu ka.
B: I walk there.
{歩いて/*散歩して/*歩んで}行きます。
*{Aruite/*Sanpo-shite/*Ayunde} ikimasu.*
(c) Through many trials and tribulations I've come to learn to walk by faith.
多くの困難や試練を通して信仰によって{歩む/*歩く/*散歩する}ことを学んだ。
*Ooku no konnan ya shiren o tooshite shinkoo ni-yotte {ayumu/*aruku/*sanpo-suru} koto o mananda.*

— vt. **[for s.o./s.a. to move on foot at a normal pace along, through, or over an area or to cause s.o./s.a. to move on foot at a normal pace]**
⟨-o⟩ a⌈ruka-se⌉ru ⟨～を⟩歩かせる /⟨causative of *aruku* ① walk/ ② **[to cause s.o./s.a. to move along at a normal pace on foot]**, **⟨-o⟩ sa⌈npo-sase⌉ru** ⟨～を⟩散歩させる /⟨causative of *sanpo-suru* ③ take a walk/ ② **[for s.o. to cause s.o./s.a. to move along at a normal pace on foot for exercise or pleasure]**

EX. I walk my dog every day.
私は犬を毎日{歩かせます/散歩させます}。
Watashi wa inu o mai-nichi {aruka-semasu/sanpo-sasemasu}.

— n. **[an act or manner of moving on foot at a normal pace; a path or street for walking along on foot]**
1. to⌉ho 徒歩 •c **[moving along at a normal pace on foot without riding a vehicle]** 《walking, pedestrianism》, **sa⌈npo** 散歩 •c **[the activity of moving along for a set distance on foot for exercise or pleasure]** 《stroll, outing, promenade》

EX. I prefer walking to riding a bicycle.
私は{散歩/徒歩}のほうが自転車に乗るより好きです。
Watashi wa {sanpo/toho} no hoo ga jitensha ni noru yori suki desu.

2. a⌈ruki-kata 歩き方 /⟨V*masu* of *aruku* ① walk + *kata* way, manner/ **[a manner or moving along on foot]**

EX. Her walk reminds me of Marilyn Monroe.
彼女の歩き方はマリリン・モンローのに似ていると思う。
Kanojo no aruki-kata wa Maririn Monroo no ni nite iru to omou.

3. ho⌈doo 歩道 •c **[a street on which people travel by foot as opposed to one where vehicles are driven]** 《sidewalk》

EX. I was hit by a bike as I was standing on the walk.

歩道で立っていたら、自転車にぶつけられたんです。
Hodoo de tatte itara, jitensha ni butsuke-rareta n desu.

PHRASE: take a walk *sanpo (o) suru* 散歩(を)する ③ SEE walk vi.

EX. Let's take a walk in the park.
公園を散歩しましょう。
Kooen o sanpo-shimashoo.

PHRASE: walk of life *shokugyoo* 職業 •c ⟪occupation, profession⟫, *mibun* 身分 ⟪status, station in life⟫

EX. People from all walks of life come to this church.
この教会には色々な{職業/身分}の人が来ます。
Kono kyookai ni wa iro-irona {shokugyoo/mibun} no hito ga kimasu.

wall n. **[a vertical structure forming one of the sides of a building or room or built as a boundary or enclosure to an area]**

1. jo˹oheki 城壁 •c [a vertical barrier surrounding a castle or town for protection] ⟪a castle wall⟫

EX. The walls of the old city are still standing.
古い町の城壁は今でも立っている。
Furui machi no jooheki wa ima demo tatte iru.

2. ka˹be 壁 [one of the vertical sides of a room, building, or area] ⟪partition⟫

EX. The Berlin Wall came down suddenly in 1989.
ベルリンの壁は1989年に突然崩壊した。
Berurin no kabe wa sen-kyuu-hyaku-hachi-juu-ku-nen ni totsuzen hookai-shita.

3. he˹i 塀 •c [an upright structure of stone, concrete, wood, brick, etc., put around a house, field, garden, etc., to keep out intruders or to keep prisoners from escaping] ⟪fence⟫

EX. In the U.S., yards of private houses are usually not surrounded by walls.
アメリカでは個人の家の庭は塀で囲まれていないのが普通だ。
Amerika de wa kojin no ie no niwa wa hei de kakoma-rete inai no ga futsuu da.

wallet n. **[a pocket-sized folding case for holding money, cards, photographs, etc.] sa˹ifu 財布 •c [a small cloth or leather container for holding paper money or change] ⟪purse, pocketbook⟫, sa˹tsu-ire˺ 札入れ [a folding pocket-book for holding paper money]**

EX. Someone pickpocketed my wallet on the bus.
バスの中で{財布/札入れ}をすられた。
Basu no naka de {saifu/satsu-ire} o sura-reta.

wander vi. **[to move about aimlessly ⟪fig. "follow a winding course," "stray in one's thoughts"⟫]**

1. a˹te-mo-na˺ku a˹ruki-mawa˺ru あてもなく歩き回る ① [for s.o. to walk around aimlessly], bu˺ra-bura a˹ruki-mawa˺ru ぶらぶら歩き回る ① [for s.o./s.a. to walk around idly]

EX. Hans likes to wander for hours in the woods.
ハンスは森の中を何時間も{あてもなく/ぶらぶら}歩き回るのが好きです。
Hansu wa mori no naka o nan-jikan mo {ate-mo-naku/bura-bura} aruki-mawaru no ga suki desu.

2. ma˹gari-kune˺tte tsuzuku 曲がりくねって続く ① [for s.t. such as a road, river, or mountain range to follow a winding course]

EX. A river wandered across the vast plain.
川が広大な平野を曲がりくねって続いていた。
Kawa ga koodaina heiya o magari-kunette tsuzuite ita.

3. to˹ritome ga na˺i 取り留めがない adj(*i*). **[lacking consistency or cohesiveness]**

EX. The old professor's thoughts tend to wander, making it hard to follow his lectures.
老教授の考えはしばしば取り留めがないため講義についていくのが大変だ。
Roo-kyooju no kangae wa shiba-shiba

W

toritome ga nai tame koogi ni tsuite iku no ga taihen da.

want vt. **[to need an object/action/state because a person/thing lacks it]**

1. **⟨-ga⟩ ho⌈shi⌉i** **⟨〜が⟩欲しい** adj(*i*). **[to be desirable to the speaker/listener]** **⟪desire⟫**, **{⟨-ga⟩/⟨-o⟩} V*masu* ta⌉i** **{⟨〜が⟩/⟨〜を⟩} V*masu*たい** adj(*i*). **[for the speaker/listener to have a desire to do s.t.]**

EX. (**a**) I want a baby of our own.
私、私たちの赤ちゃんが欲しいの。
Watashi, watashi-tachi no aka-chan ga hoshii no.
(**b**) If you want money, I'll give you some.
お金が欲しいならあげるよ。
O-kane ga hoshii nara ageru yo.
(**c**) A: What do you want to do this time, Billy?
ビリーちゃん、今度は何{が/を}したい?
Birii-chan, kondo wa nani {ga/o} shitai?
B: I want to go on the Ferris wheel.
大観覧車に乗りたい。
Dai-kanran-sha ni nori-tai.

NOTE: The feeling of desire expressed by *⟨-ga⟩* V*masu tai* is more spontaneous and immediate than that expressed by *⟨-o⟩* V*masu tai*. Thus, in a situation such as the following, where the desire expressed is immediate and strong, *⟨-ga⟩* is much more natural sounding than *⟨-o⟩*. (After running ten miles) *Aa, mizu {ga/??o} nomi-tai.* "Man, could I use, (lit, drink) some water!"

2. **⟨-o⟩ ho⌈shiga⌉ru** **⟨〜を⟩欲しがる** **/⟨adj(*i*). stem of *hoshii* want + *garu* ① show signs of/** ① **[for a third person to show signs of desiring s.t/s.o./s.a.]**, **⟨-o⟩ V*masu* ta-⌈ga⌉ru** **⟨〜を⟩V*masu*たがる** **/⟨adj(*i*). stem of V*masu tai* want + *garu* ① show signs of/** ① **[for a third person to desire to do s.t.]**

EX. (**a**) Stacy wants a new sports car.
ステーシーは新しいスポーツカーを欲しがっている。
Suteeshii wa atarashii supootsukaa o hoshigatte iru.
(**b**) My younger brother wants to study Japanese, too.
弟も日本語を勉強したがっています。
Otooto mo Nihon-go o benkyooshi-tagatte imasu.
(**c**) My children always want sweets.
うちの子供たちはいつも甘いものを欲しがります。
Uchi no kodomo-tachi wa itsu-mo amai mono o hoshigarimasu.

3. **⟨-ga⟩ ta⌈rinai** **⟨〜が⟩足りない** **/⟨Vstem of *tariru* ② sufficient + *nai* not/** **[not have enough of s.t.]**, **⟨-ga⟩ i⌈ru** **⟨〜が⟩要る** ② **[to be necessary or desirable]** **⟪need⟫**, **hi⌈tsuyoona** **必要な** adj(*na*). **[essential for s.t./s.o./s.a.]** **⟪needed, required, indispensable⟫**

EX. (**a**) These cookies want a little bit more sugar.
このクッキーはちょっと砂糖が{足りない/??要る/*必要だ}。
*Kono kukkii wa chotto satoo ga {tarinai/??iru/*hitsuyoo da}.*
(**b**) We want more money to build a house.
家を建てるのに金が{もっと要る/もっと必要だ/足りない}。
Ie o tateru no ni kane ga {motto iru/motto hitsuyoo da/tarinai}.

war n. **[a hostile conflict, esp. one between countries involving military attacks]** **se⌈nsoo 戦争 •c** **⟪warfare, battle⟫** ↔ **heiwa 平和 •c**; **ta⌈takai 戦い** **/⟨V*masu* of *tatakau* ① fight/** **[a struggle to defeat an opponent, overcome a difficulty, or achieve s.t.]** **⟪warfare, fight, battle, encounter, struggle, contest⟫**

EX. (**a**) When the war broke out I was a junior high school student.
{戦争/??戦い}が始まった時、私は中学生でした。
{Sensoo/??Tatakai} ga hajimatta toki, watashi wa chuugaku-sei deshita.
(**b**) There has still been little visible progress in modern medicine's war against cancer.
現代医学のがんに対する{戦い/*戦争}においてはまだ大した進展が見られない。
*Gendai-igaku no gan ni-taisuru {tatakai/*sensoo} ni-oite wa mada*

W

taishita shinten ga mi-rarenai.
(**c**) According to its constitution, Japan has disavowed all forms of war.
憲法によると、日本はいかなる{戦争/*戦い}をも放棄した。
*Kenpoo ni-yoru to, Nihon wa ikanaru {sensoo/*tatakai} o mo hooki-shita.*

ward[1] n. **[a person who acts as a legal guardian for a child or a child who is under the care of a legal guardian]**
1. ko⌈oken-nin 後見人 •c [a person who acts as a legal guardian for a child] **《guardian, tutor, curator》**
2. hi⌉-ko⌈oken-nin 被後見人 •c [a child who is under the care of a legal guardian]

ward[2] n. **[the state of being under guard 《fig. "a room in a hospital for a specific group of patients," "a prison cell," "an administrative division of a city"》]**
1. byo⌈otoo 病棟 •c [a hospital building containing rooms for patients that are hospitalized] 《sickroom》
EX. Mr. Yoshida's room is in the respiratory ward.
吉田さんの部屋は呼吸器疾患の病棟です。
Yoshida-san no heya wa kokyuu-ki-shikkan no byootoo desu.
2. ka⌈nboo 監房 •c [a prison cell]
3. -ku 〜区 [an administrative division of a large city]
EX. I live in the Meito ward of Nagoya.
私は名古屋の名東区に住んでいます。
Watashi wa Nagoya no Meitoo-ku ni sunde imasu.

warfare n. **[a state of armed conflict, esp. between nations]**
ko⌈osen 交戦 •c [a state of armed conflict] 《war, belligerence, battle, engagement》, se⌈nsoo 戦争 •c [a hostile conflict, esp. between countries involving military attacks] 《war, battle》
EX. (**a**) We must avoid nuclear warfare by all means.
私たちは核{戦争/*交戦}をどうしても避けなければならない。
*Watashi-tachi wa kaku-{sensoo/*koosen} o dooshite mo sakenakereba naranai.*
(**b**) A state of warfare currently exists between those two countries.
両国は今{交戦/戦争}中だ。
Ryookoku wa ima {koosen/sensoo}-chuu da.

warm adj. **[having or producing a moderately high temperature; feeling a comfortable amount of heat in one's body or in the surrounding atmosphere 《fig. "ardent", "affectionate"》]**
1. a⌈tataka⌉i あたたかい adj(*i*). **[having or producing a moderately high temperature; feeling a comfortable amount of heat in one's body or the surrounding atmosphere 《fig. "affectionate"》] 《mild, genial, cordial, kind》 ↔ samui 寒い** adj(*i*). **[sensing discomfort due to low temperature in one's body or in the surrounding atmosphere], tsumetai 冷たい** adj(*i*). **[having a low temperature physically percepfible to the touch]; a⌉tata⌉kana あたたかな** adj(*na*).
㊈ "feeling a comfortable amount of heat in one's body in the surrounding atmosphere"▷暖か, otherwise ▷温か
NOTE: *Atatakai* and *atatakana* have corresponding emphatic and colloquial versions *attakai* and *attakana*, respectively.
EX. (**a**) It's so warm it's almost like spring, isn't it?
春のようで、暖かいですね。
Haru no yoo de, atatakai desu ne.
NOTE: 温かい would not be the correct way to write *atatakai* in *kanji* in this example.
(**b**) Warm days finally arrived in mid June.
六月中旬になってやっと{暖かな/暖かい}日がやって来た。
Roku-gatsu chuujun ni natte yatto {atatakana/atatakai} hi ga yatte kita.
(**c**) I'd like something warm to eat.
何か{温かい/?温かな}ものが食べたいです。
Nani-ka {atatakai/?atatakana} mono ga tabe-tai desu.

NOTE: 暖かい would not be the correct way to write *atatakai* in *kanji* in this example.

(**d**) You really have warm hands.
{温かい/温かな}手をしていますね。
{Atatakai/Atatakana} te o shite imasu ne.
(**e**) She has a warm heart.
彼女は心が温かい。
Kanojo wa kokoro ga atatakai.

— vt. **[to cause a physical substance or an environment to have a moderately high temperature ⟪fig. "fill one's heart with good feeling"⟫]**
⟨-o⟩ a⌈tataka⌉ku suru ⟨～を⟩あたたかくする ③, **⟨-o⟩ a⌈tatame⌉ru** ⟨～を⟩あたためる ② **[for s.o. to cause a physical substance or an environment to have a moderately high temperature ⟪fig. "fill one's heart with good feeling," "keep s.t. important for a long time"⟫]** ⟪**heat up, keep**⟫ ↔ **hiyasu** 冷やす ①
㊅ "feeling a comfortable amount of heat in one's body in the surrounding atmosphere"▷暖か, otherwise ▷温か SEE the note for warm adj.

EX. (**a**) You should warm the sake before you drink it.
酒は飲む前に{温めなければ/温かくしなければ}いけない。
Sake wa nomu mae ni {atatamenakereba/atatakaku shinakereba} ikenai.
(**b**) Please warm this bread in the oven.
このパンをオーブンで{温めて/温かくして}ください。
Kono pan o oobun de {atatamete/atatakaku shite} kudasai.
(**c**) We warmed our room with a heater.
ヒーターで部屋を{暖めた/暖かくした}。
Hiitaa de heya o {atatameta/atatakaku shita}.

W

warmth n. **[the state or quality of being at a moderately high temperature]**
a⌈tata⌉ka-sa あたたかさ **[a measurable degree of moderate heat]**, **a⌈tataka-mi** あたたかみ **[a directly perceptible quality of having moderate heat]**
㊅ "feeling a comfortable amount of heat in one's body in the surrounding atmosphere"▷暖か, otherwise ▷温か SEE the note for warm adj.

EX. (**a**) I like the warmth of California's climate.
カリフォルニアの気候の{暖かさ/*暖かみ}が好きです。
*Kariforunia no kikoo no {atataka-sa/ *atataka-mi} ga suki desu.*
(**b**) I miss the warmth of your body.
あなたの体の{温かみ/?温かさ}が恋しい。
Anata no karada no {atataka-mi/ ?atataka-sa} ga koishii.
(**c**) The warmth of his character touched me.
あの人の心の{温かさ/?温かみ}に感動しました。
Ano hito no kokoro no {atataka-sa/ ?atataka-mi} ni kandoo-shimashita.

warn vt. **[to call s.o.'s attention to the potential for danger or other undesirable circumstance; to advise s.o. how to act to avoid an undesirable consequence]**
⟨-ni⟩ ⟨-to⟩ ke⌈ikoku-suru ⟨～に⟩⟨～と⟩警告する ③ **[for s.o. to cause s.o. to pay attention to some imminent danger or evil]** ⟪**caution, admonish**⟫, **⟨-ni⟩ ⟨-to⟩ i⌈mashime⌉ru** ⟨～に⟩⟨～と⟩戒める ② **[for s.o. to give advice to s.o. in advance so that he/she will not commit a mistake]** ⟪**admonish, remonstrate**⟫

EX. (**a**)The weather bureau warned the local residents that severe thunderstroms were coming.
気象庁は激しい雷雨が来ると住民に{警告した/*戒めた}。
*Kishoo-choo wa hageshii raiu ga kuru to juumin ni {keikoku-shita/ *imashimeta}.*
(**b**) I warned him against experimenting with drugs.
僕は彼に麻薬に手を出さないようにと{戒めた/?警告した}。
Boku wa kare ni mayaku ni te o dasanai yooni to {imashimeta/ ?keikoku-shita}.

warning n. **[a notice or advice regarding the potential for danger or other undesirable circumstance]**

1. ke⌈ikoku 警告 •c [an act/instance of causing s.o. to pay attention to some imminent danger or evil] ⟪caution, admonition⟫

EX. In spite of my warning, my son and his friend went on the mountain climb and nearly ended up losing their lives.
私の警告にもかかわらず息子と友達は山に登り、あやうく命をおとすところだった。
Watashi no keikoku nimo-kakawarazu musuko to tomodachi wa yama ni nobori, ayauku inochi o otosu tokoro datta.

2. i⌈mashime 戒め /⟨V*masu* of *imashimeru* ② admonish/ [an advance indication that s.t. is going to happen] ⟪admonition, remonstrance⟫

EX. I intend to abide by my father's warning never to get into debt no matter how hard pressed I am.
どんなに困っても借金をするなという父の戒めを守るつもりです。
Donna-ni komatte mo shakkin o suru na to iu chichi no imashime o mamoru tsumori desu.

3. yo⌈koku 予告 •c [an act/instance of informing s.o. of an important matter ahead of time]

EX. Landlords are required to give tenants six months' warning before raising the rent.
家賃を上げる場合、大家は借家人に六か月前に予告をしなければならない。
Yachin o ageru baai, ooya wa shakuya-nin ni rok-kagetsu mae ni yokoku o shinakereba naranai.

4. ma⌈e-bure 前触れ [an advance indication that s.t. is going to happen] ⟪preliminary announcement, herald, harbinger, forerunner⟫

EX. Were there any warning signs before the heart attack occurred?
心臓発作の前触れがあったんですか。
Shinzoo-hossa no mae-bure ga atta n desu ka.

warrior n. **[a man who fights in battle ⟨w⟩]**
bu⌉shi 武士 •c [a professional military man in ancient times ⟨w⟩] ⟪soldier, military man⟫, yu⌉ushi 勇士 [a brave man who fights in battle]

EX. Warriors in medieval Japan often pursued aesthetic activities such as the tea ceremony.
中世日本の{武士/勇士}は茶道のような美的活動をたしなむことが多かった。
Chuusei Nihon no {bushi/yuushi} wa sadoo no yoona bi-teki katsudoo o tashinamu koto ga ookatta.

warship n. **[a military ship]**
gu⌈nkan 軍艦 •c

EX. The battleship Yamato was probably one of the most powerful warships ever built.
戦艦大和は多分史上最強の軍艦の一つだっただろう。
Senkan Yamato wa tabun shijoo saikyoo no gunkan no hitotsu datta daroo.

was vi. **[affirmative past tense of the first and third person singular of the copula and of the existential verb "to be"]**

1. de⌉shita でした cop. **[formal affirmative past tense of the copula *da*] ⟪was, were⟫, datta だった** cop. **[informal/written style affirmative past tense of the copula *da*] ⟪was, were⟫, de⌈a⌉tta であった** cop. **[written style affirmative past tense of the copula] ⟪was, were⟫**

EX. Bob was then a student at Princeton University.
ボブはその時プリンストン大学の学生{でした/だった}。
Bobu wa sono toki Purinsuton-daigaku no gakusei {deshita/datta}.

2. a⌈rima⌉shita ありました [formal affirmative past tense of *aru*, for s.t. to exist] ⟪was, were, existed⟫, a⌉tta あった [informal affirmative past tense of *aru*] ⟪was, were, existed⟫, i⌈ma⌉shita いました [formal affirmative past tense of *iru* for s.o./s.a. to exist] ⟪was, were, existed⟫, i⌈ta

W

いた **[informal affirmative past tense of *iru*]** **《was, were, existed》**

EX. (**a**) There was a house on top of the hill.
丘の上に家が{ありました/あった/*いました/*いた}。
*Oka no ue ni ie ga {arimashita/atta/*imashita/*ita}.*
(**b**) There were many college students at the party.
パーティーには大学生が大勢{いました/いた/*ありました/*あった}。
*Paatii ni wa daigaku-sei ga oozei {imashita/ita/*arimashita/*atta}.*

— aux. **[an auxiliary verb used in the passive or progressive construction]**

1. {Vneg. reta/Vstem rareta/sareta} {Vneg. れた/Vstemられた/された} [for s.t./s.o./s.a. acting as the subject of a sentence to be affected in the past by the action of the verb of that sentence]

EX. When I was in elementary school I was often bullied by my classmates.
小学生のときよく級友にいじめられた。
Shoogaku-sei no toki yoku kyuuyuu ni ijime-rareta.

2. V*te* ita V*te*いた [for s.o./s.a./s.t. to be in the middle of doing s.t. in the past or to be in a state in the past resulting from s.t. that happened earlier]

EX. He was swimming in the pool.
彼はプールで泳いでいた。
Kare wa puuru de oyoide ita.

wash vt. **[to cleanse s.t. with water (and soap) 《fig. "purify," "flow over or against," "erode"》]**

1. ⟨-o⟩ a⌈rau ⟨〜を⟩洗う ① [to cleanse s.t./s.a. with water or other cleanser 《fig. "flow over or against," "expose"》] 《cleanse, rinse, wash against, expose》

EX. (**a**) I washed my pants in the washing machine.
洗濯機でズボンを洗った。
Sentak-ki de zubon o aratta.
(**b**) The waves were washing up against the shore.
波が岸を洗っていた。
Nami ga kishi o aratte ita.

2. ⟨-o⟩ a⌈rai-kiyome⌉ru ⟨〜を⟩洗い清める ② [for s.o. to make s.t. free of impurity using water or other liquid]

EX. Christianity teaches that one's sins can be washed away if one confesses them and repents.
キリスト教では罪を告白し悔い改めるなら、それを洗い清めてもらうことができると教えられている。
Kirisuto-kyoo de wa tsumi o kokuhaku-shi kui-aratameru nara, sore o arai-kiyomete morau koto ga dekiru to oshie-rarete iru.

3. a⌈rai-naga⌉su 洗い流す ① [for the action of a liquid to carry s.t. away] 《erode, wash away》

EX. The topsoil bared by deforestation was washed away by the rain.
山林伐採によってむき出しにされた山の表面の土は雨によって洗い流された。
Sanrin-bassai ni-yotte muki-dashi ni sareta yama no hyoomen no tsuchi wa ame ni-yotte arai-nagasa-reta.

washbowl n. **[a bowl holding water, usu. attached to the wall, in which to clean one's hands]**
se⌈nmen⌉-ki 洗面器 •c 《wash basin》

Washington n.

1. Wa⌈shi⌉nton ワシントン •f [Washington, D.C.]

2. Wa⌈shinto⌉n-shuu ワシントン州 •f+c [the State of Washington]

washroom n. **[a room containing one or more washbowls and toilet]**
(o-)⌈tea⌉rai (お)手洗い 《toilet》

EX. Where is the washroom?
お手洗いはどこでしょうか。
O-tearai wa doko deshoo ka.

NOTE: The prefix *o-* is used here to give the attached word a more polite, less vulgar sound.

wasn't v. **[negative past tense of the first and third person singular of the copula and of the existential verb "to be"]**

1. {dewaa⌈rimase⌉n/jaa⌈rimase⌉n} deshita {ではありません/じゃありません}でした cop.

W

[formal negative past tense of the copula *da*] ((wasn't, weren't)), {**dewa⌈na⌉katta/ ja⌈na⌉katta**} {ではなかった/じゃなかった} cop. **[informal/written style negative past tense of the copula *da*]** ((wasn't, weren't))

EX. (**a**) A: Were you a student at that time?
その時学生でしたか。
Sono toki gakusei deshita ka.
B: No, I wasn't. I had already graduated and was working.
いいえ、そう{{ではありません/じゃありません}でした/*ではなかった/*じゃなかった}。もう卒業して仕事をしていました。
*Iie, soo {{dewaarimasen/jaarimasen} deshita/*dewanakatta/*janakatta}. Moo sotsugyoo-shite shigoto o shite imashita.*
(**b**) Mary wasn't a college student yet in 1990.
1990年にメアリーはまだ大学生{{ではありません/じゃありません}でした/ではなかった/じゃなかった}。
Sen-kyuu-hyaku-kyuu-juu-nen ni Mearii wa mada daigaku-sei {{dewaarimasen/jaarimasen} deshita/ dewanakatta/janakatta}

2. a⌈rimase⌉n deshita ありませんでした **[formal negative past tense of *aru*, for s.t. to exist]**, **na⌉katta** なかった **[informal negative past tense of *aru*]**, **i⌈masen⌉ deshita** いませんでした **[formal negative past tense of *iru*, for s.o./s.a. to exist]**, **i⌈na⌉katta** いなかった **[informal negative past tense of *iru*]**

EX. (**a**) A: Was there any Japanese dictionary at the bookstore?
本屋に日本語の辞書、あった?
Hon'ya ni Nihon-go no jisho, atta?
B: No, there wasn't.
いや、{ありませんでした/なかった/*いませんでした/*いなかった}。
*Iya, {arimasen deshita/nakatta/*imasen deshita/*inakatta}.*
(**b**) A: Was there a quiz today?
今日、小テスト、あった?
Kyoo, shoo-tesuto, atta?
B: No, there wasn't.
いや、{ありませんでした/なかった/*いませんでした/*いなかった}。
*Iya, {arimasen deshita/nakatta/*imasen deshita/*inakatta}.*
(**c**) A: Was Bill upstairs?
ビルは二階にいた?
Biru wa ni-kai ni ita?
B: No, he wasn't.
いや、{いませんでした/いなかった/*ありませんでした/*なかった}よ。
*Iya, {imasen deshita/inakatta/*arimasen deshita/*nakatta} yo.*
(**d**) I wasn't home yesterday morning.
きのうの朝は家に{いませんでした/いなかった/*ありませんでした/*なかった}。
*Kinoo no asa wa ie ni {imasen deshita/inakatta/*arimasen deshita/*nakatta}.*

—— aux. **[an auxiliary verb used in the passive or progressive construction]**
1. {**Vneg. renakatta/Vstem rarenakatta/ sarenakatta**} {Vneg.れなかった/Vstemられなかった/されなかった} **[for s.t./s.o./s.a. acting as the subject of a sentence to not be affected in the past by the action of the verb of that sentence]**

EX. Luckily I wasn't hit by the car.
幸い僕はその車にはねられなかった。
Saiwai boku wa sono kuruma ni hane-rarenakatta.

2. V*te* inakatta V*te*いなかった **[for s.o./s.a./s.t. to not be in the middle of doing s.t. in the past or to not be in a state in the past resulting from s.t. that happened earlier]**

EX. Robert wasn't studying at his desk when I checked a minute ago.
さっき見たときロバートは机で勉強していなかった。
Sakki mita toki Robaato wa tsukue de benkyoo-shite inakatta.

waste vt. **[for s.o. to use or spend s.t. in a needless or careless way]**
⟨-o⟩ **ro⌈ohi-suru** ⟨〜を⟩浪費する ③ •c **[for s.o. to use s.t. unnecessarily or to no good purpose, esp. time, money, or energy]** ((use to no purpose, squander)), **mu⌈da-zu⌉kai-**

suru むだ遣いする ③ [for s.o. to use s.t. to no purpose] ⸨squander⸩

EX. (**a**) She's wasting her money buying clothes like that.
彼女はあんな風に服を買ったりして金を{浪費/むだ遣い}している。
Kanojo wa anna fuu ni fuku o kattari shite kane o {roohi/muda-zukai}-shite iru.
(**b**) I finally realized that I was wasting my time taking a class I had no interest in.
全然興味のない授業を取ったりして時間を{浪費/むだ遣い}していることにやっと気が付いた。
Zenzen kyoomi no nai jugyoo o tottari shite jikan o {roohi/muda-zukai}-shite iru koto ni yatto ki ga tsuita.

— n. **[the act of using or spending s.t. in a needless or careless way; s.t. thrown away or left over because it is not needed; land which is not suitable for productive use]**

1. ro˥ohi 浪費 •c [the act of using s.t. unnecessarily or to no good purpose, esp. time, money, or energy] ⸨dissipation, extravagance⸩, mu˥da-zu˥kai むだ遣い [using s.t. to no purpose] ⸨extravagance⸩

EX. It's a waste of electricity to leave lights turned on like that.
そんなに電気をつけっぱなしにしていては電気の{浪費/むだ遣い}だ。
Sonna-ni denki o tsuke-ppanashi ni shite ite wa denki no {roohi/muda-zukai} da.

NOTE: *Muda-zukai* can also be written as むだ使い.

2. a˥re-chi 荒れ地 [an uncultivated, barren area of land]

EX. Many Japanese cities lay in waste for a period following the war.
日本の町の多くは戦争が終わった後しばらくの間荒れ地だった。
Nihon no machi no ooku wa sensoo ga owatta ato shibaraku no aida are-chi datta.

3. ha˥iki˥-butsu 廃棄物 •c [s.t. in a broken or useless condition to be thrown away]

EX. Industrial waste is polluting the river.
産業廃棄物が川を汚染している。
Sangyoo-haiki-butsu ga kawa o osen-shite iru.

wasteful adj. **[using or spending s.t. in a needless or careless way]**
mu˥dana むだな adj(*na*). **•c [resulting in no profit or effect despite time or effort expended] ⸨futile, fruitless⸩, fu-˥ke˥izaina 不経済な** adj(*na*). **•c [not economical] ⸨unthrifty, expensive⸩**

EX. A: I spent $1,000 on this TV.
このテレビに千ドル使ったんだ。
Kono terebi ni sen-doru tsukatta n da.
B: I call that wasteful.
それは{むだ/不経済}というものだ。
Sore wa {muda/fu-keizai} to iu mono da.

watch vt. **[for s.o./s.a. to keep one's eyes fixed on s.t./s.o./s.a. that moves or changes; to guard or take care of s.t./s.o./s.a.; to be alert for an opportunity or occurrence of s.t.]**

1. ⟨-o⟩ mi˥ru ⟨〜を⟩見る ② [for s.o./s.a. to direct one's attention to s.t./s.o./s.a. in order to visually perceive its outward shape or its content] ⸨see, view, look through, examine, look up, try, read⸩

EX. I watch the news on television every day.
私は毎日テレビでニュースを見ます。
Watashi wa mai-nichi terebi de nyuusu o mimasu.

2. ⟨-o⟩ mi-˥mamoru ⟨〜を⟩見守る /⟨V*masu* of *miru* ② watch + *mamoru* ① protect/ ① [for s.o./s.a. to keep one's eyes on s.t./s.o./s.a. so that no harm comes to it/him/her] ⸨stare⸩

EX. The mother watched her child go across the street.
母親は子供が道を渡るのを見守っていた。
Haha-oya wa kodomo ga michi o wataru no o mi-mamotte ita.

3. ⟨-no⟩ ba˥n o suru ⟨〜の⟩番をする ③ [for s.o./s.a. to take one's turn keeping an eye on s.t./s.a. valuable] ⸨look after, stand guard over⸩

W

EX. Could you watch this suitcase for me for a minute?
ちょっとこの荷物の番をしてくれませんか。
Chotto kono nimotsu no ban o shite kuremasen ka.

4. ⟨-o⟩ mi-⌈haru ⟨～を⟩見張る ① [for s.o. to keep a close eye on s.o./s.t./s.a. to prevent escape or harm] ⟪open one's eyes wide, look out for, oversee⟫, ⟨-o⟩ ka⌈nshi-suru ⟨～を⟩監視する ③ •c [for s.o. to carefully monitor s.o.] ⟪oversee, keep an eye on⟫

EX. Two prison guards were watching the inmates.
二人の看守が囚人を{見張って/監視して}いた。
Futari no kanshu ga shuujin o {mi-hatte/kanshi-shite} ita.

— n. **[the act of keeping one's eyes fixed on s.t. that moves or changes or a fixed period of time during which one does this ⟪fig. "a portable timepiece"⟫]**

1. mi-⌈hari 見張り /⟨V*masu* of *mi-haru* ① look out for/ [the act of keeping a close eye on some place/s.o. to prevent escape or harm or s.o. who does this] ⟪lookout, vigilance, watchman, guard⟫, ka⌈nshi 監視 •c [the act of carefully monitoring s.o.] ⟪guard, duty, vigil, observation⟫

EX. Keeping watch over prison inmates is now largely done by electronics means.
囚人の{見張り/監視}は今は大抵電子的手段を使って行われている。
Shuujin no {mi-hari/kanshi} wa ima wa taitei denshi-teki-shudan o tsukatte okonawa-rete iru.

2. to⌈kei 時計 [a device for measuring and indicating time by means of springs, electricity, etc.] ⟪clock⟫, ka⌈ichuu-do⌉kei 懐中時計 [a timepiece kept in one's bosom or pocket] ⟪a pocket watch⟫, u⌈de-do⌉kei 腕時計 [a timepiece worn on the wrist]

PHRASE: watch over ⟨*-o*⟩ *kango-suru* ⟨～を⟩看護する ③ •c ⟪nurse, attend on⟫

EX. The nurse who watched over my father was very kind.
父を看護してくれた看護婦はとても親切だった。
Chichi o kango-shite kureta kango-fu wa totemo shinsetsu datta.

PHRASE: watch for ⟨⟨*-no*⟩⟩ *kikai o ukagau* ⟨⟨～の⟩⟩機会をうかがう ①

EX. I'm always watching for good opportunities to buy stocks.
株を買う機会をいつもうかがっている。
Kabu o kau kikai o itsu-mo ukagatte iru.

watchman n. **[a person whose job it is to guard s.t., esp. some property]**
ya⌈kei 夜警 •c [the act of keeping a lookout at night for fires, crime, etc., or a person who does this] ⟪nightwatch, night watchman⟫

EX. I'm working part-time as a watchman at a factory.
僕は工場の夜警のアルバイトをしています。
Boku wa koojoo no yakei no arubaito o shite imasu.

water n. **[the colorless liquid which falls as rain, covers the majority of the surface of the earth, and is necessary to support life]**
mi⌈zu 水 [the unheated form of the colorless liquid that falls as rain, covers the majority of the surface of the earth, and is necessary to support life]

EX. (**a**) I'd like some water to drink.
水が飲みたい。
Mizu ga nomi-tai.
(**b**) We have water, but it isn't heated.
水はありますが、お湯ではありません。
Mizu wa arimasu ga, o-yu dewaarimasen.

PHRASE: water supply *suidoo* 水道 •c, hot water *(o-)yu* (お)湯, boil water *(o-)yu o wakasu* (お)湯をわかす ①

— vt. **[to sprinkle over s.t./s.a., supply s.t./s.o./s.a. with, or dilute s.t. with the colorless liquid that falls as rain and is necessary to life]**
⟨-ni⟩ mi⌈zu o ma⌉ku ⟨～に⟩水をまく ① [for s.o. to sprinkle over s.t./s.o./s.a. the

W

colorless liquid that falls as rain and is necessary to life], ⟨-ni⟩ mi⌈zu o yaru ⟨〜に⟩ 水をやる ① [for s.o. to supply s.o./s.a./a plant with the colorless liquid that falls as rain and is necessary to life]

EX. (**a**) Did you water the flowers yet?
花にもう水を{やりました/*まきました}か。
*Hana ni moo mizu o {yarimashita/ *makimashita} ka.*
(**b**) In Japan people water the streets in front of their houses.
日本では(人々は)家の前の道に水を{まきます/*やります}。
*Nihon de wa (hito-bito wa) ie no mae no michi ni mizu o {makimasu/ *yarimasu}.*

waterfall n. [a stream that falls from a high place] ta⌈ki 滝 《rapids, cascade, cataract》

taki

EX. The power and beauty of the Niagara Falls has made them one of North America's most popular tourist sites.
ナイアガラの滝はその力強さ、また美しさのため北アメリカで最も人気のある観光地の一つとなっている。
Naiagara no taki wa sono chikara-zuyo-sa, mata utsukushi-sa no tame Kita-Amerika de mottomo ninki no aru kankoo-chi no hitotsu to natte iru.

watermelon n.
su⌈ika すいか •c

EX. Certain varieties of Japanese watermelon are yellow inside.
日本のすいかには中が黄色のがある。
Nihon no suika ni wa naka ga ki-iro no ga aru.

W

watery adj. [full of, containing too much of, or resembling moisture or liquid, esp. the colorless liquid which falls as rain 《fig. "insipid"》]

1. mi⌈zu o fuku⌉nda N 水を含んだN /⟨*mizu* water + prt. *o* + Vinf. past of *fukumu* ① contain/ [containing the colorless liquid which falls as rain], mi⌈zu o fuku⌉nde iru (N) 水を含んでいる(N) /⟨*mizu* water + prt. *o* + V*te iru* of *fukumu* ① contain/ ② [containing the colorless liquid which falls as rain]

EX. The lawn is still watery from last night's rain.
ゆうべの雨で芝生はまだ水を含んでいる。
Yuube no ame de shibafu wa mada mizu o fukunde iru.

2. a⌈wa⌉i 淡い adj(*i*). [light and weak in color, taste, or intensity 《fig. "transitory"》] 《faint, pale, passing》, a⌈ojiro⌉i 青白い adj(*i*). [bluish-white, esp. in complexion] 《pale, pallid, waxy》

EX. The walls in the house were painted with a watery color.
その家の壁は{青白い/淡い}色で塗装されていた。
Sono ie no kabe wa {aojiroi/awai} iro de tosoo-sarete ita.

3. mi⌈zuppo⌉i 水っぽい adj(*i*). [resembling the taste of the colorless liquid that falls as rain] 《sloppy, washy》, a⌈ji ga na⌉i 味がない adj(*i*). [having no flavor]

EX. This beer is too watery tasting for me.
このビールは僕には{水っぽい/味がない}ねえ。
Kono biiru wa boku ni wa {mizuppoi/ aji ga nai} nee.

4. na⌉mida ga deru (N) 涙が出る(N) [for tears to come out]

EX. My eyes get watery because of the pollen in the air.
空気中の花粉のせいで(目から)涙が出るんです。
Kuuki-chuu no kafun no sei de (me kara) namida ga deru n desu.

wave n. [a long ridge of water moving over the surface of a body of water, esp. the sea; a curve or series of curves, esp. of hair; a motion or occurrence which involves an alternating rise and fall in height or intensity, either physical or emotional]

1. na⌈mi⌉ 波 [a rising and falling movement

on the surface of a body of water due to wind or other natural forces; a physical or emotional occurrence or geographical land form which involves an alternating rise and fall in height or intensity]

EX. (**a**) The waves are high today, aren't they?
今日は波が高いですねえ。
Kyoo wa nami ga takai desu nee.
(**b**) Our country is currently riding a wave of economic prosperity.
我が国は現在経済繁栄の波に乗っている。
Waga-kuni wa genzai keizai han'ei no nami ni notte iru.

2. u⌈e⌉ebu ウエーブ •f [a curve or series of curves of hair]

EX. Jane always sets her hair so that she gets beautiful waves.
ジェーンはいつも美しいウエーブが出るように髪をセットする。
Jeen wa itsu-mo utsukushii ueebe ga deru yooni kami o setto-suru.

3. fu⌈ru koto 振ること [the act of shaking s.t. while holding it on its end]

EX. Karen left the room with a slight wave of her right hand.
カレンは右手をちょっと振って、部屋を出て行った。
Karen wa migi-te o chotto futte, heya o dete itta.

—— vi. **[for s.t. to move in an alternately rising and falling fashion 《fig. "for s.o. to signal s.t. to s.o. by moving one's hand in an alternately rising and falling or back and forth motion"》]**

1. yu⌈reru 揺れる ② [to shift back and forth or up and down in position or to be unsettled emotionally] 《sway, quake, pitch, roll, toss, vibrate, jolt》

EX. The tall prairie grass waved in the wind.
草原の背の高い牧草が風に揺れていた。
Soogen no se no takai bokusoo ga kaze ni yurete ita.

2. te⌉ o fu⌈tte a⌉izu-suru 手を振って合図する ③ [for s.o. to give a signal to s.o. by moving one's hand in an alternately rising and falling or back and forth motion]

EX. I waved to my friend when I saw him from my car.
車から友だちを見かけた時、私は手を振って合図した。
Kuruma kara tomodachi o mi-kaketa toki, watashi wa te o futte aizu-shita.

—— vt. **[to cause s.t. to move in an alternately rising and falling fashion]**

⟨-o⟩ fu⌈ru ⟨〜を⟩振る ① [for s.o./s.a. to hold a part of s.t. and cause it to move/tremble quickly to and fro or up and down 《fig. "sprinkle"》] 《shake》

EX. I'll never forget the image of her waving a handkerchief to me as my boat pulled away from the pier.
私の乗っている船が波止場を離れる時の彼女がハンカチを振っている姿はいつまでたっても忘れられない。
Watashi no notte iru fune ga hato-ba o hanareru toki no kanojo ga hankachi o futte iru sugata wa itsu-made tatte mo wasure-rarenai.

wax n. **[a fat-like substance secreted by bees or a polishing agent made of this substance]**

ro⌉o ろう, wa⌉kkusu ワックス •f [a polishing agent]

EX. (**a**) This wax figure of President Kennedy looks exactly like him.
このケネディ大統領の{ろう/*ワックス}人形は本物そっくりですね。
*Kono Kenedii Daitooryoo no {roo/ *wakkusu}-ningyoo wa hon-mono sokkuri desu ne.*
(**b**) The floor has just been polished with wax so be careful.
床は{ワックス/??ろう}で磨いたばかりですから、気を付けてください。
Yuka wa {wakkusu/??roo} de migaita bakari desu kara, ki-o-tsukete kudasai.

—— vt. **[for s.o. to use the fat-like substance secreted by bees to polish s.t.]**

⟨-ni⟩ wa⌉kkusu o ka⌈ke⌉ru ⟨〜に⟩ワックスをかける ② [for s.o. to apply the fat-like substance secreted by bees to s.t.]

EX. Storekeepers often wax fruit so it looks fresh.
店の人は新鮮に見えるように、よく果物にワックスをかける。
Mise no hito wa shinsen ni mieru yooni, yoku kuda-mono ni wakkusu o kakeru.

way n. **[a route to get to a destination or the distance covered on such a route 《fig. "a manner or method by which one does s.t."》]**

1. mi⌈chi 道 [a strip of paved or cleared ground for getting from one place to another or the distance covered in a journey 《fig. "method," "the proper way of thinking or conducting oneself," "special field"》] 《road, journey, means》

EX. This is the way to the station.
これが駅へ行く道です。
Kore ga eki e iku michi desu.

2. ⟨-no⟩ shi⌈kata ⟨〜の⟩仕方 /⟨V*masu* of *suru* ③ do + *kata* style/ [a method or manner of doing s.t.] 《method, means》, ya⌈rikata やり方 /⟨V*masu* of *yaru* ① do + *kata* style/ [a method or manner of doing s.t.] 《method, means》, ho⌈ohoo 方法 •c [the means to achieve a goal] 《method》, V*masu* ka⌈ta V*masu*方 [a method or manner of doing what is indicated by the verb in V*masu*]

EX. (**a**) The way he drives is dangerous.
彼の運転の{仕方/やり方/方法}は危ない。
Kare no unten no {shikata/yarikata/hoohoo} wa abunai.
(**b**) There's more than one way to learn a language.
ことばの勉強には色々な{仕方/やり方/方法}がある。
Kotoba no benkyoo ni wa iro-irona {shikata/yarikata/hoohoo} ga aru.
(**c**) A: He always takes the lead, but never likes to follow others.
彼はいつも人の先頭に立つのが好きで、人に従うのが嫌いだね。
Kare wa itsu-mo hito no sentoo ni tatsu no ga sukide, hito ni shitagau no ga kirai da ne.
B: Yes, that's just his way.
そうだけど、あれが彼の{やり方/??仕方/*方法}なんだよ。
*Sooda kedo, are ge kare no {yarikata/??shikata/*hoohoo} na n da yo.*
(**d**) I like the way she laughs.
僕はあの人の笑い方が好きだ。
Boku wa ano hito no warai-kata ga suki da.

PHRASE: all the way *haru-baru* はるばる, *waza-waza* わざわざ 《on purpose, expressly, take the trouble to》

EX. He came all the way to Kyushu to meet me.
彼は{わざわざ/はるばる}九州まで私に会いに来てくれた。
Kare wa {waza-waza/haru-baru} Kyuushuu made watashi ni ai ni kite kureta.

PHRASE: by the way *tokoro de* ところで 《incidentally》

EX. It's cold today. I hope spring will come soon. By the way, how's your business doing?
今日は寒いですね。早く春が来るといいんですがね。ところで、お仕事の方、いかがですか。
Kyoo wa samui desu ne. Hayaku haru ga kuru to ii n desu ga ne. Tokoro de, o-shigoto no hoo, ikaga desu ka.

PHRASE: by way of ⟨*-o*⟩ *tootte* ⟨〜を⟩通って 《via》, *-keiyu de* 〜経由で •c

EX. I went to Europe by way of the United States.
私はアメリカ{を通って/経由で}ヨーロッパに行きました。
Watashi wa Amerika {o tootte/-keiyu de} Yooroppa ni ikimashita.

PHRASE: by way of *to-shite* 〜として 《as》

EX. Let me say this by way of conclusion.
結論として次の点を言わせてください。
Ketsuron to-shite tsugi no ten o iwa-sete kudasai.

PHRASE: in one's way *jama {ni natte iru/da}* 邪魔{になっている/だ}

EX. Am I in your way?

W

邪魔{です/になっています}か。
Jama {desu/ni natte imasu} ka.

PHRASE: in a way *aru ten de wa* ある点では

EX. A: Are you unhappy at your company?
会社が面白くないんですか。
Kaisha ga omoshirokunai n desu ka.
B: In a way. The work tends to be a bit monotonous.
ある点ではね。仕事がちょっと単調になりがちでね。
Aru ten de wa ne. Shigoto ga chotto tanchoo ni nari-gachi de ne.

PHRASE: in no way *kesshite*...neg. 決して…neg. ⟪never⟫

EX. Things may be a bit slow, but we're in no way in danger of going out of business.
少し景気は悪いにしても、決して倒産する恐れはない。
Sukoshi keiki wa warui ni-shite-mo, kesshite toosan-suru osore wa nai.

PHRASE: on the way {Vinf. nonpast/N *no*} *tochuu de* {Vinf. nonpast/Nの}途中で ⟪along the route⟫

EX. I suddenly got a cramp in my foot on the way to the beach.
海岸に行く途中で突然足がつってしまった。
Kaigan ni iku tochuu de totsuzen ashi ga tsutte shimatta.

PHRASE: that way *sochira {e/ni}* そちら{へ/に}, *sotchi {e/ni}* そっち{へ/に}, *achira {e/ni}* あちら{へ/に}, *atchi {e/ni}* あっち{へ/に}, *sonna fuu (ni)* そんな風(に)

EX. (**a**) A: Where did John go?
ジョンはどこへ行きましたか。
Jon wa doko e ikimashita ka.
B: That way.
{あちら/あっち/そちら/そっち/*そんな風}{へ/に}行きましたよ。
*{Achira/Atchi/Sochira/Sotchi/*Sonna fuu} {e/ni} ikimashita yo.*
(**b**) Don't speak that way to your superiors.
目上の人に{そんな風/*あちら/*あっち/*そちら/*そっち}に話してはいけません。
*Me-ue no hito ni {sonna fuu/*achira/*atchi/*sochira/*sotchi} ni hanashite wa ikemasen.*

PHRASE: this way *kochira ({e/ni})* こちら({へ/に}), *kotchi ({e/ni})* こっち({へ/に}), *konna fuu (ni)* こんな風(に)

EX. (**a**) Please come this way.
どうぞ{こちら/こっち/*こんな風}{へ/に}。
*Doozo {kochira/kotchi/*konna fuu} {e/ni}.*
(**b**) This is the first time for me to study Japanese this way.
{こんな風に/*こちら{へ/に}/*こっち{へ/に}}日本語を勉強するのは初めてです。
*{Konna fuu ni/*Kochira {e/ni}/*Kotchi {e/ni}} Nihon-go o benkyoo-suru no wa hajimete desu.*

PHRASE: which way *dochira ({e/ni})* どちら({へ/に}), *dotchi ({e/ni})* どっち({へ/に})

EX. (**a**) Which way is it to Tokyo Station?
東京駅は{どちら/どっち}ですか。
Tookyoo-eki wa {dochira/dotchi} desu ka.
(**b**) Which way are you going?
{どちら/?どっち}{へ/に}いらっしゃいますか。
{Dochira/?Dotchi} {e/ni} irasshaimasu ka.

we pron. **[a pronoun normally used to refer to the first person plural (but used in certain cases such as by a king or editor to refer to the first person singular) or to the second person singular ø to show the speaker's strong sense of identification with the listener]**
wa⌈ta(ku)shi⌉-tachi 私たち ⟨fml⟩, bo⌉ku-tachi 僕たち, bo⌉ku-ra 僕ら ⟨s⟩ [the first person plural pronoun used by male speakers ⟨s⟩], a⌈tashi⌉-tachi あたしたち [the first person plural pronoun used by female speakers ⟨s⟩]

NOTE: "We" is often not expressed at all when it can be understood in a given context.

EX. (**a**) A: Where did you get married?
どこで結婚しましたか。
Doko de kekkon-shimashita ka.
B: We got married in Greece.
{私たちは/あたしたちは/僕たちは/僕らは/ø}ギリシアで結婚しました。

{Wata(ku)shi-tachi wa/Atashi-tachi wa/Boku-tachi wa/Boku-ra wa/ø} Girisha de kekkon-shimashita.
(**b**) Professor, do we have to do this homework by tomorrow?
先生、{私たちは/あたしたちは/僕たちは/ø/*僕らは}この宿題をあしたまでにしなければなりませんか。
*Sensei, {wata(ku)shi-tachi wa/atashi-tachi wa/boku-tachi wa/ø/*boku-ra wa} kono shukudai o ashita made ni shinakereba narimasen ka.*
(**c**) A: How are we feeling today?
{ø/*私たちは/*あたしたちは/*僕たちは/*僕らは}今日は気分いかがですか?
*{ø/*Wata(ku)shi-tachi wa/*Atashi-tachi wa/*Boku-tachi wa/*Boku-ra wa} kyoo wa kibun ikaga desu ka.*
B: Much better, thank you.
おかげさまで、とてもよくなりました。
O-kage-sama de, totemo yoku narimashita.

NOTE: Speaker A above is typically a nurse or a doctor addressing her/his patient in a sympathetic way.

weak adj. **[lacking physical, mental, or emotional strength, power, or ability; lacking intensity, esp. in taste due to a high proportion of water content]**

1. yo⌈wa⌉i 弱い adj(*i*). **[lacking physical, mental, or emotional strength, power, or ability]** **⟪weak, feeble, frail, infirm, light⟫** ↔ **tsuyoi** 強い adj(*i*).

EX. (**a**) My right leg has been weak ever since the accident.
あの事故以来、右の足が弱くなった。
Ano jiko irai, migi no ashi ga yowaku natta.
(**b**) My doctor has told me not to do excessive exercise because I have a weak heart.
心臓が弱いから過度の運動は慎むように医者に言われている。
Shinzoo ga yowai kara kado no undoo wa tsutsushimu yooni isha ni iwa-rete iru.
(**c**) I'm very weak in math.
僕は数学に弱い。
Boku wa suugaku ni yowai.
(**d**) My will is too weak for me to quit smoking.
意志が弱いからたばこがやめられない。
Ishi ga yowai kara tabako ga yame-rarenai.
(**e**) The Japanese economy has been very weak in recent years.
日本の経済はここ数年とても弱かった。
Nihon no keizai wa koko suu-nen totemo yowakatta.
(**f**) This portion of your paper is weak.
あなたの論文のこの部分は弱い。
Anata no ronbun no kono bubun wa yowai.

2. u⌈sui 薄い adj(*i*). **[having little depth or intensity, esp. in color or taste ⟪fig. "for color/taste to be weak"⟫] ⟪thin, watery, pale, scanty⟫** ↔ **atsui** 厚い adj(*i*).; **mi⌈zuppo⌉i** 水っぽい adj(*i*). **[resembling the taste of the colorless liquid that falls as rain] ⟪sloppy, watery, washy⟫**

EX. (**a**) This coffee is awfully weak.
このコーヒーはひどく{薄い/水っぽい}。
Kono koohii wa hidoku {usui/mizuppoi}.
(**b**) This beer is weak, isn't it?
このビールは{水っぽい/*薄い}ね。
*Kono biiru wa {mizuppoi/*usui} ne.*

wealth n. **[an abundant supply of material things, esp. money]**

1. to⌉mi 富 **[an abundant supply of property/money/resources ⟨w⟩], shi⌈san** 資産 **•c [property owned by an individual or a corporation] ⟪property, fortune, assets, means⟫**

EX. My uncle accumulated his wealth by buying and selling land.
叔父は土地の売買で{富/資産}を蓄えた。
Oji wa tochi no baibai de {tomi/shisan} o takuwaeta.

2. ho⌈ofuna 豊富な adj(*na*). **•c [rich or plentiful in material supply, variety, or experience] ⟪abundant, plentiful, rich,**

W

copious)), yu˥takana 豊かな adj(*na*). **[existing in more than sufficient quantities with some to spare]** ⟪**plentiful, rich, affluent, bountiful**⟫

EX. The diplomat had a wealth of international experience.
その外交官は国際的経験が{豊富/豊か}だった。
Sono gaikoo-kan wa kokusai-teki keiken ga {hoofu/yutaka} datta.

wealthy adj. **[possessing riches]**
yu˥takana 豊かな adj(*na*). SEE wealth 2, **yu˥ufukuna** 裕福な adj(*na*). •c **[having financial resources sufficient to lead a comfortable life]** ⟪**rich, affluent**⟫, **fu˹yuuna** 富裕な adj(*na*). •c **[having an abundance of possessions]** ⟪**rich, opulent**⟫

EX. (**a**) That student is from a wealthy family.
あの学生は{裕福な/富裕な/*豊かな}家の出です。
*Ano gakusei wa {yuufukuna/fuyuuna/*yutakana} ie no de desu.*
(**b**) The Japanese are generally regarded by the rest of the world as wealthy people.
日本人は概して世界の人々から{裕福な/富裕な/豊かな}国民だと思われている。
Nihon-jin wa gaishite sekai no hito-bito kara {yuufukuna/fuyuuna/yutakana} kokumin da to omowa-rete iru.

weapon n. **[an instrument used in fighting to inflict bodily harm on one's opponent]**
bu˥ki 武器 •c **[an instrument used in combat to kill or cause injury to one's opponent]** ⟪**arms**⟫, **he˥iki** 兵器 •c **[a collective noun for instruments used in combat]** ⟪**arms, weaponry**⟫

EX. (**a**) Nuclear weapons should be eliminated.
核{兵器/*武器}は廃止すべきだ。
*Kaku-{heiki/*buki} wa haishi-su-beki da.*
(**b**) It is considered a right in America to own a defensive weapons.
アメリカでは護身用の{武器/*兵器}を持つことが個人の権利と考えられている。
*Amerika de wa goshin-yoo no {buki/*heiki} o motsu koto ga kojin no kenri to kangae-rarete iru.*

wear vt. **[for s.o. to have s.t. on one's body for cover warmth, protection, or decoration ⟪fig. "cause damage to or reduce s.t. by friction or extended use"⟫]**

1. ⟨-o⟩ **ki˹ru** ⟨～を⟩着る ② **[for s.o. to dress oneself with an item of clothing that covers the torso]** ⟪**put on, slip on, have on**⟫, ⟨-o⟩ **ka˹bu˥ru** ⟨～を⟩かぶる ① **[for s.o. to cover one's head or face with s.t. such as a hat or mask or to become covered by s.t. such as water, dust, etc.]** ⟪**put on, cover, pour over oneself**⟫, ⟨-o⟩ **ha˹ku** ⟨～を⟩はく ① **[for s.o. to dress oneself with an item of clothing that covers all or part of the body below the waist]** ⟪**put on, have on**⟫, ⟨-o⟩ **tsu˹ke˥ru** ⟨～を⟩つける ② **[for s.o. to cause s.t./s.o. to adhere to s.t./s.o./s.a. else]** ⟪**join, apply s.t. to s.t. else, put ashore, light, follow, add**⟫, ⟨-o⟩ **ha˹meru** ⟨～を⟩はめる ② **[for s.o. to insert s.t. into s.t. else so that it fits tightly]** ⟪**put on, insert**⟫, ⟨-o⟩ **ka˥ke˥ru** ⟨～を⟩かける ② **[for s.o. to cause s.t. to extend to and come in contact with s.t. else ⟪fig. "cover," "hang," "call s.o. by phone," "bet," "spend," "sprinkle," "splash," "sit down," "build (a bridge)"⟫]** ⟪**hang, suspend, lay (a wire), seat, sprinkle, put on (glasses)**⟫, ⟨-o⟩ **su˥ru** ⟨～を⟩する ③ **[for s.o./s.a. to conduct an action willfully; for s.o./s.a./s.t. to cause s.t. to take on a different state; for s.t. to happen in such a way as to be perceptible to s.o./s.a.; for s.t. to be in a certain state or possess a certain attribute; for an amount of time/money to pass/be required; for some proposition to be posited as true ⟪fig. "put on a somewhat small, ornamental object"⟫]** ⟪**put on**⟫

NOTE: The antonym for *kiru, kaburu* and *haku* is *nugu* "take off (an item of clothing)" and the antonym for *tsukeru* and *kakeru* is *hazusu* "remove" or *toru* "take (off)."

㊥ "cause s.t. physical to hang"▷掛ける, "build (a bridge across a river)"▷架ける, "bet"▷かける

W

㊈ "wear footwear"▷履く, otherwise ▷はく

EX. (**a**) Most American college students wear jeans on campus.
大抵のアメリカの大学生は大学ではジーンズを{はいて/*着て/*かぶって/*つけて/*はめて/*かけて/*して}いる。
*Taitei no Amerika no daigaku-sei wa daigaku de wa jiinzu o {haite/*kite/*kabutte/*tsukete/*hamete/*kakete/*shite} iru.*
(**b**) I couldn't recognize Alice because she was wearing a skirt.
僕はアリスがスカートを{はいて/*着て/*かぶって/*つけて/*はめて/*かけて/*して}いたからだれだか分からなかった。
*Boku wa Arisu ga sukaato o {haite/*kite/*kabutte/*tsukete/*hamete/*kakete/*shite} ita kara dare da ka wakaranakatta.*
(**c**) Who's that girl wearing sandals?
サンダルを{履いて/*着て/*かぶって/*つけて/*はめて/*かけて/*して}いる女の子はだれですか。
*Sandaru o {haite/*kite/*kabutte/*tsukete/*hamete/*kakete/*shite} iru onna-no-ko wa dare desu ka.*
(**d**) The earrings you're wearing are beautiful.
きれいなイヤリングを{つけて/して/*はいて/*着て/*かぶって/*はめて/*かけて}いるね。
*Kireina iyaringu o {tsukete/shite/*haite/*kite/*kabutte/*hamete/*kakete} iru ne.*
(**e**) It's cold outside! You'd better wear gloves.
外は寒いよ。手袋を{はめた/した/*はいた/*着た/*かぶった/*つけた/*かけた}方がいいよ。
*Soto wa samui yo. Te-bukuro o {hameta/shita/*haita/*kita/*kabutta/*tsuketa/*kaketa} hoo ga ii yo.*
(**f**) That's a nice tie you're wearing!
すてきなネクタイを{して/*はいて/*着て/*かぶって/*つけて/*はめて/*かけて}いるのね。
*Sutekina nekutai o {shite/*haite/*kite/*kabutte/*tsukete/*hamete/*kakete} iru no ne.*
(**g**) I've never seen Jenny wearing lipstick before.
ジェニーが口紅を{つけて/?して/*はいて/*着て/*かぶって/*はめて/*かけて}いるのを見るのははじめてだ。
*Jenii ga kuchi-beni o {tsukete/?shite/*haite/*kite/*kabutte/*hamete/*kakete} iru no o miru no wa hajimete da.*
(**h**) Bob went to school wearing his new hat.
ボブは新しい帽子を{かぶって/*はいて/*着て/*つけて/*はめて/*かけて/*して}学校へ行った。
*Bobu wa atarashii booshi o {kabutte/*haite/*kite/*tsukete/*hamete/*kakete/*shite} gakkoo e itta.*

2. ⟨-o⟩ **ha⌈ya⌉su** ⟨〜を⟩生やす ① **[to cause s.t. to grow hair or roots]** ⦅**grow, cultivate**⦆

EX. My father wore a beard in his younger days.
父は若い時ひげを生やしていた。
Chichi wa wakai toki hige o hayashite ita.

PHRASE: wear …expression …{*kao/hyoojoo*} *o shite iru* 〜{顔/表情}をしている ②

EX. Henry wore a puzzled expression.
ヘンリーは困惑した{顔/表情}をしていた。
Henrii wa konwaku-shita {kao/hyoojoo} o shite ita.

PHRASE: wear down ⟨*-de*⟩ *suri-heru* ⟨〜で⟩すり減る ①

EX. The feet of countless pilgrims over the centuries has worn down the steps in front of the old cathedral.
大聖堂の前の階段は何百年にもわたって訪れた無数の巡礼者の足ですり減っていた。
Dai-seidoo no mae no kaidan wa nan-byaku-nen ni mo watatte otozureta musuu no junrei-sha no ashi de suri-hette ita.

PHRASE: wear out ⟨*-de*⟩ *tsukare-kiru* ⟨〜で⟩疲れ切る ①, ⟨*-de*⟩ *hiroo-konpai-suru* ⟨〜で⟩疲労困ぱいする ③ •c

EX. The hard training wore me out.

W

ハードトレーニングで私は{疲れ切った/疲労困ぱいした}。
Haado toreeningu de watashi wa {tsukare-kitta/hiroo-konpai-shita}.

— vi. **[for s.t. to keep in close contact with s.t./s.o. else over time (until it becomes damaged)]**
su⌈ri-heru すり減る ② [for s.t. to become diminished through prolonged contact with s.t. else, esp. through rubbing] ((wear out)), su⌈ri-kire⌉ru すり切れる ② [for a fabric to become threadbare through prolonged contact with s.t. else, esp. through rubbing] ((become seedy))

EX. (**a**) My jeans have begun to wear at the knees.
僕のジーンズのひざの辺りがすり{切れ/*減り}はじめた。
*Boku no jiinzu no hiza no atari ga suri-{kire/*heri}-hajimeta.*
(**b**) The tires on our car have worn down and need to be replaced.
うちの車のタイヤがすり{減った/*切れた}から取り換えなければならない。
*Uchi no kuruma no taiya ga suri-{hetta/*kireta} kara tori-kaenakereba naranai.*

PHRASE: wear well *naga-mochi-suru* 長持ちする ③

EX. American jeans usually wear well.
アメリカのジーンズは大抵長持ちする。
Amerika no jiinzu wa taitei naga-mochi-suru.

— n. **[the state/act of having s.t. on one's body as clothing or of being used as clothing; damage caused by normal use or age; clothing]**
1. cha⌈kuyoo 着用 •c [the act of putting on clothes]

EX. This tweed jacket is still like new despite years of wear.
このツイードの上着は長年の着用にもかかわらず、まだ新品同様だ。
Kono tsuiido no uwagi wa naga-nen no chakuyoo nimo-kakawarazu, mada shinpin dooyoo da.

2. ma⌈metsu 摩滅 •c [the process of a metal becoming stressed or damaged through prolonged contact with s.t. else, esp. through rubbing] ((abrasion))

EX. Use of a lubricant is essential for preventing wear on the gears.
ギアの摩滅を防ぐにはオイルの使用は不可欠だ。
Gia no mametsu o fusegu ni wa oiru no shiyoo wa fukaketsu da.

3. fu⌈ku⌉ 服 •c [a generic term for apparel, esp. that visible to the outside as opposed to underwear] ((dress, costume, clothes))

EX. A: What should I wear to the party?
パーティーには何を着て行けばいいかしら。
Paatii ni wa nani o kite ikeba ii kashira.
B: Casual wear would be fine.
普通の服でいいよ。
Futsuu no fuku de ii yo.

weary adj. **[very tired or causing tiredness or boredom]**
1. tsu⌈kare-ha⌉teta N 疲れ果てたN / ⟨Vinf. past of *tsukare-hateru* ② become completely tired/ [completely tired], tsu⌈kare-ha⌉tete iru (N) 疲れ果てている(N) / ⟨V *te iru* of *tsukare-hateru* ② become completely tired/ [to be in a state of complete fatigue]

EX. I was weary from climbing when I reached the summit.
頂上に着いた時は登るのに疲れ果てていた。
Choojoo ni tsuita toki wa noboru no ni tsukare-hatete ita.

2. ⟨-ni⟩ a⌉kita N ⟨〜に⟩飽きたN / ⟨Vinf. past of *akiru* ② get bored/ [for s.o./s.a. to be in the state of being bored with s.t./s.o./s.a.], ⟨-ni⟩ a⌉kite iru (N) ⟨〜に⟩飽きている(N) / ⟨V *te iru* of *akiru* ② get bored/ [for s.o./s.a. to be in the state of being bored with s.t./s.o./s.a.]

EX. My son seems to have gotten weary of computer games.
息子はコンピューターゲームにもう{飽きている/飽きた}らしい。
Musuko wa konpyuutaa-geemu ni moo

| {akite iru/akita} rashii.

weather n. **[the condition of the atmosphere at a particular time and place] te⌉nki 天気 •c [the condition of the atmosphere at a particular place and time or good atmospheric conditions], te⌈nkoo 天候 •c [atmospheric conditions at a particular place over an extended period of time]**

EX. (**a**) The weather is nice, so how about going on a hike today?
{天気/*天候}がいいから今日はハイキングに行きましょうか。
*{Tenki/*Tenkoo} ga ii kara kyoo wa haikingu ni ikimashoo ka.*
(**b**) The weather during the month of June is usually not very good.
六月の{天候/天気}は大抵余りよくありません。
Roku-gatsu no {tenkoo/tenki} wa taitei amari yoku arimasen.
(**c**) According to the weather forecast it's going to be a hot summer.
{天気/*天候}予報によると、暑い夏になるそうだ。
*{Tenki/*Tenkoo}-yohoo ni yoru to, atsui natsu ni naru sooda.*

weave vt. **[for s.o. to make s.t. such as a fabric by passing threads or strips of material over and under each other 《fig. "to move in a zigzag fashion through an area containing obstacles," "combine separate elements into an integrated whole, such as a story"》]**

1. ⟨-o⟩ o⌈ru ⟨～を⟩織る ① [for s.o. to make cloth by interlacing strands of material], ⟨-o⟩ a⌉mu ⟨～を⟩編む ① [for s.o. to make s.t. by joining threads of fabric, hair, bamboo, etc., into a network 《fig. "edit"》] ((knit, braid, entwine, crochet))

EX. (**a**) Have you ever seen cloth being woven?
布を{織って/*編んで}いるところを見たことがありますか。
*Nuno o {otte/*ande} iru tokoro o mita koto ga arimasu ka.*
(**b**) I remember my grandmother weaving a basket out of bamboo.
祖母が竹でかごを{編んで/*織って}いたのを覚えている。
*Sobo ga take de kago o {ande/*otte} ita no o oboete iru.*

2. ⟨-o⟩ ku⌈mi-tateru ⟨～を⟩組み立てる ② [for s.o. to build s.t. by assembling separate objects into a single whole] ((construct, fabricate, assemble))

EX. Ted is very good at weaving imaginative stories.
テッドは想像力のある話を組み立てるのがとても上手だ。
Teddo wa soozoo-ryoku no aru hanashi o kumi-tateru no ga totemo joozu da.

3. ⟨-o⟩ ⟨-ni⟩ o⌈ri-komu ⟨～を⟩⟨～に⟩織り込む ① [for s.o. to integrate a new or different element into a larger whole, such as the design in a fabric or plot of a story]

EX. A good speech usually has one or two anecdotes woven into it.
上手な話は大抵その中に一つ二つエピソードを織り込んでいる。
Joozuna hanashi wa taitei sono naka ni hitotsu futatsu episoodo o ori-konde iru.

4. ji⌈guzagu ni ⟨-o⟩ su⌈suma-seru ジグザグに⟨～を⟩進ませる /⟨causative of *susumu* ① proceed/ ② [for s.o. to cause s.t. such as a vehicle to proceed in a zigzag motion]

web n. **[s.t. that is woven 《fig. "cobweb," "network," "intricate structure"》]**

1. ku⌉mo-no-su くもの巣 [a pattern of fine threads woven by a spider or an intricate network suggestive of s.t. woven]

EX. The spider spun a beautiful web in the tree.
くもがきれいなくもの巣を木に張った。
Kumo ga kireina kumo-no-su o ki ni hatta.

2. re⌈nraku⌉-moo 連絡網 •c [a network of communication among different members of a group] ((network)), ne⌈tto-wa⌉aku ネットワーク •f [an organization of several broadcasting stations]

EX. The police have exposed an underground web of criminal organizations.

W

警察は地下犯罪組織の{連絡網/ネットワーク}を暴き出した。
Keisatsu wa chika-hanzai-soshiki no {renraku-moo/netto-waaku} o abaki-dashita.

wedding n. **[a marriage ceremony]**
ke⌈kko⌉n-shiki 結婚式 •c, **ko⌈nrei** 婚礼 •c ⟨fml⟩

EX. (**a**) Our wedding is planned for next June.
私たちの{結婚式/?婚礼}は来年の六月の予定です。
Watashi-tachi no {kekkon-shiki/?konrei} wa rainen no roku-gatsu no yotei desu.
(**b**) The prince's wedding took place at the palace.
王子様の{結婚式/婚礼}は宮殿で行われた。
Ooji-sama no {kekkon-shiki/konrei} wa kyuuden de okonawa-reta.

wedge n. **[a V-shaped piece of wood or iron used to split or force things apart 《fig. "s.t. shaped like a V"》]**
ku⌈sabi くさび

EX. We used a wedge to split the wood.
薪を割るのにくさびを使った。
Maki o waru no ni kusabi o tsukatta.

Wednesday n.
su⌉iyo⌉o(-bi) 水曜(日) •c

EX. On Wednesday evenings I usually eat out with my wife.
水曜(日)の晩は大抵妻と外食します。
Suiyoo(-bi) no ban wa taitei tsuma to gaishoku-shimasu.

weed n. **[a wild plant which is useless or harmful]**
za⌈ssoo 雑草 •c **[a wild plant of no agricultural or horticultural value]**, **ku⌈sa⌉** 草 **[a common low-growing plant with blade-shaped green leaves]**

EX. We have a lot of weeds growing in our back yard.
裏庭には{雑草/草}がたくさん生えている。
Ura niwa ni wa {zassoo/kusa} ga takusan haete iru.

— vt. **[for s.o. to remove wild plants which are useless or harmful, esp. by uprooting]**
⟨-no⟩ {za⌈ssoo/ku⌈sa⌉} o to⌉ru ⟨〜の⟩{雑草/草}を取る ①

EX. You'd better weed your lawn.
芝生の{雑草/草}を取ったほうがいいですよ。
Shiba-fu no {zassoo/kusa} o totta hoo ga ii desu yo.

week n. **[a calendar unit of seven days, esp. from Sunday through Saturday]**
shu⌉u 週 •c, **shu⌈ukan** 週間 •c **[a duration of time consisting of seven successive days]**

EX. (**a**) A: How long is the summer session at this university?
この大学の夏学期はどのぐらいですか。
Kono daigaku no natsu-gakki wa dono-gurai desu ka.
B: It runs for nine weeks.
九週(間)続きます。
Kyuu-shuu(kan) tsuzukimasu.
(**b**) A: What day is considered the first day of the week in Japan?
日本では、{週/*週間}の初めの日は何曜日だとされていますか。
*Nihon de wa, {shuu/*shuukan} no hajime no hi wa nan-yoobi da to sarete imasu ka.*
B: Monday is.
月曜日です。
Getsuyoo-bi desu.

PHRASE: day of the week *yoo(-bi)* 曜(日) •c

EX. What day of the week is it today?
今日は何曜(日)ですか。
Kyoo wa nan-yoo(-bi) desu ka.

PHRASE: every week *mai-shuu* 毎週 •c

EX. How many hours do you work every week?
毎週何時間働いていますか。
Mai-shuu nan-jikan hataraite imasu ka.

PHRASE: last week *senshuu* 先週 •c

EX. I arrived in Japan last week.
先週日本に着きました。
Senshuu Nihon ni tsukimashita.

PHRASE: the week after next *sa-raishuu* 再来週 •c

W

EX. I'm returning to Thailand the week after next.
再来週タイへ帰ります。
Sa-raishuu Tai e kaerimasu.

PHRASE: this week *konshuu* 今週 •c

EX. I'm going to Sydney this week on a business trip.
今週は出張でシドニーへ行く予定です。
Konshuu wa shutchoo de Shidonii e iku yotei desu.

weekend n. **[the period of time between Friday night and Monday morning]**
shu⌈umatsu 週末 •c [the period of time in a seven-day cycle during which businesses and schools are normally closed, usually from Saturday afternoon through Sunday evening], u⌈iikue⌉ndo ウイークエンド •f [the period of time at the end of a seven-day cycle, usually from Saturday afternoon through Sunday afternoon]

EX. (**a**) A: How was your weekend?
{週末/ウイークエンド}はどうでしたか。
{Shuumatsu/Uiikuendo} wa doo deshita ka.
B: It was fun.
楽しかったです。
Tanoshikatta desu.
(**b**) This weekend I'm going golfing.
{今週末/このウイークエンド}はゴルフをします。
{Konshuumatsu/Kono uiikuendo} wa gorufu o shimasu.

weekly adj. **[relating to a period of seven days or happening once in a seven-day cycle]**
1. ma⌈i-shuu no N 毎週のN •c [relating to or happening once in each seven-day cycle]

EX. The weekly quiz is given each Monday.
毎週の小テストは月曜ごとにあります。
Mai-shuu no shoo-tesuto wa getsuyoo-goto ni arimasu.

2. (ma⌈i-)shuu ichi-do⌉ no N (毎)週一度のN •c [happening or done once in each seven-day cycle]

EX. Weekly exercise is not enough to keep in shape.
体の調子を維持するには(毎)週一度の運動だけでは足りない。
Karada no chooshi o iji-suru ni wa (mai-)shuu ichi-do no undoo dake de wa tarinai.

— adv. **[(once) in every seven-day cycle]**
ma⌈i-shuu 毎週 •c [in every seven-day cycle], shu⌉u ni i⌈chi-do⌉ 週に一度 [once in every seven-day cycle]

EX. A: Is this magazine published weekly?
この雑誌は{毎週/週に一度}出ていますか。
Kono zasshi wa {mai-shuu/shuu ni ichi-do} dete imasu ka.
B: No, it's published monthly.
いいえ、月に一度です。
Iie, tsuki ni ichi-do desu.

PHRASE: weekly magazine *shuukan-shi* 週刊誌 •c

EX. The Japanese are avid readers of weekly magazines.
日本人は週刊誌を読むのが大好きです。
Nihon-jin wa shuukan-shi o yomu no ga dai-suki desu.

weep vi. **[for s.o. to shed tears out of strong emotion, esp. grief or joy]**
na⌈ku なく ① [for s.o./s.a. to utter sounds involuntarily out of grief or sadness, usually accompanied by tears, or for s.a. to utter its characteristic sound] 《**cry, shed tears, howl, roar, whine**》
㊥ "for an animal to utter its sound"▷鳴く, otherwise ▷泣く

EX. I wept without stopping for almost a week after I lost my mother.
私は母を亡くしてから一週間近く泣き続けた。
Watashi wa haha o nakushite kara is-shuukan chikaku naki-tsuzuketa.

weigh vt. **[for s.o. to measure the heaviness of s.t./s.o./s.a.** 《**fig. "consider carefully"**》**]**
1. ⟨-no⟩ me⌈kata o haka⌉ru ⟨〜の⟩目方をはかる ① [for s.o. to measure the heaviness of a body or s.t. smaller than a body, esp. food stuff], ⟨-no⟩ ta⌈ijuu o haka⌉ru ⟨〜の⟩体重をはかる ① [for s.o. to measure the heaviness of s.o./s.a.'s body], ⟨-no⟩ o⌈mo-sa o haka⌉ru

W

⟨～の⟩重さをはかる ① **[for s.o. to measure the heaviness of s.t.]**
㊗ "weigh"▷量る, "measure length/height/depth/speed/temperature"▷測る otherwise ▷計る

EX. (**a**) Please weigh this package.
この包みの{目方/重さ/*体重}を量ってください。
*Kono tsutsumi no {mekata/omo-sa/ *taijuu} o hakatte kudasai.*
(**b**) I'm afraid to weigh myself.
自分の{体重/重さ/目方}を量るのが怖い。
Jibun no {taijuu/omo-sa/mekata} o hakaru no ga kowai.

2. ⟨-o⟩ hi⌈kaku-kentoo-suru ⟨～を⟩比較検討する ③ •c [for s.o. to consider a matter carefully by making comparisons] ⟪**examine comparatively**⟫

EX. We have to weigh the pros and cons of this matter.
この問題の長所、短所を比較検討しなければならない。
Kono mondai no choosho, tansho o hikaku-kentoo-shinakereba naranai.

— vi. **[to have a certain degree of heaviness] me⌈kata ga...a⌉ru 目方が…ある ① [for s.t. smaller than a human body to have a specified degree of heaviness], ta⌈ijuu ga...a⌉ru 体重が…ある ① [for a body to have a specified degree of heaviness]**

EX. A: How much do you weigh?
{体重/目方}はどのぐらいありますか。
{Taijuu/Mekata} wa dono-gurai arimasu ka.
B: About sixty kilograms.
六十キロぐらいです。
Roku-juk-kiro gurai desu.

weight n. **[the degree of heaviness of s.t./s.o./s.a. ⟪fig. "heavy burden," "importance"⟫]**

1. o⌈mo-sa 重さ /⟨adj(*i*). stem of *omoi* heavy + suf. *sa* -ness/ **[the degree of heaviness of s.t.]**, **ju⌈uryo⌉o 重量 •c [the degree of heaviness, esp. of s.t. relatively heavy]**

EX. What is the weight of this parcel?
この小包の{重さ/重量}はどのぐらいですか。
Kono ko-zutsumi no {omo-sa/juuryoo} wa dono-gurai desu ka.

2. ju⌈uatsu 重圧 •c [pressure]

EX. He struggled under the heavy weight of his responsibilities.
彼は責任の重圧にあえいだ。
Kare wa sekinin no juuatsu ni aeida.

3. chi⌈kara⌉ 力 [a capacity of any kind to do s.t., including physical, intellectual, mental, or spiritual] ⟪**strength, energy, force, power, vigor, support, ability**⟫

EX. That politician's argument doesn't hold any weight.
あの政治家の議論には力がない。
Ano seiji-ka no giron ni wa chikara ga nai.

PHRASE: gain weight *taijuu ga fueru* 体重が増える ②, *futoru* 太る ① ⟪grow fat, put on weight⟫ ↔ *yaseru* やせる ②

EX. I've gained weight since I've stopped exercising.
運動をやめてから{体重が増えた/太った}。
Undoo o yamete kara {taijuu ga fueta/futotta}.

PHRASE: lose weight *taijuu ga heru* 体重が減る ②, *yaseru* やせる ② ↔ 太る ①

EX. Haven't you lost weight lately?
このごろ{体重が減った/やせた}んじゃありませんか。
Kono-goro {taijuu ga hetta/yaseta} n jaarimasen ka.

weird adj. **[strange in a bizarre way] he⌉nna 変な** adj(*na*). **•c [exhibiting an unusual characteristic/condition/behavior]** ⟪**strange, queer**⟫

EX. That guy is really weird.
あいつは本当に変な奴だ。
Aitsu wa hontoo ni henna yatsu da.

welcome int. **[an interjection used to greet a person pleasantly upon his/her arrival] yo⌉o-koso** (i⌈rasshaima⌉shita) ようこそ(いらっしゃいました)

EX. Welcome to Japan!

W

日本へようこそ。
Nihon e yoo-koso.

NOTE: *Yoo-koso* was originally an adverb similar in form and meaning to *yoku*, but is now often used by itself as an interjection. *Yoku* must be used with a verb, as in *yoku irasshaimashita.*

— adj. **[received with pleasure in a place or freely permitted to do or use s.t.]**

1. ka⌈ngei-sareru (N) 歓迎される(N) /⟨passive of *kangei-suru* ③ welcome/ •c

EX. Whenever I went to see the Tanakas, I was always welcome.
いつ田中さんたちのお宅に行っても、歓迎されました。
Itsu Tanaka-san-tachi no o-taku ni itte mo, kangei-saremashita.

2. {ji⌈yu⌉u/ka⌈tte} ni…V*te* i⌉i {自由/勝手}に…Vteいい [permitted to do s.t. as one likes]

EX. You're welcome to any food in the refrigerator.
冷蔵庫の中の食べ物は何でも{自由/勝手}に食べていいですよ。
Reizoo-ko no naka no tabe-mono wa nan-demo {jiyuu/katte} ni tabete ii desu yo.

— vt. **[for s.o. to gladly receive or accept s.o./s.t./s.a.]**

1. ⟨-o⟩ ka⌈ngei-suru ⟨〜を⟩歓迎する ③ •c, ⟨-o⟩ yo⌈roko⌉nde mu⌈kaeru ⟨〜を⟩喜んで迎える ②

EX. When I went to Seoul, my Korean friends welcomed me warmly.
ソウルに行った時、韓国人の友達は私を{温かく歓迎して/喜んで迎えて}くれた。
Souru ni itta toki, Kankoku-jin no tomodachi wa watashi o {atatakaku kangei-shite/yorokonde mukaete} kureta.

2. ⟨-o⟩ yo⌈roko⌉nde u⌈ke-ireru ⟨〜を⟩喜んで受け入れる ② [for s.o. to accept s.t. with pleasure]

EX. A: How did he take your criticism?
あなたの批判を彼はどう受け取りましたか。
Anata no hihan o kare wa doo uke-torimashita ka.
B: He welcomed it.
喜んで受け入れましたよ。
Yorokonde uke-iremashita yo.

PHRASE: You're welcome. *Iie.* いいえ。, *Doo-itashimashite.* どういたしまして。

EX. A: Thank you very much!
どうもありがとうございました。
Doomo arigatoo gozaimashita.
B: You're welcome.
いいえ、どういたしまして。
Iie, doo-itashimashite.

NOTE: "You're welcome" can be expressed by *iie* or *doo-itashimashite* alone or by the two together, as in the above example.

welfare n. **[the state of being happy and healthy or assistance provided by the government to needy persons]**
fu⌈ku⌉shi 福祉 •c [a condition of social stability where people, esp. those without independent means, are satisfied with their economic state] ((well-being)), ko⌈ofuku 幸福 •c [a state of joyful contentment] ((happiness, well-being, bliss))

EX. I intend to vote for a candidate who is truly concerned for the welfare of the people.
国民の{福祉/幸福}を本当に考えている候補者に投票します。
Kokumin no {fukushi/koofuku} o hontoo ni kangaete iru kooho-sha ni toohyoo-shimasu.

PHRASE: be on welfare *seikatsu-hogo o ukeru* 生活保護を受ける ②

EX. When I was a child my family was on welfare.
私が子供の時、うちは生活保護を受けていた。
Watashi ga kodomo no toki, uchi wa seikatsu-hogo o ukete ita.

well[1] n. **[a deep hole dug into the earth for drawing water, oil, etc., or an enclosed area shaped like this]**

1. i⌉do 井戸 •c [a deep hole dug into the earth for drawing water]

ido

EX. When I was a child, we used

W

to draw water from a well by hand.
子供のころは手で井戸から水を汲んだものだ。
Kodomo no koro wa te de ido kara mizu o kunda mono da.

2. yu⌈sei 油井 •c [a deep hole dug into the earth for drawing oil]

well² adv. **[in a good or satisfactory manner]**
1. jo⌈ozu⌉ni 上手に /⟨adj(*na*). *ni* of *joozuna* skillful/ •c [with a great deal of skill], u⌉maku うまく /⟨adj(*i*). *ku* of *umai* adj(*i*). skillful/ [with a great deal of skill in doing or thinking of s.t.], yo⌉ku よく /⟨adj(*i*). *ku* of *ii* adj(*i*). good/ [satisfactorily/carefully/ many times], shu⌈bi-yo⌉ku 首尾よく [in a smooth and successful manner throughout; with a successful result]

EX. (**a**) Bill speaks very well in front of audiences.
ビルは聴衆の前で大変{うまく/上手に/*よく/*首尾よく}話す。
*Biru wa chooshuu no mae de taihen {umaku/joozuni/*yoku/*shubi-yoku} hanasu.*

NOTE: Example (a) can also be expressed as *Biru wa Nihon-go o hanasu no ga {joozu/umai} desu.*

(**b**) He does very well at solving complex problems.
彼は複雑な問題を{うまく/上手に/*よく/*首尾よく}解決する。
*Kare wa fukuzatsuna mondai o {umaku/joozuni/*yoku/*shubi-yoku} kaiketsu-suru.*

(**c**) A: How is he handling that difficult job?
彼、あの難しい仕事、どうやってる?
Kare, ano muzukashii shigoto, doo yatte ru?
B: Very well.
{よく/上手に/うまく/?首尾よく}やってるよ。
{Yoku/Joozuni/Umaku/?Shubi-yoku} yatte ru yo.

NOTE: *Yoku* in the sense of "satisfactorily" is used only with *yaru* "to do" or with potential verbs. It cannot be freely used with other verbs.

(**d**) A: How did the meeting go?
会議はどうでしたか。
Kaigi wa doo deshita ka.
B: It all went very well.
{首尾よく/うまく/*よく/*上手に}いったよ。
*{Shubi-yoku/Umaku/*Yoku/*Joozuni} itta yo.*

PHRASE: Well done! *Yoku yatta.* よくやった。

— adj. **[in good health or in a satisfactory condition]**
1. ge⌉nkina 元気な adj(*na*). **•c [in good health or full of energy] ⟪in high spirits, healthy⟫, ke⌈nkoona 健康な** adj(*na*). **•c [in good physical condition with no bodily dysfunctions] ⟪healthy, sound⟫**

EX. You look so well these days.
このごろ{元気/健康}そうだねえ。
Kono goro {genki/kenkoo}-soo da nee.

2. yo⌉shi よし int. **[an interjection indicating acceptance or determination or used to accompany a direction or command] ⟪good, all right⟫**

EX. A: Have you finished your homework?
宿題をやったか。
Shukudai o yatta ka.
B: Yes, I've finished all of it.
うん、全部やった。
Un, zenbu yatta
A: Very well. Then you may watch television.
よし。テレビを見ていいぞ。
Yoshi. Terebi o mite ii zo.

— int. **[an interjection indicating surprise, relief, or resignation or used to introduce a new thought when hesitating]**
1. he⌈e へえ [an interjection indicating surprise or amazement]

EX. A: I've decided to go to seminary and become a minister.
神学校に入って牧師になることにしました。
Shin-gakkoo ni haitte bokushi ni naru koto ni shimashita.
B: Well, well, well.
へえ、そいつは驚いた。
Hee, soitsu wa odoroita.

W

2. (so⌈re-)ja⌉(a) （それ）じゃ（あ） **[if that is the case《fig. "a signal to indicate that s.t. is to begin or end or two people are to part"》]** **《if so, then》**

EX. A: I don't care what my boss says. I'm not going to spend a weekend going to a conference like that.
上司が何と言おうと、あんな会議に出るのに週末を使うなんてごめんです。
Jooshi ga nan to ioo to, anna kaigi ni deru no ni shuumatsu o tsukau nante gomen desu.
B: Well, suit yourself!
じゃあ、勝手にしてください。
Jaa, katte ni shite kudasai.

3. do⌉o na n desu ka どうなんですか **[a question used to press s.o. for a response, literally meaning "how is it?"]**

EX. A: Can you give me the reason why you didn't show up?
どうして来なかったのか理由を説明出来ますか。
Dooshite konakatta no ka riyuu o setsumei dekimasu ka.
B: —no reply—
A: Well?
どうなんですか。
Doo na n desu ka.

4. i⌈ya mo⌉o いやもう **[an interjection indicating resignation]**

EX. My daughter colors her hair pink and wears a super-short mini skirt. Well, I guess there's just nothing I can do about it.
娘は髪をピンクに染めたり、超ミニスカートをはいたり、いやもう、どうしようもないんですよ。
Musume wa kami o pinku ni sometari, choo-mini-sukaato o haitari, iya moo, doo-shiyoo-mo-nai n desu yo.

W

5. sa⌉a さあ **[an interjection indicating hesitation or determination or used to invite s.o. to do s.t.]** **《come, come now》**, **e⌈eto** ええと **[an interjection indicating hesitation while thinking]** **《let me see》**

EX. (**a**) A: Do you think he's going to pass his exams?
彼は試験に受かると思いますか。
Kare wa shiken ni ukaru to omoi masu ka.
B: Well, that's hard to tell.
{さあ/*ええと}、どうでしょうね。
*{Saa/*Eeto}, doo deshoo ne.*
(**b**) A: What time is it in London now?
ロンドンは今何時ですか。
Rondon wa ima nan-ji desu ka.
B: Well, let me see. I think it's 5:15 P.M.
{ええと/*さあ}、午後五時十五分だと思います。
*{Eeto/*Saa}, soo desu ne. Gogo go-ji juu-go-fun da to omoimasu.*

well-known adj. **[very familiar to many people]**
yu⌈umeina 有名な adj(*na*). **•c [having a name which is widely familiar]** **《famous, noted, renowned》**, **yo⌉ku shi⌈ra-reta N** よく知られたN **/〈Vinf. past of passive of *yoku shiru* ① know well/ [to be very familiar to many people]**, **yo⌉ku shi⌈ra-rete iru (N)** よく知られている(N) **/〈V*te iru* of passive of *yoku shiru* ① know well/ ② [to be very familiar to many people]**

EX. (**a**) Waseda University and Keio University are both well-known private universities in Japan.
早稲田大学と慶応大学はどちらも日本で{有名な/よく知られた/よく知られている}私立大学だ。
Waseda daigaku to Keioo daigaku wa dochira-mo Nihon de {yuumeina/yoku shira-reta/yoku shira-rete iru} shiritsu-daigaku da.
(**b**) *Sashimi* is a well-known part of Japanese cuisine.
刺身は日本食として{よく知られている/?有名な}ものだ。
Sashimi wa Nihon-shoku to-shite {yoku shira-rete iru/?yuumeina} mono da.

Welsh n. **[the people or the language of Wales]**
1. U⌈eeruzu⌉-jin ウェールズ人 **•f+c [a person from Wales or the people of Wales]**

2. U⸢eeruzu-go ウェールズ語 •f+c **[the language of Wales]**

— adj. **[of Wales or of its people or language]**

1. U⸢eeruzu⸣-jin no N ウェールズ人のN •f+c **[of a person from or the people of Wales]**

2. U⸢eeruzu-go no N ウェールズ語のN •f+c **[of the language of Wales]**

went vi. **[the past tense of the verb "go"]**
i⸢tta 行った /⟨Vinf. past tense of *iku* ① go/, **i⸢kima⸣shita** 行きました /⟨formal past tense of *iku* ① go/ SEE go

EX. A: Did you go to the language lab today?
今日ランゲージラボに{行った?/行きましたか。}
Kyoo rangeeji rabo ni {itta?/ikimashita ka.}
B: No, but I went yesterday.
いや、でもきのうは{行った/行きました}よ。
Iya, demo kinoo wa {itta/ikimashita} yo.

NOTE: Both Japanese *iku* and English "go" are frequently used verbs, and, as is often the case with such verbs, both are somewhat irregular in their conjugations. Japanese verbs with a dictionary form ending in *-ku* normally have an informal past tense form ending in *-ita*, such as *aku* "to open"▷*aita*, *oku* "to place"▷*oita*, *kaku* "to write"▷*kaita*, *kiku* "to listen"▷*kiita*, *saku* "to bloom"▷*saita*, *tsuku* "to arrive"▷*tuita*, and *hiku* "to pull"▷*hiita*, but the informal past tense form of *iku* is *itta*.

wept vi. **[the past tense of the verb "weep"]**
na⸢ita ないた /⟨Vinf. past tenses of *naku* ① weep, cry/, **na⸢kima⸣shita** なきました /⟨formal past tense of *naku* ① weep, cry/ SEE weep

EX. I wept when the Emperor died.
天皇陛下がお亡くなりになった時、私は{泣いた/泣きました}。
Tennoo-heika ga o-nakunari ni natta toki, watashi wa {naita/nakimashita}.

were vi. **[affirmative past tense of the second person singular and the first, second, and third person plural of the copula and of the existential verb "to be"]**

1. **da⸣tta** だった cop. **[informal/written style affirmative past tense of the copula *da*]** ⟪was⟫, **de⸣shita** でした cop. **[formal affirmative past tense of the copula *da*]** ⟪was⟫

EX. (a) Were you single when you first went to Japan?
初めて日本へ行った時独身{だった?/でしたか。}
Hajimete Nihon e itta toki dokushin {datta?/deshita ka.}
(b) Who were the people who came this morning?
今朝来た人たちはだれ{だった?/でしたか。}
Kesa kita hito-tachi wa dare {datta?/deshita ka.}

2. **a⸢rima⸣shita** ありました **[formal affirmative past tense of *aru*, for s.t. to exist]** ⟪was⟫, **a⸣tta** あった **[informal affirmative past tense of *aru*]** ⟪was⟫, **i⸢ma⸣shita** いました **[formal affirmative past tense of *iru* for s.o./s.a. to exist]** ⟪was⟫, **i⸢ta** いた **[informal affirmative past tense of *iru*]** ⟪was⟫ SEE be

EX. (a) There were a lot of Japanese books in the library.
図書館には日本の本がたくさん{あった/ありました/*いた/*いました}。
*Tosho-kan ni wa Nihon no hon ga takusan {atta/arimashita/*ita/*imashita}.*
(b) There were about twenty people at the party.
パーティーには二十人くらいの人が{いた/いました/*あった/*ありました}。
*Paatii ni wa ni-juu-nin-kurai no hito ga {ita/imashita/*atta/*arimashita}.*

— aux. **[an auxiliary verb used in the passive or progressive construction]**

1. {Vneg. **reta**/Vstem **rareta**/**sa⸢reta**} {Vneg.れた/Vstemられた/された} **[for s.t./s.o./s.a. acting as the subject of a sentence to be affected in the past by the action of the**

verb of that sentence]

EX. The burglars were arrested by the police.
強盗は警察に逮捕された。
Gootoo wa keisatsu ni taiho-sareta.

2. V*te* ita V*te*いた [for s.o./s.a./s.t. to be in the middle of doing s.t. in the past or to be in a state in the past resulting from s.t. that happened earlier]

EX. They were preparing for their trip to Japan.
彼らは日本への旅行の準備をしていた。
Karera wa Nihon e no ryokoo no junbi o shite ita.

weren't vi. **[negative past tense of the second person singular and the first, second, and third person plural of the copula and of the existential verb "to be"]**
1. {**dewa⌈na⌉katta/ja⌈na⌉katta**} {ではなかった/じゃなかった} cop. **[informal/written style negative past tense of the copula *da*],** {**dewaa⌈rimase⌉n/jaa⌈rimase⌉n**} **deshita** {ではありません/じゃありません}でした cop. **[formal negative past tense of the copula *da*]**

EX. The young people we met there weren't students.
そこで会った若い人たちは学生{ではなかった/じゃなかった/ではありませんでした/じゃありませんでした}。
Soko de atta wakai hito-tachi wa gakusei {dewanakatta/janakatta/dewaarimasen deshita/jaarimasen deshita}.

2. a⌈rimase⌉n deshita ありませんでした [formal negative past tense of *aru*, for s.t. to exist] SEE be, **na⌉katta なかった [informal negative past tense of *aru*], i⌈masen⌉ deshita いませんでした [formal negative past tense of *iru*, for s.o./s.a. to exist], i⌈na⌉katta いなかった [informal negative past tense of *iru*]** SEE be

EX. (**a**) There weren't very many coeds at the college I went to.
私が行っていた大学には女子学生はあまり{いなかった/いませんでした/*なかった/*ありませんでした}。
*Watashi ga itte ita daigaku ni wa joshi-gakusei wa amari {inakatta/imasen deshita/*nakatta/*arimasen deshita}.*
(**b**) There weren't any tall buildings in this area ten years ago.
十年前、この辺には高い建物は{なかった/ありませんでした/*いなかった/*いませんでした}。
*Juu-nen mae, kono hen ni wa takai tate-mono wa {nakatta/arimasen deshita/*inakatta/*imasen deshita}.*

— aux. **[an auxiliary verb used in the passive or progressive construction]**
1. {**Vneg. renakatta/Vstem rarenakatta/sa⌈rena⌉katta**} {**Vneg.**れなかった/**Vstem**られなかった/されなかった} **[for s.t./s.o./s.a. acting as the subject of a sentence to not be affected in the past by the action of the verb of that sentence]**

EX. We weren't given enough information on the matter.
私たちはそのことに関して十分な情報を与えられなかった。
Watashi-tachi wa sono koto ni-kanshite juubunna joohoo o atae-rarenakatta

2. V*te* inakatta V*te*いなかった [for s.o./s.a./s.t. to not be in the middle of doing s.t. in the past or not be in a state in the past resulting from something that happened earlier]

EX. Management decided that the employees in that division weren't working hard enough to deserve a pay raise last year.
経営者側はその課の社員が昨年は昇給に値するだけの仕事をしていなかったと判断した。
Keiei-sha-gawa wa sono ka no shain ga sakunen wa shookyuu ni atai-suru dake no shigoto o shite inakatta to handan-shita.

west n. **[the direction of the sunset《fig. "the occidental countries, esp. Europe and the United States"》]**
1. ni⌈shi 西 [the direction of the sunset]

EX. (**a**) The sun rises from the east and sets in the west.

W

太陽は東から出て、西に沈む。
Taiyoo wa higashi kara dete, nishi ni shizumu.
(**b**) He lives to the west of the downtown area.
彼は町の中心より西の方に住んでいる。
Kare wa machi no chuushin yori nishi no hoo ni sunde iru.

2. se˥iyoo 西洋 •c [Europe and America as viewed from the Far Eastern countries] 《the Occident, Europe》 ↔ tooyoo 東洋 •c

EX. The distinction between East and West is fast disappearing in modern times.
現代では東洋と西洋の区別が急速になくなりつつある。
Gendai de wa tooyoo to seiyoo no kubetsu ga kyuusokuni nakunari-tsutsu aru.

western adj. **[of or in the direction of the sunset 《fig. "of or coming from countries or states located in the direction of the sunset, esp. the Occidental counries"》]**

1. ni˥shi no N 西のN [of or in the direction of the sunset]

EX. There is a very beautiful park in the western part of the city.
町の西の区域にきれいな公園がある。
Machi no nishi no kuiki ni kireina kooen ga aru.

2. se˥ibu no N 西部のN •c [of or in the part of an area or country which lies in the direction of the sunset]

EX. Climate-wise the western areas of the island are quite different from its eastern areas.
島の西部の地域と東部の地域は気候が全く違う。
Shima no seibu no chiiki to toobu no chiiki wa kikoo ga mattaku chigau.

3. se˥iyoo no N 西洋のN •c [of the Occident] ↔ tooyoo no N 東洋のN •c

EX. Western and Eastern ways of thinking are different in some fundamental respects.
西洋と東洋の考え方は基本的に違うところがある。
Seiyoo to tooyoo no kangae-kata wa kihon tekini chigau tokoro ga aru.

PHRASE: a Western-style building *(sei-)yoo-kan* (西)洋館 •c, Western-style food *yooshoku* 洋食 •c ↔ *washoku* 和食 •c

EX. Which do you like better, Japanese-style food or Western-style food?
和食と洋食とどちらの方が好きですか。
Washoku to yooshoku to dochira no hoo ga suki desu ka.

PHRASE: a Western-style room *yooma* 洋間 •c ↔ *washitsu* 和室 •c

EX. Japanese houses normally have at least one Western-style room.
一般的な日本の家屋には少なくとも洋間が一つはある。
Ippan-tekina Nihon no kaoku ni wa sukunaku tomo yooma ga hitotsu wa aru.

westward adj. **[in or toward the direction of the sunset]**

1. ni˥shi no ho˥o e no N 西の方へのN [directed toward the direction of the sunset]

EX. Our westward bike trip started from Boston in May.
私たちの西の方への自転車旅行は五月にボストンから始まった。
Watashi-tachi no nishi no hoo e no jitensha-ryokoo wa go-gatsu ni Bosuton kara hajimatta.

2. ni˥shi-muki no N 西向きのN [facing the direction of the sunset]

EX. A westward wind was blowing.
西向きの風が吹いていた。
Nishi-muki no kaze ga fuite ita.

— adv. **[toward the direction of the sunset]**
ni˥shi {e/ni} 西{へ/に} [in the direction of the sunset]

EX. (**a**) Our house faces westward.
私たちの家は西{に/?へ}向いている。
Watashi-tachi no ie wa nishi {ni/?e} muite iru.
(**b**) We walked westward until we hit the river.
川に行きあたるまで西{へ/に}歩いた。
Kawa ni iki-ataru made nishi {e/ni} aruita.

W

wet adj. **[moist, covered, or soaked with liquid 《fig. "rainy," "permitting the sale or manufacture of liquor"》]**
1. 〈〈-de〉〉 **shi⌈metta N** 〈〈〜で〉〉湿ったN **/〈Vinf. past of *shimeru* ① become wet/ [moist from having absorbed liquid] 《dampened, moist》**, 〈〈-de〉〉 **shi⌈mette iru (N)** 〈〈〜で〉〉湿っている(N) **/〈V*te iru* of *shimeru* ① become wet/ [moist from having absorbed liquid]**, 〈〈-de〉〉 **nu⌈reta N** 〈〈〜で〉〉ぬれたN **/〈Vinf. past of *nureru* ② become wet/ [covered or soaked with liquid]**, 〈〈-de〉〉 **nu⌈rete iru (N)** 〈〈〜で〉〉ぬれている(N) **/〈V*te iru* of *nureru* ② get wet/ [covered or soaked with liquid]**, 〈〈-de〉〉 **u⌈ru⌉nda N** 〈〈〜で〉〉潤んだN **/〈Vinf. past of *urumu* ① become wet/ [moistened with tears 《fig. "dimmed," "clouded"》]**, 〈〈-de〉〉 **u⌈ru⌉nde iru (N)** 〈〈〜で〉〉潤んでいる(N) **/〈V*te iru* of *urumu* ① become wet/ [moistened with tears 《fig. "dimmed," "clouded"》]**

EX. (**a**) I got caught in a rain shower, so my hair is wet.
私は夕立に会って、髪の毛が{ぬれて/*湿って/*潤んで}います。
*Watashi wa yuudachi ni atte, kami-no-ke ga {nurete/*shimette/*urunde} imasu.*
(**b**) Her eyes were wet with tears as she parted with me.
私と別れた時、彼女の目は涙で{潤んで/ぬれて/*湿って}いた。
*Watashi to wakareta toki, kanojo no me wa namida de {urunde/nurete/*shimette} ita.*
(**c**) The ground was wet from the previous night's rain.
昨晩の雨で地面が{ぬれて/湿って/*潤んで}いた。
*Sakuban no ame de jimen ga {nurete/shimette/*urunde} ita.*
(**d**) The inside of the house was wet with moisture due to the rainy weather.
雨のせいで家の中は{湿って/*ぬれて/*潤んで}いた。
*Ame no sei de ie no naka wa {shimette/*nurete/*urunde} ita.*

2. a⌉me no N 雨のN **[marked by the occurrence of rain], a⌉me no o⌉oi N** 雨の多いN **[having a lot of rain]**

EX. (**a**) I like to read books on the days when the weather is wet outside.
外が{雨の/*雨の多い}日には本を読むのが好きだ。
*Soto ga {ame no/*ame no ooi} hi ni wa hon o yomu no ga suki da.*
(**b**) Tokyo typically has wet weather in June.
東京の六月は通常、{雨が多い/*雨だ}。
*Tookyoo no roku-gatsu wa tsuujoo, {ame ga ooi/*ame da}.*

PHRASE: get wet 〈*-de*〉 *nureru* 〈〜で〉ぬれる ② 《become damp, become moistened》

EX. I got caught in the rain and got all wet.
雨に降られて、ぬれてしまった。
Ame ni fura-rete, nurete shimatta.

— vt. **[to cause s.t. to become moist, covered, or soaked with liquid]**
〈-de〉 **nu⌈reru** 〈〜で〉ぬれる ② **[for s.t. to become soaked with or covered on its surface with liquid] 《moisten, dampen, soak》**, 〈-de〉 **shi⌈meru** 〈〜で〉湿る ① **[for s.t. to become moist with liquid] 《become damp》**, 〈-o〉 **nu⌈rasu** 〈〜を〉ぬらす ① **[to soak or cover the surface of s.t. with liquid] 《moisten, dampen, soak》**, 〈-o〉 **shi⌈merasu** 〈〜を〉湿らす ① **[for s.o. to moisten s.t. with liquid] 《dampen》**

EX. (**a**) The rain wet my hair.
雨で髪の毛が{ぬれた/湿った}。
Ame de kami-no-ke ga {nureta/s himetta}.
(**b**) When pulling weeds, it makes it easier to wet the ground first.
雑草を取る時は先に地面を{ぬらした/湿らした/*ぬれた/*湿った}方が取りやすい。
*Zassoo o toru toki wa saki ni jimen o {nurashita/shimerashita/*nureta/*shimetta} hoo ga tori-yasui.*

PHRASE: wet the bed *o-nesho o suru* おねしょをする ③

whale n.
ku⌈jira 鯨

W

EX. The whale is a mammal.
鯨はほ乳動物だ。
Kujira wa honyuu-doobutsu da.

wharf n. **[a structure built along or at an angle to a shore for loading and unloading ships]**
ha⌈to-ba 波止場 [a place along which ships can dock in a harbor] ⟪quay, jetty, pier⟫, **ga⌈npeki 岸壁 •c [a wall of rock or concrete along a shore where ships can dock]** ⟪rock wall, quay, pier⟫, **fu⌈too ふ頭 •c [a place along which ships can dock for loading and unloading cargo or passengers]** ⟪quay, pier⟫

EX. A boat was docked along the wharf.
船が{波止場/岸壁/ふ頭}に泊っていた。
Fune ga {hato-ba/ganpeki/futoo} ni tomatte ita.

what¹ pron. **[an interrogative pronoun which requests an identification of s.t. or a clarification of s.t. not heard or understood clearly by the speaker]**
{na⌉ni/na⌉n} 何 n. **[an interrogative pronoun which requests an identification of s.t. or which refers to s.t./s.o. that the speaker has forgotten or does not want to mention]**

NOTE: *Nan* is used when the following sound is /t/ or /d/, as in *nan to*, *nan de*, or when the following word is a counter, as in *nan-mai* (how many sheets of), *nan-nin* (how many people), *nan-satsu* (how many bound objects), etc.; otherwise, *nani* is used.

EX. (**a**) A: What do you plan to do after graduation?
卒業したら、何をするつもりですか。
Sotsugyoo-shitara, nani o suru tsumori desu ka.
B: I'm going to teach at a high school.
高校で教えるつもりです。
Kookoo de oshieru tsumori desu.
(**b**) A: What did you eat for lunch today?
今日は昼御飯に何を食べましたか。
Kyoo wa hiru-gohan ni nani o tabemashita ka.
B: I had some spaghetti.
スパゲッティを食べました。
Supagetti o tabemashita.
(**c**) What is that huge building over there?
あの巨大な建物は何ですか。
Ano kyodaina tate-mono wa nan desu ka.
(**d**) A: I'd like to borrow some money from you.
君から金を借りたいんだ。
Kimi kara kane o kari-tai n da.
B: You'd like to borrow what?
何を借りたいんだって?
Nani o kari-tai n datte?

PHRASE: So what? *da kara doo datte iu n desu ka.* だからどうだって言うんですか。

EX. A: My dad makes $80,000 a year.
おやじは年に八万ドルもらっているんです。
Oyaji wa nen ni hachi-man-doru moratte iru n desu.
B: So what?
だからどうだって言うんですか。
Dakara doo datte iu n desu ka.

PHRASE: Tell you what *ano ne* あのね

EX. A: Tell you what.
あのね。
Ano ne.
B: What?
何?
Nani ?

PHRASE: what for *nan de* 何で ⟪why, what with⟫, *dooshite* どうして ⟪why, by/with what means⟫

EX. A: What are you studying Japanese for?
{なんで/どうして}日本語を勉強しているんですか。
{Nan de/Dooshite} Nihon-go o benkyoo-shite iru n desu ka.
B: Because I want to go work in Japan someday.
いつか日本へ行って、仕事をしたいからです。
Itsu-ka Nihon e itte, shigoto o shi-tai kara desu.

— adj. **[an interrogative adjective which requests information about the number, kind, or identity of s.t./s.o./s.a.]**

do⌉nna N どんなN [an interrogative adjective that requests a description of s.t./s.o./s.a.] ⟪what kind of⟫

EX. (**a**) A: What kinds of books are you reading these days?
このごろどんな本を読んでいますか。
Kono-goro donna hon o yonde imasu ka.
B: I'm reading science fiction.
SFを読んでいます。
Esu-efu o yonde imasu.
(**b**) A: What kind of person do you think you'd like to marry?
どんな人と結婚したいと思いますか。
Donna hito to kekkon-shi-tai to omoimasu ka.
B: Someone cheerful.
明るい人がいいです。
Akarui hito ga ii desu.

PHRASE: What time is it? *Nan-ji desu ka.* 何時ですか。

what² pron. **[the thing(s) which]**

ko⌈to⌉ こと [whatever is or may be said, done, or conceived of as an event, fact, or situation occurring in time; a nominalizer forming a noun clause expressing s.t. perceived indirectly by means of one's rational faculties rather than directly through the five senses] ⟪thing⟫

EX. (**a**) Are you listening to what I'm saying?
私の言っていることを聞いているんですか。
Watashi no itte iru koto o kiite iru n desu ka.
(**b**) What has happened has happened.
起きたことは起きたことだ。
Okita koto wa okita koto da.

whatever pron. **[anything that or no matter what]**

na⌉n-demo 何でも [any kind of thing, event, fact, etc. (in an affirmative sentence)], na⌉ni + prt. V*te* mo 何+prt.V*te* も

EX. (**a**) I'll do whatever you say.
{おっしゃることは何でも/??何をおっしゃっても}やります。
{Ossharu koto wa nan-demo/??Nani o osshatte mo} yarimasu.
(**b**) Whatever he does, he's successful at it.
あの人は{何をやっても/??やることは何でも}成功する。
Ano hito wa {nani o yatte mo/??yaru koto wa nan-demo} seikoo-suru.

— adj. **[any…that… or no matter what…]**

do⌉nna N de⌉mo どんなNでも [whichever kind of object/person/animal one chooses], do⌉nna N + prt. V*te* mo どんなN+prt.V*te* も [no matter what…]

EX. (**a**) Whatever he reads he does so avidly.
{どんな本でも/*どんな本を読んでも}熱心に読む。
*{Donna hon demo/*Donna hon o yonde mo} nesshinni yomu.*
(**b**) Whatever kind of present I give her, she's never satisfied.
{どんなプレゼントを上げても/*どんなプレゼントでも}彼女は気に入ってくれたことがない。
*{Donna purezento o agete mo/*Donna purezento demo} kanojo wa ki ni itte kureta koto ga nai.*

wheat n.

ko-⌈mugi⌉ 小麦

EX. Bread is made from wheat flour.
パンは小麦粉で作ります。
Pan wa ko-mugi-ko de tsukurimasu.

wheel n. **[a round frame or solid object that revolves around its center ⟪fig. "machinery"⟫]**

1. sha⌈rin 車輪 •c [a circular object that turns on an axis and allows a vehicle to move] ⟪rundle⟫

EX. The front wheel of my bike came off.
自転車の前の車輪が外れてしまった。
Jitensha no mae no sharin ga hazurete shimatta.

2. ki⌈koo 機構 •c [the arrangement of the parts of a social system] ⟪mechanism, system, structure, organization⟫

EX. The wheels of Japanese management move differently from those in Europe and the United States.

日本の経営の機構は欧米とは違う。
Nihon no keiei no kikoo wa Oo-Bei to wa chigau.

PHRASE: steering wheel *handoru* ハンドル •f, four wheel drive *yon-rin-kudoo* 四輪駆動

when[1] adv./pron. **[at or during what time]**
iˈ**tsu** いつ **⟪at what time, how soon⟫**

EX. (**a**) A: When did you come to Tokyo, Professor Smith?
スミス先生、東京にはいついらっしゃいましたか。
Sumisu-sensei, Tookyoo ni wa itsu irasshaimashita ka.
B: I arrived just yesterday.
きのう来たばかりです。
Kinoo kita bakari desu.
(**b**) A: When does summer vacation start?
夏休みはいつ始まりますか。
Natsu-yasumi wa itsu hajimarimasu ka.
B: On July 15.
七月十五日です。
Shichi-gatsu juu-go-nichi desu.
(**c**) A: When are you and Sally getting married?
サリーといつ結婚するんですか。
Sarii to itsu kekkon-suru n desu ka.
B: Next June.
来年の六月です。
Rainen no roku-gatsu desu.
(**d**) From when to when did you live in Japan?
日本にはいつからいつまで住んでいたんですか。
Nihon ni wa itsu kara itsu made sunde ita n desu ka.

PHRASE: Say when! *dono-gurai ga ii ka itte kudasai.* どのぐらいがいいか言ってください。

EX. A: Say when!
どのぐらいがいいか言ってください。
Dono-gurai ga ii ka itte kudasai.
B: OK, that's enough.
はい、そのぐらいです。
Hai, sono-gurai desu.

NOTE: *Itsu* can never be used as the conjunction "when." Thus, for example, "when" in "When I first went to Japan, I didn't know Japanese" cannot be translated by *itsu*, but requires the use of *toki*, as in *Nihon e hajimete itta {toki/*itsu}, Nihon-go o shirimasendeshita.* SEE when[1] conj.

—— conj. **[at or during the time at which or during which]**
Sinf. toˈ**ki**ˈ **(ni) Sinf.時(に)** SEE the note for when[2].

EX. (**a**) A: What did you study when you were in Japan?
日本にいた時、何を勉強しましたか。
Nihon ni ita toki, nani o benkyoo-shimashita ka.
B: I studied Japanese.
日本語を勉強しました。
Nihon-go o benkyoo-shimashita.
(**b**) When I get a headache I take an aspirin.
頭が痛い時はアスピリンを飲みます。
Atama ga itai toki wa asupirin o nomimasu.

when[2] pron. **[a relative pronoun used to introduce a relative clause modifying "time," "occasion," or other nouns expressing a time]**
ø

NOTE: When the nonpast affirmative form of adj(*na*). or N + cop. appears before *toki*, the form used is adj(*na*). stem + *na* or N *no*, respectively.

EX. (**a**) There was a time when everybody knew everybody else in town.
町の人がみんなお互いを知っていた時があった。
Machi no hito ga minna o-tagai o shitte ita toki ga atta.
(**b**) There are occasions when I just don't feel like doing anything.
何もしたくないような時があります。
Nani mo shi-takunai yoona toki ga arimasu.

NOTE: Japanese has no relative pronouns. In Japanese relative clauses, the modifying sentence is placed immediately in front of the modified noun, with no relative pronoun intervening.

whenever conj. **[at any time that]** **i˥tsu V*te* mo いつV*te*も [no matter when one does s.t. or s.t. happens], Sinf. to˥ki˥ ni (wa) i˥tsu-demo Sinf. 時に(は)いつでも [always at a time when]**

EX. (**a**) Please come see me whenever you have time.
{暇な時にはいつでも/*いつ暇があっても}いらしてください。
*{Himana toki ni wa itsu-demo/*Itsu hima ga atte mo} irashite kudasai.*
(**b**) Whenever I have a problem, I talk about it with a close friend.
{問題のある時にはいつでも/*いつ問題があっても}それについて親しい友達と話します。
*{Mondai no aru toki ni wa itsu-demo/ *Itsu mondai ga atte mo} sore ni-tsuite shitashii tomodachi to hanashimasu.*
(**c**) Whenever I go to see him, he's always working.
{いつ会いに行っても/*会いに行く時はいつでも}、彼は仕事をしています。
*{Itsu ai-ni itte mo/*Ai-ni iku toki wa itsu-demo}, kare wa shigoto o shite imasu.*

where[1] adv./pron. **[in, at, or to which or what place, position, or situation] do˥ko どこ [which or what place, part, or position, including a place at, in, toward, or through which a motion or action occurs], do˥chira どちら [what one of a set of two possibilites; what place or direction]** **((who, which, what))**

NOTE: *Dochira* in the sense of "where" is more polite than *doko.*

EX. (**a**) A: Excuse me, but where is the washroom?
すみませんが、お手洗いは{どこ/どちら}でしょうか。
Sumimasen ga, o-tearai wa {doko/ dochira} deshoo ka.
B: Over there.
{あそこ/あちら}です。
{Asoko/Achira} desu.
(**b**) A: Where is your apartment?
アパートは{どこ/どちら}ですか。
Apaato wa {doko/dochira} desu ka.
B: It's near the station.
駅の近くです。
Eki no chikaku desu.
(**c**) A: Where did you come from today?
今日は{どこから来ましたか/どちらからいらっしゃいましたか}。
Kyoo wa {doko kara kimashita ka/ dochira kara irasshaimashita ka}.
B: I came from Osaka.
大阪から来ました。
Oosaka kara kimashita.
(**d**) A: Do you know where the party's going to be?
パーティーが{どこ/*どちら}であるか知っていますか。
*Paatii ga {doko/*dochira} de aru ka shitte imasu ka.*
B: Yes, it's going to be at my house.
ええ、僕のうちです。
Ee, boku no uchi desu.
(**e**) A: Where does it hurt?
{どこ/*どちら}が痛いんですか。
*{Doko/*Dochira} ga itai n desu ka.*
B: Right here.
ここです。
Koko desu.
(**f**) A: Where should I get off?
{どこ/?どちら}で降りたらいいですか。
{Doko/?Dochira} de oritara ii desu ka.
B: At the next station.
次の駅です。
Tsugi no eki desu.
(**g**) A: Where are you going?
{どこへ行くんですか/どちらへいらっしゃるんですか}。
{Doko e iku n desu ka/Dochira e irassharu n desu ka}.
B: To the department store.
ちょっと、デパートまで。
Chotto, depaato made.
(**h**) From where to where is traffic on Main Street blocked off during the July 4th parade?
独立記念日のパレードの間、大通りは

{どこ/*どちら}から{どこ/*どちら}まで通行止めになるんですか。
*Dokuritsu-kinen-bi no pareedo no aida, oo-doori wa {doko/*dochira} kara {doko/*dochira} made tsuukoo-dome ni naru n desu ka.*

—— conj. **[in, to, or at the place at which]**
Sinf. to⌈koro + prt. Sinf.所+prt.

EX. (**a**) There was a large crater where the meteor had landed.
いん石が落下した所には大きなクレーターがあった。
Inseki ga rakka-shita tokoro ni wa ookina kureetaa ga atta.
(**b**) I put the keys where I always do.
かぎはいつも置く所に置いたよ。
Kagi wa itsu-mo oku tokoro ni oita yo.

where[2] pron. **[a relative pronoun used to introduce a relative clause modifying "place," "area," or other nouns expressing a place]**
ø

EX. (**a**) A: Is this the place where you live?
ここが住んでいる所ですか。
Koko ga sunde iru tokoro desu ka.
B: Yes, it is.
はい、そうです。
Hai, soo desu.
(**b**) This is the house where Soseki Natsume was born.
ここは夏目漱石が生まれた家です。
Koko wa Natsume Sooseki ga umareta ie desu.

NOTE: Japanese has no relative pronouns. In Japanese relative clauses, the modifying sentence is placed immediately in front of the modified noun, with no relative pronoun intervening.

whereas conj. **[but in contrast ⟨w⟩]**
Sinf. no ni ta⌉ishi(te) Sinf.のに対し(て) [in contrast to]

NOTE: When the nonpast affirmative form of adj(*na*). or N + cop. occurs before *no ni taishi(te)*, the form used is adj(*na*). stem + *na* or N *dearu*, respectively.

EX. Japan excels in production technologies, whereas the United States excels in basic research.
日本は生産技術に秀でているのに対して、アメリカは基礎研究に秀でている。
Nihon wa seisan-gijutsu ni hiidete iru no ni taishite, Amerika wa kiso-kenkyuu ni hiidete iru.

wherever conj. **[to, at, or in any place or situation]**
do⌉ko + prt. V*te* mo どこ+prt.V*te*も [to/at any place one does s.t. or s.t. happens], do⌉ko (prt.) demo どこ(prt.)でも [any place]

EX. (**a**) Wherever you go, I know you will succeed.
{どこへ行っても/どこでも}きっと成功しますよ。
{Doko e itte mo/Doko demo} kitto seikoo-shimasu yo.
(**b**) You can sit wherever you like.
{どこでも/?どこに座っても}いいですから、座ってください。
{Doko demo/?Doko ni suwatte mo} ii desu kara, suwatte kudasai.
(**c**) I'll follow you wherever you go.
{あなたが行く所はどこへでも/あなたがどこへ行っても}ついて行きます。
{Anata ga iku tokoro wa doko e demo/Anata ga doko e itte mo} tsuite ikimasu.

whether conj. **[a conjunction indicating an alternative possibility]**
…ka (do⌉o ka) …か(どうか) [if s.t. happens/is done or not], Vvol. to…Vvol. to Vvol.と…Vvol.と [regardless of which of two alternative actions or states occurs], adj(*i*). stem ka⌈ro⌉o to adj(*i*). *ku* na⌈karo⌉o to adj(*i*). stem かろうと adj(*i*). *ku*なかろうと [regardless of if a certain state exists or not], adj(*i*). stem ka⌈ro⌉o to adj(*i*). stem ⌈karo⌉o to adj(*i*). stem かろうとadj(*i*). stem かろうと [regardless of one state existing or another], {adj(*na*). stem/N} {dea⌈ro⌉o/da⌈ro⌉o} to {adj(*na*). stem/N} dea⌈ruma⌉i to {adj(*na*). stem/N}{であろう/だろう}と{adj(*na*). stem/N}であるまいと, {adj(*na*). stem/N} {de⌈aro⌉o/da⌈ro⌉o} to {adj(*na*). stem/N} {de⌈aro⌉o/da⌈ro⌉o} to {adj(*na*).

stem/N}{であろう/だろう}と{adj(*na*). stem/N}{であろう/だろう}と, Vvol. to {Vinf. nonpast/Vstem} ma˥i to Vvol.と{Vinf. nonpast/Vstem}まいと [regardless of if an action/state occurs or not]

NOTE: In "Vvol. *to*...Vvol. *to*," the two verbs may be different, but in "Vvol. *to* {Vinf. nonpast/V*masu*}*-mai to*," the two verbs must be identical. A similar restriction also applies to adjectives and nouns. The form Vinf. nonpast *mai to* is used when the verb is ① or ③.

EX. (**a**) I don't know whether or not I can attend the meeting.
会に出られるかどうか分かりません。
Kai ni de-rareru ka doo ka wakarimasen.
(**b**) I'm not sure whether I can finish this report by next Monday.
来週の月曜日までにこのレポートを書いてしまえるかどうか自信がない。
Raishuu no getsuyoo-bi made ni kono repooto o kaite shimae-ru ka doo ka jishin ga nai.
(**c**) It doesn't matter whether we stay in a hotel or a Japanese-style inn.
ホテルに泊まろうと旅館に泊まろうとかまいません。
Hoteru ni tomaroo to ryokan ni tomaroo to kamaimasen.
(**d**) They train without fail every day whether it's raining or sunny outside.
外が雨{であろう/だろう}と晴れ{であろう/だろう}と、彼らは毎日必ずトレーニングをする。
Soto ga ame {dearoo/daroo} to hare {dearoo/daroo} to, kare-ra wa mai-nichi kanarazu toreeningu o suru.
(**e**) I have to ask you to do this whether you like it or not.
気に入ろうと、入るまいと、これをやってもらわなければなりません。
Ki-ni iroo to, iru-mai to, kore o yatte morawanakereba narimasen.
(**f**) Whether it's easy or hard I still want to give Japanese a try.
日本語は難しかろうと、難しくなかろうと、やってみたい。
Nihon-go wa muzukashikaroo to, muzukashikunakaroo to, yatte mitai.
(**g**) It's an assignment, so whether the book is interesting or boring I still have to read it.
その本は面白かろうと、つまらなかろうと、宿題だから読まなければならない。
Sono hon wa omoshirokaroo to, tsumaranakaroo to, shukudai da kara yomanakereba naranai.
(**h**) Whether I'm healthy or not I have to keep working.
元気{であろう/だろう}と元気でなかろうと、働きつづけなければならない。
Genki {dearoo/daroo} to genki denakaroo to, hataraki-tsuzuke nakereba naranai.
(**i**) Whether the apartment is convenient or not, we still have to live there.
便利{であろう/だろう}と不便{であろう/だろう}とそのアパートに住まなければならない。
Benri {dearoo/daroo} to fuben {dearoo/daroo} to sono apaato ni sumanakereba naranai

which[1] adj. **[what one or ones of a set of two or more possibilities specified by the following noun]**
do˥no N どのN [what one or ones of a set of three or more possibilities specified by the noun] ⟪**what**⟫, **do˥chira no N どちらのN [what one of a set of two possibilities specified by the noun; of or coming from what place or direction ⟨fml⟩]** ⟪**where, what place**⟫, **do˥tchi no N どっちのN** ⟨**s**⟩

EX. (**a**) A: Which car is yours, Bill?
{どの/どちらの/どっちの}車がビルさんのですか。
{Dono/Dochira no/Dotchi no} kuruma ga Biru-san no desu ka.
B: That small car over there.
あの小さい車です。
Ano chiisai kuruma desu.
(**b**) A: Which way are you going?
{どちらの/どっちの/*どの}方へ行きますか。

W

{Dochira no/Dotchi no/*Dono} hoo e ikimasu ka.*
B: I'm going this way.
{こちらの/こっちの/*この}方へ行きます。
*{Kochira no/Kotchi no/*Kono} hoo e ikimasu.*

— pron. **[what one or ones of a set of two or more possibilities]**
do˥re どれ [what one or ones of a set of three or more possibilities], do˥chira どちら [what one of a set of two possibilities; what place or direction], do˥tchi どっち ⟨s⟩, **do˥no hito どの人 [what person], do˥chira no hito どちらの人, do˥tchi no hito どっちの人** ⟨s⟩

EX. (**a**) A: Which do you like better, beer or whiskey?
ビールとウイスキーと{どちら/どっち/*どれ/*どちらの人/*どの人/*どっちの人}が好きですか。
*Biiru to Uisukii to {dochira/dotchi/*dore/*dochira no hito/*dono hito/*dotchi no hito} ga suki desu ka.*
B: I like beer better.
ビールの方が好きです。
Biiru no hoo ga suki desu.
(**b**) A: Which is Mr. Yamamoto, the man in the sweater or the man in the suit?
{どちら/どっち/どれ/どちらの人/どっちの人/どの人}が山本さんですか。セーターを着てる人ですか。背広を着ている人ですか。
{Dochira/Dotchi/Dore/Dochira no hito/Dotchi no hito/Dono hito} ga Yamamoto-san desu ka. Seetaa o kite iru hito desu ka. Sebiro o kite iru hito desu ka.
B: He's the man in the sweater.
セーターを着ている人です。
Seetaa o kite iru hito desu.

which² pron. **[a relative pronoun that takes an inanimate noun as its antecedent]**
ø

EX. (**a**) Did you attend the conference on British-Japanese economic relations which was held in London last March?
去年の三月にロンドンで開かれた日英の経済関係に関する会議に出席しましたか。
Kyonen no san-gatsu ni Rondon de hiraka-reta Nichi-Ei no keizai-kankei ni-kansuru kaigi ni shusseki-shimashita ka.
(**b**) He's using the dictionary which I gave him.
彼は私があげた辞書を使っている。
Kare wa watashi ga ageta jisho o tsukatte iru.

NOTE: Japanese has no relative pronouns. In Japanese relative clauses, the modifying sentence is placed immediately in front of the modified noun, with no relative pronoun intervening.

while n. **[a period of time, esp. that during which s.t. is being done]**
a˥ida 間 [the space between two temporal/spatial points] ⟪interval, midway, time, period, between⟫, **ji˥kan 時間 •c [the continuum from past to present into the future or a subinterval of this during which a state, action, or event occurs or continues ⟪fig. "a counter for hour"⟫]** ⟪hour, time, period⟫

EX. (**a**) I felt better after I slept for a while.
しばらくの{間/*時間}寝て、気分がよくなった。
*Shibaraku no {aida/*jikan} nete, kibun ga yoku natta.*
(**b**) I'd been reading a book for a long while and hadn't noticed that it had gotten dark outside.
{長い間/長時間}本を読んでいたので外が暗くなっていたのに気が付かなかった。
{Nagai aida/Choo-jikan} hon o yonde ita node soto ga kuraku natte ita no ni ki ga tsukanakatta.
(**c**) I haven't seen you in a long while.
長い{間/*時間}会わなかったね。
*Nagai {aida/*jikan} awanakatta ne.*

PHRASE: worth one's while Vinf. *kachi ga aru* Vinf. 価値がある ①

EX. I'm sure that studying Japanese will be worth your while.
日本語の勉強はきっと、する価値がありますよ。
Nihon-go no benkyoo wa kitto, suru kachi ga arimasu yo.

— conj. **[during or in the time that some action or state continues]**

1. Vinf. a⸢ida (ni) Vinf.間(に) [during or in the time that the action or state specified by the verb continues], V*masu* na⸣gara V*masu*ながら [a conjunction indicating that the action expressed by the preceding verb takes place concurrently with the action expressed in the main clause]

NOTE: 1. *Aida*, if followed by the particle *ni*, indicates that the timespan of the event expressed in the main clause falls within the timespan of the event expressed in the *aida*-clause, as in example (a). *Aida* without *ni*, as in example (b), indicates that the two events are assumed to cover the same span of time.
2. The action expressed by V*masu nagara* is always secondary to the action expressed in the main clause. In English, however, the action expressed by "while Ving" is not always secondary to the action of the main clause.

EX. (**a**) While you were out of the room, there was a telephone call from your wife.
部屋を出ていらっしゃる間に奥さんから電話がありました。
Heya o dete irassharu aida ni oku-san kara denwa ga arimashita.
(**b**) I don't think about anything while I swim.
泳いでいる間何も考えていない。
Oyoide iru aida nani-mo kangaete inai.
(**c**) It's not good manners to chew gum while listening to a lecture.
{ガムをかみながら講義を聞く/講義を聞いている間ガムをかむ}のは行儀が悪い。
{Gamu o kami-nagara koogi o kiku/ Koogi o kiite iru aida gamu o kamu} no wa gyoogi ga warui.
(**d**) I have a friend who works more than twenty hours a week while going to class at night.
週に二十時間以上も働きながら、夜学校に通っている友達がいる。
Shuu ni ni-juu-jikan-ijoo mo hataraki-nagara, yoru gakkoo ni kayotte iru tomodachi ga iru.

2. Sinf. ke⸣redo(mo) Sinf.けれど(も) [a disjunctive subordinate conjunction that combines two sentences] 《although, though》

EX. While I admit that he's doing his very best, his grades are still poor.
彼が一生懸命やっていることは認めるけれど(も)、成績はまだ悪い。
Kare ga isshoo-kenmei yatte iru koto wa mitomeru keredo(mo), seiseki wa mada warui.

whip n. **[a strip or cord of leather fastened to a handle used for driving on an animal or punishing a person 《fig. "a blow struck as if with such a strip or cord of leather"》] mu⸣chi むち [a strip of leather or stick of bamboo used for driving on a horse or punishing a person 《fig. "an action or word to encourage or reprimand s.o."》]**

EX. During the war, teachers often used whips to punish students.
戦争中先生は学生を罰するためにむちを使うことが多かった。
Sensoo-chuu sensei wa gakusei o bassuru tame ni muchi o tsukau koto ga ookatta.

— vt. **[for s.o. to strike a person or drive on an animal using a strip or cord or leather 《fig. "stir up"》]**

1. ⟨-o⟩ mu⸣chi de u⸣tsu ⟨〜を⟩むちで打つ ① [for s.o. to strike s.o. with a strip of leather or stick of bamboo]

EX. Don't whip your children. Talk to them.
子供をむちで打ってはいけない。言って聞かせなさい。
Kodomo o muchi de utte wa ikenai. Itte kika-senasai.

2. ⟨-ni⟩ mu⸣chi o atete to⸢basu ⟨〜に⟩むちを

W

当てて飛ばす ① **[for s.o. to drive on an animal using a strip of leather or stick of bamboo]**

EX. The jockey continuously whipped his horse on.
騎手は絶えず馬にむちを当てて飛ばした。
Kishu wa taezu uma ni muchi o atete tobashita.

3. ⟨-o⟩ **a⌈wa-date⌉ru** ⟨〜を⟩泡立てる ② **[to cause foam or bubbles to rise]** **《mix by stirring, heat up》**

EX. First whip the white of the eggs.
先ず卵の白身を泡立てます。
Mazu tamago no shiro-mi o awa-datemasu.

PHRASE: whipped cream *hoippu-kuriimu* ホイップクリーム •f

whirl vi. **[to move rapidly in a circlar motion]**
gu⌉ru-guru ma⌈waru ぐるぐる回る ① **[to move in a repeated circular motion], u⌉zu o ma⌈ku** 渦を巻く ① **[to move rapidly in such a way as to form a spiral]**

EX. (**a**) The sea at Naruto is known for its whirling waters.
鳴門の海は水が{渦を巻く/*ぐるぐるまわる}ので有名だ。
*Naruto no umi wa mizu ga {uzu o maku/*guru-guru mawaru} node yuumei da.*
(**b**) Leaves blown up by the autumn wind whirled in the air.
秋風で舞い上がった枯れ葉が空中で{ぐるぐる回って/渦を巻いて}いた。
Aki-kaze de mai-agatta kare-ha ga kuuchuu de {guru-guru mawatte/uzu o maite} ita.

— vt. **[to cause s.t. to move in a rapid circular motion]**
⟨-o⟩ **gu⌉ru-guru ma⌈wasu** ⟨〜を⟩ぐるぐる回す ① **[for s.o. to cause s.t. to move in a repeated circular motion],** ⟨-ni⟩ **u⌉zu o makasu** ⟨〜に⟩渦を巻かす ① **[to cause s.t. to move rapidly in such a way as to form a spiral]**

EX. (**a**) The cheerleader whirled her baton in the air.
チアリーダーが空中でバトン{をぐるぐる回した/*に渦を巻かせた}。
*Chiariidaa ga kuuchuu de baton {o guru-guru mawashita/*ni uzu o makaseta}.*
(**b**) When I was a boy I used to like to whirl the water around in a tub so fast that the bottom showed.
子供の時おけの中の水{に渦を巻かして/?をぐるぐる回して}底が見えるようにするのが好きだった。
Kodomo no toki oke no naka no mizu {ni uzu o makashite/?o guru-guru mawashite} soko ga mieru yooni suru no ga suki datta.

— n. **[a rapid circular motion or a state of confusion]**
u⌉zu 渦 **[a rapid spiral motion, esp. of liquid or gas 《fig. "turmoil"》], u⌈zu⌉-maki** 渦巻き **[a rapid spiral motion, esp. of liquid or gas]** **《eddy, whirlpool, swirl, spiral》**

EX. (**a**) Look at the whirls in the river.
川の{渦/渦巻き}を見てご覧。
Kawa no {uzu/uzu-maki} o mite goran.
(**b**) Recently I've been caught up in a whirl of activity at the office and for the past several days haven't even been able to break for lunch.
このごろは会社で仕事の{渦/*渦巻き}に翻ろうされて昼休みさえとれない日が続いている。
*Kono-goro wa kaisha de shigoto no {uzu/*uzu-maki} ni honroo-sarete hiru-yasumi sae tore-nai hi ga tsuzuite iru.*

whisker n. **[facial hair, esp. that which grows on the sides of the face]**
ho⌉o-hige ほおひげ

EX. I thought of letting my whiskers grow, but my wife wouldn't hear of it.
ほおひげを伸ばそうと思ったことがあるけど、妻に大反対された。
Hoo-hige o nobasoo to omotta koto ga aru kedo, tsuma ni dai-hantai-sareta.

whiskey n.
u⌈i⌉sukii ウイスキー •f

W

whisper vi. **[for s.o. to speak softly without using the vocal cords 《fig. "for wind to make a quiet, soothing sound"》]**
1. sa⌈sayaku ささやく ① [for s.o. to speak softly with little or no voice] 《murmur》, ko-⌈goe de hana⌉su 小声で話す ① [for s.o. to speak in a low voice]

EX. (**a**) He leaned over and whispered "I love you" softly in her ear.
彼は彼女の方に身を寄せて耳元で「愛してるよ」と低い声で{ささやいた/*小声で話した}。
*Kare wa kanojo no hoo ni mi o yosete mimi-moto de 'Aishite ru yo' to hikui koe de {sasayaita/*ko-goe de hanashita}.*
(**b**) The person sitting next to me suddenly started whispering something to me.
隣に座っている人が、私に急に{小声で何か話し始めた/??何かささやき始めた}。
Tonari ni suwatte iru hito ga, watashi ni kyuuni {ko-goe de nani-ka hanashi-hajimeta/??nani-ka sasayaki-hajimeta}.

2. sa⌉wa-sawa to o⌈to⌉ o ta⌈te⌉ru さわさわと音をたてる ② [for leaves to make a soft sound in the wind]

EX. The leaves of the bamboo trees whispered in the autumn wind.
竹の葉が秋の風にさわさわと音をたてていた。
Take no ha ga aki no kaze ni sawa-sawa to oto o tatete ita.

— n. **[s.t. spoken softly without using the vocal cords 《fig. "rumor"》]**
sa⌈sayaki ささやき /〈V*masu* of *sasayaku* ① whisper/ [the act of speaking softly with little or no voice]

EX. I can't teach when I hear whispers coming from my students.
学生のささやきが聞こえると教えられない。
Gakusei no sasayaki ga kikoeru to oshie-rarenai.

whistle vi. **[to make a shrill sound by blowing or drawing air through a narrow opening]**
fu⌈e o fuku⌉ 笛を吹く ① [for s.o. to play a small wind instrument by blowing], ku⌈chi-bu⌉e o fu⌈ku⌉ 口笛を吹く ① [for s.o. to make a sound by blowing or drawing air through puckered lips]

EX. (**a**) When I whistled, the cat appeared out of nowhere.
私が{笛/口笛}を吹くと、猫がどこからかやってきた。
Watashi ga {fue/kuchi-bue} o fuku to, neko ga doko kara ka yatte kita.
(**b**) The policeman whistled for the man to stop.
警官はその男を止めようと{笛/*口笛}を吹いた。
*Keikan wa sono otoko o tomeyoo to {fue/*kuchibue} o fuita.*

— n. **[a small instrument that produces a shrill sound when blown or a shrill sound produced by blowing or drawing air through a narrow opening]**
fu⌈e 笛 [a small, long wind instrument made of wood, bamboo, or metal which produces a sound or a variety of sounds when blown into, normally high in register] 《flute, pipe》, ku⌈chi-bu⌉e 口笛 [a puckered mouth used as an instrument to produce a shrill sound or the sound thus produced]

EX. (**a**) Start running when I blow the whistle, okay?
僕が{笛/*口笛}を吹いたら、走り始めるんだ。いいね。
*Boku ga {fue/*kuchi-bue} o fuitara, hashiri-hajimeru n da. Ii ne.*
(**b**) When the dog heard his master's whistle, he jumped for joy.
犬は主人の{口笛/?笛}を聞いて、飛び上がって喜んだ。
Inu wa shujin no {kuchi-bue/?fue} o kiite, tobi-agatte yorokonda.

white adj. **[having the color of fresh snow or free from color 《fig. "pale," "innocent," "Caucasian"》]**
1. shi⌈ro⌉i 白い adj(*i*). [having the color of fresh snow 《fig. "not guilty"》] 《fair, blank,

W

spotless, innocent, not guilty⟫ ↔ kuroi 黒い adj(*i*).

EX. Jane is the girl wearing a white sweater and a blue skirt.
ジェーンは白いセーターを着て、青いスカートをはいている女性です。
Jeen wa shiroi seetaa o kite, aoi sukaato o haite iru josei desu.

2. a⌈o-za⌉meta (ka⌈o) 青ざめた(顔) /⟨Vinf. past of *ao-zameru* ② become pale/ [a pale (face)]

EX. When the police arrived, there was an old woman standing at the door, her face white with terror.
警官が着いた時に、恐怖で青ざめた顔の老婦人がドアのところに立っていた。
Keikan ga tsuita toki ni, kyoofu de ao-zameta kao no roo-fujin ga doa no tokoro ni tatte ita.

3. wa⌈ru-gi no na⌉i 悪気のない adj(*i*). **[free from evil thoughts or intentions]**

EX. Even a white lie can have unintended harmful consequences.
悪気のないうそでも思いがけない害を及ぼすことがある。
Waru-gi no nai uso demo omoigakenai gai o oyobosu koto ga aru.

4. ha⌉kujin no N 白人のN •c [Caucasian]

EX. White Americans and black Americans need to make greater efforts to discard their prejudices against each other.
白人のアメリカ人と黒人のアメリカ人は、お互いの偏見を捨てるよう更に努力しなければならない。
Hakujin no Amerika-jin to kokujin no Amerika-jin wa, o-tagai no henken o suteru yoo sarani doryoku-shinakereba naranai.

who¹ pron. **[what or which person or persons]**
da⌉re だれ [what or which person or persons]

EX. (**a**) A: Who's that man talking to the good-looking girl?
きれいな女の子と話しているあの男の人はだれですか。
Kireina onna-no-ko to hanashite iru ano otoko no hito wa dare desu ka.
B: Oh, that's my father.
ああ、あれは父です。
Aa, are wa chichi desu.
(**b**) A: Who wrote *Snow Country*?
『雪国』を書いたのはだれですか。
"Yuki-guni" o kaita no wa dare desu ka.
B: Yasunari Kawabata.
川端康成です。
Kawabata Yasunari desu.
(**c**) A: That's strange—the window's open. I wonder who opened it.
おかしいねえ。窓が開いてる。だれが開けたんだろう。
Okashii nee. Mado ga aite ru. Dare ga aketa n daroo.
B: Oh, sorry. I did.
あ、ごめん。僕が開けたんだ。
A, gomen. Boku ga aketa n da.

who² pron. **[a relative pronoun indicating the subject of a relative clause and taking a person as its antecedent]**
ø

EX. (**a**) Do you remember the instructor who taught us Japanese 20 years ago?
二十年前に日本語を教えてくれた先生のこと覚えてる?
Ni-juu-nen mae ni Nihon-go o oshiete kureta sensei no koto oboete ru?
(**b**) The police caught the burglar who stole the stereo out of my car.
警察は僕の車からステレオを盗んだ泥棒を捕まえた。
Keisatsu wa boku no kuruma kara sutereo o nusunda doroboo o tsukamaeta.
(**c**) I met a guy at a party the other day who had gone to the same high school as I.
この間パーティーで私と同じ高校に行った人に会った。
Kono aida paatii de watashi to onaji kookoo ni itta hito ni atta.

NOTE: Japanese has no relative pronouns. In Japanese relative clauses, the modifying sentence is placed immediately in front of the modified noun, with no relative pronoun intervening.

whoever pron. **[whatever person, any person who]**
1. da⌉re (prt.) demo だれ(prt.)でも [any person]
EX. (**a**) Whoever wants to come is welcome.
だれでも来たい人は歓迎します。
Dare demo kitai hito wa kangei-shimasu.
(**b**) I'll gladly give advice to whoever wants it.
欲しい人にはだれにでも喜んでアドバイスをしてあげます。
Hoshii hito ni wa dare ni demo yorokonde adobaisu o shite agemasu.
2. da⌉re ga…{V/adj./cop.}*te* mo だれが…{V/adj./cop.}*te*も [no matter who does/is s.t.]
EX. Whoever wins the election, it probably won't make much difference to the country's economy.
だれが当選しても、国の経済にはさほど影響はないだろう。
Dare ga toosen-shite mo, kuni no keizai ni wa sahodo eikyoo wa nai daroo.

whole adj. **[entire, having no part missing]**
1. ze⌈ntai no N 全体のN •c [including all parts of s.t. taken together as one] ↔ bubun no N 部分のN •c; zen- 全～ •c [the entire…], maru- まる～ [the entire (numeral counter)] ⟪complete⟫
EX. (**a**) I plan to take part in the marathon even if I can't run the whole distance.
{全体の/全/*まる}行程は走れないにしてもマラソンに参加するつもりだ。
*{Zentai no/Zen-/*Maru-} kootei wa hashire-nai ni shite mo marason ni sanka-suru tsumori da.*
(**b**) It took four whole years to write this novel.
この小説を書くのに{まる/*全体の/*全}四年かかった。
*Kono shoosetsu o kaku no ni {maru-/*zentai no/*zen-} yo-nen kakatta.*
2. ma⌈ru-goto まるごと adv. **[entirely; without being divided into parts] ⟪wholly, bodily⟫**
EX. We cooked the big red snapper whole.
私たちは大きいたいをまるごと料理した。
Watashi-tachi wa ookii tai o maru-goto ryoori-shita.
—— n. **[all the parts together making up s.t.] ze⌈ntai 全体 •c [all the parts of s.t. taken together as one] ⟪the whole body⟫**
EX. The whole of the town knew the mysterious incident.
村全体がその不思議な事件のことを知っていた。
Mura zentai ga sono fushigina jiken no koto o shitte ita.

wholly adv. **[to the entire amount or extent]**
1. ma⌈ttaku 全く [in a manner so strongly that it cannot be described in any other way] ⟪quite, entirely, utterly, completely, thoroughly⟫, ka⌈nzenni 完全に /⟨adj(*na*). *ni* of *kanzenna* complete/ •c [in a way absolutely free from imperfections/ weaknesses] ⟪perfectly, thoroughly, entirely, completely⟫
EX. (**a**) We cannot wholly accept your conditions.
私たちはそちらの条件を{完全に/*全く}受け入れることはできない。
*Watashi-tachi wa sochira no jooken o {kanzenni/*mattaku} uke-ireru koto wa dekinai.*
(**b**) His speech was wholly incomprehensible.
彼の話は{全く/?完全に}分からなかった。
Kare no hanashi wa {mattaku/?kanzenni} wakaranakatta.
(**c**) I wholly agree with you.
私はあなたに{全く/?完全に}賛成だ。
Watashi wa anata ni {mattaku/?kanzenni} sansei da.
(**d**) He is wholly mistaken.
彼は{全く/完全に}間違っている。
Kare wa {mattaku/kanzenni} machigatte iru.
2. ta⌉da ただ [to the exclusion of others]

((merely, simply, solely, alone)), **mo⌉ppara 専ら [single-mindedly, to the exclusion of others]** ((entirely, wholly, solely, exclusively))

EX. They devoted themselves wholly to social work.
彼らは{ただ/専ら}社会事業のために尽くした。
Kare-ra wa {tada/moppara} shakai-jigyoo no tame ni tsukushita.

whom¹ pron. **[the objective form of the interrogative pronoun "who" ⟨fml⟩]**
da⌉re prt. だれ prt. SEE who¹ pron.

EX. (**a**) A: Whom are you looking for?
だれを探しているんですか。
Dare o sagashite iru n desu ka.
B: I'm looking for Prof. Kimura.
木村先生を探しているんです。
Kimura-sensei o sagashite iru n desu.
(**b**) A: Whom did you consult first about the matter?
そのことについてだれに最初に相談したんですか。
Sono koto ni-tsuite dare ni saisho ni soodan-shita n desu ka.
B: My section chief.
課長です。
Kachoo desu.
(**c**) A: Whom are you working for?
だれのために働いているんですか。
Dare no tame ni hataraite iru n desu ka.
B: For my own father.
うちの父です。
Uchi no chichi desu.
(**d**) A: Whom did you receive a letter from?
だれから手紙を受け取ったんですか。
Dare kara tegami o uke-totta n desu ka.
B: From my wife.
妻からです。
Tsuma kara desu.

whom² pron. **[the objective form of the relative pronoun "who" ⟨fml⟩]**
ø SEE who² pron.

EX. (**a**) Remember that Japanese businessman whom we met at the airport?
空港で会ったあの日本人のビジネスマンを覚えていますか。
Kuukoo de atta ano Nihon-jin no bijinesuman o oboete imasu ka.
(**b**) I went out last week with a girl with whom I had worked at the bank.
僕は銀行で一緒に働いていた女の子と先週デートをした。
Boku wa ginkoo de issho ni hataraite ita onna-no-ko to senshuu deeto o shita.
(**c**) Is there anyone whom you can recommend to me as a Japanese language teacher?
日本語の先生として勧められる人がいますか。
Nihon-go no sensei to-shite susume-rareru hito ga imasu ka.

NOTE: Japanese has no relative pronouns. In Japanese relative clauses, the modifying sentence is placed immediately in front of the modified noun, with no relative pronoun intervening.

whose¹ pron. **[the possessive form of the interrogative pronoun "who"]**
da⌉re no N だれのN SEE who¹ pron.

EX. (**a**) A: Whose umbrella is this?
これはだれの傘ですか。
Kore wa dare no kasa desu ka.
B: It's mine.
私のです。
Watashi no desu.
(**b**) A: Whose parents are those?
あの人たちはだれの御両親ですか。
Ano hito-tachi wa dare no go-ryooshin desu ka.
B: They're Tom's.
トムの御両親です。
Tomu no go-ryooshin desu.

whose² pron. **[the possessive form of the relative pronoun "who"]**
ø SEE who² pron.

EX. (**a**) Anyone whose hobby is composing *haiku* is a friend of mine.
俳句を作るのが趣味の人はみんな私の友達です。
Haiku o tsukuru no ga shumi no hito wa minna watashi no tomodachi desu.

(**b**) A child whose parents live long usually also lives long.
両親が長生きすると、大抵その子供も長生きする。
Ryooshin ga naga-iki-suru to, taitei sono kodomo mo naga-iki-suru.

NOTE: Japanese has no relative pronouns. In Japanese relative clauses, the modifying sentence is placed immediately in front of the modified noun, with no relative pronoun intervening.

why adv. **[for what reason or purpose]**

1. na⌉n-de 何で **[for what reason or by what means ⟨s⟩]** **《how come, how》**, **do⌉o-shite** どうして **[for what reason or by what means]** **《how come, how》**, **na⌉ze** なぜ **[for what reason or due to what cause]**

EX. A: Why are you studying Japanese?
{何で/どうして/なぜ}日本語を勉強しているんですか。
{Nan-de/Doo-shite/Naze} Nihon-go o benkyoo-shite iru n desu ka.
B: Because I want to get a good job.
いい仕事につきたいからです。
Ii shigoto ni tsuki-tai kara desu.

2. na⌉n no tame ni 何のために **[for what purpose]**

EX. A: Why are you going all the way to Atlanta for spring break?
春休みに何のためにアトランタまで行くんですか。
Haru-yasumi ni nan no tame ni Atoranta made iku n desu ka.
B: To see my girlfriend.
彼女に会うためです。
Kanojo ni au tame desu.

wick n.

to⌈oshin 灯心 **•c**

wicked adj. **[morally very bad]**

1. yo⌈koshimana よこしまな adj(*na*). **[offending against what is righteous]** **《evil, vicious, dishonest》**, **fu⌈seina** 不正な adj(*na*). **•c [not conforming to what is right]** **《bad, unjust, unfair, foul》**

EX. Most religions teach that a person who does wicked deeds will be punished sooner or later.
大抵の宗教では{よこしまな/不正な}行いをする人は遅かれ早かれ罰せられると教えられている。
Taitei no shuukyoo de wa {yokoshimana/fuseina} okonai o suru hito wa osokare hayakare basse-rareru to oshie-rarete iru.

2. i⌈ji-wa⌉runa 意地悪な adj(*na*). **[ill-tempered and deriving a perverse pleasure from doing unkind things to others, esp. ones weaker than oneself]** **《spiteful, ill-tempered, ill-natured, cantankerous》**

EX. His wicked pranks have earned him the resentment of everyone around him.
彼はその意地悪ないたずらのせいで周りの人全員の反感を買っている。
Kare wa sono iji-waruna itazura no sei de mawari no hito zen'in no hankan o katte iru.

wide adj. **[made up of a large area from side to side]**

1. hi⌈ro⌉i 広い adj(*i*). **[extensive in terms of two-dimensional space, knowledge, or vision]** **《broad, large, extensive, vast, spacious, broad-minded, generous》** ↔ **semai** 狭い adj(*i*).

EX. When I first visited America I was amazed at how wide the roads were.
初めてアメリカを訪れた時道が広いのに驚いた。
Hajimete Amerika o otozureta toki michi ga hiroi no ni odoroita.

2. ha⌈ba ga hi⌈ro⌉i 幅が広い adj(*i*). **[covering a large area from side to side]**, **ha⌈ba-hiro⌉i** 幅広い adj(*i*). **[great in extent 《fig. "broad in the range of one's activities"》]**

EX. (**a**) The cabin of a Boeing 747 is wide enough to seat twelve people across.
ボーイング747はキャビン{の幅が広くて/??が幅広くて}十二人の人が並んで座れるほどだ。
Booingu sebun-foo-sebun wa kyabin {no haba ga hirokute/??ga haba-hirokute} juu-ni-nin no hito ga narande suware-ru hodo da.

W

(**b**) My desk has gotten too small for me. I'll have to buy a wider one.
今の机では狭くなった。もっと{幅が広い/??幅広い}のを買わなくてはいけない。
Ima no tsukue de wa semaku natta. Motto {haba ga hiroi/??haba-hiroi} no o kawanakute wa ikenai.
(**c**) Prof. Sawada is sought after as a lecturer for his wide-ranging expertise in international affairs.
沢田教授は国際関係に関するその{幅広い/幅の広い}専門的知識のため講演者として人気がある。
Sawada-kyooju wa kokusai-kankei ni-kansuru sono {haba-hiroi/haba no hiroi} senmon-teki chishiki no tame kooen-sha to-shite ninki ga aru.

— adv. **[over a large area; to the full extent]**
hi⌉roku 広く /⟨adj(*i*). *ku* of *hiroi* adj(*i*). wide/ ⟪**widely**⟫, **o⌉okiku 大きく /⟨adj(*i*). *ku* of *ookii* adj(*i*). big/**

EX. Open your mouth as wide as you can.
口を出来るだけ{広く/大きく}開けて。
Kuchi o dekiru dake {hiroku/ookiku} akete.

widely adv. **[over a large area; in an extensive manner]**
1. hi⌉roku 広く /⟨adj(*i*). *ku* of *hiroi* wide/
SEE wide adv.

EX. Dr. Chang is widely known for his achievements in the field of biochemistry.
チャン博士は生化学の分野の功績で広く知られている。
Chan-hakase wa sei-kagaku no bun'ya no kooseki de hiroku shira-rete iru.

2. hi⌈jooni 非常に /⟨adj(*na*). *ni* of *hijoona* awful/ •c [to a degree or extent which is much more than average] ⟪**very, extremely, greatly**⟫

EX. Our views on politics differ widely.
私たちの政治に関する意見は非常に違う。
Watashi-tachi no seiji ni-kansuru iken wa hijooni chigau.

widespread adj. **[occurring over a large area or among many people]**
fu⌈kyuu-shita N 普及したN /⟨Vinf. past of *fukyuu-suru* ③ become disseminated/ •c [for a custom or way of thinking to become disseminated] ⟪**diffused, disseminated, propagated**⟫, **fu⌈kyuu-shite iru (N) 普及している(N) /⟨V*te iru* of *fukyuu-suru* ③ become disseminated/ •c**

EX. The use of cell phones became widespread in Japan earlier than it did in the U.S.
携帯電話の使用が普及したのはアメリカより日本の方が先だった。
Keitai-denwa no shiyoo ga fukyuu-shita no wa Amerika yori Nihon no hoo ga saki datta.

widow n. **[a woman whose husband has died and who has not remarried]**
mi⌈bo⌉ojin 未亡人 •c

EX. Poor Doris became a widow at the age of 26 when her husband was killed in an automobile accident.
かわいそうに、ドリスは御主人が自動車事故で亡くなって、二十六歳で未亡人になってしまった。
Kawai-sooni, Dorisu wa go-shujin ga jidoosha-jiko de nakunatte, ni-juu-roku-sai de miboojin ni natte shimatta.

width n. **[the measurement of s.t. from one side to another]**
1. ha⌉ba 幅 [the measurement of s.t. on a dimension at a right angle to its length]

EX. A: What's the size of your kitchen?
キッチンの大きさはどのぐらいですか。
Kitchin no ooki-sa wa dono gurai desu ka.
B: It's four meters in length and two meters in width.
長さは四メートルで、幅は二メートルです。
Naga-sa wa yon-meetoru de, haba wa ni-meetoru desu.

2. hi⌉ro-sa 広さ /⟨adj(*i*). stem of *hiroi* spacious + suf. *sa* ness/ [the extent of the two-dimensional measurements of s.t.; breadth]

W

EX. One of the selling points of this new compact car is the width of its seats.
この新しい小型車は座席の広さが売り物だ。
Kono atarashii kogata-sha wa zaseki no hiro-sa ga uri-mono da.

wife n. **[a woman married to s.o.]**
tsu⌉ma 妻 [the female member of a married couple, used as a legal term or by the husband], ka⌉nai 家内 [a humble term used to refer to one's own female partner in a marriage], o⌉ku-san 奥さん [a polite term of address used to refer to the female partner in s.o. else's marriage], o⌉ku-sama 奥様 [a very polite term of address used to refer to the female partner in s.o. else's marriage]

EX. (**a**) This is my wife, Yoshiko.
{妻/家内/*奥さん/*奥様}の良子です。
*{Tsuma/Kanai/*Oku-san/*Oku-sama} no Yoshiko desu.*
(**b**) A: How is your wife?
{奥さん/奥様/*妻/*家内}はお元気ですか。
*{Oku-san/Oku-sama/*Tsuma/*Kanai} wa o-genki desu ka.*
B: Fine, thank you.
はい、おかげ様で。
Hai, o-kage-sama de.

PHRASE: man/husband and wife *fuufu* 夫婦 •c

EX. I now pronounce you man and wife.
あなたがたが夫婦であることをここに宣言します。
Anata-gata ga fuufu dearu koto o koko ni sengen-shimasu.

wild adj. **[occurring or existing in a natural state; not tamed, civilized, or disciplined]**
1. ya⌈sei no N 野生のN •c [growing or living in a natural state] ⟪ferine, feral, savage, undomesticated, uncultivated⟫, no- 野～ [growing as a plant in a natural state]

EX. (**a**) Have you ever seen a wild horse?
{野生の/*野}馬を見たことがありますか。
*{Yasei no/*No-} uma o mita koto ga arimasu ka.*
(**b**) Have you ever eaten wild strawberries?
{野生の/野}いちごを食べたことがありますか。
{Yasei no/No-} ichigo o tabeta koto ga arimasu ka.

2. shi⌈zen no mama⌉ no N 自然のままのN [existing in a natural, unchanged state]

EX. I love to spend time alone in the wild surroundings of the outdoors.
戸外の自然のままの環境の中で一人で時間を過ごすのが好きだ。
Kogai no shizen no mama no kankyoo no naka de hitori de jikan o sugosu no ga suki da.

3. ya⌈banna 野蛮な adj(*na*). **•c [having a natural and uncivilized character] ⟪savage, barbarous, unrefined, uncivilized, untamed⟫**

EX. Even modern man has a wild nature in him that cannot be fully suppressed by civilization.
現代人も文明によって抑え切れない、野蛮な性質を有している。
Gendai-jin mo bunmei ni-yotte osae-kire-nai yabanna seishitsu o yuushite iru.

4. ra⌈nboona 乱暴な adj(*na*). **•c [rough and careless in one's words, actions, or behavior] ⟪violent, rude, rough, hard, outrageous⟫**

EX. My husband tends to get a bit wild when he drinks.
夫はお酒が入ると、少しばかり乱暴になるところがあるんです。
Otto wa o-sake ga hairu to, sukoshi bakari ranbooni naru tokoro ga aru n desu.

5. ha⌈ge⌉shiku ko⌈ofun-shita N 激しく興奮したN /⟨Vinf. past of *hageshiku koofun-suru* ③ become very excited/ [for s.o./s.a. to be frantically excited], ha⌈ge⌉shiku ko⌈ofun-shite iru (N) 激しく興奮している(N) /⟨V *te iru* of *hageshiku koofun-suru* ③ become very excited/ ② [for s.o./s.a. to be frantically excited]

EX. When my cat saw the bird, it went wild.
うちの猫は鳥を見て、激しく興奮した。
Uchi no neko wa tori o mite, hageshiku koofun-shita.

W

wild boar n.
i⌈noshi⌉shi いのしし

EX. In Japan, the wild boar is considered to represent recklessness because of its tendency to dash straight forward at full speed.
全力でまっすぐ走る習性から、いのししは日本では向こう見ずの象徴とされている。
Zenryoku de massugu hashiru shuusei kara, inoshishi wa Nihon de wa mukoo-mizu no shoochoo to sarete iru.

wilderness n. **[an uncultivated, uninhabited area of land in its natural state]**
ge⌉n'ya 原野 •c [an uncultivated field] ((wasteland, moor)), a⌈re-chi 荒れ地 [an uncultivated, barren land] ((wasteland, barren land)), sa⌈baku 砂漠 •c [a large, barren area of rock and sand] ((desert))

EX. We flew for hours over the vast wilderness of the Sahara.
アフリカのサハラの広大な{原野/荒れ地/砂漠}の上を何時間も飛び続けた。
Afurika no Sahara no koodaina {gen'ya/are-chi/sabaku} no ue o nan-jikan-mo tobi-tsuzuketa.

wildlife n. **[animals living in their natural, undomesticated state]**
ya⌈sei-se⌉ibutsu 野生生物 •c

EX. I'd like to go to Africa to see the wildlife there.
野生生物を見にアフリカに行きたい。
Yasei-seibutsu o mini Afurika ni iki-tai.

will aux. **[an auxiliary verb indicating the speaker's judgment about the occurrence of a future event or state or intention to do s.t. in the future]**
1. Sinf. {da⌈ro⌉o/de⌈sho⌉o} Sinf.{だろう/でしょう} [an auxiliary indicating the speaker's conjecture about the occurrence of an event or state in the past, present, or future which is not based on any particular information or evidence] ((probably))

NOTE: *Daroo* is an informal version of *deshoo*. When the nonpast affirmative form of adj(*na*). or N + cop. appears before *daroo* or *deshoo*, the form used is adj(*na*). stem or N, respectively.

EX. (**a**) I'm sure the rain will stop soon.
雨はきっともうすぐやむ{だろう/でしょう}。
Ame wa kitto moo sugu yamu {daroo/deshoo}.
(**b**) I'm sure you'll find Japanese interesting.
日本語はあなたにとって面白い{だろう/でしょう}。
Nihon-go wa anata ni-totte omoshiroi {daroo/deshoo}.
(**c**) If another world war breaks out, it'll be the end of the world.
もし世界大戦がまた起きれば、世界は滅びる{だろう/でしょう}。
Moshi sekai-taisen ga mata okireba, sekai wa horobiru {daroo/deshoo}.

2. ø, Vinf. nonpast tsu⌈mori da Vinf. nonpastつもりだ [for s.o. to propose in his/her mind ahead of time to do s.t.] ((intend to)), Vvol. to o⌈mo⌉u Vvol.と思う ① [for s.o. to determine in his/her mind to do s.t.]

NOTE: When the nonpast affirmative form of adj(*na*). or N + cop. occurs before *tsumori da*, the form used is adj(*na*). stem + *na* or N *no*, respectively.

EX. I'll accept the job if it's offered to me.
もしその仕事の話が私の所に来たら{引き受けます/引き受けるつもりです/引き受けようと思います}。
Moshi sono shigoto no hanashi ga watashi no tokoro ni kitara {hiki-ukemasu/hiki-ukeru tsumori desu/hiki-ukeyoo to omoimasu}.

PHRASE: Will you...? *{Vneg./Vstem/ko/shi} nai?* {Vneg./Vstem/来/し}ない?, V*masu masen ka* V*masu*ませんか, Will you...for me? V*te {kureru?/kudasaru?/kure/kudasai}* {くれる?/くださる?/くれ/ください}

NOTE: *Kureru* and *kure* are informal versions of *kudasaru* and *kudasai*, respectively. *Kudasaru* and *kure* are used by female and male speakers, respectively.

EX. (**a**) A: Will you come see me this weekend?
今週末、遊びに来ませんか。
Konshuu-matsu, asobi ni kimasen ka.

W

B: With pleasure.
ええ、喜んで伺います。
Ee, yorokonde ukagaimasu.
(**b**) A: Will you answer this letter for me?
この手紙の返事、書いて{くれる?/くださる?/くれ。/ください。}
Kono tegami no henji, kaite {kureru?/kudasaru?/kure./kudasai.}
B: Certainly.
かしこまりました。
Kashikomarimashita.

3. ø [a zero auxiliary (no auxiliary attached to the verb) indicating that an event or action occurs habitually or universally]

EX. (**a**) No matter how sad you may be now, time will heal your sorrows.
どんなに悲しくても(悲しみを)時間がいやしてくれるよ。
Donnani kanashikute mo, (kanashi-mi o) jikan ga iyashite kureru yo.
(**b**) Drink wine and the truth will come out.
酒が入れば、本音が出る。
Sake ga haireba, honne ga deru.

— n. **[the mental ability to decide to do s.t. and act accordingly]**

1. i˥shi 意志 •c [the mental faculty by which one determines a course of action for oneself and directs one's efforts toward that end] ((volition, intention purpose)), ki 気 •c [an energy that permeates the body and soul of every living being] ((spirit, mind, soul))

NOTE: *Ishi* is usually written as 意志 but may also alternatively be written as 意思, especially in legal documents.

EX. (**a**) Where there's a will, there's a way.
{意志/*気}があれば、出来る。
*{Ishi/*Ki} ga areba, dekiru.*
(**b**) Do you have the will to quit smoking?
たばこをやめる{意志/気}がありますか。
Tabako o yameru {ishi/ki} ga arimasu ka.

2. ke˥tsui 決意 •c [the act of setting one's mind to follow a particular course of action or to adopt a particular attitude toward s.t.] ((resolution, determination)), ke˥sshin 決心 •c [the act of making up one's mind firmly to take a particular course of action] ((determination, resolution))

EX. My son is set in his will to become a doctor and won't be persuaded otherwise.
医者になろうという息子の{決意/決心}は固くて、反対の意見には耳を貸そうともしない。
Isha ni naroo to iu musuko no {ketsui/kesshin} wa katakute, hantai no iken ni wa mimi o kasoo to mo shinai.

willing adj. **[ready or wanting to do s.t. of one's own choice]**
su˥sunde V 進んでV [readily of one's own initiative or volition], yo˥roko˥nde V 喜んでV [with pleasure]

EX. My math teacher was always willing to help me whenever I had trouble solving a problem.
数学の先生は僕が問題を解けなかった時はいつでも{進んで/喜んで}手伝ってくださった。
Suugaku no sensei wa boku ga mondai o toke-nakatta toki wa itsu demo {susunde/yorokonde} tetsudatte kudasatta.

willow n.
ya˥nagi 柳

win vi. **[for s.o./s.a. to gain victory in a race, contest, or war]**
⟨-ni⟩ ka˥tsu ⟨〜に⟩勝つ ① [for s.o./s.a. to fight against and gain victory over an enemy or opponent] ((gain a victory, be a winner, overcome, defeat, beat)) ↔ makeru 負ける ②

EX. (**a**) Bill won in a game of chess with Paul.
ビルはチェスでポールに勝った。
Biru wa chesu de Pooru ni katta.
(**b**) In the Olympic Games winning is said to be secondary in importance to participating.
オリンピック競技では勝つことより参加することが大事だと言われている。
Orinpikku-kyoogi de wa katsu koto yori sanka-suru koto ga daiji da to iwa-rete iru.

W

— vt. **[for s.o./s.a. to gain victory in a race, contest, or war or to gain s.t. of value as a result of great effort]**
1. 〈**-ni**〉 **ka⌉tsu** 〈～に〉**勝つ** ① **[for s.o./s.a. to fight against and gain victory over an enemy or opponent]** SEE win vi.

EX. (**a**) He won the bet with his friends on the soccer match.
彼はサッカーの試合をめぐる友達とのかけに勝った。
Kare wa sakkaa no shiai o meguru tomodachi to no kake ni katta.
(**b**) It's impossible to tell who will win the presidential election.
だれが大統領選挙に勝つか全く予想がつかない。
Dare ga daitooryoo-senkyo ni katsu ka mattaku yosoo ga tsukanai.

2. 〈**-o**〉 **ka⌈chi-toru** 〈～を〉**勝ち取る** ① **[for s.o. to gain s.t. of value as a result of great effort]**, 〈**-o**〉 **ka⌈kutoku-suru** 〈～を〉**獲得する** ⓪ **•c [for s.o. to succeed in getting hold of s.t. abstract or of value through effort]** ⟪**gain, acquire, obtain, secure**⟫

EX. (**a**) Julie won first prize in the Japanese speech contest.
ジュリーは日本語のスピーチコンテストで一等賞を{勝ち取った/獲得した}。
Jurii wa Nihon-go no supiichi kontesuto de it-too-shoo o {kachi-totta/kakutoku-shita}.
(**b**) I was on cloud nine when I won her hand in marriage.
彼女の結婚の承諾を{勝ち取った/?獲得した}時には、僕は天にも昇る気持ちだった。
Kanojo no kekkon no shoodaku o {kachi-totta/?kakutoku-shita} toki ni wa, boku wa ten ni mo noboru kimochi datta.
(**c**) She won the prize money at the golf tournament.
彼女はゴルフトーナメントで賞金を{獲得した/*勝ち取った}。
*Kanojo wa gorufu-toonamento de shookin o {kakutoku-shita/*kachi-totta}.*

— n. **[victory in a race or contest]**
sho⌉ori 勝利 •c ⟪**victory, triumph**⟫

EX. We celebrated our win by throwing a big party.
盛大なパーティーをして勝利を祝った。
Seidaina paatii o shite shoori o iwatta.

wind¹ n. **[a movement of air in the atmosphere, usu. created by natural forces ⟪fig. "destructive force," "direction"⟫]**
1. ka⌉ze 風 [a natural movement of air in the atmosphere ⟪fig. "a cold, as if caused by a cold draft of air drawn into the body"⟫]
㊤ "natural movement of air"▷風, "cold"▷風邪

EX. A strong, cold wind was blowing from the north.
強くて冷たい風が北から吹いていた。
Tsuyokute tsumetai kaze ga kita kara fuite ita.

2. do⌈okoo 動向 •c [the direction in which s.t. is moving, esp. the psychology of a social group] ⟪**tendency, trend, movement**⟫, **ke⌈ikoo 傾向 •c [a natural propensity to develop or act in a certain way]** ⟪**tendency, trend, drift**⟫

EX. It's very difficult to divine the political winds currently blowing in the country.
この国の現在の政治的{動向/傾向}は大変つかみにくい。
Kono kuni no genzai no seiji-teki {dookoo/keikoo} wa taihen tsukami-nikui.

wind² vi. **[to move in a curving motion back and forth or along a twisting course, esp. around another object]**
1. ma⌈gari-kune⌉tte na⌈gare⌉ru 曲がりくねって流れる ② **[for a body of water such as a river to flow in a meandering way]** ⟪**meander, curve**⟫

EX. A river winds through the center of town.
川が町の中を曲がりくねって流れている。
Kawa ga machi no naka o magari-kunette nagarete iru.

2. 〈**-ni**〉 **ma⌈ki-tsu⌉ku** 〈～に〉**巻き付く** ① **[for s.t. to become coiled around s.t. else]** ⟪**coil around, twine around**⟫, 〈**-ni**〉 **ka⌈ra⌉mi-tsuku**

〈〜に〉絡み付く ① **[for a narrow and long object to twine around s.t.] 《twine around, cling》**

EX. (**a**) The morning glory vine wound around the bamboo pole.
朝顔のつるが竹の棒に{巻き付いた/絡み付いた}。
Asagao no tsuru ga take no boo ni {maki-tsuita/karami-tsuita}.
(**b**) The snake wound around the leg of the dozing camper.
蛇が昼寝をしているキャンパーの足に{巻き付いた/絡み付いた}。
Hebi ga hiru-ne o shite iru kyanpaa no ashi ni {maki-tsuita/karami-tsuita}.

— vt. **[for s.o. to cause s.t. to wrap around itself or s.t. else 《fig. "tighten the spring which powers a device"》]**

1. 〈-o〉〈-ni〉 ma⌈ki-tsuke⌉ru 〈〜を〉〈〜に〉巻き付ける ② **[for s.o. to coil s.t. around s.t. else] 《twine/coil s.t. around s.t. else》**

EX. The nurse wound the bandage around my foot.
看護婦は包帯を僕の足に巻き付けた。
Kango-fu wa hootai o boku no ashi ni maki-tsuketa.

2. (to⌈kei no) ne⌉ji o ma⌈ku (時計の)ねじを巻く ① **[for s.o. to tighten the spring of a watch]**

EX. This watch is battery-operated, so it doesn't need to be wound.
この時計は電池で動くから、ねじを巻かなくてもいいんです。
Kono tokei wa denchi de ugoku kara, neji o makanakute mo ii n desu.

PHRASE: wind down *kutsurogu* 寛ぐ ① 《make onself comfortable, relax, unbend oneself》

EX. I like to wind down after a long day at work with a good book.
一日中仕事をした後では、本を読んで寛ぐのが好きです。
Ichi-nichi-juu shigoto o shita ato de wa, hon o yonde kutsurogu no ga suki desu.

windmill n. **[a tower-like building containing a machine powered by the action of the wind on a rotating set of sails attached to its top]**
fu⌈usha 風車 **•c**

EX. Holland is known for its many windmills.
オランダは風車が多いので知られている。
Oranda wa fuusha ga ooi no de shira-rete iru.

window n. **[an opening in the wall or roof of a house to let in light and air, usu. fitted with framed glass, or an opening resembling this]**

1. ma⌉do 窓 **[an opening in the wall or roof of a house to let in light and air, usu. fitted with framed glass]**

EX. (**a**) Could you open the window, please?
窓を開けてくださいませんか。
Mado o akete kudasaimasen ka.
(**b**) I don't like rooms without windows. They make me feel claustrophobic.
窓のない部屋は嫌いです。閉じ込められたような気持ちになるので。
Mado no nai heya wa kirai desu. Toji-kome-rareta yoona kimochi ni naru node.
(**c**) The eyes are often called the windows of the mind.
目は心の窓だとよく言われる。
Me wa kokoro no mado da to yoku iwa-reru.

2. ma⌈do⌉-guchi 窓口 **[an opening through which some transaction takes place] 《wicket》**

EX. A: Where can I buy a season pass for the bus?
バスの定期券はどこで買えますか。
Basu no teiki-ken wa doko de kaemasu ka.
B: Please go to window 5.
五番の窓口に行ってください。
Go-ban no mado-guchi ni itte kudasai.

windshield n. **[the glass in the forward window of a motor vehicle]**
fu⌈ronto-ga⌉rasu フロントガラス **•f**

EX. Many injuries are caused in automobile accidents by people hitting their heads against windshields.

自動車事故で頭をフロントガラスにぶつけてけがをする人が多い。
Jidoosha-jiko de atama o furonto-garasu ni butsukete kega o suru hito ga ooi.

PHRASE: windshield wiper *waipaa* ワイパー •f

EX. The windshield wipers on my car are getting worn out and make a terrible noise each time I use them.
私の車のワイパーが古くなって、使うたびにひどい音がする。
Watashi no kuruma no waipaa ga furuku natte, tsukau tabi ni hidoi oto ga suru.

windy adj. **[having or exposed to much (high) wind]**

1. ka⌈ze ga tsuyo⌉i 風が強い adj(*i*). **[having strong winds]**

EX. It's windy today, isn't it?
今日は風が強いですね。
Kyoo wa kaze ga tsuyoi desu ne.

2. ka⌈ze-atari ga tsuyo⌉i 風あたりが強い adj(*i*). **[exposed to much (strong) wind ⟪fig. "exposed to sharp criticism"⟫]**

EX. The mountain peak was so windy I could hardly keep standing.
山の頂上は風あたりが強くて、立っていられないほどだった。
Yama no choojoo wa kaze-atari ga tsuyokute, tatte i-rarenai hodo datta.

wine n. **[an alcoholic beverage made from fermented grapes]**

bu⌈do⌉o-shu ぶどう酒, wa⌉in ワイン •f

EX. (**a**) Which do you prefer, wine or beer?
{ぶどう酒/ワイン}とビールと、どちらがお好きですか。
{Budoo-shu/Wain} to biiru to, dochira ga o-suki desu ka.
(**b**) I'd like to have some white wine with my fish.
魚料理といっしょに{白ぶどう酒/ホワイトワイン}が飲みたいです。
Sakana-ryoori to issho ni {shiro-budoo-shu/howaito-wain} ga nomi-tai desu.

PHRASE: rice wine *sake* 酒

EX. Have you ever had rice wine?
酒を飲んだことがありますか。
Sake o nonda koto ga arimasu ka.

wing n. **[one of the movable body parts of a bird or insect used in flying or s.t. similar to this in shape or function]**

1. tsu⌈basa 翼 [one/both of the projecting feathered parts of a bird used in flying or a similar part of an airplane], ha⌈ne 羽 [one/all of the coverings that grow from a bird's skin or one/both of a pair of projecting structures by which a bird/airplane flies] ⟪feather, plume⟫

EX. (**a**) A crane's wings look particularly beautiful when it is flying through falling snow.
鶴の{翼/羽}は雪の中を飛ぶ時特に美しい。
Tsuru no {tsubasa/hane} wa yuki no naka o tobu toki tokuni utsukushii.
(**b**) The wings on this plane are each about 10 meters long.
この飛行機の{翼/?羽}はそれぞれ十メートルぐらいです。
Kono hikoo-ki no {tsubasa/?hane} wa sore-zore juu-meetoru-gurai desu.

2. so⌈de そで [the part of a piece of clothing that covers the arms or a part of s.t. such as a building, chair, or highway which extends to either side of the main part] ⟪sleeve⟫, u⌈i⌉ngu ウイング •f [the parts of a building extending symmetrically to the right and left]

EX. My office is in the right wing of this building.
私の事務所はこの建物の右{袖/ウイング}にあります。
Watashi no jimu-sho wa kono tate-mono no migi-{sode/uingu} ni arimasu.

wink vi. **[for s.o. to close and open one eye quickly, esp. as a signal of affection to s.o.]**
u⌈i⌉nku-suru ウインクする ③ •f [for s.o. to close and open one eye quickly, esp. as a signal to catch the attention of a member of the opposite sex]

EX. A young guy sitting across from me on the bus winked at me.
バスの中で向かいに座っていた男の子

W

が私にウインクした。
Basu no naka de mukai ni suwatte ita otoko-no-ko ga watashi ni uinku-shita.

—— n. [a quick closing and opening movement of the eye]
ma⌈ba⌉taki まばたき /⟨V*masu* of *mabataku* ① wink/ [a quick closing and opening movement of the eye], u⌈i⌉nku ウインク •f

winner n. [a person who gains victory in a race or contest]
1. yu⌈usho⌉o-sha 優勝者 •c [a person who receives first prize in a competition] ⟪victor, champion⟫
EX. The winner of the tennis match received $50,000.
テニスの試合の優勝者は五万ドルもらった。
Tenisu no shiai no yuushoo-sha wa go-man-doru moratta.
2. ju⌈sho⌉o-sha 受賞者 •c [a person who receives a prize in a competition]
EX. There will be a lecture tomorrow by last year's winner of the Nobel Peace Prize.
去年のノーベル平和賞の受賞者による講演会が明日開かれます。
Kyonen no Nooberu-heiwa-shoo no jushoo-sha ni-yoru kooen-kai ga asu hiraka-remasu.

winter n. [the season between autumn and spring]
fu⌈yu⌉ 冬
EX. (**a**) A: How are the winters here?
ここの冬はどうですか。
Koko no fuyu wa doo desu ka.
B: They're very cold.
大変寒いですよ。
Taihen samui desu yo.
(**b**) A: When does winter vacation start?
冬休みはいつ始まりますか。
Fuyu-yasumi wa itsu hajimarimasu ka.
B: It starts on December 22.
十二月二十二日に始まります。
Juu-ni-gatsu ni-juu-ni-nichi ni hajimarimasu.

wipe vt. [to remove s.t. from a surface by rubbing s.t. over it ⟪fig. "blot out s.t. from one's memory"⟫]
⟨-o⟩ fu⌈ku ⟨〜を⟩ふく ① [for s.o. to rub a surface with cloth or paper to clean it] ⟪mop, swab⟫, nu⌈gu⌉u ぬぐう ① [for s.o. to rub a dirty spot or object off a surface with s.t. soft ⟪fig. "blot out"⟫] ⟪mop⟫
EX. (**a**) You're sweating. Here—use this handkerchief to wipe your forehead.
汗をかいていますよ。どうぞ、このハンカチで額を{ふいて/ぬぐって}ください。
Ase o kaite imasu yo. Doozo, kono hankachi de hitai o {fuite/nugutte} kudasai.
(**b**) I wiped my car with a soft cloth after washing it.
車を洗ってから柔らかい布で{ふいた/?ぬぐった}。
Kuruma o aratte kara yawarakai nuno de {fuita/?nugutta}.
(**c**) God will in his mercy wipe away all your sins.
神は慈悲深いのであなたの罪をすべて{ぬぐって/*ふいて}くれます。
*Kami wa jihi-bukai node anata no tsumi o subete {nugutte/*fuite} kuremasu.*

wire n. [a flexible metal thread ⟪fig. "telegraph"⟫]
1. ha⌈rigane 針金 [a metalic thread]
EX. My shirt sleeve got caught on a wire.
シャツの袖が針金に引っ掛かってしまった。
Shatsu no sode ga harigane ni hikkakatte shimatta.
2. de⌈nsen 電線 •c [an electric power line]
EX. Three sparrows were perched on a telephone wire.
すずめが三羽、電線に止まっていた。
Suzume ga san-ba, densen ni tomatte ita.
3. de⌈npoo 電報 •c [a telegram]
EX. I sent a wire to my friend on his wedding day.

W

結婚式の日に友達に電報を打った。
Kekkon-shiki no hi ni tomodachi ni denpoo o utta.

—— vt. [to use a flexible metal wire thread for some purpose ⟪fig. "send a telegram"⟫]
1. ⟨-ni⟩ ha⌈rigane o tsukau ⟨〜に⟩針金を使う ① [for s.o. to use a flexible metal wire for some purpose]
EX. I wired the loose shutter down.
外れそうになっていたシャッターを、針金を使ってしっかり留めた。
Hazure-sooni natte ita shattaa o, harigane o tsukatte shikkari tometa.
2. de⌈npoo o u⌉tsu 電報を打つ ① [for s.o. to send a telegram]

Wisconsin n.
U⌈isuko⌉nshin ウイスコンシン •f [the State of Wisconsin]

wisdom n. **[intelligence and sound judgment, esp. regarding what is right and wrong or an action or saying based on such judgment]**
chi⌈e 知恵 •c [the mental ability to understand the logic of things and to distinguish between good and evil] ⟪sense, wits, sagacity, intelligence⟫, ke⌈nmei-sa 賢明さ •c /⟨adj(*na*). stem of *kenmeina* wise + suf. *sa* ness⟩/ [the quality of being knowledgeable and having good judgment about the logic of things] ⟪intelligence, sagacity, judiciousness⟫
EX. You cannot buy wisdom; you have to earn it through experience.
{知恵/賢明さ}を買うことは出来ない。経験を通して身に付けなければならない。
{Chie/Kenmei-sa} o kau koto wa dekinai. Keiken o tooshite mi ni tsukenakereba naranai.
PHRASE: good wisdom *kashikoi okonai* 賢い行い
EX. It is good wisdom to put health first.
健康第一にすることは賢い行いだ。
Kenkoo dai-ichi ni suru koto wa kashikoi okonai da.

wise adj. **[having intelligence and sound judgment, esp. regarding what is right and wrong]**
ka⌈shiko⌉i 賢い adj(*i*). [outstanding in talent, intelligence, or judgment] ⟪intelligent, sagacious, clever, bright⟫ ↔ bakana ばかな adj(*na*)., orokana おろかな adj(*na*).; ke⌈nmeina 賢明な adj(*na*). •c [knowledgeable and having sound judgment in making decisions] ⟪intelligent, sagacious, judicious⟫ ↔ orokana おろかな adj(*na*).
EX. (**a**) It would be wise to have your children begin their study of foreign languages at an early age.
子供に小さい時から外国語の勉強を始めさせるのは{賢い/賢明だ}。
Kodomo ni chiisai toki kara gaikoku-go no benkyoo o hajime-saseru no wa {kashikoi/kenmei da}.
(**b**) I think he's a wise enough person not to offend his boss.
あの人は{賢い/賢明な}人だから、上役の気を悪くさせるようなことはしないと思う。
Ano hito wa {kashikoi/kenmeina} hito da kara, uwa-yaku no ki o waruku saseru yoona koto wa shinai to omou.
(**c**) It was a wise decision of yours to stop smoking.
たばこをやめることにしたのは{賢明な/賢い}決断だ。
Tabako o yameru koto ni shita no wa {kenmeina/kashikoi} ketsudan da.

wish vt. **[for s.o. to desire s.t. to happen or desire to do s.t.]**
1. ({⟨-ga⟩/⟨-o⟩}) V*masu* ta⌉i ({⟨〜が⟩/⟨〜を⟩}) V*masu*たい adj(*i*). [for the speaker/listener to have a desire to do s.t.]
NOTE: *-tai* is an auxiliary adjective which expresses the desire of the speaker to do s.t. or, in a question, asks what the listener desires to do. The topic noun with *wa*, when it occurs in this construction is either the first/second person singular or s.o. with whom the speaker identifies closely.
EX. (**a**) I wish to make an appointment with the Director of the Center for Japanese Studies.

日本研究センターの所長との面会を申し込みたいのですが。
Nihon Kenkyuu Sentaa no shochoo to no menkai o mooshi-komi-tai no desu ga.
(**b**) I wish to see Mt. Fuji during my stay in Japan.
私は日本にいる間に富士山が見たいと思います。
Watashi wa nihon ni iru aida ni Fuji-san ga mi-tai to omoimasu.

2. ⟨-o⟩ V*masu* ta-ˈgaˈru ⟨～を⟩V*masu*たがる ① [for a third person to show signs of desiring to do s.t.]

EX. Mr. Smith wishes to become a computer programmer.
スミスさんはコンピュータープログラマーになりたがっている。
Sumisu-san wa konpyuutaa puroguramaa ni nari-ta-gatte iru.

3. ⟨-ni⟩ V*te* morai-tai ⟨～に⟩V*te*もらいたい adj(*i*). **[for s.o. to want s.o. else to do s.t.]**

EX. I wish my son to become a doctor.
私は息子に医者になってもらいたい。
Watashi wa musuko ni isha ni natte morai-tai.

4. Vinf. nonpast {no o/koˈtoˈ o/yoˈoni} iˈnoˈru Vinf. nonpast{のを/ことを/ように}祈る ① [for s.o. to pray that s.t. favorable will happen] ⟪**pray**⟫

EX. I wish you good luck on your exam.
試験がうまく行く{のを/ことを/ように}祈っているよ。
Shiken ga umaku iku {no o/koto o/yoonI} inotte iru yo.

PHRASE: I wish you a happy new year. *Shinnen omedetoo (gozaimasu).* 新年おめでとう(ございます)。, *Akemashite omedetoo (gozaimasu).* 明けましておめでとう(ございます)。

NOTE: The above new year's greetings should only be used after the new year has actually arrived. Prior to midnight on December 31, the new year's greeting which should be used is *Yoi o-toshi o (o-mukae kudasai).* よいお年を(お迎えください)。.

5. Sinf. past ra iˈi {n da ke(re)do/noˈni} Sinf. pastらいい{んだけ(れ)ど/のに} [a conditional expression indicating a desire for s.t. which is currently not the case (a counterfactual desire)], Sinf. past ra naˈa Sinf. pastらなあ

EX. (**a**) I wish I were brighter than I am.
もっと頭がよかったら{いいんだけ(れ)ど/いいのに/なあ}。
Motto atama ga yokattara {ii n da ke(re)do/ii noni/naa}.
(**b**) I wish I could go to Japan this summer.
今年の夏日本へ行けたら{いいんだけ(れ)ど/いいのに/なあ}。
Kotoshi no natsu Nihon e ike-tara {ii n da ke(re)do/ii noni/naa}.
(**c**) I wish I were healthy again.
また元気になれたら{いいんだけ(れ)ど/いいのに/なあ}。
Mata genki ni naretara {ii n da ke(re)do/ii noni/naa}.

— n. **[a strong feeling of desiring s.t. or s.t. that is strongly desired]**

1. noˈzomi 望み /⟨V*masu* of *nozomu* ① hope for/ [an indication or desire of future success] ⟪**desire, expectation, hopes, chances, prospects**⟫, **kiˈboo 希望 •c [s.t. which one desires will happen in the future or desiring that s.t. in the future will turn out a certain way]**

EX. My wish is to get well and to start working again.
私の{望み/希望}は元気になって、また働き始めることです。
Watashi no {nozomi/kiboo} wa genki ni natte, mata hataraki-hajimeru koto desu.

2. neˈgaˈi 願い /⟨V*masu* of *negau* ① request/ [an act/instance of asking s.o. or God for s.t. or asking s.o. or God to do s.t.] ⟪**desire, hope, request, petition**⟫

EX. My wish is to get a good job.
私の願いはいい仕事をもらうことです。
Watashi no negai wa ii shigoto o morau koto desu.

witch n. **[a woman who practices sorcery] maˈjo 魔女 •c** ⟪**she-devil, she-demon**⟫

with prep. **[in the company or care of s.o.; in a (mutual) action involving s.o.; by means of s.t.; having or characterized by s.t.; because of s.t.]**

1. to と prt. **[a particle marking a noun phrase which is in a reciprocal relationship with the subject of the clause]**

EX. (**a**) I went to Japan with my father.
私は父と日本に行きました。
Watashi wa chichi to Nihon ni ikimashita.
(**b**) I'm playing tennis with Yoshiko tomorrow morning.
僕はあしたの朝、好子さんとテニスをします。
Boku wa ashita no asa, Yoshiko-san to tenisu o shimasu.
(**c**) Our company is dealing with a bank in Hong Kong.
うちの会社は香港にある銀行と取引しているんです。
Uchi no kaisha wa Honkon ni aru ginkoo to tori-hiki-shite iru n desu.
(**d**) My car collided with another car at a crowded intersection.
僕の車が交通量の多い交差点でほかの車とぶつかった。
Boku no kuruma ga kootsuu-ryoo no ooi koosa-ten de hoka no kuruma to butsukatta.
(**e**) When I was a kid, I often quarreled with my younger brother.
子供の時に弟とよくけんかしました。
Kodomo no toki ni otooto to yoku kenka-shimashita.
(**f**) I agree with you there.
そこは君と意見が同じだ。
Soko wa kimi to iken ga onaji da.

2. de で prt. **[using s.t.]** **⟪by, for, using⟫**

EX. (**a**) Can I write my answers with a ball-point pen?
答えをボールペンで書いてもいいですか。
Kotae o booru-pen de kaite mo ii desu ka.
(**b**) It is said that the Japanese first eat with their eyes and then with their mouth.
日本人はまず目で食べ、それから口で食べると言われる。
Nihon-jin wa mazu me de tabe, sore kara kuchi de taberu to iwa-reru.

NOTE: In formal Japanese cuisine, foods are arranged artistically in beautiful plates and bowls, so that one is tempted to look first, and then eat. How a meal looks is as important as how it tastes.

3. ⟨-no⟩ N ⟨〜の⟩N [a particle which, with a preceding noun phrase, forms a phrase to modify the noun phrase that follows] **⟪'s, of, in, at, for, by, from⟫, {⟨-o⟩ motte/V*te*} (iru N) {⟨〜を⟩持って/V*te*}(いるN)**

EX. (**a**) Who's the girl with the broom in her hand?
手にほうき{を持っている/*の}女性はだれですか。
*Te ni hooki {o motte iru/*no} josei wa dare desu ka.*
(**b**) The villagers stared at Sally as if they'd never seen someone with blue eyes before.
村人は初めて青い目{の/をしている/*を持っている}人を見たかのようにサリーをじっと見つめていた。
*Mura-bito wa hajimete aoi me {no/o shite iru/*o motte iru} hito o mita ka no yooni Sarii o jitto mitsumete ita.*
(**c**) The lady told me her sad story with tears in her eyes.
婦人は目に涙を浮かべて、悲しい話をした。
Fujin wa me ni namida o ukabete, kanashii hanashi o shita.

4. de で prt. **[indicating a weak causal relationship]** **⟪and, because of, due to, because⟫**

EX. (**a**) When I learned that I had passed the entrance exam, I was overcome with joy.
入学試験に受かったことが分かった時、私は喜びで興奮した。
Nyuugaku-shiken ni ukatta koto ga wakatta toki, watashi wa yorokobi de koofun-shita.
(**b**) Yesterday I was down with the flu or something.

私は昨日流感かなんかで寝込んでしまった。
Watashi wa kinoo ryuukan ka nan-ka de ne-konde shimatta.
(**c**) The highway was jammed with vacationing cars.
高速道路は休暇をとって出かける車で込んでいた。
Koosoku-dooro wa kyuuka o totte dekakeru kuruma de konde ita.

PHRASE: Are you with me? *Watashi no iu koto ga wakarimasu ka.* 私の言うことが分かりますか。

PHRASE: What's the matter with you? *Doo shita n desu ka.* どうしたんですか。

wither vi. **[for a plant to dry up and shrivel; for s.o./s.t. to lose freshness or vigor]** **ka⌈reru** かれる ② **[for s.t. to become dry and lacking in vigor, such as a plant, wellspring, voice, s.o.'s creativity, s.o.'s performance, s.o.'s handwriting, etc.]** **((dry up, run dry, get hoarse, be seasoned))**, **shi⌈bomu** しぼむ ① **[for s.t. fully open or expanded, such as a flower blossom or hope, to dry up and shrink]** **((fade, droop, shrivel))**

㊥ "dry up"▷枯れる, "for a voice to become hoarse"▷かれる

NOTE: When the subject of *kareru* is s.o.'s artistic performance or handwriting, the verb does not necessarily indicate "dryness" in a negetive sense, but rather a more positive quality of being "seasoned." For example: *Kare no gei wa toshi to tomoni karete kita.* "His art has become seasoned with age."

EX. (**a**) The flower withered in the sun.
その花は日に当たって{枯れた/*しぼんだ}。
*Sono hana wa hi ni atatte {kareta/*shibonda}.*
(**b**) His hopes of attending college withered with the death of his father .
父の死で、彼の大学進学の希望は{しぼんで/*枯れて}しまった。
*Chichi no shi de, kare no daigaku-shingaku no kiboo wa {shibonde/*karete} shimatta.*

W

within prep. **[inside of or enclosed by s.t.; not exceeding a certain amount, degree, or scope]**

1. **⟨-no⟩ na⌉ibu ⟨ni⟩** ⟨～の⟩内部⟨に⟩ n.(+prt.) **•c [inside of s.t.]** **((interior, inner parts))**, **⟨-no⟩ na⌉ka ⟨ni⟩** ⟨～の⟩中⟨に⟩ n.(+prt.) **[to/at a point which is part of a space surrounded by s.t.]** **((interior, inside, in))**, **-inai ⟨ni⟩** ～以内⟨に⟩ **•c [not going beyond a temporal or spatial limit]** **((less than, no more than, inside of))**, **-nai ⟨ni⟩** ～内⟨に⟩ **•c [internal to s.t. spatial or temporal]**

EX. (**a**) There was nothing contained within the box.
箱{の中/の内部/*以内/*内}には何もなかった。
Hako {no naka/no naibu/-inai/*-nai} ni wa nani-mo nakatta.*
(**b**) The school is within two miles of our house.
学校は家から二マイル{以内/??内/*の中/*の内部}のところにあります。
*Gakkoo wa ie kara ni-mairu{-inai/??-nai/*no naka/*no naibu} no tokoro ni arimasu.*
(**c**) The station is within walking distance.
駅は家から歩ける距離{内/*以内/*の中/*の内部}にあります。
Eki wa ie kara aruke-ru kyori {-nai/-inai/*no naka/*no naibu} ni arimasu.*
(**d**) Please do this work within the specified time.
この仕事は指定された時間{内/以内/*の中/*の内部}にしてください。
*Kono shigoto wa shitei-sareta jikan {-nai/-inai/*no naka/*no naibu} ni shite kudasai.*

2. **-inai ni** ～以内に **•c** SEE within prep. 1

EX. Can you translate this Japanese manual into English within a week?
一週間以内にこの日本語の説明書を英語に翻訳出来ますか。
Is-shuukan-inai ni kono Nihon-go no setsumei-sho o ei-go ni hon'yaku dekimasu ka.

—— n. **[the inside]**
na˥ibu 内部 •c [the interior (part) of s.t.] ((**interior, inner part, inside**)), **u˥chi-gawa 内側 [the inner side of s.t.]** ((**inside, inner part**))

EX. (**a**) Homestay provides an excellent opportunity to observe a foreign culture from within.
ホームステイは外国の文化を{内部/内側}から見るいい機会だ。
Hoomu-sutei wa gaikoku no bunka o {naibu/uchi-gawa} kara miru ii kikai da.
(**b**) Someone from within has apparently been leaking company secrets to the press.
だれか{内部/*内側}の者が報道機関に社内の秘密をもらしているようだ。
*Dare-ka {naibu/*uchi-gawa} no mono ga hoodoo-kikan ni shanai no himitsu o morashite iru yooda.*

without prep. **[not having or showing s.t.; not accompanied by some event or action]**
1. -nashi {**ni/de**} **-なし{に/で} [not having s.t.],** ⟨**-o**⟩ {**mo˥ta˥nai de/mo˥ta˥zu ni**} ⟨〜を⟩{持たないで/持たずに} **[not holding or possessing s.t.]**

EX. (**a**) One cannot be happy without good health.
健康{なし{に/で}/*を持たないで/*を持たずに}は幸福にはなれない。
*Kenkoo {-nashi {ni/de}/*o motanai de/*o motazu ni} wa koofuku ni wa nare-nai.*
(**b**) How can a person survive after retirement without a pension?
定年後年金{なし{に/で}/*を持たないで/*を持たずに}どうやって暮らせますか。
*Teinen-go nenkin {-nashi {ni/de}/*o motanai de/*o motazu ni} doo yatte kurase-masu ka.*
(**c**) You can run into serious trouble if you go abroad for study without sufficient money.
お金{を十分持たないで/を十分持たずに/*なし{に/で}}海外へ留学すると大変なことになるかもしれない。
O-kane {o juubun motanai de/o juubun motazu ni/-nashi {ni/de}} kaigai e ryuugaku-suru to taihenna koto ni naru kamoshirenai.*

2. Vinf. nonpast ko˥to˥ (**mo**) {**na˥ku/na˥shi ni**} **Vinf. nonpastこと(も){なく/なしに} [not accompanied by the act of doing s.t. or by the occurrence of s.t.],** {{**Vneg./Vstem/ko/shi**} **nai de/**{**Vneg./Vstem/ko/se**} **zu ni**} {{**Vneg./Vstem/来/し**}ないで/{**Vneg./Vstem/来/せ**}ずに}

EX. (**a**) Tony spent two years in Japan without ever studying Japanese.
トニーは日本語を一度も勉強{しないで/せずに/することなく/覚えることなしに}日本で二年間過ごした。
Tonii wa Nihon-go o ichi-do mo benkyoo-{shinai de/sezu ni/suru koto naku/suru koto nashi ni} Nihon de ni-nenkan sugoshita.
(**b**) I came to school without eating breakfast today and I'm starving.
今日は朝御飯を{食べないで/食べずに/*食べることもなく/*食べることもなしに}学校に来たので、おなかがぺこぺこなんだよ。
*Kyoo wa asa-gohan o {tabenai de/tabezu ni/*taberu koto mo naku/*taberu koto mo nashi ni} gakkoo ni kita node, o-naka ga peko-peko na n da yo.*

witness n. **[a person who sees or hears s.t. noteworthy (and is called upon later to testify about it in court)]**
1. mo˥kugeki˥-sha 目撃者 •c [s.o. who actually sees or hears the occurrence of s.t. noteworthy]

EX. There were two witnesses to the traffic accident.
その交通事故の目撃者は二人いた。
Sono kootsuu-jiko no mokugeki-sha wa futari ita.

2. sho˥onin 証人 •c [a person who testifies in court]

EX. Two witnesses came to court to testify in the bribery case.

贈収賄事件で二人の証人が証言をしに出廷した。
Zooshuuwai-jiken de futari no shoonin ga shoogen o shi ni shuttei-shita.

— vt. [for s.o. to be present to see or hear s.t. noteworthy]
1. ⟨-o⟩ mo⌈kugeki-suru ⟨～を⟩目撃する ③ •c [for s.o. to actually see or hear the occurrence of s.t. noteworthy]

EX. I witnessed an automobile accident today at an intersection downtown.
今日私は町の交差点で自動車事故を目撃した。
Kyoo watashi wa machi no koosa-ten de jidoosha-jiko o mokugeki-shita.

2. sho⌈onin to-shite sho⌈mei-suru 証人として署名する ③ •c [for s.o. to provide one's signature attesting to having seen or heard s.t. significant]

wolf n.
o⌉okami おおかみ

woman n. **[an adult female person]**
o⌈nna no hito 女の人 ↔ otoko no hito 男の人; jo⌈sei 女性 •c [the human sex which gives birth] ⟪femininity, womanhood⟫ ↔ dansei 男性 •c; fu⌈jin 婦人 •c [an adult, often married female person] ⟪lady, dame⟫ ↔ shinshi 紳士 •c; jo⌉shi 女子 •c [a female person] ⟪female, lady, girl, daughter⟫ ↔ danshi 男子 •c; o⌈nna⌉ 女 [an adult female person, esp. as seen in the role of a dating/marriage/sexual partner ⟨s⟩] ⟪female, the fairer sex, sweetheart⟫ ↔ otoko 男

EX. (**a**) Women tend to live longer than men.
{女性/女/女の人/女子/*婦人}は大抵{男性/男/男の人/男子/*紳士}より長生きする。
*{Josei/Onna/Onna no hito/Joshi/ *Fujin} wa taitei {dansei/otoko/otoko no hito/danshi/*shinshi} yori naga-iki-suru.*
(**b**) The women's liberation movement is not as influential in Japan as it is in the U.S.
{女性/*婦人/*女/*女の人/*女子}解放運動は日本ではアメリカほど勢力がない。
*{Josei/*Fujin/*Onna/*Onna no hito/ *Joshi}-kaihoo-undoo wa Nihon de wa Amerika hodo seiryoku ga nai.*
(**c**) I graduated from a women's college in Tokyo.
私は東京の{女子/*婦人/*女性/*女/*女の人}大(学)を出ました。
*Watashi wa Tookyoo no {joshi-/*fujin/ *josei/*onna/*onna no hito} dai(gaku) o demashita.*
(**d**) What sort of woman do you want to marry?
どんな{女の人/女性/??婦人/??女/*女子}と結婚したいんですか。
*Donna {onna no hito/josei/??fujin/ ??onna/*joshi} to kekkon-shi-tai n desu ka.*
(**e**) He's always flirting with women.
彼はいつも{女性/女/女の人/*婦人/*女子}とふざけている。
*Kare wa itsu-mo {josei/onna/onna no hito/*fujin/*joshi} to fuzakete iru.*
(**f**) Who's that woman standing over there?
あそこに立っておいでの{御婦人/女の人/女性/*女/*女子}はどなたですか。
*Asoko ni tatte oide no {go-fujin/onna no hito/josei/*onna/*joshi} wa donata desu ka.*

wonder n. **[a feeling of surprise combined with admiration or curiosity; s.t. which causes such a feeling]**
1. kyo⌉oi 驚異 •c [a feeling of sheer astonishment or s.t. which causes such a feeling] ⟪marvel⟫, kyo⌈otan 驚嘆 •c [a feeling of astonishment combined with admiration] ⟪admiration⟫, o⌈doroki⌉ 驚き /⟨V*masu* of *odoroku* ① be surprised/ [a feeling of surprise or s.t. which causes such a feeling] ⟪surprise, astonishment, amazement⟫

EX. (**a**) The ability of man to land a rocket on the moon never ceases to be a wonder to me.
ロケットを月面着陸させた人類の能力はいつまでたっても私にとって{驚異/驚き/*驚嘆}だ。
Roketto o getsumen-chakuriku-saseta jinrui no nooryoku wa itsu made tatte

W

*mo watashi ni-totte {kyooi/odoroki/ *kyootan} da.*
(**b**) The Japanese post-war economic recovery was something worthy of wonder.
日本の戦後の経済復興は{驚嘆/?驚異/ ?驚き}に値するものだった。
Nihon no sengo no keizai-fukkoo wa {kyootan/?kyooi/?odoroki} ni atai-suru mono datta.

2. fu⌈shigi 不思議 •c [s.t. that goes beyond human comprehension] ⟪wonderfulness, mystery, miracle, marvel⟫, o⌈doroku-be⌉ki koto 驚くべきこと [s.t. that merits astonishment], kyo⌉oi 驚異 •c SEE wonder n. 1; **ki⌈se⌉ki 奇跡 •c [a mysterious phenomenon that goes beyond human comprehension] ⟪miracle, marvel⟫**

EX. The fact that anyone survived the plane crash is a wonder.
飛行機事故で生き残った人がいることは{驚くべきこと/驚異/奇跡/不思議}だ。
Hikoo-ki-jiko de iki-nokotta hito ga iru koto wa {odoroku-beki koto/kyooi/ kiseki/fushigi} da.

PHRASE: no wonder *doori de* 道理で

EX. A: Jim has been living in Japan for five years, you know.
ジムは日本に五年間も住んでいますよ。
Jimu wa Nihon ni go-nenkan mo sunde imasu yo.
B: No wonder his Japanese is so good.
道理で日本語が上手なわけですね。
Doori de Nihon-go ga joozuna wake desu ne.

— vi./vt. **[for s.o. to feel curiosity, doubt, or surprise about s.t.]**

1. ⟨-ni⟩ o⌈doro⌉ku ⟨〜に⟩驚く ① [for s.o./ s.a. to be suddenly aroused out of a state of calmness by encountering s.t. unexpected] ⟪be surprised, be astonished, be amazed⟫

EX. (**a**) The young prince wondered at Cinderella's beauty.
若い王子はシンデレラの美しさに驚いた。
Wakai ooji wa Shinderera no utsukushi-sa ni odoroita.
(**b**) I wonder that he wasn't killed in that terrible accident.
あんなひどい事故なのに彼が死なずにすんだとは驚きましたね。
Anna hidoi jiko na noni kare ga shinazu ni sunda to wa odorokimashita ne.

2. (ho⌈ntoo ni) Sinf. {ka⌈na/ka⌉shira} (本当に)Sinf.{かな/かしら} [an expression indicating the speaker's curiosity or doubt as to the truthfulness of s.t.]

NOTE: Sinf. *kashira* is used primarily by female speakers, but Sinf. *kana* can be used by either male or female speakers. When the nonpast affirmative form of adj(*na*). or N + cop. occurs before *kana* or *kashira*, the form used is adj(*na*). stem or N, respectively.

EX. (**a**) I wonder if Mr. Yoshida is coming to Sapporo this summer.
吉田さんは今年の夏札幌に来る{かな/ かしら}。
Yoshida-san wa kotoshi no natsu Sapporo ni kuru {kana/ka-shira}.
(**b**) I wonder if it's going to rain today.
今日は雨が降る{かな/かしら}。
Kyoo wa ame ga furu {kana/kashira}.

PHRASE: I was wondering if… …*ka doo ka mayotte ita* …かどうか迷っていた

EX. I was wondering if I should tell Bob's mother about his behavior at school recently.
ボブのお母さんにボブの学校での最近のふるまいについて話そうかどうか迷っていたんです。
Bobu no o-kaa-san ni Bobu no gakkoo de no saikin no furumai ni-tsuite hanasoo ka doo ka mayotte ita n desu.

wonderful adj. **[remarkable, surprisingly good or fine]**

1. fu⌈shigina 不思議な adj(*na*). **•c [going beyond human comprehension] ⟪marvelous, strange, mysterious, magical⟫, o⌈doroku-be⌉ki N 驚くべきN [causing astonishment]**

EX. For me the beauty of Bach's music is in the wonderful sense of proportion it conveys.
バッハの音楽の美しさはそこから伝わ

W

ってくる{不思議な/驚くべき}調和の感覚にあると思う。
Bahha no ongaku no utsukushi-sa wa soko kara tsutawatte kuru {fushigina/odoroku-beki} choowa no kankaku ni aru to omou.

2. su⌈barashi⌉i すばらしい adj(*i*). **[causing great wonder/admiration/pleasure due to being extremely good] 《splendid, excellent, superb, great, smashing》, su⌈tekina** すてきな adj(*na*). **•c [giving a favorable impression to the observer on the basis of outward appearance such as dress, color, pattern, etc.] 《great, cute, lovely, splendid, stunning》**

NOTE: *Sutekina* is normally used by female speakers, as in example (a).

EX. (**a**) What a wonderful house you have!
なんて{すばらしい/すてきな}お宅でしょう。
Nante {subarashii/sutekina} o-taku deshoo.
(**b**) I heard from your teachers about your wonderful academic record in school.
あなたの学校での成績は{すばらしい/*すてきだ}って先生方から聞きましたよ。
*Anata no gakkoo de no seiseski wa {subarashii/*suteki da} tte sensei-gata kara kikimashita yo.*
(**c**) The weather's wonderful. Let's go out for a walk.
{すばらしい/??すてきな}天気ね。散歩に行きましょうよ。
{Subarashii/??Sutekina} tenki ne. Sanpo ni ikimashoo yo.
(**d**) That's a wonderful *kimono* Masako is wearing, isn't it?.
雅子さんが着ている着物は{すてき/すばらしい}ですね。
Masako-san ga kite iru kimono wa {suteki/subarashii} desu ne.

wood n. **[the hard material making up the trunk and branches of trees, esp. when cut for use as fuel or building material; an area densely covered with trees growing naturally]**

1. mo⌈ri 森 **[an area with many old, tall trees, often regarded as a holy place inhabited by Shinto deities] 《grove, woodland》**

EX. In Japan one often finds Shinto shrines in the woods.
日本ではよく森に神社がある。
Nihon de wa yoku mori ni jinja ga aru.

2. mo⌈ku⌉zai 木材 **•c [trees cut down and processed for use in building things such as houses and furniture] 《lumber》, za⌈imoku** 材木 **•c**

EX. The wood used in building this house is mostly white cedar.
この家を建てるのに使った{木材/材木}はほとんどがひのきだ。
Kono ie o tateru no ni tsukatta {mokuzai/zaimoku} wa hotondo ga hinoki da.

3. ma⌈ki まき **[the hard material from trees used as fuel for heating and cooking] 《firewood》**

EX. Many people in Vermont burn wood to heat their homes.
バーモントでは家を暖めるためにまきを燃やす人が多い。
Baamonto de wa ie o atatameru tame ni maki o moyasu hito ga ooi.

PHRASE: woodblock print *hanga* 版画 **•c**

EX. The woodblock prints of the Edo period are known as *ukiyoe.*
江戸時代の版画は『浮世絵』として知られている。
Edo-jidai no hanga wa "ukiyo-e" to-shite shira-rete iru.

wooden adj. **[made from the hard material taken from trees 《fig. "lacking in expressive quality"》]**

ki⌉ no N 木のN **[relating to or made from the hard material taken from trees], ki⌉ de dekita N** 木で出来たN **[made from the hard material taken from trees], mo⌈ku-sei no N** 木製のN **•c [made from the hard material taken from trees]**

EX. I bought a wooden spoon and fork to go along with my new salad bowl.
私は新しいサラダボールに合わせて

{木の/木で出来た/木製の}スプーンとフォークを買った。
Watashi wa atarashii sarada-booru ni awasete {ki no/ki de dekita/moku-sei no} supuun to fooku o katta.

woodland n. **[land covered by many trees]**
shi⌈nrin-chi⌉tai 森林地帯 •c [an area covered by forests]
EX. The fire apparently started in the woodlands of California.
火事はカリフォルニアの森林地帯で始まったらしい。
Kaji wa Kariforunia no shinrin-chitai de hajimatta rashii.

wool n. **[the soft hair of mammals, esp. sheep, or yarn made from this]**
1. ke 毛 [a fine threadlike growth that emerges from the skin of humans and certain animals] ((hair, fur)), yo⌈omoo 羊毛 •c [the soft hair of sheep], u⌉uru ウール •f
EX. This sweater is made of wool.
このセーターは{羊毛/ウール/毛}です。
Kono seetaa wa {yoomoo/uuru/ke} desu.
2. ke-⌈ito 毛糸 [the soft hair of sheep processed for knitting] ((worsted yarn, woolen yarn))
EX. I'm knitting wool mufflers for my grandchildren.
孫にあげるために毛糸のマフラーを編んでいます。
Mago ni ageru tame ni ke-ito no mafuraa o ande imasu.

woolen adj. **[similar to or made of the soft hair of sheep]**
u⌉uru no N ウールのN •f
EX. (**a**) I bought a woolen jacket for my father.
父にウールのジャケットを買ってあげた。
Chichi ni uuru no jaketto o katte ageta.
(**b**) I like the feel of woolen clothes.
私はウールの衣服の着心地が好きです。
Watashi wa uuru no ifuku no ki-gokochi ga suki desu.

word n. **[the minimal sequence of linguistic sounds that carries meaning and that is not bound to another form]**
1. go⌉ 語 •c [a technical term for the shortest linguistic unit which carries meaning], ta⌈ngo 単語 •c [the smallest linguistic unit which is not bound to another form] ((vocabulary))
EX. (**a**) I know only a few Japanese words and cannot speak the language well.
日本語は{単語/*語}を少ししか知らなくて、上手に話せません。
*Nihon-go wa {tango/*go} o sukoshi shika shiranakute, joozuni hanase-masen.*
(**b**) A sentence consists of a string of words.
文は一連の{語/単語}で出来ている。
Bun wa ichiren no {go/tango} de dekite iru.
2. ko⌈toba⌉ 言葉 [the system or one of a number of systems used for communicating among humans whereby meaning is expressed in vocal sounds or written letters; a sequence of linguistic sounds forming a unit of meaning in human communication] ((language, speech))
EX. (**a**) I don't understand how he could say words like that to me.
どうしてあの人が私にあんな言葉を言えたのか分かりません。
Dooshite ano hito ga watashi ni anna kotoba o ie-ta no ka wakarimasen.
(**b**) One should use polite words when speaking to a superior.
目上の人に話す時は丁寧な言葉を使わなければいけません。
Meue no hito ni hanasu toki wa teineina kotoba o tsukawanakereba ikemasen.
3. ya⌈kusoku 約束 •c [an explicit statement that one will or will not do s.t. or s.t. that one has explicitly said one will or will not do (including a date, engagement, or appointment)] ((promise, engagement, appointment, contract, convention))
EX. I don't like it when people don't keep their word.
約束を守らないなんていやですね。

Yakusoku o mamoranai nante iya desu ne.

PHRASE: have a word with ⟨-to⟩ *chotto hanasu* ⟨〜と⟩ちょっと話す ①

EX. Can I have a word with you?
ちょっとあなたと話したいことがあるんですが。
Chotto anata to hanashi-tai koto ga aru n desu ga.

PHRASE: in a word *{hito-kuchi/hito-koto} de ieba* {一口/一言}で言えば

EX. In a word, the movie was dull.
{一口/一言}で言えば、あの映画はつまらなかった。
{Hito-kuchi/Hito koto} de ieba, ano eiga wa tsumaranakatta.

work vi. **[for s.o./s.a. to use one's energy productively to accomplish s.t.; for s.t. such as a machine to function as intended]**

1. ha⌈taraku 働く ① [for s.t./s.o., esp. a laborer, mechanical device, or biological organ, to operate properly or use one's energy productively to acomplish an intended purpose/goal] ⟪labor, function⟫, shi⌈goto o suru 仕事をする ③ [for s.o. to expend time and effort on an activity performed for some purpose other than amusement]

EX. (**a**) I work eight hours a day at my office.
会社で毎日八時間{働いて/仕事をして}います。
Kaisha de mai-nichi hachi-jikan {hataraite/shigoto o shite} imasu.
(**b**) My brain doesn't work well in the morning.
僕の頭は朝はよく{働かない/*仕事をしない}。
*Boku no atama wa asa wa yoku {hatarakanai/*shigoto o shinai}.*

2. ⟨-o⟩ be⌈nkyoo-suru ⟨〜を⟩勉強する ③ •c [for s.o. to incorporate as part of oneself knowledge or a skill through careful reading, consideration, or practice or to sell merchandise at a discount price]

EX. You'd better work harder or you're going to flunk the course.
もっと勉強しないと、落第してしまうよ。
Motto benkyoo-shinai to, rakudai-shite shimau yo.

3. ki⌈ku 効く ① [for s.t. to have a clear effect on s.t. else in the way intended] ⟪have an effect⟫

EX. I took some medicine for the headache, but it didn't work.
頭痛がしたので薬を飲みましたが効きませんでした。
Zutsuu ga shita node kusuri o nomimashita ga kikimasen deshita.

— vt. **[for s.o. to cause s.o./s.a. to use its/his/her energy productively to accomplish s.t.; for s.o. to cause s.t. such as a machine to function]**

1. ⟨-o⟩ ha⌈taraka-seru ⟨〜を⟩働かせる /⟨causative of *hataraku* ① work/, ⟨-o⟩ tsu⌈kau ⟨〜を⟩使う ① [for s.o. to put s.t./s.o./s.a. into service for a particular purpose, including as an instrument or as material which is consumed] ⟪use, employ, spend, speak, exploit⟫, ⟨-o⟩ ko⌈ki-tsukau ⟨〜を⟩こき使う ① [for s.o. to cause one's subordinate to do so much that he/she becomes exhausted] ⟪sweat, slave-drive⟫

EX. I hate my boss because he works me like a slave.
上司は僕を奴隷みたいに{働かせる/使う/こき使う}から、大嫌いだ。
Jooshi wa boku o dorei mitai ni {hataraka-seru/tsukau/koki-tsukau} kara, dai-kirai da.

2. ⟨-o⟩ u⌈goka⌉su ⟨〜を⟩動かす ① [for s.o. to cause s.t./s.o./s.a. to change in position or location or to function properly], ⟨-o⟩ so⌈ojuu-suru ⟨〜を⟩操縦する ③ •c [for s.o. to operate a machine, esp. an airplane ⟪fig. "control"⟫] ⟪fly (a plane), steer, operate⟫, ⟨-o⟩ so⌉osa-suru ⟨〜を⟩操作する ③ •c [for s.o. to cause a relatively complex machine to function, excluding a car or airplane] ⟪operate, manipulate, manage⟫

NOTE: Unlike other short causatives, *ugokasu* does not have a longer causative version.

Ugokaseru means not "to cause s.o./s.a./s.t. to move" but "can move s.t./s.o./s.a.".

EX. I don't know how to work this robot machine.
この産業ロボットをどうやって{動かす/操縦する/操作する}のか分かりません。
Kono sangyoo-robotto o doo yatte {ugokasu/soojuu-suru/soosa-suru} no ka wakarimasen.

— n. **[the use of one's energy productively to accomplish s.t.; s.t. which is done or accomplished; a literary or artistic creation]**
1. shi⌈goto 仕事 [an activity performed for a particular purpose other than amusement and on which one expends time and effort] ((job, task, labor, business)), ro⌈odoo 労働 •c [activity performed in order to earn wages] ((labor)), sho⌈ku⌉gyoo 職業 •c [an activity one pursues in order to make a living] ((occupation, profession))

EX. (**a**) A: Which do you love more, me or your work?
どちらを愛しているの、私、それとも{仕事/*労働/*職業}?
*Dochira o aishite iru no, watashi, sore tomo {shigoto/*roodoo/*shokugyoo}?*
B: I love both.
両方ともだよ。
Ryoohoo tomo da yo.
(**b**) A: What is your line of work?
{お仕事/御職業/*労働}は何ですか。
*{O-shigoto/Go-shokugyoo/*Roodoo} wa nan desu ka.*
B: I'm a bank clerk.
銀行員です。
Ginkoo-in desu.

2. shi⌈waza 仕業 [s.t. one has done], ko⌉oi 行為 •c [s.t. one does intentionally to accomplish some purpose, esp. for the benefit of another] ((action, act, behavior, deed))

EX. (**a**) The glass in the window is broken. I wonder whose work this was.
窓ガラスが割れている。だれの{仕業/??行為}だろう。
Mado-garasu ga warete iru. Dare no {shiwaza/??kooi} daroo?
(**b**) This murder was the work of the devil.
この殺人は悪魔の{仕業/行為}だ。
Kono satsujin wa akuma no {shiwaza/kooi} da.

3. sa⌈kuhin 作品 •c [an artistic creation by s.o.], cho⌈saku 著作 •c [the act of composing a book for publication or a book so composed by s.o.] ((writing, book, publication))

EX. (**a**) I like Picasso's work.
私はピカソの{作品/*著作}が好きだ。
*Watashi wa Pikaso no {sakuhin/*chosaku} ga suki da.*
(**b**) I'm currently reading one of Camus's works.
私は今カミュの{作品/著作}の一つを読んでいる。
Watashi wa ima Kamyu no {sakuhin/chosaku} no hitotsu o yonde iru.
(**c**) I've heard every work composed by Verdi.
ベルディの作った{作品/*著作}を全部聞いたことがある。
*Berudii no tsukutta {sakuhin/*chosaku} o zenbu kiita koto ga aru.*

worker n. **[a person who expends time and energy on an activity for a purpose other than amusement]**
ha⌈taraite iru hito 働いている人 [a person who is engaged in some productive activity, esp. for the purpose of earning a living], ro⌈odo⌉o-sha 労働者 •c [a person who performs an activity in order to earn wages] ((working man, laborer)), ke⌈nkyu⌉u-sha 研究者 •c [a person who is professionally engaged in research] ((researcher)), ke⌈nkyu⌉u-in 研究員 •c [a member of a research institute who is engaged in research] ((researcher))

EX. (**a**) The number of female workers is on the increase in Japan.
日本では女性{労働者/*研究者/*研究員}の数が増えている。
Nihon de wa josei-{roodoo-sha/

W

**kenkyuu-sha/*kenkyuu-in} no kazu ga fuete iru.*
(**b**) How many workers are there at this research center?
この研究所には{研究員/研究者/働いている人/*労働者}が何人いますか。
*Kono kenkyuu-jo ni wa {kenkyuu-in/kenkyuu-sha/hataraite iru hito/*roodoo-sha} ga nan-nin imasu ka.*

working adj. **[functioning properly]**
1. ha⌈taraku N 働くN [N that engages in some productive activity, esp. for the purpose of earning a living], ji⌈tsuyoo-tekina 実用的な adj(*na*). **•c [suitable to be readily put to use in actual situations]** **《practical》**

EX. (**a**) Working females are beginning to suffer from the same stresses that working males suffer from.
{働く/*実用的な}女性は{働く/*実用的な}男性と同じストレスに悩むようになってきた。
*{Hataraku/*Jitsuyoo-tekina} josei wa {hataraku/*jitsuyoo-tekina} dansei to onaji sutoresu ni nayamu yooni natte kita.*
(**b**) Do you have a working knowledge of Japanese?
日本語の{実用的な/*働く}知識がありますか。
*Nihon-go no {jitsuyoo-tekina/*hataraku} chishiki ga arimasu ka.*

2. tsu⌈kae-ru (N) 使える(N) /〈potential form of *tsukau* ① use/ [able to be used], kinmu- 勤務～ •c [relating to a job or professional activity], shigoto no N 仕事のN

EX. (**a**) Is this telephone in working order?
この電話は{使える/*勤務/*仕事の}状態になっていますか。
*Kono denwa wa {tsukae-ru/*kinmu-/*shigoto no} jootai ni natte imasu ka.*
(**b**) Our working hours at this office are from 9 a.m. to 5 p.m.
この会社の{勤務/仕事の/*使える}時間は午前九時から午後五時までです。
*Kono kaisha no {kinmu-/shigoto no/*tsukae-ru} jikan wa gozen ku-ji kara gogo go-ji made desu.*

world n. **[the earth and all its nations and peoples; a particular sphere of activity, interest, or life with all the things and individuals included in it]**
1. se⌈ka⌉i 世界 •c 《earth》, -kai ～界 •c [a particular field or domain of activity or interest]

EX. (**a**) The Japanese appear to have the longest life expectancy in the world.
日本人の平均寿命は世界で一番長いようだ。
Nihon-jin no heikin-jumyoo wa sekai de ichiban nagai yooda.
(**b**) In the world of medicine, the conquest of cancer is probably the issue currently receiving the greatest attention.
{医学の世界/医学界}ではがんの征服が現在一番の関心事だ。
{Igaku no sekai/Igak-kai} de wa gan no seifuku ga genzai ichiban no kanshin-ji da.

2. yo-⌈no⌉-naka 世の中 [the totality of inter-personal networks constituting human society] 《society》, se⌉ken 世間 •c [people who belong to the same community] 《public》

EX. (**a**) The Japanese appear to be very sensitive to how a person is viewed by the surrounding world.
日本人は{世間/*世の中}にどう思われるかを大変気にするようだ。
*Nihon-jin wa {seken/*yo-no-naka} ni doo omowa-reru ka o taihen ki-ni-suru yooda.*
(**b**) You know Jiro Hayashi? What a small world!
林二郎を知っているんですか。{世の中/世間}は狭いですねえ。
Hayashi Jiroo o shitte iru n desu ka. {Yo-no-naka/Seken} wa semai desu nee.

PHRASE: Wh-word + in the world *ittai* 一体 •c
EX. What in the world are you eating?

W

一体何を食べているんですか。
Ittai nani o tabete iru n desu ka.

worm n. **[a small elongated animal with a soft body and no back bone or legs]**
mu⌈shi 虫 [a small organism which breeds its young by hatching and crawls on the ground or flies about] **((insect, bug, moth, vermin))**

EX. A: Mom, look! A worm!
お母さん、ほら、虫が。
O-kaa-san, hora, mushi ga.
B: Oh, that's an earthworm.
ああ、あれはみみずよ。
Aa, are wa mimizu yo.

worry vt. **[to cause one to feel uneasy or anxious]**
1. {⟨-de⟩/⟨-ni⟩} na⌈ya⌉mu {⟨〜で⟩/⟨〜に⟩}悩む ① [for s.o. to feel physical/psychological pain] **((be worried, be troubled))**, **⟨-de⟩ shi⌈npai-suru ⟨〜で⟩心配する ③ •c [for s.o. to feel uneasy or anxious about s.t.]** **((be afraid of, fear))**

EX. My daughter's future worries me.
娘の将来のことで{悩んで/心配して}いる。
Musume no shoorai no koto de {nayande/shinpai-shite} iru.

—— vi. **[for s.o. to feel uneasy or anxious about s.t.]**
({⟨-de⟩/⟨-ni⟩}) na⌈ya⌉mu ({⟨〜で⟩/⟨〜に⟩})悩む ① [for s.o. to feel physical/psychological pain] **((be worried, be troubled))**, **⟨-o⟩ shi⌈npai-suru ⟨〜を⟩心配する ③ •c [for s.o. to feel uneasy or anxious about s.t. in the future]** **((be afraid of, fear))**

EX. (**a**) I worry about my son's health.
私は息子の体のこと{を心配して/で悩んで}いる。
Watashi wa musuko no karada no koto {o shinpai-shite/de nayande} iru.
(**b**) Don't worry! Your friends will take good care of you.
{心配しない/*悩まない}でいいよ。友達が面倒を見てくれるから。
*{Shinpai-shinai/*Nayamanai} de ii yo. Tomodachi ga mendoo o mite kureru kara.*

—— n. **[a state of mental unease or anxiety or s.t. that causes this]**
1 shi⌈npai 心配 •c [an uncomfortable feeling caused by uncertainty or by the expectation of danger/evil/s.t. troublesome] **((care, concern, anxiety, fear))**

EX. (**a**) Worry about my upcoming exams has been keeping me up at night.
今度の試験のことが心配でこのごろは夜あまりよく寝られません。
Kondo no shiken no koto ga shinpai de kono-goro wa yoru amari yoku ne-raremasen.
(**b**) Worry is an enemy of good health.
心配は健康の敵だ。
Shinpai wa kenkoo no teki da.

2. shi⌈npai no ta⌉ne 心配の種 [a cause or source of unease or anxiety], **shi⌈npai-goto 心配事 [a matter which causes one unease or anxiety]**

EX. (**a**) My greatest worry is my daughter studying abroad.
留学している娘が一番の{心配の種/*心配事}なんです。
*Ryuugaku-shite iru musume ga ichiban no {shinpai no tane/*shinpai-goto} na n desu.*
(**b**) His many worries have caused him to become depressed.
あの人は{心配の種/心配事}が多くて、落ち込んでいるんです。
Ano hito wa {shinpai no tane/shinpai-goto} ga ookute, ochi-konde iru n desu.

worse adj./adv. **[less good, favorable, or healthy; less well]**
⟨-yori⟩ wa⌈ru⌉i ⟨〜より⟩悪い adj(*i*). ↔ **⟨-yori⟩ ii ⟨〜より⟩いい** adj(*i*).

EX. (**a**) A: How is the pain in your shoulder today?
肩の痛みは今日はどうですか。
Kata no ita-mi wa kyoo wa doo desu ka.
B: It's worse than yesterday.
昨日より悪いです。
Kinoo yori warui desu.
(**b**) My new boss is worse than the last one.

今度の上司はこの前のより悪い。
Kondo no jooshi wa kono mae no yori warui.

PHRASE: make matters worse *motto warui koto ni wa* もっと悪いことには

EX. The apartment is small. To make matters worse, it doesn't even have a window.
アパートは小さいです。もっと悪いことには、窓が一つもないんです。
Apaato wa chiisai desu. Motto warui koto ni wa, mado ga hitotsu mo nai n desu.

worship vi./vt. **[for s.o. to pay respect to a deity or to treat s.o. with adoration]**
1. ⟨⟨-o⟩⟩ **ra⌈ihai-suru** ⟨⟨〜を⟩⟩礼拝する ③ •c **[for s.o. to clasp one's hands before or kneel down to pray to a Buddha],** ⟨⟨-o⟩⟩ **re⌈ihai-suru** ⟨⟨〜を⟩⟩礼拝する ③ •c **[for s.o. to praise and offer prayers to God at a Jewish synagogue or a Christian church],** ⟨-o⟩ **o⌈ga⌉mu** ⟨〜を⟩拝む ① **[for s.o. to clasp one's hands and pray to God or Buddha]** ⟪**pray, bow to**⟫

EX. (**a**) On Sundays, more than 40% of all Americans attend church to worship.
日曜日にはアメリカ人の40％以上が教会に行って{礼拝して/*礼拝して/*拝んで}いる。
*Nichiyoo-bi ni wa Amerika-jin no yon-jup-paasento-ijoo ga kyookai ni itte {reihai-shite/*raihai-shite/*ogande} iru.*
(**b**) Buddhists worship Buddha.
仏教徒はおしゃか様を{拝む/礼拝する/*礼拝する}。
*Bukkyooto wa O-shaka-sama o {ogamu/raihai-suru/*reihai-suru}.*

2. ⟨-o⟩ **su⌈uhai-suru** ⟨〜を⟩崇拝する ③ •c **[for s.o. to admire and idolize s.o.]** ⟪**admire, adore**⟫

EX. No human being should be worshiped, as no one is perfect.
人間を崇拝するのは誤りだ。だれも完全ではないのだから。
Ningen o suuhai-suru no wa ayamari da. Dare-mo kanzen dewanai no da kara.

— n. **[an act performed in honor of a deity, including prayer, praise, and/or religious ceremony]**
1. ra⌈ihai 礼拝 •c **[an act of paying respect to or offering prayers to a Buddha], re⌈ihai** 礼拝 •c **[an act or service conducted in honor of the Judeo-Christian God, including prayer, praise, and/or religious ceremony]**
2. re⌈iha⌉i-shiki 礼拝式 •c **[a religious service conducted in honor of the Judeo-Christian God]**

worth adj. **[having the specified (monetary) value; good enough for or deserving of doing s.t.]**
{Vinf. nonpast/N no} ka⌉chi ga a⌉ru (N)
{Vinf. nonpast/Nの}価値がある(N)

EX. (**a**) This antique car is worth $80,000.
この時代ものの車は八万ドルの価値がある。
Kono jidai-mono no kuruma wa hachi-man-doru no kachi ga aru.
(**b**) Is it worth spending $1,000 on such a tiny machine?
こんな小さな機械に千ドルも使う価値があるんですか。
Konna chiisana kikai ni sen-doru mo tsukau kachi ga aru n desu ka.
(**c**) Japanese is a language well worth studying.
日本語は勉強する価値が十分ある言語です。
Nihon-go wa benkyoo-suru kachi ga juubun aru gengo desu.

— n. **[the quality of being good, useful, or exchangeable for money or other commodity]**
ka⌉chi 価値 •c **[the degree to which s.t./s.o./s.a. is useful, good, or exchangeable for money]** ⟪**value**⟫

EX. (**a**) The worth of an education lies not only in the career training it provides but also in its effectiveness in building character.
教育の価値は職業訓練を施すという点だけでなく人格の形成に役立つという点にもある。

W

Kyooiku no kachi wa shokugyoo-kunren o hodokosu to iu ten dake denaku jinkaku no keisei ni yaku-datsu to iu ten ni mo aru.
(**b**) The worth of a human being cannot be measured solely by how much he earns.
人の価値は収入だけでは計れない。
Hito no kachi wa shuunyuu dake de wa hakare-nai.

would aux. **[the form of the auxiliary verb "will" used in polite expressions or to express a future event anticipated in the past or an event that might have occurred if another event had occurred first]**

1. ø

EX. John said he would come to the party.
ジョンはパーティーに来ると言った。
Jon wa paatii ni kuru to itta.

2. Sinf. n de˥su ga Sinf.んですが [a form indicating willingness to do s.t. if a certain condition were met], Sinf. de˥sho˥o Sinf.でしょう [a form indicating the probability of an event occurring]

NOTE: Note the following exceptional patterns involving these forms: 1. when the informal nonpast form of {adj(*na*)./N + cop.} occurs in front of *n desu ga*, the form used is {adj(*na*). stem/N} *na n desu ga*; 2. when the informal nonpast form of adj(*na*). occurs in front of *deshoo*, the form used is adj(*na*). stem + *deshoo*; 3. when the informal nonpast form of N + cop. occurs in front of *deshoo*, the form used is N *deshoo*.

EX. (**a**) If I had the money, I would go to Japan.
もしもお金があったら、日本へ行く{んですが/でしょう}。
Moshi mo o-kane ga attara, Nihon e iku {n desu ga/deshoo}.
(**b**) If I hadn't studied Japanese I would never have gotten married to a Japanese man.
日本語を勉強しなかったら、日本人の男性と結婚しなかった{でしょう/んですが}。
Nihon-go o benkyoo-shinakattara, Nihon-jin no dansei to kekkon-shinakatta {deshoo/n desu ga}.

PHRASE: Would you mind if I...? V*te mo kamaimasen ka* V*te*も構いませんか。

EX. A: Would you mind if I opened the window?
窓を開けても構いませんか。
Mado o akete mo kamaimasen ka.
B: No, please go ahead.
ええ、どうぞ。
Ee, doozo.

3. (yo˥ku)…Vinf. past mo˥no˥ da (よく)…Vinf. pastものだ [a form indicating an action performed repeatedly or habitually in the past]

EX. (**a**) When I was a child, my father would often play catch with me.
子供の時、父は私とよくキャッチボールをしてくれたものだ。
Kodomo no toki, chichi wa watashi to yoku kyatchi-booru o shite kureta mono da.
(**b**) Back in those days I would write a letter to her every other day.
あのころ僕は一日おきに彼女に手紙を書いたものだ。
Ano koro boku wa ichi-nichi oki ni kanojo ni tegami o kaita mono da.

4. Vvol. to shi˥na˥katta Vvol.としなかった [for s.o. not to show a willingness to do s.t.], neg. of Vinf. past. [s.o. did not do s.t.]

EX. My five-year-old son wouldn't leave the toy department.
五つの息子はおもちゃ売り場を{離れようとしなかった/離れなかった}。
Itsutsu no musuko wa omocha-uri-ba o {hanareyoo to shinakatta/hanarenakatta}.

wouldn't aux. **[the negative form of "would"]**

SEE would 4

wound[1] n. **[an injury to the body caused by a cut, stab, blow, or tear《fig. "emotional hurt"》]**

1. ki˥zu 傷 [a tear or cut on a surface《fig. "shame," "emotional hurt"》]

EX. The wound I got during the war still causes me pain.
戦争で受けた傷がまだ痛む。
Sensoo de uketa kizu ga mada itamu.

2. (ko⌈koro no) i⌈tade (心の)痛手 [an emotional injury]

EX. It took Mari a year to recover from the wounds of her broken love affair.
マリは失恋の(心の)痛手から回復するのに一年かかった。
Mari wa shitsuren no (kokoro no) itade kara kaifuku-suru no ni ichi-nen kakatta.

—— vt. **[to inflict a physical or psychological injury on s.o./s.a.]**
⟨-o⟩ ki⌈zu-tsuke⌉ru ⟨〜を⟩傷つける ② [to inflict physical or mental harm on s.o./s.t./s.a.] ⟪injure, hurt, harm, damage, impair⟫, ⟨-o⟩ fu⌈shoo-saseru ⟨〜を⟩負傷させる /⟨causative of *fushoo-suru* ③ be wounded/ ② •c [to cause s.o. injury esp. in a war or accident], ⟨-ni⟩ ke⌈ga⌉ o saseru ⟨〜に⟩けがをさせる ② /⟨causative of *kega o suru* ③ be wounded/ [for s.o. to inflict physical damage on s.o.] ⟪injure⟫

EX. (**a**) The drunken driver hit and wounded a pedestrian.
酔っ払った運転手が歩行者をひいて{けがをさせた/負傷させた/*傷つけた}。
*Yopparatta unten-shu ga hokoo-sha o hiite {kega o saseta/fushoo-saseta/*kizu-tsuketa}.*
(**b**) His words wounded her feelings.
彼の言葉は彼女の気持ち{を傷つけた/*にけがをさせた/*を負傷させた}。
*Kare no kotoba wa kanojo no kimochi {o kizu-tsuketa/*ni kega o saseta/*o fushoo-saseta}.*

W

wound[2] vt. **[the past or past participle of "wind"]**
SEE wind[2] vt.

woven vt. **[the past participle of "weave"]**
SEE weave

wrap vt. **[to cover s.t. by folding s.t. around it]**
⟨-o⟩ (⟨-de⟩) tsu⌈tsu⌉mu ⟨〜を⟩(⟨〜で⟩)包む ① [for s.o. to cover or pack s.t. in its entirety with cloth or paper or to enclose s.o./s.t./s.a. with warmth] ⟪envelop, pack up, veil⟫, ⟨-o⟩ ⟨-ni⟩ ma⌈ki-tsuke⌉ru ⟨〜を⟩⟨〜に⟩巻き付ける ② [for s.o. to coil s.t. around s.t. else] ⟪wind, bandage, bind, roll up, reel⟫

EX. (**a**) Would you wrap this in some nice wrapping paper, please?
きれいな包装紙で{包んで/*巻き付けて}くれませんか。
*Kireina hoosoo-shi de {tsutsunde/*maki-tsukete/*ootte} kuremasen ka.*
(**b**) It was cold outside so I wrapped a scarf around my neck.
外はとても寒かったので、スカーフ{を首に巻き付けた/*で首を包んだ}。
*Totemo samukatta node, sukaafu {o kubi ni maki-tsuketa/*de kubi o tsutsunda}.*

PHRASE: be wrapped up in ⟨*-ni*⟩ *muchuu ni natte iru* ⟨〜に⟩夢中になっている ②

EX. I was so wrapped up in my work that I didn't notice it had become dark outside.
私は仕事に夢中になっていて、外が暗くなっていたことに気がつかなかった。
Watashi wa shigoto ni muchuu ni natte ite, soto ga kuraku natte ita koto ni ki-ga-tsukanakatta.

wreck vt. **[to destroy or ruin s.t., esp. a vehicle, in an accident]**
(⟨-de⟩) ta⌉iha-suru (⟨〜で⟩)大破する ③ •c [for s.t. to sustain serious damage] ⟪be wrecked, be heavily damaged⟫, (⟨-de⟩) na⌈npa-suru (⟨〜で⟩)難破する ③ •c [for a boat to capsize, sink, or run aground due to high seas, submerged rocks, etc.] ⟪shipwreck⟫, (⟨-de⟩) ha⌈metsu-suru (⟨〜で⟩)破滅する ③ •c [for s.t./s.o. to be totally ruined] ⟪ruin⟫

EX. (**a**) The boat was wrecked in the typhoon.
船は台風で{難破した/大破した/*破滅した}。
*Fune wa taifuu de {nanpa-shita/taiha-shita/*hametsu-shita}.*
(**b**) Drugs wrecked his life.

麻薬で彼の人生は{破滅した/*大破した/*難破した}。
*Mayaku de kare no jinsei wa {hametsu-shita/*taiha-shita/*nanpa-shita}.*
(**c**) The car was wrecked by the impact of the collision.
衝突の衝撃で車が{大破した/*難破した/*破滅した}。
*Shoototsu no shoogeki de kuruma ga {taiha-shita/*nanpa-shita/*hametsu-shita}.*

— n. **[an instance of s.t. such as a vehicle sustaining major damage and disablement; the remains of s.t. such as a vehicle which has sustained major damage and disablement]**
1. ta⌉iha 大破 •c [an act/instance of destroying s.t. or of s.t. being completely destroyed] ((ruin, serious damage))
2. na⌈npa 難破 •c [a disabling accident involving a ship]
3. za⌈ngai 残がい •c [the remains of an object which has been destroyed beyond use] ((wreckage))

EX. My car was a wreck after the accident.
僕の車は、事故の後、残がい同様だった。
Boku no kuruma wa, jiko no ato, zangai dooyoo datta.

wriggle vi. **[for s.o./s.a. to twist one's body in a writhing motion]**
no⌈taku⌉ru のたくる ① [for s.o./s.a. to creep forward using twisting motions of the body] ((writhe, squirm)), u⌈gome⌉ku うごめく ① [for a worm or worm-like creature to move about in a constant crawling motion] ((squirm)), mo⌉zo-mozo-suru もぞもぞする ③ [for a worm or worm-like creature to creep about or for s.o. to squirm] ((squirm))

EX. (**a**) Little worms were wriggling under the stone.
石の下で、小さな虫が{うごめいて/のたくって/もぞもぞして}いた。
Ishi no shita de, chiisana mushi ga {ugomeite/notakutte/mozo-mozo-shite} ita.
(**b**) A snake was wriggling through the grass in our backyard.
蛇が裏庭の芝生で{のたくって/*うごめいて/*もぞもぞして}いた。
*Hebi ga ura-niwa no shibafu de {notakutte/*ugomeite/*mozo-mozo-shite} ita.*
(**c**) The first-graders wriggled impatiently in their seats as the teacher gave them instructions.
一年生の子供たちは席について先生の説明を聞いている間中、じっとしていられなくて{もぞもぞして/*うごめいて/*のたくって}いた。
*Ichi-nensei no kodomo-tachi wa seki ni tsuite sensei no hanashi o kiite iru aida-juu, jitto shite i-rarenakute {mozo-mozo-shite/*ugomeite/*notakutte} ita.*

wring vt. **[for s.o. to twist and squeeze s.t., esp. to force liquid out ((fig. "force s.t. out of s.o."))]**
⟨-o⟩ shi⌈bo⌉ru ⟨~を⟩しぼる ① [for s.o. to squeeze liquid out of s.t. or force s.t. out of s.o. such as taxes or ideas ((fig. "focus on s.t."))] ((squeeze, press, extract)), ⟨-o⟩ ne⌈ji⌉ru ⟨~を⟩ねじる ② [for s.o. to apply a rotating force to s.t. straight and narrow which is fixed at one end so that it turns or to turn the opposite ends of s.t. straight and narrow in opposite directions] ((twist, screw, wrench)), ⟨-o⟩ hi⌈ne⌉ru ⟨~を⟩ひねる ① [for s.o. to hold s.t. with one's fingers and twist it ((fig. "put great thought into s.t.," "beat s.o. easily"))] ((turn, switch, twist)), ⟨-o⟩ tsu⌉yoku ni⌈giru ⟨~を⟩強く握る ① [for s.o. to hold s.t. very tightly, esp. s.o.'s hands]
㊮ "squeeze milk/oil/lemon"▷搾る, otherwise ▷絞る

EX. (**a**) Don't wring my arm! It hurts!.
腕を{ねじらない/ひねらない/強く握らない/*しぼらない}でください。痛いから。
*Ude o {nejiranai/hineranai/tsuyoku nigiranai/*shiboranai} de kudasai. Itai kara.*

W

(**b**) If you don't tell me the truth I'll wring your neck, young man.
本当のことを言わないなら、おまえの首を{ひねる/*絞る/*ねじる/*強く握る}ぞ。
*Hontoo no koto o iwanai nara, omae no kubi o {hineru/*shiboru/*nejiru/*tsuyoku nigiru} zo.*
(**c**) You'd better wring out the towel. It's dripping water.
タオルを{絞った/*ねじった/*ひねった/*強く握った}方がいいですよ。水が垂れているから。
*Taoru o {shibotta/*nejitta/*hinetta/*tsuyoku nigitta} hoo ga ii desu yo. Mizu ga tarete iru kara.*
(**d**) She wrung my hand with joy when we met.
会ったとき、彼女は喜んで私の手を{強く握った/*ねじった/*絞った/*ひねった}。
*Atta toki, kanojo wa yorokonde watashi no te o {tsuyoku nigitta/*nejitta/*shibotta/*hinetta}.*

wrinkle n. **[a small crease or ridge on a smooth surface such as skin, paper, or cloth]** ((**line, crease, furrow, crumple**))
shi⌈wa しわ ((**lines, furrows**))

EX. (**a**) The old man's forehead was covered with wrinkles.
老人は額にたくさんしわがあった。
Roojin wa hitai ni takusan shiwa ga atta.
(**b**) I flattened out the wrinkles in my pants with an iron.
ズボンのしわをアイロンでのばしました。
Zubon no shiwa o airon de nobashimashita.

— vt. **[to make one or more creases or ridges on a smooth surface such as skin, paper, or cloth]**
shi⌈wa o tsu⌈ku⌉ru しわを作る ①, **shi⌈wa (-kucha) ni suru** しわ(くちゃ)にする ③ **[to cause one or more creases or ridges on a small surface]**

EX. The cat slept on my newly-laundered shirt and wrinkled in.
猫が洗濯したばかりのシャツの上に寝て{しわ(くちゃ)にした/しわを作った}。
Neko ga sentaku-shita bakari no shatsu no ue ni nete {shiwa(-kucha) ni shita/shiwa o tsukutta}.

— vi. **[for one or more creases or ridges to form on a smooth surface such as skin, paper, or cloth]**
shi⌈wa ni na⌉ru しわになる ① **[for a surface to develop one or more creases or ridges]**, **⟨-ni⟩ shi⌈wa ga de⌈ki⌉ru** ⟨〜に⟩しわが出来る ② **[for one or more creases or ridges to form on a surface]**

EX. Why don't you put on rubber gloves when you wash the dishes so that your hands don't wrinkle.
手{がしわにならない/にしわが出来ない}ように、食器を洗う時にゴム手袋をはめたらどうですか。
Te {ga shiwa ni naranai/ni shiwa ga dekinai} yooni, shokki o arau toki ni gomu-te-bukuro o hametara doo desu ka.

wrist n. **[the joint between the hand and the arm]**
te⌉-kubi 手首

EX. A baseball pitcher has to have a strong wrist.
野球のピッチャーは手首が強くなければならない。
Yakyuu no pitchaa wa te-kubi ga tsuyoku nakereba naranai.

write vi./vt. **[for s.o. to form letters, words, or symbols on a surface, esp. on paper using a pen or pencil]**
⟨-o⟩ ka⌉ku ⟨〜を⟩かく ① **[for s.o. to make a short line on a surface with a pointed object]** ((**scratch, draw (a line)**))
㊥ "write"▷書く, "draw a picture/scratch"▷かく

EX. (**a**) I can read *hiragana*, but I can't write it.
平仮名は読めますが、書けません。
Hira-gana wa yome-masu ga, kake-masen.
(**b**) Write me a letter when you get over there, will you?

W

向こうに着いたら手紙を書いてね。
Mukoo ni tsuitara tegame o kaite ne.
(**c**) What are you writing your thesis on?
論文は何について書いているんですか。
Ronbun wa nani ni-tsuite kaite iru n desu ka.
(**d**) Could you show me how to write this *kanji*?
この漢字をどう書くか教えていただけませんか。
Kono kanji o doo kaku ka oshiete itadake-masen ka.

writer n. **[the author of s.t. or a person who makes a living by composing things such as books, articles, etc., for others to read]**
1. ka⌉ita hito 書いた人 [the author of s.t.]
EX. Who is the writer of this article?
この記事を書いた人はだれですか。
Kono kiji o kaita hito wa dare desu ka.
2. cho⌉sha 著者 •c [the creator of a particular book/thesis/essay] ((author)), hi⌉ssha 筆者 •c [a person who is currently composing or has composed a particular book/thesis/essay] ((author, the present writer)), sa⌈kka 作家 •c [one who creates artistic works as an occupation, such as a novelist, a painter, etc.] ((author, novelist, painter, sculptor)), sa⌈kusha 作者 •c [the creator of a particular poem, novel, painting, sculpture, etc.] ((author, novelist, sculptor, painter))
EX. (**a**) I once interviewed the writer of this book.
この本の{著者/作者/筆者/*作家}にインタビューしたことがある。
*Kono hon no {chosha/sakusha/hissha/*sakka} ni intabyuu-shita koto ga aru.*
(**b**) According to the views of this writer, Japan should adopt a cautious attitude toward opening its markets.
この{筆者/著者/*作家/*作者}は、日本は市場開放に対して慎重な態度を取るべきだとしている。
*Kono {hissha/chosha/*sakka/*sakusha} wa, Nihon wa shijoo-kaihoo ni-taishite shinchoona taido o toru beki da to shite iru.*
(**c**) A: Who do you like best among currently popular Japanese writers?
現代の日本の人気{作家/*筆者/*作者/*著者}の中でだれが一番好きですか。
*Gendai no Nihon no ninki-{sakka/*hissha/*sakka/*chosha} no naka de dare ga ichiban suki desu ka.*
B: I like Haruki Murakami best.
村上春樹が一番好きです。
Murakami Haruki ga ichiban suki desu.

writing n. **[the act of composing s.t. to be read; literary work(s); letters or words formed by s.o.'s hand]**
1. ka⌉ku ko⌈to⌉ 書くこと [an act/instance of composing s.t. to be read], cho⌈jutsu 著述 •c [an act/instance of composing a book] ((book, literary production))
EX. The popular writer said in an interview that he couldn't live without writing.
その人気作家はインタビューの中で{書くこと/著述}なしには生きていけないと語った。
Sono ninki-sakka wa intabyuu no naka de {kaku koto/chojutsu} nashi ni wa ikite ikenai to katatta.
2. cho⌈saku 著作 •c [the act of composing a book for publication or a book so composed by s.o.] ((literary work, authorship)), sa⌈kuhin 作品 •c [an artistic creation by s.o.] ((work, opus)), kaita mo⌈no⌉ 書いたもの [s.t. composed to be read]
EX. (**a**) Have you ever read Pascal's writings?
パスカルの{著作/作品/書いたもの}を読んだことがありますか。
Pasukaru no {chosaku/sakuhin/kaita mono} o yonda koto ga arimasu ka.
(**b**) I like to read his writing.
私は彼の{書いたもの/著作/作品}を好んで読んでいる。
Watashi wa kare no {kaita mono/chosaku/sakuhin} o kononde yonde iru.
3. mo⌉ji 文字 •c [the symbol of a sound or other linguistic unit in a human language]

EX. Japanese writing is unique in that it is made up of three systems: *hiragana, katakana* and *kanji.*
日本の文字は三つの表記法、すなわち、平仮名、片仮名、漢字からなる点でユニークだ。
Nihon no moji wa mittsu no hyooki-hoo, sunawachi, hira-gana, kata-kana, kanji kara naru ten de yuniiku da.

PHRASE: writing brush *fude* 筆

EX. When we do calligraphy we use a writing brush.
書道をする時は筆を使います。
Shodoo o suru toki wa fude o tsukaimasu.

PHRASE: writing materials *bunboo-gu* 文房具 •c ⟪stationery⟫, *hikki-yoogu* 筆記用具 •c

EX. (**a**) At the beginning of each semester, we place an order for any necessary writing materials.
学期の初めには必要な{文房具/??筆記用具}を注文します。
Gakki no hajime ni wa hitsuyoona {bunboo-gu/??hikki-yoogu} o chuumon-shimasu.
(**b**) Bring any writing materials you need with you to the test.
テストには必要な{筆記用具/*文房具}を持って来なさい。
*Tesuto ni wa hitsuyoona {hikki-yoogu/*bunboo-gu} o motte kinasai.*

written adj. **[the past participle of "write"] ka⌈ka⌉reta N 書かれたN /⟨Vinf. past tense of the passive form of *kaku* ① write/**

EX. There are a lot of written materials dealing with that incident.
その事件については書かれた資料がたくさんあります。
Sono jiken ni-tsuite wa kakareta shiryoo ga takusan arimasu.

PHRASE: written language *bungo* 文語 •c ↔ *koogo* 口語 •c

wrong adj. **[not in conformity with what is just, morally good, true, correct, or proper] 1. fu⌈sei no N 不正のN •c [not comforming to an ethical or legal standard] ⟪unjust, unfair, wicked, dishonest, unlawful, illegal⟫, fu⌈seina 不正な** adj(*na*). **•c, ma⌈chiga⌉tta N 間違ったN /⟨Vinf. past of *machigau* ① err/ [not consistent with what is true or factual or with a socially established convention], ma⌈chiga⌉tte iru (N) 間違っている(N) /⟨V*te iru* of *machigau* ① err/ ② [not consistent with what is true or factual or with a socially established convention] ⟪incorrect⟫ ↔ tadashii 正しい** adj(*i*).; **⟨-ni⟩ fu-⌈te⌉kitoona ⟨〜に⟩不適当な** adj(*na*). **•c [not right for a given situation, purpose, or requirement] ⟪unsuitable, unfit, inadequate, improper⟫ ↔ tekitoona 適当な** adj(*na*). **•c**

EX. (**a**) The man appears to have made large sums of money through his ethically wrong business practices.
男は{不正な/*間違った/*間違っている/*不適当な}取引で多額の金をもうけたらしい。
*Otoko wa {fuseina/*machigatta/*machigatte iru/*fu-tekitoona} torihiki de tagaku no kane o mooketa rashii.*
(**b**) A: I believe that a married woman should stay at home and care for her family.
結婚した女の人はうちにいて家族の面倒を見た方がいいと思いますよ。
Kekkon-shita onna no hito wa uchi ni ite kazoku no mendoo o mita hoo ga ii to omoimasu yo.
B: You're totally wrong on that.
それは完全に{間違っています/*不正です/*不適当です}よ。
*Sore wa kanzenni {machigatte imasu/*fusei desu/*fu-tekitoo desu} yo.*
(**c**) Where did you get the wrong idea that Japanese people are the hardest working in the world?
日本人が世界一よく働くという{間違った/間違っている/*不正の/*不適当な}考えをどこで聞いて来たんですか。
*Nihon-jin ga sekai-ichi yoku hataraku to iu {machigatta/machigatte iru/*fusei no/*fu-tekitoona} kangae o doko de kiite kita n desu ka.*
(**d**) Living in a different culture one is at

times bound to make wrong assumptions about people's behavior.
違う文化で生活すると人の行動について{間違った/不適当な/間違っている/*不正の}判断をすることは避けられない。
*Chigau bunka de seikatsu-suru to hito no koodoo ni-tsuite {machigatta/fu-tekitoona/machigatte iru/*fusei no} handan o suru koto wa sakerarenai.*

2. ma⌈chiga⌉tta N 間違ったN /⟨Vinf. past of *machigau* ① err/ [not consistent with what is true or factual or with a socially established convention], ma⌈chiga⌉tte iru (N) 間違っている(N) /⟨V *te iru* of *machigau* ① err/ ② [not consistent with what is true or factual or with a socially established convention] ⟪incorrect⟫ ↔ tadashii 正しい adj(*i*).; **gya⌈ku no N 逆のN •c [opposite in order or direction to s.t. else or to what is normal or expected] ⟪reverse, opposite⟫, u⌈ra (no) N 裏(の)N [located on the side which is not exposed to view] ⟪on the back, on the reverse side⟫**

EX. (**a**) A car was driving in the wrong lane.
車が{間違った/逆の/間違っている/*裏の}車線を走っていた。
*Kuruma ga {machigatta/gyaku no/machigatte iru/*ura no} shasen o hashitte ita.*
(**b**) I signed my name on the wrong side of the sheet of paper.
私は紙の{裏側/{*間違った/*逆の/*間違っている}面}に名前を書いてしまった。
*Watashi wa kami no {ura-gawa/{*machigatta/*gyaku no/*machigatte iru} men} ni namae o kaite shimatta.*

3. gu⌈ai ga wa⌈ru⌉i 具合が悪い adj(*i*). **[in bad condition physically or mechanically; undesirable in timing or manner of execution], cho⌈oshi ga wa⌈ru⌉i 調子が悪い** adj(*i*). **[out of order physically, mechanically, or psychologically]**

EX. Something's wrong with the engine on my car.
車のエンジンの{具合/調子}が悪い。
Kuruma no enjin no {guai/chooshi} ga warui.

— adv. **[in a manner not in conformity with what is just, morally good, true, correct, or proper]**
fu⌈seini 不正に /⟨adj(*na*). *ni* of *fuseina* unjust/ [in a manner not conforming to an ethical or legal standard], ma⌈chiga⌉tte 間違って /⟨V *te* of *machigau* ① to make an error/ ⟪by mistake⟫, cho⌈oshi wa⌉ruku 調子悪く /⟨adj(*i*). *ku* of *chooshi (ga) warui* adj(*i*). in bad condition/, gu⌈ai wa⌉ruku 具合悪く /⟨adj(*i*). *ku* of *guai (ga) warui* adj(*i*). in bad condition/

PHRASE: get s.o. wrong ⟨*-o*⟩ *gokai-suru* ⟨〜を⟩誤解する ③ •c

EX. Don't get me wrong. I'm all for the feminist movement.
誤解しないでください。女性解放運動には大賛成なんですから。
Gokai-shinaide kudasai. Josei-kaihoo-undoo ni wa dai-sansei na n desu kara.

— n. **[s.t. which is not in conformity with what is just, morally good, true, correct, or proper]**
a⌉ku 悪 •c [s.t. bad or undesirable], fu⌈sei 不正 •c [the state of not conforming to an ethical or legal standard; s.t. which does not so conform] ⟪injustice, dishonesty, illegality⟫, hi⌈koo 非行 •c [behavior that runs counter to reason or moral standards] ⟪misdeed, misconduct⟫

Wyoming n.
Wa⌈iomi⌉ngu ワイオミング •f [the state of Wyoming]

W

X

Xmas n. **[an abbreviation for "Christmas"]**
Ku⌈risu⌉masu クリスマス •f

EX. Merry Xmas! And a Happy New Year!
メリークリスマス。そして、よいお年を。
Merii Kurisumasu. Soshite, yoi o-toshi o.

X-ray n.
e⌈kkusu-sen X線 •f+c, re⌈nto⌉gen レントゲン •f

NOTE: *Rentogen* comes from the name of the German scientist who discovered X-rays.

EX. The X-ray of my mouth revealed that I have three cavities.
口の中の{X線/レントゲン}で、虫歯が三つもあることが分かった。
Kuchi no naka no {ekkusu-sen/rentogen} de, mushi-ba ga mittsu mo aru koto ga wakatta.

Y

Yankee n.
ya⌉nkii ヤンキー •f

yard[1] n. **[a unit of length equal to 0.9144 meter]**
ya⌉ado ヤード •f

EX. In football, the goal lines for each team are 100 yards apart.
フットボールでは相対するチームのゴールラインは百ヤード離れている。
Futto-booru de wa ai-taisuru chiimu no gooru-rain wa hyaku-yaado hanarete iru.

yard[2] n. **[the area of ground next to or surrounding a house or other building 《fig. "shipyard"》]**
ni⌈wa 庭 [a plot of ground next to a house, often used to grow flowers and other plants] 《garden》, u⌈ra-niwa 裏庭 [a plot of ground on the opposite side of a house from the main entrance] 《back yard》, a⌈kichi 空き地 [an empty piece of land available for use] 《vacant land, unoccupied land》, na⌈ka-niwa 中庭 [a space between buildings on an estate] 《courtyard, court》, ko⌉onai 構内 •c [the area within the boundaries of a piece of property, esp. that of an institution] 《premises, precincts, compound》

EX. (**a**) The children are out playing baseball in the yard.
子供たちが{庭/裏庭/空き地/構内/中庭}で野球をしている。

Kodomo-tachi ga {niwa/ura-niwa/akichi/koonai/naka-niwa} de yakyuu o shite iru.
(**b**) This campus has a beautiful yard.
このキャンパスは{中庭/*庭/*裏庭/*構内/*空き地}がきれいだ。
*Kono kyanpasu wa {naka-niwa/*niwa/*ura-niwa*koonai/*akichi} ga kirei da.*

yarn n. **[fibers of thread spun into strands, esp. for the purpose of knitting or weaving]**
ke⌈ito 毛糸 [the soft hair of sheep processed for knitting], i⌉to 糸 [a very fine cord made of strands of spun silk or other fiber] ((**thread**))

EX. I need some yarn to knit a sweater for my fiance.
未来の夫にセーターを編んで上げるのに、{毛糸/*糸}が要ります。
*Mirai no otto ni seetaa o ande ageru no ni, {ke-ito/*ito} ga irimasu.*

yawn vi. **[for s.o./s.a. to open one's mouth wide from sleepiness or boredom]**
a⌈kubi o suru あくびをする ③

EX. Several students were yawning while listening to the teacher's lecture.
先生の話を聞きながらあくびをしている学生が数人いた。
Sensei no hanashi o kikinagara akubi o shite iru gakusei ga suu-nin ita.

—— n. **[an involuntary act of opening the mouth wide from sleepiness or boredom]**
a⌈kubi あくび

yeah adv. **[an informal version of "yes"]**
u⌉n うん int. **[an interjection indicating agreement with or acceptance of what has been said** ⟨s⟩**]**

EX. (**a**) A: Did you eat your breakfast yet?
朝御飯、もう食べた?
Asa-gohan, moo tabeta?
B: Yeah, I did.
うん、食べたよ。
Un, tabeta yo.
(**b**) A: Do you want to take a shower?
シャワー、浴びたい?
Shawaa, abi-tai?
B: Yeah.
うん。
Un.

year n. **[a 12-month period as measured by the Gregorian calendar]**
to⌈shi⌉ 年 [a 12-month period as measured by the Gregorian calendar or the age of s.o.], -nen ～年 •c [a counter for a 12-month period as measured by the Gregorian calendar], -sai ～歳 •c [a counter for the number of 12-month periods that have elapsed since one's birth]

EX. (**a**) Last year was an eventful year for our family.
去年は我が家にとって出来事の多い年でした。
Kyonen wa waga-ya ni-totte deki-goto no ooi toshi deshita.
(**b**) A: How old is your daughter?
娘さんは(年は)いくつですか。
Musume-san wa (toshi wa) ikutsu desu ka.
B: She's 17 years old.
十七({歳/*年})です。
*{Juu-nana-({sai/*nen})} desu.*
(**c**) I've lived in Tokyo for five years.
僕は東京に五年(間)住んでいます。
Boku wa Tookyoo ni go-nen(-kan) sunde imasu.

PHRASE: the year after next *sarai-nen* 再来年 **•c**, the year before last *{ototoshi/otodoshi}* {おととし/おとどし}, every year *{mai-toshi/mai-nen}* **•c** 毎年

EX. I go to New York once every year.
私はニューヨークへ毎年一回行っています。
Watashi wa Nyuuyooku e mai-toshi ik-kai itte imasu.

PHRASE: last year *kyonen* 去年 **•c**, *sakunen* 昨年 **•c** ⟨fml⟩

EX. I graduated from college last year.
{去年/昨年}大学を卒業しました。
{Kyonen/Sakunen} daigaku o sotsugyoo-shimashita.

PHRASE: next year *rainen* 来年 **•c**

EX. The construction of that building is

Y

expected to be completed in June of next year.
あの建築中の建物は来年の六月に完成する予定です。
Ano kenchiku-chuu no tate-mono wa rainen no roku-gatsu ni kansei-suru yotei desu.

PHRASE: twenty years old *hatachi* 二十(歳)

NOTE: *Hatachi* is a numeral counter used only for the twentieth year of a person's life.

PHRASE: this year *kotoshi* 今年

EX. (**a**) My daughter entered college this year.
娘が今年大学に入りました。
Musume ga kotoshi daigaku ni hairimashita.
(**b**) I have to finish writing my book before the end of this year.
今年中に本を書き終わらなければならないんです。
Kotoshi-juu ni hon o kaki-owaranakereba naranai n desu.

yearly adj. **[occurring once in every 12-month period]**
ne⌉n i⌈k-ka⌉i no N 年一回のN [occurring once every 12-month period], ma⌈i-toshi no N 毎年のN [occurring, done, etc., in every 12-month period]

EX. The alumni gathering for my class is a yearly event.
僕の学年の同窓会は{毎年/年一回}の催しものです。
Boku no gakunen no doosoo-kai wa {mai-toshi/nen ik-kai} no moyooshi mono desu.

yell vi. **[for s.o. to utter a loud cry]**
wa⌈me⌉ku わめく ① [for s.o. to utter a loud and hideous cry] ⟪**shout, scream**⟫, ⟨⟨**-to**⟩⟩ **sa⌈ke⌉bu** ⟨⟨〜と⟩⟩**叫ぶ ① [for s.o. to utter in a loud voice (spontaneously) in order to bring attention to s.t.]** ⟪**shout, cry (out), scream, shriek, exclaim**⟫

EX. (**a**) The child began yelling when his mother refused to buy him a toy.
子供は母親がおもちゃを買ってくれなかったので{わめき/*叫び}出した。
*Kodomo wa haha-oya ga omocha o katte kurenakatta node {wameki/*sakebi} dashita.*
(**b**) He yelled into the crowd to get everyone's attention.
彼は注意を引こうとして、群衆に向かって{叫んだ/*わめいた}。
*Kare wa chuui o hikoo to shite, gunshuu ni mukatte {sakenda/*wameita}.*
(**c**) As we sat watching the night sky, my son suddenly yelled out, "Look, a shooting star!"
みんなで座って夜空を眺めている時、突然息子が「流れ星だ」と{叫んだ/*わめいた}。
*Minna de suwatte yo-zora o nagamete iru toki, totsuzen musuko ga 'Nagare-boshi da' to {sakenda/*wameita}.*

yellow adj. **[having the color of egg yolk]**
ki⌈iroi 黄色い adj(*i*).

EX. (a) The color of taxicabs in the U.S. is often yellow.
アメリカのタクシーの色は黄色いことが多い。
Amerika no takushii no iro wa kiiroi koto ga ooi.
(b) The leaves have already turned yellow.
木の葉がもう黄色くなった。
{Ki/Ko} no ha ga moo kiiroku natta.

—— n. **[the color of egg yolk]**
ki-⌈iro 黄色

Yellowstone n.
I⌈eroosuto⌉on イエローストーン •f

yen n. **[the monetary unit in Japan]**
e⌉n 円 •c

EX. A: What is the exchange rate today between the yen and the dollar?
今日の円とドルの為替相場はどうなっていますか。
Kyoo no en to doru no kawase-sooba wa doo natte imasu ka.
B: It's 98 yen to the dollar.
一ドル、九十八円です。
Ichi-doru, kyuu-juu-hachi-en desu.

yes adv. **[an adverb indicating an affirmative reply to a question or request or used to**

make known the speaker's presence in response to a summons]

1. ha⌉i はい int. **[an interjection indicating an affirmative reply to a question or request or acknowledging what has been said by the other party or used to make known the speaker's presence in response to a summons] ↔ iie** いいえ int.; **e⌉e** ええ int. **[an interjection indicating an affirmative response to a question or acknowledging]**

NOTE: *Ee*, which is less formal than *hai*, is often avoided in formal situations such as conversations with one's superior. *Ee* cannot be used as a response when one's name is called in a roll call. When one's name is called out informally as in "Yoshiko!", the normal response is "*Nani?*" (What is it?).

EX. (**a**) A: Have you read this book?
この本を読んだことがありますか。
Kono hon o yonda koto ga arimasu ka.
B: Yes, I have.
{はい/ええ}、あります。
{Hai/Ee}, arimasu.
(**b**) A: Haven't you seen *Cats* yet?
『キャッツ』をまだ見ていませんか。
"Kyattsu" o mada mite imasen ka.
B: Yes, I have.
いいえ、もう見ました。
Iie, moo mimashita.
B (alternative answer): No, I haven't seen it.
{はい/ええ}、まだです。
{Hai/Ee}, mada desu.

NOTE: In answering a negative question, "no" is used in English if one agrees with the negative statement and "yes" if one disagrees with the negative statement and wishes to express the opposite, affirmative statement, Japanese is just the reverse in this respect, as seen in examples (b) and (d): *hai/ee* is used to indicate agreement with the negative statement and *iie* to express the opposite, affirmative statement. But if the negative question is itself understood to make an affirmative assertion, as in example (c), agreement with this assertion is expressed in both English and Japanese by "yes"/*hai/ee* and disagreement by "no"/*iie*.

EX. (**c**) A: —Showing something to B that B has left behind— Isn't this yours?
これ、あなたのじゃありませんか。
Kore, anata no jaarimasen ka.
B: Yes, that's right.
{はい/ええ}、そうです。
{Hai/Ee}, soo desu.
B (alternative answer): No, it isn't.
いいえ、違います。
Iie, chigaimasu.
(**d**) A: Didn't you go to the party?
パーティーへ行かなかったんですか。
Paatii e ikanakatta n desu ka.
B: Yes, I did.
いいえ、行きました。
Iie, ikimashita.
B (alternative answer): No, I didn't.
{はい/ええ}、行きませんでした。
{Hai/Ee}, ikimasen deshita.

yesterday n. **[the day before the present day]**
ki⌈no⌉o きのう **↔ ashita** あした, **asu** あす; **sa⌈ku⌉jitsu** 昨日 **•c** ⟨**fml**⟩ **↔ myoonichi** 明日 **•c** ⟨**fml**⟩

EX. (**a**)Yesterday was the Emperor's birthday.
{きのう/昨日}は天皇陛下のお誕生日でした。
{Kinoo/Sakujitsu} wa tennoo-heika no o-tanjoo-bi deshita.
(**b**) Yesterday was my birthday.
{きのう/*昨日}は僕の誕生日だったんだ。
*{Kinoo/*Sakujitsu} wa boku no tanjoo-bi datta n da.*

—— adv. **[on the day before the present day]**
ki⌈no⌉o きのう **↔ ashita** あした, **asu** あす; **sa⌈ku⌉jitsu** 昨日 **•c** ⟨**fml**⟩ **↔ myoonichi** 明日 **•c** ⟨**fml**⟩

NOTE: Just as English "yesterday" takes no preposition, Japanese *kinoo* takes no particle, including *ni*. For example, {Yesterday/*On yesterday} I saw a movie.▷ *{Kinoo/*Kinoo ni} eiga o mimashita.*

EX. (**a**) The prime minister paid a visit to the American Embassy yesterday.
首相は{きのう/昨日}アメリカ大使館を訪れた。

Y

Shushoo wa {kinoo/sakujitsu} Amerika-taishikan o otozureta.
(**b**) We had a *kanji* quiz yesterday in Japanese class.
{きのう/*昨日}日本語の授業で漢字の小テストがあったんだ。
*{Kinoo/*Sakujitsu} Nihon-go no jugyoo de kanji no shoo-tesuto ga atta n da.*

NOTE: *Kuizu* in Japanese cannot be used to mean "a small test"; it means a game in which people compete by answering a set of questions.

yet adv. **[at the present time]**
mo˥o もう [to be no longer in the same state as at some previous time] ⟪(not) any longer, already, yet, now⟫, **ma˥da まだ [to be in the some state as all previous points in time under consideration]** ⟪still, (not) yet⟫

EX. (**a**) A: Has your friend arrived in Tokyo yet?
友達は{もう/*まだ}東京に着きましたか。
*Tomodachi wa {moo/*mada} Tookyoo ni tsukimashita ka.*
B: No, not yet.
いいえ、{まだ/*もう}です。
*Iie, {mada/*moo} desu.*
(**b**) A: Have you eaten lunch yet?
{もう/*まだ}昼御飯を食べましたか。
*{Moo/*Mada} hiru-gohan o tabemashita ka.*
B: Yes, I already have.
ええ、{もう/*まだ}食べました。
*Ee, {moo/*mada} tabemashita.*
(**c**) A: Have you done your homework yet?
{もう/*まだ}宿題をしましたか。
*{Moo/*Mada} shukudai o shimashita ka.*
B: No, I haven't yet.
いいえ、{まだ/*もう}していません。
*Iie, {mada/*moo} shite imasen.*
(**d**) A: Have you ever been to Okinawa?
沖縄へ行ったことがありますか。
Okinawa e itta koto ga arimasu ka.
B: No, not yet.
いいえ、{まだ/*もう}です。
*Iie, {mada/*moo} desu.*

yield vi. **[to give way to another, esp. under force or compulsion, or to bear fruit]**
⟨-ni⟩ ma˥keru ⟨〜に⟩負ける ② [to be defeated by some concrete or intangible force] ⟪be defeated, be beaten, lose, go under⟫, **⟨-ni⟩ {o˥ojiru/o˥ozuru} ⟨〜に⟩{応じる ②/応ずる} [to respond (positively) to an outside stimulus]** ⟪answer, reply to, respond to, obey, comply with, apply for⟫, **⟨-ni⟩ ku˥ssuru ⟨〜に⟩屈する ③ •c [for s.o. to bend to s.t./s.o. physically or psychologically]** ⟪bend, give in to, bow to⟫

NOTE: *Oozuru* is used only in its nonpast affirmative form.

EX. (**a**) He is not the type of person to yield to temptation.
彼は誘惑に{負ける/屈する/*応じる/*応ずる}ような人じゃない。
*Kare wa yuuwaku ni {makeru/kussuru/*oojiru/*oozuru} yoona hito janai.*
(**b**) If someone asks me to do something insistently, I usually yield to the request.
だれかに何かをしつこく頼まれると、私は大抵その要求に{応じて/*負けて/*屈して}しまう。
*Dare-ka ni nani-ka o shitsukoku tanoma-reru to, watashi wa taitei sono yookyuu ni {oojite/*makete/*kusshite} shimau.*

— vt. **[for s.o. to give control or possession of s.t. to another; for s.t. to produce or bring about s.t.]**

1. ⟨-ni⟩ ⟨-o⟩ yu˥zuru ⟨〜に⟩⟨〜を⟩譲る ① [for s.o. to hand over to another s.t. such as a possession, right, or position] ⟪transfer, give way, offer⟫

EX. (**a**) My father yielded all his property to me.
父は私に全財産を譲ってくれた。
Chichi wa watashi ni zen-zaisan o yuzutte kureta.
(**b**) At this intersection, cars have to yield right of way to pedestrians.
この交差点では車は歩行者に道を譲らなければならない。
Kono koosa-ten dewa kuruma wa hokoo-sha ni michi o yuzuranakereba naranai.

2. ⟨-o⟩ sa˥n-su˥ru ⟨〜を⟩産する ③ •c [to

produce s.t.] ((produce)), ⟨-o⟩ sa⌈nshutsu-suru ⟨〜を⟩産出する •c [to produce s.t. natural, such as an agricultural product] ((produce, turn out))

EX. This area used to yield a lot of rice.
この地方は昔は米をたくさん{産して/産出して}いた。
Kono chihoo wa mukashi wa kome o takusan {san-shite/sanshutsu-shite} ita.

3. ⟨-ni⟩ ⟨-o⟩ mo⌈tara⌉su ⟨〜に⟩⟨〜を⟩もたらす ① [to bring about s.t.] ((bring about, cause))

EX. The cold air from the north yielded snow.
北からの冷たい風が雪をもたらした。
Kita kara no tsumetai kaze ga yuki o motarashita.

4. mi⌉ o tsu⌈ke⌉ru 実をつける ② [to bear fruit]

EX. This apple tree yields a lot of fruit.
このりんごの木はよく実をつける。
Kono ringo no ki wa yoku mi o tsukeru.

— n. [the amount of s.t. produced]

1. sa⌈nshutsu 産出 •c [an art/instance of producing s.t. or s.t. produced] ((production, output))

EX. The yield of rice this year was greater than average.
今年の米の産出は例年より多かった。
Kotoshi no kome no sanshutsu wa reinen yori ookatta.

2. ri-⌈ma⌉wari 利回り [return on an investment] ((interest, profits, returns))

EX. The yield on regular deposits at this bank is less than two percent.
この銀行の普通預金の利回りは二%以下です。
Kono ginkoo no futsuu-yokin no ri-mawari wa ni-paasento-ika desu.

you pron. [the second person singular or plural pronoun]

1. a⌈na⌉ta あなた [the second person singular pronoun used to refer to a conversational partner of socially equal rank, esp. one's husband, or of inferior rank or to a general audience such as in a survey], ki⌈mi 君 [the second person singular pronoun used normally by male speakers to refer to a conversational partner of socially equal rank, such as a girlfriend, or of inferior rank], a⌉nta あんた [the second person singular pronoun used to refer to a conversational partner of socially inferior rank ⟨s⟩], o-⌈mae お前 [an informal second person singular pronoun usually used by men to refer to a conversational partner of socially equal rank, such as one's wife, or of inferior rank ⟨s⟩]

NOTE: The second person pronoun is usually omitted completely in Japanese because the second person is immediately present in the conversation, and referents whose identity is obvious are typically not mentioned in the language. If the addressee's name is known to the speaker, the name + *wa* will normally be used in place of a second person pronoun.

EX. (a) A: Where do you come from?
{ø/あなたは/君は/*あんたは/*お前は}どこから来ましたか。
*{ø/Anata wa/Kimi wa/*Anta wa/*O-mae wa} doko kara kimashita ka.*
B: I come from New York.
ニューヨークから来ました。
Nyuuyooku kara kimashita.
(b) You're a slob! You know that?
{ø/お前は/君は/あんたは/*あなたは}薄汚いな。分かってるのか。
*{ø/O-mae wa/Kimi wa/Anta wa/*Anata wa} usu-gitanai na. Wakatte ru no ka.*

2. a⌈nata-ga⌉ta あなたがた [the second person plural pronoun used to refer to one's social equals or inferiors ⟨fml⟩], a⌈na⌉ta-tachi あなたたち [the second person plural pronoun used to refer to one's social equals or inferiors ⟨s⟩], a⌉nta-tachi あんたたち [the second person plural pronoun used to refer to one's social inferiors ⟨s⟩], ki⌈mi⌉-tachi 君たち •c [the second person plural pronoun normally used by male speakers to refer to social equals or inferiors], o-⌈mae⌉-tachi お前たち [the second person plural pronoun used by male speakers to

Y

refer to social inferiors ⟨s⟩]

EX. (**a**) What time are you all leaving tomorrow?
{ø/あなたがたは/あなたたちは/君たちは/*お前たちは/*あんたたちは}あした何時に出かけますか。
*{ø/Anata-gata wa/Anata-tachi wa/Kimi-tachi wa/*O-mae-tachi wa/*Anta-tachi wa} ashita nan-ji ni dekakemasu ka.*
(**b**) What are you guys doing here?
{ø/あんたたちは/お前たちは/*君たちは/*あなたたちは/*あなたがたは}ここで何をしていやがるんだ。
*{ø/Anta-tachi wa/O-mae-tachi wa/*Kimi-tachi wa/*Anata-tachi wa/*Anata-gata wa} koko de nani o shite iyagaru n da?*

young adj. **[in a relatively early stage of life or existence or appearing so]**
wa⌈ka⌉i 若い adj(*i*). **[having lived for only a short time relative to some norm ⟪fig. "immature"⟫]** **⟪juvenile, youthful, immature⟫**, **wa⌈ka-waka-shi⌉i 若々しい** adj(*i*). **[appearing to be at an early stage in life relative to some norm and in good health]** **⟪youthful, fresh⟫**, **mi⌈jukuna 未熟な** adj(*na*). **•c [unripe ⟪fig. "immature"⟫]** **⟪unripe, immature, green⟫**

EX. (**a**) When I was young, I wanted to become a pianist.
私は{若い/*若々しい/*未熟な}時ピアニストになりたかった。
*Watashi wa {wakai/*waka-waka-shii/*mijukuna} toki pianisuto ni naritakatta.*
(**b**) My father looks young for his age.
父は年の割に{若く/若々しく/*未熟に}見えます。
*Chichi wa toshi no wari ni {wakaku/waka-waka-shiku/*mijukuni} miemasu.*
(**c**) She's still too young to know how to deal with this kind of problem.
彼女はまだ{若い/未熟な/*若々しい}のでこのような問題をどうしたらいいか分かっていません。
*Kanojo wa mada {wakai/mijukuna/*waka-waka-shii} node kono yoona mondai o dooshitara ii ka wakatte imasen.*
(**d**) Jane is younger than Michelle.
ジェーンはミシェルより{若い/*若々しい/*未熟だ}。
*Jeen wa Misheru yori {wakai/*waka-waka-shii/*mijuku da}.*

young man n. **[a male person who has lived only a relatively short time, esp. used as an address form]**
1. se⌈inen 青年 •c [a person who is between the late teens and early 30s in age] **⟪youth⟫**

EX. Your son has turned into a nice young man.
息子さんは立派な青年になりましたね。
Musuko-san wa rippana seinen ni narimashita ne.

2. ø [an address form for a male person who has live only a relatively short time]

EX. How are you doing, young man?
どうだい?
Doo dai?

youngster n. **[a child or person who has lived only a relatively short time]**
wa⌈ka-mono 若者 [a person who has lived only a relatively short time] **⟪lad, youth⟫**, **ya⌉ngu ヤング •f**

EX. Shibuya in Tokyo is a popular place for youngsters to gather.
東京の渋谷は{若者/ヤング}を引き付ける街だ。
Tookyoo no Shibuya wa {waka-mono/yangu} o hiki-tsukeru machi da.

your pron. **[the possessive form of the second person singular or plural pronoun "you"]**
NOTE: "Your" is often not expressed at all when it can be understood in a given context.
1. a⌈na⌉ta no N あなたのN, ki⌈mi no N 君のN, a⌉nta no N あんたのN, o-⌈mae no N お前のN SEE you

EX. (**a**) What's your address?
{ø/あなたの/?君の/?あんたの/*お前の}住所はどこですか。
*{ø/Anata no/?Kimi no/?Anta no/*O-mae no} juusho wa doko desu ka.*
(**b**) Could you let me use your car?

Y

{ø/君の/あんたの/お前の/?あなたの}車を使わせてくれないか。
{ø/Kimi no/Anta no/O-mae no/?Anata no} kuruma o tsukawa-sete kurenai ka.

2. a⌈nata-ga⌉ta no N あなたがたのN, a⌉nata-tachi no N あなたたちのN, ki⌈mi-tachi⌉ no N 君たちのN, a⌉nta-tachi no N あんたたちのN, o-⌈mae-ta⌉chi no N お前たちのN SEE you

EX. (**a**) Who's your Japanese teacher?
{ø/あなたがたの/あたなたたちの/君たちの/??あんたたちの/*お前たちの}日本語の先生はだれですか。
*{ø/Anata-gata no/Anata-tachi no/Kimi-tachi no/??Anta-tachi no/*O-mae-tachi no} Nihon-go no sensei wa dare desu ka.*
(**b**) Where are those brats of yours?
{ø/あんたたちの/お前たちの/*君たちの/*あなたたちの/*あなたがたの}がきどもはどこにいるんだ?
*{ø/Anta-tachi no/O-mae-tachi no/*Kimi-tachi no/*Anata-tachi no/*Anata-gata no} gaki-domo wa doko ni iru n da?*

yourself pron. **[the reflexive or emphatic form of the second person singular or plural pronoun]**
ji⌉bun 自分 •c [a reflexive or emphatic pronoun that refers back to a human subject with whom the speaker identifies closely, including himself/herself]

EX. (**a**) Look at yourself in the mirror. You look so tired.
鏡で自分を見てご覧。疲れた顔をしているよ。
Kagami de jibun o mite goran. Tsukareta kao o shite iru yo.
(**b**) Say this to yourself the first thing every morning: "This is going to be the best day of my life."
朝一番に、自分にこう言いなさい。「今日は私の人生で一番いい日になる」と。
Asa ichi-ban ni, jibun ni koo iinasai. 'Kyoo wa watashi no jinsei de ichiban ii hi ni naru' to.
(**c**) You did it yourself, didn't you?
あなたが自分でしたんじゃないですか。
Anata ga jibun de shita n janai desu ka.

PHRASE: Help yourself to *doozo* ⟨*-o*⟩ *go-jiyuu ni o-tori kudasai* どうぞ⟨〜を⟩御自由にお取りください

EX. Help yourself to some fruit.
どうぞ果物を御自由にお取り下さい。
Doozo kuda-mono o go-jiyuu ni o-tori kudasai.

youth n. **[the time of life between childhood and adulthood; the quality of having lived only a relatively short time or a (male) person who has that quality]**
1. wa⌈ka⌉i toki 若い時 [the time when the years one has lived are relatively few], se⌈inen-ji⌉dai 青年時代 •c [the period of life between childhood and maturity], se⌈ishun-ji⌉dai 青春時代 •c [a period in life comparable to spring time] ⟪adolescence, puberty⟫

EX. In my youth I used to go rowing often.
{若い時/青年時代/青春時代}はよくボートをこいでいたものだ。
{Wakai toki/Seinen-jidai/Seishun-jidai} wa yoku booto o koide ita mono da.

2. wa⌉ka-sa 若さ /⟨adj(*i*). stem *wakai* young + suf. *sa* ness/, **se⌈ishun 青春 •c [the springtime of one's life]** ⟪adolescence⟫

EX. Youth is a thing of inherent beauty.
{若さ/青春}はそれだけで美しい。
{Waka-sa/Seishun} wa sore dake de utsukushii.

3. wa⌈ka-mono 若者 [a person who has lived only a relatively short time], se⌈inen 青年 •c [a person who is between the late teens and early 30s in age] ⟪young man, young people⟫

EX. I couldn't recognize him at first because he had turned into such a splendid youth.
立派な{若者/青年}になっていたので、最初は彼のことが分からなかった。
Rippana {waka-mono/seinen} ni natte ita node, saisho wa kare no koto ga wakaranakatta.

Z

Z

zero n. **[a number representing nothingness]**
re˥i 零 •c, ze˥ro ゼロ •f

EX. (**a**) His ability in management is almost zero.
彼は経営の才能はほとんど{ゼロ/*零}だ。
*Kare wa keiei no sainoo wa hotondo {zero/*rei} da.*
(**b**) Today it's forecast to go down to ten degrees below zero.
天気予報では今日は{零/*ゼロ}下十度まで気温が下がるそうです。
*Tenki-yohoo de wa kyoo wa {rei/*zero}-ka juu-do made kion ga sagaru soodesu.*

zinc n.
a┌en 亜鉛 •c

zone n. **[an area having a special character, purpose, or use distinguishing it from other areas]**
chi┌ta˥i 地帯 •c [a belt-like area with specific characteristics] ((area, region, belt)), ku˥iki 区域 •c [an area artificially distinguished from other areas for some purpose] ((limits, boundary, domain, sphere, area, district, territory)), chi˥iki 地域 •c [a geographic division characterizable in terms of climate/culture/natural environment] ((region, area, territory)), -tai ～帯 •c [a belt-like area], chi┌ku˥ 地区 •c [an area specially designated for some purpose], -ken ～圏 •c [a cultural or economic sphere] ((sphere, circle, range))

EX. (**a**) This is a residential zone where factories cannot be built.
ここは住宅{地域/地帯/区域/地区/*帯/*圏}ですから工場を建てることは出来ません。
*Koko wa juutaku-{chiiki/chitai/kuiki/chiku/*tai/*ken} desu kara koojoo o tateru koto wa dekimasen.*
(**b**) As long as you travel within this zone the bus fare is the same.
この{区域/?地域/*地帯/*圏}内でバスを利用するかぎり、バス料金は同じです。
*Kono {kuiki/?chiiki/*chitai/*ken}-nai de basu o riyoo-suru kagiri, basu-ryookin wa onaji desu.*
(**c**) Japan is in a totally different time zone from that of China.
日本は中国とはまったく異なる時間{帯/*区域/*地域/*地区/*地帯/*圏}に属しています。
*Nihon wa Chuugoku to wa mattaku kotonaru jikan-{tai/*kuiki/*chiiki/*chiku/*chitai/*ken} ni zokushite imasu.*

—— vt. **[for s.o. to designate an area for a special purpose or use]**
⟨-o⟩ ⟨-ni⟩ ku˥bun-suru ⟨～を⟩⟨～に⟩区分する ③ [to divide an area into subareas] ((classify, sort, itemize))

EX. The government proposed to zone the district into commercial, educational, and residential areas.
政府はその地域を商業、教育、住宅地区に区分することを提案した。
Seifu wa sono chiiki o shoogyoo, kyooiku, juutaku-chiku ni kubun-suru koto o teian-shita.

zoo n. **[a park or other public place where living animals are displayed]**
do┌obutsu˥-en 動物園 •c

EX. There are Chinese pandas at the Ueno Zoo in Tokyo.
東京の上野動物園には中国のパンダがいる。
Tookyoo no Ueno-doobutsu-en ni wa Chuugoku no panda ga iru.

APPENDICES

I

MAJOR CHARACTERISTICS OF THE JAPANESE LANGUAGE

For a more detailed discussion of Japanese grammar, see Makino and Tsutsui (1986) *A Dictionary of Basic Japanese Grammar*, Tokyo: The Japan Times.

A: WORD ORDER

Important information comes toward the end of a sentence in Japanese.

The basic word order of a Japanese sentence is Subject + Object + Verb (=SOV). Important markers that define the basic informational character of a sentence, such as the question marker *ka*, the negative marker *nai*, the persuasion marker *yo*, the involvement marker *no da*, etc., come toward the end of a sentence. Each sentence is, so to speak, a suspense story. This characteristic implies that less important information comes toward the beginning of a sentence. A typical example of less important information is a noun phrase marked by *wa* (=topic marker).

Examples

(1) スミスさんはすしを食べます。
Sumisu-san wa sushi o tabemasu.
(Mr. Smith eats *sushi.*)

(2) スミスさんはすしを食べますか。
Sumisu-san wa sushi o tabemasu ka.
(Does Mr. Smith eat *sushi*?)

(3) スミスさんはすしを食べません。
Sumisu-san wa sushi o tabemasen.
(Mr. Smith doesn't eat *sushi.*)

(4) スミスさんはすしを食べますよ。
Sumisu-san wa sushi o tabemasu yo.
(I tell you Mr. Smith eats *sushi.*)

(5) スミスさんはすしを食べるんです。
Sumisu-san wa sushi o taberu n desu.
(It's that Mr. Smith eats *sushi.*)

(6) スミスさんはすしを食べますね。
Sumisu-san wa sushi o tabemasu ne.
(Mr. Smith eats *sushi*, doesn't he?)

In every meaningful constituent of the sentence, the modifier (i.e., the less important information) precedes the modified element (i.e., the more important information), as shown in the following chart. The modified element in each case appears in boldface.

Note: In 2., 3. and 5. on the following page the modifier is obligatory.

1.

Adjective	Noun
おもしろい *omoshiroi* (an interesting dictionary)	**辞書** ***jisho***

2.

Noun	Particle
花子 *Hanako* (Hanako (topic))	**は** ***wa***
花子 *Hanako* (Hanako (subject))	**が** ***ga***
花子 *Hanako* (Hanako (object))	**を** ***o***
花子 *Hanako* (to/by/from Hanako)	**に** ***ni***
花子 *Hanako* (from Hanako)	**から** ***kara***

3.

Sentence	Conjunction
太郎が来る *Taro ga kuru* (Because Taro is coming)	**から** ***kara***
太郎が来る *Taro ga kuru* (Although Taro is coming)	**けれど** ***keredo***
太郎が来る *Taro ga kuru* (If Taro comes)	**と** ***to***

4.

Relative Clause	Noun
トムが買った *Tomu ga katta* (The dictionary that Tom bought)	**辞書** ***jisho***

5.

Sentence	Nominalizer
辞書を使う *Jisho o tsukau* (To use/Using a dictionary)	**こと/の** ***koto/no***

B: CONJUGATIONS (Verbs and Adjectives)

Unlike English, Japanese adjectives conjugate in a way similar to Japanese verbs. The following charts illustrate Japanese conjugations. As you can see, both verbs and adjectives have two forms: a formal form to be used in formal situations such as when speaking with a superior (esp. in terms of age) and an informal form to be used in informal situations such as when speaking with people who are not one's superiors. Informal forms are more basic than formal forms.

1. *i*-adjectives (adj(*i*).)

	Informal	Formal
Nonpast/Aff.	おもしろい *omoshiroi* (interesting)	おもしろいです *omoshiroi desu*
Past/Aff.	おもしろかった *omoshirokatta* (was/were interesting)	おもしろかったです *omoshirokatta desu*
Nonpast/Neg.	おもしろくない *omoshirokunai* (not interesting)	おもしろく{ないです/ありません} *omoshiroku{nai desu/arimasen}*
Past/Neg.	おもしろくなかった *omoshirokunakatta* (was/were not interesting)	おもしろく{なかったです/ありませんでした} *omoshiroku{nakatta desu/arimasen deshita}*

Ii (good) is an irregular adjective. Its conjugation is:

	Informal	Formal
Nonpast/Aff.	いい *ii* (good)	いいです *ii desu*
Past/Aff.	よかった *yokatta* (was/were good)	よかったです *yokatta desu*
Nonpast/Neg.	よくない *yokunai* (not good)	よく{ないです/ありません} *yoku{nai desu/arimasen}*
Past/Neg.	よくなかった *yokunakatta* (was/were not good)	よく{なかったです/ありませんでした} *yoku{nakatta desu/arimasen deshita}*

2. *na*-adjectives (adj(*na*).)

	Informal	Formal
Nonpast/Aff.	元気だ *genki da* (healthy)	元気です *genki desu*
Past/Aff.	元気だった *genki datta* (was/were healthy)	元気でした *genki deshita*
Nonpast/Neg.	元気{では/じゃ}ない *genki {dewa/ja}nai* (not healthy)	元気{では/じゃ}{ないです/ありません} *genki {dewa/ja}{nai desu/arimasen}*
Past/Neg.	元気{では/じゃ}なかった *genki {dewa/ja}nakatta* (was/were not healthy)	元気{では/じゃ}{なかったです/ありませんでした} *genki {dewa/ja}{nakatta desu/arimasen deshita}*

Note: Adj(*na*). takes *-na* before a noun as in: 元気な人 *genkina hito* (a healthy person)

3. Verb Conjugations

The formal verb conjugations are simple, because the stem stays the same for every verb.

かき	ます	*kaki-masu*	(formal, nonpast, affirmative)
	ません	*-masen*	(formal, nonpast, negative)
	ました	*-mashita*	(formal, past, affirmative)
	ませんでした	*-masendeshita*	(formal, past, negative)
	ましょう	*-mashoo*	(formal, volitional (let's…))

The informal verb conjugation is slightly more complicated. Rules for deriving an informal nonpast (dictionary) form from its formal, nonpast form are provided below.

Rule 1
If a formal, nonpast verb form ends in an [i] sound right before *-masu* (e.g. *yom-i-masu, kak-i-masu, nom-i-masu, mach-i-masu, nor-i-masu, oyog-i-masu*), and if the sound preceding the *masu* is not monosyllabic then the verb belongs to Group 1.

Note: There are some exceptions to this rule, such as the verb *okimasu* (get up). It is a Group 2 verb, although it should be in Group 1 according to the above rule.

Rule 2
If a formal, nonpast verb form ends in an [e] sound right before *-masu* (e.g. *n-e-masu, mi-e-masu, kiko-e-masu*) or if the sound preceding the *-masu* is monosyllabic (e.g. *m-i-masu, i-masu*), then the verb belongs to Group 2.

The irregular verbs are *kuru* (come), *suru* (do), *iku* (go), and *-ssharu* (polite verbs).

Group 1 Conjugations
If a verb belongs to Group 1, then the following rule is used to derive its basic conjugated forms.

Rule 3
Start from the formal, nonpast, affirmative form (the so-called *masu* form). First identify the *hiragana* that comes right before *-masu*. This *hiragana* should be in the second row of the *hiragana* chart. Replace this with the first, third, fourth and fifth row *hiragana*.

Take *kakimasu* (write) as an example. This verb is a Group 1 verb, because [i] comes right before *-masu* and *kaki* is not monosyllabic. (SEE Rule 1) The *hiragana* that comes right before *-masu* is *ki*, so you should replace this with the first row *hiragana ka*, the third row *hiragana ku*, the fourth row *hiragana ke* and the fifth row *hiragana ko*, as shown below. (SEE Rule 3)

Each replacement will give you different meanings as indicated in the parentheses.

かか ない	*ka-ka-nai*	(informal, nonpast, negative)
かき ます	*ka-ki-masu*	(formal, nonpast, affirmative)
かく	*ka-ku*	(informal, nonpast, affirmative)
かけ ば	*ka-ke-ba*	(informal/formal, conditional (if…))
かこ う	*ka-ko-o*	(informal, volitional (let's…))

The same method of deriving conjugations is applicable to other Group 1 verbs. Another example follows:

のま ない	*no-ma-nai*	(informal, nonpast, negative)
のみ ます	*no-mi-masu*	(formal, nonpast, affirmative)
のむ	*no-mu*	(informal, nonpast, affirmative)
のめ ば	*no-me-ba*	(informal/formal, conditional (if…))
のも う	*no-mo-o*	(informal, volitional (let's…))

The derivational rules for V*te* and the informal past form are as follows:

Rule 4
V*te* can be derived from the informal, nonpast form (=dictionary form). If the dictionary form ends in: [u] (as in *kau* (buy), *arau* (wash), *tsukau* (use)), then replace [u] with [tte] (って) (as in *katte, aratte, tsukatte*), if [mu] (as in *nomu* (drink), *komu* (be crowded)), or [bu] (as

in *tobu* (fly), *asobu* (play)), then replace [mu] or [bu] with [nde] (んで) (as in *nonde, konde, tonde, asonde*); if [su] (as in *kasu* (loan), *kosu* (get across), *korosu* (kill)), then replace [su] with [shite]; if [ku] (as in *kaku* (write), *saku* (bloom)) or [gu] (as in *kogu* (row a boat), *isogu* (hurry), then replace [ku] or [gu] with [ite] or [ide] respectively (as in [kaite] [saite], [koide], [isoide]).

Rule 5
The informal past tense form can be derived from V*te* by replacing *-te* with *-ta* and *-de* with *-da.* (e.g. *kaite* → *kaita, yonde* → *yonda*, etc.)

Group 2 Conjugations (Group 2 Verbs)
The derivational rules for V*te* and the informal past form are as follows:

Rule 6
V*te* of verbs can be derived from their informal, nonpast, affirmative form by replacing the *-ru* with *-te.* (e.g. *tabe-ru* → *tabe-te, mi-ru* → *mi-te*)

Rule 7
The informal past form can be derived from V*te* by replacing *-te* with *-ta.* (e.g. *tabe-te* → *tabe-ta, mi-te* → *mi-ta*, etc.)

C: PERSONAL PRONOUNS

There is more than one first person and second person pronoun, but there is no basic third person pronoun.
It is as if the Japanese were carrying masks (=persona) in the form of personal pronouns so that they can choose a situationally correct one at any given time. There are at least eight variations of the first person singular pronoun *watakushi* created by omitting or transforming various sounds: *watashi, atakushi, atashi, washi, wai, atai, asshi, ate.* In addition to these variations there are other first person singular pronouns such as *boku* and *ore.* The following chart illustrates the basic personal pronouns.

Note: each pronoun can take a plural suffix as shown in parentheses. The letters "m" and "f" stand for male and female respectively.

First Person
わたくし(ども/たち) *watakushi* (*domo/tachi*) (very fml.)
わたし(たち) *watashi* (*tachi*) (fml.)
あたし(たち) *atashi* (*tachi*) (fml., f)
ぼく(たち/ら) *boku* (*tachi/ra*) (inf., m)
あたし(たち/ら) *atashi* (*tachi/ra*) (inf., f)
おれ(たち) *ore* (*tachi*) (very inf.)

Second Person
あなた(がた/たち) *anata* (*gata/tachi*) (fml. but not honorific)
きみ(たち/ら) *kimi* (*tachi/ra*) (inf., m)
おまえ(たち/ら) *omae* (*tachi/ra*) (inf., m)
あんた(たち/ら) *anta* (*tachi/ra*) (inf.)

D: VIEWPOINTS

There are both subjective and objective ways to express a situation; the Japanese prefer to use the former.
In any language there are ways to express ideas in a subjective way and in an objective way. The Japanese, however, prefer in most cases to express themselves in a subjective way, using such constructions as the passive construction, the donative construction, the involving construction (esp. *no da*), and others.

Examples
(1) a. 先生は小林をほめた。
Sensei wa Kobayashi o hometa.
(The teacher praised Kobayashi.)
b. 小林は先生にほめられた。
Kobayashi wa sensei ni home-rareta.
(Kobayashi was praised by the teacher.)

(2) a. 山田は部下にボーナスを与えた。
Yamada wa buka ni boonasu o ataeta.
(Yamada gave her subordinate a bonus.)

b. 部下は山田にボーナスをもらった。
Buka wa Yamada ni boonasu o moratta.
(The subordinate received a bonus from Yamada.)

(3) a. きのう東京駅で火事があった。
Kinoo Tookyoo-eki de kaji ga atta.
(There was a fire at Tokyo station yesterday.)

b. きのう東京駅で火事があったんだ。
Kinoo Tookyoo-eki de kaji ga atta n da.
(It's that there was a fire at Tokyo station yesterday.)

(4) a. 宿題を忘れた。
Shukudai o wasureta.
((I) forgot (my) homework.)

b. 宿題を忘れてしまった。
Shukudai o wasurete shimatta.
((I) unfortunately forgot (my) homework.)

Example sentences (1)b, (2)b, and (3)b are a passive, donative and involving construction, respectively. Sentences (1)a, (2)a, and (3)a are the corresponding objective versions. Sentences (1)b and (2)b are more subjective than (1)a and (2)a, because in the former the speaker takes the viewpoint of the subject (i.e., Kobayashi in (1)b and *buka* in (2)b). Sentence (3)b sounds very involving and can never be used in a text that requires an objective statement or description such as a newspaper article. Sentence (4)b is another case of a subjective expression that corresponds to the objective expression of (4)a.

E: SOUND SYMBOLISM

There are abundant sound-symbolic words in Japanese, used not only by children but also by adults.

Sound-symbolic words, referred to as *giseigo* (onomatopoeia) or *gitaigo* (pheno-mimes/psycho-mimes), are frequently used in colloquial speech to express something by appealing directly to a person's senses.

Examples

(1) a. 雨が静かに降っている。
Ame ga shizukani futte iru.
(It's raining quietly.)

b. 雨がしとしと降っている。
Ame ga shito-shito futte iru.
(It's raining quietly.)

(2) a. 男が遠慮なく部屋に入って来た。
Otoko ga enryo naku heya ni haitte-kita.
(A man intruded into the room.)

b. 男がずかずかと部屋に入って来た。
Otoko ga zuka-zuka to heya ni haitte-kita.
(A man intruded into the room.)

(3) a. 老人が危なっかしそうに歩いている。
Roojin ga abunakkashi-soo ni aruite iru.
(An old man is walking in a staggering manner.)

b. 老人がよたよたと歩いている。
Roojin ga yota-yota to aruite iru.
(An old man is walking in a staggering manner.)

Example sentences (1)b, (2)b, and (3)b are sound-symbolic versions of (1)a, (2)a and (3)a. They are more expressive and more direct in the sense that the meaning is intertwined with sound.

F: POLITE EXPRESSIONS

In Japanese, expressions of politeness are built into the grammar and vocabulary.

One can certainly speak politely in English, or in any language for that matter. In Japanese, though, polite speech is more stylized and grammaticized. Particularly when one is speaking to or about a superior or when one is speaking to a customer, polite speech is required by social norm. All things being equal, the longer the honorific expression is, the more polite it is.

Examples

(1) a. その本は鈴木先生が**お**読み**です**。
Sono hon wa Suzuki-sensei ga ***o****-yomi* ***desu****.*
(Prof. Suzuki will read/is reading that book.)

b. その本は鈴木先生が読ま**れます**。
*Sono hon wa Suzuki-sensei ga yoma-****remasu****.*
(Prof. Suzuki will read that book.)

c. その本は鈴木先生が**お**読み**になります**。
Sono hon wa Suzuki-sensei ga ***o****-yomi* ***ni narimasu****.*
(Prof. Suzuki will read that book.)

The sentences in (1) are all honorific polite expressions, but (1)c is the most polite of these. The parts in boldface are each a fixed grammatical pattern for expressing politeness.

(2) a. 鈴木先生が**見えました**。
Suzuki-sensei ga ***miemashita****.*
(Prof. Suzuki came here.)

b. 鈴木先生が**いらっしゃいました**。
Suzuki-sensei ga ***irasshaimashita****.*
(Prof. Suzuki came here.)

The sentences in (2) include lexical honorific polite expressions. Basic verbs such as "to see" (*go-ran-ni naru*), "to know" (*go-zonji da*), "to come/go/be" (*irassharu*), "to eat" (*meshiagaru*), "to do" (*nasaru*), "to die" (*nakunaru*), etc. all have special lexical forms for expressing honorific polite meaning.

(3) 私がスーツケースを**お**持ち{**します/いたします**}。
Watashi ga suutsu-keesu o ***o****-mochi* ***{shimasu/itashimasu}****.*
(I will carry your suitcase.)

Sentence (3) is a standard humble polite expression. Just as in the case of lexical honorific polite expressions, there are lexical humble polite expressions for basic verbs such as "to see" (*haiken-suru*), "to drink/eat/receive" (*itadaku*), "to go/come" (*mairu*), "to do" (*itasu*), "to meet" (*o-me ni kakaru*), "to know" (*zonjiru*), etc.

G: DELETIONS

The Japanese language tends to omit whatever is understood from the linguistic or non-linguistic context.

All languages make use of omission when the omitted information can be recovered from the context. However, what makes Japanese different from English is that Japanese has so many subject-less sentences, whereas in English a subject cannot normally be omitted.

Examples

(1) a. A: 夏休みに(あなたは)どこに行きますか。
Natsu-yasumi ni (anata wa) doko ni ikimasu ka.
(Where are you going during summer vacation?)
B: (私は)カナダに行きます。
(Watashi wa) Kanada ni ikimasu.
(I'm going to Canada.)

b. A: (私たちは)テニスでもしましょうか。
(Watashi-tachi wa) tenisu demo shimashoo ka.
(Shall we play tennis?)
B: (私たちは)そうしましょう。
(Watashi-tachi wa) soo shimashoo.
(Yes, let's.)

c. Looking at a photo:
A: (これは)だれですか。
(Kore wa) dare desu ka
(Who is this?)
B: (これは)妹です。
(Kore wa) imooto desu.
(This is my younger sister.)

So-called impersonal constructions, which are used to express situations not subject to human control, are subject-less, whereas in English "it" must be used here as a subject.

(2) a. 今八時です。
Ima hachi-ji desu.
(It's eight o'clock now.)
b. いい天気ですねえ。
Ii tenki desu nee.
(It's a fine day, isn't it?)
c. 今日は暑いなあ。
Kyoo wa atsui naa.
(It's hot today.)

As a matter of fact, any sentential element which can be recovered from context, other than the main verbs, can be omitted in Japanese.

(3) a. A: 宿題をした?
Shukudai o shita?
(Did you do your homework?)
B: うん、したよ。
Un, shita yo.
(Yes, I did.)
b. A: お母さんに手紙を出した?
O-kaa-san ni tegami o dashita?
(Have you sent the letter to your mother?)
B: ああ、出したよ。
Aa, dashita yo.
(Yes, I have.)

As these examples show, as long as the main verb is retained, the rest of the recoverable elments (the direct object, the indirect object) can be omitted.

H: RESTRICTIONS ON THE GRAMMATICAL PERSON OF SUBJECT WORDS

There are some strict rules about the grammatical person of the subject noun—that is, whether the subject noun can be in the first, second, or third person—with certain predicates.

This is especially so with adjectives that express psychological or emotional states, such as *ureshii* (happy), *kanashii* (sad), *tanoshii* (fun), *sabishii* (lonely), *-tai* (want to do), etc. The subject noun with these predicates must be in the first person in statements or in the second person in questions, as seen in the examples below. However, this restriction does not hold if the predicate is followed by a modal form, that is, a form which indicates that the speaker is making some kind of judgment (such as a conjecture) or is basing the sentence on some kind of evidence (such as hearsay). Modal forms include sentence-final forms such as *daroo, -no da, -sooda, -rashii, -yoo da*, etc.

Examples

(1) a. 彼女がいないと{僕/*あなた/*彼}はさびしい。
*Kanojo ga inai to {boku/*anata/*kare} wa sabishii.*
(When she isn't around {I feel/?you feel/he feels} lonely.)
b. 彼女がいないと{(あなたは)/*彼は}さびしいですか。
*Kanojo ga inai to {(anata wa)/*kare wa} sabishii desu ka.*
({Do you/Does he} feel lonely when she isn't around?)

(2) a. {僕/*あなた/*父}は韓国語を勉強したい。
*{Boku/*Anata/*Chichi} wa Kankoku-go o benkyoo-shi-tai.*
({I/?You/My father} would like to study Korean.)
b. {あなた/*お父さん}も韓国語を勉強したいですか。
*{Anata/*O-too-san} mo Kankoku-go o benkyoo-shi-tai desu ka.*
({Would you/Would your father} like to study Korean, too?)

(3) a. {僕/*あなた/*母}は犬がこわい。
*{Boku/*Anata/*Haha} wa inu ga kowai.*
({I'm/?You're/My mother is} scared of dogs.)
b. {(あなたは)/*彼は}犬がこわいですか。
*{(Anata wa)/*Kare wa} inu ga kowai desu ka.*
({Are you/Is he} scared of dogs?)

In order for the third person subject to be used with these kinds of predicates, the predicate must either be followed by a modal form, as explained earlier, or followed by the suffix *-garu/-gatte iru* (show/is showing signs of being…), as seen in (4).

(4) a. 彼女がいないと{彼/*僕/*あなた}はさびしがります。(cf. (1)a)
*Kanojo ga inai to {kare/*boku/*anata} wa sabishi-garimasu.*
(When she isn't around {he misses/ I miss/?you miss} her.)

b. {父/*僕/*あなた}は韓国語を勉強したがっている。(cf. (2)a)
*{Chichi/*Boku/*Anata} wa Kankoku-go o benkyoo-shi-ta-gatte iru.*
({My father wants (Lit. "is showing signs of wanting")/I want/?You want} to study Korean.)

c. {母/*僕/*あなた}は犬をこわがっている。(cf. (3)a)
*{Haha/*Boku/*Anata} wa inu o kowa-gatte iru.*
({My mother is/I'm/?You're} scared of dogs.)

II

COUNTERS IN JAPANESE

The following chart lists some commonly-used counters.

	Type A	Type B	Type C
	枚 *-mai* (thin object: *paper, ticket*, etc.)	本 *-hon* (long object) *pencil, stick*, etc.)	課 *-ka* (lesson)
1	一枚 *ichi-mai*	一本 *ip-pon*	一課 *ik-ka*
2	二枚 *ni-mai*	二本 *ni-hon*	二課 *ni-ka*
3	三枚 *san-mai*	三本 *san-bon*	三課 *san-ka*
4	四枚 *yo(n)-mai*	四本 *yon-hon*	四課 *yon-ka*
5	五枚 *go-mai*	五本 *go-hon*	五課 *go-ka*
6	六枚 *roku-mai*	六本 *rop-pon*	六課 *rok-ka*
7	七枚 *nana* } *-mai* *shichi*	七本 *nana* } *-hon* *shichi*	七課 *nana* } *-ka* *shichi*
8	八枚 *hachi-mai*	八本 *hachi-hon* *hap-pon*	八課 *hachi* } *-ka* *hak*
9	九枚 *kyuu-mai*	九本 *kyuu-hon*	九課 *kyuu-ka*
10	十枚 *juu-mai*	十本 *jup-pon*	十課 *juk-ka*

Adopted from *A Dictionary of Basic Japanese Grammar* (The Japan Times, 1986) by courtesy of The Japan Times, Ltd.

Type D	Type E	Type F	Irregular Types			
冊 *-satsu* (volume)	頁 *-peeji* (page)	頭 *-too* (head of cattle)	人 *-nin* (people)	日 *-ka* (day of the month)	日 *-nichi* (day)	晩 *-ban* (night)
一冊 *is-satsu*	一頁 *ip* / *ichi* } *-peeji*	一頭 *it-too*	一人 *hitori*	一日 *tsuitachi*	一日 *ichi-nichi*	一晩 *hito-ban*
二冊 *ni-satsu*	二頁 *ni-peeji*	二頭 *ni-too*	二人 *futari*	二日 *futsu-ka*	二日 *futsu-ka*	二晩 *futa-ban*
三冊 *san-satsu*	三頁 *san-peeji*	三頭 *san-too*	三人 *san-nin*	三日 *mik-ka*	三日 *mik-ka*	三晩 *mi-ban*
四冊 *yon-satsu*	四頁 *yon-peeji*	四頭 *yon-too*	四人 *yo-nin*	四日 *yok-ka*	四日 *yok-ka*	四晩 *yo-ban*
五冊 *go-satsu*	五頁 *go-peeji*	五頭 *go-too*	五人 *go-nin*	五日 *itsu-ka*	五日 *itsu-ka* *go-nichi*	五晩 *go ban*
六冊 *roku satsu*	六頁 *roku* / *rop* } *peeji*	六頭 *roku-too*	六人 *roku-nin*	六日 *mui-ka*	六日 *mui-ka* *roku-nichi*	六晩 *roku-ban*
七冊 *nana* / *shichi* } *-satsu*	七頁 *nana* / *shichi* } *-peeji*	七頭 *nana* / *shichi* } *-too*	七人 *nana* / *shichi* } *-nin*	七日 *nano-ka*	七日 *nano-ka* *shichi-nichi*	七晩 *nana-ban*
八冊 *has-satsu*	八頁 *hachi* / *hap* } *-peeji*	八頭 *hat-too*	八人 *hachi-nin*	八日 *yoo-ka*	八日 *yoo-ka* *hachi-nichi*	八晩 *hachi-ban*
九冊 *kyuu-satsu*	九頁 *kyuu-peeji*	九頭 *kyuu-too*	九人 *kyuu* / *ku* } *-nin*	九日 *kokono-ka*	九日 *kokono-ka* *ku-nichi*	九晩 *kyuu-ban*
十冊 *jus-satsu*	十頁 *jup-peeji*	十頭 *jut-too*	十人 *juu-nin*	十日 *too-ka*	十日 *too-ka*	十晩 *juu-ban*

Notes

1. Depending on the initial sound of a counter, the pronunciation of the number and/or the counter changes. Counters are classified according to the phonetic modifications they undergo. Type A counters are straightfoward cases of *Sino-Japanese Number + Counter*, with no phonetic modifications. The following is a chart of phonetic modifications for Type B through Type F. If there is no entry for a given number it indicates that there is no phonetic modification for that particular number. As for the remaining irregular types, they must be memorized individually.

	Type B	Type C	Type D	Type E	Type F
	h-	*k-*	*s-*	*p-*	*t-*
1	[*ipp-*]	[*ikk-*]	[*iss-*]	[*ipp-*]	[*itt-*]
3	[*sanb-*]				
6	[*ropp-*]	[*rokk-*]		([*ropp-*])	
8	([*happ-*])	([*hakk-*])	[*hass-*]	([*happ-*])	[*hatt-*]
10	[*jupp-*]	[*jukk-*]	[*juss-*]	[*jupp-*]	[*jutt-*]

([ ]) indicates that [ ] is optional.

2. The 20th day of the month and 20 days are not *nijuu-nichi* but *hatsuka*. "Twenty years old" is expressed by *hatachi*.

3. The following is a list of other examples of each type:

Type A:

倍 *-bai* time　番 *-ban* ordinal number
度 *-do* frequency　畳 *-joo* tatami mat
部 *-bu* part　面 *-men* newspaper page

Type A′:

(Exactly the same as Type A except that number 4 is pronounced *yo*, not *yon*.)

時 *-ji* o'clock　時間 *-jikan* hour
年 *-nen* year

Type A″:

(Exactly the same as Type A except that numbers 4, 7 and 9 are pronounced *shi*, *shichi* and *ku*, respectively.)

月 *-gatsu* name of the month

Type A‴:

(Exactly the same as Type A except that the initial sound of the counter with number 3 changes from *wa* to *ba*.)

羽 *-wa* bird

Type B:

杯 *-hai* cup of　匹 *-hiki* animal

Type B′:

(Exactly the same as Type B except that the initial sound of the counter with number 3 is not *b-* but *p-*.)

泊 *-haku* stay (overnight)
分 *-fun* minute

Type C:

か月 *-kagetsu* month
回 *-kai* frequency　巻 *-kan* volume
個 *-ko* piece

Type C′:

(Exactly the same as Type C except that the initial sound of the counter with number 3 can be either *k-* or *g-*.)

階 *-kai* floor

Type D:

歳 *-sai* -year old　隻 *-soo* boat

Type D′:

(Exactly the same as Type D except that the initial sound of the counter with number 3 is *z-* not *s-*.)

足 *-soku* footgear

Type E:

ポンド *-pondo* pound

Type F:

等 *-too* class, grade
トン *-ton* ton　通 *-tsuu* letter

III

A LIST OF TECHNICAL TERMS

BUISINESS

A

absenteeism
keikaku-teki kekkin 計画的欠勤

accountability
kekka ni taishite ou-beki gimu
結果に対して負うべき義務

accounting department
keiri-bu 経理部

action plan
koodoo-hooshin 行動方針

administrative cost
kanri-hi 管理費

administrative overheads
kanri-sho-keihi 管理諸経費

advertising campaign
senden-katsudoo, kyanpeen 宣伝活動、キャンペーン

affiliate company
ko-gaisha 子会社

after-sales service
afutaa-saabisu アフターサービス

after-tax profit
zeihiki-rieki 税引き利益

amalgamation
gappei 合併

answerphone
rusuban-denwa 留守番電話

appraisal
satei 査定

appreciation of yen
en-daka 円高

aptitude test
tekisei-shiken 適性試験

arbitration
chuusai, saitei 仲裁、裁定

artificial intelligence
jinkoo-chinoo 人工知能

assembly line
kumi-tate-rain, nagare-sagyoo 組立てライン、流れ作業

assets
shisan 資産

assistant manager
fuku-shihai-nin 副支配人

associate company
mochikabu-gaisha 持ち株会社

at par
gakumen de 額面で
audio-visual aids
shi-choo-kaku-kizai 視聴覚機材
audit
kaikei-kansa 会計監査
auditor
kansa-yaku 監査役
authorized capital
juken-shihon 授権資本

B

backlog
juchuu-zan 受注残
back-to-back loan
soosai-roon 相殺ローン
bad-debt losses
kashi-daore-sonshitsu 貸し倒れ損失
bad debts
furyoo-saiken 不良債権
bad times
fu-keiki 不景気
balance sheet
taishaku-taishoo-hyoo 貸借対照表
bank rate
ginkoo-kinri 銀行金利
bar chart
boosen-zuhyoo 棒線図表
bar code
shoohin-coodo 商品コード
bear
yowaki-suji 弱気筋
bear market
yowaki-sooba 弱気相場
behavioral science
koodoo-kagaku 行動科学
bill of credit
shin'yoo-joo 信用状
blue-chip stock
ne-gasa-kabu 値がさ株
blue-collar worker
roodoo-sha 労働者
blueprint
sekkei-zu 設計図
board meeting
torishimari-yaku-kai 取締役会
board of directors
juuyaku-kai 重役会
boardroom
kaigi-shitsu 会議室
book value
bojoo-kakaku 簿上価格
boom
kookyoo 好況
bottleneck
shoogai 障害
bottom line
saishuu-kekka 最終結果
brainstorming
bureen-sutoomingu ブレーンストーミング
branch office
shisha 支社
brand
burando ブランド
brand image
burando-imeeji ブランドイメージ
break even
kinkoo ni naru 均衡になる
break-even analysis
son'eki-bunki-bunseki 損益分岐分析
break-even point
son'eki-bunki-ten 損益分岐点
breakthrough
toppa 突破
briefing
gaiyoo-setsumei 概要説明
broker
naka-gai-nin, burookaa 仲買人、ブローカー
brokerage
shuusen-ryoo 周旋料
budget
yosan 予算
budget constraint
yosan-teki-seiyaku 予算的制約
budgetary control
yosan-kanri 予算管理
bug
bagu バグ
built-in
kumi-komi 組み込み
bull
tsuyoki-suji 強気筋
bulletin board
koohoo-keiji-ban 公報掲示板

bull market
kai-te-sooba 買い手相場
business corporation
eiri-hoojin 営利法人
business cycle
keiki-junkan 景気循環
business forecasting
keiki-yosoku 景気予測
business management
kigyoo-keiei 企業経営
business outlook
bijinesu-mi-tooshi ビジネス見通し
business relations
tori-hiki-kankei 取引関係
business strategy
keiei-senryaku 経営戦略
business trend
keiki-dookoo 景気動向
buyers' market
kai-te-shijoo 買い手市場
buying behavior
koobai-koodoo 購買行動
buy out
kai-toru 買い取る
buzz-word
bazu-waado (aru bun'ya de tsukawa-reru tokushu-yoogo) バズワード(ある分野で使われる特殊用語)
bypass
ukai-suru 迂回する
by-product
fuku-sanbutsu 副産物

C

CAD (computer-aided design)
konpyuutaa-riyoo-sekkei コンピューター利用設計
CAL (computer-aided learning)
konpyuutaa-riyoo-gakushuu コンピューター利用学習
capability
nooryoku 能力
capital allowance
shihon-hikiate-kin 資本引当金
capital assets
kotei-shisan 固定資産
capital commitment
shihon-itaku 資本委託
capital expenditure
shihon-shishutsu 資本支出
capital gain
shihon-teki-rijun 資本的利潤
capital goods
shihon-zai 資本財
capital-intensive
shihon-shuuyaku-teki 資本集約的
capitalize
shihon ni kumi-ireru 資本に組み入れる
capital loss
shihon-teki-sonshitsu 資本的損失
capital raising
shikin-chootatsu 資金調達
capital structure
shihon-koosei 資本構成
car phone
jidoosha-denwa 自動車電話
cartel
karuteru カルテル
case study
keesu-sutadi, jirei-kenkyuu ケーススタディ、事例研究
cash flow
genkin-ryuudoo, shikin-guri 現金流動、資金繰り
CBA (cost-benefit analysis)
hiyoo-ben'eki-bunseki 費用便益分析
cellphone
keitai-denwa 携帯電話
centralization
shuuchuu-ka 集中化
centralize
shuuchuu-ka-suru 集中化する
central processing unit (CPU)
chuuoo-shori-soochi 中央処理装置
chain of command
meirei-keitoo 命令系統
chain of distribution
ryuutsuu-keitoo 流通系統
chain store
cheen-sutoa チェーンストア
chairman
kaichoo 会長
channels of communication
tsuushin-channeru 通信チャンネル
channels of distribution
ryuutsuu-channeru 流通チャンネル
chief executive
saikoo-keiei-sekinin-sha 最高経営責任者
chip
chippu チップ

circulating capital
ryuudoo-shihon 流動資本
clearing house
tegata-kookan-jo 手形交換所
clerical worker
jimu-shokuin 事務職員
closed loop
tojita ruupu 閉じたループ
cold storage warehouse
reitoo-sooko 冷凍倉庫
collateral
tanpo(-shooken) 担保(証券)
collective bargaining
dantai-kooshoo 団体交渉
collusion
dangoo 談合
commercial bank
shoogyoo-ginkoo 商業銀行
commodity
shoohin 商品
commodity exchange
shoohin-tori-hiki 商品取引
commodity market
shoohin-shijoo 商品市場
common currency
kyootsuu-tsuuka 共通通貨
common language
kyootsuu-go 共通語
Common Market
Yooroppa-keizai-kyoodoo-tai ヨーロッパ経済共同体
communications network
tsuushin-moo 通信網
communications theory
tsuushin-riron 通信理論
company philosophy
kigyoo-tetsugaku 企業哲学
company policy
kaisha no hooshin 会社の方針
company profile
kigyoo-gaiyoo 企業概要
compatibility
gokan-sei 互換性
compatible
gokan-sei ga aru 互換性がある
competency
koodoo-nooryoku 行動能力
competitive price
kyoosoo-kakaku 競争価格
competitive
kyoosoo-teki 競争的
competitive advantage
kyoosoo-joo no yuui 競争上の優位
competitive edge
kyoosoo-teki-yuui 競争的優位
competitiveness
jiyuu-kyoosoo 自由競争
competitive position
kyoosoo-teki-shisei 競争的姿勢
comptroller
kaikei-kansa-kan 会計監査官
computer
konpyuutaa コンピューター
computer-aided design (CAD)
konpyuutaa-riyoo-sekkei コンピューター利用設計
computer-aided learning (CAL)
konpyuutaa-riyoo-gakushuu コンピューター利用学習
computerize
konpyuutaa-ka-suru コンピューター化する
computer language
konpyuutaa-gengo コンピューター言語
computer literate
konpyuutaa ga wakaru コンピューターがわかる
computer memory chip
kioku-chippu 記憶チップ
computer simulation
konpyuutaa-shumireeshon
コンピューターシュミレーション
computer storage
konpyuutaa-kioku-soochi コンピューター記憶装置
computer terminal
konpyuutaa tanmatsu-ki コンピューター端末機
computer virus
konpyuutaa-uirusu コンピューターウイルス
confidentiality
kimitsu-sei 機密性
conglomerate
konguromaritto コングロマリット
consensus
gooi 合意
consortium
gooben-gaisha 合弁会社
consult
soodan-suru 相談する
consultant
konsarutanto コンサルタント

consumables
shoomoo-hin 消耗品
consumer behavior
shoohi-sha-koodoo 消費者行動
consumer durables
taikyuu-shoohi-zai 耐久消費財
consumer goods
shoohi-zai, shoohi-busshi 消費財、消費物資
consumer orientation
kokyaku-shikoo 顧客志向
consumer price index
shoohi-sha-bukka-shisuu 消費者物価指数
consumer protection
shoohi-sha-hogo 消費者保護
consumer spending
kojin-shoohi 個人消費
containerization
kontena-ka コンテナ化
contingency
guuhatsu 偶発
contract hire
keiyaku-koyoo 契約雇用
contract out
gaibu ni hatchuu-suru 外部に発注する
control
kanri 管理
convenience store
konbiniensu-sutoa (konbini)
コンビニエンスストア(コンビニ)
convertible currency
koukan-kanoo-tsuuka 交換可能通貨
corporate advertising
kigyoo-kookoku 企業広告
corporate culture
kigyoo-bunka 企業文化
corporate growth
kigyoo no seichoo 企業の成長
corporate image
kigyoo-imeeji 企業イメージ
corporation tax
hoojin-zei 法人税
correlation
sookan-kankei 相関関係
cost accounting
genka-kaikei 原価会計
cost analysis
genka-bunseki 原価分析
cost-benefit analysis (CBA)
hiyoo-ben'eki-bunseki 費用便益分析
cost consciousness
genka-ishiki 原価意識
cost control
genka-kanri 原価管理
cost-effective
hiyoo-tai-kooka 費用対効果
cost-effectiveness
hiyoo-kooka 費用効果
cost-efficiency
hiyoo-kooka 費用効果
cost of living
seikei-hi 生計費
cost reduction
genka-hiki-sage 原価引き下げ
cost structure
genka-koosei 原価構成
CPU (central processing unit)
chuuoo-shori-soochi 中央処理装置
creative thinking
soozoo-teki-shikoo 創造的思考
credit management
shin'yoo-kanri 信用管理
credit rating
shin'yoo-kaku-zuke 信用格付け
credit squeeze
kin'yuu-hikishime 金融引き締め
crisis management
kiki-kanri 危機管理
critical mass
genkai-ryoo 限界量
cross-licensing
soogo-tokkyo-shiyoo-ken 相互特許使用権
culture
bunka 文化
currency
tsuuka 通貨
currency convertibility
(tsuuka no) koukan-sei (通貨の)交換性
current assets
ryuudoo-shisan 流動資産
customer orientation
kokyaku-joohoo-teikyoo 顧客情報提供
customized
chuumon-seisan-shita 注文生産した
custom-made
chuumon-seisan 注文生産

cut-off point
uchikiri-gendo 打ち切り限度
cut prices
ne-biki-suru 値引きする
cutting edge
kattingu-ejji カッティング・エッジ

D

data bank
deeta-bank データバンク
data base
deeta-beesu データベース
data retrieval
deeta-kensaku データ検索
deadline
shime-kiri 締め切り
deal
tori-hiki 取引
debrief
joohoo o ukeru 情報を受ける
debriefing
taiken no kiki-tori 体験の聞き取り
decentralize
bunsan-ka-suru 分散化する
declaration
shinkoku 申告
decline
keiki no kakoo 景気の下降
deficit financing
akaji-zaisei 赤字財政
deflation
defureeshon デフレーション
delivery time
nooki 納期
demand
juyoo 需要
department store
hyakka-ten 百貨店
depreciate
genka-shookyaku-suru 減価償却する
depreciation of yen
en-yasu 円安
depression
kyookoo 恐慌
deregulate
kisei o kanwa-suru 規制を緩和する
deregulation
kisei-kanwa 規制緩和
desktop computer
takujoo-gata-konpyuutaa 卓上型コンピューター
desktop publishing
denshi-shuppan 電子出版
devaluation
heika kiri-sage 平価切下げ
differentiate
sabetsu-ka-suru 差別化する
digital
dejitaru デジタル
direct costs
chokusetsu-genka 直接原価
direct expenses
chokusetsu-keihi 直接経費
direct mail
dairekuto-meeru ダイレクトメール
direct marketing
chokusetsu-hanbai 直接販売
director
yakuin 役員
disbursement
genkin-shiharai 現金支払
discount house
yasu-uri-ten 安売店
discriminate
sabetsu-suru 差別する
discrimination
sabetsu(-taiguu) 差別(待遇)
disintegration
hookai 崩壊
disk drive
disuku-doraibu ディスクドライブ
dismissal
kaiko 解雇
disposable income
ka-shobun-shotoku 可処分所得
dissolution
kaisan 解散
distance learning
gakugai de no gakushuu 学外での学習
distribution
ryuutsuu, hanbai 流通、販売
distribution channel
ryuutsuu-kikoo, ryuutsuu-keiro 流通機構、流通経路
distribution costs
ryuutsuu-keihi 流通経費

distribution industry
ryuutsuu-gyoo 流通業
distribution network
ryuutsuu-kikoo, ryuutsuu-keiro 流通機構、流通経路
diversification
tayoo-ka 多様化
diversify
tayoo-ka-suru 多様化する
dividend
haitoo 配当
double-digit inflation
futa-keta-infure 2桁インフレ
down time
kyuushi-jikan 休止時間
due date
shiharai-kijitsu 支払期日
durable goods
taikyuu-zai 耐久財

E

early retirement
sooki-teinen 早期定年
econometric
keiryoo-keizai-gaku-teki 計量経済学的
economic climate
keizai kishoo 経済気象
economic fluctuation
keiki no hendoo 景気の変動
economic mission
keizai-shisetsu-dan 経済使節団
economic outlook
keiki mi-tooshi 景気見通し
economic plateau
koogen-keiki 高原景気
economic stagnation
keiki-teitai 景気停滞
economic adjustment
keiki-choosei 景気調整
economy of scale
kibo no keizai 規模の経済
ECU (European Currency Unit)
Ooshuu-tsuuka-tan'i 欧州通貨単位
EDPS (electronic data processing system)
denshi-deeta-shori-shisutemu 電子データ処理システム
effective demand
yuukoo-juyoo 有効需要
efficiency
nooritsu 能率
electronic data processing system (EDPS)
denshi-deeta-shori-shisutemu 電子データ処理システム
electronic mail (e-mail)
denshi-meeru 電子メール
electronic publishing
denshi-shuppan 電子出版
e-mail
denshi-meeru 電子メール
employment
koyoo 雇用
enterprise
kigyoo 企業
enterprising
kigyoo-seishin ni tomu 企業精神に富む
entrepreneur
kigyoo-ka 企業家
environment
kankyoo 環境
equal employment opportunity
kintoo-koyoo-kikai 均等雇用機会
equality
byoodoo 平等
equal pay
dooitsu-chingin 同一賃金
estimate
mi-tsumoru 見積る
Eurodollars
Yuuro-daraa ユーロ・ダラー
European Currency Unit (ECU)
Ooshuu-tsuuka-tan'i 欧州通貨単位
evaluate
hyooka-suru 評価する
exchange rate
kawase-reeto 為替レート
executive board
joomu-kai 常務会
executive compensation
yakuin-hooshuu 役員報酬
executive director
senmu-torishimari-yaku 専務取締役
expand
kakudai-suru 拡大する
expected date
yotei-kijitsu 予定期日
expense account
koosai-hi 交際費

expert system

senmon-ka-keiei-shisutemu 専門家経営システム

explore

tansaku-suru 探索する

F

facsimile

fakkusu ファックス

factor

yooso 要素

fair competition

kooseina kyoosoo 公正な競争

family tree

keizu 系図

fax

fakkusu, fakkusu de okuru ファックス、ファックスで送る

fax machine

fakkusu-kiki ファックス機器

feasibility

shoorai-sei 将来性

feasibility study

junbi-choosa 準備調査

feedback

fiido-bakku フィードバック

field research

jitchi-choosa 実地調査

field test

jitchi-shiken 実地試験

finance

shikin-chootatsu 資金調達

financial administration

zaimu-gyoosei 財務行政

financial analysis

zaimu-bunseki 財務分析

financial appraisal

zaimu-satei 財務査定

financial control

zaimu-toosei 財務統制

financial management

zaimu-kanri 財務管理

financial statements

zaimu-shohyoo 財務諸表

financial year

kaikei-nendo 会計年度(英)

fire

kaiko-suru 解雇する

fire fighting

toraburu o kaiketsu-suru kinkyuu-sochi
トラブルを解決する緊急措置

fiscal policy

zaisei-seisaku 財政政策

fiscal year

kaikei-nendo 会計年度(米)

fixed assets

kotei-shisan 固定資産

fixed costs

kotei-hi 固定費

fixed (exchange) rate system

kotei-sooba(-sei) 固定相場(制)

flexitime

furekkusu-taimu フレックス・タイム

float

furooto フロート

floppy disk

furoppii フロッピー

flowchart

sagyoo-kootei-zu, furoochaato
作業工程図、フローチャート

flow diagram

sagyoo-kootei-zu 作業工程図

focus

shooten, shooten o awaseru 焦点、焦点を合わせる

follow-up

tsuiseki-choosa 追跡調査

forecast

yosoku 予測

foreign currency

takoku-tsuuka 他国通貨

foreign exchange reserves

gaika-junbi 外貨準備

forward exchange rate

saki-mono-kawase-sooba 先物為替相場

franchise

eigyoo-menkyo, furanchaizu 営業免許、フランチャイズ

freelance

jiyuu-keiyaku 自由契約

freeze

tooketsu-suru 凍結する

fringe benefits

fuka-kyuufu 付加給付

full capacity

zen-nooryoku 全能力

full-time employee

jookin-sha 常勤者

full-time employment
jookin-koyoo 常勤雇用
functional
kinoo-teki 機能的
function key
kinoo-kii 機能キー
futures
saki-mono-tori-hiki 先物取引
futures market
saki-mono-shijoo 先物市場

G

game theory
geemu no riron ゲームの理論
GDP (gross domestic product)
kokunai-soo-seisan 国内総生産
general manager
buchoo 部長
gentleman's agreement
shinshi-kyootei 紳士協定
globalization
sekai-ka 世界化
globalize
sekai-ka-suru 世界化する
GNP (gross national product)
kokumin-soo-seisan 国民総生産
going rate
genkoo-kinri 現行金利
gold exchange standard system
kin-kawase-hon'i-sei 金為替本位制
gold reserve
kin jumbi 金準備
go public
kabushiki o kookai-suru 株式を公開する
gross domestic product (GDP)
kokunai-soo-seisan 国内総生産
gross national product (GNP)
kokumin-soo-seisan 国民総生産
gross profit
soo-rijun 総利潤
group dynamics
shuudan-rikigaku 集団力学
growth area
seichoo-chiiki 成長地域
growth industry
seichoo-sangyoo 成長産業
growth potential
senzai-seichoo-ryoku 潜在成長力
guideline
shidoo-kijun 指導基準

H

hacker
hakkaa ハッカー
hard copy
haado-kopii ハード・コピー
hard disk
haado-disuku ハード・ディスク
hard sell
gooinna uri-kata 強引な売り方
hard selling
gooinna hambai 強引な販売
harmonize
choowa-saseru 調和させる
head-hunt
jinzai o atsumeru 人材を集める
head-hunter
jinzai-boshuu-gakari 人材募集係
head-hunting
jinzai-chootatsu 人材調達
head office
honsha 本社
heuristics
tansaku-hoohoo 探索方法
high-tech
haiteku ハイテク
hire
yatou 雇う
hiring and firing
koyoo oyobi kaiko 雇用および解雇
holding company
mochikabu-gaisha 持ち株会社
home country
jikoku 自国
host country
shusai-koku 主催国
HRD (human resource development)
jin-teki-shigen-kaihatsu 人的資源開発
HRM (human resource management)
jin-teki-shigen-kanri 人的資源管理
human engineering
ningen-koogaku 人間工学

human relations
ningen-kankei 人間関係
human resource development (HRD)
jin-teki-shigen-kaihatsu 人的資源開発
human resource management (HRM)
jin-teki-shigen-kanri 人的資源管理
human resources
jin-teki-shigen 人的資源

I

idle capacity
yuukyuu-shisetsu 遊休施設
IMF (International Monetary Fund)
kokusai-tsuuka-kikin 国際通貨基金
impact
eikyoo 影響
implement
jisshi-suru 実施する
import
yunyuu 輸入
imported inflation
yunyuu-infure 輸入インフレ
impulse buying
shoodoo-gai 衝動買い
income
shotoku 所得
income tax
shotoku-zei 所得税
in-depth interview
shinsoo-mensetsu-hoo 深層面接法
indirect costs
kansetsu-hiyoo 間接費用
indirect expenses
kansetsu-keihi 間接経費
indirect labor
kansetsu-roodoo(-hi) 間接労働(費)
industrial espionage
sangyoo-supai 産業スパイ
industrial psychology
sangyoo-shinri-gaku 産業心理学
industrial relations
rooshi-kankei 労使関係
inflation
infure インフレ
inflationary economy
infure-keizai インフレ経済
informatics
joohoo-kagaku 情報科学
information flow
joohoo no nagare 情報の流れ
information network
joohoo-moo 情報網
information retrieval
joohoo-kensaku 情報検索
information theory
joohoo-riron 情報理論
infrastructure
shakai-teki-seisan-kiban 社会的生産基盤
in-house
shanai 社内
innovate
kaikaku-suru 改革する
innovative
kaikaku-teki 改革的
input
inputto インプット
integration
toogoo-ka 統合化
interactive
taiwa-shiki, kuri-kaeshi 対話式、繰り返し
interface
intaafeesu インターフェース
internal audit
naibu-kansa 内部監査
international currency
kokusai-tsuuka 国際通貨
internationalize
kokusai-ka-suru 国際化する
International Monetary Fund (IMF)
kokusai-tsuuka-kikin 国際通貨基金
international monetary system
kokusai-tsuuka-seido 国際通貨制度
inventory control
zaiko-kanri 在庫管理
investment
tooshi 投資
investment bank
tooshi-ginkoo 投資銀行

J

J-curve effect
jee-kaabu-kooka Jカーブ効果

job assignment
ninmu 任務
job classification
shokkai 職階
job compensation
shokumu-hooshuu 職務報酬
job description
shokumu-kijutsu-hyoo 職務記述表
job improvement
shokumu no kaizen 職務の改善
job opportunity
koyoo-kikai 雇用機会
job rotation
haichi-tenkan 配置転換
job security
shokumu-hoshoo 職務保証
joint consultation
rooshi-kyoogi 労使協議
joint venture
gooben-kigyoo 合弁企業
joint venture company
gooben-gaisha 合弁会社

K

key currency
kijiku-tsuuka 基軸通貨
know-how
nou-hau ノウハウ

L

labor
roodoo 労働
labor costs
roomu-hi 労務費
labor dispute
rooshi-funsoo 労使紛争
labor-intensive
roodoo-shuuyaku-teki 労働集約的
labor mobility
roodoo-ryuudoo-sei 労働流動性
labor relations
rooshi-kankei 労使関係
LAN (local area network)
kyokuchi-tsuushin-moo 局地通信網
landing
chakuriku 着陸
laptop computer
rappu-toppu-gata-konpyuutaa
ラップトップ型コンピューター
lay off
ichiji-kaiko-suru 一時解雇する
layoff
ichiji-kaiko 一時解雇
leadership
shidoo-ryoku 指導力
leading edge
riidingu-ejji リーディング・エッジ
lease
chingashi-suru 賃貸しする
liabilities
saimu 債務
liberalization
jiyuu-ka 自由化
license
menkyo 免許
life cycle (of a product)
(seihin no) jumyoo (製品の)寿命
lifestyle
seikatsu-yooshiki 生活様式
lifetime employment
shuushin-koyoo 終身雇用
line of command
meirei-keitoo 命令系統
liquid assets
ryuudoo-shisan 流動資産
liquidate
seisan-suru 精算する
liquidation
seisan 精算
listed
joojoo(-shita) 上場(した)
local area network (LAN)
kyokuchi-tsuushin-moo 局地通信網
local-content
genchi-chootatsu o kitei-shita, genchi-seihin shiyoo-kitei no aru
現地調達を規定した、現地製品使用規定のある
local content rules
genchi-buhin-shiyoo-kisoku 現地部品使用規則
local currency
genchi-tsuuka 現地通貨
logistics
rojisutikusu ロジスティクス
logo
rogo, shoohyoo ロゴ、商標

low-tech
tei-gijutsu 低技術
lump sum
ichiji-kin 一時金

M

mailbox
yuubin-posuto 郵便ポスト
mail order
tsuushin-hanbai 通信販売
mainframe
hontai 本体
management
keiei(-jin) 経営(陣)
management accounting
kanri-kaikei 管理会計
management consultant
keiei-konsarutanto 経営コンサルタント
management information system (MIS)
keiei-joohoo-shisutemu 経営情報システム
managerial
kanri-sareta 管理された
managing director (MD)
joomu-torishimari-yaku 常務取締役
M&A (mergers and acquisitions)
kigyoo no kyuushuu-gappei 企業の吸収合併
manpower
jinzai 人材
manpower resource
jin-teki-shigen 人的資源
manufacture
seizo-suru 製造する
manufacturing capacity
seisan-nooryoku 生産能力
margin of safety
anzen-yoyuu-ritsu 安全余裕率
market appraisal
shijoo-hyooka 市場評価
marketing
shijoo-tori-hiki 市場取引
market potential
shijoo-senzai-ryoku 市場潜在力
market price
shijoo-kakaku 市場価格
market research
shijoo-choosa 市場調査
market share
shijoo-sen'yuu-ritsu 市場占有率
market structure
shijoo-koozoo 市場構造
market value
shijoo-kachi 市場価値
mark-up
ne-age 値上げ
mass production
tairyoo-seisan 大量生産
MD (managing director)
joomu-torishimari-yaku 常務取締役
media
baitai 媒体
mediate
chuusai-suru 仲裁する
memory
kioku-soochi 記憶装置
merge
heigoo-suru 併合する
merger
gappei 合併
mergers and acquisitions (M&A)
kigyoo no kyuushuu-gappei 企業の吸収合併
micro
bishi-teki 微視的
middle management
chuukan-kanri-shoku 中間管理職
minimum wage
saitei-chingin 最低賃金
MIS (management information system)
keiei-joohoo-shisutemu 経営情報システム
modem
modemu モデム
monetary control
kin'yuu-choosetsu 金融調節
money laundering
shikin-senjoo 資金洗浄
money supply
tsuuka-kyookyuu(-ryoo) 通貨供給(量)
monitor
kanshi-suru 監視する
monopoly market
dokusen-shijoo 独占市場
motivate
dooki o ataeru 動機を与える
motivation
dooki 動機

mouse
mausu マウス

N

national brand
zenkoku-burando 全国ブランド
needs analysis
niizu-bunseki ニーズ分析
negotiate
kooshoo-suru 交渉する
net assets
jun-shisan 純資産
net profit
jun'eki 純益
net worth
jiko-shihon 自己資本
newly industrialized country (NIC)
shinkoo-sangyoo-koku 新興産業国
NIC (newly industrialized country)
shinkoo-sangyoo-koku 新興産業国
night shift
yakin 夜勤
non-tariff barrier (NTB)
hi-kanzei-shooheki 非関税障壁
non-verbal communication
hi-gengo-komyunikeeshon 非言語コミュニケーション
no-strike clause
sutoraiki-kinshi-jookoo ストライキ禁止条項
NTB (non-tariff barrier)
hi-kanzei-shooheki 非関税障壁
numerical control
suuchi-seigyo 数值制御

O

occupational hazard
shokugyoo-joo no kiken 職業上の危険
on-line
on-rain オンラインの
operating division
jigyoo-bumon 事業部門
operations research (OR)
gyoomu-choosa 業務調查
optimal condition
saiteki-jooken 最適条件
OR (operations research)
gyoomu-choosa 業務調查
organization chart
soshiki-zu 組織図
organization structure
soshiki-koosei 組織構成
output
shutsuryoku 出力
OVA (overhead value analysis)
soo-keihi-kachi-bunseki 総経費価値分析
overheads
keihi 経費
overhead value analysis (OVA)
soo-keihi-kachi-bunseki 総経費価値分析
overheated economy
kanetsu-keiki 過熱景気
overtime
zangyoo 残業

P

package deal
hookatsu-kooshoo 包括交涉
packaging
hoosoo 包装
parallel import
heikoo-yunyuu 平行輸入
parameter
parameetaa パラメーター
parent company
oya-gaisha 親会社
participation
sanka 参加
partner
kyoodoo-keiei-sha 共同経営者
partnership
kyoodoo-keiei 共同経営
part-time employment
hi-jookin-koyoo 非常勤雇用
part-timer
hi-jookin-juugyoo-in 非常勤従業員
patent
tokkyo(-ken) 特許(権)
payroll
chingin-meisai-hyoo 賃金明細表
payroll deductions
chingin-koojo 賃金控除
PC (personal computer)
pasokon パソコン

performance evaluation
gyooseki-satei 業績査定
peripheral device
shuuhen-kiki 周辺機器
personal computer (PC)
pasokon パソコン
personal growth
kojin-teki-seichoo 個人的成長
personnel management
jinji-kanri 人事管理
personnel manager
jinji-tantoo-sha 人事担当者
petty cash
koguchi-genkin 小口現金
phase out
dankai-tekini haishi-suru 段階的に廃止する
planned obsolescence
keikaku-teki-chinpu-ka 計画的陳腐化
plant capacity
seizoo-nooryoku 製造能力
Plaza Accord
Puraza-gooi プラザ合意
point-of-sale (POS)
hanbai-jiten no 販売時点の
POS (point-of-sale)
hanbai-jiten no 販売時点の
post-industrialization
datsu-koogyoo-ka 脱工業化
potential demand
senzai-juyoo 潜在需要
PR (public relations)
koohoo-katsudoo 公報活動
premium
uwanose-kinri 上乗せ金利
president
shachoo 社長
price differential
kakaku-kakusa 価格格差
price index
kakaku-shisuu 価格指数
print out
insatsu-suru 印刷する
printout
insatsu-shutsuryoku 印刷出力
private enterprise
minkan-kigyoo 民間企業
privatize
min'ei-ka-suru 民営化する
probability theory
kakuritsu-riron 確率理論
problem analysis
mondai-bunseki 問題分析
problem area
mondai-ryooiki 問題領域
problem solving
mondai-kaiketsu 問題解決
procedure
te-tsuzuki 手続き
process
kakoo-suru 加工する
procurement
chootatsu 調達
product analysis
seihin-bunseki 製品分析
product development
seihin-kaihatsu 製品開発
product differentiation
seihin-sabetsu-ka 製品差別化
product improvement
seihin-kaizen 製品改善
production complex
seisan-fukugoo-tai 生産複合体
production control
seisan-kanri 生産管理
production engineering
seisan-koogaku 生産工学
production planning and control
seisan-keikaku-kanri 生産計画管理
production schedule
seisan-keikaku 生産計画
productivity
seisan-sei 生産性
product life
seihin-jumyoo 製品寿命
product line
seisan-rain 生産ライン
profit
rieki 利益
profit margin
shooko-kin 証拠金
profit outlook
rieki-mi-tooshi 利益見通し
promotion
shooshin 昇進
pro rata
hirei-shite 比例して

prosperity
kookyoo 好況
public enterprise
kooei-kigyoo 公営企業
publicly listed company
joojoo-kigyoo 上場企業
public relations (PR)
koohoo-katsudoo 公報活動
public utility
kookyoo-jigyoo 公共事業
purchasing power
koobai-ryoku 購買力
purchasing power parity
koobai-ryoku heika 購買力平価

Q

QC (quality control)
hinshitsu-kanri 品質管理
quality assurance
hinshitsu-hoshoo 品質保証
quality circle
hinshitsu-kanri-shoo-guruupu 品質管理小グループ
quality control (QC)
hinshitsu-kanri 品質管理
quantitative analysis
keiryoo-bunseki 計量分析
quarter
shi-hanki 四半期
quota
wariate 割当て

R

R&D (research and development)
kenkyuu-kaihatsu 研究開発
rationale
riron-teki 理論的
rationalization
goori-ka 合理化
read-only memory (ROM)
kotei-kioku-soochi 固定記憶装置
real income
jisshitsu-shotoku 実質所得
real time
riaru-taimu リアルタイム
recession
keiki-kootai 景気後退
recruit
shinki-saiyoo-suru 新規採用する
recruitment
saiyoo 採用
recycle
sai-riyoo-suru 再利用する
recycling
sai-riyoo 再利用
redundancy
juufuku 重複
registered trademark
tooroku-shoohyoo 登録商標
regulate
kisei suru 規制する
regulation
kisei 規制
reliability
shinrai-do 信頼度
remuneration
hooshuu 報酬
reorganization
sai-hensei 再編成
replacement costs
sai-shutoku-genka 再取得原価
replacement demand
kaikae-juyoo 買替需要
resale price
saihan-kakaku 再販価格
research and development (R&D)
kenkyuu-kaihatsu 研究開発
reserve currency
junbi-tsuuka 準備通貨
restructuring
sai-hensei 再編成
retail store
kouri-ten 小売店
retirement
taishoku 退職
revaluation
heika kiri-age 平価切上げ
revolving credit
kaiten-shin'yoo-kanjoo 回転信用勘定
risk analysis
kiken-bunseki 危険分析
risk management
kiki-kanri 危機管理
robotize
robotto-ka-suru ロボット化する

ROM (read-only memory)
kotei-kioku-soochi 固定記憶装置
royalty
tokkyo-shiyoo-ryoo 特許使用料
running expenses
unten-keihi 運転経費

S

sales department
eigyoo-bu 営業部
sales forecast
hanbai-yosoku 販売予測
sales manager
hanbai-sekinin-sha 販売責任者
sales network
hanbai-moo 販売網
sales policy
hanbai-seisaku 販売政策
sales potential
hanbai-kanoo-sei 販売可能性
sales promotion
hanbai-sokushin 販売促進
sales turnover
hanbai-kaiten-ritsu 販売回転率
SDR, SDRs (special drawing rights)
tokubetsu-hikidashi-ken 特別引出権
securities
yuuka-shooken 有価証券
segmentation
saibun-ka 細分化
self-appraisal
jiko-hyooka 自己評価
sellers' market
uri-te-shijoo 売り手市場
sell out
uri-tsukusu 売り尽くす
semiconductor
han-dootai 半導体
severance pay
taishoku-kin 退職金
sexual harassment
sei-teki-iyagarase 性的いやがらせ
shipment
shukka 出荷
shortfall
akaji 赤字
simulation
mogi-renshuu 模擬練習
single currency
tan'itsu-tsuuka 単一通貨
skilled labor
jukuren-koo 熟練工
slump
fushin 不振
socio-cultural
shakai-bunka-teki 社会文化的
socio-economic
shakai-keizai(-gaku) 社会経済(学)
software
sofuto-uea ソフトウエア
sole agent
soo-dairi-ten 総代理店
special drawing rights (SDR, SDRs)
tokubetsu-hikidashi-ken 特別引出権
spreadsheet
tenkai-hyoo 展開表
staff management
shokuin-kanri 職員管理
stagflation
sutagufureeshon スタグフレーション
stagger
jisa-shukkin 時差出勤
standard
kijun 基準
standard deviation
hyoojun-hensa 標準偏差
standardization
hyoojun-ka 標準化
standardize
hyoojun-ka-suru 標準化する
standard time
hyoojun-jikan 標準時間
state of the art
koodo-gijutsu-suijun 高度技術水準
stock control
zaiko(-hin)-kanri 在庫(品)管理
stock market
shooken-shijoo 証券市場
stock option
kabushiki-kai-ire-sentaku-ken 株式買い入れ選択権
store
kioku 記憶
strategy
senryaku 戦略

streamline
kooritsu-ka-suru 効率化する
strike
sutoraiki o suru ストライキをする
strong currency
tsuyoi tsuuka 強い通貨
structural recession
koozoo-fukyoo 構造不況
subcontract
shita-uke-keiyaku o suru 下請け契約をする
subcontractor
shita-uke-gyoosha 下請け業者
subliminal advertising
senzai-ishiki-kookoku 潜在意識広告
subsidiary
hojo-teki-gyoomu 補助的業務
subsidiary company
ko-gaisha 子会社
supermarket
suupaa スーパー
supervise
kantoku-suru 監督する
supervisor
kanri-sha 管理者
supply
kyookyuu 供給
supply-demand gap
jukyuu-gyappu 需給ギャップ
supply-demand relationship
jukyuu-kankei, jukyuu-jootai 需給関係、需給状態
swap
swappu スワップ
symposium
shinpojiumu シンポジウム
systems analysis
shisutemu-bunseki システム分析
systems engineering
shisutemu-koogaku システム工学

T

take-home pay
te-dori-kyuuryoo 手取り給料
take-off
ririku 離陸
take-over
nottori 乗っ取り
take-over bid (TOB)
kabushiki no kookai-kai-tsuke 株式の公開買い付け
target
mokuhyoo 目標
tariff barrier
kanzei-shooheki 関税障壁
task force
purojekuto-chiimu, tasuku-foosu
プロジェクトチーム、タスクフォース
tax
kazei-suru 課税する
tax-deductible
zeikin-koojo, kazei-koojo 税金控除、課税控除
tax incentive
zeisei-joo-no yuguu-sochi 税制上の優遇措置
tax relief
genzei 減税
technology transfer
gijutsu-iten 技術移転
terminal
tanmatsu(-soochi) 端末(装置)
think-tank
shinku tanku シンクタンク
time-sharing
jibunkatsu(-shori) 時分割(処理)
TOB (take-over bid)
kabushiki no kookai-kai-tsuke 株式の公開買い付け
top-down
jooi-katatsu-hooshiki 上意下達方式
top management
saikoo-keiei-sha 最高経営者
total quality control (TQC)
soogoo-teki-hinshitsu-kanri 総合的品質管理
total quality management (TQM)
soogoo-teki-hinshitsu-keiei 総合的品質経営
TQC (total quality control)
soogoo-teki-hinshitsu-kanri 総合的品質管理
TQM (total quality management)
soogoo-teki-hinshitsu-keiei 総合的品質経営
trade imbalance
booeki-fu-kinkoo 貿易不均衡
trade restriction
booeki-seigen 貿易制限
trade union
(shokushu-betsu no) roodoo-kumiai (職種別の)労働組合
transportation
un'yu 運輸

trend
dookoo 動向
troubleshooting
koshoo-hakken-shuuri 故障発見修理

U

unfair competition
fu-kooseina kyoosoo 不公正な競争
unlisted company
hi-joojoo-kigyoo 非上場企業
update
kooshin-suru 更新する
user-friendly
kooi-teki-shiyoo-sha 好意的使用者

V

value
kachi 価値
value added
fuka-kachi 付加価値
value added tax (VAT)
fuka-kachi-zei 付加価値税
VAT (value added tax)
fuka-kachi-zei 付加価値税
VDU (visual display unit)
hyooji-soochi 表示装置
venture capital
benchaa-shihon ベンチャー資本
verbal communication
gengo-komyunikeeshon 言語コミュニケーション
vested interest
kakutei-kenri, kitoku-ken'eki 確定権利、既得権益
vice-president
fuku-shachoo 副社長
visual display unit (VDU)
hyooji-soochi 表示装置
vocational training
shokugyoo-kunren 職業訓練
volume
ryoo 量

W

wage
chingin 賃金
wage freeze
chingin-tooketsu 賃金凍結
warehousing industry
sooko-gyoo 倉庫業
weak currency
yowai tsuuka 弱い通貨
weighted average
kajuu-heikin 加重平均
white-collar (worker)
howaito-karaa ホワイトカラー
white goods
daidokoro-yoo-denki-seihin 台所用電器製品
whiz-kid
kiremono 切れ者
word processor (WP)
waapuro ワープロ
working capital
unten-shikin 運転資金
working hours
kinmu-jikan 勤務時間
work in progress
shikake-hin 仕掛け品
workload (work load)
hyoojun-sagyoo-ryoo 標準作業量
works council
rooshi-gyoogi-kai 労使協議会
work stress
shigoto no sutoresu 仕事のストレス
workplace
shokuba 職場
WP (word processor)
waapuro ワープロ
write off
chookeshi ni suru 帳消しにする

Y

yardstick
kijun-shakudo 基準尺度

Z

zero defects
mu-kekkan-undoo 無欠陥運動
zero-sum game
zero-samu-geemu ゼロサムゲーム

ECONOMY

A

accounts payable
kaikake-kin 買掛金
accounts receivable
urikake-kin 売り掛け金
accrual basis
hassei-shugi 発生主義
across-the-board reduction of tariff
kanzei no ikkatsu-hiki-sage 関税の一括引き下げ
active openings ration
yuukoo-kyuujin-bairitsu 有効求人倍率
allowance for bad debts
kashi-daore-hikiate-kin 貸し倒れ引き当て金
APEC (Asian Pacific Economic Cooperation)
Ajia-Taihei-yoo-keizai-kyooryoku-kaigi
アジア太平洋経済協力会議
appreciation of the Yen
en-daka 円高
arbitrage
saitei-tori-hiki 裁定取引
Asian Development Bank
Ajia-kaihatsu-ginkoo アジア開発銀行
Asian Pacific Economic Cooperation (APEC)
Ajia-Taihei-yoo-keizai-kyooryoku-kaigi
アジア太平洋経済協力会議
at the market
nariyuki-chuumon 成り行き注文

B

balance of (international) payments
kokusai-shuushi 国際収支
balance of payment statistics
kokusai-shuushi-tookei 国際収支統計
bank debenture
kin'yuu-sai 金融債
Bank for International Settlements
Kokusai-kessai-ginkoo 国際決済銀行
Bank of Japan
Nihon-ginkoo (Nichi-gin) 日本銀行(日銀)
bankruptcy
toosan 倒産
barrier to entry
sannyuu-shooheki 参入障壁
bilateralism
ni-koku-kan-shugi 2国間主義
bill discount market
tegata-baibai-shijoo 手形売買市場
bloc economy
burokku-keizai ブロック経済
blue chip
buruu-chippu ブルーチップ
Board of Governors of the Federal Reserve System (FRB)
Renpoo-junbi-seido-riji-kai 連邦準備制度理事会
bond with warrant
waranto-sai ワラント債
break-even point
son'eki-bunki-ten 損益分岐点
budget cycle
yosan-junkan 予算循環
business cycle
keiki-junkan 景気循環
business fluctuation
keiki-hendoo 景気変動

C

call by sinking fund
teiji-shookan 定時償還
capital balance
shihon-shuushi 資本収支
capital gains taxation
kyapitarugein-kazei キャピタルゲイン課税
capital market
shihon-shijoo 資本市場
capital stock
shihon-kin 資本金
cash transaction
jitsumono-tori-hiki 実物取引
certified public accountant
koonin-kaikei-shi 公認会計士
collective bargaining
dantai-kooshoo 団体交渉
common agricultural policy
kyootsuu-noogyoo-seisaku 共通農業政策
competitive wage rate
chingin-sooba 賃金相場
composite index
keiki-soogoo-shisuu 景気総合指数
concerted intervention
kyoochoo-kainyuu 協調介入

construction bond
kensetsu-kokusai 建設国債
consumer behavior survey
shoohi-dookoo-choosa 消費動向調査
consumer price
shoohi-sha-kakaku 消費者価格
consumer price index (CPI)
shoohi-sha-bukka-shisuu 消費者物価指数
contingency plan
fusoku-jitai-taioo-keikaku 不測事態対応計画
controlled economy
toosei-keizai 統制経済
convertible bond
tenkan-shasai 転換社債
corporate debenture
shasai 社債
CPI (consumer price index)
shoohi-sha-bukka-shisuu 消費者物価指数
credit rating
saiken-kaku-zuke 債券格付け
current account balance of payment
keijoo-shuushi 経常収支
current assets
ryuudoo-shisan 流動資産
current liabilities
ryuudoo-fusai 流動負債
custom(s) house
zeikan 税関
customs clearance
tsuukan 通関
customs duty
kanzei 関税

D

debt accumulation
ruiseki-saimu 累積債務
debt deflation
fusai-defureeshon 負債デフレーション
default
saimu-fu-rikoo 債務不履行
deficit
kokusai-shuushi akaji 国際収支赤字
deficit-covering bond
akaji-kokusai 赤字国債
deflation
defure デフレ
demand for money
kahei-juyoo 貨幣需要
denomination
denomi デノミ
deposit insurance corporation
yokin-hoken-kikoo 預金保険機構
depreciation
genka-shookyaku 減価償却
deregulation
kisei-kanwa 規制緩和
derivative
kin'yuu-hasei-shoohin 金融派生商品
diffusion index
keiki-dookoo-shisuu 景気動向指数
disclosure system
disukuroojaa-seido ディスクロージャー制度
discount debenture
waribiki-sai 割引債
discounting of bill
tegata-waribiki 手形割引
diversification
takaku-ka 多角化
dividend
haitoo 配当
divisionalized organization
jigyoo-bu-sei-soshiki 事業部制組織
dollar crash
doru booraku ドル暴落

E

EC (European Community)
Ooshuu-kyoodoo-tai 欧州共同体
econometrics
keiryoo-keizai-gaku 計量経済学
economic interdependence
keizai-teki soogo-izon 経済的相互依存
economic cooperation organization
keizai-kyooryoku-kikoo 経済協力機構
economic crash
keizai-kyookoo 経済恐慌
economic crisis
keizai-kiki 経済危機
economic growth
keizai-seichoo 経済成長
economic low
keizai-hoosoku 経済法則

economic maladjustment
keizai no hizumi 経済のひずみ
economic panic
keizai-kyookoo 経済恐慌
economic planning
keizai-keikaku 経済計画
economic policy
keizai-seisaku 経済政策
economic power
keizai-taikoku 経済大国
economics
keizai-gaku 経済学
economic standard
keizai-suijun 経済水準
economic summit
keizai shunoo-kaigi 経済首脳会議
economic superpower
keizai-cho-taikoku 経済超大国
economic system
keizai-taisei 経済体制
economies of scale
kibo no keizai 規模の経済
economies of scope
han'i no keizai 範囲の経済
EFTA (European Free Trade Association)
Ooshuu-jiyuu-booeki-rengoo 欧州自由貿易連合
electronic commerce
denshi-tori-hiki 電子取引
employment adjustment
koyoo-choosei 雇用調整
Employment Security Law
shokugyoo-antei-hoo 職業安定法
EMS (European Monetary System)
Ooshuu-tsuuka-seido 欧州通貨制度
escape clause
menseki-jookoo 免責条項
EU (European Union)
Ooshuu-rengoo 欧州連合
Euro-bond
Yuuro-sai ユーロ債
European Community (EC)
Ooshuu-kyoodoo-tai 欧州共同体
European Council
Ooshuu-riji-kai 欧州理事会
European Economic Area
Ooshuu-keizai-chiiki 欧州経済地域
European Free Trade Association (EFTA)
Ooshuu-jiyuu-booeki-rengoo 欧州自由貿易連合
European Monetary System (EMS)
Ooshuu-tsuuka-seido 欧州通貨制度
European Union (EU)
Ooshuu-rengoo 欧州連合
expenses
hiyoo 費用
export insurance
booeki-hoken 貿易保険
extra territorial application
iki-gai-tekiyoo 域外適用

F

fair trade
koosei-booeki 公正貿易
financial accounts
kin'yuu-kanjoo 金融勘定
financial deregulation
kin'yuu-jiyuu-ka 金融自由化
financial futures transaction
kin'yuu-saki-mono-tori-hiki 金融先物取引
financial market
kin'yuu-shijoo 金融市場
financial statements
zaimu-shohyoo 財務諸表
first section, the
shijoo-dai-ichi-bu 市場第1部
fixed assets
kotei-shisan 固定資産
fixed liabilities
kotei-fusai 固定負債
fixed rate
kotei-kinri 固定金利
floating rate
hendoo-kinri 変動金利
foreign currency reserves
gaika-junbi-daka 外貨準備高
foreign exchange fluctuation insurance
kawase-hendoo-hoken 為替変動保険
foreign exchange market
gaikoku-kawase-shijoo 外国為替市場
foreign exchange rate
gaikoku-kawase-sooba 外国為替相場
FRB (Board of Governors of the Federal Reserve System)
Renpoo-junbi-seido-riji-kai 連邦準備制度理事会
free economy
jiyuu-keizai 自由経済

free trade principle
jiyuu-booeki-shugi 自由貿易主義
friction
booeki-masatsu 貿易摩擦
fundamentals
fandamentaruzu ファンダメンタルズ
futures contract
saiken-saki-mono-tori-hiki 債券先物取引

G

GATT (General Agreement on Tariffs and Trade)
Gatto, kanzei-booeki-ippan-kyootei
ガット、関税貿易一般協定
general account
ippan-kaikei 一般会計
General Agreement on Tariffs and Trade (GATT)
Gatto, kanzei-booeki-ippan-kyootei
ガット、関税貿易一般協定
general expenditure
ippan-saishutsu 一般歳出
GNP (gross national product)
kokumin-soo-seisan 国民総生産
government bond
kokusai 国債
gross domestic product
kokunai-soo-seisan 国内総生産
gross national expenditure
kokumin-soo-shishutsu 国民総支出
gross national product (GNP)
kokumin-soo-seisan 国民総生産
growth economy
seichoo-keizai 成長経済

H

holding company
mochikabu-gaisha 持株会社
horizontal division of labor
suihei-bungyoo 水平分業

I

IMF (International Monetary Fund)
Kokusai-tsuuka-kikin 国際通貨基金
import quota system
yunyuu-wariate-sei 輸入割当制
import restriction
yunyuu-seigen 輸入制限
import surcharge
yunyuu-kachoo-kin 輸入課徴金
import usance
yunyuu-yuuzansu 輸入ユーザンス
increase of capital
zooshi 増資
industrial dispute
roodoo-soogi 労働争議
industrial organization
sangyoo-soshiki 産業組織
industrial structure
sangyoo-koozoo 産業構造
industrial structure council
sangyoo-koozoo-shingi-kai 産業構造審議会
inflation
infure インフレ
infrastructure
kabu-koozoo, keizai-kiban 下部構造、経済基盤
insurance company
hoken-gaisha 保険会社
interest-bearing bond
ritsuki-sai 利付債
international currency
kokusai-tsuuka 国際通貨
international financial market
kokusai-kin'yuu-shijoo 国際金融市場
International Monetary Fund (IMF)
Kokusai-tsuuka-kikin 国際通貨基金
international policy cooperation
kokusai-seisaku-kyoochoo 国際政策協調
inventories
tana-oroshi-shisan 棚卸し資産
inventory investment
zaiko-tooshi 在庫投資
investment company
tooshi-shintaku-itaku-kaisha 投資信託委託会社
invisible trade
booeki-gai-tori-hiki 貿易外取引
issue of government bonds, the
kokusai-hakkoo 国債発行

J

Japan bashing
Nihon-tataki 日本たたき

Japan Chamber of Commerce and Industry
Nihon-shookoo-kaigi-sho 日本商工会議所

Japan Committee for Economic Development
Keizai-dooyuu-kai 経済同友会

Japan Federation of Employers' Association
Nihon-keiei-sha-dantai-renmei (Nikkeiren)
日本経営者団体連盟(日経連)

job rotation
haichi-tenkan 配置転換

joint-stock corporation
kabushiki-gaisha 株式会社

joint venture
goohen-gaisha 合弁会社

K

key industry
kikan-sangyoo 基幹産業

kitty
kyoodoo-shusshi-kin 共同出資金

L

labor force
roodoo-ryoku 労働力

labor productivity
roodoo-seisan-sei 労働生産性

Labor Standards Law
roodoo-kijun hoo 労働基準法

law of demand
juyoo no hoosoku 需要の法則

legal reserve
hootei-junbi-kin 法定準備金

lifelong employment system
shuushin-koyoo-seido 終身雇用制度

listing standard
joojoo-kijun 上場基準

list price
teika 定価

long-term rate of interest
chooki-kinri 長期金利

M

macroeconomics
makuro-keizai-gaku マクロ経済学

management creed
keiei-rinen 経営理念

margin transaction
shin'yoo-tori-hiki 信用取引

market equilibrium
shijoo-kinkoo 市場均衡

market price
shika 市価

merchandise trade
booeki-tori-hiki 貿易取引

microeconomics
micuro-keizai-gaku ミクロ経済学

money market
tanki-kin'yuu-shijoo 短期金融市場

money supply
manee-sapurai マネー・サプライ

monopoly price
dokusen-kakaku 独占価格

mortgage company
teitoo-shooken-gaisha 抵当証券会社

most-favored-nation treatment
saikei-koku-taiguu 最恵国待遇

MTN (the multilateral tariff negotiations)
takoku-kan-kanzei-hiki-sage-kooshoo
多国間関税引き下げ交渉

multilateralism
ta-koku-kan-shugi 多国間主義

multilateral tariff negotiations, the (MTN)
takoku-kan-kanzei-hiki-sage-kooshoo
多国間関税引き下げ交渉

municipal bond
chihoo-sai 地方債

N

NAFTA (North American Free Trade Agreement)
Hoku-Bei-jiyuu-booeki-kyootei 北米自由貿易協定

National Economic Council
Kokka-keizai-kaigi 国家経済会議

national economy
kokumin-keizai 国民経済

national income
kokumin-shotoku 国民所得

natural rate of unemployment
shizen-shitsugyoo-ritsu 自然失業率

negotiable certificate of deposit
jooto-sei-yokin 譲渡性預金

net national product
jun-kokumin-seisan 純国民生産

New York Stock Exchange (NYSE)
Nyuuyooku-shooken-tori-hiki-jo
ニューヨーク証券取引所
non-resident
hi-kyojuu-sha 非居住者
non-tariff barrier (NTB)
hi-kanzei-shooheki 非関税障壁
North American Free Trade Agreement (NAFTA)
Hoku-Bei-jiyuu-booeki-kyootei 北米自由貿易協定
notes payable
shiharai-tegata 支払い手形
notes receivable
uketori-tegata 受け取り手形
NTB (non-tariff barrier)
hi-kanzei-shooheki 非関税障壁
NYSE (New York Stock Exchange)
Nyuuyooku-shooken-tori-hiki-jo
ニューヨーク証券取引所

O

ODA (Official Development Assistance)
seifu-kaihatsu-enjo 政府開発援助
OECD (Organization for Economic Cooperation and Development)
Keizai-kyooryoku-kaihatsu-kikoo 経済協力開発機構
OEM (original equipment manufacturing agreement)
aite-kata-burando-shoohin-seizoo-kyookyuu-kyootei
相手方ブランド商品製造供給協定
Official Development Assistance (ODA)
seifu-kaihatsu-enjo 政府開発援助
operating loss
eigyoo-sonshitsu 営業損失
operating profit
eigyoo-rieki 営業利益
orderly marketing
tekisei-yushutsu 適正輸出
ordinary bank
futsuu-ginkoo 普通銀行
ordinary loss
keijoo-sonshitsu 経常損失
ordinary profit
keijoo-rieki 経常利益
Organization for Economic Cooperation and Development (OECD)
Keizai-kyooryoku-kaihatsu-kikoo 経済協力開発機構
original equipment manufacturing agreement (OEM)
aite-kata-burando-shoohin-seizoo-kyookyuu-kyootei
相手方ブランド商品製造供給協定
out-sourcing
auto-sooshingu アウトソーシング
overall balance
soogoo-shuushi 総合収支
over-the-counter market
tentoo-kabushiki-shijoo 店頭株式市場

P

personal consumption expenditures
kojin-shoohi 個人消費
PL (product liability)
seizoo-butsu-sekinin 製造物責任
planned economy
keikaku-keizai 計画経済
plant and equipment investment
setsubi-tooshi 設備投資
plant export
puranto-yushutsu プラント輸出
Plaza Accord
Puraza-gooi プラザ合意
preference treatment tariff
tokukei-kanzei 特恵関税
price control
kakaku-toosei 価格統制
price fall
bukka-kakoo 物価下降
price freeze
kakaku-tooketsu 価格凍結
price increase rate
bukka-jooshoo-ritsu 物価上昇率
price index
bukka-shisuu 物価指数
price level
bukka-suijun 物価水準
price rise
bukka-jooshoo 物価上昇
prices
bukka 物価
price stability
bukka-antei 物価安定
prime rate
puraimu-reeto プライムレート

private bonds
minkan-sai 民間債
private sector
minkan-bumon 民間部門
processing trade
kakoo-booeki 加工貿易
product innovation
seihin-kakushin 製品革新
product liability (PL)
seizoo-butsu-sekinin 製造物責任
profit maximization
rijun saidai-ka 利潤最大化
project system
purojekuto-seido プロジェクト制度
provisional budget
zantei-yosan 暫定予算
public bond
koosai, kookyoo-sai 公債、公共債
public debt securities
kookyoo-sai 公共債
public goods
kookyoo-zai 公共財
public investment
kookyoo tooshi 公共投資
public offering
koobo 公募
public sector
kookyoo-bumon 公共部門
public utility rate
kookyoo-ryookin 公共料金

Q

quadrilateral trade talks
yon-kyoku-tsuushoo-kaigi 4極通商会議
quantity theory of money
kahei-suuryoo-setsu 貨幣数量説

R

rate of potential growth
senzai-seichoo-ritsu 潜在成長率
ratio of net worth
jiko-shihon-hiritsu 自己資本比率
reciprocity principle
soogo-shugi 相互主義
regionalism
chiiki-shugi 地域主義
regular way
futsuu-tori-hiki 普通取引
resale price
saihan-kakaku 再販価格
resident
kyojuu-sha 居住者
retail price
kouri-kakaku 小売価格
retaliatory tariff
hoofuku-kanzei 報復関税
revenues
shuueki 収益

S

SEC (Securities & Exchange Commission)
Amerika-shooken-tori-hiki-jo アメリカ証券取引所
Securities & Exchange Commission (SEC)
Amerika-shooken-tori-hiki-jo アメリカ証券取引所
Securities and Exchange Law
shooken-tori-hiki-hoo 証券取引法
securities firm
shooken-gaisha 証券会社
security analyst
shooken-anarisuto 証券アナリスト
services balance
booeki-gai-shuushi 貿易外収支
service trade
saabisu-booeki サービス貿易
session
tachiai 立ち会い
share
kabushiki 株式
short-term rate of interest
tanki-kinri 短期金利
social overhead capital
shakai-shihon 社会資本
special account
tokubetsu-kaikei 特別会計
special drawing rights
tokubetsu-hikidashi-ken 特別引き出し権
speculative stocks
shite-kabu 仕手株
Spring Labor Offensive
shuntoo 春闘
stabilized growth
antei-seichoo 安定成長

stock
kabushiki 株式
stock adjustment
sutokku-choosei ストック調整
stock exchange
shooken-tori-hiki-jo 証券取引所
stock futures transaction
kabushiki-saki-mono-tori-hiki 株式先物取引
stock market
kabushiki-shijoo 株式市場
stock option transaction
kabushiki-opushon-tori-hiki 株式オプション取引
stock price index
kabuka-shisuu 株価指数
strong stockholder
antei-kabunushi 安定株主
structural adjustment
koozoo-choosei 構造調整
structural impediments initiative
Nichi-Bei-koozoo-kyoogi 日米構造協議
subscription rights
shinkabu-hikiuke-ken 新株引き受け権
summit
samitto, shuyoo-senshin-koku-shunoo-kaigi
サミット、主要先進国首脳会議
superstructure
joobu-koozoo 上部構造
supplementary budget
hosei-yosan 補正予算
supply-side economics
kyookyuu-juushi-gata no keizai-gaku
供給重視型の経済学
surplus
jooyo-kin 剰余金
surplus country
kokusai-shuushi-kuroji-koku 国際収支黒字国

T

takeover bid
kabushiki-kookai-kaitsuke 株式公開買付け
tariff
kanzei 関税
tariff barrier
kanzei-shooheki 関税障壁
tariff rate
kanzei-ritsu 関税率
taxable goods
kazei-hin 課税品
taxpayer numbering system
noozei-sha-bangoo-seido 納税者番号制度
technology export
gijutsu-yushutsu 技術輸出
technology transfer
gijutsu-iten 技術移転
terms of trade
kooeki-jooken 交易条件
third party allocation
dai-san-sha-wariate 第三者割り当て
trade agreement
booeki-kyootei 貿易協定
trade balance
booeki-shuushi 貿易収支
trade dispute
booeki-masatsu 貿易摩擦
trade friction
booeki-masatsu 貿易摩擦
trade imbalance
booeki-fu-kinkoo 貿易不均衡
trade liberalization
booeki-jiyuu-ka 貿易自由化
trade protectionism
hogo-booeki-shugi 保護貿易主義
trade restriction
booeki-seigen 貿易制限
trade secret
eigyoo-himitsu 営業秘密
transit trade
tsuuka-booeki 通過貿易
treasury bill market
tanki-kokusai-shijoo 短期国債市場
treasury investment and loan
zaisei-tooyuushi 財政投融資
Treaty of Maastricht
Maasutorihito-jooyaku マーストリヒト条約
triangular trade
sankaku-booeki 三角貿易
trust bank
shintaku-ginkoo 信託銀行

U

UNCTAD (United Nations Conference of Trade and Development)
Kokuren-booeki-kaihatsu-kaigi 国連貿易開発会議

unemployment
shitsugyoo 失業
United Nations Conference of Trade and Development (UNCTAD)
Kokuren-booeki-kaihatsu-kaigi 国連貿易開発会議
unit of trading
baibai-tan'i 売買単位
Uruguay Round
Uruguai-raundo ウルグアイ・ラウンド
U.S.-Japan Framework Talks on bilateral trade
Nichi-Bei-hookatsu-keizai-kyoogi 日米包括経済協議

V

visiting employee
shukkoo 出向
voluntary export curb
yushutsu no jishu-kisei 輸出の自主規制
voluntary restriction on exports
yushutsu-jishu-kisei 輸出自主規制

W

Western European Union
Sei-Oo-doomei 西欧同盟
wholesale price
oroshi-uri-kakaku 卸売価格
wholesale price index (WPI)
oroshi-uri-bukka shisuu 卸売物価指数
World Bank
sekai-ginkoo 世界銀行
world economy
sekai-keizai 世界経済
world trade
sekai-booeki 世界貿易
World Trade Organization (WTO)
Sekai-booeki-kikoo 世界貿易機構
WPI (wholesale price index)
oroshi-uri-bukka-shisuu 卸売物価指数
WTO (World Trade Organization)
Sekai-booeki-kikoo 世界貿易機構

Y

yield to maturity
saishuu-ri-mawari 最終利回り

SCIENCE

A

abnormal weather
ijoo-kishoo 異常気象
acid rain
sansei-u 酸性雨
acquired immunodeficiency syndrome (AIDS)
eizu エイズ
active oxygen
kassei sanso 活性酸素
AI (artificial intelligence)
jinkoo-chinoo 人工知能
AIDS (acquired immunodeficiency syndrome)
eizu エイズ
algebra
daisuu-gaku 代数学
algorithm
arugorizumu アルゴリズム
antibiotic
koosei-busshitsu 抗生物質
arteriosclerosis
doomyaku-kooka-shoo 動脈硬化症
artificial intelligence (AI)
jinkoo-chinoo 人工知能
artificial organ
jinkoo-zooki 人工臓器
artificial satellite
jinkoo-eisei 人工衛星
astrophysics
tentai-butsuri-gaku 天体物理学
atmosphere
taiki 大気
atmospheric pressure
kiatsu 気圧
atom
genshi 原子
atomic energy
genshi-ryoku 原子力
atomic nucleus
genshi-kaku 原子核
automaton
ootomaton オートマトン
avalanche
nadare 雪崩

axiom
koori 公理

B

big bang theory
biggu-ban-riron ビッグバン理論
biochemistry
sei-kagaku 生化学
biophysics
seibutsu-butsuri-gaku 生物物理学
biotechnology
baio-tekunorojii バイオテクノロジー
black hole
burakku-hooru ブラックホール
blood type
ketsueki-gata 血液型

C

calorie
karorii カロリー
catalyst
shokubai 触媒
cell
saiboo 細胞
cerebral hemorrhage
noo-shukketsu 脳出血
chaos
kaosu カオス
chemical reaction
kagaku-hannoo 化学反応
chromosome
senshoku-tai 染色体
civil engineering
doboku-koogaku 土木工学
clone
kuroon クローン
cognitive engineering
ninchi-koogaku 認知工学
cognitive linguistics
ninchi-gengo-gaku 認知言語学
cognitive psychology
ninchi-shinri-gaku 認知心理学
cognitive science
ninchi-kagaku 認知科学
cold wave
kanpa 寒波
communication satellite
tsuushin-eisei 通信衛星
computational linguistics
keisan-gengo-gaku 計算言語学
computer network
konpyuutaa-netto-waaku コンピューター・ネットワーク
computer science
joohoo-kagaku 情報科学
constellation
seiza 星座
continental shelf
tairiku-dana 大陸棚
cosmic ray
uchuu-sen 宇宙線
cosmology
uchuu-ron 宇宙論
crustal movement
chikaku-hendoo 地殻変動
cybernetics
saibanetikusu サイバネティクス

D

data base
deeta-beesu データベース
detergent
senzai 洗剤
diabetes
toonyoo-byoo 糖尿病
dinosaur
kyooryuu 恐竜

E

earthquake magnitude
magunichuudo マグニチュード
ecosystem
seitai-kei, ekoshisutemu 生態系、エコシステム
ecotechnology
ekotekunorojii エコテクノロジー
electric engineering
denki-koogaku 電気工学
electrocardiogram
shinden-zu 心電図
electron
denshi 電子
elementary particle
so-ryuushi 素粒子

energy saving
shoo-enerugii (shoo-ene) 省エネルギー(省エネ)
entropy
entoropii エントロピー
environmental study
kankyoo-gaku 環境学
enzyme
kooso 酵素
euthanasia
anraku-shi 安楽死

F

facsimile
fakushimiri, fakkusu ファクシミリ、ファックス
fault
dansoo 断層
fermentation
hakkoo 発酵
floppy disk
furoppii フロッピー
fluid dynamics
ryuutai-rikigaku 流体力学
foehn
feen-genshoo フェーン現象
font
fonto フォント
front
zensen 前線
function
kansuu 関数
fuzzy theory
fajii-riron ファジー理論

G

galaxy
ginga 銀河
gene
iden-shi 遺伝子
generative grammar
seisei-bunpoo 生成文法
gene recombination
iden-shi-kumi-kae 遺伝子組み換え
genetic engineering
iden-shi-koogaku 遺伝子工学
geology
chiri-gaku, chishitsu-gaku 地理学、地質学
geomagnetism
chi-jiki 地磁気
geometry
kika-gaku 幾何学
geophysics
chikyuu-butsuri-gaku 地球物理学
global warming
chikyuu-ondan-ka 地球温暖化

H

heart transplant
shinzoo-ishoku 心臓移植
heat wave
neppa 熱波
hemoglobin
hemogurobin ヘモグロビン
high polymer
koo-bunshi 高分子
human geography
jinbun-chiri-gaku 人文地理学
hypertension
koo-ketsuatsu 高血圧

I

ICU (intensive care unit)
shuuchuu-chiryoo-bu 集中治療部
immunity
men'eki 免疫
industrial robot
sangyoo-robotto 産業ロボット
information engineering
joohoo-koogaku 情報工学
information science
joohoo-kagaku 情報科学
information theory
joohoo-riron 情報理論
informed consent
infoomudo-konsento インフォームド・コンセント
inorganic chemistry
muki-kagaku 無機化学
integrated circuit
shuuseki-kairo 集積回路
intensive care unit (ICU)
shuuchuu-chiryoo-bu 集中治療部
internet
intaanetto インターネット

L

laser
reezaa レーザー
linear motor
rinia-mootaa リニアモーター
liquid crystal display
ekishoo-disupurei 液晶ディスプレイ

M

machine translation
kikai-hon'yaku 機械翻訳
mechanical engineering
kikai-koogaku 機械工学
metabolism
taisha 代謝
metastasis
ten'i 転移
microorganism
bi-seibutsu 微生物
mineralogy
koobutsu-gaku 鉱物学
modem
modemu モデム
molecular biology
bunshi-seibutsu-gaku 分子生物学
molecular formula
bunshi-shiki 分子式
molecule
bunshi 分子
monsoon
monsuun モンスーン
multimedia
maruchimedia マルチメディア
mutation
totsuzen-hen'i 突然変異

N

nebula
seiun 星雲
neuron
nyuuron ニューロン
nuclear energy
kaku-enerugii 核エネルギー
nuclear fuel
kaku-nenryoo 核燃料
nuclear fusion
kaku-yuugoo 核融合
nuclear power generation
genshi-ryoku-hatsuden 原子力発電
nuclear reactor
genshi-ro 原子炉

O

ohm
oomu オーム
optical fiber
hikari-faibaa 光ファイバー
organic chemistry
yuuki-kagaku 有機化学
origin of life
seimei no kigen 生命の起源
oxidation
sanka 酸化
ozone layer depletion
ozon-soo hakai オゾン層破壊

P

personal computer
paasonaru-konpyuutaa (pasokon)
パーソナルコンピューター(パソコン)
personal computer communication
pasokon-tsuushin パソコン通信
pharmacology
yakuri-gaku 薬理学
pheromone
feromon フェロモン
plastics
goosei-jushi, purasuchikku 合成樹脂、プラスチック
probability of precipitation
koosui-kakuritsu 降水確率
probability theory
kakuritsu-ron 確率論
programming
puroguramingu プログラミング
protein
tanpaku-shitsu 蛋白質
psychiatry
seishin-igaku 精神医学
psychoanalysis
seishin-bunseki 精神分析

Q

quantum mechanics
ryooshi-rikigaku 量子力学
quasar
kueesaa クエーサー

R

radiation
hoosha-sen 放射線
radioactive waste
hoosha-sei-haiki-butsu 放射性廃棄物
radioactivity
hoosha-noo 放射能
regional geography
chishi-gaku 地誌学

S

satellite
eisei 衛星
seismology
jishin-gaku 地震学
semiconductor
han-dootai 半導体
snow storm
fubuki 吹雪
sociobiology
shakai-seibutsu-gaku 社会生物学
software
sofuto-uea ソフトウエア
solar car
sooraa-kaa ソーラーカー
solar system
taiyoo-kei 太陽系
speech recognition
onsei-ninshiki 音声認識
stress
sutoresu ストレス
sunspot
taiyoo-kokuten 太陽黒点
supercomputer
suupaa-konpyuutaa (supakon)
スーパーコンピューター(スパコン)
superconductivity
choo-dendoo 超伝導
symbiosis
kyoosei 共生
synthetic fiber
goosei-sen'i 合成繊維

T

terminal
tanmatsu 端末
theory of relativity
sootai-sei-riron 相対性理論
thermodynamics
netsu-rikigaku 熱力学
topology
isoo 位相
tornado
tatsumaki 竜巻
transistor
toranjisutaa トランジスター

V

virtual reality
baacharu-riaritii, kasoo-genjitsu-kan
バーチャルリアリティー、仮想現実感
virus
uirusu ウイルス
volt
boruto ボルト

W

watt
watto ワット
word processor (WP)
waapuro ワープロ
WP (word processor)
waapuro ワープロ

MEDICAL SCIENCE

A

Achilles tendon
Akiresu-ken アキレス腱
Ad, Adr (adrenaline)
adorenarin アドレナリン
addiction
chuudoku 中毒
Addison's disease
Ajison-byoo アジソン病
adrenaline (Ad, Adr)
adorenarin アドレナリン
alcoholic cardiomyopathy
arukooru-sei-shinkin-shoo アルコール性心筋症
alcoholism
arukooru-chuudoku アルコール中毒
alkalinity
arukari-sei アルカリ性
ampule
anpuru アンプル
anamnesis
kioo-shoo 既往症
anatomy
kaiboo-gaku 解剖学
aneurysm
doomyaku-ryuu 動脈瘤
angina pectoris
kyooshin-shoo 狭心症
anorexia nervosa
shinkei-sei-mu-shokuyoku-shoo
神経性無食欲症
antibiotics
koosei-busshitsu 抗生物質
antihypertensive agent drug
kooatsu-zai 降圧剤
aorta
dai-doomyaku 大動脈
apnea
mu-kokyuu 無呼吸
arteriosclerosis
doomyaku-kooka-shoo 動脈硬化症
artery
doomyaku 動脈
arthritis
kansetsu-en 関節炎
ascites
fukusui 腹水
aspirin
asupirin アスピリン
asthenia
muryoku-shoo 無力症
atrophy
ishuku 萎縮
audibility
chooryoku 聴力
auscultation
chooshin 聴診

B

baroreceptor
atsu-juyoo-tai 圧受容体
benign
ryoosei 良性
birthmark
bohan, aza 母斑、あざ
bleeding
shukketsu 出血
blood clot
gyooketsu 凝血
blood pressure (BP)
ketsuatsu 血圧
blood test
ketsueki-kensa 血液検査
blotch
aza あざ
body temperature (BT)
taion 体温
BP (blood pressure)
ketsuatsu 血圧
brain death
nooshi 脳死
breast cancer
nyuugan 乳癌
bronchial asthma
kikan-shi-zensoku 気管支喘息
bronchus
kikan-shi 気管支
bruise
daboku-shoo 打撲傷
BT (body temperature)
taion 体温

C

capillary blood pressure
moosai-kan-atsu 毛細管圧
cardiac function performance
shin-kinoo 心機能
cardiovascular system
junkan-kei 循環系
carotid artery
kei-doomyaku 頸動脈
cast
gipusu ギプス
CH (cholesterol)
koresuterooru コレステロール
chapped skin
akagire あかぎれ
chest X-ray
kyoobu-ekkusu-sen-shashin 胸部X線写真
chill
okan 悪寒
cholesterol (CH)
koresuterooru コレステロール
chromosome
senshoku-tai 染色体
chronic
mansei no 慢性の
clinic
shinryoo-jo, shinryoo-shitsu 診療所、診療室
clinical medicine
rinshoo-igaku 臨床医学
coagulation
gyooko 凝固
common cold
kanboo 感冒
computed tomography (CT)
konpyuuta-dansoo-satsuei コンピュータ断層撮影
congestion
ukketsu うっ血
constipation
benpi 便秘
contraception
hinin, jutai-choosetsu, sanji-seigen
避妊、受胎調節、産児制限
contusion
zasoo, zashoo 挫創、挫傷
convulsion
keiren, hikitsuke けいれん、ひきつけ
coronary artery
kanjoo-doomyaku 冠状動脈
costa
rokkotsu 肋骨
cracks
hibiware ひびわれ
critical condition
kitoku 危篤
CT (computed tomography)
konpyuuta-dansoo-satsuei コンピュータ断層撮影
cyanosis
chianooze チアノーゼ

D

damage
shoogai 傷害
debility
suijaku 衰弱
dehydration
dassui 脱水
dentistry
shika 歯科
diabetes mellitus (DM)
toonyoo-byoo 糖尿病
diagnosis
shindan 診断
dialysis
tooseki 透析
diaphragm
ookaku-maku 横隔膜
diarrhea
geri 下痢
dietician
eiyoo-shi 栄養士
diet therapy
shokuji-ryoohoo 食餌療法
difficult breathing
kokyuu-konnan 呼吸困難
disease
shikkan 疾患
diuretic
rinyoo-yaku 利尿薬
DM (diabetes mellitus)
toonyoo-byoo 糖尿病
dyspnea
kokyuu-konnan 呼吸困難

E

eardrum
komaku 鼓膜
ECG (electrocardiogram)
shinden-zu 心電図
echocardiogram
shin-ekoo-zu 心エコー図
egg
ranshi 卵子
electrocardiogram (ECG)
shinden-zu 心電図
emphysema
hai-kishu 肺気腫
enema
kanchoo 浣腸
enzyme
kooso 酵素
epidemic
ryuukoo-sei 流行性
eruption
hosshin 発疹
erythrocyte sedimentation rate (ESR)
sekkekkyuu-chinkoo-sokudo, ketchin
赤血球沈降速度、血沈
ESR (erythrocyte sedimentation rate)
sekkekkyuu-chinkoo-sokudo, ketchin
赤血球沈降速度、血沈
external injury
gaishoo 外傷

F

factor
inshi 因子
fatal dose
chishi-ryoo 致死量
febrile
netsu-sei no 熱性の
first aid
ookyuu-teate 応急手当
forceps
kanshi 鉗子
foreign body
ibutsu 異物
fracture
kossetsu 骨折

G

gangrene
eso 壊疽
gastric cancer
igan 胃癌
gastric irrigation
i-senjoo 胃洗浄
gastric juice
ieki 胃液
gastric lavage
i-senjoo 胃洗浄
gastric ulcer
i-kaiyoo 胃潰瘍
gastroscope
i-naishi-kyoo, i-kamera 胃内視鏡、胃カメラ
gastroscopy
i-naishi-kyoo-kensa 胃内視鏡検査
gauze
gaaze ガーゼ
germ
saikin 細菌
German measles
fuushin, mikka-bashika 風疹、三日ばしか

H

hardening
kooka-shoo 硬化症
HD (hemodialysis)
ketsueki-tooseki 血液透析
hearing
chooryoku 聴力
heart
shinzoo 心臓
heartburn
mune-yake 胸やけ
heat sensation
netsukan 熱感
hematemesis
toketsu 吐血
hematology
ketsueki-gaku, ketsueki-byoo-gaku
血液学、血液病学
hemiplegia
hanshin-fuzui 半身不随
hemodialysis (HD)
ketsueki-tooseki 血液透析

hemoptysis
kakketsu 喀血
hemorrhage
shukketsu 出血
hemorrhoid
ji 痔
heredity
iden 遺伝
hernia
herunia ヘルニア
hives
jinma-shin じんま疹
house call
ooshin 往診
hygiene
eisei-gaku, yoboo-eisei 衛生学、予防衛生
hyperlipemia
kooshikes-shoo 高脂血症
hypertension
koo-ketsuatsu 高血圧
hypnotism
saimin-jutsu 催眠術
hypotension
tei-ketsuatsu 低血圧

I

incubation period
senpuku-ki 潜伏期
infection
kansen 感染
infertility
funin-shoo 不妊症
inflammation
enshoo 炎症
injury
sonshoo, gaishoo 損傷、外傷
inspection
shishin 視診
intoxication
chuudoku 中毒
irregular pulse
fu-seimyaku 不整脈
ischemia
kyoketsu 虚血
itching sensation
sooyoo-kan 掻痒感

J

jugular vein
kei-joomyaku 頸静脈

K

kidney
jinzoo 腎臓

L

lacrimal gland
ruisen 涙腺
lipid
shishitsu 脂質
loss of appetite
shokuyoku-fushin 食欲不振
low back pain
yootsuu 腰痛
lung
hai 肺
lung edema
hai-suishu 肺水腫

M

malignant
akusei 悪性
menstruation
gekkei 月経
metastasis
ten'i 転移
microbe
bi-seibutsu 微生物
mortality
shiboo-ritsu 死亡率
motor nerve
undoo-shinkei 運動神経
mucous membrane
nenmaku 粘膜
muscle cramp
komura-gaeri, kin-keiren 腓返り、筋けいれん
myoma
kinshu 筋腫
myopia
kinshi 近視

N

narcotics
mayaku 麻薬
nausea
ooki 嘔気
necrosis
eshi 壊死
neurology
shinkei-ka-gaku, shinkei-byoo-gaku 神経科学、神経病学
neurosis
noirooze ノイローゼ
neutral fat
chuusei-shiboo 中性脂肪
newborn
shinsei-ji 新生児
nitroglycerin (NTG)
nitoroguriserin ニトログリセリン
NTG (nitroglycerin)
nitoroguriserin ニトログリセリン

O

obesity
himan 肥満
obstruction
heisoku 閉塞
operation
shujutsu 手術
oral administration
keikoo-tooyo 経口投与
orthopedic surgery
seikei-geka 整形外科
ovary
ransoo 卵巣
oxidize
sanka 酸化
oxygen
sanso 酸素

P

pacemaker
peesumeekaa ペースメーカー
palpation
shokushin 触診
palsy
fuzen-mahi 不全麻痺
paralysis
kanzen-mahi 完全麻痺
parasites
kisei-chuu 寄生虫
pathology
byoori-gaku 病理学
pelvis
kotsuban 骨盤
percussion
dashin 打診
pharynx
intoo 咽頭
physiology
seiri-gaku 生理学
pinworm
gyoochuu 蟯虫
plasma
kesshoo 血漿
plastic surgery
keisei-geka 形成外科
pleurisy
kyoomaku-en 胸膜炎
pregnancy
ninshin 妊娠
prescription
shohoo-sen 処方せん
pressure load
atsu-fuka 圧負荷
pus
noo 膿

R

radiation
hoosha-sen 放射線
rale
ra-on ラ音
rehabilitation
rihabiriteeshon リハビリテーション
remedy
iyaku-hin, chiryoo-yaku 医薬品、治療薬
RHD (rheumatic heart disease)
riumachi-sei-shin-shikkan リウマチ性心疾患
rheumatic heart disease (RHD)
riumachi-sei-shin-shikkan リウマチ性心疾患
rib
rokkotsu 肋骨

S

sarcoma
nikushu 肉腫
sclerosis
kooka-shoo 硬化症
sepsis
haiketsu-shoo 敗血症
shortness of breath (SOB)
iki-gire 息切れ
SOB (shortness of breath)
iki-gire 息切れ
sperm
seishi 精子
sterile
mekkin no, mu-kin no 滅菌の、無菌の
sterilize
sakkin-suru 殺菌する
strict bed rest
zettai-ansei 絶対安静
stroke
noo-sotchuu 脳卒中
sudden death
totsuzen-shi 突然死
suppuration
kanoo 化膿
surgery
geka, geka-shujutsu, shujutsu 外科、外科手術、手術
symptom
shoojoo 症状
syphilis
baidoku 梅毒

T

TB (tuberculosis)
kekkaku 結核
therapy
ryoohoo 療法
thrombus
kessen 血栓
tonsillitis
hentoo-en 扁桃炎
trachea
kikan 気管
transplantation
ishoku 移植
treatment
chiryoo 治療
tuberculosis (TB)
kekkaku 結核
tumor
shuyoo 腫瘍

U

urinary bladder
bookoo 膀胱
urination
hainyoo 排尿
urticaria
jinma-shin じんま疹

V

vaccination
yoboo-sesshu 予防接種
vein
joomyaku 静脈
visual acuity
shiryoku 視力
visual examination
shishin 視診
vomit
ooto 嘔吐

W

waste product
roohai-butsu 老廃物
white blood cells
hakkekkyuu 白血球

Y

yawn
akubi あくび

IV

KANJI IN COMMON USE

開階解塊壊懐貝外劾害涯街慨該概垣各角拡革格核殻郭覚較隔閣

靴寡歌箇稼課蚊我画芽賀雅餓介回灰会快戒改怪拐悔海界皆械絵

温穏**カ**下化火加可仮何花佳価果河科架夏家荷華菓貨渦過嫁暇禍

猿遠鉛塩演縁**オ**汚王凹央応往押欧殴桜翁奥横屋億憶虞乙卸音恩

エ永泳英映栄営詠影鋭衛易疫益液駅悦越謁閲円延沿炎宴援園煙

維慰遺緯域育一壱逸芋引印因姻員院陰飲隠韻**ウ**右宇羽雨運雲

ア亜哀愛悪握圧扱安案暗**イ**以衣位囲医依委威胃為尉異移偉意違

語誤護口工公孔功巧広甲交光向后好江考行坑孝抗攻更効幸拘肯

減源厳**コ**己戸古呼固孤弧故枯個庫湖雇誇鼓顧五互午呉後娯悟碁

兼剣軒健険圏堅検嫌献絹遣権憲賢謙繭顕験懸元幻玄言弦限原現

継慶憩警鶏芸迎鯨劇撃激欠穴血決結傑潔月犬件見券肩建研県倹

訓勲薫軍郡群**ケ**兄刑形系径茎係型契計恵啓掲渓経蛍敬景軽傾携

均近金菌勤琴筋禁緊謹襟吟銀**ク**区句苦駆具愚空偶遇隅屈掘繰君

協況峡挟狭恐恭胸脅強教郷境橋矯鏡競響驚仰暁業凝曲局極玉斤

急級糾宮救球給窮牛去巨居拒拠挙虚許距魚御漁凶共叫狂京享供

義疑儀戯擬犠議菊吉喫詰却客脚逆虐九久及弓丘旧休吸朽求究泣

季紀軌既記起飢鬼帰基寄規喜幾揮期棋貴棄旗器輝機騎技宜偽欺

緩憾還館環簡観艦鑑丸含岸岩眼頑顔願**キ**企危机気岐希忌汽奇祈

官冠巻看陥乾勘患貫寒喚堪換敢棺款間閑勧寛幹感漢慣管関歓監

確獲嚇穫学岳楽額掛潟括活喝渇割滑褐轄且株刈干刊甘汗缶完肝

昭宵将消症祥称笑唱商渉章紹訟勝掌晶焼焦硝粧詔証象傷奨照詳

所書庶暑署緒諸女如助序叙徐除小升少召匠床抄肖尚招承昇松沼

縦叔祝宿淑粛縮塾熟出述術俊春瞬旬巡盾准殉純循順準潤遵処初

舟秀周宗拾秋臭修終習週就衆集愁酬醜襲十汁充住柔重従渋銃獣

借酌釈爵若弱寂手主守朱取狩首殊珠酒種趣寿受授需儒樹収囚州

識軸七失室疾執湿漆質実芝写社車舎者射捨赦斜煮遮謝邪蛇勺尺

嗣試詩資飼誌雌賜諮示字寺次耳自似児事侍治持時滋慈辞磁璽式

四市矢旨死糸至伺志私使刺始姉枝祉肢姿思指施師紙脂視紫詞歯

察撮擦雑皿三山参桟蚕惨産傘散算酸賛残暫**シ**士子支止氏仕史司

細菜最裁債催歳載際在材剤財罪崎作削昨索策酢搾錯咲冊札刷殺

婚混紺魂墾懇**サ**左佐査砂唆差詐鎖座才再災妻砕宰栽彩採済祭斎

酵稿興衡鋼講購号合拷剛豪克告谷刻国黒穀酷獄骨込今困昆恨根

侯厚恒洪皇紅荒郊香候校耕航貢降高康控黄慌港硬絞項溝鉱構綱

遅痴稚置竹畜逐蓄築秩窒茶着嫡中仲虫沖宙忠抽注昼柱衷鋳駐著

棚丹担単炭胆探淡短嘆端誕鍛団男段断弾暖談壇**チ**地池知値恥致

帯泰袋逮替貸隊滞態大代台第題滝宅択沢卓拓託濯諾濁但達脱奪

俗族属賊続卒率存村孫尊損**タ**他多打妥堕惰駄太対体耐待怠胎退

装僧想層総遭槽操燥霜騒藻造像増憎蔵贈臓即束足促則息速側測

措粗組疎訴塑礎双壮早争走奏相荘草送倉捜挿桑掃曹巣窓創喪葬

染扇栓旋船戦践銭銑潜線遷選薦繊鮮全前善然禅漸繕**ソ**阻祖租素

惜責跡積績籍切折拙窃接設雪摂節説舌絶千川仙占先宣専泉浅洗

斉政星牲省逝清盛婿晴勢聖誠精製誓静請整税夕斥石赤昔析隻席

遂睡穂錘随髄枢崇数据杉寸**セ**畝瀬是井世正生成西声制姓征性青

森診寝慎新審震薪親人刃仁尽迅甚陣尋**ス**図水吹垂炊帥粋衰推酔

食植殖飾触嘱織職辱心申伸臣身辛侵信津神唇娠振浸真針深紳進

彰障衝賞償礁鐘上丈冗条状乗城浄剰常情場畳蒸縄壌嬢錠譲醸色

普腐敷膚賦譜侮武部舞封風伏服副幅復福腹複覆払沸仏物粉紛雰

苗秒病描猫品浜貧賓頻敏瓶**フ**不夫父付布扶府怖附負赴浮婦符富

飛疲秘被悲扉費碑罷避尾美備微鼻匹必泌筆姫百氷表俵票評漂標

板版班畔般販飯搬煩頒範繁藩晩番蛮盤**ヒ**比皮妃否批彼披肥非卑

拍泊迫舶博薄麦漠縛爆箱畑肌八鉢発髪伐抜罰閥反半犯帆伴判坂

ハ把波派破覇馬婆拝杯背肺俳配排敗廃輩売倍梅培陪媒買賠白伯

難**ニ**二尼弐肉日入乳尿任妊忍認**ネ**寧熱年念粘燃**ノ**悩納能脳農濃

動堂童道働銅導峠匿特得督徳篤毒独読凸突届屯豚鈍曇**ナ**内南軟

島桃討透党悼盗陶塔搭棟湯痘登答等筒統稲踏糖頭謄闘騰同洞胴

伝殿電**ト**斗吐徒途都渡塗土奴努度怒刀冬灯当投豆東到逃倒凍唐

逓停偵堤提程艇締泥的笛摘滴適敵迭哲鉄徹撤天典店点展添転田

沈珍朕陳賃鎮**ツ**追墜通痛塚漬坪**テ**低呈廷弟定底抵邸亭貞帝訂庭

貯丁弔庁兆町長挑帳張彫眺釣頂鳥朝脹超腸跳徴潮澄調聴懲直勅

腕

裂恋連廉練錬**ロ**炉路露老労郎朗浪廊楼漏六録論**ワ**和話賄惑枠湾

厘倫輪隣臨**ル**涙累塁類**レ**令礼冷励戻例鈴零霊隷齢麗暦歴列劣烈

律略柳流留竜粒隆硫旅虜慮了両良料涼猟陵量僚領寮療糧力緑林

欲翌翼**ラ**裸羅来雷頼絡落酪乱卵覧濫欄**リ**吏利里理痢裏履離陸立

ヨ与予余誉預幼用羊洋要容庸揚揺葉陽溶腰様踊窯養擁謡曜抑浴

厄役約訳薬躍**ユ**由油愉諭輸癒唯友有勇幽悠郵猶裕遊雄誘憂融優

命明迷盟銘鳴滅免面綿**モ**茂模毛妄盲耗猛網目黙門紋問匁**ヤ**夜野

幕膜又末抹万満慢漫**ミ**未味魅岬密脈妙民眠**ム**矛務無夢霧娘**メ**名

棒貿暴膨謀北木朴牧僕墨撲没堀本奔翻凡盆**マ**麻摩磨魔毎妹枚埋

胞俸倣峰砲崩訪報豊飽褒縫亡乏忙坊妨忘防房肪某冒剖紡望傍帽

遍編弁便勉**ホ**歩保捕浦補舗母募墓慕暮簿方包芳邦奉宝抱放法泡

噴墳憤奮分文聞**ヘ**丙平兵併並柄陛閉塀幣弊米壁癖別片辺返変偏

V

SELECTED ENGLISH NAMES IN *KATAKANA*

MALE NAMES	NICKNAMES
Adam *Adamu* アダム	
Andrew *Andoryuu* アンドリュー	Andy *Andii* アンディー
Anthony *Ansonii* アンソニー	Tony *Tonii* トニー
Benjamin *Benjamin* ベンジャミン	Ben *Ben* ベン
Bradley *Buraddorii* ブラッドリー	Brad *Buraddo* ブラッド
Brian *Buraian* ブライアン	
Chad *Chaddo* チャッド	
Charles *Chaarusu* チャールス	Chuck *Chakku* チャック
	Charlie *Chaarii* チャーリー
Christopher *Kurisutofaa* クリストファー	
	Chris *Kurisu* クリス
Daniel *Danieru* ダニエル	Dan *Dan* ダン
David *Deibiddo/Debiddo* デイビッド/デビッド	
	Dave *Deebu* デーブ
Dennis *Denisu* デニス	Denny *Denii* デニー
Donald *Donarudo* ドナルド	Don *Don/Dan* ドン/ダン
Douglas *Dagurasu* ダグラス	Doug *Daggu/Dagu* ダッグ/ダグ
Edward *Edowaado* エドワード	Ted *Teddo* テッド
	Ned *Neddo* ネッド
	Eddie *Edii* エディー
Eric *Erikku* エリック	
George *Jooji* ジョージ	
Gregory *Guregorii* グレゴリー	Greg *Gureggu* グレッグ
James *Jeemuzu* ジェームズ	Jim *Jimu* ジム
	Jamie *Jeimii* ジェイミー
Jason *Jeison* ジェイソン	
Jeffrey *Jefurii* ジェフリー	Jeff *Jefu* ジェフ
Jeremy *Jeramii* ジェラミー	
John *Jon* ジョン	Johnny *Jonii* ジョニー
Jonathan *Jonasan* ジョナサン	
Joseph *Josefu* ジョセフ	
Joshua *Joshua* ジョシュア	
Justin *Jasutin* ジャスティン	
Keith *Kiisu* キース	
Kenneth *Kenesu* ケネス	Ken *Ken* ケン
Kevin *Kebin* ケビン	
Matthew *Mashuu* マシュー	
Michael *Maikeru* マイケル	Mike *Maiku* マイク
Nathan *Neisan* ネイサン	
Nicholas *Nikorasu* ニコラス	Nick *Nikku* ニック
Patrick *Patorikku* パトリック	Pat *Patto* パット
Paul *Pooru* ポール	
Peter *Piitaa* ピーター	Pete *Piito* ピート
Richard *Richaado* リチャード	Dick *Dikku* ディック
Robert *Robaato* ロバート	Bob *Bobu* ボブ
Ryan *Raian* ライアン	

Scott *Sukotto* スコット
Sean *Shoon* ショーン
Shane *Sheen* シェーン
Steven *Sutiibun* スティーブン Steve *Sutiibu* スティーブ
Thomas *Toomasu* トーマス Tom *Tomu* トム
Timothy *Timoshii* ティモシー Tim *Timu* ティム
Todd *Toddo* トッド
William *Uiriamu* ウイリアム Bill *Biru* ビル

FEMALE NAMES **NICKNAMES**

Alison *Arison* アリソン
Amanda *Amanda* アマンダ
Amy *Eimii* エイミー
Andrea *Andorea* アンドレア
Angela *Anjera* アンジェラ
Ann(e) *An* アン
Carrie *Kyarii* キャリー
Catherine *Kyasarin* キャサリン Cathy *Kyashii* キャシー
Christina *Kurisutiina* クリスティーナ
Christine *Kurisutiin* クリスティーン
Christy *Kurisutii* クリスティー
Danielle *Danieru* ダニエル
Elizabeth *Erizabesu* エリザベス Elsa *Erusa/Eruza* エルサ/エルザ
Bess/Beth *Besu* ベス
Betsy *Bettsii* ベッツィー
Betty *Betii* ベティー
Lisa *Risa/Riza/Raiza* リサ/リザ/ライザ
Liz *Rizu* リズ
Emily *Emirii* エミリー
Erica *Erika* エリカ
Erin *Erin* エリン
Heather *Hezaa* ヘザー
Heidi *Haidii* ハイディー
Jennifer *Jenifaa* ジェニファー
Jessica *Jeshika* ジェシカ
Jill *Jiru* ジル
Jodi *Jodii* ジョディー
Kara *Kaara* カーラ
Karen *Karen* カレン
Kathleen *Kyasariin* キャサリーン
Kelly *Kerii* ケリー
Kimberly *Kinbarii* キンバリー Kim *Kimu* キム
Kristen *Kurisutin* クリスティン
Laura *Roora* ローラ
Lori *Roori* ローリ
Mary *Merii/Mearii* メリー/メアリー
Melanie *Meranii* メラニー
Melissa *Merissa* メリッサ
Michelle *Misheru* ミシェル
Nicole *Nikooru* ニコール
Rachel *Reicheru* レイチェル
Rebecca *Rebekka* レベッカ
Robin *Robin* ロビン
Sarah *Sara/Seira* サラ/セイラ
Shannon *Shanon* シャノン
Stacy *Suteishii* ステイシー
Stephanie *Sutefanii* ステファニー
Susan *Suuzan* スーザン
Tammy *Tamii* タミー
Tanya *Tania* タニヤ
Tara *Taara* ターラ
Theresa *Teresa* テレサ
Tonya *Toniya* トニヤ
Tracy *Toreishii* トレイシー
Wendy *Uendii* ウエンディー

FAMILY NAMES

Anderson *Andaason* アンダーソン
Brown *Buraun* ブラウン
Clark *Kuraaku* クラーク
Davis *Deibisu* デイビス
Edwards *Edowaazu* エドワーズ
Evans *Ebansu* エバンス
Green *Guriin* グリーン
Hall *Hooru* ホール
Harris *Harisu* ハリス
Jackson *Jakuson* ジャクソン
Johnson *Jonson* ジョンソン
Jones *Joonzu* ジョーンズ
Lewis *Ruisu* ルイス
Martin *Maatin* マーティン
Miller *Miraa* ミラー
Moore *Muua* ムーア
Roberts *Robaatsu* ロバーツ
Robinson *Robinson* ロビンソン
Smith *Sumisu* スミス
Taylor *Teiraa* テイラー
Thomas *Toomasu* トーマス
Thompson *Tonpuson* トンプソン
Walker *Uookaa* ウオーカー
White *Howaito* ホワイト
Williams *Uiriamuzu* ウイリアムズ
Wilson *Uiruson* ウイルソン
Wright *Raito* ライト

VI

THE HUMAN BODY AND A TYPICAL JAPANESE HOME

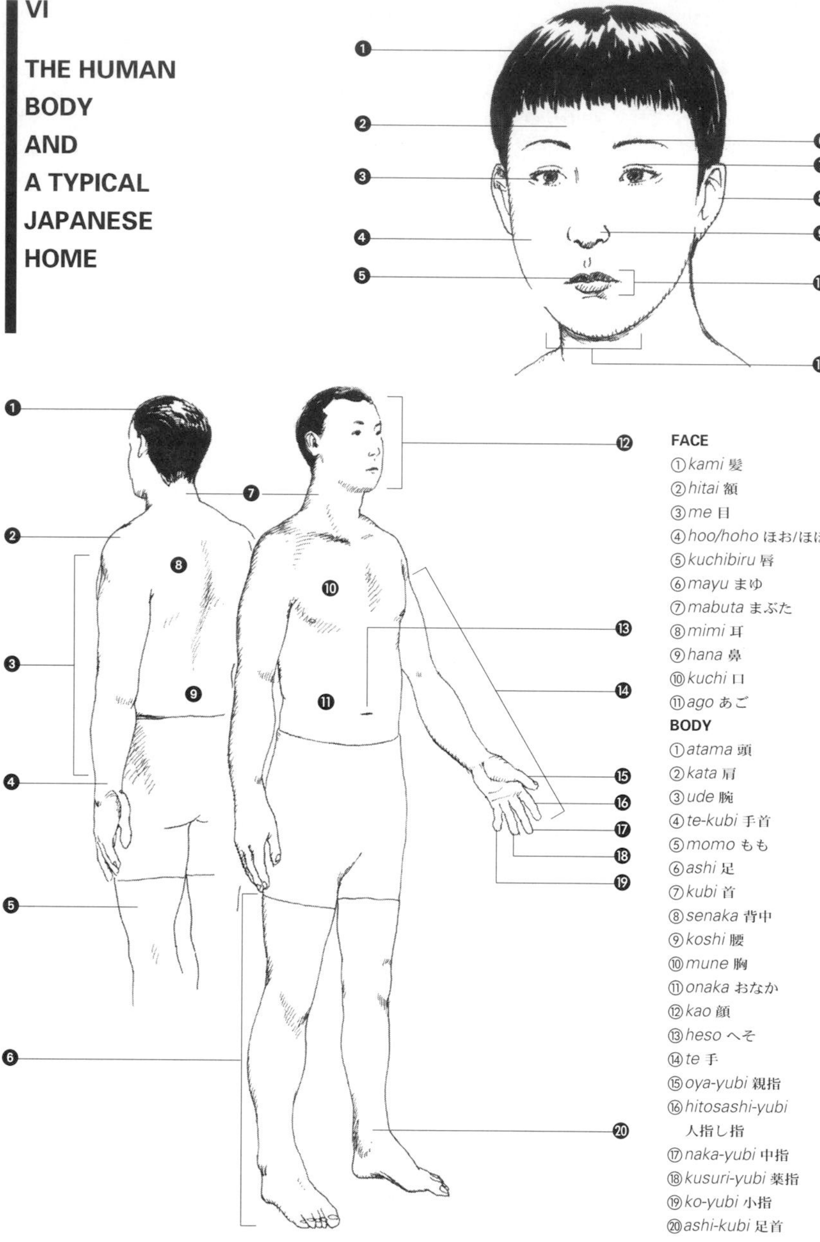

FACE

①kami 髪
②hitai 額
③me 目
④hoo/hoho ほお/ほほ
⑤kuchibiru 唇
⑥mayu まゆ
⑦mabuta まぶた
⑧mimi 耳
⑨hana 鼻
⑩kuchi 口
⑪ago あご

BODY

①atama 頭
②kata 肩
③ude 腕
④te-kubi 手首
⑤momo もも
⑥ashi 足
⑦kubi 首
⑧senaka 背中
⑨koshi 腰
⑩mune 胸
⑪onaka おなか
⑫kao 顔
⑬heso へそ
⑭te 手
⑮oya-yubi 親指
⑯hitosashi-yubi 人指し指
⑰naka-yubi 中指
⑱kusuri-yubi 薬指
⑲ko-yubi 小指
⑳ashi-kubi 足首

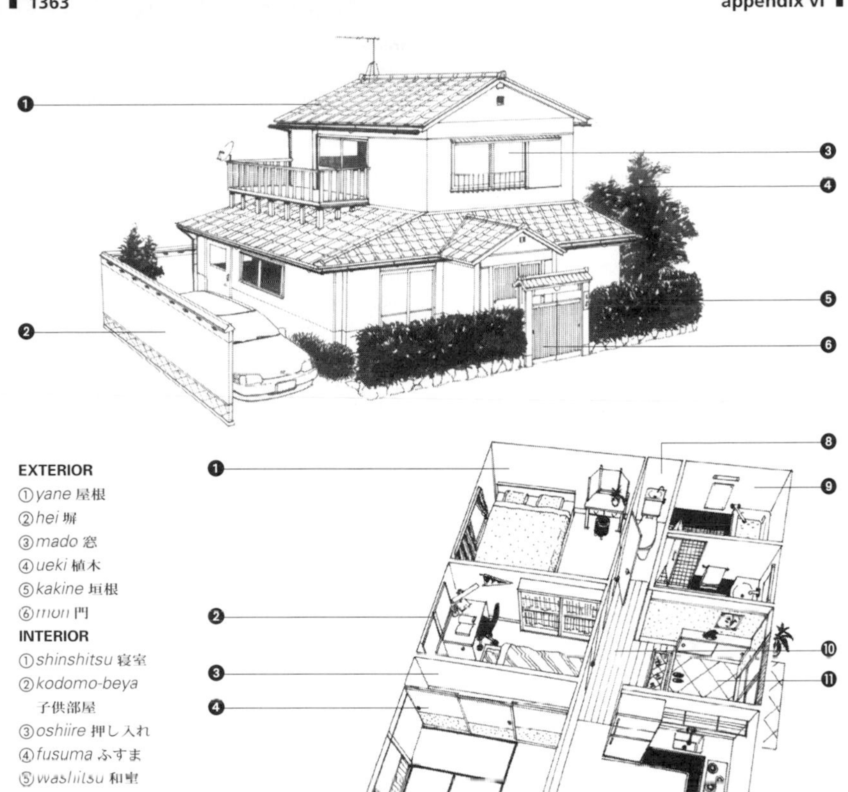

EXTERIOR

① *yane* 屋根
② *hei* 塀
③ *mado* 窓
④ *ueki* 植木
⑤ *kakine* 垣根
⑥ *mon* 門

INTERIOR

① *shinshitsu* 寝室
② *kodomo-beya* 子供部屋
③ *oshiire* 押し入れ
④ *fusuma* ふすま
⑤ *washitsu* 和室
⑥ *kyaku-ma* 客間
⑦ *tokonoma* 床の間
⑧ *(o-)te-arai* お手洗い
⑨ *furo-ba* ふろ場
⑩ *rooka* 廊下
⑪ *genkan* 玄関
⑫ *dainingu-kitchin* ダイニングキッチン
⑬ *yooshitsu* 洋室
⑭ *ima* 居間

VII

A LIST OF *KANJI* NOTES

A given word can sometimes be represented by different characters having the same *kun*-reading. In that case, the different characters often represent different nuances of the same word. Refer to this section for help in choosing the right character when more than one choice is available.

abura あぶら : liquid oil 油, solid animal fat 脂

agaru あがる : rise to a higher location 上がる, (for a kite) to fly/(for a flag) to be raised/(for cargo) to be unloaded/(for food) to be deep-fried 揚がる, (for a hand) to be raised 挙がる, otherwise あがる

ageru あげる : raise s.t. 上げる, deep-fry/fly (a kite)/raise (a flag)/unload (cargo) 揚げる, raise one's hand 挙げる, otherwise あげる

aita あいた : empty 空いた, open 開いた

aiteiru あいている : for a window/door to be open 開いている, vacant 空いている

akeru あける : leave space vacant 空ける, open 開ける, dawn/begin 明ける

aku あく : become empty 空く, open 開く

arai あらい : coarse 粗い, violent 荒い

arawareru あらわれる : appear/come into view 現れる, be expressed 表れる

arawasu あらわす : indicate/express 表す, write (a book) 著す, cause s.t. to appear 現す

ashi あし : for animals/living things 足, for other inanimate objects 脚

atataka あたたか : atmospheric/comfortable heat 暖か, otherwise 温か

atatamaru あたたまる : a physical substance heats up 温まる, the environment or one's body heats up to the point that one feels warm and comfortable 暖まる

atatameru あたためる : heat a physical substance 温める, heat an environment or a part of the body so that one feels warm and comfortable 暖める

ateru あてる : appropriate 充てる, otherwise 当てる

ato あと : after 後, mark/trace 跡

atsui あつい : sensing discomfort throughout one's body due to the presence of a great amount of heat 暑い, for s.t. to have a high temperature physically perceptible to the touch 熱い

atsusa あつさ : heat one feels with one's entire body 暑さ, heat of a physical object 熱さ

au あう : meet s.o./see s.o. 会う, agree/fit/match/suit 合う, otherwise あう

ayamari あやまり : apology 謝り, error/mistake 誤り

ayamaru あやまる : err 誤る, apologize 謝る

■

hakaru はかる : measure time/value 計る, measure distance/speed/ability 測る, measure weight 量る, scheme 図る, deceive/plot 謀る, consult 諮る

haku はく : wear footwear 履く, otherwise はく

hanareru はなれる : become free 放れる, leave/separate 離れる

hanasu はなす : let go 放す, part 離す

haru はる : spread out 張る, post はる

hayai はやい : early/soon 早い, fast/quick/speedy 速い

hayaku はやく : early/soon 早く, quickly/speedily 速く

hi ひ : light 灯, fire 火, sun/day 日

hiki-nobasu ひきのばす : pull s.t. and elongate it 引き伸ばす, cause s.t. to take more time 引き延ばす

hiku ひく : play a stringed instrument 弾く, otherwise 引く

■

itameru いためる : damage s.t. 傷める, cause physical pain 痛める

itamu いたむ : for a part of one's body to produce a feeling of pain 痛む, get damaged 傷む, grieve いたむ

■

kaerimiru かえりみる : look back on/think of 顧みる, reflect on 省みる

kaeru かえる : cause s.t./s.o./s.a. to change 変える, cause s.t./s.o./s.a. to replace s.t./s.o./s.a. else 代える, exchange s.t. for s.t. else 換える

kaeru かえる : come/go back (from a place) to the original place 帰る, come/go back to the original state/owner 返る

kaesu かえす : cause s.t./s.o./s.a. to come/go back (from a place) to the original place 帰す, cause s.t./s.o./s.a. to come/go back to the original state/owner 返す

kage かげ : shade 陰, image/shadow 影

kakaru かかる : for a bridge to be built or ladder to be set up 架かる, hang 掛かる, otherwise かかる

kakeru かける : build a bridge or set a ladder 架ける, hang 掛ける, otherwise かける

kaku かく : write 書く, scratch/draw a picture かく

karai からい : spicy 辛い, otherwise からい

kareru かれる : dry up 枯れる, for a voice to become hoarse かれる

katai かたい : stiff/inflexible 硬い, solid/firm/tight 固い, rigid/unyielding (in character) 堅い

kawa かわ : tanned skin (=leather) 革, skin 皮

kawaku かわく : for s.o. to become thirsty 渇く, dry 乾く

kawaru かわる : change/shift 変わる, take the place of 代わる, be replaced 替わる/換わる

kaze かぜ : wind 風, a virus infection 風邪

kiku きく : listen to s.t. carefully 聴く, ask/hear/listen 聞く

kiku きく : take effect 効く, work 利く

koeru こえる : go over s.t. spatially 越える, surpass/exceed 超える

kotaeru こたえる : respond verbally 答える, respond non-verbally こたえる

■

machi まち : town/city 町, a busy area of a city/streets 街

miru みる : for a doctor to see his/her patient 診る, otherwise 見る

■

naka なか : inside 中, relationship 仲

naku なく : for an animal to utter its sound 鳴く, otherwise 泣く

nakusu なくす : lose s.t./s.a. 無くす, lose s.o. 亡くす

naoru なおる : be repaired/for s.t. broken to be fixed 直る, be cured/heal 治る

naosu なおす : cure disease/injury 治す, correct/fix/mend 直す

nobasu のばす : postpone/prolong (in time) 延ばす, grow/straighten/stretch 伸ばす

nobi のび : prolongation 延び, stretch 伸び

nobiru のびる : be postponed/prolonged (in time) 延びる, grow 伸びる

noboru のぼる : climb 登る, for the sun/moon/smoke to rise 昇る, otherwise 上る

noru のる : be on/appear/get onto s.t./s.o./s.a. that is immobile/be recorded 載る, ride/get onto s.t./s.o./s.a. that is perceived to be mobile 乗る

■

oba おば : aunt older than one's parent 伯母, aunt younger than one's parent 叔母

oji おじ : older brother/brother-in-law of one's parents 伯父, younger brother/brother-in-law 叔父, older male person 小父

okasu おかす : commit/violate/sin against 犯す, risk/defy/illness strikes a specific part of body 冒す, invade/transgress/illness strikes s.o. 侵す

okosu おこす : restore おこす, arouse 起こす

okuru おくる : send 送る, give (a gift) 贈る

orosu おろす : let s.o. off a vehicle 降ろす, wholesale merchandise 卸す, drop s.o. off 下ろす

osaeru おさえる : press down physically 押さえる, control 抑える

osamaru おさまる : be soothed/be at peace 治まる, fit into 収まる

osameru おさめる : pay 納める, gain/put into 収める, govern 治める, study 修める

osu おす : recommend 推す, otherwise 押す

■

sabaku さばく : control s.t. skillfully with one's hands, deal with a problem さばく, judge s.o. to find if he/she is guilty or not guilty 裁く

sagasu さがす : look for s.t./s.o./s.a. that a person needs 探す, look for s.t./s.o./s.a. that one has lost (sight of) 捜す

sakana さかな : fish 魚, food to be eaten with alcoholic beverages さかな

saku さく : tear 裂く, spare 割く

sasu さす : point 指す, sting/stab 刺す, put in/become visible 差す, put a flower in/stick in 挿す

semeru せめる : striking an opponent in order to beat him 攻める, accuse 責める

shiboru しぼる : squeeze milk/oil/lemon 搾る, wring 絞る

shimaru しまる : close 閉まる, tighten 締まる

shimeru しめる : close 閉める, tighten/fasten 締める, wring/strangle 絞める

shio しお : salt 塩, tide 潮

sukuu すくう : deliver/help/save 救う, scoop up すくう

sumu すむ : become clear 澄む, live 住む, become completely done 済む

suru する : print 刷る, rub 擦る

susumeru すすめる : move forward 進める, recommend s.o. (as a candidate) 薦める, otherwise 勧める

■

tama たま : ball 球, gem/jewel 玉, bullet たま

tatakai たたかい : a fight in war or a sports events 戦い, a fight against disease, poverty, etc. 闘い

tatakau たたかう : fight in war or in a sports event 戦う, fight against disease, poverty, etc. 闘う

tateru たてる : build a building 建てる, otherwise 立てる

tatsu たつ : stand up 立つ, for time to elapse 経つ

tayori たより : letter 便り, reliance 頼り

tazuneru たずねる : ask 尋ねる, visit 訪ねる

tobu とぶ : jump 跳ぶ, fly 飛ぶ, in compounds such as *tobi-agaru*, *tobi-oriru*, etc. とぶ

tokasu とかす : dissolve/melt 溶かす, comb (hair) とかす

tokeru とける : dissolve/melt 溶ける, be solved/come untied 解ける

toku とく : figure out the answer to a question/problem 解く, dissolve s.t. 溶く

tomaru とまる : stay overnight 泊まる, be fastened 留まる, stop moving 止まる

tomeru とめる : give lodging to s.o. 泊める, fasten 留める, bring s.o./s.a./s.t. to a halt 止める

toru とる : take a picture 撮る, catch an animal 捕る, employ/adopt 採る, take charge of 執る, otherwise 取る

tsukeru つける : attach/fix/spread 付ける, wear 着ける, otherwise つける

tsukeru つける : steep foodstuffs in liquid/salt/sugar/paste 漬ける, otherwise つける

tsuku つく : arrive 着く, become attached 付く, go to bed/take a job/study under 就く, otherwise つく

tsukuru つくる : build/manufacture 造る, otherwise 作る

tsutomeru つとめる : try 努める, act as 務める, be employed 勤める

■

umu うむ : give birth to an offspring 産む, give birth to an offspring/artistic work or give rise to an accident, rumor, interest, etc. 生む

utsu うつ : shoot s.o./s.a./s.t. with a gun or fire a bullet 撃つ, hit/strike 打つ

utsuru うつる : be reflected 映る, be photographed 写る, move physically from one place to another 移る

utsusu うつす : photograph/copy 写す, project an image on the surface of a screen/water 映す, move s.t./s.o./s.a. physically from one place to another 移す

■

wakareru わかれる : divide itself 分かれる, separate from s.o. 別れる

waku わく : bubble up from heat 沸く, spring up spontaneously as from under the ground わく

■

yabureru やぶれる : be torn 破れる, be defeated 敗れる

yaburu やぶる : tear 破る, defeat 敗る

yameru やめる : quit a job/resign 辞める, cease/abandon/stop やめる

yasashii やさしい : easy 易しい, tender 優しい

yomu よむ : compose haiku/waka 詠む, read 読む

VIII

JAPANESE-ENGLISH INDEX

A

a!	あっ!	Oh
aa	ああ	ah
aa	ああ	alas
aa, ii tomo	ああ、いいとも	sure
Aakansoo	アーカンソー	Arkansas
abara-bone	あばら骨	rib
abunai	危ない	dangerous
abura	あぶら	fat
abura	あぶら	grease
abura	あぶら	oil
abura ga ooi	脂が多い	fat
aburakkoi	脂っこい	fat
abura-mi	脂身	fat
aburu	あぶる	toast[1]
achi-kochi ({de/ni/o})	あちこち({で/に/を})	around
achi-kochi (to)	あちこち(と)	around
achira e	あちらへ	away
adana	あだ名	nickname
adaputaa	アダプター	adapter
adobaisu	アドバイス	advice
adobanteeji	アドバンテージ	advantage
aen	亜鉛	zinc
afureru	あふれる	swim
Afurika	アフリカ	Africa
Afurika no N	アフリカのN	African
agaku, (Vvol. to shite)	あがく, (Vvol.として)	struggle
agaru	あがる	increase
agaru	あがる	rise
agaru	あがる	up
ageru	あげる	fry
ageru	あげる	give
ageru	あげる	increase
ageru	あげる	raise
ageru to iu, V*te*	あげると言う, V*te*	offer
ago	あご	chin
ago	あご	jaw
ago-hige	あごひげ	beard
ai	愛	love
aichaku o motte iru	愛着をもっている	attach
aida	間	for
aida	間	while
aida de	間で	among
aidagara	間柄	relation
Aidaho	アイダホ	Idaho
aida {ni/de/o/etc.}	間{に/で/を/etc.}	between

aida (ni), Vinf.	間(に), Vinf.	while
aida ni, {Vinf. nonpast/N no}	間に, {Vinf. nonpast/Nの}	during
aida, ⟨-no⟩	間, ⟨〜の⟩	by
aida zutto, ⟨-no⟩	間ずっと, ⟨〜の⟩	during
aidea	アイデア	idea
aidentitii	アイデンティティー	identity
ai-fuda	合い札	check
aigan-doobutsu	愛がん動物	pet
aijin	愛人	lover
aijoo	愛情	affection
a, ikenai!	あっ、いけない!	oops
aimaina	あいまいな	vague
ai ni {iku/kuru}	会いに{行く/来る}	visit
ainiku	あいにく	unfortunately
Ainshutain	アインシュタイン	Einstein
Aiowa	アイオワ	Iowa
airon	アイロン	iron
airon o kakeru	アイロンをかける	iron
airon o kakeru	アイロンをかける	press
Airurando	アイルランド	Ireland
Airurando no N	アイルランドのN	Irish
aisatsu	あいさつ	greeting
aisatsu-suru	あいさつする	greet
aisatsu-suru	あいさつする	salute
aishite iru	愛している	attach
aisu-kuriimu	アイスクリーム	ice cream
Aisurando	アイスランド	Iceland
aisuru	愛する	love
aita N	あいたN	open
aite	相手	partner
aite iru (N)	空いている(N)	free
aite iru (N)	あいている(N)	vacant
ai-tsugu N	相次ぐN	successive
aizu	合図	sign
aizu	合図	signal
aji	味	flavor
aji	味	taste
Ajia	アジア	Asia
aji ga ii	味がいい	tasty
aji ga nai	味がない	tasteless
aji ga nai	味がない	watery
aji-mi	味見	taste
aji o tsukeru	味を付ける	season
ajiwau	味わう	taste
aka	赤	red
aka-aka-to kagayaku	赤々と輝く	blaze

aka-aka-to moeru	赤々と燃える	blaze
aka-chan	赤ちゃん	baby
akademii	アカデミー	academy
akai	赤い	red
akaku naru, (kao ga)	赤くなる, (顔が)	flush
akanboo	赤ん坊	baby
akarameru	赤らめる	flush
akari	明かり	light[1]
akarui	明るい	bright
akarui	明るい	clear
akarui	明るい	gay
akarui	明るい	light[1]
akarui	明るい	radiant
akaruku	明るく	brightly
akaru-mi ni deru	明るみに出る	surface
akaru-sa	明るさ	brightness
akeru	あける	open
aki	秋	autumn
aki	秋	fall
aki-	空き〜	empty
akichi	空き地	clearing
akichi	空き地	yard[2]
akirakana	明らかな	apparent
akirakana	明らかな	clear
akirakana	明らかな	evident
akirakana	明らかな	obvious
akirakani	明らかに	apparently
akirakani	明らかに	clearly
akireru	あきれる	shock
akiru	飽きる	tire[1]
akita N	飽きたN	tired
akita N	飽きたN	weary
akite iru (N)	飽きている(N)	tired
akite iru (N)	飽きている(N)	weary
akkan	悪漢	villain
akoodeon	アコーデオン	accordion
aku	悪	evil
aku	あく	open
aku	悪	wrong
akubi	あくび	yawn
akubi o suru	あくびをする	yawn
akui	悪意	spite
akuma	悪魔	devil
akuseku (to) hataraku	あくせく(と)働く	toil
akusento	アクセント	accent
akutai o tsuku	悪態をつく	swear
amachua	アマチュア	amateur
ama-gasa	雨傘	umbrella

amai	甘い	sweet
amai-mono	甘い物	sweet
amari	余り	spare
amayakasu	甘やかす	spoil
Amazon	アマゾン	Amazon
Amazon-gawa	アマゾン川	Amazon
ame	あめ	candy
ame	雨	rain
Amefutto	アメフット	football
ame ga furu	雨が降る	rain
ame ga ooi	雨が多い	rainy
ame no N	雨のN	rainy
ame no N	雨のN	wet
ame no ooi N	雨の多いN	wet
Amerika	アメリカ	America
Amerika Gasshuu-koku	アメリカ合衆国	United States of America
Amerika-Indian	アメリカインディアン	Indian
Amerika-jin	アメリカ人	American
Amerikan-futto-booru	アメリカンフットボール	football
Amerika no N	アメリカのN	American
ami	網	net
amido	網戸	screen
ami-mono o suru	編み物をする	knit
ami(-no)-me	網(の)目	network
amu	編む	knit
amu	編む	weave
Amusuterudamu	アムステルダム	Amsterdam
ana	穴	burrow
ana	穴	cavity
ana	穴	hole
ana	穴	slot
anaake-ki	穴開け器	punch[2]
ana o akeru, (anaake-ki de)	穴を開ける,(穴開け器で)	punch[2]
anata	あなた	sweetheart
anata	あなた	you
anata-gata	あなたがた	you
anata-gata no N	あなたがたのN	your
anata no N	あなたのN	your
anata-tachi	あなたたち	you
anata-tachi no N	あなたたちのN	your
Andesu-sanmyaku	アンデス山脈	Andes
Anguro-Sakuson	アングロサクソン	Anglo-Saxon
ani	兄	brother
anki-suru	暗記する	memorize
annai-joo	案内状	circular

annai-sho	案内書	guide
annai-suru	案内する	direct
annai-suru	案内する	guide
annai-suru	案内する	lead
anna N	あんなN	such
annani	あんなに	that[1]
ano hito-tachi	あの人たち	they
ano hito-tachi {o/ni}	あの人たち{を/に}	them
ano N	あのN	that[1]
anshin	安心	peace
anshin-kan	安心感	security
anshinna	安心な	secure
anshoo-suru	暗唱する	recite
anta	あんた	you
anta no N	あんたのN	your
anta-tachi	あんたたち	you
anta-tachi no N	あんたたちのN	your
antei(-sei)	安定(性)	stability
antei-shita N	安定したN	stable
antena	アンテナ	antenna
anzen	安全	safety
anzen	安全	security
anzen hoshoo	安全保障	security
anzenna	安全な	safe
anzenna	安全な	secure
anzenni	安全に	safely
anzen o kakuho-suru	安全を確保する	secure
ao	青	blue
aogu	あおぐ	fan[1]
aoi	青い	blue
aoi	青い	green
aojiroi	青白い	pale
aojiroi	青白い	watery
ao (no N)	青(のN)	green
ao-zameta (kao)	青ざめた(顔)	white
apaato	アパート	apartment
apaato	アパート	flat[2]
apaato-dai	アパート代	rent
Aparachia-sanmyaku no N	アパラチア山脈のN	Appalachian
apiiru	アピール	appeal
Aporo	アポロ	Apollo
aposutorofi	アポストロフィ	apostrophe
apuroochi	アプローチ	approach
ara	あら	my
ara!	あら!	Oh
ara-ara-shii	荒々しい	rough
Arabama	アラバマ	Alabama

Arabia	アラビア	Arabia
Arabia-go	アラビア語	Arabic
Arabia-jin	アラビア人	Arab
Arabia-jin	アラビア人	Arabian
Arabia-jin no N	アラビア人のN	Arabian
Arabia no N	アラビアのN	Arabian
Arabu-jin	アラブ人	Arab
Arabu-jin	アラブ人	Arabian
Arabu-jin no N	アラブ人のN	Arabian
Arabu no N	アラブのN	Arabian
arai	粗い	coarse
arai-guma	あらいぐま	raccoon
arai-kiyomeru	洗い清める	wash
arai-nagasu	洗い流す	wash
arakajime	あらかじめ	previously
ara-maa	あらまあ	dear
arare	あられ	hail
arare ga furu	あられが降る	hail
arashi	嵐	storm
arashi no N	嵐のN	stormy
arashi no yoona	嵐のような	stormy
arasou	争う	compete
ara-suji	荒筋	outline
Arasuka	アラスカ	Alaska
aratamatta N	改まったN	formal
arau	洗う	wash
arawareru	現れる	appear
arawareru	現れる	emerge
arawareru	あらわれる	reveal
arawareru	あらわれる	show
arawasu	あらわす	express
arawasu	あらわす	illustrate
arawasu	あらわす	indicate
arawasu	あらわす	reflect
arawasu	あらわす	represent
arayuru N	あらゆるN	all
arayuru N	あらゆるN	every
are	あれ	that[1]
areba…pot.	あれば…pot.	entitle
are-chi	荒れ地	waste
are-chi	荒れ地	wilderness
areta N	荒れたN	rough
arete iru (N)	荒れている(N)	rough
ari	あり	ant
ari-ari-to miseru	ありありと見せる	visible
ari-enai	あり得ない	impossible
ari-{eru/uru}	あり得る	possible
ari-{eru/uru}	あり得る	probable
arigatai to omotte iru	ありがたいと思っている	thankful
arigatai to omou	ありがたいと思う	grateful
arigatai to omou	ありがたいと思う	thankful
arigatoo to iu	ありがとうと言う	thank
arimasen	ありません	isn't
arimasen deshita	ありませんでした	wasn't
arimasen deshita	ありませんでした	weren't
arimashita	ありました	was
arimashita	ありました	were
ari-soo mo nai (N)	ありそうもない(N)	unlikely
ari-sooni (mo) nai (N)	ありそうに(も)ない(N)	unlikely
ari-{uru/eru} koto	あり得る事	possibility
Arizona	アリゾナ	Arizona
aru	ある	are
aru	ある	be
aru	ある	bear[2]
aru	ある	consist
aru	ある	exist
aru	ある	happen
aru	ある	have
aru	ある	is
aru	ある	lie[1]
aru	ある	locate
aru	ある	offer
aru	ある	own
aru	ある	possess
aru	ある	stand
aru	ある	there's
arubamu	アルバム	album
arufabetto	アルファベット	alphabet
arufabetto-jun ni	アルファベット順に	alphabetically
aruite {iku/kuru}	歩いて{行く/来る}	wade
aruite wataru	歩いて渡る	wade
aruiwa, (ka)	あるいは, (か)	or
aruka-seru	歩かせる	walk
aruki-kata	歩き方	step
aruki-kata	歩き方	walk
aruki-mawaru	歩き回る	roam
aruki-mawaru	歩き回る	tramp
aruki-mawaru, ate-mo-naku	歩き回る, あてもなく	wander
aruki-mawaru, bura-bura	歩き回る, ぶらぶら	wander
arukooru	アルコール	alcohol
arukooru-chuudoku	アルコール中毒	alcoholic
arukooru no haitta N	アルコールの入ったN	alcoholic

aru koto	あること	presence
aruku	歩く	walk
aruminyuumu	アルミニウム	aluminum
arumi-sasshi	アルミサッシ	sash[2]
aru N	あるN	certain
Arupusu-sanmyaku	アルプス山脈	Alps
aru, Sinf. nonpast koto {ga/mo}	ある, Sinf. nonpastこと{が/も}	sometimes
aru, Vinf. past koto ga	ある, Vinf. pastことが	have
Aruzenchin	アルゼンチン	Argentina
asa	麻	linen
asa	朝	morning
asa-gohan	朝ご飯	breakfast
asai	浅い	shallow
ase	汗	perspiration
ase	汗	sweat
ase ga deru	汗が出る	perspire
ase-mizu nagashite hataraku	汗水流して働く	sweat
ase o kaku	汗をかく	perspire
ase o kaku	汗をかく	sweat
ashi	あし	feet
ashi	あし	foot
ashi	あし	leg
ashi	あし	paw
ashi	あし	reed
ashi-ato	足跡	footstep
ashi-ato	足跡	trace
ashi-ato	足跡	track
ashi-ato	足跡	trail
ashi-ato o tsukeru	足跡を付ける	track
ashi-dai	足台	stool
ashi de fumi-tsukeru	足で踏み付ける	stamp
ashi-kubi	足首	ankle
ashi no ura	足の裏	sole[2]
(ashi no) yubi	(足の)指	toe
ashi o fumi-dasu	足を踏み出す	step
ashi o hikizutte yukkuri aruku	足を引きずってゆっくり歩く	trail
ashi-oto	足音	footstep
ashita	あした	tomorrow
asobi	遊び	game
asobi	遊び	play
asobi-ba	遊び場	playground
asobi ni {iku/kuru}	遊びに{行く/来る}	visit
asobu	遊ぶ	idle
asobu	遊ぶ	play
asoko	あそこ	there
asoko {ni/de/e/o/ga}	あそこ{に/で/へ/を/が}	there
assari-shita N	あっさりしたN	mild
assari-shite iru (N)	あっさりしている(N)	mild
asshoo-suru	圧勝する	overwhelm
asu	明日	tomorrow
ataeru	与える	allow
ataeru	与える	award
ataeru	与える	give
ataeru	与える	provide
ataeru	与える	render
atama	頭	head
atama	頭	intelligence
atama	頭	mind
atama ga ii	頭がいい	bright
atama ga ii	頭がいい	brilliant
atama ga ii	頭がいい	intelligent
atama ga ii	頭がいい	smart
atama no jihada	頭の地肌	scalp
atarashii	新しい	fresh
atarashii	新しい	new
atarashiku-suru	新しくする	renovate
atari	辺り	neighborhood
atarimae no N	当たり前のN	natural
ataru	当たる	guess
ataru	当たる	hit
ataru	当たる	strike
atashi	あたし	I
atashi no N	あたしのN	my
atashi-tachi	あたしたち	we
atashi-tachi no N	あたしたちのN	our
atatakai	あたたかい	warm
atatakaku suru	あたたかくする	warm
atataka-mi	あたたかみ	warmth
atatakana	あたたかな	warm
atataka-sa	あたたかさ	warmth
atatamaru	あたたまる	heat
atatameru	あたためる	heat
atatameru	あたためる	warm
atchi e	あっちへ	away
atehamaru	あてはまる	apply
ate-mo-naku aruki-mawaru	あてもなく歩き回る	wander
Atene	アテネ	Athens
ate ni naranai (N)	当てにならない(N)	uncertain
ate-ni-suru	当てにする	depend

ateru	あてる	devote
ateru	あてる	guess
ateru	あてる	hit
ato	あと	another
ato	あと	mark
ato	あと	trace
ato de	後で	after
ato de	後で	afterward(s)
ato de	後で	later
ato ga tsuku	跡が付く	mark
ato made nokoru, ⟨-yori⟩	後まで残る, ⟨〜より⟩	survive
ato ni	後に	behind
ato ni tsuzuku	後に続く	succeed
ato o tsugu	後を継ぐ	succeed
atorakushon	アトラクション	attraction
atorie	アトリエ	studio
atsugami	厚紙	cardboard
atsui	あつい	hot
atsui	厚い	thick
atsukai	扱い	treatment
atsukau	扱う	handle
atsukau	扱う	treat
atsumaru	集まる	gather
atsumaru	集まる	rally
atsumeru	集める	collect
atsumeru	集める	gather
atsumeru	集める	raise
atsumeru koto	集めること	collection
atsu-mi	厚み	thickness
atsuryoku	圧力	pressure
atsuryoku	圧力	stress
atsuryoku o kakeru	圧力をかける	pressure
atsu-sa	あつさ	heat
atsu-sa	厚さ	thickness
atsu-sa no N, (Amount) no	厚さのN, (Amount)の	thick
atta	あった	was
atta	あった	were
attoo-suru	圧倒する	overwhelm
attoo-tekina	圧倒的な	overwhelming
au	あう	agree
au	あう	fit
au	あう	match[1]
au	あう	meet
au	あう	see
au	あう	suitable
auto	アウト	out

autoputto	アウトプット	output
auto-rain	アウトライン	outline
au yakusoku	会う約束	date
awa	泡	bubble
awa	泡	foam
awa-dateru	泡立てる	whip
awai	淡い	watery
awanai	合わない	disagree
awaremi	哀れみ	sympathy
ayamari	あやまり	error
ayamari	あやまり	mistake
ayamaru	あやまる	apologize
ayashii	怪しい	suspicious
ayashimu, Sinf. no dewanai (daroo) ka to	怪しむ, Sinf.のではない(だろう)かと	suspect
ayatsuri-ningyoo	操り人形	puppet
ayumu	歩む	walk
azarashi	あざらし	seal[1]
azayakana	鮮やかな	vivid
azukeru	預ける	check
azukeru	預ける	deposit
azukeru	預ける	put

B

ba	場	scene
baa	バー	bar
baagen	バーゲン	sale
baagen-hin	バーゲン品	bargain
baai	場合	case[2]
baai	場合	occasion
Baajinia	バージニア	Virginia
baareru	バーレル	barrel
baggu	バッグ	purse
-bai	〜杯	cup
-bai	〜倍	time
bai-bai	売買	trade
bai-bai-suru	売買する	trade
baikingu	バイキング	Viking
baiku	バイク	motorcycle
bai ni naru	倍になる	double
bai ni suru	倍にする	double
bai no N	倍のN	double
baiorin	バイオリン	violin
baishin-in	陪審員	jury
baitai	媒体	vehicle
baiten	売店	stall
baiyaa	バイヤー	buyer

baka	ばか	fool
bakabakashii	ばかばかしい	stupid
baka-banashi	ばか話	chatter
baka-geta koto	ばかげたこと	nonsense
baka-geta koto	ばかげたこと	rubbish
baka-geta N	ばかげたN	ridiculous
baka-geta N	ばかげたN	stupid
baka-gete iru	ばかげている	stupid
baka-gete iru (N)	ばかげている(N)	ridiculous
baka-mitaina	ばかみたいな	foolish
bakana	ばかな	foolish
bakana	ばかな	silly
bakana	ばかな	stupid
bakana hanashi	ばかな話	trash
baka-ni-suru	ばかにする	slight
...bakari	…ばかり	only
bakari da, Vinf. past	ばかりだ, Vinf. past	only
baketsu	バケツ	bucket
baketsu	バケツ	pail
bakkin	罰金	fine
bakkin-tsuuchi	罰金通知	ticket
bakku-guraundo	バックグラウンド	background
bakudaina	ばく大な	huge
bakudaina	ばく大な	vast
bakudan	爆弾	bomb
bakuha-suru	爆破する	blast
bakuha-suru	爆破する	blow
bakuhatsu	爆発	explosion
bakuhatsu-suru	爆発する	explode
bakuro-suru	暴露する	expose
bakuro-suru	暴露する	reveal
bakuteria	バクテリア	bacteria
bakuzen to shita N	漠然としたN	vague
bakuzen to shite iru (N)	漠然としている(N)	vague
bamen	場面	scene
bamen	場面	situation
ban	晩	evening
ban	番	turn
ban	バン	van
-ban	～番	place
-ban	～版	version
banana	バナナ	banana
banbutsu	万物	universe
bando	バンド	band
bando	バンド	belt
bane	ばね	spring
ban-gohan	晩御飯	dinner
ban-gohan	晩御飯	supper
bangoo	番号	number
bangoo o tsukeru	番号を付ける	number
bangumi	番組	program
ban-kuruwase de makasu	番狂わせで負かす	upset
ban o suru	番をする	watch
-ban-sen	～番線	track
bansoo	伴奏	accompaniment
bansoo o suru, (uta no)	伴奏をする, (歌の)	accompany
bara	ばら	rose
baraetii	バラエティー	variety
baransu	バランス	balance
baree	バレエ	ballet
baree-booru	バレーボール	volleyball
bareru	バレル	barrel
barieeshon	バリエーション	variation
barubu	バルブ	valve
barukonii	バルコニー	balcony
basha	馬車	carriage
basho	場所	location
basho	場所	place
basho	場所	seat
basho	場所	site
basho	場所	space
basho	場所	stand
basho, (shimeru-beki)	場所, (占めるべき)	slot
bassui	抜粋	selection
bassuru	罰する	punish
basu	バス	bass
basu	バス	bus
basuketto	バスケット	basket
basu-tei	バス停	stop
bataa	バター	butter
batan	ばたん	bang
batan to shimeru	ばたんと閉める	bang
batan to shimeru	ばたんと閉める	slam
batsu	罰	punishment
batsugun no N	抜群のN	outstanding
batsu-jirushi	×印	cross
battaa	バッター	batter
batterii	バッテリー	battery
battingu	バッティング	batting
batto	バット	bat
-ba, Vcond.	～ば, Vcond.	if
bearingu	ベアリング	bearing
bebii-shittaa	ベビー・シッター	baby-sitting
beddo	ベッド	bed

beddoruumu	ベッドルーム	bedroom
beekon	ベーコン	bacon
beesu	ベース	base
beesu	ベース	bass
beesu-booru	ベースボール	baseball
Beikoku	米国	America
Beikoku-jin	米国人	American
Beikoku no N	米国のN	American
beki da, Vinf. nonpast	べきだ, Vinf. nonpast	ought
ben	弁	valve
bengo-shi	弁護士	lawyer
bengo-suru	弁護する	defend
benjo	便所	lavatory
benjo	便所	toilet
benki	便器	stool
benkyoo	勉強	study
benkyoo-suru	勉強する	study
benkyoo-suru	勉強する	work
benrina	便利な	convenience
benrina	便利な	convenient
benrina	便利な	handy
berii	ベリー	berry
beru	ベル	bell
berubetto	ベルベット	velvet
berubetto no N	ベルベットのN	velvet
Berugii	ベルギー	Belgium
Berurin	ベルリン	Berlin
beruto	ベルト	belt
besuto	ベスト	best
beta-beta-suru	べたべたする	sticky
Betonamu	ベトナム	Vietnam
betsu-betsu ni	別々に	apart
betsu-betsu no N	別々のN	separate
betsu ni	別に	particularly
betsu no hoohoo de	別の方法で	differently
betsu no mono	別のもの	another
betsu no N	別のN	another
betsu no N	別のN	else
bi	美	beauty
bibu	尾部	tail
bideo	ビデオ	video
bideo-disuku	ビデオディスク	video-disk
bideo-teepu	ビデオテープ	tape
bideo-teepu	ビデオテープ	videotape
bifuteki	ビフテキ	beefsteak
biibaa	ビーバー	beaver
biichi	ビーチ	beach
biifu	ビーフ	beef
Biinasu	ビーナス	Venus
biiru	ビール	beer
biirusu	ビールス	virus
biito	ビート	beet
biizu	ビーズ	bead
bijin	美人	beauty
bijinesu-man	ビジネスマン	businessman
bijon	ビジョン	vision
bijutsu	美術	art
bijutsu-kan	美術館	museum
bikko no N	びっこのN	lame
bikko o hiku	びっこを引く	limp
bikkuri-saseru	びっくりさせる	amaze
bikkuri-saseru	びっくりさせる	astonish
bikkuri-saseru	びっくりさせる	startle
bikkuri-suru yoona	びっくりするような	amazing
bikkuri-suru yoona	びっくりするような	astonishing
bikkuri-suru yoona N	びっくりするようなN	incredible
bikoo	鼻孔	nostril
bikoo-suru	尾行する	tail
bimyoona	微妙な	delicate
bimyoona	微妙な	subtle
bimyoona chigai	微妙な違い	shade
bin	瓶	bottle
bin	瓶	jar
bin	瓶	pot
binboo	貧乏	poverty
binboona	貧乏な	poor
biniiru	ビニール	vinyl
binkanna	敏感な	sensitive
binsokuna	敏速な	speedy
bira	ビラ	poster
biroodo	ビロード	velvet
biroodo no N	ビロードのN	velvet
biru	ビル	building
birudingu	ビルディング	building
bi-seibutsu	微生物	microbe
bisho-nure ni naru	びしょぬれになる	soak
bisho-nure ni suru	びしょぬれにする	soak
bisuketto	ビスケット	biscuit
bitamin	ビタミン	vitamin
biyoo-in	美容院	beauty parlor
boin	母音	vowel
boiraa	ボイラー	boiler
bokkusu	ボックス	booth
boku	僕	I

boku no N	僕のN	my
boku-ra	僕ら	we
bokushi	牧師	minister
bokushi	牧師	pastor
bokusoo	牧草	pasture
bokusoo-chi	牧草地	field
bokusoo-chi	牧草地	meadow
bokusoo-chi	牧草地	pasture
boku-tachi	僕たち	we
boku-tachi no N	僕たちのN	our
bon	盆	tray
bonchi	盆地	basin
bon'yari-shita N	ぼんやりしたN	vague
bon'yari-shite iru (N)	ぼんやりしている(N)	vague
bonyuu	母乳	milk
boo	棒	pole[1]
boo	棒	staff
boodaina	膨大な	huge
booei	防衛	defense
booei	防衛	security
booeki	貿易	trade
booeki	貿易	traffic
booeki-gyoosha	貿易業者	trader
booeki-suru	貿易する	trade
booen-kyoo	望遠鏡	telescope
boofuu	暴風	storm
boofuu-u	暴風雨	storm
boofuu(-u) no N	暴風(雨)のN	stormy
boogai	妨害	stop
boogai suru	妨害する	block
boogai-suru	妨害する	disturb
boogai-suru, {Vinf. nonpast no/N} o	妨害する, {Vinf. nonpastの/N}を	prevent
boogyo	防御	defense
boogyo-suru	防御する	defend
booi	ボーイ	waiter
bookan-sha	傍観者	spectator
bookaru	ボーカル	vocal
booken	冒険	adventure
booken	冒険	risk
booken	冒険	venture
booken-zuki no N	冒険好きのN	adventurous
bookoo	暴行	violence
boonasu	ボーナス	bonus
booru	ボール	ball
booru	ボール	bowl
booru-gami	ボール紙	cardboard
booru o utsu	ボールを打つ	stroke[1]
boorupen	ボールペン	ball-point pen
booryoku	暴力	violence
booryoku-dan	暴力団	gang
booshi	帽子	cap
booshi	帽子	hat
booshi	防止	prevention
booshi-kake	帽子掛け	hook
booto	ボート	boat
booto	ボート	rowboat
bootoku	冒とく	violation
bootoo-suru	暴騰する	soar
borantia	ボランティア	volunteer
boro	ぼろ	rag
boro-fuku	ぼろ服	rag
borokire	ぼろきれ	rag
Boruchimoa	ボルチモア	Baltimore
boruto	ボルト	bolt
boryuumu	ボリューム	volume
boseki	墓石	stone
boshuu-suru	募集する	recruit
bosu	ボス	boss
Bosuton	ボストン	Boston
botan	ボタン	button
botsuraku	没落	ruin
botsuraku-saseru	没落させる	ruin
botsuraku-saseru	没落させる	sink
bu	部	club
-bu	〜部	copy
-bu	〜部	part
bubun	部分	part
bubun	部分	passage
bubun	部分	piece
bubun	部分	section
bubun	部分	segment
bubun-tekini	部分的に	partly
Budda	仏だ	Buddha
budoo	ぶどう	grape
budoo no ki	ぶどうの木	vine
budoo-shu	ぶどう酒	wine
buhin	部品	part
buji	無事	safety
bujini	無事に	safely
buki	武器	arms
buki	武器	weapon
bu-kiyoona	不器用な	awkward
bu-kiyoona	不器用な	clumsy
bu-kiyoona	不器用な	unskillful

bukka	物価	price
Bukkyoo	仏教	Buddhism
bumon	部門	division
bun	文	sentence
bun	分	share
bunboo-gu	文房具	stationery
bun-bun iu oto	ブンブンいう音	buzz
bungaku	文学	literature
bungaku-tekina	文学的な	literary
bungei-	文芸〜	literary
bungei-fukkoo	文芸復興	renaissance
bunka	文化	culture
bunka no N	文化のN	cultural
bunka-tekina	文化的な	cultural
bunkatsu	分割	division
bunkatsu	分割	split
bunkatsu-suru	分割する	divide
bunken	文献	literature
bunmei-ka-shita N	文明化したN	civilized
bunpai-suru	分配する	distribute
bunpai-suru	分配する	divide
bunpoo	文法	grammar
bunpu	分布	distribution
bunretsu	分裂	split
bunrui	分類	classification
bunrui-suru	分類する	classify
bunrui-suru	分類する	sort
bunryoo	分量	quantity
buntai	文体	style
buntan	分担	share
buntsuu	文通	correspondence
bun'ya	分野	field
bura-bura aruki-mawaru	ぶらぶら歩き回る	wander
bura-bura aruku	ぶらぶら歩く	stroll
buraindo	ブラインド	blind
burando	ブランド	brand
bura-sagaru	ぶら下がる	swing
burashi	ブラシ	brush
burashi o kakeru	ブラシをかける	brush
burausu	ブラウス	blouse
bureeki	ブレーキ	brake
bureina	無礼な	rude
burendo	ブレンド	blend
buriifukeesu	ブリーフケース	briefcase
burijji	ブリッジ	bridge[2]
burokku	ブロック	block
burondo no N	ブロンドのN	blond
buroochi	ブローチ	pin
Buroodouei	ブロードウエイ	Broadway
bushi	武士	warrior
busho	部署	post[2]
bussei	物性	physics
busshitsu	物質	substance
busshitsu no N	物質のN	substantial
busshitsu-tekina	物質的な	material
buta	豚	pig
butai	舞台	stage
buta-niku	豚肉	pork
butoo-kai	舞踏会	ball
butsu	ぶつ	hit
butsu	ぶつ	strike
butsukaru	ぶつかる	crash
butsukaru	ぶつかる	hit
butsukeru	ぶつける	bump
butsukeru	ぶつける	hit
butsuri(-gaku)	物理(学)	physics
butsuri-gakusha	物理学者	physicist
butsuri-tekina	物理的な	physical
buttai	物体	object
buttekina	物的な	material
buttooshi no N	ぶっ通しのN	unbroken
but(t)sukaru	ぶ(っ)つかる	strike
buttsuzuke no N	ぶっ続けのN	unbroken
buumu	ブーム	boom
buumu no N	ブームのN	booming
buusu	ブース	booth
buutsu	ブーツ	boot
buzoku	部族	tribe
buzoku no N	部族のN	tribal
byoo	秒	second[2]
byoo	びょう	tack
byoobu	びょうぶ	screen
byoo de tomeru	びょうで留める	tack
byoodoo	平等	equality
byoodooni	平等に	alike
byoodooni	平等に	equally
byoodooni	平等に	evenly
byoodoo no N	平等のN	equal
byooin	病院	hospital
byooki	病気	disease
byooki	病気	illness
byooki	病気	sickness
byooki	病気	trouble
byooki no N	病気のN	ill
byooki no N	病気のN	sick

byoonin	病人	patient
byoosha-suru	描写する	describe
byoosha-suru	描写する	represent
byoosha-suru	描写する	sketch
byootoo	病棟	ward[2]

C

cha	茶	tea
chaaminguna	チャーミングな	charming
chaato	チャート	chart
cha-iro	茶色	brown
cha-iro no N	茶色のN	brown
-chaku	～着	place
chaku-chaku-to	着々と	steadily
chakuriku-suru	着陸する	land
chakuyoo	着用	wear
channeru	チャンネル	channel
chanpion	チャンピオン	champion
chansu	チャンス	chance
chansu	チャンス	occasion
chansu	チャンス	opportunity
chan-to	ちゃんと	right
chan-to shita N	ちゃんとしたN	square
chanto shita N	ちゃんとしたN	substantial
charenji	チャレンジ	challenge
charenjinguna	チャレンジングな	challenging
chataku	茶たく	saucer
chawan	茶わん	cup
chawan	茶わん	teacup
chein	チェイン	chain
cheen	チェーン	chain
chekku	チェック	check
chekku no shirushi	チェックの印	check
chekku-suru	チェックする	check
chesu	チェス	chess
chi	血	blood
chichi	父	father
chichi	乳	milk
chichi o shiboru	乳をしぼる	milk
chichi-oya	父親	father
chie	知恵	wisdom
chi ga deru	血が出る	bleed
chigai	違い	difference
chigai	違い	distinction
chigai ga wakaru	違いが分かる	tell
chigatta N	違ったN	different
chigatte iru (N)	違っている(N)	different
chigatte iru (N)	違っている(N)	unequal
chigatte, ⟨-to⟩	違って, ⟨～と⟩	unlike
chigau	違う	differ
chigau hoohoo de	違う方法で	differently
chigau N	違うN	different
chigau N	違うN	distinct
chigau (N)	違う(N)	unequal
chihei-sen	地平線	horizon
chihoo	地方	district
chihoo	地方	region
chihoo no N	地方のN	local
chii	地位	place
chii	地位	position
chii	地位	post[2]
chii	地位	rank
chii	地位	state
chii	地位	status
chiifu	チーフ	chief
chiiki	地域	area
chiiki	地域	district
chiiki	地域	neighborhood
chiiki	地域	quarter
chiiki	地域	region
chiiki	地域	zone
chiiki-kyoodoo-tai	地域共同体	community
chiiki-shakai	地域社会	community
chiimu	チーム	team
chiimu o tsukuru	チームを作る	team
chiisai	小さい	small
chiisai koe de	小さい声で	softly
chiisai tochi	小さい土地	plot
chiisana koe de	小さな声で	softly
chiisana N	小さなN	little
chiisana N	小さなN	small
chiizu	チーズ	cheese
chiji	知事	governor
chijimeru	縮める	shorten
chika-chozoo-{ko/shitsu}	地下貯蔵{庫/室}	cellar
chika-doo	地下道	tunnel
chikagoro	近ごろ	recently
chikagoro no N	近ごろのN	recent
chikai	地階	basement
chikai	近い	close[2]
chikai	近い	near
chikai	誓い	oath
chikai koto	近いこと	vicinity
chikaku	近く	neighborhood
chikaku	近く	vicinity

chikaku {ni/de/o}	近く{に/で/を}	beside
chikaku ni	近くに	toward(s)
chikaku no N	近くのN	near
chika {ni/de/o}	地下{に/で/を}	underground
chika no N	地下のN	underground
chikara	力	force
chikara	力	power
chikara	力	steam
chikara	力	weight
chikara ga aru (N)	力がある(N)	strong
chikara-zuyoi	力強い	powerful
chikara-zuyoi	力強い	vigorous
chika-shitsu	地下室	basement
chika-tetsu	地下鉄	subway
chikau, ({kami/seisho} ni kakete)	誓う, ({神/聖書}に掛けて)	swear
chikazuku	近付く	approach
chikazuku hoohoo	近付く方法	access
chikei	地形	terrain
chiketto	チケット	ticket
chiku	地区	district
chiku	地区	neighborhood
chiku	地区	zone
chikyuu	地球	earth
chikyuu	地球	globe
chikyuu-gi	地球儀	globe
chimei-tekina	致命的な	fatal
chi-namagusai	血なまぐさい	bloody
chinande, na ni	ちなんで, 名に	after
chingin	賃金	wage
chinjutsu	陳述	statement
chinjutsu-suru	陳述する	state
chinmoku	沈黙	silence
chinmoku-saseru	沈黙させる	silence
chinoo	知能	intelligence
chinretsu	陳列	display
chinretsu-suru	陳列する	display
chippokena	ちっぽけな	tiny
chippu	チップ	tip[2]
chippu o {ageru/yaru}	チップを{あげる/やる}	tip[2]
chiratto miru	ちらっと見る	glance
chiratto miru	ちらっと見る	peek
chiri	ちり	dust
chiri	地理	geography
chirigami	ちり紙	tissue
chiru	散る	fall
chiru	散る	scatter

chiryoo	治療	cure
chiryoo(-hoo)	治療(法)	remedy
chiryoo(-hoo)	治療(法)	treatment
chiryoo-suru	治療する	treat
chisei	治世	reign
chisei	地勢	terrain
chishiki	知識	knowledge
chishiki-jin	知識人	intellectual
chishitsu-gaku	地質学	geology
chisso	窒素	nitrogen
chitai	地帯	area
chitai	地帯	zone
chitchai	ちっちゃい	tiny
chitchana N	ちっちゃなN	tiny
chitekina	知的な	intellectual
chiten	地点	point
chiten	地点	spot
chitsujo	秩序	order
chizu	地図	map
chojutsu	著述	writing
chokin-suru	貯金する	save
chokin to iu oto	ちょきんという音	snap
chokkan	直観	instinct
chokoreeto	チョコレート	chocolate
chokumen-suru	直面する	face
chokusetsu	直接	directly
chokusetsu no N	直接のN	direct
chokuzoku no N	直属のN	immediate
chomeina	著名な	distinguished
chomeina	著名な	prominent
Chomoranma	チョモランマ	Everest
choo	ちょう	butterfly
-choo	～長	chair
-choo	～長	chief
choobo	帳簿	book
chooboo	眺望	prospect
choocho	ちょうちょ	butterfly
choochoo	町長	mayor
choodai-suru	ちょうだいする	eat
choodo	ちょうど	exactly
choodo	ちょうど	just
choodo	ちょうど	right
choohei	徴兵	draft
choohei-suru	徴兵する	draft
choo-hookei	長方形	rectangle
choo-hookei no N	長方形のN	rectangular
choojin	超人	superman
choojoo	頂上	summit

choojoo	頂上	top
choojoo no N	頂上のN	top
chooka	超過	excess
chookoku-suru	彫刻する	carve
chookoo	兆候	symptom
chooku	チョーク	chalk
chooku-boodo	チョークボード	chalkboard
choosa	調査	investigation
choosa	調査	survey
choosa-suru	調査する	explore
choosa-suru	調査する	investigate
choosa-suru	調査する	survey
choosei	調整	adjustment
choosei-suru	調整する	adjust
choosen	挑戦	challenge
Choosen	朝鮮	Korea
choosen-suru	挑戦する	challenge
chooshi	調子	condition
chooshi	調子	pace
chooshi	調子	tone
chooshi	調子	vein
chooshi ga warui	調子が悪い	wrong
chooshi no ii aruki-kata	調子のいい歩き方	swing
chooshi o awaseru	調子を合わせる	tune
chooshi waruku	調子悪く	wrong
choosho	長所	merit
chooshoku	朝食	breakfast
chooshuu	聴衆	audience
chooten	頂点	peak
chooten	頂点	summit
choowa	調和	harmony
choowa	調和	proportion
choowa	調和	unity
chooyaku	跳躍	spring
choozai	調剤	pharmacy
choozoo	彫像	statue
choppu	チョップ	chop
chosaku	著作	work
chosaku	著作	writing
chosha	著者	author
chosha	著者	writer
chotto	ちょっと	bit
chotto	ちょっと	little
chotto	ちょっと	minor
chotto	ちょっと	slight
chotto	ちょっと	slightly
chotto aruku	ちょっと歩く	step

chotto-shita {mono/mon}	ちょっとした{もの/もん}	something
chotto-shita N	ちょっとしたN	some
chozoo	貯蔵	preservation
chozoo	貯蔵	stock
chozoo	貯蔵	storage
chozoo-butsu	貯蔵物	provision
chozoo-suru	貯蔵する	preserve
chuu	注	note
-chuu	～中	duration
-chuu	～中	middle
chuuburarin	宙ぶらりん	suspense
chuucho	ちゅうちょ	hesitation
chuucho-suru	ちゅうちょする	hesitate
chuu-chuu naku	ちゅうちゅう鳴く	squeak
chuugaeri o saseru	宙返りをさせる	tumble
chuugaeri o suru	宙返りをする	tumble
Chuugoku	中国	China
Chuugoku-go	中国語	Chinese
Chuugoku-go no N	中国語のN	Chinese
Chuugoku-jin	中国人	Chinese
Chuugoku-jin no N	中国人のN	Chinese
Chuugoku no	中国のN	Chinese
chuu-gurai no N	中ぐらいのN	medium
chuu-gurai no N	中ぐらいのN	moderate
chuui	注意	attention
chuui	注意	care
chuui	注意	caution
chuui	注意	eye
chuui	注意	note
chuui-bukai	注意深い	careful
chuui-bukaku	注意深く	cautiously
chuui o harau	注意を払う	attend
chuui-shite	注意して	carefully
chuui-suru	注意する	advise
chuui-suru	注意する	caution
chuui-suru	注意する	note
chuui-suru, ⟨-no⟩ koto o	注意する、⟨～の⟩ことを	remind
chuujitsuna	忠実な	loyal
chuujitsuni	忠実に	truly
chuukan no N	中間のN	intermediate
chuukei	中継	relay
chuukoku	忠告	advice
chuukoku-suru	忠告する	advise
chuuko no N	中古のN	secondhand
chuuko no N	中古のN	used[2]
chuukyuu no N	中級のN	intermediate

chuumoku-subeki N	注目すべきN	remarkable
chuumon	注文	order
chuumon-suru	注文する	order
chuuoo	中央	center
chuuoo no N	中央のN	central
chuu o tsukeru	注を付ける	note
chuuritsu no N	中立のN	neutral
Chuuseibu	中西部	Midwest
chuusei no N	中世のN	medieval
chuusei no N	中性のN	neutral
chuusha	駐車	parking
chuusha	注射	shot
chuushin	中心	center
chuushin	中心	heart
chuushin no N	中心のN	central
chuushi-suru	中止する	cancel
chuushoku	昼食	lunch
chuutoo-kyooiku no N	中等教育のN	secondary
chuuzoo-suru	鋳造する	cast

D

da	だ	am
da	だ	be
da	だ	is
daasu	ダース	dozen
daburusu	ダブルス	double
dachoo	だちょう	ostrich
daen-kei	楕円形	oval
dageki	打撃	blow
dageki	打撃	shock
dageki	打撃	stroke[1]
dai	題	theme
dai-	大〜	great
dai-	大〜	major
-dai	〜代	charge
-dai	〜代	fare
daian	代案	alternative
daiaroogu	ダイアローグ	dialogue
dai-bokujoo	大牧場	ranch
dai-bokujoo-keiei-sha	大牧場経営者	rancher
daibu	大分	considerably
dai-bubun	大部分	majority
dai-bubun	大部分	most
dai-bubun wa	大部分は	mostly
Dai-buriten-too	大ブリテン島	Britain
daidokoro	台所	kitchen
daidokoro-yoohin	台所用品	utensil
daietto	ダイエット	diet[1]
daigaku	大学	college
daigaku	大学	university
daigaku no kyooin	大学の教員	professor
dai-hachi	第八	eighth
daihyoo(-sha)	代表(者)	representative
daihyoo-suru	代表する	represent
daihyoo-tekina N	代表的なN	representative
dai-ichi(-i) no N	第一(位)のN	prime
dai-ichi no N	第一のN	primary
daijin	大臣	minister
daijina	大事な	important
daijini suru	大事にする	cherish
daijini suru	大事にする	treasure
daijoobu da	大丈夫だ	OK
(dai-)juu-ban-me (no N)	(第)十番目(のN)	tenth
dai-juu-hachi	第十八	eighteenth
(dai-)juu-nana-ban-me (no N)	(第)十七番目(のN)	seventeenth
(dai-)juu-roku-ban-me (no N)	(第)十六番目(のN)	sixteenth
(dai-)juu-shichi-ban-me (no N)	(第)十七番目(のN)	seventeenth
daika	代価	price
daika	代価	value
dai-kiraina	大嫌いな	hate
dai-ku	第九	ninth
daiku	大工	carpenter
daimei	題名	title
dai(mei) o tsukeru	題(名)を付ける	title
dai-meishi	代名詞	pronoun
daimoku	題目	theme
daimoku	題目	topic
(dai-)nana-ban-me (no N)	(第)七番目(のN)	seventh
dai-nashi ni naru	台無しになる	spoil
dai-ni	第二	second[1]
(dai-)ni-juu-ban-me (no N)	(第)二十番目(のN)	twentieth
dai-ni no N	第二のN	second[1]
-dairi	〜代理	acting
dairi-nin	代理人	agent
dairi(-nin)	代理(人)	substitute
dairi-ten	代理店	agency
(dai-)roku-ban-me (no N)	(第)六番目(のN)	sixth
(dai-)roku-juu-ban-me (no N)	(第)六十番目(のN)	sixtieth

dai-san no mono	第三のもの	third
dai-seidoo	大聖堂	cathedral
dai-seikoo	大成功	triumph
(dai-)shichi-ban-me (no N)	(第)七番目(のN)	seventh
daishoo	代償	price
dai-sukina	大好きな	favorite
dai-sukina	大好きな	fond
dai-sukina	大好きな	love
daitai	大体	approximately
daitai	大体	much
daitai	大体	roughly
daitai no N	大体のN	rough
daitanna	大胆な	bold
daitanni	大胆に	boldly
dai-tasuu	大多数	majority
daitooryoo	大統領	president
daiya	ダイヤ	diamond
daiyaku	代役	substitute
daiyamondo	ダイヤモンド	diamond
daiyaru	ダイヤル	dial
daiyoo-hin	代用品	substitute
dajun	打順	bat
dakara	だから	so
dakara	だから	therefore
dake	だけ	just
dake	だけ	very
-dake da	～だけだ	merely
dake da, Sinf. no wa N	だけだ, Sinf.のはN	only
daki-shimeru	抱き締める	embrace
daki-shimeru	抱き締める	hug
daki-shimeru	抱き締める	press
daki-shimeru	抱き締める	squeeze
daku	抱く	embrace
daku	抱く	hold
dakyoo	妥協	compromise
dakyoo-suru	妥協する	compromise
damara-seru	黙らせる	silence
damasu	だます	cheat
damasu	だます	deceive
damasu	だます	trap
damasu	だます	trick
damatte iru (N)	黙っている(N)	silent
dame ni naru	駄目になる	spoil
damu	ダム	dam
dan	団	company
dan	段	level
dan	段	step
danboo	暖房	heating
dan-booru	段ボール	carton
dan-booru-bako	段ボール箱	carton
dan-dan	だんだん	gradual
dan-dan	だんだん	gradually
dangan	弾丸	bullet
dangan	弾丸	shot
dangen	断言	affirmation
dangen-suru	断言する	affirm
dangen-suru	断言する	assert
dangen-suru	断言する	pronounce
danjo-kyoogaku	男女共学	coeducation
dankai	段階	stage
dankai	段階	step
danketsu-shita N	団結したN	united
danko to shita N	断固としたN	firm
danko to shita N	断固としたN	sturdy
dannen-suru	断念する	abandon
danpen	断片	fragment
danraku	段落	paragraph
danro	暖炉	fireplace
danryoku-sei ga aru N	弾力性があるN	flexible
dansei	男性	man
dansei no N	男性のN	male
dansu	ダンス	dance
dansu o suru	ダンスをする	dance
dansu-paatii	ダンスパーティー	ball
dantai	団体	group
dantai	団体	organization
dan'yaku	弾薬	ammunition
-dara	～だら	if
darakete iru (N)	だらけている(N)	slack
darashi ga nai (N)	だらしがない(N)	untidy
dare	だれ	who[1]
dare-demo	だれでも	anybody
dare-demo	だれでも	anyone
dare ga…{V/adj./cop.}*te* mo	だれが…{V/adj./cop.}*te*も	whoever
dare-ka	だれか	any
dare-ka	だれか	anybody
dare-ka	だれか	anyone
dare-ka	だれか	somebody
dare-ka	だれか	someone
dare-mo	だれも	anyone
dare-mo…neg.	だれも…neg.	any
dare-mo…neg.	だれも…neg.	anybody
dare-mo…neg.	だれも…neg.	nobody

dare-mo…neg.	だれも…neg.	none
dare no N	だれのN	whose[1]
dare prt.	だれ prt.	whom[1]
dare (prt.) demo	だれ(prt.)でも	whoever
dare-sore	だれそれ	so-and-so
daroo to {adj(*na*). stem/N} dearumai to, {adj(*na*). stem/N}	だろうと{adj(*na*). stem/N}であるまいと, {adj(*na*). stem/N}	whether
daroo, Sinf.	だろう, Sinf.	will
daroo to {adj(*na*). stem/N} {dearoo/daroo} to, {adj(*na*). stem/N}	だろうと{adj(*na*). stem/N}{であろう/だろう}と,{adj(*na*). stem/N}	whether
dasaku	駄作	rubbish
dasha	打者	batter
dasu	出す	issue
dasu	出す	produce
dasu	出す	serve
dasu	出す	shoot
datta	だった	was
datta	だった	were
datte	だって	even
de	で	at
de	で	by
de	で	for
de	で	from
de	で	in
de	で	on
de	で	through
de	で	via
de	で	with
de-ai	出会い	encounter
dearoo to {adj(*na*). stem/N} dearumai to, {adj(*na*). stem/N}	であろうと{adj(*na*). stem/N}であるまいと, {adj(*na*). stem/N}	whether
dearoo to {adj(*na*). stem/N} {dearoo/daroo} to, {adj(*na*). stem/N}	であろうと{adj(*na*). stem/N}{であろう/だろう}と, {adj(*na*). stem/N}	whether
dearu	である	am
dearu	である	be
dearu	である	is
de-au	出会う	encounter
de-dokoro	出所	source
deeta	データ	data
deeto	デート	date
deeto no aite	デートの相手	date
deeto-suru	デートする	date
degozaimasu	でございます	am
degozaimasu	でございます	be
deguchi	出口	exit
deirassharu	でいらっしゃる	are
deirassharu	でいらっしゃる	be
de-iri-guchi	出入り口	door
deki-goto	出来事	event
deki-goto	出来事	incident
deki-goto	出来事	occurrence
dekinai	出来ない	unable
dekinai, Sinf. tame (ni)	出来ない, Sinf.ため(に)	prevent
dekiru	出来る	can[1]
dekiru	出来る	possible
dekiru-dake	出来るだけ	possibly
dekiru, Vinf. nonpast koto ga	出来る, Vinf. nonpastことが	can[1]
dekita N	できたN	made
dekite iru	できている	consist
deko-boko no N	凸凹のN	rough
deko-boko no N	凸凹のN	rugged
deko-boko no N	凸凹のN	uneven
demae	出前	delivery
demo	でも	but
demo	デモ	demonstration
demo	でも	even
demo	でも	however
demo	でも	though
de mo naku {N/adj(*na*). stem} de mo nai, {N/adj(*na*). stem}	でもなく{N/adj(*na*). stem}でもない, {N/adj(*na*). stem}	neither
demonsutoreeshon	デモンストレーション	demonstration
demo o suru	デモをする	demonstrate
de nai to, (moshi) {adj(*na*). stem/N}	でないと, (もし){adj(*na*). stem/N}	unless
de nakereba, (moshi) {adj(*na*). stem/N}	でなければ, (もし){adj(*na*). stem/N}	unless
denchi	電池	battery
denchi	電池	cell
denden-mushi	でんでんむし	snail
dengon	伝言	message
denki	電気	electricity
denki	電気	light[1]
denki-kamisori	電気かみそり	shaver
denki no N	電気のN	electric
denki no N	電気のN	electrical
denki-sutando	電気スタンド	lamp
denkyuu	電球	bulb
Denmaaku-go	デンマーク語	Danish

Denmaaku-go no N	デンマーク語のN	Danish
Denmaaku-jin no N	デンマーク人のN	Danish
Denmaaku no N	デンマークのN	Danish
de, ((-no) naka)	で, ((〜の)中)	in
denpa	伝ぱ	spread
denpa-suru	伝ぱする	transmit
denpoo	電報	cable
denpoo	電報	telegram
denpoo	電報	telegraph
denpoo	電報	wire
denpoo o utsu	電報を打つ	wire
densen	電線	wire
densetsu	伝説	legend
densha	電車	train
denshi-keesan-ki	電子計算機	computer
denshi-koogaku	電子工学	electronics
denshi-koogyoo	電子工業	electronics
denshin-ki	電信機	telegraph
denshi no N	電子のN	electronic
denshoo	伝承	tradition
dentatsu	伝達	communication
dentatsu-sha	伝達者	transmitter
dentatsu-suru	伝達する	communicate
dentatsu-suru	伝達する	convey
dentoo	電灯	light[1]
dentoo	伝統	tradition
dentoo-tekina	伝統的な	traditional
denwa	電話	call
denwa	電話	phone
denwa	電話	ring[2]
denwa	電話	telephone
(denwa-)kookan-shu	(電話)交換手	operator
denwa o kakeru	電話をかける	dial
denwa o kakeru	電話をかける	phone
denwa-suru	電話する	call
denwa-suru	電話する	dial
denwa-suru	電話する	phone
depaato	デパート	department store
derikeetona	デリケートな	delicate
deru	出る	attend
deru	出る	graduate
deru	出る	leave
deru	出る	shoot
deru	出る	up
deshita	でした	was
deshita	でした	were
deshoo, Sinf.	だろう, Sinf.	will
deshoo, Sinf.	でしょう, Sinf.	would
desu	です	am
desu	です	be
desu	です	is
desukara	ですから	therefore
desuku	デスク	desk
detarame	でたらめ	random
detaramena	でたらめな	random
detarame no N	でたらめのN	random
dete-kuru	出てくる	emerge
Detoroito	デトロイト	Detroit
dewaarimasen	ではありません	aren't
dewaarimasen	ではありません	isn't
dewaarimasen deshita	ではありませんでした	wasn't
dewaarimasen deshita	ではありませんでした	weren't
dewanai	ではない	aren't
dewanai	ではない	isn't
dewanai, {adj(*na*). stem/N}	ではない, {adj(*na*). stem/N}	not
dewanakatta	ではなかった	wasn't
dewanakatta	ではなかった	weren't
dezaato	デザート	dessert
dezain	デザイン	design
dezain-suru	デザインする	design
dibeeto	ディベート	debate
difensu	ディフェンス	defense
diiraa	ディーラー	dealer
direkutaa	ディレクター	director
disuku	ディスク	disk
do	度	degree
do	〜度	time
doa	ドア	door
dochira	どちら	where[1]
dochira	どちら	which[1]
dochira-ka	どちらか	either
dochira(-ka) no N	どちら(か)のN	either
dochira ka to ieba	どちらかと言えば	rather
dochira-mo…neg.	どちらも…neg.	either
dochira no hito	どちらの人	which[1]
dochira no N	どちらのN	which[1]
dochira no N mo…neg.	どちらのNも…neg.	either
dochira prt. V*te* mo	どちらprt. V*te*も	either
dodai	土台	foundation
dogi-magi-saseru	どぎまぎさせる	embarrass
Doitsu	ドイツ	Germany

Doitsu-go	ドイツ語	German
Doitsu-jin	ドイツ人	German
Doitsu no N	ドイツのN	German
dojoo	土壌	soil
doko	どこ	where[1]
doko de mo…neg.	どこでも…neg.	nowhere
doko ({de/ni}) demo	どこ({で/に})でも	everywhere
doko-ka hoka no tokoro {de/ni/e} どこかほかの所{で/に/へ}		elsewhere
doko-ka {ni/e/de}	どこか{に/へ/で}	anywhere
doko-ka ({ni/e/de})	どこか({に/へ/で})	somewhere
doko-ka yoso {de/ni/e} どこかよそ{で/に/へ}		elsewhere
doko {ni/e} demo	どこ({に/へ})でも	anywhere
doko ({ni/e}) mo	どこ({に/へ})も	anywhere
doko {ni/e} mo {ikanai/konai} どこ{に/へ}も{行かない/来ない}		nowhere
doko ni mo…neg.	どこにも…neg.	nowhere
doko (prt.) demo	どこ(prt.)でも	wherever
doko+prt. V*te* mo	どこ+prt.V*te*も	wherever
doku	毒	poison
doku no N	毒のN	poisonous
dokuritsu	独立	independence
dokuritsu-shin ga tsuyoi	独立心が強い	independent
dokuritsu-shita N	独立したN	independent
dokuritsu-shite iru (N)	独立している(N)	independent
dokusha	読者	reader
dokushin no N	独身のN	single
dokusho	読書	reading
dokusoo-tekina	独創的な	original
dokutokuna	独特な	particular
dokutokuna	独特な	peculiar
dokutokuna	独特な	proper
dokutokuna	独特な	special
dokutokuna	独特な	unique
dokutoku no N	独特のN	particular
dokutoku no N	独特のN	peculiar
dokutoku no N	独特のN	proper
dokutoku no N	独特のN	special
dokutoku no N	独特のN	unique
domoru	どもる	stumble
donaru	怒鳴る	shout
donaru	怒鳴る	shout
donburi	どんぶり	bowl
donchoo	どんちょう	curtain
don-don to tataku	どんどんとたたく	pound[2]
donna…demo	どんな…でも	any
donna N	どんなN	what[1]
donna N demo	どんなNでも	whatever
donna N+prt. V*te* mo	どんなN+prt.V*te*も	whatever
donna-ni…{V/adj./cop.}*te*} mo どんなに…{V/adj./cop.}*te*}も		however
dono hito	どの人	which[1]
dono N	どのN	which[1]
doo	どう	how
doo	胴	trunk
doobutsu	動物	animal
doobutsu	動物	creature
doobutsu-en	動物園	zoo
doo-doo to shita N	堂々としたN	stately
doofuu-suru	同封する	enclose
doogi	道義	principle
doogi-go	同義語	synonym
doogi ni sansei-suru	動議に賛成する	second[1]
doogu	道具	instrument
doogu	道具	tool
doogu	道具	utensil
doogu isshiki	道具一式	outfit
doogyoo-sha	同業者	trade
dooi	同意	agreement
dooi-go	同意語	synonym
dooi-suru	同意する	agree
dooi-suru	同意する	consent
doo-jidai no N	同時代のN	contemporary
dooji no N	同時のN	simultaneous
doojoo	同情	feeling
doojoo	同情	pity
doojoo	同情	sympathy
dooka	どうか	please
dooke(-yakusha)	道化(役者)	clown
dookoo	動向	wind[1]
dookoo-suru	同行する	accompany
dookutsu	洞くつ	cave
dookyuu-sei	同級生	classmate
dookyuu-sei	同級生	fellow
doomoona	どう猛な	fierce
doo nan desu ka	どうなんですか	well[2]
doo ni ka (koo ni ka)	どうにか(こうにか)	somehow
doonyuu-suru	導入する	introduce
doori ni awanai (N)	道理に合わない(N)	unreasonable
dooro	道路	road
dooro-waki	道路わき	roadside
dooryoo	同僚	associate
dooryoo	同僚	mate
dooryoo	同僚	peer
dooseiaisha no N	同性愛者のN	gay

dooshi	動詞	verb
doo-shite	どうして	why
dooshitsu-sha	同室者	roommate
doo-shiyoo-mo-nai	どうしようもない	hopeless
doosoo-kai	同窓会	reunion
doo yatte	どうやって	how
dooyoona	同様な	parallel
dooyoo-saseru	動揺させる	upset
doozen da	同然だ	virtually
doozo	どうぞ	please
doozo, doozo	どうぞ、どうぞ	sure
dorafuto	ドラフト	draft
doraibaa	ドライバー	driver
doraibaa	ドライバー	screwdriver
doraibu	ドライブ	drive
dorama	ドラマ	drama
dorama	ドラマ	theater
doramachikkuna	ドラマチックな	dramatic
dore	どれ	which[1]
dore-mo…neg.	どれも…neg.	none
doresu	ドレス	dress
doriru	ドリル	drill
doriru de ana o akeru	ドリルで穴を開ける	drill
doriru o saseru	ドリルをさせる	drill
doroboo	泥棒	robber
doroboo	泥棒	thief
doru	ドル	dollar
doryoku	努力	effort
dosatto iu oto	どさっという音	thump
dosha-buri da, (ame ga)	どしゃ降りだ, (雨が)	pour
doshin	どしん	bang
doshin-doshin to aruku	どしんどしんと歩く	tramp
doshin-doshin to V	どしんどしんとV	thump
doshin to iu oto	どしんという音	thump
doshin to oku	どしんと置く	bang
doshin to tsuku	どしんと突く	thump
dosun	どすん	bang
dota-dota to aruku	どたどたと歩く	tramp
dotchi	どっち	which[1]
dotchi-ka	どっちか	either
dotchi(-ka) no N	どっち(か)のN	either
dotchi-mo…neg.	どっちも…neg.	either
dotchi no hito	どっちの人	which[1]
dotchi no N	どっちのN	which[1]
dotchi no N mo…neg.	どっちのNも…neg.	either

dotchi prt. V*te* mo	どっちprt. V*te*も	either
dotoo	怒涛	rage
dotto	ドット	dot
dotto nagare-komu	どっと流れ込む	pour
doyoo(-bi)	土曜(日)	Saturday

E

e	絵	drawing
e	柄	handle
e	絵	painting
e	絵	picture
e	へ、	to
Eberesuto-san	エベレスト山	Everest
ebi	えび	shrimp
eda	枝	branch
ee	ええ	sure
ee	ええ	yes
eejenshii	エージェンシー	agency
eejento	エージェント	agent
eekaa	エーカー	acre
eeto	ええと	well[2]
egaku	描く	draw
egaku	描く	represent
egao	笑顔	smile
eien ni	永遠に	forever
eien no N	永遠のN	eternal
eiga	映画	film
eiga	映画	movie
eiga	映画	picture
eiga-kan	映画館	theater
(eiga-)satsuei-jo	(映画)撮影所	studio
eigo	英語	English
eigo no N	英語のN	English
Eikoku	英国	England
Eikoku-jin	英国人	British
Eikoku-jin	英国人	Englishman
Eikoku-jin no N	英国人のN	British
Eikoku no N	英国のN	British
Eikoku no N	英国のN	English
eikyoo	影響	influence
eikyoo o oyobosu	影響を及ぼす	influence
eikyoo-ryoku	影響力	influence
eikyoo-suru	影響する	affect
eikyoo-suru	影響する	influence
eikyuu ni	永久に	forever
eikyuu ni	永久に	permanently
eikyuu no N	永久のN	permanent

eisei	衛星	satellite
eiyuu	英雄	hero
eizoo	映像	picture
Ejiputo	エジプト	Egypt
Ejiputo-go	エジプト語	Egyptian
Ejiputo-jin no N	エジプト人のN	Egyptian
Ejiputo no N	エジプトのN	Egyptian
Ejison	エジソン	Edison
e-kaki	絵かき	painter
eki	益	profit
eki	駅	station
ekisupaato	エキスパート	expert
ekitai	液体	fluid
ekitai (no N)	液体(のN)	liquid
ekkusu-sen	X線	X-ray
eko-hiiki-suru	えこひいきする	favor
emono	獲物	game
e, N	へ, N	toward(s)
en	円	circle
en	円	yen
enban	円盤	disk
enchoo	延長	extension
enchoo-sen	延長戦	overtime
enchoo-suru	延長する	prolong
enchuu	円柱	column
endai	演題	theme
endan	演壇	platform
endoo(-mame)	えんどう(豆)	pea
enerugii	エネルギー	energy
enerugii	エネルギー	vigor
enerugisshuna	エネルギッシュな	energetic
engeki	演劇	drama
engeki	演劇	play
engeki	演劇	stage
engeki	演劇	theater
engi	演技	acting
engi	演技	performance
engi ga adj.	演技がadj.	play
enjeru	エンジェル	angel
enjin	エンジン	engine
enjin ga tomatte shimau	エンジンが止まってしまう	stall
enjinia	エンジニア	engineer
enjin o teishi-saseru	エンジンを停止させる	stall
enjin-teishi	エンジン停止	stall
enjiru	演じる	perform
enjiru	演じる	play

enjo	援助	aid
enjo	援助	assistance
enjo-suru	援助する	aid
enkai	宴会	party
enkei-gekijoo	円形劇場	bowl
enkei no N	円形のN	circular
enki	延期	stay
enki-suru	延期する	delay
enkyokuna	えん曲な	indirect
enogu	絵の具	paint
e, (〈-no〉 ue)	へ, (〈～の〉上)	up
enpitsu	鉛筆	pencil
enryo	遠慮	modesty
enryo-suru	遠慮する	hesitate
ensoku	遠足	picnic
ensoo	演奏	performance
ensoo ga adj.	演奏がadj.	play
ensoo-ka	演奏家	player
ensoo-sha	演奏者	player
ensoo-suru	演奏する	perform
ensui no N	塩水のN	saltwater
ensuto	エンスト	stall
en-suto-suru	エンストする	stall
entotsu	煙突	chimney
entotsu	煙突	stack
enzeru	エンゼル	angel
enzetsu	演説	address
enzetsu	演説	speech
enzetsu o suru	演説をする	speak
enzetsu-sha	演説者	speaker
e o kaku	絵をかく	paint
e o kaku {koto/no}	絵をかく{こと/の}	painting
eppei	閲兵	parade
epuron	エプロン	apron
eraba-reta N	選ばれたN	select
erabu	選ぶ	choose
erabu	選ぶ	elect
erabu	選ぶ	pick
erabu	選ぶ	select
erabu	選ぶ	take
erai	偉い	great
eranda {mono/hito/tokoro}	選んだ{物/人/ところ}	choice
erebeetaa	エレベーター	elevator
eregantona	エレガントな	elegant
erekutoronikusu	エレクトロニクス	electronics
eri	襟	collar
erinuki no N	えり抜きのN	select

eru	得る	acquire
eru	得る	gain
eru	得る	obtain
Erusaremu	エルサレム	Jerusalem
esa	えさ	bait
esa	えさ	food
esa o yaru	えさをやる	feed
eshaku-suru	会釈する	nod
essee	エッセー	essay
Esukimoo-jin	エスキモー人	Eskimo
Esukimoo no N	エスキモーのN	Eskimo
eyoo to tsutomeru	得ようと努める	reach

F

fan	ファン	fan[2]
fasshon	ファッション	fashion
ferii(-booto)	フェリー(ボート)	ferry
fiito	フィート	foot
Finrando	フィンランド	Finland
Firaderufia	フィラデルフィア	Philadelphia
firumu	フィルム	film
fooku	フォーク	fork
fuan	不安	anxiety
fuan	不安	fear
fuanna	不安な	uneasy
fu-annai no N	不案内のN	unfamiliar
fubenna	不便な	inconvenient
fubuki	吹雪	snowstorm
fuchi	縁	border
fuchi	縁	edge
fuchi	縁	frame
fuchi	縁	rim
fuchi-nashi-booshi	縁なし帽子	cap
fu-chuuina	不注意な	careless
fu-chuuina	不注意な	thoughtless
fu-chuuini-mo	不注意にも	carelessly
fuda	札	tag
fudan	普段	usually
fuda o tsukeru	札を付ける	tag
fude-zukai	筆使い	touch
fue	笛	whistle
fue o fuku	笛を吹く	whistle
fueru	増える	grow
fueru	増える	increase
fueru	増える	swell
fuhei	不平	complaint
fuhei o iu	不平を言う	complain
fuhen no N	不変のN	constant
fuhen no N	不変のN	permanent
fuhen-tekina	普遍的な	universal
fu-hitsuyoona	不必要な	unnecessary
fu-hon'i-nagara	不本意ながら	unwillingly
fui ni	不意に	suddenly
fujin	婦人	lady
fujin	夫人	Mrs.
fujin	婦人	woman
fukai	深い	deep
fukai	深い	profound
fukai	深い	thick
fukai kanashi-mi	深い悲しみ	grief
fukai kanmei o ataeru (N)	深い感銘を与える(N)	impressive
fu-kanoona	不可能な	impossible
fuka-sa	深さ	depth
fukasu	ふかす	steam
fu-keiki	不景気	depression
fu-keikina	不景気な	slow
fu-keizaina	不経済な	wasteful
fukeru	ふける	sink
fuketsuna	不潔な	filthy
fu-kigenna	不機嫌な	sour
fukin	ふきん	cloth
fukin	付近	neighborhood
fukin	付近	vicinity
fu-kisokuna	不規則な	irregular
fuki-tobasu	吹き飛ばす	blow
fuki-tsukeru	吹きつける	spray
fukkoo	復興	restoration
fukkoo-suru	復興する	restore
fukku	フック	hook
fukoo	不幸	misery
fu-kooheina	不公平な	unequal
fukoona	不幸な	unfortunate
fukoona	不幸な	unhappy
fukooni-mo	不幸にも	unfortunately
fuku	吹く	blow
fuku	服	clothes
fuku	服	wear
fuku	ふく	wipe
fukugen	復{元/原}	restoration
fukugen-suru	復{元/原}する	restore
fuku isshiki	服一式	outfit
fukuji	服地	cloth
fukujuu-saseru	服従させる	subject
fukujuu-suru	服従する	subject

fukumu	含む	contain
fuku o ki-seru	服を着せる	dress
fuku o shitateru	服を仕立てる	tailor
fukuramu	膨らむ	swell
fukuranda N	膨らんだN	swollen
fukuro	袋	bag
fukuro	袋	sack
fukuroo	ふくろう	owl
fukusei-suru	複製する	reproduce
fukusha	複写	reproduction
fukusha-suru	複写する	reproduce
fukushi	副詞	adverb
fukushi	福祉	welfare
fukushuu-suru	復習する	review
fukusoo	服装	dress
fukusoo	服装	outfit
fukusuu no N	複数のN	plural
fukutsu no N	不屈のN	stout
fukutsuu	腹痛	stomachache
fukuyokana	ふくよかな	plump
fukuzatsuna	複雑な	complex
fukuzatsuna	複雑な	complicated
fukyoo(-ji)	不況(時)	slack
fukyuu-shita N	普及したN	widespread
fukyuu-shite iru (N)	普及している(N)	widespread
fu-meiryoona	不明瞭な	vague
fumi-tsukeru	踏み付ける	tramp
fumoo no N	不毛のN	barren
fumoto	ふもと	bottom
-fun	〜分	minute
funa-nori	船乗り	seaman
fu-narena	不慣れな	unfamiliar
funa-tabi	船旅	voyage
funbetsu	分別	sense
funbetsu ga aru N	分別があるN	sensible
fune	船	boat
fune	船	ship
fune	船	vessel
fune de iku	船で行く	sail
fune de wataru	船で渡る	sail
fune ni tsumu	船に積む	ship
fun'iki	雰囲気	atmosphere
fun'iki	雰囲気	mood
funkyuu-suru	紛糾する	tangle
funmatsu	粉末	powder
funmu-ki	噴霧器	spray
funsai	粉砕	smash
funshitsu	紛失	loss
funsoo	紛争	trouble
funsui	噴水	fountain
funtoo	奮闘	struggle
funtoo-suru, (Vvol. to shite)	奮闘する, (Vvol.として)	struggle
Furansu	フランス	France
Furansu-go	フランス語	French
Furansu-jin	フランス人	French
Furansu-jin	フランス人	Frenchman
Furansu no N	フランスのN	French
furasuko	フラスコ	flask
fureru	触れる	mention
fureru	触れる	touch
fureru-koto	触れること	reference
furi	ふり	pretense
furi-kakeru	振り掛ける	sprinkle
furi-kata	振り方	swing
furi-mawasu	振り回す	swing
furi-mawasu koto	振り回すこと	swing
furi-muku	振り向く	turn
furina	不利な	handicap
furina ten	不利な点	drawback
furi o suru	ふりをする	assume
furi o suru, Sinf.	ふりをする, Sinf.	pretend
furo	ふろ	bath
furo-ba	ふろ場	bathroom
furo ni hairu	ふろに入る	bathe
furonto	フロント	reception desk
furonto-garasu	フロントガラス	windshield
furo-oke	ふろおけ	tub
Furorida	フロリダ	Florida
furu	降る	fall
furu	振る	shake
furu	振る	swing
furu	振る	wave
furue	震え	tremble
furueru	震える	shake
furueru	震える	shiver
furueru	震える	tremble
furueru	震える	vibrate
furue-saseru	震えさせる	vibrate
furui	古い	old
furui	古い	old-fashioned
furui-tata-seru	奮い立たせる	inspire
furu koto	振ること	swing
furu koto	振ること	wave
furumai	振るまい	behavior
furumai	振るまい	conduct

furumau	振るまう	behave
furumau	振るまう	conduct
furu-sato	ふるさと	home
furu-sato	ふるさと	hometown
fusa	房	bunch
fusa	房	cluster
fusa	房	strand
fusagu	ふさぐ	block
fusagu	ふさぐ	stop
fusai	負債	debt
fusawashii	ふさわしい	proper
fusegu, {Vinf. nonpast no/N} o	防ぐ, {Vinf. nonpastの/N}を	prevent
fusei	不正	wrong
fuseina	不正な	wicked
fuseina	不正な	wrong
fuseini	不正に	wrong
fusei no N	不正のN	wrong
fushi	節	tune
fushigi	不思議	mystery
fushigi	不思議	wonder
fushigina	不思議な	mysterious
fushigina	不思議な	strange
fushigina	不思議な	wonderful
fu-shinsetsuna	不親切な	unfriendly
fushoo-saseru	負傷させる	wound[1]
fusoku-shite iru (N)	不足している(N)	scarce
fusoku-shite iru (N)	不足している(N)	short
futa	ふた	cap
futa	ふた	lid
futa-go	双子	twin
futa-go no N	双子のN	twin
futari	二人	couple
futatabi	再び	again
futatsu (+counter) (no N)	二つ(+counter)(のN)	two
fu-teiki no N	不定期のN	occasional
fu-tekitoona	不適当な	unequal
fu-tekitoona	不適当な	wrong
futoi	太い	thick
futoi tsuna	太い綱	cable
futoo	ふ頭	pier
futoo	ふ頭	wharf
futoona	不当な	unreasonable
futo-sa	太さ	thickness
futotta N	太ったN	fat
futotte iru (N)	太っている(N)	fat
fu-tsuriai no N	不釣り合いのN	unequal
futsuu	普通	commonly
futsuu	普通	usually
futsuu {denai/janai} (N)	普通{でない/じゃない}(N)	unusual
futsuu denai (N)	普通でない(N)	abnormal
futsuu no N	普通のN	common
futsuu no N	普通のN	normal
futsuu no N	普通のN	ordinary
futsuu no N	普通のN	usual
fuu	風	manner
-fuu	～風	fashion
fuuchoo	風潮	current
fuudo	風土	climate
fuufu	夫婦	couple
fuu-gawarina	風変わりな	odd
fuu-giri	封切り	release
fuu-giru	封切る	release
fuujiru	封じる	seal[2]
fuukei	風景	landscape
fuukei	風景	scenery
fuukei-ga	風景画	landscape
fuumi	風味	flavor
fuunna	不運な	unfortunate
fuun-ni-mo	不運にも	unfortunately
fuusen	風船	balloon
fuusha	風車	windmill
fuushuu	風習	practice
fuutoo	封筒	envelope
fuyasu	増やす	increase
fuyoo	扶養	support
fuyoo-kazoku	扶養家族	dependent
fuyoo-suru	扶養する	support
fuyu	冬	winter
fu-yukaina	不愉快な	obnoxious
fu-yukaina	不愉快な	stink
fu-yukaina	不愉快な	ugly
fu-yukaina	不愉快な	uncomfortable
fu-yukaina	不愉快な	unpleasant
fuyuuna	富裕な	wealthy
fu-zoroi no N	不ぞろいのN	irregular

G

ga	が	although
ga	が	but
ga	が	for
ga	が	though
-gachi da, V*masu*	～がちだ, V*masu*	subject

-gachi da, V*masu*	～がちだ, V*masu*	tend
-gachina, V*masu*	～がちな, V*masu*	apt
gachoo	が鳥	goose
gai	害	harm
-gai	～街	quarter
gaido	ガイド	guide
gaijin	外人	foreigner
gaikan	外観	surface
gaikan	概観	survey
gaikan-suru	概観する	survey
gaiken	外見	appearance
gaiken-joo dake no N	外見上だけのN	apparent
gaikoku-jin	外国人	alien
gaikoku-jin	外国人	foreigner
gaikoku no N	外国のN	alien
gaikoku no N	外国のN	foreign
gaikoo	外交	diplomacy
gaikoo-kan	外交官	diplomat
gaikotsu	がい骨	skeleton
gaimen	外面	surface
gainen	概念	concept
gairyaku	概略	sketch
gaitoo	外とう	coat
gaka	画家	painter
gake	がけ	cliff
gakka-choo	学科長	chairman
gakkai	学会	social
gakka-naiyoo	学科内容	program
gakkari-saseru	がっかりさせる	discourage
gakki	学期	session
gakki	学期	term
gakkoo	学校	school[1]
gaku	額	amount
gaku	額	frame
gaku	額	sum
gakubu	学部	school[1]
gaku-buchi	額縁	frame
gakuchoo	学長	president
gakufu	楽譜	music
gakufu	楽譜	score
gakui	学位	degree
gakuin	学院	academy
gakumon	学問	learning
gakumon	学問	scholarship
gakumon (no) bun'ya	学問(の)分野	discipline
gakunen	学年	grade
gakusei	学生	student
gakusha	学者	scholar

gakusha	学者	student
gakushi-in	学士院	academy
gakushiki	学識	scholarship
gakushoo	楽章	movement
gakushuu	学習	study
gakutai	楽隊	band
gaman	我慢	patience
gaman-suru	我慢する	patient
gaman-suru	我慢する	stand
gaman-suru	我慢する	stomach
gaman-zuyoi	我慢強い	patient
gami-gami donaru	がみがみどなる	thunder
gan	がん	cancer
ganchiku ga aru (N)	含蓄がある(N)	pregnant
ganjitsu	元日	New Year's Day
ganjoona	頑丈な	stout
ganjoona	頑丈な	strong
ganjoona	頑丈な	sturdy
gankin	元金	principal
gankin no N	元金のN	principal
gankona	頑固な	persistent
gankona	頑固な	rigid
gankona	頑固な	stubborn
gankona	頑固な	tough
gankyoona	頑強な	stubborn
gankyoona	頑強な	tough
ganpeki	岸壁	wharf
gan'yaku	丸薬	pill
gappei	合併	union
gappei-shita N	合併したN	united
gara	柄	pattern
garakuta	がらくた	junk
garakuta	がらくた	rubbish
garakuta	がらくた	stuff
garasu	ガラス	glass
gareeji	ガレージ	garage
gashi-suru	餓死する	starve
gasorin	ガソリン	gas[2]
gasorin	ガソリン	gasoline
gasorin	ガソリン	petrol
gasorin-sutando	ガソリンスタンド	garage
gasshiri-shita N	がっしりしたN	rugged
gasshiri-shita N	がっしりしたN	solid
gasshiri-shita N	がっしりしたN	square
gasshiri-shita N	がっしりしたN	stout
gasshiri-shite iru (N)	がっしりしている(N)	rugged
gasshiri-shite iru (N)	がっしりしている(N)	solid
gasshoo	合唱	chorus

gasu	ガス	gas[1]
(gasu-)renji	(ガス)レンジ	stove
gasu-tanku	ガスタンク	tank[1]
-gawa	〜側	side
gazoo	画像	picture
geemu	ゲーム	game
geijutsu	芸術	art
geijutsu-tekina	芸術的な	artistic
geka	外科	surgery
geka-byooin	外科病院	surgery
geki	劇	drama
geki	劇	play
gekido	激怒	rage
gekijoo	激情	passion
gekijoo	劇場	theater
gekirei	激励	cheer
geki-tekina	劇的な	dramatic
gekitotsu-suru	激突する	slam
gekkoo	月光	moonlight
gekkyuu-tori no N	月給取りのN	salaried
gen	弦	string
genba	現場	scene
genbun	原文	text
gendai no	現代の	contemporary
gendai no N	現代のN	current
gendai no N	現代のN	modern
gengo	言語	language
gengo	言語	tongue
gen'in	原因	cause
gen'in to naru	原因となる	cause
gen'in to naru (N)	原因となる(N)	responsible
genjitsu	現実	reality
genjitsu-mi	現実味	reality
genjuuna	厳重な	severe
genkai	限界	limit
genkakuna	厳格な	rigid
genkan	玄関	hall
genki	元気	energy
genki ga nai (N)	元気がない(N)	blue
genkin	現金	cash
genkina	元気な	energetic
genkina	元気な	fine
genkina	元気な	fit
genkina	元気な	healthy
genkina	元気な	vigorous
genkina	元気な	well[2]
genkin ni {kaeru/suru}	現金に{替える/する}	cash

genki-zukeru	元気づける	cheer
genkoo	原稿	draft
genkoo	原稿	manuscript
genkoo o kaku	原稿を書く	draft
genkyuu-suru koto	言及すること	reference
genmei-suru	言明する	declare
genmei-suru	言明する	protest
genmei-suru	言明する	state
gen o haru	弦を張る	string
genpon	原本	original
genri	原理	principle
gensaku	原作	original
gensen	源泉	spring
genshi	原子	atom
genshi-kaku no N	原子核のN	nuclear
genshi no N	原子のN	atomic
genshi no N	原始のN	primitive
genshi-ryoku no N	原子力のN	nuclear
genshi-tekina	原始的な	primitive
genshoo	減少	decrease
genshoo	現象	phenomenon
genshukuna	厳粛な	solemn
genso	元素	element
gensoku	原則	principle
genson no N	現存のN	existing
gen'ya	原野	wilderness
genzai	現在	now
genzai	現在	present[1]
genzai	現在	presently
genzai no N	現在のN	present[1]
genzon no N	現存のN	existing
genzoo	現像	development
genzoo-suru	現像する	develop
geta	げた	clog
getsuyoo(-bi)	月曜(日)	Monday
gia	ギア	gear
gichoo	議長	chairman
gijutsu	技術	technique
gijutsu	技術	technology
gijutsu-tekina	技術的な	technical
gikai	議会	parliament
giketsu-suru	議決する	vote
gikochinai	ぎこちない	awkward
gikoo	技巧	technique
-gimi, {Vmasu/N}	〜気味, {Vmasu/N}	touch
gimon	疑問	doubt
gimon da, 〈-ka〉 doo ka	疑問だ, 〈〜か〉どうか	doubt

gimu	義務	duty
gimu	義務	obligation
gimu-tekina	義務的な	obligatory
gin	銀	silver
ginki	銀器	silver
ginkoo	銀行	bank[1]
ginoo	技能	craft
ginoo	技能	skill
giri	義理	duty
giri	義理	obligation
giri no N	義理のN	obligatory
Girisha	ギリシア	Greece
Girisha-go	ギリシア語	Greek
Girisha-go no N	ギリシア語のN	Greek
Girisha-jin	ギリシア人	Greek
Girisha-jin no N	ギリシア人のN	Greek
Girisha no N	ギリシアのN	Greek
giron	議論	argument
giron	議論	discussion
giron-suru	議論する	argue
giron-suru	議論する	debate
giron-suru	議論する	discuss
gisei	犠牲	sacrifice
gisei ni suru	犠牲にする	sacrifice
gisei-sha	犠牲者	victim
giseki	議席	seat
gishi	技師	engineer
gitaa	ギター	guitar
go	語	word
-go	～語	language
go-ban-me no N	五番目のN	fifth
gochamaze ni suru	ごちゃ混ぜにする	scramble
go-chisoo	ごちそう	feast
go-chisoo-suru	ごちそうする	treat
go+counter me no N	五+counter目のN	fifth
go (+counter) (no N)	五(+counter)(のN)	five
goei	護衛	guard
go-gatsu	五月	May
gogo	午後	afternoon
gogo	午後	p.m.
gohan	御飯	meal
gohan	御飯	rice
goi	語い	vocabulary
goi-hyoo	語い表	vocabulary
go-juu (+counter) (no N)	五十(+counter)(のN)	fifty
gokai	誤解	misunderstanding
gokai-suru	誤解する	mistake
gokai-suru	誤解する	misunderstand
gokan	語幹	stem
-gokochi ga yokunai (N), V*masu*	～心地がよくない(N), V*masu*	uncomfortable
gomakasu	ごまかす	cheat
gomi	ごみ	garbage
gomi	ごみ	rubbish
gomi	ごみ	trash
gomu	ゴム	rubber
gomu-seihin	ゴム製品	rubber
-go ni	～後に	later
-goo	～号	number
goodoo no N	合同のN	joint
goohoo-tekina	合法的な	legal
gooinna	強引な	pushy
goojoona	強情な	stubborn
gookaku	合格	pass
gookaku-suru	合格する	pass
gookan	強かん	violation
gookan-suru	強かんする	violate
gookei	合計	total
gookei (ga) ⟨-ni⟩ naru	合計(が)⟨～に⟩なる	total
goori-tekina	合理的な	rational
gooru	ゴール	goal
-goo-sen	～号線	route
gootoo	強盗	robber
goraku	娯楽	amusement
goraku	娯楽	entertainment
goraku	娯楽	recreation
goraku	娯楽	sport
gorin-taikai	五輪大会	Olympic Games
-goro	～ごろ	about
-goro	～ごろ	around
gorufu	ゴルフ	golf
goshi-goshi arau	ごしごし洗う	scrub
goshi-goshi kosuru	ごしごしこする	scrub
goshippu	ゴシップ	gossip
go-shujin	ご主人	husband
goten	御殿	palace
-goto ni	～ごとに	a
-goto (ni)	～ごと(に)	every
gozaimasu	ございます	are
gozaimasu	ございます	be
gozen	午前	a.m.
guai ga warui	具合が悪い	wrong
guai waruku	具合悪く	wrong
gunbu	軍部	military
gunji-	軍事～	military

gunjin	軍人	serviceperson
gunji-ryoku	軍事力	strength
gunkan	軍艦	warship
gunshuu	群衆	crowd
guntai	軍隊	armed forces
guntai	軍隊	military
guntai	軍隊	troop
gurafu	グラフ	graph
gura-gura-shita N	ぐらぐらしたN	loose
gura-gura-shite iru (N)	ぐらぐらしている(N)	loose
-gurai	～ぐらい	about
-gurai	～ぐらい	somewhere
guramu	グラム	gram
gurasu	グラス	glass
guree no N	グレーのN	gray
guriin (no N)	グリーン(のN)	green
guru-guru maita mono	ぐるぐる巻いた物	coil
guru-guru mawaru	ぐるぐる回る	whirl
guru-guru mawasu	ぐるぐる回す	whirl
gurutto mawaru	ぐるっと回る	swing
guruupu	グループ	group
gutai-tekina	具体的な	concrete
gutto kandoo-saseru	ぐっと感動させる	thrill
guusuu no N	偶数のN	even
guuzen	偶然	chance
guuzen ni	偶然に	accidentally
guuzen+verb	偶然+verb	happen
gyaku	逆	reverse
gyaku ni	逆に	backward
gyaku ni suru	逆にする	reverse
gyaku no N	逆のN	reverse
gyaku no N	逆のN	wrong
gyangu	ギャング	gang
gyappu	ギャップ	gap
gyo-kai-rui	魚介類	seafood
gyokuza	玉座	throne
gyoo	行	line
gyoogi	行儀	manners
gyoogi-yoku suru	行儀よくする	behave
gyooji	行事	event
gyookan o akeru	行間を空ける	space
gyooko	凝固	setting
gyoomu	業務	affair
gyooretsu	行列	train
gyoosei	行政	administration
gyooseki	業績	achievement
gyooshi-suru	凝視する	regard
gyooten-saseru	仰天させる	startle
gyotto-suru	ぎょっとする	frighten
gyu tto nigiru	ぎゅっと握る	squeeze
gyuuniku	牛肉	beef
gyuunyuu	牛乳	milk
gyuunyuu-kakoo-jo	牛乳加工所	dairy
gyuunyuu o shiboru	牛乳をしぼる	milk

H

ha	刃	blade
ha	刃	edge
ha	葉	leaf
ha	葉	leaves
ha	歯	tooth
-ha	～派	family
haato	ハート	heart
haba	幅	width
haba ga hiroi	幅が広い	broad
haba ga hiroi	幅が広い	wide
haba-hiroi	幅広い	wide
habamu	阻む	restrain
habuke-ru, {(-no) o-kage de/Sinf. nonpast to}…	省ける, {(～の)おかげで/Sinf. nonpastと}…	save
habuku	省く	eliminate
habuku	省く	omit
ha-burashi	歯ブラシ	toothbrush
hachi	はち	bee
hachi	鉢	bowl
hachi-ban-me	八番目	eighth
hachi-ban-me no N	八番目のN	eighth
hachi (+counter) (no N)	八(+counter)のN	eight
hachi-gatsu	八月	August
hachi-juu (+counter) (no N)	八十(+counter)(のN)	eighty
hachi-mitsu	はちみつ	honey
hachi-no-su	はちの巣	hive
hachi-ue	鉢植え	plant
hachuu-rui	はちゅう類	reptile
hadaka ni suru	裸にする	strip
hadaka no N	裸のN	bare
hada o sasu yoona	肌を刺すような	biting
hadashi de	はだしで	barefoot
hadashi no N	はだしのN	barefoot
hae	はえ	fly
haeru	生える	grow

hagaki はがき postcard
hagane 鋼 steel
hagasu はがす peel
hagemasu 励ます encourage
hagemasu 励ます support
hagemu 励む attend
hageshii 激しい acute
hageshii 激しい intense
hageshii 激しい rough
hageshii 激しい towering
hageshii 激しい violent
hageshii kanjoo 激しい感情 passion
hageshii koi 激しい恋 passion
hageshiku 激しく bitterly
hageshiku 激しく sharply
hageshiku arasou 激しく争う struggle
hageshiku koofun-shita N 激しく興奮したN wild
hageshiku koofun-shite iru (N) 激しく興奮している(N) wild
hageshiku uchi-tsukeru 激しく打ちつける beat
hageshi-sa 激しさ violence
hageta N はげたN bald
haha 母 mother
haha-oya 母親 mother
hahen 破片 fragment
hahen 破片 piece
hai 灰 ash
hai 肺 lung
hai はい yes
-hai 〜杯 cup
haiboku 敗北 defeat
haibun 配分 distribution
haichi-suru 配置する set
haigo ni 背後に behind
hai-iro no N 灰色のN gray
hai-iro no N 灰色のN neutral
haikei 背景 background
haikei 背景 setting
haikei ni 背景に against
haiki-butsu 廃棄物 trash
haiki-butsu 廃棄物 waste
haikingu ハイキング hike
haikingu ni iku ハイキングに行く hike
haiki-suru 廃棄する scrap
hairu 入る enter
hairu 入る fit
hairu 入る include
hairu 入る join
hairu koto o yurusu 入ることを許す admit
ha-isha 歯医者 dentist
ha-ita 歯痛 toothache
haitatsu 配達 delivery
haitatsu-kuiki 配達区域 route
haitatsu-nin 配達人 carrier
haitatsu-suru 配達する deliver
haitte iru 入っている contain
haiyaku 配役 cast
haiyuu 俳優 actor
haiyuu 俳優 player
hai-zara 灰皿 ashtray
haji 恥 shame
hajimari 始まり beginning
hajimari 始まり origin
hajimari 始まり start
hajimaru 始まる begin
hajimaru 始まる open
hajimaru 始まる start
hajime 初め beginning
hajime 初め start
hajime 初め top
hajime ni 初めに first
hajime no N 初めのN first
hajime no N 初めのN initial
hajimeru 始める begin
hajimeru 始める open
hajimeru 始める start
hajimete 初めて first
hajimete no N 初めてのN first
hajimete no N 初めてのN new
haka 墓 grave
hakai 破壊 ruin
hakai-suru 破壊する destroy
hakai-suru 破壊する ruin
hakari はかり balance
hakari はかり scale[2]
hakari-shire-nai 計り知れない immense
hakaru はかる measure
hakaru はかる reckon
hakaru, mekata o はかる, 目方を weigh
hakaru, omo-sa o はかる, 重さを weigh
hakaru, taijuu o はかる, 体重を weigh
hakase 博士 doctor
hake はけ brush
haki-ke 吐き気 sickness

haki-soona	吐きそうな	sick
hakkan	発汗	perspiration
hakkan-suru	発汗する	perspire
hakken	発見	discovery
hakken-suru	発見する	detect
hakken-suru	発見する	discover
hakkiri iu	はっきり言う	pronounce
hakkiri kikoenai (N)	はっきり聞こえない(N)	vague
hakkiri mienai (N)	はっきり見えない(N)	vague
hakkiri-shita N	はっきりしたN	clear
hakkiri-shita N	はっきりしたN	distinct
hakkiri-shite inai (N)	はっきりしていない(N)	uncertain
hakkiri-shite iru (N)	はっきりしている(N)	clear
hakkiri to	はっきりと	clearly
hakkoo	発行	issue
hakkoo-busuu	発行部数	circulation
hakkoo-sha	発行者	publisher
hakkoo-suru	発行する	issue
hako	箱	box
hako	箱	case[1]
hakobu	運ぶ	carry
hakobu	運ぶ	transport
-hako, Japanese Number	～箱, Japanese Number	pack
haku, tsuba o	吐く, つばを	spit
haku	掃く	sweep
haku	はく	wear
hakuboku	白墨	chalk
hakubutsu-kan	博物館	museum
hakuchoo	白鳥	swan
hakujin no N	白人のN	white
hakusei ni suru	はく製にする	stuff
hakushi no N	白紙のN	blank
hakushu	拍手	applause
hakushu o okuru	拍手を送る	applaud
hakushu-suru	拍手する	clap
hama	浜	beach
hamaguri	はまぐり	clam
ha-maki	葉巻	cigar
hamaki o suu	葉巻を吸う	smoke
hamaru	はまる	fit
hameru	はめる	wear
hametsu	破滅	ruin
hametsu	破滅	smash
hametsu-saseru	破滅させる	ruin
hametsu-suru	破滅する	wreck
ha-migaki	歯磨き	toothpaste
hamu	ハム	ham
han	判	seal[2]
-han	～半	half
hana	花	bloom
hana	花	blossom
hana	花	flower
hana	鼻	nose
hana-bi	花火	fireworks
hanabira	花びら	petal
hana no ana	鼻の穴	nostril
hana o narasu	鼻をならす	snort
hanareru	離れる	leave
hanareru	離れる	separate
hanareta N	離れたN	separate
hanarete	離れて	aside
hanarete	離れて	away
hanare waza	離れ業	stunt
hanashi	話	account
hanashi	話	news
hanashi	話	speech
hanashi	話	story[1]
hanashi	話	talk
hanashi-ai	話し合い	discussion
hanashi-au	話し合う	discuss
hanashi-buri	話振り	speech
hanashi-buri	話振り	style
hanashi-chuu	話し中	busy
hanashi-kata	話し方	speech
hanashi-kata	話し方	tone
hanashi o mochi-kakeru, Vinf. nonpast	話を持ちかける, Vinf. nonpast	approach
hanashi o suru	話をする	address
hanashi o suru	話をする	visit
hanashi-te	話し手	speaker
hanasu	話す	address
hanasu	話す	relate
hanasu	放す	release
hanasu	話す	speak
hanasu	話す	talk
hanasu	話す	tell
hanasu chikara	話す力	speech
hanasu koto	話すこと	speech
hanasu, ⟨-no⟩ koto o kuwashiku	話す, ⟨～の⟩ことを詳しく	recite
hanasu nooryoku	話す能力	speech

hana-ya	花屋	florist
hanayome	花嫁	bride
hanbai	販売	sale
hanbai-gyoosha	販売業者	dealer
hanbun	半分	half
handan	判断	judgment
handan-ryoku	判断力	judgment
handan-suru, {⟨-o⟩/⟨-to⟩/Sinf. ka doo ka}	判断する, {⟨〜を⟩/⟨〜と⟩/Sinf.かどうか}	judge
handikyappu	ハンディキャップ	handicap
hando-baggu	ハンドバッグ	handbag
hane	羽	feather
hane	羽	wing
han'ei	繁栄	prosperity
han'ei shite iru (N)	繁栄している(N)	prosperous
han'ei-suru	繁栄する	flourish
han'ei-suru	反映する	reflect
hane-kaeri	跳ね返り	reflection
hane-kaeru	跳ね返る	bounce
hane-kaeru	跳ね返る	spring
hane-kaesu	跳ね返す	reflect
hane-kakeru	跳ねかける	splash
hane-kasu	跳ねかす	splash
hane-kasu koto	跳ねかすこと	splash
haneru	跳ねる	spring
han'i	範囲	extent
han'i	範囲	ground
han'i	範囲	range
han'i	範囲	scope
han'i	範囲	sphere
hanikami-ya no N	はにかみやのN	bashful
hanjoo-suru	繁盛する	flourish
hankachi	ハンカチ	handkerchief
hanka-gai	繁華街	downtown
hanka-gai {e/ni}	繁華街{へ/に}	downtown
hankei	半径	radius
hanken	半券	check
hanketsu	判決	sentence
hanko	判子	seal[2]
hankyuu	半球	hemisphere
hanmaa	ハンマー	hammer
hannoo	反応	reaction
hannoo	反応	response
hannoo-suru	反応する	react
hannoo-suru	反応する	respond
han o osu	判を押す	seal[2]
han o osu	判を押す	stamp
hanpuku	反復	repetition
hanran o okosu	反乱を起こす	revolt
hanran-suru	氾濫する	flood
hansamuna	ハンサムな	handsome
hansen	帆船	sailboat
(hansen no yoo ni) {susumu/iku}	(帆船のように){進む/行く}	sail
hansha	反射	reflection
hansha-suru	反射する	reflect
han-shite	反して	against
hanshoku-suru	繁殖する	breed
hansoku	反則	violation
hansoo-suru	帆走する	sail
hantai	反対	objection
hantai	反対	opposition
hantai	反対	reverse
hantai da	反対だ	object
hantai da	反対だ	oppose
hantai-gawa no N	反対側のN	opposite
hantai ni suru	反対にする	reverse
hantai no N	反対のN	opposite
hantai no N	反対のN	reverse
hantai-suru	反対する	object
hantai-suru	反対する	oppose
hantai-suru	反対する	resist
hantoo	半島	peninsula
hanzai	犯罪	crime
han-zubon	半ズボン	short
happa	葉っぱ	leaf
happa	葉っぱ	leaves
happoo	発砲	shot
happoo-suru	発砲する	shoot
happyoo	発表	announcement
happyoo	発表	release
happyoo-suru	発表する	announce
happyoo-suru	発表する	release
hapuningu	ハプニング	incident
hara	腹	belly
hara ga tatsu	腹が立つ	angry
harande iru (N)	はらんでいる(N)	pregnant
hara o tatete iru (N)	腹を立てている(N)	angry
harau	払う	pay
hare	晴れ	fair
hareru	晴れる	clear
hareta N	晴れたN	clear
hareta N	はれたN	swollen
haretsu-suru	破裂する	burst
hari	針	needle
-hari	〜針	stitch

hari-au	張り合う	rival
harigane	針金	wire
harigane o tsukau	針金を使う	wire
harikeen	ハリケーン	hurricane
hari-tsukeru	はりつける	glue
haru	張る	pitch
haru	はる	post[1]
haru	春	spring
haru koto	張ること	tension
hasamaru	挟まる	catch
hasami	はさみ	scissors
hasamu	挟む	pinch
hasamu	挟む	sandwich
hashi	橋	bridge[1]
hashi	はし	chopsticks
hashi	端	edge
hashi	端	tip[1]
hashigo	はしご	ladder
hashike	はしけ	barge
hashira	柱	hashira
hashira	柱	post[1]
hashira-seru	走らせる	run
hashiru	走る	run
hashiru	走る	shoot
hashiru	走る	travel
hassei	発生	occurrence
hassei-suru	発生する	occur
hassei-suru	発生する	spring
hassha	発車	departure
hassha	発射	shot
hassha-suru	発車する	depart
hassha-suru	発射する	project
hassha-suru	発射する	shoot
hasshin-on	発信音	tone
hasuu no nai N	端数のないN	round
hata	旗	flag
hatachi (no N)	二十(歳)(のN)	twenty
hatake	畑	field
hatake	畑	patch
hata-meku	はためく	flap
hataraite iru hito	働いている人	worker
hataraka-seru	働かせる	work
hataraka-se-sugiru	働かせ過ぎる	overwork
hataraki-sugiru	働き過ぎる	overwork
hataraku	働く	function
hataraku	働く	work
hataraku N	働くN	working
hata-zao	旗竿	staff

hato	はと	dove
hato	はと	pigeon
hato-ba	波止場	pier
hato-ba	波止場	wharf
hato-ha (no hito)	はと派(の人)	dove
hatsubai	発売	release
hatsubai-suru	発売する	release
hatsudoo-ki	発動機	motor
hatsuka-nezumi	はつかねずみ	mouse
hatsumei	発明	invention
hatsumei-ka	発明家	inventor
hatsumei-suru	発明する	invent
hatsuon	発音	pronunciation
hatsuon-suru	発音する	pronounce
hattatsu	発達	development
hattatsu	発達	progress
hattatsu-saseru	発達させる	develop
hattatsu-suru	発達する	develop
hatten	発展	development
hatten	発展	expansion
hatten	発展	progress
hatten-saseru	発展させる	expand
hatten-saseru, jojoni	発展させる, 徐々に	evolve
hatten-suru	発展する	develop
hatten-suru	発展する	expand
hatten-suru	発展ずる	progress
hau	はう	creep
hau	はう	scramble
hau	はう	trail
Hawai	ハワイ	Hawaii
Hawai no N	ハワイのN	Hawaiian
hayai	はやい	early
hayai	はやい	fast
hayai	はやい	quick
hayai	はやい	rapid
hayai	はやい	speedy
hayai	はやい	swift
hayai koto	速いこと	speed
hayaku	はやく	early
hayaku	はやく	fast
hayaku	はやく	quickly
hayaku	はやく	rapidly
hayaku	はやく	soon
hayaku aruku	速く歩く	trot
haya-sa	速さ	speed
haya-sa	速さ	velocity
hayasu	生やす	wear
hazu da, Sinf.	はずだ, Sinf.	ought

hazu da, Sinf.	はずだ, Sinf.	should
hazu ga nai, {(-no)/adj(*na*). stem na/{adj(*i*)./V}inf.}	はずがない, {(〜の)/adj(*na*). stemな/{adj(*i*)./V}inf.}	can[1]
hazukashi-gari-ya no N	恥ずかしがりやのN	bashful
hazukashii	恥ずかしい	ashamed
hazukashi-sa	恥ずかしさ	shame
hazumu	弾む	bounce
hazure	はずれ	outskirts
hazureru	外れる	miss
hazusu	外す	remove
hebi	蛇	snake
hee	へえ	gee
hee	へえ	well[2]
hee, soo desu ka	へえ、そうですか	really
hei	塀	fence
hei	塀	wall
heibonna	平凡な	ordinary
heichi	平地	plain
heieki	兵役	service
heiina	平易な	plain
heiki	兵器	weapon
heikin	平均	average
heikina	平気な	calm
heikin no N	平均のN	average
heikoona	平行な	parallel
heiryoku	兵力	strength
heisa-on	閉鎖音	stop
heisa-suru	閉鎖する	shut
heisha	兵舎	quarter
heitanna	平たんな	flat[1]
heiwa	平和	peace
heiwana	平和な	peaceful
heiwa-tekina	平和的な	peaceful
heiya	平野	plain
hen	辺	neighborhood
hendoo	変動	movement
hendoo	変動	variation
henji	返事	answer
henji	返事	reply
henji o suru	返事をする	reply
henka	変化	change
henka	変化	shift
henka	変化	transition
henka	変化	turn
henka	変化	variation
henka	変化	variety
henka-saseru	変化させる	transform
henka-suru	変化する	change
henkei-suru	変形する	transform
henken	偏見	prejudice
henkoo	変更	change
henkyaku-suru	返却する	return
henna	変な	funny
henna	変な	odd
henna	変な	peculiar
henna	変な	queer
henna	変な	strange
henna	変な	weird
hensen	変遷	transition
henshu	変種	variation
henshuu	編集	editing
henshuu-sha	編集者	editor
henshuu-suru	編集する	edit
hensoo(-kyoku)	変奏(曲)	variation
hensuu	変数	variable
herasu	減らす	decrease
herasu	減らす	less
herasu	減らす	reduce
herasu	減らす	trim
heri	へり	edge
herikoputaa	ヘリコプター	helicopter
herikudaru	へり下る	stoop
heri o tooru	へりを通る	skirt
heru	減る	decrease
herumetto	ヘルメット	helmet
hetana	下手な	bad
hetana	下手な	badly
hetana	下手な	poor
hetana	下手な	unskillful
heya	部屋	chamber
heya	部屋	room
heya-dai	部屋代	rent
hi	日	date
hi	日	day
hi	火	fire
hi	日	sun
hi-aburi no hashira	火あぶりの柱	stake
hi-aburi no kei	火あぶりの刑	stake
hi-atari ga ii	日当たりがいい	sunny
hibachi	火鉢	brazier
hi-bana	火花	spark
hi-bana ga chiru	火花が散る	spark
hibi	ひび	crack
hibi ga hairu	ひびが入る	crack

hibiki-wataru	響き渡る	vibrate
hidari-gawa no N	左側のN	left-hand
hidari ni	左に	left
hidari (no N)	左(のN)	left
hidoi	ひどい	awful
hidoi	ひどい	bad
hidoi	ひどい	dreadful
hidoi	ひどい	mean[1]
hidoi	ひどい	severe
hidoi	ひどい	terrible
hidoku	ひどく	bitterly
hidoku	ひどく	terribly
hidoku osoreru	ひどく恐れる	terrify
hie-bie-suru	冷え冷えする	chilly
hifu	皮膚	skin
hifu o hi-yake-saseru	皮膚を日焼けさせる	tan
hi ga ataranai (N)	日が当たらない(N)	shady
higai	被害	damage
higai o ataeru	被害を与える	damage
higai-sha	被害者	victim
higashi	東	east
higashi no hoo ni	東の方に	east
higashi no N	東のN	east
higashi no N	東のN	eastern
higeki	悲劇	tragedy
higeki no N	悲劇のN	tragic
hige o soru	ひげをそる	shave
hihan	批判	criticism
hihan tekina	批判的な	critical
hihyoo	批評	criticism
hihyoo	批評	review
hihyoo-ka	批評家	critic
hihyoo o kaku	批評を書く	review
hiiki	ひいき	patronage
hiiki-kyaku	ひいき客	patron
hi(-iro)	ひ(色)	scarlet
hi(-iro) no N	ひ(色)のN	scarlet
hiiroo	ヒーロー	hero
hiiru	ヒール	heel
hiji	ひじ	elbow
hi-jookin no N	非常勤のN	part-time
hijooni	非常に	badly
hijooni	非常に	extremely
hijooni	非常に	greatly
hijooni	非常に	highly
hijooni	非常に	unusually
hijooni	非常に	very
hijooni	非常に	widely
hikae-mena	控え目な	modest
hikage	日陰	shade
hikaku	比較	comparison
hikaku-kentoo-suru	比較検討する	weigh
hikaku no N	比較のN	comparative
hikaku suru	比較する	compare
hikaku-taishoo-suru	比較対照する	oppose
hikaku-teki	比較的	comparatively
hikaku-teki	比較的	relatively
hikara-seru	光らせる	shine
hikari	光	light[1]
hikari	光	shine
hikaru	光る	shine
hiken-sha	被験者	subject
hiketsu	秘けつ	mystery
hiketsu	秘けつ	secret
hiketsu	秘けつ	trick
hiki-ageru	引き上げる	salvage
hiki-au	引き合う	pay
hiki-dashi	引き出し	drawer
hiki-gaeru	ひきがえる	toad
hiki-hanasu	引き離す	separate
hiki-komoru {ie/tokoro}	引きこもる{家/所}	retreat
hiki-nobasu	引き伸ばす	enlarge
hiki-nobasu	引きのばす	prolong
hiki-nuku	引き抜く	pluck
hiki-nuku	引き抜く	pull
hiki-okosu	引き起こす	bring
hiki-saku	引き裂く	tear[1]
hiki-shimeru	引き締める	string
hiki-tsukeru	引き付ける	attract
hiki-tsukeru mono	引き付けるもの	attraction
hiki-ukeru	引き受ける	assume
hiki-ukeru	引き受ける	undertake
hiki-ukeru koto	引き受けること	assumption
hiki-wake	引き分け	draw
hiki-wake	引き分け	tie
hiki-wake ni naru	引き分けになる	tie
hiki-watasu	引き渡す	surrender
hiki-zan	引き算	subtraction
hiki-zuru	引きずる	drag
hiki-zuru	引きずる	trail
hikkaku	引っかく	scratch
hikkosu	引っ越す	move
hikkuri-kaesu	ひっくり返す	turn
hikkuri-kaesu	ひっくり返す	upset
hikoo	非行	wrong

hikoo-joo	飛行場	airport
hi-kooken-nin	被後見人	ward[1]
hikoo-ki	飛行機	aircraft
hikoo-ki	飛行機	airplane
hikoo-ki	飛行機	flight
hikoo-ki	飛行機	plane
hikoo-ki de iku	飛行機で行く	fly
hikoo-ki ni noru	飛行機に乗る	fly
hi-kooshiki no N	非公式のN	informal
hiku	引く	draw
hiku	ひく	grind
hiku	ひく	play
hiku	ひく	pull
hiku	引く	subtract
hikui	低い	low
hikui	低い	short
hima	暇	time
himana	暇な	free
himaraya-sugi	ヒマラヤ杉	cedar
himitsu	秘密	secret
himitsu no N	秘密のN	secret
himitsu no N	秘密のN	underground
himo	ひも	band
himo	ひも	string
himo de shibaru	ひもで縛る	string
himo o tsukeru	ひもを付ける	string
hinan	避難	refuge
hinan	避難	shelter
hinan-jo	避難所	refuge
hinan-jo	避難所	shelter
hinan no mato	非難の的	target
hinan-suru	非難する	accuse
hinata	日なた	sunshine
hineru	ひねる	wring
hin ga ii	品がいい	elegant
hinkon	貧困	poverty
hi-no-de	日の出	sunrise
hi no hikari	日の光	sun
hi no hikari	日の光	sunlight
hi-no-iri	日の入り	sunset
hi no uchi-dokoro ga nai	非の打ちどころがない	thorough
hinshitsu	品質	quality
hinshu	品種	breed
hinto	ヒント	hint
hi o tsukeru	火をつける	light[1]
hipparu	引っ張る	haul
hipparu	引っ張る	pull
hipparu	引っ張る	strain
hipparu	引っ張る	stretch
hippatte iku	引っ張って行く	tow
hiraita N	開いたN	open
hiraku	開く	hold
hiraku	開く	open
hira-te-uchi	平手打ち	slap
hiretsuna	卑劣な	base
hiri-hiri-suru N	ひりひりするN	sore
hiritsu	比率	proportion
hiritsu	比率	ratio
hiro-ba	広場	square
hiro-biro-to shita N	広々としたN	spacious
hiro-biro-to shite iru (N)	広々としている(N)	spacious
hirogari	広がり	sheet
hirogari	広がり	spread
hirogaru	広がる	reach
hirogaru	広がる	spread
hirogeru	広げる	spread
hiroi	広い	sweeping
hiroi	広い	wide
hiroku	広く	wide
hiroku	広く	widely
hiromaru	広まる	run
hiromeru	広める	spread
hiroo-en	披露宴	reception
hiro-sa	広さ	width
hiru	昼	day
hiru	昼	daytime
hiru	昼	noon
hiru-gohan	昼御飯	lunch
hiru-ma	昼間	day
hiru-ma	昼間	daytime
hiru-ne	昼寝	nap
hiryoo	肥料	fertilizer
hiryoo	肥料	food
hisan	悲惨	misery
hisanna	悲惨な	miserable
hisanna	悲惨な	tragic
hisashi	ひさし	peak
hishi-gata	菱形	diamond
hisho	秘書	secretary
hisoka ni	ひそかに	secretly
hissha	筆者	writer
hisshi de	必死で	desperately
hisshi no N	必死のN	desperate
hitai	額	forehead

hitan	悲嘆	grief
hitan	悲嘆	sorrow
hitei no N	否定のN	negative
hitei-suru	否定する	deny
hitei-tekina	否定的な	negative
hito	人	man
hito	人	person
hito-ban	一晩	overnight
hito-bito	人々	folk
hito-bito	人々	people
hito-bito	人々	those
hitode	ひとで	starfish
hito-de	人手	hand
hito-doori	人通り	traffic
hito-gara	人柄	person
hito-gara	人柄	personality
hito-gomi	人ごみ	crowd
hito-kado no ningen	ひとかどの人間	somebody
hito-kage	人影	figure
hito-kaki	一かき	stroke[1]
hito-katamari	一塊	cluster
hito-kawa mukeba	一皮むけば	underneath
hito kire	一切れ	slice
hito-kuchi	一口	bite
hito-me	一目	glance
hito-me o hikanai (N)	人目を引かない(N)	unnoticed
hito-mure no N	一群れのN	pack
hito-natsu(k)koi	人なつ(っ)こい	friendly
hito-nigiri	一握り	handful
hitori	一人	single
hitori de	一人で	alone
hitori-hitori	一人一人	each
hitori-hitori no N	一人一人のN	each
hitori-hitori no N	一人一人のN	individual
hitori mo...neg.	一人も…neg.	no
hitori no N	一人のN	a
hitori no N	一人のN	single
hitoshii	等しい	equal
hitoshiku	等しく	equally
hito-tachi	人たち	folk
hito-tachi	人たち	people
hito-toki no N	一時のN	transitory
hitotsu	一つ	loaf
hito-tsumami	一つまみ	pinch
hitotsu mo...neg.	一つも…neg.	no
hitotsu (ni-tsuki)	一つ(につき)	apiece
hitotsu ni wa	一つには	partly
hitotsu no N	一つのN	a
hitotsu (no N)	一つ(のN)	one
hitsuji	羊	sheep
hitsuji-kai	羊飼い	shepherd
hitsuyoo	必要	necessity
hitsuyoo	必要	need
hitsuyoo {denai/janai}	必要{でない/じゃない}	unnecessary
hitsuyoo ga aru, Vinf. nonpast	必要がある, Vinf. nonpast	need
hitsuyoo-jooken	必要条件	requirement
hitsuyoona	必要な	involve
hitsuyoona	必要な	necessary
hitsuyoona	必要な	need
hitsuyoona	必要な	take
hitsuyoona	必要な	want
hitsuyoona mono	必要なもの	necessity
hitsuyoona mono	必要なもの	need
hitsuyoo to suru	必要とする	demand
hitsuzen-sei	必然性	necessity
hitteki-suru	匹敵する	compare
hiyakasu	冷やかす	tease
hi-yake	日焼け	tan
hiyasu	冷やす	cool
hi-yoke	日よけ	blind
hiyokuna	肥沃な	fertile
hiyoo	費用	cost
hiyoo	費用	expense
hi-yuukoo-tekina	非友好的な	unfriendly
hiza	ひざ	knee
hi-zuke	日付	date
hizume	ひづめ	hoof
ho	帆	sail
hoan-kan	保安官	sheriff
hochoo	歩調	pace
hodo	ほど	extent
hodokoshi-mono	施し物	hand-out
hodo...neg.	ほど…neg.	less
hodoo	歩道	sidewalk
hodoo	歩道	walk
hoeru	ほえる	bark
hoeru	ほえる	roar
hogo	保護	preservation
hogo	保護	protection
hogo-	保護～	protective
hogo-ikusei	保護育成	patronage
hogo-suru	保護する	preserve
hogo-suru	保護する	protect
hoho	ほほ	cheek

hohoemi-kakeru	ほほえみかける	smile
hohoemu	ほほえむ	smile
hoiku-en	保育園	nursery
hoiku-jo	保育所	nursery
hoiru	ホイル	foil
hojikuru	ほじくる	pick
hojiru	ほじる	pick
hoji-suru	保持する	retain
hokan	保管	preservation
hoka ni	外に	besides
hoka ni	外に	else
hoka ni	外に	further
hoka ni	外に	than
hoka no	外の	others
hoka no N	外のN	another
hoka no N	外のN	else
hoka no N	外のN	other
hokan-suru	保管する	preserve
hoken	保険	insurance
(hoken ga) kikanai N	(保険が)きかないN	uncovered
hoken o kakeru	保険をかける	insure
Hokkyoku-chihoo	北極地方	arctic
Hokkyoku no N	北極のN	arctic
hokoo-sha	歩行者	pedestrian
hokori	ほこり	dust
hokori ni shite iru	誇りにしている	pride
hokori ni shite iru	誇りにしている	proud
hoku-	北～	northern
hokuro	ほくろ	mole[2]
hoku-sei	北西	northwest
hoku-sei no N	北西のN	northwest
hoku-too	北東	northeast
hoku-too no N	北東のN	northeast
homeru	ほめる	praise
homeru koto	ほめること	praise
home-tataeru	ほめたたえる	praise
home-tataeru koto	ほめたたえること	praise
hon	本	book
hon	本	volume
-hon	～本	roll
hon'an	翻案	adaptation
hon-bako	本箱	bookcase
honbu	本部	headquarters
honbun	本文	text
hon-dana	本棚	bookshelf
hone	骨	bone
hone-ori	骨折り	toil
honki no N	本気のN	serious
hon-mono no N	本物のN	real
hon-mono no N	本物のN	solid
honnoo	本能	instinct
honomekasu	ほのめかす	hint
honoo	炎	flame
honsha	本社	headquarters
honshitsu	本質	substance
honshitsu-tekina	本質的な	essential
honshitsu-tekini	本質的に	essentially
hontoo ni	本当に	indeed
hontoo ni	本当に	really
hontoo ni	本当に	truly
hontoo ni	本当に	very
(hontoo ni) Sinf. {kana/kashira}	(本当に)Sinf.{かな/かしら}	wonder
hontoo no koto	本当のこと	truth
hontoo no N	本当のN	real
hontoo no N	本当のN	true
hontoo-rashii	本当らしい	probable
hontoo wa	本当は	really
ho-nuno	帆布	canvas
hon-ya	本屋	bookstore
hon'yaku	翻訳	translation
hon'yaku-suru	翻訳する	translate
hon'yaku-suru	翻訳する	turn
honyuurui	ほ乳類	mammal
hoo	ほお	cheek
hoo	ほう	really
-hoo	～法	method
hoobi	褒美	prize
hoodoo	報道	report
hoofuna	豊富な	abundant
hoofuna	豊富な	wealth
hoofu-sa	豊富さ	abundance
hoo ga ii, {Vinf. past affirmative/Vinf. nonpast negative}	方がいい, {Vinf. past affirmative/Vinf. nonpast negative}	should
hoogaina	法外な	unreasonable
hoogaku	方角	bearing
hoogaku	方角	direction
hoogeki-suru	砲撃する	shell
hoogen	方言	dialect
hoogen	方言	speech
hoo-hige	ほおひげ	whisker
hoohoo	方法	approach
hoohoo	方法	method
hoohoo	方法	way
hooi-suru, teki o	包囲する, 敵を	surround

hoojiru	報じる	report
hooki	ほうき	broom
hookoku	報告	statement
hookoku(-sho)	報告(書)	report
hookoku-suru	報告する	report
hookoo	方向	course
hookoo	方向	direction
hookoo-tenkan	方向転換	turn
hookyuu	俸給	salary
hoomon	訪問	visit
hoomon-{sha/kyaku}	訪問{者/客}	visitor
hoomu	ホーム	platform
hoo {ni/e}	方{に/へ}	toward(s)
hoori-nageru	ほうり投げる	hurl
hooritsu	法律	law
hooru	ホール	hall
hooru	ほうる	throw
hooru	ほうる	toss
hooseki	宝石	jewel
hoosha-sen	放射線	radiation
hooshi	奉仕	service
hooshin	方針	policy
hooshi-sha	奉仕者	servant
hooshoo-kin	報奨金	reward
hooshoo(-kin) o ataeru	報奨(金)を与える	reward
hooshuu	報酬	reward
hoosoku	法則	law
hoosoo	放送	broadcast
hoosoo	放送	broadcasting
hoosoo-kyoku	放送局	station
hoosoo-moo	放送網	network
hoosoo-suru	放送する	broadcast
hoosu	ホース	hose
hoo-tekina	法的な	legal
hoppeta	ほっぺた	cheek
hora	ほら	there
horaana	洞穴	cave
horu	掘る	dig
horyo	捕虜	prisoner
horyuu-suru	保留する	reserve
hoshi	星	star
hoshigaru	欲しがる	want
hoshii	欲しい	want
hoshi-kusa	干し草	hay
hoshoo	保証	guarantee
hoshoo	保証	seal[2]
hoshoo-suru	保証する	assure
hoshoo suru	保証する	guarantee

hoshoo-suru	保証する	secure
(hoso-)himo	(細)ひも	string
hosoi	細い	narrow
hosoi	細い	thin
hoso-nagai	細長い	slender
(hoso-nagai) ana	(細長い)穴	slot
hoso-nagai boo	細長い棒	rod
hoso-nagai mono	細長いもの	stalk
hosoo	舗装	pavement
hosoo-suru	舗装する	pave
hossa	発作	fit
hossori-shita N	ほっそりしたN	slender
hossori-shita N	ほっそりしたN	slim
hossori-shite iru (N)	ほっそりしている(N)	slender
hossori-shite iru (N)	ほっそりしている(N)	slim
hosu	干す	dry
hoteru	ホテル	hotel
hotobashiri-deru	ほとばしり出る	spring
hotoke	仏	Buddha
hotondo	ほとんど	almost
hotondo	ほとんど	nearly
hotondo	ほとんど	virtually
hotondo…neg.	ほとんど…neg.	hardly
hotondo (neg.)	ほとんど(neg.)	scarcely
hotondo no N	ほとんどのN	most
hottate-goya	掘立小屋	shack
hotto-shita kimochi	ほっとした気持ち	relief
hoyoo	保養	feast
hozon	保存	preservation
hozon-butsu	保存物	reserve
hozon-suru	保存する	preserve
hyakka-jiten	百科事典	encyclopedia
hyaku (+counter) (no N)	百(+counter)(のN)	hundred
hyaku-man (+counter) (no N)	百万(+counter)(のN)	million
hyakushoo	百姓	farmer
hyoo	表	chart
hyoo	ひょう	hail
hyoo	ひょう	leopard
hyoo	表	schedule
hyoo	ひょう	stone
hyoo	表	table
hyooban	評判	credit
hyooban	評判	reputation
hyoodai o tsukeru	表題をつける	entitle

hyoo ga furu	ひょうが降る	hail
hyoogen	表現	expression
hyoogen-suru	表現する	express
hyoogen-suru	表現する	represent
hyoogen-suru	表現する	speak
hyoogen-yooshiki	表現様式	style
hyoogi-in	評議員	senator
hyoogi-in-kai	評議員会	senate
hyoohaku-suru	漂泊する	roam
hyoohon	標本	sample
hyoohon	標本	specimen
hyooji-suru	表示する	read
hyooji-suru	表示する	record
hyoojun	標準	standard
hyoojun-tekina	標準的な	standard
hyooka-suru	評価する	estimate
hyooka-suru	評価する	rate
hyooketsu-suru	票決する	vote
hyoomen	表面	surface
hyooron-ka	評論家	critic
hyooshi	表紙	cover
hyooshiki	標識	sign
hyooteki	標的	target
hyotto shitara…(kamoshirenai)	ひょっとしたら…(かもしれない)	perhaps

I

i	胃	stomach
-i	～位	place
ibiki	いびき	snore
ibiki o kaku	いびきをかく	snore
ibusu	いぶす	smoke
ichi	位置	bearing
ichi	市	market
ichi	位置	position
ichi+animal counter mo…neg.	一+animal counterも…neg.	no
ichiba	市場	market
ichiban	一番	best
ichiban	一番	most
ichi-ban	一番	first
ichiban ii	一番いい	best
ichiban juuyoona	一番重要な	prime
ichiban ki-ni-itte iru (N)	一番気に入っている(N)	favorite
ichi-ban mae	一番前	front
ichiban ookii	一番大きい	biggest
ichiban ookina N	一番大きなN	biggest
ichiban sukina	一番好きな	favorite
ichiban {sukunai, chiisana, etc.} N	一番{少ない, 小さな, etc.}N	least
ichiban takusan no N	一番たくさんのN	most
ichiban tooi	一番遠い	utmost
ichi-ban toshi-ue no N	一番年上のN	eldest
ichiban ue	一番上	head
ichibu	一部	fragment
ichi-bu	一部	piece
ichi-bu	一部	portion
ichi+counter mo…neg.	一+counterも…neg.	no
ichi (+counter) (no N)	一(+counter)(のN)	one
ichi-da	一打	stroke[1]
ichi-do	一度	once
ichi-do mo Vinf. past koto ga nai	一度もVinf. pastことがない	never
ichi-do…{Vinf. nonpast to/Vcond.+ba/Vstem+reba/sureba/kureba}	一度…{Vinf. nonpast to/Vcond.+ば/Vstem+れば/すれば/来れば}	once
ichi-gatsu	一月	January
ichigo	いちご	strawberry
ichi-gun no N	一群のN	pack
ichiji azukeru	一時預ける	check
ichi-ji teishi-saseru	一時停止させる	suspend
ichiji-tekina	一時的な	temporary
ichi-joo no hikari	一条の光	shaft[1]
ichi-jun	一巡	round
ichi-mai no kami	一枚の紙	sheet
ichimi	一味	gang
ichi-nen-sei	一年生	freshman
ichi-nichi	一日	day
ichi o mitsukeru	位置を見つける	locate
ichioo	一応	tentatively
ichioo no N	一応のN	tentative
ichi-ren	一連	string
ichi-ren no N	一連のN	streak
ichi, (shimeru-beki)	位置, (占めるべき)	slot
ichiyoo denai (N)	一様でない(N)	uneven
ichizoku	一族	family
idaina	偉大な	great
ido	緯度	latitude
ido	井戸	well[1]
idoo	移動	migration
idoo	移動	passage
idoo	移動	transfer
idoo-suru	移動する	migrate

idoo-suru	移動する	move
ie	家	house
Ieroosutoon	イエローストーン	Yellowstone
ifuku	衣服	dress
igaina	意外な	unexpected
-igai (wa)	～以外(は)	except
igaku	医学	medicine
igaku no N	医学のN	medical
igen	威厳	dignity
igen ga aru N	威厳があるN	stately
igi	異議	objection
igi	意義	significance
igi ga aru N	意義があるN	significant
Igirisu	イギリス	England
Igirisu-jin	イギリス人	British
Igirisu-jin	イギリス人	Englishman
Igirisu-jin no N	イギリス人のN	British
Igirisu-jin no N	イギリス人のN	English
Igirisu no N	イギリスのN	British
Igirisu no N	イギリスのN	English
ihan	違反	violation
ihan-suru	違反する	violate
ii	いい	favorable
ii	いい	fine
ii	いい	good
ii	いい	nice
ii	いい	sweet
ii-arawasu	言い表す	speak
iie	いいえ	no
ii-haru	言い張る	insist
ii-haru	言い張る	persist
ii-kata	言い方	phrase
ii-kiru	言い切る	pronounce
(ii) ne	(いい)ね	OK
iin-kai	委員会	board
iin-kai	委員会	committee
ii, Sinf. to	いい, Sinf.と	hope
ii tenki no N	いい天気のN	shiny
ii, {V/adj./cop.}*te* mo	いい, {V/adj./cop.}*te*も	can[1]
ii, {V/adj./cop.}*te* mo	いい, {V/adj./cop.}*te*も	may
ii, Vinf. past ra	いい, Vinf. pastら	should
ii, V*te* mo	いい, V*te*も	mind
iiwake	言い訳	excuse
ijimekko	いじめっ子	bully
ijimeru	いじめる	bully
ijimeru	いじめる	tease
iji-suru	維持する	maintain
iji-waruna	意地悪な	mean[1]
iji-waruna	意地悪な	wicked
-ijoo	～以上	over
-ijoo	～以上	upward
ijoona	異常な	abnormal
ijoona	異常な	unusual
ijooni	異常に	unusually
ijooni nagaku tsuzuku	異常に長く続く	persist
ijuu	移住	migration
ijuu-suru	移住する	migrate
-ika	～以下	below
ikada	いかだ	raft
ikaga	いかが	how
ikagawashii	いかがわしい	shady
ikameshii	いかめしい	solemn
-ika no N	～以下のN	under
ikari	怒り	fury
ika-seru	行かせる	send
ike	池	pond
ikei	い敬	awe
iken	意見	opinion
iken	意見	remark
iken	意見	sentiment
iken	意見	thinking
iken	意見	thought
iken	意見	view
iken	意見	voice
ikenai N	いけないN	bad
ikenai, {V/adj./cop.}*te* wa	いけない, {V/adj./cop.}*te*は	must
ikenai, {V/adj./cop.}*te* wa	いけない, {V/adj./cop.}*te*は	should
iken ga awanai	意見が合わない	disagree
iken ga itchi-suru	意見が一致する	agree
ikenie	いけにえ	sacrifice
ikenie	いけにえ	victim
ikenie ni suru	いけにえにする	sacrifice
ikenie o sasageru koto	いけにえを捧げること	sacrifice
iken o mooshi-ageru	意見を申し上げる	submit
iken o noberu	意見を述べる	comment
iki	息	breath
-iki	～行き	bound for
ikidoori	憤り	resentment
iki-iki-shita N	生き生きしたN	lively
iki-iki-shita N	生き生きしたN	vital
iki-iki-shita N	生き生きしたN	vivid

iki-iki-shite iru (N)	生き生きしている(N)	lively
iki-iki-shite iru (N)	生き生きしている(N)	vital
iki-iki-shite iru (N)	生き生きしている(N)	vivid
ikimashita	行きました	went
iki-mono	生き物	being
iki-mono	生き物	creature
ikinari	いきなり	suddenly
iki-nobiru	生き延びる	survive
iki-nokoru	生き残る	survive
iki-nokoru koto	生き残ること	survival
ikinuki	息抜き	relaxation
ikioi	勢い	power
ikioi	勢い	vigor
iki o suru	息をする	breathe
iki o tsugu	息を継ぐ	pause
ikiru	生きる	live
ikite iru (N)	生きている(N)	alive
ikite iru (N)	生きている(N)	living
ik-kai	一回	once
ikken	一見	view
ikki	一気	stretch
ik-ko	一個	loaf
ik-ko	一個	single
ikkoo	一行	party
ikoo	移行	transition
iku	行く	bound for
iku	行く	come
iku	行く	go
iku	行く	visit
ikubun	幾分	somewhat
iku, (hansen no yoo ni)	行く, (帆船のように)	sail
ikura-ka	いくらか	any
ikura-ka	いくらか	some
ikura-ka	いくらか	somewhat
ikura…{V/adj./cop.}*te*} mo	いくら…{V/adj./cop.}*te*}も	however
ikutsu-ka	いくつか	some
ikutsu-ka no N	いくつかのN	several
ikutsu-ka (no) N	いくつか(の)N	some
ima	居間	living room
ima	今	now
ima-made ni	今までに	ever
imagoro wa	今ごろは	now
ima no N	今のN	current

ima no N	今のN	present[1]
imasen	いません	isn't
imasen deshita	いませんでした	wasn't
imasen deshita	いませんでした	weren't
imashime	戒め	warning
imashimeru	戒める	warn
imashita	いました	was
imashita	いました	were
imeeji	イメージ	image
imi	意味	meaning
imi	意味	sense
imi	意味	significance
imi ga aru N	意味があるN	significant
imin	移民	immigrant
imin	移民	immigration
imi no aru N	意味のあるN	meaningful
imi-suru	意味する	represent
imiteeshon	イミテーション	imitation
in	韻	rhyme
inabikari	稲光	lightning
inai	いない	aren't
inai	いない	free
inai	いない	isn't
-inai ni	～以内に	within
-inai (ni)	～以内(に)	within
inai, V*te*	いない, V*te*	aren't
inai, V*te*	いない, V*te*	isn't
inaka	田舎	country
inaka	田舎	countryside
inaka no N	田舎のN	rural
inakatta	いなかった	wasn't
inakatta	いなかった	weren't
inakatta, V*te*	いなかった, V*te*	wasn't
inakatta, V*te*	いなかった, V*te*	weren't
inazuma	稲妻	lightning
inbun	韻文	verse
inchi	インチ	inch
Indio	インディオ	Indian
Indo	インド	India
Indo-jin	インド人	Indian
Indo no N	インドのN	Indian
i-nemuri-suru	居眠りする	nod
infomeeshon	インフォメーション	information
infure	インフレ	inflation
infureeshon	インフレーション	inflation
inkan	印鑑	seal[2]
inkina	陰気な	somber
inku	インク	ink

inochi	命	life
inochi ni kakawaru (N)	命にかかわる(N)	vital
in o fumu	韻を踏む	rhyme
in o osu	印を押す	stamp
inoru, Sinf. yooni	祈る, Sinf.ように	pray
inoru, Vinf. nonpast {no o/koto o/yooni}	祈る, Vinf. nonpast{のを/ことを/ように}	wish
inoshishi	いのしし	wild boar
inpakuto	インパクト	impact
inryoku	引力	gravity
insatsu	印刷	printing
insatsu-butsu	印刷物	hand-out
insatsu-jutsu	印刷術	printing
insatsu-ki	印刷機	press
insatsu-suru	印刷する	print
insei no N	陰性のN	negative
inshoo	印象	image
inshoo	印象	impression
inshoo-tekina	印象的な	impressive
insutorakutaa	インストラクター	instructor
intabyuu	インタビュー	interview
intai	隠退	retreat
intai-shita N	引退したN	retired
intai-suru	引退する	retire
interi	インテリ	intellectual
inu	犬	dog
inu no ko	犬の子	puppy
in'yoo	引用	quotation
in'yoo-suru	引用する	quote
ippai ni naru	いっぱいになる	fill
ippai ni suru	いっぱいにする	fill
ippai no N	いっぱいのN	full
ip-paku no N	一泊のN	overnight
ippan-gainen	一般概念	universal
ippan ni	一般に	commonly
ippan ni	一般に	generally
ippan no N	一般のN	general
ippan-tekina	一般的な	general
ippan-tekina	一般的な	universal
ip-pitsu	一筆	stroke[1]
ip-po	一歩	pace
ip-po	一歩	step
ippoo-tsuukoo no N	一方通行のN	one-way
ira-ira-suru	いらいらする	impatient
irai, V*te*	以来, V*te*	since[1]
iranai	要らない	unnecessary
irassharu	いらっしゃる	are
irassharu	いらっしゃる	be

irassharu	いらっしゃる	come
irassharu	いらっしゃる	go
ireru	入れる	add
ireru	入れる	cast
ireru	入れる	fit
ireru	入れる	include
ireru	入れる	insert
ireru	入れる	pour
ireru	入れる	put
ireru, (naka ni)	入れる, (中に)	number
iriguchi	入り口	entrance
iri-majitta N	入り混じったN	mixture
Irinoi	イリノイ	Illinois
iro	色	color
iroai	色合い	shade
iro ga aseru	色があせる	fade
iro-irona	色々な	different
iro-irona	色々な	varied
iro-irona	色々な	various
irojiro	色白	fair
iron	異論	objection
ironna	いろんな	various
irori	囲炉裏	fireplace
iru	いる	am
iru	いる	be
iru	要る	demand
iru	いる	exist
iru	いる	have
iru	要る	need
iru	いる	own
iru	いる	roast
iru	射る	shoot
iru	いる	stay
iru	いる	there's
iru	要る	want
irui	衣類	clothing
iru koto	いること	presence
(iru N), V*te*	(いるN), V*te*	with
iru, Sinf. hito mo	いる, Sinf.人も	some
iru tokoro	いる所	presence
iru, V*te*	いる, V*te*	am
iru, V*te*	いる, V*te*	are
iru, V*te*	いる, V*te*	be
iru, V*te*	いる, V*te*	is
isai o hanatsu	異彩を放つ	shine
isamashii	勇ましい	brave
isamashiku	勇ましく	bravely
ise-ebi	いせえび	lobster

isei yoku aruku	威勢よく歩く	swing
iseki	遺跡	site
isha	医者	doctor
isha	医者	physician
ishi	医師	doctor
ishi	医師	physician
ishi	石	rock
ishi	石	stone
ishi	意志	volition
ishi	意志	will
ishiki	意識	consciousness
ishiki-fumei no N	意識不明のN	unconscious
ishiki ga aru (N)	意識がある(N)	conscious
ishiki-shite iru (N)	意識している(N)	conscious
ishin	維新	restoration
ishi no sotsuu o hakaru	意志の疎通をはかる	communicate
isoga-seru	急がせる	hurry
isogashii	忙しい	busy
isogi	急ぎ	haste
isogi-ashi	急ぎ足	trot
isogu	急ぐ	hurry
isogu	急ぐ	rush
isoide	急いで	hurriedly
isoide	急いで	quickly
is-setsu	一節	passage
issho ni	一緒に	together
issho ni iku	一緒に行く	accompany
(issho ni) V	(一緒に)V	share
isshoo	一生	life
isshoo-kenmei (ni)	一生懸命(に)	hard
isshun	一瞬	instant
issoo	いっそう	even
issoo-suru	一掃する	sweep
issoo-suru (N)	一掃する(N)	sweeping
isu	いす	chair
isu	いす	stool
Isuraeru	イスラエル	Israel
ita	板	board
ita	いた	was
ita	いた	were
itadaki	頂	top
itadaki no N	頂のN	top
itadaku	いただく	eat
itadaku	いただく	get
itadaku	いただく	receive
itade	痛手	wound[1]
itagane	板金	plate
itai	痛い	ache
itai	痛い	hurt
itai	痛い	painful
itai	痛い	pinch
itai	遺体	remain
itai	痛い	sore
itai tokoro	痛い所	sore
itamae	板前	cook
itameru	いためる	fry
itameru	いためる	hurt
ita-mi	痛み	pain
itamu	痛む	ache
itamu	いたむ	hurt
itamu	いたむ	spoil
itanda N	傷んだN	bad
Itaria	イタリア	Italy
Itaria-go	イタリア語	Italian
Itaria-go no N	イタリア語のN	Italian
Itaria-jin	イタリア人	Italian
Itaria-jin no N	イタリア人のN	Italian
Itaria no N	イタリアのN	Italian
itaru-tokoro {de/ni}	いたるところ{で/に}	everywhere
ita-sa	痛さ	pain
itasu	いたす	do
ita, V*te*	いた, V*te*	was
ita, V*te*	いた, V*te*	were
itazura	いたずら	mischief
itazura	いたずら	trick
itchi	一致	agreement
itchi	一致	correspondence
itchi-shinai	一致しない	disagree
itchokusen ni	一直線に	straight
iten	移転	shift
ito	意図	intention
ito	意図	thought
ito	糸	thread
ito	糸	yarn
itoko	いとこ	cousin
ito o toosu	糸を通す	thread
itoshii	いとしい	beloved
itoshii	いとしい	dear
itoshii	いとしい	precious
itsu	いつ	when[1]
itsu-demo, Sinf. toki ni (wa)	いつでも, Sinf.時に(は)	whenever
itsu-demo yorokonde V	いつでも喜んでV	ready
itsu-ka	いつか	ever
itsu-ka	いつか	someday

itsu-ka	いつか	sometime
itsu-made-mo	いつまでも	forever
itsu-mo	いつも	always
itsu-mo	いつも	constantly
itsu-mo	いつも	ever
itsu-mo, ⟨-ni⟩ wa	いつも, ⟨〜に⟩は	every
itsu-mo no N	いつものN	regular
itsu-mo no N	いつものN	usual
itsutsu-me no N	五つ目のN	fifth
itsutsu (no N)	五つ(のN)	five
itsuu	胃痛	stomachache
itsu *Vte* mo	いつ*Vte*も	whenever
itta	行った	went
ittai	一体	ever
ittai…ka	一体…か	should
ittai ni	一帯に	throughout
ittei no N	一定のN	constant
ittei no N	一定のN	uniform
iu	言う	mention
iu	言う	remark
iu	言う	say
iu	言う	speak
iu hito, ⟨-to⟩	いう人, ⟨〜と⟩	a
iu mono, ⟨-to⟩	いうもの, ⟨〜と⟩	a
iu, {⟨-o⟩/⟨-to⟩}	言う, {⟨〜を⟩/⟨〜と⟩}	bid
iu, {⟨-o⟩/⟨-to⟩/Vinf. nonpast yooni}	言う, {⟨〜を⟩/⟨〜と⟩/Vinf. nonpastように}	tell
iu, Sinf. to	言う, Sinf.と	imply
iu, Vinf. nonpast yooni (to)	言う, Vinf. nonpastように(と)	instruct
iu, Vinf. past+ra doo ka to	言う, Vinf. past+らどうかと	suggest
iwa	岩	rock
iwa de dekita N	岩で出来たN	rocky
iwai	祝い	celebration
iwai	祝い	congratulation
iwai	祝い	present[2]
iwa no ooi N	岩の多いN	rocky
iwa no yoona	岩のような	rocky
iwau	祝う	celebrate
iwayuru N	いわゆるN	so-called
iya	いや	no
iya-iya(-nagara)	いやいや(ながら)	unwillingly
iya moo	いやもう	well[2]
iyana	嫌な	awful
iyana	嫌な	harsh
iyana	嫌な	obnoxious
iyana	嫌な	unpleasant
iyana nioi ga suru	嫌なにおいがする	stink
iya-ni-naru	いやになる	tired
iyashii	卑しい	humble
iyashimu-beki N	卑しむべきN	pitiful
iyasu	いやす	remedy
iyoku	意欲	volition
izen (ni)	以前(に)	formerly
izen (ni)	以前(に)	previously
izumi	泉	spring

J

ja(a)	じゃ(あ)	well[2]
jaaku	邪悪	darkness
jaanarizumu	ジャーナリズム	press
jaarimasen	じゃありません	aren't
jaarimasen	じゃありません	isn't
jaarimasen deshita	じゃありませんでした	wasn't
jaarimasen deshita	じゃありませんでした	weren't
jagaimo	じゃがいも	potato
jaketto	ジャケット	jacket
jama	邪魔	hindrance
jama ni naru	邪魔になる	hinder
jama o suru	邪魔をする	disturb
jama o suru	邪魔をする	hinder
jama o suru	邪魔をする	interrupt
jama-suru	邪魔する	violate
jama-suru, {Vinf. nonpast no/N} o	邪魔する, {Vinf. nonpastの/N}を	prevent
jamu	ジャム	jam[2]
janai	じゃない	aren't
janai	じゃない	isn't
janai, {adj(*na*). stem/N}	じゃない, {adj(*na*). stem/N}	not
ja nai to, (moshi) {adj(*na*). stem/N}	じゃないと, (もし){adj(*na*). stem/N}	unless
janakatta	じゃなかった	wasn't
janakatta	じゃなかった	weren't
ja nakereba, (moshi) {adj(*na*). stem/N}	じゃなければ, (もし){adj(*na*). stem/N}	unless
janguru	ジャングル	jungle
jari	砂利	gravel
jazu	ジャズ	jazz
jetto-ki	ジェット機	jet
ji	字	character
ji	字	letter

-ji	〜時	o'clock
-ji	〜時	time
jibiki	字引	dictionary
jibun	自分	self[1]
jibun	自分	yourself
jibun de	自分で	herself
jibun de	自分で	himself
jibun de, (watashi ga)	自分で, (私が)	myself
jibun(-jishin)	自分(自身)	herself
jibun(-jishin)	自分(自身)	himself
jibun(-jishin)	自分(自身)	myself
jibun(-jishin)	自分(自身)	oneself
jibun(-jishin)	自分(自身)	ourselves
jibun(-jishin)	自分(自身)	self[2]
jibun(-jishin) no N	自分(自身)のN	own
jibun no N	自分のN	her
jibun no N	自分のN	his
jibun-tachi	自分たち	themselves
jidai	時代	age
jidai	時代	era
jidai	時代	period
jidai	時代	time
jidoo	児童	student
jidoo no N	自動のN	automatic
jidoosha	自動車	auto
jidoosha	自動車	automobile
jidoosha	自動車	car
(jidoosha-)shuuri-koojoo	(自動車)修理工場	garage
jidoo-tekini	自動的に	automatically
jiei-tai	自衛隊	Self-Defense Force
jigen	次元	dimension
jigoku	地獄	hell
jiguzagu ni ⟨-o⟩ susuma-seru	ジグザグに⟨〜を⟩進ませる	weave
jigyoo	事業	enterprise
jigyoo	事業	undertaking
jigyoo (keikaku)	事業(計画)	project
jiin	寺院	temple
jiinzu	ジーンズ	jeans
jiipan	ジーパン	jeans
jijitsu	事実	fact
jijitsu-joo	事実上	virtually
jijoo	事情	case[2]
jijoo	事情	circumstance
jijoo	事情	state
ji-joo	二乗	square
jikaku	自覚	awareness
jikan	時間	hour
jikan	時間	time
jikan	時間	while
-jikan	〜時間	hour
jikan-gai ni	時間外に	overtime
jikan o hakaru	時間を計る	time
jikan(-tai), (shimeru-beki)	時間(帯), (占めるべき)	slot
jikan-wari	時間割り	schedule
jika-sei no N	自家製のN	homemade
jiken	事件	case[2]
jiken	事件	event
jiken	事件	occurrence
jiki	磁器	china
jiki	時季	season
jikken	実験	experiment
jikken	実験	test
jikken o suru	実験をする	test
jikken (o) suru	実験(を)する	experiment
jikken-shitsu	実験室	laboratory
jikken-tekina N	実験的なN	experimental
jikkoo	実行	practice
jikkoo-suru	実行する	practice
jiko	事故	accident
jikoku no N	自国のN	native
ji(ko-boo)ei	自(己防)衛	self-defense
jiku	軸	axis
jiku	軸	shaft[1]
jiku-uke	軸受け	bearing
jiman	自慢	pride
jiman no N	自慢のN	proud
jiman no N	自慢のN	vain
jiman-suru	自慢する	pride
jiman-suru	自慢する	proud
jimen	地面	ground
jimina	地味な	plain
jimina	地味な	simple
jimina	地味な	somber
jimini	地味に	simply
jimu	事務	office
jimu-in	事務員	clerk
jimu-shitsu	事務室	office
jimu-sho	事務所	office
jinbutsu	人物	figure
jin'in	人員	personnel
jinja	神社	shrine
jinkoo	人口	population

jinniku	人肉	flesh
jinrui	人類	mankind
jinsei	人生	life
jinsei-kan	人生観	philosophy
jinsen	人選	selection
jinsokuna	迅速な	rapid
jinsokuni	迅速に	rapidly
jiritsu	自立	independence
jiritsu-shin ga tsuyoi	自立心が強い	independent
jiritsu-shita N	自立したN	independent
jiritsu-shite iru (N)	自立している(N)	independent
jisei	時制	tense
jishaku	磁石	magnet
jishin	自信	confidence
jishin	地震	earthquake
-jishin	〜自身	oneself
-jishin	〜自身	self[2]
jishin ni michita N	自信に満ちたN	confident
jishin ni michite iru (N)	自信に満ちている(N)	confident
jisho	辞書	dictionary
jisho	地所	plot
jishoo	事象	phenomenon
jison-shin	自尊心	pride
jissai no N	実際のN	actual
jissai wa	実際は	actually
jissen	実践	practice
jissen-suru	実践する	practice
jissen-tekina	実践的な	powerful
jisshitsu-tekina	実質的な	substantial
ji-suberi	地滑り	slide
-jitai	〜自体	oneself
jitai-suru	辞退する	decline
jiten	辞典	dictionary
jiten	時点	point
jitensha	自転車	bicycle
jitensha	自転車	bike
jitsuen	実演	demonstration
jitsugen-suru	実現する	realize
jitsugyoo-ka	実業家	businessman
jitsuni	実に	indeed
jitsuyoo-tekina	実用的な	powerful
jitsuyoo-tekina	実用的な	working
jitsuzai	実在	reality
jitsuzai no N	実在のN	real
jitto miru	じっと見る	gaze
jitto miru	じっと見る	regard
jitto miru	じっと見る	stare
jiyoo hoofuna	滋養豊富な	substantial
jiyuu	自由	freedom
jiyuu	自由	liberty
jiyuuna	自由な	free
jiyuuna	自由な	liberal
jiyuuni	自由に	freely
jiyuuni kushi-suru chikara	自由に駆使する力	command
jiyuu ni...*Vte* ii	自由に…*Vte*いい	welcome
jiyuu-shugi-tekina	自由主義的な	liberal
jizoku-suru	持続する	sustain
jogingu (o) suru	ジョギング(を)する	jog
-joo	〜場	field
jooba	乗馬	riding
joobuna	丈夫な	solid
joobuna	丈夫な	stout
joobuna	丈夫な	strong
joobuna	丈夫な	sturdy
joocho-fu-anteina	情緒不安定な	emotional
joodan	冗談	joke
jooen	上演	production
jooen-suru	上演する	produce
jooen-suru	上演する	stage
joogi	定規	ruler
jooheki	城壁	wall
joohinna	上品な	elegant
joohinna	上品な	graceful
joohinna	上品な	polite
joohinna	上品な	refined
joohoo	情報	information
jooin	上院	senate
jooin-giin	上院議員	senator
jookei	情景	scene
jooken	条件	condition
jooken	条件	reservation
jooki	蒸気	steam
jooki	蒸気	vapor
jookoo	条項	article
jookoo	条項	clause
jookoo	条項	provision
jookyaku	乗客	fare
jookyaku	乗客	passenger
jookyoo	状況	circumstance
jookyoo	状況	condition
jookyoo	状況	picture
jookyoo	状況	situation
joomu-in	乗務員	crew
joomyaku	静脈	vein

joonetsu	情熱	passion
jooo	女王	queen
jooren	常連	regular
jooriku-suru	上陸する	land
jooryuu no N	上流のN	upper
joosha	乗車	riding
jooshitsu no N	上質のN	superior
jooshoo no (N)	上昇の(N)	upward
jootai	状態	condition
jootai	状態	state
jootatsu	上達	improvement
jooto	譲渡	transfer
jootoona	上等な	superior
jootoo no N	上等のN	superior
jooto-suru	譲渡する	transfer
jooyaku	条約	treaty
jooyoku	情欲	passion
joozuna	上手な	good
joozuna	上手な	skillful
joozuni	上手に	skillfully
joozuni	上手に	well[2]
joozuni naru	上手になる	improve
joryoku	助力	assistance
josei	女性	female
josei	女性	lady
josei	女性	woman
josei no N	女性のN	female
joshi	助詞	particle
joshi	女子	woman
jo-ten'in	女店員	salesgirl
joyuu	女優	actress
judaku	受諾	acceptance
judoo-tai	受動態	passive
jueki	樹液	sap
jugyoo	授業	class
jugyoo	授業	lesson
jukkoo	熟考	reflection
jukuren	熟練	skill
jukuren-shite iru (N)	熟練している(N)	skillful
jukuryo	熟慮	reflection
jukushita N	熟したN	ripe
jukutatsu	熟達	perfection
jukutatsu	熟達	proficiency
jukutatsu-do	熟達度	proficiency
jukutatsu-shita N	熟達したN	proficient
jukutatsu-shite iru (N)	熟達している(N)	proficient
junbi	準備	arrangement
junbi	準備	preparation
junbi	準備	provision
junbi ga dekita N	準備が出来たN	ready
junbi-suru	準備する	prepare
jungyoo	巡業	tour
jungyoo-suru	巡業する	tour
jun'i o tsukeru	順位を付ける	rank
junjo	順序	order
junjo	順序	procedure
junjo	順序	sequence
junkai-suru	巡回する	patrol
junkan	循環	circulation
jun ni naraberu	順に並べる	sequence
junrei-sha	巡礼者	pilgrim
junsuina	純粋な	pure
junsuina	純粋な	sheer
junsui no N	純粋のN	pure
juryoo	受領	receipt
jushin	受信	reception
jushoo-sha	受賞者	winner
jutsubu	述部	predicate
juu	銃	gun
juuatsu	重圧	pressure
juuatsu	重圧	stress
juuatsu	重圧	weight
juubun	十分	enough
juubunna	十分な	adequate
juubunna	十分な	enough
juubunna	十分な	sufficient
juubun(ni)	十分(に)	enough
juubun(ni)	十分(に)	fully
juubun(ni)	十分(に)	sufficiently
juu-bun no ichi	十分の一	tenth
juu (+counter) (no N)	十(+counter)(のN)	ten
juudaina	重大な	grave
juu-dai no N	十代のN	teenage
juudai-sa	重大さ	gravity
juuden-suru	充電する	charge
juu-gatsu	十月	October
juu-go (+counter) (no N)	十五(+counter)(のN)	fifteen
juugyoo-in	従業員	employee
juu-hachi-ban-me	十八番目	eighteenth
juu-hachi-ban-me no N	十八番目のN	eighteenth
juu-hachi (+counter) (no N)	十八(+counter)(のN)	eighteen
juu-ichi (+counter) (no N)	十一(+counter)(のN)	eleven
juu-ichi-gatsu	十一月	November

juuji-ka	十字架	cross
juuji-shite iru	従事している	engage
juujunna	従順な	obedient
juujunni	従順に	passively
juu-ku (+counter) (no N)	十九(+counter)(のN)	nineteen
juu-kyuu (+counter) (no N)	十九(+counter)(のN)	nineteen
juu-nana-ban-me (no N)	十七番目(のN)	seventeenth
juu-nana (+counter) (no N)	十七(+counter)(のN)	seventeen
juunanna	柔軟な	flexible
-juu (ni)	～中(に)	throughout
juu-ni (+counter) (no N)	十二(+counter)(のN)	twelve
juu-ni-gatsu	十二月	December
juuniku	獣肉	flesh
-juu o	～中を	through
juu-oku	十億	billion
juu-roku-ban-me (no N)	十六番目(のN)	sixteenth
juu-roku (+counter) (no N)	十六(+counter)(のN)	sixteen
juuryoku	重力	gravity
juuryoo	重量	weight
juu-san (+counter) (no N)	十三(+counter)(のN)	thirteen
juusha	従者	train
juushi	重視	emphasis
juu-shichi-ban-me (no N)	十七番目(のN)	seventeenth
juu-shichi (+counter) (no N)	十七(+counter)(のN)	seventeen
juu-shi (+counter) (no N)	十四(+counter)(のN)	fourteen
juusho	住所	address
juusu	ジュース	juice
juutan	じゅうたん	carpet
juuten	重点	emphasis
juuyaku	重役	director
juuyaku	重役	executive
juu-yon (+counter) (no N)	十四(+counter)(のN)	fourteen
juuyoo {denai/janai} (N)	重要{でない/じゃない}(N)	unimportant
juuyoona	重要な	important
juuyoona	重要な	significant
juuyoo-sei	重要性	consequence
juuyoo-sei	重要性	importance
juuyoo-sei	重要性	note
juuyoo-sei	重要性	significance
-juu zutto	～中ずっと	through
juwa-ki	受話器	receiver
juwa-ki	受話器	telephone
juyoo	需要	demand
juyo-suru	授与する	award
juzu-dama	数珠玉	bead

K

ka	か	or
-ka	～科	family
kaabon-shi	カーボン紙	carbon
kaabu	カーブ	curve
kaado	カード	card
kaanibaru	カーニバル	carnival
kaapetto	カーペット	carpet
kaaten	カーテン	curtain
kaato	カート	cart
kaaton	カートン	carton
kaba	かば	hippopotamus
kabaa	カバー	cover
kabaa-suru	カバーする	cover
kaban	かばん	bag
kabau	かばう	protect
kabau	かばう	shelter
kabau	かばう	shield
kabe	壁	wall
kabi	かび	mildew
kabi	かび	mold[1]
kabin	花瓶	vase
kabin-shiki	花瓶敷	mat
kabocha	かぼちゃ	pumpkin
kabu	株	share
kabu	株	stock
kabu	かぶ	turnip
kaburu	かぶる	wear
kabuto	かぶと	helmet
kachi	価値	value
kachi	価値	worth
kachi ga aru (N)	価値がある(N)	valuable
kachi ga aru (N), {Vinf. nonpast/N no}	価値がある(N), {Vinf. nonpast/Nの}	worth
kachiku	家畜	stock
kachi-toru	勝ち取る	win
kachitto iu oto	カチッという音	click
kadai	課題	assignment
kadai	課題	challenge

kado	角	corner
kado-batta N	角張ったN	square
kado no N	過度のN	excessive
…ka (doo ka)	…か(どうか)	whether
ka doo ka, Sinf.	かどうか, Sinf.	if
kaede	かえで	maple
kae-rareru	変えられる	variable
kaeru	かえる	alter
kaeru	かえる	change
kaeru	かえる	frog
kaeru	かえる	return
kaeru	変える	shift
kaeru	かえる	transform
kaeru	かえる	turn
kaeru	かえる	vary
kaesu	かえす	return
kafeteria	カフェテリア	cafeteria
kagaku	化学	chemistry
kagaku	科学	science
kagaku no N	化学のN	chemical
kagaku-sha	化学者	chemist
kagaku-sha	科学者	scientist
kagaku-tekina	化学的な	chemical
kagaku-tekina	科学的な	scientific
kagaku-yakuhin	化学薬品	chemical
kagami	鏡	mirror
kagayaite iru (N)	輝いている(N)	radiant
kagayakashii	輝かしい	glorious
kagayakashii	輝かしい	splendid
kagayaki	輝き	splendor
kagayaku	輝く	shine
kagayaku (N)	輝く(N)	radiant
kage	かげ	reflection
kage	陰	shade
kage	影	shadow
kageki	歌劇	opera
-kagetsu	～か月	month
kagi	かぎ	key
kagi	かぎ	lock
kagi ga kakaru	かぎがかかる	lock
kagi o kakeru	かぎをかける	lock
kagiru	限る	limit
kagi-tsukeru	かぎつける	smell
kago	かご	basket
kagu	家具	furniture
kagu koto	かぐこと	smell
kagu o ireru	家具を入れる	furnish
kahei	貨幣	money

kai	会	board
kai	階	floor
kai	かい	oar
kai	かい	paddle
kai	貝	shellfish
kai	階	story[2]
-kai	～回	time
-kai	～界	world
kaibutsu	怪物	monster
kaichiku	改築	renovation
kaichiku-suru	改築する	renovate
kaichoo	会長	president
kaichuu-dokei	懐中時計	watch
kaidan	階段	stairs
kaifuku	回復	rally
kaifuku-suru	回復する	rally
kaifuku-suru	回復する	recover
kaiga	絵画	painting
kaigai-denpoo	海外電報	cable
kaigan	海岸	beach
kaigan	海岸	coast
kaigan	海岸	seashore
kaigan	海岸	seaside
kaigan-zoi no N	海岸沿いのN	coastal
kai-gara	貝殻	shell
kaigi	会議	conference
kaigi	会議	meeting
kaigi-shitsu	会議室	chamber
kaigi-sho	会議所	chamber
kaigoo	会合	assembly
kaigun	海軍	navy
kaigun no N	海軍のN	naval
kaigun-taishoo	海軍大将	admiral
kaihatsu	開発	development
kaihatsu-suru	開発する	develop
kaihei	海兵	marine
kaihi-suru	回避する	avoid
kaihoo	会報	bulletin
kaihoo	解放	release
kaihoo-suru	解放する	release
kaiin	会員	member
kaikaku	改革	reform
kaikaku-suru	改革する	reform
kaiken	会見	interview
kaiketsu	解決	settlement
kaiketsu	解決	solution
kaiketsu-hoo	解決法	solution
kaiketsu-saku	解決策	remedy

kaiketsu-suru	解決する	resolve
kaiketsu-suru	解決する	settle
kaiketsu-suru	解決する	solve
kaiketsu-suru {hito/mono}	解決する{人/物}	settler
kaiki	会期	session
kaiki-sen	回帰線	tropic
kaikyoo	海峡	channel
kaikyoo	海峡	strait
kaikyuu	階級	class
kaimen	海綿	sponge
kai-mono	買い物	shopping
kai-mono ni iku	買い物に行く	shop
kai-mono o suru	買い物をする	shop
kai-narasa-rete iru (N)	飼い慣らされている(N)	tame
kai-narasu	飼い慣らす	tame
kainin	解任	recall
kainin-suru	解任する	recall
kairai	かいらい	puppet
kairaku	快楽	pleasure
kairyoo	改良	improvement
kairyoo-suru	改良する	improve
kaisan-	海産〜	marine
kaisan-butsu	海産物	seafood
kaisha	会社	company
kaisha	会社	concern
kaisha-in	会社員	company employee
kaishaku	解釈	interpretation
kaishaku-suru	解釈する	interpret
kaishi	開始	start
kaishuu	回収	recall
kaishuu-suru	回収する	recall
kaisoo	海藻	seaweed
kaisui no N	海水のN	saltwater
kaita hito	書いた人	writer
kaitaku-sha	開拓者	pioneer
kaitaku-sha	開拓者	settler
kaita mono	書いたもの	writing
kai-te	買い手	buyer
kaite aru	書いてある	read
kaitei-kikan	開廷期間	session
kaitekina	快適な	comfortable
kaiten	回転	revolution
kaiten	回転	turn
kaiten-saseru	回転させる	turn
kaiten-suru	回転する	rotate

kaitoo	回答	reply
kaitoo	解答	solution
kaitoo-suru	回答する	reply
kaiwa	会話	conversation
kaiwa	会話	talk
kaiyoo	海洋	ocean
kaiyoo-	海洋〜	marine
kaizen	改善	improvement
kaizen	改善	reform
kaizen-suru	改善する	improve
kaizen-suru	改善する	reform
kaizen-suru	改善する	remedy
kaizoku	海賊	pirate
kaizoo	改造	renovation
kaizoo-suru	改造する	renovate
kaji	火事	fire
kaji o toru	かじを取る	steer
kajiru	かじる	bite
kaji-ya	かじ屋	blacksmith
kaju-en	果樹園	orchard
…ka…ka {dochira-ka/dotchi-ka}	…か…か{どちらか/どっちか}	either
kakaeru	抱える	hold
kakaku	価格	price
kakaku	価格	value
kakareta N	書かれたN	written
kakaru	かかる	catch
kakaru	かかる	cost
kakaru	かかる	hang
kakaru	かかる	span
kakaru	かかる	take
kakaru	かかる	trail
kakato	かかと	heel
kakatte iru	かかっている	depend
kakawari-ai	かかわりあい	association
kakawaru	かかわる	concern
kake	かけ	bet
kake	かけ	stake
-kake	〜掛け	rack
kake-dokei	掛け時計	clock
kakei	火刑	stake
kakeru	かける	bet
kakeru	かける	hang
kakeru	かける	play
kakeru	かける	pour
kakeru	かける	spend
kakeru	かける	venture
kakeru	かける	wear

kaki	かき	oyster
kaki	かき	persimmon
kaki-atsumeru	かき集める	scrape
kaki-mawasu	かき回す	stir
kaki-mazeru	かき混ぜる	scramble
kaki-mazeru	かき混ぜる	stir
kaki-naosu	書き直す	rewrite
kaki-ne	垣根	fence
kaki-tomeru	書き留める	note
kaki-tomeru	書き留める	record
kakki ga aru (N)	活気がある(N)	lively
kakko	括弧	parenthesis
kakkoo	格好	shape
kako	過去	past
kakomu	囲む	enclose
kakomu	囲む	surround
kako no N	過去のN	past
kakou	囲う	surround
kaku	かく	draw
kaku	かく	remark
kaku	かく	scratch
kaku	かく	write
kaku-	各～	each
-kaku	～覚	sense
kakuchoo	拡張	expansion
kakuchoo-suru	拡張する	expand
kakudai-suru	拡大する	enlarge
kakudo	角度	angle
kakugo ga dekite iru (N)	覚悟が出来ている(N)	ready
kakuho-suru	確保する	secure
kakujitsuna	確実な	certain
kakujitsuna	確実な	sure
kakujitsuni	確実に	surely
kaku koto	書くこと	writing
kaku koto ga dekinai (N)	欠くことができない(N)	essential
kakumei	革命	revolution
kakumei no N	革命のN	revolutionary
kakumei-tekina	革命的な	revolutionary
kakunin-suru	確認する	identify
kaku no N	核のN	nuclear
kakure-basho	隠れ場所	nest
kakureru	隠れる	hide
kakuri	隔離	isolation
kakuritsu	確立	establishment
kakuritsu	確率	probability
kakuritsu-suru	確立する	establish
kakushin	核心	heart
kakushin	確信	trust
kakushin-shite iru (N)	確信している(N)	confident
kakusu	隠す	cover
kakusu	隠す	hide
kakutei-tekina	確定的な	tangible
kakutoku	獲得	acquisition
kakutoku-suru	獲得する	acquire
kakutoku-suru	獲得する	obtain
kakutoku-suru	獲得する	take
kakutoku-suru	獲得する	win
kakuu no N	架空のN	imaginary
kakyoku	歌曲	song
kama	かま	boiler
kamau	構う	bother
kamau	構う	care
kamawanai, {V/adj./cop.}*te* mo	構わない, {V/adj./cop.}*te* も	can[1]
kamawanai, {V/adj./cop.}*te* mo	構わない, {V/adj./cop.}*te* も	may
kamawanai, V*te* mo	構わない, V*te*も	mind
kame	かめ	pot
kame	かめ	turtle
kamen	仮面	mask
kamera	カメラ	camera
kami	神	god
kami	髪	hair
kami	神	heaven
kami	紙	paper
kaminari	雷	thunder
kaminari ga naru	雷が鳴る	thunder
kami ni kakete chikau	神に掛けて誓う	swear
kami-sama	神様	god
kami-sori	かみそり	razor
kamoku	{科/課}目	subject
…kamoshirenai	…かもしれない	perhaps
kamoshirenai, {adj(*na*). stem/N} {ø/datta}	かもしれない, {adj(*na*). stem/N}{ø/だった}	may
kamoshirenai, {adj(*na*). stem/N} {ø/datta}	かもしれない, {adj(*na*). stem/N}{ø/だった}	maybe
kamoshirenai, {adj(*na*). stem/N} {ø/datta}	かもしれない, {adj(*na*). stem/N}{ø/だった}	might
kamoshirenai, {adj(*na*). stem/N} {ø/datta}	かもしれない, {adj(*na*). stem/N}{ø/だった}	possibly
kamoshirenai, {V/adj(*i*).}inf.	かもしれない, {V/adj(*i*).}inf.	may
kamoshirenai, {V/adj(*i*).}inf.	かもしれない, {V/adj(*i*).}inf.	maybe

kamoshirenai, {V/adj(*i*).}inf.	かもしれない, {V/adj(*i*).}inf.	might
kamoshirenai, {V/adj(*i*).}inf.	かもしれない, {V/adj(*i*).}inf.	possibly
kamotsu	貨物	cargo
kamotsu	貨物	freight
kamu	かむ	bite
kamu	かむ	chew
kamu, (hana o)	かむ, (鼻を)	blow
kan	缶	can[2]
-kan	～感	feeling
-kan	～間	for
-kan	～管	pipe
-kan	～感	sense
-kan	～巻	volume
Kanada	カナダ	Canada
Kanada-jin	カナダ人	Canadian
Kanada no N	カナダのN	Canadian
kana, (hontoo ni) Sinf.	かな, (本当に)Sinf.	wonder
kanai	家内	wife
kanakiri-goe no N	金切り声のN	shrill
kana-kiri-goe o {ageru/dasu}	金切り声を{あげる/出す}	scream
kanarazu	必ず	surely
kanarazu-shimo…neg.	必ずしも…neg.	necessarily
kanarazu…V	必ず…V	promise
kanari	かなり	comparatively
kanari	かなり	considerably
kanari	かなり	fair
kanari	かなり	fairly
kanari	かなり	pretty
kanari no N	かなりのN	comparative
kanashi-{geni/sooni}	悲し{げに/そうに}	sadly
kanashii	悲しい	sad
kanashi-mi	悲しみ	regret
kanashi-mi	悲しみ	sadness
kanashi-mi	悲しみ	sorrow
kanashimu	悲しむ	mourn
kanashi-sa	悲しさ	sadness
kana-zuchi	金づち	hammer
kanban	看板	sign
kanban	看板	signboard
kanbasu	カンバス	canvas
kanboku	潅木	bush
kanboku	潅木	shrub
kanboo	監房	ward[2]
kanbu	幹部	executive
kanchoo	艦長	captain
kandaina	寛大な	generous
kandan-kei	寒暖計	thermometer
kandoo-saseru	感動させる	affect
kandoo-saseru	感動させる	touch
kandoo-saseru, gutto	感動させる, ぐっと	thrill
kane	鐘	bell
kane	金	money
kane-mochi no N	金持ちのN	rich
kane o kakeru	金をかける	bet
kane o kifu-suru	金を寄付する	subscribe
kangae	考え	idea
kangae	考え	thinking
kangae	考え	thought
kangae-kata	考え方	philosophy
kangae o hakkiri iu	考えをはっきり言う	vocal
kangaeru	考える	regard
kangaeru	考える	think
kangaeru	考える	view
kangaeru koto	考えること	thinking
kangaeru koto	考えること	thought
kangaruu	カンガルー	kangaroo
kangei	歓迎	reception
kangei-kai	歓迎会	reception
kangei-sareru (N)	歓迎される(N)	welcome
kangei-suru	歓迎する	welcome
kangen-gaku-dan	管弦楽団	orchestra
kangen-suru	還元する	reduce
kango-fu	看護婦	nurse
kango o suru	看護をする	attend
kanja	患者	patient
kanja	患者	subject
kanji	感じ	sensation
kanji	感じ	sense
kanji	感じ	sentiment
kanji	感じ	touch
kanji ga ii	感じがいい	pleasing
kanjiru	感じる	feel
kanjiru	感じる	sense
kanjoo	勘定	bill
kanjoo	感情	emotion
kanjoo	感情	feeling
kanjoo-gaki	勘定書	check
kanjoo ni ireru	勘定に入れる	count
kanjoo-tekina	感情的な	emotional
kanju-sei	感受性	feeling
kankaku	感覚	feeling
kankaku	感覚	sensation

kankaku	感覚	sense
kankaku	間隔	interval
kan-kan ni natte okoru	かんかんになって怒る	furious
kankei	関係	bearing
kankei	関係	concern
kankei	関係	connection
kankei	関係	relation
kankei	関係	relationship
kankei ga aru N	関係があるN	relative
kankei-suru	関係する	relate
kankei-zukeru	関係付ける	relate
kanketsuna	簡潔な	brief
kanketsuni	簡潔に	briefly
kanki	寒気	chill
kanki-sen	換気扇	fan[1]
kanki-suru	喚起する	arouse
kankitsu-rui	かんきつ類	citrus
kankoku	勧告	recommendation
kankoo	刊行	publication
kankoo	観光	sightseeing
kankoo-butsu	刊行物	publication
kankoo-kyaku	観光客	sightseer
kankoo-kyaku	観光客	tourist
kankoo-kyaku	観光客	visitor
kankoo-suru	刊行する	publish
kankyaku	観客	spectator
kankyoo	環境	environment
kankyoo	環境	setting
kankyoo	環境	surrounding
kanningu-suru	カンニングする	cheat
kanntan ni	簡単に	readily
kannuki	かんぬき	bar
kanojo	彼女	she
kanojo no	彼女の	hers
kanojo no N	彼女のN	her
kanojo+prt.	彼女+prt.	her
kanojo-ra	彼女ら	they
kanojo-ra no N	彼女らのN	their
kanojo-ra {o/ni}	彼女ら{を/に}	them
kanojo-tachi	彼女たち	they
kanojo-tachi no N	彼女たちのN	their
kanojo-tachi {o/ni}	彼女たち{を/に}	them
kanoona	可能な	possible
kanoo-sei	可能性	possibility
kanoo-sei	可能性	probability
kanpai	乾杯	toast[2]
kanpai-sareru hito	乾杯される人	toast[2]

kanpeki	完ぺき	perfection
kanpekini	完ぺきに	perfectly
kanpekini	完ぺきに	thoroughly
kanpeki-shugi-sha	完ぺき主義者	perfectionist
kanri	管理	control
kanri-un'ei	管理運営	administration
Kanzasu	カンザス	Kansas
kansatsu	観察	observation
kansatsu-suru	観察する	observe
kansei	完成	completion
kansei	完成	perfection
kansei-suru	完成する	complete
kansei-suru	完成する	perfect
kansen	感染	infection
kansen-suru	感染する	infect
kansetsu-sei	間接性	indirectness
kansetsu-tekina	間接的な	indirect
kansha	感謝	appreciation
kansha	感謝	gratitude
kansha	感謝	recognition
kansha	感謝	thanks
kansha no hyoogen	感謝の表現	thanksgiving
kansha no inori	感謝の祈り	thanksgiving
kansha-shite iru	感謝している	thankful
kansha-suru	感謝する	appreciate
kansha-suru	感謝する	grateful
kansha-suru	感謝する	thank
kanshi	冠詞	article
kanshi	監視	watch
kanshin-ji	関心事	concern
kanshin-suru	感心する	impress
kanshi-suru	監視する	watch
kanshoku	感触	texture
kanshoo	鑑賞	appreciation
kanshoo-suru	鑑賞する	appreciate
kanshuu	観衆	audience
kanshuu	慣習	convention
kanshuu	慣習	practice
kanshuu	観衆	spectator
kanso-ka-suru	簡素化する	simplify
kansoku	観測	observation
kansoku-suru	観測する	observe
kansona	簡素な	simple
kansoni	簡素に	simply
kansoo	感想	sentiment
kansoo	感想	thought
kansoo-shita N	乾燥したN	dry
kansuru	関する	concern

kantanna	簡単な	minor
kantanna	簡単な	simple
kantanni	簡単に	easily
kantanni	簡単に	simply
kantanni suru	簡単にする	simplify
kanten	観点	standpoint
kanten	観点	viewpoint
kantoku	監督	charge
kantoku	監督	director
kantoku	監督	manager
kantoku	監督	supervision
kantoku-suru	監督する	supervise
kanuu	カヌー	canoe
kan'yo	関与	share
kan'yoona	肝要な	vital
kanzenna	完全な	complete
kanzenna	完全な	perfect
kanzenna	完全な	solid
kanzenna	完全な	strict
kanzenna	完全な	thorough
kanzenna	完全な	total
kanzenna mono ni suru	完全なものにする	perfect
kanzenni	完全に	altogether
kanzenni	完全に	completely
kanzenni	完全に	fully
kanzenni	完全に	perfectly
kanzenni	完全に	thoroughly
kanzenni	完全に	through
kanzenni	完全に	utterly
kanzenni	完全に	wholly
kanzoo	肝臓	liver
kanzume	缶詰	can[2]
kanzume	缶詰	canned food
kao	顔	face
kao	顔	feature
kaori	香り	smell
kappatsuna	活発な	vigorous
kapuseru	カプセル	capsule
kara	から	as
kara	から	from
kara	殻	shell
kara	から	through
karaa	カラー	collar
karada	体	body
karada ga fu-jiyuuna	体が不自由な	handicapped
karada no N	体のN	physical
karada-tsuki	体つき	shape
karai	からい	salty

karai	からい	spicy
kara kara dasu	殻から出す	shell
karakau	からかう	tease
karama-seru	絡ませる	tangle
karami-tsuku	絡み付く	wind[2]
karamu	絡む	tangle
kara no N	空のN	empty
karappo no N, naka ga	空っぽのN, 中が	hollow
kara, S	から, S	because
kara, S	から, S	since[2]
kara, Sinf.	から, Sinf.	that[3]
karasu-mugi	からす麦	oats
kara, V*te*	から, V*te*	since[1]
kare	彼	he
kare	彼	husband
karee	カレー	curry
karei-sa	華麗さ	splendor
karendaa	カレンダー	calendar
kare no	彼の	his
kare no N	彼のN	his
kare+prt.	彼+prt.	him
kare-ra	彼ら	they
kare-ra no N	彼らのN	their
kare-ra {o/ni}	彼ら{を/に}	them
kareru	かれる	wither
Kariforunia	カリフォルニア	California
kari-komu	刈り込む	trim
kari ni	仮に	tentatively
kari no N	仮のN	tentative
kari o suru	狩りをする	hunt
kariru	借りる	borrow
kariru, kane o haratte	借りる, 金を払って	rent
karite iru	借りている	owe
-karoo to adj(*i*). *ku* nakaroo to, adj(*i*). stem	～かろうと adj(*i*). *ku*なかろうと, adj(*i*). stem	whether
-karoo to adj(*i*). stem karoo to, adj(*i*). stem	～かろうと adj(*i*). stemかろうと, adj(*i*). stem	whether
karu	刈る	clip
karu	刈る	mow
karui	軽い	light[2]
karui	軽い	mild
karuku suru koto	軽くすること	relief
karuku tataku	軽くたたく	pat
karuku tataku	軽くたたく	tap
karuku tataku koto	軽くたたくこと	pat
karuku tataku koto	軽くたたくこと	tap
karuku tataku oto	軽くたたく音	tap
karushiumu	カルシウム	calcium

kasa	傘	umbrella
kasa-kasa to oto o tateru	かさかさと音を立てる	rustle
kasan	加算	addition
kasanaru	重なる	overlap
kasaneru	重ねる	pile
kasegu	稼ぐ	earn
kasen	下線	underline
kasen o hiku	下線を引く	underline
kasetsu	仮説	assumption
kasetsu	仮説	hypothesis
kasetto	カセット	cassette
kashi	菓子	cake
kashi	華氏	Fahrenheit
kashi	かし	oak
kashi-kan	下士官	soldier
kashikoi	賢い	clever
kashikoi	賢い	wise
Kashikomarimashita	かしこまりました	certainly
kashikomarimashita	かしこまりました	sir
kashira, (hontoo ni) Sinf.	かしら, (本当に)Sinf.	wonder
kashitsu	過失	fault
kashu	歌手	singer
kassai	喝さい	cheer
kassha	滑車	tackle
kassoo-ro	滑走路	runway
kasu	貸す	lend
kasu	貸す	loan
kasukana	かすかな	faint
kasumi	かすみ	mist
kata	型	mold[2]
kata	型	pattern
kata	肩	shoulder
kata	型	type
katachi	形	form
katachi	形	shape
katachi-zukuru	形作る	shape
kata-dotte tsukuru	型取って作る	pattern
kata-gaki	肩書き	title
kata-gami	型紙	pattern
katai	かたい	firm
katai	かたい	hard
katai	かたい	rigid
katai	かたい	stiff
katai	かたい	tough
kata-kake	肩掛け	shawl
kataku	かたく	firmly
katakuri-ko	かたくり粉	starch
kata-kurushii	堅苦しい	stiff
katamari	塊	block
katamari	塊	chunk
katamari	塊	lump
katamari	塊	mass
kata-mi	形見	souvenir
kata-michi no N	片道のN	one-way
katamukeru	傾ける	tilt
katamuku	傾く	decline
katamuku	傾く	lean
katamuku	傾く	slant
katamuku	傾く	tilt
katana	刀	sword
kata o sukumeru	肩をすくめる	shrug
katatsumuri	かたつむり	snail
kata, V*masu*	方, V*masu*	fashion
-kata, V*masu*	～方, V*masu*	way
kata-zukeru	片付ける	clear
kata-zukeru	片付ける	tidy
katchuu	甲ちゅう	armor
katei	仮定	assumption
katei	家庭	home
katei	過程	process
katei	課程	program
katei no N	家庭のN	domestic
katei-suru	仮定する	assume
katsu	勝つ	overcome
katsu	勝つ	win
katsudoo	活動	action
katsudoo	活動	activity
katsudoo	活動	motion
katsudoo-tekina	活動的な	active
katsuji	活字	type
katsuji-tai de kaku	活字体で書く	print
katsuryoku	活力	energy
katsuryoku	活力	spring
katsuryoku	活力	vigor
katsute	かつて	once
katsuyoo-sarete inai (N)	活用されていない(N)	unemployed
katte iru	飼っている	own
katte ni…V*te* ii	勝手に…V*te*いい	welcome
katto	カット	cut
katto-suru	カットする	cut
kau	買う	buy
kau	買う	purchase
kauntaa	カウンター	counter

kawa	革	leather
kawa	川	river
kawa	皮	shell
kawa	皮	skin
kawa-gishi	川岸	bank[2]
kawa-himo	革ひも	strap
kawa-himo de kukuru	革ひもでくくる	strap
kawa-himo de tataku	革ひもでたたく	strap
kawai-garu	かわいがる	love
kawaii	かわいい	cute
kawai-soona	かわいそうな	pitiful
kawai-soona	かわいそうな	poor
kawai-soona	かわいそうな	sorry
kawaita N	乾いたN	dry
kawakasu	乾かす	dry
kawaku	かわく	dry
kawa o hagu	皮をはぐ	skin
kawa o muku	皮をむく	skin
kawa o namesu	皮をなめす	tan
kawara	かわら	tile
kawari	代わり	substitute
kawari ni	代わりに	for
kawari ni	代わりに	instead
kawari ni (-o) tsukau	代わりに(〜を)使う	substitute
kawari no hito	代わりの人	replacement
kawari o saseru	代わりをさせる	substitute
kawari o tsutomeru	代わりを務める	substitute
kawari-yasui	変わりやすい	variable
kawari-yasui mono	変わりやすいもの	variable
kawaru	かわる	change
kawaru	かわる	shift
kawaru	かわる	vary
kawase	為替	exchange
kawatte iru	変わっている	peculiar
kayaku	火薬	powder
kayoo(-bi)	火曜(日)	Tuesday
kayou	通う	commute
ka-yowai	か弱い	tender
kayui	かゆい	itchy
kazan	火山	volcano
kazan (no) N	火山(の)N	volcanic
kazan no yoona	火山のような	volcanic
kazari	飾り	decoration
(kazari-)obi	(飾り)帯	sash[1]
kazaru	飾る	adorn
kazaru	飾る	decorate
kazaru	飾る	trim
kaze	かぜ	cold
kaze	風	wind[1]
kaze-atari ga tsuyoi	風あたりが強い	windy
(kaze ga) fuku	(風が)吹く	blow
kaze ga tsuyoi	風が強い	windy
kazoe-kire-nai hodo no N	数えきれないほどのN	infinite
kazoeru	数える	count
kazoku	家族	family
kazoku	家族	household
kazu	数	number
kazu ni ireru	数に入れる	count
ke	毛	fur
ke	毛	hair
ke	毛	wool
ke-ashi ga nagai	毛足が長い	shaggy
kechina	けちな	mean[1]
kedamono	けだもの	beast
keeburu-sen	ケーブル線	cable
keeki	ケーキ	cake
keesu	ケース	case[1]
kega	けが	injury
ke ga nagai	毛が長い	shaggy
kega o saseru	けがをさせる	wound[1]
kega o suru	けがをする	hurt
kega o suru	けがをする	injure
kegasu	汚す	compromise
kegasu	汚す	stain
kegasu	汚す	violate
ke-gawa	毛皮	fur
keibatsu	刑罰	punishment
keibi	警備	guard
keibi-in	警備員	guard
keibi-suru	警備する	guard
keiei	経営	management
keiei-jin	経営陣	management
keiei-sha	経営者	manager
keiei-suru	経営する	manage
keiei-suru	経営する	run
keigo	敬語	honorific
keihoo	警報	alarm
keii	敬意	regard
keiji	掲示	bulletin
keika	経過	passage
keikaku	計画	plan
keikaku	計画	project
keikaku	計画	scheme
keikaku da, Vinf. nonpast	計画だ, Vinf. nonpast	plan

keikan	警官	officer
keikan	警官	policeman
keiken	経験	experience
keiken	経験	taste
keiken-suru	経験する	taste
keiken-suru	経験する	undergo
keiki	計器	instrument
keikoku	警告	caution
keikoku	警告	notice
keikoku	警告	warning
keikoku-suru	警告する	caution
keikoku-suru	警告する	warn
keikoo	傾向	current
keikoo	傾向	stream
keikoo	傾向	tendency
keikoo	傾向	wind[1]
keikoo ga aru, Vinf. nonpast	傾向がある, Vinf. nonpast	tend
keimu-sho	刑務所	jail
keimu-sho	刑務所	prison
keirei-suru	敬礼する	salute
keireki	経歴	career
keiro	経路	channel
keisan	計算	calculation
keisan-suru	計算する	calculate
keisan-suru	計算する	reckon
keisatsu	警察	police
keisei	形成	formation
keisha	傾斜	slant
keisha	傾斜	slope
keishiki	形式	form
keishi-suru	軽視する	neglect
keitai-yoo no N	携帯用のN	portable
ke-ito	毛糸	wool
ke-ito	毛糸	yarn
keiyaku	契約	contract
keiyaku-jooken	契約条件	term
keiyoo-shi	形容詞	adjective
-keiyu de	～経由で	via
keiyu-shite	経由して	by
keizai	経済	economy
keizai-gaku no N	経済学のN	economic
keizai-joo no N	経済上のN	economic
keizai-tekina	経済的な	economical
keizai-tekina	経済的な	financial
kekka	結果	consequence
kekka	結果	effect
kekka	結果	outcome
kekka	結果	result
kekkan	欠陥	fault
kekkan	血管	vein
kekkan	血管	vessel
kekki-taikai	決起大会	rally
kekkon	結婚	marriage
kekkon-saseru	結婚させる	unite
kekkon-shiki	結婚式	wedding
kekkon-shite iru	結婚している	married
kekkon-suru	結婚する	marry
kekkoona	結構な	fine
kekkyoku	結局	eventually
kemono	獣	beast
kemui	けむい	smoky
kemuri	煙	smoke
kemuri ga deru	煙が出る	smoke
kemutai	けむたい	smoky
ken	県	prefecture
-ken	～圏	zone
kenbi-kyoo	顕微鏡	microscope
kenbutsu	見物	sightseeing
kenbutsu-nin	見物人	spectator
kenchiku	建築	architecture
kenchiku-ka	建築家	architect
ken'i	権威	authority
Kenia	ケニア	Kenya
ken'in-suru	けん引する	tow
ken'i(-sha)	権威(者)	authority
kenjuu	拳銃	pistol
kenka	けんか	fight
kenka	けんか	quarrel
kenkai	見解	theory
kenkai	見解	thought
kenkai	見解	view
kenka-suru	けんかする	fight
kenka-suru	けんかする	quarrel
kenkoo	健康	health
kenkoona	健康な	healthy
kenkoona	健康な	well[2]
kenkyona	謙虚な	humble
kenkyona	謙虚な	modest
kenkyuu	研究	research
kenkyuu	研究	study
kenkyuu-in	研究員	worker
kenkyuu-jo	研究所	institute
kenkyuu-jo	研究所	laboratory
kenkyuu-ronbun	研究論文	study
kenkyuu-sha	研究者	student

kenkyuu-sha	研究者	worker
kenkyuu-shitsu	研究室	office
kenkyuu-suru	研究する	study
kenmeina	賢明な	wise
kenmei-sa	賢明さ	wisdom
kenpoo	憲法	constitution
kenri	権利	claim
kenri	権利	right
kenryoku	権力	authority
kenryoku	権力	power
kenryoku ga aru (N)	権力がある(N)	powerful
kensa	検査	check
kensa	検査	examination
kensa	検査	search
kensa	検査	test
kensa-hoo	検査法	test
kensa-suru	検査する	examine
kensa-suru	検査する	inspect
kensa-suru	検査する	test
kensetsu	建設	construction
kensetsu-suru	建設する	construct
kenshoo-kin	懸賞金	prize
Kentakkii	ケンタッキー	Kentucky
kentoo ga tsuku	見当が付く	guess
kentoo-suru	検討する	study
kenzenna	健全な	healthy
kerai	家来	servant
-kereba, adj(*i*). stem	～ければ, adj(*i*). stem	if
ke(re)do	け(れ)ど	though
ke(re)do(mo)	け(れ)ど(も)	although
ke(re)do(mo)	け(れ)ど(も)	as
ke(re)do(mo)	け(れ)ど(も)	but
keredomo	けれども	though
keredo(mo), Sinf.	けれど(も), Sinf.	while
keru	ける	kick
keshi-gomu	消しゴム	eraser
keshiki	景色	landscape
keshiki	景色	scenery
keshiki	景色	sight
keshoo	化粧	make-up
keshoo	化粧	toilet
keshoo-shitsu	化粧室	toilet
kesseki	結石	stone
kesseki-shite	欠席して	absent
kesshin	決心	decision
kesshin	決心	determination
kesshin	決心	resolution
kesshin	決心	will
kesshin (o) suru	決心(を)する	determine
kesshin-suru	決心する	decide
kesshin-suru, Vvol. to	決心する, Vvol.と	resolve
kesshite…(nanka ja) nai	決して…(なんかじゃ)ない	no
keta	桁	figure
ketsudan	決断	volition
ketsueki	血液	blood
ketsugi	決議	resolution
ketsugoo	結合	union
ketsugoo-suru	結合する	combine
ketsugoo-suru	結合する	unite
ketsui	決意	determination
ketsui	決意	will
ketsuron	結論	conclusion
ketsuron-zukeru	結論づける	conclude
kettei	決定	decision
kettei-suru	決定する	determine
ketten	欠点	drawback
ketten	欠点	fault
kewashii	険しい	steep
kezuru	削る	sharpen
kezuru	削る	shave
ki	木	tree
ki	気	will
-ki	～期	stage
kiba	きば	tusk
kibatsuna	奇抜な	fantastic
kibinna	機敏な	alert
kibishii	厳しい	grim
kibishii	厳しい	harsh
kibishii	厳しい	severe
kibishii	厳しい	stern
kibishii	厳しい	stiff
kibishii	厳しい	strict
kibishiku	厳しく	sternly
kibo	規模	scale[3]
kiboo	希望	hope
kiboo	希望	wish
kiboo-suru	希望する	hope
kibun	気分	mood
kichi	基地	base
ki-chigai	気違い	nut
ki-chigai (no N)	気違い(のN)	mad
kichin-to	きちんと	neatly
kichin-to	きちんと	properly
kichin-to shita N	きちんとしたN	neat

kichin-to shita N	きちんとしたN	orderly
kichin-to shita N	きちんとしたN	tidy
kichin-to shite iru (N)	きちんとしている(N)	neat
kichin-to shite iru (N)	きちんとしている(N)	orderly
kichin-to shite iru (N)	きちんとしている(N)	tidy
kichin-to suru	きちんとする	organize
kichin-to suru	きちんとする	tidy
kichoo-hin	貴重品	treasure
kichoo-hin	貴重品	valuable
kichoona	貴重な	precious
kichoona	貴重な	valuable
ki de dekita N	木で出来たN	wooden
kidoo	軌道	orbit
kieru	消える	disappear
kieru	消える	fade
kieru	消える	vanish
kifu	寄付	contribution
kifu	寄付	subscription
kifu-suru	寄付する	contribute
ki-{gaeru/kaeru}	着替える	change
ki ga hikeru	気が引ける	reluctant
kigai o kuwaeru	危害を加える	harm
(ki-ga-)kurutte iru (N)	(気が)狂っている(N)	crazy
ki ga mijikai	気が短い	impatient
ki ga mijikai	気が短い	short-tempered
ki ga tooku naru	気が遠くなる	faint
ki-ga-tsuite inai (N)	気がついていない(N)	unconscious
ki-ga-tsukanai	気がつかない	unaware
ki-ga-tsuku	気がつく	notice
ki-ga-tsuku	気がつく	occur
ki-ga-tsuku	気がつく	perceive
kigen	紀元	A.D.
kigen	機嫌	mood
kigen	起源	origin
kigen	機嫌	temper
kigen to suru	起源とする	stem
kigen-zen	紀元前	B.C.
ki-gire	木切れ	stick
kigoo	記号	symbol
kigu	器具	instrument
kigyoo	企業	enterprise
kihin	気品	style
kihon	基本	basis
kihon-tekina	基本的な	basic
kihon-tekina	基本的な	cardinal
kii	キー	key
kii-kii iu	きいきい言う	squeak
kii-kii iu N	きいきい言うN	shrill
ki-iro	黄色	yellow
kiiroi	黄色い	yellow
kiji	記事	article
ki-ji	生地	material
ki-ji	生地	texture
kijun	きじゅん	standard
kijutsu	記述	description
kijutsu-suru	記述する	describe
kika(-gaku)	幾何(学)	geometry
kikai	機会	chance
kikai	機械	machine
kikai	機会	occasion
kikai	機会	opportunity
(kikai ga) naku naru	(機会が)なくなる	slip
kikai-koo	機械工	mechanic
kikai no N	機械のN	mechanical
kikai-tekina	機械的な	mechanical
kika-ki	気化器	carburetor
kikan	期間	duration
kikan	機関	establishment
kikan	器官	organ
kikan	期間	period
kikan	期間	term
kikan-shi	機関士	engineer
kikei no doobutsu	奇形の動物	monster
kikei no shokubutsu	奇形の植物	monster
kiken	危険	danger
kiken	危険	risk
kikenna	危険な	dangerous
kiken ni sarasu	危険にさらす	risk
kiki-morasu	聞き漏らす	miss
kikin	基金	foundation
kikin	基金	fund
kiki-narenai N	聞き慣れないN	strange
kiki-te	聞き手	listener
kiki-tekina	危機的な	critical
kiki-wake ga ii	聞き分けがいい	reasonable
kikoeru	聞こえる	audible
kikoeru	聞こえる	hear
kikoo	気候	climate
kikoo	寄稿	contribution
kikoo	機構	mechanism
kikoo	機構	wheel

kikoo-suru	寄稿する	contribute
kiku	きく	ask
kiku	菊	chrysanthemum
kiku	きく	hear
kiku	きく	inquire
kiku	きく	listen
kiku	効く	work
kiku, ⟨-de⟩ wa doo ka to	聞く, ⟨〜で⟩はどうかと	offer
kiku no hana	菊の花	chrysanthemum
kiku, {⟨-no⟩ koto o/⟨-ni-tsuite⟩}	聞く, {⟨〜の⟩ことを/⟨〜について⟩}	question
kikyuu	気球	balloon
kikyuu	危急	pinch
ki-mae ga ii	気前がいい	generous
kimaru	決まる	fix
kime	きめ	texture
kimeru	決める	decide
kimeru	決める	determine
kimeru	決める	fix
kimeru	決める	settle
kimi	君	you
kimi no N	君のN	your
kimi-tachi	君たち	you
kimi-tachi no N	君たちのN	your
kimochi	気持ち	emotion
kimochi	気持ち	feeling
kimochi	気持ち	sensation
kimochi	気持ち	sense
kimochi	気持ち	sentiment
kimochi ga ii	気持ちがいい	comfortable
kimochi ga ii	気持ちがいい	pleasing
kimochi (ga) ii	気持ち(が)いい	pleasant
ki-mono	着物	kimono
kimyoona	奇妙な	curious
kimyoona	奇妙な	odd
kimyoona	奇妙な	queer
kimyoona	奇妙な	strange
kin	金	gold
kinbenna	勤勉な	diligent
kinchoo	緊張	strain
kinchoo	緊張	tension
kinchoo-shita N	緊張したN	nervous
kinchoo-shita N	緊張したN	tense
kinchoo-shite iru (N)	緊張している(N)	tense
kinchoo-suru	緊張する	strain
kindai-ka	近代化	modernization
kindai-ka-suru	近代化する	modernize

kindai no N	近代のN	modern
kindai-tekina	近代的な	modern
kinen	記念	remembrance
kinen-hin	記念品	souvenir
kinen-suru	記念する	commemorate
kingyo	金魚	goldfish
kin-iro no N	金色のN	golden
ki-ni-sawaru	気に障る	offend
ki-ni-suru	気にする	care
kin'itsu no N	均一のN	uniform
kinjiru	禁じる	forbid
kinjiru	禁じる	prohibit
kinjo	近所	neighborhood
kinjo	近所	vicinity
kinjo no hito	近所の人	neighbor
kinko	金庫	safe
kinkoo	近郊	suburb
kinkoo	近郊	vicinity
kinkyuu-hasshin-saseru	緊急発進させる	scramble
kinkyuu-hasshin-suru	緊急発進する	scramble
kinkyuu(jitai)	緊急(事態)	emergency
kinkyuu no N	緊急のN	urgent
kinmu	勤務	service
kinmu-	勤務〜	working
kinniku	筋肉	muscle
kin no N	金のN	golden
ki-no-dokuna	気の毒な	pitiful
ki-no-dokuna	気の毒な	poor
ki no dokuna	気の毒な	regret
ki-no-dokuna	気の毒な	sorry
kinoko	きのこ	mushroom
ki no N	木のN	wooden
kinoo	機能	function
kinoo	きのう	yesterday
kinori ga shinai	気乗りがしない	reluctant
kinpatsu	金髪	fair
kinpatsu no N	金髪のN	blond
kinpen	近辺	vicinity
kinrei	禁令	prohibition
kinsei	均整	proportion
kinsen	琴線	chord
kinshi	禁止	prohibition
kinshi-suru	禁止する	forbid
kinshi-suru	禁止する	prohibit
kinshitsu denai (N)	均質でない(N)	uneven
kintoona	均等な	equal
kinu	絹	silk
kin'yoo(-bi)	金曜(日)	Friday

kinzoku	金属	metal
kioku	記憶	memory
kioku-ryoku	記憶力	memory
kion	気温	temperature
ki-o-tsukeru	気を付ける	careful
ki o ushinau	気を失う	faint
ki o waruku-suru	気を悪くする	offend
kippu	切符	ticket
kiraina	嫌いな	dislike
kira-kira hikatte iru (N)	きらきら光っている(N)	brilliant
kira-kira (to) hikaru	きらきら(と)光る	twinkle
kirameki	きらめき	spark
kirameku	きらめく	shine
kirameku	きらめく	spark
kirameku N	きらめくN	sparkling
kirau	嫌う	dislike
kire	きれ	cloth
kire-hashi	切れ端	chip
kire-hashi	切れ端	scrap
kireina	きれいな	beautiful
kireina	きれいな	clean
kireina	きれいな	pretty
kireina	きれいな	pure
kireina mono	きれいなもの	beauty
kireini	きれいに	beautifully
kireini suru	きれいにする	clean
kireini suru	きれいにする	clear
kireru	切れる	break
kireru	切れる	cut
kiri	きり	drill
kiri	霧	fog
kiri	霧	mist
kiri	霧	vapor
kiri-fuki	霧ふき	spray
kiri ga fukai	霧が深い	foggy
kiri ga kakatta N	霧がかかったN	foggy
kiri-hanasu	切り離す	separate
kiri-kabu	切り株	stump
kiri-kizamu	切り刻む	chop
kiri-kizu	切り傷	cut
kiri-kuchi, (hoso-nagai)	切り口, (細長い)	slit
kirin	きりん	giraffe
kiri-nuku	切り抜く	clip
Kirisuto	キリスト	Christ
Kirisuto-kyoo	キリスト教	Christianity
Kirisuto-kyoo no N	キリスト教のN	Christian
Kirisuto-kyooto	キリスト教徒	Christian
Kirisuto-kyooto no N	キリスト教徒のN	Christian
kiri-toru	切り取る	trim
kiritsu	規律	discipline
kiri-tsumeru	切り詰める	cut
kiri-wakeru	切り分ける	carve
kiro	キロ	kilogram
kiro	キロ	kilometer
kiro-guramu	キログラム	kilogram
kiroku	記録	record
kiroku-sha	記録者	recorder
kiroku-suru	記録する	record
kiroku-tekina	記録的な	record
kiro-meetaa	キロメーター	kilometer
kiro-meetoru	キロメートル	kilometer
kiru	切る	clip
kiru	切る	cut
kiru	着る	wear
kiru mono	着るもの	dress
-kiru, V*masu*	～切る, V*masu*	through
kisei	規制	regulation
kisei-suru	規制する	control
kiseki	奇跡	miracle
kiseki	奇跡	wonder
kisen	汽船	steamboat
kisen	汽船	steamer
kisetsu	季節	season
kisha	記者	reporter
kisha	汽車	train
kishi	岸	shore
kishi {ni/de/e}	岸{に/で/へ}	ashore
kishira-seru	きしらせる	scrape
kishitsu	気質	streak
kishu	機首	nose
kishu	騎手	rider
kishuu	奇襲	surprise
kishuu-suru	奇襲する	surprise
kiso	基礎	base
kiso	基礎	basis
kiso	基礎	foundation
kisoku	規則	regulation
kisoku	規則	rule
kisoku-tadashii	規則正しい	regular
kisoku-tadashiku	規則正しく	regularly
kisoku-tekina	規則的な	regular
kisoku-tekini	規則的に	regularly
kiso o oku	基礎を置く	base
kiso-tekina	基礎的な	basic
kisou	競う	compete

kissui no N	生粋のN	pure
kisu	キス	kiss
kisu (o) suru	キス(を)する	kiss
kita	北	north
kita-	北～	northern
kitaeru	鍛える	train
kitai	期待	expectation
kitai	気体	gas[1]
kitai-suru	期待する	expect
kita kara no N	北からのN	northern
kitanai	汚い	dirty
kitanai	汚い	filthy
kita no N	北のN	north
kita no N	北のN	northern
kitchin	キッチン	kitchen
kitei-suru	規定する	state
kitoku no N	危篤のN	critical
kitsui	きつい	tight
kitsune	きつね	fox
kitte	切手	stamp
kitte o haru	切手をはる	stamp
kitte wakeru	切って分ける	carve
kitto	きっと	bet
kiwadoi	きわどい	tricky
kiwame-te juuyoona	極めて重要な	vital
kiyoona	器用な	clever
kizami-me	刻み目	score
kizami-me o tsukeru	刻み目をつける	score
kizamu	刻む	chop
kizen to shita N	毅然としたN	firm
kizetsu-suru	気絶する	faint
kizu	傷	injury
kizu	傷	wound[1]
ki-zuite iru koto	気付いていること	awareness
ki-zuite iru (N)	気付いている(N)	aware
ki-zuka-renai (N)	気づかれない(N)	unnoticed
ki-zuka-renai (N)	気づかれない(N)	unobserved
kizuna	きずな	bond
kizu-tsukeru	傷つける	compromise
kizu-tsukeru	傷つける	damage
kizu-tsukeru	傷つける	hurt
kizu-tsukeru	傷つける	injure
kizu-tsukeru	傷つける	wound[1]
kizu-tsuki-yasui	傷つきやすい	sensitive
ko	弧	arc
ko	子	child
-ko	～個	bar
ko-bashiri ni aruku	小走りに歩く	trot
koboreru	こぼれる	spill
kobosu	こぼす	spill
kobushi de naguru koto	こぶしで殴ること	punch[1]
ko-byakushoo	小百姓	peasant
kochira {ni/e/de/o}	こちら{に/へ/で/を}	here
ko-dachi	木立	grove
kodai Rooma-jin	古代ローマ人	Roman
kodai Rooma-jin no N	古代ローマ人のN	Roman
kodai Rooma no N	古代ローマのN	Roman
kodomo	子供	child
kodomo	子供	family
kodomo	子供	kid
kodomo-jimita N	子供じみたN	childish
kodomo no koro	子供のころ	childhood
kodomo-ppoi	子供っぽい	childish
kodoo-suru	鼓動する	beat
koe	声	voice
ko-eda	小枝	stick
ko-eda	小枝	twig
koe ni dashite	声に出して	aloud
koe no N	声のN	vocal
koeta N	肥えたN	fertile
koeta tokoro {ni/de/no}	こえたところ{に/で/の}	beyond
koete	越えて	over
koete iru	こえている	beyond
kogasu	焦がす	burn
kogeru	焦げる	burn
kogitte	小切手	check
ko-goe de hanasu	小声で話す	whisper
kogu	こぐ	row[2]
ko-hitsuji	子羊	lamb
koi	濃い	dark
koi	濃い	dense
koi	恋	love
koi	濃い	thick
koi-bito	恋人	lover
koi-bito	恋人	steady
koi-bito	恋人	sweetheart
koi-gataki	恋敵	rival
koin	コイン	coin
koi ni	故意に	deliberately
ko-inu	子犬	puppy
koiru	コイル	coil
ko-ishi	小石	pebble
kojiki	こじき	beggar
kojin	個人	individual
kojin no N	個人のN	personal

Kokakoora	コカコーラ	coke
koke	こけ	moss
koki-tsukau	こき使う	overwork
koki-tsukau	こき使う	work
kokka	国家	nation
kokka	国家	state
kokkai	国会	diet[2]
Kokkai-giji-doo	国会議事堂	Capitol
kokkaku	骨格	skeleton
kokka no N	国家のN	national
kokkeina	こっけいな	ridiculous
kokki	国旗	flag
kokku	コック	cook
kokkyoo	国境	border
kokoa	ココア	cocoa
kokonatsu	ココナツ	coconut
koko {ni/e/de/o}	ここ{に/へ/で/を}	here
ko-ko no N	個々のN	individual
kokonotsu (no N)	九つ(のN)	nine
kokoro	心	heart
kokoro	心	mind
kokoro	心	spirit
kokoro kara	心から	truly
kokoro kara no N	心からのN	hearty
kokoromi	試み	attempt
kokoromiru	試みる	attempt
kokoromiru	試みる	try
(kokoro no) itade	(心の)痛手	wound[1]
kokoro no ita-mi	心の痛み	sting
kokoro no N	心のN	spiritual
kokoro o ubau	心を奪う	fascinate
kokoro-zuke	心付け	tip[2]
kokoro-zuke o {ageru/yaru}	心付けを{あげる/やる}	tip[2]
koko-yashi (no mi)	ココやし(の実)	coconut
kokuban	黒板	blackboard
kokuban	黒板	chalkboard
kokuban-fuki	黒板拭き	eraser
kokufuku	克服	victory
kokufuku-suru	克服する	overcome
kokuji	告示	notice
kokujin	黒人	black
kokumin	国民	citizen
kokumin	国民	people
kokumotsu	穀物	cereal
kokumotsu	穀物	grain
kokunai no N	国内のN	domestic
kokuoo	国王	king

kokuoo no N	国王のN	royal
kokuritsu no N	国立のN	national
kokusai-tekina	国際的な	international
kokuseki	国籍	nationality
kokyoo	故郷	home
kokyoo	故郷	hometown
kokyuu	呼吸	breath
kokyuu	呼吸	breathing
kokyuu o suru	呼吸をする	breathe
komaasharu	コマーシャル	commercial
komakai	細かい	fine
komakai	細かい	nice
komakaku suru	細かくする	change
komakana N	細かなN	nice
komara-seru	困らせる	annoy
komara-seru	困らせる	embarrass
komara-seru	困らせる	puzzle
komara-su	困らす	puzzle
kome	米	rice
komento	コメント	comment
komento-suru	コメントする	comment
ko-michi	小道	alley
komi-itta N	込み入ったN	complicated
komi-itte iru (N)	込み入っている(N)	complicated
ko-mugi	小麦	wheat
komyunikeeshon	コミュニケーション	communication
komyunitii	コミュニティー	community
kona	粉	flour
kona	粉	powder
kona-gona ni kowasu	粉々に壊す	smash
kona-gona ni naru	粉々になる	smash
kona-gona ni {waru/suru}	粉々に{割る/する}	shatter
konban	今晩	tonight
konbineeshon	コンビネーション	combination
konboo	こん棒	club
konboo	こん棒	stick
konchuu	昆虫	insect
(konchuu no) mure	(昆虫の)群れ	swarm
(konchuu no) taigun	(昆虫の)大群	swarm
kon-date	献立	menu
konde iru	込んでいる	crowded
kone	コネ	connection
Konechikatto	コネチカット	Connecticut
ko-neko	子猫	kitten
kongan-suru, Sinf. yooni	懇願する, Sinf.ように	pray
kongen	根源	root

kongoo-butsu	混合物	blend
konki-zuyoi	根気強い	persistent
konkuriito	コンクリート	concrete
konkyo	根拠	basis
konkyo	根拠	foundation
konkyo	根拠	ground
konna N	こんなN	such
konnan	困難	difficulty
konnani	こんなに	this
konnanna	困難な	difficult
konnichi	今日	today
konnichi de wa	今日では	nowadays
konnichi-tekina	今日的な	current
konnichi-wa	こんにちは	hello
konnichi-wa	こんにちは	hi
kono-aida	この間	recently
kono-goro	このごろ	recently
kono-goro no N	このごろのN	recent
kono mae	この前	last
kono mae no N	この前のN	last
konomi	好み	taste
kono N	このN	past
kono N	このN	this
kono tame ni	このために	thus
kono yooni	このように	thus
konpon	根本	root
konpon-tekina	根本的な	ultimate
konpyuutaa	コンピューター	computer
konran	混乱	confusion
konran-saseru	混乱させる	confuse
konran-shi-yasui	混乱しやすい	confusing
konrei	婚礼	wedding
konseki	痕跡	trace
konshin-kai	懇親会	social
kontesuto	コンテスト	contest
kontorasuto	コントラスト	contrast
kontorooru-suru	コントロールする	control
kon'ya	今夜	tonight
kon'yaku-shite iru	婚約している	engage
-koo	～口	mouth
kooba	工場	factory
koobai	こう配	slope
kooban	交番	police box
koobutsu	鉱物	mineral
koocha	紅茶	tea
koochi	コーチ	coach
koochi-sho	拘置所	jail
koochi-suru	コーチする	coach

koochoo	校長	headmaster
koochoo	校長	principal
koodaina	広大な	vast
koodo	コード	chord
koodoku-ryoo	購読料	subscription
koodoku-suru	購読する	take
koodoni	高度に	highly
koodoo	行動	action
koodoo	行動	behavior
koodoo	坑道	tunnel
koodoo-suru	行動する	act
koodoo-suru	行動する	do
kooei	光栄	honor
kooeki-jigyoo	公益事業	service
kooen	講演	lecture
kooen	公園	park
kooen	講演	talk
kooen-sha	後援者	patron
kooen-sha	講演者	speaker
koofuku	幸福	happiness
koofuku	幸福	welfare
koofukuna	幸福な	happy
koofuku-suru	降伏する	surrender
koofun	興奮	excitement
koofun-sase-rareru N	興奮させられるN	exciting
koofun-saseru	興奮させる	stir
koofun-shita N	興奮したN	excited
koofun-shite	興奮して	excitedly
koogai	郊外	outskirts
koogai	郊外	suburb
koogaku	工学	engineering
koogei	工芸	craft
koogeki	攻撃	attack
koogeki	攻撃	strike
koogeki-mokuhyoo	攻撃目標	target
koogeki-suru	攻撃する	attack
koogi	講義	lecture
koogi	抗議	protest
koogi-naiyoo	講義内容	program
koogi-suru	抗議する	protest
koogo ni suru	交互にする	alternate
koogo no N	交互のN	alternate
koogyoo	工業	industry
koogyoo	興行	show
koogyoo no N	工業のN	industrial
koohan	公判	trial
koo-han'i ni wataru N	広範囲にわたるN	extensive
kooheina	公平な	fair

koohii	コーヒー	coffee
kooho-sha	候補者	candidate
koohyoo	公表	announcement
koohyoo	好評	reputation
kooi	行為	action
kooi	好意	favor
kooi	行為	work
kooi-tekina N	好意的な	favorable
kooji	工事	construction
koojitsu	口実	pretense
koojitsu	口実	pretext
koojo	皇女	princess
koojoo	工場	factory
kooka	硬貨	coin
kooka	効果	effect
kookai	後悔	regret
kookai-suru	後悔する	regret
kookan	交換	exchange
kookana	高価な	precious
kookana	高価な	valuable
kookan-shu	交換手	operator
kookan-suru	交換する	change
kookan-suru	交換する	exchange
kookan-suru	交換する	trade
kooka-tekina	効果的な	effective
kooka-tekini	効果的に	effectively
kookei	光景	sight
kookei-sha ni naru	後継者になる	replace
kooken	貢献	contribution
kooken	貢献	share
kooken-nin	後見人	ward[1]
kooken-suru	貢献する	contribute
kooki-shin	好奇心	curiosity
kooki-shin ga tsuyoi	好奇心が強い	curious
kookoku	広告	advertisement
kookoku-suru	広告する	advertise
(kookoo-)san-nen-sei	(高校)三年生	senior
kooku	コーク	coke
kookuu-bin	航空便	airmail
kookuu-bin de okuru	航空便で送る	airmail
kookuu-gaisha	航空会社	airline
kookyoo-kyoku	交響曲	symphony
kookyoo no N	公共のN	public
kookyuuna	高級な	superior
koomoku	項目	item
koomori	こうもり	bat
koomu-in	公務員	official
koomuru	被る	suffer
koomuru	被る	sustain
koomyaku	鉱脈	streak
koomyaku	鉱脈	vein
koonai	構内	yard[2]
koonin {ni/to} naru	後任{に/と}なる	succeed
koonyuu	購入	purchase
koonyuu-hin	購入品	purchase
koonyuu-suru	購入する	purchase
koora	コーラ	cola
koora	甲羅	shell
koorasu	コーラス	chorus
koori	氷	ice
koori-tsuku	凍りつく	freeze
koori-tsuku-yoona	凍りつくような	freezing
koori-tsuku-yoona	凍りつくような	frosty
kooritsu no N	公立のN	public
kooron	口論	argument
kooron-suru	口論する	argue
kooru	凍る	freeze
kooryo	考慮	consideration
koosai	交際	association
koosai	交際	company
koosai	交際	contact
koosai-suru	交際する	associate
koosan	公算	probability
koosa-ten	交差点	intersection
koosei	構成	composition
kooseina	公正な	fair
kooseina	公正な	square
koosei-sarete iru	構成されている	consist
koosei-suru	構成する	compose
koosei-zuri	校正刷り	proof
kooseki	功績	achievement
kooseki	鉱石	ore
koosen	光線	ray
koosen	鉱泉	spa
koosen	交戦	warfare
koosha	後者	latter
koosha	校舎	schoolhouse
kooshi	講師	instructor
kooshi-jima	格子じま	check
kooshiki	公式	formula
kooshiki ni	公式に	officially
kooshiki no N	公式のN	official
kooshin	行進	parade
kooshin-ryoo	香辛料	spice
kooshin-ryoo ga kiita N	香辛料がきいたN	spicy
kooshin-suru	行進する	march

kooshin-suru	更新する	renew
koosoku-dooro	高速道路	highway
koosu	コース	course
koosui	香水	perfume
kootai	後退	retreat
kootai(jikan)	交替(時間)	shift
kootai-sha	交代者	replacement
kootai-suru	後退する	retreat
kootai-suru	交替する	rotate
Kootan-setsu	降誕節	Christmas
kootei	肯定	affirmation
kootei	工程	process
kootei-suru	肯定する	affirm
kootetsu	鋼鉄	steel
kootetsu-sei no mono	鋼鉄製のもの	steel
kooto	コート	coat
kooto	コート	court
kooto	コート	overcoat
kootoo no N	口頭のN	oral
kootsuu	交通	traffic
kootsuu-kikan	交通機関	transportation
kootta N	凍ったN	icy
kootte iru (N)	凍っている(N)	icy
koounna	幸運な	fortunate
(koo)u-ryoo	(降)雨量	rainfall
kooza	口座	account
kooza	講座	course
koozan	鉱山	mine[2]
koozoo	構造	structure
koozoo(-joo) no N	構造(上)のN	structural
koozoo-tekina	構造的な	structural
koozui	洪水	flood
kopii	コピー	copy
kopii-suru	コピーする	copy
kopii-suru	コピーする	reproduce
koppu	コップ	glass
koraeru	こらえる	sustain
kore	これ	this
korekushon	コレクション	collection
kore-ra	これら	these
kore-ra no N	これらのN	these
koritsu	孤立	isolation
koritsu-shita N	孤立したN	isolated
koritsu-shite iru (N)	孤立している(N)	isolated
koro	ころ	around
korobu	転ぶ	fall
koroga-su	転がす	roll
korogaru	転がる	roll
korogaru	転がる	tumble
Koronbia	コロンビア	Columbia
Koronbusu	コロンブス	Columbus
korosu	殺す	kill
korosu	殺す	murder
ko-sa	濃さ	thickness
ko-saseru	来させる	cause (to come)
ko-saseru	来させる	force (to come)
ko-saseru	来させる	get (to come)
ko-saseru	来させる	let (come)
ko-saseru	来させる	make (come)
ko-saseru	来させる	permit (to come)
koshi	腰	hip
koshi	腰	waist
koshi-kake	腰掛け	chair
koshi o mageru	腰を曲げる	stoop
koshi (o) kakeru	腰(を)掛ける	sit
koshitsu	個室	stall
koshoo	こしょう	pepper
koshoo	故障	trouble
koshoo-suru	故障する	fail
koso-doro	こそ泥	thief
kosshi	骨子	substance
kossori to	こっそりと	secretly
kossori to	こっそりと	underground
kosu	こす	strain
kosuri-toru	こすり取る	scrape
kosuru	こする	rub
kotae	答え	answer
kotae	答え	reply
kotaeru	こたえる	answer
kotaeru	答える	entertain
kotaeru	こたえる	reply
kotaeru	こたえる	respond
kotai	固体	solid
kotai no N	固体のN	solid
koten	古典	classic
koten-tekina	古典的な	classical
koto	こと	affair
koto	こと	matter
koto	こと	thing
koto	こと	what[2]
kotoba	言葉	language
kotoba	言葉	tongue
kotoba	言葉	word
koto-gara	事柄	affair
koto (mo) {naku/nashi ni}, Vinf. nonpast	こと(も){なく/なしに}, Vinf. nonpast	without

kotonaru	異なる	differ
kotonaru N	異なるN	different
kotonaru N	異なるN	distinct
kotonatta N	異なったN	different
kotonatte iru (N)	異なっている(N)	different
koto-ni-yottara…(kamoshirenai)	ことによったら…(かもしれない)	perhaps
koto, Sinf. (to iu)	こと, Sinf.(という)	that[3]
kotowaru	断る	decline
kotowaru	断る	refuse
kotowaza	ことわざ	proverb
koto-zuke	言付け	message
kotsu	こつ	secret
kotsu	こつ	trick
kotsu-kotsu to tataku	こつこつとたたく	tap
kotte iru	凝っている	stiff
kottoo-hin	骨とう品	antique
kottoo-hin	骨とう品	curio
kou	請う	beg
ko-uri	小売り	retail
ko-uri-suru	小売りする	retail
kouri-ten	小売店	shop
ko-ushi	子牛	calf
kowagara-seru	怖がらせる	scare
kowa-garu	怖がる	dread
kowa-garu	怖がる	fear
kowa-gatte iru	怖がっている	fearful
kowai	怖い	dreadful
kowai	怖い	fear
kowai	怖い	fearful
kowai	怖い	frightening
kowai	怖い	scared
kowai	怖い	scary
kowai	怖い	stern
kowareru	壊れる	break
kowarete inai (N)	壊れていない(N)	unbroken
kowasu	壊す	break
kowasu	壊す	destroy
koya	小屋	cabin
koya	小屋	hut
koya	小屋	shelter
koyashi	肥やし	fertilizer
koyomi	暦	calendar
koyoo	雇用	employment
koyuu no N	固有のN	proper
ko-zeni	小銭	change
ko-zeni-ire	小銭入れ	purse
kozue	こずえ	treetop
ko-zukai	小遣い	allowance
ko-zutsumi	小包	package
ko-zutsumi	小包	parcel
ku	句	phrase
-ku	～区	ward[2]
ku-ban-me (no N)	九番目(のN)	ninth
kubaru	配る	distribute
kubetsu	区別	distinction
kubetsu-suru	区別する	distinguish
kubi	首	neck
kubi-kazari	首飾り	necklace
kubi ni suru	首にする	fire
kubire (no bubun)	くびれ(の部分)	waist
kubi-wa	首輪	collar
kubun-suru	区分する	zone
kuchi	口	mouth
kuchi-arasoi	口争い	argument
kuchi-arasoi-suru	口争いする	argue
kuchibashi	くちばし	beak
kuchibiru	唇	lip
kuchi-bue	口笛	whistle
kuchi-bue o fuku	口笛を吹く	whistle
kuchi-buri da, Sinf. yoona	口ぶりだ, Sinf.ような	sound
kuchi-gomoru	口ごもる	stumble
kuchi-hige	口ひげ	mustache
ku (+counter) (no N)	九(+counter)(のN)	nine
kuda	管	pipe
kuda	管	tube
kudaketa N	くだけたN	informal
kuda-mono	果物	fruit
kudaranai	くだらない	small
kudaranai	くだらない	stupid
kudaranai koto	くだらないこと	rubbish
kudaranai mono	くだらない物	stuff
kudari no N	下りのN	down
kudasaru	くださる	give
ku-gatsu	九月	September
kugi	釘	nail
kugi-zuke ni naru	釘付けになる	freeze
kui	くい	post[1]
kui	くい	stake
kuiki	区域	zone
kujaku	くじゃく	peacock
kujikenai	くじけない	unbroken
kujira	鯨	whale
kujoo	苦情	complaint
kukaku	区画	block

kuki	茎	stalk
kuki	茎	stem
kukkiri to	くっきりと	sharply
kuma	熊	bear[1]
kuma-de	熊手	rake
kuma-de de kaki-atsumeru	熊手でかき集める	rake
kuma-seru	組ませる	pair
kumi	組	class
kumiai	組合	union
kumi-awase	組み合わせ	combination
kumi-awa-seru	組み合わせる	combine
kumi ni naru	組になる	pair
kumi ni suru	組にする	pair
kumi-tateru	組み立てる	weave
kumo	雲	cloud
kumo	くも	spider
kumo-no-su	くもの巣	web
kumotte iru (N)	曇っている(N)	cloudy
kumu	組む	cross
kuni	国	country
kuni	国	home
kuni	国	hometown
kuni	国	state
kuni no N	国のN	national
kuni zentai no N	国全体のN	national
kun-kun kagu	くんくんかぐ	sniff
kun-kun kagu koto	くんくんかぐこと	sniff
kunoo	苦悩	sting
kunren	訓練	discipline
kunren	訓練	training
kunren-suru	訓練する	train
kunsei ni suru	くん製にする	smoke
kunshoo	勲章	decoration
kunshoo o sazukeru	勲章を授ける	decorate
kuootaa-bakku	クォーターバック	quarterback
kuooto	クォート	quart
kuppuku-suru	屈服する	surrender
kuraberu	比べる	compare
kuraberu	比べる	contrast
kurabu	クラブ	club
kuragari	暗がり	dark
kurai	暗い	dark
-kurai	～くらい	somewhere
kuraimakkusu	クライマックス	climax
kura-sa	暗さ	darkness
kurasu	クラス	class
kurasu	暮らす	live
kurasu-kai	クラス会	reunion
kurasu-meeto	クラスメート	classmate
kuratchi	クラッチ	clutch
kura-yami	暗やみ	dark
kura-yami	暗やみ	darkness
kurejitto	クレジット	credit
kureru	くれる	give
kureru to iu, V*te*	くれると言う, V*te*	offer
kuriimu	クリーム	cream
kuriiningu-ya	クリーニング屋	laundry
kuri-kaeshi	繰り返し	repetition
kuri-kaeshi	繰り返し	round
kuri-kaeshite iu	繰り返して言う	repeat
kuri-kaesu	繰り返す	parrot
kuri-kaesu	繰り返す	repeat
kurippu	クリップ	clip
Kurisuchan	クリスチャン	Christian
Kurisuchan no N	クリスチャンのN	Christian
Kurisumasu	クリスマス	Christmas
Kurisumasu	クリスマス	Xmas
kurisutaru	クリスタル	crystal
kuro	黒	black
kuroi	黒い	black
kuroi	黒い	dark
kuroo	苦労	hardship
kuroo	苦労	trouble
kuroobaa	クローバー	clover
kuroo-shite susumu	苦労して進む	toil
kuroo-shite V	苦労してV	wade
kurooto	玄人	professional
kuroozetto	クローゼット	closet
kuroppoi	黒っぽい	somber
kuro-zunda N	黒ずんだN	somber
kuru	来る	come
kuru	来る	visit
kurubushi	くるぶし	ankle
kuruma	車	auto
kuruma	車	automobile
kuruma	車	car
kuruma de okuru	車で送る	drive
kuruma o tomeru	車をとめる	park
kurumu	くるむ	tuck
kurushii	苦しい	painful
kurushimeru	苦しめる	sting
kurushimeru	苦しめる	trouble
kurushi-mi	苦しみ	pain
kurushimu	苦しむ	suffer
kurushi-sa	苦しさ	pain

kurutte iru (N)	狂っている(N)	crazy
kusa	草	grass
kusa	草	weed
kusabi	くさび	wedge
kusai	くさい	stink
kusa o kuu	草を食う	graze[2]
kusa o taberu	草を食べる	graze[2]
kusa o toru	草を取る	weed
kusara-seru	腐らせる	spoil
kusari	鎖	chain
kusaru	腐る	rot
kusaru	腐る	spoil
kusatta N	腐ったN	bad
kuse	癖	habit
kuse ga nai (N)	くせがない(N)	mild
kushami	くしゃみ	sneeze
kushami o suru	くしゃみをする	sneeze
kusshon	クッション	cushion
kussuru	屈する	surrender
kussuru	屈する	yield
kusu-kusu-warai	くすくす笑い	chuckle
kusu-kusu warau	くすくす笑う	chuckle
kusuri	薬	medicine
kusuri-ya	薬屋	drugstore
kusuri-ya	薬屋	pharmacy
kutoo	句読	punctuation
kutoo-ten	句読点	punctuation
kutsu	靴	shoe
kutsuroga-seru	くつろがせる	relax
kutsurogu	くつろぐ	relax
kutsu-shita	靴下	hose
kutsu-shita	靴下	sock
kutsu-shita	靴下	stockings
kutsuu	苦痛	pain
kutsuu da	苦痛だ	painful
kutsu-zoko	靴底	sole[2]
kuttsuite-iku	くっついて行く	trail
kuttsukeru	くっつける	glue
kuttsukeru	くっつける	stick
kuttsuku	くっつく	cling
kuttsuku	くっつく	stick
kuudoo	空洞	cavity
kuugun	空軍	air force
kuuhaku	空白	vacuum
kuuhaku no N	空白のN	blank
kuukan	空間	space
kuuki	空気	air
kuukoo	空港	airport
kuuran	空欄	blank
kuuran	空欄	space
kuuruna	クールな	cool
kuusoo	空想	vision
kuwadate	企て	attempt
kuwadate	企て	scheme
kuwadateru	企てる	attempt
kuwadateru	企てる	undertake
kuwaeru	加える	add
kuwaete	加えて	plus
kuwashii	詳しい	detailed
kuwashii koto	詳しいこと	detail
kuwashiku hanasu, ⟨-no⟩ koto o	詳しく話す, ⟨〜の⟩ことを	recite
kuwawaru	加わる	join
kuwawaru	加わる	participate
kuyamu	悔やむ	regret
kuzu	くず	trash
kuzusu	くずす	change
kuzutetsu	くず鉄	scrap
kyaa tto iu	きゃあっと言う	scream
kyabetsu	キャベツ	cabbage
kyabinetto	キャビネット	cabinet
kyabureetaa	キャブレーター	carburetor
Kyaderakku	キャデラック	Cadillac
kyakkan-tekina	客観的な	objective
kyaku	客	company
kyaku	客	customer
kyakusha	客車	coach
kyakushitsu	客室	cabin
kyandee	キャンデー	candy
kyandee	キャンデー	sweet
kyanpeen	キャンペーン	campaign
kyanpu	キャンプ	camp
kyanpu-seikatsu	キャンプ生活	camping
kyanpu-suru	キャンプする	camp
kyanseru-suru	キャンセルする	cancel
kyappu	キャップ	cap
kyaputen	キャプテン	captain
kyaria	キャリア	career
kyarijji	キャリッジ	carriage
kyasshu	キャッシュ	cash
kyasuto	キャスト	cast
kyodaina	巨大な	huge
kyodaina	巨大な	massive
kyodaina	巨大な	vast
kyohi-suru	拒否する	refuse
kyojin	巨人	giant

kyojuu-chi	居住地	settlement
kyojuu-sha	居住者	occupant
kyoka	許可	admission
kyoka	許可	license
kyoka	許可	permission
kyoka-negai	許可願い	petition
kyoka-negai(-sho)	許可願い(書)	petition
kyoka-sho	許可書	ticket
kyoka-shoo	許可証	permit
kyoka-suru	許可する	permit
kyoku	局	bureau
kyoku	極	pole[2]
kyoku	曲	tune
-kyoku	～局	office
kyokudo no hiroo	極度の疲労	fatigue
kyokumen	局面	aspect
kyokumen	局面	phase
kyokusen	曲線	curve
kyokutanna	極端な	extreme
kyokutanna	極端な	utmost
kyokutanni	極端に	extremely
kyoo	今日	today
kyoochoo	強調	stress
kyoochoo-suru	強調する	emphasize
kyoochoo-suru	強調する	stress
kyoodai	兄弟	brother
kyoodoo-keiei-sha	共同経営者	associate
kyoodoo-keiei-sha	共同経営者	partner
kyoodoo no N	共同のN	joint
kyoodoo-shikin	共同資金	pool
kyoodoo-tooshi	共同投資	pool
kyooen	饗宴	feast
kyoofu	恐怖	dread
kyoofu	恐怖	fear
kyoofu	恐怖	fright
kyoofu	恐怖	horror
kyoofu	恐怖	terror
kyoofu-kan	恐怖感	dread
kyoogi	競技	competition
kyoogi-kai	競技会	contest
kyoogi-kai	協議会	council
kyoogi no N	競技のN	athletic
kyooguu	境遇	situation
kyooi	驚異	marvel
kyooi	驚異	wonder
kyooiku	教育	education
kyooiku	教育	training
kyooiku-gaku	教育学	pedagogy
kyooiku no N	教育のN	educational
kyooiku o uketa N	教育を受けたN	educated
kyooiku-tekina	教育的な	educational
kyooi-tekina	驚異的な	marvelous
kyooju	教授	professor
kyooju-hoo	教授法	pedagogy
kyooju-suru	享受する	enjoy
kyookai	協会	association
kyookai	境界	boundary
kyookai	教会	church
kyookai	協会	social
kyookai no seki	教会の席	stall
kyookai o sadameru	境界を定める	define
kyookan	共感	sympathy
kyooka-sho	教科書	textbook
kyooka-suru	強化する	strengthen
kyookoku	峡谷	canyon
kyookoo	恐慌	panic
kyookun	教訓	lesson
kyookyaku	橋脚	pier
kyookyuu	供給	supply
kyookyuu-butsu	供給物	supply
kyookyuu-gen	供給源	resource
kyookyuu-suru	供給する	provide
kyookyuu-suru	供給する	supply
kyoomi	興味	interest
kyoomi ga aru (N)	興味がある(N)	interested
kyooretsuna	強烈な	intense
kyooryoku	協力	cooperation
kyooryokuna	強力な	powerful
kyooryoku-suru	協力する	cooperate
kyo o sadameru	居を定める	settle
kyoosan-shugi	共産主義	communism
kyoosei	強勢	accent
kyoosei	矯正	reform
kyooshi	教師	instructor
kyooshi	教師	teacher
kyooshitsu	教室	classroom
kyooshitsu	教室	schoolroom
kyooshoku	教職	pedagogy
kyoosoo	競争	competition
kyoosoo	競争	race
kyoosoo	競走	race
kyoosoo-aite	競争相手	rival
kyoosoo-suru	競争する	compete
kyoosoo-suru	競争する	race
kyoosoo-suru	競走する	race
kyoosoo-suru	競争する	rival

kyootan	驚嘆	wonder
kyootei	協定	agreement
kyootei	協定	understanding
kyootsuu no N	共通のN	common
kyootsuu no N	共通のN	mutual
kyoowa-koku	共和国	republic
kyooyoo	教養	culture
kyooyoo ga aru N	教養があるN	educated
kyooyoo no aru N	教養のあるN	civilized
kyooyuu-suru	共有する	share
kyori	距離	distance
kyozetsu-suru	拒絶する	refuse
kyuu	球	globe
kyuu-ban-me (no N)	九番目(のN)	ninth
kyuu-bun no ichi	九分の一	ninth
kyuu (+counter) (no N)	九(+counter)(のN)	nine
kyuuden	宮殿	palace
kyuufu-kin	給付金	benefit
kyuuji-suru	給仕する	serve
kyuuji-suru	給仕する	wait
kyuujitsu	休日	holiday
kyuujo	救助	relief
kyuujo	救助	rescue
kyuu-juu (+counter) (no N)	九十(+counter)(のN)	ninety
kyuuka	休暇	vacation
kyuukai	休会	recess
kyuukaku	きゅう覚	nose
kyuukaku	きゅう覚	smell
kyuukei	休憩	recess
kyuukei	休憩	rest[1]
kyuukei-shitsu	休憩室	lounge
kyuukei-suru	休憩する	rest[1]
kyuukon	球根	bulb
kyuukoo	急行	express
kyuu-koobai no N	急勾配のN	steep
kyuukoo-ressha	急行列車	express
kyuukutsuna	窮屈な	tight
kyuukutsuna	窮屈な	uneasy
kyuukyoku no N	究極のN	ultimate
kyuuna	急な	sharp
kyuuna	急な	sudden
kyuuni	急に	suddenly
kyuuni V*masu* hajimeru	急にV*masu*始める	burst
kyuuryoo	給料	salary
kyuuryoo	給料	wage
kyuushiki no N	旧式のN	old-fashioned
kyuushutsu	救出	rescue
kyuushutsu-suru	救出する	rescue
kyuushuu-suru	吸収する	absorb
kyuushuu-suru	急襲する	raid
kyuusokuna	急速な	rapid
kyuusokuni	急速に	rapidly
kyuutei	宮廷	court
kyuuyoo	休養	relaxation

M

maagarin	マーガリン	margarine
mabataki	まばたき	wink
maboroshi	幻	vision
machi	まち	town
machiai-shitsu	待合室	waiting room
machi {e/ni}	街{へ/に}	downtown
machigaeru	間違える	mistake
machigai	間違い	error
machigai	間違い	mistake
machigai nai to omou, (Sinf. no wa)	間違いないと思う, (Sinf.のは)	positive
machigainaku	間違いなく	sure
machigainaku	間違いなく	undoubtedly
machigainaku ⟨-to⟩ omou	間違いなく⟨〜と⟩思う	sure
machigatta N	間違ったN	false
machigatta N	間違ったN	incorrect
machigatta N	間違ったN	mistaken
machigatta N	間違ったN	wrong
machigatte	間違って	wrong
machigatte iru (N)	間違っている(N)	false
machigatte iru (N)	間違っている(N)	incorrect
machigatte iru (N)	間違っている(N)	mistaken
machigatte iru (N)	間違っている(N)	wrong
mada	まだ	remain
mada	まだ	still
mada	まだ	yet
mada mite inai (N)	まだ見ていない(N)	unseen
made	まで	till
made	まで	to
made	まで	until
made mo	までも	very
made-ni	までに	by
made, Vinf. nonpast affirmative	まで, Vinf. nonpast affirmative	till
made, Vinf. nonpast affirmative	まで, Vinf. nonpast affirmative	until

mado	窓	window
mado-guchi	窓口	window
mado-waku	窓枠	sash[2]
mae	前	front
mae-bure	前触れ	warning
mae {e/ni}	前{へ/に}	forward
mae-kake	前掛け	apron
mae-motte	前もって	previously
mae ni	前に	before
mae ni	前に	previously
-mae (ni)	～前(に)	ago
mae ni, Vinf. nonpast	前に, Vinf. nonpast	before
mae no N	前のN	ex-
mae no N	前のN	former
mae no N	前のN	previous
mae wa…Vinf. past (mono da) ga ima wa…neg.	前は…Vinf. past(ものだ)が、今は…neg.	used[3]
magari-kunette nagareru	曲がりくねって流れる	wind[2]
magari-kunette tsuzuku	曲がりくねって続く	wander
magaru	曲がる	bend
magatta tokoro ni	曲がったところに	around
mageru	曲げる	bend
mago	孫	grandchild
mago-tsuka-seru	まごつかせる	embarrass
maguro	まぐろ	tuna
mahoo	魔法	magic
mahoo-tsukai	魔法使い	magician
mai-	毎～	every
-mai	～枚	sheet
mai agaru	舞い上がる	soar
Maiami	マイアミ	Miami
mai+counter of time	毎+counter of time	per
maigo no N	迷子のN	stray
maiku	マイク	microphone
maikurofon	マイクロフォン	microphone
maikurokonpyuutaa	マイクロコンピューター	microcomputer
mainasu	マイナス	minus
mai-nichi	毎日	daily
mai-nichi no N	毎日のN	daily
mai-nichi no N	毎日のN	everyday
mairu	参る	come
mairu	参る	go
mairu	マイル	mile
mai-shuu	毎週	weekly
mai-shuu ichi-do no N	毎週一度のN	weekly
mai-shuu no N	毎週のN	weekly
maite aru mono	巻いてある物	roll
mai-toshi	毎年	annually
mai-toshi no N	毎年のN	annual
mai-toshi no N	毎年のN	yearly
mai-tsuki no N	毎月のN	monthly
majimena	まじめな	earnest
majimena	まじめな	serious
majiru	混じる	mix
majo	魔女	witch
majutsu-shi	魔術師	magician
makanai	賄い	board
makaroni	マカロニ	macaroni
makaseru	任せる	leave
makasu	負かす	beat
makasu	負かす	defeat
makeru	負ける	lose
makeru	負ける	yield
makezu-girai	負けず嫌い	fighter
maki	まき	firewood
maki	まき	wood
maki-chirasu	まき散らす	scatter
maki-jaku	巻尺	tape
maki-komu	巻き込む	involve
maki-tsukeru	巻き付ける	twist
maki-tsukeru	巻き付ける	wind[2]
maki-tsukeru	巻き付ける	wrap
maki-tsuku	巻き付く	twist
maki-tsuku	巻き付く	wind[2]
makka ni naru, (kao ga)	真っ赤になる, (顔が)	flush
makki no N	末期のN	terminal
maku	幕	act
maku	幕	curtain
maku	まく	plant
maku	巻く	roll
maku	まく	scatter
maku	まく	sprinkle
makura	枕	pillow
mama de iru	ままでいる	remain
mame	豆	bean
mametsu	摩滅	wear
ma-mo-naku	間もなく	shortly
ma-mo-naku	間もなく	soon
mamora-renai (N)	守られない(N)	unobserved
mamoru	守る	defend
mamoru	守る	guard
mamoru	守る	keep

mamoru	守る	preserve
mamoru	守る	protect
mamoru	守る	respect
mamoru	守る	save
mamoru	守る	shelter
mamoru	守る	shield
manaa	マナー	manners
mane	まね	imitation
maneejaa	マネージャー	manager
mane o suru	まねをする	imitate
mane o suru	まねをする	parrot
maneru	まねる	imitate
mane-suru	まねする	copy
manga	漫画	cartoon
Manhattan	マンハッタン	Manhattan
ma-ni-au	間に合う	catch
ma-ni-au	間に合う	do
man'ichi Sinf. past ra	万一Sinf. pastら	should
mannaka	真ん中	center
mannaka	真ん中	halfway
mannaka	真ん中	middle
manshon	マンション	apartment
manshon	マンション	flat[2]
manto	マント	cloak
manzoku ga iku (N)	満足が行く(N)	satisfactory
manzoku-kan	満足感	satisfaction
manzokuna	満足な	satisfactory
manzoku-saseru	満足させる	please
manzoku-saseru	満足させる	satisfy
manzoku-shite iru	満足している	pleased
manzoku-suru	満足する	satisfy
manzoku-suru	満足する	settle
marena	まれな	rare
maru	丸	circle
maru-	まる〜	whole
maru-goto	まるごと	whole
marui	丸い	circular
marui	丸い	round
marui mono	丸いもの	round
maru-ki	丸木	log
maruki-bune	丸木舟	canoe
maru-maru to shita N	丸々としたN	plump
maruta	丸太	log
masaka	まさか	no
masaka	まさか	really
masaka-no-toki	まさかの時	need
masani...da	正に…だ	very
masatsu-suru	摩擦する	rub
masshuruumu	マッシュルーム	mushroom
massuguna	真っすぐな	straight
massugu(ni)	真っすぐ(に)	directly
massugu(ni)	真っすぐ(に)	straight
massugu ni naru	真っすぐになる	straighten
massugu tatta N	真っすぐ立ったN	upright
massugu tatte iru (N)	真っすぐ立っている(N)	upright
masu	ます	trout
masuku	マスク	mask
masutaa	マスター	master
masutaa-suru	マスターする	master
masuto	マスト	mast
mata	また	again
mata, ...mo	また, …も	also
mata-to-nai (N)	またとない(N)	unique
matchi	マッチ	match[2]
mato	的	focus
mato	的	target
matomo ni naru	まともになる	straighten
matsu	松	pine
matsu	待つ	stay
matsu	待つ	wait
matsuri	祭り	festival
mattaku	全く	completely
mattaku	全く	entirely
mattaku	全く	quite
mattaku	全く	totally
mattaku	全く	utterly
mattaku	全く	wholly
mattaku (neg.)	全く(neg.)	simply
mattaku no N	全くのN	complete
mattaku no N	全くのN	sheer
(mattaku) sono toori da	(全く)その通りだ	exactly
mattan	末端	terminal
matto	マット	mat
mausu	マウス	mouse
mawari	周り	around
mawari-michi	回り道	detour
mawari {ni/de/o}	周り{に/で/を}	around
mawari {ni/o}	周り{に/を}	around
mawari no N	周りのN	surrounding
mawaru	回る	circle
mawaru	回る	turn
mawasu	回す	pass
mawasu	回す	spin
mawasu	回す	turn
ma-yonaka	真夜中	midnight

mayu	まゆ	brow
mayu o hisomeru	まゆをひそめる	frown
mazari-mono no nai N	混ざり物のないN	plain
mazaru	混ざる	mix
maze-awaseta mono	混ぜ合わせたもの	mixture
mazeru	混ぜる	blend
mazeru	混ぜる	mix
mazui	まずい	badly
mazui	まずい	tasteless
mazui	まずい	unfortunate
mazu (saisho ni)	先ず(最初に)	first
mazushii	貧しい	poor
me	芽	bud
me	目	eye
me-ate	目当て	view
mecha-kucha	めちゃくちゃ	mess
medatanai (N)	目立たない(N)	unnoticed
medatsu	目立つ	visible
meekaa	メーカー	manufacturer
meetoru	メートル	meter
me ga mienai	目が見えない	blind
megane	めがね	eye glasses
megane	めがね	glasses
me ga sameru	目が覚める	awake
me ga sameru	目が覚める	wake
mei	めい	niece
meidai	命題	thesis
meido	メイド	maid
meihakuna	明白な	apparent
meihakuna	明白な	evident
meihakuna	明白な	obvious
meijin	名人	master
meijiru	命じる	order
meijiru, {(-o)/Vinf. nonpast yoo ni}	命じる, {(〜を)/Vinf. nonpastように}	require
meijiru, Vinf. yooni	命じる, Vinf.ように	command
meikaina	明快な	transparent
meikakuna	明確な	definite
meikoo	名工	craftsman
mei-mei	めいめい	each
meirei	命令	command
meirei	命令	order
meirei-suru	命令する	order
meisei	名声	fame
meishi	名詞	noun
meishi	名士	personality
meiwaku	迷惑	annoyance
meiwaku	迷惑	nuisance
meiwaku	迷惑	trouble
meiwakuna hito	迷惑な人	nuisance
meiwaku o kakeru	迷惑をかける	bother
meiwaku o kakeru	迷惑をかける	trouble
meiyo	名誉	honor
meizuru, {(-o)/Vinf. nonpast yoo ni}	命ずる, {(〜を)/Vinf. nonpastように}	require
mekanizumu	メカニズム	mechanism
mekata ga…aru	目方が…ある	weigh
mekata o hakaru	目方をはかる	weigh
Mekishiko	メキシコ	Mexico
mekuru	めくる	turn
me-mori	目盛	scale[3]
memo-yooshi	メモ用紙	pad
men	面	mask
men	面	phase
men	面	side
menbaa	メンバー	member
mendoona	面倒な	annoying
mendoona	面倒な	troublesome
mendori	めんどり	hen
(me ni) mienai	(目に)見えない	invisible
me ni mieru (N)	目に見える(N)	visual
menjo-suru	免除する	excuse
menkyo	免許	license
menkyo shoo	免許証	license
menmitsuna	綿密な	close[2]
menmitsuni	綿密に	closely
me no naka ni irete mo itakunai ko	目の中にいれても痛くない子	treasure
men(-rui)	めん(類)	noodle
menseki	面積	space
mensetsu	面接	interview
men-suru	面する	face
men-suru	面する	look
menyuu	メニュー	menu
me o samashite iru (N)	目を覚ましている(N)	awake
me o samasu	目を覚ます	awake
me o samasu	目を覚ます	wake
Meriirando	メリーランド	Maryland
merodii	メロディー	melody
meron	メロン	melon
meshi-agaru	召しあがる	eat
meshitsukai	召し使い	servant
mesu	雌	female
mesu no N	雌のN	female
mettani…neg.	めったに…neg.	seldom

me-ue	目上	superior
mezurashii	珍しい	rare
mezurashii	珍しい	unique
mezurashii	珍しい	unknown
mezurashii	珍しい	unusual
mi	身	position
mi-awaseru	見合わせる	suspend
miboojin	未亡人	widow
mibun	身分	place
mibun	身分	position
mibun	身分	state
mibun	身分	station
mibun	身分	status
miburi	身振り	gesture
mi-burui	身震い	shiver
michi	道	path
michi	道	road
michi	道	route
michi	道	trail
michi	道	way
michibata	道端	roadside
michibiku	導く	lead
michibiku	導く	steer
michi, genkan kara toori made no	道, 玄関から通りまでの	driveway
michi ni mayotta N	道に迷ったN	lost
michi ni mayotta N	道に迷ったN	stray
michi ni mayou	道に迷う	stray
michi no N	未知のN	unknown
michi o oshieru	道を教える	direct
michi o yuzuru	道を譲る	yield
midashi	見出し	headline
midasu	乱す	disturb
midasu	乱す	violate
midori(-iro) (no N)	緑(色)(のN)	green
mienai	見えない	invisible
mienai (N)	見えない(N)	unseen
mienaku suru	見えなくする	screen
mieru	見える	show
mieru	見える	visible
mie-suita N	見え透いたN	obvious
mie-suita N	見え透いたN	transparent
mie-suite iru (N)	見え透いている(N)	transparent
migaku	磨く	brush
migaku	磨く	polish
migaku	磨く	shine
migi(-gawa)	右(側)	right
migi(-gawa) no N	右(側)のN	right
migi-kiki no N	右利きのN	right-handed
migotona	見事な	impressive
migotona	見事な	magnificent
migotona	見事な	nice
mi-hari	見張り	guard
mi-hari	見張り	watch
mi-haru	見張る	guard
mi-haru	見張る	watch
mihiraki	見開き	spread
mihon	見本	sample
mihon	見本	specimen
miitingu	ミーティング	meeting
mijikai	短い	brief
mijikai	短い	short
mijikaku naru	短くなる	shorten
mijikaku suru	短くする	shorten
mijikana	身近な	personal
mijimena	惨めな	miserable
mijimena	惨めな	unhappy
mijin-giri ni suru	みじん切りにする	chop
mijukuna	未熟な	young
mikake	見かけ	surface
mikaku	味覚	taste
mikan	みかん	mandarin orange
mikan	みかん	tangerine
mi-kansei no N	未完成のN	incomplete
mikata	味方	friend
mi-kata	見方	philosophy
mi-kata	見方	viewpoint
mikata o suru	味方をする	side
miki	幹	stem
miki	幹	stock
miki	幹	trunk
mikiri-hin	見切り品	sacrifice
mikomi	見込み	chance
mikomi	見込み	probability
mikomi	見込み	promise
mikomi	見込み	prospect
mikomi	見込み	view
mi-mamoru	見守る	watch
miman	未満	under
mimi	耳	ear
mimi ga kikoe-nai	耳が聞こえない	deaf
mi-mono	見もの	spectacle
mi-mono no N	見もののN	spectacular
mi-moto	身元	identity
minami	南	south
minami {e/ni}	南{へ/に}	south

minami kara no N	南からのN	southern
minami-muki no N	南向きのN	southern
minami ni aru (N)	南にある(N)	southern
minami no N	南のN	south
minami no N	南のN	southern
minamoto	源	origin
minamoto	源	source
mi-naosu	見直す	review
mi-narenai N	見慣れないN	strange
mi-nareta N	見慣れたN	familiar
mi-nasu	見なす	count
mi-nasu	見なす	regard
minato	港	harbor
minato	港	port
minato-machi	港町	port
mineraru	ミネラル	mineral
minikui	醜い	ugly
minna	みんな	all
minna	みんな	everybody
minna	みんな	everyone
mi-nogasu	見逃す	miss
minori ga ooi	実りが多い	productive
minshu-shugi	民主主義	democracy
minshu-tekina	民主的な	democratic
mi o kagameru	身をかがめる	stoop
mi o kiru yoona	身を切るような	sharp
mi o makaseru	身を任せる	surrender
mi o tsukeru	実をつける	yield
mirai	未来	future
mirai-zoo	未来像	vision
miri	ミリ	millimeter
miri-meetoru	ミリメートル	millimeter
miru	みる	look
miru	みる	see
miru	見る	view
miru	見る	watch
miru koto	見ること	sight
miruku	ミルク	milk
miru-me	見る目	eye
miru, V*te*	みる, V*te*	try
miryoku	魅力	appeal
miryoku	魅力	attraction
miryoku	魅力	charm
miryoku-tekina	魅力的な	appealing
miryoku-tekina	魅力的な	attractive
miryoku-tekina	魅力的な	charming
miryoo-suru	魅了する	fascinate
misairu	ミサイル	missile

misaki	岬	cape
misaki	岬	point
mise	店	shop
mise-birakashi	見せびらかし	show
mi-seinen-sha	未成年者	minor
misekake	見せかけ	assumption
miseru	見せる	show
miseru, (jissai ni) V*te*	みせる, (実際に)V*te*	demonstrate
Mishigan	ミシガン	Michigan
mi-shiranu N	見知らぬN	strange
Mishishippii	ミシシッピー	Mississippi
miso	味そ	beanpaste
missetsuni	密接に	closely
misshuu-shita N	密集したN	dense
misshuu-shite iru (N)	密集している(N)	dense
misu	ミス	Miss
misuterii	ミステリー	mystery
mi-suteru	見捨てる	desert
mitaina, N	みたいな, N	like[2]
mitaina, Sinf.	みたいな, Sinf.	evidently
mitaina, Sinf.	みたいな, Sinf.	seem
mita-tokoro…yooda	見たところ…ようだ	apparently
mite morau	見てもらう	consult
mite sore to wakaru koto	見てそれと分かること	recognition
mitomeru	認める	acknowledge
mitomeru	認める	admit
mitomeru	認める	appreciate
mitomeru	認める	recognize
mitomeru koto	認めること	recognition
mi-tooshi	見通し	prospect
mitsudo	密度	density
mitsukaru	見つかる	find
mitsukeru	見つける	detect
mitsukeru	見つける	discover
mitsukeru	見つける	find
mitsukeru	見つける	spot
mitsukeru, V*te* iru tokoro o	見付ける, V*te*いるところを	catch
mi-tsumeru	見つめる	gaze
mi-tsumeru	見つめる	regard
mitsumeru	見つめる	stare
mi-tsumori	見積もり	estimate
mi-tsumoru	見積もる	estimate
mi-tsumoru	見積もる	project
mitsurin	密林	jungle
mitsu-zoroi	三つ揃い	suit[2]

mittsu-me no N	三つ目のN	third
mittsu (no N)	三つ(のN)	three
mi-uchi	身内	relative
mi-wakeru	見分ける	identify
mi-watasu koto	見渡すこと	survey
miyage	土産	gift
miyage	土産	souvenir
miyo	御世	reign
mizu	水	water
mizu-bitashi ni naru	水浸しになる	flood
mizu o fukunda N	水を含んだN	watery
mizu o fukunde iru (N)	水を含んでいる(N)	watery
mizu o kiru	水をきる	strain
mizu o maku	水をまく	water
mizu o yaru	水をやる	water
mizuppoi	水っぽい	watery
mizuppoi	水っぽい	weak
mizusaki-annai-nin	水先案内人	pilot
mizu-sashi	水差し	pitcher[2]
mizu-tamari	水たまり	pool
mizuumi	湖	lake
mo	も	even
mo	も	too
mochi-ageru	持ち上げる	lift
mochi-dasu	持ち出す	salvage
mochi-hakobi ga dekiru (N)	持ち運びが出来る(N)	portable
mochiiru	用いる	use
mochi-nushi	持ち主	owner
mochiron	もちろん	sure
mochi-tsuzukeru	持ち続ける	retain
moderu	モデル	model
modoru	戻る	rally
modoru	戻る	return
modosu	戻す	return
moeru	燃える	burn
mogaki	もがき	struggle
mogaku, (Vvol. to shite)	もがく, (Vvol.として)	struggle
mogu	もぐ	pick
mogu	もぐ	pluck
mogura	もぐら	mole[1]
moguru	潜る	plunge
mohan	模範	model
mohan-tekina	模範的な	model
moji	文字	writing
moji	文字	letter
moji-doori no N	文字通りのN	literal
mokei	模型	model
mokka	目下	now
mokka	目下	presently
mokugeki-sha	目撃者	witness
mokugeki-suru	目撃する	witness
mokuhyoo	目標	aim
mokuhyoo	目標	goal
mokuhyoo	目標	object
mokuhyoo	目標	objective
mokuromi	もくろみ	scheme
moku-sei no N	木製のN	wooden
mokuteki	目的	cause
mokuteki	目的	end
mokuteki	目的	object
mokuteki	目的	objective
mokuteki	目的	point
mokuteki	目的	purpose
mokuteki-go	目的語	object
mokuyoo(-bi)	木曜(日)	Thursday
mokuzai	木材	timber
mokuzai	木材	wood
...mo mata	…もまた	also
momiji	もみじ	maple
momo	桃	peach
momo-iro	桃色	pink
momo-iro no N	桃色のN	pink
...mo(...mo)...neg.	…も(…も)…neg.	nor
mo N2 mo...neg., N1	もN2も…neg., N1	neither
mon	門	gate
mo naku, adj(*i*). *ku* mo nai, adj(*i*). *ku*	もなく、adj(*i*). *ku* もない, adj(*i*). *ku*	neither
mondai	問題	issue
mondai	問題	matter
mondai	問題	problem
mondai	問題	question
...mo...neg.	…も…neg.	either
...mo...neg. shi, ...mo...neg.	…も…neg.し、…も…neg.	nor
monku	文句	phrase
mono	物	object
mono	物	stuff
mono	物	thing
mono da, (yoku)...Vinf. past	ものだ, (よく)…Vinf. past	would
mono-gatari	物語	story[1]
mono-goshi	物腰	bearing

mono ni doojinai	ものに動じない	stable
mono-oki	物置	barn
mono, ⟨-o⟩ ⟨-ni⟩ shita	もの, ⟨〜を⟩⟨〜に⟩した	version
mono-oto	物音	sound
mono-sashi	物差し	ruler
mono-sugoi	ものすごい	awful
mono-sugoi	ものすごい	fierce
(mono-)sugoi	(もの)すごい	tremendous
mono-warai no tane	物笑いの種	target
mono-yawarakana	もの柔らかな	smooth
moo	もう	already
moo	もう	now
moo	もう	yet
moodo	モード	mode
moofu	毛布	blanket
moo hitori	もう一人	another
moo hitotsu	もう一つ	another
moo ichi-do	もう一度	again
moojoo-soshiki	網状組織	network
mooke	もうけ	gain
mooke	もうけ	profit
mookeru	もうける	profit
moomoku no N	盲目のN	blind
mooretsuna	猛烈な	violent
mooshi bun (ga) nai	申し分(が)ない	perfect
mooshi-bun (ga) nai	申し分(が)ない	satisfactory
mooshi-de	申し出	offer
mooshi-deru	申し出る	petition
mooshi komi	申し込み	application
mooshi-komu	申し込む	apply
mooshi-komu	申し込む	propose
mooshi-komu, V*masu* tai to	申し込む, V*masu*たいと	propose
mooshi-tate	申し立て	petition
mooshi-tateru	申し立てる	petition
mooshi-tateru	申し立てる	plead
mooshi-tate-sho	申し立て書	petition
moo sugu	もうすぐ	soon
moo sukoshi de	もう少しで	nearly
mootaa	モーター	motor
mootaa-saikuru	モーターサイクル	motorcycle
mooteru	モーテル	motel
moo tsukawa-rete inai (N)	もう使われていない(N)	dead
moppara	専ら	wholly
morai-tai, V*te*	もらいたい, V*te*	wish
morasu	漏らす	leak

morau	もらう	get
morau	もらう	receive
morau, V*te*	もらう, V*te*	get
moreru	漏れる	leak
mori	森	forest
mori	森	wood
moru	漏る	leak
mo sezu, V*masu* mo shinai, V*masu*	もせず、V*masu*もしない, V*masu*	neither
(moshi) {adj(*na*). stem/N} {de/ja} {nakereba/nai to}	(もし){adj(*na*). stem/N}{で/じゃ}{でなければ/でないと}	unless
moshi-moshi	もしもし	hello
moshi-moshi	もしもし	sir
(moshi) Sinf. to shitara	(もし)Sinf.としたら	suppose
(moshi soo) shinakattara	(もしそう)しなかったら	otherwise
(moshi) {Vneg./Vstem/ko/shi/adj(*i*). *ku*} {nakereba/nai to}	(もし){Vneg./Vstem/来/し/adj(*i*). *ku*}{なければ/ないと}	unless
Mosukuwa	モスクワ	Moscow
motanai de	持たないで	without
motarasu	もたらす	bring
motarasu	もたらす	yield
motareru	もたれる	lean
motase-kakeru	もたせかける	lean
motazu ni	持たずに	without
mote-asobu	もてあそぶ	toy
motenasu	もてなす	entertain
moto	元	origin
moto	元	source
moto de	もとで	under
moto e modosu koto	元へ戻すこと	replacement
motomeru	求める	pursue
motomeru	求める	request
motomete	求めて	after
moto no ichi e	元の位置へ	back
moto no yooni	もとのように	again
moto-zuku	基づく	base
motsu	持つ	have
motsu	持つ	own
motsu	持つ	possess
motsure-saseru	もつれさせる	tangle
motte-iku	持って行く	take
motte iru	持っている	hold
motte (iru N)	持って(いるN)	with
motte-koi no N	持って来いのN	perfect

motte-kuru	持って来る	bring
motto	もっと	even
motto	もっと	further
motto	もっと	more
mottomona	もっともな	reasonable
mottomo ookii	最も大きい	biggest
mottomo ookina N	最も大きなN	biggest
motto saki	もっと先	further
motto {saki/mukoo} ni	もっと{先/向こう}に	farther
moya	もや	vapor
moyasu	燃やす	burn
moyoo	模様	design
moyoo	模様	pattern
moyoo o tsukeru	模様を付ける	print
mozo-mozo-suru	もぞもぞする	wriggle
mozoo-hin	模造品	imitation
muchi	むち	rod
muchi	むち	whip
muchi de utsu	むちで打つ	whip
muchina	無知な	ignorant
muchi o atete tobasu	むちを当てて飛ばす	whip
muchuu ni saseru	夢中にさせる	absorb
muchuu no N	夢中のN	crazy
mudana	むだな	wasteful
muda-zukai	むだ遣い	waste
muda-zukai-suru	むだ遣いする	waste
muekina	無益な	useless
mugaina	無害な	harmless
mugen no N	無限のN	infinite
mugon	無言	silence
mu-imina	無意味な	vain
mu-imina koto	無意味なこと	nonsense
mu-ishiki no N	無意識のN	unconscious
mu-jakina	無邪気な	innocent
muji no N	無地のN	plain
mu-jooken no N	無条件のN	unconditional
mu-jooken no N	無条件のN	unqualified
mukaeru	迎える	greet
mukaeru	迎える	meet
mukaeru, yorokonde	迎える, 喜んで	welcome
mukai(-gawa) no N	向かい(側)のN	oppose
mukanai (N), (-ni)	向かない(N), (〜に)	unfriendly
mukashi	昔	formerly
mukashi	昔	once
mukashi hayatta N	昔はやったN	old-fashioned
mukashi kara aru	昔からある	old
mukashi kara iru	昔からいる	old

mukatte	向かって	at
mukau	向かう	face
mukau	向かう	tend
mukeru	向ける	direct
mukeru	向ける	point
mukeru	向ける	turn
-muki dewanai	〜向きではない	unfriendly
mukoo(-gawa) ni	向こう(側)に	across
mukoo(-gawa) ni	向こう(側)に	over
mukoo-gawa no N	向こう側のN	farther
mukoo {ni/de/no}	向こう{に/で/の}	beyond
mukoo ni suru	無効にする	cancel
muku	向く	face
muku	向く	fit
muku	向く	look
muku	むく	peel
mumi-kansoona	無味乾燥な	dry
mune	胸	chest
mune ga ippai ni naru	胸がいっぱいになる	swell
mune ni osameru	胸に納める	swallow[1]
mura	村	village
mura-bito	村人	villager
muragaru	群がる	crowd
muragaru	群がる	swarm
muragatte tonde iku	群がって飛んで行く	swarm
mura no hito	村の人	villager
murasaki(-iro)	紫(色)	purple
murasaki-iro no N	紫色のN	purple
murasaki no N	紫のN	purple
mure	群れ	flock
mure	群れ	herd
mure	群れ	school[2]
mure	群れ	troop
mure, (konchuu no)	群れ, (昆虫の)	swarm
murina	無理な	unreasonable
muri ni {Vneg.+seyoo/Vstem+saseyoo/ko-saseyoo/saseyoo} to suru	無理に{Vneg.+せよう/Vcond.+させよう/来させよう/させよう}とする	press
muri o suru	無理をする	sweat
muryokuna	無力な	helpless
muryoo-joosha-ken	無料乗車券	pass
muryoo-nyuujoo-ken	無料入場券	pass
mu-sakui no N	無作為のN	random
mushi	虫	bug
mushi	虫	insect
mushi	虫	worm
mushi-atsui	蒸し暑い	sticky

mushi-ba	虫歯	cavity
mushi-ki	蒸し器	steamer
mushiro	むしろ	rather
mushiro, …to iu yori wa	むしろ, …と言うよりは	rather
mushiru	むしる	pluck
mushiru	むしる	pull
mushi-suru	無視する	ignore
mushi-suru	無視する	neglect
mushi-suru	無視する	regardless
musu	蒸す	steam
musubi	結び	closing
musubi-tsukeru	結び付ける	combine
musubi-tsukeru	結び付ける	unite
musubu	結ぶ	conclude
musubu	結ぶ	connect
musubu	結ぶ	tie
musubu, (mi o)	結ぶ, (実を)	bear[2]
musubu mono	結ぶもの	tie
musuko	息子	son
musume	娘	daughter
musume	娘	girl
musume-san	娘さん	girl
mutto-suru	むっとする	revolt
muttsu (no N)	六つ(のN)	six
muzai no N	無罪のN	innocent
muzukashii	難しい	difficult
muzukashii	難しい	hard
muzukashii	難しい	tough
muzukashii-sa	難しさ	difficulty
myaku(-haku)	脈(拍)	pulse
myakuraku	脈絡	train
myoogi	妙技	stunt
myooji	名字	surname
myuujikaru	ミュージカル	musical

N

nabe-shiki	なべ敷	mat
nadare	雪崩	slide
naderu	なでる	pat
naderu	なでる	stroke[2]
naderu koto	なでること	pat
nade-tsukeru	なで付ける	smooth
-nado	～など	etc.
nae-doko	苗床	nursery
nagabika-seru	長引かせる	prolong
naga-biku	長引く	drag
naga-gutsu	長靴	boot
nagai	長い	long
naga-iki-suru, ⟨-yori⟩	長生きする, ⟨～より⟩	survive
nagaku	長く	long
nagame	眺め	prospect
nagame	眺め	view
nagameru	眺める	look
-nagara, V*masu*	～ながら, V*masu*	while
nagare	流れ	current
nagare	流れ	flow
nagare	流れ	stream
nagare-komu	流れ込む	flow
nagare-ochiru	流れ落ちる	flow
nagareru	流れる	float
nagareru	流れる	flow
nagareru	流れる	run
nagareru	流れる	stream
naga-sa	長さ	length
naga-sa	長さ	long
nagashi	流し	sink
nagasu	流す	float
nagasu	流す	flush
nagasu	流す	shed
nagasu	流す	spill
nage-dasu	投げ出す	fling
nageru	投げる	cast
nageru	投げる	pitch
nageru	投げる	throw
nageru	投げる	toss
nage-suteru	投げ捨てる	surrender
nage-taosu	投げ倒す	throw
nage-tsukeru	投げつける	hurl
nage-uri	投げ売り	sacrifice
naguru	殴る	beat
naguru	殴る	hit
naguru	殴る	knock
naguru	殴る	punch[1]
naguru	殴る	strike
nagusame	慰め	comfort
nagusameru	慰める	comfort
nai	ない	absent
nai	ない	aren't
nai	無い	free
nai	ない	isn't
nai	無い	lack
naibu	内部	within
naibu (ni)	内部(に)	within
naibu no N	内部のN	internal

-nai de, {Vneg./Vstem/ko/shi} 〜ないで, {Vneg./Vstem/来/し} without
naifu ナイフ knife
naika-i 内科医 physician
naikaku 内閣 cabinet
nai koto ないこと absence
-nai (ni) 〜内(に) within
nairiku no N 内陸のN inland
nairon ナイロン nylon
naisen 内線 extension
naita ないた wept
nai to, (moshi) {Vneg./Vstem/ko/shi/adj(*i*). *ku*} ないと, (もし){Vneg./Vstem/来/し/adj(*i*). *ku*} unless
nai, {Vneg./Vstem/shi/ko/adj(*i*). *ku*} ない, {Vneg./Vstem/し/来/adj(*i*). *ku*} not
-nai, Vstem of pot. 〜ない, Vstem of pot. unable
naiya 内野 diamond
naiyoo 内容 content
naiyoo 内容 program
naiyoo 内容 substance
naiyoo, ({koogi-/gakka-}) 内容, ({講義/学科}) program
najimi no nai なじみのない strange
naka 中 inside
naka 中 under
nakaba 半ば middle
naka {de/ni} 中{で/に} among
nakama 仲間 associate
nakama 仲間 circle
nakama 仲間 companion
nakama 仲間 company
nakama 仲間 fellow
nakama 仲間 friend
nakama 仲間 gang
nakama 仲間 partner
nakama 仲間 peer
naka-mi 中身 content
naka-mi 中身 substance
naka-naka なかなか considerably
naka (ni) 中(に) within
naka {ni/de/o} 中{に/で/を} amid
naka {ni/de/o} 中{に/で/を} under
naka ({ni/de/o}) 中({に/で/を}) under
naka-niwa 中庭 court
naka-niwa 中庭 yard[2]
naka o 中を through
naka o saku 仲を裂く split
nakatta なかった wasn't
nakatta なかった weren't
nakereba {ikenai/naranai}, {adj(*na*). stem/N} {de/ja} なければ{いけない/ならない}, {adj(*na*). stem/N}{で/じゃ} must
nakereba {ikenai/naranai}, {adj(*na*). stem/N} {de/ja} なければ{いけない/ならない}, {adj(*na*). stem/N}{で/じゃ} ought
nakereba {ikenai/naranai}, {adj(*na*). stem/N} {de/ja} なければ{いけない/ならない}, {adj(*na*). stem/N}{で/じゃ} owe
nakereba {ikenai/naranai}, {adj(*na*). stem/N} {de/ja} なければ{いけない/ならない}, {adj(*na*). stem/N}{で/じゃ} should
nakereba {ikenai/naranai}, {Vneg./Vstem/shi/ko/adj(*i*). *ku*} なければ{いけない/ならない}, {Vneg./Vstem/し/来/adj(*i*). *ku*} must
nakereba {ikenai/naranai}, {Vneg./Vstem/shi/ko/adj(*i*). *ku*} なければ{いけない/ならない}, {Vneg./Vstem/し/来/adj(*i*). *ku*} need
nakereba {ikenai/naranai}, {Vneg./Vstem/shi/ko/adj(*i*). *ku*} なければ{いけない/ならない}, {Vneg./Vstem/し/来/adj(*i*). *ku*} ought
nakereba {ikenai/naranai}, {Vneg./Vstem/shi/ko/adj(*i*). *ku*} なければ{いけない/ならない}, {Vneg./Vstem/し/来/adj(*i*). *ku*} owe
nakereba {ikenai/naranai}, {Vneg./Vstem/shi/ko/adj(*i*). *ku*} なければ{いけない/ならない}, {Vneg./Vstem/し/来/adj(*i*). *ku*} should
nakereba, (moshi) {Vneg./Vstem/ko/shi/adj(*i*). *ku*} なければ, (もし){Vneg./Vstem/来/し/adj(*i*). *ku*} unless
-nakereba, {Vneg./Vstem/adj(*i*). *ku*/{adj(*na*). stem/N}{de/ja}} 〜なければ, {Vneg./Vstem/adj(*i*). *ku*/{adj(*na*). stem/N}{で/じゃ}} if
nakimashita なきました wept
naku なく cry
naku なく weep
naku naru, (kikai ga) なくなる, (機会が) slip
nakunatte iru (N) なくなっている(N) missing
nakushita N 無くしたN lost
nakusu なくす lose
nakute wa {ikenai/naranai}, {adj(*na*). stem/N} {de/ja} なくては{いけない/ならない}, {adj(*na*). stem/N}{で/じゃ} must
nakute wa {ikenai/naranai}, {adj(*na*). stem/N} {de/ja} なくては{いけない/ならない}, {adj(*na*). stem/N}{で/じゃ} ought

nakute wa {ikenai/naranai}, {adj(*na*). stem/N} {de/ja}	なくては{いけない/ならない}, {adj(*na*). stem/N}{で/じゃ}	owe
nakute wa {ikenai/naranai}, {adj(*na*). stem/N} {de/ja}	なくては{いけない/ならない}, {adj(*na*). stem/N}{で/じゃ}	should
nakute wa {ikenai/naranai}, {Vneg./Vstem/shi/ko/adj(*i*). *ku*}	なくては{いけない/ならない}, {Vneg./Vstem/し/来/adj(*i*). *ku*}	must
nakute wa {ikenai/naranai}, {Vneg./Vstem/shi/ko/adj(*i*). *ku*}	なくては{いけない/ならない}, {Vneg./Vstem/し/来/adj(*i*). *ku*}	ought
nakute wa {ikenai/naranai}, {Vneg./Vstem/shi/ko/adj(*i*). *ku*}	なくては{いけない/ならない}, {Vneg./Vstem/し/来/adj(*i*). *ku*}	owe
nakute wa {ikenai/naranai}, {Vneg./Vstem/shi/ko/adj(*i*). *ku*}	なくては{いけない/ならない}, {Vneg./Vstem/し/来/adj(*i*). *ku*}	should
namae	名前	name
na(mae) o tsukeru	名(前)を付ける	name
nama-gomi	生ごみ	garbage
namake-mono no N	怠け者のN	lazy
nama-namashii	生々しい	vivid
nama no N	生のN	fresh
nama no N	生のN	raw
nama-nurui	生ぬるい	lukewarm
namari	なまり	accent
namerakana	滑らかな	smooth
namerakani suru	滑らかにする	smooth
nameru	なめる	lick
nameru	なめる	suck
nami	波	wave
-nami	～並	range
namida	涙	tear[2]
namida ga deru (N)	涙が出る(N)	watery
nami-hazureta N	並外れたN	extraordinary
nami-hazurete iru (N)	並外れている(N)	extraordinary
nami-nori o suru	波乗りをする	surf
nan	何	what[1]
nana-ban-me (no N)	七番目(のN)	seventh
nana (+counter) (no N)	七(+counter)(のN)	seven
nana-juu (+counter) (no N)	七十(+counter)(のN)	seventy
naname ni	斜めに	sideways
naname ni naru	斜めになる	slant
naname no	斜めの	oblique
nanatsu (no N)	七つ(のN)	seven
nanbu	南部	south
nanbu no N	南部のN	southern
nan+counter ka	何+counterか	some
nan+counter ka no N	何+counterかのN	several
nan+counter ka (no) N	何+counterか(の)N	some
nandai	難題	puzzle
nan-de	何で	why
nan-demo	何でも	anything
nan-demo	何でも	whatever
nando-mo	何度も	and
nan-do-mo iku	何度も行く	haunt
nani	何	what[1]
nani-ka	何か	any
nani-ka	何か	anything
nani-ka	何か	something
nani-mo dekinai, (jibun de wa)	何もできない, (自分では)	helpless
nanimo-kamo	何もかも	everything
nani-mo…neg.	何も…neg.	any
nani-mo…neg.	何も…neg.	anything
nani-mo…neg.	何も…neg.	none
nani-mo…neg.	何も…neg.	nothing
nani-mo shinai de iru	何もしないでいる	idle
nani-mo shiranai N	何も知らないN	ignorant
nani+prt. V*te* mo	何+prt.V*te*も	whatever
nanji	なんじ	thou
nanji no N	なんじのN	thy
Nankyoku no N	南極のN	Antarctic
Nankyoku-tairiku	南極大陸	Antarctica
nanmon	難問	puzzle
nan no tame ni	何のために	why
na-noru	名乗る	identify
nanpa	難破	wreck
nanpa-suru	難破する	wreck
nan-sei	南西	southwest
nan-sei chihoo	南西地方	southwest
nan-sei {e/ni}	南西{へ/に}	southwest
nan-sei no N	南西のN	southwestern
nansensuna koto	ナンセンスなこと	nonsense
nan-toka…verb	なんとか…verb	manage
nan-too	南東	southeast
nantoo chihoo	南東地方	southeast
naoru	なおる	heal
naoru	なおる	recover
naosu	なおす	correct
naosu	なおす	fix
naosu	なおす	mend

naosu	なおす	repair
naozari ni suru	なおざりにする	slight
napukin	ナプキン	napkin
narabe-kata	並べ方	arrangement
narabu	並ぶ	compare
nara, Sinf. (no)	なら, Sinf.(の)	if
narasu	慣らす	accustom
narasu	鳴らす	sound
narau	習う	learn
narawashi	習わし	practice
-narenai N, V*masu*	~慣れないN, V*masu*	new
narete iru (N)	慣れている(N)	used[1]
nari-soona, (ima-nimo) ⟨-ni⟩	なりそうな, (今にも)⟨~に⟩	threaten
nari-yuki	成り行き	course
naru	鳴る	blow
naru	成る	consist
naru	なる	grow
naru	なる	number
naru	鳴る	ring[2]
naru, {adj(*i*). *ku*/adj(*na*). *ni*/⟨-ni⟩}	なる, {adj(*i*). *ku*/adj(*na*). *ni*/⟨~に⟩}	drive
naru, {adj(*i*). *ku*/adj(*na*). *ni*/⟨-ni⟩}	なる, {adj(*i*). *ku*/adj(*na*). *ni*/⟨~に⟩}	get
naru, {adj(*i*). *ku*/adj(*na*). *ni*/⟨-ni⟩}	なる, {adj(*i*). *ku*/adj(*na*). *ni*/⟨~に⟩}	turn
naru, {⟨-ni⟩/adj(*i*). *ku*/adj(*na*). *ni*}	なる, {⟨~に⟩/adj(*i*). *ku*/adj(*na*). *ni*}	become
naru, (⟨-no⟩ o-kage de)…pot. yooni	なる, (⟨~の⟩おかげで)…pot.ように	enable
(naru) oto	(鳴る)音	ring[2]
naru, tame ni {Vinf. nonpast yoo ni/adj(*i*). *ku*/adj(*na*). *ni*}	なる, ために{Vinf. nonpastように/adj(*i*). *ku*/adj(*na*). *ni*}	render
naru, Vinf. yooni	なる, Vinf.ように	come
nasake	情け	mercy
nasake-nai	情けない	miserable
nasaru	なさる	do
nashi	梨	pear
nashi de sumasu, N	なしで済ます, N	spare
-nashi {ni/de}	~なし{に/で}	without
nashi-togeru	成し遂げる	achieve
natoriumu	ナトリウム	sodium
natsu	夏	summer
natsukashii	なつかしい	miss
nattoku-saseru	納得させる	convince
nattsu	ナッツ	nut
nawa	縄	rope
naya	納屋	barn
nayama-sareru	悩まされる	suffer
nayama-seru	悩ませる	trouble
nayami	悩み	trouble
nayamu	悩む	suffer
nayamu	悩む	worry
naze	なぜ	why
nazo-nazo	なぞなぞ	riddle
n desu ga, Sinf.	んですが, Sinf.	would
ne	ね	OK
ne	根	root
ne-agari-suru	値上がりする	up
Nebada	ネバダ	Nevada
neba-neba-suru	ねばねばする	sticky
nedan	値段	price
negai	願い	request
negai	願い	wish
negai-goto	願い事	request
negau	願う	request
negau, Sinf. yooni	願う, Sinf.ように	pray
negau, Vinf. nonpast yoo (ni)	願う, Vinf. nonpastよう(に)	request
ne-iro	音色	tone
neji	ねじ	screw
neji de shimeru	ねじで締める	screw
neji-mawashi	ねじ回し	screwdriver
neji o maku	ねじを巻く	wind[2]
nejireru	ねじれる	twist
nejiru	ねじる	twist
nejiru	ねじる	wring
nekko	根っ子	root
nekkuresu	ネックレス	necklace
neko	猫	cat
neko-ze	猫背	stoop
nekutai	ネクタイ	necktie
nekutai	ネクタイ	tie
nemui	眠い	sleepy
nemuri	眠り	sleep
nemuru	眠る	sleep
nemutai	眠たい	sleepy
nemutte	眠って	asleep
-nen	~年	year
nendo	粘土	clay
nen ik-kai no N	年一回のN	yearly
nen-irini tsukurareta N	念入りに作られたN	elaborate
nenkin	年金	pension
nenkoo-joretsu	年功序列	seniority

nenrei	年齢	age
nenryoo	燃料	fuel
ne o tsukeru	値を付ける	value
nerai o sadameru	ねらいを定める	aim
(neri-)ha-migaki	(ねり)歯磨き	toothpaste
neru	寝る	sleep
ne, Sinf. n {desu/da}	ね, Sinf.ん{です/だ}	understand
ne-soberu	寝そべる	lie[1]
nesshinna	熱心な	eager
nesshinna	熱心な	earnest
nesshinna	熱心な	enthusiastic
nesshinna	熱心な	keen
nesshinni negatte iru	熱心に願っている	eager
netamu	ねたむ	jealous
netsu	熱	fever
netsu	熱	heat
netsuboo-shite iru	熱望している	eager
netsui	熱意	enthusiasm
netsui	熱意	passion
netsuretsuna koi	熱烈な恋	passion
nettai no N	熱帯のN	tropical
netto	ネット	net
netto waaku	ネットワーク	network
netto-waaku	ネットワーク	web
nezumi	ねずみ	mice
nezumi	ねずみ	mouse
nezumi	ねずみ	rat
nezumi-iro no N	ねずみ色のN	gray
ni	に	among
ni	に	and
ni	に	at
ni	に	by
ni	に	for
ni	に	in
ni	に	into
ni	に	on
ni	に	to
ni	に	toward(s)
ni-au	似合う	suit[2]
ni-bai	二倍	twice
(ni-)bai ni naru	(二)倍になる	double
(ni-)bai ni suru	(二)倍にする	double
(ni-)bai no N	(二)倍のN	double
ni-ban-me	二番目	second[1]
ni-ban-me no N	二番目のN	second[1]
ni-basha	荷馬車	wagon
nibui	鈍い	dull
nichibotsu	日没	sunset

ni chigai-nai, {adj(*na*). stem/N} {ø/datta}	にちがいない, {adj(*na*). stem/N}{ø/だった}	must
ni chigai-nai, {V/adj(*i*).}inf.	にちがいない, {V/adj(*i*).}inf.	must
nichijoo no N	日常のN	daily
nichijoo no N	日常のN	everyday
nichiyoo(-bi)	日曜(日)	Sunday
nichiyoo-hin	日用品	groceries
ni (+counter) (no N)	二(+counter)(のN)	two
ni-do	二度	twice
ni-do to ...neg.	二度と…neg.	never
nieru	煮える	cook
ni-fuda	荷札	label
ni-fuda	荷札	tag
ni-fuda o tsukeru	荷札を付ける	tag
nigai	苦い	bitter
nigai kao o suru	苦い顔をする	frown
ni-gatsu	二月	February
nigeru	逃げる	escape
nigeru	逃げる	flee
nigiru	握る	hold
nigiyakana	にぎやかな	bustling
nigiyakana	にぎやかな	busy
nigiyakana	にぎやかな	lively
Nihon	日本	Japan
Nihon-go	日本語	Japanese
Nihon-go no N	日本語のN	Japanese
Nihon-jin	日本人	Japanese
Nihon-jin no N	日本人のN	Japanese
Nihon no N	日本のN	Japanese
niji	にじ	rainbow
ni-ji-tekina	二次的な	secondary
ni-juu	二十	score
ni-juu-ban-me (no N)	二十番目(のN)	twentieth
ni-juu (+counter) (no N)	二十(+counter)(のN)	twenty
ni-juu-go sento	二十五セント	quarter
ni-kai	二回	twice
nikai+prt.	二階+prt.	upstairs
ni-kanshite	に関して	on
ni-kanshite	に関して	regarding
ni-kanshite no N	に関してのN	on
ni-kanshite (no N)	に関して(のN)	concerning
ni-kansuru N	に関するN	concerning
ni-kansuru N	に関するN	on
nikki	日記	diary
nikkoo	日光	sun
nikkoo	日光	sunlight

nikkoo	日光	sunshine
nikkuneemu	ニックネーム	nickname
niko-niko-suru	にこにこする	smile
nikoyakana	にこやかな	radiant
niku	肉	flesh
niku	肉	meat
nikui	憎い	hate
nikumu	憎む	hate
niku-tai	肉体	body
niku-ya	肉屋	butcher
ni-kyuu-hin	二級品	second[1]
nimo-kakawarazu, (sore)	にもかかわらず, (それ)	nevertheless
ni-motsu	荷物	load
ningen	人間	being
ningen	人間	man
ningen no kuzu	人間のくず	trash
ningen no N	人間のN	human
ningen-tekina	人間的な	human
ningyoo	人形	doll
ningyoo	人形	puppet
nin'i no N	任意のN	random
ninjin	にんじん	carrot
ninki	人気	popularity
ninki ga aru (N)	人気がある(N)	popular
ninki-mono	人気者	favorite
ninmei-suru	任命する	appoint
ninmu	任務	mission
ni, ((-no) naka)	に, ((〜の)中)	in
ni, ((-no) naka)	に, ((〜の)中)	into
ni, ((-no) ue)	に, ((〜の)上)	onto
ni, ((-no) ue)	に, ((〜の)上)	up
ninshin-shite iru (N)	妊娠している(N)	pregnant
ninshoo	人称	person
nintai	忍耐	patience
nintai-zuyoi	忍耐強い	patient
nioi	におい	odor
nioi	におい	scent
nioi	におい	smell
nioi ga suru	においがする	smell
nioi o kagu	においをかぐ	smell
niou	におう	smell
Nippon	日本	Japan
niru	煮る	boil
niru	煮る	cook
ni-rui	二塁	second[1]
ni-ryuu no N	二流のN	second-class
nise no N	にせのN	false
nishi	西	west
nishi {e/ni}	西{へ/に}	westward
nishi-muki no N	西向きのN	westward
nishi no hoo e no N	西の方へのN	westward
nishi no N	西のN	western
ni-shite wa	にしては	for
ni-taishite	に対して	for
nitchuu	日中	day
nite inai (N)	似ていない(N)	unlike
nite iru	似ている	resemble
nite iru (N)	似ている(N)	alike
nite iru (N)	似ている(N)	similar
ni-too no N	二等のN	second[1]
ni-too no N	二等のN	second-class
ni(-totte) wa	に(とって)は	for
ni-tsuite	について	about
ni-tsuite	について	on
ni-tsuite	について	regarding
ni-tsuite no N	についてのN	on
ni-tsuite (no N)	について(のN)	concerning
ni-tsuki	につき	a
ni-tsuki	につき	to
ni-tsuki	につき	per
niwa	庭	garden
niwa	庭	yard[2]
niwaka-ame	にわか雨	shower
niwatori	鶏	chicken
niyari to {warau/suru}	にやりと{笑う/する}	smile
niyatto {warau/suru}	にやっと{笑う/する}	smile
ni-yotte	によって	by
ni-yotte	によって	through
ni-zukuri	荷造り	packing
ni-zukuri o suru	荷造りをする	pack
no	の	of
no	の	's
no-	野〜	wild
nobasu	のばす	delay
nobasu	のばす	extend
nobasu	のばす	grow
nobasu	のばす	prolong
nobasu	のばす	smooth
nobasu	のばす	straighten
nobasu	のばす	stretch
noberu	述べる	describe
noberu	述べる	express
noberu	述べる	observe
noberu	述べる	relate
noberu	述べる	state

noberu, sarani kuwashiku	述べる, 更に詳しく	elaborate
nobi	のび	stretch
nobiru	のびる	extend
nobiru	のびる	grow
noboru	のぼる	climb
noboru	のぼる	rise
node	ので	as
node, Sinf.	ので, Sinf.	because
node, Sinf.	ので, Sinf.	since[2]
node, Sinf.	ので, Sinf.	that[3]
nodo	のど	throat
nodo ga kawaita N	のどが渇いたN	thirsty
nodo ga kawaite iru (N)	のどが渇いている(N)	thirsty
nodo no kawaki	のどの渇き	thirst
nogareru	逃れる	escape
noizu	ノイズ	noise
no janai ka to omou, {{V/adj(*i*).}inf./{adj(*na*). stem/N}}{na/datta}	のじゃないかと思う, {{V/adj(*i*).}inf./{adj(*na*). stem/N}}{な/だった}	fear
nokku-suru	ノックする	knock
nokogiri	のこぎり	saw
nokogiri de kiru	のこぎりで切る	saw
nokori	残り	remainder
nokori	残り	rest[2]
nokori-mono	残り物	remain
nokoru	残る	leave
nokoru	残る	remain
nokoru, (-yori) ato made	残る, (～より)後まで	survive
nokosu	残す	leave
noma-seru	飲ませる	feed
nomi-komu	飲み込む	swallow[1]
nomi-mono	飲物	beverage
nomi-mono	飲物	drink
nomu	飲む	drink
nomu	飲む	swallow[1]
nomu	飲む	take
nomu	飲む	use
noni	のに	although
noni	のに	as
nonoshiru	ののしる	swear
noo	脳	brain
noogyoo	農業	agriculture
noogyoo o suru	農業をする	farm
noojoo	農場	farm
nooka	農家	farmer
noomaruna	ノーマルな	normal
noomin	農民	farmer
nooritsu	能率	efficiency
nooritsu-tekina	能率的な	efficient
nooryoku	能力	ability
nooryoku	能力	capacity
nooryoku	能力	competence
nooryoku	能力	power
nooryoku ga aru (N), {Vinf. nonpast/N no}	能力がある(N), {Vinf. nonpast/Nの}	capable
nooto	ノート	notebook
nori	のり	glue
nori	のり	paste
nori	のり	starch
nori de hari-tsukeru	のりではりつける	glue
nori de haru	のりではる	paste
nori-kae	乗り換え	transfer
nori-kaeru	乗り換える	change
nori-kaeru	乗り換える	transfer
nori-kumi-in	乗組員	crew
nori-mono	乗り物	transportation
nori-mono	乗り物	vehicle
nori-okureru	乗り遅れる	miss
noroi	のろい	slack
noro-noro	のろのろ	slowly
noru	のる	board
noru	のる	carry
noru	のる	ride
noru hito	乗る人	rider
Noruuee	ノルウェー	Norway
no, Sinf. (to iu)	の, Sinf.(という)	that[3]
notakuru	のたくる	wriggle
notte, ({hikoo-ki/fune} nado ni)	乗って, ({飛行機/船}などに)	aboard
notte-iku	乗って行く	ride
notte-{iku/kuru}	乗って{行く/来る}	take
no, {{V/adj(*i*).}inf./adj(*na*). stem na}	の, {{V/adj(*i*).}inf./adj(*na*). stemな}	one
nozoku	除く	eliminate
nozoku	のぞく	peek
nozomashii	望ましい	desirable
nozomi	望み	hope
nozomi	望み	promise
nozomi	望み	wish
nozomu	望む	desire
nozomu	望む	hope
nugu, (kite iru mono o)	脱ぐ, (着ている物を)	strip

nuguu	ぬぐう	wipe
nui-awaseru	縫い合わせる	sew
nui-me	縫い目	seam
nukasu	抜かす	omit
-nukeru, V*masu*	～抜ける, V*masu*	through
nukete iru bubun	抜けている部分	gap
nukete iru (N)	抜けている(N)	missing
nuku	抜く	pick
nuku	抜く	pull
-nuku, V*masu*	～抜く, V*masu*	through
numa	沼	pond
numa-chi	沼地	swamp
nuno	布	cloth
nurasu	ぬらす	wet
nureru	ぬれる	wet
nureta N	ぬれたN	wet
nurete iru (N)	ぬれている(N)	wet
nuru	塗る	spread
nurui	ぬるい	lukewarm
nusumi	盗み	steal
nusumu	盗む	rob
nusumu	盗む	steal
nusumu	盗む	take
nusumu, naka no mono o	盗む, 中の物を	rob
nutte-iku	縫って行く	thread
nuu	縫う	sew
nuu	縫う	stitch
nyuugaku	入学	entrance
nyuuin-saseru	入院させる	hospitalize
nyuujoo	入場	entrance
nyuujoo-ryoo	入場料	admission
nyuumon	入門	introduction
nyuunenna	入念な	elaborate
nyuusatsu-suru	入札する	bid
nyuu-seihin-hanbai-jo	乳製品販売所	dairy
nyuusu	ニュース	news
nyuuyoku	入浴	bath
nyuuyoku-saseru	入浴させる	bathe
nyuuyoku-suru	入浴する	bathe
nyuuyoo-ji	乳幼児	infant
Nyuuyooku	ニューヨーク	New York

O

o	を	down
o	尾	tail
o!	おっ!	Oh
oba	おば	aunt
o-baa-chan	おばあちゃん	grandma
o-baa-san	おばあさん	grandmother
oba-san	おばさん	aunt
obi	帯	band
obi	帯	belt
obi	帯	sash[1]
obieru	おびえる	terrify
oboe-gaki	覚書	note
oboeru	覚える	learn
oboeru	覚える	memorize
oboeru	覚える	remember
oboete iru	覚えている	remember
(o-)cha	(お)茶	tea
ochiiru	陥る	sink
ochi-komu	落ち込む	sink
ochiru	落ちる	drop
ochiru	落ちる	fail
ochiru	落ちる	fall
ochitsuita N	落ち着いたN	calm
ochitsuite	落ち着いて	calmly
ochitsuite iru (N)	落ち着いている(N)	calm
ochitsukanai	落ち着かない	uneasy
ochitsuka-seru	落ち着かせる	settle
ochitsuki ga nai (N)	落ち着きがない(N)	restless
ochitsuku	落ち着く	calm
ochitsuku	落ち着く	relax
ochitsuku	落ち着く	settle
odayakana	穏やかな	mild
odayakana	穏やかな	peaceful
odayakani	穏やかに	quietly
odokasu	おどかす	scare
odori	踊り	dance
odoroite tobi-agaru koto	驚いて飛び上がること	start
odoroka-seru	驚かせる	alarm
odoroka-seru	驚かせる	amaze
odoroka-seru	驚かせる	astonish
odoroka-seru	驚かせる	startle
odoroka-seru	驚かせる	surprise
odoroka-su	驚かす	astonish
odoroka-su	驚かす	startle
odoroka-su	驚かす	surprise
odoroka-su koto	驚かすこと	surprise
odoroki	驚き	astonishment
odoroki	驚き	surprise
odoroki	驚き	wonder
odoroku	驚く	frighten
odoroku	驚く	wonder

odoroku-beki koto	驚くべきこと	surprise
odoroku-beki koto	驚くべきこと	wonder
odoroku-beki N	驚くべきN	amazing
odoroku-beki N	驚くべきN	astonishing
odoroku-beki N	驚くべきN	wonderful
odoru	踊る	dance
odoshi	脅し	threat
odosu	脅す	threaten
oeru	終える	conclude
oeru	終える	end
oeru	終える	finish
ofisu	オフィス	office
o-fukuro	お袋	mother
ogamu	拝む	worship
ogawa	小川	brook
ogawa	小川	stream
ogori	おごり	treat
ogoru	おごる	treat
Ohaio	オハイオ	Ohio
o-hitsuji	雄羊	ram
oi	おい	nephew
oi-harau	追い払う	drive
oi-harau	追い払う	scatter
oi-kakeru	追いかける	chase
oi-kakeru	追いかける	hunt
oi-kosu	追い越す	overtake
oi-kosu	追い越す	pass
oi-nuku	追い抜く	pass
oiru	オイル	oil
oishii	おいしい	delicious
oishii	おいしい	good
oishii	おいしい	tasty
oi-tateru	追い立てる	urge
oi-tsuku	追いつく	overtake
o-iwai	お祝い	celebration
o-iwai	お祝い	congratulation
o-iwai	お祝い	present[2]
oji	おじ	uncle
o-jigi	お辞儀	bow
o-jigi o suru	お辞儀をする	bow
o-jii-chan	おじいちゃん	grandpa
o-jii-san	おじいさん	grandfather
oji-san	おじさん	uncle
o-joo-san	お嬢さん	daughter
o-joo-san	お嬢さん	girl
oka	丘	hill
oka	おか	shore
o-kaa-sama	お母様	mother

o-kaa-san	お母さん	mother
o-kage da	お陰だ	owe
o-kage de…habuke-ru	おかげで…省ける	save
o-kage de…setsuyaku-dekiru	おかげで…節約出来る	save
o-kanjoo	お勘定	check
oka no chuufuku	丘の中腹	hillside
okashii	おかしい	funny
okashii	おかしい	queer
okashina N	おかしなN	funny
okashina N	おかしなN	queer
okasu	おかす	commit
okasu	おかす	violate
o-kawari	お代わり	second[1]
oke	おけ	pail
oke	おけ	tub
oki-dokei	置き時計	clock
o-ki-ni-iri	お気に入り	favorite
okiru	起きる	arise
okiru	起きる	awake
okiru	起きる	occur
okiru	起きる	rise
okiru	起きる	spring
okiru	起きる	start
okiru	起きる	wake
okkanai	おっかない	scary
okonai	行い	conduct
okonai o aratame-saseru	行いを改めさせる	reform
okonau	行う	conduct
okonau	行う	perform
okonau	行う	practice
okora-seru	怒らせる	offend
okori-{eru/uru}	起こり得る	possible
okori-{eru/uru}	起こり得る	probable
okoru	起こる	arise
okoru	起こる	happen
okoru	起こる	occur
okoru	起こる	stem
okoru koto	起こること	occurrence
okosu	おこす	arouse
okosu	起こす	raise
okosu	起こす	wake
okotaru	怠る	neglect
okotta N	怒ったN	mad
okotte iru (N)	怒っている(N)	angry
oku	置く	lay
oku	置く	leave
oku	置く	place

oku	置く	put
oku	奥	rear
oku	置く	set
okugai no N	屋外のN	outdoor
okunai {de/ni/o}	屋内{で/に/を}	indoors
oku ni	奥に	farther
oku no N	奥のN	rear
Okurahoma	オクラホマ	Oklahoma
okure	遅れ	delay
okureru	遅れる	hinder
okureru	遅れる	late
okurete	遅れて	behind
okuri-mono	贈り物	gift
okuri-mono	贈り物	present[2]
okuri-te	送り手	transmitter
okuru	おくる	present[2]
okuru	おくる	send
okuru	おくる	transmit
okuru, (fune de)	送る, (船で)	ship
oku-sama	奥様	wife
oku-sama, N no	奥様, Nの	Mrs.
oku-san	奥さん	wife
oku-san, N no	奥さん, Nの	Mrs.
oku, V*te*	おく, V*te*	leave
(o-)kyaku	(お)客	customer
o-mae	お前	son
o-mae	お前	you
o-mae no N	お前のN	your
o-mae-tachi	お前たち	you
o-mae-tachi no N	お前たちのN	your
o-mago-san	お孫さん	grandchild
o-mawari(-san)	お巡り(さん)	policeman
o-miya	お宮	shrine
(o-)miyage	(お)土産	souvenir
omocha	おもちゃ	toy
omoi	重い	heavy
omoi	重い	serious
omoi-dasu	思い出す	recall
omoi-dasu	思い出す	recollect
omoi-dasu	思い出す	remember
omoi-dasu, {miru/kiku} to	思い出す, {見る/聞く}と	remind
omoi-de	思い出	memory
omoi-de	思い出	recall
omoi-de	思い出	remembrance
omoigakenai	思いがけない	sudden
omoigakenai	思いがけない	unexpected
omoigakenaku	思いがけなく	suddenly
omoi-kitte V	思い切ってV	venture
omoi-todomara-seru	思い止まらせる	discourage
omoi-todomara-seyoo to suru	思い止まらせようとする	discourage
omoitsuki	思いつき	idea
omoi-yari	思いやり	consideration
omoi-yari ga aru (N)	思いやりがある(N)	tender
omoi-yari ga aru (N)	思いやりがある(N)	thoughtful
omoi-yari ga nai (N)	思いやりがない(N)	thoughtless
omoi-yaru	思いやる	consider
omoki o oku	重きをおく	stress
omomuki	趣	flavor
omona	主な	chief
omona	主な	main
omona	主な	principal
omoni	主に	chiefly
omoni	主に	mainly
omoni	主に	mostly
omo-ni	重荷	burden
omo-ni	重荷	tax
omo-ni o owa-seru	重荷を負わせる	burden
omo-sa	重さ	weight
omo-sa o hakaru	重さをはかる	weigh
omoshiro-gara-seru	面白がらせる	amuse
omoshiroi	面白い	fun
omoshiroi	面白い	interesting
omoshirokunai	面白くない	dull
omoshirokunai (N)	面白くない(N)	uninteresting
omotai	重たい	heavy
omote	表	front
omotte mo inai, Sinf. nado to wa	思ってもいない, Sinf.などとは	pretend
omou	思う	believe
omou	思う	consider
omou	思う	expect
omou	思う	feel
omou	思う	figure
omou	思う	find
omou	思う	reckon
omou	思う	strike
omou	思う	submit
omou	思う	think
omou, neg. of Sinf. to	思う, neg. of Sinf.と	doubt
omou, (-no koto o) (machigatte) ⟨-to⟩	思う, (〜のことを) (間違って)⟨〜と⟩	take
omou, Sinf. daroo to	思う, Sinf.だろうと	suppose
omou, Sinf. no dewanai (daroo) ka to	思う, Sinf.のではない(だろう)かと	suspect

omou, Sinf. (no/n) {dewanai/ja nai} ka to	思う, Sinf.(の/ん){ではない/じゃない}かと	question
omou, Sinf. to	思う, Sinf.と	gather
omou, Sinf. to	思う, Sinf.と	guess
omou, Vvol. to	思う, Vvol.と	plan
omou, Vvol. to	思う, Vvol.と	will
omowa-reru, Sinf. yooni	思われる, Sinf.ように	seem
omuretsu	オムレツ	omelet
on	音	note
onaji da	同じだ	parallel
onaji hito	同じ人	same
onaji janai (N)	同じじゃない(N)	unlike
onaji koto	同じこと	same
onaji-kurai	同じくらい	as
onaji mono	同じ物	same
onaji N	同じN	identical
onaji (N)	同じ(N)	same
onaji yoona	同じような	similar
onaji yoona	同じような	uniform
o-naka	おなか	belly
o-naka	おなか	stomach
o-naka ga peko-peko da	おなかがぺこぺこだ	starve
o-naka ga suku	おなかがすく	hungry
ondo	温度	temperature
ondo-kei	温度計	thermometer
ondori	おんどり	rooster
one	尾根	ridge
ongak-ka	音楽家	musician
ongaku	音楽	music
ongaku ga sukina	音楽が好きな	musical
ongaku-ka	音楽家	musician
ongaku no N	音楽のN	musical
ongaku no sainoo ga aru (N)	音楽の才能がある(N)	musical
ongaku o tomonau (N)	音楽を伴う(N)	musical
ongi	恩義	debt
onkai	音階	scale[3]
onkei	恩恵	benefit
onkenna	穏健な	moderate
onkoona	温厚な	mild
onna	女	female
onna	女	woman
onna no hito	女の人	lady
onna no hito	女の人	woman
onna-no-ko	女の子	girl
onna no N	女のN	female

ono	おの	ax
o, (⟨-no⟩ naka)	を, (⟨〜の⟩中)	in
ononoki	おののき	shiver
ononoku	おののく	shiver
ono-ono	各々	each
ono-ono no N	各々のN	each
onryoo	音量	volume
onsei-gaku	音声学	phonetics
onsei-gaku no N	音声学のN	phonetic
onsei no N	音声のN	phonetic
onsen	温泉	spa
onsen-chi	温泉地	spa
onsetsu	音節	syllable
onsetsu-moji-hyoo	音節文字表	syllabary
onshitsu	温室	greenhouse
onsu	オンス	ounce
oo	王	king
oo!	おお!	aw
oobaa	オーバー	coat
oobaa	オーバー	overcoat
oobaa-kooto	オーバーコート	coat
oobaa-kooto	オーバーコート	overcoat
oobo-sha	応募者	applicant
oo-bukuro	大袋	sack
oobun	オーブン	oven
ooda	殴打	strike
oo-doori	大通り	avenue
oofuku	往復	trip
oofuku(-ryokoo)	往復(旅行)	round-trip
oo-goe de hanasu	大声で話す	shout
ooi	多い	frequent
ooi	多い	lot
ooi	多い	many
ooi	王位	throne
(oo)in	(押)韻	rhyme
ooi no nai (N)	覆いのない(N)	uncovered
ooji	王子	prince
ooji	皇子	prince
oojiru	応じる	accept
oojiru	応じる	yield
oojo	王女	princess
ookami	おおかみ	wolf
oo-kasshoku	黄褐色	tan
ookesutora	オーケストラ	orchestra
ookii	大きい	big
ookii	大きい	large
ookii	大きい	loud
ookiku	大きく	wide

ookiku hirogeta N	大きく広げたN	widespread
ookiku naru	大きくなる	swell
ookiku suru	大きくする	enlarge
(ookina) hon	(大きな)本	volume
ookina N	大きなN	big
ookina N	大きなN	large
ooki-sa	大きさ	scale[3]
ooki-sa	大きさ	size
ookoku	王国	kingdom
oomakana	大まかな	rough
oomizu	大水	flood
oo-moji	大文字	capital
oomu	おうむ	parrot
oomugi	大麦	barley
oonaa	オーナー	owner
oorai	往来	traffic
ooru	オール	oar
Oorubanii	オールバニー	Albany
oo-sawagi	大騒ぎ	fuss
ooshin-suru	往診する	visit
ooshitsu no N	王室のN	royal
Ooshuu	欧州	Europe
Ooshuu no N	欧州のN	European
Oosutoraria	オーストラリア	Australia
Oosutoraria-jin	オーストラリア人	Australian
Oosutoria	オーストリア	Austria
Oosutoria-jin	オーストリア人	Austrian
ootobai	オートバイ	motorcycle
ootomachikku no N	オートマチックのN	automatic
ootomiiru	オートミール	cereal
ootomiiru	オートミール	oatmeal
ootoo	応答	response
ootoo-suru	応答する	respond
oou	覆う	cover
oou	覆う	screen
ooya	大家	landlady
ooya	大家	landlord
ooyake ni	公に	officially
ooyake no N	公のN	official
ooyake no N	公のN	public
oo-yasu-uri	大安売り	sale
ooyoo	応用	application
ooyoo-suru	応用する	apply
ooyoso no N	おおよそのN	approximate
oozappana	大雑把な	sweeping
oozei	大勢	many
oozei	大勢	troop
oozei no hito	大勢の人	crowd
oozuru	応ずる	yield
opera	オペラ	opera
opereetaa	オペレーター	operator
oppo	尾っぽ	tail
Oranda	オランダ	Holland
Oranda	オランダ	Netherlands
Oranda-go	オランダ語	Dutch
Oranda-go no N	オランダ語のN	Dutch
Oranda-jin	オランダ人	Dutch
Oranda-jin no N	オランダ人のN	Dutch
Oranda no N	オランダのN	Dutch
ore	おれ	I
Oregon	オレゴン	Oregon
orenji	オレンジ	orange
ore no N	おれのN	my
oreru	折れる	break
ore-tachi no N	おれたちのN	our
oreta ha no ne	折れた歯の根	stump
ori	おり	cage
ori	折	occasion
oriento	オリエント	Orient
ori-guai	織り具合	texture
oriibu	オリーブ	olive
oriibu-iro	オリーブ色	olive
orijinaruna	オリジナルな	original
ori-komu	織り込む	weave
ori-mageru	折り曲げる	bend
orimasu	おります	am
orimasu	おります	are
orimasu	おります	be
ori-mono	織物	cloth
ori-mono	織物	textile
ori-mono-genryoo	織物原料	textile
Orinpikku	オリンピック	Olympic Games
ori-tatame-ru	折り畳める	fold
ori-tatamu	折り畳む	fold
orosokani suru	おろそかにする	neglect
oru	折る	break
oru	折る	fold
oru	織る	weave
orugan	オルガン	organ
osaeru	おさえる	control
osaeru	おさえる	restrain
osae-tsukeru	押さえ付ける	pin
o-seji o iu	お世辞を言う	flatter
osen	汚染	pollution
o-shaberi	おしゃべり	chat
o-shaberi	おしゃべり	chatter

o-shaberi	おしゃべり	talk
o-shaberi (o) suru	おしゃべり(を)する	chat
oshi	押し	thrust
oshieru	教える	instruct
oshieru	教える	show
oshieru	教える	teach
oshi ga tsuyoi	押しが強い	pushy
oshii	惜しい	regret
oshiire	押し入れ	closet
oshi-komeru	押し込める	jam[1]
oshi-komu	押し込む	jam[1]
oshi-komu	押し込む	tuck
oshi-{komu/komeru}	押し{込む/込める}	squeeze
oshimu	惜しむ	spare
oshite nobasu	押してのばす	press
oshi-tsubusu	押しつぶす	squash
oshi-tsukeru	押し付ける	press
oshi-tsukeru koto	押しつけること	press
osoi	遅い	late
osoi	遅い	slow
osoku	遅く	late
osoku	遅く	slowly
osoku suru	遅くする	slow
osoraku	恐らく	probably
osore	恐れ	dread
osore	恐れ	threat
osoreru	恐れる	dread
osoreru	恐れる	fear
osorete iru	恐れている	fearful
osoroshii	恐ろしい	awful
osoroshii	恐ろしい	dreadful
osoroshii	恐ろしい	fear
osoroshii	恐ろしい	fearful
osoroshii	恐ろしい	frightening
osoroshii	恐ろしい	scare
osoroshii	恐ろしい	terrible
osoroshii	恐ろしい	tremendous
osoroshii hodo no N	恐ろしいほどのN	tremendous
osoroshiku	恐ろしく	terribly
osoroshi-sa	恐ろしさ	fear
osoroshi-sa	恐ろしさ	horror
osou	襲う	attack
osou	襲う	storm
osou	襲う	strike
osu	おす	press
osu	おす	push
osu	押す	shove
osu koto	押すこと	press

osu no N	雄のN	male
(o-)tagai no N	(お)互いのN	mutual
o-taku	お宅	house
o-taku	お宅	residence
(o-)tearai	(お)手洗い	bathroom
(o-)tearai	(お)手洗い	lavatory
(o-)tearai	(お)手洗い	toilet
(o-)tearai	(お)手洗い	washroom
oten	汚点	stain
(o-)tera	(お)寺	temple
o-tetsudai-san	お手伝いさん	maid
oto	音	ring[2]
oto	音	sound
otoko	男	fellow
otoko	男	guy
otoko	男	man
otoko no hito	男の人	man
otoko-no-ko	男の子	boy
otoko no N	男のN	male
o-tomo	お供	train
otona	大人	adult
otona no N	大人のN	mature
otonashii	おとなしい	gentle
otonashii	おとなしい	quiet
otonashii	おとなしい	tame
otonashiku	おとなしく	passively
otonashiku	おとなしく	quietly
o-too-chan	お父ちゃん	pa
(o-)too-chan	(お)父ちゃん	papa
oto o dasu	音を出す	sound
o-too-sama	お父様	father
o-too-san	お父さん	father
otooto	弟	brother
otoroeru	おとろえる	decline
otoshi-ana	落とし穴	trap
otosu	落とす	drop
otosu	落とす	fail
otosu	落とす	reduce
otosu	落とす	shed
(o-)tsukai	(お)使い	errand
o-tsuri	お釣り	change
(o-)tsuya	(お)通夜	wake
otto	夫	husband
otto!	おっと!	oops
ou	追う	hunt
ou	追う	pursue
o-ushi	雄牛	ox
owari	終わり	close[1]

owari	終わり	closing
owari	終わり	conclusion
owari	終わり	end
owari no nai N	終わりのないN	endless
owaru	終わる	end
owaru	終わる	finish
owaru	終わる	over
owaru	終わる	result
owaru	終わる	through
owatta N	終わったN	past
oya	親	parent
oya!	おや!	Oh
oya-maa	おやまあ	dear
oya-yubi	親指	thumb
oyobu	及ぶ	extend
oyobu	及ぶ	reach
oyogi	泳ぎ	swimming
oyogu	泳ぐ	swim
o-yome-san	お嫁さん	bride
oyoso	およそ	about

P

paasento	パーセント	percent
paasonaritii	パーソナリティ	personality
paatii	パーティー	party
paatonaa	パートナー	partner
paato(-taimu) no N	パート(タイム)のN	part-time
pachin to iu oto	ぱちんという音	snap
paddo	パッド	pad
pafoomansu	パフォーマンス	performance
pai	パイ	pie
-pai	～杯	cup
painappuru	パイナップル	pineapple
painto	パイント	pint
paionia	パイオニア	pioneer
paipu	パイプ	pipe
paipu-orugan	パイプオルガン	organ
pairotto	パイロット	pilot
pajama	パジャマ	pajamas
pakkingu	パッキング	packing
pan	パン	bread
panchi	パンチ	punch[1]
panchi	パンチ	punch[3]
paneru	パネル	panel
panikku	パニック	panic
pantsu	パンツ	pants
pantsu	パンツ	trousers
pan-ya	パン屋	bakery
papa	パパ	papa
paragurafu	パラグラフ	paragraph
pareedo	パレード	parade
Pari	パリ	Paris
pari-pari-shita N	パリパリしたN	crisp
pari-pari-shite iru (N)	パリパリしている(N)	crisp
parupu	パルプ	pulp
pasu	パス	pass
pasupooto	パスポート	passport
pasu-suru	パスする	pass
pataan	パターン	pattern
patoron	パトロン	patron
patorooru	パトロール	patrol
patorooru-suru	パトロールする	patrol
pawaa	パワー	power
pazuru	パズル	puzzle
pea	ペア	pair
pea ni naru	ペアになる	pair
pea ni suru	ペアにする	pair
pea o kumu	ペアを組む	pair
pecha-kucha shaberu	ぺちゃくちゃしゃべる	chatter
pedaru	ペダル	pedal
peeji	ページ	page[1]
peesu	ペース	pace
peesuto	ペースト	paste
pen	ペン	pen
penchi	ペンチ	pliers
pengin	ペンギン	penguin
penii	ペニー	penny
penki	ペンキ	paint
penki o nuru	ペンキを塗る	paint
penki o nuru {koto/no}	ペンキを塗る{こと/の}	painting
penki-ya	ペンキ屋	painter
Penshirubania	ペンシルバニア	Pennsylvania
Perusha	ペルシア	Persia
petto	ペット	pet
piano	ピアノ	piano
piero	ピエロ	clown
piiku	ピーク	peak
piinatsu	ピーナツ	peanut
piinattsu	ピーナッツ	peanut
pika-pika no N	ぴかぴかのN	shiny
pika-pika (to) hikaru	ぴかぴか(と)光る	twinkle
pikatto hikaru	ぴかっと光る	flash
pikunikku	ピクニック	picnic

pikurusu	ピクルス	pickle
pin	ピン	pin
pinchi	ピンチ	pinch
pin de tomeru	ピンで留める	pin
pinku	ピンク	pink
pinku no N	ピンクのN	pink
pinto	ピント	focus
pin-to	ぴんと	tightly
pin-to hatta N	ぴんと張ったN	tense
pin-to hatta N	ぴんと張ったN	tight
pin-to hatte iru (N)	ぴんと張っている(N)	tense
pin to hatte iru (N)	ぴんと張っている(N)	tight
piramiddo	ピラミッド	pyramid
piriodo	ピリオド	period
piru	ピル	pill
pishari to shimeru	ぴしゃりと閉める	slam
pishari to utsu	ぴしゃりと打つ	slap
pishin to iu oto	ぴしんという音	snap
pisuton	ピストン	piston
pisutoru	ピストル	pistol
pitchaa	ピッチャー	pitcher[1]
pittari to	ぴったりと	tightly
pittari tsuita N	ぴったり付いたN	tight
pittari tsuite iru (N)	ぴったり付いている(N)	tight
Pittsubaagu	ピッツバーグ	Pittsburgh
pointo	ポイント	point
pojishon	ポジション	position
poketto	ポケット	pocket
pokin to iu oto	ぽきんという音	snap
pokin to oreru koto	ぽきんと折れること	snap
pokitto oru	ぽきっと折る	snap
ponchi	ポンチ	punch[3]
pondo	ポンド	pound[1]
ponpu	ポンプ	pump
poochi	ポーチ	porch
Poorando	ポーランド	Poland
pootaburu no N	ポータブルのN	portable
poozu	ポーズ	pause
...poozu o toru	…ポーズを取る	strike
poppukoon	ポップコーン	popcorn
porio	ポリオ	polio
Porutogaru	ポルトガル	Portugal
Porutogaru-go	ポルトガル語	Portuguese
Porutogaru-go no N	ポルトガル語のN	Portuguese
Porutogaru jin	ポルトガル人	Portuguese
Porutogaru-jin no N	ポルトガル人のN	Portuguese
Porutogaru no N	ポルトガルのN	Portuguese
posutaa	ポスター	poster
posuto	ポスト	mailbox
poteto	ポテト	potato
potto	ポット	pot
-ppanashi ni suru, V*masu*	〜っぱなしにする, V*masu*	leave
-pun	〜分	minute
puraibeetona	プライベートな	private
puraido	プライド	pride
puramu	プラム	plum
puran	プラン	plan
puranto	プラント	plant
purasu	プラス	plus
purasuchikku	プラスチック	plastic
purasu no N	プラスのN	positive
(puratto)hoomu	(プラット)ホーム	platform
puree	プレー	play
pureeto	プレート	plate
pureeyaa	プレーヤー	player
puresshaa	プレッシャー	pressure
puresu	プレス	press
puresu-suru	プレスする	press
purezento	プレゼント	gift
purezento	プレゼント	present[2]
purinto	プリント	hand-out
purizumu	プリズム	prism
puro	プロ	professional
puroguramu	プログラム	program
purojekuto	プロジェクト	project
puro no N	プロのN	professional
puropera	プロペラ	propeller
puropooshon	プロポーション	proportion
purosesu	プロセス	process
purotto	プロット	plot
putsun to kireru	ぷつんと切れる	snap
puttsuri to kireru koto	ぷっつりと切れること	snap
puuru	プール	pool
pu(u)tto	ぷ(う)っと	puff

R

raberu	ラベル	label
raibaru	ライバル	rival
raifuru	ライフル	rifle
raifuru-juu	ライフル銃	rifle

raihai	礼拝	worship
raihai-suru	礼拝する	worship
raihoo-{sha/kyaku}	来訪{者/客}	visitor
-ra ii {n dake(re)do/noni}, Sinf. past	～らいい{んだけ(れ)ど/のに}, Sinf. past	wish
raikyaku	来客	visitor
raimu	ライム	lime
rai-mugi	ライ麦	rye
raion	ライオン	lion
raisu	ライス	rice
raitaa	ライター	lighter
rajio	ラジオ	radio
raketto	ラケット	paddle
rakka	落下	fall
rakka-suru	落下する	drop
rakuda	らくだ	camel
rakudai-ten o tsukeru	落第点を付ける	fail
rakuna	楽な	easy
rakutan	落胆	disappointment
rakutan-saseru	落胆させる	discourage
ramu	ラム	lamb
ran	欄	column
ran	欄	section
-ra naa, Sinf. past	～らなあ, Sinf. past	wish
ranboona	乱暴な	rude
ranboona	乱暴な	violent
ranboona	乱暴な	wild
ranbooni nage-komu	乱暴に投げ込む	fling
ranbooni nage-tsukeru	乱暴に投げつける	fling
rangai	欄外	margin
rannaa	ランナー	runner
ranningu	ランニング	running
ranzatsuna	乱雑な	untidy
-rarenai, Vstem	～られない, Vstem	aren't
-rarenai, Vstem	～られない, Vstem	isn't
-rarenakatta, Vstem	～られなかった, Vstem	wasn't
-rarenakatta, Vstem	～られなかった, Vstem	weren't
-rareru, Vstem	～られる, Vstem	am
-rareru, Vstem	～られる, Vstem	are
-rareru, Vstem	～られる, Vstem	be
-rareru, Vstem	～られる, Vstem	is
-rareru, Vstem	～られる, Vstem	on
-rareta, Vstem	～られた, Vstem	was
-rareta, Vstem	～られた, Vstem	were
rarii	ラリー	rally
rasen	らせん	spiral
rasen-kei no mono	らせん形の物	spiral
rasen-(kei) no N	らせん(形)のN	spiral
rashii, N	らしい, N	like[2]
rashii, Sinf.	らしい, Sinf.	evidently
rashii, Sinf.	らしい, Sinf.	seem
rashikunai (N)	らしくない(N)	unlike
-ra, Sinf. past	～ら, Sinf. past	if
raundo	ラウンド	round
raunji	ラウンジ	lounge
rebaa	レバー	liver
Rebanon	レバノン	Lebanon
-reba, Vstem	～れば, Vstem	if
reberu	レベル	level
reedaa	レーダー	radar
reeru	レール	rail
reesu	レース	lace
reesu	レース	race
reeyon	レーヨン	rayon
regyuraa	レギュラー	regular
rei	例	example
rei	例	illustration
rei	零	zero
reigai	例外	exception
reigi	礼儀	courtesy
reigi-tadashii	礼儀正しい	civil
reigi-tadashii	礼儀正しい	polite
reihai	礼拝	worship
reihai-shiki	礼拝式	worship
reihai-suru	礼拝する	worship
reikon	霊魂	spirit
reikon no N	霊魂のN	spiritual
rein-kooto	レインコート	raincoat
reiseina	冷静な	cool
reitoo-suru	冷凍する	freeze
reizoo-ko	冷蔵庫	refrigerator
reji(sutaa)	レジ(スター)	register
rekishi	歴史	history
rekishi-joo no N	歴史上のN	historical
rekishi-tekina	歴史的な	historic
rekoodaa	レコーダー	recorder
rekoodo	レコード	disk
rekoodo	レコード	record
rekurieeshon	レクリエーション	recreation
remon	レモン	lemon
remoneedo	レモネード	lemonade
ren'ai	恋愛	love
-renai, Vneg.	～れない, Vneg.	aren't
-renai, Vneg.	～れない, Vneg.	isn't

-renakatta, Vneg.	～れなかった, Vneg.	wasn't
-renakatta, Vneg.	～れなかった, Vneg.	weren't
renga	れんが	brick
rengoo-shita N	連合したN	united
renji	レンジ	range
renji	レンジ	stove
renmei	連盟	league
renpoo no N	連邦のN	federal
renraku	連絡	communication
renraku	連絡	contact
renraku-moo	連絡網	web
renraku-sen	連絡船	ferry
renraku-suru	連絡する	communicate
renraku-suru	連絡する	contact
renraku-suru	連絡する	reach
renshoo-suru	連勝する	sweep
renshuu	練習	drill
renshuu	練習	exercise
renshuu	練習	practice
renshuu o saseru	練習をさせる	drill
renshuu-suru	練習する	practice
rensoo	連想	association
rensoo-suru	連想する	associate
renta-kaa	レンタカー	rent-a-car
rentogen	レントゲン	X-ray
renzoku	連続	sequence
renzoku	連続	series
renzoku	連続	succession
renzu	レンズ	lens
repootaa	レポーター	reporter
repooto	レポート	paper
repooto	レポート	report
repooto-yooshi	レポート用紙	pad
-reru, Vneg.	～れる, Vneg.	am
-reru, Vneg.	～れる, Vneg.	are
-reru, Vneg.	～れる, Vneg.	be
-reru, Vneg.	～れる, Vneg.	is
-reru, Vneg.	～れる, Vneg.	on
resepushon	レセプション	reception
reshiibaa	レシーバー	receiver
reshiito	レシート	receipt
ressha	列車	train
ressun	レッスン	lesson
resutoran	レストラン	restaurant
retasu	レタス	lettuce
-reta, Vneg.	～れた, Vneg.	was
-reta, Vneg.	～れた, Vneg.	were
retsu	列	line
retsu	列	row[1]
retsu	列	train
retsu ni naraberu	列に並べる	rank
riaritii	リアリティー	reality
riberaruna	リベラルな	liberal
ribon	リボン	ribbon
rieki	利益	benefit
rieki	利益	gain
rieki	利益	plus
rieki	利益	profit
rieki o eru	利益を得る	profit
rihatsu-ten	理髪店	barber
riidaa	リーダー	leader
riigu	リーグ	league
riji	理事	director
rikai	理解	understanding
rikai-ryoku	理解力	understanding
rikisetsu-suru	力説する	urge
rikkooho-suru	立候補する	run
rikoona	利口な	bright
rikoona	利口な	clever
rikoona	利口な	smart
rikooru	リコール	recall
rikooru-suru	リコールする	recall
riko-shugi	利己主義	selfishness
riko-shugi no N	利己主義のN	selfish
riko-tekina	利己的な	selfish
riku	陸	land
riku-age-suru	陸揚げする	land
riku-gun	陸軍	army
rikugun-gunjin	陸軍軍人	soldier
rikutsu ni awanai (N)	理屈に合わない(N)	unreasonable
ri-mawari	利回り	yield
ringo	りんご	apple
rinji no N	臨時のN	extra
rinji no N	臨時のN	temporary
Rinkaan	リンカーン	Lincoln
rinkaku	輪郭	outline
rinkaku o egaku	輪郭を描く	trace
rinkaku o kaku	輪郭をかく	outline
ripootaa	リポーター	reporter
ripooto	リポート	paper
ripooto	リポート	report
rippana	立派な	grand
rippana	立派な	royal
rippana	立派な	splendid

rippana	立派な	stately
rippoo-tai	立方体	cube
rirakkusu-suru	リラックスする	relax
riree	リレー	relay
riron	理論	theory
risei-teki {denai/janai} (N)	理性的{でない/じゃない}(N)	unreasonable
risei-tekina	理性的な	rational
rishi	利子	interest
risoo	理想	ideal
risoo no N	理想のN	ideal
risoo-tekina	理想的な	ideal
risshoo	立証	demonstration
risshoo-suru	立証する	demonstrate
risshoo-suru	立証する	prove
risu	りす	squirrel
risuto	リスト	list
risuto-appu-suru	リストアップする	list
ritsu	率	percentage
ritsu	率	rate
rittoru	リットル	liter
riyoo	利用	use
riyoo-dekiru (N)	利用できる(N)	available
riyoo-hoo	利用法	use
riyoo-sha	利用者	patron
riyoo-suru	利用する	use
riyuu	理由	cause
riyuu	理由	ground
riyuu	理由	reason
rizumikaruna	リズミカルな	rhythmical
rizumu	リズム	rhythm
robii	ロビー	lobby
robotto	ロボット	robot
robusutaa	ロブスター	lobster
roji	路地	alley
roketto	ロケット	rocket
roketto-hassha-dai	ロケット発射台	pad
rokkotsu	肋骨	rib
roku-ban-me (no N)	六番目(のN)	sixth
roku (+counter) (no N)	六(+counter)(のN)	six
rokuga	録画	recording
rokuga-suru	録画する	record
rokuga-suru	録画する	tape
roku-gatsu	六月	June
roku-juu-ban-me (no N)	六十番目(のN)	sixtieth
roku-juu (+counter) (no N)	六十(+counter)(のN)	sixty
rokuon	録音	recording
rokuon-suru	録音する	record
rokuon-suru	録音する	tape
rokuon-teepu	録音テープ	tape
romanchikkuna	ロマンチックな	romantic
romen-densha	路面電車	streetcar
ronbun	論文	dissertation
ronbun	論文	paper
ronbun	論文	study
ronbun	論文	thesis
Rondon	ロンドン	London
rongi	論議	discussion
ronji-kata	論じ方	treatment
ronjiru	論じる	discuss
ronjutsu	論述	treatment
ronpoo	論法	reasoning
ronpyoo	論評	comment
roo	ろう	wax
roobu	ローブ	robe
Roodo-airando	ロードアイランド	Rhode Island
roodoo	労働	labor
roodoo	労働	work
(roodoo-)kumiai	(労働)組合	union
roodoo-sha	労働者	laborer
roodoo-sha	労働者	worker
roohi	浪費	waste
roohi-suru	浪費する	waste
rooka	廊下	hall
Rooma	ローマ	Rome
roon	ローン	loan
roopu	ロープ	rope
roosoku	ろうそく	candle
roosuto	ロースト	roast
roosuto-biifu	ローストビーフ	roast
roosuto-niku	ロースト肉	roast
Rosanzerusu	ロサンゼルス	Los Angeles
Roshia	ロシア	Russia
Roshia-go	ロシア語	Russian
Roshia-jin	ロシア人	Russian
Roshia no N	ロシアのN	Russian
rui	塁	base
ruiji	類似	similarity
ruiji-ten	類似点	similarity
runes(s)ansu	ルネ(ッ)サンス	renaissance
rusu	留守	absence
rusu ni suru	留守にする	away
ruumu-meito	ルームメイト	roommate
ruuru	ルール	rule

ryaku-go	略語	abbreviation
ryokan	旅館	inn
ryoken	旅券	passport
ryokoo	旅行	journey
ryokoo	旅行	tour
ryokoo	旅行	travel
ryokoo	旅行	trip
ryokoo no N	旅行のN	traveling
ryokoo o suru	旅行をする	tour
ryokoo-sha	旅行者	tourist
ryokoo-sha	旅行者	traveler
ryokoo-suru	旅行する	travel
ryokoo-yoo no N	旅行用のN	traveling
ryoo	量	amount
ryoo	寮	dormitory
ryoo	量	quantity
ryoo	量	volume
ryoodo	領土	territory
ryoogae-suru	両替する	change
ryoohoo	療法	cure
ryoohoo no N	両方のN	both
ryoohoo no N	両方のN	either
ryoohoo-tomo	両方共	both
ryooiki	領域	range
ryooji-kan	領事館	consulate
ryooken	猟犬	hunter
ryookin	料金	charge
ryookin	料金	fare
ryookin	料金	fee
ryookin	料金	rate
ryookin	料金	toll
ryoo o suru	漁をする	fish
ryoori	料理	cooking
ryoori	料理	cuisine
ryoori	料理	dish
ryoori-hoo	料理法	recipe
ryoori-nin	料理人	cook
ryoori-suru	料理する	cook
ryoori-ya	料理屋	restaurant
ryooshi	漁師	fisherman
ryooshi	猟師	hunter
ryooshin	両親	parent
ryooshin-tekina	良心的な	religious
ryooshuu-sho	領収書	receipt
-ryuu	～流	school[1]
ryuuiki	流域	valley
ryuukoo	流行	fashion
ryuukoo	流行	style
ryuukoo no N	流行のN	stylish
ryuukoo okure no N	流行遅れのN	old-fashioned
ryuushi	粒子	particle
ryuutsuu	流通	distribution

S

saa	さあ	well[2]
saabisu	サービス	service
saafin o suru	サーフィンをする	surf
saakuru	サークル	circle
sabaibaru	サバイバル	survival
sabaku	砂漠	desert
sabaku	さばく	try
sabaku	砂漠	wilderness
sabi	さび	rust
sabiru	さびる	rust
sabishii	寂しい	lonely
sabishii	寂しい	miss
sabita N	さびたN	rusty
sabite iru (N)	さびている(N)	rusty
sabi-tsuku	さびつく	rusty
saboru	サボる	cut
sae	さえ	even
saegiru	さえぎる	screen
saezuru	さえずる	sing
sagaru	下がる	drop
sagaru	下がる	fall
sagaru	下がる	lower
sagaru	下がる	sink
sagashi-motomeru	さがし求める	seek
sagasu	さがす	search
sagasu	さがす	seek
sagatte iru	下がっている	down
sageru	下げる	cut
sageru	下げる	drop
sageru	下げる	lower
sageru	下げる	reduce
sagyoo	作業	operation
sagyoo	作業	task
-sai	～歳	year
saiai no N	最愛のN	beloved
saibai-suru	栽培する	cultivate
saiban	裁判	trial
saiban-kan	裁判官	judge
saiban ni kakeru	裁判にかける	try
saiban-sho	裁判所	court
saiboo	細胞	cell

sai-choosa	再調査	review
sai-choosa-suru	再調査する	review
saichuu	最中	middle
saichuu ni	最中に	amid
saidai-gen no N	最大限のN	utmost
saidai no N	最大のN	biggest
saidan-suru	裁断する	tailor
saifu	財布	wallet
saigai	災害	disaster
saigo	最後	last
saigo ni	最後に	finally
saigo ni wa	最後には	eventually
saigo no N	最後のN	final
saigo no N	最後のN	last
saijin	才人	talent
sai-jookyuu-sei	最上級生	senior
saijoo no mono	最上のもの	best
saijoo no N	最上のN	best
saijoo no N	最上のN	supreme
saiken	債券	bond
saiken-suru	再建する	restore
saikin	最近	lately
saikin	最近	recently
saikin no N	最近のN	recent
saikoo-	最高～	maximum
sai-koochoo	最高潮	climax
saikoo-kyuu no N	最高級のN	prime
saikoo no mono	最高のもの	best
saikoo no N	最高のN	best
saikoo no N	最高のN	super
saikoo no N	最高のN	supreme
saikuru	サイクル	cycle
sainan	災難	disaster
sainan	災難	tragedy
-sai no N	～歳のN	old
sainoo	才能	ability
sainoo	才能	capacity
sainoo	才能	facility
sainoo	才能	gift
sainoo	才能	power
sainoo	才能	talent
sain o suru	サインをする	sign
sairen	サイレン	siren
sairyoo no N	最良のN	best
saisei	再生	reproduction
saisei-suru	再生する	reproduce
saishin no N	細心のN	close[2]
saisho	最初	first
saishoku-shugi-sha	菜食主義者	vegetarian
saisho ni	最初に	first
saisho no N	最初のN	first
saisho no N	最初のN	initial
saisho no N	最初のN	original
saishoo-gen no N	最小限のN	minimum
saishuu-tekina	最終的な	final
saishuu-tekina	最終的な	ultimate
saitei no N	最低のN	minimum
saiwai(ni mo)	幸い(にも)	fortunate
saiyoo-suru	採用する	adopt
saizen	最善	best
saizu	サイズ	size
saji	さじ	spoon
saka	坂	slope
saka-ba	酒場	bar
sakaeru	栄える	flourish
sakai	境	boundary
sakai o sessuru	境を接する	bounded
sakana	さかな	fish
sakanna	盛んな	flourishing
sakari	盛り	bloom
sakari-ba	盛り場	downtown
sakari-ba {e/ni}	盛り場{へ/に}	downtown
sakasama ni	逆さまに	upside-down
sake	酒	drink
sake	酒	sake[2]
sake	さけ	salmon
sakebi-goe	叫び声	call
sakebu	叫ぶ	cry
sakebu	叫ぶ	shout
sakebu	叫ぶ	yell
sake-rarenai	避けられない	inevitable
sakeru	避ける	avoid
saki	先	ahead
saki	先	end
saki	先	point
saki	先	tip[1]
saki-data-reru	先立たれる	survive
sakka	作家	author
sakka	作家	writer
sakkaa	サッカー	football
sakkaku	錯覚	illusion
sakkyoku	作曲	composition
sakkyoku-suru	作曲する	compose
saku	咲く	bloom
saku	柵	fence
saku	裂く	split

sakubun	作文	composition
sakufuu	作風	style
sakugen	削減	cut
sakuhin	作品	piece
sakuhin	作品	work
sakuhin	作品	writing
sakuin	索引	index
sakujitsu	昨日	yesterday
saku koto	裂くこと	split
sakumotsu	作物	crop
sakuranbo	さくらんぼ	cherry
sakura (no hana)	桜(の花)	cherry blossom
sakuryaku	策略	plot
sakuryaku	策略	trick
sakuryaku ga umai (N)	策略がうまい(N)	tricky
sakusha	作者	author
sakusha	作者	writer
sakyuu	砂丘	sand
-sama	～様	Mr.
samasu	冷ます	cool
samatageru	妨げる	stop
samatageru, {Vinf. nonpast no/N} o	妨げる, {Vinf. nonpastの/N}を	prevent
sama-zamana	様々な	different
sama-zamana	様々な	vary
same	さめ	shark
sameru	冷める	cool
samo-nai-to	さもないと	otherwise
samu-ke	寒気	chill
samu-sa	寒さ	cold
samui	寒い	cold
san	酸	acid
-san	～さん	Miss
-san	～さん	Mr.
-san	～さん	Mrs.
-san	～さん	Ms.
san-bashi	桟橋	pier
sanbun	散文	prose
san-bun no ichi	三分の一	third
sanbutsu	産物	product
sanchoo	山頂	peak
san+counter me no N	三+counter目のN	third
san (+counter) (no N)	三(+counter)(のN)	three
sandaru	サンダル	sandal
sandoitchi	サンドイッチ	sandwich
Sanfuranshisuko	サンフランシスコ	San Francisco
san-gatsu	三月	March
sangyoo	産業	industry
(sangyoo-)gijutsu	(産業)技術	technology
sangyoo no N	産業のN	industrial
sanji	惨事	tragedy
san-juu (+counter) (no N)	三十(+counter)(のN)	thirty
sanka	参加	participation
sankakkei	三角形	triangle
sankakkei no N	三角形のN	triangular
sankaku-joogi	三角定規	triangle
sankan-nin	参観人	visitor
sanka-suru	参加する	participate
san-koku-kan no N	三国間のN	triangular
sankoo	参考	reference
sankoo-bunken	参考文献	reference
sanmi ga aru (N)	酸味がある(N)	acid
sannen	三年	junior
sannen-sei	三年生	junior
sanpai-sha	参拝者	visitor
sanpo	散歩	walk
sanpo-saseru	散歩させる	walk
sanpo-suru	散歩する	walk
sansei	賛成	approval
sansei	賛成	favorable
sansei	賛成	sympathy
sansei da	賛成だ	for
sansei-suru	賛成する	agree
sansei-suru	賛成する	approve
sansei-suru	賛成する	support
san-sha-kan no N	三者間のN	triangular
sanshoo-suru	参照する	refer
sanshutsu	産出	yield
sanshutsu-suru	算出する	reckon
sanshutsu-suru	産出する	yield
sanso	酸素	oxygen
san-suru	産する	yield
sansuu	算数	arithmetic
sansuu	算数	mathematics
sanzai-suru	散在する	scatter
sara	皿	dish
sara	皿	plate
sarada	サラダ	salad
sarani	さらに	even
sararii	サラリー	salary
sararii-man	サラリーマン	company employee
sara-sara to oto o tateru	さらさらと音を立てる	rustle
sarasu	さらす	expose
sarenai	されない	aren't (past participle)

sarenai	されない	isn't (past participle)
sarenakatta	されなかった	wasn't (past participle)
sarenakatta	されなかった	weren't (past participle)
sareru	される	am (past participle)
sareru	される	are (past participle)
sareru	される	be (past participle)
sareru	される	is (past participle)
sareru	される	(do) on
sareta	された	was (past participle)
sareta	された	were (past participle)
saru	猿	monkey
sarubeeji	サルベージ	salvage
sasae	支え	staff
sasae	支え	support
sasaeru	支える	support
sasaeru	支える	sustain
sasageru	捧げる	devote
sasayaki	ささやき	whisper
sasayaku	ささやく	whisper
saseru	させる	cause (to do)
saseru	させる	force (to do)
saseru	させる	get (to do)
saseru	させる	keep (doing)
saseru	させる	let (do)
saseru	させる	make (do)
saseru	させる	permit (to do)
-saseru, Vcond.	～させる, Vcond.	permit
-saseru, Vstem	～させる, Vstem	cause
-saseru, Vstem	～させる, Vstem	force
-saseru, Vstem	～させる, Vstem	get
-saseru, Vstem	～させる, Vstem	keep
-saseru, Vstem	～させる, Vstem	let
-saseru, Vstem	～させる, Vstem	make
sashi-ageru	差し上げる	give
sashie	挿絵	illustration
sashie o kaku	挿絵をかく	illustrate
sashi-hiku	差し引く	subtract
sashi-komu	差し込む	insert
sashi-komu	差し込む	stick
sashimi	刺身	sashimi
sashi-osaeru	差し押さえる	seize
sashi-sematta N	差し迫ったN	urgent
sashite iu, ⟨-no⟩ koto o	指して言う, ⟨～の⟩ことを	refer
sashizu	指図	direction
sashizu	指図	order
sashizu-suru	指図する	direct
sashizu-suru	指図する	order
sasou	誘う	invite
sasshin	刷新	renovation
sasshu	サッシュ	sash[1]
sasu	差す	indicate
sasu	刺す	stab
sasu	刺す	stick
sasu	刺す	sting
sasu koto	刺すこと	sting
sasu, ⟨-no⟩ koto o	指す, ⟨～の⟩ことを	refer
sasupensu	サスペンス	suspense
sasu yoona ita-mi	刺すような痛み	sting
satoo	砂糖	sugar
satsu	札	bill
-satsu	～冊	volume
satsuei	撮影	shot
satsuei-jo	撮影所	studio
satsugai-suru	殺害する	murder
satsu-ire	札入れ	wallet
satsujin	殺人	murder
satte	去って	away
satto me o toosu	さっと目を通す	glance
sattoo-suru	殺到する	flood
satto V	さっとV	shoot
Sausu-dakota	サウスダコタ	South Dakota
Sausu-karoraina	サウスカロライナ	South Carolina
saware-ru (N)	触れる(N)	tangible
sawaru	触る	handle
sawaru	触る	touch
sawa-sawa to oto o tateru	さわさわと音をたてる	whisper
sawatte miru	触ってみる	feel
sawayakana	さわやかな	crisp
saya-saya to oto o tateru	さやさやと音を立てる	rustle
sayuu-suru	左右する	govern
se	背	height
se-bone	背骨	spine
se-bone no N	背骨のN	spinal
sedai	世代	generation
seeraa	セーラー	sailor
seerusu-man	セールスマン	salesperson
seetaa	セーター	sweater
segamu	せがむ	beg
segamu, Vinf. nonpast yooni	せがむ, Vinf. nonpastように	press
segare	せがれ	son

sei	せい	fault
sei	背	height
sei-	聖～	St.
seibetsu	性別	sex
seibi-koo	整備工	serviceperson
seibun	成分	element
seibu no N	西部のN	western
seibutsu-gaku	生物学	biology
seichoo	成長	growth
seichoo-suru	成長する	grow
seido	精度	precision
seido	制度	system
seidoo	聖堂	shrine
seifu	政府	government
seifuku	制服	uniform
se(i) ga…da	背が…だ	tall
seigaku-kyoku	声楽曲	vocal
seigaku no N	声楽のN	vocal
seigan	請願	petition
seigan-sho	請願書	petition
seigan-suru	請願する	petition
(se(i) ga) takai	(背が)高い	tall
seigen	制限	limit
seigen-suru	制限する	limit
seigen-suru	制限する	restrict
seihin	製品	product
seihoo-kei	正方形	square
seihoo-kei no N	正方形のN	square
sei-ibutsu-ire	聖遺物入れ	shrine
seijaku(-sa)	静寂(さ)	silence
seiji	政治	government
seiji	政治	politics
seiji-gaku	政治学	politics
seiji-ka	政治家	politician
seijin	成人	adult
seijin	聖人	saint
seiji no N	政治のN	political
seiji-tekina	政治的な	political
seiji-ya	政治屋	politician
seijoona	正常な	normal
seikaku	性格	character
seikaku	性格	personality
seikakuna	正確な	accurate
seikakuna	正確な	exact
seikakuna	正確な	precise
seikakuna	正確な	straight
seikakuna	正確な	strict
seikakuni	正確に	accurately

seikakuni	正確に	correctly
seikakuni	正確に	exactly
seikaku-sa	正確さ	accuracy
seikaku-sa	正確さ	precision
seikatsu	生活	life
seikatsu-suru	生活する	live
seikei	生計	bread
seikei	生計	living
seiken	政権	government
seiki	世紀	century
seiki	生気	spirit
seikoo	性交	sex
seikoo	成功	success
seikoo shi-soo mo nai (N)	成功しそうもない(N)	unlikely
seikoo-shi-sooni (mo) nai (N)	成功しそうに(も)ない(N)	unlikely
seikoo-shite iru (N)	成功している(N)	successful
seikoo-suru	成功する	succeed
seikotsu-ire	聖骨入れ	shrine
(sei-)kyooju	(正)教授	professor
seikyuu-sho	請求書	bill
seikyuu-sho	請求書	check
seikyuu-suru	請求する	charge
seimei	生命	life
seimei	声明	protest
seimei	声明	statement
seimei ni kakawaru (N)	生命にかかわる(N)	vital
seimei-sho	声明書	statement
seimitsuna	精密な	precise
seimitsu-sa	精密さ	precision
seinen	青年	young man
seinen	青年	youth
seinen-jidai	青年時代	youth
sei no N	正のN	positive
-sei no N	～製のN	made
sei o dasu	精を出す	attend
seion	声音	vocal
seirai no N	生来のN	native
seirei	精霊	spirit
seirei no N	聖霊のN	spiritual
seireki	西暦	A.D.
seiri	整理	arrangement
seiri (no kikan)	生理(の期間)	period
seiri-suru	整理する	organize
seiryoku	精力	energy
seiryoku	精力	steam

seiryoku	精力	vigor
seiryoku ga aru (N)	勢力がある(N)	powerful
seiryoku o furuu	勢力をふるう	reign
seiryoku-tekina	精力的な	energetic
seiryoku-tekina	精力的な	vigorous
seiryoo-inryoo-sui	清涼飲料水	cola
seisaku	政策	policy
seisaku	政策	tack
seisan	生産	production
seisan-daka	生産高	output
seisan-suru	生産する	produce
seisan-tekina	生産的な	productive
seisei-shita N	精製したN	refined
seiseki	成績	grade
seiseki	成績	record
seishi	精子	sperm
seishikina	正式な	formal
seishiki no N	正式のN	formal
seishin	精神	soul
seishin	精神	spirit
seishin no N	精神のN	spiritual
seishin-tekina	精神的な	mental
seishin-tekina	精神的な	spiritual
seishi-suru	制止する	restrain
seishitsu	性質	nature
seishitsu	性質	quality
seisho-hoo	正書法	spelling
seishoku	生殖	reproduction
seisho ni kakete chikau	聖書に掛けて誓う	swear
seishun	青春	youth
seishun-jidai	青春時代	youth
sei-tekina	静的な	static
seito	生徒	pupil
seito	生徒	student
seiton	整とん	arrangement
seitoo	政党	party
seitoona	正当な	fair
seiyoku	性欲	sex
seiyoo	西洋	Occident
seiyoo	静養	rest[1]
seiyoo	西洋	west
(seiyoo-)nashi	(西洋)梨	pear
seiyoo no N	西洋のN	western
seiyoo-sumomo	西洋すもも	plum
seizen to shita N	整然としたN	orderly
seizen to shita N	整然としたN	tidy
seizen to shite iru (N)	整然としている(N)	orderly
seizen to shite iru (N)	整然としている(N)	tidy

seizon	生存	survival
seizon-sha	生存者	survival
seizoo-suru	製造する	manufacture
seizoo-suru	製造する	produce
seizui	精髄	soul
sekai	世界	world
sekai-kan	世界観	philosophy
sekando	セカンド	second[1]
seken	世間	social
seken	世間	world
seki	席	place
seki	席	seat
sekinin da	責任だ	responsible
sekinin ga aru (N)	責任がある(N)	responsible
sekinin ga omoi	責任が重い	responsible
sekinin-sha	責任者	charge
sekitan	石炭	coal
sekiyu	石油	oil
sekiyu	石油	petroleum
sekizai	石材	stone
sekkachina	せっかちな	impatient
sekkai	切開	section
sekkei	設計	design
sekkei-suru	設計する	design
sekkei-zu	設計図	plan
sekken	石けん	soap
sekkin	接近	access
sekkin	接近	approach
sekkin-suru	接近する	approach
sekkoo(-hei)	斥候(兵)	scout
sekkusu	セックス	sex
sekkyoku-tekina	積極的な	active
sekkyoku-tekina	積極的な	positive
seko-han no N	セコハンのN	secondhand
semai	狭い	narrow
semaru	迫る	push
seme-komu	攻め込む	raid
semento	セメント	cement
semeru	せめる	accuse
semeru	責める	charge
seminaa	セミナー	seminar
sen	線	line
sen	栓	plug
senaka	背中	back
senchi	センチ	centimeter
senchi-{meetoru/meetaa}	センチ{メートル/メーター}	centimeter
senchoo	船長	captain

sen (+counter) (no N)	千(+counter)(のN)	thousand
sengen	宣言	declaration
sengen-suru	宣言する	declare
sengo no N	戦後のN	postwar
sen'i	繊維	fiber
sen'in	船員	sailor
sen'in	船員	seaman
senkoo	専攻	major
senkoo-suru	専攻する	major
senkoo-suru	専攻する	specialize
senku-sha	先駆者	pioneer
senkyaku	船客	passenger
senkyo	選挙	election
senkyoo-shi	宣教師	missionary
senmen-ki	洗面器	basin
senmen-ki	洗面器	washbowl
senmon	専門	field
senmon	専門	major
senmon	専門	specialty
senmon-ka	専門家	expert
senmon-ka	専門家	professional
senmon-ka	専門家	specialist
senmon-tekina	専門的な	professional
senmon-tekina	専門的な	technical
sennen-suru	専念する	concentrate
sennyuu-kan	先入観	prejudice
sen o kaku	線をかく	stroke[1]
senpai	先輩	senior
senpai	先輩	superior
senpai no N	先輩のN	senior
senpuu-ki	扇風機	fan[1]
senro	線路	track
senryoo	占領	occupation
senryoo-suru	占領する	occupy
sensaina	繊細な	delicate
sensaina	繊細な	subtle
senseeshon	センセーション	sensation
sensei	先生	instructor
sensei	先生	Mr.
sensei	先生	teacher
sensha	戦車	tank[2]
senshitsu	船室	cabin
senshoku-tai	染色体	chromosome
senshu	選手	player
sensoo	戦争	war
sensoo	戦争	warfare
sensu	扇子	fan[1]
sensui-kan	潜水艦	submarine

sentaa	センター	center
sentaku	選択	choice
sentaku	洗濯	laundry
sentaku	選択	selection
sentaku-mono	洗濯物	laundry
sentaku ni yakamashii	選択にやかましい	selective
sentaku no N	選択のN	selective
sentaku-suru	選択する	choose
sentaku-ya	洗濯屋	cleaner
sentaku-ya	洗濯屋	laundry
sentan	先端	peak
sento	セント	cent
sentoo-ki	戦闘機	fighter
senzai-tekina	潜在的な	potential
senzen no N	戦前のN	prewar
senzo	先祖	stock
seron	世論	opinion
serori	セロリ	celery
-seru, Vneg.	～せる, Vneg.	cause
-seru, Vneg.	～せる, Vneg.	force
-seru, Vneg.	～せる, Vneg.	get
-seru, Vneg.	～せる, Vneg.	keep
-seru, Vneg.	～せる, Vneg.	let
-seru, Vneg.	～せる, Vneg.	make
-seru, Vneg.	～せる, Vneg.	permit
sesshoku	接触	contact
sesshoku	接触	touch
sesshoku-suru	接触する	touch
sessuru	接する	touch
setai	世帯	household
setchaku-zai	接着剤	glue
seto-mono	瀬戸物	china
setsu	節	clause
setsu	節	section
setsubi	設備	equipment
setsubi	設備	facility
setsubi-ji	接尾辞	suffix
setsuboo-shite iru	切望している	eager
setsuboo-shite iru (N)	切望している(N)	anxious
setsumei	説明	account
setsumei	説明	description
setsumei	説明	direction
setsumei	説明	explanation
setsumei	説明	version
setsumei-suru	説明する	account
setsumei-suru	説明する	brief
setsumei-suru	説明する	describe
setsumei suru	説明する	explain

setsumei-suru, rei o agete　説明する，例を挙げて		
		illustrate
setsuritsu	設立	establishment
setsuritsu-suru	設立する	establish
setsuyaku-dekiru, {(-no) o-kage de/Sinf. nonpast to}…		
節約出来る，{(〜の)おかげで/Sinf. nonpastと}…		
		save
setsuzoku	接続	connection
settoku-shite causative of V　説得してcausative of V		
		persuade
settoku-suru	説得する	convince
settoku-suru	説得する	persuade
settoo-ji	接頭辞	prefix
sewa	世話	care
sewa	世話	charge
sewa o suru	世話をする	attend
-sha	〜車	car
shaberu	シャベル	shovel
shaberu	しゃべる	speak
shaberu	しゃべる	talk
shaberu de horu	シャベルで掘る	shovel
shaberu de sukuu	シャベルですくう	shovel
shachoo	社長	president
shafuto	シャフト	shaft[1]
shafuto	シャフト	shaft[2]
shageki	射撃	shoot
shageki	射撃	shot
shageki-kai	射撃会	shoot
shahei-butsu	遮へい物	shield
shai	謝意	thanks
shain	社員	staff
shajiku	車軸	axle
shakai	社会	social
shakai-gaku	社会学	sociology
shakai no N	社会のN	social
Shaka-muni	しゃか牟尼	Buddha
shake	しゃけ	salmon
shakkin	借金	debt
shako	車庫	garage
shakoo-kai	社交界	social
shakoo-kai no N	社交界のN	social
shakoo-tekina	社交的な	social
shakuhoo	釈放	release
shakuhoo-suru	釈放する	release
shamen	斜面	slant
shamen no heichi	斜面の平地	terrace
shamen-suru	赦免する	pardon
shaniku-sai	謝肉祭	carnival
sharin	車輪	wheel
shasatsu-suru	射殺する	shoot
shasei	写生	sketch
shashin	写真	photo
shashin	写真	picture
shashin-ki	写真機	camera
(shashin o) hiki-nobasu　(写真を)引き伸ばす		
		enlarge
shashin o toru	写真を撮る	photo
(shashin o) toru	(写真を)撮る	take
shashin-satsuei-shitsu	写真撮影室	studio
shatei-kyori	射程距離	range
shatei(-kyori)	射程(距離)	shot
shatsu	シャツ	shirt
shawaa	シャワー	shower
Sheekusupia	シェークスピア	Shakespeare
sherii	シェリー	sherry
shi	市	city
shi	死	death
shi	詩	poem
shi	詩	poetry
shi	詩	song
shi	詩	verse
-shi	〜氏	Mr.
-shi	〜姉	sister
shi-ageru	仕上げる	complete
shiai	試合	competition
shiai	試合	game
shiai	試合	match[1]
Shiatoru	シアトル	Seattle
shiawase	しあわせ	happiness
shiawasena	しあわせな	happy
shiba-fu	芝生	grass
shiba-fu	芝生	lawn
shiba-fu	芝生	sod
shibai	芝居	play
shibari-tsukeru	縛り付ける	fasten
shibaru	縛る	fasten
shibaru	縛る	tie
shibaru mono	縛るもの	tie
shiba-shiba	しばしば	often
shiba-tsuchi	芝土	sod
shibomu	しぼむ	wither
shiboo	脂肪	fat
shiboo ga ooi	脂肪が多い	fat
shiboru	しぼる	wring
shibui	渋い	astringent
shibuki	しぶき	spray

shibu-shibu(-nagara)	渋々(ながら)	reluctantly
shichi-ban-me (no N)	七番目(のN)	seventh
shichi (+counter) (no N)	七(+counter)(のN)	seven
shichi-gatsu	七月	July
shichi-juu (+counter) (no N)	七十(+counter)(のN)	seventy
shichimen-choo	七面鳥	turkey
shichoo	市長	mayor
shichoo-sha	視聴者	audience
shichuu	シチュー	stew
shi (+counter) (no N)	四(+counter)(のN)	four
-shidai da	~次第だ	depend
-shidai da	~次第だ	dependent
-shidai da	~次第だ	subject
shiden	市電	streetcar
shidoo	指導	guidance
shidoo	指導	supervision
shidoo-ken	指導権	leadership
shidoo-ryoku	指導力	leadership
shidoo-sha	指導者	director
shidoo-sha	指導者	leader
shidoo-suru	指導する	coach
shidoo-suru	指導する	direct
shidoo-suru	指導する	steer
shidoo-suru	指導する	supervise
shieki	使役	causative
shifuto-rebaa	シフトレバー	stick
shigaa	シガー	cigar
shigami-tsuku	しがみつく	cling
shigan-hei	志願兵	volunteer
shigan-sha	志願者	applicant
shigaretto	シガレット	cigarette
shi-gatsu	四月	April
shigeki	刺激	stimulus
shigeki-suru	刺激する	stimulate
shigemi	茂み	bush
shigemi	茂み	thicket
shigen	資源	resource
shigoto	仕事	business
shigoto	仕事	chore
shigoto	仕事	employment
shigoto	仕事	job
shigoto	仕事	occupation
shigoto	仕事	task
shigoto	仕事	trade
shigoto	仕事	undertaking
shigoto	仕事	work
shigoto-ba	仕事場	shop
shigoto-buri	仕事ぶり	performance
shigoto ga nai (N)	仕事がない(N)	unemployed
shigoto no N	仕事のN	working
shigoto o suru	仕事をする	work
shihai-ken	支配権	control
shihai-nin	支配人	manager
shihai-sha	支配者	ruler
shihai-suru	支配する	control
shihai-suru	支配する	govern
shihai-suru	支配する	reign
shihai-suru	支配する	rule
shiharai	支払い	payment
shiharau, (daikin o)	支払う, (代金を)	pay
shihon(-kin)	資本(金)	capital
shiiku-suru	飼育する	breed
shiin	シーン	scene
shi-ireru	仕入れる	stock
shiiru	シール	seal[2]
shiitsu	シーツ	sheet
Shiizaa	シーザー	Caesar
shiizun	シーズン	season
shiji	指示	direction
shiji	支持	support
shijin	詩人	poet
shiji-shite	支持して	behind
shiji-suru	指示する	direct
shiji-suru	支持する	second[1]
shiji-suru	支持する	support
shiji-suru, Vinf. nonpast yooni (to)	指示する, Vinf. nonpastように(と)	instruct
shijoo	市場	market
shi-juu (+counter) (no N)	四十(+counter)(のN)	forty
shika	鹿	deer
Shikago	シカゴ	Chicago
shika-i	歯科医	dentist
shikaku	資格	requirement
shikaku	視覚	sight
shikaku	四角	square
shikaku	視覚	vision
shikaku ga nai (N)	資格がない(N)	unqualified
shikakui	四角い	square
shikaku no N	四角のN	square
shikaku (no) N	視覚(の)N	visual
shikaku o ataeru	資格を与える	entitle
shikaku-tekina	視覚的な	visual
shika…neg.	しか…neg.	only

shikari-tsukeru	しかりつける	scold
shikaru	しかる	scold
shikashi	しかし	but
shikashi	しかし	however
shikata	仕方	way
shiken	試験	examination
shiken	試験	test
shiken-hoo	試験法	test
shiken-mondai	試験問題	test
shiken o suru	試験をする	test
shiken-suru	試験する	examine
shiken-tekina	試験的な	experimental
shiken-tekini	試験的に	tentatively
shiki	式	ceremony
shikichi	敷地	plot
shikichi	敷地	site
shikichoo	色調	tone
shiki-mono	敷物	rug
shikin	資金	fund
shikirini…*Vmasu* ta-gatte iru (N)	しきりに…*Vmasu*たがっている(N)	anxious
shikiru	仕切る	screen
shiki-sha	指揮者	director
shiki-suru	指揮する	conduct
shiki-utsushi o suru	敷き写しをする	trace
shikkari	しっかり	fast
shikkari	しっかり	firmly
shikkari shimeru	しっかりしめる	secure
shikkari-shita N	しっかりしたN	firm
shikkari-shita N	しっかりしたN	secure
shikkari-shita N	しっかりしたN	stable
shikkari-shita N	しっかりしたN	steady
shikkari-shita N	しっかりしたN	sturdy
shikkari-shite iru (N)	しっかりしている(N)	alert
shikkari-shite iru (N)	しっかりしている(N)	firm
shikkari-shite iru (N)	しっかりしている(N)	stable
shikkari-shite iru (N)	しっかりしている(N)	strong
shikkari-shite iru (N)	しっかりしている(N)	sturdy
shikkari(-to)	しっかり(と)	steadily
shikke	湿気	moisture
shikke ga ooi	湿気が多い	humid
shikki	湿気	moisture
shikoo	思考	thinking
shikoo	思考	thought
shikori	しこり	lump
shiku	敷く	lay
shiku	敷く	spread
shikujiru	しくじる	fail

shi-kumi	仕組み	mechanism
shikyuu	支給	provision
shikyuu-suru	支給する	provide
shima	島	island
shima	しま	streak
shima	しま	stripe
shimai	姉妹	sister
shimaru	しまる	close[1]
shimaru	しまる	shut
shimatta!	しまった!	oops
shimau, V*te*	しまう, V*te*	finish
shimau, V*te*	しまう, V*te*	have
shimei	使命	mission
shimei-suru	指名する	appoint
shime-kukuru	締めくくる	conclude
shimerasu	湿らす	wet
shimeru	しめる	close[1]
shimeru	しめる	fasten
shimeru	占める	occupy
shimeru	しめる	shut
shimeru	しめる	tie
shimeru	湿る	wet
(shimeru-beki) {basho/ichi/jikan(-tai)}	(占めるべき){場所/位置/時間(帯)}	slot
shimesu	示す	display
shimesu	示す	indicate
shimesu	示す	point
shimesu	示す	record
shimesu	示す	show
shime-tsukeru	締め付ける	squeeze
shimetta N	湿ったN	wet
shimette iru (N)	湿っている(N)	wet
shimi	染み	spot
shimi	染み	stain
shimi-komu	しみ込む	soak
shimin	市民	citizen
shimin no N	市民のN	civil
shimo	霜	frost
shina-mono	品物	article
shinboo	辛抱	patience
shinboo	心棒	shaft[1]
shinboo-suru	辛抱する	patient
shinboo-zuyoi	辛抱強い	patient
shinboru	シンボル	symbol
shinbun	新聞	newspaper
shinbun	新聞	paper
shinbun(-shi)	新聞(紙)	newspaper
shinchoo	身長	height

shinchoo ga...da	身長が…だ	tall
shinchoona	慎重な	deliberate
shinchooni	慎重に	deliberately
shinchuu	真ちゅう	brass
shindai	寝台	bed
shinda N	死んだN	dead
shindan-hoo	診断法	test
shinde iru (N)	死んでいる(N)	dead
shinden	神殿	temple
shindoo	振動	vibration
shindoo	震動	vibration
shindoo-saseru	しんどうさせる	vibrate
shindoo-suru	振動する	vibrate
shindoo-suru	震動する	vibrate
shin'enna	深遠な	profound
shinfonii	シンフォニー	symphony
shingoo	信号	sign
shingoo	信号	signal
shingurusu	シングルス	single
shinjin-bukai	信心深い	religious
shinji-rarenai	信じられない	unbelievable
shinji-rarenai yoona N	信じられないようなN	incredible
shinjiru	信じる	believe
shinjitsu	真実	truth
shinju	真珠	pearl
shinka	臣下	subject
shin-kaiin	新会員	recruit
shinka-suru	進化する	evolve
shinkei	神経	nerve
shinkei no N	神経のN	nervous
shinkoku	申告	declaration
shinkokuna	深刻な	grave
shinkokuna	深刻な	serious
shinkoku-suru	申告する	declare
shinkoo	信仰	belief
shinkoo	信仰	faith
shinkoo	進行	progress
shinkookei no N	進行形のN	progressive
shinkoo-suru	進行する	proceed
shinkoo-suru	進行する	progress
shinkuu	真空	vacuum
shinmai	新米	stranger
shinnen	信念	belief
shin no N	真のN	true
shinnyuu	侵入	invasion
shinnyuu-sha	侵入者	invader
shinnyuu-suru	侵入する	invade

shi no N	詩のN	poetic
shinpai	心配	anxiety
shinpai	心配	care
shinpai	心配	concern
shinpai	心配	fear
shinpai	心配	trouble
shinpai	心配	worry
shinpai de tamaranai	心配でたまらない	nervous
shinpai-goto	心配事	worry
shinpaina	心配な	fear
shinpaina	心配な	fearful
shinpaina	心配な	uneasy
shinpai no tane	心配の種	worry
shinpai-saseru	心配させる	concern
shinpai-shite	心配して	anxiously
shinpai-shite iru	心配している	fearful
shinpai-shite iru (N)	心配している(N)	anxious
shinpai-suru	心配する	worry
shinpei	新兵	recruit
shinpi	神秘	mystery
shinpin no yoo ni suru	新品のようにする	renew
shinpi-tekina	神秘的な	mysterious
shinpo	進歩	advance
shinpo	進歩	improvement
shinpo	進歩	progress
shinpo-suru	進歩する	advance
shinpo-suru	進歩する	progress
shinpo-tekina	進歩的な	progressive
shinpu	新婦	bride
shinrai	信頼	belief
shinrai	信頼	confidence
shinrai	信頼	faith
shinrai	信頼	trust
shinrai-dekiru (N)	信頼出来る(N)	dependable
shinrai-suru	信頼する	rely
shinrai-suru	信頼する	trust
shinratsuna	辛らつな	bitter
shinratsuna	辛らつな	spicy
shinri	心理	psychology
shinri	真理	truth
shinri-gaku	心理学	psychology
shinrin	森林	forest
shinrin-chitai	森林地帯	woodland
shinro	進路	course
shinro	進路	tack
shinro	進路	track
shinrui	親類	relative
shinryaku	侵略	invasion

shinryaku-sha	侵略者	invader
shinryaku-suru	侵略する	invade
shinsa-in	審査員	judge
shinsa-suru	審査する	judge
shinseina	神聖な	holy
shinseina	神聖な	sacred
shinseina	神聖な	solemn
shinseki	親せき	relative
shinseki no atsumari	親せきの集まり	reunion
shinsenna	新鮮な	fresh
shinsetsu	親切	kindness
shinsetsuna	親切な	friendly
shinsetsuna	親切な	kind
shinsetsuna	親切な	sweet
shinsetsuna	親切な	tender
shinshi	紳士	gentleman
shinshitsu	寝室	bedroom
shinshitsu	寝室	chamber
shintai	身体	body
shintaku	信託	trust
shintaku-suru	信託する	trust
Shintoo	神道	Shinto
shinu	死ぬ	die
shinwa	神話	myth
shin'yoo	信用	confidence
shin'yoo	信用	credit
shin'yoo	信用	faith
shin'yoo-suru	信用する	trust
shinzoku-kankei	親族関係	relationship
shinzoo	心臓	heart
shio	塩	salt
shio	しお	tide
shio-karai	塩からい	salty
shio-mizu no N	塩水のN	saltwater
shio ni nagasu	潮に流す	tide
shio no N	潮のN	tidal
shioreru	しおれる	fade
shippai	失敗	failure
shippai-suru	失敗する	fail
shippai-suru	失敗する	trip
shippo	しっぽ	tail
shirabe	調べ	check
shiraberu	調べる	check
shiraberu	調べる	consult
shiraberu	調べる	examine
shiraberu	調べる	inspect
shiraberu	調べる	investigate
shiraberu	調べる	search
shira-kaba	白かば	birch
shiranai hito	知らない人	stranger
shiranai N	知らないN	strange
shiranai (N)	知らない(N)	unknown
(shiranai uchi ni jikan ga) tatsu	(知らないうちに時間が)たつ	slip
shirase	知らせ	notice
shiraseru	知らせる	acquaint
shiraseru	知らせる	announce
shira-seru	知らせる	communicate
shira-seru	知らせる	inform
shiraseru	知らせる	transmit
shirei-bu	司令部	headquarters
shiren	試練	trial
shiri	尻	hip
shiri-ai	知り合い	acquaintance
shiriaru	シリアル	cereal
shiriizu	シリーズ	series
shiritsu no N	私立のN	private
shirizoku	退く	retreat
shiro	城	castle
shiroi	白い	white
shirooto	素人	amateur
shiroppu	シロップ	syrup
shiru	汁	juice
shiru	知る	learn
shiru, {(-o)/Sinf. ka doo ka}	知る, {(〜を)/Sinf.かどうか}	know
shirushi	印	mark
shirushi	印	sign
shirushi	印	symptom
shirushi	印	token
shirushi o tsukeru	印を付ける	mark
shiryo ga nai (N)	思慮がない(N)	thoughtless
shiryoku	視力	sight
shiryoku	視力	vision
shiryoo	資料	data
shiryoo	資料	material
shisai	司祭	priest
shisan	資産	wealth
shisatsu ni {iku/kuru}	視察に{行く/来る}	visit
shisei	姿勢	posture
shisetsu	施設	facility
shisetsu-dan	使節団	mission
shisho	司書	librarian
shishoku	試食	taste
shishoku-suru	試食する	taste
shishoosha-suu	死傷者数	toll

shishutsu	支出	expenditure
shison	子孫	descendant
shisoo	思想	thought
shi, (sore ni), S	し、(それに), S	furthermore
shissona	質素な	simple
shissoni	質素に	simply
shissoo-suru	疾走する	speed
shisutaa	シスター	sister
shisutemu	システム	system
shisuu	指数	index
shita	舌	tongue
shita-birame	舌平目	sole[3]
shita de	下で	under
shita e	下へ	down
shita-e	下絵	drawing
shita-gaki	下書き	draft
shitagatte	従って	consequently
shitagatte	従って	so
shitagatte	従って	therefore
shitagau	従う	follow
shitagau	従う	obey
shitagau	従う	submit
shita-gi	下着	underwear
shitai	死体	remain
shitaku	支度	arrangement
shitaku	支度	preparation
shitaku-suru	支度する	prepare
shita ni	下に	underneath
shita {ni/de/o}	下{に/で/を}	beneath
shita ({ni/de/o})	下({に/で/を})	under
shita {ni/e}	下{に/へ}	under
shita no hoo	下の方	bottom
shita no hoo ni	下の方に	below
shita no hoo {ni/de/o}	下の方{に/で/を}	beneath
shita (no) N	下(の)N	under
shitashii	親しい	close[2]
shitashii	親しい	dear
shitashii	親しい	familiar
shitchi	湿地	swamp
shi-tekina	詩的な	poetic
shi-tekina	私的な	private
shiten	支店	branch
shitoyakana	しとやかな	graceful
shitsu	質	quality
shitsuboo	失望	disappointment
shitsuboo-saseru	失望させる	disappoint
shitsuboo-saseru	失望させる	fail
shitsudo ga takai	湿度が高い	humid

shitsugyoo	失業	unemployment
shitsugyoo-shita N	失業したN	unemployed
shitsugyoo-shite iru (N)	失業している(N)	unemployed
shitsuke	しつけ	discipline
shitsuke	しつけ	training
shitsukoi	しつこい	persistent
shitsumon	質問	question
(shitsumon nado ni) kotaeru	(質問などに)答える	entertain
shitsumon-suru, {(-no) koto o/(-ni-tsuite)}	質問する, {(〜の)ことを/(〜について)}	question
shitsureina	失礼な	impolite
shitsureina	失礼な	rude
shitsuyoona	しつようなな	stubborn
shitte iru	知っている	realize
shitto-suru	しっとする	jealous
shiwa	しわ	wrinkle
shiwa ga dekiru	しわが出来る	wrinkle
shiwa(-kucha) ni suru	しわ(くちゃ)にする	wrinkle
shiwa ni naru	しわになる	wrinkle
shiwa o tsukuru	しわを作る	wrinkle
shiwaza	仕業	work
shiya	視野	view
shiyoo	使用	employment
shiyoo	使用	use
shiyoo-hoo	使用法	use
shiyoo no N	私用のN	private
shiyoo-suru	使用する	use
shiyuu no betsu	雌雄の別	sex
shizen	自然	nature
shizen-kagaku	自然科学	physical science
shizen ni	自然に	naturally
shizen no mama no N	自然のままのN	wild
shizen no N	自然のN	natural
shizen no N	自然のN	physical
shizukana	静かな	calm
shizukana	静かな	quiet
shizukana	静かな	silent
shizukana	静かな	soft
shizukana	静かな	still
shizukani	静かに	quietly
shizukani	静かに	softly
shizuke-sa	静けさ	silence
shizuku	しずく	drop
shizumeru	沈める	sink
shizumu	沈む	sink
shizumu koto	沈むこと	setting

-sho	～署	station
shodoo	書道	calligraphy
shoho no N	初歩のN	elementary
shohyoo	書評	review
shohyoo o kaku	書評を書く	review
shoji	所持	possession
shoki(-choo)	書記(長)	secretary
shoki no N	初期のN	early
shokkaku	触角	antenna
shokkaku	触覚	touch
shokki-dana	食器棚	cupboard
shokkinguna	ショッキングな	shocking
shokku	ショック	shock
shoku	食	diet[1]
shoku	職	employment
shoku	職	position
shoku	職	post[2]
shokubutsu	植物	plant
shokubutsu	植物	vegetation
shokubutsu-ningen	植物人間	vegetable
shokudoo	食堂	cafeteria
shokugyoo	職業	business
shokugyoo	職業	occupation
shokugyoo	職業	profession
shokugyoo	職業	trade
shokugyoo	職業	work
shokugyoo-joo no N	職業上のN	professional
shokuin	職員	personnel
shokuin	職員	staff
shokuin o ireru	職員を入れる	staff
shokuji	食事	board
shokuji	食事	diet[1]
shokuji	食事	dining
shokuji	食事	meal
shokuji o suru	食事をする	dine
shokuji-seigen	食事制限	diet[1]
shokuji-suru	食事する	eat
shokumu	職務	task
shokunin	職人	craftsman
shokuryoo	食糧	food
shokuryoo(-hin)	食料(品)	groceries
shokuryoo-hin-ten	食料品店	grocery
shokutaku	食卓	table
shokuyoku	食欲	appetite
shomei-suru	署名する	sign
shomei-suru, (bunsho ni)	署名する, (文書に)	subscribe
shomotsu	書物	volume

shoo	賞	award
shoo	章	chapter
shoo	省	ministry
shoo	賞	prize
shoo	ショー	show
shoobai	商売	business
shoobai	商売	trade
shooboo-shi	消防士	fireman
Shoochi-shimashita	承知しました	certainly
shoochoo	象徴	symbol
shoochoo-suru	象徴する	represent
shoodaku-suru	承諾する	consent
shoodoo	衝動	impulse
shoo-fuda	正札	tag
shoo-fuda o tsukeru	正札を付ける	tag
shooga	しょうが	ginger
shoogai	生涯	career
shoogai	障害	handicap
shoogai-butsu	障害物	barrier
shoogai ga aru (N)	障害がある(N)	handicapped
shoogaku-kin	奨学金	scholarship
shoogatsu	正月	New Year('s)
shoogeki	衝撃	impact
shoogeki	衝撃	shock
shoogeki-tekina	衝撃的な	shocking
shoogo	正午	noon
shoogoo	称号	title
shoogyoo	商業	business
shoogyoo	商業	commerce
shoogyoo-chiku	商業地区	downtown
shoogyoo-chiku {e/ni}	商業地区{へ/に}	downtown
shoogyoo no N	商業のN	commercial
shooheki	障壁	barrier
shoohin	商品	goods
shoohin	小品	sketch
shoohyoo	商標	brand
shoojikina	正直な	honest
shoojikina	正直な	straight
shoojikina	正直な	upright
shoojikini	正直に	honestly
shoojikini	正直に	straight
shoojiru	生じる	arise
shoojiru	生じる	result
shoojiru	生じる	stem
shoojo	少女	girl
shoojoo	症状	symptom
shooka	消化	digestion
shookai	紹介	introduction

shookai-suru	紹介する	introduce
shookai-suru	紹介する	present[2]
shookai-suru	紹介する	refer
shookan-suru	召喚する	summon
shooko	証拠	evidence
shooko	証拠	proof
shooko	証拠	trace
shookoo	将校	officer
shoo-kyuushi	小休止	pause
shoomei	証明	demonstration
shoomei-suru	証明する	demonstrate
shoomei-suru	証明する	prove
shoonen	少年	boy
shooni-mahi	小児まひ	polio
shoonin	承認	acknowledg(e)ment
shoonin	承認	approval
shoonin	商人	merchant
shoonin	商人	trader
shoonin	証人	witness
shoonin-suru	承認する	acknowledge
shoonin-suru	承認する	approve
shoonin to-shite shomei-suru	証人として署名する	witness
shoorai	将来	future
shoorai 〈-ni〉 naru kamoshirenai	将来〈〜に〉なるかもしれない	potential
shoorai-sei	将来性	promise
shoorei	奨励	patronage
shoori	勝利	triumph
shoori	勝利	victory
shoori	勝利	win
shoori o iwau	勝利を祝う	triumph
shoori o osameru	勝利を収める	triumph
shooru	ショール	shawl
shooryaku	省略	abbreviation
shooryaku	省略	skip
shooryaku-suru	省略する	omit
shoosai	詳細	detail
shoosan	賞賛	admiration
shoosan	賞賛	applause
shoosan	賞賛	praise
shoosan no mato	賞賛の的	admiration
shoosan-suru	賞賛する	admire
shoosan-suru	賞賛する	applaud
shoosetsu	小説	fiction
shoosetsu	小説	novel
shooshin-suru	昇進する	advance
shoo-shoo	少々	bit
shooshuu-suru	召集する	draft
shooshuu-suru	召集する	summon
shootai	招待	invitation
shootai-suru	招待する	invite
shooten	焦点	focus
shooten	商店	shop
shoototsu	衝突	crash
shoototsu-suru	衝突する	crash
shootsu	ショーツ	short
shooyo	賞与	bonus
shooyu	しょう油	soy (sauce)
shoozuru	生ずる	result
shoppai	しょっぱい	salty
shoppingu	ショッピング	shopping
shori-kakoo-suru	処理加工する	process
shorui	書類	document
shorui	書類	paper
shorui-kaban	書類かばん	briefcase
shosai	書斎	study
shotai	所帯	household
shotchuu	しょっちゅう	constantly
shoten	書店	bookstore
shotoku	所得	income
shotto	ショット	shot
shoyuu	所有	ownership
shoyuu	所有	possession
shoyuu-butsu	所有物	possession
shoyuu-butsu	所有物	property
shoyuu-ken	所有権	ownership
shoyuu-ken	所有権	title
shoyuu-sha	所有者	owner
shoyuu-suru	所有する	own
shoyuu-suru	所有する	possess
shozai-chi	所在地	seat
shozoku-suru	所属する	belong
shozon da, Vinf. nonpast	所存だ, Vinf. nonpast	shall
shu	種	species
shubi-yoku	首尾よく	well[2]
shuchoo	主張	claim
shuchoo-suru	主張する	assert
shuchoo-suru	主張する	claim
shuchoo-suru	主張する	insist
shuchoo-suru	主張する	persist
shuchoo-suru	主張する	plead
shudai	主題	subject
shudai	主題	theme
shudan	手段	means

shudan	手段	vehicle
shuei	守衛	guard
shufu	主婦	housewife
shugi	主義	cause
-shugi	～主義	-ism
shugo	主語	subject
shui	首位	top
shui no N	首位のN	top
shujin	主人	host
shujin	主人	husband
shujin	主人	master
shujinkoo	主人公	hero
shujutsu	手術	operation
shujutsu	手術	surgery
shujutsu-dai	手術台	table
shujutsu o suru	手術をする	operate
shujutsu-shitsu	手術室	surgery
shujutsu-suru	手術する	operate
shukketsu-suru	出血する	bleed
shukkoo	出港	departure
shukudai	宿題	assignment
shukudai	宿題	homework
shukuga	祝賀	celebration
shukuga-kai	祝賀会	celebration
shukuhaku	宿泊	lodging
shukuhaku	宿泊	stop
shumi	趣味	hobby
shumi	趣味	taste
shumi ga warui	趣味が悪い	tasteless
shumoku	種目	event
shunkan	瞬間	moment
shunkan	瞬間	point
shuppan	出版	publication
shuppan-butsu	出版物	press
shuppan-butsu	出版物	publication
shuppan-gyoosha	出版業者	publisher
shuppan-sha	出版社	publisher
shuppan-suru	出版する	publish
shuppatsu	出発	departure
shuppatsu	出発	start
shuppatsu-suru	出発する	depart
shuppatsu-suru	出発する	leave
shurui	種類	kind
shurui	種類	sort
shurui	種類	species
shurui	種類	type
shurui	種類	variety
shushoo	主将	captain

shusse	出世	success
shusseki	出席	attendance
shusseki	出席	presence
shusseki-sha-suu	出席者数	attendance
shusseki-shite iru (N)	出席している(N)	present[1]
shusseki-suru	出席する	attend
shusse-suru	出世する	succeed
shusse-suru	出世する	successful
shutai	主体	subject
shuto	首都	capital
shu-to-shite	主として	chiefly
shu-to-shite	主として	primarily
shutsugen	出現	appearance
shutten	出典	source
shuttoo-suru	出頭する	report
shuu	州	state
shuu	週	week
shuubun	醜聞	scandal
shuuchaku-eki	終着駅	terminal
shuuchi no N	周知のN	public
shuuchuu	集中	concentration
shuuchuu-suru	集中する	concentrate
shuudan	集団	group
shuudoo-jo	修道女	sister
shuugeki	襲撃	raid
shuugeki-suru	襲撃する	storm
shuugoo-tai	集合体	unit
shuuhen	周辺	rim
shuui	周囲	around
shuui no N	周囲のN	surrounding
shuuji	習字	calligraphy
shuujin	囚人	prisoner
shuukai	集会	assembly
shuukaku	収穫	crop
shuukaku	収穫	harvest
shuukan	習慣	custom
shuukan	習慣	habit
shuukan	習慣	practice
shuukan	週間	week
shuuki	周期	cycle
shuuki	臭気	odor
shuukuriimu	シュークリーム	puff
shuukyoo	宗教	religion
shuukyoo no N	宗教のN	religious
shuukyoo-tekina	宗教的な	religious
shuumatsu	週末	weekend
shuu ni ichi-do	週に一度	weekly
shuunyuu	収入	income

shuuri	修理	renovation
shuuri	修理	repair
shuuri-koo	修理工	mechanic
shuuri-koojoo	修理工場	garage
shuuri-suru	修理する	mend
shuuri-suru	修理する	renovate
shuuri-suru	修理する	repair
shuushi-fu	終止符	period
shuushi-fu	終止符	stop
shuushuu	収集	collection
shuushuu-suru	収集する	collect
shuuten	終点	terminal
shuuten no N	終点のN	terminal
shuutoku-suru	習得する	acquire
shuutoku-suru	習得する	master
shuuyoo-nooryoku	収容能力	capacity
shuuzen	修繕	repair
shuuzen-suru	修繕する	repair
shuyoona	主要な	major
shuyoona	主要な	primary
shuyoona	主要な	principal
(shuzai-)kisha	(取材)記者	reporter
shuzoku	種族	tribe
shuzoku no N	種族のN	tribal
soakuna	粗悪な	coarse
soba	そば	buckwheat
soba	そば	noodle
soba {ni/de/o}	そば{に/で/を}	beside
soba {ni/de/o}	そば{に/で/を}	by
sobo	祖母	grandmother
sodateru	育てる	raise
sode	そで	sleeve
sode	そで	wing
sofaa	ソファー	sofa
sofu	祖父	grandfather
sokkusu	ソックス	sock
soko	底	bottom
soko	そこ	there
soko-de	そこで	so
soko(i)ra-juu {de/ni}	そこ(い)ら中{で/に}	everywhere
sokonau	損なう	shatter
soko {ni/de/e/o/ga}	そこ{に/で/へ/を/が}	there
sokubaku	束縛	bond
sokudo	速度	speed
sokudo	速度	velocity
sokudo o otosu	速度を落とす	slow
sokuho	速歩	trot
sokuryoo	測量	survey
sokuryoo-suru	測量する	survey
sokuseki	足跡	trace
sokutei	測定	measurement
sokuza ni	即座に	promptly
son	損	loss
sonae-tsukeru	備え付ける	furnish
sonae-tsukeru	備え付ける	install
sonchoo	村長	mayor
sonchoo	尊重	respect
sonchoo suru	尊重する	respect
sonchoo-suru	尊重する	value
songai	損害	damage
songai	損害	loss
songai o ataeru	損害を与える	damage
songen	尊厳	dignity
sonkei	尊敬	regard
sonkei	尊敬	respect
sonkei-suru	尊敬する	respect
sonmin	村民	villager
sonna N	そんなN	such
sonnani	そんなに	so
sonnani	そんなに	that[1]
sonnara	そんなら	then
sono	その	its
sono-go	その後	thereafter
sono hito-tachi	その人たち	they
sono hito-tachi {o/ni}	その人たち{を/に}	them
sono kekka (to-shite)	その結果(として)	therefore
sono-mama shinjiru	そのまま信じる	swallow[1]
sono mono, N	そのもの, N	very
sono N	そのN	that[1]
sono tame ni	そのために	thus
sono tochi no N	その土地のN	local
sono-toki	その時	then
sono-toki	その時	then
sono toori da	その通りだ	exactly
sono-uchi(-ni)	そのうち(に)	soon
sono ue	その上	besides
sono ue, (shi)	その上, (し)	moreover
sono yooni	そのように	thus
sonshitsu	損失	loss
sonzai	存在	being
sonzai	存在	existence
sonzai	存在	presence
sonzai-suru	存在する	exist
soo	相	aspect
soo	層	layer
soo	そう	so

soo	層	streak
soo-	総～	total
soochi	装置	apparatus
soochi	装置	device
soochoo	総長	president
sooda	ソーダ	soda
soodan	相談	conference
soodan	相談	consultation
soodan-suru	相談する	consult
sooda-sui	ソーダ水	soda
soo dewanai	そうではない	otherwise
soo-gaku	総額	sum
soogaku	総額	total
soogaku (ga) ⟨-ni⟩ naru	総額(が)⟨～に⟩なる	total
soogoo-daigaku	総合大学	university
sooguu	遭遇	encounter
sooguu-suru	遭遇する	encounter
sooi-ten	相違点	difference
sooi-ten	相違点	distinction
soo janai	そうじゃない	otherwise
soo {janai/shinai} to, (moshi)	そう{じゃない/しない}と,(もし)	otherwise
sooji-ki o kakeru	掃除機をかける	vacuum
sooji-suru	掃除する	clean
sooji-suru	掃除する	sweep
soojuu-dekiru	操縦出来る	steer
soojuu-shi	操縦士	pilot
soojuu-suru	操縦する	fly
soojuu-suru	操縦する	work
sookan	壮観	spectacle
sookan no N	壮観のN	spectacular
sookei (ga) ⟨-ni⟩ naru	総計(が)⟨～に⟩なる	total
sookei-suru	総計する	total
sooko	倉庫	storage
sooko	倉庫	storehouse
sookoo	草稿	draft
sookoo o kaku	草稿を書く	draft
sookutsu	巣くつ	nest
sookyuuna	早急な	early
-soona, V*masu*	～そうな, V*masu*	probable
-soona, {V*masu*/adj(*i*/*na*). stem}	～そうな, {V*masu*/adj(*i*/*na*). stem}	likely
-soona, {V*masu*/adj(*i*/*na*). stem}	～そうな, {V*masu*/adj(*i*/*na*). stem}	look
-sooni naru, V*masu*	～そうになる, V*masu*	almost
sooon	騒音	noise
sooritsu	創立	foundation
sooryo	僧りょ	priest
sooryoo	総量	total
soosa	捜査	investigation
soosa	操作	operation
soosa	捜査	search
soosaku	創作	creation
soosaku-butsu	創作物	creation
soosaku-suru	創作する	create
soosaku-suru	捜索する	search
soosa-suru	捜査する	investigate
soosa-suru	操作する	operate
soosa-suru	操作する	work
soosetsu-suru	創設する	create
soosha	走者	runner
sooshiki	葬式	funeral
sooshin-ki	送信機	transmitter
sooshoku	装飾	decoration
soosu	ソース	sauce
soo-sure-ba	そうすれば	and
soosuu	総数	total
soosuu (ga) ⟨-ni⟩ naru	総数(が)⟨～に⟩なる	total
sootai-tekina	相対的な	relative
sootoo	相当	considerably
sootoo-suru	相当する	equivalent
soozoku	相続	succession
soozoku-suru	相続する	inherit
soozoo	創造	creation
soozoo	想像	guess
soozoo	想像	imagination
soozoo-butsu	創造物	creation
soozoo-joo no N	想像上のN	imaginary
soozoo-ryoku	想像力	imagination
soozoo-ryoku ni tonda N	想像力に富んだN	imaginative
soozoo-ryoku ni tonde iru (N)	想像力に富んでいる(N)	imaginative
soozoo-ryoku no yutakana	想像力の豊かな	imaginative
soozoo-ryoku-yutakana	創造力豊かな	fertile
soozoo-suru	創造する	create
soozoo-suru	想像する	dream
soozoo-suru	想像する	imagine
soozoo-tekina	創造的な	creative
sora	空	sky
sora	そら	there
sora no tabi	空の旅	voyage
sore	それ	it

sore	それ	that[1]
sore demo yahari	それでもやはり	nevertheless
sore-dewa	それでは	then
sore-igai de wa	それ以外では	otherwise
sore igo	それ以後	since[2]
sore irai	それ以来	since[2]
sore-jaa	それじゃあ	then
(sore-)ja(a)	(それ)じゃ(あ)	well[2]
sore-kara	それから	then
sore made	それまで	meanwhile
sore-nara	それなら	then
sore ni	それに	besides
sore ni	それに	furthermore
sore ni, (shi)	それに, (し)	moreover
sore ni-yotte	それによって	thereby
sore-ra	それら	they
sore-ra	それら	those
sore-ra no N	それらのN	their
sore-ra no N	それらのN	those
sore-ra {o/ni}	それら{を/に}	them
sore-tomo	それとも	or
soreto-naku iu	それとなく言う	hint
sore to onaji yooni	それと同じように	so
sore-zore	それぞれ	each
sore-zore	それぞれ	respectively
sore-zore no N	それぞれのN	each
sore-zore no N	それぞれのN	own
soro	ソロ	solo
soru	そる	shave
soshiki	組織	organization
soshiki	組織	structure
soshiki	組織	system
soshiki	組織	tissue
soshiki(-joo) no N	組織(上)のN	structural
soshiki-suru	組織する	organize
soshi-suru	阻止する	check
soshite	そして	and
soshoo	訴訟	suit[1]
sosogu	注ぐ	pour
sotchokuna	率直な	direct
sotchokuna	率直な	frank
sotchokuna	率直な	honest
sotchokuna	率直な	straight
sotchokuna	率直な	transparent
sotchokuni	率直に	directly
sotchokuni	率直に	freely
sotchokuni	率直に	honestly
sotchokuni	率直に	straight

sotchuu	卒中	stroke[1]
soto	外	outside
soto-gawa	外側	outside
soto-gawa no N	外側のN	outer
soto {ni/e}	外{に/へ}	out
soto no N	外のN	outer
sotsugyoo	卒業	graduation
sotsugyoo-sei	卒業生	graduate
sotsugyoo-shiki	卒業式	graduation
sotsugyoo-suru	卒業する	graduate
sotte	沿って	along
sotte	沿って	down
sotte iku	沿って行く	follow
soyana	粗野な	coarse
soyo-kaze	そよ風	breeze
su	巣	burrow
su	巣	nest
su	酢	vinegar
subarashii	すばらしい	beautiful
subarashii	すばらしい	brilliant
subarashii	すばらしい	fantastic
subarashii	すばらしい	fascinating
subarashii	すばらしい	glorious
subarashii	すばらしい	grand
subarashii	すばらしい	great
subarashii	すばらしい	magnificent
subarashii	すばらしい	marvelous
subarashii	すばらしい	rare
subarashii	すばらしい	remarkable
subarashii	すばらしい	royal
subarashii	すばらしい	spectacular
subarashii	すばらしい	splendid
subarashii	すばらしい	terrific
subarashii	すばらしい	wonderful
subayai	すばやい	rapid
subayaku	すばやく	promptly
subayaku	すばやく	rapidly
subayaku V	すばやくV	shoot
suberi-dai	滑り台	slide
suberu	滑る	slide
suberu	滑る	slip
suberu yooni {iku/tobu}, (-no) ue o	滑るように{行く/飛ぶ}, (〜の)上を	skim
sube-sube-shita N	すべすべしたN	smooth
sube-sube-shite iru (N)	すべすべしている(N)	smooth
subete	すべて	everything
subete no N	すべてのN	all

subete no N	すべてのN	every
subette korobu, (surutto)	滑って転ぶ, (するっと)	slip
suchiiru	スチール	steal
suchiiru(-shashin)	スチール(写真)	still
sudeni	すでに	already
Sueeden	スエーデン	Sweden
Sueeden-go	スエーデン語	Swedish
Sueeden-go no N	スエーデン語のN	Swedish
Sueeden-jin	スエーデン人	Swedish
Sueeden-jin no N	スエーデン人のN	Swedish
Sueeden no N	スエーデンのN	Swedish
sueru	据える	plant
sugata	姿	figure
sugata	姿	form
sugata	姿	reflection
sugata	姿	shape
-sugi	～過ぎ	past
suginai	過ぎない	mere
suginai	過ぎない	merely
sugiru	過ぎる	pass
-sugiru, {adj(*i*/*na*). stem/V*masu*}	～すぎる, {adj(*i*/*na*). stem/V*masu*}	too
-sugiru, V*masu*	～すぎる, V*masu*	over-
sugoi	すごい	fascinating
sugoi	すごい	spectacular
sugoi	すごい	tremendous
sugoku	すごく	awfully
sugoku hara ga tatsu	すごく腹が立つ	furious
sugoku hara o tateru	すごく腹を立てる	furious
sugosu	過ごす	spend
sugu	すぐ	immediate
sugu	すぐ	immediately
sugu	すぐ	instantly
sugu	すぐ	shortly
sugu (ni)	すぐ(に)	directly
sugu (ni)	すぐ(に)	promptly
sugu (ni)	すぐ(に)	readily
sugureta N	優れたN	excellent
sugureta N	優れたN	outstanding
sugureta N	優れたN	remarkable
sugureta N	優れたN	superior
sugurete iru	優れている	superior
sugu soba ni	すぐそばに	close[2]
sugu soba no N	すぐそばのN	immediate
sugu, (-to)	すぐ, (～と)	upon
suichoku no N	垂直のN	perpendicular
suichoku no N	垂直のN	vertical
suichuu no N	水中のN	underwater
suiden	水田	field
suiden	水田	paddy
suiei	水泳	swimming
suigen	水源	source
suigin	水銀	mercury
suigyuu	水牛	buffalo
suihei-sen	水平線	horizon
suiheina	水平な	level
suii	推移	passage
suii	推移	transition
suijooki	水蒸気	vapor
suijun	水準	standard
suika	すいか	watermelon
suimen	水面	surface
suimin	睡眠	sleep
suingu	スイング	swing
suiri-shoosetsu	推理小説	mystery
suiro	水路	channel
suiron	推論	reasoning
suisan-	水産～	marine
suisei no o	すい星の尾	tail
suisen	推薦	recommendation
suisen-suru	推薦する	recommend
suishoo	水晶	crystal
suiso	水素	hydrogen
suisoku	推測	guess
suisoo	水そう	aquarium
Suisu-jin	スイス人	Swiss
Suisu-jin no N	スイス人のN	Swiss
Suisu no N	スイスのN	Swiss
suiyoo(-bi)	水曜(日)	Wednesday
suizoku-kan	水族館	aquarium
suji	筋	plot
suji	筋	story[1]
suji	筋	thread
sukaafu	スカーフ	scarf
sukaato	スカート	skirt
Sukanjinabia	スカンジナビア	Scandinavia
sukanku	スカンク	skunk
sukauto	スカウト	scout
sukauto-suru	スカウトする	scout
sukeeru	スケール	scale[3]
sukeeto	スケート	skate
sukeeto o suru	スケートをする	skate
sukejuuru	スケジュール	schedule
suketchi	スケッチ	sketch
suki	すき	plow

suki da, ⟨-yori⟩ ⟨-no hoo ga⟩ 好きだ，⟨～より⟩⟨～の方が⟩ prefer
suki de ⟨-o⟩ tagayasu すきで⟨～を⟩耕す plow
sukii o suru スキーをする ski
suki-ma 透き間 gap
suki-ma 透き間 space
sukina 好きな like[1]
sukippu スキップ skip
sukippu-suru スキップする skip
suki-tootta N 透き通ったN transparent
suki-tootte iru (N) 透き通っている(N) transparent
sukkari すっかり altogether
sukkari すっかり completely
sukkari すっかり entirely
sukkari すっかり quite
sukkari すっかり utterly
sukoa スコア score
sukoshi 少し bit
sukoshi 少し few
sukoshi 少し little
sukoshi 少し slight
sukoshi 少し slightly
sukoshi 少し some
sukoshi-mo…neg. 少しも…neg. any
sukoshi (no) 少し(の) some
sukoshi wa 少しは any
Sukottorando スコットランド Scotland
sukui-dasu 救い出す rescue
sukui-toru すくい取る skim
sukunai 少ない few
sukunai 少ない little
sukunai 少ない slim
sukunai 少ない small
sukurappu スクラップ scrap
sukurappu ni suru スクラップにする scrap
sukuriin スクリーン screen
sukuu すくう rescue
sukuu すくう save
sukuunaa スクーナー schooner
sukyandaru スキャンダル scandal
suma-seru すませる finish
sumasshu スマッシュ smash
sumi 炭 charcoal
sumi 隅 corner
sumi 墨 ink
sumire すみれ violet
sumire-iro すみれ色 violet
sumu すむ end
sumu すむ finish
sumu 住む live
sumu 住む reside
sumu すむ through
sumu, o-kage de {Vneg.+zu/Vstem+zu/sezu/kozu} ni 済む，おかげで{Vneg.+ず/Vstem+ず/せず/来ず}に save
sumu yooni suru, {Vneg./Vstem/shi/ko} nai de 済むようにする，{Vneg./Vstem/し/来}ないで spare
suna 砂 sand
suna-darake no N 砂だらけのN sandy
suna-iro no N 砂色のN sandy
suna no N 砂のN sandy
sunappu スナップ snap
sunda N 澄んだN clear
sunpoo 寸法 dimension
sunpoo 寸法 measurement
supaaku スパーク spark
supai スパイ spy
supaisu スパイス spice
supea-taiya スペアタイヤ spare
Supein スペイン Spain
Supein-go スペイン語 Spanish
Supein-go no N スペイン語のN Spanish
Supein-jin スペイン人 Spanish
Supein-jin no N スペイン人のN Spanish
Supein no N スペインのN Spanish
supekutoramu スペクトラム spectrum
supiido スピード speed
supiido o dasu スピードを出す speed
suponji スポンジ sponge
supootsu スポーツ game
supootsu スポーツ sport
supootsu-man rashii スポーツマンらしい athletic
suppai 酸っぱい sour
supuree スプレー spray
supuun スプーン spoon
suraido スライド slide
surakkusu スラックス slack
suratto-shita N すらっとしたN slender
suratto-shite iru (N) すらっとしている(N) slender
sure-chigau すれ違う cross
suri-heru 擦り減る wear
suri-kireru 擦り切れる wear
suri-muku すりむく graze[1]
surippa スリッパ slipper
suriru スリル thrill
suritto スリット slit

surotto	スロット	slot
suru	する	cost
suru	する	decide
suru	する	deliver
suru	する	determine
suru	する	do
suru	する	grind
suru	する	perform
suru	する	play
suru	する	set
suru	する	shape
suru	する	wear
suru, {adj(*i*). *ku*/adj(*na*). *ni*/〈-ni〉}	する, {adj(*i*). *ku*/adj(*na*). *ni*/〈〜に〉}	drive
surudoi	鋭い	acute
surudoi	鋭い	sharp
surudoku	鋭く	sharply
surudoku suru	鋭くする	sharpen
suru, {〈-ni〉/adj(*i*). *ku*/adj(*na*). *ni*}	する, {〈〜に〉/adj(*i*). *ku*/adj(*na*). *ni*}	make
suru, {〈-ni〉/adj(*i*). *ku*/adj(*na*). *ni*}	する, {〈〜に〉/adj(*i*). *ku*/adj(*na*). *ni*}	render
(surutto) subette korobu	(するっと)滑って転ぶ	slip
suru, {Vneg./Vstem/shi/ko} nai yooni	する, {Vneg./Vstem/し/来}ないように	stop
susume	勧め	recommendation
susumeru	勧める	offer
susumeru, {〈-o〉/Sinf. nonpast yooni}	勧める, {〈〜を〉/Sinf. nonpastように}	recommend
susumeru, {〈-o〉/Sinf. nonpast yooni}	勧める, {〈〜を〉/Sinf. nonpastように}	urge
susumu	進む	advance
susumu	進む	proceed
susumu	進む	steer
susumu	進む	travel
susumu, (hansen no yoo ni)	進む, (帆船のように)	sail
susunde iru (N)	進んでいる(N)	fast
susunde, (saki e)	進んで, (先へ)	along
susunde V	進んでV	willing
sutaa	スター	star
sutaato	スタート	start
sutairu	スタイル	figure
sutairu	スタイル	style
sutajio	スタジオ	studio
sutando	スタンド	lamp
sutanpu o osu	スタンプを押す	stamp
suteeji	ステージ	stage
suteeki	ステーキ	beefsteak
suteeki	ステーキ	steak
sutekina	すてきな	beautiful
sutekina	すてきな	lovely
sutekina	すてきな	wonderful
suteppu	ステップ	step
suteppu o fumu	ステップを踏む	step
suteru	捨てる	abandon
suteru	捨てる	desert
suteru	捨てる	discard
sutokkingu	ストッキング	stockings
sutokku	ストック	stock
sutoobu	ストーブ	heater
sutoobu	ストーブ	stove
sutoorii	ストーリー	story[1]
sutooru	ストール	stole
sutoraiki	ストライキ	strike
sutoraiki o suru	ストライキをする	strike
sutoraiku	ストライク	strike
sutoreeto de	ストレートで	straight
sutoreeto ni	ストレートに	straight
sutoreeto no N	ストレートのN	straight
sutoresu	ストレス	stress
sutsuuru	スツール	stool
suu	数	number
suu	吸う	smoke
suu	吸う	suck
suugaku	数学	mathematics
suuhai-suru	崇拝する	worship
suuji	数字	figure
suuji	数字	number
suupaa	スーパー	supermarket
suupaaman	スーパーマン	superman
suupu	スープ	soup
suushi	数詞	number
suutsu	スーツ	suit[2]
suutsukeesu	スーツケース	suitcase
suwaru	座る	sit
suzu	すず	tin
suzume	すずめ	sparrow
suzushii	涼しい	cool

T

ta	田	field
ta	田	paddy
ta-	他〜	transitive

taaminaru	ターミナル	terminal
taaru	タール	tar
taba	束	bunch
taba	束	bundle
tabako	たばこ	cigarette
tabako	たばこ	tobacco
tabako o suu	たばこを吸う	smoke
tabe-mono	食べ物	food
tabe-rareru	食べられる	stomach
taberu	食べる	eat
taberu	食べる	have
taberu	食べる	take
tabe-saseru	食べさせる	feed
tabi	旅	journey
tabi	旅	travel
tabi	旅	trip
tabi-bito	旅人	traveler
tabi no N	旅のN	traveling
tabi-shoonin	旅商人	traveler
tabi-tabi	たびたび	frequently
tabi-tabi	たびたび	often
tabun	多分	probably
tachi-agaru	立ち上がる	rise
tachi-agaru	立ち上がる	stand
tachiba	立場	position
tachiba	立場	situation
tachiba	立場	stand
tachiba	立場	standpoint
tachi-domaru	立ち止まる	stop
tachi-itta N	立ち入ったN	personal
tachi-mukau	立ち向かう	face
tachi-naoru	立ち直る	recover
tachi-oojoo-suru	立ち往生する	stall
tada	ただ	wholly
tadachini	直ちに	immediate
tadachini	直ちに	readily
tada…dake	ただ…だけ	only
tada hitotsu no N	ただ一つのN	sole[1]
tada no N	ただのN	free
tada…no N	ただ…のN	only
tadashii	正しい	correct
tadashii	正しい	proper
tadashii	正しい	right
tadashii	正しい	true
tadashii koto	正しいこと	right
tadashiku	正しく	correctly
tadashiku	正しく	properly
tadashiku	正しく	right
tadashiku	正しく	truly
tadoru	たどる	trace
taema-nai	絶え間ない	constant
taema-nai	絶え間ない	continuous
tae-nuku	耐え抜く	survive
taeru	耐える	bear[2]
taeru	耐える	stand
taeru	耐える	undergo
taezu	絶えず	constantly
tagai no N	互いのN	mutual
tagai no ryookai	互いの了解	understanding
-tagaru, V*masu*	～たがる, V*masu*	curious
-ta-garu, V*masu*	～たがる, V*masu*	want
-ta-garu, V*masu*	～たがる, V*masu*	wish
tagayasu	耕す	cultivate
ta-hata	田畑	field
tai	対	to
tai-	大～	great
-tai	～帯	zone
taido	態度	attitude
taido	態度	bearing
taido	態度	behavior
taido	態度	reaction
taido ni deru	態度に出る	react
taieki	体液	sap
taifuu	台風	typhoon
taigun, (konchuu no)	大群, (昆虫の)	swarm
taiha	大破	wreck
taiha-suru	大破する	wreck
Taihei-yoo	太平洋	Pacific Ocean
taihen	大変	much
taihen	大変	quite
taihen	大変	very
taihen da	大変だ	dear
taihenna	大変な	grave
taihenna	大変な	tough
taihi-suru	対比する	contrast
taihoo	大砲	cannon
taiho-suru	逮捕する	arrest
taiiku-kan	体育館	gymnasium
taijuu ga…aru	体重が…ある	weigh
taijuu o hakaru	体重をはかる	weigh
taikai	大会	convention
taikaku	体格	build
taikaku	体格	constitution
taikei	体系	system
taiki-chuu no N	大気中のN	atmospheric
taiki-ken	大気圏	atmosphere

taikin	大金	fortune
taiki no N	大気のN	atmospheric
taikutsuna	退屈な	boring
taikutsuna	退屈な	dry
taikutsuna	退屈な	dull
taikutsu-saseru	退屈させる	bore
taikutsu-shinogi	退屈しのぎ	refuge
taikutsu-shite iru (N)	退屈している(N)	bored
taimoo	大望	ambition
taimoo aru N	大望あるN	ambitious
-tai, (nan-to shite demo) V*masu*	～たい, (何としてでも) V*masu*	hungry
taion	体温	temperature
taion-kei	体温計	thermometer
taipu	タイプ	type
taipu(raitaa)	タイプ(ライター)	typewriter
taipu(raitaa) de utsu	タイプ(ライター)で打つ	type
taipu(raitaa) o utsu	タイプ(ライター)を打つ	type
taira denai (N)	平らでない(N)	uneven
tairana	平らな	even
tairana	平らな	flat[1]
tairana	平らな	level
tairani suru	平らにする	scrape
tairani suru	平らにする	level
tairiku	大陸	continent
tairu	タイル	tile
tairyoku	体力	power
tairyoku	体力	strength
tairyoo no N	大量のN	mass
Taiseiyoo no N	大西洋のN	Atlantic
taisetsuna	大切な	important
taisetsu ni suru	大切にする	value
taishi	大使	ambassador
taishi-kan	大使館	embassy
taishi(te), Sinf. no ni	対し(て), Sinf.のに	whereas
taishoku-shita N	退職したN	retired
taishoku-suru	退職する	retire
taishoo	対照	comparison
taishoo	対照	contrast
taishoo	対象	object
taishoo-suru	対照する	contrast
taishuu-muki no N	大衆向きのN	popular
taishuu no N	大衆のN	popular
taishuu-sei	大衆性	popularity
taisoo	体操	calisthenics
taisoo	体操	exercise

taisoo	体操	gymnastics
taisuru N, (-ni)	対するN, (～に)	toward(s)
taitei	大抵	generally
taitei	大抵	mostly
taitei	大抵	usually
taitei no N	大抵のN	most
-tai to omou, V*masu*	～たいと思う, V*masu*	hope
-tai, V*masu*	～たい, V*masu*	curious
-tai, V*masu*	～たい, V*masu*	like[1]
-tai, V*masu*	～たい, V*masu*	want
-tai, V*masu*	～たい, V*masu*	wish
taiwa	対話	dialogue
taiya	タイヤ	tire[2]
taiya no chuubu	タイヤのチューブ	tube
taiyoo	太陽	sun
taiyoo no N	太陽のN	solar
taiyoo no N	太陽のN	sunny
taiyoo no yoona	太陽のような	sunny
taizai	滞在	stay
taizai	滞在	stop
taizai	滞在	visit
taizai-suru	滞在する	stay
taka	たか	hawk
taka-ha	たか派	hawk
takai	高い	costly
takai	高い	dear
takai	高い	expensive
takai	高い	high
takai	高い	superior
takai	高い	tall
takaku	高く	high
takaku	高く	highly
takaku agaru	高く上がる	soar
takaku sobieru	高くそびえる	tower
takaku sobieru (N)	高くそびえる(N)	towering
takaku suru	高くする	raise
takara(-mono)	宝(物)	treasure
taka-sa	高さ	height
take	竹	bamboo
taki	滝	waterfall
takkuru	タックル	tackle
takkuru-suru	タックルする	tackle
tako	たこ	octopus
takuji-sho	託児所	nursery
takurami	たくらみ	plot
takurami	たくらみ	scheme
takusan	たくさん	lot

takusan	たくさん	many
takusan	沢山	plentiful
takusan	沢山	plenty
takusan deru	たくさん出る	pour
takusan hairu	たくさん入る	pour
takusan (no) N	たくさん(の)N	much
takushii	タクシー	taxi
takuwae	蓄え	stock
takuwaeru	蓄える	save
takuwacru	蓄える	stock
tama	たま	ball
tama	たま	bullet
tama	たま	shot
tamageru	たまげる	shock
tamago	卵	egg
tamago-gata	卵型	oval
tamago-gata no N	卵型のN	oval
(tamago o) iri-tamago ni suru	(卵を)いり卵にする	scramble
tamanegi	玉ねぎ	onion
tamaru	たまる	gather
tamashii	魂	soul
tamashii	魂	spirit
tame	ため	point
tame	ため	purpose
tame	ため	sake[1]
tame-ike	ため池	tank[1]
tame-iki	ため息	sigh
tame-iki o tsuku	ため息をつく	sigh
tame (ni)	ため(に)	for
tame {(ni)/no N}, {Vinf. nonpast/N no}	ため{(に)/のN}, {Vinf. nonpast/Nの}	for
tame (ni), {(-no)/Sinf.}	ため(に), {(〜の)/Sinf.}	so
tame ni, Vinf. nonpast	ために, Vinf. nonpast	that[3]
tamerau	ためらう	hesitate
tameru	ためる	save
tameshi	試し	trial
tamesu	試す	test
tamesu	試す	try
tana	棚	rack
tana	棚	shelf
tana-biku	棚引く	trail
tanbo	たんぼ	paddy
tandoku no N	単独のN	sole[1]
tandoku no N	単独のN	solid
tane	種	seed

tane	種	stone
tane o maku	種をまく	sow
tane-uma	種馬	stallion
tangan	嘆願	petition
tangan	嘆願	suit[1]
tangan-sho	嘆願書	petition
tangan-suru	嘆願する	petition
tango	単語	vocabulary
tango	単語	word
tango-hyoo	単語表	vocabulary
tani	谷	valley
tan'i	単位	credit
tan'i	単位	unit
tani-{ma/ai}	谷{間/あい}	valley
tan'itsu-sei	単一性	unity
tanjoo	誕生	birth
tanjoo-bi	誕生日	birthday
tanjunna	単純な	simple
tanjunni suru	単純にする	simplify
tanken	探険	exploration
tanken-suru	探険する	explore
tanki	短気	temper
tankina	短気な	short-tempered
tankoo	炭坑	pit
tanku	タンク	tank[1]
tanku	タンク	tank[2]
tanmatsu(-ki)	端末(機)	terminal
tan-naru N	単なるN	mere
tanni	単に	simply
tannoona	たんのうな	proficient
tanomi	頼み	request
tanomi-goto	頼み事	request
tanomu	頼む	ask
tanomu, Vinf. nonpast yoo (ni)	頼む, Vinf. nonpastよう(に)	request
tanoshii	楽しい	delightful
tanoshii	楽しい	enjoyable
tanoshii	楽しい	fun
tanoshii	楽しい	jolly
tanoshii	楽しい	pleasant
tanoshii koto	楽しいこと	treat
tanoshima-seru	楽しませる	amuse
tanoshima-seru	楽しませる	entertain
tanoshima-seru	楽しませる	please
tanoshima-su	楽します	please
tanoshimi	楽しみ	amusement
tanoshimi	楽しみ	delight
tanoshimi	楽しみ	enjoyment

tanoshimu	楽しむ	enjoy
tanoshi-sa	楽しさ	pleasure
tanpaku-shitsu	蛋白質	protein
tansho	短所	drawback
tanso	炭素	carbon
tansu	たんす	chest
tansui-kabutsu	炭水化物	starch
tansuu no N	単数のN	singular
tantei	探偵	detective
taoreru	倒れる	fall
taoru	タオル	towel
taosu	倒す	overthrow
-tara	～たら	if
tarai	たらい	basin
tarai	たらい	tub
tarinai	足りない	lack
tarinai	足りない	want
tarinaku naru	足りなくなる	fail
tariru	足りる	enough
taru	たる	barrel
tasaku no N	多作のN	productive
tasan no N	多産のN	fertile
tasan no N	多産のN	productive
tashikameru	確かめる	check
tashikana	確かな	sure
tashikani	確かに	certainly
tashikani	確かに	surely
tashikani	確かに	undoubtedly
tashikani…to iu	確かに…と言う	assure
tashi-zan	足し算	addition
tashoo	多少	some
tashoo (no)	多少(の)	some
tasogare(-doki)	たそがれ(時)	twilight
tassei	達成	achievement
tassei-suru	達成する	achieve
tasshana	達者な	proficient
tassuru	達する	reach
tasu	足す	add
tasukaru	助かる	survive
tasuke	助け	help
tasukeru	助ける	aid
tasukeru	助ける	assist
tasukeru	助ける	help
tasukeru	助ける	save
tasukete {ageru/yaru}	助けて{あげる/やる}	spare
tasuu no N	多数のN	numerous
tatakai	たたかい	fight
tatakai	戦い	battle
tatakai	戦い	war
tatakau	戦う	battle
tatakau	たたかう	fight
tataki-kiru	たたき切る	chop
tataki-tsukeru	たたきつける	knock
tataku	たたく	beat
tataku	たたく	hit
tataku	たたく	knock
tataku	たたく	strike
tatamu	畳む	fold
tata-seru	立たせる	raise
tata-seru	立たせる	stand
tatchi	タッチ	touch
tate	縦	length
tate	盾	shield
tate-ana	たて穴	pit
tate-koo	立坑	shaft[2]
tate-mono	建物	building
tate-mono no naka {de/ni/o}	建物の中{で/に/を}	indoors
tateru	たてる	build
tateru	たてる	erect
tateru	たてる	raise
tateru	たてる	stand
tatoeru	たとえる	compare
tatsu	たつ	pass
tatsu koto	立つこと	stand
tatsumaki	竜巻	tornado
tatsu, (shiranai uchi ni jikan ga)	たつ, (知らないうちに時間が)	slip
tatta hitori no N	たった一人のN	sole[1]
tatta hitotsu no N	たった一つのN	single
tatta no ichi+counter mo	たったの一+counterも	single
tatta…no N	たった…のN	only
tatte iru	立っている	stand
tawaa	タワー	tower
tayasuku	たやすく	easily
tayori	たより	news
tayori ni naru (N)	頼りになる(N)	dependable
tayori ni suru	頼りにする	rely
tayoru	頼る	depend
tayoru	頼る	rely
tayotte iru (N)	頼っている(N)	dependent
tazuna	手綱	rein(s)
tazuneru	たずねる	visit
tazuneru	尋ねる	ask
tazuneru	尋ねる	inquire

tazuneru, {(-no) koto o/(-ni-tsuite)}	尋ねる, {(〜の)ことを/(〜について)}	question
te	手	hand
tearai	手洗い	bathroom
tearai	手洗い	lavatory
tearai	手洗い	toilet
tearai	手洗い	washroom
te-araku	手荒く	roughly
te-arani	手荒に	roughly
te-biki	手引	guide
te-bukuro	手袋	glove
teburi	手振り	gesture
techoo	手帳	notebook
teeburu	テーブル	table
teeburu-kurosu	テーブルクロス	cloth
teema	テーマ	subject
teema	テーマ	theme
teepu	テープ	tape
teepu o maku	テープを巻く	tape
teepu o tsukeru	テープをつける	tape
teepu-rekoodaa	テープレコーダー	recorder
teepu-rekoodaa	テープレコーダー	tape recorder
te ga aite iru (N)	手が空いている(N)	available
te-gakari	手掛かり	clue
tegami	手紙	letter
tegiwa no iru (N)	手際の要る(N)	tricky
tegorona	手ごろな	reasonable
tehon	手本	example
tehon	手本	model
teian-suru	提案する	advance
teian-suru	提案する	propose
teian-suru, Vinf. past+ra doo ka to	提案する, Vinf. past+らどうかと	suggest
teido	程度	degree
teido	程度	extent
teien	庭園	garden
teigaku ni suru	停学にする	suspend
teigi	定義	definition
teigi-suru	定義する	define
teijuu-suru	定住する	settle
teika	低下	depression
teika	低下	drop
teika	低下	fall
teiketsu-suru	締結する	conclude
teiki-koodoku-suru	定期購読する	subscribe
teiki-tekina	定期的な	regular
teiki-tekini	定期的に	regularly
teikoku	帝国	empire

teikoo	抵抗	resistance
teikoo	抵抗	stand
teikoo-ryoku	抵抗力	resistance
teikoo-suru	抵抗する	resist
teikyoo-suru	提供する	provide
teineina	丁寧な	polite
teinen-taishoku-shita N	定年退職したN	retired
teinen-taishoku-suru	定年退職する	retire
teire	手入れ	raid
teire o suru	手入れをする	trim
teire (o) suru	手入れ(を)する	raid
teiryuu-jo	停留所	stop
teisatsu-kan	偵察艦	scout
teisatsu-ki	偵察機	scout
teisatsu-suru	偵察する	scout
teisei	訂正	correction
teisei-suru	訂正する	correct
teishi	停止	halt
teishoku ni suru	停職にする	suspend
teishutsu-suru	提出する	submit
teitaku	邸宅	residence
tejina	手品	trick
te-jun	手順	procedure
teki	敵	enemy
tekido no N	適度のN	moderate
tekii o motta N	敵意を持ったN	hostile
tekii o motte iru (N)	敵意を持っている(N)	hostile
teki o hooi-suru	敵を包囲する	surround
tekioo	適応	adaptation
tekioo-saseru	適応させる	adapt
Tekisasu	テキサス	Texas
tekiseina	適正な	fair
tekisetsuna	適切な	adequate
tekisetsuna	適切な	apt
tekisetsuni	適切に	properly
teki-suru	適する	fit
tekisuto	テキスト	text
tekisuto	テキスト	textbook
tekitoona	適当な	appropriate
tekitoona	適当な	proper
tekitoona	適当な	suitable
te-kubi	手首	wrist
tekunikku	テクニック	technique
tekunorojii	テクノロジー	technology
temijikani	手短に	briefly
ten	点	dot
ten	点	feature

ten	点	grade
ten	天	heaven
ten	点	point
ten	点	respect
ten	点	score
-ten	～店	shop
tenbin	天びん	balance
tenbin	天びん	scale[2]
tenbin de hakaru	天びんで量る	scale[2]
tenboo	展望	prospect
Teneshii	テネシー	Tennessee
tengoku	天国	heaven
te ni hairu (N)	手に入る(N)	available
te ni ireru	手に入れる	obtain
te ni ireru	手に入れる	secure
te ni ireru	手に入れる	take
te-nimotsu	手荷物	baggage
ten'in	店員	clerk
ten'in	店員	salesperson
tenisu	テニス	tennis
tenji	展示	display
tenji	展示	exhibit
tenji-hin	展示品	exhibit
tenji-kai	展示会	show
tenji-suru	展示する	display
tenji-suru	展示する	exhibit
tenjoo	天井	ceiling
tenkei-tekina	典型的な	typical
tenki	天気	weather
tenki ga areru	天気が荒れる	storm
tenki ga ii	天気がいい	sunny
tenkin-suru	転勤する	transfer
tenkoo	天候	weather
tenkyuu	天球	sphere
tenmetsu-saseru	点滅させる	flash
tenmon-gaku	天文学	astronomy
tenmon-gakusha	天文学者	astronomer
tennoo	天皇	emperor
tennoo-sei	天王星	Uranus
te-no-hira	手のひら	palm
ten o toru	点を取る	score
ten o tsukeru	点をつける	score
tenpi	天火	oven
tenpo	テンポ	pace
tenpo	テンポ	tempo
tenpu no sai	天賦の才	genius
tenpura	てんぷら	tempura
tenran-kai	展覧会	show
tensai	てん菜	beet
tensai	天才	genius
tensha-ga	転写画	transfer
tenshi	天使	angel
tenshu	店主	storekeeper
tensoo-suru	転送する	forward
tensu	テンス	tense
tento	テント	tent
(tento o) haru	(テントを)張る	pitch
tenugui	手ぬぐい	towel
te o futte aizu-suru	手を振って合図する	wave
(te-)oke	(手)おけ	pail
te o nobasu	手を伸ばす	reach
teppen	てっぺん	top
teppen no N	てっぺんのN	top
tera	寺	temple
terasu	照らす	shine
terasu	テラス	terrace
terebi	テレビ	television
terebi	テレビ	TV
teru	照る	shine
te-saguri de sagasu	手探りで捜す	feel
te-sei no N	手製のN	homemade
tesuto	テスト	test
tesuto-hoo	テスト法	test
tesuto o suru	テストをする	test
tetsu	鉄	iron
tetsubun	鉄分	iron
tetsudai	手伝い	help
tetsudau	手伝う	assist
tetsudau	手伝う	help
tetsudoo	鉄道	rail
tetsudoo	鉄道	railroad
tetsugaku	哲学	philosophy
tetsu-kabuto	鉄かぶと	helmet
te-tsuzuki	手続き	procedure
tettei-tekina	徹底的な	sweeping
tettei-tekina	徹底的な	thorough
tettei-tekini	徹底的に	thoroughly
te-zawari	手ざわり	touch
te-zukuri no N	手作りのN	homemade
tiin-eijaa	ティーンエージャー	teenager
tisshu	ティッシュ	tissue
to	と	and
to	戸	door
to	と	with
tobasu	飛ばす	skip
tobi-agaru	飛び上がる	jump

tobi-agaru	飛び上がる	spring
tobi-dasu	飛び出す	jump
tobi-koeru	飛び越える	clear
tobi-koeru	飛び越える	leap
tobi-komu	飛び込む	jump
tobi-komu	飛び込む	plunge
tobi-mawaru	跳び回る	hop
tobi-noru	飛び乗る	leap
tobi-oriru	飛び降りる	jump
tobira	扉	door
toboshii	乏しい	poor
tobu	とぶ	fly
tobu	とぶ	jump
tobu	とぶ	spring
tobu, kata-ashi de pyon-to	跳ぶ, 片足でぴょんと	hop
tochi	土地	ground
tochi	土地	land
tochi	土地	property
tochuu	途中	halfway
To-den	都電	streetcar
todokeru	届ける	deliver
todoku	届く	carry
todoku	届く	reach
togarasu	尖らす	sharpen
toge	とげ	spine
toge	とげ	thorn
toge no N	とげのN	spinal
toge-toge-shii	とげとげしい	harsh
togu	研ぐ	grind
togu	研ぐ	sharpen
toho	徒歩	walk
toire	トイレ	bathroom
toire	トイレ	lavatory
toire	トイレ	toilet
to iu	という	of
to-iu imi da	という意味だ	mean[2]
to-iu koto da	ということだ	mean[2]
to-iu koto da, Sinf.	ということだ, Sinf.	imply
to iu koto {desu/da} ne, Sinf.	ということ{です/だ}ね, Sinf.	understand
to iu N, S	というN, S	that[3]
toji-komeru	閉じ込める	trap
tojiru	閉じる	close[1]
tokage	とかげ	lizard
tokai	都会	city
tokai	都会	town
tokai no N	都会のN	urban

tokai-tokuyuu no N	都会特有のN	urban
tokasu	とかす	dissolve
tokasu	とかす	melt
tokei	時計	clock
tokei	時計	watch
tokei ga -ji o utsu	時計が〜時を打つ	strike
(tokei no) neji o maku	(時計の)ねじを巻く	wind[2]
tokeru	とける	dissolve
tokeru	とける	melt
toki	時	occasion
toki	時	time
toki-doki	時々	occasionally
toki-doki	時々	sometimes
toki (ni), Sinf.	時(に), Sinf.	when[1]
toki ni (wa) itsu-demo, Sinf.	時に(は)いつでも, Sinf.	whenever
toki o mi-hakarau, Vinf. nonpast affirmative	時を見計らう, Vinf. nonpast affirmative	time
toki-ori	時折	occasionally
toki-ori no N	時折のN	occasional
tokka-hin	特価品	bargain
tokkyo	特許	patent
tokkyo-hin	特許品	patent
tokkyo-shoo	特許証	patent
toko-no-ma	床の間	alcove
tokoro	ところ	just
tokoro	所	place
tokoro	所	point
tokoro+prt., Sinf.	所+prt., Sinf.	where[1]
toko-ya	床屋	barber
toku	とく	solve
toku	得	profit
tokubetsuna	特別な	special
tokubetsuni	特別に	specially
tokuchoo	特徴	characteristic
tokuchoo	特徴	feature
tokuchoo	特徴	trait
tokuchoo o arawasu	特徴を表す	characterize
tokuchoo-tekina	特徴的な	typical
tokuchoo {to natte iru/dearu} (N)	特徴{となっている/である}(N)	characteristic
tokuchoo-zukeru	特徴づける	characterize
tokuina	得意な	proud
tokui ni natte iru	得意になっている	proud
tokui no N	得意のN	proud
tokuni	特に	especially
tokuni	特に	particularly
toku o suru	得をする	benefit

toku o suru	得をする	profit
tokusei	特性	property
tokushoku	特色	characteristic
tokushoku	特色	specialty
tokushuna	特殊な	special
tokushuna	特殊な	specific
tokushuu	特集	feature
tokutei no N	特定のN	particular
tokutei no N	特定のN	specific
tokuten	得点	score
tokuyuuna	特有な	peculiar
tokuyuu no N	特有のN	peculiar
tomari-gi	止まり木	perch
tomaru	とまる	halt
tomaru	とまる	lodge
tomaru	とまる	perch
tomaru	とまる	settle
tomaru	とまる	sit
tomaru	とまる	stay
tomaru	とまる	stop
tomaru koto	止まること	stop
tomato	トマト	tomato
tomeru	とめる	fasten
tomeru	とめる	halt
tomeru	留める	pin
tomeru	とめる	restrain
tomeru	とめる	stop
tomi	富	riches
tomi	富	wealth
tomodachi	友達	friend
tomodachi	友達	mate
ton	トン	ton
tonakai	トナカイ	caribou
tonakai	トナカイ	reindeer
tonari-atta N	隣あったN	adjacent
tonari ni	隣に	next
tonari no hito	隣の人	neighbor
tonda N	富んだN	rich
tonde iru (N)	富んでいる(N)	rich
tonikaku	とにかく	anyhow
tonikaku	とにかく	anyway
tonneru	トンネル	tube
tonneru	トンネル	tunnel
too	とう	cane
too	塔	pagoda
too	塔	tower
-too	〜等	class
-too	〜等	place

too-boe (o) suru	遠ぼえ(を)する	howl
tooboo-sha	逃亡者	runaway
toobu	東部	East
toochaku	到着	arrival
toochaku-suru	到着する	arrive
too-chan	父ちゃん	pa
too-chan	父ちゃん	papa
toochi	統治	reign
toochi	統治	rule
toochi-kikan	統治期間	reign
toochi-sha	統治者	ruler
toochi-suru	統治する	govern
toochi-suru	統治する	reign
toochi-suru	統治する	rule
toodai	灯台	lighthouse
tooei-suru	投影する	project
tooge	峠	pass
toogi	討議	discussion
toogi-suru	討議する	discuss
toohoo ni	東方に	east
toohyoo	投票	vote
toohyoo de kimeru	投票で決める	vote
toohyoo-hoohoo	投票方法	vote
toohyoo-soosuu	投票総数	vote
toohyoo-suru	投票する	vote
toohyoo-suru hito	投票する人	voter
tooi	遠い	distant
tooi	遠い	far
tooi	遠い	faraway
tooi	遠い	remote
tooitsu	統一	unity
tooitsu-suru	統一する	unify
too-jiki	陶磁器	pottery
too(-ji)ki-seizoo	陶(磁)器製造	pottery
too(-ji)ki-seizoo-sho	陶(磁)器製造所	pottery
tooji-sha	当事者	party
toojoo-kyaku	搭乗客	passenger
tooketsu-suru	凍結する	freeze
tooki	陶器	china
tooki	陶器	pottery
tooki	投機	venture
tooku	遠く	far
Tookyoo	東京	Tokyo
tookyuu	等級	grade
tookyuu o tsukeru	等級を付ける	rank
too-mawashi no N	遠回しのN	oblique
toomeina	透明な	sheer
toomeina	透明な	transparent

toomen no N	当面のN	present[1]
too (no N)	十(のN)	ten
(too no yooni) takaku sobieru	(塔のように)高くそびえる	tower
toori	通り	street
toori-koshite	通り越して	past
toori-kosu	通り越す	pass
toori ni	とおりに	as
toori-sugiru	通り過ぎる	pass
tooroku	登録	registration
tooroku-bo	登録簿	register
tooroku-suru	登録する	register
tooron	討論	debate
tooron-suru	討論する	debate
tooru	通る	lead
tooru	通る	pass
toorui	盗塁	steal
toosanai	通さない	tight
toosetsu wa	当節は	nowadays
tooshi	闘士	soldier
tooshin	灯心	wick
tooshi-suru	投資する	invest
tooshite	通して	through
toosho no N	当初のN	initial
toosu	通す	pass
toosu	通す	transmit
toosutaa de pan o yaku	トースターでパンを焼く	toast[1]
toosuto	トースト	toast[1]
toosuto ni suru	トーストにする	toast[1]
-toosu, V*masu*	～通す, V*masu*	through
tootoo	とうとう	finally
tootta ato	通った跡	track
tootte	通って	by
tootte	通って	through
tootte	通って	via
toowaku-saseru	当惑させる	puzzle
Tooyoo	東洋	East
tooyoo	東洋	Orient
tooyoo-jin	東洋人	oriental
tooyoo no N	東洋のN	oriental
tooyoo-tekina	東洋的な	oriental
tooza no N	当座のN	temporary
toozen	当然	naturally
topikku	トピック	topic
toppu	トップ	top
toppu no N	トップのN	top
tora	とら	tiger

toraeru	捕らえる	capture
toraeru	捕らえる	catch
toraeru	捕らえる	seize
toraeru	捕らえる	take
torakku	トラック	truck
torakutaa	トラクター	tractor
toranku	トランク	trunk
toranpetto	トランペット	trumpet
torasuto	トラスト	trust
toreeningu	トレーニング	training
toreeraa	トレーラー	trailer
tori	鳥	bird
(tori-)atsukai	(取り)扱い	treatment
tori-atsukau	取り扱う	treat
tori-chigaeru	取り違える	confuse
toride	とりで	fort
tori-hiki	取引	bargain
tori-hiki	取引	deal
tori-hiki	取引	trade
tori-hiki	取引	traffic
tori-hiki-suru	取引する	trade
tori-kae	取り替え	replacement
tori-kaeru	取り替える	change
tori-kaeru	取り換える	exchange
tori-kaeru	取り替える	replace
tori-kaesu	取り返す	recover
tori kago	鳥かご	cage
tori-kesu	取り消す	cancel
tori-kime	取り決め	arrangement
tori-kimeru	取り決める	arrange
tori-kumu	取り組む	tackle
tori-maku	取り巻く	crowd
tori-maku	取り巻く	surround
tori-modosu	取り戻す	rally
tori-modosu	取り戻す	recover
tori-modosu	取り戻す	restore
tori-niku	とり肉	chicken
tori-nozoku	取り除く	remove
tori-nozoku	取り除く	rid
toritome ga nai	取り留めがない	wander
tori-tsukeru	取り付ける	attach
tori-tsukeru	取り付ける	fix
tori-tsukeru	取り付ける	install
toritsuku	取り付く	possess
tori-tsukurou	取り繕う	patch
toru	とる	hand
toru	取る	rob
toru	とる	steal

toru	とる	subscribe
toru	とる	take
toru	撮る	take
Toruko	トルコ	Turkey
Toruko-jin	トルコ人	Turk
toru, naka no mono o	取る, 中の物を	rob
toshi	年	age
toshi	都市	city
toshi	年	year
to shinakatta, Vvol.	としなかった, Vvol.	would
toshi o totte iru (N)	年を取っている(N)	aged
toshi o totte iru (N)	年を取っている(N)	old
toshi-shita	年下	junior
to shitara, (moshi) Sinf.	としたら, (もし)Sinf.	suppose
to-shite	として	as
to-shite wa	としては	for
toshi-totta N	年取ったN	aged
toshi-totta N	年取ったN	old
toshi-ue	年上	senior
toshi-ue	年上	seniority
toshi-ue no N	年上のN	old
toshi-ue no N	年上のN	senior
tosho-kan	図書館	library
tosho-kan-in	図書館員	librarian
tosho-shitsu	図書室	library
to, Sinf. nonpast	と, Sinf. nonpast	if
tosoo	塗装	coating
tosoo	塗装	painting
tosshin	突進	rush
tosshin-suru	突進する	rush
to suru	とする	attempt
to suru, Vvol.	とする, Vvol.	try
tosu-suru	トスする	toss
totemo	とても	awfully
totemo	とても	much
totemo	とても	quite
totemo	とても	so
totemo…neg.	とても…neg.	possibly
totemo V*masu* ta-gatte iru	とてもV*masu*たがっている	eager
totonoeru	整える	arrange
totsuzen	突然	suddenly
totsuzen no N	突然のN	sudden
totte	取っ手	handle
totte-kawaru	取って代わる	replace
totte-kawaru	取って代わる	substitute
totte-kuru	取って来る	fetch
totte-kuru	取って来る	get
to(t)temo	と(っ)ても	very
totte-oku	取っておく	keep
totte-oku	取っておく	save
to {Vinf. nonpast/Vstem} mai to, Vvol.	と{Vinf. nonpast/Vstem}まいと, Vvol.	whether
to…Vvol. to, Vvol.	と…Vvol. と, Vvol.	whether
to wa kagiranai, Sinf.	とは限らない, Sinf.	necessarily
tsuaa	ツアー	tour
tsuaa de ⟨-ni⟩ iku	ツアーで⟨〜に⟩行く	tour
tsubame	つばめ	swallow[2]
tsubasa	翼	wing
tsubo	つぼ	jar
tsubo	つぼ	pot
tsubomi	つぼみ	bud
tsubu	粒	grain
tsuchi	土	earth
tsuchi	土	ground
tsuchi	土	soil
tsue	つえ	cane
tsue	つえ	staff
tsugi	つぎ	patch
tsugi da	次だ	follow
tsugi-komu	つぎ込む	invest
tsugi-me	継ぎ目	seam
tsugi ni	次に	next
tsugi no koto	次のこと	this
tsugi no N	次のN	next
tsugi no yoona N	次のようなN	this
tsugi o ateru	つぎをあてる	patch
tsugoo	都合	convenience
tsugoo ga ii	都合がいい	convenient
tsugoo ga ii	都合がいい	suit[2]
tsugoo ga warui	都合が悪い	inconvenient
tsugu	つぐ	pour
tsui	対	pair
tsui	つい	unintentionally
tsuika	追加	addition
tsuika no N	追加のN	additional
tsuikyuu	追求	pursuit
tsuikyuu-suru	追求する	pursue
tsui ni	ついに	finally
tsui no hitotsu	対の一つ	twin
tsui no N	対のN	twin
tsuiraku	墜落	crash
tsuiraku-suru	墜落する	crash
tsuiseki	追跡	pursuit
tsuiseki-suru	追跡する	pursue

tsuiseki-suru	追跡する	track
tsuiseki-suru	追跡する	trail
tsuitate	ついたて	screen
tsuite-iku	ついて行く	follow
tsuite-iku	ついて行く	trail
tsuite inai (N)	ついていない(N)	unfortunate
tsuite-kuru	ついて来る	follow
tsuite-kuru	ついて来る	trail
tsuiyasu	費やす	spend
tsukaeru	仕える	serve
tsukae-ru (N)	使える(N)	working
tsukai	使い	errand
tsukai-furushi no N	使い古しのN	used[2]
tsukai-kata	使い方	usage
tsukai-kata	使い方	use
tsukai-michi	使い道	use
tsukai-sugi	使い過ぎ	strain
tsukai-sugiru	使い過ぎる	strain
tsukamaeru	捕まえる	capture
tsukamaeru	捕まえる	catch
tsukamaeru	捕まえる	seize
tsukamaeru	捕まえる	take
tsukamu	つかむ	grab
tsukamu	つかむ	grasp
tsukamu	つかむ	seize
tsukamu	つかむ	take
tsuka-no-ma no N	束の間のN	transitory
tsukare-hateta N	疲れ果てたN	weary
tsukare-hatete iru (N)	疲れ果てている(N)	weary
tsukareru	疲れる	try
tsukareru, {(-de)/V*te*}	疲れる, {(〜で)/V*te*}	tire[1]
tsukareru, V*te*	疲れる, V*te*	try
tsukare-saseru	疲れさせる	weary
tsukareta N	疲れたN	tired
tsukarete iru (N)	疲れている(N)	tired
tsukau	使う	employ
tsukau	使う	occupy
tsukau	使う	spend
tsukau	使う	use
tsukau	使う	work
tsuke-fuda	付け札	ticket
tsuke-mono	漬物	pickle
tsukeru	つける	apply
tsukeru	つける	attach
tsukeru	付ける	fit
tsukeru	付ける	put
tsukeru	つける	set
tsukeru	つける	soak
tsukeru	つける	wear
tsuki	月	month
tsuki	月	moon
tsuki	突き	thrust
tsuki-au	つきあう	date
tsuki-deru	突き出る	project
tsuki-deta N	突き出たN	prominent
tsuki-dete iru (N)	突き出ている(N)	prominent
tsuki ichi-do no N	月一度のN	monthly
tsuki-matou	つきまとう	haunt
tsuki-matou	つきまとう	pursue
tsuki no hikari	月の光	moonlight
tsuki no N	月のN	lunar
tsuki-sasaru	突き刺さる	strike
tsuki-sasu	突き刺す	plunge
tsuki-sasu	突き刺す	stick
tsuki-sasu	突き刺す	thrust
tsukkomu	突っ込む	plunge
tsuku	つく	arrive
tsuku	突く	poke
tsuku	つく	reach
tsuku	突く	shove
tsuku	突く	stab
tsuku	つく	stick
tsuku	突く	thrust
tsukue	机	desk
tsukuri-banashi	作り話	fiction
tsukuru	つくる	build
tsukuru	つくる	compose
tsukuru	つくる	fix
tsukuru	つくる	form
tsukuru	つくる	grow
tsukuru	つくる	make
tsuma	妻	wife
tsumannai	つまんない	unimportant
tsumaranai	つまらない	boring
tsumaranai	つまらない	stupid
tsumaranai	つまらない	tasteless
tsumaranai	つまらない	unimportant
tsumaranai	つまらない	uninteresting
tsumaranai mono	つまらないもの	nothing
tsuma-yooji	つまようじ	toothpick
tsumazuite korobu	つまずいて転ぶ	stumble
tsumazuka-seru	つまずかせる	stumble
tsumazuka-seru	つまずかせる	trip
tsumazuku	つまずく	stumble
tsumazuku	つまずく	trip
tsume	つめ	claw

tsume	つめ	nail
tsume-kakeru	詰め掛ける	crowd
tsume-komu	詰め込む	crowd
tsume-komu	詰め込む	jam[1]
tsume-komu	詰め込む	pack
tsume-komu	詰め込む	stuff
tsume-mono	詰め物	packing
tsume-mono o suru	詰め物をする	stuff
tsumeru	詰める	fill
tsumeru	詰める	shorten
tsumeru	詰める	stuff
tsumetai	冷たい	cold
tsumetai, koori no yooni	冷たい, 氷のように	icy
tsumeta-sa	冷たさ	chill
tsumi	罪	crime
tsumi	罪	sin
tsumi ga nai (N)	罪がない(N)	harmless
tsumi ga nai (N)	罪がない(N)	innocent
tsumi-kasaneru	積み重ねる	stack
tsumi-ni	積み荷	cargo
tsumi o okasu	罪を犯す	stumble
tsumori	つもり	intention
tsumori	つもり	thought
tsumori da, Sinf.	つもりだ, Sinf.	intend
tsumori da, Sinf.	つもりだ, Sinf.	shall
tsumori da, {{V/adj(*i*).}inf./adj(*na*). stem {na/datta}/N {no/datta}}	つもりだ, {{V/adj(*i*).}inf./adj(*na*). stem{な/だった}/N{の/だった}}	mean[2]
tsumori da, Vinf. nonpast	つもりだ, Vinf. nonpast	plan
tsumori da, Vinf. nonpast	つもりだ, Vinf. nonpast	will
tsumoru	積もる	pile
tsumu	積む	load
tsumu	摘む	pick
tsumu	積む	pile
tsumu	摘む	pinch
tsumu	摘む	pluck
tsumugu	紡ぐ	spin
tsuna	綱	rope
tsunagari	つながり	link
tsunagari	つながり	train
tsunagi-awaseru	つなぎ合わせる	piece
tsunagu	つなぐ	connect
tsunagu	つなぐ	join
tsunagu	つなぐ	tie
tsunagu mono	つなぐもの	tie
tsundora	ツンドラ	tundra
tsune ni	常に	always
tsune ni	常に	constantly
tsune ni	常に	ever
tsuneru	つねる	pinch
tsuno	角	horn
tsunoru	募る	recruit
tsuppashiru	突っ走る	speed
tsurai	つらい	hard
tsurai	つらい	painful
tsura-sa	つらさ	pain
tsure	連れ	companion
tsure	連れ	partner
tsure-ai	連れあい	partner
tsurete-iku	連れて行く	guide
tsurete-iku	連れて行く	lead
tsurete-iku	連れて行く	take
tsurete-kuru	連れて来る	bring
tsurete-kuru	連れて来る	lead
tsurete, Vinf. nonpast ni	つれて, Vinf. nonpastに	as
tsuri	釣り	fishing
tsuri-ai	釣り合い	balance
tsuri-ai	釣り合い	proportion
tsuri-bari	釣り針	hook
tsuri-doogu	釣り道具	tackle
tsuri-kawa	つり革	strap
tsuri o suru	釣りをする	fish
tsuri-sen	釣銭	change
tsuru	釣る	fish
tsuru	つる	vine
tsurugi	剣	sword
tsuru no aru shokubutsu	つるのある植物	vine
tsurusu	つるす	hang
tsurusu	つるす	suspend
tsurusu	つるす	swing
tsutaeru	伝える	carry
tsutaeru	伝える	communicate
tsutaeru	伝える	convey
tsutaeru	伝える	transmit
tsutome	勤め	service
tsutome-guchi	勤め口	position
tsutomeru, eyoo to	努める, 得ようと	reach
tsutsu	筒	tube
tsutsumi	包み	package
tsutsumi	包み	parcel
tsutsumu	包む	wrap
tsutsushimi-buka-sa	慎み深さ	reserve

tsu(t)tsuku	突(っ)つく	pick
tsu(t)tsuku	突(っ)つく	poke
tsuuchi	通知	notice
tsuugaku-suru	通学する	commute
tsuujiru	通じる	lead
tsuujiru	通じる	run
tsuuka	通貨	currency
tsuukin-suru	通勤する	commute
tsuukoku	通告	notice
tsuukoo	通行	passage
tsuukoo-nin	通行人	pedestrian
tsuukoo-ryoo	通行料	toll
tsuuretsuna	痛烈な	bitter
tsuurisuto	ツーリスト	tourist
tsuuro	通路	passage
tsuushin	通信	communication
tsuushin	通信	correspondence
tsuuwa-ryoo	通話料	toll
tsuuyaku	通訳	interpretation
tsuuyaku-suru	通訳する	interpret
tsuya	つや	shine
tsuya	通夜	wake
tsuyoi	強い	powerful
tsuyoi	強い	sharp
tsuyoi	強い	strong
tsuyoi	強い	sturdy
tsuyoi	強い	tough
tsuyoi sake	強い酒	spirit
tsuyoi shoodoo	強い衝動	urge
tsuyoi, ⟨-yori⟩	強い, ⟨〜より⟩	superior
tsuyoku hipparu	強く引っ張る	tug
tsuyoku hipparu koto	強く引っ張ること	tug
tsuyoku nigiru	強く握る	wring
tsuyoku suru	強くする	strengthen
tsuyo-mi	強み	strength
tsuyo-sa	強さ	strength
tsuyo-sa	強さ	stress
tsuzuite ⟨-ga⟩ aru	続いて⟨〜が⟩ある	successive
tsuzukeru	続ける	continue
tsuzukeru	続ける	sustain
-tsuzukeru, V*masu*	〜続ける, V*masu*	persist
-tsuzukeru, V*masu*	〜続ける, V*masu*	keep
tsuzuku	続く	continue
tsuzuku	続く	follow
tsuzuku	続く	run
tsuzuku, ijooni nagaku	続く, 異常に長く	persist
tsuzuri	つづり	spelling
tsuzuru	つづる	spell

U

ubau	奪う	strip
uchi	うち	home
uchi	うち	house
uchiawase	打ち合わせ	meeting
uchi {e/ni}	うち{へ/に}	home
uchi-gawa	内側	inside
uchi-gawa	内側	within
uchi-gawa no N	内側のN	inner
uchi-katsu	打ち勝つ	overcome
uchikina	内気な	bashful
uchikina	内気な	shy
uchi-komu	打ち込む	drive
uchi-kudaku	打ち砕く	pound[2]
uchi-kudaku	打ち砕く	smash
uchi ni, ⟨-no⟩	うちに, ⟨〜の⟩	by
uchi no hito	うちの人	husband
uchi-nomesu	打ちのめす	overcome
uchi no naka {de/ni/o}	うちの中{で/に/を}	indoors
uchi-taosu	打ち倒す	overthrow
uchiwa	うちわ	fan[1]
uchi-yoseru nami	打ち寄せる波	surf
uchooten ni naru	有頂天になる	transport
uchuu	宇宙	space
uchuu	宇宙	universe
uchuu-hikoo-shi	宇宙飛行士	astronaut
uchuu-sen	宇宙船	spacecraft
uchuu-sen	宇宙船	spaceship
ude	腕	arm
ude-dokei	腕時計	watch
udon	うどん	noodle
ue	上	top
ueebu	ウエーブ	wave
Ueeruzu	ウエールズ	Wales
Ueeruzu-go	ウェールズ語	Welsh
Ueeruzu-go no N	ウェールズ語のN	Welsh
Ueeruzu-jin	ウェールズ人	Welsh
Ueeruzu-jin no N	ウェールズ人のN	Welsh
ueetaa	ウエーター	waiter
ueetoresu	ウエートレス	waitress
ue {ni/de}	上{に/で}	upon
ue {ni/de/o}	上{に/で/を}	above
ue {ni/de/o}	上{に/で/を}	on
ue {ni/de/o}	上{に/で/を}	over
ue {ni/e}	上{に/へ}	up
ue (no hoo) {e/ni}	上(の方){へ/に}	upward
ue no hoo {ni/de/o}	上の方{に/で/を}	above

ue no N	上のN	top
ue no N	上のN	upper
ue no N, ⟨-yori⟩	上のN, ⟨〜より⟩	superior
ueru	植える	plant
uesuto	ウエスト	waist
ugokanai	動かない	still
ugokasu	動かす	move
ugokasu	動かす	operate
ugokasu	動かす	run
ugokasu	動かす	stir
ugokasu	動かす	work
ugoki	動き	motion
ugoki	動き	movement
ugoki-hajimeru	動き始める	start
ugoku	動く	behave
ugoku	動く	move
ugoku	動く	operate
ugoku	動く	run
ugoku	動く	stir
ugomeku	うごめく	wriggle
uiikuendo	ウイークエンド	weekend
uingu	ウイング	wing
uinku	ウインク	wink
uinku-suru	ウインクする	wink
uirusu	ウイルス	virus
uisukii	ウイスキー	whiskey
Uisukonshin	ウイスコンシン	Wisconsin
ukaberu	浮かべる	float
ukabi-agaru	浮かび上がる	surface
ukabu	浮かぶ	float
ukabu	浮かぶ	occur
ukabu	浮かぶ	swim
ukagau	伺う	come
ukai-ro	迂回路	detour
uke-ire-rareru	受け入れられる	acceptable
uke-ireru	受け入れる	accept
uke-ireru	受け入れる	receive
uke-ireru, yorokonde	受け入れる, 喜んで	welcome
uke-mi-kei	受け身形	passive
uke-mi no N	受け身のN	passive
ukeou	請け負う	undertake
ukeru	受ける	get
ukeru	受ける	receive
ukeru	受ける	suffer
ukeru	受ける	sustain
ukeru	受ける	take
ukeru	受ける	undergo
uketori-nin	受取人	receiver
uke-toru	受け取る	accept
uke-toru	受け取る	receive
uke-toru koto	受け取ること	receipt
uke-toru koto	受け取ること	reception
uke-tsugu	受け継ぐ	inherit
uketsuke	受付	reception
ukeuri no N	受け売りのN	secondhand
uke-zara	受け皿	saucer
ukkari	うっかり	carelessly
ukkari	うっかり	unintentionally
uku	浮く	float
uku	浮く	swim
ukurere	ウクレレ	ukulele
uma	馬	horse
uma-goya	馬小屋	stable
umai	うまい	delicious
umai	うまい	good
umaku	うまく	well[2]
umaku iku	うまくいく	flourish
umaku iku	うまくいく	relate
uma o umaya ni ireru	馬をうまやに入れる	stall
umareru	生まれる	born
umareta N	生まれたN	native
umaretsuki	生まれつき	naturally
umaretsuki no N	生まれつきのN	natural
umaru	埋まる	fill
umaya	うまや	stable
ume-awaseru	埋め合わせる	supply
umeki-goe	うめき声	moan
umeku	うめく	groan
umeku	うめく	moan
umeru	埋める	bury
umeru	埋める	fill
umi	海	ocean
umi	海	sea
umi-be	海辺	seashore
umi-be	海辺	seaside
umi-game	海がめ	turtle
umi-no-sachi	海の幸	seafood
umu	うむ	bear[2]
umu	うむ	breed
umu	うむ	produce
umu	うむ	reproduce
un	運	fortune
un	運	luck
un	うん	yeah
unagi	うなぎ	eel
unaru	うなる	snarl

unazuku	うなずく	nod
unchin	運賃	fare
undoo	運動	campaign
undoo	運動	exercise
undoo	運動	motion
undoo	運動	movement
undoo	運動	travel
undoo-joo	運動場	playground
undoo-senshu	運動選手	athlete
undoo-suru	運動する	exercise
un'ei	運営	politics
unga	運河	canal
un ga ii	運がいい	fortunate
un ga ii	運がいい	lucky
un ga warui	運が悪い	unfortunate
unkoo	運行	motion
unkoo	運行	movement
unmei	運命	fate
unpan	運搬	transport
unpan	運搬	transportation
unpan-hoo	運搬法	transportation
unpan-nin	運搬人	carrier
unten	運転	driving
unten-dekiru	運転出来る	steer
unten-shu	運転手	driver
unten-suru	運転する	drive
unten-suru	運転する	operate
unten-suru	運転する	steer
unu-bore	うぬぼれ	pride
unu-boreru	うぬぼれる	swell
unu-borete iru	うぬぼれている	pride
un waruku	運悪く	unfortunately
un-yoku	運よく	fortunate
unzari-suru	うんざりする	sick
ura	裏	inside
uragiru	裏切る	sell
urami	うらみ	spite
ura-niwa	裏庭	backyard
ura-niwa	裏庭	yard[2]
ura (no) N	裏(の)N	wrong
uranyuumu	ウラニウム	uranium
urayamashi-gatte iru	うらやましがっている	envious
urayamashii	うらやましい	envious
urayamashii	うらやましい	jealous
urayamashiku omotte iru	うらやましく思っている	envious
ureru	売れる	sell
ureshii	うれしい	glad
ureshii	うれしい	happy
ureshii	うれしい	pleased
ureshii koto	うれしいこと	treat
ureshi-sa	うれしさ	joy
ure-yuki	売れ行き	sale
uri-ba	売り場	counter
uri-kire	売り切れ	sellout
uri-komu	売り込む	sell
uroko	うろこ	scale[1]
uru	得る	acquire
uru	得る	gain
uru	売る	sell
urunda N	潤んだN	wet
urunde iru (N)	潤んでいる(N)	wet
urusai	うるさい	noisy
urusai	うるさい	particular
urusai	うるさい	selective
u-ryoo	雨量	rainfall
usagi	うさぎ	rabbit
ushi	牛	cattle
ushi	牛	cow
ushi	牛	ox
ushinau	失う	lose
ushinawasu	失わす	sink
ushiro	後ろ	back
ushiro	後ろ	rear
ushiro e	後ろへ	back
ushiro muki ni	後ろ向きに	backward
ushiro ni	後ろに	behind
ushiro no N	後ろのN	rear
uso	うそ	lie[2]
uso o tsuku	うそをつく	lie[2]
usu-	薄～	pale
usu-gurai	薄暗い	somber
usui	薄い	subtle
usui	薄い	thin
usui	薄い	weak
usui ori-mono	薄い織物	tissue
usu-ita	薄板	sheet
usuku kiru	薄く切る	slice
usura-samui	薄ら寒い	chilly
usureru	薄れる	fade
uta	歌	song
utagai	疑い	doubt
utagai	疑い	suspicion
uta ga joozuna	歌が上手な	singer
utagau	疑う	doubt

utagau 疑う question
utagau, Sinf. no dewanai (daroo) ka to 疑う, Sinf.のではない(だろう)かと suspect
utagawashi-gena 疑わしげな suspicious
utagawashii 疑わしい suspicious
utata-ne うたた寝 nap
utau 歌う sing
uto-uto-suru うとうとする nod
utsu 撃つ fire
utsu うつ hit
utsu うつ shoot
utsu うつ strike
utsubyoo うつ病 depression
utsu, ({kana-zuchi/hanmaa} de) 打つ, ({金づち/ハンマー}で) hammer
utsukushii 美しい beautiful
utsukushii 美しい pretty
utsukushii hito 美しい人 beauty
utsukushiku 美しく beautifully
utsukushi-sa 美しさ beauty
utsu oto 打つ音 stroke[1]
utsuri-kawari 移り変わり transition
utsuru うつる move
utsuru うつる reflect
utsuru うつる shift
utsuru うつる spread
utsuru うつる transfer
utsushi 写し copy
utsusu うつす infect
utsusu うつす move
utsusu うつす pass
utsusu うつす project
utsusu うつす reflect
utsusu うつす remove
utsusu うつす shift
utsusu うつす transfer
utsusu うつす translate
uttae 訴え appeal
uttaeru 訴える appeal
uttaeru 訴える complain
uttaeru 訴える sue
utte aruku 売って歩く travel
uun ううん no
uuru ウール wool
uuru no N ウールのN woolen
uwa-be 上辺 surface
uwa-gi 上着 coat
uwa-gi 上着 jacket
uwa-muki no N 上向きのN upward
uwa-nuri 上塗り coating
uwasa うわさ rumor
uwasa うわさ talk
uwasa-banashi うわさ話 gossip
uwasa-banashi o suru うわさ話をする gossip
uwa-yaku 上役 boss
sukui-toru すくい取る skim
uyo-uyo-shite iru うようよしている swarm
uzu 渦 whirl
uzu-maki 渦巻き whirl
uzu o maku 渦を巻く whirl

W

wa 輪 circle
wa 輪 link
wa 輪 loop
wa 輪 ring[1]
wabiru わびる apologize
wadai 話題 topic
wagamama わがまま selfishness
wagamamana わがままな selfish
wagon ワゴン wagon
wain ワイン wine
Waiomingu ワイオミング Wyoming
waishatsu ワイシャツ shirt
wakai 若い young
wakai toki 若い時 youth
waka-mono 若者 youngster
waka-mono 若者 youth
wakare 別れ farewell
wakareru 分かれる divide
wakareru 別れる leave
wakareru わかれる part
wakareru わかれる segment
wakareru わかれる separate
wakari-yasui 分かりやすい plain
wakaru 分かる discover
wakaru 分かる feel
wakaru 分かる find
wakaru 分かる identify
wakaru 分かる know
wakaru 分かる prove
wakaru 分かる recognize
wakaru 分かる reveal
wakaru 分かる see
wakaru 分かる show

wakaru	分かる	teach
wakaru	分かる	understand
waka-sa	若さ	youth
wakasu	沸かす	boil
waka-te	若手	junior
wakatte iru	分かっている	realize
waka-waka-shii	若々しい	young
wake	訳	reason
wake-mae	分け前	portion
wake-mae	分け前	share
wakeru	分ける	divide
wakeru	分ける	part
wakeru	分ける	segment
wakeru	分ける	separate
wakeru	分ける	split
waki ni	わきに	aside
wakkusu	ワックス	wax
wakkusu o kakeru	ワックスをかける	wax
waku	わく	boil
waku	枠	frame
wakuchin	ワクチン	vaccine
waku-gumi	枠組み	framework
waku-waku-suru N	わくわくするN	exciting
wameku	わめく	yell
wan	湾	bay
wan	わん	bowl
wan	湾	gulf
wana	わな	trap
wana ni kakeru	わなにかける	trap
wani	ワニ	alligator
wan-wan	ワンワン	bow-wow
waon	和音	chord
warai-mono	笑い物	sport
warau	笑う	laugh
ware-me	割れ目	crack
ware-me ga dekiru	割れ目ができる	crack
ware o wasurete yorokobu	我を忘れて喜ぶ	transport
wareru	割れる	break
ware-ware-jishin	我々自身	ourselves
ware-ware no N	我々のN	our
wariai	割合	fairly
wariai	割合	proportion
wariai (ni)	割合(に)	relatively
wariai(ni)	割合(に)	comparatively
wari-ate	割り当て	assignment
wari-ateru	割り当てる	assign
warini	割に	fairly

wari-zan	割り算	division
waru	割る	break
waru	割る	crack
waru	割る	divide
waru	割る	split
waru-gashikoi	悪賢い	smart
waru-gi no nai	悪気のない	white
warui	悪い	bad
warui	悪い	evil
warui, 〈yori〉	悪い,〈~より〉	worse
waru koto	割ること	split
waruku-suru	悪くする	upset
waru-mono	悪者	villain
washa	話者	speaker
Washinton	ワシントン	Washington
Washinton-shuu	ワシントン州	Washington
washi-zukami ni suru	わしづかみにする	grab
wasureru	忘れる	forget
wasureru	忘れる	omit
watakushi	私	I
wata(ku)shi-domo no N	私どものN	our
wata(ku)shi-tachi	私たち	we
wata(ku)shi-tachi-jishin	私たち自身	ourselves
wata(ku)shi-tachi no N	私たちのN	our
wataru	渡る	cross
watashi	わたし	I
watashi-bune	渡し船	ferry
watashi no	私の	mine[1]
watashi no N	私のN	my
watashi+prt.	私+prt.	me
watashi-tachi ni	私たちに	us
watashi-tachi o	私たちを	us
watasu	渡す	hand
watatte iku	渡って行く	migrate
watatte kuru	渡って来る	migrate
waza-to	わざと	deliberately
wazuka	わずか	few
wazurawasu	煩わす	trouble

Y

ya	や	and
ya	矢	arrow
-ya	~屋	shop
yaa	やあ	hi
yaado	ヤード	yard[1]
yaban-jin	野蛮人	savage

yabanna	野蛮な	savage
yabanna	野蛮な	wild
yabu	やぶ	bush
yabu	やぶ	thicket
yabuku	破く	tear[1]
yabura-rete inai (N)	破られていない(N)	unbroken
yabureru	破れる	break
yaburu	破る	break
yaburu	破る	defeat
yaburu	破る	tear[1]
yaburu	破る	violate
yachin	家賃	rent
yagai no N	野外のN	outdoor
yagate	やがて	directly
yagate	やがて	soon
yagi	山羊	goat
yagyuu	野牛	buffalo
ya-jirushi	矢印	arrow
yakamashii	やかましい	noisy
yakamashii	やかましい	particular
yakan	やかん	kettle
yakei	夜警	watchman
yakeru	焼ける	broil
yakeru	焼ける	burn
yaki-mono	焼き物	china
yaki-mono	焼き物	pottery
yaki-suteru	焼き捨てる	destroy
yakkaina	厄介な	annoying
yakkaina	厄介な	awkward
yakkaina	厄介な	troublesome
yakkyoku	薬局	drugstore
yakkyoku	薬局	pharmacy
yakkyoo	薬きょう	shell
yaku	約	about
yaku	約	approximately
yaku	焼く	bake
yaku	焼く	broil
yaku	焼く	burn
yaku	役	character
yaku	焼く	fry
yaku	役	part
yaku	焼く	roast
yaku	役	role
yaku	訳	translation
-yaku	～訳	version
yaku-bun	訳文	translation
yakuin	役員	officer
yakume	役目	role

yakumi	薬味	spice
yakumi ga kiita N	薬味がきいたN	spicy
yakunin	役人	official
yaku ni tatanai (N)	役に立たない(N)	useless
yaku ni tatsu	役に立つ	helpful
yaku ni tatsu	役に立つ	serve
yaku ni tatsu (N)	役に立つ(N)	powerful
yaku ni tatsu (N)	役に立つ(N)	useful
yaku o ateru	役を当てる	cast
yaku o tsutomeru	役を務める	act
yakusha	役者	actor
yakusha	役者	actress
yakusha	役者	player
yakusoku	約束	promise
yakusoku	約束	undertaking
yakusoku	約束	word
yakusoku o suru, Vinf. nonpast	約束をする, Vinf. nonpast	promise
yakusoku-suru	約束する	commit
yakusoku-suru	約束する	undertake
yakusoku-suru, Vinf. nonpast to と	約束する, Vinf. nonpast	promise
yakusu	訳す	translate
yakusu	訳す	turn
yakusuru	訳する	turn
yakuwari	役割	function
yakuwari	役割	role
yakuzai-shi	薬剤師	chemist
yakuzai-shi	薬剤師	pharmacist
yakyuu	野球	ball
yakyuu	野球	baseball
yama	山	heap
yama	山	mountain
yama	山	pile
yama	山	stack
yameru	やめる	abandon
yameru	やめる	cease
yameru	やめる	quit
yameru	やめる	stop
yamu	やむ	cease
yamu	やむ	stop
yamu-o-enai	止むを得ない	necessary
yanagi	柳	willow
yane	屋根	roof
yane-ura	屋根裏	attic
yangu	ヤング	youngster
yankii	ヤンキー	Yankee
yanushi	家主	landlady

yanushi	家主	landlord
yari	やり	spear
yari-gai ga aru (N)	やりがいがある(N)	challenging
yarikata	やり方	style
yarikata	やり方	way
yari-kata	やり方	policy
yari-sokonau	やり損なう	stumble
yarite	やり手	operator
yari-togeru	やり遂げる	accomplish
yaru	やる	do
yaru	やる	give
yaru	やる	play
yaru	やる	send
yasai	野菜	vegetable
yasashii	やさしい	easy
yasashii	やさしい	gentle
yasashii	やさしい	kind
yasashii	優しい	tender
yasashiku	優しく	gently
yasashi-sa	優しさ	kindness
yasei no doobutsu	野生の動物	savage
yasei no N	野生のN	savage
yasei no N	野生のN	wild
yasei-seibutsu	野生生物	wildlife
yashin	野心	ambition
yashinau	養う	cultivate
yashinau	養う	support
yashinau	養う	sustain
yashi (no ki)	やし(の木)	palm tree
yashin-tekina	野心的な	ambitious
yasui	安い	cheap
-yasui, V*masu*	〜やすい, V*masu*	subject
yasume-nai (N)	休めない(N)	restless
yasumi	休み	holiday
yasumi	休み	pause
yasumi	休み	recess
yasumi	休み	rest[1]
yasumi	休み	vacation
yasumi-basho	休み場所	perch
yasumu	休む	rest[1]
yasunde	休んで	absent
yasu-ppoi	安っぽい	cheap
yasu-uri	安売り	sale
yatai	屋台	stall
yatotte iru	雇っている	retain
yatou	雇う	employ
yatou	雇う	engage
yatou	雇う	hire

yatsu	やつ	creature
yatsu	やつ	fellow
yatsu	やつ	guy
yatsu	やつ	thing
yatsugibaya ni abise-kakeru	矢継ぎ早やに浴びせ掛ける	shoot
yatto	やっと	barely
yatto	やっと	finally
yattoko	やっとこ	pliers
yattsu (no N)	八つ(のN)	eight
yawarageru koto	和らげること	relief
yawarakai	柔らかい	soft
yawarakai	柔らかい	tender
yawarakaku	柔らかく	softly
yawarakana	柔らかな	soft
yawarakani	柔らかに	softly
yaya	やや	somewhat
yayakoshii	ややこしい	confusing
yo-ake	夜明け	dawn
yobi-atsumeru	呼び集める	rally
yobi-dasu	呼び出す	page[2]
yobi-dasu	呼び出す	summon
yobi-goe	呼び声	call
yobi-{kaesu/modosu}	呼び{返す/戻す}	recall
yobi no N	予備のN	preliminary
yobi no N	予備のN	spare
yobi-shitsu	予備室	spare
yobi-tekina	予備的な	preliminary
yobi-tsukeru	呼び付ける	summon
yoboo	予防	prevention
yoboo	予防	protection
yoboo-suru, {Vinf. nonpast no/N} o	予防する, {Vinf. nonpastの/N}を	prevent
yobu	呼ぶ	call
yobu	呼ぶ	invite
yobun no N	余分のN	extra
yobun no N	余分のN	spare
yochi	余地	room
yogen	予言	prediction
yogen-suru	予言する	predict
yogore	汚れ	stain
yogoreta N	汚れたN	dirty
yogoreta N	汚れたN	filthy
yogorete iru (N)	汚れている(N)	dirty
yogorete iru (N)	汚れている(N)	filthy
yogosu	汚す	stain
yohaku	余白	blank
yohaku	余白	margin

yojireru	よじれる	twist
yojiru	よじる	twist
yoka	余暇	leisure
yokattari, warukattari no N	良かったり、悪かったりのN	uneven
-yoke	～よけ	protection
yokin-suru	預金する	deposit
yokka	四日	fourth
yokkyuu	欲求	thirst
yoko	横	length
yoko-bara	横腹	side
yoko-boo	横棒	bar
yoko-boo	横棒	rail
yoko-gi	横木	rail
yokoku	予告	notice
yokoku	予告	warning
yoko-michi ni soreru	横道にそれる	stray
yoko ni	横に	sideways
yoko ni naru	横になる	lie[1]
yoko no N	横のN	horizontal
yoko-ppara	横っ腹	side
yokoshimana	よこしまな	wicked
yokosu	よこす	send
yokotaeru	横たえる	lay
yoko-yure	横揺れ	roll
yoku	欲	desire
yoku	よく	frequent
yoku	よく	frequently
yoku	よく	hard
yoku	よく	often
yoku	欲	thirst
yoku	よく	well[2]
yokuboo	欲望	desire
-yoku ga aru (N)	～欲がある(N)	thirsty
yoku kangaeru	よく考える	consider
yoku kata-zuita N	よく片付いたN	neat
yoku kata-zuite iru (N)	よく片付いている(N)	neat
yoku naru	良くなる	improve
yoku shiranai (N)	よく知らない(N)	unfamiliar
yoku shira-reta N	よく知られたN	well-known
yoku shira-rete iru (N)	よく知られている(N)	well-known
yokushitsu	浴室	bathroom
yoku shitte iru	よく知っている	familiar
yokusoo	浴槽	bathtub
yoku suru	良くする	improve
yomu	よむ	read
yomu hito	読む人	reader
yon-ban-me no N	四番目のN	fourth
yon-bun-no-ichi	四分の一	quarter
yon (+counter) (no N)	四(+counter)(のN)	four
yon (+counter) no N	四(+counter)のN	fourth
yonde kuru	呼んで来る	fetch
yo-nen-sei	四年生	senior
yon-juu (+counter) (no N)	四十(+counter)(のN)	forty
yo-no-naka	世の中	world
yooboo	容ぼう	feature
yoochi-en	幼稚園	kindergarten
yooeki	溶液	solution
yoofuku	洋服	clothes
yoofuku	洋服	dress
yoofuku-ya	洋服屋	tailor
yoogi-sha	容疑者	suspect
yoogo	用語	term
yooi	用意	arrangement
yooi	用意	preparation
yooi	用意	provision
yooi ga dekita N	用意が出来たN	ready
yooiku	養育	support
yooin	要因	factor
yooi-suru	用意する	prepare
yooji	用事	business
yooji	ようじ	toothpick
yoojin	用心	care
yoojin	用心	caution
yoojin-bukaku	用心深く	cautiously
yookai	溶解	solution
yooken	用件	business
yooki	陽気	sunshine
yooki	容器	vessel
yookina	陽気な	cheerful
yookina	陽気な	gay
yookina	陽気な	merry
yookina	陽気な	sunny
yookini	陽気に	cheerfully
yoo-koso (irasshaimashita)	ようこそ(いらっしゃいました)	welcome
yoo(-kyoku) no N	陽(極)のN	positive
yookyuu	要求	claim
yookyuu	要求	demand
yookyuu-sareru	要求される	require
yookyuu-suru	要求する	claim
yookyuu-suru	要求する	demand

yookyuu-suru	要求する	require
yoomoo	羊毛	wool
yoona, N no	ような, Nの	like[2]
yoona, Sinf.	ような, Sinf.	appear
yoona, Sinf.	ような, Sinf.	as
yoona, Sinf.	ような, Sinf.	evidently
yoona, Sinf.	ような, Sinf.	seem
yoonen-jidai	幼年時代	childhood
yoonen-ki	幼年期	childhood
yooni	ように	as
yoonin	容認	acceptance
yooni, neg. of Vinf. nonpast	ように, neg. of Vinf. nonpast	lest
yoo(ni), Vinf.	よう(に), Vinf.	so
Yooroppa	ヨーロッパ	Europe
Yooroppa no N	ヨーロッパのN	European
yoosai	要塞	fort
yoosei	要請	request
yoosei	養成	training
yoosei-jo	養成所	nursery
yoosha	容赦	pardon
yoosha-suru	容赦する	pardon
yooshi	用紙	form
yooshiki	様式	mode
yooshiki	様式	pattern
yooshi ni suru	養子にする	adopt
yooso	要素	element
yoosu	様子	aspect
yoosu	様子	show
yoosu	様子	sign
yoosuru	要する	require
yooten	要点	point
yooyaku	ようやく	finally
yooyaku	要約	outline
yooyaku	要約	summary
yooyaku-suru	要約する	outline
yooyaku-suru	要約する	sum
yoreba Sinf. sooda	よればSinf.そうだ	according to
yori	より	strand
yori adj., N	よりadj., N	less
yori-kakatte	寄り掛かって	against
yori (mo), {N/adj(*na*). stem/{V/adj(*i*).} inf. nonpast}}	より(も), {N/adj(*na*). stem/{V/adj(*i*).} inf. nonpast}}	than
yoroi-kabuto	よろいかぶと	armor
yorokoba-seru	喜ばせる	delight
yorokoba-seru	喜ばせる	please
yorokoba-su	喜ばす	please
yorokobi	喜び	delight
yorokobi	喜び	joy
yorokobi	喜び	pleasure
yorokobu	喜ぶ	delighted
yorokobu	喜ぶ	glad
yorokonde	喜んで	gladly
yorokonde iru	喜んでいる	pleased
yorokonde mukaeru	喜んで迎える	welcome
yorokonde uke-ireru	喜んで受け入れる	welcome
yorokonde V	喜んでV	willing
yoromeku	よろめく	stumble
yoron	世論	opinion
yoru	よる	depend
yoru	夜	night
yoru	よる	twist
yoru juu-ni-ji	夜十二時	midnight
yoru to Sinf. sooda	よるとSinf.そうだ	according to
yosan	予算	budget
yoshi	よし	well[2]
yosoku	予測	forecast
yosoku	予測	prediction
yosoku-suru	予測する	forecast
yosoku-suru	予測する	predict
yosoo	予想	expectation
yosoo	予想	prospect
yosoou	装う	assume
yosu	よす	quit
yotei	予定	schedule
yotei-hyoo	予定表	calendar
yotsu-ashi no doobutsu	四足の動物	beast
yotte chigau	よって違う	depend
yotte iru (N)	酔っている(N)	drunk
yottsu-me no N	四つ目のN	fourth
yottsu (no N)	四つ(のN)	four
yowai	弱い	weak
yowaru	弱る	fail
yowa-yowa-shii	弱々しい	faint
yoyaku	予約	reservation
yoyaku-koodoku	予約購読	subscription
yoyaku-suru	予約する	book
yoyaku-suru	予約する	reserve
yoyuu	余裕	room
yubi	指	finger
yubi	指	toe
yubi-sasu	指差す	indicate
yubi-sasu	指差す	point
yubi-wa	指輪	ring[1]
yubune	湯舟	bathtub

yudan naku ki o kubatte iru (N)	油断なく気を配っている(N)	alert
Yudaya-jin	ユダヤ人	Jew
Yudaya-jin no N	ユダヤ人のN	Jewish
Yudaya-kyookaidoo	ユダヤ教会堂	synagogue
yuderu	ゆでる	boil
yugameru	ゆがめる	twist
yuge	湯気	steam
yuge	湯気	vapor
yuiitsu no N	唯一のN	sole[1]
yuka	床	floor
yukaina	愉快な	cheerful
yukaina	愉快な	enjoyable
yukaina	愉快な	jolly
yukaini	愉快に	cheerfully
yuki	雪	snow
-yuki	～行き	bound for
yuki ga furu	雪が降る	snow
yuki ga furu	雪が降る	snowy
yuki ga ooi	雪が多い	snowy
-yuki no N	～行きのN	for
yuki no yoona	雪のような	snowy
yuki no yoona mono	雪のようなもの	snow
yukkuri	ゆっくり	slow
yukkuri (to)	ゆっくり(と)	slowly
yukue-fumei no N	行方不明のN	missing
yume	夢	dream
yume	夢	vision
yume-miru-yoona	夢見るような	faraway
yume ni omou	夢に思う	dream
yunifoomu	ユニフォーム	uniform
yuniikuna	ユニークな	unique
yunyuu	輸入	import
yunyuu-hin	輸入品	import
yunyuu-suru	輸入する	import
yureru	揺れる	move
yureru	揺れる	shake
yureru	揺れる	stir
yureru	揺れる	swing
yureru	揺れる	tremble
yureru	揺れる	vibrate
yureru	揺れる	wave
yuri	ゆり	lily
yurumeru	緩める	relax
yurumi	緩み	slack
yurunda N	緩んだN	slack
yurunde iru (N)	緩んでいる(N)	slack
yurushi	許し	pardon
yurushi	許し	permission
yurusu	許す	allow
yurusu	許す	excuse
yurusu	許す	pardon
yurusu	許す	permit
yusaburu	揺さぶる	toss
yusei	油井	well[1]
yushutsu	輸出	export
yushutsu-hin	輸出品	export
yushutsu-suru	輸出する	export
yusoo	輸送	transport
yusoo	輸送	transportation
yusoo-hoo	輸送法	transportation
yusoo-suru	輸送する	transport
yusuru	揺する	shake
yusuru	揺する	swing
Yuta	ユタ	Utah
yutakana	豊かな	abundant
yutakana	豊かな	rich
yutakana	豊かな	wealth
yutakana	豊かな	wealthy
yutori	ゆとり	room
yuttari-shita N	ゆったりしたN	loose
yuttari-shite iru (N)	ゆったりしている(N)	loose
yuubin	郵便	mail
yuubin-kyoku	郵便局	post office
yuubin-ryookin	郵便料金	postage
yuubin-uke	郵便受け	mailbox
yuuboona	有望な	probable
yuuekina	有益な	advantageous
yuuekina	有益な	useful
yuufukuna	裕福な	rich
yuufukuna	裕福な	wealthy
yuugaina	有害な	harmful
yuugaina	有害な	poisonous
yuugana	優雅な	graceful
yuugana	優雅な	refined
yuugata	夕方	evening
yuugi	遊戯	sport
yuujin	友人	friend
yuujoo	友情	friendship
yuukanna	勇敢な	brave
yuukanni	勇敢に	bravely
yuuka-shooken	有価証券	security
yuukei no N	有形のN	tangible
yuuken-sha	有権者	voter
yuuki	勇気	courage

yuuki-tai	有機体	organism
yuuki-zukeru	勇気づける	encourage
yuumeina	有名な	distinguished
yuumeina	有名な	famous
yuumeina	有名な	well-known
yuumoa	ユーモア	humor
yuumoa ni tonda N	ユーモアに富んだN	humorous
yuunoona	有能な	capable
yuurei	幽霊	ghost
yuurei	幽霊	spirit
yuurei ga deru	幽霊が出る	haunt
yuurina	有利な	advantageous
yuurina	有利な	favorable
yuurina tachiba	有利な立場	advantage
yuuseina	優勢な	dominant
yuuseina, ⟨-yori⟩	優勢な, ⟨〜より⟩	superior
yuushi	勇士	soldier
yuushi	勇士	warrior
yuushoku	夕食	dinner
yuushoku	夕食	supper
yuushoo-sha	優勝者	winner
yuushuuna	優秀な	excellent
yuuutsu	憂うつ	melancholy
yuuutsuna	憂うつな	blue
yuuutsuna	憂うつな	melancholy
yuu-yake	夕焼け	sunset
yuuzai no N	有罪のN	guilty
yuuzuu ga kikanai (N)	融通がきかない(N)	rigid
yuuzuu ga kiku N	融通が利くN	flexible
yuwaeru	結わえる	tie
yuwaeru mono	結わえるもの	tie
yuzuri-watasu	譲り渡す	surrender
yuzuru	譲る	give
yuzuru	譲る	yield

Z

zaa-zaa	ざあざあ	fast
za-buton	ざぶとん	cushion
zaidan	財団	foundation
zaigen	財源	resource
zaiko	在庫	supply
zaimoku	材木	lumber
zaimoku	材木	timber
zaimoku	材木	tree
zaimoku	材木	wood
zairyoo	材料	material
zaisan	財産	fortune
zaisan	財産	riches
zaisan	財産	treasure
zaisan o yuzuru	財産を譲る	transmit
zaisei	財政	finance
zaisei-tekina	財政的な	financial
zakka	雑貨	groceries
zakka-ten	雑貨店	grocery
zakka-ya	雑貨屋	grocery
zangai	残がい	wreck
zangyoo	残業	overtime
zankokuna	残酷な	cruel
zannenna	残念な	pity
zannenna	残念な	regret
zannenna	残念な	sorry
zannenna	残念な	unfortunate
zannenna koto ni	残念なことに	unfortunately
zannen ni omou, {⟨-o⟩/Vstem of pot. nakute}	残念に思う, {⟨〜を⟩/Vstem of pot.なくて}	regret
zanzon-butsu	残存物	survival
zara-zara-shita N	ざらざらしたN	rough
zara-zara-shita N	ざらざらしたN	rugged
zara-zara-shite iru (N)	ざらざらしている(N)	rough
zara-zara-shite iru (N)	ざらざらしている(N)	rugged
zaseki	座席	seat
zasshi	雑誌	magazine
zassoo	雑草	weed
zassoo o toru	雑草を取る	weed
zatsudan	雑談	chat
zatsuji	雑事	chore
zatsuon	雑音	noise
zattoo	雑踏	jam[1]
zatto yomu	ざっと読む	skim
zei	税	tax
zeikin	税金	duty
zeikin	税金	tax
zeitaku	ぜいたく	luxury
zeitakuna	ぜいたくな	luxury
zemi	ゼミ	seminar
zeminaaru	ゼミナール	seminar
zen-	前〜	ex-
zen-	全〜	total
zen-	全〜	whole
zenbu	全部	all
zenbu de	全部で	altogether
zenbu no N	全部のN	all

zenbu no N	全部のN	entire
zenchi-shi	前置詞	preposition
zenchoo	全長	span
zen-juumin	全住民	population
zenpoo	前方	ahead
zen-senkan	全戦艦	navy
zenshin	前進	progress
zenshin-suru	前進する	progress
zenshin-suru N	前進するN	progressive
zenshoo-meidai	全称命題	universal
zentai	全体	whole
zentai no N	全体のN	entire
zentai no N	全体のN	total
zentai no N	全体のN	whole
zenzen	全然	quite
zenzen…neg.	全然…neg.	no
zenzen…neg.	全然…neg.	totally
zeppeki	絶壁	cliff
zerii	ゼリー	jello
zero	ゼロ	nothing
zero	ゼロ	zero
zesuchaa	ゼスチャー	gesture
zetsuboo	絶望	despair
zetsuboo-tekina	絶望的な	desperate
zetsuboo-tekina	絶望的な	hopeless
zettai ni	絶対に	absolutely
zettai ni	絶対に	swear
zettai ni …neg.	絶対に…neg.	never
-zoku	～族	family
zokusuru	属する	belong
zokusuru	属する	reside
zoku-zoku-suru kanji	ぞくぞくする感じ	thrill
zoo	象	elephant
zoo	像	statue
zoogan	象眼	setting
zooka	増加	growth
zooka	増加	increase
zookin	雑きん	cloth
zoo no hana	象の鼻	trunk
zoosen(-jutsu)	造船(術)	shipbuilding
zotto-saseru	ぞっとさせる	thrill
zu	図	diagram
zu	図	figure
zuan	図案	pattern
zubon	ズボン	pants
zubon	ズボン	trousers
zudon	ずどん	bang
zugai-kotsu	頭蓋骨	skull
zuhyoo	図表	chart
zuhyoo	図表	diagram
zuihitsu	随筆	essay
zujoo {ni/o/de}	頭上{に/を/で}	overhead
zukku	ズック	canvas
zumen	図面	drawing
-zu ni, {Vneg./Vstem/ko/se}	～ずに, {Vneg./Vstem/来/せ}	without
zunoo	頭脳	brain
zurui	ずるい	cunning
zurui	ずるい	tricky
zutsuu	頭痛	headache
zutsuu no tane	頭痛の種	headache
zutto	ずっと	far
zutto	ずっと	stay
zutto	ずっと	steady
zutto	ずっと	through

日本語学習 基礎英日辞典
Kodansha's Basic English-Japanese Dictionary

2002年11月 第1刷発行
2006年8月 第4刷発行

編　者　牧野成一、中田清一、大曽美恵子

発行者　富田 充

発行所　講談社インターナショナル株式会社
〒112-8652 東京都文京区音羽 1-17-14
電話 03-3944-6493（編集部）
03-3944-6492（マーケティング部・業務部）
ホームページ www.kodansha-intl.com

印刷・製本所　大日本印刷株式会社

Printed in Japan
ISBN4-7700-2895-4

1	一	丨	丶	丿	乙	乚	亅	
2	二	亠	人	𠆢	亻	儿	入	八
冂	冖	冫	几	凵	刀	刂	力	勹
匕	匚	十	卜	卩	㔾	厂	厶	又
了	3	口	囗	土	士	夂	夕	大
女	子	宀	寸	小	⺍	尢	尸	山
川	工	己	巾	干	幺	广	廴	廾
弋	弓	彡	彳	艹	辶	阝	阝	忄
扌	犭	氵	4	心	⺗	戈	戸	手
支	攵	文	斗	斤	方	无	日	曰
月	月 (肉)	木	欠	止	歹	殳	毋	比
毛	氏	气	水	火	灬	爫	父	片
牛	犬	王	礻	耂	5	玄	玉	瓦